DINOSAURS
THE ENCYCLOPEDIA

NOSAURS
THE ENCYCLOPEDIA

by Donald F. Glut

Foreword by MICHAEL K. BRETT-SURMAN,
PH.D., VERTEBRATE PALEONTOLOGY

McFarland & Company, Inc., Publishers
Jefferson, North Carolina, and London

For Ned Colbert,
who inspired so many

British Library Cataloguing-in-Publication data are available

Library of Congress Cataloguing-in-Publication Data

Glut, Donald F.
Dinosaurs: the encyclopedia / by Donald F. Glut : foreword by
Michael K. Brett-Surman.
p.   cm.
Includes bibliographical references and index.
ISBN 0-89950-917-7 (library binding : 50# alkaline paper) ∞
1. Dinosaurs—Encyclopedias.   I. Title.
QE862.D5G652   1997
567.9'1'03—dc20   95-47668
                                                                          CIP

Manufactured in the United States of America

*McFarland & Company, Inc., Publishers
Box 611, Jefferson, North Carolina 28640*

Acknowledgments

I am indebted to the following paleontologists for their critical reviewing of selected portions of the manuscript, and for their invaluable criticisms, opinions, evaluations, corrections, notations, additions, deletions and suggestions: (For hadrosaurids, iquanodontids, the introductory and systematics sections, and for serving as chief scientific advisor in critically reviewing the major portion of the final draft) Michael K. Brett-Surman of the Smithsonian Institution, and George Washington University, Washington, D.C.; (ankylosaurs) Walter P. Coombs, Jr., of Western New England College, Springfield, Massachusetts; (pachycephalosaurs, non-hadrosaurid ornithopods, stegosaurs, introductory and systematics sections) Hans-Dieter Sues of the Royal Ontario Museum; (ceratopsians) Peter Dodson of the School of Veterinary Medicine, Philadelphia, and The Academy of Natural Sciences of Philadelphia; (dinosaur footprints) James O. Farlow, Jr., of Earth and Space Science, Indiana-Purdue University at Fort Wayne, Indiana, and Martin G. Lockley of the geology department, University of Colorado at Denver; (prosauropods) Peter M. Galton of the University of Bridgeport, Connecticut; (sauropods) John S. McIntosh of Wesleyan University, Middletown, Connecticut; and (theropods and miscellaneous genera and species) Ralph E. Molnar of the Queensland Museum, Queensland, Australia.

Also, I would especially like to thank sincerely the following workers for so generously allowing me to examine and photograph specimens and for providing articles from paleontological journals, and also for their overall help, support, guidance, advice and encouragement over the years: Harley J. Armstrong, Museum of Western Colorado; Donald Baird, formerly of Princeton University; Robert T. Bakker, Tate Museum, Casper, Wyoming; Michael J. Benton, University of Bristol; William T. Blows, Isle of Wight Dinosaur Project; John R. Bolt, John J. Flynn and William F. Simpson, The Field Museum; José F. Bonaparte and Fernando Novas, Museo Argentino de Ciencias Naturales; George Callison, California State University, Long Beach, and Dinamation International Corp.; Kenneth Carpenter, Denver Museum of Natural History; Alan G. Charig and Angela Milner, The Natural History Museum, London; Sankar Chatterjee, Texas Tech University; Daniel J. Chure, Dinosaur National Monument; Edwin H. Colbert and Michael Morales, Museum of Northern Arizona; Philip J. Currie, Royal Tyrrell Museum of Paleontology;

Mary R. Dawson, the Carnegie Museum of Natural History; Dougal Dixon; Gordon Edmund, formerly of the Royal Ontario Museum; Andrzej Elzanowski, Max-Planck Institut für Biochemie; Catherine A. Forster; Eugene S. Gaffney, American Museum of Natural History; Marc R. Gallup; William B. Gallagher, New Jersey State Museum; David D. Gillette, Division of State History and Antiquities, Utah; William R. Hamme, Augustana College; Thomas R. Holtz, Jr., Branch of Paleontology and Stratigraphy, United States Geological Survey; James A. Hopson and Paul C. Sereno, University of Chicago; John R. Horner, Museum of the Rockies; Nicholas Hotten, III, National Museum of Natural History; Stephen Hutt, Museum of Geology, Isle of Wight; James A. Jensen, formerly of Brigham Young University Earth Sciences Museum; Zofia Kielan-Jaworoska, Paleontologisk Museum, University of Oslo; James I. Kirkland (who also provided editorial review) and Michael L. Perry of the Dinamation International Society; D. P. Lane and R. M. Owens of the Palaeontological Association; Robert A. Long, Museum of Paleontology, University of California, Berkeley; James H. Madsen, Jr., Dinolab; Wade E. Miller and Kenneth Stadtman, Earth Science Museum, Brigham Young University; David B. Norman, Sedgwick Museum, University of Cambridge; Mary J. Odano, Valley Anatomical Preparations; Everett C. Olson, University of California, Los Angeles; John H. Ostrom, Yale Peabody Museum of Natural History; J. Michael Parrish, Northern Illinois University; Gregory S. Paul, Baltimore; H. Philip Powell, University Museum, Oxford; Robin E. H. Reid, Queen's University of Belfast; Thomas H. V. Rich, National Museum of Victoria; Dale A. Russell, National Museum of Canada; Frederick R. Schram, Zoologisch Museum, Amsterdam; Masahiro Tanimoto, Osaka, Japan; Philipe Taquet, Museum National d'Histoire Naturelle; Daniel W. Varner; Rupert Wild, Staatliches Museum für Natur, Paläontologische Abteilung; Peter Wellnhofer, Bayerische Staatssammlungen für Palao. & Hist. Geol.; Michael Williams, Cleveland Museum of Natural History; and Rainer Zangerl, formerly of the Field Museum.

Finally, thanks to Bob Allen; Chris and Paula Andress, and L. Edward Gastellum, all formerly of Petrified Forest National Park; Charlie, Ed and Stephen Chiodo of Chiodo Brothers Productions, Inc.; Coni Constantine, an inspiration; Nina N. Cummings, Monica Mikulski, Ron Testa and John Weinstein of The Field Museum; Stephan

Acknowledgments

A. and Sylvia J. Czerkas; Jim Danforth of Pterodactyl Productions; Allen A. Debus of the U.S. Environmental Protection Agency; Roger Dicken; Thomas R. Dickens; The Dinosaur Club of Southern California; Tracy Ford ("Dinosaur Hunter"); Brian Franczak; my mother, Julia Glut (for not diverting me from an obsession that began almost half a century ago); Mae Hai and Peter Pan (for translating into English passages from Chinese journals, Ania Bober for Russian); Mark Hallett; Dean Hannotte; Ray Harryhausen; Douglas Henderson; Greg Holmes; Jack Janzen; Hollister Knowlton, formerly of The Academy of Natural Sciences of Philadelphia; Joe Kubert; William Roddy Lozowski; Chris Mays and Michael Converse of Dinamation International Corp.; Melinda McNaughter of The Carnegie Museum of Natural History; Richard Mirissis; George Olshevsky of Mesozoic Meanderings and Archosaurian Articulations (for countless services, including the translation into English of Russian papers); David Peters; Raymond Rye of the National Museum of Natural History; the late Edward Schneider; Dave Tribble; the Peters Von Sholly; William G. Stout; David Thomas; Gordon Thomas; and George Turner.

I apologize to anyone I may have missed.

I have done my best to credit all illustrations used in this project to their original sources and to obtain permissions for their use when such permissions are required. In the case of scientific journals, I have made at least two written attempts to acquire permission to reprint illustrations originally appearing therein. Photographs of museum specimens and exhibits (except those taken by the author or other private photographers) are assumed to be owned by the respective institution housing that material, and are thus credited in the captions. The copyright for each privately taken photograph is presumably held by its respective photographer. Unless otherwise stated, the copyright for original artwork is held by the artist.

Foreword

When Sir Richard Owen coined the word *dinosaur* in 1842, he had no way of anticipating the chain reaction of "dinomania" that would continue to capture the world for over 150 years. Dinosaur science has completely changed within our own generation. New dinosaurs have been named at such an expanding rate that, by the year 2000, about half of all known dinosaurs will have been named in the reader's lifetime.

Dinosaurs are the most popular animals of all time because they represent everything humans love—adventure, power, lost worlds, mystery, and science. Since 1979, I have preached the word that, with dinosaurs, professors and teachers have in their grasp the best possible method to introduce the sciences to both adults and the young. Where else can one find a topic that practically guarantees perfect attention in every age group?

More books have been written about dinosaurs than any other group of fossils. It was not until 1972, however, that a new kind of book was written—the first *Dinosaur Dictionary*. It was written by Donald F. Glut. This format has subsequently been copied by other writers many times. Unfortunately, these copies are less critical in content, are written for young adults, and lack the depth of research that has gone into the present work. Previous books in this vein can all be replaced by this volume.

This current book is Don Glut's third, and most comprehensive contribution. It is one of the few books reviewed by the many international professional experts in the science of dinosaur paleontology. It contains a wealth of information for both the layman and the professional and is one of a handful of books that also includes the history of dinosaur nomenclature. It contains the best compilation of illustrations and data available anywhere about the original specimens that paleontologists have used to name species of dinosaurs. One of the most extensive bibliographies of the original literature on dinosaurs is contained herein as well.

Although there are many new pieces of dinosaur software on the computer market, both on CD-ROM and on the World Wide Web, this encyclopedia is far and away the best information source for any school, university, or public library, and for the dedicated lay individual. The media (because dinosaurs are always in the news), students and scholars, teachers and professors will save hours of research time with this one volume.

MICHAEL K. BRETT-SURMAN, PH.D.
George Washington University

Tyrannosaurus rex the classic "King Tyrant Lizard," reconstructed mounted skeleton (AMNH 5627). Photo by Anderson, courtesy Department of Library Services, American Museum of Natural History (neg. #315110).

Table of Contents

Preface

This compendium of dinosaur information is an outgrowth of my earlier books, *The Dinosaur Dictionary* (1972) and *The Complete Dinosaur Dictionary* (1992, originally published in 1982 with the title *The New Dinosaur Dictionary*). To readers familiar with those books, the differences between this encyclopedic work and those others should be obvious. The text of this work is far more detailed, complete and technical than either of those previous books ever attempted to be.

The virtually simultaneous idea and decision to do this project in its present format were spawned while I was attending talks at the "Dinosaurs Past and Present" symposium held in February, 1986, at the Museum of Natural History of Los Angeles County. (For the record, I "officially" announced the project while a number of symposium speakers and attendees were ordering dinners at the El Cholo Mexican restaurant in Los Angeles. Among the vertebrate paleontologists present at this gathering, if my memory is accurate, were Phil Currie, Jack Horner, Rob Long and Dale Russell.) The project has been ongoing since then.

The purpose of this book is twofold: To provide a handy reference tool for use by paleontologists, students, and libraries, and to offer information of a less technical nature to the amateur paleontologist, casual dinosaur enthusiast or interested general reader.

Regarding the first intent, this book does not presume to be part of that vast body of writings known as the "paleontological literature," which is based upon the original research of paleontologists, presented in peer-reviewed articles published in accredited scientific journals; nor is it an organ for formal taxonomic purposes. Rather, it is a compendium providing basic information and a synthesis of the writings of paleontologists based upon their work. I have throughout the text cited authors and dates referring to the original articles, which are listed in the bibliography. The approach I have taken in this project is fairly conservative. My own opinions should be taken as personal observations and not as any "official" pronouncements.

As to the second intent, I have tried to include enough less technical information to satisfy the more casual reader (the glossary helping these readers to understand the more advanced sections of the book). Perhaps this book will also serve to induce those dinosaur enthusiasts to seek out the professional journals and read the original papers.

One of the more visible ways this book differs from the two earlier "dictionaries" is in the approach to life restorations. All such illustrations (except those included for historical reasons) have been prepared by artists recognized in the field of vertebrate paleontology, who have based their restorations on the original fossil material. Missing from this book are "life restorations" of numerous dinosaur genera based on scrappy fossil remains (depicted in my own books as well as in popular books by other authors), such as *Acanthopholis* and *Palaeoscincus*, both known from very incomplete fossil material (*Palaeoscincus*, for example, founded upon a single tooth). Many misconceptions about dinosaurs have been perpetuated via the distribution of such mostly hypothetical and often fanciful illustrations. Rather than contribute further to such misinformation, I have included restorations of only those dinosaurian genera known from fossil remains sufficient to make a reasonably accurate picture of how that animal looked when alive.

Vertebrate paleontology is a perpetually evolving science. New dinosaur fossils are constantly being discovered, and new taxa, new or revised descriptions of genera and species, revisions in dinosaurian systematics, and other information regarding these extinct animals unceasingly appear in the literature. What is generally accepted as correct today may be regarded as inaccurate tomorrow. Since this book went to press, some of the material it contains will almost certainly have gone out of date.

Revising a book of this size every few years to keep it "up to date" would be a monstrous (and quite expensive, both to the publisher as well as the purchaser) undertaking. Therefore, it is the intent of the author not necessarily to revise this book *per se* for future editions; instead, new genera and species, revised classifications, corrections, deletions and other such information may be dealt with supplementary volumes. If such a plan is carried out (and done so successfully), this project should remain current and open-ended.

I ask the reader to understand that, in a project of this magnitude involving such a mass of names, dates and facts, errors—especially those of the typographical species—are likely to creep into the text. I ask that the reader kindly point out such errors to me by letter in care of the publisher, so that they can be corrected in some future edition.

DONALD F. GLUT
Burbank, California

I: A Background

Dinosaurs, in the "classical" sense (*i.e.*, excluding their apparent descendants, the birds), comprise one of the most successful terrestrial vertebrate groups ever to rule this planet, having occupied many terrestrial niches for approximately 150 million years. These fascinating animals ranged in size from the diminutive to the gigantic, and often assumed spectacular appearances. They are known today only from their fossil remains and traces and from what information can be extrapolated from these fossils.

Ever since their bones were first discovered and recognized as such, dinosaurs have been objects of fascination for both scientists and laymen. Dinosaurian remains may be regarded as clues in a "who done it?" mystery, global in scope and spanning an entire geological era, requiring the efforts, interpretations and speculations of a scientist-detective (*i.e.*, a vertebrate paleontologist) to solve at least part of that mystery. The study and classification of dinosaurs contribute to piecing together the complete and puzzling history of our Earth. The interpretation of the preserved remains of dinosaurs and other extinct organisms also stimulates the public's imagination as paleontologists attempt to decipher what these creatures might have been like as living animals.

Dinosaurian bones have probably been known for many centuries, although their origins had generally been attributed to dragons, human giants, and other fanciful monsters. Indeed, human beings probably encountered unidentified dinosaur fossils throughout history and prehistory. Dong (1987), in his book *Dinosaurs from China*, cited a probable discovery of dinosaurian bones in the present area of Santai, at Wucheng, in the vicinity of the southern Qinling Mountains, in the Province of Sichuan, during the Western Jin Dynasty (A.D. 265–317), recorded in a book by Chang Qu. Dong noted that, in earlier centuries, fossilized vertebrate remains found in that

Photo by the author

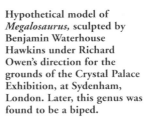

Hypothetical model of *Megalosaurus*, sculpted by Benjamin Waterhouse Hawkins under Richard Owen's direction for the grounds of the Crystal Palace Exhibition, at Sydenham, London. Later, this genus was found to be a biped.

country were referred to as "dragon bones," the dragon being a Chinese symbol for both justice and power.

In 1676, the Reverend Robert Plot figured what appears to have been the distal end of a femur of the theropod dinosaur, *Megalosaurus* (see *Megalosaurus* entry). Plot, however, believed that the specimen had human origins. Not until the first half of the nineteenth century were dinosaurian remains identified as those of an entirely new group of reptiles.

Simpson (1942), in a review detailing the beginnings of vertebrate paleontology in North America, cited a passage from an unpublished manuscript intended for the *Proceedings of the American Philosophical Society*. This piece, dated October 5, 1787, reported "A large thigh bone found near Woodbury creek in Glocester [*sic*] county, N.J." which was described "by Mr. Matlack and Dr. Wistar." There were plans at the time for Matlack and Wistar, with a Dr. Rodgers, to search for more of the skeleton. This specimen could have belonged to *Hadrosaurus* (not named until 1858; see *Hadrosaurus* entry). If so, this would have constituted the first dinosaurian remains discovered in North America. Unfortunately, as Simpson pointed out, the paper describing the fossil was never printed and the results of any subsequent search never recorded.

Comparative anatomist Sir Richard Owen (1802–94), who coined the word *Dinosauria*.

Courtesy The Field Museum (neg. #66187).

Traditional depiction of *Apatosaurus excelsus* as a ponderous amphibious animal, with tail dragging, head based on that of *Camarasaurus*, from a mural (circa. 1926–31) by Charles R. Knight.

A Background

Courtesy Queensland Museum

Top: Painting of *Rhoeto-saurus brownei* by Douglas S. Annand during the late 1920s under direction of Heber A. Longman, Largely based on a sculpture of *Camarasaurus* by E. S. Christman, again portraying sauropods living in swamps and dragging their tails. Right: Hypothetical life restorations of *Iguanodon*, sculpted by Hawkins between 1882–84 under Owen's direction, for the Crystal Palace Exhibition. The "hose horn" was later found to be a spiked thumb.

Photo by the author

quite unlike modern lizards. On August 2, 1841, in an address to the British Association for the Advancement of Science, Owen proposed that all of these forms be recognized as a "distinct tribe or suborder of Saurian reptiles." In 1942, Owen termed this new group *Dinosauria*, combining the superlative form of the Greek words *deinos* (for "fearfully great," the adjective form meaning "terrible") with *sauros* (for "lizard").

Following Owen's embracing of the then known forms of dinosaurs into a single group, more dinosaur discoveries were made in other countries. Before the turn of the century, a wealth of dinosaurian remains had been collected in North America as well as Belgium[*]. Today, dinosaur specimens have been

---

[*]*The early days of dinosaur discoveries have been discussed in more detail in many popular books including* Dinosaurs: Their Discovery and World *(1961),* Men and Dinosaurs *(1968) and* Dinosaurs: An Illustrated History *(1983), all by Edwin H. Colbert;* The Hot-Blooded Dinosaurs *(1975), by Adrian J. Desmond;* The Day of the Dinosaur *(1978), by John Man; and* The Illustrated Encyclopedia of Dinosaurs *(1986), by David B. Norman.*

Courtesy National Museum of Natural History, Smithsonian Institution (neg. #28531)

Traditional but outmoded interpretation of *Stegosaurus stenops,* one of a series of dinosaur models sculpted by paleontologist Charles Whitney Gilmore, and distributed to museums during the early 1900s.

The first dinosaurian genus to be formally named and described was the carnivorous *Megalosaurus*, the remains of which included an incomplete lower jaw found near Stonesfield in north Oxfordshire, England (see *Megalosaurus* entry). The fossils were described in 1824 by William Buckland. Following this historical find, the remains of two other large and equally fantastic reptiles, both herbivores, *Iguanodon* and the armored *Hylaeosaurus* (see individual entries), were named in England.

These and additional early British discoveries of a fragmentary nature prompted Sir Richard Owen (1802–1894), a leading comparative anatomist who would eventually become the first superintendent of the British Museum (Natural History) (now The Natural History Museum, London), to regard *Iguanodon*, *Megalosaurus*, and *Hylaeosaurus* as elephantine reptiles

Courtesy The Field Museum (neg. #59442)

Classic confrontation of horned dinosaur *Triceratops horridus* and carnivorous *Tyrannosaurus rex,* from a mural (circa. 1926–1930) by Charles R. Knight. Although somewhat inaccurate today, this interpretation correctly depicts a theropod with tail off the ground.

During the 1960s, artist Zdenek Burian's "modernized" life restorations strongly influenced public awareness of dinosaurs, although some of the ideas portrayed in his paintings (*e.g.* sauropods such as *Brachiosaurus brancai* deeply submerged in water) were later refuted.

Stegosaurus stenops, mural painted circa 1926–31 by artist Charles R. Knight (1874–1953), whose interpretations of extinct life forms most strongly influenced the public for almost a century.

collected from every continent on the globe, including, more recently, Antarctica.

It must be stressed, however, that although it is a commonly believed that all or most kinds of large prehistoric reptiles fall under an umbrella category "dinosaur," the Dinosauria only includes those reptiles that meet certain diagnostic criteria. Various contemporaneous marine reptiles (such as mosasaurs,

Late Triassic scene by artist Rudolph Zallinger ("cartoon") for Pulitzer Prize-winning mural painted circa 1940, including large prosauropod *Plateosaurus engelhardti,* small theropod *Podokesaurus holyokensis,* (middle) cynodont *Cynognathus,* and (right foreground) sphenosuchian archosaur *Saltoposuchus.*

plesiosaurs, and ichthyosaurs), flying reptiles (pterosaurs), so-called "thecodontians," pelycosaurs, therapsids, crocodilians, lizards, snakes, chelonians (turtles and tortoises) and other reptilian forms are *not* dinosaurs and will, therefore, not be dealt with in this text.

By the 1930s, although the dinosaurs had become an icon in the consciousness of the general public, formal studies of dinosaurian remains had become rather neglected by the paleontological community. Dinosaurs, then regarded in the traditional sense as slow and sluggish dim-witted reptiles, were generally viewed by scientists as evolutionary dead ends, leaving behind no descendants and serving as interesting curiosities hardly worth much serious study. That view was dramatically altered when Ostrom (1969*a*) published his discovery in Montana of a quite bird-like new genus of carnivorous dinosaur, which he named *Deinonychus* (see *Deinonychus* entry). Ostrom showed that *Deinonychus* deviated greatly from the older image of dinosaurs that scientists and laymen alike had come to expect. To the contrary, the evidence strongly suggested that *Deinonychus* was an active creature with a relatively large brain. Its skeletal structure brought to light the very close relationship between at least some dinosaurs and birds, and also prompted new, sometimes radical speculations regarding dinosaurian physiology and behavior. Thanks largely to Ostrom's work on *Deinonychus,* the study of dinosaurs had again become an active pursuit among vertebrate paleontologists.

The discovery of *Deinonychus* inspired modern vertebrate paleontologists to regard dinosaurs as something far more significant than curiosities of an ancient world. Scientists again began hunting for the fossilized remains of these fabulous creatures. Some of the most spectacular dinosaur discoveries have been made since 1970. Indeed, a review of the publication dates of dinosaur names used extensively in this encyclopedia reveals the great number of new genera and species that have been described since the early 1970s. These past decades have seen a veritable explosion of ideas and speculations regarding dinosaurs. Consequently the study of dinosaurs again occupies a vital niche in the field of vertebrate paleontology.

The Mesozoic Era

Dinosaurs thrived during a geological expanse of time called the Mesozoic era (approximately 248 to about 64 million years ago). The Mesozoic (meaning "middle life") is the second in a series of three geological eras during which complex life forms with hard parts like shells and bone diversified, representing the last 600 million years on earth. The first era is the Paleozoic (meaning "ancient life," consisting of numerous invertebrates and vertebrates); the last era is the Cenozoic ("recent life," in which mammals and birds were the dominant land vertebrates). As the Mesozoic Era was dominated by numerous reptilian forms, it is often referred to as the "Age of Reptiles."

In addition to the appearance of the dinosaurs, it was during the Mesozoic Era that birds and mammals first appeared, as well as a number of modern insect groups and the first flowering plants.

During the Mesozoic, the world's continents gradually broke apart from a single supercontinent (named Pangaea by the German geographer Alfred

Courtesy The Field Museum (neg. #GEO79514).

Skull of the Late Cretaceous crocodilian *Leidyosuchus riggsi*.

Early Triassic (pre-dinosaur) scene painted by Charles R. Knight in 1931 of several carnivorous cynodant *Cynognathus* and herbivorous *Kannemeyeria*, dicynodonts from the Karroo beds of South Africa.

Marine reptiles of the Early Jurassic: The long-necked plesiosaur *Plesiosaurus* and ichthyosaur ("fish lizard") *Stenopterygius*, painted circa 1926–31 by Charles R. Knight.

Courtesy The Field Museum (neg. #75016).

Courtesy The Field Museum (Neg. #72379).

Illustration by Doug Henderson.

The Late Triassic in what is now the Petrified Forest in Arizona: Giant phytosaur *Rutiodon lithodendrorum* and group of small and primitive ornithischian dinosaurs. Flora includes horsetails (*Equisetites bradyi*, foreground), ferns (*Clathropteris walkerii*, extreme foregound, also covering roots of left-center log), cycad (*Lyssoxylon grigsbyi*, lower right) stem, tree fern (*Itopsidema vancleavei*, left center) stem, and conifer (*Brachyphyllum hegewaldia*) branches.

Wegener, who first proposed this idea of "continental displacement" in 1915) in which all the large land masses were joined together. Moving as part of tectonic plates (great plates of the Earth's crust) floating on magma heated by the Earth's core, the continents shifted several centimeters per year throughout the Mesozoic.

The Mesozoic era is divided into three geological periods, the Triassic, the Jurassic, and the Cretaceous:

The Triassic period (about 245 to 208 million years ago) was named after the threefold geological sequence in Germany, formed by rocks of this age. During this period, the Paleozoic supercontinent Pangaea still existed. By the end of the period, Pangaea was starting to break up into two parts, Laurasia (North America, Europe, and much of Asia) and Gondwana (South America, Africa, Antarctica, Australia, and India).

The Triassic climate of North America, Europe, and much of Asia was consistently warm and included large areas that were quite arid, with extensive deserts and sand dunes not uncommon.

Courtesy The Field Museum (neg. #P.C. 182-G).

Skull of Late Cretaceous mosasaur *Tylosaurus dyspelor*.

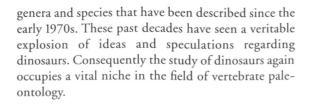

Skeletons of Late Cretaceous mosasaurs *Tylosaurus proriger* and (upper right) *Platecarpus.*

Skeleton (cast) of *Rutiodan* sp., giant (about 5.6 meters or 19 feet long, .9 meters or about three feet high) phytosaur collected from the badlands of Petrified Forest National Park, Arizona, displayed at Rainbow Forest Museum. Such predators, the dominant animal forms of the Late Triassic, coexisted with the earliest dinosaurs.

In the seas, modern groups of invertebrates replaced the archaic forms of the Paleozoic era. All of the major present-day groups of echinoderms existed by this time, while hexacorals made their first appearance. More advanced types of fishes appeared, as did the first ichthyosaurs, plesiosaurs, and other reptiles.

On land, reptiles of various kinds dominated the land as well as the air (the most primitive pterosaurs). Nonmammalian synapsids ("mammal-like reptiles") were especially abundant at the beginning of the Triassic. By the Middle Triassic, however, these were partially replaced by the earliest archosaurs. In turn, by the latter part of the Triassic period, these primitive archosaurs had been replaced by the dinosaurs.

Late Jurassic sea life, northern Rocky Mountain area, including squid-like belemnites. Diorama by George Marchand.

A Background

Skeleton of *Diplodocus carnegii* (CM 84, 94 and 307; skull based on CM 662 and USNM 2673), recovered from the Morrison Formation at Sheep Creek, Wyoming.

Huene (1907–07) and other workers reported numerous supposed dinosaurian remains, including teeth and postcranial bones, from the Middle Triassic of Europe. These specimens, however, have all been subsequently identified as belonging to non-dinosaurian reptiles (mostly prolacertiforms, "thecodontians" or placodonts; see Colbert 1970*b*; Wild 1973; Chatterjee 1985; Galton 1985*a*) or as indeterminate reptiles. Furthermore, some dinosaur-yielding South American formations once believed to be of Middle Triassic (Ladinian) age have since been dated more accurately as Late Triassic (Carnian; below) (see Anderson and Cruickshank 1981; Anderson 1981; Tucker and Benton 1982; Benton 1983, 1984*a*).

However, as noted by Rogers, Swisher, Sereno, Monetta, Forster and Martínez (1993), dinosaurs

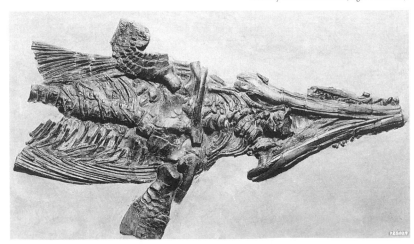

Partial skeleton Early–?Late Jurassic ichthyosaur *Leptopterygius tenuirostris*.

Late Cretaceous dinosaur egg from the Gobi Desert, Mongolia.

Tracks of Late Jurassic dinosaur named *Gigandipus caudatus*, foot correspoonding to that of *Allosaurus*.

seem to have originated sometime during the Middle to Late Triassic. The most complete skeletal remains of early dinosaurs (the small, possible theropods *Herrerasaurus* and *Eoraptor*, and ornithischian *Pisanosaurus*) have been found in the Ischigualasto Formation of Argentina. Using radiometric dating methods, Rogers *et al.* concluded that the Ischigualasto rocks were some 227.8± 0.3 million years old, of middle Carnian age. By 228 million years ago, the major dinosaurian lineages—Theropoda, Sauropodomorpha and Ornithischia— were already established, with theropods already among the important carnivorous tetrapods. Small to large prosauropods made their debut in the Late Triassic and ornithischians remained quite primitive through the end of this period.

The three periods of the Mesozoic Era have been further divided into various geological stages, all of which have been based on sequences of marine sedimentary rocks and dated through various scientific means (the best dating technique involving the analysis of radioactive isotopes, present in many elements, which decay at a constant rate).

The Late Triassic period is divided into the major stages of Carnian and Norian (geologic time scales from Harland, Cox, Llewellyn, Smith and

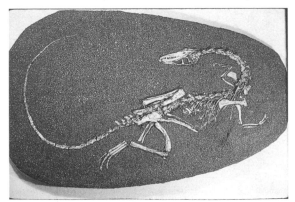

Cast of holotype (AMNH 7224) skeleton of Late Triassic carnivorous dinosaur *Rioarribasaurus colberti*.

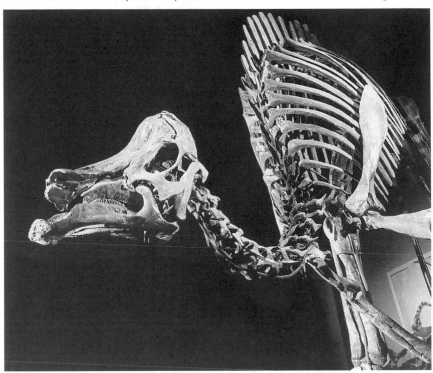

Skeleton of Late Cretaceous duckbilled dinosaur *Hypacrosaurus altispinus*.

Jim Adams removes sandstone from *Camarasaurus* coracoid on the Great Wall of Dinosaurs, at Dinosaur National Monument, richest North American site (Morrison Formation) for Late Jurassic dinosaur fossils.

A Background

Thanks to D. Baird, courtesy Württemberg, National History Collection, Stuttgart, Germany.

Skeleton of Late Triassic prosauropod dinosaur *Plateosaurus engelhardti* (originally *P. trossingensis*).

Courtesy The Field Museum (neg. #66186).

Late Cretaceous Kansas sea populated by such reptiles as the pterosaur *Pteranodon,* mosasaur (Marine lizard) *Tylosaurus,* and turtle *Protostega,* mural by Charles R. Knight, painted circa 1926–1931.

Courtesy The Field Museum (neg. #GEO79878).

Skull of giant Late Cretaceous mosasaur *Tylosaurus dyspelor.*

Skeleton of Early-Late Jurassic mesosuchian crocodile *Steneosaurus.*

Courtesy The Field Museum (neg. #63219).

Illustration by Doug Henderson, From *Dinosaurs: A Global View,* by Czerkas and Caerkas, published by Dragon's World Ltd. and its copublishers.

Carnivorous dinosaur *Ornitholestes hermanni* in Late Jurassic Colorado.

Courtesy Institute of Paleobiology, Warsaw (neg. #LB38720).

Skeleton of Late Cretaceous carnivorous dinosaur *Tyrannosaurus bataar* (originally referred to *Tarbosaurus*) found during the Polish-Mongolian Paleontological Expedition in 1964 at Tsagan Khushu, Nemegt Basin, Gobi Desert, Mongolia.

Late Jurassic coral island of southern Germany, scene painted in 1931 by Charles R. Knight, fauna including the small theropod dinosaur *Compsognathus longipes,* bird *Archaeopteryx lithographica,* and pterosaur *Rhamphor-hynchus bucklandi.*

Courtesy The Field Museum (neg. #75017).

Walters, 1989), the earliest unquestionable dinosaurs being of Carnian age (see right).

The Jurassic Period (about 203 to 145.6 million years ago) was named for the Jura Mountains on the borders of France and Switzerland, an area in which marine rocks from this period are especially well represented. At the beginning of the Jurassic, Pangaea continued to split into several large segments, with Europe moving away from North America, forming a narrow northern Atlantic Ocean. By the Middle Jurassic, another body of water, the Turgai Sea, had

Late Triassic
NORIAN (223 to 208 million years ago)
CARNIAN (235 to 223 million years ago)

separated Europe from Asia.

By the Jurassic, most ancient Paleozoic mountain ranges had weathered down to low ranges of hills. The desert regions, so common during the Triassic, still existed but were reduced in size during the wetter Early Jurassic. The rather stable climate was generally mild and subtropical. Vegetation included conifers (which grew in thick forests), numerous cycads and cycadeoids, tree ferns, and ginkgo trees.

New forms of insects appeared during the Jurassic. Sea life included a vast number

Courtesy National Museum of Natural History, Smithsonian Institution (neg. #78138).

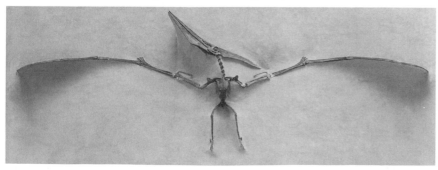

Skeleton of Late Cretaceous pterosaur *Pteranodon ingens,* wingspan approximately 7 meters (23 feet).

Courtesy Royal Tyrrell Museum/Alberta Community Development.

Skull of Late Cretaceous duckbilled dinosaur *Lambeosaurus lambei.*

A Background

Skeleton of Late Cretaceous plesiosaur *Morenosaurus stocki*. Inset: Skull of Late Cretaceous duckbilled dinosaur *Edmontosaurus*.

Skeleton of medium-sized pterosaur *Nyctosaurus gracilis*, wingspan 2.4 meters or 7–9 feet, from the Upper Cretaceous, Niobrara Formation of West Kansas.

of ammonites, shelled cephalopods that dominated all other invertebrate forms, with plesiosaurs and ichthyosaurs as the dominant marine reptiles. Primitive birds first appeared during this period, although the skies were dominated by pterosaurs.

Dinosaurs proliferated during the Jurassic, appearing in great numbers and forms. Giant theropods had been well established by this time, and sauropods replaced the last of the prosauropods, often attaining gigantic size. The Ornithischia mainly consisted of ornithopods, more advanced than those of the Triassic but not yet as advanced as the hadrosaurids of the next period, the plated and spined stegosaurs, as well as the earliest of the armored ankylosaurs.

The Jurassic period is divided into the major stages (shown on the following page).

The Cretaceous period (145.6 to 65 million years ago), the longest of the three Mesozoic periods, was named for the chalk that was laid down during this time in Europe. The continents were further separated from one another at the start of this period, with shallow seas starting to divide the southern continents. As South America and Africa were driven farther apart, the South Atlantic Ocean began to open up. At the same time, the Labrador Sea appeared

(Bottom of display) skull of Early-Middle Jurassic ichthyosaur *Ichthyosaurus communis.*

Skeletons of Late Cretaceous carnivorous dinosaur *Albertosaurus libratus* (FMNH PR 308; skull cast of FMNH PR87469) and duckbilled dinosaur *Lambeosaurus lambei* (FMNH PR380; skull formerly CNHM UC1479), mounted in 1956 by Orville L. Gilpin.

A Background

Late Cretaceous underwater scene, Coon Creek, Tennessee, including seaweed, oysters, clams, scallops, snails, and ammonites.

LATE
TITHONIAN (152.1 to 145.6 million years ago)
KIMMERIDGIAN (154.7 to 152.1 million years ago)
OXFORDIAN (157.1 to 154.7 million years ago)

MIDDLE
CALLOVIAN (161.3 to 157.1 million years ago)
BATHONIAN (166.1 to 161.3 million years ago)
BAJOCIAN (173.5 to 166.1 million years ago)
AALENIAN (178 to 173.5 million years ago)

EARLY
TOARCIAN (187 to 178 million years ago)
PLIENSBACHIAN (194.5 to 187 million years ago)
SINEMURIAN (203.5 to 194.5 million years ago)
HETTANGIAN (208 to 203.5 million years ago)

in the Northern Hemisphere. By the Late Cretaceous, Africa and South America were separating with the intrusion of a spreading South Atlantic Ocean. North America and Europe were also separating further. Europe and Asia became divided by seaways, while North America was likewise divided by a large body of water called the Western Interior Seaway, extending from the present-day Gulf of Mexico into the Canadian North-West Territories. Such seaways isolated the various kinds of fauna which had spread everywhere. To the west of the Western Interior Seaway, the Rocky Mountains were beginning to rise. The Earth's great land masses were beginning to assume their present-day outlines.

Almost complete skeleton (USNM 4842) of *Triceratops horridus* (originally referred to as *T. prorsus*), collected under the supervision of John Bell Hatcher at Converse County, Wyoming, mounted by Charles Whitney Gilmore, missing parts supplied from other specimens or restored in plaster, hindfeet those of a duckbilled dinosaur.

Skull (ROM 1215) of Late Cretaceous armored dinosaur *Edmontonia rugosidens*.

In situ holotype skull (NMC 8535) of Late Cretaceous horned dinosaur *Anchiceratops longirostris.* Horseshoe Canyon Formation, Alberta.

Skeleton of *Mosasaurus conodon,* an 8.5-meter (29-foot) long Late Cretaceous marine lizard from South Dakota, skeleton of *Edmontosaurus annectens* in background.

Skeleton (cast of ROM 5091) of Late Jurassic theropod *Allosaurus fragilis,* collected from the Morrison Formation, Cleveland Lloyd Dinosaur Quarry, Utah. To the right is *Stegosaurus.*

The opening of the Cretaceous marked a continuation of the mild climate of the Jurassic, although dry areas existed in southern North America and Europe, while parts of eastern Asia seem to have been arid. More marked seasons began to occur during this period. By the end of the Cretaceous, the temperatures had become more variable, possibly the result of altered ocean currents and wind patterns caused by the "drifting" continents and spreading seas.

With this cooler climate, the flora of the Cretaceous also began to change. Towards the end of the period, the once abundant tropical and subtropical gymnosperm plant species were being replaced by flowering plants.

In the seas, the ammonites and belemnites were very abundant. Modern teleost fishes underwent a

Skeleton of Early-Middle Jurassic ichthyosaur *Stenopterygius gradricissus.*

spectacular evolutionary diversification. Amphibians were represented by the present-day groups (frogs, salamanders, and apodans). Although icthyosaurs were declining, plesiosaurs continued to prosper. Sea turtles had evolved to gigantic sizes, while mosasaurs, giant marine lizards, had become the seas' most vicious predators. Birds had evolved substantially since the Jurassic and were represented both by flying and flightless forms, but the skies continued to be the domain of the larger pterosaurs, some of which attained giant size.

The land was still ruled by dinosaurs, which included some groups that had persisted from the Jurassic. Theropods often attained gigantic sizes, and many of them evolved highly specialized adaptations. Sauropods were relatively rare in the Northern Hemisphere, and stegosaurs became extinct in the Early Cretaceous. The latter were replaced by a variety of ankylosaurs. The dominant herbivores in the Northern Hemisphere were the most derived of the ornithopods, the duckbilled hadrosaurs, which appeared and flourished during the Late Cretaceous. The Late Cretaceous also marked the arrival of the dome-headed pachycephalosaurs and the horned ceratopsians, both groups representing some of the last dinosaurs to survive until the end of the period.

Illustration by Doug Henderson. From *Dinosaurs: A Global View*, by Czerkas and Czerkas, published by Dragon's World Ltd., and its co-edition publishers.

Scene of Late Cretaceous Montana featuring carnivorous dinosaur *Albertosaurus*.

Thanks to D. Baird, photo by Sidney Prentice, courtesy Carnegie Museum of Natural History.

Skull (CM 1219) of Late Cretaceous horned dinosaur *Triceratops prorsus* (originally referred to *T. brevicornis*).

The Cretaceous period is divided, in descending order, into the following major stages:

LATE
MAASTRICHTIAN (74 to 65 million years ago)
CAMPANIAN (83 to 74 million years ago)
SANTONIAN (86.6 to 83 million years ago)
CONIACIAN (88.5 to 86.6 million years ago)
TURONIAN (90.4 to 88.5 million years ago)
CENOMANIAN (97.5 to 90.4 million years ago)

EARLY
ALBIAN (112 to 97.5 million years ago)
APTIAN (124.5 to 112 million years ago)
BARREMIAN (131.8 to 124.5 million years ago), possibly including the Weald clay division of the Wealden series
HAUTERIVIAN (135 to 131.8 million years ago), possibly, with the Valganinian stage, including the Hatsings beds division of the Wealden series
VALANGINIAN (140.7 to 135 million years ago)
BERRIASIAN (145.6 to 140.7 million years ago)

Courtesy J. H. Madson, Jr. and Utah Museum of Natural History, University of Utah.

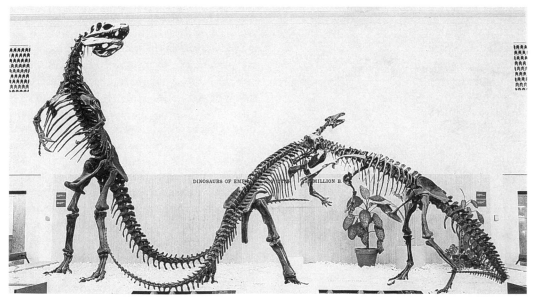

DINOSAURS OF EMP   MILLION B

Skeletons of Late Jurassic dinosaurs, the theropod *Allosaurus fragilis* and (center) ornithopod *Camptosaurus dispar*, from the Cleveland-Lloyd Dinosaur Quarry.

Dinosaur Origins and Relationships

Dinosaurs, as well as other forms of extinct (and extant) life, have traditionally been classified according to the Linnaean system of classification, named for its originator, Swedish naturalist Carolus Linnaeus (Carl von Linné [1707–1778]. In his system, organisms are grouped together into a hierarchical system of taxa, each of which are characterized by specific characters or sets of characters. The Linnaean system reflects divisions among these groups in a nested or hierarchical arrangement, based on a similarity of form (later modified to reflect evolutionary theories). The name of a single taxon represents a suite of characters that characterize all its constituent taxa. Each taxon is assigned a *rank* (*i.e.* suborder, family, *etc.*).

In recent years, most biologists have reclassified dinosaurs and other life forms using the newer method of cladistics, which does *not* assign a *rank* to any taxon (although the term "family" is still generally used). Developed by the German entomologist Willi Hennig, cladistics is concerned with the establishment of monophyletic taxa (see Hennig 1966) or "clades." A clade constitutes a real genetic entity in the history of life. It can be diagnosed by "synapomorphies," or derived characters shared by all the original members of a group. Synapomorphies are the sole criterion for delineating monophyletic taxa, and only from synapomorphies can phylogenetic affinity

be inferred. A common ancestor for a taxon must exhibit all of its synapomorphies. Traditional Linnaean classification have often relied upon the concept of the "grade" that can be diagnosed by both primitive and derived characters that delineate a certain grade, or level, of evolution.

When assessing phylogenetic relations among fossil taxa, synapomorphies are identified by a method called "outgroup comparison" (see Hennig). When a character exhibits two or more states within a monophyletic group (or "ingroup"), the state also found in its relatives ("outgroup") is regarded as a shared ("plesiomorphic") character, and that occurring only within the group as derived ("apomorphic"). However, a cladistic analysis of most living taxa shows that no single hierarchic arrangement is entirely congruent with all characters. Not all synapomorphies accompany the appearance of each new lineage during the phylogenetic history of a clade and are manifest in all descendants. Hence, incongruence or "homoplasy" (an evolutionary reversal, convergence, or parallelism) is present in many such arrangements. In choosing between alternate arrangements, cladists usually invoke the criterion of "parsimony" to arrive at the arrangement that requires the least number of homoplasies.

An example of the classification of one genus of dinosaur, *Triceratops*, using both Linnaean and cladistic methods, is shown in the diagram at left:

From a Linnaean perspective, within the kingdom Animalia, is the phylum Chordata, which includes all animals with a notochord, central nervous system above the notochord, gill slits, and a usually closed vascular system with contractible sections. Among the Chordata, the subphylum Vertebrata comprises all animals with backbones.

True reptiles first appeared during the Pennsylvanian Period (the upper part of the so-called "Coal Age"). The most important group, Diapsida, is characterized by the presence of two openings in the skull behind each orbit. Included within this diverse group are Squamata (lizards and snakes), Archosauromorpha, and all the marine reptiles other than turtles. From cladistic analyses by various workers (Gauthier 1984; Benton 1983, 1984*a*, 1985; Evans 1984, 1988), Archosauromorpha includes *Trilophosaurus*, Rhynchosauria (highly specialized, beak-snouted herbivores), Prolacertilia (superficially lizard-like forms), and Archosauria.

Archosauria ("ruling reptiles") has been defined by different authors who have included within it various sets of lower taxa. Benton (1990) diagnosed the group by the following characters: Possession of antorbital fenestra; postfrontal reduced; postparietals absent or fused; caudal border of infratemporal fenestra bowed; laterally compressed serrated teeth; loss

LINNAEAN

Class REPTILIA
  Subclass ARCHOSAURIA
    Order ORNITHISCHIA
      Suborder CERATOPSIA
        Family CERATOPSIDAE
          Subfamily CHASMOSAURINAE
            Genus *Triceratops*

CLADISTIC

DINOSAURIA
  ORNITHISCHIA
    CERAPODA
      MARGINOCEPHALIA
        CERATOPSIA
          NEOCERATOPSIA
            CERATOPSIDAE
              CHASMOSAURINAE
                Triceratops

of trunk intercentra; laterosphenoid ossification in the braincase; no ectepicondylar groove or foramen on humerus; femur with fourth trochanter. Archosauria includes Crocodylotarsi (phytosaurs, aetosaurs, rausichians, and crocodylomorphs [crocodilians and crocodile-like forms]) and Ornithosuchia (the dinosaur-bird line).

For many years, dinosaurs had been generally regarded as descended during the Late Triassic from a group of archosaurs traditionally lumped together as a group called Thecodontia ("socket-toothed"). Gauthier (1984) pointed out that "Thecodontia" represents an artificial grouping of many archosaurian groups that evolved teeth in sockets in the jaws. The name should be abandoned. [Note: Although now regarded as an obsolete and undefinable term, "Thecodontia"—flagged by quotation marks—may appear from time to time in the text.] (For a complete discussion of how dinosaurs are classified cladistically, see pages 11–30 [by Benton] in *The Dinosauria*, edited by Weishampel, Dodson and Osmólska, 1990.)

Belonging to the Archosauria, the genus *Euparkaria*, from the Early Triassic of South Africa, seems to have been near a pivotal spot in the division of two archosaurian groups, Crocodylotarsi (leading to crocodiles) and Ornithosuchia (leading to dinosaurs and birds). The systematic placement of this small, primitive reptile has been problematic. Early archosaurs possess a primitive ankle. In the derived ankle, the ankle bends along a simple hinge between the astragalus-calcaneum and the rest of the foot, called a mesotarsal ankle. Cruickshank and Benton (1985) have interpreted the ankle structure in *Euparkaria* as simply being a modified primitive mesotarsal (or MPM) type, while Gauthier (1986) and Parrish (1986) regarded it as the more derived crocodile-reversed (CR) type (in which a peg on the astragalus fits into the open acetabulum of the ilium). Gauthier also pointed out that *Euparkaria* shares with Ornithosuchia (see below) a reduced gracile squamosal and an astragalus lacking a ventral flange. These latter interpretations suggest that *Euparkaria* may be close to both ornithosuchids and dinosaurs.

Among the various archosaurian taxa that had been grouped into the "Thecodontia," one group is the Ornithosuchia (see Gauthier 1986), which includes archosaurs possessing the crocodile-reversed ankle structure and those with an advanced mesotarsal (astragalus and calcaneum are strongly attached to the tibia and fibula, the ankle bending along the astragalus-calcaneum and the rest of the foot), both of which allowed for an erect gait rather than the sprawling or variable gait of more primitive reptiles. The

ankle structure in dinosaurs (as well as birds and pterosaurs) was of the advanced mesotarsal condition.

Ornithosuchians first appeared in the Early Triassic. Gauthier characterized the Ornithosuchia as having a long and narrow pubis, ischium with reduced contacts, femur with lesser trochanter and sharp fourth trochanter, and reduced fifth toe. As now regarded, the Ornithosuchia includes the Late Triassic Ornithosuchidae (superficially very dinosaur-like bipedal forms with a crocodile-reversed ankle), *Lagosuchus*, Pterosauria, and Dinosauria (including birds). Based upon a cladistic analysis of archosaurs, Sereno (1991b) divided the Archosauria into two groups, the Crurotarsi and the Ornithodira (see systematics section), Ornithodira including such taxa as Pterosauria and Dinosauromorpha, the latter including *Lagosuchus* and Dinosauria [and Aves]).

Pterosaurs, a group of winged archosaurs sometimes mislabeled "flying dinosaurs" in popular books, have been known since at least 1784, when a small skeleton (of the genus *Pterodactylus*) from a limestone quarry in Eichstátt, was described by naturalist Cosmo Alessandro Collini. Traditionally, Pterosauria has been classified as a separate archosaurian order related to the dinosaurian "orders" Saurischia and Ornithischia, as well as to Crocodylia and "Thecodontia." Gauthier (1984) argued that Pterosauria should be regarded as the sister-group of Dinosauria, apparently possessing very dinosaur-like hindlimbs. More recently, Sereno (1991b) argued that Pterosauria should occupy a basal position within Ornithodira.

Lagosuchus was originally described by Romer (1971) on the basis of an isolated hindlimb from the Chañares Formation (Triassic) in La Rioja Province, Argentina. It was referred by Romer to the Pseudosuchia, then a suborder of "Thecodontia." Romer observed that the tarsal joints (the proximal tarsals functionally part of the lower leg, the distal tarsals united with the foot) is the kind found in dinosaurs. Though Romer found that the tarsal construction suggested a connection with a radiation leading toward "coelurosaurian" dinosaurs, he doubted that *Lagosuchus* could be placed close to the direct line leading to such dinosaurs.

Bonaparte (1975a) placed *Lagosuchus* into its own family Lagosuchidae, suggesting that this genus could have been the ancestor from which all other dinosaurs evolved. *Lagosuchus* does, in fact, possess some characters shared with all dinosaurs (*e.g.* advanced mesotarsal joint and distinct cervical and dorsal vertebra). Some workers have, therefore, regarded *Lagosuchus* as the earliest known dinosaur. More recent work by Bonaparte has shown that the ankle joint in *Lagosuchus* may not be as dinosaur-like as once interpreted. For the present, at least, *Lagosuchus* remains referred to the Ornithosuchia.

Birds and Dinosaurs

The relationship of dinosaurs to birds has been a matter of debate since the nineteenth century, when dinosaur footprints were first misinterpreted as having been made by birds.

Traditionally, the genus *Archaeopteryx* has been celebrated as the earliest known bird, albeit one with teeth and other reptilian features. Recently this genus was referred to as "the earliest undisputed bird" (Currie and Zhao 1993).

The first fossil specimen of type species *Archaeopteryx lithographica* was a single feather discovered in 1860 in the fine-grained lithographic Solnhofen Limestone (Upper Jurassic) of Franconia, Bavaria. The find was significant in constituting the first evidence that birds had existed as far back as the Jurassic period.

Shortly after this discovery was made, a complete skeleton of *Archaeopteryx* including well-preserved feather impressions was found in the same quarry, just two years after the publication of Charles Darwin's *On the Origin of Species* (1859). This specimen seemed to be a so-called "missing link" or intermediate form between two groups of animals. While some skeletal characters distinguish this genus from maniraptoran theropods (those excluding aves), certain other features are clearly avian. Moreover, some of the avian features of this specimen are indicative of modern birds, with the identical count of primary and secondary flight feathers and the structure of the fight feathers (Heilmann 1926). This "London specimen," described by Meyer (1861*b*), is today regarded by most vertebrate paleontologists as the single most important vertebrate fossil that has ever been collected.

After reexamining the five then known specimens of *Archaeopteryx* (to date, seven specimens representing this genus have been collected), Ostrom (1973) observed that the genus is more similar to certain Jurassic and Cretaceous theropods than to any known "thecodontian" (so-called "thecodontians," now regarded as an artificial assemblage, but then believed to be ancestral to birds). Furthermore, the "Eicstätt specimen," identified as *Archaeopteryx* by Mayr (1973), had for more than two decades been mislabeled as *Compsognathus*, a theropod dinosaur contemporaneous with *Archaeopteryx*. Ostrom pointed out that, had the "London" and "Berlin"

Archaeopteryx specimens not included well-defined feather impressions, they too would have been mistaken for small theropods.

Ostrom (1973; 1975*a*, 1975*b*, 1976, 1985; 1990) observed numerous anatomical features common both to *Archaeopteryx* and dromaeosaurids and other small theropods. Included in this list was the striking similarity between the forelimb bones, particularly of the manus, of *Archaeopteryx* and such theropods as *Ornitholestes*, *Deinonychus*, and *Velociraptor*, these suggesting that the many derived characters common to this genus and "coelurosaurs" support the theory that an Early or Mid-Jurassic theropod was ancestral to *Archaeopteryx* and later birds. In his review of the Dromaeosauridae, Ostrom (1990) stressed that these similarities "strongly indicate a close phyletic relationship between dromaeosaurids and primitive birds," but did not label *Archaeopteryx* as a theropod.

Thulborn (1984), in his own study of the avian relationships of *Archaeopteryx* and the origin of birds, concluded that this genus is no more closely related to modern birds than are several types of theropod dinosaurs (including tyrannosaurids and ornithomimids). Believing that *Archaeopteryx* was not ancestral to modern birds, nor was it a convincing "intermediate" between reptiles and birds, Thulborn recommended transferring *Archaeopteryx* to the Theropoda.

Following the work begun by Ostrom in the 1970s, it has become generally (though not universally; see below) accepted that birds descended from a small theropod ancestor. From a cladistic perspective, then, the group Aves must be classified within Dinosauria; or, perhaps more dramatically stated, all birds, both extinct and living, *are dinosaurs*.

Although *Archaeopteryx* has traditionally been included within Aves, Gauthier (1986) proposed that the later taxon be restricted to the crown group of living birds, thereby excluding *Archaeopteryx*. To embrace *Archaeopteryx* and all other birds, Gauthier (1986) erected the new theropod group Aviale, also including the Dromaeosauridae and Troodontidae.

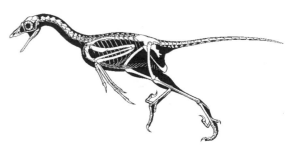

Skeletal reconstruction of the avialian theropod *Archaeopteryx lithographica* by Gregory S. Paul.

Gauthier (1986) diagnosed Avialae by the following synapomorphies: Premaxillae elongate, narrow, more pointed anteriorly, nasal processes longer; maxillary process of premaxilla reduced so that maxilla contributes broadly in external naris; enlarged brain/basicranium; bicondyled quadrate displaced from distal position on opisthotic to more anteromedial position in contact with prootic; maxillary and dentary teeth reduced in size and number (or lost), crowns unserrated, roots enlarged, completely enclosing replacement teeth within them; furcula robust (for hypertrophied flight musculature); scapula with more or less well-developed acromion process (for ligamentous connection to clavicle); length to breadth ratio of scapula at midlength exceeding nine (except in penguins), scapula tapering distally; acrocoracoid tuberosity larger than in other coelurosaurs; coracoid enlarged, inflected posteromedially more so than in other coelurosaurs; forelimbs and hands very long, forearm more than 87 percent humerus length, metacarpal II approaching or exceeding one half humerus length; ischium compressed, dorsoventrally deep; tibia, fibula, and metatarsals relatively more elongate relative to femur that in other theropods, regardless of body size; fibula attenuate distally, may not extend to end of tibia; proximal tarsals fused to tibia–fibula and (in adults) to each other; distal tarsals and metatarsals fused at least distally in mature adults, metatarsal I attached to distal quarter of metatarsal II; tail reduced to no more than 23 free caudal vertebrae; feathers cover limbs and tail, feathers on lateral margins of tail and posterior margins of arms enlarged, curved and asymmetrically veined.

Also, Gauthier (1986) listed 70 characters shared by all maniraptorans (see systematics section), with dromaeosaurids sharing five characters uniquely with birds, and troodontids sharing one. Other workers (Paul 1984a; Currie 1985, 1987a) have suggested closer affinities to troodontids than dromaeosaurids, based on a number of proposed synapomorphies (periotic pneumatic cavities, pneumatic cavities associated with internal carotid, more medially placed quadrate condyle than in larger theropods, fenestra pseudorotunda, loss of interdental plates, presence of a constriction between crown and root of teeth).

A second and smaller species of *Archaeopteryx*, *A. bavarica*, was named and described by Wellnhofer (1993), based upon a skeleton with feather impressions, found in 1992 at Solhofen. Wellnhofer noted that this specimen exhibited the first evidence of interdental plates, interpreted by that author as a distinctive theropod character. Nevertheless, Wellnhofer retained the systematic placement of *Archaeopteryx* within Aves.

Archaeopteryx has come to be alternately regarded as either a primitive bird or a feathered dinosaur, often depending upon where one chooses to separate birds from dinosaurs. Holtz (1994a), in a cladistic analysis of various groups within Theropoda, considered *Archaeopteryx* to be a theropod based on "strong morphological evidence" (Ostrom 1973; Gauthier 1986; Sereno and Rao 1992), part of an unnamed dromaeosaurid-bird clade within Maniraptora and diagnosed by the following unambiguous synapomorphies: Pubic boot projecting only posteriorly; pelvis opisthopubic; loss of fourth trochanter on femur; caudal vertebrae highly modified (neural spines limited to caudals I-IX; box-like centra in caudals I-V; zygapophysial facets vertically oriented); chevrons longer than deep; lesser trochanter extended by lamella of bone separate from main body of femur.

More recently, Perle, Norell, Chiappe and Clark (1993) described *Mononychus olecranus*, a thrush-sized Upper Cretaceous flightless bird with a single manual digit, and a number of theropod features. This new genus and species was based on an incomplete skeleton collected in Mongolia in the 1920s, during American Museum of Natural History expeditions led by Roy Chapman Andrews and Walter Granger. Following Gauthier (1986), Perle *et al.* regarded both *Mononychus* and *Archaeopteryx* as avialian theropod dinosaurs, with the former closer to extant birds than is *A. lithographicus*.

In a later nontechnical article, Norrell, Chiappe and Clark (1993) regarded *Mononykus* (revised spelling) as a bird based on the presence of various derived characteristics, including the presence of a breastbone with a strong median keel, a fibula reduced to a small spike, and fused wrist bones, these traits shared with modern birds. Primitive features in this genus also found in theropods include teeth, the long tail, and foot bones that are separate from one another.

In an article on *Mononychus*, *Archaeopteryx*, and other Mesozoic birds, Milner (1993) noted that, developmentally, feathers and reptilian scales are homologous structures and that feathers must have originated as a means of insulation in the maniraptoran lineage from which birds arose. Milner speculated, based on earlier cladistic schemes, that the bird lineage branched off the theropod line before the advent of a range of advanced dinosaurs, and that feathers could have been a common insulating outer layer among bipedal theropods.

However, not all workers accept that birds descended directly from theropod dinosaurs. Most vociferous in this opposing view, Martin (1991), a fossil bird specialist, argued that birds did not evolve from theropods and stated that the ancestor of birds possessed ten diagnostic characters. According to Martin, theropods possess but four of these ten characters, showing a scattered distribution that suggests independent derivation.

In a more recent study of a newly collected troodontid braincase (RTMP 86.36.457), Currie and Zhao (1993*b*) noted that seven of the ten characters listed by Martin seem to have been present in troodontids, the remaining characters—pneumatic articular; teeth with ventrally closed replacement pits; and root cementum—are not now known in troodontids. Currie and Zhao pointed out that tyrannosaurids possess pneumatic articulars, so a future discovery of this feature in troodontids would not be surprising. Also, between birds and crocodiles there is no special relationship regarding replacement pits in teeth. All archosaur teeth have replacement pits that start above the tooth base, progressing proximally and distally until the tip is reabsorbed. Currie and Zhao also stated that the fact that teeth of *Archaeopteryx* seem to have drifted away from the jaws does not support Martin's interpretation that the teeth were held in place by cementum. Currie and Zhao concluded that troodontids and birds are more closely related to one another than either of them are to certain more primitive theropods (see *Troodon* entry).

Further evidence supporting dinosaur-bird relationships was offered by Barreto, Albrecht, Bjorling, Horner, and Wilsman (1993), who compared cells within the growth plates (*i.e.*, discs of cartilage near the ends of growing long bones that generate bone elongation) of juvenile individuals of the ornithischian *Maiasaura* with those of the modern monitor lizard, dog and chicken. Barretto *et al.* found that the growth plates of this dinosaur strikingly resembles those of the chicken and differed dramatically from those of modern reptiles. Barreto *et al.* discovered that the remnants of dinosaur chondrocytes (cells that make up growth plates) resemble those of birds; in birds and *Maiasaura*, these cells are rather short and ovoid in shape, while in mammals and reptiles they are tall and have four distinct sides. Also, a scanning electron microscope (SEM) revealed in the *Maiasaura* bone calcified walls as well as calcospherites (calcified lumps), a pattern identical to that in birds a very different from that in mammals and reptiles. According to Barreto *et al.*, the foregoing evidence suggests that both birds and dinosaurs—ornithischians as well as saurischians—evolved from a common ancestor, growth plates being too complex to have evolved twice.

Interpreting all birds as maniraptorans takes on special significance when we consider that at least one theropod line has survived on a global level and as an enormously diversified group, with almost nine thousand living species. In this sense, dinosaurs are not extinct. However, for purposes of this book, the avialians *Archaeopteryx* and *Mononykus* (as well as all other extinct and extant vertebrates generally identified as birds) have been excluded from the listing of genera and species and from the general discussion. The author of this book has opted to follow others (*e.g.*, Chure and McIntosh 1989; Weishampel, Dodson and Osmólska 1990) in including only those taxa usually regarded as "dinosaurs." If and when *Archaeopteryx*, *Mononychus*, and perhaps other bird genera become accepted as "dinosaurian" in the more common usage of that term, those taxa will be accordingly dealt with in future volumes.

Dinosaur Success

Dinosaurs differ from other archosaurs in a number of features, some involving the structures of the ankle joint, knee and hip. Among these differences, the dinosaurian femur possesses a distinct head by which this bone fits into the perforated acetabulum at a right angle, so that the femoral shaft extends downward, rather than outward from the hip socket. The knee is a simple open hinge joint. This combination of morphological features resulted in a hindlimb that was tucked directly beneath the body, providing both pillar-like support and also enhancing walking and running abilities. This liberation of dinosaurs from the sprawling life styles of earlier reptilian groups was most advantageous, affording them many new evolutionary opportunities, most especially larger size ranges.*

Various reasons have been offered to explain the rise of the dinosaurs to supplant the more abundant

---

*Peczkis (1994), in a study of the implications of body-mass estimates for dinosaurs, made such estimates for 220 of the more than 300 generally accepted dinosaur genera. From this database, Peczkis found that the 1–10 ton body mass is the modal weight range for all dinosaurian genera, those on almost every continent, those during most Mesozoic stages, and those in two of the three major historical periods (1870–1900, 1900–1940, and 1970–present) of dinosaur discoveries; that theropods were considerably smaller than herbivorous dinosaurs during the Late Jurassic and again in the Late Cretaceous (while at other times they were approximately equal in mass); and that, regarding the discovery of dinosaur genera over time, there has been a simultaneous proportional increase in very small forms (less than 10 kilograms) and relative decrease in giant forms (10–100 tons), the latter suggesting that early researchers were biased toward collecting large dinosaurs.

and diverse mammal-like reptile groups that had previously dominated the Earth. Most of these explanations have involved competition and the notion that the morphological and physiological advancements in dinosaurs garnered for them a superiority in design better to survive over other animal groups.

One of the most prominent of these competition theories was offered by Charig (1980), who hypothesized that the fully erect walking posture in dinosaurs, resulting in superior walking and running abilities, led directly to their success. According to Charig, this superiority made the earliest flesh-eating dinosaurs very efficient hunters, which brought to extinction the various nondinosaurian herbivores of the time. This sudden lack of plant-eating forms then could have hastened the evolution of herbivorous dinosaurs (prosauropods, "fabrosaurids" and heterodontosaurids) to exploit the existing vegetation and also to counterbalance the presence of carnivores.

An alternative explanation for the success of dinosaurs was proposed by Benton (1979*a*; see also Tucker and Benton 1982; Benton 1983, 1984*b*). Benton (1979*a*) doubted that large-scale competition between erect-posture animals (dinosaurs) and sprawling animals, over tens of millions of years, could result in dinosaurs outcompeting their contemporaries. Benton found a pattern of extinctions involving mammal-like reptiles and other reptilian forms toward the end of the Triassic following floral changes, particularly a global extension of the conifers. Benton suggested that the early dinosaurs simply took over the many niches left vacant by their extinct predecessors, just as the mammals would occupy those niches much later abandoned by the last of the dinosaurs.

Later, Benton (1983, 1991) suggested that the early dinosaurs radiated, not because of competition with other vertebrates, but after a mass extinction of other reptile groups at about the Carnian-Norian boundary. Following more recent work by Rogers, Swisher, Sereno, Monetta, Forster and Martínez (1993), in which the oldest known dinosaur-bearing rocks (the Ischigualasto Formation) were found to have a radiometric date of 228 million years ago, Benton (1993) concluded that the origin and early evolution of the dinosaur may have been more of a "low-key affair." According to Benton (1993), the study by Rogers *et al.* confirms the opinion that the earliest dinosaurs did not replace more primitive tetrapods after long-term competition, as members of both assemblages coexisted without any evidence of a decline in one and rise of the other. Benton (1993) further pointed out that, according to recent studies by Sereno, Forster, Rogers and Monetta (1993) and Sereno and Novas (1993), the main lines (*i.e.*,

Thanks to D. Baird, photo by Willard Starks, courtesy Museum of Natural History, Princeton University

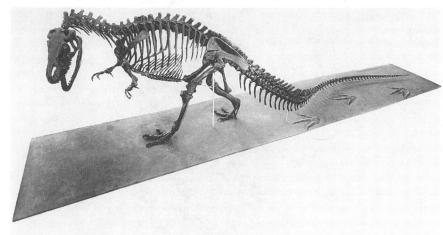

Theropoda, Sauropodomorpha, and Ornithischia) of dinosaurian evolution were established by Carnian times, all modest-sized, light-weight, bipedal animals, and all having seemingly diverged from a single common ancestor after just several million years.

Skeleton (PU 14554) of *Allosaurus fragilis,* from the Cleveland Lloyd Dinosaur Quarry, Emery County, Utah, mounted in antiquated tail-dragging pose.

"Warm-Blooded" versus "Cold-Blooded" Dinosaurs

A controversial and popular theory attempting to explain dinosaur success during the Triassic is that they were endothermic/homiothermic (*i.e.*, generating body heat internally) and keeping the level constant like most birds and mammals, rather than

Life-sized model made for the U.S. Government exhibit, World's Fair (1904), St. Louis, depicting *Stegosaurus stenops* with front legs splayed-out lizard style.

Courtesy National Museum of Natural History, Smithsonian Institution (neg. #28156).

A Background

Camptosaurus dispar and *Allosaurus fragilis* skeletons, from the Cleveland Lloyd Dinosaur Quarry, poses designed by James A. Jensen to display symmetrical reptilian sinuosity, balanced on two legs. Only three points (one foot of *Camptosaurus* and both of *Allosaurus*) contact platform.

Thanks to D. Baird, courtesy Brigham Young University.

Courtesy J. O. Farlow.

Theropod ichnite from F6 Ranch, Kimble County, Texas, from a trail recording a running dinosaur.

ectothermic/poikolothermic (maintaining body temperature at fluctuating levels with heat mostly from external sources) as are all other living reptiles. A fair amount of evidence, both supporting and denying this idea, has surfaced in recent years. The chief advocate that all dinosaurs were "warm-blooded" has been Robert T. Bakker, author of numerous scientific and popular articles on this intriguing possibility. Bakker (1980) pointed out that both dinosaurs and mammals evolved in the Late Triassic and postulated that dinosaurs must have been as efficient as mammals in order to enjoy complete dominance over them during the Mesozoic. Consequently, according to Bakker, dinosaurs must have been endothermic.

In 1969, at the first North American Paleontological Convention in Chicago, Ostrom argued that,

among all living vertebrates, only mammals and birds are endothermic and have an upright posture, and that high metabolic rates and high uniform body temperatures are needed to maintain an upright posture. As all dinosaurs maintained such a posture, Ostrom concluded that they seemed to have been quite active creatures with high metabolic rates (see also Ostrom 1980a).

In a technical paper, Bakker (1971) associated a fully erect posture and locomotion with the continuous levels of activity needed by living birds and mammals to get the required amounts of food to sustain their metabolism. According to Bakker, an erect gait allowed the body weight to be supported with less muscle power than a sprawling gait, thus saving energy.

Ostrom found it striking that both theropod and ornithopod dinosaurs independently achieved a

Skeleton of *Camptosaurus dispar* mounted in an action pose suggestive of a possibly warm-blooded animal.

fully bipedal posture, while a third group, the prosauropods, were at least semibipedal. Pointing out that all living bipeds are warm-blooded, Ostrom stated that this fact strengthened (but did not prove) the argument that posture is controlled by physiological factors.

Seymour (1976) noted that the larger dinosaurs must have had fully divided four-chambered hearts that could produce great differences in pressure between the pulmonary and systemic tracts. The greater the distance between heart and brain, the greater the required systemic pressure. In a form such as *Brachiosaurus*, with the neck and head upright, there would be an approximate distance of 6 meters between the heart and brain. The three-chambered heart of a modern reptile would be incapable of handling the action required to pump blood up the elongated neck to the brain. Only birds and mammals among living animals possess a fully divided four-chambered heart. As both Seymour and Ostrom pointed out, however, this establishes that many (but not all) dinosaurs must have possessed an advanced circulatory system capable of maintaining endothermy, but is not a proof for endothermy.

In 1968, Bakker published a nontechnical article wherein he argued that the current reconstructions of dinosaur forelimb posture was incorrect. Bakker pointed out that the shoulder socket in dinosaurs faces downward as in mammals rather than outward as in sprawling reptiles and stated that the dinosaurian forelimb should, therefore, be positioned upright instead of sprawling. He further suggested that dinosaurian locomotor patterns compared favorably with those of mammals and that dinosaurs must have been fast, agile, and energetic animals with a physiological level not unlike that of mammals.

Late Cretaceous dinosaurs of western Canada, painted by Charles R. Knight in 1931, incorrectly interpreted as sluggish, swamp-bound, tail-dragging animals (left to right, half-submerged *Corythosaurus casuarius,* group of *Parasaurolophus walkeri,* armored *"Palaeoscincus" costatus* [based on remains of *Edmontonia rugosidens*], pair of *Struthiomimus altus,* and three *Edmontosaurus regalis*).

A Background

Courtesy D. A. Thomas.

Bakker (1968, 1971, 1972, 1974) interpreted certain features in the shoulders and pelvises in theropods, ornithopods and ceratopsians, present in fast-running birds and mammals, as indications of high levels of activity and high running speeds, and consequently, evidence for endothermy. Ostrom (1978c, 1980a) agreed that many smaller dinosaurs, especially lightly built theropods, seemed to be agile and capable of rapid movement, but Ostrom (1980a) was not convinced of Bakker's assessment of the locomotor abilities of the larger dinosaurs. Ostrom (1980a) suggested that only the small theropods, especially in their relationship to birds, were candidates for endothermic dinosaurs.

Brain size has been used as an argument to support both ectothermy and endothermy in dinosaurs. Birds and mammals, having relatively large brains, engage in more sophisticated activity than ectothermic reptiles, which have comparatively small brains. Food, oxygen and a consistent body temperature are required to supply the larger and more complex avian and mammalian brains. As observed by Feduccia (1973), the relatively small brains in dinosaurs seem to be clear indications of ectothermy. By contrast, the relatively large brains in ornithomimid or "ostrich" dinosaurs (Russell 1972) offer support to the argument for endothermy (Dodson 1974; Ricqlès

1974]; Bakker 1974, 1975). However, Jerison (1973) noted that internal thermoregulation requires a smaller brain than that required by cold-blooded animals for the behavioral control of internal temperature. In a newspaper article, Halstead (1975b) interpreted these larger brains in ornithomimids as being associated with balance and good eyesight rather than body temperature.

In a study of the relative brain size in archosaurs, Hopson (1977) found that most dinosaurs had a brain that compared favorably in size with that of a typical reptile, although the brain of the dinosaur *Troodon* [=*Stenonychosaurus* of his usage] was comparatively as large as that in some birds and mammals. Hopson concluded that dinosaurs exhibited a spectrum of activity levels intermediate between those of living ectotherms and living endotherms, that most dinosaurs were less active than modern endotherms, that the metabolic rates of dinosaurs were below those of living birds and mammals and that metabolic rates varied greatly among different kinds of dinosaurs (a view shared by many specialists today; see also Farlow 1990). Based on skeletons designed for high speed running in conjunction with very large brains, Hopson, as would Ostrom (1980a), deduced that only the small theropods were fully warm-blooded.

Ostrom (1980a) noted that bird- and mammal-like physiology in dinosaurs would naturally lead to the supposition that dinosaurs must have behaved somewhat like birds and mammals. Indeed there is evidence that at least some kinds of dinosaurs may have engaged in rather sophisticated activity atypical of living reptiles. Bird (1944) was the first author to report multiple fossil trackways, in Bandera County, Texas, as evidence of apparent sauropod group activity. Huene (1928) regarded a concentration of *Plateosaurus* skeletons discovered near Trossingen, West Germany, as possible evidence of migratory herding. Studies of the duckbilled dinosaur *Maiasaura* (Horner and Makela 1979; Horner 1986; Horner and Weishampel 1988) showed that at least this form may have maternally cared for its young and seemingly migrated (see *Maiasaura* entry). Although such activity usually does seem to coincide with an endothermic regime, it does not prove endothermy; nor are all ectothermic animals devoid of such complex social behavior (*e.g.* crocodiles care for their young).

Bakker (1975) noted that dinosaur bones from northern Yukon and footprints from Spitzbergen originate in latitudes much too high for cold-blooded animals. Also, Bakker (1972, 1973, 1974, 1975, 1980, 1986) noted that ectothermic and endothermic animals of the same body mass, in order to survive, must take in different amounts of food. Endotherms require more food than ectotherms, much of it

Diplodocus carnegii, painted by Zdenek Burian during the late 1950s, depicted as a sluggish, swamp-dwelling behemoth, its bulk buoyantly supported by water.

utilized to produce body heat. Full ectotherms need roughly about 10 percent of the food taken in by full endotherms. A balance exists in nature between the number of predator and prey animals and a census of the fossil record could reveal a predator-prey ratio indicative of the physiology of those animals. Bakker found that among ectothermic Permian vertebrate communities herbivorous and carnivorous forms were about equally represented, while among dinosaurian and Tertiary mammalian communities the predator-prey ratio was fairly low (5 percent predators to 90 percent prey) with comparatively smaller numbers of herbivores supporting a given number of carnivores.

This perspective was challenged by Charig (1976), who listed various objections to Bakker's approach, most notably collector bias, the incompleteness of the fossil record, the interactions of other animals in food chains, and relative life spans. Thulborn (1973a) as well as other workers (Farlow 1980; Russell and Béland 1979) pointed out that ratios of large cold-blooded predators to prey closely approach those for warm-blooded predators. Halstead (1976) suggested that the low predator-prey ratios in dinosaurs could be related to the large size of the animals. Tracy (1976) suggested that the ratios could have different meanings if the predators ate their young, other carnivores or were partly scavengers. Benton (1979b) added that some of the larger herbivores, because of their size (like modern elephants), may have been unavailable for predation, and their inclusion would greatly lower the predator-prey ratio. Ostrom (1980a) further pointed out that the food requirements per unit weight decrease with increasing body size, thereby

resulting in a lower predator-prey ratio than Bakker's.

Various workers (Gross 1934); Enlow and Brown 1956, 1957, 1958; Currey 1960, 1962); de Ricqlès 1976, 1980) showed that dinosaurian bone often resembles mammalian bone histologically, rather than that of other kinds of reptiles. The primary compact bone in dinosaurs and mammals is highly vascularized with many Haversian canals. In cross-section, the bones of living "cold-blooded" reptiles display well developed growth rings, while those of warm-blooded animals, including mammals and apparently most dinosaurs,

Protoceratops andrewsi, painted by Charles R. Knight in 1927, portrayed with lizard-like sprawling posture.

Courtesy The Field Museum (neg. #55563).

A Background

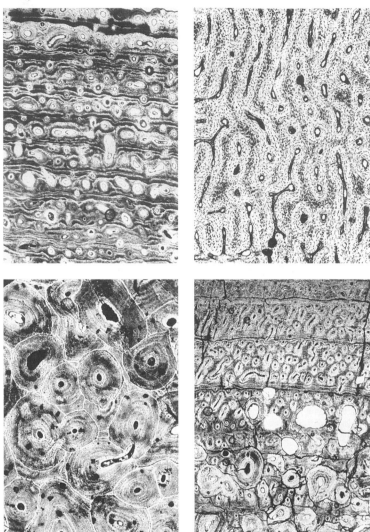

Top, left: Microscopic study of zonal (growth right) bone from a sauropod pubis (BMNH R9472), evidence possibly supporting ectothermy. Top, right: Microscopic view of fiber-lammelar bone (irregular laminar type) in a sauropod limb bone. Bottom, left: Microscopic view of dense Haversian bone in *Tyrannosaurus* rib. Bottom, right: Microscopic study of *Megalosaurus* pubis exhibiting Haversian reconstruction in three distinct parts: Top part with zonal bone (growth ring) with small primary osteones, middle with resorption lacunae (spaces between cells), lower with secondary osteones (Haversian system).

show less well-developed growth rings. The high vascularization, Haversian canals and poorly developed growth rings have been associated with high activity and endothermy in mammals and, therefore by implication, also in dinosaurs (see Bakker 1972; de Ricqlès 1974, 1976).

The use of dinosaurian bone as evidence to support endothermy was challenged by workers such as Reid (1984). From Reid's detailed microscopic studies it appears that highly vascular bone can also be found in many reptiles, while poorly vascular bone can also be seen in small birds and mammals. The primary compact bone in dinosaurs is of two principal types (see de Ricqlès 1974, 1975): 1. Fibrolamellar bone, being fast-growing to allow for the rapid growth of the animal, and 2. lamellar-zonal bone, the most typical of which is divided into growth rings, designed to help the bones to carry heavy loads. While de Ricqlès (1974) associated fibrolamellar bone

with endothermy, Reid found the former only to be related to sustaining rapid growth. Reid also pointed out that this type of compact bone had first appeared in therapsids (which need not have been endothermic, occurring in the same fauna as pareiasaurs such as *Bradysaurus*, which has bones typical of ectotherms) and, in incipient form, in the primitive Late Permian therapsid *Biarmosuchus*. In one dinosaurian form (*Rhabdodon*), Reid observed that the primary compact bone was quite similar to the kind usually found in crocodiles. Reid also observed typically reptilian growth rings in such diverse forms of dinosaurs as *Iguanodon*, megalosaurids and sauropods.

According to Reid, Haversian bone was often developed in dinosaurs to the level of that in mammals but not as extensively as implied by some workers, while no Haversian systems were perceived in some bone (*e.g.* a femur section of "*Aristosuchus*"). In *Iguanodon*, which offered the widest range of study samples, Reid found variations in Haversian bone between different bones, different specimens of a given bone, and different portions of the same bone. In some cases, Reid noted, the local development of Haversian bone could be related to bone remodeling associated with muscle insertions rather than endothermy.

In the early 1990s, Barrick and Showers used a newly developed test involving the two different isotopic forms of oxygen (oxygen-18 and the vastly more common oxygen-16) in nature to study the bones of modern animals. The ratio of oxygen-18 to oxygen-16 is indicative of the temperature at which the bones were formed while the animal was growing. In endotherms the body temperature should be rather uniform. In ectotherms, the limbs and tail should be cooler. Barrick and Showers found that the chemical composition of the bones from the ribs and legs of endothermic animals was identical, while that from the comparable bones in ectotherms revealed distinct chemical differences. Of five dinosaurian species studied, the isotopic composition pattern of those bones was the same as in modern mammals, the ratios in the limbs and tail almost identical to those in the ribs and pelvis. Of the dinosaurs studied, the one exception was the adult *Camarasaurus*, a sauropod that may have been endothermic while young, becoming more ectothermic as it grew to giant size.

One hypothesis attempting to explain the success of large dinosaurs like sauropods was proposed long before the advent of the ideas about endothermy. Based upon their studies of living alligators, Colbert, Cowles and Bogert (1946) introduced the theory of "mass (or "inertial" or "bulk") homeothermy." According to this theory, the body temperatures of medium- to large-sized ectothermic animals remain relatively constant during normal subtropical-type daytime temperature fluctuations. Extrapolating on this idea, Cloudsley-Thompson (1972) theorized that dinosaurs achieved constant body temperatures by virtue of their large size. Bennett and Dawson (1976) added that high metabolic rates may have been produced in dinosaurs by activity metabolism and large size, instead of solely by thermoregulation. As inertial homeotherms, big dinosaurs could have lived life styles not unlike those of mammals without themselves being endothermic. Turning this idea around, some dinosaurs may have achieved gigantic size to sustain an efficient endothermic-like metabolism via mass homeothermy. Taking this idea further, McNab and Auffenberg (1976) pointed out that large endothermic dinosaurs would have suffered from overheating.

Benton (1979b) pointed out that the climates of the Mesozoic were generally warmer than those of today and were quite arid during the Late Triassic. Endothermy could have been both disadvantageous and unnecessary to dinosaurs (except for small theropods) which could have achieved homeothermy simply because of their large size. Benton argued that ectothermy, rather than endothermy as Bakker (1968) suggested, could have accounted for the takeover of therapsids by ectothermic archosaurs during the Triassic. Mammals, although continuing throughout the Mesozoic, did not become a significant group until the final extinction of the dinosaurs. This suggested to Benton that being an ectotherm with a constant body temperature, without the need to consume large quantities of food as in endotherms, may have assured the dinosaurs' success and diversification in the Jurassic and Cretaceous.

The problems regarding dinosaur energetics and thermal biology were examined by Farlow (1990). Farlow speculated that some dinosaurs may have had ontogenetically and seasonally variable rates of metabolism, allowing them to exploit the benefits of both ectothermy and endothermy.

Spotila, O'Connor, Dodson and Paladino (1991) acknowledged that portraying dinosaurs as avian- or mammalian-style endotherms has a certain intuitive appeal to the layperson, who prefers this new image to the old cultural symbols of sluggishness, stupidity, extinction, and failure; this new dinosaur image is both partisan and flawed, is derived from a philosophy that endothermy is superior to ectothermy (see Bakker 1986), that endothermic dinosaurs are necessary for a comprehensive evolutionary theory (Bakker 1980), and from an insistence that all dinosaurs were equally endothermic (Bakker 1986).

Spotila et al. reviewed the concept of "gigantothermy," by which living reptiles utilize large body size, low metabolic rates, peripheral tissues as insulation, and active control of blood circulation to maintain high body temperatures. As an example, Spotila et al. used the example of the leatherback turtle that migrates 10,000 kilometers per year while keeping warm in cold Arctic waters. Employing computer models to predict the thermal behavior of dinosaurs under both steady-state and transient conditions, Spotila et al. concluded: 1. Sauropods with mammalian-level metabolic rates could not have tolerated warm conditions without fatal overheating; 2. very small insulated dinosaurs would have been near environmental temperature whether they were ectotherms or endotherms; 3. moderate- to large-sized Arctic dinosaurs probably migrated away from cold winter conditions while small dinosaurs would have hibernated; and 4. gigantothermy allowed for lifestyles combining the benefits of homeothermy and mechanical performance with the energy economy afforded by lower metabolic rates.

Can we unequivocally arrive at a verdict as to whether all—or some—dinosaurs were warm- or cold-blooded, or perhaps something intermediate? Unfortunately, without a living dinosaur to examine, there may never be such a final determination. When dealing with extinct animals we are limited to the skeletal remains preserved as fossils. Comparisons of dinosaurs to modern animals must be done with caution. Weighing the evidence pro and contra, it seems reasonable to regard at least the smaller theropod dinosaurs apparently ancestral to birds as quite possibly endothermic in the strict sense of the word. However, other forms of dinosaurs could have been ectothermic while still maintaining warm bodies and having active lifestyles.[*]

Dinosaur Extinctions

Oddly enough, the most fascinating aspect of dinosaurs for the general public seems to be not that they ruled a planet for 150 million years or that they were one of the most successful of all the terrestrial vertebrates, but that they became extinct. "Why did

---

*The controversy has been covered in detail in other books, the first popular volume dealing with dinosaur endothermy being Desmond's (1976) biased treatment The Hot-Blooded Dinosaurs. For more technical arguments favoring ectothermy in most dinosaurs, see A Cold Look at the Hot Blooded Dinosaurs, edited by Thomas and Olson (1980a). Supporting endothermy in all dinosaurs was the persuasively written book The Dinosaur Heresies by Bakker (1986) and Predatory Dinosaurs of the World by Paul (1988c). For a more current summary, see Farlow (1990).

the dinosaurs die out?" must surely be one of the most often asked question by interested laypersons.

Certainly the extinction of these animals at the end of the Cretaceous period has taken on such interest that writers of popular books about dinosaurs are usually compelled to include discussions on this topic, while the media are quick to bring to the public the "latest theories" attempting to explain their demise. The public's obsession for this topic is, perhaps, understandable. Dinosaurs, interesting creatures all, are gone. With the threat of humanity's own extinction looming in its future, the idea that these former rulers of the Earth perished "mysteriously," "suddenly," and *en masse* holds a strange perhaps even morbid attraction.

To many paleontologists, however, the extinction of the dinosaurs holds far less importance as well as fascination. As paleontologist John R. Horner has emphatically stated in a number of media interviews, the fact that the dinosaurs died out is relatively unimportant (see Horner and Lessem 1993). What is important is that the dinosaurs were so successful.

Nevertheless, the dinosaurs are extinct—unless, as do many paleontologists, we classify birds as dinosaurs, in which case only the "classic" lineages disappeared.

Many possible explanations have been offered over the years to explain the extinction of the dinosaurs. They include: Inability to adapt to a cooling climate, changes in oceanographic conditions and atmospheric pressure; floods or poisonous water; eggs developing malformed shells, developing into one sex, or eaten by small mammals; unsuccessful competition for food with mammals and leaf-eating caterpillars; brains too small; inability to mate, sexual frustration, suicide; overabundance of predatory forms; magnetic reversal of the Earth's poles, allowing a flood of cosmic radiation, or shift of rotational poles; inability to handle the flowering plants that first appeared during the Cretaceous; flowering plants photosynthesized additional oxygen, enriching the

atmosphere beyond the dinosaurs' metabolic capacities; poisoning by plants that had absorbed selenium from decaying rocks; absence of food plants resulting from segregation of plant communities that previously coexisted; collapse of food chain; poisonous minerals, or an absence of needed trace substances such as selenium and calcium; lineages becoming racially senile; weather becoming too dry (or wet); body size too great to satisfy appetites, to adapt to change or to hibernate; increased size resulting in clumsiness; sperm death from excessive heat, resulting in sterilization; excessive reproductive rates checked by runaway effects of group selection; death by disease spread by insects or marine reptiles, or parasites; absence of natural laxatives, of redundant DNA, or aberrant chromosomal realignments; overspecialization; malfunction of endocrine systems; too high natural radiation level; deadly cosmic rays from an exploding supernova; blinding solar radiation; sunspot activity, sea-floor breaking up supercontinents, mountain-building, rise of sea level, fall of sea level and the resultant rise of the average height of continents, presence of volcanic dust, a hypothetical worldwide fire, or Arctic Ocean water spilling into warm southern seas.

None of these hypotheses is without flaws and none explains why numerous other nondinosaurian groups (crocodiles, lizards, snakes, turtles, rhynchocephalians, frogs, salamanders, and birds) survived.

In the media, the most popular, spectacular and tidy of modern theories regarding dinosaur extinctions has cosmic origins. In 1978, geologist Luis W. Alvarez and his son Walter Alvarez, with a geology team from the University of California (Berkeley), discovered sudden high levels of iridium (or iridium "spike"), a rare heavy element found in meteorites, asteroids and comets (but also known in the Earth's molten core) in Upper Cretaceous rocks just at the Cretaceous-Tertiary boundary near Gubbio, Italy. This iridium "spike" was interpreted as evidence of a colossal meteorite impact at the end of the Mesozoic Era.

This theory (see Alvarez, Alvarez, Asaro and Michel 1980; W. Alvarez, Kauffman, Surlyk, Alvarez, Asaro and Michel 1984) presents the scenario that a huge (6 to 9 miles in diameter) celestial body collided with the Earth, vaporizing on impact and throwing up an enormous cloud of dust and steam. This cloud blocked out the sunlight essential for plant growth with dramatic biological repercussions leading, after less than one year, to mass extinction. Evidence from paleobotany suggests a sudden change in the pollen record in the same layer as the iridium spike at the K-T [Cretaceous-Tertiary] boundary (see Pillmore, Tschundy, Orth, Gilmore and Knight 1984; Nichols,

Photo by the author, courtesy Cleveland Museum of Natural History.

Holotype skull (CMNH 7541) of *Nanotyrannus lancensis,* a late Maastrichtian carnivorous dinosaur.

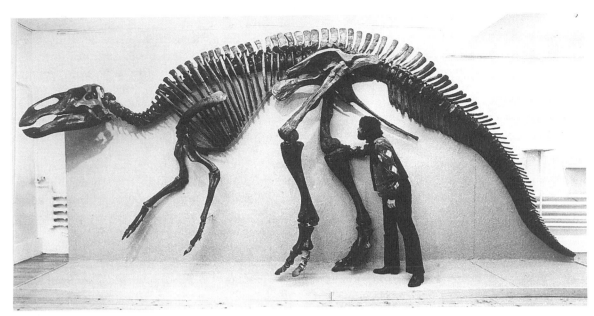

Skeleton of *Edmontosaurus,* a duckbilled dinosaur that survived into late Maastrichtian times.

Courtesy Ulster Musem.

Jarzen, Orth and Oliver 1986; Saito, Yamanoi and Kaiho 1986; Tschundy, Pillmore, Orth, Gilmore and Knight 1984; Rschundy and Tschundy 1986.

Some scientists known to the general public through popular writings and media appearances have endorsed this "impact theory" of dinosaur extinction, seeing it as a blueprint for a possible "nuclear winter," the threat of which overhangs the survival of our own species. Other explanations for the iridium layer have included a rain of comets (see W. Alvarez *et al.* 1988) and, in contrast, excessive volcanic activity (Officer, Hallam, Drake and Devine 1987).

As with the other theories, the catastrophic impact theory has had detractors. In opinion poles conducted among paleontologists attending both the Society of Vertebrate Paleontology meetings in Rapid City, South Dakota, and the Dinosaur Systematics Symposium at the Royal Tyrrell Museum of Palaeontology, Drumheller, Alberta (both held in 1986), the overwhelming majority of participants favored a more conservative "gradual" explanation over the more spectacular "cosmic" explanation for dinosaur extinction.

Weakening the theory that dinosaur extinction was caused by the skies darkening due either to an extraterrestrial impact or to volcanic activity is the fossil evidence that dinosaurs did, in fact, exist in regions where long periods of night and low temperatures were the norm. Rich, Rich, Wagstaff. Mason, Douthitt, Gregory and Felton (1988) showed that a diverse biota (including theropod and hypsilophodontid dinosaurs, labyrinthodont amphibians, and also numerous other vertebrates, invertebrates, and plants) existed in polar latitudes during the Cretaceous along what is today Australia's southeast coast. The climate in that area would have been seasonal, nontropical and cool, the mean annual temperature most likely less than 5 degrees centigrade; the location near the South Pole would also mean prolonged periods of darkness. Rich *et al.* concluded that, as some dinosaurs obviously thrived in such conditions for at least tens of millions of years (Valanginian-Albian time in Australia, Campanian-Maastrichtian time in Alaska), darkness and cold may not have directly related to their extinction. (See discussions on this subject in the entries for *Allosaurus,*

Skull (FMNH P12003) of *Triceratops horridus* (originally referred to *T. calicornis*), one of the last dinosaur species to become extinct.

Courtesy The Field Museum (neg. #17464).

Atlascopcosaurus and *Leaellynasaura*; also see Vickers-Rich and Rich 1993.)

Also weakening the theory that dinosaur extinction resulted from the impact of a celestial body is evidence that such an assumed impact at the K-T boundary was not necessarily unique to the Mesozoic. At approximately the end of the Triassic period, an asteroid or comet measuring some 6 miles in diameter seemingly struck eastern Quebec, leaving a crater measuring over 40 miles in diameter (see Olsen and Sues 1986; Olsen, Shubin and Anders 1987), while another asteroid seems to have collided with the Earth during the Jurassic (Boslough 1987; McLaren 1988). Obviously, neither of these earlier impacts had much effect on dinosaurian success or failure.

In a criticism of theories that meteoritic impacts, comet showers or volcanic eruptions killed off the Late Cretaceous dinosaurs, Paul (1989) pointed out that dinosaurs (and pterosaurs) survived earlier such events without discernible losses and actually increased in diversity. Paul noted a number of possible survival mechanisms implemented by dinosaurs including a large number of species, the abundant populations of some species, the toughness of many species, and cold- and dark-adapted polar dinosaurs acting as reserve populations.

Paladino, Dodson, Hammond and Spotila (1987), noting that the recent hypotheses concerning catastrophic causes for dinosaur extinction have not been generally accepted by paleontologists, offered another hypothesis. Paladino *et al.* pointed out that sex in most turtles, apparently all crocodilians, and some lizards is determined by the temperature of the egg during incubation, and that temperature could also have determined the sex of hatchling dinosaurs. Dinosaur eggs found in upland sites in western Montana would have been exposed to fluctuating or lower temperatures as the climate deteriorated and seasonality increased during in late Maastrichtian times, producing hatchlings of mostly the same sex. Such an imbalance would have drastically changed the population breeding structure and driven these animals toward extinction. This scenario, in conjunction with other biological factors (*e.g.* changing food supply and available niches), could explain dinosaur extinction without the intrusion of any celestial *deus ex machina*. It would not, however, explain why crocodiles and turtles did not die out along with these dinosaurs. Paladino *et al.* emphasized caution in critical acceptance of any extinction hypothesis, theirs included, noting that a hypothesis that cannot be tested has but limited scientific value.

Zhao, Ye, Li, Zhao and Yan (1990), in a brief report pending a yet to be published systematic study, offered a theory concerning dinosaur extinction across the Cretaceous-Tertiary boundary. Their work was based upon interdisciplinary investigations (including the examination of the general geology, isotopes, magnetostratigraphy, trace elements and the microstructure of dinosaur eggshells) conducted by a Sino-German team since 1983 on the redbed facies of Late Cretaceous to Early Tertiary passage beds in Nanxiong Basin, Guangdong Province, China.

First, Zhao *et al.* placed the Cretaceous-Tertiary boundary at an argillaceous siltstone between the Pingling Formation and the Shanghu Formation, which can be clearly observed from east Kongcun to west Fengmenao. According to Zhao *et al.*: (1) The color changes throughout the boundary, with purplish red siltstone below the boundary and dark red siltstone above; (2) the calcareous concretions are small below the boundary, and large, with irregular shapes and hollow centers, above it; and (3) dinosaur eggshells appear only below this boundary, while a rich Paleocene fauna appears above it.

Second, Zhao *et al.* found abnormalities in dinosaur eggshells from the Nanxiong Basin. Of those specimens large enough to be sufficiently evaluated, some shells were found to vary considerably in thickness, with a temporary tendency towards a reduction in shell thickness revealed in specimens from the Yuanpu Formation to the Pingling Formation. Other eggshells show abnormally varying proportional thicknesses between the cone and columnar layers, double-layered or multilayered cones, irregular spaces, or disorderly arranged crystalline calcite of the columnar layer. Such abnormalities seem to have a connection with the effect of trace elements, an assumption confirmed by analysis of such elements in the examined dinosaur eggshells. Some of these trace elements can be attributed to variations in eggshell mineral content related to environmental changes, others to drastic changes of a very dry climate.

Zhao *et al.* postulated the scenario that trace elements polluted the South China area during the geologically brief time of from 200,000 to 300,000 years before the Cretaceous-Tertiary boundary when the climate became extremely dry. These trace elements, taken in abundance into dinosaurs' bodies via the food chains, caused imbalances of the trace element levels, affecting the animals' reproduction and leading to pathologic eggshells. Such eggshells would have been too meager to protect the developing embryos. An excess of trace elements transmitted from the parent's food could have eventually resulted in abnormal embryonic development and much reduced hatchability. As envisioned by Zhao *et al.*, the number of progeny so affected would have dwindled until the final population entirely collapsed.

In regarding the extinction of the dinosaurs (except for birds), some points should be considered:

(1) People who have not studied dinosaurs often tend to think of these animals as all living in the same place and at the same time, with all of them dying out simultaneously. The fact is, however, that during their 150 million-year reign, dinosaur extinction was ongoing, with species going extinct to be replaced by other kinds of dinosaurs. (Putting this more into perspective, more time elapsed between the extinction of the last stegosaurus and the hatching of the first tyrannosaurus than between the extinction of the last dinosaur and the birth of the first human being.)

(2) There is nothing strange or unusual about all of the dinosaurs dying out. Extinction is the natural fate of all groups of life forms. More than 99 percent of every species that has ever lived is now extinct.

(3) The Earth and its diverse life forms are affected by such occurrences as moving land masses, the opening and closing of large bodies of water, the subsequent altering of climates, changes in atmospheric content, the appearance of new forms of vegetation and animals to feed upon that vegetation.

(4) Animal groups, including dinosaurs, tend to evolve from forms that are relatively small and generalized to those that are large and specialized. When a certain maximum size and high degree of specialization is attained within a group, adapting to geologically sudden environmental and geographical change becomes increasingly difficult. Also, birth rates tend to be lower in large animals. Many dinosaurs, within their respective groups, had evolved to great size and a high level of specialization.

(5) Although many forms of animals did not survive beyond the end of the Cretaceous (including dinosaurs, sauropterygians, mosasaurs, pterosaurs, toothed birds, and various cephalopods), many more kinds did—fishes, amphibians, birds, turtles, lizards, snakes, and multituberculates.

(6) Dinosaurs have been interpreted by some paleontologists as being on the decline toward the end of the Cretaceous. The number of dinosaurian species seems to have substantially declined during the final stage, with few newer species evolving to exploit the changing ecosystem (although, as observed by Russell 1984a, 1984b, dinosaurs were not waning, and according to Paul 1989, dinosaurian diversity was at its peak). Various studies indicate that the ankylosaurs comprised the first dinosaurian group to vanish during the Cretaceous (see Carpenter 1983), successively followed by hadrosaurids, theropods, and ceratopsians (Carpenter and Breithaup 1986; Clemens 1986). By about the last two million years of the Cretaceous, the number of species was relatively low compared to that in the earlier Cretaceous or in the Jurassic. As noted by Dodson (1990a), dinosaurian diversity appears to decline between the Campanian and the Late Maastrichtian when between-formation comparisons are made based upon skulls or articulated skeletons, but remains, at least in the early Maastrichtian as high as in preceding stratigraphic levels when including taxa founded upon isolated teeth. However, major decline in a group's diversity does not necessarily result in extinction, as some groups (including coelacanths and lungfish) surviving today had undergone such declines.

(7) Fossil evidence shows that some Late Cretaceous dinosaurs lived well within the Arctic and Antarctic circles, thereby surviving in colder climates (see Rich and Rich 1989). Other evidence (dinosaur teeth found in Montana mixed with mammalian bones above the iridium anomaly at the Cretaceous-Tertiary border) might suggest that some dinosaurs survived beyond the culmination of the Cretaceous and into the Paleocene period (see Rigby, Newman, Smit, Van der Kaars, Sloan and Rigby 1987; Sloan, Rigby, Van Valen and Gabriel 1986). In an experiment testing the degree of abrasion and weathering of enamel-coated teeth (from the tyrannosaurid *Albertosaurus* and a crocodilian) from the Paleocene portion of the Hell Creek Formation due to sediment transport, Argast, Farlow, Gabet and Brinkman (1987) found that transport alone does not seem to cause rapid or extensive changes in the morphology of such teeth, and concluded that it was not possible to infer limited transport or nontransport for such teeth based upon its fresh or unabraded appearance. According to these authors, then, the amount of wear on such teeth did not constitute convincing evidence either to support or deny that dinosaur teeth in the Paleocene part of the Hell Creek Formation had been reworked from older, dinosaur-bearing levels. However, Eaton, Kirkland and Doi (1989), after recovering Cretaceous shark teeth that had been redeposited in younger deposits, showed that the mixing of taxa from differing ages and environments by fluvial processes is not uncommon, especially during tectonically active periods like the Early Tertiary.

Why, then, did the dinosaurs die out? That question will most likely not have an entirely satisfactory answer anytime soon, although it will undoubtedly continue to be asked. It seems plausible that any credible explanation for dinosaur extinction would involve more than one theory, none of which can be thoroughly tested. All theories will, unfortunately, be affected by the incompleteness of the fossil record. Regardless of the causes of the final extinction of the dinosaurs, the topic seems far less important than the far more interesting topics relating to the success of these fascinating animals. When adding the birds to this very diverse and successful group, dinosaur extinction seems to be even less significant.

II: Dinosaurian Systematics

As paleontology depends upon the recovery, preparation, and interpretation of fossils, attempts to determine a genealogy of any extinct animals must always be imperfect and preliminary due to the fragmentary and incomplete fossil record.

In a cladistic analysis of basal archosaurs, Sereno (1991*b*) defined Archosauria as including two clades, Crurotarsi plus Ornithodira, plus all the descendants of their common ancestor. Sereno defined Ornithodira as including Pterosauria (flying reptiles) plus the genus *Sclermochlus*, Dinosauromorpha (including dinosaurs plus Aves) plus all the descendants of their common ancestor. Consequently Sereno noted that the Pterosauria occupy a basal position within Ornithodira and are not the sister-group to the Dinosauria as is often suggested. As defined by Sereno, Dinosauromorpha includes *Lagerpeton chanarensis* plus *Lagosuchus talampayensis* plus *Pseudolagosuchus major* plus Dinosauria (including Aves), plus all the descendants of their common ancestor.

The term "Dinosauria," when created in 1842 by Sir Richard Owen, was intended to embrace all of the then known very large Mesozoic terrestrial reptiles with "elephant-like" bodies (*Megalosaurus*, *Iguanodon*, and *Hylaeosaurus*) under a single natural grouping. In the late 1800s, however, this view had changed with the accumulation of considerably more dinosaurian remains.

In 1887, Seeley had observed that all the then known dinosaurs could be divided into two separate groups based on the structure of their hips. Seeley considered the Dinosauria to be an unnatural group actually comprising two separate orders, Saurischia and Ornithischia, each with its own separate ancestry within the Archosauria. Saurischia comprise the so-called "lizard-hipped" group, so named because of the more or less "lizard-like" structure of the pelvis (pubis pointing forward and downward), Ornithischia comprise the "bird-hipped" group because of the "birdlike" structure of the pelvis (pubis pointing backward). These two orders were further subdivided by other differences (see diagnoses of Saurischia and Ornithischia below).

This notion of the artificiality of the Dinosauria has been challenged only in the last two decades. Bakker and Galton (1974), based largely on Galton's ideas concerning a possible affinity between the

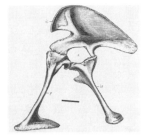

Saurischian pelvis (*Allosaurus fragilis*). Scale = 4 cm. (After Marsh 1896).

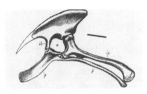

Ornithischian pelvis (*Camptosaurus dispar*). Scale = 12 cm. (After Marsh 1896).

Skeletons of saurischian dinosaur *Allosaurus fragilis* (LACM 3729/46030) and ornithischian *Camptosaurus dispar* (LACM 3729/46031), collected in 1966 by the University of Utah, mounted during the mid-1960s by Leonard Bessem.

Dinosaurian Systematics

Thansk to D. Baird, photo by Willard Starks, courtesy Museum of Natural History, Princeton University.

Skeleton (PU 14554) of allosaurid theropod *Allosaurus fragilis* from the Cleveland Lloyd Dinosaur Quarry.

recovery, preparation, and study of fossils, and by reinterpretations of previously known taxa. Thus, any attempt at organizing an accurate dinosaurian phylogeny must, at best, be regarded as tentative. (The classification of the Theropoda [see below] is the most unstable and is presently undergoing the most extensive revisions. For example, the taxon Ceratosauria may be eliminated after this book goes to press.)

The following systematic break-down of the Dinosauria constitutes a conservative attempt to organize the various taxa above the generic level into a convenient and usable system. It was based upon currently available published data, using as a starting point the system arrived at through cladistic analyses by various dinosaur specialists and published in *The Dinosauria*, the benchmark work edited by Weishampel, Dodson and Osmólska (1990). The organization of the Theropoda presented below is also based upon more recent cladistic studies of that problematic group, largely the reorganization proposed by Holtz (1994*a*), including characters observed by previous authors (see Holtz 1994*a*, Appendices 1 and 2).

This attempted organization of the Dinosauria is not an "official" classification created by or necessarily endorsed or advocated by this writer. In cases where there exist conflicts or inconsistencies between various published classifications, or differences of opinion by different authors, this writer has sometimes made a subjective decision as to which version to follow, while also including some of the more recent opposing views. Certainly, this organization is tentative. Parts of it may be severely outdated before this book is published; the inevitable changes will be attended to in future volumes. As there is no consensus among cladists regarding all relationships between dinosaurian taxa, the present writer has preferred to avoid controversy by not including in this book cladograms attempting to illustrate these relationships.

saurischian *Anchisaurus* and the later ornithischians, reinstated the taxon Dinosauria, recognizing it as a natural clade and monophyletic group, and regarding the Saurischia and Ornithischia as two closely related orders. As noted by Benton (1990), the Dinosauria is now universally recognized as monophyletic, a single naturally occurring group of closely related animals.

Dinosaurian systematics are in a perpetual state of flux, with classifications and revisions influenced by new discoveries and more taxa being subjected to cladistic analysis, by more advanced techniques in the

Courtesy The Field Museum (neg. #12781).

Theropod fossil footprints.

Courtesy American Museum of Natural History.

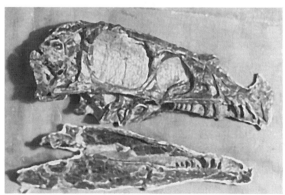

Holotype skull (AMNH 619) of coelurosaurian theropod *Ornitholestes hermanni*, right lateral view. Photo by R. A. Long and S. P. Welles.

Readers familiar with more "traditional" dinosaur books will notice the absence of such higher-taxa designations as "suborder," "infraorder," *etc.* Cladistic classification has eliminated these descriptive terms, with the exception of "genus" and "species." The taxon immediately above the genus level, formerly designated a "family," still retains the Greek-based suffix "-idea" indicative of that group. Continents listed for each of the following categories are those as they exist today and indicate where fossil evidence has been found. Genera listed are arranged in alphabetical order.

For a convenient reference, the divisions of the Dinosauria are arranged according to the following tentative scheme:

DINOSAURIA

I. SAURISCHIA
  A. THEROPODA
    1. ?*Eoraptor*
    2. ?HERRERASAURIDAE
    3. ?CERATOSAURIA
      a. COELOPHYSOIDEA
      b. NEOCERATOSAURIA
        1. ?*Ceratosaurus*
        2. ABELISAUROIDEA
          i. ABELISAURIDAE
          ii. *Noasaurus*
          iii. *Elaphrosaurus*
    4. TETANURAE [excluding AVES]
      a. ?SPINOSAURIDAE
      b. ?EUSTREPTOSPONDYLIDAE
      c. ?MEGALOSAURIDAE
      d. AVETHEROPODA
        1. ALLOSAUROIDEA
          i. SINRAPTORIDAE
          ii. ALLOSAURIDAE
        2. COELUROSAURIA
          i. *Compsognathus*
          ii. MANIRAPTORA
            a. *Ornitholestes*
            b. DROMAEOSAURIDAE
              1. VELOCIRAPTORINAE
              2. ?DROMAEOSAURINAE
            c. ARCTOMETATARSALIA
              1. OVIRAPTOROSAURIA
                OVIRAPTORIDAE
                OVIRAPTORINAE
                INGENIINAE
                ?CAENAGNATHIDAE
              2. ELMISAURIDAE
              3. *Avimimus*
              4. TYRANNOSAURIDAE
              5. BULLATOSAURIA

5. BULLATOSAURIA (cont.)
    TROODONTIDAE
    ORNITHOMIMOSAURIA
    ?*Shuvosaurus*
    HARPYMIMIDAE
    GARUDIMIMIDAE
    ORNITHOMIMIDAE
    d. ?THERIZINOSAUROIDEA
      1. ALXASAURIDAE
      2. THERIZINOSAURIDAE
  B. SAUROPODOMORPHA
    1. PROSAUROPODA
      a. THECODONTOSAURIDAE
      b. ANCHISAURIDAE
      c. MASSOSPONDYLIDAE
      d. YUNNANOSAURIDAE
      e. PLATEOSAURIDAE
      f. MELANOROSAURIDAE
      g. BLIKANASAURIDAE
    2. SAUROPODA
      a. VULCANODONTIDAE
      b. CETIOSAURIDAE
        1. CETIOSAURINAE
        2. SHUNOSAURINAE
      c. BRACHIOSAURIDAE
      d. CAMARASAURIDAE
        1. CAMARASAURINAE
        2. ?OPISTHOCOELICAUDINAE
      e. DIPLODOCIDAE
        1. DIPLODOCINAE
        2. DICRAEOSAURINAE
      f. MAMENCHISAURIDAE
      g. TITANOSAURIA
        1. ANDESAURIDAE
        2. TITANOSAURIDAE
II. ORNITHISCHIA
  A. *Pisanosaurus*
  B. *Technosaurus*
  C. *Lesothosaurus*
  D. GENASAURIA
    1. THYREOPHORA
      a. *Emausaurus*
      b. *Scutellosaurus*
      c. *Scelidosaurus*
      d. ?*Tatisaurus*
      e. ?*Echinodon*
      f. STEGOSAURIA
        1. HUAYNAGOSAURIDAE
        2. STEGOSAURIDAE
      g. ANKYLOSAURIA
        1. NODOSAURIDAE
        2. ANKYLOSAURIDAE
    2. CERAPODA
      a. ORNITHOPODA
        1. HETERODONTOSAURIDAE
        2. HYPSILOPHODONTIDAE
        3. IGUANODONTIA

3. IGUANODONTIA (cont.)
4. *Tenontosaurus*
5. DRYOSAURIDAE
6. CAMPTOSAURIDAE
7. IGUANODONTIDAE
8. *Probactrosaurus*
9. HADROSAURIDAE
   i. *Telmatosaurus*
   ii. *Claosaurus*
   iii. *Secernosaurus*
   iv. HADROSAURINAE
   v. LAMBEOSAURINAE
b. MARGINOCEPHALIA
  1. *Stenopelix*
  2. PACHYCEPHALOSAURIA
   i. HOMALOCEPHALIDAE
   ii. PACHYCEPHALOSAURIDAE
  3. CERATOPSIA
   i. PSITTACOSAURIDAE
   ii. NEOCERATOPSIA
     a. PROTOCERATOPSIDAE
     b. CERATOPSIDAE
       1. CENTROSAURINAE
       2. CHASMOSAURINAE

Explanations of Higher Taxa of the Dinosauria

DINOSAURIA   Owen 1842—(=PACHYPODES Meyer 1845, ORNITHOSCELIDA Huxley 1869)

Emended diagnosis: Vomers elongate, reaching caudally at least to level of antorbital fenestra; two or more fully incorporated sacral vertebrae (Novas 1992*b*; Sereno and Novas 1992 [although most spe-

(Foreground) skeleton (IVPPV8738) of melanorosaurid prosauropod *Lufengosaurus hueni* [originally referred to *L. magnus*], (background) sauropod *Datousaurus bashanensis* (IVPPV72262), exhibited in 1989 at the Natural History Museum of Los Angeles County. Photo by the author.

cialists required three or more vertebrae for inclusion in the Dinosauria); glenoid facing fully backward; deltapectoral crest low, running one-third or one-half the length of shaft of humerus; fourth manual digit with three or fewer phalanges; acetabulum perforated; head of femur fully offset proximally, with distinct neck and ball; fibula greatly reduced; astragalus with ascending process (Benton 1990, based upon characters noted previously by other authors).

General description: Small to gigantic terrestrial archosaurs, with erect gait, various diets.

Geographic range: Worldwide.

Age: Late Triassic (Carnian)–Late Cretaceous (Maastrichtian).

Taxa: Ornithischia plus Saurischia.

Dinosauria *incertae sedis*: *Aliwalia*, ?*Macrodontophion*, *Sanpasaurus*, ?*Spondlyosoma*, *Tichosteus*, *Walkeria*.

SAURISCHIA   Seeley 1888

Emended diagnosis: Quadratojugal overlaps laterally on to caudal process of jugal; elongate caudal

Courtesy J. O. Farlow.

Theropod ichnite from trail, Huckabay Site, Texas.

Skeleton (ROM 5091) of allosaurid theropod *Allosaurus fragilis* collected from the Cleveland Lloyd Dinosaur Quarry, Utah. To the left is *Stegosaurus.*

Courtesy Royal Ontario Museum.

Courtesy J. O. Farlow.

Large theropod footprint trail from Thayer Site, Comal County, Texas. Scale = 1 meter.

cervical vertebrae resulting in relatively longer neck than in other archosaurs; axial postzygapophyses set lateral to prezygapophyses; epipophyses present on cranial cervical postzygapophyses; accessory intervertebral articulations (hyposphene-hypantrum) present in dorsal vertebrae; manus over 45 percent length of the humerus; manus distinctly asymmetrical, digit II longest; proximal ends of metacarpals IV and V lying on palmar surfaces of manual digits III and IV, respectively; pollex heavy, with very broad metacarpal (Benton 1990).

Generalized description: Small to gigantic, bipedal, semibipedal and quadrupedal forms, carnivorous, herbivorous and possibly omnivorous forms, with skull and pelvis relatively less remodeled as compared to the Ornithischia.

Age: Late Triassic (Carnian)–Late Cretaceous (Maastrichtian).

Geographic range: Worldwide.

Taxa: Theropoda plus Sauropodomorpha.

THEROPODA Marsh 1881—(=GONIOPODA Cope 1866)

Emended diagnosis: Reduced overlap of dentary on to base of postdentary, and reduced mandibular symphysis; lacrimal exposed on skull roof; maxilla with accessory fenestra; rostrally fused vomers; expanded ectopterygoid with ventral fossa; first

Dinosaurian Systematics

Anchisauripus minusculus (originally *Brontozoum minusculum*), one of three theropod tracks (AC 45/2) in trail.

intercentrum having large fossa and small odontoid notch; second intercentrum having broad crescent-shaped foss for reception of the first intercentrum; pleurocoel (openings to hollow centrum) in presacral vertebrae; tail with transition point having marked changes in the form of the articular processes; enlarged distal first carpal overlapping the bases of first and second metacarpals; manual digit I absent or reduced to a vestige; manual digit IV absent or reduced; penultimate manual phalanges elongate; manual digit III with short first and second phalanges; manual unguals enlarged, sharply pointed, strongly recurved, with enlarged flexor tubercles; ilium with long preacetabular process; caudal part of ilium with a pronounced brevis fossa; cranially convex femur; fibula closely appressed to tibia, articulated with tibial crest; metatarsus narrow and elongate; pedal digit IV reduced; pedal digit V represented by a very strong reduced metatarsal; metatarsal I reduced, not contacting tarsus, attached halfway or further down side of metatarsal II; long bones thin-walled, hollow (Benton 1990, based upon other workers, including Gauthier 1986 and Osmóska 1990).

Generalized description: Small to giant, bipedal, carnivorous, with small to very large head, either with sharp teeth or toothless, usually with either greatly reduced or elongated forelimbs and birdlike feet, the first digit of which is reduced and spurlike; toothless forms possibly herbivorous or omnivorous.

Age: Late Triassic–Late Cretaceous.

Geographic range: Worldwide.

Taxa: ?*Eoraptor* plus ?Herrerasauridae plus ?Ceratosauria plus Tetanurae*.

Paleontologist Elmer S. Riggs (right) and field laboratory assistant H. W. Menke (left) with Grand Junction, Colorado sauropod remains, early 1900s, at the Field Columbian Museum.

Paleontologist Fátima C. F. Santos with sauropod ichnites from the Antnor Navarro Formation, Sousa, Paraibe, Brazil.

Theropoda *incertae sedis*: *Archaeornithoides, Asiamerica, Avisaurus, Betasuchus, Calamosaurus, Cal-*

Huene (1920) divided the Theropoda into two major groups, Carnosauria (then understood as basically including large theropods with big heads and short necks) and Coelurosauria (mostly smaller forms with small heads and long necks). This classification remained in general usage until later workers (e.g., Colbert and Russell 1969; Ostrom 1969b) showed that the two groups could not adequately be separated based upon Huene's criteria. Thus, the terms "Carnosauria" and "Coelurosauria" in their original context were generally abandoned until new taxa were erected within Theropoda (e.g., Ceratosauria, Tetanurae, etc.) and Gauthier (1986) reinstated and redefined these two groups, after which Molnar, Kurzanov and Dong (1990) again rediagnosed Carnosauria. Holtz (1994a), after a cladistic reevaluation of the Theropoda, demonstrated that "Carnosauria" is a polyphyletic grouping and abandoned this and other theropod taxa. The present organization of Theropoda has been largely based upon Holtz's (1994a) phylogeny. Various other workers (e.g., Currie 1995), however, have continued to use "Carnosauria" in the more modern interpretation introduced by Gauthier (1986). In more recent preliminary reports, Holtz and Padian (1995a, 1995b) announced a forthcoming revised analysis of theropod phylogeny which, to date of this writing, has not yet been published. In this new analysis, Carnosauria may resurface, with Tetanurae split into two stem-taxa—Carnosauria, defined by Holtz as tetanurans closer to Allosaurus than to birds, and Coelurosauria, defined as those closer to birds than to Allosaurus. Holtz's forthcoming reorganization of the Theropoda may establish new taxa and will reposition and redefine various existing taxa (including the Ornithomimosauria), establish a coelurosaurian clade consisting of Oviraptorosauria and Therizinosauroidea, and produce other changes that will invariably affect the present scheme. For the above reasons, and because much of what has been written in the literature regarding large theropods has been based upon the older notions of "Carnosauria" and "carnosaur," those terms, as used in the present document, will be flagged by quotation marks.

*amospondylus, Chuandongocoelurus, Coeluroides, Cry-
olophosaurus, Dandakosaurus, Deinocheirus, Dolichosuchus, Embasaurus, Genyodectes, ?Halticosaurus, ?Ino-
saurus, Itemirus, Jubbulpuria, Kakuru, Laevisuchus,
?Likhoelesaurus, Lukousaurus, Microvenator, Podokesaurus, Prodeinodon, ?Protoavis, Pterospondylus, Rapator, ?Saltopus, Sinocoelurus, Sinosaurus, Teinurosaurus, Thecocoelurus, Thecospondylus, Tugulusaurus,
?Velocipes, Wyleia, ?Zatomus.*

HERRERASAURIDAE Benedetto 1973—(=HER-
RERASAURIA Galton 1985, STAURIKOSAURI-
DAE Galton 1977)

Emended diagnosis: Posterior dorsal vertebrae
with centra anteroposteriorly shortened (*e.g.* dorsal
13–15 with length/height ratio less than 0–8); posterior dorsal and sacral vertebrae with robust neural
spines axially shortened, square-shaped in cross-section; sacrals with very deep ribs, especially that of
second sacral, which covers almost entire medial
surface of iliac blade; proximal caudals with vertical
neural spines; distal caudals with elongated prezygapophyses, overlapping almost 50 percent of pre-
ceeding vertebra; acromial process extends distally
with respect to scapular glenoid lip, forms nearly right
angle with scapular blade; distal expansion of scapular blade strongly reduced; pubis with distal half
anteroposteriorly expanded; pubic "foot" distinct,
axially broadened, more than 25 percent of pubic
length (Novas 1992*b*).

General description: Small, bipedal, 1–5 meters
long, with large head, typically theropod-type teeth,
short neck, rather long forelimbs, relatively long
thighs.

Occurrence: South America? North America.

Courtesy Buenos Aires Museum.

Courtesy The Field Museum (neg. #GEO81665).

Skeleton (FMNH PR308; skull cast of FMNH PR87469) of tyrannosaurid theropod *Albertosaurus libratus,* collected by Barnum Brown in 1914 along Red Deer River, Alberta. This was the first dinosaur skeleton to be exhibited mounted from within, without external supports.

Skeleton of cetiosaurid sauropod *Patagosaurus fariasi.* Thanks to D. Baird.

Skeleton of diplodocid sauropod *Diplodocus hayi*, including holotype CM 662, referred material CM 94, skull (cast) CM 1161, mounted under direction of Wann Langston, Jr.

Right forelimb of *Camarasaurus grandis* [originally referred to *Morosaurus impar*].

Age: Late Triassic.

Genera: ?*Chindesaurus, Herrerasaurus, Staurikosaurus.*

CERATOSAURIA   Marsh 1884

Emended diagnosis: [Unambiguous synapomorphies] Distal end of fibula flaring to overlap ascending process of astragalus; two pairs of cervical pleurocoels; cervical transverse process strongly back-turned, triangular in dorsal view; ilium fused with pubish and ischium in adults (Holtz 1994*a*). [Note: This taxon may prove to be invalid; see *ceratosaurus* entry.]

Generalized description: Small to large, some with cranial horns or crests.

Age: Late Triassic–Late Cretaceous.

Geographic range: North America, ?South America, Europe, Asia, Africa.

Taxa: Coelophysoidea plus Neoceratosauria.

Ceratosauria *incertae sedis*: *Sarcosaurus, ?Velocisaurus.*

COELOPHYSOIDEA Holtz (1994*a*)—(=CERATOSAUROIDEA Bonaparte 1991 [in part], COELOPHYSIDAE Paul 1988, COELOPHYSINAE Nopcsa 1928, PODOKESAURIDAE Huene 1914, PODOKESAURINAE Nopcsa 1923, SEGI-

H. W. Menke, early 1900s, with holotype femur (FMNH P25107) of brachiosaurid sauropod *Brachiosaurus altithorax*.

Courtesy Cleveland Museum of Natural History (neg. #G-2956).

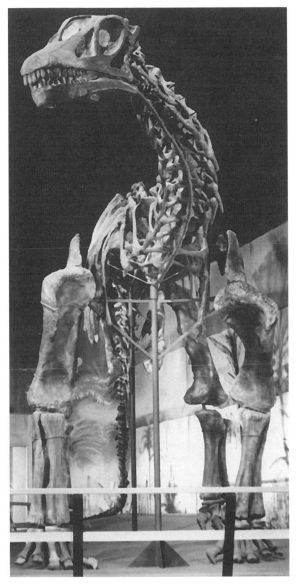

Skeleton of cetiosaurid sauropod *Haplocanthosaurus delsfi*, anterior half largely restored after *Camarasaaurus*.

SAURIDAE Camp 1936, SEGISAURINAE Kalandadze and Rautian 1991)

Diagnosis: Unambiguous synapomorphies include pronounced subnarial gap (indicating possibly mobile premaxilla-maxilla joint); reduction of axial parapophysis; loss of diapophysis; loss of axial pleurocoels (Holtz 1994*a*).

Generalized description: Small to large, similar to but larger than Coeluridae, lightly built, gracile, with rather elongated head, some more specialized forms bearing cranial crests, moderately long neck, short and slender forelimbs with four-fingered hand, foot birdlike with three functional toes.

Age: Late Triassic–Early Jurassic.

Geographic range: North America, Europe, Africa.

Genera: *Coelophysis, Dilophosaurus, Liliensternus, ?Procompsognathus, Rioarribasaurus, Segisaurus, Syntarsus.*

Ceratosauria *incertae sedis: Genusaurus.*

NEOCERATOSAURIA Novas 1992—(=CERATOSAURIDAE Marsh 1884, CERATOSAUROIDEA Bonaparte 1991 [in part])

Diagnosis: [Unambiguous synapomorphies] femoral head directed anteromedially; premaxilla very deep subnarially; parietal projected dorsally; infratemporal fenestra very large; deeply posteroventrally projected articulation of quadrate (Holtz 1994*a*).

Generalized description: Medium to very large, massively-built, large head, short neck, short forelimbs.

Age: Late Jurassic–Late Cretaceous.

Geographic range: North America, South America, Europe, Asia, Africa.

Taxa: ?*Ceratosaurus* (see entry) plus Abelisauroidea.

ABELISAUROIDEA Novas and Bonaparte 1991—(=ABELISAURIA Novas 1992)

Emended diagnosis: [Unambiguous synapomorphies] pleurocoelous dorsal vertebrae; humerus straight; cnemial process arising out of lateral surface of tibial shaftl pronounced pubic "boot"; aliform lesser trochanter; more than five sacral vertebrae (Holtz 1994*a*).

Generalized description: Small, sometimes gracile forms to large, massive forms.

Age: Middle–Late Cretaceous.

Geographic range: South America, Asia.

Taxa: Abelisauridae plus *Noasaurus* plus *Elaphrosaurus.*

ABELISAURIDAE Bonaparte and Novas 1985[*]—(=ABELISAURIA Novas 1992, ABELISAURINAE Paul 1988

Diagnosis: Similar to Tyrannosauridae in long preorbital region and rugosity on nasals, differing

---

[*]*Bonaparte (1986*d*) originally believed the Abelisauridae could be the sister-group to Allosauridae, both sharing a common ancestry in the Jurassic. Bonaparte, Novas and Coria (1990) subsequently regarded Abelisauridae, along with Ceratosauridae and Noasauridae (=Noasaurinae Paul 1988), as belonging to new taxon Ceratosauroidea, which they put into "Carnosauria," based upon their definition of that taxon. Later, Molnar (1990) postulated that abelisaurids constituted a theropod lineage that evolved independently of "Carnosauria," possibly from ceratosaur ancestors.*

Courtesy J. O. Farlow.

Anomoepus curvatus, AC 52/20, fossil footprint made by an Early Jurassic (Norian) small, bipedal ornithischian dinosaur.

Courtesy J. O. Farlow.

Eubrontes platypus (originally *Amblonyx giganteus*), single theropod track in AC 13/4.

Courtesy J. O. Farlow.

Anchisauripus sillimani (originally *A. dananus*), footprint (YPM 2118) of small, Early Jurassic theropod from the Connecticut Valley.

Dinosaurian Systematics

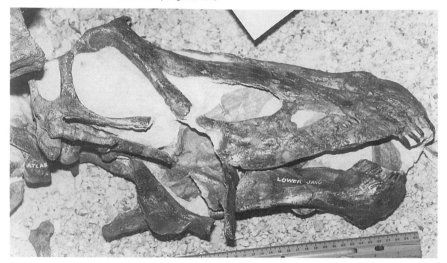

Skull (CM 3452) of diplodocid sauropod *Diplodocus* sp.,
right lateral view. Photo by
R. A. Long and S. P. Welles
(neg. #73-114-21).

Moraeischnium barbernae
Leonardi 1979, paratype ?hyp-
silophodontid tracks, from the
Late Cretaceous Sousa Forma-
tion, District of Sousa,
Paráiba State, northeastern
Brazil.

in following features: broad interorbital roof, very wide infratemporal fenestra, huge preorbital opening, large orbital opening with postorbital intruding into orbit.

Generalized description: Large, with a high and broad head, rather long snout and large eyes.

Age: Middle–Late Cretaceous.

Geographic range: South America, Asia.

Genera: *Abelisaurus, Carnotaurus, ?Indosaurus, ?Indosuchus, ?Majungasaurus, Tarascosaurus, ?Xenotarsosaurus*

TETANURAE   Gauthier 1986

Emended diagnosis: [Unambiguous synapomorphies] pronounced horizontal groove across anterior face of astragalar condyles; pleurocoelous dorsal vertebrae; presacral column reduced anteroposteriorly relative to length of femur; sharp ridge on tibia anterolaterally for clasping fibula; antorbital tooth row (Holtz 1994*a*).

Generalized description: Small to giant, wide range of diversity, including all theropods that are more closely allied with birds than to Ceratosauria.

Age: Middle Jurassic–Late Cretaceous.

Geographic distribution: North America, South America, Europe, Asia, Australia, Africa.

Taxa: ?Spinosauridae plus ?Eustreptospondylidae plus ?Megalosauridae plus Avetheropoda.

Tetanurae *incertae sedis*: *Bahariasaurus, Bruhathkayosaurus, Carcharodontosaurus, Coelurus, Dryptosauroides, Gasosaurus, Giganotosaurus, Iliosuchus, Kaijiangosaurus, Kelmayisaurus, Labocania, Ornithomimoides, Orthogoniosaurus, Shanshanosaurus, Stokesosaurus, ?Unquillosaurus, Walgettosuchus.*

SPINOSAURIDAE   Stromer 1915

Diagnosis: Dentary with marked dorso-ventral constriction behind fourth tooth; teeth elongate, relatively straight, subcylindrical, nonserrated; presacral vertebrae opisthocoelous; dorsal neural spines greatly elongate.

Generalized description: Large, with three-fingered hand, and dorsal "sail" supported by long spines, possibly quadrupdal, neck relatively long.

Age: Late Cretaceous.

Geographic range: Africa, ?Europe, ?Asia.

Genera: ?*Baryonyx*, ?*Siamosaurus, Spinosaurus.*

EUSTREPTOSPONDYLIDAE   Paul   1988— (=EUSTREPTOSPONDYLINAE Paul 1988, ILIOSUCHIDAE   Paul   1988, METRIACANTHO-

Courtesy The Field Museum (neg. #GEO81874).

Composite skeleton (anterior part FMNH P27021, posterior part FMNH P25112, skull (cast) CM 12020 of *Camarasaurus*) of diplodocid sauropod *Apatosaurus excelsus*.

SAURINAE Paul 1988, STREPTOSPONDYLIDAE Kurzanov 1989)[*]

Diagnosis: Skull low, long; frontals long; postfrontals shifted forward; dorsal vertebrae with long

Courtesy G. Leonardi.

Souseichnium pricei Leonardi 1979, holotype iguanodontid footprints from the Late Cretaceous, Sousa Foundation, district of Sousa, Paráiba State, northeastern Brazil.

centra, more opisthocoelous than in megalosaurids and allosaurids; pleurocoels more estensively developed.

Generalized description: Long heads with low snout.

Age: Middle–Late Jurassic.

Geographic range: Europe.

Genera: *Becklespinax, Eustreptospondylus, ?Piveteausaurus.*

MEGALOSAURIDAE Huxley 1869—(=CERATOSAUROIDEA Bonaparte 1991 [in part], ERECTOPODIDAE Huene 1932, ILIOSUCHIDAE Paul 1988, MEGALOSAURI fitzinger 1843, MEGALOSAURINAE Paul 1988, MEGALOSAUROIDES Gervais 1853, TORVOSAURIDAE Jensen 1985, UNQUILLOSAURIDAE Powell 1986)[†] Diagnosis: [There is currently no adequate published diagnosis

---

[*]*Novas (1992a) proposed the new taxon Avipoda to include* Eustreptospondylus *plus* Compsognathus *plus Tetanurae, diagnosed by such derived traits as follows: Maxillary fenestra; femoral head offset from femoral shaft, slightly inclined dorsally, lacking of anterior depression for muscular attachment; femur with anterodistal intercondylar groove; femur with crista tibiofibularis transversely compressed and vertically oriented; tibia with crista fibularis prominent and more distally located than in Ceratosauria; astragular ascending process transversely widened.*

[†]*The term "megalosaur" has traditionally been used to identify virtually any large theropod based on fragmentary remains from Europe, many of these forms having only large sizes in common. British megalosaurids are currently being restudied by Welles and Powell and continental megalosaurs by Taquet and Powell. To date, these myriad "megalosaur" taxa have yet to be sufficiently sorted out. Gauthier (1986) tentatively referred Megalosauridae to the "Carnosauria" due to lack of data; Britt (1991) regarded the Megalosauridae as a group within Ceratosauria, based upon numerous similarities between* Ceratosaurus, Megalosaurus, *and* Torvosaurus. *This assessment was not accepted by Holtz (1994a), who regarded both* Torvosaurus *and* Megalosaurus *as tetanurans.*

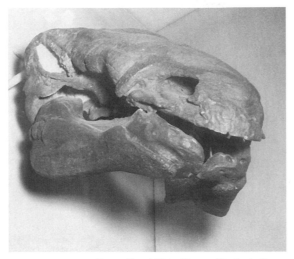

Skull (cast) of nodosaurid thyreophoran *Edmontonia rugosidens*, right three-quarter view. Photo by the author.

Courtesy Natural History Museum of Los Angeles County.

of Megalosauridae. Kurzanov (1989) pointed out that, if all the remains described, much of which is poorly preserved, do pertain to *Megalosaurus*, they exhibit numerous characteristic features, some applicable to allosaurids, some to Tyrannosaurids, some probably plesiomorphic; some European megalosaurids are characterized by an atypical increase in height of neural spines.]

Generalized description: Including most generalized forms; large, head with long jaws, teeth with double edges, very short forelimbs with three-fingered hands, powerful hindlimbs, toes with large talons.

Age: Late Jurassic–?Late Cretaceous.

Geographic range: North America, South America, Europe, Asia.

Genera: *Afrovenator, Altispinax, Edmarka, Erectopus, Magnosaurus, Megalosaurus, ?Metriacan-*

Skeleton (MIWG) of iguanodontid ornithopod *Iguanodon atherfieldensis*. Photo by the author.

Courtesy Museum of Isle of Wight Geology.

thosaurus, ?Monolophosaurus, Poekilopleuron, Torvosaurus, ?Wakinosaurus, ?Xuanhanosaurus.

AVETHEROPODA   Paul 1988

Emended diagnosis: [Unambiguous synapomorphies] Loss of obturator foramen; proximally placed lesser trochanter; basal half of metacarpal I closely appressed to II; cnemial process arising out of lateral surface of tibial shaft; pronounced pubic "boot"; coracoid tapering posteriorly; U-shaped premaxillary symphysis; premaxillary tooth crowns asymmetrical in cross-section (Holtz 1994a).

Generalized description: Very small to giant, with wide range of diversity and specializations.

Age: Late Jurassic–Late Cretaceous.

Geographic range: ?Worldwide[*].

Taxa: Allosauroidea plus Coelurosauria.

ALLOSAUROIDEA   Currie and Zhao 1993

Diagnosis: Large theropods; more derived than megalosaurids, similar to allosaurids in various features (last maxillary tooth anterior to orbit; antorbital sinus extending into interior of lacrimal, nasal, and jugal; ventral end of postorbital above ventral margin of orbit; upper quadratojugal prong of jugal shorter than lower prong; quadrate-quadratojugal fenestra present with associated sinus; pneumatic basisphenoidal recess; braincase box opened up posteriorly between tubera, which are no longer pedunculate; oval muscular attachment on basioccipital; down-turned paroccipital processes; posteroventral limit of exoccipital-opisthotic contacts basisphenoid, but is separated from basal tubera by notch; at least incipient separation of opthalmic from other branches of trigeminal nerve); tenth presacral vertebra in process of incorporation into dorsal rather than cervical region; triangular neurapophysis; axial neural spine reduced; axial centrum without ventral keel; parapophyses reduced in lateral extension from primitive condition; anteroposteriorly thin rib heads; elongate scapular blade sharply set off from acromial

---

[*]*Molnar (1989) speculated that large theropods (as well as primitive sauropods, hypsilophodontians, iguanodontids, ankylosaurs, and various nondinosaurian groups) may have occurred in Antarctica, although most of these groups have not yet been found on that continent. Molnar's conclusion was through indirect inference using the reconstructed positions of the continents during the Mesozoic. In the Cretaceous, Antarctica was a "bridge" offering the only link between Australia (where Allosaurus is known from the Early Cretaceous) and the other continents. According to Molnar, continental terrestrial taxa must have dispersed into Australia overland across Antarctica.*

process and glenoid lip; obturator fenestra of ischium opens into notch, producing distinct obturator process; metatarsal V relatively shorter than in more primitive genera (Currie and Zhao 1993).[*]

Generalized description: Large to giant, with large head, short neck, short forelimbs bearing three fingers with formidable claws.

Age: Middle Jurassic–Early Cretaceous.
Geographic range: ?Worldwide.
Taxa: Sinraptoridae plus Allosauridae.

SINRAPTORIDAE   Currie and Zhao 1993

Diagnosis: [Same as for Allosauroidea, plus the following] more primitive than allosaurids in that quadrate is more elongate; paroccipital processes not as strongly downturned; and distal end of scapula not expanded; autapomorphies include presence of two or more sets of accessory openings in antorbital fossa connected to maxillary sinus; low lacrimal horn; ventral margin of axial intercentrum rotated above ventral margin of axial centrum (Currie and Zhao 1993).

Generalized description: Large forms, low "horns" above eyes.

Age: Late Jurassic.
Geographic range: Asia.
Genera: *Sinraptor, Yangchuanosaurus.*

ALLOSAURIDAE   Marsh 1878—(=ALLOSAURINAE Paul 1988, ANTRODEMIDAE Stromer 1934, LABROSAURIDAE Marsh 1882)

Emended diagnosis: [Unambiguous synapomorphies] pubic "boot" longer anteriorly than posteriorly, triangular (apex posterior) in ventral aspect (Holtz 1994*a*).

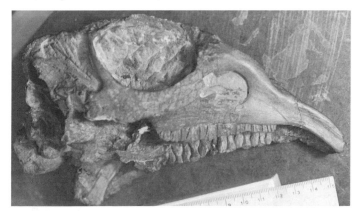

Skull (CM 3390) of dryosaurid ornithopod *Dryosaurus altus.* Photo by R. A. Long and S. P. Welles (neg. #73-472-29).

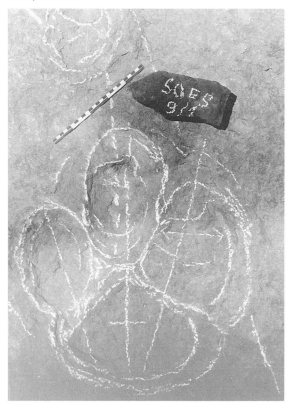

Caririchnium magnificum Leonardi 1984, holoytpe ichnite of ?advanced iguanodontid or ?primitive hadrosaurid, from the Rio do Peixe group, Antenor Navarro Formation, Serroti de Pimente, Paráiba, Brazil.

Generalized description: Large forms, more derived than sinraptorids.

Age: Middle Jurassic–Early Cretaceous.
Geographic range: ?Worldwide.
Genera: *Acrocanthosaurus, Allosaurus, Chilantaisaurus, ?Compsosuchus, Piatnitzkysaurus, Saurophagus, Szechuanosaurus, ?Valdoraptor.*

COELUROSAURIA   Huene 1914

Emended diagnosis: [Unambiguous synapomorphies] Ischium only two-thirds or less length of pubis; loss of ischial "foot"; expanded circular orbit; ischium with triangular obturator process; ascending process of astragalus greater than one-fourth length of epipodium; 15 or fewer

---

[*]*Currie and Zhao united Sinraptoridae and Allosauridae into the taxon Allosauroidea, which they defined by the synapomorphies separating these groups from Ceratosaurus, abelisaurids, megalosaurids, and other primitive theropods, adding that some of those characters may eventually be also found in megalosaurids. According to Currie and Zhao, abelisaurids and perhaps some poorly known African and European forms apparently split off the evolutionary line of "carnosaurs" leading to allosaurids before Sinraptor.*

Skeleton (ROM 5090) of camptosaurid ornithopod *Camptosaurus* cf. *dispar.*

caudal vertebrae with transverse processes (Holtz 1994*a*).[*]

Generalized description: Small to giant, with large eyes, birdlike feet.

Age: Late Jurassic–Late Cretaceous.

Geographic range: North America, South America, Europe, Asia, Africa.

Taxa: *Compsognathus* plus Maniraptora plus ?Therizinosauridae.

Coelurosauria *incertae sedis*: ?*Diplotomodon*, ?*Dryptosaurus.*

MANIRAPTORA   Gauthier 1986

Emended diagnosis: Ulna bowed posteriorly; metacarpal III long, slender; posterodorsal margin of ilium curving ventrally in lateral aspect; cervical zygapophyses flexed; jugal expressed on rim of antorbital fenestra; metacarpal I one-third or less length of II (Holtz 1994*a*, based on Gauthier 1986[†]).

Generalized description: More birdlike in form than other theropods.

Age: Late Jurassic–Late Cretaceous.

Geographic range: North America, South America, Europe, Asia, Africa.

Taxa: *Ornitholestes* plus Dromaeosauridae plus Arctometatarsalia plus ?Therizihosauroidea.

Maniraptora *incertae sedis*: *Alvarezsaurus*, ?*Irritator*, *Ricardoestesia.*

DROMAEOSAURIDAE Russell 1969—(=ELOPTERYGIDAE Lambrecht 1933, ELOPTERYGINAE Le Loeuff, Buffetaut, Mechin and Mechin-Salessy 1992)

Emended diagnosis: Long but shallow premaxillary process excludes maxilla from margin of external naris, separates anterior ends of maxilla and nasal; lacrimal slender, T-shaped; frontal process of postorbital upturned, meets a pronounced and posteroventrally inclined postorbital process of frontal; T-shaped quadratojugal different from L-shaped ones in most theropods; pronounced ventrolatral process of squamosal is sutured to top of paroccipital process, extends conspicuously lateral to intertemporal bar and quadratojugal; distal end of paroccipital process twisted to face posterodorsally; pneumatopore in anterior surface of paroccipital process opens into pneumatic sinus within the process; relatively short basipterygoid processes extending ventrally onto level of basal tubera; pterygoid lacking ventral extension that, with ectopterygoid, forms "pterygoid flange" in theropods as diverse as *Rioarribasaurus, Allosaurus,* and *Sinraptor* (Currie and Zhao, 1993*a*); palatine contacting ectopterygoid, separating palatine fenestra from subsidiary palatine fenestra; dentary relatively tall, labiolingually thin, Meckelian groove shallow; splenial with relatively large, triangular process exposed on lateral surface of mandible between dentary and angular; relatively large, triangular internal mandibular fenestra (infra–Meckelian fenestra); retroarticular process broad, shallow, shelf-like, with vertical, columnar process rising from posteromedial corner; interdental plates in premaxilla, maxilla, and dentary fused to each other and to margins of jaws; pubis presumably retroverted; specialized (sickle-clawed) pedal digit II (Currie 1995).

Generalized description: Rather small to medium, lightly built, large heads with narrow snout, moderately deep and straight lower jaw, backwardly curved teeth, with unusually long forelimbs, hand with a very mobile wrist, three long fingers and large curved claws, foot with second toe developed into a highly raptorial "sickle claw," and a long, stiff tail.

Age: Early–Late Cretaceous.

Geographic range: North America, Asia.

Taxa: ?Dromaeosaurinae plus Velociraptorinae.

---

[*] *As defined by Gauthier (1986), Coelurosauria includes birds and those theropods closer to birds than they are to the "Carnosauria," with Tyrannosauridae assigned to the latter taxon.*

[†] *As originally defined by Gauthier (1986), Maniraptora also embraces birds and was erected to emphasize that certain characters were shared by a common ancestor of Aves and Dromaeosauridae. As pointed out by Holtz (1994a), based on his own phylogenetic analysis, most of the manual characters that Gauthier (1986) used to diagnose Maniraptora were plesiomorphic at the dromaeosaurid-bird clade level. Gauthier (1986) also erected the new maniraptoran taxon Aviale, to embrace Dromaeosauridae, Troodontidae and also the bird Archaeopteryx (see section on "Dinosaurs and Birds")*

Dromaeosauridae *incertae sedis*: ?*Adasaurus*, ?*Euronychodon, Hulsanpes*, ?*Phaedrolosaurus*.

Taxa: Oviraptorosauria plus Elmisauridae plus *Avimimus*, Tyrannosauridae plus Bullatosauria.

VELOCIRAPTORINAE   Barsbold 1978

Emended diagnosis: Denticles on anterior carina of maxillary and dentary teeth significantly smaller than posterior denticles; second premaxillary tooth significantly larger than third and fourth premaxillary teeth; nasal depressed in lateral view (Paul 1988*b*) (this bone unknown in *Dromaeosaurus*) (Currie 1995).

Generalized description: More gracile and agile than in dromaeosaurines.

Age: Early–Late Cretaceous.

Geographic range: North America, Asia.

Genera: *Deinonychus, Koreanosaurus*, ?*Saurornitholestes, Utahraptor, Velociraptor*.

DROMAEOSAURINAE   Matthew and Brown 1922

Emended diagnosis: Fewer maxillary teeth (9) than in other dromaeosaurids; anterior carina of maxillary tooth close to midline of tooth near tip, but not far from tip tooth twists toward lingual surface; differs from velociraptorines in following features: premaxillar deeper, thicker; quadratojugal stouter; top of frontal flatter, margin of supratemporal fossa not as pronounced; postorbital process of frontal more sharply demarcated from dorsomedial orbital margin; posteromedial process of palatine more slender; anterior and posterior tooth denticles subequal in size (Currie 1995).

Generalized description: Head more massive than in velociraptorines.

Age: Late Cretaceous.

Geographic distribution: North America.

Genus: ?*Dromaeosaurus*.

ARCTOMETATARSALIA   Holtz (1994*a*)

Diagnosis: [Unambiguous synapomorphies] tibia and metatarsus elongate; metatarsals deeper anteroposteriorly than mediolaterally; acrtometatarsus; metatarsus gracile; reversal of flexed cervical zygapophyses (Holtz 1994*a*).*

Generalized description: Small to very large, feet birdlike.

Age: Late Cretaceous.

Geographic distribution: North America, Asia.

OVIRAPTOROSAURIA   Barsbold 1976

Emended diagnosis: Mandible extensively fenestrated, medial process on articular; dentary with two long caudal processes, ventral process bordering mandibular fenestra; splenial very shallow; prearticular extending rostrally along more than half length of mandible; jaws toothless, rostral portions probably covered by horny bill (Barsbold, Maryańska and Osmólska 1990).

Generalized description: Small, toothless with beak, neck moderately long, hand with three fingers; possibly herbivorous or omnivorous.

Age: Late Cretaceous.

Geographic range: North America, Asia.

Taxa: Oviraptoridae plus ?Caenagnathidae.

OVIRAPTORIDAE Barsbold 1976—(=?CAENAGNATHIDAE Sternberg 1940)

Emended diagnosis: Derived characters of short

Holtz (1994b) pointed out that the Cretaceous theropod families Ornithomimidae, Tyrannosauridae, Troodontiadae, Elmisauridae, and Avimimidae share an unusual condition of the metatarsus not shared by underived theropod families (e.g., Ceratosauridae and Allosauridae). Metatarsal III (central metatarsal) is greatly reduced proximally, almost entirely excluded from anterior view, and nearly to entirely excluded in dorsal view, and forms a wedge shape distally, is triangular in transverse cross-section, which is buttressed against the more columnar second and fourth metatarsals. For this morphology, forming a tightly bound structure, Holtz (see also 1994a) coined the term "arctometatarsalian condition."

Utilizing morphometric analysis comparing numerous theropod taxa, Holtz (1994b) showed that this structure is significantly more elongate and gracile than the metatarsi of underived theropods, and that it is associated with relatively elongate distal hind limbs per unit femoral length. These limb proportions, when compared with those of modern and extinct mammals and flightless birds, were interpreted as consistent with the hypothesis of enhanced cursoriality in derived theropods. Through biomechanical analysis, Holtz (1994b) found that this kind of relatively gracile foot was not substantially weaker than the feet of underived theropods, but rather that these metatarsi were well designed to withstand the forces and stresses that accompany enhanced cursorial ability. Thus, even giant predators such as Tyrannosaurus (sometimes regarded as a slow-moving animal), with significantly more gracile metatarsi for a given femoral length, appear to have been better adapted for enhanced cursorial ability than underived genera such as Ceratosaurus and Allosaurus. Holtz (1994b) cautioned that, although the proportions of the arctometatarsalian forms suggest trends toward increased speed relative to underived theropods, the actual speeds attainable by these dinosaurs were unknown.

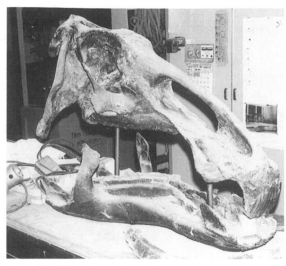

Skull (LACM 23502) of hadrosaurine ornithopod *Edmontosaurus annectens*, a rare specimen preserving the beak. Photo by the author.

Courtesy Natural History Museum of Los Angeles County.

deep mandible; dentary with short, concave rostral portion thickened at symphysis; two widely separated caudal dentary processes that border vertically enlarged external mandibular fenestra ventrally and dorsally; external mandibular fenestra subdivided by spine-like rostral process of surangular; skull deep with shortened snout, palate with pair of median, tooth-like processes on maxillae (Barsbold, Maryańska and Osmólska 1990).

Generalized description: Small forms, head with short jaws with parrot-like beak and relatively large braincase, frontlimbs very long, similar to those in ornithomimids, differing from latter in that claws are more sharply curved and first finger somewhat longer than other two fingers.

Age: Late Cretaceous.
Geographic range: Asia.
Taxa: Oviraptorinae plus Ingeniinae.

OVIRAPTORINAE   Barsbold 1981

Diagnosis: Manus with comparatively long, slender digits; digit I shortest; penultimate phalanges longest; unguals strongly curved, with strong flexor tubercles and dorsoposterior "lips."

Generalized description: More gracile than ingeniines, cranial crest in some forms.

Age: Late Cretaceous.
Geographic range: Asia.
Genera: *Conchoraptor, Oviraptor.*

INGENIINAE Barsbold 1981

Diagnosis: Manual digit I longest, very strong; digits II and III much shorter, thinner due to strongly reduced phalanges, especially penultimate phalanges, which are shorter than preceding phalanx; unguals of digits II and III short, weakly curved, with small flexor tubercles; unguals without "lips."

Generalized description: More robust than oviraptorines, apparently crestless head, relatively smaller claws on second and third fingers.

Age: Late Cretaceous.
Geographic range: Asia.
Genus: *Ingenia.*

CAENAGNATHIDAE   Sternberg 1940—(=CAENAGNATHINAE Paul 1988; =?OVIRAPTORIDAE Barsbold 1976)

Emended diagnosis: Derived characters of mandible with long, narrow fenestra; rostral portion of mandible with dorsal curvature; dentary with two shallow grooves along lateral edges on dorsal surface of symphysis; (from shape of mandible) skull apparently not shortened (Barsbold, Maryańska and Osmólska 1990).

Generalized description: More primitive than oviraptorids.

Age: Late Cretaceous.
Geographic range: North America, Asia.
Genera: *Caenagnathasia, Caenagnathus.*

ELMISAURIDAE   Osmólska 1981—(=?CAENAGNATHIDAE Sternberg 1940)

Emended diagnosis: Manual digit III longer than I; proximodorsal "lip" on manual unguals; metatarsal III pinched proximally between II and IV, only proximal tip excluded from the extensor surface of metatarsus; second to fourth distal tarsals and metatarsals tightly associated, tending to coosify into tarsometatarsus; back of metatarsus deeply emarginated; ilium with postacetabular blade shorter than preacetabular blade (Currie 1990).

Generalized description: Small, lightly built, with gracile hands and large feet.

Age: Late Cretaceous.
Geographic range: North America, Asia.
Genera: *Chirostenotes, Elmisaurus.*

TYRANNOSAURIDAE   Osborn 1905—(=AUBLYSODONTIDAE Nopcsa 1928, AUBLYSODONTINAE Nopcsa 1928, DEINODONTIDAE Brown 1914, DEINODONTINAE Matthew and Brown 1922, DINODONTIDAE Cope 1866,

Skull (NMC 2870) of hadrosaurine ornithopod *Prosaurolophus maximus.* Photo by M. K. Brett-Surman.

DEINODONTOIDEA Tatarinov 1964, TYRANNOSAURINAE Matthew and Brown 1922)[*]

Emended diagnosis: Head large relative to body size; neck, trunk and forelimbs short; nasals very rugose, often fused along midline, constricted between lacrimals; frontals excluded from orbits by lacrimals; jugal pierced by large foramen; premaxillary teeth D-shaped in cross-section, carinae along posteromedial and posterolateral margins; vomer with diamond-shaped process between maxillae; ectopterygoid with large ventral opening; surangular foramen large; cervical centra slightly opisthocoelous, anteroposteriorly compressed, and broad; scapula long, slender; humerus with weakly- to moderately well-developed deltopectoral crest; manus reduced to two function digits (II and III), digit IV reduced to splint; pubis with well-developed anterior "foot"; distal end of ischium not expanded; astragalus with broad and tall ascending ramus (Carpenter 1992).

Generalized description: Largest of theropods as a group, and more massive and powerful, with extremely small forelimbs with functionally two-fingered hand, digit III a splint-like vestige.

Age: Late Cretaceous.

Geographic range: North America, South America, Asia.

Genera: *Albertosaurus, Alectrosaurus, ?Alioramus, Aublysodon, Chingkankousaurus, Daspletosaurus, Deinodon, Maleevosaurus, Nanotyrannus, Tyrannosaurus.*

BULLATOSAURIA Holtz (1994*a*)

Diagnosis: [Unambiguous synapomorphies] parasphenoid capsule bulbous; pterygoid canal; frontals long, triangular; occipital region deflected ventrally; endocranium enlarged; orbit with pronounced rim; reversal of pleurocoelous dorsal vertebrae (Holtz 1994*a*).

The Tyrannosauridae has traditionally been positioned within the "Carnosauria" (in its original meaning; also sensu *Gauthier 1986, and Molnar, Kurzanov and Dong 1990) along with other large theropods (e.g. megalosaurids and allosaurids). However, based on the derived condition of the tyrannosaurid pes (see Holtz 1994a, below), Huene (1920, 1926b) regarded these dinosaurs as large "coelurosaurs" sharing a common ancestor with ornithomimids separated from other theropods. This assessment was also reached, over the years, by other authors, although tyrannosaurids were generally kept nestled within "Carnosauria."*

More recent (and independent) cladistic analyses by various workers have shown tyrannosaurids to be derived members of the Coelurosauria. For example, Novas (1992a) noted that the Tyrannosauridae, Ornitholestes, Ornithomimidae, and Maniraptora share several derived features not present in Allosaurus, this suggesting that tyrannosaurids are very large coelurosaurs.

Holtz (1994a) referred the Tyrannosauridae to the Coelurosauria (an assessment also reached by Bakker and Currie in an as yet unpublished study), regarding the latter taxon as a group of otherwise small theropods and as the sister-group of ornithomimids and troodontids. Holtz (1994a, [in press]) found that tyrannosaurids share with certain coelurosaurian groups (i.e., ornithomimids, troodontids, elmisaurids, and avimimids) an unusual condition of the pes (termed "the arctometatarsalian condition" by that author), wherein the central metatarsal is pinched proximally and thereby obscured from view anteriorly and reduced or excluded from contact with the tibiotarsus; the three functional metatarsals in most other theropods are generally cylindrical in form, of subequal length, and subequal in diameter throughout the length. The atrophied carpal structure in tyrannosaurids derived from a maniraptoran manus possessing a semilunate carpal. According to Holtz (1994a), characters found in tyrannosaurids previously recognized as diagnostic of the "Carnosauria" (e.g. increased development of attachment surfaces for cranial musculature and hindlimb proportion) are related to size (found also in sauropods and other large predatory archosaurs) rather than having phylogentic importance.

Skull (FMNH P15003) of hadrosaurine ornithopod *Edmontosaurus regalis.*

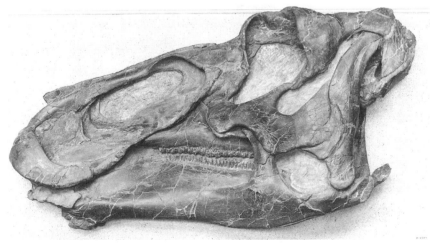

Generalized description: Small to medium, lightly built, birdlike, long face, long, slender hindlimbs.

Age: ?Late Triassic–Late Cretaceous.

Geographic range: North America, Asia.

Taxa: Troodontidae plus Ornithomimosauria.

TROODONTIDAE   Gilmore 1924—(=SAUROR-NITHOIDIDAE Barsbold 1974; =?BRADYCNE-MIDAE Harrison and Walker 1975)

Emended diagnosis: Skull long, with narrow snout, large endocranial cavity; external naris bounded by maxilla caudoventrally; basioccipital and periotic sinus systems; parasphenoid capsule bulbous; braincase with lateral depression on lateral wall, containing enlarged middle ear cavity; basipterygoid process enlarged, hollow; mandible with rostrally tapering dentary that exposes laterally a row of foramina located within groove beneath alveolar margin; up to 25 premaxillary and maxillary teeth and 35 dentary teeth; all teeth small, recurved, spaced closely together; distal and often mesial edges of teeth with large, hooked denticles pointing toward tip of crown; distal and mesial denticles of subequal size; calcaneum thin, fused with astragalus; metatarsus long to very long, with longitudinal, proximal trough along extensor face of metatarsal III; metatarsal III slightly longer than IV, reduced to bone splinter for about half proximal length; on extensor side, proximal end of metatarsal III hidden by tightly adhering ends of metatarsals II and IV; distal end of metatarsal III with tongue-like articular surface extending proximocaudally; metatarsal IV most robust, occupying more than half width of metatarsus in caudal view (Osmól-ska and Barsbold 1990); all six sacral vertebrae fully anklosed; pneumatic foramina present on first two sacrals; ventral surface of sacrals flattened with medial groove developing shallowly on sacral 2, very pronounced on 3–6; neural platform present (Howse and Milner 1993).

Generalized description: Small, with long, narrow head, with largest relative brain size of all dinosaurs, long, slender and delicate jaws, small, closely-spaced teeth, very long, slender hindlimbs, second toe enlarged with claw sometimes straight.

Age: Late Jurassic[*]–Late Cretaceous.

Geographic distribution: North America, Asia.

Genera: *Borogovia*, ?*Bradycneme*, ?*Heptasteornis*, *Koparion*, ?*Lisboasaurus*, ?*Ornithodesmus*, *Saurornithoides*, *Sinornithoides*, *Tochisaurus*, *Troodon*.

ORNITHOMIMOSAURIA   Barsbold 1976

Emended diagnosis: Femur distinguished from those of "carnosaurs" by head being anteroposteri-orly compressed rather than oval or round, and by lesser trochanter being slightly higher (not lower) than greater trochanter (Rich and Rich 1994).

Generalized description: Small to rather large, lightly built, superficially resembling modern ground birds, with long snout, beak-like and usually toothless jaws (small teeth present in primitive forms), toothless jaws probably covered by horny beak, large eyes, long neck, relatively long forelimbs (about half length of hindlimbs), nonraptorial hand with three long fingers, slender hindlimbs, thigh shorter than shin, three-four toes, cursorial, possibly omnivorous or herbivorous, among fleetest of cursorial dinosaurs.

Age: ?Late Triassic–Late Cretaceous.

Geographic range: North America, Europe, Asia.

Taxa: ?*Shuvosaurus* plus Harpymimidae plus Garudimimidae plus Ornithomimidae.

Orniithomimosauria *incertae sedis*: *Pelecanimimus*.

HARPYMIMIDAE   Barsbold and Perle 1984

Emended diagnosis: Derived characters include front of dentary, with six small, blunt, cylindrical teeth; short humerus, measuring about length of skull and almost that of scapula; metacarpal I just slightly more than half length of II, III longest (Barsbold and Osmólska 1990).

Generalized description: Very primitive, the only known forms to have teeth, with relatively large hand, feet probably three-toed; moderately fast locomotion. Having blunt, cylindrical teeth.

Age: Middle Cretaceous.

Geographic range: Asia.

Genus: *Harpymimus*.

GARUDIMIMIDAE   Barsbold 1981—(=GARU-DIMIMINAE Paul 1988)

Emended diagnosis: Derived characters include dorsal and sacral vertebrae lacking pleurocoels; ilium shorter than pubis; metatarsal III strongly narrowed along proximal part, visible throughout extensor face of metatarsus, separating metatarsals II and IV entirely; proximal phalanx of pedal digit II as long as in digit III; pedal digit III just slightly longer than IV (Barsbold and Osmólska 1990).

Generalized description: Very primitive, with

Chure (1994) postulated that the origins of the Troodontidate may be earlier than the Late Jurassic, this hypothesis based upon the fact that the Late Jurassic genus Koparion (see entry) already possesses several troodontid dental specializations.

four-toed foot that retains a short first toe; moderately fast locomotion.

Age: Late Cretaceous.

Geographic distribution: Asia.

Genus: *Garudimimus.*

ORNITHOMIMIDAE Marsh 1890—(=ORNITHOMIMINAE Nopcsa 1923)

Emended diagnosis: Femur distinguished from that of *Chirostenotes pergracilis* (Elmisauridae) by more proximally situated base of lesser trochanter (femora of Harpymimidae and Garudimidae not described) (Rich and Rich 1994).

Generalized description: Medium, fingers of subequal length, no first toe, third toe longer than second and fourth; fastest locomotion among ornithomimosaurians.

Age: Early–Late Cretaceous.

Geographic range: North America, Asia.

Genera: *Archaeornithomimus, Dromiceiomimus, Gallimimus, Ornithomimus, Struthiomimus.*

THERIZINOSAUROIDEA Russell and Dong 1993—(=ENIGMOSAURIDAE Barsbold and Perle 1989, SEGNOSAURIA Barsbold and Perle 1980, SEGNOSAURIDAE Perle 1979)[*]

Diagnosis: Ala from jugal embracing ventrolateral corner of lateral temporal fenestra; heavy crest rising from anterior third of dentary dorsoposteriorly toward anterodorsal end of surangular; teeth becoming larger anteriorly; zygapophyses widely spaced on cervical vertebrae, zygapophyseal pedicels well spaced, zygapophyseal extremities defining shape intermediate between right-angeled "X" in dorsal outline; shaft of posterior cervical ribs bifurcating anteriorly; neural arches of anterior dorsal vertebrae elevated so that distance between arch suture and level of zygapophyseal articulations are greater than three-fourths height of centrum; shaft of dorsal ribs straight, oriented at right angle to capitular ramus; rectangular buttress from metacarpal underlying metacarpal II; manual unguals flat-sided, deep proximally; rim of ilium dorsal to sacral transverse processes strongly elevated; pubic peduncle of ilium reduced; ischium strap-like, laterally bowed; posterior trochanter of femur prominent, crest on femur proximally situated; proximomedial fossa on fibula shallow or absent; metatarsus less than one-third length of tibia; facet on metatarsal I for articulation with metatarsal II enlarged, deeply concave; first digit of first toe (and entire first toe) slightly enlarged so that I-1 is longer than IV-1 (Russell and Dong 1993a).

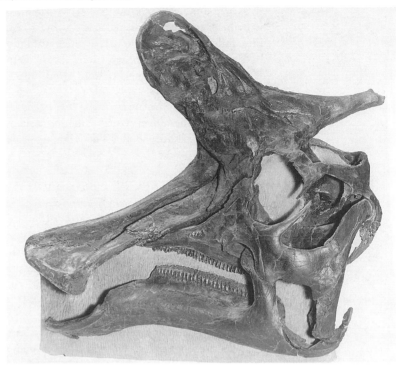

Skull (CNHM UC1479) of lambeosaurine ornithopod *Lambeosaurus lambei.*

[*]*Perle (1979), then Barsbold and Perle (1980), regarded the Segnosauria as belonging to the Theropoda. Paul (1985) observed that neither the "segnosaurians" Segnosaurus nor Erlikosaurus meet the criteria required for inclusion in Theropoda (as then defined by Romer 1966). Paul further argued that the small beaked skull, spatulate teeth, opisthopubic pelvis, and broad, tetradactyl hind feet in segnosaurids indicate affinities with prosauropods or ornithischians, concluding that segnosaurians made up a dinosaurian clade intermediate between prosauropods and ornithischians.*

Gauthier (1986) suggested that "segnosaurians" were closely related to broad-footed sauropodomorphs. In their review of Segnosauria, Barsbold and Marya'nska (1990) found Gauthier's assessment more probable than those earlier proposed, stated that this relationship requires a detailed analysis, and found it best then to regard Segnosauria as Saurischia incertae sedis.

On the basis of better remains collected from Aptian-Albian rock of Inner Mongolia, Russell and Dong (1993a) later argued that "segnosaurs" were herbivores that descended from tetanuran theropods, the oldest family-group name available for this group being Therizinosauridae Maleev 1954 (see Therizinosaurus *entry). Russell and Dong proposed the new monotypic family Alxasauridae which was combined with the Therizinosauridae ("segnosaurs") to establish new "superfamily" Therizinosauroidea, which they placed within Tetanurae.*

Based on a preliminary analysis of therizinoid theropods, Russell and Dong further suggested that Tetanurae contains two subordinate groups, "Carnosauria" (including Allosaurus, *dromaeosaurids, and tyrannosaurids) and Oviraptorosauria (including therizinosauroids, ornithomimids, troodontids, and oviraptorids), this classification dramatically contradicting the recent organization proposed by Holtz (1994a). Maniraptora was regarded by Russell and Dong as possibly an unnatural group for troodontids and dromaeosaurids contained within separate branches of their proposed "Carnosauria"-Oviraptorosauria dichotomy.*

Generalized description: Herbivorous, medium to large, somewhat resembling prosauropods, but with beak (probably covered with horny sheath in life), followed by a toothless area, which was followed by series of cheek teeth, with long arms, theropod type hands, clawed fingers, stout hindlimbs, and broad feet with claws, short tail.

Age: Late Cretaceous.

Geographic range: ?North America, Asia.

Taxa: Alxasauridae plus Therizinosauridae.

ALXASAURIDAE Russell and Dong 1993

Diagnosis: Approximately forty dentary teeth; teeth in symphyseal region of dentary; ribs not fused to cervical centra; ligament pits often well developed in manual phalanges; ilium not greatly shortened anteroposteriorly; preacetabular ala moderately expanded; ungual shorter than or subequal to first phalanx in pedal digits II-IV (Russell and Dong 1993).

Generalized description: Apparently superficially resembling moderately large prosauropod, with small head, relatively long neck, long arms, short tail.

Age: Late Cretaceous.

Geographic range: Asia.

Genus: *Alxasaurus*.

THERIZINOSAURIDAE Maleev 1954

Emended diagnosis: Skull and mandible shallow, long, toothless rostrally; external nares greatly elongate; highly vaulted palate, with elongate, caudally shifted vomers and palatines, rostrally reduced pterygoids; well-developed premaxillary-maxillary secondary palate; strongly enlarged and pneumaticized basicranium and ear region; mandible downwardly curved rostrally; six firmly coalesced sacrals with long transverse processes and sacral ribs; humerus with strongly expanded proximal and distal ends; pelvis opisthopubic, ilia separated from each other; ilium with deep, long preacetabular process, with pointed cranioventral extremity that flares outward at right angle to sagittal plane; very short postacetabular process with strong, knob-like caudolateral protuberance; astragalus with tall ascending process, reduced astragalar condyles, just partly covering distal end of tibia; pedal claws comparatively large, narrow, decurved (Barsbold and Maryańska 1990).

Generalized description: Medium to large.

Age: Late Cretaceous.

Geographic range: ?North America, Asia.

Genera: *Enigmosaurus, Erlikosaurus, Nanshiungosaurus, Segnosaurus, Therizinosaurus*.

SAUROPODOMORPHA Huene 1932

Emended diagnosis: Skull relatively small (approximately five percent of body length); dentary ventrally deflected in front; teeth lanceolate, with coarsely serrated crowns; at least ten cervical vertebrae (each about twice as long as high), forming very long neck; one to three extra sacral vertebrae, modified from dorsals and caudals; enormous pollex with enlarged claw; manual digits IV and V without claws; iliac blade with reduced postacetabular process and short preacetabular process (brachyiliac condition); pubes fused, deep, apron-like, twisted proximally; pubis with very large obturator foramen; elongate femur (longer than tibia); astragalus with ascending process that keys into tibia, the latter with matching descending process (Benton 1990, based in part on Colbert 1964, Charig, Attridge and Crompton 1965, Paul 1984a, and Gauthier 1986).

Generalized description: Herbivorous, bipedal, semibipedal and quadrupedal forms, small to gigantic, with small head, relatively longest neck, heavy bones, stocky hindlimbs, five-fingered forefoot and five-toed hindfoot.

Age: Late Triassic–Late Cretaceous.

Geographic range: Worldwide*.

Taxa: Prosauropoda plus Sauropoda†.

Sauropodomorpha *incertae sedis*: *Dachungosaurus, ?Thotobolosaurus*.

PROSAUROPODA Huene 1920—(=PALAEOPODA Colbert 1964 [in part], PLATEOSAURIA Colbert 1964)

Emended diagnosis: Skull about half length of femur; jaw articulation located slightly below maxillary tooth row level; teeth small, homodont or weakly heterodont, spatulate, with coarse, obliquely angled marginal serrations; manual digit I bearing a twisted first phalanx and enormous, trenchant ungual medially directed when hyperextended; digits II and III of subequal length, with small, slightly recurved ungual

---

Hammer and Hickerson (1993) reported the first Antarctic prosauropod material, represented by a partial pes including the astragalus and four articulated metatarsals. The remains, not yet described as of this writing, indicate a large form. (See Cryolophosaurus *entry for further information regarding locality, etc.).*

†*Traditionally sauropods have been regarded as descendents of prosauropods. More recently, however, that relationship has become clouded. Even very primitive prosauropods (e.g.* Thecodontosaurus) *have feet more derived than of any sauropod in having a reduced digit V, while prosauropods also appear to be more derived than sauropods in having elongated cervical vertebrae. Galton (1990) concluded that Sauropoda is the sister-group of Prosauropoda.*

phalanges; digits IV and V reduced, lacking ungual phalanges; typical phalangeal formula 2-3-4-(3 or 4)-3; blade-like distal parts of pubes forming broad, flat apron; fifth pedal digit vestigial (Galton 1990*a*); femur with longitudinal crest proximal to lateral condyle, situated in continuation of posterior end of condyle; lesser trochanter a weak ripple proximo-distally lying on latero-anterior surface, main part of trochanter below level of femoral head (Gauffre 1993).

Generalized description: Small to large, bipedal, facultatively bipedal or quadrupedal, with small head, leaf-shaped teeth, elongate neck, first finger powerfully developed, fourth and fifth fingers reduced and clawless, fifth toe very small, herbivorous.

Age: Late Triassic–Early Jurassic.

Geographic range: Worldwide.

Taxa: Thecodontosauridae plus Anchisauridae plus Massospondylidae plus Yunnanosauridae plus Plateosauridae plus Melanorosauridae plus Blikanasauridae.

Prosauropoda *incertae sedis*: ?*Agrosaurus*, ?*Arctosaurus*, *Azendohsaurus*, *Fulengia*, ?*Halticosaurus*, *Tawasaurus*.

THECODONTOSAURIDAE   Lydekker 1890

Emended diagnosis: Skeleton with fully bipedal proportions; primitively structured skull; derived characters of relatively long retroarticular process of mandible, closure of interpterygoid vacuity (Galton 1990*a*).

Generalized description: Small, erect-postured forms, only fully bipedal prosauropods.

Age: Late Triassic.

Geographic distribution: Europe, Africa.

Genus: *Thecodontosaurus.*

ANCHISAURIDAE   Marsh   1885—(=AMPHISAURIDAE Marsh 1882, ANCHISAURINAE Kalandadze and Rautian 1991)

Emended diagnosis: Derived characters of large basisphenoid tubera projecting farther ventrally than very small basipterygoid processes, proportionally elongate cranial process of ilium, ventral emargination of proximal part of pubis, and size reduction of first pedal ungual so it is smaller than second (Galton 1990*a*).

Generalized description: More primitive, small and slender-limbed.

Age: Early Jurassic.

Geographic range: North America.

Genera: *Anchisaurus.*

MASSOSPONDYLIDAE   Huene 1914 (=GRYPONYCHIDAE Huene 1932)

Emended diagnosis: Derived character of centrally situated, almost vertical dorsal process of maxilla (Galton 1990*a*).

Generalized description: Medium, with relatively small head and jaws.

Age: Early Jurassic.

Geographic range: Africa.

Genus: *Massospondylus.*

NANOSAURIDAE   Yang [Young] 1942

Emended diagnosis: Maxillary and dentary teeth weakly spatulate and noticeably asymmetrical, apices slightly medially directed; only a few coarse apically directed marginal (Galton 1990*a*).

Generalized description: Large, relatively tall and narrow, short snout, teeth similar to those in sauropods.

Age: Early Jurassic.

Geographic range: Asia.

Genus: *Yunnanosaurus.*

PLATEOSAURIDAE   Marsh   1895—(=AMMOSAURIDAE Huene 1914, PLATEOSAURAVIDAE Huene 1914, PLATEOSAURIDEN Huene 1929, PLATEOSAURINAE Kalandadze and Rautian 1991, PLATEOSAURINI Kalandadze and Rautian 1991,
SELLOSAURIDAE Huene 1908)

Emended diagnosis: Jaw articulation ventrally offset, well below level of dentary tooth row (Galton 1990*a*).

Generalized description: Medium to large, stout limbs, some forms heavily built.

Age: Late Triassic–Early Jurassic.

Geographic range: North America, South America, Europe, Asia, Africa.

Genera: *Ammosaurus, Coloradisaurus, Euskelosaurus, Lufengosaurus, Mussaurus, Plateosaurus, Sellosaurus.*

MELANOROSAURIDAE   Huene 1929—(=MELANOROSAURINI Kalandadze and Rautian 1991, PLATEOSAURAVIDAE Huene 1932)

Emended diagnosis: Ilium with ischial peduncle shorter than pubic peduncle (Galton 1990*a*); latero-medial width of femur greater than antero-posterior width (width measured at middle of length of femur) (Gauffre 1993).

Generalized description: More advanced, large, with tendency toward quadrupedal locomotion, some fully quadrupedal.

Age: Late Triassic.

Plesiotype skull (NMC 8887) of protoceratopsid neoceratopsian *Leptoceratops gracilis* (neg. #103488).

Reproduced with permission of Canadian Museum of Nature, Ottawa, Canada.

Geographic range: Europe, Asia, Africa.

Genera: *Camelotia, Melanorosaurus, Riojasaurus, ?Roccosaurus.*

BLIKANASAURIDAE Galton and Heerden 1985—(=BLIKANOSAURINI Kalandadze and Rautian 1991 [*sic*])

Emended diagnosis: Hindlimb extremely stocky; proportionately very short and broad metatarsus; proximal end of metatarsal III and especially II expanded craniocaudally; distal tarsals contact metatarsals I and III so calcaneum contacts metatarsal IV instead of distal tarsal (Galton 1990*a*).

Generalized description: Medium, stockily built, with proportions similar to those in sauropods, and a backwardly directed "spur" on the hindfoot.

Age: Late Triassic.

Geographic range: Africa.

Genus: *Blikanasaurus.*

SAUROPODA Marsh 1878

Emended diagnosis: Largest body size, skull relatively smallest, neck and tail relatively longest; skull having large dorsally located nares; greatly reduced jugal excluded from ventral border of skull; quadratojugal large; endocranial capacity relatively small; palate highly vaulted, pterygoids large; centra of presacral vertebrae lightened by deep pleurocoels and/or cancellous bone; vertebrae with neural arches and spines largely reduced to a complex of thin laminae; 12–19 cervical vertebrae, 8–14 dorsals; scapula oriented more nearly horizontal than vertical; ilium with broadly expanded preacetabular process, pubic

peduncle much longer than ischial; limb bones robust, solid; femur with no notch between head and greater trochanter; carpus and tarsus reduced to one or two elements each in all but perhaps earliest forms; metacarpals longer than metetarsals; number of manual phalanges greatly reduced, only digit I retaining claw; pedal digits IV and V with reduced number of phalanges (McIntosh 1990*b*).

Generalized description: Very large to gigantic (including largest tetrapods of all time), quadrupedal, with small head, smallest brain-to-body sizes of all dinosaurs, long neck, strong and upright limbs, broad feet, first toe of forefoot with claw, very short to very long tail, some with dermal ossifications or tail clubs.

Age: ?Late Triassic–Late Cretaceous.

Geographic range: North America, South America, Europe, Asia, Africa, Australia, ?Antarctica.

Taxa[*]: ?Vulcanodontidae plus Cetiosauridae plus Brachiosauridae plus Camarasauridae plus Diplodocidae plus Titanosauridae.

Sauropoda *incertae sedis*: *Aepisaurus, Asiatosaurus, Atlantosaurus, Austrosaurus, Chinshakiangosaurus, Clasmodosaurus, Damalasaurus, ?Kotasaurus, Kunmingosaurus, Lancanjiangosaurus, Macrurosaurus, Mongolosaurus.*

VULCANODONTIDAE Cooper 1984—(=?BARAPASAURIDAE Halstead and Halstead 1981)

Emended diagnosis: Teeth with coarse denticles on both edges; presacral vertebrae without pleurocoels; narrow sacrum with four functional sacral vertebrae; sacrocostal yoke not contributing to acetabulum; caudal vertebrae deeply furrowed beneath with strong chevron facets; pubes primitive, forming apron (as in prosauropods); ischium noticeably longer than pubis; relatively long forelimb, femur slender; calcaneum; metatarsals elongated (McIntosh 1990*b*)[†].

Generalized description: Large, primitive, with sauropod-like limbs, forelimbs almost as long as hindlimbs, prosauropod features including an enlarged thumb claw on the first toe.

Age: Early Jurassic.

Some workers (Gauthier 1986; Benton 1990) consider such forms as Vulcanodon *and* Barapasaurus *to be derived prosauropods rather than primitive sauropods.*

*Bonaparte (1986d) accepted Dicraeosauridae as a valid sauropod group (*contra *Berman and McIntosh 1978). The Mamenchisauridae is regarded by some authors as a valid taxon, although McIntosh (1990b) lowered both taxa to "subfamily" level within Diplodocidae.*

†*McIntosh (1990b) noted that this diagnosis is tentative, incorporating characters of* Vulcanodon, *the condition of other members of this group unknown.*

Geographic range: Asia, Africa.

Genera: ?*Barapasaurus*, ?*Ohmdenosaurus*, *Vulcanodon*, *Zizhongosaurus*.

CETIOSAURIDAE Lydekker 1888—(=?BELLUSAURINAE Dong 1990, BOTHROSAUROPODIDAE Janensch 1929 [in part], BOTHROSAUROPODOIDEA Kuhn 1965 [in part], CARDIODONTIDAE Lydekker 1895, CETIOSAURIA Seeley 1874 [in part])

Emended diagnosis: Teeth small, spatulate, more slender and numerous than in brachiosaurids and camarasaurids; centra of cervical vertebrae with relatively simple pleurocoels; caudals short, simple, with large chevron facets; humerofemoral ratio moderate (McIntosh 1990*b*).

Generalized description: Primitive and rather unspecialized, moderate to large, front and hind legs of equal or subequal length; group possibly ancestral to later sauropod families.

Age: Early–Late Jurassic.

Geographic range: North America, South America, Europe, Asia, Africa.

Taxa: Cetiosaurinae plus Shunosaurinae.

Cetiosauridae *insertae sedis*: ?*Bellusaurus*, ?*Protognathosaurus*.

CETIOSAURINAE Janensch 1929

Emended diagnosis: Chevrons conventional (McIntosh 1990*b*).

Generalized description: More generalized forms.

Age: Middle–Late Jurassic.

Geographic distribution: North America, South America, Europe, Australia, Africa.

Genera: *Amygdalodon*, *Cardiodon*, *Cetiosaurus*, *Haplocanthosaurus*, *Patagosaurus*.

SHUNOSAURINAE McIntosh 1990

Diagnosis: Chevrons forked.

Generalized description: At least some forms apparently bearing a bony tail club.

Age: Early–Late Jurassic.

Geographic range: Australia, Asia.

Genera: *Datousaurus*, *Omeisaurus*, *Rhoetosaurus*, *Shunosaurus*.

BRACHIOSAURIDAE Riggs 1904—(=ASTRODONTIDAE Huene 1948, ASTRODONTINAE Huene 1932, BOTHRIOSPONDYLIDAE Lydekker 1895, BOTHROSAUROPODIDAE Janensch 1929

[in part], BOTHROSAUROPODOIDEA Kuhn 1965 [in part], BRACHIOSAURINAE Janensch 1929, ?CHUBUTISAURIDAE Corro 1974, PLEUROCOELIDAE Marsh 1888)

Emended diagnosis: Skull moderately long, with elevated nasals and large external nares; cervical ribs elongate, slender; very low neural spines in sacral region; tail relatively short, with low spines and simple chevrons; forelimb greatly elongate, humerus to femur ratio 0.9 to 1.05; metacarpals long, slender; ilium with deep preacetabular process, long pubic peduncle, longitudinal axis directed upward; ischium directed downward, shaft twisted with unexpanded distal ends meeting edge to edge; upper lateral margin of femur with prominence (McIntosh 1990*b*).

Generalized description: Gigantic, with short and low snout, very long neck, front legs almost as long as, or longer than, hind legs, and relatively short tail.

Age: Middle Jurassic–Early Cretaceous.

Geographic range: North America, South America, Europe, ?Asia, Africa.

Genera: *Bothriospondylus*, *Brachiosaurus*, ?*Chubutisaurus*, *Dystylosaurus*, ?*Gigasctosaurus*, *Ischyrosaurus*, *Klamelisaurus*, *Lapparentosaurus*, *Morinosaurus*, *Oplosaurus*, *Pelorosaurus*, *Pleurocoelus*, *Ultrasauros*, *Volkeimeria*.

CAMARASAURIDAE Cope 1877—(=BOTHROSAUROPODIDAE Janensch 1929 [in part], BOTHROSAUROPODOIDEA Kuhn 1965 [in part], EUHELOPODIDAE Kuhn 1965, EUHELOPODINAE Romer 1956, HELOPODINAE Huene 1932, MOROSAURIDAE Marsh 1882)

Emended diagnosis: Basipterygoid processes short and sturdy; jugal excluded from lower rim of skull; midpresacral vertebrae with U-shaped divided spine (McIntosh 1990*b*).

Generalized description: Rather stocky sauropods of relatively medium to very large size, having a short snout, nostrils in front of the eyes, heavy, thick-rooted spatulate teeth that extend along the jaw margins, front- and hindlimbs about same length, back rather horizontal, tail long to very short.

Age: Late Jurassic–Late Cretaceous.

Geographic range: North America, Europe, Asia.

Taxa: Camarasaurinae plus ?Opisthocoelicaudinae.

Camarasauridae *incertae sedis*: ?*Chiayüsaurus*, *Neosodon*.

CAMARASAURINAE Nopcsa 1928

Emended diagnosis: Caudal vertebrae with relatively short amphicoelous centra (McIntosh 1990*b*).

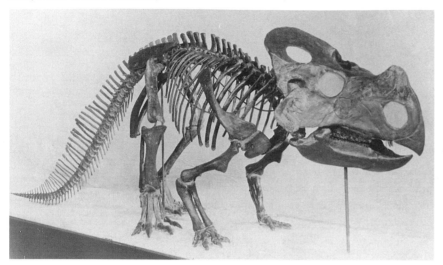

Skeleton (AMNH 5464) of protoceratopsid ceratopsian *Montanoceratops cerorhynchus.* Photo by R. A. Long and S. P. Welles (neg. #731213-10).

Generalized description: [As for Camarasauridae.]

Age: Late Jurassic–Early Cretaceous.

Geographic distribution: North America, Europe, Asia.

Genera: *Aragosaurus, Camarasaurus, ?Chondrosteosaurus, Euhelopus, Nurosaurus, ?Tienshanosaurus.**

OPISTHOCOELICAUDINAE   McIntosh 1990

Diagnosis: Opisthocoelous caudal vertebrae; tail very short.

Generalized description: Similar to camarasaurines, but with relatively short tail.

Age: Late Cretaceous.

Geographic distribution: Asia.

Genus: *Opisthocoelicaudia.*

DIPLODOCIDAE   Marsh 1884—(=AMPHICOELIDAE Cope 1877, APATOSAURIDAE Huene 1927, APATOSAURINAE Janensch 1929, ATLANTOSAURIDAE Marsh 1877, ATLANTOSAURINAE Steel 1970, HOMALOSAUROPODIDAE Janensch 1929 [in part])

Emended diagnosis: Skull relatively long; quadrate inclined rostroventrally; external nares opening dorsally; basipterygoid process slender, elongate; mandible light; teeth slender, peg-like; proximal caudal vertebrae with procoelous centra and wing-like transverse processes; middle caudal vertebrae with forked chevrons; ischia with expanded distal ends, meeting side by side (McIntosh 1990*b*).

Generalized description: Very large to gigantic, both massive and slender forms, some extremely long, with rather long head, nostrils located at top, delicate, pencil-like teeth at front of mouth, and with very long, tapering tail.

Age: Middle Jurassic–Late Cretaceous.

Geographic range: North America, Europe, Asia, Africa.

Taxa: Diplodocinae plus Dicraeosaurinae.

Diplodocidae *incertae sedis*: ?*Antarctosaurus,* ?*Megacervixosaurus.*

DIPLODOCINAE   Janensch 1929

Emended diagnosis: Twenty-five presacral vertebrae; cervical vertebrae increase in number at expense of dorsal vertebrae; sacral neural spines very high; forelimbs short (humerus to femur ratio 0.6:0.7); metatarsals III and IV longest; no calcaneum; plantar edge of lateral surface of metatarsal I with small process (McIntosh 1990*b*).

Generalized description: Very large, some with tails ending in a "whiplash."

Age: Middle Jurassic–Early Cretaceous.

Geographic distribution: North America, Europe, Africa.

Genera: *Amphicoelias, Apatosaurus, Barosaurus, ?Cetiosauriscus, Diplodocus, Dystrophaeus, Seismosaurus, Supersaurus.*

DICRAEOSAURINAE   Janensch (1929)—(=DICRAEOSAURIDAE Huene 1956, HOMALOSAUROPODIDAE Janensch 1929 [in part], HOMALOSAUROPODOIDEA Kuhn 1965 [in part])

Emended diagnosis: Twenty-four presacral vertebrae; cervical vertebrae not increasing in number at expense of dorsal vertebrae; dorsals without pleurocoels; neural spines very high, especially in sacral region, those of presacral region bifid to extreme degree (McIntosh 1990*b*).

Generalized description: Similar to diplodocids, especially in form of head and teeth, with short neck and high back.

Age: Late Jurassic–Late Cretaceous.

Peczkis (1994), in a study of the implications of body-mass estimates for dinosaurs, made such estimates for 220 of the more than 300 generally accepted dinosaur genera. From this database, Peczkis found that the 1–10 ton body mass is the modal weight range for all dinosaurian genera, those on almost every continent, those during most Mesozoic stages, and those in two of the three major historical periods (1870–1900, 1900–1940, and 1970–present) of dinosaur discoveries; that theropods were considerably smaller than herbivorous dinosaurs during the late Jurassic and again in the Late Cretaceous (while at other times they were approximately equal in mass); and that, regarding the discovery of dinosaur genera over time, there has been a simultaneous proportional increase in very small forms (less than 10 kilograms) and relative decrease in giant forms (less than the latter, suggesting that early researches were biased toward collecting large dinosaurs [i.e., sauropods]).

Geographic range: South America, Asia, Africa.

Genera: *Amargasaurus, Dicraeosaurus, ?Dyslocosaurus, Nemegtosaurus, Quaesitosaurus, Rebbachisaurus.*

MAMENCHISAURIDAE Russell and Zheng 1993—(=MAMENCHISAURINAE Young [Yang] and Chao 1970)*

Emended diagnosis: Cervical vertebrae increased in number to 18 or 19 (McIntosh 1990*b*).

Generalized description: Neck extremely long.

Age: Late Jurassic.

Geographic range: Asia.

Genus: *Mamenchisaurus.*

TITANOSAURIA Bonaparte and Coria 1993

Diagnosis: Sauropods with small pleurocoels located in anterior area of ovoid depression, anteroposteriorly extended, situated in upper half and midanterior of vertebral centrum; lateral surface of lower half of neural arch with two more well-defined deep and angular depressions (Bonaparte and Coria 1993).

Generalized description: Slender to heavy, relatively small, rather primitive forms, with wide, sloping heads, peg-like teeth, frontlimbs about three-fourth as long as hindlimbs, long "whiplash" tail, some or all forms possessing dermal armor in the form of bony plates or ossicles imbedded in the skin.

Age: Late Jurassic–Late Cretaceous.

Geographic range: North America, South America, Europe, Asia, Africa.

Taxa: Andesauridae plus Titanosauridae.

ANDESAURIDAE Bonaparte and Coria 1993—(=ANDESAURINAE Calvo and Bonaparte 1991)

Diagnosis: Titanosaurs with small pleurocoels located in anterior region of ovoid depression; two or three deep, triangular depressions on lateral surface of neural arch; neural arch and neural spine of dorsal vertebrae higher than in Titanosauridae; hyposphene-hypantrum very developed, some genera with extra articular surfaces; middle and distal caudal vertebrae with short prezygapophyses (Bonaparte and Coria 1993).

Generalized description: More primitive than Senonian titanosaurids, with back relatively taller, group quite diversified.

Age: Early–Late Cretaceous.

Geographic Distribution: South America.

Genera: *Andesaurus, Argentinosaurus, Epachthosaurus.*

TITANOSAURIDAE Lydekker 1885—(=ANTARCTOSAURIDAE Olshevsky 1978, ANTARC-TOSAURINAE Powell 1986 *see in* Bonaparte 1987, ARGYROSAURINAE Powell 1986 *see in* Bonaparte 1987, HOMALOSAUROPODIDAE Janensch 1929 [in part], HOMALOSAUROPODOIDAE Kuhn 1965 [in part], SALTASAURINAE Powell 1986 *see in* Bonaparte 1987, TITANOSAURINAE Nopcsa 1928)[†]

Emended diagnosis: Most derived characters including transversely expanded ischium and strongly procoelous anterior caudal vertebrae (those with caudal ribs or transverse processes); in more derived titanosaurids, middle and posterior caudals also procoelous; teeth narrow, flattened in more primitive forms, may be more pencil-like in derived forms; sternal plates robust; neural spines of cervical vertebrae undivided, cervical ribs extending beyond centrum to overlap following vertebra (both primitive characters); teeth not limited to anterior portion of jaw, at least primitively; external nares far anterior (Jacobs, Winkler, Downs and Gomani 1993).

Generalized description: Titanosaurs displaying variety of tooth forms, some or all genera with armor.

Age: Late Jurassic–Late Cretaceous.

Geographic range: North America, South America, Europe, Asia, Africa.

Genera: *Aegyptosaurus, Aeolosaurus, Alamosaurus, Ampelosaurus, ?Antarctosaurus, Argyrosaurus, Hypselosaurus, Iucitosaurus, ?Janenschia, Laplatosaurus, Loricosaurus, Magyarosaurus, Neuquensaurus, Saltasaurus, Titanosaurus.*§

---

*As the skull was then unknown in mamenchisaurines, McIntosh (1990b) tentatively referred the Mamenchisaurinae to the Diplodocidae. Later, Russell and Zheng (1993) removed the Mamenchisaurinae from its former tentative placement within the Diplodocidae and raised it to the higher level Mamenchisauridae, this reassessment based largely upon the recovery of nondiplodocid cranial material belonging to the genus Mamenchisaurus (see entry).

†Bonaparte and Powell (1980) recognized four "subfamilies" within Titanosauridae (Titanosaurinae, Saltasaurinae, Antarctosaurinae and Argyrosaurinae, based upon vertebral and appendicular anatomy.

§Le Loueff (1993), in a review of the titatnosaurids of Europe (see Aepisaurus, Hypselosaurus, Iucitosaurus, Macrurosaurus, Magyarosaurus, and Titanosaurus entries) concluded that many isolated titanosaurid remains from the Cretaceous of southern Europe, previously referred to existing taxa, can best be regarded as undetermined titanosaurids, and suggested that only complete skeletons or at least disatriculated partial skeletons should be named and can be adequately diagnosed. Furthermore, Le Loeuff pointed out the long interval (approximately 10 million years) separating the earliest known titanosaurid (the Cenomanian Iucitosaurus) from the later Early Campanian forms. This gap suggested to Le Loeuff that titanosaurids may have become extinct in Europe during the Late Cretaceous, and that their later reappearance during the late Campanian could be attributed to an immigration from Africa.

Posterior part of skull (FMNH P15004) of chasmosaurine ceratopsian *Anchiceratops ornatus.*

Courtesy The Field Museum (neg. #GEO79876).

ORNITHISCHIA Seeley 1888—(=ORTHOPODA Cope 1866, PRAEDENTA Hennig 1915, PREDENTATA Marsh 1894)*

Emended diagnosis: Synapomorphies include premaxilla with toothless and roughened (except in *Technosaurus*) rostral tip; palatal process of premaxilla horizontal or broadly arched; large lateral process of premaxilla excluding maxilla from margin of external naris; antorbital fenestra reduced; ventral margin of antorbital fenestra paralleling maxillary tooth row; palpabral in orbit; prefrontal with long caudal ramus overlapping frontal; subrectangular quadratojugal lying behind infratemporal fenestra; quadrate massive, elongate; predentary bone at front of mandible; dorsal border of coronoid eminence formed by dentary; mandibular condyle set below tooth row; upper and lower jaws with buccal emargination suggesting possession of cheeks; cheek teeth with low triangular crowns with well-developed cingulum beneath; cheek teeth with crowns having low and bulbous base, margins with enlarged denticles; maxillary and dentary teeth with overlapping adjacent crowns; maxillary and dentary teeth not recurved; maximum tooth size near middle of maxillary and dentary tooth rows; at least five true sacral vertebrae; no gastralia; ossified tendons at least above sacral region; pelvis opisthopubic, pubis with small prepubic process; lateral swelling of ischial tuberosity of ilium; iliac blade with long, thin preacetabular process and deep caudal process; pubis with obturator notch instead of foramen, obturator foramen formed between pubis and ischium; distal pubic and ischial symphyses; pubic symphysis and ischial sympyses only at their distal ends; femur with pendant fourth trochanter and fringe-like lesser trochanter; pedal digit V reduced to small metatarsal with no phalanges (Benton 1990, based on Maryańska and Osmólska 1984, 1985, Norman 1984*a*, 1984*b*, Sereno 1984, 1986, and Gauthier 1986).

Generalized description: Herbivorous, small to very large, bipedal, semibipedal, and quadrupedal forms, head with presumably horn-covered beak, most forms with cheek teeth, some forms bearing cranial crests, horns or other ornamentation, head more remodeled than in saurischians, some with dermal armor, and with a larger gut than in saurischians.

Age: Late Triassic–Late Cretaceous.

Geographic range: Worldwide.

Taxa: *Pisanosaurus* plus *Technosaurus* plus *Lesothosaurus* plus Genasauria[†].

Ornithischia *incertae sedis*: *Agilisaurus, Alocodon, Fabrosaurus, Galtonia, Gongbusaurus, Lucianosaurus, ?Revueltosauus, ?Taveirosaurus, Tecoviasaurus, Trimucrodon, Xiaosaurus.*

GENASAURIA Sereno 1986

Diagnosis: Cheeks; maxillary dentition offset medially; mandibular symphysis spout-shaped; coronoid process moderate; premaxilla with edentulous anterior portion; antorbital fossa with entire margin sharply defined or extended as secondary lateral wall that encloses fossa; external mandibular foramen relatively smaller; ilium with pubic peduncle relatively less robust than ischial peduncle.

---

*In a cladistic study of Ornithischia based on the patterns of unique characters among its members, Sereno (1986) concluded that all ornithischians descended from a common Late Triassic ancestor. Sereno offered a revised phylogeny for Ornithischia and introduced new higher taxa to cluster monophyletic clades.

[†]In the past, various primitive ornithischian genera (e.g. Alocodon, Fabrosaurus, Lesothosaurus, Nanosaurus, Tawasaurus, Technosaurus, Trimucrodon, Xiaosaurus, etc.) were grouped together into the family Fabrosauridae Galton 1972 (=Lesothosauridae Halstead and Halstead 1981, Nanosauridae Marsh 1978, Nanosaurinae Abel 1991), supposedly comprising a group of related basal ornithopods. Sereno (1984, 1986) and Gauthier (1986) denied that "fabrosaurids" were ancestral ornithopods and questioned the taxonomic validity of Fabrosauridae, stating that this taxon, as defined, was an unnatural paraphyletic assemblage with no unique, derived characters. This document follows Weishampel and Witmer (1990a), based on Sereno (1986) and Gauthier (1986), with Lesothosaurus, Pisanosaurus, and Technosaurus regarded as among the most primitive members of Ornithischia, and Lesothosaurus the sister-taxon of Genasauria.

Generalized description: All except very primitive ornithischians, all with cheek teeth and true cheeks.

Age: Early Jurassic–Late Cretaceous.
Geographic range: Worldwide.
Taxa: Thyreophora plus Cerapoda.

THYREOPHORA Nopcsa 1915—(=EURYPODA Sereno 1986, SCELIDOSAURIA Cooper 1985, SCELIDOSAURIDAE Cope 1869, SCELIDO-SAURINAE Nopcea 1923, THYREOPHOROIDEA Nopcsa 1928)

Emended diagnosis: Jugal orbital bar with transversely broad orbital rim, transversely broader than dorso-ventrally tall; dorsal body surface with parasagittal row of keeled scutes, lateral rows of low keeled scutes (Sereno 1986).

Generalized description: Small to very large, mostly quadrupedal but including bipedal forms, all possessing body armor or spikes or plates.

Age: Early Jurassic–Late Cretaceous.
Geographic range: Worldwide.
Taxa: *Emausaurus* plus *Scuttelosaurus* plus *Scelidosaurus* plus ?*Tatisaurus* plus ?*Echinodon* plus Stegosauria plus Ankylosauria*.
Thyreophora: *incertae sedis*: *Lusitanosaurus*.

STEGOSAURIA Marsh 1877—(=STEGOSAURI Gadow 1896, STEGOSAUROIDEAE Hay 1902, STEGOSAUROMORPHA Cooper 1985)

Emended diagnosis: Quadrupedal, armored, derived cranial characters of large oval fossa on pterygoid ramus of quadrate and subrectangular, plate-like quadrate head; derived postcranial characters: dorsal neural arch pediceles at least 1.5 times height of centrum; mid-dorsal vertebrae with transverse processes 50 to 60 degrees above horizontal; anterior dorsal vertebrae with spacious neural canal equal to more than half diameter of face of centrum; distal caual centra subquadrate; absence of ossified epaxial tendons; acromion broad, plate-like; triceps tubercile prominent, humerus with descending ridge; proximal carpals large, blocklike; intermedium and ulnare coossified; distal carpals absent; acetabular surface of pubis oval, laterally directed; prepubic process more than half length of postpubic process; digit I absent; digit III with only three phalanges (one phalanx lost); prominent osteoderms angling slightly away from saggital plane, grading in form from short, erect plates anteriorly to longer posterodorsally angling spines posteriorly; proportionately narrow terminal spine pair projecting beyond last caudal vertebra; characteristic parascapular spine projecting postero-laterally from shoulder (Sereno and Dong 1992).

Generalized description: Medium to large, quadrupedal, with proportionally small head and short neck, short and massive forelimbs, columnar hind legs longer than front legs, front feet with five toes, toes hoof-like, and with two rows of back-directed spines, some forms with shoulder spines.

Age: Middle Jurassic–Late Cretaceous.

Reuniting Stegosauria and Ankylosauria and others in the Thyreophora (as had Nopcsa in 1915), Sereno (1986) also erected the Eurypoda, which he diagnosed as follows: Skull with two lateral supraorbitals forming dorsal margin of orbit; quadrate condyle strongly angled ventromedially; quadrate shaft not laterally distinct from pterygoid ramus; absence of otic notch between quadrate and paroccipital process; vertical median portion of pterygoid palatal ramus developed posteriorly, median palatal keel extending to posterior end of palate; exoccipital border of foramen magnum with short recessed section on each side, supraoccipital and dorsal portion of border overhanging recess from above, occipital condyle floors recess from below; dentary with symphseal portion very slender relative to ramus at midlength; atlas with neural arches fused to atlar intercentrum; dorsal and ventral borders of scapular blade parallel, distal expansion of blade minor or absent; femur with fourth trochanter as muscle scar or absent entirely; in adult, lesser trochanter entirely fused to greater trochanter; ilium with preacetabular process directed about 40 degrees lateral to axial column, postacetabular process relatively shorter; ischial blade without distal expansion and ventromedial slant; pedal digit IV with no more than four phalanges; metacarpals and metatarsals relatively short. This taxon has not been generally adopted.

Courtesy Natural History Museum of Los Angeles County.

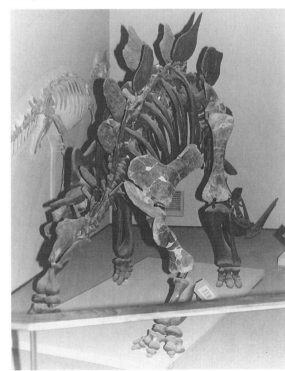

Reconstructed partial skeleton (LACM 3719/16440) of stegosaurid thyreophoran *Stegosaurus*. Photo by the author.

Skeleton (ROM 843) of chasmosaurine ceratopsian *Chasmosaurus belli*.

Geographic range: North America, ?South America, Europe, Asia, Africa.

Taxa: Huayangosauridae plus Stegosauridae[*].

HUAYANGOSAURIDAE Galton 1990—(=HUAYANGOSAURINAE Dong, Tang and Zhou 1982)

Emended diagnosis: Cranial dorsal ribs with prominent hamularis process; distal end of pubic rod much enlarged.

Generalized description: Medium size, with premaxillary teeth, apparently two rows of small, paired dorsal plates, tail spines.

Age: Middle Jurassic.

Geographic range: Asia.

Genera: *Huayangosaurus, Regnosaurus*.

STEGOSAURIDAE Marsh 1877—(=HYPSIRHOPHIDAE Cope 1898, OMOSAURIDAE Lydekker 1888, STEGOSAURINAE Nopcsa 1917, STEGOSAUROIDAE Hay 1930, STEGOSAUROIDEA Hay 1901 [in part])

Emended diagnosis: Skull with orbit caudal to maxillary tooth row; femorohumeral ratio of at least 145 percent (modified from Sereno 1986), coracoid higher than wide, width just slightly more than half ventral part of scapula; scapula with prominent acromial process; ilium with prominent antitrochanter, reduced ischial peduncle (Galton 1990*b*).

Generalized description: Large, feet with three toes, plates small to very large, arranged in two paired or alternating rows.

Age: Middle Jurassic–Late Cretaceous.

Geographic range: North America, Europe, Asia, Africa.

Genera: *Changdusaurus, Chialingosaurus, Chungkingosaurus, Craterosaurus, Dacentrurus, Dravidosaurus, Kentrosaurus, Lexovisaurus, Monkonosaurus, Paranthodon, Stegosaurus, Tuojiangosaurus, Wuerhosaurus*.

ANKYLOSAURIA Osborn 1923

Emended diagnosis: Low, flat cranium, rear of skull more wide than high; closed antorbital and supratemporal fenestrae; in adults, sutures between cranial bones of skull roof obliterated; maxilla with deep, dorsally arched cheek emargination; passage between the space above the palate and that below the braincase closed by pterygoid; accessory antorbital ossification(s) and postocular shelf partially or completely enclosing orbital cavity; bony median septum extending from ventral surface of skull roof into palate as fused vomers; quadratojugal contacting postorbital; quadrate with dorsoventrally narrow pterygoid process; quadrate slants rostroventrally from underside of the squamosal; mandible having coosified keeled plate along ventrolateral margin; caudal dorsal ribs tending to fuse to vertebrae at centrum and along transverse process, may also underlie and fuse to the expanded preacetabular segment of ilium; at least three caudal dorsal vertebrae fuse to sacral vertebrae, forming presacral rod, ribs of former contacting preacetabular process of ilium; neural and hemal spines of distal caudals elongate along axis of tail, with contact between adjacent hemal spines; ilium rotated into horizontal plane; secondarily closed acetabulum; small pubis with quite short extension of shaft adjacent to ischium; pubis almost entirely excluded from acetabulum; no prepubic

---

[*]*Dong (1990*b*) recognized two stegosaurian "subfamilies," Huayangosaurinae and Stegosaurinae, on the basis of both cranial and postcranial features, and postulated that stegosaurs originated in Asia, arising from a small Later Triassic ornithopod ("a fabrosaur or heterodontosaur"). Dong diagnosed Huayangosaurinae as follows: Small to medium size, primitive; high skull with facial region relatively shorter than in stegosaurines; antorbital fenestra; unspecialized jugal; one-three supraorbitals; slight heterodonty; compressed premaxillary teeth with deep marginal serrations and enamel on both surfaces; lower jaw with small mandibular fenestra. Dong diagnosed Stegosaurinae as follows: Medium to large, advanced; very small skull relatively low in proportion to body; jugal reduced; two-three supraorbital elements; closed antorbital fenestra; no premaxillary teeth; poorly developed coronoid process. According to J. I. Kirkland (personal communication 1993), the Stegosauria may prove to comprise three distinct subgroups, Huayangosauridae plus a group represented by forms lacking shoulder spines and having tall neural spines over pelvis plus that represented by* Stegosaurus.*

process; body covered dorsally by armor plates of three or four shapes (including flat, oval to rectangular plates bearing a keel, ridge or short spine externally; larger armor plates commonly symmetrically arranged in transverse rows (Coombs and Maryańska 1990).

Generalized description: Stocky, quadrupedal, forelimbs about two-thirds to three-fourths as long as hindlimbs, with short, broad feet, a broad, head carried low and covered by a mosaic of armor plates, small leaf-shaped teeth, with body armor usually made up of small rounded plates in parallel strips, forming a continuous bony shield on the back, tail making up about one half body length.

Age: Late Jurassic–Late Cretaceous.
Geographic range: Worldwide.
Taxa: Nodosauridae plus Ankylosauridae[*].

Ankylosauria *incertae sedis: Brachypodosaurus, Danubiosaurus, ?Peishansaurus, Sauroplites,*

NODOSAURIDAE   Marsh 1890—(=ACANTHO-PHOLIDIDAE Nopcsa 1902, ACANTHOPHO-LIDINAE Huene 1956, EDMONTONIINAE Russell 1940, HYLAEOSAURIDAE Nopcsa 1902, NODOSAURINAE Abel 1919, PALAEOSCINCI-DAE Nopcsa 1918, PANOPLOSAURINAE Nopcsa 1929, PANOPLOSAURINES Lapparent and Lavocat 1955, POLACANTHIDAE Wieland 1911, POLA-CANTHINES Lavocat 1955, STEGOSAUROIDEA Hay 1901 [in part], STRUTHIOSAURIDAE Kuhn 1966, STRUTHIOSAURINAE Nopcsa 1923)

Emended diagnosis: Palate hourglass-shaped; basipterygoid processes consisting of pair of rounded, rugose stubs; occipital condyle hemispherical, composed of basioccipital only, set off from braincase on short neck and angled about 50 degrees downward from line of maxillary tooth row; skull roof with a large plate between orbits, rostrocaudally narrow plate along caudal edge of snout rostral to orbits; scapular spine displaced toward glenoid; large coracoid, craniocaudally long relative to dorsoventral width; ischium ventrally flexed at midlength (Coombs and Maryańska, modified after Sereno 1986)

Generalized description: Body more upright than in Ankylosauridae, with relatively longer, gracile pear-shaped, ?usually hornless head fortified with bony plates, with bone-covered side openings and small teeth, carapace sometimes bearing large lateral spikes, ?no tail club.

Age: Late Jurassic–Late Cretaceous.
Geographic range: Worldwide.
Genera: *Acanthopholis, Crataeomus, ?Cryptodraco, Dracopelta, Edmontonia, Hierosaurus, Hylaeosaurus, ?Lametasaurus, Leipsanosaurus, Minmi, Mymoorapelta, Niobrarasaurus, Nodosaurus, Palaeo-*

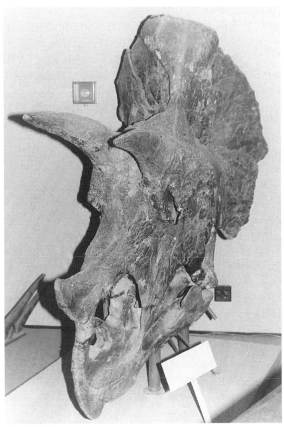

Somewhat compressed skull (LACM 7207/59049) of chasmosaurine ceratopsian *Triceratops prorsus.* Photo by the author.

Photo by the author, courtesy Natural History Museum of Los Angeles County.

scincus, Panoplosaurus, Pawpawsaurus, Polacanthus, Priconodon, ?Priodontognathus, Rhodanosaurus, Sarcolestes, Sauropelta, Silvisaurus, Struthiosaurus, Texastes.

Bakker (1988) proposed that Nodosauridae be divided into Panoplosaurinae Nopcsa 1929, including forms with short, plump snouts, lumpy armor and wide premaxillary bar between external nares, and Edmontoniinae Russell 1940, including forms with narrow internarial bars, unswollen snouts of varying length and flat osteoderms, and lack of lumpy armor. He also proposed that new taxon Edmontoniinae be erected to embrace all Late Cretaceous "nodosaurians" characterized by a wider spoon-like beak rim, more extensive secondary palate with posterior displacement of the internal nares and in the absence of premaxillary teeth. After a cladistic comparison of ankylosaurs and stegosaurs, Bakker concluded that stegosaurs and "nodosaurs" might be more related to one another than either is to Ankylosauridae. Bakker suggested that stegosaurs, "nodosaurs," ankylosaurids and possibly pachycephalosaurs constitute a monophyle clade, all perhaps belonging to an expanded Stegosauria. This assessment has not been generally adopted. According to J. I. Kirkland (personal communication 1993), based upon new undescribed Upper Jurassic and Lower Cretaceous ankylosaur remains recovered from the Cedar Mountain Formation of the east-central Colorado plateau region (see Mymoorapelta entry), the Ankylosauria may represent three distinct groups, Nodosauridae plus a second group represented by Polacanthus-like forms plus Ankylosauridae.

ANKYLOSAURIDAE Brown 1908—(=ANKY-LOSAURINAE Nopcsa 1918, SHAMOSAURINAE Tumanova 1983, SYRMOSAURIDAE Maleev 1952)

Emended diagnosis: Skull with maximum width equal to or greater than length; snout arches above level of the postorbital skull roof; premaxillary septum dividing external nares, ventral or lateral opening leading into maxillary sinus; caudal process of premaxilla along margin of beak extending lateral to most mesial teeth; premaxillary palate wider than long; no ridge separating premaxillary palate from lateral maxillary shelf; premaxillary beak with edge continuous with lateral edge of maxillary shelf; secondary palate complex, twisting respiratory passage into vertical S-shaped bend; paired sinuses in premaxilla, maxilla and nasal; postorbital shelf comprising postorbital and jugal bones extends farther medially and ventrally than in nodosaurids; near-horizontal epipterygoids contacting pterygoid and prootic; quadratojugal dermal plate prominent, wedge-shaped, caudolaterally projecting; squamosal dermal plate large, wedge-shaped, caudolaterally projecting; infratemporal fenestra, paroccipital process, quadratojugal, and all but quadrate condyle hidden in side view by united quadratojugal and squamosal dermal plates; each lateral supraorbiotal element with sharp lateral rim and low dorsal prominence; flat lateral supraorbital margin above orbit; skull roof covered by numerous small scutes (including paired premaxillary scutes, a median nasal scute, two scutes laterally between orbit and external nares, scutes on each supraorbital element, single scute on squamosal and on quadratojugal dermal plates); scute pattern poorly defined in supraorbital region; lower, more rounded coronoid process than in nodosaurids; centra of distal caudal vertebrae partially or completely fused, with elongate, dorsoventrally broad prezygapophyses and elongate postzygapophyses united to form a single dorsoventrally flattened, tongue-like process; distal caudal vertebrae with hemal arches having zygapophysis-like overlapping processes and elongate bases that contact, forming fully encased hemal canal; sternal plates fused; deltopectoral crest and transverse axis through distal humeral condyles in same plane; ilium with short postacetabular process; ischium almost vertical below acetabulum; pubis reduced to very small bone fused to ilium and ischium; femur with fourth trochanter on distal half; tail terminating with club comprising large pair of lateral plates and two smaller terminal plates; distal caudal vertebrae surrounded by ossified tendons (Coombs and Maryańska, modified after Sereno 1986).

Generalized description: Body more robust than in Nodosauridae, head triangular and bearing horns, carapace with small lateral spikes (when present), tail terminating in a club.

Age: Late Cretaceous.

Geographic range: North America, ?South America, Asia.

Genera: ?*Amtosaurus, Ankylosaurus, Euoplocephalus, Heishansaurus,* ?*Maleevus, Pinacosaurs, Saichania, Sangonghesaurus, Shamosaurus, Talarurus, Tarchia,* ?*Tianchisaurus, Tsagantegia.*

CERAPODA Sereno 1986

Emended diagnosis: Mandibular symphysis spout-shaped; entire margin of antorbital fossa sharply defined or extending as a lateral wall enclosing fossa (Benton 1990).

Generalized description: All primitive to advanced ornithopods, dome-headed and horned ornithischians, with thicker enamel on one side of cheek teeth.

Age: Early Jurassic–Late Cretaceous.

Geographic distribution: North America, South America, Europe, Asia, Africa, Australia.

Taxa: Ornithopoda plus Marginocephalia.

ORNITHOPODA Marsh 1871—(ORNITHO-PODIDAE Zittel 1895, ORNITHOPOIDEA Nopcsa 1928)

Emended diagnosis: Pronounced ventral offset of maxillary and dentary tooth rows; caudal elongation of lateral process of premaxilla contacting lacrimal and/or prefrontal, thereby covering articulation of maxilla and nasal (absent in hypsilophodontids) (Weishampel 1990, modified from Sereno 1986).

Generalized description: Most diverse of dinosaurian herbivorous groups, from small to very large, the former bipedal, latter sometimes semibipedal to quadrupedal.

Age: Early Jurassic–Late Cretaceous.

Geographic range: North America, South America, Europe, Asia, Africa, Australia.

Taxa: Heterodontosauridae plus Hypsilophodontidae plus Iguanodontia.

Ornithopoda *incertae sedis: Drinker, Othnielia.*

HETERODONTOSAURIDAE Kuhn 1966—(=TIANCHUNGOSAUROIDEA Zhao 1983, XIPHOSAURIDAE Sereno 1986)[*]

Emended diagnosis: Cheek teeth high-crowned; crowns chisel-shaped, with denticles restricted to apical most third of crown; caniniform tooth present in

---

[*]*According to Sereno (1986), Heterodontosauridae is sister-group of higher ornithopods on the basis of four synapomorphies (projection of premaxillary tooth row below level of maxillary tooth row, paroccipital processes strongly pendant laterally, very tall quadrates making occipital profile taller than wide and depressing jaw joint far below tooth row, and prexamilla with elongate lateral process contacting lacrimal and covering nasal-maxilla contact). Weishampel and Witmer (1990b) accepted Sereno's assessment, adding that the reduction or loss of cingulum may constitute another feature.*

both premaxilla and dentary (Weishampel and Witmer 1990*b*).

Generalized description: Among smallest and earliest ornithischians, predentary probably covered with horn, followed by of cheek teeth, closely packed.

Age: Early Jurassic.

Geographic range: North America, Asia, Africa.

Genera: *Abrictosaurus, Dianchungosaurus, Geranosaurus, Heterodontosaurus, Lanasaurus, Lycorhinus, ?Oshanosaurus*.

HYPSILOPHODONTIDAE   Dollo 1882—(=HYPSILOPHODONTINAE Abel 1919, LAOSAURIDAE Marsh 1879, LAOSAURINAE Abel 1919, THESCELOSAURIDAE Sternberg 1937, THESCELOSAURINAE Sternberg 1940)

Emended diagnosis: Maxilla with rostral process fitting into groove on posteromedial aspect of premaxilla; frontal with lateral peg fitting into socket on medial surface of postorbital; scapula shorter than or as long as humerus; pubis with rod-shaped prepubic process, generally wider mediolaterally than deep dorsoventrally; sheath of epaxial and hypaxial ossified tendons surrounding distal portion of tail (Sues and Norman 1990).

Generalized description: Small to medium, slender, probably horny premaxillary beak, short forelimbs with five-fingered hand, long hindlimbs with four-toed feet.

Age: Middle Jurassic–Late Cretaceous.

Geographic range: North America, Europe, Asia, Australia, ?Antarctica.

Genera: *Atlascopcosaurus, Bugenasaura, Fulgurotherium, Hypsilophodon, Laosaurus, Leaellynasaura, Nanosaurus, Orodremus, Parksosaurus, Phyllodon, Thescelosaurus, Yandusaurus, Zephyrosaurus*.

IGUANODONTIA   Dollo 1888—(=ANKYLOPOLLEXIA Sereno 1986, EUORNITHOPODA Sereno 1986)[*]

Emended diagnosis: Major characters include loss of premaxillary teeth; eversion of oral margin of premaxilla; antorbital fossa relatively small or absent; external naris enlarged relative to orbit; predentary having bilobate ventral process; predentary with denticulate oral margin; manual digit III reduced to three phalanges; femur with deep flexor groove between distal condyles (Weishampel 1990, modified from Sereno 1986).

Generalized description: Small to very large, bipedal, semibipedal, and quadrupedal forms.

Age: Late Jurassic–Late Cretaceous.

Geographic range: North America, South America, Europe, Asia, Africa, Australia, ?Antarctica[†].

Taxa: *Tenontosaurus* plus Dryosauridae plus Camptosauridae plus Iguanodontidae plus *Probactrosaurus* plus Hadrosauridae.

Iguanodontia *incertae sedis*: *Callovosaurus, Craspedodon, Muttaburrasaurus, Parahrabdodon, Rhabdodon.*

Sereno (1986) erected the taxon Euornithopoda to embrace Camptosauridae, Dryosauridae, Hadrosauridae, Iguanodontidae, Probactrosaurus, Tenontosaurus. Euornthopoda was diagnosed as follows: Skull with moderate-size antorbital fossa; loss of external mandibular fenestra; ilium with prepubic process elongated beyond preacetabular process; ischium with a tabular obturator process (Weishampel 1990, modified from Sereno 1986). Sereno (1986) created Ankylopolexia, to include Probactrosaurus, Camptosauridae, Hadrosauridae, Iguanodontidae, diagnosed as follows: Differs from more primitive ornithopods in dentary tooth crowns with lingual surface having distally offset and reduced primary ridge separated by shallow, vertical trough from a low, broad secondary ridge (small number of tertiary ridges developed from base of marginal denticles); carpals partially fused into two blocks, one associated with distal radius, one with distal ulna; manual ungual modified into spur; pubis with prepubic process transversely flattened and broadened; rhomboidal latticework of ossified tendons (Norman and Weishampel 1990, based on Sereno 1986). Neither Euornithopoda nor Ankylopolexia have been generally adopted.

†Horne (1994) reported a typical but small ornithopod femur (USNM 181339) measuring 32 centimeters in length. The specimen was spotted by Horne in January, 1971 cropping out of a road cut, in the lower redbed sequence of the Valle de Angeles Group (Late Cretaceous; latest Aptian–late Albian), between Rancho Grande and San Luis, in the central highlands of Honduras. The specimen, probably from a hadrosaurid or another kind of iguanodont ornithopod, is the only fossil known from this sequence, and notable for being the only dinosaurian bone yet found in Central America.

Iguanodontian (probably hadrosaurid) footprint.

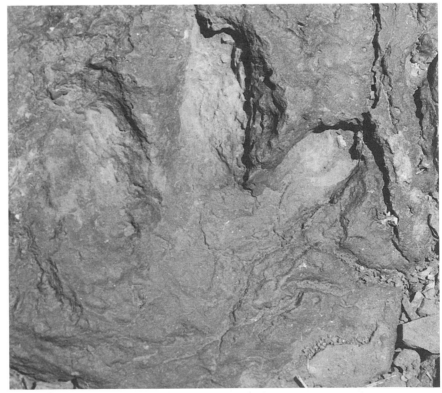

Courtesy G. Leonardi.

DRYOSAURIDAE Milner and Norman 1984—(=DRYOSAURINAE Cooper 1985)

Emended diagnosis: Skull with premaxilla not enclosing external naris dorsally; ilium with wide brevis shelf; distal articular end of femur with deep extensor groove; femur with deep pit (for insertion of M. caudifemoralis longus) developed at base of fourth trochanter; metatarsal I vestigial (Sues and Norman 1990).

Generalized description: Small to medium, bipedal, unspecialized ornithopod forms, with sharp ridged cheek teeth, five-fingered hand, long, stiffened tail.

Age: Late Jurassic–Early Cretaceous.

Geographic range: North America, Africa.

Genera: *Dryosaurus, Kangnasaurus, Valdosaurus.*

CAMPTOSAURIDAE Marsh 1885—(=CAMPTONOTIDAE Marsh 1881, CAMPTOSAURINAE Abel 1919)

Emended diagnosis: Scapular blade constricted with strong flare at coracoid articulation and at distal end; acromion prominent, with clavicular facet; coracoid short relative to scapular length; coracoid subquadrate, with abrupt craniodistal angle; coracoid foramen near scapular articular surface, opening mesially at scapulacoracoid articulation; humerus relatively short, narrow; deltopectoral crest weak, giving humerus a proximal to distal taper; radius rounded and distally compact; carpus compact, heavily ossified; carpal atricular relationships well defined; three proximal and five distal carpals; ilium massive, with straight dorsal margin; postacetabular ventral margin of ilium with moderate medial reflection; prepubis deep, flat, postpubis stout and decurved ventrally; ischial shaft rounded, decurved, with distal expansion; femur curved, with prominent lesser trochanter; femur with well-defined anterior intercondylar sulcus; pes short, stocky, with broad metatarsus and digits (Dodson 1980).

Generalized description: Rather robust, medium to semi-large, bipedal to semibipedal, tail without tall spines, hand with large wrist and short, spur-like first finger, foot broad and stocky.

Age: Middle–Late Jurassic–?Early Cretaceous.

Geographic range: North America, Europe.

Genus: *Camptosaurus.*

IGUANODONTIDAE Cope 1869—(=IGUANODONTINAE Abel 1919, IGUANODONTOIDAE Hay 1930, IGUANODONTOIDES Gervais 1853, KALODONTIDAE Nopcsa 1901, KALODONTOIDEA Huene 1948, ORNITHOPODIDAE Nopcsa 1915 [in part])[*]

Emended diagnosis: Pollex ungual enlarged and conical; maxilla with well-developed and obliquely projecting jugal process; maxilla with prominent lacrimal process forming rostral margin of antorbital fenestra; lacrimal block-like, bearing distinctive pattern of recesses on internal surface, forming lateral wall of tubular passage leading to antorbital fenestra; quadratojugal narrow, overlain by jugal rostrally, embayed caudally where it forms rostral margin of paraquadrate foramen (Norman and Weishampel 1990).

Generalized description: Medium to large, bipedal, semibipedal, and quadrupedal, skull long with long snout (broader than in camptosaurids) horny beak and numerous grinding teeth, large shoulders and forelimbs, second and third fingers blunt and hoof-like, thumb developed into a "spike," hindlimbs and feet broad.

Age: Late Jurassic–Early Cretaceous.

Geographic range: North America, Europe, Asia, Africa, Australia.

Genera: ?*Anoplosaurus, Bihariosaurus, Iguanodon, Ouranosaurus.*

HADROSAURIDAE Cope 1869—(=HADROSAURIA Huene 1908, KRITOSAURINES Lapparent and Lavocat 1955, ORNITHOPODIDAE Nopcsa 1915 [in part], PROTRACHODONTIDAE Nopcsa 1915, SAUROLOPHIDAE Nopcsa 1917, SAUROLOPHINAE Brown 1914, TRACHODONTOIDEA Huene 1948, TRACHODONTIDAE Lydekker 1888)

Emended diagnosis: Dental battery jaws consisting of closely packed tooth families, three-five replacement per tooth position, one-three functional teeth per position; supraorbitals fused with dorsal rim of orbit; maxilla with elevated dorsal process resulting in displacement of antorbital fenestra to rostrodorsal surface of maxilla; loss of paraquadrate and surangular foramina; mesiodistal narrowing of maxillary teeth; carpus reduced; loss of manual digit I; ilium with large antitrochanter; pubic shaft reduced (Weishampel and Horner 1990); cervical vertebrae opisthocoeloes; presacrals 30–34; "synsacrum" with six (juvenile) to ten (adult) sacrals; 60+ caudals; vertebral neural spines taller than in other ornithopods, underside of midsacral vertebrae depressed; lattice-

Traditionally, Iguanodontidae has been regarded as a family defined on the basis of various primitive characters mostly having to do with limb bone proportions. As noted by Norman and Weishampel (1990), iguanodontids used to be generally regarded as any large ornithopods with "so-called graviportal hindlimbs," but without the skull specializations of hadrosaurids.

work of ossified tendons in two series on each side, eight–nine tendons per neural spine per series; scapula elongate, broad; humerus with parallel-sided deltopectoral process; radius and ulna elongate; metacarpals reduced, rod-like, with poorly ossified ends; manus covered with fleshy "mitten," not webbed; digits not divergent; unguals hoof-like; forearms relatively longer than in other ornithopods; pelvic elements unfused; ilium with decurved preacetabular process; iliac postacetabular process elongate, rectacular with parallel dorsal and ventral borders; antitrochanter most robust of all ornithopods; prepubis elongate, ventrally deflected, blade greatly expanded, prepubic neck elongate; postpubis much reduced, rod-like; ischium straight; fourth trochanter of femur shaped like isosceles triangle, located at midpoint of shaft; hindlimb/forelimb ratio averaging 1.66; pedal unguals hoof-like; pedal phalangeal formula 0,3,4,5,1 (Brett-Surman 1975, 1988; Chapman and Brett-Surman 1990).

Generalized description: Large, body plan quite similar to that in iguanodontids (without the "spiked thumb"), bipedal and semibipedal, heads with "duckbills" formed by flat, broad jaws, some forms with cranial crests, some (or all) with dorsal dermal "frill," forelimbs relatively long with long forearms, fingers covered in a fleshy "mitten," fingers and toes hooved.

Age: Late Cretaceous.

Geographic range: North America, South America, Europe, Asia.

Taxa: *Telmatosaurus* plus Hadrosaurinae plus Lambeosaurinae[*].

Hadrosauridae *incertae sedis*: *Arstanosaurus?*, *Cionodon, Claosaurus, Diclonius, Dysganus, Hypsibema, Mandschurosauus, Microhadrosaurus, Ornithotarsus, ?Orthomerus, Pneumatoarthrus, Secernosaurus, Thespesius, ?Tsintaosaurus.*

HADROSAURINAE Lambe 1918—(=CLAOSAURIDAE Marsh 1890, PROHADROSAURIDAE Abel 1919, PROTRACHODONTIDAE flower 1928, PROTRACHODONTINAE Nopcsa 1923, TRACHODONTINAE Brown 1914)

Emended diagnosis: Transversely expanded premaxilla; development of a circumnarial depression; and a ventrally grooved sacrum (Weishampel and Horner 1990); nasal elements folded (except in *Saurolophus* clade [see footnote under HADROSAURIDAE]; fossa (presumably for salt glands) in *Edmontosaurus* clade [see footnote under HADROSAURIDAE]; nasal passages direct; skull long and low, with no hollow crests; preorbital portion of skull elongate; edentulous part of skull longer than in the

Reproduced with permission of Canadian Museum of Nature, Ottawa, Canada.

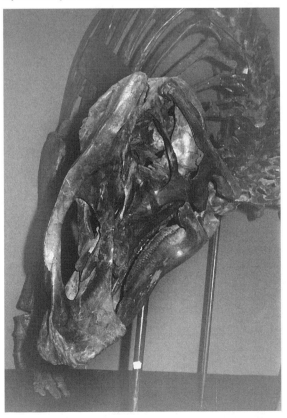

Mounted skeleton (including holotype (NMC 8893) of hadrosaurid ornithopod *Brachylophosaurus canadensis*. Photo by M. K. Brett-Surman.

Lambeosaurinae; scapula relatively longer than in the Lambeosaurinae but not as wide; deltopectoral process of humerus with larger length/width ratio than in lambeosaurines; ilium longer but not as tall as (dorsoventrally); ilium with largest length/width ratio and longest postacetabular process of all ornithopods; pubis with longest prepubic "blade" and prepubic "neck" of all ornithopods; ischium unfooted but clubbed in *Gilmoreosaurus*; tarsus relatively wider than in lambeosaurines; appendicular elements generally more gracile than in lambeosaurines; neural spines not as tall as in lambeosaurines; neural spines of sacrals with length/width ratio generally less than 4.5 (Brett-Surman 1988).

Generalized description: More gracile forms, with longer head, either "flat-headed" or with a solid cranial crest.

Geographic range: North America, South America, Europe, Asia.

Genera: *Anasazisaurus, Anatotitan, Aralosaurus, Brachylophosaurus, Edmontosaurus, Gilmoreosaurus, Gryposaurus, Hadrosaurus, Kritosaurus, Lophorhothon, Maiasaura, Naashoibitosaurus, Saurolophus Shantungosaurus, Tanius.*

LAMBEOSAURINAE Parks 1923—(=CHENEOSAURIDAE Huene 1956, CHENEOSAURINAE Lull and Wright 1942, LAMBEOSAURIDAE Huene 1948, ORNITHOPODIDAE Nopcsa 1915 [in part], STEPHANOSAURINAE Lambe 1920)

Emended diagnosis: Modified nasal cavity which overlies position of supraorbital; jugal with truncated, rounded articulation with maxilla; dentary teeth with crown-root angle exceeding 45 degrees; elongate neural spines; robust appendicular bones; (Weishampel and Horner 1990); skull shorter, narrower than in the Hadrosaurinae; muzzle not as long nor wide as in hadrosaurines (except in *Saurolophus* clade [see footnote under HADROSAURIDAE]; preorbital region shorter; external nares simpler, not as expanded and not folded; nasal apparatus greatly expanded into hollow crests with multiple chambers and looped narial passages; mandible more strongly developed ventrally; edentulous portion of mandible proportionally shorter than in the Hadrosaurinae; scapula shorter but wider than in hadrosaurines; deltopectoral process of humerus more robust than in the Hadrosaurinae; forearms shorter but thicker than in hadrosaurines; ilium more robust, postacetabular process with smaller length/height ratio, ilium with lowest length/width ratio and shortest postacetabular process; pubis with shorter prepubic "blade" and "neck," "blade" expanded dorsoventrally, "neck" shorter than in hadrosaurines; ischium footed except in *Bactrosaurus*, where it is clubbed; ischial shaft thicker; tarsus relatively less wide and taller than in the Hadrosaurinae; sacral centra with ventral ridge running longitudinally; sacral neural spines with length/width ratio generally greater than 4.5 (Brett-Surman 1975, 1988; Chapman and Brett-Surman 1990).

Generalized description: More robust forms, head with hollow crest, shorter head, taller in region of the back because of more elongate sacral neural spines, forelimbs shorter but stouter.

Geographic range: North America, South America, Asia.

Genera: *Bactrosaurus, ?Barsboldia, Corythosaurus, Hypacrosaurus, ?Jaxartosaurus, Lambeosaurus, Nipponosaurus, Parasaurolophus.*

MARGINOCEPHALIA Sereno 1986

Emended diagnosis: Ischium lacking obturator process; derived characters include formation of parietosquamosal shelf (or incipient frill) overhanging occiput; pubis reduced, lacks symphysis (from Sereno 1986); greater separation of acetabula than the dorsal borders of ilia (from Maryańska and Osmólska 1985) (Dodson 1990*b*).

Generalized description: Small to large, bipedal and quadrupedal, mostly Late Cretaceous forms, including "dome-headed," parrot-beaked, "frilled," and horned ornithischians.

Age: Early–Late Cretaceous.

Geographic range: North America, Europe, Asia.

Taxa: Pachycephalosauria plus Ceratopsia[*].

Marginocephalia *incertae sedis*: *Stenopelix*.

PACHYCEPHALOSAURIA Maryańska and Osmólska 1974

Emended diagnosis: Skull roof thickened, tablelike or domed; jugal and quadratojugal strongly extended ventrally toward articular surface of quadrate; jugal meeting quadrate ventral to quadra-

---

[*]*Traditionally, pachycephalosaurs were classified as ornithopods (see Gilmore 1924a), mostly because they were bipedal, although they have also been assigned to Stegosauria (Lambe 1918b), Ankylosauria (Romer 1927), and Ceratopsia (Nopcsa 1904).*

More recent work (Sereno 1984, 1986; Marya´nska and Osmólska 1985) suggests that Pachycephalosauria and Ceratopsia, both regarded as monophyletic taxa, share a suite of diagnostic characters, although these taxa may superficially seem to represent two very different groups of ornithischian dinosaurs. Sereno erected Marginocephalia to include Pachycephalosauria and Ceratopsia, but added that the monophyletic status of the larger taxon is not entirely secure.

tojugal; orbit with ossified rostral and medial walls; orbital roof having two supraorbitals, contact between first supraorbital and nasal excluding prefrontal-lacrimal contact; basicranial region strongly shortened sagitally, thin and plate-like basal tubera, contact between prootic-basisphenoid plate and quadrate ramus of pterygoid; squamosal broadly expanded on occiput; external surfaces of cranial bones strongly ornamented, prominent osteoderms on rim of squamosal; dorsal and caudal vertebrae with ridge-and-groove articulation between zygapophyses; sacral and proximal caudal vertebrae with long ribs; forelimb about 25 percent length of hindlimb; humerus slightly bowed and twisted, with rudimentary deltopectoral crest; cranially broad and horizontal preacetabular process of ilium, medial flange on postacetabular process; reduced pubis excluded from acetabulum; ischium having long dorsoventrally flattened cranial peduncle that contacts pubic peduncle of ilium and sacral ribs (instead of pubis); middle portion of tail with multiple rows of fusiform ossified tendons (Maryańska 1990).

Generalized description: Small to medium, bipedal, heads with relatively short facial region, thickened skull roof, small leaf-like teeth, and bony ornamentation of varying degrees on snout and in back of the skull.

Age: Early–Late Cretaceous.

Geographic range: North America, Europe, Asia, Africa.

Taxa: Homalocephalidae plus Pachycephalosauridae.

Pachycephalosauria *incertae sedis*: *Chaoyoungosaurus, Micropachycephalosaurus*.

HOMALOCEPHALIDAE Dong 1978—(=HOMALOCEPHALERIDAE Dong 1978)

Emended diagnosis: Derived character of a flat, table-like skull roof; relatively large, primitive supratemporal fenestra (Maryańska 1990).

Generalized description: Small to medium, flatheaded.

Age: Late Cretaceous.

Geographic range: Asia.

Genera: *Goyocephale, Homalocephale, Wannanosaurus*.

PACHYCEPHALOSAURIDAE Sternberg 1945—(=DOMOCEPHALINAE Sereno 1986, PSALISAURIDAE Lambe 1918, THOLOCEPHALIDAE Sereno 1986)

Emended diagnosis: More or less extensive, dome-like thickening of frontals and parietals (Sues and Galton 1987).

Generalized description: Small to medium, heads with domes of various sizes.

Age: Early–Late Cretaceous.

Geographic range: North America, Europe, Asia, Africa.

Genera: *Gravitholus, Ornatotholus, Pachycephalosaurus, Prenocephale, Stegoceras, Stygimoloch, Tylocephale, Yaverlandia*.

CERATOPSIA Marsh 1890—(=CERATOPSOIDEA Hay 1902; PONDEROPODA Huene 1952)

Emended diagnosis: Head triangular in dorsal view; median rostral bone on anterior snout overlying premaxilla; snout tall with relatively tall premaxillae; external nares high on snout; better developed biplanar lateral surface of jugal; proportionately tall maxilla (at least two-thirds as tall as long); premaxilla vaulted (deep, transversely arched); mandibular symphysis immobile, symphysis broad, strong union between dentary rami and predentary; jugal orbital bar broader dorsoventrally than posterior ramus below laterotemporal fenestra; parietal transversely broad, overhanging most of occipital margin (Sereno 1986).

Generalized description: Small to giant, mostly quadrupedal forms, head triangular in top view, snout high, hooked, parrot-like beak probably horn-covered in life, head usually with large frill and facial horns, front feet with five toes.

Age: Late Cretaceous.

Geographic range: North America, ?South America, Asia.

Taxa: Psittacosauridae plus Neoceratopsia.

Ceratopsia *incertae sedis*: *Claorhynchus, Trachodon*.

PSITTACOSAURIDAE Osborn 1923—(=PROTIGUANODONTINAE Osborn 1923, PSITTACOSAURINES Lavocat 1955)[*]

Emended diagnosis: Ceratopsians with short preorbital skull segment (equal to less than 40 percent length of skull); external naris very high on snout; nasal extending rostroventrally below external

---

Originally classified within Ornithopoda, Psittacosauridae was transferred by Maryańska and Osmólska (1975) to Ceratopsia, mostly because of the presence of the rostral bone in the psittacosaurid skull. Sereno (1990) suggested that Psittacosauridae might warrant a subgroup because two of the best known psittacosaurid species (Psittacosaurus sinensis and P. xinjiangensis) share the potential synapomorphy of a prominent, laterally projecting jugal horn, a character absent in the two other best known species (P. mongoliensis and P. meileyingensis), and also in Neoceratopsia, the nearest outgroup.

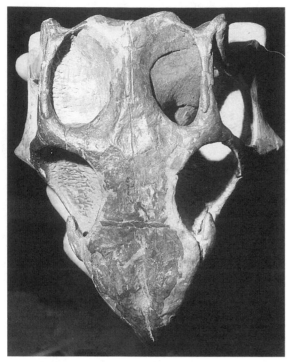

Psittacosaurid ceratopsian *Psittacosaurus mongoliensis*, AMNH 6253, holotype skull (dorsal view) of *Protiguanodon mongoliensis*. Photo by R. A. Long and S. P. Welles (neg. #73E-344-26).

Courtesy American Museum of Natural History.

naris, establishing contact with rostral; extremely broad caudolateral premaxillary process, separating maxilla from external naris by wide margin, extending dorsally to form a tall, parrot-like rostrum; premaxilla, maxilla, lacrimal, and jugal sutures converging to a point on snout; absence of antorbital fenestra and antorbital fossa; unossified gap in wall of lacrimal canal; eminence on rim of buccal emargination of maxilla near junction with jugal; pterygoid mandibular ramus elongate; bulbous primary ridge of dentary crown; manual digit IV with one simplified phalanx; absence of manual digit V (Sereno 1990).

Generalized description: Small, facultatively bipedal, with a tall parrot-like beak comparatively shorter than in any other ornithischians, rather long forelimbs with four fingers, feet with four functional toes, superficially resembling primitive ornithopods in general body proportions.

Age: Early Cretaceous.

Geographic range: Asia.

Genus: *Psittacosaurus*.

NEOCERATOPSIA   Sereno 1986

Diagnosis: Head very large relative to body; rostral and predentary sharply keeled, ending in a point; quadrate sloping rostrally; cranial frill prominently broad, confluent with supratemporal fossa; exoccipitals excluding basioccipital from foramen magnum; predentary with bifurcated caudoventral process and laterally sloping triturating surface; teeth with ovate crowns in buccal aspect; maxillary teeth with prominent buccal primary ridge; one-three or four fused cervicals forming syncervical; gently decurved ischium (Sereno 1986).

Generalized description: Small to large, mostly quadrupedal, head very large relative to body size, with a prominent beak probably covered with horny material in life, frills of varying shapes and sizes, some bearing bony processes, larger forms with horns.

Age: Late Cretaceous.

Geographic range: North America, Asia.

Taxa: Protoceratopsidae plus Ceratopsidae.

PROTOCERATOPSIDAE   Granger and Gregory, 1923—(=ASIACERATOPSINAE Nessov and Kaznyshkina 1989 *see in* Nessov, Kaznyshkina and Cherepanov 1989, LEPTOCERATOPSINAE Nopcsa 1923, PROTOCERATOPIDAE Steel 1970, PROTOCERATOPSINAE Nessov *et al.* 1989, STENOPELIXIDAE Kuhn, STENOPELYXIDAE Kuhn 1917)[*]

Emended diagnosis: Skull with sharp, keeled, pendent rostral that occludes with sharp, keeled predentary; jugals widely flaring; downward- and forward-sloping quadrate; some degree of development of parietal frill; large circular antorbital fossa with small antorbital fenestra; palate vaulted, with small rostral external nares; syncervical; tibia as long as or longer than femur; nearly straight or gently decurved ischium lacking obturator process; unguals with form of either acute or bluntly tapering claws (Dodson and Currie 1990).

Generalized description: Small, relatively primitive, mostly quadrupedal, basically hornless (though in adults the region above the snout and eyes can be raised and roughened, with a rudimentary nasal horn sometimes present), with a somewhat developed neck frill, some forms possibly capable of rapid and bipedal locomotion.

Although Protoceratopsidae is generally regarded as monophyletic (see Dodson and Currie 1990), Sereno (1986) questioned this status. Sereno suggested that the Protoceratopsidae constitute a paraphyletic group of successively derived species culminating with Montanoceratops cerorhynchus, *and that Protoceratopsidae is the sister-group to Ceratopsidae. Dodson and Currie more or less rejected that idea, pointing out that the skull of* M. cerorhynchus *is not well enough known to propose more than a hypothetical relationship between this species and ceratopsids, and that possible future work based upon the description by Osmólska (1986) of Asiatic protoceratopsids may demonstrate synapomorphies within Protoceratopsidae. According to Dodson and Currie, the monophyly of Protoceratopsidae may ultimately be demonstrated by characters including a shallow, circular antorbital fossa, inclined parasagittal process of the palatine, and maxillary sinus.*

Age: Late Cretaceous.

Geographic range: North America, ?South America, Asia.

Genera: *Asiaceratops, Bagaceratops, Breviceratops, Kulceratops, Leptoceratops, Microceratops, Montanoceratops, Protoceratops, Udanoceratops*[*].

CERATOPSIDAE Marsh 1888—(=AGATHAU-MIDAE Cope 1890, AGATHAUMANTIDAE Cope 1890, CERATOPIDAE Lydekker 1889, CERATOPSOIDAE Hay 1930, CERATOPSOIDEA Hay 1901, PACHYRHINOSAURIDAE Sternberg 1950)

Emended diagnosis: Head large, with prominent parietosquamosal frill, and variably yet often strongly-developed nasal or postorbital horns; external nares enlarged, set in narial fossae; prefrontals meeting on midline to separate nasals from frontals; frontals folding to form secondary skull roof expressed as frontal fontanelle; infratemporal fenestrae reduced; squamosal with strong postquadrate expansion; free border of squamosal often ornamented with or without epidermal ossifications; broad contact of jugal and squamosal above infratemporal fenestra; quadrate with pocket to receive wing of pterygoid; enlarged choanae; reduced palatine, longitudinal process lost; reduced ectopterygoid, eliminated from exposure on palate; palatine foramen lost; eustachian canal impressed on pterygoids; supraoccipital excluded from foramen mangum by exoccipitals, which form two-thirds of ossipital condyle; one-third of condyle formed by basioccipital; dentary with expanded apex of coronoid process; dental batteries; teeth with split roots; tendency to add epidermal ossifications to squamosal and parietal; centra of cervical vertebrae expanded in width to support head; usually ten fused sacral vertebrae; humerus with robust deltopectoral crest; ilium with everted dorsal border; ischium decurved; femur considerably longer than tibia; unguals blunt, rounded and hoof-like (Dodson and Currie 1990).

Generalized description: Relatively small to giant, quadrupedal, with prominent frill sometimes developed to very large size, horns of varying sizes, largest brains compared to body size of all quadrupedal dinosaurs, forelimbs slightly shorter than hindlimbs, hind feet short, toes on front and hind feet spreading, hoof-like.

Age: Late Cretaceous.

Geographic range: North America, ?South America, ?Asia.

Taxa: Centrosaurinae plus Chasmosaurinae[†].

Ceratopsidae *incertae sedis*: ?*Notoceratops, Turanoceratops*.

CENTROSAURINAE Lambe 1915—(EUCENTROSAURINAE Olshevsky 1991, MONOCLONINAE Nopcsa 1923, MONOCLONINAE Nopcsa 1923, PACHYRHINOSAURIDAE Sternberg 1950, PACHYRHINOSAURINAE Olshevsky 1992)

Emended diagnosis: Large forms, with short, deep facial region (preorbital length/height = 1.2 to 2.4); no inter-premaxillary fossae; nasal bones with finger-like processes projecting into narial apertures; premaxilla and predentary bones with wide laterally inclined shearing surfaces; nasal horncore, when present, large, formed primarily by upgrowth of nasal bones; supraorbital horns poorly developed; no postfrontal foramen; postfrontal fontanelle walled primarily by large frontal bones; prefrontal bones large; cranial frill short (0.54–1.00 basal length of skull); squamosal quadrangular (length/height about 1.0); first sacral rib expanded ventrally, forming triangular web of bone; ventral surface of sacrum with poorly developed longitudinal channel; reduced olecranon process of ulna; ischium relatively straight (Lehman 1990).

Generalized description: Relatively small to medium, with relatively short and high face, usually with longer nasal horn and shorter to nonexistent brow horns, and frill that is usually (possibly always) fenestrated, usually shorter than length of the basal part of the head, and with a generally scalloped border with epoccipital processers sometimes present, frill having a more derived degree but not as

[*]Nessov and Kaznyshkina 1989 (see in Nessov, Kaznyshkina and Cherepanov 1989) split Protoceratopsidae into two new taxa, Asiaceratopsinae and Protoceratopsinae. Asiaceratopsinae was diagnosed as follows: Maxilla long, without fossa, including antorbital fenestra; relatively large, narial opening, situated low; jugal massive and thick; surangular (?epigugal) process protruding strongly laterally; part of lower dentary shelf straight, not curved in side view; lateral temporal bones short, widened laterally relatively strongly; narrow phalanges; no premaxillary teeth, nine–ten maxillary teeth, six–seven dentary teeth, enamel usually present on both sides of teeth. Protoceratopsinae were regarded as more derived than asiaceratopsines. This division has not been adopted.

[†]Lehman (1990) divided Ceratopdiae into Centrosaurinae and Chasmosaurinae. However, as later pointed out by Olshevsky (1992), Article 37(a) of the International Code of Zoological Nomenclature states specifies that the "subfamily" including the nominotypical genus of the family must bear the same name. Olshevsky, therefore, renamed the first of these taxa Pachyrhinosaurinae for the next available taxon containing the unequivocally valid genus Pachyrhinosaurus. For the second "subfamily," Olshevsky reinstated Ceratopsinae Abel 1919, this taxon including the questionably valid genus Ceratops (see entry). Olshevsky added that if Ceratops is ever shown to be an unquestionable junior synonym of Chasmosaurus (see Dodson 1990), then, by the same ICZN rule, Ceratopsidae will have to be renamed Chasmosauridae, Ceratopsinae reverting to Chasmosaurinae. The renaming was not adopted.

prominently as in chasmosaurines, and which has a more derived degree of border ornamentation than in ceratopsines.

Age: Late Cretaceous.

Geographic range: North America.

Genera: *Achelousaurus, Avaceratops, Brachyceratops, Centrosaurus, Einiosaurus, Monoclonius, Pachyrhinosaurus, Styracosaurus.*

CHASMOSAURINAE Lambe 1915—(=CERATOPSINAE Abel 1919, EOCERATOPSINAE Lambe 1915, TOROSAURIDAE Nopcsa 1915)

Emended diagnosis: Large to giant, with long, low facial region (preorbital length/height = 1.4–3.0); inter-premaxillary fossae; premaxilla and predentary with horizontal or poorly developed lateral cutting flange; nasal horncore, when present, small, formed in part by separate ossification; usually large supraorbital horns; postfrontal foramen; postfrontal fontanelle walled mostly by postorbital bones; reduced frontal bones; small prefrontal bones; long cranial frill (0.94–1.70 basal length of skull, except *Triceratops*); squamosal bones triangular (length/height = 2.0–3.5); ventral surface of sacrum with prominent longitudinal channel; ulna with large olecranon process; ischium strongly curved (Lehman 1990).

Generalized description: Larger and more highly developed than centrosaurines, with long and low facial region, pronounced beak, shorter nasal horn (when present) and longer paired brow horns, and with a long usually fenestrated frill longer than the basal part of the head, frill border with more prominent epoccipitals than in centrosaurines.

Age: Late Cretaceous.

Geographic range: North America.

Genera: *Agathaumas, Anchiceratops, Arrhinoceratops, Ceratops, Chasmosaurus, Dysganus, Pentaceratops, Polyonax, Torosaurus, Triceratops.*

In 1960, Neave Parker illustrated this scene depicting members of various dinosaurian groups extant in Late Cretaceous Mongolia: (Left to right) tyrannosaurid theropod *Tyrannosaurus bataar,* psittacosaurid ceratopsian *Psittacosaurus mongoliensis,* unidentified sauropods, hadrosaurid *Saurolophus angustriostris,* protoceratopsid ceratopsian *Protoceratops andrewsi,* and a hypothetical giant ceratopsian (based on an ankylosaurian bone fragment). Parker's illustrations, though somewhat inaccurate by today's standards, were largely responsible for the public's image of dinosaurs during the 1960s.

III: The Dinosaurian Genera

T his section comprises an alphabetically arranged compilation of dinosaurian generic names. Each genus name is followed by its author(s) and the year that name was first published in the paleontological literature. (Diagnoses and generalized descriptions of higher taxa with broader applications to each genus, explanations of geological ages, and explanations of abbreviations used to designate institutions where specimens are housed, can be found in preceding sections.) Species at the end of each entry are arranged chronologically according to date of publication.

Where two or more genera may be synonymous, but that synonymy has not been compellingly demonstrated, I have chosen to err on the side of inclusion, retaining their generic separation at least tentatively. Doubtful genera (*nomina dubia*) based upon meager or indeterminate fossil remains are likewise retained within their own genus. When these genera have been formally synonymized in the literature but their synonymy has not been generally accepted, or there is sufficient uncertainty or controversy regarding their synonymy, I have used my own judgment in whether or not to give a genus individual-entry treatment. As more original research is done in the field and new fossil specimens are collected, the arrangement of the genera in this work will undoubtedly be affected. Thus, in future editions, genera now grouped together may be "split" into separate taxa, while genera now regarded as distinct could be "lumped" together into a single taxon.

Whenever possible, entries for genera include original as well as modern or best emended diagnoses. However, some genera, especially older taxa, have never been properly or adequately diagnosed or, in many cases, not diagnosed at all. Many taxa have never been diagnosed using cladistic methods. It is beyond the scope of this compendium to generate new diagnoses, and so these entries, mostly older taxa, may include noncladistic as well as cladistic diagnoses. Some entries for which diagnoses have not been published include brief descriptions instead. Following the newer cladistic methodology, Linnaean ranks (*e.g.* "order," "superfamily," *etc.* above the rank of family) will generally not be used.

Genera that were once (but no longer are) regarded as dinosaurian, as well as *nomina nuda*, can be found in the sections following this compilation.

ABELISAURUS   Bonaparte and Novas 1985
Saurischia: Theropoda: Ceratosauria: Neoceratosauria: Abelisauroidea: Abelisauridae.
Name derivation: "[Roberto] Abel" + Greek *sauros* = "lizard."

Type species: *A. comahuensis* Bonaparte and Novas 1985.
Other species: [None.]
Occurrence: Allen Formation, Rio Negro Province, Argentina.
Age: Late Cretaceous (early Maastrichtian).
Known material/holotype: MC 11098, nearly complete skull.

Diagnosis of genus (as for type species): Skull large, deep, with broad interorbital roof; nasal with prominent rugosity; preorbital fenestrae huge (much larger than in tyrannosaurids); interorbital region wider than in other large theropods, contacts outside of lacrimals and postorbitals; infratemporal openings very wide; orbits large and very high; squamosal almost horizontal, projecting posteriorly; quadratojugal process ventrally directed (not forward as in tyrannosaurids and to a lesser degree than in *Allosaurus*); quadrate quite long (much larger than in tyrannosaurids, comparable to *Ceratosaurus*); portion of maxilla accommodating teeth laterally compressed; braincase with laterosphenoids conspicuous processes, and basisphenoids with a marked transverse constriction (similar to *Piatnitzkysaurus*) (Bonaparte and Novas 1985).

Comments: *Abelisaurus*, a theropod with a head superficially resembling that of tyrannosaurids, was the basis for the new family Abelisauridae Bonaparte and Novas 1985.

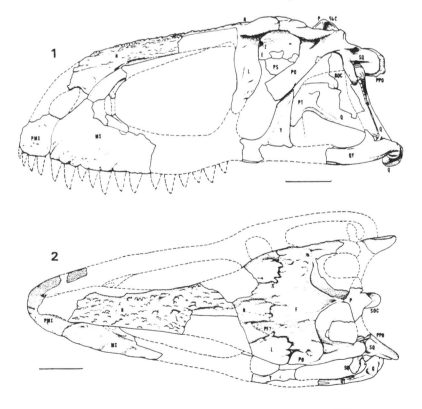

Abelisaurus comahuensis, MC 11098, holotype skull in lateral and dorsal view. Scale = 10 cm. (After Bonaparte and Novas 1985).

The holotype skull measures about 85 centimeters (33 inches) in length (Bonaparte and Novas 1985), indicating a rather large theropod.

Bonaparte (1985), and Bonaparte and Novas, suggested that *A. comahuensis* and *Carnotaurus sastrei* were closely related forms that evolved independently of "carnosaurs." Kurzanov (1989) nestled *Abelisaurus* (and the Abelisauridae) within "Carnosauria," placing it close to the "allosaurid-tyrannosaurid" line [tyrannosaurids now regarded as large, derived coelurosaurs; see Holtz 1994*a*]. Molnar (1990) suggested that *A. comahuensis* (and *C. sastrei*) may have evolved from ceratosaurian stock. Novas (1992*a*) later referred the Abelisauridae to his new ceratosaurian taxon Neoceratosauria, an assessment agreed to more recently by Holtz after a cladistic analysis of the Theropoda.

Key references: Bonaparte (1985); Bonaparte and Novas (1985); Holtz (1994*a*); Kurzanov (1989); Molnar (1990); Novas (1992*a*).

ABRICTOSAURUS   Hopson 1975

Ornithischia: Genasauria: Cerapoda: Ornithopoda: Heterodontosauridae.

Name derivation: Greek *abriktos* = "wide awake" + Greek *sauros* = "lizard."

Type species: *A. consors* (Thulborn 1974).

Other species: [None.]

Occurrence: Upper Elliot Formation [formerly Upper Stormberg Series], South Africa; Paballong, South Africa.

Age: Early Jurassic (Hettangian–?Sinemurian; Olsen and Galton 1984).

Known material: Partial skeleton with skull; fragmentary skull, ?juvenile, ?adult.

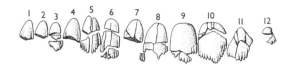

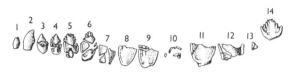

Abrictosaurus consors, UCL B54, holotype teeth of *Lycorhinus consors,* left maxillary teeth (above), left mandibular teeth (below), in buccal view, teeth numbered front-back. (After Thulborn 1974).

Holotype: UCL B54, skull and partial skeleton.

Diagnosis of genus (as for type species): Primitive heterodontosaurid; lower cheek teeth with relatively symmetrical crowns with narrow basal cingula; roots unswollen, well set off from crowns; middle vertical ridge lies centrally on external face of crown; posterior ridges of about same prominence; caniniform teeth present in referred specimens but not in holotype; lower caniniform only serrated on anterior cutting edge (Hopson 1975*b*).

Comments: The genus *Abrictosaurus* was founded upon a moderately well-preserved heterodontosaurid skull (UCL B54) lacking the caniniform teeth found in *Heterodontosaurus*, and a partial skeleton from the Upper Elliot Formation of South Africa. This material was originally described by Thulborn (1974) as a new species of *Lycorhinus*, which he named *L. consors*. Subsequently, Hopson (1975*b*), recognizing this material as generically distinct from and more derived than *Lycorhinus*, made it the holotype of the new genus *Abrictosaurus*. At the same time, Hopson provisionally referred a fragmentary skull (UCL A.100) from Paballong, Mount Fletcher District, Cape Province to the type species and diagnosed *Abrictosaurus* based on the holotype and the referred specimen.

Thulborn had suggested that the presence or lack of tusks could constitute sexual dimorphism, the tuskless *Abrictosaurus* being female and tusked *Heterodontosaurus* male morphs of the same species.

Sereno (1986) suggested that apparently only members of a subgroup of "Heterondontosauria" more derived than *Abrictosaurus* possess caniniform teeth; and that this genus is the primitive sister-taxon among "heterodontosaurs."

Weishampel and Witmer (1990*b*), in their review of the Heterodontosauridae, speculated that the lack of a caniniform tooth, while perhaps suggesting a female morph, might also represent a juvenile condition. Additional ?juvenile features include

Abrictosaurus consors, UC B54, holotype skull. (After Thulborn 1974.)

⊢———⊣ 1 cm

the four unfused sacral vertebrae (reported by Thulborn) and the short, steeply sloping facial skeleton (perhaps a uniquely derived feature).

Key references: Hopson (1975*b*); Sereno (1986); Thulborn (1974); Weishampel and Witmer (1990).

ACANTHOPHOLIS Huxley 1867—(=*Eucercosaurus, Syngonosaurus;=?Hylaeosaurus.*)
Ornithischia: Genasauria: Thyreophora: Ankylosauria: Nodosauridae.
Name derivation: Greek *akantha* = "thorn" + Greek *pholis* = "scale."
Type species: *A. horridus* Seeley 1867.
Other species: ?*A. eucercus* Seeley 1869 [*nomen dubium*], *A. macrocercus* Seeley 1869 [*nomen dubium*], *A. stereocercus* Seeley 1869 [*nomen dubium*].
Occurrence: Cambridge Greensand, Cambridge, England. Age: Early Cretaceous (Late Albian–Cenomanian).
Age: Early-Late Cretaceous (late Aptian-Cenomanian).
Known material: Incomplete and fragmentary remains, including armor, of various individuals.
Cotypes: GSM 109046-GSM 109058, including an occiput, 3 teeth, vertebral centra, distal end of a humerus, and armor plates.
Diagnosis of genus: [None published.]
Comments: The genus *Acanthopholis* was established on poor material found by a "Mr. Griffiths" in the Chalk Marl of Folkestone, Cambridge Greensand, near Cambridge, England.

Huxley (1876*b*) originally described type species *A. horridus* based upon vertebral features: Dorsal centrum with articular end measuring about 5.6 centimeters (2.1 inches) long, over 5 centimeters (2

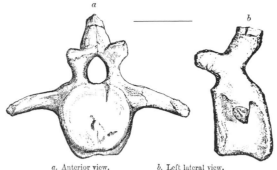

a. Anterior view. *b.* Left lateral view.

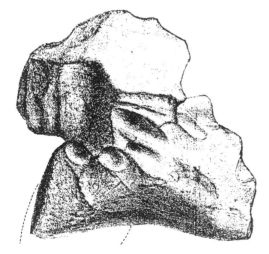

Acanthopholis horridus, GSM 109046-109058, holotype right side of occiput of skull, showing united basioccipital and basisphenoid. (After Seeley 1881.)

inches) deep, vertically ovate in outline, almost 5 centimeters (1.9 inches) wide at middle, over 3.5 centimeters (1.4 inches) wide at upper part under pedicles of neural arches; ?third caudal vertebra with fairly short centrum; caudal ribs transverse, anchylosed, compressed downward from above, directed outward and downward; mid-caudal centrum almost 4 centimeters (about 1.5 inches), base having a deep, narrow, concave median groove; neural arch laterally compressed, elongated backward beyond centrum into a neural spine; most distally located caudal centrum almost 4 centimeters (1.55 inches) long, with shorter neural arch.

Two additional species, *A. stereocercus* and *A. eucercus*, were based on material collected for the Woodwardian Museum, University of Cambridge by W. Farren from the Cambridge Greensand. *A. stereococercus* was based on a series of twelve vertebrae and a dermal-spine fragment (SMC B55588-B55609). Seeley (1879) observed that only four of these vertebrae belonged to *Acanthopholis*, referring the other elements to the iguanodontian *Anoplosaurus*.

Huxley (1867*b*) described *A. stereocercus* as follows: Two dorsal vertebrae with centra with more deeply concave articular faces; sacral or caudal vertebra with large neural canal and oblong centrum defined by six sides; proximal caudal with neural arch anchylosed to centrum, well-marked short transverse processes, and unusually large facets divided from each other for chevrons; dermal fragment, a nearly smooth plate, probably referable to this species.

A. eucercus was based on a series of six caudal vertebrae (SMC 55551-SMC 55557). Seeley (1979) distinguished this species from *A. horridus* by more elongated caudals, more constricted centra, ridges on sides of centra, rapid decrease in length of centra, and in generally larger size of elements (implying a larger species than *A. horridus*). In their review of the Ankylosauria, Coombs and Maryańska regarded this species as a *nomen dubium* and probably non-ankylosaurian.

Two type species erected by Seeley are now regarded as conspecific with *A. horridus*: *Eucercosaurus tanyspondylus* was based on an associated series of

Acanthopholis horridus, GSM 109046-109058, holotype anterior caudal vertebra, anterior and left lateral views. Scale = 1 cm. (After Seeley 1881.)

Acanthopholis horridus, GSM 109046-109058, holotype middle caudal vertebra, right lateral, and ventral views. Scale = 1 cm. (After Seeley 1881.)

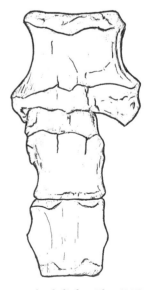

Acanthopholis horridus, SMC collection, holotype sacral vertebrae of *Eucercosaurus tanyspondylus*. (After Seeley 1879.)

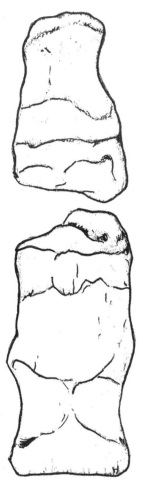

Acanthopholis horridus, SMC, holotype sacral vertebrae of *Syngonosaurus macrocerus.* (After Seeley 1879.)

nineteen dorsal, sacral and caudal vertebrae, and a neural arch (SMC collection), from the upper Cambridge Greensand at Trumpington, near Cambridge. Poorly preserved, some of these remains were incrusted with phosphate of lime, several quite decomposed, and some worn. Seeley incorrectly inferred that this dinosaur was bipedal. Seeley also suggested that the skull and neck may have been small, as the four preserved dorsal vertebrae decrease markedly towards the neck.

Syngonosaurus macrocercus was based on a series of nineteen cervical, dorsal, sacral and caudal vertebrae (SMC collection) from the Cambridge Greensand. Seeley likened these elements to those in *Eucercosaurus.* Some dermal plates were found in association with the vertebrae, leading Seeley to assume that this species might have been armored.

Romer (1956) surmised that dinosaurs like *Acanthopholis* were more lightly armored than North American nodosaurids, but Coombs (1978) showed that all nodosaurids were virtually equally covered with body armor. Coombs regarded *A. horridus* as a relatively small nodosaurid, possibly a *nomen dubium.* Later, Coombs and Maryańska (1990) assigned *Acanthopholis* to the Nodosauridae mostly on the basis of tooth structure and the presence of tall, conical spines and flat or slightly convex medially keeled plates.

Notes: During the 1950s, artist Neave Parker attempted a life restoration of *Acanthopholis* as a relatively slender dinosaur with varying-spaced rows of armor plates and with dorsal spines in the neck and shoulder region. This imaginative restoration was first published in Swinton's *Dinosaurs* (1962), subsequently appeared in numerous other popular books about dinosaurs, was reproduced on posters and in other formats, and has been often copied by other artists. However, the remains of *Acanthopholis* are too meager to create any life restoration beyond a fabrication.

Seeley (1878) referred the species *A. macrocercus* Seeley 1869 [*nomen dubium*; in part] to *Anoplosaurus* and *A. platypus* Seeley 1871 to the sauropod *Macrurosaurus.*

Key references: Coombs (1978); Coombs and Maryańska (1990); Huxley (1867); Seeley (1867, 1869, 1879).

ACHELOUSAURUS   Sampson 1995

Ornithischia: Genasauria: Cerapoda: Marginocephalia: Ceratopsia: Neoceratopsia: Ceratopsidae: Centrosaurinae.

Name derivation: "Achelous" [transforming character from Greek mythology] + Greek *sauros* = "lizard."

Type species: *A. horneri* Sampson 1995.

Other species: [None].

Occurrence: Two Medicine Formation, Montana, United States.

Age: Late Cretaceous (late Campanian).

Known material: Skull, partial skulls with partial postcrania, subadult, partial skull with associated partial postcrania.

Holotype: MOR 485, partial skull including nasal boss, supraorbital bosses, parietal.

Diagnosis of genus (as for type species): Centrosaurine with relatively thin, heavily pitted nasal boss (in adults); relatively large, high-ridged supraorbital bosses rather than true horns (in adults); subadults having true supraorbital horncores with concave surfaces medially; parietal with single pair of curved spikes projecting posterolaterally from rear margin (Sampson 1995).

Comments: The genus *Achelousaurus* was founded upon an incomplete skull (MOR 485) collected from the Two Medicine Formation, Landslide Butte field Area, northwest of Cut Bank, Glacier County, Montana. Referred remains include a well-preserved subadult specimen (MOR 591), with partial skull, an almost complete vertebral column, entire pelvis and sacrum, and, recovered from a nearby locality, one femur, collected on Black Tail Creek, Glacier County; and a partial skull with associated vertebrae and ribs (MOR 485) (Sampson 1995).

As described by Sampson, *Achelousaurus* is similar in size and morphology to a second centrosaurine from the Two Medicine Formation, *Einiosaurus* (see entry), with parietal ornamentation (usually diagnostic in centrosaurines) almost identical in both forms. The parietal spikes in *Achelousaurus* are

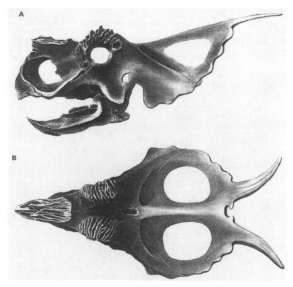

Achelousaurus horneri, skull reconstruction based on holotype MOR 485, A. left lateral, B. dorsal view. (After Sampson 1995.)

directed more laterally than in *Einiosaurus*, but not nearly to the degree seen in *Pachyrhinosaurus*. This possession of nasal and orbital bosses in *Achelousaurus* suggested to Sampson a relationship with *Pachyrhinosaurus*. *Achelousaurus* differs from *Pachyrhinosaurus* in having a relatively smaller nasal bone which does not extend onto the frontals, but shares with that genus these synapomorphises: Expanded supracranial cavity with cornual sinuses; low, rounded supraorbital horns (in subadults); and similar though distinct posterior margins of the parietal.

Given the similarities between the type species *Achelousaurus horneri* and *Einiosaurus procurvicornis*, Sampson considered the possibility of their representing sexual dimorphs of a single species, but rejected this hypothesis because of the following: 1. No evidence in any *Einiosaurus* specimen of the well-developed cranial bosses present in *A. horneri*; 2. the stratigraphical separation of both morphs (though both were found in the same area); 3. the possession by both of these centrosaurines of independent secondary sexual characters.

Sampson further expressed that, had *Achelousaurus* been the only ceratopsid found in the Two Medicine Formation, it might have been referred to *Pachyrhinosaurus*, based on the shared possession of nasal and supraorbital bosses. However, the parietal, arguably the most diagnostic element among centrosaurines, is derived and almost identical to that of *Einiosaurus*. In Sampson's opinion, therefore, the cranial morphology of *Einiosaurus* (including nasal and supraorbital horns) is too different from *Pachyrhinosaurus* to warrant referring *Achelousaurus* to that genus.

Key reference: Sampson (1995).

ACROCANTHOSAURUS Stovall and Langston 1950

Saurischia: Theropoda: Tetanurae: Avetheropoda: Allosauroidea: Allosauridae.

Name derivation: Greek *akro* = "high" + Greek *akantha* = "spine" + Greek *sauros* = "lizard."

Type species: *A. atokensis* Stovall and Langston 1950.

Other species: [None.]

Occurrence: Antlers Formation, Oklahoma, Texas, United States.

Age: Early Cretaceous (Late Aptian–Early Albian).

Known material: Several incomplete skeletons, cranial remains, ?isolated teeth.

Holotype: MUO 8-0-59, incomplete skull and partial postcranial including ninth cervical and sixth dorsal vertebrae, and a dorsal spine.

Diagnosis of genus (as for type species): Giant, heavily-built, with massive, greatly elongated neural spines; skull massive, with moderately heavy arcades; orbits and postorbital fenestrae somewhat reduced; jugular foramen much enlarged. frontals and parietals solidly fused; quadratosquamosal movement in the skull somewhat lessened; centra of cervical vertebrae moderately long and opisthocoelous, pleurocoels deep; anterior dorsal vertebrae distinctly opisthocoelous; medial caudal vertebrae with supplementary neural processes; chevrons closed proximally by a transverse bar, on each ramus showing an anterior upward-projecting process; pelvic bones not coossified; pubis slender, with wide distal end; ischium slender, straight, elongate, somewhat widened distally; tibia strongly bowed outward; third metatarsal somewhat constricted proximally by lateral elements (Stovall and Langston 1950).

Comments: The genus *Acrocanthosaurus* was established on an incomplete skull and postcranial skeleton (MUO 8-0-59), found in the Trinity sands of Atoka County, Oklahoma. A second incomplete skeleton, lacking the skull and including a medial and the eleventh caudal vertebrae, designated the paratype (MUO 8-0-58), was collected from the same locality. Referred to this genus was a postorbital bone from Wise County, Texas (Stovall and Langston 1950).

According to Stovall and Langston, the most unusual feature in *Acrocanthosaurus* is the greatly elongated neural spines, which make this genus unique among North American theropods. The anterior caudal spines are flat, broad plates, each succeeding plate becoming broader, attaining maximum expanse in the sixth, which is more elongate and has a broad, rounded summit. Succeeding spines become longer, transversely much thicker, and decreased in antero-posterior dimension. During life, these spines were probably imbedded in muscles, creating a thick dorsal ridge that would have extended from behind the head, down the back, approximately to mid-tail.

Stovall and Langston observed that the known postcranial remains suggested a standard "carnosaurian" morphology, a complete skeleton probably measuring some 13 meters (42.6 feet) in length. They also found similarities between *A. atokensis* and a specimen (UUVP 6000) of *Allosaurus fragilis*. Walker (1964) referred *Acrocanthosaurus* to the Tyrannosauridae. Langston (1974) later suggested that the genus is related to the early Oxfordian *Metriacanthosaurus*, another long-spined form, and that *Acrocanthosaurus* might be descended from that form.

Madsen (1976*a*) noted that comparison of cranial material of *A. atokensis* with additional skull elements of *A. fragilis* collected from the Cleveland-Lloyd Dinosaur Quarry reveals close similarities between these two species. Madsen stated that the

Acrocanthosaurus atokensis, MUO 8-0-59, holotype partial skull, restored parts of skull based on *Allosaurus*. (After Stovall and Langston 1950.)

Photo by R. A. Long and S. P. Welles (neg. #73/41-12).

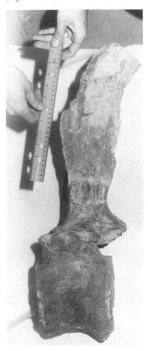

Acrocanthosaurus atokensis, MUO 8-0-59, holotype anterior caudal vertebra.

Ichnite attributed to a theropod like *Acrocanthosaurus*, holotype of *Eubrontes* (?) *glenrosensis* Shuler 1936. This now-dilapidated track is mounted in the bandstand of the town square at Glen Rose, Texas.

Glen Rose trackway sometimes interpreted as a record of a large theropod (?*Acrocanthosaurus*) stalking a sauropod (?*Pleurocoelous*; sauropod tracks named *Brontopodus birdi*).

lacrimal of *A. atokensis* with its two dorsal cavities (reported by Stovall and Langston) is similar to that in *A. fragilis* (see Gilmore 1920). The postcranial skeletons differ most notably in the elongation of the neural spines in *Acrocanthosaurus*.

Also, Madsen speculated that these spines may have constituted one of at least two options for accommodating a disproportionately large skull in larger theropods: In dinosaurs like *Acrocanthosaurus*, the elongated spines could accommodate greater muscle mass needed to support the skull; in forms like *Allosaurus*, the cervicals become shorter (see Charig and Crompton 1965). The posture of the neck could be related to the development of the cervical vertebrae, the head of *Acrocanthosaurus* carried at the end of an outstretched neck in which the neural spines had become longer, that of *Allosaurus* on an "S"-curve neck comprising shortened cervicals.

Molnar, Kurzanov and Dong (1990), in a cladistic review of "Carnosauria," agreed that *A. atokensis* shares with *Allosaurus* (in addition to those shared features observed by Stovall and Langston) the following: Jugal foramen prominent, postorbital bar broadened, pleurocoels progressing into caudal dorsal vertebrae series, and the fibular bar (these features also known in tyrannosaurids). Molnar *et al.* suggested that certain shared features (broad postorbital bar, caudal dorsal pleurocoels, and fibular process, the latter apparently for muscle attachment) in this genus could be convergent, related to large size, and that there was no reason to regard *A. atokensis* as a tyrannosaurid.

Excavation of a skeleton identified as *Acrocanthosaurus* began in November, 1992 from a 15-foot deep creek on a ranch owned by the Hobson family, in Parker County, Weatherford, Texas. The specimen, publicized as the most complete dinosaur skeleton and largest theropod yet found in Texas, is to be prepared at Southern Methodist University, after which it will be exhibited at the Fort Worth Museum. Newspapers (including the Houston *Chronicle*, November 15, 1992) announced the find.

This first relatively complete skeleton of *Acrocanthosaurus* was collected from a calcite-cemented siliceious sandstone. Due to the site of the multi-ton blocks containing the material, traditional museum methods for exposing fossil bone and removing matrix (*e.g.*, acid baths and air scribes) were eschewed in favor of using diamond saws. The skeleton will offer a more accurate picture as to how this dinosaur appeared in life (Yarborough 1995).

Notes: Isolated ?*Acrocanthosaurus* teeth were reported from the Paluxy River area, Wise County, Texas (M. R. Gallup, personal communication 1988).

Large fossil footprints originally named *Eubrontes glenrosensis* (see Shuler 1917; referred by Langston to *Irenesauripus*), from the Glen Rose Formation, Comanchean Series, Paluxy River, near Glen Rose, Texas, seem to have been made by a theropod like *Acrocanthosaurus*. The tracks are semidigitigrade and functionally tridactyl, the toes well separated, heel always impressed, among other features (Sternberg 1932*b*). During the late 1930s and early 1940s, these tracks became publicized as a dinosaur "stamping ground" (Bird 1944). One particularly famous trackway, excavated for the American Museum of Natural History, apparently recorded a large theropod stalking a sauropod (Bird 1941; Langston 1979). Although that interpretation is maintained by some workers, it has been questioned by others. Farlow (1987*b*), for example, doubted that a lone theropod weighing about 2 metric tons (approximately 2.25 tons) would be stalking a sauropod weighing some 20 metric tons (about 20.25 tons).

Key references: Langston (1974; 1979); Madsen (1976*a*); Molnar, Kurzanov and Dong (1990); Stovall and Langston (1950).

ADASAURUS Barsbold 1977
Saurischia: Theropoda: Tetanurae: Avetheropoda: Coelurosauria: Maniraptora: ?Dromaeosauridae *incertae sedis*.

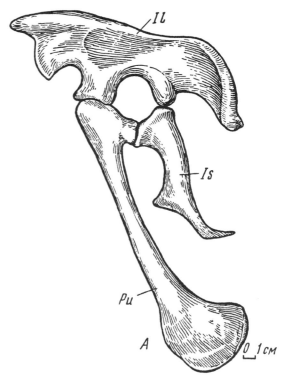

Adasaurus mogoliensis, GIN 100/200, holotype pelvis. (After Barsbold 1983.)

Name derivation: Mongolian "Ada [god of the underworld]" + Greek *sauros* = "lizard."

Type species: *A. mongoliensis* Barsbold 1977.

Other species: [None.]

Occurrence: Nemegtskaya Svita, Nemegt Formation, Bayankhongor, Mongolian People's Republic.

Age: Late Cretaceous (?late Campanian or early Maastrichtian).

Known material: Partial skull; partial skeleton; fragmentary postcrania.

Holotype: GIN 100/20, incomplete cranium and partial skeleton.

Diagnosis of genus (as for type species): Pelvis birdlike, with ilia (as in segnosaurids) well separated from each other, anterior wings deflected outwards; pubis with a long, narrow shaft posteroventrally directed, parallel to ischium; pubic "foot" small and narrow, dorsal surface with a deep, longitudinal depression at symphysis that separates pubes; ischium elongated, with a narrow shaft and narrow, distally placed obturator process that coossifies with pubis some distance away from its distal end (Barsbold 1979; Barsbold and Perle 1980).

Comments: The genus *Adasaurus* was established on an incomplete skeleton and skull from the Nemegt Formation, Khara Khutul locality in southeast Mongolia. Barsbold (1977) first published a drawing of the unusual pelvis of *Adasaurus* without assigning the genus a specific name.

Later, Barsbold (1979), then Barsbold and Perle (1980), showed that this pelvis differs from that in segnosaurids in that the obturator process of the pubis is distally located, narrow and firmly coalesced with the pubic shaft just above the distal end of the shaft. Barsbold and Perle suggested that *Adasaurus* warranted its own family.

A partial second skeleton subsequently referred by Barsbold (1983) to *Adasaurus* includes both hind-feet. The foot bears a "killer claw" smaller than that of *Velociraptor*, implying that *Adasaurus* was similar to that genus, *Deinonychus* and *Dromaeosaurus*.

Osmólska (1981), showing how certain theropod features may relate to the origin of birds, observed that the pelvis of *Adasaurus* barely differs from that figured by Walker (1977) of *Archaeopteryx*.

In his review of the Dromaeosauridae, Ostrom (1990) commented that the pelvis in *A. mongoliensis* is opisthopubic, the second metacarpal slender, and the second ungual claw reduced in comparison to *Deinonychus*, adding that no other characters diagnostic of Dromaeosauridae permit the certain assignment of *Adasaurus* to this group.

Key references: Barsbold (1977, 1979, 1983); Barsbold and Perle (1980); Osmólska (1981); Ostrom (1990).

AEGYPTOSAURUS Stromer 1932

Saurischia: Sauropodomorpha: Sauropoda: Titanosauria: Titanosauridae.

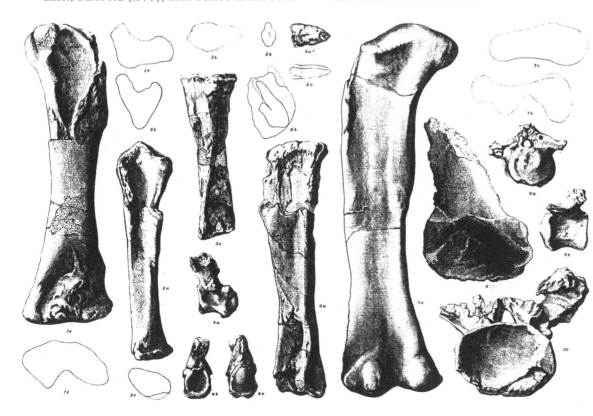

Aegyptosaurus baharijensis, IPGH, holotype 1. left humerus, 2. left radius, 3. right ulna, 4., 9. and 10., vertebral centra, 6., left tibia, 7., left femur. (After Stromer 1932.)

Name derivation: "Egypt" + Greek *sauros* = "lizard."
Type species: *A. baharijensis* Stromer 1932.
Other species: [None.]
Occurrence: Baharija Formation, Marsa Matruh, Southern Sahara, Egypt.
Age: Late Cretaceous (?Early Cenomanian).
Known material: Incomplete postcrania.
Holotype: IPGH collection [lost or destroyed], three vertebral centra, incomplete left scapula, left humerus, left radius, right ulna, left tibia, and left femur.

Diagnosis of genus: [None published.]

Comments: The discovery of *Aegyptosaurus* documents the occurrence of sauropods in Late Cretaceous Africa. The genus was founded upon incomplete postcranial remains apparently representing a single individual, collected in October, 1911 by R. Markgraf at Baharijie, Egypt (Stromer 1932).

(Apparently the type specimen was destroyed during World War II.)

Stromer originally described this genus as follows: Vertebral centra higher than wide; first centrum (apparently from dorsal series) opisthocoelous, second (apparently an anterior caudal) and third pleurocoelous; scapula (if complete) probably about 60 centimeters (approximately 23 inches) in length, (as preserved) closely agrees with that in titanosaurids; limb proportions suggest affinities with titanosaurids, femur almost one-fourth longer than humer process similar to that in *Alamosaurus*.

Lapparent (1957, 1960) also reported the occurrence of *A. baharijensis* in the Lower Cretaceous of the Southern Sahara, south of Hoggar, this material including caudal vertebrae, the distal end of a thoracic rib, and the proximal portions of two metatarsals.

McIntosh (1990*b*), in reviewing the Sauropoda, described *Aegyptosaurus* as follows: Bones very similar to those in other titanosaurids; (best preserved) caudal vertebra with more elevated arch than in *Alamosaurus*, *Titanosaurus* and *Saltasaurus*; limbs similar to but much less robust than in *Titanosaurus*; humerus narrower proximally than in *Alamosaurus*, *Argyrosaurus* and *Saltasaurus*; femur with fourth trochanter just above half length (instead of one-third way down from head as in *Titanosaurus*); humerus-femur ratio 0.78; ulna-humerus ratio 0.75; tibia-femur ratio 0.69. McIntosh noted that bones of *Aegyptosaurus* display only minor differences from those of other titanosaurids.

Key references: Lapparent (1957, 1960); McIntosh (1990*b*); Stromer (1932).

AEOLOSAURUS Powell 1986—(=*Eolosaurus*.)
Saurischia: Sauropodomorpha: Sauropoda: Titanosauria: Titanosauridae.
Name derivation: "Aeolus [in Greek mythology, god of the winds]" + Greek *sauros* = "lizard."
Type species: *A. rionegrinus* Powell 1986.
Other species: [None.]
Occurrence: Angostura Colorado Formation, ?Los Alamitos Formation, Patagonia, Allen Formation, Rio Negro Province, Argentina.
Age: Late Cretaceous (Late Senonian; Early Maastrichtian, or Campanion–Maastrichtian).
Known material: Incomplete postcranial remains.
Holotype: MJG-R 1, seven anterior caudal vertebrae, right and left incomplete scapulae, right and left humeri, radius and ulna, right and left ischia, five metacarpals, right fibula and tibia, astragalus, and various indeterminate fragments.

Diagnosis of genus (as for type species): Caudal vertebrae with compressed centra, with high lateral wall and narrow ventral face from third to fourth caudal; neural arch inclining anteriorly; prezigapophysis longer than in any known titanosaurid, projecting forwardly and upwardly with the same inclination of neural arch as in the anterior caudals, inclining anteriorly only at medioposterior part of caudals; articular facets of prezygapophyses much enlarged in anterior caudals; postzygapophyses located in middle-anterior part of vertebral centrum at beginning of midcaudal series; neural spine inclining forward in anterior caudals, less so in early midcaudals; hemaphophysis with extreme separation proximally, with broad articular facets that become distinctly level; scapula broad, with expanded distal end; short,

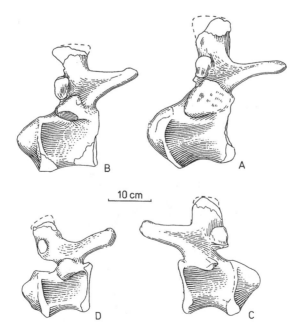

Aeolosaurus rionegrinus, MJG-R 1, holotype caudal vertebrae. (After Powell 1987.)

10 cm

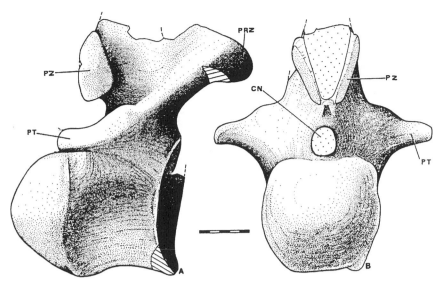

Aeolosaurus sp., MPCA 27174, anterior caudal vertebra lateral and posterior views. Scale = 5 cm. (After Salgado and Coria 1993.)

prominent ridge for muscle attachment, near upper border of internal face of scapula; (as in *Saltasaurus loricatus*); humerus robust, deltoid crest with prominent apex for insertion of pectoral muscle; metacarpals short and robust (as in *Titanosaurus*); (Salgado and Coria 1993, modified after Powell 1986).

Comments: The name *Aeolosaurus* was first mentioned (spelled *Eolosaurus*) in a preliminary faunal list published by Bonaparte (1985), the genus to be described at a later date by Powell. The genus was founded on partial postcranial remains (MJG-R 1) collected from the Angostura Colorada Formation, Casa de Piedra, Estancia Maquinchao, Río Negro Province, Argentina (Powell 1986*b*). The occurrence of *Aeolosaurus* (and the hadrosaurid "*Kritosaurus*" australis; see *Gryposaurus* entry) contributed to dating the Los Alamitos Formation as of Campanian age

(Powell 1986*a*; Bonaparte 1986*e*).

Powell (1986*b*) diagnosed the genus (and type species *A. rionigrinus*) as follows: Caudal vertebrae with compressed centra, with high lateral wall and narrow ventral face from third to fourth caudal; caudal prezigapophysis longer than in any known titanosaurid, forwardly and upwardly projecting in most anterior caudals; articular surfaces of postzigapophysis facing nearly laterally, located almost halfway relative to axis of centrum; caudal neural spine situated over anterior border of centrum, axis long, sloping slightly forward on anterior caudals; scapula broad with expanded distal end; short, prominent ridge (for muscle attachment, as in *Saltasaurus loricatus*) near upper border of internal face of scapula; humerus robust, deltoid crest with prominent apex for insertion of pectoral muscle;

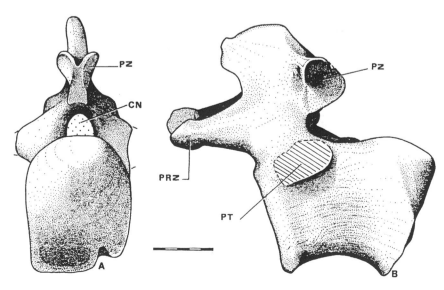

Aeolosaurus sp., MPCA 27174, middle-posterior caudal vertebra, posterior and lateral views. Scale = 5 cm. (After Salgado and Coria 1993.)

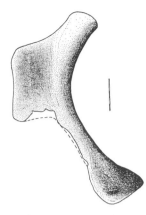

Aeolosaurus sp., MPCA 27174, right ischium, medial view. Scale = 10 cm. (After Salgado and Coria 1993.)

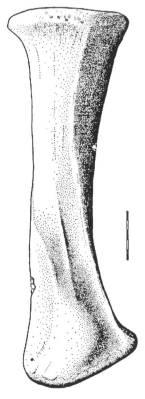

Aeolosaurus sp., MPCA 27174, right radius, ulnar view. Scale = 5 cm. (After Salgado and Coria 1993.)

metacarpals short and robust (as in *S. Loricatus*); pubis with broad but not bulky distal end without ventral longitudinal elevation.

Powell (1986*b*) observed that *Aeolosaurus* caudals closely resemble those of *Titanosaurus*, differing in having much longer prezygapophyses with wider facets, and the more forward placement of the neural spine and the postzygapophyses facets. A peculiar caudal feature is that the last preserved vertebra corresponds to an amphycoelic vertebral body.

Tentatively referred to the type species was a series of fifteen articulated caudal vertebrae (MACN-RN 147) from the Los Alamitos Formation of northeastern Patagonia. Powell preferred assigning this material to *A. rionegrinus*? until more fossil evidence becomes available to confirm species determination.

Powell reported that broken pieces of several cylindrical teeth were also found at the Los Alamitos locality. The teeth can be divided into three groups: 1. Larger teeth with a diameter of about 12.0 millimeters; 2. (including most of these teeth) those with a diameter ranging from 8 to 5 millimeters; and 3. (smallest) those with a diameter ranging from 1.5 to 2.2 millimeters. These teeth could represent two taxa, some possibly belonging to *Aeolosaurus*.

Additional specimens, collected from the Inferior Member of the Allen Formation, at Salitral Moreno, Province of Rio Negro, Argentina, were described by Salgado and Coria (1993) and assigned by them to the genus *Aeolosaurus*. These specimens include MPCA 27174, comprising five caudal vertebrae, a right ulna, metacarpal, left pubis, and right ischium, MPCA 27175, a right ulna and right radius; and MPCA 27176 and 27177, two dermal plates.

Salgado and Coria (1993) observed differences in this material from the holotype (MJG-R 1, consisting of incomplete postcranial remains) of the type species *A. rionegrinius*. These differences include the proportions of the prezygapophyses (shorter and more robust in the Salitral Moreno material), relative position of the postzygapophyses (located not as far forward as in the holotype), and the morphology of the radius (gracile in the new material; robust in the holotype) and ischium (distal end more robust and acetabular outline considerably more concave than in the holotype).

As noted by Salgado and Coria, the Salitral Moreno material is significant as representing the first Patagonian titanosaurid in which the possession of dermal armor has been documented.

Note: Powell (1986*b*) also reported fragments of fossil eggshells recovered from the Los Alamitos site. They are relatively thick (compared to European dinosaur eggshells), ranging in thickness from 1.8 to 5 millimeters, and externally ornamented with small, quite convex domes, each dome corresponding to a long, needle-shaped, crystalline unit.

Key reference: Bonaparte (1985); Powell (1986*b*); Salgado and Coria (1993).

AEPISAURUS Gervais 1853 [*nomen dubium*]
Saurischia: Sauropodomorpha: Sauropoda *incertae sedis*.

Name derivation: Latin *apex* = "summit [tall]" + Greek *sauros* = "lizard."

Type species: *A. elephantius* Gervais 1853 [*nomen dubium*].

Other species: [None.]

Occurrence: Monte Ventoux, France.

Age: Early Cretaceous (Aptian–?Albian).

Known material/holotype: MNHN 1868-242, humerus.

Diagnosis: [None published.]

Comments: The new genus and species *Aepisaurus elephantius* (generic name sometimes misspelled *Aepysaurus* [Gervais 1859] in the literature) was founded on a humerus from the Grès Verts of Mont Ventoux, near Bédoin (Vaucluse, France). The type specimen (MNHN 1868-242), a humerus, is apparently now lost (see Le Loeuff 1993).

The genus was originally described by Gervais (1853) as follows: Humerus 90 centimeters (about 35 inches) long, 33 centimeters (over 12.5 inches) wide across proximal end, 15 centimeters (about 5.8

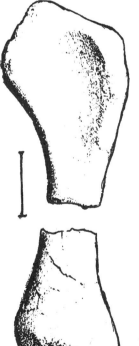

Aepysaurus elephantinus, MNHN 1868-242, holotype humerus. Scale = 8 cm. (After Gervais 1853.)

inches) wide at mid-shaft, and 25 centimeters (about 9.5 inches) wide across the distal end.

Because the holotype resembled the humerus of titanosaurid *Laplatasaurus*, Gervais classified *Aepisaurus* with the Titanosauridae. However, in his review of the Sauropoda, McIntosh (1990*b*) pointed out that the slender humerus, though bearing some resemblance to *Laplatasaurus*, also resembles that of some brachiosaurids and the camarasaurid *Camarasaurus*.

According to Le Loeuff in a review of the titanosaurids of Europe, the humerus, as figured by Gervais, is that of an undetermined sauropod, its proportions suggesting affinities with neither camarasaurids nor titanosaurids, the type specimen undiagnostic.

Note: Gervais also reported a conical tooth recovered from the same locality as *A. elephantius*. Gervais believed that the tooth represented a larger sauropod and a possible second species of *Aepisaurus*. Le Loeuff observed that this tooth is seemingly that of a crocodilian.

Other bones referred by Gervais to *Aepisaurus* sp., apparently the distal part of a humerus and distal part of a possible ulna, should, according to Le Loeuff, be regarded as belonging to an undetermined sauropod.

Key references: Gervais (1853); Le Loeuff (1993); McIntosh (1990*b*).

AETONYX Broom 1911—(See *Massospondylus*.)
Name derivation: Latin *aetatis* = "old" + Greek *onyx* = "claw."
Type species: *A. palustris* Broom 1911.

AFROVENATOR Sereno, Wilson, Larsson, Duthell and Sues 1994
Saurischia: Theropoda: ?Tetanurae: Megalosauridae.
Name derivation: *Afro* = "African" + Latin *venator* = "hunter."
Type species: *A. abakensis* Sereno, Wilson, Larsson, Dutheil and Sues 1994.
Other species: [None].
Occurrence: Tiouraréen beds (Lower Cretaceous), Sahara Desert.
Age: Early Cretaceous (?Barremian–Hauterivian).
Known material/holotype: (Originally catalogued as UC OBA 1), relatively complete skeleton including skull lacking most of lower jaws, cervical vertebrae (most anterior cervicals articulated), incomplete dorsal and caudal series, ribs, pelvic girdle, almost complete forelimbs, hindlimbs.
Diagnosis of genus (as for type species): Diagnosed by these autapomorphies: maxilla with lobe-shaped anterior margin of antorbital fossa; third cer-

vical vertebra with low, rectangular neural spine; very flat semilunate carpal; metacarpal I with broad flange for articulation against metacarpal II (Sereno *et al.* 1994).

Comments: In 1990, Paul C. Sereno, as part of a British Museum (Natural History) [now The Natural History Museum, London] survey expedition, traced a route across 500 miles of the southern Saharan Desert, Africa. Sereno knew that the journey would lead to a site which, 50 years earlier, a French priest and paleontologist had called "the dinosaurs' graveyard." Beyond this site by some 20 kilometers, Sereno had observed a row of massive sauropod vertebrae emerging from the desert sands. In September, 1994, after many delays, most of them political in nature, Sereno returned to that site (called "In Abaka" in the language of local Touareg inhabitants of the area) with a caravan of six Land Rovers, there to collect several previously unknown dinosaurian species from approximately 130 million years ago (Morell 1994).

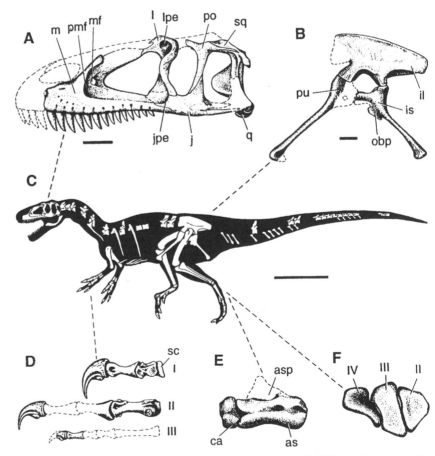

Afrovenator abakensis, UC OBA 1, holotype A. reconstructed skull, left lateral view; B. pelvis, left lateral view; C. skeleton, D. partial left manus, lateral view; E. right astragalus and calcaneum, anterior view (ascending process based on articular depression on distal tibia); F. left metatarsus, proximal view. Scale (A, B, D, E, F) = 10 cm; (C) = 1 m. (After Sereno, Wilson, Larsson, Duthell and Sues 1994.)

Among the remains recovered by Sereno's group in 1994 were those of a broad-toothed sauropod (see "Introductory" section on sauropods) and the first relatively complete skeleton of an African theropod (found by amateur fossil hunter Ruben D. Carolini) from the Cretaceous. All of these remains were found buried in shallow, mud-filled channel deposits on a floodplain and display evidence of fluvial transport. Associated nondinosaurian vertebtrate fossils included remains of the coelocanth *Mawsonioa*, dipnoan *Ceratodus*, semionotid *Lepidotes*, a pleurodiran turtle, and crocodyliforms. Lack of caliche deposits and lack of periodic growth in fossilized wood is indicative of a relatively uniform climate (Sereno *et al.* 1994).

The theropod was named *Afrovenator abakensis* by Sereno *et al.* In describing this new genus and species, the authors observed that the skull is low compared to that of other large-headed theropods such as *Allosaurus*, with a maximum height at the orbits equal to less than one-third the skull length, but (unlike *Allosaurus* and some other carnivorous dinosaurs) only poorly developed cranial crests and rugosities, the lacrimal crest having a low, rounded profile. The maxilla has sockets for a total of 14 blade-shaped teeth. The skeleton is relatively gracile. The forelimbs are apparently similar to those in *Allosaurus* but with different limb proportions (humerus in *Afrovenator* comparatively longer, metacarpal I with stouter proportions, ungual on digit III especially small). The distal segments of the hindlimb are more elongate than those of *Allosaurus*, with the femur only slightly longer than the tibia.

Afrovenator was referred by Sereno *et al.* to the theropod group Tetanurae because of the following tetauran synapomorphies: Skull with opening in antorbital fossa (maxillary fenestra); pneumatic excavation in jugal; position of posteriormost maxillary tooth (anterior to orbit); specialized wrist bones that constrain motion of hand to a transverse plane (semi-lunate carpal with articular trochlea for disc-shaped radiale. Also, the hand resembles that in other tetanurans, having a smaller digit III relative to digits I and II; the femur possesses a blade-shaped trochanter; and the astragalus has a plate-shaped ascending process.

Sereno *et al.* referred *Afrovenator* to the tetanuran theropod taxon Torvosauridae [=Megalosauridae] (a group sharing such cranial features as the long anterior ramus of the maxilla and the transversely

Photo by Allen A. Debus (neg. #1A).

Afrovenator abakensis, skeleton (cast, reconstructed from holotype UC OBA 1 and *Allosaurus* material) mounted at Harold Washington Library Center, Chicago.

Afrovenator

broad ventral process of the postorbital) as apparently representing a basal lineage of that family, because this genus lacks the sickle-shaped ungual on manual digit I which characterizes more advanced torvosaurids.

As pointed out by Sereno *et al.*, a coherent picture of dinosaurian biogeography during the Cretaceous of Africa has not been possible due to the paucity of substantial fossil evidence. The discovery of *Afrovenator* and other fossil vertebrate remains from Lower Cretaceous Saharan rocks has yielded important data regarding the understanding of dinosaurian biogeography of the late Mesozoic.

In the past, most authors have recognized distinct Laurasian and Gondwanan biotas. However, the occurrence of *Afrovenator* and a broad-toothed sauropod in Cretaceous Africa during the early stage of the break-up of the supercontinent Pangaea does not support the existence of a distinct Gondwanan fauna. *Afrovenator* shares a close relationship to tetanuran theropods, which are known from both northern and southern continents, while the sauorpod is more closely related to broad-toothed forms, also known from both continents. This suggested to Sereno *et al.* that several lineages of tetanuran theropods and broad-toothed sauropods had achieved a cosmopolitan distribution before the break-up of the supercontinent.

In the Late Jurassic, relatively uniform dinosaurian faunal exchange was permitted via a persistent land connection from the north through Europe, this connection apparently becoming fragmented during the Early Cretaceous, approximately when the southern continents were becoming biogeographically isolated. Sereno *et al.* postulated that, during this time of increasing isolation, these cosmopolitan dinosaurian groups experienced different fates. In Africa during the Cretaceous, "torvosaurids" [=megalosaurids] such as *Afrovenator*, as well as spinosaurids, survived as the dominant large carnivores, while tetanuran allosaurids and then coelurosaurs became dominant in Asiamerica, and ceratosaurian abelisaurids achieved dominance in South America. Sereno *et al.* concluded that the distinct dinosaurian faunas of all three land masses arose during the Cretaceous, when continental isolation reached its zenith, by differential survival of once widespread lineages with origins that can be traced back to the Early Jurassic.

A mounted skeleton of *A. abakensis*, cast from the type material with the missing portions based on *Allosaurus*, was exhibited in 1994-95 at Harold Washington Library Center in Chicago. As mounted, the skeleton measured about 8 meters (27 feet) in length.

Photo by Allen A. Debus (neg. #5A).

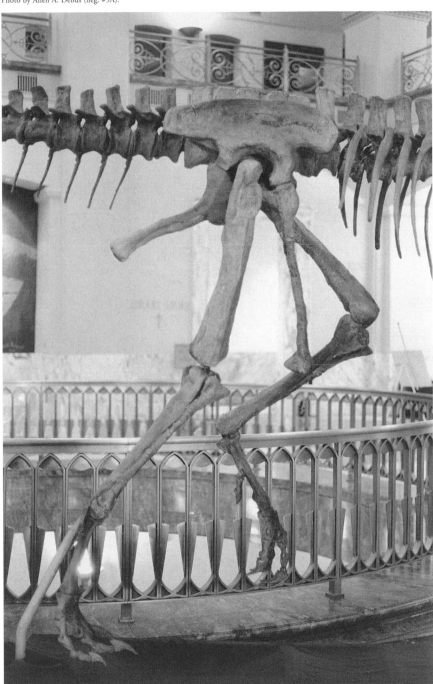

Afrovenator abakensis, posterior part of skeleton (cast, reconstructed from holotype UC OBA 1 and *Allosaurus* material) mounted at Harold Washington Library Center, Chicago.

Note: In October, 1994, prior to the official publication of the name, "Afrovenator" appeared in various newspaper articles about the discovery of this dinosaur (*e.g.*, the Chicago *Tribune* and Chicago *Sun-Times*).

Key references: Morell (1994); Sereno *et al.* 1994 (1994).

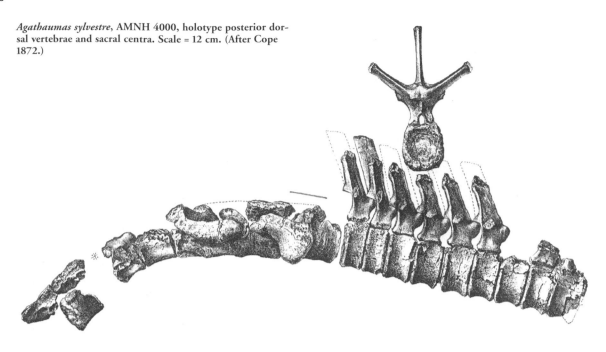

Agathaumas sylvestre, AMNH 4000, holotype posterior dorsal vertebrae and sacral centra. Scale = 12 cm. (After Cope 1872.)

AGATHAUMAS Cope 1872 [*nomen dubium*]—
(=? *Torosaurus*, ? *Triceratops*)

Ornithischia: Genasauria: Cerapoda: Marginocephalia: Ceratopsia: Neoceratopsia: Ceratopsidae: Chasmosaurinae.

Name derivation: Greek *agan* = "much" + Greek *thauma* = "marvel" [or "marvelous"].

Type species: *A. sylvestris* (Cope 1872) [*nomen dubium*].

Other species: [None.]

Occurrence: ?Lance Formation, Wyoming, United States.

Age: Late Cretaceous (Maastrichtian).

Known material/holotype: AMNH 4000, incomplete postcranial skeleton, including nine posterior dorsal vertebrae, sacrum with ilia (one almost complete), ribs, other elements.

Diagnosis of genus: [No modern diagnosis published.]

Comments: *Agathaumas* was founded upon an incomplete postcranial skeleton (AMNH 4000), found in 1872 by F. B. Meek apparently in the Lance Formation, at Black Buttes, Sweetwater County, Wyoming (Hatcher, Marsh, and Lull 1907). This material represented the first ceratopsian known from remains other than merely teeth or fragments.

Originally, Cope (1872) diagnosed *Agathaumas* as follows: Dorsal vertebrae with no indication of capitular facet for rib, centra slightly concave posteriorly; neural canal very small; neural arch short, distinct from centrum; eight to nine sacral vertebrae, the last reduced and rather elongate; base of ischium fused with ilium; ribs compressed.

Cope (1872) diagnosed *A. sylvestris* as follows: Last nine dorsal vertebrae with somewhat short centra and high, compressed neural spine; eight sacral vertebrae flattened below.

(Although the above features were once considered to have diagnostic significance, subsequent ceratopsian discoveries revealed that postcrania of Chasmosaurines are very much the same. Lacking a skull, it cannot be determined whether *Agathaumas* is a valid genus or, more likely, synonymous with *Triceratops* or *Torosaurus*.)

Fragmentary remains from South Dakota and Colorado have been assigned to *Agathaumas*, although without justification.

Notes: A fanciful life restoration of *Agathaumas* was made, first as a statuette and then a painting, by artist Charles R. Knight working under Cope's direction (based on *Monoclonius sphenocerus*, then thought to be a species of *Agathaumas*). Imaginatively, Knight depicted the animal with spiked frill, two small orbital horns and one long nasal horn. Both pieces were completed shortly after Cope's death in 1897.

Agathaumas sylvestre, AMNH 4000, holotype right ilium. Scale = 12 cm. (After Cope 1872.)

Agathaumas sylvestre, AMNH 4000, holotype vertebrae.

The painting accompanied an article by Ballou (1897) in *The Century Illustrated Monthly Magazine*. Photographs of both statuette and painting were subsequently published in periodicals and popular books.

A. milo Cope 1874 [*nomen dubium*] is generally regarded as belonging to hadrosaurid *Edmontosaurus regalis* (see Weishampel and Horner 1990).

Key reference: Cope (1872).

AGILISAURUS   Peng 1990

Ornithischia *incertae sedis*.

Name derivation: Latin *agilis* = "agile" + Greek *sauros* = "lizard."

Type species: *A. louderbacki* Peng 1990.

Other species: *A. multidens* (He and Cai 1983).

Occurrence: Lower Shaximiao Formation, Dashanpu, Zigong, Sichuan Province, China.

Age: Middle Jurassic.

Known material: Incomplete skeletons.

Holotype: ZDM6011, almost complete skeleton.

Diagnosis for genus (as for type species): Small cursorial ornithopod with a short, deep skull; middle part of parietal strongly contracted; nasal long, with suture part concave longitudinally at midline; posterior process of premaxilla not contacting lacrimal; depression for M. buccinatoris on maxilla and dentary marked; antorbital fenestra situated high on skull; orbit posterolaterally located; palpebral very well-developed; quadrate robust, with transversely expanded mandibular condyle; mandible with high coronoid process, low-situated articular cavity, but no external fenestra; five premaxillary, 14 maxillary and 20 dentary teeth; premaxillary and anterior three dentary teeth recurved and caniniform; remaining crowns of dentary and maxillary teeth from triangular- to diamond-shaped; nine cervical, 15 dorsal, five sacral and 44 caudal vertebrae, tail equal to more than one-half body length; ossified tendons present only in trunk and hip areas; scapula shorter than humerus; ilium long, postpubis long and rod-like, obturator process proximally located; femur shorter than tibia; lesser trochanter situated lower than greater trochanter, separated from greater trochanter by a deep cleft; fourth trochanter pendent; nutritive foramina present on femoral shaft; third metatarsal longer than one-half length of femur; pedal phalangeal formula 2-33-4-5-0; toes clawed (Peng 1992).

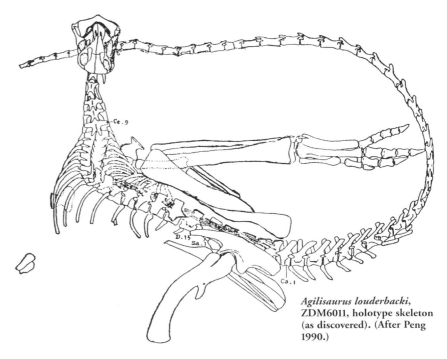

Agilisaurus louderbacki, ZDM6011, holotype skeleton (as discovered). (After Peng 1990.)

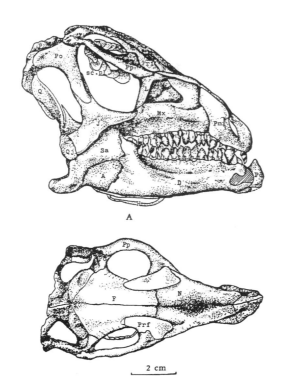

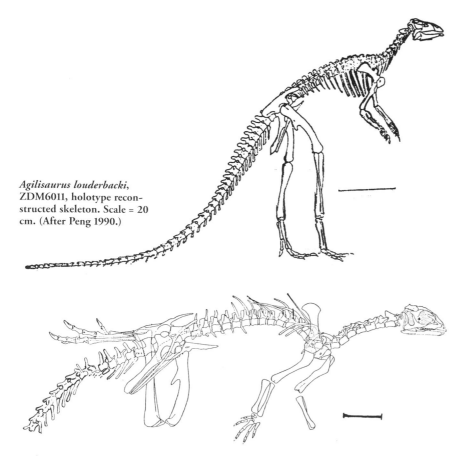

Diagnosis of *A. multidens*: Skull distinguished by rounded, relatively large orbit; quadrajugal long and narrow; sagittal crest of parietal weakly-developed; occipital crest well-developed; eighteen maxillary and twenty mandibular teeth (premaxillary teeth unknown); lateral ridge and approximately three denticulations present at anterior and posterior margins on maxillary and dentary teeth; nine amphiplated cervical vertebrae with well-developed ventral keels and triangular neural spines, 15 amphiplated dorsals with rectangular spines, and five co-ossified sacrals; first sacral rib slender, situated so as not to contact ilium (He and Kaiji 1983).

Comments: *Agilisaurus* was founded upon an almost complete skeleton (ZDM6011) discovered in 1984 in the Lower Shaximiao Formation of Dashanpu, Zigong, China. Ironically, the discovery was made during the course of digging the foundation of the building of the Zigong Dinosaur Museum. The type specimen, the most complete ornithopod skeleton known from China, was first briefly described by Peng (1990) as the new genus and species *Agilisaurus louderbacki* (Peng 1992).

Peng (1990, 1922) referred *Agilisaurus* to the Fabrosauridae [abandoned] because of what he considered "typical traits" of Fabrosauridae: 1. Marginally positioned dentition; 2. tooth crowns with two uniformly enamelled surfaces, each with faint vertical ridges and no occlusial wear surfaces; 3. greatly reduced forelimb, hindlimb elongated and sturdy; and 4. lesser trochanter lower than the greater trochanter, separated from the latter by a deep cleft.

The species originally named *Yandusaurus multidens* was based upon an incomplete skeleton (T6001) collected from the red bed of the Lower Shaximiao Formation of Dashanpu, Zigong, and described by He and Kaiji (1983). Sues and Norman (1990) regarded this taxon as a junior synonym of the type species of *Yandusaurus*. Later, Peng (1992) observed that the skeletal features of *Y. multidens* resemble those of *A. louderbacki*, differing only in some [unspecified] subtle features, suggesting that this taxon be referred, as a second species, to *Agilisaurus*.

Key references: He and Kaiji (1983); Peng (1990, 1992); Sues and Norman (1990).

AGROSAURUS Seeley 1891 [*nomen dubium*]
Saurischia: Sauropodomorpha: ?Prosauropoda *incertae sedis*.
Name derivation: Greek *agros* = "field" + Greek *sauros* = "lizard."
Type species: *A. macgillivrayi* Seeley 1891 [*nomen dubium*].
Other species: [None.]

Agilisaurus louderbacki, ZDM6011, holotype skull, right lateral and dorsal views. (After Peng 1990.)

Agilisaurus louderbacki, ZDM6011, holotype reconstructed skeleton. Scale = 20 cm. (After Peng 1990.)

Agilisaurus multidens, T6001, holotype skeleton of *Yandusaurus multidens*. Scale = 8 cm. (After He and Kaiji 1983.)

Occurrence: North Queensland, Australia.

Age: ?Late Triassic or ?Early Jurassic.

Known material/holotype: BMNH 49984, tooth, claw, tibia.

Diagnosis: [None published.]

Comments: The genus *Agrosaurus* was founded upon isolated elements including a broken tooth, a claw, and tibia (BMNH 49984), reported by Seeley (1891*a*), collected during the voyage of HMS *Fly* from unrecorded sediments (?Upper Triassic; Molnar 1982*b*) on the coast of North Queensland, Australia.

As measured by Seeley, the tibia is approximately 21 centimeters (8 inches) long.

This genus has been classified over the years as both a prosauropod (Galton and Cluver 1976) and "coelurosaur." *Agrosaurus* was listed as an indeterminate prosauropoda in *The Dinosauria* (Galton 1990*a*; Weishampel 1990*a*).

The discovery of *Agrosaurus* in Australia establishes the occurrence there of prosauropods similar to those on other continents.

Key references: Galton and Cluver (1976); Seeley (1891).

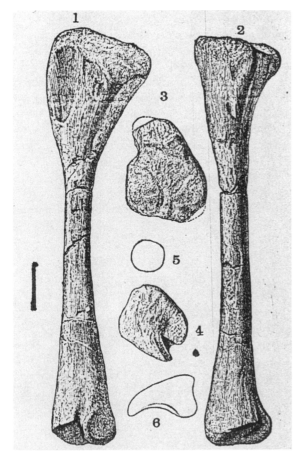

Agrosaurus macgillivrayi, BMNH R49984, holotype left tibia (1. posterior, 2. anterior, 3. dorsal, and 4. distal views, 5. cross-section of shaft), 6. claw phalange. Scale = 2 cm. (After Seeley 1891.)

ALAMOSAURUS   Gilmore 1922

Saurischia: Sauropodomorpha: Sauropoda: Titanosauria: Titanosauridae.

Name derivation: "[Ojo] Alamo" + Greek *sauros* = "lizard."

Type species: Species: *A. sanjuanensis* Gilmore 1922.

Other species: [None.]

Occurrence: Upper Kirtland Shale, New Mexico, North Horn Formation, Utah, Javalina Formation, Texas, United States.

Age: Late Cretaceous (Maastrichtian).

Known material: Partial postcranial skeleton, isolated postcrania.

Holotype: USNM 10,486, left scapula.

Diagnosis of genus: [None published.]

Comments: *Alamosaurus* was one of the last sauropods and is the titanosaurid known from the most complete articulated skeletal remains. The genus was established on a well-preserved left scapula (USNM 10,486) discovered by United States Geological Survey geologist John B. Reeside, Jr. in [what was then called] the Ojo Alamo Formation of San Juan County, New Mexico. The paratype (USNM collection), a right ischium found almost 200 feet away from the scapula, may be from the same individual (Gilmore 1922).

Gilmore originally described the scapula as follows: Shaft gradually widening from below toward proximal end, with no special expansion of the anterior border and no rapid superior expansion of both borders, this portion heavy, but thinner and less massive than in *Camarasaurus*. Gilmore distinguished the ischium by its extreme shortness and lack of the long, slender posterior extension typical of sauropods.

Subsequently, Gilmore (1946*b*) referred to *Alamosaurus* a caudal centrum (USNM 15658) and caudal neural spine from the same locality as the type specimens, and 30 articulated caudals (beginning with the first), 25 chevrons, both ischia, left scapula and coracoid, right humerus, ulna, radius and metacarpus, two sternal plates, and pieces of three ribs

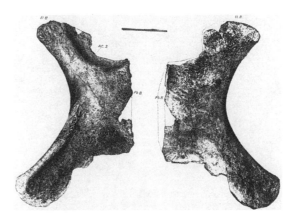

Alamosaurus sanjuanensis, USNM 10,486, holotype left scapula. Scale = 20 cm. (After Gilmore 1922.)

Alamosaurus sanjuanensis, USNM 10,486, paratype right ischium, external and internal views. Scale = 20 cm. (After Gilmore 1922.)

(USNM 15560), collected by Gilmore in 1937 from the lower North Horn Formation of Utah. (A sacrum, observed in the ground but not collected, belonged to this specimen.)

McIntosh (1990b), in his review of the Sauropoda, briefly described *Alamosaurus* as follows: first caudal centrum biconvex, the other centra in this series strongly procoelous, lacking pleurocoels; neural arches and spines on cranial half of centrum, rapidly diminishing in height; prezygapophyses long, transverse processes disappear after eighth caudal; chevrons simple, prominent chevron facets suggesting some ventral excavation; sternal plates very large; scapula large, with but a slight distal expansion, large angle between shaft and ridge on proximal plate; scapula-coracoid straight, except margin is broken in the middle by a marked upward deflection, forward rim of coracoid projecting beyond scapula (but not as much as in *Magyarosaurus* and *Saltasaurus*); forelimb relatively long, includes somewhat stout humerus expanded greatly at both ends, and stout radius expanded at both ends, especially at distal end; ulna to humerus ratio of 0.65, humerus ratio 0.59, indicating short forearm; metacarpus to humerus ratio 0.30; ischia short, stout, united edge to edge for their complete length, shaft of ischium broad with broad but thin distal ends.

As noted by Lehman (1987), sauropods seem to have become extinct on the North American continent by the end of the Early Cretaceous. The occurrence of *Alamosaurus* in Texas, New Mexico, and Utah indicates that sauropods were reintroduced from South America during the Maastrichtian.

Alamosaurus, a genus with rather long and robust forelimbs, perhaps measured some 15 meters (50 feet) in length.

Key references: Gilmore (1922, 1946b0; McIntosh (1990b).

ALBERTOSAURUS Osborn 1905—(=*Gorgosaurus*; = ?*Daspletosaurus*, ?*Deinodon*).

Saurischia: Theropoda: Tetanurae: Avetheropoda; Coelurosauria: Maniraptora: Arctometatarsalia: Tyrannosauridae.

Name derivation: "Alberta [Canada]" + Greek *sauros* = "lizard."

Type species: *A. sarcophagus* Osborn 1905.

Other species: *A. libratus* (Lambe 1914).

Occurrence: ?Lance Formation, Wyoming, Dinosaur Park [Judith River] Formation (Eberth and Hamblin 1993), Montana, Fruitland Formation, Kirtland Shale, New Mexico, United States; Horseshoe Canyon Formation, Alberta, Canada.

Age: Late Cretaceous (late Campanian-early Maastrichtian).

Known material: five fragmentary skulls with postcrania, nine partial skulls, three incomplete skeletons, six skulls, postcrania, fragmentary remains.

Holotype: NMC 5600, incomplete skull.

Diagnosis of genus: Premaxilla contacts nasal below the external nares; compared with *Tyrannosaurus*, lacrimal horn often better developed, postorbital considerably smoother, posterior portion of dentary not as deep; wrist comprising five elements; ilium with deep postacetabular blade; pubic shaft straight (Carpenter 1992).

Diagnosis of *A. sarcophagus*: Premaxilla very short and broad anteroposteriorly, little visible in side view; pro-maxillary fenestra located well anterior to the maxillary opening, visible in lateral aspect; maxillary opening taller than long, separated from antorbital opening by a thin bar of the maxillary; lacrimal horn moderately-developed; surangular foramen comparatively small (for a tyrannosaurid); body apparently shorter than that of *A. libratus*; distal end

Albertosaurus sarcophagus, NMC 5600 holotype skull. Scale = 6 cm. (After Lambe 1914.)

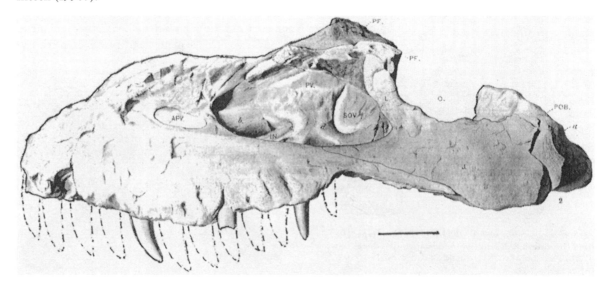

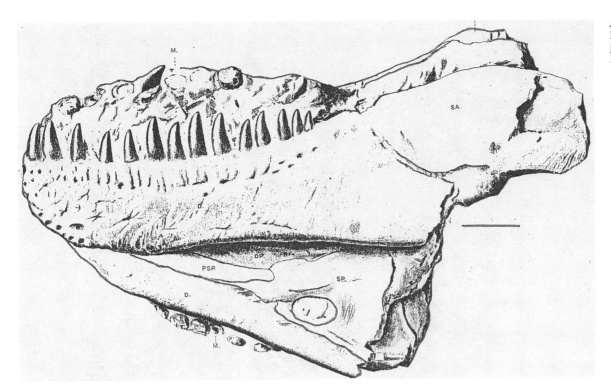

Albertosaurus sarcophagus, NMC 5600, holotype lower jaw. Scale = 6 cm. (After Lambe 1914.)

Photo by the author, courtesy Royal Tyrrell Museum/Alberta Community Development.

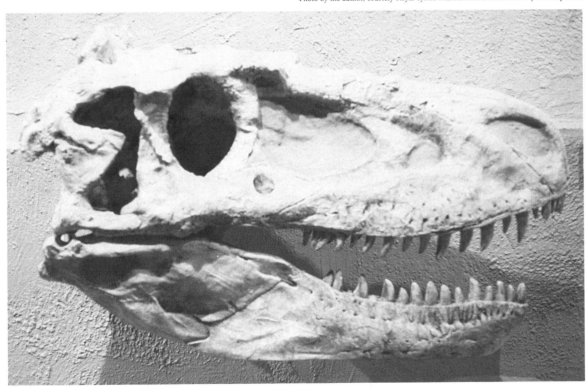

Albertosaurus sarcophagus, referred skull.

of scapular blade strongly inflected forward; tibia more gracile than in *A. libratus* (Carpenter 1992).

Diagnosis of *A. libratus*: Pro-maxillary openings close to maxillary fenestra; maxillary opening oval, separated by wide bar of maxillary from antorbital fenestra; lacrimal horn very well-developed; surangular very large; distal end of scapula broadening gradually; acromion process of scapula very deep; tibia more robust than in *A. sarcophagus* (Carpenter 1992).

Albertosaurus

Skeleton of *Albertosaurus libratus* (FMNH PR308, postcrania missing large portions of posterior half, restored; FMNH PR87469, cast of skull), collected by Barnum Brown in 1914 along Red Deer River, Alberta, as originally mounted in 1956.

Comments: *Albertosaurus* is the tyrannosaurid genus known from the most specimens, many fossils of this dinosaur having been recovered including complete skeletons and specimens representing various growth stages.

The genus was founded on an incomplete skull including the palatal region, braincase, and lower jaws (NMC 5600), collected from the [then so-called] "Laramie" Formation [=Horseshoe Canyon Forma-

tion; the true Laramie Formation is in Colorado] at Kneehills Creek, Red Deer River, Alberta, Canada. This skull, plus a smaller incomplete skull (NMC 5601) with lower jaws, and some postcranial material (fragments of sacral vertebrae and an ilium, the distal end of a tibia with astragalus, a fourth metatarsal, and three pedal ungual phalanges), collected by the Geological Survey of Canada from the Kneeshill Creek locality, were later referred by Cope (1892*a*) to

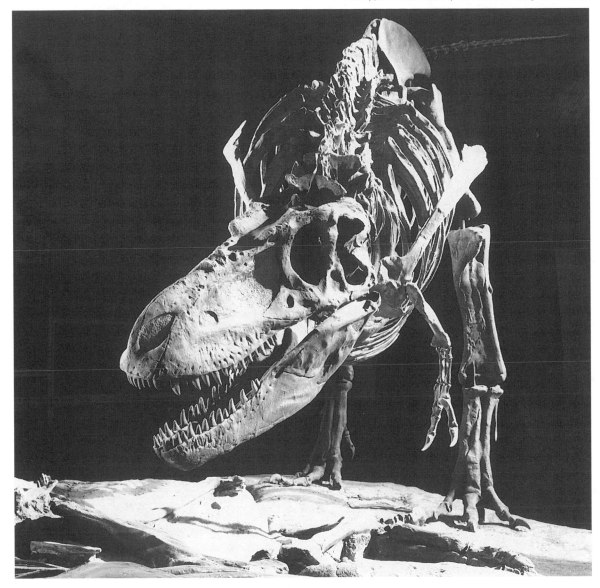

Skeleton of predator *Albertosaurus libratus* (FMNH PR308; skull cast of FMNH PR87469) posed over that of prey *Lambeosaurus lambei* (FMNH PR380), remounted in correct pose for The Field Museum's "DNA to Dinosaurs" exhibit (opened June, 1994).

his species *Laelaps incrassatus*. Cope acknowledged that this material differed from other then known theropods, but did not realize that it represented a new family,

As the name *Laelaps* was preoccupied and was replaced by *Dryptosaurus*, Lambe (1903, 1904c) later described these fossils in greater detail as *D. incrassatus*. Osborn (1905) then removed this material from *Dryptosaurus*, erecting the new genus and species *Albertosaurus sarcophagus*, with NMC 5600 designated as the holotype and NMC 5601 the paratype. Briefly, Osborn diagnosed *A. sarcophagus* as having fifteen mandibular teeth, including one small anterior tooth.

Albertosaurus is best understood from fossil material originally named *Gorgosaurus*. Prior to the discovery of this genus, Cope (1876a) proposed the name *Laelaps incrassatus* [*nomen dubium*] for teeth

collected from supposed Fort Union beds (later referred to the Judith River Formation) in Montana. Cope described (but did not figure) these teeth (the features regarded by him as distinctive now known to be typical of tyrannosaurids).

In summer 1913, Charles H. Sternberg discovered a well-preserved, almost complete theropod skeleton (NMC 2120) in the Judith River Formation, near Berry Creek, at Red Deer River, Alberta, Canada. The material included the skull, most of the vertebral column, pectoral and pelvic arches, at least one forearm, hindlimbs, and possibly an entire series of abdominal ribs. This was the first specimen of a Cretaceous theropod in which either the manus or a complete set of ventral ribs were preserved.

Lambe (1914a) briefly described the forearm in this specimen, noting that the manus clearly showed

Albertosaurus

Illustration by Gregory S. Paul.

Two *Albertosaurus libratus* (left) charging *Styracosaurus albertensis* group in a cattail marsh, "Judith River" Formation.

only two digits (with the tiny remnant of digit III appressing II). Lambe (1914c) designated this specimen as the type of new genus and species *Gorgosaurus libratus*. The approximate length of the animal was estimated at 8.25 meters (about 29 feet). Later, Lambe (1917c) deduced that this individual had become entombed in a water-laid deposit, and that its floating carcass had become stranded in shallow water where it settled into the sand.

In his review of Late Cretaceous tyrannosaurs of western Canada, Russell (1970b) suggested that cranial material of *A. sarcophagus* so closely resembles *G. libratus* that *Albertosaurus* and *Gorgosaurus* were almost certainly congeneric. Suggesting that *G. libratus* was probably immediately ancestral to *A. sarcophagus*, Russell placed the former species into the genus *Albertosaurus* as new binomial *A. libratus*, a status it has since generally retained in the literature.

However, more recently Russell's synonymy of *Albertosaurus* and *Gorgosaurus* has been questioned by some workers. According to Bakker (*see in* Bakker, Williams and Currie 1988), skull material of *A. sarcophagus* is so crushed that positive verification of resemblance is difficult to confirm. Bakker *et al.* suggested that *Gorgosaurus* may be a valid genus distinct from *Albertosaurus*. Molnar, Kurzanov and Dong (1990) accepted Russell's synonymy. Contrarily, Currie (1992) listed *Gorgosaurus* as a distinct genus among other large tyrannosaurids, pointing out the need for further description and revision. Holtz (1994), in his analysis of the Tyrannosauridae, stated that further work in preparation by Bakker, Currie and Carpenter may eventually justify resurrection of *Gorgosaurus*, although no formal synonymy has been made to date of this writing.

Furthermore, Carpenter (19920, noting that the holotype and paratype skulls of *A. sarcophagus* are

Albertosaurus libratus (juvenile), AMNH 5664, holotype skeleton of *Gorgosaurus sternbergi.*

incomplete and crushed, questioned their comparison with skulls referred to *A. libratus*. According to Carpenter, one incomplete and disarticulated skull (AMNH 5222, now rearticulated) shares with the holotype and paratype such features as short, broad premaxillaries, pre-maxillary opening visible in side view and widely separated from maxillary opening, and narrow maxillary bar separating the maxillary from antorbital openings. Specimen AMNH 5222 is short and deep (as in *Tyrannosaurus*) instead of long and low (as in *Albertosaurus*). *A. sarcophagus* also differs from *A. libratus* in such features as the pro-maxillary opening clearly visible in side view, broad

bar of the maxillary separating maxillary from antorbital openings, possible extension of the postorbital into the orbit, and in the more gracile limbs and short *Tyrannosaurus*-like trunk. Carpenter concluded that *A. sarcophagus* and *A. libratus* seemed different enough from one another to suggest generic separation, but cautioned that a final verdict on this issue should await a complete review of *A. sarcophagus*, based upon new skeletons, by Currie (1992).

Other taxa have also been referred to *A libratus*: "*Laelaps*" *falculus* [*nomen dubium*], based on several teeth found by J. C. Isaac in the Union beds" of Fergus County, described (but not figured) by

?*Albertosaurus libratus*, AMNH 3957, holotype teeth of *Laelaps hazenianus*.

?*Albertosaurus libratus*, AMNH 3959, holotype teeth of *Laelaps falculus*.

Cope (1876a); also *L. hazenianus* Cope 1876 [*nomen dubium*], *Ornithomimus grandis* Marsh 1890 [*nomen dubium*], and *Dryptosaurus kenabekides* Hay 1899 [*nomen dubium*].

"*G.*" *sternbergi* was based on the most completely known specimen (AMNH 5664) (missing the tail) of a North American tyrannosaurid. The skeleton was collected from the "Judith River" Formation at Red Deer River. Matthew and Brown (1923) distinguished this species as being smaller and more slender than *G. libratus*, with less massive jaws, a more slender muzzle, more shallow and elongate maxilla, and more circular orbits, the femur considerably shorter than the tibia. Matthew and Brown recognized these and other differences between this species and *A. libratus* as possibly age related, also noting other juvenile signs (widely open sutures between skull roof bones and non-co-ossified pelvic elements). Russell regarded *G. sternbergi* as a young *A. libratus*.

A. arctunguis was described by Parks (1928) based on a sacrum and adjacent vertebrae, left scapula-coracoid and forelimb, left half of the pelvis, and associated limb bones (ROM 807), from the Edmonton Formation near Red Deer River, along Kneehills Creek. Russell regarded the supposed distinguishing features of ROM 807 as pathologic and referred this species to *A. sarcophagus*.

Albertosaurus reached an approximate maximum length, according to Russell, of about 8.8 meters (30 feet).

Examining six specimens (AMNH 5423, 5458, 5664, USNM 12814, NMC 11593, and 2120) of *A. libratus* from the Belly River Formation near Steveville, Russell correlated changes in bodily proportions with the animal's size, and established growth trends from hatchling individuals to adults. Using femur length as an arbitrary standard, Russell proposed that, as the animal increases in size from half-grown to adult, the skull, sacrum, humerus, and radius-ulna grow at the same rate as the femur; presacral vertebral column, ribs, scapula-coracoid, pubis, and ischium increase more rapidly; and the caudal vertebral column, manus, tibia, metatarsus, and pes grow at a slower rate. With those results as a guide, Russell reconstructed a conjectural hatchling, depicted with claws and generally slender and delicate proportions.

More gracile limbs would, according to Russell (1977), permit a juvenile to catch smaller and fleeter prey.

Among the first paleontologists to comment on the probable lifestyle of a tyrannosaurid, Lambe (1917c) imagined *Albertosaurus* [=*Gorgosaurus* of his usage] as a lazy giant spending most of its life squatting, sitting or lying on the ground in a prone position. The well-developed "ventral ribs" or "gastralia" and footed pubis seemed to him to be adaptations for lying prostrate. Hunger may have inspired the animal to stand, assuming a somewhat stooped pose upon its somewhat bowed hind legs. Lambe believed that a creature so massive and seemingly ponderous as *Albertosaurus* could not have been an active predator and must have been a veritably harmless scavenger. Today, however, many paleontologists regard large theropods as active predators. Brown (*see in* Matthew and Brown 1923) had a referred skeleton (AMNH 5458) of *G. libratus* mounted at the American Museum of Natural History in a running pose as if pursuing a group of hadrosaurs.

Russell (1970b, 1977) surmised that *Albertosaurus* was probably the fleetest of large theropods in its environment, well suited to prey upon hadrosaurs, the more formidable ceratopsians left to its heavier and more powerful contemporary *Daspletosaurus*. This scenario was supported by the occurrence in the "Judith River" Formation of more "albertosaurs" and hadrosaurs than "daspletosaurs" and ceratopsians.

Rarely are tyrannosaurid humeri found and, in five specimens of *A. libratus* where the humerus is preserved, it had apparently been damaged during life. Russell (1970b), pointing out similar damage in the distal end of a *Daspletosaurus* humerus, speculated that the forelimbs of such dinosaurs may have been crushed by the weight of their bodies.

Notes: The species ?*A. periculosus* Riabinin 1930 [*nomen dubium*] was tentatively referred by Molnar (1990) to *Tyrannosaurus* [=*Tarbosaurus* of his usage] *bataar*. Note: *G. lancinator* Maleev 1955 was referred to *T. bataar*; *G. novojilovi* Maleev 1955 by Carpenter (1992) to new genus *Maleevosaurus*; *G. lancensis* Gilmore 1946 was made the type species of new genus *Nanotyrannus* by Bakker *et al.* (1988).

Fossil footprints attributed to *Albertosaurus* were found in coal mines in the Mesaverde Group, including the DeBeque landslide locality east of Grand Junction, Colorado (Lockley, Young and Carpenter 1983).

Key references: Bakker, Williams and Currie (1988); Carpenter (1992); Cope (1876a, 1892a); Currie (1992); Lambe (1903, 1904c, 1914a, 1914c, 1917c); Lockley, Young and Carpenter (1983); Matthew and Brown (1923); Molnar, Kurzanov and Dong (1990); Osborn (1905); Parks (1928); Russell (1970b, 1977).

ALECTROSAURUS   Gilmore 1933

Saurischia: Theropoda: Tetanurae: Avetheropoda: Coelurosauria: Maniraptora: Arctometatarsalia: Tyrannosauridae.

Name derivation: Greek *alektros* = "rooster" = Greek *sauros* = "lizard."

Type species: *A. olseni* Gilmore 1933.

Other species: [None.]

Occurrence: Iren (Erlien) Dabasu Formation, Nei Mongol Zizhqu, People's Republic of China; Baynshirenskaya Svita, Omnogov, Mongolian People's Republic.

Age: Late Cretaceous (?early Cenomanian).

Known material: Incomplete lower jaw and partial postcrania apparently representing at least three individuals.

Holotype: AMNH 6554, nearly complete right hind leg and foot, pubic fragment.

Diagnosis of genus (as for type species): Small- to medium-sized tyrannosaurid, with third pedal digit relatively shorter relative to length of the third metatarsal than in most other tyrannosaurids; posterior border of distal condyle of the third metatarsal demarcated by a distinct lip, so that distal articulatory surface is not medially continuous with shaft (as it is in tyrannosaurids *Albertosaurus* and *Tyrannosaurus* and ornithomimid *Struthiomimus*); flexor tubercles on third, probably second (incompletely preserved in AMNH 6554), and on fourth pedal digits are comparatively larger than in "*Gorgosaurus*" [=*Albertosaurus libratus*] and probably "*Tarbosaurus*" [=*Tyrannosaurus bataar*] extending posteriorly to be almost flush with ventral margin of the articular facet (Mader and Bradley 1989).

Comments: The name *Alectrosaurus* has appeared in the literature for more than half a century. Only recently, however, has this genus become more adequately understood through studies by Mader and Bradley (1989).

Alectrosaurus was founded on cotype specimens from two individuals discovered by George Olsen, assistant paleontologist to chief paleontologist Walter Granger, during the Third Asiatic Expedition of the American Museum of Natural History in 1923, in the former Iren Dabasu Formation (?early Cenomanian; see Currie and Eberth 1993) in Mongolia (now Inner Mongolian Autonomous Region). As chronicled by Mader and Bradley, the first specimen (AMNH 6554) of *Alectrosaurus*, found by Olsen on April 25, 1923, included a nearly complete right hindlimb comprising a right femur (missing the proximal end), tibia, fibula, astragalus, calcaneum, complete pes though missing the distal tarsal bones, three metatarsals of the left hind foot, two manual unguals, manus, and a portion of the distal pubic foot. The second specimen (catalogued several years later as AMNH 6368), discovered by Olsen on May 4 about 30 meters away from the first, included a right humerus, the first phalanx of a second digit, an ungual of a first manual digit, four fragmentary caudal vertebrae, and two very poorly preserved unidentified elements (the latter reported in Granger's field record of the expedition, catalogued in 1984 as AMNH 21784). It was Granger's unsubstantiated opinion that both specimens belonged to the same individual.

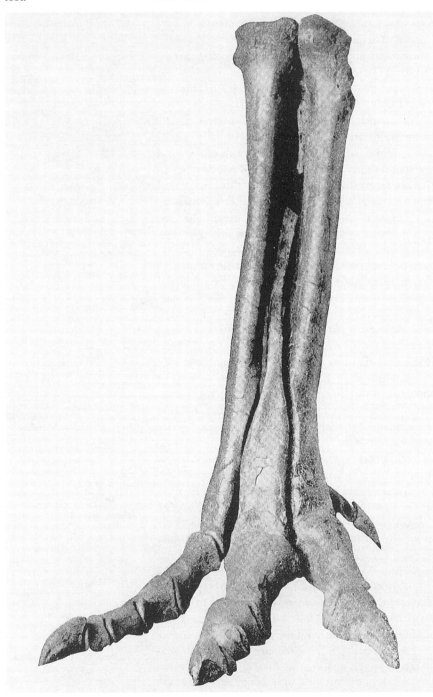

Alectrosaurus olseni, AMNH 6554, holotype right hind foot.

When Gilmore eventually described the material in 1933, he regarded both AMNH 6554 and AMNH 6368 as syntypes belonging to the same genus, which he named *Alectrosaurus*, because the manual unguals appeared to be morphologically similar in both specimens. Gilmore maintained that two individuals were represented by these remains (but did not mention the caudal vertebrae [AMNH 21784]).

Based on those two specimens, Gilmore originally diagnosed the monotypic *A. olseni* as follows: "Deinodont" [=tyrannosaurid] with long, slender limbs and a long, slender humerus; ungual and phalanx of first digit robust, laterally compressed and strongly curved; femur and tibia subequal in length; astragalus one-fourth combined length of that element and the tibia.

Although Gilmore's assessment of AMNH 6368 was mostly accepted by subsequent authors (*e.g.* White 1973 in his catalogue of dinosaur genera), the generic identity of the forelimbs (relatively large for a tyrannosaurid) and the unusual foreclaw have raised questions in lieu of more recent discoveries.

The large size of these manual claws led Rozhdestvensky (1970) to suggest that *Alectrosaurus* was congeneric with, or at least very closely related to, another Mongolian form with large foreclaws, *Chilantaisaurus*. Baird and Horner (1977) suggested possible affinities between *Alectrosaurus* and the North American *Dryptosaurus*, another form with large manual claws. Perle (1977), while referring new theropod material from the Mongolian Bashin-Tsab locality to *Alectrosaurus*, tentatively referred the large manual ungual to the "Segnosauridae" [Therizinosauroidea].

In reevaluating *Alectrosaurus*, Mader and Bradley removed the forelimb material (AMNH 6368) from the genus and transferred it to the "Segnosauridae" as "segnosaur *incertae sedis*," at the same time designating the hindlimb and pubis (AMNH 6554) as the most reasonable lectotype for *A. olseni*. Mader and Bradley tentatively included in this specimen the two manual unguals, and, described for the first time, the caudal vertebrae (AMNH 21784).

Gilmore interpreted the hindlimb and foot in *Alectrosaurus* as similar to those in the holotype (AMNH 5664) of "*Gorgosaurus sternbergi*," but also, though comprising more massive elements, similar to those in ornithomimids. As shown by Mader and Bradley, this resemblance (proportions and the constriction of the third metatarsal) to ornithomimids is superficial. The lectotype of *A. olseni* exhibits several morphological characters which preclude classification with Ornithomimidae, including 1. possession of a bipartite protuberance of the fibula (a character regarded by Mader and Bradley as a synapomorphic character of tyrannosaurids), 2. possession of a hallux (not present in ornithomimids), and 3. possession of sharply recurved and trenchant pedal claws (triangular, unrecurved, somewhat hoof-like in ornithomimids).

Alectrosaurus was regarded by Mader and Bradley as a typical tyrannosaurid of small to medium size, mostly differing from other known forms (except the similarly proportioned *Maleevasaurus novojilov*) by the unusual proportions of the hindlimbs: The femur is subequal in length to the tibia, and the metatarsals are relatively long compared to the tibia and femur.

Material referred by Perle to *Alectrosaurus* included remains of one or more individuals (PST GIN AN MNR 100/50 and 100/51). As pointed out by Mader and Bradley, only specimen 100/51 includes limb material that can be compared to AMNH 6554, while specimen 100/50 has only a partial maxilla in common with 100/51. Perle, who did not personally examine the AMNH material and was limited in his own assessment by the paucity of the syntypes and brevity of Gilmore's description, referred the Bashin-Tsab specimens to *Alectrosaurus* on the basis of similar hindlimb morphology. Mader and Bradley stated that, given the possibly correct assignment by Perle of the Bashin-Tsab material to *Alectrosaurus*, perhaps some other characters observed by Perle and diagnostic of the genus may perhaps be noted, though not evident in AMNH 6554. These include: 1. Nasal (in specimen 100/50) smooth and lacking rugosities found in all other known tyrannosaurids, and 2. anterior limb girdle and manual ungual (in 100/50) larger compared to those in other tyrannosaurids. Perle had also observed that the skull of the Bashin-Tsab *Alectrosaurus*, compared to other known tyrannosaurids, is lower, has a more rounded orbit, a greater number of teeth, and that the ilium has a more rounded posterior border. (Mader and Bradley questioned the diagnostic significance of those features.)

According to Mader and Bradley, due to the general lack of diagnostic characters in the lectotype, there may yet be some degree of uncertainty regarding the status of *Alectrosaurus*.

Molnar, Kurzanov and Dong (1990) stated that *Alectrosaurus* shows various features diagnostic of the Tyrannosauridae (squamosal-quadratojugal wing, large surangular opening, confluent supratemporal recesses, and a proximally attenuated third metatarsal). Molnar *et al.* noted that *Alectrosaurus* and another Asian form *Alioramus* are different from other tyrannosaurids, both apparently relatively slender, with gracile limb bones, lower skulls and a non-reduced tooth count.

Note: The caudal vertebrae were regarded by Mader and Bradley as "theropod *incertae sedis*,"

described as small, with elongated and platycoelous centra, each with a less pronounced reptilian spoon-shaped configuration than in *Allosaurus*, *Albertosaurus*, *Deinonychus*, *Plateosaurus* and *Ornithomimus*. Three of these vertebrae are approximately the same size, the fourth considerably smaller.

Key references: Gilmore (1933); Mader and Bradley (1989); Molnar *et al.* (1990); Perle (1977); Rozhdestvensky (1970).

ALGOASAURUS   Broom 1904

Saurischia: Sauropodomorpha: Sauropoda *incertae sedis.*

Name derivation: "Algo [Basin]" + Greek *sauros* = "lizard."

Type species: *A. bauri* Broom 1904.

Other species: [None.]

Occurrence: Upper Kirkwood Formation, Cape Province, South Africa.

Age: ?Late Jurassic-?Early Cretaceous.

Known material/holotype: Port Elizabeth Museum collection, fragmentary vertebrae, femur, incomplete scapula, phalanx.

Diagnosis of genus: [None published.]

Comments: The genus *Algoasaurus* was established upon incomplete postcranial remains collected from a quarry of the Sunday River Formation (now Upper Kirkland Formation; see Galton and Coombs 1981; Rich, Molnar and Rich 1983) at Uitenhage, Cape Province, South Africa. As the specimen only mildly interested the quarry workers, many bones were made into bricks before what remained of the material could be collected by the Port Elizabeth Museum (Broom 1904).

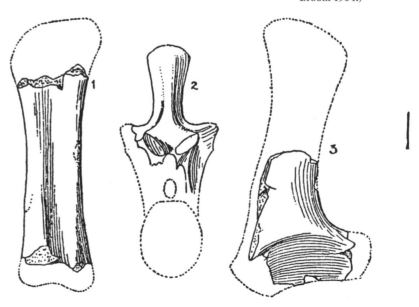

Algoasaurus bauri, Port Elizabeth Museum, holotype 1. left femur, 2. dorsal vertebra (posterior view), 3. right scapula. Scale = 7 cm. (After Broom 1904.)

Broom described this genus as follows: Vertebrae resembling those in *Diplodocus*, when complete measuring about .4 meters (1.35 feet); scapula, though much smaller, resembling that in *Apatosaurus* [=*Brontosaurus* of his usage]; femur apparently resembling that in *Diplodocus* and, if complete, measuring about 500 millimeters (over 19 inches) long; femur with fourth trochanter comparatively much smaller than in *Apatosaurus, Diplodocus* and *Camarasaurus* [=*Morosaurus* of his usage] (Broom 1904).

Key reference: Broom (1904).

ALIORAMUS   Kurzanov 1976
Saurischia: Theropoda: Tetanurae: Avethropoda:
   Coelurosauria: Maniraptora: Arctometatarsalia:
   Tyrannosauridae.
Name derivation: Latin *alius* = "different" + Latin
   ramus = "branch."
Type species: *A. remotus* Kurzanov 1976.
Other species: [None.]
Occurrence: Nogon Tsav beds, Bayankhongor,
   Mongolian People's Republic.
Age: Early Late Cretaceous (early Maastrichtian).
Known material/holotype: GI 3141/1, fragmentary
   skull, lower jaw, three metatarsals.

Diagnosis of genus (as for type species): Skull elongate; two rows of relatively large crest-like blades on upper part of nasal; three more teeth in both upper and lower jaws than usual for tyrannosaurids (Kurzanov 1976).

Comments: *Alioramus* was founded on an incomplete skull and three metatarsals (GI 3141/1), collected from the beds of Nogon-Tsav, Mongolian People's Republic, discovered during the 1971 joint Polish-Mongolian Expedition to Mongolia (Kurzanov 1976).

Molnar, Kurzanov and Dong (1990) regarded *Alioramus* as a tyrannosaurid because of the follow-

Alioramus remotus, GI 314/1, holotype metatarsals. (After Kurzanov 1976.)

ing features diagnostic of the Tyrannosauridae: Squamosal-quadratojugal wing; large surangular opening; confluent supratemporal recesses; and a proximally attenuated third metatarsal. Molnar *et al.* pointed out that this genus, along with *Alectrosaurus*, differs from other known tyrannosaurids in being more slender, with more gracile limb elements, and a lower skull with tooth count not reduced.

Alioramus, which probably measured some 6 meters (20 feet) in length, was most distinguished by the two rows of small, rather jagged cranial crests located behind the snout and up to the eyes.

Key references: Kurzanov (1976); Molnar *et al.* (1990).

ALIWALIA   Galton 1985
Dinosauria *incertae sedis*.
Name derivation: "Aliwal [locality]."
Type species: *A. rex* Galton 1985
Other species: [None.]
Occurrence: Lower Elliot Formation, Cape
   Province, South Africa.
Age: Late Triassic (late Carnian-lower Norian).
Known material/Cotypes: NMW 1886-XV-39 and
   1876-VII-B124, proximal and distal ends of left
   femur.

Diagnosis of genus (as for type species): Femur with medially directed head separated from shaft by a well-defined neck region; lesser trochanter with

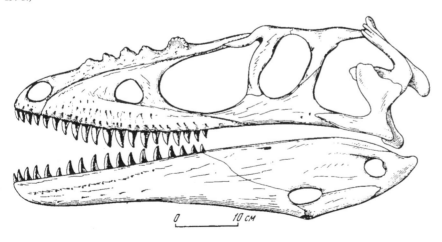

Alioramus remotus, GI 3141/1, holotype skull (restored). (After Kurzanov 1976.)

prominent crest; fourth trochanter large, pendant-shaped, very proximally located (Galton 1976e).

Comments: The genus *Aliwalia* was established on both ends of a an incomplete left femur (NMW 1886-XV-39 and MNW 1876-VII-B124), recovered from beds assumed to be lower Elliot Formation (Late Triassic [upper Carnian-lower Norian]), at Barnard's Spruit, Ward, south of Aliwal North, Cape Province, Karoo basin, South Africa. The only data accompanying these pieces informed that the proximal end of the femur was donated by Consul Adler of Port Elizabeth, South Africa, in 1873, and that the distal end was donated by Alfred Brown via Adler along with twenty-six other reptile bones. Presumably Brown collected both ends which apparently were collected from the same excavation site that yielded the holotype of the prosauropod *Euskelosaurus brownii*. The material was first described by Huene (1906) as possibly belonging to *Euskelosaurus* (Galton 1976e).

According to Galton, the femur differs from that in prosauropods and resembles that in theropods in 1. possessing a well-defined and medially directed caput femoris that connects to the shaft by a constricted neck region, 2. the prominence of the lesser trochanter (very similar to that in *Halticosaurus* and *Liliensternus*), and 3. the very proximal position of the fourth trochanter.

Galton regarded *Aliwalia* as a possible herrerasaurid. Sues (1990), however, observed that *A. rex*, except for the position of the fourth trochanter, shares no derived characters with *Herrerasaurus* in the few known comparable features and should be regarded as ?Dinosauria *incertae sedis*. Novas (1992) regarded *A. rex* as Dinosauria indet. and lacking any autapomorphic features.

Tentatively referred by Galton to *A. rex* was a large left maxilla (BMNH R3301) with replacement teeth *in situ*, collected from the same lower Elliot Formation excavation site that yielded the lectotype femur of *E. brownii*. The specimen, measured by Seeley (1894), is more than 40 millimeters (almost 1.55 inches) in length. Galton's tentative referral of this specimen was based on its appropriate size (compared with the holotype of *A. rex*) and also on its apparently coming from the same excavation site, but added that it could also represent a rausuchid "thecodontian" (see also Olsen and Galton 1984).

Note: Galton pointed out similarities between the femoral fragments of *Aliwalia* to a previously undescribed portion of a left femur, collected from the middle Stubensandstein (Norian) in southern Germany, but too fragmentary for classification.

Key references: Galton (1976e); Huene (1906); Novas (1992); Olsen and Galton (1984); Sues (1990).

ALLOSAURUS Marsh 1877—(=*Antrodemus*, *Apatodon*, *Creosaurus*, *Hypsirophus* [in part], *Labrosaurus*; =?*Epantarius*)

Saurischia: Theropoda: Tetanurae: Avetheropoda: Allosauroidea: Allosauridae.

Name derivation: Greek *hallos* = "different" + Greek *sauros* = "lizard."

Type species: *A. fragilis* Marsh 1877.

Other species: *A. atrox* (Marsh 1878), ?*A. trihedron* (Cope 1877), ?*A. atrox* (Marsh 1878), ?*A. ferox* Marsh 1894, ?*A. stechowi* (Janensch 1925), ?*A. tendagurensis*, Janensch 1925 [*nomen dubium*].

Occurrence: Morrison Formation, Colorado, Montana, New Mexico, Oklahoma, South Dakota, Utah, Wyoming, United States; ?Tendaguru Beds, Mtwara, Tanzania; Australia.

Age: Late Jurassic–Early Cretaceous (Kimmeridgian–Tithonian; ?Neocomian–?Aptian).

Known material: At least three complete skulls, many incomplete skulls and cranial elements, complete and partial postcranial skeletons of at least sixty individuals, isolated elements.

Holotype: YPM 1930, two dorsal centra, tooth, proximal phalanx of right pedal digit III.

Diagnosis of genus (as for type species): Robust, very large theropod; head large; skull and mandible elongate, robust, and subequal in length to femora and ilia (within 5 percent); five or more premaxillary teeth, 14 to 16 maxillary teeth, 15 to 17 dentary teeth; maxilla with complex sinus, perforate laterally, dorsally, and medially; vomers fused in an anteriorly elongated shaft divided posteriorly; supraoccipital

Allosaurus fragilis, YPM 1930, holotype including portion of humerus.

Photo by J. H. Madsen, Jr., courtesy Yale Peabody Museum of Natural History.

Allosaurus

Photo by R. A. Long and S. P. Welles (neg. #72-893).

Allosaurus fragilis, "neotype" UUVP 6000, complete skull, part of incomplete articulated skeleton collected from Dinosaur National Monument, near Jensen, Utah.

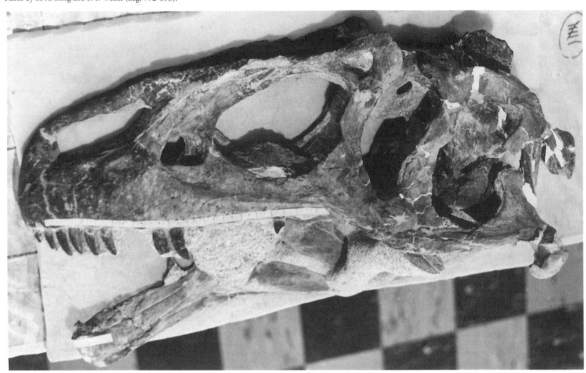

Allosaurus fragilis skeleton (AMNH 4753; skull cast from another specimen), mounted over pelvis, hind limb bones, and tail vertebrae of *Apatosaurus*. (In his privately published newsletter [April, 1996], Stephen Pickering proposed a new species, *A. whitei*, for this skeleton, characterized by a long, low skull, lacrimals with bluntly rounded apexes, and slender limb bones.)

Photo by Anderson, courtesy Library Services, American Museum of Natural History (neg. #35422).

Allosaurus fragilis, restored skull. (After Madsen 1976.)

unpaired, enters margin of foramen magnum; quadrate slanted forward to almost vertical position; mandible with three accessory bones including a true coronoid; pubis strong, with a large distal expansion which may or may not be fused distally and medially; distal end of ischium expanded asymmetrically; nine cervical, 14 dorsal, five sacral, and 48 to 51 caudal vertebrae; cervical and first two dorsal vertebrae strongly opisthocoelous, third dorsal platycoelous, posterior dorsals amphyplatyan; sacral vertebrae locked by grooves and ridges on articular faces of centra; anterior caudals moderately amphicoelous, becoming more so posteriorly; haemal arches borne on second through about the next 40 caudals; caudal centra neither cavernous nor hollow; forearm and manus long, manus with three strong digits; digital formula 2-3-4-0-0; hindlimbs robust, with four (?five) pedal digits; digits II–IV evenly spaced or tridactyl anteriorly, digit I diminutive, posterolater in approximate opposition to II, III, and IV; V may be represented only by proximal half; digital formula 2-3-4-5-0 (Madsen 1976*b*).

Diagnosis of *A. atrox*: (Compared to *A. fragilis*, skull relatively larger, lower and more rectangular; preorbital horns smaller, less triangular; neck shorter; forelimbs more robust (Paul 1988*c*).

Diagnosis of ?*A. stechowi*: Teeth stout in proportion (measuring 3.5 to 4.5 centimeters, or about 1.35 to 1.75 inches, in length), with distinctive longitudinal grooves (Janensch 1925).

Comments: One of the largest North American Late Jurassic theropods, *Allosaurus* was founded on a tooth and very incomplete postcranial remains (YPM 1930) discovered in the Morrison Formation at Fremont County, Garden Park, Colorado.

However, prior to the naming of the genus, the new type species *Antrodemus valens* had been based on the posterior half of a sixth caudal vertebra (USNM 218), discovered by Ferdinand Vandiveer Hayden in the Morrison Formation of Grand County, Middle Park, Colorado. Leidy (1870) originally referred this specimen to the European genus *Poicilopleuron* as new species *P. valens*. Leidy gave no precise stratigraphic information regarding the origin of the specimen, but simply stated that it had come from Middle Park, Colorado, and that Hayden (incorrectly) thought the site to have been of Cretaceous age.

Originally, Leidy diagnosed *P. valens* as follows: Medullary cavity of vertebral body divided into smaller recesses by trabeculae. Leidy proposed that, if other characters not included in his diagnosis were ever found to be significant, the Colorado taxon should be renamed *Antrodemus*. In a subsequent paper, Leidy (1873), though still calling the species *P. valens* in the text, captioned the accompanying plate illustrations *Antrodemus*.

Allosaurus

Allosaurus fragilis skeleton (ROM 12868).

Allosaurus fragilis, USNM 218, holotype posterior half of sixth caudal vertebra of *Poicilopleuron* [=*Antrodemus*] *valens*.

?*Allosaurus fragilis*, YPM 1879, holotype left pes of *Camptonotus amplus*.

Because of the resemblance of the holotype to the corresponding element in *Allosaurus fragilis*, Gilmore (1920) considered *A. fragilis* and *A. valens* to be conspecific. In his monograph on *A. fragilis*, Madsen (1976*b*) pointed out that Leidy's description of *A. valens* was given with only broad geographic reference and no exact stratigraphic data; that Leidy had received the holotype third hand; and that the holotype of *A. valens* is but questionably diagnostic generically, certainly indeterminate specifically. Thus, Madsen (1976*b*) argued that synonymy between *A. valens* with *A. fragilis* could not be established. Subsequently, however, most authors have abandoned the name *Antrodemus* and regarded *A. valens* as a junior synonym of *A. fragilis* (*e.g.*, see Molnar, Kurzanov and Dong 1990).

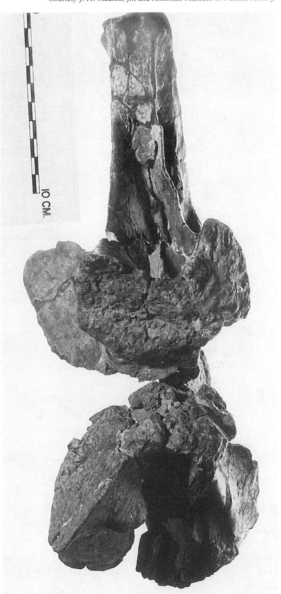

Epanterias amplexus, AMNH 5767, holotype neural arch, first dorsal vertebra, possibly referrable to *Allosaurus*.

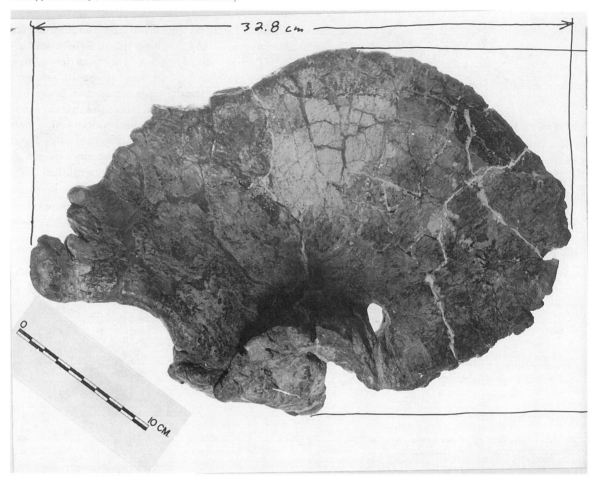

Epanterias amplexus, AMNH 5756, holotype right coracoid, possibly referrable to *Allosaurus*.

The genus *Allosaurus* was briefly described (but not figured) by Marsh (1877*d*), who distinguished it (and type species *A. fragilis*) from other then known theropods by the following: Vertebrae modified for lightness by deep pleurocoels; vertebrae biconcave; some centra of "hour-glass" shape; bones of pes slender. The type material indicated to Marsh an animal some 4.5 to 6 meters (about 15 to 20 feet) in length. Subsequently, Marsh (1878*a*) made *Allosaurus* the type genus of the new family Allosauridae.

Although a number of species have been referred to *Allosaurus*, Madsen recognized only one valid American species of the genus, *A. fragilis*, the others regarded by him as junior synonyms:

Apatodon mirus [*nomen dubium*] was based on part of a lower jaw with a tooth (type specimen lost) recovered from the Jurassic or Early Cretaceous of the "Rocky Mountain region." Marsh (1877*b*) originally interpreted this tooth as having a mammalian "appearance" and described it as belonging to a tapir-sized Jurassic mammal. Later, Bauer (1890) identified the specimen as a piece of weathered dinosaur vertebra.

Allosaurus lucaris was based on a few cervical, six dorsal and two sacral vertebrae, two humeri, incomplete radius and ulna, scapula-coracoid, and phalanx (YPM 1931), collected from the Morrison Formation at Como Bluff, and described by Marsh (1878*b*). Marsh concluded that an anterior dorsal vertebra exhibited specifically distinct features, including a convex anterior articulation of the centrum and concave posterior face. Subsequently, Marsh (1879*a*) interpreted these remains as generically distinct and referred them to the new genus and species *Labrosaurus lucaris*. Marsh (1884*b*) later referred to *Labrosaurus* the new species *L. ferox*, based on a left dentary with twelve teeth (USNM 2315). Marsh (1884*b*) distinguished this species as having more triangular teeth and what he interpreted as a partially edentulous dentary. Gilmore found a deep (?pathologic) notch in this toothless portion to be a peculiar feature. Hay (1909) later questioned Marsh's (1884*b*) observations regarding the teeth, pointing out that the crowns are missing and the roots almost entirely covered with matrix; furthermore, as no teeth were found with the holotype of *L. lucaris*, Marsh (1884*b*) had referred *L. ferox* to *Labrosaurus* without sufficient grounds. Later, Marsh (1896) referred (but did not describe) a tooth to this genus, erecting third species *L. sulcatus* [*nomen dubium*]. (This tooth is apparently an anterior tooth of the genus *Ceratosaurus*; J. H. Madsen, personal communication, 1986.)

Hypsirophus discursus Cope 1878 was based in part on a neural spine (AMNH 5731) now known to belong to *A. fragilis* intermixed with material belonging to *Stegosaurus armatus*. ?*A. tendagurensis* was based on an allosaurid tibia from the Upper Jurassic (Tendaguru) beds of Tanzania, described by Janensch (1925) and measuring 91 centimeters (about 35 inches) long.

Type species *Epanterias amplexus* was based on two anterior dorsal vertebrae (AMNH 5767), one represented by a centrum, the other by most of the neural arch and spine, an associated axis, vertebra, coracoid, and fragmentary limb bone (misinterpreted as a metatarsal), from the uppermost Morrison Formation at Garden Park, Fremont County, Colorado. Originally identified as sauropod by Cope (1878*e*), the remains were shown by Osborn and Mook (1921) to be those of an exceptionally large *A. fragilis*, about one-fifth larger than any then known Morrison theropod, measuring perhaps some 13 meters (44 feet) long and 5 meters (17 feet) tall. Bakker (1990) resurrected the name *Epanterias*, noting that this form has a skeletal size 20 percent greater than any other "allosaur" sample, and mentioned that James I. Kirkland and Jeff Stephenson had discovered a new third locality for *E. amplexus* high in the Morrison Formation, near Masonville, Colorado. Chure, Madsen and Britt (1993) later noted that *Epanterias* is invalid, its type material indistinguishable from *Allosaurus* or *Saurophagus* (see entry).

In recent years, some paleontologists have questioned the single-species interpretation of *Allosaurus*, especially regarding the species *A. atrox*. Marsh (1878*a*) originally described this taxon as the type species of new genus *Creosaurus*, founded on a jugal, premaxilla, two sacral caudal vertebrae, ilium, astragalus, two claws, and two phalanges (YPM 1890) from a smaller (?younger) form, collected from the Morrison Formation, Como Bluff, Wyoming. Marsh (1878*a*) offered few characters for distinguishing *Creosaurus*, including possessing a greater number of premaxillary teeth than *Allosaurus*. Gilmore observed that none of the significant elements of YPM 1890 showed generic differences from *Allosaurus* [=*Antrodemus* of his usage] and argued that the name *Creosaurus* should be abandoned, with YPM 1890 tentatively designated the type of new species *Antrodemus atrox* (the validity of this taxon yet to be tested). *A. atrox* seemingly represents a somewhat

?*Allosaurus fragilis*, AMNH 5756, holotype distal end of left metatarsal IV of *Epanterias amplexus*.

more abundant and gracile morph than the rarer and more robust *A. fragilis*, although their differences may inevitably prove to constitute a sexual dimorphism (see *Tyrannosaurus* entry).

Over the years since discovery of the type material, many *Allosaurus* specimens have been collected. In his classic review of the theropod specimens in the National Museum collection, Gilmore (1920) diagnosed *Allosaurus* based on ten specimens: A nearly complete skeleton (USNM 4734), regarded as the topotype by Gilmore, collected in 1883–84 by M. P. Felch from Canyon City, Fremont County, Colorado, and exhibited at the National Museum; nine cervical, ten dorsal, two sacral and seven caudal vertebrae, cervical and dorsal ribs, six chevrons, pubes, ischia, and portions of the ilium (USNM 8367), collected in 1886 by Fred Brown from Albany County, Wyoming; eight cervical centra, 11 dorsal centra, two sacral centra, many neural process of cervical and dorsal vertebrae, a right ilium, two ischia, a right femur, and parts of ribs (USNM 2323), collected by Brown in 1888 from Como, Albany County; two maxillae, five dorsal centra, five co-ossified sacral vertebrae, three caudal centra, parts of ilia, two broken ischia, two broken pubes, two femora, a left pes, and a few bones of the manus (USNM 8423), collected by Felch in 1884 from Canon City; a right maxillary with teeth and dentary (USNM 8335), collected in 1884 by Felch from Canon City; the holotype of *A. valens* (USNM 218); five coossified sacral centra, a lateral metatarsal, and phalanges of the fore and hind feet (USNM 8405) collected by Brown in 1884 from Como; a left astragalus (USNM 7336) collected by Felch in 1886 from Canon City; an ungual (USNM 8302) from the third digit from the right manus, collected in 1884 by Ed Kennedy from Como; and an ungual (USNM 8257) from the second digit of the right manus, collected in 1883 by Felch near Canon City.

A wealth of material assigned to *A. fragilis* has been reported from various continents. The most abundant yields have come from Utah, from the northeastern area of the state now called Dinosaur National Monument, and from the central-eastern region at the Cleveland-Lloyd Dinosaur Quarry. In fact, most of the dinosaurian remains collected from Cleveland-Lloyd have been those of *Allosaurus*. Since 1927, well-preserved specimens representing at least 44 individuals, ranging from juveniles to various-

Photo by R. A. Long and S. P. Welles, courtesy Yale Peabody Museum of Natural History.

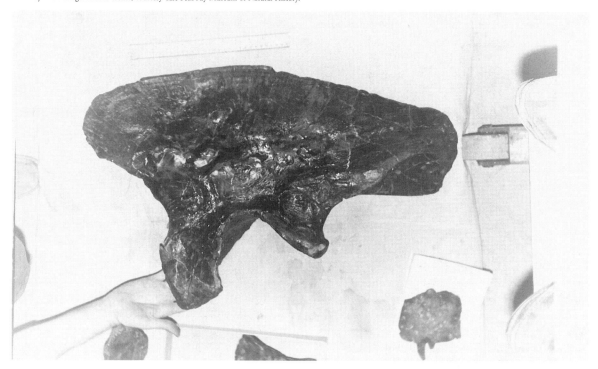

Allosaurus fragilis, YPM 1890, holotype left ilium and premaxilla (right) of *Creosaurus atrox*.

Photo by the author, courtesy National Museum of Natural History Smithsonian Institution.

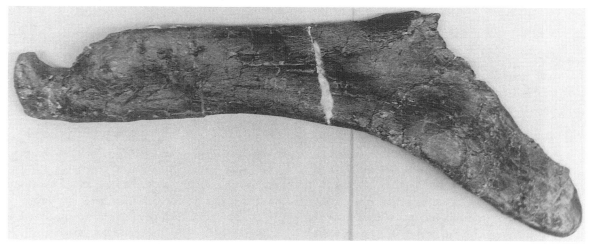

Allosaurus fragilis, USNM 2315, holotype left dentary of *Labrosaurus ferox*, posterior portion restored in plaster.

sized adults, have been retrieved from the Cleveland-Lloyd site, making *Allosaurus* the most common theropod known in the Morrison Formation, indeed the one of the best known and researched of all theropods. Some of the Cleveland-Lloyd specimens, especially those of older individuals, exhibit evidence of pathology. Because of the size distribution and range of *A. fragilis* remains from this quarry, Stokes (1985) speculated that, like modern reptiles, this species grew continuously throughout life.

The atypical concentration of predator bones as opposed to those of prey at Cleveland-Lloyd may suggest that the location was once a deathtrap for the animals preserved there, or that some catastrophic event occurred (Madsen 1976*a*). However, as pointed out by Molnar and Farlow (1990), a detailed scenario of the formation of this deposit has yet to be worked out. Molnar and Farlow noted that the orientation of the elements suggests that they were disarticulated and scattered before burial, and there is evidence of scavenging.

In his monograph on *A. fragilis*, Madsen, who had examined the Cleveland-Lloyd material, added more diagnostic characters to those listed by Gilmore. Madsen's new diagnosis of *Allosaurus* (and the type species) was based on the holotype (YPM 1930), on the National Museum skeleton (USNM 4734), regarded by Madsen as the paratype, and the neotype (UUVP 6000), a complete skull and partial skeleton lacking all but the first caudal vertebra, chevrons ribs, forearms, and some pedal digital elements, collected from Dinosaur National Monument.

Photo by R. A. Long and S. P. Welles (neg. #73/436-4), courtesy American Museum of Natural History.

Allosaurus fragilis, AMNH 5731, holotype neural spine of *Hypsirophus discursus.*

Allosaurus fragilis, life restoration by Mark Hallett.

Allosaurus

Allosaurus ferox, skull from Garden Park, Colorado, which Marsh had intended to describe.

Allosaurus ferox, YPM 1893, holotype left dentary.

Madsen observed that the "ear"-shaped lacrimal in *Allosaurus* is deeply excavated, possibly a housing for one or more glands, such as a salt gland, as Norman (1985) speculated in his book, *The Illustrated Encyclopedia of Dinosaurs*. The lacrimal probably supported a low dermal horn, as first suggested by Osborn (1903b). Madsen theorized that, since the very thin walls of the lacrimal could have been easily injured, this horn may have served as a sunshade as well as a buttress. Molnar (1977) further suggested that the lacrimal horns might have been used in intraspecies display or combat.

Madsen noted that the number of caudal vertebrae may very among individuals. Also, Madsen speculated that the infrequent occurrence of abdominal ribs found in specimens from the Cleveland-Lloyd Dinosaur Quarry could indicate that these bones were eaten by scavengers or that most of these ele-

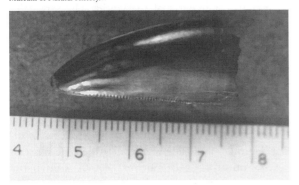

Labrosaurus sulcatus, YPM 1936, ?ceratosaurian holotype tooth.

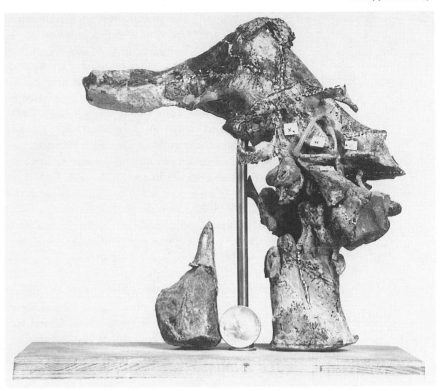

Allosaurus endocast.

ments consisted of cartilage; and that manual digit I, having no apparent use to an adult individual, may have been used by juveniles as a somewhat opposable grasping appendage.

An adult *Allosaurus* attained an average length of 8.5 meters (approximately 30 feet) and weighed (calculated by Colbert 1962) some 2.09 metric tons (2.3 tons). One skull collected by Madsen was about 90 centimeters (36 inches) long, with teeth, including roots, attaining lengths of up to 12.5 centimeters (5 inches). Some *Allosaurus* individuals attained giant size, one Cleveland-Lloyd specimen measured by Madsen indicating an individual 12 meters (about 40 feet long) and 4.5 meters (about 15 feet) tall.

Allosaurus was one of the most formidable of all Jurassic predators, its large head and body designed for preying upon the various herbivorous dinosaurs of its community. Its three-fingered foreclaws, the largest about 25 centimeters (10 inches) long, were powerful devices for grasping and ripping prey. Gilmore believed that the foreclaws constituted an effective grasping organ. According to Gilmore, the first manual digit, directed away from the other digits when at rest, could move toward the axis of the manus when that digit was flexed. The claws so articulated with the penultimate phalanges that, especially on the first and second digits, they were held almost at right angles to the axes of the phalanges, and could have functioned as hooks. Most likely, *Allosaurus* attacked its victims using both jaws and claws working together.

Though the saber-like teeth were ideal for tearing and cutting flesh, feeding was facilitated by the somewhat loose attachment of the quadrate with its adjacent bones. Molnar and Farlow pointed out that in *A. fragilis* the "loose" joints are not distributed so as to divide the skull into mobile segments, as in snakes, but rather to resist tensional forces, allowing passive motion as long as the elements are not sepa-

rated. Therefore, cranial kinesis was not likely, while slight movement between some elements may have been possible (see also Osborn 1912*a*; Russell 1970*b*). In a functional analysis of the *Allosaurus* skull, McClelland (in press) will show that only lateral movement of the conjoined quadratojugal-quadrate was feasible, requiring a hinge joint at the contact of squamosal and quadrate, and a lap joint of the quadratojugal over the jugal. McClelland will further show that, coupled with intramandibular kinesis, this mobility would allow (as in some modern reptiles) for the expansion of the gullet in swallowing large chunks of meat.

An updated hindlimb muscle reconstruction of *A. fragilis* was submitted by Saitta (1995) who criticized, as inadequate or incompatible, earlier reconstructions made after previous studies of the muscles of birds and, especially, crocodiles. Saitta noted that the "muscles lining the highly retroverted pubis/ischium" of birds are difficult, if not impossible, to apply to the distinct allosaurian, or theropod pubis/ischium; and that, in crocodilians, only the deep pelvic muscles (M. puboischio-femoralis externus and M. ischic trochantericus) can be reasonably drawn upon when doing a hindlimb reconstruction of *A. fragilis*. Saitta stated that "birds are more tenable as homologous in reconstructing the superficial ilium-femur based muscles (M. tensor facia latae, M.

biceps femoris, M. sartorius, M. adductors),'" this idea "advancing the birdlikeness of the theropod hindlimb, and rejecting a direct application to theropods of the many fragmented muscle groups of sprawling crocodiles." Saitta found that strong conclusions can be drawn pertaining to the morphology and function in the hindlimb of *A. fragilis* based on evidence drawn from the extant chicken *Gallus domesticus* and extinct giant flightless bird *Diatryma steni*; and noted that bone scarring is the most reliable method of approximating the size and relative functions of a muscle in specimens of *A. fragilis*.

The discovery of an allosaurid left astragalus (NMV Pl50070), from the Early Cretaceous of Victoria, Australia, extends allosaurid distribution to all continents except Antarctica, and confirms the survival of Allosauridae beyond the Jurassic-Cretaceous boundary (Molnar, Flannery and Rich 1980). To date, this specimen, designated *Allosaurus* sp. by Molnar *et al.* and belonging to a rather small species, represents the latest known surviving *Allosaurus* individual. Molnar *et al.* suggested that, as Victoria was within the Antarctic Circle during the Cretaceous,

the region could have sheltered animals already extinct in other parts of the world. The astragalus was distinguished from that in other "allosaurs" by greater robustness, suggesting a more sturdily built animal. The absence of a pronounced pit posterior to the base of the ascending process and presence of a well-defined vertical groove on the posterior face of the ascending process distinguish this form from *A. fragilis*. Although Welles (1883*a*) regarded the Australian specimen as most likely non-allosaurid, Molnar, Flannery and Rich (1985) defended their assessment, pointing out various shared similarities between *Allosaurus* sp. and *A. fragilis*.

Notes: Crushed ?*Allosaurus* eggs (Museum of Western Colorado collection) were found in the Young Egg Locality, Dominguez Canyon, Delta County, Colorado.

Labrosaurus stechowi Janensch 1925 [*nomen dubium*], based on teeth from the Upper Jurassic of Tendaguru, is probably referable to *Ceratosaurus roechlingi* (Madsen, personal communication). Apparently not *Allosaurus* are ?*A. sibericus*, originally *Antrodemus sibericus* Riabinin 1914, based on the dis-

Photo by Jerry Van Wyngarden, courtesy Museum of Western Colorado.

Crushed egg, possibly referrable to *Allosaurus*, from Young Egg Locality, Dominguez Canyon, Delta County, Colorado.

tal portion of a *Ceratosaurus nasicornis*-like metatarsal IV, from the Lower Cretaceous of Udinsk, Siberia; and ?*A. meriani*, based on a tooth from the Upper Jurassic of Moutier, Savoy, originally described by Greppin (1870) as *Megalosaurus meriani*.

From South Africa, Mateer (1987) reported a large, well-preserved, ungual (SAM 1475), apparently from the pes and missing the proximal articular facet, collected from the Late Jurassic–Early Cretaceous Sundays River Formation. The specimen is identical to claws of *A. fragilis*. Mateer also reported two Late Jurassic theropod teeth from the Enon Formation, one 2.8 centimeters (about 1.1 inches), being sharply recurved with serrations on its posterior side. Both teeth have ?18–20 posterior serrations per 5 millimeters, but lack the vertical striations found in *Allosaurus*. These specimens establish the presence of Late Jurassic–Early Cretaceous theropods in South Africa.

Dong, Hasegawa and Azuma (1990), in the dinosaur exhibition guidebook *The Age of Dinosaurs in Japan and China*, described as an indeterminate allosaurid the informally named "Katsuyamasaurus,"

Courtesy J. O. Farlow.

Gigandipus caudatus Hitchcock 1855 [formerly *Gigantitherium caudatum*], AC 9/10, holotype footprints conforming to feet of *Allosaurus fragilis*, from the Late Jurassic (Hettangian-Pleinsbachian), Newark Supergroup, Connecticut Valley, Lily Pond, Turners Falls, Massachusetts.

a large theropod from Japan reported by Lambert (1990) in *Dinosaur Data Book*. In the latter, Lambert also mentioned the informally named "Madsenius," a Morrison Formation allosaurid based on cranial remains previously referred to *Allosaurus* and *Creosaurus* to be described by Bakker.

The species *A. medius* Marsh 1888 [*nomen dubium*; *partim*] has been referred to *Archaeornithomimus affinis*, and *Creosaurus potens* Lull 1911 [*nomen dubium* to ?*Dryptosaurus medius*.

Key references: Bakker (1990); Bauer (1890); Chure, Madsen and Britt (1993); Colbert (1962); Cope (1878*e*); Gilmore (1920); Hay (1909); Madsen (1976*b*); Marsh (1877*b*, 1877*d*, 1878*a*, 1878*b*, 1879*a*, 1884*b*, 1896); Molnar (1977); Molnar and Farlow (1990); Molnar, Kurzanov and Dong (1980, 1985); Osborn (1903*b*; 1912*a*); Osborn and Mook (1921); Paul (1988*c*); Russell (1970*b*); Saitta (1995); Stokes (1985); Welles (1983*a*).

ALOCODON Thulborn 1973 [*nomen dubium*]
Ornithischia *incertae sedis*.
Name derivation: Greek *arotroun* = "furrow" + Greek *odous* = "tooth."
Type species: *A. kuehnei* Thulborn 1973 [*nomen dubium*].
Other species: [None.]
Occurrence: Província do Beira Litoral, Portugal.
Age: Late Jurassic (Late Callovian).
Known material: Teeth.
Holotype: LPFU P X 2, left maxillary tooth crown.

Diagnosis of genus (as for type species): Teeth with ornamentation of fine vertical ribs and irregular cingula sometimes bearing small denticles; ratio of crown height to width varies in central cheek teeth from 1.1, in posterior teeth 1.2; anterior and posterior denticles and large apex of each crown bluntly rounded (Galton 1978).

Comments: The genus *Alocodon* was founded upon an incomplete tooth (LPFU P X 2) found in soft gray and brownish-gray marls of a small pit south of the village of Pedrogao, on the west coast of Portugal. (The presence of various ostrocods [*Bisulcocypris* spp., *Cytherella* sp., *Darwinula* sp., ?*Klieana* sp., *Lophocythere composita*, *L.* cf. *flexicosta*, *Monoceratina trepti*, *M.* aff. *ungulina*, *Schuleridea* sp. and *Theriosynoecum wyomingense* var. *pedrogaoense*], directly comparable with types found elsewhere in Europe, indicate these beds are of Late Callovian age.) Collected from the same locality was a premaxillary tooth crown (P X 1), designated the paratype, and one hundred fifty-six teeth or parts of teeth (Thulborn 1973*b*).

Thulborn originally diagnosed the genus (and type species, *A. kuehnei*) as follows: Dentition het-

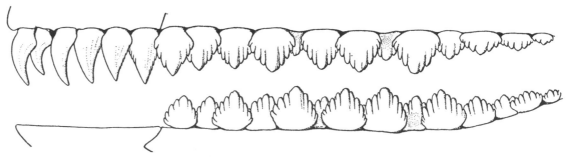

Alocodon kuehnei, **dental series (reconstructed) including holotype tooth LPFU P x 2. (After Thulborn 1973.)**

erodont; tooth crowns fully and uniformly enamelled, with smooth, inflated buccal surfaces; lingual surfaces ornamented with fine vertical ribs; anterior premaxillary tooth crowns tall, acutely conical, recurved, often with a shoulder-like swelling of the distal margin near the cervix; similar posterior premaxillary crowns with small denticles on the distal margin (sometimes also on mesial margin); cheek tooth crowns with triangular profile, about as high as long; occlusal tip formed by a single large denticle; lingual ribbing often irregular; mesial and distal edges with large, bluntly rounded denticles; lingual surface with a short cingulum near the distal margin, sometimes also with cingulum near the mesial margin; posterior cheek crown depressed, much longer than high, yet having large marginal denticles; posterior cheek teeth with cingula weak or absent; all cingula irregular, often carrying small denticles.

According to Thulborn, the preserved teeth in *Alocodon* seem to form a definite series running in a backward progression. Based on proportions of the crowns and the numbers of marginal denticles of isolated teeth, Thulborn conjecturally reconstructed the dentition of *Alocodon*: An edentulous predentary (reconstructed as extending almost to the suture between maxilla and premaxilla) was probably present. This predentary may have been intermediate in form between that in *Fabrosaurus australis* and *Hypsilophodon foxii*.

Thulborn believed that *Alocodon* was a fairly direct descendant of *Fabrosaurus*. This idea was challenged by Galton (1978), who stated that there are too many differences between the teeth of both genera to assume a close relationship between these taxa. Galton concluded that the diagnostic features of *Alocodon* (not found in *Fabrosaurus*) imply that the genus may have descended from a Late Triassic or Early Jurassic form similar to *Fabrosaurus* or *Lesothosaurus*.

Thulborn identified the holotype as a cheek tooth. Galton (1983*b*), however, showed that this specimen is a left maxillary tooth, as the taller lateral surface is on the convex side of the crown and the asymmetrical apical denticle is located on the more posterior part of the crown. Galton (1983*b*) also pointed out that both *Alocodon* and *Othnielia* have

cheek teeth in which the enamel is textured, intimating that either such texturing occurred independently in both genera, or that the two forms may be closely related to one another, more so than any ornithopods yet described.

In a review of primitive ornithischians, Weishampel and Witmer (1990*a*) regarded *Alocodon* and tooth genus *Trimucrodon* as *nomena dubia*, but (as later noted by Sereno 1991) did so without comparison. Sereno referred both genera to Ornithischia *incertae sedis* based on two ornithischian synapomorphies—low, subtriangular crowns separated from their roots by a basal constriction, and absence of recurvature in maxillary and dentary crowns (see Sereno 1986).

Key references: Galton (1987, 1983*b*); Sereno (1986, 1991); Wieshampel and Witmer (1990*a*); Thulborn (1973*b*).

ALTISPINAX Huene 1922 [*nomen dubium*]
Saurischia: Theropoda: ?Tetanurae: Megalosauridae.
Name derivation: Latin *altus* = "high" + Latin *spina* = "spine."
Type species: *A. dunkeri* (Dames 1884) [*nomen dubium*].
Other species: [None.]

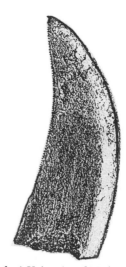

Altispinax dunkeri, **University of Marburg, No. 84, holotype tooth. (After Dames 1884.)**

Occurrence: Wealden, Hannover, Germany.

Age: Early Cretaceous (Barremian).

Known material/holotype: University of Marburg collection, No. 84, tooth.

Diagnosis of genus: [No modern diagnosis published.]

Comments: The genus *Altispinax* was erected by Huene (1922) to embrace the type specimens of two new species of *Megalosaurus*, *M. dunkeri* Dames 1884 and *M. oweni* Lydekker 1889, along with several other theropod specimens (including three dorsal vertebrae). *M. dunkeri* had been originally established by Dames (1884), based on a worn tooth (University of Marburg collection, no. 84; see Huene 1926c), collected from the Wealden of Deister, Hannover, Germany.

Huene (1922) did not designate a type species for *Altispinax*, Huene (1926c) later stating that the generic name was reserved for *M. dunkeri* in the event that it was ever proven that the tooth and vertebrae belonged to the same species. Subsequently, White (1973), in his catalog of dinosaur genera, fixed the type species of this form as *A. dunkeri*, making it a *nomen dubium*, and leaving the vertebrae without a generic name.

Altispinax, as based on the tooth, was diagnosed by Huene (1922, 1926c) as follows: Tooth falciformally curved; serrated cutting longitudinal edge at posterior margin; anterior border thickened, obtuse.

The dorsal vertebrae included in *Altispinax* were later made the type specimen of new genus and species *Becklespinax huenei* by Olshevsky (1991).

Key references: Dames (1884); Huene (1922, 1926b); White (1973).

ALVAREZSAURUS Bonaparte 1991

Saurischia: Theropoda: Tetanurae: Avetheropoda: Coelurosauria: Maniraptora *incertae sedis*.

Name derivation: "[Don Gregorio] Alvarez" + Greek *sauros* = "lizard."

Type species: *A. calvois* Bonaparte 1991.

Other species: [None.]

Occurrence: Rio Colorado Formation, Neuquén Group, Argentina.

Age: Late Cretaceous (Maastrichtian).

Known material/holotype: MUCPv 54, series of eight articulated but incomplete vertebrae, including five cervicals and three dorsals, one cervical centrum, two incomplete dorsal neural arches, three sacral centra in articulation with right ilium, another sacral centrum, 13 more or less complete proximal and medial caudals with haemal arches in natural position, greater part of right scapula and associated incomplete coracoid, greater part of right and fragments of left ilia,

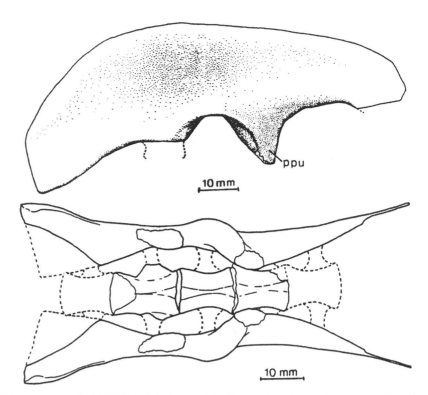

Alvarezsaurus calvoi, MUCPv 54, holotype right ilium A. lateral view, B. reconstruction of ilium united with sacrum, ventral view. (After Bonaparte 1991.)

incomplete middle proximal portions of both femora, middle distal portion of right tibia united with astragalus and calcaneum, fragments of distal part of left tibia, incomplete right metatarsus in natural position, fourth metatarsal in articulation with its five phalanges, three distal phalanges of second toe, three incomplete metatarsals of left foot with four phalanges of fourth toe, two phalanges of third, one isolated phalanx, two fragments of phalanges.

Diagnosis of genus (as for type species): Small theropod; cervical vertebrae with postzygapophyses having circular expansions, vestigial neural spines and amphicoelous centra; anterior dorsal vertebrae with vestigial neural spines; five or six sacral vertebrae, anterior sacrals with a slight axial depression at ventral border of centrum, posterior sacrals with narrow lower border; scapula small, reduced, lacking acromial expansion; ilium deep and long, with postacetabular expansion larger than preacetabular; metatarsals II-IV of subequal thickness, III comparatively narrow as seen from behind; fourth metatarsal larger than others, with smaller proximal portion; no evidence of fusion of metatarsus; astragalus not fused with tibia, with widened internal and external depression (Bonaparte 1991).

Comments: The genus *Alvarezsaurus* was founded on postcranial remains (MUCPv 54) collected from the Bajo de la Carpa Member of the Rio

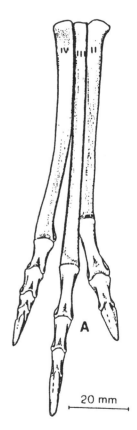

Alvarezsaurus calvoi, MUCPv 54, holotype right pes in dorsal view. (After Bonaparte 1991.)

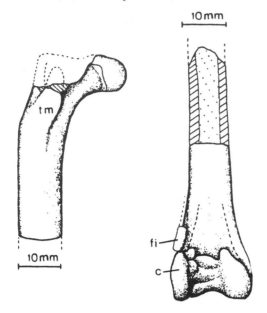

Alvarezsaurus calvoi, MUCPv 54, holotype proximal portion of right femur (dorsal view) and distal portion of right tibia united with astragalus, calcaneum, and fibular fragment (anterior view). (After Bonaparte 1991.)

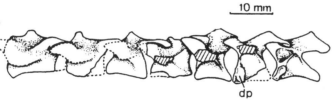

Alvarezsaurus calvoi, MUCPv 54, holotype cervical and dorsal vertebrae, lateral view. (After Bonaparte 1991.)

Alvarezsaurus calvoi, MUCPv 54, holotype caudal vertebrae, lateral view. (After Bonaparte 1991.)

Colorado Formation, Neuquén Group, Argentina (Bonaparte 1991).

According to Bonaparte, the vertebrae, pelvis and hindlimbs of *Alvarezsaurus* resemble, in some ways, those in ornithomimosaurs, these similarities apparently due to parallelism. The uniqueness of this taxon's characters warranted its placement into two new groups, respectively, Alvarezsauria Bonaparte 1991 and Alvarezsauridae Bonaparte 1991, neither of which have been generally adopted.

Note: The postacetabular expansion being larger than the preacetabular is also a condition of the ilium referred to *Carcharodontosaurus* (R. E. Molnar, personal communication 1992).

Key reference: Bonaparte (1991).

ALXASAURUS Russell and Dong 1993

Saurischia: Theropoda: Tetanurae: ?Coelurosauria: Therizinosauroidea: Alxasauridae.

Name derivation: "Alxa [Desert]" + Greek *sauros* = "lizard."

Type species: *A. elesitaiensis* Russell and Dong 1993.

Other species: [None.]

Occurrence: Bayin Gobi Formation, Alxa Desert, Inner Mongolia, People's Republic of China.

Age: Early Cretaceous.

Known material: Disarticulated partial remains of at least three (?five) individuals.

Holotype: IVPP 88402 (larger individual), right dentary, five crushed cervical vertebrae, two cervical ribs, seven crushed ?posterior dorsal vertebrae, three right and three left relatively complete dorsal ribs, numerous rib fragments, sacrum, anterior sacral ribs, about 20 caudal vertebrae preserved in series.

Diagnosis of genus (as for Alxasauridae and type species): Approximately 40 dentary teeth; teeth in symphysial region of dentary; ribs not fused to cervical centra; ligament pits often well developed in manual phalanges; ilium not greatly shortened anteroposteriorly; preacetabular ala moderately expanded; ungual shorter than or subequal to first phalanx in pedal digits II–IV (Russell and Dong 1993).

Comments: Representing the most complete remains of any yet known Asian theropod and the basis for the new family Alxasauridae, *Alxasaurus* was founded upon a partial skeleton (IVPP 88402; larger individual) found in 1985 by Xi-Jin Zhao, in steeply inclined exposures (site discovered by Cui Guihai) of the Bayin Gobi Formation, west of the abandoned village of Elesitai, west of Tukemu Village, Wulanbuhe Desert, eastern sector of the Alxa Desert, Inner Mongolia. Referred specimens include three articulated posterior cervical or anterior dorsal vertebrae and four disarticulated dorsals (IVPP 88402; smaller individual), and a partial postcranial skeleton (IVPP 88501), including five crushed and disarticulated dorsal vertebrae, first sacral vertebra, incomplete second sacral, metacarpals I (right) and III (left), four manual phalanges, ungual phalanges I-2, II-3, and III-4, posterior tip of left ilium, both ends of the right and proximal end of left femora, both ends of left and proximal end of right tibiae, proximal ends of both fibulae, ?right pedal phalanges II-1 and 2, III-1, 2, and 3, IV-1, 2, and 4, and three pedal unguals of uncertain identification (specimen discovered by Richard Day). Additional as yet unexamined material which probably belongs to this species includes scattered vertebrae and ribs, and appendicular remains (IVPP 88301), and appendicular material

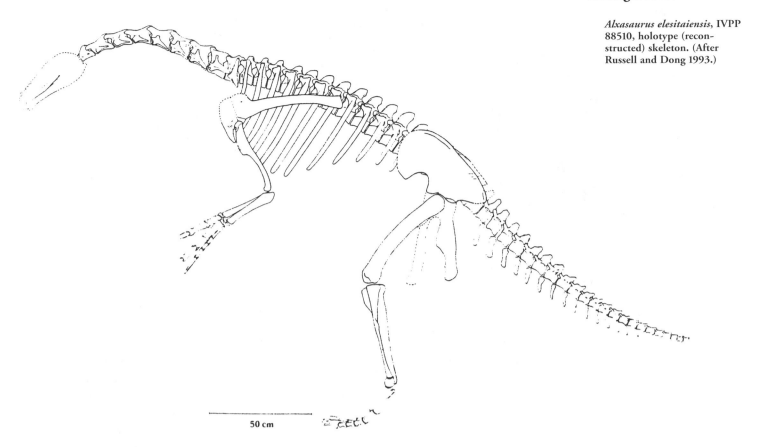

50 cm

(IVPP 88510). The material was collected by expeditions of the Sino-Canadian Dinosaur Project from between August 21 and September 2, 1988 (Russell and Dong 1993).

As reconstructed by Russell and Dong, the skeleton of type species *Alxasaurus elesitaiensis*, based on the type specimen, generally resembles that of a moderately large prosauropod, having a small skull, relatively long neck, long arms, and short tail. Russell and Dong estimated the adult dinosaur to be approximately 3.8 meters (about 13 feet) long, about 1.5 meters (5.2 feet) high at the hips, with a weight of about 380 kilograms (about 750 pounds).

As observed by Russell and Dong, the Alxa specimens exhibit various features that imply a relationship to what were then called "segnosaurs" (*e.g.* small skull–ilium length ratio; presence of a recurved symphysial process and prominent dorsolateral shelf on dentary; relatively large number of dentary teeth; amphyplatyan nature of cervical centra, and low cervical neural arches; morphology of proximal end of scapula and coracoid; presence of three manual digits; unusually deep preacetabular process of ilium; short postacetabular process of ilium, bearing lateral tuberosity; greater trochanter of femur expanded anteroposteriorly, separated from lesser trochanter by deep cleft).

According to Russell and Dong, skeletal materials of *A. elesitaiensis* represent the oldest and most complete "segnosaur" specimens yet described. The morphology of these materials suggested to them that taxa previously described as "segnosaurs" or therizinosaurids may represent the same assemblage (named Therizinosauroidea by the authors) of endemic Asian dinosaurs.

Comparing *Alxasaurus* to other theropods, Russell and Dong found attributes suggesting a relationship of therizinosauroids with the Tetanurae, with several character reversals, associated with a shortening and simplification of the tail and broadening of the foot, having taken place. According to Russell and Dong (see systematic section, this volume), characters of the Therizinosauroidea also imply a dichotomy between the "Carnosauria" and Oviraptorosauria (including ornithomimids, therizinosauroids, troodonts, and oviraptorosaurids).

Key reference: Russell and Dong (1993).

AMARGASAURUS Salgado and Bonaparte 1991
Saurischia: Sauropodomorpha: Sauropoda:
  Diplodocidae: Dicraeosaurinae.
Name derivation: "[La] Amarga [zone of Formation]" + Greek *sauros* = "lizard."

Amargasaurus

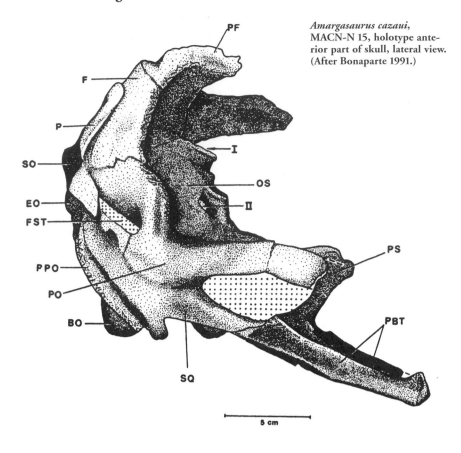

Amargasaurus cazaui, MACN-N 15, holotype anterior part of skull, lateral view. (After Bonaparte 1991.)

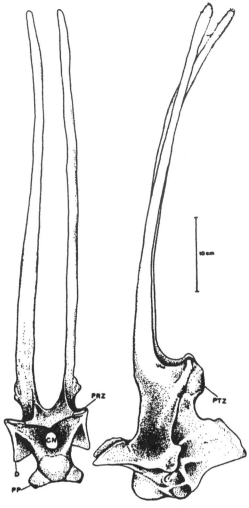

Amargasaurus cazaui, MACN-N 15, holotype cervical vertebra, anterior and lateral views. Scale = 10 cm. (After Bonaparte 1991.)

Amargasaurus cazaui, MACN-N 15, holotype atlas and axis, lateral and anterior views. (After Bonaparte.)

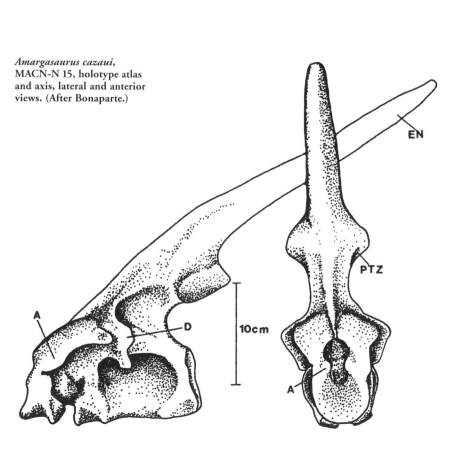

Type species: *A. cazaui* Salgado and Bonaparte 1991.
Other species: [None.]
Occurrence: La Amarga Formation, Neuquén, Patagonia, Argentina.
Age: Early Cretaceous (Hauterivian).
Known material: Incomplete skeletons of three individuals.
Type specimen: MACN-N 15, almost complete skeleton with partial skull (including basicranial and temporal regions), 22 articulated presacral vertebrae joined with skull and sacrum, partially eroded sacrum with five fused sacral vertebrae, three medial-to-anterior caudal vertebrae, one posterior caudal, three hemal arches, one very proximal cervical vertebra, some incomplete proximal dorsals, numerous parts of caudal vertebrae, right scapula-coracoid, humerus, left radius, ulna, ilium, femur, tibia, fibula, one astragalus two metatarsals.

Photo by B. Franczak.

Amargasaurus cazaui, reconstructed skeleton MACN-N 15
mounted at the Museo
Argentino de Ciencias Naturales, Buenos Aires.

Diagnosis of genus (as for type species): Dicrae-osaurine [=dicraeosaurid of their usage] about size of *Dicraeosaurus hansemanni*; presacral vertebrae with neural spines much taller and more pronouncedly bifurcated than in *Dicraeosaurus*, this condition continuing almost to penultimate presacral; cervical neural spines much longer than in *Dicraeosaurus*, subcylindrical in cross-section; secondary pleurocoels not present (as in *Dicraeosaurus*); five fused sacral vertebrae; pelvis and appendicular skeleton compare favorably with *Dicraeosaurus*; temporal region of skull with parietal and postparietal fenestrae as in *Dicraeosaurus*; basipterygoid processes quite long, fused; position and form of external nares comparable to *D. hansemanni*; orbit large with large opening for olfactory nerve, bordered by a bony process (Salgado and Bonaparte 1991).

Comments: Type species *Amargasaurus groeberi* was first mentioned, but neither diagnosed nor described, by Bonaparte (1984a) in *Sulle Orme dei Dinosauria*, an Italian book about dinosaurian remains and traces, edited by Giancarlo Ligabue. In this original and informal notice, Bonaparte stated that the new taxon was known from fragmentary remains of three moderate-sized individuals.

This unusual sauropod, renamed *A. cazaui*, was founded upon an almost complete skeleton with partial skull (MACN-N 15), discovered in March 1984,

by Bonaparte, Guillermo Rougier and other members of the 8th Paleontological Expedition to Patagonia, under the auspices of the National Geographic Society's program to investigate Jurassic and Cretaceous South American vertebrate faunas. The remains were found in Late Necomanian beds of the lower part of the La Amarga Formation, in the central-western Province of Neuquén, Neuquén Basin, northwestern Patagonia, Argentina (Salgado and Bonaparte 1991).

Comparing *A. cazaui* to other sauropods, Salgado and Bonaparte concluded that this species is similar to yet more derived than the African *Dicraeosaurus hansemanni*. Comparing *Amargasaurus-Dicraeosaurus* with *Diplodocus*, they listed a suite of salient differences: In *Amargasaurus-Dicraeosaurus*, the frontals are fused (not fused in *Diplodocus*); parietal and postparietal fenestrae present (absent in *Diplodocus*); supraoccipital narrow with no participation in the posttemporal fossa (wide in *Diplodocus*, contributing to the posttemporal pit); supraoccipital crest robust (vestigial in *Diplodocus*); basipterygoid processes very large (moderately large in *Diplodocus*); cervical vertebrae have neither pleurocoels nor a system of osseous bars (both present in *Diplodocus*); secondary dorsal vertebrae lack pleurocoels (marked pleurocoels present in *Diplodocus*); and proximal caudal vertebrae robust, heavy and lack pleurocoels (lightly constructed, with pleurocoels, in *Diplodocus*). Because of

Amargasaurus

Photo by B. Franczak.

Amargasaurus cazaui, anterior part of mounted skeleton MACN-N 15 (skull reconstructed after that of *Diplodocus*) displayed at the Museo Argentino de Ciencias Naturales, Buenos Aires.

these differences, Salgado and Bonaparte suggested that *Amargasaurus* and *Dicraeosaurus* represent their own taxon Dicraeosauridae, regarded as more derived than and with significant differences to Diplodocidae.

The extremely long and bifurcated neural spines, especially those of the neck, would have made *Amargasaurus* a visually spectacular animal, some of these spines having an approximate length of some 50.50 centimeters (about 21 inches). Salgado and Bonaparte speculated that the spines may have had some defensive function, presenting an obstacle to a theropod attacker seeking out its neck. The spines would have enhanced the sauropod's profile, possibly for intimidating rivals during mating season. Also, tall neural spines would have helped to keep the dinosaur cool by increasing the surface-to-volume ratio, especially if they supported twin sails.

Key reference: Salgado and Bonaparte (1991).

Amargasaurus cazaui, life restoration by Brian Franczak.

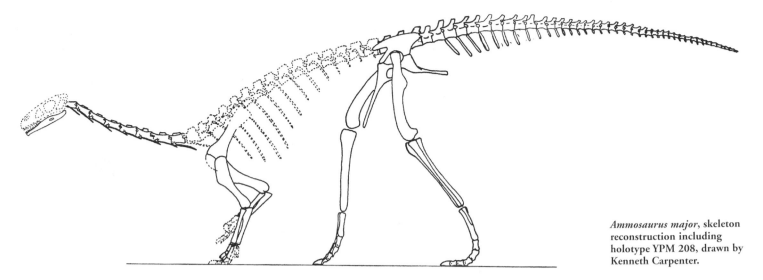

AMMOSAURUS   Marsh 1891

Saurischia: Sauropodomorpha: Prosauropoda: Plateosauridae.

Name derivation: Greek *ammos* = "sand" + Greek *sauros* = "lizard."

Type species: *A. major* (Marsh 1889).

Other species: [None.]

Occurrence: Upper (Portland) Beds, Newark Supergroup, Connecticut, Navajo Sandstone, Arizona, United States.

Age: Early Jurassic (Pleinsbachian or Toarcian).

Known material: Four incomplete skeletons.

Holotype: YPM 208, three presacral vertebrae, sacrum, pelvis, both hindlimbs.

Diagnosis of genus: Broad-footed prosauropod, distinguished by such derived characters as long anterior process of ilium, and ventral emargination on subacetabular part of the ischium, and the primitive form of the third sacral rib, with transverse process and rib separated (Galton 1976).

Comments: The genus *Ammosaurus*, founded on incomplete postcranial remains (YPM 208), was originally described by Marsh (1889) as a new species of *Anchisaurus* and incorrectly classified as a "coelurosaurian" theropod. The holotype, preserved in the animal's death pose, was discovered in 1884 in a quarry in the Newark Series, Portland Sandstone (apparently Pleinsbachian; see *Anchisaurus* entry), Connecticut Valley, near Manchester, Connecticut. Although the specimen was apparently complete at the time of its discovery, Marsh only collected the posterior portion of the skeleton. Subsequently, Marsh (1891) recognized these remains as belonging to a new genus which he named *Ammosaurus*.

Marsh (1889) originally diagnosed this genus as follows: Three sacral vertebrae; dorsal vertebrae with biconcave or almost plane articular ends; ilium with slender preacetabular process; ischia very slender, backwardly directed, closely adapted to one another for the posterior half of their length. The preserved remains indicate an animal from almost 1.8 to nearly 2.4 meters (about 6 to 8 feet) long.

Later, Huene (1914) used *Ammosaurus* as basis for the new [abandoned] family Ammosauridae, which he believed represented the most primitive "coelurosaurs." This interpretation of *Ammosaurus* as a theropod was long accepted by other authors (*e.g.*, Romer 1956, 1966; Colbert 1961). Colbert and Baird (1958) suggested that *Ammosaurus* might not be a theropod but a prosauropod with affinities to *Anchisaurus*. Colbert (1964) later concluded that the Ammosauridae and other "Triassic carnosaurs" represented an early radiation of carnivorous dinosaurs distinct from "Coelurosauria" and "Carnosauria" and limited to the Triassic. Walker (1964), pointing out that postcranial material of Triassic "carnosaurs" was not positively associated with cranial material, suggested that the former be classified with the Prosauropoda.

In reevaluating this genus, Galton (1971b), observed a suite of characters shared by *Ammosaurus* and prosauropods, including: 1. Seemingly 25 presacral vertebrae (in YPM 209, the type specimen of *A. solus*; 23 to 24 in theropods); 2. modification of the third sacral vertebra to a modified caudal vertebra (YPM 208); 3. pelvic girdle of the brachyiliac type (dolichoiliac type in theropods); 4. pubic peduncle of the iliac broad and much longer than the ischial head; 5. acetabulum large with elliptical outline (YPM 208, 209); 6. ratio of 2.0 of the length of the ilium to its height at the ischiadic head (YPM 208) (1.3 in the prosauropod *Plateosaurus*, 2.5 in theropod *Rioarribasaurus* [=*Coelophysis* of his usage]); 7. femur (YPM 208) lacking prominent lesser trochanter

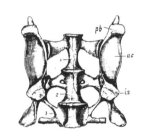

Ammosaurus major, YPM 208, holotype sacrum and ilia. (After Marsh 1986.)

Ammosaurus major, YPM 208, holotype right pes. (After Marsh, 1891, 1896.)

(characteristic of theropods) and longer than the tibia (YPM 208, 209); and 8. pes (YPM 208, 209) broad with a shortened but complete first metatarsal (long but slender in theropods, with the proximal section of the shaft unossified). Based on these synapomorphies, Galton (1971b) removed *Ammosaurus* from Theropoda and reassigned it to the Prosauropoda.

Noting that none of the characters diagnostic to *Ammosaurus* warranted the retention of Ammosauridae, Galton (1976) referred *Ammosaurus* to the Anchisauridae. In a later review of Prosauropoda, Galton (1990a) assigned the type species *A. major* to the Plateosauridae.

A second species, *A. solus*, was based on a pelvic arch and both feet (YPM 209), these remains collected from the same quarry as the holotype of *A. major*. Marsh (1892a), noting its smaller size (1.75 to 2.4 meters, or 6 to 8 feet, in length), referred this material to *Anchisaurus*. Galton (1976), observing that the holotype of this species cannot be distinguished from *A. major* except by size, designated *A. solus* a junior synonym of *A. major*, the former possibly representing a juvenile.

Prosauropod material from the Navajo Sandstone of the Navajo Indian Reservation in northeastern Arizona was described by Brady (1935) as resembling *A. major*. This material includes the lower parts of a skeleton (MNA G2 7233), the upper parts lost by erosion, found on the plateau between Navajo and Shonto Canyons, between Tuba City and Navajo Mountain. The animal apparently was buried in its death posture, prone with hind legs doubled under the body, the feet extended and claws bent down as if grasping the sand. Galton (1971b) referred this specimen to *Ammosaurus*, noting that it might represent a new species, the obturator process of the pubis being apparently smaller than in *A. major*. Galton (1971b) designated these remains as *Ammosaurus* cf. *major*; later, Galton (1976) suggested they might represent a new genus.

Key references: Brady (1935); Colbert (1964); Colbert and Baird (1958); Galton (1971b, 1976, 1990a); Huenei (1914); Marsh (1889, 1891, 1892a); Walker (1964).

AMPELOSAURUS Le Loeuff 1995

Saurischia: Sauropodomorpha: Sauropoda: Titanosauria; Titanosauridae.

Name derivation: Greek *ampelos* = "gravevine" + Greek *sauros* = "lizard."

Type species: *A. atacis* Le Loeuff 1995.

Other species: [None].

Occurrence: Marnes Rouges Inferieurs Formation, Departement de l'Aude, France, Europe.

Age: Late Cretaceous (Early Maastrichtian).

Known material: Disarticulated remains including a tooth, partial postcranial material, including osteoderms, representing various individuals.

Holotype: MDE-C3-247, three articulated middle dorsal vertebrae.

Diagnosis of genus (as for type species): Teeth slightly spatulate; neural spines of dorsal vertebrae with expanded distal part; dorsal neural spines directed strongly backward; scapular blade unexpanded; osteoderms of various shapes present (Le Loeuff 1995).

Comments: Among the best documented European sauropods, the genus *Ampelosaurus* was founded

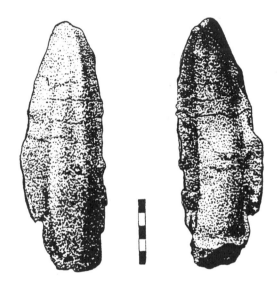

Ampelosaurus atacis, MDE-C3-52, tooth, (left) labial and (right) lingual views. Scale = 5 mm. (After Le Loeuff 1995.)

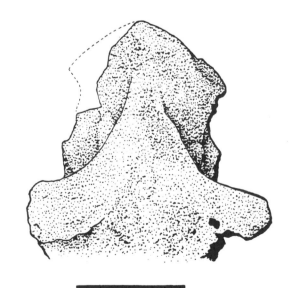

Ampelosaurus atacis, MDE-C3-59, neural spine of dorsal vertebra, anterior view. Scale = 10 cm. (After Le Loeuff 1995.)

upon several vertebrae (MDE-C3-247) recovered during excavations begun in 1989 on a bonebed in the Marnes Rogues Inferieurs Formation, Maurine member (Bilotte 1985), at Bellevue, Campagne-sur-Aude, Departement de l'Aude, France, by a team of the Musée des Dinosaures in Espéraza (Jean le Loeuff and Valérie Martin), the Centre National de la Recherche Scientifique in Paris (Eric Buffetaut, Haiyan Tong, and Lionel Cavin), and the Muséum d'Histoire Naturelle in Boulogne-sur-Mer (Michel Martin). Referred material, collected from the same locality, includes one tooth (MDE-C3-52), dorsal vertebrae (MDE-C3-38, C3-59, C3-92 to 94, and C3-148), caudal vertebrae (MDE-C3-24 to 27, C3-46, C3-55, C3-58, C3-63 to 65, C3-95 to 101, C3-124, C3-127, and C3-147), ribs (MDE-C3-60), chevrons (MDE-C3-72 and C3-139), sternal plates (MDE-C3-23 and C3-80), scapulae (MDE-C3-21 and C3-145), coracoids (MDE-C3-22, C3-161, and C3-351), humeri (MDE-C3-1, C3-79, C3-81, C3-86, C3-175, and C3-312), ulnae (MDE-C3-56, C3-83, and C3-300), a radius (MDE-C3-85), pubis (MDE-C3-57), ilium (MDE-C3-123), ischium (MDE-C3-84), femora (MDE-C3-20, C3-40, C3-44, C3-61, C3-61, C3-78, C3-210, C3-201, and C3-261), tibiae (MDE-C3-137 and 138, C3-144, and C3-173), fibulae (MDE-C3-48 and C3-137), phalanges (MDE-C3-88), and osteoderms (MDE-C3-136, C3-192, C3-204, and C3-325) (Le Loeuff 1995).

In a preliminary description of the type species *A. atacis*, Le Loeuff noted that the recovered tooth is 21 millimeters high with a maximum width of 6 millimeters, that its axial part is cylindrical, with thin rostral and caudal expansions, and that it is very different from the cylindrical titanosaurid teeth found at Laño in northwestern Spain (Sanz 1986; Astibia, Buffetaut, Buscalioni, Cappetta, Corral, Estes, Garcia-Garmilla, Jaeger, Jimenez-Fuentes, Le Loeuff, Mazin, Orue-Extebarria, Pereda-Suberbiola, Powell, Rage, Rodriguez-Lazaro, Sanz, and Tong 1990). The four osteoderms referred to this species have various shapes (scutes, spines, and bulbs). (As of this writing, Le Loeuff's description of these scutes along with hypotheses regarding their paleobiological significance is in press.)

As observed by Le Loeuff, *A. atacis* clearly differs from other Late Cretaceous European titanosaurids and confirms their diversity. Le Loeuff linked the decline of titanosaurids during the Late Maastrichtian (Le Loeuff 1993) to climatic changes from the subtropical to temporate (Bardossy and Dercourt 1990).

(To date of this writing, a monograph on *A. atacis* is in preparation by Le Loeuff.)

Key reference: Le Loeuff (1995).

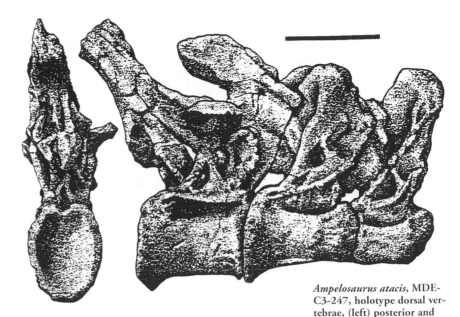

Ampelosaurus atacis, MDE-C3-247, holotype dorsal vertebrae, (left) posterior and (right) right lateral views. Scale = 17 cm. (After Le Loeuff 1995.)

AMPHICOELIAS Cope 1877 [*nomen dubium*]— (=?*Diplodocus*)

Saurischia: Sauropodomorpha: Sauropoda: Diplodocidae: Diplodocinae.

Name derivation: Greek *amphi* = "both" + Greek *koilos* = "hollow" or "concave."

Type species: *A. altus* Cope 1877 [*nomen dubium*].

Other species: [None.]

Occurrence: Morrison Formation, Colorado, United States.

Age: Late Jurassic (Kimmeridgian-Tithonian).

Known material: Partial postcrania.

Holotype: AMNH 5764, two dorsal vertebrae, pubis, femur, tooth.

Diagnosis of genus: [No modern diagnosis published.]

Comments: *Amphicoelias* was established upon postcranial remains (AMNH 5764) collected from the uppermost beds of the Morrison Formation, Garden Park, Fremont County, northeast of Canyon City, Colorado. On this genus, Cope (1877b) erected the [abandoned] family Amphicoelidae. In their classic review of Cope's sauropods, Osborn and Mook (1921) arbitrarily assigned a scapula, coracoid, and ulna (AMNH 5764a) to the type specimen.

Cope originally diagnosed the genus as follows: Centra with unequally amphicoelous articular ends; posterior end more concave, with prominent concave margins; anterior end less expanded, slightly concave; pubis stout, with slightly concave, thicker border and opposite strongly convex, thinner margin; femur elongate, with strong third trochanter at mid-shaft, head not separated by a well marked neck, greater trochanter not projecting beyond the head.

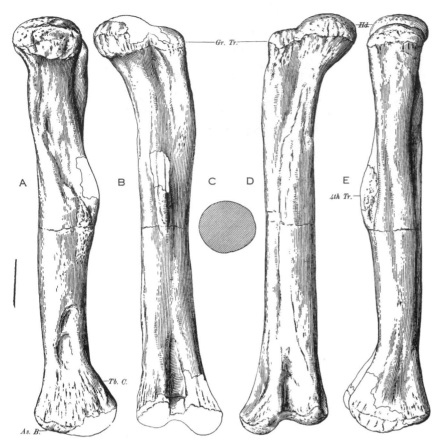

Amphicoelias altus, AMNH 5764, holotype right femur, A.–B. internal and posterior views, C. cross-section, D.–E. anterior and external views. Scale = 20 cm. (After Osborn and Mook 1921.)

Photo by R. A. Long and S. P. Welles (neg. #73-451-9), courtesy American Museum of Natural History.

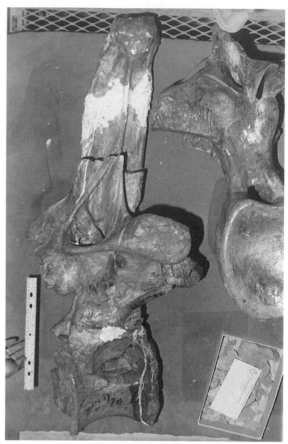

Amphicoelias altus, AMNH 5764, holotype dorsal vertebra, lateral view.

Later, Osborn and Mook rediagnosed the genus as follows: Slender-limbed sauropod with tall, slender vertebral spines closely resembling those in *Diplodocus*. At the same time, they diagnosed *A. altus* as follows: Dorsal centrum contracted laterally and inferiorly; dorsal neural arch highly elevated to zygapophyses; neural spine thin, with thickened and double anterior and posterior borders; femur very slender.

Second species, *A. fragillimus*, was based on an almost complete neural arch from the ninth or tenth dorsal vertebra, collected from the same locality as the holotype of *A. altus*. As the specimen was lost during transference of Cope's collection to the Academy of Natural Sciences of Philadelphia, Osborn and Mook noted that the characters of this species could not be clearly determined. In describing this vertebra, Cope (1878*f*) noted that it was larger than that of *A. altus* (or any other sauropod that had yet been described), the bone when complete about 1.8 meters (over 6 feet) high. From the size of this specimen, Cope (1878*f*) estimated that the femoral length could have been more than 3.5 meters (12 feet). Osborn and Mook, doubting that this specimen warranted the erection of a new species, provisionally referred *A. fragillimus* to *A. altus* (synonymy accepted by McIntosh 1990*b* in his review of the Sauropoda).

Osborn and Mook suggested that *Amphicoelias* could be congeneric with *Diplodocus* or some other genus, though not enough of its skeleton was known to make a synonymy. McIntosh observed that the very slender femur in *Amphicoelias* is quite similar to that of *Diplodocus*, but noted that the separation of these two genera was based upon Osborn and Mook's interpretation of the former having an erect rather than caudoventrally inclined spine in the tenth dorsal vertebra. McIntosh regarded *Amphicoelias* as a genus of doubtful validity included in the diplodocid "subfamily" Diplodocinae.

Note: *Amphicoelias* was the first sauropod dinosaur for which a life restoration was published. The illustration, prepared by Charles R. Knight under Cope's direction and published in an article by Ballou (1897) for *The Century Illustrated Monthly Magazine*, depicted the animal entirely submerged in a lake, its head protruding above the water's surface. Ballou envisioned the animal as completely aquatic, supposedly too massive to walk on land, utilizing the water for buoyancy and also to hold together its colossal frame. In Ballou's estimation, *Amphicoelias*

Amphicielias altus, AMNH 5764, holotype dorsal vertebra (top) and right femur (bottom).

Photo by the author, courtesy American Museum of Natural History.

would have reached almost 18 to nearly 24 meters (60 to 80 feet) in length and weighed from about 2.7 to 3.6 metric tons (3 to 4 tons). (A more accurate estimation was made by Paul 1988*a*, who calculated the weight to be about 16 metric tons, or almost 18 tons.) Ballou surmised that *Amphicoelias* was an omnivore, using its long neck to help secure a diet of fish in addition to vegetation from the lake bottom and from overhanging branches. (This image of water-bound

sauropods has persisted for decades, but has been abandoned by modern paleontologists.)

The species *A. latus* Cope 1877 was referred by Osborn and Mook to Camarasaurus supremus.

Key references: Ballou (1897); Cope (1877*b*, 1878*f*); McIntosh (1990*b*); Osborn and Mook (1921); Paul (1988*a*).

AMPHISAURUS Marsh 1882—(Preoccupied, Barkas 1870; see *Anchisaurus*.)
Name derivation: Greek *amphi* = "both" + Greek *sauros* = "lizard."
Type species: *A. polyzelus* Marsh 1882.

AMTOSAURUS Kurzanov and Tumanova 1978—(=*Maleevus, Talarurus, ?Tarchia*) Ornithischia: Genasauria: Thyreophora: Ankylosauria: Ankylosauridae.
Name derivation: "Amtgay [site]" + Greek *sauros* = "lizard."
Type species: *A. magnus* Kurzanov and Tumanova 1987.
Other species: [None.]

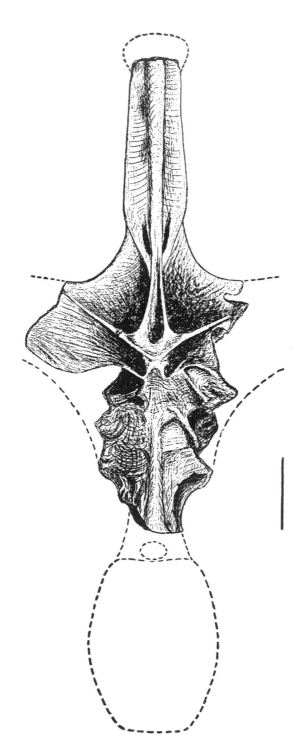

Amphicoelias fragillimus, holotype dorsal vertebra, posterior view, estimated by Osborn and Mook (1921) as dorsal 9 or 10. Scale = 20 cm. (After Cope 1878.)

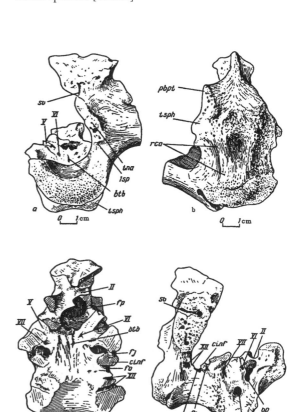

Amtosaurus magnus, No. 3780/2, holotype braincase in posterior, ventral, dorsal, and lateral views. (After Kurzanov and Tumanova 1978.)

Occurrence: Baynshirenskaya Svita, Omnogov, Mongolian People's Republic.

Age: Late Cretaceous (Cenomanian–Lower Santonian).

Known material/holotype: Partial braincase.

Diagnosis of genus (as for type species): Occiput and braincase high; occipital condyle appearing as narrow oval; on surface between condyle and sphenoccipital protuberances are two longitudinal, gently sloping elevations that are symmetric relative to median depression; interior part of floor of braincase slightly inflected; dorsum sellae with triangular process to sides of the pituitary fossa on continuation of the basis trabeculi basalis; fenestra ovalis lying considerably above jugular fenestra; outlets of nerve XII on same level (Kurzanov and Tumanova 1978).

Comments: The genus *Amtosaurus* was founded upon a partial braincase collected from the Bayan-Shireh suite (see Maleev 1952a), (Cenomanian to lower Santonian age; Barsbold 1972), in Amtgay, Eastern Mongolia. The type specimen indicates that *Amtosaurus* was a dinosaur similar to but larger than its contemporary *Talarurus*, also differing in various proportions and details (Kurzanov and Tumanova 1978; Tumanova 1987).

Note: Coombs (personal communication 1988) regarded both *Amtosaurus* and *Maleevus* as trivial variants of *Talarurus plicatospineus*, at best only marginally justifiable as distinct species. Later, Coombs and Maryańska (1990) noted that this taxon might be hadrosaurid, retaining it with reservations as an ankylosaurid.

Key references: Coombs and Maryańska (1990); Kurzanov and Tumanova (1978); Tumanova (1987).

AMYGDALODON Cabrera 1947

Saurischia: Sauropodomorpha: Sauropoda: Cetiosauridae: Cetiosaurinae.

Name derivation: Greek *amygdale* = "almond" + Greek *odous* = "tooth."

Type species: *A. patagonicus* Cabrera 1947.

Other species: [None.]

Occurrence: Cerro Carnerero Formation, Chubut, Argentina.

Age: Middle Jurassic (Bajocian).

Known material/holotype: MLP 46-VIII-21-1, four complete and three incomplete teeth, poorly preserved cervical, dorsal and caudal vertebrae, partial scapula, incomplete pubis, rib fragments.

Diagnosis of genus: Large, particularly primitive sauropod; dorsal vertebrae noncancellous, lack pleurocoels (Cabrera 1947).

Comments: The genus *Amygdalodon* was established on a partial skeleton (MLP 46-VIII-21-1), collected from the Cerro Carnerero Formation, Bayocian (see Stipanicic, Rodrigo, Baulies and Martínez 1968), Pampa de Agnia, province of Chubut, Argentina.

Cabrera (1947) found the preserved portion of the pubis of special interest, being a solid though slender piece of bone terminating in a heavy, convex process that curves more backward than forward. From the shape of the vertebrae and especially the slightness of the pleurocoels, Cabrera assigned *Amygdalodon* to the Cetiosauridae, a group including the then most primitive known sauropods.

As noted by Casamiquela (1963), *Amygdalodon* is the most primitive sauropod known from South America. In some ways it is morphologically similar to prosauropods and is a model that seems to have given rise to many more derived sauropod forms.

McIntosh (1990b), observing that the teeth in *A. patagonicus* are heart-shaped, closely resembling those of the English cetiosaurid *Cardiodon*, assigned *Amygdalodon* to the cetiosaurid subfamily Cetiosaurinae.

Key references: Cabrera (1947); Casamiquela (1963); McIntosh (1990b).

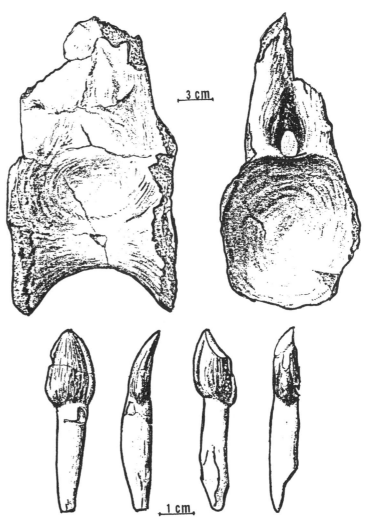

Amygdalodon patagonicus, MLP 46-VIII-21-1, holotype, (top) dorsal vertebra in lateral and posterior views, (bottom) two teeth, labial and anterior views of one, labial and posterior views of another. (After Cabrera 1947.)

3 cm

1 cm

ANASAZISAURUS Lucas and Hunt 1993
Ornithischia: Genasauria: Cerapoda: Ornithopoda:
  Iguanodontia: Hadrosauridae: Hadrosaurinae.
Name derivation: "Anasazi [prehistoric people
  indigenous to Chaco Canyon near type locality]"
  + Greek *sauros* = "lizard."
Type species: *A. horneri* Lucas and Hunt 1993.
Other species: [None.]
Occurrence: Kirtland Formation, Arroyo, Kimbeto
  New Mexico, United States.
Age: Late Cretaceous (Santonian–Early Campan-
  ian).
Known material/holotype: BYU 12950, partial
  skull.

Diagnosis of genus (as for type species): Distinguished from all other known hadrosaurids by possession of short, posteriorly folded nasal crest that is
above level of frontals but does not extend posterior
to anterior end of frontals (Lucas and Hunt 1993).

Comments: The genus *Anasazisaurus* was
founded upon a partial skull (BYU 12950) collected
by Brooks D. Britt (see Horner 1992) from strata low
(probably correlative with the Farmington Formation) in the Kirtland Formation (Upper Cretaceous;
Santonian–Early Campanian; see Lucas and Hunt
1992) of Kimbeto Arroyo, northwestern New Mexico (Lucas and Hunt 1993).

The holotype skull was originally regarded by
Horner (1992) as belonging to *Kritosaurus navajovius*,

Anasazisaurus horneri, BYU 12950, reconstructed
holotype skull, left lateral (top) and
dorsal (bottom) views. (After
Hunt and Lucas 1993.)

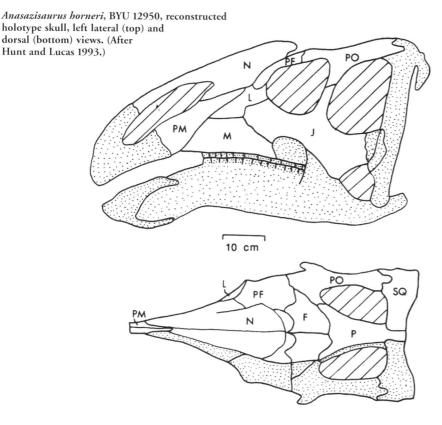

10 cm

based upon two features: 1. Junction where nasals
meet frontals appears to show nasals bifurcated, anterior end of frontal at midline therefore being
extended between nasals; 2. extensive lateral wing of
prefrontal extends over posterior end of nasal. As
pointed out by Lucas and Hunt, Horner observed
that these features only "appear" to be present in
K. navajovius. Furthermore, Lucas and Hunted noted
these features are not synapomorphies of *K. navajovius*, the first feature occurring in *Prosaurolophus*
and *Saurolophus*, the second in *Prosaurolophus*
(Horner 1992).

According to Lucas and Hunt, BYU 12950 represents a new genus possessing a nasal morphology
that is unique among hadrosaurids. The nasals arch
posterodorsally, terminating above and between
orbits (Horner 1992).

Key references: Horner (1992); Lucas and Hunt
(1993).

ANATOSAURUS Lull and Wright 1942—(See
  Edmontosaurus.)
Name derivation: Latin *anatos* = "duck" + Greek
  sauros = "lizard."
Type species: *A. annectens* Marsh 1892.

ANATOTITAN Brett-Surman 1990, *in* Chapman
  and Brett-Surman 1990
Ornithischia: Genasauria: Cerapoda: Ornithopoda:
  Iguanodontia: Hadrosauridae: Hadrosaurinae.
Name derivation: Latin *anatos* = "duck" + "Titan
  [mythological Greek giant]."
Type species: *A. copei* (Cope 1876).
Other species: *A. longiceps* (Marsh 1890).
Occurrence: Hell Creek Formation, Montana, Lance
  Formation, Hell Creek Formation, South Dakota,
  Lance Formation, Wyoming, United States.
Age: Late Cretaceous (Late Maastrichtian).
Known material: At least two articulated skulls
  with postcrania, isolated cranial remains.
Holotype: AMNH 5730, complete skeleton.

Diagnosis of genus (as for type species): Skull
longer, lower, wider than in any other hadrosaurid;
quadrate length/mandibular length ratio smallest,
edentulous portion of mandible longest, of any
hadrosaurid; appendicular elements comparatively
longer, more gracile than in any comparably-sized
hadrosaurine; limb bones up to 10 percent longer
than in *Edmontosaurus* of same ontogenetic age; neck
of prepubic blade longer, shallower than in any other
hadrosaurid; borders of postacetabular process tending not to be parallel (Brett-Surman 1990, *in* Chapman and Brett-Surman 1990).

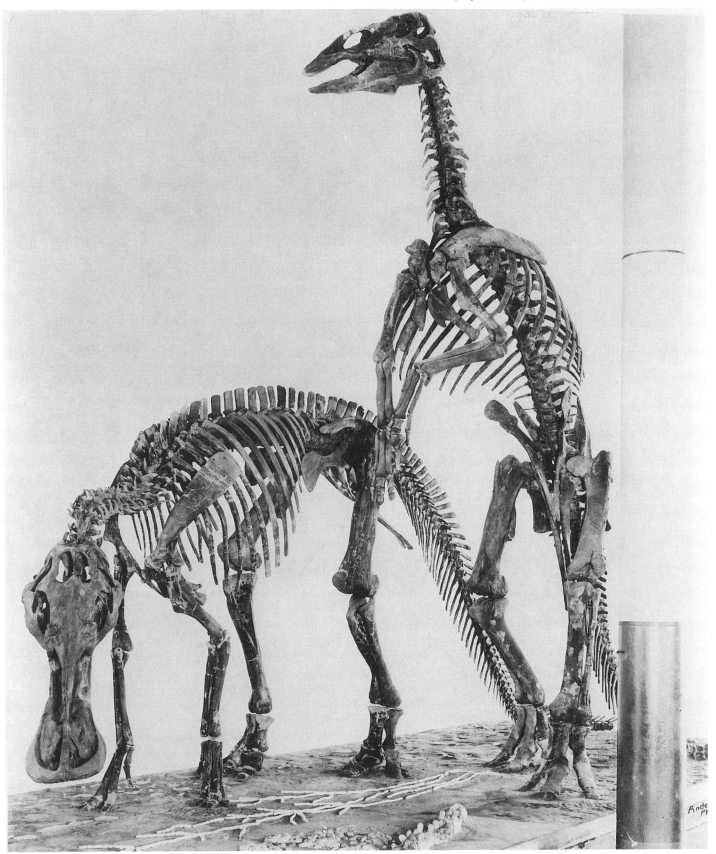

Anatotitan copei, AMNH 5730, holotype skeleton (quadrupedal pose), and ANMH 5886, paratype skeleton, of *Anatosaurus copei.*

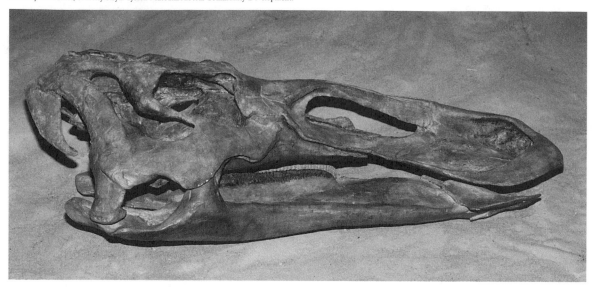

Anatotitan copei, cast of AMNH 5730, holotype skull of *Anatosaurus copei*.

Comments: The genus now called *Anatotitan* was established on a complete skeleton (AMNH 5730), collected by J. L. Wortman and R. S. Hill during the Edward Drinker Cope expedition of 1882, from the Lance Formation near Moreau River, north of the Black Hills, South Dakota. The paratype (AMNH 5886), another almost complete skeleton, was found by Oscar Hunter in 1904, collected two years later by Barnum Brown and Peter Kaisen from the Lance Formation of Crooked Creek, Montana. Both skeletons were put on display at the American Museum of Natural History, the holotype originally mounted in a quadrupedal pose, the paratype in a bipedal stance.

Cope (1876) regarded these skeletons as referable to Leidy's *Trachodon mirabilis*, a tooth genus then believed to be hadrosaurid (see *Trachodon* entry). Believing that Leidy had abandoned the name *Trachodon* entirely, Cope (1883) then referred the new material to another of Leidy's species *Diclonius mirabilis*. Lull and Wright (1942), in their classic review of duckbilled dinosaurs, subsequently referred Cope's material to *Anatosaurus*, a new genus they erected to eliminate some of the confusion regarding numerous very similar yet differently named flat-headed hadrosaurs, the two skeletons representing their new species *A. copei*.

Eventually, Brett-Surman (1975, 1979) recognized type species *A. annectens* as a junior synonym of *Edmontosaurus regalis*. Finding *A. copei* to be generically distinct from *Edmontosaurus*, Brett-Surman referred it to the new genus *Anantotitan* (Brett-Surman 1990, *in* Chapman and Brett-Surman 1990).

Cope (1876) originally diagnosed this species as follows: Skull remarkably contracted at anterior portion of maxillae, unusually deep posteriorly, with uniquely flat and transversely expanded premaxillae; posterior edges of occipital produced far posteriorly, forming a thin roof over anterior region of the neck; orbit posteriorly located, with horizontal oblong outline, posterior border flat with slight rugosities at pre- and postfrontal sutures; frontal region somewhat concave, superior face of prefrontal convex anterior to line of the orbit.

As measured by Wortman, the holotype skeleton is about 11 meters (38 feet) in length, the skull 1.18 meters (about 4 feet) long. Brett-Surman (personal communication 1987) noted that the height at the hip in this skeleton is approximately 2.1 meters (about 7 feet). The weight of *Anatotitan* was about 3 metric tons (almost 3.4 tons) (G. S. Paul, personal communication 1988).

Lull and Wright referred to *A. copei* the species *Trachodon longiceps* Marsh 1890 [*nomen dubium*], based on a right dentary with teeth (YPM 616), collected in 1889 by John Bell Hatcher from the Lance Formation of Niobrara County, Wyoming. Marsh (1890) estimated the length of this dentary, if complete, to be 1.1 meters (3.6 feet). At the time of its description, this was the largest hadrosaur dentary on record. According to Weishampel and Horner (1990), this species may be referable to the type species. Brett-Surman (1989) regarded *Anatotitan* as the epitome of hadrosaurine evolution, the muzzle area increased both anteriorly and laterally into a shovel-like structure perhaps adapted to gathering in more plants per mouthful.

Key references: Brett-Surman (1975, 1979, 1989, 1990), Cope 1876, 1883; Lull and Wright (1942); Marsh (1890); Weishampel and Horner (1990).

Anatotitan copei **herd.**

ANCHICERATOPS   Brown 1914

Ornithischia: Genasauria: Cerapoda: Marginocephalia: Ceratopsia: Neoceratopsia: Ceratopsidae: Chasmosaurinae.

Name derivation: Greek *anchion* = "similar" +
Greek *keratos* = "horn" + Greek *ops* = "face."

Type species: *A. ornatus* Brown 1914.

Other species: *A. longirostris* Sternberg 1929.

Occurrence: Dinosaur Park Formation, Oldman
Formation (both formerly Judith River Forma-
tion; see Eberth and Hamblin 1993); Horseshoe
Canyon Formation, Alberta, Canada.

Age: Late Cretaceous (Late Campanian–Maastrichtian).

Known material: Complete skeleton, six skulls.

Holotype: AMNH 5251, incomplete skull.

   Diagnosis of genus (as for type species): Skull
large; supraorbital horns massive at their bases, divergent, rising closely together, curving outward then
forward; crest large, flat, thick, with small fontanelles
and large epoccipital bones ornamenting the border;
pair of short knob-like processes on posterior end of
the crest; squamosal intermediate in length between
Centrosaurus and *Triceratops* (Brown 1914*b*); brow
horns larger than nasal horn; crest more or less rec-

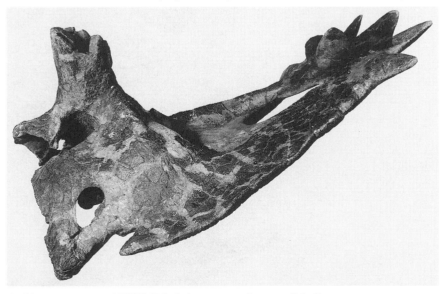

Anchiceratops ornatus, **AMNH 5251, holotype posterior part of skull.**

Anchiceratops

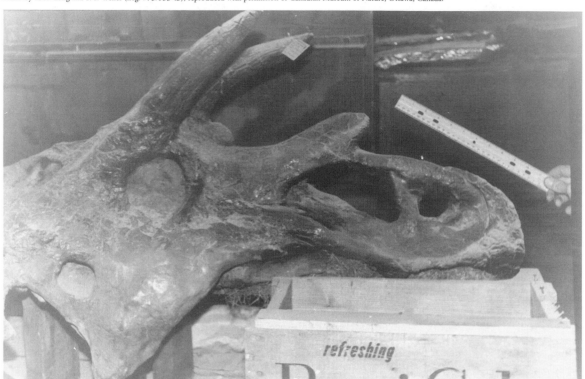

Anchiceratops longirostris,
NMC 8535, holotype
anterior part of skull.

Anchiceratops longirostris,
NMC 8535, holotype
posterior of skull.

tangular; epoccipitals on parietals larger than on squamosal (Sternberg 1929).

Diagnosis of *A. longirostris*: Differs from *A. ornatus* mostly by form of the brow horns, which are relatively longer, less slender, more divergent laterally (Russell and Chamney 1967).

Comments: A moderately large ceratopsian (4.8 meters or 16 feet), *Anchiceratops* was established on the incomplete skull (AMNH 5251) of an old individual lacking the anterior end and top of the supraorbital horn cores. The specimen was collected in 1912 by the American Museum of Natural History expedition from the Horseshoe Canyon (then Edmonton) Formation, below Tolman Ferry, Red Deer River, Alberta, Canada. A paratype specimen (AMNH 5259), consisting of braincase and nearly complete brow horns, was collected about the same time a few miles distant from where the holotype had been found (Brown 1914*a*).

A second species, *A. longirostris*, described by Sternberg (1929), was based on an almost complete skull (NMC [formerly GSC] 8535), lacking lower jaws, collected by Sternberg in 1924 at Red Deer River, northwest of Morin.

In his classic revision of the Ceratopsia, Lull (1933) observed that the most distinctive generic characters of *Anchiceratops* involve the crest, which has a somewhat rectangular shape. Lull agreed that the small fontanelles and large epoccipitals were diagnostically significant, adding that a large pair of these processes of unusual form and size are situated on the squamosals posteriorly; and that the prominences described by Brown as "knob-like" are actually somewhat flattened and curved so as to be upwardly convex.

Lull observed that the skull of *Anchiceratops* is morphologically very similar to that of the smaller and geologically older *Chasmosaurus*. In both genera, the face is long and there are three horns. The nasal horn is short, located about midway between nares and orbits, and directed forward. The brow horns are large as in *Triceratops*, differing in rising upward and outward for a distance of half their length before curving forward. Lull speculated that the nasal horn apparently shifts forward in ceratopsid evolution, resulting in the lengthening of the facial region. In *Anchiceratops*, the position of this horn is about intermediate. Crest ornamentation lessens as ceratopsids evolve, the relatively early *Anchiceratops* displaying the most crest ornamentation of the Chasmosaurinae [="long-frilled" forms of his usage], the parietal fen-

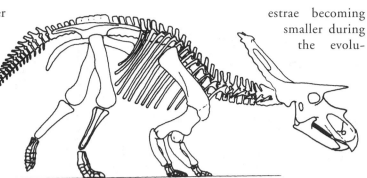
Skeleton of *Anchiceratops*, drawn by Kenneth Carpenter.

estrae becoming smaller during the evolution of this line. *Anchiceratops*, with relatively small parietal openings, could represent a precocious sideline of this lineage stemming from *Chasmosaurus belli* and reaching a dead end in the "Edmonton" Formation.

Because *Anchiceratops* fossils occur only in coaly beds, Sternberg suggested that this form dwelt in swamps. Russell and Chamney (1967), however, pointed out that Sternberg's suggestion was based upon uncollected specimens in the field without notation of their precise stratigraphic position. No evidence supports the notion that *Anchiceratops* is more common to any particular horizon, this genus probably having lived in varied environments.

Russell and Chamney observed that one small skull (UW 2419) of *Anchiceratops* has relatively heavier brow horn cores similar to those in the paratype of *A. ornatus*, a feature indicating a specific rather than ontogenetic difference. Another specimen (ROM 802), if it can be referred to *A. ornatus*, seems to have heavier brow horns and a shorter snout than *A. longirostris*. Such differences exhibit a potential for sexual dimorphism (P. Dodson, personal communication 1987).

As pointed out by Russell and Chamney, *Anchiceratops* is the most abundantly known ceratopsian in the lower Horseshoe Canyon Formation, some fourteen specimens having been collected, ranging in stratigraphic position from the upper part of member A of the formation to the lower half of member B. These specimens include the only postcranial remains, a complete skeleton (NMC [formerly GSC] 8538) lacking the skull, collected by Sternberg in 1925 at Red Deer River, near Ramsey, on display at the Canadian Museum of Nature, Ottawa.

In their review of the Neoceratosauria, Dodson and Currie (1990) stated that *Anchiceratops* appears to be the most generalized of all chamosurine taxa.

Key references: Brown (1914*b*); Dodson and Currie (1990); Lull (1933); Russell and Chamney (1967); Sternberg (1929).

Anchisaurus polyzelus, YPM 201, holotype skeleton.

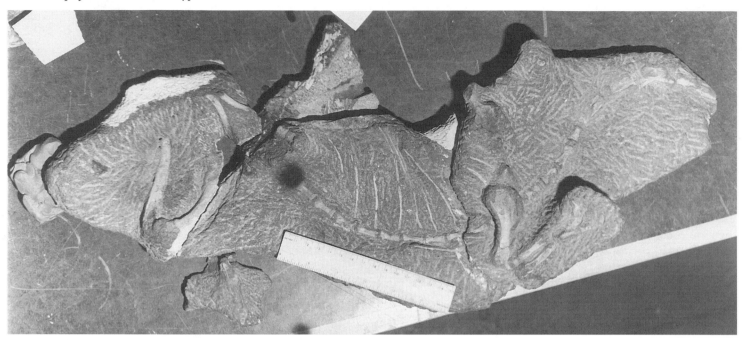

Photo by R. A. Long and S. P. Welles (neg. #73/487-44), courtesy Yale Peabody Museum of Natural History.

ANCHISAURUS Marsh 1885—(=*Amphisaurus*, *Megadactylus*, *Yaleosaurus*)

Saurischia: Sauropodomorpha: Prosauropoda: Anchisauridae.

Name derivation: Greek *anchion* = "similar" + Greek *sauros* = "lizard."

Type species: *A. polyzelus* (Hitchcock 1865).

Other species: [None.]

Occurrence: Upper (Portland) Beds, Newark Supergroup, Connecticut, Massachusetts, United States.

Age: Early Jurassic (Pleinsbachian or Toarcian).

Known material: Almost complete skeleton with skull, fragmentary skeleton.

Holotype: AC 41/109, one dorsal and four caudal vertebrae, right manus, distal ends of right radius and ulna, left femur, proximal end of left tibia, left fibula and pes, two ischia.

Diagnosis of genus: About nine maxillary and 16 dentary teeth; basipterygoid process very small; cervical vertebrae elongate; dorsal centra low; neural spines of anterior caudal vertebrae with broad bases; first metacarpal broad; manual digits I and II of subequal length; ilium with long anterior process; pubis with an open obturator foramen, distal part relatively narrow and not apron-like (Galton 1976).

Comments: The basis for the taxon Anchisauridae Marsh 1885, *Anchisaurus* was founded on a partial postcranial skeleton (AC 41/109), collected from the Longmeadow Sandstone, Newark Series, of Springfield, Hampden County, Massachusetts. The bones were discovered during blasting operations at the water shops of the United States Armory.

The discovery of these fossils was announced by E. Hitchcock (1855) and first described (but not named) by Wyman in Hitchcock's (1858*a*, 1858*b*) classic study of fossil footprints in New England. The remains were subsequently described and figured by E. Hitchcock, Jr. (1865) as *Megadactylus polyzelus* in a supplement to his father's volume. As the name *Megadactylus* proved to be preoccupied (Fitzinger 1843), the taxon was renamed *Amphisaurus* by Marsh (1877). When that name was also found to be preoccupied (Barkas 1870), Marsh (1885) renamed the genus *Anchisaurus*.

Galton (1990*a*), in a review of the Prosauropoda, observed that primitive characters exhibited in the type species *A. polyzelus* include the following: Jaw articulation of the slenderly constructed skull just slightly below the maxillary tooth-row level; small nasal; narrow lacrimal; thin prefrontal; and proportionally narrow distal apron-like part of pubis. Also, unlike the more primitive prosauropod *Thecodontosaurus*, *Anchisaurus* and the other prosauropods shared these derived characters: Dentary more than half length of mandible; trunk at least subequal to length of hindlimb (femur + tibia + third metatarsal); and massive manual digit I.

A second species, *A. colurus*, was founded upon a skull with jaws, eighteen presacral vertebrae, scapu-

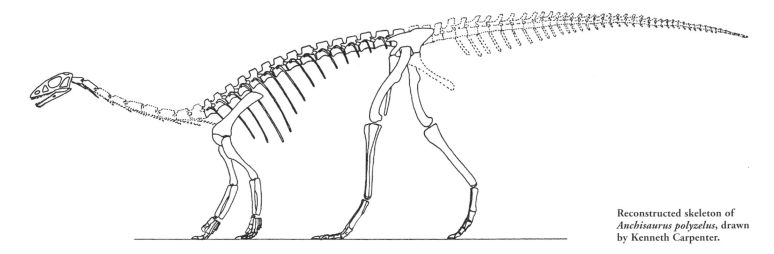

Reconstructed skeleton of *Anchisaurus polyzelus*, drawn by Kenneth Carpenter.

lacoracoid, left forelimb with manus, ilium, pubes, and right hindlimb with pes (YPM 1883), recovered from the Portland Sandstone, Newark Series, of Manchester, Hartford County, Connecticut. As noted by Marsh (1891b, 1896), this specimen constituted one of the most-perfect dinosaur skeletons that had yet been discovered, the fairly well-preserved skull and limbs still in natural position. Huene (1932) genus and species, *Yaleosaurus colurus*, which Ostrom (1970) later referred back to *Anchisaurus*. Galton (1976) interpreted the differences between both taxa as constituting sexual dimorphism, *A. polyzelus* representing the male morph and *Y. colurus* the female. At the same time, Galton (1976) referred the mate-

Anchisaurus polyzelus, life restoration by Brian Franczak.

rial from the Lower Jurassic Portland Formation of the Connecticut Valley to two monospecific genera and species, the slender-footed morph to *Anchisaurus polyzelus*, and the broad-footed morph to *Ammosaurus major*. *Anchisaurus* attained a length of about 2.5 meters (8 feet).

Notes: The first prosauropod specimen discovered in the United States (and the first fossil bone from the Triassic of the Connecticut Valley) was uncovered during blasting operations in 1818 for a well in Portland Beds, Newark Series, at East Windsor, Connecticut. The specimen (YPM 2125) includes eight pieces of matrix with fragmentary remains of caudal vertebrae, and the distal end of a left femur, with traces of the fibula and a natural mold of a portion of the tibia. Smith (1820) reported these fragmentary remains as possibly human, although tail bones were later also identified. Wyman (1855) identified these remains as reptilian, after which Lull (1912) referred them to *A. colurus*.

Galton (1976) described the femur of YPM 2125 as having a distal width of about 40 millimeters (approximately 1.55 inches) and almost no intercondylar groove. One manual carpal is very large, the first enormous. The size of the bones are intermediate between the holotypes of *A. polyzelus* and *A. colurus*. Although the forelimb is prosauropod in structure, the second through fifth metacarpals are too fragmentary to determine whether the manus belongs to *Anchisaurus* or *Ammosaurus*. According to Galton (1976), this specimen should be regarded as both generically and specifically indeterminate.

Key references: Galton (1976, 1990*a*); Hitchcock (1855, 1858*a*, 1858*b*,1865); Huene (1932); Marsh (1887, 1885, 1891b, 1896); Ostrom (1970).

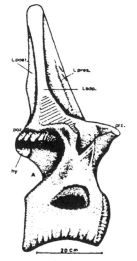

Andesaurus delgadoi, MUCPv 132, holotype posterior dorsal vertebra, lateral view. (After Calvo and Bonaparte 1991.)

ANDESAURUS
Calvo and Bonaparte 1991
Saurischia:
Sauropodomorpha:
Sauropoda:
Titanosauria:
Andesauridae.
Name derivation: "Andes [Mountains]" + Greek *sauros* = "lizard."
Type species: *A. deladoi* Calvo and Bonaparte 1991.
Other species: [None.]

Occurrence: Rio Limay Formation, Patagonia, Argentina.
Age: Late Cretaceous (Albian–Cenomanian).
Known material/holotype: MUCPv 132, partial skeleton including four articulated posterior dorsal vertebrae, 21 articulated caudal vertebrae in two corresponding sections (from anterior part and last half of tail), nearly complete left ischium, incomplete right humerus and femur, various incomplete elements.

Diagnosis of genus (as for type species): Large titanosaurid; posterior dorsal vertebrae high, with slightly opisthocoelous centrum relatively low and long (somewhat resembling that of *Argyrosaurus*); tall neural spine (as in other titanosaurids); additional hyposphene-hypantrum articulations; well-developed lamina bifurcated at inferior part; medial and distal caudal vertebrae amphyplatyan, with wide, flat, quadrangular neural spines, neural arch oriented more posteriorly than in other titanosaurids; humerus large, proportionally more gracile than in *Argyrosaurus*; pubis with relatively large proximolateral process, pubic foramen a good distance away from lateral border; ischium with small iliac peduncle (Calvo and Bonaparte 1991).

Comments: The genus *Andesaurus* was established upon a partial postcranial skeleton (MUCPv 132). Discovered by Alejandro Delgado in May 1987, the material was collected by the Museo de Ciencias Naturales of the Universidad Nacional del Comahue, in cooperation with Museo Argentina de Ciencias Naturales, from the Rio Limay Formation (Grupo Neuquén) (Albian-Cenomanian) of Neuquén, Patagonia, Argentina (Calvo and Bonaparte 1991).

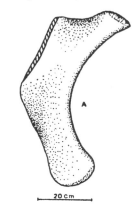

Andesaurus delgadoi, MUCPv 132, holotype left ischium, ventral view. (After Calvo and Bonaparte 1991.)

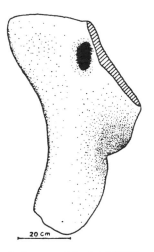

Andesaurus delgadoi, MUCPv 132, holotype right pubis, dorsoanterior view. (After Calvo and Bonaparte 1991.)

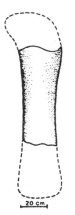 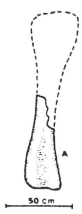

Andesaurus delgadoi,
MUCPv 132, holotype
incomplete femur, anterior
view. (After Calvo and
Bonaparte 1991.)

Andesaurus delgadoi,
MUCPv 132, holotype
incomplete right humerus,
posterior view. (After Calvo
and Bonaparte.)

Although observing similarities between some characters of the dorsal vertebrae and pubis in this species with those of a specimen referred to ?*Argyrosaurus superbus* (see Powell 1986*a*), Calvo and Bonaparte were not able to recognize any direct relationship between the two taxa. Furthermore, Calvo and Bonaparte regarded the relative primitive condition of *A. delgadoi* as warranting its own new taxon Andesaurinae, to represent a stage of titanosaurid evolution less derived than typical Senonian forms.

Key reference: Calvo and Bonaparte (1991).

ANKYLOSAURUS Brown 1908

Ornithischia: Genasauria: Thyreophora: Ankylosauria: Ankylosauridae.

Name derivation: Greek *ankulosis* = "stiffening of the joints" + Greek *sauros* = "lizard."

Type species: *A. magniventris* Brown 1908.

Other species: [None.]

Occurrence: Hell Creek Formation, Montana, Lance Formation, Wyoming, United States; Scollard Formation, Alberta, Canada.

Age: Late Cretaceous (Late Maastrichtian).

Known material: Remains of three individuals, including skulls and postcrania.

Holotype: AMNH 5895, partial skeleton with skull, scapulacoracoid, seven cervical, ten dorsal and four caudal vertebrae, ribs, dermal plates.

Diagnosis of genus (as for type species): Rostral and lateral expansion of dermal armor of nasal bones covering premaxillae and restricting external nares to small round openings located far laterally near premaxillary-maxillary suture at the margin of the mouth; beak narrower than the distance between caudalmost maxillary teeth; premaxillary area of palate

subequal in length and width; horn-like projections at caudolateral corners of the skull roof, formed by large pyramidal squamosal dermal plates; massive tail club (Coombs and Maryańska 1990).

Comments: *Ankylosaurus*, the most famous ankylosaur, and the similar *Euoplocephalus* are the only ankylosaurids known from North America.

The genus *Ankylosaurus* was founded upon an incomplete skeleton including the skull (AMNH 5895), found by Peter Kaisen in Hell Creek Beds near Gilbert Creek, north of Miles City, Valley County, Montana (Brown 1908).

As ankylosaurs were poorly understood at the time, Brown presumed that his new armored dinosaur was a Late Cretaceous member of the Stegosauria. Consequently, Brown's original skeletal reconstruction of *Ankylosaurus* was patterned after the posture of *Stegosaurus*, with a strongly arched vertebral column. Brown hypothetically, arranged the dermal plates in longitudinal rows of armor. (The holotype did not show any indication of a clubbed tail). Because of the rather obvious differences between *Ankylosaurus* and *Stegosaurus*, Brown placed the former into its own family Ankylosauridae. Armored

Ankylosaurus magniventris,
AMNH 5895, holotype skull,
dorsal view.

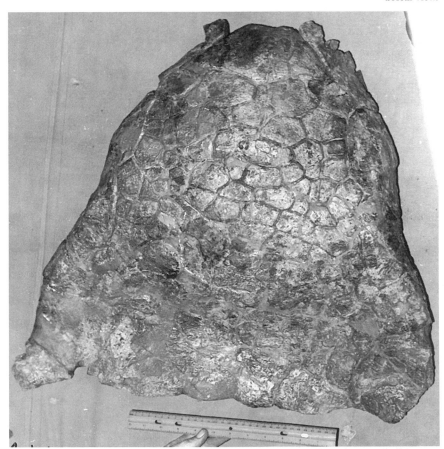

Photo by R. A. Long and S. P. Welles (neg. #73/251-28), courtesy American Museum of Natural History.

dinosaurs such as *Ankylosaurus* were later referred to the higher taxon Ankylosauria Osborn 1923.

Brown originally diagnosed *Ankylosaurus* as follows: Skull with plates of bone coossified into a continuous sculptured shield; parietal crest quite short, bordering plates embossed; nares far anteriorly; vertebral spines not greatly elevated above their respective centra; parapophysis not rising above neural canal; anterior ribs with area for attachment of uncinate processes; posterior ribs firmly coossified with their respective vertebrae; scapula and coracoid curved, coossified.

(Not all of Brown's characters are now regarded as having diagnostic significance. Coombs [1978a], in his revision of ankylosaurian families, showed that the presence of coossified dermal plates in the skull, moderately high neural spines, and the fusion of scapula and coracoid [except in *Struthiosaurus* and *Hylaeosaurus*] are common to all members of Ankylosauria.)

Brown described the dermal plates as uniformly low, ranging from one inch square to 14 inches long and 10 inches wide. All plates are asymmetrical and resembled an inverted "V" in cross-section. The larger plates are nearly flat with a low dorsal ridge near one border. In some plates, this ridge extends the entire length of the plate near the midline. Another kind of plate, which Brown positioned at the neck and posterior area of the body, has a dorsal ridge rising from its posterior end, terminating near the center at its apex. Two of the largest plates are coossified at their ventral surfaces with a thick, covered plate of bone. Two more large plates are solidly fused to heavy bone and seem to represent part of a continuous shield. All plates are channeled by vascular grooves.

Coombs observed that the nasal bone or a dermal plate fused to the dorsal margin of the nostril has

***Ankylosaurus magniventris*, AMNH 5214, tail club, dorsal view.**

laterally and anteriorly expanded over the narial opening and premaxillae, so that the small and circular nostril lies far laterally on the snout, and the premaxillae are entirely covered by bony plates.

Specimen AMNH 5214 of *A. magniventris* revealed that the large distal caudal vertebrae are modified to accommodate a bony tail club, which consists of several large bones, fused together and imbedded in the skin. Coombs observed that the long prezygapophyses and long flattened postzygapophyses of these vertebrae extensively overlap each other to immobilize the distal third of the tail. Long neural arches and low haemal arches in the distal caudals contribute to strengthening this part of the tail.

Although traditionally depicted in life restorations as a squat dinosaur with armor including large lateral spikes, and dragging a heavy clubbed tail, *Ankylosaurus* walked in a more upright position with the tail carried off the ground. As shown by Coombs,

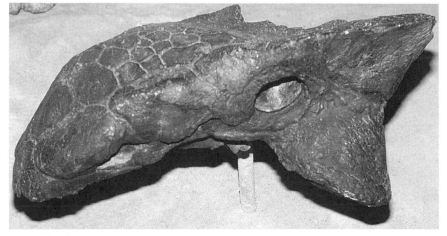

***Ankylosaurus magniventris* skull.**

no known ankylosaurids bear large lateral spikes, although the dorsal region is covered with dermal plates. These plates are set into a continuous pattern of small, flat interlocking ossicles. This armor increases in size, weight and density near the pelvic region.

In life, the armor in *Ankylosaurus* (and other ankylosaurs) probably served as a deterrent to and provided protection from even the largest tyrannosaurids. If attacked, *Ankylosaurus* could utilize its tail club as a weapon, swinging it by means of the long tail muscles to lash forcibly into the ankles of these giant predators.

As Coombs pointed out, *Ankylosaurus* is the last known ankylosaur and the largest, the maximum skull length 760 millimeters (almost 30 inches). The entire length of the animal was about 7.5 meters (25 feet), height 1.2 meters (4 feet).

Carpenter (1982*a*) referred two teeth from apparent baby ankylosaurs to *A. magniventris*. One tooth (UCMP 124399), from the Lance Formation, is unworn and undamaged. The specimen is 3.2 millimeters high and 2.7 millimeters wide, with six denticles on each side of the crown. The second specimen, a heavily worn tooth (UCMP 120195), from the Hell Creek Formation, measures 3.3 millimeters high and 2.9 millimeters wide. According to Carpenter, the heavy wear implies that baby ankylosaurids did not bite off and swallow food whole, but used their teeth to process it.

Key references: Brown (1908); Carpenter (1982*a*); Coombs (1978*a*); Coombs and Maryańska (1990); Osborn (1923).

ANODONTOSAURUS Sternberg 1929—(See *Euoplocephalus*.)
Name derivation: Greek *an* = "without" + Greek *odontos* = "teeth" + Greek *sauros* = "lizard."
Type species: *A. lambei* Sternberg 1929.

ANOPLOSAURUS Seeley 1879 [*nomen dubium*]
Ornithischia: Genasauria: Cerapoda: Ornithopoda: Iguanodontia: ?Iguanodontidae.
Name derivation: Greek *an* = "without" + Greek *oplos* = "armed" + Greek *sauros* = "lizard."
Type species: *A. curtonotus* Seeley 1879 [*nomen dubium*].
Other species: *A. major* Seeley 1879 [*nomen dubium*, in part].
Occurrence: Cambridge Greensand, England.
Age: Late Cretaceous.
Known material: Vertebrae, fragmentary postcrania, fragmentary skull material.
Holotype: SMC collection, anterior end of anterior extremity of left ramus of lower jaw, five or six cervical centra, twelve dorsal vertebrae, six sacral centra, neural arches of mostly dorsal vertebrae, portions of both coracoids, proximal end of scapula, pieces of ribs, both ends of right humerus and left femur, pieces of metatarsals, phalanges, left tibia, other fragments.
Diagnosis of genus: [None published.]
Comments: The genus *Anoplosaurus* was established upon worn fragmentary remains (SMC collection), collected from the Greensand of Cambridge, England, and obtained in 1872 by Henry Keeping for the Woodwardian Museum of the University of Cambridge.

Seeley (1879) described the genus (and type species, *A. curtonotus*) as follows: Lower jaw no more than 6 centimeters (almost 2.4 inches) long (small size suggesting a ?juvenile); symphysial union of mandibular rami apparently very narrow and short; alveolar margin almost straight; first five cervical vertebrae of similar size (about 19 centimeters, or 7.25 inches, long), the most anterior ones with somewhat depressed centrum; cervical centra becoming slightly deeper, decreasing in length posteriorly; dorsal centra of similar form, becoming slightly longer poste-

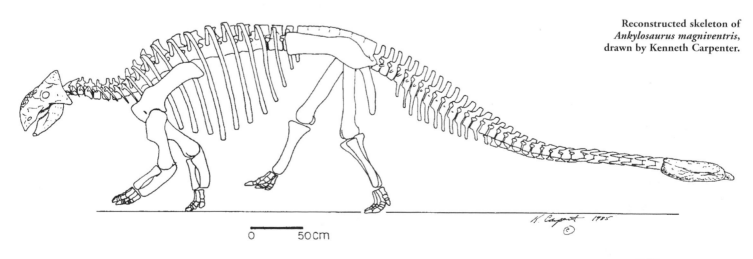

Reconstructed skeleton of *Ankylosaurus magniventris*, drawn by Kenneth Carpenter.

0   50cm

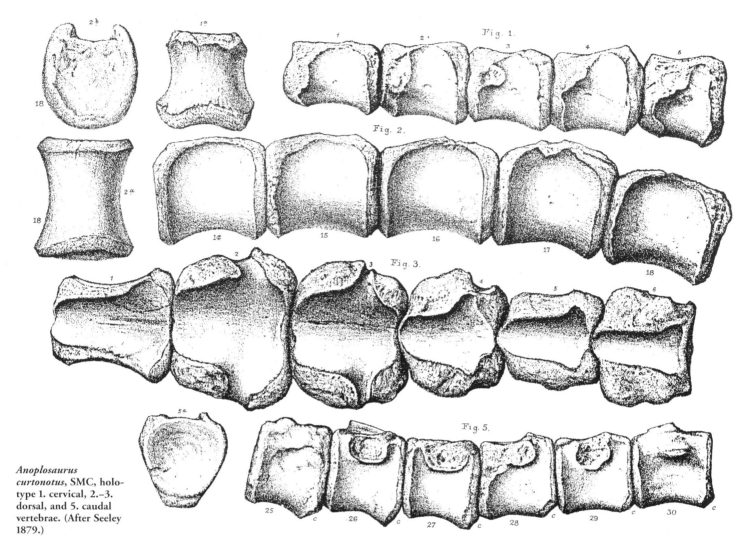

Anoplosaurus curtonotus, SMC, holotype 1. cervical, 2.–3. dorsal, and 5. caudal vertebrae. (After Seeley 1879.)

riorly, forming upward arch when in sequence; dorsal ribs all somewhat curved; six sacral vertebrae not ankylosed to sacrum (?juvenile feature) (Seeley 1879).

Seeley estimated that the humerus, when complete, was about 24 centimeters (9 inches) long, with a long and compressed radial crest running at least halfway along the length of the bone. The small, well-preserved metacarpal is about 3.6 centimeters (1.4 inches) long. The femur was probably about 30.5 centimeters (12 inches) when complete. The tibia appears to have been relatively slender.

A second species, *A. major*, was based on a cervical centrum and three caudal vertebrae, material originally included in the holotype of *Acanthopholis stereocercus* Seeley 1869, but which Seeley (1879) removed because of its similarity to *Anoplosaurus*. This material, collected from the Cambridge Greensand by W. Farren for the Woodwardian Museum, includes a cervical vertebra and three caudal vertebrae. Seeley (1879) described this species as follows: Relatively longer than *A. curtonotus*; presence of neu-

ral canal in a deep groove of vertebral centrum (suggesting this species is larger than the type species).

In their review of the Iguanodontidae and related ornithopods, Norman and Weishampel (1990) regarded both *A. curtonotus* and *A. major* as *nomina dubia*.

Key references: Norman and Weishampel (1990); Seeley (1869, 1879).

ANSERIMIMUS Barsbold 1988

Saurischia: Theropoda: Tetanurae: Coelurosauria: Maniraptora: Arctometatarsalia: Bullatosauria: Ornithomimosauria: Ornithomimidae.

Name derivation: Latin *anser* = "goose" + Greek *mimos* = "mimic."

Type species: *A. planinychus* Barsbold 1988.

Other species: [None.]

Occurrence: Nemegtskaya Svita, Bayankhongor, Mongolian People's Republic.

Age: Late Cretaceous (Late Senonian).

Known material/holotype: SPS GIN AN MPR 100/300, incomplete postcranial skeleton including scapula, partial manus, partial pes.

Diagnosis of genus (as for type species): Humerus with high, prominent deltopectoral crest; manus with dorso-ventrally compressed ungual phalanges (Barsbold 1988).

Comments: The genus *Anserimimus* was founded upon an incomplete skeleton (SPS GIN AN MPR 100/300) lacking the skull from the Nemegt Formation of Bugeen-Tsav, southwest Mongolia. The material was discovered during the late 1970s by a Joint Soviet-Mongolian Paleontological Expedition (Barsbold 1988).

According to Barbold, *A. planyhychus* differs from all other known ornithomimid species. The reinforced forelimb with a manus possessing hoof-like (widened, pointed, and flattened) unguals may have been adapted to perform more active functions usually atypical of ornithomimisaurs, in which the forelimbs were generally rather weak and probably were not used constantly in obtaining food. The forelimbs in *Anserimimus* may have offered broadened ecological possibilities, possibly adapted to scraping off relatively loose substrate or matter that could be shifted, scattered, or displaced (including soft and loose soil, and remnants of riverside and aquatic vegetation).

Barsbold noted that the occurrence of this form attests to the diversity of the Mongolian branches of the Ornithomimidae, the Asian genera (also including *Harpymimus, Archeornithomimus, Garudimimus,* and *Gallimimus*) providing a far wider morphological series in comparison to the North American forms. This series corresponds to the various Mongolian niches and also reflects the various stages of the evolution of the Ornithomimosauria.

Key reference: Barsbold (1988).

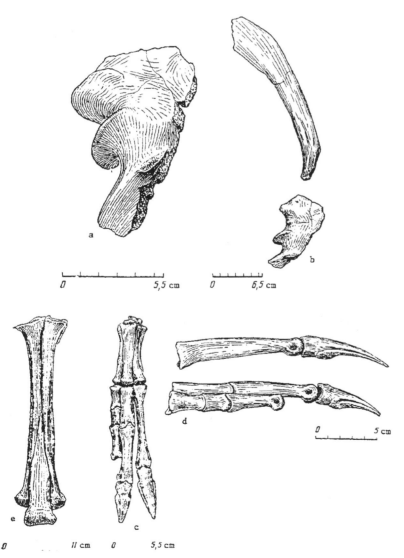

Anserimimus planinychus, SPS GINAN MAR 100/300, holotype a. fragment of left scapulacoracoid, b. fragments of left scapulacoracoid (above—dorsal process of scapula), c. right manus with distal carpus, d. right manual digits, e. right metatarsus. (After Barsbold 1988.)

Antarctosaurus

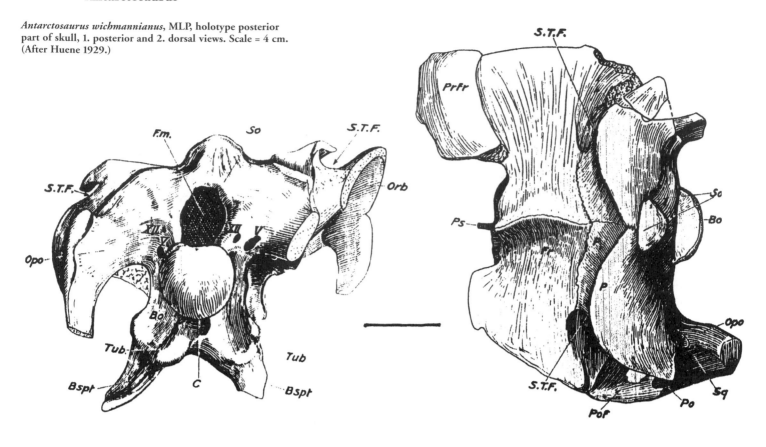

Antarctosaurus wichmannianus, MLP, holotype posterior part of skull, 1. posterior and 2. dorsal views. Scale = 4 cm. (After Huene 1929.)

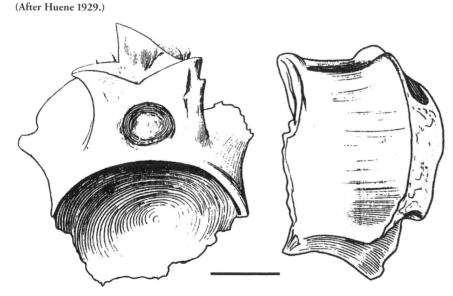

Antarctosaurus wichmannianus, MLP, holotype cervical vertebra, posterior and ventral views. Scale = 8 cm. (After Huene 1929.)

ANTARCTOSAURUS   Huene 1927

Saurischia: Sauropodomorpha: Sauropoda:
  Titanosauria: Titanosauridae.

Name derivation: "Antarctic" + Greek *sauros* =
  "lizard."

Type species: *A. wichmannianus* Huene 1929.

Other species: ?*A. giganteus* Huene 1929, ?*A. septen-trionalis* Huene 1932, ?*A. jaxarticus* Riabinin 1938 [*nomen dubium*], ?*A. brasiliensis* Arid and Vizotto 1972.

Occurrence: Castillo Formation, Bajo Barreal Formation, Laguna Palacios Formation, Allen (or Rio Colorado) Formation, Rio Negro, Rio Neuquen Formation, Neuquen, Bajo Barreal Formation, Chubut, Argentina; Asencio Formation, Palmites, Uruguay; Vinitas Formation, Coquimbo, Chile; Bauru Formation, Sao Paulo, Goias, Minas, Gerais, Brazil.

Age: Late Cretaceous (Campanian–Maastrichtian).

Known material: Partial skeleton, with some cranial material and most of limbs, femora, pubis, fragmentary postcrania.

Holotype: National Museum (Buenos Aires) 6804, partial skull including braincase and mandible, cervical vertebra, scapula, radius, ulna, pelvis, hindleg bones.

  Diagnosis of genus: [No modern diagnosis published.]

  Comments: *Antarctosaurus* is the largest known sauropod from South America. The generic name was first published by Huene (1927) in a review of then known sauropods; at the time, Huene neither described the genus nor assigned it a specific name.

  The genus was founded upon a very incomplete skull and some postcranial material (National Museum 6804), supposedly belonging to the same very large individual, recovered from Rio Negro, General Roca, Argentina (Huene 1929).

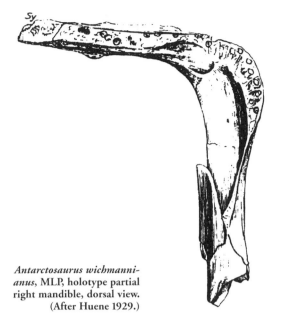

Antarctosaurus wichmannianus, MLP, holotype partial right mandible, dorsal view. (After Huene 1929.)

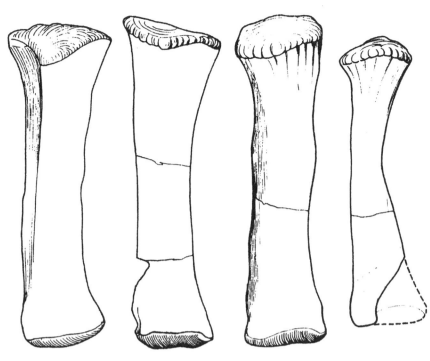

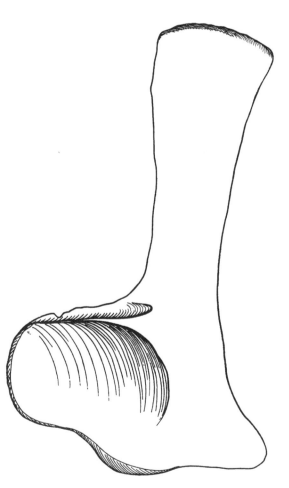

Antarctosaurus wichmannianus, MLP, holotype left scapula. (After Huene 1929.)

Huene (1929) originally diagnosed *Antarctosaurus* as follows: Relatively slender; skull high posteriorly, with large orbits and apparently short facial region with a broad snout; parietals and frontals short, wide; basipterygoid process long; scapula narrow, with straight posterior border and prominent deltoid process; humerus rather slender; metacarpals increasing in length from first to fourth, fifth slightly shorter than the fourth; hindlimb bones slim; femur with fourth trochanter slightly above mid-shaft; double muscle insertions on fibula located side by side at upper two-thirds of the bone; fourth metacarpal most slender in metatarsal series. Type species, *A. wichmannianus*, was described by Huene (1929) as a moderately heavy form that reached a length of about 18 meters (about 60 feet).

A second species, *A. giganteus*, was based on a right and left femur, incomplete left pubis, two distal caudal vertebrae, distal portion of a tibia, numerous rib fragments, and six unidentifiable, poorly preserved bones from the Neuquén Formation of Neuquén, Argentina. As measured by Huene (1929), the right femur is 2.22 meters (about 7.5 feet) long, left humerus 2.31 meters (about 8 feet), distinguishing this species as one of the largest [then] known dinosaurs. Paul (1988*a*) calculated the weight of this species to be from about 40–50 metric tons (about 45–nearly 56 tons).

The species *A. septentrionalis* was based on an incomplete braincase, scapulae, forelimb, and possible sternal bone, from the Lameta Beds of Madhya Pradesh, India (Huene 1932). Huene (in Huene and

Antarctosaurus wichmannianus, MLP, holotype metacarpals V, IV, III, II. (After Huene 1929.)

Courtesy The Field Museum (neg. #50630).

Antarctosaurus wichmannianus, left tibia.

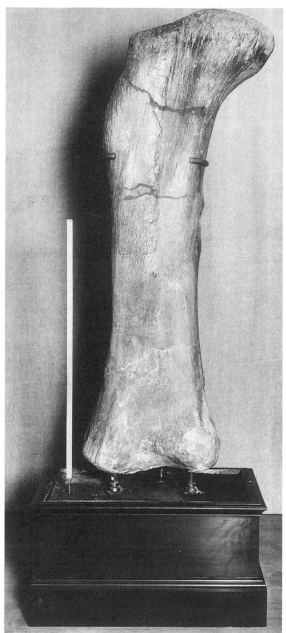

*Antarctosaurus wichmanni-
anus*, FMNH P13019
[P13326], right femur.

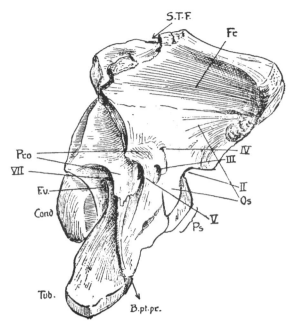

"*Antarctosaurus*" *septentrionalis*, holotype basicranium.
(After Huene and Matley 1933.)

Matley 1933) diagnosed this species as follows: Large
but slender; skull with very short base, especially the
basisphenoid, latter characterized by large, broadly-
oval median channel; supraoccipital and frontal crest
flatter than in *A. wichmannianus*; eighth caudal vertebra intermediate in shape between *Titanosaurus* and
Argyrosaurus; anterior hemapophyses deeply bifurcated, very long, with broader blade than *Argyrosaurus*; only anterior hemapophysial facets visible in
centrum; ribs very broad; scapula very long (relatively
much longer and with quite different shape than in
A. wichmannianus), slender, with blade forming slight
angle at middle of its upper border; humerus very

long and slender; lower forelimb and femur similar
to those in *A. wichmannianus*.

According to McIntosh (1990*b*) in his review of
sauropod dinosaurs, the assignment of both *A. giganteus* and *A. spetentrionalis* to *Antarctosaurus* is doubtful; also, a large associated caudal vertebra referred to
A. septentrionalis has a flat-sided centrum not unlike
that in *Titanosaurus*, this form possibly representing
a large species of that genus.

McIntosh pointed out that the skull figured by
Huene as belonging to this genus is largely hypothetical, restored after that of *Diplodocus*, mostly based
upon similarities in the mandible and weak teeth.
According to McIntosh, from what cranial material
is preserved, the skull of *Antarctosaurus* is distinguished by a very slender parasphenoid, large prefrontal whose articular surface with the frontal takes
up more than half of that bone's rostral margin (suggesting a nasal very different from that of *Camarasaurus* and *Diplodocus*), and a mandible that is
square in front.

McIntosh briefly described the postcrania of
A. wichmannianus as follows: Scapula with long, slender shaft little expanded distally; large angle between
axis and muscle ridge; coracoid articulation with a
short, sharp central deflection; humerus apparently
long and slender; metacarpals relatively slender;
ischium with a long, slender shaft, not nearly as broad
a distal end as in *Alamosaurus*; ratio of tibia to femur
0.67; metatarsals relatively stout, third and fourth
longest, second relatively much shorter, first much
longer than in *Macrurosaurus*.

More recently, Jacobs, Winkler, Downs and Gomani (1993), in their paper on the titanosaurid *Malawisaurus* (see entry), questioned the traditional assignment of *Antarctosaurus* to the Titanosauridae, which had been so done because Huene assigned the lower jaw fragment and teeth to that group. This led to the persistent misconception that titanosaurid and diplodocid skulls were similar in their morphology. In *Antarctosaurus*, the teeth are pencil-like but slightly flattened, and the jaw has an anteriorly restricted tooth row with an abrupt angle toward the symphysis, characters similar to *Diplodocus*. However, in the jaw of *Malawisaurus*, the teeth are narrow but not pencil-like. Jacobs *et al.* considered it less likely that titanosaurids and diplodocids evolved characters such as these in parallel, while also noting that none of the elements of *Antarctosaurus* figured by Huene exhibit any derived characters of titanosaurids. For these reasons, Jacobs *et al.* regarded *Antarctosaurus* as a possible diplodocid, a group not otherwise known from the Late Cretaceous of South America.

Excavations in 1975 by Bonaparte (1982) into the Laguna Palacios Formation (Senonian) of southern Chubut, Patagonia, yielded fossils of a very large *Antarctosaurus* individual. These remains constitute the first complete and associated bones recorded pertaining to this genus, including six dorsal vertebrae (revealing for the first time the vertebral morphology of this genus), scapula, humerus, both radii and ulnae, complete pubis, incomplete femur, tibia, fibula, and astragalus.

Notes: Jacobs *et al.* suggested that a sauropod maxilla, with a short and very high snout, figured but not identified by Huene and Matley in their paper on *A. septentrionalis*, is that of a titanosaurid. In this specimen, the maxillary-premaxillary suture is entirely beneath the external nares, a feature known only in one other sauropod specimen, the premaxilla of *Malawisaurus*.

Fossil eggs from Deccan, Peninsular India, attributed to *Antarctosaurus* by Vianey-Liaud, Jain and Shani (1988) were assigned by Mikhailov (1991) to the egg family Megathoolithidae, which Mikhailov diagnosed as follows: Tubospherulithic morphotype; tubocanaliculate pore system; sculptured surface; compactituberculate ornamentation; subspherical eggs; "thick" eggshell of 1.5 to 2.5 (possibly more) millimeters.

A portion of a large radius was collected from the Los Blanquitos Formation, Arroya Morterito, southern end of La Candelaria Hills region, Province of Salta, Argentina. Bonaparte and Bossi (1967) referred this specimen to *Antarctosaurus* sp. Powell (1979) noted that the bone differs significantly from the radius of *Antarctosaurus*, apparently representing a new genus of sauropod belonging to an undetermined higher taxon.

Key references: Bonaparte (1982); Bonaparte and Bossi (1967); Huene (1929, 1932, 1956); Huene and Matley (1933); Jacobs, Winkler, Downs and Gomani (1993); McIntosh (1990*b*); Paul (1988*a*); Vianey-Liaud, Jain and Shani (1988).

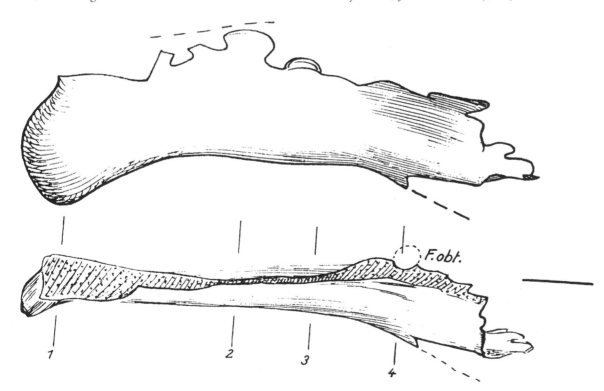

Antarctosaurus giganteus, AC 2300, holotype partial left pubis, dorsal and lateral views. Scale = 20 cm. (After Huene 1929.)

ANTRODEMUS   Leidy 1870 [*nomen dubium*]—
(See *Allosaurus*.)

Name derivation: Greek *antron* = "cavern" [or
Greek *antros* = "strong"] + Greek *demas* =
"framed."

Type species: *A. valens* (Leidy 1870) [*nomen
dubium*].

APATODON   Marsh 1877 [*nomen dubium*]—(See
Allosaurus.)

Name derivation: Greek *apatelos* = "deceptive" +
Greek *odous* = "tooth."

Type species: *A. mirus* Marsh 1877 [*nomen
dubium*].

APATOSAURUS   Marsh 1877—(=*Brontosaurus*,
Elosaurus; =?*Atlantosaurus*)

Saurischia: Sauropodomorpha: Sauropoda:
Diplodocidae: Diplodocinae.

Name derivation: Greek *apatelos* = "deceptive" +
Greek *sauros* = "lizard."

Type species: *A. ajax* Marsh 1877.

Other species: *A. excelsus* (Marsh 1879), *A. louisae*
Holland 1915, *A. yahnahpin* Filla and Redman
1994.

Occurrence: Morrison Formation, Colorado,
Wyoming, Utah, Oklahoma, United States.

Age: Late Jurassic–?Early Cretaceous (Kimmeridgian–Tithonian; ?Neocomian–?Hauterivian).

Apatosaurus ajax, YPM 1860,
holotype sacrum.

Photo by R. A. Long and S. P. Welles (neg. #73/464-47), courtesy Yale Peabody
Museum of Natural History.

Photo by R. A. Long and S. P. Welles (neg. #73/493-34), courtesy Yale Peabody
Museum of Natural History.

Aptosaurus ajax, **YPM 1860, holotype cervical vertebra.**

Known material: Ten partial skeletons, two with
partial crania, hundreds of postcranial elements,
adults and juveniles.

Holotype: YPM 1860, sacrum, vertebrae.

Diagnosis of genus: Similar to *Diplodocus* and
Barosaurus, though bones (especially those of neck
and forelimb) are much more robust, caudal vertebrae
shorter and less specialized, forked chevrons less
developed (McIntosh 1990*b*).

Diagnoses of *A. excelsus* and *A. louisae* [no modern diagnoses published].

Diagnosis of *A. yahnahpin*: Closest to *A. excelsus*, differing in retention of following primitive characters: greatly expanded upper scapular blade; scapular spine (deltoid ridge) perpendicular to long axis of
scapular blade; coracoid shallow, not enlarged centrally; humerus with very long narrow shaft; ?addi-
tional primitive character, retention of very long cervical ribs (Filla and Redman 1994).

Comments: *Apatosaurus* represents the classic
popular conception a dinosaur, usually appearing in
nontechnical books (and in the media) under the better known though incorrect name "*Brontosaurus*."
The genus was established on a sacrum and some vertebrae (YPM 1860), discovered by Arthur Lakes in the
Morrison Formation at Jefferson County, Morrison,
Colorado. This material was subsequently described
(though not figured) by Marsh (1877*d*).

Apatosaurus ajax, YPM 1840, holotype f *Atlantosaurus immanus*, 1. left pubis and ischium (scale = 40 cm.), 2. left femur, inner view, 2a., proximal end, 3. left femur, front view, 3a., distal end (scale = 32 cm). (After Marsh 1878.)

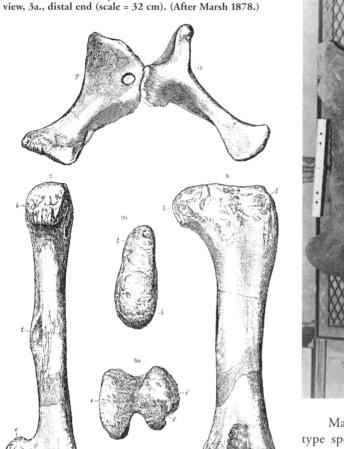

Photo by R. A. Long and S. P. Welles (neg. #73/464-3), courtesy Yale Peabody Museum of Natural History.

Apatosaurus excelsus, YPM 1981, holotype sacrum of *Brontosaurus amplus*.

Marsh originally distinguished *Apatosaurus* (and type species, *A. ajax*) from the earlier-described *Atlantosaurus* by the sacrum, *Atlantosaurus* having three coossified vertebrae, *Apatosaurus* four. Marsh estimated the length of *A. ajax* to be between 50 and 60 feet, the height over 30 feet.

Apatosaurus ajax, life restoration by Brian Franczak.

Paleontologist G. R. Wieland with skeleton of *Apatosaurus excelsus*, YPM 1980, holotype of *Brontosaurus excelsus*, skull hypothetical. In foreground is skeleton of juvenile *Camarasaurus*, to right giant sea turtle *Archelon*.

Marsh (1878*a*) then described a partial skeleton (YPM 1840) from Colorado, including a femur measuring about 1.7 meters (nearly 6 feet), as *Atlantosaurus immanis*, stating that the femur represented the largest land animal yet known, possibly approaching a total length of more than 29 meters (100 feet). Later, Berman and McIntosh (1978) regarded this specimen as belonging to *A. ajax*.

In 1879, W. H. Reed and E. G. Ashley found the remains of two quite large adult sauropods at Como Bluff, Wyoming. The more perfect of these specimens was a nearly complete skeleton (YPM 1980) found in about the same position the animal was in when it died. The skeleton, which lacked a skull, included the first few cervical vertebrae, the posterior half of the tail, both ulnae, left radius, and bones of both manus and pes except for the astragalus. (This, one of the most complete sauropod skeletons discovered up to that time, was mounted for display at the Yale Peabody Museum of Natural History.) Marsh (1879*b*) used these two skeletons as the basis for the new sauropod genus *Brontosaurus*, naming the more complete skeleton *B. excelsus* and the other *A. amplus*. The latter species was based on the greater portion of

a skeleton (YPM 1981). Marsh (1881c), who did not figure the specimen, later distinguished *A. amplus* from *B. excelsus* by four characters no longer considered diagnostic.

Marsh (1879*b*) accompanied his original description of *Brontosaurus* with the first published reconstruction of a sauropod skeleton, the missing bones based on *Camarasaurus*. Marsh (1879*b*, 1896) distinguished *Brontosaurus* from other sauropods by various features including its immense size. However, Marsh (1879*b*) did not realize the true length of the tail, estimating the total number of caudal vertebrae as slightly more than half the number known today. As later revealed by Holland (1915*a*), there were up to 82 caudals, resulting in an extremely long tail terminating in a "whiplash."

Riggs (1903*b*) reexamined the type specimens of both *Apatosaurus* and *Brontosaurus*, as well as an incomplete but well-preserved skeleton (FM 7163). The latter specimen had been collected by a Field Columbian Museum field team led by H. W. Menke in 1901 from the Grand River Valley (at a site that became known as "Dinosaur Hill," commemorated in 1938 by a stone monument with a bronze dedica-

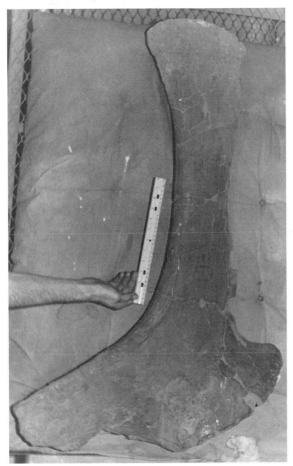

Apatosaurus excelsus, YPM 1981, holotype ischium of *Brontosaurus amplus*.

tion plaque) near Fruita, Colorado. This skeleton (FM P25112) lacked the skull, neck, forelimbs, feet, and latter part of the tail. The right fifth rib had an enlargement of the shaft because of an imperfectly healed fracture, while the adjacent rib showed the result of an unhealed similar fracture. (According to Moodie 1923, this injury may have been caused by falling, bumping a tree, or colliding with another dinosaur.) This skeleton was mounted for exhibition at the Field Columbian Museum. In 1933, the skeleton was moved to the institution's (now The Field Museum) new location. The missing parts, most of them from another individual (FM P27021), were added to the skeleton in 1958.

Based on the above three specimens, Riggs concluded that the holotype of *A. ajax* represented a young individual and that the differences between *Apatosaurus* and *Brontosaurus* were ontogenetic. Riggs observed that the sacrum in both forms comprises three primary and two secondary sacral vertebrae.

The primary sacrals are coossified at their centra, zygapophyses, and spines. The secondary sacrals remain free until the animal reaches maturity, when they coossify by centra and zygapophyses with the true sacrals. In the adult "*Brontosaurus*" (but not the juvenile *Apatosaurus*) all five sacrals connect by sacral ribs and diapophyses with the ilia. Riggs made *Brontosaurus* a junior synonym of *Apatosaurus* and referred the Fruita skeleton to *A. excelsus*, the latter generic name having priority according to the rules of the International Code of Zoological Nomenclature. Still, the name "*Brontosaurus*" persists in public usage. Indeed, because the name "*Brontosaurus*" is so well known, both "*Brontosaurus*" and *Apatosaurus* have the same author, and the type specimen defining *Brontosaurus* is so nearly complete, Bakker (1986), in his book *The Dinosaur Heresies*, argued that the rule should be waived in this case in favor of the slightly newer name (it has not been).

Over the years, a total of seven species have been referred to *Apatosaurus* and "*Brontosaurus*." According

Apatosaurus excelsus, YPM 1981, holotype humerus of *Brontosaurus amplus*.

Apatosaurus excelsus, YPM 1981, holotype tibia of *Brontosaurus amplus*.

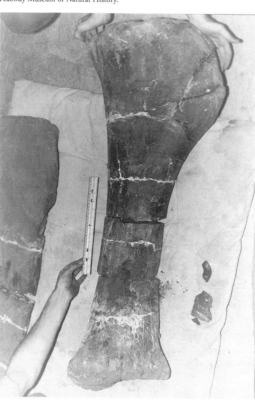

Apatosaurus excelsus, CM 566, holotype scapula, fibula, and femur of *Elosaurus parvus*.

to McIntosh (1990*b*) in his review of the Sauropoda, the relatively slender, adult Upper Morrison Formation species, *A. ajax* (from measurements of the immense holotype of "*Atlantosaurus*" *immanis*), may have been as much as 15 percent larger than the more massive, Lower Morrison Formation *A. excelsus*, and should provisionally be considered a separate species. Also, according to McIntosh (1990*a*), three species (*A. laticollis* Marsh 1879, *A. minimus* Mook 1917, and ?*A. alenquerensis* Lapparent and Zbyszewski 1957) should no longer be regarded as valid species of *Apatosaurus*. McIntosh (1990*b*) noted that "*A. minimus*" seems to be a cetiosaurid, while ?*A. alenquerensis* should be tentatively referred to *Camarasaurus*.

A. yahnahpin was based on a partial postcranial skeleton (TATE-001) collected from the Bertha Quarry, in the lower third (Brushy Basin Member) of the Morrison Formation, in southeastern Wyoming. (This quarry has also yielded the single shed tooth of a crocodile and a metatarsal of an adult dryosaur.) The holotype constituted the first sauropod specimen to possess definite gestralia ribs. Due to the burial position of the specimen, the gestralia were preserved virtually in place, situated behind a pair of sternal plates, just anterior to the distal end of the pubis. (Earlier sauropod excavations had yielded disarticulated bones that were described as probable ges-

tralia [Marsh 1888; Hatcher 1901, 1903], although no definite association with an animal or placement of the bones in a skeleton were possible.) As the sand grains of the quarry were tightly packed and resisted vertical compression following burial, most of the elements in the type specimen suffered only a small amount of post-depositional distortion (Filla and Redman 1994).

Filla and Redman noted that the set of gestralia indicate that the dinosaur's body was further strengthened by a very muscular, reinforced rectus abdominus muscle; that the long cervical ribs, heavy split neural spines, and bihemispherical shape of the posterior cervical centra combined to enhance the lateral bracing of the neck; and that extensive shoulder musculature, determined by humerus and scapulacoracoid structure, implies a quite powerful and flexible forelimb. These features would have resulted in a stoutly built animal capable of such dynamic and forceful behavior as running, rearing up on the hind legs to feed, engaging in territorial or defensive combating, and neck "butting" during courtship (Bakker 1986).

Furthermore, Filla and Redman speculated that the gestralia basket may have served as a protective shield, but also have contributed to the workings of the respiratory system.

Sauropod skulls are rarely preserved in association with their postcranial skeletons. Since the type specimen of *Brontosaurus excelsus* did not include the skull, Marsh (1879*b*) arbitrarily gave it a *Camarasaurus* type skull found some four miles away from the postcranial remains. Thus, until more recent years, *Apatosaurus* has been traditionally portrayed with a boxy *Camarasaurus*-like head. However, as shown by Berman and McIntosh (1978), features of the skeleton, including the very long neck and "whiplash" tail, suggest affinities with *Diplodocus*.

In 1909, Earl Douglass began excavating a mostly articulated (and the most complete) skeleton (CM 3018) of *Apatosaurus*, at the Carnegie Quarry, later to become Dinosaur National Monument, near Jensen, Utah. Holland (1915*b*) described this skeleton as the holotype of new species *A. louisae*. A second skeleton (CM field no. 40) of the same species, though a 20 percent smaller adult, was found next to the first specimen. Above the neck of the smaller skeleton was found a more narrow *Diplodocus*-like skull (CM 11162). Holland (1915*b*) challenged the classic Marsh reconstruction with its *Camarasaurus*-type skull, concluding that the *Diplodocus*-like skull was actually that of *Apatosaurus*.

Holland had contemplated using the *Diplodocus*-like skull when the type skeleton of *A. louisae* was mounted at the Carnegie Museum of Natural History, but was apparently dissuaded from doing so by Henry Fairfield Osborn, who favored Marsh's *Camarasaurus*-like skull interpretation. Rather than mount the skeleton with a skull he believed wrong, Holland

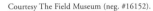

Courtesy The Field Museum (neg. #16152).

Holotype articulated vertebrae (FMNH 25107) of *Brachiosaurus altithorax* as found *in situ*; this and *Apatosaurus excelsus* were two giant sauropods from Western Colorado described by Elmer S. Riggs.

Apatosaurus

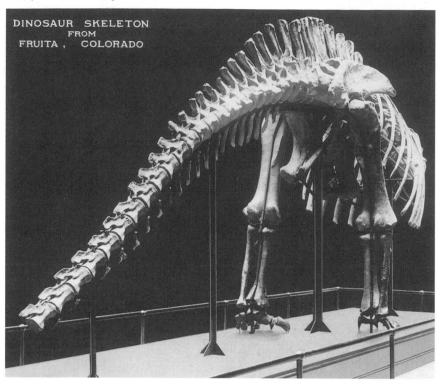

DINOSAUR SKELETON
FROM
FRUITA, COLORADO

Apatosaurus excelsus, FMNH P25112, partial skeleton from Fruita, Colorado, mounted at the Field Columbian Museum.

left it headless. The skeleton remained without a head for twenty years until, after Holland's death in 1932, it was given the traditional cast of a *Camarasaurus* skull (CM 12020).

Berman and McIntosh eventually settled the controversy by demonstrating that the diplodocid skull (CM 11162) was indeed the probable skull of *Apatosaurus*, perhaps belonging to the type specimen of *A. louisae*. The skull, lacking teeth and the lower jaw, closely resembles that of *Diplodocus*. The main differences between the skulls are in subtle proportions mostly in the palate, quadrate and braincase, and in structure, although some differences in CM 11162 could be due to postmortem distortion.

McIntosh (1990*b*) briefly described the genus *Apatosaurus* as follows: Skull similar to that in *Diplodocus*, with slightly broader muzzle, shorter quadrate and basipterygoid process (see below); teeth apparently typically peg-like; 15 cervical vertebrae; atlas with single-headed rib; centra opisthocoelous with well-developed pleurocoels, short (compared to other diplodocids), cervical vertebrae 10 and 11 longest; V-shaped cleavage in neural spine beginning at about cervical 6, becoming very pronounced in rest of cervical series; cervical ribs strikingly robust; ten dorsal vertebrae, with centra having well-developed pleuro-

coels, opisthocoelous except beyond the first where cranial ball is much reduced, appearing only on upper half of centrum; spines increasing in height, becoming very high at sacrum; transverse processes directed horizontally; parapophysis below pleurocoel on dorsal 1, migrates upward on centrum reaching arch by dorsal 4; five sacral centra firmly fused in adult, with deep pleurocoels; (as in *Diplodocus*, spines very high, sacrals 2 and 3 fusing clear to top; tail with 82 caudal vertebrae (Holland 1915*b*); first few caudals with elaborate wing-like ribs, ?perforated; amphicoelous centra without pleurocoels; proximal ones with rounded V-shape below; midcaudals elongate (not as markedly as in *Diplodocus* and *Barosaurus*); neural arch decreasing regularly in size, disappearing between caudals 35 and 40; last 40 caudals biconvex bony rods of "whiplash"; proximal chevrons bridged over hemal canal; middle chevrons forked, diplodocid type but smaller; scapula with long slender blade only slightly expanded at distal end; angle between ridge and blade broader than in *Diplodocus*; coracoid quadrangular; forelimb bones relatively short and massive, humerus to femur ratio of 0.64, ulna to humerus 0.70; ulna with proximal more greatly expanded than in *Diplodocus*; carpus (Hatcher 1902) replaced by single element lying above metacarpals II-IV; metacarpals short, heavy (metacarpus to humerus ratio of 0.25); phalangeal formula of manus 2-2-1-1-1, with small phalanx 1–2 present in some individuals; pelvis resembling that in *Diplodocus*, but more robust; slightly-developed (less so than in *Diplodocus* and *Barosaurus*) ambiens process on upper border of pubis; distal ends of ischia meet side by side, thickened dorsoventrally to greater extent than in any other known sauropod; hindlimb bones sturdy, tibia to femur ratio of 0.60; calcaneum absent; metatarsals short, robust, metatarsus to tibia ratio 0.21.

Apatosaurus is one of the larger sauropods, averaging more than 23 meters (76.5 feet) in length, the holotype of "*B.*" *excelsus* 4.5 meters (over 15 feet) high at the hips. Colbert (1962), based on the mounted skeleton displayed at the American Museum of Natural History and the relative amount of water displaced by a submersed scale model, estimated a living adult *Apatosaurus* to average from 27.87 to 32.42 metric tons (30.80 to 35.80) tons. Anderson, Hall-Martin and Russell (1985) estimated the weight of the animal represented by the holotype of *A. louisae*, using a model based on that skeleton, as 35 metric tons (almost 40 tons) (see also Russell 1987). Paul (1988*a*), again utilizing skeletal material (including the largest *Apatosaurus* specimen, incomplete femur YPM 1840), and also more accurate and less bulky scale models, calculated the maximum weight as about 20.5 metric tons (23 tons).

Chief Preparator of Fossils Orville L. Gilpin ca. 1958 reconstructing *Apatosaurus excelsus* cervical series (FMNH P27021), with *Camarasaurus* skull (cast of CM 12020).

In a study of the paleoecology of the Morrison Formation, Dodson, Bakker and Behrensmeyer (1983) found that skeletons of *Apatosaurus* are the least abundant in that formation and the least likely to be found near other individuals of that genus, this suggesting that these dinosaurs lived alone rather than in herds.

Traditionally, *Apatosaurus* had been portrayed as mostly aquatic. According to this idea, introduced by Marsh (1884*a*) based on the narial placement in *Diplodocus*, such animals were so heavy that they could not walk on land. Presumably, the water buoyantly supported their massive bulk while also offering protection from land-roaming theropods. Modern paleontologists, however, tend to regard sauropods as primarily land-based. In a study of sauropod habits and habitats, Coombs (1975) showed that the pillar-like legs and (following Riggs 1904) short, stout feet were not designed for swimming but rather to support great weight on land. Coombs added that, as

Apatosaurus louisae, CM 3018, holotype skeleton, with probable skull CM 11162.

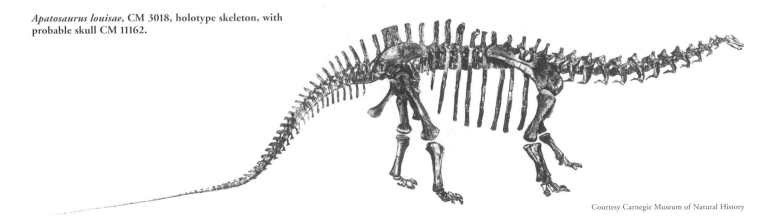

Apatosaurus

Apatosaurus louisae, CM 11162, probable skull on mounted holotype skeleton CM 3018.

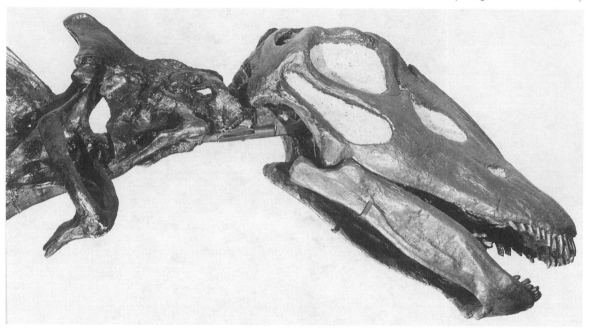

Apatosaurus excelsus partial skeleton (FMNH P25112) exhibited during the late 1940s–early 1950s in the old "Hall 38," (formerly named) "Chicago Natural History Museum." Among other specimens displayed is holotype (FMNH 25107) of *Brachiosaurus altithorax*.

Composite skeleton (FMNH P27021 and P25112, skull cast of CM 11162) of *Apatosaurus excelsus*, remounted in more dynamic pose for new "DNA to Dinosaurs" exhibit.

Apatosaurus excelsus **skeleton (FMNH P25112) being remounted in 1921 for exhibition at the new Field Museum of Natural History.**

shown by trackways, sauropods did wade and swim on occasion.

Further evidence supporting a mostly terrestrial lifestyle was offered by Dodson *et al.*, who pointed out that large Morrison Formation herbivorous dinosaurs like *Apatosaurus* (also *Camarasaurus*, *Diplodocus*, *Stegosaurus* and, to a lesser extent, *Camptosaurus*) occur throughout the complete range of fossiliferous sedimentary environments, strongly suggesting that the activities of such dinosaurs were not restricted to permanent bodies of water. More likely, an adult *Apatosaurus*, the highly articulated remains of which were discovered in well-oxidized overbank sediments, was active on a dry floodplain just before its death. Unlikely was the possibility of its bulky remains having been transported from a body of water eventually to reach a floodplain. Bakker (1986), noted that *Apatosaurus* remains are almost always found in deposits where those of water animals are rare or altogether absent, and that frequently mixed among their fossil bones are the shed or broken teeth of terrestrial predators.

In his book *Dinosaurs*, Hotton (1963) noted that an animal the size of a sauropod would require substantial energy to move its massive body, and suggested that the long neck might have evolved as a mechanism to provide a means of conserving body movement. The neck, moving about in the fashion of a vacuum cleaner hose, could have covered a wide feeding area, allowing the creature to consume more food, while the body remained in a stationary position. Bakker (1971) envisioned *Apatosaurus* living in forests and on plains, feeding on coarse terrestrial vegetation. The dinosaur's lifestyle may be compared to that of the elephant, its long neck utilized like a construction crane, enabling *Apatosaurus* to consume plants from the edge of rivers and lakes without having to step into the mud.

Osborn (1915b) was the first author to postulate that *Apatosaurus* could rise up on its hind legs, a concept now accepted by some modern paleontologists. Osborn imagined sauropods rearing up to defend themselves against theropod aggressors, utilizing their frontlimbs as weapons. Assuming a bipedal pose, as depicted by Bakker (1971), would also raise the animal for high browsing. However, this concept of bipedal sauropods has more recently been challenged by Rothschild and Berman (1991) (see *Diplodocus* entry).

As the *Apatosaurus* head is so diminutive in comparison to the rest of body, there has been speculation as to how the animal could take in enough fodder to sustain its size, and then, as sauropods did not masticate, how that food was processed. Bakker (1986) noted that highly polished pebbles, found [by William L. Stokes] scattered around the rib cages of some sauropod skeletons, may be gizzard stones. Swallowed, these stones would have lined the gizzard, becoming a powerful grinding mill to process the food. A huge sauropod could, utilizing a sophisticated gizzard, process enough fodder to sustain a high metabolism, good evidence, according to Bakker (1986), to support true endothermy in dinosaurs. Bakker (1986) argued that *Apatosaurus* could very well have eaten very tough vegetation and was possibly also equipped with a rearward fermentation vat. As with modern-day rearward fermenters (like elephants), the abdominal ribcage in *Apatosaurus* is compact, and the ribs over the belly arch widely outward from their respective vertebrae, indications that this dinosaur may have been similarly equipped.

Farlow (1987a) suggested that very large dinosaurs like *Apatosaurus* probably ate rather coarse and fibrous fodder. The animals' large size was most likely enhanced by having very low mass-specific daily metabolic needs, their food probably digested by a symbiotic microflora housed in the fermentation

Photo by R. A. Long and S. P. Welles (neg. #73-96), courtesy Carnegie Museum of Natural History.

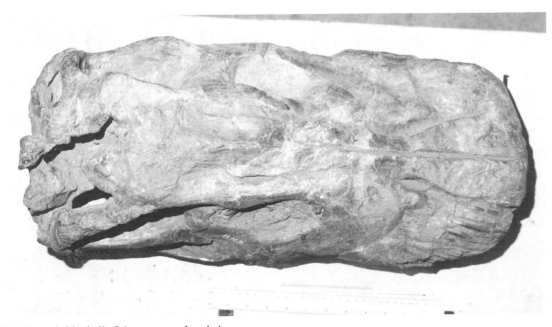

CM 11162, probable skull of *Apatosaurus*, dorsal view.

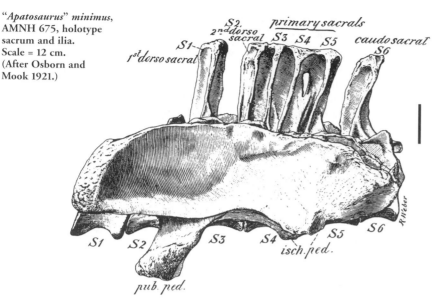

"*Apatosaurus*" *minimus*, AMNH 675, holotype sacrum and ilia. Scale = 12 cm. (After Osborn and Mook 1921.)

chamber that broke down the fodder's soluble cellular contents and readily fermentable cell-wall constituents. The rate of fermentation depended on the animal's body temperature which, in sauropods, was probably quite high, even if they were not strictly endothermic, but inertial homeotherms. As a by-product of fermentation, sufficient heat could have been generated to provide a significant proportion of the animal's thermoregulatory warmth. Farlow speculated on the possibility that sauropods achieved such enormous sizes in order to reach high digestive efficiencies through such fermentation.

Remains of four *Apatosaurus* juveniles have been found. The first originally described by Peterson and Gilmore (1902) as *Elosaurus parvus*, based on an incomplete skeleton including right scapula, humerus and ulna, left humerus, right femur, left fibula, distal end of the right pubis, part of an anterior cervical neural arch, dorsal neural arch, two sacral vertebrae, and proximal ends of three ribs (CM 566), from a quarry at Sheep Creek, Wyoming. In life, this individual might have been 5 meters (16 feet) in length. The other three specimens were collected from Dinosaur National Monument.

Apatosaurus is also known from the Dry Mesa Quarry (Morrison Formation, Upper Jurassic [Tithonian] or Lower Cretaceous [Neocomian or Hauterivian]), near the southwest corner of Dry Mesa, in west central Colorado (see Britt 1991).

Notes: The name *Brontosaurus giganteus* appeared in an anonymous article published in the November 1898 issue of the *New York Journal* for a large, nondiagnostic femur discovered by William Harlow Reed. The specimen was never formally described.

White (1958) referred the species *A. grandis* to *Camarasaurus*.

As no *Apatosaurus* hatchlings had been found, nor eggs or nests positively referable to sauropod skeletal remains, Bakker (1971, 1987) suggested that such dinosaurs did not lay eggs but gave live birth to their young. Bakker (1987) noted that the remains of the smallest individuals are about one fourth the size of the adults, and that the pelvic canals of an adult *Apatosaurus* were sufficiently wide to give live birth. A newborn *Apatosaurus*, in Bakker's (1987) estimation, would be approximately one fifth the height and one hundredth the weight (about 225 kilograms, or 500 pounds) of an adult. In 1910, the bones of a juvenile individual were found near the skeleton of an adult, evidence, argued Bakker, that the adult was bearing a fetus. As there are limits to the size an egg can reach (the Pleistocene flightless bird *Aepyornis maximus*, largest of the so-called "elephant birds," seemingly having laid the largest eggs, measuring about .3 meters [over one foot] in length), it seemed reasonable that a baby *Apatosaurus* would have a better chance at survival and growing to adult proportions beginning life at a size substantially larger than a hatchling. However, this idea of live-birthing

Photo by R. A. Long and S. P. Welles (neg. #73-48-26), courtesy American Museum of Natural History.

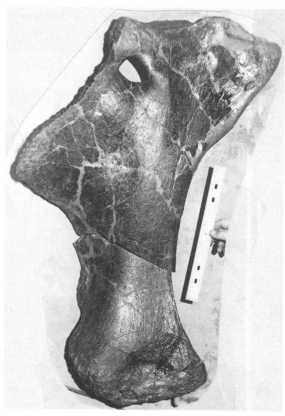

"*Apatosaurus*" *minimus*, AMNH 675, holotype right pubis, lateral view.

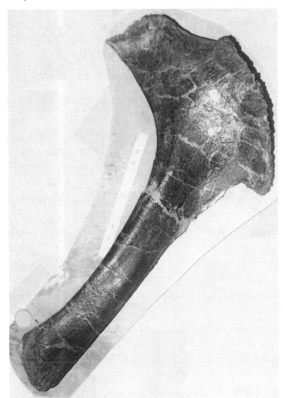

"*Apatosaurus*" *minimus*, AMNH 675, holotype right ischium, lateral view.

sauropods has been challenged. Apparent hatchling sauropod individuals have been discovered (see *Camarasaurus* entry); also, according to Dunham, Overall, Porter and Forster (1989), nothing about the pelvic structure in sauropods suggests live birth as opposed to laying eggs.

Key references: Anderson, Hall-Martin and Russell (1985); Bakker (1971, 1986, 1987); Berman and McIntosh (1978); Britt (1991); Colbert (1962); Coombs (1975); Dodson, Bakker and Behrensmeyer (1983); Farlow (1987*a*); Filla and Redman (1994); Gilmore (1936*a*); Hatcher (1902); Holland (1915*a*, 1915*b*); Hotton (1963); Marsh (1877*d*, 1878*a*, 1879*b*, 1896); McIntosh (1990*a*, 1990*b*); Moodie (1923); Osborn (1915*b*); Peterson and Gilmore (1902); Paul (1988*a*); Riggs (1903*b*, 1904).

ARAGOSAURUS Sanz, Buscalioni, Casanovas and Santafé 1987

Saurischia: Sauropodomorpha: Sauropoda: Camarasauridae: Camarasaurinae.

Name derivation: "Aragón" + Greek *sauros* = "lizard."

Type species: *A. ischiaticus* Sanz, Buscalioni, Casanovas and Santafe 1987.

Other species: [None.]

Occurrence: Las Zabacheras Beds, Teruel, Spain.

Age: Early Cretaceous (?Hauterivian).

Known material: Partial postcrania.

Holotype: ZH-1-19, right scapula (ZH-1), left femur (ZH-2), right ischium (ZH-3), chevrons (ZH-4, ZH-5, ZH-9 and ZH-14), chevron fragments (ZH-7, ZH-8, ZH-9, ZH-11 and ZH-13), pes bone (ZH-6), proximal phalange of pes (ZH-10), posterior caudal vertebrae (ZH-12, ZH-16 and ZH-18), medium caudal vertebra (ZH-17), phalangeal ungual (ZH-19).

Diagnosis of genus (as for type species): Caudal vertebra with great transversal (club-like) development of neurophysis; scapular blade expanded terminally, with intermediate development (*e.g.*, between cetiosaurids and *Brachiosaurus* or *Rebbachisaurus*); anterior scapular zone with great dorso-ventral development (acromio-glenoideus), 0.27 ratio of minimal width of scapular blade to maximal acromio-glenoideus height; ischium with well-developed iliac process; pubic process with great dorso-ventral development; 0.63 ratio of anteroposterior length of pubic process to length of ischiadic contact with pubis; ischiadic process of ilium with conspicuous terminal expansion; 0.82 ratio of length of humerus to femur; lateral bulge just distal to greater trochanter of femur; femur with relatively well-developed medial condyle, 0.77 ratio of maximal antero-posterior diameter of latter to the maximal transversal distal femoral width (Sanz, Buscalioni, Casanovas and Santafé 1987).

Comments: The genus *Aragosaurus* was founded upon material originally reported by Lapparent (1960*b*), plus new material (ZH-1-19), collected from the Las Zabacheras outcrop of the syncline of Galve (Lower Cretaceous, ?Hauterivian), Teruel, Spain (Sanz *et al.* 1987).

McIntosh (1990*b*), in a review of the Sauropoda, observed that the caudal vertebrae in *A. ischiaticus* are almost identical in form to those of *Camarasaurus*; the forelimb is relatively longer than in *C. lentus* and *C. grandis*, but similar to that in ?*C. alenquerensis*; the humerus, though more slender and with a less expanded proximal end, is similar to that in *Camarasaurus*; that the ulna and radius, though somewhat more slender, resemble that in *Camarasaurus*; the femur is almost identical to that in the latter genus, though its head is less protruding than in ?*C. alenquerensis*; and that the pubis seems to be less robust and the ischium shorter than in *Camarasaurus*.

Key references: Lapparent (1960*b*); (McIntosh (1990*b*); Sanz, Buscalioni, Casanovas and Santafé (1987).

ARALOSAURUS Rozhdestvensky 1968

Ornithischia: Genasauria: Cerapoda: Ornithopoda:
Iguanodontia: Ankylopollexia: Hadrosauridae:
Hadrosaurinae.

Name derivation: "Aral [Lake, U.S.S.R.]" + Greek
sauros = "lizard."

Type species: *A. tuberiferus* Rozhdestvensky 1968.

Other species: [None.]

Occurrence: Beleutinskaya Svita, Kazachskaya S.S.R.

Age: Late Cretaceous (?Turonian–Early Santonian).

Known material/holotype: PEN AN SSR 2229/I,
almost complete articulated skull.

Diagnosis of genus: Skull moderately widened in jugal area; nasals arciform, forming a thickened crest at midline; frontals contributing slightly in formation of orbit; well-developed, ellipse-like fontanels at boundary of nasals and frontals, between them; lacrimal very large; orbit rounded-oval in outline, considerably wider than smaller lateral temporal fenestra; postorbital trident-shaped at posterior end; upper part of quadrate curved; maxilla, including ?thirty tooth rows, very wide at its apex, rising anteriorly at almost right angles; mandibular teeth with a supplementary crest; upper epiphysis of humerus narrow, delto-pectoral crest slightly developed; inner and outer distal condyles of femur well-developed, not closing at front; third metatarsal noticeably widened laterally at proximal end; second and fourth metatarsals widened at distal end, far more antero-posteriorly than laterally (Rozhdestvensky 1968).

Diagnosis of *A. tuberiferus*: "Average-sized" hadrosaur; dorsal surface of skull with low tuberculate thickening of nasal bones and well-developed opening; length of supratemporal fenestra about one third width of the skull in orbital area, exceeding its width in occipital area by less than one and one half times; orbit subtriangular, broader at upper border;

lateral temporal opening narrow, barely exceeding width of quadrate; 7.4 ratio of length of this opening to length of orbit; maxilla twice as long as high, with thirty tooth rows; tooth crown three times taller than wide; mandibular teeth with supplementary crest anterior to the medial crest, rising above middle of crown; humerus with epiphyses of same width; delto-pectoral crest beginning slightly above middle of humeral shaft; distal condyles of femur of equal width, slightly smaller than distance between anterior and posterior sides of the femur along lower surface; third metatarsal widened at proximal end, constituting half its length; distal ends of second and fourth metatarsals about twice as large in anterior-posterior direction than in lateral direction (Rozhdestvensky 1968).

Comments: The genus *Aralosaurus* was founded upon an incomplete skull (PEN AN SSR 2229/I), discovered in 1957 in the Beleutinskiaia Formation, Shakh-Shakh site, Central Kazakhstan S.S.R., north of Karmakchi (Dzhusaly Station), Central Asia [formerly Union of Soviet Socialist Republics]. The specimen was found in an excellently intact condition with the brain cavity opened, allowing a detailed study of the braincase. A correlation of type species, *A. tuberiferus*, with other hadrosaurids allows a very general assignment of its geological age to the Cenomanian–Early Senonian interval (Rozhdestvensky 1968).

Rozhdestvensky observed that, in general outline, the skull of *Aralosaurus* resembles that of *Kritosaurus*, differing from that genus only in the small temporal fossae, very high and greatly expanded lacrimal, broad apex of the maxilla, curved quadrate, and the fewer number of teeth.

From the material preserved, Rozhdestvensky estimated the complete length of the skull to be about 65 centimeters (almost 27 inches) and that of the animal some 6.5 meters (about 22 feet). The type specimen seems to represent a relatively young (or at least not the largest) individual as evidenced by the easily disarticulated, nonknitted sutures between the bones.

With the dentition entirely preserved in the holotype of *A. tuberiferus*, Rozhdestvensky observed differences between the lower and upper teeth. Basically, the mandibular teeth can be differentiated from the maxillary teeth by the presence of the supplementary crest. These differences can also be applied to other hadrosaurs, serving as criteria to identify previously unidentifiable hadrosaurid teeth.

Note: The ellipse-like opening at boundary of nasals and frontals is an important growth feature; the supplementary crest of the mandibular teeth is a primitive feature more like iguanodontids than hadrosaurids (M. K. Brett-Surman, personal communication 1988).

Key reference: Rozhdestvensky (1968).

Aralosaurus tuberiferus, PEN AN SSR 2229/I, holotype partial skull. (After Rozhdestvenksy 1968.)

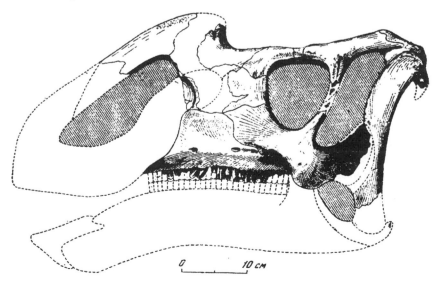

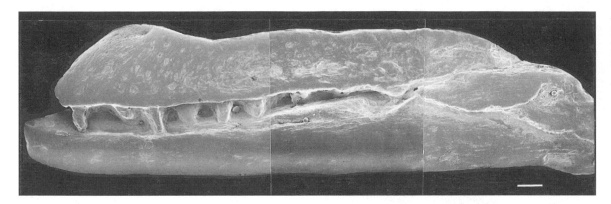

Archaeornithoides deinosauriscus, ZPAL MgD-II/29, holotype incomplete skull, left lateral view. Scale = 1 cm. SEM photo (After Elźanowski and Wellnhofer 1993.)

ARCHAEORNITHOIDES Elźanowski and Wellnhofer 1992

Saurischia: Theropoda *incertae sedis*.

Name derivation: Greek *Archaeornis* (a junior synonym of *Archaeopteryx*) + Greek *oides* = "resembling, like."

Type species: *A. deinosauriscus* Elźanowski and Wellnhofer 1992.

Other species: [None.]

Occurrence: Djadokhta Formation, Bayn Dzak, Mongolia.

Age: Late Cretaceous (Middle–Late Campanian).

Known material/holotype: ZPAL MgD-II/29, fragmentary skull, including maxillae, dentaries, crushed palatal bones.

Diagnosis of genus (as for type species): Maxilla with major pit on lateral surface of nasal process; rostromedial process recurved ventrally; large dorsal opening to supraalveolar canal behind base of nasal process; broad palatal shelf enclosing small rostral and large caudal sinus; dentary with interdental septa descending labio-lingually, separated from lingual wall by paradental groove (Elźanowski and Wellnhofer 1992).

Comments: The genus *Archaeornithoides* was founded upon the partial skull (ZPAL MgD-II/29) of a juvenile individual, discovered by the Polish-Mongolian Palaeontological Expedition, in the Djadokhta Formation (Middle–Late Campanian; see Currie 1991; Dong 1993*a*), Bayn Dzak (formerly Shabarakh Usu), District Dalandzadgag, Mongolia. The premaxilla had fallen off before burial. The jaws had probably been bitten off from the braincase, as evidenced by the presence of bite marks located about opposite each other on the left dentary and right jugal ramus of the right maxilla (Elźanowski and Wellnhofer 1992).

The total complete length of the skull, estimated by the authors, is 5 centimeters (over 1.75 inches).

According to Elźanowski and Wellnhofer, the broad palatal shelf with its pneumatic sinuses best distinguishes *Archaeornithoides* from all other known theropods. The skull presents a novel combination of theropod and primitive avian characters. The tetraradiate palatine, with a medial embayment for the subsidiary palatal fenestra, is a feature of all dromaeosaurids and some tyrannosaurids. The premaxilla-maxilla articulation resembles that in the theropod *Baryonyx*. There are no interdental plates (secondary ossifications that enclose dental alveoli on the lingual side), present in all known theropods except *Baryonyx*, *Spinosaurus* and Troodontidae). A feature shared by *Archaeornithoides* with these three taxa is the presence of the paradental groove. Birdlike characters include the maxillary palatal shelf and dentition. *Archaeornithoides* also resembles *Spinosaurus* in the shape of the rostral alveoli of the dentary and in the irregular arrangement of the widely spaced caudal teeth. *Archaeornithoides* is similar to the bird Late Jurassic bird *Archaeopteryx* in having widely spaced, pointed maxillary teeth.

The avian features of the maxillary palatal shelf and dentition indicated to the authors that this genus is distinguished from all other potential sister-groups of birds, with *Archaeornithoides* the closest known nonavian relative of *Archaeopteryx* and other birds.

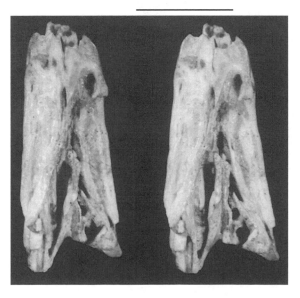

Archaeornithoides deinosauriscus, ZPAL MgD-II/29, holotype skull in dorsal stereo view. Scale = 20 mm. (After Elźanowski and Wellnhofer 1992.)

Archaeornithoides deinosauriscus, ZPAL MgD-II/29, holotype skull, detail of rostral ends of right maxillary and dentary, showing unfinished surface of bones, covered with primary vascular canals. (After Elźanowski and Wellnhofer 1993.)

Elźanowski and Wellnhofer further stated that the ramifications of this corollary for the origin of birds depends upon the phylogenetic importance of a paradental groove, lack of interdental plates, and other similarities to *Baryonyx*, *Spinosaurus* and troodontids. If ceratosaurs (with opposite character states; see Welles 1984) are correctly identified as plesiomorphic sister-taxa of all other theropods (Gauthier 1986; Benton 1990), then the similarities of *Archaeornithoides* and these three taxa are synapomorphic, suggesting that they (and perhaps *Lisboasaurus;* see entry) form a monophyletic group.

Elźanowski and Wellnhofer placed this genus into its own monotypic group Archaeornithoididae.

Key reference: Elźanowski and Wellnhofer (1992).

ARCHAEORNITHOMIMUS Russell 1972

Saurischia: Theropoda: Tetanurae: Avetheropoda: Coelurosauria: Maniraptora: Arctometatarsalia: Bullatosauria: Ornithomimosauria: ?Ornithomimidae.

Name derivation: Greek *archaio* = "ancient" Greek *ornithos* = "bird" + Greek *mimos* = "mimic."

Type species: *A. asiaticus* (Gilmore 1933).

Other species: ?*A. bissektensis* Nessov 1995.

Occurrence: Djadochta Formation, Bayn Dzak, Mongolia; "Northern Eurasia" [?*A. bissketensis*].

Age: Late Cretaceous (Middle–Late Campanian).

Known material/holotype: ZPAL MgD-II/29, fragmentary skull, including maxillae, dentaries, crushed palatal bones; N 479/12457 [holotype femur of ?*A. bissektensis*].

Diagnosis of genus (as for type species): Maxilla with major pit on lateral surface of nasal process; rostromedial process recurved ventrally; large dorsal opening to supraalveolar canal behind base of nasal process;

Archaeornithomimus bissketensis, N 479/12457, holotype femur. (After Nessov 1995.)

broad palatal shelf enclosing small rostral and large caudal sinus; dentary with interdental septa descending labio-lingually, separated from lingual wall by paradental groove (Elźanowski and Wellnhofer 1992).

Diagnosis of ?*A. bissektensis*: [Unavailable as of this writing].

Comments: The genus *Archaeornithomimus* was founded upon the two cotype specimens (AMNH 6569, AMNH 6565), collected in 1923 by Peter Kaisen, from the Iren Dabasu Formation (?Cenomanian; Weishampel and Horner 1986), Mongolia. This material was originally referred by Gilmore to the genus *Ornithomimus* as new species *O. asiaticus*. Referred material included a sacrum (AMNH 6576) with four coossified sacral vertebrae.

Gilmore originally diagnosed the monotypic *O. asiaticus* as follows: Smaller than "*O.*"[=*Struthiomimus*] *altus*; cervical ribs free from vertebrae; pelvic bones not coossified; tarsus with two bones in a distal row; first metacarpal relatively shorter than in "*O.*" *altus*; postcranial skeleton closely resembling "*O.*" *altus*; (few preserved) cervical vertebrae elongate, strongly amphicoelus (perhaps due to age rather than structure); dorsal vertebrae amphicoelus, with relatively low neural spines; two flattened bones constituting distal row of tarsus fitting tightly over ends of metatarsals, articulating with articular ends of posterior half of metatarsals, leaving remaining portion clear (unlike the more completely covered ends in "*O.*" *altus*).

Superficially, this species resembles a smaller version of *Struthiomimus altus*, but with relatively shorter hind legs. Gilmore attributed the small size of this dinosaur to immaturity but added that, given the fossil evidence, even the adult would be smaller than "*O.*" *altus*. Gilmore observed that the differences between the then-known ornithomimids, compared bone by bone, are so minimal that, had they not been found in Asia and North America, they might have been interpreted as intraspecific variations.

In a study of ostrich dinosaurs from the Late Cretaceous of Western Canada, Russell (1972) made *O. asiaticus* the type species of new genus *Archaeornithomimus*.

A second species, *A. affinis*, was based on various meager syntype specimens (USNM 6107), including a recurved pedal ungual, two distal caudal vertebrae, vertebral centrum, astragalus, and two incomplete hollow metatarsals, collected from the Arundel Formation (Hauterivian or Barremian) of Maryland, and originally described by Gilmore (1920) as a species of "*Coelosaurus*"[=*Ornithomimus*]. The material was tentatively referred by Russell to *Archaeornithomimus* on the basis of a curved pedal ungual. However, Smith and Galton pointed out that the

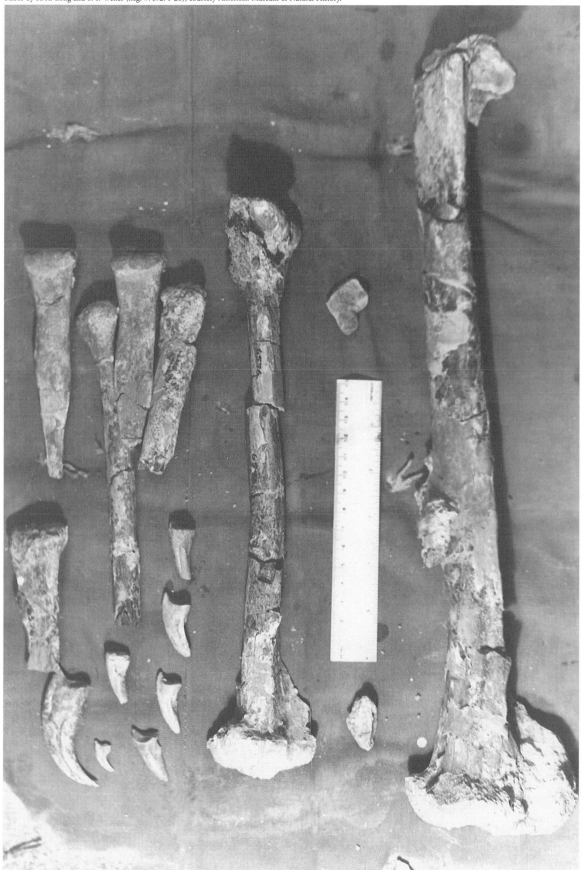

Archaeornithomimus asiaticus, AMNH 6569 and 6565 cotypes, partial manus, metatarsus, limb bones of *Ornithomimus asiaticus*.

pedal unguals of *A. asiaticus* and other ornithomimids are straight, so the recurved Asian phalanges are probably referable to *Alectrosaurus*, the only other theropod known from Iren Dabasu Formation, and the recurved pedal ungual from Maryland probably to ?*Dryptosaurus*. The Arundel material, with the exception of the incomplete metatarsals which can only be referred to Coelurosauria, is too poor to classify beyond theropod *incertae sedis*. In their review of the Ornithomimosauria, Barsbold and Osmólska (1990) considered this species to be a *nomen dubium*.

Smith and Galton (1990) rediagnosed *Archaeornithomimus* (and type species *A. asiaticus*) and fully described the known elements, based upon the lectotype specimen (AMNH 6565), paralectotype (AMNH 6569), and various referred specimens, all from the same locality as AMNH 6565: A ?fifth cervical vertebra (AMNH 21786); ?eighth cervical (AMNH 21787); tenth dorsal and first-fourth dorsal vertebrae (AMNH 21788); ?fifth-tenth dorsals (AMNH 21789); ilium, first-fifth sacral vertebrae, and first-fifth proximal caudals (AMNH 21790);

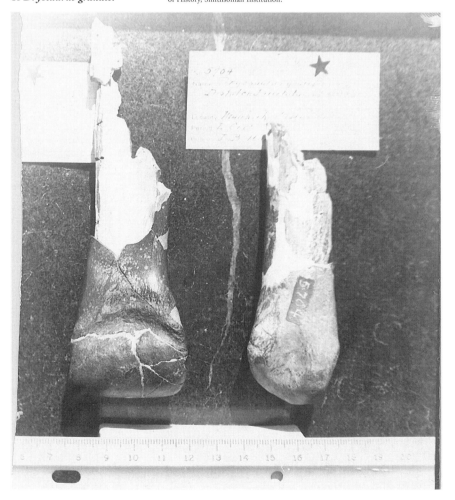

Archaeornithomimus asiaticus, referred specimen USNM 5703, holotype distal ends of metatarsals IV and III of *Dryosaurus grandis*.

Photo by R. A. Long and S. P. Welles (neg. #73/139-29), courtesy National Museum of History, Smithsonian Institution.

?third-eleventh caudals (AMNH 21791); ?eleventh-fifteenth proximal caudals (AMNH 21802); proximal caudal spines (AMNH 21889); distal causals (AMNH 21792); seven distal caudals (AMNH 21793); eight distal caudals (AMNH 21794, formerly AMNH 6576); scapulacoracoid and humerus (AMNH 21795, formerly AMNH 6566); humerus, radius, and ulna (AMNH 21796, formerly AMNH 6567); radius, ulna, metacarpals I-III, and phalanges (AMNH 6569); first metacarpal (AMNH 21889, formerly AMNH 6570); metacarpal II (AMNH 21888, formerly AMNH 65570); ischium (AMNH 21798, formerly AMNH 6558); pubis (AMNH 21799, formerly AMNH 6570); femur (AMNH 21800, formerly AMNH 6570); tibia, astragalus (AMNH 21801), formerly AMNH 6576); pedal ungual (AMNH 21803); and manual unguals (AMNH 21884, 21885, 21886 and 21887, all formerly AMNH 6570).

Barsbold and Osmólska observed that in *A. asiaticus* metatarsals II and IV contact one another on the extensor face of the metatarsus, but just for a short distance (as in *Ornithomimus*), and that the metatarsus in this species is slightly stouter than in any other known ornithomimid, its width 18 percent of its length (as opposed to 11 to 13 percent in other ornithomimids). Contrary to other ornithomimids, metatarsal III in *A. asiaticus* does not overlap the adjoining metatarsals on the extensor face of the metatarsus.

As noted by Barsbold and Osmólska, *A. asiaticus* is the stratigraphically oldest ornithomimid species, having a less derived metatarsus than other members of Ornithomimidae. The third metacarpal is distinctly and uniquely reduced in thickness and length, reason possibly for questioning the assignment of *Archaeornithomimus* to this group.

Notes: The proximal third of metatarsal IV, a dorsal centrum, parts of two caudal centra, and two phalanges (AMNH 6593), described by Gilmore (1933*b*), collected in 1928 in Tairum Nor Basin (recording a new locality for Mongolian ornithomimids), closely resembles those elements in *A. asiaticus*.

Sattler (1993), in her book *The Illustrated Dinosaur Dictionary*, included the undescribed and unofficially named genus *Arkanosaurus*, reportedly founded upon foot bones found in Cretaceous rocks in Arkansas, United States, and resembling *Ornithomimus*. According to D. J. Chure (personal communication to Olshevsky 1992), these remains, to be described as new genus and species "Arkansaurus fridayi," represent a primitive ornithomid that may prove to be a species of *Archaeornithomimus*.

Key references: Barsbold and Osmólska (1990); Gilmore (1933*b*); Russell (1972); Smith and Galton (1990).

ARGENTINOSAURUS Bonaparte and Coria
1993

Saurischia: Sauropodomorpha: Sauropoda:
Titanosauria: Andesauridae.

Name derivation: "Argentina" + Greek *sauros* =
"lizard."

Type species: *A. huenculensis* Bonaparte and Coria
1993.

Other species: [None.]

Occurrence: Rio Limay Formation, Neuquén
Province, Argentina, South America.

Age: Early–Late Cretaceous (Albian–Cenomanian).

Known material/holotype: PVPH-1, three incomplete anterior and three posterior dorsal vertebrae,
ventral region of almost complete sacrum including centra 1–5, without last sacral, with greater

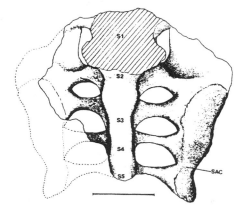

Argentinosaurus huinculensis, PVPH-1, holotype sacrum,
ventral view. Scale = 50 cm. (After Bonaparte and Coria
1993.)

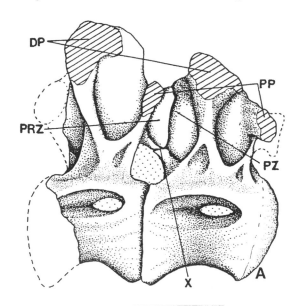

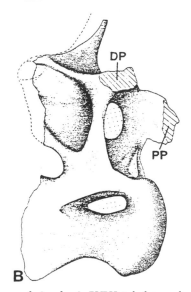

Argentinosaurus huinculensis, PVPH-1, holotype dorsal vertebrae. Scale = 50 cm. (After Bonaparte and Coria 1993.)

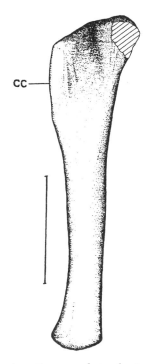

Argentinosaurus huinculensis,
PVPH-1, holotype right tibia,
medial view. Scale = 50 cm.
(After Bonaparte and Coria
1993.)

portions of right sacral ribs, large portion of dorsal rib fragment, and almost complete right tibia.

Diagnosis of genus (as for type species): Giant
titanosaur; dorsal vertebrae with large hyposphene-
hypantrum bearing extra articulations; neural spines
of anterior dorsal vertebrae expanded transversely, flat
anteroposteriorly, surface for prespinal lamina robust;
middle and posterior dorsals with low and wide centra, with ventral surface almost flat, pleurocoels
located in anterior half of centrum; bodies of sacral
vertebrae 2–5 much reduced; dorsal ribs of tubular
structure, cylindrical and hollow; most dense bone in
presacral and sacral vertebrae; tibia with slender with
short cnemial crest (Bonaparte and Coria 1993).

Comments: The genus *Argentinosaurus* was
established upon various vertebral remains, and a
tibia (PVPH-1), collected from the Huincul Member
of the Rio Limay Formation, east of Plaza Huincul,
Province of Neuquén, Argentina (Bonaparte and
Coria 1993).

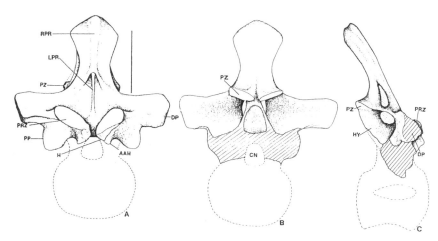

Argentinosaurus huinculensis, PVPH-1, holotype anterior dorsal vertebra, A. anterior, B. posterior, C. lateral views. Scale = 50 cm. (After Bonaparte and Coria 1993.)

Preparator J. B. Abbott with right femur (FMNH P130018 [P13532]) of *Argyrosaurus superbus*. Left and center are right femur and left tibia of *Antarctosaurus wichmannianus.*

Bonaparte and Coria described *Argentinosaurus* as a gigantic sauropod, with the tibia, as measured by the authors, totaling 155 centimeters (approximately 58 inches) in length.

Key reference: Bonaparte and Coria (1993).

ARGYROSAURUS   Lydekker 1893
Saurischia: Sauropodomorpha: Sauropoda:
    Titanosauria: Titanosauridae.
Name derivation: Greek *argyros* = "silver" + Greek
    sauros = "lizard."
Type species: *A. superbus* Lydekker 1893.
Other species: [None.]
Occurrence: Cerro Castillo Formation, Bajo Barreal
    Formation, Laguna Palacios Formation, Rio
    Negro, Laguna Palacios Formation, Bajo Barreal
    Formation, Chubut; ?[unnamed formation],
    Santa Cruz, Argentina; Asencio Formation,
    Uruguay.
Age: Late Cretaceous (Campanian–Maastrichtian).
Known material/holotype: MLP 20 [old catalogue
    number], left humerus, radius, ulna, metacarpals,
    carpal.
    Diagnosis of genus: [No modern diagnosis published.]

    Comments: The genus *Argyrosaurus* was founded on a fairly well preserved forelimb (MPL 20), discovered at Rio Chico, Chubut, Argentina, South America.

    Other material referred to this genus has been collected from the Rio Colorado Formation (Bonaparte and Gasparini 1978; Powell 1986*a*), Provincia de Neuquén, Rio Senguer, Sierra de San Bernardo, and Rio Neuquén Formation (Huene 1929; Bonaparte and Gasparini 1978), Chubut, Rio Leona, Santa Cruz, Rio Uruguay, Entre Rios, and, represented by fragments reported by Lambert (1942) from the Late Cretaceous Asencio Formation (Mones 1980), Departamento Palmitas, Uruguay. However, as cautioned by McIntosh (1990*b*) in his sauropod review, the association of a femur and large titanosaurid caudal vertebra from localities other than the type locality is conjectural.

    Originally, Lydekker (1893*b*) diagnosed *Argyrosaurus* as follows: Very massive sauropod, larger than *Apatosaurus*; caudal vertebrae very short, wide, procoelous; humerus and forearm powerful; metacarpals elongate, second longest, fifth reduced; femur extremely broad, fourth trochanter at mid-shaft.

    As described by Lydekker, the humerus of *A. superbus* is approximately 140 centimeters (about 4.75 feet) long; metacarpals IV and V are fused through their entire length. Lydekker estimated *Argyrosaurus* to be one of the largest of then known

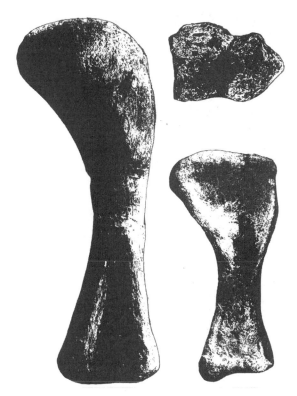

Argyrosaurus superbus, MLP, holotype (clockwise) A. left humerus, B. carpal, C. ulna. (After Lydekker 1893.)

dinosaurs and suggested that it was allied with *Titanosaurus*.

    McIntosh briefly described *A. superbus* as follows: Humerus relatively robust, with square proximal end (similar to that in *Saltasaurus* and *Opisthocoelicaudia*); radius and ulna comparatively more slender, ratio of ulna to humerus 0.69; relatively very long metacarpals comparable to those of brachiosaurids and camarasaurids, much longer than in diplodocids.

    Key references: Lydekker (1933*b*); McIntosh (1990*b*).

ARISTOSAURUS   van Hoepen 1920—(See
    Massospondylus.)
Name derivation: Greek *aristo* = "best" + Greek
    sauros = "lizard."
Type species: *A. erectus* van Hoepen 1920.

ARISTOSUCHUS   Seeley 1887—(See
    Calamospondylus.)
Name derivation: Greek *aristo* = "best" + Greek
    souchos = "crocodile."
Type species: *A. pusillus* (Owen 1876).

ARRHINOCERATOPS   Parks 1925

Ornithischia: Genasauria: Cerapoda: Marginocephalia: Ceratopsia: Neoceratopsia: Ceratopsidae: Chasmosaurinae.

Name derivation: Greek *a* = "without" + Greek *keratos* = "horned" + Greek *ops* = "face."

Type species: *A. brachyops* Parks 1925.

Other species: [None.]

Occurrence: Horseshoe Canyon Formation,
Alberta, Canada.

Age: Late Cretaceous (Maastrichtian).

Known material/holotype: ROM 796 (original
number ROM 5135), nearly complete skull with
jaws.

Diagnosis of genus: Brow horn cores large,
anterolaterally directed; nasal horn core short, massive, apex anterodorsally directed, posterior edge
merging smoothly with dorsal profile of the face; face
relatively short; rostral small; premaxilla forms a septum with shallow depressions on each side, with two
posterior flanges projecting into external narial opening; epijugal large, ventrolaterally directed; lateral
temporal opening subtriangular in outline; antorbital
opening, if present, reduced; squamosal long, tapering, reaching posterior border of frill; frill short,
broad, with moderately-sized oval fenestrae (Tyson
1980).

Comments: The genus *Arrhinoceratops* was
founded upon a nearly complete skull with jaws
(ROM 796 [formerly ROM 5135]), collected during
the University of Toronto Expedition of 1923, from
the Horseshoe Canyon [then Edmonton] Formation,
above Bleriot Ferry, at Red Deer River, Alberta,
Canada.

Originally, Parks (1925) diagnosed the genus
(and type species *A. brachyops*) as follows: Large
supraorbital horn cores directed outwards and forward; facial region short, with no nasal horn; crest relatively large, subquadrate in shape, flat, with moderate-sized, oval fontanelles; squamosals long; jugal
with unusually long anterior process.

Parks believed that *Arrhinoceratops* lacked a nasal
horn, speculating that the sharp and somewhat rugose
nasal may have borne a horny sheath. Lull (1933), in
his revision of the Ceratopsia, observed that more of
an indication of a nasal horn is present in the holotype of *Arrhinoceratops* than in the holotype (USNM
4720) of *Triceratops obtusus*. Lull added that the horn-
like area in both forms lies above the anterior margin of the narial openings, arguing that the nasal horn
core in *Arrhinoceratops* was simply not preserved.

A revised diagnosis of *Arrhinoceratops* and its
type species was proposed by Tyson (1981) after
reevaluating the holotype, the only specimen that
could unequivocally be assigned to this genus. Tyson
demonstrated that a horn core is present and that the
jugal is not characterized by an atypically long anterior process. Tyson (*contra* Parks) further showed that

Arrhinoceratops brachyops, ROM 796, holotype skull, lateral view.

Courtesy Royal Ontario Museum.

Arrhinoceratops brachyops,
ROM 796, holotype skull,
three-quarter view.

there is no nasal-rostral contact in *Arrhinoceratops* or in any other known ceratopsian.

Superficially, *Arrhinoceratops* resembles *Triceratops*, though having parietal fontanelles. As noted by Lull, the facial region of *Arrhinoceratops* resembles that of *Chasmosaurus*, though with smaller parietal fenestrae, and with narrower though relatively longer parietal fenestrae than in *Torosaurus*; length of the skull is 1.52 meters (over 5 feet).

Sternberg (1949) divided the Ceratopsidae into two lineages, one (now called Chasmosaurinae) comprising genera with short squamosals, the other genera (now pachyrhinosaurines) with long squamosals that reach or closely approach the posterior margin of the frill. In the past, most authors (including Parks and Lull) have associated *Arrhinoceratops* with the long-squamosaled forms, particularly *Chasmosaurus* and *Torosaurus*. Tyson argued that *Arrhinoceratops* cannot be related to *Chasmosaurus*, the latter having large parietal openings and an indented posterior frill margin. Lawson (1986) speculated that *Arrhinocer-* *atops* shares some characteristics with *Anchiceratops*, *Torosaurus* and *Triceratops*, including broad frills with either elliptical or circular openings, or a condition derived from that pattern. Tyson agreed with Lawson that there exists a graded series of frill shapes, from the short and broad frill of *A. brachyops* to the long narrow frills of large specimens of *Torosaurus latus*, but concluded that *Arrhinoceratops* cannot be closely related to any other genus within that lineage.

The left squamosal of the holotype of *A. brachyops* is marked by an additional opening that Lull interpreted as pathologic. Molnar (1977) noted that similar possible cranial injuries were also reported by Hatcher, Marsh and Lull (1907) in *Triceratops elatus*, *T. hatcheri*, *T. serratus* [all = *T. horridus*] and *Pentaceratops fenestratus* [= *P. sternbergii*]. These openings, found in the lateral portion of the crest, could represent wounds inflicted by the horns of rivals during intraspecific combat.

Note: The species *A. utahensis* Gilmore 1946 was referred by Lawson to the species *Torosaurus latus*.

Key references: Hatcher, Marsh and Lull (1907); Lawson (1986); Lull (1933); Molnar (1977); Parks (1925); Tyson (1980).

ARSTANOSAURUS   Suslov 1982 [*nomen dubium*]

Ornithischia: Genasauria: Cerapoda: Ornithopoda: Iguanodontia: Hadrosauridae *incertae sedis*.

Name derivation: "Arstan [for ancient Arstan well and benchmark near locality, at Arstan, area in Asia]" + Greek *sauros* = "lizard."

Type species: *A. akkurganensis* Suslov 1982.

Other species: [None.]

Occurrence: Bostobinskaya Formation, Kazakhstan, S.S.R.

Age: Late Cretaceous (Santonian–Campanian).

Known material: Partial maxilla, ?incomplete femur.

Holotype: IZ 1/1, posterior half of left maxilla.

Diagnosis of genus (as for type species): Maxilla massive, low, with almost straight dorsal edge, horizontal process above shelf; triangular in cross-section; with downward-pointing apex (Suslov and Shilin 1982).

Comments: The genus *Arstanosaurus* was established on an incomplete left maxilla (IZ 1/1) from sandy-shaly deposits of the Bostobinskaya Formation (Santonian-Campanian; see Martinson, Nikitin, Teplova and Vasil'yev 1966; Nikitin and Vasil'yev 1977), southern Kazakhstan, northeastern Aral region, Dzhusalin uplift, in what was formerly part of the Union of Soviet Socialist Republics. Associated with the type specimen was the distal end of a femur IZ 1/2 possibly referable to this genus (Suslov and Shilin 1982).

Suslov and Shilin referred *Arstanosaurus* to the Hadrosauridae. However, Brett-Surman (1989) noted that the massiveness and lowness of the maxilla is hardly of diagnostic importance, given the partial and worn nature of the holotype, and because these features are plesiomorphic for hadrosaurids; that both sides of the obtuse angle formed by the dorsal edge of the maxilla are relatively straight in all known hadrosaurids; and that the horizontal edge above the shelf may reflect ontogenetic or populational variation.

Suslov and Shilin described tooth replacement in *Arstanosaurus*: There are nine vertical tooth rows preserved, four more in the transverse fracture, each vertical series containing one functioning tooth in the alveolar groove. Replacement teeth are located within the thickness of the bone, the outer replacement tooth directly above the functional tooth, its crown within the branching roots [a ceratopsian feature, according to Brett-Surman] of the functional tooth. The outermost tooth of the replacement row, pushing outward, gradually replaced the functional tooth as the latter was worn down. Apparently the entire jaw contained from 26 to 30 vertical tooth rows.

Note: Suslov and Shilin stated that the associated femur fragment could only be identified as representative of Hadrosauridae, having met the diagnostic criteria of Lull and Wright (1942), especially in the outline of the condyles and the form of the intercondylar groove. The specimen is distinct in that 1) practically all of the anterior surface of the tibial condyle is represented by a deep hemispherical depression, overhung by the edge of the condyle and its ventrolateral process, and 2) the posterior segments of the condyles are extremely elongated dorsally and considerably exceed in height their maximum (ventral) transverse width. (Brett-Surman, however, noted that these features are true for many ornithopods and are no longer regarded as diagnostic of hadrosaurs.)

Key references: Brett-Surman (1989); Suslov and Shilin (1982).

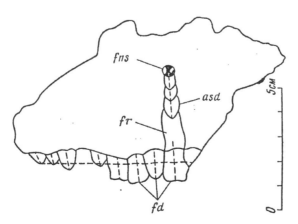

Arstanosaurus akkurganensis, IZ 1/1, holotype posterior half of left maxilla. (After Suslov 1982.)

ASIACERATOPS   Nessov and Kaznyshkina 1989 *see in* Nessov, Kaznyshkina and Cherepanov 1989

Ornithischia: Genasauria: Cerapoda: Marginocephalia: Ceratopsia: Neoceratopsia: Protoceratopsidae.

Name derivation: "Asia" + Greek *keratops* = "horn face."

Type species: *A. salsopaludalis* Nessov and Kaznyshkina 1989.

Other species: [None.]

Occurrence: Kysyk-Kum, Asia.

Age: Late Cretaceous (Cenomanian–?Early Turonian).

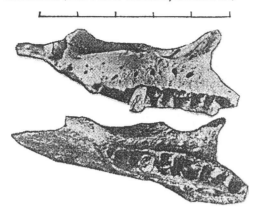

Asiaceratops salsopaludalis, holotype partial maxilla. Scale in centimeters. (After Nessov and Kaznyshkina 1989.)

Known material/holotype: Skull and some postcranial remains.

Diagnosis of genus (as for type species): Maxilla long, without fossa, includes antorbital fenestra; narial opening relatively large, low; jugal massive, thick; surangular (?epijugal) process strongly protruding laterally; portion of lower dentary shelf short, strongly widened laterally comparatively; teeth with enamel on both sides; no premaxillary teeth; from nine to ten maxillary teeth, six to seven dentary teeth; phalanges narrow (Nessov and Kaznyshkina 1989).

Comments: The genus *Asiaceratops* was founded upon skull and some postcrania from the Cenomanian-?Early Turonian of southwestern Kysyl-Kum, Asia (Nessov and Kaznyshkina, *see in* Nessov, Kaznyshkina and G. O. Cherepanov 1989).

Nessov and Kaznyshkina put this genus into its own group Asiaceratopsinae, which has not yet been adopted. The authors speculated that the Chinese species ?*Microceratops sulcidens* Bohlin 1953 could represent a possible second species of *Asiaceratops*.

Key reference: Nessov and Kaznyshkina (1989).

Asiamericana asiatica, N 460, holotype tooth. (After Nessov.)

ASIAMERICANA

Nessov 1995
Saurischia *incertae sedis*.
Name derivation: "Asia" + "America."
Type species: *A. asiatica* Nessov 1995.
Other species: [None].
Occurrence: "Northern Eurasia."

Age: Late Cretaceous.
Known material/holotype: N 460, tooth.
Diagnosis of genus (as for type species): [Unavailable as of this writing].

Comments: The new type species *Asiamericana asiatica*, based upon a tooth (N 460), was described by Nessov (1995) in a paper [English translation not yet available] discussing new data about the assemblages, ecology, and paleobiology of dinosaurs of "Northern Eurasia." According to Nessov, *A. asiatica* may be a spinosaurid, although affinities with even the Theropoda could not be confirmed.

Key reference: Nessov (1995).

ASIATOSAURUS Osborn 1924 [*nomen dubium*]—(=?*Euhelopus*)

Saurischia: Sauropodomorpha: Sauropoda *incertae sedis*.
Name derivation: "Asia" + Greek *sauros* = "lizard."
Type species: *A. mongoliensis* Osborn 1924 [*nomen dubium*].
Other species: *A. kwangshiensis* Hou, Yeh and Chow 1975 [*nomen dubium*].
Occurrence: Oshih Formation, Mongolia.
Age: Early Cretaceous.
Known material: Teeth.
Holotype: AMNH 6264, tooth.

Diagnosis of genus: Relatively large sauropod; tooth spatulate, with basically symmetrical crown and very shallow, spatulate fovea; anterior process of dor-

Asiatosaurus mongoliensis, (left) AMNH 6294, paratype ?anterior dentary tooth, (right) AMNH 6264, holotype ?posterior dentary tooth.

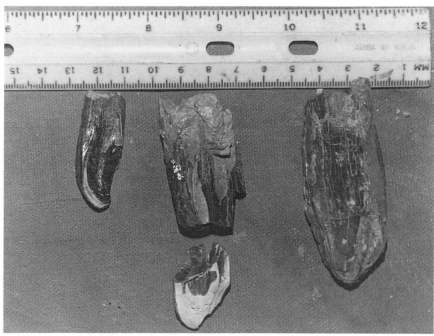

Photo by R. A. Long and S. P. Welles (neg. #73/407-22), courtesy American Museum of Natural History.

sal centrum very quite strong, semispherical; lateral fovea of centrum well-developed (Dong 1973).

Comments: The discovery of *Asiatosaurus* marked the occurrence of sauropods in Mongolia during the Early Cretaceous. The genus was established upon a tooth (AMNH 6264) selected by Osborn (1924*b*) from two teeth collected in 1922 from the Oshih [Ashile] Formation, Red Mesa, Oshih Basin, Mongolia. Osborn was not certain that the holotype and the other tooth (paratype AMNH 6294) belonged to the same individual, but did regard them as conspecific. Osborn deduced the holotype to be a possible posterior dentary tooth and the paratype a possible anterior dentary tooth.

Osborn originally diagnosed *Asiatosaurus* as follows: Tooth small and concavo-convex; crown subspaulate, slightly expanded superiorly; two lateral external and one median internal vertical groove; paratype tooth much larger than holotype, transverse equaling anteroposterior diameter of the fang; summit expanded; internal section convexo-concave; shallow lateral and internal vertical grooves.

Because the teeth seemed similar to those of *Camarasaurus*, Osborn assigned *Asiatosaurus* to the Camarasauridae.

Dong (1973) referred to the type species *A. mongoliensis* a complete dorsal vertebra (field number 64041), collected from the Lower Cretaceous of Wuerho, Sinkiang, China. Although a vertebra cannot unequivocally be referred to a genus based on a tooth, Dong designated this bone the paratype of cf. *A. mongoliensis*. As the dorsal centrum resembles that in another Chinese genus, *Euhelopus*, in the development of the anterior process and lateral fovea, Dong suggested that *Asiatosaurus* and *Euhelopus* are congeneric.

The species *A. kwangshiensis* Yeh and Zhao 1975 [*nomen dubium*] was based upon teeth from Mongolia.

Key references: Dong (1973); Osborn (1924); Hou, Yeh and Chow (1975).

ASTRODON Johnston 1859 [*nomen dubium*]—(See *Pleurocoelus*.)
Name derivation: Greek *astro* = "star" + Greek *odous* = "tooth."
Type species: *A. johnstoni* Leidy 1865 [*nomen dubium*].

ATLANTOSAURUS Marsh 1877 [*nomen dubium*]—(=?*Apatosaurus*)
Saurischia: Sauropodomorpha: Sauropoda *insertae sedis*.
Name derivation: "Atlas [god of strength]" + Greek *sauros* = "lizard."
Type species: *A. montanus* (Marsh 1877).
Other species: [None.]
Occurrence: Morrison Formation, Colorado, United States.
Age: Late Jurassic (Kimmeridgian–Tithonian).
Known material: Partial postcrania.
Holotype: YPM 1835, last two sacral vertebrae, hindlimb elements, fragments.
Diagnosis of genus: [No modern diagnosis published.]

Comments: Marsh (1877*a*) established what he believed was a new genus and species, *Titanosaurus montanus*, on a large incomplete sacrum and other postcranial remains (YPM 1835), found by Arthur Lakes in the Morrison Formation in what came to be known as the "*Atlantosaurus* beds," at Jefferson County, near Morrison, Colorado. As the name *Titanosaurus* was preoccupied Lydekker (1877), Marsh (1877*d*) erected for this material the new generic name *Atlantosaurus*, at the same time basing upon it the new [abandoned] sauropod taxon Atlantosauridae.

Marsh (1877*a*) diagnosed *Atlantosaurus* as follows: Sacral centra with concave inferior surfaces; transverse processes very stout, moderately long, with firmly coossified distal ends, separated by large oval openings. (These characters are of no diagnostic significance today.)

From the dimensions of the sacrum, Marsh (1877*a*) estimated the length of *Atlantosaurus* as 15 to 18 meters (50 to 60 feet), making this genus, at the time of its original description, the largest known terrestrial animal. From the length of the femur (about

Atlantosaurus montanus, YPM 1835, holotype sacral vertebrae. (After Marsh 1896.)

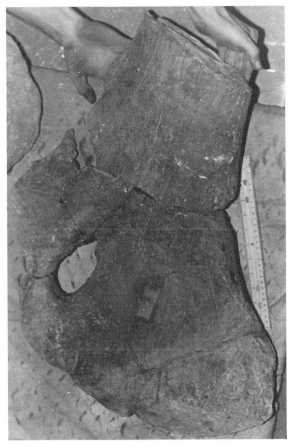

Atlantosaurus montanus, YPM 1002, pubis.

7 feet or almost 2.1 meters), Marsh (1877*d*) later estimated the length of this dinosaur to be at least 80 feet or nearly 24 meters, incorrectly basing this guess on the proportions of a crocodile.

As pointed out by Berman and McIntosh (1978), the sacrum of *A. montanus* exhibits features characteristic of a number of sauropods including those in other families. *Atlantosaurus* may be congeneric with *Apatosaurus*, though a conclusive synonymy, based on the former's type material, cannot be made.

Note: The species *A. immanis* was referred by Berman and McIntosh to *Apatosaurus ajax*.

Key references: Berman and McIntosh (1978); Marsh (1877*a*, 1877*d*).

ATLASCOPCOSAURUS   Rich and Rich 1989
Ornithischia: Genasauria: Cerapoda: Ornithopoda: Hypsilophodontidae.
Name derivation: "Atlas Copco Corporation [providors of video equipment for the Riches' excavations]" + Greek *sauros* = "lizard."
Type species: *A. loadsi* Rich and Rich 1989.

Other species: [None.]
Occurrence: Otway Group, Victoria, Australia.
Age: Early Cretaceous (Latest Aptian–Early Albian).
Known material: Maxilla, teeth.
Holotype: NMV P166409, fragmentary left maxilla with one erupted cheek tooth, three unerupted cheek teeth.

Diagnosis of genus (as for type species): Differs from all other hypsilophodontids (except *Zephyrosaurus*) in that apex of upper cheek teeth is located close to rear of the tooth (instead of about midway between anterior and posterior borders) (Rich and Rich 1989).

Comments: The genus *Atlascopcosaurus* was founded upon a fragmentary cranial remains with teeth (NMV P166409), found at Dinosaur Cove, Otway Group (see Drinnan and Chambers 1986; combined by some authors with the Strzelecki Group into the Korumburra Group; see Wagstaff and Mason 1989 for methods of dating faunas), Point Lewis, southeastern Australia, an area located at the time well within the Antarctic Circle. Referred material includes a left maxilla with seven cheek teeth (NMV P157390) from the same locality and stratigraphic position as the type specimen; isolated, left lower cheek tooth (NMV P177934) from Dinosaur Cove West, Dinosaur Cove; from Dinosaur Cove East, Dinosaur Cove, an isolated, left upper cheek tooth (NMV P181679), left dentary fragment with eleven empty alveoli along the buccal margin and three unerupted teeth lingual to them (NMV P182967), and left maxilla fragment with ten empty alveoli along the buccal margin and three unerupted teeth lingual to them (NMV P185970); and from Slippery Rock, Dinosaur Cove, an isolated, left upper cheek tooth (NMV P181677) of a juvenile, lacking the crown posterior to the primary ridge, isolated, left lower cheek tooth (NMV P186003), right anterior, dentary fragment with the tips of three unerupted teeth showing (NMV P186847), and an isolated, right upper cheek tooth (NMV P187116) (Rich and Rich 1989).

The upper cheek teeth in *Atlascopcosaurus* were distinguished by Rich and Rich from another Aus-

Atlascoposaurus loadsi, NMV P166409, holotype partial maxilla.

Courtesy T. H. Rich.

tralian polar hypsilophodontid, *Leaellynasaura* (Rich and Rich 1989), by the presence of a minimum of eight ridges instead of a maximum of five, the ridges being of two distinct sizes rather than grading between those of maximum and minimum strength, and confined to the buccal surface instead of being developed equally on both sides of unworn teeth; cheek teeth differing *Rhabdodon* [=*Mochlodon* of their usage] (Nopcsa 1904) by a weaker primary ridge, upper cheek teeth distinguished further by the primary ridge near the posterior margin instead of central on the buccal surface of the crown; lower cheek teeth differing from *Kangnasaurus* (Cooper 1985) by a much weaker primary ridge; cheek teeth differing from *Dryosaurus* (Galton 1983*b*) and ?*Valdosaurus* (Galton and Taquet 1982) by the lack of a lozenge-shaped crown and possession of stronger secondary ridges and ridges covering all the buccal surface of the upper cheek teeth and the lingual surface of the lowers instead of being confined to the tooth margins; cheek teeth differing from *Camptosaurus* (Galton and Powell 1980) and *Tenontosaurus* (Galton 1974*b*; Morris 1976) for the same reasons as differing from *Dryosaurus* and ?*Valdosaurus*, but also being notably smaller; cheek differing from *Othnielia* (Galton 1983*b*) by a well-defined primary ridge with stronger secondary ridges that extend almost to the base of the crown; cheek teeth differing from *Phyllodon*, *Nanosaurus* and *Alocodon* (Galton 1983*b*) by their markedly larger size, and in the possession of well-defined primary and secondary ridges instead of only marginal denticles; upper cheek teeth differing from *Hypsilophodon* (Galton 1974*a*) by a distinct secondary ridge and more numerous and prominent secondary ridges; cheek teeth differing from *Parksosaurus* (Galton 1973*a*) in having a distinct and markedly larger primary ridge, from *Zephyrosaurus* (Sues 1980*b*) by a stronger primary ridge and more difference between it and other ridges; upper cheek teeth differing from the isolated hypsilophodontid cheek tooth (QM F9505) from Lightning Ridge, Australia (figured Molnar 1980*d*), by the primary ridge being located near the posterior margin of the buccal surface of the tooth and not near the midpoint; the lower cheek teeth differing from the Lightning Ridge tooth in that the ventral margins of the crown diverge from each other proceeding apically from the root at an approximate 70-degree rather than 45-degree angle.

Rich and Rich observed that both *Atlascopcosaurus* and *Leaellynasaura* were rather small forms, the adults measuring only from about 2 to three meters (about 6.75 to over 10 feet) in length. The authors also noted that no large dinosaurs have been recorded from Victoria, a situation that might either be attributed to prevailing conditions in the area during the Early Cretaceous, or to a bias of collection.

Key reference: Rich and Rich (1989).

AUBLYSODON Leidy 1868

Saurischia: Theropoda: Tetanurae: Avetheropoda: Coelurosauria: Maniraptora: Arctometatarsalia: Tyrannosauridae.

Name derivation: Greek *au* = "backward" + Greek *blysis* = "spout" + Greek *odous* = "tooth."

Type species: *A. mirandus* Leidy 1868.

Other species: ?*A. lateralis* Cope 1876 [*nomen dubium*].

Occurrence: Judith River Formation, Two Medicine Formation, Hell Creek Formation, Montana, Lance Formation, Denver Formation, Wyoming, Kirtland Shale, ?Fruitland Formation, New Mexico, United States.

Age: Late Cretaceous (Late Campanian–Maastrichtian).

Known material: Isolated teeth, incomplete skull, fragmentary skull and postcrania.

Holotype: ANSP 9535, three teeth.

Diagnosis of genus (as for type species): Moderate-sized theropod, apparently with a long and low skull; some (probably premaxillary) teeth D-shaped in cross-section and lacking serrations along posterolateral and posteromedial carinae; posterolateral carina shifted progressively further posteriorly, giving tooth crown a twist in progressively more lateral premaxillary teeth; dentaries slender, with a "step" in alveolar border just posterior to third tooth, and with anteroventral border with acute angle relative to alveolar border; first dentary tooth with medially-displaced anterior carinae, but not D-shaped in cross-section; dentary teeth (except first) and maxillary teeth laterally compressed blades; serrations extending about half-way down anterior edge and to crown base on anterior edge; anterior serrations finer than posterior serrations (Molnar and Carpenter 1989).

Comments: Leidy (1868) established the genus *Aublysodon* on three teeth (ANSP 9535), collected by Ferdinand Vandiveer Hayden from the Judith River Formation at Fort Benton, Choteau County, Montana.

Leidy first described these teeth as incisiform, with a D-shaped cross-section. Cope (1876*b*), Lambe (1902) and Osborn (1905) later observed that two of these teeth, which were serrated, resembled the premaxillary teeth of *Deinodon*. Hence, *Aublysodon* is generally considered to be a junior synonym of that genus. However, as the third tooth in this series is unserrated, Lambe tentatively referred it to the ornithomimid species "*Ornithomimus*" [=*Struthiomimus*] *altus*.

In 1966, a fragmentary skull (LACM 28471) of a moderate-sized theropod was found near a large ?*Triceratops* skull, and collected by Harley Garbanii from a dark clay of the Hell Creek Formation, Garfield County, Montana (Molnar 1978). Later, the specimen was temporarily put on display at the Natural History Museum of Los Angeles County, labeled as a possible juvenile *Tyrannosaurus rex*. However, a juvenile *T. rex* maxilla described by Lawson (1975) differs from this specimen in being deeper, with the maxillary fenestra adjacent to the anterior margin of the antorbital recess.

The Montana specimen, consisting of the front part of the snout and jaws, was described by Molnar who, rather than assigning it a name, referred to it informally as the "Jordan theropod." Molnar noted that the snout is longer, relative to height, than in any known tyrannosaurid, and that the maxilla most closely resembled that of the immature *Albertosaurus libratus* in the American Museum of Natural History collection. The partial endocranial mold from this specimen is similar to those of tyrannosaurids and to *Ceratosaurus*, suggesting well-developed optic lobes and a relatively wide olfactory passage. At that time, Molnar concluded that the "Jordan theropod" was a dromaeosaurid.

Teeth resembling the unserrated tooth assigned to *Aublysodon* were collected from Lance and Hell Creek formations (UCM 43447, 73091, 124367, 124399, 124406, 124978, 124980, 124981 and 124982). These teeth are from juvenile individuals and range from 6.1 (UCMP 124367) to 7 millimeters (UCMP 124981) high from crown tip to crown base, and from 2 (UCMP 124367) to 2.9 millimeters

(UCMP 124978) wide across the face of the tooth near the base. As in the tooth figured by Leidy, these specimens are D-shaped in cross-section, have parallel sides and paired posterior lateral ridges lacking serrations. From these teeth, Carpenter (1982*a*) concluded that *Aublysodon* is a valid genus and designated the unserrated tooth figured by Leidy the lectotype. Carpenter observed that all of these teeth differ from those of other known theropod premaxillary teeth in that the lateral ridges curve toward each other, without meeting, near the base.

Paul (1988*c*), in his book *Predatory Dinosaurs of the World*, had referred the "Jordan theropod" to a new species of *Aublysodon, A. molnaris*, distinguished as somewhat larger than the type species, with larger teeth and a more robust snout, although no other *Aublysodon* specimens have a snout preserved (R. E. Molnar, personal communication 1988).

Molnar and Carpenter (1989), pointing out that Paul's referral of the "Jordan theropod" to *A. molnaris* was founded upon its larger teeth and similarity to undescribed remains from the Judith River Formation, did not attempt to evaluate that species. Instead, they referred the "Jordan theropod" to *Aublysodon* cf. *A. mirandus*, also referring to this genus the following teeth: NMC 116a and 1822, and RTMP 66.31.93, 80.8.192, 80.16.485, 80.16.1202, 81.16.197, 81.19.79, 82.20.457, 85.6.134, 86.77.122–123, 87.36.81, 87.46.24, and 88.4.7, from the Judith River Formation at Dinosaur Provincial Park, Alberta, Canada; YPM-PU 22252, 23328, 23385, 23389, and 23390, from the Judith River Formation of Hill County, Montana; YPM-PU 23391 from the Judith River Formation of Choteau County, Montana;

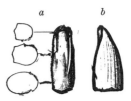

Aublysodon mirandus, ANSP 9335, holotype tooth, a. anterior and b. lateral views. (After Marsh 1892.)

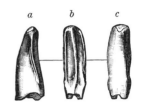

Aublysodon mirandus, YPM 297, holotype tooth of *A. cristatus*, a. side, b. back, and c. front views. (After Marsh 1892.)

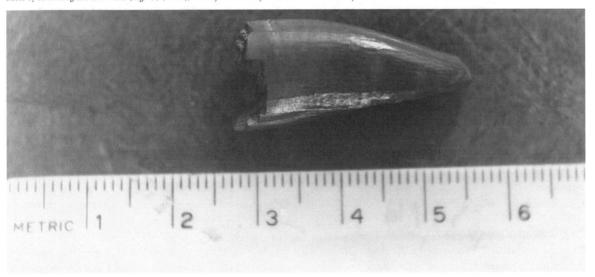

Aublysodon mirandus, YPM 296, holotype tooth of *A. amplus*.

Aublysodon cf. *A. mirandus*, LACM 2847, anterior part of skull.

YPM-PU 23387 from the Two Medicine Formation, Teton County, Montana; UCMP 124367, 124399, 124406, 124978-124982, and 124994, from the Hell Creek Formation at Garfield County and McCone County, Montana; RTMP 87.112.33 and 87.114.7, from the Hell Creek Formation, Montana; UCM 37878 and 43447, UCMP 73091, 73101, 85141, 124993, 124995, 124996, 125229, 125230, 125233, 125234, and 125237, and YPM 296 (holotype of *A. amplus*) and 297 (holotype of *A. cristatus*), from the Lance Formation, Niobrara County, Wyoming; UCM 38060 from the Denver Formation, Arapahoe County, Colorado; KU 12419, from the Kirtland Formation, San Juan County, New Mexico; and ?frontal RTMP 80.16.485 (see Currie 1987*c*).

Later, Lehman and Carpenter (1990), adding that Paul did not give an adequate diagnosis of his species and that the larger size of LACM 28471 was attributed by Molnar and Carpenter to ontogenetic variation, regarded *A. molnaris* as a junior synonym of *A. mirandus*.

Other taxa now regarded as junior synonyms of *A. mirandus* include ?*A. lateralis* Cope 1876 [*nomen dubium*] based on teeth from the Judith River [Oldman] Formation of Montana, and *A. amplus* Marsh 1892 and *A. cristatus* Marsh 1892, both *nomina dubia* based on teeth.

Currie (1987*c*) placed *Aublysodon* in the Tyrannosauridae. Currie, Rigby and Sloan (1990), in a study demonstrating that theropod teeth from the Judith River Formation are diagnostic at the taxon through species levels, observed that the originally figured *Aublysodon* tooth is identical to teeth of the Asian tyrannosaurid *Alectrosaurus*. Other unidentified Judithian teeth (NMC 41104), possibly belonging to a gracile or juvenile tyrannosaurid (or ?dromaeosaurid) could belong to *Aublysodon*. Because of subtle differences in tooth morphology, Currie *et al.* assigned *Aublysodon* to the group Aublysodontinae Nopcsa 1928.

Molnar and Carpenter regarded *Aublysodon* as a primitive genus related to tyrannosaurids. Later, Molnar, Kurzanov and Dong (1990) observed that the "Jordan theropod" skull had appressed against it a premaxillary tooth that matched the lectotype tooth of *A. mirandus,* stating that this skull may pertain to *Aublysodon.* The apparent dromaeosaurid features (*e.g.*, elongate contact between prefrontal and frontal) of the skull once perceived by Molnar (1978) are actually plesiomorphies or otherwise dubious. Although the frontals are long, the confluence of the supratemporal recesses across the parietals, as well as other features, suggest a relationship to tyrannosaurids.

Lehman and Carpenter referred to *Aublysodon* cf. *A. mirandus* a fragmentary skull and postcranial skeleton (OMNH 10131) collected in June 1940 by J. W. Stovall and D. E. Savage in San Juan County, New Mexico, northeast of Chaco Canyon. The material, representing the most complete and diagnostic "carnosaur" remains yet found in the San Juan basin, includes several cranial fragments, an incomplete dentary, parts of both femora, tibia, pubis, metatarsals, several ribs, and gastralia. Although, according to Oklahoma Museum of Natural History records, an ilium was also recovered, that element could not be located. According to Lehman and Carpenter, the mode of preservation of the specimen and the adhering matrix suggest that it came from the Fruitland Formation or lower part of the Kirtland Shale, and probably belongs to the Hunter Wash local fauna (see Lehman 1981; Lucas 1981).

Lehman and Carpenter referred this specimen to the Tyrannosauridae because of its size, general form and proportions, "D-shaped premaxillary tooth, rugose postorbital, well-developed pubic foot, and proximally constricted third metatarsal," and to *Aublysodon* on the basis of the "narrow, elongated, and deeply notched frontals, wide V-shaped frontal-parietal suture, and nonserrated incisiform premaxillary tooth" that compares well with skull specimen LACM 28471.

As described by Lehman and Carpenter, the limb bones of OMNH 10131 are gracile and have

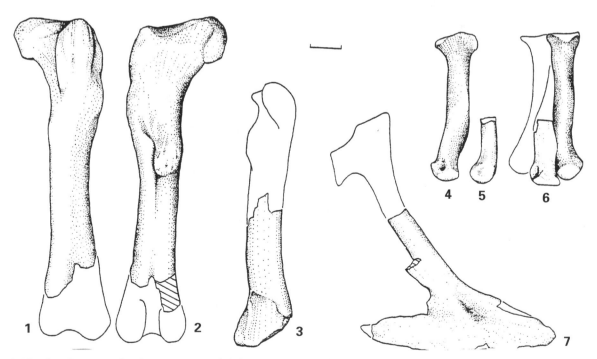

Aublysodon cf. *A. mirandus*, OMNH 10131, 1. left femur, anterior view, 2. same bone, posterior view, 3. right tibia, anterior view, 4. left metatarsal IV, lateral view, 5. left metatarsal III, lateral view, 6. left metatarsals III and IV articulated, anterior view, 7. pubic foot, right lateral view. Scale = 10 cm. (After Lehman and Carpenter 1990.)

Aublysodon mirandus, AMNH 3956, holotype teeth of *A. lateralis*.

AUSTROSAURUS   Longman 1933

Saurischia: Sauropodomorpha: Sauropoda *incertae sedis*.

Name derivation: Latin *auster* = "south" + Greek *sauros* = "lizard."

Type species: *A. mckillopi* Longman 1933.

Other species: [None.]

Occurrence: Allaru Formation, ?Wilton Formation, Queensland, Australia.

Age: Early Cretaceous (Albian).

Known material: Dorsal vertebrae, ?partial limb bones from several individuals.

Holotype: QM F2316, approximately six dorsal centra, neural arches, lower parts of spine, rib fragments.

Diagnosis of genus: [No modern diagnosis published.]

Comments: The second sauropod known from Australia (after *Rhoetosaurus*), the genus *Austrosaurus* was established from very incomplete postcranial remains (QM F2316), recovered from the Allaru Formation [Tambo Series], Clutha, Queensland.

Longman (1933) originally diagnosed *Austrosaurus* as follows: primitively structured dorsal vertebrae similar to those in middle-Jurassic sauropods from other continents; dorsal centra spongy-boned, with poorly-developed pleurocoels and thick walls, the latter filled with small, connecting and closed cav-

proportions similar to those in *Albertosaurus*, though the tibia and metatarsals are shorter relative to the femur. Also, the distal end of the tibia shows a medial emargination thus far not known in other tyrannosaurids. According to Lehman and Carpenter, OMNH 10131 represents a large individual, comparable in size to other tyrannosaurid adults. Many of its postcranial features are indistinguishable from those in *Albertosaurus*.

Based upon Rosenzweig's (1966) concept of the hunting set (introduced for mammals), Molnar offered a possible hunting set for the Hell Creek Formation theropods. This hypothetical set, arranged according to a sequence of skull sizes in descending order, included *T. rex*, *Nanotyrannus* [=*Albertosaurus* of his usage] *lancensis*, the "Jordan theropod" and, representing dromaeosaurids known only from isolated and unnamed teeth, the nonpresent *Saurornithoides mongoliensis*, the "Jordan theropod" filling a gap in the sequence by feeding on small prey.

Key references: Carpenter (1982*a*); Cope (1876); Currie (1987*b*); Currie, Rigby and Sloan (1990); Lambe (1902); Lehman and Carpenter (1990); Leidy (1868); Molnar (1978); Molnar and Carpenter (1989); Paul (1988*c*).

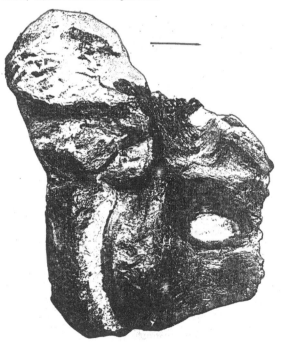

Austrosaurus mckillopi, QM F2316, holotype incomplete dorsal vertebra, "Specimen A," lateral view. Scale = approximately 6 cm.

Photo by W. J. Sanderson. (After Longman 1933.)

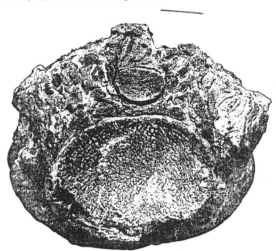

Austrosaurus mckillopi, QM F2316, holotype dorsal vertebra, "Specimen B," posterior view. Scale = approximately 4 cm.

ities; caudal vertebrae of simple structure, no struts, buttresses or laminae in the arches; coracoid with a notch instead of foramen; metacarpals exceptionally long relative to other forelimb elements and to those in other sauropods; forelimb very long, especially distally.

Five specimens from a relatively primitive sauropod, found in the middle Cretaceous Wilton Formation (Late Albian to Early Cenomanian; Dettmann 1973) of Queensland, were described by Coombs and Molnar (1981) and designated *Austrosaurus* sp. These specimens include the proximal and distal ends of a humerus, proximal and distal ends of a femur, proximal ends of three metacarpals (QM F3390); nine caudal vertebrae, an incomplete neural arch, three partial dorsal vertebrae, an incomplete scapula, proximal ends of the ischium, and pieces of ribs (QM F6737); a metacarpal, distal end of a possible ulna, and the distal end of a femur (QM F7291); 18 caudal vertebrae, one possible carpal, two incomplete ulnae, two partial radii, two partial humeri, an incomplete scapular blade, possible ilium fragment, four metacarpals, and rib pieces (QM F7292); and possible coracoid and femoral head (QM F7880). The specimens are too fragmentary to make good comparisons with other sauropods, though the similarities between this material and *Rhoetosaurus* are few. The material was described due to the paucity of Australian dinosaur fossils.

As shown by Coombs and Molnar, *Austrosaurus* has features similar to those in both cetiosaurs and brachiosaurs. However, despite the long forelimb in *Austrosaurus*, this genus more closely resembles a cetiosaurid [=cetiosaurine of their usage]. Though the metacarpals are elongate, the humerus is not, suggesting that *Austrosaurus* may not be a brachiosaurid [=brachiosaurine of their usage] but some other type of sauropod paralleling Brachiosauridae.

In his review of sauropods, McIntosh (1990*b*) briefly described *A. mckillopi* as follows: Dorsal vertebrae strongly opisthocoelous, with large balls and cups, deep pleurocoels bored into centrum rather than expanding inside it; rest of centrum lightened by labyrinthine complex of small intramural cavities separated by very thin plates of bone; centra unlike those in other known sauropods. McIntosh noted that, although *Austrosaurus* is sometimes classified as a camarasaurid, the close cancellous structure of the bones in camarasaurids precludes that assignment.

Note: The referral of the Wilton Formation specimens to *Austrosaurus*, though likely, is highly conjectural (J. S. McIntosh, personal communication 1987).

Possibly referable to *Austrosaurus* is the so-called "Hughenden sauropod," an undescribed Australian form ?20 meters (about 86 feet) long, known from material collected near Hughenden. Molnar (1982*b*) noted that this material may involve two different specimens representing a single taxon, including an incomplete humerus (QM L349) from Silver Hills, and the posterior portion of a cervical vertebra (QM F6142) from Pelican, the latter closely resembling the same element in *Brachiosaurus brancai*. Since the neck of *Austrosaurus* is not known, an exact identification of it with the Hughenden material cannot be made.

Key references: Coombs and Molnar (1981); Longman (1933); McIntosh (1990*b*); Molnar (1982*b*).

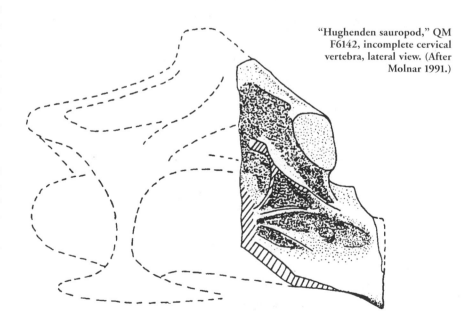

"Hughenden sauropod," QM F6142, incomplete cervical vertebra, lateral view. (After Molnar 1991.)

AVACERATOPS   Dodson 1986

Ornithischia: Genasauria: Cerapoda: Margin-ocephalia: Ceratopsia: Neoceratopsia: Ceratopsidae: Centrosaurinae.

Name derivation: "Ava [Cole]" + Greek *keratops* = "horn face."

Type species: *A. lammersi* Dodson 1986.

Other species: [None.]

Occurrence: Dinosaur Park [Judith River] Formation, Montana, United States.

Age: Late Cretaceous (Late Campanian).

Known material/holotype: ANSP 15800, incomplete skull, most of appendicular skeleton, some vertebrae, ribs, ?subadult.

Diagnosis of genus (as for type species): Squamosal distinctive, robust, with long rostral portion; squamosal prominent in outline of the frill, but does not continue the smooth curve of the parietal border; parietal thin, fan-shaped, with no sagittal emargination along caudal margin; apparently no parietal openings; jugal thin, lacks central ridge; premaxilla relatively long, with long ventral edge; maxilla robust, with strong medial ridge (Dodson 1986).

Comments: The genus *Avaceratops* was established on an incomplete skull and partial postcranial skeleton (ANSP 15800), belonging to a young individual. The specimen was collected between 1981 and 1986 by field parties from the University of Pennsylvania and the Academy of Natural Sciences of Philadelphia, from the Careless Creek bonebed (discovered earlier that year by Eddy Cole, husband of Ava Cole), "Judith River" Formation, near Shawmut, Wheatland County, Montana (about 160 kilometers south of localities worked by Edward Drinker Cope and Joseph Leidy on the Missouri River.) Thus far, *Avaceratops* represents the most complete dinosaur spec-

Avaceratops lammersi, ANSP 5800, holotype skeleton, skull almost complete, nasals, frontals, postorbitals among elements not preserved.

Photo by David Bennett, courtesy Library, The Academy of Natural Sciences of Philadelphia.

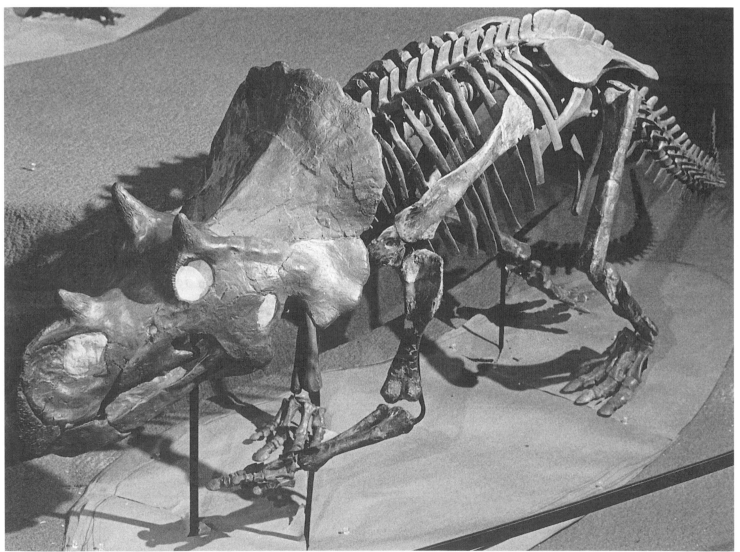

imen collected from Montana's "Judith River" Formation. The discovery was first reported by Dodson (1984a), who published a preliminary description of the still unnamed new genus.

As observed by Dodson (1986), the squamosal in *Avaceratops* has more than the usual prominence in the composition of the frill. The imperfectly preserved left jugal shows no evidence of thickening of the distal tip as in *Centrosaurus* or *Brachyceratops*. The maxilla is apparently relatively longer than in *Brachyceratops*. There is no preserved evidence suggesting the pattern of the horns. The ulna seems less robust than in *Brachyceratops*, with a less pronounced olecranon process. The unguals are not hoof-like, as in large ceratopsids, but flattened, tapering and bluntly rounded at the apex, suggestive of the manual unguals in *Leptoceratops* and pedal unguals in *Protoceratops*.

Dodson (1986) estimated the length of the holotype skeleton, when complete, to be about 2.3 meters (almost 8 feet) ± 83 millimeters (over 3.5 inches), but inferred that the length of a fully grown adult would be about 4 meters (about 13.5 feet), relatively less than that of typical "Judith River" Formation ceratopsids. To support this idea, Dodson pointed out that the occipital condyle in immature ceratopsids is clearly divided into the paired exoccipitals and median basioccipital (see Hatcher, Marsh and Lull 1907), while these three components, in adults, fuse into a single sphere-shaped structure, as in *Avaceratops*. Also, the pedal unguals in this genus have a protoceratopsid-like rather than ceratopsid-like character. These two lines of evidence suggest a different growth pattern in *Avaceratops*, resulting in a possibly smaller adult size.

In their review of the Neoceratosauria, Dodson and Currie (1990) suggested that *A. lammersi* is a relatively primitive centrosaurine, more so than *Brachyceratops*.

Not all workers have been convinced that *Avaceratops* is a young adult. Fiorillo (1987) suggested that the remains might belong to a juvenile. Penkalski (1993), in a preliminary report, believed that the type specimen belongs to a subadult. Furthermore, Penkalski stated that cladistic analysis shows that *Avaceratops* is the most primitive known ceratopsid, plesiomorphies including the following: Adult size relatively small; squamosal with distinct shape and long rostral half; tooth count low; limb elements gracile overall; ulna with small olecranon process; deltopectoral crest of humerus not as distally expanded as in later ceratopsids; tibia/femur ratio higher; unguals tapering instead of rounded. Penkalski also noted that this genus shares two characters with *Triceratops* (*i.e.*. solid frill and lack of sagittal indentation along posterior frill border.

Note: Olshevsky (1991) pointed out that, since the species *A. lammersi* was named after various members of a family rather than an individual, the species name, according to Article 31[a][ii] of the International Code of Zoological Nomenclature, should take the plural-ending spelling, the species thereby corrected to *A. lammersorum*. The ICZN has not ruled on this new name, nor has the name been adopted.

Key references: Dodson (1984a, 1986); Dodson and Currie (1990); Fiorillo (1987); Penkalski (1993).

AVIMIMUS Kurzanov 1981

Saurischia: Theropoda: Tetanurae: Avetheropoda: Coelurosauria: Maniraptora: Arctometatarsalia *incertae sedis.*

Name derivation: Latin *avis* = "bird" + Greek *mimos* = "mimic."

Type species: *A. portentosus* Kurzanov 1981.

Other species: [None.]

Occurrence: "Barungoyotskaya" Svita, Omnogov, "Djadochtinskaya" Svita, Ovorkhangai, Mongolian People's Republic.

Age: Late Cretaceous (?Early Cenomanian).

Known material: Three incomplete skeletons.

Holotype: PIN 3907/1, incomplete skeleton including humerus, shoulder girdle, partial pelvic girdle, four consecutive dorsal vertebrae.

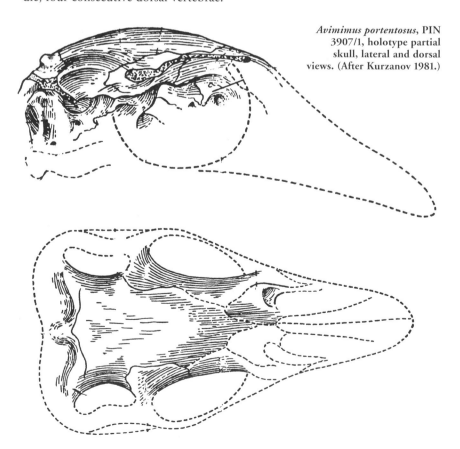

Avimimus portentosus, PIN 3907/1, holotype partial skull, lateral and dorsal views. (After Kurzanov 1981.)

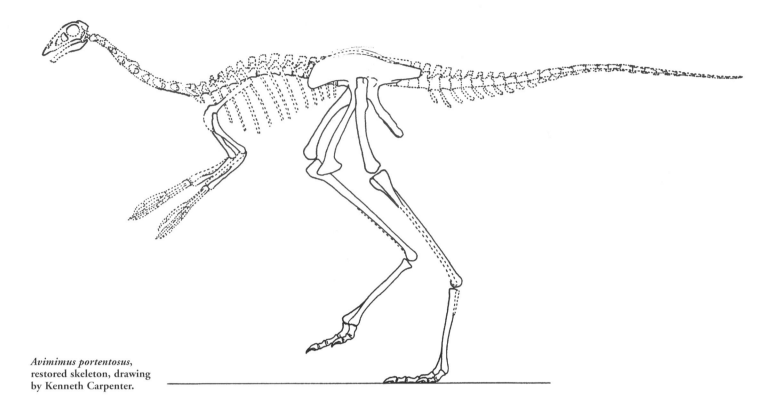

Avimimus portentosus,
restored skeleton, drawing
by Kenneth Carpenter.

Diagnosis of genus (as for type species): Skull with edentulous premaxillae, bony denticulation (as in lambeosaurine hadrosaurids), narial openings that extend to above orbit (as in sauropods), and fused braincase (as in birds and some theropods); ?hypapophysis on cervical vertebrate (birdlike feature of maniraptorans); ilium markedly inclined medially (birdlike feature); metatarsal V retained (as in primitive dinosaurs); shaft of ulna with crest (unique feature, ?birdlike); metacarpals I-III fused at their bases (birdlike) (Norman 1990).

Comments: The genus *Avimimus* was founded upon an incomplete skeleton (PIN 3907/1), recovered from the Gobi Desert in Mongolia, during the Soviet-Mongolian Expedition of 1971 (Kurzanov 1981).

Kurzanov originally diagnosed *Avimimus* as very birdlike, with such avian characters as a slender body, long and slender birdlike neck, slim legs, and birdlike feet.

Considering *Avimimus* to be distinctive enough to warrant its own higher taxon, Kurzanov erected for it the monotypic Avimidae.

Discovery of a pelvic fragment of *A. portentosus*, during the Joint Soviet-Mongolian Paleontological Expedition in 1980 at Udan-Sayr, shed new data on the pelvic structure of this species. The specimen (PIN 3907/2) consisted of the proximal part of the left pubic and ischial bones, which had grown together into a single unit. Kurzanov (1983) noted

that the proximal part of the pubic bone in the holotype had been misidentified in his original diagnosis. Based on these new remains, *Avimimus* seems to have been over one to about 1.5 meters (3.5 to 5 feet) in length.

Considering its birdlike features, Kurzanov (1981) suggested that *Avimimus* might have had feathers, though no feather impressions were found with any remains. (The presence of feathers in dinosaurs is, at present, a speculative notion. No certain feather impressions have yet been found with any specimen conclusively identified as dinosaurian [excluding Aves].) Kurzanov speculated that the very birdlike humerus possessed ridges to which flight muscles might have been attached. The ulna has a bony crest which, as in birds, may have been a place for feather attachment. If feathers were present in *Avimimus*, they were more likely used for body insulation than flight. *Avimimus* was probably a cursorially active creature that caught insects and small reptiles for food. As some paleontologists believe today, if cursorial dinosaurs like *Avimimus* were endothermic, feathers would have helped prevent loss of body heat.

Reviewing problematic "coelurosaurs," Norman (1990) pointed out that many of the features of the braincase of this genus resemble the condition in sauropods; the skull and lower jaw seem to resemble oviraptorids; the vertebral column is basically typical of most small theropods; except for the avian feature

of the ilium, the rest of that element seems to be typically theropod; and the hindlimb is typical of theropods in most respects. *Avimimus* exhibits a small number of tetanuran and ornithomimid characters, while the development of hypapophyses on the cervical vertebrae is a maniraptoran character.

Owing to the unique combination of characters displayed in *Avimimus* that suggest affinities with theropods, sauropods, ornithopods and birds, Norman (1990) advised against attempting to determine the precise affinities of this genus with currently recognized higher taxa. Holtz (1994*a*), in his revision of the Theropoda, assigned *Avimimus* to the maniraptoran group Arctometatarsalia.

Note: The tibia in *A. portentosus* is quite slender, as in *Kakuru*, but with a tibiotarsus (R. E. Molnar, personal communication 1987).

The former Cenomanian age suggested for the Iren Dabasu Formation (Upper Cretaceous) at Iren Nor Inner Mongolia, People's Republic of China, was questioned by Currie and Eberth (1993) as possibly being too old. As noted by Currie and Eberth, the fossil assemblage of the Iren Dabasu Formation is close to that of the Bayn Shire Formation of Mongolia. However, the presence in the Iren Dabasu Formation of *Avimimus* and *Saurornithoides* and their absence in the Bayn Shire Formation, both theropods (as well as *Velociraptor*) characteristic of the Dja-

dochta Formation (Campanian) and younger Mongolian sediments, indicate that the Iren Dabasu Formation is younger than Cenomanian. According to Currie and Eberth, the best age now considered for this formation is Early Cenomanian, although preliminary data suggest that it may later prove to be as young as Campanian.

Key references: Kurzanov (1981, 1983); Norman (1990).

AZENDOHSAURUS   Dutuit 1972 [*nomen dubium*]

Saurischia: Sauropodomorpha: Prosauropoda *incertrae sedis*.

Name derivation: "Azendoh [village]" + Greek *sauros* = "lizard."

Type species: *A. laaroussii* Dutuit 1972 [*nomen dubium*].

Other species: [None.]

Occurrence: Argana Formation, Atlas Mountains, Marrakech, Morocco.

Age: Late Triassic (Carnian).

Known material: Fragment of mandible, isolated teeth, dentaries and dentary fragments, maxillae.

Holotype: MNHN MTD XVI 1, incomplete dentary with teeth.

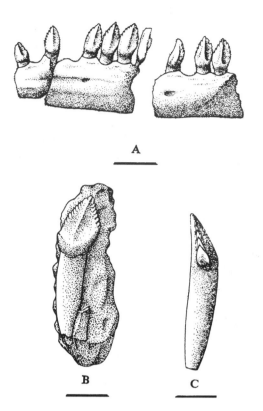

Azendohsaurus laaroussii, MNHN MTD XVI 1, holotype
A. incomplete lower jaw with teeth (buccal view; scale = 1
cm.), B. tooth in buccal view (scale = .50 cm.) and C. distal
view (scale = .33 cm). (After Dutuit 1972.)

Diagnosis of genus (as for type species): Prosauropod with following autapomorphies: neck between crown and root of tooth consistently present; antero-posterior expansion of crown always beginning at its base; prominent longitudinal keel on medial face of maxillary; fossa posterior to dorsal process on medial face of maxillary; entire anterior rim of dentary inclining ventrally, forming angle with dorsal rim of dentary. Other significant characters: Series of foramanina on medial face of maxillary, each situated at base of a tooth; truncate cone-shaped maxillary process with wide base (Gauffrey 1993).

Comments: The genus *Azendohsaurus* was established upon an incomplete dentary with teeth (MNHN MTD XVI 1), collected in 1965–66 from the northern part of the Argana Formation, near and east of the village of Azendoh, "Argana corridor," Morocco. Cotype specimens consist of two teeth (MNHN MTD XVI 2, MTD XVI 3) (Dutuit 1972).

Incorrectly interpreting these remains to be ornithischian, Dutuit originally diagnosed *Azendohsaurus* (and type species *A. laaroussii*) as an ornithischian similar to *Fabrosaurus australis*.

Galton (1990*a*) observed that the dentary teeth and a loose tooth of *Azendohsaurus* are actually from a prosauropod, as the crowns are symmetrical in mesiodistal views and the marginal serrations are finer and more numerous, as in the primitive prosauropod *Thecodontosaurus antiquus*. Galton interpreted *A. laaroussii* as a thecodontosaurid prosauropod.

The holotype was evaluated again by Guaffre (1993) after study of additional specimens from the type locality. These further remains include two isolated teeth (paratypes MNHN-ALM 424-5 [MTD XVI 2] and ALM 424-4 [MTD XVI 3]), both consisting of isolated teeth, and various referred specimens. Other referred material include an almost complete left dentary (MNHN-ALM 351) visible only in external view; right dentary (MNHN-ALM 365-20), visible in lingual view, missing the ends; dentary fragments (MNHN-ALM 353, ALM 365-17, and ALM 365-18); left maxillary (MNHN-ALM 355-3), visible in lingual view, with posterior region missing, and with damaged dorsal part of dorsal process; and an isolated right maxillary (MNHN-ALM 365-21).

After comparing the above material with various nondinosaurian groups of comparable age, Gauffrey observed that the morphology of the teeth closely resembles that of prosauropods and ornithischians. Gauffrey concluded that this material belongs to a valid taxon and a single dinosaurian genus and species possessing the following taxonomically significant characters: Well-developed dorsal process of maxillary, well individualized with base situated at bone's anterior half (prosauropod feature); teeth without wear surfaces (nonyunnanosaurid prosauropod); maximum height of dentition reaching between anterior quarter and anterior third of tooth row (sauropodomorph); no evidence of predentary (nonornithischian); no buccal emargination on maxillary (nonornithischian). Gauffrey placed *A. laaroussii* within Prosauropoda, but was unable to assign the species to any further subgroup, other than to determine its nonyunnanosaurid status.

Dated as of Carnian age, *A. laaroussii*, Gauffrey noted, is one of the earliest prosauropods as well as one of the earliest dinosaurs.

Key references: Dutuit (1972); Galton (1990*a*); Gauffrey (1993).

Azendohsaurus laaroussii, MNHN-ALM 351, left dentary, external view. Scale = 10 mm. (After Gauffrey 1993, courtesy The Palaeontological Association.)

BACTROSAURUS   Gilmore 1933

Ornithischia: Genasauria: Cerapoda: Ornithopoda: Iguanodontia: Hadrosauridae: Lambeosaurinae.

Name derivation: "Bactria [province of Asia]" + Greek *sauros* = "lizard."

Type species: *B. johnsoni* Gilmore 1933.

Other species: *B. kysylkumensis* (Riabinin 1931).

Occurrence: Iren (Erlien) Dabusu Formation, Nei Mongol, Zizhiqu, People's Republic of China; Kazakstan, Russia; "Northern Eurasia" [*B. kyslykumensis*].

Age: Late Cretaceous (?early Cenomanian).

Known material: Associated disarticulated cranial and postcranial material representing at least six individuals, juvenile to adult, other cranial and postcranial remains [for type species], jaw fragments, teeth, and vertebrae.

Holotype: AMNH 6553, left maxilla, dentary, ten dorsal vertebrae, ridged sacrum with seven sacral vertebrae, 36 caudal vertebrae, left scapula, left sternum, both pubes, both ischia, ilium, left femur, fibula, complete left and partial right pes.

Diagnosis of genus (as for type species): Reduced dentition, with 23 vertical rows of dentary teeth, 28 maxillary teeth; spines of posterior dorsal vertebrae tall and (in front view) "club-shaped"; five coossified sacral vertebrae; ilium arched strongly, with decurved preacetabular process; ischium stout, with expanded "foot"; pubis short with extended blade; terminal pedal phalanges with thickened truncate anterior borders (Gilmore 1933b). [Note: Not all of these characters are regarded today as diagnostic, applying either to all lambeosaurines or to hadrosaurids in general. Brett-Surman (1989) pointed out that thickened and sometimes fluted anterior borders of the toes and clubbed vertebral spines are an old age character.]

Diagnosis of *B. kyslykumensis*: [Modern diagnosis unavailable as of this writing].

Comments: The oldest known true lambeosaurine, the genus *Bactrosaurus* was established upon incomplete crania and postcrania (AMNH 6553), collected in 1923 by Albert F. Johnson from "Johnson's Quarry," in the Iren Dabasu Formation (defined by and dated Lower Cretaceous by Granger and Berkey 1922; ?early Cenomanian; see Currie and Eberth 1993) of Mongolia. Found at the same locality were the posterior parts (skull roof and neurocranium) of two hadrosaurid skulls (AMNH 6365 and 6366).

Photo by the author, courtesy American Museum of Natural History.

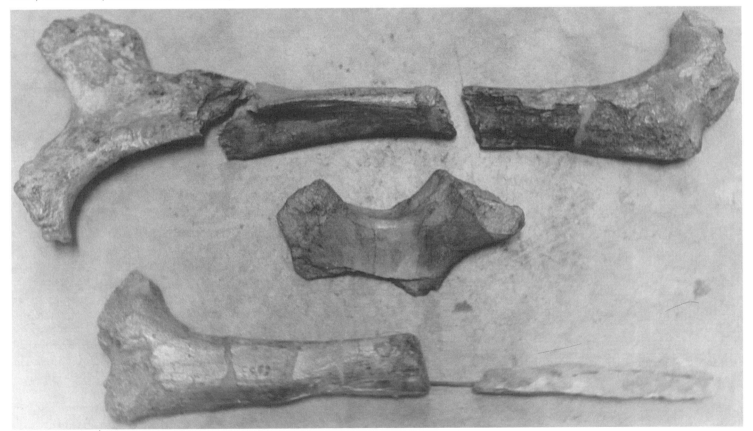

Bactrosaurus johnsoni, AMNH 6553, holotype ischia and fragments.

Bactrosaurus

Bactrosaurus johnsoni, AMNH 6553, holotype pubes.

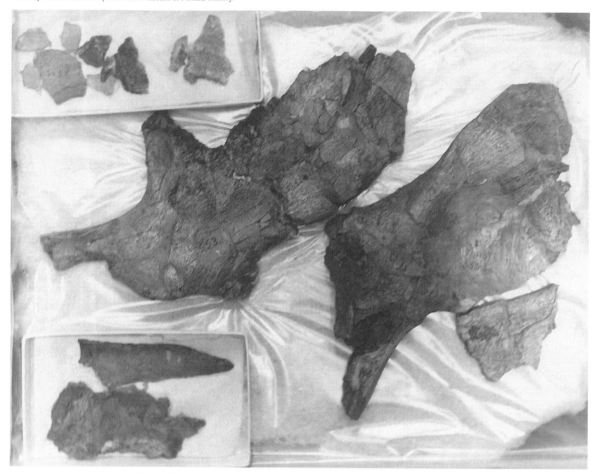

Gilmore was puzzled that the better preserved of the two associated skulls (AMNH 6365) did not possess a hollow crest, while other features, particularly of the postcrania, indicated that *Bactrosaurus* was a lambeosaurine. These features include the characteristic reduced dentition, footed ischium, widely expanded prepubis, and highly arched ilium. As shown by Brett-Surman (1975), curvature of the outline of the ilium and pubis in *Bactrosaurus* is diagnostically characteristic of lambeosaurines. Despite the apparently paradoxial skull, Gilmore regarded *B. johnstoni* as belonging to the Lambeosaurinae, noting that its discovery fully established the occurrence of the Lambeosaurinae in the Iren Dabasu region.

A second species, *B. prynadai* (*nomen dubium*) Riabinin 1937, was based on right and left mandibles (PEN AN SSR 32/5009 and 33/5009), and part of the upper jaw (PEN AN SSR 31/5009), found in 1923 at Kyrk-kuduk, Alym-Tau Range, near the Sary-Agach railway station, Kazakhstan, Russia. This species has been referred to *B. johnsoni.*

Because of its "flat-headed" skull (AMNH 6365), Rozhdestvensky (1966) transferred *Bactrosaurus* to the Hadrosaurinae. Yang [Young] (1958) referred the AMNH 6365 skull, along with the holotype (PEN AN SSR 31/5009, 32/5009, and 33/5009) of *B. prynadai* Riabinin 1939 [*nomen dubium*], to hadrosaurine *Tanius sinensis.* Maryańska and Osmólska (1981) disputed the assignment of the AMNH 6365 skull to *Bactrosaurus,* noting that it did not belong to the type specimen, and, pointing out the close resemblance between this skull and that of *T. sinensis,* tentatively referred it to that species. Weishampel and Horner recognized this skull as hadrosaurine and referred it to another Iren Dabasu hadrosaur, *Gilmoreosaurus mongoliensis.*

Examining one left and three right previously undescribed prefrontal bones (respectively AMNH 6584, 6585, 6586 and 6587) not reported by Gilmore, from the same formation, Weishampel and Horner (1986) observed that a hollow lambeosaurine crest is indeed present in the skull of *Bactrosaurus.* These four prefrontals are morphologically similar to each other. In each case, the lateral wall extends dorsally to form a thin, vertically oriented and caudally elongate wall that is somewhat crescent-shaped in outline and bounded ventrally by the rugose orbital margin. Several shallow and faintly striated cavities

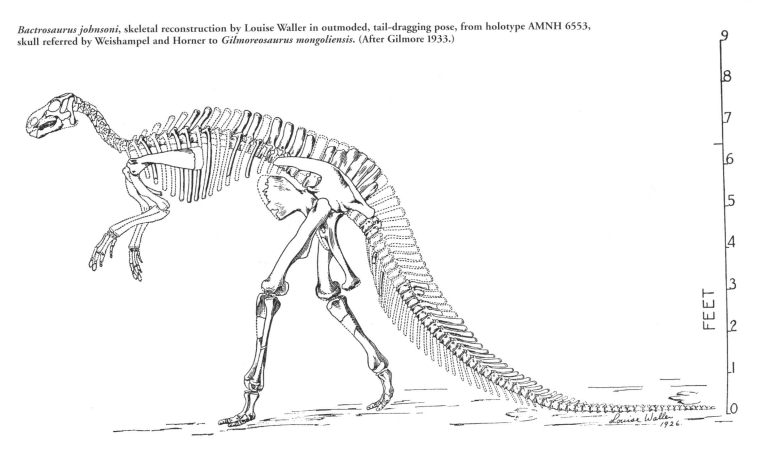

Bactrosaurus johnsoni, skeletal reconstruction by Louise Waller in outmoded, tail-dragging pose, from holotype AMNH 6553, skull referred by Weishampel and Horner to *Gilmoreosaurus mongoliensis*. (After Gilmore 1933.)

(including the rostral cavity which contacts the lacrimal) are borne on this wall medially, directly above the orbit for the premaxilla, and caudally for what Weishampel and Horner interpreted as the nasal portion of a hollow crest. As no evidence has been found to suggest the presence of any other lambeosaurine in the Iren Dabasu or Iren Nor localities, Weishampel and Horner referred all of the above lambeosaurine material to *B. johnsoni*.

Bactrosaurus was a relatively heavy animal, massive and powerful, more so than its hadrosaurine contemporary *Gilmoreosaurus*. From measurements made by Gilmore, this dinosaur attained an approximate length of 6 meters (20 feet) and was more than 1.9 meters (6.5 feet) high at the hips. Its weight was about 1.11 metric tons (almost 1.25 tons) (G. S. Paul, personal communication 1988).

Though superficially resembling an iguanodontid, *Bactrosaurus* is one of the earliest known primitive hadrosaurs. Brett-Surman (1975, 1989) observed that *Bactrosaurus* is most similar to the more derived *Parasaurolophus*, both having a greatly expanded, "footed" ischium, very thick ischial shaft, prepubes with greatest length-to-width ratio of the pubic blade, and smallest length-to-width ratio of the pubic neck. This suggests that, due to similarities of their pelvic girdles but because of the difference in

geologic age, *Bactrosaurus* may be ancestral to *Parasaurolophus*.

The species *B. kysylkumensis* (Riabinin 1931) was founded on a fragmentary left dentary, four vertebrae, and a tibia from Djira-Kuduk, and two caudal vertebrae from the shores of Lake Khodja-Kul, Sultan-uis-dag (of Turonian or Cenomanian age), Amu-Daria River, Kysyl-Kum Desert, Russia, this material originally referred to *Cionodon*. Rozhdestvensky (1977) referred *C. kysylkumensis* to "*Thespesius*," after which Nessov (1995), following the collection of new material from "Northern Eurasia," referred this species to *Bactrosaurus*.

Key references: Brett-Surman (1975, 1989); Gilmore (1933*b*); Maryańska and Osmólska (1981); Nessov (1995); Riabinin (1931, 1937); Rozhdestvensky (1966); Weishampel and Horner (1986); Yang [Young] (1958).

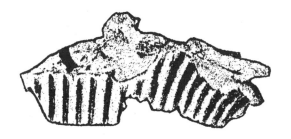

Bactrosaurus Kysylkumensis, holotype fragmentary dentary of Cionodon *Kysylkumensis*. (After Riabinin 1931.)

BAGACERATOPS Osmólska and Maryańska 1975
Ornithischia: Genasauria: Cerapoda: Ceratopsia: Neoceratopsia: Protoceratopsidae, Protoceratopsinae.

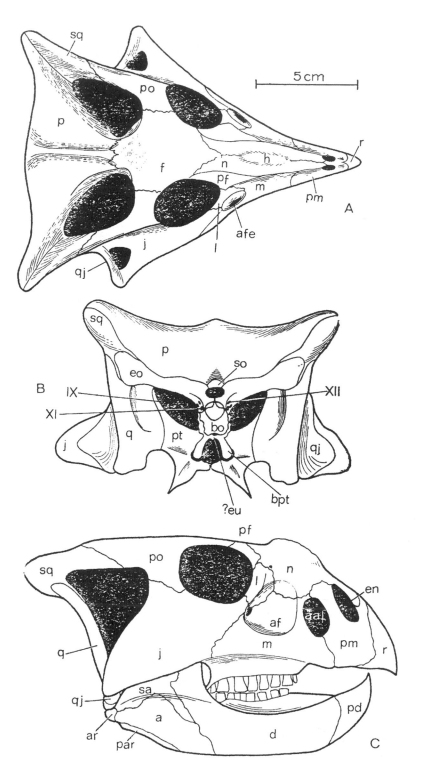

Bagaceratops rozhdestvenskyi, ZPAL MgD-I/125, holotype skull in A. dorsal, B. posterior, and C. lateral views. (After Maryańska and Osmólska 1975.)

Name derivation: Mongolian *baga* = "small" + Greek *keratos* = "horned" + Greek *ops* = "face."

Type species: *B. rozhdestvenskyi* Maryańska and Osmólska 1975.

Other species: [None.]

Occurrence: Red of Beds of Khermeen Tsav, Omnogov, Mongolian People's Republic.

Age: Late Cretaceous (middle–late Campanian).

Known material: Five complete and 17 fragmentary skulls, postcranial skeletons, juvenile to adult.

Holotype: ZPAL MgD-I/126, nearly complete skull with mandible, lacking anterior part of snout, adult.

Diagnosis of genus (as for type species): Frill short; nasal horn core prominent, moderate-sized; additional antorbital openings present in premaxilla-maxilla suture (this character unique among other known protoceratopsids); preorbital part of snout short; no premaxillary teeth, ten maxillary teeth; anterior part of upper jaw long, toothless; mandible shallow, with straight ventral margin (Maryańska and Osmólska 1975).

Comments: *Bagaceratops* was founded on an almost complete skull with lower jaw (ZPAL MgD-126), collected from Khermeen Tsav (Red Beds, middle-late Campanian; see Currie 1991; Dong 1993a), southwest of the Nemegt Basin, Gobi Desert, Mongolia. Referred to this genus from the same locality were the skull with dentary (ZPAL MgD-I/123) of an immature individual, lacking palatal, basicranial and occipital regions, an almost complete adult skull (ZPAL MgD-I 127, 129, and 133) missing nasals and posterior cranial portions, 17 fragmentary skulls (ZPAL 137-140), eight mandibles (ZPAL MgD-I/152-154), loose teeth (ZPAL MgD-I/141 and 151), and various postcranial fragments (ZPAL MgD-I/142, 146, 152 and 154) (Maryańska and Osmólska 1975).

As described by Maryańska and Osmólska, the skull of *B. rozhdestvenskyi* is triangular shape and somewhat narrow, the frill nearly horizontal in position. *Bagaceratops* resembles both *Leptoceratops gracilis* and *Microceratops gobiensis*, differing from the former in having a developed nasal horn and slightly longer frill. The various collected skulls range in length from 4 to 25 centimeters (1.5 to 10 inches), with adult *Bagaceratops* measuring about 90 centimeters (3 feet) long.

Maryańska and Osmólska observed ontogenetic differences in various *Bagaceratops* skulls, five apparently representing mature individuals. Only one skull (ZPAL MgD-I/125) exhibits any significant morphological variation—a relatively slight widening of the frill and a comparatively larger horn core, characters which Brown and Schlaikjer (1940) interpreted as sexual dimorphic features in sexually mature adults. As this skull is smaller than the other four and apparently younger, Maryańska and Osmólska attributed their differences either to ontogenetic or individual variability.

Maryańska and Osmólska compared an immature *Bagaceratops* skull (ZPAL MgD-I/123), measuring 47 millimeters (about 1.8 inches) long (then the smallest known dinosaur skull reported), with mature specimens, noting various growth changes that may be applied to different species within the Protoceratopsidae. These changes include a decrease in relative length of the orbit, slight increase in length of the snout, temporary lengthening of the frill which eventually stops as the rest of the skull continues to grow, increase in width of the frill, and increase in width across the quadrates and jugals.

Dodson and Currie (1990) noted that *Bagaceratops*, although coming from younger strata than *Protoceratops andrewsi* and possessing a nasal horn, is more primitive in most respects than that species; more primitive than *L. gracilis* as the squamosal and jugal are separated by the postorbital; and that its ten maxillary teeth constitutes the lowest tooth count in any known neoceratopsian species.

Note: Originally, Maryańska and Osmólska included an ?unfenestrated parietal in their suite of diagnostic characters of *B. rozhdestvensky*. However, in a later personal communication to Dodson, Osmólska stated that the parietal does possess a fenestra (see Dodson and Currie), that character, therefore, having been deleted from their diagnosis.

Key references: Dodson and Currie (1990); Maryańska and Osmólska (1975).

BAHARIASAURUS Stromer 1934

Saurischia: Theropoda: Tetanurae *incertae sedis.*

Name derivation: "Baharija [Oasis]" + Greek *sauros* = "lizard."

Type species: *B. ingens* Stromer 1934.

Other species: [None.]

Occurrence: Baharija Formation, Marsa Matruh, Egypt; Faraka Formation, Tahousa, "Continental intercalaire," [unnamed formation], Agadez, Niger.

Age: Early–Late Cretaceous, (?late Albian–?early Cenomanian).

Known material: Isolated postcrania.

Holotype: IPHG 1922 [?destroyed], two dorsal vertebrae, three sacral vertebrae, two pubes, ischium.

Diagnosis of genus (as for type species): Three sacral vertebrae solidly fused, fourth free; sacrals platycoelous, about twice as long as wide, about length of those in the larger "*Gorgosaurus;*" ischium considerably smaller than in *Carcharodontosaurus*, similarly deeply pitted; acetabulum with small concave edge proportionally longer, pubic articulation not as high as in *Carcharodontosaurus*; pubes inclined toward each other, fused for most of their length, about size of those in "*Gorgosaurus*," with shafts opposing one another (as in *Carcharodontosaurus*) (Stromer 1934).

Comments: The genus *Bahariasaurus* was founded upon various postcranial elements (IPHG 1922), discovered in the Baharija Basin of Egypt. Referred material from the same locality includes pelvic elements, caudal vertebrae, a femur, and fibula (IPHG 1912), and an ischium, and caudals (IPHG 1911) from juvenile individuals (Stromer 1934). (The type specimen, no longer in the Institut für Paläontologie und Historische Geologie collection, was apparently destroyed in 1944 during World War II by an American bombing raid.)

Bagaceratops rozhdestvenskyi, ZPAL MgD-I/123, immature skull., A. lateral and B. dorsal views. (After Maryańska and Osmólska 1975.)

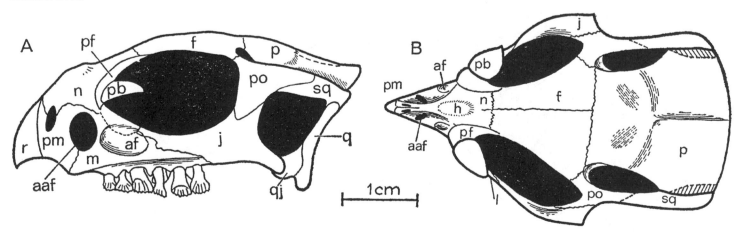

caudals as 6 and 5.5 centimeters (about 2.3 and 2.2 inches) respectively, the second having prominent chevrons; the remaining three caudals respectively 6, 5.5 and 5 centimeters (about 1.95 inches) in length.

Usually, *Bahariasaurus* has been classified as a megalosaurid, although Lapparent suggested that it belongs in the Tyrannosauridae. Molnar, Kurzanov and Dong (1990) observed that *B. ingens* (and *Carcharodontosaurus saharicus*) share these synapomorphies with tyrannosaurids: Supratemporal recesses confluent over parietals, amphicoelous instead of opisthocoelous cranial dorsal centra, neural spine central instead of distal in distal caudal vertebrae, nearly perpendicular expansion of the glenoid margin of the scapula from that of the scapular blade, apparently subtriangular obturator process of the ischium, and cranial tubercle of the fibula. *B. ingens* also shares other features with the Allosauridae.

As both *B. ingens* and *C. saharicus* are known from incomplete and unassociated material, Molnar *et al.* treated them together, noting that, with the exception of the form of the dorsal centra, all of the features characteristic of Tyrannosauridae (regarded by Holtz 1994 as derived coelurosaurs) are probably related to muscle attachments.

Key references: Lapparent (1960); Molnar, Kurzanov and Dong (1990); Stromer (1934).

Bahariasaurus ingens, holotype ischium. (After Stromer 1934.)

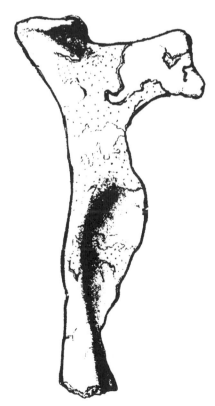

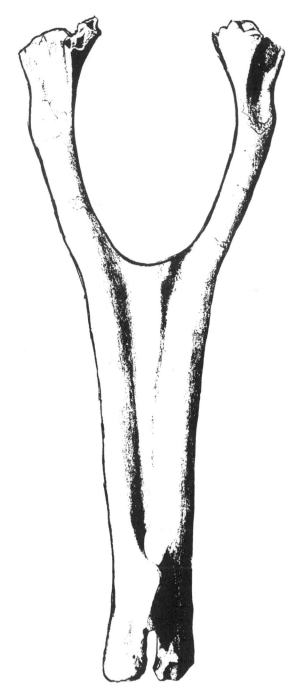

Bahariasaurus ingens, holotype pubes. (After Stromer 1934.)

From the size of the referred material, Stromer envisioned *B. ingens* as a theropod larger and more powerfully built than *Spinosaurus*, *Carcharodontosaurus*, and "*Gorgosaurus*."

Lapparent (1960) referred six caudal vertebrae from the Lower Cretaceous of the southern Sahara to *B. ingens*. Lapparent described an anterior caudal as amphicoelous, more excavated anteriorly than posteriorly, measuring 6.5 centimeters (about 2.5 inches) long, with a very excavated neural canal; two mid-

BARAPASAURUS Jain, Kutty, Roy-Chowdhury
and Chatterjee 1975

Saurischia: Sauropodomorpha: Sauropoda: Vulcanodontidae.

Name derivation: Indian *bara* = "big" + Indian *pa-*
= "leg" + Greek *sauros* = "lizard."

Type species: *B. tagorei* Jain, Kutty, Roy-Chowdhury and Chatterjee 1975.

Other species: [None.]

Occurrence: Kota Formation, Andhra Pradesh, India.

Known material: Six partial disarticulated skeletons, missing skulls, manus and pedes.

Age: Early Jurassic.

Holotype: ISI R.50, sacrum.

Diagnosis of genus: Large sauropod with relatively slender limbs; teeth spoon-shaped, with coarse
denticles on anterior and posterior keels; cervical and
dorsal centra opisthocoelous, other centra approximately platycoelous; hyposphene-hypantrum articulation in middle and posterior dorsal vertebrae; cervical centra apparently slightly less than twice length
of dorsal centra; centra not cavernous, but with oval
or ovoidal depressions in lateral or laterodorsal surfaces; neural spines apparently not bifurcate, those of
posterior dorsals very high; sacrum with four
coossified vertebrae, high spines, amphiplatyan centra, sacrocostal yokes set close together; scapula with
narrow blade, anterior border passing by somewhat
shallow, gradual curve into a conservatively broad
proximal expansion; coracoid subcircular, with foramen; ilium with blade with well-developed anterior
process; acetabulum with deep medial wall, not part
of sacrocostal yoke; ischiadic peduncle of ilium short;
pubic peduncle long, ventrally and somewhat anteriorly directed; pubes rod-like distally, with well-developed terminal expansions that could contact each

Partially mounted skeleton of
Barapasaurus tagorei at the
Indian Statistical Institute,
Calcutta. From left to right,
two unidentified men, T. S.
Kutty, Edwin H. Colbert, Mr.
Dickins, Sohan Jain,
unidentified man.

Barapasaurus

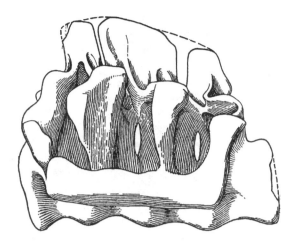

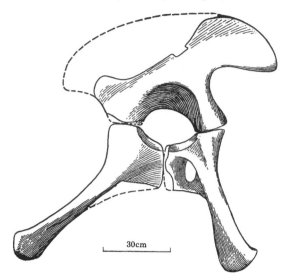

30cm

other; ischium slender, distally rod-shaped and expanded, longer than pubis; femur with straight shaft, head at about 90-degree angle to shaft; femur with central cavity, lacking lesser trochanter, with well-developed, ridge-like fourth trochanter that could bear an acute declined tip; tibia rather short and stout, with somewhat well-developed cnemial crest; humerus almost equally expanded proximally and distally, with pronounced deltopectoral crest; ulna stouter than radius, shaft slender (Jain *et al.* 1975).

Comments: One of the earliest known apparent sauropods, *Barapasaurus* was founded upon a sacrum (ISI R.50) from the Kota Formation (Lower Jurassic, based on fossil fishes discovered during the nineteenth century in limestone with new specimens; see Jain 1973), Gondwana Group, Pranhita-Godavari Valley, Deccan of Peninsular India. The type specimen was discovered in 1959, after which it and some 300 sauropod specimens (ISI collection) were excavated in 1961 by S. L. Jain, P. L. Robinson and Tapan Roy-

Chowdhury (1962). From the numerous specimens collected, much is known regarding the postcranial osteology of *Barapasaurus*, although the precise relative proportions of the limbs is still questionable (Jain, Kutty, Roy-Chowdhury and Chatterjee (1975).

Halstead and Halstead (1981) placed *Barapasaurus* into its own family Barapasauridae. Bonaparte (1986a) later referred *Barapasaurus* to the Cetiosauridae because of morphological agreement of vertebrae, scapula, humerus, pubis and ischium with what is known of those elements in *Cetiosaurus*. In his review of Sauropoda, McIntosh (1990b) regarded *Barapasaurus* as a primitive sauropod having pubes (shafts twisted to form a transverse apron) resembling those

Barapasaurus tagorie skeleton mounted at the Indian Statistical Institute.

Photo by R. A. Long and S. P. Welles (neg. #73/456-39), courtesy Yale Peabody Museum of Natural History.

Barosaurus lentus, YPM 429, holotype cervical vertebra.

in prosauropods; however, Benton (1990; same volume) believed its affinities to be with prosauropods.

Contra Jain *et al.*, McIntosh observed that the femur in *Barapasaurus* does retain a reduced but well-marked lesser trochanter, a feature by which this genus is unique among sauropods; the fourth trochanter is more prominent than in later sauropods; also, the third metatarsal is relatively longer than in any other known sauropod.

McIntosh noted that, once the skull and feet of *Barapasaurus* are recovered, this genus has the potential of being the best-known Early Jurassic sauropod. Because of its narrow sacrum, McIntosh tentatively classified *Barapasaurus* with the Vulcanodontidae rather than Cetiosauridae, cautioning that a final decision would have to await a more complete description of this genus.

In life, *Barapasaurus* probably resembled the more primitive *Vulcanodon*. It attained a length of about 14 meters (47 feet) and a height of almost 4.5 meters (15 feet).

Colbert (1973), in the book *Wandering Lands and Animals*, noted that *Barapasaurus* (then unnamed) is an important form in understanding the geographical distribution of dinosaurs in Early and Middle Jurassic times, contributing to the history of the break-up of Gondwana and the time at which the fragments began to "drift" apart, particularly in regards to India and other Gondwana continents.

Key references: Benton (1990); Bonaparte (1986*a*); Halstead and Halstead (1981); Jain, Kutty, Roy-Chowdhury, and Chatterjee (1975); McIntosh (1990*b*).

BAROSAURUS Marsh 1890—(=?*Dystrophaeus*, ?*Janenschia*)

Saurischia: Sauropodomorpha: Sauropoda: Diplodocidae: Diplodocinae.

Name derivation: Greek *baros* = "heavy" + Greek *sauros* = "lizard."

Type species: *B. lentus* Marsh 1890.

Other species: ?*B. africanus* (Fraas 1908), *B. gracilis* (Janensch 1961).

Occurrence: Morrison Formation, South Dakota, Colorado, Utah, United States; Upper Tendaguru Beds, Mtwara, Tanzania.

Age: Late Jurassic–?Early Cretaceous (Kimmeridgian–Tithonian; ?Neocomian–?Hauterivian).

Known material: More than eight incomplete skeletons missing skulls, skull elements, many isolated limb bones, much isolated postcranial material, adults and juvenile.

Holotype: YPM 429, incomplete skeleton, including cervical, dorsal, and caudal vertebrae, chevrons, sacrum with partial centrum and coalesced neural spines, ribs and rib fragments, left sternal plate, incomplete scapula, portions of ilium, right pubis, left ischium, femur and tibia fragments, ends of left fibula.

"Diagnosis" of Genus: Distinguished mostly from *Diplodocus* by enormously elongated cervical vertebrae and slightly less developed caudal neural arches and spines; cervicalization of midpresacrals evident; anterior caudals with wing-like transverse processes, midcaudals with *Diplodocus*-like fore and aft processes; distal ends of ischia expanded, contacting each other on their ventromedial surfaces; metatarsal I with distinct process on posteroventral edge of its lateral surface (Berman and McIntosh 1978).

"Diagnosis" of ?*B. africanus*: Hindlimbs very similar in construction to those of *Diplodocus* (Fraas 1980).

Barosaurus lentus, YPM 429, holotype caudal vertebra.

Comments: A very long and somewhat rare sauropod that is structurally quite similar to *Diplodocus*, the genus *Barosaurus* was founded upon a partial postcranial skeleton (YPM 429), collected from the (then "*Atlantosaurus*" beds) Morrison Formation of Meade County, Piedmont, South Dakota.

Marsh (1890) originally distinguished this genus mostly by the caudal vertebrae, which, generally resembling those of *Diplodocus*, are concave below, as in that genus, but with deeply excavated pleurocoels.

A second specimen of *Barosaurus*, comprising the first and second metacarpals of a left manus, and representing a smaller individual, was found at the same site. This second specimen was later made the holotype of new species *B. affinis* [*nomen dubium*], which was briefly described by Marsh (1890) as belonging to a "smaller species" of *Barosaurus*. Marsh did not state the distinguishing characters of this species, nor did he provide identifying labels for the type remains. Completion of Marsh's monograph on sauropods, wherein he had planned to elaborate on *Barosaurus*, was interrupted by his death in 1899. (*B. affinis* is now considered to represent a younger *B. lentus* individual.)

After being fully prepared for study during the winter of 1917 at the old Peabody Museum at Yale University, the holotype skeleton of *B. lentus* was redescribed by Lull (1919). Few additional specimens of *B. lentus* have been found, with three partial skeletons collected from the Morrison Formation at Dinosaur National Monument, Utah.

The type species originally named *Gigantosaurus africanus* was based on incomplete remains of several individuals from the Upper Jurassic of Tendaguru (Upper Kimmeridgian; see Aiken 1961), Tanzania, Africa. These remains, first described by Fraas (1908), include parts of a skull, vertebrae, limb, and girdle bones. As the generic name *Gigantosaurus* proved to be preoccupied (Seeley 1869), Sternfield (1911) referred *G. africanus* to the new genus *Tornieria* as *T. africana*. This taxon was subsequently referred by Janensch (1922) to *Barosaurus*. McIntosh (1990*b*) commented that the evidence for that referral is not compelling and should be regarded as tentative. *B. gracilis* Russell, Béland and McIntosh 1980 (originally *B. africanus* var. *gracilis* Janensch 1961) was based upon numerous isolated limb elements from the Tendaguru Beds at Mtwara.

In a review of the Sauropoda, McIntosh (1990*b*) observed that, from what skeletal parts are known of *Barosaurus*, this genus is very closely related to

Barosaurus lentus, YPM 429, holotype partial axial skeleton and pelvic girdle. (After Lull 1917.)

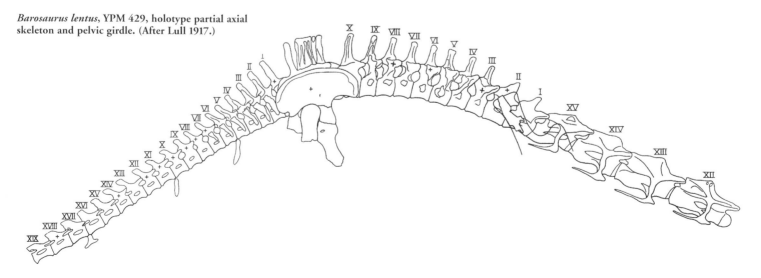

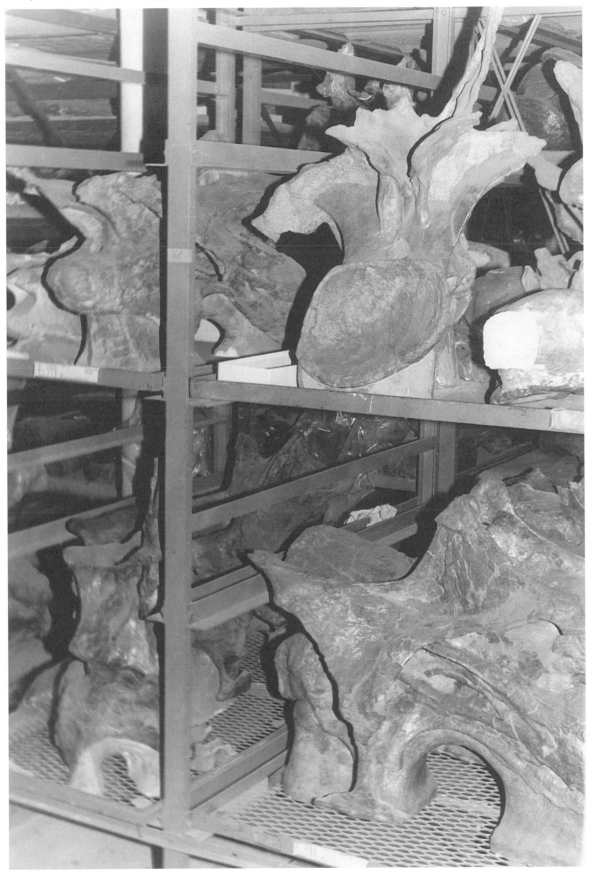

Barosaurus lentus cervical
and dorsal vertebrae in
storage.

Barosaurus

Barosaurus lentus skeleton mounted in controversial bipedal pose, defending young from *Allosaurus fragilis.*

Diplodocus. Their mutual limb bones virtually indistinguishable, *Barosaurus* primarily differs in its cervical vertebrae, which measure relatively about 33 percent longer than in *Diplodocus.*

McIntosh briefly described *Barosaurus* as follows: Enormously elongated cervical vertebrae (similar to those in *Diplodocus*, if stretched); neural spines forked in middle and caudal part of neck, arch virtually covering centrum and not set forward; cervical ribs, though long and slender, extending only to back end of centrum; forked spines beginning farther back in column, becoming very deep "V"s at rear end of neck, notch then disappearing more rapidly than in *Diplodocus*; small auxiliary central spine present (as in *Diplodocus*); ?nine dorsal vertebrae, dorsal #1 resembling cervical, elongated with parapophysis on bottom of centrum, rib apparently not fused to it; parapophysis on bottom of centrum in dorsal #2, moves up just in front of pleurocoel in dorsal #3, reaches base of arch on dorsal #4; dorsals beyond #1 closely resemble those in *Diplodocus*, with same well-defined thin laminae, opisthocoelous centra with prominent balls on front through dorsal #5, large pleurocoels throughout; all five sacral vertebrae entering into yoke formation; caudals resembling, but less specialized than, those in *Diplodocus*, some shorter, especially in midcaudal region; wing-like transverse processes and caudal ribs modified to more normal form by caudal #7; proximal caudal centra less procoelous; pleurocoel disappearing after caudal #14, ventral excavation a broad, gentle concavity; proximal caudal neural spines broad transversely, tops not bifid; chevrons from midcaudal

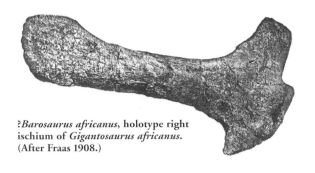

?*Barosaurus africanus*, holotype right ischium of *Gigantosaurus africanus*. (After Fraas 1908.)

region like, but smaller than, in *Diplodocus*; tail probably smaller than that of *Diplodocus* (McIntosh 1990b).

Barosaurus was a highly specialized, slender-limbed sauropod reaching a maximum length of 27 meters (90 feet). The animal probably resembled *Diplodocus*, though with comparatively heavier hind limbs, a shorter tail, and longer neck. Lull speculated that the obliqueness of the posterior cervical centra and the first dorsal centrum implied a different carriage of neck in *Barosaurus*, probably giraffe-like as in the Tendaguru species *Brachiosaurus brancai*.

Barosaurus has also been reported from the Dry Mesa Quarry (Morrison Formation, Upper Jurassic [Tithonian] or Lower Cretaceous [Neocomian or Hauterivian]; Britt 1991), near the southwest corner of Dry Mesa, west central Colorado.

The occurrence of *Barosaurus* and *Brachiosaurus* on opposite sides of juxtaposed continents (western United States and Tanzania), during a time when Pangaea was still a single land mass, suggests that at least some of these giant dinosaurs, like modern African elephants, migrated over vast distances seeking food (Galton 1977).

Note: A cast of the original holotype of *B. lentus*, with the missing elements restored, was mounted in 1992 at the American Museum of Natural History. The skeleton was mounted rearing up on its hind legs over that of an *Allosaurus*, as if defending its young against the attacking predator. The mount has been controversial. According to newspaper accounts, some paleontologists (*e.g.,* Kevin Padian) have agreed with the pose of the *Barosaurus* skeleton, while others (*e.g.,* Paul Sereno and Peter Dodson) have criticized the display, stating that the bipedal posture was impossible. American museum paleontologist Michael Novacek was quoted as stating that the exhibit was meant to stimulate discussion and debate.

Key references: Fraas (1908); Janensch (1922); Lull (1919); Marsh (1890, 1896, 1899); McIntosh (1990b); Russell, Béland and McIntosh (1980); Sternfield (1911).

?*Barosaurus africanus*, A. holotype right femur (anterior view), B. holotype left fibula (lateral view) of *Gigantosaurus africanus*. (After Fraas 1908.)

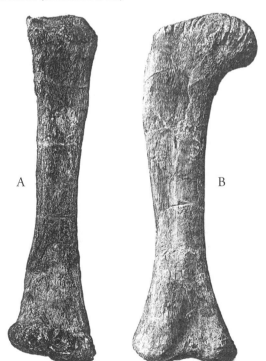

A   B

?*Barosaurus africanus*, holotype mid-caudal (16–20) vertebra (lateral views) of *Gigantosaurus africanus*. (After Fraas 1908.)

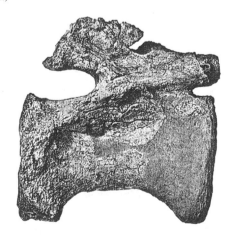

?*Barosaurus africanus*, holotype rib (from mid-trunk region) of *Gigantosaurus africanus*. (After Fraas 1908.)

BARSBOLDIA Maryańska and Osmólska 1981
[*nomen dubium*]

Ornithischia: Genasauria: Cerapoda: Ornithopoda:
Iguanodontia: Hadrosauridae: Lambeosaurinae.

Name derivation: "[Rinchen] Barsbold."

Type species: *B. sicinskii* Maryańska and Osmólska
1981 [*nomen dubium*].

Other species: [None.]

Occurrence: Nemegt Formation, Omnogov, Mongolian People's Republic.

Age: Late Cretaceous (Maastrichtian).

Known material/holotype: ZPAL MgD-I/110, vertebrae including series of nine posterior dorsals,
nine coalesced sacrals and 15 caudals, left ilium, six
to seven thoracic ribs, tibia and fibula fragments,
third and fourth left metatarsals, third phalanx
and ungual of third pedal digit, several fragments
of dorsal and caudal neural spines, fragments of
left and right pubis, fragments of ossified tendons.

Diagnosis of genus (as for type species): Lambeosaurine with relatively high neural spines, highest at
middle of synsacrum, decreasing in height more
abruptly forwards than backwards; neural spines of
anterior caudals club-like; ilium very deep above
acetabulum (Maryańska and Osmólska 1991*b*).

Comments: The first lambeosaurine known
from the Nemegt Formation, *Barsboldia* was founded
upon an incomplete postcranial skeleton (ZPAL
MgD-I/110), collected from sandy deposits at Northern Sayr, Nemegt, Nemegt Basin, Gobi Desert, Mongolia. The holotype was found with the articulated
vertebral column lying on its right side, the other elements disarticulated but not greatly displaced, the
anterior and posterior portions of the skeleton eroded
and lost (Maryańska and Osmólska 1981*b*).

As described by Maryańska and Osmólska, the
synsacrum, comprising nine vertebrae, measures 960
millimeters (about 37 inches) in length. The sacral
neural spines and anterior caudal spines are approximately three times higher than their respective centra. From the length of the sacral spines, *Barsboldia*
is among lambeosaurines in which these are most
developed, surpassed only by *Hypacrosaurus altispinax*
in their length.

Brett-Surman (1989), who regarded this genus
as a *nomen dubium*, noted that the type material is
unlike any other Asian hadrosaurid, closely resembling corresponding elements in *Hypacrosaurus*, and
that the club-like distal ends of the neural spines
could be an old age condition. In their review of the
Hadrosauridae, Weishampel and Horner (1990), noting that *Barsboldia* is very poorly known, regarded
this genus as Lambeosaurinae *incertae sedis*.

Note: The mounted skeleton of an undescribed
hadrosaurid from Mongolia was published by Saito
(1979) in the book *Wonder of the World's Dinosaurs*.
This skeleton, measuring about one meter (39.37
inches) long and 71 centimeters (almost 28 inches)
high, was exhibited in Japan by the [then] Union of
Soviet Socialist Republics with the label "Gadolosaurus." According to Masahiro Tanimoto (personal
communication), "Gadolosaurus" is a Japanese term
meaning "baby dinosaur," or is a Japanese phoneti-
cization of the Cyrillic word *gadrosavr*, meaning
"hadrosaur" (see Brett-Surman 1989). Apparently a
number of the "features" perceived in this skeleton are
plaster fabrications.

Key references: Brett-Surman (1989); Maryańska
and Osmólska (1981*b*); Weishampel and Horner
(1990).

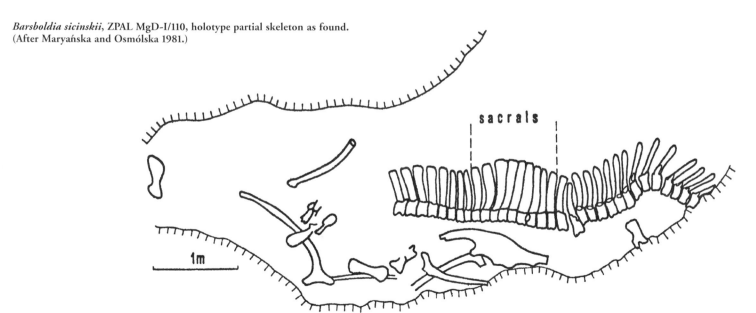

Barsboldia sicinskii, ZPAL MgD-I/110, holotype partial skeleton as found.
(After Maryańska and Osmólska 1981.)

sacrals

1m

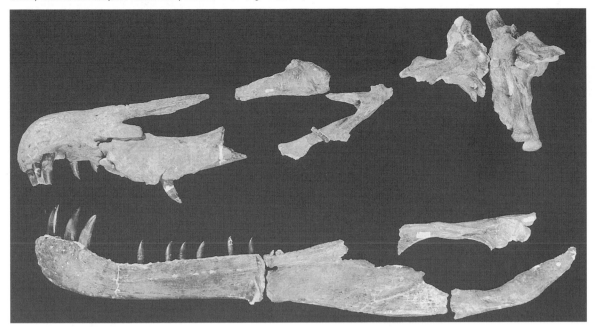

Baryonx walkeri, BMNH R9951, holotype incomplete skull.

BARYONYX   Charig and Milner 1986

Saurischia: Theropoda: ?Tetanurae: ?Spinosauridae.

Name derivation: Greek *barus* = "heavy" + Greek *onux* = "claw."

Type species: *B. walkeri* Charig and Milner 1986.

Other species: [None.]

Occurrence: Wealden, Surrey, England; ?Niger, Africa.

Age: Early Cretaceous (Barremian).

Known material/holotype: BMNH R9951, conjoined premaxillae, front of left maxilla, conjoined nasals, lacrimal and parts of adjacent elements, frontals, anterior part of braincase, some post-dentary bones of mandible, teeth, axis, most other cervical, some dorsal and one caudal vertebrae, cervical rib, dorsal ribs, gastralia, chevrons, scapulae, coracoids, ?clavicle, humeri, manual phalanges with unguals, pieces of ilia, pubes, and ischium, proximal end of left femur, distal end of right femur, left fibula lacking distal end, right calcaneum; distal ends of metatarsals, pedal phalanges with unguals, fragments, ?gastroliths.

Diagnosis of genus (as for type species and Baryonychidae): Snout extended into very narrow rostrum, ending with spatula-shaped, horizontal expansion; external naris long, low, resembling triangle with apex forwardly directed, situated back from front of snout to ascend gently toward posteriorly; premaxilla and maxilla with apparently mobile articulation above subrostral notch; small median knob at posterior end of nasals, cross-shaped in dorsal view, its anterior limb drawn forwards into thin, low median crest; occiput deep, with horizontally outwardly-directed paroccipital processes; basipterygoid processes descend far below basioccipital, slightly diverging laterally; tooth count unusually high, seven teeth in premaxilla, unknown number in maxilla, 32 in dentary; teeth with lightly fluted crowns on lingual side, anterior and posterior keels with very fine serrations approximating seven per millimeter, and long, slender roots; third premaxillary tooth and third and fourth dentary teeth largest; no obvious interdental plates; cervical vertebrae long, strongly opisthocoelous, with short neural spines and well-developed epipophyses; neck without typical theropod upward curve; humerus relatively well-developed, with massive and nearly straight shaft, broadly expanded and very flattened ends; ilium with long, straight posterior process; at least one pair of very large talons, apparently belonging to forefeet; (other unstated more esoteric characters) (Charig and Milner 1986).

Comments: This unusual theropod was discovered in January, 1983 by William J. Walker, who found an extremely large claw bone in a claypit at Ockley, near Dorking, Surrey, England. (The new dinosaur to which the specimen belonged received worldwide media recognition under the popular name "Claws.") The following month, the British Museum (Natural History) [now Natural History Museum, London] began excavations on the site, which yielded much of the well-preserved skeleton of the first large theropod found in Britain in over a century. The remains also constituted the first reasonably complete large theropod discovered in Lower Cretaceous rocks in Europe. (Mixed with this material were unrelated fossil remains including fish teeth and scales, an *Iguanodon* humerus and phalanx, and

Baryonyx

Baryonyx walkeri, BMNH R9951, holotype ?manual claw.

numerous insects.) The basis for a new monotypic taxon Baryonychidae, the new genus, named *Baryonyx*, was founded on cranial and postcranial remains (BMNH R9951) (Milner and Charig 1986).

As noted by Charig and Milner, *Baryonyx* shows an odd combination of both primitive and derived characters. As in Triassic "thecodonts," the downward tip of the snout, seeming mobility between premaxilla and maxilla and subrostral notch, the atypically greater number of teeth, long vertebrae, and form of the posterior process of the ilium are all primitive characters remarkable for an Early Cretaceous form. *Baryonyx* also displays various specializations indicative of an advanced theropod, including the terminal expansion of the upper jaw and, just posterior to it, the extreme narrowness of the skull; also the median knob and crest of the nasals, lack of an "S" curve to the neck, and enormous talon.

The probable life style of *Baryonyx* was not clear to Charig and Milner. Suggestive of quadrupedality were the elongated snout, long neck, and form and strong development of the humerus, though the slender and flattened ends of the humerus indicate that the animal was mostly bipedal. The position of the nares and form of the postcranial skeleton indicate a terrestrial animal, although the long snout and abundance of teeth suggest a fish eater. Charig and Milner deduced that *Baryonyx* could have been a land-dweller that crouched into a quadrupedal pose on river banks, from where it fed on fish. Possibly this dinosaur was a scavenger.

The huge ungual, one of the most striking features of *Baryonyx*, is in form exactly like that of *Allosaurus*, albeit of larger size. It was not unequivocally determined whether the talon in *Baryonyx* belongs to the manus or pes. If a manual claw, it would probably have been held clear of the ground if the animal were walking on all fours. The claw has the appearance of an offensive or defensive weapon and may have been used, suggested Charig and Milner, to catch fish as would that of a grizzly bear.

Prior to the first published accounts of *Baryonyx*, Taquet (1984) had reported two fragmentary snouts from the Aptian of Niger. Taquet described these specimens as the mandibular symphyses of a spinosaurid. Charig and Milner noted that these specimens might be assigned to the Baryonychidae, being almost identical to the conjoined premaxillae of *Baryonyx*, though not comparing favorably with *Spinosaurus*.

Although more is known about *Baryonyx* than many other theropods, the systematic position of *B. walkeri* has presented problems. Superficially, the skull displays similarities with crocodilians. In their contribution to the Dinosaur Systematics Symposium volume of papers (see Dodson 1986), written after more (but not all) of the *Baryonyx* material had been prepared, Charig and Milner (1990) demonstrated that this genus is not crocodilian, because the type specimen lacks the following crocodylomorph/crocodilian synapomorphies (Gauthier 1984, 1986): 1. Coracoid ventromedially elongated, 2. reduction in pubis size and its near-exclusion from acetabulum, 3. shortening of ischium to half length of the pubis, and 4. development of a crurotarsal ankle-joint, calcaneum with an enlarged tuber and socket (the latter for reception of the peg of the astragalus).

Charig and Milner (1990) established that *Baryonyx* is dinosaurian as demonstrated by the following features, some of which have rarely (if ever) been observed in crocodilians: 1. Teeth generally similar to those of most other theropods, being recurved, serrated, laterally compressed blades; 2. "fully improved" stance and gate (Charig 1965), with mesotarsal ankle-joint, 3. huge ungual suggesting at least a partial biped, and 4. ischium with an obturator process. As *Baryonyx* is obviously not an ornithischian, nor is the dentition the kind known in sauropodomorphs, Charig and Milner (1990) found no evidence contrary to their conclusion that the genus is theropod.

In his book *Predatory Dinosaurs of the World*, Paul (1988c) regarded *Baryonyx* as a member of the Spinosauridae mostly because of the slender, semiconical, crocodile-like teeth with very tiny serrations, crocodile-like lower jaw with expanded tips, and apparent lack of S-curve in the neck. Paul speculated that the long and slender fingers were not suitable for walking, and the relatively long arms and large claws were possibly used as defensive weapons. Charig and Milner (1990) criticized Paul's interpretation of this genus on various grounds, including that Paul had not examined the holotype of *B. walkeri*, and that he had made reference to material yet neither fully understood nor described in that specimen.

Baryonyx walkeri, life restoration by Gregory S. Paul.

Based upon Gauthier's criteria for Theropoda, Charig and Milner (1990) determined that *Baryonyx* could not be assigned with certainty either to the Ceratosauria or Tetanurae, possessing some characters diagnostic of both taxa. Molnar (1990), while agreeing that *Baryonyx walkeri* probably represents a distinct family, pointed out that this species is not yet well enough known (the holotype of *B. walkeri* yet to be fully described) to assign that taxon to some higher group.

Charig and Milner (1990) reported the discovery of a single isolated, rather tall neural spine that suggests that a ridge was present down the center of this dinosaur's back. Unlike *Becklespinax*, in which the three preserved neural spines are relatively heavier and longer and have an enormous lateral thickening toward their upper ends [possibly a pathological condition; R. E. Molnar, personal communication 1991], the spine in *Baryonyx* is flat and slender.

Charig and Milner (1990) concluded that *Baryonyx* is a theropod that does not seem to fit into Gauthier's definition of Theropoda; the characters found in this genus, some unique, and its unusual combination of characters, indicate that this form neither belongs in Spinosauridae nor any other theropod group; and the genus warrants its own family.

Note: A maxillary fragment from southern Morocco was described by Buffetaut (1989) as pertaining to *Spinosaurus* (see entry). Because of its similarity to the maxilla in *Baryonyx*, Buffetaut concluded that the two genera were closely related. Charig and Milner (1990) acknowledged that the Moroccan specimen is quite similar in general shape to the maxilla of *Baryonyx*, though almost twice the size, so much that they regarded this specimen as an indeterminate genus and species of baryonychid. What Buffetaut had done, in their opinion, was simply compare one baryonychid with another rather than a baryonychid with a spinosaurid. After comparing in detail the *Baryonyx* and *Spinosaurus* type material, Charig and Milner (1990) concluded that, although characters shared by both of these genera do suggest a phylogenetic relationship, it is not close enough to warrant including them within the same group, the differences between these forms outweighing the similarities.

Key references: Buffetaut (1989); Charig and Milner (1986, 1990), Paul (1986c).

BECKLESPINAX Olshevsky 1991

Saurischia: Theropoda: ?Tetanurae:
    Eustreptospondylidae.

Name derivation: "[Samuel H.] Beckles" + Latin
    spina = "spine."

Type species: *B. altispinax* (Paul 1988).

Other species: [None.]

Occurrence: Wealden, Hanover, Germany.

Age: Early Cretaceous (Barremian).

Known material/holotype: BMNH R1828, dorsal
    vertebrae.

Diagnosis of genus (as for type species): [No modern diagnosis published.]

Comments: The genus now called *Becklespinax* has had an involved taxonomic history. Dames (1884) based new species *Megalosaurus dunkeri* on a worn and probably indeterminate tooth from the Wealden of Hannover, Germany. Lydekker (1890) arbitrarily assigned more material, including an unusual metatarsus (see *Valdoraptor* entry), to this taxon. Huene (1923) later proposed the new genus and species combination *Altispinax dunkeri* for the tooth. As *M. dunkeri* was the only species referred to *Altispinax*, Kuhn (1939) later designated the tooth to be the lectotype of *Altispinax*.

Huene (1926) described the vertebrae as follows: Dorsals with spines about five times longer than diameter of centra, four times longer than centra are long; vertebrae opisthocoelous.

To *M. dunkeri*, Huene had referred three articulated massive dorsal vertebrae (BMNH R1828; specimen 74 in Huene 1926) with extremely high neural spines. This material was discovered in the Lower Wealden of Battle-near-Hastings, East Sussex, England, during the early 1850s, by Samuel H. Beckles, and originally described by Owen (1853–1864) as belonging to *M. bucklandi*, the type species of *Megalosaurus*. Because of the atypical height of these spines, Huene separated them generically from *Megalosaurus*, proposing for them the new generic name of *Altispinax*. Huene (1926), while including the indeterminate tooth in this genus, stated that *Altispinax* had been founded upon material referred "from arguments of probability" by Lydekker to *M. dunkeri*. At the same time, Huene stated that the name *Altispinax* was reserved for *M. dunkeri* should it someday be confirmed that the vertebrae and tooth belonged to the same species.

However, in erecting *Altispinax*, Huene (1923) failed to designate formally a type species; nor did he designate any of the material attributed to this genus as a type specimen. Stovall and Langston (1950) pointed out the lack of a valid reason to regard all of the material assigned to *Altispinax*—all having come from various localities and found at different times—as belonging to the same genus. Stovall and Langston, as well as other authors (*e.g.*, Steel 1970), avoided designating a type species for *Altispinax*.

Because these dorsal spines are similar to those in the later North American theropod *Acrocanthosaurus*, Stovall and Langston speculated that "*Altispinax*" and that genus developed along similar lines, but added that the European form was not necessarily ancestral to *Acrocanthosaurus*. Molnar (1990) observed that the dorsals in "*Altispinax*" show no particular similarity to those of *Spinosaurus* other than being elongate. In the former, the spines are constricted above the arch; in the latter, they are dilated above the arch.

As the source of the name *Altispinax* is the series of tall-spined dorsal vertebrae; Olshevsky (1991) later proposed that these remains should constitute the holotype. Olshevsky noted that White (1973), in his catalogue of dinosaur genera, perhaps inadvertently listed *M. dunkeri* as the type species of *Altispinax*, thereby fixing that type species for the genus, brand-

Becklespinax altispinax, BMNH R1828, holotype dorsal neural spines (figure reversed by Owen). (After Owen 1853–64.)

Partially mounted skeleton of *Bellusaurus sui.* (After Dong 1987).

ing the genus a *nomen dubium* and leaving the vertebrae without a generic name. Olshevsky formally designated the vertebrae as the holotype of a new theropod genus distinct from *Megalosaurus*. Because Paul (1988*b*) had referred this specimen to *Acrocanthosaurus* (as new species *A. altispinax*), Olshevsky proposed the new genus and species combination of *Becklespinax altispinax.* (The name *Altispinax dunkeri* remained for the tooth described by Dames.)

According to Olshevsky, the vertebrae are posterior dorsals, probably the eighth–tenth; except for the neural spines, they most closely match those in *Piatnitzkysaurus* in the conformation of the apophyses and laminae, and in the position of the neural spine atop the neural arch; the firm contact between apexes of the ninth and tenth neural spines is a uniquely diagnostic feature; and ?eighth neural spine is not broken but naturally shorter than the ninth, perhaps another diagnostic feature.

Note: Olshevsky speculated that Owen had possession of this specimen when he supervised the design of the "humpbacked" *Megalosaurus* built by Benjamin Waterhouse Hawkins for the Crystal Palace in London.

Key references: Dames (1884); Huene (1923, 1926); Kuhn (1939); Lydekker (1890); Molnar (1990); Olshevsky (1991); Owen (1853–64); Steel (1970); Stovall and Langston (1950); Paul (1988*b*); White (1973).

BELLUSAURUS Dong 1990

Saurischia: Sauropodomorpha: Sauropoda:
  ?Cetiosauidae *incertae sedis.*

Name derivation: Latin *bellus* = "beautiful" + Greek *sauros* = "lizard."

Type species: *B. sui* Dong 1990.

Other species: [None.]

Occurrence: Wacaiwan Formation, Xinjiang, China.

Age: Middle Jurassic.

Known material: Disarticulated remains of at least 17 juvenile individuals.

Holotype: Incomplete skeleton, juvenile.

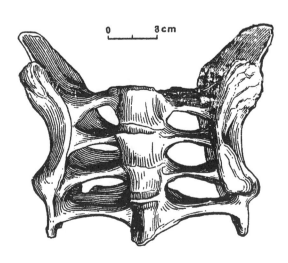

Bellusaurus sui, ?holotype sacrum. (After Dong 1990.)

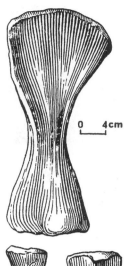

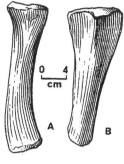

Bellusaurus sui, ?holotype humerus, ulna, and radius. (After Dong 1990.)

Diagnosis of genus (as for type species): Small sauropod; upper and lower teeth spoon-shaped; skull lightly constructed, moderately deep, nares located laterally; neck surpassing trunk in length; cervical vertebrae short, opisthocoelous, 1.5 times length of dorsals, similar to those of *Pleurocoelous,* but with simpler, lower neural spines; dorsal vertebrae opisthocoelous, with large pleurocoels, neural spines moderately high and nonbifurcated; four sacral vertebrae, first three sacral neural spines fused and plate-like; sacrum lacking "sacrocostal blade"; anterior caudal vertebrae procoelous, first caudal with fanlike transverse processes; mid-caudals amphicoelous; chevrons simple, unforked; scapula with well-developed proximal plate (Dong 1990a).

Comments: The genus *Bellusaurus* was founded on a partial skeleton, discovered in the Middle Jurassic Wucaiwan Formation of the Junggar Basin, between the Altai and Tianshan Mountains, Xinjiang, China. The specimen was found in a bonebed containing numerous remains of at least 17 juveniles. The site, south of Kelamaili mountain, was discovered in 1954 by petroleum geologists and named Konglong-gou, meaning "dinosaur valley" (Dong 1990a).

Originally, Dong (1987a) informally described *Bellusaurus* as a relatively small cetiosaurid measuring about 4.8 meters (more than 16 feet) in length, with a rather short neck. A photograph of its reconstructed mounted skeleton (lacking ribs) first appeared in Dong's (1987b) book *Dinosaurs from China.*

Dong (1990a) put *Bellusaurus* in the Brachiosauridae within its own "subfamily" Bellusaurinae. McIntosh (1990b), on the basis of the short forelimb, suggested that *Bellusaurus* could be a cetiosaurid.

In *Dinosaurian Faunas of China,* Dong (1992) speculated that the remains of 17 individuals found at Konglong-gou suggest that a herd of these animals may have been overwhelmed in a flash flood.

Note: Regarding Dong's (1990a) comparison of *Bellusaurus* with *Pleurocoelus,* the cervical and dorsal neural spines in the latter are unknown (S. J. McIntosh, personal communication 1990).

Key references: Dong (1987a, 1987b, 1990a, 1992); McIntosh (1990b).

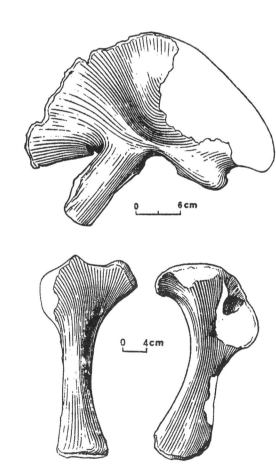

Bellusaurus sui, ?holotype scapula (both sides) and coracoid. (After Dong 1990.)

Bellusaurus sui, ?holotype ilium, pubis, and ischium. (After Dong 1990.)

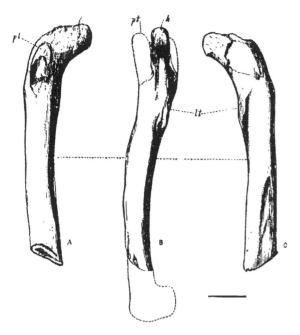

Betasuchus bredai, BMNH 32997, holotype femur of *Megalosaurus bredai*, A. anterior, B. inner, C. posterior views. Scale = 4 cm. (After Seeley 1883.)

BETASUCHUS   Huene 1932 [*nomen dubium*]— (=*Ornithomimidorum* [in part])

Saurischia: Theropoda *incertae sedis*.
Name derivation: Greek *beta* = "beta ['b', second letter of Greek alphabet]" + Greek *souchos* = "crocodile."
Type species: *B. bredai* (Seeley 1883) [*nomen dubium*].
Other species: [None.]
Occurrence: Maastricht Beds, Netherlands.
Age: Late Cretaceous (upper Senonian).
Known material/holotype: BMNH 42997, incomplete right femur.

Diagnosis of genus: [None published].

Comments: The species *Betasuchus bredai* was originally described by Seeley (1883) as a new species of *Megalosaurus*, *M. bredai* [*nomen dubium*], based on an incomplete right femur (BMNH 42997) from the Maastricht Beds, Netherlands. Huene (1926*b*) identified this specimen as pertaining to a "coelurosaur," which he referred to as "*Ornithomimidorum* genus b," then (1932) subsequently referred it to the new genus and species *Betasuchus bredai*.

Huene (1932) described the femur as follows: Closely resembles that in *Elaphrosaurus* and *Sarcosaurus*; significantly differs from that of *Struthiomimus* in its higher-situated fourth trochanter.

Norman (1990), reviewing a number problematic "coelurosaurs," regarded this genus as indeterminate.

Key references: Huene (1926*b*, 1932); Norman (1990); Seeley (1888).

BIHARIOSAURUS   Marinescu 1989

Ornithischia: Genasauria: Cerapoda: Ornithopoda: Iguanodontia: Iguanodontidae.
Name derivation: "[Department of] Bihor" + Greek *sauros* = "lizard."
Type species: *B. bauxiticus* Marinescu 1989.
Other species: [None.]
Occurrence: Brusturi-Cornet, Romania.
Age: Late Jurassic–Early Cretaceous (?upper middle Tithonian).
Known material/holotype: Maxillary tooth, post crania remains including basioccipital, cervical vertebra, partial sacrum, proximal caudal vertebra, mid-distal caudal vertebra, distal caudal vertebra.

Diagnosis of genus (as for type species): Primitive characters including sacrum with vertebrae free, only two coossified, neural arch weakly fused with centrum; derived characters including teeth having very fine denticles (Marinescu 1989).

Bihariosaurus bauxiticus, holotype (left to right, top row) maxillary teeth, basioccipital with basisphenoid, cervical vertebra (anterior view); (middle row) sacral fragments; (bottom row) proximal caudal, median-distal caudal, and distal caudal vertebrae (lateral view). (After Marinescu 1989.)

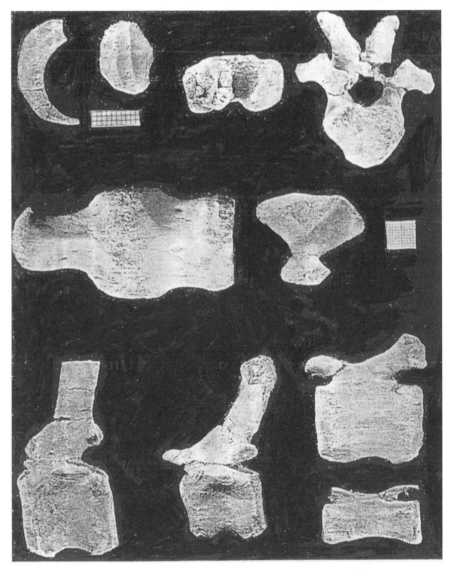

Comments: The genus *Bihariosaurus* was founded on partial postcranial remains and a tooth, discovered in 1978, at Brusturi-Cornet (Padurea Cariului—Muntii Apuseni, département de Bihor), Romania. Found with the holotype were a number of gastrolites (Marinescu 1989).

Marinescu found these remains to resemble most closely those of *Camptosaurus*, and for that reason referred *Bihariosaurus* to the Iguanodontidae.

According to Marinescu, the position in which the bones were found indicate that the remains had been transported by lake mud, probably swept away during flood season.

Note: Olshevsky (1992) provisionally listed this taxon with the Camptosauridae, as Marinescu had based his identification with Iguanodontidae on resemblances to *Camptosaurus* rather than *Iguanodon*.

Key references: Marinescu (1989); Olshevsky (1992).

BLIKANASAURUS Galton and Van Heerden 1985

Saurischia: Sauropodomorpha: Prosauropoda: Blikanasauridae.

Name derivation: "Blikana [Trading Store]" + Greek *sauros* = "lizard."

Type species: *B. cromptoni* Galton and Van Heerden 1985.

Other species: [None.]

Occurrence: Lower Elliot Formation, Leribe, Lesotho.

Age: Late Triassic (late Carnian or early Norian).

Known material/holotype: SAM K403, left epipodals, tarsus, pes missing two or three phalanges.

Diagnosis of genus (as for type species): Tibia with maximum proximal width 48 percent of maxi-

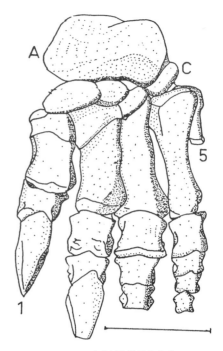

Blikanasaurus cromptoni, SAM K403, holotype tarsus and pes, posterior view. Scale = 10 cm. (After Galton and Van Heerden 1985.)

mum length; relatively robust and deep descending process; distal end of fibula with large oval, ventromedially directed articular surface; astragalus transversely relatively short, ascending process high, prominent; calcaneum small, ventrolateral to astragalus; metatarsal I short, robust, metatarsals II–IV subequal in length, V much reduced; metatarsals I–V with ratio of maximum proximal width to maximum length of 0.91, 0.72, 0.53, 0.53 and 0.74 (Galton and Van Heerden 1985).

Comments: Basis for the new family Blikanosauridae, the genus *Blikanasaurus* was founded upon a partial right hindlimb (SAM K403), discovered in the basal Elliot Formation (Red Beds) (late Carnian or early Norian; Galton and Olsen 1984), Stormberg Group, Karoo Supergroup, Herschel district, Transkei, Lesotho, Africa (Galton and Van Heerden 1985). The specimen was first described, though briefly and without name and illustration, by Charig, Attridge and Crompton (1965), as the "Blikana dinosaur."

Charig *et al.* originally distinguished the "Blikana dinosaur" from other prosauropods by the shortness and robustness (comparable to proportions in sauropods) of the bones, and by the anteriorly oriented hallux.

This dinosaur was heavily built and probably quadrupedal, not unlike the later sauropods. However, Charig *et al.* regarded it as not ancestral to Sauropoda, as metatarsal V is reduced, while V and I in

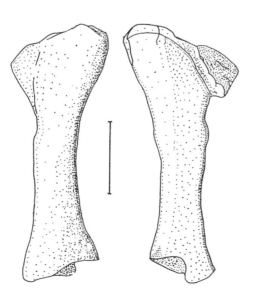

Blikanasaurus cromptoni, SAM K403, holotype tibia, anterior and lateral views. Scale = 10 cm. (After Galton and Van Heerden 1985.)

sauropods are relatively long (see Cruickshank 1975; Van Heerden 1978).

Galton and Van Heerden erected upon this material the new genus and species *Blikanasaurus cromptoni*, noting that this dinosaur was unique to all Triassic saurischians, being an early experiment toward heavy, saurischian quadrupeds. This condition resulted from the combination of heavily-built limbs with a short astragalus, and the need to spread body mass to three central metatarsals.

Key references: Charig, Attridge and Crompton (1965); Galton and Van Heerden (1985).

BOROGOVIA Osmólska 1987
Saurischia: Theropoda: Tetanurae: Avetheropoda: Coelurosauria: Maniraptora: Arctometatarsalia: Bullatosauria: Troodontidae.

Name derivation: "Borogove [fantastic creature in Lewis Carroll's *Alice in Wonderland*]".

Type species: *B. gracilicrus* Osmólska 1987.

Other species: [None.]

Occurrence: Nemegt Formation, Omnogov, Nemegtskaya Svita, Bayankhongor, Mongolian People's Republic.

Age: Late Cretaceous (?late Campanian or ?early Maastrichtian).

Known material/holotype: ZPAL MgD-I/174, incomplete left and right tibiotarsi, proximal portion of fibula, distal parts of left metatarsals II and IV, distal portions of articulated right metatarsals II–IV.

Diagnosis of genus (as for type species): Medium-sized troodontid; tibiotarsus very long, slender; second toe with very short phalanx II–2 and straight ungual; third toe much thinner and weaker than second and fourth (Osmólska 1987).

Comments: Originally described by Osmólska (1982) as *Saurornithoides* sp., the genus *Borogovia* was established upon hindlimb fragments (ZPAL MgD-I/174) found in 1971 by the Polish-Mongolian Palaeontological Expedition, in the Nemegt Formation, Altan Ula IV locality, Nemegt Basin, Omnogov, Mongolian People's Republic (Osmólska 1987).

According to Osmólska (1987), the holotype of *B. gracilicrus* is unique in constituting the largest albeit fragmentary shin portion known in a troodontid, measuring at least 280 millimeters (approximately 11 inches) if complete. This length exceeds by 13 percent the 243 millimeters (almost 9.5 inches) estimated by Russell (1969) for the tibia in *Saurornithoides mongoliensis*, although the pes in the latter is slightly larger.

Comparing *B. gracilicrus* to other troodontids, Osmólska (1987) showed that this form is unique in

that digit III is the thinnest of three functional pedal digits. The second pedal digit has a very short phalanx II-2; the second ungual is straight with an almost non-existent flexor tuber, indicating that this toe was placed on the ground for support. (In all other known troodontids, the second digit has a strongly curved ungual and a distinct flexor tuber, this toe presumably usually carried off the ground and used as a weapon.)

Osmólska (1987) postulated that the thickness and firm articulation between the phalanges of pedal digit IV are suggestive of circumstances taking place during the animal's life, causing the stress on the foot to be asymmetrically distributed. Although the second toe touched the ground, the sharpness of the ungual could indicate that it was sometimes used in functions other than support, perhaps during courtship behavior.

Key reference: Osmólska (1982, 1987).

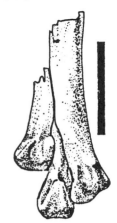

Borogovia gracilicrus, ZPAL MgD-I/174, holotype distal end of right metatarsus. Scale = 3 cm. (After Osmólska 1987.)

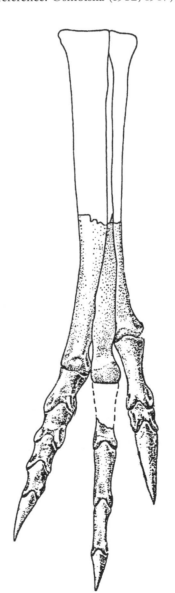

Borogovia gracilicrus, ZPAL MgD-I/174, holotype fragmentary right pes, anterior view. (After Osmólska 1987.)

BOTHRIOSPONDYLUS Owen 1875—
(=*Marmarospondylus*)

Saurischia: Sauropodomorpha: Sauropoda:
Brachiosauridae.

Name derivation: Greek *bothrion* = "trench" + Latin
spondylus = "vertebrae."

Type species: *B. suffosus* Owen 1875 [*nomen dubium*].

Other species: *B. robustus* (Owen 1875) [*nomen dubium*], ?*B. madagascariensis* Lydekker 1895.

Occurrence: Kimmeridge Clay, Wiltshire, England,
Forest Marble, Wiltshire, England; ?Isalo Formation, Majunga, Madagascar.

Age: Late Jurassic (early Kimmeridgian–late
Bathonian).

Known material: Vertebrae, and isolated limb elements from at least ten individuals.

Cotypes: BMNH 44592-5, three sacral vertebrae,
44589-91, four dorsal centra.

Diagnosis of genus: [No modern diagnosis published.]

Comments: The genus *Bothriospondylus* was established on two cotype specimens, (BMNH 4458-91) and (BMNH 44592-5), collected from the Kimmeridge Clay of Swindon, Wiltshire, England (found in association with bones of the marine reptile *Pliosaurus bradydeirus*).

The genus was diagnosed by Owen as follows: Sacral vertebrae very broad, somewhat flattened horizontally, with large pleurocoels [these characters then unknown in other dinosaurs]. Owen diagnosed *B. suffosus* as follows: (Four) dorsal centra with larger and longer pleurocoels than have the sacrals.

Second species, *B. robustus*, originally the type species of new genus *Marmarospondylus* Owen 1875 [*nomen dubium*], was based on fragmentary vertebrae or vertebral centra (BMNH R22428) from the Forest-marbel of Wiltshire, England. Owen diagnosed *B. robustus* as follows: Pleurocoel more shallow; centrum relatively shorter (in proportion to breadth and height); trunk comparatively larger than in *B. suffosus*. [These characters are no longer regarded as diagnostic.]

B. madagascariensis Lydekker (1895) was based on cervical, dorsal, sacral and caudal vertebrae, and fragmentary limb and girdle bones from Northwest Madagascar. Lydekker briefly diagnosed this species as follows: Front and hind legs of about equal length. Other material referred to this species include remains described by Thevenis (1907); six teeth, seven vertebrae, some large broken vertebral processes, sacrum, rib fragments, limb bones, and girdle elements from the Sequanian of Damparis, described by Lapparent (1943); and an articulated manus bear-

Bothriospondylus suffosus, BMNH R44592-5, holotype dorsal centra. (After Owen 1875.)

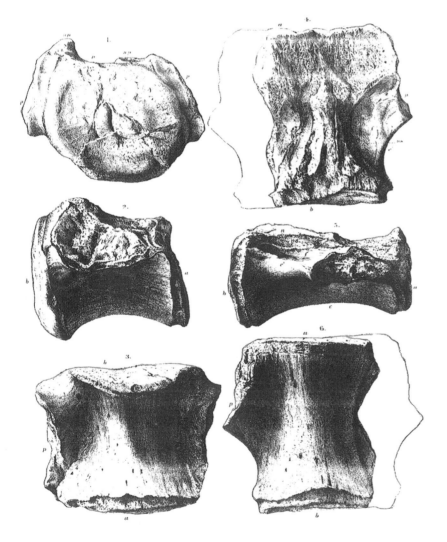

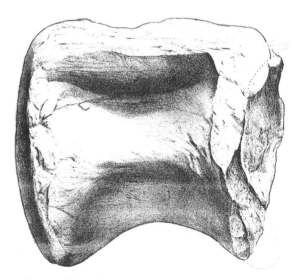

Bothriospondylus robustus, BMNH R22428, holotype dorsal vertebra of *Marmarospondylus robustus*. (After Owen 1875.)

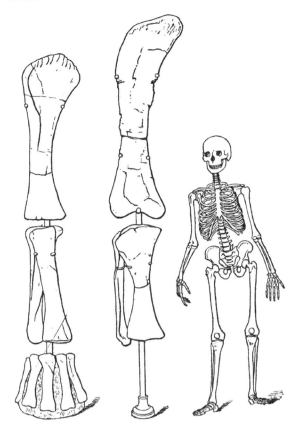

?*Bothriospondylus madagascariensis*, right front and hind limbs.

ing a single ungual phalanx from Madagascar, described by Lavocat (1955*a*). In his review of Sauropoda, McIntosh (1990*b*) stated that the assignment of the Madagascar species is dubious, especially as the status of the type species is doubtful, but cautioned against removing it from *Bothriospondylus* until a full review can be made of the species.

Note: *B. elongatus* Owen 1875 [*nomen dubium*] and *B. magnus* Owen 1875 [*nomen dubium*] were referred by McIntosh (1990*b*) to *Pelorosaurus conybearei*.

Key references: Lapparent (1943); Lavocat (1955*a*); Lydekker (1895); McIntosh (1990*b*); Owen (1875); Thevenis (1907).

BRACHIOSAURUS Riggs 1903—(=?*Oplosaurus*, ?*Pelorosaurus*; ?*Ultrasauros*)

Saurischia: Sauropodomorpha: Sauropoda: Brachiosauridae.

Name derivation: Latin *bracchium* = "arm" + Greek *sauros* = "lizard."

Type species: *B. altithorax* Riggs 1903.

Other species: *B. brancai* Janensch 1914, ?*B. atalaiensis* Lapparent and Zbyszewski 1957, *B. nougaredi* Lapparent 1960.

Occurrence: Morrison Formation, Colorado, Utah, United States; Tendaguru Beds, Mtwara, Tanzania; ?[unnamed formation], Estremadura, Portu-

Courtesy The Field Museum (neg. #GEO-16152.)

Brachiosaurus altithorax, FMNH 25107, holotype right ilium.

Brachiosaurus

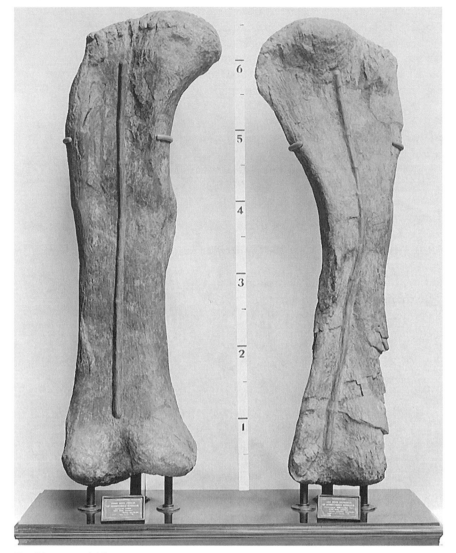

Brachiosaurus altithorax,
FMNH 25107, holotype right
femur and humerus.

gal; "Continental intercalaire," Wargla, Algeria.

Age: Late Jurassic–Early Cretaceous (Kimmeridgian–Tithonian; ?Necomian–?Hauterivian–Albian).

Known material: Partial skeletons from seven individuals, more than three skulls, sacrum, vertebrae, ischia, pubes, isolated limb bones, forelimb and hindlimb bones.

Holotype: FM 25107, seven presacral vertebrae, sacrum, two anterior caudal vertebrae, coracoid, right humerus, ilium, femur, some more or less complete ribs.

Diagnosis of genus (as for type species): Robust overall; mid-dorsal centra, anterior dorsal spines, and transverse processes not much taller or wider than those of posterior dorsals; neural arches long, tall, narrow; transverse processes flat; dorsal centra pleurocoels large; dorsal column more than twice

humerus length, very long relative to vertebrae height; body massive relative to limbs (Paul 1988*a*).

Diagnosis of *B. brancai*: Gracile overall; 25 presacral and 12 dorsal vertebrae; length of mid-dorsal centra approximately that of posterior dorsal centra; anterior dorsal spines and transverse processes much taller and wider than those of posterior dorsals, forming shoulder withers; neural arches short vertically and fore and aft; transverse processes broad transversely, forming shallow "V"; pleurocoels of dorsal centra of moderate size; length of dorsal column less than twice that of humerus, short relative to vertebral height; mass of body, relative to limbs, relatively modest (Paul 1988*a*).

Diagnosis of *B. nougaredi*: Distinguished by great height of sacrum and extreme elongation of metacarpals (Lapparent 1960).

Comments: *Brachiosaurus*, rarest of the Morrison Formation sauropods, is among the largest and most massive terrestrial animals known from good fossil remains. With its raised nostrils, very long neck, long forelimbs, shorter hindlimbs, downward sloping back, and short tail, this is one of the relatively small number of dinosaurian genera known to the general public.

The genus was established on a partial postcranial skeleton (FM 25707), collected in 1900 by the Field Columbian Museum from a hill in the Morrison Formation of Grand River valley, Fruita, Mesa County, overlooking Grand Junction, Colorado. The material had apparently settled into a river or lake sediment, the missing parts having been disturbed sometime later, perhaps by a flood. As discovered, the vertebral column showed little displacement from its position in life.

Dinosaur bones had been found by a dentist, Dr. S. M. Bradbury, who was president of the Western Colorado Academy of Science in Grand Junction, and who had been collecting fossil bones as curios. In 1899, when Elmer S. Riggs, Assistant Curator of Paleontology at the Field Columbian Museum, began to send inquiries regarding fossil finds to various rural towns in the western United States, Bradbury replied, noting that dinosaur bones had been known and collected by local residents since 1885. Riggs, who had been successfully digging up fossil material in Wyoming, decided to spend his next field season in the Grand Junction area, arriving there in spring, 1900, with field assistants H. W. Menke and V. H. Bennett. On July 4 of that year, Menke found an exposure of bones on a small hill (about 200 feet above the surrounding valley) that would become known as Riggs Hill. (In 1938, a stone monument with bronze plaque was dedicated at the quarry site to commemorate the discovery, the dinosaur's name

Brachiosaurus altithorax, reconstructed skeleton including cast of holotype FMNH 25107, in the Field Museum's Stanley Field Hall.

misspelled "Brachyosaurus" on the plaque.) These remains, the holotype of *B. altithorax*, were sent to the Field Columbian Museum. (The bones were exhibited there, and later at the Field Museum of Natural History, for approximately half a century, after which they were stored for more than four decades with the museum's collections. In 1993, the Field Museum [renamed again] mounted a sculpted skeleton of *Bra-*

chiosaurus including casts of the original holotype elements; the following year, the original type material was again put out for public display.)

Riggs (1903*a*) briefly described the genus from the humerus, femur, coracoid and parts of the sacrum and vertebral centra as visible before the specimen had been extracted from the matrix. After the specimen was prepared at the Field Columbian Museum

Brachiosaurus

by J. B. Abbott and C. T. Kline, Riggs (1904) published a more complete description of the holotype, recognizing that *Brachiosaurus* represented a new and unusual family of sauropods, which he named Brachiosauridae.

Brachiosaurus was originally diagnosed by Riggs (1904) as follows: Gigantic; thorax immense; vertebrae with highly specialized hyposphene-hypantrum articulation; vertebral pedicles low, broadly structured; sacrum unusually broad. Riggs (1904) diag-

Brachiosaurus brancai, composite skeleton including holotype SI and SII, mounted at the Humboldt Museum für Naturkunde.

nosed the type species as follows: Dorsal vertebrae distinguished by light construction, long centra with large lateral cavity, and singular neural spines; dorsal centra less pronouncedly opisthocoelous in anterior vertebrae than is common in most other sauropods; thoracic ribs unusually long, one of more slender ribs from mid-thoracic region 2.75 (9 feet) long, another with shaft measuring .2 meters (8 inches) in width; humerus relatively slender, measuring 2.04 meters (80 inches) long; femur slightly shorter, measuring some 2.03 meters (79.5 inches) in length.

Additional information regarding *Brachiosaurus* surfaced with the discovery of more complete material in Tendaguru (upper Kimmeridgian; Aiken 1961), some 40 miles inland from the seaport of Lindi on the eastern coast of Tanzania (formerly German East Africa). Upon these remains was based *B. brancai*, best known of all brachiosaurid species.

As recounted by Colbert (1968) in his book *Men and Dinosaurs*, some weathered sauropod bone-fragments originally named *Gigantosaurus robustus* [now *Janenschia robusta*] were found by W. B. Sattler, an engineer working for the Lindi Prospecting Company in Tendaguru. Word of Sattler's find reached Eberhard Fraas, a paleontologist from Stuttgart, Germany, who happened to be in the colony at the time. Sattler collected some of these remains, which aroused the interest of W. Branca, director of the Berlin Museum of Natural History. Branca organized an expedition to retrieve the fossils, with Werner Janensch and Edwin Henning eventually taking charge of the project. From 1908–12 the expedition worked the site, which yielded the bones of numerous African Jurassic reptiles, including some of the best *Brachiosaurus* material collected, upon which Janensch (1914) founded the species *B. brancai*.

These remains represented a number of individuals (SI, SII [types], R, na, Bo, *etc.*), enough to mount a composite skeleton (the largest mounted dinosaur skeleton in the world) of *B. brancai* for display in the Humboldt Museum für Naturkunde, at Humboldt University in [what would temporarily become East] Berlin. This skeleton measures some 22.5 meters (74 feet) long and 12 meters (39 feet) tall, though there are bones in the museum collection that indicate an even larger individual. (The mounted skeleton had to be dismantled and stored away to escape destruction during World War II air raids.)

Janensch (1914) described *B. brancai*, though not in great detail. The African material revealed the skull of *Brachiosaurus* to be somewhat similar to that of *Camarasaurus*, with its stout, strong jaws and large chisel-shaped teeth. Large openings are located both anterior and posterior to the orbits. Most unusual is the flat snout that rises into enormous nasal openings anterior to the orbits. However, as pointed out by Lull (1919), Janensch referred the Tendaguru material to *Brachiosaurus* mainly because of its elongated forelimbs, apparently not making comparisons of the dorsal vertebrae of the American and African forms. As there was no reason to assume that the American *Brachiosaurus* possessed huge cervical vertebrae as did *B. brancai*, Lull questioned including the African form in this genus.

Apparently belonging to *B. brancai* is specimen BMNH 23 (mostly destroyed), consisting of plectrum, teeth, cervical, dorsal, and caudal vertebrae, ribs, humeri, ilium, incomplete pubis, ischium, incomplete femur, and calcaneum, from Tendaguru, near Kindope, informally described in 1931 in the British publication *Natural History* (volume 3, number 19). The cervicals in this specimen are long, with moderately well-developed and (unlike previously known *Brachiosaurus* specimens) moderately high neural spines.

Paul (1988*a*), in a paper in which he published a new skeletal reconstruction of *B. brancai* (based on the mounted Berlin skeleton and BMNH M23), discovered errors in earlier reconstructions of this species. Paul noted that the Berlin mount included bones from individuals of different sizes and also bones modeled in plaster (including the presacral ver-

Brachiosaurus brancai, holotype skull. Scale = 10 cm. (After Janensch 1935.)

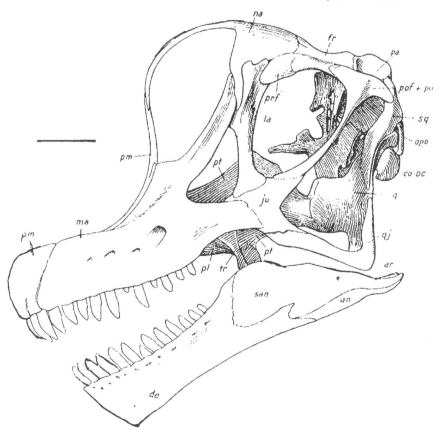

Brachiosaurus brancai, life restoration by Brian Franczak.

tebrae) and that Janensch's figures were sometimes in error. According to Paul, Janensch's figures (and the Berlin mount) show the dorsal centra as significantly larger than the actual remains, vertical and anterior dorsal ribs and shoulder girdle as too high and far forward on the ribcage, scapula and humerus too short, forelimb sprawling, and tail overly long, heavy and drooping.

Paul noted that corrections in the reconstructed skeleton of *B. brancai* revealed that this species differs from *B. altithorax* most significantly in the morphology of the dorsal column. There should be a total of 12 dorsal vertebrae (in BMNH M23), not eleven (as illustrated by Janensch.) The trunk should be shorter than previously restored, forelimbs taller, with "withers" or tall neural spines over the shoulders (a common feature among mammals but not known in other dinosaurs except save for chasmosaurine ceratopsids). *B. brancai* is shorter-bodied, more gracile and giraffe-like than had been realized, while *B. altithorax* is more heavily-bodied and possibly more derived in the shoulder region, with unusually long anterior dorsals. The Morrison and Tendaguru forms are seemingly derived phylogenetically in various ways, perhaps even representing distinct genera. However, because of the incompleteness of *B. altithorax* remains as well as the small sample size of Morrison and Tendaguru dorsal columns, Paul did not attempt to separate both forms on a generic basis, but rather proposed that the two forms be separated for the present on a subgeneric (a division usually employed regarding invertebrates) level as *Brachiosaurus* (*Brachiosaurus*) *altithorax* and *Brachiosaurus* (*Giraffatitan*) *brancai*. This subgeneric name has not been generally accepted, although Olshevsky (1991, 1992) listed *Giraffatitan* as a distinct genus based on the vertebral column as figured by Paul.

From what is known of the African form, the average length of *Brachiosaurus* would have been almost 24 meters (80 feet) from snout to tip of the relatively short tail, the head generally carried at a sharp angle to the extremely long neck almost 12 meters (40 feet) above ground. The back slopes downwards due to the longer front legs, so long, in fact, that Riggs (1903*a*) originally misidentified the humerus as the femur. (The slope of the back in the Berlin mounted skeleton is exaggerated, due to the hind feet having been mounted in a plantigrade position, and with the hind legs belonging to a slightly smaller individual.)

The species *B. fraasi*, described by Janensch (1914), was based upon fragmentary remains (HMN collection) from the Late Jurassic to Early Cretaceous of Tendaguru, Africa. A humerus from this species measures about 1.75 meters (almost 6 feet) in length. Janensch (1961) subsequently synonymized this species with *B. brancai*. Paul later referred all Tendaguru brachiosaurid specimens, including *B. fraasi*, to *B. (Giraffatitan) brancai*.

?*B. atalaiensis* Lapparent and Zbyszewski 1957 was based on 28 vertebrae, some ribs, a scapula, sternal fragment, proximal portion of the right humerus, ilium fragment, nearly complete pubis, portion of the left femur, and left tibia, from the Kimmeridgian of Portugal. Lapparent and Zbyszewski described this species as follows: Longest cervical centrum 20 centimeters (about 7.75 inches) in length, 12 centimeters (over 4.5 inches) high; proximal caudal with diameter of 18.5 centimeters (about 7 inches); humerus remarkably slender and, if complete, probably approximately 101 centimeters (almost 4 feet) in length; ilium proportionately less robust and pubis comparatively stronger than in *Apatosaurus*; femur, if complete, about 200 centimeters (almost 6.5 feet) long, tibia 112 centimeters (about 3.5 feet); distinguished from *B. altithorax* mostly by relatively longer forelimbs, from *B. brancai* by comparatively shorter cervical vertebrae and less gigantic front limbs.

B. nougaredi Lapparent (1960) was based on a sacrum and limb bones from the Upper Jurassic, Taouratine horizon, Sahara Desert.

The weight of *Brachiosaurus* has traditionally been estimated at ranging from about 36 to 45 metric tons (40 to 50 tons). Colbert (1962) estimated the probable weights of dinosaurs based, in part, upon the amount of water displaced by scale-models. Utilizing a model of *Brachiosaurus* sculpted by Vincent Fusco under the supervision of Barnum Brown, Colbert calculated the weight of the living animal to be approximately 66 to 77 metric tons (80 to 85 tons). Paul, water-immersing a more accurate model with shorter body and more slender musculature, calculated the weight of the largest "lean" (toward the end of the dry season, when the animal lacked fat reserves) *B. brancai* to be closer to the earlier 45-metric tons estimation.

At the time that Riggs first described *Brachiosaurus*, sauropods were already regarded as semiaquatic or at least swamp-dwelling animals. This idea was mostly inspired by the great bulk of these dinosaurs, which seemed to imply that they were too heavy for terrestrial locomotion, and also on the structure of the teeth, which were interpreted as best suited to soft and succulent vegetation. Some paleontologists had even observed that the vertebrae in some sauropods bore certain similarities to those of whales. Riggs (1904), however, could not single out any aquatic or semiaquatic mammal or reptile in which the vertebrae possessed the fluting or hollowing of opisthocoelous sauropods.

Riggs (1904) hypothesized that *Brachiosaurus* was mostly terrestrial, his idea based mainly on the structure of the limbs and on the feet (unknown in the *B. altithorax* holotype) of other opisthocoelian sauropods. Riggs (1904) pointed out that amphibious animals like the hippopotamus have relatively short legs and broad feet. In dinosaurs such as *Brachiosaurus*, the straight hind legs are indicative of terrestrial animals that inhabit uplands. The short, stout metapodials and blunted phalanges in opisthocoelian dinosaurs, a foot structure similar to that of elephants, and the reduction in the number of claws, would have been ill-adapted for aquatic locomotion. Furthermore, the presumed relatively short tail (unknown in the holotype) of *Brachiosaurus*, plus the long and slender limbs, the deep thorax, broad sacrum, and expanded ilium, all seemed to indicate good adaptations for the land-dwelling life style for a quite agile dinosaur. Riggs (1904) concluded that *Brachiosaurus* was a highly specialized terrestrial sauropod.

These conclusions were mostly disregarded by contemporary paleontologists who clung to the model of an amphibious *Brachiosaurus*, a conception that persisted into modern times. Zdenek Burian's painting, first published in Augusta's (1960) book *Prehistoric Animals*, has, despite various anatomical errors, become a classic much copied or imitated by other artists. The painting depicts a *B. brancai* pair submerged in water, one entirely below the surface.

Kermack (1951), based upon earlier work by German physiologists including Stigler (1911) attempting to determine the maximum pressure a human being could endure underwater while still breathing, applied the same methods to sauropods. Kermack's calculations revealed that a dinosaur like *Brachiosaurus*, if fully submerged with only the raised nostrils breaking the water's surface, would have had at least 8 pounds per square inch of water pressure exerted upon its lungs, thereby preventing their expansion and probably crushing the trachea. Assuming that the animal could have remained thusly submerged and still resist collapse of the lungs, the blood would have had to flow at incredible speeds. With the air inside the lungs at normal atmospheric pressure,

Brachiosaurus nougaredi, holotype left metacarpal and phalange of manual digit III. Scale = 3 cm. (After Lapparent 1960.)

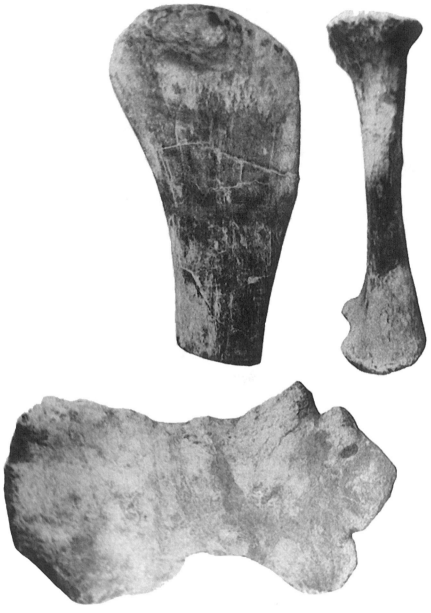

?*Brachiosaurus atalaiensis*, holotype partial left humerus, left tibia, and left pubis. (After Lapparent and Gbyszewski 1957.)

Further considering an aquatic versus terrestrial life style for *Brachiosaurus*, Dodson, Bakker and Behrensmeyer (1983) showed that the North American species is known only in flood plain deposits notably lacking lakeside sediments and the remains of turtles and crocodiles, suggesting that these sauropods may not have lived in association with bodies of standing water. However, the authors also pointed out that, according to Lull (1915*b*) and Schubert (1918), the abundant Tendaguru species is apparently associated with water.

Still puzzling is the high position of the nostrils in *Brachiosaurus*. When sauropods were considered as mostly aquatic animals, the raised nostrils were seen as a kind of snorkel, letting the dinosaur feed while submerged underwater. Marsh (1884*a*) compared the narial openings in *Diplodocus* to those of the phytosaur "*Belodon*," their similar locations suggesting aquatic habits. Although modern workers usually view these dinosaurs as basically terrestrial animals (see *Apatosaurus* entry), Coombs (1975), in a study of sauropod habits and habitats, cautioned that data pertaining to sauropod narial morphology was inconclusive and dependent on the choice of analog.

With *Brachiosaurus* viewed as a terrestrial creature, Bakker (1986) suggested that the nostrils were covered in life by a fleshy chamber that amplified sound. In his book *The Illustrated Encyclopedia of Dinosaurs*, Norman (1985) mentioned that they may have also served to increase the olfactory sense or functioned as a cooling surface for the blood.

Riggs (1904) examined the possibilities of *Brachiosaurus* assuming a bipedal pose. Sauropods like *Camarasaurus*, *Apatosaurus* and *Diplodocus* were fitted for rearing up on their hind legs by virtue of their elevated sacral spines and strong dorsal vertebrae, while *Brachiosaurus* possessed short sacral spines. The articulation of these spines would have rendered impossible the lateral movement of the body necessary to elevate the anterior part of the body. Also in *Brachiosaurus*, the structure of the strong thoracic ribs strengthened the vertebral column in this region for quadrupedal locomotion. For these reasons and because the forelimbs were so heavy, Riggs (1904) concluded that *Brachiosaurus* was limited to walking on all fours.

Paul, however, argued that brachiosaurids, like other dinosaurs, were hindlimb dominant, the center of gravity toward the rear, the hindlimbs more robust and supporting more weight than the forelimbs. With this arrangement, according to Paul, dinosaurs like *Brachiosaurus* could rear up on their hind limbs more easily than can elephants, which can rear up despite their forelimb dominance.

the blood in the pulmonary vessels would have exploded into the lungs, resulting in hemorrhage and probably heart damage.

Bakker (1971) also argued that *Brachiosaurus* was a terrestrial animal physically suited to a land-based life style. Bakker showed that the pillar-like legs, comparatively narrow feet, deep and narrow rib-cage and reinforced back were all indicative of a creature designed for living on land. Bakker favored a high-browsing life style in which the neck, like a giraffe's, raised the head to the tallest trees to feed. More evidence favoring terrestrial habits is the heavily-abraided teeth, signs that *Brachiosaurus* ate tough or gritty vegetation (*e.g.,* branches, twigs, and cycadoid-tree fronds) rather than soft water plants.

Notes: Jensen (1987) discussed various brachiosaurid remains possibly belonging to *B. altithorax* and having diagnostic significance. This material includes a highly eroded, incomplete skeleton discovered about 1943 by Daniel E. and Vivian Jones on the Uncompahgre Upwarp, at a site that was named the Potter Creek Quarry (about 70 kilometers away from Riggs' locality), near Delta, in western Colorado (part of the humerus having been collected about the time of discovery and donated to the United States National Museum, although the specimen was not described), in about the middle of the Brushy Basin Member of the Morrison Formation. After working for two seasons (1971 and 1975) at this site, Jensen recovered such elements as part of the originally collected humerus, a medial dorsal vertebra, incomplete left ilium, left radius, and metacarpal. Jensen (1987) also reported *Brachiosaurus* remains (possibly belonging to a new species) including a rib, distal cervical vertebra, proximal half of a scapula, and coracoid, collected in 1962 and 1966 from the Jensen/Jensen Quarry, discovered by him in 1960 in the basal Brushy Basin Member, Morrison Formation, near Jensen, Utah, south of Green River several miles away from the Dinosaur National Monument Quarry.

Also, Jensen reported the proximal third of a sauropod femur, which he had discovered in 1985 in a uranium miner's front yard at the Recapture Creek Member of the Morrison Formation, southern Utah. Jensen (1987) observed this to be the largest bone he had ever seen (measuring 1.67 meters, or 5.5 feet, in circumference). Because of the resemblance of its profile to the same bone in *Brachiosaurus*, this specimen was referred to the Brachiosauridae but not to any genus.

Key references: Bakker (1971, 1986); Dodson, Bakker and Behrensmeyer (1983); Janensch (1914); Jensen (1987); Kermack (1951); Lapparent (1960); Lapparent and Zbyszewski (1957); Lull (1919); Paul (1988*a*); Riggs (1903*a*, 1904).

BRACHYCERATOPS Gilmore 1914—(=?*Centrosaurus*)

Ornithischia: Genasauria: Cerapoda: Marginocephalia: Ceratopsia: Neoceratopsia: Ceratopsidae: Centrosaurinae.

Name derivation: Greek *brachy* = "short" + Greek *keratos* = "horned" + Greek *ops* = "face."

Type species: *B. montanensis* Gilmore 1914.

Other species: [None.]

Occurrence: Two Medicine Formation, Montana, United States.

Age: Late Cretaceous (Campanian–Maastrichtian).

Brachyceratops montanensis, USNM 7951, holotype restored skeleton.

Known material: Six incomplete skulls, skeletons, adult, juveniles.

Holotype: USNM 7951, incomplete, disarticulated skull.

Diagnosis of genus (as for type species): Small; skull with much abbreviated and vertically deep facial portion; brow horns small, united firmly with postorbitals; nasal horn core large, slightly recurved, laterally compressed, longitudinally divided by median suture, outgrowth of nasals; frill with comparatively sharp median crest, apparently small fenestrae located entirely within median element; border of frill scalloped, lacking epoccipitals; teeth reduced; pes with five digits, digit V vestigial; anterior blade of ilium greatly expanded, strongly curving outward (Gilmore 1917, emended from Gilmore 1914a).

Comments: The genus *Brachyceratops* was founded on a partial skull (USNM 7951), collected in 1913 by Charles Whitney Gilmore from the Two Medicine Formation, Milk River, Blackfeet Indian Reservation, Glacier County, Montana. Provisionally associated with the holotype was a fragmentary part of the crest, a right dentary, and predentary.

Gilmore (1914a) originally diagnosed *Brachyceratops* (and type species *B. montanensis*) based on the

holotype and three paratypes, the latter consisting of a rostral and portions of premaxillaries (USNM 7952); sacrum, pelvis, and an articulated series of 50 caudal vertebrae, associated with dorsal ribs and vertebrae (USNM 7953); and a tibia, fibula, and partly articulated left hind foot, including astragalus, calcaneum, two tarsals of the distal row, four metatarsals, portion of a fifth tarsal, and 11 phalanges (USNM 7957).

Gilmore (1914a, 1917) observed that the narial opening of the skull is situated forward and under the nasal. This, according to Lull (1933), positioned *Brachyceratops* midway between the Belly River Formation and Lance Formation ceratopsians. As Lull noted, the nasal horn arises over the posterior border of the nares in more primitive forms, and, evolving progressively, over the opening itself in later forms.

Gilmore (1917) speculated that the small size of the animal (the total length of the composite skeleton displayed at the National Museum of Natural History being some 1.7 meters or 6 feet) was indicative of an immature individual. Lull added that the general proportions, plus the open sutures, indicate that this individual is not even half grown.

Later, Gilmore (1939) described the first adult specimen (USNM 14765) of *Brachyceratops*, consisting of disarticulated skull elements (right half of the frill lacking the squamosal; articulated postorbital, jugal, postfrontal and prefrontal, lacrimal and supraorbital; right maxillary with several teeth; left premaxillary, rostral, part of the right half of the nasal horn core; a basioccipital fragment; and various fragments), both femora, left scapula, first rib, one dorsal vertebra, and two phalangeal bones collected from northern Montana. As the greatest growth changes were evident in the frill of this individual, Gilmore (1939) substantiated his earlier speculation that, rather than separate epoccipital processes, direct outgrowths of the frill itself, prominently developed in the adult skull, were present on the frill margin to create a scalloped appearance.

Usually, *Brachyceratops* has been regarded as a juvenile *Monoclonius* or *Centrosaurus*. Lambe (1915) referred the genus to *M. dawsoni*, though Lull maintained that their synonymy could not be unequivocably demonstrated. According to Lull, the fenestrae in *Brachyceratops* are apparently smaller than those in *Monoclonius* and the parietals lack the hook-like processes diagnostic of *Centrosaurus*. Unlike *Monoclonius*, *Brachyceratops* possesses a longitudinally divided nasal horn.

Dodson (1990d) pointed out other differences between *Brachyceratops* and *Monoclonius*, citing the relatively short face, long frill, and small fenestrae in *Brachyceratops*, but noting other distinguishing characters. In *Brachyceratops* the jugal is erect, while in

Brachyceratops montanensis, USNM 14765, partial frill (adult), dorsal view, posterior part at left. Scale = 14 cm. (After Gilmore 1939.)

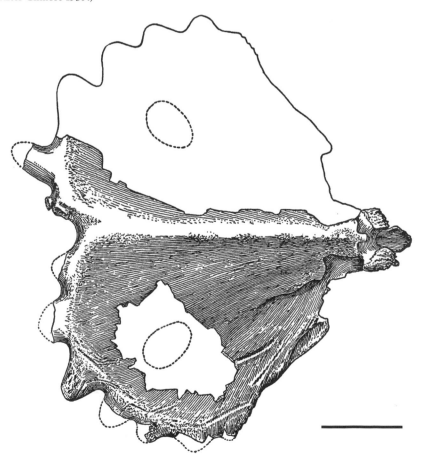

Monoclonius (and *Centrosaurus*) it is swept backwards. The maxilla in *Brachyceratops* is relatively short with alveolar grooves for only 20 teeth. Gilmore (1917) had considered twenty alveoli to be a juvenile character, Lull adding that the jaws become longer during growth with the number of tooth rows possibly increasing. Dodson found the number of alveoli not to be an ontogenetic character.

Dodson questioned the presence of fenestrae in the crest. Gilmore (1917), in restoring the crest of *Brachyceratops*, had based his reconstruction on inadequate material from which, Lull noted, the exact shape and size of the fontanelles cannot be determined. Lull added that Gilmore's reconstruction only incorporated a small portion of the antero-internal margin of the right fenestra. Dodson concluded that *Brachyceratops* cannot be ontogenetically transformed into *Monoclonius* and is seemingly distinct from other centrosaurines (see Dodson and Currie 1990).

Dodson further stated that John R. Horner had collected a series of juvenile and adult centrosaurine skulls between 1986 and 1987 from the Two Medicine Formation. As the juveniles resemble *B. montanensis*

and the adults *Styracosaurus ovatus*, and since this locality is near the type locality of the former species, Dodson questioned whether *Brachyceratops* might be a juvenile *S. ovatus*.

Key references: Dodson (1990*d*) Dodson and Currie (1990); Gilmore (1914*a*, 1917, 1939); Lambe (1915); Lull (1933).

BRACHYLOPHOSAURUS   Sternberg 1953

Ornithischia: Genasauria: Cerapoda: Ornithopoda: Iguanodontia: Hadrosauridae: Hadrosaurinae.

Name derivation: Greek *brachy* = "short" + Greek *lophos* = "crest" + Greek *sauros* = "lizard."

Type species: *B. canadensis* Sternberg 1953.

Other species: *G. goodwini* Horner 1988.

Occurrence: Oldman Formation, Alberta, Canada; Oldman Formation, Montana, United States.

Age: Late Cretaceous (late Campanian).

Known material: Skull with associated postcrania, partial skull, nearly complete skull with associated postcrania.

Photo by R. A. Long and S. P. Welles (neg. #74/10-B17), reproduced with permission of Canadian Museum of Nature, Ottawa, Canada.

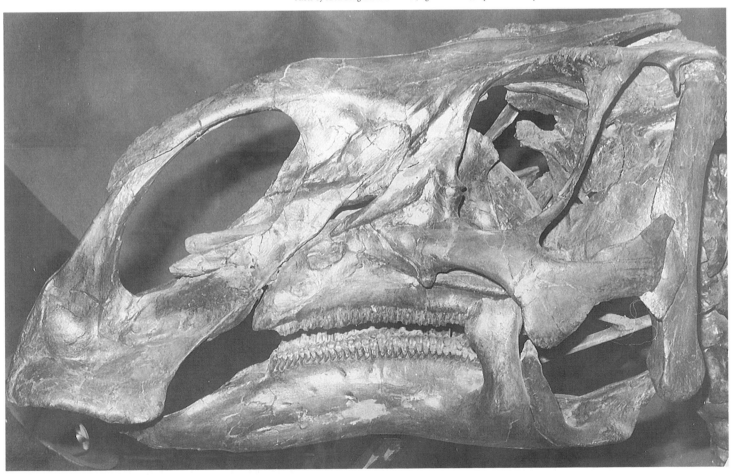

Brachylophosaurus canadensis, NMC 8893, holotype skull, left lateral view.

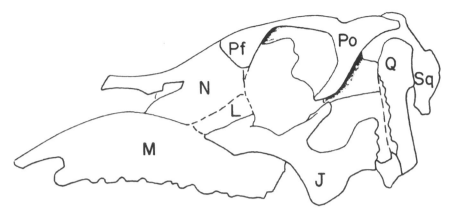

Brachylophosaurus goodwini, UCMP 130139, holotype skull. Length = 65 cm. (After Horner 1988.)

Holotype: NMC 8893, complete skull, cervical and anterior dorsal vertebrae, ribs, scapulae, coracoids, humeri, left ulna, radius.

Diagnosis of genus (as for type species): Hadrosaurid with a solid, posteriorly directed flat and widened, solid nasal crest; nasal depression not extended to crest; jugal lightly constructed, with large ventrally projecting boss; anteroposteriorly short supraoccipital-exoccipital roof posterior to foramen magnum (Horner 1988).

Diagnosis of *B. goodwini*: Deep and rounded dorsal pit or depression at near junction of frontal and postorbital; upper process of nasal dorsally concave; posterolateral surface of nasal reaching orbital rim; quadratojugal process of jugal paralleling postorbital process (Horner 1988).

Comments: The genus *Brachylophosaurus* was founded upon a skull with incomplete postcranial remains (NMC 8893), collected in 1936 by Charles M. Sternberg from the Oldman Formation, in a thin sandstone bed at Little Sandhill Creek near Red Deer River, Alberta, Canada. While recovering the specimen, Sternberg interpreted it to be a new species of *Gryposaurus*, although further study revealed it to be generically distinct (Sternberg 1953).

Originally, Sternberg diagnosed *Brachylophosaurus* (and type species *B. canadensis*) as follows: Skull relatively high (in lateral view), subrectangular; beak subrectangular in outline, turned down anteriorly, not reflected; nares oval in outline, located relatively high, with no depressed area to accommodate vomero-nasal organ; nasal parallel to tooth row, extending posteriorly over frontals to form a somewhat *Saurolophus*–like, paddle-shaped crest that overhangs parietals; frontals short, mid-portion covered by nasals, outer aspect contributing to rim of the orbit; maxilla relatively high anteriorly, with elongate anterior maxillary process fitting into a groove in the maxilla; lacrimal large, triangular, with far anteriorly extending tip; orbit positioned highly; lateral temporal openings approximately three times high as wide; quadrate moderately long, slightly curved; prevomer very thin, subtriangular, much longer than high; dentary moderately high, edentulous portion about half length of the tooth magazine; upper edge of dentary progresses anteriorly at about same level as the grinding surface, then turns down very sharply; dentary teeth with enamel face about three times high as wide; lingual-buccal diameter greater than fore-and-aft breadth; about 49 vertical rows of teeth in maxilla, about 39 in dentary; postcranial skeleton extremely gracile; forearm relatively longer than in other hadrosaurines; cervical vertebrae low, broad; anterior dorsal vertebrae with moderately high neural spines with great fore-and-aft diameter.

As measured by Sternberg, the holotype skull is about 800 millimeters (31 inches) in length between perpendiculars, and about 420 millimeters (about 16 inches) high taken through the orbit.

Sternberg observed that the down-turned beak of *Brachylophosaurus*, with no reflection of the anterior edge, and the elongated forearm, were suggestive of the Lambeosaurine, but referred the genus to the Hadrosaurinae because the premaxillae and nasals are not folded and extend to surround the elongated and looped narial passages. Because of its incipient crest, Ostrom (1961) reassigned *Brachylophosaurus* to the [abandoned] "subfamily" Saurolophinae. Brett-Surman (1975, 1989) and Weishampel and Horner (1990) placed this genus in the Hadrosaurinae. Weishampel and Horner, as did Brett-Surman (1975, 1989), speculated that the accentuated nasal arch in *B. canadensis* was utilized in head-pushing during intraspecific combat (although Brett-Surman believed the premaxilla-nasal junction was too weak to be used in combat).

A second species, *B. goodwini*, was based upon a partial skull, cervical vertebrae, scapulae, coracoids, sternals, humeri, and rib fragments (UCMP 130139), recovered from a unit of gray fluted sandstone about 15 meters above a coal bed (assumed equivalent to the uppermost "Foremost Formation" of Alberta, about middle of the Oldman Formation, ?late Campanian). The specimen was discovered in 1981 by Mark Goodwin during field work under the direction of William Clemens of the University of California Museum of Paleontology, Berkeley (Horner 1988).

As observed by Horner, the skulls of both species of *Brachylophosaurus* are virtually identical with the exception of the frontal depressions and depressed nasals in *B. goodwini*. Covering all possibilities that could result in a contradictory justification, Horner noted that the differences between the two species

Thanks to D. Baird, reproduced with permission of Canadian Museum of Nature, Ottawa, Canada (neg. #J-638).

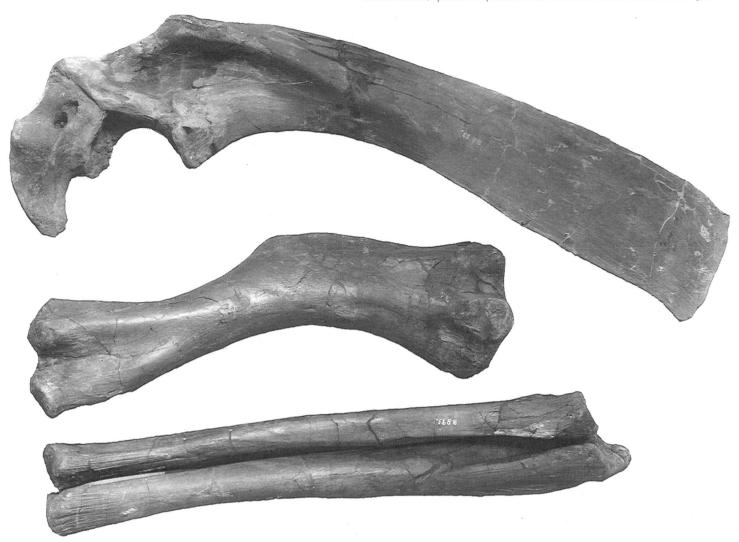

Brachylophosaurus canadensis, NMC 8893, holotype scapulacoracoid, humerus, radius, and ulna.

might someday prove to constitute sexual dimorphic characters, or that *B. goodwini* may be reinterpreted as a new genus. However, Horner cautioned that additional specimens must be collected and more precisely dated before such simplistic "splitting" can be justified.

Key references: Brett-Surman (1975, 1989); Horner (1988); Sternberg (1953); Weishampel and Horner (1990).

BRACHYPODOSAURUS   Chakravarti 1934
[*nomen dubium*]
Ornithischia: Thyreophora: Ankylosauria *incertae sedis.*
Name derivation: Greek *brachy* = "short" + Greek *podos* = "foot" + Greek *sauros* = "lizard."
Type species: *B. gravis* Chakravarti 1934 [*nomen dubium*].

Other species: [None.]
Occurrence: Mottled Nodular Beds–Upper Limestone, Jabalpur, India.
Age: Late Cretaceous (Upper Senonian or Danian).
Known material/holotype: Geological Museum Collection V9, Benares Hindu University, left humerus.

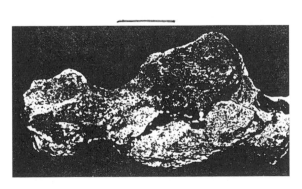

Brachypodosaurus gravis, IM V9, holotype humerus. Scale = 6 cm. (After Chakravarti 1934.)

Diagnosis of genus: [None published.]

Comments: The genus *Brachypodosaurus* was established upon a left humerus (IM collection), recovered from the "Junction of Mottled Nodular beds and Upper Limestone" (upper part of Lameta Beds) (Late Cretaceous; Matley 1921), at Chota Simla, Jubbulpore (now Jabalpur), Madhya-Pradesh, India (Chakravarti 1934).

Chakravarti described the humerus as short, robust, probably belonging to a short-footed and heavy dinosaur allied to stegosaurids, but warranting a new family.

Lapparent (1957) regarded the type species as an indeterminate stegosaur. Coombs and Maryańska (1990), in their review of the Ankylosauria, regarded this taxon as an ankylosaurian *nomen dubium*.

Key references: Chakravarti (1934); Lapparent (1957).

BRADYCNEME   Harrison and Walker 1975

Saurischia: Theropoda: Tetanurae: Avetheropoda: Coelurosauria: Maniraptora: Arctometatarsalia: Bullatosauria: ?Troodontidae.

Name derivation: Greek *bradys* = "slow" + Greek *cneme* = "leg."

Type species: *B. draculae* Harrison and Walker 1975.

Other species: [None.]

Occurrence: Szentpeterfalva, Transylvania, Romania.

Age: Late Cretaceous (?Maastrichtian).

Known material/holotype: BMNH A1588, distal end of right tibiotarsus.

Diagnosis of genus (as for type species): Tibiotarsus with broad and antero-posteriorly flattened distal end; distal projection of external condyle beyond internal condyle is quite well marked; projection of inner condyle directed internally to some extent; both condyles projecting to some extent anteriorly; anterior intercondylar fossa deep, transverse; well-developed groove on outer side, terminating at a large external ligamental prominence, proximally located at the external surface of outer condyle (Harrison and Walker 1975).

Comments: The genus *Bradycneme* was founded upon a partial right tibiotarsus (BMNH A1588), collected in 1923 by Lady Smith-Woodward, from the Szentpeterfalva, Hafzeg, Transylvania [then in Hungary]. The genus established the Bradycnemidae, a new taxon proposed by Harrison and Walker (1975), which they regarded as a family of owls of the "order" Strigiformes.

According to Brodkorb (1978), the type specimen almost surely represents, not a bird, but a theropod dinosaur.

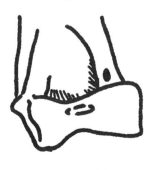

Bradycneme draculae, BMNH A1588, holotype right tibiotarsus. (After Harrison and Walker 1975.)

Note: Based upon the degree of robustness of the astragalus, *Bradycneme* may belong to the Troodontidae (R. A. Molnar, personal communication 1988).

Key reference: Harrison and Walker (1975).

BREVICERATOPS   Kurzanov 1990

Ornithischia: Genasauria: Cerapoda: Marginocephalia: Ceratopsia: Neoceratopsia: Protoceratopsidae.

Name derivation: Latin *brevis* = "short" + *Ceratops* [Greek *keratos* = "horned" + Greek *ops* = "face"].

Type species: *B. kozlowskii* (Maryańska and Osmólska 1975).

Other species: [None.]

Occurrence: Barun Goyot Formation, Nemegt Basin, Mongolia.

Age: Late Cretaceous (Middle Campanian).

Known material: Mostly cranial and some postcranial remains representing at least five individuals, juvenile.

Holotype: ZPAL MgD-1/117, almost complete skull with mandible, partial postcrania including cervical, dorsal, and sacral vertebrae, right scapula, left humerus, ulna, radius, incomplete left ilium, fragmentary left ischium, right and part of left femora, fragmentary right tibia and fibula, fragments of right metatarsus, and pieces of ribs, subadult.

Diagnosis of genus (as for type species): Medium-sized protoceratopsids, with narrow and fairly short snout; nasal bones forming short, flattish horn; postorbital bones flat, smooth, with long descending branches, which even in young specimens already reach lower margin of orbits; squamosals in all age stages entirely forming upper margin of lower temporal depression; anterior margin of upper temporal depression formed by parietal and postorbital bones; frill short relative to total length of skull, low, in adults rising slightly (up to 15 degrees) relative to skull roof, widening moderately in caudal directions; squamosals almost parallel in anterior half (in young, parallel along entire length); sacrum with eight fused vertebrae; humerus short, thick; anterior end of ilium distinctly twisted (Kurzanov 1990).

Comments: The new genus *Breviceratops* was established on an incomplete skull with poorly preserved partial skeleton (ZPAL MgD-1/117), found by Teresa Maryańska and Halszka Osmólska in 1970, during the 1964–1971 Polish-Mongolian Paleontological Expeditions (Kielan-Jaworoska and Dovchin 1969; Kielan-Jaworoska and Barsbold 1972), in the red sands of the Barun Goyot Formation (Gradziński and Jerzykiewicz 1972; tentatively dated Middle

Campanian; by Kielan-Jaworoska 1974), Khulsan locality, Nemegt Basin, Gobi Desert, southern Mongolia. Referred remains from the same locality include a distorted skull with lower jaw from an immature individual, two almost complete dentaries, postcranial fragments from a young adult, fragments of dentaries, teeth, various skull elements, and three neural arches of caudal vertebrae. Maryańska and Osmólska (1975) tentatively referred this material to the genus *Protoceratops* as new species *?P. kozlowski*.

Originally, Maryańska and Osmólska diagnosed *?P. kozlowskii* as follows: Skull with anteriorly sloping profile, very long, narrow prefrontal; posterior ala extending behind midpoint of orbit; jugal deep, below postorbital bar; mandible deep, with straight lower edge; nasal-frontal suture behind anterior margin of orbit; eight vertebrae coalesced into sacrum; humerus short, stout; ilium with distinctly everted anterior process.

Maryańska and Osmólska acknowledged that this material, though fragmentary and based on immature specimens, could represent a new genus, this opinion shared by Dodson and Currie (1990) in their review of the Neoceratopsia. Kurzanov (1990) referred to this species two small skulls (PIN collection) excavated several years before the type material at Kherman-Tsav and originally referred to *P. andrewsi*. From all of this material, Kurzanov noted that the differences between *P. andrewsi* and *?P. kozlowski* were sufficient to propose that the latter represented a new genus, which he named *Breviceratops*.

As observed by Kurzanov, *Breviceratops* essentially differs from *Protoceratops* in two ways: 1. The snout of *Breviceratops* has a small but distinct horn, as opposed to the nasal tubercle of *Protoceratops*, and 2. the frill is short, narrow, and low in the former genus, but much larger in all dimensions in the latter. Also, supraorbital tubercles are not present in *Breviceratops* (present in *Protoceratops*); the upper temporal depressions are framed equally by the parietal and postorbital bones (frontal bones also participating in this structure in *Protoceratops*); anterior branch of the squamosal is developed more strongly and is not straight (curved inward in the middle in *Protoceratops*); and the sacrum is formed by eight (not seven, as in *Protoceratops*) vertebrae.

Comparing *Breviceratops* to other protoceratopsid genera (*Protoceratops*, *Microceratops*, *Bagaceratops*, *Leptoceratops*, and *Montanoceratops*), Kurzanov saw *Breviceratops* as representing a clear example of a transition from one form to another in formations successively replacing one another (*i.e.*, the Djadokht and Barun Goyot formations). In this sequence of forms, Kurzanov was able to trace the evolutionary tendencies involving the nasal horn and frill, the two

most salient features of ceratopsids. The sample population of five *Breviceratops* skulls (PIN 3142/1, 1, 4, and 5, almost complete skulls, and PIN 3142/3, right side of skull) allowed for the study of certain aspects of the age variation of the new genus and to compare it with the well-known variation of its most closely related genus, *Protoceratops*.

Kurzanov noted the following most marked allometric changes in the *Breviceratops* skulls: Shape changes from high triangle (first and fourth specimens) to equilateral; nasal bones become longer, narrower, nasal horn gradually developing to 3 centimeters in height, internasal suture disappearing even in earliest growth stages; horn in juveniles located well anterior of orbits, at middle of nasal bones, gradually shifting with age rearward toward anterior margin of orbits; frill lengthens and widens posteriorly (the widening more intensive in adults) and from plane of

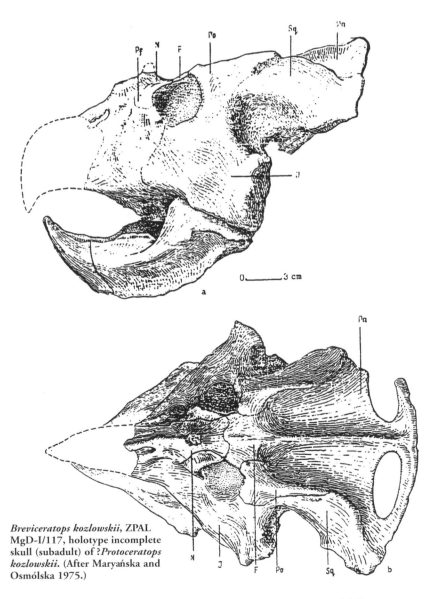

Breviceratops kozlowskii, ZPAL MgD-I/117, holotype incomplete skull (subadult) of *?Protoceratops kozlowskii*. (After Maryańska and Osmólska 1975.)

skull roof gradually rises relative to it; median ridge of frill, initially not manifested at all, becomes clearly visible (second specimen), reaching height of almost 2 centimeters along its entire length (fifth specimen); frontal-parietal depression in juveniles gradually becomes purely frontal depression in adults; relative area of frontal bones and their participation in forming orbits decrease, surface of these bones changing from slightly convex to flat or even somewhat concave; frontal-parietal suture moves from early position opposite posterior margin of orbits to level of anterior margin of lower temporal depression; lacrimals widen, taking on more vertical orientation; prefrontal bones become shorter, narrower; and anterior branch of squamosal becomes higher, longer.

Also, Kurzanov noted that some of the above age changes can be seen to occur to one degree or another in all known protoceratopsids, the most important of which are these: Orbits change from elongated-round to subquadratic or subrectangular (in addition to decreasing in size); skull roof changes from slightly convex to flat or slightly concave, frontal-parietal depression forming; skull becomes shorter, snout becomes longer (features observed by Maryańska and Osmólska); frill length and width increases; angle of inclination of frill to plane of skull roof increases; ventral margin of lower jaw changes from straight to rounded.

Kurzanov agreed with Maryańska and Osmólska that this new species was the direct ancestor of *P. andrewsi*. As noted by Kurzanov, this suggestion is supported by the closeness in the skulls of these two species, by their similar allometric changes, and also by the fact that the Barun Goyot deposits with *Breviceratops* directly replace the Djadokhta deposits yielding *Protoceratops*.

Key references: Kurzanov (1990); Maryańska and Osmólska (1975).

BRONTOSAURUS Marsh 1879—(See *Apatosaurus.*)

Name derivation: Greek *bronte* = "thunder" + Greek *sauros* = "lizard."

Type species: *B. excelsus* Marsh 1879.

BRUHATHKAYOSAURUS Yadagiri and Ayyasami 1989

Saurischia: Theropoda: Tetanurae: Avetheropoda *incertae sedis*.

Name derivation: Sanskrit *bruhatkaya* = "huge body" + Greek *sauros* = "lizard."

Type species: *B. matleyi* Yadagiri and Ayyasami 1989.

Other species: [None.]

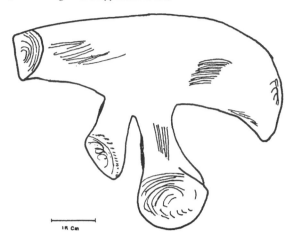

Bruhathkayosaurus matleyi, GSI PAL/SR/20, holotype ilium. (After Yadagiri and Ayyasami 1989.)

Occurrence: Kallamedu Formation, Tamilnadu, India.

Age: Late Cretaceous (Maastrichtian).

Known material: Ilium, tibia, femur, caudal vertebra.

GSI PAL/SR/20: Ilium.

Diagnosis of genus (as for type species): Huge theropod with heavy limb bones, tibia the largest; ilium large, with heavy puboischiac peduncle, posteriorly massive (Yadagiri and Ayyasami 1989).

Comments: The discovery of *Bruhathkayosaurus* records the occurrence of large "carnosaurs" in sandstones of the Kallamedu Formation (Upper Cretaceous) of the Ariyalu Group (characterized by the presence of dinosaurian bones; devoid of marine invertebrate fossils; underlain by Ottakkoil Formation, overlain by Niniyur Formation), Tiruchirapalli district Tamil Nadu, northeast of Kallamedu Village, India. The genus is known from scattered postcranial remains including the well-preserved holotype ilium (Yadagiri and Ayyasami 1989).

As measured by Yadagiri and Ayyasami, the ilia are 1200 millimeters (over 46 inches) in length, with a median width of 250 millimeters (over 9.5 inches). The tibia is significantly large, with a length of 2000 millimeters (over 75 inches) and shaft width of 380 millimeters (about 15 inches). The femur has a width of 750 millimeters (about 29 inches) across the condyles.

Key reference: Yadagiri and Ayyasami (1989).

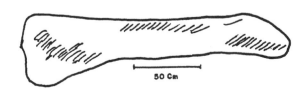

Bruhathkayosaurus matleyi, GSI PAL/SR/20, holotype tibia. (After Yadagiri and Ayyasami 1989.)

Photo by R. A. Long and S. P. Welles
(neg. #82-6-2), courtesy Natural History
Museum of Los Angeles County.

BUGENASAURA Galton 1995

Ornithischia: Genasauria: Cerapoda: Ornithopoda:
  Hypsilophodontidae.

Name derivation: Latin *bu* = "large" + Latin *gena*
  [feminine] = "cheek" + Greek *saura* [feminine] =
  "lizard."

Type species: *B. infernalis* Galton 1995

Other species: [None].

Occurrence: Hell Creek Formation, South Dakota,
  United States.

Age: Late Cretaceous (Late Maastrichtian).

Known material: Incomplete skull with partial
  postcrania; ?vertebrae and incomplete hindlimb.

Holotype: SDSM 7210, incomplete skull, four dorsal vertebrae, two manual phalanges.

  Diagnosis of genus (as for type species): Cheek
tooth rows very deeply recessed, with transversely

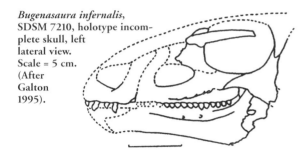

Bugenasaura infernalis,
SDSM 7210, holotype incom-
plete skull, left
lateral view.
Scale = 5 cm.
(After
Galton
1995).

Photo by R. A. Long and S. P. Welles (neg. #82-6-3), courtesy Natural History
Museum of Los Angeles County.

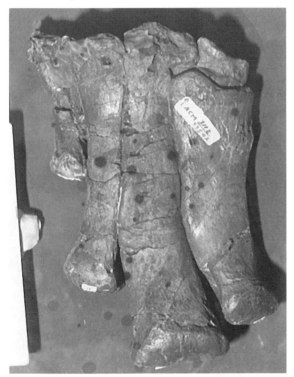

?*Bugenasaura infernalis*, holotype left metatarsus, anterior
view (LACM 33542) of ?*Thescelosaurus garbanii*.

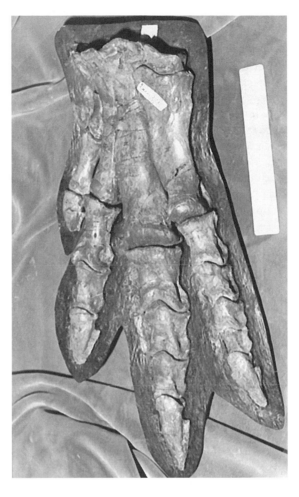

?*Bugenasaura infernalis*,
holotype left pes, dorsal view
(LACM 33542) of
?*Thescelosaurus garbanii*.

wide and deep dentary; ventral part of maxilla with
very prominent overhanging ridge, much of which
has a braided appearance [see below for possible additional character] (Galton 1995).

  Comments: *Bugenasaura* was founded upon partial skeletal remains, including an incomplete skull,
collected from the Olson locality of the Hell Creek
Formation, Harding County, South Dakota (Galton
1995).

  As observed by Galton, the skull of this genus
differs from all other known hypsilophodontids by an
elongate and slender supraorbital (the retention of
the primitive state for the Hypsilophodontidae).

  Galton tentatively referred to type species
B. infernalis 16 vertebrae and an incomplete hindlimb
(LACM 33542) from the Hell Creek Formation,
Garfield County, Montana, originally described by
Morris (1976) as the holotype of ?*Thecelosaurus garbanii*. Galton noted that, if this referral is correct,
then *Bugenasaura* also possesses the additional autapomorphic character of a proportionally small calcaneum that is excluded from the articular surface of
the midtarsal joint by a large astragalus.

  Key references: Galton (1995); Morris (1976).

CAENAGNATHASIA   Currie, Godfrey and
  Nessov 1993

Saurischia: Theropoda: Tetanurae: Avetheropoda:
  Coelurosauria: Maniraptora: Arctometatarsalia:
  Oviraptorosauria: Caenagnathidae.

Name derivation: Greek *kainos* = "recent" + Greek
  gnathos = "jaw" + "Asia."

Type species: *C. matinsoni* Currie, Godfrey and
  Nessov 1993.

Other species: [None.]

Occurrence: Bissekty Formation, Uzbekistan, Asia.

Age: Late Cretaceous (Late Turonian).

Known material: Two incomplete mandibles.

Holotype: CMGP 401/12457, anterior region of
  fused dentaries.

Diagnosis of genus (as for type species): Depression on postventral margin of symphysis not hourglass-shaped [as in some *Caenagnathus* specimens]; no circular pit or notch in dentary for reception of anterior tip of prearticular [character variable in *Caenagnathus*]; fluting on lingual margin of occlusal edge not distinct, no tooth-like apical projection on ridges; first anterior occlusal groove relatively larger than in *Caenagnathus*, first pair of lateral occlusal ridges not meeting ventrally to separate it from concavity in dorsal surface of symphysial shelf; no second anterior occlusal groove, no tubercles on midline or at base of first lateral occlusal ridge; deeper, narrower lateral groove, foramina in floor more obvious; vascular grooves less conspicuous than in *Caenagnathus*, floor of midline depression without foramina; region

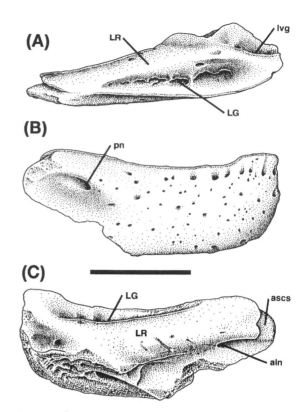

Caenagnathasia martinsoni, CMGP 402/12457, right dentary, A. dorsal, B. lateral, and C. medial views.
Scale = 10mm. (After Currie, Godfrey and Nessov 1993.)

underneath anterior occlusal margin, though hollow, seems infilled with cancellous bone (Currie, Godfrey and Nessov 1993).

Comments: The genus *Caenagnathasia* was based upon two relatively small caenagnathid dentaries, discovered in the lower part of the Bissekty Formation, Dzhyrakaduk locality, north of Bukhara, in the central Kyzylkum Desert, Uzbekistan. The first of these specimens, an incomplete dentary (CMGP 401/12457), was collected in 1979; the second (CMGP 401/12457) consisted of most of a right dentary. CMGP 401/12457, the more complete of these specimens, was designated the holotype of type species *C. martinsoni* (Currie *et al.* 1993).

Currie *et al.* basically distinguished *Caenagnathasia* from other caenagnathids by its relatively smaller size (lacking symphysial sutures, indicating maturity), and by its geographic separation and greater geologic age.

As noted by Currie *et al.*, these remains represent the smallest caenagnathid specimens yet found, their discovery establishes the first record of oviraptorosaurians from Uzbekistan, the first record of the Caenagnathidae in Asia, and extending the temporal range of caenagnathids back to the Late Turanian.

Key references: Cracraft (1971); Currie, Godfrey and Nessov (1993).

Caenagnathasia martinsoni, CMGP 401/12457, holotype dentaries, A. dorsal, B. ventral, C. posterior, and D. right lateral views. Scale = 10 cm. (After Currie, Godfrey and Nessov 1993.)

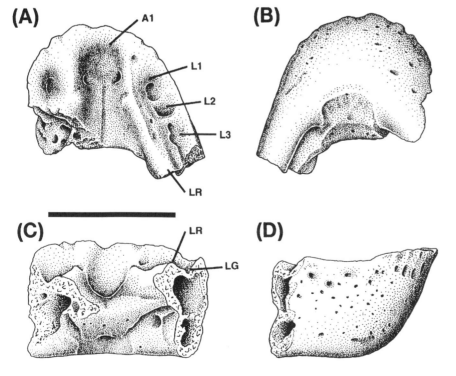

CAENAGNATHUS Sternberg 1940—(=?*Chirostenotes*)

Saurischia: Theropoda: Tetanurae: Avetheropoda: Coelurosauria: Maniraptora: Arctometatarsalia: Oviraptorosauria: ?Caenagnathidae.

Name derivation: Greek *kainos* = "recent" + Greek *gnathos* = "jaw."

Type species: *C. collinsi* Sternberg 1940.

Other species: *C. sternbergi* Cracraft 1971.

Occurrence: Oldman Formation, Alberta, Canada; Hell Creek Formation, South Dakota, United States.

Age: Late Cretaceous (Campanian–Maastrichtian).

Known material: Mandibles, isolated fragmentary cranial and postcranial remains.

Holotype: GSC 8776, mandible missing ventral border of left ramus.

Diagnosis of genus (as for type species): Toothless; dentaries fused at symphysis; pars symphysis relatively long and broad; mandibular fossa large; articular surface of jaw large, oval, concave, with ridged axis parallel to direction of the ramus; mandibular process short (Sternberg 1940).

Diagnosis of *C. sternbergi*: Species somewhat smaller but more robust than *C. collinsi* (Cracraft 1971).

Comments: The genus *Caenagnathus* was established upon a nearly complete lower jaw (GSC 8776), discovered in the "Belly River" Formation [now Oldman Formation], at Sand Creek, at the former Steveville Ferry, Alberta, Canada. The specimen was collected in 1936 by a National Museum of Canada field party under the direction of C. M. Sternberg (R. M. Sternberg 1940).

Because of various birdlike features of the type specimen (especially fusion of the dentaries into an absolutely smooth symphysis, absence of internal, external and posterior mandibular processes, and the ridged articular surface), Sternberg originally classified *Caenagnathus* as avian, erecting for it the new [abandoned] order Caenagnathiformes and family Caenagnathidae. From its large size, Sternberg speculated that *Caenagnathus* could have been a running bird.

Whetmore (1960) later identified the holotype of *C. collinsi* as reptilian, after which Romer (1966) tentatively assigned *Caenagnathus* to the "Coelurosauria."

Caenagnathus sternbergi Cracraft 1971 was based on the posterior end of a right mandibular ramus from Steveville.

Currie and Russell (1988), observing many similarities in the postcrania of *Chirostenotes* and *Oviraptor* and suggesting that both genera are related, inferred that *Caenagnathus* is also related to *Chirostenotes*, and may even be conspecific with *Chirostenotes pergracilis*. However, additional data are needed before a formal synonymy can be made between *Caenagnathus* and *Chirostenotes*.

In their review of the Oviraptorosauria, Barsbold, Maryańska and Osmólska (1990) concluded that *Caenagnathus* is a more primitive oviraptorosaur, warranting its own group Caenagnathidae, and speculated that, although this genus is only known from lower jaws, their shape suggests that the skull was not shortened.

New caenagnathid specimens, fragmentary and isolated though better preserved than the holotypes of *Caenagnathus collinsi* (CMN 8776) and *C. sternbergi* (CMN 2690), were described by Currie, Godfrey and Nessov (1993). The specimens were recovered from the Dinosaur Park Formation (Campanian) of southern Alberta, Canada, and Hell Creek For-

Photo by R. A. Long and S. P. Welles (neg. #73/538-14), reproduced with permission of Canadian Museum of Nature, Ottawa, Canada.

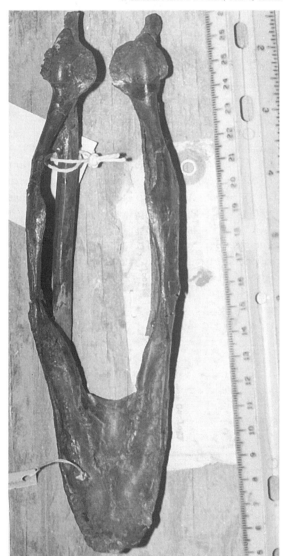

Caenagnathus collinsi, NMC P-3606/8776, holotype lower jaws, superior view.

mation (Maastrichtian) of South Dakota. This new material included: (Hell Creek Formation) left articular-surangular-coronoid complex (BHM 2033); (Dinosaur Park Formation) anterior portion of fused dentaries (RTMP 79.8.622), the smallest specimen yet known of *Caenagnathus*, collected by Hope Johnson, nearly complete pair of fused dentaries (RTMP 90.56.6), collected by M. Marsovsky, almost complete pair of fused dentaries (RTMP 91.144.1), collected by Wendy Sloboba on the south side of the Bow River, near Hays (Alberta), anterior caudal vertebra (RTMP 92.36.390), collected by Susan Currie, almost complete pair of fused dentaries (RTMP 92.36.390), the best-preserved pair known, collected by Sloboba; and (Dinosaur Park Formation, Sandy Point) anterior region of fused dentaries, collected by Wayne Marshall (East Coulee, Alberta) (Currie *et al.* 1993).

Utilizing these new and other specimens (also those belonging to *Caenagnathasia*; see entry), Currie *et al.*. found that in caenagnathids (as well as other oviraptorosaurs) the upright orientation of the head, position of the throat beneath the middle of the jaws, high lateral margin of the lower jaws, and insertion of the "upper jaws" between the lower jaws all suggest a mechanism by which food was pushed down the throat, this pushing enhanced by the sliding back and forth of the mandible utilizing specialized jaw joints. The jaws could not expand to the sides, as they do in most theropods, which would have limited the size of food portions. These jaws seem to have been well adapted for processing eggs, which could have been pushed to the wide area at the center of the jaws, and there broken by teeth and lateral ridges, the high jaw margins preventing loss of the contents of the eggs. All caenagnathid jaws exhibit a highly vascularized concavity on the postero-lingual surface of the symphysial shelf, this perhaps indicating the presence of a tongue that could have manipulated the food and helped to prevent the loss of fluid.

However, Currie *et al.* cautioned that, although jaw anatomy supports the theory that oviraptorids were adapted for eating eggs, they probably ate other foods as well. A sharp-edged rhamphotheca (not preserved on any specimen) at the front of their jaws could produce a strong nipping bite, which may have allowed these animals to cut up smaller prey, which could be swallowed without further processing. According to Currie *et al.*, the jaws, though strong, were not powerful enough to crush mollusks or grind plant material. Also, considering the relationship of these dinosaurs to dromaeosaurids and other theropods, and the fact that the oviraptorid skeleton displays no adaptations typical of herbivores, the authors found the notion that they had become herbivores unlikely.

As noted by Currie *et al.*, the South Dakota remains extend the temporal range of caenagnathids in North America. Also, most of these specimens differ from the holotype of *C. collinsi* and may be referable to *C. sternbergi*. However, the Hell Creek specimen, conservatively referred to *Caenagnathus* sp., is larger than any of the other "Judithian" specimens, with a mandibular articulation sufficiently different to regard it as a new species.

Note: Currie (1992) described an isolated caudally incomplete parietal (RTMP 81.19.252), collected from Dinosaur Provincial Park in Alberta, that may belong to a caenagnathid. The specimen (as in *Oviraptor*) is more expanded than in other known theropods, with no sagittal crest. Currie assigned this parietal to the Oviraptorosauria but could not, without the discovery of better specimens, refer it to *Caenagnathus*, *Chirostenotes* or *Elmisaurus*.

Key references: Barsbold, Maryańska and Osmólska (1990); Cracraft (1971); Currie (1992); Currie, Godfrey and Nessov (1993); Currie and Russell (1980); Sternberg (1940).

CALAMOSAURUS Lydekker 1891 [*nomen dubium*]—(=?*Calamospondylus*)
Saurischia: Theropoda *incertae sedis*.
Name derivation: Latin *calamus* = "reed" + Greek *sauros* = "lizard."
Type species: *C. foxi* (Lydekker 1889) [*nomen dubium*].
Other species: [None.]
Occurrence: Wealden, Isle of Wight, England.
Age: Early Cretaceous (?Barremian).
Known material: Vertebrae, tibia.
Holotype: BMNH R901, two associated cervical vertebrae, one almost complete, the other missing the neural arch.

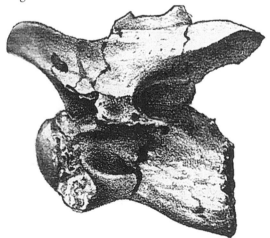

Calamosaurus foxi, BMNH R901, holotype cervical vertebra of *Calamospondylus foxi*. (After Seeley 1891.)

Diagnosis of genus: [None published.]

Comments: Before the naming of this genus, the species *Calamospondylus foxi* Lydekker 1889 [*nomen dubium*] had been founded on two cervical vertebrae (BMNH R901) belonging to a small theropod, this material discovered by William Fox on the Isle of Wight. Lydekker described these vertebrae as opisthocoelus, with oblique central faces and honeycombed interiors. As the name *Calamospondylus* was preoccupied (Fox 1866), Lydekker (1891*a*) renamed this species *Calamosaurus foxi*.

Although *Calamosaurus* is often regarded as a junior synonym of *Calamospondylus*, Norman (1990) pointed out that the former, based on two cervical vertebrae and a referred tibia, cannot be directly compared to *Calamospondylus*.

Key references: Lydekker (1889, 1891*a*); Norman (1990).

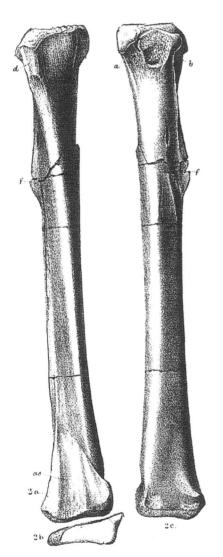

Calamosaurus foxi, right tibia originally referred to *Calamospondylus foxi*, anterior and posterior views. (After Seeley 1891.)

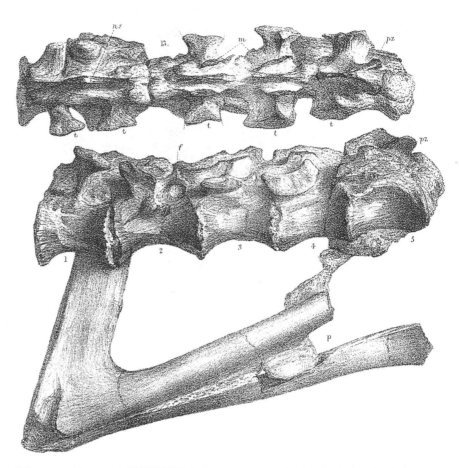

Calamospondylus oweni, BMNH R901, holotype sacrum and pubis, (top) dorsal and (bottom) lateral views. (After Seeley 1887.)

CALAMOSPONDYLUS Fox 1866 [*nomen dubium*]—(=*Aristosuchus*; =?*Calamosaurus*, ?*Thecocoelurus*, ?*Thecospondylus*)

Saurischia: Theropoda *incertae sedis*.

Name derivation: Latin *calamus*/Greek *kalamos* = "reed" + Greek *spondylos* = "vertebrae."

Type species: *C. oweni* Fox 1866 [*nomen dubium*].

Other species: [None.]

Occurrence: Wealden, Isle of Wight, England; Romania.

Age: Early Cretaceous (Upper Barremian).

Known material: Postcrania.

Holotype: BMNH R901, two dorsal, five sacral and two caudal vertebrae, fused distal portions of both pubes, ungual phalanx.

Diagnosis of genus: [No modern diagnosis published.]

Comments: The genus *Calamospondylus* was established upon various postcranial remains (BMNH R178), discovered and collected by William Fox from Wealden shales of Brook, southern coast of the Isle of Wight, England. Fox (1866) named this material *Calamospondylus oweni* [*nomen dubium*] but

Calamospondylus

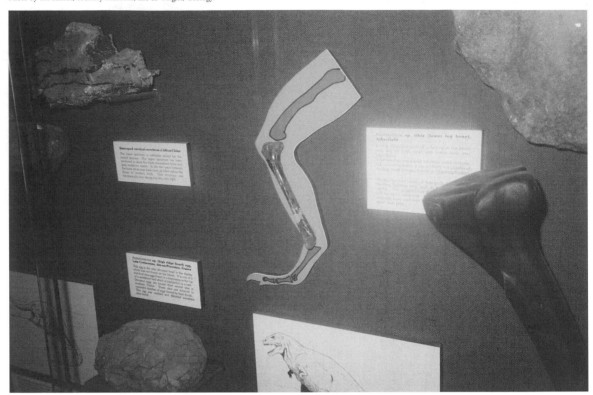

Calamospondylus oweni, hindlimb elements originally referred to *Aristosuchus pusillus.*

did not diagnose the new taxon. Additional remains including a small dorsal vertebra and two incomplete caudals (BMNH R178a), and two relatively large terminal phalanges (BMNH R179 and 899) from the manus, were found by Fox at the same locality.

Later, Owen (1876) diagnosed the type species as follows: Vertebrae with compact osseous texture and smooth exterior; dorsal centrum with large medullary cavity.

Owen saw these characters as diagnostic of the Oolitic genus "*Poikilopleuron*" [=*Poekilopleuron*], a large theropod which Owen believed to be crocodilian. For the Wealden material, Owen erected the new species *P. pusillus*. Owen distinguished *P. pusillus* as smaller than type species *P. bucklandi*. Foreseeing objections that the material might someday prove to belong to a young *P. bucklandi* individual, Owen stated that no signs of immaturity were perceived in *P. pusillus*. Owen described the vertebral centra of *P. pusillus* as long relative to depth and width, and the ungual phalanx as remarkably curved, with a strong lever-process and deep lateral grooves.

Seeley (1887*b*), pointing out that Owen's criterion regarding the medullary cavity in the vertebrae was not diagnostic, proposed that this species warranted its own genus, renaming the taxon *Aristosuchus*

pusillus. Generally, *Aristosuchus* is regarded as a senior synonym of *Calamospondylus*, although, as pointed out by Norman (1990), the latter name, despite Fox's meager original description of *C. oweni*, clearly has priority.

The species *Calamosaurus foxi*, *Thecocoelurus daviesi*, and *Thecospondylus horneri* were regarded by Ostrom (1970) as junior synonyms of *C. oweni* [=*A. pusillus* of his usage]. According to Norman, this synonymy cannot be adequately demonstrated, and *Calamospondylus* should best be considered a *nomen dubium*.

Calamospondylus has been classified as a "coelurosaur" based on the relative size of the ungual. The five sacral vertebrae measure only 12 centimeters (about 4.7 inches) in length. The distal "foot" of the pubis is apparently much longer than in many other theropods.

Other remains referred to *C. oweni* include the proximal portion of a femur from Barnes High, Isle of Wight, reported by Galton (1973*d*), and a specimen from the Padurea Craiului Mountains of Bihor, Romania, reported and referred to *Aristosuchus* sp. by Jurcsak and Popa (1985).

Key references: Fox (1866); Galton (1973*d*); Jurcsak and Popa (1985); Norman (1990); Ostrom (1970); Owen (1876); Seeley (1887*b*).

CALLOVOSAURUS Galton 1980 [*nomen dubium*]
Ornithischia: Genasauria: Cerapoda: Ornithopoda:
Iguanodontia *incertae sedis*.
Name derivation: "Callovian" + Greek *sauros* =
"lizard."
Type species: *C. leedsi* (Lydekker 1889) [*nomen
dubium*].
Other species: [None.]
Occurrence: Lower Oxford Clay, England.
Age: Middle Jurassic (Middle Callovian).
Known material/holotype: BMNH R1993, almost
complete left femur.

Diagnosis of genus (as for type species): Femur
characterized by proportionally narrow greater trochanter; lesser trochanter expanded anteroposteriorly; flattened transversely; distal end unexpanded,
with shallow anterior intercondylar groove (Galton
1980*c*).

Comments: The genus now called *Callovosaurus*
represents the earliest record of Iguanodontia.

Lydekker (1889) had described a nearly complete femur (BMNH R1993) collected from the
Lower Oxford Clay (Middle Callovian) of Peterborough, England, as a new species of the Kimmeridgian
genus *Camptosaurus*, named *C. leedsi*. Later, Gilmore
(1909) believed it more likely that, if *C. leedsi* was
referable to an American genus, it should be *Dryosaurus*.

Galton (1975), observing diagnostically significant differences between the femur of *C. leedsi* and
those of *C. dispar*, *C. prestwichi*, and *Dryosaurus*, suggested that BMNH R1993 could represent a new
genus. Owing to the difference in both anatomy and
stratigraphic horizon, Galton (1980*c*) made *C. leedsi*
the type species of new genus *Callovosaurus*.

In a review of the Iguanodontidae and related
ornithopods, Norman and Weishampel (1990) considered the type material of this form as indeterminate, with *C. leedsi* a *nomen dubium* regarded as
Iguanodontia *incertae sedis*.

Key references: Galton (1975, 1980*c*); Gilmore
(1909); Lydekker (1889); Norman and Weishampel
(1990).

CAMARASAURUS Cope 1877—(=?*Catheto-
saurus, Caulodon, Morosaurus, Uintasaurus*)
Saurischia: Sauropodomorpha: Sauropoda:
Camarasauridae: Camarasaurinae.
Name derivation: Greek *kamara* = "chamber" +
Greek *sauros* = "lizard."
Type species: *C. supremus* Cope 1877.
Other species: *C. grandis* Marsh 1877, *C. lentus*
Marsh 1889, ?*C. alenquerensis* (Lapparent and
Zbyszewski 1957), *C. lewisi* Jensen 1988.

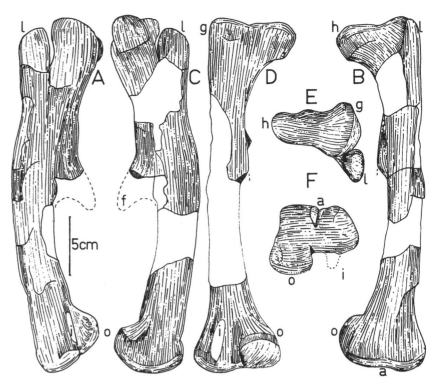

Callovosaurus leedsi, BMNH
R1993, holotype left femur of
Camptosaurus leedsi, A. lat-
eral, B. anterior, C. medial,
D. poseterior, E. proximal,
and F. distal views. (After
Galton 1980.)

Occurrence: Morrison Formation, Wyoming,
Colorado, New Mexico, Montana, Utah, United
States; [unnamed formation], Estremadura, Portugal.

Age: Late Jurassic (?Oxfordian–Kimmerd-
gian–Tithonian).

Known material: More than 18 partial skeletons,
some with associated skulls, hundreds of postcranial
elements, from adults, subadults, and juveniles.
Holotype: AMNH 5760, one cervical, three dorsal,
and four caudal vertebrae.

Diagnosis of genus: Massively proportioned, all
bones except ischium stoutly constructed; cervical
vertebrae with bifurcated neural spines; dorsal vertebrae stout, with low, broad, strong spines possessing
distinct lamination; spines grading from divided to
single, seventh dorsal either single or only slightly
notched; zygapophyses large, far apart in anterior
dorsals, close together in articulation of third, fourth,

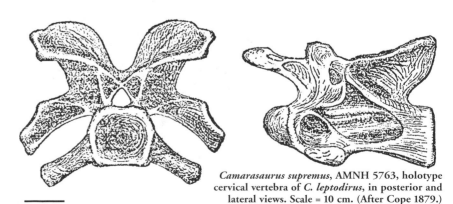

Camarasaurus supremus, AMNH 5763, holotype
cervical vertebra of *C. leptodirus*, in posterior and
lateral views. Scale = 10 cm. (After Cope 1879.)

Photo by R. A. Long and S. P. Welles (neg. #73/310-4), courtesy American Museum of Natural History.

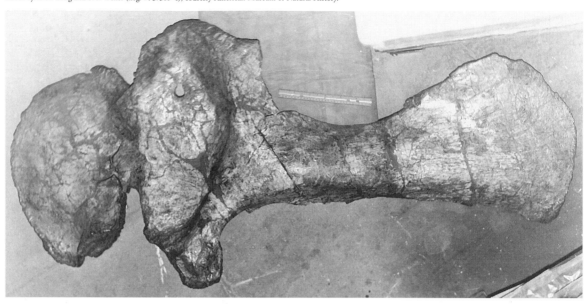

Camarasaurus supremus, AMNH 814, paratype right scapula coracoid.

then succeeding dorsals; diapophyses long; parapophyses low in first three dorsals, becoming and remaining consistently high; dorsal centra of medium length, those near sacrum slightly shorter, opisthocoelus; sacrum with short spines, includes vertebra posterior to tenth dorsal as functional dorso-sacral, tending toward retardation; caudal vertebrae with short spines with expanded summits and slightly developed ribs; scapula large, massive, expanded at both ends; coracoid subcircular in outline; ischium slender, with long shaft; pubis massive, more angular in outline, median border more twisted than in *Apatosaurus* (Osborn and Mook 1921).

Diagnosis of *C. lewisi*: Cervical vertebrae with bifurcated neural spines (with exception of atlas and axis); prominent preepiophyseal ridges (not reported in other sauropods) present on superior surfaces of all cervical postzygapophyses; suprapostzygapophy-

Photo by R. A. Long and S. P. Welles (neg. #73/407), courtesy American Museum of Natural History.

Camarasaurus supremus, AMNH 5768, holotype teeth of *Caulodon diversidens*.

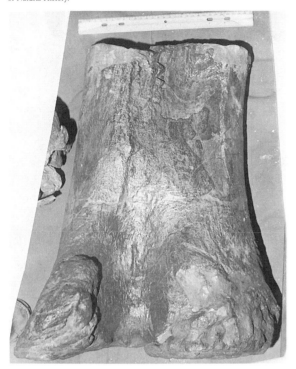

Camarasaurus supremus, AMNH 5765, holotype distal end of right femur of *Amphicoelias latus.*

seal laminae on cervical vertebrae neither alligned nor confluent with epiophyses (as in other sauropods); all except last dorsal vertebrae bifurcated; anterior iliac processes rotated ventrally around transverse axis of the acetabulum, lowering anterior point of the iliac blade from 18 to 20 degrees below axis of the vertebral column; metapophyseal spurs directed lateroventrally on all dorsal and sacral neural spines; prediapophyseal spurs projecting from anterior face of diapophyses on dorsal transverse processes; metapophyseal spurs on second and third sacral neural spines connected with subhorizontal supracostal plates on dorsal ridge of third and fourth sacral ribs by diagonal struts of bone (such plates, spurs and bone-struts not present in other North American Jurassic sauropods); chevrons on anterior third of tail one-third longer than in *Camarasaurus supremus* (as arranged by Osborn and Mook 1921) (Jensen 1988).

Comments: The best known North American sauropod and most abundant Morrison Formation dinosaur, the genus *Camarasaurus* was founded on vertebrae (AMNH 5760) collected by O. W. Lucas in Garden Park, Canyon City, Fremont County, Colorado. The material, sent to the Cope Museum in Philadelphia, was first described by Cope (1877*a*) as new genus and species *C. supremus.* In the wake of this discovery, various sauropod taxa have been

erected that are now known to be junior synonyms of *Camarasaurus.*

Cope originally diagnosed *Camarasaurus* as follows: Vertebral centra opisthocoelian and hollow; neural arches very high, with greatly expanded zygapophyses; neural spines transverse to the long axis of the centrum, one spine bifurcate; rib articulations supported by widely extended diapophyses; capitular articular facets not present on centra, but in some vertebrae are found on basal region of diapophyses; ?cervical vertebra depressed and remarkably long; caudal amphicoelian but not deeply so; caudal neural spines of usual form, those on anterior two caudals elongate. *C. supremus* was diagnosed by Cope as follows: Centra with thin external walls; processes composed of lamina united by narrow margins, and by vertebrae proportionally lighter relative to their bulk than in any [then known] terrestrial vertebrate.

Cope (1877*c*) also named the new genus and species *Caulodon diversidens,* based on ten teeth (AMNH 5768) collected from the uppermost beds of the Morrison Formation at Garden Park. Cope (1877*c*) described but did not figure these teeth, at the

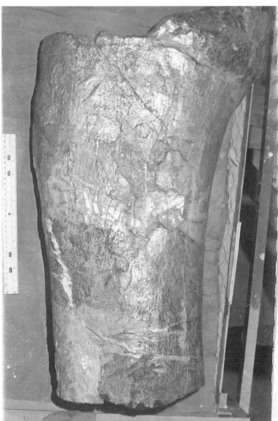

Camarasaurus supremus, AMNH 5765, holotype proximal end of right femur of *Amphicoelias latus.*

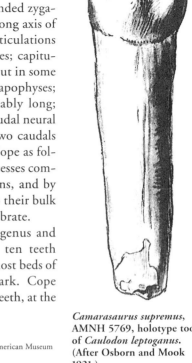

Camarasaurus supremus, AMNH 5769, holotype tooth of *Caulodon leptoganus.* (After Osborn and Mook 1921.)

Camarasaurus supremus, life restoration by Brian Franczak.

same time describing (but not figuring) new species *C. leptoganus*, based on a single tooth (AMNH 5769) from the same horizon, northeast of Canyon City. A second tooth found with the holotype of *C. leptoganus* apparently belonged to the same species.

Marsh (1877*d*), Cope's professional rival, later described (but did not figure) a well-preserved incomplete skull and some postcranial material (YPM 1905) collected from Como Bluff, Wyoming, representing an immature sauropod individual. Marsh believed this material belonged to a new species of *Apatosaurus*, which he named *A. grandis*. This species was diagnosed by Marsh as follows: Cervical vertebrae thin-walled; caudals elongate and slender (indicating long tail); femur short, lacking third trochanter, great trochanter much lower on femoral head and continuous with it, foot seemingly of medium length. The length of this animal, Marsh estimated, was at least 30 feet or close to nine meters.

Later, Marsh (1878*b*) described more Como Bluff sauropod remains under the new generic name of *Morosaurus*. Type species *M. impar* was based on a sacrum (YPM 1900) and indicated an animal of almost 7.5 meters (about 25 feet) long. Referred species *M. robustus* was based on an ilium (YPM 1902).

Marsh (1889*b*) erected new species *M. lentus* upon on an incomplete skeleton (YPM 1910) lacking the skull, found in the so-called "*Atlantosaurus* beds" in Wyoming, the specimen representing a subadult individual much smaller than *M. grandis*. This species was diagnosed by Marsh (1889*b*) as follows: Smaller than *C. grandis*, with relatively shorter legs; shorter, more massive vertebrae with smaller pleurocoels; cervical and dorsal centra more depressed; neural arch resting on centrum rather than (as in other species) elevated atop pedestals above the articular faces.

Noting similarities between *Camarasaurus* and *Morosaurus* specimens, Osborn (1898) suggested that they were congeneric. Riggs (1901) acknowledged these similarities, but thought *Morosaurus* was more closely related to *Atlantosaurus*. Mook (1914) believed the two forms were congeneric. In their classic review of Cope's sauropods, Osborn and Mook (1921), interpreted the differences between *Camarasaurus* and *Morosaurus* as ontogenetic and referred *Morosaurus* to the former genus.

Osborn and Mook, while acknowledging the difficulty in discussing taxa based on teeth, observed the resemblance between the various *Caulodon* specimens and the maxillary teeth of *C. supremus*, in the smaller skull of "*Morosaurus*" [=*Camarasaurus*]

Jim Adams and Tobe Williams reliefing scapulae of *Camarasaurus supremus* at quarry visitor center, Dinosaur National Monument, Utah.

Mounted skeleton of *Camarasaurus supremus*.

***Camarasaurus grandis*, YPM 1907, holotype metatarsals.**

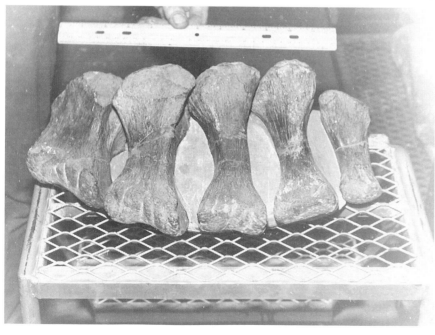

(AMNH 467), and in the skull of a cotype of "*M.*" *grandis* (YPM 1905). Accepting the possibility of two sauropod genera having the same types of teeth, Osborn and Mook provisionally referred *Caulodon* to *Camarasaurus*. Today these teeth are usually regarded as belonging to *C. supremus*.

Two other species were referred by Osborn and Mook to *C. supremus*:

Amphicoelias latus Cope 1877 had been based on a right femur and four caudals (AMNH 5765) from the uppermost beds of the Morrison Formation at Garden Park. Cope (1878*a*) observed that the mass of this individual was great relative to its height, and also that the femur is very robust. Osborn and Mook, noting that the material lacked the slender proportions characteristic of *Amphicoelias*, regarded it as a young individual.

C. leptodirus Cope 1879 was based on three cervical vertebrae (AMNH 5763) and ?other fossils, from the uppermost Morrison Formation beds at Garden Park. Osborn and Mook, noting that the proportional differences observed by Cope (1879) in *C. leptodirus* were due to the bones' coming from a different part of the neck of *C. supremus* than was

Photo by R. A. Long and S. P. Welles (neg. #73/463-23), courtesy Yale Peabody Museum of Natural History.

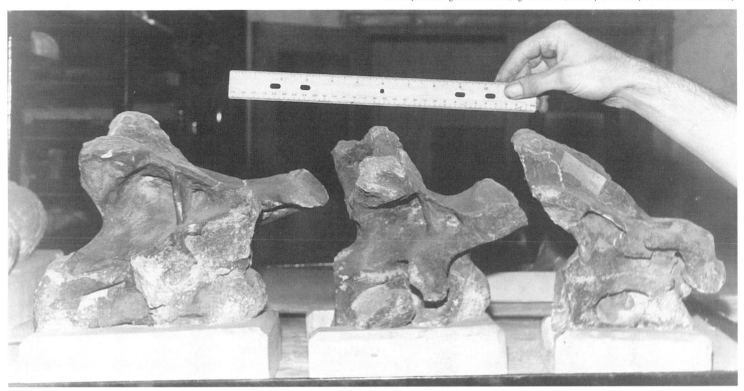

Camarasaurus grandis, YPM 1905, cervical vertebrae.

Courtesy the Field Museum (neg. #4017a).

Camarasaurus grandis, scapulacoracoid *in situ* [originally referred to *Morosaurus impar*].

Photo by R. A. Long and S. P. Welles (neg. #73/459-16), courtesy Yale Peabody Museum of Natural History.

Camarasaurus grandis, YPM 1900, holotype sacrum of *Morosaurus impar*.

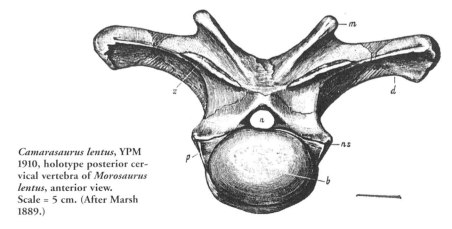

Camarasaurus lentus, YPM 1910, holotype posterior cervical vertebra of *Morosaurus lentus*, anterior view. Scale = 5 cm. (After Marsh 1889.)

known at the time, provisionally referred it to that species.

Holland (1924*b*) later described five posterior cervical vertebrae (CM 11069) collected from the Morrison Formation, Dinosaur National Monument, Utah. Upon these remains Holland founded yet another new sauropod taxon, *Uintasaurus douglassi*.

In a paper describing in detail the braincase and internal aspects of several cranial bones of *C. lentus*, White (1958) reviewed the taxa *C. grandis*, *M. robustus*, *C. supremus*, *C. lentus*, *C. agilis* and *U. douglassi*. White concluded that only *C. supremus* and *C. lentus* are valid species. White regarded as junior synonyms of *C. supremus* the species *C. leptodirus*, *C. diversidens*, *C. leptoganus*, *A. grandis*, *M. impar*, and *M. robustus*, with *U. douglassi* made a junior synonym of *C. lentus*.

McIntosh (1990*b*), in his review of the Sauropoda, accepted *C. supremus*, *C. grandis* and *C. lentus* as valid species of *Camarasaurus*; and *C. annae* Ellinger 1950 [*nomen dubium*] and *Uintasaurus douglassi* Holland 1919 as junior synonyms of *C. lentus*. Also, McIntosh reassessed the species ?*Apatosaurus alenquerensis* Lapparent and Zbyszewski 1957, based upon a large part of a postcranial skeleton missing the vertebral arches, collected from the Upper Jurassic of Portugal. As this species agrees in various characters (12 dorsal vertebrae, even the caudals having strong ball and socket articulation; scapula with distal end broadly expanded; humerus long and slender; ischium with unexpanded distal end) with *Camarasaurus*, and basically in the robustness indices (ratios of least circumference of shaft to length) with the American and European camarasaurids but not with *Apatosaurus*, McIntosh tentatively referred this species to *Camarasaurus* as ?*C. alenquerensis*.

The new genus and species *Cathetosaurus lewisi* was founded on a well preserved incomplete articulated, postcranial skeleton (BYU 9047) with atlas, axis, ten cervical vertebrae with ribs, 12 dorsal vertebrae, dorsosacral vertebra, 20 dorsal ribs, 43 anterior caudal vertebrae with many articulated chevrons, ribs coossified with ilium, right humerus, radius, ulna, partial manus, pubis, and ischia. It was collected in 1967 by James A. Jensen from the Brushy Basin Member (Late Jurassic [Tithonian] or Early Cretaceous [Neocomian or Hauterivian]; Britt 1991, based on Kowallis, Heaton and Bringhurst 1986) of the Morrison Formation, Dominguez-Jones Quarry, Uncompahgre Upwarp, Mesa County, Colorado (Jensen 1988). The name *Cathetosaurus* first appeared in the March, 1987 issue of *Discover* magazine, after which it was published in a paper by Jensen (1987) on new brachiosaurid finds.

Jensen (1988) regarded *Cathetosaurus* as a novel sauropod, apparently the only North American form

Camarasaurus lentus, skeleton in death pose.

Camarasaurus lentus, CM 11338, skeleton of immature individual, one of the most complete sauropod specimens collected.

Camarasaurus lewisi, BYU 9047, holotype of *Cathetosaurus lewisi*, (left) presacral vertebrae, lateral view, (right) dorsosacral or first presacral vertebra, anterior view. (After Jensen 1988.)

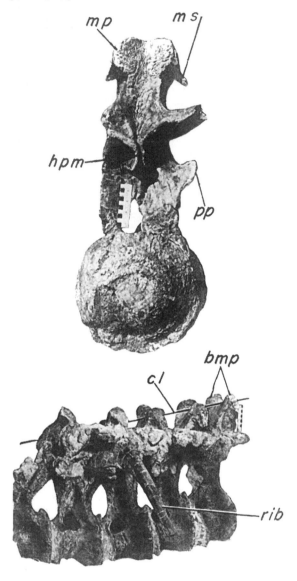

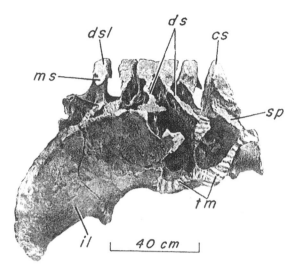

Camarasaurus lewisi, BYU 9047, holotype sacrum of *Cathetosaurus lewisis*, left lateral view. (After Jensen 1988.)

?*Camarasaurus alenquerensis*, holotype left and right ischia of *Apatosaurus alenquerensis*. (After Lapparent and Zbyszewski 1957.)

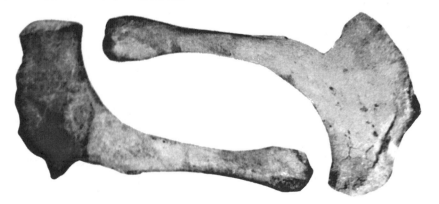

yet identified capable of voluntary bipedalism. Jensen (1988) interpreted the various vertebral projections and processes as serving as points of attachment for strong supporting ligaments which allowed *Cathetosaurus* to rear up on its hind legs and tail. This idea seemed to be supported by the unusually inclined pelvis, which is unlike that in other sauropods. Based on a biomechanical analysis of the *Cathetosaurus* remains, as well as those of brontotheres, Jensen concluded that heavier sauropods like *Brachiosaurus*, *Apatosaurus*, and *Barosaurus* were probably incapable of rearing-up to a tripodal position; also, that life restorations depicting more massive sauropods voluntarily raised to a bipedal stance are fanciful, the artists ignoring the empirical demands of biomechanics.

The holotype skeleton of *C. lewisi* offered taphonomic evidence from which Jensen (1988) envisioned a possible *post mortem* scenario. The skeleton seems to have been scavenged before burial. Teeth marks in the left ilium and the displacement of the front limb bones suggest that the remains were fed upon by a large theropod equal in size to *Torvosaurus tanneri*. Apparently the carcass was later overturned and dismembered by the same or another carnivore of equal size which tore off the hindlimbs. The intact preservation of the neck and rib cage indicated that the carnivore favored the more heavily muscled pelvic-rear limb region as the best source of food. Smaller teeth marks on the ilium imposed over the larger marks reveal the presence of small scavengers that apparently intruded and fed upon the carcass between feeding periods of the large theropod(s). An unknown period of time after the scavenging, an overbank flood could have floated the bloated body an unknown distance to its eventual burial site.

Miller, McIntosh, Stadtman and Gillette (1992) made *C.lewisi* a new species of *Camarasaurus*, regarding four features (involving struts, plates, and spurs) recognized by Jensen (1988) as characters diagnostic of *Cathetosaurus* as representing advanced age, two (neural spine bifurcation extending from third cervical vertebra beyond mid-dorsals to sacrum; extensive counterclockwise rotation of ilium beneath inferior borders of sacrals, the latter a major character not reported in other sauropods) as of taxonomic significance.

Camarasaurus had a shorter, thicker neck than most sauropods, its "box-like" head directed at a distinct angle from the neck. The forelimbs were comparatively long, the humerus four-fifths the length of the femur, resulting in a back that is nearly horizontal. The relatively short tail was somewhat flat and higher than wide.

In addition to adult specimens, some fine immature *Camarasaurus* individuals have been collected and show the larger heads and shorter necks typical of young sauropods. Photographs of some of these specimens, published in popular books about dinosaurs, have led to the misconception that *Camarasaurus* was a comparatively small sauropod. To the contrary, adult individuals reached an approximate length of 18 meters (more than 60 feet) and weighed from about 19.5 to more than 23 metric tons (22 to 26 tons) (G. S. Paul, personal communication 1988).

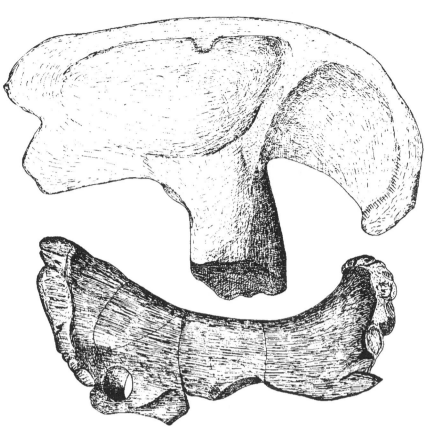

?*Camarasaurus alenquerensis*, holotype of *Apatosaurus alenquerensis*, (top) ilium, (bottom) pubis. (After Lapparent and Zbyszewski 1957.)

The most complete sauropod skeleton yet discovered is that of an immature *C. lentus*, collected at Dinosaur National Monument, Utah, by the Carne-

Photo by R. A. Long and S. P. Welles (73/139-36), courtesy National Museum of Natural History, Smithsonian Institution.

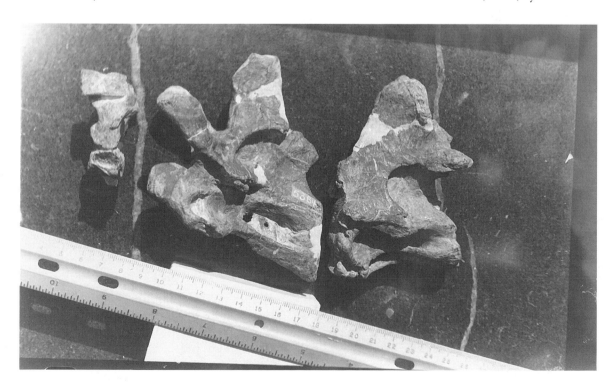

"*Morosaurus*" *agilis*, USNM 5384, holotype anterior caudal vertebrae of unnamed cetiosaurid.

gie Museum of Natural History. The specimen (CM 11338), described by Gilmore (1925a), was preserved in the animal's death pose and lacks only the left ilium and ischium and some ribs. Associated with these bones was a thin carbon layer that may represent fossilized skin impressions.

Fiorillo (1987) made the first attempt at utilizing dental microwear data to interpret dinosaur diets, examining the two basic tooth types of sauropods (the robust, spatulate form exhibited by *Camarasaurus*, and gracile, peg-like form of *Diplodocus* [see entry for more details]). Fiorillo, after studying eleven *Camarasaurus* teeth from two Morrison Formation localities (Freezeout Hills, Wyoming, and Carnegie Quarry, Dinosaur National Monument, Utah), found that these teeth exhibited coarser scratch patterns than did those of *Diplodocus*. This suggested that the diet of *Camarasaurus* contained more grit than that of *Diplodocus*. As there was some overlapping in the scratch morphology of both genera, Fiorillo inferred that, to some degree, both *Camarasaurus* and *Diplodocus* ate the same kinds of food.

Notes: Britt and Stadtman (in preparation) will describe a tiny premaxilla from the Dry Mesa Quarry, Colorado, with four unerupted teeth resembling teeth in *Camarasaurus*. The premaxilla measures 38 millimeters (about 1.35 inches) in height and 18 millimeters (almost 7 inches) wide. Besides the small size, the bone texture suggests a hatchling or extremely young individual (see "Abstracts of Papers, Forty-Eighth Annual Meeting, Society of Vertebrate Paleontology, Tyrrell Museum of Paleontology, Drumheller, Alberta, 13–15 October 1988," Journal of Vertebrate Paleontology 8, Supplement to no. 3, September 23, 1988).

Lambert (1990) reported the informally named "Sugiyamasaurus," a sauropod from Japan based on spatulate teeth. Dong, Hasegawa and Azuma (1990), in the book *The Age of Dinosaurs in Japan and China*, regarded this form as an indeterminate camarasaurid.

The species "*M.*" *agilis* Marsh 1889 was referred by McIntosh to Cetiosauridae *incertae sedis*.

Key references: Cope (1877a, 1877c, 1878a, 1889); Fiorillo (1987); Gilmore (1925a); Holland (1924b); Jensen (1987, 1990); Marsh (1877d, 1878b, 1889a); McIntosh (1990b); Mook (1914); Osborn (1898); Osborn and Mook (1921); White (1958).

CAMELOTIA Galton 1985
Saurischia: Sauropodomorpha: Prosauropoda: Melanorosauridae.
Name derivation: "Camelot."
Type species: *C. borealis* Galton 1985.
Other species: [None.]

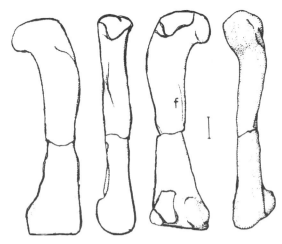

Camelotia borealis, BMNH R2870, holotype left femur, in anterior, medial, posterior, and lateral views. Scale = 10 cm. (After Galton 1985.)

Occurrence: Westbury Formation, Somerset, England.
Age: Late Triassic.
Known material/cotypes: BMNH R2870–R2874, R2876–R2878, four dorsal and five caudal vertebrae, fragments of ribs, a hemal arch, pubis, ischium, right femur, proximal end of tibia, two pedal phalanges.

Diagnosis of genus (as for type species): Large melanorosaurid; posterior dorsal and posterior caudal centra higher than long; lesser trochanter extending close to proximal end of femur; proximal end of tibia only slightly expanded anteroposteriorly, relative to shaft (Galton 1985).

Comments: The genus *Camelotia* was established on postcranial remains (BMNH R2870–R2874, R2876–R2878) collected during the nineteenth century from the Wedmore Stone, Westbury Formation, Penarth Grou of Wedmore, Somerset, England.

Seeley (1898) referred this material to *Avalonia sanfordi* (preoccupied; the type species of *Avalonianus* Kuhn 1961) and *Picrodon herveyi*, after which Huene (1907–08) referred it to *Gresslyosaurus ingens* [=*Plateosaurus engelhardti*]. Eventually, Galton (1985) designated these remains (BMNH R2870–R2874, R2876–R2878) the holotype of the new genus *Camelotia*.

Key references: Galton (1985); Seeley (1989).

CAMPTONOTUS Marsh 1879—(Preoccupied, Uhler 1864; see *Camptosaurus*.)
Name derivation: Greek *kamptos* = "bent" + Greek *notos* = "south."
Type species: *C. dispar* Marsh 1879.

CAMPTOSAURUS Marsh 1885—
(=*Brachyrophus, Camptonotus, Cumnoria, Symphyrophus*)

Ornithischia: Genasauria: Cerapoda: Ornithopoda: Iguanodontia: Camptosauridae.

Name derivation: Greek *kamptos* = "bent" + Greek *sauros* = "lizard."

Type species: *C. dispar* (Marsh 1879).

Other species: *C. prestwichii* (Hulke 1880), ?*C. depressus* Gilmore 1909.

Occurrence: Morrison Formation, Wyoming, Utah, Colorado, Oklahoma, ?Morrison Formation, Wyoming, Lakota Formation, South Dakota, United States; Kimmeridge Clay, Oxfordshire, England.

Age: Late Jurassic–?Early Cretaceous (Kimmeridgian–Barremian; ?Neocomian–?Hauterivian).

Known material: 25 to 30 skull elements, some with associated postcrania, about ten incomplete articulated skeletons, fragmentary skeleton with skull, miscellaneous postcrania, juvenile to adult.

Holotype: YPM 1877, seven cervical and first dorsal vertebrae, femora, tibia, fibula, manus, pes.

Diagnosis of genus: [Crania] skull low and wide; premaxilla edentulous, with large posterior process overlapping nasal dorsally; antorbital openings small; frontal forming small part of orbital margin; supraoccipital bordering foramen magnum; maxilla and den-

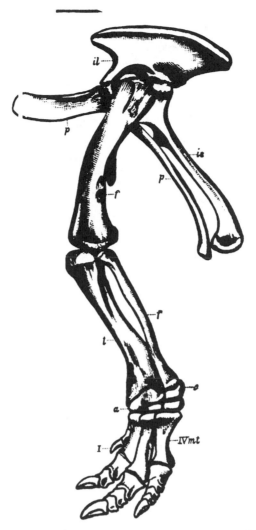

Camptosaurus dispar, YPM 1877, holotype (including left femur, tibia, fibula, and pes) of *Camptonotus dispar*. Scale = 6 cm. (After March 1879.)

Camptosaurus dispar, YPM 1877, holotype right pes of *Camptonotus dispar*.

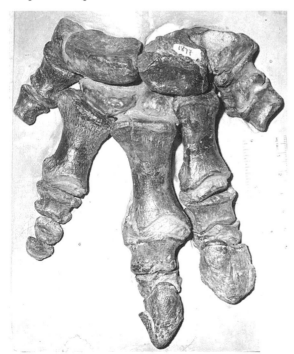

Photo by R. A. Long and S. P. Welles (neg. #73-473-38), courtesy Yale Peabody Museum of Natural History.

tary each bearing 15 or 16 lozenge-shaped, functional teeth, and, per aveolus, one replacement tooth; maxillary teeth with more strongly developed vertical keel than dentary teeth; surface of maxillary-tooth crown sculptured, bearing several secondary vertical ridges; nondenticulate half bordered by anterior and posterior ridges; equivalent part of dentary tooth with posterior ridge (Galton and Powell 1980); [postcrania] scapular blade constricted, with strong flare at the coracoid articulation; acromion prominent, with clavicular facet; coracoid short relative to length of the scapula, subquadrate, with an abrupt craniodistal angle; coracoid foramen at articular surface of scapula, opening at middle of articulation of scapulacoracoid; humerus relatively short and narrow; deltopectoral crest weak, so that humerus tapers distally; radius distally compact and rounded; carpus compact, heavily ossified; carpals with well-defined artic-

Camptosaurus

Courtesy National Museum of Natural History, Smithsonian Institution (neg. #43496).

Camptosaurus dispar skeletons [originally referred to *C. nanus* and *C. browni*, respectively], juvenile and adult.

Photo by R. A. Long and S. P. Welles (neg. #73/315-26), courtesy American Museum of Natural History.

Camptosaurus dispar, AMNH 5772, holotype fragments of *Symphyrophus musculosus*.

ular relationships; three proximal and five distal carpals; ilium massive, with a straight dorsal margin; postacetabular ventral margin of ilium with a moderate medial reflection; prepubis deep, flat; postpubis stout, decurved; femur curved, with prominent lesser trochanter, well-defined anterior intercondylar sulcus; pes short, stocky; metatarsus and digits broad (Dodson 1980).

Diagnosis of *C. dispar*: Skull with large intramaxillary cavity; posterior process of premaxilla reaching prefrontal; three or four secondary ridges reaching middle of tooth crown anterior to a pronounced keel; third cervical centrum platycoelous; lower edge of anterior ends of fourth-to-ninth cervical centra gently rounded; carpus well-ossified; radiale fused with first metacarpal; manus with five short, stocky digits; long bones and pes massive (Galton and Powell 1980).

Diagnosis of *C. prestwichii*: Skull with small intramaxillary cavity; five secondary ridges reaching middle of tooth crown anterior to a prominent keel; anterior ends of fourth-to-ninth cervical centra with subrhomboid outline; long bones and pes slender (Galton and Powell 1980).

Diagnosis of ?*C. depressus*: Ilium low, with shallow acetabulum, and narrow preacetabular notch; anterior end of pubis broad; sacrals with rounded ventral surfaces (Galton and Powell 1980).

Comments: Marsh (1879) based the new genus and species *Camptonotus dispar* upon a partial skeleton (YPM 1877) collected from a quarry in the Morrison Formation, near Como, Albany County, Wyoming. As the name *Camptonotus* proved to be preoccupied (Uhler 1864), Marsh (1885) renamed the genus *Camptosaurus*, upon which he founded the new ornithopod family Camptosauridae.

Marsh (1879) originally diagnosed *Camptonotus* as follows: Edentulous premaxillaries with horny beak; teeth large, irregular in number; skull with supraorbital opening; cervical vertebrae long, opisthocoelous; sacrum with five vertebrae with peg-and-notch articulation; sternum not ossified; limb bones hollow; forelimbs about one half size of hindlimbs; five functional manual digits; prepubis long, broad; postpubis elongate; femur longer than tibia; metatarsals short; pes with three functional digits, rudimentary first digit, "wanting" fifth.

However, some of the above characters are no longer regarded as diagnostic or correct. For example, the femur is longer than the tibia in most Cretaceous adult ornithopods (M. K. Brett-Surman, personal communication). Also, Dodson (1980) showed that the sternum in *Camptosaurus* is, in fact, ossified, and that the hollow limb bones are indicative of juveniles.

Three possibly valid species of *Camptosaurus* (*C. dispar*, *C. prestwichii*, and ?*C. depressus*) were recognized by Galton and Powell (1980), who rediagnosed the type species based on the holotype and the paratypes (partial sacrum, YPM 1877a, and pelvic girdle and forelimb YPM 1878).

?*C. depressus*, originally described by Gilmore (1909*a*), was based on ilia, pubis, and vertebrae (USNM 4753) from the Lakota Sandstone, "Calico Canyon," near Buffalo Gap Station, South Dakota. Galton and Jensen (1978) tentatively referred to this species the partial crown of a right dentary tooth (USGS D262) collected by D. E. Walcott in 1957 from the locality that yielded the holotype of *C. depressus*. This specimen has a thick enamel and ornamented surface and corresponds to the dentary teeth in other *Camptosaurus* specimens. Subsequently, Galton and Powell (1980) regarded this species as provisionally valid.

Galton and Powell (1980) determined that the remaining *Camptosaurus* remains from the Morrison Formation (*i.e.*, *C. medius* Marsh 1894, *C. nanus* Marsh 1894, and *C. browni* Gilmore 1909) belong to the same species, *C. dispar*, their differences attributable to individual variation or ontogeny.

Galton and Powell (1980) referred *Iguanodon prestwichii* (Hulke 1880; renamed *Cumnoria prestwichii* Seeley 1888) to *Camptosaurus* as the new species *C. prestwichii*. This species is based on an almost complete skeleton (OUM J.3303) from the Lower Kimmeridge Clay, near Oxford, England. *C. prestwichii* is very similar to *C. dispar*, though more gracile. Examination by Galton and Powell of a pit-like intramaxillary cavity in this species revealed that it did not involve the attachment of muscles, but may have housed a salt gland.

Illustration by Gregory S. Paul.

Camptosaurus dispar (left) and two *Dryosaurus altus*.

Camptosaurus

C. prestwichii represents the only undisputed remains of *Camptosaurus* known from outside North America, providing evidence for a Late Jurassic land connection between that continent and Europe. Although such a connection has long been presumed to have existed (Charig 1973; Colbert 1974; Cox 1974), supporting faunal evidence has been slight. The high degree of evolutionary divergence between

Photo by the author, courtesy University Museum, Oxford.

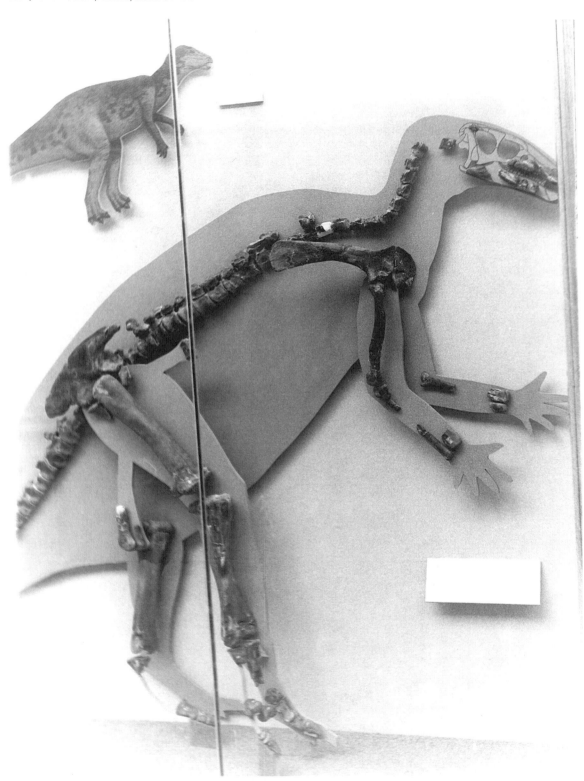

Camptosaurus prestwichii,
OUM J.3303, holotype partial skeleton of *Iguanodon prestwichii.*

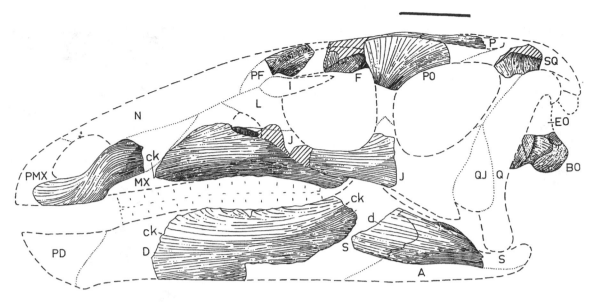

Camptosaurus prestwichii, OUM J. 3303, holotype fragmentary skull of *Iguanodon prestwichii*, left lateral view. Scale = 4 cm. (After Galton and Powell 1980, after Gilmore 1909; courtesy The Palaeontological Association.)

C. prestwichii and *C. dispar*, according to Galton and Powell, seems not due to geographical distance but to the length of time of their mutual isolation.

Other skeletal material, mostly recovered from Wyoming, has since been referred to this genus, these specimens exhibiting much individual variation in size and ontogenetic development. *Camptosaurus* is also known from the Dry Mesa Quarry (Morrison Formation, Upper Jurassic [Tithonian] or Lower Cretaceous [Neocomian or Hauterivian]; see Britt 1991), near the southwest corner of Dry Mesa, in west central Colorado.

Camptosaurus somewhat resembles *Iguanodon*, although the head is less deep and the manus is more primitive. The first finger in *Camptosaurus*, unlike the large spike in *Iguanodon*, is reduced to a spur-like finger, and the unguals on digits II and III are more curved and less hoof-like. The heavy hindlimbs and relatively shortened forelimbs indicate that *Camptosaurus* was mostly bipedal. However, the length of the forelimbs, about half that of the hindlimbs, and the large bony wrist, allowed for a quadrupedal stance, probably when the animal dropped down to eat.

Camptosaurus was a small- to medium-sized and rather conservative-looking ornithopod. Marsh (1896) estimated the length of *C. dispar* to be about 6 meters (20 feet). Colbert (1962), in a study of possible weights in dinosaurs employing water-immersed scale models, estimated the average *Camptosaurus* to weigh about 383 kilograms (842 pounds). However, more recent weight estimates are higher, an adult possibly totaling about 1.53 metric tons (about 1.7 tons) (G. S. Paul, personal communication 1988).

Camptosaurus is important as an intermediate form, more derived than hypsilophodontids yet more primitive than the later hadrosaurids.

Usually regarded as junior synonyms of *C. dispar* are the type species "*Brachyrophus*" *altarkansanus* Cope 1878 [*nomen dubium*] and "*Symphyrophus*" *musculosus* Cope 1878 [*nomen dubium*].

"*Brachyrophus*" was established on four vertebral centra (AMNH 5776) collected from the Morrison Formation, at Canyon City, Colorado. Apparently Cope (1878*b*), who collected the specimen, neither described nor figured it, but regarded it as sauropod. The specimen was identified by William Diller Matthew at the time of cataloguing, after the 1902 transferal of the Cope collection to the American Museum of Natural History. Osborn and Mook (1921) observed that the position of the type specimen is uncertain. Osborn and Mook noted that the centra, in cross-section, are hexagonal, a typical feature of ornithischians, and suggested that *Brachyrophus* could be referable to *Camptosaurus*. (In a paper explaining the etymology of Cope's dinosaurian taxa, Creisler 1992 pointed out that the name "*Brachyrophus*" predates *Camptosaurus* and "*B.*" *altarkansanus* predates *C. dispar*.)

"*Symphyrophus*" was founded on a vertebral centrum and distal end of a femur (AMNH 5772) apparently from an immature individual, recovered from the uppermost beds of the Morrison Formation, Garden Park, north to northeast of Canyon City. Cope misidentified the femur for a humerus in his original description of the material, again incorrectly regarding the remains as sauropod. Osborn and Mook con-

?*Camptosaurus depressus*, USNM 4753, holotype ilia and vertebrae.

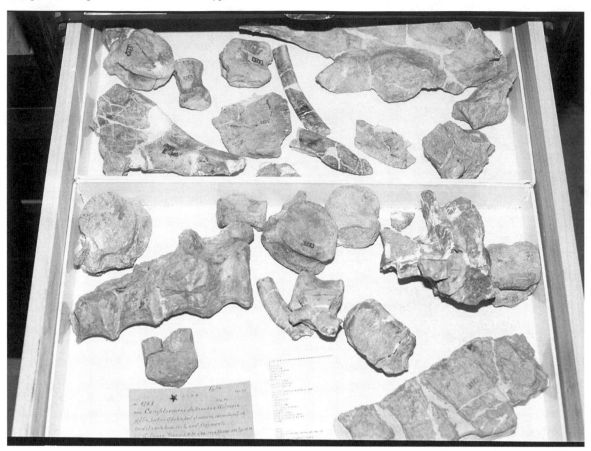

Photo by the author, courtesy National Museum of Natural History, Smithsonian Institution.

sidered this material to be indeterminate, suggesting that it probably not belong to a sauropod and might actually be crocodilian.

Notes: A nearly complete *Camptosaurus*-like right femur (UA 22) and the head and median portion of the shank of a left femur (UA 23), in a large nodule discovered by E. P. Hilton in Lower Cretaceous sediments south of the Empire Mountains, southeast of Tucson, Arizona, were reported by Miller (1964). Part of the shank of another femur was found about ten miles east of that locality. As described by Miller, the nearly complete femur measures 700 millimeters (about 2.4 feet) long. This material most resembles that in *Iguanodon atherfieldensis*, but differs in being wider, the head not at a right angle to the shaft, and shaft concave distally on the posterior surface. Its length suggests an animal from almost 6 to 6.7 meters (20 to 25 feet) long, within the size range of *Camptosaurus*. According to Miller, the Arizona femur shares many features with *Camptosaurus*, indicating a close relationship to that genus. As *Camptosaurus* is strictly a Jurassic form, it may belong to a related but as of yet unnamed genus.

Camptonotus amplus Marsh 1879 was based on an almost complete left pes (YPM 1879) which apparently belongs to the theropod *Allosaurus fragilis*. Other European ornithopod species once referred to *Camptosaurus* were reevaluated by Galton and Powell: *C. inkeyi* Nopcsa (1900) was referred by them to *Rhabdodon priscus* and *C. valdensis* Lydekker (1889) to *Valdosaurus*. ?*C. leedsi* Lydekker (1889) was made the type species of new genus *Callovosaurus* by Galton (1980c).

Key references: Britt (1992); Cope (1878b); Creisler (1992); Dodson (1980); Galton and Jensen (1978); Galton and Powell (1980); Gilmore (1909a); Hulke (1880); Marsh (1879, 1885, 1896).

CAMPYLODON Huene 1929 [*nomen dubium*] — (Preoccupied, Cuvier and Valenciennes 1832; see *Campylodoniscus*.)
Name derivation: Greek *kampylos* = "curved" + Greek *odous* = "tooth."
Type species: *C. ameghinol* Huene 1929 [*nomen dubium*].

CAMPYLODONISCUS Kuhn 1961 [*nomen dubium*]—(=*Campylodon* Huene)

Saurischia: Sauropodomorpha: Sauropoda *incertae sedis*.

Name derivation: Greek *kampylos* = "curved" + Greek *odous* = "tooth" + *iscus* = "like."

Type species: *C. ameghinoi* (Huene 1929) [*nomen dubium*].

Other species: [None.]

Occurrence: Chubut, Argentina.

Age: Late Cretaceous (Campanian–Maastrichtian).

Known material/holotype: MPL collection, partial maxilla with tooth.

Diagnosis of genus: [No modern diagnosis published.]

Comments: Huene (1929) described the species *Campylodon ameghinoi*, founded upon an incomplete maxilla with one tooth (MPL collection), recovered from the Upper Cretaceous of Sierra de San Bernardo, Chubut, Argentina. As the name *Campylodon* proved to be preoccupied (Cuvier and Valenciennes 1832), Kuhn (1961) later proposed for Huene's species the new generic name *Campylodoniscus*.

Originally, Huene diagnosed the monotypic *C. ameghinoi* as follows: Teeth peg-like, crown slightly spatulate and pointed; point curved, laterally flattened, roughly sculptured; maxilla very deep and, if complete, possibly similar to that of more advanced titanosaurids.

Huene tentatively assigned this taxon to the Titanosauridae. Steel (1970) pointed out that the type specimen of *Campylodoniscus* could represent any South American sauropod except *Amygdalodon* or *Antarctosaurus*.

In a review of the Sauropoda, McIntosh (1990*b*) described *C. ameghinoi* as follows: Teeth with broader

Campylodoniscus ameghinoi, MLP collection, holotype tooth of *Campylodon ameghinoi*, in labial lateral, anterior, and lingual lateral views. (After Huene 1929.)

crowns than in diplodocids, but not as broad as in camarasaurids; quite different from tiny slender teeth of *Antarctosaurus* and those referred to *Alamosaurus*. According to McIntosh, this species is mostly significant in documenting the existence of Late Cretaceous sauropods with nondiplodocid type skulls.

Key references: Huene (1929); Kuhn (1961); McIntosh (1990*b*); Steel (1970).

CARCHARODONTOSAURUS Stromer 1931

Saurischia: Theropoda: Tetanurae *incertae sedis*.

Name derivation: Greek *karcharo* = "shark" + Greek *sauros* = "lizard."

Type species: *C. saharicus* (Depéret and Savornin 1927).

Other species: [None.]

Occurrence: Baharija Formation, Marsa Matruh, Egypt; Tegana Formation, Ksares-Souk, Morocco; Chemini Formation, "Continental intercalaire," Medinine, Tunisia; "Continental intercalaire," Adrar, Tamenghest, Wargla, Algeria;

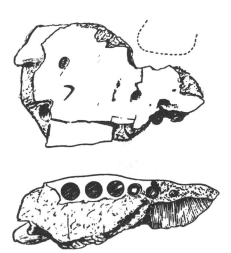

Campylodoniscus ameghinoi, MLP, holotype left maxilla of *Campylodon ameghinoi*, in side and ventral views. (After Huene 1929.)

Carcharodontosaurus saharicus, holotype teeth of *Megalosaurus saharicus*, labial (left) and lingual (right) surfaces. (After Deperet and Savornin 1928.)

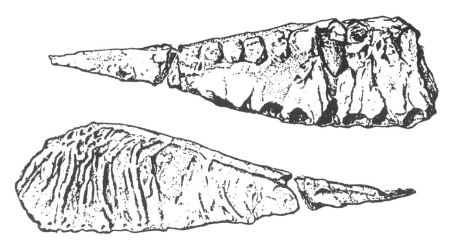

Carcharodontosaurus saharicus, referred left maxilla, internal and external views. (After Stromer 1931.)

"Continental intercalaire," Medenine, Tunisia;
"Continental intercalaire," Gharyan, Lybia;
"Continental intercalaire," Agadez, Niger.

Age: Early–Late Cretaceous (Late Albian–Early Cenomanian).

Known material: Fragmentary skull, associated postcrania, isolated teeth, isolated postcrania.

Holotype: [Destroyed], two teeth.

Diagnosis of genus: [None published to date of this writing.]

Comments: The genus now known as *Carcharodontosaurus* was first described by Depéret and Savornin (1927) as a new species of *Megalosaurus*, which they named *M. saharicus*, established on two somewhat "shark-like" teeth found in a subterranean water channel or tunnel near at Baharija-Oasis, Timimoun, Algiers, North Africa. (The type specimen was destroyed during World War II by an American bombing raid of Munich in 1944.)

More fossil material was assigned to this genus, collected by the Munich museum expedition in 1911 from the Cenomanian Baharija Beds (Stromer 1931) in Egypt. These remains included teeth similar to those described by Depéret and Savornin and imperfect skull material (from which the making of an endocranial cast was attempted), massively proportioned vertebrae, pelvic elements, limb bones, and other elements. Upon this material and the type specimen of *M. saharicus*, Stromer erected the new genus *Carcharodontosaurus*. Other remains referred to the type species include material reported by Stromer (1934), teeth from Morocco (Lavocat 1954), and from the "Continental intercalaire," central Sahara desert region, teeth and bone fragments (Lapparent 1960).

Stromer (1931) described the original and referred material as follows: Teeth sharp, double-ridged, usually not curved; forelimbs greatly reduced but (as evidenced by manual ungual phalanx) with powerful claws; dorsal vertebral spines unusually high; approximate total length 8 meters, or about 27 feet.

Carcharodontosaurus seems to have measured at least 8 meters (26 feet) in length. In his book *Predatory Dinosaurs of the World*, Paul (1988c) speculated that the unusual shape of the teeth in *Carcharodontosaurus* suggests that this dinosaur did not slice its prey's flesh, but rather employed a unique way of cutting out wounds.

Carcharodontosaurus seems to have been a more derived and specialized form than the Jurassic megalosaurids. *C. saharicus* has usually been classified with the Megalosauridae, although Lapparent (1960) argued that its true affinities (as well as those of *Bahariasaurus ingens*, another Baharija species) were with the Tyrannosauridae. Molnar, Kurzanov and Dong (1990) noted that both *C. saharicus* and *B. ingens* share synapomorphic features with tyrannosaurids (see *Bahariasaurus* entry) and others shared with allosaurids. *C. saharicus* also exhibits autapomorphic features (*e.g.*, broad, nonrecurved teeth, ilium with a low preacetabular process) suggesting that some independent "carnosaurian" evolution occurred in Gondwana after the arrival of ancestors of *C. saharicus*. As

Carcharodontosaurus saharicus, (left to right) referred dorsal centrum, consecutive caudal vertebrae, anterior caudal vertebra, anterior caudal centrum. Scale = 2 cm. (After Lapparent 1960.)

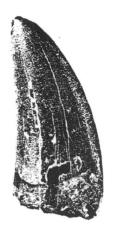

Carcharodontosaurus sahari-cus, referred teeth. Scale = 1 cm. (After Lapparent 1960.)

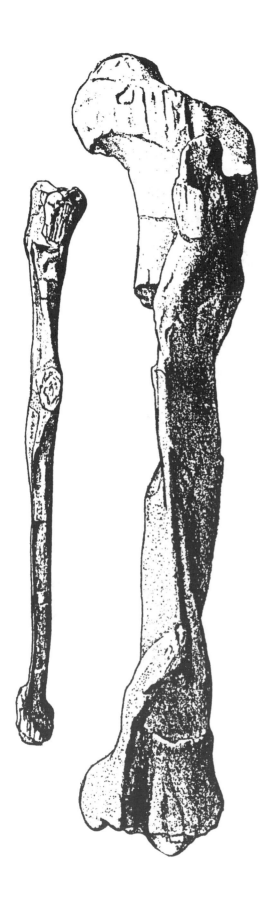

both Baharija species are represented by incomplete and unassociated elements, Molnar *et al.*. treated *C. saharicus* and *B. ingens* together, postulating that, except for the dorsal central form, all features shared with tyrannosaurids are most likely associated with muscle attachments. Both taxa were regarded by Molnar *et al.* as "Carnosauria *incertae sedis*."

More recently, Rauhut (1995) reconsidered the systematic position of *Carcharodontosaurus* and *Bahariasaurus*. As the material belonging to these two taxa was destroyed, Rauhut had to rely on data originally published by Stromer (1931, 1934, 1936). Rauhut referred both of these genera to their own allosauroid family, Carcharodontosauridae Stromer 1931, which, according to Rauhut, probably had its origins in the primitive allosaurids of the Middle to Late Jurassic (Kimmeridgian) of Tendaguru (Tanzania). Rauhut characterized carcharodontosaurids as large allosauroids possessing pleurocoelous proximal caudal vertebrae.

Comparing *Carcharodontosaurus* and *Bahariasaurus* with other allosauroids, Rauhut concluded that Carcharodontosauridae may be the sister-group to Allosauridae, both families sharing the following characters: Maxillary with fused interdental plates; obturator-notch wide; and ischium with slender "neck" at pubic peduncle. Rauhut also observed the

?*Carcharodontosaurus sahari-cus*, referred ilium (After Stromer 1931.)

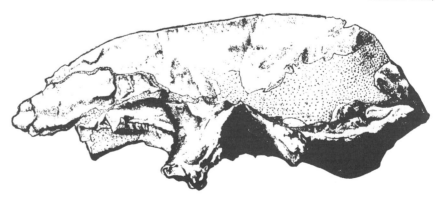

Carcharodontosaurus saharicus, referred left fibula and femur. (After Stromer 1931.)

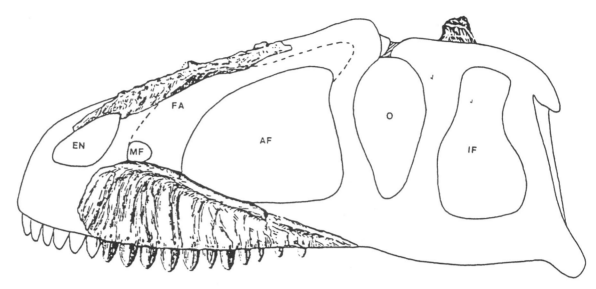

Carcharodontosaurus saharicus, reconstructed skull, left lateral view, modified after Stromer (1936), made after comparisons with *Sinraptor* and *Allosaurus.* Scale = 50 cm. (After Rauhut 1995.)

following similarities between *Carcharodontosaurus* and *Bahariasaurus* and the allosauroids *Sinraptor* and *Allosaurus:* Participation of nasal bone in antorbital fossa; reduction of distal symphysis of public shafts; presence of obturator notch; presence of small notch at distal end of obturator process (possibly plesio-morphic); and shape and height of lesser trochanter.

Rauhut noted various similarities between *Car-charodontosauridae* and *Bahariasaurus,* most notably the possession of pleurocoels in the anterior caudal vertebrae, a character unique to these among all known theropods; also, strongly opisthocoelous cer-vical vertebrae (probably a size-related feature), with only one pair of pleurocoels; pubis-symphisis found only in middle parts of pubic shafts, but reduced proximally and distally; pubis bowed anteriorly; obturator process offset from pubic process of isch-ium; and wing-like lesser trochanter.

Note: Fossil dinosaur footprints possibly attrib-utable to *Carcharodontosaurus* were reported from the Niger Republic by Ginsburg, Lapparent, Loiret and Taquet (1966).

Key references: Depéret and Savornin (1927); Lapparent (1960); Molnar, Kurzanov and Dong (1990); Paul (1988c); Rauhut (1995); Stromer (1931, 1934, 1936).

CARDIODON   Owen 1841 [*nomen dubium*]—
   (=?*Cetiosaurus*)
Saurischia: Sauropodomorpha: Sauropoda:
   Cetiosauridae: Cetiosaurinae.
Name derivation: Greek *kardia* = "heart" + Greek
   odous = "tooth."

Type species: *C. rugolosus* Owen 1845 [*nomen
   dubium*].
Other species: [None.]
Occurrence: Wiltshire, England.
Age: Middle Jurassic (Late Bathonian).
Known material/holotype: BMNH R1527, tooth.
   Diagnosis of genus: [None published.]
   Comments: The genus *Cardiodon* was founded upon a "heart-shaped" tooth (BMNH R1527) col-lected from the Forest Marble, Bradford, Wiltshire, England, described (but not illustrated) by Owen (1841).

Although the type species *C. rugulosus* is often classified as a junior synonym of *Cetiosaurus oxonien-sis,* McIntosh (1990b) noted that a synonymy cannot be established.

Key references: McIntosh (1990b); Owen 1845.

CARNOTAURUS   Bonaparte 1985
Saurischia: Theropoda: Ceratosauria:
   Neoceratosauria: Abelisauroidea: Abelisauridae.
Name derivation: Latin *carnis* = "flesh" + Greek
   tauros = "bull."
Type species: *C. sastrei* Bonaparte 1984.
Other species: [None]
Occurrence: Gorro Frigio Formation, Chubut,
   Argentina.
Age: Middle Cretaceous (Albian–Cenomanian).
Known material/holotype: MACN-CH 894,
   almost complete skeleton with associated skull,
   integument.
   Diagnosis of genus (as for type species): Large theropod [="carnosaur" of Bonaparte's usage]; skull

with deep, narrow snout, and salient supraorbital horns; orbits divided into an upper, rounded section anterolaterally projected for the eyes, with a posterodorsal wall, and lower, dorsoventrally elongated section; supratemporal opening small, its posterior wall high, formed by parietal and squamosal, and with a low, lateral border; infratemporal and preorbital fenestrae similar to those in *Abelisaurus*, larger than in tyrannosaurids; quadrate very high; squamosal with short, rod-shaped projection (as in *Abelisaurus*); reduced forelimbs with very short and stout radius and ulna, distal ends large and convex (Bonaparte 1985); skull shorter and higher than in *Abelisaurus* and other theropods; infratemporal and preorbital openings smaller than in *Abelisaurus*; contact between dentary and postdentary loose, forming large mandibular fenestra; cervical vertebrae behind axis bearing reduced neural spines and high, well-developed epipophyses; seven fused sacral vertebrae; ilia long, square-shaped; pubes, ischia, and femora long, slender (Bonaparte, Novas and Coria 1990).

Comments: This unusual theropod was found on the Estancia Pocho Sastre, near Bajada Moreno, Telsen Department of Chubut Province, Patagonia, Argentina, during the 8th Paleontological Expedition to Patagonia. *Carnotaurus* was established on a well-preserved, nearly complete skeleton (MACN-CH 894) lacking only the feet, distal half of tibiae and

Carnotaurus sastrei, MACN-CH 894, holotype skull, right lateral view.

Carnotaurus sastrei, MACN-CH 894, holotype skeleton.

fibulae, and distal half of the tail, which were lost due to weathering (Bonaparte 1985).

The genus was originally diagnosed and described by Bonaparte. The skull is 57 centimeters (22 inches) long, comparatively quite short for a theropod. Its most remarkable feature is the prominent horns, surmounting the orbits, projecting out laterally and upwards. The function of these horns is unknown, although they may have been used for intraspecific display or intimidation. The upper, rounded part of the orbits indicates that the eyes could at least partially focus on the same field of vision.

According to Bonaparte, *Carnotaurus* represents a unique theropod evolutionary lineage apparently indigenous only to the Southern Hemisphere.

In a joint paper, Bonaparte, Novas and Coria (1990) rediagnosed and fully described the type species *C. sastrei*.

Comparing *C. sastrei* with other theropods, Bonaparte *et al.* concluded that *Carnotaurus* should be classified with the Abelisauridae, the skulls of *Carnotaurus* and *Abelisaurus*, though very different in proportions, sharing several features diagnostic of that group: 1. Plesiomorphic characters in the squamosal and general shape of the infratemporal opening; 2. postorbital almost enclosing the orbit ventrally; lacrimal posteriorly convex; 3. preorbital opening large; 4. maxillary fenestra small and slightly separated from the main preorbital opening, yet still within the same general depression; 5. characters in the parietal crest and proportions of the supratemporal openings; and 6. ornamentation of the nasal with rugosities suggesting a corneous covering.

Comparing *Carnotaurus* with *Ceratosaurus*, Bonaparte *et al.* showed that both forms share the following cranial characters: 1. Skulls similar in the height of the premaxilla in narial region; 2. small maxillary fenestra located near the preorbital opening; 3. jugal lacking an anterior projection overlying the maxilla, and which does not border the preorbital opening; 4. large infratemporal opening with no anterior projection of the quadratojugal and squamosal; 5. dorsoventrally long quadrate; and 6.

Carnotaurus sastrei, MACN-CH 894, detail of left scapulacoracoid and forelimb.

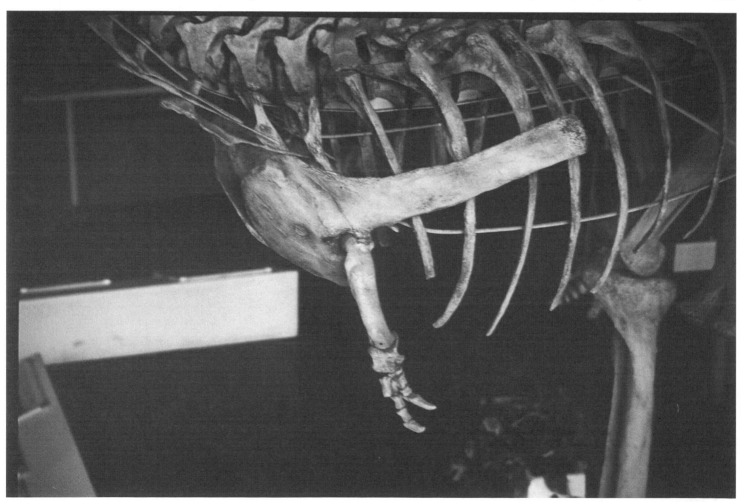

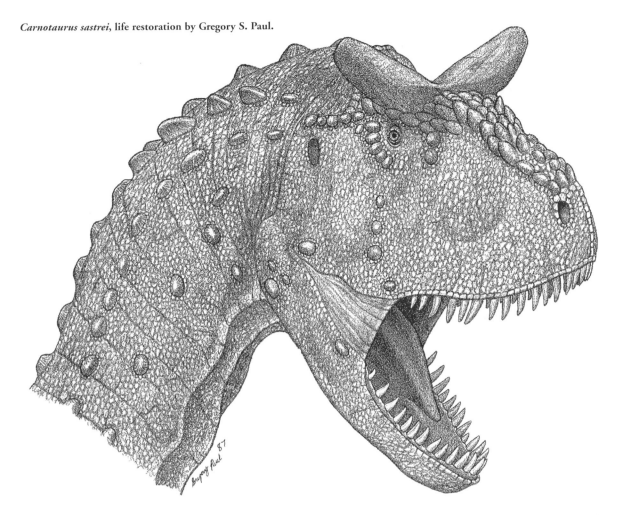

Carnotaurus sastrei, life restoration by Gregory S. Paul.

squamosal with a slender, rod-like ventral projection not oriented anteroventrally.

Regarding postcrania of *Carnotaurus* and *Cerotosaurus*, the following shared characters were observed: 1. Centra well fused to sacrum and secondarily reduced; 2. pelvis axially elongated; 3. obturator foramen of pubis surrounded by bone; 4. large laminar contact between pubis and ischium; 5. ischium with distal expansion; 6. femoral head directed anteromediad, lower than major trochanter; 7. lesser trochanter poorly developed dorsally; and, 8. manual digits with short phalanges.

Bonaparte *et al.* also listed various differences between these two genera, some (including the nasal and lacrimal protuberances and only three premaxillary teeth in *Ceratosaurus*) precluding the possibility that *Ceratosaurus* may have been ancestral to *Carnotaurus*. Other characters (*e.g.,* more derived cervical caudal vertebrae in *Carnotaurus*) show no morphological similarities with *Ceratosaurus*. However, Bonaparte *et al.* suggested a close and significant relationship between *Ceratosaurus* and *Carnotaurus* without defining that relationship, also noting that this relationship is closer than it might be with any other

"carnosaurian" group, with Ceratosauridae and Abelisauridae possibly united within a higher taxon Ceratosauroidea. Since this assessment, Holtz (1994*a*) referred Abelisauridae to the ceratosaurian taxon Neoceratosauria (see also Holtz and Padian 1995; Currie 1995).

Found with the type specimen were several fragments of fossil skin impressions, the best yet known in any theropod, showing rows of relatively large and nonbony semiconical scales (Bonaparte 1985). As observed by Bonaparte *et al.*, the fragments, found under the right side of the skeleton, correspond to several parts of the body (anterior cervical region, scapular area near the glenoid cavity, thoracic region, and proximal part of the tail), with only slight variation between the different fragments. The surface of the skin consists of somewhat low, conical protuberances measuring from 4 to 5 centimeters in diameter. They are separated from one another by about 8 to 10 centimeters. The surface between them is rough and has somewhat low, small and rounded granules approximately 5 millimeters in diameter separated from each other by narrow furrows. Each protuberance has a modest keel.

The holotype skull and a mounted skeleton of *C. sastrei* have been exhibited at the Buenos Aires Museum.

Key references: Bonaparte (1985); Bonaparte, Novas and Coria (1990).

CATHETOSAURUS Jensen 1987—(See *Camarasaurus.*)

Name derivation: Greek *kathetos* = "upright/perpendicular" + Greek *sauros* = "lizard."

Type species: *C. lewisi* Jensen 1987.

CAUDOCOELUS Huene 1932 [*nomen dubium*]—(See *Teinurosaurus.*)

Name derivation: Latin *cauda* = "tail" + Greek *coelis* = "hollow."

Type species: *C. sauvagei* Huene 1932 [*nomen dubium*].

CAULODON Cope 1877 [*nomen dubium*]—(See *Camarasaurus.*)

Name derivation: Greek *kaulos* = "stalk" + Greek *odous* = "tooth."

C. diversidens Cope 1877 [*nomen dubium*].

CENTROSAURUS Lambe 1904/Fitzinger 1834—(=?*Brachyceratops*, ?*Monoclonius*, ?*Styracosaurus*)

Ornithischia: Genasauria: Cerapoda: Marginocephalia: Ceratopsia: Neoceratopsia: Ceratopsidae: Centrosaurinae.

Name derivation: Greek *kentron* = "horn" + *sauros* = "lizard."

Type species: *C. apertus* Lambe 1904.

Other species: *C. nasicornis* Brown. 1917.

Occurrence: Oldman Formation, Alberta, Canada; ?Oldman Formation, Montana, United States.

Age: Late Cretaceous (Late Campanian).

Known material: Fifteen skulls, several adult skeletons, much bone bed material with adults, subadults and juveniles.

Holotype: NMC 971, parietal crest.

Diagnosis of genus (as for type species): Parietal characterized by thickened border, pair of hook-like structures that project caudally, and pair of horns that project rostrally over parietal fenestrae (Dodson and Currie 1990).

Diagnosis of *C. nasicornis*: Nasal horn erect; brow horns rudimentary, with heavy rugosity above orbits; moderately curved crest; muzzle with distinct shape, rugose (Lull 1933).

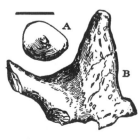

Centrosaurus recurvicornis, postfrontal with supraorbital horn core, figured but unidentified by Cope in 1877, A. dorsal and B. lateral views. Scale = 4 cm.

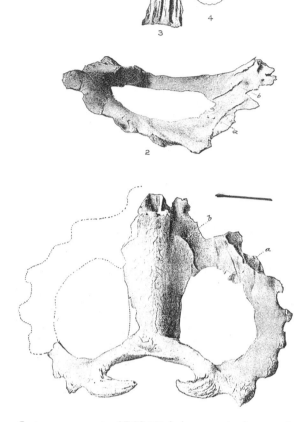

Centrosaurus apertus, NMC 971, holotype parietal crest and nasal horn core. Scale = 16 cm. (After Lambe 1904.)

Comments: The genus *Centrosaurus* was founded upon a parietal crest (NMC 971), collected by Lawrence M. Lambe in 1901 from the Belly River [now Oldman] Formation, below "Steveville," in Alberta, Canada. Since the discovery of the type specimen, numerous other *Centrosaurus* specimens, including complete skeletons, have been collected, mostly from the Red Deer River area of Alberta.

Centrosaurus was first described by Lambe (1904a) in conjunction with describing the holotype (GSC 1173) of *Monoclonius dawsoni*. Originally, Lambe diagnosed *Centrosaurus* as follows: Frill saddle-shaped, with curved, hook-like process at back. Lambe (1904a, 1904b) distinguished the type species as follows: Large fontanelles; central portion of parietal expansion of crest relatively broad, high in front, concave longitudinally, transversely convex on upper surface; border of crest regularly scalloped, outer margin with sharp-edged epoccipital processes that decrease in size anteriorly.

C. apertus, AMNH 5427,
holotype skeleton with
integument of *C. cutleri*,
dorsal view.

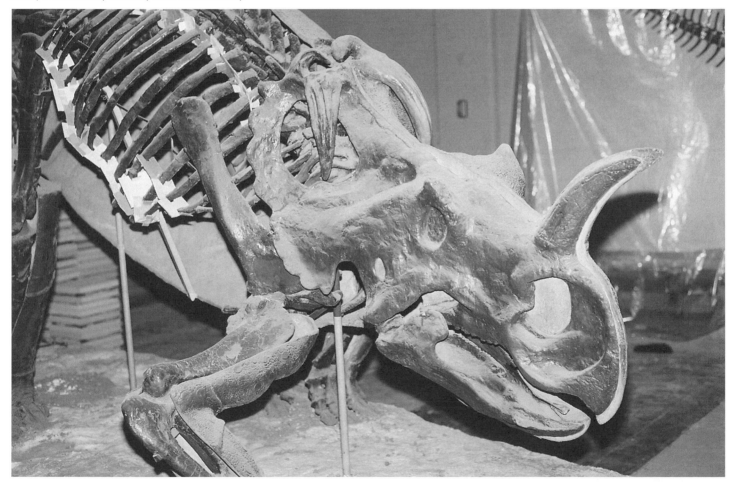

C. apertus, YPM 2015, skeleton [originally referred to *Monoclonius flexus*].

Centrosaurus

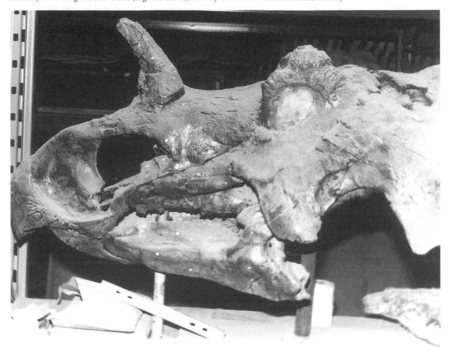

C. apertus, NMC 8795, holotype skull of *C. longirostris*, left lateral view.

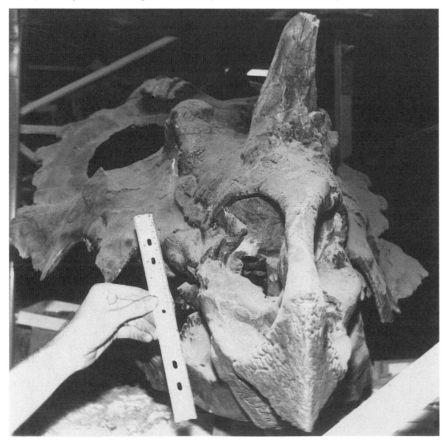

Centrosaurus apertus, NMC 8795, holotype skull, three-quarter view.

Other taxa relating to *Centrosaurus* were subsequently named and described: *C. flexus* Brown 1914 was based on a skull (AMNH 5239) collected by the American Museum of Natural History expedition of 1912, below "Steveville" at Red Deer River. Later, Lull (1933), in his classic revision of the Ceratopsia, distinguished this species by the long, forwardly-curving nasal horn. *Monoclonius cutleri* Brown 1917 (later referred to *Centrosaurus*) was based on the posterior half of a skeleton with integument (AMNH 5427) collected in 1913 from the same locality as *C. flexus* for the American Museum of Natural History. *Monoclonius nasicornis* Brown 1917 was based on a skull and skeleton (AMNH 5351) collected in 1914 by an American Museum team, from Sand Creek, twelve miles below "Steveville."

Lull regarded *Centrosaurus* as a subgenus of *Monoclonius*, this assessment based on a skeleton with skull (YPM 2015; formerly AMNH 5341) referred to the species *C. flexus*, the specimen collected in 1914 for the American Museum of Natural History at Sand Creek, below "Steveville" and later mounted at the Yale Peabody Museum of Natural History. In his osteology of *Centrosaurus flexus* based upon this display specimen, Lull stated that the skeleton is over 5 meters (or 17 feet, 4 inches) in length and is smaller and less stoutly built than *Triceratops*. According to Lull, the nasal horn varies in curvature between individuals and can reach a length of up to about 47 centimeters (18 inches). Lull placed *Centrosaurus* early in the evolution of what were then called "short-frilled" ceratopsids.

Sternberg (1940*b*) later published a revised diagnosis of the genus *Centrosaurus* based on the holotype of a new species *C. longirostris*, comprising a skull with lower jaws (GSC 8795), discovered by G. E. Lindblad and collected in 1917 by Sternberg from the Oldman [now Dinosaur Park] Formation south of Sand Creek, Red Deer River.

Centrosaurus apertus, GSC 1173, holotype frill of *Monoclonius dawsoni*, ventral view. Scale = approximately 8 cm. (After Lambe 1902.)

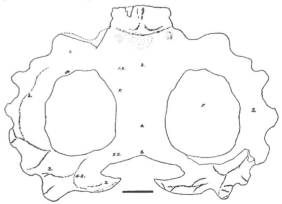

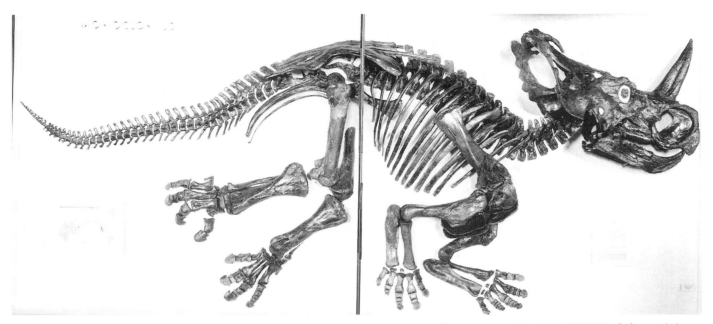

Centrosaurus nasicornis, AMNH 5351, holotype skeleton.

In their review of the Neoceratopsia, Dodson and Currie (1990) regarded *C. longirostris*, *C. flexus*, *C. cutleri*, and *M. dawsoni* as junior synonyms of *C. apertus*.

According to Dodson (1990*d*), some variations in *Centrosaurus* specimens are due to sexual dimorphism. Males can be differentiated from females by a deeper face, higher nasal horn, more prominent orbital horns (Lehman 1990) and longer frill, among other differences. (According to Lehman, males also generally tend to attain larger body size.) Dodson also noted that the species *Styracosaurus albertensis* is so close to *C. apertus* that both taxa may be congeneric, though not necessarily conspecific (see *Styracosaurus* entry; also Dodson and Currie 1990).

?*C. recurvicornis*, AMNH 3999, holotype snout.

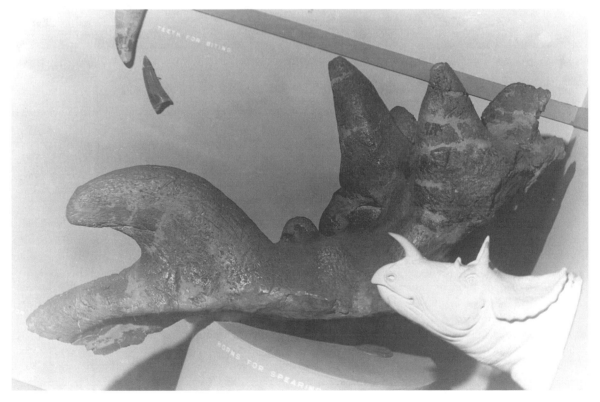

Centrosaurus

Illustration by Doug Henderson. From *Dinosaurs: A Global View*, by Czerkas and Czerkas, published by Dragon's World Ltd. and its co-edition publishers.

A *Centrosaurus* herd fords a flooded Alberta river, flora including flowering plants, and a hardwood tree covered with magnolia, ivy, and stag ferns.

Centrosaurus skin impressions, described by Brown (1917), were part of the holotype of *Monoclonius cutleri*, found overlying the right flank and femur. These impressions consist of small polygonal and large tubercles, all low and of the same height. The small tubercles are five- or six-sided, set closely together, and do not grade up to the larger round ones. Large tubercles are uniformly round and defined by a circumscribing groove, arranged in rows apparently over the ventral surface of the body.

Bone beds, as pointed out by Currie and Dodson (1984), are common in Late Cretaceous strata throughout Alberta, Canada. These provide information about dinosaurs not possible through the study of single skeletons. In Dinosaur Provincial Park, near Brooks, Alberta, numerous bone bed accumulations of various types of large ceratopsians show that the genera *Centrosaurus*, *Chasmosaurus*, and

Monoclonius were contemporaneous, but seemingly moved in their own respective herds. In their report on Quarry 143, a 3,000-square meter (approximately 350-square yard) bone bed opened in 1979, Currie and Dodson noted that about twenty bones, mostly belonging to *Centrosaurus*, were found per square meter. As the *Centrosaurus* remains were found in three major growth stages, Currie and Dodson concluded that these dinosaurs seem to have bred at certain times each year, growth rates were extremely rapid during the first year of life, and individuals represented in this bone bed died at the same time.

Currie and Dodson speculated that, given the numerous bones of a single species of animal, this herd made up of such well defended dinosaurs probably suffered some catastrophic demise. Currie (1987*b*), in the book *Dinosaurs Past and Present*, speculated that the herd may have attempted to cross a river during a flood, many individuals drowning as they crowded together. Currie and Dodson postulated that the *Centrosaurus* carcasses were washed downstream onto sand bars, point bars, or river banks. There, as indicated by shed theropod teeth, the carcasses were scavenged by both small and large carnivorous dinosaurs. The carcasses decomposed in the sun for the duration of the dry season and the skeletons became disarticulated. When the river flooded its banks again, the small bones were washed downstream, while the larger bones were buried in mud and sand.

In the paleontological literature, as well as in popular books, *Centrosaurus* is often regarded as congeneric with *Monoclonius*, the two forms having been synonymized by Brown (1914*b*). Most life restorations labeled *Monoclonius* have, in fact, been based on the more completely known *Centrosaurus*, with its short brow horns, long nasal horn, and the frill with its hook-like process, forwardly directed horns, and scalloped edge. Lull's regarding *Centrosaurus* as a subgenus of *Monoclonius* was based both on cranial differences and on their geographic separation of some 250 miles. Sternberg (1938, 1940*b*), while maintaining the generic separation of these two forms, distinguished *Centrosaurus* by the hook-like processes on the frill, in addition to the rugose bone bordering on the antedorsal border of the orbits, and the different structure of the nasal horn.

As Chure and McIntosh (1989) pointed out, the name *Centrosaurus* was first coined by Fitzinger (1843) for a lacertilian genus, although the name as first intended is apparently not in current usage. If *Centrosaurus* and *Styracosaurus* are found to be congeneric, then the latter name would replace *Centrosaurus*. If *Centrosaurus* remains generically distinct from *Styracosaurus* and the name *Centrosaurus* is held valid in its original usage, then Chure and McIntosh proposed that this genus (or subgenus) be renamed *Eucentrosaurus* (for "true *Centrosaurus*").

Key references: Brown (1914*b*, 1917); Chure and McIntosh (1989); Currie (1987*b*); Currie and Dodson (1984); Dodson (1990*d*); Dodson and Currie (1990); Lambe (1904*a*, 1904*b*); Lehman (1990); Lull (1933); Sternberg (1938, 1940).

CERATOPS Marsh 1888/Rafinesque 1815
Ornithischia: Genasauria: Cerapoda: Marginocephalia: Ceratopsia: Neoceratopsia: Ceratopsidae: Chasmosaurinae
Name derivation: Greek *keratos* = "horned" + Greek *ops* = "face."
Type species: *C. montanus* Marsh 1888 [*nomen dubium*].
Other species: [None.]
Occurrence: Judith River Formation, Montana, United States.
Age: Late Cretaceous (Campanian).

Ceratops montanus, USNM 2411, holotype supraorbital horncores and occipital condyle.

Photo by M. K. Brett-Surman, courtesy National Museum of Natural History, Smithsonian Institution.

Known material: Cranial remains. Holotype: USNM 2411, occipital condyle, pair of supraorbital horn cores.

Diagnosis of genus: [No modern diagnosis published.]

Comments: The genus *Ceratops* was founded upon an occipital condyle and a pair of horn cores (USNM 2411), collected in 1888 by John Bell Hatcher from the Judith River Formation of Fergus County, Montana. For this material, Marsh (1888*b*) erected the new genus and species *Ceratops montanus*.

Marsh diagnosed this genus as follows: Horn-cores of modest length, subtriangular, slightly hollowed at base, almost round in cross-section.

As horned dinosaurs were virtually unknown at that time, Marsh incorrectly believed this form to be closely allied with the plated dinosaur *Stegosaurus*, though regarding it as sufficiently distinct to erect for it the new family Ceratopsidae. From the markings on the horn cores, Marsh knew that they had once been covered with true horn. Marsh (1888*b*) envisioned *Ceratops* as a massive creature measuring from almost 7.5 to about 9 meters (25 to 30 feet) in length. As some large dermal plates not found with the holotype were incorrectly referred to this genus, Marsh (1888*b*) surmised that *Ceratops* also possessed paired dorsal ossifications, thereby creating a chimera that was in fact part ceratopsian and part ankylosaurian.

Lull (1906), believing the name *Ceratops* to be preoccupied (Rafinesque 1815), renamed the genus *Proceratops*, an unnecessary change, as the 1815 name proved to be a *nomen oblitum*. Subsequently, Lull (1933) noted that, in the absence of other cranial features, *Ceratops* was too inadequately represented to diagnose.

Ceratops, generally considered a *nomen dubium* (*e.g.*, Dodson 1990, Lehman 1990), seems to be a valid genus. Trexler (1990), in a preliminary report, announced the recent discovery of the disarticulated remains of a horned chasmosaurine in a bone bed deposit along Milk River in the Judith River Formation of North-Central Montana. Diagnostic elements of this specimen include two robust, procurved brown horns with brain case, parietal bar, right squamosal, and right jugal. The only known ceratopsian similar to this material is *C. montanus*.

Key references: Dodson (1990); Lehman (1990); Lull (1906, 1933); Marsh (1888*a*, 1888*b*); Trexler (1995).

CERATOSAURUS Marsh 1884

Saurischia: Theropoda: ?Ceratosauria: ?Neoceratosauria.

Name derivation: Greek *keratos* = "horned" + Greek *sauros* = "lizard."

Type species: *C. nasicornis* Marsh 1884.

Other species: ?*C. ingens* (Janensch 1920) [*nomen dubium*], *C. roechlingi* Janensch 1925.

Occurrence: Morrison Formation, Colorado, Utah, ?Oklahoma, United States; ?Tendaguru Formation, East Africa.

Age: Late Jurassic–?Early Cretaceous (Kimmeridgian–Tithonian; ?Necomanian–?Hauterivian).

Known material: Five individuals, including almost complete adult skeleton; ?isolated tooth, quadrate, vertebrae, fragmentary fibula.

Holotype: USNM 4735, nearly complete skeleton with skull.

Diagnosis of genus (as for type species): Median nasal "horne"; fusion between metatarsals II–IV; epaxial osteoderms (Rowe and Gauthier 1990).

Comments: *Ceratosaurus* is one of the relatively small number of dinosaurs known to the general public. Its image, with the nasal horn, bony eye ridge, four-fingered hand, and row of small ossicles along the neck, back and tail, is a familiar one in popular books about dinosaurs.

The basis for both the "infraorder" Ceratosauria Marsh 1884 and family Ceratosauridae Marsh 1884, *Ceratosaurus* was founded on an almost complete skeleton with skull (USNM 4735), recovered from the Morrison Formation at Garden Park, Canyon City, Fremont County, Colorado. The remains were collected in 1883–84 by M. P. Felch in the same quarry that yielded the first skeleton of the generally larger and quite different theropod *Allosaurus*. The holotype skeleton was mounted and put on display at the [then United States] National Museum of Natural History.

Ceratosaurus was first described by Marsh (1884), who considered the genus sufficiently different to warrant its own "suborder." Marsh originally diagnosed *Ceratosaurus* as follows: Nasal horn core; cervical vertebrae flat on anterior end, strongly cupped on posterior end [=opisthocoelous], apparently forming weak articulation joint; pelvis birdlike, all bones ankylosed. The genus was regarded by Marsh (1896) as the most "interesting" of all American Jurassic theropods; it was also, at the time of Marsh's (1884) original description, the best known. Marsh (1884) incorrectly figured the pubis as terminating in a distal expansion because, as Gilmore (1920) noted in his osteology of theropods in the United States National Museum collection, he had restored it after that of *Allosaurus*.

Gilmore regarded the nasal horn in *Ceratosaurus* as a familial rather than generic character, perhaps having sexual significance; pointed out that the "prefrontal" bone identified by Marsh (1884) is actually the lacrimal; observed that the tips of the lacrimal

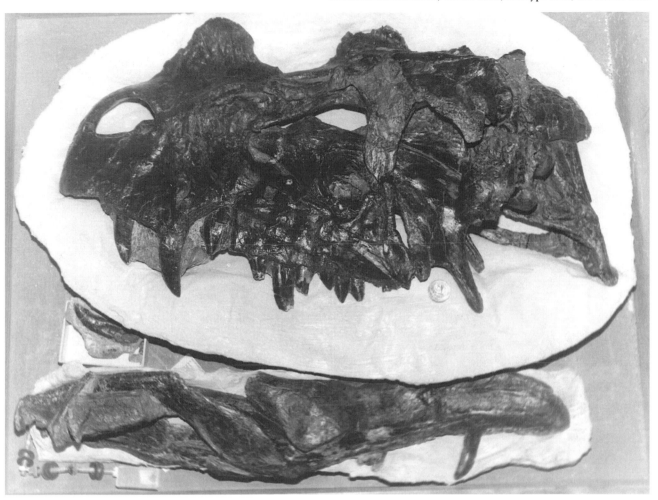

Photo by the author, courtesy National Museum of Natural History, Smithsonian Institution.

horns in *Ceratosaurus* are more sharply pointed than in *Allosaurus* [=*Antrodemus* of his usage], and that the lacrimals were lightened by pneumatic cavities as in the latter genus.

Several dermal ossifications were found with the type specimen of *C. nasicornis*, some in the matrix suggesting their position in the living animal. Gilmore described these ossifications as irregularly shaped, those of the tail region from 25 to 38 millimeters above the summits of the neural spines, those of the neck positioned nearer the vertebrae, indicating a thickness of the skin and muscles between them and the bones. Gilmore suggested that these protuberances comprised a continuous row that extended from the base of the skull along the median line of the back, then down the greater length of the tail. Also found with the type specimen was a small, subquadrangular skin plate with a somewhat smooth ventral and a roughened dorsal surface. The plate measures 58 by 70 millimeters. As the plate had been

freed from the matrix, Gilmore could not determine its probable location in the skin, though its presence did suggest that *Ceratosaurus* possessed other dermal ossifications.

Marsh (1884) suggested that the nasal horn of *C. nasicornis* may have been utilized as both an offensive and defensive weapon, which seems unlikely in that other theropods of comparable size and proportions existed quite adequately without the need for such accouterment. As no other horned theropods were then known, Marsh (1884) surmised that the horn might have been a sexual character. According to Rowe and Gauthier (1990), the cranial ornaments in *C. nasicornis* are so delicately constructed that they, as well as the epaxial osteoderms, were probably used for display rather than combat.

Marsh (1892*e*) observed that the brain of *Ceratosaurus* was very elongate, of medium size, relatively larger than the brains of plant-eating dinosaurs, and situated in the cranium rather obliquely. Huene

Ceratosaurus

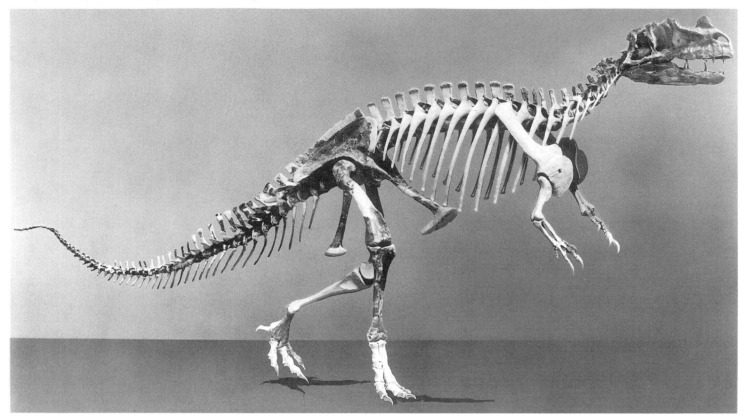

Ceratosaurus nasicornis, USNM 4735, holotype skeleton (with cast of skull).

(1926*b*) later commented that the cerebral hemispheres of the *Ceratosaurus* brain were large, as were the optic lobes. Paul (1988*c*), in his book *Predatory Dinosaurs of the World*, observed that the skull of *Ceratosaurus* is more lightly constructed than in any other known large theropod.

As interpreted by Marsh (1892*e*), the tail in the holotype is quite long (more than half the animal's entire length), high and thin, the anterior caudal vertebrae (except the first) supported by long chevrons, good adaptations for swimming.

The metatarsals are fused together (an avian feature), forming the basis of an extremely strong hind foot. Gilmore proposed that this fusion was a natural though unusual condition, observing that there is little evidence of outgrowths of bone on the metatarsals in the holotype, and that in some theropods, including *Tyrannosaurus* (see Osborn 1906), there is a natural tendency toward such fusion. (Brett-Surman, personal communication 1993, believes that the fusion in USNM 4735 is pathologic.) Believing the type specimen of *C. nasicornis* to be subadult, Gilmore speculated that such fusion would probably indicate an exceedingly aged *Ceratosaurus* individual. USNM 4753 may represent an old animal, also evidenced by

apparent osseous growths of the neural spines (R. E. Molnar, personal communication 1987). Regarding *Ceratosaurus* as a ceratosaur (see below), Rowe and Gauthier noted that the tibia, astragalus, and calcaneum are often separate elements in juveniles, but fused in adults to form a birdlike tibiotarsus.

Based on a review of eight theropod species (*C. nasicornis*, *Syntarsus kayentakatae*, *S. rhodesiensis*, *Rioarribasaurus colberti* [=*Coelophysis bauri* of their usage], *Liliensternus liliensterni*, *Dilophosaurus wetherilli*, *Sarcosaurus woodi*, and *Segisaurus halli*), Rowe and Gauthier (see Rowe 1989; Rowe and Gathier 1990) concluded that these taxa share numerous derived characters that unite them in a newly diagnosed Ceratosauria. *C. nasicornis* was regarded by Rowe and Gauthier as the sister-taxon to other ceratosaurs, the latter more derived though occurring earlier in time. This discordance was attributed to the limited number and incompleteness of the fossil materials referable to *C. nasicornis*, and also to the incompleteness of available morphological data pertaining to this species.

However, more recent cladistic analyses indicate that *Ceratosaurus* may not belong in the Ceratosauria (see Holtz and Padian 1995) at all. Currie

(1995) found the taxon Ceratosauria definable only by plesiomorphic characters if it includes *Ceratosaurus*. According to Currie, the cervical centra of *Ceratosaurus* approach the opisthocoelic condition found in "Carnosauria" (as defined by Currie) one of the reasons, in his opinion, that this genus should be removed from Ceratosauria, redefined, and regarded as the sister-taxon of the "Carnosauria." Through phylogenetic analysis, Currie concluded that most remaining well-known theropods (including avimimids, caenagnathids, dromaeosaurids, ornithomimids, oviraptorids, troodontids, and birds) belong to the monophyletic group Coelurosauria. Supporting Currie's opinion was a study of theropod vertebrae by Britt (1995), who identified a complex (or camellate) internal structure found only in avetheropods and *Ceratosaurus*.

Disassociated bones (UUVP 81), presumably from the same individual, of a much larger *Ceratosaurus* (the average-sized individual presumably about 6 meters [20 feet] long and 2 meters [6.5 feet] high), currently referred to *C.* sp., were removed from the Cleveland-Lloyd Dinosaur Quarry, near Cleveland, Emery County, Utah, during the early 1960s, under the direction of James H. Madsen, Jr. (1976*b*). Madsen and Chure (in preparation) will describe this material as pertaining to an apparently new species of *Ceratosaurus* measuring about 8.8 meters (30 feet) in length (Madsen, personal communication 1993).

Intraspecific conflict between two *Ceratosaurus nasicornis* individuals.   Illustration by Gregory S. Paul.

Ceratosaurus

Ceratosaurus, **anterior teeth of left dentary, lingual view.**

(Late Jurassic; Tithonian) of East Africa. Janensch (1925) also described the species *C. roechlingi,* based on several caudal vertebrae, a left quadrate, the proximal portion of a left fibula, and undescribed vertebral and rib fragments, collected from the upper "saurian bed" northeast of Tendaguru hill in Tendaguru, Africa. According to Rowe and Gauthier (1990), neither ?*C. ingens* nor *C. roechlingi* preserve any diagnostic characters beyond those of Theropoda ancestrally, and should best be regarded as *nomina dubia.* Caudal vertebrae from the middle "saurian" beds of Stegosaurier-Graben, Kindope, north of Tendaguru, referred to *Labrosaurus stechowi,* probably belong to *C. roechling* (Molnar, personal communication).

Stovall (1938) reported a fragmentary specimen attributed to *Ceratosaurus* from the Morrison Formation of Oklahoma. Rowe and Gauthier stated that, although this material may belong to *Ceratosaurus,* it shows no diagnostic characters to justify its classification beyond Theropoda.

Key references: Britt (1991, 1995); Currie (1995); Gilmore (1920); Huene (1926*b*); Janensch (1920, 1925); Marsh (1884, 1892*e,* 1896); Paul (1986*c*); Rowe and Gauthier (1990); Stovall (1938).

A new specimen (MWC 0001) of *Ceratosaurus,* presumably belonging to *C. nasicornis,* was found in 1976 by Thor Erikson, son of paleontologist Lance Erikson, in the area of Fruita, Colorado. It will be described by Madsen and Welles in a forthcoming revised osteology of *Ceratosaurus.* The specimen, which includes the most complete *Ceratosaurus* skull yet recovered, is from a large individual, apparently about as big as an average-sized *Allosaurus.* A cast of the skull was displayed at the Dinosaur Valley exhibit of the Museum of Western Colorado, in Grand Junction.

The first occurrence of *Ceratosaurus* from the Dry Mesa Quarry (Morrison Formation, Upper Jurassic [Tithonian] or Lower Cretaceous [Necomanian or Hauterivian], west central Colorado) was reported by Britt (1991). Britt tentatively referred this material, consisting of six dorsal vertebrae (BYUVP 4951–4952, 8907, 9142–9144), 17 caudals (BYUVP 4838, 4853, 4908, 5092, 8910, 8937–8938), and two left third metatarsals (BYUVP 5020 and 5008), to *C. ?nasicornis.*

Notes: ?*C. ingens* was originally described by Janensch (1920) as a new species of *Megalosaurus,* founded on flat-bladed teeth (HMN MB. R1050), measuring about 15.5 centimeters (nearly 6 inches) in length, recovered from the Tendaguru Formation

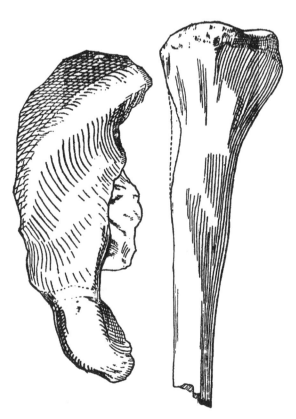

Ceratosaurus roechlingi, **holotype (left) partial left quadrate, (right) partial left fibula (lateral view). (After Janensch 1925.)**

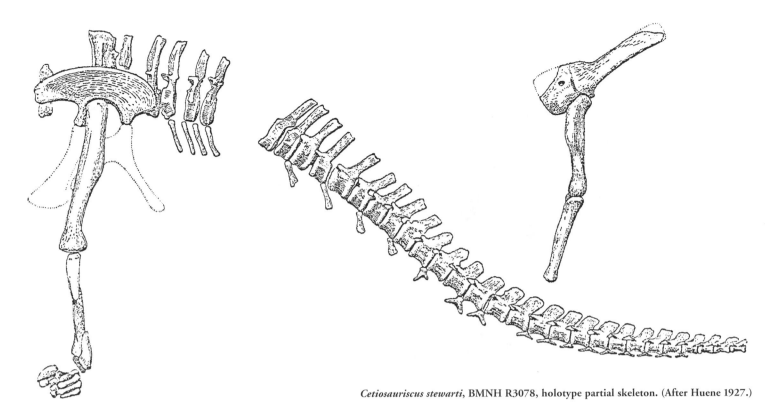

Cetiosauriscus stewarti, BMNH R3078, holotype partial skeleton. (After Huene 1927.)

CETIOSAURISCUS   Huene 1927

Saurischia: Sauropodomorpha: Sauropoda:
  Diplodocidae: ?Diplodocinae.

Name derivation: Greek *ketios* = "sea monster
  [whale]" + Greek *sauros* = "lizard" + *iscus* = "like."

Type species: *C. stewarti* Charig 1980.

Other species: ?*C. longus* (Owen 1842) [*nomen
  dubium*], ?*C. glymptonensis* (Phillips 1871) [*nomen
  dubium*], ?*C. greppini* (Huene 1922) [*nomen
  dubium*].

Occurrence: Oxford Clay, Cambridgeshire, Inferior
  Oolite, West Yorkshire, Forest Marble,
  Northamptonshire, England; Unter-Virgula-
  Schichten, Bern, Switzerland.

Age: Middle–Late Jurassic (Bajocian–Late Bathonian–Callovian–?Tithonian).

Known material: Postcrania, at least five partial
  skeletons without skulls.

Holotype: BMNH R3078, posterior half of incomplete skeleton.

  Diagnosis of genus: [No modern diagnosis published.]

  Comments: The genus *Cetiosauriscus* was first
established upon a pelvis (BMNH R3078) recovered
from the Oxford Clay of Peterborough, Cambridgeshire, England. The specimen was originally
referred by Woodward (1905) to *Cetiosaurus leedsii*,
based on postcranial remains (BMNH R1988) originally described by Hulke (1887) as a new species of

Ornithopsis [=*Pelorosaurus*].

  Later, Owen (1842*a*), upon caudal vertebrae
from the Upper Jurassic of West Yorkshire, erected a
new species of *Cetiosaurus*, *C. epioolithicus*, after
which he (1842*b*) renamed that taxon *C. longus*, referring to it a metatarsal from Blechingdon, England. In
1848, Owen was informed by William Buckland of a
femur (OUM J13617) 1.25 meters (4.25 feet) long. As
this bone corresponded in texture with that of the
Blechingdon metatarsal and also with that of some
long bone fragments from Blisworth, Northamptonshire, Owen (1875) referred that also to *C. longus*.

  Owen (1875) described *C. longus* as follows:
Postzygapophyses represented by hollow pits; both
articular ends of centrum slightly concave, ends
expanded and subcircular, sides between them moderately compressed; undersurface of centrum concave
lengthwise, marked by partial articular surfaces, indicating that hemal arches articulate over vertebral
interspaces; coracoid broad, subquadrate, rounded.

  Later, Huene (1927) erected the new genus
Cetiosauriscus to receive BMNH 3078 in addition to
incomplete postcrania which Huene (1922) had originally described as *Ornithopsis greppini*. However, as
previously noted by Seeley (1889), there were not
sufficient grounds for assuming that R3078 and
R1988 belonged in the same genus, the only common
bone between them being an ilium too poorly preserved for adequate comparison.

Cetiosauriscus

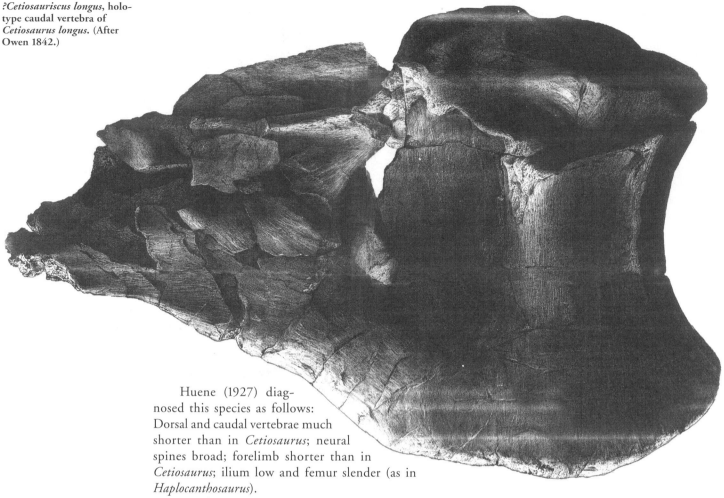

Huene (1927) diagnosed this species as follows: Dorsal and caudal vertebrae much shorter than in *Cetiosaurus*; neural spines broad; forelimb shorter than in *Cetiosaurus*; ilium low and femur slender (as in *Haplocanthosaurus*).

Another species, *Cetiosaurus glymtonensis*, was originally described by Phillips (1871), based on relatively long caudal vertebrae from Northamptonshire. In his reassessment of the Sauropoda, McIntosh (1990*b*) referred this species and *C. longus* to *Cetiosauriscus*.

Eventually, Charig (1980) designated a specimen consisting of the rear half of a skeleton (BMNH R3078) as the holotype of *Cetiosauriscus* and assigned it a new specific name, the genus and species combination becoming *C. stewarti*. This skeleton was exhibited at the British Museum (Natural History) [now Natural History Museum, London] until the late 1970s, when renovation of the museum's dinosaur hall necessitated its removal to the collections.

In his book *Vertebrate Paleontology*, Romer (1956) listed *Cetiosauriscus* as a junior synonym of *Cetiosaurus*, a designation it has generally maintained in the paleontological literature (Steel 1969) and in nontechnical books (Swindon 1970; Norman 1985) ever since. However, Berman and McIntosh (1978) showed that *Cetiosauriscus* shares these diagnostic characters with diplodocids: Wing-like transverse process on anterior caudal vertebrae; apparent *Diplodocus*–like midcaudal chevrons with fore and aft-directed distal ends; "whip-lash" development of the tail; 2.3 humerus-to-femur length ratio; and metatarsals III and IV longest, I clearly showing posteroventral margin on lateral surface. *Cetiosauriscus* was regarded by Berman and McIntosh as a primitive member of the Diplodocidae.

Later, McIntosh noted that it was not entirely clear whether to assign *Cetiosauriscus* to one of two diplodocid "subfamilies," Diplodocinae or Mamenchisaurinae. Pointing out several diplodocine characters exhibited by this genus but not *Mamenchisaurus* (humerofemoral ratio of two-thirds, distal end of metatarsal I with projecting process, apparently no calcaneum), but also noting that the forked chevrons are more like those in *Mamenchisaurus* than in *Diplodocus* and that the bone texture is more sponge-like as in cetiosaurid *Cetiosaurus*, McIntosh tentatively assigned *Cetiosauriscus* to the Diplodocinae.

Key references: Berman and McIntosh (1978); Charig (1980), Huene (1922, 1927); Hulke (1887); McIntosh (1990*b*); Owen (1841*a*, 1842*b*, 1875); Phillips (1871); Romer (1956); Seeley (1889).

CETIOSAURUS Owen 1841—(=?*Cardiodon*)

Saurischia: Sauropodomorpha: Sauropoda:
  Cetiosauridae: Cetiosaurinae.

Name derivation: Greek *ketios* = "sea monster
  [whale]" + Greek *sauros* = "lizard."

Type species: *C. medius* Owen 1842.

Other species: *C. oxoniensis* Phillips 1871, *C. leedsii*
  (Hulke 1887), ?*C. mogrebiensis* Lapparent 1955.

Occurrence: Inferior Oolite, West Yorkshire, Great
  Oolite, Nottinghamshire, Chipping Norton Formation, Great Oolite, Forest Marble, Glouceser-
  shire, Chipping Norton Formation, Forest Marble, Oxfordshire, Great Oolite, Buckinghamshire,
  Great Oolite, Wiltshire, England; Guettious
  Sandstones, Beni Mellal, Morocco.

Age: Middle Jurassic (Bajocian–Late Bathonian).

Known material: Vertebrae and limb bones, two
  partial skeletons without skulls, isolated postcrania, fragmentary limb elements.

Holotype: UMO collection, various postcranial
  remains including caudal vertebrae.

  Diagnosis of genus: [No modern diagnosis published.]

  Comments: *Cetiosaurus* was the first sauropod to
be discovered and described and is one of the geologically oldest known sauropods.

  In 1757, nearly a century before the first description of *Cetiosaurus* was published, a partial femur was
discovered by slate miners working in the Stonesfield
Slate near Woodstock, Oxford, England. The fossil
was turned over to Joshua Platt who, two years earlier, had found three large unidentified vertebrae at
the same location. Platt (1758) figured and described
the specimen, which measured about 75 centimeters
(29 inches) in length, had a minimum width across
the shaft of more than 10 centimeters (4 inches) and
a maximum width of about 21 centimeters (8 inches).
To Platt's thinking, the bone was that of a rhinoceros
or hippopotamus that had perished in the Deluge of
the Old Testament.

  This femur, though proportionately slightly
longer, corresponded in shape and proportions to the
left femur later described and figured by Phillips
(1871), eventually named *Cetiosaurus oxoniensis* by
Lydekker (1888*a*). The specimen has been generally
regarded as a possible early *Cetiosaurus* discovery,
although this bone may not be sauropod and could
belong to a megalosaurid theropod (J. S. McIntosh,
personal communication 1988).

  The genus *Cetiosaurus* was established on various specimens comprising some massive bones
including vertebrae (UMO collection) from the Isle
of Wight, Tilgate Forest in Sussex, Buckingham and
Oxford, England. Owen (1841) named these collective remains *Cetiosaurus* (no species designated), pre-

suming them to represent some huge crocodilian with
strictly aquatic habits. Later, in distinguishing
Cetiosaurus from other then-known dinosaurian genera, Owen (1875) observed that an anterior dorsal
vertebra exhibits a uniformly close though coarse texture as in whales, Owen thereby assuming *Cetiosaurus*
to be aquatic.

  Owen (1842*b*) erected the species *C. medius*
(first announced as *C. hypoolithicus* Owen 1841),
based on caudal vertebrae from the Upper Jurassic
of West Yorkshire. Though the type material is poor,
this was the first valid species and the accepted type
species of *Cetiosaurus* (Steel 1970; McIntosh
(1990*b*).

  In 1868–70, a reasonably complete *Cetiosaurus*
skeleton (approximately one hundred different OUM
numbers, one for each bone, most of them catalogued
from J13622 to J13689 and J13741 to J13748 [McIn-
tosh, personal communication 1987]) was collected
from the Great Oolite (Bathonian), Enslow, north of
Oxford. Upon this skeleton Phillips established the
species *C. oxoniensis*. Owen (1875) noted that the size
of this species almost equaled that of *C. longus*.
Lydekker later selected the more completely known
C. oxoniensis as the type species of *Cetiosaurus*, a designation it still maintains in some modern texts
(Olshevsky 1978, 1991, 1992).

  C. leedsii was based on several vertebrae, ribs,
incomplete pelvis, and many fragments (BMNH
R1988) from the Oxford Clay of Peterborough,
described by Hulke (1887) as *Ornithopsis leedsii*. A
restored femur, according to Hulke, would measure
1.36 meters (over 4.5 feet) in length. Seeley (1889)
suggested that this species was identical to *C.
oxoniensis*. It may, however, belong to the Brachiosauridae (McIntosh, personal communication
1988).

  Described by Lapparent (1955), *C. mogrebiensis*
was based on material representing a large form, collected from Bathonian-age deposits near El Mers, in
the Moyen Atlas of Morocco. These remains include
cervical and dorsal vertebrae, shoulder and forelimb
bones, ribs, pieces of the manus, and a poorly-preserved incomplete pelvic girdle from Tamguert
n'Tarit, the humerus measuring 1.37 meters (more
than 4.5 feet); and scapula, humerus, ulna, ischia,
eight dorsal vertebrae, poorly-preserved ilium, and
right femur from Taghrout, apparently representing
an even larger individual than that collected from
Tamguert n'Tarit. The femur measures 1.60 meters
(almost 5.5 feet) long. An incomplete left femur from
Tamguert n'Tarit is comparable in size to that of the
Taghrout specimen. According to McIntosh, the relationship of this species to *Cetiosaurus* has yet to be
established, *C. mogrebiensis* exhibiting a number of

oxoniensis

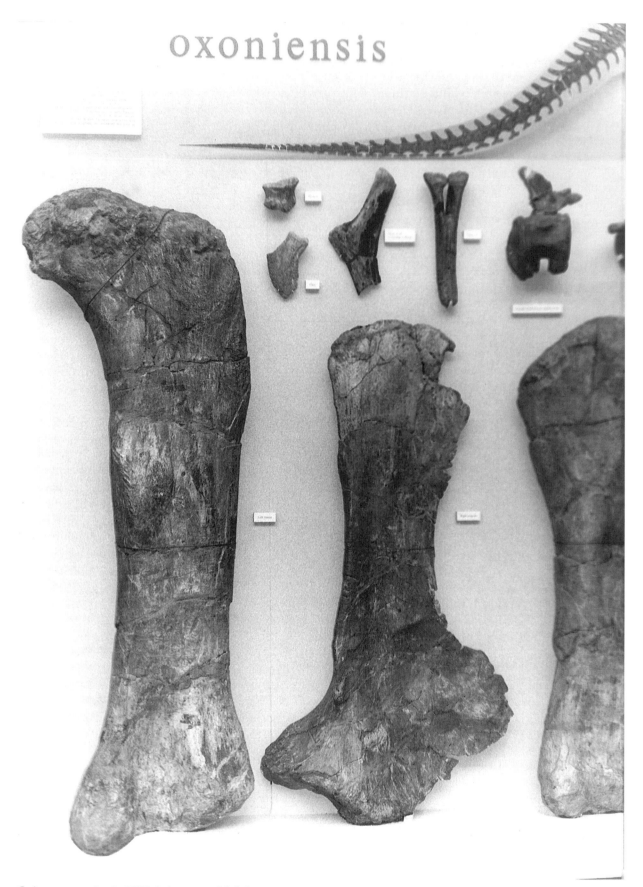

Cetiosaurus oxoniensis, OUM, holotype partial skeleton.

Photo by the author, courtesy University Museum, Oxford.

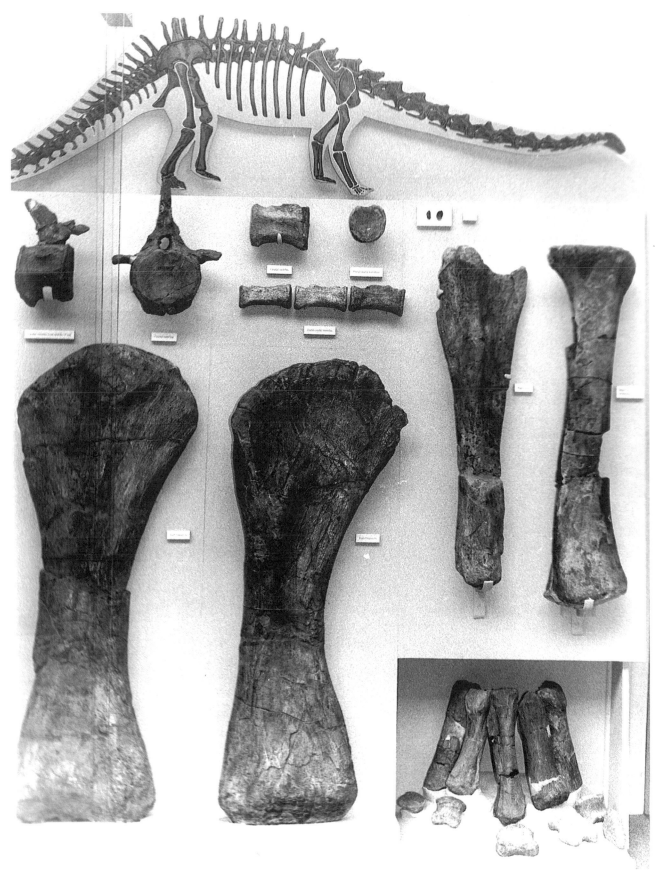

Cetiosaurus oxoniensis, OUM, holotype partial skeleton.

Photo by the author, courtesy University Museum, Oxford.

anatomical differences including a relatively longer forelimb, its respective bones comparatively shorter and more slender.

McIntosh briefly described *Cetiosaurus* as follows: Cervical centra of moderate length; pleurocoels elongated and rather shallow, not complicated by dividing septa known in more derived sauropods; vertebrae with undivided neural spines; middle and caudal dorsal vertebrae amphicoelous or platycoelous, with pleurocoels; neural arches high; spines low; diapophyses directed upward and outward; caudal centra relatively short, amphicoelous, lacking pleurocoels, displaying prominent chevron facets; proximal and middle caudal vertebrae with arches and spines resembling those in *Camarasaurus*; no forked chevrons yet reported; scapula with proximal portion less broad than in most later genera, but with widely expanded distal end; forelimbs moderately long forelimbs, forearm bones relatively long compared to hindlimb; pubis relatively broad; ischium slender, only slightly expanded distally.

Cetiosaurus was a large sauropod with an approximate maximum length of at least 15 meters (over 50 feet).

Swindon (1970) stated in his book *The Dinosaurs* that the deposits from which *Cetiosaurus* remains have been retrieved show evidence of coastal waters, small lakes and lagoons, suggesting a possible environment of this genus.

Notes: Regarded by McIntosh as an unnamed cetiosaurid is "*Morosaurus*" *agilis* Marsh 1889, based on the posterior half of a skull (USNM 5384), and (as depicted in a field sketch accompanying the type specimen) probably atlas, axis, and third cervical vertebra, collected by M. P. Felch from the Morrison Formation at Garden Park. This material was briefly described by Marsh (1889*b*), who, erroneously it seems, listed "other parts of the skeleton" including a hind foot (apparently a right manus collected in 1888, possibly belonging to a different individual or even species), now missing, as part of the type specimen. Gilmore (1907) described this species in greater detail, estimating the animal's length to be more than twice that determined by Marsh.

C. brevis Owen 1842 [*nomen dubium*] was referred to *Iguanodon anglicus* and *C. brachyurus* Owen 1842 [*nomen dubium*] to *I.* "*mantelli*" [=*I. anglicus*] by McIntosh (not yet published, referred to by Ostrom 1970, and so listed by Olshevsky 1978, 1989). According to Chure and McIntosh (1989), *C. rigauxi* Sauvage 1874 [*nomen dubium*] is nondinosaurian.

Key references: Hulke (1887); Lapparent (1955); Lydekker (1888*a*); McIntosh (1990*b*); Owen ((1970).

CHASMOSAURUS Lambe 1914—(=*Eoceratops*)
Ornithischia: Genasauria: Cerapoda: Marginocephalia: Ceratopsia: Neoceratopsia: Ceratopsidae: Chasmosaurinae.
Name derivation: Latin *chasma* = "opening" + Greek *sauros* = "lizard."
Type species: *C. belli* (Lambe 1914).
Other species: *C. russelli* Sternberg 1940, *C. mariscalensis* Lehman 1989.
Occurrence: Belly River [now Oldman] Formation, Alberta, Canada; Aguja Formation, Texas, United States.
Age: Late Cretaceous (Campanian).
Known material: Fifteen complete or partial skulls, several skeletons, integument.
Holotype: NMC 491, median bar and part of posterior transverse bar of crest.

Diagnosis of genus: Premaxillary flange along anterior margin of external naris; supraorbital horncores curving posteriorly; posterior border of parietal fenestra strap-like, with transverse dimension at least twice proximodistal width; frill broadening posteriorly to form triangular shield with maximum width more than twice width of skull at orbits (Forster, Sereno, Evans and Rowe 1993).

Diagnosis of *C. belli*: Parietal frill with almost straight transverse posterior bars, each bearing one large triangular epoccipital process on its posterolateral corner; other parietal epoccipitals variable in

Chasmosaurus belli, GSC 491, holotype parietals, dorsal view. Scale = 18 cm. (After Lambe 1914.)

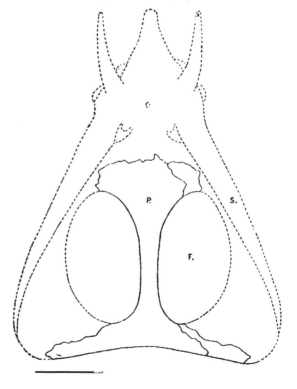

Chasmosaurus belli, skeletons, plesiotype GSC 2245 at right.

number and degree of coossification with parietal, but much smaller; lateral bar of parietal entirely enclosing parietal fenestra (Godfrey and Holmes 1995).

Diagnosis of *C. russelli*: Posterior margin of parietal frill broadly arched on either side of median emargination; each side bearing three low triangular, roughly equal-sized epoccipital processes; lateral ramus of parietal reduced, does not completely encircle fenestra (in all but one specimen), allowing squamosal to form part of its lateral border (Godfrey and Holmes 1995).

Diagnosis of *C. mariscalensis:* Strong anteromedian nasal process extending between premaxillae on internarial bar; supraorbital horncores erect, attaining 85-degree angle to maxillary tooth row (in adults); squamosal with convex lateral frill margin (Forster, Sereno, Evans and Rowe 1993).

Comments: *Chasmosaurus* seems to be the most geographically widespread chasmosaurine genus (Dodson and Currie 1990). The earliest known chasmosaurine, the genus was established a portion of a crest (NMC [formerly GSC] 491) collected in 1891 by Lawrence Lambe from the Belly River [now Oldman] Formation at Red Deer River, in Alberta. Since that discovery, much *Chasmosaurus* material has been collected, including nearly perfect skulls and postcranial remains.

Lambe (1902) originally referred specimen NMC 491 to a new species of *Monoclonius*, which he named *M. belli.* Later, Lambe (1914*a*) described this species in detail based on the plesiotype (NMC [formerly GSC] 2245), consisting of a large part of the skull and skeleton collected in 1913 by Charles H. Sternberg and later displayed at the National Museum of Canada [=Canadian Museum of Nature], Ottawa. Lambe (1914*a*), convinced that this species was ancestral to the Lancian *Torosaurus*, gave it the new name *Protorosaurus.* That same year, when *Protorosaurus* proved to be preoccupied (Meyer 1830), Lambe (1914*b*) renamed the genus *Chasmosaurus*, with *C. belli* designated the type species.

From the plesiotype, Lambe (1914*b*) diagnosed *Chasmosaurus* as follows: Skull large, broadly triangular in superior aspect; facial portion abbreviated, narrow; crest greatly expanded, ending squarely behind face, with epoccipital processes; fontanelles large, subtriangular, enclosed by slender framework formed by coalesced parietals; squamosals very long, narrow, with scalloped free border; supraorbital horn cores small and erect; supratemporal fossae of moderate size; postfrontal fontanelles; jaws robust, with large teeth; body covered with small, nonoverlapping, plate-like scales and smaller tubercle-like scales.

Another species, *C. kaiseni* Brown 1933, was based on a well-preserved skull (AMNH 5401) lacking lower jaws, collected during the American Museum of Natural History expedition of 1913, near "Steveville," Red Deer River. Lull (1933) believed that

Chasmosaurus

Chasmosaurus belli, parietal crest, dorsal view.

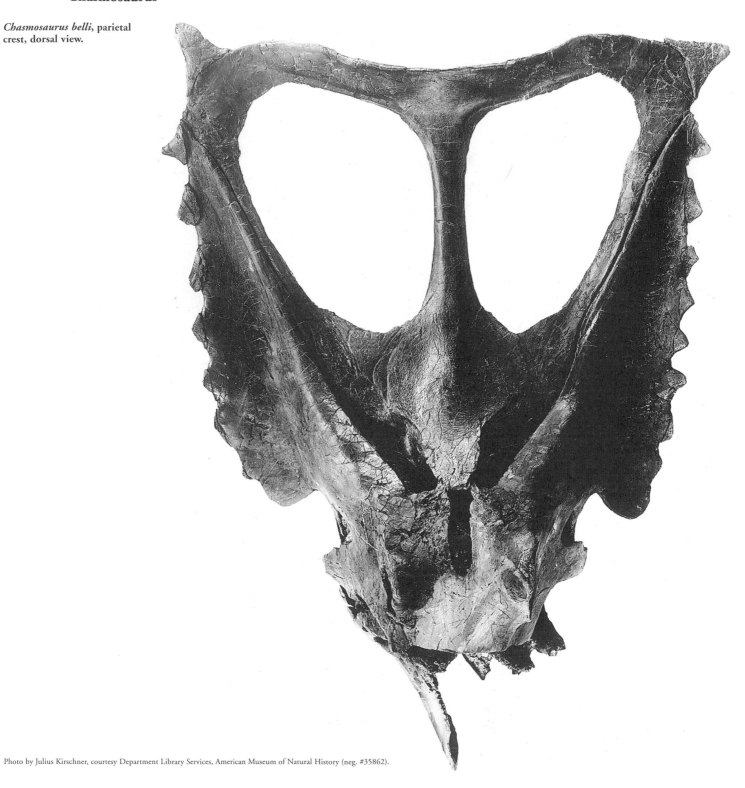

Photo by Julius Kirschner, courtesy Department Library Services, American Museum of Natural History (neg. #35862).

this species was more progressive in brow horn development than the more generalized *C. belli*. Lehman (1989, 1990), recognizing sexual dimorphism in the pattern of brow horns, postulated that those forms with forwardly directed and laterally divergent horns (*e.g., C. kaiseni*) are female, those with erect horns (*e.g., C. belli*) male. In their review of the Neocer-

atopsia, Dodson and Currie regarded *C. kaiseni* as conspecific with *C. canadensis*.

The species *C. brevirostris* Lull 1933 was based on a skull without lower jaws (ROM 5436) collected in 1926 for the University of Toronto at Red Deer River, near "Steveville." Lehman (1989) referred this skull to *C. belli*.

C. russelli was based on a skull missing lower jaws (NMC [formerly GSC] 8800), collected in 1938 by Loris S. Russell from the upper part of the Oldman Formation, east of Manyberries, Alberta, and named by C. M. Sternberg (1940*b*). Two more specimens from the Oldman Formation were referred by Sternberg to this species. These include a skull with lower jaws (NMC [formerly GSC] 8801), much of the crest eroded away, found by D. R. Lowe in 1928, south of "Steveville," plus a skull (NMC [formerly GSC] 8802) collected by Sternberg in 1937 near the same horizon, east of Manyberries, Alberta. The posterior part of the parietals (NMC [formerly GSC] 8803) of another skull was collected by Sternberg, from a bone bed located in 1935 by Roy Graham on the South Saskatchewan River. Sternberg designated these specimens to be paratypes of *C. russelli*. Sternberg diagnosed this species from the holotype and paratype specimens.

C. mariscalensis, the only species of this genus known outside of Alberta, was based upon an accumulation of disarticulated remains representing from 10 to 15 individuals. The fossils were discovered in a bone bed in the upper part of the Aguja Formation (Campanian), Big Bend National Park, Brewster County, Texas. The material included the holotype (UTEP P.37.7.086), consisting of a braincase, left supraorbital horncore, left maxilla, and right dentary; right coracoid P.37.7.142); right pubis (UTEP P.37.7.146); and other remains from the same locality. As the material was all collected from the same locality and stratigraphic horizon and constitute a morphologically homogeneous assemblage, it seems to represent a population sample of a single species (Lehman 1989).

Before *Chasmosaurus* was so named, Lambe (1902) erected the new species *M. canadensis*, based on the right half of a skull with right lower jaw (NMC [formerly GSC] 1254), collected in 1901 by

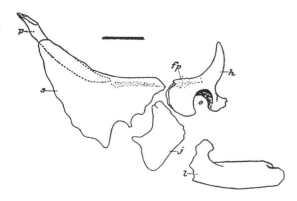

Chasmosaurus belli, NMC 1254, holotype incomplete skull of *Monoclonius canadensis*, right lateral view. Scale = 16 cm. (After Lambe 1902.)

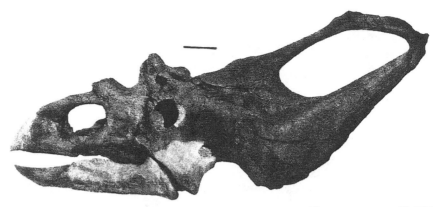

Chasmosaurus russelli, GSC 8800, holotype skull, left lateral view. Scale = approx. 14 cm. (After Sternberg 1940.)

Lambe from the Belly River Series [now Oldman] Formation, Red Deer River. Lambe (1915) subsequently referred this taxon to a new genus *Eoceratops*. Lull (1933) observed that the type material of *Eoceratops* represented an immature individual, some of its perceived specific characters (*e.g.,* small nasal horn and lack of epoccipitals) ontogenetic features. Lull also pointed out that Lambe's (1915) reconstruction of the skull was highly conjectural, the muzzle restored as short and very deep as that condition in ceratopsians typically goes with a short, broad squamosal. Lull found it noteworthy that only one *Eoceratops* skull had been found at a locality so otherwise rich in *Centrosaurus* and *Chasmosaurus* skulls. Lehman (1990) believed *Eoceratops* to be a junior synonym of *Chasmosaurus*, but reserved the possibility of *E. canadensis* representing a distinct species, *C. canadensis*. Lehman (1989, 1990) observed that, since the horncores are erect, the holotype of this species could represent a juvenile or subadult male. Dodson and Currie concurred with Lehman (1990) that *Eoceratops* seems to be congeneric with *Chasmosaurus*.

Chasmosaurus was a modest-sized ceratopsian, the skeleton (NMC [formerly GSC] 2280) exhibited alongside the mounted plesiotype at the Canadian Museum of Nature measuring about 4.8 meters (16 feet) long. The skull, as measured by Lambe (1915), is about .9 meters (3 feet) long. Preserved integument impressions show that the hide consisted of small, closely set, five- or six-sided tubercles that grade up to larger, rounded tubercles.

Though the frill in *Chasmosaurus* is strikingly long, totaling more than half the length of the entire skull, it is not particularly strongly constructed. The fontanelles of the crest are enormous and the posterior edge is quite thin, resulting in a relatively weak structure that was probably not very effective as a defensive shield. More likely, the frill was utilized for the attachment of jaw muscles and for identification than for defense. Farlow and Dodson (1975), in reviewing the function of ceratopsian frills, proposed

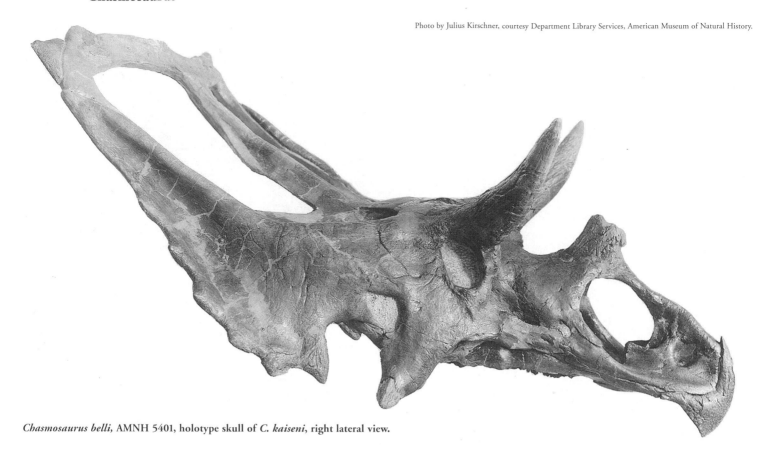

Chasmosaurus belli, AMNH 5401, holotype skull of *C. kaiseni,* **right lateral view.**

that dinosaurs like *Chasmosaurus* probably simply nodded the head forward, or swung it from side to side, to make an impressive threat display.

The *C. mariscalensis* material recovered from the Aguja Formation bone bed revealed a wide range of ontogenetic (from juvenile to adult) and sexual variation. From this variation, Lehman (1989) described fully, for the first time, the postcranial skeleton of *Chasmosaurus,* and also observed that some of the apparent specific differences originally perceived in earlier-named species were actually due to age or sexual dimorphism. Lehman (1989) also observed that *Chasmosaurus* differs from other ceratopsines in having posteriorly curved brown horn cores, postfrontal fontanelle open throughout life, very slender bar-like parietal framework, smaller adult body, and very slender limb bones.

More recently, an almost complete, well-preserved skull (TMM 43098-1) of *C. mariscalensis* was found during a field trip from the University of Chicago to Big Bend National Park, Windy City locality (a site which also yielded some hadrosaurid remains), southwest of Rattlesnake Mountain, Brewster County, Texas. The skull, buried in a small sandstone lens in the "upper shale member" of the Aguja Formation (Late Campanian), was discovered with its left side partially exposed, with the distal portion

of the left brow horn and left half of the frill and jugal weathered away. The specimen reveals that the brow horns in this species are long and erect (Forster, Sereno, Evans and Rowe 1993).

Paul (1987), in the book *Dinosaurs Past and Present,* implied that *Chasmosaurus* was congeneric with *Pentaceratops,* this possibility not disregarded by Dodson and Currie. Lehman (1989) noted that although the adult-sized *C. mariscalensis* does share some diagnostic characters (abbreviated premaxilla, flat-sided maxilla, and larger brow horncores) with *P. sternbergii,* the two genera should be regarded as separate.

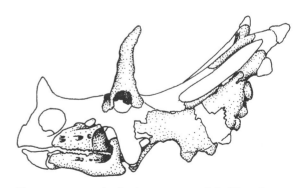

Chasmosaurus mariscalensis, **reconstructed skull based on type specimen UTEP P.37.7.086, and 046, 065, and 066, left lateral view. (After Lehman 1987.)**

Fossilized skin of *Chasmosaurus* showing scalation.

Lehman (1989) found it unlikely that *P. sternbergii* is a direct descendant of *C. mariscalensis*, as the latter species has a shortened and more triangular squamosal, and therefore a comparatively shorter frill than in other less derived *Chasmosaurus* species, a condition possibly derived secondarily from the more elongate squamosal of *C. belli*. Lehman (1989) regarded *C. mariscalensis* as intermediate in many respects between *C. canadensis* and *P. sternbergii*.

Comparing *Chasmosaurus* with other ceratopsids including *Pentaceratops*, Forster *et al.* identified three characters (1. posterior process of premaxilla with blunt, finger-shaped distal end inset on nasal, 2. large parietal fenestra, 3. marked median embayment in posterior parietal margin) that support a sister-group relationship between this genus and southern chasmosaurine *P. sternbergii*. Forster *et al.* concluded that the southern species *C. mariscalensis* displays

characters (1. thin premaxillary flange along anterior margin of external naris, 2. brow horns curved posteriorly, 3. strap-like posterior border of parietal fenestra, 4. posterior frill very broad) indicating a closest relationship to northern species *C. belli* and *C. russelli*; and that the biogeographic history inferred from these relationships suggests that a single southward dispersal event cannot explain the biogeographic exchange between the northern and southern species.

The genus and Canadian species were recently reviewed again by Godfrey and Holmes (1995), based upon an examination of previously collected materials, including all but two known Albertan skulls (BMNH R 4948, a disarticulated skull and postcranial elements, and a skull in Buenos Aires, Argentina, sent there by the Royal Ontario Museum; see Lull 1933), and also upon their description of recently collected *Chasmosaurus* cranial remains from the Belly River [now Oldman] Formation of Alberta, Canada. Previously described skulls reexamined by Godfrey and Holmes include NMC 2245 and ROM 839 (originally 5436), referred to *C. belli*, and NMC 2280 and 8800, referred to *C. russelli*; newly collected skulls, referred to *C. russelli*, were RTMP 81.19.175 (isolated skull preserving right half of cranium and frill except distal segment of parietal bar) and 83.25.1 (frill of large individual).

In describing this newly collected material, Godfrey and Holmes expressed that "lack of detailed cranial descriptions, inconsistent or confused use of diagnostic characters, incompleteness of the material used to diagnose some species, as well as insufficient consideration given to the possibility of sexual dimorphism, geographic and stratigraphic distribution, intraspecific ontogenetic variation, or postmortem distortion in limited sample size have cast doubts on the validity of some species." Godfrey and Holmes attributed most, if not all, of the characters used to diagnose several *Chasmosaurus* species to the following:

1. *Chasmosaurus* skulls were particularly susceptible to postmortem distortion: Height of snout is often exaggerated by lateral compression (as in the species *C. brevirostris*); the expanded frill is especially susceptible to mediolateral crushing and dorsoventral flattening, making establishment of width or even approximate shape difficult; shapes of the orbit, lateral temporal opening, naris, and jugal notch (all commonly used in diagnosing species) are easily distorted.

2. Some *Chasmosaurus* species were named based on misinterpretations of structure: *C. russelli* was characterized in part by a rostral with a straight inferior margin (Sternberg 1940), though the critical part of this element was not preserved; a separate epinasal was thought to diagnose *C.* ("*Eoceratops*") *canadensis* (Lull 1915) and *C. kaiseni* (Brown 1933), though this could only be confirmed by Godfrey and Holmes in the former species.

3. Most taxonomic obfuscation in *Chasmosaurus* can be attributed to intraspecific variation; certain skull dimensions (*e.g.*, frill and length/height ratio of snout) are subject to strong positive allometric growth; small individuals have cranial proportions quite distinct from larger or older individuals.

Godfrey and Holmes explicitly recognized two more or less distinct morphs in the examined *Chasmosaurus* skulls from Alberta: As the differences between these two morphs could not be explained by allometry or sexual dimorphism, the authors further suggested that each morph represents a distinct species: *C. belli* (including junior synonyms *C. canadensis*, *C. kaiseni*, and *C. brevirostris*), characterized in part by a basically unemarginated posterior parietal margin, and *C. russelli*, characterized by a deeply emarginated posterior parietal margin.

These valid species were found by Godfrey and Holmes to be sexually dimorphic apparently in the length of the orbital horncores (males possessing longer brow horns), this being the most frequently cited indicator of gender (Lehman 1989, 1990; Dodson and Currie 1990), although both sexes of *C. mariscalensis* possess long supraorbital horns (Lehman 1989).

Key references: Dodson and Currie (1990); Farlow and Dodson (1975); Forster, Sereno, Evans and Rowe (1993); Godfrey and Holmes (1995); Lambe (1902, 1914*a*, 1914*b*); Lehman (1989, 1990); Lull (1933); Sternberg (1940*b*).

CHENEOSAURUS   Lambe 1917—(See *Hypacrosaurus*.)

Name derivation: Greek *chen* = "goose" + Greek *sauros* = "reptile."

Type species: *C. tolmanensis* Lambe 1917.

CHIALINGOSAURUS   Yang [Young] 1959

Ornithischia: Genasauria: Thyreophora: Stegosauria: Stegosauridae.

Name derivation: "Chialing River" + Greek *sauros* = "lizard."

Type species: *C. kuani* Yang [Young] 1959.

Other species: [None.]

Occurrence: Shangshaximiao Formation, Sichuan, People's Republic of China.

Age: Middle or earliest Late Jurassic (Oxfordian or Kimmeridgian).

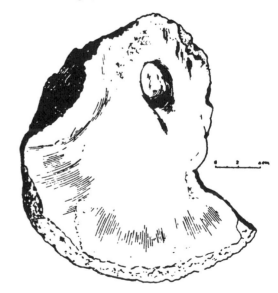

Chialingosaurus kuani, IVPP V2300, holotype coracoid. Scale in centimeters. (After Yang [Young] 1959.)

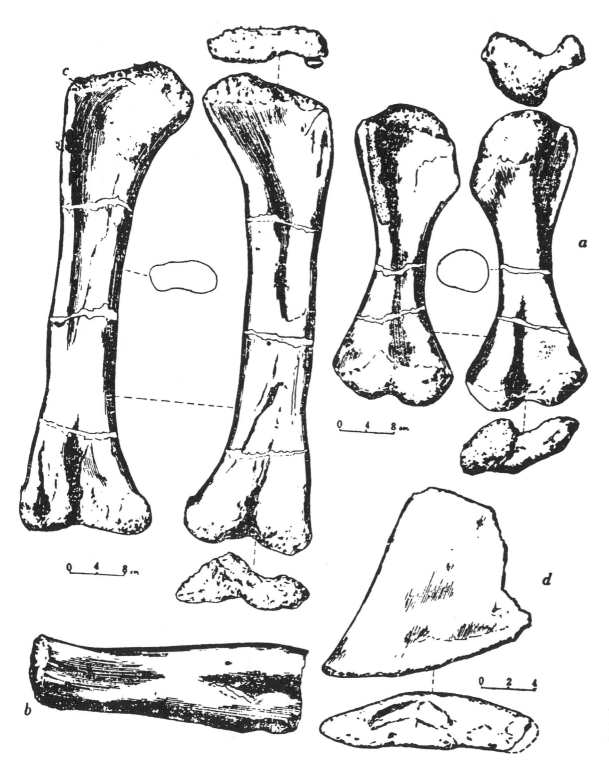

Known material: Incomplete postcranial
remains.

Holotype: IVPP V2300, six vertebrae, three dermal spines, middle portion of left scapula, coracoids,
humeri, right radius, distal portion of right ischium,
left femur, metatarsal III, limb-bone fragments.

Diagnosis of genus (as for type species):

Medium-size stegosaur of slender proportions; skull
higher and narrower than in *Stegosaurus* and *Tuojiangosaurus*, with vertical quadrate, fewer teeth than
in later forms, teeth not overlapping each other, and
thick, deep lower jaw; femoral length-humeral
height ratio relatively high (1.62); femur slender,
straight, with no fourth trochanter; dermal

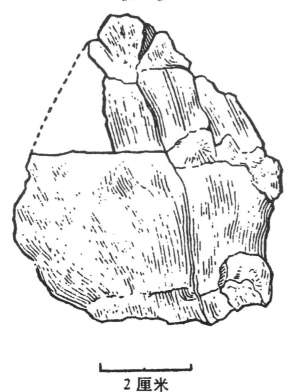

Chialingosaurus kuani, CV 202, referred dermal plate. Scale in centimeters. (After Yang [Young] 1959.)

2 厘米

ossifications include rather small, plate-like spines (Dong 1990*b*).

Comments: *Chialingosaurus*, the first stegosaur to be found and named in Asia, was established on a partial postcranial skeleton (IVPP V2300) collected from Taipingstai, Yunghsing, Chuhsien, Szechuan [now Sichuan] province, China. A referred specimen (CV 202) consists of a fragmentary skull with lower jaws, a few vertebrae, incomplete limb bones, and four dermal plates.

Yang [formerly Young] (1959*a*) originally diagnosed *Chialingosaurus* as follows: Relatively primitive stegosaur of slender proportions; forelimb relatively long, humerus-to-femur length ratio 1.62; femur straight, slender, lacking fourth trochanter; dermal spines somewhat small and plate-like, seemingly arranged in two paired rows extending from neck to tail.

Chialingosaurus seems to be less specialized in its dermal ossifications than such later stegosaurs as *Kentrosaurus* and *Stegosaurus*.

In a review of the Stegosauria, Galton (1990*b*) stated that the only unique derived character shown by this form is in the femur (triangular lesser trochanter with broad base).

Key references: Dong (1990*b*); Galton (1990*b*); Yang [Young] (1959*a*).

CHIAYÜSAURUS Bohlin 1953 [*nomen dubium*]

Saurischia: Sauropodomorpha: Sauropoda: ?Camarasauridae *insertae sedis*.

Name derivation: "Chia-yu-kuan" [place in China] + Greek *sauros* = "lizard."

Type species: *C. lacustris* Bohlin 1953 [*nomen dubium*].

Other species: [None.]

Occurrence: Keilozo Formation, Xinjiang Uygur Ziziqu, People's Republic of China.

Age: Late Jurassic (Oxfordian–Kimmeridgian).

Known material/holotype: IVPP collection, posterior tooth.

Diagnosis of genus: [None published.]

Comments: The genus *Chiayüsaurus* was established upon a single tooth (IVPP collection), recovered at Chia-yu-kuan in northwestern China (Keilozo Formation, Dong 1977; Oxfordian–Kimmeridgian, Dong, personal communication to Weishampel 1990*a*).

The tooth was described by Bohlin (1953) as follows: Spatulate; concavity on inner side occupying only distal half of height, proximal half broadly convex; pronounced rib near posterior border within concavity; "wing" shorter and thinner than main part of crown, posterior to rib; external side of tooth strongly convex; enamel surface densely covered with almost microscopical ridges and "warts."

Bohlin observed that the tooth crown agrees in size with average-sized teeth of the geologically younger *Euhelopus* [=*Helopus* of his usage], measuring 27 millimeters along the middle, 13 millimeters anteroposteriorly, and 8 millimeters lateromedially. In *Chiayüsaurus* (and *Asiatosaurus*), the internal rib is removed backwards; in *Camarasaurus* and *Euhelopus* it is more symmetrically located. Bohlin distinguished this tooth from other camarasaurid teeth by a very high basal portion on its lingual side.

Key reference: Bohlin (1953).

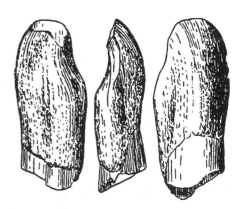

Chiayüsauros lacustris, IVPP, holotype tooth, lingual, posterior, and labial views. Scale = 1 cm. (After Bohlin 1953.)

CHILANTAISAURUS Hu 1964

Saurischia: Theropoda: Tetanurae: Avetheropoda: Allosauroidea: Allosauridae.

Name derivation: "[Lake] Chilantai" + Greek *sauros* = "lizard."

Type species: *C. tashuikouensis* Hu 1964 (Type).

Other species: *C. maortuensis* Hu 1964, ?*C. sibiricus* (Riabinin 1914), ?*C. zheziangensis* Dong 1979.

Occurrence: [Unnamed formation], Nei Mongol Zizhiqu, People's Republic of China; ?Turgingskaya Svita, Buriat-mongolskaya Avtonommays S.S.R.

Age: Late Cretaceous (Albian).

Known material: Incomplete skull with postcranial skeleton, fragmentary postcrania, isolated metatarsal.

Holotype: IVP AS 2884, right humerus, first ungual phalanx of manus, fragmentary ilium, femora, right fibula, right metatarsals II–IV, left metatarsals III–IV.

Diagnosis of genus (as for type species): Long and massive humerus; foreclaws unusually large, digit I with strongly recurved ungual; femur longer than tibia, with moderately-developed fourth trochanter; metatarsals short, not coalesced (Hu 1964).

Diagnosis of *C. tashuikouensis*: Skull of moderate size, with proportionately large occipital condyle, relatively small quadrate; twelve maxillary teeth (Hu 1964).

Comments: The genus *Chilantaisaurus*, type species *C. tashuikouensis*, was founded upon postcranial remains (IVP AS 2884), collected from Alashan, Chilantai, Tashuikou, People's Republic of China. The material was collected at the Tao Suei-Kou site during the Soviet-Chinese Paleontological Expedition to Inner Mongolia in 1960 (Hu 1964).

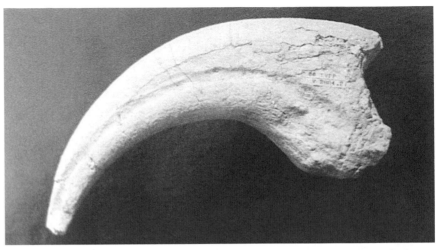

Chilantaisaurus tashnikouensis, IVP AS 2884.2, holotype manual claw. (After Dong 1987.)

Also described by Hu was a second species, *C. maortuensis*, based on the posterior part of the skull, right maxilla, axis, and six caudal vertebrae, recovered from Maortu, north of Chilantai, Alashan, referred to *Chilantaisaurus* because of similarities in the caudal vertebrae.

Molnar, Kurzanov and Dong (1990) observed that the two species of *Chilantaisaurus* have few elements in common, thereby making their mutual relationship yet to be determined.

A third species, originally named *Allosaurus [?] sibiricus* Riabinin 1914 was based on the distal portion of a fourth metatarsal from the Turga Formation (Lower Cretaceous), Tarbagatay Mines, Transbaikal, Udinsk, Siberia. As this specimen in distal view is almost identical to the metatarsal of *C. tashuikouensis* in form and proportions of the distal condyle, because both differ in these features from other theropods, and given the similarity of locality and

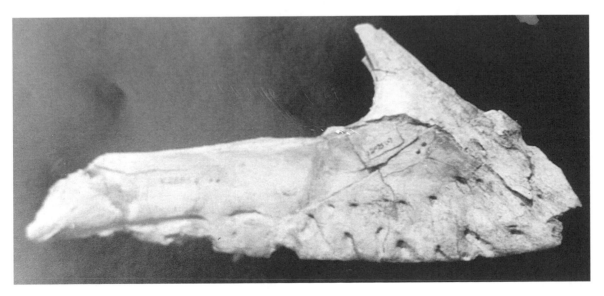

Chilantaisaurus maortuensis, IVP AS 2885.4, holotype right maxilla, right lateral view. (After Dong 1987.)

age, Molnar *et al.*. tentatively referred this species to *Chilantaisaurus*.

Rozhdestvensky (1970), observing similarities between *Chilantaisaurus* and *Alectrosaurus*, proposed that the two forms might be congeneric. However, while the two genera are more or less similar, their synonymy has not been accepted (Mader and Bradley 1989; Molnar *et al.*. 1990).

Paul (1988*b*) suggested that *Chilantaisaurus* was an allosaurid included with *Allosaurus* in the subfamily Allosaurinae. As observed by Molnar *et al.*., *Chilantaisaurus* shares with *A. fragilis* a declined paroccipital process and shortened axial centrum, the latter feature also seen in tyrannosaurids. The caudal attenuation of the proximal portion of metatarsal III is seemingly intermediate between the nonattenuate condition in *A. fragilis* and attenuate in tyrannosaurids, indicating that, at least in the morphology of the metatarsals, *Chilantaisaurus* may be a form intermediate between typical allosaurids and tyrannosaurids. The shortened axis in *C. maortuensis* could be a feature related to size, convergent with tyrannosaurids; but the promixal attenuation of metatarsal III in *Chilantaisaurus* is probably not size related, perhaps intimating a closer kinship with tyrannosaurids than allosaurids. Molnar *et al.*. concluded that *Chilantaisaurus* belonged in the Allosauridae.

C. zheziangensis, a species described by Dong (1979), was based upon a manual claw (NIGP collection) from the Upper Cretaceous (Santonian–Campanian) of Nanshiung province, China. Dong (personal communication to Molnar 1984) noted that this may have been based on part of the holotype of *Nanshiungosaurus brevispinus*. As suggested by Barsbold and Maryańska (1990), *C. zheziangensis* is probably a "segnosaurian" [=therizinosaur], the structure of the pedal phalanges and large decurved claws quite similar to *Segnosaurus galbinensis*.

Key references: Dong (1979); Hu (1964); Mader and Bradley (1989); Molnar, Kurzonov and Dong (1990); Riabinin (1914); Rozhdestvensky (1970).

CHINDESAURUS Long and Murry 1995

Saurischia: Theropoda: ?Herrerasauridae.

Name derivation: "Chinde [Point]" + Greek *sauros* = "lizard."

Type species: *C. bryansmalli* Long and Murry 1995.

Other species: [None.]

Occurrence: Chinle Formation, Arizona, Bull Canyon Formation, New Mexico, "PreTecovas" and Tecovas Formation, Dockum Group, Texas, United States.

Age: Late Triassic (?Middle Carnian–Early Norian).

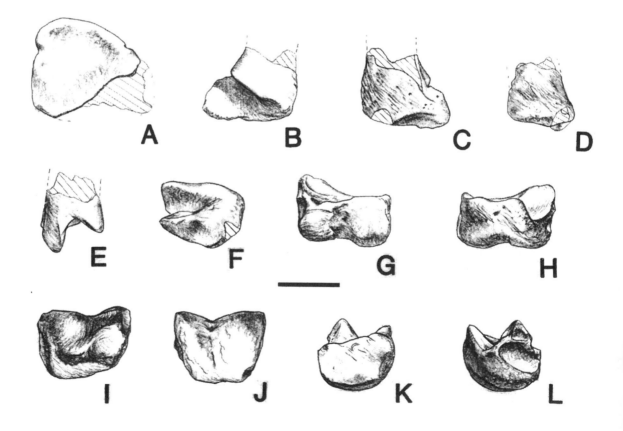

Chindesaurus bryansmalli, PEFO 10395, holotype A, right tibia, proximal view; B–F, distal end of tibia, (B) anterior, (C) posterior, (D) medial, (E) lateral, and (F) distal views; G–L, right astragalus, (G) anterior, (H) posterior, (I) proximal, (J) distal, (K) medial, and (L) lateral views. Scale = 2 cm. (After Long and Murry 1995.)

Known material: Incomplete skeleton, also numerous postcranial elements representing at least eight individuals.

Holotype: PEFO 10395, partial skeleton including incomplete cervical centrum, posterior dorsal vertebrae, two sacral vertebrae, caudal vertebrae, portions of fragmentary right and left ilia, proximal extremity of right pubis, considerable portion of left pubic shaft, complete (crushed) right and fragmentary left femora, fragmentary right tibia, complete right astragalus, rib fragments, chevron.

Diagnosis of genus (as for type species): Autapomorphies include astragalus bearing prominent cleft anteriorly, continuing posteriorly across distal astragalar surface as a groove; distal astragalar surface glutealform in outline, with anterior margin much wider than posterior margin; astragalus with prominent posteroproximal projection beyond proximal articular surface (Long and Murry 1995).

Comments: The genus *Chindesaurus* was founded upon a poorly preserved, incomplete postcranial skeleton (about 50 bones apparently representing a single individual) found in August, 1984 by Bryan Small, and collected during that and the following year by him and a University of California, Berkeley, Museum of Paleontology party led by Robert A. Long from the lower and upper Petrified Forest Member of the Chinle Formation, at Chinde Point, Petrified Forest National Park, Arizona. The bones were found in this isolated pocket along with those of the nondinosaurian reptile *Chatterjeea elegans*.

Remains referred to the type species *C. bryansmalli* include the following material: From Arizona, from the lower Petrified Forest Member, Chinle Formation (Late Carnian), Apache County, five dorsal centra (UCMP collection) recovered from the *Placerias* Quarry, and from the upper Petrified Forest Member, Chinle Formation (Early Norian), Apache County, two co-ossified sacral vertebrae (UCMP) from a larger individual than the holotype from Dinosaur Hollow, and a dorsal vertebra (PEFO 4849) from Chinde Point; from New Mexico, the Bull Canyon Formation (Early Norian), Bull Canyon, Guadeloupe and Quay Counties, the proximal end of a left femur (NMMNH P4415), from Revuelto Creek various dorsal and caudal centra (NMMNH P16656), and from Barranca a complete dorsal centrum (NMMNH P17325); and from the Dockum Group, in Texas, from the "PreTecovas Horizon" (?Middle Carnian), TMM Site 3, Quarry 3, Howard County, the proximal portion of a left femur, and from the Tecovas Formation (Late Carnian), Crosby County, a right ilium (Long and Murry 1995).

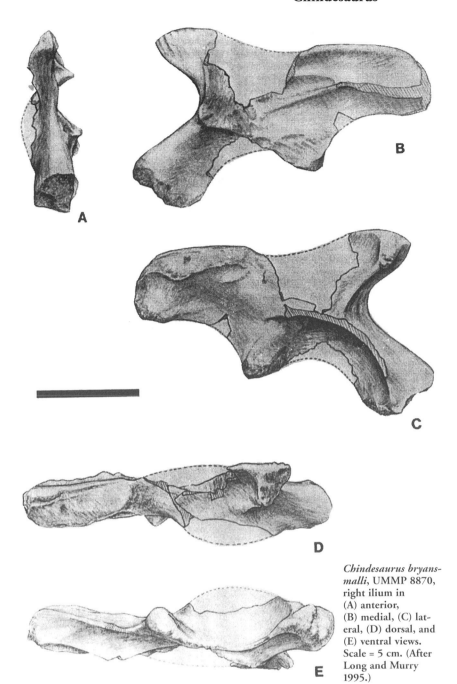

Chindesaurus bryansmalli, UMMP 8870, right ilium in (A) anterior, (B) medial, (C) lateral, (D) dorsal, and (E) ventral views. Scale = 5 cm. (After Long and Murry 1995.)

Prior to the above discoveries, Case (1927) had figured a small right ilium (UMMP 8870) recovered from an unknown locality in Crosby County, Texas, which he referred, along with other material, to the ceratosaur genus "*Coelophysis*" [=*Rioarribasaurus*], found in abundance at the Ghost Ranch quarry in New Mexico. As observed by Long and Murry, this ilium differs significantly from that of *Rioarribasaurus* (=Ghost Ranch "*Coelophysis*" of their usage) and any other known ceratosaur, but compares most closely with that of *Staurikosaurus pricei* and, to a lesser extent, *Herrerasaurus ischigualastensis*, two her-

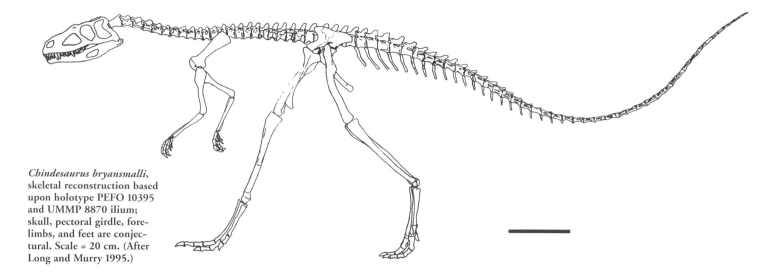

Chindesaurus bryansmalli, skeletal reconstruction based upon holotype PEFO 10395 and UMMP 8870 ilium; skull, pectoral girdle, fore-limbs, and feet are conjectural. Scale = 20 cm. (After Long and Murry 1995.)

rerasaurids from Brazil. Furthermore, although the ilium of PEFO 10395 is represented only by fragments, its preserved posterior blade and pubic peduncle are virtually identical to Case's specimen. On this basis, Long and Murry referred the ilium described by Case to *C. bryansmalli*.

In diagnosing *C. bryansmalli*, Long and Murry noted that the following features are useful in defining this genus and species, although the authors admittedly had not assessed their cladistic importance: Moderately large herrerasaurid (3–4 meters [approximately 10–13.5 feet] long); neck apparently rather long, lightly built; preserved dorsal vertebrae indicating short, compact body relative to greatly-elongate hind limbs (femur = length of nine dorsal centra); dorsal vertebrae amphiplatyan, pleurocoels present (absent in *Staurikosaurus*); probably two sacral vertebrae; mid-caudal neural spines erect (inclined in *Staurikosaurus*), relatively tall, restricted to posterior one-third of vertebra; mid- to distal caudal prezygapophyses long, slender, but not approaching elongation exhibited in *Herrerasaurus*; anterior portion of iliac blade with vertical ridge that "swells" near dorsal margin of blade; anterior blade small, with wide-open notch between anterior blade and pubic process, anterior iliac blade acutiform; posterior iliac blade long and (unlike *Staurikosaurus* and *Herrerasaurus*) about equivalent to length of acetabulum; ventral portion of posterior iliac blade not possessing prominent longitudinal furrow (=brevis fossa); pubic process long and slender (short and thick in *Herrerasaurus*) with anterolateral expansion at distal end; ischial process terminating in relatively sharp point; pubis slender, pubic apron very thin, probably poorly developed medially (wider in *Staurikosaurus*); femur very long and slender, with greatest proximal breadth about equal to one-sixth length

of femur; femoral head well set-off from shaft (considerably more prominent than in *Herrerasaurus*); anterior (lesser) trochanter forming bulbous ridge but with no developed ascending process; trochanteric ridge prominent; fourth trochanter confined to upper half of femur; distal end of femur with no indication of transverse expansion; tibia slender, shallow posterior notch separating medial and lateral tuberosities into unequal parts, lateral tuberosity larger than medial; distal tibial extremity subrectangular, transverse diameter exceeding longitudinal diameter as in *Staurikosaurus* (distal extremity transversely expanded in *Herrerasaurus*), notch for ascending process of astragalus wide anteroposteriorly and deep medially, cutting across two-thirds of distal surface of tibia; astragalus compact, with little anteroposterior compression; ascending process restricted to lateral half of proximal surface; ascending process short, thick anteroposteriorly, beveled anteriorly; ascending process depressing into base of tibia instead of projecting dorsally along anterior surface of tibia.

Long and Murry noted that the astragalus of *C. bryansmalli* differs greatly from that of early ceratosaurs as well as sauropodomorphs, but its compact shape and form of the ascending process compares very closely with the reconstructed astragalus of *S. pricei*. (The authors pointed out that the astragalus in this Brazilian dinosaur has not been preserved, although the distal surface of the tibia shows that the astragalus must have been compact [rather than transversely expanded] as in *C. bryansmalli*, its ascending process deeply imbedded within the under-surface of the tibia. In more advanced theropods, the ascending process wraps around anterior surface of the tibia.) The astragalus in *Chindesaurus* compares most favorably with that of *Herrerasaurus*. However, there are differences between the astragalus in both genera: [Compare with above diagnosis of *C. bryans-malli*] in *H. ischigualastensis*, anterior margin of distal surface is shallowly concave, with no groove transversing ventral surface; outline of distal surface is subrectangular; distinct fibular facet (lacking or not preserved in *C. bryansmalli*) on astragalus is present lateral to ascending process; posteroproximal projection is laterally situated and far less extensive than in *Chindesaurus*. These differences prompted the authors to use caution in assigning *Chindesaurus* to a family.

Long and Murry provisionally referred *Chindesaurus* to the Herrerasauridae on the basis of the following synapomorphies: Reduction of sacral vertebrae to two; reduction of brevis shelf and fossa; presence of iliac tuberosity; and deepening of posterior dorsal centra. The long, low posterior iliac blade and acutely pointed anterior iliac blade suggested to Long and Murry that, at least in terms of characters of the ilium, *Chindesaurus* was less derived than *Staurikosaurus*.

On the basis of the very long and slender femur (approximately nine times the length of the dorsal centra), Long and Murry envisioned *Chindesaurus* as a very long-limbed, short bodied cursorial dinosaur having a primitive pelvis and tarsus.

Note: Popular accounts (*e.g.,* in newspaper and magazine articles, television news and talk shows, video documentaries, *etc.*) of the discovery of this dinosaur had appeared for almost a decade before the new genus was formally named, some of which incorrectly heralded it as the most primitive dinosaur yet known. Long first referred to this dinosaur as a "plateosaur" and nicknamed it "Gertie" (after the animated character created by cartoonist Winsor McCay for a short film first shown in 1912). In a preliminary announcement, Murry and Long (1989) stated that the new genus would be later described as "Chindesaurus bryansmalli."

Key references: Case (1927); Long and Murry (1995); Murry and Long (1989).

CHINGKANKOUSAURUS   Yang [Young] 1958

Saurischia: Theropoda: Tetanurae: Avetheropoda: Coelurosauria: Maniraptora: Arctometatarsalia: Tyrannosauridae.

Name derivation: "Chingkankou [village]" + Greek *sauros* = "lizard."

Type species: *C. fragilis* Yang [Young] 1958.

Other species: [None.]

Occurrence: Wangshi Series, Shandong, People's Republic of China.

Age: Late Cretaceous (Campanian–Early Maastrichtian).

Known material/holotype: IVP AS 636, right scapula.

Diagnosis of genus (as for type species): Scapula basically resembling that of *Allosaurus*, but smaller, with very weak distal expansion (Yang [Young] 1958).

Comments: The genus *Chingkankousaurus* was established on a right scapula, collected from the Wangshi Series, Shantung [now spelled Shandong], Chingkankou, China (Young [Yang] 1958).

Molnar, Kurzanov and Dong (1990) referred *C. fragilis* to the Tyrannosauridae on the basis of its very slender scapular blade.

Key references: Molnar, Kurzanov and Dong (1990); Yang [Young] (1958).

Chingkankosaurus zhongheensis, **IVP AS 636 holotype right scapula. (After Yang [Young] 1958.)**

CHIROSTENOTES Gilmore 1924—
(=*Macrophalangia*; =?*Caenagnathus*, ?*Dromaeosaurus*, ?*Ricardoestia*)
Saurischia: Theropoda: Tetanurae: Avetheropoda: Coelurosauria: Maniraptora: Arctometatarsalia: Elmisauridae.
Name derivation: Greek *cheir* = "hand" + Greek *steno* = "narrow."
Type species: *C. pergracilis* Gilmore 1924.
Other species: [None.]

Occurrence: Oldman Formation, Dinosaur Park Formation, Horseshoe Canyon Formation, Alberta, Canada.
Age: Late Cretaceous (Middle Campanian–Early Maastrichtian).
Known material: Incomplete skeleton, pes, two manus, sacrum, isolated elements.
Holotype: NMC 2367, right manus, left manus.
    Diagnosis of genus (as for type species): Medium-sized theropod weighing, when mature,

Chirostenotes pergracilis, NMC 2367, holotype right and left manus.

Photo by the author, courtesy Royal Tyrrell Museum/Alberta Community Development.

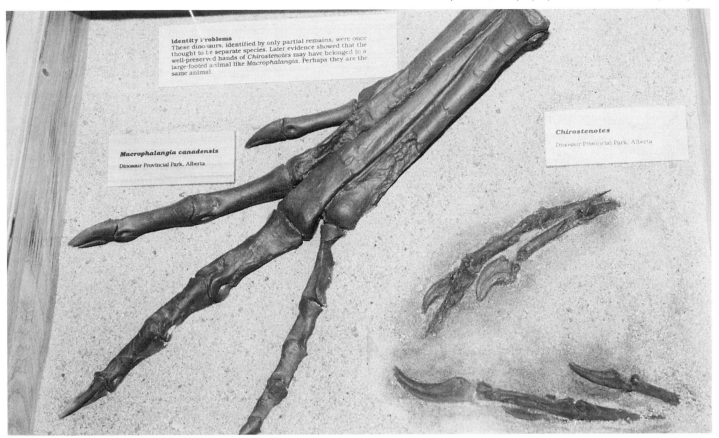

Identity Problems
These dinosaurs, identified by only partial remains, were once thought to be separate species. Later evidence showed that the well-preserved hands of *Chirostenotes* may have belonged to a large-footed animal like *Macrophalangia*. Perhaps they are the same animal.

Macrophalangia canadensis
Dinosaur Provincial Park, Alberta

Chirostenotes
Dinosaur Provincial Park, Alberta

Chirostenotes pergracilis, NMC 8538, (cast) holotype right pes of *Macrophalangia canadensis*, with NMC 2367, (cast) holotype right and left manus of *C. pergracilis*.

between 35 and 40 kilograms (about 76 to 88 pounds); six sacral vertebrae with pleurocoels; manual digit III longer than I, phalanges of III slender, with diameter of less than one half that of phalanges of other digits; manual unguals with well-developed "lip" (as in *Elmisaurus* and *Oviraptor*); pelvis dolichoiliac and prepubic, preacetabular portion of iliac blade longer than postacetabular portion; metatarsal III proximally pinched between metatarsals II and IV, only the proximal tip excluded from anterior surface of the metatarsus (as in *Elmisaurus* and ?*Oviraptor*); tarsometatarsus in old individuals ?fused (as in *Elmisaurus*) (Currie and Russell 1988).

Comments: The taxonomic history of the genus now understood to be *Chirostenotes* involves a number of genera and species:

Prior to the naming of *Chirostenotes*, Marsh (1888*a*) described some elongated, thin-walled metapodials and an ungual phalanx, collected by John Bell Hatcher from the Potomac Formation (Lower Cretaceous) of Maryland. Marsh referred this material to the genus *Coelurus* as the holotype of new species *C. gracilis*.

The genus *Chirostenotes* was founded upon a left and right three-digit manus (NMC 2367) collected from the former Belly River [now Oldman] Formation at Little Sandhill Creek, Red Deer River, "Steveville," Alberta, Canada.

Gilmore (1924) originally diagnosed *Chirostenotes* as follows: Digit II greatly elongate; metacarpals and phalanges laterally compressed.

At the same time noticing the close similarity between the *C. gracilis* type material and unguals of *Chirostenotes*, Gilmore referred Marsh's species to this genus. Later, Ostrom (1980), able to locate only the ungual (USNM 4973), stated that "*C. gracilis*," established on inadequate material, should be regarded as a *nomen dubium*.

Another new genus, *Macrophalangia*, was founded on the distal end of a right tibia with part of the astragalus, two incompletely preserved distal tarsals, and complete right pes missing only the proximal halves of metatarsals III and IV. The material (NMC [formerly GSC] 8538) was collected from the Dinosaur Park Formation, southwest of the mouth of Berry Creek ("Steveville"), Red Deer River, and described by Sternberg (1932a).

As the foot of *Macrophalangia* resembles that of *Ornithomimus* and *Struthiomimus*, particularly in the greatly elongated phalanges and decurved unguals, and in the lateral compression of the proximal end of metatarsal III, Sternberg (1923a) proposed that this genus be placed in the Ornithomimidae.

Yet another taxon, a species originally referred to *Ornithomimus* as new species *O. elegans*, was based on a left metatarsus (ROM 4758) collected in 1926 by the University of Toronto, from the Dinosaur Park Formation, Sand Creek, Red Deer River. The specimen was described by Parks (1933), who, comparing its size to *Struthiomimus altus* and *C. pergracilis*, believed that the smaller species *O. elegans* was a valid taxon. Sternberg (1934), however, suggested that *O. elegans* could belong to *Macrophalangia* or *Chirostenotes*. Russell (1972), in his review of Canadian ostrich dinosaurs, regarded *O. elegans* as a more gracile species of *Macrophalangia*.

Osmólska (1981) later described the remains of *Elmisaurus*, another small theropod with a pes similar to that of *Macrophalangia*. Osmólska erected the family Elmisauridae to receive the new genus as well as *Macrophalangia* and *Chirostenotes*.

Because the pes of *Marcophalangia* and manus of *Chirostenotes* were found in the same formation, it was long suspected that these two forms could be congeneric, although no matching bones had been

collected to substantiate a synonymy. The question was resolved in the summer of 1979, after a field party of the Provincial Park Museum of Alberta found a partial skeleton (RTMP 79.20.1) in a canyon of the Dinosaur Park Formation in Dinosaur Provincial Park, Alberta. Gilles Dannis of the Provincial Museum found a small theropod sacrum weathering out of a cliff in a hard grayish sandstone matrix. The recovered specimen includes sacrum, ribs, coracoid, partial left manus, ilium, ischium, femur, tibia, metatarsus, and pedal phalanges I-I and III-I (Currie and Russell 1988). Also in the bedding plane that yielded this specimen was a considerable amount of fossilized wood, presumably *Metasequoia* (Eberth, Currie and Braman 1988).

At first, Currie (1980) tentatively referred this skeleton to the genus *Dromaeosaurus*, at the same time pointing out that the forelimbs in the specimen resembled those in *Chirostenotes*. With the more complete skeleton from Dinosaur Provincial Park available for comparison, the elements duplicated from both the *C. pergracilis* and *M. canadensis* holotypes revealed to Currie and Russell that *Chirostenotes* and *Macrophalangia* were congeneric.

Based on these more complete remains along with the previously collected specimens, Currie and Russell rediagnosed *Chirostenotes*. Pointing out that *Chirostenotes* shares numerous diagnostic characters with *Elmisaurus*, Currie and Russell concluded that both forms are closely related, differing mainly in the fusion of the tarsometatarsus in the latter genus. Currie and Russell also listed a suite of similarities between *Chirostenotes* and *Oviraptor*, including the relative proportions of manual digits I and III, the dorsoposterior "lip" on manual unguals, shape of the ilium, arrangement of the metatarsus, and six pleurocoelous sacral vertebrae, suggesting a strong relationship between these three genera, all of which seem to have been derived from dromaeosaurid ancestors.

Currie and Russell recognized two morphs pertaining to *Chirostenotes*, one represented by a gracile foot (ROM 781 and RTMP 79.20.1), the second by a more robust metatarsus (NMC 8538). Assuming that these two forms, both closely related and from the same formation, represent a sexual dimorphism, Currie and Russell concluded that all specimens of *Chirostenotes* can be referred to a single species, *C. pergracilis*.

According to Currie and Russell, the long hind limbs and large feet of *Chirostenotes* could be interpreted as wading adaptations, the hands suitable for collecting mollusks, other invertebrates, and eggs. The tail was probably relatively short, as suggested by the short postacetabular iliac blade, short ischium,

Chirostenotes pergracilia, left ilium (TMP 79.20), in a. lateral and b. medial views. (After Currie and Russell 1988.)

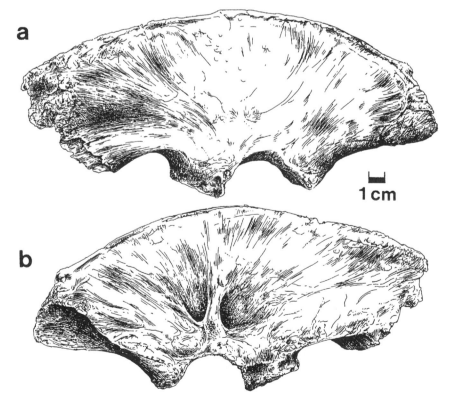

a

b

1 cm

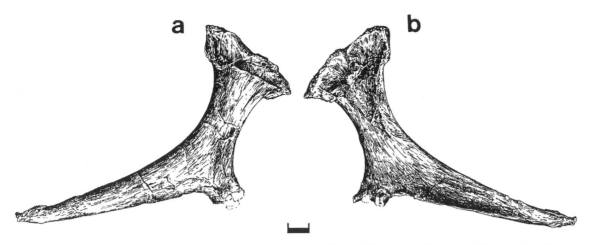

Chirostenotes pergracilis, right ischium (TMP 79.20.1), in a. lateral and b. medial views. Scale = 1 cm. (After Currie and Russell 1988.)

ventrally positioned (more so than in any other known theropod) lesser trochanter of the femur, and long sacrum. The long and slender third manual digit is reminiscent of the syndactylous [or fused, as in many birds] digits in marsupial mammals, but also seems to have been capable of a wide range of adduction and abduction movement independent of the second digit. This suggested to Currie and Russell that the specialized finger of this dinosaur may have been utilized in prying insects and other invertebrates from crevices in trees or streams, or may even have been used in "grooming."

Currie and Russell speculated that *Chirostenotes* may be synonymous with the oviraptorosaur *Caenagnathus*, observing many similarities between the postcrania of elmisaurids and *Oviraptor* (*e.g.,* relative proportions of manual digits I and III, presence of a proximodorsal "lip" on the manual unguals, shape of the ilium, and six sacral vertebrae with pleurocoels). Currie (1990) concluded that these similarities at least suggest that Elmisauridae and Oviraptorosauria are sister-taxa.

Ostrom (1990) observed that the holotype of *C. pergracilis* displays digital proportions and a manus configuration comparable to those in the dromaeosaurids *Deinonychus antirrhopus* and *Velociraptor mongoliensis*, and further suggested that *Chirostenotes* and *Dromaeosaurus*, a dromaeosaurid also from the Dinosaur Park Formation of Alberta, may be congeneric.

Note: The jaws referred by Gilmore to *C. pergracilis* were made the holotype of new genus and species *Ricardoestesia gilmorei* by Currie, Rigby and Sloan (1990).

Key references: Currie (1990); Currie and Russell (1988); Gilmore (1924); Marsh (1988*a*); Osmólska (1981); Ostrom (1980, 1990); Parks (1933); Russell (1972); Sternberg (1932*a*, 1934).

CHONDROSTEOSAURUS Owen 1876 [*nomen dubium*]—(=*Chondrosteus, Eucamerotus*)
Saurischia: Sauropodomorpha: Sauropoda: ?Camarasauridae: ?Camarasaurinae.
Name derivation: Greek *chondros* = "cartilage" +
Greek *osteon* = "bone" + Greek *sauros* = "lizard."
Type species: *C. gigas* Owen 1876 [*nomen dubium*].
Other species: [None.]
Occurrence: Wealden, Isle of Wight, England.
Age: Lower Cretaceous (Hauterivian–Barremian).
Known material/cotypes: BMNH 46869 and
46870, centra of posterior cervical vertebrae.

Diagnosis of genus: [None published.]

Comments: The genus *Chondrosteosaurus* was founded upon two cervical centra (BMNH 46869 and 46870) recovered from the Wealden of the south shore of the Isle of Wight.

Owen (1876) described these vertebrae as follows: Broad ventral surface, with gentle transverse concavity; deep pleurocoel on each side of centrum, between parapophyses and diapophyses (as in *Bothriospondylus*); parapophysis projecting from undersurface; neurophysis beginning to rise about two inches

Chondrosteosaurus gigas, BMNH 46869, holotype posterior cervical vertebral centra. Scale = 4 cm. (After Owen 1876.)

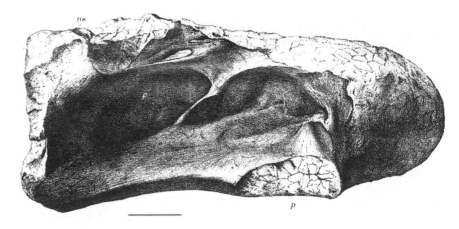

in anterior to posterior cup; base of diapophysis with fore and aft extent of about 9 centimeters (3.75 inches), vertical diameter of about 5.3 centimeters (2 inches); estimated length of complete centrum about .41 meters (1.4 feet); deep oblong depression occupying entire side of centrum; neural canal with diameter about one-fourth the transverse diameter of the vertebral column.

At first not certain of the dinosaurian affinities of *Chondrosteosaurus*, Owen inferred from the neural canal that the center of origin of the motory nerves made *Chondrosteosaurus* a sluggish creature best adapted to living in watery environments (an incorrect conclusion regarding sauropods that has persisted for a century). From that supposition, Owen surmised that the animal, when on land, must have been supported by "limbs of dinosaurian proportions." Owen commented that the vertebrae equaled the length of the vertebra of any known living or fossil whale.

In reviewing the Sauropoda, McIntosh (1990*b*) observed that the large pleurocoel in the type specimen, divided in two by a vertical ridge, is suggestive of brachiosaurids or camarasaurids, although in the former the centrum is short and ventrally flat. Finding the closest resemblance of the specimen to be with the tenth cervical vertebra in *Camarasaurus*, McIntosh tentatively referred *Chondrosteosaurus* to the Camarasauridae.

The genus *Eucamerotus* [no specific name assigned] Hulke 1872 [*nomen dubium*], based on a vertebral neural arch from the Wealden, Isle of Wight, was referred to *Chondrosteosaurus*.

Key references: Hulke (1872); McIntosh (1990*b*); Owen (1876).

Chuandongocoelurus primitivus, CCG 20010, holotype right pes. Scale = .67 cm. (After He 1984.)

CHUANDONGOCOELURUS He 1984 [*nomen dubium*]

Saurischia: Theropoda: Tetanurae *incertae sedis*.

Name derivation: "Chuandong [place in China]" + *Coelurus*.

Type species: *C. primitivus* He 1984 [*nomen dubium*].

Other species: [None.]

Occurrence: Sichuan, China.

Age: Late Jurassic.

Known material/holotype: CCG 20010, axis, caudal vertebrae, partial left ?scapula, fragmentary ilium, pubis and ischium, almost complete right hindlimb comprising femur, tibia, astragalus, calcaneum, and partial pes.

Diagnosis of genus (as for type species): Vertebrae rather concave; cervical vertebrae hollow extensively; scapula somewhat broad; acetabulum rather

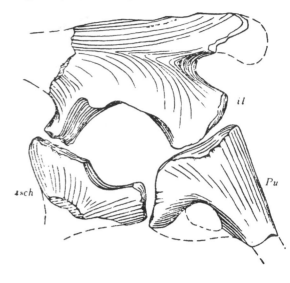

Chuandongocoelurus primitivus, CCG 20010, holotype partial pelvis. (After He 1984.)

large, with marked supraacetabular rim; tibia longer than femur (He 1984).

Comments: The genus *Chuandongocoelurus* was founded upon postcranial material (CCG 20010) from the Kaijiang District, Golden Chicken Commune, Sichuan Province, China (He 1984).

Norman (1990), in his review of problematic "coelurosaurs," observed that the type material of *C. primitivus* may belong to a juvenile individual, as some of the vertebrae seem to have unfused neurocentral sutures. The hindlimb suggests theropod affinities (femur with a simple dorsal curvature to the shaft, prominent cranial trochanter, crested fourth trochanter), but the ascending process of the astragalus is not very prominent, suggesting an ornithopod; rather than strap-like (as in most theropods), the scapula seems atypically broad; the long and slender

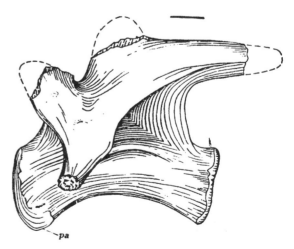

Chuandongocoelurus primitivus, CCG 20010, holotype cervical vertebra. Scale = 1 cm. (After He 1984.)

metatarsus is unfused and exhibits no lateral compression of the proximal end of metatarsal III; metatarsals are symmetrical, II and IV of subequal length; the articulated phalanges of the pedal digit IV are apparently preserved in association with the metatarsus. Norman regarded *C. primitivus* as a *nomen dubium*, the type material being too poor to provide diagnostic characters that justify referring to a binomial taxon.

Key references: He (1984); Norman (1990).

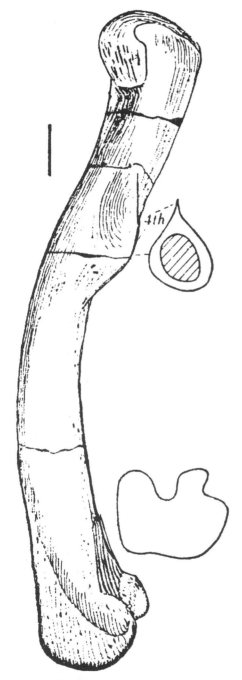

Chuandongocoelurus primitivus, CCG 20010, holotype right femur. Scale = 1.43 cm. (After He 1984.)

CHUBUTISAURUS   Corro 1974

Saurischia: Sauropodomorpha: Sauropoda: ?Brachiosauridae.

Name derivation: "Chubut [Province]" + Greek *sauros* = "lizard."

Type species: *C. insignis* Corro 1974.

Other species: [None.]

Occurrence: Gorro Frigio Formation, Chubut, Argentina.

Age: Early Cretaceous (Albian).

Known material: Two incomplete skeletons, with most limb bones and caudal vertebrae.

Holotype: MACN 18.222, humerus, femur, vertebrae, fragments.

Diagnosis of genus (as for type species): Large, heavily-built sauropod; cervical vertebrae concave-

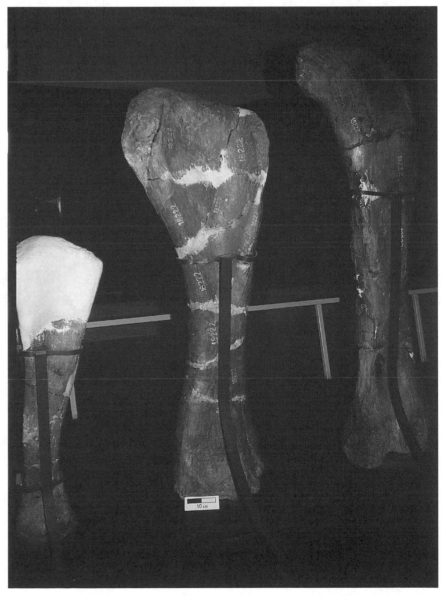

Chubutisaurus insignis, MACN 18.222, holotype tibia, humerus, and femur.

Chubutisaurus

Chubitisaurus insignis, MACN 18.222, holotype proximal caudal vertebrae, lateral view.

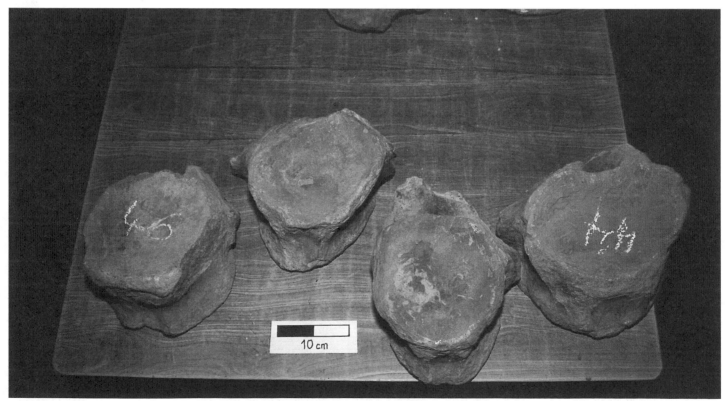

Chubitisaurus insignis, MACN 18.222, holotype proximal caudal vertebrae, anterior view.

convex, with great pleurocoels separated by a bony bar in both upper halves; dorsal vertebrae probably large, flattened anterioposteriorly, great neural spines, large, deep pleurocoels; proximal caudal vertebrae large and compact, with flattened proximal and concave distal surfaces, large transverse apophyses, short, stout and separate neural spines; more distal caudals slightly amphicoelic, lacking such an apophysis; forelimbs shorter than hind limbs; radius short with triangular-shaped distal end; femur large, solidly constructed, with slightly prominent fourth trochanter (Corro 1975).

Comments: The genus *Chubutisaurus* was founded upon postcranial remains (MACN 18.222) collected from the Departamento de Paso de Indios (Late Chubutian), province of Chubut, Argentina (Corro 1975).

Corro placed *Chubutisaurus* in its own family, Chubutisauridae. McIntosh (1990b), however, observed that various characters (including the form of the caudal centra and 0.85 humerofemoral length ratio) suggest assignment of this genus to the Brachiosauridae.

Key references: Corro (1974); McIntosh (1990b).

CHUNGKINGOSAURUS Dong, Zhou and Zhang 1983

Ornithischia: Genasauria: Thyreophora: Stegosauria: Stegosauridae.

Name derivation: "Chungking or Chungqing City" + Greek *sauros* = "lizard."

Type species: *C. jiangbeiensis* Dong, Zhou and Zhang 1983 (Type).

Other species: [None.]

Occurrence: Shangshaximiao Formation, Sichuan, People's Republic of China.

Age: Middle to Late Jurassic (Oxfordian or Kimmeridgian).

Known material: Incomplete skeleton with skull, three fragmentary postcranial skeletons.

Holotype: CV 206, anterior half of skull, teeth, sacral vertebrae, humerus, femur, two almost complete dermal spines.

Diagnosis of genus (as for type species): Small, with high, narrow skull, lower jaw with small teeth; teeth with symmetrical crowns, arranged in single row, teeth not overlapping; five sacral vertebrae, the first abdominal, with three small fenestrae between sacral ribs; femur rounded in cross-section; 1.61 to 1.68 ratio of femoral to humeral length; bony dermal spines thick and plate-like (Dong, Zhou and Zhang 1983); tooth crowns sharp and compressed; femur straight, lacks fourth trochanter; large, thick bony plates with shape intermediate between plates and spines; terminal tail spines (Dong 1990b).

Comments: The genus *Chungkingosaurus* was founded upon an incomplete skeleton with partial skull (CV 206), collected from the Middle–Late Jurassic of Sichuan Basin, Sichuan province, China (Dong, Zhou and Zhang 1983).

Dong *et al.* also described three specimens from the Upper Shaximiao Formation which they referred to *Chungkingosaurus* sp. These specimens include: Sacrum and both ischia (CV 207), recovered from Oilin Park, Chungking City, with ischia "different" from that in the type species; a specimen comprising four caudal vertebrae, right humerus, both femora, and fragmentary bony plates, from the Hua-ei-pa quarry in Chungking City; and ten caudal vertebrae from the distal end of the tail, along with three pairs of caudal spines and traces of the first pair of spines (CV 208) (with the suggestion of a total of four pairs of spines), from Lungshi, Hechuan County, Sichuan Province (see also Dong 1990b).

Galton (1990b), in a review of the Stegosauria, noted that *C. jiangbeiensis* is derived in having a humerus with very broad ends and in the possession of four pairs of terminal tail spines (Dong 1990b); primitive in that the sacrum retains three pairs of large foramina between the transverse processes, and the humerus retains a very proximal deltopectoral crest; and that some dermal osteoderms are intermediate in form between plates and spines.

Key references: Dong (1990); Dong *et al.* (1983); Galton (1990b).

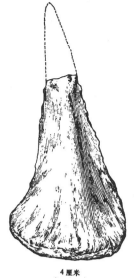

4 厘米

Chungkingosaurus jiangbeiensis, CV00206, holotype incomplete dermal spines. (After Dong, Zhou and Zhang 1983.)

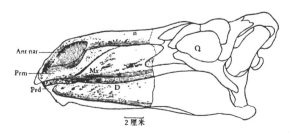

2 厘米

Chungkingosaurus jiangbeiensis, CV00206, holotype partial skull, left lateral view. (After Dong, Zhou and Zhang 1983.)

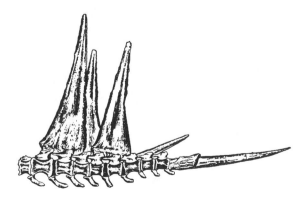

Chungkingosaurus sp., CV00208, anterior part of tail with dermal spines. (After Dong, Zhou and Zhang 1983.)

CIONODON Cope 1874 [*nomen dubium*]

Ornithischia: Genasauria: Cerapoda: Ornithopoda: Iguanodontia: Hadrosauridae *incertae sedis*.

Name derivation: Greek *kionos* = "column" + Greek *odous* = "tooth."

Type species: *C. arctatus* Cope 1874 [*nomen nudum*].

Other species: *C. stenopsis* Cope 1875 [*nomen dubium*].

Occurrence: Denver or Arapahoe Formation, Colorado, United States; Dinosaur Park Formation, Alberta, Canada.

Age: Late Cretaceous.

Known material: Fragmentary crania, vertebrae, fragmentary postcrania, tibia.

Holotype: AMNH 3951, portion of right maxilla, two dorsal vertebrae, distal end of metatarsal III, distal end of ulna.

Diagnosis of genus: [No modern diagnosis published.]

Comments: This poorly known, doubtful genus was founded on a partial snout (AMNH 3978), apparently from what is now the Dinosaur Park Formation (Eberth and Hamblin 1993), at Judith River, Fergus County, Montana.

Type species, *C. arctatus*, was originally diagnosed by Cope (1874) as follows: Long bones with solid, cancellous; teeth rod-like, inner face of tooth shielded by an enamel plate, no stem; dorsal vertebrae opisthocoelian; anterior end of dorsal more compressed than posterior end; dorsal vertebrae with transverse fossa on articular faces (for ligament attachment); caudal vertebra somewhat elongate and depressed.

From what he misinterpreted as the distal end of a femur and head and distal end of a tibia, Cope (1874) surmised that the hind limbs were comparatively smaller than in *Hadrosaurus foulkii*, *Cionodon* apparently a horse-sized animal. Lull and Wright (1942) later pointed out that Cope's perceived "femur" is actually the distal end of metatarsal III, and that his "tibia" is probably the proximal end of an ulna.

Cope observed that the dentition in *Cionodon* was the most complex of all [then] known reptiles, suited to pulverizing vegetation and mechanically comparable to the molar structure in mammals that chew their food. Cope allied *Cionodon* closely with "*H.*" *occidentalis* [=*Thespesius occidentalis*], but having a more complicated dental structure.

Cionodon arctatus, AMNH 3951, holotype portion of right maxilla, distal end of metatarsal III, dorsal vertebrae, distal end of ulna.

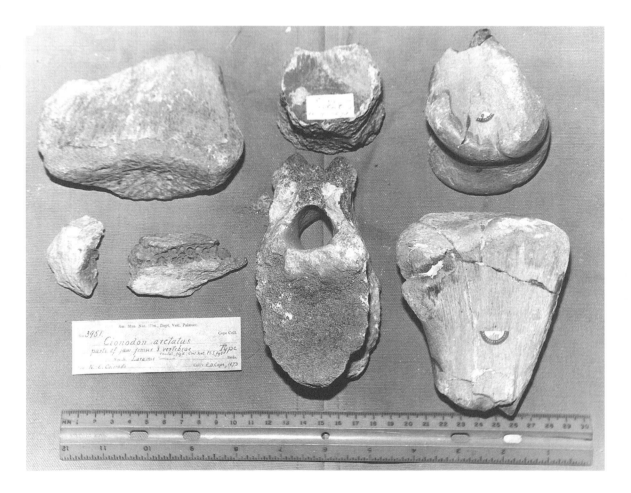

A referred species, *C. stenopsis*, was based upon fragments of maxillary bones (AMNH collection; lost or misplaced), a few containing teeth, found by George M. Dawson in the Dinosaur Park Formation, Milk River region, Alberta, Canada. Cope (1875*b*) diagnosed this species as follows: Teeth about same size as in *C. arctatus*, but lacking carina on enamel-face at base of crown; less pronounced longitudinal protuberance on inner side of maxillary bone.

In their review of hadrosaurs, Lull and Wright (1942), reevaluating *Cionodon*, found that, with the exception of the maxilla, there seem to be no generic or specific characteristics of taxonomic value in the holotype; the type material is therefore incapable of sustaining a diagnostic standing. Also, the characters used to diagnose *C. stenopsis* are not sufficient criteria for establishing a species. *Cionodon* may be synonymous with other Campanian hadrosaurid, but the material pertaining to this genus is too poor to make a positive referral to any taxon.

Note: The species *C. kysylkumense* Riabinin 1931 [*nomen dubium*], was referred by Rozhdestvenskii (1977) to "*Thespesius*."

Key references: Cope (1874, 1875); Lull and Wight (1942).

CLAORHYNCHUS   Cope 1892 [*nomen dubium*]
Ornithischia: Genasauria: Ceratopsia: Ceratopsidae *incertae sedis*.
Name derivation: Greek *klao* = "broken" + Greek *rhynchos* = "beak."
Type species: *C. trihedrus* Cope 1892 [*nomen dubium*].

Other species: [None.]
Occurrence: Dinosaur Park Formation, Montana, United States.
Age: Late Cretaceous (Campanian).
Known material/holotype: AMNH 3978, anterior portion of combined premaxillary and predentary.

Diagnosis of genus: [No modern diagnosis published.]

Comments: This poorly known and doubtful genus was founded on a partial snout (AMNH 3978), apparently from the Dinosaur Park Formation, Judith River, Fergus County, Montana.

Claorhynchus was distinguished by Cope (1892*b*) from other [then] known dinosaurs by premaxillae with entirely flat inferior faces and lack of alveolar ridges. He originally referred this material to the [abandoned] ceratopsian family Agathaumidae 1872. Cope described but did not figure the type specimen, although the characters in his diagnosis are no longer regarded as significant. Correctly, Cope postulated that the predentary beak must have been covered in life by a horny sheath and was adapted to crush hard substances.

Claorhynchus may be congeneric with some other Late Cretaceous ceratopsid, although its type material is too poor for a synonymy to be made.

Note: Referred to *Claorhynchus* were a tooth and frill fragment from South Dakota. Reanalysis of this material by Michael K. Brett-Surman and Douglas A. Lawson in 1973 indicate that the fragment could be part of the squamosal of *Triceratops* (M. K. Brett-Surman, personal communication 1987).

Key reference: Cope (1892*b*).

***Claorhynchus trihedrus*,
AMNH 3978, holotype frill
fragments.**

Claosaurus

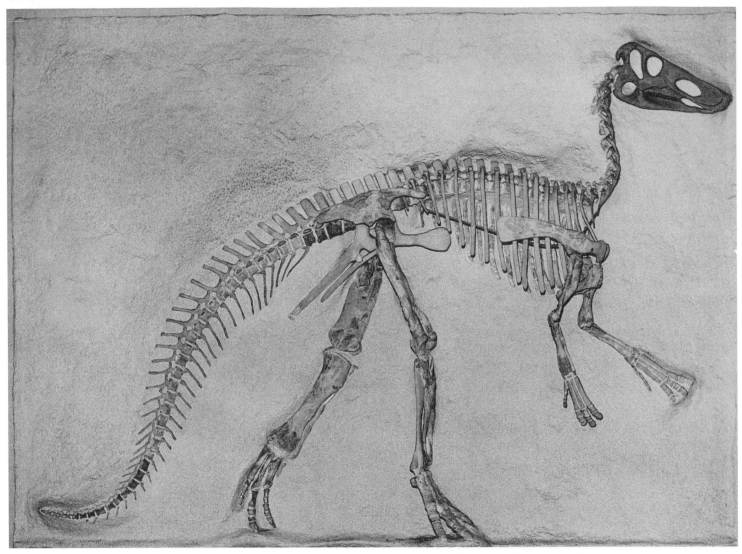

Claosaurus agilis, YPM 1190, holotype incomplete skeleton of *Hadrosaurus agilis* (most of skull and part of tail reconstructed).

CLAOSAURUS Marsh 1890

Ornithischia: Genasauria: Cerapoda: Ornithopoda: Iguanodontia: Hadrosauridae.

Name derivation: Greek *klaos* = "broken" + Greek *sauros* = "lizard."

Type species: *C. agilis* (Marsh 1872).

Other species: ?*C. affinis* Wieland 1903 [*nomen dubium*].

Occurrence: Niobrara Chalk, Kansas, ?Fort Pierre Formation, South Dakota, United States.

Age: Late Cretaceous (Middle Santonian–Early Campanian).

Known material/holotype: YPM 1190, postcranial skeleton with associated skull fragments, missing tail.

Diagnosis of genus (as for type species): Distinguished by short acetabular process of ilium (unique to this taxon within context of "higher" iguanodontians, including hadrosaurids) (Carpenter, Dilkes and Weishampel 1995).

Comments: The genus *Claosaurus* was founded upon a postcranial skeleton with fragments of the skull (YPM 1190), collected by Othniel Charles Marsh on July 30, 1871, from Smoky Hill Chalk Member, Niobrara Chalf Formation, on the north side of Smoky Hill River, Logan County, in western Kansas. Marsh (1872) originally believed that these remains represented a new species of *Hadrosaurus*, which he named *H. agilis*. With the later discovery of more hadrosaurid material, Marsh (1890) recognized that YPM 1190 represented a new genus and species which he renamed *Claosaurus agilis*.

Marsh described this species as about one-third the size of *Hadrosaurus foulkii*, but of more slender proportions, with proportionately shorter cervical vertebrae.

In their classic review of North American hadrosaurids, Lull and Wright (1942) noted that, without the skull, little can be diagnosed regarding *Claosaurus*. Lull and Wright pointed out that the vestigial first metatarsal, absent in all other hadrosaurs but present in iguanodontids, is a primitive feature of this dinosaur. *Claosaurus* may have descended from iguanodontids and been ancestral to later North American hadrosaurids, but without a skull, its precise position cannot be determined.

Brett-Surman (1989) later pointed out that diagnosing genera based on size has little or no taxonomic utility. Brett-Surman also stated that the length-to-width ratio of the ilium is smaller, and the postacetabular process relatively shorter and less developed, than in other hadrosaurines, only *Secernosaurus* having a more primitive appearing ilium.

To date, *Claosaurus* is the most primitive North American hadrosaurid known from comparative evidence. Though smaller, this genus superficially resembles in bodily proportions the later and more derived hadrosaurids. The holotype skeleton o of *C. agilis* (heavily restored, with a plaster skull and tail added and mounted at Yale Peabody Museum of Natural History) measures some 3.5 meters (12 feet) in length.

The species ?*C. affinis* Wieland 1903 [*nomen nudum*] was based on three toe bones from the right pes, collected from the Upper Fort Pierre Formation of South Dakota. The bones resemble corresponding bones in *Edmontosaurus*. This species is best regarded as Hadrosauridae *incertae sedis* (M. K. Brett-Surman, personal communication 1988).

In their review of the Hadrosauridae, Weishampel and Horner (1990) included *Claosaurus* within Hadrosauridae, but regarded the material as too poor to assign this taxon either to Hadrosaurinae or Lambeosaurinae.

Note: The remains of an unnamed juvenile hadrosaurine, apparently older than *C. affinis*, were collected from the Eutaw Formation (Santonian) in the bed of the Tombigbee River, near the Mooreville Member of the Selma Chalk, Mississippi. Reported by Kaye and Russell (1973), this specimen (USNM 175583) consists of a predentary fragment, four sacral and three caudal centra, neural arches of four dorsal and one caudal vertebrae, distal ends of right radius and ulna, proximal ends of left radius and right ulna, posterior end of right ilium, left femur, tibia, third and fourth metatarsals and proximal phalanx of digit IV, distal end of right femur, and numerous small bone fragments. The specimen differs from *Claosaurus* in that the tibia and median metatarsal are longer relative to the femur.

Key references: Brett-Surman (1989); Carpenter, Dilkes and Weishampel (1995); Lull and Wright (1942); Marsh (1872, 1892); Weishampel and Horner (1990); Wieland (1903).

CLASMODOSAURUS Ameghino 1899 [*nomen dubium*]

Saurischia: Sauropodomorpha: Sauropoda *incertae sedis*.

Name derivation: Greek *klasma* = "fragment" + Latin *modulatus* = "measured" + Greek *sauros* = "lizard."

Type species: *C. spatula* Ameghino 1899 [*nomen dubium*].

Other species: [None.]

Occurrence: Cardiel Formation, Santa Cruz, Argentina.

Age: Late Cretaceous (Upper Senonian).

Known material/holotype: Three teeth.

Diagnosis of genus: [None published.]

Comments: The genus *Clasmodosaurus* was founded on three teeth from Rio Sehuen, Santa Cruz, Argentina (Ameghino 1899).

Ameghino briefly described the material as follows: Sauropod teeth measuring from 5 to 6 centimeters (about 1.95 to 2.3 inches) long.

Huene (1929) regarded these teeth as nondinosaurian, belonging rather to an animal related to the crocodilian *Teleosaurus*; Steel (1969) listed *Clasmodosaurus* as a junior synonym of the theropod *Genyodectes*; Molnar (1980c) considered *Clasmodosaurus* to be a sauropod.

Key references: Ameghino (1899); Molnar (1980c).

CLEVELANOTYRANNUS Currie 1987—(See *Nanotyrannus.*)

Name derivation: "Cleveland [Ohio]" + Greek *tyrannos* = "tyrant."

Type species: (No specific name given).

Clasmodosaurus spatula, holotype teeth in lateral and anterior views. (After Ameghino 1899.)

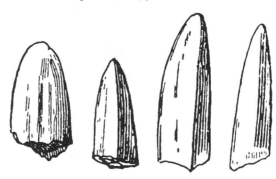

COELOPHYSIS Cope 1889 [*nomen dubium*] — (=*Longosaurus*; =?*Podokesaurus*, ?*Rioarribasaurus*, ?*Syntarsus*)

Saurischia: Theropoda: Ceratosauria: Coelophysoidea.

Name derivation: Greek *koilos* = "hollow" + Greek *physis* = "form."

Type species: *C. bauri* (Cope 1887).

Other species: *C. longicollis* (Cope 1887) [*nomen dubium*], *C. willistoni* (Cope 1889) [*nomen dubium*].

Occurrence: Chinle Formation, Petrified Forest National Park, New Mexico, United States.

Age: Late Triassic (Late Carnian–Early Norian).

Known material: Postcrania, fragments.

Holotype: AMNH 2722, partial postcranial skeleton.

Diagnosis of genus: [No modern diagnosis published.]

Comments: In 1881, David Baldwin, working for Edward Drinker Cope, collected the skeleton of a small dinosaur from the Petrified Forest Member of the Chinle Formation, Rio Arriba County, in northwestern New Mexico. As pointed out by Colbert (1989), Baldwin collected these remains from three localities in the area, two of which were in Arroyo Seco, the third described by Baldwin as "Gallina Canyon." (The stratigraphic unit which yielded Baldwin's specimens probably constitutes the Petrified Forest Member that is demonstrably older than the Rock Point Member of the Late Triassic Chinle Formation; see Hunt and Lucas 1989*b*; 1991.)

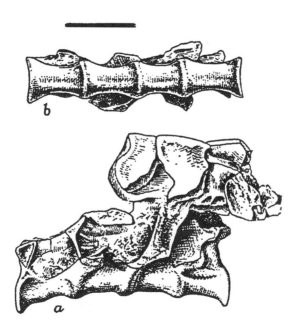

Coelophysis bauri, AMNH 2722, lectotype four fused sacral vertebrae with pubic process of ilium, in a. left lateral and b. ventral views. Scale = 2 cm. (After Huene 1915.)

Baldwin's collection of fragmentary dinosaurian remains were originally described (though not figured) by Cope (1887*a*), who regarded them as new species of *Coelurus*, which he named *C. longicollis* and *C. bauri*. Cope based *C. longicollis* on questionably associated material including cervical, dorsal, and caudal vertebrae, fragments of an ilium, pubis, femur, proximal phalanx, and claw, collected from an unspecified locality in New Mexico. From these remains, Cope estimated the individual's size to be comparable to that of a greyhound, slightly larger than the animal represented by the type specimen of *C. fragilis*. *C. bauri*, based on a cervical vertebra, sacrum, and the distal end of a femur, was apparently a smaller species than *C. longicollis*. Cope assigned no specimen numbers to this material.

Subsequently, Cope (1887*b*) described more New Mexico theropod remains as a new species of the nondinosaurian genus *Tanystropheus*, *T. willistoni*, at the same time removing *C. bauri* and *C. longicollis* from *Coelurus* on the basis of their amphicoelous cervicals, referring these species also to *Tanystropheus*. Cope (1887*b*) also acknowledged specimens later assigned to both of these species (including a fragmentary right ilium, later catalogued AMNH 2708) apparently from the original collection (see Padian 1986), but which had not been mentioned in his original paper. Later, Cope (1889) referred all three species to the newly erected genus *Coelophysis*, but neither established a type species nor designated any type specimens.

Cope (1889) originally diagnosed *Coelophysis* as follows: Differs from *Coelurus* in having biconcave cervical vertebrae, simple femoral condyles, as well as other [unspecified] points.

Much of Cope's *Coelophysis* material was later figured by Huene (1906; 1915), who tried to sort out the taxonomic status of material not referred to by Cope. According to Padian, Huene (1915) reassigned some of these remains from one species to another mostly based upon size (AMNH 2708 referred to *C. bauri*), while not designating any of these fossils as type specimens. For no obvious reason, Hay (1930) later designated *C. bauri* as the type species of *Coelophysis*.

After the Cope collection was relocated to the American Museum of Natural History, the *Coelophysis* material was catalogued as AMNH 2701–2708. As noted by Padian (1986), new catalogue numbers were assigned in 1973 to Cope's specimens (AMNH 2701–2708, 2715, 2716 for the type material of *C. longicollis*, AMNH 2717–2725 for *C. bauri*, and AMNH 2726–2727 for *C. willistoni*).

The partial ilium (AMNH 2708) was apparently later designated a lectotype for *C. bauri* by

Welles (1984). However, as pointed out by Hunt and Lucas (1991), this specimen, previously transferred by Huene from *C. longicollis* to *C. bauri*, had also been identified by Huene (1915) as part of the "type" of *C. longicollis*. Also, AMNH 2708 was not one of the original syntypes of *C. bauri*, nor was this specimen a syntype of *C. longicollis*, not having been referred to in Cope's (1887*a*) original description. Therefore, according to Articles 74 and 73, respectively, of the International Code of Zoological Nomenclature (ICZN 1985), AMNH 2708 is ineligible to be a lectotype of *C. bauri*.

Numerous theropod specimens recovered from the Whitaker (or "*Coelophysis*") quarry in the Rock Point Member of the Chinle Formation at Ghost Ranch, New Mexico, were assigned by Colbert (1947, 1964, 1989) to *Coelophysis*. Padian (1987), in reevaluating Cope's original *Coelophysis* type material, noted that *Coelophysis* had been founded upon scrappy remains, the genus neither adequately diagnosed nor compared with other taxa; and that the Ghost Ranch specimens, in all of their completeness (indeed, because of it), have obscured the paucity of the type material of *Coelophysis*. Padian argued that the *Coelophysis* type material does sustain its validity on the basis of possessing certain synapomorphies and lacking others. *Coelophysis*, not exhibiting the synapomorphies present in other early theropods (crests, horns, *etc.*), seems to represent the closest known representative of an ancestral theropod species. These basal similarities may be seen in both the meager specimens described by Cope and by the excellent specimens collected at Ghost Ranch.

In response to Padian (1987), Colbert (1989) pointed out that a genus is based upon a type species, not upon fossil materials, and that the type species is based upon a specimen or specimens; also, that Cope's original *Coelophysis* materials are adequate to carry the name and need not be diagnostic to represent the species. Colbert (1989) further argued that many of the theropod bones collected at Ghost Ranch can be matched in morphological details and measurements (as well as on their geographic and stratigraphic occurrences) with specimens described by Cope as *Coelurus bauri*, *Coelurus longicollis* and *Tanystropheus willistoni*. For these reasons, Colbert (1989) favored retaining *Coelophysis* as a valid genus to which the Ghost Ranch specimens could be referred. At the same time, Colbert (1989), apparently unaware of Welles' designating a lectotype for *C. bauri*, named specimen AMNH 2722, consisting of four fused sacral vertebrae and an associated pubic process of an ilium, as the lectotype for that species.

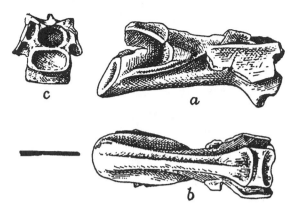

Coelophysis longicollis, AMNH 2701, lectotype cervical vertebra, in a. right lateral, b. ventral and c. anterior views. Scale = 2 cm. (After Huene 1915.)

More recently, Hunt and Lucas (1991) argued that specimen AMNH 2722, though a valid lectotype for *C. bauri* being one of Cope's (1887*a*) original syntypes for that species, is not diagnostic; that the sacral vertebrae are morphologically unremarkable, indistinguishable from some other Late Triassic and Early Jurassic theropods (*e.g.*, *Liliensternus* and *Syntarsus*); that fusion of sacral vertebrae is typical of the Ceratosauria as well as some ornithurine theropods (Rowe 1989); that the iliac portion is also undiagnostic; and that the specimen, based upon size and gross morphology, cannot be distinguished from *Syntarsus*. Hunt and Lucas (1991) also argued that, according to the spirit and letter of Article 61 of International Code of Zoological Nomenclature, the type specimen bearing the name "provides the objective standard of reference by which the application of the name it bears is determined." Hunt and Lucas (1989*b*, 1991) showed that the Ghost Ranch quarry is probably geologically younger than the rocks from which Baldwin's original *Coelophysis* bones were recovered. For these reasons, Hunt and Lucas (1991) removed the Ghost Ranch specimens from the genus *Coelophysis*, creating for their reception the new genus *Rioarribasaurus* (see entry), and regarded the name *Coelophysis* (including the remains collected by Baldwin and described by Cope) as a *nomen dubium*.

Welles (1984) had made *C. longicollis* the type of new genus *Longosaurus*, designating the ilium (AMNH 2705) as the lectotype, and describing this species as follows: Ilium differs from "*C. bauri*" [=*Rioarribasaurus colberti*] in being considerably longer (189 millimeters as restored), wider across peduncles (82 millimeters), slightly greater between notches (59 millimeters), with spine almost twice as high (32 millimeters) posteriorly; other [unspecified] differences.

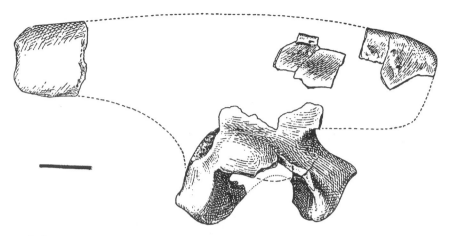

Coelophysis willistoni, AMNH 2726, lectotype fragmentary right ilium. Scale = 2 cm. (After Huene 1915.)

As noted by Hunt and Lucas (1991), however, specimen AMNH 2705, not one of the original syntypes of *C. longicollis*, was not eligible to become a lectotype of that species, according to Article 74 of the ICZN. Hunt and Lucas (1991) designated a cervical vertebra (AMNH 2701) as the lectotype of *C. longicollis*, but pointed out that this specimen is not diagnostic beyond the level of primitive theropod. As none of the syntypes of this taxon can be diagnosed, Hunt and Lucas (1991) regarded *C. longicollis* as a *nomen dubium*.

Hunt and Lucas (1991) designated a partial right ilium (AMNH 2726) as the lectotype of *C. willistoni*, noting that this specimen, as well as the syntype dorsal centrum (AMNH 2727), are not diagnostic, and that this taxon also should be considered a *nomen dubium*.

Notes: *Coelophysis* is the official state fossil of New Mexico, although the name, in this case, actually refers to the dinosaur presently known as *Rioarribasaurus*.

An appeal, supported by many paleontologists, is currently underway to the ICZN for reinstating the name *Coelophysis* as representing the Ghost Ranch specimens (see *Rioarribasaurus* entry).

Key references: Colbert (1946, 1964, 1989); Cope (1887*a*, 1887*b*, 1889); Hay (1930); Huene (1906, 1915); Hunt and Lucas (1989*b*, 1991); Padian (1986); Welles (1984).

COELOSAURUS Owen 1854 [*nomen oblitum*]—(See *Ornithomimus*.)

Name derivation: Greek *koilos* = "hollow" + Greek *sauros* = "lizard."

Type species: *C. antiquus* Leidy 1865 [*nomen oblitum*].

COELUROIDES Huene 1932 [*nomen dubium*]

Saurischia: Theropoda *incertae sedis*.

Name derivation: Greek *koilos* = "hollow" + Greek *oeides* = "form."

Type species: *C. largus* Huene 1932 [*nomen dubium*].

Other species: [None.]

Occurrence: Lameta Formation, Madhya Pradesh, India.

Age: Late Cretaceous (Coniacian–Santonian).

Known material/cotypes: IM K27/562, K27/574 and K27/595, isolated incomplete caudal vertebrae.

Diagnosis of genus: [No modern diagnosis published.]

Comments: The genus *Coeluroides* was founded upon caudal vertebrae (IM K27/562, K27/574 and K27/595) collected from the Lameta Formation of Madhya Pradesh, near Jabalpur, India. Huene (1932; *see in* Huene and Matley 1933) misidentified these caudals as dorsal vertebrae. Huene (1932) classified this genus with the Coeluridae, although its affinities may be elsewhere.

Huene (*see in* Huene and Matley) diagnosed this genus as follows: Vertebrae very large, from 9–11 centimeters (about 3.5–4.25 inches) in length; centrum well-rounded in transverse section near articular face and at middle, where it is also somewhat narrow; diapophysis quite broad and plate-like, thickened below, without real buttress, directed backward; postzygapophyses meeting at middle of bone; dorsal neural spine with very long, steeply rising base. The remains indicate a large theropod about the size of *Allosaurus*.

As observed by Molnar (1990), the caudals in *C. largus* are primitive in that the transverse processes are linked by laminae with both prezygapophyses and postzygapophyses.

Key references: Huene (1932); Huene and Matley (1933); Molnar (1990).

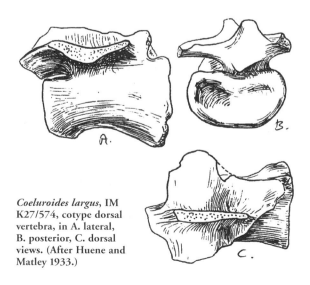

Coeluroides largus, IM K27/574, cotype dorsal vertebra, in A. lateral, B. posterior, C. dorsal views. (After Huene and Matley 1933.)

COELURUS Marsh 1879 [*nomen dubium*]
Saurischia: Theropoda: Tetanurae *incertae sedis*.
Name derivation: Greek *koilos* = "hollow."
Type species: *C. fragilis* Marsh 1879.
Other species: [None.]
Occurrence: Morrison Formation, Wyoming, Utah, United States.
Age: Late Jurassic–?Early Cretaceous (Kimmeridgian–Tithonian; ?Neocomian–?Hauterivian).
Known material/holotype: YPM 1991, caudal vertebra.

Diagnosis of genus (as for type species): Small coelurosaurian (*sensu* Gauthier 1986), with "footed" pubis and fused cervical ribs; cervical vertebrae opisthocoelous, with shallowly convex cranial surfaces; lateral dyapophyseal shelf very broad and decurved (Norman 1990).

Comments: The genus *Coelurus* was founded upon unspecified material including sacral and caudal vertebrae, collected from the so-called "*Atlantosaurus* Beds," Morrison Formation, Quarry 13, Como Bluff, Wyoming. The genus and type species, *C. fragilis*, were briefly described but not illustrated by Marsh (1879*b*). Marsh briefly described these remains as representing a very small reptile with extremely hollow vertebrae. At the time, Marsh was not certain that the fossils pertained to a dinosaur.

Subsequently, Marsh (1881*b*) diagnosed *C. fragilis* as follows: Cervical vertebrae large and elongate, with large neural canal; "dorsals" [actually a caudal; see below] much shorter; caudals long; all bones extremely lightweight, excavations more extensive than in skeleton of any other known vertebrate.

At the same time, Marsh (1881*b*) made *Coelurus* the type genus of a new order Coeluria, with its own family Coeluridae, and published figures of a cervical vertebra (YPM 1993), [supposed] dorsal (YPM 1991) vertebra, and caudal (YPM 1992) vertebra.

A second species, *C. agilis*, was later described by Marsh (1884), allegedly based only upon a pair of pubes (YPM 2010) from Quarry 13. The type specimen of this species actually comprises more than these pubes. In a letter to Gilmore (1920), Richard Swann Lull stated that the specimen also includes a femur, tibia, fibula, humerus, radius, ulna, coracoid, an ungual, some foot bones, and a few vertebrae. Marsh (1884) incorrectly stated that this species "was at least three times the bulk of" *C. fragilis*. The two forms are now regarded as conspecific (Norman 1990).

Noting the separate cataloguings of Marsh's specimens and that only the supposed "dorsal" was marked as the type specimen in Marsh's handwriting, Gilmore designated the other two vertebrae as plesiotypes. Gilmore regarded *Coelurus* as synonymous with the better known genus *Ornitholestes*. Indeed,

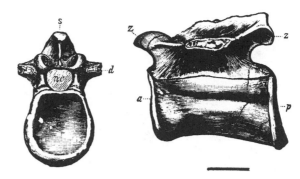

Coelurus gracilis, YPM 1991, holotype caudal vertebra, in anterior and lateral views. Scale = 1 cm. (After Marsh 1896.)

since Gilmore's synonymy, these two forms have been generally regarded as such in the literature as well as in the popular press. However, as later noted by Ostrom (1980*b*), no formal comparison of the specimens upon which *Coelurus* and *Ornitholestes* had been published; nor was there a complete published record of the existing material that had been, or could be, referred to either taxon.

In a detailed reevaluation of the genus *Coelurus*, Ostrom traced the histories of the various type specimens, while including a comprehensive listing of all material pertaining to this taxon in the Yale Peabody Museum of Natural History collections. Ostrom showed that the vertebra (YPM 1991) identified as a dorsal by Marsh (1879*b*) is really a caudal, and noted that the complete type specimen of *C. agilis* consists of at least 54 elements, including at least 11 vertebrae, some neural arches, and other material. Emphasizing the fact that all *C. fragilis* and *C. agilis* type specimens were collected from the same part of the same quarry, with no duplication of elements, Ostrom concluded that the four types probably represent the same individual.

Though Gilmore had contended that, given the paucity of the *Coelurus* type material, it was not feasible to compare this genus with *Ornitholestes*, such a comparison was made possible using additional materials listed by Ostrom. Comparing the type remains of both forms, Ostrom found that: 1. Cervicals in *Coelurus* are much longer and more complex than in *Ornitholestes*; 2. metapodials in *Coelurus* are at least 50 percent longer than in *Ornitholestes*, though the femora are nearly equal in length; 3. dorsal centra and arches are morphologically different in both forms; 4. differences in the hollowness of the bones in both forms are significant; and 5. caudal prezygapophyses are extremely elongate in *Ornitholestes* and not in *Coelurus*, though this feature is of questionable importance. From these findings Ostrom concluded that *Coelurus* and *Ornitholestes* are not congeneric.

Photo by R. A. Long and S. P. Welles (neg. #73/139-17), courtesy National Museum of Natural History, Smithsonian Institution.

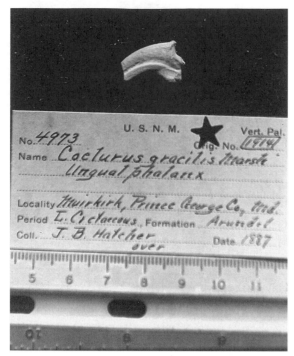

Coelurus gracilis, USNM 4973, referred ungual phalanx.

Norman regarded *Coelurus* as a highly cursorial dinosaur. On the basis of the semilunate form of the carpal, Gauthier (1986) assigned *Coelurus* to the Maniraptora. Norman, however, pointed out that this genus lacks the key maniraptoran character of hypapophyses on the cervicals.

Note: Britt (1991) reported miscellaneous, indeterminate, small-theropod remains, possibly *Coelurus* or *Ornitholestes* (or juvenile theropods), collected from the Dry Mesa Quarry (Morrison Formation, Upper Jurassic [Tithonian] or Lower Cretaceous [Neocomian or Hauterivian]) in west central Col-

Coloradisaurus brevis, PVL 3967, holotype skull of *Coloradia brevis*, right lateral view. (After Bonaparte 1978.)

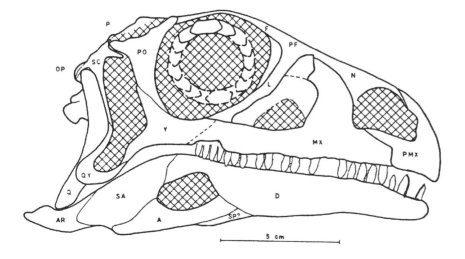

5 cm

orado. This material includes a fibula (BYUVP 4876) and complete metatarsal I (measuring 50 millimeters in length).

The species *C. bauri* Cope 1887 and *C. longicollis* Cope 1887 were transferred by Cope (1889) to the genus *Coelophysis*. *C. gracilis* Marsh 1888 [*nomen dubium*], based on an isolated ungual phalanx from the Arundel Formation (Hauterivian–Barremian) of Maryland, was referred by Gilmore (1924) to *Chirostenotes* (although Norman regards *C. gracilis* as generically and specifically indeterminate). Osborn (1903) made *C. hermanni* the type species of *Ornitholestes*.

Key references: Britt (1991); Gauthier (1986); Gilmore (1920); Marsh (1879*b*, 1881*b*, 1884); Norman (1990); Ostrom (1980*b*).

COLORADIA   Bonaparte 1978—(Preoccupied, Blake 1863; see *Coloradisaurus*.)
Name derivation: "[Los] Colorados [Formation]."
Type species: *C. brevis* Bonaparte 1978.

COLORADISAURUS   Lambert 1983
Saurischia: Sauropodomorpha: Prosauropoda: Melanorosauridae.
Name derivation: "[Los] Colorados [Formation]" + Greek *sauros* = "lizard."
Type species: *C. brevis* (Bonaparte 1978).
Other species: [None.]
Occurrence: Upper Los Colorados Formation, La Rioja, Argentina.
Age: Late Triassic (Norian).
Known material/holotype: PVL 3967, skull with jaws, three cervical, two dorsal and three caudal vertebrae, fragments of scapula, coracoid and humerus, portions of ulna and radius, isolated incomplete carpals and metacarpals, various manual phalanges, complete astragalus, pedal phalanege.

Diagnosis of genus (as for type species): Derived characters include maxilla with wide dorsal process and large medial lamina to the maxilla; lacrimal with large medial lamina; braincase with large ventral step so that occipital is located well above the parasphenoid (Galton 1990*a*).

Comments: The genus *Coloradisaurus* was established on a skull and postcranial remains (PVL 3967) originally described by Bonaparte (1978*a*) as new genus *Coloradia*. This material collected from the Los Colorados Formation (Upper Triassic) of La Rioja, in northern Argentina. As the name *Coloradia* proved to be preoccupied (Blake 1863), Lambert (1983) renamed the genus *Coloradisaurus*.

Bonaparte originally diagnosed the monotypic *C. brevis* as follows: Related to *Plateosaurus* and *Lufengosaurus*, with shorter snout, but with frontal portion rather long; preorbital opening located partially below snout; orbits relatively large, with sclerotic ring; nasals short; frontals elongate; occiput partially exposed in dorsal view; cervical vertebrae low, large, with long, thin ribs.

As these remains were found in a lower level but in the same sedimentary environment as those of melanorosaurids, Bonaparte suggested that prosauropod families were not restricted to a particular and different habitat.

In a review of the Prosauropoda, Galton (1990*a*) assigned *Coloradisaurus* to the Plateosauridae [see note].

Note: In the February, 1996 (No. 166) issue of the *Society of Vertebrate Paleontology New Bulletin*, Galton stated that, through an editorial mishap in the first (1990) edition of *The Dinosauria* (whereby he was never sent complete galley proofs for correction of his chapter titled "Basal Sauropodomorpha"), the genera *Coloradisaurus, Euskelosaurus,* and *Lufengosaurus*, melanorosaurids all, were incorrectly listed with the Plateosauridae. This mistake was subsequently corrected for the revised paperback edition (1992) of that book.

Key references: Bonaparte (1978*a*); Galton (1990*a*); Lambert (1983).

COMPSOGNATHUS Wagner 1859

Saurischia: Theropoda: Tetanurae: Avetheropoda: Coelurosauria.

Name derivation: Greek *komposs* = "elegant" + *gnathos* = "jaw."

Type species: *C. longipes* Wagner 1859.

Other species: [None.]

Occurrence: Ober Solnhofen Plattenkalk, Bavaria, Germany; Lithographic Limestone, Canjuer, Var, France.

Age: Late Jurassic (Kimmeridgian–Tithonian).

Known material: Two skulls and associated postcrania, eggs.

Holotype: BSP 1563, almost complete skeleton, juvenile.

Diagnosis of genus (as for type species): No mandibular fenestra; skull slender, equal to about 30 percent of body length; pleurocoels restricted to cervical vertebrae; dorsal centra spool-shaped, neural spines fan-shaped; caudal vertebrae without transverse processes; forelimb extremely short (37 percent length of hindlimb); digital manual formula 2-2-0-0-0; pubic "foot" expanded rostrally; ischium with prominent obturator process, distal portion of ischial shaft

fused to its neighbor; pedal digit I reduced (entire digit shorter than metatarsal II) (Norman 1990).

Comments: One of the smallest known dinosaurs (made famous in popular books as the "size of a chicken"), the genus *Compsognathus* (basis for the group Compsognathidae Marsh 1882) was founded upon the well-preserved, virtually complete skeleton (BSP 1563) of a juvenile individual, collected during the late 1850s apparently by physician and amateur fossil collector Dr. Oberndorfer, from a locality near Kelheim, Bavaria, Germany. One of the first almost complete dinosaur skeletons ever found, the type specimen was preserved lying on its right size in a death pose (exhibited in many dinosaur skeletons), the head and neck strongly arched over the back apparently due to the contraction of the neck muscles in *rigor mortis*.

Oberndorfer did not reveal the precise location of his discovery, perhaps as security against the many amateurs who collected fossils from the lithographic limestone quarries. As recounted by Ostrom (1978*b*) in a paper on the osteology of type species *C. longipes*, a more recent label associated with the type specimen mentions the small village of Jachenhausen, located some 15 kilometers northwest of the town of Kelheim where Oberndorfer resided. Ostrom and Peter Wellnhofer attempted to reestablish the precise source of the holotype, but were only able to conclude that it came from lithographic facies of the Solnhofen Limestone, probably from the Riedenburg-Kelheim area.

Compsognathus was first reported by Andreas Wagner (1859), who did not recognize it as a dinosaur. Later, Huxley (1868*a*, 1870*b*), in speculating about the affinities between dinosaurs and birds, referred to *Compsognathus* as a birdlike reptile. The type specimen of *C. longipes* was subsequently restudied and redescribed by Nopcsa (1903*a*) and Huene (1925, 1926*c*, 1932), as well as by other scientists.

In his early descriptions of the type species, Huene noted that the skull of *C. longipes* is low and measures 6.5 centimeters (about 2.5 inches) in length. Cervical vertebrae measure from 11 to 12 millimeters (about .42 to .47 inches) long, dorsals about 9 millimeters (.35 inches), distal caudals slightly longer than 1 millimeter each. The scapula measures 40 millimeters (about 1.55 inches) long. The ilium measures 64 millimeters (about 2.5 inches) in length. The pubis is relatively small, measuring about 70 millimeters (2.7 inches), with a large distal "foot." The ischium is 36 millimeters (1.4 inches) long. The humerus, measuring 52 millimeters (about 2 inches in length), is longer than the radius, measuring 24 millimeters (over .9 inches) or ulna. The manus [as

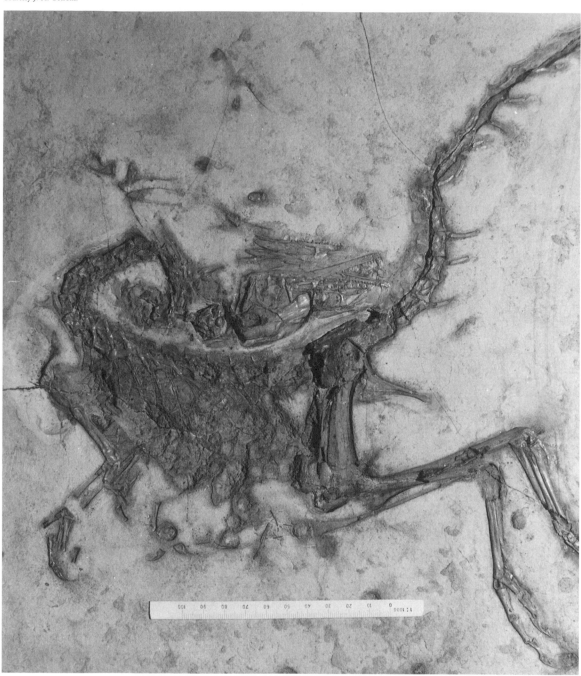

Compsognathus longipes, BSP 1563, holotype skeleton.

originally interpreted by Wagner] has "three" digits [see below] equipped with powerful claws, with a rudimentary "fourth" digit. The femur is rather massively constructed and measures 76 millimeters (about 2.8 inches) long. The tibia measures 83 millimeters (about 3.4 inches). The fibula becomes very slender distally. The proximal tarsals tend to form a birdlike tibio-tarsus with the tibia. The astragalus has a long ascending process. There are three functional toes, metatarsals greatly elongate, distal tarsals represented by three flattened bones.

Based on the holotype, *Compsognathus* reached an approximate length of 70 centimeters (about 28 inches), or, as noted by Ostrom, about the size of a small partridge, and weighing approximately 3 to 3.5 kilograms (about 6.6 to about 7.75 pounds).

From an analysis of the type specimen, Ostrom published the first real diagnosis of *Compsognathus.* Ostrom interpreted the manus of *Compsognathus* as having two digits, a derived condition seen in Late Cretaceous tyrannosaurids and which would separate *Compsognathus* from other known Late Jurassic theropods. Ostrom stated that, in both right and left manus of the holotype, seven elements (represented either by bones or impressions) are present, each duplicated exactly with no unmatched or extra bones. (Huene 1926c had assumed that some elements were missing. Paul (1987), in the book *Dinosaurs Past and Present*, questioned Ostrom's interpretation, noting that the hands in the type specimen were poorly-preserved and disarticulated. Ostrom speculated that the slightly scattered hand bones had probably been moved by water currents during decomposition of the carcass.

As to the suggestion by some modern workers and artists that small theropods may have been feathered, Ostrom stated that the holotype of *C. longipes* is the critical specimen to examine. This specimen comes from the same limestones (but not same facies) that yielded such fine specimens of the bird *Archaeopteryx* showing distinct feather impressions. As the slab containing the *C. longipes* holotype specimen shows no impressions suggestive of feathers, but otherwise reveals in an almost undisturbed manner the fine details of the skeleton, Ostrom concluded that *Compsognathus* almost certainly did not have feathers.

A second possible species, *C. "corallestris,"* was based on a well-preserved, nearly complete skeleton from the lithographic Portlandian (early Cretaceous, Barremian) limestone, "Petit Plan," Canjuers, west of Nice, France. Bidar, Demay and Thomel (1972) distinguished this species mostly by its larger size and the forelimbs. Bidar *et al.* interpreted several wrinkle-like linear undulations, paralleling the anterior margin of the forelimb, as an impression of soft parts representing a flipper-like appendage, suggesting to them an adaptation to a semiaquatic life style for this species.

Ostrom, however, questioned the latter interpretation, pointing out that the forelimb was so poorly preserved in the specimen from France that it is impossible even to discern the various individual elements with certainty, and noting that most of these elements are represented only by impressions. Identical impressions occur elsewhere on the limestone slab; the flipper interpretation is therefore highly improbable. Ostrom noted that this specimen is nearly identical to the smaller *C. longipes* holotype, finding no reason to regard them as separate species (synonym accepted by Norman 1990).

Compsognathus longipes, and flock of *Pterodactylus*, illustration by Brian Franczak.

The second specimen (Humboldt Museum für Naturkunde, East Berlin) to be assigned to *C. longipes* consists of four bones (apparently three metatarsals and a proximal phalanx), preserved on counterpart slabs, first reported by Dames (1884). This specimen indicates an individual intermediate in size between the holotypes of *C. longipes* and *C. "corallestris."* According to Ostrom, the relative lengths of bones in these latter two specimens compare rather closely, although neither compares with the lengths in the Humboldt specimen. Ostrom (as had Dames) concluded that the Humboldt specimen should not be assigned to the type species.

Huene envisioned *Compsognathus* as a fast-moving predator, able to run, hop, and jump after prey that probably consisted of insects and small vertebrates. Ostrom cautioned that attempted reconstructions of extinct animals are at best educated guesses, but agreed that, due to its small size, *Compsognathus* was most likely partially insectivorous, as evidenced by its dentition, and may also have preyed upon small vertebrates. This latter idea was supported by examination of the stomach contents in the holotype of *C. longipes*, which revealed a tiny, well-pre-

served reptilian skeleton.

Marsh (1881*b*, 1883, 1895, 1896), the first paleontologist to notice this tiny second skeleton, identified it as an embryonic *Compsognathus*, supposedly evidence that dinosaurs were viviparous. Nopcsa later pointed out numerous features identifying these remains as lacertilian. Ostrom listed more features supporting Nopcsa's conclusion and identified the ingested remains as those of the small lizard *Bavarisaurus*. From the proportions of the tail and limbs of *Bavarisaurus*, Ostrom surmised that this was a swift ground-dwelling lizard and that, consequently, *Compsognathus* must have had keen vision, fast acceleration, quick reactions, speed, and maneuverability to have caught it.

Regarding the probable ontogenetic stage of the known specimens of *Compsognathus*, Ostrom listed three distinctive features (1. relatively large skull, 2. disproportionately large orbit, and 3. relatively long hindlimbs) that suggested that the holotype of *C. longipes* represented an individual that was not fully mature. Noting the

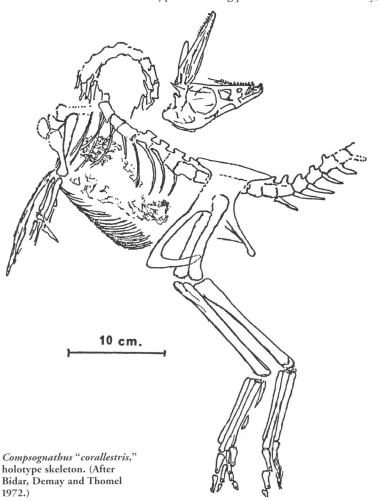

larger size and fully ossified state of the holotype of *C. "corallestris,"* Ostrom concluded that the German specimen belonged to a subadult (although not juvenile) individual.

Also addressing this question as to whether the specimens of *Compsognathus* represented fully grown individuals, Callison and Quimby (1984) utilized several species of modern day bipedal cursorial birds as models because of their sharing various similarities with "coelurosaurian" dinosaurs. Callison and Quimby observed that different proportions are exhibited in the hindlimbs of young and old individuals and large and small species of birds. A baby ostrich, for example, has a femur approximately the same length as that of an adult chicken. The distal width of the ostrich's femur is, however, proportionately wider relative to its length, creating a knobby knee effect. This seems to anticipate the ostrich growing larger by beginning its life with such greater knee widths. By measuring the lengths of an associated femur and tibia, diameter and length of a tibia, and length and distal width of a femur, and taking into consideration ossification, Callison and Quimby used growth patterns in approximately determining ontogenetic stage and adult size in cursorial birds. Applying their findings to bipedal dinosaurs, Callison and Quimby determined that the known *Compsognathus* specimens rep-

Compsognathus "corallestris," holotype skeleton. (After Bidar, Demay and Thomel 1972.)

10 cm.

resent subadult to adult individuals, probably growing no larger than domestic chickens. This method could also be applied to predict the general ontogenetic stage and adult size of a bipedal cursorial dinosaur.

Norman observed that signs of immaturity in *Compsognathus* include the disproportionately large head and orbit, the disarticulation of the skull bones in an otherwise mostly undisturbed skeleton, and perhaps the absence of detailed anatomical features in some limb bones.

Norman listed a suite of characters (large caudally placed antorbital fenestra, maxillary teeth restricted rostrally to orbit, absence of manual digit IV, ischium with obturator process, pubis with expanded "foot," and short metatarsal I) by which *Compsognathus* can be assigned to Tetanurae, but could not precisely establish the systematic position of the genus with regard to other theropods.

More recently, Holtz (1994*a*), after a cladistic analysis of various theropod groups, concluded that *Compsognathus* belongs to Coelurosauria as the sister-taxon to all other coelurosaurs.

Huene (1901) interpreted a series of polygonal surface irregularities, located in the holotype in depressions along the ventral regions of the abdomen and trunk, as evidence of horny dermal armor in *Compsognathus*, comparing them to the dorsal dermal ossicles described by Gilmore (1920) in association with the genus *Ceratosaurus*. This interpretation was rejected by Nopcsa. Ostrom, after studying the original slab under high magnification and various lighting conditions, concluded that the "polygon" irregularities perceived by Huene may actually be cavities etched by solution, as ground water percolated through fractures in the slab. More recently, Griffith (1993) interpreted these irregularities as eggs.

Key references: Bidar *et al.* (1972); Callison and Quimby (1984); Dames (1884); Griffith (1993); Holtz (1994*a*); Huene (1925, 1926*c*, 1932); Huxley (1868*a*, 1870*b*); Marsh (1881*b*, 1883, 1895, 1896); Nopcsa (1903*a*); Ostrom (1978*b*); Paul (1987); Wagner (1859).

COMPSOSUCHUS Huene 1932 [*nomen dubium*]

Saurischia: Theropoda: Tetanurae: ?Avetheropoda: ?Allosauroidea: ?Allosauridae.

Name derivation: Greek *kompsos* = "elegant" + Greek *souchos* = "crocodile."

Type species: *C. solus* Huene 1932 [*nomen dubium*].

Other species: [None.]

Occurrence: Lameta Formation, Bara Simla Hill, Madhya Pradesh, India.

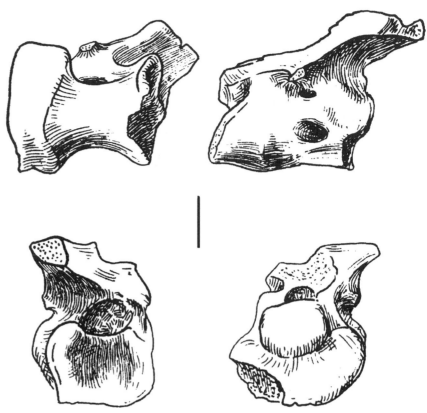

Composuchus solus, IM K27/578, holotype axis, four views. Scale = 2 cm. (After Huene and Matley 1933.)

Age: Late Cretaceous (Middle–Late Maastrichtian).

Known material/holotype: IM K27/578, cervical vertebra, ?axis with articulated axial intercentrum, atlas centrum.

Diagnosis of genus: [None published.]

Comments: The genus *Compsosuchus* was founded upon vertebrae (IM K27/578) collected from the Lameta Formation of Bara Simla, near Jabalpur, India (Huene 1932).

Huene (*see in* Huene and Matley 1933) described the type species *C. solus* as follows: Cervical vertebra 4 centimeters (about 1.55 inches) in length (Huene 1932); centrum with two pleurocoels, one above the other; diapophysis rather small and blunt, with prominent margin proceeding obliquely to postzygapophysis; postzygapophysis extending beyond centrum.

Huene (1932) classified *Compsosuchus* with the Compsognathidae. Molnar, Kurzanov and Dong (1990), however, observed that the axis of *C. solus* resembles that of *Allosaurus fragilis* in position of the upper pleurocoel, with a cylindrical axial intercentrum in ventral aspect, axial pleurocentrum that is less than twice as long as the axial intercentrum, and a broad neural canal; these features suggesting that *Compsosuchus* could be an allosaurid.

Key references: Huene (1932); Huene and Matley (1933); Molnar, Kurzanov and Dong (1990).

CONCHORAPTOR   Barsbold 1986
Saurischia: Theropoda: Tetanurae: Avetheropoda:
   Coelurosauria: Maniraptora: Arctometatarsalia:
   Oviraptorosauria: Oviraptoridae: Oviraptorinae.
Name derivation: Greek *kongche* = "shell" + Latin
   raptor = "robber."
Type species: *C. gracilis* Barsbold 1986.
Other species: [None.]
Occurrence: Red Beds of Khermeen Tsav, Omno-
   gov, Mongolian People's Republic.
Age: Late Cretaceous (Middle Campanian).
Known material: Skull, associated postcranial skele-
   ton, three fragmentary postcrania.
Holotype: GI 100/20, skull.

   Diagnosis of genus (as for type species): Relatively small oviraptorid lacking cranial crest (Barsbold 1986).

   Comments: The genus *Conchoraptor* was
founded upon a skull (GI 100/200) from Mongolia.
Because it lacked a cranial crest, this specimen originally thought to be that of a juvenile *Oviraptor*.
Later, it was identified as that of a small adult individual representing a new genus (Barsbold 1986).

   The holotype skull was measured by Barsbold as
10 centimeters (approximately 3.8 inches) in length.
Barsbold interpreted the skull of *Conchoraptor* as possessing a horny beak that was possibly utilized in
crushing mollusks (see also Barsbold, Maryańska and
Osmólska 1990).

   Key references: Barsbold (1986); Barsbold,
Maryańska and Osmólska (1990).

Corythosaurus casuarius,
**AMNH 5240, holotype skele-
ton with integument.**

CORYTHOSAURUS   Brown 1914—(=*Pteropelyx*;
   Procheneosaurus [in part] =?*Hypacrosaurus*)
Ornithischia: Genasauria: Cerapoda: Ornithopoda:
   Iguanodontia: Hadrosauridae: Lambeosaurinae.

Name derivation: Greek *korythos* = "Corinthian
   [helmet]" + Greek *sauros* = "lizard."
Type species: *C. casuarius* Brown 1914.
Other species: "*C. convincens*" [juvenile; not yet
   described].
Occurrence: Dinosaur Park Formation, Alberta,
   Canada; ?Judith River Formation, Montana,
   United States.
Age: Late Cretaceous (Middle–Late Campanian).
Known material: Over ten articulated skulls with
   associated postcrania, 10–15 articulated skulls,
   isolated cranial elements, juvenile to adult.
Holotype: AMNH 5240, skeleton missing fore-
   limbs and end of tail, with fossilized integument.

   Diagnosis of genus (as for type species): Skull
large, with high, full rounded crest, superficially
resembling that of a cassowary (Dodson 1975).

   Comments: The genus *Corythosaurus* was
founded on a nearly complete skeleton (AMNH
5240), collected in 1914 by Barnum Brown for the
American Museum of Natural History, from the
"Belly River" group (now Dinosaur Park Formation),
near "Steveville," Red Deer River, Alberta, Canada.
A plesiotype specimen (AMNH 5338), an almost
complete skeleton with integument and missing the
latter part of the tail, most of the left manus, and a
few phalanges of the right manus, was collected the
same year from about the same location. Both skeletons were displayed at the American Museum of Natural History.

   Originally, Brown (1914*d*) diagnosed *Corythosaurus* as follows: Large hadrosaur measuring
about 9 meters (31 feet) long; skull with high, narrow, laterally compressed, helmet-like crest, its summit directly above orbit; muzzle short, narrow,
slightly expanded anteriorly, and deflected, profile
and that of crest forming approximate 115-degree

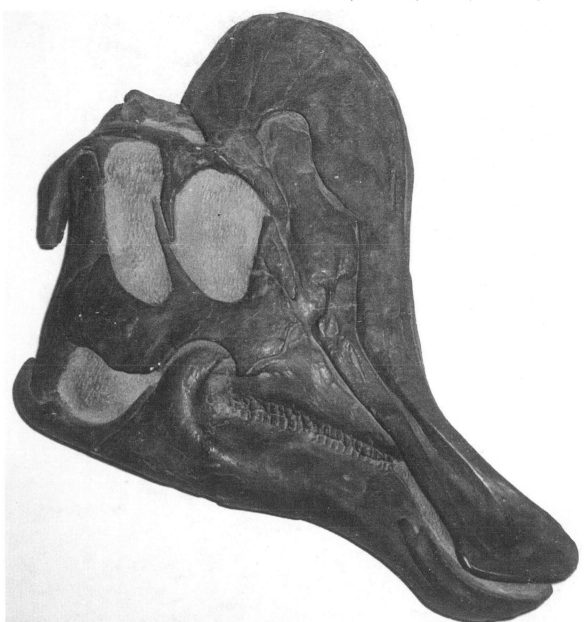

Corythosaurus casuarius, restored holotype skull (cast) of *C. brevicristatus*.

angle; nasal passages closed in adults, open on sides of crest in juveniles where there are variable vacuities; nasals have receded posteriorly, forming summit and rear of crest in outline and part of its lateral surface, separating the two premaxillary branches, with narial tube loop extending into upper branch; edentulous portion of muzzle short; 43 maxillary-tooth rows; dentary deep, massive, 37 tooth rows.

Brown diagnosed type species *C. casuarius* as follows: Rear of crest overhanging occiput, contacting squamosals immediately over symphysis; posterior margin without indentation, no development of

spur-like posterio-inferior process; upper branch of premaxillae not reaching summit of crest; lower branch moderately expanded above premaxillary sulcus; external nares not completely enclosed; orbit broad and oval in outline, apex downward, long axis 30 to 45 degrees from the perpendicular; lacrimal just meeting ascending process of maxilla; mandible robust, sharply decurved but variable.

As measured by Colbert (1962), the holotype skeleton of *C. casuarius* is 3.01 meters (over 10 feet) tall at the hips. An adult *Corythosaurus* probably weighed approximately 2.16 metric tons (more than

Corythosaurus casuarius,
ROM 845, skeleton.

2.4 tons) (G. S. Paul, personal communication 1988).

Although now only one described species of *Corythosaurus* is recognized as valid, various other species have been referred to this genus: *C. excavatus* was based on a skull (No. 13, University of Alberta collection) lacking maxilla, lacrimal, jugal, quadratojugal, and quadrate bones, collected by Levi Sternberg in 1919 at Sand Creek, Red Deer River. This species was described by Gilmore (1923), who distinguished it by its large and rounded crest among other features. *C. intermedius* was based on a nearly complete skull (ROM 776, formerly GSC 4670) collected in 1920 by the University of Toronto at Red Deer River, above Happy Jack Ferry. Parks (1923) distinguished this species by its very quite high and short crest among other features. (Both the type and paratype [ROM 777, formerly GSC 4671] specimens of this species also have a perforation in the thin part of the crest, at the suture between the upper branch of the premaxilla and nasal.)

Three more species, based on specimens from Red Deer River, were named and described by Parks (1935), who suggested that their holotype skulls might represent sexual dimorphism, growth stages or individual variation within the same species: *C. bicristatus*, based on a skull with jaws (ROM 868, formerly GSC 5852), lacking the predentary, collected in 1933 by Sternberg 2 miles southwest of Steveville, one half mile west of Red Deer River, was distinguished by the crest, which rises almost vertically posterior to the external nares, among other features; *C. bevicristatus*, founded upon an incomplete skull missing the anterior part of the snout and pos-terior portion of the squamosal, was distinguished mainly by its low crest.

Dodson (1975), after measuring numerous lambeosaurine skulls, speculated that the crest served as a visual signal for identification of individuals of the same species, and that the size and shape of the crest represented different growth stages or sexual dimorphism among individuals and did not reflect specific differences. From this study, Dodson reduced the number of species referred to *Corythosaurus* down to one, *C. casuarius*, the holotype representing an adult male, *C. excavatus* and *C. intermedius* females, *C. bicristatus* a female, and *C. brevicristatus* a juvenile male. (At the same time, Dodson referred *C. frontalis* to *Lambeosaurus lambei*; see *Lambeosaurus* entry.)

Other taxa are also now regarded as junior synonyms of *C. casuarius*: Matthew (1920) had named and briefly described *Procheneosaurus*, a genus founded on a skull, vertebrae, and a right scapula from the Judith River [Oldman] Formation. Parks (1931), noting that Matthew did not assign this genus a specific name and therefore the taxon had no sci-

Corythosaurus casuarius, mounted skeleton.

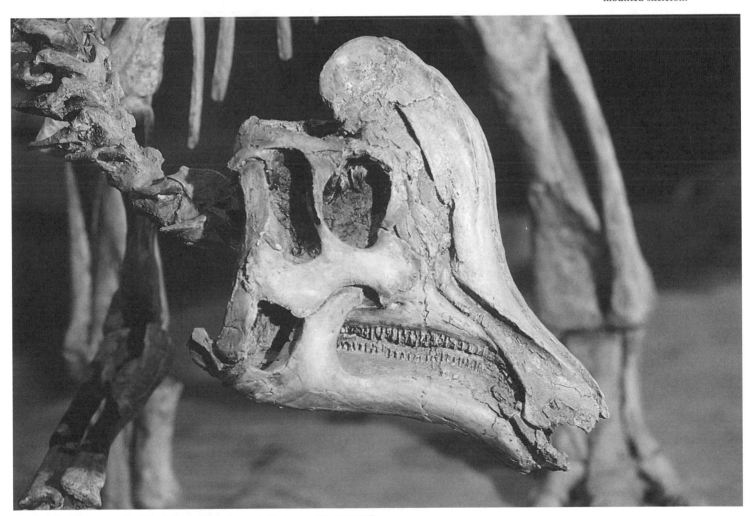

Photo by Collin Orthner, courtesy Royal Tyrrell Museum/Alberta Community Development (slide #10.005.02d).

entific value, referred it to his new genus and species *Tetragonosaurus erectofrons*, founded on a skull with jaws (ROM 7558, formerly 3577), collected in 1927 by L. Sternberg from the Judith River [=Oldman] Formation, west of Red Deer River, below the mouth of Sand Creek. Lull and Wright, noting the definability of Matthew's material and the priority of the name, resurrected *Procheneosaurus*. To *Procheneosaurus*, Lull and Wright referred *T. cranibrevis* Sternberg 1935, based on an incomplete skull with jaws (NMC 8633) collected by Charles M. Sternberg in 1928 from the Judith River [Oldman] Formation, above Red Deer River, south of the mouth of Berry Creek; to *P.? altidens*, they referred *Trachodon altidens* [*nomen dubium*], based on a left maxilla with teeth (NMC 1092) from Red Deer River, and first described by Lambe (1902), observing that the form and size of NMC 1092 most strongly resembled *P. cranibrevis*. In both *P. erectofrons* and *P. cranibrevis*, Lull and Wright noted that the skulls are small and

deep and the crests small. According to Dodson, the features apparently distinguishing these species are of ontogenetic importance, all species of *Procheneosaurus* interpreted by him to be juveniles of *C. casuarius*.

Finally, the genus *Pteropelyx* Cope 1889 had been founded on the greater part of a skeleton (AMNH 3971) lacking the skull, collected in 1876 by J. C. Isaac from the Judith River [Oldman] Formation), near Cow Island, on the upper Missouri River, Montana. Lull and Wright found *Pteropelyx* to be of conventional form and suggested that it could be synonymous with other contemporaneous forms. Brett-Surman (1975, 1979) provisionally referred *Pteropelyx* to *Corythosaurus* because the postcrania in both genera are inseparable. Subsequently, after studying the postcrania of both forms and finding that their pelvic and limb elements are identical, Brett-Surman (1989) suggested that *Pteropelyx* and *Corythosaurus* are congeneric. Although the name *Pteropelyx* has priority over *Corythosaurus*, Brett-Sur-

Corythosaurus casuarius (juvenile), NMC 8633, holotype skull of *Tetragonosaurus cranibrevis*.

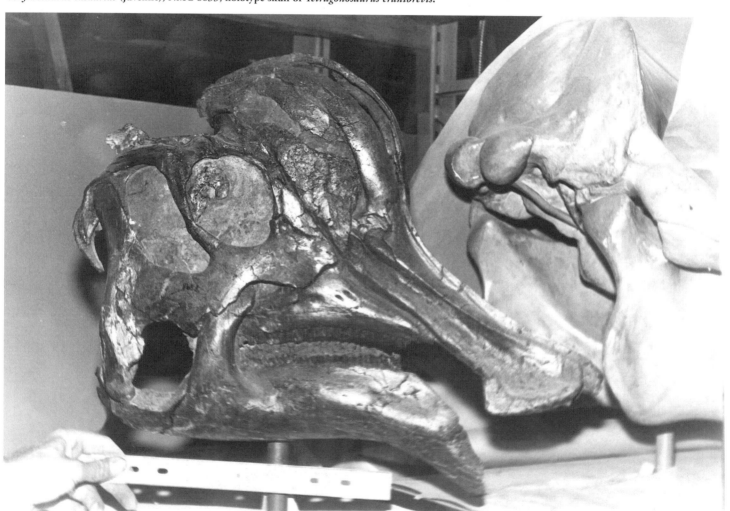

Photo by R. A. Long and S. P. Welles (neg. #73/537-10), reproduced with permission of Canadian Museum of Nature, Ottawa, Canada.

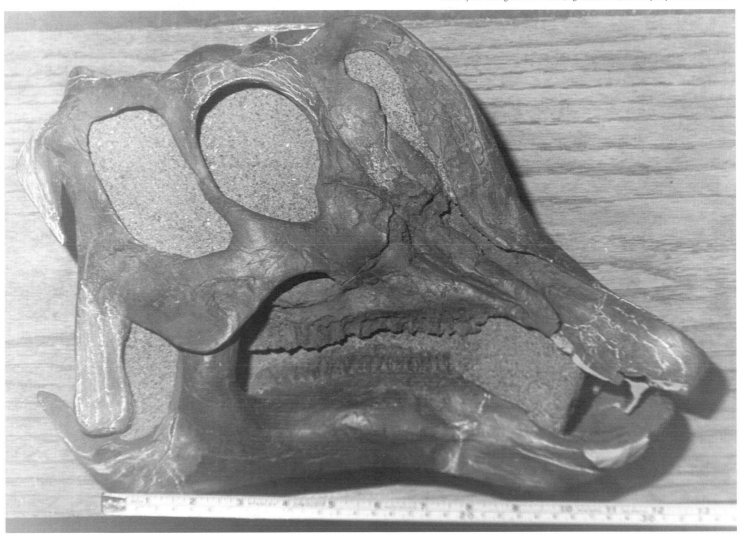

Corythosaurus casuarius (juvenile), ROM 579, holotype skull of *Tetragonosaurus erectofrons.*

man (1989) argued that *Pteropelyx* should be abandoned to avoid confusion, the latter a taxon lacking a skull and with but a single specimen referred to it.

Fossilized integument impressions in some *Corythosaurus* specimens reveal that the skin was remarkably thin, and that numerous limpet-like scutes were present in the epidermis. These scutes were either circular or elliptical and distinctly pyramidal in shape. As observed by Lull and Wright (1942), the largest scutes attain an approximate length of 38 millimeters (about 1.5 inches), breadth of 32 millimeters (1.3 inches) and height of 8 millimeters (3.1 inches). These scutes are confined to the ventral surface of the abdomen below the pelvis. On the neck and sides of the body are uniform tubercles of polygonal shape, not arranged in any specific order. The abdominal region features longitudinal rows of oval-shaped, limpet-like tubercles separated by uniformly large, polygonal tubercles, these rows parallel to one another. Fleshy pads covered with large, low tubercles are present beneath the metatarsals and proximal phalanges. There are no signs of webbing.

As reported by Lull and Wright, preserved in the matrix of plesiotype specimen (NMC 8676) of species *C. excavatus* is a good impression of the horny beak. This impression extends in front and on the sides of the predentary for 36 millimeters (over 1.45 inches). (See *Edmontosaurus* entry, and Morris 1970, for data regarding the hadrosaurid beak.)

Sternberg (1939) found the beak in NMC 8676 to be evidence refuting Wilfarth's (1938) idea that the beak and hood in lambeosaurines accommodated the attachment of powerful muscles for controlling a proboscis. (Wilfarth admitted that many German paleontologists lacked the opportunity to study the various hadrosaur species or their published descrip-

Corythosaurus

tions.) Sternberg explained that all hadrosaurs seemingly had a beak, which would have been quite useless to an animal with a proboscis. Sternberg also pointed out that: 1. No evidence of an imagined proboscis has ever been found in any hadrosaur specimen; 2. it is unlikely that animals with such highly developed narial passages would also develop a breathing proboscis; and 3. in proboscis-bearing mammals, the anterior part of the skull is not roofed by nasal bones and the "nares" are located far back, contrary to the conditions in lambeosaurines.

Corythosaurus and other (if not all) hadrosaurids had an integumentary dorsal frill above the dorsal spines. In this genus, the frill extended backwards over the dorsals, sacrals and caudals and, according to Lull and Wright, may have continued forward to the skull. The frill was uniformly covered with a patternless arrangement of large polygonal tubercles and, above the sacrals and anterior caudals, reached a height of 125 millimeters (5 inches) (see *Edmontosaurus* entry; also Horner 1984*c*).

Brown (1916*b*) originally posed *Corythosaurus* as a bipedal animal. Sternberg (1965) challenged that interpretation, arguing that in all naturally articulated skeletons of hadrosaurs the femora always point forward and downward. If an upright pose was natural to the animal, at least some skeletons should feature femora pointing directly downward or backward. Consequently, Sternberg brought *Corythosaurus* down to all fours. Galton (1970), however, from skeletons of *C. casuarius, Edmontosaurus annectens* and other hadrosaurids, demonstrated that *Corythosaurus* was

certainly bipedal, its body balanced horizontally over the femur and locked into position by the ossified tendons on the tail (see *Edmontosaurus* entry), the best set of these tendons on AMNH 5338.

Superficially, the cranial crest of *Corythosaurus* resembles a Corinthian soldier's helmet, hence its name. The crest is hollow with passages running from the nostrils to the throat. There has been much speculation as to the function of these canals (see *Parasaurolophus* entry), including being used as a reserve air chamber when the animal was underwater, a popular notion introduced by Romer (1933). However, Ostrom (1962*a*) demonstrated that the maximum air that a *Corythosaurus* crest could hold was only about four percent total lung capacity, hardly an efficient respiratory adaptation.

Ostrom stated that the nasal bone in skull NMC 8676 forms a major part of the crest. Separate, paired narial passages ascend from the external nares, running posteriorly through the nasals, turning anteriorly and dorsally anterior to the orbits, then posteriorly again, to form separate S-shaped curves within the crest. These canals lead into paired lateral openings above and behind the S-shaped loops. This medial crest cavity apparently extends ventrally to the olfactory canal of the braincase. Ostrom suggested that this cavity was the most appropriate site for the olfactory bulbs and that this increase in surface tissue area allowed for the enhancement of the sense of smell. For an animal lacking other means of defense, a heightened olfactory sense could be crucial for survival, alerting these dinosaurs of impending danger.

In a detailed study of the nasal cavity of lambeosaurines, Weishampel (1981) observed that there are three differences between adult individuals of *C. casuarius* and the quite similar species *Hypacrosaurus altispinus*: 1. Premaxillae-nasal openings present in *C. casuarius* but absent in the latter species; 2. *C. casuarius* with S-shaped loops along the course of the ascending track, apparently lacking in *H. altispinus*; and 3. fenestrae present in *C. casuarius* on the medial walls of the lateral diverticula, allowing free communication between these openings, not present in *H. altispinus*. Weishampel also showed that the nasal cavity in *C. casuarius* changes in form concomitant with the growth of the crest during ontogeny.

Brett-Surman (1989), observing similarities between *Corythosaurus* and *Hypacrosaurus*, postulated that *Corythosaurus* is ancestral to, and might even be congeneric with the latter. This potential synonymy would result in all species of *Corythosaurus* and *Hypacrosaurus* being reduced to two species, *H. casuarius* and its "chronospecies" (a descendant species more derived, after the passage of time) *H. altispinus*.

Also, Brett-Surman (1989) observed that postcranial elements in *Corythosaurus* and the rarer *Lambeosaurus* are indistinguishable from each other, both

Corythosaurus casuarius, AMNH 3971, holotype pubis of *Pteropelyx grallipes*.

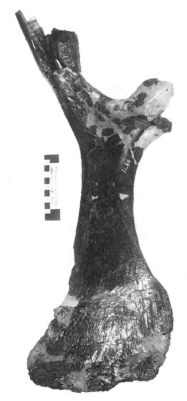

Photo by J. H. Horner, courtesy D. Baird, and American Museum of Natural History.

Corythosaurus casuarius, AMNH 3971, holotype two left femora of *Pteropelyx grallipes*.

Photo by R. A. Long and S. P. Welles (neg. #73/302-6), courtesy American Museum of Natural History.

forms possibly representing different species of the same genus, with *L. magnicristatus* and *L. lambei* the male and female morphs of *C. casuarius*, and *C. intermedius* the male and female of the other species. However, Brett-Surman (1989) cautioned against synonymizing these forms until more *Lambeosaurus* specimens can be found and studied.

Note: A mounted skeleton from the Late Cretaceous (Santonian), of South Kazakhstan, Central Asia, labeled "Corythosaurus convincens," was exhibited as part of "The Great Russian Dinosaurs Exhibition." A juvenile, it measures about 4 meters (about 13.5 feet) long. A photo of the skeleton appeared in *The ICI Australia Catalogue of the Great Russian Dinosaur Exhibition, 1993–1995*, by Patricia Vickers-Rich and Thomas Rich, published in 1993. To date of this writing, the species has not been formally named or described. The specimen represents the first *Corythosaurus* discovery in Asia.

Key references: Brett-Surman (1975, 1979, 1989); Brown (1914*d*, 1916*b*); Colbert (1962); Cope (1889*b*); Dodson (1975); Galton (1970); Gilmore (1923); Lambe (1902); Lull and Wright (1942); Matthew (1920); Ostrom (1962*a*); Parks (1923, 1931, 1935); Romer (1933); Sternberg (1939, 1965); Weishampel (1981).

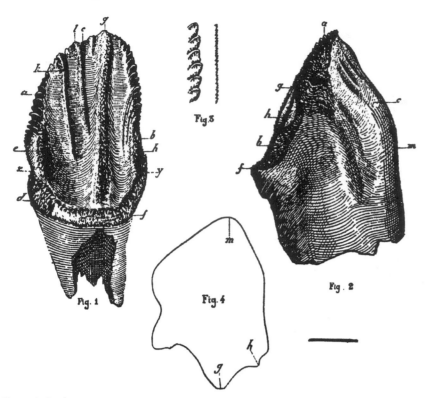

Craspedodon lonzeensis, IRSNB 390, holotype teeth, scale = 2 cm.; fig. 3 showing enlargement of serrations. (After Dollo 1883.)

CRASPEDODON   Dollo 1883 [*nomen dubium*]

Ornithischia: Genasauria: Cerapoda: Ornithopoda: Iguanodontia *incertae sedis*.

Name derivation: Greek *kraspedon* = "edge" + Greek *odous* = "tooth."

Type species: *C. lonzeensis* Dollow 1883 [*nomen dubium*].

Other species: [None.]

Occurrence: Glauconie argileuse, Namur, Belgium.

Age: Late Cretaceous (Santonian).

Known material: Three teeth.

Holotype: IRSNB 390, two teeth missing roots.

Diagnosis of genus: [No modern diagnosis published.]

Comments: The genus *Craspedodon* was founded upon two incomplete teeth (IRSNB 390) collected from the Upper Cretaceous of Lonzee, Namur, Belgium.

The genus was diagnosed by Dollo (1883) as follows: Teeth strongly compressed anteroposteriorly, asymmetrical in side view; crowns rounded at summit, separated from the root on internal surface; external surface with five ridges, first very marked, second and third weakest.

Dollo observed that these teeth were more advanced in development of their ridges than in *Iguanodon*, thereby representing a specialized descendent of that genus in Late Cretaceous Europe.

In their review of iguanodontids and related ornithopods, Norman and Weishampel (1990) regarded *C. lonzeensis* as Iguanodontia *insertae sedis*.

Note: Steel (1969) suggested that *Iguanodon hilli*, a species based on a tooth from the Totternhoe Stone (Lower Chalk) of Hitchin, Hertfordshire, and described by Newton (1892), may be referable to *Craspedodon*.

Key references: Dollo (1883); Norman and Weishampel (1990).

CRATAEOMUS   Seeley 1881 [*nomen dubium*]— (=?"*Struthiosaurus*" [entry notes])

Ornithischia: Thyreophora: Ankylosauria: Nodosauridae.

Name derivation: Greek *krater*/Latin *crater* = "mixing vessel" + Latin *omasum* = "pouch."

Type species: *C. lepidophorous* Seeley 1881 [*nomen dubium*].

Other species: *C. pawlowitschii* Seeley 1881 [*nomen dubium*].

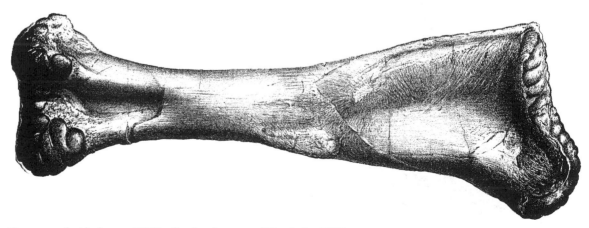

Crataeomus lepidophorous, GIUV collection, humerus. (After Seeley 1881.)

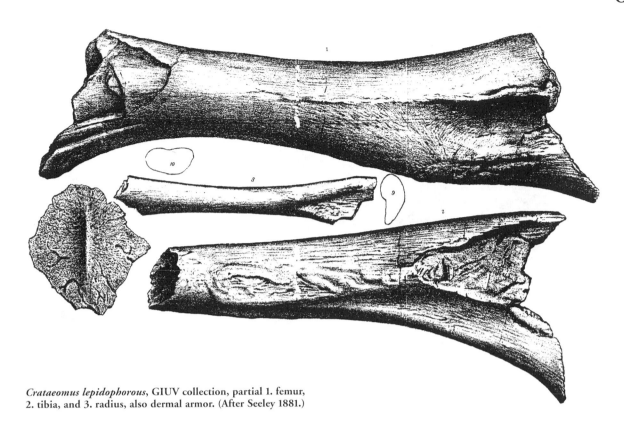

Crataeomus lepidophorous, GIUV collection, partial 1. femur,
2. tibia, and 3. radius, also dermal armor. (After Seeley 1881.)

A. *Crataeomus pawlowitschii*, GIUV collection, left scapula,
compared with B. right scapula (reversed for comparison) of
C. lepidophorous. Scale = 2 cm. (After Seeley 1881.)

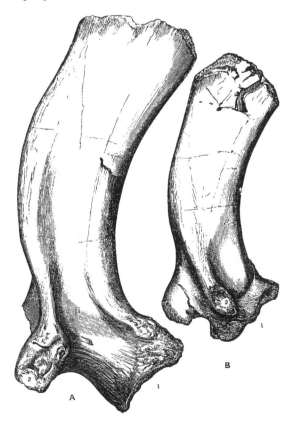

Occurrence: Gosau Formation, Siebenbergen,
   Hungary.
Age: Late Cretaceous (Turonian).
Known material: Partial mandibles, teeth, postcra-
   nia, dermal scutes, dermal spines, miscellaneous
   fragments.
Holotype: GIUV collection, anterior ends of three
   left mandibles.

   Diagnosis of genus: [None published.]

   Comments: The genus *Crataeomus* was founded
upon fragmentary left mandibles (GIUV collection)
from the Gosau Formation of Siebenburgen, Hungary. Referred material includes portions of lower
jaws, teeth, vertebrae, ribs, scapula-coracoid, ilium,
radius, ulna, tibia, armor consisting of plates, spines
and scutes, and various fragments. Seeley (1881)

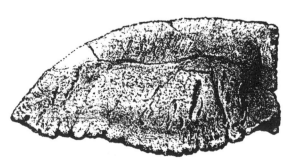

Crataeomus lepidophorous, GIUV collection, dermal armor.
(After Seeley 1881.)

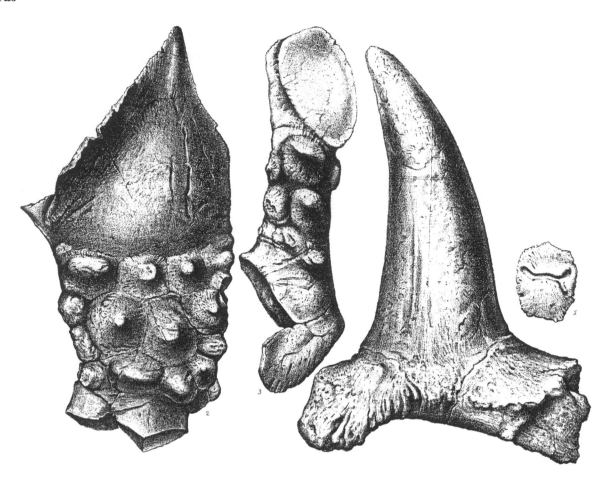

Dermal armor (GIUV collection) referred to *Crataeomus*. (After Seeley 1881.)

described but did not figure the type specimen, nor did he assign the genus a specific name.

Seeley described this genus as small (about 2 meters or 6.8 feet in length) and similar to "*Struthiosaurus*" (see entry notes).

From the same locality, Seeley also described *C. pawlowitschii*, based upon material including a dorsal and caudal vertebra, dorsal rib, left scapula, incomplete right femur and right tibia, and dorsal armor; material referred to this species includes the distal end of a humerus.

Romer (1956) referred *Crataeomus* to "*Struthiosaurus*," this synonymy repeated over the years by other writers (Steel 1969; Olshevsky 1978; 1989; 1991; 1992). Coombs (1978*a*), however, regarded this referral as tentative.

Key references: Coombs (1978*a*); Seeley (1881).

CRATEROSAURUS Seeley 1874 [*nomen dubium*]
Ornithischia: Genasauria: Thyreophora:
  Stegosauria: Stegosauridae.
Name derivation: Greek *krater*/Latin *crater* = "mixing vessel" + Greek *sauros* = "lizard."
Type species: *C. pottonensis* Seeley 1874 [*nomen dubium*].

Other species: [None.]
Occurrence: Wealden (Woburn Sands; reworked), Bedfordshire, England.
Age: Early Cretaceous (?Valanginian–?Barremian).
Known material/holotype: SMC B.28814, incomplete neural arch of dorsal vertebra.

Diagnosis of genus (as for type species): Dorsal vertebra with unique deep excavation on dorsal sur-

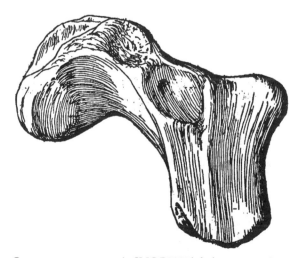

Craterosaurus pottonensis, SMC B28814, holotype neural arch of dorsal vertebra. (After Seeley 1874.)

face immediately caudal to the prezygapophyses (Galton 1985*b*; 1990*b*).

Comments: *Craterosaurus* was founded on an incomplete dorsal vertebra recovered from the Potton Nodule Bed, in the upper part of Woburn Sands (probably reworked from beds of Neocomian age; see Casey 1961), near Potton, Bedfordshire, England. The holotype (SCM B.28814) was first described by Seeley (1874), who mistook it for part of a braincase. Later, the specimen was restudied and correctly identified by Nopcsa (1912).

Key references: Galton (1985*b*, 1990*b*); Nopcsa (1912); Seeley (1874).

CREOSAURUS Marsh 1878—(See *Allosaurus*.)
Name derivation: Greek *kreas* = "flesh" + Greek *sauros* = "lizard."
Type species: *C. atrox* Marsh 1878.

CRYOLOPHOSAURUS Hammer and Hickerson 1994
Saurischia: Theropoda *incertae sedis.*
Name derivation: Greek *kryos* = "frost" + Greek *lophos* = "crest" + Greek *sauros* = "lizard."
Type species: *C. ellioti* Hammer and Hickerson 1994.
Other species: [None.]
Occurrence: Falla Formation, Transantarctic Mountains, Antarctica.
Age: Late Triassic or Early Jurassic (Pliensbachian).
Known material/holotype: Partial skull with articulated mandibles, ?partial postcrania including femur, ilium, ischium, pubis, tibiotarsus, fibula, two articulated metatarsals, 30 vertebrae.

Diagnosis of genus (as for type species): Skull deep, narrow, approximately 65 centimeters (25 inches) long; nasals extend posteriorly as high ridges that join with large furrowed lacrimal crest, which runs above orbits approximately perpendicular to skull length, curving anteriorly as it rises; furrowed surface of crest apparently separating into what would be small vertical projections along dorsal surface; orbital horn fused to crest on each side; in postorbital region, jugal crossing lower lateral temporal opening and sutures with squamosal, splitting opening into two parts (Hammer and Hickerson 1994).

Comments: *Cryolophosaurus*, a large theropod distinguished by an unusual crest rising from its head above the orbits, is one of the few dinosaurs of any kind yet discovered in Antarctica, the first carnivorous dinosaur found on that continent, and one of the small number of carnivorous forms known from any Gondwana continent. The dinosaur is also unusual

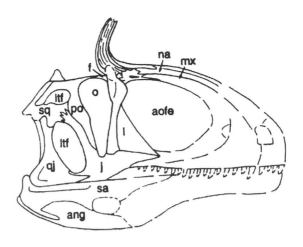

Cryolophosaurus ellioti, holotype (restored) skull, right lateral view. (After Hammer and Hickerson 1994.)

in bearing some resemblance to large Middle–Late Jurassic tetanurans, while also displaying certain primitive ceratosaurian features.

The new genus and species *C. ellioti* was founded upon a skull and associated incomplete skeleton (found during the austral summer of 1990–91; see Hammer and Hickerson 1993) collected from tuffaceous sandstone high in the Falla Formation at Mount Kirkpatrick, near the Beardmore Glacier, in the Central Transantarctic Mountains, Antarctica, about 360 kilometers from the geographic South Pole. The right side of the skull was better preserved than the left, the front of the skull had been glacially eroded away, and the top of the cranial crest was broken (Hammer and Hickerson 1994).

Hammer and Hickerson noted that two broken theropod teeth, apparently the result of scavenging and found near the shaft of a limb bone, may belong to another theropod or to another individual of this genus. At least two other nontheropod dinosaurs (including a probable prosauropod) and two nondinosaurian taxa (a pterosaur and large tritylodont) made up the fauna at this locality. Plant fossils found include tree trunks indicating forested areas.

The authors pointed out that the holotype of *C. ellioti* provides important data on the earlier evolutionary stages of large theropods, exhibiting a mixture of primitive and derived features, indicating that Early Jurassic large theropods had diverged significantly from Triassic ancestors. The deep, narrow skull with its large antorbital fenestra is similar to that of Late Middle to Late Jurassic tetanurans from other continents (*e.g.*, *Allosaurus* and *Yangchuanosaurus*); however, although the new genus possesses pneumatic lacrimals as in tetanurans, it lacks the large lacrimal opening and deep surangular typical of larger "carnosaurian" tetanurans. Though the skull shows derived characteristics, the associated postcrania exhibits more primitive features. The femur has a highly bowed shaft, declined head from the greater trochanter, and lacks a deep extensor groove, features typical of more primitive theropods including the ceratosaur *Dilophosaurus*; tibia, astragalus, and calcaneum seem to be fused as in most ceratosaurs and abelisaurs. Allowing that the cranial and postcranial remains may not go together, Hammer and Hickerson observed that the latter are definitely theropod and are the correct size for an association with the skull. The pelvis is quite similar to megalosaurid-grade theropods like *Gasosaurus*, *Monolophosaurus*, and *Yangchuanosaurus*.

Given the likelihood that the cranial and postcranial elements of *Cryolophosaurus* belong together, Hammer and Hickerson speculated that this genus could either be a ceratosaur with features convergent with those of some large tetanurans, an earlier large tetanuran possessing some primitive features, or an early abelisaur, its highly derived skull features indicating that Early Jurassic Gondwana theropods had diverged much from the smaller basal Triassic forms.

Hammer and Hickerson noted that the existence of this fauna suggests that the Earth's climatic conditions were at least seasonally temperate at high latitudes during the early part of the Jurassic, perhaps as high as 65 to 70 degrees south with a low temperature of at least 60 degrees.

Key reference: Hammer and Hickerson (1993, 1994).

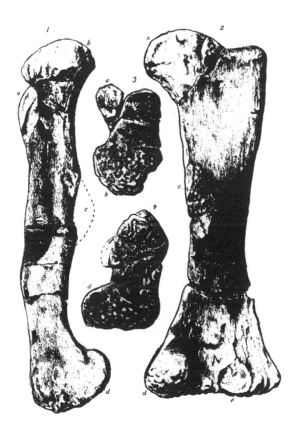

Cryptodraco eumerus, OUM J.46882, holotype right femur of *Cryptosaurus eumerus*, in 1. lateral, 2. anterior, 3. dorsal, and 4. ventral views. (After Seeley 1875.)

CRYPTODRACO Lydekker 1889 [*nomen dubium*]—(=*Cryptosaurus* Seeley 1875)

Ornithischia: Genasauria: Thyreophora: Ankylosauria: ?Nodosauridae.

Name derivation: Greek *kruptos* = "hidden" + Latin *draco* = "dragon."

Type species: *C. eumrus* (Seeley 1875) [*nomen dubium*].

Other species: [None.]

Occurrence: Amphill Clay, Cambridgeshire, England.

Age: Late Jurassic (Upper Oxfordian).

Known material/holotype: OUM J.46882, right femur.

Diagnosis of genus (as for type species): Femur massive, with prominent head; lesser trochanter large, anteroposteriorly wide, separated from greater trochanter by cleft much deeper laterally than medially; anterior intercondylar groove shallow distally; condyles very quite prominent posteriorly (Galton 1980*b*).

Comments: The genus *Cryptodraco* was originally described by Seeley (1875) as the type species *Cryptosaurus eumerus*, which had been based on a femur (OUM J.46882) collected from Amphill Clay (Upper Oxfordian), in Cambridgeshire, England. The specimen was presented in 1869 by L. Ewbank of Clare College, Cambridge, to the Woodwardian Museum.

Observing that the position of the "inner [=lesser] trochanter" of the femur was in "close agreement" with that of *Iguanodon*, Seeley believed *Cryptodraco* to be an iguanodontid.

Seeley originally "diagnosed" this genus as follows: Femur 1.25 feet (more than .46 meters) long, with slight anteroposterior and forward flexure at lower third of shaft; gently concave in longitudinal outline on outer side, much more concave on inner side; both ends of femoral shaft triangular.

As the name *Cryptosaurus* proved to be preoccupied (Saint-Hillaire 1833), Lydekker (1889*a*) proposed the new generic name *Cryptodraco* for this taxon.

Upon reexamining the type specimen, Galton (1980*b*) identified it as ankylosaurian, recognizing in it certain characters listed by Coombs (1978*a*) as diagnostic of nodosaurids. Because of these features and also the similarity of the holotype to the femur of nodosaurid *Hoplitosaurus*, Galton tentatively transferred *Cryptodraco* to the Nodosauridae. Also, Galton noted that the lesser trochanter in *Cryptodraco* is larger than that of *Hoplitosaurus*.

Key references: Coombs (1978*a*); Galton (1980*b*); Lydekker (1889*a*); Seeley (1875).

CRYPTOSAURUS Seeley 1875—(Preoccupied, Geoffrey Saint-Hillaire 1833; see *Cryptodraco*.)

Name derivation: Greek *kruptos* = "hidden" + Greek *sauros* = "lizard."
Type species: *C. eumerus* Seeley 1875 [*nomen dubium*].

CUMNORIA Seeley 1888—(See *Camptosaurus*.)
Name derivation: "Cumnor [Hurst, near Oxford, England]."
Type species: *C. prestwichii* (Hulke 1880).

DACENTRURUS Lucas 1902—(=*Omosaurus* Owen 1875)
Ornithischia: Genasauria: Thyreophora: Stegosauria: Stegosauridae.
Name derivation: Greek *da* = "very" + Greek *kentron* = "spiny" + Greek *ouros* = "tail."
Type species: *D. armatus* (Owen 1875).
Other species: ?*D. phillipsi* (Seeley 1893) [*nomen dubium*].
Occurrence: Lower Kimmeridge Clay, Cambridgeshire, Dorset, Wiltshire, Corralian Oolite Formation, Dorset, England; Argiles d'Octeville, Seine-Maritime, France; [unnamed formation], Beira Litoral, [unnamed formation], Estremadura, Portugal.
Age: Late Jurassic (Oxfordian–Kimmeridgian).
Known material: Almost complete postcranial skeleton, partial postcranial skeleton, isolated and fragmentary postcrania, juvenile to adult.

Holotype: BMNH 46013, incomplete postcranial skeleton, including three cervical and 14 dorsal vertebrae, sacrum, 12 caudal vertebrae, left humerus, radius, ulna, carpus, metacarpus, a phalanx, ilia and ischia, right pubis, a femur, tibia, distal end of fibula and calcaneum, left metatarsal IV, right dermal nuchal plate, left dermal caudal spine.

Diagnosis of genus (as for type species): Derived characters include dorsal vertebrae with massive centra wider than long, with lateral pleurocoelous depressions; sacrum with almost solid dorsal plate; pubis with deep prepubic process; long dermal tail spines, with sharp lateral and medial edges (Galton 1990*b*).

Comments: *Dacentrurus* was the first stegosaurid genus to be described. This dinosaur was of the general proportions of *Stegosaurus*, though with slightly longer front legs, two rows of small dermal plates and paired dermal spines, and measuring approximately

Dacentrurus armatus, BMNH 46013, holotype partial skeleton (ventral view) of *Omosaurus armatus*, including pelvis, vertebrae, right femur. (After Owen 1875.)

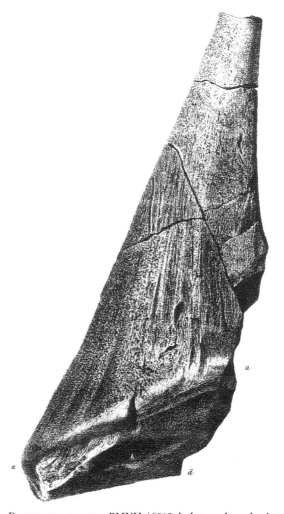

Dacentrurus armatus, BMNH 46013, holotype dermal spine, lateral view, of *Omosaurus armatus*. (After Owen 1875.)

Dacentrurus armatus, holotype proximal end of right femur of *Astrodon pusillus*. (After Lapparent and Zbyszewski 1957.)

The species *O. hastiger* was based on two very large spines (BMNH 46321) with quite massive bases, discovered near one another in a Kimmeridge Clay pit, at Wooton Bassett, Wiltshire. Owen (1877) noted that these spines form a pair, though he incorrectly believed them to be "carpal spines" because of their resemblance to the thumb spikes in *Iguanodon*, and because they were found in proximity to the manus. The right (and longest) spine is over 36 centimeters (14 inches) long. Galton (1990*b*) referred this species to *D. armatus*, Galton (1985*b*) suggesting that these spines probably came from a more anterior position on the tail than in the holotype of "*O.*" *armatus*.

?*O phillipsi* was based on an incomplete femur (YM 498) from the Malton Oolite Member of the Coralline Oolite Formation, Slingsby, North York-

4.4 meters (15 feet) in length. The genus was established on an incomplete skeleton lacking the skull (BMNH 46013), collected in 1874 by the Swindon Brick and Tile Company, from the Kimmeridge Clay at Swindon, Wiltshire, England.

Owen (1875) originally described this material as new genus and species *Omosaurus armatus*. After Marsh (*see in* Lydekker 1888) pointed out that name *Omosaurus* was preoccupied (Leidy 1856), Lucas (1901*b*) renamed the genus *Dacentrurus*.

Owen, observing that the base of the preserved dermal spine is asymmetrical, deduced that this spine was one of a pair. Commenting on the superior strength of the spine, Owen postulated that a series of spines, if located dorsally along the tail, may have served as an attack weapon.

The first modern diagnosis of *Dacentrurus*, based on the holotype of *D. armatus*, was published almost a century after Owen's description by Galton (1985*b*), in a review of British stegosaurs. At the same time, Galton described the only preserved dermal plate as asymmetrical, with a transversely oblique base measuring 150 millimeters (about 5.8 inches) long and 70 millimeters (about 2.7 inches) wide. Comparing this plate to a comparable plate in *Stegosaurus*, Galton located it on the left side of body, possibly the anterior part of the back. As preserved, the left dermal caudal spine (measured by Owen) has a maximum length of 456 millimeters (over 1.5 feet). Galton noted that this spine has a slightly expanded base measuring 118 millimeters (about 4.5 inches) wide and a strongly sculptured surface.

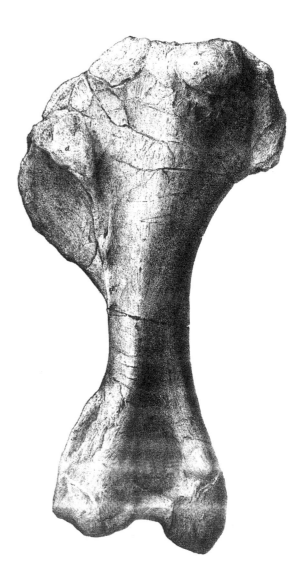

Dacentrurus armatus, BMNH 46013, holotype left humerus of *Omosaurus armatus*. (After Owen 1875.)

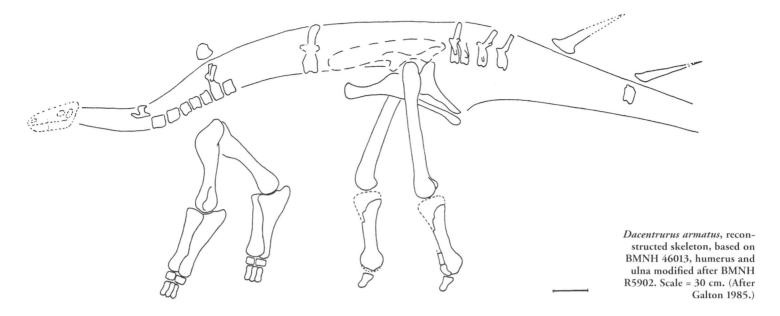

Dacentrurus armatus, reconstructed skeleton, based on BMNH 46013, humerus and ulna modified after BMNH R5902. Scale = 30 cm. (After Galton 1985.)

shire, England. The femur, in three pieces, was first described by Seeley (1893). Galton (1983) redescribed this femur as that of a juvenile stegosaur, as shown by the columnar-like form of the shaft. As the specimen exhibits no diagnostic characters and because it was not possible to determine whether the specimen was more similar to that of *Lexovisaurus* or the comparably-sized *Dacentrurus*, Galton tentatively referred it to the latter. ?*D. phillipsi* is significant in having been founded on the only evidence thus far known of Oxfordian stegosaurs.

D. lennieri was founded on several cervical and dorsal vertebrae, all sacrals, one caudal, fragment of a femur, one ilium, and distal portions of pubes and ischia, from France, this material originally described by Nopcsa (1911b) as a species of *Omosaurus*. To this species, Lapparent and Zbyszewski referred a specimen including two distal caudal vertebrae, three dorsals, sacrum, eight caudals, some ribs, ilium, fragments of pubis and ischium, left femur, humeri, right tibia, and two large dermal spines (MGSP), from the Kimmeridgian of Foz do Arelho, Portugal. Galton (1990b) also referred this species to D. armatus.

The species originally named *Astrodon pusillus* was described as a sauropod by Lapparent and Zbyszewski (1957), based upon the proximal end of a femur, ?calcaneum, probable third metatarsal, pos-

sible pubis, a radius, ?proximal end of metacarpal I, ungual phalanx, scapula, posterior dorsal centrum, anterior sacral centrum, distal portions of two sacral ribs, and a caudal centrum (MGSP), apparently from the same individual, collected from the Kimmeridgian of the Canal du Pedreira, Louriñha, Portugal. These remains were identified as stegosaurian by Galton and Boine (1980). Galton (1981c) subsequently showed that these fossils represent either a valid small species of *Dacentrurus* or a juvenile individual D. armatus.

Also to D. [=*Omosaurus* of their usage] armatus, Lapparent and Zbyszewski referred some vertebrae, ribs, a right ilium, right ischium, right pubis, and right femur (MGSP), recovered from the Lusitanian–Kimmeridgian of Baleal, Portugal. According to Galton, the so-called "nuchal plate" referred to this species is actually the dorsal part of a neural arch, with the eroded base of a neural spine, and the tail spine is the eroded proximal end of a hemal arch.

According to Galton (1990b) in a review of the Stegosauria, primitive characters in D. armatus include dorsal vertebrae with a low pedicle of the neural arch, transverse processes elevated at 45 degrees, and femur to humerus ratio of 147 percent.

Notes: Lapparent and Lavocat (1955) reported an egg believed by them to be that of O. lennieri from

Dacentrurus armatus, BMNH 46013, holotype dermal spine of *Omosaurus armatus*. (After Owen 1875.)

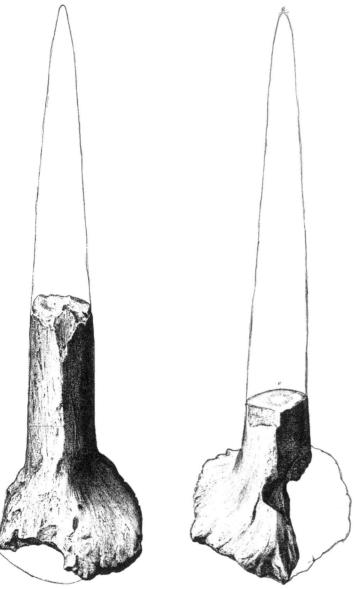

Dacentrurus armatus, BMNH 46321, holotype right and left dermal spines of *Omosaurus hastiger*. (After Owen 1877.)

DANUBIOSAURUS Bunzel 1871 [*nomen dubium*]—(=*Pleuropeltus*; =?*"Struthiosaurus"* [notes])

Ornithischia: Genasauria: Thyreophora: Ankylosauria *incertae sedis*.

Name derivation: "Danube [river]" + Greek *sauros* = "lizard."

Type species: *D. anceps* Bunzel 1871 [*nomen dubium*].

Other species: [None.]

Occurrence: Gosau Formation, Siebenburgen, Transylvania.

Age: Late Cretaceous (Turonian).

Known material/holotype: GIUV collection, composite fragmentary remains, including scapula, plates, scutes.

Diagnosis of genus: [None published.]

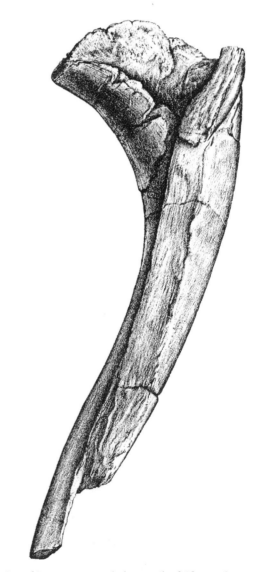

Danubiosaurus anceps, holotype rib of *Pleuropeltus suessi*. (After Seeley 1881.)

Alfeizerao, Portugal. The egg has a long diameter of 19 centimeters (almost 7.4 inches) and a short diameter of 13 centimeters (over 5 inches). It is oval, smaller than [theropod] eggs attributed to sauropods, similar in dimensions to those [incorrectly] associated with the ceratopsian *Protoceratops*, but less slenderly elongated.

O. vetustus Huene 1910 was tentatively referred by Galton and Powell (1983) to *Lexovisaurus*.

Key references: Galton (1981*c*, 1983, 1985*b*, 1990*b*); Lucas (1901*b*); Galton and Boine (1980); Lapparent and Lavocat (1955); Lapparent and Zbyszewski (1957); Lucas (1901*b*); Lydekker (1888); Nopcsa (1911*b*); Owen (1875), 1877); Seeley (1893).

Comments: The new type species *Danubiosaurus anceps* was established on fragmentary postcranial material (GIUV collection), recovered from the Gosau Formation of Siedenbergen, Transylvania, Hungary [now in Romania]. Bunzel (1871) originally described these remains as those of an extinct lizard, misidentifying the dermal elements as an ungual phalanx and left ilium.

Later, Seeley (1881) described the new dinosaurian species *Crataeomus pawlowitschii*, the type material of which included a scapula originally included in the holotype of type species *D. anceps*. Seeley designated part of the former material as the type specimen of new species *Pleuropeltus suessi*, which was founded upon two specimens (apparently GIUV collection) from the Gosau Formation of Transylvania. (This material was misidentified by Seeley as a pair of postfrontal bones belonging to a large chelonian.)

P. suessi was considered by Romer (1956, 1966) to be synonymous with "*Struthiosaurus*" *transilvanicus* (see *Struthiosaurus* entry notes), a species known from the same formation. Although this synonymy has been repeated by other authors (Steel 1969; Olshevsky 1978, 1991, 1992), it was regarded by Coombs and Marya´nska, in their review of the Ankylosauria, as a *nomen dubium* belonging in *D. anceps*.

D. anceps has also generally been accepted as a junior synonym of "*Struthiosaurus*" *transilvanicus* (Romer 1956, 1966; Steel 1969; Olshevsky 1978, 1991, 1992), a nodosaurid from the same formation, although Coombs (1978*a*) regarded that synonymy as tentative. The scapula may represent a distinct genus. Coombs and Marya´nska considered this taxon to be indeterminate.

Key references: Bunzel (1871); Coombs (1978*a*); Coombs and Marya´nska (1990); Seeley (1881).

DASPLETOSAURUS Russell 1970—(=?*Albertosaurus*)

Saurischia: Theropoda: Tetanurae: Avetheropoda: Coelurosauria: Maniraptora: Arctometatarsalia: Tyrannosauridae.

Name derivation: Greek *daspletos* = "frightful" + Greek *sauros* = "lizard."

Type species: *D. torosus* Russell 1970.

Other species: [None.]

Occurrence: Oldman Formation, Alberta, Canada.

Age: Late Cretaceous (Late Campanian).

Known material: Three incomplete skulls, complete skull with associated partial skeleton, three partial skeletons.

Holotype: NMC 8506, skull, postcranial skeleton missing hindlimbs.

Diagnosis of genus (as for type species): Premaxilla not contacting nasals under external nares; lacrimal horn well-developed, postorbital rugose (less than in *Tyrannosaurus*); pro-maxillary opening very small; surangular foramen very large; ilium with very long postacetabular blade; ischium straight; scapula broadens gradually posteriorly; acromion process of scapula forming continuous arc with coracoid (Carpenter 1992).

Comments: *Daspletosaurus* was founded on an incomplete skeleton with skull (NMC 8506) and limbs, collected by Charles M. Sternberg in 1921, from the Oldman (formerly Judith River) Formation at "Steveville," Alberta, Canada. The paratype (AMNH 5438) includes a sacrum and adjacent thoracic and caudal vertebrae, pelvis, right femur, left tibia, and second metatarsal, recovered from Little Sandhill Creek basin. Originally, Sternberg believed that both specimens represented an undescribed species of *Albertosaurus* [=*Gorgosaurus* of his usage] (Russell 1970*b*).

Additional *Daspletosaurus* remains subsequently collected include a left hind limb (NMC 350), max-

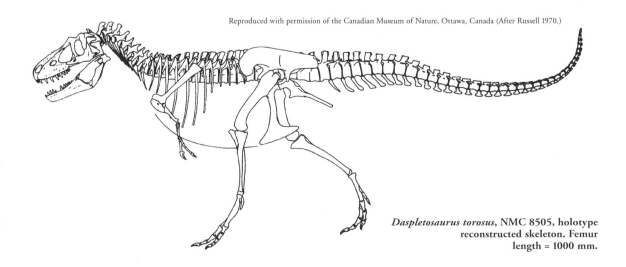

Reproduced with permission of the Canadian Museum of Nature, Ottawa, Canada (After Russell 1970.)

Daspletosaurus torosus, NMC 8505, holotype reconstructed skeleton. Femur length = 1000 mm.

Daspletosaurus

illa (AMNH 3546) from Little Sandhill Creek basin, right femur and metatarsal IV (UA 11), weathered incomplete skull with lower jaws (NMC 11594) from the "Judith River" Formation, near Manyberries, Alberta, and premaxilla, maxilla and dentary (BMNH R4863).

Upon the above specimens Russell erected the new genus and species *Daspletosaurus torosus,* which he originally diagnosed as follows: Premaxilla not contacting nasal below external naris; maxillary teeth large, not greatly reduced posteriorly; anteriormost antorbital opening within the maxilla minute, hardly visible in lateral view; first antorbital opening almost as high as long; nasals between the lacrimals, slightly constricted and interrupted on each side by long, slender tongue of the frontal; frontal broadly exposed on skull roof, with no deep vertical cleft above orbit; prefrontal broadly exposed dorsally between nasal, lacrimal, and frontal; lacrimal "horn" triangular in side view, exceeding in development the postorbital "horn," apex centered above the antorbital ramus; anteroexternal edge of antorbital ramus of lacrimal not continuing across lateral surface of jugal; jugular process and ventral process of extopterygoid inflated, the latter with a large, ventrally opening sinus; angular ending posteriorly beneath center of surangular foramen; main ventral opening of basisphenoid sinus located on midline of skull beneath transverse wall linking basipterygoid processes; presphenoid not medially bridging optic fenestra; single pit on anterior surface of the laterosphenoid to allow exit of third and fourth cranial nerves, fifth exiting from lateral surface of the laterosphenoid; neural spine of the fourth cervical vertebra much larger than fifth; spine of the fifth distally pointed; spine of sixth smaller, sharply pointed; diapophysis of twelfth thoracic vertebra covered by anterior blade of the ilium; forelimb strongly developed, humerus in adults estimated at about 38 percent length of femur; anterodistal condyle of metacarpal I reduced, digit I diverging distally from second; first phalanx (in adults) of digit II robust; dorsal edge of ungual of manual digit I passing through an approximately 90-degree arc; circumference of femur (in adults) from 38 to 41 percent of length.

According to Russell, *Daspletosaurus* attained an approximate length of 8.3 to 8.9 meters (28 to 30 feet) and weighed about 2.2 metric tons (2.5 tons).

Comparing this genus to *Albertosaurus*, Russell showed that in *Daspletosaurus* the presacral vertebrae are generally shorter and higher, basal caudals become smaller less rapidly posteriorly, thoracic ribs are slightly longer, forelimb, ilium and sacrum longer, and metatarsus slightly shorter.

Russell discounted the possibility that *Daspletosaurus* might be the more mature adult stage of the smaller *Albertosaurus*, pointing out that *Daspletosaurus* was generally heavier and more powerfully developed than the latter, adding that the body at the base of the tail is heavier and the hips and hindlimbs are more powerfully developed.

Also, Russell argued that two so similar large theropods could well have coexisted by preying upon two distinct groups of fauna. Fewer "daspletosaurs" and ceratopsians are known from the "Judith River" Formation than "albertosaurs" and hadrosaurs, implying that the heavier and more powerful *Daspletosaurus* preyed on the large horned dinosaurs; the lighter and more fleet-footed *Albertosaurus* were better suited to hunt duck-billed dinosaurs. Later, Russell (1977) noted that *Daspletosaurus* inhabited marshlands adjacent to the courses of streams, an environment also inhabited by hadrosaurids (such as *Brachylophosaurus, Parasaurolophus,* and *Kritosaurus*), ceratopsians (like *Centrosaurus*), and pachycephalosaurs.

Comparing *Daspletosaurus* with other members of Tyrannosauridae, Russell (1970*b*) noted that this genus has the largest forelimb of any known tyrannosaurid, and that the foramina of the skull are smaller and surrounded by denser struts of bone than in *Tyrannosaurus*.

A specimen including scattered cranial bones, abdominal ribs, left forelimb, pelvis, and hindlimbs (NMC 11315), collected near the south bank of Red Deer River, was designated *Daspletosaurus* cf. *D. torosus* by Russell (1970*b*). The humerus, radius-ulna, ilium, and circumference of the femur are longer, relative to the length of the femur, than would be expected in a similar femur length in *Albertosaurus*; the claw of manual digit I is apparently less recurved; and the foot is very similar though the metatarsus is slightly shorter than in *Albertosaurus*. Russell (1970*b*) noted that this specimen reveals that ontogenetic changes in limb proportions in both genera were about the same.

Key references: Carpenter (1992); Russell (1970*b*, 1977).

Illustration by Brian Franczak.

Two *Daspletosaurus torosus* against the armored *Edmontonia rugosidens.*

DATOUSAURUS Dong and Tang 1984—
(=*Lancangosaurus*)

Saurischia: Sauropodomorpha: Sauropoda:
Cetiosauridae: Shunosaurinae.

Name derivation: "Datou [place in China]" +
Greek *sauros* = "lizard."

Type species: *D. bashenensis* Dong and Tang 1984.

Other species: [None.]

Occurrence: Xiashaximiao Formation, Sichuan,
People's Republic of China.

Age: Middle Jurassic (Bathonian–Callovian).

Known material: Two incomplete skeletons, one
without skull, possible jaws.

Holotype: Skeleton, ?skull.

Diagnosis of genus (as for type specimen): Primitive, huge sauropod, measuring 14 meters (about 47 feet) long; skull large, short, heavy, nares set at front, quadrate slanted less forward ventrally; jaw high, heavily built, no lateral jaw vacuity; teeth large, spatulate; four premaxillary, 10–12 maxillary and 12–14 dentary teeth; presacral vertebrae solidly constructed; 13 cervical vertebrae, opisthocoelous cervical centra

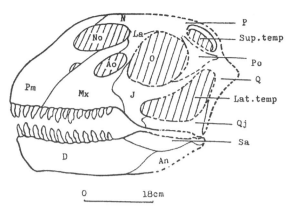

Reconstructed skull possibly belonging to *Datousaurus bashenensis*. (After Dong 1987.)

with rather large pleurocoels, 12 dorsals with platycoelous centra, four sacrals with fused anterior neural spines; length of cervical centrum 2.5 times that of dorsal centrum; neural spines low, with reduced lamellar structure; chevrons of caudal vertebrae forked; shoulder and pelvic girdles heavy, sacriostal

Photo by the author.

Datousaurus bashenensis, skeleton on temporary display at the Natural History Museum of Los Angeles County.

Datousaurus bashanensis, cervical vertebra. (After Dong 1987.)

yoke well developed; limbs robust; manus and pes both with five digits (Dong and Tang 1984).

Comments: Originally named *Lancangosaurus* (Dong, Zhou and Zhang 1983), the genus *Datousaurus* was founded upon a skeleton collected during 1979–1981 from the Xiashaximiao Formation, Dashanpu quarry, Zigong, Sichuan Province, China (Dong and Tang 1984).

Datousaurus reached a length of about 15 meters (more than 50 feet).

McIntosh (1990*b*), in his review of the Sauropoda, pointed out that the skull referred to *D. bashanensis*, while probably belonging to this species, was found isolated from the postcranial skeleton and should therefore be viewed with caution; and, if not for this skull, *Datousaurus* could be considered a possible ancestor of diplodocids.

Note: In his book *Dinosaurs from China*, Dong (1987) reported teeth of a primitive sauropod similar to those of *Datousaurus* from the Middle Jurassic Chaya Group, Changdu Basin, Tibet.

Key references: Dong and Tang (1984); McIntosh (1990*b*).

Datousaurus bashanensis, sacrum and pelvis. (After Dong 1987.)

DEINOCHEIRUS Osmólska and Roniewicz 1967

Saurischia: Theropoda *incertae sedis*.

Name derivation: Greek *deinos* = "terrible" + Greek *cheir* = "hand."

Type species: *D. mirificus* Osmólska and Roniewicz 1969.

Other species: [None.]

Occurrence: Nemegt Formation, Omnogov, Mongolian People's Republic.

Age: Late Cretaceous (?Late Campanian or Early Maastrichtian).

Known material: Forelimb elements.

Holotype: ZPAL MgD-1/6, two damaged scapulacoracoids, complete left humerus, crushed right humerus, complete left ulna, damaged right ulna, left and right radii, complete left and right metacarpi, all phalanges excluding unguals of right manus.

Diagnosis of genus (as for type species): Forelimbs gigantic; scapula 25 percent longer than humerus; humerus with robust and proximally located deltopectoral crest; manus equal in length to half that of humerus and radius; manual unguals robust, strongly curved, with flexor tubera close to the proximal articular face (Norman 1990).

Comments: This unusual genus was founded on a forelimb (ZPAL MgD-1/6); also found were two supposed ceratobranchials, four or five dorsal ribs, one or two left ribs, three vertebrae fragments, and several unidentifiable fragments of bone, all apparently belonging to the individual represented by the holotype. The material was found by Zofia Kielan-Jaworoska during the 1965 Polish-Mongolian Paleontological Expedition, in the Upper Nemegt Beds of the Gobi Desert, Mongolia (Osmólska and Roniewicz 1967).

Osmólska and Roniewicz originally diagnosed the monotypic species *D. mirificus* as follows: Scapula long, slender; coracoid large; forelimbs long, slender; humerus straight, twisted, with a pronounced, triangular deltopectoral crest; humerus about three-fourths as long as scapula; length of radius slightly more than half that of humerus; manus slightly longer than humerus, with comparatively long metacarpus; three long, equally developed manual digits terminating in claws.

Osmólska and Roniewicz placed the genus into its own monotypic family Deinocheiridae.

Apparently, *Deinocheirus* is a gigantic theropod with remarkably long forelimbs. As described by Osmólska and Roniewicz, these forelimbs are approximately 240 centimeters (about 8 feet) long. In life, the foreclaws were probably fortified by a horny sheath. Osmólska and Roniewicz noted that the limb

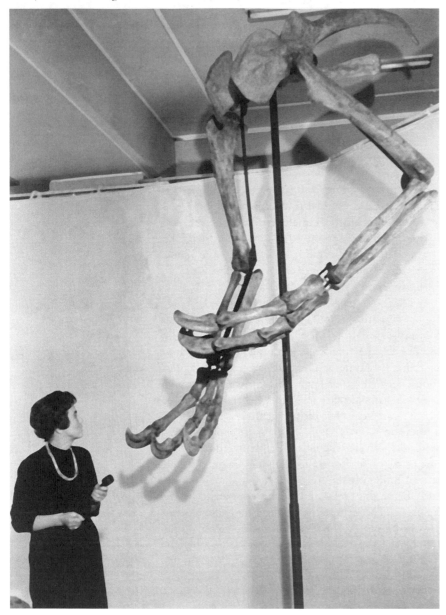

Courtesy Institute of Paleobiology.

Deinocheirus mirificus, MGD-I/6, holotype right and left forelimbs and shoulder girdles, with paleontologist Zofia Kielan-Jaworoska.

are impossible to execute given the paucity of remains now available. However, Rozhdestvensky (1970), in a study of giant claws of Asian and African carnivorous dinosaurs, attempted an admittedly controversial speculation regarding those of *Deinocheirus*. Noting comparisons between the claws in this genus and those in *Ornithomimus*, Rozhdestvensky took the idea a step further, showing that the claws in *Deinocheirus* bear an even stronger resemblance to those in both extinct and recent sloths, noting also that Osborn (1917) had compared the forelimb structure of sloths and *Struthiomimus*. With the sloth as a model, Rozhdestvensky envisioned *Deinocheirus* with a trunk and hind limbs no longer (and perhaps shorter) than the forelimbs, and capable of climbing trees and hanging from their thick branches.

Although *Deinocheirus* has come to be thought of as possibly some kind of gigantic ornithomimid, Norman (1990), while agreeing that the limbs of this genus and ornithomimids are similar in general proportions, disagreed with that interpretation. As pointed out earlier by Nichols and Russell (1985), the scapulacoracoid in this genus has a more typically theropod structure (no flange on supraglenoid buttress, coracoid very deep dorsoventrally, posterior coracoid process rather poorly developed) than that of most ornithomimids. Norman also pointed out that *Deinocheirus* possesses a disproportionately long scapula, when compared to ornithomimids, and that the manual unguals are raptorial, unlike those in ornithomimids.

Because of the lack of further diagnostic material assignable to this taxon, and also because of the extraordinarily large size of the known remains, Norman regarded *Deinocheirus* as Theropoda *incertae sedis*.

Key references: Nichols and Russell (1985); Norman (1990); Osmólska and Roniewicz (1969).

bones in this genus are hollow, thick-walled and adapted for grasping. Size notwithstanding, the structure of the manus and humerus strongly resemble that of *Ornithomimus*, implying to some workers that *Deinocheirus* might be a gigantic ornithomimid. However, the manus in *Deinocheirus* is broader than in *Ornithomimus*, and digit I, unlike that in *Ornithomimus*, was seemingly unable to fold inward for effective grasping.

Postcrania belonging to this genus have provided little information concerning the dinosaur's appearance in life. Accurate life restorations of *Deinocheirus*, attempted in some popular books about dinosaurs,

DEINODON   Leidy 1856 [*nomen dubium*]—
   (=?*Albertosaurus*, ?*Daspletosaurus*)
Saurischia: Theropoda: Tetanurae: Avetheropoda;
   Coelurosauria: Maniraptora: Arctometatarsalia:
   Tyrannosauridae.
Name derivation: Greek *deinos* = "terrible" + Greek
   odous = "tooth."
Type species: *D. horridus* Leidy 1856 [*nomen
   dubium*].
Other species: [None.]
Occurrence: Dinosaur Park Formation, Montana,
   United States.
Age: Late Cretaceous (Late Campanian).
Known material/holotype: ANSP collection, two
   isolated fragmentary premaxillary teeth.

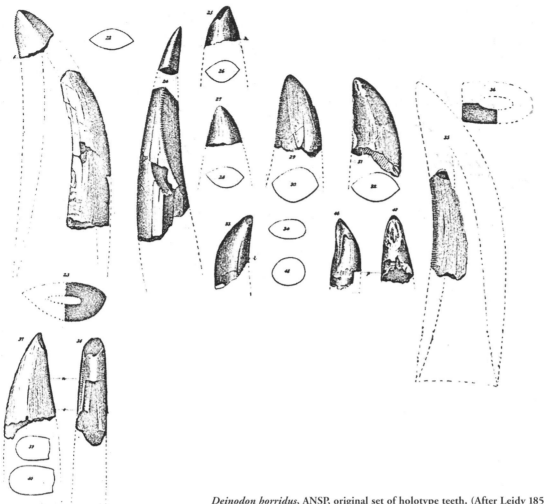

Deinodon horridus, ANSP, original set of holotype teeth. (After Leidy 1856.)

Diagnosis of genus: [No modern diagnosis published.]

Comments: The first tyrannosaurid to be named and described, this poorly known genus was established on twelve fragmentary isolated teeth (ANSP collection) recovered from the former Judith River [=Dinosaur Park] Formation, in Choteau County near the Missouri River, Fort Benton, Montana. The material was first described (but not illustrated) by Leidy (1856). The genus later became the basis for the [abandoned] family Deinodontidae Cope 1866.

Leidy originally described these teeth as resembling those of *Megalosaurus*, being compressed, conical, and curved, with trenchant, dentated borders, but generally thicker relative to breadth than in that genus. The largest of these teeth is 1.25 inches (about 37 centimeters) long from the apex, two-thirds inches broad (about 1.75 centimeters) broad at the base, and "5 lines" thick. Leidy observed that, if these teeth had been discovered in four different localities rather than together, he would have considered them to represent four different genera.

Subsequently, Leidy (1860) applied the name *Deinodon* to all of these teeth but failed to designate any of them as the type specimen. The material included small dentary teeth having a D-shape cross-section and large saber-shaped maxillary teeth. Though Cope (1866) applied the name *Deinodon* only to the D-sectioned teeth, Leidy (1868*a*) used all of the teeth to establish the new genus and species *Aublysodon mirandus*. Later, Hay (1908*b*) observed that *Aublysodon* should only be regarded as a genus distinct from *Deinodon* if it could be clearly demonstrated that both sets of teeth came from different kinds of dinosaurs (see *Aublysodon* entry).

Deinodon is usually considered to be congeneric with *Albertosaurus*. However, as nothing is known of the mandible and maxilla of *D. horridus* nor of the structure of the premaxillary teeth, this taxon cannot sufficiently be compared with *Albertosaurus* for an unequivocal synonymy to be made.

Key references: Cope (1866); Hay (1908*b*); Leidy (1856, 1860, 1868*a*).

DEINONYCHUS   Ostrom 1969—

(=?*Koreanosaurus*, ?*Saurornitholestes*)

Saurischia: Theropoda: Tetanurae: Avetheropoda:
  Coelurosauria: Maniraptora: Dromaeosauridae:
  Velociraptorinae.

Name derivation: Greek *deinos* = "terrible" + Greek
  onyx = "claw."

Type species: *D. antirrhopus* Ostrom 1969.

Other species: [None.]

Occurrence: Cloverly Formation, Montana,
  Wyoming, United States.

Age: Early Cretaceous (Aptian–Albian).

Known material: More than eight articulated and
  disarticulated skeletons and skulls, isolated teeth.

Holotype: YPM 5205, complete left and incomplete right pes.

Diagnosis of genus (as for type species): Small
and bipedal, with moderately large head; skull with
three antorbital openings; orbits large, circular; nasals
long, narrow, not fused; lower margin of external
naris formed by inferior premaxillary process; supraorbital rugosities on postorbital and lacrimal; preorbital bar slender, in weak contact with thin and plate-
like jugal; quadratojugal very small, T-shaped,
apparently not contacting squamosal; pterygoid long
and slender; ectopterygoid complex, pocketed ventrally; palatines expanded medially, with subsidiary
palatine openings; teeth with anterior and posterior
serrations; denticles on posterior serrations twice as
large as on anterior serrations; four asymmetrical,
sub-incisiform premaxillary teeth, 15 maxillary teeth,
and 16 dentary teeth of subequal size; 22 to 23 presacral vertebrae, three to four sacrals, about 40 caudals; pleurocoels of presacral vertebrae small, deep;
cervical vertebrae moderately long, massive, platycoelous, sharply angled; dorsals short, platycoelous
to amphiplatyan, with well-developed hyposphene-
hypantrum; dorsal neural spines short, stout; caudal
vertebrae long, platycoelous, all but the first eight or
nine with extremely long, rod-like prezygapophyseal
processes; chevrons elongated into paired, double
bony rods that extend forward beneath preceding
eight or nine segments; forelimbs not reduced; carpus comprising radiale and ulnare only, the former
with well defined, asymmetrical ginglymus proximally for articulation with the radius; humerus and
radius-ulna not reduced; manus long, slender, with
three very long digits having a 2-3-4 formula, digits
IV and V lost; metacarpal III long, slender, divergent
from II; ischium with triangular obturator process;
hindlimbs moderately long, well-developed; pes of
medium length, with four digits, V a vestigial
metatarsal, digital formula 2-3-4-5-0; digits III and
IV of equal length, II specialized in having a large,
trenchant and strongly recurved ungual, I reduced

and backwardly-directed; distal end of metatarsal II
deeply grooved; metatarsal III not greatly compressed
proximally; articular facets of metatarsal II developed
to allow unusual extension though little flexion
between first and second phalanges (Ostrom 1969).

Comments: The remarkable genus *Deinonychus*,
the best known and reported dromaeosaurid, was
established on fossil material collected in summer,
1962, by John H. Ostrom, Grant Meyer and other
workers during the first of six expeditions, undertaken by the Peabody Museum of Natural History,
Yale University, to northern Wyoming and central
Montana. The type material included a complete left
pes and incomplete right pes (YPM 5205) collected
from sandstones and shales of the Cloverly Formation
(defined by Darton 1906; invertebrate and plant fossil evidence suggesting probably Late Aptian–Early
Albian age) of Carbon County, near Bridger, Montana (Ostrom 1969*a*).

Other specimens referred by Ostrom to *Deinonychus* include three series of articulated caudal vertebrae (YPM 5201, 5202, and 5203), part of the atlas,
axis, seventh and ninth dorsal vertebrae (YPM 5204),
almost complete left and right manus (YPM 5206),
incomplete skull with jaws, atlas, axis, the seventh
cervical vertebra, first and tenth dorsals, and anterior
caudal (YPM 5210), incomplete skull (YPM 5232),
some isolated and fragmentary elements (YPM 5207,
5208, 5209, 5211-5231, 5231–5265), incomplete
skeleton lacking skull and jaws (AMNH 3015), and
fragmentary bones of manus and pes (AMNH 3037).

Based on the holotype and these referred specimens, Ostrom diagnosed the monotypic species
D. antirrhopus, tentatively identifying an isolated
bone as a right pubis, then incorrectly interpreting it
as short and greatly expanded into a scoop-shaped
element with a distinct obturator process.

Deinonychus was referred by Ostrom to the Dromaeosauridae, after which Colbert and Russell (1969)
created for *Deinonychus* and related forms the "infraorder" Deinonychosauria (this taxon more recently
shown to be a polyphyletic grouping by Holtz 1994).

Ostrom (1969*b*) subsequently published an osteology of *D. antirrhopus*, although his description was
not complete until the discovery in 1974 of more
material, including femora, pubes, complete ilia and
sacrum (MCZ4371), elements missing in the type
specimen. Ostrom (1974) correctly identified the supposed pubis as an unusually large right coracoid and,
at the same time, redescribed the pubes as being of
the usual theropod design, though of unusual length
relative to the short ischium (pubis over twice as long
as ischium).

With this additional material, Ostrom (1976)
redescribed *D. antirrhopus*, noting that the femur is

about 10 percent shorter than the tibia; metatarsal I is not fused to II, and seems to have been joined by ligaments to the metatarsus, suggesting that its preserved position (reverted extremely toward the rear) may not have been such in life; and that the difference in curvature in the sickle claw in various specimens might be attributable to individual variation, sexual dimorphism or ontogeny.

The teeth in *Deinonychus*, as described by Ostrom (1969*b*), are mostly backwardly-directed, unlike the downwardly-directed stabbing teeth of most theropods, apparently adaptations for feeding rather than killing.

Ostrom (1976) stated that, although the femur to tibia-length ratio might suggest that *Deinonychus* was a fast runner, the length of metatarsus relative to tibia indicate that the animal was not one of the most fleet-footed of car-nivorous dinosaurs. Various-sized specimens of apparently different age indicate an increase in fore-limb length of 20 percent with a tibia length 18 percent longer, but only a 12 percent increase in metatarsus length. Ostrom (1976) suggested that if metatarsal growth did not keep pace with that of the other long bones as the animal aged, its cursorial ability declined.

According to Ostrom (1969*d*), *Deinonychus* attained a length of almost 3 meters (about 10 feet), was slightly more than 1 meter (3.5 feet) in height, and weighed from almost 70 to nearly 80 kilograms (150–175 pounds).

Ostrom (1969*a*) observed that the most distinctive features of this genus are the pes, carpus, manus and caudal vertebrae, indications that *Deinonychus* was a creature of great speed and agility suggesting a highly predacious lifestyle.

As shown by Ostrom (1969*a*, 1969*b*, 1969*d*), the pes of *Deinonychus* differs from that of nondromaeosaurid theropods in that the fourth or outside toe is equal in length to the middle toe. (In other

Illustration by Gregory S. Paul.

Deinonychus antirrhophus pack attacks herd of *Tenontosaurus tilleti*.

Deinonychus

Deinonychus antirrhopus, skeleton.

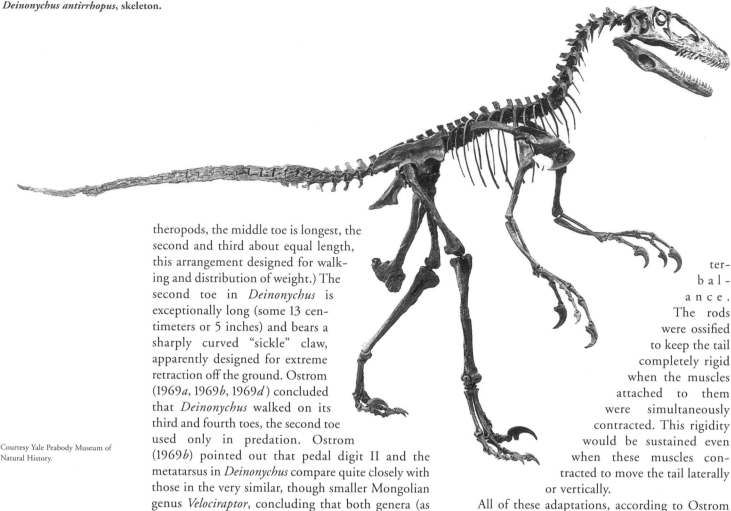

theropods, the middle toe is longest, the second and third about equal length, this arrangement designed for walking and distribution of weight.) The second toe in *Deinonychus* is exceptionally long (some 13 centimeters or 5 inches) and bears a sharply curved "sickle" claw, apparently designed for extreme retraction off the ground. Ostrom (1969*a*, 1969*b*, 1969*d*) concluded that *Deinonychus* walked on its third and fourth toes, the second toe used only in predation. Ostrom (1969*b*) pointed out that pedal digit II and the metatarsus in *Deinonychus* compare quite closely with those in the very similar, though smaller Mongolian genus *Velociraptor*, concluding that both genera (as well as *Dromaeosaurus*) are closely related.

According to Ostrom (1969*a*, 1969*b*, 1969*d*), the hand of *Deinonychus* is unusual, being long and raptorial, thus adapted for grasping prey. In the wrist, the proximal facet of the radiale is a strongly asymmetrical ginglymus that allowed the hand to rotate about a longitudinal axis. This condition afforded the animal a remarkable degree of wrist mobility, the hands able to flex at the wrist while turning toward each other.

Ostrom (1969*a*, 1969*b*, 1969*d*) showed that the tail structure in *Deinonychus* is unusual because of the bundles of long ossified tendons that are attached to the prezygapophyses. These tendons are identical to those in the tails of modern lizards and some mammals. The tendons in *Deinonychus* enclose the caudal vertebrae to surround the tail above and below (except in the region near the hips). Despite the tail's seeming inflexibility due to these bony rods, all caudal vertebrae exhibit normal articular facets. These ossified tendons connect a series of muscles at the base of the tail to the vertebrae, providing movement and indicating that the tail served as a dynamic counterbalance. The rods were ossified to keep the tail completely rigid when the muscles attached to them were simultaneously contracted. This rigidity would be sustained even when these muscles contracted to move the tail laterally or vertically.

All of these adaptations, according to Ostrom (1969*a*, 1969*b*, 1969*d*), seem to be suggestive of predation behavior. *Deinonychus* probably hunted prey such as the much larger *Tenontosaurus*, an ornithopod whose bones were found in abundance in the same quarries that yielded *Deinonychus* remains. *Deinonychus*, perhaps hunting in a pack (see Ostrom 1969*b*; Farlow 1976), pursued its prey at rapid speed, its body stabilized by the stiffened tail. Then, seizing its victim with its powerful taloned front claws, *Deinonychus* could draw one foot forward, kicking out and disemboweling the prey with its sickle-claw.

Some authors (Carpenter 1982; Paul 1984*a*, 1987) have suggested that *Deinonychus* is a North American species of *Velociraptor*. Paul (1988*b*) argued that the skull of *Deinonychus*, if restored correctly with nasals depressed, would be very similar to *V. mongoliensis*, both species sharing long and low maxillae, with a ventrally convex lower border (giving the snout an elongate, upcurved shape), and that the nasals are L-shaped in transverse section. Other similarities include the peculiar T-shaped quadratojugals; lacrimals with similar dorsal bosses and preorbital bars with U-shaped cross-sections; shallow depression arising from second preorbital opening, terminating in a kinked maxillary-nasal suture; postorbital with upturned frontal process; lower jaws with a long, parallel-edged dentary having multiple rows of small foramina and an especially large foramen at the tip; teeth with reduced anterior serrations and little heterodonty between premaxillary and anterior teeth; retroverted coracoids and pubes; ribcage with uncinate processes. Paul (1988*b*) referred *D. antirrhophus* to *V. antirrhophus*, a synonymy that has not been generally accepted, and was flatly rejected by Ostrom (1990), based on unspecified anatomical and temporal stratigraphic grounds. Currie, Rigby and Sloan (1990) stated that new material in the collections of the Tyrrell Museum of Paleontology may exhibit enough differences to support distinction between these genera.

Notes: Bakker (1986), in his book *The Dinosaur Heresies*, compared the skeleton of *Deinonychus* with that of the bird *Archaeopteryx*, observing strikingly avian features in the former. Bakker stated that *Deinonychus* can be regarded either as a birdlike dinosaur or a dinosaur-like bird. This speculation included the idea that dinosaurs like *Deinonychus* had feathers (although no evidence of feathers have, to date of this writing, been found with any dinosaurian remains).

Another dinosaur-bird association was suggested by Molnar, who speculated that the sickle claw in *Deinonychus* may also have been used in intraspecific combat, as in cassowaries and fowl (R. E. Molnar, personal communication 1988).

The first record of the Velociraptorinae on Cretaceous Gondwanian continents was reported by Rauhut and Werner (1995) from among a wealth of continental vertebrate fossils collected from the Wadi Milk Formation (Cenomanin) of northern Sudan, Africa, this fauna including the following: Other theropods such as an ?ornithomimid and at least one larger form, a titanosaurid sauropod, hypsilophodontid and iguanodontid ornithopod; reptiles including crocodiles, snakes, and turtles; amphibians such as frogs, caecilians (Werner 1994*b*); and fishes including polypterids, lepisosteids, osteoglossids, teleosts, lungfishes, and (rarely) cartilaginous forms (Werner 1993, 1994*a*). Fragmentary velociraptorine remains found on the weathered surface at this locality consist of isolated teeth and postcranial elements. Because of the poorly preserved condition of this material, only some of the remains were transported for deposit in the collection of the Special Research Project 69 of the Technical University of Berlin. The recovered material comprises one tooth (Vb-875) and five phalangeal elements (Vb-713 and 714, Vb-860, Vb-866, and Vb-868).

Of the studied material, Rauhut and Werner noted the following characters linking the Sudanese theropod to the Dromaeosauridae: 1. Difference between denticle size of anterior and posterior serration of tooth Vb-875, similar to that in velociraptorines *Deinonychus, Velociraptor*, and *Saurornitholestes* (Currie, *et al.* 1990), in combination with morphology of posterior serrations, similar to *Deinonychus* (Ostrom 1969*b*) and *Saurornitholestes* (Currie *et al.* 1990); 2. prominent ventral "heel" and deeply grooved ginglymoidal distal articular facet of pedal phalanx Vb-713, similar to those in *Deinonychus* (Ostrom 1969*b*); and 3. shape of ungual Vb-714 and Vb-860 in combination with asymmetrical arrangement of claw grooves, as in dromaeosaurids *Utahraptor* (Kirkland, Gaston, and Burge 1993), *Deinonychus* (Ostrom 1969*a*), and in an as yet undescribed dromaeosaurid (MOR 660), and a sharp ven-

Deinonychus antirrhopus, YPM 5205, holotype left pes.

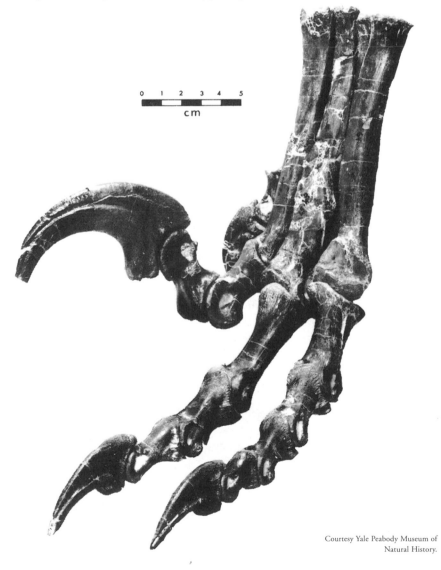

tral margin, both of these features presently known only in dromaeosaurids.

Rauhut and Werner found the Sudanese material to be too fragmentary for the proposal of a new genus and species name, but pointed out that it demonstrates a wider distribution and diversification of the Dromaeosauridae than was previously known.

Key References: Carpenter (1982); Colbert and Russell (1969); Currie, Rigby and Sloan (1990); Farlow (1974); Ostrom (1969a, 1969b, 1969d, 1974, 1976); Paul (1984a, 1987, 1988b).

DELTADROMEUS Sereno, Dutheil, Iarochene, Larsson, Lyon, Magwene, Sidor, Varricchio and Wilson 1996

Saurischia: Theropoda: Tetanurae: Avetheropoda: Coelurosauria *incertae sedis*.

Name derivation: Greek *delta* = "delta" + Greek *dromeus* = "runner."

Type species: *D. agilis* Sereno, Dutheil, Iarochene, Larsson, Lyon, Magwene, Sidor, Varricchio and Wilson 1996.

Other species: [None.]

Occurrence: "Kem Kem beds," Morocco; Baharija Formation, Marsa Matruh, Egypt.

Age: Late Cretaceous (Cenomanian).

Known material: Incomplete postcrania, various postcranial bones.

Holotype: SGM-Din 2 (Ministère de l'Energie et des Mines collection, Rabat, Morocco), partial postcranial skeleton [illustration not available at press time].

Diagnosis of genus (as for type species): Anterior caudal vertebrae having broad quadrangular neural spines; coracoid and acromion broadly expanded anteroposteriorly; coracoid having shallow notch in anterior region; ischial midshaft compressed dorsoventrally; distal shaft of femur with accessory trochanter; femoral medial distal condyle having anterior extension; metatarsal IV distal condyles reduced (Sereno, Dutheil, Iarochene, Larsson, Lyon, Magwene, Sidor, Varricchio and Wilson 1996).

Comments: The first remains of *Deltadromeus* were discovered in the summer of 1995 by American writer Gabrielle Lyon, during a joint U.S.-Moroccan expedition led by Paul C. Sereno of the University of Chicago (Lemonick 1996). The type species *D. agilis* was founded upon a largely complete postcranial skeleton (SGM-Din 2), collected that same year from the Kem Kem region of southeastern Morocco (Sereno *et al.,* 1996). According to Sereno *et al.,* several elements (corocoid, femur, and fibula) belonging to SGM-Din 2 are identical to bones (IPHG 1912, including a left coracoid, pubes, a right femur, prox-

imal right tibia, and left fibula) referred by Stromer (1931) to *Bahariasaurus ingns* (see *Bahariasaurus* entry) but which do not belong to the fragmentary holotype of that Egyptian species; therefore, the authors designated the Moroccan remains as the holotype of the new genus and species *D. agilis*, to which they referred several of the Egyptian elements.

The probable length of the holotype skeleton, if complete, was estimated by the authors to be approximately 9 meters (about 30 feet).

Sereno *et al.,* observed the following in *Deltadromeus*: Limb bones are remarkably slender, with length-to-diameter ratios similar to those in the smaller *Ornithomimus*, but just 50 to 60 percent of those in the same-sized *Allosaurus*; plate-shaped coracoid and proximal scapula are broader than in theropods that also exhibit expansion of acromial region; based on preserved portions of humerus, radius, and ulna, forelimb seems not to have been substantially reduced in length; and cursorial proportions of limb bones are between those for *Allosaurus* and *Ornithomimus*.

Deltadromeus was referred by Sereno *et al.,* to the Coelurosauria based on the following synapomorphies: Expansion of coracoid; reduction of fourth trochanter of femur to a low ridge; and presence of large, deep fossa on proximal end of fibula. Phylogenetic analysis of *Deltadromeus* further suggested that the genus is an early derivative of the radiation of the Coelurosauria, most closely resembling the smaller and older *Ornitholestes*.

The discoveries of *Deltadromeus* and new remains belonging to *Carcharodontosaurus*, and comparisons of these taxa with Cretaceous theropods from other parts of the world, inspired questions regarding the long accepted view that Laurasia and Gondwana were entirely separated by Late Cretaceous times (see section on Mesozoic Era), leading Sereno *et al.,* to the following biogeographic conclusions:

1. Several large theropods (*e.g., Deltadromeus, Carcharodontosaurus,* and *Spinosaurus*) achieved a trans–African distribution during the Late Cretaceous.

2. Large carcharodontosaurids underwent a global radiation during the Early Cretaceous.

3. Basal coelurosaurs achieved global distribution by the Late Jurassic (the early divergence of a lineage that gave rise to *Deltadromeus*, suggesting the presence of primitive coelurosaurs on southern continents before the end of that period).

4. A distinctive dinosaur fauna (including basal coelurosaurs like *Deltadromeus*) was present in Africa at the beginning of the Late Cretaceous (Cenomanian).

5. Substantial faunal exchange may have persisted between major land areas well into the Early

Dianchungosaurus lufengensis, 7205, holotype fragmentary maxilla, in a. external, b. internal, and c. ventral views. Scale = 3 cm. (After Yang [Young] 1982.)

Cretaceous, with marked isolation of North and South American, and African dinosaurian faunas apparently rising abruptly early in the Late Cretaceous when dispersal land connections between northern and southern land masses were finally severed.

Key references: Sereno, Dutheil, Iarochene, Larsson, Lyon, Magwene, Sidor, Varricchio and Wilson (1996); Stromer (1931).

DENVERSAURUS Bakker 1988—(See *Edmontonia*.)

Name derivation: "Denver [city of Colorado]" + Greek *sauros* = "lizard."

Type species: *D. schlessmani* Bakker 1988.

DIANCHUNGOSAURUS Yang [Young] 1982 [*nomen dubium*]

Ornithischia: Genasauria: Cerapoda: Ornithopoda: Heterodontosauridae.

Name derivation: "Dianchung [place in China]" + Greek *sauros* = "lizard."

Type species: *D. lufengensis* Yang [Young] 1982 [*nomen dubium*].

Other species: *D. elegans* Zhao 1986 [*nomen nudum*].

Occurrence: Lower Lufeng Series, Yunnan, People's Republic of China.

Age: Early Jurassic.

Known material: Jaw fragments.

Holotype: 7205, fragmentary maxilla with teeth.

Diagnosis of genus (as for type species): Maxilla somewhat rugose, anterior portion thin, low, edentulous; maxillary dentition including prominent canine teeth, remaining teeth small and rounded, separated rather widely from one another, becoming progressively larger posteriorly; nares apparently large and low (Yang [Young] 1982b).

Comment: The genus *Dianchungosaurus* was founded on part of a maxilla with teeth (7205), discovered in 1972 in the Dark Red Beds of the Lower Lufeng Formation, Lufeng, Yunnan, People's Repub-

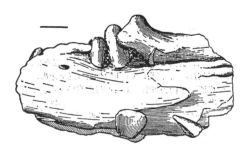

Dianchungosaurus lufengensis, 7211, referred jaw fragment. Scale = 3 cm. (After Yang [Young] 1982.)

lic of China. A second jaw fragment (7211) was referred to the type species, *D. lufengensis* (Yang [formerly Young] 1982b).

A second species, *D. elegans*, was mentioned though not described by Zhao (1986) in an article about the Jurassic reptiles of China.

In their review of the Heterodontosauridae, Weishampel and Witmer (1990b) regarded *D. lufengensis* as a *nomen dubium*.

Key references: Weishampel and Witmer (1990b); Yang (1982b); Zhao (1986).

DICERATOPS Lull *see in* Hatcher 1905

Ornithischia: Genasauria: Cerapoda: Marginocephalia: Ceratopsia: Neoceratopsia: Ceratopsidae: Chasmosaurinae.

Name derivation: Greek *di* = "two" + Greek *keratos* = "horn" + Greek *os* "face."

Type species: *D. hatcheri* Lull 1905.

Other species: [None.]

Occurrence: Lance Formation, Wyoming, United States.

Age: Late Cretaceous (Maastrichtian).

Known material/holotype: USNM 2412, skull missing lower jaws.

Diagnosis of genus: Possession of both parietal and squamosal fenestrae; shares with *Torosaurus* unique frontal fontanelle configuration (a shallow channel extending posterolaterally from frontal to fontanelle towards anterior margin of each upper temporal fenestra, each channel ending at a foramen in parietal medial to upper temporal fenestra); skull with greater frill/basal length than in *Triceratops* (Forster 1996b).

Comments: *Diceratops* was based on an almost complete skull (USNM 2412) collected by John Bell Hatcher from the Lance Formation of Converse [now Niobrara] County, Wyoming. Hatcher (1905), in a prequel to his first Ceratopsia monograph, described the specimen but did not name it. In an editorial note following Hatcher's short paper, published posthumously and two years before the classic monograph edited and rewritten by Lull, Lull (*see in* Hatcher) erected the new genus *Diceratops* for this specimen. Hatcher saw these generic cranial characters in USNM 2412: Absence of nasal horn; large fenestrations in squamosal bones, small fenestrations

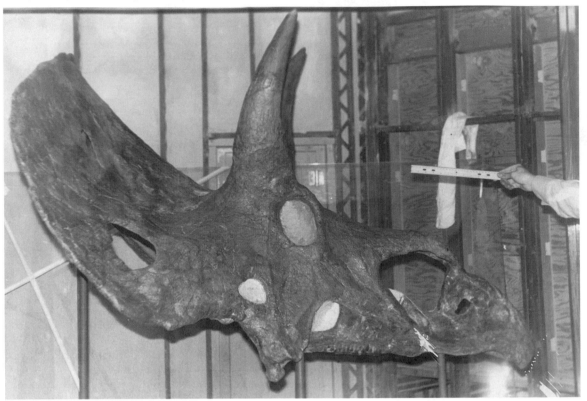

Diceratops hatcheri, USNM 2412, holotype skull.

in parietals; squamosal without quadrate notch. Hatcher cited these specific characters: Brow horns short, robust, erect, slightly curved, almost circular in cross-section; orbits anterior to horns; concave frontal region between horns; exoccipital processes slender, widely expanded.

Lull (in an editorial note, 1907) made this skull the holotype of *D. hatcheri*, but in an appended footnote suggested that the "fenestrations" in the frill were pathologic, possibly due to disease, injury, or preservation. Later, Lull (1933) argued that Hatcher's generic characters were simply differences of degree and referred *D. hatcheri* to *Triceratops*, allowing that the former might represent a subgenus. Ostrom and Wellnhofer (1986) later regarded *D. hatcheri* as a probable junior synonym of *T. horridus*.

More recently, Forster (1996*b*) reinterpreted *Diceratops* as a valid genus. Forster noted that nasal horns are sometimes missing from *Triceratops* skulls due to lack of fusion between epinasal ossification and nasal boss (Forster 1996*a*), this condition possibly explaining the lack of a nasal horn in *D. hatcheri*. Regarding the "fenestrae" in USNM 2412, Forster (1996*b*) stated that such openings, present in all known chasmosaurines except *Triceratops*, are: 1. Located posterior to the contact with the paroccipi-

tal processes; 2. either uni- or bilateral; 3. almost uniform in shape; and 4. have smoothly rounded margins. Also, a large fenestra occurs in the left squamosal of *Diceratops* immediately posterior to the paroccipital processes; a smaller oval fenestra occurs in the right squamosal. Their margins, where preserved, are smoothly rounded, without any outward sign of trauma. A pathologic area of bone was observed along the left squamosal-parietal suture, just posterior to the left fenestra; but the margin of the fenestra near this area is smooth and even, seemingly unaffected by the injury. According to Forster (1996*b*), the even nature of the squamosal fenestrae in *Diceratops* and presence of such openings in all chasmosaurines except *Triceratops* indicate that they are a real morphological feature.

Forster (1996*b*) also noted that Diceratops also possesses parietal fenestrae (right parietal having a narrow opening 16 centimeters in length), a character shared with other chasmosaurines except *Triceratops*; and that *Diceratops* shares with *Torosaurus* a configuration, found in no other ceratopsid, of the frontal fontanelle (frontal fontanelle singular in *Diceratops*, paired in *Torosaurus*).

Key References: Forster (1996*a*, 1996*b*); Hatcher (1905); Lull (1905, 1933); Ostrom and Wellnhofer (1986).

DICLONIUS Cope 1876 [*nomen dubium*]

Ornithischia: Genasauria: Cerapoda:
   Ornithopoda: Iguanodontia: Hadrosauridae
   incertae sedis.

Name derivation: Greek *di* = "double" + Greek *klon*
   = "stem" + Greek *ios* = [adjectival ending].

Type species: *D. pentagonus* Cope 1876 [*nomen
   dubium*].

Other species: *D. calamarius* Cope 1876 [*nomen
   dubium*], *D. perangulatus* Cope 1876 [*nomen
   dubium*].

Occurrence: Dinosaur Park Formation, Montana,
   United States.

Age: Late Cretaceous (Campanian).

Known material/holotype: AMNH 3972, teeth.

   Diagnosis of genus: [No modern diagnosis published.]

   Comments: The doubtful genus *Diclonius* was
founded upon fragmentary detached teeth, all collected from the Dinosaur Park Formation [then "Fort
Union beds"], apparently at Dog Creek, east of Judith
River, Montana.

   Diclonius was diagnosed by Cope (1876*a*) as follows: Teeth elongate, lacking a distinct root; dense
material only on front of crown, producing cutting
edge; back of tooth coated with cementum, absorbed
from below during successional protrusion of teeth.

   Cope (1876*a*) referred three species, each based
on a single tooth, to this genus—*D. pentagonus* (holotype AMNH 3972), *D. perangulatus* (AMNH 5737),
and *D. calamarius* (AMNH 5733). Originally, the
type material of *D. pentagonus* also included an additional tooth and two teeth fragments, that of
D. perangulatus 12 additional fragmentary teeth and
a caudal vertebra (not mentioned by Cope), and that
of *D. calamarius* four more fragmentary teeth. Cope
neither figured these teeth, nor did he designate any
of the three species as the type species. Later, Hay
(1902) designated the type species to be *D. pentagonus.*

   Cope diagnosed type species *D. pentagonus* as
follows: Front of tooth crown divided longitudinally
by a prominent median keel, moderately prominent
at lower part of crown; borders of crown not serrate;
back of crown divided into three faces by two parallel, longitudinal solid angles; crown contracted near
base by lateral bevels for adjacently growing teeth;
faces covered by cementum with granular roughness.

   Lull and Wright (1942), unable to find the type
specimens and basing their opinion upon Cope's
published descriptions only, regarded the type material of *D. pentagonus* and *D. calamarius* as apparently
hadrosaurid, but suspected incorrectly (Coombs
1988) that *D. perangulatus* could be ceratopsian, Cope
having been misled by a ceratopsian tooth included

Diclonius pentagonus,
AMNH 3972, neotype tooth
in stereo pair crown and
anterior-posterior views.
Scale in mm.

Photo by W. P. Coombs, Jr., courtesy
Americna Museum of Natural History.

Diclonius perangulatus,
AMNH 5737, neotype tooth
in stereo pair crown and
anterior-posterior views.
Scale in mm.

Photo by W. P. Coombs, Jr., courtesy
American Museum of Natural History.

in the type of Leidy's (1865) *Trachodon mirabilis* (see
Trachodon entry).

   In reassessing the status of *Diclonius*, Coombs
(1988) pointed out that hadrosaurid teeth, because
they show too much variability within a single individual and too much morphologic overlap between
species that can be distinguished by other anatomical
features, cannot provide reliable sources of taxonomic
characters at the specific, generic, and perhaps even
"subfamilial" levels. Coombs recommended that any
hadrosaur taxon based upon isolated teeth be regarded
as a *nomen dubium*. The material of all three of Cope's
Diclonius species consist of hadrosaurid teeth, none
of which can be adequately defined as a taxon, and
all of which should be regarded as *nomen dubia*.
Coombs removed the caudal vertebra from the holotype of *D. perangulatus*, assigning it new catalog
number AMNH 9144 and tentatively identifying it
as belonging to the nondinosaurian genus *Opisthotriton*. Also, Coombs published the first illustrations of
Cope's original *Diclonius* material.

   Note: According to Brett-Surman (1989), the
fact that the teeth of *D. pentagonus* are heavily worn
and isolated from their dental battery makes them
useless for purposes of diagnosis. Although Lull and
Wright had stated that two of the three cotypes of
D. pentagonus were lost, Brett-Surman found some

Photo by W. P. Coombs, Jr., courtesy
American Museum of Natural History.

Diclonius calamarius, AMNH
5733, neotype tooth in stereo
pair crown and anterior-posterior views. Scale in mm.

heavily worn hadrosaurid teeth in the basement of the American Museum of Natural History. The teeth had the word *Diclonius* in faded ink in handwriting resembling Cope's. They had no taxonomic value below family level.

Key references: Brett-Surman (1989); Coombs (1988); Cope (1976); Hay (1902); Lull and Wright (1942).

DICRAEOSAURUS Janensch 1914

Saurischia: Sauropodomorpha: Sauropoda:
 Diplodocidae: Dicraeosaurinae.
Name derivation: Greek *dikros* = "forked" + Greek
 sauros = "lizard."
Type species: *D. hansemanni* Janensch 1914.
Other species: *D. sattleri* Janensch 1914.
Occurrence: Middle and upper Tendaguru Beds,
 Mtwara, Tanzania.
Age: Late Jurassic (Kimmeridgian).
Known material: Skeleton without skull and fore-
 limbs, two partial skeletons, two partial skeletons
 without skulls, isolated vertebrae, limb elements
 and other postcranial remains.
Holotype: HMN collection, partial postcranial
 skeletons including second through nineteenth
 caudal vertebrae, pelvis, hindlimbs.

"Diagnosis" of genus: Orbit of same shape as in *Diplodocus*; small fontanelle between frontal and parietal on midline, smaller opening between parietal and supraoccipital (*postparietale hucke* of Janensch, similar to supposed pineal opening in *Diplodocus*); [preserved] rostral parts of premaxilla and maxilla like *Diplodocus*, dentary more massive; teeth slender, peglike; four predentary, 12 dentary and 16 dentary teeth; 11 or 12 cervical and 12 or 13 dorsal vertebrae; presacral vertebral centra opisthocoelous, with typical articulation in cervical and dorsal regions, ball becoming reduced to gentle convexity after dorsal vertebra 4; pleurocoels notably weak; side of centrum in cranial and middle caudals concave behind with no distinct rim of pleurocoel, concavity developing into small pleurocoel beneath diapophysis; relatively small but more typical pleurocoel on last two cervicals, disappearing on cranial and later dorsals, replaced by small well-marked cavity on lateral face of neural arch just below transverse process; parapophysis directed outward from bottom of centrum of first ten cervicals in normal fashion, migrating upward from cervical 11 onward to reach boundary of centrum and neural arch by dorsal 2, thereafter located on arch; cervical centra relatively short, longest cervical 8, decreasing in length to cervical 12, remaining presacral centra about same length; spines beginning with cervical 3 unusually tall, gradually increasing in height throughout presacral region, height of last dorsal four times that of centrum; spines deeply divided beginning with cervical 3, this condition enhanced backward to maximum development on dorsals 3 and 4, after which degree of division decreases rapidly, small notch remaining in dorsal 7, none thereafter; caudal dorsal spines consisting of four thin laminae set at right angles to each other, cross shaped in cross-section, with transversely directed laminae exceeding longitudinal directed ones (spine division reaching maximum development in this genus); slender trans-

Dicraeosaurus hansemanni, HMN, composite skeleton including holotype material, mounted at the Humboldt Museum für Naturkunde.

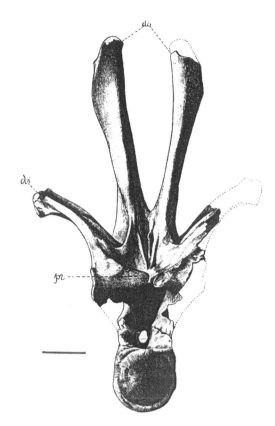

Diagnosis of *D. sattleri*: Distinguished from *D. hansemanni* by more slender pubis, wider neural arch with taller neural spines and longer diapophyses (these features probably progressive, as *D. sattleri* occurs in upper rather than middle "Dinosaur Beds" (Janensch 1914).

Comments: The genus *Dicraeosaurus* was founded upon incomplete postcranial remains (HMN collection) collected from the middle Tendaguru beds of Tendaguru, at the settlement of Kindope, Mtwara, Tanzania, East Africa. Other incomplete remains from various individuals were collected from the same locality, including portions of skull, vertebrae, limb, and girdle bones. From all of these

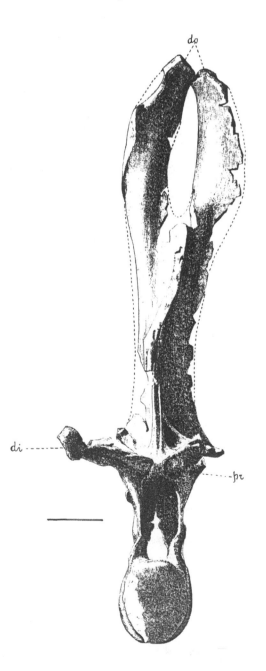

Draeosaurus sattleri, HMN, holotype caudal vertebra. Scale = 8 cm. (After Janensch 1914.)

Dicraeosaurus hansemanni, HMN, holotype caudal vertebra. Scale = 8 cm. (After Janensch 1914.)

verse process of dorsal vertebrae directed upward and outward; cervical ribs short, reaching rear of centrum throughout most of neck, last one very long (over half length of thoracic rib 1) and directed downward; sacrum typical, all five vertebrae contributing to sacrocostal yoke; sacral spines 2 to 4 fused; proximal caudal centra procoelous, this condition soon modifying to planoconcave, then amphicoelous, with no pleurocoels or ventral excavations; proximal centra relatively short, middle ones slightly longer, distal ones considerably longer than broad; "whiplash" of rod-like distal caudal vertebrae; chevrons forked by caudal 17; hemal canal bridged over; scapula with distal end moderately expanded, angle between shaft and ridge fairly acute, small jog on scapulacoracoid border above foramen; forelimb short, humerus to femur ratio of 0.62; humerus stouter than in other known sauropods (except *Apatosaurus Opisthocoelicaudia,* and *Saltasaurus*), ulna to humerus ratio of 0.66; ilium resembling those in *Diplodocus* and *Apatosaurus*; pubis with rather long, slender shaft, with prominent hook-like ambiens process; distal end of ischium broadened dorsoventrally to articulate with mate side by side; femur less slender than in *Diplodocus*, shaft almost circular; tibia to femur ratio of 0.62 (McIntosh 1990*b*).

Dicraeosaurus

From *Dinosaurs: A Global View*, by Czerkas and Czerkas, published by Dragon's World Ltd. and its co-edition publishers.

Dicraeosaurus hansemanni,
life restoration by Mark
Hallett.

remains, a composite skeleton was reconstructed and placed on exhibit at the Humboldt Museum für Naturkunde, Humboldt University, in what was once East Berlin.

Based on the holotype, Janensch originally diagnosed the genus (and type species *D. hansemanni*) as follows: Neck short; cervical, dorsal, and sacral vertebrae with high spines, cervical and anterior dorsal spines bifurcate; dorsal centra lacking pleurocoels. Later, Janensch (1929) augmented his first diagnosis and described the reconstructed skeleton.

Second species *D. sattleri* was based upon fragmentary material representing a number of individuals. These remains, from Tendaguru, include vertebrae, ribs, and girdle bones (HMN collection).

Upon *Dicraeosaurus*, Janensch (1929) erected the new "subfamily" Dicraeosaurinae, after which Huene (1956) proposed the new family Dicraeosauridae.

Berman and McIntosh (1978) tentatively referred *Dicraeosaurus* to the Diplodocidae, noting that the skull and teeth are distinctly diplodocid, and that this genus shares other features with Diplodocidae: Presacral neural spines cleft (more deeply than in other known sauropods); sacral spines high; anterior caudals with wing-like transverse processes; mid-caudal chevrons like those in *Diplodocus*; distal ends of ischia greatly expanded; and forelimb short with possible humerofemoral length ratio close to 2:3. Atypically of Dipolodocidae, the neck is short; only 12 cervical and 12 dorsal vertebrae; and dorsals lack pleurocentral cavities. McIntosh (1990*b*) later regarded *Dicraeosaurus* as an aberrant diplodocid.

Bonaparte (1986*d*) stressed the validity and distinctness of Dicraeosauridae, based upon vertebral features. McIntosh (1990*b*) classified *Dicraeosaurus* as a diplodocid belonging to the subfamily Dicraeosaurinae. More recently, Salgado and Bonaparte (1991), in describing *Amargasaurus*, argued that that genus and *Dicraeosaurus* are more derived than, and have significant differences to, Diplodocidae and, therefore, warrant their own family.

Key references: Berman and McIntosh (1978); Bonaparte (1986*d*); Huene (1956); Janensch (1914, 1929); McIntosh (1990*b*); Salgado and Bonaparte (1991).

DILOPHOSAURUS   Welles 1970

Saurischia: Theropoda: Ceratosauria:
   Coelophysoidea.

Name derivation: Greek *di* = "two" + Greek *lophos*
   = "crest" + Greek *sauros* = "lizard."

Type species: *D. wetherilli* (Welles 1954).

Other species: *D. sinensis* Hu 1993.

Occurrence: Kayenta Formation, Arizona, United
   States; Lower Lufeng Formation, Yunnan, China.

Age: Early Jurassic (?Sinemurian–Pliensbachian).

Known material: Two associated skeletons,
   subadult, incomplete skeleton, four fragmentary
   specimens, articulated complete skeleton.

Holotype: UCMP 37302, almost complete skeleton
   with skull.

   Diagnosis of genus (as for type species): Skull
with highly arched, paired nasolacrimal crest; neural
spines with cross-like distal extremities; scapula blade
with square distal expansion (Rowe and Gauthier
1990).

   Diagnosis of *D. sinensis*: Most characteristic features are skull with pair of bony crests, and deep
notch separating dentiginous margins of premaxilla
and maxilla; skull large relative to 5.5-meter (approximately 19-foot long) body (these features shared with

D. wetherilli); distinct in that bony crests are higher,
thicker, converging posteriorly to contact on midline, snout rather short; teeth of upper and lower jaws
shorter, stronger; five premaxillary, 13 maxillary, and
13 dentary teeth (4/12/17 in *D. wetherilli*); one antorbital fenestra in maxilla, second represented by foramen (Hu 1993).

   Comments: The taxon now known as *Dilophosaurus* was originally described as a new species of
Megalosaurus, named *M. wetherilli*, founded on an
almost complete skeleton (UCMP 37302) measuring
about 6 meters (20 feet) in length, and parts of a second skeleton (UCMP 37303), the latter found 10 feet
away from the holotype. Both specimens were discovered in summer, 1942, by a party from the University of California (Berkeley) Museum of Paleontology. The material was recovered from rocks above
the Chinle Formation, in a valley of purplish blocky
shale in the Kayenta Formation (a broadly distributed
geological unit on the Colorado Plateau named by
Baker, Dane and Reeside 1936 after rocks originally
described by Gregory 1917 as a sandy facies of the
Todilto Formation; redefined and dated as Early
Jurassic by Averitt, Detterman, Harshbarger, Repenning and Wilson 1955), Gold Springs, about 20 miles

Dilophosaurus wetherilli,
**UCMP 37302, restored holo-
type (subadult) skeleton of**
Megalosaurus wetherilli.

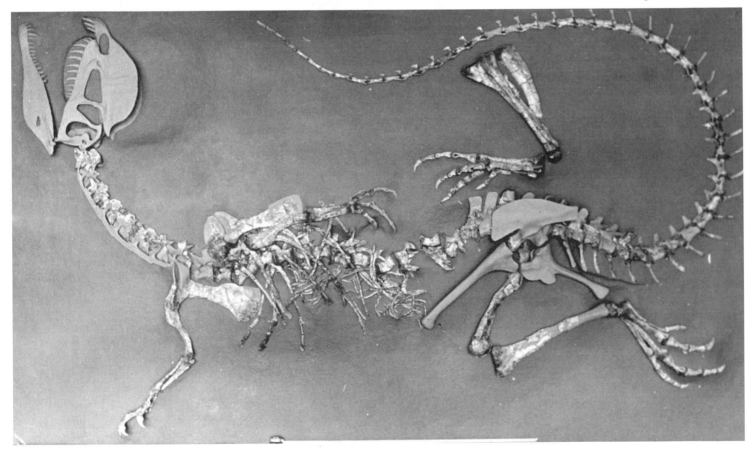

Courtesy Museum of Paleontology, University of California, Berkeley (neg. #69-89).

Dilophosaurus

Dilophosaurus wetherilli, reconstructed mounted skeleton (cast of UCMP 37302).

Dilophosaurus wetherilli, first three-dimensional standing skeleton, mounted by Allen Tedrow, based upon UCMP 37302.

north of Cameron, near Tuba City, Navajo Indian Reservation, Arizona (Welles 1964).

The bones were collected by Samuel P. Welles, W. H. Rush and H. E. Cott, then prepared under the supervision of Welles and later by Wann Langston, Jr. Langston prepared a plaque mount of the holotype skeleton for display at the University of California Museum of Paleontology.

Welles, mostly to distinguish the species and establish its valid name, originally diagnosed *M. wetherilli* as follows: "Megalosaur" with forelimbs comparatively longer than in *M. bucklandi* or *Eustreptospondylus oxoniensis* [="*M. cuvien*" of his usage], limb proportions closer to these species than to any other known form; tibia relatively longer than in other megalosaurs, almost same length as femur; ascending process of the astragalus low, peg-like.

In 1964, near the type locality, Welles (1970) found another skeleton (UCMP 77270) corresponding to that of *M. wetherilli,* though about one-third larger. With new information provided by UCMP 77270, Welles (1970) restudied the original specimens and, assisted by Robert A. Long, restored the missing parts. Welles (1970) discovered that the first two skeletons were those of juveniles (regarded by Rowe and Gauthier 1990 as juvenile to subadult individuals), that this dinosaur was not a megalosaurid and, most surprising, that it bore two cranial crests. Welles (1970), therefore, removed this species from *Megalosaurus,* erecting for it the new genus *Dilophosaurus,* transferring *D. wetherilli* to the Coeluridae. Subsequently, Welles (1983*b*) discovered a suture running around the base of the dorsal process of the astragalus, the first such suture ever noticed on a dinosaur astragalus.

Based on all three skeletons, Welles (1984) published a new and more detailed diagnosis of *D. wetherilli* and a detailed osteology of the skeleton. Comparing *Dilophosaurus* with 47 other taxa, Welles (1984) observed that it compared most favorably with *Halticosaurus*, but was different enough to merit generic distinction, and transferred it to the Halticosauridae.

As *Dilophosaurus* seemed to exhibit both "coelurosaurian" features (skull delicately constructed, lightly built with weak articulation of premaxilla; cervical vertebrae extremely hollowed by pleurocoels, centrocoels and chonoses, plano-concave or slightly convexo-concave; forearm sturdy, hand well-developed for grasping; metatarsals slightly more than half femoral length) and "carnosaurian" features (relatively large skull; more than seven long anterior caudal vertebrae; femur stout, epipodials nearly as long as femur), in addition to some features unique to this genus, Welles (1984) questioned the validity of grouping theropods into two "infraorders," Coelurosauria and "Carnosauria," *Dilophosaurus* apparently a form intermediate between these two groups. Gauthier (1984), later redefining these and other theropod taxa, placed *Dilophosaurus* in the Ceratosauria, a referral supported by other authors (*e.g.,* Rowe 1989; Padian 1989*a*; Weishampel, Dodson and Osmólska 1990; Molnar, Kurzanov and Dong 1990).

Welles (1984) observed that the skull of *Dilophosaurus*, though large relative to body size, was rather delicately constructed. The supposedly weakly-attached premaxilla and subnarial gap, as well as the long and slender teeth, were interpreted as precluding a powerful bite. Welles (1984) surmised that the animal plucked at its prey rather than tore into it and was more of a scavenger than a hunter (although, scavengers such as hyenas require a more powerful bite than do hunters; R. E. Molnar, personal communication 1988). According to Welles (1984), if *Dilophosaurus* did attack and kill a large animal, it probably utilized its powerful grasping hands and feet instead of jaws. The smaller anteriorly located teeth could have bitten off flesh, while the back teeth performed the cutting and slicing. Also, the teeth are considerably smaller than their alveoli and must have been held in their jaws rather loosely, the latter further evidenced by the large number of isolated teeth found lying around the skull in odd places. However, as pointed out by Rowe and Gauthier, articulated remains show that the palatal process of the premaxilla interdigitates with the maxillary process, resulting in a firm junction.

The high cranial crests may have had some behavioral significance such as individual recognition. Their delicate construction, according to Rowe

Illustration by Mark Hallett. From *Dinosaurs: A Global View*, by Czerkas and Czerkas, published by Dragon's World Ltd. and its co-edition publishers.

Two *Dilophosaurus wetherilli* and their prey, the primitive armored dinosaur *Scutellosaurus lawleri*.

and Gauthier, suggests that they were used only for display purposes.

Welles (1984) postulated that *Dilophosaurus* individuals traveled in herds. This was apparently confirmed by thickly-crossed trackways of footprints named *Dilophosauripus* (Welles 1971) found at Tuba City, Arizona, ichnites from Connecticut attributed to dinosaurs such as *Dilophosaurus*, and from the three skeletons having been found close together. Rowe and Gauthier agreed that ceratosaurs may have known complex social behavior.

The first Asian species of this genus, *D. sinensis*, was founded upon a nearly complete skeleton (KMV 8701), discovered and collected in 1987 by a team from the Kunming Municipal Museum, from Lower Jurassic sediments of the Lower Lufeng Formation, at Xiyang Village, on the outskirts of Kunming City, in Jinning County, Yunnan Province, China. The holotype was associated with a skeleton of the theropod *Yangchuanosaurus* (Hu 1993).

The discovery of this species was first reported in the Japanese newspaper *Asahi Shinbun* for May 29, 1989, wherein the dinosaur was referred to by its popular name "Kunming-long" ("long" being the Chinese word for "dragon"). The skull was first illustrated by Dong, Hisa and Azuma (1990) in the book *The Hunt for the Asian Dinosaurs*, in which was published the new species name. The holotype skeleton was mounted at Kunming.

The skull is relatively smaller and shorter than that of *D. wetherilli*, and is 40 centimeters (15 inches) long, 30 centimeters (about 11.5 inches) high, with each crest 11 centimeters (about 4.25 inches) high and 5 centimeters (almost 1.95 inches) thick.

According to Hu, the presence of *Dilophosaurus* in both China and North America suggests that close land connections existed between the latter continent and Asia during the Early Jurassic.

Key references: Dong, Hisa and Azuma (1990); Gauthier (1984); Hu (1993); Molnar *et al.* (1990); Padian (1989*a*); Rowe (1989); Rowe and Gauthier (1990); Weishampel, Dodson and Osmólska (1990); Welles (1954, 1970, 1971, 1983*b*, 1984).

DIMODOSAURUS Pidancet and Chopard 1862—(See *Plateosaurus*.)
Name derivation: Greek *di* = "two" + Latin *modus* = "measure" + Greek *sauros* = "lizard."
Type species: *D. poligniensis* Pidancet and Chopard 1862.

DINODOCUS Owen 1884 [*nomen dubium*]—(See *Pelorosaurus*.)
Name derivation: Greek *deinos* = "terrible" + Greek *dokos* = "beam."
Type species: *D. mackesoni* Owen 1884 [*nomen dubium*].

DINOSAURUS Rutimeyer 1856—(Preoccupied, Waldheim 1847; see *Plateosaurus*.] Name derivation: Greek *deinos* = "terrible" + Greek *sauros* = "lizard."
Type species: *D. gresslyi* Rutimeyer 1856.

DIPLODOCUS Marsh 1878—(=?*Dystrophaeus*)
Saurischia: Sauropodomorpha: Sauropoda: Diplodocidae: Diplodocinae.

Name derivation: Greek *diplos* = "double" + Greek *dokos* = "beam."
Type species: *D. longus* Marsh (1878).
Other species: *D. lacustris* Marsh 1884 [*nomen dubium*], *D. carnegii* Hatcher 1901, *D. hayi* Holland 1924.
Occurrence: Morrison Formation, Colorado, Utah, Wyoming, United States.
Age: Late Jurassic–Early Cretaceous (Kimmeridgian–Tithonian; ?Neocomian–?Hauterivian).
Known material: Four skulls, caudal vertebrae, five postcranial skeletons without manus, partial skeleton with braincase, jaw with teeth, hundreds of postcranial elements.
Holotype: YPM 1920, two complete caudal vertebrae, some incomplete caudals, chevrons.

"Diagnosis" of genus: Snout elongated, teeth confined to very front of jaws; nares located on very top of skull and confluent; dorsal process of maxilla long and broad to its upper end; jugal excluded by quadratojugal from lower rim of skull; basipterygoid processes very long; mandible squared in front; peglike teeth particularly weak; 4 premaxillary, 9–11 maxillary and 10 dentary teeth; 15 cervical and 10 dorsal vertebrae; all presacral centra opisthocoelous, cervicals and dorsals markedly so, caudal dorsals weakly so; cervical centra moderately elongated, with large pleurocoels divided by complex series of laminae; large simple pleurocoels throughout dorsal series; spines of presacral vertebrae bifid starting with small notch in third cervical, soon developing into deep V-shaped cleft reaching extreme development at cervicodorsal boundary; small secondary spine developed at base of cleft of thirteenth cervical, persisting

Photo by R. A. Long and S. P. Welles (neg. #73/459-23), courtesy Yale Peabody Museum of Natural History.

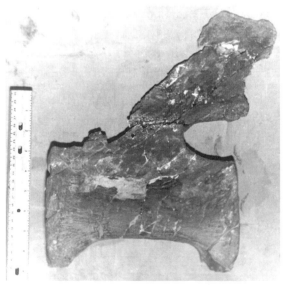

Diplodocus longus, YPM 1920, holotype caudal vertebra.

Diplodocus longus, referred skeleton.

through first five dorsals; cleft spines in shoulder region relatively elevated, but not nearly as much as in *Dicraeosaurus*; cervicodorsal transition marked by abrupt change from slender horizontal cervical ribs, extending backward just to rear of centra, to elongated heavy downwardly projecting thoracic rib of dorsal 1; dorsal centra progressively decreasing in length from elongated dorsal 1-4; dorsal 1 with parapophysis on bottom of lateral face of centrum well below pleurocoel; dorsal 2 with parapophysis just below and in front of pleurocoel; dorsal 3 with parapophysis just above pleurocoel, reaching border of centrum and arch on dorsal 4 and arch itself on dorsal 5; cleft in spine decreasing progressively backward to small notch on dorsal 8, nothing on dorsals 9 and 10; spine height increasing regularly, highest at sacrum where total height of vertebra is four times centrum; transverse processes directed laterally; five sacral centra fused in adults, ribs entering sacrocostal yoke; all sacrals with deep pleurocoels, that on caudosacral somewhat reduced; spines on sacrals 2 and 3 always united, that of sacral 4 sometimes entering plate; small ossicle often found between tips of sacral spines 1 and 2; proximal caudal centra short, gently procoelous, with deep pleurocoels back to caudal 19; centra excavated ventrally with two parallel grooves separated by central ridge; ridge disappearing farther back, excavation becoming deep trough; spines high, slender, first eight or so slightly bifid; caudal ribs attached by thin laminae to transverse processes, pro-

ducing wing-like structures similar to sacral ribs, continuing backward about to caudal 13 before gradually assuming more normal form, finally disappearing about caudal 20; middle caudals greatly elongated, 30 or so distal caudals reduced to biconvex rods forming "whip-lash"; caudals numbering at least 70, ?more than 80; proximal chevrons normal, hemal canal bridged over; chevrons more typically forked after caudal 12, with appearance of cranial process at front margin; in superior view chevrons assuming diamond shape, with two articular facets at two central apices, other two occurring where lateral branches join cranially and caudally (this development, typical of diplodocids, most extreme in this genus); branches farther back more detached, chevrons developing into two parallel rows; scapula with large proximal plate, angle between ridge on it and shaft more acute than in *Apatosaurus*; distal end of scapula more expanded than in other diplodocids; forelimb bones very slender (humerus to femur ratio 0.65, humerus to metacarpus 0.23); metacarpals slender, short; pubis with relatively long, slender shaft, with prominent hook-like process on cranial margin for attachment of ambiens muscle; ischium with slender shaft which expands and thickens distally (ischia appearing to meet somewhat between side-by-side arrangement of *Apatosaurus* and edge-to-edge articulation of *Camarasaurus* and *Brachiosaurus*); femur straight, very slender; tibia to femur ratio 0.65 to 0.69, metatarsus to tibia ratio 0.23;

Diplodocus

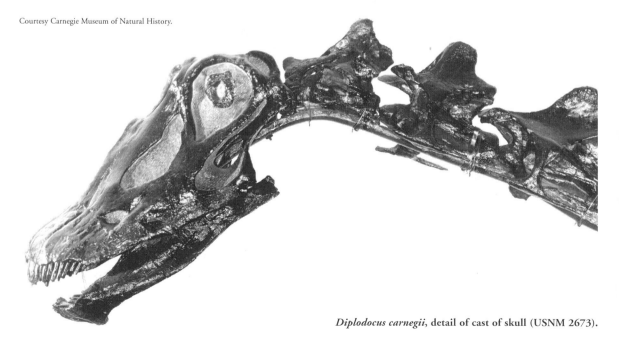

Diplodocus carnegii, composite skeleton including holotype CM 84, referred specimens CM 94 and 307, and skull (cast of USNM 2673).

astragalus with medially directed projection relatively shorter than in *Camarasaurus*; no calcaneum; metatarsals more slender than in *Apatosaurus*; metatarsals III and IV longest; phalangeal formula 2-3-4-2-1 or 2-3-3-2-1 (McIntosh 1990b).

Diagnosis of *D. carnegii*: Distinguished from *D. longus* by smaller cervical ribs and much more strongly backward-directed caudal spines (Hatcher 1901).

Diagnosis of *D. lacustris*: Smaller than *D. longus*, with more slender jaws (Marsh 1884*a*).

Diagnosis of *D. hayi*: Distinguished by cranial features, including placement and direction of parasphenoid in comparison with skull of *D. carnegii*, and by absence of a parietal foramen (Holland 1924*a*).

Comments: One of the longest dinosaurs, *Diplodocus* established both the family Diplodocidae Marsh 1884 and subfamily Diplodocinae Janensch 1929. The genus was founded upon caudal vertebrae (YPM 1920) from the mid-caudal region, discovered in 1877 by Samuel Wendell Williston in the Morrison Formation, at Garden Park, Canyon City, Fremont County, Colorado. These vertebrae were first described by Osborn (1899). Although Osborn expressed strong hopes of extracting an entire skeleton, only the neural arches were retrieved.

More information regarding *Diplodocus* resulted from work sponsored by industrialist and philanthropist Andrew Carnegie. As recounted by McGinnis (1982) in her book *Carnegie's Dinosaurs*, Carnegie had been intensely interested in acquiring dinosaur skeletons for exhibition in the then new Carnegie Museum of Natural History. Carnegie's interest was supposedly fired up by the headline of a Sunday, November, 1898 edition of the *New York Journal* reporting on the "Most Colossal Animal Ever on Earth Just Found Out West!" The find was made by William H. Reed of the American Museum of Natural History. Accompanying the article was an illustration depicting a towering sauropod rearing up on its hind legs to peer into an eleventh-story window of the New York Life Building.

Carnegie contacted William J. Holland, recently appointed director of the Carnegie Museum, to purchase the remains of the dinosaur. Holland then dispatched paleontologists J. L. Wortman and Arthur S. Coggeshall to Medicine Bow, Wyoming, where this "Most Colossal Animal" had been found, only to

Diplodocus carnegii, detail of cast of skull (USNM 2673).

Diplodocus carnegii, CM 3452, skull with several cervical vertebrae, displayed as found.

learn from Reed that the only part of the skeleton retrieved was the upper portion of a limb bone. Undaunted, Wortman and Coggeshall began their own search for dinosaur remains, soon finding themselves some 30 miles away from Reed's original site. On July 4, 1899, at Sheep Creek, the Carnegie Museum scientists uncovered a bone from the hind foot of a huge dinosaur. More excavation produced more bones, revealing that the remains were that of a *Diplodocus* individual that had apparently perished in the mud of some Late Jurassic lake or stream. Thus far, this constituted the most complete *Diplodocus* skeleton (CM 84) known. The quarry that yielded the bones became known as "Camp Carnegie."

In spring of 1900, a second field party to the site expanded the quarry, producing a second skeleton (CM 94) of a somewhat smaller *Diplodocus* individual. The remains were collected by O. A. Peterson. Elements from both skeletons were combined in a composite skeleton put on display at the Carnegie Museum. As the front limbs of *Diplodocus* were not known, these were restored after the somewhat different forelimbs of *Camarasaurus*. Plaster casts of this skeleton, including the incorrect *Camarasaurus* forelimbs, were distributed to museums the world over until 1957, when the final replica was produced, the molds, by that time, having deteriorated with age and use.

Diplodocus carnegii, life restoration by Mark Hallett.

Hatcher (1901) based his osteology of the postcranial skeleton of *Diplodocus* on the Carnegie Museum specimens, disassociated *Diplodocus* bones in that museum's collection, and caudal vertebrae in the American Museum of Natural History collections (AMNH 222). Hatcher, regarding the Carnegie Museum skeletons as belonging to a separate species from type species *D. longus*, named his new species *D. carnegii*. McIntosh (1990*a*), however, noted that Hatcher's reasons for recognizing these two species as distinct may not be entirely valid and that more material is required before the problem of their specific separation can be unequivocally resolved.

In describing *Diplodocus*, Hatcher noted that the vertebrae are designed for maximum strength with minimum weight. The centra throughout the vertebral column have large pleurocoels, the interior consisting of numerous cavities enclosed by thin bony plates that meet, cross, and abut against the thin outer centra walls to provide the maximum resistance to external stress. Hatcher estimated a total of 37 caudal vertebrae [73 generally accepted today, though there might even be more; J. S. McIntosh, personal communication 1988], terminating in a "whip-lash."

A third and smaller species, *D. lacustris* Marsh 1884, was based on a maxilla, lower jaws, and teeth (YPM 1922), collected by Arthur Lakes from the Morrison Formation in Colorado. Hatcher, noting that sauropods, like crocodilians and other reptiles, probably continued to grow throughout their lifespan, questioned the use of size as a criterion for specific determination.

D. hayi was based on the cranium and greater part of the skeleton (CM 662) (the only specimen including forefoot material) of a young individual, collected from Dinosaur National Monument. Postcranial remains include cervical, dorsal, sacral and caudal vertebrae, scapula, humeri, left radius, ulna and metacarpals, pelvis, distal end of the right femur, bones of the right pes, and left tibia and fibula. The

skeleton, supplemented with material from other specimens including a left femur and caudal vertebrae (CM 94) and a skull cast (CM 1161), was mounted under the direction of Wann Langston at the Houston Museum of Natural Science.

Diplodocus remains have also been recovered from the Dry Mesa Quarry (Morrison Formation, Upper Jurassic [Tithonian] or Lower Cretaceous [Neocomian or Hauterivian]), near the southwest corner of Dry Mesa, in west central Colorado (Britt 1991).

The skull of *Diplodocus* was first completely and accurately described by Berman and McIntosh (1978), based on the only known skull (CM 3452) directly associated with postcranial remains (assigned to *D. carnegii*), and also a more complete skull (CM 11161), both from Dinosaur National Monument. Berman and McIntosh also provided the first accurate and detailed description of the braincase of *Diplodocus*.

Diplodocus was a slender sauropod, the extremely long neck and tail contributing to its approximate 28-meter (87-foot) length, its estimated weight (Colbert 1962; Paul 1988*a*) totaling 10.5 to 10.7 metric tons (less than 12 tons).

Although Hatcher had correctly restored *Diplodocus* in an upright posture, it became somewhat fashionable during the early Twentieth Century to depict the animal with its limbs sprawled out reptile style. This attitude was apparently precipitated by English artist F. W. Frohawk (1905), who, regarding *Diplodocus* as simply an enormous lizard, restored it as such with the legs directed outward. Among the scientists accepting this curious notion was Hay (1908*a*), who published a life restoration of two *Diplodocus* in crocodile-like posture on a riverbank. The issue of upright versus sprawling posture raged in both North America and Europe. In Germany, Gustav Tornier restored the dinosaur's skeleton in the lizard pose, though in doing so he had to dislocate virtually every joint. The controversy was finally settled by Holland (1908) who, in criticizing Tornier's "skeletal monstrosity," showed that such an animal would require, when crawling, a deep trench to accommodate its ribcage. Supplementing Holland's conclusion was Roland T. Bird's (1954) discovery in 1938 of sauropod ichnites at Glen Rose, Texas. The trackmaker had a twelve-foot stride but a rail only six feet wide. Obviously, the width would have been much greater for an animal crawling like a lizard.

Because of the high location of the narial openings, Marsh (1884*a*) theorized that this dinosaur may have been aquatic. Marsh's professional rival Cope (1884) based his own theory of aquatic habits for sauropods mostly on the narial position in *Diplodocus*, presuming that dinosaurs like *Diplodocus* could breathe while submerged with just the nostrils part of the head above the surface. Coombs (1975), in a paper on possible sauropod habits, following earlier studies (Williston 1914; Romer 1956; Walker 1968; Bakker 1971), demonstrated that the narial arrangement of *Diplodocus* is not necessarily indicative of aquatic habits in tetrapods.

Bakker observed that the general cranial contour of sauropods like *Diplodocus*, the size, shape, and placement of the external nares in particular, resemble those in mammals either possessing or apparently possessing a very large nose or even a proboscis. Coombs objected to this rather controversial image of a proboscis-bearing sauropod, pointing out that no living reptiles possess anything similar to such an elephantine or tapiroid adaptation, while reptiles have little superficial musculature anteriorly on the snout to accommodate such an adaptation.

Hatcher, like many paleontologists before and after him, regarded *Diplodocus* and other sauropods as amphibious, though the modern interpretation is that they were essentially terrestrial (see *Apatosaurus* entry). Hatcher viewed the modifications in the bones, providing maximum strength though minimum weight, as an adaptation to increase quite considerably the animal's buoyancy in water. However, because of the relative slenderness of *Diplodocus* as opposed to much bulkier sauropods like *Apatosaurus*, Hatcher allowed that this animal was quite capable of terrestrial locomotion. Hatcher envisioned *Diplodocus* as spending most of its time in freshwater lakes or rivers, venturing perhaps frequently onto the land in search of food or in migrating to some other body of water.

Because the jaws of *Diplodocus* are almost edentulous, the weak rake-like teeth restricted to the front of the mouth, Hatcher saw *Diplodocus* as having a diet limited to soft and succulent plants detached by these teeth, like prehensile organs, from the floors of lakes and rivers and along the shores. However, the teeth of *Diplodocus* are worn flat at right angles to their length, abrasions which cannot be attributed to such soft vegetation. Tornier posited that *Diplodocus* was not a herbivore but rather ate fishes and bivalve molluscs, its teeth becoming abraded against mussel shells. Holland (1924*a*) remained agnostic to Tornier's proposal, noting that no traces of shells had ever been found in the stomach region of *Diplodocus* specimens. Commenting that the fragile teeth in this genus has led to the questionable theory that it ate only soft vegetation, Coombs noted that a modern horse or bovoid artiodactyl, stripped of its molariform teeth, would seem to have a cropping dentition about as powerful as that of *Diplodocus*. This suggested that *Diplodocus* and other sauropods with pencil-like teeth could nip off and ingest a wide variety of plants that would be broken down either through chemicals, bacteria, or by gizzard stones.

When viewed as a terrestrial rather than aquatic animal, the form and placement of the teeth in *Diplodocus* offer new interpretation. As suggested by Bakker (1971, 1986), the model for dinosaurs such as *Diplodocus* could be the giraffe, which utilizes its long neck to reach treetops for feeding. Fiorillo (1991) made the first study of sauropod teeth utilizing dental microwear data to interpret dinosaur diets. Pointing out that sauropod dentitions fall into two basic tooth categories (gracile, peg-like teeth as in *Diplodocus* and robust, spatulate teeth as in *Camarasaurus*), Fiorillo examined 22 teeth from Two Morrison Formation localities, Freezeout Hills (Wyoming) and Carnegie Quarry, eleven of which belonged to two individuals of *Diplodocus* (the others to *Camarasaurus*). Fiorillo found that *Diplodocus* teeth generally displayed finer scratch patterns than did those of *Camarasaurus*, although some of the deeper scratches in the former approximated some of the medium-sized scratches observed in the latter. These findings

Diplodocus hayi, CM 662, holotype (subadult) left ilium.

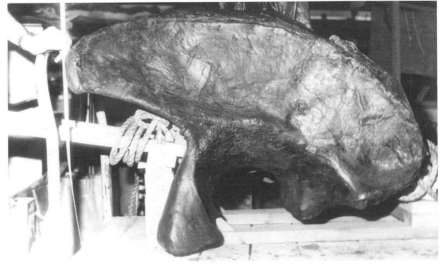

Photo by R. A. Long and S. P. Welles (neg. #73/38-13), courtesy Carnegie Museum of Natural History.

indicated that both dinosaurs ate different kinds of food; that the finer markings on the *Diplodocus* teeth suggest lesser amounts of grit in the diet, grit being related to browsing height (see Janis 1988), this genus therefore possibly having browsed at a higher level than *Camarasaurus*; and that the overlap in scratch morphology suggests that both dinosaurs may have sometimes eaten the same food.

Supposed fractured and fused caudal vertebrae (consistently in the vicinity of the twentieth caudal) have been found in some *Diplodocus* specimens. Blumberg and Sokoloff (1961) interpreted this phenomenon as the result of injury-related arthritis (traumatic osteoarthritis). Such breakage and fusion has been perceived by some paleontologists to be the result of these gigantic animals rearing up on their hind legs in a tripodal position, perhaps to lift their heads even closer to the treetops. Coombs agreed that sauropods, as do such unlikely modern quadrupeds as elephants and bighorn sheep, could have, on occasion, reared up on their hind limbs to get at high branches, but generally found this to be an unlikely stance. Bakker (1986) argued that, because of the animal's head-to-neck orientation, the *Diplodocus* snout was horizontally directed with the neck raised. Interpreted as a high feeder, *Diplodocus* might be visualized as probing among the branches of tall trees, its teeth well suited to such abrasive food as conifer needles.

Continuing this idea of *Diplodocus* assuming a tripodal stance, Paul (1987), in the book *Dinosaurs Past and Present*, envisioned diplodocids as rearing up for purposes of combat. Paul (1987) noted the divergent, large-clawed thumb in diplodocids. This digit, separate from the main united finger unit in the diplodocid manus, could have served as a weapon, wielded against attacking theropods while the sauropod was reared up bipedally.

Although bipedally-rearing sauropods have become common subjects for modern dinosaur art,

this notion was challenged by Rothschild (1987), who suggested that these fused caudal vertebrae were the result of the physiologic phenomenon called diffuse idiopathic skeletal hyperostosis, or DISH (a tendency toward ligamentous, tendinous or capsular ossification) (see Rothschild 1982; Resnick and Niwayama 1988).

Later, Rothschild and Berman (1991), in a study of fused caudal vertebrae of the Late Jurassic sauropods *Diplodocus*, *Apatosaurus,* and *Camarasaurus*, pointed out that DISH is not uncommon in mammals (including humans, usually those of advanced age) as well as many species of dinosaurs. This condition in sauropods seems to be uniquely restricted to a small region of the end of the tail. In this region, ligaments affected by DISH span the vertebral centra, producing a massive osseous overgrowth that does not involve the intervertebral space or the annulus fibrosus of the disc, thereby representing true bridging of the vertebrae. Rothschild and Berman examined all the preserved tail sections of specimens of *Diplodocus*, *Apatosaurus,* and *Camarasaurus* in North America (with the exception of those exposed at the Dinosaur National Monument quarry), particular attention given to the seventeenth to twenty-third caudals. (The first apparent ligamentous bridging of caudal vertebrae in *Camarasaurus* was reported by Rothschild and Berman in two specimens, CM 312 and UUVP 4317, collected from the Cleveland-Lloyd Quarry in Utah.) Subjecting these caudal elements to computerized axial tomography (CAT) analysis, Rothschild and Berman examined the alterations of their vertebral centra internal to the osseous overgrowth fusing the caudals together, rather than just the gross external appearance generally available to previous workers. Direct conformation of their CAT scan findings was provided by a longitudinally sectioned representative fused pair of *Diplodocus* caudals (AMNH 655).

Rothschild and Berman observed that all specimens showing vertebral bridging were large and apparently fully mature individuals. The bridging of the intervertebral spaces is composed of continuous, coalesced, and usually smooth longitudinal bands, and is generally circumcentral, save for perhaps a narrow midventral and middorsal area. CAT scan analysis revealed a clear separation between the ends of the vertebral centra and the joining overgrowth of ossified bands. This observation (confirmed by examination of AMNH 655) indicated that ossification did not involve the clearly definable disc space and was extrinsic to the area of the annulus fibrosus, the latter confirming that the fusion represents true ligamentous bridging. No evidence was found suggesting that this fusion resulted from bone breakage or disease.

Uncatalogued metatarsals (YPM acquisition #1045) of a very large, unknown sauropod, incorrectly regarded by Marsh as referable to *Diplodocus longus*.

Photo by R. A. Long and S. P. Welles (neg. #73/455A-21), courtesy Yale Peabody Museum of Natural History.

Courtesy Houston Museum of Science.

Diplodocus hayi, skeleton (subadult) including holotype CM 662, supplemented with CM 94 and *D. carnegii* skull (cast) CM 1161.

Rothschild and Berman concluded that the fused caudal vertebrae in these sauropods resulted from DISH. Regarding the concept of a sauropod rearing up on its hind legs, Rothschild and Berman noted that the tail, as observed by earlier workers (Gilmore 1906; Hatcher 1901; Holland 1906), probably did not make first contact with the ground until the twenty-eighth or twenty-ninth caudal, well beyond the part of the tail where fusion occurs. More likely, the caudal bridging may have facilitated keeping the tail elevated off the ground. In considering the possibility that vertebral fusion facilitated using the tail as a whip-like defense weapon, Rothschild and Berman noted that this fusion occurs in only half of the adult specimens of the three sauropods studied, a phenomenon that had led Rothschild (1987) to speculate that whip-lash behavior might be a sexually dimorphic feature utilized by males during intraspecific combat. Taking into account Beverly Halstead's unpublished theories (see Fritz 1988) regarding dinosaur mating (*i.e.,* the male twisted his tail under the female's to affect an exact meeting of

their sex organs), Rothschild and Berman added that the caudal bridging may have been a female characteristic, representing an adaptation allowing for upward and sideways arching of her thick and powerful tail to facilitate copulation.

Notes: On May 21, 1975, a well-preserved, mid-caudal chevron (BMNH R8924) pertaining to a diplodocid was found and collected by Stephen Hutt in the Lower Cretaceous, Wealden Formation, near Grange Chine on the Isle of Wight, England. Charig (1978) reported the find, then subsequently (1980) described the specimen as measuring 19.6 centimeters (about 7.4 inches) long, with a maximum width of 8.1 centimeters (more than 3 inches).

Czerkas (1992) introduced the idea that in diplodocids (and perhaps all sauropods) a median row of dermal spines was present over the tail and perhaps along the neck and body as well. The idea was based upon numerous apparently "conical or spine-like elements" discovered when the Howe Quarry, in Wyoming, was reopened in 1990 by professional collector Kirby Siber. Czerkas interpreted

Diplodocus

CM 11255, skull (right lateral view) referred to *Diplodocus* sp.

these elements as dermal spines attributed "to diplodocids resembling *Diplodocus* and *Barosaurus*."

Lambert (1990), in his *Dinosaur Data Book*, listed the informally named "Hisanohamasaurus," based on remains found in Japan; Dong, Hasegawa and Azuma (1990), in *The Age of Dinosaurs in Japan and China*, regarded this form as an indeterminate diplodocid.

From sauropod trackways, mostly those in the Morrison Formation (United States) and Wealden beds (England), combined with the skeletal record of sauropods from those localities, Farlow (1992) arrived at conclusions regarding the habitats in which these dinosaurs may have been most common. Though Dodson (1990) suggested that sauropods generally prospered in humid conditions, with Morrison sauropods atypically adapted to seasonally dry environments, Farlow (1992) found that Morrison sauropods may have been more the rule than exception. Farlow pointed out, however, that this conclusion does not necessarily apply to all sauropods, as they are known in fossil faunas that accumulated in regions that probably had fairly wet climates; and that sauropods were a diverse group of animals able to adapt successfully to a wide range of terrestrial environments.

Foster (1995), utilizing the ratio of minimum circumference to length to quantify the limb-bone robustness in some sauropod dinosaurs, found that, along with other characters of individual bones, robustness may aid in taxonomic identification of limb bones not associated with vertebrae. Results from Foster's study showed that minimum ratios of circumference to length "are only valuable for some elements and genera, but that in some cases two genera can only be distinguished by other characteristics of the bones." According to Foster, the forelimb bones of *Apatosaurus* have consistently higher ratios than other genera; those of *Diplodocus* are often similar to *Camarasaurus* but lower than *Apatosaurus*; ratios of the humerus in *Brachiosaurus* are significantly lower than in other genera, with little indication of allometric change; femora and fibulae of *Camarasaurus* and *Apatosaurus* have similar ratios, with those of *Diplodocus* just slightly lower; tibiae of *Diplodocus*, *Barosaurus,* and *Pleurocoelous,* more notably slender than in *Apatosaurus* and *Camarasaurus*; slight allometric change is suggested for the radius, tibia, and fibula, "expressed as a lowering in minimum circumference/length ratios of a few percent from the smallest specimen of an element to the largest," humerus and femur apparently not showing this trend.

Key references: Bakker (1971, 1986); Berman and McIntosh (1978); Bird (1954); Blumberg and Sokoloff (1961); Britt (1991); Colbert (1962); Coombs (1975); Cope (1884); Fiorillo (1991); Gilmore (1906, 1986); Hatcher (1901); Hay (1908*a*); Holland (1906, 1908, 1924*a*); Marsh (1878, 1884, 1888*a*); McGinnis (1982); McIntosh (1990*a*, 1990*b*); Osborn (1899); Paul (1988*a*, 1887); Rothschild (1987); Rothschild and Benson (1991).

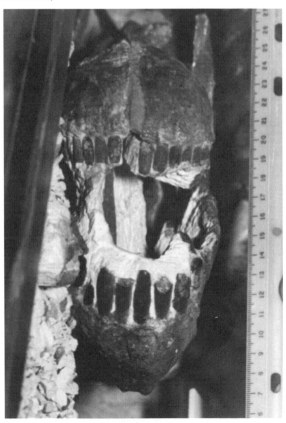

CM 11255, skull (anterior view) referred to *Diplodocus* sp.

DIPLOTOMODON Leidy 1868 [*nomen dubium*]—(=?*Dryptosaurus*)

Saurischia: Theropoda: Tetanurae: ?Avetheropoda: ?Coelurosauria *incertae sedis*.

Name derivation: Greek *diplos* = "double" + Greek *tome* = "cutting" + Greek *odous* = "tooth."

Type species: *D. horrificus* (Leidy 1865) [*nomen dubium*].

Other species: [None.]

Occurrence: "Green-sand formations," New Jersey, United States.

Age: Late Cretaceous.

Known material/holotype: Tooth.

　　Diagnosis of genus: [None published.]

　　Comments: Leidy (1865) founded the new genus and species *Tomodon horrificus* on a single tooth collected from the "Green-sand formations" of Gloucester County, New Jersey. Leidy originally misidentified the tooth as that of a plesiosaur and observed that the base of the specimen showed an irregular porous condition possibly caused by erosion.

　　Leidy (1868*b*) subsequently changed his opinion, believing the specimen to belong to a fish, at the same time noting that the name of *Tomodon* was preoccupied (Duméril 1853) for a genus of snake; he referred the tooth to the new genus *Diplotomodon*.

　　The tooth was eventually identified as that of a theropod by Welles (1952), who provisionally referred it to the Megalosauridae. Later, Molnar (1990) observed that the tooth most closely resembles the tooth third from the front in the jaw of *Dryptosaurus aquilunguis* and suggested that it may belong to that species.

　　Key references: Leidy (1865, 1868*b*); Molnar (1990); Welles (1952).

Diplotomodon horrificus, ANSP 9680, holotype tooth.

DIRACODON Marsh 1881 [*nomen dubium*]— (See *Stegosaurus*.)

Name derivation: Greek *di* = "two" + Greek *rachis* = "ridge" + Greek *odous* = "tooth."

Type species: *D. laticeps* Marsh 1881 [*nomen dubium*].

DOLICHOSUCHUS Huene 1932 [*nomen dubium*]

Saurischia: Theropoda *incertae sedis*.

Name derivation: Greek *dolichos* = "long" + Greek *souchos* = "crocodile."

Type species: *D. cristatus* Huene 1932 [*nomen dubium*].

Other species: [None.]

Occurrence: Mittlerer Stubensandstein, Baden-Württemberg, Germany.

Age: Late Triassic (Middle Norian).

Known material/holotype: BMNH 38058, imperfect left tibia.

　　Diagnosis of genus: [None published.]

　　Comments: The genus *Dolicosuchus* was founded upon an incomplete tibia collected from the Upper Keuper, Stubensandstein of Württemberg, Kaltenthal (near Stuttgart), [former Federal Republic of] Germany.

　　Huene (1932) described this tibia as very slender, thin-walled, with a strong outwardly-developed lateral crest unknown in other Triassic forms; 29 centimeters (about 11 inches) in length.

　　Though originally referred by Huene to the Podokesauridae, Norman (1990), in reassessing various problematic "coelurosaurs," found the type material of *D. cristatus* too fragmentary to be of any descriptive or comparative use.

　　Key references: Huene (1932); Norman (1990).

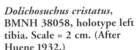

Dolichosuchus cristatus, BMNH 38058, holotype left tibia. Scale = 2 cm. (After Huene 1932.)

DRACOPELTA Galton 1980

Ornithischia: Genasauria: Thyreophora: Ankylosauria: Nodosauridae.

Name derivation: Latin *draco* = "dragon" + Greek *pelta* = "[small] shield."

Type species: *D. zbyszewskii* Galton 1980.

Other species: [None.]

Occurrence: [Unnamed formation], Estremadura, Portugal.

Age: Late Jurassic (Kimmeridgian).

Known material/holotype: SGP collection, partial rib cage with armor.

　　Diagnosis of genus (as for type species): At least five distinct types of dermal scutes from thoracic region, including: 1. Very small isolated flat scutes; 2. small medial paired circular plates with raised centers

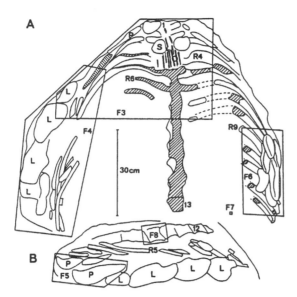

Dracopelta zbyszewskii, SGP, holotype partial skeleton, in A. dorsal and B. ventral views. (After Galton 1980.)

Name derivation: "Dravidanadu [common name for southern part of Indian Peninsula]" + Greek *sauros* = "lizard."
Type species: *D. blanfordi* Yadagiri and Ayyasami 1979.
Other species: [None.]
Occurrence: Trichinopoly Group, Tirchirapalli District, Tamil Nadu, India.
Age: Late Cretaceous (Coniacian).
Known material: Partial skull, tooth, postcranial remains, dermal plates and spine.
Holotype: GSI SR PAL 1, fragmentary skeleton with partial skull.

Diagnosis of genus (as for type species): Small stegosaur distinguished by two supraorbitals, the anterior opening large; postorbital thin, expanded anteriorly, with straight margin; absence of postfrontal; small tooth with three crenulations; sacrum with four co-ossified amphiplatyan centra with fused neural arches; neural canal expanded, sometimes excavated into centrum; sternum plate-like, with proximal expansion; iliac blade curved posteriorly; ischial peduncle narrow, weak; generally thin (10 millimeters), triangular dermal plates with stout bases; dermal spine curved with medial expansion (Dong 1990*b*).

Comments: *Dravidosaurus*, the first and only stegosaur positively dated as of Upper Cretaceous age (see Galton 1981*a*), was founded on a partly preserved skull (GSI SR PAL 1) from the [Late Cretaceous ammonite] *Kossmaticeras theobaldianum* zone (see Kossmatt 1895; Sastry, Rao and Mamgain 1969) of the Trichinopoly Group (Rao 1956), at Siranattam village, in the Tiruchirapalli district of southern India, the rocks from which the material was recovered corresponding to the European Coniacian stage. Referred material from the same locality includes a tooth (GSI SR PAL 2), sacrum (GSI SR PAL 3), ilium (GSI SR PAL 4), ischium (GSI SR PAL 5), armor plate (GSI SR PAL 6), and dermal spine (GSI SR PAL 7) (Yadagiri and Ayyasami 1979).

Yadagiri and Ayyasami originally diagnosed the monotypic *D. blanfordi* as follows: Small stegosaur

and rims; 3. very long anterolateral plates; 4. narrow nonprojecting dorsolateral plates that do not overlap; and 5. laterally-projecting lateral plates that overlap (Galton 1980*a*).

Comments: The first known Late Jurassic ankylosaur, *Dracopelta* was established on postcranial remains (SGP collection), much of which had eroded away, recovered from the Kimmeridgian of Ribomar, Estremadura region, on the west coast of Portugal (Galton 1980*a*).

As described by Galton, the smallest preserved scute, one from the first grouping, measures 31 millimeters by 21 millimeters. The largest preserved scute, of the fifth group, was at least 190 millimeters long and 110 wide.

Key reference: Galton (1980).

DRAVIDOSAURUS   Yadagiri and Ayyasami 1979
Ornithischia: Genasauria: Thyreophorea:
   Stegosauria: Stegosauridae.

Dravidosaurus blanfordi, GSI SR PAL 1, holotype fragmentary skull in lateral and dorsal views. (After Yadagiri and Ayyasami 1979.)

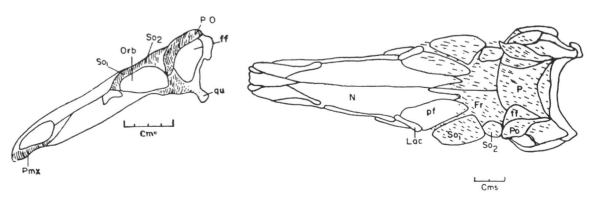

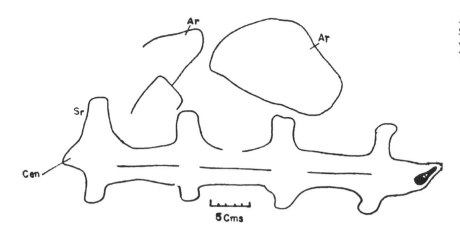

Dravidosaurus blanfordi, GSI SR PAL 1, holotype sacrum with armor plates. (After Yadagiri and Ayyasami 1979.)

with relatively smaller skull than in other known stegosaurs; skull with two ?supraorbital openings, anterior opening large; no postfrontal; postorbital a thin bone expanded anteriorly, with straight margin; sacrum with four co-ossified amphiplatyan centra; neural canal expanded, sometimes excavated into the centrum; neural arches fused to centrum; illial plate curved posteriorly, narrow at the weak ischiac peduncle; sternum plate-like, proximally expanded; dermal plates triangular, with stout base; tail spine curved, uniquely expanded medially (Yadagiri and Ayyasami 1979).

As measured by Yadagiri and Ayyasami, the skull is 200 millimeters (about 7.6 inches) in length. The plates are mostly thin (about 10 millimeters in thickness), the smallest 50 millimeters high and 30 millimeters long, the larger plate 250 millimeters high and 150 millimeters long. The dermal spine is 150 millimeters in length, bulged at mid-length with a diameter of 30 millimeters, tapering near the base to a diameter of 22 millimeters.

Yadagiri and Ayyasami observed that the skull of *Dravidosaurus*, narrow and depressed with two supraorbital openings, resembles that of *Stegosaurus*, differing mainly in the absence of a postfrontal, the thin straight postorbital, and thick rectangular ptery-

goid. It also differs from *Stegosaurus* in the form of the beak, consisting of the anterior portion of the premaxilla, which ends in a point. The referred tooth [see below] generally resembles teeth in *Kentrosaurus*. *Dravidosaurus* differs from other known stegosaurs in the illial plate, which has a less expanded posterior end, in the weak ischial peduncle, and in the form of the sacrum.

As noted by Yadagiri and Ayyasami, the occurrence of *Dravidosaurus* in Upper Cretaceous rocks of India extends stegosaurian presence beyond the early Cretaceous, clearly documenting the survival of Stegosauria to almost the end of the Mesozoic.

In a review of Asian stegosaurs, Dong (1990*b*) pointed out that the tooth referred to as *D. blanfordi* had been obtained during preparation when the rock matrix was being washed away from the skull. As this tooth, which measures only 3 millimeters long, seems to be too small for a stegosaurian skull measuring 250 millimeters in length, and because it shows three small and simple crenulations on the crown similar to those of Late Cretaceous ankylosaurs, Dong speculated that it may eventually prove to belong to an ankylosaur.

Key references: Dong (1990*b*); Galton (1981*a*); Yadagiri and Ayyasami (1979).

Dravidosaurus blanfordi, GSI SR PAL 1, holotype anterior sacral vertebra. (After Yadagiri and Ayyasami 1979.)

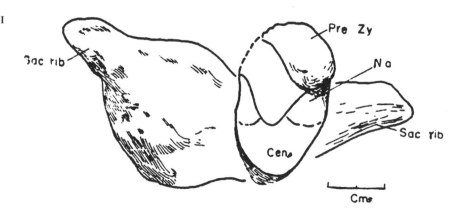

DRINKER Bakker, Galton, Siegwarth and Filla 1990

Ornithischia: Ornithopoda *incertae sedis*.

Name derivation: "[Edward] Drinker [Cope]."

Type species: *D. nisti* Bakker, Galton, Siegwarth and Filla 1990.

Other species: [None.]

Occurrence: Morrison Formation, Wyoming, United States.

Age: ?Late Jurassic–?Early Cretaceous (?Purbeckian).

Known material: Incomplete skeleton, subadult, miscellaneous postcranial remains, juveniles and half-grown individuals, tooth.

Holotype: CPS 106, partial skeleton including parts of both upper and lower jaws, centra from all sections of vertebral column, partial fore and hindlimbs, subadult.

Diagnosis of genus (as for type species): Closest to *Othnielia*, differing in much greater complexity of maxillary and dentary tooth crowns; each cusp divided into three cusplet units, a central cusp, with a low ridge running toward base of crown; crown edge developed into sharp blade fore and aft of main cusplet, with thickened edge making a narrow ridge; ridges pass from edge of crown toward base, merging with low swelling made by ridge of the central cusplet; maxillary teeth with accessory row of cusps developed along edge of very prominent cingulum, along posterior half of base of inner crown (Bakker, Galton, Siegwarth and Filla 1990).

Drinker nisti, CPS 106, holotype left metatarsal I and first hallucal phalanx, in outer, dorsal (anterior), inner, and ventral (posterior) views. (After Bakker, Galton, Siegwarth and Filla 1990.)

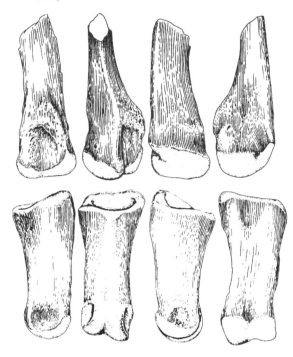

Comments: The genus *Drinker* was founded upon a partial subadult skeleton (CPS 106), discovered by James Siegwarth and James Filla in the Big Nose locality of the Morrison Formation, Breakfast Bench Beds (located by Robert T. Bakker in 1978), below the Dakota Sandstone, at West Como Bluff, Albany County, Wyoming (Bakker, Galton, Siegwarth and Filla 1990).

Referred material from the same locality includes vertebral centra, promixal radius, distal third metatarsal, and astragalus (CPS 107) from a very young individual, and vertebral centra, distal humerus, and hind-foot phalanges (CPS 108) and

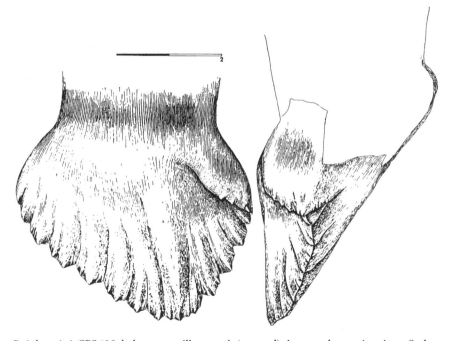

Drinker nisti, CPS 106, holotype maxillary tooth (reversed), inner and posterior views. Scale in mm. (After Bakker, Galton, Siegwarth and Filla 1990.)

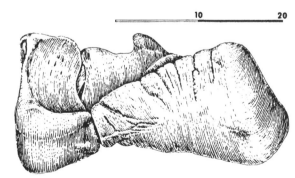

Drinker nisti, CPS 106, holotype left astragalus and fourth distal tarsal, posterior view. Scale in mm. (After Bakker, Galton, Siegwarth and Filla 1990.)

dorsal vertebral centrum (CPS 109) from two half-grown individuals; from the Breakfast Bench Beds at East Como Bluff, Albany County, a dentary tooth, caudal vertebrae, and partial phalanges of the hind foot (CPS 197) of a fully adult individual, and a one-fifth grown femur head; and from West Como Bluff below the Dakota Sandstone (see Ostrom and McIntosh 1966), a femur (USNM 5808) belonging to a juvenile individual (Gilmore 1909*b*), and an anterior maxillary tooth (YPM 9524) (Galton 1983*b*) (Bakker *et al.*, 1990).

Drinker was regarded by Bakker *et al.*, as an "hypsilophodontoid," with *Othnielia* too primitive (maxillary and posterior dentary teeth lacking the derived character of a strong, central, vertical ridge found in dryosaurids, hypsilophodontids, camptosaurids, iguanodontids and hadrosaurids) to allocate to the Hypsilophodontidae (see Galton 1983*b*).

According to Bakker *et al.*, *Drinker* and *Othnielia* constitute a more primitive ornithopod group differing from other Late Jurassic–Cretaceous forms in: 1. Lack of a wide, horizontal shelf on the posterior part of the ilium; 2. less elongated cervical vertebrae foreto-aft; 3. less expanded anterior-outer (or "lesser") trochanter of the femoral head; and 4. less reduced inner hindtoe.

Bakker (1990) regarded the Breakfast Bench horizon as the youngest of the Morrison faunal epoch, possibly dating to the Jurassic–Cretaceous transition. Common are small ornithopods such as *Drinker*, with broad, spreading hindfeet, while sauropods are rare. The Breakfast Bench environment may have been that of a swampy lake shore or delta better suited to supporting animals like *Drinker* than

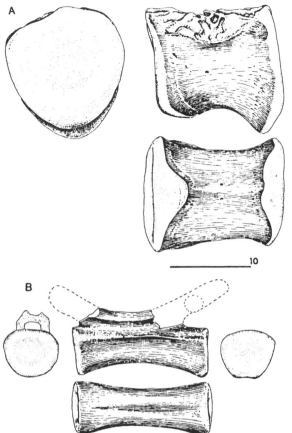

Drinker nisti, CPS 106, holotype A. anterior (?third) caudal and B. distal caudal vertebra in anterior, lateral, ventral, and posterior views. Scale in mm. (After Bakker, Galton, Siegwarth and Filla 1990.)

large animals with compact feet such as sauropods and stegosaurs.

Key references: Bakker (1990); Bakker, Galton, Siegwarth and Filla (1990); Galton (1983*b*); Gilmore (1909*b*); Ostrom and McIntosh (1966).

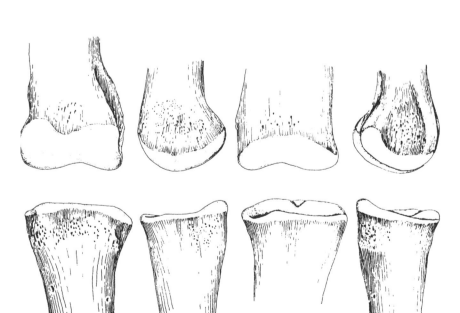

Drinker nisti, CPS 106, holotype right metatarsal III, distal end, and first phalanx, proximal end, in ventral (posterior), inner, dorsal (anterior), and outer views. (After Bakker, Galton, Siegwarth and Filla 1990.)

DROMAEOSAURUS Matthew and Brown 1922—(=?*Chirostenotes*)

Saurischia: Theropoda: Tetanurae: Avetheropoda: Coelurosauria: Maniraptora: Dromaeosauridae: ?Dromaeosaurinae.

Name derivation: Greek *dramaios* = "swift-running" + Greek *sauros* = "lizard."

Type species: *D. albertensis* Matthew and Brown 1922.

Other species: ?*D. explanatus* (Cope 1876), ?*D. minutus* (Marsh 1892) [*nomen dubium*],

Occurrence: Dinosaur Park Formation, Alberta, Canada; Judith River Formation, Montana, United States.

Age: Late Cretaceous (Late Campanian–Early Maastrichtian).

Known material: Incomplete skull, isolated cranial and postcranial elements, fragments, teeth.

Holotype: AMNH 5356, partial skull with lower jaws, hyoids, associated footbones.

Diagnosis of genus (as for type species): Fewer maxillary teeth (9) than in other dromaeosaurids; anterior carina of maxillary tooth close to midline of tooth near tip, but not far from tip tooth twists toward lingual surface (this twist presently not known in other theropods); differs from velociraptorines in following features: premaxilla deeper, thicker; quadratojugal stouter; top of frontal flatter, margin of supratemporal fossa not as pronounced; postorbital process of frontal more sharply demarcated from dorsomedial orbital margin; posteromedial process of palatine more slender; anterior and posterior tooth denticles subequal in size (Currie 1995).

Diagnosis of ?*D. explanatus*: Teeth with strongly compressed and curved crowns; one side flat, the other gently convex; posterior cutting edge median and concave (Cope 1876*a*).

Comments: *Dromaeosaurus* was founded on a partial skull with some postcranial remains (AMNH 5356) from the Belly River series [now Oldman Formation], Red Deer River, at the former Steveville Ferry, in Alberta, Canada, discovered by Barnum Brown during the 1910–15 American Museum of Natural History excavations.

As *Dromaeosaurus* seemed to bear similarities to both "carnosaurs" and "coelurosaurs," while also being unusually different, and because no similar forms were yet known, Matthew and Brown (1922)

Dromaeosaurus albertensis, AMNH 5356, holotype skull, right lateral view, much restored for museum display.

Courtesy Royal Tyrrell Museum/Alberta Community Development (slide #10.002.02b).

Dromaeosaurus albertensis, mounted skeleton.

provisionally referred this genus to the [abandoned] family Deinodontidae Cope 1866. Matthew and Brown erected for the genus the new subfamily Dromaeosaurinae on the basis of differences in the skull, number of teeth, form of the premaxillary teeth, and differences in the feet.

Matthew and Brown originally diagnosed the genus (and type species *D. albertensis*) as follows: Comparable in size to *Ornithomimus,* with well-developed teeth; teeth compressed or asymmetrically oval, sharply pointed, recurved, serrate on anterior and posterior borders; at least three premaxillary, nine maxillary, and ten dentary teeth; snout rounded and deep; top of skull (fragmentary in the holotype) slightly smaller than in *Struthiomimus,* with general proportions of larger theropods; brain cavity relatively large; jaws long but not massive; skull about 21 centimeters (8 inches) in length.

In describing the fragmentary foot bones, Matthew and Brown observed that the second toe in *Dromaeosaurus* is only slightly smaller than in *Albertosaurus* [=*Deinodon* of their usage], despite the vast differences in the sizes of their skeletons, and slightly larger than the second toe of *Struthiomimus.* (Not until the discovery of *Deinonychus* [see entry] in 1964 was a more salient interpretation of the *Dromaeosaurus* foot realized.)

Over the years, other authors assigned *Dromaeosaurus* to different higher taxa until Colbert and Russell (1969), recognizing that this genus represented a distinct stage in theropod evolution, put it into its own family Dromaeosauridae. Colbert and Russell proposed that Dromaeosauridae be included in a new "infraorder" Deinonychosauria (regarded by Holtz 1994 as a polyphyletic taxon), characterized by many cranial, forelimb, and hindlimb specializations suggesting strong predacious habits.

Noting the strikingly broad braincase, particularly in the medullary region, Colbert and Russell suggested that *Dromaeosaurus* had an unusually large brain (by dinosaurian standards). The skull was kinetic as in birds (particularly *Archaeopteryx*), the braincase fused to the skull roof. Though only about 1.8 meters (6 feet) long, *Dromaeosaurus,* with its relatively large brain, large eyes, and grasping hands, must have been a swift, skillful, and formidable hunter.

Colbert and Russell speculated that this dinosaur utilized its enlarged digit (8 centimeters or 3 inches long) as a tearing or digging weapon. More likely, this claw was used to disembowel prey, probably small ornithischians, captured with its three-clawed foreclaws (see *Deinonychus* entry).

Russell (1972) later referred *Ornithomimus minutus,* based on a partial metatarsus from the Laramie

Dromaeosaurus albertensis, AMNH 3961, holotype teeth of *Laelaps laevirons.*

Photo by R. A. Long and S. P. Welles (neg. #73/320–43), courtesy American Museum of Natural History.

Dromaeosaurus albertensis,
AMNH 3958, holotype teeth
of *Laelaps explanatus*.

Photo by R. A. Long and S. P. Welles (neg. #73/320-36), courtesy American Museum of Natural History.

Formation of Colorado and originally described by Marsh (1892c), to *Dromaeosaurus* as new species *D. minutus*. Possibly referable to *D. albertensis* is *Laelaps explanatus*, based on teeth collected by J. C. Isaac from the Dinosaur Park Formation ("Fort Union beds") of Fergus County, Montana. Cope (1876a) described (but did not figure) these teeth, observing that they were about the size of those of the largest of living varanid lizards.

More recently, Currie (1995) reexamined the holotype skull of *A. albertensis*, pointing out that it had been heavily reconstructed for display purposes, many of its details having been obscured by colored plaster. Following separation of the largely reconstructed skull roof, and repreparation and restudy of the skull (including the use of CT scans), Currie offered a revised diagnosis of the taxon, noting that, contrary to earlier reports, the premaxillary teeth are not D-shaped in cross-section, the cranium is not pneumatic, interdental plates are present, and the braincase bones are not pneumatized.

According to Currie, dromaeosaurids form a distinct clade of specialized theropods that are not closely related to other Late Cretaceous "coelurosaurs."

Note: Lambert (1990), in the *Dinosaur Data Book*, reported the unofficially named "Kitandanisaurus." According to Dong, Hasegawa and Azuma (1990), in the guidebook *The Age of Dinosaurs in Japan and China*, this new form is an indeterminate dromaeosaurid.

In a more recent preliminary notice, Azuma and Currie (1995) reported that this theropod is a giant dromaeosaurid that was discovered among other dinosaurian remains at the Karsuyama quarry, in the Kitandani Formation (Lower Cretaceous; Albian) in the Tetori Group in Fukui Prefecture, Japan. According to Zuma and Currie, this new genus was identified in 1991 as a dromaeosaurid from jaw fragments on the basis of fused interdental plates. More dromaeosaurid material (right ?first manual ungual, right astragalus, and left metatarsal III) was found two years later. These remains could represent part of an associated skeleton.

As briefly described by Azuma and Currie, the manual ungual is strongly recurved, laterally compressed, and tapers to a sharp point; in a straight line, it measures 10.5 centimeters from the dorsal edge of the proximal articulation to the tip, and along the outer curvature it measures 15 centimeters. The third metatarsal measures 29.5 centimeters in length. Azuma and Currie estimated the total size of this dromaeosaurid to be about twice that of *Deinonychus* and 25 percent smaller than *Utahraptor* in linear dimensions. The authors further pointed out that the presence of giant dromaeosaurids in Japan, Mongolia, and the United States constitutes evidence that faunal interchange between the northern continents was occurring during Albian times.

Key references: Colbert and Russell (1969); Cope (1876a); Marsh (1892); Matthew and Brown (1922).

Photo by R. A. Long and S. P. Welles (neg. #73/501-19), courtesy Yale Peabody Museum of Natural History.

?*Dromaeosaurus minutus*, YPM 1049, holotype metatarsal III of *Ornithomimus minutus*.

Photo by R. A. Long and S. P. Welles (neg. #73/320-32), courtesy American Museum of Natural History.

Dromaeosaurus albertensis,
AMNH 3954, holotype teeth
of *Laelaps cristatus*.

DROMICEIOMIMUS   Russell 1972

Saurischia: Theropoda: Tetanurae: Avetheropoda:
   Coelurosauria: Maniraptora: Arctometatarsalia:
   Bullatosauria: Ornithomimosauria:

Name derivation: Latin *Dromiceius* = "[generic
   name for] emu" + Latin *mimus* = "mimic."

Type species: *D. brevitertius* (Parks 1926).

Other species: *D. samueli* (Parks 1928).

Occurrence: Horseshoe Canyon Formation,
   Dinosaur Park Formation, Alberta, Canada.

Age: Late Cretaceous (Latest Campanian–Early
   Maastrichtian).

Known material: Partial skull with associated
   postcranial skeleton, six fragmentary postcranial
   skeletons, skull with partial postcrania.

Holotype: ROM 797, sacrum and adjacent caudal
   vertebrae, several distal caudals, pelvis, hind
   limbs.

Diagnosis of genus (as for type species): Presacral
vertebral column not as long as combined lengths of
femur, tibiaastragalus, and metatarsal III; posterior
width of anteriormost 15 caudal less half its central
length; transition point between proximal and distal
tail segments located between twelfth and thirteenth
caudals; scapula longer than humerus; antebrachium
approximately 70 percent length of femur; manus not
as powerfully developed as in *Struthiomimus*, unguals
apparently like those in *Ornithomimus edmontonicus*;
antilium, tibia, metatarsus, and third toe longer relative to femur than in *Ornithomimus* and
Struthiomimus (Russell 1972).

Diagnosis of *D. samueli*: Differs from *D. brevitertius* in that humerus is about five times longer
than average-sized anterior dorsal centrum (almost
six times longer in type species); cranial bones are
more heavily constructed (a difference which may or
may not have taxonomic significance) (Russell 1972).

Comments: The genus *Dromiceiomimus* was
founded upon incomplete postcrania (ROM 797)
collected from the Edmonton [now Horseshoe
Canyon] Formation, member A, east of Red Deer
River, Alberta, Canada, and originally described by
Parks (1926*b*) as *Struthiomimus brevitertius*.

In his original description of the holotype, Parks
observed that the proximal end of metatarsal III is
not fused, a condition Russell (1972) later regarded as
an individual abnormality.

Russell, recognizing this material as representing
a new genus, renamed Parks' species *Dromiceiomimus
brevitertius*, referring to it additional specimens from
the same and nearby localities. These remains
included humeri, pubes and ischia, left femur, tibiae
and fibulae, metatarsal fragments, and phalangial elements of the left foot (AMNH 5201), from the Horseshoe Canyon Formation, member B, west of Red
Deer River; sacrum and adjacent dorsal vertebrae,
caudals, left ilium, pubes and ischia, and hindlimbs
(NMC 12068), from the Horseshoe Canyon Formation, member B, east of Red Deer River; proximal
and distal ends of the tail, distal ends of pubes and
ischia, left femur, both tibiae and fibulae, and feet
(NMC 12069), from the same locality; distal ends of

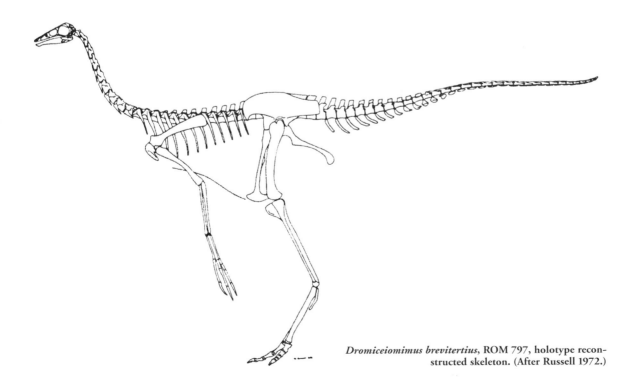

Dromiceiomimus brevitertius, ROM 797, holotype reconstructed skeleton. (After Russell 1972.)

tibiae, metatarsi, and pedal phalanges (NMC 12070) from the same locality; posterodorsal region of the skull, left temporal region, anterior half of left and posterior half of right mandibles, incomplete presacral vertebral column, almost complete caudal series, left ilium, pubes and ischia, left femur and tibia-fibula, left metatarsus, and two pedal phalanges (NMC 12228), from the Horseshoe Canyon Formation, member B, west of Red Deer River; and possibly a specimen (ROM 840) from the Oldman (now Dinosaur Park) Formation of Alberta.

The species *S. ingens* Parks 1933 was based on a sacrum and adjacent dorsals, pelvis, complete left hind limb, right femur and tibia, and the proximal end of a right fibula (ROM 852), collected from the Horseshoe Canyon Formation, member B, east of Red Deer River. Russell attributed the differences between the relative proportions of the pelvic girdle and hindlimb in this species to ontogeny, regarding *S. ingens* as representing a larger, heavier, and more mature *D. brevitertius*.

S. samueli Parks (1928*b*) was based on a skull with lower jaws, cervical and anterior dorsal vertebrae, scapulae-coracoids and humeri, right radius-ulna, proximal end of the right metacarpus, and two ungual phalanges (ROM 840), recovered from the Judith River [now Dinosaur Park] Formation, Dinosaur Provincial Park, Alberta. Russell regarded this taxon as conspecific with *D. brevitertius*, although Barsbold and Osmólska (1990), in their review of the Ornithomosauria, accepted *D. samueli* as a valid species.

Russell described the skull of *Dromiceiomimus* as having a remarkably large orbit, the rim measuring about 72 millimeters (about 2.75 inches) in diameter. The skull is kinetic, the distal end of the quadrate apparently capable of limited anteroposterior movement. An endocranial mold revealed that the brain was relatively large, the general relation of brain to body weight similar to that of a comparable-sized ostrich. The brain had short and thin olfactory bulbs and cerebral hemispheres slightly wider than in *Troodon* [=*Stenonychosaurus* of his usage].

Dromiceiomimus has long limbs, a slender forearm and hand, and a relatively short back, and an approximate length of 2.9 meters (10 feet).

Comparing this genus and other ornithomimids to an ostrich, Russell envisioned a possible lifestyle for *Dromiceiomimus*: The lightly-built body and powerful hindlimbs represent a cursorial mode of living and a running speed surpassing that of the ostrich, though with less dodging ability. Lacking adaptations for defense, dinosaurs like *Dromiceiomimus* could only rely on speed or perhaps camouflage coloration to escape predators such as dromaeosaurids or juvenile tyrannosaurids. The large eyes, which may have been color sensitive, would have been crucial in alerting *Dromiceiomimus* of danger while also serving as an important adaptation to cursorial habits.

The shape of the muzzle, which may have been covered by a horny beak, plus features of the secondary palate and the transverse axis of flexure in the skull roof, suggested to Russell that *Dromiceiomimus* was insectivorous. The weak jaw adductor muscles in *Dromiceiomimus* and other ornithomimids were adapted for soft foods, perhaps soft animal parts and eggs, while the hands were possibly suited for uncovering food objects on the ground. Diet may not have been limited to only one kind of food. As gastric stones have never been associated with ornithomimid skeletons and given that all other theropods seemingly were carnivorous, Russell denounced the notion that dinosaurs like *Dromiceiomimus* were at least partially herbivorous.

Russell suggested that the very wide pelvic canal and small body size in ornithomimids, especially *Dromiceiomimus*, may indicate that these animals were either oviparous or ovovivaporous, perhaps producing fewer young at a given time than other

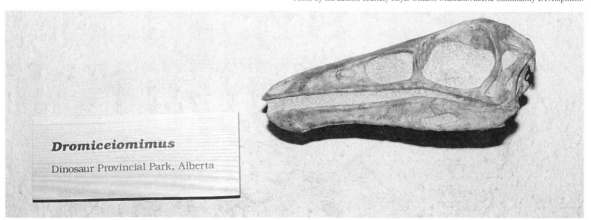

Dromiceiomimus brevitertius, skull (cast of NMC 12228).

Illustration by Gregory S. Paul.

**Dromiceimimus brevitertius,
hypothetically depicted with
downy feather covering.**

theropods. The remains of both adult and half-grown individuals found at one site suggest that *Dromiceiomimus* may have had some kind of a social structure, perhaps living together with the adults caring for their young.

According to Russell, environmental pressures from a lifestyle similar to that of ground birds produced a generally similar body form in *Dromiceiomimus* and other ornithomimids, including large eyes, kinetic skull, secondary palate, large brain, and presumably about an equal level of intelligence.

Dromiceiomimus was quite common in the lower Horseshoe Canyon Formation, at least as common as *S. altus* was in the earlier "Oldman" Formation along Red Deer River.

As observed by Barsbold and Osmólska, the tibiotarsus in *Dromiceiomimus* is relatively longer than in any known ornithomimid, from 18 to 25 percent longer than the femur (depending on the individual's size).

Key references: Barsbold and Osmólska (1990); Parks (1926*b*, 1928*b*); Russell (1972).

DROMICOSAURUS Hoepen 1920 — (See
Massospondylus.)
Name derivation: Latin *Dromiceius* = "[generic name for] emu" + Greek *sauros* = "lizard."
Type species: *D. gracilis* Hoepen 1920.

DRYOSAURUS Marsh 1894 — (=*Dysalotosaurus*)
Ornithischia: Genasauria: Cerapoda: Ornithopoda: Iguanodontia: Dryosauridae.
Name derivation: Greek *dryos* = "oak" + Greek *sauros* = "lizard."
Type species: *D. altus* (Marsh 1878).
Other species: *D. lettowvorbecki* (Virchow 1919).
Occurrence: Morrison Formation, Colorado, Wyoming, Utah, United States; Middle Saurian

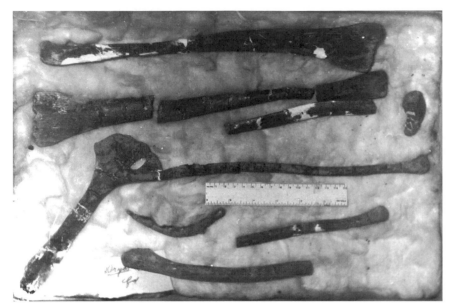

Photo by R. A. Long and S. P. Welles (neg. #73/472-3), courtesy Yale Peabody Museum of Natural History.

Dryosaurus altus, YPM 1876D, holotype fibula, pubis, and miscellaneous elements of *Laosaurus altus*.

ing a horizontal sheet under braincase; squamosal bordering dorsally the remnant of posttemporal fenestra; anteroventral edge of paroccipital process deeply excavated; posteroventral process of predentary bifurcated; dorsal articular cotylus of surangular fits into notch on posterior surface of coronoid process; premaxilla edentulous; lateral surface of maxillary tooth ornamented, showing more prominent primary vertical ridge than medial surface of corresponding dentary tooth; two-four secondary vertical ridges anterior to primary ridge in both maxillary and dentary teeth, up to three posterior to that ridge (Galton 1983*b*).

Diagnosis of *D. altus*: Wide contact between premaxilla and prefrontal; palpebral elongate, with large base; prominent angle projecting on anterior edge of postorbital; squamosal with long anterior process; dorsomedial edge of maxilla squarish at level

Photo by R. A. Long and S. P. Welles (neg. #73/72-12), courtesy Yale Peabody Museum of Natural History.

Bed, Tendaguru Beds, Mtwara, Tanzania; ?Oxford Clay, Northamptonshire, England.

Age: Late Jurassic–?Early Cretaceous (Late Kimmeridgian–Early Tithonian; ?Neocomian–?Hauterivian).

Known material: Almost complete skeleton, seven partial skeletons, postcranial elements, teeth, many disassociated cranial and postcranial elements.

Holotype: YPM 1876, tooth, pelvis, hind leg.

Diagnosis of genus: Neural spines with maximum height greater than dorsal length of dorsal vertebrae, with elongate transverse processes; base of small fifth sacral rib short anteroposteriorly; caudal vertebrae with neural spines 45 degrees or less to top of their centra; first 12 caudals with transverse processes; humerus with low deltopectoral crest; main body of ilium low, brevis shelf wide, ratio posteriorly 0.5; obturator process on proximal fourth of ischium; distal half of ischium bar-shaped, curved in side view; femur with deep cleft between lesser and greater trochanters, deep depression on medial surface of the shaft separated from base of fourth trochanter, and deep anterior intercondylar groove distally; pes with vestigial metatarsal I (Galton 1981*b*); premaxilla with short anterior process not contacting with nasal, and long posterior process that contacts lacrimal; anterior end of maxilla with lateral process; frontals broad; medial length of parietal about one fourth its entire length; postventral projection on proximal end of quadrate, large notch on anterior edge; jugal large, with V-shaped margin for lower temporal opening; lower portion of quadrate flange of pterygoid form-

Dryosaurus altus, YPM 1876D, holotype femur of *Laosaurus altus*.

of the palatine suture; lateral margin of trigeminal foramen (V) with triangle-shaped outline and mostly acute edge; humerus with shallow distal intercondylar grooves; ulna with small olecranon process; radius and ulna with rounded edges in distal view (Galton 1983*b*).

Diagnosis of *D. lettowvorbecki*: Narrow contact between premaxilla and prefrontal; short palpebral with small base; postorbital with straight anterior edge; anterior process to squamosal short; dorsomedial edge of maxilla gently convex at level of palatine suture; lateral margin of trigeminal foramen (V) circular in outline, with gently convex edge; humerus with deep distal intercondylar grooves; ulna with large olecranon process; radius and ulna with acute edges in distal view (Galton 1983*b*).

Comments: This small, conservative appearing ornithopod was founded upon a tooth, pelvis, and hind leg (YPM 1876) collected from the Morrison Formation, at Como Bluff, Wyoming. The material was originally described by Marsh (1878) as the holotype of *Laosaurus altus*. After studying additional material referred to this species and observing the long, amphicoelous cervical vertebrae and long, narrow prepubis, Marsh (1894) concluded that this form was generically distinct from *Laosaurus* and intermediate between that genus and *Camptosaurus*. Marsh (1894) referred this species to the new genus *Dryosaurus*.

Marsh (1894, 1896) diagnosed "*L.*" [=*Dryosaurus*] *altus* as follows: Skull with long supraorbital, horny beak, edentulous premaxillaries, moderate-sized teeth; cervical vertebrae long, amphicoelous; six coossified sacral vertebrae; limbs bones slender and long; forelimbs especially small; five manual digits; prepubis long and narrow; postpubis elongate, slender; hindlimbs very long, tibia longer than femur; metatarsals long and hollow.

Marsh (1894) envisioned *Dryosaurus* as one of the most slender and gracile members of the Ornithopoda, with a length up to about 3 to 3.5 meters (10 to 12 feet).

Since Marsh's original diagnosis, better specimens of this dinosaur have been found, including juveniles and an almost complete skeleton (CM 3392) collected around 1922 from Dinosaur National Monument, Utah. This latter specimen, on display at the Carnegie Museum of Natural History, includes a crushed skull, the only skull known from this species. The specimen, as described by Gilmore (1925*b*), reveals that the snout is slim and the orbits large, the latter to accommodate a large eye reinforced by a sclerotic ring. The cheek teeth are elongated, with coarse, serrated cutting edges and vertical ridges, articulated for simultaneously coming together to chew tough vegetation. The second through fourth toes were used

for walking, the first toe apparently held off the ground, the fifth substantially reduced.

Galton and Jensen (1973*b*) reported numerous fragments (ESM-171R) representing juvenile individuals referred to *D. altus*, collected by Rodney Scheetz and family in the Morrison Formation, Montrose County, Colorado. Shepherd, Galton and Jensen (1977) referred four additional incomplete specimens to *D. altus*. These remains were collected from Bone Cabin Quarry in Wyoming; the Elk Mountains, in Johnson County, Wyoming; Moffat County, Colorado; and the exhibit cliff at Dinosaur National Monument, Utah. *Dryosaurus* is also known from the Dry Mesa Quarry (Morrison Formation, Upper Jurassic [Tithonian] to Lower Cretaceous [Neocomian or Hauterivian]), near the southwest corner of Dry Mesa, in west central Colorado (Britt 1991).

Shepherd, Galton and Jensen compared *D. altus* to *Dysalotosaurus lettowvorbecki* Virchow 1919 (not Pombecki 1920; see Galton 1983*b*), a genus and species founded on the remains (destroyed during World War II) of several individuals (none designated the type specimen), from the Tendaguru Formation (Upper Kimmeridgian; see Aiken 1961), settlement of Kindope, Tendaguru, East Africa. The material was sufficient to mount a composite skeleton at the Humboldt Museum für Naturkunde in what used to be East Berlin. A neotype specimen (HM dy A) consists of an associated braincase, parietal, frontals, postfrontals, and lacrimal from the middle Saurian Bed (upper Kimmeridgian) of Tendaguru Hill, near Kindope. Shepherd *et al.*, noted that the skulls and postcrania of this species and *D. altus* are virtually identical, the supraorbital longer in *D. altus*. Noting that no two skulls are alike in other hypsilophodontids,

Dryosaurus altus, CM 3390, skull, left lateral view.

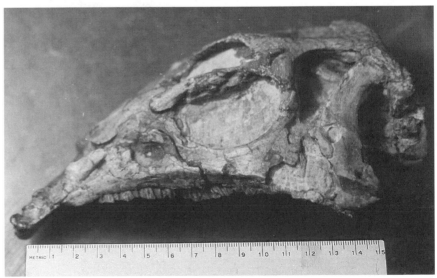

Photo by R. A. Long and S. P. Welles (neg. #73-472-27), courtesy Carnegie Museum of Natural History.

and pointing out the nearly identical postcranial features shared by these genera, Shepherd *et al.*, referred the African species to *Dryosaurus*. Galton (1983*b*) subsequently listed a suite of 21 cranial characters shared by both *D. altus* and *D. lettowvorbecki*.

The presence of *Dryosaurus* in North America and East Africa supports the theory that Laurasia and Gondwana were linked by a land route during the late Jurassic (Galton 1977*b*).

Galton (1977*b*) also reported fragmentary material probably referable to *Dryosaurus* from Europe, including a slender tibia (SMC J46889) from the early Oxford Clay (Middle Callovian) of Fletton, near Peterborough, Northamptonshire.

Milner and Norman (1984) placed *Dryosaurus* in its own family Dryosauridae. Cooper (1985) erected for *Dryosaurus* and related forms the [abandoned] subfamily Dryosaurinae, a taxon which he included in Hypsilophodontidae, with *Dryosaurus* regarded as an "aberrant hypsilophodontid."

In reviewing both the Hypsilophodontidae and Dryosauridae, Sues and Norman (1990) observed that *Dryosaurus* closely resembles hypsilophodontid ornithopods, significantly differing in the following features: Absence of premaxillary teeth; prominent median vertical ridge present on buccal aspect of maxillary tooth crowns; contact between premaxilla and both prefrontal and lacrimal; small quadratojugal

Dryosaurus altus, CM 3392, skeleton.

Photo by Sydney Prentice, courtesy Carnegie Museum of Natural History (neg. #20875).

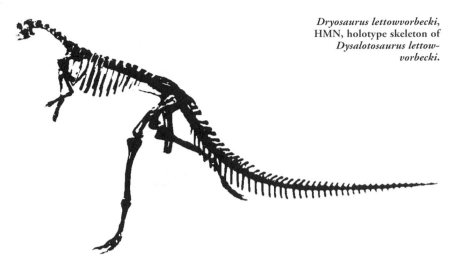

Dryosaurus lettowvorbecki,
HMN, holotype skeleton of
*Dysalotosaurus lettow-
vorbecki*.

overlapped extensively by quadrate and jugal; predentary with bilobed ventral process; relatively long and slender humerus with low deltopectoral crest; ischium with proximally located obturator process, and curved (caudodorsally convex) shaft and rostrocaudally expanded distal end. Sues and Norman suggested that Dryosauridae is the sister-group of all other taxa within Iguanodontia (see Sereno 1986; Norman and Weishampel 1989).

New incites into the physiologies and growth patterns in dinosaurs resulted from a study by Chinsamy (1995) of *D. lettowvorbecki*. As it was not possible to section a complete skeleton, 13 incomplete femora (GPIT 1713/138, 150, 85, 137, 113, 12, 46, 51, 86, 105, 3, 106, 103, and 88) were used in Chinsamy's study, which was standardized by examining and comparing the histology of these specimens only at midshaft (the area least affected by remodeling). The bones represented a range of ontogenetic development (from juvenile to adult) and size (10 to 32 centimeters). Thin sections of bone from these specimens were analyzed by Chinsamy using light micropsy (ordinary and polarized light).

According to Chinsamy, the most notable feature of *Dryosaurus* bone tissue is the absence of any pauses in the deposition of fibro-lamellar bone, occurring continuously as in mammals and birds, and indicating independence from cyclicity or seasonality. (This pattern differs uniquely from the histological descriptions of earlier studies of growth series of other dinosaurian taxa, wherein pauses in the deposition of bone tissue has been observed.) The uninterrupted deposition of fibro-lamellar bone in *Dryosaurus* suggested to Chinsamy that this genus grew rapidly during ontogeny without pauses in its rate of bone disposition. However, the lack of closely spaced lines in the peripheral regions of the largest individuals used in this study suggested that *D. lettowvorbecki* displayed an indeterminate growth pattern as in most reptiles.

Chinsamy concluded that this study offered supporting evidence to the hypothesis that there was no particular pattern of bone tissue in the Dinosauria; rather, different kinds of dinosaurs probably exhibited a range of physiologies and growth patterns.

Notes: A small tooth and phalanx (AM F66771) from the Griman Creek Formation at Lightning Ridge, New South Wales, Australia, were reported by Molnar (1980*b*), who noted that the tooth resembles teeth of *Dryosaurus*. (Molnar also reported unidentifiable dinosaur remains, including an ornithopod-like jaw lacking teeth, with a crocodile-like sculpture, from the Strzelecki Group in southern Victoria.)

Wiffen and Molnar (1989) described the posterior portion of an ilium (CD529) of a *Dryosaurus*-like dinosaur, recovered in February, 1987, from the Upper

Cretaceous (Piripauan–Haumurian [equivalent to Campian–Maastrichtian]; see Wellman 1959) Mata Series (including the informally named Maungatani-wha Sandstone; Moore 1987), at Mangahouanga Stream, North Island, New Zealand. Representing the second undisputed ornithopod from New Zealand (Molnar 1981) and the first to be recognized at the family level, the specimen, as preserved and broken vertically at the acetabulum, measures 102 millimeters long and 59 millimeters deep at the ischial peduncle. According to Wiffen and Molnar, the specimen seems to have derived from a "hypsilophodontian ornithopod" as evidenced by the tuberosity at the posterior end of the dorsal blade, the lateral tuberosity of the ischial peduncle, and its similar overall form.

Wiffen and Molnar stated that the occurrence of this small ornithopod in an area that was near the Ross Sea region of Antarctica (near 60 degrees South latitude) suggests that the animal could live in polar regions, perhaps Antarctica itself. During the Late Cretaceous, this region would have had a cool to cold-temperate climate with well-defined seasons (see Stevens 1985), with mean sea level air temperatures of about 14 degrees Centigrade (Clayton and Stevens 1965; Bramwell and Whitfield 1974), as well as periods of prolonged summer daylight and winter night. Such conditions resulted in an environment quite different from those in which most dinosaurs lived.

D. grandis Lull 1911 [*nomen dubium*] was referred to theropod *Archaeornithomimus affinis*. The femur (BMNH R167) which Galton (1975) referred to *D.? canaliculatus* was subsequently referred by Galton (1977*b*) to *Valdosaurus*.

Key references: Britt (1991); Galton (1977*b*, 1981*b*, 1983*b*); Galton and Jensen (1973*b*); Gilmore (1925*b*); Marsh (1878, 1894, 1896); Milner and Norman (1984); Shepherd, Galton and Jensen (1977); Sues and Norman (1990); Virchow (1919).

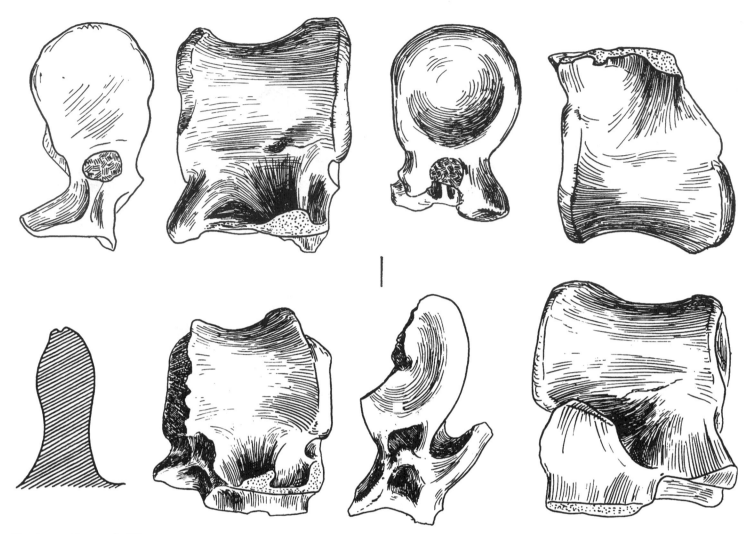

Dryptosauroides grandis, IM K20/334, K20/609, K27/549, K27/601, K27/626, and K27/602, cotype caudal vertebrae. Scale = 2 cm. (After Huene and Matley 1933.)

DRYPTOSAUROIDES   Huene 1932 [*nomen dubium*]

Saurischia: Theropoda: Tetanurae *incertae sedis*.

Name derivation: Greek *dryptos* = "to rend" + Greek *sauros* = "lizard" + Greek *oeides* = "form."

Type species: *D. grandis* Huene 1932 [*nomen dubium*].

Other species: [None.]

Occurrence: Lameta Formation, Jabalpur, India.

Age: Late Cretaceous (Coniacian–Santonian).

Known material: Caudal vertebrae, ribs.

Cotypes: IM K20/334, K20/609, K27/549, K27/601, K27/626, and K27/602, incomplete caudal vertebrae.

Diagnosis of genus: [No modern diagnosis published.]

Comments: The genus *Dryptosauroides* was founded upon six large incomplete caudal vertebrae (IM K20/334, K20/609, K27/549, K27/601, K27/626, and K27/602), a referred caudal vertebra, and fragmentary ribs, from the Lameta Beds of Madhya Pradesh, Jabalpur, India (Huene 1932).

The type species, *D. grandis,* was diagnosed by Huene (*see in* Huene and Matley 1933) as follows: Vertebrae with centra from 13–14 centimeters (about 5–5.4 inches) in length, about 10 centimeters (approximately 3.8 inches) in height, indicating a large theropod; centra lacking pleurocoels, broadly rounded below, narrow in the middle, with slightly concave articular faces; prezygapophyses directed obliquely upwards, but not projecting beyond length of centrum.

Huene thought that these vertebrae seemed to be closest to those in the North American genus *Dryptosaurus*. Lapparent (1957) noted that bones from the above locality (and other localities in India) are usually poorly preserved, so that sometimes their identification can only be hypothetical. According to Molnar (1990), the vertebrae of *C. grandis* do not exhibit any "carnosaurian" features.

Key references: Huene (1932); Lapparent (1957); Molnar (1990).

DRYPTOSAURUS Marsh 1877—(=*Laelaps*; =?*Diplotomodon*)

Saurischia: Theropoda: Tetanurae: ?Avetheropoda: ?Coelurosauria *incertae sedis*.

Name derivation: Greek *dryptos* = "to rend" + Greek *sauros* = "lizard."

Type species: *D. aquilunguis* (Cope 1866).

Other species: ?*D. medius* (Marsh 1888) [*nomen dubium*], ?*D. potens* (Lull 1911) [*nomen dubium*].

Occurrence: New Egypt Formation, New Jersey, United States.

Age: Late Cretaceous (Late Maastrichtian).

Known material: Partial skeleton.

Holotype: ANSP 9995, partial jaws with teeth, portions of scapular arch, humeri, left femur, right tibia and fibula, dorsal and caudal vertebrae, astragalus, metatarsals, phalanges, various fragments.

Diagnosis of genus: [No modern diagnosis published.]

Comments: The first theropod described from North America and the only large theropod known from eastern North America, the genus that would later be named *Dryptosaurus* was founded upon poorly-preserved incomplete cranial and postcranial remains (ANSP 9995), collected from marl pits in the green sand of Barsborough, Glouster County, New Jersey. These remains were discovered by workmen under the direction of J. C. Voorhies of the West Jersey Marl Company.

On August 21, 1866, Cope (1866) exhibited these specimens (upon which he erected the genus *Laelaps*) at the Academy of Natural Sciences of Philadelphia, to a gathering of 22 members of that institution.

Cope assigned his *Laelaps* to a new [abandoned] family "Dinodontidae," and estimated the total length of this dinosaur as about 5.3 meters (18 feet) in length. Later, Cope (1870) redescribed the type species, *L. aquilunguis*, in greater detail and illustrated the holotype.

Cope (1866) originally diagnosed the genus as follows: Differs from the European *Megalosaurus* in having femur with head not projecting far beyond the shaft, not constricted below, and with more slender tibia; unlike *Deinodon*, teeth are serrated on both edges; mandibular teeth recurved, compressed, crowns transversely oval; ungual phalanx remarkably large, especially compressed at tip.

Marsh (1877a), Cope's professional rival, pointing out that the name *Laelaps* was preoccupied (Koch 1839 and Walker 1843), renamed Cope's genus *Dryptosaurus*, subsequently (1890) making *Dryptosaurus* (a name Cope never accepted) the type genus of the new family Dryptosauridae.

The most striking feature of *D. aquilunguis* is the very large, eagle-like, ungual phalanx of the first digit. Cope (1866, 1870) erred in assuming that this phalanx, actually a manual claw, belonged to the pes. The length of the upper surface of this claw is about 75 percent that of the humerus, the entire claw measuring at least 21 centimeters (8 inches) long. Huene (1926) later suggested that this claw was used as a tool to sever blood vessels and pry between the armor plates of ankylosaurs.

Other species were subsequently referred to *Dryptosaurus*: *Allosaurus medius* Marsh 1888 [*nomen dubium*], tentatively assigned to *Dryptosaurus*, was based on a broken tooth, along with bones of the limbs and feet (USNM 4972), collected by John Bell Hatcher from the Arundel Formation (Early Cretaceous), near Muirkirk, Prince Georges County, Maryland. Marsh (1888a) described this tooth as remarkably flat and sharp, with smooth surfaces, serrated edges; crown height 30 millimeters, anteroposterior diameter at base 15 millimeters, transverse diameter 7 millimeters. Marsh (1888a) regarded the tooth as the most significant part of the specimen. Most of the other elements believed by Marsh (1888a) to belong to this specimen were later transferred by Lull (1911) to the ornithischian *Dryosaurus*. Gilmore (1920), finding this specimen to be indeterminate, tentatively referred it to *Dryptosaurus* "largely on geographic considerations." Gilmore noted that, among various separate bones from Prince Georges County, described by Lull as belonging to this species, are some large claws, represented by the proximal half of the first phalanx (USNM 8504) of pedal digit II and the complete and

Dryptosaurus aquilunguis, ANSP 9995, holotype manual claw and dentary tooth of *Laelaps aquilunguis.*

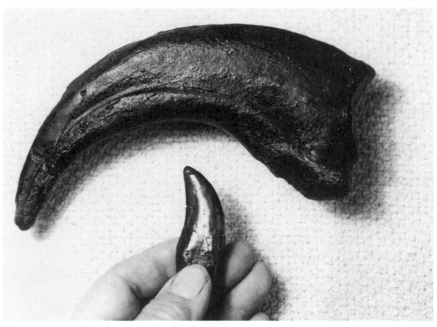

Photo by D. Baird, courtesy Academy of Natural Sciences of Philadelphia.

Dryptosaurus

?Dryptosaurus medius, USNM 4972, holotype split tooth and tooth fragment of *Allosaurus medius*.

well-preserved phalanx I (formerly Goucher College collection, number 2521, apparently lost during transferal to the National Museum of Natural History) of digit III. As described by Lull, the first specimen is rather high, with two prominent ridges on the inner face; the second specimen resembles *A. fragilis*, differing in being more depressed proximally, especially in the broader and flatter undersurface.

Creosaurus potens Lull 1911 [*nomen dubium*], based on a vertebral centrum (USNM 3049) from the anterior caudal series, collected by J. K. Murphy from a sewer in Washington, D.C., was tentatively referred by Gilmore to *Dryptosaurus*.

According to Molnar (1990), *D. medius* and *D. potens* may be conspecific.

Some paleontologists have regarded *Dryptosaurus* as belonging to the Megalosauridae or Tyrannosauridae. A more recent study by Denton (1990) of the holotype skeleton of *D. aquilunguis* and of new fossil material from the Ellisdale site (Monmouth County, New Jersey), incorporating both skeletal comparisons and allometric scaling of osteological data, resulted in a reevaluation of the taxonomic standing of *Dryptosaurus*. In a preliminary report, Denton suggested that *Dryptosaurus* may be classified within the coelurosaur clade, exhibiting such coelurosaurian features as a generally gracile skeleton, laterally compressed teeth having strong poste-

rior serrations, fourth metatarsal like that in dromaeosaurs, enormous recurved manual claw, poorly developed fourth trochanter, relatively large forelimbs, and phalanges and tarsus like those in ornithomimids.

Notes: Cope (1866) conceived of *Dryptosaurus* as the most formidable predator that had ever lived, filling a gap in the Cretaceous fauna occupied by the herbivorous *Hadrosaurus*, and being the deadly enemy of the latter. Cope (1866, 1870) argued that this theropod was capable of taking tremendous kangaroo-like leaps, pouncing upon its prey and ripping into it with its claws. However, although this notion of leaping dinosaurs has long been rejected, Molnar and Farlow (1990) did not rule out the possibility entirely, citing a dinosaur trackway from the Upper Jurassic of Ain, France, reported by Bernier, Barale, Bourseau, Buffetaut, Demathieu, Gaillard, Gall and Wenz (1984), and interpreted as the trace of a giant leaping theropod.

A famous painting made in 1897 by artist Charles R. Knight under Cope's direction portrays two *Dryptosaurus* individuals in battle, one on its back, the other in mid-leap. The painting (based on an earlier sculpture by Knight also directed by Cope) depicts these theropods in standard "carnosaur" mold, with the characteristic talon misplaced on the hindfoot. This restoration is significant in depicting

?Dryptosaurus potens, USNM 3049, holotype vertebral centrum of *Creosaurus potens*, with remains of crocodilians and the mosasaur *Clidastes*.

theropods as active and rapidly moving animals, an idea that was lost over the years, resurfacing some three-quarters of a century later when dinosaurs again came to be viewed as other than sluggish and slow-moving.

A well-preserved metatarsal measuring about 44 centimeters (17 inches), attributed to *Dryptosaurus*, was found in 1987 by David R. Schwimmer in a bank of a stream near the Chattahoochee River in Stewart County, Georgia. The specimen, as yet undescribed, constitutes the largest dinosaur bone ever found in that state.

Three fragmentary femora collected by Halsey Miller, Jr., during the middle 1960s from the Black Creek Formation (Late Cretaceous [Tayloran or Campanian]; Baird and Horner 1979), at Phoebus Landing, on the Cape Fear River in North Carolina, were redescribed by Baird and Horner as representing a medium-sized theropod comparable to *Dryptosaurus* or *Albertosaurus*. Two of these femora, forming part of Cope's holotype (USNM 7189) for *Hypsibema crassicauda*, came from marl pits of James King in Sampson County. The distal third of a right femur (ANSP 15330) morphologically resembles that in *Dryptosaurus* and *Albertosaurus*. Two teeth (ANSP 15332), also from Phoebus Landing, are similar to those in of both of these genera, but otherwise display no characteristics to permit a positive identification.

L. gallicus Cope 1867 [*nomen dubium*] was based on various theropod specimens including vertebrae, pubis, distal end of a tibia with astragalus, calcaneum, and some fragments, collected from the Upper Jurassic of Normandy, France, figured by Cuvier (1812). Molnar, Kurzanov and Dong (1990) observed that the tarsals are characteristic of Allosauridae and exhibit the oldest example of a separate but interlocked astragalus and calcaneum (see Welles and Long 1990); also that the cervical and dorsal vertebrae are strongly opisthocoelous. Molnar *et al.,* agreed that this species is not *Dryptosaurus* and may be an allosaurid.

L. macropus Cope 1868 is part of the holotype of *Coelosaurus antiquus*; *L. incrassatus* Cope 1876 [*nomen dubium*], *L. falculus* Cope 1876 [*nomen dubium*], *L. hazenianus* Cope 1876 [*nomen dubium*], and *D. kenabekides* Hay 1899 [*nomen dubium*] were referred to *Albertosaurus sarcophagus*, and *L. cristatus* Cope 1876 [*nomen dubium*], *L. explanatus* Cope 1876 [*nomen dubium*], and *L. laevifrons* Cope 1876 [*nomen dubium*] to *Dromaeosaurus albertensis* (see Matthew and Brown 1922). *L. trihedrodon* Cope 1877 [*nomen dubium*] was tentatively referred to *Allosaurus.*

Key references: Cope (1866, 1867); Cuvier (1812); Gilmore (1920); Huene (1926); Lull (1911); Marsh (1888); Molnar and Farlow (1990); Molnar, Kurzanov and Dong (1990).

DYNAMOSAURUS Osborn 1905—(See *Tyrannosaurus.*)
Name derivation: Greek *dunamis* = "power" + Greek *sauros* = "lizard."
Type species: *D. imperiosus* Osborn 1905.

DYOPLOSAURUS Parks 1934—(See *Euoplocephalus.*)
Name derivation: Greek *dyo* = "double" + Greek *oplos* = "armed" + Greek *sauros* = "lizard."
Type species: *D. acutosquameus* Parks 1924.

DYSALOTOSAURUS Pompecki 1920—(See *Dryosaurus.*)
Name derivation: Greek *dys* = "bad" + Greek *aloto* = "difficult to catch" + Greek *sauros* = "lizard."
Type species: *D. lettow-vorbecki* Pompecki 1920.

DYSGANUS Cope 1876 [*nomen dubium*]
Ornithischia: Genasauria: Cerapoda: Marginocephalia: Ceratopsia: Neoceratopsia: Ceratopsidae: Ceratopsinae.
Name derivation: Greek *dys* = "bad" + Greek *ganos* = "brightness."
Type species: *D. encaustus* Cope 1876 [*nomen dubium*].
Other species: *D. bicarinatus* Cope 1876 [*nomen dubium*], *D. haydenianus* Cope 1876 [*nomen dubium*], *D. peiganus* Cope 1876 [*nomen dubium*].
Occurrence: Judith River Formation, Montana, United States.
Age: Late Cretaceous (Campanian).
Known material: Teeth.
Holotype: AMNH 5739, fragmentary teeth.
Diagnosis of genus: [No modern diagnosis published.]
Comments: *Dysganus*, a poorly known genus named during the early days of dinosaur discoveries, was established upon various detached, worn, and fragmentary indeterminate teeth collected in 1876 by

Dysganus encaustus, AMNH 5739, neotype tooth in stereo pair crown and occlusal views.

Photo by W. P. Coombs, Jr., courtesy American Museum of Natural History.

Dysganus

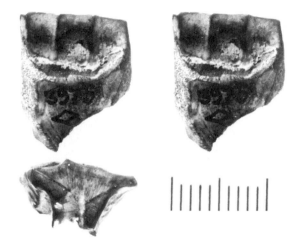

Matthew (*see in* Lull and Wright 1942) later designated *D. encaustus* as the type species of *Dysganus*, with one tooth (AMNH 5739) singled out from the four groups of teeth as the type specimen.

Cope expressed doubts that the *D. peiganus* teeth belonged to a hadrosaurid, observing similarities in the crown and base with Leidy's *Palaeoscincus*. Lull and Wright, in reevaluating this species, pointed out that the tooth should be excluded from the Hadrosauridae on the basis of the enamel entirely surrounding the crown and suggested that it belonged with the Ankylosauridae.

Later, Cope (1890) suggested that *Dysganus* was ceratopsian, an assignment agreed to Nopcsa (1901). Lull and Wright identified the teeth of *D. encaustus* and *D. bicarinatus* as ceratopsian, possibly belonging either to *Ceratops* or *Monoclonius*.

More recently, Coombs and Galton (1988) stated that the four species of *Dysganus* are all ceratopsian, that neither the genus nor any of its species can be adequately defined, and that all should be regarded as *nomen dubia*. Since the type species of *Monoclonius* (*M. crassus*) and *Ceratops* (*C. montanus*) were established upon specimens (AMNH 3998 and USNM 2411, respectively) lacking teeth, *Dysganus* cannot be referred to either species. According to Coombs and Galton, these teeth are all from the extreme anterior end of the dental battery of a ceratopsian dinosaur. (Coombs and Galton published the first illustrations of all of the material upon which Cope founded the four *Dysganus* species.) Brett-Surman (1989) added that none of the teeth assigned by Cope to *Dysganus* are diagnostic below family level.

Key references: Brett-Surman (1989); Coombs and Galton (1988); Cope (1876*a*, 1890); Lull and Wright (1942); Nopcsa (1901).

Charles H. Sternberg from the [formerly] "Fort Union beds" (now Judith River [=Oldman] Formation) along Dog Creek, east of Judith River, in Fergus County, Montana.

These teeth were originally described (but not figured) by Cope (1876*a*), who believed them to be of hadrosaurid origin and representing four distinct species, which he named *D. encaustus*, *D. bicarinatus* (based on teeth of three individuals), *D. haydenianus*, and *D. peiganus* (AMNH 3974).

Dysganus was diagnosed by Cope as follows: Teeth with compressed crowns; body of crown a flattened shaft of dentine, one denser face producing the cutting edge.

Cope diagnosed each species as follows: (*D. encaustus*) teeth with cutting face more or less concave and sunken, lateral borders and cement of the base projecting beyond; inferior border oblique, uncurved; weak asymmetrically located keel dividing face into wide and narrow concavity; dentine delicately rugose in unworn teeth; external basal cementum rising highest on incurved border of crown; edge unserrated in unworn teeth; (*D. bicarinatus*) differs from *D. encaustus* by smaller size (two representing immature stages), absence of lateral incurved angle, and presence of two median ones; (*D. peiganus*): crown compressed and base contracted.

Dysganus peiganus, AMNH 3974, neotype tooth in stereo crown, opposite side, anterior, and occlusal views. Scale in mm.

DYSLOCOSAURUS McIntosh, Coombs and
Russell 1992

Saurischia: Sauropodomorpha: Sauropoda:
Diplodocidae: ?Dicraeosaurinae.

Name derivation: Greek *dys* = "bad" + Latin *locus* =
"place" + Greek *sauros* = "lizard."

Type species: *D. polyonychius* McIntosh, Coombs
and Russell 1992.

Other species: [None.]

Occurrence: ?Lance Formation, Wyoming, United
States.

Age: ?Late Cretaceous (?Maastrichtian).

Known material/holotype: AC 663, distal ends of
?left ulna and radius, partial head of left femur,
proximal end of left tibia, distal end of right
tibia, left astragalus, left metatarsi I, II, and III,
proximal half of IV, left phalanges I-1, III-1, and
IV-1, unguals of I, II, III (proximal half), and IV,
possible ungual of V (AC 663).

Diagnosis of genus (as for type species): Small
diplodocid; astragalus with proximodistal length
equal to or about 50 percent of transverse breadth
(higher percentage than in other known diplodocids);
metatarsals with greater circumference relative to
length than in other known diplodocids; pedal digit
IV terminating with an ungual phalanx; ?V bears
ungual phalanx (McIntosh, Coombs and Russell
1992).

Comments: An unusual diplodocid and the
first to be discovered in the Upper Cretaceous of
North America, *Dyslocosaurus* was founded upon
limb and feet elements (AC 663), recovered by F. B.
Loomis from an uncertain formation, allegedly the
Lance Formation but probably the Morrison Formation (see below), in the vicinity of Lance Creek,
eastern Wyoming (McIntosh, Coombs, and Russell
1992).

As related by McIntosh *et al.,* the as yet undescribed specimen had been mounted and displayed at
the Pratt Museum, Amherst College, where about
1963 it was noticed by McIntosh. Although Loomis'
field notes were examined by McIntosh and subsequently by Coombs, no mention of the specimen was
found therein, the only data pertaining to the material being that recorded on the exhibit label. The existence of the specimen had been acknowledged, however, by Sloan (1970), Russell (1985), and Sloan,
Rigby, Van Valen and Gabriel (1986).

McIntosh *et al.,* noted that the elements are similar to those in diplodocids, their dimensions indicating an animal approximately three fourths the size
of *Diplodocus carnegii* (the latter about 10 percent
smaller than the largest known *Diplodocus* individuals), with a live mass of about five metric tons (see
Anderson, Hall-Martin and Russell 1985).

According to
McIntosh *et al., D.
polyonychius* is unique
among the Diplodocidae
in having four definite
claws on the pes (all other
known diplodocids have
three). The only other
sauropods known to have
four pedal claws are the
camarasaurid *Camarasaurus*
(reported by Jensen 1988)
and ?brachiosaurid *Pleurocoelus* (a pes referred to that
genus and described by
Gallup 1975, 1989). The
original museum mount-
ing of the *D. polyonychius*
material, which had been
directed by Loomis,
included a bony nub-
bin which McIn-
tosh *et al.,* could
not definitely
associate with
AC 663, but
which, they
speculated,
might be inter-
preted as a fifth pedal ungual. If, in fact, the hind foot
of *D. polyonychius* does bear five claws, that feature
would make this species unique among all other
known sauropods.

As noted by McIntosh *et al.,* the unsatisfactory
provenance data for the type material of *D. polyonychius* raises a major question regarding the specimen's
significance. The only locality information found at
the Pratt Museum stated that the material had been
collected from the Lance Formation (Upper Cretaceous, of Maastrichtian age), in the vicinity of Lance
Creek in eastern Wyoming. Diplodocids had only
been known in North America from the Jurassic. No
Cretaceous sauropods are known on that continent
from the Cenomanian through Campanian, with
Maastrichtian sauropods represented there only by
Alamosaurus, an immigrant form derived from South
American titanosaurids. Lucas and Hunt (1989)
argued that the Cenomanian–Campanian absence of
sauropods is real and not an artifact of preservational
or collecting biases. While acknowledging that
Loomis' stratigraphic determination for the provenance of *D. polyonychius* could be correct, McIntosh
et al., presented evidence supporting the possibility
that AC 663 was collected from a Maastrichtian-age
provenance in the Lance Formation, derived from a

Dyslocosaurus polyonychius,
**AC 663, holotype partial left
hindlimb.**

Courtesy University of Massachusetts.

small exposure of the Morrison Formation within Niobrara County.

According to McIntosh *et al.*, if *D. polyonychius* is from the Lance Formation, it is either the last survivor of an otherwise unknown line of North American diplodocids, or it is a Maastrichtian immigrant derived from diplodocids from another continent. McIntosh *et al.* favored the latter possibility, suggesting that this species could be an immigrant form derived from Late Cretaceous diplodocids (?dicraeosaurines, represented in the Maastrichtian on that continent by *Nemegtosaurus* and *Quaesitosaurus*) of Asia. If the provenance information for AC 663 is correct, then *D. polyonychius* represents the only known North American diplodocid, the northernmost occurrence of North American Cretaceous sauropods, and perhaps the last occurrence worldwide of both diplodocids and sauropods.

Key references: McIntosh, Coombs and Russell (1992); Russell (1988); Sloan (1970); Sloan, Rigby, Van Valen and Gabriel (1986).

DYSTROPHAEUS   Cope 1877 [*nomen dubium*]—(=?*Barosaurus*, ?*Diplodocus*)
Saurischia: Sauropodomorpha: Sauropoda: Diplodocidae: Diplodocinae.
Name derivation: Greek *dys* = "bad" + Greek *tropheus* = "joint."
Type species: *D. viaemalae* Cope 1877 [*nomen dubium*].
Other species: [None.]
Occurrence: Morrison Formation, Utah, United States.
Age: Late Jurassic (Kimmeridgian–Tithonian).

Dystrophaeus viamalae, USNM 2364, holotype metacarpals. (After Cope 1877.)

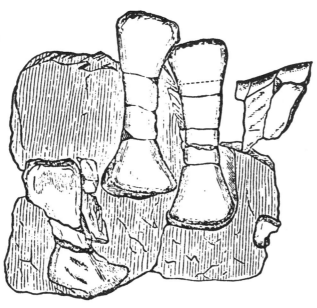

Known material/holotype: USNM 2364, postcrania including ulna, metacarpals, distal end of radius, sternal ossification, ?scapula fragment.
Diagnosis of genus: [No modern diagnosis published.]
Comments: The first sauropod discovered in the New World and the second dinosaur found in the western United States, new genus and species *Dystrophaeus viaemalae* was established upon scanty but well-preserved remains (USNM 2364) found in 1859 by John S. Newberry, in the Morrison Formation of Painted Canyon, Wayne County, Utah. Newberry had been a geologist for the Engineer Exploring Expedition under command of Captain J. N. Macomb, United States Army. Gillette, Barnes, Gillette and McIntosh (1989) announced that the site locality has been identified through reconnaissance in San Juan County, Utah, in the lower part of the Tidwell Member of the Morrison Formation and that more bones apparently belonging to the type specimen remain *in situ* (see also Gillette 1993).

Cope (1877*b*) diagnosed this genus as follows: Distinguished from other dinosaurs by form of the articular distal extremity of the humerus; ulna [misidentified as a humerus (J. S. McIntosh, personal communication 1988)] .765 meters (about 2.5 feet) long; articular ends of tarsals markedly rough or pitted to accommodate a cartilaginous cap, suggesting less than usual movement of bones upon one another.

Incorrectly believing the Upper Jurassic beds from which this material came to be of Triassic age, Cope found the specimen of unusual interest as the first found in so-called "Triassic" beds of the Rocky Mountain area. Cope envisioned *Dystrophaeus* as a gigantic terrestrial animal with powerful, subequally developed limbs.

In reviewing the Sauropoda, McIntosh (1990*b*) referred *Dystrophaeus* to the Diplodocidae, noting that of the known elements, the relatively short metacarpals precluded assignment to Brachiosauridae or Camarasauridae and suggest a diplodocid instead of cetiosaurid relationship. McIntosh further suggested that this genus might actually be *Barosaurus* or *Diplodocus*, but pointed out that such a relationship cannot now be determined.

Key references: Cope (1877*b*); Gillette (1993); Gillette *et al.,* (1989); McIntosh (1990*b*).

DYSTYLOSAURUS   Jensen 1985
Saurischia: Sauropodomorpha: Sauropoda: Brachiosauridae.
Name derivation: Greek *di* = "two" + Greek *stylos* = "beam" + Greek *sauros* = "lizard."
Type species: *D. edwini* Jensen 1985.

Other species: [None.]

Occurrence: Morrison Formation, Colorado, United States.

Age: Late Jurassic–Early Cretaceous (?Tithonian; ?Neocomian–?Hauterivian).

Known material/holotype: BYU 5750, anterior dorsal vertebra.

Diagnosis of genus (as for type species): Sauropod unique to all known North American forms in that each hypantrozygapophysal arch is supported by two parallel, diagonal infraprezygapophysal laminae; lower half of neural arch massive, neurocentral suture occupying almost seven-eighths length of centrum; neural spine transversely broad, thin, and fragile anteroposteriorly; supraprezygapophysal laminae not converging; neural arch, including spine, transverse processes and zygapophyses, entirely pneumatic (Jensen 1985*a*).

Comments: The genus *Dystylosaurus* was founded upon a dorsal vertebra (BYU 5750), collected by James A. Jensen in 1972 from the base of the Brushy Basin Member (Late Jurassic [Tithonian] or Early Cretaceous [Neocomian or Hauterivian]; Britt 1991, based on Kowallis, Heaton and Bringhurst 1986) of the Morrison Formation, near Dry Mesa, Mesa County, 35 miles west of Delta, Colorado.

Jensen (1985*a*) deduced that the specimen should be located anterior to the third dorsal vertebrae, as determined by the position of the parapophyses at the neurocentral suture and strongly-developed hyposphene/hypantrum articulation.

Pointing out that the type specimen bears little resemblance to any known sauropod, Jensen proposed that *Dystylosaurus* represents a new family,

Photo by J. A. Jensen.

A   **B**

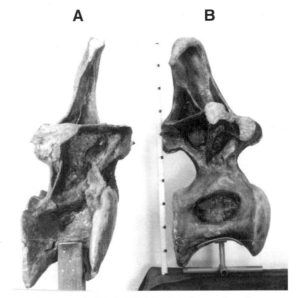

Dystylosaurus edwini, A. BYU 5750, holotype dorsal vertebra, lateral view, compared with that of B. *Brachiosaurus.*

adding that many disarticulated elements relating to this genus were probably collected from the Dry Mesa quarry over the years though not recognized as such.

As noted by McIntosh (1990*b*) in a review of the Sauropoda, *Dystylosaurus* is clearly a brachiosaurid, differing from *Brachiosaurus* mostly in the spine, which is broader transversely (?preservation), much shorter axially (perhaps because of its position in the series), and of lesser height (if the spine is as complete as it seems to be).

Key references: Jensen (1985*a*); McIntosh (1990*b*).

A   **B**   **C**

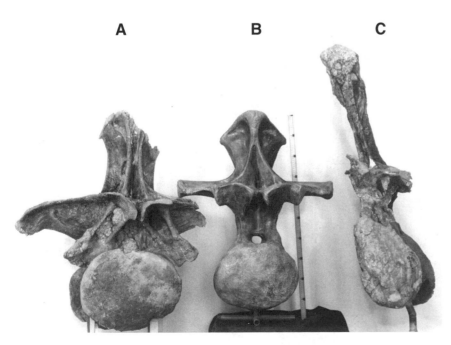

Dystylosaurus edwini, A. BYU 5750, holotype dorsal vertebra, anterior view, compared with B. those of *Brachiosaurus* and C. *Ultrasauros macintoshi.*

Photo by J. A. Jensen.

ECHINODON Owen 1861

Ornithischia: Genasauria: ?Thyreophora *incertae sedis*.

Name derivation: Greek *echinos* = "spiny" + Greek *odous* = "tooth."

Type species: *E. becklesii* Owen 1861.

Other species: [None.]

Occurrence: Middle Purbeck Beds, Dorset, England.

Age: Late Jurassic (Late Tithonian).

Known material: Isolated crania of at least three individuals, scutes.

Holotype: BMNH 48209-12, two maxillary fragments and two imperfect dentaries.

Diagnosis of genus: Maxilla with antorbital vacuity covered by a lateral sheet pierced by foramina; premaxillae forming secondary palate; lacrimal overlaps anterior end of jugal, most likely tapering to fine point; mandibular point of quadrate transversely expanded; coronoid eminence high; three premaxillary teeth lacking denticles, ?11 maxillary teeth, 10 dentary teeth, the latter with slight horizontal ridge adjacent; first maxillary tooth caniniform, remaining teeth diamond-shaped to pentagonal; most anterior and posterior denticles connected to their crown bases by well-developed ridges; no special foramina (for replacement teeth) on medial surface of jaws (Galton 1978).

Comments: *Echinodon* was first described by Owen (1861*b*), founded on incomplete skull material (BMNH 48209-12) discovered by Samuel Beckles in quarries of the freshwater Dirt Bed, lower part of the Lulworth Beds (Middle Purbeck Beds), at Durlston Bay, near Swanage, Dorset, England. Subsequently referred to this genus were more fragmentary jaws with teeth.

Galton (1978) diagnosed *Echinodon* based on the sparse cranial material referred to this genus, regarding *E. becklesii* as "the most progressive fabrosaurid," originally assigning the species to the [abandoned] family Fabrosauridae (see Weishampel and Witmer 1990) because of the supposedly slender dentary, flat maxilla, and cheek teeth lacking wear facets.

A left maxillary fragment with a complete tooth, mandible fragment, vertebrae, and various limb fragments, collected by George Callison from the Fruita Paleontological Area, Grand Junction, Colorado, were identified as *Echinodon* (see Callison 1987) and may represent a new species of that genus (Callison, personal communication 1986).

Galton (1986) believed that small dermal scutes, found in the Purbeck Feather-bed marl and originally described by Owen (1879) as "granicones" of *Nuthetes* (see excluded taxa), are most likely referable to *Echinodon*. Galton observed that *Echinodon* seems to be related to thyreophoran *Scutellosaurus*, a judgement reinforced by the presence of scutes. Agreeing with Galton's (1978, 1986) observations, Coombs, Weishampel and Witmer (1990) tentatively referred *Echinodon* to the Thyreophora.

In a review of basal ornithischians, Sereno (1991*a*) observed (*contra* Galton) that the dentary of *E. becklesii* is not slender compared to that in other ornithischians, maxilla not flat but has a gentle emargination along the entire length of the tooth row, and that the teeth do not lack tooth-to-tooth wear facets. According to Sereno, this species shares apomorphic characters with heterodontosaurids (Sereno, in preparation).

Key references: Coombs, Weishampel and Witmer (1990); Galton (1978, 1986); Owen (1861*b*, 1879); Sereno (1991*a*).

EDMARKA Bakker, Kralis, Siegwarth and Filla 1992

Saurischia: Theropoda: ?Tetanurae: Megalosauridae.

Name derivation: "[Dr. Bill] Edmark."

Type species: *E. rex* Bakker, Kralis, Siegwarth and Filla 1992.

Other species: [None.]

Occurrence: Morrison Formation, Wyoming, United States.

Age: Late Jurassic (Middle–Late Tithonian).

Known material: Various cranial and postcranial remains, adult and subadult.

Holotype: CPS 1005, incomplete left jugal; ?also CPS 1004, dorsal ribs, CPS 1002, left scapulacoracoid, caudal vertebra.

Diagnosis of genus (as for type species): Closest to *Torvosaurus tanneri*, differing in retention of primitive condition of jugal that is thin mediallaterally, relatively longer and lower in lateral aspect, with orbital margin wider front-to-back; further differing in derived character of much wider postorbital process on jugal, with enlarged, recessed facet on outer surface for expanded ventral ramus of postorbital (Bakker, Kralis, Siegwarth and Filla 1992).

Echinodon becklesi, BMNH 48209-12, holotype fragmentary maxilla. (After Owen 1861.)

Comments: New genus and species *Edmarka rex* was founded upon three specimens recovered from the Nail Quarry (discovered in mid-summer of 1990 by Robert T. Bakker and Donald Kralis), in middle levels of the Morrison Formation, Como Bluff outcrop region, Wyoming. These bones include a left jugal CPS 1005 (CPS collections temporarily at University of Colorado; to be transferred to Wyoming institutions for permanent repository) lacking only the extreme dorsal tip of the postorbital process and posterior tip of the lower quadratojugal process, and possibly dorsal ribs (CPS 1004), and an adult scapulacoracoid (CPS 10020 with closed suture, all of these remains having been found in a 3 meter by 2 meter area in the quarry. A proximal caudal vertebra (CPS 1006) with tightly coossified centrum-arch suture, discovered 5 meters away from CPS 1005, may also belong to the type individual. Referred material includes six right

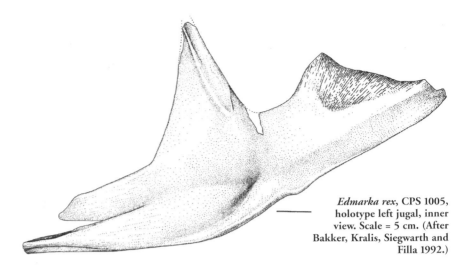

Edmarka rex, CPS 1005, holotype left jugal, inner view. Scale = 5 cm. (After Bakker, Kralis, Siegwarth and Filla 1992.)

dorsal ribs (CPS 401) from the Louise Quarry, and subadult left coracoid (CPS 1003) from the Nail Quarry, the latter found beneath the anterior edge of the type jugal. The scapulacoracoid was discovered by Kralis; in 1991, Kralis and members of a Dinamation International Society field course found and excavated the type jugal (Bakker *et al.*, 1992).

Bakker *et al.* described *E. rex* as a gigantic "torvosaurine" megalosaurid, rivaling in length *Tyrannosaurus rex*. As observed by the authors, the type jugal of *E. rex* is close in size to that of *T. tanneri*, the skull having an estimated premaxilla-quadrate length of

Edmarka rex, CPS 1010, left pubis (reversed), A. medial-anterior, B. anterior-lateral, and C. inner views. Scale in cm. (After Bakker, Kralis, Siegwarth and Filla 1992.)

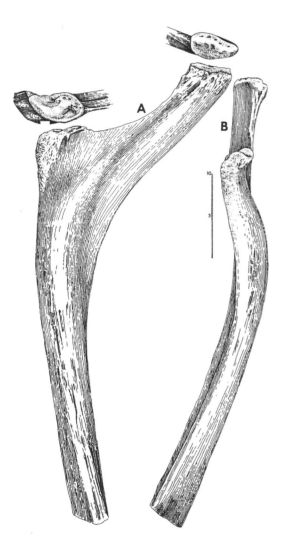

Edmarka rex, CPS 1001, third thoracic (dorsal) rib, A. detail of head, anterior-lateral view, B. external-posterior view. Scale in cm. (After Bakker, Kralis, Siegwarth and Filla 1992.)

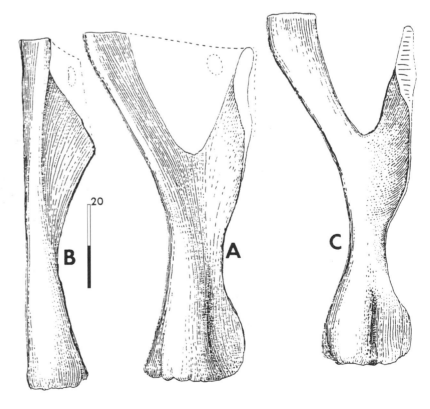

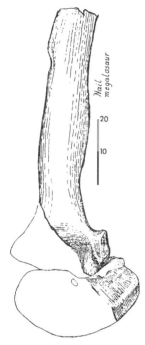

Edmarka rex, CPS 1002, ?holotype scapulacoracoid. Scale in cm. (After Bakker, Kralis, Siegwarth and Filla 1992.)

1223 millimeters (more than 4 feet); but the postcrania associated with the former species is 30 percent larger than most remains referred to the latter, this disparity suggesting that the Como Bluff vertebrae and hindlimb material do not belong to *T. tanneri*.

Consideration of the presence of a giant, Como Bluff/Morrison megalosaurid led Bakker *et al.* to postulate the following revisions of "standard views about dinosaur evolution": 1. Body size category (as occupied by *T. rex*) was filled repeatedly and successively by species from five to six separate families, this size (imposed by some intrinsic feature of the bauplan) probably being the maximum size a theropod could attain (with top femur length of 1100–1350 millimeters); 2. two giant theropods from different families never coexisted in the same place; 3. usually, when one family replaced another as giant carnivore, the largest form progressively became more advanced than the old in skull and limb characters, and came closer to an avian level of organization; and 4. the incumbent giant predator species went extinct before the appearance of the replacement giant species; occupancy of this top predator role, therefore, seemingly conferring an advantage in suppressing the evolution of another giant carnivore belonging to any other family.

Key references: Bakker, Kralis, Siegwarth and Filla (1992).

EDMONTONIA Sternberg 1928—(=*Denversaurus*; =?*Palaeoscincus*)

Ornithischia: Genasauria: Thyreophora: Ankylosauria: Nodosauridae.

Name derivation: "Edmonton [Formation]."

Type species: *E. longiceps* Sternberg 1928.

Other species: *E. rugosidens* (Gilmore 1930).

Occurrence: Dinosaur Park Formation, Horseshoe Canyon Formation, St. Mary River Formation, Two Medicine Formation, Montana, Lance Formation, South Dakota, Wyoming, Hell Creek Formation, Montana, South Dakota, Aguja Formation, Texas, Matanuska Formation, Matanuska-Susitna Borough, Alaska, United States; Oldman Formation, Alberta, Canada.

Age: Late Cretaceous (Campanian–Early Maastrichtian).

Known material: Eight specimens, including complete skulls, much of postcranial skeletons, armor.

Holotype: NMC 8531, skull with right jaw, vertebral column, pelvis, forelimb, hindlimb.

Diagnosis of genus: Skull with snout parallel or almost parallel in dorsal aspect, "smooth" cranial armor, and keeled vomer; neural pedicles of vertebrae short; neural spines shorter, more robust than in *Panoplosaurus*; three sacral vertebrae; coracoid large, almost square, not coossified with scapula; manus with four digits; medial cervical and anterior dorsal armor consisting of transverse bands comprising subrectangular and oval low keeled plates; lateral armor consisting of spines (Carpenter 1990).

Diagnosis of *E. longiceps*: Skull without postorbital prominence and with narrow palate; tooth rows moderately divergent; synsacrum robust, lateral spine smaller than in *E. rugosidens* (Carpenter 1990).

Diagnosis of *E. rugosidens*: Skull with distinct postorbital prominence; wide palate; widely divergent tooth rows; synsacrum less robust, lateral spines considerably longer than in *E. longiceps* (Carpenter 1990).

Comments: The genus *Edmontonia* was founded upon a skull with incomplete postcrania (NMC 8531), found by G. Paterson in 1924 in the Lower Edmonton (now Horseshoe Canyon) Formation at Morrin, Red Deer River, Alberta, Canada.

Originally, Sternberg (1928) diagnosed *Edmontonia* as follows: Skull with maximum width not exceeding three-fourths its length; dorsal surface of skull relatively flat; palatal bones, especially prevomers, downwardly produced to form pronounced median keel; teeth with well-developed rugose cingulae; approximately sixteen dentary teeth.

Sternberg diagnosed type species *S. longiceps* as follows: Skull three-fifths as wide as long; relatively long cranial elements; prevomers with keel terminating in a sharp edge; teeth with fluting extending down entire side of crowns.

Gilmore (1930) then described a new species of the genus *Panoplosaurus*, which he named *P. rugosidens*, based on a disarticulated and scattered specimen (USNM 11868) comprising a skull with right

Photo by R. A. Long and S. P. Welles (neg. #73/537-7), reproduced with permission of Canadian Museum of Nature, Ottawa, Canada.

Edmontonia longiceps, NMC 8531, holotype skull, right lateral view.

mandibular ramus, five cervical vertebrae, ten dorsals, synsacrum (with four dorsal, three sacral, and two caudal vertebrae), 11 caudals, 17 ribs, a portion of the right ilium, ischia, right pubis, and 50 scutes. The specimen was collected from the upper Two Medicine Formation on the Blackfeet Indian Reservation, in northwestern Montana. Later, Russell (1940*b*) referred *P. rugosidens* to *Edmontonia*.

As measured by Gilmore, the skull of this species has a maximum width of 400 millimeters (about 15.5 inches). Colbert (1962), basing calculations on AMNH 5665, estimated the weight of this individual during life to be about 3.47 metric tons (3.82 tons).

In his revision of ankylosaurian families, Coombs (1978*a*) synonymized *Edmontonia* with the genus *Panoplosaurus* but did not justify the synonomy. Carpenter and Breithaupt (1986), after reevaluating *Edmontonia* and *Panoplosaurus*, concluded that both genera are valid, *Edmontonia* mostly distinguished by a more elongated skull shape and less lumpy armor, *Panoplosaurus* by a more plump skull profile and lumpy (colloform) armor on the skull table. Later, Carpenter (1990) stated that both genera can be distinguished from each other by features in the cranial armor, palate, vertebrae, ?manus, and body armor (compare Carpenter's new diagnoses for *Edmontonia* and *Panoplosaurus* [see entry]). Coombs (1990*a*), in a study of ankylosaur teeth, and Coombs and Maryańska (1990), in their review of the Ankylosauria, did not reject this generic separation. Two species of *Edmontonia*, *E. longiceps* and *E. rugosidens*, were recognized by Carpenter as valid.

Carpenter and Breithaupt reported a number of Maastrichtian nodosaurid specimens, including four teeth (DMNH collection) from the Hell Creek Formation, Corson County, South Dakota; a tooth (UCM 42663) lacking enamel from the Lance Formation, Niobrara County, Wyoming; three teeth (UCM 48369) without enamel from the "Lance" Formation, Park County, Wyoming; a tooth (UCMP 120002) lacking enamel from the Hell Creek Forma-

Edmontonia rugosidens, ROM 1215, skull, dorsal view.

Photo by R. A. Long and S. P. Welles (neg. #73/369-9), courtesy Royal Ontario Museum.

tion, Garfield County, Montana; two teeth (UW 14095 and 14096) without enamel from the Lance Formation, Sweetwater County, Wyoming; and a basioccipital (UCM 7572) from the Laramie Formation, Weld County, Colorado. Also, Carpenter and Breithaupt reported a lateral body spine (USNM 5793) from the Lance Formation, Niobrara County, Wyoming, which they referred to *Edmontonia* sp. According to Carpenter and Breithaupt, all of these specimens confirm the presence of nodosaurids in the Lance, Hell Creek and Laramie formations and extend the geochronological range of the Nodosauridae into the Maastrichtian ("Lancian"). This establishes *Edmontonia* as the last known nodosaurid.

Comparing the amount of nodosaurid material from the Campanian with that from the Maastrichtian, Carpenter and Breithaupt observed that this

Courtesy National Museum of Natural History, Smithsonian Institution (neg. #14339-K).

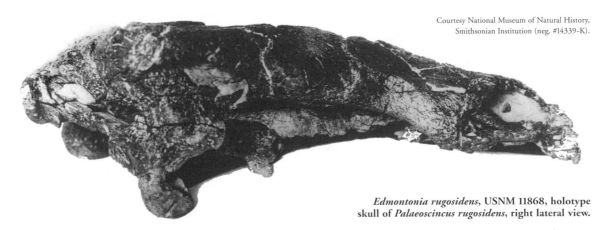

Edmontonia rugosidens, USNM 11868, holotype skull of *Palaeoscincus rugosidens*, right lateral view.

group of dinosaurs was relatively less abundant in the Maastrichtian. This suggests that nodosaurids were already extinct before the end of the Cretaceous and tends to support the hypothesis that the final dinosaur extinction was gradual rather than catastrophic.

In a proposed revision of Late Cretaceous nodosaurids, Bakker (1988) suggested that a new group, Edmontoniidae, be erected to embrace a clade of Late Cretaceous "nodosaurs" characterized by lack of premaxillary teeth, wider spoon-like beak, and more extensive secondary palate with a posterior displacement of the internal nares. At the same time, Bakker assigned new taxonomic names to two specimens previously referred to *Edmontonia*:

Bakker removed from *Edmontonia* an unusually complete skull (DMNH 468) without lower jaws, preserved crushed from top to bottom and slightly sheared from left to right. The material had been recovered in 1924 from the Lance Formation, Corson County, in the South Dakota Badlands. Carpenter and Breithaupt had designated this specimen *Edmontonia* sp. Bakker declared these remains to be the holotype of new genus and species *Denversaurus schlessmani*, regarding this taxon as the only "nodosaurian" dinosaur known from the latest Cretaceous "Lancian Faunal Age." Bakker defended the new genus' validity on the basis of cranial features perceived as differing from those in *E. rugosidens*, and from its being geologically too young to belong to *Edmontonia*. Observing that *Edmontonia* skulls are either short-headed (*E. longiceps*) or long-headed (*E. rugosidens*), Bakker assigned to the skull (NMC 8531) described by Gilmore (1930) as *E. rugosidens* a new subgeneric name, the combination becoming *E. (Chassternbergia) rugosidens*. To this subgenus, Bakker referred two specimens, a skull with partial skeleton (AMNH 5665) exhibited at the American Museum of Natural History, and a skull (AMNH 5381), both from the Oldman For-

mation of southern Alberta as a new species or subspecies.

Carpenter, however, noted that Bakker's diagnosis for *Denversaurus* relied upon his reconstruction of the skull in an uncrushed state, which Carpenter doubted was accurate, observing that if the size of the lateral temporal fenestra were increased and the quadrate more erect as in less crushed skulls of *Edmontonia*, the postorbital prominences would not be backwardly displaced. Carpenter pointed out that at least one of the characters in Bakker's diagnosis (*i.e.*, "greater spread of the basituberal rugosities over the basisphenoid and basioccipital") appears in the largest known *Edmontonia* skull (AMNH 5665) and may be related to the individual animal's age or size. Concerning Bakker's reasons for separating the subgenus *E. (Chassternbergia) rugosidens* from *Edmontonia*, Carpenter noted that the relatively shorter snout in this species is more apparent than real, due to the wide palate and divergent tooth rows, and also that Bakker was incorrect in suggesting that "smooth teeth" constitute a good specific character in nodosaurids (see Coombs 1990*a*). Carpenter found no sufficient grounds for separating *Denversaurus* from *Edmontosaurus*

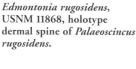

Edmontonia rugosidens, USNM 11868, holotype dermal spine of *Palaeoscincus rugosidens.*

Courtesy National Museum of Natural History, Smithsonian Institution (neg. #14339-K).

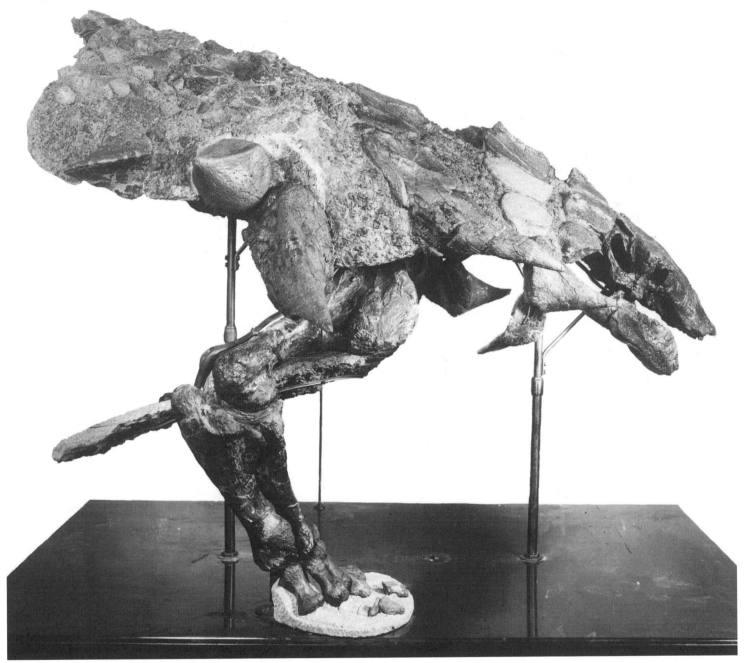

Edmontonia rugosidens, AMNH 5665, partial skeleton, right lateral view.

sp. or *E. (Chassternbergia) rugosidens* from *E. rugosidens.*

The occurrence of *Edmontonia* in the fossil record was extended by the discovery, by John A. Luster and John Joe Luster, of a partial skull (DPMWA 90-25) in Late Cretaceous fine-grained marine claystone and siltstone sediments (assigned to the upper part of the Matanuska Formation; see Grantz 1961; Jones 1963) at Matanuska-Susitna Borough, Alaska, United States. The specimen, which includes two well-preserved maxillary teeth, and lacks lower jaws, most of the premaxillary beak, and postorbital region,

was designated *Edmontonia* sp. The find constituted the first North American record of an ankylosaur north of Alberta, Canada, the first record of dinosaurian skeletal remains in Alaska outside of the North Slope, and the first report of this genus from marine rocks (Gangloff 1995).

Gangloff noted that the general shape and proportions of the cranium (including the structure of the palate) supports referring this specimen to *Edmontonia,* and that the tooth rows in DPMWA 90-25 are parallel for nearly half of their exterior extent, and the (incomplete) vomer seems to be

Edmontonia

keeled rather than grooved, as in that genus. Gangloff also pointed out that this specimen, though far from complete, is significant for its possession both of two relatively complete tooth rows and two almost complete teeth that display very little wear, the latter condition being rare among published accounts of North American nodosaurids.

Because of the fragmentary nature of this specimen, Gangloff could not refer it to any species of *Edmontonia*; however, general skull proportions strongly suggest *E. longiceps,* while tooth structure suggests *E. rugosidens* in shape and distinctness of the cusps.

Gangloff pointed out that this discovery contributes to the increasing number of nodosaurid finds from Upper Cretaceous marine formations in North America and Europe (summarized by Horner 1979; Coombs and Maryańska 1990), this growing body of evidence suggesting strongly that nodosaurids preferred coastal or pericoastal environments, while ankylosaurids did interior or upland habitats.

Dinosaurian bones from marine units significantly exceed those of fossil terrestrial mammals for a comparable area, which Fiorillo (1990) attributed as possibly due to the more durable nature of dinosaurian carcasses in watery environments. Expanding on Fiorillo's idea, Gangloff further postulated that nodosaurids and some hadrosaurs had adapted to a life along the coasts by the Late Cretaceous. Thus, their remains were more likely to have been preserved in near-shore marine sediments due to their proximity and durability.

Key references: Bakker (1988); Carpenter (1990); Carpenter and Breithaupt (1986); Colbert (1962); Coombs (1978*a*); Coombs and Maryańska (1990); Gangloff (1955); Gilmore (1930); Russell (1940*b*); Sternberg (1928).

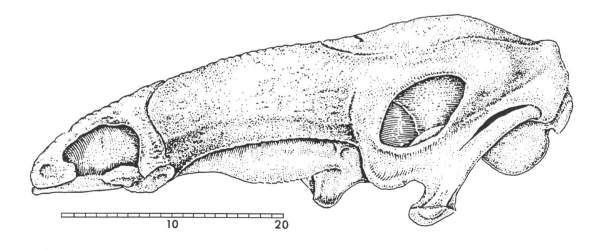

10   20

EDMONTOSAURUS Lambe 1917—(=*Anato-saurus*, in part; =?*Shantungosaurus*; =?*Thespesius*, in part)

Ornithischia: Genasauria: Cerapoda: Ornithopoda: Iguanodontia: Hadrosauridae: Hadrosaurinae.

Name derivation: "Edmonton [Formation]" + Greek *sauros* = "lizard."

Type species: *E. regalis* Lambe 1917.

Other species: *E. annectens* (Marsh 1892), *E. saskatchewanensis* (Sternberg 1926).

Occurrence: Horseshoe Canyon Formation, St. Mary River Formation, Scollard Formation, Alberta, Frenchman Formation, Saskatchewan, Canada; Hell Creek Formation, Lance Formation, South Dakota, Hell Creek Formation, North Dakota, Lance Formation, Wyoming, Laramie Formation, Colorado, Hell Creek Formation, Montana, United States.

Age: Late Cretaceous (Early–Late Maastrichtian).

Known material: At least 12 articulated skulls with associated postcrania, five to seven articulated skulls, associated and isolated cranial elements.

Holotype: NMC 2288, skull with jaws, vertebrae to caudal 6, humerus, hindlimb, pubes, ischium, right ilium.

Diagnosis of genus: Robust; premaxilla highly folded in external nares, with most highly reflected anterior border; postorbital swollen into pocket (largest in any hadrosaur), containing large cavity that extends to rear of orbit; 13 cervical, 18 dorsal, 8 sacral, and at least 29 caudal vertebrae (Brett-Surman 1989).

Diagnosis of *E. regalis*: Skull more robust, with low length-to-height ratio (?male) (Brett-Surman 1989).

Diagnosis of *E. annectens*: Skull longer, lower, less robust (?female) (Brett-Surman 1989).

Diagnosis of *E. saskatchewanensis*: Smaller (about 7 meters or 23 to 24 feet in length) (Sternberg 1926).

Comments: *Edmontosaurus*, frequently and incorrectly called "*Trachodon*" (see entry) and "*Anatosaurus*" in popular books, is the classic noncrested "duck-billed dinosaur" and is one of the relatively small number of dinosaur genera familiar to the general public. With the discovery of numerous specimens of *Edmontosaurus*, including some excellent skeletons, *Edmontosaurus* is one of the best known dinosaur genera. However, this genus is often confused with other taxa, especially *Anatosaurus*, which was established nearly two decades after *Edmontosaurus* was named.

The taxonomic history of *Anatosaurus* begins with the collection of two skeletons with skulls (USNM 2414 and YPM 2182) in 1891 by John Bell Hatcher, from the Lance Formation, Niobrara County, Wyoming. Later, these specimens were mounted, respectively, at the United States National Museum [now National Museum of Natural History], Smithsonian Institution, and at the Yale Peabody Museum of Natural History. Marsh (1892c) referred both skeletons to the genus *Claosaurus* as the types of new species *C. annectens*. The skeleton designated USNM 2414 was found in an unusually fine

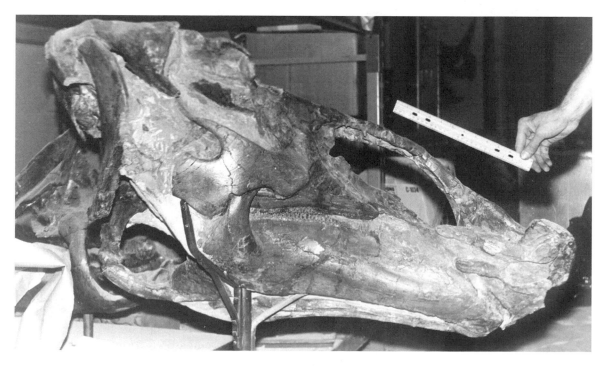

Edmontosaurus regalis, NMC 2288, holotype skull, right ventrolateral view.

Edmontosaurus

Illustration by Brian Franczak.

Three *Tyrannosaurus rex* individuals attacking herd of *Edmontosaurus regalis*.

state of completeness. Lucas (1904) attributed this condition to the fact that the animal had either perished in quicksand or that its yet undecomposed carcass was covered with sand due to a cloudburst or freshet. Accordingly, the skeleton remained articulated, the ribs attached to their respective vertebrae, femora still in their sockets, legs in walking position. In the surrounding matrix were preserved samples of the animal's fossilized skin, revealing small, irregularly six-sided, horny plates.

Marsh originally diagnosed this new species as follows: Long, narrow skull, anterior part moderately expanded transversely; muzzle blunt, rugose, formed above by premaxilla and below by predentary; premaxilla and predentary especially massive and prominent; orbit very large, subtriangular; nasals slender and long; frontals very short, almost as wide as long; parietals very small, a narrow ridge on upper surface of skull, separating supratemporal fossae, ending between median processes of squamosals; squamosals robust; main portion of jugal robust, much compressed, externally convex; maxilla of moderate size; lower jaws long and massive; 30 presacral nine sacral (in adults) and ?60 caudal vertebrae; cervical, dorsal, and anterior caudal vertebrae opisthocoelous; chevrons very long; scapula large and much curved; humerus comparatively short, with prominent radial crest; radius and ulna much elongated, the former about same length as humerus, latter longer; manus

long, with three functional digits, digit I rudimentary, V entirely wanting; pubis with very large expanded prepubis and rudimentary postpubis; shaft of ischium greatly lengthened; femur long, with almost straight shaft; tibia shorter than femur, with prominent cnemial crest; fibula very straight; calcaneum large; pes with three digits, II-IV massive, terminal phalanges covered with broad hooves, digits I and V wanting.

The genus *Edmontosaurus* was founded upon a complete skull and most of the postcranial skeleton (unprepared, most of the postcrania still in plaster jackets, NMC 2288). The material was discovered in 1912 by Levi Sternberg in the Horseshoe Canyon [then lower Edmonton] Formation, at Red Deer River near Three Hills Creek, Alberta, Canada. The paratype specimen (NMC 2289) of *E. regalis* consists of a skull lacking premaxillae and predentary, all vertebrae to the fifth caudal, and fore and hindlimbs, missing some foot bones, collected by George F. Sternberg in 1916 from the Horseshoe Canyon Formation.

Lambe (1917*b*) originally diagnosed type species *E. regalis* as follows: Skull relatively longer than in other hadrosaurines, high and broad posteriorly, flat anteriorly, laterally compressed behind low and greatly expanded snout; large pocket-like recess developed within postorbital, leading to large orbit; lateral temporal fossa restricted dorsally; ectopterygoid intervenes between maxilla and pterygoid, connects them; mandible deep, strong, slightly decurved

Edmontosaurus annectens, USNM 2414, holotype skeleton of *Anatosaurus annectens.*

anteriorly; teeth with rounded apical outline in lateral view, keeled, with relatively smooth borders; up to 49 vertical rows of dentary teeth, up to 53 rows in maxilla; moderate-sized dorsal spines increase slightly in height posteriorly in series; up to eight sacral vertebrae in adults; ischium long, thin, blunted distally; femur slightly exceeding tibia in length; humerus almost as long as ulna; animal robustly built, measuring almost 12 meters (about 40 feet) in length.

A half century after Marsh described *C. annectens*, Lull and Wright (1942), in their classic monograph on North American hadrosaurs (in which they identified all then known North American hadrosaur fossil localities), pointed out that there was much confusion regarding hadrosaur nomenclature, many taxa having been based on poor material. Intending to start fresh, they erected the new generic name *Anatosaurus* to embrace the two excellent specimens collected by Hatcher, as well as additional referred material.

Lull and Wright recognized three species of *Anatosaurus*: *A. annectens*, their new name for Marsh's

C. annectens; *A. copei*, based on material originally named *Diclonius mirabilis*; and *A. saskatchewanensis*, based on a skull and disarticulated skeleton (NMC 8509) collected by Charles M. Sternberg in 1921 from the Frenchman Formation at Rocky Creek, Saskatchewan, Canada, originally described by Sternberg (1926) as a new species of *Thespesius*. Sternberg distinguished this species by its smaller size and other characters no longer regarded as diagnostic.

Lull and Wright believed *Edmontosaurus* and *Anatosaurus* to be valid genera, the former distinguished by larger size, more robust muzzle and lower jaws, greater number of teeth, and other cranial features. Brett-Surman (1975, 1979), after examining material referred to both genera, concluded that the differences noted by Lull and Wright had ontogenetic origins and that both taxa were congeneric, the older name *Edmontosaurus* having priority. Brett-Surman (1989) recognized two possibly valid species, the rarer, more robust *E. regalis* and the more common and gracile *E. annectens*, although their differences could be sexual. Brett-Surman (1975, 1979)

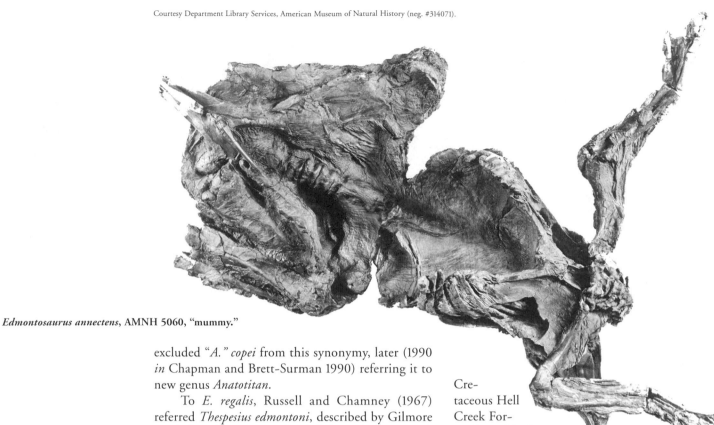

Edmontosaurus annectens, AMNH 5060, "mummy."

excluded "*A.*" *copei* from this synonymy, later (1990 *in* Chapman and Brett-Surman 1990) referring it to new genus *Anatotitan*.

To *E. regalis*, Russell and Chamney (1967) referred *Thespesius edmontoni*, described by Gilmore 1924*c*, based on an articulated skeleton (NMC 8399) complete to the sixth caudal vertebra, from the Horseshoe Canyon Formation of Alberta, interpreting this species' characters as due to ontogeny or individual variation; they also considered *E. saskatchewanensis* to be conspecific with *E. regalis*. Brett-Surman (1989) accepted *E. saskatchewanensis* as a valid species, but found *E. edmontoni* morphologically indistinguishable from *E. annectens*.

Lull and Wright referred to *E. regalis* the species *Trachodon selwyni* Lambe 1902 [*nomen dubium*], based on teeth and mandibular rami (NMC 290) collected by Lambe in 1898 (or 1901), from the Judith River (Oldman) Formation, at Red Deer River, Alberta; they also provisionally referred a femur to this species. Also referred to *E. regalis* were *Trachodon avatus* Cope 1871 [*nomen dubium*] and *Agathaumas milo* Cope 1874 [*nomen dubium*]. *A. milo* had been based on a sacral centrum and fragment of the proximal end of the tibia (AMNH collection) from Colorado, mentioned (but not described) by Cope (1874*a*), subsequently identified by Cope (1874*b*) as *Hadrosaurus occidentalis*.

Rohrer and Konizeski (1960) described a left dentary (USNM 22102) which they designated *Edmontosaurus* sp., collected in 1957 by Rohrer from the Hell Creek Formation at Garfield County, Montana. Rohrer and Konizeski noted that the presence of this fossil substantiates the correlation of the Upper Cretaceous Hell Creek Formation with the Upper Edmonton [now Horseshoe Canyon Formation] member of Alberta and the survival of *Edmontosaurus* into the latest Cretaceous.

Edmontosaurus has body proportions not unlike those of other hadrosaurs. This was a large form, a referred skeleton (ROM 801) mounted at the Royal Ontario Museum measuring almost 12 meters (about 40 feet) long, with a height at the hips of about 1.8 meters (6 feet). The head of *Edmontosaurus* is typically hadrosaurine, including a beak that was, during life, covered by a horny sheath. G. S. Paul (personal communication 1988) calculated the weight of an adult *Edmontosaurus* to be from about 2.1 to 2.78 metric tons (almost 2.4 to about 3.2 tons).

Leidy (1858) originally proposed that hadrosaurs were mostly aquatic, apparently basing this assumption on the flattened tail which, Leidy believed, could have been utilized as a swimming organ. This notion was generally accepted by workers, the presence of the "webbed" (actually paddle-like) covering in the hand of the Senckenberg "mummy" and, to a lesser extent, the superficially duck-like head, seemingly supporting it. Traditionally the image of *Edmontosaurus* and other hadrosaurids has been of a huge, duck-like dinosaur spending most of its time in water. Only in more recent years has this view dramatically changed.

Ostrom (1964c) stated that, as our understanding of modern animals is dependent to a large degree on our knowledge of their environment, the same should also apply to our understanding of extinct animals. Ostrom pointed out that most hadrosaurid remains have been collected from deposits that are terrestrial in origin. Geologic evidence indicates that the physical setting in which these dinosaurs lived seems to have been a near-sealevel coastal plain, with rivers and swamps meandering across estuarine deltas and wide floodplains. Anatomical evidence nonsupportive of a primarily aquatic life style include the dental batteries in hadrosaurids, adapted for efficiently grinding plant foods (perhaps including woody tissues) of the woodland types associated with hadrosaur-bearing formations, and also the stomach contents of the Senckenberg "mummy."

Ostrom demonstrated that hadrosaurs were accomplished bipeds, though the vertebral column was held rather horizontally (a conclusion also reached by Lull and Wright). Ostrom observed that the structure of the hind foot and ankle is adapted for terrestrial locomotion, that the very prominent fourth trochanter of the femur is characteristic of almost all bipedal archosaurs, and that the ossified tendons seem to have strengthened the vertebral column in the region of maximum stress (pelvis and hind limbs) for walking with the body horizontally posed. Ostrom concluded that hadrosaurids were primarily terrestrial foragers and that the well-known "aquatic adaptations" were protective adaptations, evolved in lieu of armor or weaponry, providing these animals with swimming abilities adequate to escape from terrestrial dangers.

The posture of hadrosaurs such as *Edmontosaurus* was further investigated by Galton (1970), who compared various hadrosaurid skeletons, including the holotype (USNM 2414) and plesiotype (YPM 2182) of *A. annectens,* and a skeleton of *Corythosaurus casuarius* (AMNH 5240), with those of quadrupedal dinosaurs, graviportal mammals, and the ostrich *Struthio camelus* (YPM 2125). Galton, like Ostrom, concluded that hadrosaurids were bipedal, as revealed by the length of the hindlimb relative to trunk and forelimb, nongraviportal structure of the forelimb with its elongated radius, ulna and metacarpals, lack of epidermal calluses or tubercle enlargements on the "mitten," well-developed fourth trochanter, progressive changes in the size of the centra and height of the neural arches on either side of the sacrum, upward turn of the centra at the base of the tail, and ossified tendons. Galton suggested that arguments supporting a quadrupedal pose in hadrosaurids only indicate that, as in many birds, the thoracic and tail sections of the vertebral column were held more or less horizontally. The flattened tail, once thought to have been utilized in swimming, was reinterpreted as a balancing organ for bipedal terrestrial locomotion.

Many paleontologists have noted that dinosaurs like *Edmontosaurus*, descended from terrestrial running forms (*e.g.,* iguanodontids), were even better anatomically adapted for a mostly land-based lifestyle. In aquatic animals, the toes are long and widely spread; the tail requires a wide base and vertebrae with wide transverse processes to accommodate strong muscles for swinging the tail against the water's resistance; and the caudal spines are vertically directed to support a ligament utilized in flexing the tail

Edmontosaurus annectens, skull (right lateral view) including sclerotic ring and beak, now at Senckenburg Museum.

Photo by R. A. Long and S. P. Welles (neg. #73/210-7).

underwater. Contrarily, hadrosaurids have quite short toes on both front and hind feet; the tail base and transverse processes are only of relatively moderate width; and the caudal spines are directed strongly backward, the latter feature characteristic of terrestrial reptiles. The trellis of bony rods attached to the back and tail spines would have so stiffened the animal's backside as to make swimming by tail propulsion difficult at best.

The bony tendons attached to the vertebral spines in *Edmontosaurus* and similar genera strengthened the vertebral column, keeping the body from swaying from side to side during walking. The pillar-like legs are designed to support great weight on land. The foot, with its three robust, splayed-out toes, is engineered to afford good balance and grip, and the powerfully built ankle is designed for walking. The hand, though first interpreted as webbed and paddle-like, has an enlarged, hoof-like digit III, apparently designed to provide additional support for the animal when it came down on all fours. The supposed "webbings" of the manus were simply the foreclaw mittens that had, after the animal's death, become dried-out and flattened bags of skin. Also, fossil iguanodont footprints found in Canada reveal crescent-shaped forepaw impressions, indicating that in hadrosaurid ancestors the toes were also imbedded in such a mitten.

In *Edmontosaurus* (and other hadrosaurids) are hundreds of strong teeth, held together by bony tissue in upper and lower dental batteries. Each battery forms a long grinding surface that, when the jaws chewed with an up and down action, could crush tough vegetation. This action was facilitated by powerful jaw muscles. Teeth were constantly being worn down by coarse vegetation to be replaced by new teeth growing up from below. With about 500 teeth in each battery, *Edmontosaurus* may have had a total of some 700 active and replacement teeth (contrary to the supposed "two thousand teeth" often referred to in popular books), about 80 actively used, for chewing at one time.

Morris (1970) described the hadrosaur bill from the excellently preserved bill mold of the skull (LACM 23902) of a mature individual. Referred by Morris to *A.* cf. *annectens*, this skull was recovered from the Hell Creek Formation, south of Fort Peck Reservoir, Montana. The skull, belonging to an individual almost 12 meters (about 40 feet) long, is similar to but differs somewhat from the holotype of *E. annectens*, and was found further north. The specimen, preserved as a mold in gray, lithic siltstone, is approximately 110 millimeters (4.2 inches) long where it joins the premaxillary bone. Extending downwards about 50 millimeters (approximately 1.9 inches) below the anterior margin of the predentary, the bill overlaps the front of the lower jaw. Morris suggested that the horny bill was affixed anterior to the bill, secured by extending upwards and onto the surface of the premaxillaries. The poorly-preserved predentary offered no evidence for a bill on the lower jaw.

Morris pointed out that hadrosaurs may have eaten a variety of foods. This idea was supported by a mummified specimen (SM R4036; see below) of

Edmontosaurus saskatchewanensis, NMC 5509, holotype skull, of *Thespesius saskatchewanensis* (left lateral view.)

Courtesy Royal Ontario Museum.

E. regalis discovered by Charles H. Sternberg in Converse County, Wyoming, and displayed at the Senckenberg Museum. As shown by Krausell (1922), the stomach contents of this specimen included conifer needles, seeds, twigs, and other unidentified fossilized vegetation.

Hadrosaurid specimens (including USNM 2414) with fossilized soft parts are not uncommon, two of the finest examples being the so-called *Edmontosaurus* "mummies." These specimens have provided much information as to the life appearance of *Edmontosaurus*. One "mummy" (AMNH 5060), discovered in Kansas in 1908 by C. M. Sternberg, lying on its back with impressions of fossilized dehydrated skin covering the articulated bones, was displayed at the American Museum of Natural History (Osborn 1912*b*). The specimen reveals that the hide was remarkably thin and leathery, with an imbedded mosaic of horny variably sized tubercles, the largest along the back and legs. Tubercles clustered over the throat, neck, and sides are round or oval and sometimes arranged in definite patterns. Spaced between these clusters are small, polygonal tubercles averaging about 2.5 millimeters (about .1 inch) in diameter, becoming larger toward the central mass around which a ring is formed by larger tubercles. The skin on the abdomen underlying the pelvis is covered with small, round, or oval-shaped clusters of pavement tubercles arranged in longitudinal, irregular lines. Large, pavement tubercles also cover the skin over the outer and lower part of the fibula.

In a popular article, C. H. Sternberg (1929) told of his accidental discovery of the Senckenberg Museum "mummy" (SM 4036) while he was resting on a sandstone ledge (his trousers torn by the end of the fossilized tail). Sternberg surmised that the animal had become trapped in quicksand. As the neck was stretched to its full length with feet pointed downward, Sternberg envisioned the live animal as

trying to swim out of a deathtrap. The manus in this specimen has preserved the mitten-like covering that encloses all digits and extends beyond the terminal phalanges by several centimeters. Small, flattened, polygonal tubercles, measuring about 2 to 3 millimeters (less than .3 inches) in size, are present on the palmar surface.

Some *Edmontosaurus* specimens show what appears to be a dorsal frill (Osborn 1912*b*) surmounting the back and tail above the neural spines, a feature that might, according to Lull and Wright, have been present in all hadrosaurs. Horner (1984*c*) described such a frill from a tail section (MOR V 007) of a presumed *Edmontosaurus* from the Hell Creek Beds of Montana. This section, consisting of eighteen articulated posterior caudal vertebrae encased in siltstone, was part of an entire skeleton, the rest of which is now in Switzerland. Horner observed that the frill consists of "segments," each located directly above the dorsal tip of a corresponding neural spine. Each "segment" has a flat dorsal edge and is about 50 millimeters wide and 45 millimeters deep dorsoventrally. Rather than the tubercles seen on the sides of the tail, the surfaces of the "segments" show vertically oriented striations. The skin was seemingly thickened between the "segmented" portion of the frill and the summits of the dorsal spines, as a groove with a surface studded with small tubercles extends almost the complete length of the specimen. Horner speculated that this "segmented" frill extended from the cervical region to near the base of the tail, that the "segments" served a display function, and that the thickened part of the frill supported the individual segments.

More recently, the existence of the hadrosaurid dorsal frill was denied by Czerkas (1993), who stated that its identification as such was incorrect. According to Czerkas, the frill was incorrectly based upon skin from the side of the neck, which, in life, would have resulted in a deep, muscular neck analogous to that of a horse.

Notes: Baird (1979) referred to *Edmontosaurus* sp., with "reasonable probability," an ungual phalanx (ANSP 8947) associated with the holotype of *Tylosteus ornatus* [=*Pachycephalus wyomingensis*] collected by Ferdinand Vandiveer Hayden, apparently in 1859-60, in the "Black Foot country at the head of the Missouri River," and first described by Leidy (1872, 1873). Later, Baird (1986) also described two hadrosaurid specimens, a femur fragment (PU 22413), cited by Weishampel and Weishampel (1983), and a juvenile tibia fragment (USNM 336469), both from the Severn Formation of Maryland, as hadrosaurid. Baird noted that the Maryland specimens are too imperfect for positive identification.

Carpenter (1982*a*) reported two isolated Lancian teeth of baby hadrosaurids perhaps referable to *Edmontosaurus*. One tooth (UCM 45060) is 3.6 millimeters high and 3 millimeters wide, the other (UCM 45061) 2.9 millimeters high and 3 millimeters wide. Both teeth show heavy usage wear.

Derstler (1995) reported a bone bed, discovered in 1990, at the Dragon's Grave site in the Lance Formation (Uppermost Cretaceous, Upper Maastrichtian) of Niobrara County, Wyoming, and containing numerous remains belonging to the hadrosaur *Edmontosaurus annectens.* The remains, representing third-grown juveniles to large adults, were buried on a floodplain near the site of carcass accumulation. As noted by Derstler, the bonebed also contains shed theropod teeth, from scavengers (mostly ?*Dromaeosaurus,* others from *Tyrannosaurus rex,* ?*Nanotyrannus, Ricardestes,* ?*Saurornitholestes,* and *Troodon formosus*), and typical Lance background fossils (mostly plant debris, a few turtle and fish bones, and freshwater bivalves; the site also contains bones from a juvenile theropod and eggshell scraps, possibly representing a single species of troodontid, this evidence suggesting that a nearby *Troodon* nesting area suffered the same event that buried the hadrosaurs).

Ryan, Bell and Eberth (1995) reported the first detailed description of a long known dinosaur bone bed from the Horseshoe Canyon Formation (Edmonton Group) of Alberta, Canada. The bone bed contains an abundance of coalified plant fragments and small amber beads. Among the 565 vertebrate elements recovered from this bonebed is an abundance of remains belonging to the hadrosaur *Edmontosaurus,* identified as such by cranial elements. Most of these remains are from adults. About 50 percent of the recovered elements show theropod teeth marks, indicating that the hadrosaur carcasses were scavenged before reworking and burial, probably by *Albertosaurus,* the only other common large carnivore known (from a dentary and unassociated teeth) from this bone bed. (Ryan *et al.* noted that rare microvertebrate material recovered via screen washing from this bone bed includes *Opisthotriton, Scapherperon, Myledaphus, Lepisosteus,* and an indeterminate turtle; during the early 1960s, an articulated, partial skull of ceratopsian *Pachyrhinosaurus canadensis* was extracted there, its quadrates having only recently been collected.)

Key references: Brett-Surman (1975, 1979, 1989, 1990); Cope (1874*a*, 1874*b*); Czerkas (1993); Derstler (1995); Galton (1970); Gilmore (1924*c*); Horner (1984*c*); Krausell (1922); Lambe (1902, 1917*b*, 1942); Leidy (1872, 1873); Lucas (1904); Lull and Wright (1942); Marsh (1892*a*); Morris (1970); Osborn (1912*b*); Ostrom (1964*c*); Russell and Chamney (1967); Ryan, Bell and Eberth (1995); C. H. Sternberg (1929); C. M. Sternberg (1926).

EFRAASIA Galton 1973—(See *Sellosaurus.*)
Name derivation: "[Eberhard] Fraas."
Type species: *E. diagnostica* (Huene 1932).

EINIOSAURUS Sampson 1995
Ornithischia: Genasauria: Cerapoda: Marginocephalia: Ceratopsia: Neoceratopsia: Ceratopsidae: Centrosaurinae.
Name derivation: Blackfeet Indian *Eini* = "buffalo" + Greek *sauros* = "lizard."
Type species: *E. procurvicornis* Sampson 1995.
Other species: [None.]
Occurrence: Two Medicine Formation, Montana, United States.
Age: Late Cretaceous (Late Campanian).
Known material: Three incomplete adult skulls, cranial and postcranial elements of various age classes.
Holotype: MOR 456-8-9-6-1, incomplete skull with nasal horn, supraorbital regions, partial parietal.

Diagnosis of genus (as for type species): Centrosaurine with long-based, laterally compressed nasal horn; supraorbital horns (if present) low, rounded with convex medial surfaces; parietal with single pair of large, curved spikes projecting posteriorly from posterior margin (Sampson 1995).

Comments: The new type species *Einiosaurus procurvicornis* was established on an incomplete skull (MOR 456-8-9-6-1) recovered from the Two Medicine Formation, Canyon Bonebed, Landslide Butte Area, northwest of Cut Bank, Glacier County, Montana. Referred material from the same locality includes two more adult skulls and various elements representing different growth stages (catalogued collectively as MOR 456); material from Dino Ridge Quarry, also in the Landslide Butte Area, includes more than 200 dissociated cranial and postcranial elements (collectively, MOR 373) from several age classes (Sampson 1995). Both sites may represent independent, drought-related mass death events (Rogers 1990).

Before this taxon was officially named and described, it was referred to as a new species of *Styracosaurus*, called *S. makeli* [*nomen nudum*] by Czerkas and Czerkas 1990 in their book, *Dinosaurs: A Global*

Einiosaurus procurvicornis, skull reconstruction based on holotype MOR 456 8-9-6-1, left lateral and dorsal views. Scale = 10 cm. (After Sampson 1995.)

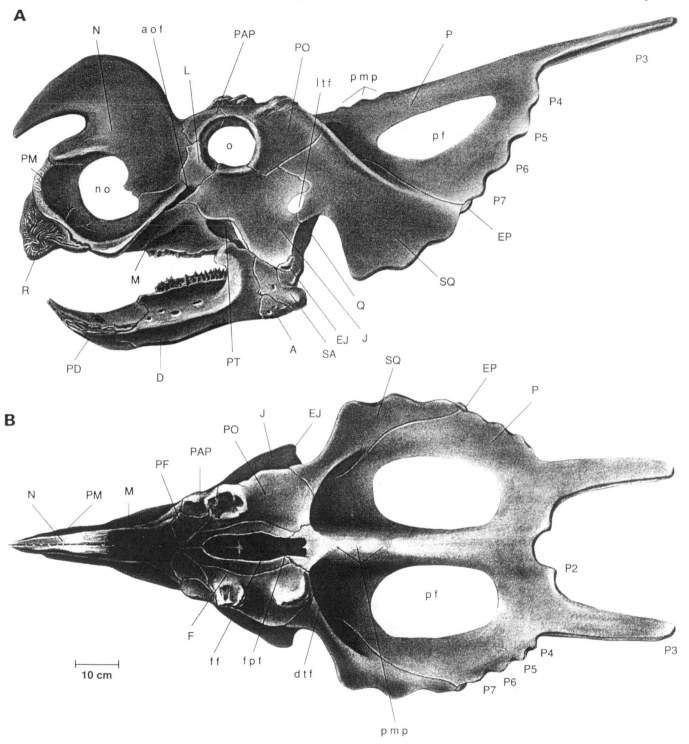

Einiosaurus procurvicornis, cast of holotype skull (MOR 456 8-9-6-1) exhibited at Dinofest International (1996), University of Arizona, Tempe.

View. Subsequently, the name "Einiosaurus" informally appeared in various popular publications (*e.g., Natural History*).

As described by Sampson, the most striking features of the holotype of *E. procurvicornis* are the forward- and downward-turned nasal horn and presence of a single long epoccipital horn on each parietal. The nasal horncore in this species is longer-based and more forward-curved, and the supraorbital horncores longer-based and more rounded in side view, than in other centrosaurines. Examination by Sampson of various nasals referred to *E. procurvicornis,* representing different ontogenetic stages, demonstrate that the nasal horn in this species "developed as in other centrosaurines, from sagitally-divided horncore halves that later fused from the tip down to form a single median structure." Nasal horncores of subadults are relatively small (about 120 millimeters high), laterally compressed, and sagittally divided; those in adults are long-based, laterally compressed, extend posteriorly almost to the frontals, and occur in two morphs, 1. small and erect, and 2. large and strongly recurved. Although these two morphs could represent sexual dimorphism, Sampson cautioned that any such claim would be completely speculative given the small sampling of material.

Sampson noted that *Einiosaurus* is similar in size and morphology to *Achelousaurus* (see entry) and falls within the general size range of other Campanian centrosaurines (*e.g.,* *Styracosaurus* and *Centrosaurus*).

Notes: Recently, the Centrosaurinae was reassessed by Sampson, based on *Einiosaurus procurvicornis* and *Achelousaurus horneri* and other known adult centrosaurine taxa. Sampson's phylogenetic review suggests that the Centrosaurinae contains two monophyletic clades, one containing *Centrosaurus* and *Styracosaurus,* the other *Achelousaurus, Einiosaurus,* and *Pachyrhinosaurus.* Both clades are supported by a single unambiguous character: The *Centrosaurus–Styracosaurus* clade by the presence of a prefrontal-prefrontal contact; the *Archelousaurus–Einiosaurus–Styracosaurus* clade by a long-based nasal horncore (in subadults).

Two evolutionary trends in the Centrosaurinae were apparent to Sampson: 1. In at least one lineage, the primitive nasal horncore (as in *Centrosaurus, Styracosaurus,* and *Einiosaurus*) underwent phylogenetic transformation into a nasal boss (*Achelousaurus*), which subsequently became hypertrophied (*Pachyrhinosaurus*); and, 2. supraorbital horncores (as in adult *Centrosaurus, Styracosaurus,* and *Einiosaurus*) transformed in at least one lineage into a highly rugose boss (as in *Achelousaurus* and *Pachyrhinosaurus*).

Horner, Varricchio and Goodwin (1992) speculated that dinosaur evolution may have been driven, in part, by shoreline fluctuations of the Late Cretaceous Interior Seaway, with maximum transgression of the Bearpaw Seaway in the Late Campanian reducing severely areal habitats as it moved westward toward the Rocky Mountains; and that some dinosaurs met this ecological "stress" through rapid modifications of sexual ornamentations. Sampson pointed out that all characters in his phylogenetic analysis involved elements of the skull roof, and all but one (premaxilla internal shelves) seemed to be associated with cranial ornamentation (particularly the horns and parietosquamosal frill) in what appear to be secondary sexual characters, most likely the result of sexual selection. Given the similarity in morphologies common to all ceratopsians, Darwinian natural selection (for survival success) seems to have been a less important factor in ceratopsian evolution and speciation than sexual selection (for reproductive success).

Key reference: Sampson (1995).

ELAPHROSAURUS   Janensch 1920

Saurischia: Theropoda: Ceratosauria: Neoceratosauria: Abelisauroidea.

Name derivation: Greek *elaphros* = "light-weight" +
Greek *sauros* = "lizard."

Type species: *E. bambergi* Janensch 1920.

Other species: ?*E. iguidiensis* Lapparent 1960, ?*E.
gautieri* Lapparent 1960.

Occurrence: Tendaguru Beds, Mtwara, Tanzania;
Ebechko, Tedreft, North Africa; ?Baharija, Egypt;
Boulogne-sur-Mer, France; Morocco.

Age: Late Jurassic (Kimmeridgian), Early Cretaceous, (?Cenomanian).

Known material: Fragmentary postcrania, teeth,
miscellaneous postcranial remains.

Holotype: HMN collection, incomplete postcranial
skeleton, associated teeth.

Diagnosis of genus (as for type species): Elongate cervical and posterior caudal vertebrae, with
strongly developed prezygapophyses; forelimbs
short; tibia, fibula, and metatarsals very elongate;
tibia longer than femur; manus and pes tridactyl
(Janensch 1920).

Diagnosis of ?*E. iguidiensis*: Distinguished from
E. bambergi by relative lesser height of caudal vertebrae (Lapparent 1960).

Diagnosis of ?*E. gautieri*: Distinguished by larger
size (measuring about 6 meters [over 20 feet] long)
and form of vertebrae (Lapparent 1960).

Comments: The genus *Elaphrosaurus* was
founded on a partial postcranial skeleton (HMN collection) found in the Tendaguru Formation, in
Tendaguru, Tanzania, East Africa (Janensch 1920).

Lapparent (1960) referred two additional species
of Lower Cretaceous (Cenomanian) age to *Elaphrosaurus*: *E. iguidiensis*, first reported by Lapparent
(1957), was based on teeth, vertebrae, ungual phalanx,
distal portion of a femur, and partial tibia from the
Lower Cretaceous of Ebrechko, southern Tunisia in
North Africa; *E. gautieri* was based on vertebrae and
fragmentary limb bones from the Lower Cretaceous
of Tedreft, North Africa.

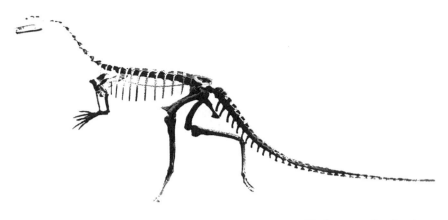

Elaphrosaurus bambergi,
HMN, holotype restored
skeleton.

Other specimens tentatively assigned to *Elaphrosaurus* include a tibia from the Cenomanian-
Turonian of Baharija (Stromer 1934); caudal vertebra from the Kimmeridgian of Boulogne-sur-Mer
(Lapparent and Lavocat 1955); and tibia from the
Lower Cretaceous of Morocco, this specimen measuring 63 centimeters (about 25 inches) long (Lavocat 1954).

Janensch classified *Elaphrosaurus* as a "coelurid."
Nopcsa (1928) perceived morphological similarities
between this genus and ornithomimids, including the
form of presacral and anterior caudal vertebrae, presence of elongated anterior prezygapophyses on distal
caudals, absence of a crest on the anteroproximal surface of the pubis, and abbreviated phalanges on pedal
digit IV. Russell (1972) found nothing in the known
morphology of *Elaphrosaurus* to exclude it from the
ancestry of later ornithomimids, also suggesting that
this dinosaur, with its short ilium and hindlimbs rel-

Elaphrosaurus bambergi, HMN, holotype caudal vertebra.
Scale = 2 cm. (After Janensch 1920.)

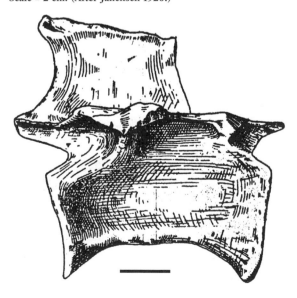

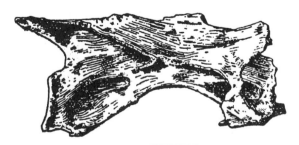

Elaphrosaurus bambergi, HMN, holotype dorsal vertebra.
Scale = 2 cm. (After Janensch 1920.)

Elaphrosaurus bambergi,
HMN, holotype cervical ver-
tebra. Scale = 2 cm. (After
Janensch 1920.)

• 399 •

Elaphrosaurus

Illustration by Gregory S. Paul.

Elaphrosaurus bambergi pursuing *Dryosaurus lettowvorbecki.*

ative to size of vertebral elements, was not as well adapted to a cursorial life style as were Late Cretaceous ornithomimids. Later, Russell and Galton (1982c) listed characters in *E. bambergi* that are more primitive than in ornithomimids (*e.g.*, shortness of ilium and hindlimbs compared to vertebral elements; relatively short humerus; metatarsal III not shrouded by the II and IV proximally (the latter two not contacting one another on the extensor face of the metatarsus); low ascending process of the astragalus; more distally located deltopectoral crest of the humerus; and possibility of teeth).

Other authors (*e.g.*, Barsbold and Osmólska 1990) have regarded this genus as an ornithomimid. However, in his book *Predatory Dinosaurs of the World*, Paul (1988c) stated that *Elaphrosaurus* is not an ornithomimid, pointing out that the humerus is more like (though less strongly constructed than) that of *Rioarribasaurus* [=*Coelophysis* of his usage], and that the lightness of build of the skeleton is of "coelophysid" proportions. (Paul also noted that, among known theropods, *Elaphrosaurus* seems to have the

lowest trunk and shallowest chest, the tail appearing to have an unusual downward bend.) More recently, Holtz (1994a), using cladistic analysis, showed that *Elaphrosaurus* possesses shared derived characters with abelisaurids and suggested that this genus is the sister-taxon of the ceratosaurian group Abelisauridae. According to Holtz, the similarity between this genus and Ornithomimosauria, in the strict sense, are the result of convergence.

Note: Fossil footprints have been attributed to *Elaphrosaurus*, though inconclusively, including tracks from the lower Cenomanian of Jerusalem (Avnimelech 1962) and from the Niger Republic (Ginsburg, Lapparent, Loiret and Taquet 1966).

Key references: Barsbold and Osmólska (1990); Janensch (1920); Lapparent (1957, 1960); Lapparent and Lavocat (1955); Lavocat (1954); Nopcsa (1924); Russell and Galton (1982c); Smith and Galton (1990); Stromer (1934).

?*Elaphrosaurus gautieri*, holotype distal end of right pubis (scale = 2 cm.), left humerus, right tibia (scale = 4 cm.). (After Lapparent 1960.)

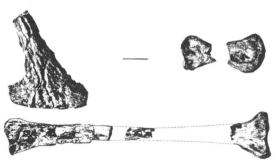

?*Elaphrosaurus iguidiensis*, holotype caudal vertebra. Scale = 2 cm. (After Lapparent 1960.)

?*Elaphrosaurus gautieri*, referred teeth. Scale = 1 cm. (After Lapparent 1960.)

ELMISAURUS Osmólska 1981—
(=?*Caenagnathus*, ?*Ricardoestesia*)
Saurischia: Theropoda: Tetanurae: Avetheropoda:
Coelurosauria: Maniraptora: Arctometatarsalia:
Elmisauridae.
Name derivation: Mongolian *elmyi* = "pes" + Greek
sauros = "lizard."
Type species: *E. rarus* Osmólska 1981.
Other species: *E. elegans* (Parks 1933).
Occurrence: Nemegt Formation, Omnogov, Mon-
golian People's Republic; Dinosaur Park Forma-
tion, Alberta, Canada.
Age: Late Cretaceous (Campanian).
Known material: Six pedes, manus, limb bones,
foot bones representing several individuals.
Holotype: ZPAL MgD-I/172, left tarsometatarsus
lacking metatarsal I.

Diagnosis of genus: *Chirostenotes*–like manus;
metacarpal I more than one-half length of II; distal
tarsals III and IV completely coossified with one
another and with metatarsus to form tarsometatarsus;
tarsal IV with upward process at lateral margin;
metatarsus semicrescent-shaped in cross-section;
metatarsals II-IV fused proximally (Osmólska 1981).

Diagnosis of *E. rarus*: Metatarsal III visible for
about 90 percent of its length; length-to-width ratio
of metatarsus 0.18; metacarpal I approximately two-
thirds length of first phalanx of this digit; digits I and
II equally thick, thicker than III; ventroposterior portions of manual phalanges thickened at proximal surfaces (Osmólska 1981).

Diagnosis of *E. elegans*: More gracile than
E. rarus or *Chirostenotes pergracilis*; in dorsal view,
posteromedial corner of tarsometatarsus more deeply
emarginated than in *E. rarus*; longitudinal, ridge-like
posterolateral margin of metatarsal IV not as powerfully developed proximally as in *E. rarus*; small processes of metatarsals II and IV overlapping metatarsal
III close to articular surfaces (Currie 1989).

Comments: The basis for the group Elmisauridae Osmólska 1981, *Elmisaurus* was founded upon an
incomplete left tarsometatarsus (ZPAL MgD-I/172),
collected during the Polish-Mongolian Paleontological Expedition to Mongolia in 1970, from the northern part of the Nemegt locality, Nemegt Formation,
Gobi Desert, Mongolian People's Republic. Referred
specimens from the same locality are a right phalanx
including the distal portion of the metatarsus, various pedal phalangial elements and two fragmentary
unguals, right manus including metacarpal I and distal portion of II, various manual phalangial elements
and unguals, and indeterminable fragments of long
bones of limbs (ZPAL MgD-I/98), and proximal
portion of the right tarsometatarsus (ZPAL MgD-
I/20) (Osmólska 1981).

In describing *Elmisaurus*, Osmólska noted that
the most striking character of the foot is the tarsometatarsus. This coossification of metapodials had
been generally regarded as an avian character. The
presence of a tarsometatarsus in *Elmisaurus* and some
other theropods, however, indicates that this character is not exclusive to birds. Osmólska concluded that
the tarsometatarsus was not an avian acquisition but
that of certain theropods as early as the Late Triassic.
This feature supports the hypothesis that birds
descended from coelurosaurian dinosaurs.

E. elegans, a second species, was founded upon
complete left metatarsals II and IV, incomplete distal tarsal III, distal tarsal IV, and metatarsal III (ROM
781), collected in 1926 along Little Sandhill Creek
(now Dinosaur Provincial Park), in Alberta. The

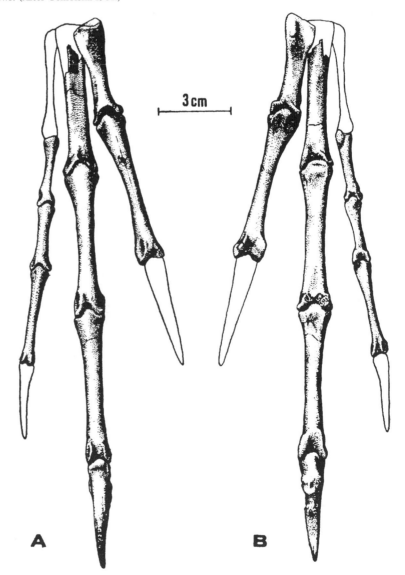

Elmisaurus rarus, ZPAL MgD-I/98, reconstruction of right manus, in A. dorsal and B. palmar views. (After Osmólska 1981.)

3 cm

A   B

material, originally described by Parks (1933) as a new species of *Ornithomimus*, represents the first record of the genus in North America. Remains referred to *E. elegans* include the proximal end of a fused right tarsometatarsus (RTMP 82.39.4), collected by Linda Strong-Watson in 1982 in Dinosaur Provincial Park; and the shaft and distal end of a left metatarsal II (ROM 37163), collected between 1920 and 1954 by a University of Toronto-Royal Ontario Museum expedition to the badlands (now Dinosaur Provincial Park), this specimen smaller than the holotype (Currie 1989).

Currie noted that RTMP 82.39.4 compares closely with the Asian Type species *E. rarus* in size and morphology. ROM 781, more complete than RTMP 82.39.4, displays other features diagnostic for *Elmisaurus*. Also, the more recently collected specimen indicates that this genus and *Chirostenotes*, though very similar in structure of the manus, are distinct taxa.

According to Currie, analysis of the *Elmisaurus* remains suggests that faunal interchange between Asia

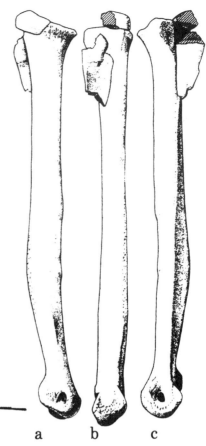

Elmisaurus elegans, ROM 781, holotype metatarsal II, A. medial, B. posterior, C. lateral views. Scale = 1 cm. (After Currie 1989.)

and North America continued during the Late Cretaceous.

Note: The proximal portion of a tarsometatarsus (ZPAL MgD-I/85) was collected from the same locality as the remains of *E. rarus*. Osmólska observed that this specimen differs from *Elmisaurus* in having a much stronger fusion of its elements and in the posterior face of the tarsometatarsus, both in proportions of its contributing bones and in the lack of an upward process of tarsal IV. Osmólska regarded this specimen as pertaining to a theropod of uncertain "infraorder" and family, genus and species indeterminate.

Key references: Currie (1989); Osmólska (1981); Parks (1933).

ELOSAURUS Peterson and Gilmore 1902—(See *Apatosaurus*.)

Name derivation: Greek *elops* = "fish" + Greek *sauros* = "lizard."

Type species: *E. parvus* Peterson and Gilmore 1902.

Elmisaurus rarus, reconstruction of left pes based on ZPAL MgD-I/172 (holotype tarsometatarsus) and ZPAL MgD-I/98 (digits, reversed from right side), in A. dorsal and B. palmer views, C. proximal articular surface of tarsometatarsus. (After Osmólska 1981.)

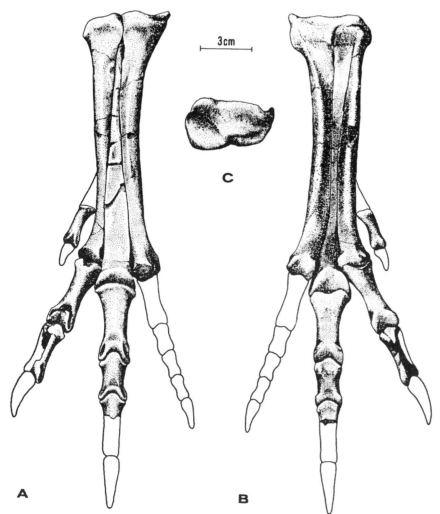

EMAUSAURUS Haubold 1990

Ornithischia: Genasauria: Thyreophora.

Name derivation: "EMAU [Ernst-Moritz-Arndt-Universität in Greifswald] + Greek *sauros* = "lizard."

Type species: *E. ernsti* Haubold 1990.

Other species: [None.]

Occurrence: [Unnamed Formation], Germany.

Age: Early Jurassic (Lower Toarcien).

Known material/holotype: SGWG 85, almost complete skull, associated postcranial remains.

Diagnosis of genus (as for type species): Primitive thyreophoran distinguished by following autapomorphies: body of moderate size, approximately 2 meters (about 6.6 feet) long; osteoderms relatively small, conical-to-plate-shaped; skull broad; five premaxillary teeth; narrow premaxillary snout and palate; buccal shelf on dentary and maxillary initiated at tenth tooth position; broad triangular palpebral; W-shaped contact of jugal and quadratojugal; postorbital with prominent dorsolateral crest; rounded, upturned retroarticular process (Haubold 1990).

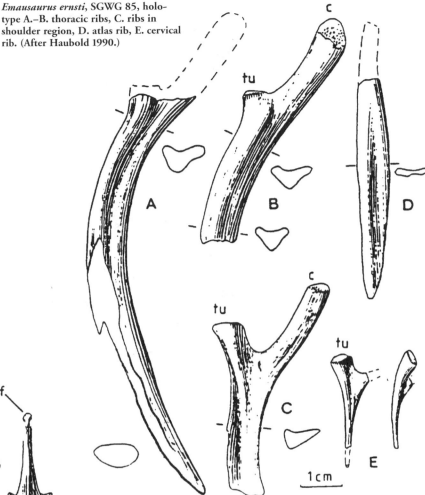

Emausaurus ernsti, SGWG 85, holotype A.–B. thoracic ribs, C. ribs in shoulder region, D. atlas rib, E. cervical rib. (After Haubold 1990.)

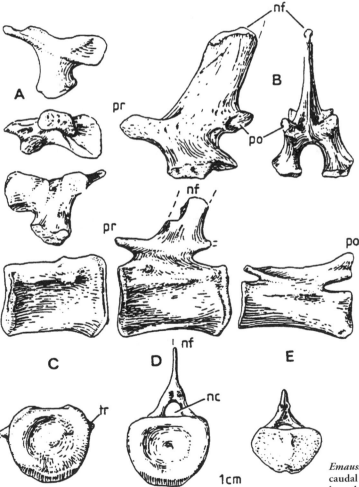

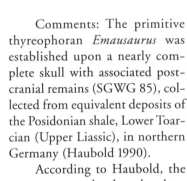

Comments: The primitive thyreophoran *Emausaurus* was established upon a nearly complete skull with associated postcranial remains (SGWG 85), collected from equivalent deposits of the Posidonian shale, Lower Toarcian (Upper Liassic), in northern Germany (Haubold 1990).

According to Haubold, the genera most closely related to *Emausaurus* are *Scutellosaurus* and *Scelidosaurus*, these representing successive sister-taxa to the common and unknown ancestor of both the Stegosauria and Ankylosauria.

Key reference: Haubold (1990).

Emausaurus ernsti, SGWG 85, holotype A. neural arch, B. neural arch of anterior caudal vertebra in lateral and posterior views, C.–E. mid caudal (12–24) vertebrae, in lateral and posterior views. (After Haubold 1990.)

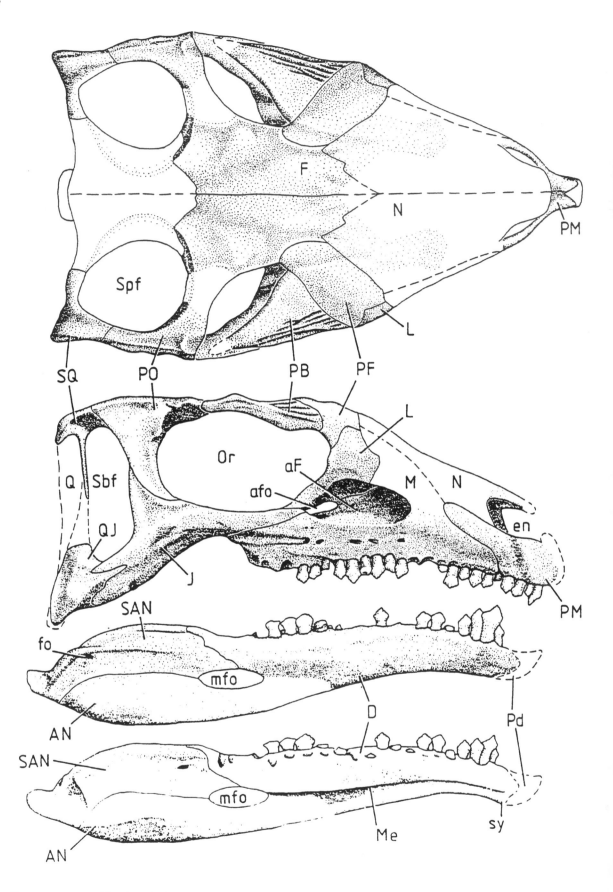

Emausaurus ernsti, SGWG 85, holotype skull, in dorsal and left lateral views. (After Haubold 1990.)

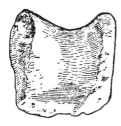

Embasaurus minax,
holotype dorsal verte-
bra. (After Riabinin
1931.)

EMBASAURUS Riabinin
1931 [*nomen dubium*]
Saurischia: Theropoda *incer-
tae sedis.*
Name derivation: "Emba
[River]" + Greek *sauros* =
"lizard."
Type species: *E. minax*
Riabinin 1931 [*nomen
dubium*].
Other species: [None.]
Occurrence: Neocomian
Sands, Gurievsk.
Age: ?Early to Late Cretaceous.
Known material/holotype: Posterior dorsal verte-
bra, incomplete ?anterior dorsal vertebra, both
missing neuropophyses.

Diagnosis of genus: (More complete) dorsal vertebra with almost platycoelous articular face (unusual
and atypical of Early Cretaceous theropod) (Riabinin
1931).

Comments: The genus *Embasaurus* was founded
on incomplete dorsal vertebrae collected from the
"Neocomian" Sands (Lower Cretaceous) of Mount
Koi-Kara, Transcaspian Steppes, Gurievsk (formerly
Union of Soviet Socialist Republics) (Riabinin 1931).

According to Molnar (1990), *E. minax* seems to
be a relatively primitive form, as platycoelous vertebrae often occur in older taxa but are not known in
"carnosaurs."

Key references: Molnar (1990); Riabinin (1931).

ENIGMOSAURUS Barsbold and Perle 1983
Saurischia: Theropoda: Tetanurae: ?Coelurosauria:
Therizinosauroidea: Therizinosauridae.
Name derivation: Greek *ainigma* = "puzzling" +
Greek *sauros* = "lizard."
Type species: *E. mongoliensis* Barsbold and Perle 1983.
Other species: [None.]
Occurrence: Baynshirenskaya Svita, Dornogov,
Mongolian People's Republic.
Age: Late Cretaceous (?Cenomanian or ?Turonian).
Known material/holotype: GIN 100/84, incomplete
pelvic girdle missing upper portion of ilia.

Diagnosis of genus (as for type species): Pubis
with uncompressed, narrow shaft; ischium with
small, shallow obturator process (Barsbold and
Maryańska 1990).

Comments: Originally described by Barsbold
and Perle (1980) as an indeterminate "segnosaurian"
[=therizinosauroid] the genus *Enigmosaurus* was
founded upon an incomplete pelvic girdle (GIN
100/84) collected from the Upper Cretaceous Bayan
Shireh suite at Khara Khutul, southeastern Mongolia.

Barsbold and Perle originally diagnosed this
taxon as follows: Ilia apparently with bases broadly
separated from each other, anterior wings seemingly
outwardly deflected; ilium apparently with pubic projection; pubis postventrally directed, parallel to
ischium, with long, narrow shaft; pubic "foot" small,
narrow; dorsal surface of pubis with deep longitudinal depression at symphysis separating pubes; ishium
elongate, with narrow shaft and narrow, distally
located obturator process, the latter fusing with pubis
some distance above its distal end.

In their monograph on Mongolian theropods,
Barsbold and Perle (1983) referred GIN 100/84 to
the new genus *Enigmosaurus*. Barsbold (1983) placed
the genus into its own higher taxon Enigmosauridae.

Key references: Barsbold (1983); Barsbold and
Maryańska (1990); Barsbold and Perle (1981, 1983).

EOCERATOPS Lambe 1915—(See
Chasmosaurus.)
Name derivation: Greek *eos* = "dawn" + Greek
keratos = "horned" + Greek *ops* = "face."
Type species: *E. canadensis* (Lambe 1902).

EORAPTOR Sereno, Forster, Rogers and Monetta
1993
?Dinosauria: ?Saurischia: ?Theropoda.
Name derivation: Greek *eos* = "dawn" + Latin *raptor*
= "thief."
Type species: *E. lunensis* Sereno, Forster, Rogers
and Monetta 1993.
Other species: [None.]

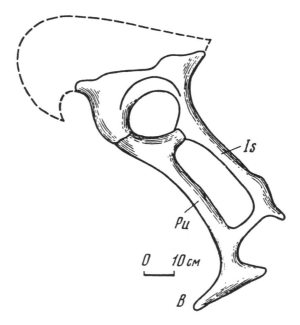

Enigmosaurus mongoliensis,
GIN 100/84, holotype pelvis.
(After Barsbold and Perle
1983.)

Eoraptor

Occurrence: Ischigualasto Formation, Valley of the Moon, Argentina.

Age: Late Triassic (Middle Carnian).

Known material/holotype: PVSJ 512, articulated skeleton with skull, missing distal caudal vertebrae.

Diagnosis of genus (as for type species): Small, 1-meter-long theropod; external nares slightly enlarged; premaxilla with slender posterolateral process; leaf-shaped premaxillary and anterior maxillary crowns (Sereno, Forster, Rogers and Monetta, 1993).

Comments: The name "Eoraptor" was first published in the January 1993 issue of *National Geographic* magazine, in an article about dinosaurs written by Rick Gore.

The most primitive apparent dinosaur yet discovered, the genus *Eoraptor* was founded on an almost complete, well-preserved skeleton including the skull, discovered in October 1991, by student Ricardo Martinez, in the foothills of the Andes, Ischigualasto Formation, Valley of the Moon, Ischigualasto Provincial Park, Ischigualasto–Villa Unión Basin, northwest Argentina. The specimen had been preserved in a muddy siltstone and was closely associated with other common Ischigualasto vertebrates (including *Herrerasaurus*, *Saurosuchus*, *Exaeretodon*, *Ischigualastia*, *Aetosauroides*, and an undescribed cynodont) (Sereno, Forster, Rogers and Monetta 1993). Collection of the holotype took almost a year, after which it was sent to Chicago for preparation by William F. Simpson and Bob Masek at Field Museum of Natural History (now the Field Museum). There it was first displayed before being returned to the Museum of Natural Science in San Juan, Argentina.

Sereno *et al.* interpreted *Eoraptor* as close to the predicted structure and size of the common dinosaurian ancestor. Among the derived skull characters present in theropods, sauropodomorphs, and ornithischians (the main dinosaurian clades) but absent in *Eoraptor* are development of an intermandibular joint (theropods) and greatly enlarged external naris and narial fossa (sauropodomorphs). The forelimbs are less than half as long as the hindlimbs, indicating that the animal was an obligatory biped.

The skull is primitively saurischian in design, having transversely narrow proportions, relatively large antorbital fenestra, small subnarial foramen beneath the external naris, and forked posterior process on the jugal. Absent are the derived skull specializations of Theropoda, Sauropodomorpha, and Ornithischia. The skull has a unique heterodont dentition: The posterior half of the upper tooth row has

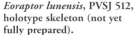

Eoraptor lunensis, PVSJ 512, holotype skeleton (not yet fully prepared).

Photo by John Weinstein, courtesy the Field Museum (neg. #G-85672.12c).

Eoraptor lunensis, PVSJ 512, holotype skull, right lateral view.

serrated, recurved crowns (as in theropods), the anterior half has leaf-shaped crowns with a basal constriction (as in basal sauropodomorphs).

The postcranial skeleton also lacks many of the derived features present in dinosaurs. The sacrum possesses only three vertebrae. The manus retains digit V, which has been reduced to a short metacarpal. The sacral vertebrae lack pleurocoels (often present in saurischians), but the long bones are strongly hollowed (as in theropods).

According to Sereno *et al. Eoraptor* exhibits key synapomorphies that identify this genus as saurischian (*e.g.*, subnarial opening; epipophyseal processes and slender, interconnecting ribs for increased flexibility of the neck). Also, *Eoraptor* possesses features that link this genus with other theropods (predatory hand with trenchant unguals; elongate distal phalanges and metacarpal pits for phalangeal hyperextension, enhancing raking and grasping capabilities).

As Sereno *et al.* pointed out, the occurrence of *Eoraptor* with such contemporaries as the more derived *Herrerasaurus* and ornithischian *Pisanosaurus* supports the hypothesis that small dinosaurs diverged rapidly from a common Early Carnian ancestor, the main carnivorous and herbivorous lineages already established by the Middle Carnian.

More recently, the phylogenetic status of *Eoraptor* was questioned by Holtz (1995*a*, 1995*b*) in preliminary reports announcing his new revision (not yet published) of the Theropoda. According to Holtz (1995*a*, 1995*b*), *Eoraptor* and also the Herrerasauridae are not theropods, are probably not saurischians, and may not be dinosaurian.

Note: Fraser and Padian (1995) reported possible basal dinosaur remains found at a recent excavation at Cromwell Quarry in Great Britain. The animal is an ornithodiran represented by varied elements including well-preserved ilia and a humerus, and also fragmentary postcranial elements. Recovered elements bear numerous features often regarded as dinosaurian synapomorphies: Humerus with low deltopectoral crest extending about one-third way down the shaft; ilium semiperforate, with well-pronounced supraacetabular buttress; iliac blade with short anterior process but well-developed posterior process and shallow but distinct brevis shelf; ?two sacral vertebrae. Fraser and Padian reported that Cromwell Quarry has also yielded other abundant archosaurian remains, including the sphenosuchian crocodylomorph *Terrestrisuchus*.

Key references: Holtz (1995*a*, 1995*b*); Sereno, Forster, Rogers and Monetta (1993).

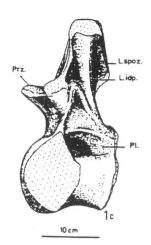

Epachthosaurus sciuttoi, MACN-CH 1317, holotype dorsal vertebra. (After Powell 1990.)

EPACHTHOSAURUS Powell 1990
Saurischia: Sauropodomorpha: Sauropoda: Titanosauria: Andesauridae.
Name derivation: Greek *epachthos* = "heavy" or "slow" + Greek *sauros* = "lizard."
Type species: *E. sciuttoi* Powell 1990.
Other species: [None.]
Occurrence: Bajo Barreal Formation, Sierra de San Bernardino, Argentina.
Age: Late Cretaceous (?Senonian).
Known material: Isolated dorsal vertebra, articulated dorsal vertebrae with partial sacrum.
Holotype: MACN-CH 1317, incomplete dorsal vertebra.

Diagnosis of genus (as for type species): Dorsal vertebrae with relatively large, wide, depressed centra and very large, deep pleurocoels (as in titanosaurids); posterior dorsal neural spines compressed anteroposteriorly, with thick prespinal laminae with forked lower portion; end of diapophysis of neural arch uneven (Powell 1990).

Comments: The genus and species originally spelled *Epachtosaurus* [sic] *sciuttoi* was first mentioned (but not described) by Powell in a paper authored by Martínez, Giménez, and Bochatey (1986).

With the spelling altered to *Epachthosaurus*, this genus was founded on an isolated vertebra (MACN-CH 1317) from the Upper Cretaceous (?Senonian) of the Ocho Hermanos site, Upper Member of the Bajo Barreal Formation (Chubut Group; Sciutto 1981), at Sierra de San Bernardo (Chubut province), in the San Jorge Basin, Argentina. The paraplastotype (MACN 18689) comprises an articulated series of six posterior dorsal vertebrae with part of the sacrum, and fragments of the pubic peduncle of the ilium (Powell 1990).

The collected material belonging to *E. sciuttoi* is very incomplete. However, titanosaurids are known to occur in the Upper Cretaceous of South America, and features of the dorsal vertebrae of this species, primarily the nature of the pleurocoels, are indicative of titanosaurids. For these reasons, Powell (1990) tentatively assigned this genus to the Titanosauridae.

Key references: Martínez, Giménez and Bochatey (1986); Powell (1990).

EPANTERIAS Cope 1878—(See *Allosaurus*; also, see *Saurophagus*.)
Name derivation: Greek *epi* = "upon" + Greek *anteris* = "buttress" + Greek *ias* = "characterized by."
Type species: *E. amplexus* Cope 1878.

ERECTOPUS Huene 1923
Saurischia: Theropoda: ?Tetanurae: Megalosauridae.
Name derivation: Latin *erectus* = "upright" + Greek *pous* = "foot."
Type species: *E. sauvagei* (Huene 1923).
Other species: ?*E. superbus* (Huene 1932).
Occurrence: [Unnamed formations], Meuse, Pas-de-Calais, France; ?Boca do Chapim, Portugal.
Age: Late Early Cretaceous (Albian).
Known material: Fragmentary skeleton, teeth, ?tooth and bone fragments.
Syntypes: [?Lost] two teeth, posterior portion of lower jaw, several dorsal centra, part of sacrum, caudal vertebrae, ribs, femur, tibia, part of articulated manus, phalanges, ?calcaneum, presumably from the same individual.

Diagnosis of genus: [No modern diagnosis published.]

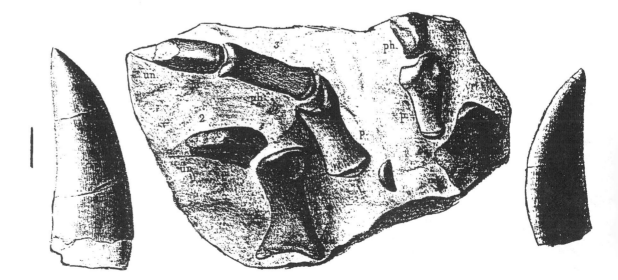

Erectopus sauvagei, syntype teeth and partial manus of *Megalosaurus superbus*. Scale = 1 cm. (After Sauvage 1876.)

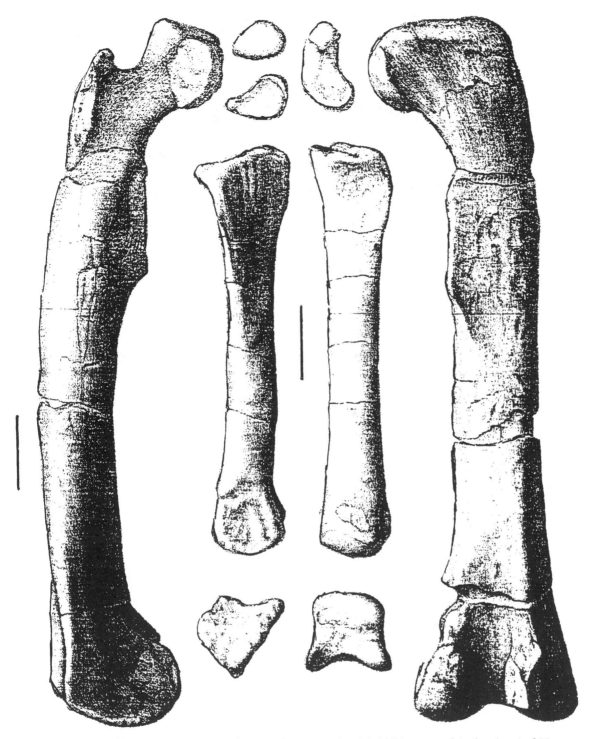

Erectopus sauvagei, syntype (left and right) right femur (scale = 3.33 cm.) and (middle) metatarsal (scale = 4 cm.) of *Megalosaurus superbus*. (After Sauvage 1876.)

Comments: This modest-sized theropod was founded upon teeth and postcranial material collected from a well in the Albian Gault Sand, Bois de la Panthière, Meuse River, Ardennes, northern France, originally referred by Sauvage (1876) to a new species of *Megalosaurus*, which he named *M. superbus*.

Huene (1923), noting that the teeth in this form resemble those in *Megalosaurus*, but that most of the bones differ, created the new combination *Erectopus sauvagei* to receive the latter material.

Huene diagnosed this genus (and type species) as follows: Femur exceptionally long, greatly curved

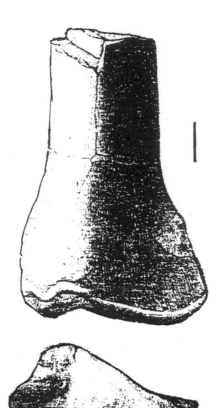

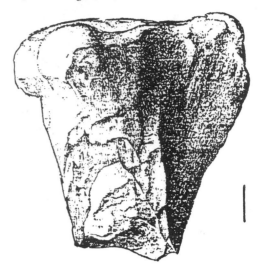

Erectopus sauvagei, syntype proximal end of tibia. Scale = 2 cm. (After Sauvage 1876.)

Erectopus sauvagei, syntype distal end of tibia, caudal and distal views. Scale = 2 cm. (After Sauvage 1876.)

medially; fibular condyle considerably larger than tibial condyle; distal portion of femoral shaft less curved than proximal half; femur apparently straighter than in *Megalosaurus*; tibia with prominent cnemial crest; crista lateralis atypically near proximal end of tibia; metatarsal III almost half length of femur; phalanges of manus very slender; first phalanx of pollex short, bearing a small claw; dorsal centra relatively high.

According to Huene (1926c), *E. sauvagei* has a five-fingered hand (although the manus is not completely known) and is a rather small theropod, the femur measuring 50 centimeters (about 19.5 inches) in length.

Later, Huene (1932) described teeth originally included by Sauvage (1882) in the type material of *M. superbus*, these regarded by Huene (1932) as too large to be associated with *E. sauvagei*. Huene (1932) retained the specific name but did not assign them to any genus. *E. superbus* has come to be regarded as a possible second species of *Erectopus*.

Stromer (1934) referred a femur and tibia (IPHG 1912) from the lower Cenonian of Gebel el Dist, Egypt, to the type species. Lapparent and Zbyszewski (1957) reported a piece of tooth, and two other fragments of tooth and bone, from Boca do Chapim (Cap d'Espichel), Portugal, that may be

referable to *S. superbus*. The tooth has a basal diameter of 20 centimeters (more than 7.75 inches). (This material establishes the occurrence of large theropods in Portugal during the earliest Cretaceous.)

As observed by Kurzanov (1989), the first phalange of manual digit I in *E. sauvagei* is short and massive, the lateral condyle of the femur no larger than the medial condyle. Molnar (1990) added that the manual claws of *E. sauvagei* are small and the relative length of metatarsal III indicates a long foot. According to Molnar, the figures published by Sauvage reveal odd skeletal elements, including the femoral head displaced caudally from the midline of the shaft; also, Sauvage mentioned (but did not illustrate) a presumed jaw fragment with a coronoid process. These features are unknown in other theropods. Molnar pointed out that neither the femur nor tibia display any "carnosaurian" features, while the distal tibia is virtually identical to that of *Poekilopleuron bucklandii*.

Key references: Huene (1923, 1926c); Kurzanov (1989); Lapparent and Zbyszewski (1957); Molnar (1990); Sauvage (1882); Stromer (1934).

ERLIKOSAURUS Barsbold and Perle 1980
Saurischia: Theropoda: Tetanurae: ?Coelurosauria: Therizinosauroidea: Therizinosauridae.
Name derivation: Mongolian "Erlik [lamaist deity, king of the dead]" + Greek *sauros* = "lizard."
Type species: *E. andrewsi* Barsbold and Perle 1980.
Other species: [None.]
Occurrence: Bayenshirenskaya Svita, Omnogov, Mongolian People's Republic; ?Bayan Shireh,

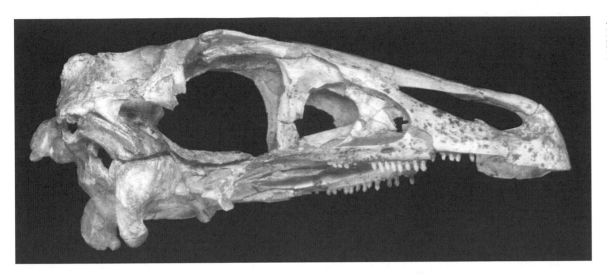

Erlikosaurus andrewsi, GI 100/111, holotype skull, right lateral view. (After Clark, Perle and Norell 1994.)

Khara Khutul, Mongolia; ?Dinosaur Park Formation, Alberta, Canada.

Age: Late Cretaceous (?Cenomanian or ?Turonian).

Known material: Skull, pes, fragmentary postcrania, ?pelvic girdle.

Holotype: GI 100/111, skull with mandible, left humerus, pedes, and disarticulated cervical vertebrae.

Diagnosis of genus (as for type species): Medium-sized "segnosaurid" [=Therizinosaur] with laterally compressed pedal unguals (Barsbold and Perle 1980).

Comments: The genus *Erlikosaurus* was established on a skull and some postcranial remains (GI 100/111), collected from the Bayan Shireh [Baynshirenskaya Svita] suite, Baysheen Tsav, southeastern Mongolia (Barsbold and Perle 1980). The skull represents the most complete and best preserved skull of any therizinosaurid (Clark, Perle and Norell 1993).

In describing *Erlikosaurus*, Barsbold and Perle observed that, in general morphology of the jaws, teeth, cervical vertebrae, and feet, this genus is quite similar to *Segnosaurus*. *Erlikosaurus* differs from that genus in smaller size, longer edentulous portion of the mandible, greater number of mandibular teeth, and lateral compression of the pedal unguals.

Originally, Barsbold and Perle tentatively assigned *Erlikosaurus* to the Segnosauridae [now Therizinosauroidea; see Russell and Dong 1993; Russell and Russell 1993] because its pelvis was unknown (the unusual structure of the pelvis being a diagnostic character of "segnosaurids"). Later, Barsbold and Maryańska (1990) observed that the mandibular teeth in *Erlikosaurus* are small, straight, and only slightly flattened; at the same time, they assigned this genus both to the Segnosauria and Segnosauridae.

In a preliminary report, Clarke *et al.* noted that the skull of *Erlikosaurus* is similar to that of other known theropods (except *Eoraptor*) in the possession of an intramandibular joint; the braincase has features (*e.g.*, penetration of caudal tympanic recess into paroccipital process; inflated parabasisphenoid; deep subarcurate fossa; fused braincase bones; large forebrainendocast) otherwise known only in birds and some nonbirdlike maniraptorans; as in birds and tyrannosaurids, the articular has a foramen aërum; however, some features are unlike Maniraptora (*e.g.*, prefrontal covers lacrimal; antorbital fossa rimmed; accessory antorbital fenestrae absent; pterygo-palatine fenestra absent; braincase roof flat instead of

Erlikosaurus andrewsi, GI 100/111, holotype left humerus. (After Barsbold and Perle 1980.)

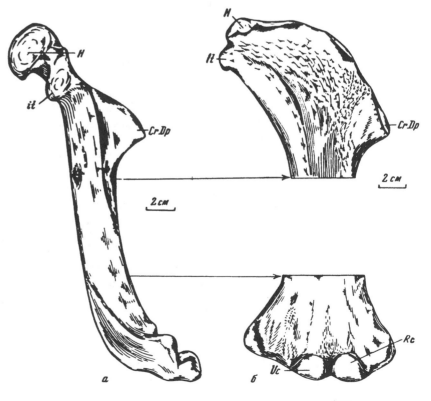

Erlikosaurus andrewsi, GI 100/111, holotype right pes. (After Barsbold and Perle 1980.)

EUCAMEROTUS Hulke 1872 [*nomen dubium*]—(See *Chondrosteosaurus*.)

Name derivation: Greek *eu* = "good" + Greek *kamara* = "vault" + Greek *ous* = "ear."

Type species: *E.* [no specific name assigned] Hulke 1872 [*nomen dubium*].

EUCERCOSAURUS Seeley 1879 [*nomen dubium*]—(See *Acanthopholis*.)

Name derivation: Greek *eu* = "good" + Greek *kerkos* = "tail" + Greek *sauros* = "lizard."

Type species: *E. tanyspondylus* Seeley 1879 [*nomen dubium*].

EUCNEMESAURUS Van Hoepen 1920 [*nomen dubium*]—(See *Euskelosaurus*.)

Name derivation: Greek *eu* = "good" + Greek *kneme* = "tibia" + Greek *sauros* = "lizard."

Type species: *E. fortis* van Hoepen 1920 [*nomen dubium*].

vaulted). Clark *et al.* observed that the skull of *Erlikosaurus* is unlike that of all other known theropods in various features (*e.g.*, great size of inflated parabasiphenoid; small cubconical lanceolate teeth; inset tooth rows; extremely long vomer articulating posteriorly with cultriform process.

According to Clark *et al.*, *Erlikosaurus* lacks cranial synapomorphies of ceratosaurs and "carnosaurs," but shares some features with ornithomimids (*e.g.*, broad, edentulous premaxilla; downturned mandibular symphysis).

Possibly referable to *Erlikosaurus* is an indeterminate pelvic girdle (GI 100/84) missing the upper portions of the ilia, recovered from the Bayan Shireh suite at the Khara Khutul locality in southeastern Mongolia. Barsbold and Perle described the specimen as apparently having broadly separated ilia, anterior wings outwardly deflected; pubic shaft long, narrow, directed posteroventrally, parallel to ischium; pubic "foot" small and narrow, dorsal surface of "foot" with a deep longitudinal depression at symphysis separating pubes; ischium long, with a narrow shaft, and narrow, distally placed obturator process that coossifies with the pubis above distal extremity of the latter. According to Barsbold and Perle, this specimen differs from that of *Segnosaurus galbinensis* in its slightly smaller size and in the structure of the pubis, ischium, and obturator process.

Currie (1992) suggested that a frontal (NMC 12349) from Alberta, Canada, described as belonging to a theropod by Sues (1978), may represent *Erlikosaurus*, and that another, more recently discovered frontal (RTMP 81. 16. 231), from the Dinosaur Park Formation of Dinosaur Provincial Park, Alberta, may also be that of a therizinosaur [=segnosaurid of their usage].

Key references: Barsbold and Perle (1980); Barsbold and Maryańska (1990); Clark, Perle and Norell (1993); Currie (1992); Sues (1978).

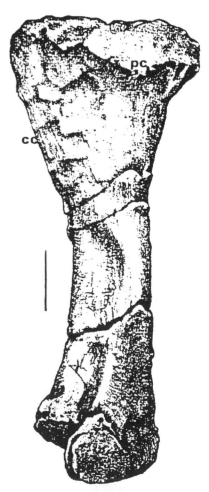

Euskelosaurus browni, PMU.R119, holotype left tibia of *Eucnemesaurus fortis*. Scale = approximately 6 cm. (After Hoepen 1920.)

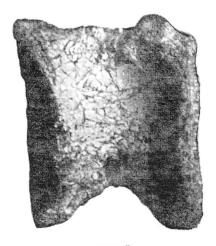

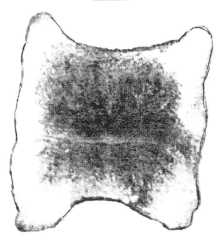

Eucnemesaurus fortis, PMU.R233, cotype centrum of dorsal vertebra, right lateral view, and dorsal vertebra, dorsal view. Scale = 1 cm. (After Hoepen 1920.)

EUHELOPUS Romer 1956—(=*Helopus*; =?*Asiatosaurus*)

Saurischia: Sauropodomorpha: Sauropoda: Camarasauridae: Camarasaurinae.

Name derivation: Greek *eu* = "good" + Greek *helos* = "marsh" + Greek *pous* = "foot."

Type species: *E. zdanskyi* (Wiman 1929).

Other species: [None.]

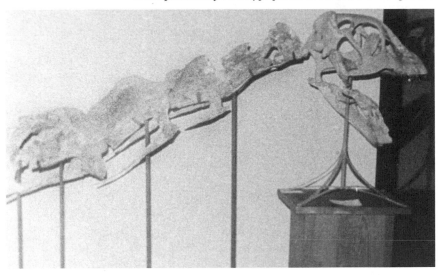

Euhelopus zdanskyi, holotype partial skeleton. (After Dong 1987.)

Occurrence: Men-Yin Formation, Shandong, People's Republic of China.

Age: Late Jurassic (?Kimmeridgian).

Known material/cotypes: PMU.R233, anterior portion of skeleton including incomplete skull with lower jaws, almost complete presacral column, fragmentary coracoid, left femur, and PMU.R234, series of articulated dorsal and sacral vertebrae, pelvis, right femur, tibia, fibula, astragalus, metatarsals I-IV, three phalangeal elements, three unguals.

Diagnosis of genus (as for type species): Skull generally similar to that of *Camarasaurus*, but more delicate; frontal somewhat flat; squamosal resembles that of *Camarasaurus*, almost identical to *Brachiosaurus*; quadratojugal, though more slender, similar to *Camarasaurus* and *Brachiosaurus*; lacrimal

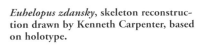

Euhelopus zdansky, skeleton reconstruction drawn by Kenneth Carpenter, based on holotype.

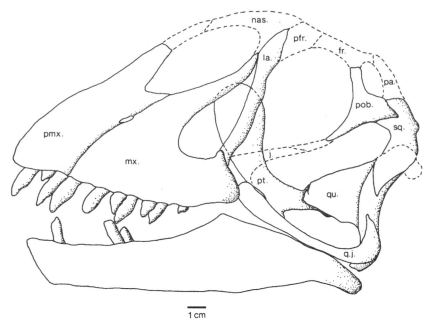

Euhelopus zdanskyi, PMU.R233a, holotype reconstructed skull, left lateral view. (After Mateer and McIntosh 1985.)

1 cm

slender, straight; teeth directed anteriorly (precise position unknown); vertebral column almost 8.3 meters (29 feet) long, consisting of 17 cervical and 14 dorsals (formula closest to *Mamenchisaurus*, with 19 cervicals and 11–12 dorsals); neck extremely long; neural spines bifurcated widely with small process between spines of shoulder region (similar to diplodocids); humerus to femur ratio higher (0.99) than in any known sauropod except *Brachiosaurus*, forelimbs as long as hindlimbs (Mateer and McIntosh 1985).

Comments: The genus and species now known as *Euhelopus zdanskyi* was the first Chinese sauropod to be described. Originally named *Helopus*, it was established upon two partial supplementary skeletons (with which were mixed several theropod fragments), collected in 1923 by Otto Zdansky from the Mengyin Group (apparently Late Jurassic; Mateer and McIntosh 1985, based on studies by Chen 1982 of fossil conchostracans), Ninjiagou, Mengyin County, Shandong. The two skeletons were found about 2 to 3 kilometers apart. Wiman designated the first specimen example "a," the second "b."

The genus was first described by Wiman (1929) in his monograph on the dinosaurs of Shantung [now spelled Shandong], China. Huene (1932) made *Helopus* the type genus of the [abandoned] subfamily Helopodinae. Noting that the name *Helopus* was preoccupied (Wagler 1832), Romer (1956) proposed that the genus be renamed *Euhelopus*, at the same time erecting for it the new subfamily Euhelopodinae. Kuhn (1965) later referred

Euhelopus to its own [abandoned] family Euhelopodidae.

Based on both specimens, Wiman first diagnosed *Euhelopus* [=*Helopus* of his usage] (and the type species) as follows: Skull resembling that of *Camarasaurus*; vertebral column atypically long; cervical and dorsal neural spines slightly forked; estimated length of animal about 10 meters (approximately 34 feet).

Yang [originally spelled Young] (1935) later described more dinosaurian remains from the same locality, including a left scapula and coracoid, and right humerus, possibly pertaining to one of Wiman's syntypes. (According to Mateer and McIntosh, some of this material almost certainly belongs to example "a.")

As later pointed out by Mateer and McIntosh, Wiman did not describe all of the *Euhelopus* material and misinterpreted some cranial features. Although Wiman believed that the pes had four digits, metatarsal V was obviously missing, all sauropod hindfeet being pentadactyl.

Noting that *Euhelopus* is camarasaurid-like (especially in the box-like skull, spoon-shaped teeth, and form of the presacral vertebrae), but also exhibits features characteristic of dinosaurs only distantly related to camarasaurids, Mateer and McIntosh did not assign this genus to any particular sauropod family. More recently, McIntosh (1990*b*), in his review of the Sauropoda, noted that the pelvis of *Euhelopus* is similar to that of the cetiosaurid *Omeisaurus*, but with a less robust pubis and broader blade and distal end of the ischium. McIntosh pointed out that *Euhelopus* represents a form possessing characters between *Omeisaurus* and the camarasaurid *Camarasaurus*, and that the skull and tooth characters and beginning of bifurcation of the neural spine suggest that *Euhelopus* belongs in the Camarasauridae. McIntosh also placed this genus into the subfamily Camarasaurinae.

Note: Early life restorations erroneously depicted *Euhelopus* as bipedal, this posture based upon an illustration in Wiman's monograph portraying the animal in a marsh underwater with its forelimbs buoyantly lifted. These subsequent restorations, while retaining the animal's pose, neglected to include the water from the original illustration.

Key references: Huene (1932); Kuhn (1965); Mateer and McIntosh (1985); McIntosh (1990*b*); Romer (1956); Wiman (1929); Yang [Young] (1935).

EUOPLOCEPHALUS Lambe 1910—(=*Anodontosaurus, Dyoplosaurus, Scolosaurus, Stereocephalus*)

Ornithischia: Genasauria: Thyreophora: Ankylosauria: Ankylosauridae.

Name derivation: Greek *euoplo* = "well-protected" + Greek *kephale* = "head."

Type species: *E. tutus* (Lambe 1902).

Other species: [None.]

Occurrence: Judith River Formation, Two Medicine Formation, Montana, United States; Dinosaur Park Formation, Horseshoe Canyon Formation, Alberta, Canada.

Age: Late Cretaceous (Late Campanian–Early Maastrichtian).

Known material: Over 40 skulls (15 partial), isolated teeth, nearly complete skeleton with armor *in situ*, adults and juveniles.

Holotype: NMC 210, upper part of cranium, transverse series of five scutes.

Diagnosis of genus (as for type species): Premaxillae not covered by dermal ossifications; slit-like external nostril facing rostrally, divided by vertical septum; beak with width equal to or greater than distance between caudalmost maxillary teeth; pes with three digits (Coombs and Maryańska 1990).

Comments: The best known of all ankylosaurs in terms of the amount of collected remains, the genus *Euoplocephalus* was founded upon a partial skull and five scutes (NMC 210), collected from the Belly River [now Dinosaur Park] Formation at "Steveville," Alberta, Canada. Lambe (1902) originally described this material as *Stereocephalus tutus*. As that generic name was preoccupied (Arribalzaga 1884), Lambe (1910) subsequently renamed it *Euoplocephalus*.

Lambe (1902) described this genus as follows: Skull (as preserved) strongly convex transversely, moderately so from anteroposteriorly; entire upper surface and vertical sides bearing coossified plates arranged with a degree of bilateral symmetry, plates somewhat small at center and toward the back, larger in front and on sides, mostly five- or six-sided, with surfaces marked by raised and irregular structural cross-hatchings; scutes with irregularly oval basal outline, sharply keeled with sloping sides, fitting together to form an arch with sides that curve both forward and downward; scutes ossified to a thickness of bone constituting inner surface of the scutes-bearing arch; median scute apparently symmetrical, others asymmetrical; sides of scutes scarred by vascular markings.

Following the naming of *Euoplocephalus*, three additional ankylosaurian genera were erected, all later to be recognized as junior synonyms of *Euoplocephalus* but representing various areas of the body. These new taxa, taken together, offered a more complete understanding of the genus:

Dyoplosaurus (type species *D. acutosquameus*) was founded on a fragmentary skull, ilium, ischium, femur, tibia, and greater part of the posterior part of the axial skeleton, including tail and tail club (ROM 784). The specimen was collected in 1920 by a University of Toronto expedition from the badlands of the Dinosaur Park Formation, at "Steveville." Preserved with the skeleton were scutes and skin impressions. This individual had apparently fallen into a prone position when it died. The skeleton provided the first information regarding the structure of the ankylosaurian tail. As measured by Lambe (1924), the skull is about 350 millimeters (13.5 inches) wide. Preserved integument was studded with bony tubercles and large scutes.

Scolosaurus (type species *S. cutleri*) was founded on a well-preserved, almost complete skeleton (BMNH R5161) from the Dinosaur Park Formation, at Red Deer River. This specimen, lacking most of the skull and somewhat flattened dorsoventrally due to postmortem crushing, was described by Nopcsa (1928a). The armor includes large, heavy plates in the neck region; segments bearing six longitudinal rows of blunt spines and ridged plates, with numerous smaller scutes, in the dorsal region; pointed spines and crests in the forelimb region; and spines becoming fewer in number towards the end of the tail, increasing in size and terminating in two large spikes. The holotype skeleton measures 5 meters (almost 17 feet) long and 1.70 meters (about 5.8 feet) wide.

Anodontosaurus was founded upon a skull, left mandibular ramus, and many dermal scutes (NMC 8530), collected by George F. Sternberg in 1916, from the Horseshoe Canyon [then Edmonton] Formation at Morrin, Red Deer River, Alberta (C. M. Sternberg 1929). Charles M. Sternberg incorrectly believed that this specimen represented the first known toothless stegosaur.

Among other taxa referred to *E. tutus*, *Palaeoscincus asper* was based on a tooth (NMC 1349) discovered in 1901 in the Belly River Series below Berry creek, and described by Lambe (1902).

Euoplocephalus tutus, NMC 210, holotype dermal plate (A. side and B. dorsal views) of *Stereocephalus tutus*. Scale = 6 cm. (After Lambe 1902.)

Euoplocephalus tutus, referred skull, right lateral view.

Photo by R. A. Long and S. P. Welles, courtesy American Museum of Natural History.

After reevaluating numerous specimens of the above taxa in collections of the National Museum of Canada [now Canadian Museum of Nature] British Museum (Natural History) [now Natural History Museum, London], American Museum of Natural History, and National Museum of Natural History, Coombs (1978*a*) concluded that they all represented *Euoplocephalus*. Based on known specimens of *Euoplocephalus*, Coombs (1986) postulated a mid–Campanian to mid–Maastrichtian age range for this genus.

From the various specimens referred to *Euoplocephalus*, Carpenter (1982*c*) prepared the first accurate composite skeletal reconstruction and life restoration of this dinosaur (in fact, the first such restoration of any ankylosaur). Carpenter restored

Euoplocephalus with limbs in an upright posture (not splayed out as in earlier depictions) and the tail off the ground. The head is protected by sheets of surface bone. The tough skin is generally studded with small ossicles. Bands of large, variously-shaped plates run across the body in the back and tail regions. Two bands are set over the neck, the first consisting of large, slightly ridged plates, the second of large and blunt spikes. Four bands studded with rows of large, low, keeled plates are on the back behind the neck. The hips are covered by bands bearing disc-shaped studs. Plates of various size are (probably) present in unknown arrangement in the areas of the forelimbs, shoulders, and thighs. The anterior part of the tail has bands with four rows of keeled spikes, the latter becoming progressively smaller, the last two spikes in this series being relatively large. The tail is studded with small nodules of bone but without bands. The tail culminates in a heavy club of bone.

Haas (1960) made a study of the jaw muscles of ankylosaurs based on two undescribed skulls (AMNH 5337 and 5405) probably belonging to *Euoplocephalus*. Haas found that the musculature system in such massive skulls was relatively weak. This suggests that dinosaurs like *Euoplocephalus* probably ate relatively soft vegetation.

Coombs (1978*a*) regarded *Euoplocephalus* as a rather advanced ankylosaurid, noting that pedal digit I (lost in the more primitive ankylosaurid *Pinacosaurus*), including the metatarsal, has been lost in this genus. In both *Euoplocephalus* and *Pinacosaurus*, the nostril is an elongate slit divided by a vertical septum and the premaxillae are not covered by dermal plates. (In the more derived *Ankylosaurus*, the nostril

Euoplocephalus tutus, NMC 8530, holotype skull of *Anodontosaurus lambei*, left lateral view.

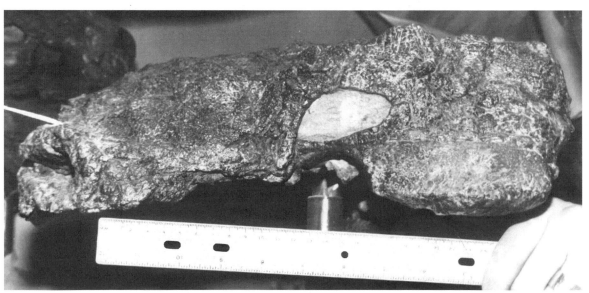

Photo by R. A. Long and S. P. Welles (neg. #73/536-29), reproduced with permission of Canadian Museum of Nature, Ottawa, Canada.

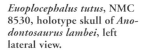

is a small circular opening located far laterally on the snout and the premaxillae are covered by dermal plate.)

Among ornithischians, endocranial anatomy is the most poorly known in ankylosaurs. Coombs (1978*b*) prepared an endocranial cast of *Euoplocephalus* (from skull AMNH 5337) and discovered that the brain was similar to that of other totally quadrupedal ornithischians, but possessed short, divergent olfactory stalks. These stalks, unique among Ornithischia, may have developed according to the general widening and shortening of the ankylosaurid skull. The brain of *Euoplocephalus* had small cerebral hemispheres and a poorly developed cerebellum, primitive characters when compared to the larger cerebrum and cerebellum in orinithischians with bipedal or cursorial habits. Coombs (1978*b*) concluded that differences in the brain of *Euoplocephalus* and other ornithischians may be less the result of brain architecture than of the external shape of the cranium.

Coombs (1986) described a juvenile *Euoplocephalus* specimen (AMNH 5266), consisting of five vertebral centra, neural arch, one dorsal and two sacral ribs, right ischium, complete right hindlimb and pes, almost complete left pes, and various fragments, collected by Barnum Brown, Peter Kaisen, George Olsen and Charles M. Sternberg in 1912 from the Horseshoe Canyon Formation, at Red Deer River.

Photo by R. A. Long and S. P. Welles (neg. #73/536-29), reproduced with permission of Canadian Museum of Nature, Ottawa, Canada.

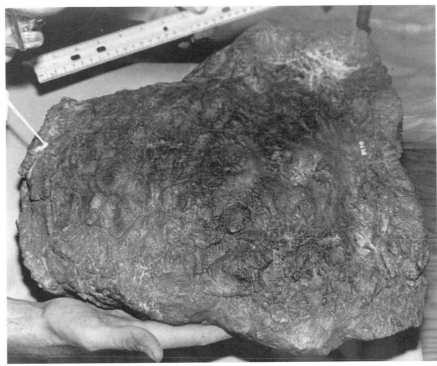

Euoplocephalus tutus, NMC 8530, holotype skull of *Anodontosaurus lambei*, dorsal view.

This specimen includes a relatively complete right and left pes, from which Coombs (1986) presented the first description of the hindfoot in this genus. As described by Coombs (1986), the pes is compact; with

Euoplocephalus tutus, BMNH R5161, holotype skeleton of *Scolosaurus cutleri*.

Photo by the author, courtesy the Natural History Museum, London.

Euoplocephalus tutus, ROM 784, holotype partial skeleton with integument of *Dyoplosaurus acutisquameus*. Scale = 20 cm. (After Parks 1924.)

short, heavily built digits and greatly reduced tarsal elements; toes apparently splayed out; three complete metatarsals with phalanges, but no sign of metatarsals I or V.

Applying Galton's (1982b) list of qualitative differences in postcranial skeletons of juvenile and adult stegosaurs to *Euoplocephalus*, Coombs (1986) observed in the juvenile specimen the following conditions: 1. Lack of fusion between vertebral centrum and neural arches and of sacral ribs to vertebrae and ilium; 2. surfaces of long bones smooth (surface markings and rugosities in subadults and adults); 3. femoral head less spherical and less clearly delimited from adjacent part of the shaft; 4. distal ends of tibia and fibula not fused to astragalus and calcaneum in juveniles and subadults; and, 5. ungual phalanx of manus widest somewhat down from proximal articular end (widest at the proximal end in adults). Coombs (1986) also noted that the juvenile *Euoplocephalus* differs from adults in having less expanded articular faces of the dorsal centra, less compressed and blade-like diapophyses, and a less compressed and flattened ischium.

In their review of the Ankylosauria, Coombs and Maryańska (1990) commented that *Euoplocephalus* is the most common Campanian and Early Maastrichtian ankylosaurid of western North America. The fact that *E. tutus* specimens are usually found as isolated elements or partial skeletons (see Dodson 1971; Béland and Russell 1978) suggested in *Euoplocephalus* solitary habits or small group clusters, although some species could have at least sometimes formed larger groups (see *Pinacosaurus* entry).

Coombs (1995) reviewed the structure and probable functions of the tail club in *Euoplocephalus*, based upon a study of numerous specimens of Late Campanian to Early Maastrichtian age, and assigned to this genus. The material consists of the following specimens collected from the Dinosaur Park Formation, vicinity of Red Deer River, Alberta, Canada: AMNH 5211, major plate, above Tolman, above left

bank of Red Deer River; AMNH 5216, tail club, below Tolman, above left bank; AMNH 5245, sacrum, pelvis, ribs, tail club; AMNH 5405, skull, mandible, predentary, humerus, ulna, terminal caudal plates, south of "Steveville;" CMN 349, tail club; CMN 2251, ?left major plate of tail club, west of mouth of Little Sandhill Creek; CMN 2252 and 2253, partial tail clubs; CMN 40605, distal caudals and tail club, southwestern extremity of badlands of Little Sandhill Creek; ROM 784, holotype of *Dyoplosaurus acutosquameus*, partial skull, mandible, teeth, ilium, tibia, femur, pes, posterior axial skeleton with tail club; ROM 788, tail club with coossified distal caudal vertebrae; probably from the Dinosaur Park Formation, CMN 2234, partial tail club broken into two pieces; from the Horseshoe Canyon Formation, Alberta, Canada: RTMP 71.40.1, isolated major plate; USNM 10753, tail club, northwest of Morrin; and from Montana; USNM 16747, three coossified distal caudal vertebrae, Two Medicine Formation, Blackfeet Indian Reservation, Glacier County; and AMNH 5471, two caudal vertebrae, partial tail club, St. Mary Formation, Two Medicine River, near Holy Family Mission. Coombs also described the smallest known ankylosaurid tail club (ROM 7751), probably belonging to a subadult individual, recovered from the Dinosaur Park Formation of Alberta.

As observed by Coombs, most of these tail clubs can be placed into one of three shape categories—round, bluntly pointed, or elongate. Coombs offered several possible explanations for this diversity:

1. The shape and size of the tail club knob (*i.e.,* the complete set of dermal plates) might be attributable to sexual dimorphism if the club had a sex-linked intraspecific function as in antagonistic behavior. However, sexual dimorphism intimates roughly equal numbers of two distinct size-shape categories, which is not shown by the data; and if the knobs of one sex were generally larger, these might be (but are not) more commonly preserved and found than the small ones.

2. The tail clubs may represent different phases of ontogeny, although growth cannot explain all of the variation. Known clubs cannot be arranged into a convincing single growth series: arranging them by increasing length results in a different sequence than by increasing width or increasing thickness.

3. Some of the variability in the knobs must be attributed to individual variation, the differences in the number and arrangement of minor plates (*i.e.*, small plates that form the posterior terminus of a knob, but sometimes also present between major plates) making virtually every knob unique.

4. The two tail clubs (AMNH 5245 and 5216) with bluntly pointed knobs could represent a genus other than *Euoplocephalus*, although the apparent similarity may be related to the small sample size of these specimens.

Coombs concluded that the variation in tail club morphology "is partially ontogenetic-allometric, partially individual, possibly taxonomic, and doubtfully sexually dimorphic."

In analyzing the length of the hindlimb and tail (from 2100 to 2500 millimeters in an adult *Euoplocephalus*, about twice the length of the hindlimb), and considering the downward angle (about 35 degrees at the first caudal vertebra) of the tail from the hips, Coombs concluded that the tail must have been normally carried above the ground (approximately 178 millimeters). The structure of the caudal vertebrae, made stronger and more rigid by ossified tendons, restricted the flexibility of the tail laterally and especially vertically.

Coombs suggested that the tail was used primarily for defense, swung just above the ground, striking

Euoplocephalus tutus, skeletal reconstruction drawn by Kenneth Carpenter, in a. lateral and b. dorsal views, c. cross-section at sixth presacral vertebra. (After Carpenter 1982.)

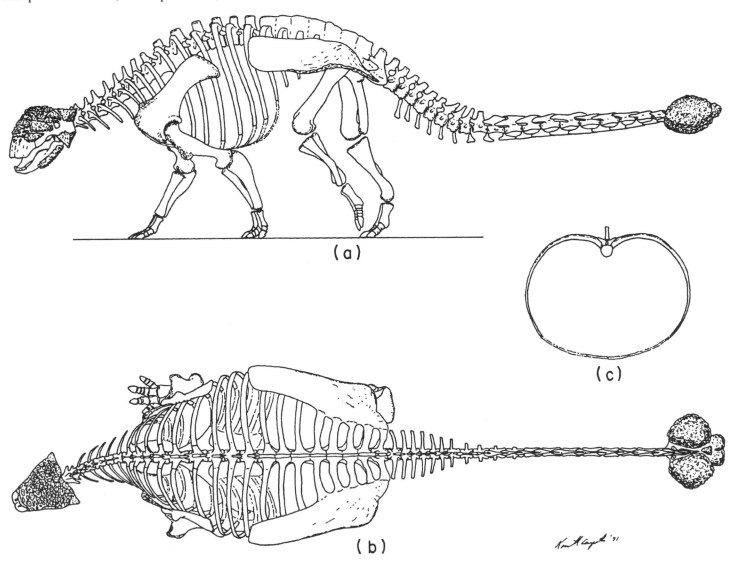

(a)

(c)

(b)

Euoplocephalus

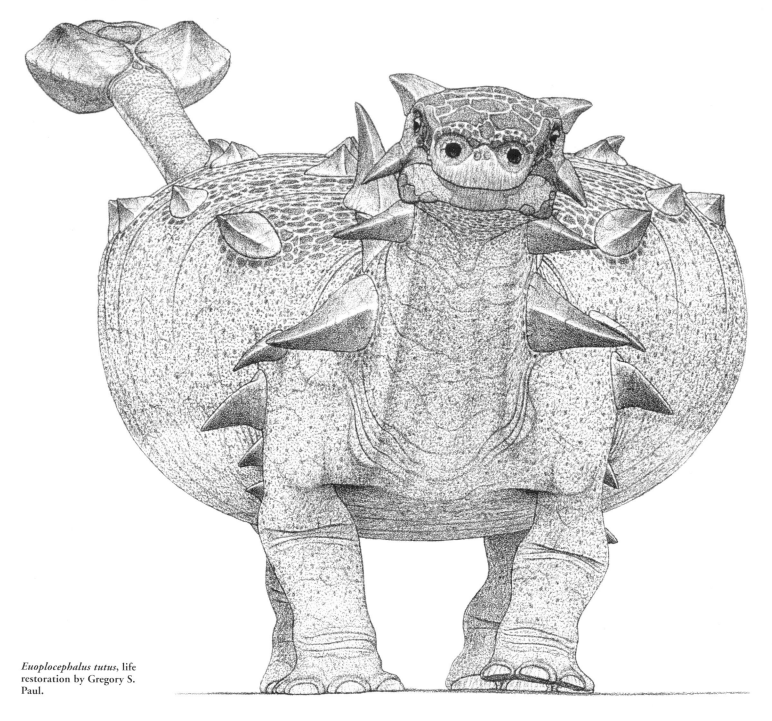

Euoplocephalus tutus, life restoration by Gregory S. Paul.

at the fragile metatarsals of an attacking theropod. The armored knob, the largest known having a mass of 20 kilograms (about 44 pounds), at the end of a 2-meter (about 6.8 feet) lever arm, swung by an animal weighing from 1 to 2 metric tons (1.1–2.25 tons), doing irreparable bone-crushing damage. Coombs discounted the notion of an ankylosaurid swinging its tail against a theropod's thigh, pointing out that the tail lacked sufficient musculature to so raise the tail, and that such a blow would cause little damage to a predator.

Although intraspecific antagonistic functions of the tail were possible, Coombs found the posturing required for such behavior to be clumsy and implausible, noting that no modern tetrapod uses its tail for this purpose.

Note: Maryańska (1977) referred the species *Dyoplosaurus giganteus* Maleev 1956 to new genus *Tarchia*.

Key references: Carpenter (1982c); Coombs (1978a, 1978b, 1986, 1995); Coombs and Maryańska (1990); Haas (1960); Lambe (1902, 1910, 1924); Nopcsa (1928a); Sternberg (1929).

EURONYCHODON   Antunes and Sigogneau-
Russell 1991

Saurischia: Theropoda: Tetanurae:
Avetheropoda: Coelurosauria:
Maniraptora: ?Dromaeosauridae.

Name derivation: "[European form of
Paronychodon]."

Type species: *E. portucalensis* Antunes and
Sigogneau-Russell 1991.

Other species: *E. asiaticus* Nessov 1995.

Occurrence: District of Coimbra, Portugal;
"Northern Eurasia" [*E. asiaticus*].

Age: Late Cretaceous (?Late Campanian–
Maastrichtian).

Known material/holotype: Centro de Estratigrafia e
Paleobiologia da Universidade Nova de Lisboa
collection, number TV 20, tooth; N 9/12454,
holotype [material not known as of this writing]
of *E. asiaticus*.

Diagnosis of genus (as for type species): Small
theropod distinguished by unserrated teeth, with
recurved crown divided into a convex libial face and
flat lingual face, latter crossed by one to several ridges
(subject to strong wear) (Antunes and Sigogneau-
Russell 1992).

Diagnosis of *E. asiaticus*: [Unavailable as of this
writing].

Comments: The genus *Euronychodon* was
founded upon a tooth (Centro de Estratigrafia e Paleobiologia da Universidade Nova de Lisboa collection,
number TV 20), from the Upper Cretaceous (?Late
Campanian–Maastrichtian) sand and clay at the village of Taveiro, District of Coimbra, Portugal
(Antunes and Sigogneau-Russell 1991).

Antunes and Sigogneau-Russell found that their
description of this tooth corresponded most closely
to descriptions of teeth of the North American dromaeosaurid *Paronychodon* published by Carpenter
(1982) and Currie, Rigby and Sloan (1990). Antunes
and Denise Sigogneau-Russell tentatively referred the
type species *E. portucalensis* to the Dromaeosauridae,
considering it to represent a new genus related to
Paronychodon.

The ridges on the ligual side of the tooth are
obliquely striated, evidence, the authors noted, of
wear.

Antunes and Sigogneau-Russell noted that the
tooth of *E. portucalensis* mainly differs from the
North American genus in the absence of longitudinal depressions and a median ridge. As the tooth lacks
serrations (atypical of theropods), the authors quoted
Carpenter who had stated that such denticulations
can be either present or absent on the posterior edge
of the tooth of *Paronychodon*, with no serrations
occurring on the anterior edge.

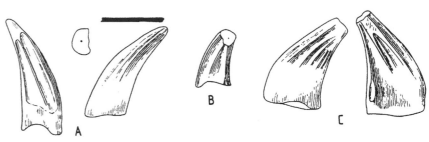

Note: For Antunes and Sigogneau-Russell's
comments on dinosaur extinction regarding *Euronychodon*, see *Taveirosaurus* entry.

Key reference: Antunes and Sigogneau-Russell
(1991).

Euronychodon portucalensis,
A. TV20, holotype tooth in
lingual and labial views, and
cross-section, B. TV19, tooth
in lingual view, C. TV18,
tooth in labial and lingual
views. Scale = 40 cm. (After
Antunes and Sigogneau-Russell 1991.)

EUSKELOSAURUS   Huxley 1866—(=*Eucnemesaurus, Gigantoscelus, Orinosaurus, Orosaurus,
Plateosauravus*)

Saurischia: Sauropodomorpha: Prosauropoda:
Plateosauridae.

Name derivation: Greek *eu* = "good" + Greek *skelos*
= "leg" + Greek *sauros* = "lizard."

Type species: *E. browni* Huxley 1866.

Other species: *E. capensis* (Lydekker 1889) [*nomen
dubium*], *E. molengraaffi* Van Hoepen 1916
[*nomen dubium*], *E. fortis* (Van Hoepen 1920).

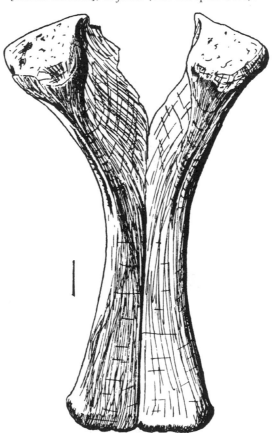

Euskelosaurus browni, SAM
3602-3 and 3607-9, holotype
ischia of *E. africanus*.
Scale = 5 cm. (After
Haughton 1924.)

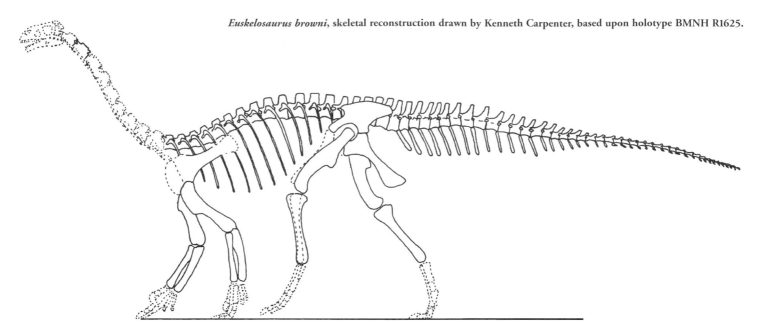

Euskelosaurus browni, skeletal reconstruction drawn by Kenneth Carpenter, based upon holotype BMNH R1625.

Occurrence: Lower Elliot Formation, Orange Free State, Cape Province, Bushveld Sandstone, Transvaal, South Africa; Lower Elliot Formation, Leribe, Lesotho; Mpandi Formation, Matabeleland South, Zimbabwe.

Age: Late Triassic (Late Carnian or Early Norian).

Known material: Seventeen fragmentary skeletons, isolated postcranial elements.

Holotype: BMNH R1625, femur, tibia, fibula, pubis, vertebrae fragments.

Diagnosis of genus (as for type species): Anterior cervical vertebrae low, long, with strong dorsal ridge on postzygapophyses; anterior dorsal vertebrae with a well-developed ventral keel; presacral vertebrae with concave sides; all dorsal and sacral vertebrae with hyposphene-hypantrum articulations; all vertebrae amphicoelous; scapula expanded proximally, with a broad blade; humerus very broad proximally, with well-developed, sigmoidal deltopectoral ridge, measuring 77–79 percent length of femur; distal end of ischium much expanded; acetabulum relatively long, lower end of fourth trochanter at distal half of shaft; long axes of proximal and distal expansions of tibia forming more than 45-degree angle with each other (Heerden 1979).

Comments: The genus *Euskelosaurus* was founded upon partial postcranial remains (BMNH R1625) collected from the lower Elliot Formation (Late Triassic [Late Carnian or Early Norian]; see Olsen and Galton 1984), formerly Stormberg Series, at the base of the Red Beds, in Aliwal North, at Kraai River, Cape Province, South Africa.

Huxley (1866) originally diagnosed *Euskelosaurus* as follows: Dorsal centra high; caudal vertebrae

relatively short; tibia powerfully-developed proximally; femur rather short, with prominent greater trochanter, fourth trochanter at distal portion of shaft; pedal phalanges short and compressed. The holotype of *E. browni* was described by Huxley as representing a large form, the femur one meter (39.37 inches) in length.

Heerden (1979) later reviewed the morphology and taxonomy of *Euskelosaurus*, based on the holotype of *E. browni*, as well as two additional specimens (the latter incorrectly designated paratypes by Heerden) collected from the basal Elliot Formation of Kromme Spruit, Transkei (formerly part of Cape Province), representing the new species *Plateosaurus cullingworthi* (SAM 3341-3356) and *E. africanus* (SAM 3602-3 and 3607-9). Haughton (1924) had considered *E. africanus* to be smaller than *E. browni* (although Heerden found that criterion to be of no diagnostic importance), and *P. cullingworthi* as of heavier build than *Euskelosaurus*. Huene (1932), observing that these two species were based on the remains of more robustly proportioned prosauropods than the European *Plateosaurus*, erected for them the new genus *Plateosauravus*. Heerden regarded both *E. africanus* and *P. cullingworthi* as junior synonyms of *E. browni*.

To *Euskelosaurus*, Heerden referred *Orosaurus capensis* (Lydekker 1889) [*nomen dubium*], *Plateosaurus stormbergensis* Broom 1915 [*nomen dubium*], *Gigantocoelus molengraaffi* Hoepen 1916 [*nomen dubium*], *Eucnemesaurus fortis* Hoepen 1920 [*nomen dubium*], and *Melanorosaurus readi* Haughton 1924, but without determining a species owing to the incompleteness of their holotypes:

Orosaurus capensis was based on a much distorted proximal end of a tibia (BMNH R1626), from the base of the Elliot Formation, probably found with the holotype of *E. browni*. Huxley (1867) originally misidentified this specimen as the distal end of a femur. Huxley named the material *Orosaurus* but did not assign it a specific name. As the genus was preoccupied (Peters 1862), Lydekker (1889b) renamed it *Orinosaurus*. Huene, regarding the type material as indeterminate, referred this species to *Euskelosaurus*.

Gigantoscelus molengraaffi was based on the weathered distal end of a femur (TM 65) from Haakdoornbult 344, Waterberg district, Transvaal, South Africa. Hoepen (1916) considered *G. molengraaffi* to be a distinct genus and species because the femur is somewhat larger than in *Euskelosaurus*, with a narrower sulccus between the two distal condyles.

Eucnemesaurus fortis was based on weathered material including some fragmentary vertebrae, proximal ends of a pubis, femur and tibia, and a distorted but more complete tibia (TM 119), collected from about halfway up the Elliot Formation, at Zonderhout, in the district Slabberts, Orange Free State, South Africa. Hoepen (1920) distinguished *E. fortis* from *E. browni* because of slight differences in the pubis and femur.

Plateosauravus stormbergensis was based on a right femur, metacarpal I, and fragments of vertebrae and the pubis (AMNH 5605), from the base of the Elliot

Formation at Witkop, near Jamestown, Cape Province.

Melanorosaurus readi was later shown by Galton (1985c) to be a valid genus and species distinct from *E. browni*.

Cooper (1980b) referred to *Euskelosaurus* cf. *browni* material from Zimbabwe, Rhodesia, including a tooth, fragmentary dorsal centrum (QG 1363), caudal vertebra (QG 1386), portion of the distal head of the scapula (QG 1370), two ischium specimens (QG 1364 and 1365), distal fragment of a femur (QG 1387), partial tibia (QG 1306), proximal head of fibula (QG 1307), well-preserved metatarsal (QG 1326), and isolated phalanx (QG 1342). The remains were collected by the seventeenth expedition of the Rhodesian Schools Exploratory Society, led by C. K. Cooke and J. Bistow, from the Mpandi Formation of the Karoo succession in the Limpopo Valley. Cooper noted that the find constituted the first substantiated record of *Euskelosaurus* from Zimbabwe, thereby allowing a direct litho-and chronostratigraphic correlation with the lowest part of the Elliot Formation in the main Karoo Basin.

Note: Huene reported fossil footprints (which he named *Ichnites Euskelosauroides*), found in the Cave Sandstone of Lesotho, as possibly those of *Euskelosaurus*.

Key references: Broom (1915); Cooper (1980b); Galton (1985c); Haughton (1924); Heerden (1979); Huene (1932); Huxley (1866); Lydekker (1889b); Van Hoepen (1916, 1920).

Euskelosaurus browni, SAM 3341-3356, holotype right ischium of *Plateosauravus cullingworthi*. Scale = 5 cm. (After Haughton 1924.)

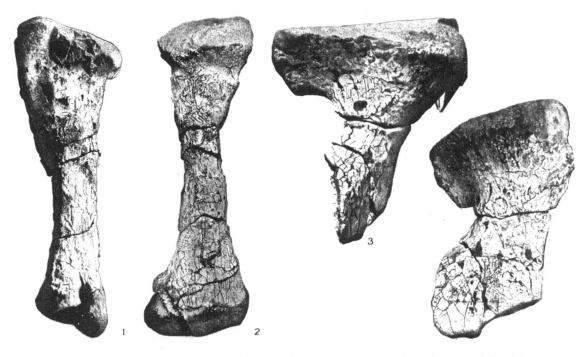

Euskelosaurus browni, TM 119, holotype left tibia (1. lateral and 2. posterior views) and left pubis (3. medial and 4. anterior views) of *Eucnemesaurus fortis*. (After Hoepen 1920.)

EUSTREPTOSPONDYLUS Walker 1964—
(=*Streptospondylus* Owen 1842)

Saurischia: Theropoda: ?Tetanurae: Eustreptospondylidae.

Name derivation: Greek *eu* = "well" + Greek *streptos* = "reversed" [*i.e.,*, "opisthocoelous," or "reversed procoelous"] + Greek *spondylos* = "vertebrae."

Type species: *E. oxoniensis* Walker 1964.

Other species: [None.]

Occurrence: Chipping Norton Formation, Oxford Clay, Oxfordshire, Middle Oxford Clay, Buckinghamshire, England.

Age: Late Jurassic (Late Callovian).

Known material: Disarticulated skull with skeleton, limb elements.

Holotype: UMO J13558, anterior half of anterior dorsal vertebra, part of tooth, various long bone fragments, unidentified bone, subadult.

Diagnosis of genus (as for type species): Skull roof similar to that of *Allosaurus*, but of more primitive construction; frontals, though shortened, longer than wide; prefrontals more anteriorly located and farther apart than in *Allosaurus*; upper part of orbit less compressed (Walker 1964).

Comments: The taxonomic history of *Eustreptospondylus* was chronicled by Walker (1964) in his paper on *Ornithosuchus* and the origin of "carnosaurs":

The species *Streptospondylus cuvieri* was founded on incomplete remains including a partial vertebra, a compressed, cone-shaped, a hollow tooth resembling that of *Megalosaurus*, part of a "broad, flat bone," and various fragments, presumably from the Great Oolite Series (Early Bathonian), near Chipping Norton Limestone, near Oxford, England. Owen (1841) described but did not figure these specimens, which seem to have been lost. Earlier, Cuvier (1836) had described and figured (but did not name) various fossil bones from the Upper Jurassic of Normandy [see *Dryptosaurus* entry]. Although it was generally assumed (because of the specific name) that Owen referred these specimens to *S. cuvieri*, at least the vertebrae, such was not the case.

An incomplete, well-preserved skeleton (UMO J13558) was later collected from the Middle Oxford Clay (Late Callovian) of a Summertown brick pit, in Wolvercote, near Oxford, England. This skeleton was first written about by Phillips (1871). The Oxford skeleton was restudied by Huene (1923), who redescribed it as a new species of *Megalosaurus*, *M. cuvieri*, doubting that the differences between Owen's and this species were great enough to warrant generic separation.

Huene originally diagnosed *M. cuvieri* as follows: Skull differing from *M. bucklandi* in only minor points; cervical vertebrae relatively high and short, dorsals comparatively low; cervicals and anterior dorsals deeply opisthocoelous, less so posteriorly in the series; shoulder girdle, though relatively smaller, resembles that of *M. bucklandi*; humerus more slender, less than half length of femur or tibia; ilium and pubis resembling those of *M. bucklandi*, but with deeper brevis below iliac blade; pubis straight, rod-like, with small terminal expansion; ischium straighter; femur slimmer than in *M. bucklandi*, lesser tro-

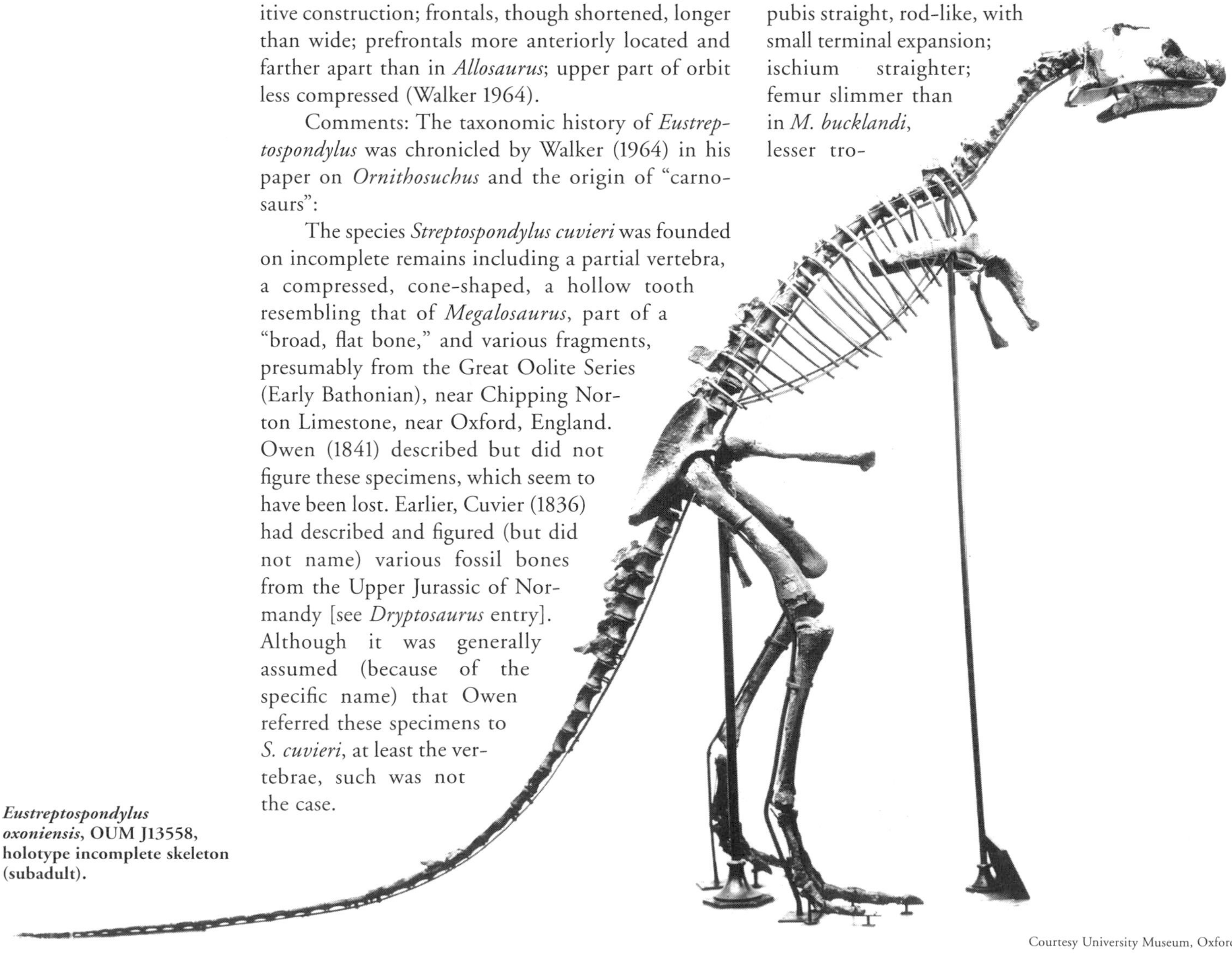

Eustreptospondylus oxoniensis, OUM J13558, holotype incomplete skeleton (subadult).

Courtesy University Museum, Oxford.

chanter more proximal; tibia with well-developed lateral crest; fibula very slender; ascending process of astragalus resembling that of *Poekilopleuron bucklandi*; metatarsals and phalanges more slender than in *M. bucklandi*.

As Walker pointed out, Owen's description of the vertebra indicates only that it is either a posterior cervical or anterior dorsal vertebra of a "carnosaur." This vertebra cannot, therefore, be adequately compared with those of the Oxford skeleton and the Normandy specimens. Considering these points, and because of the lack of figures and the absence of the original type material, Walker regarded *S. cuvieri* as indeterminable. Both the Oxford skeleton and Normandy specimens, then, lacked valid generic and specific names. The Normandy specimens cannot be necessarily grouped together under a single species.

Recognizing the Oxford skeleton as generically distinct from *Megalosaurus*, Walker proposed for it the new genus and species combination of *Eustreptospondylus oxoniensis*. As Walker pointed out, *Streptospondylus* was a *nomen nudum* first introduced by Meyer 1830, who had intended to raise a species of *Steneosaurus*, a fossil crocodile, to the rank of genus bearing this new name. The original name, however, must be retained in such a procedure, *Streptospondylus* thereby becoming a junior synonym of *Steneosaurus*.

The type skeleton of *E. oxoniensis*, mounted at the University Museum at Oxford, is that of a rather small, apparently lightly-built, immature individual animal approximately 5 to 6 meters (16.5 to 20 feet) in length.

Molnar, Kurzanov and Dong (1990) noted that *E. oxoniensis* exhibits various similarities with *Allosaurus fragilis* (*e.g.*, lacrimal ornamentation, enlarged lacrimal foramen, strongly opisthocoelous cervical vertebrae, and a notched astragalus for the calcaneum [see Welles and Long 1974]). As to the differences listed by Walker, Molnar *et al.* pointed out that the condition of the dorsal portion of the orbit is a ?juvenile character; and that other differences, including the "curved" ischium observed by Walker, are dubious.

Molnar *et al.* observed in *E. oxoniensis* the presence of such "carnosaurian" features as the reduced atlantal neural spine and wing-like lesser trochanter of the femur, and the obturator notch of the pubis (as in *A. fragilis*, reported by Walker). Admitting to a possible relationship of *E. oxoniensis* to the ancestry of "Carnosauria," and that this species probably belongs to that taxon, Molnar *et al.* advised against determining its detailed affinities until further study of the material can be made.

Note: The species *S. altodorfensis* Meyer 1832 and *S. lyciensis* Costa 1864 [*nomen dubium*] are croc-odilian (E. Buffetaut, personal communication to Olshevsky). *E. divesensis* Walker 1964 was made the Type species of new genus *Piveteausaurus* by Taquet and Wells (1977). *S. major* Owen 1842 [*nomen dubium*] was referred by Lydekker (1888a) to *Iguanodon bernissartensis*. *S. geoffroyi* Meyer 18?? [*nomen nudum*] and *S. jurinensis* ?Gray 18?? [*nomen nudum*] are nondinosaurian (Chure and McIntosh 1989).

Key references: Cuvier (1836); Huene (1923); Molnar, Kurzanov and Dong (1990); Owen (1841); Phillips (1871); Walker (1964).

FABROSAURUS Ginsburg 1964 [*nomen dubium*]
Ornithischia *incertae sedis*.

Name derivation: [Jean Henri] "Fabre" + Greek *sauros* = "lizard."

Type species: *F. australis* Ginsburg 1964 (Type) [*nomen dubium*].

Other species: [None.]

Occurrence: Upper Elliot Formation, Mafateng District, Lesotho.

Age: Early Jurassic (Hettangian-Pliensbachian).

Known material/holotype: MNHN LES9, posterior portion of right dentary with nine alveolia and three teeth.

Diagnosis of genus (as for type species): Dentary ramus broader than in other "fabrosaurids," with special foramen in medial surface for replacement teeth [see below; Sereno 1991a]; dentary teeth with crowns ranging from triangular to diamond shape (Galton 1978).

Comments: The genus *Fabrosaurus* was founded upon a partial dentary with three teeth (MNHN LES 9), recovered from the upper Elliott Formation (formerly upper Stormberg Series ["Red Beds"]; dated by Olsen and Galton 1984 as Late Jurassic [Hettangian-Pliensbachian]), Mafateng District of Lesotho, in southern Africa.

Ginsburg (1964) originally diagnosed the monotypic *F. australis* as follows: Small dinosaur; teeth with long vertical roots; crowns small, narrow crowns,

Fabrosaurus australis, MNHN LES9, holotype fragment of right dentary, in dorsal and lateral views. Scale = 2 cm. (After Ginsburg 1964.)

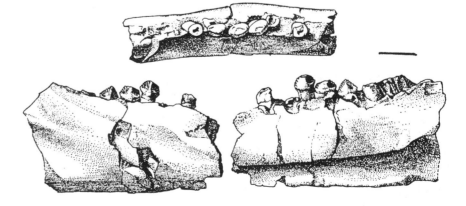

about same size in lateral view, with regular crenellations on anterior and posterior edges.

The teeth measure from 3.3 to 3.5 millimeters in length.

Fabrosaurus was first referred by Ginsburg to the Scelidosauridae. On the basis of referred specimens now called *Lesothosaurus diagnosticus*, Thulborn (1970, 1971, 1972) referred *Fabrosaurus* to the Hypsilophodontidae. Galton (1972), because of the distinct form of this referred material, placed this genus into its own family Fabrosauridae (abandoned; see Weishampel and Witmer 1990*a*).

When Galton (1978) rediagnosed the type species, he believed that the perceived diagnostic characters were sufficient to maintain *Fabrosaurus* as a probably valid genus. However, Sereno (1991*a*) pointed out that the "special foramina," regarded by Galton as a progressive feature, is actually known in all other ornithischians, including *L. diagnosticus*. In reexamining the holotype of *F. australis*, Sereno found Galton's interpretation of a "broader" dentary ramus to be unsupported. Also, Sereno pointed out that the characters noted in Ginsburg's original diagnosis are now known to be present in many ornithischians and seem to be primitive within Ornithischia.

After studying new so-called "fabrosaurid" remains, Gow (1981) questioned the generic separation of *Fabrosaurus* and *Lesothosaurus*, suggesting that the differences between them might be attributed to ontogenetic changes, sexual dimorphism, or the effects of post-burial pressure. Gow concluded that

the *F. australis* holotype could be from an older individual generically identical to *L. diagnosticus*.

In reassessing various primitive ornithischians, Weishampel and Witmer regarded *F. australis* as a *nomen dubium*. Sereno, unable to discern any autapomorphic characters in the holotype dentary or teeth on this species, also regarded it as *nomen dubium*, the specimen indeterminate.

Note: A so-called "fabrosaurid" from Nova Scotia, known only from a scrap of jaw, was mentioned in *Guidebook A59, 24th International Geological Congress* (1972) as being turkey-sized and similar to *Fabrosaurus*.

Key references: Galton (1972, 1978); Ginsburg (1964); Gow (1981); Sereno (1991*b*); Thulborn (1970, 1971, 1972); Weishampel and Witmer (1990*a*).

FRENGUELLISAURUS   Novas 1986—(See *Herrerasaurus*.)
Name derivation: "[Joaquìn] Frenguelli" + Greek *sauros* = "lizard."
Type species: *F. ischigualastensis* Novas 1986.

FULENGIA   Carrol and Galton 1977 [*nomen dubium*]—(=?*Lufengosaurus*)
Saurischia: Sauropodomorpha: Prosauropoda *incertae sedis*.
Name derivation: "[Anagram for] Lufeng."
Type species: *F. youngi* Carrol and Galton 1977 [*nomen dubium*].

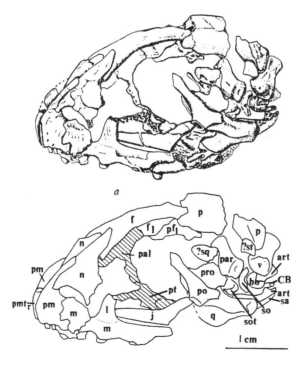

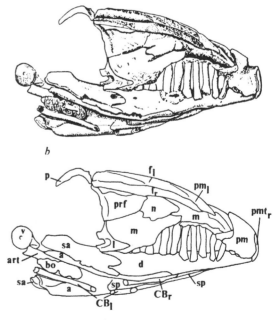

Fulgenia youngi, CUP 2037, holotype skull, in a. left and b. right lateral views. (After Carroll and Galton 1977.)

Fulgurotherium

Other species: [None.]
Occurrence: Lower Lufeng Formation, Yunnan, China.
Age: Lower Jurassic (Hettangian-Pliensbachian).
Known material: Skull, vertebrae, partial upper and lower jaws, bone fragments, representing at least three individuals.
Type specimen: CUP 2037 (now in FMNH collection), skull.

Diagnosis of genus (as for type species): [No appropriate diagnosis published.]

Comments: New genus and species *Fulengia youngi* was named by Carroll and Galton (1977), based upon a small prosauropod skull (CUP 2037) collected by Father E. Oehler, SVD, in 1948 or 1949 (see Simmons 1965), at Ta Ti, Lufeng Basin (Dark Red Beds), Lower Lufeng Formation (dated in a volume published by the Paleontological Institute of Nanking in 1975 as Early Jurassic; see also Olsen and Galton 1977, 1984), near K'un-ming, Yunnan Province, China. The specimen was originally referred to the prosauropod *Yunnanosaurus huangi* (see Simmons).

Carroll and Galton, who placed *Fulengia* into its own family, Fulengidae, described this genus as representing a new and quite primitive lizard, and diagnosed it by the following six lepidosaurian features: 1. Pleurodont teeth with iguanid-like serrations, 2. small lacrimal, 3. posterior jugal process absent, 4. configuration of bones in temporal region and expanded quadrate, 5. median frontal and parietal, and 6. association of those characters with a procoelous vertebra.

Evans and Milner (1989) reidentified this specimen (along with referred specimen CUP 2308) as pertaining to a juvenile prosauropod because the possession of a single supporting synapomorphy (teeth with denticulate blade-shaped crowns). Evans and Milner further suggested that *F. youngi* could be synonymous with *Lufengosaurus huenei*.

Evans and Milner referred to *F. hueni* two additional specimens, discovered in the Lufeng collection and found at Ta Ti the same time as the *F. youngi* holotype, and placed together under CUP catalogue number 2038. These specimens constituted what Evans and Milner designated CUP 2038*a*, made up of various bone fragments including a vertebra and hyoid element, and CUP 2038*b*, including a quadrate, ?exoccipital, maxillary fragments, and dentaries belonging to two different-sized individuals. Both specimens, originally identified as *Y. huangi*, are similar in size and general preservation to the type specimen of *F. youngi*.

As later noted by Sereno (1991*a*), other prosauropod synapomorphies seen in the type skull of

F. youngi include the broad anteroventral process on the nasal and down-turned anterior end of the dentaries. Pointing out that denticulate tooth crowns are plesiomorphic within Prosauropoda, Sereno regarded *F. youngi* as a *nomen dubium*, and specimens CUP 2037 and 2038 as indeterminate prosauropod remains.

Key references: Carroll and Galton (1977); Evans and Milner (1989); Sereno (1991*a*); Simmons (1965).

FULGUROTHERIUM   Huene 1932

Ornithischia: Genasauria: Cerapoda: Ornithopoda: Hypsilophodontidae.
Name derivation: Latin *fulgur* = lightning [Lightning Ridge]" + Greek *theros* = "beast."
Type species: *F. australe* Huene 1932.
Other species: [None.]
Occurrence: Griman Creek Formation, New South Wales, Australia.
Age: Early Cretaceous (Albian).
Known material: Femoral fragments, isolated postcrania, ?teeth.
Holotype: BMNH 3719, distal end of right femur.

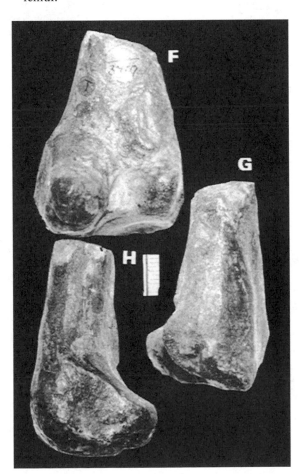

Fulgurotherium australe, BMNH R3719, holotype distal portion of femur, in posterior, lateral, and medial views. Scale in mm. (After Molnar and Galton 1986.)

Fulgurotherium

Diagnosis of genus (as for type species): Femur with distally curved shaft; rod-like lesser trochanter lower than greater trochanter, separated from it by shallow (or no) cleft; anterior intercondylar groove very narrow distally; lateral condyle thin, smaller than the medial (Molnar and Galton 1986).

Comments: *Fulgurotherium* was established upon a partial femur (BMNH 3719) collected from an opal field at Lightning Ridge, New South Wales, Australia. The holotype and other vertebrate fossils from this site were derived from the Wallangulla Sandstone Member of the Griman Creek Formation, which was had apparently been deposited into an estuary (Byrnes 1977), seemingly that of a river that flowed westward into an inland sea (Molnar and Galton 1986).

Huene (1932) originally described the monotypic *F. australe* as follows: Specimen (as preserved) 5 centimeters (about 1.95 inches) long [he could not estimate the complete length]; diameter at distal condyle 35 millimeters (about 1.35 inches).

Huene incorrectly regarded *Fulgurotherium* as a "coelurosaur," a classification it long sustained.

The real affinities of *Fulgurotherium* were not realized until the recovery of six opalized hypsilophodontid femora (QM F10220, QM F10221, QM F12673, AM 66764, AM F66765, and AM F66775) from the Griman Creek Formation at Lightning Ridge. Molnar and Galton pointed out the hypsilophodontid affinities of these specimens, noting that among ornithopods taxonomic assessments can be made on the basis of the femur. The Lightning Ridge femora display characters diagnostic of Hypsilophodontidae, including (as in QM F10220) the fourth trochanter at above mid-shaft.

As the Lightning Ridge femora agree with the holotype of *F. australe* in the structure of the medial condyle and region behind and above the knee-joint, Molnar and Galton referred those specimens to that taxon. Based on a composite of the Lightning Ridge femora and assuming them to belong to the same species, Molnar and Galton diagnosed this species.

Rich and Rich (1989) described various hypsilophodontid specimens, referred to *A. australe*, collected from the Otway Group (see Drinnan and Chambers 1986) in southwestern Australia, an area well located during the Early Cretaceous within the Antarctic Circle. From the Eagles Nest locality of that region, this material included a right femur (NMP P150054) lacking condyles and proximal regions of the head and greater and lesser trochanters; anterointernal third of midshaft with the base of the capitulum of the right femur (NMV P185948); and a partial left femur with capitulum, partial fourth trochanter, and distal end (NMV P187094), missing the shaft between capitulum and fourth trochanter; from The Arch near Kilkunda locality, a left femur (NMV P164998) lacking the head and medial of greater and lesser trochanters;

and from Dinosaur Cove East, Dinosaur Cove, a right femur (NMV P177935) missing its distal fourth with much of the capitulum worn away, and left femur fragment with capitulum, with greater and lesser trochanters worn (NMV P185961), but with the fourth trochanter and all of the bone distal to that point missing.

Notes: Molnar and Galton noted that a seventh femur (AM F66767) from Lightning Ridge may represent another and rarer hypsilophodontid taxon. This specimen differs from the other Lightning Ridge femora by its more distinct anterior intercondylar groove and conical condyles.

Rich and Rich also described other unidentified hypsilophodontid remains from the Otway Group. Labeled as "Victorian Hypsilophodontid Femur Type 1," the material includes two left femora (NMV P185986 and P185995) lacking condyles, and a left femur (NMV P185999), missing the distal tip of the internal condyle and most posterior part of the capitulum, from Dinosaur Cove East; right femur (NMV P186004) lacking most of the condyles and proximal tips of greater trochanter and capitulum, from the Slipper Rock locality; and distal half of a left femur (NMV P187115), either from Slipper Rock or Dinosaur Cove East.

According to Rich and Rich, the distal end of this type of femur differs markedly from femora of *Leaellynasaura amicagraphica* by not being anteroposteriorly compressed to the same degree, and in ridges not extending as far along the shaft proximally; from that of *F. australe*, in the medial condyle projecting much farther posteriorly from the shaft than the lateral condyle, instead of both condyles being subequal in this regard, and also in the absence of a groove external to the lateral condyle. The proximal ends differ from those of all other known hypsilophodontids in that the greater and lesser trochanters are notably expanded anteroposteriorly and compressed mediolaterally into a blade-like structure.

The material called "Victorian Hypsilophodontid Femur Type 2" consists of a very damaged right femur (NMV P156980) missing the head, much of the greater trochanter, tip of the lesser trochanter, and condyles. Rich and Rich noted that this femur is markedly larger than that of other Victorian hypsilophodontids, differing in two ways: 1. The distal end is "twisted" by 45 degrees, and 2. the lateral corner of the shaft changes abruptly rather than gradually from a smooth, rounded surface near the greater and lesser trochanters to a very sharp surface midway between those and the fourth trochanter.

Key references: Huene (1932); Molnar and Galton (1986); Rich and Rich (1989).

GALLIMIMUS Osmólska, Roniewicz and Barsbold 1972

Saurischia: Theropoda: Tetanurae: Avetheropoda: Coelurosauria: Maniraptora: Arctometatarsalia: Bullatosauria: Ornithomimosauria: Ornithomimidae.

Name derivation: Latin *gallus* = "chicken" + Greek *mimos* = "mimic."

Type species: *G. bullatus* Osmólska, Roniewicz and Barsbold 1972.

Other species: [None.]

Occurrence: Nemegt Formation, Omnogov, Mongolian People's Republic.

Age: Late Cretaceous (?Late Campanian or Early Maastrichtian).

Known material: Two almost complete skeletons, complete postcranial skeleton, skull with associated fragmentary postcrania, fragmentary postcrania.

Holotype: GI DPS 100/11, nearly complete skeleton including skull with somewhat distorted snout and well-preserved braincase, incomplete mandible, well-preserved, incomplete cervical vertebrae, fragments of dorsal centra, five sacral centra, almost complete series of 38 caudal vertebrae, fragments of cervical ribs, fragments of dorsal ribs and hemal arches, slightly damaged scapulae and coracoids, almost complete forelimbs, radiale of right manus, incomplete ungual of digit I and incomplete second phalanx of digit II of left manus, incomplete ilium and ischium, nearly complete hindlimb bones, pedal elements.

Diagnosis of genus (as for type species): Presacral vertebral column equal in length to hindlimb; manus (shortest among ornithomimids) 35 percent length of combined humerus and radius; metacarpal I shortest (somewhat shorter than in *Struthiomimus*), adhering to II along about its proximal half, though diverging distally; metacarpal II longest; manual digit II somewhat longer than other two digits; manual unguals relatively short (approximately 19 percent length of manus), rather curved, with strong flexor tubercles; contact between proximal parts of metatarsals II and IV, on extensor side of metatarsus, relatively extensive (Barsbold and Osmólska 1990).

Comments: *Gallimimus* is the largest known ornithomimid and the only member of the Ornithomimidae for which good skull material is known. The genus was founded by Osmólska, Roniewicz and Barsbold (1972) upon an almost complete skeleton (GI DPS 100/11), collected during the Polish-Mongolian Palaeontological Expeditions (Kielan-Jaworoska and Dovchin 1968/1969; Kielan-Jaworoska and Barsbold 1972) from the Upper Nemegt Beds (Gradziński, Kaźmierczak and Lefeld 1969; Grad-

Gallimimus

Courtesy Institute of Paleobiology, Polish Academy of Sciences.

Gallimimus bullatus, skeletons of young individuals, from Tsayan Whushu, Nemegt Basin, Gobi Desert, Mongolian People's Republic, collected during the 1964 Polish Mongolian Palaeontological Expedition.

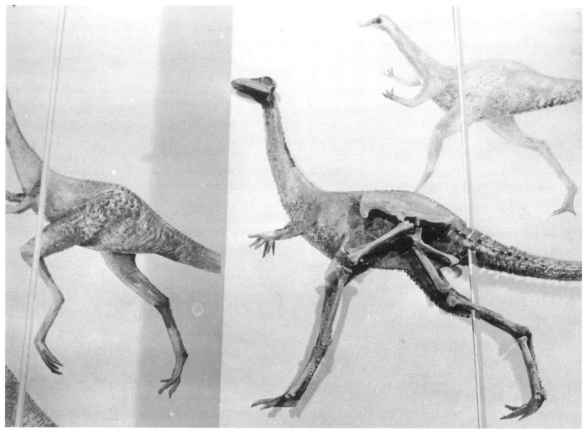

Illustration by Gregory S. Paul.

Gallimimus bullatus group walking their chicks.

Gallimimus bullatus, GI DPS 100/11, holotype skull (cast).

Photo b y Skarzynski, courtesy Institute of Paleobiology, Polish Academy of Sciences.

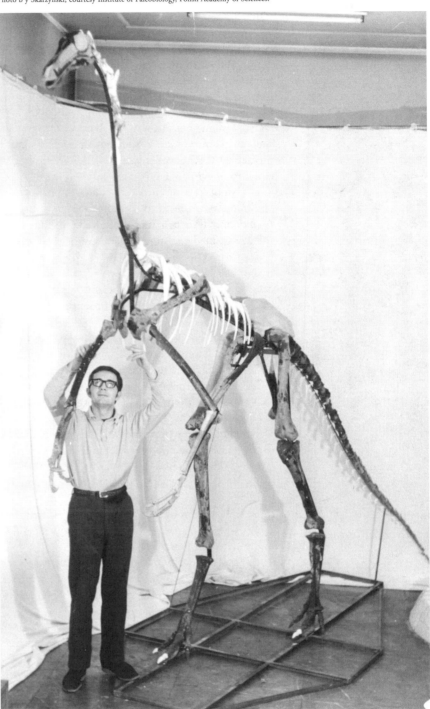

Photo by the author, courtesy The Natural History Museum, London.

ziński and Jerzykiewicz 1972), Gobi Desert, Mongolia.

Osmólska *et al.* based their diagnosis of the monotypic *G. bullatus* on the holotype and other specimens collected from Upper Nemegt Beds during the joint expeditions, including a fragmentary skeleton with skull and mandible (ZPAL Mg.D-I/1), and various isolated elements and fragmentary specimens (ZPAL Mg.D-I/10, ZPAL Mg.D-I/24, and ZPAL Mg.D-I/33) from Tsagan Khushu, (ZPAL Mg.D-I/7, ZPAL Mg.D-I/8, ZPAL Mg.D-I/15, ZPAL Mg.D-I/77, and ZPAL Mg.D-I/94) from Nemegt, (ZPAL Mg.D-I/32 and ZPAL Mg.D-I/74) from Atlan Ula IV, (ZPAL Mg.D-I/78) from Naran Bulak, a nearly complete skeleton with skull (GI DPS 100/10) from Bugeen Tsav, and additional single bones (ZPAL Mg.D-I/: 14, 17, 18, 20, 51, 55, 58, 73

Photo by the author, courtesy The Natural History Museum, London.

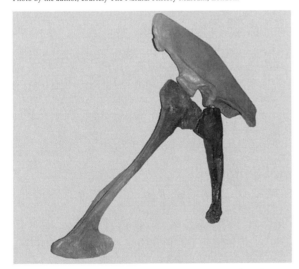

Gallimimus bullatus, GI DPS 100/11, holotype pelvis (cast).

Gallimimus bullatus, GI DPS 100/11, holotype skeleton.

and 75) from different localities within the Nemegt Basin.

Originally, Osmólska *et al.* diagnosed *G. bullatus* as follows: Large ornithomimid species with very long snout flattened dorsoventrally at tip; infratemporal opening subtriangular in outline, jugal not included in borders; exit for third and fourth nerves merging with optic fissure; mandible shovel-like anteriorly, with elongate external openings; presacral vertebral column same length as femur; tibia-astragalus and metatarsal III combined; anteriormost fifteen caudal centra with posterior width exceeding half length; fifteenth and sixteenth caudals constituting boundary between anterior and posterior caudals; humerus longer than scapula; manus about one-fourth length of forelimb; ungual of manual digit III shorter than penultimate phalanx of digit III; metatarsus more than 70 percent as long as shanks; metatarsal II 97 percent length of IV; pedal digit III equal to one-third length of shank.

Osmólska *et al.* discovered an odd, pear-shaped "bulbous structure" in the braincase of two skulls of *G. bullatus*. This structure, hollowed and formed by the thin-walled parasphenoid, opening broadly at the base of the skull, may represent an apparent derivative of the "Rathke's pouch," a sac from the mouth cavity present during the embryonic stage in mammals but otherwise not known in reptiles.

Osmólska *et al.* speculated on the life style of *Gallimimus*: The orbits are very laterally positioned. The snout is reminiscent of the bill of a goose or duck. As shown by the articular surfaces of the cervical vertebrae, the neck was held slightly obliquely, inclining up at about a 35-degree angle to the line of the anterior dorsals. The proximal portion of the neck seems to have been quite mobile. The fingers allowed for limited flexion and extension and the humerus is relatively feeble, implying that the forelimbs were used for raking or digging light material on the ground to acquire food rather than for carrying food to the mouth. All of these features suggest that *Gallimimus* searched the ground for primarily small living prey which it swallowed whole.

The largest *Gallimimus* skull collected (part of the holotype) is 320 millimeters (about 12.5 inches) long, indicating to Osmólska *et al.* a total length for the animal of about 4 meters (13 feet).

Note: *Utan Scientific Magazine* 4 (24), 1988, reported the informally named "Sanchusaurus," based on a partial caudal vertebra from Japan, and possibly representing the largest and oldest known ornithomimid. Dong, Hasegawa and Azuma (1990) referred to this form as *Gallimimus* sp. in *The Age of Dinosaurs in Japan and China*.

Key references: Barsbold and Osmólska (1990); Osmólska, Roniewicz and Barsbold (1972).

Galtonia gibbidens, AMNH 2339, lectotype premaxillary tooth, lingual view. Scale = 1 mm. (After Hunt and Lucas 1994.)

Occurrence: New Oxford Formation, Pennsylvania, United States.
Age: Late Triassic (Upper Carnian).
Known material: Premaxillary teeth.
Lectotype: AMNH 2339, almost complete premaxillary tooth.

Diagnosis of genus (as for type species): Ornithischian that differs from others (except *Fabrosaurus australis*) in possessing narrow, elongate premaxillary teeth (width/height ratio = 2.5/6.5) with denticulated margins that are nearly symmetrical in lingual view; distinguished from *F. australis* in lacking thinner mesial than distal margins (Sereno 1991) and in being less recurved (Thulborn 1970) (Hunt and Lucas 1994).

Comments: As chronicled by Lucas and Hunt (1994), a new species of *Thecodontosaurus*, *T. gibbidens*, had been erected by Cope (1878*g*) upon syntypes, comprising teeth collected by C. M. Wheatley from strata now referred to the New Oxford Formation, near Emiggsville, York County, Pennsylvania, and which Huene (1921) incorrectly implied were found in the Lockatong Formation at Phoenixville, in Chester County, Pennsylvania. Although Cope did not establish a holotype for this material, Hunt and Lucas designated the almost complete tooth (AMNH 2339) figured by Huene as the lectotype, pointing out that two teeth are included in this catalogue number, the second being a broken premaxillary tooth now lacking most of the upper half of the crown. The third syntype (AMNH 2327) consists of a premaxillary tooth. At the same time, Hunt and Lucas made *T. gibbidens* the type species of a new genus, *Galtonia*.

Hunt and Lucas noted that these teeth, originally believed to be those of a prosauropod, were identified by Peter M. Galton as those of an ornithischian. The teeth differ from those of type species *Thecodontosaurus antiquus* (see Galton 1984) in being bulbous and asymmetrical (narrow and symmetrical in *Thecodontosaurus*) in mesial or distal aspects and in having a broad, ovoid basal (narrow-basal in *Thecodontosaurus*) cross-section.

As measured by Hunt and Lucas, the lectotype tooth has a height of up to 6.5 millimeters, basal-crown width of 2.5 millimeters, and basal-crown length of 5 millimeters.

Key references: Cope (1878*g*); Hunt and Lucas (1994).

GALTONIA Hunt and Lucas 1994
Ornithischia *incertae sedis*
Name derivation: "[Peter M.] Galton."
Type species: *G. gibbidens* (Cope 1878).
Other species: [None].

GARUDIMIMUS Barsbold 1981
Saurischia: Theropoda: Tetanurae: Avetheropoda: Coelurosauria: Maniraptora: Arctometatarsalia: Bullatosauria: Ornithomimosauria: Garudimimidae.

Name derivation: "Garuda [in Hindu mythology, a heavenly bird, part eagle and part man, symbolic of strength and speed]" + Greek *mimos* = "mimic."

Occurrence: Baynshirenskaya Svita, Omnogov, Mongolian People's Republic.

Type species: *G. brevipes* Barsbold 1981.

Other species: [None.]

Age: Late Cretaceous (Cenomanian–Turonian).

Known material/holotype: GI 100/13, incomplete skull, fragments of axial skeleton, pelvis, incomplete hindlimbs.

Diagnosis of genus (as for type species): Infratemporal fenestra less reduced and quadrate more vertical than in other ornithomimid species; pubis longer than ilium; tibiotarsus approximately 3 percent shorter than femur; pes tetradactyl, retaining short digit I; metatarsus compact, relatively short and stout, only slightly more than half length of tibiotarsus, width about 22 percent of length; pedal phalanges short, robust (Barsbold and Osmólska 1990).

Comments: Basis for the family Garudimidae Barsbold 1981, *Garudimimus* was established upon an incomplete skeleton with partial skull (GI 100/13), collected from the Bayan Shireh Suite (Baynshirenskaya Svita Bayshin-Tsav), in southeastern Mongolia (Barsbold 1981).

Barsbold originally diagnosed *Garudimimus* as follows: Ilium with high anterior portion and markedly narrow and slender flange; tarsal element III united with proximal surface of metatarsal III.

According to Barsbold, the unconstricted metatarsal III and development of prominent pedal digit I distinguishes *Garudimimus* from all other known ornithomimosaurs. The skull is quite similar to that of *Gallimimus* in the development of the basisphenoid capsule. An unusual feature of the skull is a small backwardly-directed horn anterior to the orbit.

Key references: Barsbold (1981); Barsbold and Osmólska (1990).

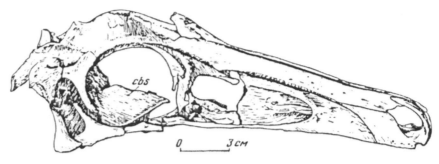

Garudimimus brevipes, GI 100/13, holotype skull. (After Barsbold 1981.)

GASOSAURUS   Dong and Tang 1985—

(=?*Kaijangosaurus*)

Saurischia: Theropoda: Tetanurae: *incertae sedis.*

Name derivation: "Gas [company]" + Greek *sauros* = "lizard."

Type species: *G. constructus* Dong and Tang 1985.

Other species: [None.]

Occurrence: Lower Shaximiao Formation, Sichuan, People's Republic of China.

Age: Middle Jurassic (Bathonian–Callovian).

Known material/holotype: IVPP V7265, postcrania including four cervical, seven dorsal, five sacral, and seven caudal vertebrae, part of limb, left pelvic girdle.

Diagnosis of genus (as for type species): Small "megalosaur" with approximate length of 3.5 meters (12 feet); teeth of megalosaurid form; cervical vertebra platycoelus, with incipient weak ventral keel; five, strongly-fused sacral vertebrae with nonfused neural spines; distal end of pubis and ischium forming somewhat expanded process lacking a "foot" (Dong and Tang 1985); femoral head extending more medially than in other taxa (possibly pathological or due to distortion); lesser trochanter of femur well above proximal end of shaft, leaving sulcus between it and

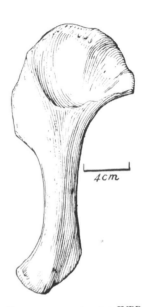

Gasosaurus constructus, IVPP V7265, holotype humerus. (After Dong and Tang 1985.)

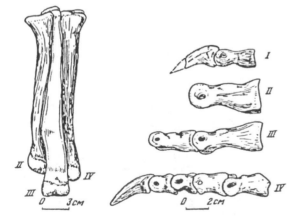

Garudimimus brevipes, GI 100/13, holotype left metatarsus (flexor side) and left pedal digits. (After Barsbold 1981.)

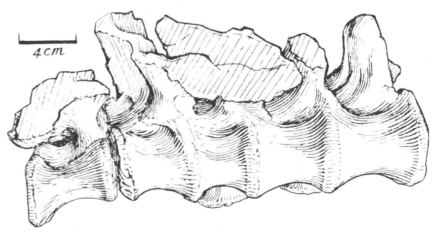

Gasosaurus constructus, IVPP V7265, holotype sacrum. (After Dong and Tang 1985.)

Gasosaurus

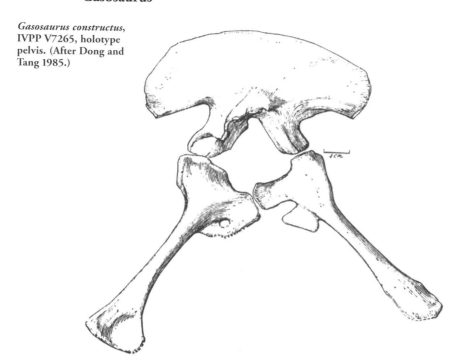

Gasosaurus constructus, IVPP V7265, holotype pelvis. (After Dong and Tang 1985.)

femoral head; ilium short, with strongly-arched dorsal margin (Molnar, Kurzanov and Dong 1990).

Comments: The genus *Gasosaurus* was established on an incomplete postcranial skeleton (IVPP V7256), found in a large sandstone block collected from the dinosaurian quarry of Dashanpu, Lower Shaximiao Formation, Zigong, Sichuan Basin, China. The paratype comprises three teeth (Dong and Tang 1985).

Dong and Tang considered *G. constructus* to belong to the Megalosauridae, then regarded as "carnosaurian," but more recently also tentatively grouped with the Ceratosauria (see Britt 1991). Molnar, Kurzanov and Dong (1990) observed that the elevation of the femoral head is this taxon's only apparent "carnosaurian" feature.

In his book *Dinosaurs from China,* Dong (1987) envisioned *Gasosaurus* as an active predator.

The type skeleton, the missing elements hypothetically restored, was part of the world-traveling exhibit of Chinese dinosaurs in 1987.

Key references: Dong and Tang (1985); Molnar, Kurzanov and Dong (1990).

Gasosaurus constructus, reconstructed skeleton including holotype IVPP V7265, temporarily exhibited at the National Museum of Wales.

Photo by the author.

GENUSAURUS Accarie, Beaudoin, Dejax, Friès, Michard and Taquet 1995

Saurischia: Theropoda: Ceratosauria *incertae sedis*.

Name derivation: Latin *genu* [shortened form of *geniculum*] = "little knee" + Greek *sauros* = "lizard."

Type species: *G. sisteronis* Accarie, Beaudoin, Dejax, Friès, Michard and Taquet 1995.

Other species: [None].

Occurrence: Haute-Provence, France.

Age: Early Cretaceous (Middle Albian).

Known material/holotype: MNHN, Bev. 1, left ilium, proximal end of right pubis, right femur, proximal ends of right tibia and fibula, tarsal element, centrum of sacral vertebra, seven centra of dorsal vertebrae.

Diagnosis of genus (as for type species): Ceratosaur characterized by extreme development of cnemial crest of tibia (Accarie, Beaudoin, Dejax, Friès, Michard and Taquet 1995).

Comments: The new type species *Genusaurus sisteronis* was based upon a partial postcranial skeleton (MNHN, Bev.1) discovered in marine Middle Albian outcrops at Bevons, 4,250 kilometers southwest of Sisteron (Alpes de Haute-Provence), France (Accarie, Beaudoin, Dejax, Friès, Michard and Taquet 1995).

The specimen was identified by Accarie *et al.* as ceratosaurian by the following characters: 1. Pubic shaft bowed forwards; 2. pubis and ischium fused; 3. trochantric shelf marked on anterior trochanter of femur; 4. deep sulcus along side of base of crista tibiofibularis; and 5. deep sulcus on medial surface of proximal end of fibula.

The authors observed that the pubis and ischium resemble those of ceratosaurians *Sarcosaurus woodi* and *Rioarribasaurus colbertii* [=*Coelophysis bauri* of their usage]. Also, they suggested that the hypertrophy of the tibial cnemial crest could be explained by the forward inclination of the femur, this morphology being similar to that of the femur in the extant bird *Struthio* and extinct *Aepyornis*.

Accarie *et al.* noted that the discovery of this new ceratosaur in the Cretaceous indicates that the spatial and temporal distribution of different dinosaurian taxa is yet far from being completely known (although the Late Cretaceous taxon Abelisauridae is generally regarded today as belonging in Ceratosauria).

As pointed out by Accarie *et al.*, the type specimen was found lying in a detric level associated with oysters and silicified wood fragments, and was associated with an abundant microflora comprising pollen and spores. The latter indicates the nearness of the seashore, the presence of a wooded country consisting primarily of ferns and conifers, and a temperate-to-warm and somewhat humid paleoenvironment on the nearby continent.

Key reference: Accarie, Beaudoin, Dejax, Friès, Michard and Taquet (1995).

GENYODECTES Woodward 1901—
  (=?*Loncosaurus*)

Saurischia: Theropoda *incerta sedis*.

Name derivation: Greek *genyos* = "jaw" + Greek *dektes* = "biting."

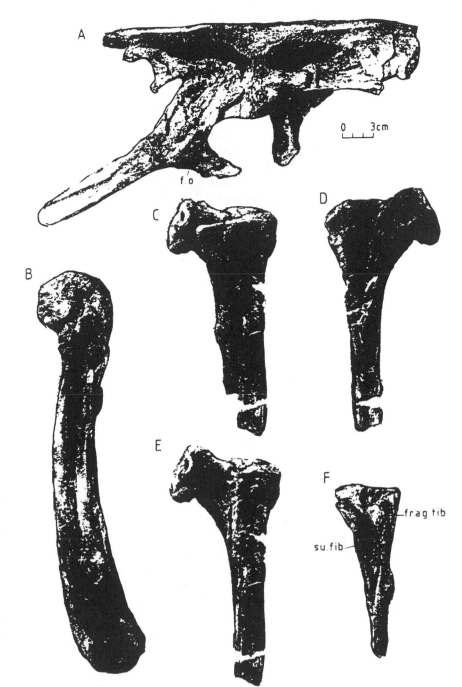

Genusaurus sisteronis, MNHN, Bev. 1, holotype A. left ilium and left proximal pubis, lateral view; B. left femur, lateral view; C. left tibia and fibula, lateral view; D. left tibia, medial view; E. left tibia, lateral view; F. left fibula, medial view. (After Accarie, Beaudoin, Dejax, Friès, Michard and Taquet 1995).

Type species: *G. serus* Woodward 1901.

Other species: [None.]

Occurrence: [Unnamed formation], Chubut, Argentina.

Age: ?Late Cretaceous.

Known material: Incomplete skull, ?postcrania.

Holotype: MLP 26–39, partial skull including premaxillae, portions of maxillae and dentaries, lower jaws with most teeth in position.

Diagnosis of genus: [None published.]

Comments: The genus *Genyodectes* was established on an incomplete, brittle and very fractured skull (MLP collection) from the "areniscas rojas" (?Upper Cretaceous) of Canadon Grande, Chubut, Argentina.

Woodward (1901) described the dentary teeth as relatively small, none being larger than any premaxillary tooth.

Later, Huene (1926) reported postcranial remains that may belong to *Genyodectes*.

Bonaparte, Novas and Coria (1990) observed that the holotype skull of *G. serus* shows significant similarities to that of *Carnotaurus*, but lacks sufficient diagnostic characters to identify it with or differentiate it from *C. sastrei*. (Although *Genyodectes* is regarded as of Middle or Upper Cretaceous age, the geographic and stratigraphic provenance that yielded the type specimen of *G. serus* is not precise, so that Bonaparte *et al.* were unable to date it more accurately than Jurassic or Cretaceous.)

Molnar (1990) observed that, although sometimes classified with the Tyrannosauridae, *Genyodectes* displays no characters diagnostic of that family (premaxillary teeth not D-shaped in cross-section).

Note: Bonaparte and Powell (1980) reported isolated theropod teeth from the Lecho Formation, El Brete, southern Salta province, Northwestern Argentina, similar to those of *G. serus* or the species *Majungasaurus crenatissimus*, though positive identification of these specimens was not possible even at the family level.

Key references: Bonaparte, Novas and Coria (1990); Huene (1926); Molnar (1990); Woodward (1901).

GERANOSAURUS Broom 1911 [*nomen dubium*]

Ornithischia: Genasauria: Cerapoda: Ornithopoda: Heterodontosauridae.

Type species: *G. atavus* Broom 1911 [*nomen dubium*].

Other species: [None.]

Name derivation: Greek *gerabodes* = "crane-like" + Greek *sauros* = "lizard."

Occurrence: Clarens Formation, Cape Province, South Africa.

Age: Early Jurassic (Hettangian-Pliensbachian).

Known material: Partial skull, ?incomplete postcrania.

Holotype: SAM 1871, skull fragments including anterior portion of mandible with fairly complete dentary and almost perfect predentary, portions of premaxilla and maxilla.

Diagnosis of genus: [None published.]

Comments: *Geranosaurus* was founded upon badly crushed skull fragments (SAM 1871) recovered from the Clarens Formation (Early Jurassic [Hettangian-Pliensbachian]; see Olsen and Galton 1984), Base of Cave Sandstone (formerly upper Stormberg Series), at Barkley Pass, Cape Province, South Africa (Broom 1911).

Broom described *Geranosaurus* as follows: Predentary with concave upper surface, 12 millimeters long, 12 millimeters wide, with sharp outer and anterior edges that once formed horny beak; dentary (as preserved) 73 millimeters long; nine anterior dentary teeth with rounded roots in sockets; maxillary teeth with flat chisel-shaped crowns, outer face feebly ridged; teeth most distinctive in that most anterior [presumably canine] tooth is larger than others, with diameter of 5 millimeters, the others with diameter 3–4 millimeters.

Associated with the type material were some imperfect vertebrae and some slender and birdlike hindlimb bones, including a tibia, fibula, and partial foot. Broom, doubting that these bones all represented a single animal and observing that the vertebrae seemed to be too large for association with the skull, described only the jaw bones, which he designated the holotype of *G. atavus*. (These associated remains have never been identified as belonging to *Geranosaurus*.)

Crompton and Charig (1962) reported that preparation of the *G. atavus* type material confirmed

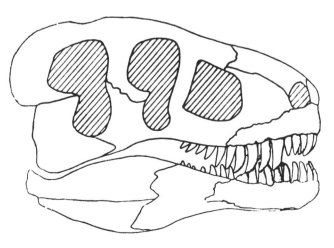

Genyodectes serus, reconstructed skull based on holotype (MLP 26–39) incomplete premaxillae and partial maxillae. (After Bonaparte 1978.)

the presence of a predentary, and also the occurrence in both jaws of caniniform elements and the lack of replacement teeth medial to the functional dentition. They also showed that *Geranosaurus* differs from *Heterodontosaurus* in lacking both a diastema in the upper jaw and a shelf separating the maxillary teeth from the lateral surface of the maxilla.

Weishampel and Witmer (1990*b*), in their review of the Heterodontosauridae, considered *G. atavus* to be a *nomen dubium*.

Key references: Broom (1911); Crompton and Charig (1962); Weishampel and Witmer (1990*b*).

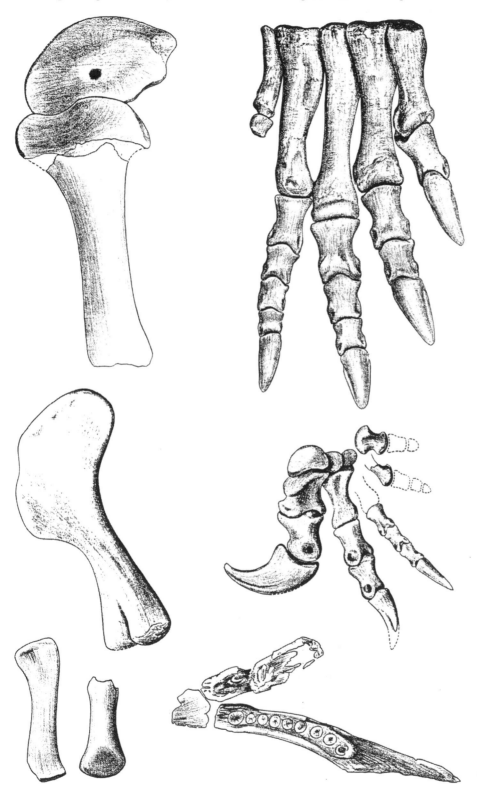

Geranosaurus harriesi, SAFM 1871, holotype scapulacoracoid, pes, humerus, manus, radius, ulna, lower jaws. (After Broom 1911.)

GIGANOTOSAURUS Coria and Salgado 1995
Saurischia: Theropoda: Tetanurae *incertae sedis*.
Name derivation: Latin *gigan* = "giant" + Greek
 notos = "austral" + Greek *sauros* = "lizard."
Type species: *G. carolinii* Coria and Salgado 1995.
Other species: [None.]
Occurrence: Rio Limay Formation, Neuquén
 Province, Argentina, South America.
Age: Late Cretaceous (Albian–Cenomanian).
Known material/holotype: MUCPv-CH-1,
 disarticulated skeleton including partial skull,
 almost complete vertebral column, complete pec-
 toral and pelvic girdles, femora, left tibia and
 fibula.

Diagnosis of genus (as for type species): Main
body of maxilla dorsoventrally wide, dorsal and ventral edges subparallel; supraorbital lacrimal-post-
orbital contact eave-like; two pneumatic foramina in
internal side of quadrate; symphysial end of dentary
dorsoventrally expanded, bearing ventral process;
proximal end of scapula forwardly projected above
coracoid; tubercle-like insertion for triceps in ventral
border of scapula; ischium with lobule-shaped obturator process; femoral head dorsally projected; posterior intercondylar groove in proximal end of tibia
(Coria and Salgado 1995).

Comments: The largest theropod recorded from
the Southern Hemisphere and possibly the largest of
all carnivorous dinosaurs, the type species *Giganotosaurus carolinii* was founded upon an incomplete
skeleton collected from the Candeleros Member, Rio
Limay Formation, Neuquén Group, south of Villa
El Chocón, Neuquén Province, in northwestern
Patagonia (Argentina). The remains were entombed
in floodplain deposits also known to have preserved
abundant sauropod remains (Coria and Salgado
1995).

In their preliminary report on this taxon, Coria
and Salgado noted that this theropod, with its proportionally low skull, reduced shoulder girdle, and
robust vertebrae and hind limbs, "represents a primitive evolutionary iteration of large theropods, and
provides an opportunity to examine the Gondwana
dinosaur palaeocommunities and their relationships
to those from Laurasia."

According to Coria and Salgado, *Giganotosaurus*
shares with the Tetanurae the following unequivocal
synapomorphies: Tibia with fibular crest, anterior
tubercle in fibula, and ascending process of astragalus
more than 20 percent of the tibial length.

As measured by the authors, this giant theropod
totals 12.5 meters (about 42 feet) in length and had
an estimated weight of from 6 to 8 metric tons (about
6.8 to 9 tons). The skull, approximately twice the
size of that of *Abelisaurus*, measures about 1.53 meters
(about 5.2. feet) long. Coria and Salgado speculated
that the enormous size of this genus as well as the
comparably sized and independently evolved *Tyrannosaurus rex* suggest that gigantism may be associated
with common environmental conditions of their
respective ecosystems.

Key reference: Coria and Salgado (1995).

GIGANTOSAURUS Seeley 1869 [*nomen
 dubium*]
Saurischia: Sauropodomorpha: Sauropoda:
 ?Brachiosauridae.
Name derivation: Greek *gigas* = "giant" + Greek
 sauros = "lizard."
Type species: *G. megalonyx* Seeley 1869 [*nomen
 dubium*].
Other species: [None.]
Occurrence: Kimmeridge Clay, Cambridgeshire,
 England.
Age: Late Jurassic (Kimmeridgian).
Known material: Unassociated sacral vertebrae,
 limb elements.

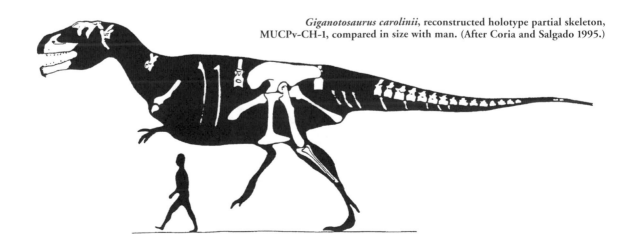

Giganotosaurus carolinii, reconstructed holotype partial skeleton,
MUCPv-CH-1, compared in size with man. (After Coria and Salgado 1995.)

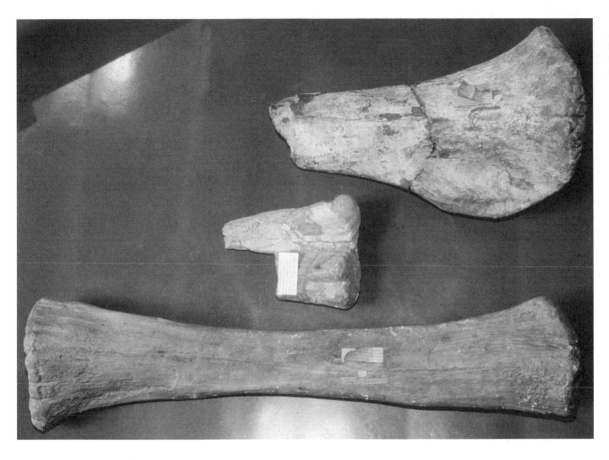

Gigantosaurus megalonyx, cast of BMNH R32498-99, holotype proximal end of tibia, distal end of femur, radius, in Sedgwick Museum.

Courtesy R. E. Molnar.

Holotype: BMNH R32498-99, sacral centrum, cast of fibula, proximal half of tibia, radius, terminal phalanx.

Diagnosis of genus: [No modern diagnosis published.]

Comments: Among the various poorly known sauropods named and described during the early years of dinosaur discoveries, *Gigantosaurus* was established on very incomplete postcranial remains (BMNH R32498-99) collected from the Kimmeridge Clay of Ely, Cambridgeshire, England. Two caudal vertebrae and two casts of a claw-like ungual phalanx were referred to type species *G. megalonyx*. The caudals and phalanx casts were put on display at the British Museum (Natural History) [now Natural History Museum, London]. Hulke (1869) also referred to this species the cast of a large tibia. This material was described (but not figured) by Seeley (1869).

Seeley described the genus (and type species *G. megalonyx*) as follows: One caudal vertebra [tentatively reidentified as cervical] very slightly concave anteriorly, very slightly convex posteriorly; other caudal "hour-glass"-shaped, about 15.5 centimeters (6 inches) long; ungual phalanx much compressed from side to side, articular surface laterally convex and rugose; fibula about 70 centimeters (27 inches) in length, somewhat flattened, curved slightly towards tibia, expanded laterally at rugose articular ends; proximal end of fibula reniform, distal end ovate; tibia portion with rugose sub-rhomboid and flattened articular end.

G. megalonyx is sometimes included in the species *Pelorosaurus humerocristatus* (Steel 1970; Olshevsky 1978, 1989, 1992). Though this taxon may be congeneric with *Pelorosaurus*, *Brachiosaurus* or *Ischyrosaurus*, its material is too poor to make a synonymy or even to identify positively as brachiosaurid (J. S. McIntosh, personal communication 1987).

Note: Fraas (1908), unaware that the name *Gigantosaurus* was preoccupied, used it as the basis for new titanosaurid species *G. robustus*, which Sternfield (1911) later referred to a new genus *Tornieria* and Wild (1991) to the new genus *Janenschia* (see entry). *G. africanus* Fraas 1908 has been referred to *Barosaurus*.

Key reference: Hulke (1869); Seeley (1869).

GIGANTOSCELUS Van Hoepen 1916 [*nomen dubium*]—(See *Euskelosaurus*.)

Name derivation: Greek *gigas* = "giant" + Greek *skelos* = "leg."

Type species: *G. molengraaffi* Van Hoepen 1916 [*nomen dubium*].

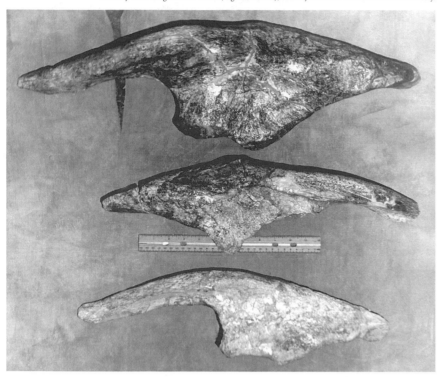

Gilmoreosaurus mongoliensis,
AMNH 6551, holotype ilia.

GILMOREOSAURUS   Brett-Surman 1979

Ornithischia: Genasauria: Cerapoda: Ornithopoda:
  Iguanodontia: Hadrosauridae: Hadrosaurinae.

Name derivation: "[Charles Whitney] Gilmore" +
  Greek *sauros* = "lizard."

Type species: *G. mongoliensis* (Gilmore 1933).

Other species: *G. arkhangelskyi* Nessov and
  Kaznyshkina 1995 [see in Nessov 1995], ?*G.
  atavus* Nessov 1995.

Occurrence: Iren Dabasu Formation, Nei Mongol,
  People's Republic of China; "Northern Eurasia"
  [*G. arkhangelskyi* and ?*G. atavus*].

Age: Late Cretaceous (?Cenomanian–
  ?Maastrichtian).

Known material: Isolated crania, associated disarticulated postcranial remains, representing at
  least eight individuals.

Holotype: AMNH 6551, incomplete cranial and
  postcranial skeleton; N 664/12457, holotype
  fragmentary remains, crania including jaw fragments and teeth, postcrania including vertebrae,
  femur, portions of limbs, of *G. arkhangelskyi*; N
  576/12457, holotype tooth of ?*G. atavus*.

Diagnosis of genus (as for type species): Maxilla
triangular with apex near mid-length; only 29 vertical tooth rows; teeth distinguished by less robust
carina, sharper edge, denticles on all maxillary teeth;
predentary with decided transverse depression crossing ventral surface on anterior side; no posteriorly

directed process developed on median line of predentary; four cervical, ten dorsal, seven sacral, and 33
caudal vertebrae, with relatively short spines without
transverse thickening except at upper extremity; centra relatively short, opisthocoelous, anterior ends
almost flat; two median sacral spines unusually wide
fore and aft (widest 82 millimeters); scapula gently
curved from one end to other horizontally, blade only
moderately expanded; humerus relatively short, stout,
subequal in length with radius; ilium with comparatively shorter and narrower postacetabular extension;
pubis with moderately long neck and gradually
expanded blade (as in hadrosaurines) (Gilmore 1933*a*).

Diagnoses of *G. arkhangelskyi* and *G. atavus*:
[Unavailable as of this writing].

Comments: The material upon which *Gilmoreosaurus* was founded was originally described by
Gilmore (1933*a*) as a tentative new species of *Mandschurosaurus*, *M. mongoliensis*. This species was based
upon cotype specimens (AMNH 6551 and 6371) representing almost all skeletal elements from at least
four adult individuals. The scattered remains were
collected by George Olsen in May 1923, during the
Asiatic Expeditions of the American Museum of Natural History, from the Iren Dabasu [Erlien Dabsu]
Formation (*see in* Granger and Berker 1922; dated as
Late Cretaceous by Gilmore; ?Cenomanian by
Weishampel and Horner 1986; Senonian by Currie
and Eberth 1993) in Mongolia.

Observing basic generic similarities between the
new specimens and the type of *Mandschurosaurus*, yet
failing to see the possibility of suitably comparing
them, Gilmore referred the cotype material to that
genus for "expediency." Gilmore recognized inconsistencies between *M. mongoliensis* and the type
species *M. amurensis*, but did not consider them to
be of generic importance.

Brett-Surman (1975) performed the first extensive analysis of hadrosaur postcrania as their morphology reflects on taxonomy and systematics. Brett-
Surman regarded *Mandschurosaurus* as a *nomen
dubium* (see *Mandschurosaurus* entry) and (1979) recognized *M. mongoliensis* as representing a distinct
genus exhibiting both iguanodont and hadrosaurine
features. Brett-Surman (1979) made *M. mongoliensis*
the type species of new genus *Gilmoreosaurus*, designating AMNH 6551 as the holotype, and noting that
the diagnosis of this species conforms with that of
Gilmore.

According to Brett-Surman (1979), *Gilmoreosaurus* exhibits an early trend from iguanodontid to
true hadrosaurine and represents (Brett-Surman
1989) the most primitive of the Hadrosaurinae (contemporaneous with *Bactrosaurus*, the first true lambeosaurine). Brett-Surman (1979) observed that

Gilmoreosaurus is more lightly built and gracile than contemporary hadrosaurids. The arms, hands, and legs, however, are relatively more robust than in later hadrosaurids, the latter feature suggesting a possible adaptation for good maneuverability during bipedal running. Signs of muscle attachment indicate that *Gilmoreosaurus* had strong legs well suited for rapid acceleration.

Most of the transitional features between iguanodontids and hadrosaurids observed by Brett-Surman (1989) in *Gilmoreosaurus* pertain to the pelvis: Curved ischium with clubbed (but not fully "footed") distal end (as in iguanodontids); ilium with postacetabular process smaller than in other hadrosaurids (except *Claosaurus agilis*), twisted dorsomedially (as in *Secernosaurus*); rudimentary antitrochanter and large, thick pubic peduncle (as in *Bactrosaurus*); and ventrally curved pubic blade (as in true hadrosaurids). In the proximal row of pedal phalanges, the proximal margins of the phalanges are wider than the distal margins. The unguals are more claw-like (as in iguanodontids) than hoof-like (as in hadrosaurids).

Weishampel and Horner, in reevaluating the hadrosaurid dinosaurs from the Iren Dabasu Formation, observed that some of the cranial material originally referred by Gilmore to *Bactrosaurus* represents a hadrosaurine. This material includes two skull portions (AMNH 6365 and 6366) comprising the skull roof and neurocranium. Weishampel and Horner referred these specimens to *G. mongoliensis*, the only hadrosaurine known from that locality.

In their subsequent review of the Hadrosauridae, Weishampel and Horner (1990) noted that *G. mongoliensis* is the second most primitive known hadro-

saurid (after *Telmatosaurus*), apparently sharing with all higher hadrosaurids relatively narrow dentary teeth and a strong single median carina on their enamel face.

Note: According to Pasch (1995), the known geographic range in Alaska for the Hadrosauridae was extended with the discovery of hadrosaur remains in the accreted terrains of the Matanuska Formation, northeast of Anchorage, in southern Alaska. A Turonian age was given to this material, established by the presence of the invertebrates *Mesopuzoia*, *Muramotoceras*, *Gaudryceras*, *Tetragonites*, *Yezoites* or *Otoscaphites*, and *Inoceramus* in the same quarry. Hadrosaurid material includes isolated and articulated vertebrae, and portions of all four limbs (humeri, metatarsals, phalanges, and portions of a tibia, fibula, astragalus, and ulna). The closely associated remains constitute the first assemblage belonging to a single individual found in Alaska. Discovery of this dinosaur in Alaska offers evidence of a Turonian-age link between Asia and North America, and may also provide an evolutionary link between the Iguanodontidae and Hadrosauridae.

Key references: Brett-Surman (1975, 1979, 1989); Gilmore (1933a); Nessov (1995); Weishampel and Horner (1986, 1990).

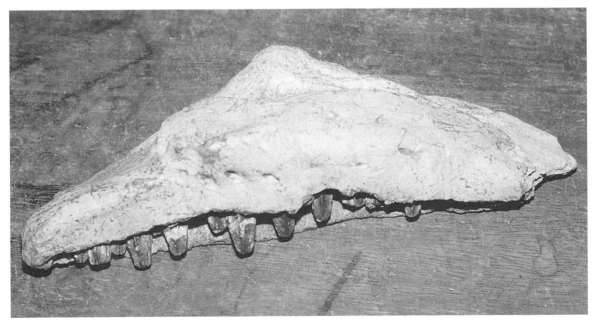

GONGBUSAURUS Dong, Zhou and Zhang 1983 [*nomen dubium*]

Ornithischia *incertae sedis.*

Name derivation: "[Yu] Gong [of Zigong Dinosaur Museum]" + Greek *sauros* = "lizard."

Type species: *G. shiyii* Dong, Zhou and Zhang 1983 [*nomen dubium*].

Other species: *G. wucaiwanensis* Dong 1989.

Occurrence: Shangshaximiao Formation, Sichuan, Sishugou Formation, Xinjianp, China.

Age: Late Jurassic.

Known material: Teeth, fragmentary mandible and associated partial postcrania.

Holotype: IVPP V9069, premaxillary tooth, cheek tooth.

Diagnosis of genus (as for type species): Small, primitive "ornithopod" with pointed, asymmetrical premaxillary tooth; cheek tooth symmetrical, similar to *Fabrosaurus*; both teeth lacking wear surfaces (Dong, Zhou and Zhang 1983); crown of cheek teeth enameled both inside and outside (Dong 1989).

Diagnosis of *G. wucaiwanensis*: Small "ornithopod," 1.3–1.5 meters (about 4.4 to over 5 feet) in length; probably 12–14 dentary teeth; cheek teeth similar to, though larger and thicker, than in *G. shiyi*; prepubis blade-like, with anterior tip process; four distal tarsals; metatarsal III longest and stoutest, about twice length of I; metatarsal I slender, shorter than other metatarsals; metatarsal V reduced to small, rod-like bone, under and fused with IV; digital formula 2,3,4,5, 0 (Dong 1989).

Comments: The genus *Gongbusaurus* was established upon two isolated teeth (CV V9069) collected from the early Upper Jurassic of the Shangshaximiao Formation, at Hunjuoshi, Jungshi (Rongxian), Sichuan Basin, Sichuan Province, China (Dong Zhou and Zhang 1983).

In their review of primitive ornithischians, Weishampel and Witmer (1990*a*) regarded *G. shiyii* as a *nomen dubium*.

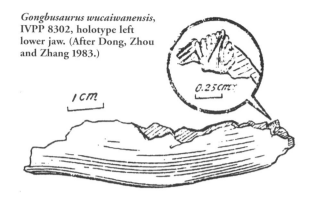

Gongbusaurus wucaiwanensis, IVPP 8302, holotype left lower jaw. (After Dong, Zhou and Zhang 1983.)

Dong (1989) described a second species, *G. wucaiwanensis*, based upon a fragmentary left mandible (with twelve preserved alveoli, and with two replacing teeth in the fourth and twelfth alveoli, two teeth probably missing from the specimen), three caudal vertebrae, and incomplete forelimb (IVPP 8302), from the Shishugou Formation (early Late Jurassic) of Wucaiwan, Kelamali region, Junggar Basin, Xinjianp, China. Two sacral and eight caudal vertebrae, and a pair of complete hindlimbs constitute the paratype specimen (IVPP 8303).

From the structure of the hindlimb and foot, Dong deduced that *G. wucaiwanensis* was cursorial and not arboreal.

Key references: Dong (1989); Dong, Zhou and Zhang (1983); Weishampel and Witmer (1990*a*).

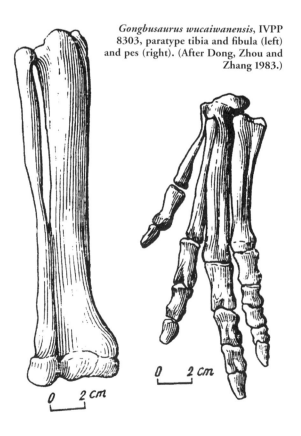

Gongbusaurus wucaiwanensis, IVPP 8303, paratype tibia and fibula (left) and pes (right). (After Dong, Zhou and Zhang 1983.)

Gongbusaurus shiyii, IVPP V9069, holotype teeth. (After Dong 1987.)

GORGOSAURUS Lambe 1914—(See *Alberto-saurus*.)

Name derivation: Greek *gorgos* = "terrible" + Greek *sauros* = "lizard."

Type species: *G. libratus* Lambe 1914.

GOYOCEPHALE Perle, Maryańska and Osmól-ska 1982

Ornithischia: Genasauria: Cerapoda: Margin-ocephalia: Pachycephalosauria: Homalo-cephalidae.

Name derivation: Mongolian *goyo* = "decorated; elegant" + Greek *cephale* = "head."

Type species: *G. lattimorei* Perle, Maryańska and Osmólska 1982.

Other species: [None.]

Occurrence: [Unnamed formation], Ovorkhangai, Mongolian People's Republic.

Age: Late Cretaceous (?Late Santonian or Early Campanian).

Known material/holotype: GI SPS 100/1501, complete skull roof, damaged occiput (comprising fragments of parietals, squamosals, and exoccipitals), basicranial region (basioccipital, with condyle and fragmentary basisphenoid), left postorbital bar, fragments of quadrates and jugals, premaxillae and maxillae with teeth, mandible with teeth, atlas intercentrum, two dorsal spinal processes, sacrum with fragments of neural arches, almost complete caudal series (comprising seven posterior caudals with fragmentary neural arches), ilia with damaged acetabular regions, left humerus, fragmentary left ulna and radius, fragments of indeterminate phalanges, sterna, distal portion of left tibia, proximal portion of ?left fibula, two left distal tarsals, proximal and distal parts of left metatarsals II-IV, distal end of right metatarsal IV, left pedal digit IV (missing phalanx IV-4), right pedal phalanx IV-2, left phalanx II-1, unguals of left digits II and III, many caudal tendons, fragments of thoracic ribs, indeterminable remains.

Diagnosis of genus (as for type species): [Same as Perle, Maryańska and Osmólska 1982 (below), deleting references to maxilla and sacrum] (Maryańska 1990).

Comments: Presumably the oldest known homalocephalid genus and one of the few for which good postcrania is known, *Goyocephale* was founded upon a disarticulated skeleton (GI SPS 100/1501) collected from Upper Cretaceous red sandstones (no precise age determined) of Boro Khovil, west of Dzamyn Khond, South Gobi Desert, Mongolia (Perle *et al.* 1982).

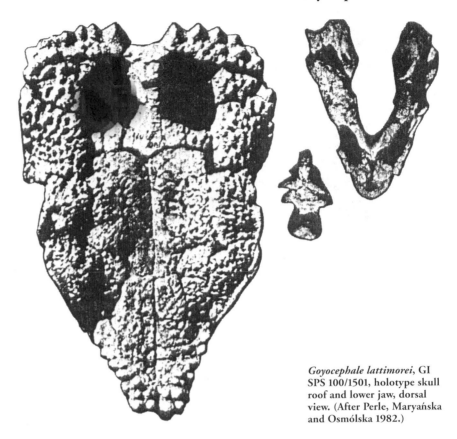

Goyocephale lattimorei, GI SPS 100/1501, holotype skull roof and lower jaw, dorsal view. (After Perle, Maryańska and Osmólska 1982.)

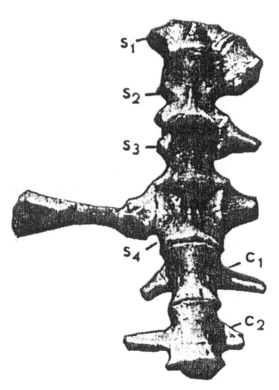

Goyocephale lattimorei, GI SPS 100/1501, holotype sacrum. (After Perle, Maryańska and Osmólska 1982.)

Goyocephale lattimorei, GI SPS 100/1501, holotype articulated caudal vertebrae. (After Perle, Maryańska and Osmólska 1982.)

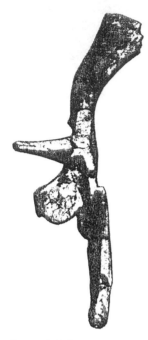

Goyocephale lattimorei, GI SPS 100/1501, holotype ilium. (After Perle, Maryańska and Osmólska 1982.)

Perle *et al.* originally diagnosed the monotypic *G. lattimorei* as follows: Longitudinally oval supratemporal fenestra and narrow interfenestral bridge, the latter about one third transverse width of the fenestra; occiput weakly concave with relatively small occipital condyle; ventral maxillary edge weakly arched laterally along posterior portion; medial portion of skull roof indistinctly ornamented; sacrum with four weakly coossified vertebrae; preacetabular process of ilium with flat dorsal surface bent angularly along medial and lateral margins; medial iliac flange short anteroposteriorly; postacetabular process straight, subrectangular in side view.

As noted by Perle *et al.*, the holotype of *G. lattimorei* is almost the same size as specimens of the pachycephalosaurs *Homalocephale calathocercos* and *Prenocephale prenes*, but differs from the preserved portion of the skull in *H. calathocercos* in having a larger and elongated supratemporal fenestra, narrower interfenestral bridge, narrower portions of the parietals bounding anteriorly the supratemporal fenestrae, less concave occiput with smaller occipital condyle, shallower neurocranium, narrower infratemporal fenestra, and quadrate with an anteroposteriorly narrower mandibular condyle.

Perle *et al.*, observed that both cranial and postcranial characters of *G. lattimorei*, particularly the large supratemporal opening and short sacrum, indicate that this form was more primitive than *H. calathocercos*, perhaps implying that the deposits which yielded the *G. lattimorei* specimen are older than the Nemegt Formation rocks from which *H. calathocercos* was recovered.

Key references: Maryańska (1990); Perle, Maryańska and Osmólska (1982).

GRAVITHOLUS   Wall and Galton 1979
Ornithischia: Genasauria: Cerapoda: Marginocephalia: Pachycephalosauria: Pachycephalosauridae.
Name derivation: Latin *gravis* = "heavy" + Latin *tholus* = "dome."
Type species: *G. albertae* Wall and Galton 1979.
Other species: [None.]
Occurrence: Oldman Formation, Alberta, Canada.
Age: Late Cretaceous (Late Campanian).

Known material/holotype: RTMP 72.27.1, frontoparietal dome.

Diagnosis of genus (as for type species): Very wide and massive frontoparietal dome; parietal with large depression; braincase relatively smaller than in *Stegoceras* (Sues and Galton 1987).

Comments: The genus *Gravitholus* was established on a single frontoparietal dome (RTMP 72.27.1), collected from the Oldman Formation, near Jenner Ferry, Alberta, Canada.

Wall and Galton (1979) originally diagnosed the monotypic *G. albertae* as follows: Skull roof thickened to a very wide dome (comparatively larger than in any known *Stegoceras* specimen); parietal with a large depression and many smaller pits; braincase (compared to even large specimens of *S. validum*) significantly smaller relative to size of dome; dome lacking node-like ornamentation.

As pointed out by Wall and Galton, the relatively small size of the endocranial cavity of the dome is the most important diagnostic feature in *Gravitholus*. Later, in their monograph on North American dome-headed dinosaurs, Sues and Galton (1987) noted that the type species seems to be distinguished from all other contemporaneous pachycephalosaurs by the extreme width of the frontoparietal. Reviewing the Pachycephalosauria, Maryańska (1990) suggested that the shape of the dome in this poorly documented species could be pathologic.

Key references: Maryańska (1990); Sues and Galton (1987); Wall and Galton (1979).

Gravitholus albertae, PMA 72.27, holotype dome, dorsal and lateral views. Scale = 1 cm. (After Wall and Galton 1979.)

GRESSLYOSAURUS Rütimeyer 1857 [*nomen dubium*]—(See *Plateosaurus*.)
Name derivation: "[Amanz] Gressly" + Greek *sauros* = "lizard."
Type species: *G. ingens* Rütimeyer 1857 [*nomen dubium*].

GRYPONYX Broom 1911—(See *Massospondylus*.)
Name derivation: Latin *gryphus* = "curved" + Latin *onyx* = "claw."
Type species: *G. africanus* Broom 1911.

GRYPOSAURUS Lambe 1914—(=?*Hadrosaurus*, ?*Kritosaurus*)
Ornithischia: Genasauria: Cerapoda: Ornithopoda: Iguanodontia: Hadrosauridae: Hadrosaurinae.
Name derivation: Latin *gryphus* = "griffin" + Greek *sauros* = "lizard."
Type species: *G. notabilis* Lambe 1914.
Other species: *G. latidens* Horner 1992.
Occurrence: Oldman Formation, Alberta, Canada, Lower Two Medicine Formation, Montana, United States.
Age: Late Cretaceous (Late Santonian-Early Campanian).
Known material: About ten complete skulls, 12 fragmentary skulls, associated postcrania, almost complete skeleton with partial skull, other material.
Holotype: NMC 2278, skull with associated incomplete postcranial skeleton.

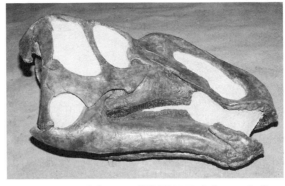

***Gryposaurus notabilis*,** cast of NMC 2278, holotype skull.

Diagnosis of genus: Derived characters of arched nasal located anterior to orbit, circumnarial depression above anterior end of lacrimal, broad posterior nasal processes that insert into frontals at midline (Horner 1992).

Diagnosis of *G. notabilis*: Nasal arch rising above plane of dorsal surface of frontals; posterior ends of external nares with narrow U-shape (Horner 1992).

Diagnosis of *G. latidens*: Dentary extremely wide, short (dorsoventral length to anteroposterior width ratio about 2.1); excavations on ventral surfaces of premaxillae for union of anteroventral maxillary processes of maxilla (Horner 1992).

Comments: The genus *Gryposaurus* was founded upon an incomplete skeleton with skull (NMC 2278), collected in 1913 by George F. Sternberg from

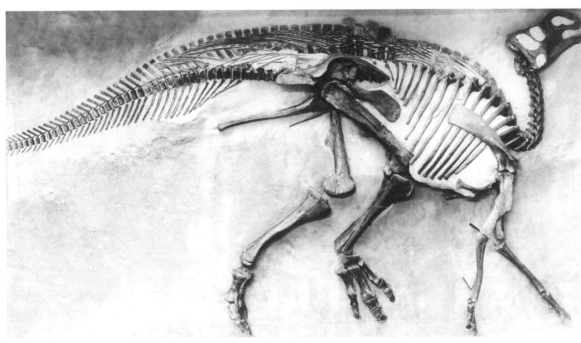

"Gryposaur," ROM 4614, holotype skeleton of *Kritosaurus incurvimanus*.

Gryposaurus notabilis, life restoration by Brian Franczak.

the Belly River Formation (now Oldman Formation) at Red Deer River, Alberta, Canada.

Lambe (1914*b*) originally diagnosed *Gryposaurus* as follows: Large, narrow, very deep skull with highly-arched nostrils; lower anterior border of premaxillae laterally expanded; orbit much smaller than lateral temporal fossa; high quadrate partially separated from jugal by small quadrato-jugal; mandible robust; predentary laterally expanded, deflected in posterior half and posteriorly bifurcated below at midline; anterior dorsal vertebrae with long neural spines; ischia not expanded distally; epidermal scales small, polygonal, nonimbricating, tuberculate, about same size.

Lambe found the most characteristic feature of the skull of this genus to be the nasal bones, which rise to an extraordinary height a short distance anterior to the orbits. The summit of this "hump" is as high as the highest point in the posterior area of the skull. This rise was probably covered in life by skin and may have been a sexual character utilized for identification.

In their classic work on North American duck-billed dinosaurs, Lull and Wright (1942), after com-

paring feature by feature the type skulls of *Kritosaurus navajovius* and *Gryposaurus notabilis*, concluded that these two species belonged in the same genus. Lull and Wright distinguished the so-called "northern" species *G. notabilis* from the "southern" species *K. navajovius* mostly by the former's somewhat smaller skull, relatively shorter quadrate (due either to growth, populational variation, or preservation; M. K. Brett-Surman, personal communication 1988) and laterally expanded predentary.

Waldman (1969) described a poorly-preserved, nearly complete skeleton (NMC 8784) of an immature *K. notabilis* individual from the Oldman Formation, near Sand Creek, above Red Deer River. The specimen lacks the distal forelimb region, has incomplete tibiae and fibulae, and was estimated by Waldman to be 3.3 meters (almost 11.5 feet) when complete. From this specimen, Waldman drew information regarding growth changes in hadrosaurids. In postero-lateral view, the skull is slightly higher compared to length than in an adult, the jaw and jugal less than or about one half the length of that in an adult. The composition of the skull roof differs from that in the adult, the frontal (in an animal otherwise less than half grown) almost three-quarters the length of the adult. Waldman concluded that the greatest rate of lateral growth would have occurred in the postorbital and frontal regions and that broadening of the skull roof did not take place until the animal was approximately half grown.

For nearly half a century, *Gryposaurus* was regarded as a junior synonym of *Kritosaurus*, until Horner (1990) resurrected the former taxon, restricting its use to the species from Alberta, *G. notabilis*, with *K. navajovius* limited to the material from the San Juan Basin of New Mexico. Horner (1990) based this separation mainly on tooth structure. In their review of the Hadrosauridae, Weishampel and Horner (1990) retained the generic name *Gryposaurus*, pointing out that the type species of *Kritosaurus* had been based upon very poor and questionably useful material. Weishampel and Horner (1980), and Brett-Surman (1989), independently grouped both of these genera, together with *Aralosaurus* and *Hadrosaurus*, into an "unnamed taxon" consisting of "gryposaurs" (=Kritosaurini of Brett-Surman). At the same time, Weishampel and Horner speculated that the accentuated nasal arch in *G. notabilis* (and in *Aralosaurus tuberiferus*) was probably used as a broadside weapon in intraspecific contests.

Horner (1992) erected a new species of *Gryposaurus*, *G. latidens*, founded upon an almost complete skeleton with skull (AMNH 5465, tail section formerly AMNH 5467), from the Lower Two Medicine Formation, Pondera County, Montana. Referred by Horner (1992) to this species were numerous elements (MOR 478) from a monospecific bonebed at the same locality. Horner (1992) regarded this species as rather primitive, as the median carina of the dentary teeth are quite wide, and some teeth have carina that are grooved (similar to teeth of primitive hadrosaur *Claosaurus* and of *Iguanodon*).

Skin impressions from the abdomen underlying the pelvis in the holotype of *K. notabilis* show smooth polygonal scales arranged in no particular pattern, averaging about three-sixteenths of an inch in diameter. The neck and sides of the body seem to have had uniform, polygonal-shaped tubercles arranged in apparently random order.

Lull and Wright stated that fossilized integument impressions, preserved in the holotype of *K incurvimanus,* reveal that the skin was quite thin, with limpet-like scutes, either circular or elliptical in shape and distinctly pyramidal. These scutes measure up to 38 millimeters (1.5 inches) in length, 32 millimeters (1.3 inches) in breadth and 8 millimeters (3.1 inches) in height. Associated with this specimen was a dermal element found lying on the midline of the back, over the posterior dorsal and anterior sacral spinous processes. This structure is laterally compressed with a shortened summit and an elliptical base surrounded by a folded-in line of skin. The skin in the immediate vicinity of the scute is covered by simple, low-coned tubercles.

The holotype (NMC 419) of *Trachodon marginatus* Lambe 1902 [*nomen dubium*] (generally regarded as a junior synonym of *G. notabilis*) was preserved with fossil skin. As described by Lull and Wright, the skin features round, limpet-like conical plates in the tail region. These plates are from 5.2 to 6.8 centimeters (2 to 3 inches) apart, separated by small, polygon-shaped tubercles, and are about 1.3 centimeters (.5 inch) in diameter.

Notes: Parks (1919, 1920) described a skull (ROM 764; formerly GSC 4514) from the Oldman Formation, at Sand Hill Creek above Red Deer River, as a new species of *Kritosaurus*, which he named *K. incurvimanus*, distinguished by a smaller and lighter skull. Waldman suggested that this species could represent an immature *K. navajovius*. Weishampel and Horner assessed "*K.*" *incurvimanus* as representing an "unnamed gryposaur." Horner (1992) later determined that this species and *G. notabilis* were distinct taxa. Lucas and Hunt (1993), however, found the cited differences between these species (nasal arch at or above plane of frontals, posterior nares broad or narrow U-shaped) not to be of taxonomic significance.

Hadrosaurus notabilis, a species reported by Horner (1979) from the Bearpaw Shale of both Stillwater County and Wheatland County, Montana, was regarded by Weishampel and Horner as another "unnamed gryposaur."

"Gryposaur," holotype skeleton of "*Kritosaurus*" *australis.*

Photo by F. E. Novas, courtesy Museo Argentino de Ciencias Naturales.

Gyposaurus

Photo by F. E. Novas, courtesy Museo Argentino de Ciencias Naturales.

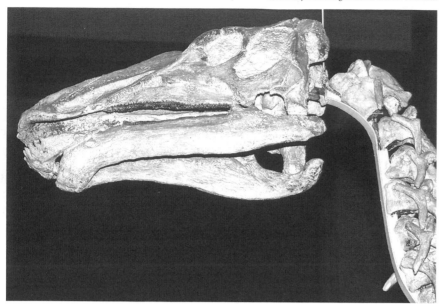

"Gryposaur," holotype skeleton of "*Kritosaurus*" *australis*, detail of skull.

hadrosaurids to roam into South America (see Brett-Surman 1979), while South American titanosaurids were moving into North America. This species was also considered by Weishampel and Horner to represent an "unnamed gryposaur."

The first juvenile hadrosaurid specimen (possibly belonging to *Gryposaurus*) from New Mexico was a fragmentary left dentary (KUVP 96980) with part of the tooth battery, described by Hall (1933). The specimen was discovered in 1985 in the Fruitland Formation (Upper Cretaceous), Fossil Forest area, San Juan County. The specimen, as preserved and measured by Hall, is 79 millimeters, including the symphysis and tooth-bearing portion of the bone.

Key references: Bonaparte (1974, 1985); Brett-Surman (1979); Hall (1993); Horner (1979, 1990, 1992); Lambe (1914b); Lucas and Hunt (1993); Lull and Wright (1942); Parks (1919, 1920); Weishampel and Horner (1990); Waldman (1969).

Bonaparte (1975, 1984) reported about 23 hadrosaurid specimens, including a broken, incomplete skull, several vertebrae, ribs, and scapula identified as a new species of *Kritosaurus*, *K. australis*, from the southeastern Rio Negro of Patagonia. The find supports the idea that a land connection existed during the Cretaceous that allowed North American

GYPOSAURUS Broom 1911—(See *Massospondylus*.)

Name derivation: Greek *gyp* = "vulture" + Greek *sauros* = "lizard."

Type species: *G. capensis* Broom 1911.

Photo by F. E. Novas, courtesy Museo Argentino de Ciencias Naturales.

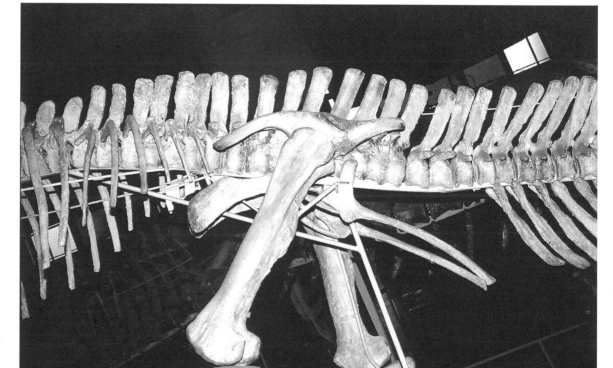

"Gryposaur," holotype skeleton of "*Kritosaurus*" *australis*, detail of pelvic region.

HADROSAURUS   Leidy 1858—(=?*Gryposaurus*, ?*Kritosaurus*)

Ornithischia: Genasauria: Cerapoda: Ornithopoda: Iguanodontia: Hadrosauridae: Hadrosaurinae.

Name derivation: Greek *hadros* = "sturdy" + Greek *sauros* = "lizard."

Type species: *H. foulkii* Leidy 1858.

Other species: *H. minor* Marsh 1870 [*nomen dubium*], *H. cavatus* Cope 1871 [*nomen dubium*], *H. breviceps* Marsh 1889 [*nomen dubium*].

Occurrence: Woodbury Formation, New Egypt Formation, Greensand, New Jersey, Dinosaur Park Formation, Montana, United States.

Age: Late Cretaceous (Campanian).

Known material: Articulated ?postcranial skeleton, teeth, isolated postcranial remains.

Holotype: ANSP 10005, mandibular teeth, postcrania including 28 vertebrae, humerus, radius, ulna, ilium, ischium, femur, tibia, fibula, two metatarsals.

Diagnosis of genus: [No modern diagnosis published.]

Comments: *Hadrosaurus* was the second dinosaur named in North America and the first known from good skeletal material. The type specimen (ANSP 10005) was found just two years after the first fragmentary dinosaur specimens were discovered in South Dakota and Montana.

In 1858, as recounted by Leidy (1858), William Parker Foulke heard of bones that had been excavated from a marl pit on the farm of John E. Hopkins, in Haddonfield, Camden County, New Jersey, some two decades earlier. Hopkins told Foulke that the bones were of large size and quite numerous. Being younger and not particularly interested in such matters, Hopkins had allowed visitors to carry off all of these collected fossil remains without recording who had taken what. Hopkins allowed Foulke to attempt relocating the original pit which was within the Matawan Formation. Found by Foulke and reopened, the pit yielded more remains pertaining to the same kind of animal, including an incomplete postcranial skeleton (ANSP 10005). The bones were all ebony black from the infiltration of iron and were well-preserved. Foulke presented these bones, in addition to fossil shells and wood, to the Philadelphia Academy on December 14, 1858. Leidy, informed of the discovery, visited the excavation, observing similarities between the teeth of the newly recovered specimen and those of the European genus *Iguanodon*, reason for him to assume that both forms were closely related. For the New Jersey material, Leidy erected the new genus and species *Hadrosaurus foulkii*.

Leidy diagnosed *H. foulkii* as follows: Cervical vertebrae opisthocoelous; humerus about 60 centimeters (23 inches) long, ulna about 23 inches long, radius about 52 centimeters (20 inches) [Leidy was impressed by the very great disproportion between the fore- and hindlimbs, which, he commented, was greater than in *Iguanodon*]; femur with large fourth

Photo by the author, courtesy Academy of Natural Sciences of Philadelphia.

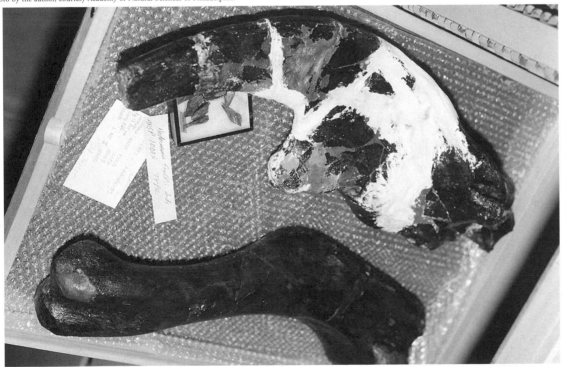

Hadrosaurus foulkii, ANSP 10005, holotype left ilium and left humerus.

Hadrosaurus

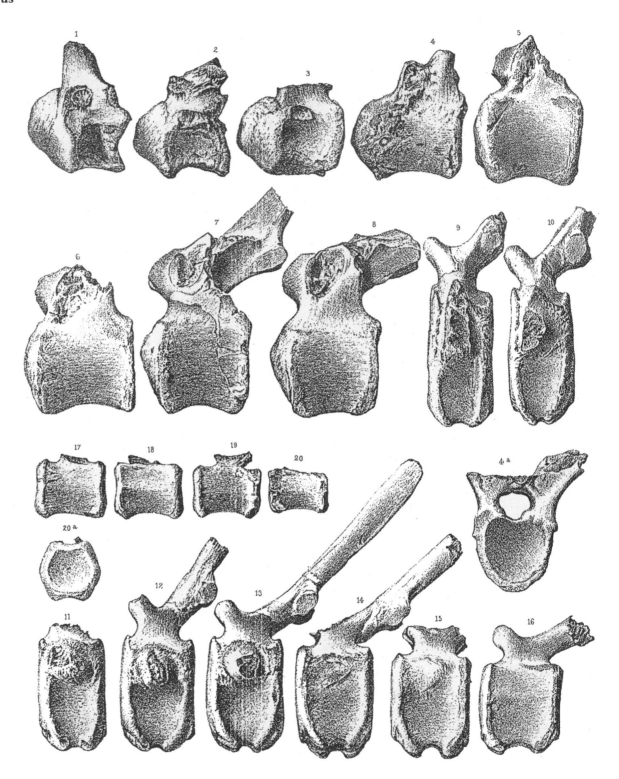

Hadrosaurus foulkii, ANSP
10005, holotype vertebrae.
(After Leidy 1858.)

trochanter at mid-shaft; femur more than 100 centimeters (40 inches) long; tibia with narrow shaft, more than 90 centimeters (36.5 inches) long; metatarsals of robust proportions. Using the modern crocodile and iguana as models, Leidy incorrectly estimated *Hadrosaurus* to have had a total of 50 caudal vertebrae, the entire vertebral series sup-

posedly to have numbered 80. Leidy estimated the length of *Hadrosaurus* to have been about 7.2 meters (25 feet).

At this time, *Iguanodon* was still incorrectly believed to be an entirely quadrupedal animal with a stocky, rhinoceros-like body. Leidy, having more substantial skeletal material to study, arrived at his own,

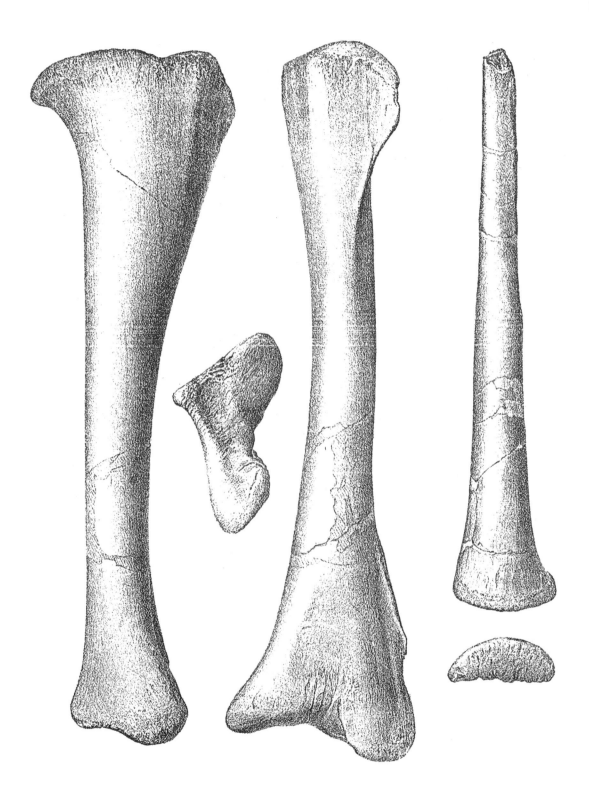

Hadrosaurus foulkii, ANSP 10005, holotype tibia, in internal and external views, and distal end of fibula, external view. (After Leidy 1858.)

more accurate reconstruction of *Hadrosaurus*. With little known during the nineteenth century regarding dinosaur lifestyles, Leidy imaginatively envisioned *Hadrosaurus* as a mostly amphibious animal that spent some of its time on land browsing, maintaining a kangaroo-like erect posture resting on hind legs and tail. (Today hadrosaurs are regarded as basically terrestrial animals; see *Edmontosaurus* entry.) Although inaccurate by modern standards, Leidy's concept was a significant development in the evolution of paleontological theory in depicting *Hadrosaurus* as a biped with an upright posture.

In late 1868, English sculptor Benjamin Waterhouse Hawkins, who had taken up residence in Phila-

Hadrosaurus

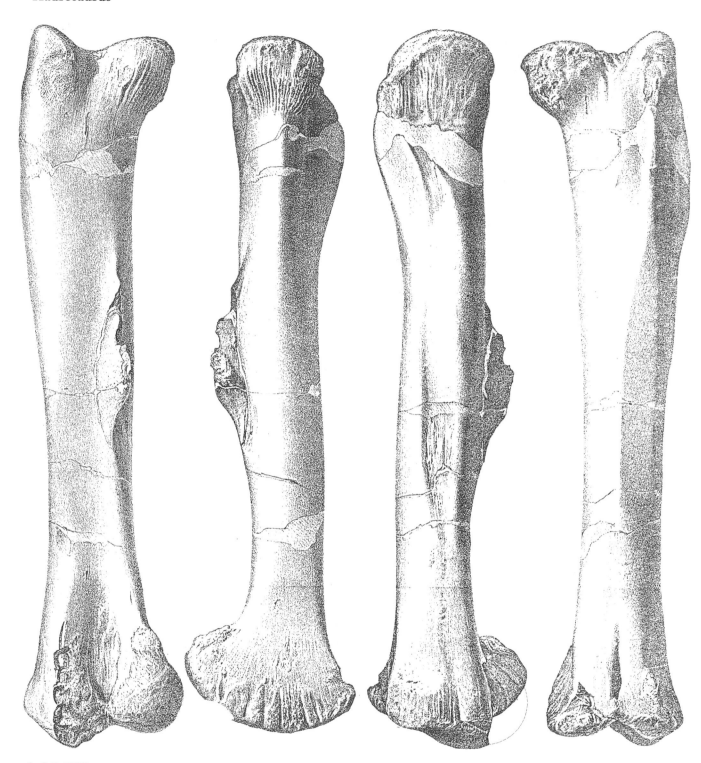

Hadrosaurus foulkii, ANSP 10005, holotype left femur, in posterior, internal, external, and anterior view. (After Leidy 1858.)

delphia, endeavored to mount, at his own expense, the bones of *H. foulkii* for the Academy of Natural Sciences of Philadelphia. Hawkins utilized both supposition and imagination to fill in the missing elements. As dinosaurs were still thought of as huge lizard-like animals and since the teeth in *Hadrosaurus* resembled those in *Iguanodon*, the unknown skull was sculpted to resemble that of a modern day iguana. The posture adopted for the reconstructed skeleton was based upon Leidy's idea of a giant kangaroo-posed animal. Part real bone and part plaster, this specimen became the world's first mounted dinosaur skeleton. Hawkins made four copies of this skeleton for display at other museums.

In later years, after more fossil material similar to *Hadrosaurus* was collected, the genus would become the basis for the family Hadrosauridae Cope 1869 (and also the subfamily Hadrosaurinae Lambe 1918), embracing this group of so-called "duckbilled" dinosaurs, designated as such because their long and flat snouts superficially resemble the beak of a duck.

Other species were later referred to *Hadrosaurus*. *Edmontosaurus minor*, now regarded as belonging in *Hadrosaurus*, was based upon several dorsal and sacral vertebrae (YPM 1600) from the New Egypt Formation of Sewell, New Jersey, collected by Othniel Charles Marsh in 1869. The specimen was briefly "described" by Marsh (1870) as a reptile similar to *H. foulkii,* but only half the size. This species was designated by Lull and Wright (1942) a *nomen nudum* in their classic monograph on North American hadrosaurs; it was later described by Colbert (1948*a*). *H. cavatus* Cope 1871, regarded as a *nomen nudum* by Lull and Wright, was based on four mid-caudal vertebrae (AMNH 1390) from the Greensand of New Jersey. *H. breviceps* Marsh 1889 was based on a fragmentary dentary from the Dinosaur Park Formation, Montana.

Lull and Wright stated that the genus *Hadrosaurus* is difficult to diagnose as the holotype lacks a skull. *Hadrosaurus* had been classified as a flat-headed form, lambeosaurines being unknown at the time its remains were first described. According to Lull and Wright, the most diagnostic evidence supporting the hadrosaurine status of this genus is the maintained slenderness toward the distal end of the ischium and relative length of humerus and radius (latter character shown to be irrelevant by Brett-Surman 1975, 1989).

Notes: Dinosaurian remains from the Black Creek Formation (Campanian), Phoebus Landing, North Carolina, too poor to identify on the generic

Photo by Thomas W. Smillie, thanks to D. Baird, courtesy National Museum of Natural History, Smithsonian Institution.

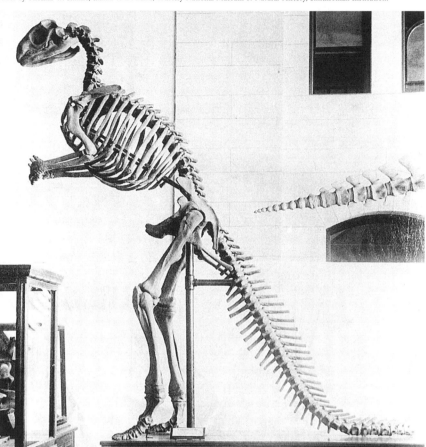

Hadrosaurus foulkii, **cast of restored skeleton (including holotype ANSP 10005), made by Benjamin Waterhouse Hawkins in 1874.**

level, were described and identified as probably hadrosaurid by Baird and Horner (1979). These include two mandibular fragments (ANSP 15306 and USNM 7096) described by Miller (1967), and a right

Hadrosaurus breviceps, **YPM 1779, holotype fragmentary dentary with teeth.**

Photo by J. R. Horner, courtesy D. Baird.

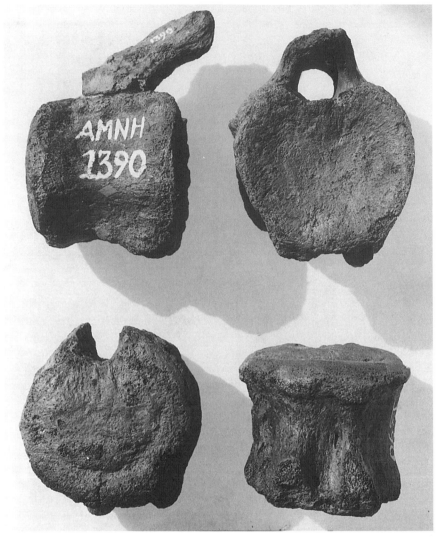

Hadrosaurus cavatus, AMNH 1390, holotype caudal vertebrae.

Photo by D. Baird, courtesy American Museum of Natural History.

coronoid process (ANSP 15329) (described by Miller as a large postzygapophysis) possibly from the same individual as ANSP 15306; two shed (maxillary and dentary) teeth (ANSP 15333) described for the first time by Baird and Horner, the dentary tooth having a diamond-shaped crown measuring 18.0 millimeters high and 8.7 millimeters wide; an incomplete right scapula (ANSP 15322) with nonexpanding blades, originally described by Miller; and two limb bones, a fragment of a small left tibia, and right metatarsal II (USNM 7189) originally referred by Cope (1875*a*) to *Hypsibema crassicauda*. Baird and Horner also described the distal half of a large right humerus (UNC 5735), with proportions similar to those of *Hadrosaurus* and measuring about 415 millimeters (almost 17 inches) long, from the Peedee Formation, mentioned by Brett and Wheeler (1961). This latter, specimen, if complete, would have measured approximately 830 millimeters (almost 33 inches) long,

being the third largest hadrosaurid humerus known. The vertebra once called *H. tripos* Cope 1869, from the Black Creek Formation of North Carolina, was identified by Baird and Horner (1979) as pertaining to a Pliocene whale.

Baird and Horner (1977), observing close affinities between dinosaurs of the New Jersey–Delaware area and those of the Western United States and Canada, suggested that *H. foulkii* and the Western species *Kritosaurus navajovius* belonged in the same genus, the latter becoming new genus and species combination *H. navajovius*. Brett-Surman (1989) favored keeping *Hadrosaurus* and *Kritosaurus* generically separate, at least until a complete skeleton or skull of *Hadrosaurus* can be compared to *Kritosaurus* from the same geologic and ontogenetic age. Brett-Surman could not separate the two forms based on postcrania.

H. paucidens Marsh 1889 [*nomen dubium*] was referred by Ostrom (1964*a*) to *Lambeosaurus*. *H. agilis* Marsh 1872 was made the type species of *Claosaurus* by Marsh (1890).

"Hironosaurus," informally named by Hisa in *Utan Scientific Magazine* 4 (24), 1988, was based on teeth and a ?caudal vertebra found in Japan. Dong, Hasegawa and Azuma (1990), in the dinosaur exhibition guidebook *The Age of Dinosaurs in Japan and China*, regarded this form as an indeterminate hadrosaurid.

Key references: Baird and Horner (1977); Brett-Surman (1975, 1989); Colbert (1948*a*); Leidy (1858); Lull and Wright (1942); Marsh (1870, 1889); Miller (1967).

HALTICOSAURUS Huene 1908

Saurischia: ?Theropoda or ?Sauropodomorpha *incertae sedis*.

Name derivation: Greek *haltos* = "hold" + Greek *sauros* = "lizard."

Type species: *H. longotarsus* Huene 1908.

Other species: *H. orbitoangulatus* Huene 1932.

Occurrence: Stubensandstein, Württemberg, Pfaffenhofen, Germany.

Age: Late Triassic (Middle Norian).

Known material: Fragmentary skeleton, partial skull.

Holotype: SMNS collection, fragments of lower jaw and teeth, three cervical vertebrae, second and third sacral vertebrae lacking spines, two dorsal centra (one half complete), proximal caudal vertebra, two fragments of left ilium, proximal portion of left humerus, metatarsal III, proximal half of right femur, middle portion of left femur with fourth trochanter.

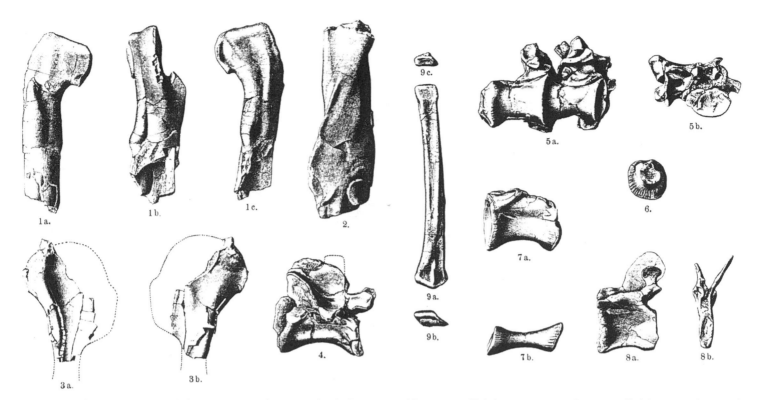

Halticosaurus longotarsus, SMNS, holotype 1. proximal portion of right femur, 2. middle portion of left femur, 3. proximal portion of left humerus, 4. cervical vertebra, 5. second and third sacral vertebrae, 6.–8. caudal vertebrae, 9. metatarsal. (After Huene 1908.)

Diagnosis of genus: [None published.]

Comments: This poorly known genus was founded upon a fragmentary skeleton (SMNS collection) discovered in the summer of 1906 by Professor Eberhard Fraas in the Stubensandstein of Pfaffenhofen, Württemberg, Germany (Huene 1908).

Huene described type species *H. longotarsus* as follows: Cervical vertebrae with long and compressed centra with slight dorsal curve, deep ventral cavity, short zygapophysis, moderately broad spine; dorsal centrum 4.3 centimeters (about 1.65 inches) long and 1.1 centimeters (about .42 inches) at mid-portion; sacral centra 3.5 centimeters (about 1.35 inches) long, 2.2 centimeters (about .83 inches) high anteriorly, 3 centimeters (about 1.25 inches) wide; caudal vertebra 3.6 centimeters (over 1.35 inches) long, with centrum measuring 2.8 centimeters (more than 1.1 inches) high; estimated length of ilium, if complete, 13–15 centimeters (about 5 to 5.75 inches), height about 7 centimeters (about 2.4 inches); femur, if complete, at least 30 centimeters (about 11.5 inches) long; metatarsal 14.3 centimeters (about 12.5 inches) in length.

Later, Huene (1921, 1932) referred additional remains from the same horizon and locality to *H. longotarsus*.

A second species, *H. orbitoangulatus,* was based on part of a skull (Number 12-353b) from the Stubensandstein at Pfaffenhofen, Germany. Huene (1932) distinguished this species from *H. longotarsus* mostly by slight differences in squamosal, prefrontal, suprangular, and posterior portions of the dentary.

Halticosaurus reached an approximate length of 18 feet (about 5.4 meters).

As observed by Norman (1990) in his review of various problematic "coelurosaurs," the material pertaining to *H. longotarsus* is quite poorly-preserved and displays no features suitable for diagnostic purposes. According to Norman, this taxon could represent a theropod (the unusually long and slender metatarsal associated with the other remains resembles that of a theropod), but also a small prosauropod (in structure of the ilium, if that element has been restored correctly, form of the femur, presence

Halticosaurus orbitoangulatus, Number 12 353b, holotype restored skull, left lateral view. (After Huene 1932.)

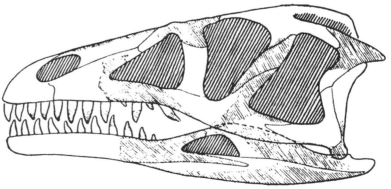

of but two fused sacral vertebrae, and lack of pleurocoels on the cervicals).

Note: Third species *H. liliensterni* Huene 1934
was made the type species of the new genus *Liliensternus* by Welles (1984). The specimen referred by
Larsonneur and Lapparent (1966) to *Halticosaurus* sp.
was referred by Cuny and Galton (1993) to that
genus.

Key references: Huene (1908, 1921, 1932); Norman (1990).

HAPLOCANTHOSAURUS Hatcher 1903—
(=*Haplocanthus* Hatcher 1903).

Saurischia: Sauropodomorpha: Sauropoda:
  Cetiosauridae: Cetiosaurinae.
Name derivation: Greek *haplos* = "single" + Greek
  akantha = "spine" + Greek *sauros* = "lizard."
Type species: *H. priscus* (Hatcher 1903).
Other species: *H. delfsi* McIntosh and Williams
  (1988).
Occurrence: Morrison Formation, Colorado,
  Wyoming, United States.
Age: Late Jurassic (Kimmeridgian–Tithonian).
Known material: Three partial postcranial skeletons.
Holotype: CM 572, incomplete skeleton including
  two posterior cervical vertebrae, ten dorsal verte-

Photo by R. A. Long and S. P. Welles (neg. #73-120-18), courtesy Cleveland Museum of Natural History.

Haplocanthosaurus priscus, CM 879, holotype coracoid (lateral view) of *H. utterbacki*.

brae, five sacral vertebrae with pelvis, 19 anterior
caudals, two chevrons, almost complete series
of ribs, femur.

Diagnosis of genus: Cervical vertebrae moderately long, with prominent but simple pleurocoels;
posterior cervical and anterior dorsal neural spines
not divided; dorsal centra comparatively small, with
prominent pleurocoels; dorsal arches high, diapophyses extending upward at 45 degrees and also outward;
dorsal neural spines short, broad; sacrum with usual
dorso-sacral, three primary sacrals, and caudo-sacral
with centra coossified, as are the sacral ribs, forming
yoke; at least some centra with small pleurocentral
cavities; neural spines relatively low, tending toward
coalescence of all, but especially first–third; caudal
centra short, amphicoelous, without pleurocentral
cavities; chevron facets of caudals very prominent,
giving sculptured look to underside of centrum; caudal spines slender, of moderate height anteriorly, low
further back, those of anterior region curved backward; distal end of scapula thin, broadly splayed,
proximal plate comparatively smaller than in most
sauropods; sternal plates large and subquadrangular;
ischium with relatively small proximal portion,
straight shaft, slightly broadened but not thickened
distal end; femur not overly stout or slender, shaft
with latero-medial diameter significantly greater than
in *Brachiosaurus* (McIntosh and Williams 1988).

Diagnosis of *H. priscus*: Medium-sized species;
femur and pelvic girdle comparatively slender; ischia
with narrowed distal ends rotated inward, fused to
their opposite in midline (McIntosh and Williams
1988).

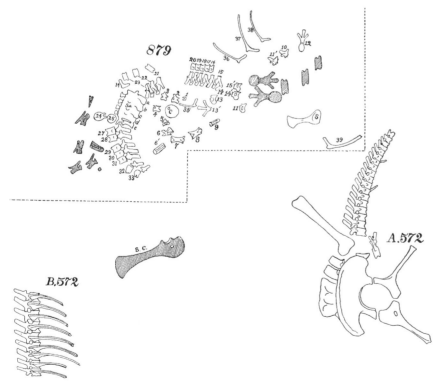

Haplocanthosaurus priscus, field drawing of CM 572, holotype skeleton of *Haplocanthus priscus*, as discovered.
Scale = approximately 1.25 meters. (After Hatcher 1903.)

Diagnosis of *H. delfsi*: Very large species (35–50 percent larger than fully adult *H. priscus*); pelvic girdle bones and femur more robust than in type species, pubis especially much heavier distally; distal end of ischium broader than in type species, not rotated inward, not fused to its opposite; mid-dorsal neural spines with V-shaped, anterolaterally projecting laminae; posterior dorsal spines with more greatly developed median laminae than *H. priscus* (McIntosh and Williams 1988).

Comments: Hatcher (1903*a*) erected the new genus and species *Haplocanthus priscus* on two partial, excellently-preserved sauropod skeletons. The specimens were discovered by W. H. Utterback at one of Othniel Charles Marsh's old sites, the so-called Marsh-Felch quarry, which was reopened by Hatcher in 1901. The Morrison Formation quarry was located about eight miles north of Canyon City, Colorado. The more

Haplocanthosaurus priscus, CM 672, holotype cervical vertebrae "a" and "b," lateral view.

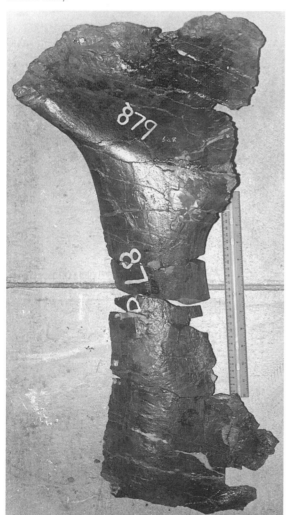

Haplocanthosaurus priscus, CM 879, holotype scapula (lateral view) of *H. utterbacki*.

complete of these two skeletons (CM 572) was designated the holotype.

In a post-publication note attached to the short paper in which he described these remains, Hatcher stated that the name *Haplocanthus* had proven to be preoccupied (Agassiz 1833-44) for a genus of acanthodian fossil fish. Hatcher then proposed that the genus be renamed *Haplocanthosaurus*.

Hatcher originally diagnosed the genus (and type species *H. priscus*) as follows: Short, "absolutely simple" [not bifurcated] neural spines [the most distinguishing feature, according to Hatcher]; anterior and mid-dorsal vertebrae with transverse processes inclined upward and outward instead of directly outward; neural arches in posterior dorsals high, exceeding length of neural spines; anterior sacral vertebrae with neural spines firmly coossified to form elongate bony plate.

Hatcher regarded this form as the most generalized sauropod yet discovered in North America.

The same year that he founded the type species, Hatcher (1903*b*) published a monograph on the osteology of the genus. In this publication he also erected a new species, *H. utterbacki*, for the second skeleton (CM 879), which included ten cervical, 13 dorsal, five sacral, and seven caudal vertebrae, left scapula, right coracoid, and a few ribs. Hatcher (1903*b*) distinguished this species by features of the sacral vertebrae.

An incomplete, largely articulated sauropod skeleton (CMNH 10380) was found in Canyon City in early summer 1954 by a field party dispatched by William E. Scheele, then director of the Cleveland Museum of Natural History. The specimen, discovered lying on its left side, included the first four cervical vertebrae, nine posterior dorsal vertebrae with

Haplocanthosaurus

Haplocanthosaurus delfsi, CMNH 10380, holotype caudal vertebrae.

Haplocanthosaurus delfsi, reconstructed skeleton, including holotype CMNH 10380, and elements of *Camarasaurus.*

ribs of the left side, five sacrals, the first 14 caudals, the shaft and distal end of the left scapula, fragmentary ?coracoid, right sternal plate, proximal end of the left radius, proximal end of the left ulna, ilia, left pubis, left ischium, and left femur. These remains were excavated between 1954 and 1957 and prepared for exhibition by George Whitaker at the American Museum of Natural History in New York. In 1961, the skeleton was displayed at the Cleveland Museum in the pose in which it was found, and in 1963 was mounted in a standing position. Bones modeled or cast from other specimens, along with real *Camarasaurus* (AMNH 825) bones, substituted for the missing elements. The restored skeleton, according to Williams (1982), measures almost 21 meters (70 feet) in length.

The Cleveland Museum of Natural History skeleton was not described for more than two decades, when McIntosh and Williams (1988) recognized it as belonging to a new species which they named *H. delfsi.* Based upon this skeleton and earlier described remains referred to *Haplocanthosaurus,* McIntosh and Williams rediagnosed the genus (and type species) as well as the new species.

In reevaluating the two species described by Hatcher (1903*a*, 1903*b*), McIntosh and Williams observed that the difference between *H. priscus* and slightly smaller (by 5 percent) *H. utterbacki,* namely the degree of coossification of the sacral spines, is an allometric feature, and suggested that "*H. utterbacki*" is simply a younger *H. priscus* individual.

Defending the validity of the Cleveland Museum specimen as a distinct species, McIntosh and Williams pointed out the great disparity in size between the relatively small adult *H. priscus* and gigantic adult *H. delfsi* (following the contention of Mook 1917 that

size may be an important factor in determining species) and also the various differences between CMNH 10380 and earlier described specimens.

Notes: The name given to the fossil fish was *Haplocanthus.* According to Article 56(b) of the International Code of Zoological Nomenclature, a one-letter difference between two genus-group names does not constitute homonymy, *Haplocanthus* thereby being an available name and technically a senior synonym of *Haplocanthosaurus.* In an appeal to the ICZN (Case 2684) noted in the *Bulletin of Zoological Nomenclature,* 46 (4), December 1989, Lucas and Hunt proposed that the well known and often used name *Haplocanthosaurus* be placed on the Official List of Generic Names in Zoology, and that the previously published name *Haplocanthus,* apparently not used as a valid name since 1903, be placed on the Official Index of Rejected and Invalid Generic Names in Zoology.

A skeleton (nicknamed the "Carling Giant") attributed to *Haplocanthosaurus* was discovered by physicist James Filla in summer 1990. Newspaper accounts (including the *Houston Chronicle* for June 24, 1991) stated that the skeleton represents an animal approximately 70 feet long and 25 feet tall. The specimen is to be displayed at the University of Wyoming museum in Laramie.

Key references: Hatcher (1903*a*, 1903*b*); McIntosh and Williams (1988); Williams (1982).

HAPLOCANTHUS Hatcher 1903—(Preoccupied, Agassiz 1833-44; see *Haplocanthosaurus.*)
Name derivation: Greek *haplos* = "spine" + Greek *akanthos* = "spine."
Type species: *H. priscus* Hatcher 1903.

HARPYMIMUS Barsbold and Perle 1984

Saurischia: Theropoda: Tetanurae: Avetheropoda: Coelurosauria: Maniraptora: Arctometatarsalia: Bullatosauria: Ornithomimosauria: Harpymimidae.

Name derivation: Greek *harpy* [mythical bird] + Greek *mimos* = "mimic."

Type species: *H. okladnikovi* Barsbold and Perle 1984.

Other species: [None.]

Occurrence: Shinekhudukskaya Svita, Dundgov, Mongolian People's Republic.

Age: Middle Cretaceous (Aptian–Albian).

Known material/holotype: GI 100/29, distorted skull including left mandibular ramus, incomplete postcranial skeleton including parts of left manus and left pes lacking digits III-IV.

Diagnosis of genus (as for type species): Manus 38 percent length of forelimb; four unfused distal carpals; metacarpal I much shorter than and appressed to II; distal surfaces of both metacarpals glymoid, metacarpal I derived in constituting some-what more than half length of II; manual unguals about 22 percent length of manus; ungual of digit II approximately length of its penultimate phalanx; pes apparently tridactyl (no evidence of digit I); metatarsus moderately slender, width about 20 percent its length; metatarsal III uniformly narrows proximally, separating II and IV throughout extensor face of metatarsus; metatarsal III not overlapping adjoining metatarsals distally; pedal digits relatively short and massive; proximal phalanges of pedal digits II and III short, stout, subequal in length (Barsbold and Osmólska 1990).

Comments: The genus *Harpymimus* was founded upon a partial skeleton (GI 100/29), discovered in 1981 by the Joint Soviet-Mongolian Paleontological Expedition in the Shinekhuduk Formation at Huren-duh, in southeastern Mongolia. The find constituted the first record of a primitive ornithomimosaur from the Middle Cretaceous of Mongolia (Barsbold and Perle 1984).

Originally, this genus was briefly diagnosed by Barsbold and Perle as having unequally elongated metacarpal bones.

Barsbold and Perle noted that the elongation of the metacarpal bones distinguish this genus from most other ornithomimosaurs (which are characterized by metacarpal bones of about the same length). This condition in *Harpymimus* is similar to that in toothed theropods.

As observed by Barsbold and Perle, the ornithomimosaurs of Central Asia comprise a series of genera that possess different characters exhibiting an evolutionary sequence. In *Ornithomimus*, there is slight unevenness in the elongation of the metacarpal bones; in *Garudimimus*, pedal digit I is preserved; and in *Harpymimus*, the metacarpal bones are unevenly elongated, and a dentition, though reduced, is present. These differences suggest that ornithomimosaurs originated in Central Asia, with *Harpymimus*, still exhibiting most features of a general theropod character, lying close to the origin of the Ornithomimosauria.

Because of the presence of teeth, Barsbold and Perle excluded *Harpymimus* from the Ornithomimidae and placed the genus into its own family, Harpymimidae. Smith and Galton (1990) included *Harpymimus* in the Ornithomimidae, pointing out that having teeth is not a diagnostic feature, teeth probably also being present in *Elaphrosaurus*, and expected in a conservative ornithomimid. In a review of the Ornithomimosauria, Barsbold and Osmólska (1990) retained Harpymimidae, regarding it as the most primitive of ornithomimosaur families.

Key references: Barsbold and Osmólska (1990); Barsbold and Perle (1984); Smith and Galton (1990).

Harpymimus okladnikovi, GI 100/29, holotype a. left ramus of lower jaw (partially reconstructed), interior view, b. left manus (partially reconstructed), dorsal view, c. left pes (distal parts of digits III and IV not preserved), dorsal view. (After Barsbold and Perle 1984.)

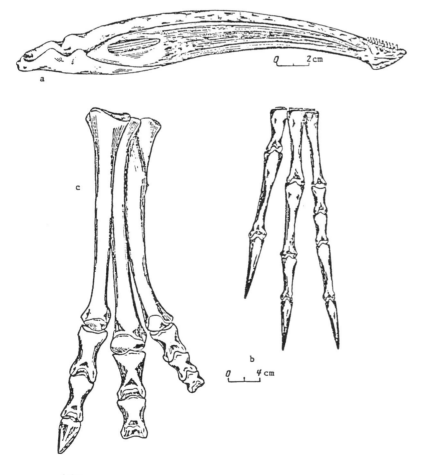

HECATASAURUS Brown 1910—(See *Telmatosaurus*.)

Name derivation: "Hecate [Greek fertility goddess]" + Greek *sauros* = "lizard."

Type species: *H. transsylvanicus* (Nopcsa 1899).

HEISHANSAURUS Bohlin 1953 [*nomen dubium*]

Ornithischia: Genasauria: Thyreophora: Ankylosauria: Ankylosauridae.

Name derivation: "Heishan [place in China]" + Greek *sauros* = "lizard."

Type species: *H. pachycephalus* Bohlin 1953 [*nomen dubium*].

Other species: [None.]

Occurrence: Minhe Formation, West Gansu, China.

Age: Late Cretaceous.

Known material/holotype: IVPP collection (destroyed), dislocated skull with teeth, rib fragments, crushed vertebrae, dermal plates.

Diagnosis of genus: [No modern diagnosis published.]

Comments: The genus *Heishansaurus* was established upon badly crushed skull and postcranial remains, collected from the Djadokhta equivalent of Chia-Yu-Kuan, West Kansu [now spelled Gansu], in northwest China (Bohlin 1953). The type specimen has apparently "disintegrated."

Bohlin diagnosed the monotypic *H. pachycephalus* as follows: Base of skull apparently broad, occipital condyle large; height of tooth crowns (when unworn) probably consistent in all teeth; teeth generally resembling those in *Pinacosaurus grangeri*; vertebrae from posterior cervical or anterior dorsal region more or less amphicoelous, very rugose, with wide neural canal; anterior caudal vertebrae with broad, relatively short centra and very long transverse processes.

Dermal armor seems to have consisted of plates varying in size and form. The most common plates are flat, moderately thick, and circular or tetragonal. The largest plate measures about 10 centimeters in diameter. The smallest dermal ossifications are small nodules barely greater than pea-size. Also present are small elongate plates. Bohlin found no evidence to indicate where these ossifications would be located on the animal.

Key references: Bohlin (1953).

Photo by the author, courtesy American Museum of Natural History.

Heishansaurus pachycephalus, cast of IVPP, holotype partial skull, vertebrae, and dermal armor.

HELOPUS Wiman 1929—(Preoccupied, Wagler 1832; see *Euhelopus*.)
Name derivation: Greek *helos* + Greek *pous* = "foot."
Type species: *H. zdanskyi* Wiman 1929.

Heptasteornis andrewsi,
BMNH A4359, holotype
tibiotarsi, anterior and distal
view. (After Harrison and
Walker 1975.)

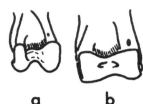

a   b

HEPTASTEORNIS Harrison and Walker 1975
Saurischia: Theropoda: Tetanurae: Avetheropoda: ?Coelurosauria: ?Maniraptora: ?Arctometatarsalia: ?Bullatosauria: ?Troodontidae.
Name derivation: Greek *hepta* = "seven [towns, in reference to Siebenburgen, German name for Transylvania]" + Greek *asty* = "town" + Greek *ornis* = "bird."
Type species: *H. andrewsi* Harrison and Walker 1975.
Other species: [None.]
Occurrence: Sinpetru Beds, Judethean Hunedoara, Romania.
Age: Late Cretaceous (?Maastrichtian).
Known material: Two partial tibiotarsi.
Holotype: BMNH A4359, distal end of left tibiotarsus.

Diagnosis of genus: Tibiotarsus with distal end less broad and flattened antero-posteriorly than in *Bradycneme*; very small distal projection of outer condyle beyond internal condyle; internal condyle projecting much farther anteriorly than external condyle; anterior intercondylar fossa not as marked as in *Bradycneme* (Harrison and Walker 1975).

Comments: The genus now called *Heptasteornis* was founded upon an incomplete tibiotarsus (BMNH A4359) collected from Szentpeterfalva, Hatszeg, Transylvania, Romania. The specimen was presented to the British Museum (Natural History) [now Natural History Museum, London] in 1913 by Baron Franz Nopcsa. A paratype specimen (BMNH A1528), consisting of the distal end of another left tibiotarsus, was presented by Nopcsa in 1922. The holotype was referred to *Elopteryx nopcsai*, apparently a large bird, by Charles W. Andrews (1913), who in the same paper named that genus and type species; the paratype was subsequently referred to *E. nopcsai* by Kálmán Lambrecht (1929) in his handbook of fossil birds.

Both specimens were later identified by Harrison and Walker (1975) as belonging to a new genus which they named *Heptasteornis*, referring it to new taxon Bradycnemidae (originally believed by them to represent very large Upper Cretaceous owls of the "order" Strigiformes).

Brodkin (1978) later pointed out that the specimen almost certainly represents a theropod dinosaur. Based on the relative robustness of the astragalus, *Heptasteornis* may belong to the Dromaeosauridae (R. E. Molnar, personal communication 1988).

Key references: Brodkin (1975); Harrison and Walker (1978).

HERRERASAURUS Reig 1963—(=*Frenguellisaurus, Ischisaurus*)
?Dinosauria: ?Saurischia: Herrerasauridae.
Name derivation: "[Victorino] Herrera" + Greek *sauros* = "lizard."
Type species: *H. ischigualastensis* Reig 1963.
Other species: [None.]
Occurrence: Ischigualasto Formation, San Juan, Argentina.
Age: Late Triassic (Middle Carnian).

0 1 2 3 4 5 cm

Herrerasaurus ischigualastensis, PVL 2566, holotype (partially reconstructed) right pes, dorsal view. (After Reig 1963.)

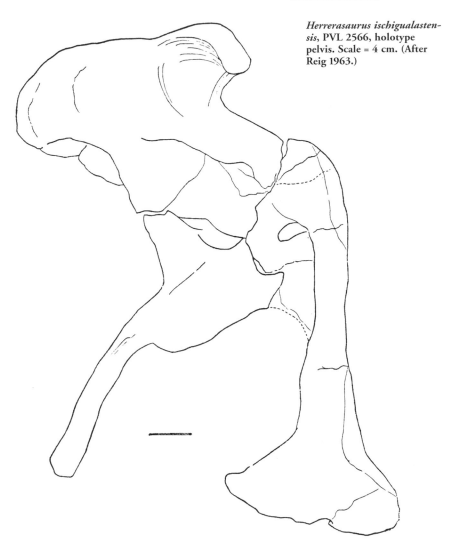

Known material: Several skeletons, partial skeletons of five individuals, isolated postcrania, skull with associated cervical vertebrae.

Holotype: PVL 2566, articulated skeleton including articulated vertebrae (dorsal 7 to distal caudal ?50), pelvis lacking distal half of ischia, almost complete hindlimb missing calcaneum, proximal half of metatarsal I, several pedal phalanges, left astragalus.

Diagnosis of genus (as for type species): Premaxillary-maxillary fenestra posterior to external naris; anterior end of both antorbital fenestra and antorbital fossa semicircular; ventral border of maxilla sinuous, particularly at level of jugal articulation; ridge on lateral surface of jugal; upper part of lower temporal fenestra less than one-third as broad as lower part; deeply incised upper temporal fossa that extends across medial process of postorbital; ventral process of squamosal subquadrate with lateral depression; quadratojugal overlapping posterodorsal face of quadrate; pterygoid ramus of quadrate with inturned, trough-shaped ventral margin; dentary with slender posterodorsal process, T-shaped in cross-section; surangular with forked anterior process for articulation with posterodorsal process of dentary; apices of neural spines of posterior trunk vertebrae with pronounced lateral borders; internal tuberosity of humerus projecting proximally, separated from humeral head by deep groove; humeral entepicondyle ridge-like, with anterior and posterior depressions; manus 60 percent of humerus plus radius length; pubis proximally curved, ventrally oriented; lateral margins sinuous in anterior view; posterior border of postacetabular pedicle of ischium forming right angle with dorsal border of ischial shaft; femur with anteroproximal keel and subcircular muscle scar on anterolateral distal shaft; tibia shorter than femur (tibial length representing 87 to 91 percent of femur length (Novas 1993).

Comments: One of the earliest apparent dinosaurs, *Herrerasaurus* was founded on four well-preserved cotype specimens (PVL 2558, 2054, 2264, and 2588; see below) representing the incomplete remains of five individuals, two by numerous bones and articulated partial skeletons. The material was collected, in addition to other fossil vertebrate remains, during four successive expeditions (1959, 1960, 1961, and 1962) organized by various Argentinean institutions, mainly the Instituto Miguel Lillo of Tucumian, from the lower third of the Ischigualasto Formation (Ischigualastian; Late Triassic [Middle Carnian; see Rogers, Swisher, Sereno, Monetta, Forster and Martínez 1993]), Hoyada de Ischigualasto, San Juan and La Rioja Provinces, Argentina. The remains were found in association with the typical Mesotriassic Cynodont-Rhynchosaur assemblage (Reig 1963).

As noted by Novas (1993), PVL 2054 comprises fragments of pubes and gastralia, almost complete femora, and tibia (Novas 1989). PVL 2588 was separated by Novas (1989) into two specimens: PVL 2588 comprises fragments of femora and tibiae, and an isolated manual ungual, PVL 2588b material lacking apomorphic features of either *Herrerasaurus* or Herrerasauridae. The latter, as well as PVL 2264 (left femur missing proximal and distal ends, collected from the Los Colorados Formation) were regarded by Novas (1993) as indeterminate archosaurian remains.

Reig originally diagnosed *Herrerasaurus* as follows: "Carnosaur" of medium size, with deep, robust premaxilla and robust teeth; three premaxillary, eight maxillary, and 12 dentary teeth; sacrum with three vertebrae; ilium short, high, spine very robust anteriorly; pubis as large as tibia, directed almost perpendicularly to vertebrae, distal end expanded;

Herrerasaurus

Courtesy J. F. Bonaparte.

Herrerasaurus ischigualasten-sis, restored articulated skeleton including holotype partial postcrania (PVL 2566), modeled skull hypothetical (and incorrect), as originally mounted at Paleontologia de Vertebrados de la Fundación Miguel Lillo, Argentina.

Herrerasaurus ischigualasten-sis, skeleton, including skull PVSJ 407 and specimens PVSJ 53 and 373.

ischium shorter than pubis; humerus more than half size of femur; femur slender, sigmoid; tibia shorter than femur, stoutly constructed and robust; astragalus without ascending process; calcaneum very small; metatarsal III elongate, I and V reduced and about two-thirds length of II and III.

According to Reig, the skull would be about 29 centimeters (approximately 11 inches) long, femur 47.3 centimeters (more than 18 inches), and tibia 41.1 centimeters (about 15.5 inches). (The entire animal measured from about 1.75 to 2.4 meters, or 6 to 8 feet, and weighed about 135 kilograms, or 300 pounds.)

Two more type species were founded upon material of the same age and collected from the same horizon as *H. ischigualastensis*: In the paper in which he introduced *Herrerasaurus*, Reig named and described *Ischisaurus cattoi*, erected upon the bones of two individuals, including a fragmentary left premaxilla and maxillae with teeth, incomplete frontals, dentaries with teeth, splenials, posterior articular ends of lower jaws, vertebrae (several cervicals, dorsals, and caudals), humeri, proximal ends of ulnae, left radiale, portions of left ilium, femur, tibia, astragalus, proximal half of left metatarsal I, left metatarsals II and III, some left pedal phalanges, right tibia and calcaneum (MACN 18.060). The material, along with the remains of other taxa, was recovered in 1959, 1960, 1961, and 1962, respectively, in four expeditions organized by Argentinean institutions mostly by the Instituto Miguel Lillo of Tucumián. Later, Novas (1986) named and described *Frenguellisaurus ischigualastensis*, based on the greater part of a skull, including right premaxilla, both maxillae, left jugal, temporal and occipital regions of the braincase, mandibular rami, axis, portion of an anterior cervical vertebra, and some distal caudal vertebrae (PVL UNSJ 53). Novas (1986) regarded *Frenguellisaurus* as an early probable theropod closely allied with *Staurikosaurus*, speculating that *Frenguellisaurus* and *Herrerasaurus* may be components of the oldest radiation of moderately-sized bipedal, carnivorous archosaurs.

New interpretations of the above three taxa resulted from the collection of additional *Herrerasaurus* material. In 1988, Paul C. Sereno and Alfredo Monetta discovered a well-preserved, almost complete articulated skeleton, including a skull (PVSJ 407), in the Andes foothills of the Ischigualasto Formation (Sereno, Novas, Arcucci and Yu 1988). The skull includes articulated lower jaws, incomplete partial sclerotic ring in the right orbit, and left stapes with the footplate lodged in the fenestra ovalis

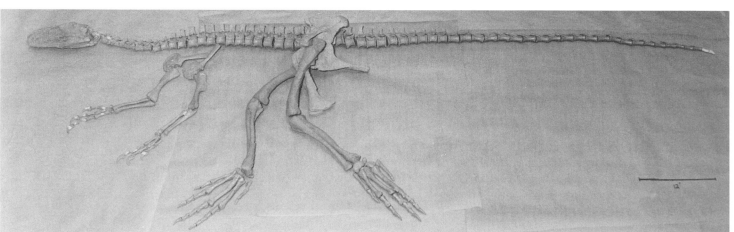

Courtesy the Field Museum (neg. #GN86435.23).

(Sereno and Novas 1993). Other *Herrerasaurus* remains collected at this time included a nearly complete, poorly-preserved skeleton (PVSJ 461) (Novas 1993; Sereno 1993; Sereno and Novas 1993); articulated postcrania (PVSJ 373) including a portion of scapular blade and complete left forelimb; right scapula and almost complete, articulated right carpus and manus (PVSJ 380) (Sereno 1993).

Sues (1990) observing *Ischisaurus* to be quite similar to *Herrerasaurus* in various skeletal features, suggested that the two forms could be congeneric. From the more recently collected *Herrerasaurus* material (Sereno *et al.*, 1988), Novas (1992*b*; 1993) found both *I. cattoi* and *F. ischigualastensis* to be conspecific with *H. ischigualastensis*. Novas (1993; see also Sereno 1993; Sereno and Novas 1993) referred a partial postcranial skeleton (MCZ 7064), originally referred to as cf. *Staurikosaurus* by Brinkman and Sues (1987), to *Herrerasaurus*. This specimen, collected in 1958 by Alfred Sherwood Romer from the Ishigualasto Formation, northwest of Arroyo de Agua, San Juan Province, includes atlas-axis complex, parts of at least five dorsal vertebrae, fragments of both scapulacoracoids, both ends of humeri, incomplete left ilium, proximal ends of ischia, distal end of right femur, proximal and distal ends of right tibia, proximal end of right fibula, and some pedal phalanges.

From the above referred material, Novas rediagnosed the monotypic *H. ischigualastensis* and redescribed the postcranium; Sereno (1993) described the

pectoral girdle and forelimb, primarily based on PVSJ 373; Sereno and Novas (1993) redescribed the skull and neck primarily based upon the skull and articulated cervical vertebrae of PVSJ 407.

As described by Sereno and Novas (1993), the skull has a rectangular profile and transversely narrow snout. The neck is relatively slender, with prominent epipophyses on all cervical vertebrae. According to Sereno and Novas, marked supratemporal depressions for jaw adductor muscles on the skull roof and a well-developed, sliding intra-mandibular joint suggest that *H. ischigualastensis* was an active predator. The latter feature, allowing the tooth anterior segment to rotate about 15 degrees, was interpreted as a mechanism enhancing the capture of prey, a feature analogous to that in some extant anguimorph lizards.

Herrerasaurus ischigualastensis, reconstructed mounted skeleton, including casts of specimens PVSJ 407, PVSJ 53, and 373.

Herrerasaurus ischigualastensis, PVSJ 407, skull, right lateral view.

As described by Sereno (1993), the forelimb is less than one-half the length of the hindlimb, the manus with a phalangeal formula of 2-3-4-1-0, manual digits IV and V much reduced. Sereno observed that the forearm is stiff and incapable of significantly turning the palm upward or downward. The carpus seems to have been able to flex the manus against the forearm at an approximately 45-degree angle, and inversion and reversion of the manus seems to have been restricted. Sereno interpreted the manus as being specialized for grasping and raking (as in other theropods), with the trenchant unguals of digits I–III converging during flexion and extension.

Classifying *Herrerasaurus* has been controversial. Because its pubis resembles that of *Allosaurus*, Reig originally regarded *Herrerasaurus* as a "carnosaur" more advanced in some respects, though older, than other Triassic "megalosaurids." Walker (1964) acknowledged that the pubis of *Herrerasaurus* resembles that of Late Jurassic and Cretaceous "carnosaurs," but did not imply any relationship between this genus and other taxa. Benedetto (1973) assigned *Herrerasaurus* and the more primitive *Staurikosaurus* to a new family Herrerasauridae. Galton (1985e) later placed the Herrerasuridae (and Staurikosauridae) into a new taxon, Herrerasauria, within Theropoda. Both *Herrerasaurus* and *Staurikosaurus* were later reevaluated by Brinkman and Sues (1987), who concluded that both genera should not be included within Saurischia (as strictly defined by Gauthier and Padian

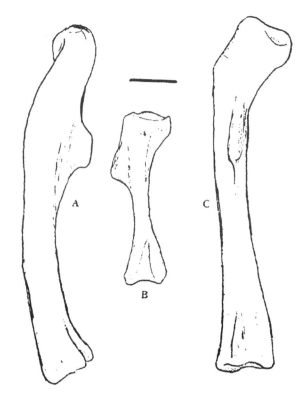

Herrerasaurus ischigualastensis, MACN 18.060, holotype femur in A. lateral and C. posterior views, and B. humerus of *Ischisaurus cattoi*. Scale = 3 cm. (After Reig 1963.)

1985), but be regarded as successive sister-taxa to the Saurischia.

Sereno and Novas (1992) believed that the more recently collected specimens revealed a fairly complete picture of this genus and clarified the sequence of anatomical changes that occurred during early dinosaur evolution. Sereno and Novas (1992) interpreted features suggesting to them that *Herrerasaurus* was not a basal dinosaur outside of Saurischia and Ornithischia; rather, the skull, neck, and, particularly, forelimb exhibit characters present only in saurischians (*e.g.*, subnarial foramen between premaxilla and maxilla, hyposphene-hypantrum articulations of dorsal vertebrae, epipophyses on mid- and posterior cervicals, and elongate manus approaching or exceeding half length of more proximal part of the forelimb). Features suggesting affinity with the Theropoda include the footed pubis and elongate prezygapophyses in distal caudal vertebrae. From the original and more recently collected material, Novas (1993) interpreted the following features as theropod synapomorphies: Cervical epipophyses prong-shaped (Sereno and Novas 1992); trochanteric shelf on proximal femur; humerus almost 50 percent length of femur; metacarpals I-III with deep extensor pits; metacarpal IV strongly reduced, with less than two phalanges; metacarpal V strongly reduced, phalanges

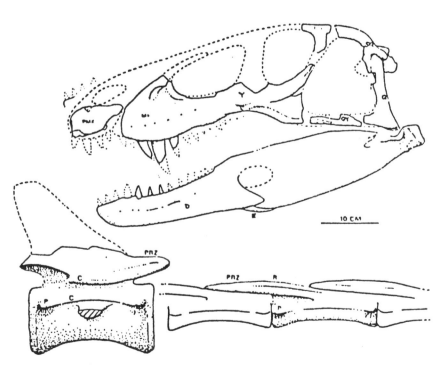

Herrerasaurus ischigualastensis, PVL UNSJ 53, holotype skull and caudal vertebrae of *Frenguellisaurus ischigualastensis*. (After Novas 1986.)

of V absent; splenial posterior process spoon-shaped, horizontally placed below angular, angular anteriorly hooked; lacrimal exposed on skull roof; distal caudal prezygapophyses elongate; penultimate manual phalanges elongate; manual unguals of digits II and III enlarged; pubis enlarged distally.

More recently, however, Holtz (1995*a*, 1995*b*), in preliminary reports, announced a new phylogenetic analysis of herrerasaurids, concluding that *Herrerasaurus* (also *Staurikosaurus* and *Eoraptor*; see entries) are not theropods, probably not saurischians, and possibly not dinosaurs, suggesting that *Eoraptor* and the Herrerasauridae make up the sister-group to either the theropod-sauropodomorph clade or the Dinosauria *stricto sensu*.

According to Sereno and Novas (1992), the possession of only two fully incorporated sacral vertebrae in *Herrerasaurus* (and *Staurikosaurus*) suggests that full incorporation into the sacrum of at least one more dorsal vertebra must have occurred in Saurischia and Ornithischia independently; the narrow distal end of the tibia in these genera (also in the basal ornithischian *Pisanosaurus*) likewise suggest inde-

pendent broadening of tibia and astragalus in both major dinosaurian groups.

Note: Reig referred to *Herrerasaurus* an incomplete left femur from the Los Colorados beds, this specimen later interpreted by Bonaparte (1960) as belonging to an ornithosuchid "thecodontian."

Key references: Benedetto (1973); Brinkman and Sues (1987); Galton (1985*e*); Holtz (1995*a*, 1995*b*); Novas (1986, 1989, 1992*b*, 1993); Reig (1963); Sereno (1993); Sereno and Novas (1992, 1993); Sereno, Novas, Arucci and Yu (1988); Sues (1990); Walker (1964).

HETERODONTOSAURUS Crompton and Charig 1962 Ornithischia: Genasauria: Cerapoda: Ornithopoda: Heterodontosauridae.

Name derivation: Greek *hetero* = "different" + Greek *odous* = "tooth" + Greek *sauros* = "lizard."

Type species: *H. tucki* Crompton and Charig 1962.

Other species: [None.]

Occurrence: Upper Elliot Formation, Clarens Formation, Cape Province, South Africa.

Heterodontosaurus tucki, SAM K1332, skeleton.

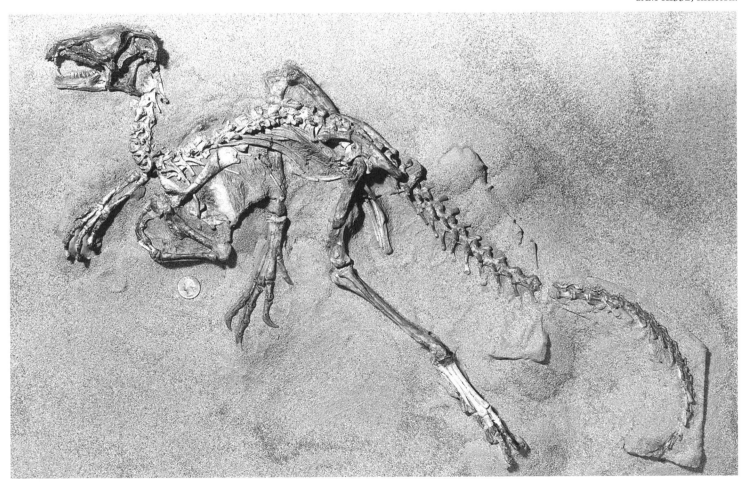

Courtesy Museum of Comparative Zoology, Harvard University.

Age: Early Jurassic (Hettangian–Sinemurian).

Known material: Two complete skulls, one with associated complete postcranial skeleton, fragmentary jaw.

Holotype: SAFM K337, partial skeleton with almost complete skull and lower jaw.

Diagnosis of genus (as for type species): Skull with accessory antorbital fenestra within antorbital fossa; distinctive jugal boss; dorsal vertebrae with bifid transverse processes; loss of ossified tendons in the tail; humerus with well-developed entepicondyle; ulnare and intermedium fused; elongate manus; femur lacking cleft-like separation between lesser and greater trochanters; femur having lost caudal intercondylar fossa; fusion of distal tibia, distal fibula, astragalus and calcaneum; fibula very slender, lacking distal expansion (from Sereno 1986); fusion of distal tarsals and proximal metatarsus; pits on heads of proximal pedal phalanges (Weishampel and Witmer 1990*b*).

Comments: Basis for the family Heterodontosauridae Kuhn 1966, the genus *Heterodontosaurus* was founded upon a partial skeleton with almost complete skull (SAFM K337), discovered in 1962 by Alan J. Charig, John Attridge, and Barry Cox, in the upper Elliot Formation (Early Jurassic [Hettangian–Pliensbachian]; see Olsen and Galton 1984) (formerly upper Stormberg Series), Cave Sandstone, Herschel district, Cape Province, South Africa.

Crompton and Charig (1962) gave a preliminary description of the skull, provisionally referring *Heterodontosaurus* to the Ornithopoda. Originally, Crompton and Charig diagnosed *Heterodontosaurus* as follows: Facial region of skull short; orbit large, supraorbital projecting into orbit; squamosal backwardly produced beyond postero-dorsal corner of quadrate; jugal with flange; premaxilla deep ventral to naris, with three carnivorous type teeth posteriorly, third large and caniniform; wide diastema, followed by series of approximately 12 close-set, very specialized maxillary teeth, the latter medial to lateral surface of maxilla; maxillary teeth with vertical distal ridges but no cingulum development; lower jaw apparently with prominent coracoid process; first mandibular tooth large, caniniform, projecting upward to diastema; remaining dentary teeth resembling maxillary teeth, enamel present only on inner surface of crowns [some of these characters now known to apply to all heterodontosaurids].

The holotype skull, as measured by Crompton and Charig, is about 92 millimeters (approximately 35 inches) long.

An articulated, virtually complete skeleton (SAM K1332) of *Heterodontosaurus*, the first such specimen of any heterodontosaurid, was found in December 1966 in the Upper Red Beds, Stormberg Series, on the northern slopes of Krommespruit Mountain, in the District of Herschel, South Africa. This specimen was briefly described by Santa Luca, Crompton and Charig (1976). The first detailed description of the postcranial skeleton of this specimen was subsequently offered by Santa Luca (1980), who calculated the length of the individual as just over one meter (3.4 feet).

According to Santa Luca *et al.*, *Heterodontosaurus* was probably a cursorial biped, that opinion based on the structure of the hand and foot, and the length ratio of tibia to femur. Paul (1987) envisioned *Heterodontosaurus* as capable of galloping on all fours. However, this notion was rejected by Weishampel and Witmer (1990*b*) in their review of the Heterodontosauridae on the grounds that the morphology of the claws and relations of scapula, coracoid, and sternum to limit scapular rotation argue against such rapid quadrupedal locomotion.

As observed by Santa Luca *et al.*, the manus, with its long, slender fingers and well-developed claws, seems primarily adapted to grasping, tearing and, perhaps, digging. The forelimbs, though relatively robust, were probably only used for locomotion when the animal was moving slowly, as in feeding. The elongated lower leg bones and metatarsals are features suited to rapid locomotion. The tail is long and tapering and counterbalanced the animal when it ran. Santa Luca (1980) theorized that, when the animal came down on all fours to forage, the elbow might have allowed a semisprawling attitude, and that the structure of the pelvis may have created in *Heterodontosaurus* a stance similar, but not identical, to that of birds. According to Weishampel and Witmer, the attitude of the axial skeleton is largely horizontal and the lever-arm mechanics suggest a powerful femoral retraction. *Heterodontosaurus*, then, though mostly bipedal, probably adopted a quadrupedal stance when standing still or when foraging, and used its powerful forelimbs and large claws to dig up roots and termites or tear apart the nests of insects.

Charig (1979) suggested that the small, simple teeth in the front of the upper jaw, biting against a horny and toothless beak, were used in nipping off leaves. The tall, closely packed, grooved, and ridged cheek teeth, working like scissors, cut up the food, which was held in the fleshy cheek pouches. If need be, the food could be chewed a second time before the cheek muscles pushed it back into the mouth to be swallowed. Weishampel and Witmer noted that the lack of teeth along the rostral part of the premaxilla, the probable presence of a horny beak, and the narrowing of the oral margins of the premaxillae imply comparatively selective cropping abilities. Therefore, *Heterodontosaurus* and other heterodontosaurids may have been active, agile and cursorial herbivores that mostly foraged on ground cover and shrubby vegetation.

The large canine tusks may have been utilized as defensive weapons or in sexual or social display. It has been suggested that these tusks could also constitute a sexual dimorphism, being only present in males. Molnar (1977) speculated that the jugal boss of the skull may have been used in intraspecies combat, the boss serving as a horn-like weapon to deliver blows. With both combatants standing parallel to each other, such blows could have been delivered to the opponent's flanks. Coombs (1972) postulated that the palpebral in *Heterodontosaurus*, which had developed as a partial bar across the orbit, could have protected the eye during such combat.

Santa Luca (1980) suggested that *Heterodontosaurus*, though a bipedal ornithischian, might not be an ornithopod, possibly representing an early nonornithopod radiation which is, at yet, too poorly known for "subordinal" or "infraordinal" definition. Sereno (1986), however, demonstrated that *Heterodontosaurus* is clearly ornithopod, with Heterodontosauridae the sister-taxon of higher ornithopods (see systematics section). Sereno stated that additional unpublished fossil material from both the Stormberg Series [=Elliot Formation] and Kayenta Formation of Arizona confirm that many of the unusual features of *Heterodontosaurus* are shared by other heterodontosaurids, and noted that the posterior premaxillary and anterior dentary caniniform teeth seem to be restricted to a heterodontosaurid subgroup more advanced than the genus *Abrictosaurus*.

Key references: Charig (1979); Coombs (1972); Crompton and Charig (1962); Molnar (1977); Santa Luca (1980); Sereno (1986); Weishampel and Witmer (1990*b*).

HETEROSAURUS Cornuel 1850—(See *Iguanodon.*)

Name derivation: Greek *hetero* = "different" + Greek *sauros* = "lizard."

Type species: *H. necomiensis* Cornuel 1850 [*nomen dubium*, in part].

HIEROSAURUS Wieland 1909 [*nomen dubium*]—(= ?*Nodosaurus.*)

Ornithischia: Genasauria: Thyreophora: Ankylosauria: Nodosauridae.

Heterodontosaurus tucki drawing of skull based on holotype SAFM K337. (After Galton.)

Hierosaurus sternbergi, YPM 1847, holotype dermal elements.

Photo by the author, courtesy Yale Peabody Museum of Natural History.

Name derivation: Greek *hieros* = "sacred" + Greek *sauros* = "lizard."

Type species: *H. sternbergii* Wieland 1909 [*nomen dubium*].

Other species: [None.]

Occurrence: Niobrara Chalk Formation, Kansas, United States.

Age: Late Cretaceous (Middle Santonian–Early Campanian).

Homalocephale calathocercos, life restoration by Gregory S. Paul.

Known material/holotype: YPM 1847, at least 34 scutes, skull and rib fragments.

Diagnosis of genus (as for type species): [None published].

Comments: The type species *Hierosaurus sternbergi* [*nomen dubium*] was based on a pair of dermal ?caudal elements and six scutes (YPM 1847), collected from the Smoky Hill Chalk Member, Niobrara Chalk Formation, Gove County, in western Kansas. Because these latter remains were found in marine deposits, Wieland (1909) incorrectly speculated that the dinosaur may have been aquatic. Although he never diagnosed this taxon, Wieland regarded the armor as distinctive, including dermal plates "characterized by deep and broad horn shield sulci."

Coombs (1978*a*), in his reorganization of the Ankylosauria, referred this taxon to *Nodosaurus*. However, as later pointed out by Carpenter, Dilkes and Weishampel (1995), the elongated, keeled scutes which Wieland found to be distinctive also occur in other nodosaurids. Coombs and Maryańska (1990), as well as Carpenter *et al.*, best considered *H. sternbergii* to be a *nomen dubium*. Carpenter *et al.* added that, if the skeleton of this taxon were better known, it might otherwise offer diagnosable characters for this species.

A second species, *H. coleii*, was referred by Carpenter *et al.* to new genus *Niobrarasaurus* (see entry).

Key references: Carpenter, Dilkes and Weishampel (1995); Coombs (1978*a*); Coombs and Maryańska (1990); Wieland (1909).

HIKANODON Keferstein 1825 [*nomen oblitum*]—(See *Iguanodon*.)

Type species: (?No specific name designated).

HOMALOCEPHALE Maryańska and Osmólska 1974

Ornithischia: Genasauria: Cerapoda: Marginocephalia: Pachycephalosauria: Homalocephalidae.

Name derivation: Greek *homalos* = "even" + Greek *cephale* = "head."

Type species: *H. calathocercos* Maryańska and Osmólska 1974.

Other species: [None.]

Occurrence: Nemegt Formation, Omnogov, Mongolian People's Republic.

Age: Late Cretaceous (?Late Campanian or Early Maastrichtian).

Known material/holotype: GI SPS 100/51, almost complete skeleton including incomplete skull without lower jaws, two sternal plates, ten posterior dorsal vertebrae with attached ribs, six sacrals lacking neural arches and with nearly complete right sacral ribs and fragmentary left ribs, 29 caudal vertebrae with caudal ribs, several incomplete chevrons, right ilium, left ischium, distal parts of prepubes, damaged incomplete left femur, fragmentary right femur, distal ends of tibiae and fibulae, left astragalus, left and right distal tarsal III, right metatarsal II, distal portion of right metatarsal III, distal parts of left metatarsals I-III, first phalanx of left pedal digit ?IV, numerous isolated caudal ossified tendons, ossified tendons ensheathing distal caudals.

Diagnosis of genus (as for type species): Supratemporal fenestra rounded; interfenestral bridge broad, about equal in size to transverse width of supratemporal fenestra; occiput moderately concave; cranial roof roughly ornamented (*i.e.*, pitted); preacetabular process of ilium with gently convex surface; craniocaudally long medial iliac flange; downwardly curved acetabular iliac process (Maryańska 1990).

Comments: Basis for the family Homalocephalidae Dong 1987 (emended, Perle, Maryańska and Osmólska 1983), the genus *Homalocephale* was founded by Maryańska and Osmólska (1974) on the most complete cranial and postcranial material of any known pachycephalosaur (GI SPS 100/51). The material was collected during a Polish-Mongolian Paleontological Expedition (Kielan-Jaworoska and Dovchin 1969; Kielan-Jaworoska and Barsbold 1972) from the Nemegt Formation, Nemegt, Nemegt Basin, Gobi Desert, Mongolia People's Republic (Gradziński, Kaźmierczak and Lefeld 1969).

Originally, Maryańska and Osmólska diagnosed the monotypic *H. calathocercos* as follows: Cranial roof thick but completely flat; sutures of interfrontal and frontoparietal distinct; infratemporal openings low, long; orbit large, almost round; quadrate backwardly deflected along upper half of length; occipital area moderately concave, centrally deepened, occipital condyle large; foramen magnum large and round; basal tubera flat anteroposteriorly, ventral edges very close to quadrate wings of pterygoids; ventral edge of maxilla arched outward; cranial roof roughly ornamented; maxillary teeth with small crowns.

Maryańska and Osmólska described the skull of *H. calathocercos* as having a greatest width of 138 millimeters (almost 5.5 inches) and maximum height of 118 millimeters (about 4.5 inches). Deep, large pits cover the cranial roof on its periphery, this ornamentation becoming weaker and denser towards the medial line. Moderate-sized nodes are present along the posterolateral and posterior edges of the skull roof.

Considering differences between *Homalocephale* and another Mongolian pachycephalosaur, *Prenocephale,* that might constitute sexual dimorphism,

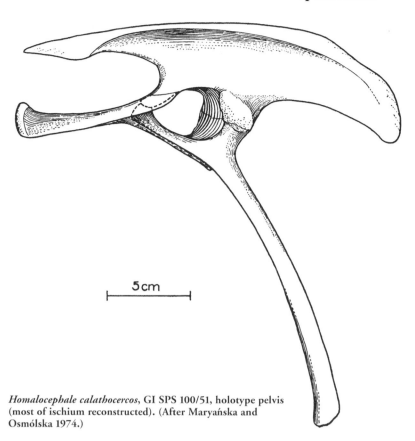

Homalocephale calathocercos, GI SPS 100/51, holotype pelvis (most of ischium reconstructed). (After Maryańska and Osmólska 1974.)

Maryańska and Osmólska concluded that these seemed to be of a generic nature.

In a review of the Pachycephalosauria, Maryańska (1990) noted that, in relative size of the supratemporal fenestra, *Homalocephalus* is the most derived of pachycephalosaurids.

Key references: Maryańska (1990); Maryańska and Osmólska (1974).

Photo by the author.

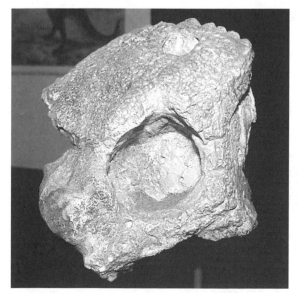

Homalocephale calathocercos, GI SPS 100/51, holotype partial skull, posterior view, in "The Great Russian Dinosaurs" exhibit (1996), Mesa Southwest Museum, Mesa, Arizona.

HOPLITOSAURUS Lucas 1902 [*nomen dubium*
Ornithischia: Genasauria: Thyreophora:
   Ankylosauria: Nodosauridae.
Name derivation: Greek *hoplites* = "armed" + Greek
   sauros = "lizard."
Type species: *H. marshi* (Lucas 1901) [*nomen
   dubium*].
Other species: [None.]
Occurrence: Lakota Formation, South Dakota,
   United States.
Age: Early Cretaceous (Barremian).
Known material/holotype: USNM 4752, partial
   postcrania, including right femur, proximal half
   of left humerus, distal half of right humerus,
   proximal portion of right scapula and coracoid,
   dorsal centrum, caudal centra, numerous dermal
   plates, fragments of ribs, other remains.

Hoplitosaurus

Diagnosis of genus (as for type species): Plates and spines generally massive, with relatively large basal surfaces, tapering abruptly, edges sharp (Lucas 1901).

Comments: The genus *Hoplitosaurus* was established on a much distorted, partial postcranial skeleton (USNM 4752) collected in 1898 by N. H. Darton from the Lakota Formation, in "Calico County," near Buffalo Gap Station, South Dakota. Lucas (1901) originally described USNM 4752 as representing a new species of *Stegosaurus*, which he named *S. marshi*.

Lucas originally characterized *S. marshi* "by the general massive appearance of the plates and spines, the comparatively large extent of their basal surfaces, their abrupt taper, and sharp edges."

Lucas (1902), subsequently recognizing certain similarities between this form and *Polacanthus*, referred it to the new genus *Hoplitosaurus*.

Gilmore (1914*b*), in his classic "Osteology of the Armored Dinosauria," published a revised description of *H. marshi* and assigned it to the Scelidosauridae. Gilmore described at least five kinds of dermal armor: 1. Thin, simple, flattened, rectangular scutes with rounded corners and no sculpture or ornamentation; 2. (most abundant) ossicle-like scutes that vary considerably in size (10–50 millimeters in greatest diameter) and shape (rounded, elliptical, and subrectangular); 3. numerous keeled scutes that vary greatly in size (one 32 millimeters thick through center) and shape (button-like kind with center raised as a blunt, conical projection, and more abundant elongated, angularly rounded kind, with sharp, asymmetrically placed keel on dorsal side); 4. large, subtriangular, plate-like structures with blood-vessel impressions [apparently from the tail], largest of these with greatest antero-posterior diameter of 210 millimeters, greatest vertical diameter 175 millimeters, greatest width 65 millimeters; 5. spined scutes, roughly triangular, almost all long and asymmetrical, including

Hoplitosaurus marshi, USNM 4752, holotype right femur, anterior view, right scapula-coracoid, and dermal armor of *Stegosaurus marshi*.

Photo by the author, courtesy National Museum of Natural History, Smithsonian Institution.

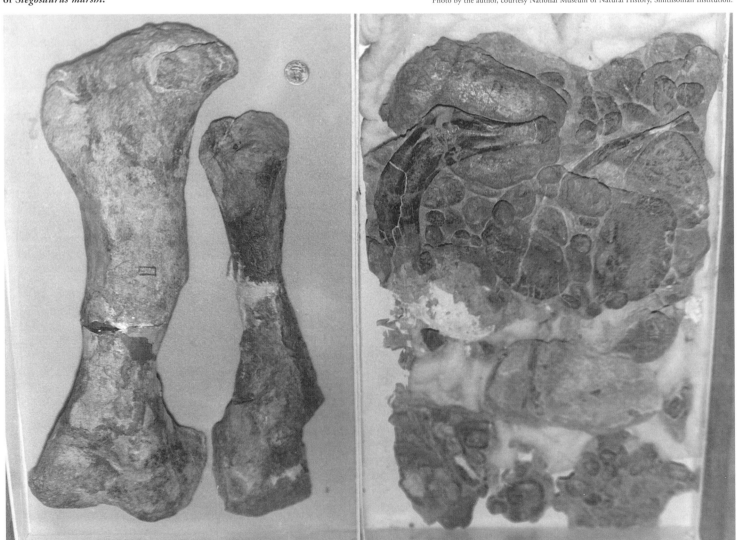

Hoplitosaurus marshi, USNM 4752, holotype dermal plate of *Stegosaurus marshi*. Scale = 4 cm. (After Lucas 1902.)

Hoplitosaurus marshi, USNM 4752, holotype dermal plate of *Stegosaurus marshi*. Scale = 3 cm. (After Lucas 1902.)

Hoplitosaurus marshi, USNM 4752, holotype dermal plate of *Stegosaurus marshi*. Scale = 3 cm. (After Lucas 1902.)

those (apparently from the tail) with median, anteroposteriorly expanded bases, contracting to a rounded spine that tapers to a blunt upper extremity, with a greatest length of 390 millimeters and a greatest anteroposterior length of 280 millimeters, those with compressed, grooved bases and spine with greatest height 330 millimeters and greatest anteroposterior length approximately 210 millimeters, and those with heavy, massive, expanded bases and compressed spines with sharp edges in front and back, greatest height in excess of 270 millimeters, greatest anteroposterior length 175 millimeters, with base having maximum width of 150 millimeters.

Gilmore envisioned *Hoplitosaurus* as an animal of low stature, measuring about 1.2 meters (4 feet) high at the hips. Lucas had placed the second grouping of scutes in the throat region, but Gilmore, noting that the femur was found attached to the lower side of the sandstone block containing the specimen, suggested they might have formed a carapace-like covering over the pelvic region. Although Lucas had also speculated as to the placement of other armor structures on the body, Gilmore noted that these elements were found disassociated and mingled with various skeletal elements, stating that placement of them was mostly a matter of conjecture.

In recent years, the validity of *Hoplitosaurus* as a distinct genus has been questioned by various workers. Blows (1987), after an examination of *Polacanthus* specimen BMNH R9293, perceived close

affinities between that genus and *Hoplitosaurus*. Blows observed that both genera have flat and standing dermal elements that compare well with each other. However, no Polacanthus-like sacral shield is known in the North American form. Blows postulated that, if this shield is considered sufficient grounds for species differentiation, the new combination of *P. marshi* be reserved for the American form.

Coombs and Maryańska (1990) regarded Blows' synonymy of these two genera as tentative, noting that the presence of a lesser trochanter distinct from the greater trochanter in the holotype of *H. marshi* is a feature otherwise only known in *Cryptodraco* (see Galton 1980*b*, 1983*c*); the lesser and greater trochanters in the femora of all other known ankylosaurs (and stegosaurs) are fused (see Sereno 1986).

Pereda-Suberbiola (1991) also considered *Hoplitosaurus* to be synonymous with *Polacanthus*, mostly based upon a perceived similarity in the shape of the proximal end of the femur. More recently, however, Coombs (1995) rejected this synonymy, pointing out that there is greater similarity between *Polacanthus* and *Texasetes*, and that the distal ends of the femora of *Polacanthus* and *Hoplitosaurus* are quite different. Coombs further noted that the femur of *Hoplitosaurus* is unique and somewhat anomalous among ankylosaurs, primarily in the flexure of the shaft.

Key references: Blows (1987); Coombs (1995); Coombs and Maryańska (1990); Gilmore (1914*b*); Lucas (1901, 1902); Pereda-Suberbiola (1991).

HOPLOSAURUS Seeley 1881 [*nomen dubium*]—
(See *Struthiosaurus* [notes])
Name derivation: Greek *hoplon* = "weapon" + Greek
sauros = "lizard."
Type species: *H. ischyrus* Seeley 1881 [*nomen
dubium*].

HORTALOTARSUS Seeley 1894 [*nomen
dubium*]—(See *Massospondylus*.)
Name derivation: Greek *hora* = "right time" + Latin
talus = "ankle bone" + Greek *tarsos* = "sole of
foot."
Type species: *H. skirtopodius* Seeley 1881 [*nomen
dubium*].

Huayangosaurus taibaii, CV00720, referred dermal shoulder plate. (After Dong, Zhou and Tang 1982.)

HUAYANGOSAURUS Dong, Zhou and Tang
1982
Ornithischia: Genasauria: Thyreophora:
Stegosauria: Huayangosauridae.
Name derivation: *Hua Yang Guo Zhi* [book from
Jin Dynasty (A.D. 265–317), Huayang being
early name for Sichuan] + Greek *sauros* =
"lizard."
Type species: *H. taibaii* Dong, Zhou and Tang
1982.
Other species: [None.]
Occurrence: Xiashaximiao Formation, Sichuan,
People's Republic of China.
Age: Middle Jurassic (Bathonian–Callovian).
Known material: Complete skeleton with skull,
complete skull, five fragmentary postcranial
skeletons.

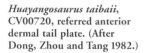

Huayangosaurus taibaii, CV00720, referred anterior dermal tail plate. (After Dong, Zhou and Tang 1982.)

Holotype: IVPP V6728, complete skull, fragmentary postcrania (presumably belonging to the
same individual) including five vertebrae, fragmentary limbs, three plates.

Diagnosis of genus (as for type species): Cranium distinguished by oval depression between premaxilla and maxilla, small horn core on dorsal aspect
of postorbital, and high maxillary tooth count (25–30
in adults); postcranium distinguished by anterior
dorsal ribs with intercostal flanges and flared distal
ends, and coossified, subcylindrical carpal block
(Sereno and Dong 1992).

Comments: The best represented Middle Jurassic stegosaur and one of the only genera known from
cranial remains, *Huayangosaurus* was founded upon

Photo by M. Tanimoto.

Huayangosaurus taibaii, skeleton exhibited at Zigong Dinosaur Museum.

a partial skeleton with a well-preserved skull (IVPP V6728), discovered in 1980 in the Xiashaximiao (Lower Shaximiao) Formation of Dashanpu, Zigong City, Sichuan Province, China. Referred to the type species *H. taibaii* were the imperfectly-preserved, disarticulated remains of six individuals from the same locality (ZDM T7001, an almost complete skeleton with complete skull [see below], 64 vertebrae, limbs, and 12 plates, from a smaller individual; ZDM T7002, comprising several vertebrae; ZDM T7003, including vertebrae and pelvic girdle; ZDM T1004, caudal vertebrae; CV 00720, including fragmentary skull, 28 vertebrae, and 20 plates; and CV 00721, comprising seven vertebrae). Upon this genus and species was erected the subfamily Huayangosaurinae (Dong, Zhou and Tang 1982).

Zhou (1984) first diagnosed the monotypic *H. taibaii* as follows: Small to medium sized, primitive stegosaur; skull with two supraorbital openings; premaxillary teeth simple, pitted; jugal elongated; antorbital fenestrae small and triangular; mandible with prominent coronoid process and small foramen; eight cervical and 17 dorsal vertebrae, four coossified sacrals, about 35 caudals; processes of anterior dorsal ribs well-developed, hook-like; limb bones at least partially hollow; femur about 113 percent length of humerus; pedal digits II and III with three phalanges each; dermal plate lance-shaped.

As originally reconstructed by Zhou, the skeleton of *Huayangosaurus* bears two rows of small, paired, heart-shaped dermal plates which grade to

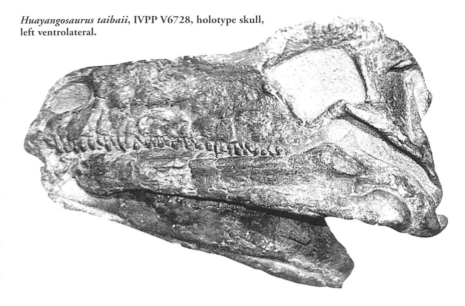

Huayangosaurus taibaii, IVPP V6728, holotype skull, left ventrolateral.

less rounded and more narrow and spine-shaped plates toward the shoulder region, diminishing in size past the hips, and terminating approximately half-way along the tail where there are presumably four large spines. The length of the animal was estimated at about 4 meters (13.5 feet). In his book *Dinosaurs from China*, Dong (1987) added that *Huayangosaurus* also possessed bony scutes on both sides of the body, the shoulders bearing a pair of large dermal spines [as in *Kentrosaurus* and *Tuojiangosaurus*].

To date, *Huayangosaurus* is the most primitive known stegosaur. The snout, unlike the long and narrow edentulous snouts of later stegosaurs, exhibits the more primitive feature of seven premaxillary teeth on each side (see Sereno 1986). The form and size of the dermal plates, grading into spines, support the hypothesis that large plates in more advanced stegosaurs may have evolved from spines (Hoffstetter 1957; Steel 1969).

Based upon studies of the holotype and specimen ZDM 7001, Sereno and Dong (1992) rediagnosed *H. taibaii*; offered a detailed description of the skull, noting cranial features not previously observed; and also offered a revised cladistic diagnosis of the Stegosauria (see systematics section).

In comparing *Huayangosaurus* to *Stegosaurus*, Sereno and Dong noted that the former retains premaxillary teeth and a moderate-sized antorbital fossa; forelimb not shortened relative to hindlimb (humerus to femur ratio of 0.91); side of trunk armored with one parascapular [new term suggested by Sereno and Dong] spine; and at least one row of keeled scutes.

Sereno and Dong noted that the diagnostic character of the postorbital horn (not occurring in

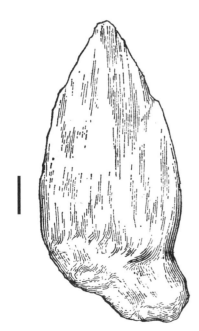

Huayangosaurus taibaii, ZDM T7001, referred dermal nucal plate. Scale = 2 cm. (After Dong, Zhou and Tang 1982.)

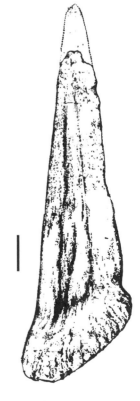

Huayangosaurus taibaii, CV00720, referred dermal sacral plate. Scale = 3 cm. (After Dong, Zhou and Tang 1982.)

Huayangosaurus taibaii,
T7001, referred tail spine.
Scale = 4 cm. (After Dong,
Zhou and Tang 1982.)

Stegosaurus, the only other stegosaur for which the postorbital is known) is either variable, sexually dimorphic, or perhaps a maturation feature.

As described by Sereno and Dong, the preserved plate, associated with the type skull and probably positioned over the cervical vertebrae, is diamond-shaped, broadest below mid-height, the base beveled to one side indicating that it angled dorsolaterally away from the axial plane (as in *Stegosaurus*). Other larger plates (ZDM 7001 and CV 00720; see Zhou) are intermediate in size and shape (lanceolate) between the cervical plate and caudal spines, thickened along the anterior margin, with a median prominence on the medial side, and with a sharper axis. The type caudal spine (closely resembling those of ZDM 7001) is transversely compressed with sharp anterior and posterior edges, the lateral and medial sides resembling the lance-shaped plates, with a thickened anterior margin, flattened lateral surface, and gently convex medial surface. The beveled base indicates that the spine angled posterodorsally away from the sagittal plane. Parasacral spines (Dong 1990), found in association with the pectoral girdle, are distinguished from caudal spines and resemble those in *Tuojiangosaurus,* with a narrow, cylindrical shaft projecting from an expanded plate-shaped base (Hennig 1924; Galton, Brun and Rioult 1980; Galton 1982*a*). The scutes (in IVPP V6728, ZDM 7001 and CV 00720) are solid, oval-shaped and keeled and seem to have been aligned in a parasagittal row, the spacing between them greater than the length of one scute. Apparently these scutes were embedded in the epidermis.

Sereno and Dong regarded *Huayangosaurus* as the sister-taxon of all other stegosaurs (which have lost premaxillary teeth, have a smaller antorbital fossa, pubis with larger prepubic process, and lost the lateral rows of scutes). *Huayangosaurus* is united with other stegosaurs by 19 (see diagnosis of Stegosauria, systematics section). This suite of characters indicate that stegosaurs had already acquired most of their conspicuous skeletal modifications by the Middle Jurassic. Sereno and Dong pointed out that the earliest known ankylosaur (*i.e.*, the Callovian *Sarcolestes*; see Galton 1983*a*) is also known from the Middle Jurassic, a time perhaps close to the divergence of these two groups.

Key references: Dong (1987); Dong, Zhou and Tang (1982); Sereno and Dong (1992); Zhou (1984).

HULSANPES Osmólska 1982

Saurischia: Theropoda: Tetanurae: Avetheropoda:
 Coelurosauria: Maniraptora: Dromaeosauridae
 incertae sedis.

Name derivation: "Khulsan [locality]" + Latin *pes* = "foot."

Type species: *H. perlei* Osmólska 1982.

Other species: [None.]

Occurrence: Barun Goyot Formation, Omnogov, Mongolian People's Republic.

Age: Late Cretaceous (Middle Campanian).

Known material/holotype: ZPAL MgD-I/173, opposed metatarsals II–IV lacking proximal articular ends, with second phalanx of digit I, proximal portion of second phalanx of digit II, proximal portion of third phalanx of digit I, ?octico-occipital fragment of skull (probably pertaining to type specimen), juvenile.

Diagnosis of genus (as for type species): Pes functionally tridactyl; metatarsus slender, width-to-length ratio 0.16; metatarsal III not wedged in anterior view, II–IV subequally thick; pedal digit II specialized (Osmólska 1982).

Comments: The genus *Hulsanpes* was founded upon an incomplete hindfoot (ZPAL MgD-I/173) collected during the 1970 Polish-Mongolian Paleontological Expedition (Kielan-Jaworoska and Barsbold 1972).

Osmólska (1982) noted similarities between the pedal structure in *Hulsanpes* and that in dromaeosaurids. However, owing to the incompleteness of the *H. perlei* type material and the fact that it represents a juvenile individual, Osmólska only tentatively referred this genus to the Dromaeosauridae.

Ostrom (1990), in a review of the Dromaeosauridae, judged that *H. perlei* does appear to display the modified form of the second toe diagnostic to that group, but noted that other diagnostic features have not yet been reported in this taxon.

Key references: Osmólska (1982); Ostrom (1990).

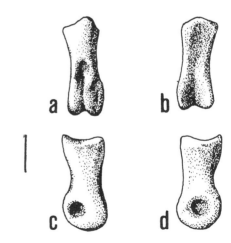

Hulsanpes perlei, ZPAL MgD-I/173, holotype right pedal phalanx II, in a. dorsal, b. ventral, c. medial, and d. lateral views. Scale = 4 cm. (After Osmólska 1982.)

HYLAEOSAURUS   Mantell 1833—

(=?*Acantholpholis*)

Ornithischia: Genasauria: Thyreophora: Ankylosauria: Nodosauridae.

Name derivation: Greek *hyiaos* = "belonging to the
forest [Weald]" + Greek *sauros* = "lizard."

Type species: *H. armatus* Mantell 1833.

Other species: [None.]

Occurrence: Wealden (Tunbridge Wells Sand/Grin-
stead Clay), West Sussex, East Sussex, England;
unnamed formation, Ardennes, France; ?Salas de
los Infantes, Province of Burgos, Spain.

Age: Early Cretaceous (Late Valanginian–
Barremian).

Known material: Two partial postcranial skeletons,
isolated postcranial elements.

Holotype: BMNH R3775, ten anterior and some
loose vertebrae, two coracoids, two distal portions of scapulae, several ribs, dermal spines.

Diagnosis of genus (as for type species): Moderate to large size (3–5 meters, or about 11–17 feet);
scapular spine slanting obliquely across entire scapular blade (Coombs and Maryańska 1990).

Comments: *Hylaeosaurus* is historically important as the third dinosaurian genus and first known
ankylosaur to be described. The genus was established
on partial postcranial remains with armor (BMNH
R3775), found in 1832 in a block of stone, in a
Wealden quarry at Tilgate Forest, Sussex, England.
The material was discovered by Gideon Algernon
Mantell, who noticed indications of fossil bone in a
large chunk of stone that had been broken up and
discarded on the roadside.

The type species, *H. armatus,* was first described
by Mantell (1833) as follows: Anterior dorsal vertebrae with broad centra having thick hemal ridge; posterior dorsal centra compressed, with pronounced lateral hollow [=pleurocoel]; posterior chevrons
becoming elongate inferiorly; dermal spines much
compressed, sometimes relatively narrow, with convex anterior and posterior margins.

Owen (1858) later redescribed *Hylaeosaurus*, his
description augmented by the discovery of additional
material including part of a tail (BMNH 3789),
found in 1837 in Tilgate Forest, and a tibia (BMNH
2615), phalangeal bone, and scapula (BMNH 2584)
from a Wealden stone quarry at Bolney, Sussex.

Owen described the dermal scutes of the tail as
elliptical or circular, convex with the summit developed into a tubercle most prominent in smaller

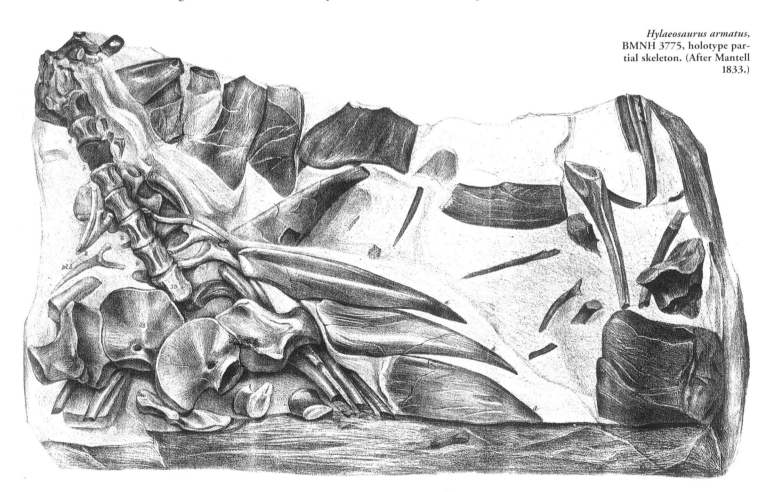

Hylaeosaurus armatus,
BMNH 3775, holotype par-
tial skeleton. (After Mantell
1833.)

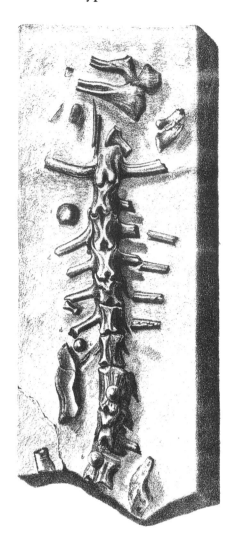

Hylaeosaurus armatus, BMNH 3775, holotype vertebrae. (After Mantell 1833.)

scutes, and with an outer surface studded by very small tubercles. The largest scute is less than 8 centimeters (under 3 inches) in diameter, the smallest over 2.5 centimeters (about 1 inch) in diameter. The scutes decrease in size as they approach the end of the tail. Since there was no evidence that these scutes overlapped each other, Owen speculated that they may have studded the skin in random arrangement.

Discovered with the holotype of *H. armatus* were some large elongated, flattened, pointed plates of bone, three found in succession on the left side of the thorax partly overlaying the left scapula and vertebral ribs. One spine is long and triangular with a thickened base. Mantell incorrectly imagined these spines as forming a single serrated fringe along the animal's back. Owen, however, noted that the spines were asymmetrical, having a slight concavity, this nonsymmetry implying that they may have projected in two rows from the dorsal region. (It was not until later nodosaurid discoveries were made that these spines were more correctly positioned laterally along the body.)

The holotype of *H. armatus* has never been entirely exposed from its rock matrix, and so an accurate life restoration of the animal has yet to be made. Nevertheless, in the early 1850s, sculptor Benjamin Waterhouse Hawkins, under Owen's direction, attempted a life-sized model of the animal for the grounds of the Crystal Palace exhibition center at Sydenham, London. Hawkins imaginatively and fancifully restored the dinosaur with a prickly back and a row of dorsal spines.

Sanz (1983) reported fragmentary nodosaurid remains, possibly referrable to *H. armatus,* from the Lower Cretaceous of Salas de los Infantes, Province of Burgos, Spain.

Note: Perhaps representing a new nodosaurid genus are four dermal scutes, similar to those of *Hylaeosaurus,* recovered from the Kimmeridge Clay of Rodbourne, Wiltshire, England, and reported by Delair (1973).

Key references: Coombs and Maryańska (1990); Mantell (1833); Owen (1858).

HYPACROSAURUS Brown 1913—
(=*Cheneosaurus*; =?*Corythosaurus*)
Ornithischia: Genasauria: Cerapoda:
   Ornithopoda: Iguanodontia: Hadrosauridae:
   Lambeosaurinae.
Name derivation: Greek *hy* = "very" + Greek *akros* = "high" + Greek *sauros* = "lizard."
Type species: *H. altispinus* Brown 1913.
Other species: *H. stebingeri* Horner and Currie 1993.
Occurrence: Horseshoe Canyon Formation, Alberta, Canada; Two Medicine Formation, Montana, United States, Alberta, Canada.
Age: Late Cretaceous (Early Maastrichtian).
Known material: Vertebrae, 5–10 articulated skulls, some with associated postcrania, adult and juvenile, isolated skull elements, numerous skeletal elements, embryo to adult, associated eggs.
Holotype: AMNH 5204, last eight dorsal and two anterior caudal vertebrae, ilia, right ischium, right pubis, several ribs, adult.

Diagnosis of genus (as for type species): Differs from *Corythosaurus* in following features: more robust "toes" and "heel" in "foot" of ischium; taller neural spines (caused in old individuals by bone deposition?); crest more pointed, without S-shaped narial loop; fenestra missing on medial wall of lateral diverticula (from Weishampel 1981) (Brett-Surman 1989).

Diagnosis of *H. stebingeri*: (No autapomorphies); long, thin lacrimal morphologically intermediate between species of *Lambeosaurus* and *H. altispi-*

nus, narial crest with apex directly over anterior ends of orbits, similar to those two taxa; shares with *Hypacrosaurus,* restricted external naris, wide narial crest, and restricted dorsal centra with very tall neural spines; with species of *Lambeosaurus,* narial crest, mostly composed of premaxillae (Horner and Currie 1993).

Comments: The genus *Hypacrosaurus* was founded upon postcranial remains (AMNH 5204) collected in 1910 by the American Museum of Natural History from the Horseshoe Canyon [then Edmonton] Formation, above Red Deer River, near Tolman Ferry, Alberta, Canada.

Paratypes from approximately the same horizon and locality consist of three mid-dorsal vertebrae (AMNH 5206); sacrum and last ten dorsal vertebrae, nine ribs, left ilium, right pubis, left femur, left tibia, both fibulae, four metatarsals, five phalanges, and pieces of epidermis (AMNH 5217); and a front limb, nine cervical vertebrae, left tibia, fibula, and pes (AMNH 5272). Subsequent discoveries included a plesiotype (designated as such by Lull and Wright 1942) collected by George F. Sternberg in 1915 below Tolman Ferry, consisting of a skull with right mandible, articulated series of dorsal, sacral, and caudal vertebrae, numerous ribs, right humerus, ulna, radius, pelvic arch, and complete right hindlimb with pes (NMC 8501). Other referred material includes a skull (AMNH 5278; formerly GSC 8500), lacking crest and both dentaries, collected in 1915 by P. A. Bungart north of Tolman Ferry on the east side of Red Deer River, above Rumsey Ferry, plus a skull (ROM 4974) collected in 1922 by Levi Sternberg, from the east side of Red Deer River, above Rumsey Ferry.

With the skull not yet known, Brown (1913*b*) originally diagnosed the type species, *H. altispinus,* based on the holotype and paratypes, as follows: Cervical vertebrae strongly opisthocoelus, with spines reduced or absent, ribs stout; dorsal centra reduced in size, spines high and massive, from five to seven times higher than respective centra; eight sacral vertebrae; scapula long, very broad; radius greatly exceeding humerus in length; ilium deep, strongly curved; ischium long, terminating in foot-like expansion; pubis with short and broadly expanded anterior blade; femur, tibia, and fibula almost equal in length; pes long and massive.

Based upon the plesiotype skull, Gilmore (1924*e*) later supplemented Brown's original diagnosis mostly adding cranial characters, many of which are no longer regarded as significant. The skull closely resembles that of *Corythosaurus,* with a lower, narrower, and less rounded cranial crest. Another striking feature of *Hypacrosaurus* is the elongated vertebral

spines. During life these spines were probably surrounded by musculature and ossified tendons to create a hump-like rise along the dorsal region of the animal at the base of the vertebral spines, as in some mammals.

Based on remains referred to the type species, *Hypacrosaurus* was a large lambeosaurine, an adult measuring approximately 9 meters (30 feet) in length.

The second species of this genus, *H. stebingeri,* described by Horner and Currie (1993), was founded upon the nearly complete skeleton (MOR 549) of a nestling, recovered from the Two Medicine Formation, at Badger Creek, Glacier County, Montana, with numerous specimens referred to this new species. As related by Horner and Currie, the material (including eggs, nests, some of them complete, and hundreds of skeletal elements) was discovered in greenish-gray sandstones of the uppermost part of

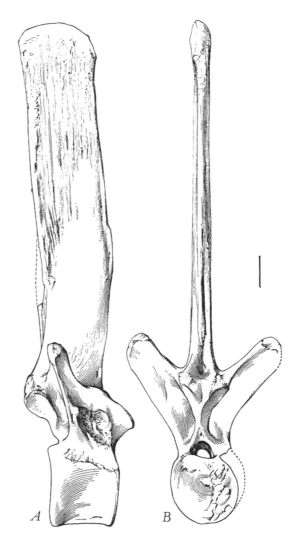

Hypacrosaurus altispinus, AMNH 5206, paratype mid-dorsal vertebrae. Scale = 4 cm. (After Brown 1913.)

the Two Medicine Formation, on both sides of the United States–Canadian border, in Montana and Alberta. Specimens from Montana were collected at two major nesting horizons in Glacier County, one located near Landslide Butte. Sites along this horizon, yielding randomly strewn crushed eggs, include those designated Egg Baby Butte, Egg Baby West, Baby Slide, Egg Explosion Hill, North Dome, and Egg Baby North. Another horizon, on Blacktail Creek, "yielded a nest with broken eggs, a clutch of eggs with embryos (MOR 559), and a fluvial concentration of disarticulated skeletal remains (MOR 548)." An isolated embryonic or nepionic individual (MOR 562) was found at Badger Creek.

According to Horner and Currie, several nests were found at a variety of sites in the Devil's Coulee area of Alberta. Most of the specimens used in Horner and Currie's study of this species came from a single nest at a locality called Little Diablo's Hill. Five nests were yielded by this locality, one (RTMP 89.79.53) containing eight eggs, some eggs found at this site containing embryonic specimens. Horner and Currie stated that the collected material represents "the largest collection of baby skeletal material of any single species of hadrosaur known from any area in the world."

A reconstruction of one egg (RTMP 90.130.1) by Horner and Currie shows an almost spherical egg measuring about 20 centimeters by 18.5 centimeters,

among the largest of all known dinosaur eggs. Horner and Currie described an embryo measuring 60 centimeters in length and a hatchling 1.7 meters long.

In describing this material, Horner and Currie noted that the morphology of nestlings resembles that of adults, but observed the following ontogenetic changes between embryos and nestlings: Early development of nasal crest (from a slight dome, with beginning of formation of S-loop narial passage, to vertical vaulting as skull size increases); increase in tooth rows in both maxilla and dentary, with probably an addition of at least one tooth to each vertical row; changes in proportion of orbits (becoming proportionally smaller) to increasing skull size; deepening of articular rugosities at union junctions; and changes in osteohistological structures; neural canal becoming proportionally smaller as neural spines increase in height; circumference-to-width ratios of femora and tibiae change during ontogeny, the elements becoming less robust with age; ends of all bones ossify, processes and muscle scars becoming more distinct; ossified tendons become more compact, less flexible.

Horner and Currie also noted that the embryos possess worn teeth, this suggesting that the teeth in hatchlings of this species were functional; and that histological studies indicate very rapid growth during this species' stay in the nest.

Courtesy Royal Tyrrell Museum/Alberta Community Development (slide #10.025.06a).

Hypacrosaurus altispinus,
skeleton.

According to Horner and Currie, *H. stebingeri* seems to be an intermediate taxon, phylogenetically, between a species of *Lambeosaurus* and *H. altispinus*.

Lambe (1917*a*) described the type species *Cheneosaurus tolmanensis*, based on a skull, limb bones, pelvic arch, and vertebrae (NMC 2246), collected by G. F. Sternberg in 1915 from the Horseshoe Canyon [then Edmonton] Formation, northwest of Big Valley Creek at Red Deer River above Tolman Ferry, in Alberta. Nopcsa (1933) first proposed that *Cheneosaurus* was a juvenile of *Hypacrosaurus*, after which Lull and Wright also recognized juvenile characters in the former genus. Later, Dodson (1975) demonstrated that *C. tolmanensis* represents a juvenile stage of *H. altispinus*, a synonymy accepted by most subsequent authors (*e.g.*, Brett-Surman 1979; Weishampel 1981).

According to Brett-Surman (1979, 1989), *Hypacrosaurus* and *Corythosaurus* are very similar osteologically and may someday be shown to be congeneric (chronospecies in the same lineage according to Brett-Surman 1975, 1979, 1989), the differences between them specific, *Hypacrosaurus* representing the more derived species of the genus. However, Brett-Surman favored keeping *Hypacrosaurus* and *Corythosaurus* generically separate until a sufficient series of *Hypacrosaurus* skulls may be found falling within the range of *Corythosaurus*.

Note: Gilmore (1933*b*) reported a specimen (AMNH 6594) consisting of the mid-portion of a dentary, fragment of a surangular, pedal phalangeal bone and portions of three anterior caudal vertebrae, collected in 1929 by Walter Granger from the Dohoin Usu Formation, about 75 miles northeast of Shabarakh Usu, in Outer Mongolia. The large caudal centra of this specimen resemble, in both length and form, those in *Hypacrosaurus*. These bones, seemingly from the same individual, marked the most ancient occurrence of Mongolian hadrosaurids known at that time.

Arguing for ectothermy in dinosaurs, Ruben, Leitch and Hillenius (1995) noted that nasal olfactory turbinate bones or cartilages are present in all extant tetrapods, but only warm-blooded animals—birds and mammals—possess both respiratory and olfactory turbinate structures; and that respiratory turbinates (RT) in these two groups, regardless of body mass, mostly function "to restrict excessive pulmonary evaporative water loss that would otherwise be associated with high lung ventilation rates in endothermic species." Reviewing a variety of rostral features in some saurischian dinosaurs, Ruben *et al.*, concluded that respiratory turbinates were probably not present in tyrannosaurids, dromaeosaurids, and

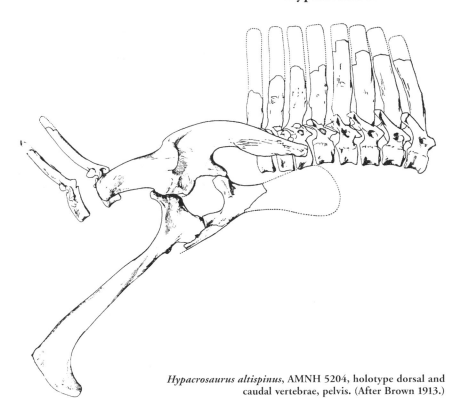

Hypacrosaurus altispinus, AMNH 5204, holotype dorsal and caudal vertebrae, pelvis. (After Brown 1913.)

ornithomimids (among the most likely candidates for endothermy among the Dinosauria), as well as probably *Archaeopteryx*, this interpreted as direct evidence for ectothermic or near-ectothermic metabolic status in these taxa; and that without respiratory turbinates, "unacceptably high rates of respiratory water loss would probably always have posed a chronic obstacle to maintenance of bulk lung ventilation rates consistent with endothermy, or with metabolic rates approaching endothermy."

Horner (1995) debated the hypothesis of Ruben *et al.*, suggesting that the enclosed narial chambers of lambeosaurine [=lambeosaurid of Horner's usage] dinosaurs, though usually interpreted as resonating chambers for sound production and possibly having this function, may also have had functions related to olfaction and water retention. As Horner pointed out, earlier descriptions and drawings of the narial chambers of lambeosaurines show them as smooth-walled, tube-like passages. However, more recent CT-Scan studies of the skull of a half-grown lambeosaurine of the genus *Hypacrosaurus* have revealed the presence of a highly complex internal network of bone within these chambers, possibly having RT implications. The walls are "wrinkled, furrowed and corrugated throughout the entire passage from the s-loop to near the external nares. Within the lower, bifurcated chambers, just posterior to s-loops, exists an extensive section of extremely thin, twisted, and curved struts of bone, most similar to what has been

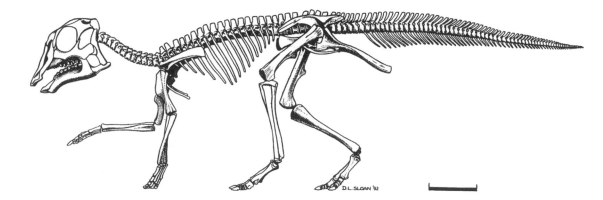

Hypacrosaurus stebingeri, reconstructed embryonic skeleton (RTMP 88.3.2). Scale = 5 cm. (After Horner and Currie 1993.)

described as nasal respiratory turbinate bones. These turbinal-like structures extend laterally from the 'wall' between the right and left lower chambers of the premaxillae and are thus within both air passages." Horner concluded that the presence of these structures, interpreted as RT, suggest high ventilation rates and endothermy in *Hypacrosaurus*.

Key references: Brett-Surman (1975, 1979, 1989); Brown (1913*b*); Dodson (1975); Gilmore (1924*e*); Horner (1995); Horner and Currie (1993); Lull and Wright (1942); Nopcsa (1933); Weishampel (1981).

HYPSELOSAURUS   Matheron 1869 [*nomen dubium*]

Saurischia: Sauropodomorpha: Sauropoda: Titanosauria: Titanosauridae.

Name derivation: Greek *hypsi* = "high" + Greek *sauros* = "lizard."

Type species: *H. pricsus* Matheron (1869).

Other species: [None.]

Occurrence: Grès de Labarre, Ariège, Grès de Saint-Chinian, Couches de Rognac, Bouches-du-Rhône, Grès à Reptiles, Var, France.

Age: Late Cretaceous (Maastrichtian).

Known material: Isolated postcrania representing at least ten individuals, ?eggs.

Holotype: AIS collection, three portions of left femur, distal portion of left tibia, greater portion of fibula, two consecutive caudal vertebrae.

Diagnosis of genus: [No modern diagnosis published.]

Comments: A relatively small sauropod, the genus *Hypselosaurus* was established upon partial postcranial remains (AIS collection), recovered from Fuveau, Bouches-du-Rhône Department, in Rognac, Provence, France. According to Le Loeuff (1995) in a review of European titanosaurids, this material seems to have been lost from the Muséum d'Histoire Naturelle, Marseilles.

Hypselosaurus was "diagnosed" by Matheron (1869) as follows: Quadrate large, massive; teeth small, slender, cylindrical, apparently rather weak; caudal vertebrae large (one 11 centimeters, or about 4.25 inches in breadth, 7 centimeters, or about 2.7 inches, high), with one articular end concave and other convex [=opisthocoelous condition], especially distinguished by lateral compression (as in crocodiles); (from limb-bone fragments) animal more than 8 meters (about 27 feet) long.

Matheron incorrectly imagined *Hypselosaurus* to be a "gigantic" and "monstrous saurian," an aquatic creature with a life style like that of some gigantic crocodile.

Other material referred to *Hypselosaurus* includes remains from Begudian on the banks of the Arc north of Trets (Collot 1891); cranial fragments, teeth, caudal vertebrae, ribs, scapulae, coracoid, pubes, limb and metapodial elements, from the "Danian" of central France (Lapparent 1947*a*); a large rib and the proximal portion of the end of a right ulna from the Upper Cretaceous of Hérault (Montouliers) (Lapparent [1954]); posterior caudal from the Upper Cretaceous of Orcau, Spain (Lapparent and Aguirre 1956); and a humerus from the Begudian of Basse-Provence (Dughi and Sirugue 1960). There is, however, no evidence to support that the material from Spain (and also that reported from Transylvania) belongs to this genus (R. E. Molnar, personal communication).

In his review of the Sauropoda, McIntosh (1990*b*) commented that the type species, *H. priscus,* differs in the robustness of its limbs from all other known European titanosaurids.

Le Loeuff stated that the scattered type specimen for *H. priscus* cannot be diagnosed by autapomorphies and can only be referred to an undetermined titanosaurid. The vertebrae exhibit no distinguishing characters; the lateral tuberosity of the fibula is typical among titanosaurids, resembling that of *Saltasaurus loricatus,* but does not exhibit the typical structure seen in titanosaurines. Le Loeuff regarded *H. priscus* as a *nomen dubium*.

According to Le Loeuff, scattered bones (housed at the Muséum d'Histoire Naturelle, Paris) referred by Lapparent (1947) to *H. priscus* and *Titanosaurus indicus*, mostly because of differences in size, should be regarded as representing an undetermined titanosaurid.

A small number of specimens recovered in Spain have been referred to *Hypselosaurus*:

Lapparent, Quintero and Tregueros (1957) described an isolated posterior caudal vertebra from Cubilla, Province de Soria. Le Loeuff considered this specimen as belonging to an undetermined titanosaurid sauropod.

Casanovas, Santafe, Sanz and Buscalioni (1987) referred to *Hypselosaurus* sp. two vertebrae (IPSN-19 and IPSN-23), collected from the Upper Maastrichtian of Els Nerets, and a proximal humerus fragment from Orcau. As observed by Le Loeuff, IPSN-19 is a laterally compressed dorsal (not caudal, as suggested by Casanovas *et al.*) centrum (height/width ratio = 0.49) and IPSN-23 is a laterally compressed posterior caudal centrum (height/width ratio = 1.1). Le Loeuff considered this material as provisionally representing an undetermined titanosaurid.

Masiera and Ullastre (1988) referred to the type species, *H. priscus,* the proximal part of a large (proximal width of 40 centimeters) humerus (housed at the Museo Municipal de Geologia in Barcelona) recovered from l'Estanyo (Tremp Basin). Le Loeuff regarded this specimen as belonging to an undetermined titanosaurid.

Hypselosaurus priscus, AIS collection, holotype including 1. portions of left femur, 2. portion of fibula, 3. distal portion of left tibia, 4.–5. caudal vertebrae. Scale = 10 cm. (After Matheron 1869.)

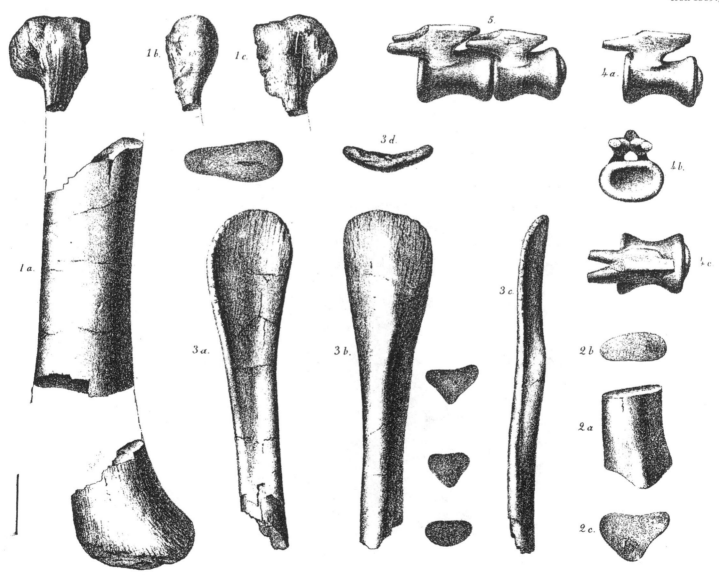

Various dinosaur bones were found during the 1980s in Late Cretaceous (Early Maastrichtian) rocks of Southwestern France, east of Le Mas d'Azil in the neighborhood of Lavelanet. Among these remains was the proximal portion of humerus, which Villatte, Taquet and Bilotte (1986) referred to *H. priscus*. Le Loeuff regarded this specimen as belonging to an undetermined titanosaurid.

Notes: Dinosaur bones collected by local priest Abbé J. J. Pouech (1881*a*, 1881*b*) during the 1870s, from the Grè de Labarre Formation (Early Maastrichian) in southwestern France, have recently been rediscovered. The collection, housed at the Museum of the Collège Jean XXIII in Pamiers, includes two different types of caudal vertebrae and two very different tibiae belonging to titanosaurid sauropods (see Le Loeuff 1991), suggesting to Le Loeuff (1993) that two different kinds of titanosaurids lived in this area. The material is too poor, however, to be referred to any titanosaurid species.

Buffetaut, Clottes, Cuny, Ducroco, Le Loeuff, Martin, Powell, Raynaud and Tong (1989) reported on a titanosaurid bonebed in the Bellevue locality at Campagne-sur-Aude. Several hundred disarticulated bones (housed at the Espéraza Dinosaur Museum at Aude) have been recovered from this site, allowing the reconstruction of a partial skeleton. Although Clottes and Raynaud (1983) and Bilotte, Duranthon, Clottes

and Raynaud (1986) referred these remains to *Hypselosaurus*, Le Loeuff (1993) identified them as clearly representing a new form with the following features: Teeth slightly spatulate; distal end of dorsal neural spines enlarged; caudal vertebrae laterally compressed; anterior caudals with very large prezygapophysial facets supported by very short prezygapophyses; neural spine of anterior caudals high, thin, with pre- and postspinal laminae.

Associated with the type specimen of *H. priscus* were numerous fragments of fossilized eggshells (now egg genus *Megathoolithus* Mikhailov 1991), these being the first apparent dinosaur egg specimens ever discovered. When describing *Hypselosaurus*, Matheron suggested with caution that these eggs could belong either to this dinosaur or to some large bird. To date, however, these eggs have not been attributed with certainty to *Hypselosaurus* and were, in fact, also referred by Voss-Foucart (1968) to the theropod *Megalosaurus*.

The finding and collecting of these eggs were chronicled by Colbert (1961) in his book *Dinosaurs: Their Discovery and World*: In 1930, a French farmer dug up a complete fossil egg while plowing in his vineyard near Aix-en-Provence, after which several more eggs were found. More discoveries, including entire batteries of eggs, some of them complete with fragmentary remains numbering in the thousands, were made during the late 1950s by botanist M. Dughi. As a result of Dughi's work, about a hundred eggs were collected, some of them crushed, others revealing their original shape. Some eggs were found in groups of five, suggesting nests. The eggs vary in shape (possibly representing more than one kind of reptile). Generally, the eggs assumed to be those of *Hypselosaurus* are almost round in shape with rugged surfaces. The largest eggs are about twice the size of ostrich eggs. Almost 60 years after the discovery of these eggs, Victor van Straelen (who had already described dinosaur eggs from Mongolia) became convinced that the French specimens belonged to *Hypselosaurus*.

Identical fossil eggs found at Renne-Le-Chateau, in France, were interpreted by Cousin, Breton, Fournier and Watte (1986) as belonging to *Hypselosaurus* and the ornithopod *Rhabdodon*, the sole criterion for identification being the arrangement of the eggs (those attributed to *Hypselosaurus* eggs laying in rather arbitrarily chosen circles, those to *Rhabdodon* forming clusters intertwined with circles). Sabath (1991), doubting that eggs laid by two such different kinds of dinosaurs could be morphologically identical after more than 100 million years of independent evolution, suggested that the eggs pertained solely to the sauropod. The patterns in which

Photo by Logan, courtesy Department Library Services, American Museum of Natural History (neg. #2A5378).

Fossil egg associated with *Hypselosaurus priscus*, compared with hen's egg.

the eggs were laid could reflect incubation temperature differences among the two groups of eggs for the purpose (as in modern crocodiles and other reptiles) of determining sex. Also, Sabath noted, the differing patterns could have some taphonomical significance or even be reflective of different nesting seasons.

Borgomanero and Leonardi (1981) reported a fossil dinosaur egg of the kind generally referred to *H. priscus* from the Aix area of Provence, France. As described by Borgomanero and Leonardi, this egg measures 15 centimeters (almost 5.8 inches) high and 15 by 10 centimeters (almost 5.8 by about 3.85 inches) wide, with a shell thickness of 1.8 millimeters.

Key references: Bilotte, Duranthon, Clottes and Raynaud (1986); Borgomanero and Leonardi (1981); Buffetaut, Clottes, Cuny, Duroco, Le Loeuff, Martin, Powell, Raynaud and Tong (1989); Casanovas, Santafe, Sanz and Buscalioni (1987); Clottes and Raynaud (1986); Colbert (1961); Cousin, Breton, Fournier and Watte (1986); Lapparent (1947); Le Loeuff (1991, 1993); Matheron (1869); McIntosh (1990*b*); Mikhailov (1991); Pouech (1881*a*, 1881*b*); Sabbath (1991); Villatte, Taquet and Bilotte (1986).

HYPSIBEMA   Cope 1869—(=*Neosaurus, Parrosaurus*)

Ornithischia: Genasauria: Cerapoda: Ornithopoda: Iguanodontia: Hadrosauridae *incertae sedis*.

Name derivation: Greek *hypsi* = "high" + Latin *bema* = "platform [stride]."

Type species: *H. crassicauda* Cope 1869 [*nomen dubium*].Other species: [None.]

Occurrence: Black Creep Formation, North Carolina, Ripley Formation, Missouri, United States.

Age: Late Cretaceous (Campanian).

Known material: Caudal vertebrae, fragmentary humerus, fragmentary tibia, metatarsal II.

Lectotype: USNM 7189, caudal vertebra.

Diagnosis of genus: [None published.]

Comments: Cope (1869*b*) founded the new genus and species *Hysibema crassicauda* upon five bones representing three dinosaurian groups (Ornithopoda, Sauropodomorpha, and Theropoda). This

material was collected by W. C. Kerr from James King's marl pits in the Black Creek Formation (deposited during "Taylor" time; see Heron and Wheeler 1964; therefore of Campanian age; see Baird and Horner 1979), Sampson County, North Carolina.

As pointed out by Baird and Horner, Cope assumed that these fossils (included under the single catalogue number USNM 7189) were all associated with each other. Among this collected material, one element (now missing) was seemingly the incomplete left femur of a large theropod. Two hadrosaurian limb bones, an incomplete right metatarsal, and a fragment of a small left tibia are actually indeterminate hadrosaurine elements.

Baird and Horner designated as the lectotype of *H. crassicauda* a single caudal vertebra (USNM 7189), this bone, some referred caudals (USNM 7093 and 7094; ANSP 15307A-C and 15338), and a ?referable caudal spine (USNM 10312) corresponding to the series of 13 caudal vertebrae (USNM 16735) from the Ripley Formation of Bollinger County, Glen Allen, Missouri. This material was originally described as a sauropod by Gilmore and Stewart (1945) as the species *Neosaurus missouriensis*; when the generic name *Neosaurus* proved to be preoccupied (Nopcsa 1923), Gilmore (1945) renamed this taxon *Parrosaurus missouriensis*. For no apparent reason other than general morphology, Gilmore tentatively referred this material to the sauropod family Camarasauridae. Gilmore never realized the similarities between the two specimens. Baird and Horner, then believing the type material of *H. crassicauda* pertained to a large sauropod, made *Parrosaurus* a junior synonym of *Hypsibema*.

H. crassicauda was described by Baird and Horner as follows: Largest (and apparently most anterior) vertebra (ANSP 15338) slightly longer than height of its centrum; caudal vertebrae becoming increasingly elongate posteriorly; ends of centra hexagonal, wider than high, slightly amphicoelous, with beveled rims; no pleurocoels.

Baird and Horner observed that the lectotype shares certain features with hadrosaurids, including a slightly amphicoelous centra, central position of the neural arch, and short anterior zygapophyses. Because

Hypsibema crassicauda, USNM 16735, holotype caudal vertebrae of *Neosaurus missouriensis.*

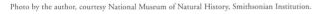

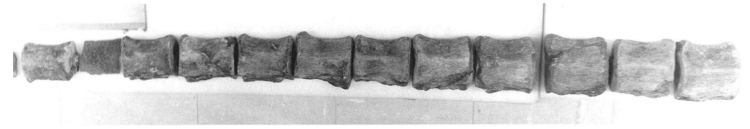

Hypsibema crassicauda, USNM 1789, lectotype caudal vertebra, left lateral view.

of these features, some paleontologists have assigned *Hypsibema* to the Ornithischia. There are similarities between the *Hypsibema* caudal and a caudal series assigned by Nopcsa (1928) to "*Orthomerus*" [= *Telmatosaurus*] *transsylvanicus* (J. S. McIntosh, personal communication). McIntosh, as well as Brett-Surman (1989), suggested that *Hypsibema* is not a sauropod but a very large hadrosaurid. More recent independent studies by Brett-Surman, Parris, Weishampel and Horner have verified that this taxon is indeed hadrosaurid (M. K. Brett-Surman, personal communication 1989). *Hypsibema* does seem to represent a hadrosaurid, not all of the original material having been available to Baird and Horner at the time of their earlier assessment (D. Baird, personal communication 1990).

Key references: Baird and Horner (1979); Brett-Surman (1989); Cope (1869*b*); Gilmore (1945); Gilmore and Stewart (1945).

HYPSILOPHODON   Huxley 1869

Ornithischia: Genasauria: Cerapoda: Ornithopoda: Hypsilophodontidae.

Name derivation: Greek *Hypsilophus* [genus of iguana lizard] + Greek *odous* = "tooth."

Type species: *H. foxii* Huxley 1869.

Other species: ?*H. wielandi* Galton and Jensen 1978.

Occurrence: Wealden Marls, Isle of Wight, England; Las Zabacheras Beds, Treul, Spain; ?Morrison Formation, South Dakota, United States; ?Porto Pinheiro, Portugal.

Age: Late Jurassic–Early Cretaceous (?Kimmeridgian–pre–Aptian Wealden or Barremian).

Known material: Three almost complete skeletons, about ten partial skeletons, cranial and postcranial remains, ?dermal armor, adults, juveniles.

Holotype: BMNH R197, incomplete skull with lower jaw, centrum of dorsal vertebra.

Diagnosis of genus (as for type species): Five premaxillary teeth separated from maxillary row of ten or 11 teeth by step; 13 or 14 dentary teeth, each with strong central ridge, ridge not on maxillary tooth; anterior processes of premaxilla separating narial openings entirely; maxilla with large antorbital depression, below that a row of large foramina; jugal and quadrate not contacting each other; quadratojugal large, perforated, borders lower temporal opening; five or six ribs in sacrum; scapula and humerus of equal length; obturator process at middle of ischium; fourth trochanter on proximal half of femur; lesser trochanter triangular in cross-section, separated from greater trochanter by shallow cleft; almost no anterior condylar groove; outer condyle almost as large as inner condyle posteriorly (Galton 1974*a*).

Diagnosis of ?*H. wielandi*: Differs from *H. foxii* in 0.45 ratio of minimum distance between proximal end of femur and distal edge of fourth trochanter, and slight anterior intercondylar groove distally (Galton and Jensen 1978).

Comments: Basis for the family Hypsilophodontidae Dollo 1882, the genus *Hypsilophodon* was founded on an incomplete skull and dorsal centrum (BMNH R197), discovered in 1849 in a sandstone slab by workmen excavating a cliff in the pre–Aptian Wealden Beds (probably Barremian [Allen 1955] or ?Early Aptian [Hughes 1958]; see Galton 1974*a*), Cowleaze Chine, near Atherfield, on the Isle of Wight, England.

Workmen broke the stone and, finding the remains imbedded into two halves, gave one half to fossil collector Gideon Algernon Mantell, the other to collector James Scott Bowerbank. As hypsilophodontids were unknown at that time, Mantell originally believed the specimen represented a juvenile *Iguanodon*. When the British Museum (Natural History) [now the Natural History Museum, London] acquired both the Mantell and Bowerbank collections in 1853, the two parts of the block were reunited. Some 23 additional specimens, including three almost complete skeletons collected in 1868 by Reverend William Fox, were recovered from this original site which came to be known as the "*Hypsilophodon* Bed."

Fox, too, regarded these remains as pertaining to young *Iguanodon* individuals. As the material exhibited features not present in *Iguanodon*, Sir Richard

Owen believed that they represented a new species of that genus which he called *I. foxii*. Huxley (1869), briefly describing one of the skulls collected by Fox and observing that the remains were generically distinct from *Iguanodon*, referred them to a new genus, *Hypsilophodon*. Huxley (1870a) erected the genus and species combination *H. foxii*; later, Huxley (1883a) attempted the first complete osteology of the type species.

A modern diagnosis and description of *H. foxii* was published by Galton (1974a), based upon specimens in the collection of the Natural History Museum, London. These specimens include those in the Mantell Collection, including the paratype (BMNH 28707, 39560-1); an articulated skeleton consisting of a partial vertebral column contained in a sandstone slab from a cliff west of Cowleaze Chine; the material in the Fox Collection, including the holotype; that in the Hooley Collection, including the nearly complete mounted skeleton (BMNH R5829) on exhibit at the Natural History Museum, collected near Cowleaze Chine; and other material.

A North American specimen possibly representing *Hypsilophodon* was reported by Galton and Jensen (1975). The specimen, a left femur (AMNH 2585), was collected from the Morrison Formation, Lakota Sandstone, near Piedmont, in western South Dakota. Later, Galton and Jensen (1978) referred this specimen to a new species, *H. wielandi*. The presence of this genus in North America supports the theory that a land connection existed between that continent and Europe during the Jurassic-Cretaceous transition. However, in their review of the Hypsilophodontidae, Sues and Norman (1989) did not regard the presently available material pertaining to *H. wielandi* as diagnostic at either generic or specific level. Sues and Norman, noting that this species could prove to be valid at some future date, regarded it for the present as a *nomen dubium*.

Associated with one specimen (BMNH R2477) of the type species were traces of thin, irregularly polygonal bony scutes, suggesting that the animal's skin was embedded with well-developed but delicate armor plates (Nopcsa 1905a). Galton (1974a) pointed out that, while these ossifications could represent dermal armor, they have not been preserved in any other specimens, including the more complete skeleton (BMNH R196), and that dermal armor is not known in any other ornithopod.

Hypsilophodon was a lightly built animal. Estimates of its size have been given as approximately 1.5 meters (5 feet) in length, its head measuring about 10 centimeters (4 inches) long and, due to its horizontal posture, carried no more than about .6 meters (2 feet) above the ground. Such estimates are not

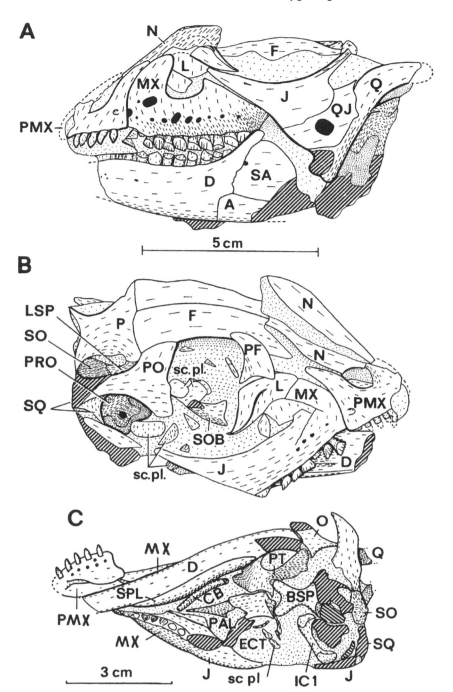

Hypsilophodon foxi, BMNH R197, holotype skull, in A. lateral, B. dorsal, and C. palatal views. (After Galton 1975.)

entirely accurate, however, as much *Hypsilophodon* material represents immature individuals. Galton (1975) pointed out that much of the Wealden fossils assigned to *Iguanodon* actually represent larger hypsilophodontid individuals. These include a fragmentary right pubis (BMNH 36538) from Cuckfield, Sussex, fragmentary right pubis (BMNH R169) from the Isle of Wight, and incomplete left pubis (BMNH R720), all listed as *Iguanodon* by Lydekker (1888a); a right tibia (BMNH 36506) measuring 332 millimeters (about 13 inches) long, from Cuckfield; and left tibia (BMNH 36508) measuring 168 millimeters

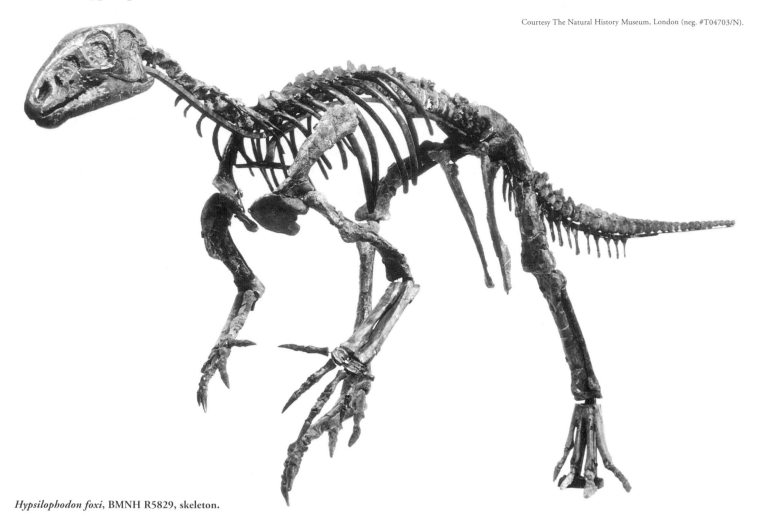

Hypsilophodon foxi, BMNH R5829, skeleton.

(about 6.2 inches) long, and right tibia (BMNH R124) measuring 280 millimeters (almost 11 inches) long, both from the Isle of Wight.

Because of its long fingers and toes, Hulke (1882) concluded that *Hypsilophodon* was adapted to climbing. Following that notion, Abel (1912) misinterpreted the first toe as being reversed, evidence to Abel that the foot was capable of grasping tree limbs. Other perceived evidence supporting this idea of tree climbing included the sharp and arched hind claws (interpreted as impeding ground locomotion), the bowed forearm bones resembling those of the Australian tree-kangaroo *Dendrolagus*, hindlimb muscles that supposedly would have restricted running speed but enhanced climbing, and the tail (apparently a balancing organ) made rigid by ossified tendons. Abel (1922, 1925) compared the animal's lifestyle to that of *Dendrolagus*. Although Heilmann (1926) dissented from this opinion, the concept of an arboreal *Hypsilophodon* has persisted to this day in popular books about dinosaurs. The perpetuation of this image was due, to some extent, to a life restoration made during the latter 1950s by artist Neave Parker, first pub-

lished in Swinton's (1967) book *Dinosaurs*, then reprinted in numerous other popular books, and oftentimes copied or used for inspiration by other artists.

Galton (1971*c*, 1971*d*) exploded this notion by demonstrating that the supposed grasping toe in *Hypsilophodon* is not reversed and that Abel (1912) had inadvertently restored it the wrong way around, the hind claws, in actuality, not being strongly arched. As shown by Galton (1971*c*, 1971*d*), the forelimbs are not unusually bowed, the muscles of the hindlimbs are arranged to enhance locomotive speed, and the rigid posterior half of the tail would have served as a dynamic stabilizer during running. Furthermore, the hindlimb proportions in *Hypsilophodon* are comparable to those of modern, rapidly running mammals, such as the horse and gazelle. In reinterpreting the possible habits of this genus, Galton (1971*c*, 1971*d*) showed that *Hypsilophodon* exhibits no specific arboreal adaptations, finally bringing this dinosaur down from the trees as a cursorial ground-dweller.

Sanz, Santa Fe and Casanovas (1983) referred to *Hypsilophodon* (presumably *H. foxii*) a metatarsal and phalangeal collected from the Capas Rojas Formation (Early Aptian) at Morella (Province of Castellón, Spain). Sanz *et al.* noted that the presence of this specimen reinforces the similarity between Wealden and Capas Rojas faunas. *Hypsilophodon* may also be represented by isolated teeth from Late Kimmeridgian rocks of Porto Pinheiro, Portugal.

Notes: A tooth (YPM 7367) collected before 1870 by G. J. Chesler from the Stonesfield Slate of the Great Oolite Series (Bathonian) at Stonesfield, Oxfordshire, England, may, according to Galton (1975), represent the oldest hypsilophodontid described to date. The tooth is similar to premaxillary teeth in *Hypsilophodon* (Galton 1974a), lacks small denticles on the anterior and posterior edges of the crown, but has a concave wear surface. The tooth is almost identical to isolated premaxillary teeth of *Thescelosaurus*.

Galton (1975) mentioned that a dentary tooth (UCMP 49611), questionably from the Kimmeridge Clay (Kimmeridgian) of Weymouth, Dorset, England, represents a hypsilophodontid dinosaur of uncertain affinities. The thickly enameled surface of the crown has a strong central ridge. Longitudinal ridges on both sides of the crown are more pronounced and numerous than in *Hypsilophodon*, *Laosaurus,* and *Dryosaurus*.

Kim (1983) reported a ?hypsilophodontid femur recovered from a cliffside in the Gugyedong Formation, Hayang Group, near Bongam Pass, southwest of Tabri station, Geumseong-myeon, Euiseong-gun, North Gyeongsang-do, South Korea.

The first neonate dinosaurian material and dinosaurian eggshell fossils found in the Cloverly For-

mation, at a site located east of Bridger, Carbon County, Montana, were reported by Maxwell and Horner (1994). The remains consist of the proximal (MOR 722-1) and distal (MOR 722-2) ends of a right tibia, and a distal third left metatarsal (MOR 722-3). MOR 722-1 and 3 are very similar to those elements in the hypsilophodontids *Hypsilophodon* and *Orodromeus*, and may, therefore, represent a newly hatched hypsilophodontid. The bone ends measure 12 and 11 millimeters across, respectively. MOR 722-3 differs from metatarsal III in *H. foxii*, *O. makelai*, and juveniles of *Tenontosaurus tilletti*, in that the shaft tapers from the distal end more markedly, and the distal articular surface is more elongate. The distal surface of this specimen is 9 millimeters across, the estimated length of the metatarsal 40–55 millimeters. The affinities of this specimen are unknown. The eggshells, represented by several indistinct fragments and confirmed as eggshell by thin sectioning, were collected by the Museum of the Rockies in 1986 from Middle Dome, Montana.

Key references: Abel (1912, 1922, 1925); Galton (1971c, 1971d, 1974a, 1975); Galton and Jensen (1975, 1978); Heilmann (926); Hulke (1882); Huxley (1869, 1870a, 1883a); Nopcsa (1905a); Sues and Norman (1989).

HYPSIROPHUS Cope 1878 [*nomen dubium*] — (composite; see *Allosaurus, Stegosaurus*.)
Name derivation: Greek *hypsi* = "high" + Greek *orophe* = "roof" + Greek *os* = [adjectival ending].
Type species: *H. discursus* Cope 1978 [*nomen dubium*].

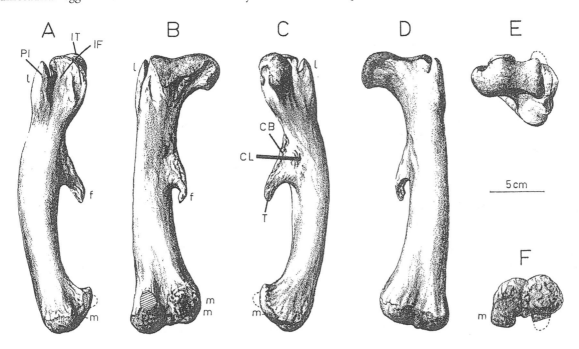

?*Hypsilophodon wielandi,* AMNH 2585, holotype left femur (distal end crushed, restored), in A. lateral, B. posterior, C. medial, and D. anterior views, E. proximal end, F. distal end, muscles after Galton (1969, 1975). PI, dorsal part of M. puboischiofemoralis, IT, M. iliotrochantericus, IF, M. iliofemoralis, CB, M. caudifemoralis brevis, CL, M. caudi-femoralis longus. (After Galton and Jensen 1979.)

I

IGUANODON Mantell 1825—(=*Heterosaurus*, *Hikanodon*, *Procerosaurus*, *Sphenospondylus*, *Therosaurus*, *Vectisaurus*)

Ornithischia: Genasauria: Cerapoda: Ornithopoda: Iguanodontia: Iguanodontidae.

Name derivation: "Iguana [lizard]" + Greek *odous* = "tooth."

Type species: *I. anglicus* Holl 1829.

Other species: *I. hoggi* Owen 1874, *I. bernissartensis* Boulenger 1881, *I. dawsoni* Lydekker 1888, *I. fittoni* Lydekker 1889, *I. atherfieldensis* Hooley 1925, ?*I. ottingeri* Galton and Jensen 1978 [*nomen dubium*], *I. lakotaensis* Weishampel and Bjork 1989.

Occurrence: Wealden, West Sussex, East Sussex, Isle of Wight, Surrey, Kent, Lower Greensand, Kent, Upper Purbeck Beds, Dorset, England; Wealden, Hainaut, Belgium; Las Zacbacheras Beds, Capas Rojas, Teruel, Castellon, [unnamed formation], Cuenca, Spain; Wealden, Nordrhein-Westphalen, [former Federal Republic of] Germany; Lakota Formation, South Dakota, United States; "Continental intercalaire," Sahara Desert, Africa.

Age: Early Cretaceous (Berriasian–Albian).

Known material: Teeth and postcranial fragments, at least 31 skeletons, some complete, most with complete or partial skulls, many complete and partial skulls, isolated teeth and postcranial remains, juvenile to adult.

Holotype: BMNH 2392, seven teeth.

Diagnosis of genus: Iguanodontid from Bernasian–Lower Aptian of Eurasia; skull long and tall in occipital aspect; supraoccipital not included in foramen magnum; premaxillary bones moderately expanded in lateral aspect, dorsal median process of premaxillae extending backward between and under nasals; palpebrals long, loose, slender, sometimes with

small accessory, articulating only at frontal; predentary strongly denticulate anteromedially; 11 cervical, 17 dorsal, 6–7 sacral, and more than 45 caudal vertebrae; neural spines of mid-dorsal series two to three times height of centrum, not expanded apically; sternal bones hatchet-shaped, with tendency for cartilage of median sternal plate to ossify; carpus with ossified ligaments; ?ungual of manual digit IV lost, those of digits II and III flattened; metatarsal I splint-like; posterior ramus of pubis slender, shorter than ischium (Norman 1986).

Diagnosis of *I. anglicus*: [No modern diagnosis published.]

Diagnosis of *I. bernissartensis*: Maximum length 11 meters (about 37 feet); double supraorbital openings; maximum of 29 vertical tooth rows in maxilla, maximum of 25 in dentary; sacrum with eight fused vertebrae; scapula unexpanded distally, shaft with very thickened proximal region; intersternal ossification between anterior ends of sternal bones and between coracoids; forelimb stout, about 70 percent length of hindlimbs; carpals coossified, first metacarpal fused to carpals; phalangeal formula of manus 2-3-3-2-4; first phalanx of digit I consisting of a thin, warped bony plate in shallow recess of proximal surface of ungual phalanx, with form of curved, cone-shaped spine that can articulate freely against fused carpo-metacarpus; ungual phalanges of digits II and III broad, hoof-like, longitudinally twisted; posterior end of ilium pointed in side view, brevis shelf broad; anterior ramus of pubis relatively narrow, transversely flattened proximally, distal end moderately expanded; pes with three distal tarsals, first metatarsal reduced and flattened transversely, fifth absent (Norman 1980).

Diagnosis of *I. atherfieldensis*: Small (gracile) species (6–7 meters, or from about 20 to 24 feet, in length); skull long, low, with slender lower jaw; palpebral long, slender (with no accessory); (poorly ossified) supraoccipital plate lacking postdorsal expansion; maxilla with maximum of 23 vertical tooth positions, dentary 20; posterior dorsal and anterior caudal vertebrae not strongly compressed anteroposteriorly, dorsals and caudals with tall, slender neural spines; six true sacral vertebrae, one sacrodorsal; scapula moderately expanded distally; phalangeal formula of 2-3-3-3-3; brevis shelf of ilium not well developed; anterior pubic ramus very deep, laterally compressed; first metatarsal narrow and spine-like (Norman 1986).

Diagnosis of ?*I. ottingeri*: Prominent vertical depressions on anterior and posterior edges of root and base of tooth crown (Galton and Jensen 1979*b*).

Diagnosis of *I. lakotaensis*: Skull with supraoccipital incised beneath parietal and squamosals,

Iguanodon lakotaensis, SDSM 8656, restored holotype skull, left lateral view. Scale = 5 cm. (After Weishampel and Bjork 1989.)

without median ridge [possibly absent in life or lost through erosion]; single aperture for both branches of facial nerve (c.n. VII) [character shared by other ornithopods]; antorbital fenestra relatively large; no contact between maxilla and lacrimal at jugal-maxilla articulation; maxillary and dentary teeth relatively small; few maxillary tooth families combined with low tooth density; dentary tooth replacement consisting of reduced z-spacing, with longer wave of alternating teeth from back of jaws ["z-spacing" and "waves" being theoretical constructs] (Weishampel and Bjork 1989).

Diagnosis of *I. dawsoni*: Species intermediate in size between *I. anglicus* and *I. bernissartensis*, differing in having only five sacral vertebrae and in characters of vertebrae and pelvis (Lydekker 1888*b*).

Comments: The second dinosaur to be described (after *Megalosaurus*), the genus *Iguanodon* was founded on seven worn teeth (BMNH 2392), discovered in the early 1820s in Kent, England. Long misplaced, five of these teeth were eventually found by David B. Norman (1977) in the British Museum (Natural History) [now The Natural History Museum, London] collection.

A traditional (though unconfirmed) story attributes the discovery of these teeth to Mary Ann Mantell, wife of family doctor and amateur geologist Gideon Algernon Mantell. According to this account, Mary Ann, while accompanying her husband on one of his doctor's calls, spotted the fossil teeth in a roadside gravel pile. Gideon Mantell then traced the gravel to quarries located in the Cuckfield area of Tilgate Forest (a conglomerate called Tilgate Grit), where he collected more teeth in addition to some large fossil bones. In his book *The Fossils of South Downs* (published in 1822), Mantell described these teeth and also credited their discovery to his wife.

The teeth puzzled Mantell. They were apparently suited for cutting vegetation like the teeth of some mammals. Contemporary scientists such as William Buckland of Oxford University and Baron Georges Cuvier of Paris regarded the teeth as those of a large fish or mammal. Cuvier went as far as to label one tooth as belonging to a rhinoceros and some ankle bones as hippopotamus. If, however, Cuvier were right and the remains were mammalian, then Mantell must have erred in his dating the rocks that yielded them as of Cretaceous age. The possibility also existed that Mantell's specimens actually came from geologically younger overlying rocks that had become mixed with the more ancient Mesozoic rocks.

Mantell, though, remained adamant that the rocks were of Mesozoic age and that the fossils must therefore be reptilian rather than mammalian. Samuel

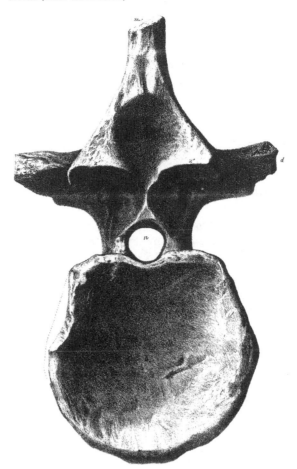

Iguanodon anglicus, holotype dorsal vertebra of *Cetiosaurus brevis*. (After Owen 1842.)

Stutchbury, a naturalist at the Hunterian Museum at the Royal College of Surgeons, noticed the resemblance in the teeth to those of a South American iguana lizard. This observation prompted Mantell (1825) to describe the teeth as belonging to an extinct, plant-eating lizard related to the iguana, but one attaining a length of about 12 meters (40 feet). Mantell used these teeth as the basis for a new genus which he named *Iguanodon*. Holl (1829) later assigned Mantell's genus a specific name, the new combination becoming *I. anglicum* [*sic*—the correct spelling should be *anglicus*].

Whether this traditional story of the discovery of these teeth is accurate or apocryphal, the first material collected pertaining to *Iguanodon* might actually be traced to an even earlier date. According to Charig (1979) in his book *A New Look at the Dinosaurs*, an unidentified *Iguanodon* bone was discovered by William Smith in 1808 at Cuckfield, in Sussex, this constituting one of the earliest properly recorded dinosaur finds. Charig also reported that Buckland allegedly found *Iguanodon* material on the Isle of Wight some years before the Mantell discovery.

In 1834, more *Iguanodon* material was discovered, including a partial skeleton found in a slab of Kentish Rag (Lower Greensand) rock, blown out of a quarry at Maidstone, Kent. According to quarry-master W. H. Bensted's account, reprinted in *The Dinosaurs*, by Swinton (1970), the specimen included two femora (33 inches long each), a tibia, metatarsal and pedal phalanges, two claws, two metacarpals (each 14 inches long), radius, several dorsal and caudal vertebrae, several rib fragments, two clavicles, two large lilia, a chevron, and tooth portion. Among these preserved elements was a singular bony "spike." Upon this material, Meyer (1832) erected the new species *I. mantelli*. Mantell (1834) subsequently described this specimen and, about 1835, reconstructed the skeleton as resembling that of a gigantic iguana-like reptile with tree-climbing abilities, its length overestimated as more than 17.5 meters (60 feet) long, the "spike" misinterpreted as a horn above the snout.

According to Swinton's account, Mantell offered to buy the Maidstone slab from Bensted, who wanted more money for it than Mantell could afford. Later, the specimen was purchased by a group of Sussex gentlemen and eventually came to reside in Mantell's Museum in Brighton, originally intended as a never-realized county museum. In 1839, Mantell sold his collection, the Maidstone specimen included, to the Trustees of the British Museum. Lydekker designated the specimen, now catalogued as BMNH R. 3791, as holotype of the new species *I. mantelli*. The slab was put on display in the old Dinosaur Gallery. (It can still be seen to-

Iguanodon atherfieldensis, **BMNH R5764, holotype skeleton.** Courtesy the Natural History Museum, London (neg. #T01143/N).

day at the renamed Natural History Museum, London.)

Comparative anatomist Richard Owen (1841), however, pointed out that *Iguanodon* (as well as the two other genera of giant Mesozoic reptiles, later to be called dinosaurs, known at the time) were unlike living lizards and proposed that they were more elephantine than lizard-like in appearance. Following Owen's interpretation, sculptor Benjamin Waterhouse Hawkins fashioned life-sized reconstructions of *Iguanodon* for the Great Exhibition of 1851 outside the Crystal Palace at Sydenham, near London. Hawkins' *Iguanodon* sculptures (which can still be viewed today at the old Crystal Palace location) resembled horned, quadrupedal, rhinoceros-like monsters supported by massive, upright limbs. Subsequent *Iguanodon* discoveries revealed that this animal was not like a lizard and that the supposed nasal horn was, in fact, a pollex or spiked thumb. Life restorations began to stray from Hawkins' elephantine interpretation, portraying the dinosaur up on its hind legs in a kangaroo-like posture, resting on the tail in a tripodal stance.

Later referred to *I. anglicus* were the species *Cetiosaurus brevis* Owen 1842 [*nomen dubium*], based on dorsal vertebrae from the submerged Wealden beds, deposited at Sandover Bay, on the shores of the Isle of Wight; *Streptospondylus major* Owen 1842 [*nomen dubium*], based on a vertebra from the Wealden of the Isle of Wight; *C. brachyurus* Owen 1842 [*nomen dubium*]; *S. recentior* Owen 1851 [*nomen dubium*]; *I. seeleyi* Hulke 1882, based on an almost complete right hind limb, right humerus, left ilium, left pes, three caudal vertebrae, and several chevrons from the Wealden of the Isle of Wight; and *Sphenospondylus gracilis* Lydekker 1888 [*nomen dubium*], a type species based on dorsal vertebrae from the Wealden of the Isle of Wight, originally given a generic but not a specific name by Seeley (1882).

The species *I. hoggi* was based on an incomplete mandibular ramus with teeth, collected from the middle Purbeck of Swanage, England, and named by Owen (1874). *I. dawsoni* [*nomen dubium*] was founded upon fragmentary remains from the Wealden of southern England. *I. hollingtonensis* Lydekker 1889, a junior synonym of *I. dawsoni*, is known from incomplete material from the Wealden of Hollington, Sussex, including a right femur, proximal portion of a right tibia, right third metatarsal, imperfect sacrum, incomplete ischia, fragmentary ilium, and dorsal vertebrae. *I. fittoni* Lydekker 1889 [*nomen dubium*] was based on a left ilium from the Wadhurst Clay of Sussex. Associated with this specimen was an imperfect sacrum and part of a pubis.

Iguanodon has become better known through specimens of the larger and more robust *I. bernissartensis*, a species represented by 24 more or less complete, articulated skeletons, plus several incomplete individuals, discovered in 1878 in a wide, marl-filled fissure, 322 meters (1,056 feet) deep at the coal mine in Bernissart, in South-West Belgium. Many of these specimens were mounted at the Institut Royal des Sciences Naturelles de Belgique, where they can be seen and studied today. (No excavations have been made at this site since World War I, but more *I. bernissartensis* material undoubtedly remains to be uncovered.) Although it was long the consensus that these fossils represented a herd of animals that had suffered a mass demise resulting from some catastrophic event, it is now generally believed that the collective Bernissart specimens represent the end result of many years of unrelated deaths (see Norman 1985). Norman (1987), in evaluating the various scenarios that could have caused a mass death, pointed out the high degree of articulation of the Bernissart skeletons, suggesting that they seem to have been buried in groups at intervals. Norman (1987) concluded that these animals may have been buried rapidly in mud brought down by flash floods.

Although various authors, most notably Dollo (1882), published brief descriptions of these specimens, the first substantial description did not appear in the literature until more than half a century after their discovery. Norman (1980) published a revised diagnosis of *I. bernissartensis* after a thorough study of the Bernissart material, including the holotype (IRSNB 1534) and other specimens (IRSNB 1561 and 1536, and the so-called "Individual S." from the conservatoire collections).

During the late 1870s, the first of the Bernissart skeletons was reconstructed under the direction of Dollo, who had subscribed to Leidy's (1858) theory that the pelvis and hindlimbs of dinosaurs were similar to those in birds. With the Emu and Wallaby serving as models, the skeletons of *I. bernissartensis* were mounted resembling those of a herd of resting kangaroos. Norman (1980) deduced that, to produce Dollo's kangaroo-like curvature of the tail, the proximal part of the tail had to be broken. In specimens preserved *in situ*, the tail can be clearly viewed as held straight. Norman observed from these specimens that Dollo's supposed swan-like curvature of the neck had been artificially produced, and, toward the sacrum

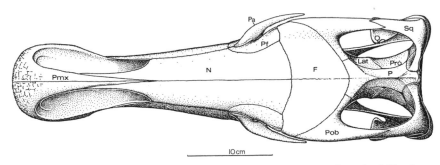

Iguanodon atherfieldensis, restored skull, based on BMNH R5764, holotype, and IRSNB 1551, lateral view. (After Norman 1986.)

on either side, the vertebral column is structured to accommodate a normally horizontal pose; on either side of the sacrum the vertebral centra become progressively taller and broader with their neural spines also becoming taller; in posterior dorsal and anterior caudal centra, there is a gradual upward curve that seems to be designed to counteract the sag-tendency of the vertebral column; and ossified tendons are most greatly concentrated over the sacrum and adjacent dorsal and sacral vertebrae.

Based upon this evidence and his own description of the postcrania, Norman (1980) reconstructed the skeleton of *I. bernissartensis* as having a normally horizontal posture, the vertebral column held at a somewhat low angle during locomotion. The forelimb is suitable for quadrupedal walking, the manus serving several functions. The hand is not only designed to support the animal's weight during walking; the pollex was probably equipped with a well developed, slightly curved claw that could have been used as a weapon during close-quarters fighting, a tool to move food and other objects, and also been utilized for intraspecific identification or combat. The fifth digit is flexible and could have been used for grasping.

As little individual variation and no evidence of sexual dimorphism has been observed in the suite of Bernissart skeletons, Van Beneden (1881) suggested that *I. bernissartensis* represented the male and "*I. mantelli*" the female of the same species. Steel (1969) regarded *I. mantelli* as a junior synonym of

Iguanodon atherfieldensis, restored skull based on IRSNB 1551, dorsal view. (After Norman 1986.)

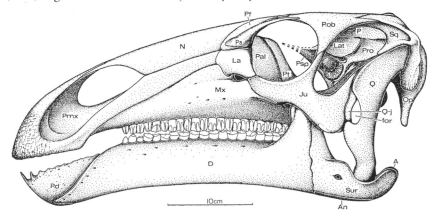

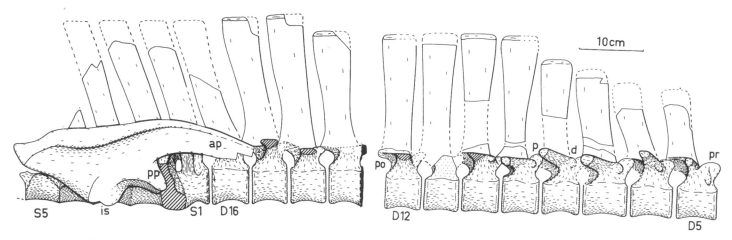

Iguanodon atherfieldensis, BMNH R8549, holotype dorsal vertebrae (5–16), sacrum, and right ilium of *Vectisaurus valdensis.* (After Galton 1976.)

Iguanodon anglicus, BMNH 2392, worn tooth, part of holotype allegedly discovered by Mary Ann Mantell in 1822. Scale = 1 cm.

I. anglicus. Norman (1980), acknowledging the feasibility of Van Beneden's suggestion, pointed out that both species, though large and closely related, could be valid, separated ecologically and therefore not in competition for the same niche.

Norman (1980) concluded that the more gracile species of *Iguanodon* present at Bernissart, represented by a skeleton (IRSNB 1551) described by Meyer as *I. mantelli,* was primarily (though not exclusively) a biped more agile than the more robust *I. bernissartensis.* This would account for the more developed pollex spine in the latter species, which, being less robust, would more require such a defensive adaptation. Norman (1980) showed that juvenile *I. bernissartensis* individuals had relatively shorter forelimbs than adults, their forelimb-to-hindlimb ratio closer to that of *I. mantelli.* This suggested that *I. bernissartensis* went from a bipedal to quadrupedal lifestyle as the animal aged. As large, agile theropods probably preyed upon the smaller immature individuals of this species, agility would have been crucial to the survival of young *I. bernissartensis.* Later, Norman (1986) regarded *I. anglicus* and *I. mantelli* as conspecific.

Norman (1977; 1985; 1987) referred to *I. bernissartensis* the genus *Vectisaurus,* which had been founded on parts of six dorsal vertebrae, a caudal centrum, and a partial left ilium (BMNH R2494), from the Wealden Marls of Brixton Chine on the Isle of Wight. Hulke (1879) originally described these remains but did not illustrate them. Other remains were later referred to type species *V. valdensis,* including 13 apparent dorsal vertebrae, most of the sacrum, ilia, and fragments of left pubis and ischium (BMNH R8649), collected by Hooley in 1916 from the Wealden Marls near Chilton Chine; incomplete sacrum with first-fourth centra and first-fifth fused sacral ribs of the right side (BMNH R8650), found by Hooley on a beach between Barnes High and Cowleaze Chine; and a small dentary (BMNH R180)

from the Wealden beds near Brixton, first described by Owen (1864) as that of a young *I. mantelli.* Galton (1976c) considered *Vectisaurus* to be a valid genus. Norman (1987) demonstrated that the holotype of *V. valdensis* is, in all probability, the fragmentary skeleton of a juvenile *Iguanodon,* and that remains referred to *Vectisaurus* sp. also represent juvenile *Iguanodon* individuals. As shown by Norman (1987), the suite of features upon which Hulke originally characterized this species relate to the ontogenetic immaturity of the type specimen.

I. bernissartensis is also known from the Hauterivian–Early Aptian of Southern England; Early Cretaceous of Central Asia; ?France, ?Portugal. ?North Africa. (Footprint evidence extends the possible appearance of this species to Spitsbergen and South America.)

The species *I. atherfieldensis* was based on a well-preserved, partial skeleton (BMNH R5764) of a small species of *Iguanodon* from the Wealden Shales near Atherfield Point, Isle of Wight. Originally, Hooley (1912) referred this specimen to *I. mantelli,* after which Hooley (1917) referred it to *I. bernissartensis.* The skeleton, eventually made the type specimen of a new species, *I. atherfieldensis,* by Hooley (1925), measures 5 meters (approximately 17 feet) in length. It was long displayed in the Dinosaur Gallery at the [then] British Museum (Natural History). Norman (1986) referred to this species the small and almost complete skeleton (IRSNB 1551) called "*I. mantelli*" from the Bernissart suite of *Iguanodon* specimens. (This skeleton had been partially cleared of matrix and put on display at the Institut Royal des Sciences Naturelles in 1884.) Norman (1986) diagnosed this taxon from two specimens, as well as material in the Natural History Museum, London collection referrable to this species.

The first North American remains of *Iguanodon* were reported by Galton and Jensen (1975), consist-

Iguanodon

Iguanodon bernissartensis, cast of IRSNB 1534, holotype skeleton, mounted in out-moded tail-dragging pose.

Photo by the author, courtesy University Museum, Oxford.

Iguanodon

Iguanodon bernissartensis, cast of IRSNB 1534, holotype skull, left lateral view.

questioned by Weishampel and Bjork (1989) in a paper describing the first indisputable remains of a North American species of *Iguanodon.* Weishampel and Bjork noted that the characters observed by Galton and Jensen are nondiagnostic even at the generic level, applying to both *I. atherfieldensis* and *I. bernissartensis,* as well as to other ornithopods including *Ouranosaurus nigeriensis* (MNHN GDF 300, 305, 340, 342, 344, GAD204; see Taquet 1976), to a slight degree to *Camptosaurus dispar* (YPM 7416, UVP 5946), and possibly to *C. prestwichii* (OUM J.3303).

Weishampel and Bjork named a new species *I. lakotaensis,* based upon an almost complete skull (SDSM 8656) comprising the braincase (missing presphenoid and parasphenoid) and most of the facial region (lacking quadratojugal, quadrate, and palpebrals), portions of the palate (missing pterygoid), a fragment including the jugal-postorbital articulation, the predentary, fragments of right and left dentaries (missing postdentary bones), and a dorsal and caudal vertebra. The specimen was collected by Dale Rossow in the Lakota Formation (?Barremian; Sohn 1979) in Lawrence County, South Dakota.

The skull of *I. lakotaensis,* as measured by Weishampel and Bjork, is approximately 550 millimeters (about 21 inches) long, 210 millimeters (8 inches) high at the orbit (excluding mandibles), and 202 millimeters (about 7.75 inches) wide across the frontals. As noted by Weishampel and Bjork, the presence of *Iguanodon* in the Lakota Formation offers further evidence in support of a possible Barremian age for that unit, and also confirms the hypothesis by Galton and Jensen (1979*b*) of Early Cretaceous faunal ties between North America and Eurasia.

Mantell (1848) first speculated that the tongue in *Iguanodon* was large, muscular, and prehensile, envisioning it issuing from the mouth through a

ing of the posterior portion of a right maxilla (BYU 2000), collected from the Cedar Mountain Formation near Grand County, in southeastern Utah. Galton and Jensen (1979*b*) subsequently erected the new species *I. ottingeri* for the material. Galton and Jensen (1979*b*) observed that these teeth are quite similar to those of *Iguanodon* specimens from Britain, having a prominent keel on the thickly enamelled lateral surface of the crown. As noted by Galton and Jensen (1979*b*), the presence of this genus in North America supports the theory that a land connection existed between that continent and Europe during or just before the Jurassic–Cretaceous transition.

Norman (1986), noting that this species was based only on teeth, designated *I. ottingeri* to be a *nomen dubium.* The status of *I. ottingeri* was further

Iguanodon bernissartensis, restored skeleton in normal walking pose. (After Norman 1980.)

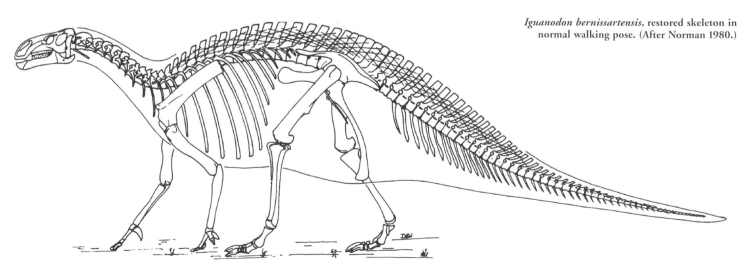

Skeleton of *Iguanodon bernissartensis* (cast of IRSNB 1534) as exhibited in the old "Dinosaur Gallery" at the formerly named British Museum (Natual History). In recent years, the hall has been updated.

spout-like opening in the anterior end of the mandible. Mantell (1848) pictured this dinosaur feeding as would a giraffe, by wrapping its tongue around arboreal vegetation. Norman, however, pointed out that the hyoid apparatus, to which the tongue-operating muscles are attached, is large and well ossified in *Iguanodon*, implying that the tongue was strongly muscularized. Such a tongue would have been required to move food around in the mouth as the animal chewed.

In describing the skull of *I. bernissartensis*, Norman (1980) pointed out that no direct evidence yet exists to support the presence of a horny beak. However, a beak is present in the later hadrosaurs, there is evidence of bony tissue associated with the beak region in *Iguanodon*, and the occlusal margins of the premaxillae and predentary are edentulous, evidence suggesting a possible beak.

In a study of the possible weights of dinosaurs, G. S. Paul (personal communication) calculated that an average-sized *I. anglicus* totaled about 1.09 metric tons (more than 1.2 tons), and *I. bernissartensis* about 3.08 metric tons (almost 3.5 tons). In their review of Iguanodontidae and related ornithopods, Norman and Weishampel (1990) envisioned *Iguanodon* as the dominant medium- to large-size plant eating dinosaur, *I. atherfieldensis* and *I. bernissartensis* being consistently found with such small and less abundant species as the ornithopods *Hypsilophodon foxii* and *Valdosaurus canaliculatus*, pachycephalosaur *Yaverlandia bitholus*, and ankylosaur *Polacanthus foxii*.

Over the decades, more British *Iguanodon* material has been reported from Dorset (Owen 1874), Surrey (M. J. Benton, personal communication to Weishampel and Bjork 1989) and Bedfordshire (D. B. Norman, personal communication to Weishampel and Bjork). Other places in Europe from which *Iguanodon* has been reported are Niedersachsen and Nordrhein-Westphalen, [former Federal Republic of] Germany (Koken 1887; Huckreide 1982; Holder and Norman 1986; Norman 1987; Norman, Hilpert and Holder 1987); and Tereul, Burgos and Castellon Provinces of Spain (Estes and Sanchez 1982; Santafé, Casanovas, Sanz and Calzada 1982; Sanz, Casanovas and Santafé 1984).

Lapparent (1951) referred a tooth from an Albian or lower Cenomanian continental horizon in southern Tunisia to "*I. mantelli*;" fragmentary remains including two large teeth, two anterior caudal vertebrae, and distal end of a right femur, collected from the Aptian of Boca do Champim, Portugal, were referred to this species by Sauvage (1896, 1897/1898) and Lapparent and Zbyszewski (1957), marking the occurrence of *I. anglicus* in that country. Lapparent (1960) also assigned to "*I. mantelli*" a tooth from the "Continental intercalaire" of the central Sahara Desert region.

Notes: The species "*I.*" *orientalis*, described by Rozhdestvensky (1952), was based on a maxilla with 27 teeth, a scapula measuring 97 centimeters (about 37 inches) long, and some ribs (PIN 559/1) collected from Khmarin-Khural, in the eastern Gobi Desert, Mongolia. A skull (PIN 3386/50) referred to this species is unusual for its large and bulbous snout, a feature not present in any other *Iguanodon* specimen. As this species is otherwise indistinguishable postcranially from *I. bernissartensis*, Norman (1986) regarded it as a *nomen dubium*. Norman and Weishampel considered this species as representing an as yet unnamed iguanodontid genus.

I. phillipsi Seeley 1869 [*nomen dubium*] was made the type species of *Priodontognathus* by Seeley (1875); *I. praecursor* Sauvage 1876 [*nomen dubium*] is a junior synonym of sauropod *Pelorosaurus humerocristatus*; *I. prestwichii* Hulke 1880 was referred to *Camptosaurus* by Galton and Powell (1980) and *I. hilli* Newton 1892 [*nomen dubium*] to *Craspedodon lonzeensis*. *I. exogirarum* Fritsch 1878 [*nomen dubium*], based on a possible marrow-cavity cast of a partial tibia from the Cenomanian (Exogyrenkalk) of Holubitz, Bohemia, and *I. albinus* Fritsch 1893 are probably nondinosaurian (Chure and McIntosh 1989).

Large, three-digit footprints associated with *Iguanodon* skeletal remains, found on the Isle of Wight, provide some information as to the probable behavior of this dinosaur. Some trackways reveal several animals traveling together in the same direction, suggesting that *Iguanodon* herded. Norman (1985) offered a speculative scenario (probably derived from interpretations of dinosaur tracks by Bird 1944, 1985; M. G. Lockley, personal communication 1989) in

Iguanodon bernissartensis (left) and ***I. atherfieldensis*** (right).   Illustration by Gregory S. Paul.

Courtesy J. I. Kirkland.

?*Iguanodon ottingeri*, BYU 2000, holotype partial right maxilla with teeth.

which the *Iguanodon* herd was structured with the more vulnerable young or much older individuals keeping toward the center, the larger adults, perhaps just the males, patrolling the edges to serve as "lookouts." As *Iguanodon* remains are oftentimes found in lowland, marshy or estuary regions, Norman suggested (1985) that these dinosaurs fed on such indigenous vegetation as horsetails, cycads, ferns, conifers, and bennettitaleans.

Tracks generally attributed to *Iguanodon* were first discovered in the Wealden sandstone of the Sussex coast. The footprints, marking the earliest known discovery of dinosaur tracks in the British Wealden (see Delair 1989 for a comprehensive history of dinosaur track discoveries in the British Wealden), were originally reported by the Reverend Edward Tagart (1846), who noted that "Dr. Harwood" suspected that they were made by an *Iguanodon* (see Taylor 1862). More than a century after their discovery, these tracks were figured for the first time by Sarjeant (1974). Between 1846 and 1850, numerous specimens, including impressions and natural casts, were found along the Sussex coast.

As pointed out by Woodhams and Hines (1989), nearly every dinosaur footprint found in Sussex has been almost automatically referred to *Iguanodon*, ignoring the presence of other Wealden dinosaurs. Poor preservation of many of these tracks should preclude classifying them below family level; some of these tracks are theropods.

Other tracks, believed to have been made by *Iguanodon*, were found in the Purbeck Beds (latest

Jurassic to earliest Cretaceous) of Dorset, the Wealden of Belgium (Dollo 1906), and sands of Hastings, Germany (Struckmann 1880; Ballerstedt 1905). In fact, the name *Iguanodon* has atypically often been used to designate the tracks themselves as well as the genus based upon skeletal remains.

Footprints attributed to *Iguanodon* were reported by Lapparent (1962) from the Lower Cretaceous of the Svalbard Archipelago, at Festningen, and also in lower part of the Helvetiafjelet Formation, southern Heer Land, island of Spitsbergen. Tracks attributed to *Iguanodon* sp. were reported by Antunes (1976) from the Lower Cretaceous (Hauterivian) of Lagosteiros, Portugal. These include impressions of hindfeet and tail, indicative of an animal resting. From the same area, Antunes reported tracks of a quite small bipedal dinosaur that may have been made by a juvenile *Iguanodon* or by an ornithopod related to *Camptosaurus*. Woodhams and Hines (1986) reported two intersecting ?*Iguanodon* tracks, found in 1980 in the Tunbridge Wells Sand (uppermost Valanginian) at Cooden, Sussex. Lim, Yang and Lockley (1989) reported multiple horizons, with ornithopod tracks, in the Jindong Formation of Korea, several of these horizons indicating iguanodontids traveling in herds.

The first quadrupedal ornithopod trackway discovered in the Spanish Wealden and the first in Europe was reported and described by Moratalla, Sanz, Jimenez and Lockley (1992). The trackway, made by a dinosaur very similar to *Iguanodon*, was found in the Lower Cretaceous (probably Hauteriv-

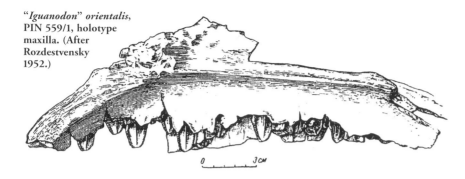

"Iguanodon" orientalis, PIN 559/1, holotype maxilla. (After Rozdestvensky 1952.)

ian) Valdemayor site in the Cabezín de Cameros township of La Rioja, Spain. Moratalla *et al.* interpreted the following from the trackway: The trackmaker was moving at an estimated speed of 4 kilometers per hour. The center of gravity (as suggested by lesser depth of manus imprint) was located near the hindlimbs; a similar kind of locomotion was used in both bipedal and quadrupedal gaits, with hindfoot rotated inward, suggesting that either mode of locomotion did not significantly modify the role of the tail during walking. Finally, digit II was almost free, while III and IV were included in a single structure of soft tissue.

Currie, Nadon, and Lockley (1991) published new information regarding large ornithopods resulting from the discovery of Late Cretaceous dinosaur trackways in the J. Sandstone of the South Platte Formation, Dakota Group (Albian–Cenomanian), Turkey Creek, west of Denver, in Colorado, and the St. Mary Formation (Late Campanian–Early Maastrichtian) of southwestern Alberta, Canada. The

South Platte Formation hindfoot tracks (best example, MWC 201), discovered in the fall of 1987 (see Lockley 1989), referred to ichnotaxon *Caririchnium leonardii*, appear as natural impressions and seem to have been made by iguanodontids. The St. Mary Formation tracks (RTMP 87.86.7), discovered in 1986 and 1987, appearing as casts, were apparently made by hadrosaurs. They resemble in overall shape the poorly preserved footprints found in Britain and Europe generally assigned to *Iguanodon* (Norman 1980); but, as the handprints are more closely associated with the corresponding footprints (less widely divergent from the trackway midline), they also resemble the *Caririchnium* trackways of Colorado. Both trackways are significant in that they represent the first reported large ornithopod tracks showing foot pad impressions.

As described by Currie *et al.* (1991), only one footprint in the Colorado series shows skin impressions. These impressions indicate tubercles of subcircular to oval shapes that average from 3 to 5 millimeters in diameter in the toe region and to a maximum dimension of 10 millimeters under the heel. The heel displays a distinctive asymmetrical bilobed morphology. In the Alberta tracks, the tubercles for any area of the foot are oval in shape and relatively uniform in size. Underneath the metatarsus, the tubercles are larger, ranging from 3.5 to 5.0 millimeters in maximum diameter; tubercles underneath the toes range from 1.5 to 3.5 millimeters in maximum diameter.

Key references: Ballderstedt (1905); Boulenger (1881); Charig (1979); Dollo (1882, 1906); Estes and Sanchez (1982); Galton (1976*c*); Galton and Jensen (1975, 1979*b*, 1987); Holder and Norman (1986); Holl (1829); Hooley (1912, 1917, 1925); Huckreide (1982); Hulke (1879); Koken (1987); Lapparent (1951, 1960, 1962); Lapparent and Zbyszewski (1957); Lydekker (1888, 1889); Mantell (1822, 1825, 1848); Meyer (1832); Norman (1977, 1980, 1985, 1986, 1987); Norman and Weishampel (1990); Norman *et al.* (1987); Owen (1842, 1851, 1864, 1874); Rozhdestvensky (1952); Santafé, Casanovas, Sanz and Calzada (1982); Sanz, Casanovas and Santafé (1989); Sarjeant (1974); Sauvage (1896, 1897/1898); Seeley (1882); Struckmann (1880); Taylor (1862); Van Beneden (1887); Weishampel and Bjork (1989); Woodhams and Hines (1989).

Photo by the author.

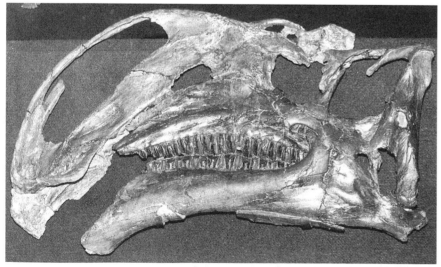

"Iguanodon" orientalis, PIN 3386/50, referred skull (apparently representing a new unnamed genus), left lateral view, in "The Great Russian Dinosaurs" exhibit (1996), Mesa Southwest Museum, Mesa, Arizona.

ILIOSUCHUS Huene 1932

Saurischia: Theropoda: Tetanurae: *incertae sedis.*

Name derivation: "Ilium" + Greek *souchos* = "crocodile."

Type species: *I. incognitus* Huene (1932).

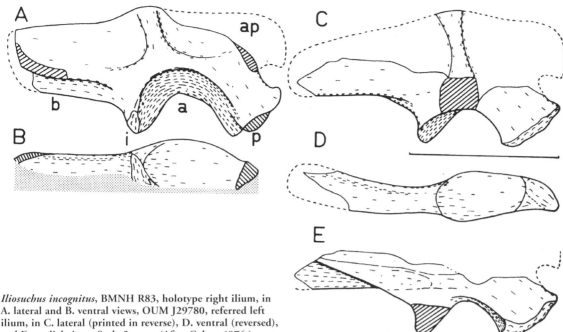

Iliosuchus incognitus, BMNH R83, holotype right ilium, in A. lateral and B. ventral views, OUM J29780, referred left ilium, in C. lateral (printed in reverse), D. ventral (reversed), and E. medial views. Scale 5 = cm. (After Galton 1976.)

Other species: [None.]
Occurrence: Stonesfield Slate, Oxfordshire, England.
Age: Middle Jurassic (Middle Bathonian).
Known material/holotype: BMNH R83, two ilia.

Diagnosis of genus (as for type species): Ilium with prominent ridge flaring out anteriorly and posteriorly above margin of acetabulum (Galton 1976*b*).

Comments: The genus *Iliosuchus* was founded upon two isolated ilia (BMNH R83), collected in 1880 by G. W. Masson from the Bathonian Great Oolite, Stonesfield Slate, Oxfordshire, England.

The small (and only partially prepared) holotype was originally described by Huene (1932) as belonging to a new "megalosaur" genus and species which he named *Iliosuchus incognitus*. Later, Romer (1966) listed *Iliosuchus* as a junior synonymy of *Megalosaurus*.

After the type specimen was prepared, Galton (1976*b*) recognized that it did represent a valid genus. To *I. incognitus*, Galton referred a small ilium (OUM J29780) from Stonesfield, Oxfordshire, originally described by Phillips (1871) as a young "megalosaur." From both specimens, Galton diagnosed the monotypic *I. incognitus*.

Galton suggested that the North American *Stokesosaurus*, then presumed to be the only other known theropod to have such a ridged ilium, is congeneric with *Iliosuchus*. The presence of both European and North American forms would provide additional faunal evidence that a transatlantic land connection existed during Middle to Late Jurassic times. (This connection had already been suggested, though faunal evidence [see Charig 1973; Cox 1974]

supporting its existence had been slight.) Later, Galton (*see in* Galton and Jensen 1979), having become aware of a vertical ridge in the ilia of other theropods (*e.g.*, *Megalosaurus bucklandi* and *Tyrannosaurus rex*), decided that the grounds for his earlier synonymy were insufficient, reinstating *I. incognitus* as a valid taxon distinct from *M. bucklandi,* restricted to the Middle Jurassic of southern England.

Molnar, Kurzanov and Dong (1990), noting that only in "carnosaurs" has an ilium with a vertical ridge been convincingly associated with other skeletal material, regarded the assignment of *I. incognitus* to the "Carnosauria" as tenuous in lieu of the absence of further characters.

Key references: Galton (1976*b*); Galton and Jensen (1979); Huene (1932); Molnar, Kurzanov and Dong (1990); Phillips (1871).

INDOSAURUS Huene and Matley 1933
Saurischia: Theropoda: Ceratosauria:
   Neoceratosauria: ?Abelisauroidea:
   ?Abelisauridae.
Name derivation: "India" + Greek *sauros* = "lizard."
Type species: *I. matleyi* Huene and Matley 1933.
Other species: [None.]
Occurrence: Lameta Formation, Madhya Pradesh,
   India.
Age: Late Cretaceous (Middle–Late Maastrichtian).
Known material: Partial skull, fragmentary post-
   crania.
Holotype: IM K27/565 [lost or misplaced],
   braincase with most of frontals.

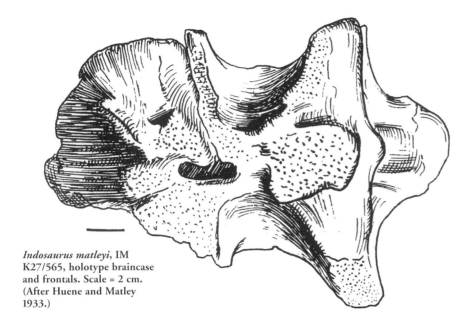

Indosaurus matleyi, IM K27/565, holotype braincase and frontals. Scale = 2 cm. (After Huene and Matley 1933.)

Diagnosis of genus (as for type species): Braincase heavily-built (for a theropod), apparently implying very massive animal; structure of fronto-parietal region resembling that of *Allosaurus*; supratemporal fossa seemingly very short and broad; apparently a pair of recessed areas anterior to supratemporal fossae; parietals broad, possibly accommodating postorbital horns (Huene *see in* Huene and Matley 1933).

Comments: The genus *Indosaurus* was founded on a braincase (IM K27/565) discovered by Charles Alfred Matley of the Geological Survey of India, during the 1917–19 expeditions to the Lameta Group (mapped in detail by Chanda and Bhattacharyya 1966, who recognized three formations within the Lameta Group, the lower third (Lameta Formation) which yielded *Indosaurus*, consisting of greensand; dated as Maastrichtian; A. Sahni, personal communication to Norman 1990) of Jabalpur, in Central India. The original type material, in the collection of the Geological Survey of India, has apparently been misplaced or lost (P. P. Satsangi, personal communication to Chatterjee 1978).

Huene and Matley (1933) described all the dinosaurian material found at this locality in a monograph, Huene focusing on the theropods. Because of the fronto-parietal structure, Huene believed *Indosaurus* was allied with *Allosaurus* [=*Antrodemus* of his usage]. Walker (1964) agreed with Huene's assessment of *Indosaurus* and assigned the genus to the Megalosauridae, commenting that the recessed areas anterior to the supratemporal fossae almost meet at midline, implying a greater degree of specialization in *Indosaurus* than in *Allosaurus*.

Bonaparte and Novas (1985) contended that *Indosaurus* could be an abelisaurid, observing striking similarities between the frontals in this form and in *Abelisaurus*, particularly in the interorbital region. Agreeing with this assignment, Molnar (1990) pointed out various similarities between the frontals of *Indosaurus* and the abelisaurid *Carnotaurus*, including 1. thickenings at the bases of horn cores, and 2. elevated parietals behind the supratemporal fossae. Molnar observed that, in dorsal view, the frontals of *Abelisaurus* and another Indian form, *Indosuchus,* share 1. supratemporal fossae of similar form, and 2. a posterior "wedge" at the supratemporal fossae. Bonaparte and Novas, in a joint paper with Coria (1990), stated that not enough information was available to arrive at a full systematic evaluation of *Indosaurus*, suggesting that this genus may represent a new and as yet unknown family.

Other cranial and postcranial materials referred to *I. matleyi* by Walker (1964) and Chatterjee (1978) were not accepted by Molnar, as two additional large theropods (*Compsosuchus solus* and *Indosuchus raptorius*) are also known from the same discovery site.

Key references: Bonaparte and Novas (1985); Bonaparte, Novas and Coria (1990); Chatterjee (1978); Huene and Matley (1933); Molnar (1990); Walker (1964).

INDOSUCHUS Huene 1932

Saurischia: Theropoda: Ceratosauria: Neoceratosauria: ?Abelisauroidea: ?Abelisauridae.

Name derivation: "India" + Greek *souchos* = "crocodile."

Type species: *I. raptorius* Huene and Matley 1933.

Other species: [None.]

Occurrence: Lameta Formation, Madhya Pradesh, India.

Age: Late Cretaceous (Middle–Late Maastrichtian).

Known material: Fragmentary skull, fragmentary postcrania.

Lectotype: IM K27/685, front part of skull, including incomplete frontals and parietals.

Diagnosis of genus (as for type species): Medium size "large theropod" [=tyrannosaurid of his usage]; four premaxillary and 14 maxillary teeth, with low tooth crowns; first premaxillary tooth and first dentary teeth incisiform, with oblique carinae; second of these teeth transitional; no preantorbital openings in maxilla; lingual wall of maxilla smooth and vertical above fused interdental plate, with slight overhanging shelf (Chatterjee 1987).

Comments: The genus *Indosuchus* was established upon a partial skull (IM K27/685) recovered

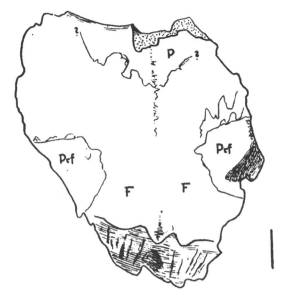

Indosuchus raptorius, IM K20/350, holotype frontal region of skull. Scale = 2 cm. (After Huene and Matley 1933.)

from the Lameta Group [Lameta Formation level; see *Indosaurus* entry] of Jabalpur [then spelled Jubbulpore], in Central India. The material was discovered by Charles Alfred Matley during the 1917–19 expeditions of the Geological Survey of India.

Indosuchus was first described by Huene in a joint monograph with Matley (Huene and Matley 1933) on various Lameta Group dinosaurs. Huene originally diagnosed the monotypic *I. raptorius* as follows: Fronto-parietal region with narrow crest; skull roof flat between orbits; postfrontal smooth. Because of the structure of the fronto-parietal region, Huene believed *Indosuchus* was closely allied with *Allosaurus* [=*Antrodemus* of his usage].

As later noted by Chatterjee (1978), Huene did not designate any of his *Indosuchus* material specimens as the type specimen. Since only one specimen, the posterior part of the skull (IM K27/685), could be found in the Geological Survey of India (P. P. Satsangi, personal communication to Chatterjee), Chatterjee designated that as the lectotype.

Excellently preserved theropod material was collected in 1922 by Barnum Brown for the American Museum of Natural History from the Lameta Group at Jabalpur. This material, consisting of a pair of premaxillae (AMNH 1753), left maxilla (AMNH 1955), and right dentary (AMNH 1960), from the ?same individual, was regarded by Chatterjee as pertaining to *Indosuchus*. However, Molnar (1990) pointed out that there are at least six theropods (*Indosuchus*, *Indosaurus*, *Orthogoniosaurus*, *Coeluroides*, *Compsosuchus*, and *Dryptosauroides*) in the Lameta Formation, this material conceivably belonging to any one of them.

Walker (1964), in reevaluating the Lameta material, had observed that the narrow crest, flattened skull roof, and smooth post-frontal in K27/685 suggest a close affinity with the tyrannosaurids *Tyrannosaurus* and *Albertosaurus*. As in *Tyrannosaurus*, the sphenethmoids in *Indosuchus* are paired. According to Walker, *Indosuchus* is a tyrannosaurid, though one less advanced than *Tyrannosaurus*, with more widely separated prefrontals and a broader median frontal ridge. At the same time, Walker stated that the ilia originally described by Matley as belonging to *Lametasaurus indicus* are probably referrable to *Indosuchus*, while the sacrum and tibia cannot be definitely assigned either to *Indosuchus* or *Indosaurus*.

Chatterjee accepted Walker's assignment of *I. raptorius* to the Tyrannosauridae and diagnosed the type species based on the lectotype and American Museum material.

Indosuchus was again reevaluated by Bonaparte and Novas (1985) with their erection of new theropod family Abelisauridae. Bonaparte and Novas observed that *Abelisaurus* shares certain characters with *Indosuchus*, especially in the region of the preorbital opening. Further studies by Buffetaut, Mechin and Mechin-Salessy (1988) found strong similarities between *Indosuchus* and *Abelisaurus*. Bonaparte, Novas and Coria (1990) pointed out that the maxilla of *Indosuchus* lacks the maxillary fenestra typical of tyrannosaurids, interpreting this genus as a possible abelisaurid, with the maxillary fenestra existing in a reduced form within the main preorbital vacuity. Supporting referring *Indosuchus* to the Abelisauridae, Molnar noted that the frontals of this genus share features with *Abelisaurus* and another Indian theropod, *Indosaurus*.

Note: Walker suggested that a frontal (K20/350) assigned to *Indosuchus* by Huene and Matley, reported from the same horizon as the other material, may belong to the ankylosaur *Lametasaurus*.

Key references: Bonaparte and Novas (1985); Bonaparte, Novas and Coria (1990); Buffetaut, Mechin and Mechin-Salessy (1988); Huene and Matley (1933); Molnar (1990); Walker (1964).

INGENIA Barsbold 1981

Saurischia: Theropoda: Tetanurae: Avetheropoda: Coelurosauria: Maniraptora: Oviraptorosauria: Oviraptoridae: Ingeniinae.

Name derivation: "Ingenia [locality]."

Type species: *I. yanshini* Barsbold 1981.

Other species: [None.]

Occurrence: Red Beds of Khermeen Tsav, Omnogov, Beds of Bugeen Tsav, Bayankhongor, Mongolian People's Republic.

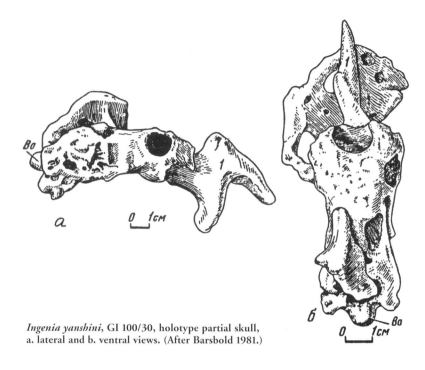

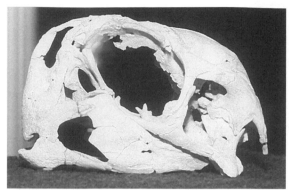

Ingenia yanshini referred skull, left lateral view, in "The Great Russian Dinosaurs" exhibit (1996), Mesa Southwest Museum, Mesa, Arizona.

Ingenia yanshini, GI 100/30, holotype partial skull, a. lateral and b. ventral views. (After Barsbold 1981.)

Age: Late Cretaceous (Middle Campanian–Early Maastrichtian).

Known material: Skulls and complete postcrania representing six individuals.

Holotype: GI 100/30, lower jaw, almost complete postcrania.

Diagnosis of genus (as for type species): Oviraptorid having manus with reduced, strongly curved digits II and III, with weakly curved and compressed ungual phalanges (Barsbold 1981).

Comments: The genus *Ingenia* was founded on a fairly complete (but mostly unfigured) postcranial skeleton and lower jaw (GI 100/30), discovered in the upper part of the Barun-Goyot Formation of Ingenia-khudur, Mongolia. Referred specimens include skull and postcranial remains (GI 100/31 and 100/33) from two more individuals (Barsbold 1981).

Barsbold placed *Ingenia* into its own subfamily, Ingeniinae. Subsequently, Barsbold (1986) raised that taxon to family level, Ingeniidae, although Ingeniinae, along with Oviraptorinae Barsbold 1981, were retained in Oviraptoridae by Barsbold, Maryańska and Osmólska (1990) in their review of the Oviraptorosauria.

According to Barsbold *et al.*, the manus (but not jaws) in *Ingenia* is more powerfully-constructed than in oviraptorines, suggesting that ingeniines may have had a different mode of life, although both lived on the same territory at the same time.

From a study of the palate of *Ingenia yanshini*, Blźanowski (1995) perceived the following cranial evidence for the avian relationships of oviraptorosaurs: Palatine composed of choanal conch and single rostral process; caudomedial processes of maxillary corresponding to avian maxillopalatina; and a bone connecting palatine (and pterygoid) to lacrimal, probably representing avian lacrimopalatine (previously mistaken for ectopterygoid). Comparing the latter with that in *Archaeopteryx* suggested to Elźanowski that this element derives from the lateral component of the pterygoid.

Other avian features observed by Elźanowski in the skull of *I. yanshini* include: Lack of ectopterygoid bridge; thin jugal bars; medial curvature of coronoid process; and deep caudal bifurcation of dentary. Elźanowski suggested that these and other avian characters present in *I. yanshini* are probably synapomorphic for oviraptorosaurians and birds.

Note: Additional material originally referred by Barsbold (1981) to this genus was made the holotype of *Oviraptor mongoliensis*.

Key references: Barsbold (1981, 1986); Barsbold, Maryańska and Osmólska (1990); Elźanowski (1995).

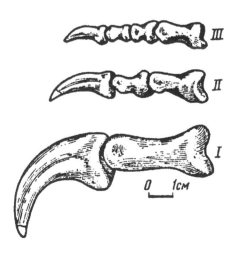

Ingenia yanshini, GI 100/30, holotype digits of right manus. (After Barsbold 1981.)

INOSAURUS Lapparent 1960 [*nomen dubium*]
Saurischia: ?Theropoda *incertae sedis.*
Name derivation: Latin *in* = "in" + Greek *sauros* = "lizard."
Type species: *I. tedreftensis* Lapparent 1960 [*nomen dubium*].
Other species: [None.]
Occurrence: "Continental intercalaire," Niger, Africa.
Age: Early Cretaceous.
Known material: Vertebrae, partial tibia.
Holotype: Caudo-sacral vertebra, anterior caudal vertebra, midcaudal vertebra.

Diagnosis of genus: [No modern diagnosis published.]

Comments: The genus *Inosaurus* was founded upon three vertebrae collected from the "Continental intercalaire" in Abangarit, Niger, in the central Sahara desert region, Africa. The genus is known from three different localities and represented by a total of 25 vertebrae and the proximal portion of a left tibia (Lapparent 1960).

The monotypic *I. tedreftensis* was diagnosed by Lapparent as follows: Small, with massively constructed "dorso-lumbar" vertebrae; mid-caudal vertebrae higher than wide; caudal centra with two ventral keels.

Lapparent described the "dorso-lumbar" vertebra as measuring 3.3 centimeters (about 12.5 inches) long; mid-caudal vertebra 10 centimeters (about 3.8 inches) high; tibia relatively small.

In a reevaluation of various problematic "coelurosaurs," Norman (1990) pointed out that no evidence supports the association of the materials collected from the three localities, adding that if *Inosaurus* is a theropod, it is a very unusual form.

Key references: Lapparent (1960); Norman (1990).

IRRITATOR Martill, Cruickshank, Frey, Small and Clarke 1996
Saurischia: Theropoda: Tetanurae: Avetheropoda: Coelurosauria: ?Maniraptora: ?Arctometatarsalia: ?Bullatosauria: Irritatoridae.
Name derivation: "Irritation."
Type species: *I. challengeri* Martill, Cruickshank, Frey, Small and Clarke 1996.
Other species: [None.]
Occurrence: Santana Formation, Ceará, Brazil, South America.
Age: Early Cretaceous (?Albian or ?Cenomanian).
Known material/holotype: SMNS 58022, almost complete skull.

Diagnosis of genus (as for type species and family): Theropod with skull with overall length of up to 840 millimeters; teeth much elongate with posterior reduction in crown height; anterior maxillary teeth straight, elongate, sub-oval in cross-section, anterior and posterior carinae unserrated; posterior maxillary teeth orthoconical; tooth replacement mesolingual, replacement teeth alternating between functional teeth; tooth rows occupying almost entire depth of maxilla; maxilla straight, with more than 11 teeth; snout laterally compressed, triangular in cross-section; nasal opening oval, located some way back from tip of snout; frontals and parietals extended posterodorsally to form saggital crest; supratemporal fenestra very small; infratemporal fenestra almost as large as orbit; orbit ovoid; quadrate massive, almost vertical; stapes very thin, stick-like, with expanded and flattened ends; lower jaw twice as deep posteriorly as anterior ramus, angular extending only short distance anterior to mandibular fenestra; mandibular fenestra an inverted triangle, twice as long as high; surangular with prominent, thin lateral shelf; at least posterior half of dentary probably edentulous (Martill, Cruickshank, Frey, Small and Clarke, 1996).

Comments: A very unusual theropod, *Irritator* represents the first identifiable specimen from the Lower Cretaceous of Brazil and the first non-avian maniraptoran to be described from the Cretaceous of South America. The genus was founded upon a skull (SMNS 58022), in the collection of the Staatliches Museum für Naturkunde Stuttgart, Germany. Though precise details on the locality which yielded this specimen are not known, the skull was identified as coming from an early diagenetic concretion, typical of those from the Romualdo Mem-

Inosaurus tedreftensis, holotype caudal vertebra. Scale = 2 cm. (After Lapparent 1960.)

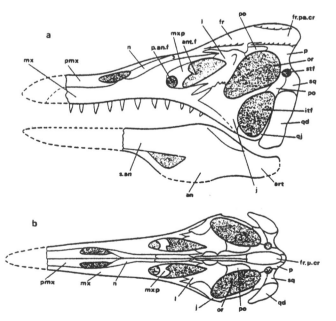

Irritator challengeri, SMNS 58022, holotype reconstructed skull, a. left lateral and b. dorsal views. (After Martill, Cruickshank, Frey, Small and Clarke 1996.)

ber of the Santana Formation (Martill 1993), closely resembling "those dug commercially in and around Porteiras and the Serra da Maozina, at the eastern most outcrop of the Chapada do Araripe, in [southern] Ceará State, northeast Brazil" (stratigraphic horizon confirmed by associated fish remains, including scales of *Cladocyclus* sp.; based on fish fauna, possibly of Albian age, though perhaps Cenomanian; see Martill). The skull had been damaged in several places, mostly do to poor preparation by commercial fossil diggers before its purchase by the museum. During examination in the United Kingdom of SMNS 58022, it was found (through CAT scan imaging and also more thorough mechanical preparation) that "the tip of the rostrum had been artificially reconstructed to increase its length by reassembly of portions of the maxilla on to the premaxilla." This discovery led to the unusual name given to the new genus, referring to "the feeling the authors felt (understated here) when discovering that the snout had been artificially elongated" (Martill *et al.* 1996).

By itself, the occurrence of the type species *I. challengeri* in Santana Formation rocks constitutes a rare find. As pointed out by Martill *et al.*, dinosaurs are rare in this formation (otherwise well known for the abundance and diversity of its fossil vertebrates, but with dinosaurs known only from remains too meagerly preserved to justify formal description), while theropods in general are very rarely found in the Southern Hemisphere.

Martill *et al.* observed that the saggital crest in *Irritator* is unique among cranial crests possessed by a relatively small number of theropods. The crest's massive construction and posterior position indicates that it served as an enlarged attachment area for the dorsal neck musculature, the latter providing strong, dorsally directed forces. According to Martill *et al.*, this indicates an ability to raise the head with reasonable force or to resist drag if the lower jaw was inserted into water. Such movement, and also the dental pattern and great elongation of the maxilla and premaxilla, suggested to the authors that *Irritator* may have been a fish eater.

In comparing (in terms of skull-character morphology) *Irritator* with other theropods and theropod groups, Martill *et al.* interpreted this genus as a tetanuran and probably maniraptoran, morphologically very distinct from other theropods known from skull material. The genus exhibits similarities with both the Dromaeosauridae (united with *Archaeopteryx* as an unnamed clade; see Holtz 1994*a*) and Bullatosauria, more so with the latter taxon, sharing identical characters with both of its subgroups, Troodontidae and Ornithomimosauriae [=Ornithomimosauridae of their usage]. As no troodontids, ornithomimosaurs, or even arctometatarsalians have been reported to date from South America, and because a number of features separate this genus from other known maniraptorans, Martill *et al.* referred *Irritator* to its own new family, the Irritatoridae, distinguished mostly by the saggital crest comprising frontals and parietals, unique dental pattern, and extreme elongation of the laterally compressed rostrum.

As pointed out by Martill *et al.*, the occurrence of *Irritator* in South America confirms the existence of a land link between that continent and the dinosaur faunas of North America and Asia, apparently via Africa, during the Cretaceous period.

Key reference: Martill, Cruickshank, Frey, Small and Clarke (1996).

ISCHISAURUS   Reig 1963—(See *Herrerasaurus.*)
Name derivation: "Ischigualasto [Beds]" + Greek *sauros* = "lizard."
Type species: *I. cattoi* Reig 1963.

ISCHYROSAURUS   Hulke 1874 [*nomen dubium*]—(=?*Pelorosaurus*)
Saurischia: Sauropodomorpha: Sauropoda: Brachiosauridae.
Name derivation: Greek *isos* = "equal" + Greek *cheir* = "hand" + Greek *sauros* = "lizard."
Type species: *I. manseli* Hulke 1874 [*nomen dubium*].
Other species: [None.]

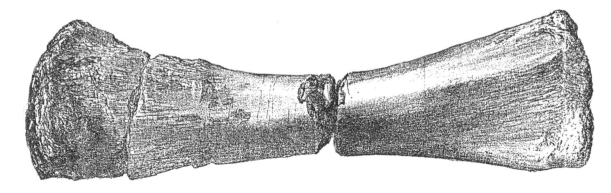

Ischyrosaurus manseli, BMNH 41626, holotype incomplete left humerus. (After Hulke 1874.)

Occurrence: Kimmeridge Clay, Dorset, Cambridgeshire, England.

Age: Upper Jurassic (Kimmeridgian).

Known material/holotype: BMNH R41626, left humerus.

Diagnosis of genus: [None published.]

Comments: The genus *Ischyrosaurus* was founded upon a left humerus missing the deltoid crest (BMNH R41626), discovered in 1868 in layers of shale, just above the band of cement stone on the west side of Clavell's Tower, between Kimmeridge Bay and Clavell's Head, in the Kimmeridge Clay of the Dorset Coast, Dorsetshire, England. The material was obtained by J. C. Mansel Pleydell, a member of the Geological Society of London (Hulke 1869).

Hulke, without naming this material, described it as follows: Humerus with subcylindrical shaft and elongated extremities; terminal surfaces rugose, studded with small protuberances, only slightly abraded; surface of bone smooth, polished, made up of dense cortex almost 13 centimeters (about 5 inches) thick.

Later, Hulke (1874) made the humerus the type specimen of new genus and species *Ischyrosaurus manseli*.

Although *Ischyrosaurus* may be congeneric with *Pelorosaurus*, the former's type material is too meager for a positive synonymy to be made.

Note: As pointed out by Chure and McIntosh (1989), the name *Ischyrosaurus* is preoccupied (Cope 1870); a name change may be unnecessary, however, as several taxa could be synonymous.

Key references: Hulke (1869, 1874).

ITEMIRUS   Kurzanov 1976

Saurischia: Theropoda: Tetanurae *incertae sedis*.

Name derivation: "Itemri [classical name for site]."

Type species: *I. medullaris* Kurzanov 1976.

Other species: [None.]

Occurrence: Beleutinskaya Svita, Uzbeckskaya, S.S.R.

Age: Late Cretaceous (Late Turonian).

Known material/holotype: PIN 327/699, braincase.

Diagnosis of genus (as for type species): Braincase with basisphenoid sinus divided basally in two; anterior outlet of middle cerebral vein separated from trigeminal foramen; auditory nerve dividing inside osseous labyrinth (Kurzanov 1976a).

Comments: Basis for the family Itemiridae, the genus *Itemirus* was founded upon the braincase (PIN 327/699) of an old individual, collected in 1958 by Anatoly Konstantinovich Rozhdestvensky from the upper Turonian Substage (dated by Pyatkov, Pyanovska, Bukharin and Bykovskiy 1967, based on an assembly of pelecypods) of the Dzhara-Kuduk (Itemir) site, Central Kyzylkum sands of Uzbeckskaya,

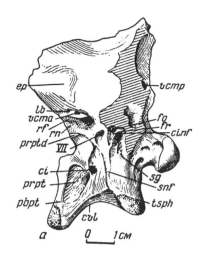

Itemirus medullaris, PIN 327/699, holotype braincase, lateral view. (After Kurzanov 1976.)

S.S.R. [former Union of Soviet Socialist Republics] (Kurzanov 1976a).

In describing the holotype, Kurzanov observed that the inner ear in *Itemirus* does not fundamentally differ from that in modern reptiles, although the lagena is much more weakly-developed than in present-day archosaurs [=crocodiles]. The semicircular canals in *Itemirus* are very high and much larger than those in hadrosaurids. The very large vestibule has a quite distinctive shape, extending lengthwise from the posterior margin of the trigeminal foramen to that of the jugular foramen. Kurzanov concluded that the ear in *Itemirus* (and ?other totally bipedal theropods) served more as a balancing than hearing organ.

According to Molnar (1990), the braincase of *I. medullaris* displays no specializations of either ornithomimids or saurornithoidids, nor does it closely resemble that of "carnosaurs." Molnar agreed that this species probably warrants its own family, but is not well enough known to refer that group to some higher-level taxon.

Key references: Kurzanov (1976a); Molnar (1990).

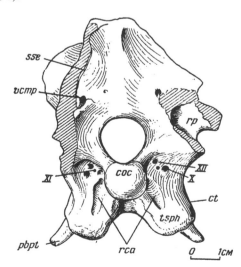

Itemirus medullaris, PIN 327/699, holotype braincase, posterior view. (After Kurzanov 1976.)

IUTICOSAURUS   Le Loeuff 1993

Saurischia: Sauropodomorpha: Sauropoda:
   Titanosauria: Titanosauridae.

Name derivation: Latin *Iuticus* [related to Jutes,
   who invaded Isle of Wight during 5th century] +
   Greek *sauros* = "lizard."

Type species: *I. valdensis* (Lydekker 1887).

Other species: [None.]

Occurrence: Wealden, Isle of Wight, England.

Age: Early Cretaceous (Barremian–Lower Aptian).

Known material: Caudal vertebrae.

Lectotype: BMNH R151, incomplete caudal vertebra.

Diagnosis of genus (as for type species): Base of
neural arch with centrum rising to constitute pro-
montory, associated to posterior ridge on lateral surface of centrum; postzygapophyses extremely long
(Le Loeuff 1993).

Comments: A new species of *Ornithopsis*,
O. valdensis, was erected by Lydekker (1887) upon
two incomplete middle caudal vertebrae (BMNH
R151 and R146a), from the Wealden of the Isle of
Wight. BMNH R151 consists of a laterally compressed, water-worn centrum; BMNH R146a is the
anterior half of a second unworn centrum.

Originally part of the William Fox collection,
the specimens were purchased in 1882 by the British
Museum (Natural History), now known as The Natural History Museum, London. Lydekker (1888*a*)
subsequently referred these remains to *Titanosaurus*
sp. a, after which Huene (1929) referred them to new
species *T. valdensis*. A third and similar caudal vertebra (BMNH R1886), collected from an unknown
Wealden locality on the Isle of Wight by Samuel H.
Beckles, shares features with R151 and R146a and
belongs to the same species (Le Loeuff 1993).

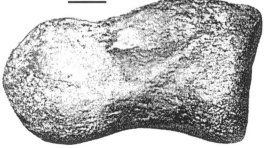

Iuticosaurus valdensis,
BMNH R151, lectotype cau-
dal vertebra, dorsal and lateral views. Scale = 2 cm.
(After Le Loeuff 1993.)

As described by Le Loeuff, R1886, the best preserved specimen, is approximately 135 millimeters
long, the centrum anteriorly 70 millimeters high and
65 millimeters wide. The centra of all three vertebrae
are deeply procoelous and the neural arches are
forwardly placed, these features indicating that the
specimens are titanosaurid.

Le Loeuff observed that the autapomorphic features of this titanosaurid are clearly different from
those of *T. indicus,* the type species of *Titanosaurus,*
and suggested that BMNH R151, R146a, and R1886
be referred to the new genus *Iuticosaurus* and the type
species *I. valdensis.*

This taxon is, Le Loeuff pointed out, the oldest
known European titanosaurid.

Key references: Huene (1929); Le Loeuff (1993);
Lydekker (1887, 1888*a*).

JANENSCHIA   Wild 1991

Saurischia: Sauropodomorpha: Sauropoda:
   ?Titanosauria: ?Titanosauridae.

Name derivation: "[Werner] Janensch."

Type species: *J. robusta* (E. Fraas 1908).

Other species: [None.]

Occurrence: Upper Tendaguru Beds, Mtwara,
   Tanzania; Chiweta Beds, Northern Province,
   Malawi.

Age: Late Jurassic (Kimmeridgian).

Known material: Postcranial remains, including
   three hindlimbs, two forelimbs, manus, 72 dorsal
   vertebrae, caudal series, caudal vertebrae.

Holotype: Distal end of right femur, tibia, pes.

Diagnosis of genus (as for type species): Very
very large titanosaurid, as much as about 20 percent
longer than other titanosaurids, with robust skeleton; cervical vertebrae with deep pleurocoels over
which are formed postzygapophyses, and thick neural
spines; dorsal vertebrae with pleurocoels and low,
nonbifurcated neural spines; sacral vertebrae with
very reduced spines, proximal sacrals with very strong
diapophyses; proximal caudal vertebrae strongly procoelous, very concave in front, very convex behind,
with no pleurocoels; middle caudals laterally strong,
articular surfaces weakly biconcave, with slightly distinct upper edge, rounded ventral side, high ellipse-
like cross-section; hindlimbs very robust, humerus,
ulna, and radius massive, becoming markedly wider
at their ends; metacarpals compact; phalangeal formula of third and longest manual digit 2-2-1-1-1;
only manual digit I bearing very long claw; pubis and
ischium robust, distal end of pubis with large surface;
femur stout, upper margin prominently deflected,
distal end strongly expanded; tibia and fibula with
expanded ends; astragalus low, flatter underneath

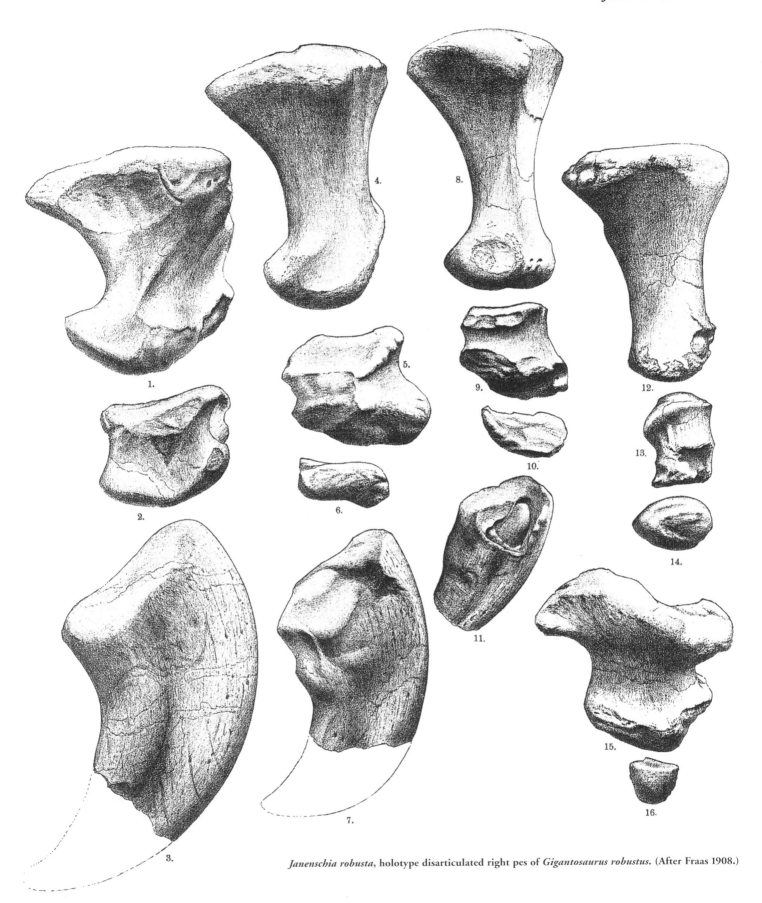

Janenschia robusta, holotype disarticulated right pes of *Gigantosaurus robustus*. (After Fraas 1908.)

Janenschia robusta, holotype partial right hindlimb and pes of *Gigantosaurus robustus.* (After Fraas 1908.)

generic species *T. robusta* could not be referred to any other known sauropod genus, Wild (1991) referred it to the new genus and species *Janenschia robusta.*

As recounted by McIntosh (1990b) in his review of the Sauropoda, Janensch referred to *Tornieria* a pubis and right ischium from the type locality, also two very large dorsal vertebrae, and a series of 30 articulated caudal vertebrae from other localities, on the basis that they were not similar to any of the other three Tendaguru sauropods (*i.e.*, *Brachiosaurus, Dicraeosaurus,* and *Barosaurus*).

Fraas originally diagnosed "*G.*" *robustus* [=*J. robusta*] as very massively constructed, with very strong hindlimbs. As measured by Fraas, the total length of the holotype femur is 1.38 meters (about 4.75 feet). Wild rediagnosed *J. robusta,* based on earlier work by Fraas, and also Janensch (1922, 1929, 1961).

According to McIntosh, the presence of pleurocoels in the caudal vertebrae constitutes the principal evidence that this genus is a titanosaurid (if these vertebrae do indeed belong to *Janenschia*), although this evidence is not, at present, convincing.

Note: The species *T. dixeyi* has been made the type species of a new genus, *Malawisaurus.*

Key references: Fraas (1908); Janensch (1922, 1929, 1961); McIntosh (1990b); Sternfield (1911); Wild (1991).

JAXARTOSAURUS   Riabinin 1939 [*nomen dubium*]—(=?*Nipponosaurus*)

Ornithischia: Genasauria: Cerapoda: Ornithopoda: Iguanodontia: Hadrosauridae: Lambeosaurinae.

Name derivation: "Jaxartes [from Yaxart, ancient name for the Syr-Daria River (formerly U.S.S.R.)]" + Greek *sauros* = "lizard."

Type species: *J. aralensis* Riabinin 1939 [*nomen dubium*].

Other species: ?*J. convincens* (Rozhdestvensky 1968), ?*J. fuyunensis* Wu 1984.

Occurrence: Dabrazinskaya Svita, Kazakhskaya, Kazakhstan, Russia, ?Wulungo Formation, Xianjiang Uygur Ziziqu, People's Republic of China.

Age: Late Cretaceous (?Turonian–Santonian).

Known material: Partial skull, partial postcrania, adult, juvenile.

Holotype: PEN AN SSR 1/5009, posterior part of skull.

Diagnosis of genus: Hadrosaur of "average size"; skull wide, low, with helmet-like crest; frontals and prefrontals not partaking in formation of crest; frontals large, inflated, separated from upper edge of orbit; supratemporal fossae not small; upper temporal arches straight, oriented parallel to sagittal line of skull (Rozhdestvensky 1968).

than in all other known sauropods; pes robust, first three toes with claws, phalangeal formula 2-3-3-2-1; metatarsal V short, very wide proximally; first toe with large claw (Wild 1991).

Comments: Perhaps the oldest known titanosaurid, the species originally named *Gigantosaurus robustus* was established on a right hind limb, discovered in 1907 by W. B. Sattler in Tendaguru, about 40 miles inland from the seaport city of Lindi, on the eastern coast of Tanzania, East Africa (see *Brachiosaurus* entry). These remains were first described by Fraas (1908), who referred them to the genus *Gigantosaurus* Fraas 1908, the type species of which was *G. africanus.*

When the name *Gigantosaurus* proved to be preoccupied (Seeley 1869), Sternfield (1911) subsequently erected the new genus *Tornieria* to receive Fraas' material, the new type species becoming *T. africana,* with *T. robusta* a referred species. Later, *T. africana* was referred to *Barosaurus.* As the remaining nonsyn-

?*Jaxartosaurus fuyubensis*, lower jaw.
(After Dong 1987.)

Diagnosis of *J. aralensis*: Cranium narrowing sharply behind orbits; short, slightly-developed sagittal crest formed by parietals; frontals wedged in between nasals away from orbital rim, separated from it by wide band of prefrontal and postorbital; parietals between frontals, the latter forwardly broadened by a process; cranium about one fifth wider posteriorly than in occipital area; occiput wider by two and one half times, on level of paroccipital processes, than high from lower point of occipital foramen; upper part of orbit wide; subtemporal fossae narrow, slit-like; orbits about four and one half times wider than subtemporal fossae; supratemporal fossae rhombus; orbital width more than one and one half times length; from 34 to 35 dentary tooth rows (Rozhdestvensky 1968).

Comments: The genus *Jaxartosaurus* was founded on the posterior part of a skull, a mandible, supraangular, four cervical vertebrae, two dorsal vertebrae, humerus, ischium, femur, and tibia, representing several individuals. This material was collected at Kyrkkuduk in the region of the Alym-tau Range, west of the Sary-Agach railroad station in the area of the Jaxartes River, Kazakhstan, Russia (Riabinin 1939). Riabinin incorrectly regarded all of these syntypes as the holotype. As there seemed to be no evidence of a lambeosaurine crest, Riabinin classified *Jaxartosaurus* with the Hadrosaurinae.

Riabinin first diagnosed the type species as follows: Mandible with obtuse and slightly downwardly directed anterior portion; edentulous portion of upper margin notched, with protuberance; from 34 to 35 vertical rows of dentary teeth; ischium with closed, oval-shaped fenestra; humerus with narrow proximal end.

Rozhdestvensky (1968) later criticized Riabinin's diagnosis, stating that it was too brief to allow a clear ascertainment of this species and its phylogenetic relation with other hadrosaurids, contained several errors, and omitted certain cranial features essential for a diagnosis of dinosaurs. Rozhdestvensky designated the more complete skull (PEN AS SSR 1/5009) as the holotype. Taking advantage of the uniquely intact condition of this specimen (*e.g.*, distinct sutures between bones, openings for passage of blood vessels and nerves, and other details), Rozhdestvensky rediagnosed the genus and type species.

Two other species were tentatively referred to this genus: ?*J. fuyunensis* Wu 1984 [*nomen dubium*] was founded upon a dentary from the Wulungo Formation, Xianjiang Uygur Ziziqu, People's Republic of China. Regarded by some paleontologists as a junior synonym of *J. aralensis*, a taxon originally named ?*Procheneosaurus convincens* Rozhdestvensky 1986, based on an almost complete juvenile skeleton (PIN 2230) missing the anterior part of the skull, distal parts of the anterior and left hindlimbs, and most posterior caudal vertebrae. The specimen was collected from the Dabrazinskaya Formation (?Senonian) of Southern Kazakhstan, Syuk-Syuk, north of Tashkent. According to Brett-Surman (1989), although *Jaxartosaurus* has achieved status as "the Asian lambeosaurine," ?*P. convincens* is indeterminate and a *nomen dubium* best not referred to the genus.

As observed by Rozhdestvensky (1968), the skull of *J. aralensis* displays some primitive features particularly notable in understanding hadrosaurid evolution. Rozhdestvensky assigned this taxon to the Lambeosaurinae because it exhibits some lambeosaurine features (*e.g.*, swelling of frontals and separation of frontals from upper margin of orbit by wide band of prefrontals and occipitals). However, *Jaxartosaurus* also has features characteristic of the Hadrosaurinae (*e.g.*, wide skull with low occiput and long, low

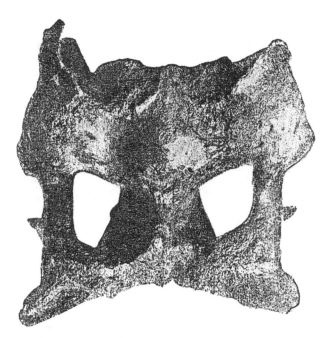

Jubbulpuria tenuis, IM K27/612, cotype dorsal vertebra, in posterior, right lateral, and dorsal views. Scale = 2 cm. (After Huene and Matley 1933.)

Jaxartosaurus aralensis, PEN AN SSR 1/5009, holotype skull roof, dorsal view. (After Rozhdestvensky 1968.)

supraoccipital). This combination of features could indicate that lambeosaurines were derived from hadrosaurines, with *Jaxartosaurus* possibly at the beginning of lambeosaurine genealogy.

As shown by Rozhdestvensky, the skull roof in *Jaxartosaurus* (also *Aralosaurus* and other hadrosaurs) displays a unique articulation. The contact of laterosphenoid with postorbital does not have the usual suture, but rather an articulation socket on the postorbital into which the laterosphenoid enters with a rounded end. This kind of joint, not previously reported in hadrosaurids, is also seen in *Saurolophus angustirostris* and other hadrosaurines, as well as in theropods and (particularly long-snouted) crocodiles. The remaining sutures of laterosphenoids and postorbitals with the adjacent bones are serrated, rendering them nonkinetic. There is a gap between the articular process of the laterosphenoid and the depression of the postorbital, which may have been filled with cartilage during the animal's life. This arrangement (L. I. Khozatskii, personal communication to Rozhdestvensky) could have functioned as a shock absorber to protect the braincase from jarring during sudden closing of the jaws.

In their review of the Hadrosauridae, Weishampel and Horner (1990) noted that the material upon which this genus was founded is quite poor and regarded *Jaxartosaurus* as Lambeosaurinae *incertae sedis.*

Key references: Brett-Surman (1989); Riabinin (1939); Rozhdestvensky (1968, 1986); Weishampel and Horner (1990); Wu (1984).

JUBBULPURIA Huene 1932 [*nomen dubium*]
Saurischia: Theropoda *incertae sedis.*
Name derivation: "Jubbulpore [town in Central India]."
Type species: *J. tenuis* Huene 1932 [*nomen dubium*].
Other species: [None.]
Occurrence: Lameta Formation, Madhya Pradesh, India.
Age: Late Cretaceous (Maastrichtian).
Known material/cotypes: IM K27/614 and K20/612, two dorsal vertebrae.

Diagnosis of genus (as for type species): Dorsal vertebrae high, slightly narrowed at middle, thin-walled; centrum slightly constricted; diapophysis relatively narrow and very flat, lacking almost any indication of buttresses; neural arch a flat plate; dorsal neural spine posteriorly located, postzygapophyses behind and stretched backward; one dorsal 4.2 centimeters (about 1.6 inches) in length (Huene 1932; Huene and Matley 1933).

Comments: The genus *Jubbulpuria* was established upon dorsal vertebrae (IM K27/614 and K20/612) collected from the so-called "Carnosaur Bed" of the Lameta Formation [Maastrichtian; see *Indosaurus* entry] at Bara Simla Hill, Jabalpur (formerly spelled Jubbulpore), Madhya Pradesh, in the Central Provinces of India.

Huene (1932) referred *Jubbulpuria* to the Coeluridae, although, as noted by Norman (1990), the type material is insufficient to regard as anything beyond the indeterminate dorsal vertebrae of a small theropod.

Key references: Huene (1932); Huene and Matley (1933); Norman (1990).

Jubbulpuria tenuis, IM K27/614, cotype dorsal vertebra, posterior and lateral views. Scale = 2 cm. (After Huene and Matley 1933.)

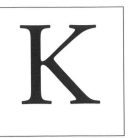

KAIJIANGOSAURUS He 1984—
(=?*Gasosaurus*)
Saurischia: Theropoda: Tetanurae *incertae sedis.*
Name derivation: "Kaijiang [District]" + Greek
sauros = "lizard."
Type species: *K. lini* He 1984.
Other species: [None.]
Occurrence: Xiashaximiao Formation, Sichuan,
People's Republic of China.
Age: Late Jurassic (Bathonian–Callovian).
Known material: Partial skeletal material represent-
ing several individuals.
Holotype: CCG 20020, seven cervical vertebrae.

Diagnosis of genus (as for type species): Teeth
flat with slightly curved inner surface; cervical vertebrae short and broad; mid-portion of cervical more
narrow, anterior portion about equal in length and
width, posterior portion smooth; caudal vertebrae
concave at anterior and mid-parts; distal caudals
strongly pneumatized; scapula rather straight, much
expanded proximally; ulna with prominent olecranon process; manual unguals strongly curved; strong
flexor tubercles on manual claws (He 1984).

Comments: *Kaijiangosaurus* was established on
incomplete cranial and postcranial remains (CCG
20020), including cervical vertebrae, discovered by a
Mr. Lin in the Kaijiang District, near Golden
Chicken Commune, in Sichuan, China. Referred to
the type species were remains of several individuals
including jugal, teeth, dorsal, sacral and caudal vertebrae, scapula, coracoid, forelimb bones, incomplete
manus bones, and hindlimb elements (He 1984).

Molnar, Kurzanov and Dong (1990) observed
that the "noncarnosaurian" characters of *K. lini* (*e.g.,*
nonelevated femoral head) are plesiomorphic, which
together with its "carnosaurian" features (*e.g.,* narrow
scapular blade expanded at glenoid region) may place
this species near the ancestry of "Carnosauria." Also,
Molnar *et al.* noted that *Kaijiangosaurus* could be
synonymous with *Gasosaurus,* a theropod from the
same formation.

Key references: He (1984); Molnar, Kurzanov
and Dong (1990).

KAKURU Molnar and Pledge 1980
Saurischia: Theropoda *incertae sedis.*
Name derivation: "Kakuru [ancestral 'serpent' of
Guyani tribe]."
Type species: *K. kujani* Molnar and Pledge 1980.
Other species: [None.]
Occurrence: Maree Formation, Andamooka South
Australia, Australia.
Age: Late Cretaceous (Aptian).
Known material/holotype: SAM P17926, fragmen-
tary right tibia.

Diagnosis of genus (as for type species): Small
but very long, slender tibia, with very high, narrow
astragalus facet (Norman 1990).

Comments: The genus *Kakuru* was established
upon a fragmentary, opalized tibia from the Marree
Formation, in the opal-bearing deposits of the Andamooka area of South Australia.

The type specimen, which had been severely
broken during excavation, was acquired in 1973 by an
Adelaide opal shop. Later that same year, the shop
acquired a slightly crushed, opalized theropod pedal
phalanx. Both specimens were eventually sold at auc-
tion, but not before casts of them were made. The
tibia cast was designated the "plastoholotype" (SAM
P17926) of the type species *K. kujani,* to which the
phalanx cast (SAM P18010) was referred (Molnar and
Pledge 1980).

Kaijiangosaurus lini, CCG
20020, holotype cervical
vertebrae. (After He 1984.)

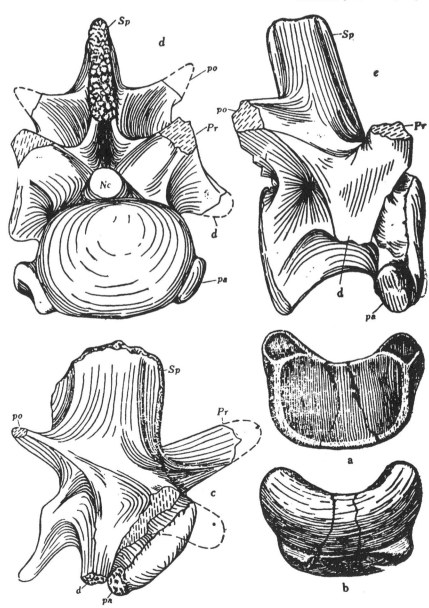

Molnar and Pledge noted that, though fragmentary, the material was worth describing given the paucity of Australian dinosaur remains.

Originally, Molnar and Pledge diagnosed the monotypic *K. kujani* as follows: Tibia with high astragalar facet; facet becoming slender dorsally to a distinct apex, but not broad enough to extend across entire width of anterior face of tibia at any point; facet limited medially by pronounced anterior ridge that runs dorsally from medial malleolus, the latter strongly produced medially.

As described by Molnar and Pledge, the preserved length of the tibia is 323 millimeters (more than 12 inches), distal breadth 40 millimeters (over 1.5 inches), and greatest thickness 20 millimeters (about .78 inches). The medial malleolus is more drawn out than in most theropods. The astragalar facet, if complete, would have resembled a somewhat narrower version of that of *Struthiomimus altus*.

The tibia, though larger, closely resembles in general proportions that of *Avimimus portentosus* (R. E. Molnar, personal communication 1988).

Molnar and Pledge observed that the most significant feature of the tibia is the astragalar ascending process which, if properly interpreted, does not fit into any of the five classes of theropod tarses established by Welles and Long (1974). The fragment is crescent-shaped in cross-section, with a diameter of approximately 53.3 by 2.7 millimeters (about 2.1 by more than .1 inches). An almost complete phalanx, provisionally referred by Molnar and Pledge to *K. kujani*, is 44 millimeters (about 1.7 inches) long, with a proximal width of 23 millimeters (about .85 inches) and proximal height of 19 millimeters (about .73 inches). Its proximal articular face is slightly concave, with only a slight median ridge.

In reviewing various problematic "coelurosaurs," Norman (1990) reevaluated *Kakuru*. While regarding this taxon as a useful record of South Australian Aptian-age theropods, Norman found the material lacking in sufficient quality for comparisons with other species and referred it to Theropoda *incertae sedis*.

Key references: Molnar and Pledge (1980); Norman (1990).

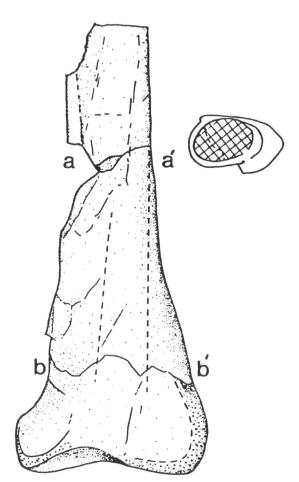

Kakuru jujani, SAM P17926, holotype partial right tibia. (After Molnar and Pledge 1980.)

KANGNASAURUS Haughton 1915 [*nomen dubium*]

Ornithischia: Genasauria: Cerapoda: Ornithopoda: Iguanodontia: Dryosauridae.

Name derivation: "[Farm] Kangnas" + Greek *sauros* = "lizard."

Type species: *K. coetzeei* Haughton 1915 [*nomen dubium*].

Other species: [None.]

Occurrence: Kalahari Deposits, Cape Province, South Africa.

Age: ?Cretaceous.

Known material: Tooth, partial postcranial remains.

Holotype: 2732, right dentary tooth.

Diagnosis of genus (as for type species): Tooth spatulate, enameled on both sides, lacking cingulum or constriction between root and crown; root seemingly long, tapering; crown longitudinally curved with subrhomboidal medio-lateral profile; convex surface strongly ridged (as in *Hypsilophodon*), median keel forming spike to cutting edge; cervical vertebrae apparently relatively long, strongly waisted at midlength, with prominent ventral keel, and (as in *Hypsilophodon* and *Camptosaurus*) apparently opisthocoelous; dorsal vertebrae platycoelous, nearly amphiplatyan, with suboval anterior and posterior profiles; caudal vertebrae with no transverse processes and much reduced neural spines; ribs with short tubercular pedicle with elliptical tuberculum; femur rather gracile, sigmoid (as in *Dryosaurus*) in medial

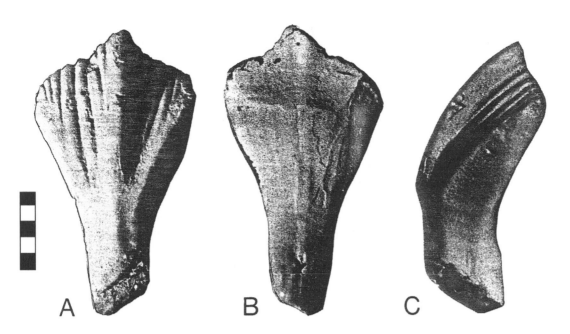

Kangnasaurus coetzeei, SAM
2732, holotype dentary
tooth, in A. labial, B. lingual,
and C. anterior views.
Scale = 5 mm. (After
Haughton 1915.)

aspect, strongly expanded at each end; depression for insertion of caudifemoralis longus muscle well separated from fourth trochanter (as in *Dryosaurus*); moderately-developed anterior intercondylar groove distally; medial surface of inner condyle flat (as in *Dryosaurus* and *Hypsilophodon*); tibia with strongly expanded proximal head, well-developed cnemial crest that curves outward markedly, separated by broadly concave groove from accessory condyle; pronounced accessory condyle on lateral surface of outer condyle for articulation with fibula (similar to *Dryosaurus*; see Galton 1981*b*, and *Hypsilophodon*; see Galton 1978); astragalus a thin cup of bone with shallowly biconcave dorsal surface; calcaneum with slightly concave, nearly flat lateral surface (closely resembling *Hypsilophodon*; see Galton 1974*a*, *Camptosaurus*; see Galton and Powell 1980; and *Dryosaurus*; see Galton 1981); distal tarsal apparently elongate hemicylinder; pes apparently tridactyl; pedal ungual asymmetrical, dorsoventrally compressed (Cooper 1985).

Comments: The genus *Kangnasaurus* was founded upon a dentary tooth (SAM 2732) found in a well at Farm Kangnas, in the Orange River valley, south of Henkries Mond, Little Bushmanland, at the base of the Kalahari succession in northernmost Cape Province, South Africa.

Possibly referable to the type species are a right femur (SAM 2731), proximal end of a right femur (SAM 2731a), distal end of a right femur (SAM 2731b), distal end of a left femur (SAM 2731c), proximal end of a right femur (SAM 2731d), articulated distal left femur and proximal portion of a tibia (SAM 2731f), distal end of a left metatarsal (SAM 2731g), distal portion of a right tibia with articulated tarsus

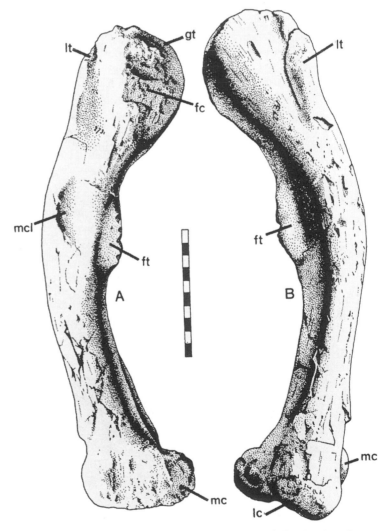

?*Kangnasaurus coetzeei*, SAM 2731, right femur in A. medial and B. lateral views. Scale = 100 mm. (After Haughton 1915.)

and proximal portion of a metatarsus (SAM 2731j), and some unidentified remains (SAM 2731h and 2731i). The foot bones and vertebrae were apparently found in a different deposit than the holotype. As noted by Cooper (1985), there is no reason to believe with certainty that these referred specimens all belong with the holotype tooth.

Kangnasaurus was first described by Haughton (1915) as an iguanodontid (this status sustaining for many decades). However, Cooper pointed out that Haughton had incorrectly identified the holotype as a right maxillary tooth because it bore (as do teeth in iguanodontids) a strong median keel. Because of the depositional separation between the tooth and ?referable material, Haughton questioned the latter's inclusion in the genus. Cooper was of the opinion that, when dealing with such disarticulated remains, it is highly probable that all pertain to the same taxon, leaving to the dissenter the burden of proof that more than a single taxon is involved. Cooper diagnosed *K. coetzeei*, treating all of these remains as the hypodigm.

Because of similarities between this genus and *Hypsilophodon* and especially *Dryosaurus*, Cooper removed *Kangnasaurus* from Iguanodontidae and reassigned it to Hypsilophodontidae. However, as *Dryosaurus* is now classified with Dryosauridae rather than Hypsilophodontidae, Milner and Norman (1984) tentatively referred *Kangnasaurus* to the former family.

Key references: Cooper (1985); Haughton (1915); Milner and Norman (1984).

KELMAYISAURUS Dong 1983 [*nomen dubium*]
Saurischia: Theropoda: Tetanurae: *incertae sedis*.
Name derivation: "Kelmay [petroleum city]" + Greek *sauros* = "lizard."
Type species: *K. petrolicus* Dong 1983 [*nomen dubium*].
Other Spectes: [None.]
Occurrence: Lianmugin Formation, Xinjiang, Uygur Zizhiqu, People's Republic of China.

Age: Early Cretaceous (?Valanginian–Albian).
Known material/holotype: IVPP V4022, fragment of right maxilla, mandibular ramus, piece of undetermined quadrate.

Diagnosis of genus (as for type species): Relatively large "carnosaur," with relatively high skull exhibiting certain features similar to *Ceratosaurus*; large antorbital opening; teeth laterally compressed (Dong 1983).

Comments: The genus *Kelmayisaurus* was founded upon incomplete skull material (IVPP V4022) collected from the Lianmuging Formation, Tugulo Series, Dlunshan, Dsungar Basin, Wuerho district, in Sinkiang, China (Dong 1983).

As observed by Dong, the skull of *Kelmayisaurus*, though larger, resembles that of *Ceratosaurus* in the structure of lower jaw and number of teeth (16 in each dentary). The Wuerho form differs from the North American genus in lacking the supradentary of the mandible, which is very conspicuous in *Ceratosaurus*, and in the straight quadrate.

Molnar, Kurzanov and Dong (1990) noted that *Kelmayisaurus* agrees with *Megalosaurus bucklandii* in four of the mandibular characters given by Madsen (1976a) and in one with *Allosaurus fragilis*, while four cannot be determined, suggesting a closer relationship with *M. bucklandii* than the latter species.

Key references: Dong (1983); Molnar, Kurzanov and Dong (1990).

KENTROSAURUS Hennig 1915—
(=*Doryphosaurus*, *Kentrurosaurus*)
Ornithischia: Genasauria: Thyreophora: Stegosauria: Stegosauridae.
Name derivation: Greek *kentros* = "spiked" + Greek *sauros* = "lizard."
Type species: *K. aethiopicus* Hennig 1915.
Other species: [None.]
Occurrence: Tendaguru Beds, Mtwara, Tanzania.
Age: Late Jurassic (Kimmeridgian).

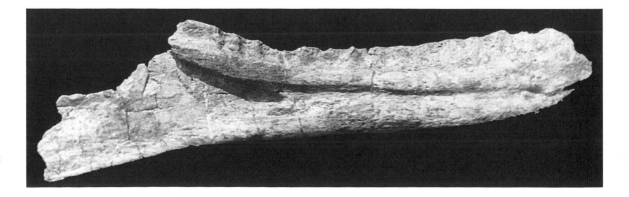

Kelmayisaurus petrolicus, IVPP V4022, holotype right mandibular ramus. (After Dong 1987.)

Kentrosaurus aethiopicus, composite skeleton including holotype ilium (21/SR/PAL), mounted at the Humboldt Museum für Naturkunde.

Known material: Two complete skeletons, four braincases, seven sacra, over 70 femora, about 25 isolated elements, juvenile to adult.

Cotypes: HMN St694 and 695, two associated mid-dorsal vertebrae.

Diagnosis of genus (as for type species): Derived characters include large neural canal within pedicle, bordered dorsally by thin transverse lamina in dorsal vertebrae; centrum with almost solid dorsal plate; neural arches leaning cranially in caudal vertebrae, transverse processes extending as far as 28 caudal; neural spines of distal two-thirds of tail with marked anticline; plow-shaped hemal arches; ilium with wide preacetabular process; primitive characters include skull with prominent paraquadrate foramen; simple cheek teeth, crowns with just seven marginal denticles; shoulder spine; neck and cranial half of back bearing six pairs of erect plates (sixth a "spine-plate"); rest of back carrying three pairs of flat spines; tail bearing five pairs of large spines including terminal pair (Galton 1990*b*).

Comments: The genus *Kentrosaurus* was founded upon two dorsal vertebrae (HMN St694 and 694, designated the holotype by Galton 1982*a*), collected from the Middle Saurian Bed at Tendaguru,

Kindope, Tanzania, East Africa, and originally described by Hennig (1915).

With the collection of a nearly complete skeleton (mounted at the Humboldt Museum für Naturkunde in what used to be East Berlin) with dentary (though lacking most of the skull), from the same locality, Hennig (1916) renamed the genus *Kentrurosaurus*, believing *Kentrosaurus* to be a homonym of Lambe's (1904) ceratopsian genus *Centrosaurus*. Nopcsa (1916) proposed *Doryphosaurus* as a replacement name. However, according to the International Code of Zoological Nomenclature, a single different letter does not constitute sufficient grounds for warranting homonymy, the original name thereby remaining valid.

Originally, Hennig (1916) diagnosed *Kentrosaurus* as follows: Small vertical dermal plates along nuchal and dorsal regions; eight pairs of elongate dermal spines in lumbar, sacral and caudal regions; spines over pelvis [see below] particularly long, with large base; eight [*sic*] pairs of tall spines at distal end of tail; summits of neural spines of anterior and mid-dorsal vertebrae not enlarged as in *Stegosaurus*, posterior members of this series forwardly inclined; limbs comparatively long, femur-to-humerus ratio ranging

Kentrosaurus aethiopicus,
life restoration by
Brian Franczak.

1.60–1.68; total length about 5 meters (approximately 17 feet).

Kentrosaurus (and type species *K. aethiopicus*) were later rediagnosed by Galton based on the holotype material, and also the following syntypes included in the mounted skeleton: Anterior caudal vertebra (HMN St856), left humerus (HMN St106), left ulna (HMN St461), right radius (HMN St77), right pubis (HMN St758), right ischium (HMN St335), left femur (HMN St463), left tibia (HMN St152), right fibula (HMN St297), eighth right flat spine (HMN St90), and right "parasacral" [see below] spine (HMN St345).

The dermal ossifications constitute the most striking features in *Kentrosaurus*. The plates are small in comparison to those in the larger and more derived genus *Stegosaurus*, the spines comparatively larger. The sixth or so-called "spine-plate" supports the idea that stegosaurian plates may have evolved from spines (see Hoffstetter 1957; Steel 1969; also *Huayangosaurus* entry).

According to Hoffstetter, *Kentrosaurus* is quite similar to British stegosaur *Lexovisaurus* and may be a descendant of that genus. Hoffstetter suggested that *Lexovisaurus* might be a subgenus of *Kentrosaurus*. Steel accepted with reservations that *Kentrosaurus* descended from *Lexovisaurus*, noting that the two genera differ mostly in dermal armor and in the former having a femur that is shorter than the ilium.

Galton offered the following evidence to support the generic validity of both forms: 1. In *Kentrosaurus*, the neural canal of dorsal vertebrae is quite tall, almost reaching to the prezygapophyses; in all other known stegosaurs, it is small, most of the neural arch below the zygapophyses consisting of solid bone; 2. in *Kentrosaurus*, the transverse processes extend as far as the 27th to 30th caudal; in other stegosaurs, they extend posteriorly just to the twelfth or thirteenth (see Hennig 1924); 3. in *Kentrosaurus*, neural spines posterior to the ninth caudal vertebra are more dorsally inclined or vertical; in other segnosaurs, from the ninth caudal, the spines are posterodorsally inclined; 4. in *Kentrosaurus*, the neural arch bordering the neural canal is anterodorsally inclined; in all other stegosaurs, this is perpendicular to the centrum; 5. in *Kentrosaurus*, the hemal arches are L-shaped; in other stegosaurs, they have a single longitudinal axis (the normal ornithischian pattern); 6. in *Kentrosaurus*, the anterior process of the ilium is deep and expands passing anteriorly; in other stegosaurs, this proportionally longer process tapers slightly passing anteriorly; 7. in *Kentrosaurus*, there is no rugose area on the lateral surface of the pubis; this is present in other stegosaurs; and, 8. in *Kentrosaurus*, there is no evidence for any large, thin plate with an only slightly expanded base transversely (as in *Lexovisaurus*).

Galton concluded that the (typically stegosaurian) solid condition of the tall region of the neural arch, between centrum and zygapophyses, was derived from one like that in *Kentrosaurus*, this genus apparently ancestral to *Lexovisaurus*.

After studying specimens of *K. aethiopicus*, *Stegosaurus stenops* and *Dacentrurus armatus*, Galton noted that various individuals had four sacral ribs while others had five, this intimating a sexual dimorphism, those individuals with four sacral ribs being male, those with five female.

Extensive *Kentrosaurus* remains were collected by the Humboldt Museum, but, as pointed out by Galton, some of this material (including two syntypes figured by Hennig 1915, a braincase HMN St460, and terminal long spine HMN St575) was either misplaced or destroyed during World War II.

Hennig restored the skeleton of *Kentrosaurus* as bearing a pair of large (then called "parasacral") spines over the hips. Thusly had this dinosaur been depicted for decades until the discovery in China, reported by Gao, Huang and Zhu (1986), of another stegosaur, *Tuojiangosaurus*, in which a pair of such spines (now called "parascapular" spines; see Sereno and Dong 1992) were found preserved very close to their correct position over the shoulders.

Note: According to Galton (1985*b*), the caudal spine (OUM J1666) reported by Delair (1973) from the Portland beds (Upper Jurassic) at Swindon, Wiltshire, England, and described by Delair as stegosaurian with affinities to *Kentrosaurus*, is unlike any stegosaurian dermal spine and is probably part of a plesiosaur.

Key references: Galton (1982*a*, 1985*b*, 1990*b*); Hennig (1915, 1916, 1924); Hoffstetter (1957); Nopcsa (1916); Steel (1969).

KENTRUROSAURUS   Hennig 1916—(See *Kentrosaurus*.)
Name derivation: Greek *kentros* = "spiked" + Greek *oura* = "tail" + Greek *sauros* = "lizard."
Type species: *K. aethiopicus* (Hennig 1915).

KLAMELISAURUS   Zhao 1993
Saurischia: Sauropodomorpha: Sauropoda:
   Brachiosauridae.
Name derivation: "Klameli" + Greek *sauros* = "lizard."
Type species: *K. gobiensis* Zhao 1993.
Other species: [None.]
Occurrence: Wucaiwan Formation, Xinjiang, China.
Age: Middle Jurassic.
Known material/holotype: IVPP V.9492, partial postcranial skeleton.

Diagnosis of genus (as for type species): [None published].

Comments: The new genus and species *Klamelisaurus gobiensis* was founded upon partial postcranial remains (IVPP V.9492), including pelvic girdle, right forelimb, and both hind limbs, collected from the Wucaiwan Formation (regarded as Middle Jurassic, based on the occurrence of the theropod *Monolophosaurus*, turtles, and crocodiles), Xinjiang, China (Zhao 1993).

Zhao briefly described the specimens as follows: Large, midtransitional kind of sauropod, measuring 17 meters (about 58 feet) in length; teeth rather massive, spatulate in form; ?16 cervical vertebrae, with opisthocoelous centra, rather high neural spines, posterior three neural spines fused; cervical centra averaging in length from 1.5–2 times that of dorsals; 13 dorsals, with opisthocoelous centra, pleurocoels rather developed on side of centrum, lamellar structure simple and massive on neural arch, spines very thick and strong; five fused sacral vertebrae; caudal neural spines stick-like, rather posteriorly directed; scapula very thin and long, coracoid slender; pelvic girdles heavy; ilium massive, with less developed upper flange; pubic peduncle occurring on front half of ilium blade; ischium rather thin, well-developed pubis distinctly flat and slightly curved; proximate end of humerus thickened, curved; ulna much longer than radius; radius somewhat straight; femur thick,

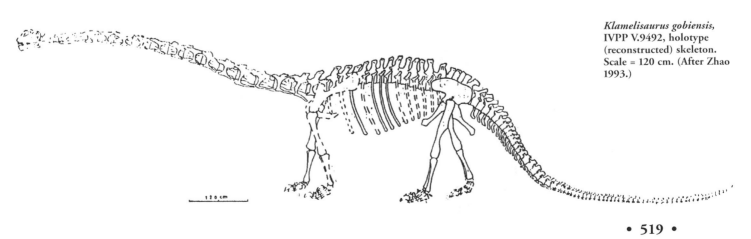

Klamelisaurus gobiensis, IVPP V.9492, holotype (reconstructed) skeleton. Scale = 120 cm. (After Zhao 1993.)

somewhat flat, with slender articular head, fourth trochanter located toward upper part of ventral surface of shaft; tibia somewhat undeveloped, shorter than fibula; forearm to "hindarm" ratio of 3 to 4.

Zhao regarded *Klamelisaurus* as an essentially advanced sauropod that otherwise displays numerous primitive features, representing an intermediate form of sauropod evolution, and erected upon this genus the new brachiosaurid subfamily Klamelisaurinae.

Key reference: Zhao (1993).

KOPARION   Chure 1994

Saurischia: Theropoda: Tetanurae: Avetheropoda: Coelurosauria: Maniraptora: Arctometatarsalia: Bullatosauria: Troodontidae.

Name derivation: Greek *koparion* ["small surgical knife"].

Type species: *K. douglassi* Chure 1994.

Other species: [None.]

Occurrence: Morrison Formation, Dinosaur National Monument, United States.

Age: Late Jurassic.

Known material/holotype: DINO 3353, nearly complete maxillary tooth crown.

Diagnosis of genus (as for type species): Tooth crown small (2 millimeters high), recurved, crown apex forming first posterior denticle; blood pits between successive denticles; constriction between crown and root; more primitive than other troodontids in lacking large posterior denticles, lacking pronounced size difference between anterior and posterior denticles, and in having posterior denticles that bend toward tooth apex but are not hooked (Chure 1994).

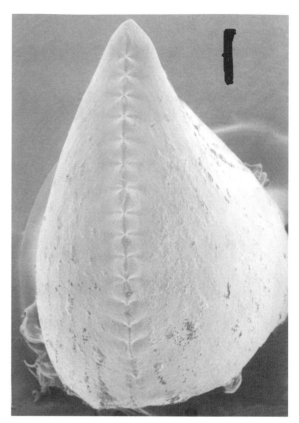

Koparion douglassi, DINO 3353, holotype maxillary tooth crown, anterior view. Scale = 100 micrometers. (After Chure 1994.)

Koparion douglassi, DINO 3353, holotype maxillary tooth crown, labial or lingual view. Scale = 1 mm. (After Chure 1994.)

Comments: The earliest known member of the Troodontidae and the first troodontid known from pre–Cretaceous sediments, the new genus and species *Koparion douglassi* was established on an isolated maxillary tooth (DINO 3353) collected from near the top of the Brushy Basin member of the Morrison Formation, at Dinosaur National Monument (Chure 1994).

Based upon features described by Currie (1987*a*) as unique to the Troodontidae, and the suggestion of Osmólska and Barsbold (1990) that tooth characters probably have taxonomic significance at the family level, Chure identified several troodontid synapomorphies in the holotype tooth of *K. douglassi* that warranted referral of this taxon to the Troodontidae. These features include 1. blood pits, 2. strongly recurved crown with apex forming most distal posterior serration, and 3. construction between crown and root. Although reluctant to name another new taxon based upon a tooth, Chure found DINO 3353 to be distinctive and separable from other Morrison Formation theropods as well as from other troodontids. Chure further noted that, as *Koparion* already possesses several dental specializations unique to the Troodontidae, the origins of this group may extend further back than the Late Jurassic.

DINO 3353 was discovered among other small specimens of small theropod teeth and other micro-vertebrate fossils collected as a result of extensive screenwashing and hand quarrying (see Chure 1992; Chure and Engelmann 1989; Chure, Engelmann and Madsen 1989; Engelmann, Chure and Madsen 1989; Engelmann, Greenwald, Callison and Chure 1990) at Dinosaur National Monument (Chure 1994). As pointed out by Chure (1994), all of these teeth are strikingly distinct from those of larger carnivorous dinosaurs in the Morrison Formation, indicating a more diverse small theropod fauna than had been previously known.

Key reference: Chure (1994).

KOTASAURUS Yadagiri 1988

Saurischia: Sauropodomorpha: ?Sauropoda *incertae sedis.*

Name derivation: "Kota [Formation]" + Greek *sauros* = "lizard."

Type species: *K. yamanpalliensis* Yadagiri 1988.

Other species: [None.]

Occurrence: Kota Formation, Andhra Pradesh, India.

Age: Early Jurassic.

Known material: Ilium, almost complete post-crania, miscellaneous postcranial remains.

Holotype: (21/SR/PAL), ilium.

Diagnosis of genus (as for type species): Large quadrupedal saurischian comparable in size and general proportions to sauropods, morphologically intermediate between prosauropods and sauropods; teeth spoon-shaped; limbs slender; centra of cervical and anterior dorsal vertebrae opisthocoelous; all other vertebral centra platycoelous, with hyposphene-hypantrum articulation present in middle and posterior dorsals; neural spines not bifurcated; posterior dorsals high; sacrum with ?three coossified vertebrae, centra amphiplatyan, sacrocostal yokes widely separated; scapula with tall, narrow blade, a twist at proximal end, and condyle; coracoid subcircular in shape with foramen; ilium with straight margin, posteriorly expanded plate, well-developed and deep anterior process that forms medial wall of acetabulum, and short ischial peduncle; pubis and ischium straight, with expansions on proximal margin; humerus more expanded at proximal end than distal end, with prominent deltopectoral crest; ulna with slender shaft, shorter than radius; femur retaining central cavity and well-developed fourth trochanter, head and straight shaft at about 90 degrees; tibia short, with stout distal face having pronounced notch; astragalus with two depressions, anterior depression deep, wide (Yadagiri 1988).

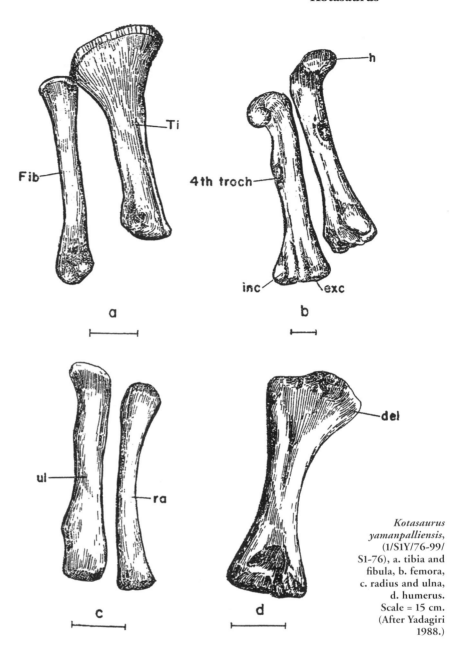

Kotasaurus yamanpalliensis, (1/S1Y/76-99/ S1-76), a. tibia and fibula, b. femora, c. radius and ulna, d. humerus. Scale = 15 cm. (After Yadagiri 1988.)

Comments: Possibly the most primitive of all known sauropods, the genus *Kotasaurus* was founded on an ilium (21/SR/PAL) collected from the Kota Formation (Lower Jurassic) in Pranhita-Godavari Valley, near the village of Yamanpalli, Andhra Pradesh, India. Referred material from the same locality includes an almost complete skeleton (1/S1Y/76-99/S1/76) missing the skull, a few meta-tarsals, and chevrons (Yadagiri 1988). These remains were collected during the late 1970s (see Yadagiri, Prasad and Satsangi 1980) but were not then recognized as belonging to a new kind of sauropod.

Yadagiri observed that *Kotasaurus*, though exhibiting many sauropod features, seems to possess

Kritosaurus

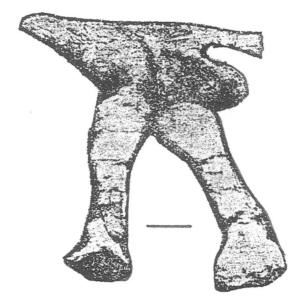

Kotasaurus yamanpalliensis, pelvic girdle including holotype (22/SR/PAL) ilium. Scale = 15 cm. (Yadagiri 1988.)

a mosaic of features pertaining both to prosauropods and sauropods. The ilium in general shape resembles that in melanorosaurid prosauropods. The sacrum has a less expanded distal end with a twisted condylar proximal end as in prosauropods. *Kotasaurus*, however, is much larger than any known prosauropod, its size comparable to true sauropods. The teeth are weak and spoon-shaped as in the sauropod *Camarasaurus*; the vertebrae are more similar to those of sauropods than prosauropods. Most significant, the ischium is elongated and straight as in sauropods.

Kritosaurus navajovius, AMNH 5799, restored holotype skull, nasal region almost entirely reconstructed.

For the above (and other) reasons, Yadagiri concluded that *Kotasaurus* is either closely related to sauropods or exhibits convergence between itself and Sauropoda and can, morphologically, be placed closer to the prosauropod-sauropod threshold than the primitive Indian sauropod *Barapasaurus* or any other known dinosaur.

Key reference: Yadagiri (1988); Yadagiri *et al.* (1980).

KRITOSAURUS   Brown 1910—(=?*Gryposaurus*, ?*Hadrosaurus*) [*nomen dubium*]

Ornithischia: Genasauria: Cerapoda: Ornithopoda: Iguanodontia: Hadrosauridae: Hadrosaurinae.

Name derivation: Greek *kritos* = "separated" + Greek *sauros* = "lizard."

Type species: *K. navajovius* Brown 1910 [*nomen dubium*].

Other species: [None.]

Occurrence: Kirtland Shale, New Mexico, ?Aguga Formation, Texas, Dinosaur Park Formation, Montana, United States, ?Oldman Formation, Alberta, Canada.

Age: Late Cretaceous (?Campanian–Maastrichtian).

Known material: Fragmentary skull with associated postcrania, skulls representing two-three individuals.

Holotype: AMNH 5799, skull missing rostrum and lower jaws.

Diagnosis of genus (as for type species): Derived characters of posteriorly folded nasal crest with lateral ridge extending out toward prefrontal (Horner 1992).

Comments: *Kritosaurus* was founded on the incomplete skull (AMNH 5799) of an old individual, collected by Barnum Brown in 1904 from the Kirtland Formation, near Ojo Alamo, San Juan County, New Mexico.

Brown (1910) diagnosed *Kritosaurus* as follows: Skull

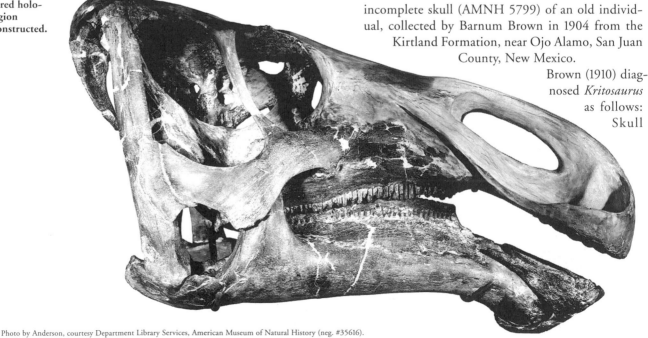

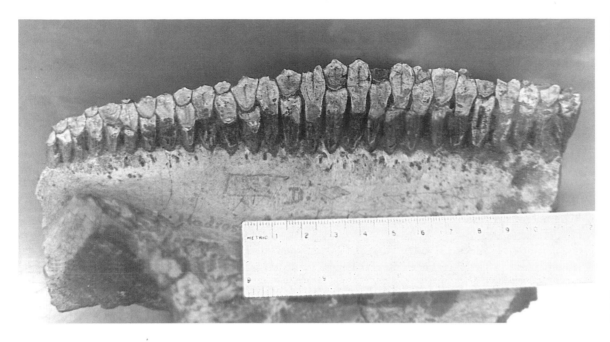

?Kritosaurus, YPM 1779, holotype lower jaw of *Hadrosaurus breviceps*.

Photo by R. A. Long and S. P. Welles (neg. #73/503-16), courtesy Yale Peabody Museum of Natural History.

deep with narrow muzzle; frontals short; orbital portion reduced, barely reaching border of orbit; nasals and premaxillaries very long; quadrate elongate; quadratojugal short anteroposteriorly, the latter entirely separating quadrate and quadratojugal; mandibular rami massive, with decurved edentulous portion; teeth in lower row spatulate.

Type species *K. navajovius* was diagnosed by Brown as follows: Maxillary teeth smooth on borders; mandibular teeth papillate on borders, with low median carina; predentary deep, massive; free edentulous portion of dentary short, not covered by predentary.

As the nasals were missing in the holotype of *K. navajovius*, Brown incorrectly restored those bones after those of *Anatotitan* [=*Diclonius* of his usage] *copei*.

In their review of North American duck-billed dinosaurs, Lull and Wright (1942) believed that *Kritosaurus* was congeneric with *Gryposaurus*, a genus for which better material had been collected. For decades, the type species *G. notabilis* was regarded as a species of *Kritosaurus*, until Horner (1990) resurrected *Gryposaurus* (see entry) as a valid taxon.

Weishampel and Horner (1990), in their review of the Hadrosauridae, regarded *K. navajovius* as belonging to a questionable genus, commenting that the type material of this form is probably not diagnostic. Later, Horner (1992) listed *Kritosaurus* as a valid genus, rediagnosing the type species based on the holotype and three additional skulls—NMMNH P-16106 (referred by Lucas and Hunt 1993 to new genus *Naashoibitosaurus*), BYU 12950 (referred by Lucas and Hunt to new genus *Anasazisaurus*), and

?YPM-PU 16970, the latter originally described by Horner (1979) as *Hadrosaurus* ["*Kritosaurus*"] *notabilis*. Lucas and Hunt regarded *K. navajovius* as a *nomen dubium*, founded on a very poor specimen missing the greater portions of the skull containing the most diagnostic features of hadrosaurs.

Notes: *H. breviceps* [*nomen dubium*] was based on the posterior part of a right dentary (YPM 1779), collected by S. F. Peckham from the Dinosaur Park Formation, Bearpaw Mountains, Montana, originally described by Marsh (1889*b*). According to Lull and Wright, these teeth differ from *Kritosaurus navajovius* in smaller size, concavity of lateral areas of the carina, and lack of papillae. Lull and Wright observed that this material is too uncharacteristic to warrant the erection of a new genus, but may be referable to *Kritosaurus*.

The species named *Trachodon marginatus* Lambe 1902 [*nomen dubium*] was based on a humerus, ulna, radius, metatarsal, pedal phalanges, cervical-vertebrae zygapophyses, ribs, teeth fragments, ossified tendons, and integument impressions (GSC 419), collected by Lambe from the Oldman Formation, Red Deer River, Alberta. Gilmore (1920) suggested that this form could be congeneric with *Kritosaurus*. The material is too meager to make a convincing synonymy.

K. incurvimanus Parks 1920 and *K. australis* Bonaparte, Franchi, Powell and Sepulveda 1984 were each regarded by Weishampel and Horner as representing an "unnamed gryposaur."

Key references: Brown (1910); Gilmore (1920); Lambe (1902*b*); Lucas and Hunt (1993); Lull and Wright (1942); Marsh (1889*b*); Parks (1920); Weishampel and Horner (1990).

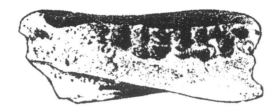

Kulceratops kulensis, N 495/12457, holotype lower jaw fragment. (After Nessov 1995.)

KULCERATOPS   Nessov 1995

Ornithischia: Genasauria: Cerapoda:
  Marginocephalia: Ceratopsia: Neoceratopsia:
  Protoceratopsidae.

Name derivation: Uzbekistani *kul'* = "Lake
  [Khodzhakul]" + Greek *keratos* = "horn" + Greek
  ops = "face."

Type species: *K. kulensis* Nessov 1995.

Other species: [None.]

Occurrence: "Northern Eurasia."

Age: Late Cretaceous.

Known material/holotype: N 495/12457, fragment
  of lower jaw with teeth.

Diagnosis of genus (as for type species):
[Unavailable as of the writing.]

Comments: The new type species *Kulceratops
kulensis* was described by Nessov (1995) in a paper
[English translation not available to date of this writ-
ing] discussing new data about the assemblages, ecology, and paleobiology of dinosaurs of "Northern
Eurasia." This dinosaur may have affinities with *Asiaceratops salsopaludalis*.

Key reference: Nessov (1995).

LABOCANIA   Molnar 1974

Saurischia: Theropoda: Tetanurae *incertae sedis*.

Name derivation: "La Bocana [Roja Formation]."

Type species: *L. anomala* Molnar 1974.

Other species: [None.]

Occurrence: "La Bocana Roja" Formation, Baja,
  California, Mexico.

Age: Late Cretaceous (?Campanian).

Known material: Fragmentary crania and postcrania.

Holotype: LACM 20877, fragmentary skull, ischium,
  right metatarsal II, pedal phalanx, chevron.

Diagnosis of genus (as for type species): Large
theropod with thick, massive frontals, with no indication of an anterior extension of supratemporal fossa
onto dermal surface; quadrate massive, mandibular
articular surface cylindrical, mandibular condyle
inclined at approximate 45-degree angle with long
axis of quadrate; dentary massive, with marked external longitudinal ridge; ischium similar to that of
tyrannosaurids (Molnar 1974).

Comments: The genus *Labocania* was established upon poorly preserved, fragmentary cranial
and postcranial remains (LACM 20877), found in
the "La Bocana Roja" Formation (presumedly Late
Campanian or older, probably no older than Cenomanian; underlying the "El Gallo Formation," which
underlies the Rosario Formation, the latter dated by
Durham and Allison 1960 as Late Campanian–Early
Maestrichtian) of Baja California, Mexico (Molnar
1974).

From the relatively large ischial scar and stout
metatarsal, Molnar estimated that *Labocania* was
probably more massive than a typical tyrannosaurid,
most likely about two-thirds the size of *Tyrannosaurus
rex*.

Labocania anomala, LACM 20877, holotype left maxilla.

Photo by R. E. Molnar, courtesy Natural
History Museum of Los Angeles County.

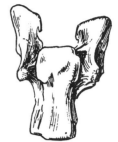

Laevisuchus indicus, IM K20/613, K20/614, K27/696, cotype cervical vertebrae. Scale 2 cm. (After Huene and Matley 1933.)

Molnar observed that *Labocania* is one of the most aberrant of all known large theropods. The cranial elements, with the exception of the maxilla, are comparatively more massive than in other known theropods, most closely resembling various Asian Cretaceous forms. The quadrate most closely resembles that of *Chilantaisaurus maortuensis*. The frontals are similar to those of *C. maortuensis* and *Indosaurus matleyi*. The maxillary teeth are typically tyrannosaurid. The massive dentary resembles that of cf. *Szechuanosaurus campi*.

According to Molnar, a fragment that seems to be the middle portion of the shaft of the right pubis closely resembles that in *T. rex*. The preserved proximal portions of the ischia are typically tyrannosaurid, most similar to *Albertosaurus libratus*. The chevron closely resembles the sixth chevron in *A. libratus*. Postcranial remains of *Labocania* are typically tyrannosaurid, but skull elements seem closer to the allosaurid *Chilantaisaurus*, abelisaurid *Indosaurus*, and cf. *Szechuanosaurus*.

Molnar noted that the similarity of *Labocania* to some Asiatic forms reinforces the general similarity between Late Cretaceous North American and Asiatic dinosaurs. Because of similarities to these forms and to tyrannosaurids, Molnar did not assign *Labocania* to any theropod family. Though not denying that the remains of two different kinds of theropods could have become mixed, Molnar inferred that, given the absence of other theropod material in the area, all elements referred to *Labocania* pertain to the same individual.

Molnar, Kurzanov and Dong (1990) observed that *L. anomala* exhibits several tyrannosaurid features (hollow quadrate, triangular obturator process of ischium, and semicircular muscle scar on caudal margin of ischium, the latter also known in ornithomimids); that cranial prongs of the chevrons are characteristic of "carnosaurs"; but also that *Labocania* is a much derived taxon very unlike any known tyrannosaurid. Though admitting to a possible relationship between *Labocania* and Tyrannosauridae [now regarded as a coelurosaurian group; see Holtz (1994a)], Molnar *et al.* reserved its referral to the "Carnosauria" in the absence of more complete remains.

Key references: Molnar (1974); Molnar, Kurzanov and Dong (1990).

LABROSAURUS Marsh 1879—(See *Allosaurus*.)
Name derivation: Latin *labrum* = "lip" + Greek *sauros* = "lizard."
Type species: *L. lucaris* (Marsh 1879).

LAELAPS Cope 1866—(Preoccupied, Koch 1839; see *Dryptosaurus*.)
Name derivation: "Laelaps [hunting dog of Greek mythology]."
Type species: *L. aquilunguis* Cope 1866.

LAEVISUCHUS Huene 1932 [*nomen dubium*]
Saurischia: Theropoda *incertae sedis*.
Name derivation: Latin *levis* = "smooth" + Greek *souchos* = "crocodile."
Type species: *L. indicus* Huene 1932 [*nomen dubium*].
Other species: [None.]
Occurrence: Lameta Formation, Madhya Pradesh, India.
Age: Late Cretaceous (Maastrichtian).
Known material: Vertebrae.
Cotypes: IM K20/613, K20/614, and K27/696, three cervical vertebrae.

Diagnosis of genus (as for type species): Vertebrae broad, solidly constructed; (most complete) vertebra measures 3.5 centimeters (about 1.35 inches) in length; centrum rather flat ventrally, with plane anterior articular surface and concave posterior surface; parapophyses much projecting laterally; centrum laterally depressed in upper portion, with three pleurocoels on each side; neural arch much expanded laterally; dorsal spine rather low (10 millimeters) above centrum, resembling four-sided pyramid (Huene 1932; see also Huene and Matley 1933).

Comments: The genus *Laevisuchus* was founded upon vertebrae (IM K20/613, K20/614 and K27/696) discovered in the "Carnosaur Bed" of the Lameta Formation (Maastrichtian; A. Sahni, personal communication to Norman 1990), at Bara Simla Hill, Jubbulpore (now spelled Jabalpur), Madhya Pradesh, Central Provinces of India.

Huene (1932) classified *Laevisuchus* with the Coeluridae, although its true higher-level theropod associations are not clearly known.

Norman commented that the type species *L. indicus* was undoubtedly small and that the form of the vertebrae is similar to that in *Calamospondylus*, adding that *L. indicus* cannot be readily distinguished from other small and theropods known from the same area and founded on equally fragmentary and uncomparable material.

Key references: Huene (1932); Huene and Matley (1933); Norman (1990).

LAMBEOSAURUS Parks 1923—(=*Didanodon*, *Stephanosaurus*; =*Procheneosaurus* [in part], *Tetragonosaurus* [in part])

Lambeosaurus

Ornithischia: *Genasauria: Cerapoda:* Ornithopoda Iguanodontia: Hadrosauridae: Lambeosaurinae.

Name derivation: "[Lawrence M.] Lambe" + Greek *sauros* = "lizard."

Type species: *L. lambei* Parks 1923.

Other species: *L. paucidens* (Marsh 1889). *L. magnicristatum* Sternberg 1935, ?*L. laticaudus* Morris 1981 [*nomen dubium*].

Occurrence: Oldman Formation, Alberta, Canada, Dinosaur Park Formation, Montana, United States.

Age: Late Cretaceous (Campanian).

Known material: About seven articulated skulls with associated postcrania, ?ten articulated skulls, isolated cranial elements, skull with articulated postcrania, skull, miscellaneous cranial and postcranial remains, integument, juvenile to adult.

Holotype: NMC 2869, incomplete skull with right mandibular ramus.

Diagnosis of genus: Modest to large size; crest of only moderate fullness, forwardly inclined, with apex anterior of orbit; posterodorsally inclined spur or spine of variable but robust dimensions (Dodson 1975).

Diagnosis of *L. lambei*: Skull relatively short, with high, narrow, somewhat parallel-sided crest; crest varies in height, proportions, and degree of rounding or angulation at summit; long axis of crest about perpendicular to axis of muzzle and posterior spine; profile of muzzle and crest forming angle that varies from 83-112 degrees; long, narrow posterior spine of crest overhanging occiput, rising above level of temporal arcade; axis of spine approximately aligned with axis of muzzle (Gilmore 1924*d*).

Diagnosis of *L. magnicristatus*: Moderately massive; crest immense, very long and high, outline broadly rounded and terminating in acute angle overhanging occiput; anterior part of profile of crest thrust forward to form approximately 75-degree angle with muzzle, extending almost over tip of beak; upper branch of maxilla high, thin, widely expanded; lower branch upturned, very large and swollen (to accommodate air passages housed within); sulcus crossing premaxilla oblique, poorly defined (perhaps due to growth or preservation); orbit broadly oval, with wide and rounded upper portion; mandible robust, very strongly decurved (Lull and Wright 1942).

Diagnosis of *L. paucidens*: Maxilla of typical hadrosaurid conformation; preserved length 235 millimeters, length if complete as much as 25 millimeters greater; shape (in side view) of shallow triangle, maximum height at midlength 85 millimeters; maximum length of tooth battery 215 millimeters, minimum length probably less than 240 millimeters; minimum of 29 transverse tooth rows recognized (total number unknown); squamosal moderately thin, triangular plate only curved along posterior limit, with straight, steeply rising anterodorsal mar-

Courtesy Royal Ontario Museum.

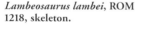

Lambeosaurus lambei, ROM 1218, skeleton.

Courtesy the Field Museum (neg. #G81559).

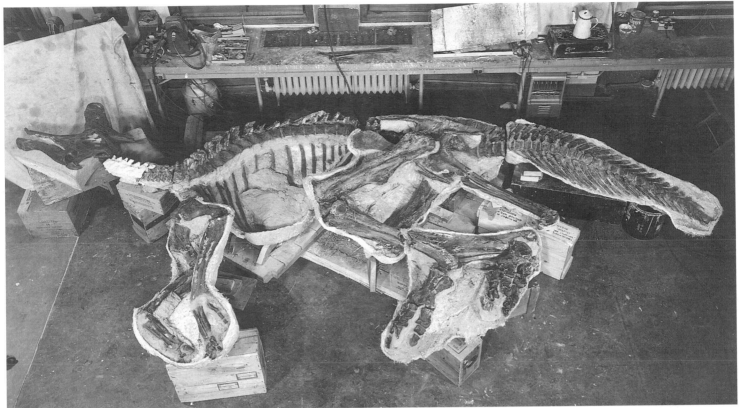

Lambeosaurus lambei, FMNH UC1479, skull, FMNH PR 380, postcrania, the latter collected by Elmer S. Riggs, George F. Sternberg, and J. B. Abbott in 1922 during the Marshall Field Expedition to Alberta.

gin; ventral margin marked anteriorly by moderately broad indentation, behind rising to prominent quadratic cotylus; squamosal most distinguished by great height (116 millimeters) above quadratic cotylus and failure of dorsal margin to bend inward over lateral portion of the supra-temporal fenestra; squamosal very similar to that of *L. lambei*, though about 20 percent larger (Ostrom 1964*a*).

Diagnosis of ?*L. laticaudus*: Distinguished by long tail and long caudal haemal arches, latter matching length of long neural spines (Morris 1981):

Comments: In 1913 and 1917, two imperfect hadrosaurid skulls (NMC 2869, ROM 794; formerly NMC 5131) were collected from the Belly River (now Oldman) Formation, at Red Deer River, south of Little Sandhill Creek, in Alberta, Canada. Lawrence M. Lambe believed, on insufficient grounds, that these skulls were conspecific with *Trachodon marginatus* [*nomen dubium*], a taxon based on some limb bones, teeth, ribs, and other fragments (NMC 419) described by Lambe (1902). Eventually realizing that these skulls did not belong to the so-called "*Trachodon*," Lambe (1914) erected for them the new genus *Stephanosaurus*, retaining the original specific name. To be a valid taxon according to the rules of scientific nomenclature, *Stephanosaurus* necessitated a new specific name. Parks (1923) later assigned the new combination *Lambeosaurus lambei* to the skulls, after which Gilmore (1924*d*) selected the better of these two specimens, a skull with right ramus (GSC 2869), as the lectotype.

Gilmore diagnosed *Lambeosaurus* as follows: Large, with relatively short skull; crest variable, expanded at right angles to profile line; summit of crest well anterior of orbit; rear of crest not contacting squamosals; spine of crest (when present) overhanging occiput in varying degrees; angle formed by muzzle and posterior part of crest about 180 degrees; premaxilla the greater portion of profile, nasals confined to back of crest and (if present) posteriorly directed spine-like process; muzzle narrow, short, anteriolaterally expanded, less than in hadrosaurines; maxilla relatively small, yet proportionately deep (slightly less than half length); edentulous portion of maxilla very short; nasals greatly receded, do not separate two branches of premaxilla; posterior portion of lower premaxillary branch widely expanded at right angles to axis of premaxilla beyond oblique sulcus; narial passage, confined to lower premaxillary branch, forming loop; lacrimal small, narrow, triangular, forming much of anterior border of orbital rim, housing conspicuous foramen; infratemporal fossa variably shaped but usually rather wide, almost equal in area to orbit; more dentary (41) than maxillary (39 to

Lambeosaurus

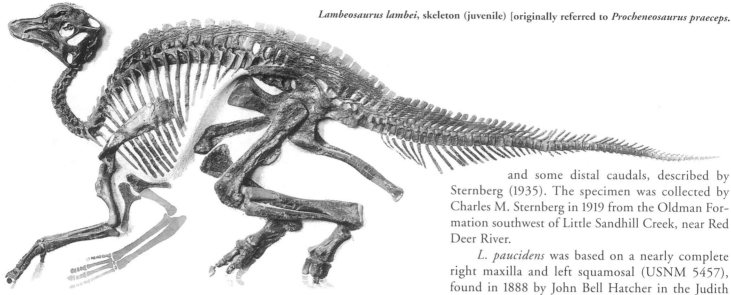

Lambeosaurus lambei, skeleton (juvenile) [originally referred to *Procheneosaurus praeceps*.

40) teeth (reverse of normal condition in hadrosaurids).

Lambeosaurus was a large hadrosaur, generally reaching a maximum length of about 12 meters (40 feet) and almost 1.8 meters (6 feet) high at the hips, some individuals substantially larger.

Three species have been referred to this genus:

L. magnicristatus was based on a skull with most of the postcrania (NMC 8705), lacking left manus, part of the forearm, right forelimb, right-side ribs,

Lambeosaurus magnicristatus, NMC 8705, holotype skull.

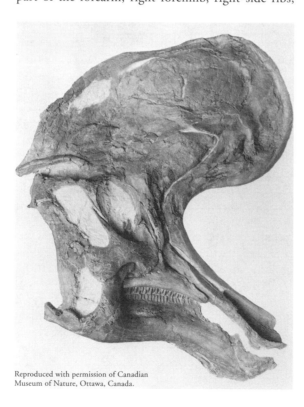

and some distal caudals, described by Sternberg (1935). The specimen was collected by Charles M. Sternberg in 1919 from the Oldman Formation southwest of Little Sandhill Creek, near Red Deer River.

L. paucidens was based on a nearly complete right maxilla and left squamosal (USNM 5457), found in 1888 by John Bell Hatcher in the Judith River beds [now Dinosaur Park Formation] on Dog Creek, in Fergus County, Montana, and originally named *Hadrosaurus paucidens* Marsh 1889. Subsequently, Marsh (1890), perceiving supposed similarities between the maxilla and that of the ceratopsian *Triceratops*, reassigned the specimen to *Ceratops* as *C. paucidencs*. Later, Ostrom (1964a) determined that the holotype of *H. paucidens* did represent a hadrosaurid and proposed that this species be transferred to *Lambeosaurus* because of striking similarities between the form of the squamosal and dimensions of the maxilla to those in *L. lambei*, particularly in the holotype of the latter. Ostrom (1964a) added that, because of the limited material, it could not be shown conclusively that the two forms are conspecific. Ostrom (1964a) proposed that this material be designated *L. paucidens*, pending future discovery of specimens from the same locality.

A tentative third species, ?*Lambeosaurus laticaudus*, was founded upon on material (LACM 17715) including a left premaxilla, maxilla, jugal, right scapula, coracoid, humerus, eight cervical vertebrae, five sacral vertebrae, three dorsal vertebrae fragments, a few caudal centra spinous processes, part of haemal arches, a few ribs, femora, left ischium, right tibia, and right metatarsal III. The material was collected from the "El Diesacado" member of the informally named "El Gallo formation," north of Arroyo Del Rosario, El Rosario, Baja California Del Norte, Mexico. Specimens referred to ?*L. laticaudus* include vertebrae, pelvic bones, limb bones, and molds of scalation. The remains indicate a large form probably measuring some 14 to 15 meters (about 47 to 51 feet) long (Morris 1981).

The deep and transversely flattened tail (a deep tail often regarded as an adaptation for aquatic locomotion) and the fragile nature of the articulation

Lambeosaurus lambei, life restoration by Brian Franczak.

between the pelvic elements implied to Morris that *?L. laticaudus* spent most of its time in water (a conclusion rejected by many other workers). Morris believed that this idea was strengthened by the occurrence of marine invertebrates at the same locality. Also, one individual seemed to have survived with a leg that had apparently been broken, then healed or become pathologically deformed during growth. Morris speculated that this limb would have been a serious handicap to a mostly terrestrial animal. Also, Morris noted that this species lived near shore estuaries along Baja California's Pacific margin. (Galton 1970 had previously argued that hadrosaurids were basically terrestrial, the high tail serving as a balancing rather than swimming organ, an idea favored by most researchers; see *Edmontosaurus* entry.)

The most remarkable feature of *?L. laticaudus* is the length of the vertebral neural spines, some of them measuring from 40 to 50 centimeters (over 15 to about 19 inches) long, the spines of the neck vertebrae smaller. Morris noted that this species might have been referred to *Hypacrosaurus*, which has both long neural spines and a tall, flattened tail, while most specimens referred to *Lambeosaurus* have had relatively short-spined tails. What identifies the Baja California hadrosaur as *Lambeosaurus*, however, is the open narial canal of the skull, extending two-thirds the length of the premaxilla, closely resembling the

Photo by R. A. Long and S. P. Welles (neg. #73/536-4), reproduced with permission of Canadian Museum of Nature, Ottawa, Canada.

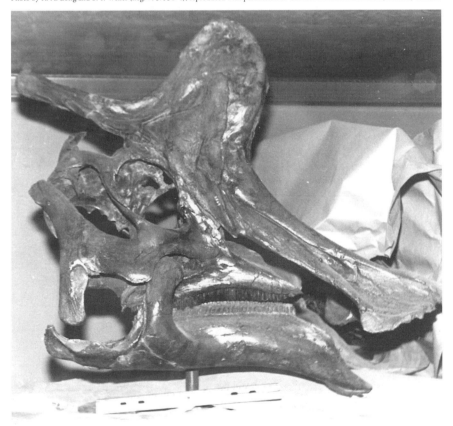

Lambeosaurus lambei, NMC 2869, holotype skull.

Lambeosaurus

Lambeosaurus magnicristatus, referred skeleton (cast).

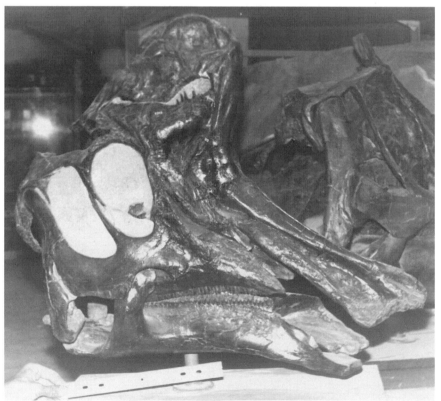

Lambeosaurus lambei, NMC 8703, holotype skull of *L. clavinitalis.*

narial crest of *L. lambei.* (A closed narial canal is a diagnostic feature of both *Hypacrosaurus* and *Parasaurolophus.*)

Scalation casts were found in association with some of the referred dorsal vertebrae of ?*L. laticaudus,* including some large bony ossicles that seem to have been randomly placed among large hexagonal and smaller rounded scales. (Portions of fossilized integument impressions in other *Lambeosaurus* specimens show an extraordinarily thin epidermis with limpet-like scutes. Lull and Wright reported uniform, polygonal-shaped tubercles arranged in no particular order, in the neck, sides of body, and also tail areas in the holotype of *L. clavinitialis.*)

In the past, various generic and specific names have been assigned to lambeosaurines based, to a degree, on size and shape of the crest. Dodson (1975), however, after measuring a wide range of lamebeosaurine skulls, concluded that variation in crest size and shape could be attributed to ontogeny and sexual dimorphism, the crest probably serving as a visual signal for intraspecific identification. Some of these species were identified by Dodson as conspecific with *L. lambei.*

L. clavinitialis had been based on an incomplete skeleton collected in 1928 by Charles M. Sternberg (1935) from the Oldman Formation above Red Deer

River. The skull has a small, rounded crest of medium fore and aft length. Dodson regarded this specimen as belonging to a female *L. lambei* while the holotype of *L. lambei* represents a male.

Procheneosaurus (no specific name originally assigned) was founded upon a skull with jaws, the vertebral column from atlas to sacrum, the right scapula, and some rib fragments (ROM 758; formerly GSC 3577), collected in 1914 by Levi Sternberg from the Oldman Formation, southeast of Sand Creek, Red Deer River. Matthew (1920) briefly described this material as representing a small form with a short, round skull having a small bill. Parks (1931), regarding Matthew's description as too meager and his generic name to have no value, erected the new genus and species *Tetragonosaurus praeceps* for this material, at the same time describing two new species: *T. erectofrons*, based on a skull and jaws (ROM 759; formerly GSC) collected in 1927 for the Royal Ontario Museum from the Oldman Formation near the mouth of Sand Creek; and *T. cranibrevis* on a skull and jaws (NMC 8633) lacking predentary, left lacrimal, jugal, quadrate, quadratojugal, and small bones of the left ramus, collected by C. M. Sternberg in 1928 above Red Deer River, south of the mouth of Berry Creek. Lull and Wright (1942), acknowledging the definability of the genus and priority of the original generic name, reinstated the name *Procheneosaurus*, the type species becoming *P. praeceps*. The skulls of all three species of *Procheneosaurus* are relatively short and high with an incipient crests. Dodson recognized all three as representing juveniles of *L. lambei*.

Didanodon altidens Osborn 1902 [*nomen nudum*] had been based on a left maxilla with teeth (GSC 1092) from the Oldman Formation at Red Deer River, but this species was neither diagnosed nor discussed. It was referred by Lull and Wright to *Procheneosaurus*.

What is now another junior synonym of *L. lambei* is *Corythosaurus frontalis* Parks 1935, based on a small juvenile skull with jaws (ROM 869; formerly GSC 5853), lacking squamosal and paroccipital process, collected by L. Sternberg in 1934 from the Oldman Formation, at Red Deer River, below Steveville Ferry, Alberta. Parks (1935) originally distinguished this species from others of *Corythosaurus* by the anterior position of the crest, which rises almost vertically to a height of approximately 80 millimeters.

The most striking feature of *Lambeosaurus* is the crest which, though varying in shape between individuals, has the general shape of a plow. There has been much speculation as to the function of such crests (see *Parasaurolophus* entry).

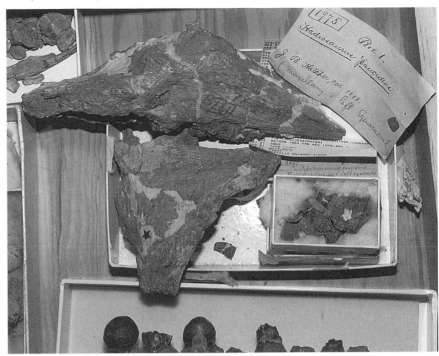

Lambeosaurus paucidens, USNM 5457, holotype right maxilla and left squamosal.

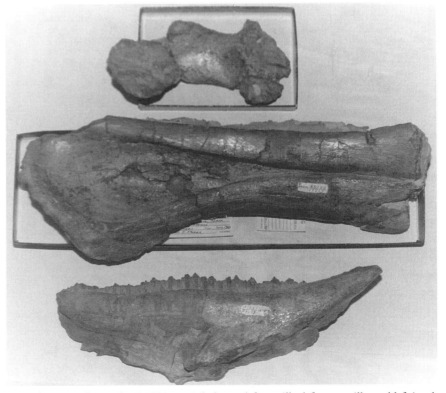

?*Lambeosaurus laticaudus*, LACM 17715, holotype left maxilla, left premaxilla, and left jugal.

Lambeosaurus

?Lambeosaurus laticaudus, LACM 17712, referred mold of scalation.

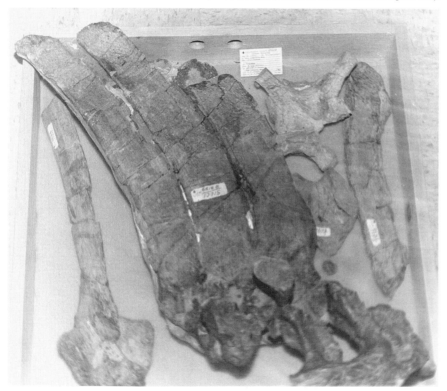

?Lambeosaurus laticaudus, LACM 17705, referred caudal vertebrae with holotype neural spines.

Ostrom (1962*a*) observed that the crest houses paired narial canals that connect with the external naris. These passages ascend within the crest making S-shaped loops, remaining separated until entering a large, undivided medial cavity at the back of the crest. In one skull (NMC 8703), originally named *L. clavinitialis,* organic material possibly representing cartilaginous turbinals was found within this cavity, perhaps the remains of a median septum that, in life, divided this chamber. This septum may have been a cartilaginous extension of the olfactory nerve canal. Ostrom noted that the posterior chamber was the only logical site for the olfactory bulbs. The crest may have augmented the sense of smell by increasing the total surface area available for the olfactory tissues. A heightened olfactory sense would have had significant survival value, alerting these virtually defenseless animals of impending danger.

Weishampel (1981) published a revision of the structure of the lambeosaurine nasal cavity, following earlier studies of lambeosaurine crests by Ostrom (1961*b*), Hopson (1975*a*), and Dodson (1975). Weishampel studied the limited sampling of lambeosaurine specimens revealing t he internal passages of the crest, including various skulls of *L. lambei* (NMC 2869, AMNH 5340, and YPM 3222). Observing that the general relationships among the specimens are quite consistent between internal and external structures, Weishampel described the internal nasal passages in all lamebeosaurines: These passages form a series of intercommunicating tubes and chambers between external and internal nares housed within specific cranial bones. The divisions are similar enough in arrangement of anatomical structures to be basically homologous with that in modern reptiles.

Dodson (1975) pointed out that *Lambeosaurus* basically differs from its nearest contemporary *Corythosaurus,* only in the forward orientation of its crest and vertically-stacked chambers in the anterior part of the crest. Otherwise they are identical, especially in postcrania (Brett-Surman 1975, 1989). As both forms occur in the same beds and *Lambeosaurus* remains are less abundant than those of *Corythosaurus,* Brett-Surman brought up the possibility that differences between these forms may be gender-related, *Lambeosaurus* being the male morph.

Notes: Morris (1978) reevaluated the partial skeleton (USNM 7948), lacking the cranium, from the Two Medicine Formation of Montana, described by Gilmore (1917) as ?*Hypacrosaurus altispinus,* suggesting that Gilmore referred the specimen to *Hypacrosaurus* on the basis of an exaggerated neural spine. Noting that all other reported *Hypacrosaurus* specimens are of Maastrichtian age, Morris concluded that the Montana specimen is indeterminate, lacking any definitive generic characters, though it may prove to be closely allied to *Lambeosaurus* sp. That assignment would affirm the outdated biostratigraphic concept limiting *Hypacrosaurus* to the Maastrichtian and *Lambeosaurus* to the geologically older Campanian.

Procheneosaurus convincens Rozhdestvensky 1968 was later regarded as a juvenile *Jaxartosaurus aralensis* by Brett-Surman (1989).

Key references: Brett-Surman (1975, 1989); Dodson (1975); Gilmore (1917, 1924*d*); Hopson (1975*a*); Lambe (1902, 1914); Lull and Wright (1942); Marsh (1889*a*); Matthew (1920); Morris (1978, 1981); Osborn (1902); Ostrom (1961*b*, 1962*a*; 1964*a*); Parks (1923, 1931, 1935); Sternberg (1935); Weishampel (1987).

LAMETASAURUS Matley 1923 [*nomen dubium*]
Ornithischia: Genasauria: Thyreophora:
    Ankylosauria: ?Nodosauridae.
Name derivation: "Lameta [Formation]" + Greek
    sauros = "lizard."
Type species: *L. indicus* Matley 1923 [*nomen
    dubium*].
Other species: [None.]
Occurrence: Lameta Formation, Madhya Pradesh,
    India.

Age: Late Cretaceous (Maastrichtian).
Known material: Partial postcrania, scutes.
Holotype: IM collection, sacrum, tibia, about
    5,000 scutes.

Diagnosis of genus (as for type species): [No modern diagnosis published.]

Comments: The genus *Lametasaurus* was founded upon very incomplete postcranial remains (IM collection) recovered from the so-called "Carnosaur Bed" of Bara Simla Hill, Lameta Formation (stratigraphic studies by Matley 1921; mapped and interpreted by Chanda and Bhattacharyya 1966 as comprising three formations) of Jubbulpore [now spelled Jabalpur], Madhya Pradesh, Central Provinces of India.

Matley originally believed these remains belonged to an armored "megalosaur," mentioning in a footnote the dermal ossifications of *Ceratosaurus* and scutes found in association with the holotype of "*Dynamosaurus*" [=*Tyrannosaurus*] *imperiosis.* After part of the Lameta collection was prepared in London, Matley (1923) changed his opinion, regarding the scutes as belonging to a new stegosaur genus and species which he named *Lametasaurus indicus.*

The Lameta dinosaur material was later described by Huene and Matley (1933), with Matley very briefly describing *Lametasaurus* as a stegosaurid. Matley (*see in* Huene and Matley) noted that tabular scutes assigned to *L. indicus* offered no new data other than indicating that the neck of this dinosaur was protected by rings of plates. Huene (*see in* Huene and Matley) speculated that the tail of *Lametasaurus* bore an *Ankylosaurus*-like club and that *Lametasaurus* was not a very highly specialized nodosaurid.

Chakravarti (1935) argued that the bones assigned to *Lametasaurus* are "megalosaurian" in form, and that most of the scutes had originally been correctly associated with "megalosaur" remains (the others probably crocodilian), again mentioning *Ceratosaurus* and "*Dynamosaurus.*"

Later, Walker (1964) examined the alleged "*Dynamosaurus*" scutes, finding them to be those of an ankylosaur such as *Hoplitosaurus.* Reevaluating the Lameta material, Walker pointed out that most noncrocodilian scutes referred by Matley (1921) to *Lametasaurus* probably belong to an armored dinosaur, since no such ossifications are known in other large theropods except *Ceratosaurus.* As Matley (1921) had at first intended to describe an armored dinosaur, Walker designated the noncrocodilian scutes as the type specimen of *L. indicus.*

Coombs (1978*a*) included ?*Lametasaurus* in the Ankylosauridae; subsequently, Coombs and Maryańska (1990) regarded *L. indicus* as both a possible nodosaurid and a *nomen dubium.*

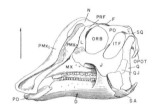

Lambeosaurus lambei, ROM 758, holotype skull of *Procheneosaurus.* Scale = 10 cm. (After Lull and Wright 1942.)

Note: Walker stated that a cranial specimen (IM K20/350), referred by Huene and Matley to the theropod *Indosuchus,* could be a portion of the skull roof of an armored dinosaur; the ilia originally described by Matley as part of the holotype of *Lametasaurus* is theropod.

Key references: Coombs (1978*a*); Coombs and Maryańska (1990); Chakravarti (1935); Huene and Matley (1933); Matley (1923); Walker (1964).

LANASAURUS Gow 1975

Ornithischia: Genasauria: Ceropoda: Ornithopoda: Heterodontosauridae.

Name derivation: Latin *lana* = "wool" [free translation, for Professor A. W. "Fuzz" Crompton] + Greek *sauros* = "lizard."

Type species: *L. scalpridens* Gow 1975.

Other species: [None.]

Occurrence: Upper Elliot Formation, Cape Province, Orange Free State, South Africa.

Age: Early Jurassic (Hettangian–?Sinemurian).

Known material/holotype: BPI 4244, almost complete isolated left maxilla with perfectly preserved teeth.

Diagnosis of genus: Distinguished from other heterodontosaurids on basis of tooth morphology; anterior labial surface of maxilla entirely devoid of pronounced pits (present in *Heterodontosaurus*); alveolar border convex towards midline of skull (toward orbit in *Heterodontosaurus*; see Charig and Crompton 1974) (Gow 1975).

Diagnosis of *L. scalpridens*: Maxillary teeth very sharp, chisel-shaped (Gow 1975).

Comments: The most primitive known heterodontosaurid, *Lanasaurus* was founded upon a maxilla with teeth (BPI 4244), collected by Christopher

E. Gow from the upper Elliot Formation (Early Jurassic; Olsen and Galton 1977), formerly upper Stormberg Series (Red Beds), at Golden Gate Highlands National Park in South Africa (Gow 1975).

From the well preserved dentition in the holotype, Gow described tooth replacement and occlusion in *Lanasaurus*, noting their close similarity to that described by Thulborn (1971) for ?"*Fabrosaurus australis*" [=*Lesothosaurus diagnosticus*]: Tooth crowns are planed off on the lingual surface into two facets. Formation of the anterior facet rapidly obliterates enamel. The posterior facet is retained to an advanced wear stage in the groove between the body of the crown and posterior proximal cusp and its ridge. Upper and lower teeth must be offset to produce these wear facets, a lower tooth constituting the posterior facet on one upper tooth and the anterior facet on the next tooth in line posteriorly.

Gow believed that *Lanasaurus* could be intermediate between the more primitive *Lesothosaurus* [=*Fabrosaurus* of his usage] and more derived *Heterodontosaurus*. Hopson (1975, 1980), however, showed that *Lanasaurus* is a heterodontosaurid similar to both *Heterodontosaurus* and *Lycorhinus*, all three genera sharing the same kind of maxillary dentition. According to Hopson (1980), wear facets on teeth and, consequently, the inferred pattern of jaw movements (essentially an open-and-shut action) do not drastically differ in these three forms nor in jaw mechanics of more derived hadrosaurids.

Key references: Gow (1975); Hopson (1975, 1980).

Lanasaurus scalpridens, BPI 4244, holotype left maxilla with teeth. (After Gow 1975.)

I cm

LAOSAURUS Marsh 1878 [*nomen dubium*]— (=?*Othnielia*)

Ornithischia: Genasauria: Cerapoda: Ornithopoda: Hypsilophodontidae.

Name derivation: Greek *laos* = "stone" + Greek *sauros* = "lizard."

Type species: *L. celer* Marsh 1878 [*nomen dubium*].

Other species: ?*L. minimus* Gilmore 1924.

Occurrence: Morrison Formation, Wyoming, United States; ?Oldman Formation, Alberta, Canada.

Age: Late Jurassic (Late Kimmeridgian–Early Portlandian).

Known material: Vertebrae, ?partial hindlimb.

Holotype: YPM 1874, two complete vertebral centra, nine half centra, ?juvenile.

Diagnosis of genus: [No modern diagnosis published.]

Comments: *Laosaurus* was founded upon vertebrae (YPM 1874) collected by Samuel Wendell Williston from the Morrison Formation at Como

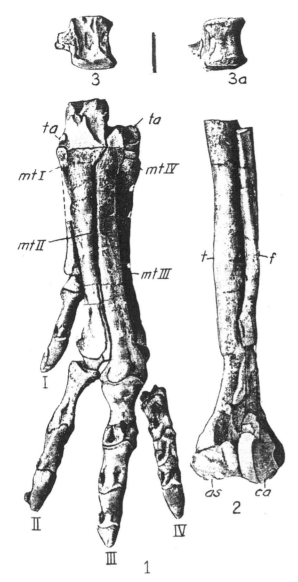

?*Laosaurus minimus*, YPM 1874, holotype 1. left forefoot, 2. distal portion of left tibia and fibula, 3. vertebral centrum. Scale = 1 cm. (After Marsh 1878.)

Bluff, Wyoming, and originally described (but not figured) by Marsh (1878*a*).

The genus (and type species, *L. celer*) were diagnosed by Marsh as follows [excluding references to referred material]: About fox-sized; vertebrae biconcave, neural arches loosely joined [perhaps juvenile feature] to centra; dorsal and anterior caudals relatively long; greatest length of median caudal centrum [see below] 24 millimeters (over .92 inches).

As recounted by Galton (1983*b*), the holotype of *L. celer* was shipped to the Yale Peabody Museum of Natural History along with remains (YPM 1875) of second species, *L. gracilis* Marsh 1878, also collected by Williston. The material may all have come from the same quarry, although this has not been confirmed by Peabody Museum records (see Ostrom

and McIntosh 1966). Marsh had listed a median caudal vertebra, presumably a centrum, as part of the type material of *L. celer*. Later, White (1973), in his catalogue of dinosaur genera, noted that the holotype (YPM 1874) of *L. celer* comprises two complete and nine partial centra and that the genus should be regarded as a *nomen dubium*.

Galton observed that all of these centra are clearly those of an hypsilophodontid. However, as they cannot be distinguished from *Hypsilophodon foxii*, Galton (1977, 1983*b*) considered the holotype of *L. celer* to be indeterminate. Galton (1983*b*) suggested that the genus *Laosaurus* be designated a *nomen nudum*.

?*L. minimus* was based on a partial left hindlimb bone and vertebral fragments from the Belly River [now Oldman] Formation (Upper Cretaceous) of Alberta, Canada. Gilmore (1924*e*), who found this species to be apparently rather similar to *Hypsilophodon*, described the material thusly: Pes lacking metatarsal V; proximal portion of metatarsal I much reduced.

In their review of the Hypsilophodontidae, Sues and Norman (1990) regarded both *L. minimus* and *L. celer* as *nomina dubia*, adding that "*L.*" *minimus* may be referable to *Orodromeus*, although type material of that species is not adequate enough for a synonymy.

Notes: Marsh (1894) made *L. altus* Marsh 1878 the type species of *Dryosaurus*.

Galton (1977), to accommodate most of the material referred to *Laosaurus* (including specimens referred to *L. gracilis* Marsh 1878 and *L. consors* Marsh 1894) and *Nanosaurus rex* Marsh 1877, erected new genus and species combination *Othnielia rex*. Bakker, Galton, Siegwarth and Filla (1990) regarded the holotype of *L. consors* as indeterminate, possibly belonging to "any one of a half-dozen ornithopod genera."

Key references: Bakker, Galton, Siegwarth and Filla (1990); Galton (1977, 1983*b*); Gilmore (1924*e*); Marsh (1978*a*); Ostrom and McIntosh (1966); Sues and Norman (1990).

LAPLATASAURUS Huene 1927
Saurischia: Sauropodomorpha: Sauropoda: Titanosauridae.
Name derivation: "La Plata [Argentina]" + Greek *sauros* = "lizard."
Type species: *L. araukanicus* Huene 1927.
Other species: [None.]
Occurrence: Castillo Formation, Bajo Barreal Formation, Laguna Formation, Rio Negro, Los Blanquitos Formation, Salta, Argentina; Asencio Formation, Palmitas, Uruguay.
Age: Late Cretaceous (Campanian–Maastrichtian).

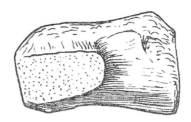

Laplatasaurus araukanicus, caudal vertebra. (After Huene 1928.)

Known material: Caudal series, other postcrania.

Cotypes: MLP CS1127, tibia, CS1128, fibula.

Diagnosis of genus: [No modern diagnosis published.]

Comments: The generic name *Laplatasaurus* was first published (without a specific name) by Huene (1927*a*) in his review of sauropods. Subsequently, Huene (1929) erected the type species *Laplatasaurus araukanicus* and described the type material. The genus was originally established on postcranial material including ten caudal vertebrae, a scapulacoracoid, sternal plates, humerus, radius, ulna, manus, ilium, tibia, and fibula (MLP collection) collected from the Upper Cretaceous of Neuquén, Argentina.

Huene (1929) tentatively diagnosed *Laplatasaurus* as follows: Much larger but more slender than "*Titanosaurus*" [=*Saltasaurus*] *robustus*; cervical vertebrae moderately long (for a titanosaurid); dorsal vertebrae with deeper pleurocoels than in "*T*." *robustus*; caudal vertebrae relatively short, with high, tapering articular ends; scapula slender, with straight posterior border and relatively smaller deltoid process than "*T*." *robustus*; ilium relatively short and high at anterior end; pubis slender, straight at mid-shaft; humerus, femur, and tibia less massive than in "*T*." *robustus*; radius of signoid configuration; ulna rather square-shaped at middle; manual phalanges rather thickened distally; femur with pronounced fourth trochanter.

Eventually, Bonaparte and Gasparini (1978) designated the fibula (MLP CS [Cinco Salta] 1127) and tibia (MLP CS1128), among the original material, as the holotype.

Powell (1979) described a humerus, ulna, radius, femur, tibia, fibula, premaxilla, and fragments of ilia, pubis, and ischium, collected from the Arroyo Morterito (Los Blanquitos Formation), southern end of La Candelaria Hills, Province of Salta, Argentina, this specimen having been originally referred by Bonaparte and Bossi (1967) to *Antarctosaurus*. Powell, noting similarities between the specimen and remains of *Laplatasaurus*, but finding the material in too poor condition for assignment to a particular species, referred it to *Laplatasaurus* sp.

Key references: Bonaparte and Bossi (1967); Bonaparte and Gasparini (1978); Huene (1927*a*, 1929); Powell (1979).

LAPPARENTOSAURUS Bonaparte 1986

Saurischia: Sauropodomorpha: Sauropoda: Brachiosauridae.

Name derivation: "[Albert F. de] Lapparent" + Greek *sauros* = "lizard."

Type species: *L. madagascariensis* (Lydekker 1895).

Other species: [None.]

Occurrence: Isalo Formation, Majunga, Madagascar.

Age: Late Jurassic (Bathonian).

Known material: More than four partial postcranial skeletons, teeth.

Holotype: MAA 91-92, almost complete juvenile skeleton.

Diagnosis of genus (as for type species): Cetiosaurid with rather flat neural spine, lacking divergent laminae found in *Cetiosaurus*, *Barapasaurus*, and *Patagosaurus* (Bonaparte 1986*a*).

Comments: The genus *Lapparentosaurus* was established upon a quite distinct juvenile specimen (MAA 91-92) from Malagasy, Madagascar, this material described by Ogier (1975) in an as yet unpublished thesis as belonging to the species *Bothriospondylus madagascariensis* Lydekker 1895 [*nomen dubium*].

Bonaparte (1986*a*) pointed out that the presence of pleurocoels in the vertebral centra of this specimen (see also Lydekker) has no serious value for comparison with other genera. Therefore, the species from Madagascar cannot be assigned to *Bothriospondylus*. Because of the completeness of this specimen and to avoid confusion regarding the systematics and stratigraphic and geographic paleodistribution of Jurassic sauropods, Bonaparte erected the new genus *Lapparentosaurus* to receive the Madagascar material.

Noting the rather primitive development of the neural spine, Bonaparte concluded that the vertebrae in *L. madagascariensis* (and in *Volkeimeria chubutensis*, regarded as a cetiosaurid by Bonaparte) represent an early stage in the development of sauropod vertebrae, more primitive than in such typical cetiosaurids as *Cetiosaurus*, but more derived than in *Vulcanodon karibaensis*.

McIntosh (1990*b*), in his review of the Sauropoda, regarded *L. madagascariensis* as a brachiosaurid, apparently very close to, if not the direct ancestor of, *Brachiosaurus*.

Key references: Bonaparte (1986*a*); Lydekker (1895); McIntosh (1990*b*); Ogier (1975).

LEAELLYNASAURA Rich and Rich 1989

Ornithischia: Genasauria: Cerapoda: Ornithopoda: Hypsilophodontidae.

Name derivation: "Leaellyn [daughter of the Riches]" + Greek *saura* [feminine] = "lizard."

Type species: *L. amicagraphica* Rich and Rich 1989.

Other species: [None.]

Occurrence: Otway Group, Victoria, Australia.

Age: Early Cretaceous (Latest Aptian or Early Albian).

Known material: Cranial fragments, teeth, isolated postcranial remains, juvenile to adult.

Holotype: NMV P185991, partial skull with teeth, juvenile.

Diagnosis of genus (as for type species): Differs from all other hypsilophodontids in femur with more anteroposteriorly compressed distal end (see Molnar and Galton 1986), and from all hypsilophodontids except *Othnielia* in ridges on both sides of unworn upper cheek teeth (Rich and Rich [now Vickers-Rich] 1989).

Comments: The genus *Leaellynasaura* was established on an incomplete skull (NMV P185991) discovered by Thomas H. V. Rich, Patricia V. Rich, and Leaellyn Rich at Slippery Rock, Dinosaur Cove, Otway Group (see Drinnan and Chambers 1986), which some authors combine with the Strzelecki Group into one unit, the Korumburra Group, near the southeastern tip of Australia. Wagstaff and Mason (1989) detailed the methods used to date the faunas (including *Leaellynasaura*, hypsilophodonts *Atlascoposaurus* and *Fulgurotherium*, two kinds of theropods including a species of *Allosaurus*, and a pterosaur) in this region. Rich and Rich (1989) pointed out that this area is located well within the Antarctic Circle of the time, possibly as far south as 80 to 85 degrees (see Embleton and McElhinny 1982; Idnurum 1985).

As noted by Rich and Rich, the holotype was the best specimen in a series of specimens collected over four summers of field work. Referred material from the same locality include left and right nasals, prefrontals, frontals, and parietals (NMV P185990), articulated proximal caudal vertebrae and about the distal seven-eighths of the femur, the proximal three-fourths of a tibia and fibula, and two articulated digits, one with two and the other three articulated phalanges (NMV P185992), and articulated distal caudal vertebrae (NMV P185993), all perhaps belonging to the same individual as the holotype. Referred material from Dinosaur Cove East, Dinosaur Cove, includes: a slightly crushed right femur (NMV P179561); a slightly crushed left femur (NMV P179564) missing the condyles; a crushed right femur (NMV P182968) missing the head, proximal part of the lesser trochanter and the distal tip of the fourth trochanter; a crushed right femur (NMV P185867) missing the medial condyle; and a right femur (NMV P185980) missing the head, proximal tip of the lesser trochanter and medial condyle. Referred material from Dinosaur Cove West,

Dinosaur Cove, includes a crushed left femur (NMV P181681), missing the internal condyle and fourth and lesser trochanters.

Rich and Rich observed that the upper cheek teeth differ from those of *Atlascopcosaurus* (Rich and Rich 1989) in lacking two discrete sizes of ridges, and in the equally developed ridges on both sides of the unworn teeth; cheek teeth differ from *Alocodon*, *Nanosaurus*, and *Phyllodon* (see Galton 1983*b*) in having ridges that cover the entire internal and external surfaces instead of denticles restricted to the crown margin; upper cheek teeth differ from those of *Camptosaurus* (Galton and Powell 1980), *Dryosaurus* (Galton 1983*b*), *Rhabdodon* [=*Mochlodon* of their usage] (Nopcsa 1904), *Atlascoposaurus* (Rich and Rich 1989), *Bugenasaura* [=*Thescelosaurus* of their usage] (Galton 1974*b*; Morris 1976), and an isolated hypsilophodontid cheek tooth (QM F9505) from Lightning Ridge, New South Wales, Australia (figured by Molnar 1980*d*), in the lack of a single primary ridge notably stronger than all other ridges; upper cheek teeth differ from those of *Atlascoposaurus*, *Othnielia* (Galton 1983*b*), *Parksosaurus* (Galton 1973*a*), *Bugenasaura*, *Zephyrosaurus* (Sues 1980*b*), and the Lightning Ridge tooth by having a maximum of five ridges instead of a minimum of eight.

The holotype of *L. amicagraphica* was interpreted by Rich and Rich as probably belonging to a juvenile individual approximately one-third the size of an adult, which would have measured from about 2 to 3 meters (about 6.5 to over 10 feet long).

In an earlier study of a partial natural endocast of the [then unnamed] holotype, Rich and Rich (1988) determined that this dinosaur had well-developed optic lobes, the eyes large. Although these characters are indicative of juveniles, Rich and Rich (1988) suggested that adults had excellent vision, and speculated that a large brain and visual acuity could

Leaellynsaura amicagraphica, **NMV P185991, holotype dentition, lateral view.**

Leaellynsaura amica-graphica, NMV P185990 (possibly part of same individual as holotype), posterior portion of frontals, plus parietals, ventral view.

Courtesy T. H. V. Rich and P. Vickers–Rich.

constitute preadaptations favorable for life during dark Antarctic winters.

In a nontechnical article, Vickers-Rich and Rich (1993) speculated that the large eyes would have allowed *Leaellynasaura* to see in the dark, enabling them to forage for food during the winter month; also, that the large eyes of these hypsilophodontids allowed them to gain a foothold in polar Australia. Vickers-Rich and Rich further speculated that these animals must have been active at freezing or subfreezing climates, suggesting that *Leaellynasaura* was warm-blooded, surviving in its environment by maintaining a constant body temperature and eating frequently in the fashion of some birds.

Note: Remains of another Antarctic hypsilophodont were reported in an Associated Press news story published on March 5, 1989. Including jaw bones, much of the vertebral column, and forelimbs, belonging to an animal measuring almost 3 meters (about 10 feet) long, these remains were discovered by Michael Thomson in the vicinity of James Ross Island in British Antarctic Territory. (Also found in the area by Thomson and his team were fossilized shells, tree trunks, leaves from conifers, and broad-leaved trees and ferns.)

Key reference: Rich and Rich (1988, 1989); Vickers-Rich and Rich (1993).

LEIPSANOSAURUS Nopcsa 1918 [*nomen dubium*] — (=?"*Struthiosaurus*" [see entry notes])
Ornithischia: Thyreophora: Ankylosauria: Nodosauridae.
Name derivation: Greek *leipsanon* = "resonant" + Greek *sauros* = "lizard."
Type species: *L. noricus* Nopcsa 1918 [*nomen dubium*].
Other species: [None.]
Occurrence: Gosau Formation, Niederöstereich, Austria.

Age: Late Cretaceous (Turonian).
Known material/holotype: [Apparently] GIUV collection, isolated tooth.

Diagnosis of genus: [None published.]

Comments: The new type species *Leipsanosaurus moricus* was erected upon a single tooth (?GIUV collection), recovered from the Gosau Formation of Niederöstereich, Austria, and described by Nopcsa (1918).

L. moricus is sometimes regarded (Romer 1956, 1966; Steel 1969; Olshevsky 1978, 1989, 1991, 1991) as a junior synonym of "*Struthiosaurus*" *transilvanicus*, a nodosaurid species from the Gosau Formation; Coombs (1978*a*) considered this synonymy to be only tentative.

Key references: Coombs (1978*a*); Nopcsa (1918).

LEPTOCERATOPS Brown 1914
Ornithischia: Genasauria: Cerapoda: Marginocephalia: Ceratopsia: Neoceratopsia: Protoceratopsidae.
Name derivation: Greek *leptos* = "slender" + Greek *keratos* = "horned" + Greek *ops* = "face."
Type species: *L. gracilis* Brown 1914.
Other species: [None.]
Occurrence: Scollard Formation, Alberta, Canada; Lance Formation, Wyoming, United States.
Age: Late Cretaceous (Late Maastrichtian).
Known material: Three complete skulls, two partial skulls, skeletons, juvenile, adult.
Holotype: AMNH 5205, nasals, maxillaries, parts of orbital border, posterior part of crest, dentary, predentary, sphlenial bones, series of articulated caudal vertebrae, complete forelimb, portions of hindlimbs.

Diagnosis of genus (as for type species): Skull with long, moderately low facial region and no parietosquamosal crest; parietals overhanging occiput, lack fenestrae, with high, thin sagittal ridge; exoccipital long, underlies parietal, bracing proximal end of quadrate; supratemporal fossa very large, not covered by postorbital and squamosal; lateral fossae large, high; squamosals short, hooking behind heads of quadrates, but not extending backwards to form crest; squamosal-postorbital bar vertical, relatively narrow, anteroinferior tip meeting posterior tip of jugal, barely excluding postorbital from lateral boundary of temporal fossa; quadrate, in lower half, almost vertical, upper half bent backward; jugal large, skull broadest through jugals; epijugal large, elongate vertically; maxillary depression deep, large, bounded by maxilla and lacrimal; nasals long, posteriorly broad, anteriorly pointed; premaxillae low, lacking teeth; rostral of moderate size, superoposterior tip between premaxillae, reaching to opposite anterior tip of nasals; palate narrow, high; maxilla large, overhanging teeth; tooth row located near center of skull at front, splaying posteriorly; (in adult) 17 maxillary and dentary teeth; mandible short, heavy; predentary broad, long, superior surface concave with narrowly rounded edges, underlapping dentaries though not wedged in between them; dentary high, short, inferiorly rounded, strongly upturned anteriorly, teeth well in from external surface, with large, low coronoid process well set out; sphlenial bone very large, reaching symphysis; 22 presacral vertebrae, first three separate in young individuals but coalesced in adults; atlas lacking neural spine; spine on axis large, that on third axis erect, slender, not fused with axis spine; ribs on atlas and twenty-second presacral vertebra single-headed, others double-headed; either sacral vertebrae are not fused or only first three are fused in immature individuals; caudal neural spines of modest length; ribs very slender, clavicles small yet well ossified; ilium erect, with thin, narrow blade and noninverted superior edge; postpubis relatively long; forelimb of modest length; humerus with well-developed pectoral crest (Sternberg 1951*a*).

Comments: The genus *Leptoceratops* was founded on incomplete cranial and postcranial remains (AMNH 5205), collected by Barnum Brown during the American Museum of Natural History expedition of 1910, from the Edmonton [now Scollard] Formation at Red Deer River, three miles above Tolman Ferry, Alberta, Canada.

Brown (1914*c*) originally diagnosed the monotypic *L. gracilis* as follows: Skeleton small, with short, deep skull lacking nasal horn; crest with high, thin sagittal ridge and smooth posterior border; squamosal extending to extreme posterior border of crest; teeth with single roots; dentary massive, short, deep, with less than 15 tooth rows; sphlenial large, extending to symphysis; predentary long, narrow; manual digits I, II, and III terminating in hoofs; carpals ossified; ulnare and radiale large; femur straight, with comparatively large fourth trochanter; tail deep, long, with high, slender spines and long chevrons.

Brown recognized *L. gracilis* as a primitive form, although some of the characters noted by him are no longer of diagnostic importance.

Other *Leptoceratops* specimens were later described, including an articulated, unusually complete skeleton (NMC 8887) found in 1947 by Sternberg (1951*a*) in the Scollard Formation, about 13.5 miles northeast of Elnora, Alberta. Sternberg published an emended diagnosis of the genus and species,

Leptoceratops gracilis, AMNH 5205, restored holotype skeleton.

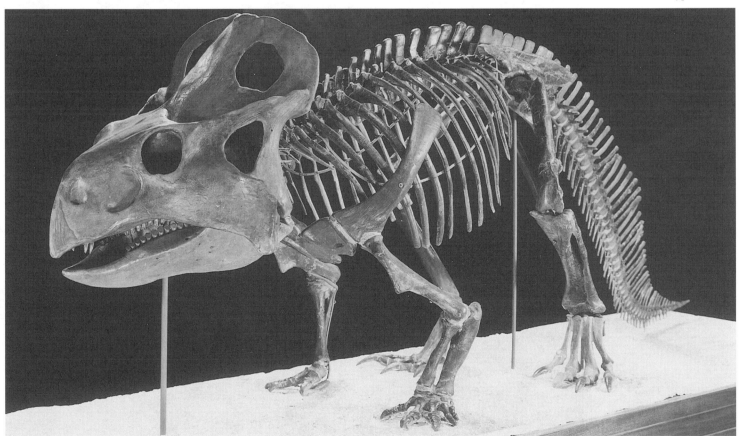

Leptoceratops gracilis, life restoration by Doug Henderson made for the Museum of the Rockies.

based on NMC 8887 (designated a plesiotype by Sternberg) and two additional plesiotype specimens from the same locality as the first, a skeleton missing most of the skull, jaws and part of a front foot (NMC 8888), and a skull and jaws, presacral vertebrae, ribs, pectoral girdle missing upper ends of scapulae, left fore and hindlimbs, sternal, and hyoid bones (NMC 8889).

In reconstructing the skeleton of *L. gracilis*, based mostly on NMC 8889, D. A. Russell (1970*a*) showed that *Leptoceratops* has an exceedingly large head, long ischium, and elongated caudal neural spines. The relative lengths of the skull, presacral, femur, and caudal-vertebral regions closely correspond to those in *Psittacosaurus sinensis*. Though *Leptoceratops* is sometimes portrayed as at least partially bipedal, Russell restored it as a quadruped, observing that the concentration of body mass in the front of the pelvis, broad abbreviated manus, and straight-shafted femur are adaptations for quadrupedalism. The skeleton has an approximate length of 181 centimeters (71.5 inches) and height at the pelvis of 73 centimeters (29 inches).

Based on osteological features of *Leptoceratops*, Coombs (1978*c*) concluded that this genus and the more derived *Protoceratops* were at least somewhat bipedal, having subcursorial to cursorial locomotor abilities, and that both genera probably were among the swiftest of quadrupedal dinosaurs (see *Protoceratops* entry).

Sternberg noted that the most surprising feature of *Leptoceratops* is the lack of a crest, as even the crests in the youngest *Protoceratops* individuals are well developed. This absence of a crest is a primitive character, as are numerous other features of the skull and postcranial skeleton, including (see Sereno 1986) the lack of the frontoparietal depression, parietal fenestrae, and greatly expanded parietal-squamosal frill. At present, *Leptoceratops* is the most primitive known protoceratopsid. This genus, the remains of which were found almost at the close of Mesozoic, seems to be an ancestor that coexisted with its own descendants.

Ostrom (1978*a*) described a partial skeleton (PU 18133) of *L. gracilis*, discovered in 1962 by Michael Ramus in Bighorn Basin strata, informally referred to as "Lance" beds

(L. S. Russell 1964), at Park County, Wyoming. The specimen, consisting of an almost complete left hindlimb, left ischium and pubis, incomplete right ischium, sacral vertebrae, and nearly complete caudal series of 46 vertebrae, lies on its right side in an extremely contorted position. As Ostrom observed, this specimen is more similar to the type specimens than are any other previously reported referred specimens. It is particularly important as evidence for correlating these Wyoming rocks with Upper Edmonton strata of central Alberta.

Leptoceratops has also been reported from Gwandong, China, and from Mongolia, though reports from Asia are vague and questionable.

Notes: Sternberg (1951) made *L. cerorhynchus* Brown and Schlaikjer 1942 the type species of *Montanoceratops*.

Rich and Rich (1994) reported the discovery of what they deduced to be unnamed neoceratopsian remains, represented by an ulna (NMV P186385, found during the early 1990s in the Strzelecki Group (Late Early Cretaceous, Late Aptian–Early Albian), along the south coast of southeastern Australia. This ulna so closely resembles that of *L. gracilis*, from the Late Cretaceous of Canada, that it is impossible to see any differences that might reveal the relative degree of advancement of the former. The authors noted that, had the Australian and Canadian forms been found at the same site, they most likely would have been regarded as the same species. Rich and Rich concluded that the Australian form's resemblance to *L. gracilis*, although both were otherwise only distantly related, may be the result of convergence. The presence of the ulna in the Australian Early Cretaceous suggested to Rich and Rich that the origin of the Neoceratopsia may be in Gondwana (see *Timimus* entry).

Key references: Brown (1914*c*); Coombs (1978*a*); Ostrom (1978*a*); Russell (1970*a*); Sternberg (1951*a*).

Leptoceratops gracilis, NMC 8889, plesiotype skull, left lateral view.

LEPTOSPONDYLUS Owen 1854 [*nomen dubium*]—(See *Massospondylus*.)
Name derivation: Greek *leptos* = "slender" + Greek *spondylos* = "vertebra."
Type species: *L. capensis* Owen 1854 [*nomenm dubium*].

LESOTHOSAURUS Galton 1978
Ornithischia.
Name derivation: "Lesotho [country in southern South Africa]" + Greek *sauros* = "lizard."
Type species: *L. diagnosticus* Galton 1978.
Other species: [None.]
Occurrence: Upper Elliot Formation, Mafeteng District, Lesotho.
Age: Early Jurassic (Hettangian-?Sinemurian).
Known material: At least four skulls and associated postcrania.
Holotype: BMNH RUB 17 [formerly UCL B17], cranial, dental, and postcranial remains, juvenile.

Diagnosis of genus (as for type species): Small-bodied basal ornithischian with cranium distinguished by anterior premaxillary foramen, and maxilla-lacrimal articulation with lacrimal inserting into slot on apex of maxilla; postcranium distinguished by proportionately short (less than 40 percent length of hindlimb) forelimbs, postacetabular process of ilium with brevis surface broadly exposed in side view, groove on dorsal margin of proximal ischial shaft, and reduced pedal digit I, with promixal end of metatarsal I splint-shaped and distal end of claw extending just beyond metatarsal II (Sereno 1991*a*).

Comments: The new genus and species combination *Lesothosaurus diagnosticus* was erected by Galton (1978) to receive material originally referred by Thulborn (1970*a*, 1972) to *Fabrosaurus australis*. Representing the most complete "fabrosaurid" fossils known to date, this material comprises the remains of at least two individuals, one (BMNH RUB17) including skull parts, teeth, and postcranial material, the other (BMNH RUB23) an incomplete, slightly damaged skull with teeth. These remains were collected from the upper Elliot Formation (Early Jurassic;

see Olsen and Galton 1984) [formerly Stormberg Series (Red Beds)] of Lesotho. The more complete specimen (BMNH RUB17) and the holotype of *F. australis* were recovered from Likhoele Mountain.

Thulborn (1970*a*) originally referred BMNH RUB23 to the Hypsilophodontidae, but later (1972) suggested that *L. diagnosticus* [=*Fabrosaurus australis* of his usage] was a very early and quite specialized hypsilophodontid. On the basis of the flat maxilla and slender dentary of this skull, Galton (1972) then erected the [abandoned] family Fabrosauridae; later, Galton (1978) assigned type species *L. diagnosticus* to this group.

Thulborn (1970*a*) diagnosed *L. diagnosticus* [=*F. australis* of his usage] as follows: Ornithischian slightly less than 1 meter (39.37 inches) in length, lacking dermal armor; skull about 10 centimeters (3.7 inches) long, triangular in profile, with large laterally positioned circular orbits; antorbital vacuity triangular, widely open; premaxilla extending behind naris, not reaching lacrimal; maxilla flat; jugal slender, without ventral flange; parietals separate, forming broad, flat zone between upper temporal openings; anterior limit of upper temporal opening marked by crescent-shaped depression of frontal; quadrate tall, extending anteriorly, with slender descending process from squamosal overlying front edge; mandible slender, with salient fingerlike retroarticular process and weak coronoid apophysis; small median edentulous predentary at mandibular symphysis; teeth of heterodont form, thecodont implantation, arranged in simple marginal row; as many as six acute, smooth, recurved teeth, last two with tiny denticles; about 14 maxillary and 14 dentary teeth; all teeth completely enameled and separate, extending to front of premaxilla; sharper premaxillary teeth and leaf-shaped cheek teeth differ, change marked by appearance of intermediately shaped transitional crowns; five sacral vertebrae with no indication of fusion between centra,

Lesothosaurus diagnosticus, skeletal reconstruction based on BMNH RUB 17, holotype, and 23. Scale = 7 cm. (After Thulborn, 1972, Galton 1978.)

within which neural canals expand ventrally; scapula tall, blade-like, with posterodorsal corner extending into short tongue-like process, and prominent, forwardly projecting "acromial" process; humerus slightly shorter than scapula; prepubis short, twisted, blade-like; femur twice length of humerus; tibia 124 percent length of femur; metatarsal I reduced and splint-like, III 52 percent length of tibia.

The validity of *Lesothosaurus* as a taxon distinct from *Fabrosaurus* was challenged by Gow (1981), who regarded as suspect the differences separating both genera. After examining new "fabrosaurid" material in the collection of the Bernard Price Institute for Paleontological Research, University of the Witwatersrand, in Johannesburg, South Africa, Gow stated that: 1. These animals continuously replaced their teeth, with tooth morphology possibly varying according to tooth position in the jaw (teeth oftentimes preserved slightly offset to affect the apparent height-to-width ratio); 2. differences in width of the dentary in both forms might not have diagnostic significance, but could be attributed to differential allometric growth, sexual dimorphism, or effects of post-burial pressure; and 3. a "special foramina" condition appears (*contra* Galton 1978) in old individuals to obliterate the groove for the dental lamina present in young individuals such as represented by the holotype of *L. diagnosticus* (the holotype of *F. australis* exhibiting an intermediate condition wherein the groove has almost disappeared, while replacement foramen are still present).

Lesothosaurus was a small, slender, and lightly-built dinosaur. Thulborn (1970a) reconstructed the tail, which is not well represented in the preserved remains, as about equal to the combined length of the head, neck and trunk. The manus, also not well preserved, may have had five short digits terminating in small claws.

Thulborn (1972) concluded that this dinosaur was probably an agile biped capable of cursorial activity, comparing favorably in locomotive ability with such modern reptiles as the basilisk. This conclusion was supported by virtually every part of the skeleton, with its light construction, slender, hollow and thin-walled bones, structure of the pelvis (set above the belly to allow freedom of leg movement), fenestrated skull, short neck and forelimbs, delicately constructed presacral vertebrae, and lack of dermal armor.

Most likely, *Lesothosaurus* was mainly herbivorous, but may occasionally have also fed on insects or carrion. Thulborn (1978) believed that this dinosaur probably chopped and crushed plant food by means of simple opening and closing movements of the jaws (see below). In their review of the most primitive ornithischians, Weishampel and Witmer (1990a) the-

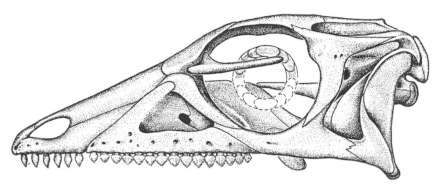

Lesothosaurus diagnosticus, restored skull, left lateral view. (After Sereno 1991.)

orized that *Lesothosaurus* probably had a horny beak in life and that the hand was probably of little use in prehension.

More recently, Sereno (1991a), in a review of *Lesothosaurus* and basal ornithischians, offered a new diagnosis of *Lesothosaurus* based upon autapomorphies present in the syntype specimens (BMNH RUB17, RUB23, and R11956). Sereno pointed out that previously published diagnoses (including Steel 1969; Thulborn 1972; Galton 1978) sometimes were in error due to misidentifications of parts of the material and did not differentiate between autapomorphies and symplesiomorphies that apply to all ornithischians or more encompassing groups, even to most other dinosaurs.

Based on the above mentioned specimens of *L. diagnosticus*, Sereno redescribed the species, observing various new details including the following: Snout proportionately long, possessing a vascularized, horn-covered tip (probably functioning as a cropping bill); postpalatine vacuities widely open (unlike the condition in many later ornithischians); dentition (contrary to inaccurate, previously published reports) marked by oblique tooth-to-tooth wear facets which, with form of the predentary-dentary articulation (predentary serving as a stable median element at symphysis), suggest (*contra* Thulborn 1978) long-axis rotation or controlled twisting of the dentary rami during mastication; pollex of forelimb partially opposable (suggesting rudimentary grasping capability); and reduced hallux held well off the ground during walking.

Sereno regarded *Lesothosaurus* as one of the earliest and most primitive ornithischians which, along with the oldest members of its sister-group Genasauria, must have diverged by the Early Jurassic (Sinemurian).

Note: Santa Luca (1984) studied three so-called "fabrosaurid" postcranial specimens (their nature and affinities very questionable; H. D. Sues, personal communication 1987), collected in Lesotho in 1967-1968 during a joint expedition from the British Museum

(Natural History) [now Natural History Museum, London], London University, Yale University, and the South African Museum (see Crompton 1968). These remains include vertebral material, right radius, left ilium, partial pubis, left femur, metatarsal IV, and phalanx (SAM K400), also vertebral, pelvic, and hindlimb material, metatarsals II-IV, and 12 right phalanges (SAM K401), from the upper Elliot Formation on Likhoele Mountain (the site that yielded both Ginsburg's and Thulborn's specimens), and vertebral material, scapula and coracoids, left and partial right humerus, left radius and ulna, pelvic material, portions of left femur and right tibia, right fibula, astragalus, calcaneum, and distal tarsal, metatarsals I-IV, 14 right phalanges, and miscellaneous centra, neural arches, and ribs (SAM K1106), from Dangershoek.

From these specimens Santa Luca observed anatomical details heretofore unknown in any "fabrosaurid" postcranial skeleton. Neither scapula nor forelimb are reduced, the radius is not robust, and (compared to other ornithopods) the manus is relatively larger and forelimb reduced only in its distal elements. The ilium differs from other ornithopod

ilia in three ways: 1. Depth of postacetabular process relatively great because of more vertical orientation of brevis shelf; 2. supra-acetabular flange forming bony hood above acetabulum; and 3. acetabular border partly ossified.

Santa Luca pointed out that the ratio of the hind limb elements is high in the range associated with rapid bipedal locomotion in ornithischians; and the fourth trochanter is located higher on the femur than in any other known ornithopod, a position more advantageous for speed than strength.

Also collected during this joint expedition were an almost complete, disarticulated skull (BMNH R8501); right ilium (BMNH R11002), left ilium (BMNH R11003), partially disarticulated posterior skull with braincase, parietals, right squamosal, right quadrate, right posterior lower jaw, and anterior neck, with axis, and third cervical vertebra (BMNH 11004) (see Weishampel 10944; Crompton and Attridge 1986).

Key references: Galton (1972, 1978); Santa Luca (1989); Sereno (1991a); Steel (1969); Thulborn (1970a, 1972); Weishampel and Witmer (1990a).

Lesothosaurus diagnosticus, life restoration by Brian Franczak.

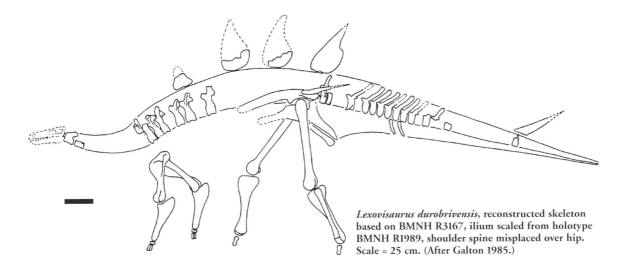

Lexovisaurus durobrivensis, reconstructed skeleton based on BMNH R3167, ilium scaled from holotype BMNH R1989, shoulder spine misplaced over hip. Scale = 25 cm. (After Galton 1985.)

LEXOVISAURUS Hoffstetter 1957

Ornithischia: Genosauria: Thyreophora: Stegosauria: Stegosauridae.

Name derivation: Greek *lexis* = "speech or word" + Greek *sauros* = "lizard."

Type species: *L. durobrivensis* (Hulke 1887).

Other species: ?*L. vetustus* (Huene 1910).

Occurrence: Lower Oxford Clay, Kimmeridge Clay, Northamptonshire, Cambridgeshire, Dorset, England; Marnes d'Argences, Calvados, France.

Age: Middle Jurassic (middle Callovian-Kimmeridgian).

Known material: Three partial postcranial skeletons, ten isolated postcranial elements, juvenile to adult.

Holotype: BMNH R1989, incomplete sacrum, ilia, left femur, metatarsal III, manual phalanx.

Diagnosis of genus (as for type species): Derived characters include: caudal centra in proximal third of tail with large proximal chevron facet uniting with distal one to give V-shaped centrum in seventh-eleventh caudal vertebrae; sacrum with almost solid dorsal plate; midcaudal vertebrae with vertical neural spines; ilium with long, thin preacetabular process; pubis with rugose central thickening; osteoderms including several very large, tall, thin plates, height more than twice craniocaudal length (Galton 1990*b*).

Comments: The genus *Lexovisaurus* was founded on partial postcranial remains (BMNH R1989) collected from the Early Oxford Clay (probably the *Kosmoceras jason* Zone; see Galton 1985*b*) of middle Callovian age, at Fletton, near Peterborough, England. The material was originally described by Hulke (1887) as *Omosaurus durobrivensis*, later redescribed (but not illustrated) by Hoffstetter and Brun (1956, 1958), then renamed *Lexovisaurus* by Hoffstetter (1957).

Specimens referred to *L. durobrivensis* (apparently from some part of the *Peltoceras athleta*, *Erymnoceras coronatum*, and *Kosmoceras jason* zones; see Galton) include the right tibia (BMNH R2854) of a juvenile individual originally described by Nopcsa (1911*a*) as *Stegosaurus priscus* [*nomen dubium*] and referred to *Lexovisaurus* by Hoffstetter (1957); incomplete postcranial skeleton (BMNH R1989-1992) collected in 1901 (Leeds 1956); the holotype (SMC J.46874) of *O. leedsi* Seeley 1901, including a large right dermal plate, distal end of a right pubis, and crushed right femur; left metatarsal II (SMC J.46885), left metacarpal I (SMC J.46886), and the distal end of a left fibula (SMC J.46888). Galton diagnosed *Lexovisaurus* based on all of these specimens.

Galton, Brun and Rioult (1980) described another specimen (MHNN collection) provisionally referred to *L. durobrivensis*, recovered from the Middle Callovian of Le Fresne d'Argences, Normandy. This generally well-preserved specimen, apparently slightly older than the holotype, includes 25 vertebrae (with 13 articulated anterior caudals), 12 hemal arches, pieces of ribs, left humerus, incomplete right femur, tibia fused to astragalus, fibula, calcaneum, and large right shoulder [then misinterpreted as a "parasacral"] spine. (These remains represented the earliest partial stegosaurian skeleton described to date.)

A poorly preserved right femur (OUM J.14000) resembling that of *L. durobrivensis*, apparently from the Lower Cornbrash (top of upper Bathonian) of Oxfordshire, was described by Huene (1910*b*) as the holotype of new species *O. vetustus*. Galton and Boine (1980) redescribed this specimen but, as it consists of just one bone, hesitated to refer it to *Lexovisaurus*.

As redescribed by Galton and Powell (1983), the femur is proportionally massive in comparison to that of other stegosaurs from England. It has a maximum length of 708 millimeters (about 27 inches), maxi-

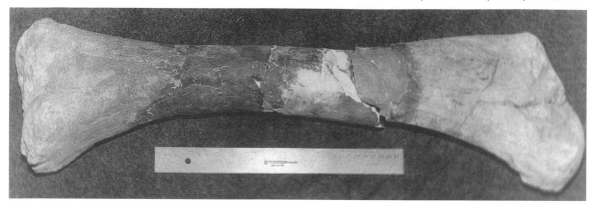

Photo by the author, courtesy University Museum, Oxford.

?Lexovisaurus vetustus, OUM J. 14000, holotype femur (juvenile) of *Omosaurus vetustus*.

mum proximal width of 201 millimeters (over 7.5 inches), and maximum distal width of 192 millimeters (about 7.25 inches). The maximum anteroposterior width of the head is 93 millimeters (about 3.5 inches). Galton and Powell speculated that this specimen might represent a new genus. However, as the femur is probably from a juvenile individual lacking diagnostic characters, and because there are no comparable-sized femora of *L. durobrivensis* with which to compare it, Galton and Powell tentatively referred the specimen to *?L. vetustus*.

Galton and Powell also provisionally referred to *?L. vetustus* a generically indeterminate cervical centrum (OUM J.29827) and anterior dorsal vertebra (OUM J.29770) from the Sharp's Hill Member of the Sharp's Hill Formation (uppermost lower Bathonian) of Oxfordshire. The dorsal centrum is longer than wide, the opposite of *Dacentrurus*. Two large dermal plates (BMNH R5838 and SDM 44.41) from the Hook Norton Member of the Hook Norton Formation (lowermost lower Bathonian) of Glouchestshire were provisionally referred to *?L. vetustus* by Galton and Powell. The plates are more massive than those in *Stegosaurus* and those known in *Lexovisaurus*.

The shoulder spine (see *Kentrosaurus* entry) is the most diagnostic feature of the Argences specimen

of *Lexovisaurus*. The spine was found close to the femur, incorrectly suggesting to Galton *et al.* its apparent placement on the living animal's hip. The base of the spine is broad with a maximum width of 275 millimeters (about 10.5 inches) and length of 450 millimeters (17 inches). The preserved length of the spine is 790 millimeters (approximately 30 inches) and, if complete, would have measured some 1.14 meters (3 feet, 9 inches), about the length of the femur. In comparison to the similar spine in the closely related genus *Kentrosaurus*, the Argences specimen is more slender and twisted along its length, the basal plate proportionally smaller and almost subcircular. Also, *Lexovisaurus* possesses more varied dermal ossifications than *Kentrosaurus*.

In a review of the Stegosauria, Galton (1990b) speculated that, given the large size and thinness of the plates in *Lexovisaurus*, and their possession of a series of grooves, they had a display or thermoregulatory function.

Key references: Galton (1985b, 1990b); Galton and Boine (1980); Galton, Brun and Rioult (1980); Galton and Powell (1983); Hoffstetter (1957); Hoffstetter and Brun (1956, 1958); Huene (1910b); Hulke (1887); Leeds (1956); Nopcsa (1911a); Seeley (1901).

Liliensternus liliensterni, reconstructed skull based on HMN R 1291, holotype partial skull of *Halticosaurus liliensternus*. Scale = 10 cm. (After Huene 1934.)

LILIENSTERNUS Welles 1984

Saurischia: Theropoda: Ceratosauria: Coelophysoidea.

Name derivation: "[Rühte von] Lilienstern."

Type species: *L. liliensterni* (Huene 1934).

Other species: *L. airelensis* Cuny and Galton 1993.

Occurrence: Knollenmergel, Bezirk Suhl, Germany; Normandy, France.

Age: Late Triassic (Late Norian)–Early Jurassic (earliest Hettangian).

Known material: Two partial skeletons, subadult; partial disarticulated skeleton.

Holotype: HMN R1291, incomplete skeleton.

Diagnosis [provisional] of Genus: Skull with large lower temporal fenestra; anterior cervical verte-

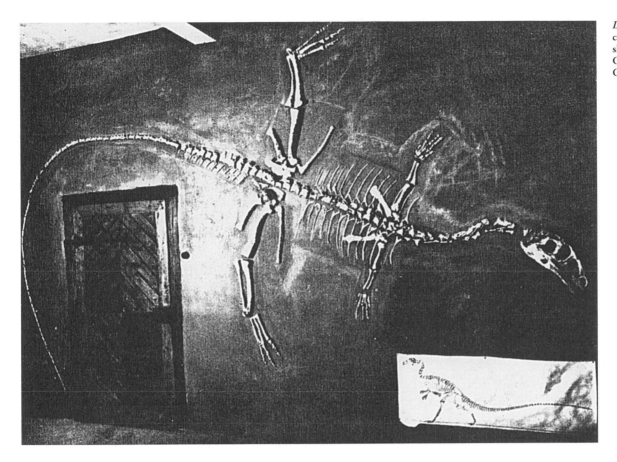

Liliensternus liliensterni,
composite reconstructed
skeleton mounted at Bedheim
Castle, Hildburghausen,
Germany.

brae elongated with two lateral buttresses from base of diapophysis; four unfused sacral vertebrae; sacral ribs fused together to form an arch; ilium with ischial peduncle posteroventrally directed; pubis with one obturator foramen (Cuny and Galton 1993).

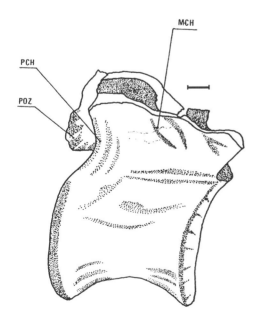

Liliensternus airelensis, holotype first caudal vertebra, right lateral view. Scale = 1 cm. (After Cuny and Galton 1993.)

Diagnosis of *P. airelensis*: First sacral vertebra with diapophysis located more anteriorly than in *L. liliensterni*, and with deep medial chonos; ilium with vertical ridge above acetabular crest; length of caudal vertebrae constant along tail (Cuny and Galton 1993).

Comments: The genus *Liliensternus* was named, but not described, by Welles (1984) in his paper on the osteology of *Dilophosaurus*.

Liliensternus was founded upon material originally described by Huene (1934) as the third species of *Halticosaurus*, which Huene had named *H. liliensterni*. The species was based upon two incomplete skeletons collected from the Knollenmergel, Upper Keuper, near Halberstadt, Thuringia, Germany. A composite of the two skeletons, much restored in plaster, was once displayed mounted on a wall in the Heimatmuseum at Bedheim Castle, in Hildburghausen, Germany. The exhibit has since been dismantled, the bones now housed in the Humboldt Museum für Naturkunde in [formerly East] Berlin.

Huene originally diagnosed this species as follows: Skull large, with triangular antorbital opening; nine elongate cervical and 15 dorsal vertebrae; tail very long; forelimbs very short; manus with five digits, I and V reduced; femur slightly longer than tibia; pedal digits II-IV very long.

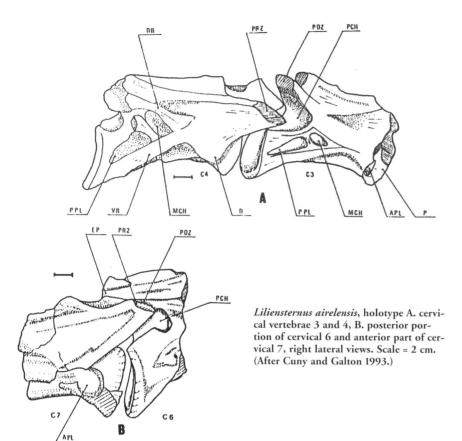

Liliensternus airelensis, holotype A. cervical vertebrae 3 and 4, B. posterior portion of cervical 6 and anterior part of cervical 7, right lateral views. Scale = 2 cm. (After Cuny and Galton 1993.)

Liliensternus airelensis, holotype pelvic girdle. Scale = 5 cm. (After Cuny and Galton 1993.)

Welles noted that the two skeletons belonging to this species were found in a lower horizon than the other two species of *Halticosaurus*, and exhibited osteological differences that warranted their own generic status. The larger of these specimens (HMN R1291) was designated as the type by Welles, who implied that a detailed description of *Liliensternus liliensterni* might be published at some later date.

In a review of the Ceratosauria, Rowe and Gauthier (1990) noted that the two skeletons of *L. liliensterni* are both from subadult gracile individuals, and that these specimens do not appear to share any derived characters that allow them to be diagnosed as a monophyletic taxon or beyond Ceratosauria.

A second species, *L. airelensis*, was referred to *Liliensternus* by Cuny and Galton (1993), based upon

Liliensternus airelensis, holotype sacrum. Scale = 5 cm. (After Cuny and Galton 1993.)

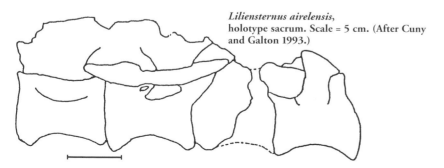

a tooth, vertebrae (five cervicals, two dorsals, four sacrals, and several caudals), and parts of the pelvic girdle, recovered from the Airel quarry, located southeast of the Cotentin peninsula, in the Carentan Basin of Normany, France. (According to Cuny and Galton, the rocks of this quarry, based on a palynological study of the sediments, seem to be of Early Hettangian age, at the Triassic-Jurassic boundary). This specimen had originally been referred to *Halticosaurus* sp. by Larsonneur and Lapparent (1966), who believed that it was close to "*Halticosaurus*" *liliensterni*.

Note: Parrish and Carpenter (1986) reported fragmentary remains of a large theropod closely related to *L. liliensterni* [=*H. liliensterni* of their usage] from the Dockum Formation of Revuelto Creek, New Mexico, and also a fragmentary scapula of a possibly related form from the Chinle Formation, lower unit of the Petrified Forest Member at Petrified Forest National Park (see also Parrish 1989).

Key references: Cuny and Galton (1993); Huene (1934); Larsonneur and Lapparent (1966); Rowe and Gauthier (1990); Welles (1984).

LIMNOSAURUS Nopcsa 1899—(Preoccupied, Marsh 1872; see *Telmatosaurus*.)
Name derivation: Greek *limne* = "lake" + Greek *sauros* = "lizard."
Type species: *L. transsylvanicus* Nopcsa 1899.

LISBOASAURUS Seiffert 1973
?Dinosauria: ?Saurischia: ?Theropoda: ?Tetanurae: ?Avetheropoda: ?Coelurosauria: ?Maniraptora.
Name derivation: Portuguese *Lisboa* = "Lisbon" [capital city of Portugal] + Greek *sauros* = "lizard."
Type species: *L. estesi* Seiffert 1973.
Other species: ?*L. microcostatus* Seiffert 1973 [*nomen dubium*].
Occurrence: Guimatora, Portugal.
Age: Late Jurassic (Oxfordian).
Known material: Maxillae, miscellaneous cranial and postcranial remains including vertebrae.
Holotype: FUB Gui.37, nearly complete right maxilla with one tooth.

Diagnosis of genus (as for type species): Small relative of troodontids and *Archaeopteryx*; maxilla either a large pit or diastema in anterior tooth-row; antorbital fossa, but with accessory antorbital fenestra either posteriorly located or absent; slender dorsal process excluded from narial margin by tall ascending process of premaxilla; teeth with mediolaterally compressed triangular crowns with lingual groove, expanded roots wider than crowns, "waist" between crown and root, anterior and posterior carinae but no serrations (Milner and Evans 1991).

Comments: A problematic genus that has recently come into question regarding its present dinosaurian status, *Lisboasaurus* was originally described by Seiffert (1973) as a new atypical anguimorph lizard related to aigialosaurs or mosasaurs. The monotypic *L. estesi* was founded upon an almost complete maxilla (FUB Gui.37) collected from the Upper Jurassic (no younger than Oxfordian; Mohr and Schmidt 1988, Erve and Mohr 1988, Mohr 1989; determination based on palynostratigraphical studies in the Iberian Peninsula) of the lignite coal mine of Guimarota, near the town of Leiria, Portugal.

Seiffert referred to the type species additional material from the same locality, including a larger left maxilla (FUB collection) several isolated teeth (FUB Gui.L.136), and two small blocks containing very poorly-preserved associated cranial and postcranial fossils (FUB Gui.L.33 and L.177), the material in these blocks interpreted by Seiffert as having fused frontals and procoelous vertebrae. At the same time, Seiffert also named and described a second species *L. microcostatus*, based on a crushed dentary (FUB Gui.34) from the same locality.

Estes (1983), in reassessing *Lisboasaurus* and other taxa named by Seiffert based upon remains collected from the Guimarota mine, commented that the holotype of *L. estesi* exhibits some similarities to the maxillae of saurischian dinosaurs.

Evans later reexamined the holotypes and all referred material in the Freie Universität, Berlin (FUB) collections belonging to both species of *Lisboasaurus*, observing the presence of thecodont teeth and an antorbital fossa, which led Evans to interpret this genus not as lacertilian but rather as a small archosaur. Furthermore, various features of the teeth (*e.g.*, labio-lingually compressed crowns with unserrated carinae, "waisting" between root and crown, and expanded roots) suggested that *Lisboasaurus* belongs within the troodontid dinosaur-bird clade, perhaps within Aviale (=*Archaeopteryx* and all later birds) as defined by Gauthier (1986). There was nothing about specimens FUB Gui.L.33 and L.177 to link them unequivocally to the holotype maxilla or the referred teeth (Milner and Evans 1991).

Comparing the holotype and accepted referred specimens of *L. estesi* with corresponding remains of other kinds of archosaurs (*i.e.*, pterosaurs, crocodylomorphs, and avialans), Milner and Evans saw them as resembling most closely those of maniraptoran theropods, the maxilla of *Lisboasaurus* most similar in shape to that of *Compsognathus* and the bird *Archaeopteryx*. In *Lisboasaurus*, the anterior maxillary teeth have a compressed asymmetrical cross-section with rounded labial and flattened lingual surfaces and carinae on the lingual corners, a character of the pre-

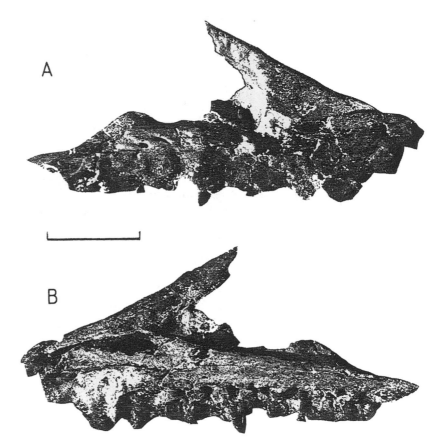

A

B

Lisboasaurus estesi, FUB Gui.37, holotype right maxilla, in A. labial and B. lingual views. Scale = 5 mm. (After Milner and Evans 1991.)

maxillary teeth in theropods (see Currie 1987*a*) which may also be a character of some maxillary teeth. Compressed asymmetrical crowns of this type are also known in *Archaeopteryx* (Howgate 1984).

According to Milner and Evans, *L. estesi* shares one derived character (teeth with constriction between crown and root) with troodontids and *Archaeopteryx*; one derived character (teeth completely unserrated) with *Archaeopteryx*, but not troodontids; one derived character (maxillary teeth with depression at base of ligual side of crown, extending as groove towards but not reaching crown tip) with troodontids, but not *Archaeopteryx*; and three derived characters (maxilla separated from naris by premaxillary and nasal processes; teeth with root wider than crown; large pocket or diastema near anterior end of maxilla suggesting presence of a lower caniniform tooth) with post–*Archeopteryx* birds, but neither troodontids nor *Archaeopteryx*.

Although Milner and Evans considered *L. estesi* to be a maniraptoran theropod, they observed that the maxilla and teeth exhibit characters that appear convergently in other archosaurs, especially crocodilians (see below).

Milner and Evans pointed out that *L. mitrocostatus* was based upon crushed material too limited for adequate comparisons with other taxa and should be regarded as a *nomen dubium*; suggested that this species be restricted to the holotype dentary; agreed with Estes that there is no certainty that this species is conspecific with *L. estesi*; and concluded that this species does not represent a lizard.

More recently, after the collection of the almost complete (as yet unnamed and undescribed) skeleton (LH-7991) of a small crocodylomorph from the Barremian of the Las Hoyas fossil site, in Cuenca province, Spain, the systematic position of *Lisboasaurus* has been questioned again by Buscalioni, Ortega, Pérez-Moreno and Evans (1996). Buscalioni *et al.* observed that this specimen has a maxillary construction and tooth morphology very similar to that of *L. estesi*, these similarities prompting them to reconsider the phylogenetic relationships of *L. estesi*. Utilizing the original description and figures pertaining to this species, Buscalioni *et al.* reinterpreted its suite of maxillary and tooth characters. Their reinterpretation was "founded on the identification of a larger number of attributes, and a phylogenetic analysis including a broad range of archosaurian taxa" (in a group including the birds *Archaeopteryx* and *Herperornis*, Troodontidae, Dromaeosauridae, Ornithomimosauria, the crocodylomorphs *Sphenosuchus*, *Notosuchus*, *Protosuchus*, and the Las Hoyas crocodylomorph), which resulted in an alternative phylogenetic hypothesis for the genus.

Buscalioni *et al.* placed *L. estesi* within Crocodylomorpha as the sister-taxon on the Las Hoyas crocodylomorph, based on various synapomorphies related to tooth morphology, tooth implantation, and maxillary construction. They further concluded that the characters shared by *Lisbosaurus* and Maniraptora may be convergences (homoplasies). Buscalioni interpreted *L. estesi* as an archosaur, but proposed that this species might be regarded as a member of Crocodyliformes rather than Maniraptora.

The holotype of *L. mitrocostatus* was found by Buscalioni *et al.* to be too fragmentary and problematical for association with *L. estesi*.

Key references: Buscalioni, Ortega, Pérez-Moreno and Evans (1996); Estes (1983); Milner and Evans (1991); Seiffert (1973).

LONCOSAURUS Ameghino 1899 [*nomen dubium*] — (=?*Genyodectes*)
Saurischia: Theropoda: ?Coelurosauria *incertae sedis*.
Name derivation: Spanish *loncha* = "slab" or "slice" + Greek *sauros* = "lizard."
Type species: *L. argentinus* Ameghino 1899 [*nomen dubium*].
Other species: [None.]

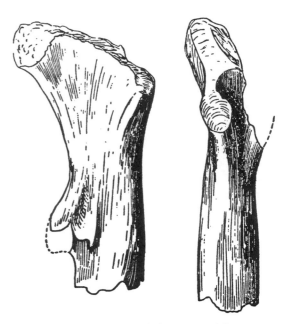

Loncosaurus argentinus, MLP, holotype partial femur, posterior lateral views. (After Huene 1929.)

Occurrence: Cardiel Formation, Provincia de Santa Cruz, Argentina.
Age: Late Cretaceous (Late Senonian).
Known material/holotype: MLP collection, incomplete femur, teeth.
Diagnosis of genus: [None published.]
Comments: The genus *Loncosaurus* was founded upon a femur and teeth (MLP collection) discovered in the Cardiel Formation of Rio Sehuen, Santa Cruz, Argentina.

Ameghino (1899) briefly described the material as follows: Femur about 50 centimeters (over 19 inches) in length; teeth 28-35 millimeters long.

Huene (1929) classified the femur as "coelurosaurian." Molnar (1980c) noted that the femur was incorrectly associated with the teeth and might pertain to an hypsilophodont or turtle. In their review of iguanodontids and related ornithopods, Norman and Weishampel (1990) regarded *L. argentinus*, sometimes classified as an Iguanodontian, as a *nomen dubium*.

Key references: Ameghino (1889); Huene (1929); Molnar (1980c); Norman and Weishampel (1990).

LONGOSAURUS Welles 1984 — (See *Coelophysis*.)
Name derivation: "[Robert A.] Long" + Greek *sauros* = "lizard."
Type species: *L. longicollis* Welles 1984.

LOPHORHOTHON Langston 1960
Ornithischia: Genasauria: Cerapoda: Ornithopoda: Iguanodontia: Hadrosauridae: Hadrosaurinae.

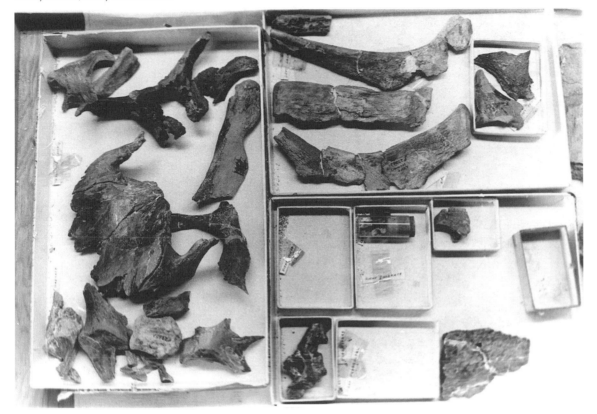

Lophorhothon atopus, FMNH P27383, holotype disarticulated skull, ischia, other elements (juvenile).

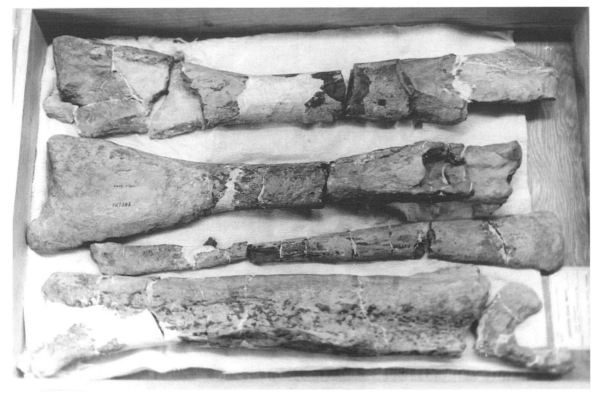

Lophorhothon atopus, FMNH P27383, holotype right tibia, left tibia, right fibula (juvenile).

Lophorhothon

Lophorhothon atopus, FMNH P27383, holotype metatarsals, vertebrae, miscellaneous elements (juvenile).

Name derivation: Greek *lophos* = "crested" + Greek *rhothon* = "nose."
Type species: *L. atopus* Langston 1960.
Other species: [None.]
Occurrence: Mooreville Chalk, Alabama, Black Creek Formation, North Carolina, United States.

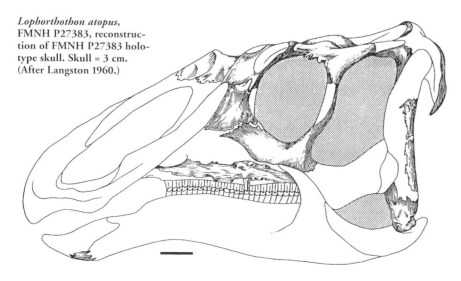

Lophorthothon atopus, FMNH P27383, reconstruction of FMNH P27383 holotype skull. Skull = 3 cm. (After Langston 1960.)

Age: Late Cretaceous (Campanian).

Known material/holotype: FM P27383, partly articulated skeleton, including much of disarticulated skull, incomplete predentary, 44 vertebrae of all kinds, many incomplete ribs and chevrons, parts of both hands including terminal phalanges, most of one ischium and part of the other, femur, almost complete lower legs and feet, several large unidentified fragments, representing very young individual.

Diagnosis of genus (as for type species): Solid-crested hadrosaurine with elevated cranium, short snout, broad orbits, wide temporal openings; nasals with pyramidal crest similar to that in *Prosaurolophus*, though situated well anterior to orbits; immature individuals with large fronto-nasal fontanel; teeth with heavily scalloped enamel surfaces and denticulate crown margins (Langston 1960).

Comments: The genus *Lophorhothon* was established upon an incomplete articulated skeleton (FM P27383) collected by Rainer Zangerl, William Turnbull, and C. M. Barber in 1946, from the Mooreville Chalk member of the Selma Formation [now Mooreville Chalk], southeast of Marion Junction and west of Selma, Dallas County, Alabama (Langston 1960).

(The formerly named Selma Formation was dated by Langston to be among the oldest, although not the oldest, Upper Cretaceous North American formations. The complete assemblage includes a theropod, nodosaurid, and also marine turtles, mosasaurs, plesiosaurs, and fishes, implying that the dinosaur remains were transported before burial to marine deposits.)

According to Langston, the *Lophorhothon* individual represented by the holotype was almost 4.5 meters (about 15 feet) long. The genus seems to be geologically antecedent to *Kritosaurus* and *Prosaurolophus*, but phylogenetically more closely (though not necessarily ancestrally) allied to the latter.

Langston noted that the holotype of *L. atopus*, as preserved, revealed a number of details regarding hadrosaur cranial anatomy that had not been previously observed, and which he believed could probably be applied to hadrosaurids in general: 1. Large supraoccipital of normal sauropsid structure and relationships, excluded by medially directed processes of exoccipitals from the dorsal margin of the foramen magnum; 2. paroccipital process composed mainly of exoccipital, opisthotic making only a minor contribution anteriorly; 3. tiny post-temporal foramen; 4. architecture of occipital face of cranium easily derived from camptosaur pattern; 5. inner ear with a vertically elongated labyrinth, with large utriculus and small sacculus, moderately developed common crus, and unusually large appendicular incipiently twisted lagena, semicircular canals of unusual proportions (other details of inner ear also observed); 6. inner ear differing from that in other dinosaurs mainly in construction of semicircular canals; 7. fenestra ovalis much smaller than had usually been depicted, lower margin slow to ossify; and 8. vagus and accessory nerves contained within exoccipital, glossopharyngeal nerve (contrary to usual interpretations) passing independently below fenestra ovalis through or just under lagenar recess.

However, in a detailed study of the cranial morphology of North American hadrosaurids, Ostrom (1961) observed (*contra* Langston) that in the plesiotype (AMNH 5338) of *Corythosaurus casuarius* and a specimen (AMNH 5461) of "*Procheneosaurus erectofrons*" [=*C. casuarius*], the supraoccipital is actually rather small, subtriangular in shape, and situated with its maximum width ventrally, tapering suddenly upward to the apex; paroccipital process seemingly consists mostly of the opisthotic (as in most reptilian groups), the exoccipital probably contributing to the medial portions of this process; vagus and glossopharyngeal nerves seem to have passed through a

common canal (in the most perfectly preserved crania, the canal for the typically small glossopharyngeal nerve being unusually large).

Key references: Langston (1960); Ostrom (1961).

LORICOSAURUS Huene 1929—
(=?*Neuquénsaurus*, ?*Saltasaurus*)
Saurischia: Sauropodomorpha: Sauropoda: Titanosauria: Titanosauridae.
Name derivation: Latin *lorica* = "corselet" + Greek *sauros* = "lizard."
Type species: *L. scutatus* Huene 1929.
Other species: [None.]
Occurrence: Allen or Rio Colorado Formation, Provincia de Rio Negro, Argentina.
Age: Late Cretaceous (Late Senonian).
Known material/holotype: MLP collection, 26 dermal plates and small osteoderms.

Diagnosis of genus: [None published.]

Comments: The genus *Loricosaurus* was established upon dermal armor (MLP collection) collected from the Allen or Rio Colorado Formation of Cinco Saltos, Rio Negro, Argentina.

Believing these ossification to be those of an armored dinosaur, Huene (1929) referred them to the Nodosauridae. Coombs (1978*a*) regarded *Loricosaurus* as Ankylosauria *incertae sedis*.

Bonaparte and Powell (1980) described similar ossifications of the genus *Saltasaurus*, an armored sauropod belonging to the Titanosauridae. Bonaparte and Powell pointed out that the *L. scutatus* material was found in the same locality that yielded the most complete remains of "*Titanosaurus australis*" [=*Neuquénsaurus* or *Saltasaurus*], implying that these plates could belong to that species.

Key references: Bonaparte and Powell (1980); Huene (1929).

LUCIANOSAURUS Hunt and Lucas 1994
Ornithischia *incertae sedis*
Name derivation: "Luciano [Mesa]" + Greek *sauros* = "lizard."
Type species: *L. wildi* Hunt and Lucas 1994.
Other species: [None.]
Occurrence: Bull Canyon Formation, New Mexico, United States.
Age: Late Triassic (?Middle Norian).
Known material: dentary/maxillary teeth.
Holotype: NMMNH P-18194, dentary/maxillary tooth.

Diagnosis of genus (as for type species): Ornithischian distinguished by dentary/maxillary teeth without cingula, and with asymmetrical basal crowns and (in some teeth) one accessory cusp (Hunt and Lucas 1994).

Lucianosaurus wildi, NMMNH P-18194, holotype tooth, buccal view. Scale = 1 mm. (After Hunt and Lucas 1994.)

Comments: The genus *Lucianosaurus* was erected upon a dentary/maxillary tooth (NMMNH P-18194) discovered in the upper portion of the Bull Canyon Formation (Late Triassic), in Guadaloupe County, near Luciano Mesa, New Mexico. Referred to type species *L. wildi* was another dentary/maxillary tooth (NMMNH P-18195) found at the same locality; although this tooth lacks an accessory cusp, it shares with the holotype the asymmetrical basal crown, a feature not observed in any other known ornithischian teeth (Hunt and Lucas 1994).

Key reference: Hunt and Lucas (1994).

LUFENGOSAURUS Yang [Young] 1941—
(=?*Fulengia*, ?*Tawasaurus*)

Saurischia: Sauropodomorpha: Prosauropoda: Melanorosauridae.

Name derivation: "Lufeng [Series]" + Greek *sauros* = "lizard."

Type species: *L. hueni* Yang [Young] 1941.

Other species: [None.]

Occurrence: Upper Lower Lufeng Series, Yunnan, People's Republic of China.

Age: Early Jurassic (Hettangian-Pliensbachian).

Known material: Over 30 skeletons, fragmentary to complete, juvenile to adult.

Holotype: LVP GSC V15, skeleton with incomplete skull, vertebrae, ribs, pectoral and pelvic girdles, all four limbs.

Diagnosis of genus (as for type species): Derived characters of skull include very large prefrontals and an expanded top to dorsal process of maxilla (Galton 1990*a*).

Comments: The genus *Lufengosaurus* was established upon an almost complete skeleton (LVP GSC V15) collected from the Upper Lower Lufeng Series, Purplish Beds, in Lufeng, Yunnan, China. The specimen represented the most complete skeleton yet collected from the Lufeng Series (missing parts includ-

Lufengosaurus huenei, skeleton, temporarily displayed in the "Dinosaurs of China" exhibit, at the National Museum of Wales.

Photo by the author.

ing the anterior part of the skull and lower jaws, parts of the last two cervical vertebrae, dorsal vertebrae and their ribs, and "a few other bones" (Yang [formerly Young] 1941a).

As noted by Sun and Cui (1986), the Lower Lufeng Formation was originally dated as "Rhaetic" [obsolete term] (Late Triassic) by Bien (1940) and Yang (1940). As there were no radiometric records of these sediments, Bien and Yang dated them based on vertebrate fossils. However, the collection of various invertebrate fossils during the "Yunnan Beds Expedition" (1966–71), led by the Paleontological Institute of Nanking, indicate these sediments are a different age. In a book published by that institution in 1975, the Lower Lufeng Formation was redated as Lower Jurassic (see also Olsen and Galton 1977, 1984).

Originally, Yang (1941b) diagnosed the monotypic *L. hueni* as follows: Prosauropod closely related to *Plateosaurus*; skull small, about 3.5 times the length of anterior caudal vertebrae; narial opening triangular; antorbital fenestra short, high, very small; orbit large, circular; upper temporal opening upwardly directed; teeth weakly compressed, of very generalized form, serrated; neck very long; cervical and dorsal vertebrae strongly constructed; tail massive; ?10 cervical, ?14 dorsal, 3 sacral, and 45 caudal vertebrae; sternum entirely ossified; pubis weakly constructed; tibia comparatively short; metatarsal III rather long; hindlimb rather short; first claws of both manus and pes especially strong.

Subsequently, Yang (1942b) described a second species, *L. magnus* [=*L. hueni*], based on remains from Ta-ch'ung, China. Later, Yang (1947) designated three posterior cervical vertebrae, six anterior dorsals, a posterior dorsal, three sacrals, eight anterior caudals with chevrons, almost complete pectoral and pelvic girdles, forelimbs, and hind limbs as the holotype

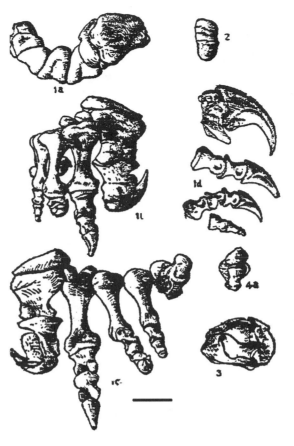

Lufengosaurus huenei, GSC V15 LVP, holotype right manus in 1a. proximal, 1b. dorsal, and 1c. ventral views, 2. proximal view of carpal III, 3. distal view of metacarpal I, 4. distal view of metacarpal V with first phalanx. Scale = 4 cm. (After Yang [Young] 1941.)

(IVPPASV 82) of this species, and the original type specimen, consisting of a pelvis, second and third sacral vertebrae, and first caudal, the co-type. Yang (1942b) regarded *L. magnus* as being about one-third larger and relatively more massive than *L. huenei*, with forelimbs comparatively shorter than hindlimbs.

Another prosauropod species originally referred to "*Gyposaurus*" [=*Massospondylus*], named *G. sinensis* Yang 1941, was based on parts of the upper and

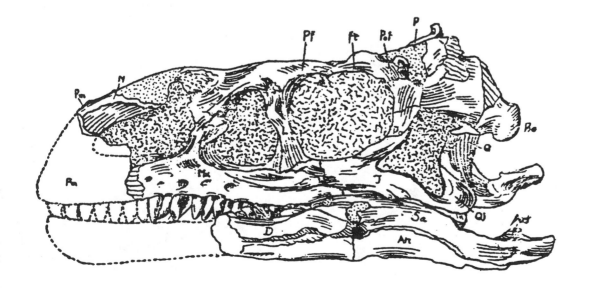

Lufengosaurus huenei, GSC V15 LVP, holotype skull. (After Yang [Young] 1941.)

Photo by M. Tanimoto.

Lufengosaurus hueni, SAFM 990, holotype partial skeleton (juvenile) of *Gyposaurus sinensis*, on exhibit at the Geological Museum of China.

lower ?left jaw with eight well-preserved teeth of both upper and lower rows (LVP GSC V24), right upper jaw fragment with teeth (V25), series of small vertebrae, pectoral girdle, and parts of the anterior and posterior limbs (V26), and most of a complete individual (V27) somewhat larger than specimen V26, recovered from the Upper Triassic badlands of Shawan, in Yunnan. Yang (1941b) noted that, according to the number of limbs and the relative size of the bones, all of these remains seemed to represent two individuals, V26 and V27, the latter including jaws with teeth catalogued as V24 and V25. Yang (1948b) also reported 11 more specimens which he referred to *G. sinensis*, including a well-preserved skeleton (LVP GSC V43), this taxon the most common of the Lufeng fossil vertebrate fauna.

Later, Galton (1976) identified the *G. sinensis* remains as representing a juvenile *L. huenei*. Cooper (1981) synonymized *Lufengosaurus* with *Massospondylus*, but Galton (1985a), in his study of dietary habits of prosauropods, argued that *Lufengosaurus* seems to represent a valid genus.

Note: Dong, Zhou and Zhang (1983) reported an indeterminate prosauropod claw from left pedal digit II, recovered from the Zhenzhunchong Formation (Lower Jurassic), at Huanshiban, Weiyun County, Sichuan Basin, Sichuan province, resembling in size and appearance that of *Lufengosaurus*.

Key references: Cooper (1981); Galton (1976, 1985a; 1990a); Yang [Young] (1941b; 1942b, 1947, 1948b).

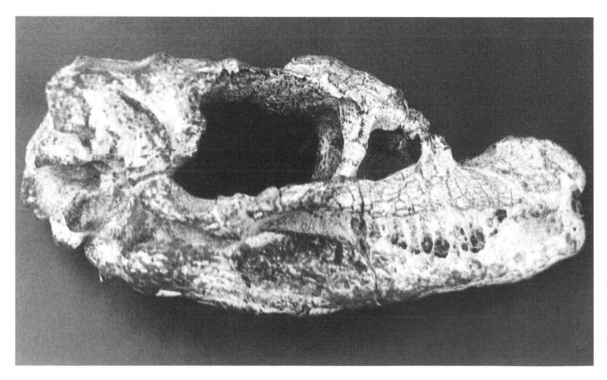

Lufengosaurus hueni, skull originally referred to *L. sinensis*. (After Dong 1987).

LUKOUSAURUS Yang [Young] 1948

Saurischia: Theropoda *incertae sedis.*

Name derivation: "Lukou [bridge]" + Greek *sauros* = "lizard."

Type species: *L. yini* Yang [Young] 1948.

Other species: [None.]

Occurrence: Lower Lufeng Series, Yunnan, People's Republic of China.

Age: Late Triassic (?Pliensbachian).

Known material: ?Three skulls, possibly isolated tooth.

Holotype: IVP AS V23, anterior part of skull with lower jaws.

Diagnosis of genus (as for type species): Skull rather small; nasal opening small, anteriorly located; preorbital opening high, triangular; orbits well-rounded; muzzle apparently slender; lower jaw slender, with straight lower margin; five premaxillary and approximately ten maxillary teeth; all teeth sharply compressed, directed backwards; fine, short serrations on posterior side of each tooth (Yang [Young] 1948*a*).

Comments: The genus *Lukousaurus* was founded on an incomplete skull (IVP AS V23) discovered in the Upper Triassic Dark Red Beds, Lower Lufeng Series, at Huangchiatien, Lufeng, Yunnan, China. Possibly referable to the type species is an isolated tooth (V263) from the same locality (Yang [formerly known in English-language publications as Young] 1948*a*).

As measured by Yang, the preserved part of the skull is 68 millimeters long on the lower left side, 77 millimeters on the upper border, 25 millimeters high anterior of the preorbital opening, and 31 millimeters anterior of the lacrimal.

Yang also described the proximal end of a right humerus (V271) with maximum breadth of 77 millimeters, collected from the Dark Purplish Beds at Ta-ch'ung, and tentatively referred by him to ?*L. yini.*

Lukousaurus was regarded by Yang as probably belonging to the "Coelurosauria," though the type specimen is larger than such "coelurosaurian" genera as *Procompsognathus* and *Podokesaurus*, and is characterized by the shortness of the premaxilla and unusual features of the nasal and maxilla. Paul (1988*c*), in his book *Predatory Dinosaurs of the World*, suggested that *Lukousaurus* may be nondinosaurian, the snout resembling that of a crocodilian or "thecodont," adding that the type material is too meager to make a positive identification. In a reassessment of problematic "coelurosaurs," Norman (1990) stated that the material pertaining to *L. yini* is theropod-like and of interest, representing an animal living in an important geographic province at the end of the Triassic or beginning of the Jurassic, but which should be retained as only a provisionally valid taxon.

Key references: Norman (1990); Paul (1988*c*); Yang [Young] (1948*a*).

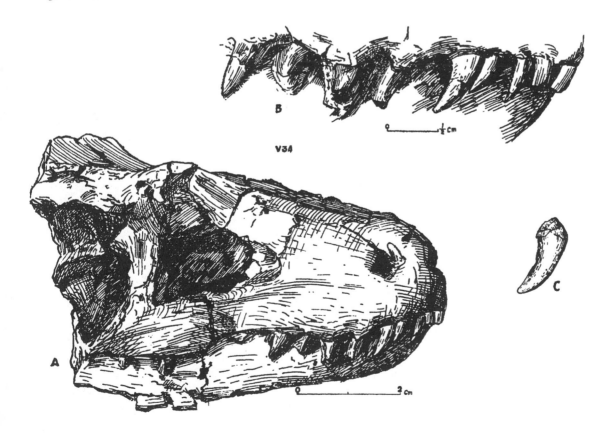

Lukousaurus yini, IVP AS V23, holotype A. skull, B. detail of right tooth row, C. isolated tooth. (After Yang [Young] 1948.)

**Lusitanosaurus liasicus,
MGSP holotype left maxilla.
(After Lapparent and
Zbyszewski 1957.)**

LUSITANOSAURUS Lapparent and Zbyszewski
1957 [*nomen dubium*]

Ornithischia: Genasauria: Tyreophora *incertae
sedis.*

Name derivation: "Lusitanian [Portuguese]" +
Greek *sauros* = "lizard."

Type species: *L. liasicus* Lapparent and Zbyszewski
1957 [*nomen dubium*].

Other species: [None.]

Occurrence: [Unnamed formation], Província do
Beira Litoral, Portugal.

Age: Early Jurassic (?Sinemurian).

Known material/holotype: MGSP collection,
fragmentary left maxilla.

Diagnosis of genus: [None published.]

Comments: The genus *Lusitanosaurus* was established upon a maxilla (MGSP collection) recovered
from the Lias (?Sinemurian) of São Pedro de Muel,
Portugal (Lapparent and Zbyszewski 1957).

Lapparent and Zbyszewski (1957) described the
maxilla as follows: About 10.5 centimeters (over 4
inches) long, 4.5 centimeters (1.75 inches) high; very
similar to the maxilla of *Scelidosaurus*, differing
mostly in dentition (eight teeth in specimen, differing
notably from *Scelidosaurus* by greater height and
points lacking scalloped margins).

In their review of basal thyreophorans, Coombs,
Weishampel and Witmer (1990) regarded this taxon
as a *nomen dubium*.

Key references: Coombs, Weishampel and Witmer (1990); Lapparent and Zbyszewski (1957).

LYCORHINUS Haughton 1924

Ornithischia: Genasauria: Cerapoda: Ornithopoda:
Heterodontosauridae.

Name derivation: Greek *lykos* = "wolf" + Greek
rhinos = "nose."

Type species: *L. angustidens* Haughton 1924.

Other species: [None.]

Occurrence: Upper Elliot Formation, Cape
Province, South Africa.

Age: Early Jurassic (Hettangian–?Sinemurian).

Known material/holotype: SAM 3606, left ramus
of left dentary with teeth.

**Lycorhinus angustidens, SAM
3606, holotype partial left
dentary with teeth. Length as
preserved = 46 mm. (After
Haughton 1924.)**

Diagnosis of genus (as for type species): Moderately advanced heterodontosaurid; lower caniniform serrated along front and back edge; lower cheek
teeth with relatively symmetrical crowns, bases with
dorsoventrally deep swelling instead of distinct cingulum; crowns with convex dorsoventral profile on
each side; middle vertical ridge on external face in or
slightly anterior to center of crown; anterior and posterior ridges approximately of equal prominence
(Hopson 1975*b*).

Comments: The genus *Lycorhinus* was founded
upon an isolated portion of a lower jaw (SAM 3606)
collected from the upper Elliot Formation (Late
Jurassic [Hettangian-Pliensbachian]; see Olsen and
Galton 1984) [formerly Stormberg Series (Red
Beds)], at Mount Fletcher, Paballong, Cape Province, South Africa. Haughton originally (1924)
believed that this specimen belonged to a cynodont.
(The holotype is now represented only by a chunk
of mudstone containing an impression of the jaw,
with a caniniform-tooth crown exposed in medial
view.)

Haughton first diagnosed the monotypic *L.
angustidens* as follows: Jaw distinguished by anteriorly
located large, pointed stabbing canine tooth; tooth
oval in cross-section, longer diameter along jaw; anterior border ridged and serrated, posterior border
ridged but not serrated; crown of canine 19.5 millimeters high, 7 millimeters long at base; jaw (as preserved) 46 millimeters long.

The type specimen was later recognized by
Crompton and Charig (1962) as belonging to an
ornithischian dinosaur.

Based upon studies of the holotype of *L.
angustidens*, and also specimens of the heterodontosaurids *Abrictosaurus consors* (UCL B54), *Heterodontosaurus tucki* (SAM K1332), *Lanasaurus scalpridens* (BPI 4244), and *Fabrosaurus australis*,
Thulborn (1978) suggested that ornithopods of the
African Red Beds responded to changing seasons by
resorting to aestivation, heterodontosaurids replacing their entire dentitions during the dry season
when the lush vegetation upon which they fed was
scarce.

Thulborn's idea was challenged by Hopson
(1980*a*), who, from studies of *Lycorhinus, Lanasaurus*,
and *Heterodontosaurus*, concluded that normal tooth
replacement was occurring during dry seasons. Hopson (1980*a*) demonstrated that teeth in heterodontosaurids were not replaced as a unit at widely spaced
time intervals, but that replacement occurred continuously in multiple waves, and that tooth replacement slowed down and eventually ceased in older
individuals. Furthermore, heterodontosaurids chewed
in typical reptile fashion, open-and-close and lateral
to medial, rather than forwards and backwards as
Thulborn had suggested. According to Hopson
(1980*a*), Thulborn based his conclusions about fore-
aft jaw movements upon older, heavily worn dentitions only.

Note: Hopson (1975*b*) designated *L. consors*
Thulborn 1974 to be the type species of a new genus,
Abrictosaurus.

Key references: Haughton (1924); Hopson
(1975*b*, 1980*a*); Thulborn (1978).

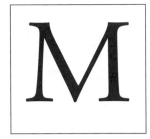

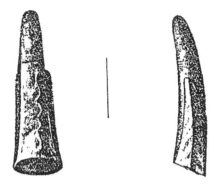

Macrodontophion, holotype tooth. Scale = 3 cm. (After Zborzewski 1834.)

MACRODONTOPHION   Zborzewski 1834
[*nomen dubium*]

?Dinosauria *incertae sedis.*

Name derivation: Greek *makros* = "long" + Greek *odous* = "tooth" + Greek *ophion* = "snake."

Type species: [No specific name designated.]

Other species: [None.]

Occurrence: Volhynia-Podolia, Ukraine.

Age: Late Jurassic or Cretaceous.

Known material/holotype: ?Tooth.

   Diagnosis of genus: [None published.]

   Comments: The genus *Macrodontophion*, included herein very provisionally, was founded upon a single ?tooth from the Volhynia-Podolia region of the [former] Ukrainian Soviet Socialist Republic.

   Zborzewski (1834) described the specimen as follows: Apparently *Megalosaurus* type tooth, large, slender, slightly recurved, almost as thick at apex as at base, rather blunt (or worn).

   Molnar (1990), in reviewing problematic "carnosaurs," observed that the tooth, unlike most theropod teeth, seems to taper only slightly or not at all from neck to tip; the specimen is indeterminate and cannot even be assigned with certainty to the Dinosauria. The rather odd "side pieces" shown in Zborweski's original figures of the specimen, as well as the abrupt flaring just at the base, are not known in archosaurian teeth, but are reminiscent of some shells (R. E. Molnar, personal communication 1991).

   The opinion of some paleontologists is that the specimen is nondinosaurian (including H. D. Sues, personal communication 1988).

   Key references: Molnar (1990); Zborzewski (1834).

MACROPHALANGIA   Sternberg 1932—(See *Chirostenotes*.)

Name derivation: Greek *makros* = "long" + [plural of] Greek *phalanx* [="toe bone"].

Type species: *M. canadensis* Sternberg 1932.

MACRUROSAURUS   Seeley 1869 [*nomen dubium*]

Saurischia: Sauropodomorpha: Sauropoda: *incertae sedis.*

Name derivation: Greek *makros* = "long" + Greek *ouros* = "tail" + Greek *sauros* = "lizard."

Type species: *M. semnus* Seeley 1869.

Other species: [None.]

Occurrence: Cambridge Greensand, Cambridgeshire, Wealden, Isle of Wight, England.

Age: Early to Late Cretaceous (Valanginian–Late Albian).

Known material: Caudal vertebrae.

Lectotype: SMC B55630, caudal centrum.

   Diagnosis of genus: [None published.]

   Comments: As chronicled by Le Loeuff (1993) in a review of European titanosaurids, the type species *Macrurosaurus semnus* was described by Seeley (1869) based upon 23 articulated caudal vertebrae (SMC B55630-B55652) collected from one of the deeper phosphate washings of the Upper Cambridge Greensand of Coldham Common, Barnwell, England (Upper Albian), and which were purchased for the Sedgwick Museum in Cambridge in 1868 from M. W. Farren. A second articulated series of smaller, more distal vertebrae (SMC B55653-B55654) were collected at Barton and obtained during the 1860s from "Rev. W." by Stokes Shaw. Although both series were found "a few miles" away from one another, Seeley (1876) claimed that they constituted the syntype specimen and may have belonged to the same individual. Seeley (1869) believed that these two vertebral series formed a continuous series of 40 vertebrae, although this assumption has never been demonstrated.

   Originally, Seeley diagnosed *Macrurosaurus* as follows: Caudal vertebrae beginning as procoelous, gradually changing until articulations of centra become almost flat, then biconcave, finally irregular toward end of tail; caudal vertebrae without chevrons;

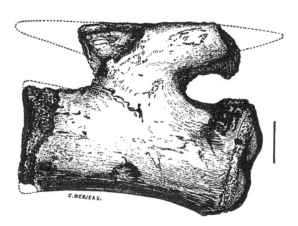

C.BERJEAU.

Macrurosaurus semnus, SM collection, holotype caudal vertebra, lateral view. Scale = 1 cm. (After Seeley 1869.)

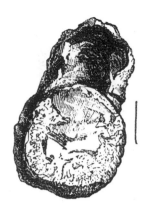

Macrurosaurus semnus, SM collection, holotype caudal vertebra, anterior view. Scale = 1 cm. (After Seeley 1869.)

neural arches in more anterior caudals supported on pedicles that rise from centrum and lack neural spine. (*Macrurosaurus* was the first giant dinosaur described to show procoelous caudal vertebrae in conjunction with the absence of chevrons.)

Seeley estimated that the tail probably included 50 vertebrae and may have been almost 4.5 meters (15 feet) long. Furthermore, Seeley suggested that large manus bones from the Cambridge Upper Greensand, previously described by him as *Acanthopholis platypus,* are too large to belong to that genus and could pertain to *Macrurosaurus.*

Le Loeuff concluded that Seeley's (1876) claims regarding one individual are unlikely. According to Le Loeuff, the first of the two "series" is a composite, while the "syntype" specimens associated with *M. semnus* seem to represent two distinct sauropods: In the first series, as described by Le Loeuff, SMC B55630, an anterior caudal centrum (no. 1 of Seeley's syntype) is deeply procoelous; in side view, ventral face of centrum is short, posterior ball well developed; neural arch was inserted on anterior part of centrum. B55631, the right side of another anterior caudal centrum is deeply concave; posterior articulation convex, but less developed than in B55360. The centra are amphicoelous from the 14th caudal (B55643) rearward; neural arch located at middle of centrum; centra dorso-ventrally compressed. According to Le Loeuff, this series does not represent a titanosaurid but rather an undetermined sauropod.

In the second series, several vertebrae (B55653, B55656, B55659-B55660) are deeply procoelous. B55654 is deeply amphicoelous, suggesting that the posterior ball was ossified with the succeeding centrum. Le Loeuff noted that these remains, as well as a well-preserved procoelous middle caudal centrum found at Barton, probably represent a titanosaurid.

Le Loeuff proposed: that the nontitanosaurid, first procoelous caudal (SMC B55630) should be regarded as the lectotype, and it is to this material that the name *M. semnus* should apply; that, displaying no autapomorphies, B55630 cannot be correctly diagnosed; and that the vertebrae from Barton and Coldham Common should be removed from the genus *Macrurosaurus* and be regarded as undetermined titanosaurids.

Ten middle caudal vertebrae (MNHN collection; formerly housed at the Institut Catholique in Paris), recovered from the Moru Quarry at Villers-Saint-Barthélémy, Oise, northern France, were described by Lapparent (1946) and referred by him to *M. semnus.* As described by Le Loeuff, the vertebrae are amphicoelous and dorso-ventrally compressed; neural arch anteriorly situated on most

proximal vertebrae, more centrally placed distally. According to Le Loeuff, these vertebrae are nontitanosaurid, although they are less elongated than the syntype material of *M. semnus,* and probably do not belong to this species.

Le Loeuff further noted that a middle caudal centrum (Bucaille collection, housed at the Musée d'Histoire Naturelle de Rouen), discovered during the nineteenth century from the Cap de la Hève, at Bléville, Seine-Maritime, northern France, is similar to the material described by Lapparent.

Key references: Lapparent (1946); Le Loeuff (1993); Seeley (1869, 1876).

MAGNOSAURUS Huene 1932—
   (=?*Megalosaurus*)
Saurischia: Theropoda: ?Tetanurae: Megalosauridae.
Name derivation: Latin *magnus* = "great" + Greek *sauros* = "lizard."
Type species: *M. nethercombensis* (Huene 1923).
Other species: ?*M. lydekkeri* Huene (1926).
Occurrence: Inferior Oolite, Dorset, England.
Age: Late Jurassic (Aalenian–Bajocian).
Known material/holotype: UMO J12143, dentaries with teeth, dorsal and caudal vertebra, part of right pubis, femora (known only from casts of internal cavities), tibiae, ?juvenile.
Diagnosis of genus: [No modern diagnosis published.]

Comments: Usually regarded as a junior synonym of *Megalosaurus,* the genus now referred to as *Magnosaurus* was founded upon incomplete material (UMO J12143) collected from the Humphriesei Zone, Lower Oolite, Nethercomb, north of Sherborne, in Dorset, England.

Huene (1923) believed the type material to belong to a new and more primitive species of *Megalosaurus,* which he named *M. nethercombensis.* Originally, Huene diagnosed this species as follows: Teeth similar (though somewhat thicker in anterior half of cross-sections) to those of *Megalosaurus bucklandii;* teeth sharply serrated at posterior edge, broad anteriorly, with blunt edge only in upper half; tibia slender, shaft with small diameter (5 centimeters or less than 1.95 inches), 48 centimeters (more than 18 inches) in length; head of tibia with forwardly projecting cnemial crest, sagittal diameter of 12 centimeters (over 4.6 inches), narrow in cross-section; width at condyle 8 centimeters (about 3.1 inches); slightly developed crista lateralis below upper end; distal portion of pubis rod-like, almost oval in cross-section.

Later, Huene (1932) assessed that this material represented a new genus, which he named *Magnosaurus.*

Waldman (1974) regarded *Magnosaurus* as basically indistinguishable from *Megalosaurus*, but commented that the tibiae of *M. nethercombensis* and *Sarcosaurus andrewsi* are quite similar. Kurzanov (1989), in a study on the origin and evolution of the "Carnosauria," listed *Magnosaurus* as a genus distinct from *Megalosaurus*. Molnar, Kurzanov and Dong (1990) pointed out that the distal tibia in *M. bucklandii* is not compressed, although the dentary of *M. nethercombensis* agrees with that of *M. bucklandii* in six out of the nine features (see Madsen 1976*a*) in which *M. bucklandii* disagrees with *Allosaurus fragilis*. Molnar *et al.* favored removing *Magnosaurus* from the genus *Megalosaurus*, at least tentatively, with both genera assigned to the Megalosauridae.

A second species, *M. lydekkeri* [originally *Megalosaurus lydekkeri* Huene 1926], was based on a tooth from the lower Lias of Lyme Regis, first described by Lydekker (1888) as differing from *Megalosaurus terquemi* by the falcimorm curvature of the tooth. *M. lydekkeri* was regarded by Molnar *et al.* as indeterminate.

Note: According to Molnar *et al.*, third species *M. woodwardi* Huene 1932 may be referable to *Sarcosaurus andrewsi*.

Key references: Huene (1923, 1926, 1932); Kurzanov (1989); Lydekker (1888); Molnar, Kurzanov and Dong (1990); Waldman (1974).

Photo by the author, courtesy University Museum, Oxford.

Magnosaurus nethercombensis, OUM J12143, holotype dentaries (?juvenile) of *Megalosaurus nethercombensis*.

MAGYAROSAURUS   Huene 1932

Saurischia: Sauropodomorpha: Sauropoda:
   Titanosauria; Titanosauridae.
Name derivation: "Magyar [ethnic group of
   Hungary]" + Greek *sauros* = "lizard."
Type species: *M. dacus* (Nopcsa 1915).
Other species: [None.]
Occurrence: Sinpetru Beds, Hunedoara, Romania.
Age: Late Cretaceous (Late Maastrichtian).
Known material: Isolated postcranial remains representing more than 12 individuals.
Lectotype: BMNH R3861a, two associated dorsal
   vertebrae.
   Diagnosis of genus (as for type species): Pleurocoels of dorsal vertebrae reduced; caudal vertebrae laterally compressed; dorsomedial protuberances at base of scapular blade; proximolateral expansion of femur very reduced (Le Loeuff 1993).
   Comments: The genus *Magyarosaurus* was founded upon various remains collected from the Upper Cretaceous of Hungary, originally referred by Nopcsa (1915) and Huene (1929) to the genus *Titanosaurus*. Later believing that the Hungarian specimens represented a genus distinct from *Titanosaurus*, Huene (1932) selected a dorsal centrum, caudal ver-

tebrae, right humerus, right ulna, and left fibula (BMNH R3861a), from the Gosau Formation of Siebenburgen, Hungary [Siebenburgen now belongs to Romania], material originally described by Nopcsa as *T. dacus*, as the type specimen of the new genus *Magyarosaurus*. At the same time, Huene (1932) referred other Hungarian remains, including two dorsal and six caudal vertebrae, right humerus, right and left ulnae, three metacarpals from the left manus, and two left fibulae (BMNH R3896) to a second species, *M. transsylvanicus*. Huene (1932) also erected the species *M. hungaricus*, based upon a left fibula (BMNH R3833), the latter measuring 47 centimeters (about 18.5 inches) long.

However, as noted by Le Loeuff (1993) in a review of European titanosaurids, Nopcsa, in describing *T. dacus*, did not designate a holotype for this new species. As Nopcsa initially described two associated dorsal vertebrae (additional material including a right humerus, right ulna, and a left fibula, collectively catalogued as BMNH R3861a), Le Loeuff designated the dorsals as the lectotype.

Huene diagnosed *M. dacus* as follows: Dorsal vertebrae deep, opisthocoelous, with relatively small pleurocoels; caudal vertebrae relatively short, broad,

Magyarosaurus dacus, BMNH R3861a, holotype caudal vertebrae, right humerus, right ulna, and left fibula of *Titanosaurus dacus*. (After Huene 1932.)

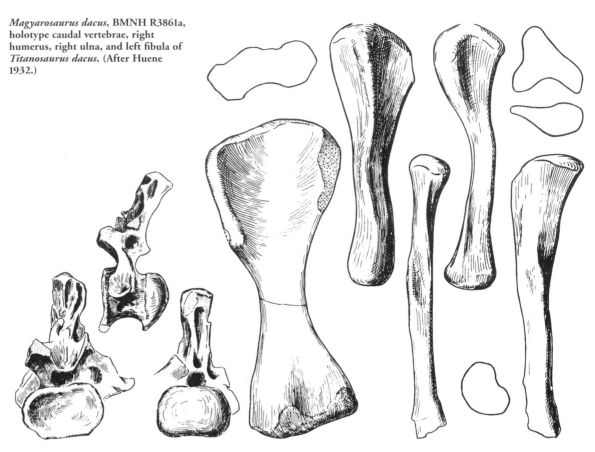

Magyarosaurus dacus, holotype metacarpals I–III, right humerus, left ulna, and left fibula of *M. transsylvanicus.*

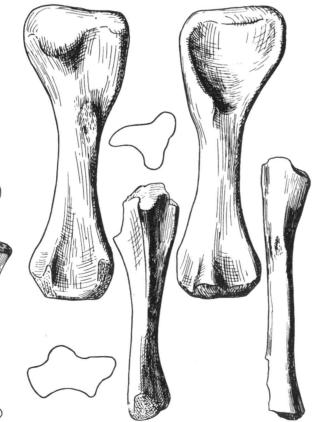

with distinct hemapophyses, longitudinal groove on ventral surface; humerus short (40 centimeters, or more than 15 inches in length), compactly built, one side broadly concave; ulna 35 centimeters (almost 13.5 inches) long, relatively slender, strongly curved, surface facing radius concave; fibula very broad proximally (Huene 1932).

The other species of *Magyarosaurus* were described by Huene (1932) as follows: (*M. transsylvanicus*) anterior dorsal vertebrae relatively large, opisthocoelous, with small pleurocoels; more anterior ?male caudal relatively short, others more elongate, all strongly pleurocoelous; ?female caudal centra about equal size, longitudinal ventral groove faint, hemapophyses very weak; humerus, ulna, and fibula about same size as in *M. dacus*, ulna more slender and less curved, fibula more slender and curved; metacarpus stout, 14 centimeters (about 5.4 inches) in length; (*M. hungaricus*) distinguished from type species mostly by wider proximal end of humerus. Le Loeuff, however, found Huene's erection of three distinct species of *Magyarosaurus* to be unjustified, and, pending a current revision of the material, suggested referring all of Nopcsa's material to *M. dacus*.

Some authors (*e.g.*, Lapparent and Lavocat 1955; Romer 1966) have regarded *Magyarosaurus* as a junior synonym of *Hypselosaurus*, others (*e.g.*, Steel

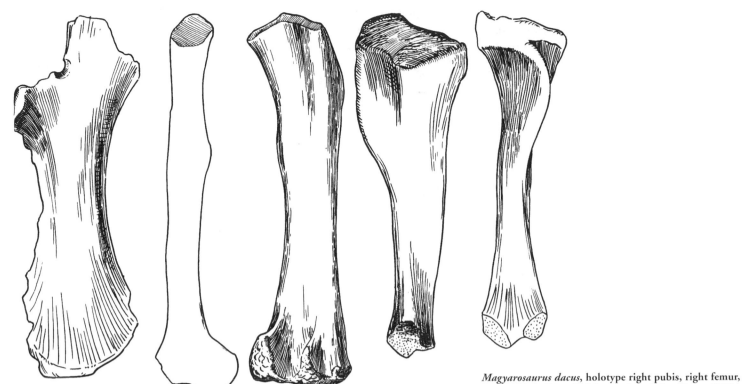

Magyarosaurus dacus, holotype right pubis, right femur, and left tibia of *M. hungaricus*. (After Huene 1932.)

1970) have viewed this genus as synonymous with the rather poorly defined *Titanosaurus*. No formal proof of these synonymies has yet been published, however, and the material grouped within the various species of *Magyarosaurus* may be too poor for a compelling synonymy to be made.

McIntosh (1990*b*) pointed out, in his review of the Sauropoda, that the various specimens that have been attributed to *Magyarosaurus* are completely dis-

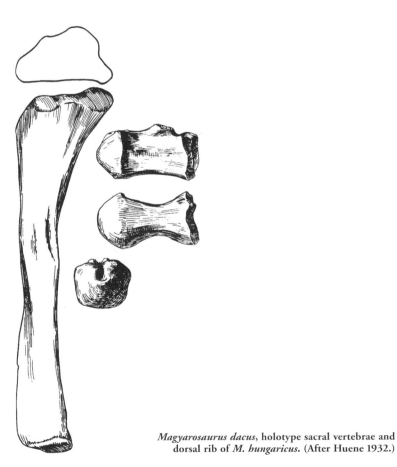

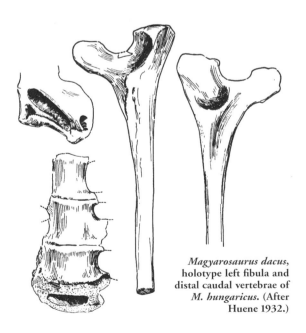

Magyarosaurus dacus, holotype left fibula and distal caudal vertebrae of *M. hungaricus*. (After Huene 1932.)

Magyarosaurus dacus, holotype sacral vertebrae and dorsal rib of *M. hungaricus*. (After Huene 1932.)

associated and could, as evidenced by both slender and robust humeri, represent more than a single genus. McIntosh briefly described *Magyarosaurus* as a slender-limbed titanosaurid, with proximal caudal vertebrae having particularly robust prezygapophyses.

Note: Fossil eggs, formerly believed by Grigorescu, Seclamen, Norman and Weishampel (1990) to be referable to *Magyarosaurus*, were transferred by Weishampel, Grigorescu and Norman (1991) to the Hadrosauridae.

Key references: Huene (1929, 1932); Lapparent and Lavocat (1955); Le Loeuff (1993); McIntosh (1990*b*); Nopcsa (1915).

MAIASAURA   Horner and Makela 1979

Ornithischia: Genasauria: Cerapoda: Ornithopoda: Iguanodontia: Hadrosauridae: Hadrosaurinae.

Name derivation: Greek *maia* = "good mother" + Greek *saura* [feminine] = "lizard."

Type species: *M. peeblesorum* Horner and Makela 1979.

Other species: [None.]

Occurrence: Upper Two Medicine Formation, Montana, United States.

Age: Late Cretaceous (Middle–Late Campanian).

Known material: Over 200 specimens, including skull and postcranial remains, embryo to adult, one specimen having skull articulated with skeleton, eggs, nests.

Holotype: PU 22405, skull with partial right dentary and predentary, adult.

Diagnosis of genus (as for type species): Skull with wide, elongate facial region; exterior naris short, on anterior end of snout; extensive facial region between posterior end of naris and anterior border of orbit; premaxillary bill short, wide; small, solid [scoop-shaped] incipient crest above and between orbits, formed by nasal and frontal bones; nasals concave to crest; long, thin quadratojugal process of jugal angling steeply upward to meet quadratojugal; dentary teeth with long, narrow enamel crown; predentary wide, very shallow, with round, evenly spaced denticulate processes around anterior border (Horner and Makela 1979).

Comments: The discovery of *Maiasaura* has led to new incites in our understanding of dinosaur growth, intelligence, and social behavior.

The genus was erected upon an almost complete skull (PU 22405), found in 1978 by Mr. and Mrs. David Trexler at the Willow Creek Anticline in the Two Medicine Formation of Teton County, Montana (Horner and Makela 1979).

Horner (1983) subsequently described the holotype skull of *M. peeblesorum* in detail, noting that it measures 820 millimeters (almost 32 inches) in length from anterior end of the premaxillae to posterior end of left exoccipital, and about 350 millimeters (almost 13.5 inches) deep, from the most dorsal end of the squamosal to ventral end of quadrate.

As noted by Horner, the massive yet depressed muzzle exhibits primitive characteristics common to both iguanodonts and early hadrosaurs, including one of the skull's most diagnostic features, the restricted narial opening and long, broad nasals at the anterior end of the muzzle. The incipient crest resembles that of *Lophorhothon* and *Prosaurolophus*. In *Maiasaura*, the area anterior and medial to the crest is convex. A circumnarial depression is restricted to the area adjacent to the nares. This depression, which may have accommodated an apparently inflatable tube or sac, apparently does not continue to the crest.

As related by Horner and Makela, at the site of the original discovery, Marion Brandvold found the skeletal remains of 11 *Maiasaura* babies, each approximately 1 meter (3.3 feet) in snout-vent length, and clustered in a nest-like structure. Remains of four more babies were found no more than 2 meters (about 6.8 feet) away from the nest. The juveniles have short snouts and relatively large feet, but otherwise agree morphologically with the adult *Maiasaura*.

Associated with these skeletons were numerous pieces of fossilized eggshell (assigned by Mihailov 1991 to the egg family Spheerolithidae). As described by Horner (1982), the restored eggs are spheroid and larger at one end than at the other. The nest, as described by Horner and Makela, is oval, concave, about 2 meters (approximately 6.8 feet) in diameter, and .75 meters (approximately 2.5 feet) deep near the center. (The later discovery of an egg containing a *Maiasaura* embryo, the first dinosaur embryo found in the United States, confirmed that these eggs belonged to this genus.)

In the years following the original discovery, more nests, eggs, and juvenile remains were collected by Horner and Makela. (For a chronological account of Horner and Makela's discoveries of the *Maiasaura* nesting grounds, see the book *Digging for Dinosaurs*; Horner and Gorman 1988.) Mineral analysis of one site indicated that some *Maiasaura* adults and juveniles had perished in a volcanic mudslide.

Until the discovery of *Maiasaura*, it was generally assumed that dinosaurs, like most modern day reptiles, abandoned their eggs to hatch, the babies forced to survive alone and unattended. Based on evidence provided by these nests, however, Horner and Makela postulated that *Maiasaura* babies had been staying together in the nest and feeding for an extended period of time. During this nesting period, when juveniles grew to almost 90 centimeters (3 feet), they must have known some parental care, the parents bringing food back to the nests rather than risk letting the juveniles go out and forage their own food.

Additional evidence supporting this theory was offered by Horner and Weishampel (1988), who reported more discoveries of *Maiasaura* embryos. As observed by Horner and Weishampel, the epiphyseal surfaces of the limbs in these embryos are poorly finished off, composed of a thin layer of calcified cartilage overlying a very spongy endochondral metaphysis. This evidence reinforced Horner and Makela's idea that *Maiasaura* individuals were late in developing, consequently spending more time in the nest being fed by parents.

Reporting a total of eight *Maiasaura* nests, Horner (1982) postulated that they, like some modern species of crocodiles and birds, nested in colonies and returned to the same nesting area annually. During the dry season, the mother *Maiasaura* made her nest on the floodplains, using fine-grained silts (see Horner 1986), then laid her eggs in a helix. The nests were then covered with reeds and other vegetation that helped to incubate the eggs. The babies may have been fed a combination of berries and seeds regurgitated by the mother.

Horner (*see in* Virginia Morell 1987) speculated that these babies were 13 inches long when they hatched and grew to ten feet by the end of their first year. (Adult *Maiasaura* measure approximately 9 meters [30 feet] long and 4.5 meters [15 feet] tall.) Such rapid growth, as fast as that of an altricial bird, requires a high metabolism and can only be sustained by endothermic animals, thus supporting the theory that dinosaurs were warm-blooded.

The rarity of juvenile dinosaurs in the fossil record has been given various explanations, including the hypothesis (see Sternberg 1956; Horner 1984) that nesting occurred in upland areas (the Two Medicine is usually regarded as the upland equivalent of the Judith River Formation), after which the dinosaurs, as adults, migrated to lowland areas; and the hypothesis (Carpenter 1982*a*) that dinosaurs also nested in lowland environments that were not ideal for preserving the remains of babies or eggshell.

Fiorillo (1987), however, cautioned that generalizations should not be made regarding dinosaur nesting. Although agreeing that evidence supports the hypothesis of upland nesting areas, Fiorillo showed that dinosaurs also nested in lowland areas, represented by the Careless Creek Quarry (Dinosaur Park Formation), in Wheatland County, Montana. About 20 percent of the dinosaurian remains from this site are juveniles, including various lambeosaurine postcranial elements such as a left and right humerus, and scapula (ANSP 15979), and a humerus (ANSP 15986) from a slightly smaller individual. As the taphonomic setting of the site indicates that the bones were not brought in over great distances, the

Maiasaura peeblesorum,
PU 22405, holotype skull
(unprepared). Scale = 12 in.

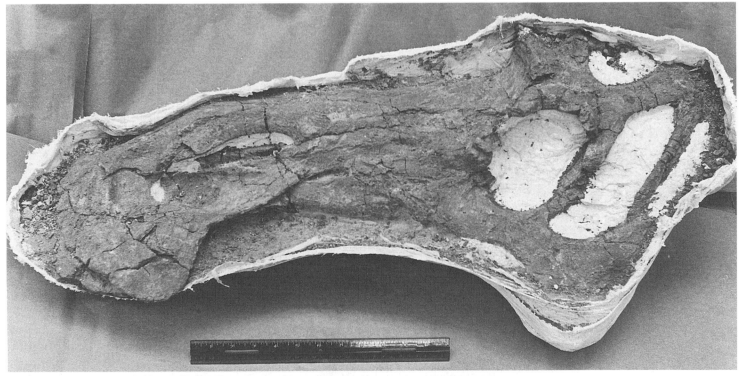

Courtesy J. R. Horner.

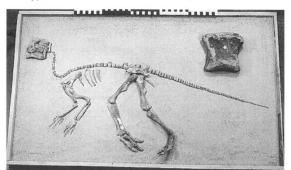

Composite juvenile skeleton (PU 224400), referred to cf. *Maiasaura peeblesorum,* compared with phalange III of adult. Scale = cm.

juveniles probably either hatched in the immediate region or migrated there. Fiorillo calculated that these remains (ANSP 15979) indicate individuals too small to have migrated from the upland region several tens of miles to the west, and suggested that at least this kind of lambeosaurine nested in coastal lowland regions. Since a lambeosaurine jaw (ANSP 16242) from the Careless Creek Quarry is about the same size as a juvenile *Maiasaura* jaw found in association with the nest (see Horner [1982]), Fiorillo further hypothesized that nesting for this Careless Creek individual occurred near the site.

However, though this genus has, for more than a decade, been regarded as the "good mother lizard," this portrayal has more recently been questioned and criticized. Deeming and Unwin (1993), from a study of embryos or neonates (hatchlings or babies) reported in various fossil vertebrates (including at least four dinosaur and two bird families), suggested that hatchling size in "*Maiasaura* may have been seriously underestimated, perhaps by up to a factor of four, thus arguments for altriciality and other proposed patterns of growth and behavior in this dinosaur may need reassessing." Compounding the issue was the description by Horner and Currie (1994, in the book *Dinosaur Eggs and Babies,* edited by Carpenter, Hirsch, and Horner) of fossils pertaining to the hadrosaur *Hypacrosaurus stebingeri* (see *Hypacrosaurus* entry), including large eggs, embryos, and babies.

In a review of *Dinosaur Eggs and Babies,* Dodson (1995) suggested that worn teeth in the *Hypacrosaurus* embryos falsifies the theory that wear facets offer evidence "that *Maiasaura* teeth were in use chewing food despite their small size." Dodson pointed out that *H. stebingeri* is presumed to have hatched at about 1 meter in length and that its authors neither claimed nor implied that the young received maternal care. Dodson questioned the credibility of

Hypacrosaurus laying eggs the size of soccer balls and hatching meter-long babies, while the closely related *Maiasaura* laid much more slender eggs (no complete *Maiasaura* eggs having been found) from which supposedly 30 centimeter-long babies hatched. Repeating Deeming and Unwin's suggestion that *Maiasaura* hatchlings may have been four times larger than reported, adding that they could have been about the size of *Hypacrosaurus* hatchlings, Dodson found the established portrayal of *Maiasaura* as the "good mother" to be "very far-fetched indeed." Furthermore, Dodson suggested that the 12-inch *Maiasaura* individuals previously identified as "hatchling" could conceivably have been embryos, and that the undeveloped limb ends reported in the smallest *Maiasaura* individual as evidence of altriciality is a feature "to be expected in an embryo far from hatching."

Also, Geist and Jones (1995), reviewing the articular surfaces on long bones of extant hatchling ratite birds and crocodilians, found that both altricial and precocial species commonly possess cartilaginous gaps similar to those seen in young *Maiasaura* individuals. This, according to Geist and Jones, opens to question the view that the poorly ossified leg bones in *Maiasaura* hatchlings indicates that these young dinosaurs required parental care in the nest.

Fiorillo (1990) reported the first occurrence of hadrosaurid remains, referred to cf. *Maiasaura,* from the marine Claggett Formation (Late Cretaceous) of south-central Montana. The material includes caudal vertebrae, phalanges, metacarpals, and metatarsals (ANSP 15805), presumably from the same individual (as no elements were duplicated and all are of appropriate size), collected between 1984–1988 by joint field parties from the Academy of Natural Sciences of Philadelphia and the University of Pennsylvania. The remains were identified as hadrosaurid on the basis of the caudals, which show a characteristic hexagonal outline in cranial and caudal views. They were referred by Fiorillo to cf. *Maiasaura* because of the presence of a keeled ungual (a character known only in *Maiasaura*; J. R. Horner, personal communication to Fiorillo).

Notes: *Maiasaura* is the state fossil of Montana.

In a study of fossil eggs and eggshell fragments from the Two Medicine Formation of Montana, Hirsch and Quinn (1990) characterized the eggshells attributed to *M. peeblesorum* as follows: One shell layer of spherulitic shell units with very small mammilae caps; shell unit made up of thin wedges that become wider while radiating toward outer shell surface; no visible boundaries between units; extinction patter sweeping; in thin sections below 50 micrometers, some individualistic extinction of wider wedges;

Maiasaura peeblesorum with hatchlings, Late Cretaceous, Montana.

Illustration by Doug Henderson.

herringbone structure crossing boundaries of wedges; porecanals of irregular shape and diameter, mostly wider in middle of shell; pore openings between ridges; shell 1.0–1.2 millimeters thick; outer surface of shell sculptured with high, steep, longitudinally-oriented ridges; inner surface with widely and irreg- ularly spaced mammilae caps and deep, large inter- stices.

Two newly discovered hadrosaur nest sites, reported by Brandvold, Brandvold, Sweeney and Boyden (1995), provided evidence of behavioral divergence in duckbilled dinosaurs. The first site, located on the Blackfeet Reservation, Pondera County, Montana, consists of a single nest, with no other nests in the nearby vicinity. The nest contained five eggs but no embryos. Found on the wall of this nest were embryonic bone fragments and eggshell pieces with rounded edges. The second site, near Choteau, Montana, and on the same horizon as the first, yielded five nests. These nests, in close proximity to each other, contained broken eggshells. Neither embryonic bones nor eggshells attributable to previous use were discovered in or around the nest. Brandvold *et al.,* suggested that the nest at the first site was used repeatedly, while those at the second may only have been used for a single season.

Possible herbivorous dinosaur coprolites from the Two Medicine Formation of Montana, reported by Chin (1990), may have a *Maiasaura* origin, based upon their size (34 by 33 by 24 centimeters) and proximity to nesting grounds and a bone bed of *M. peeblesorum.* The shapeless specimens occur as irregular blocks. Permineralized plant fragments observed in them have rough, angular edges and are less than 3 centimeters long.

Key references: Dodson (1995); Fiorillo (1987, 1990); Hirsch and Quinn (1990); Horner (1982, 1984, 1986); Horner and Gorman (1988); Horner and Makela (1979); Horner and Weishampel (1988); Mihailov (1991); Morell (1987).

MAJUNGASAURUS   Lavocat 1955
Saurischia: Theropoda: Ceratosauria:
   Neoceratosauria: ?Abelisauroidea: ?Abelisauridae.
Name derivation: "Majunga [District,
   Madagascar]" + Greek *sauros* = "lizard."
Type species: *M. crenatissimus* (Depéret 1896).
Other species: [None.]

Occurrence: Grès de Maevarano, Majunga, Maevarano Formation, Mahajanga Basin, Madagascar; ?Egypt; ?Lameta Formation, central India.
Age: Late Cretaceous (Campanian).
Known material: Partial mandible, teeth, various postcranial remains.
Holotype: Incomplete right mandible with associated teeth.

Diagnosis of genus (as for type species): Dentary moderately high but deep, lower external half strongly convex, alveolar part of lingual surface continuous (Lavocat 1955*b*).

Comments: In 1896, Depéret described two teeth, a caudal vertebra, two sacral centra, and ungual phalanx apparently from the pes, collected from the Upper Cretaceous of Majunga, Madagascar, which he referred to *Megalosaurus* as new species *M. crenatissimus.* The dorsal centra of the type specimen are distinctly pleurocoelous and measure about 6 centimeters (approximately 2.3 inches) in length.

More than a half century later, the new genus *Majungasaurus* was named by Lavocat (1955*b*), founded upon an incomplete lower jaw and teeth, collected from the Grès de Maevarano (formerly Berivotro Formation), near Majunga, Madagascar. As the teeth of this new form were identical to those included in the material described by Depéret, Lavocat referred them to his new genus and species *Majungasaurus crenatissimus.*

Gemmellaro (1921) had reported teeth, possibly attributed to *Majungasaurus* from the Maastrichtian of Egypt. Later, a sacrum and other material were found near Majunga, and teeth were collected from the Lameta Formation of central India, some or all of which may belong to *Majungasaurus.*

In a review of problematic "carnosaurs," Molnar (1990) observed that the dentary teeth of *M. crenatissimus* seem to have an unusual form in cross-section, but do not display any features diagnostic of "Carnosauria"; however, a similarly curved mandible is known in the abelisaurid *Carnotaurus sastrei,* implying a relationship of *M. crenatissimus* with the Abelisauridae.

As briefly reported by Sampson, Forster, Krause, Dodson and Ravoavy (1996), numerous well preserved dinosaurian fossils, including additional *Majungasaurus* material, were more recently recovered, over two field seasons, during joint S.U.N.Y. Stony Brook-Université d'Antananàrivo expeditions to the Upper Cretaceous (Campanian) Maevarano Formation, Mahajanga Basin, in northwestern Madagascar. According to Sampson *et al.,* these remains support the referral of *Majungasaurus* to the Abelisauridae.

Majungasaurus crenatissimus, incomplete right dentary, in a. external, b. ventral, c. dorsal views. Scale = 2 cm. (After Lavocat 1955.)

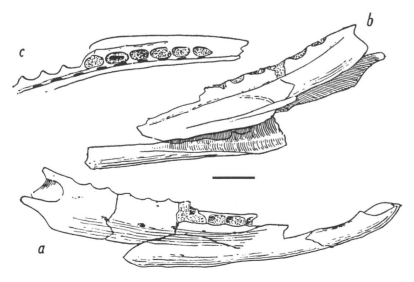

Notes: Sampson *et al.,* reported that, also collected during the S.U.N.Y. Stony Brook-Université d'Antananàrivo expeditions, were specimens of at least two species of titanosaurid sauropods (including an 80 percent complete skeleton with associated cranial elements, this being the most complete titanosaurid yet discovered); abundant theropod remains (including a small nonavian theropod and at least three taxa of birds); "and the first avian skeletal remains from the Mesozoic of Gondwana outside of South America, Australia, and Antarctica." Nondinosaurian taxa occurring at this locality include crocodilians, snakes, lizards, frogs, fishes, and mammals (Forster 1996*b*).

Theropod teeth, similar to those of *Majungasaurus crenatissimus* or *Genyodectes serus*, were reported by Bonaparte and Powell (1980) from the Lecho Formation in El Brete, southern Salta province, Northwestern Argentina. However, positive identification of these teeth, even at the family level, was not possible.

Key references: Depéret (1896); Gemmellaro (1921); Lavocat (1955*b*); Molnar (1990); Sampson, Forster, Krause, Dodson and Ravoavy (1996).

MAJUNGATHOLUS   Sues and Taquet 1979
Ornithischia: Genasauria: Cerapoda:
    Marginocephalia: Pachycephalosauria: ?Pachy-
    cephalosauridae.
Name derivation: "Majunga [District,
    Madagascar]" + Latin *tholus* = "dome."
Type species: *M. atopus* Sues and Taquet 1979.
    Other species: [None.]
Occurrence: Grès de Maevarano, Majunga,
    Madagascar.
Age: Late Cretaceous (?Campanian).
Known material/holotype: MNHN.MAJ4, skull
    roof including frontals and incomplete parietals,
    with anterior portion of braincase.

Diagnosis of genus (as for type species): Highly elevated single frontal dome irregularly ornamented by furrows and nodes; parietals not domed, with median depression and large supratemporal fenestrae (Maryańska 1990, modified after Sues 1980).

Comments: The genus *Majungatholus* was established upon part of a skull (MNHN.MAJ4; formerly École des Mines, Paris, collections), from "Grès de Maevarano" (probably Campanian), Majunga District, northwestern Madagascar. When discovered in the early 1900s, the specimen was not identified as a pachycephalosaur (Sues and Taquet 1979); nor was the locality which yielded this specimen ever recorded, although details of preservation suggest that it came from the "Grès de Maevarano" Majunga deposits (Sues 1980).

Sues and Taquet originally diagnosed the monotypic *M. atopos* as follows: Frontal region with single, dome-like thickening; frontal dome thick, with very irregular and rough dorsal surface; parietal contributing to well developed parieto-squamosal shelf, lacking any significant thickening; supratemporal fenestrae very large; braincase with long olfactory portion; olfactory lobes enclosed ventrally by bone.

Sues (1980) regarded *Majungatholus* as a fairly large pachycephalosaurid, surpassed in size only by the Maastrichtian genus *Pachycephalosaurus.*

Sues and Taquet suggested that *Majungatholus* represents a distinctive kind of pachycephalosaurid, the single dome and very large upper temporal openings being unique among that group. Sues (1980) later pointed out that the single frontal dome and very long olfactory stalks distinguish this genus from all other known pachycephalosaurids.

According to Sues and Taquet, *Majungatholus* is similar to the slightly more primitive Wealden form *Yaverlandia bitholus,* the oldest known pachycephalosaurid, in that both have large supratemporal fenestrae and thickening limited to the frontal region. *Yaverlandia* differs from *Majungatholus* in being much smaller and having a small dome on each frontal. Sues and Taquet concluded that *Majungatholus* was derived from a *Yaverlandia*-type form, probably representing a pachycephalosaurid lineage evolving independently of forms in the Northern Hemisphere. According to Sues and Taquet, the occurrence of *Majungatholus* in Madagascar and the presence of other "Laurasian" dinosaur families in the Southern Hemisphere provides evidence supporting the theory that a land connection existed between Laurasia and Gondwana at least during the first half of the Cretaceous period (and ?later).

More recently, Sampson, Forster, Krause, Dodson and Ravoavy (1996) noted that a reassessment of the holotype of *M. atopus* suggests that assignment to the Pachycephalosauridae may be incorrect, this reevaluation, if correct, thereby removing the only occurrence of pachycephalosaurids in Gondwana.

Note: Sues tentatively identified two teeth (apparently lost, according to P. Taquet, personal communication to Sues, 1978), collected by H. Perrier de la Bathie from "Grès de Maeverano" and described by Piveteau (1926), as ?*Stegosaurus madagascariensis* [*nomen dubium*], as probably belonging to *M. atopus.* Based upon Piveteau's illustrations, Sues noted that these teeth closely resembled those of

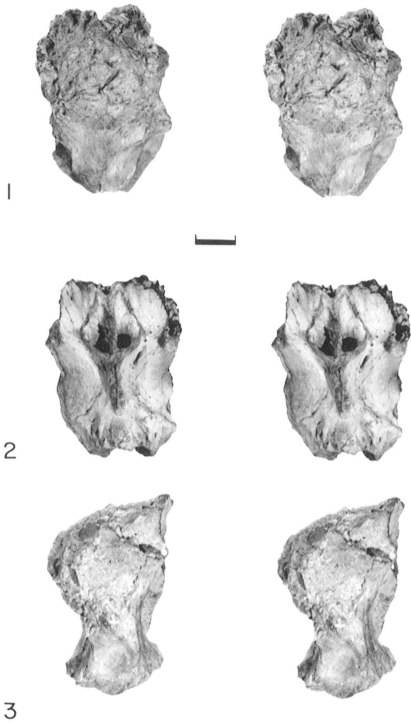

1

2

3

Majungatholus atopus,
MNHN.MAJ 4, holotype partial skull (stereographs), in 1. dorsal, 2. ventral, 3. right lateral views. Scale = 3 cm. (After Sues 1980.)

Pachycephalosaurus wyomingensis (=*P.* "*grangeri,*" as figured by Brown and Schlaikjer 1943). Owing to the loss of the original material, however, Sues did not attempt to establish with certainty their affinities and submitted that they be regarded as a *nomen dubium.*

Key references: Maryańska (1990); Piveteau (1926); Sampson, Forster, Krause, Dodson and Ravoavy (1996); Sues (1980); Sues and Taquet (1979).

MALAWISAURUS Jacobs, Winkler, Downs and Gomani 1993

Saurischia: Sauropodomorpha: Sauropoda: Titanosauria: Titanosauridae.

Name derivation: "Malawi [country in East Africa]" + Greek *sauros* = "lizard."

Type species: *M. dixeyi* (Haughton 1928).

Other species: [None.]

Occurrence: Chiweta Beds, Northern Province, Dinosaur Beds (Lupata Group), Sitwe Valley, Malawi [formerly Nyasaland], East Africa.

Age: Late Jurassic–Late Cretaceous.

Known material: Incomplete cranial and postcranial remains.

Holotype: SAM 7405, anterior caudal vertebra.

Diagnosis of genus (as for type species): [from holotype] anterior caudal vertebrae strongly procoelous, with short, vertical neural spines; [from topotypes] middle and distal caudal vertebrae not procoelous; cervical and dorsal vertebrae with undivided spines; hemal arches do not bifurcate; cervical ribs not extending beyond centrum; premaxilla blunt, external nares relatively anterior in position; teeth not restricted to anterior portion of lower jaw; at least 15 tooth positions in dentary; ischium transversely expanded; (Jacobs, Winkler, Downs and Gomani 1993).

Comments: The medium-sized sauropod now called *Malawisaurus* was founded upon material first figured by Haughton (1928) as *Gigantosaurus dixeyi*, a species based on partial postcranial remains collected from the Chiweta Beds of Malawi, East Africa. This material originally included an anterior caudal vertebra, right pubis, incomplete scapula, and sternal plates.

New information regarding this species surfaced with the collection of additional remains, including previously unknown skeletal elements (*e.g.*, premaxilla [the first known for a titanosaurid], dentary, ischium, middle and distal caudal vertebrae, cervical vertebrae), some of them articulated, collected from the upper member of the Early Cretaceous Dinosaur Beds of the Sitwe Valley, near Mwakasyunguti, northern Mawali. This latter material was collected from a single quarry in 1984 by a joint Southern Methodist University and Malawi Department of Antiquities program (Jacobs *et al.* 1993).

Jacobs *et al.* regarded only the caudal vertebra illustrated by Haughton as the holotype, the other material considered to be topotypic, at the same time referring this and the more recently collected material to the new genus and species *Maliwasaurus dixeyi.*

Although dermal armor (known in titanosaurids such as *Saltasaurus*) has not been found in association with *Maliwasaurus* remains, Jacobs *et al.* noted that calcite pseudomorphs with a shape resembling dermal armor were found in the Dinosaur Beds quarry. These pseudomorphs have a subcircular base that is flattened on one (?posterior) edge, the perimeter of which is ornamented with 12 to 13 small projections. The pseudomorphs are concave on one side and have a tall keel on the other. They are bilaterally symmetrical, with the spine compressed and inclined towards the flattened edge of the base. Observing that these pseudomorphs seem to be of biological origin, Jacobs *et al.* speculated that that could represent dermal ossicles.

Jacobs *et al.* pointed out that the premaxilla of *Malawasaurus* is primitive in having the external nares

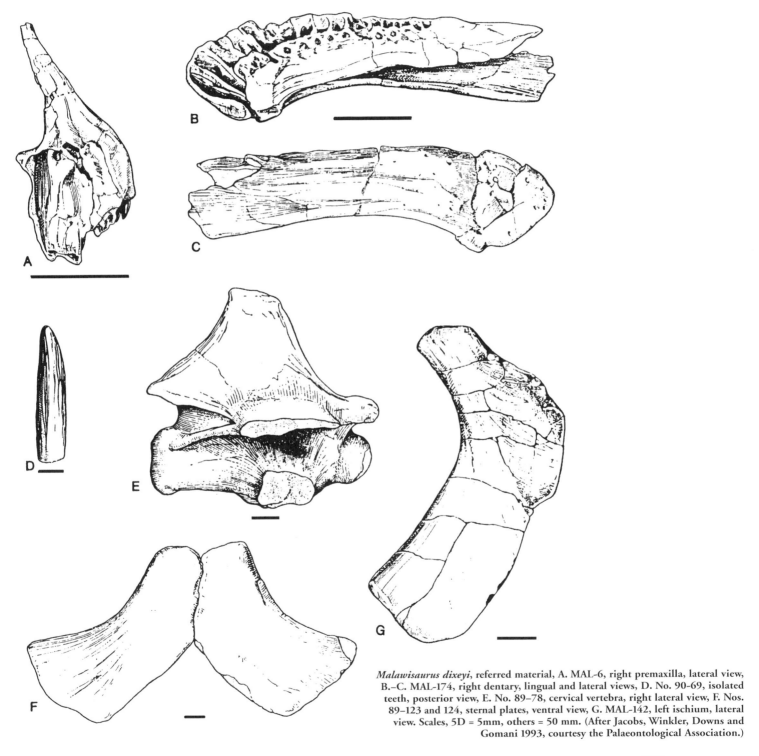

Malawisaurus dixeyi, referred material, A. MAL-6, right premaxilla, lateral view, B.–C. MAL-174, right dentary, lingual and lateral views, D. No. 90-69, isolated teeth, posterior view, E. No. 89-78, cervical vertebra, right lateral view, F. Nos. 89-123 and 124, sternal plates, ventral view, G. MAL-142, left ischium, lateral view. Scales, 5D = 5mm, others = 50 mm. (After Jacobs, Winkler, Downs and Gomani 1993, courtesy the Palaeontological Association.)

located far anterior, indicating that this genus has a blunter snout than other sauropods. The teeth are more narrow than in the brachiosaurid *Brachiosaurus*, but are not pencil-like. (In sauropods, leaf-shaped teeth and primitive, pencil-shaped teeth derived.) According to Jacobs *et al.*, the flattened teeth in *Maliwasaurus* suggest that pencil-shaped teeth (such as those in diplodocids and possibly to more derived titanosaurids) may have evolved more than once among sauropods, an example of convergence between the Diplodocidae and Titanosauridae.

Key references: Jacobs, Winkler, Downs and Gomani (1993); Haughton (1928).

MALEEVOSAURUS   Carpenter 1992
Saurischia: Theropoda: Tetanurae: Avetheropoda;
  Coelurosauria: Maniraptora: Arctometatarsalia:
  Tyrannosauridae.
Name derivation: "[Eugen Alexandrovich] Maleev"
  + Greek *sauros* = "lizard."
Type species: *M. novojilovi* (Maleev 1955).
Other species: [None.]
Occurrence: Nemegt Formation, Omnogov,
  Mongolian People's Republic.
Age: Late Cretaceous (?Late Campanian or Early
  Maastrichtian).
Known material/holotype: PIN 552-2, partial skull
  with associated postcrania.
Diagnosis of genus (as for type species): Maxillary fenestra small; premaxillary fenestra not visible in side view; antorbital fenestra very large propor-

tionally, much longer than high; lacrimal horn moderately developed, not rugose; postorbital not very rugose; lower maxillary ramus low, slender; jugal slender, resulting in very large orbit; dentary slender; cervical neural spines tall (not reduced as in other tyrannosaurids); acromial process of scapula almost nonexistent; obturator process of ischium very pronounced, spur-like, shaft curving downward distally; metatarsal IV not overlapping metatarsal III at midshaft; III not with much of overlap of II at midshaft (Carpenter 1992).

Comments: The genus *Maleevosaurus* was founded on an almost complete skeleton (PIN 552-2), originally named *Gorgosaurus novojilovi* by Maleev (1955*b*), who neither diagnosed nor described in detail this new species. The specimen was collected from the Nemegt Formation at Tsagan Ula, Mongolian People's Republic, and named along with three other tyrannosaurid taxa (see *Tyrannosaurus* entry).

The species was regarded by Rozhdestvensky (1965) as a juvenile *Tyrannosaurus* [= *Tarbosaurus* of his usage] *bataar*. Later, Osmólska (1980) noted that the structural differences of the metatarsus in "*G.*" *novojilovi* cannot be due to ontogenetic changes and suggested that this species could belong to a new genus.

More recently, Carpenter (1992) compared "*G.*" *novojilovi* with adult specimens (AMNH 5458 and 5664, respectively) of *Albertosaurus libratus*, as well as with a growth series of *T. bataar* skulls. Carpenter found that the lacrimal horn is already well-developed and jugal proportionally large in juvenile *Alber-*

Maleevosaurus novojilovi, PIN 552-2, holotype partial skull and skeleton of "*Gorgosaurus*" *novojilovi*. After Maleev 1955.)

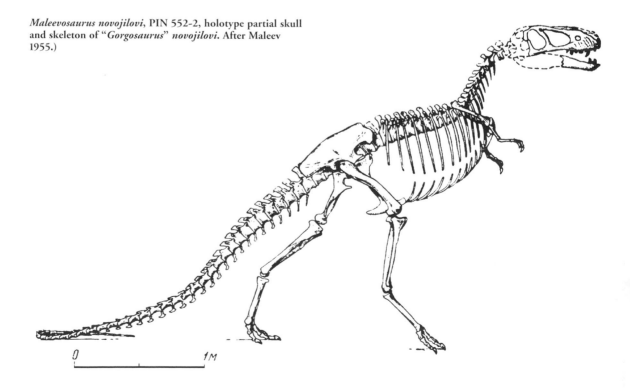

Two *Tyrannosaurus bataar* intimidate the smaller *Maleevosaurus novojilovi.*

Illustration by Brian Franczak.

tosaurus, and that in *T. bataar* there is also no change in lacrimal horn development or jugal size; the moderately-developed lacrimal and slender jugal in "*G.*" *novojilovi* are not juvenile features; also, there is no change in relative size of antorbital opening from juvenile to adult *T. bataar* individuals, indicating that this large fenestra in "*G.*" *novojilovi* is not a juvenile feature. However, the slender metatarsal III could be a juvenile feature, this being considerably more slender in juvenile than adult *Albertosaurus* individuals.

Concluding that (with the possible exception of the slenderness of metatarsal III) "*G.*" *novojilovi* is not a juvenile *T. bataar,* nor can it be referred to any other known tyrannosaurid genus (because of the large antorbital fenestra, slender jugal, very well-developed obturator process, and sharply downward curved ischium), Carpenter assigned this species to new genus *Maleevosaurus.*

Noting that the holotype of *M. novojilovi,* because of its size, may represent a juvenile individual, Carpenter pointed out that the neural arches are fused to their centra and calcaneum to astragalus, suggesting that *Maleevosaurus* is a small tyrannosaurid.

Key references: Carpenter (1992); Maleev (1955); Osmólska (1980); Rozhdestvensky (1965).

MALEEVUS Tumanova 1987—(=?*Amtosaurus,* ?*Talarurus*)
Ornithishia: Genasauria: Thyreophora: Ankylosauria: Ankylosauridae.
Name derivation: "[Eugene Alexandrovich] Maleev."
Type species: *M. disparoserratus* (Maleev 1952).
Other species: [None.]

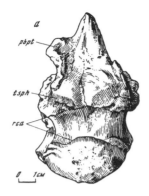
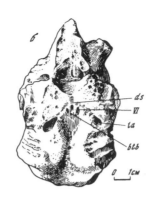

Occurrence: Baynshirenskaya Svita, Omnogov, Mongolian People's Republic.

Age: Late Cretaceous (Cenomanian–Turonian).

Known material: Fragmentary skull, cranial fragments, right ilium.

Type specimens: PIN 554/1-2, two fragments of right and left maxillae.

Diagnosis of genus: Occipital condyle subspherical, ventro-posteriorly oriented (Tumanova 1987, after [in part] Maryańska 1977).

Diagnosis of *M. disparoserratus*: Maxillary teeth with strongly developed W-shaped folding of cingulum labially (Tumanova 1987, after [in part] Maryańska 1977).

Comments: Originally described by Maleev (1952*b*) as *Syrmosaurus disparoserratus*, the genus now called *Maleevus* was founded upon two maxillary fragments (PIN 554/1-2) from the same individual, collected from the Bayn Shireh "formation," Sheeregeen Gashoon, Mongolia. (Maleev first misidentified this material as a left mandible.) Referred specimens include a basicranial fragment with occipital condyle, basioccipital, and basisphenoid (PIN 554/2-1), and

right ilium (ZPAL MgD-I/115), both specimens from the same locality as the holotype (Maryańska 1977).

Coombs (1977*a*) regarded "*Syrmosaurus*" *disparoserratus* as a synonym of *Pinacosaurus grangeri*. Maryańska, however, pointed out that the two forms are of different geological age. Also, "*S.*" *disparoserratus* differs from *Pinacosaurus* in the more primitive structure of the palate, different structure of teeth, and different distribution of cranial nerve openings. Due to the paucity of the material, Maryańska tentatively referred "*S.*" *disparoserratus* to *Talarurus*, mainly because of similarities in the general basicranial pattern, structure of the maxilla, and folding of cingulum.

Tumanova (1987) regarded this species as representing a distinct genus which Tumanova named *Maleevus*. At the same time, Tumanova split up the diagnosis for the monotypic *M. disparoserratus* proposed earlier by Maryańska, ascribing those features pertaining to the occipital condyle to this new genus, those to dentition to the type species.

In their review of the Ankylosauria, Coombs and Maryańska (1990), pointed out that, although Maryańska (1977) had regarded the differences between *M. disparoserratus* and *Talarurus plicatospineus* as grounds for specific diagnosis, she also pointed out details in the pattern of cranial foramina that are present in both of these species, but not in other known ankylosaurids. With reservation, Coombs and Maryańska retained *M. disparoserratus* as a valid taxon.

Key references: Coombs (1977*a*); Coombs and Maryańska (1990); Maleev (1952*b*); Maryańska (1977); Tumanova (1987).

MAMENCHISAURUS   Yang [Young] 1954

Saurischia: Sauropodomorpha: Sauropoda: Mamenchisauridae.

Name derivation: Chinese "Mamenchi [Ferry; from "Chi" = "brook" + "Mamen," name of brook]" + Greek *sauros* = "lizard."

Type species: *M. constructus* Yang [Young] 1954.

Other species: *M. hochuanensis* Yang [Young] and Chao 1972, *M. sinocanadorum* Russell and Zheng 1993.

Occurrence: Shangshaximiao Formation, Sichuan, Sishugou Formation, Junggar Basin, Xinjiang, People's Republic of China.

Age: Late Jurassic.

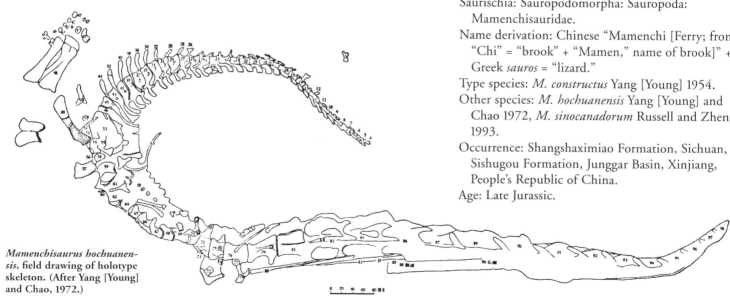

Mamenchisaurus hochuanensis, field drawing of holotype skeleton. (After Yang [Young] and Chao, 1972.)

Mamenchisaurus constructus, IVP AS, holotype incomplete skeleton.

Known material: Five skeletons, one with fragmentary skull, partial skeleton with cranial remains.

Holotype: IVP AS collection, incomplete skeleton including fragmentary skull with lower jaw, 14 cervical vertebrae, five dorsals, 30 caudals, rib, fragments of dorsal spines and chevrons, two portions of right femur, complete right tibia, fibula, and astragalus, some right metatarsals, phalanges, claws.

Diagnosis of genus: Neck greatly elongate, comprising 19 cervical vertebrae making up one half length of entire animal; cervical neural spines relatively low, posterior spines bifurcate; anterior caudal centra procoelous, chevrons of mid-caudal series forked (Dong, Zhou and Zhang 1983).

Diagnosis of *M. sinocanadorum*: Neural spines of axis and third cervical vertebra lying below crest of zygapophyseal rami; axis epipophyses powerfully developed (Russell and Zheng 1993).

Comments: *Mamenchisaurus* is the largest known dinosaur from China. The genus was founded upon an incomplete skeleton (IVP AS collection) discovered in the Shangshaximiao Formation (Red Beds) during construction of the Yitang Highway in 1952, in the vicinity of Mamenchi Ferry, Jinshajiang, along the Yangtze River, Yibin, Southwest Sichuan, China.

Though none of the neck vertebrae pertaining to *M. constructus* were complete, it was evident that the neck was remarkably long. In his original description of the type specimen, Yang [Young] (1954*b*) estimated a cervical column containing at least 16 vertebrae and measuring some 4.67 meters (almost 16 feet) long, a length approximating the total length of trunk and tail combined.

Yang [Young] originally diagnosed *Mamenchisaurus* as follows: Chevrons of anterior vertebrae similar in size and structure to those of most sauropods, especially *Omeisaurus* and *Tienshanosaurus*; at least four middle chevrons with distal ends forked upwards at their bases; chevrons toward end of tail forking so strongly as to become almost straight; limb, foot, and ankle bones resemble those of *Apatosaurus*.

As the neck was not well preserved in the type specimen (cervical vertebrae crushed), it was incorrectly reconstructed as relatively short when the skeleton, liberally supplemented with plaster, was wall-mounted at the Institute of Vertebrate Paleontology, Academia Sinica, in Peking [now Bejing].

Since the discovery of the type specimen, more *Mamenchisaurus* remains have been described. An articulated skeleton representing a second species, *M. hochuanensis*, was discovered in 1957 by the Sichuan Petroleum Expedition at Kuanmushan, Taihezhen, in Hochuan County, Sichuan Province, collected by a joint team from the Sichuan and Chongqing Municipal Museums. (The site had been known for so-called "dragon bones," fossils long used as supposed cures for various ills.) The holotype of this species, as described by Yang, Bien and Mi (1972), has a neck consisting of 19 elongated cervicals and extending 9.8 meters (33 feet). The skeleton measures some 18.5 meters (62 feet) and, if the tail were complete, would probably have totaled about 23.5 meters (80 feet), weighing, in life, approximately 36 metric tons (40 tons). This skeleton was mounted at the Chengdu College of Geology, with casts of the specimen sent to other institutions.

Yang (1958*b*) reported numerous sauropod remains from Haishihwan, Yungteng, and three spec-

Mamenchisaurus

*Mamenchisaurus hochuanen-
sis*, skeleton including cast of
holotype (cast), on temporary
exhibit in 1992 at Media
Center mall, Burbank, California, preview of new branch
of Natural History Museum
of Los Angeles County. The
skull on this mount was a
cast of a *Diplodocus* skull.

imens from Kansu, all of which he referred to *M. constructus*. The first Kansu specimen, collected in 1948 from Machiahukou, includes seven consecutive mid-caudal vertebrae, left humerus, right radius and ulna, left femur and fibula, two left and two right metatarsals, ungual, and many vertebra, rib, and other fragments; the second, from Shangyenkou, includes about ten caudal vertebrae, right humerus, left ilium, right femur, tibia, fibula, a large rib, and right astragalus from the same locality; the third, collected from Machiahukou in 1956, includes a damaged sacrum, about ten anterior caudal vertebrae with 11 almost consecutive chevrons, vertebra and rib fragments, left scapula, right coracoid, right humerus, two metacarpals, ischia, left femur, fibula, broken tibia, right astragalus, and foot bones. (Finding *Mamenchisaurus* in those localities correlates the Red Beds of Sichuan with the Kansu continental series.)

A third species of the genus, *M. sinocanadorum*, was named by Russell and Zheng (1993), based upon a well-preserved series of articulated distal cervical vertebrae, a partial atlas intercentrum, associated left mandible with teeth, and several bones from ventral surface of skull including ?vomer, pterygoid, and

quadrate (IVPP V10603). The material was discovered by Dong Zhi-Ming in August, 1987, during field activities of the Sino-Canadian Dinosaur Project (see Currie 1991; Dong 1993*a*) in the Shishugon (Stone Tree Ravine) Formation, of probable Late Jurassic Age (Dong *et al.* 1983; Russell 1993), in the eastern Junggar Basin, Xinjiang. Dong had spotted the broken end of a rib projecting from a steep exposure in a cliff about a kilometer south-southeast of the base camp of the Project. (The quarry was located within a coarse, rust-colored sandstone in a sequence of pinkish-buff sands and silts.) The neck was traced into the hillside by the end of summer, 1987, and through summer, 1988. Excavation of the specimen was completed by the summer of 1990 (Russell and Zheng 1993).

According to Russell and Zheng, that the teeth in one jaw were fully erupted yet unworn suggests that the individual may have starved. As little bone was found near the base of the exposure, the light, pneumatic cervicals may have broken away from the carcass before decomposition of the ligaments binding together the skull and vertebrae. Possibly the head and neck drifted in the stream, the head lodging in

Mamenchisaurus hochuanensis, skeleton including holotype (cast), on temporary exhibit in 1992 in at Media Center mall, Burbank, California, preview of new branch of Natural History Museum of Los Angeles County.

Photo by the author.

shallow water on a point bar, anchoring the neck until burial of the entire structure. Also, the local fossil vertebrate assemblage at the quarry site was dominated by small and large theropods, sauropods, and small ornithischians, with recovered turtle specimens as abundant as those of dinosaurs. Remains of mature forests comprising large conifers growing beside meandering streams suggest mild, perhaps monsoonal climates among the represented environments (McKnight, Graham, Carroll, Gan, Dilcher, Zhao and Liang 1990).

This material represents a large, mature animal with an estimated total length of 26 meters (almost 90 feet), and lightly proportioned (relative to *Apatosaurus* and *Brachiosaurus*), much of its length consisting of the extremely long neck.

A sauropod humerus (NSM PV17656), missing both proximal and distal ends, represented the first undisputed dinosaur known from the Japanese Islands. The specimen was discovered during the summer of 1978 by Tetsuro Hania and Tomoki Kase in the marine stratum of northern Honshu, largest of all the Japanese islands. Hanai and Kase, on a field survey of the Early Cretaceous Miyako Group, unexpectedly discovered the bone on the weathered surface of a conglomerate outcrop outside the inn at which they were staying, from a formation correlated stratigraphically with the Tanohata Formation (see Hanai, Obata and Hayami 1968) and of Middle Late Aptian–Late Early Albian age (Obata and Matsumoto 1977). Excavated by Kase, the bone was eventually identified by Yoshikazu Hasegawa of Yokohama National University as the humerus of a sauropod, probably *Mamenchisaurus*. As preserved, the specimen measures about 53 centimeters (over 20 inches) long, with maximum width of 20 centimeters (about 7.6 inches), indicating a medium-sized sauropod similar, in some respect, to *M. hochuanensis* (Hasegawa, Manabe, Hanai, Kase and Oji 1991).

Finding this specimen too poor for the erection of a new taxon, Hasegawa *et al.* referred it to ?*Mamenchisaurus* sp., also giving it a traditional Japanese informal name, "Moshi-ryu" (for "Moshi," the local name of the locality, and "ryu," meaning "dragon"). This find suggests that one group of sauropods, in addition to *Mongolosaurus haplodon* Gilmore 1933, lived in East Asia during the Early Cretaceous.

Yang and Chao (1972) put *Mamenchisaurus* into its own family, Mamenchisauridae, after which Berman and McIntosh (1978) tentatively assigned this genus to the Diplodocidae, mostly based upon diplodocid-like vertebral characters. Later, McIntosh (1990) assigned *Mamenchisaurus* to the subfamily Mamenchisaurinae, which, then owing to the lack of a skull in the type genus, he tentatively referred to the Diplodocidae.

The skull elements belonging to IVPP V10603 constitute the first cranial remains referable to *Mamenchisaurus*, now rendering this genus as one of the more completely known sauropod taxa. As Russell and Zheng pointed out, the quadrate, as in the camarasaurid *Euhelopus*, possesses an enormously deep chamber or excavation that opens into the posterior face of the quadratic shaft. The dentary gently curves toward the mandibular symphysis and the teeth are spatulate, indicating that the affinities of *Mamenchisaurus* are not with the Diplodocidae. Returning *Mamenchisaurus* to the Mamenchisauridae, Russell and Zheng noted that mamenchisaurids and diplodocids may have shared a remote common ancestry, but that the former were probably more closely related to other Asian sauropod groups.

Note: Dong, Hasegawa and Azuma (1990), in the dinosaur exhibition guidebook *The Age of Dinosaurs in Japan and China*, referred to *Mamenchisaurus* sp. sauropod material nicknamed "Moshisaurus" (or "Moshi-ryu").

Key references: Berman and McIntosh (1978); Dong, Zhou and Zhang (1983); McIntosh (1970*b*); Russell and Zheng (1993); Yang [Young] (1954*b*, 1958*b*, 1972); Yang [Young] and Chao (1972).

Mamenchisaurus hochuanensis restored, as originally interpreted, with diplodocid-type head (skull now thought to resemble that of *Euhelopus*).

Illustration by Mark Hallett.

MANDSCHUROSAURUS Riabinin 1930
[*nomen dubium*]
Ornithischia: Genasauria: Cerapoda: Ornithopoda:
Iguanodontia: Hadrosauridae *incertae sedis*.
Name derivation: "Manchuria" + Greek *sauros* =
"lizard."
Type species: *M. amurensis* (Riabinin 1925) [*nomen
dubium*]
Other species: ?*M. laosensis* Hoffet 1943 [*nomen
dubium*].
Occurrence: Yevreyskaya Avtonomnaya Oblast,
[former Rossiyskaya Sovetskaya Federativnaya
Sotsialisticheskaya Respublika, Union of Soviet
Socialist Republics]; Heilongiang, People's
Republic of China; ?[unnamed formation]
Savannakhet Khoueng, Laos.
Age: Late Cretaceous (?Maastrichtian).
Known material: Partial skeleton, postcranial
elements.
Holotype: IVP AS [in "Leningrad"] collection,
incomplete skeleton including posterior portion
of skull, lower jaw without teeth, 17 dorsal, 2
sacral, and 11 caudal vertebrae, scapulae, right
coracoid, humeri, ulna, manus bones, incomplete
pelvic girdle, femur, tibia, fibula, foot.
 Diagnosis of genus: [None published.]
 Comments: *Mandschurosaurus* was the first Chinese dinosaur to be named.

 The genus, originally named *Trachodon amurensis*, was founded upon an incomplete, scattered,
abraded, and poorly preserved skeleton (IVP AS collection), discovered in 1914 in supposed Maastricht-
ian-equivalent beds (Late Senonian), on the bank
of the Amur River, in Belye Kinchi, Manchuria.
The first fragments of the specimen were collected
the next year by geologist A. N. Kryshtofovitch of
the Museum of the Geological Committee [formerly]
U.S.S.R. (Leningrad). More material was collected
during the summers of 1916 and 1917 by the Geological Committee, led by preparator N. P. Stepanov, on
the right shore of the Amur, between the villages of
Kassatkino and Ssagibovo at the Bieyle Kroutchy
boundary (Riabinin 1925).

 Riabinin (1925) originally described the type
species as follows: Marked resemblance to *Edmontosaurus* [=*Trachodon* of his usage] *annectens*; estimated height [in upright posture resting on tail] 4.5
meters (more than 15 feet), length almost 8 meters
(almost 27 feet); mandible with reduced number (35)
of dental furrows; ischia not distally expanded.

 Later, Riabinin (1930*a*) described these remains
in greater detail, at the same time referring them to
the new genus *Mandschurosaurus*. However, as later
pointed out by Gilmore (1933), most of the remaining bones of characteristic importance are too poorly

Mandschurosaurus amurensis,
IVP AS collection, restored
holotype skeleton, mounted
at the Central Geological
Museum, Leningrad.

preserved for proper diagnosis.

 Mandschurosaurus has generally been regarded
as belonging to the Hadrosaurinae (and one of the
largest hadrosaurines). Brett-Surman (1975, 1989),
however, declared this genus a *nomen dubium*, as
none of the features present in the holotype are characteristic at the generic level, and regarded the taxon
as Hadrosauridae *incertae sedis*.

 The species *M. laoensis* was based on vertebrae,
a scapula, and femur from the ?Late Senonian of Bas-

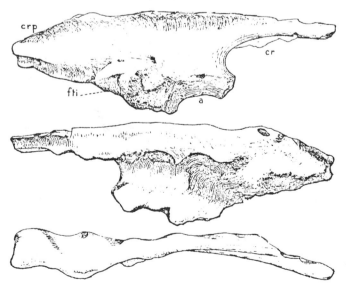

?*Mandschurosaurus
laoensis*, holotype
ilium, in external,
internal, posterior
views. (After Hoffet
1943.)

Laos, Indo-China, described by Hoffet (1937). This material may or may not belong to *Mandschurosaurus*.

Much of the mounted holotype skeleton of *Mandschurosaurus*, displayed at the Central Geological and Prospecting Museum in Leningrad, Russia, has been heavily restored in plaster.

Note: Brett-Surman (1979) made *M. mongoliensis* Gilmore 1933 the type species of a new genus, *Gilmoreosaurus*.

Key references: Brett-Surman (1975, 1989); Gilmore (1933); Hoffet (1943); Riabinin (1925; 1930a).

MANOSPONDYLUS Cope, 1892 [*nomen dubium*]—(See *Tyrannosaurus*.)

Name derivation: Greek *manos* = "porous" + Greek *spondylos* = "vertebra."

Type species: *M. gigas* Cope 1892 [*nomen dubium*].

MARMAROSPONDYLUS Owen 1875 [*nomen dubium*-]—(See *Bothriospondylus*.)

Name derivation: Greek *marmaros* = "marble" + Greek *spondylos* = "vertebra."

Type species: *M. robustus* Owen 1875 [*nomen dubium*].

Marshosaurus bicentesimus, pelvis including UUVP 2826, holotype left ilium, and UUVP 2878, paratype left ischium. (After Madsen 1976.)

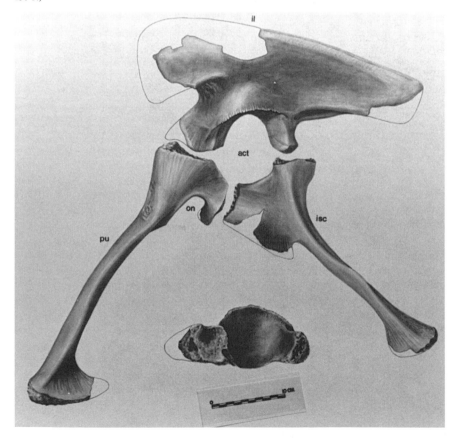

MARSHOSAURUS Madsen 1976

Saurischia: Theropoda: ?Tetanurae: ?Coelurosauria *incertae sedis*.

Name derivation: "[Othniel Charles] Marsh" + Greek *sauros* = "lizard."

Type species: *M. bicentesimus* Madsen 1976.

Other species: [None.]

Occurrence: Morrison Formation, Utah, United States.

Age: Late Jurassic-?Early Cretaceous (Kimmeridgian-Tithonian; ?Neocomian-?Hauterivian).

Known material: Partial skull and postcrania.

Holotype: UUVP 2826, left ilium.

Diagnosis of genus (as for type species): [Based on holotype] small- to medium-size theropod, about 5 meters (17 feet) or less in length; ilium heavy, with low, long posterior blade; pubic peduncle stout, with rugose articular surface divided into anterior and posterior concavities; ischiadic peduncle moderately long, rugose, with rounded surface at apex; acetabulum deep, almost symmetrical; [based on paratypes] interdental plates separated to base; premaxilla attached loosely to maxilla; maxilla with divided sinus with two fenestrae in usual position; four premaxillary, 16 maxillary, and 22 dentary teeth (total count unique among theropods), maxillary teeth with slightly expanded roots; pubis long, slender, bowed anteriorly, proximal end rugose and doubly convex to articulate with pubic peduncle; ischiadic articulation rugose, crescent-shaped, deeply notched on ventral side; shaft of pubis bowed, terminating in posteriorly expanded foot; ischium shorter than pubis, with relatively straight shaft, medially grooved at midlength, expanded distally; pubic articulation of ischium rugose, crescent-shaped; proximal end expanded, striated laterally and medially to margin of medial contact (Madsen 1976b).

Comments: The genus *Marshosaurus* was established on an ilium (UUVP 2826) collected from the Brushy Basin Member of the Morrison Formation (see Stokes 1952), Cleveland-Lloyd Dinosaur Quarry, in east central Utah. Paratype specimens include a right premaxilla (UUVP 3266); right maxillae (UUVP 1846 and 4695); left maxilla (UUVP 1864); left dentaries (UUVP 40-555 and 3454); right dentary (UUVP 3502); left ilium (UUVP 1845); right ilia (UUVP 1882 and 2742); right pubis (UUVP 4736); right ischium (UUVP 2832); and left ischium (UUVP 2878). Numerous associated elements from the Cleveland-Lloyd Dinosaur Quarry are also referable to this genus (Madsen 1976b).

As observed by Madsen, the pelvic girdle of *Marshosaurus* differs from that in other Late Jurassic theropods in various ways, including the unusually shaped pubic foot of the pubis and relative shortness

Marshosaurus bicentesimus, UUVP 3454, paratype left dentary. (After Madsen 1976.)

0   5 CM.

of the ischium, the latter about two-thirds the length of the pubis. Madsen cautioned that, until more complete skeletal remains are found, *Marshosaurus* cannot be suitably compared with other theropods or assigned to any family.

Galton and Jensen (1976*a*) noted that the ilium of *Marshosaurus* seems to have a narrow brevis shelf as in "carnosaurs." Rowe and Gauthier (1990) observed that the pubic shaft is bowed cranially as in ceratosaurs. According to Molnar (1990), the pubis of *M. bicentestimus* resembles that of *Coelurus agilis* [=*C. fragilis*] and does not belong to a "carnosaur."

The first possible occurrence of *Marshosaurus* outside of its type locality was reported by Britt (1991) from the Dry Mesa Quarry (Morrison Formation, Upper Jurassic [Tithonian] or Lower Cretaceous [Neocomian or Hauterivian]), near the southwest corner of Dry Mesa in west central Colorado. The material, a caudal vertebra (BYUVP 5201), was referred by Britt to cf. *Marshosaurus* (see also *Stokesosaurus* entry).

Key references: Britt (1991); Galton and Jensen (1976*a*); Madsen (1976*b*); Molnar (1990); Rowe and Gauthier (1990); Stokes (1952).

MASSOSPONDYLUS Owen 1854—(=*Aetonyx, Aristosaurus, Dromicosaurus, Gryponyx, Gyposaurus, Hortalotarsus, Leptospondylus, Pachyspondylus*)

Saurischia: Sauropodomorpha: Prosauropoda: Massospondylidae.

Name derivation: Greek *massa* = "bulky" + Greek *spondylos* = "vertebra."

Type species: *M. carinatus* Owen 1854.

Other species: [None.]

Occurrence: Upper Elliot Formation, Clarens Formation, Orange Free State, Cape Province, Bushveld Sandstone, Transvaal, South Africa; Upper Elliot Formation, Leribe, Quthing, Lesotho, Forest Sandstone, Matabeland North, Zimbabwe, Kayonta Formation, Arizona, United States.

Age: Lower Jurassic (Hettangian-Pliensbachian).

Known material: At least 80 partial skeletons, isolated cranial and postcranial elements, four skulls, juvenile to adult, ?eggs.

Type specimen: SAM collection (plaster cast; original specimen, RCS collection, destroyed), isolated cervical, dorsal, and caudal vertebrae, scapula, humerus, ilium, pubis, femur, tibia, numerous phalanges of manus and pes.

Diagnosis of genus: [No modern diagnosis published.]

Comments: *Massospondylus* was founded on partial postcranial remains (RCS collection) discovered in 1853 by J. M. Orpen in the Red Beds [now upper Elliot Formation, Early Jurassic (Hettangian-Pliensbachian); Olsen and Galton 1984], at Harrismith, South Africa, this material originally described by Owen (1854). (All material belonging to type species *M. carinatus* was destroyed in 1940 during bombing of the Royal College of Surgeons, London.) Owen stated that some of the material revealed dinosaurian affinities, but did not elaborate on that observation.

Huene (1906) described casts of the *M. carinatus* type material that had been sent to the South African Museum. Huene diagnosed the type species as follows: First dorsal centrum characterized by extra-

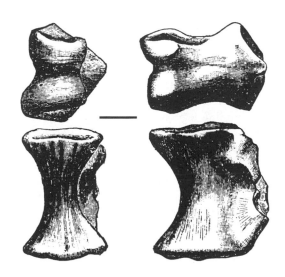

Massospondylus carinatus, RCS, holotype manual phalanx, dorsal and distal views, and dorsal centrum, lateral and ventral views. Scale = 2 cm. (After Lydekker 1888.)

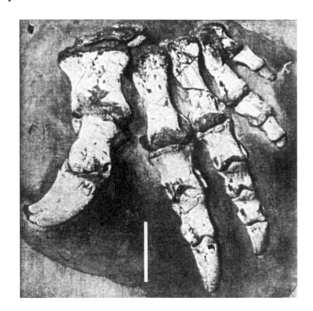

Massospondylus carinatus, BMNH, holotype left manus of *M. browni*. Scale = 3 cm. (After Van Hoepen 1920.)

for the skull, which was found some 3 feet away from the anterior part of the neck.

Cooper (1981) described in detail the skeleton of *M. carinatus*, based on a skull (SAM K1314), skull cast (BPI FN4376), and various postcranial remains (including QG 21c, 38, 46, 51, 75, 77, 1158, 1159, 1160, 1189, 1191, 1374, 1385, 1390, and 1396) from Zimbabwe. According to Cooper, the skull is typically anchisaurid and notable for the large, almost circular orbits (which would, as in *Plateosaurus*, have been reduced by the presence of a sclerotic ring), large

ordinarily high thin keel on ventral surface, scapula by high alar process at distal end on upper side; metacarpal I extraordinarily compact. Huene distinguished the genus from *Plateosaurus* by their tibiae.

A second species, *M. harriesi* Broom 1911, was founded upon forelimb bones (SAM 3394) collected from the uppermost "Red Beds" at Foutanie, Fouriesburg, South Africa. This material seemed to include an imperfect humerus, almost complete radius and ulna, perfect manus, portions of femur and tibia, and toe bones from a single individual, plus a complete pes. Broom (1911), who believed that all but the pes belonged to a single individual, provisionally referred the material to *Massospondylus* on the basis of its resemblance to *M. carinatus*. Broom mostly distinguished this species by its manus with a disproportionately large digit I, which is somewhat opposable against digits II and III, and also by the smaller digits IV and V with their reduced phalangeal count.

Haughton (1924), after reexamining this material, determined that three individuals were represented; the supposed femur was really the distal half of a humerus and should be regarded as separate from the holotype; and the forelimb should be regarded as the type of this species.

A specimen consisting of the vertebral column, front and hind legs, and pectoral and pelvic girdles, collected from the "Red Beds" on a farm between Clifton and St. Fort, was described by Van Hoepen (1920) as new species *M. browni*. Haughton later referred this material to *M. harriesi*, and also described another skeleton (SAM 5135) referred to this species from the "Red Beds," in the Herschel District of Cape Province. This specimen was almost complete, the caudal area and part of the skull having weathered off. The skeleton was articulated except

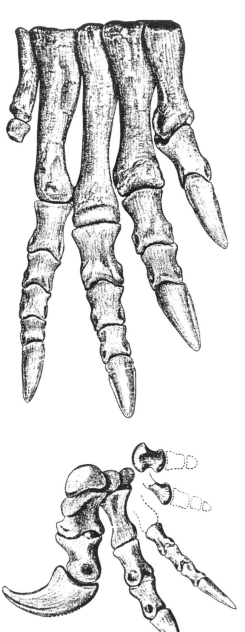

Massospondylus carinatus, SAFM 2769-2770, holotype pes and manus of *Aetonyx palustris*. (After Broom 1911.)

external nares, and relatively large teeth. Significant features of the postcranial anatomy include the presence of sternal plates, interclavicle, and incipient fourth sacral vertebra.

Cooper, postulating that the differences between *M. carinatus* and other species of *Massospondylus* (and various other prosauropod taxa) were related to intraspecific and ontogenetic variation, referred the following species to *M. carinatus*: *M. browni*, *M. harriesi*, *M. schawrzi*, and also *Leptospondylus capensis*, *Pachyspondylus orpenii*, *Hortalotarsus skirtopodus*, *Aetonyx palustris*, perhaps *Gryponyx africanus*, *G. transvaalensis*, *G. taylori*, *Thecodontosaurus dubius*, *Aristosaurus erectus*, *Dromicosaurus gracilis*, and *Gyposaurus capensis*.

M. browni Seeley 1895 was based on two femora, two cervical vertebrae, two dorsals, three caudals, and some foot bones (BMNH collection) from the "Red Beds" at Telle River. Doubting that all of these remains were from the same animal, Huene (1906) referred the vertebrae to *T.* [*Hortalotarsus*] *skirtopodus*. Galton (1976) regarded this form as indeterminate even on a generic level.

M. schwarzi Haughton 1924 [*nomen dubium*] was based on an incomplete pes, distal end of tibia, and indeterminate pieces of leg and sacrum (SAM 5134), from the "Red Beds" at Makomoreng, Mount Fletcher.

Leptospondylus capensis Owen 1854 was founded on two caudal centra (RCS collection) and *Pachyspondylus orpenii* Owen 1854 on two imperfect vertebrae (RCS collection), both from the "Red Beds" at Harrismith. Broom designated both taxa as *nomena dubia*. (These specimens were destroyed during World War II.)

Hortalotarsus skirtopodus Seeley 1894 [*nomen dubium*] was based on a tibia fragment and part of a pes (Albany Museum collection, South Africa) from the Stormberg Series [=Clarens Formation] (Cave Sandstone), Barkley East, Cape Province. To this

Massospondylus carinatus, TRM, holotype skeleton of *Aristosaurus erectus* (juvenile). Scale = approximately 5 cm. (After Hoepen 1920.)

species, Haughton referred material collected from the top of the "Red Beds," including an almost complete right scapula, complete right ulna, right ilium, distal end of left ischium, distal portion of right femur, and nearly complete tibia (SAM 3429).

Aetonyx palustris Broom 1911 was based on a few incomplete dorsal vertebrae, a humerus, radius, imperfect ulna, greater portion of each manus, upper end of a tibia, and almost complete right pes (SAM 2769, 2770), from the top of the "Red Beds" at Foutanie, Fouriesburg.

Gryponyx africanus Broom 1911 was based on vertebrae, pelvis, hind limbs, and a right and left manus (SAM 3357, 3358, 3359), from the top of the "Red Beds," Fouriesburg. Broom (1911) referred this material to a new genus as it represented an individual larger than *Massospondylus*. *G. transvaalensis* Broom

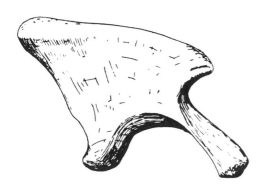

Massospondylus carinatus, holotype right ilium of *Thecodontosaurus skirtopodus*. Length of upper border = 105 mm. (After Haughton 1924.)

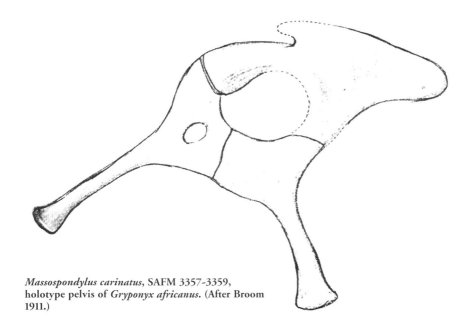

Massospondylus carinatus, SAFM 3357-3359, holotype pelvis of *Gryponyx africanus*. (After Broom 1911.)

Massospondylus carinatus, TRM, holotype ischium of *Dromicosaurus gracilis*, lateral view. Scale = 2 cm. (After Hoepen 1920.)

1912 [*nomen dubium*] was based on an ungual phalanx and distal end of a metatarsal (Transvaal Museum) from the Bushveld Sandstone. Broom (1912) distinguished this species as being about four-fifths the size of *G. africanus*, although Van Hoepen considered that the size discrepancy was due to breakage. *G. taylori* Haughton 1924 was based on a pelvic girdle and sacral vertebrae (SAM 3453) found in 1915, at the top of the "Red Beds" near Fouriesburg.

Thecodontosaurus dubius Haughton 1924 was based on the greater part of a skeleton (SAM 3712), collected in two slabs of Cave Sandstone from the "Stormberg Series" of Ladybrand, South Africa. Haughton described the specimen as larger than *T. browni*. *M. browni* Seeley 1895 [*nomen dubium*] was referred by Huene (1906) to ?*Thecodontosaurus browni*, although Galton regarded the species as indeterminate.

Aristosaurus erectus Van Hoepen 1920 was based on an incomplete skeleton (TRM collection) in a slab and its counterpart, collected from the bottom of the Clarens Formation (Cave Sandstone) at Rosendal,

Orange Free State, South Africa. Missing from the specimen are most of the skull except for part of the left maxilla, right and part of left dentaries, distal portions of forelimbs, and proximal portions of both scapulae. From the many loose sutural connections, Van Hoepen recognized this specimen as pertaining to a young individual. Based on the structure of the pelvis, relative shortness of the humerus, and greater length of the tibia, Hoepen concluded that *Aristosaurus* was an anchisaurid adapted to a normally bipedal mode of locomotion, but was highly specialized in the direction of "plateosaurids." Bonaparte (1987) assigned *Aristosaurus* to the Plateosauridae, a group now included within the family Anchisauridae (Cooper 1981).

Dromicosaurus gracilis Van Hoepen 1920 was based on a fairly complete cervical vertebra, some caudal vertebrae, fragments of humerus and radius, pubes and ischia, femur, and some pes bones (TRM collection), recovered by Van Hoepen from the "Red Beds" of Nauwport Nek, Bethlehem District, South Africa. Van Hoepen recognized this species as a larger form allied to *Massospondylus*.

Gyposaurus capensis was based on a partial skeleton (SAM 990), including 11 dorsal and six caudal vertebrae, ribs, gastralia, incomplete right scapula, ilia, right pubis and ischium, right femur and fibula, right tarsus, and right pes. The specimen was found in a sandstone slab from the Stormberg Series [=Elliot Formation] of Ladybrand, Orange Free State, South Africa, originally described by Broom (1906) as a specimen of *Hortalotarsus skirtopodus*. Broom (1911) later considered this material to be generically distinct from *Hortalotarsus* and referred it to a new genus, *Gyposaurus*.

After examination of well-preserved *Massospondylus* material (QG1254) from Zimbabwe-Rhodesia, Cooper (1980*a*) redescribed in detail the ankle of this genus. Cooper (*contra* Cruickshank 1979) interpreted the *Massospondylus* ankle as not having the peg-in-notch articulation between calcaneum and astragalus as in the "crocodile normal" (CR) condition, therefore possessing a digitigrade rather than plantigrade type ankle which, Cooper believed, was also typical of other prosauropods.

Cooper (1980*a*) noted a striking resemblance between the ankle of *Massospondylus* and that of the Early-Jurassic theropod *Dilophosaurus*, but denied any direct phyletic relationship between these two genera. The resemblance between the ankle of *Massospondylus* and that of the theropod *Syntarsus* was noticed by Cooper (1980*a*), Cruickshank, and other workers (Bakker and Galton 1974). According to Cooper, this similarity, as well as other osteological characters shared by *Massospondylus* and *Syntarsus*, supports a hypothesis that small theropods as well as sauropods descended from prosauropod stock, and that both saurischians and ornithischians descended from a common ancestral group.

The first *Massospondylus* remains known outside of Africa were reported by Attridge, Crompton and Jenkins (1985). The material consists of a well-preserved skull (MCZ 8893) collected by a Harvard University party from the Kayenta Formation (regarded by Attridge *et al.* as Lower Jurassic [Liassic]), Glen Canyon Group, on Navajo Nation land, northeastern Arizona. From this specimen Attridge *et al.* observed small palatal teeth for the first time in any *Massospondylus* skull, describing them as conical and slightly recurved, measuring about one millimeter in height.

Based on his description of the postcranial anatomy of *M. carinatus*, Cooper (1981) concluded that this species was a bipedal and active endotherm. According to Cooper (1981), bipedalism is indicated by the many essential characters listed by Romer (1966), in addition to such features as the mesotarsal ankle, commencement of chevrons so close behind sacrum, strongly cupped manus, and development of a prominent supra-acetabular buttress. Apparently *Massospondylus* could cope with dramatic temperature changes typical of a continental interior desert environment. Cooper speculated that *Massospondylus* could have avoided severe heat loss by the possession of feathers, an idea possibly supported by pedal claws which might have been used in grooming.

Cooper (1981) suggested that *Massospondylus* and other prosauropods, generally regarded as herbivorous, were carnivorous, subsisting upon carrion. Cooper (1981) based this notion on the presence of serrated, cutting teeth in *M. carinatus*, the dinosaur's inability to masticate food (maxillary teeth closing outside the dentary teeth, preventing any sideways chewing motion of the lower jaw) and accommodate resistant plant material, the lateral inflexibility of the axial skeleton, the large rapacious claw on the pollex, and relatively large teeth. Also, Cooper (1981) pointed out that, in a desert environment, vegetation must have been sparse as well as resistant.

This theory was disputed by Attridge *et al.*, who pointed out similarities between prosauropod teeth and those in unquestionably herbivorous "fabrosaurids" and ankylosaurs, as well as the herbivorous lizard *Iguana iguana*. Attridge *et al.* noted that prosauropod teeth differ markedly from those in such Triassic theropods as *Rioarribasaurus* [=*Coelophysis* of their usage], which are recurved and blade-like, with tiny serrations on anterior and posterior crests, and also from the robust, cone-shaped teeth in crocodiles and varanid lizards. Galton (1985*a*) also

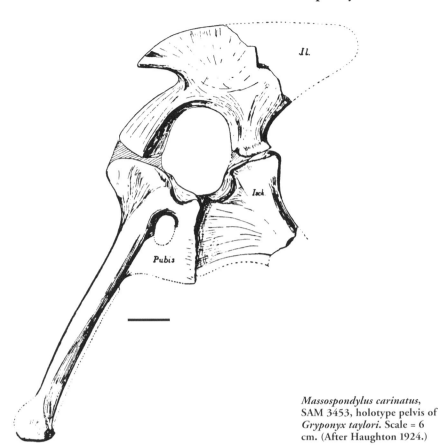

Massospondylus carinatus, SAM 3453, holotype pelvis of *Gryponyx taylori*. Scale = 6 cm. (After Haughton 1924.)

offered numerous reasons to support a strictly herbivorous diet for prosauropods (see *Plateosaurus* entry).

Crompton and Attridge (1986) remarked upon an odd feature of two adult-age skulls of *Massospondylus*. In both skulls, the lower jaw is shorter than the upper, upper teeth therefore extending anteriorly beyond the lower teeth. A small vertical wear facet is present on the lingual surface of the first upper premaxillary teeth which could not have been caused by a lower tooth. Crompton and Attridge determined that the overhang was not the result of crushing. Noting that the outer surface of the tip of the lower jaws is rugose and that many vascular canals are present, Crompton and Attridge suggested that the tips of the mandibles were covered in life with a horny beak. This supposed beak would have caused the upper-tooth wear. A beak, in conjunction with long cone-shaped upper teeth, would have equipped *Massospondylus* with a more effective cropping mechanism than in *Plateosaurus*.

In his review of the Prosauropoda, Galton (1990*a*) noted that *Massospondylus*, *Yunnanosaurus*, and other prosauropods, compared to the more primitive *Anchisaurus*, share such derived characters as a vertical or caudoventrally oriented quadrate, proportional widening of the apron-like distal part of the

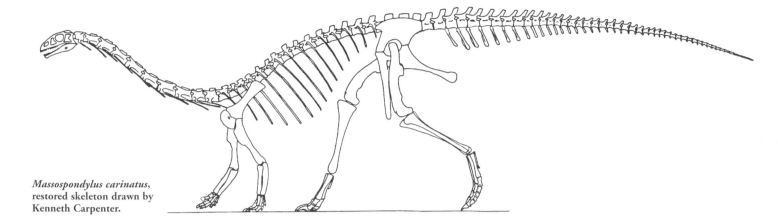

Massospondylus carinatus,
restored skeleton drawn by
Kenneth Carpenter.

pubis, more massive metacarpals II-V, and more massive metatarsals I-IV.

Notes: The rare discovery of a clutch of Triassic dinosaur eggs, found in the same horizon as isolated long bones of *Massospondylus*, was reported by Kitching (1979). The six eggs, containing foetal skeletons, were found embedded in a block of hard reddish-brown sandy mudstone, in the Elliot Formation (Red Bed Stage), Golden Gate Highlands National Park, about 17 kilometers (over 600 miles) east of Clarens, northern Orange Free State, South Africa. The eggs, as preserved, have a long axis of 65 millimeters and a short axis of about 35 millimeters. The extremely thin shell fragment of one egg has an estimated thickness of 5 millimeters. The wrinkled and somewhat flattened state of the eggs indicated to Kitching that they, as those of some modern day reptiles, were leathery and had a degree of elasticity. Among the foetal remains was a well-preserved skull measuring some 10 millimeters across the squamosals and 7 millimeters from the anterior border of the orbit to the supraoccipital. Kitching noted that, until the material could be further prepared, it was not possible to assign the specimens to any known dinosaur genus.

The species *Gyposaurus sinensis* Yang [Young] 1941, founded on material including the right upper jaw, left upper and lower jaw, cervical, dorsal, and caudal vertebrae, and sacrum, was identified by Galton (1976) as a juvenile *Lufengosaurus huenei*. *M. rawesi* Lydekker 1890 and *M. hislopi* Lydekker 1890 were apparently based on nondinosaurian remains (P. M. Galton, personal communication 1989).

Key references: Attridge, Crompton and Jenkins (1985); Bakker and Galton (1974): Bonaparte (1987); Broom (1906, 1912); Cooper (1980*a*, 1981); Crompton and Attridge (1986); Cruickshank (1979); Galton (1976, 1985*a*, 1990*a*); Haughton (1924); Huene (1906); Kitching (1979); Owen (1854); Seeley (1894*b*); Van Hoepen (1920).

MEGADACTYLUS   Hitchcock 1865/Fitzinger 1843—(See *Anchisaurus.*)
Name derivation: Greek *megalo* = "big" + Greek *daktylos* = "finger."
Type species: *M. polyzelus* Hitchcock 1865.

MEGALOSAURUS   Parkinson 1822—
(=?*Magnosaurus,* ?*Torvosaurus*)
Saurischia: Theropoda: ?Tetanurae: Megalosauridae.
Name derivation: Greek *megalo* = "big" + Greek *sauros* = "lizard."
Type species: *M. bucklandii* Meyer 1832 (=*M. conybeari* Ritgen [1826] [*nomen oblitum*]).
Other species: *M. insignis* Eudes-Deslongchamps 1870 [*nomen dubium*], ?*M. pannoniensis* Seeley 1881 [*nomen dubium*], ?*M. cambrensis* (Newton 1899) [*nomen dubium*], ?*M. hungaricus* Nopcsa 1902 [*nomen dubium*], ?*M. ingens* Janensch 1920 [*nomen dubium*], *M. lydekkeri* Huene 1926 [*nomen dubium*]; ?*M. terquemi* Huene 1926 [*nomen dubium*], ?*M. pombali* Lapparent and Zbyszewski (1957) [*nomen dubiium*], ?*M. inexpectatus* Corro 1966 [*nomen dubium*], ?*M. chubutensis* Corro 1974 [*nomen dubium*], *M. hesperis* Waldman 1974, *M. dapukaensis* Zhao 1986 [*nomen nudum*], *M. tibetensis* Zhao 1986 [*nomen nudum*].
Occurrence: Chipping Norton Formation, Stonesfield Slate, Cornbash Formation, Oxfordshire, ?Inferior Oolite, Northamptonshire, Inferior Oolite, Chipping Norton Formation, Forest Marbel, Gloucestershire, Great Oolite, Forest Marbel, Wiltshire, Corallian Oolite Formation, North Yorkshire, Upper Inferior Oolite, Dorset, England; "Rhaetic" Beds, Mid-Glamorganshire, Wales; [unnamed formation], Indre, Kimmeridge Clay, Damparis, France; ?Sinpetru Beds, Judethean Huneodoara, Romania; ?[unnamed formation], Província do Beira Litoral, Portugal;

?Gosau Formation, Niederöstereich, Austria; ?Danien, Transylvania, Romania; ?Gorro Frigio Formation, Cerro Castillo Formation, Provincia de Chubut, Argentina; ?[Jurassic] Tibet.

Age: Middle-?Late Jurassic (Bathonian-?Oxfordian).

Known material: Dentary, referred teeth and post-cranial remains, skull elements, mold of dentary, isolated teeth.

Holotype: UMO J13506, right dentary with teeth.

Diagnosis of genus: [No modern diagnosis published.]

Comments: *Megalosaurus*, basis for the family Megalosauridae Huxley 1869, was the first dinosaurian genus to be named and described.

The first existing record of an apparent *Megalosaurus* specimen relic dates back almost a century and a half before the "official" discovery of the holotype and naming of the genus. Robert Plot, in *The Natural History of Oxfordshire* (published in 1677), figured and described the distal end of a massive femur which he had unearthed from a quarry in the Parish of Cornwell, Oxfordshire, England. This bone (now lost) seems to have belonged to *Megalosaurus*. Plot, however, was unaware of the bone's nature and significance. A subscriber to the then common belief that human giants had, at some earlier time, inhabited the Earth, Plot concluded that the bone was that of a giant man or woman. In a later edition of Plot's book, the illustration of the bone, due both to its shape and an editorial mistake, was labeled as *Scrotum humanum*.

Megalosaurus was founded upon a dentary with teeth (UMO J13506), and also nonassociated mate-

rial including a series of five dorsal vertebrae, a few ribs, coracoid, clavicle, ilia, ischium, ulna, metatarsus, femur, tibia, and some fragments, collected from the Stonesfield Slates, in Woodstock, near Oxford, England. The generic (no specific name yet assigned) name was apparently coined by William Buckland and W. D. Conybeare, *Megalosaurus* therefore being the first scientific name ever officially assigned to dinosaurian remains. Buckland, who recognized the remains as reptilian, read the name on February 20, 1824, before the Geological Society of London (see Sternberg 1963).

More than a century and a half after the discovery of this material, Britt (1991) noted that the type of *Megalosaurus* is exclusively the partial dentary, the other material recovered from the same locality best regarded as co-types (J. S. McIntosh, personal communication to Britt, 1988).

On July 1, 1822, Parkinson (1822) first published the name *Megalosaurus,* but did not assign it a specific name, nor did he describe the type specimen. Parkinson, though, did state that the specimen was from the calcareous slate of Stonesfield and observed that the teeth resembled those of a monitor lizard. He surmised that *Megalosaurus* was about 2.35 meters (8 feet) high and almost 12 meters (40 feet) long.

Buckland (1824) published the first formal description of the specimen. Meyer (1832) eventually assigned a specific name to the genus, establishing these original remains as the holotype of genus and species combination *M. bucklandii*.

Owen (1856) recognized the dentary of *M. bucklandii* as reptilian because of the unequal height of the

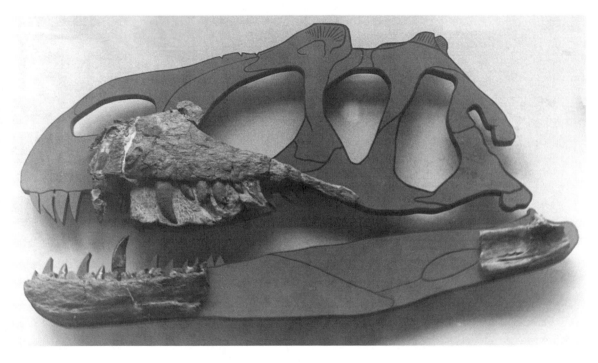

Megalosaurus bucklandii, OUM J13506, holotype left dentary with referred skull material, left lateral view.

Photo by the author, courtesy University Museum, Oxford.

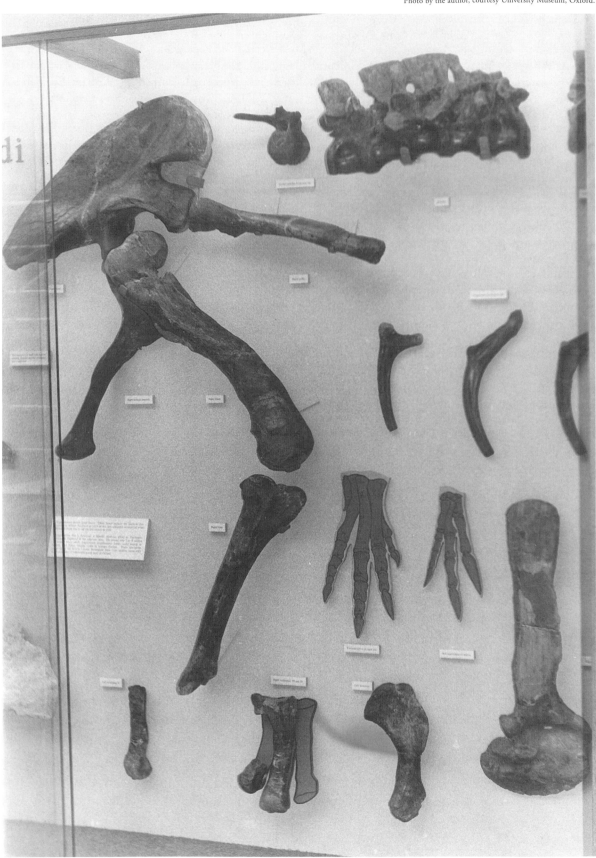

Megalosaurus bucklandi, OUM, referred pelvis, vertebrae, ribs, hindlimb, pes, humerus, and scapulacoracoid.

outer and inner alveolar walls, a feature of the jaws of modern lizards. In *Megalosaurus*, the teeth are entirely exposed in all their growth stages. Although most of the fully developed teeth had apparently been shed rather than broken off, one was preserved *in situ*. In his original diagnosis of this first dinosaur tooth ever to be described, Owen observed the following: Tooth sub-compressed, slightly recurved, minutely serrated, sharply pointed; front edge becoming blunted toward lower third of tooth near base; crown covered by smooth polished enamel, marginal serrations entirely formed by enamel.

Since *Megalosaurus* was described during the infancy of dinosaur discoveries, early conceptions of the animal's appearance in life were understandably in error. Comparing the original type material with small modern land lizards, pioneering dinosaur specialists, most notably Buckland, tended to envision *Megalosaurus* as a gigantic lizard measuring as long as 21 meters (about 70 feet).

Owen envisioned *Megalosaurus* and the small number of other dinosaurian forms known at that time as elephantine reptiles with an upright rather than sprawling, lizard-like posture, their large-to-gigantic bodies supported by four unusually developed limbs. Observing that the dorsal vertebrae in *Megalosaurus* agreed with those of the crocodile in their mode of articulation with the ribs, Owen theorized that they must also correspond with them in number. Comparing *Megalosaurus* remains to a crocodile skeleton, then shortening the tail from lacertilian to dinosaurian proportions, Owen calculated that total length of this extinct reptile to be not more than about 9 meters (30 feet).

Owen was fairly accurate in figuring the length of *Megalosaurus*, a modern estimation being about 7–8 meters (23–26 feet). His conception of an upright posture was certainly revolutionary and indeed does apply to quadrupedal dinosaurs. For many years, *Megalosaurus* continued to be portrayed in Owen's prescribed posture. That depiction was in no small way perpetuated by sculptor Benjamin Waterhouse Hawkins who, during the early 1850s under Owen's direction, created a full-scale (and highly speculative) model of *Megalosaurus* for the Crystal Palace grounds at Sydenham, London. Hawkins' recreation, still on view today, depicted *Megalosaurus* as a quadrupedal monster with a crocodile-like head and relatively short tail. Only following the discovery of more complete theropod remains was *Megalosaurus* recognized as a biped.

After restudying the material assigned to *M. bucklandii*, Huene (1923) attempted a reasonably accurate reconstruction of its skeleton, noting that

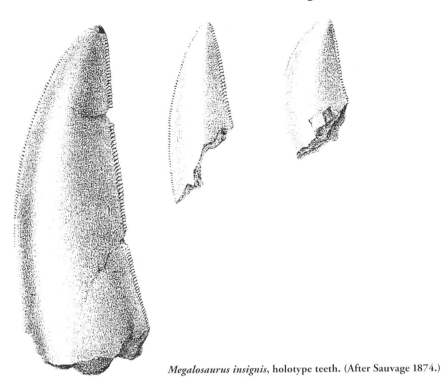

Megalosaurus insignis, holotype teeth. (After Sauvage 1874.)

the skull somewhat resembles that of *Allosaurus* [=*Antrodemus* of his usage].

As *Megalosaurus* was founded on fragmentary material, comparing it with other genera is at best difficult. To date, no modern diagnosis of the genus has been published, nor is this theropod sufficiently understood. Nevertheless, *Megalosaurus* has become a kind of dinosaurian catch basin for virtually all theropods discovered in Europe (in addition to forms from other continents). After more than a century and a half following the description of the holotype, more species have been referred to *Megalosaurus* than to any other dinosaurian genus. Most of these species were based on material too poor for positive identification.

The species ?*M. ingens* Janensch 1920 is one of many taxa based upon an isolated tooth. As pointed out by Molnar (1990) in his review of problematic "carnosaurs," it is not certain that this species is either "carnosaurian" or belongs to that genus.

M. insignis Eudes-Delongchamps 1870 [*nomen dubium*] was based on some large *Megalosaurus*-like teeth, a sacrum, and some stout phalanges, from the Kimmeridge Clay of Damparis, France. To this species Lapparent and Zbyszewski (1957) referred some specimens from Portugal, including teeth, the longest measuring 60 millimeters, or 2.3 inches, in length (Lusitanian, Kimmeridgian and Portlandian); caudal vertebrae from the Lusitanian of Fervenca (Alcobaca) and Ourém and Kimmeridgian of Praia de areia Branca, sacrals from the Lusitanian of Ourém,

Megalosaurus insignis, Praia da Areia Branca, referred caudal vertebrae. (After Lapparent and Zbysweski 1957.)

dorsals from Casal de Labrusque (Louriñha), caudals from the Lusitanian near Fervenca; fragmentary ulna from the Lusitanian of Ourém; and small manual claws of a ?juvenile from Vale de Portinheiro.

?*M. pannoniensis* Seeley 1881 [*nomen dubium*], a comparatively small form, was based on two teeth from the Upper Cretaceous (Danian) Gosau Beds near Wiener Neustadt in southern France, apparently too late for *Megalosaurus*. Lapparent and Zbyszewski tentatively referred material including three fragmentary teeth and three manual phalanges from the Upper Senonian of Viso, Portugal, to this species and described it as follows: Tooth remarkably narrow, base diameter 12 millimeters; if complete, tooth about 30 millimeters in length; phalanges small, respectively 20, 15 and 11 millimeters long. This species is also known from the Danian of Transylvania.

?*M. hungaricus* (regarded as a *nomen dubium* by Le Loeuff and Buffetaut 1991) was based on a tooth described by Nopcsa (1902). Huene (1926*b*) observed that this tooth exhibits no generic characters and is geologically too young to be *Megalosaurus*.

?*Megalosaurus pombali*, holotype anterior a. dorsal and b. caudal vertebrae. (After Lapparent and Zbyszewski 1957.)

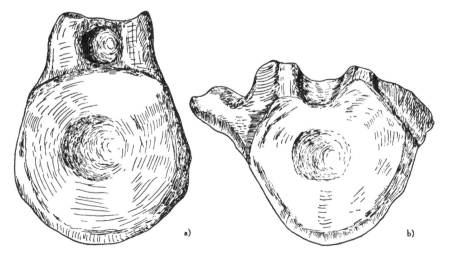

?*M. cambrensis*, originally *Zanclodon cambrensis*, was based on the natural mold of a left dentary from the "Rhaetic" [obsolete term] of Glamorganshire, Wales. The specimen was discovered in a block of hard whitish sandstone by John David while preparing stone for building a wall near Brigden, Glamorganshire. Newton (1899) described this species as follows: Dentary 275 millimeters (10.8 inches) long, 65 millimeters (2.6 inches) deep at posterior portion of alveolar margin; narrow, lower margin very straight, lower edge rounded, anterior half of outer surface comparatively flat; six strongly curved teeth with serrated posterior concave margins, largest tooth 29 millimeters (over 1.2 inches) in length above outer margin, approximately 6 millimeters (.23 inch) in thickness.

As pointed out by Molnar, Kurzanov and Dong (1990), this species, though considerably older than *M. bucklandii*, agrees in six of nine diagnostic points listed by Madsen (1976*a*), three (angular rostral margin, separate interdental plates, and exposed replacement teeth) seemingly shared derived features. The remaining three characters (mesial extent of alveolar row, form of symphysis, and form of lateral surface) cannot be determined. Accordingly, this species seems to be referable to *Megalosaurus*. Although further material is required to establish this as a valid species, its distinction is largely based upon greater age.

Huene (1926*b*) based the dubious species ?*M. terquemi* on teeth from the Angulatus beds near Hettingen, noting that their shape was different from that of other *Megalosaurus* teeth.

?*M. pombali* Lapparent and Zbyszewski 1957 [*nomen dubium*] is a later–Jurassic species based on three teeth plus eight dorsal and caudal vertebrae from the Lusitanian (Oxfordian) Vale de Portinheiro, Porto da Barcas, Portugal. Lapparent and Zbyszewski described this species as follows: Distinguished from *M. insignis* mostly by height of teeth, if complete, from 81–110 millimeters (over 3–about 4.25 inches); dorsal vertebrae large, one anterior dorsal 90 millimeters (about 3.5 inches). According to Molnar (1990), this species cannot be referred with confidence to *Megalosaurus*.

?*M. inexpectatus* and ?*M. chubutensis*, described by Corro (1966, 1974), were based upon isolated teeth from Argentina. As noted by Bonaparte, Novas and Coria (1990), these teeth lack diagnostic characters and should be regarded as *nomena dubia*.

M. hesperis Waldman (1974) was based on parts of both premaxillae, right maxilla, vomer, dentaries, and surangular (BMNH R332) from a medium-sized individual, collected from the Upper Inferior Oolite (Late Bajocian) of Sherborne, England. As noted by Molnar *et al.*, the dentaries of this species resemble those of *M. bucklandii* in six out of nine characters listed by Madsen, and differs in one (alveoli extending to extreme mesial margin), while two characters (form of symphysis and form of lateral surface) cannot be determined. As observed by Molnar *et al.*, this taxon's resemblance to ?*M. cambrensis* suggests that *M. hesperis* is a primitive species.

Zhao (1986*a*) named (but did not describe) two new species, *M. dapukaensis* and *M. tibetensis*, in an article about the Jurassic system of Tibet.

Megalosaurus has traditionally been regarded as a "carnosaur" in the old sense of that term. In their review of "Carnosauria" as more recently defined by them, Molnar *et al.* noted that the holotype of *M. bucklandii* displays no diagnostic characters of any theropod groups. The most complete referred species, *M. hesperis,* exhibits but one "carnosaurian" feature (deep surangular; see Waldman). As only one species of large theropod is known from the Stonesfield Slate, Molnar *et al.* examined the referred postcranial material, observing that the ilium has a narrow brevis shelf, the femur an elevated head, and the lesser trochanter is wing-like ("carnosaurian" features, as this group was then understood); however, the scapula lacks the abrupt acromial expansion and the femur lacks the extensor sulcus known in "carnosaurs." Molnar *et al.* acknowledged that *Megalosaurus* seems to be related to "Carnosauria," although its precise relationships to that group have yet to be determined. Britt referred Megalosauridae to the Ceratosauria, based on observed similarities between *Megalosaurus, Ceratosaurus* and *Torvosaurus.* Britt's assessment was not accepted by Holtz (1994*a*) in an analysis of the Theropoda.

Notes: Many species were originally referred to *Megalosaurus* but have subsequently been assigned to other genera: *M. meriani* Greppin (1870) [*nomen dubium*] was made the type species of *Labrosaurus meriani* by Huene (1926), although this species may be referable to *Ceratosaurus* or a related genus (R. E. Molnar, personal communication); *M. superbus* Sauvage 1882 [*partim*] was made the type species of *Erectopus sauvagei* by Huene (1923); *M. bredai* Seeley 1883 [*nomen dubium*] the type species of *Betasuchus* by Huene (1932); *M. bradleyi* Woodward 1910 the type species of *Proceratosaurus* by Huene (1926*b*); *M. parkeri* Huene 1923 the type species of *Metriacanthosaurus* by Walker (1964); *M. saharicus* Depéret and Savornin 1927 the type species of *Carcharodontosaurus* by Stromer (1931); and *M. wetherilli* Welles 1954 the type species of *Dilophosaurus* by Welles (1970).

M. dunkeri Dames 1884 was renamed *Altispinax dunkeri* (no type species designated) by Huene (1923); *M. lonzeensis* Dollo 1903 [*nomen dubium*] was renamed ?*Struthiomimus lonzeensis*, but regarded by Molnar (1990) as indeterminate; and *M. crenatissimus*

Skeleton (cast, based on holotypes MIWG 6348 and BMNH R10001, reconstructed somewhat after *Allosaurus*), exhibited as *Megalosaurus*, to be described by Steve Hutt, David M. Martill, and Michael J. Barker, as new genus and species *Neovenator salerii*.

Depéret 1896 was renamed *Majungasaurus crenatissimus* (no type species designated) by Lavocat (1955).

M. cloacinus Quenstedt 1858 [*nomen dubium*] and *M. obtusus* Henry 1876 [*nomen dubium*] were referred to *Plateosaurus engelhardti* and later regarded by Molnar (1990) as indeterminate; *M. oweni* Lydekker 1889 [*nomen dubium*] was referred by Huene (1926*b*) to "*M. dunkeri*"; and *M. africanus* Huene 1956 will be referred by Molnar (in press) to *Carcharodontosaurus saharicus. M. poikilopleuron* Huene 1923 is a junior synonym of *Poekilopleuron buck-*

?*Megalosaurus pannoniensis*, holotype tooth. (After Seeley 1881.)

landii, Huene regarding *Poekilopleuron* as a species of *Megalosaurus*. *M. merensis* Lapparent 1955 is the crocodilian *Steneosaurus*. *M. schnaitheimii* Bunzel 1871 is nondinosaurian (Chure and McIntosh 1989).

Hisa, in *Utan Scientific Magazine*, issue 4 (24), 1989, described two large theropods from Japan, informally named "Kagasaurus" and "Mifunesaurus," both regarded as indeterminate megalosaurids by Dong, Hasegawa and Azuma (1990) in the dinosaur exhibition guidebook, *The Age of Dinosaurs in Japan and China*.

Fossil footprints from the same horizon and locality as *M. pombali* were reported by Lapparent and Zbyszewski and attributed to that species. The tracks are three-toed, the largest 64 centimeters (over 20.5 inches) long, and 20 centimeters (about 7.8 inches) in diameter at its central portion. Digit III is 21 centimeters (almost 8 inches) long; I is 7 centimeters (about 2.75 inches). Also, tridactyl, subdigitigrade tracks with claw impressions, made by a bipedal dinosaur presumably *Megalosaurus*, have been found in the Upper Jurassic, at Purbeck, in Dorset, England.

Key references: Bonaparte, Novas and Corro (1990); Britt (1991); Buckland (1824); Corro (1966, 1974); Eudes-Delongchamps (1870); Huene (1926); Janensch (1920); Lapparent and Zbyszewski (1957); Le Loeuff and Buffetaut (1991); Meyer (1832); Molnar (1990); Molnar, Kurzanov and Dong (1990); Newton (1899); Nopcsa (1902, 1907); Owen (1856); Parkinson (1822); Ritgen (1826); Sauvage (1882); Seeley (1881); Waldman (1974); Zhao (1986*a*).

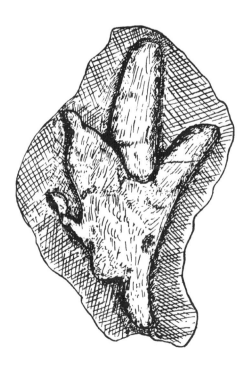

Ichnite (Fac. des Sc. de Lisbonne) attributed to *Megalosaurus*. (After Lapparent and Zbyszewski 1957.)

MELANOROSAURUS   Haughton 1924

Saurischia: Sauropodomorpha: Prosauropoda: Melanorosauridae.

Name derivation: Greek *melas* = "black" + Greek *oros* = "mountain" + Greek *sauros* = "lizard."

Type species: *M. readi* Haughton 1924.

Other species: *M. thabanensis* Gauffre 1993.

Occurrence: Lower Elliot Formation, Cape Province, South Africa; Upper Red Beds, Thabana-Morena, Lesotho.

Age: Late Triassic (Late Carnian or Early Norian); Early Jurassic (Hettangian-Pleinsbachian).

Known material: Partial skeleton, isolated femur.

Cotypes: SAM 3449, tibia, fibula, part of pelvis, vertebrae, 3450, femur, proximal half of humerus.

Diagnosis of genus (as for type species): Vertebrae smaller and lighter than in "*Gresslyosaurus*" and *Euskelosaurus* relative to femur length and size; humerus with sharply bent-over lateral process, proximal edge forming moderately high bow (less marked than in "*Gresslyosaurus*"); femur with straight shaft, lateral border approximately at right angle with proximal surface at upper, outer corner, and with lower end of fourth trochanter below mid-shaft; distal end of tibia broader anteriorly than posteriorly (Haughton 1924).

Diagnosis of *M. thabanensis*: (Based on association of following features) latero-medial width greater than antero-posterior width; fourth trochanter oblique, far from medial edge; lesser trochanter far from lateral edge (Gauffre 1993).

Comments: Basis for the family Melanorosauridae Huene 1929, the genus *Melanorosaurus* was founded on incomplete postcranial remains (SAM 3449 and 3450) recovered from the Elliot Formation (Upper Triassic [Late Carnian or Early Norian]; see Olsen and Galton 1984) (formerly Stormberg Series, basal Red Beds), found in a soft red mudstone below a sandstone band on the northern slope of Thaba 'Nyama ("Black Mountain"), district of Herschel,

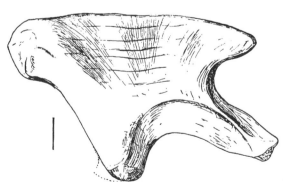

Melanorosaurus readi, SAFM 3449-3450, holotype right ilium. Scale = 5 cm. (After Haughton 1924.)

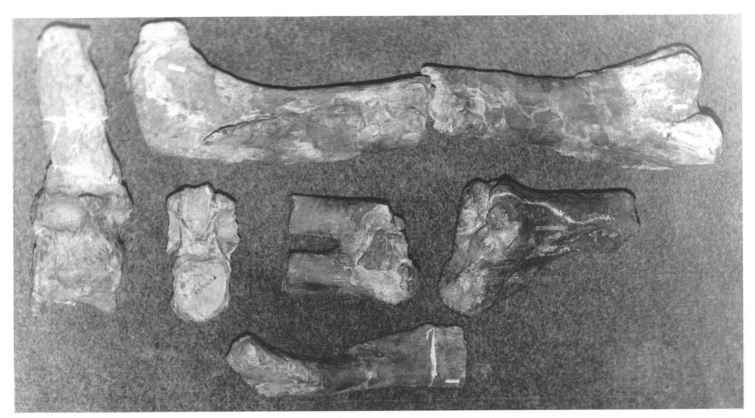

Cape Province, South Africa. A scapula and complete humerus (SAM 3532) from the same district, between Kromme Spruit and Majuba Nek, and belonging to a somewhat smaller individual, were referred to the type species *M. readi* (Haughton 1924).

In a review of the genus *Euskelosaurus*, Heerden (1979) concluded that *M. readi* was synonymous with *E. browni*. Galton (1985c), however, showed that *Melanorosaurus* is a generically distinct genus from *Euskelosaurus*: The femur of *Melanorosaurus*, in posterior view, is straight, the fourth trochanter close to the medial edge, while that in *Euskelosaurus* is sigmoid in posterior view, fourth trochanter well removed from the medial edge.

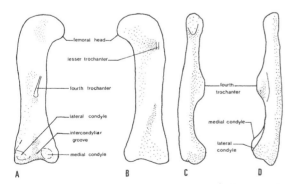

Melanorosaurus thabanensis, MNHN LE5-16, holotype right femur, A. posterior, B. anterior, C. medial, and D. lateral views. (After Gauffre 1993.)

New species *M. thabanensis* was described by Gauffre (1993), based upon an isolated complete right femur (MNHN LES-16) collected from the Upper Red Beds (strata corresponding to the Upper Elliot Formation and to the base of the Clarens Formation; see Kitching and Raath 1984; Hettangian-Pliensbachian; Galton and Olsen 1984; Olsen and Sues 1986) of the Thabana-Morena site, southeast of Mafeteng and south of Thabana-Morena village, Lesotho. Gauffre distinguished this species by the derived and distinct features of the femur, noting that it represents the only Early Jurassic melanorosaurid taxon. As measured by Gauffre, the femur is 516 millimeters in length, with a maximal distal width of 152 millimeters and maximal proximal width of 151 millimeters.

Key references: Galton (1985c); Gauffre (1993); Haughton (1924); Heerden (1979).

METRIACANTHOSAURUS   Walker 1964

Saurischia: Theropoda: ?Tetanurae: ?Megalosauridae.

Name derivation: Greek *metrios* = "moderate" + Greek *akanthos* = "spine" + Greek *sauros* = "lizard."

Type species: *M. parkeri* (Huene 1923).

Other species: [None.]

Occurrence: Corralian Oolite Formation, Dorset, England.

Metriacanthosaurus parkeri, OUM 12144, (left) holotype dorsal vertebrae, (bottom) ischium, (middle) distal ?pubis and proximal tibia (medial view), and (top) right femur of *Megalosaurus parkeri.*

Age: Late Jurassic (Early–Middle Oxfordian).

Known material/holotype: UMO 12144, pelvis, right femur, partial vertebral column.

Diagnosis of genus (as for type species): Ilium differs from *M. bucklandi* in angulation of superior margin, with comparatively deeper blade; pubis with considerably more expanded "foot," as much as ?18 centimeters (almost 7 inches) long when complete (partially eroded away in holotype); ischium more massive, but generally same as in *Allosaurus*, no posterior and downward curvature (as in *M. bucklandii*); femora comparatively more slender, lesser trochanter more proximally placed; cnemial process of tibia projecting more strongly upward than in *B. bucklandii* (Walker 1964).

Comments: The genus *Metriacanthosaurus* was named after incomplete postcranial material (UMO 12144) originally described by Huene (1923) as the holotype of a new species of *Megalosaurus*, *M. parkeri*, collected from the Lower Oxfordian, Oxford Clay, Dorset, north of Weymouth, England.

M. parkeri was originally diagnosed by Huene as follows: Spines of dorsal vertebrae very high, about 25 centimeters (almost 10 inches) long, twice length of centra; ilium differing from [that referred to] type species *M. bucklandii*; pubis very narrow, with large obturator foramen, thick, hook distal end; ischium with large longitudinal ridge on lateral surface near articular face; tibia with greatly forward-projecting cnemial crest.

Although recognizing that the characters of this genus indicated an atypical species, Huene was not willing to separate it from *Megalosaurus*.

Walker (1964), in a study of the nondinosaurian archosaur *Ornithosuchus* and the origin of "carnosaurs," stated that, based upon his own observations and having access to material unavailable to Huene, *M. parkeri* is generically distinct from *M. bucklandii*. In addition to the long dorsal neural spines, Walker pointed out other differences between the two

species. Walker referred "*M.*" *parkeri* to the new genus *Metriacanthosaurus*.

Although *M. parkeri* is usually regarded as having elongated neural spines, Molnar (1990) pointed out that these elements are not significantly longer in this species than in *Allosaurus fragilis*. The angled dorsal margin of the ilium and distinct lateral ridge of the ischium constitute the autapomorphies in this species, although no features, according to Molnar, allow its confident classification.

Key references: Huene (1923); Molnar (1990); Walker (1964).

MICROCERATOPS Bohlin 1953

Ornithischia: Genasauria: Cerapoda: Marginocephalia: Ceratopsia: Neoceratopsia, Protoceratopsidae.

Name derivation: Greek *mikros* = "small" + Greek *keratos* = "horned" + Greek *ops* = "face."

Type species: *M. gobiensis* Bohlin 1953.

Other species: [None.]

Occurrence: Minhe Formation, Gansu, Nei Mongol Zizhiqu, People's Republic of China, Sheeregeen Gashoon Formation, Omnogov, Mongolian People's Republic.

Age: Late Cretaceous (Campanian-Maastrichtian).

Known material: Partial skull, skeleton, several fragmentary specimens, juvenile and adult.

Holotype: Fragmentary dentary.

Diagnosis of genus (as for type species): Small, light-built protoceratopsid with short, fenestrated frill; jugal and mandible shallow, the latter with straight ventral border; forelimbs and hindlimbs long, slender, tibia about 16 percent longer than femur; metatarsus narrow, long, compact (Maryańska and Osmólska 1975).

Comments: A gracile animal and one of the tiniest known dinosaurian genera, *Microceratops* was established on a partial dentary collected from the Djadokhta equivalent [based upon associated dinosaur fauna, seemingly older than the Djadokhta Formation; see Maryańska and Osmólska 1975] at Tsondolein-khuduk, Wuliji, Western Kansu [now spelled Gansu], China. A few fragments of skulls and lower jaws, some vertebrae, and limb-bone fragments were referred to *M. gobiensis* (Bohlin 1953).

Originally, Bohlin diagnosed this genus (and type species, *M gobiensis*) as follows: Teeth closely resembling those of *Protoceratops*, usually asymmetrical, median rib near posterior border in upper teeth, nearer anterior border in lower teeth; better preserved and larger lower jaw with 12 teeth, smaller jaw, evidently from immature animal, with eight; cervical vertebrae differing from *Protoceratops* in no indication of small wedge-like bone at anteroinferior portion of

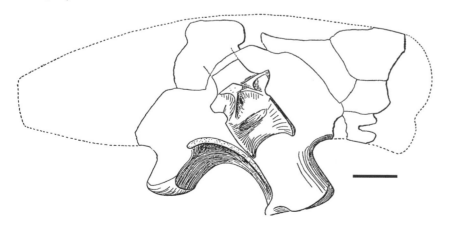

Metriacanthosaurus parkeri, OUM 12144, holotype fragmentary right ilium with dorsal vertebra of *Megalosaurus parkeri*. Scale = 8 cm. (After Huene 1926.)

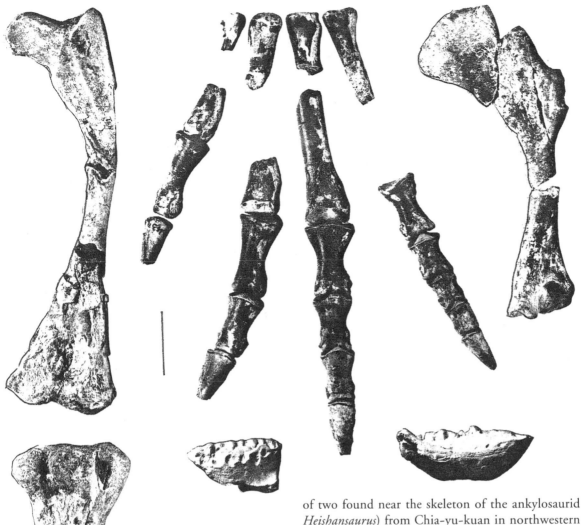

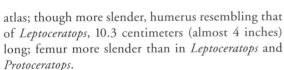

(Clockwise) *Microceratops gobiensis*, right femur, left pes [originally referred to *M. sulcidens*], left humerus, holotype (cast) fragmentary dentary (external and internal views), incomplete tibia. Scale = 2 cm. (After Bohlin 1953.)

of two found near the skeleton of the ankylosaurid *Heishansaurus*) from Chia-yu-kuan in northwestern China. Also referred to this species were vertebral centra, fragmentary limb bones, and bones from the manus and pes. Nessov and Kaznyshkina (*see in* Nessov, Kaznyshkina and Cherepanov 1989) tentatively referred ?*M. sulcidens* to a new genus, *Asiaceratops*; in their review of the Neoceratopsia, Dodson and Currie (1990) synonymized ?*M. sulcidens* with *M. gobiensis*.

Microceratops gobiensis, referred dentary. (After Dong 1987.)

atlas; though more slender, humerus resembling that of *Leptoceratops*, 10.3 centimeters (almost 4 inches) long; femur more slender than in *Leptoceratops* and *Protoceratops*.

Bohlin also described a second species, tentatively designated ?*M. sulcidens*, based on a tooth (one

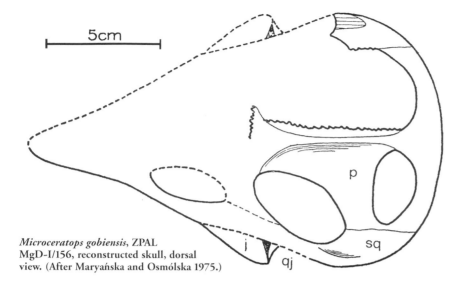

5cm

Microceratops gobiensis, ZPAL MgD-I/156, reconstructed skull, dorsal view. (After Maryańska and Osmólska 1975.)

Jaws and limb bone fragments, collected from Tzoyun, North Shansi, China, were referred to this genus by Yang [Young] (1958*a*).

More complete material, including six very immature skulls, was collected from the Djadokhta Formation in Bayn Dzak between 1964 and 1971 during the Polish-Mongolian Paleontological Expedition (see Kielan-Jaworoska and Dovchin 1969; Kielan-Jaworoska and Barsbold 1972). Kielan-Jaworoska and Barsbold reported a tiny unidentified specimen (referred to *M. gobiensis* by Maryańska and Osmólska) from the Sheeregeen Gashoon locality, Gobi Desert, collected during the Polish-Mongolian Palaeontological Expedition in 1971.

Maryańska and Osmólska rediagnosed the monotypic *M. gobiensis* based upon a new specimen (ZPAL MgD-I/156) collected from the Sheeregeen Gashoon Formation (Sheeregeen Gashoon locality). This specimen comprised a damaged skull with part of the frill and teeth, 23 vertebrae (4 posterior cervicals, 12 dorsals, and 7 sacrals), almost all with damaged neural arches, proximal portion of the left scapula, left coracoid, right humerus, radius and frag-

Microhadrosaurus nanshiungensis, IVPP V4732, holotype partial left dentary with teeth (juvenile), internal and external views. (After Dong 1987.)

mentary ulna, both extremities of the left humerus, proximal portions pubes, fragments of ilia and right ischium, right femur, tibia, almost complete pes, distal part of the left tibia, fragmentary left pes and tarsals, and ribs.

Maryańska and Osmólska noted that the fenestrated frill in this taxon is a derived character, though primitive features include a comparatively short frill, shallow jugal and mandible, and hindlimb resembling that of hypsilophodontids (especially *Hypsilophodon foxi*). The entire hindlimb is exceptionally long among ornithischians compared with trunk length. The metatarsus is long, strongly transversely arched and compact, and measures almost half the length of the tibia. Metatarsal I and probably V are very short.

These characteristics of the legs and feet indicate that *Microceratops* was bipedal and cursorial. Maryańska and Osmólska suggested that the unusually long forelimbs may have been used for a sometimes slower, quadrupedal mode of locomotion.

Key references: Bohlin (1953); Dodson and Currie (1990); Kielan-Jaworoska and Barsbold (1972); Maryańska and Osmólska (1975); Nessov, Kaznyshkina and Cherepanov (1989); Yang [Young] (1958*a*).

MICROCOELUS Lydekker 1893 [*nomen dubium*]—(See *Saltasaurus*.)
Name derivation: Greek *mikros* = "small" + Greek *koilos* = "hollow."
Type species: *M. patagonicus* Lydekker 1893 [*nomen dubium*].

MICROHADROSAURUS Dong 1979 [*nomen dubium*]
Ornithischia: Genasauria: Cerapoda: Ornithopoda: Iguanodontia: Hadrosauridae *incertae sedis*.
Name derivation: Greek *mikros* = "small" + "hadrosaur."
Type species: *M. nanshiungensis* Dong 1979 [*nomen dubium*]. Other species: [None.]
Occurrence: Nanxiong Formation, Guandong, People's Republic of China.
Age: Late Cretaceous.
Known material/holotype: IVPP V4732, partial left mandible with teeth, juvenile.
Diagnosis of genus (as for type species): [None published.]
Comments: The genus *Microhadrosaurus* was founded upon a partial mandible (NIGP V4732), collected from the Nanxiong Formation (Upper Cretaceous) of Nanshiung province, China.
The fragment has only 18 rows of tooth files. The specimen measures approximately 37 centime-

Micropachycephalosaurus hongtuyanensis, holotype ilium. Scale = 1 cm. (After Dong 1978.)

ters (17 inches) in length (as preserved) and about 41 centimeters (almost 16 inches) high at its posterior portion, indicating a tiny form otherwise quite similar to hadrosaurine genus *Edmontosaurus* (Dong 1979). In his book *Dinosaurs from China,* Dong (1987) stated that the total length of *Microhadrosaurus* would have been 2.6 meters (about 8.75 feet).

Brett-Surman (1989) noted that nothing diagnostic can be stated about the type specimen of *M. nanshiungensis.* During ontogeny the number of tooth rows increase (see Lull and Wright 1942), the skull (in lambeosaurines) changes to a great degree (Dodson 1975), and the postcranial skeleton undergoes various "preadult" changes (Brett-Surman 1975), all reasons, Brett-Surman (1989) stressed, for not using juveniles as holotypes.

Key references: Brett-Surman (1989); Dong (1979, 1987).

MICROPACHYCEPHALOSAURUS   Dong 1978

Ornithischia: Genasauria: Cerapoda: Marginocephalia: Pachycephalosauria *incertae sedis.*

Name derivation: Greek *mikros* = "small" + "pachycephalosaur."

Type species: *M. hongtuyanensis* Dong 1978.

Other species: [None.]

Occurrence: Wang Formation, Shandong, People's Republic of China.

Age: Late Cretaceous (Campanian).

Known material: Partial mandible, associated fragmentary postcrania.

Holotype: Sacrum, ilium.

Diagnosis of genus (as for type species): Differs from all other known Asian pachycephalosaurians in having femur with more proximally located fourth trochanter, ilium with caudally tapering postacetabular process (Maryańska 1990).

Comments: The genus *Micropachycephalosaurus* was founded upon fragmentary postcranial remains discovered in the Wang Formation of Laiyang, Shantung [now Shandong], China. It is one of only two pachycephalosaurian genera (with *Wannanosaurus*) known from China.

Dong (1978) neither diagnosed the genus nor described the holotype, stating simply that *Micropachycephalosaurus* is a "little" pachycephalosaur.

Dong regarded the differences between pachycephalosaurs with flatly roofed skulls and those with a rough dome and extensive shelf as of taxonomical significance, each kind belonging to one of two families, Homalocephalidae and Pachycephalosauridae.

Although the type species *M. hongtuyanensis* was classified by Dong with the Homalocephalidae, Maryańska (1990), in reviewing the Pachycephalosauria, stated that this assignment is not justified, the taxon best regarded as Pachycephalosauria *incertae sedis.*

Note: *Micropachycephalosaurus* is the longest generic name for a dinosaur published to date.

Key references: Dong (1978); Maryańska (1990).

MICROVENATOR   Ostrom 1970

Saurischia: Theropoda *incertae sedis.*

Name derivation: Greek *mikros* = "small" + Latin *venator* = "hunter."

Type species: *M. celer* Ostrom 1970.

Other species: ?*M. chagyabi* Zhao 1986 [*nomen nudum*].

Occurence: Cloverly Formation, Montana, Wyoming, United States.

Age: Early Cretaceous (Aptian–Albian).

Known material: Partial skeleton.

Holotype: AMNH 3041, incomplete postcranial skeleton.

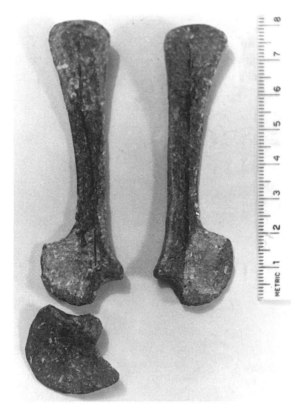

Microvenator celer, AMNH 3041, holotype scapulacoracoid.

Photo by R. A. Long and S. P. Welles (neg. #73/484-2), courtesy American Museum of Natural History.

Microvenator

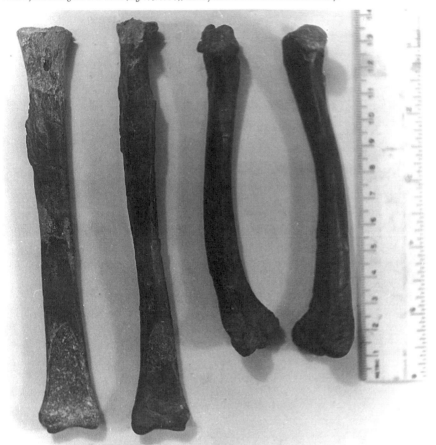

Microvenator celer, AMNH 3041, holotype femora and tibiae.

Microvenator is one of the smallest known theropods, about as large as a turkey and approximately twice the size of *Compsognathus*. Ostrom considered that these remains might pertain to a juvenile, but pointed out that the bones were well formed as in adults. As *Microvenator* seems to be most closely related to *Compsognathus*, *Ornitholestes*, and *Coelurus*, Ostrom assigned the genus to the Coeluridae.

Gauthier (1986) assigned *Microvenator* to the Maniraptora on the basis of its elongate forelimb, bowed ulna, reduced cranial part of the pubic "foot," and the absence on the femur of a fourth trochanter. Currie and Russell (1988) observed a suite of characteristics hinting that *Microvenator* may not be a coelurid, but may have affinities with the Caenagnathidae, possibly representing a primitive caenagnathid. These characteristics include proportions of a posterior sacral centrum, shape and proportions of metacarpal I, presence of a dorsoventral "lip" on one manual ungual, limb proportions, morphology of the astragalus, and presence of a distinct though small calcaneum. The absence of cervical neural spines

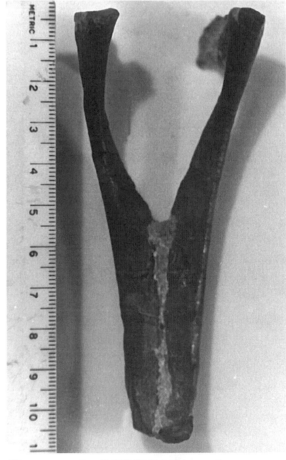

Microvenator celer, AMNH 3041, holotype pubes.

Diagnosis of genus (as for type species): Cervical vertebrae with two sequentially arranged pleurocoels; vertebrae without neural spines; forelimbs very long and slender; femur with prominent cranial trochanter, shallow pit rather than crested fourth trochanter (Norman 1990).

Comments: The genus *Microvenator* was founded upon a partial skeleton (AMNH 3041) collected from the Cloverly Formation (defined by Darton 1906; probably Late Aptian–Early Albian; see Ostrom 1970), in Wheatland County, Montana (Ostrom 1970).

Ostrom originally diagnosed the type species as follows: Very small, delicately-built coelurid, one half–two thirds size of *Ornitholestes* and *Colurus*; vertebrae and limb bones hollow with thin walls; cervical vertebrae with double pleurocoels, lacking neural spines; neural arches of dorsal vertebrae low, highly sculptured; dorsal neural spines low, rectangular, postzygapophyses far behind posterior border of centrum; astragalus with high, broad ascending process; profile of pubis concave anteriorly, distal extremities of pubis only moderately expanded; femur with short though prominent lesser trochanter and depression at fourth trochanter.

could also suggest caenagnathid affinities (R. E. Molnar, personal communication 1989).

Norman (1990), in a review of problematic "coelurosaurs," pointed out that the forelimb characters cited by Gauthier are not only suggestive of Maniraptora but also Ornithomimidae, that there is at present insufficient evidence to classify *Microvenator* as an oviraptorid, and that, until further discoveries are made, this taxon should be regarded as Theropoda *incertae sedis*.

Note: Associated with the holotype of *M. celer* were 25 teeth like those of the larger contemporary theropod *Deinonychus antirrhopus*. Although Barnum Brown had believed that these teeth belonged to AMNH 3041, Ostrom referred them to *D. antirrhopus* because of their form and much larger size.

Key references: Gauthier (1986); Currie and Russell (1988); Norman (1990); Ostrom (1970); Zhao (1986).

MINMI Molnar 1980

Ornithischia: Genasauria: Thyreophora:
    Ankylosauria: Nodosauridae.
Name derivation: "Minmi [Crossing]."
Type species: *M. paravertebra* Molnar 1980.
Other species: [None.]
Occurrence: Bungil Formation, Queensland,
    Australia.
Age: Early Cretaceous (Aptian).
Known material/holotype: QM F10329, 11 dorsal
    vertebrae with bases of ribs, five incomplete ribs,
    three "paravertebrae," incomplete manus, ventral
    armor.

Diagnosis of genus (as for type species): Small ankylosaur possessing "paravertebral" elements; ventral armor consisting of pavement of small ossicles; dorsal vertebrae of amphiplatyan condition without notocordal knobs; transverse processes slender, triangular; neural canals broad; posterior intervertebral notch shallow (Molnar 1980).

Comments: The first ankylosaur found in Australia, *Minmi* was established on an incomplete skeleton lacking a skull, including armor and a manus [misidentified as a "pes"; see below] (QM F10329), from the Minmi Member of the Bungil Formation (see Day 1964; probably Aptian; Exon and Vine 1970), north of Roma, southern Queensland, this site not having yielded any other fossil vertebrate material (Molnar 1980).

Minmi was small for an ankylosaur, its total length being only about 3 meters (approximately 10 feet).

As described by Molnar, the ventral armor (either poorly preserved or missing in other ankylosaur genera) was apparently positioned on the belly just anterior to the pelvis. This armor consists of flattened ossicles ranging from somewhat hexagonal to squarish shapes. They are relatively small, from 6 to 8 millimeters (approximately .23 to .31 inches) in diameter and 4 to 5 millimeters (approximately .151 to .19 inches) thick. The discovery of a flat and somewhat triangular element found above a rib fragment, measuring 6.5 by 5 centimeters (about 2.5 by 1.59 inches), implies the presence of dorsal armor made up of scutes larger than the ventral ossicles.

Molnar regarded *Minmi* as unique among ankylosaurs (as well as other vertebrates) because of the possession of bony elements which he termed "paravertebrae." These flat, plate-like structures are located alongside the neural arches of the dorsal vertebrae. The first two "paravertebrae" extend distally to the

Courtesy Queensland Museum (neg. #JB657).

Minmi sp., reassembled skeleton (QM F18101), the most complete dinosaurian specimen yet found in Australia, from the (Albian) Alaru Mudstone of north-central Queensland, dorsal view.

Minmi paravertebra, QM F10329, holotype ventral armor.

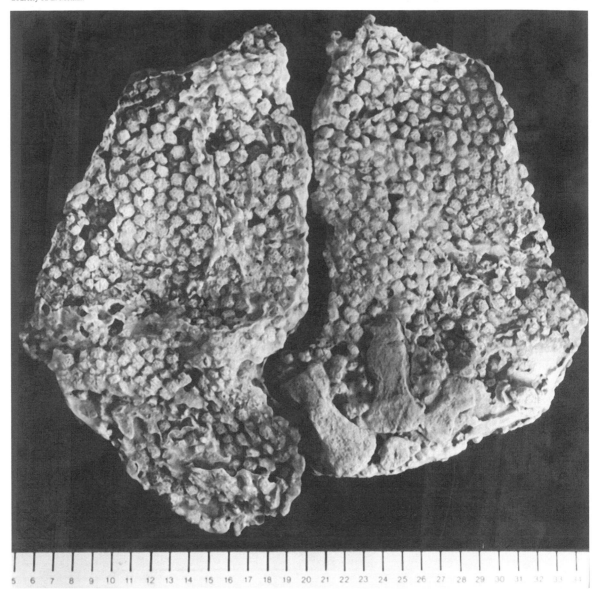

tips of the transverse processes, the third extending well beyond the tip. Elongate, posteroventrally inclined bony rods, superficially resembling ossified tendons, project posteriorly from the posteromedial corner of each "paravertebra." Originally, Molnar interpreted these paravertebral structures as possibly having been attached to supposed dorsal armor, serving either to move it or as a threat or defensive display, or to ribs, assisting in their motion presumably as a ventilation aid [see below].

Subsequent to further preparations of the type material, both mechanical and in acid, Molnar and Frey (1987) further described the remains. Molnar and Frey recognized that what was originally believed to be the pes actually represents the manus, the metacarpals differing in length as in other nodo-

saurids (see Carpenter 1984). Molnar and Frey also noted that the "paravertebrae" comprise three distinct classes of paravertebral elements, each series occurring along the neural spines, parallel to the vertebral column. The first series or "paravertebrae proper" are those originally described by Molnar, the second resemble typical ossified tendons, and the third are thin, flat, vertical blades seemingly located between the first class kind and their corresponding neural spines. The first and second class elements are associated with posterior dorsal vertebrae, the third with posterior dorsals and presacral rod.

The possible function of paravertebral elements was reconsidered by Molnar and Frey, who abandoned Molnar's earlier interpretations and compared them to the epaxial tendon-muscle systems in crocodilians. In crocodilians there are five systems of epaxial musculature, three (*i.e.,*, M. articulo-spinalis, M. spino-articularis and M. neuro-spinalis) associated with serial tendons that are similar (*e.g.*, detailed likeness in anatomical position, relationships to vertebral column, in orientation and basic form) to the "paravertebrae" in *Minmi*. Molnar and Frey reinterpreted the "paravertebrae" as homologues of the tendons in of these three muscle-tendon systems which, in crocodilians, seem to strengthen the vertebral column, especially at the pelvis, to give support and also a stiff axial framework for limb-muscle action during rapid locomotion.

According to Molnar and Frey, the absence of dorsal armor in the collected material of *Minmi*, so commonly associated with neural spines in other more heavily armored and usually larger ankylosaurs from which this genus was presumably derived, suggests that it possessed either reduced or no such armor. The paravertebral elements could then be associated with this reduced dorsal armor and perhaps have a bearing on the animal's locomotion, allowing *Minmi* greater speed and endurance than other ankylosaurs. Molnar and Frey theorized that the relatively smaller and less heavy *Minmi* may have been more of a cursor than other ankylosaurs, relying more upon active escape than passive defense.

As later interpreted by Coombs and Maryańska (1990), the "paravertebrae" in *Minmi* may be modified ossified tendons.

Molnar (1980) noted that *Minmi* is one of the only ankylosaurs known from the Gondwana continents. Its presence in the Early Cretaceous of Australia is evidence supporting the existence of a land route into the continent via South America during that time. It also attests to the widespread distribution of ankylosaurs shortly after their original appearance in the Late Jurassic.

Note: *Minmi* is the shortest generic name for a dinosaur published to date of this writing.

Key references: Coombs and Maryańska (1990); Molnar (1980); Molnar and Frey (1987).

MOCHLODON Seeley 1881 [*nomen dubium*]—
(See *Rhabdodon*.)
Name derivation: Greek *mochleuo* = "to heave up" + Greek *odon* = "tooth."
Type species: *M. suessi* (Bunzel 1881).

MONGOLOSAURUS Gilmore 1933 [*nomen dubium*]
Saurischia: Sauropodomorpha: Sauropoda *incertae sedis*.

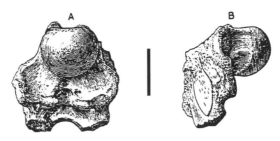

Mongolosaurus haplodon, AMNH 6710, holotype basioccipital, A. posterior and B. lateral views. Scale = 4 cm. (After Gilmore 1933.)

Name derivation: "Mongolia" + Greek *sauros* = "lizard."
Type species: *M. haplodon* Gilmore 1933 [*nomen dubium*].
Other species: [None.]
Occurrence: ?Bayanshua Formation, Nei Mongol Zizhiqu, People's Republic of China.
Age: Early Cretaceous (Berriasian-Albian).
Known material/holotype: AMNH 6710, Basioccipital, fragmentary teeth, atlas, fragmentary axis, third cervical vertebra.

Diagnosis of genus (as for type species): Teeth unlike those of all other sauropods; teeth (including portions of five crowns among other pieces) tapered, pointed obtusely, somewhat flattened on inner side, angularly rounded on outer side; low longitudinal carina, faintly serrated on one tooth, developed on either side where surfaces meet; crowns covered with thin, irregularly striated enamel; pulp cavity continuing to crown; roots cylindrical; largest (best preserved) crown with diameter of 9–7 millimeters (Gilmore 1933*b*).

Mongolosaurus haplodon, AMNH 6710, holotype tooth crown, A. labial, B. edge, C. lingual views. Scale = 2 cm. (After Gilmore 1933.)

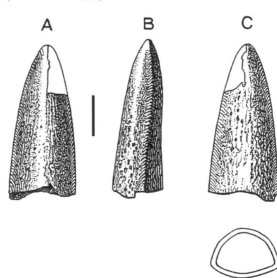

Comments: The new genus and species *Mongolosaurus haplodon* were established on very incomplete remains (AMNH 6710) collected by Walter Granger from the [then] On Gong Formation of Hu Khung Ulan, Mongolia (Gilmore 1933*b*).

Gilmore observed that the teeth of *Mongolosaurus* resemble those in *Diplodocus* and *Pleurocoelus*, but differ by the faintly serrate borders of the crown. However, he could not determine whether the teeth belonged to the upper or lower dental series. The other elements, found mingled with the teeth, are typically sauropod with no distinguishing features. Gilmore was unable to assign *Mongolosaurus* to any sauropod family.

In his review of the Sauropoda, McIntosh (1990*b*) described *M. haplodon* as follows: Basioccipital comparatively shorter than in *Brachiosaurus* and *Camarasaurus*; heavy descending processes considerably shorter than in *Camarasaurus*, shorter dorsoventrally than in *Diplodocus*; teeth unique among all known sauropods; atlas showing clear facets for articulating with cervical ribs; odontid less prominent than in other species; parapophysis of axis at mid-height on cranial end of lateral face of centrum; ridge proceeding backward from centrum, dividing lower and upper concavity, but no true pleurocoel; centrum strongly keeled ventrally; small cavities in side of third cervical suggests beginning of pleurocoel; very low spine consisting of paired incipient ridges (this feature separating *Mongolosaurus* from brachiosaurids and titanosaurids and, together with slender teeth, suggesting possible relationship with diplodocids) (McIntosh 1990*b*).

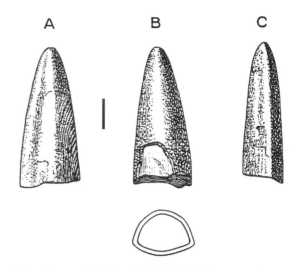

Mongolosaurus haplodon, AMNH 6710, holotype tooth crown, A. labial, B. lingual, C. edge views. Scale = 2 cm. (After Gilmore 1933.)

Note: Bohlin (1953) described a tooth discovered in the red basal conglomerates of the badland sediments at Hui-hui-pú, Mongolia. Bohlin observed that the tooth was most similar to those of *M. haplodon*, cross-sections the same, though the teeth described by Gilmore are much smaller.

Key references: Gilmore (1933*b*); McIntosh (1990*b*).

MONKONOSAURUS   Zhao 1983
Ornithischia: Genasauria: Thyreophora: Stegosauria: Stegosauridae.

Name derivation: "Monko [county in eastern part of Tibet]" + Greek *sauros* = "lizard."

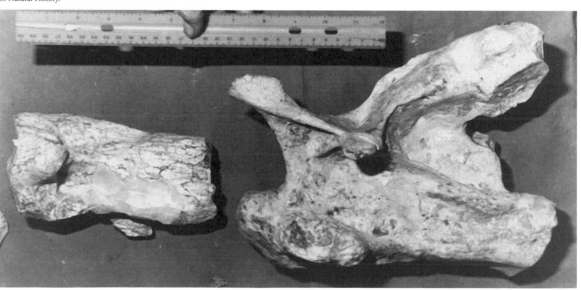

Mongolosaurus haplodon, AMNH 6710, holotype axis and third cervical vertebra.

Type species: *M. lawulacus* Zhao 1986.

Other species: [None.]

Occurrence: Loe-ein Formation, Lawulashan, Tibet.

Age: Late Jurassic or Early Cretaceous.

Known material/holotype: Two incomplete vertebrae, three dermal plates, sacrum.

Diagnosis of genus (as for type species): Medium-sized stegosaur, about 5 meters (approximately 16.75 feet) in length, with large, thin dermal plates similar in shape to those of *Stegosaurus*; five sacral vertebrae, fenestrae between sacral ribs completely closed, broad sacral neural spines lower than in *Wuerhosaurus*, *Kentrosaurus*, and *Stegosaurus* (Dong 1990*b*).

Comments: The first dinosaur found in Tibet, *Monkonosaurus* was named by Zhao [formerly Chao] (1983*a*), who did not describe the genus, assign it a specific name, or publish an illustration of the material. The type species, *M. lawulacus,* was later published without description by Zhao (1986*b*) in an article about the Cretaceous system of China.

Monkonosaurus was founded upon incomplete postcranial material collected by a team from the Chinese Academy of Sciences in 1976-77, from the Loe-ein Formation (Upper Jurassic or Lower Cretaceous), at Lawulashan, Monko County, Qamdo District, Tibet (Dong 1990*b*).

Zhao referred this genus to a proposed new "superfamily," Oligosacralosauroidea, supposedly belonging to the Pachycephalosauria and probably derived from primitive scelidosaurids from the end of the Early Jurassic or beginning of the Middle Jurassic. Zhao defined this new taxon as follows: Skull entirely covered by superficial dermal ossifications; three to five sacral vertebrae, fairly well fused; rather flat and simply-shaped armor on back of neck and trunk.

Dong later interpreted *Monkonosaurus* as a stegosaur.

Although other vertebrate fossils found in the same beds as *Monkonosaurus* are similar to those of Upper Jurassic forms from the Sichuan Basin, Dong believed that this genus was more likely of Lower Cretaceous age because of its progressive features (*i.e.,* closed sacral fenestrae and large, thin dermal plates).

Key references: Dong (1990*b*); Zhao (1983*a*, 1986*b*).

MONOCLONIUS Cope 1876—(=?*Centrosaurus*, ?*Dysganus*)

Ornithischia: Genasauria: Cerapoda: Marginocephalia: Ceratopsia: Neoceratopsia: Ceratopsidae: Centrosaurinae.

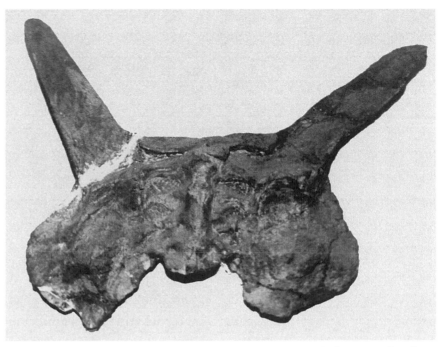

Monkonosaurus lawulocus, holotype sacrum and pelvis. (After Dong 1987.)

Name derivation: Greek *monos* = "single" + Greek *klon* = "stem" + Greek *ios* = "similarity".

Type species: *M. crassus* Cope 1876.

Other species: ?*M. sphenocerus* Cope 1889 [*nomen dubium*], *M. fissus* Cope 1889 [*nomen nudum*], *M. dawsoni* Lambe 1902, *M. lowei* Sternberg 1940.

Occurrence: Dinosaur Park Formation, Montana, United States; Oldman Formation, Alberta, Canada.

Age: Late Cretaceous (Late Campanian).

Known material: Complete skull, four incomplete skulls, isolated cranial material, horn fragments, vertebrae, isolated fragments.

Holotype: AMNH 3998, incomplete median element of crest.

Diagnosis of genus: Parietal long, relatively thin; squamosal comparatively narrower and thinner than in *Centrosaurus*, slightly shorter relative to length of

Monoclonius crassus, AMNH 3998, holotype right scapula.

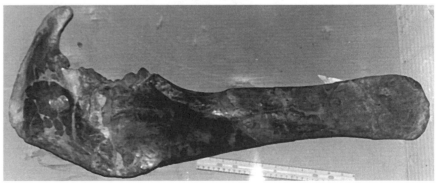

Photo by R. A. Long and S. P. Welles (neg. #73/381-36), courtesy American Museum of Natural History.

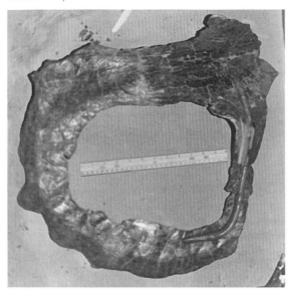

Monoclonius crassus, AMNH 3998, holotype frill, dorsal view.

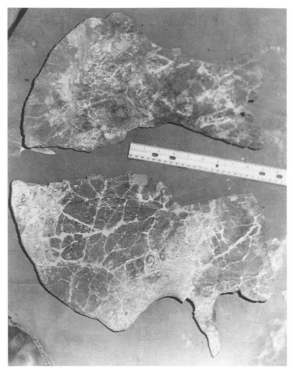

Monoclonius fissus, AMNH 3995-6, holotype squamosals.

parietal; shorter jugal than in *Centrosaurus*; nasal horn with laterally compressed base (Dodson 1990*b*).

Diagnosis of *M. dawsoni*: Large, backwardly curved nasal horn, incipient orbital horn cores, small squamosal (Lambe 1902).

Comments: *Monoclonius* is included herein provisionally. Although now regarded as a valid genus, work on this taxon presently underway by D. Tanke (personal communication, 1990) may demonstrate otherwise, resulting in a better understanding of this genus and its relationship to other centrosaurine taxa.

The genus was erected on a partial crest (AMNH 3998) collected by Edward Drinker Cope and Charles H. Sternberg in 1876, from the Judith River [now Dinosaur Park] Formation ("Fort Union beds"), between Choteau and Blaine counties, Montana. Bearing the same catalogue number as the holotype are a sacrum and other elements. This material represents a mix of individuals. However, despite the incompleteness of the type material, many additional remains have been referred to *Monoclonius*, some of them generically distinct.

Based on the holotype and referred material, Cope (1876*a*) originally diagnosed *Monoclonius* as follows: Teeth with obliquely truncate face and distinct root, the latter grooved on front for successional tooth; teeth with no cementum layer; caudal vertebrae biconcave; forelimbs large, massive.

Cope diagnosed the type species *M. crassus* as follows: Teeth with oval faces; teeth divided by elevated keel, median above, turning to one side at base; tooth margin scalloped, grooves extending more or less on convex and otherwise smooth back; ten sacral vertebrae; limb bones robust, hindlegs longer than forelegs; three anterior dorsal vertebrae coossified, first with deep cup for articulation with preceding vertebra; episternum thin, T-shaped, keeled on median line below. Cope also included measurements of various elements in his diagnosis. (Most of Cope's observed characters are no longer considered to be of diagnostic importance.)

Monoclonius crassus, NMC 8470, holotype skull of *M. lowei*, frill.

Monoclonius crassus, NMC 8470, holotype skull of *M. lowei*.

The only known complete skull of this individual is that described by Sternberg (1940*b*) as the new species, *M. lowei*. This skull (GSC 8790) was collected from the Oldman Formation southeast of Manyberries, Alberta. Sternberg noted that the skull is that of an adult, though, as shown by its open sutures, a moderately young individual.

Monoclonius is often regarded in both the paleontological literature and popular books as congeneric with *Centrosaurus*. Brown (1914*b*) synonymized the two genera, rediagnosing *Monoclonius* including characters (*e.g.*, thickening of caudal border of parietal and its hook-like processes) now known to be diagnostic of *Centrosaurus* skulls (see Dodson and Currie 1990). Lull (1933) separated *Monoclonius* and *Centrosaurus* on the basis of cranial differences and geographic isolation, but only on a subgeneric level, considering *Centrosaurus* to be a subgenus of *Monoclonius*. Adding to the confusion, most life restorations of *Monoclonius* have actually been based upon *Centrosaurus* specimens.

Sternberg (1938, 1940*b*), after studying various *Monoclonius* cranial material, particularly the holotype skull of *M. lowei*, concluded that this genus was distinct from *Centrosaurus*, with *Monoclonius* distinguished from the latter mostly by its lack of hook-like processes on the posterior border of the frill, the presence of a smoothly surfaced bone bordering the antedorsal corner of the orbits, and a compressed, posteriorly recurved nasal horn separated into two halves by a distinct longitudinal suture.

More recently, Dodson (1990*b*) reexamined specimens belonging to *Monoclonius* and *Centrosaurus* and subjected them to comparative study. Dodson pointed out that the type specimen of *M. crassus* is a composite of disarticulated and unassociated individuals, designating the well-preserved parietal (AMNH 3998) as the neotype of this species.

All additional species of *Monoclonius* considered to be valid or tentatively valid were also based upon fragmentary material: *M. sphenocerus* was erected upon a nasal horn, nasal, and left premaxilla (AMNH 3989) from the "Judith River" [Dinosaur Park] Formation, near Cow Island, on the Missouri River. According to Dodson, the nasal horn in this species is suggestive of that of *C. nasicornis* and *Styracosaurus*

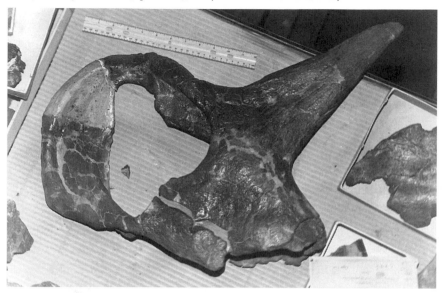

?Monoclonius sphenocerus, AMNH 3989, holotype snout with nasal horn.

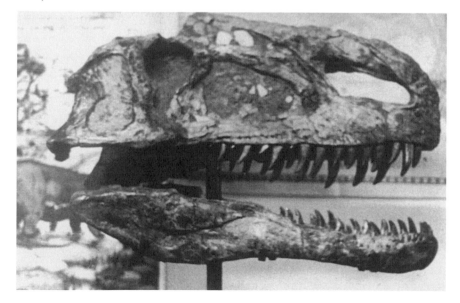

Monolophosaurus jiangi, holotype skull. (After Dong 1987.)

albertensis, but may not necessarily belong to a centrosaurine at all. *M. fissus* was founded on an incomplete, very small pterygoid (AMNH 3988) that Cope (1889) believed was a squamosal. *M. recurvicornis* Cope 1889 [*nomen dubium*] was based on a braincase, nasal with damaged horncore, two moderate-sized postorbital horns and apparently [nonfigured] squamosal found near the type material of *M. crassus*. Dodson noted that the length of the brow horns in this species suggests that it might be referable to the Chasmosaurine, although it is currently referred to *?Centrosaurus recurvicornis*. Dodson regarded all of Cope's species as *nomina dubia. M. dawsoni* Lambe 1902 was based upon an incomplete skull (GSC 1173) lacking much of the posterior portion, collected in 1901 from the "Belly River" [=Oldman] Formation of

Red Deer River, between Berry Creek and Dead Lodge Canyon, Alberta.

Isolated fragmented teeth (AMNH 5738) from two individuals, named *Dysganus haydenianus* [*nomen dubium*], collected by Charles H. Sternberg in 1876 from the "Judith River" [=Dinosaur Park] Formation ("Fort Union beds"), at Dog Creek, east of Judith River, at Fergus County, Montana, were described but not illustrated by Cope (1876*a*) as hadrosaurid. Lull and Wright (1942) showed this material to be ceratopsian, belonging to one of the "Judith River" forms. It may be referable to *M. crassus*.

Dodson (1984*a*, 1991*b*) reported the discovery of the first known skull (RTMP 82.16.11) of a juvenile ceratopsid, the smallest known of any ceratopsid, discovered and collected by T. Tokaryk from the Dinosaur Park Formation at Dinosaur Provincial Park in southern Alberta. The specimen includes an almost complete parietal, squamosals, laterosphenoids, complete right sphlenial, and possible jugal, postorbital, palatine, and pterygoid fragments. Dodson (1991) tentatively referred the remains to *Monoclonius* sp. on the basis of the parietal, which has a thin caudal edge and no parietal horns (see Sternberg 1938, 1940*b*). Based on Gilmore's (1917) reconstruction of *Brachyceratops*, Dodson (1991*b*) estimated the length of the individual to which this skull belonged as approximately 1.1 meters (almost 3.75 feet), about one fifth the size of an adult *Centrosaurus* or *Monoclonius*, no more than three times the length of a hatchling, this animal less than two years old.

Note: *M. belli* Lambe 1902 was made the type species of *Chasmosaurus* by Lambe (1914*b*), and *M. canadensis* Lambe 1902 the type species of *Eoceratops* [=*Chasmosaurus belli*] by Lambe (1915).

Key references: Brown (1914*b*); Cope (1876*a*, 1889); Dodson (1984*a*, 1991*b*); Dodson and Currie (1990); Lambe (1902); Lull (1933); Lull and Wright (1942); Sternberg (1940*b*).

MONOLOPHOSAURUS Zhao and Currie 1993
Saurischia: Theropoda: ?Tetanurae: ?Megalosauridae.
Name derivation: Greek *monos* = "single" + Greek *lophos* = "crest" + Greek *sauros* = "lizard."
Type species: *M. jiangi* Zhao and Currie 1993.
Other species: [None.]
Occurrence: Wucaiwan Formation, Junggar Basin, Xinjiang, People's Republic of China.
Age: Middle Jurassic.
Known material/holotype: IVPP 84019, complete skull, partial postcrania including all cervical vertebrae, dorsal, and sacral vertebrae, first six

caudal vertebrae, cervical, dorsal, and sacral ribs, pelvic girdle.

Diagnosis (as for type species): Skull with midline crest (formed by paired premaxillary, nasal, lacrimal, and frontal bones) extending from above external naris to a point between orbits; long, low external naris, anteroposteriorly elongate premaxilla; antorbital sinuses in nasals confluent through openings in base of crest (Zhao and Currie 1993).

Comments: Originally referred to in the popular press as "*Jiangiunmiaosaurus*," the genus *Monolophosaurus* was founded upon a skull and partial skeleton (IVPP 84019) discovered in 1981 by Xi-Jin Zhao, who was working with the Petroleum Stratigraphic Team of the Xinjiang Petroleum Bureau from Karamay, in the Middle Jurassic Wucaiwan Formation (in the highest of three members, consisting of thick units of reddish sandstones, a few showing ripple marked surfaces), northeast of Jiangjunmiao, in the Jiangiunmia Depression within the Junggar Basin, Xinjiang. In 1984, during an expedition of the Sino-Canadian Dinosaur Project (see Currie 1991; Dong 1993*a*), the specimen was excavated by a party from the Institute of Vertebrate Paleontology and Paleoanthropology. The skull and atlas neuropophyses were found separated from the rest of the skeleton, the two sides of the skull separate but associated, some of the teeth

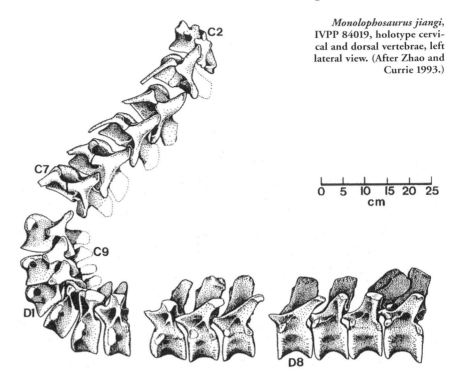

Monolophosaurus jiangi, IVPP 84019, holotype cervical and dorsal vertebrae, left lateral view. (After Zhao and Currie 1993.)

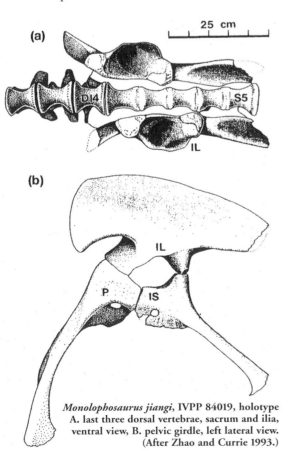

Monolophosaurus jiangi, IVPP 84019, holotype A. last three dorsal vertebrae, sacrum and ilia, ventral view, B. pelvic girdle, left lateral view. (After Zhao and Currie 1993.)

out of their alveoli, posterior cervical and dorsal vertebrae, as well as the tail, arched (Zhao and Currie 1993).

A photograph of the skull appeared in Dong's (1987*b*) book *Dinosaurs from China*.

As described by Zhao and Currie, *Monolophosaurus* is a theropod of medium size, its skull measuring 670 millimeters (about 2.25 feet) long from tip of snout to back of quadrate, the entire skeleton totaling about 5.1 meters (about 17.25 feet) in length and 1.7 meters (about 5.75 feet) high at the top of the ilium.

As pointed out by the authors, this genus is distinguished from all other known theropods by the low yet prominent medial crest extending from the bridge between the external nares back to a point between the orbits. The crest is asymmetrical, with a hollow interior connected to the antorbital fossae, showing that it is not a pathologic artifact. It represents a new kind of theropod cranial ornamentation, formed by the paired premaxillary, nasal, lacrimal, and frontal bones, which form a hollow tube with contralateral pneumatic extensions from the antorbital fossae. This crest was probably used for visual recognition by other individuals of the same species.

Lacking information on the appendicular skeleton, Zhao and Currie found it difficult to make a precise taxonomic assignment of *Monolophosaurus* to any group within Theropoda. According to the authors, this genus is best referred to as megalosaurid.

As Zhao and Currie noted, synapomorphies are shared by allosaurids and megalosaurid-grade thero-

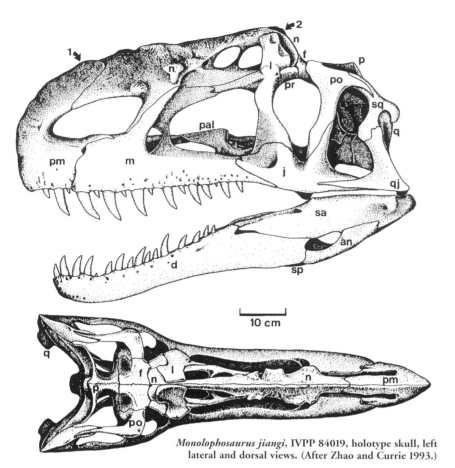

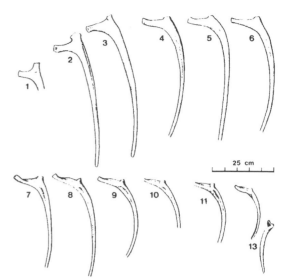

Monolophosaurus jiangi, IVPP 84019, holotype dorsal ribs, anterior views. (After Zhao and Currie 1993.)

Monolophosaurus jiangi, IVPP 84019, holotype skull, left lateral and dorsal views. (After Zhao and Currie 1993.)

pods such as *Monolophosaurus*, *Sinraptor*, and *Yangchuanosaurus* (*e.g.*, position of last maxillary tooth anterior to orbit; accessory opening conspicuous in lateral view anterior to antiorbital fenestra; nasals elongate, invaded by pneumatic diverticula from antorbital fossa; jugal pneumatized by antorbital air sac; deep basisphenoidal recess, bound posteriorly by relatively short basal tubera; axial neural spine reduced from condition in *Ceratosaurus*, *Dilophosaurus*, and other primitive theropods, lengths of cervical parapophyses shorter; brevis shelf of ilium relatively short).

Some characters suggest that *Monolophosaurus* is more advanced than *Sinraptor* and *Yangchuanosaurus*, and may be more closely related to allosaurids (*e.g.*, premaxilla not contacting nasal below external naris; length of subtemporal bar reduced from primitive condition, lateral temporal fenestra relatively small; anterior process formed by squamosal and quadratojugal constricting lateral temporal fenestra; pneumatopore of jugal very small; angular with posterior extension that reaches level of articular; epipophyses of cervical vertebrae and neural spines of dorsals relatively short; tenth presacral vertebra apparently a dorsal).

According to Zhao and Currie, the known characters suggest that *Monolophosaurus* may be closer to

allosaurids than to any other well-understood megalosaurid-grade theropods, but autapomorphies associated with the development of the crest indicate that this genus was not a suitable ancestral allosaurid.

Key references: Dong (1987*b*); Zhao and Currie (1993).

MONTANOCERATOPS Sternberg 1951

Ornithischia: Genasauria: Cerapoda: Marginocephalia: Neoceratopsia: Ceratopsia: Protoceratopsidae.

Name derivation: "Montana" + Greek *keratos* = "horned" + Greek *ops* = "face."

Type species: *M. cerorhynchus* (Brown and Schlaikjer 1942). Other species: [None.]

Occurrence: St. Mary River Formation, Montana, United States.

Age: Late Cretaceous (Early Maastrichtian).

Known material: Partial skull with associated postcrania, articulated specimen.

Holotype: AMNH 5464, incomplete skull with jaws, most of postcranial skeleton.

Diagnosis of genus (as for type species): Nasal proportionately large, deep, heavy, with very well-developed horncore; dentary long, with straight ventral margin (Brown and Schlaikjer 1942).

Comments: The genus *Montanoceratops* was named by Sternberg (1951*a*) after material originally described by Brown and Schlaikjer (1942) as a new species of *Leptoceratops*, *L. cerorhynchus*, based on an incomplete skeleton (AMNH 5464) collected in 1916 by Barnum Brown from the St. Mary River Formation, near Buffalo Lake, Blackfeet Indian reservation, Montana.

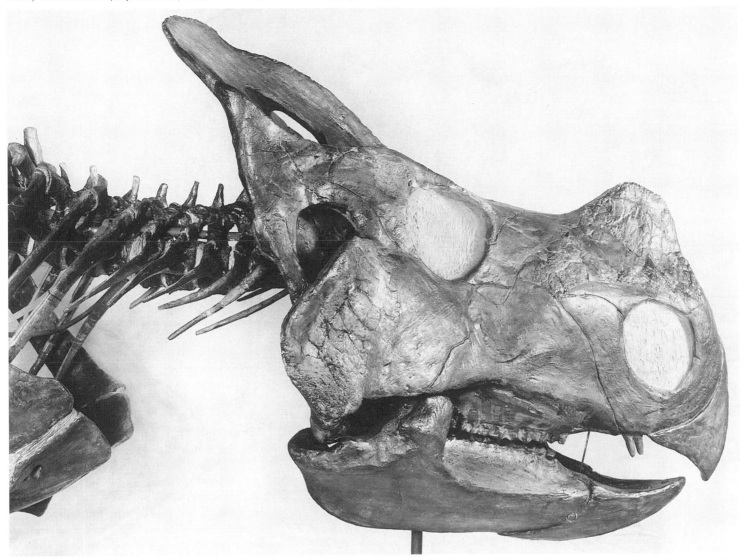

Montanoceratops cerrorhynchus, AMNH, detail of restored partial holotype skull of *Leptoceratops cerrorhynchus*.

In comparing "*L.*" *cerorhynchus* to *Protoceratops*, Brown and Schlaikjer observed that the former is more advanced in the presence of a horncore, the comparatively longer forelimbs, and generally more robust construction of the bones. The dorsal vertebrae of "*L.*" *cerorhynchus* differ in having longer neural spines, the ninth through eleventh having the greatest antero-posterior diameter instead of the fifth through seventh as in *Protoceratops*; more erect neural spines and arches; and relatively longer transverse processes, the capitular facets on the posterior dorsals showing a tendency to migrate out on the ventral surfaces of those processes. The pelvic girdle in "*L.*" *cerorhynchus* is more derived than in *Protoceratops* in that the anterior projection of the ilium is more outwardly curved, and the front of its dorsal margin is more outwardly turned; ilium has a broader ante-

rior ventral shaft to accommodate the pubo-ischio-femoralis internus; posterior ventral shaft of the ilium is more developed; anterior process of the pubis is relatively longer and less dorsoventrally expanded; posteriorly deflected portion of the pubis is relatively much shorter and more lightly built; and the ischium is comparatively more robust, shorter, and more downwardly curved. The very long phalanges and pointed claws are primitive characters.

Sternberg, however, pointed out that most of the observations made by Brown and Schlaikjer were made from referred specimens from different horizons and localities. In describing a more recently discovered complete skeleton (NMC 8889) of type species *L. gracilis*, Sternberg showed that *Leptoceratops* is more primitive than *Protoceratops*, and that the skeleton described by Brown and Schlaikjer rep-

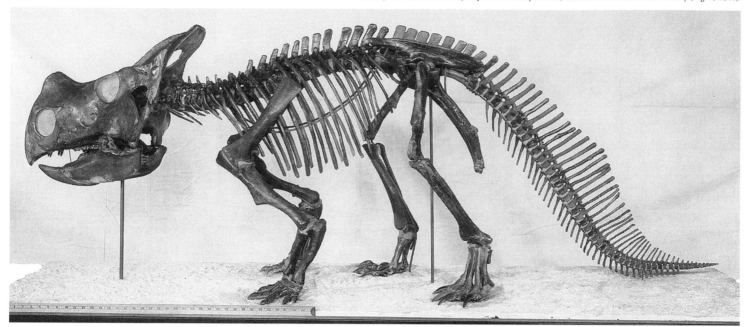

Montanoceratops cer-
rorhynchus, AMNH 5464,
restored holotype skeleton of
Leptoceratops cerrorhynchus.

resents a distinct and more advanced genus for which he proposed the new name *Montanoceratops.*

In a review of protoceratopsids, Maryańska and Osmólska (1975) noted that *Montanoceratops* is more advanced than *Protoceratops.* Following this assessment, Sereno (1984, 1986) added that *Montanoceratops* seems to be the most derived protoceratopsid, sharing with the more derived family Ceratopsidae the enlargement of external nares, broad-based nasal horncore, and at least a crescent-shaped anterior altar intercentrum.

The holotype skeleton of *M. cerorhynchus* displayed at the American Museum of Natural History is approximately the size of larger *Protoceratops* individuals.

Key references: Brown and Schlaikjer (1942); Maryańska and Osmólska (1975); Sereno (1984, 1986); Sternberg (1951*a*).

MORINOSAURUS Sauvage 1874 [*nomen*
    dubium]—(=?*Pelorosaurus*)
Saurischia: Sauropodomorpha: Sauropoda:
    Brachiosauridae.
Name derivation: Indo-European *mori* [from Latin
    mare, referring to French *Mer*] = "sea" + Greek
    sauros = "lizard."
Type species: *M. typus* Sauvage 1874 [*nomen dubium*].
Other species: [None.]
Occurrence: Département du Pas-de-Calais, France.
Age: Late Jurassic (Late Kimmeridgian).
Known material: Teeth, ?humerus.

Holotype: DutertreDelporte collection, Musée de Boulogne collection, tooth.

Diagnosis of genus: [No modern diagnosis published.]

Comments: The genus *Morinosaurus* was founded upon a much worn tooth (DutertreDelporte collection, Musée de Boulogne) from the Upper Jurassic (Kimmeridgian) of Boulogne-sur-Mer, France. A possible partial humerus may also belong to the type specimen (Sauvage 1874).

Sauvage characterized the tooth by having an internal edge with strong summit (similar to *Hypselosaurus*). As measured by Sauvage, the tooth is 50 millimeters in length, diameters at the base measuring 12 millimeters and 16 millimeters, respectively.

Key reference: Sauvage (1874).

Morinosaurus typus,
Dutertre-Delporte col-
lection, Musée de
Boulogne, holotype
tooth, lateral and edge
views. (After Sauvage
1874.)

MOROSAURUS Marsh 1878—(See
Camarasaurus.)
Name derivation: Greek *moros* = "foolish" + Greek
sauros = "lizard."
Type species: *M. impar* Marsh 1878.

MUSSAURUS Bonaparte and Vince 1979
Saurischia: Sauropodomorpha: Prosauropoda:
Plateosauridae.
Name derivation: Latin *mus* = "mouse" + Greek
sauros = "lizard."
Type species: *M. patagonicus* Bonaparte and Vince
1979.
Other species: [None.]
Occurrence: El Tranquillo Formation, Santa Cruz,
Argentina.
Age: Late Triassic (Norian).
Known material: More than ten skeletons,
complete to fragmentary, four skulls, juvenile to
adult, eggs.
Holotype: PVL 4068, nearly complete, articulated
skeleton missing rib cage and tail, juvenile.

Diagnosis of genus: [No current diagnosis published; see below.]

Comments: The genus *Mussaurus* was founded
upon an extremely small, very juvenile skeleton (PVL
44068), collected from the El Tranquillo Formation

of northern Santa Cruz, Patagonia, Argentina. The
skeleton was found in association with a nest including two fossil eggs and a number of referred specimens (PVL 4208-4215), consisting of both cranial
and postcranial remains (Bonaparte and Vince 1979).

The monotypic *M. patagonicus* was diagnosed
by Bonaparte and Vince as follows: Skull short, high,
with elongate frontals and parietals, snout very short;
preorbital opening short, high, very near orbit; teeth
long, very much rounded; mandible with thick sym-
phisis; cervical vertebrae short and high as in "thecodont" *Lagosuchus*; dorsal vertebrae, pelvis, and
hindlimbs typical of the Prosauropoda.

As described by Bonaparte and Vince, the skull
measures 3.2 centimeters (about 1.25 inches) in
length, femur 30 millimeters (about 1.15 inches), and
tibia 27 millimeters (about 1.05 inches) long.

Bonaparte and Vince observed that *Mussaurus*
exhibits such primitive features as cervical vertebrae
resembling those of *Lagosuchus*. Dorsal vertebrae,
pelvis, and hindlimbs resemble those in such prosauropods as *Plateosaurus* and *Riojasaurus*. Certain
characters of the skull suggest affinities with both
prosauropods and later sauropods such as *Camarasaurus*. This implied to Bonaparte and Vince that
both the Prosauropoda and Sauropoda share a common origin with a pre–Sauropodomorpha group,
such as "Thecodontia."

Courtesy J. F. Bonaparte

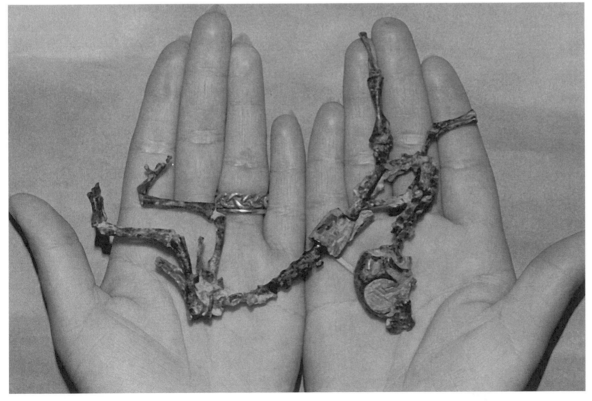

Mussaurus patagonicus, PLV
4068, holotype skeleton
(juvenile).

Mussaurus patagonicus,
referred skeleton (juvenile).

Given the extreme juvenile nature of the type skeleton, *Mussaurus* was originally assigned to its own family, Mussauridae Bonaparte and Vince 1979. Galton (1990*a*), in a review of the Prosauropoda, mentioned that a series of intermediate-sized skeletons (3 meters, or more than 10 feet in length), collected from the same site that yielded the holotype of *M. patagonicus* and described briefly by Casamiquela (1980) as *Plateosaurus* sp., link the juvenile to these larger individuals (J. F. Bonaparte, personal communication to Galton). Galton referred *Mussaurus* to the Plateosauridae, cautioning that the diagnosis of *M. patagonicus* must wait until the adult individuals have been completely described.

Key references: Bonaparte and Vince (1979); Casamiquela (1980); Galton (1990*a*).

MUTTABURRASAURUS   Bartholomai and
    Molnar 1981
Ornithischia: Genasauria: Cerapoda: Ornithopoda:
    Iguanodontia *incertae sedis.*
Name derivation: "Muttaburra [township in central
    Queensland]" + Greek *sauros* = "lizard."
Type species: *M. langdoni* Bartholomai and Molnar
    1981.
Other species: [None.]

Occurrence: Griman Creek Formation, New South
    Wales, Macunda Formation, Queensland,
    Australia.
Age: Lower Cretaceous (Albian).
Known material: Incomplete skeleton, fragmentary
    skeleton.
Holotype: QM F6140, nearly complete skeleton
    missing most of tail.

Diagnosis of genus (as for type species): Large iguanodontian [emended; =iguanodontid of their usage; see below], with inflated nasal region of snout; maxillary teeth with low ridges, lacking carina; postorbital region of skull low, broad; quadrate inclined posteriorly; frontal with lateral process; centra of dorsal vertebrae keeled; anterior caudal centra with ventral pits; four metatarsals (Bartholomai and Molnar 1981).

Comments: The genus *Muttaburrasaurus* was founded on an almost complete skeleton (QM F6140), including phalanges previously catalogued as F6095, figured by Hill, Playford and Woods (1968). The somewhat scattered remains were discovered in 1963 by D. Langdon of Muttaburra, in the Mackunda Formation (within Manuka Sub-Group, dated Lower Cretaceous [Albian]; see Vine and Day 1965; Vine, Day, Milligan, Casey, Galloway and Exon 1967; *Mut-*

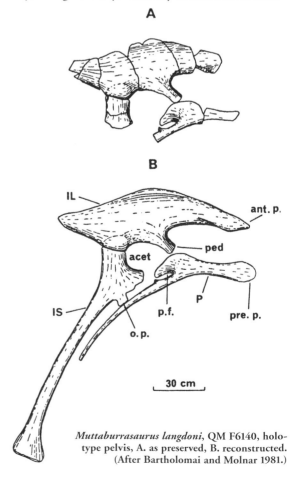

Muttaburrasaurus langdoni, QM F6140, holotype pelvis, A. as preserved, B. reconstructed.
(After Bartholomai and Molnar 1981.)

Muttaburrasaurus langdoni, QM F6140, holotype skull as preserved, left lateral view.

taburrasaurus in these deposits augmenting known fossil record of this region [Tambo Faunal Division]), Thomson River backs, southeast of Muttaburra, central Queensland, Australia (Bartholomai and Molnar 1981). The discovery was reported by Bartholomai (1966), then Hill *et al.*, after which Molnar (1980) informally referred to this dinosaur as the "Mackunda iguanodontid." Bartholomai and Molnar noted that, because *Muttaburrasaurus* was found in close association with nonabraded shallow-water marine mollusks, the type specimen was probably preserved some distance from the Albian shoreline, having floated out to sea, where it sank and became buried under marine muds.

As described by Bartholomai and Molnar, the skull of *Muttaburrasaurus* is distinguished mostly by the anterior portion of the snout, which has the appearance of a bump-like rise between the snout and orbits. This snout chamber may have been associated with enhancing the sense of smell or with amplifying sound. The dentition, unlike that of *Iguanodon* and *Camptosaurus*, seems to have functioned like a pair of shears. The unusually broad postinfratemporal bar reflects the increased volume of the adductor chamber, providing an increased area of attachment for an expanded adductor mass. Such features suggested to Bartholomai and Molnar that *Muttaburasaurus* may have been partially carnivorous (an idea not generally accepted).

An incomplete element, interpreted by Bartholomai and Molnar as a conical thumb spike, seems to have been larger, relative to metacarpals, than that of *Iguanodon.*

From measurements made by Bartholomai and Molnar, *Muttaburrasaurus* reached a length of about

7 meters (24 feet) and a height, at the hips, of 3 meters (over 10 feet). Its weight was probably about 2.59 metric tons (almost 2.9 tons) (G. S. Paul, personal communication 1988).

Bartholomai and Molnar pointed out that the 18 diagnostic features listed by Dodson (1980) to define Iguanodontidae almost constitute a description of *Muttaburrasaurus,* and consequently referred the genus to that family. However, Bartholomai and Molnar also observed that the closest affinities of this form are with *Camptosaurus,* listing 15 characteristics shared by *Muttaburrasaurus* and *Camptosaurus* (*i.e.,* constricted scapular blade flaring strongly at coracoid articulation; prominent acromion; short coracoid relative to scapula; coracoid foramen near articular surface for scapula, opening at middle of scapulacoracoid articulation; relatively narrow humerus; weak deltopectoral crest; distally compact and rounded radius; compact, heavily-ossified carpus; well-defined carpal articular relationships; massive ilium; reflected medial postacetabular ventral border of ilium; flat, deep prepubis; femur curved, with prominent lesser trochanter; anterior intercondylar sulcus on femur well

Muttaburrasaurus langdoni, QM F6140, reconstruction of holotype skull, left lateral view. (After Bartholomai and Molnar 1981.)

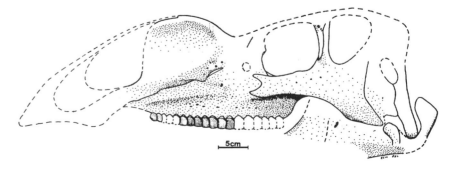

defined; and short, stocky pes, with broad metatarsus and digits.

Muttaburrasaurus shows more similarities to *Camptosaurus* than to various well-known iguanodontids (*e.g.*, *Iguanodon* and *Ouranosaurus*), reasons that *Muttaburrasaurus* is sometimes regarded as a camptosaurid. Norman and Weishampel (1990), in reassessing iguanodontids and related ornithopods, considered *Muttaburrasaurus* to be not well enough known for positive classification, designating this genus Iguanodontia *incertae sedis*.

Key references: Bartholomai (1966); Bartholomai and Molnar (1981); Hill, Playford and Woods (1968); Molnar (1980); Norman and Weishampel (1990).

MYMOORAPELTA Kirkland and Carpenter 1994

Ornithischia: Genasauria: Thyreophora: Ankylosauria: ?Nodosauridae.

Name derivation: "[Peter and Marilyn] Mygatt and [John] Moore" + Greek *pelta* = "shield."

Type species: *M. maysi* Kirkland and Carpenter 1994.

Other species: [None.]

Occurrence: Morrison Formation, Mesa County, Colorado, United States.

Age: Late Jurassic.

Known material: Numerous postcranial elements apparently pertaining to one individual, egg.

Holotype: MWC 1815, complete left ilium.

Mymoorapelta maysi, MWC 1815, holotype left ilium, A. lateral and B. dorsal views. Scale = 10 cm. (After Kirkland and Carpenter 1994.)

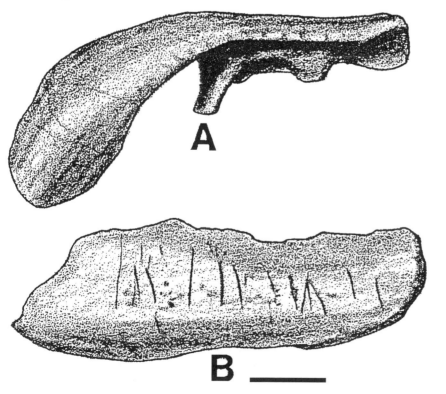

A

B

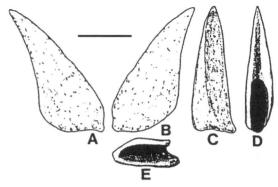

Mymoorapelta maysi, MWC 1818, cervical dermal spine, A. dorsal, B. ventral, C. anterior, D. posterior, and E. medial views. Scale = 10 cm. (After Kirkland and Carpenter 1994.)

Diagnosis of genus (as for type species): Centra of dorsal vertebrae cylindrical, less compressed laterally than in *Sauropelta*, *Edmontonia*, *Dracopelta*, *Polacanthus*, and possibly *Tianchisaurus*; anterior dorsal vertebrae with triangular pit between prezygapophyses; transverse processes not steeply angled up as in other ankylosaurs; prezygapophyses of proximal caudal vertebrae small, anteroposteriorly elongate, widely separated, and divergent (unlike joined and parallel condition in *Polacanthus*); rib triangular in cross-section (rather than T- or L-shaped as in other ankylosaurs); olecranon process broad, massive (not lateromedially compressed as in some ankylosaurs); preacetabular process of ilium curving lateroventrally (not horizontal as in other ankylosaurs), extending twice distance below ilium as pubic peduncle; ilium preacetabular process not divergent from midline; acetabulum partially closed; antitrochanter absent (as in stegosaurs); cervical dermal spine with groove extending from base to tip (in contrast to "*Polacanthus*" [=*Hoplitosaurus*] *marshi,* where it extends only about three-quarters from base to tip; caudal plates proximally tall, triangular, with base proportionally shorter relative to height than in other taxa with spine-like caudal plates (Kirkland and Carpenter 1994).

Comments: *Mymoorapelta maysi* is the first known Upper Jurassic ankylosaur from North America (see Kirkland 1993), the most complete Jurassic ankylosaur yet described, and the smallest adult, quadrupedal dinosaur identified to date in the Morrison Formation. The new genus and species was established upon a left ilium (with numerous grooves over the dorsal surface interpreted as tooth marks), with the following associated but scattered remains believed (as no elements were duplicated and the material was of the correct size and degree of ossification to represent one adult individual) to belong to the same individual: Four dorsal vertebrae (MWC 1800-03); seven caudal vertebrae (MWC 1804-08, 1839a,b); several ribs (MWC 1809-13,

1840); right ulna (MWC 1814); metacarpal (MWC 1816); phalange (MWC 1817); probable pedal ungual (MWC 939); large triangular cervical spine (MWC 1818); six caudal dermal plates (MWC 1819-24); small, solid, triangular dermal spine (MWC 1825); dorsal scutes including five circular to oval (MWC 1826-30), one wider than long (MWC 1831), two rectangular (MWC 1832-33), one massive (MWC 1834), and three large and asymmetric (MWC 1835-37); and one large sacral shield element (MWC 1838). The material was collected from the Mygatt-Moore Quarry, near the middle Brushy Basin Member of the Morrison Formation, Mesa County, in western Colorado, near the Utah-Colorado border (Kirkland and Carpenter 1994).

This quarry site was discovered in March, 1981 by Peter and Marilyn Mygatt and John D. and Vanetta Moore (see Mygatt 1991). It is one of the largest individual dinosaur sites in the region, traceable laterally in outcrop for more than 200 meters. The site was interpreted by Kirkland and Carpenter as an attritional accumulation of abundant dinosaur remains (including the sauropods *Apatosaurus, Barosaurus, Diplodocus,* and *Camarasaurus,* and theropods *Allosaurus* and *Ceratosaurus,* as well as a small unidentified theropod), based on the abundance of

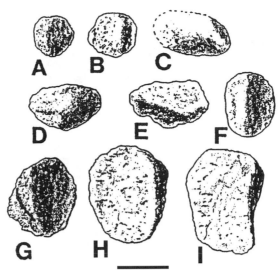

Mymoorapelta maysi, scutes, A. MWC 1828, B. MWC 1827, C. MWC 1833, D. MWC 1831, E. MWC 1832, D. MWC 1831, E. MWC 1832, F. MWC 1829, G. MWC 1834, H. MWC 1836, and I. MWC 1831. Scale = 5 cm. (After Kirkland and Carpenter 1994.)

carbonaceous plant material (including numerous *Equisetum* rhizomes with bulbils, fragments of rare fern fronds, *Brachyphyllum* leaf scales, and perhaps rare cycad seeds and frond fragments), along with the presence of freshwater snails (*Viviparus reesidei* and *Amplovalvata scabrida;* see Yen 1952) and fish (cf. *Coccolepis*).

In describing *Mymoorapelta,* Kirkland and Carpenter deduced that the triangular caudal plates (and those of *Polacanthus*) projected laterally, this hypothesis supported by a large ankylosaur, represented mostly by a tail with associated armor, described by Bodily (1968, 1969) as cf. *Hoplitosaurus.* In *Mymoorapelta,* a pair of massive scutes seem to have been present along the dorsal surface of the tail, with a triangular caudal plate projecting out laterally on each side, this arrangement of armor evidenced by the caudal vertebrae, the highly elongate caudal ribs, and low angle of the zygapophyses, possibly an adaptation for side-to-side swinging of the tail. These blade-like plates, in life possessing a keratinaceous covering, would have made an effective weapon when the tail was thusly swung. The sacral shield of *Mymoorapelta,* as in *Polacanthus,* is composed of fused dermal armor, although the individual elements of this shield are larger in the former genus. The individual ossifications began as separate centers of ossification which grew together, then fused together by a process of reabsorption and redisposition of bone on the basal surface of the shield, after which growth of the shield proceeded as a single, continuous sheet of bone (see Blows 1987; Kirkland, Carpenter and Burge 1991).

Kirkland and Carpenter found it difficult to fit *Mymoorapelta* into either of the two generally

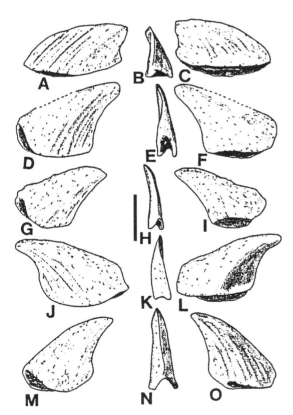

Mymoorapelta maysi, caudal plates, dorsal anterior, and ventral views: A.-C. (MWC 1824), D.-F. (MWC 1819), G.-I. (MWC 1823), J.-L. (MWC 1820), M.-O. (MWC 1822). Scale = 10 cm. (After Kirkland and Carpenter 1994.)

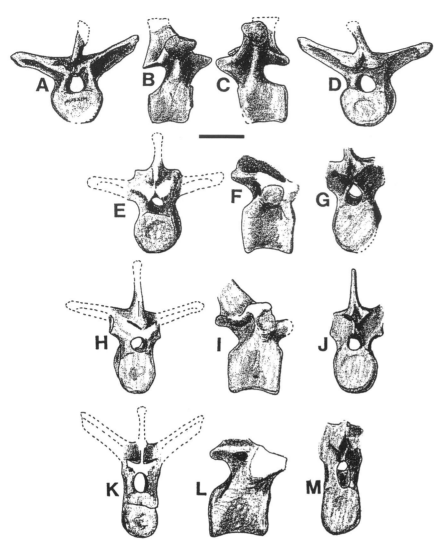

Mymoorapelta maysi, dorsal vertebrae (MWC 1800) in A. anterior, B. right lateral, C. left lateral, D. posterior views, E.–G. (MWC 1801), H.–J. (MWC 1802), K.–M. (MWC 1803). Scale = 5 cm. (After Kirkland and Carpenter 1994.)

cation to Kirkland and Carpenter, 1993). As no other ornithischians were known from the Mygatt-Moore Quarry and (with the possible exception of the small theropod) no associated saurischians were small enough to have laid the egg, Kirkland and Carpenter speculated that the egg may have been aborted by this *Mymoorapelta* at the time of its death. Kirkland and Carpenter further speculated that death may have been sudden, possibly the result of the dinosaur being trapped in mud, after which it was killed or at least scavenged.

Notes: Kirkland (1993) also reported two additional as yet undescribed "polacanthid" nodosaurs from the Cedar Mountain Formation (Lower Cretaceous [Barremian]) in eastern Utah. These new forms also seem to be related to *P. foxi* and *H. marshi*, particularly resembling them in their distinctive caudal plates. The first of these specimens is the most complete nodosaurid skeleton yet found, comprising many varied vertebrae, ribs, scapulacoracoids, ulna, femur, foot bones, almost complete pelvis with sacral shield, abundant diverse armor throughout the body, and, most significantly, a very distinctive, complete and uncrushed skull. It represents an adult approximately 4–5 meters (14–17) feet long. The other specimen (see Bodily 1968, 1969), comprising caudal vertebrae and much diverse armor recovered from higher in the Cedar Mountain Formation, represents the largest known "polacanthid" (8–9 meters or 27–30 feet long).

Key references: Kirkland (1993); Kirkland and Carpenter 1994; Kirkland, Carpenter and Burge (1991).

accepted ankylosaurian families, Nodosauridae or Ankylosauridae, based upon features noted in the preserved material, but tentatively referred it to the former, as this genus possesses a number of primitive features (*e.g.*, solid dorsal scutes). Characters shared by *M. maysi* and *Polacanthus foxi* include posteriorly grooved cervical spines, triangular caudal plates with asymmetrical hollow bases, and a co-ossified sacral shield, these similarities suggesting a close relationship between these taxa, "possibly in a separate subfamily" (Kirkland, in preparation).

As observed by Kirkland and Carpenter, extensive tooth marks are present on the posterior dorsal vertebrae, ilium, and one caudal plate, and the ribs were often preserved in short isolated lengths, indications that the animal represented by the preserved remains was fed upon.

Found in association with this material was a small dinosaurian egg measuring less than 10 centimeters in diameter (K. Hirsch, personal communi-

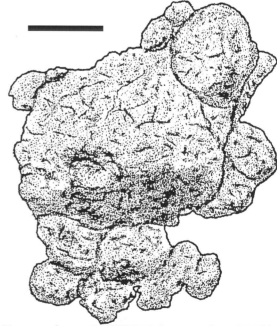

Mymoorapelta maysi, MWC 1838, fragment of sacral shield, with small scutes fused to large central scute. Scale = 2 cm. (After Kirkland and Carpenter 1994.)

NAASHOIBITOSAURUS Lucas and Hunt 1993
Ornithischia: Genasauria: Cerapoda: Ornithopoda:
  Iguanodontia: Hadrosauridae: Hadrosaurinae.
Name derivation: "Naashoibito [Member of
  Kirtland Formation] + Greek *sauros* = "lizard.""
Type species: *N. ostromi* Lucas and Hunt 1993.
Other species: [None.]
Occurrence: Kirtland Formation, New Mexico,
  United States.
Age: Late Cretaceous (Late Maastrichtian).
Known material/holotype: NMMNH P-16106,
  incomplete skull and postcrania.

Diagnosis of genus (as for type species): Differs
from other known hadrosaurids (except *Gryposaurus*)
in possessing nasal arch that rises above anterior end
of orbits; differs from *Gryposaurus* in possessing nasals
that bifurcate posteriorly so that frontals extend anteriorly between nasals along midline, and nasals with
posterior processes overlapped by extensive medial
wings of the prefrontals so that, in dorsal view, it
appears that transverse width of nasals is narrower
than that of prefrontals (Horner 1992).

Comments: The genus *Naashoibitosaurus* was
founded upon a partial skull (NMMNH P-16106) collected by David D. Gillette and David Thomas from
the Naashoibito Member of the Kirtland Formation
(Late Maastrichtian; see Lucas and Hunt 1992) in
northwestern New Mexico. Horner (1992) described
the skull roof as belonging to *Kritosaurus navajovius*,
basing his assessment on the same characters that
linked *Kritosaurus* and *Anasazisaurus* (see entry).

Unaware of Horner's study, Lucas and Hunt
(1992) described the rest of the skull and postcrania
as *Edmontosaurus saskatchewanensis*. Subsequently
finding that the specimen could not be assigned to *K.
navajovius* and that the skull roof was incompatible
with *E. saskatchewanensis*, Lucas and Hunt (1993)
referred it to the new genus and species *Naashoibitosaurus ostromi*,

Key references: Horner (1992); Lucas and Hunt
(1992, 1993).

NANOSAURUS Marsh 1877 [*nomen dubium*]
Ornithischia: Genasauria: Cerapoda: Ornithopoda:
  Hypsilophodontidae.
Name derivation: Greek *nanus* = "dwarf" + Greek
  sauros = "lizard."
Type species: *N. agilis* Marsh 1877 [*nomen dubium*].
Other species: [None.]
Occurrence: ?Morrison Formation, Colorado,
  United States.
Age: Late Jurassic (?Kimmeridgian–Tithonian).
Known material: Dentary, postcranial elements.
Holotype: YPM 1913, incomplete dentary.

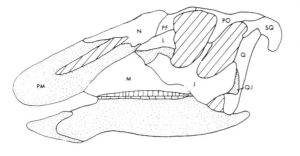

Naashoibiosaurus ostromi, NMMNH P-16106, reconstructed holotype skull, left lateral and dorsal views.
(After Hunt and Lucas 1993.)

Diagnosis of genus: [No modern diagnosis published.]

Comments: The first Late Jurassic North American ornithischian genus to be described, *Nanosaurus*
was established upon a partial dentary (YPM 1913),
poorly preserved in a slab of very fine sandstone with
indistinct impressions of 15 teeth, and postcrania

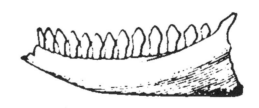

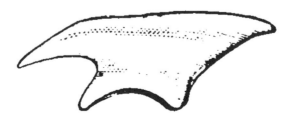

Nanosaurus agilis, YPM
1913a, lectotype incomplete
right dentary and paralectotype ilium, both left lateral
views. Scale = 5 cm. (After
Marsh 1877.)

Nanosaurus rex, YPM 1915, (smaller) femur, and YPM 4754, referred (larger) femur, the former now the holotype of *Othnielia rex* (see *Othnielia* entry).

Photo by R. A. Long and S. P. Welles (neg. #73/472-18), courtesy Yale Peabody Museum of Natural History.

including an ilium, femora, tibiae, and a fibula. The material was collected from an unknown stratigraphic level, probably from the Morrison Formation (see Galton 1987), at Garden Park, near Cañon City, Fremont County, Colorado. The remains were briefly described by Marsh (1877b), who figured the right dentary (with teeth) and the ilium. Because the dentary (as a natural mold) is more diagnostic than the ilium, Galton designated the former (YPM 1913a) as the lectotype. The associated remains, preserved in the same piece of matrix and apparently from the same individual as the lectotype, were designated paralectotypes (YPM 1913b-g) by Galton.

Marsh originally described the teeth as denticulate and resembling those of *Iguanodon*. The mandible is 3.6 centimeters (over 1.35 inches) in length, teeth .9 centimeters (almost .35 inches). Marsh erected for *Nanosaurus* its own [now abandoned] family, Nanosauridae.

Galton (1977), observing that the slender jaw is like that of *Fabrosaurus* and *Lesothosaurus*, reassigned the genus to the [abandoned] family Fabrosauridae. Later, Galton (1983b) moved *Nanosaurus* to the Hypsilophodontidae, noting that the crowns of the cheek teeth are asymmetrical (symmetry of cheek teeth once a supposed diagnostic feature of the "Fabrosauridae"; Galton 1978).

Also, Galton (1978) observed that the proportions of the dentary are similar to those in *Echinodon*; the recurved anterior teeth resemble premaxillary teeth in *Lesothosaurus*.

Galton (1978) believed *N. agilis* to be "a slightly

modified descendant of *Lesothosaurus*," although Sereno (1984) pointed out that he mentioned only general similarities in the dentition and fragmentary postcranium to support this assessment.

Sues and Norman (1990) put *Nanosaurus* into the Hypsilophodontidae as a *nomen dubium*. According to Bakker, Galton, Siegwarth and Filla (1990), the holotype of *N. agilis*, lacking well-preserved tooth crowns, cannot be defined and may well remain indeterminate. According to Sereno, there are no derived characters that can unite *N. agilis* and *Lesothosaurus diagnosticus*; there are no valid autapomorphies that can characterize the type specimen of *N. agilis*; and *N. agilis* is best regarded as Ornithischia *incertae sedis*, perhaps also a *nomen dubium*.

Notes: Bakker *et al.* stated that teeth tentatively referred by Galton (1983b) to *Manosaurus* may be referable to *Drinker*.

Galton (1977) made *N. rex* Marsh 1877 the type species of new genus *Othnielia*.

Key references: Bakker, Galton, Siegwarth and Filla (1990); Galton (1977, 1983b, 1987); Marsh (1877b); Sereno (1984); Sues and Norman (1990).

NANOTYRANNUS Bakker, Williams and Currie 1988—(=*Clevelanotyrannus, Dinotyrannus*)
Saurischia: Theropoda: Tetanurae: Avetheropoda: Coelurosauria: Maniraptora: Arctometatarsalia: Tyrannosauridae.
Name derivation: Greek *nanus* = "dwarf" + Greek *tyrannos* = "tyrant."
Type species: *N. lancensis* (Gilmore 1946).
Other species: [None.]
Occurrence: Hell Creek Formation, Montana, United States.
Age: Late Cretaceous (Maastrichtian).
Known material: Skull with associated postcranial fragments, fragmentary skeleton, teeth.
Holotype: CM 7541, almost complete skull.

Diagnosis of genus (as for type species): Skull long, low; maxillary fenestra small, separated from antorbital opening by wide bar of maxillary; antorbital fenestra longer than tall; nasals not forming wedge between frontals as in *Albertosaurus libratus* and *A. sarcophagus*; muzzle (in dorsal) aspect well differentiated from cranium (allowing for stereoscopic vision); fourth trochanter of femur more proximal than in *A. libratus*; proximal articular face of tibia nearly triangular; proximal expansion of fibula symmetrical relative to long axis of shaft (not quadrangular as in most tyrannosaurids except *Maleevosaurus*) (Carpenter 1992).

Comments: The smallest known and one of the last tyrannosaurids, *Nanotyrannus* was founded upon a well-preserved, nearly complete skull with tightly articulated lower jaws (CM 7541). The skull, originally described by Gilmore (1946) as a third species of "*Gorgosaurus*" [=*Albertosaurus*], "*G.*" *lancensis*, was collected in 1942 by David H. Dunkle from the Hell Creek Formation at Sand Creek, Carter County, eastern Montana, during an expedition for the Cleveland Museum of Natural History.

Gilmore did not strictly diagnose the new species, but observed that its closest affinities seemed to be with "*G.*" *sternbergi* [=*A. libratus*] in "its smaller size, elongate shallow maxillary, and rounder orbital fenestra." Gilmore pointed out that minor differences in skull structure had no importance on the species level, while differences in the lateral temporal fenestral region were due to postmortem distortion. The quadrate, Gilmore observed, had been crushed forward and upward, narrowing the fenestra and altering the natural angulation of the bones making up that part of the skull.

As detailed information regarding the skull character of the two previously described species of "*Gorgosaurus*" ("*G.*" *libratus* and "*G.*" *sternbergi*) was lacking, Gilmore found that properly characterizing all three species (including "*G.*" *lancensis*), based upon cranial structural features, was not possible. The smaller skull was regarded as a distinct species mostly because of the great interval of time separating it from both "*G.*" *libratus* and "*G.*" *sternbergi*. Gilmore speculated, however, that CM 7541 represented an adult individual, as suggested by the coalescence of many cranial sutures.

The skull (which was on display at the Cleveland Museum in the early 1980s) remained in open storage at the museum for decades, during which time it had never been studied in great detail, although various paleontologists did question its generic standing. In 1987, while examining a large specimen in the museum's fine collection of fossil fish, Robert T. Bakker observed that this skull more resembled *Tyrannosaurus*, having a narrow snout and wide posterior region with the orbits forwardly directed for binocular vision, than the more "lizard-like" orbital orientation of *Albertosaurus*. Bakker saw that the skull vaguely resembled that of *T. rex*, although on a much smaller scale.

Before this so-called "pygmy tyrannosaur" was formally described, it was mentioned under the generic name *Clevelanotyrannus* by Currie (1987*c*). The new genus *Nanotyrannus* was later formally introduced by Bakker, Williams and Currie (1988).

Bakker *et al.* diagnosed *Nanotyrannus* as follows: Differs from all other tyrannosaurids in derived characters of muzzle width greatly constricted to only one-fourth width of temporal region, extraordinarily wide basicranium between basitubera and basipterygoid processes, and two large pneumatic foramina situated one behind the other near midline of basiphenoid; differs from *Daspletosaurus*, "*Gorgosaurus*" [which Bakker *et al.* regarded as distinct from *Albertosaurus*, for reasons to be published later by Bakker, Currie and Williams], and *Alioramus*, but agrees with *Tyrannosaurus*, *Albertosaurus*, and "*Tarbosaurus*" [=*Tyrannosaurus*] sp. in derived features of

Nanotyrannus lancensis, CM 7541, holotype skull of *Gorgosaurus lancensis*, left lateral view.

marked expansion of width across temple relative to skull length, and basitubera forwardly displaced towards basipterygoid processes; differs from all other tyrannosaurids (except *Alioramus*) in keeping primitive characters of long, low snout [probably a size-related feature; R. E. Molnar, personal communication 1989] and strongly laterally compressed maxillary teeth; differs from all other tyrannosaurids in nasal lacking strong ridges and striae along dorsal surface [?size-related; Molnar, personal communication]; differs from *Tyrannosaurus* in retention of primitive character of smooth depressed area on antero-ventral corner of lacrimal for muscle origin.

Although the skull has features identifying it as an adult (tightly interlocking sutures between the bones of the skull roof [first observed by Gilmore], well-developed supraoccipital alae, and a clearly formed tuberosity on the ventral border of the jugal), it is approximately one half the size of an adult *A. libratus*. The type skull is the smallest adult tyrannosaurid skull known, measuring only 572 millimeters (approximately 22 inches) long.

In comparing *Nanotyrannus* with other tyrannosaurids, Bakker *et al.* emphasized that this genus exhibits both primitive and derived features, and concluded that, although illustrating marked structural convergence with *Tyrannosaurus*, *Nanotyrannus* probably evolved independently from a very primitive and as yet unknown tyrannosaurid.

The most unusual aspects of the type specimen are its size and adaptations for possible binocular vision. Bakker *et al.* noted that the orbits are directed forward, the frontal is markedly expanded, and the muzzle is constricted to a degree apparently unknown in other tyrannosaurids. The occipital condyle was carried on a con-

stricted neck which faced strongly downward, so that the head was sharply bent down on the neck. These adaptations would suggest a depth perception, favored by natural selection, that would have been advantageous in the animal's dealing with such heavily armed plant-eating contemporaries as ceratopsians (also hunting in dim light or hunting camouflaged prey; see Molnar and Farlow 1990; also Jules 1971).

However, as Molnar and Farlow pointed out, while binocular vision would certainly have been advantageous to a large carnivore, it does not necessarily follow that such vision is always present with the kind of orbital orientation found in *Nanotyrannus*. Molnar and Farlow cited studies (Konishi and Pettigrew 1981; Pettigrew 1986) of birds that have strongly overlapping visual fields but do not enjoy stereoscopic vision, and cautioned that a conclusion regarding such vision can only be verified by behavioral or neuroanatomical studies (Pettigrew 1986) impossible for an extinct dinosaur.

Three teeth (DMNH collection), broken off at the crown, found in 1924 by D. Reinheimer in the Lancian beds of Corson County, South Dakota, were referred by Bakker *et al.* to *Nanotyrannus* (these found along with five teeth of a juvenile *Tyrannosaurus*).

A fragmentary tyrannosaurid skeleton (LACM 23845), from the Hell Creek Formation in Garfield County, central Montana, originally thought to be an immature *T. rex*, was tentatively designated *Albertosaurus* cf. *A. lancensis* [=*A. megagracilis* Paul 1988] by Molnar (1980c). The remains indicate a slender, gracile form differing from *T. rex* by its smaller skull and in the form of the articulations of some cranial bones. Cranial features and proportions of the limb bone match those in *Albertosaurus*. That this was a swift-footed theropod is indicated by the development of the cnemial crest, apparent proximal position of the fourth trochanter, and general slenderness of the hindlimb bones. Molnar proposed that the rel-

Fragmentary skeleton (LACM 23845) referred to *Nanotyrannus lancensis*, drawing by Tracy L. Ford. Scale = 1 m. (After Olshevsky and Ford 1995.)

atively small skull and shape of the manual claw indicate a large theropod coexisting with *T. rex*, but feeding on smaller prey or in a different fashion. (In the Japanese popular magazine, *Dinosaur Frontline*, Olshevsky and Ford 1995 referred LACM 23845 to new genus *Dinotyrannus*; this referral has not yet been adopted.)

Carpenter (*see in* Lehman and Carpenter 1990) regarded *Nanotyrannus* as a juvenile specimen of *Tyrannosaurus*. In an apparently previously written paper, Carpenter (1992) regarded this species as prob-

lematic, observing that the skull in lateral view closely resembles that of *A. libratus*, but in dorsal aspect the muzzle is well differentiated from the cranium, a feature otherwise only known in *Tyrannosaurus*. Furthermore, in *T. bataar*, skulls of juveniles resemble *Albertosaurus* in profile. Carpenter noted that the parietals in CMNH 7541 are the only entirely coalescent bones, frontals and nasals separate anteriorly, and that fusion of cranial bones in dinosaurs is highly variable (see Brown and Schlaikjer 1940*b*) and therefore not a reliable criterion for determining ontogenetic age. Comparing CMNH 7541 to various *T. bataar* skulls, Carpenter surmised that the oval shape of the orbit could be a juvenile character. Also, the skeleton tentatively referred by Molnar to *?A. lancensis* is relatively small and gracile, indications of a juvenile animal, exhibiting nothing to prevent its being regarded as a juvenile *T. rex*.

Note: In various newspaper articles (*e.g.*, Los Angeles *Times*, May 2, 1988, Part II, p. 4), issued before publication of the official naming and description of this genus, Bakker stated that *Nanotyrannus*

weighed only 600 to 1,000 pounds, or approximately 270 to 460 kilograms. Bakker added that the comparatively small and delicate teeth are suggestive of a more delicate bite for attacking small prey probably weighing no more than 60 pounds, or about 27 kilograms.

In an article published in *Discover* magazine, Bakker (1992) reported the results of a computed axial tomography (CT or CAT scan) study of the type skull of *N. lancensis*. The skull possesses an avian-like exit (through an independent canal passing through the braincase bones, rather than, as in all modern nonavian vertebrates, sideways through a large braincase opening) for the V1 nerve. As in birds, the skull possesses air chambers which would have been helpful in cooling internal tissues, evidence, Bakker contended, supporting warm-bloodedness. Furthermore, the brain of *Nanotyrannus* was relatively larger than in other tyrannosaurids, the inner braincase bones fitting snugly together. Turbinals (paper-thin sheets of bone that are standard apparatus in some modern mammals such as dogs and hyaenas) are present in the inner snout wall, suggestive of an acute sense of smell. The inner ear bones seem to have been surrounded by air chambers, which would have increased hearing sensitivity to low-frequency sounds. The cheekbones have grooves indicating that the outer ear canals wrapped around the head so that the ears pointed forward, in a fashion which Bakker compared to an old-fashioned hearing trumpet, possibly allowing for stereo hearing. Tooth crowns in *Nanotyrannus* are almost all the same height and tightly packed together with few spaces between them, indications, Bakker stated, of an efficient, "pinking shears"-like bite.

Key references: Bakker, Williams and Currie (1988); Carpenter (1992); Currie (1987c); Gilmore (1946); Lehman and Carpenter (1990); Molnar (1980c); Molnar and Farlow (1990).

NANSHIUNGOSAURUS   Dong 1979

Saurischia: Theropoda: Tetanurae: ?Coelurosauria: Therizinosauroidea: Therizinosauridae.

Name derivation: "Nanshiung [province]" + Greek *sauros* = "lizard."

Type species: *N. brevispinus* Dong 1979.

Other species: [None.]

Occurrence: Nanxiong Formation, Guandong, People's Republic of China.

Age: Late Cretaceous (Late Campanian).

Known material/holotype: NIGP V4731, presacral vertebral column, pelvis.

Diagnosis of genus: Vertebral column if complete only about 10 meters (about 34 feet) or less in length; pelvic elements coossified; pubis and ischium in parallel orientation; ilium with very long preacetabular process, almost no postacetabular process; pubis terminating in "boot" (Dong 1979).

Comments: The genus *Nanshiungosaurus* was founded upon incomplete postcranial remains (NIGP V4731) discovered in Nanshiung, on the south coast of China.

Dong (1979) originally believed *Nanshiungosaurus* to be a "peculiar" and relatively small "sauropod." Since the pelvis described by Dong is clearly therizinosaurid, *Nanshiungosaurus* was referred by Barsbold and Maryańska (1990) to the "Segnosauria" [=Therizinosauridae] and Segnosauridae. As observed by Barsbold and Maryańska, *N. brevispinus* has cervical vertebrae similar in structure to that in Mongolian therizinosaurids [=segnosaurians of their usage]. *S. brevispinus* differs from *Segnosaurus galbinensis* in having an ilium with a shallower cranial portion of the preacetabular process.

Key references: Barsbold and Maryańska (1990); Dong (1979).

NEMEGTOSAURUS   Nowiński 1971

Saurischia: Sauropodomorpha: Sauropoda: Diplodocidae: Dicraeosaurinae.

Name derivation: "Nemegt [Formation]" + Greek *sauros* = "lizard."

Type species: *N. mongoliensis* Nowiński 1971.

Other species: *N. pachi* Dong (1977).

Occurrence: Nemegt Formation, Omnogov, Mongolian People's Republic; Subash Formation, Shashan County, China.

Age: Late Cretaceous (?Late Campanian or Early Maastrichtian).

Known material: Skull, partial postcrania, tooth.

Holotype: ZPAL MgD-I/9, nearly complete skull.

Diagnosis of genus (as for type species): Intermediate in some respects between *Dicraeosaurus* and *Diplodocus*; skull lightly constructed, strongly elongated, with long, downwardly bent snout lacking accessory preorbital foramen; palatine bones very narrow, strongly elongated longitudinally; extensive lacrimal contributing to margin of external naris; nasal not contacting maxilla; prefrontal entering margin of external naris and very large orbit; very small supratemporal fossa elongated transversely, open dorsally; squamosal contacting quadratojugal, but is not

Nanshiungosaurus brevispinus, NIGP VA7321, holotype partial skeleton. (After Dong 1987.)

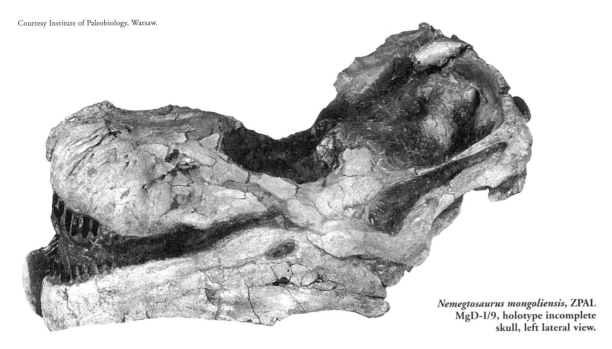

Nemegtosaurus mongoliensis, ZPAL MgD-I/9, holotype incomplete skull, left lateral view.

part of margin of supratemporal fossa; parietal crest very prominent; occipital condyle far anteriorly, sloping ventroanteriorly to form approximate 100-degree angle with horizontal plane; lower jaw very light, with mandibular vacuity present; teeth lance-shaped, crown-to-root ratio 2.1 (Nowiński 1971).

Comments: The genus *Nemegtosaurus* was established on the most complete skull yet known from a Late Cretaceous sauropod, with lower jaws (ZPAL MgD-I/9), collected in 1965 from the Uppermost Cretaceous, Upper Nemegt Beds (Gradziński, Kazmierczak, and Lefeld 1968/1969) during the third Polish-Mongolian Expedition to the Gobi Desert (Kielan-Jaworoska and Dovchin 1968/1969).

In describing *Nemegtosaurus*, Nowiński (1971) noted that the skull generally resembles that of *Dicraeosaurus* in side view, and that the teeth are particularly similar to those in the latter genus. McIntosh (1990*b*), in reviewing the Sauropoda, observed that the skull of *Nemegtosaurus* most closely resembles that of *Dicraeosaurus*, primarily differing in the length and positioning of the basipterygoid process.

Nowiński pointed out that, although fragmentary sclerotic rings are known in other sauropods (including *Camarasaurus lentus*, *Brachiosaurus brancai*, and *Diplodocus hayi*), the skull of *N. mongoliensis* has the first completely preserved example to be described. It differs from other known sclerotic rings in dinosaurs in being bilaterally symmetrical and in the arrangement of the positive and negative plates relative to the main axis of the skull. The positive plates lie posterodorsally, negative plates anterodorsally (ventrally and dorsally in other known dinosaurs and in extant birds). Nowiński allowed for the possibility that the plates in *Nemegtosaurus* should be placed in the conventional position, their preserved orientation perhaps the result of post mortem displacement. As preserved, the plates cannot be assigned to either of the two categories of sclerotic rings recognized by Lemmrich (1931) in modern birds, similar types of which were recognized by Ostrom (1961*c*) in dinosaurs.

A second species, *N. pachi* Dong 1977, was based on the pencil-like tooth of a large sauropod from the Subash Formation (Late Cretaceous) of Shanshan County, Turpan Basin, China.

Key references: Dong (1977); McIntosh (1990*b*); Nowiński (1971).

Nemegtosaurus pachi, holotype tooth. (After Dong 1987.)

NEOSAURUS Gilmore 1945—(Preoccupied, Nopcsa 1923; see *Hypsibema*.)

Name derivation: Greek *neos* = "new" + Greek *sauros* = reptile.

Type species: *N. missouriensis* Gilmore and Stewart 1945.

NEOSODON Moussaye 1885 [*nomen dubium*]

Saurischia: Sauropodomorpha: Sauropoda: Camarasauridae *incertae sedis*.

Name derivation: Greek *neos* = "new" + Greek *odous* = "tooth."

Type species: (No specific name assigned).

Other species: [None.]

Occurrence: Département du Pas-de-Calais, France.

Age: Late Jurassic (Portlandian).

Known material: Tooth, other material [to be announced].

Holotype: Incomplete tooth.

Diagnosis of genus: [None published].

Comments: The genus *Neosodon* was founded upon a large, well-worn tooth with a broken point and root, discovered in Wilmille, near Boulogne, France. The tooth was described by Moussaye (1885), who did not assign it a specific name and incorrectly believed that *Neosodon* was related to *Megalosaurus*, a theropod.

Moussaye described the tooth as follows; 60 millimeters (more than 2.3 inches) high, 35 millimeters (about 1.35 inches) wide, 20 millimeters (about .78 inches) thick (total length, if complete, estimated as about 80 millimeters [almost 3.1 inches]); blackish in color, smooth, rather flat, resembling spear head, with convex external face, slightly concave inner face with slight roughness toward point, widening towards "neck"; edges rounded and worn on both lateral surfaces toward summit; root rounded on external side.

Neosodon, holotype tooth, in 1. labial, 2. lingual, and 3. cross-sectionald views. Scale = 1 cm. (After Moussaye 1885.)

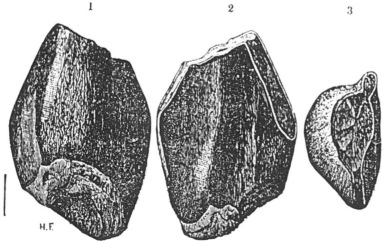

Sauvage (1888) referred the tooth to a North American sauropod species, *Caulodon praecursor*; other writers (Huene 1932; Romer 1966; Steel 1970; Olshevsky 1978, 1991, 1992) have referred *Neosodon* to the brachiosaurid *Pelorosaurus*.

More recently, Buffetaut and Martin (in preparation), having made a study of the latest Jurassic dinosaurs from the Boulonnais in northern France, will show that *Neosodon* is not a brachiosaurid, but a very large camarasaurid, and apparently the most abundant sauropod from that area.

Key references: Moussaye (1885); Sauvage (1888).

NIOBRARASAURUS Carpenter, Dilkes and Weishampel 1995

Ornithischia: Genasauria: Thyreophora: Ankylosauria: Nodosauridae.

Name derivation: "Niobrara [Chalk Formation]" + Greek *sauros* = "lizard."

Type species: *N. coleii* (Mehl 1936).

Other species: [None.]

Occurrence: Niobrara Chalk Formation, Kansas, United States.

Age: Late Cretaceous (Middle Santonian–Early Campanian).

Known material/holotype: MU 650 VP, partially articulated, fragmentary skeleton, including cranial parts, teeth, cervical, dorsal, and caudal vertebrae, chevrons, ribs, partial sacrum, partial right scapulacoracoid, partial ilia, complete right humerus, ulna, and radius, fragments of left ulna and radius, metacarpals, complete right femur, tibia, fibula, and pes, parts of left femur, tibia, and fibula, armor.

Diagnosis of genus (as for type species): Armor on snout consisting of two pairs (rather than one as in *Panoplosaurus mirus* and *Edmontonia* spp.) of elongated scutes; secondary palate extending caudally more than in other nodosaurids; neural spine of caudal vertebrae short, terminating in expanded nob; transverse processes of anterior caudal vertebrae project backwards (forwards in *Sauropelta edwardsi orum* [=*S. edwardsi* of their usage], *Edmontonia* spp., and most other nodosaurids); humerus with slender shaft (typical of most nodosaurids), differing from that of *P. mirus* and *Edmontonia* spp. in having a shallower olecranon notch between radial and ulnar condyles; deltopectoral crest undifferentiated from humeral head by a "step"; bicipital crest less pronounced than in *S. edwardsi orum*, but more than in *P. mirus* and *Edmontonia* spp.; olecranon process of ulna considerably more pronounced than in "*Stegopelta landerensis* [=*Nodosaurus textilis*]" and possibly *Edmontonia* spp., less so than in *S. edwardsiorum*; femur similar to that of *Hoplitosaurus marshi* in medial development of fourth trochanter, differs in not being S-shaped in lateral profile (Carpenter, Dilkes and Weishampel 1995).

Comments: *Niobrarasaurus coleii* was founded on a partial skeleton (MU 650 VP), discovered in 1930 by Virgil Cole in the Smoky Hill Chalk Member of the Niobrara Chalk Formation, in Gove County, western Kansas. These remains, housed at the University of Missouri, Columbia, were originally referred by Mehl (1936) to a second species of *Hierosaurus, H. coleii,* on the basis of its being recovered from the same formation that yielded the type species *H. sternbergii.* In their review of the Ankylosauria, Coombs and Maryańska (1990) regarded this species as a junior synonym of *Nodosaurus textilis.* More recently, Carpenter *et al.* recognized the remains of *H. coleii* as belonging to a new genus, which they named *Niobrarasaurus,* its relationships to other nodosaurids unknown.

Notes: Carpenter *et al.* discussed two specimens referred to Nodosauridae *incertae sedis.* The first specimen consists of a pair of elongated scutes (YPM 55419) (possibly cervical armor) collected from the Smoke Hill Chalk Member, Niobrara Chalk Formation, at Hackberry Creek, Gove County, Kansas, originally described by Wieland (1909). They are approximately twice as wide as long, joined along the midline, with heavily-pitted dorsal surfaces. The unusual elongated domed shape of the scutes superficially resembles the "intercostal plates" of *N. textilis.* The second such specimen discussed by Carpenter *et al.* was a fragmentary skeleton (KU 25150), found by J. D. Stewart on May 24, 1973, in the middle part of the Smoky Hill Member of the Niobrara Chalk Formation (*Clioscaphites choteauensis* or *C. vermiformis* zone), in Rooks County, Kansas. The specimen includes four crushed centra, ribs and rib fragments, proximal and distal ends of left scapula, complete left humerus, partial right humerus, proximal ends of right ulna and radius, partial ?pubis, ?fibula fragment, and 12 armor fragments. It represents the oldest (Middle Santonian; Hattin

Photo by R. A. Long and S. P. Welles (neg. #73/55-2).

Niobrarasaurus coleii, U. Mo. UP 650 VP, holotype tooth of *Hierosaurus coleii.*

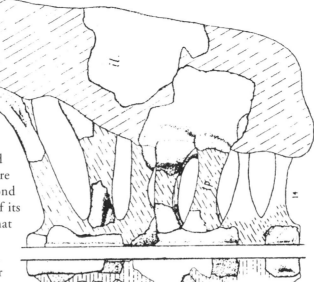

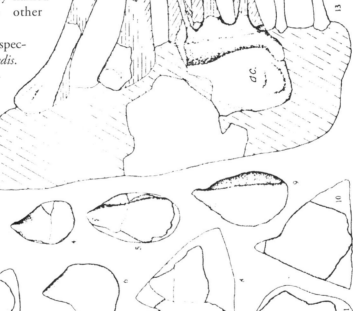

Niobrarasaurus coelii, U. Mo. UP 650 VP, holotype sacrum, pelvis, and dermal ossifications of *Hierosaurus coelii.* (After Mehl 1936.)

1982) nodosaurid from this formation. Although this specimen was too fragmentary to assign to any known genus or species, Carpenter *et al.* noted that the lack of fusion between the neural arches and centra are indicative of an immature individual.

Key references: Carpenter, Dilkes and Weishampel (1995); Coombs and Maryańska (1990); Mehl (1936).

1 m

Nipponosaurus sachalinensis,
**holotype incomplete skeleton
(juvenile).**

NIPPONOSAURUS   Nagao 1936—
(=?*Jaxartosaurus*)

Ornithischia: Genasauria: Cerapoda: Ornithopoda:
Iguanodontia: Hadrosauridae: Lambeosaurinae.
incertae sedis.

Name derivation: Japanese *Nippon* = "Japan" +
Greek *sauros* = "lizard."

Type species: *N. sachalinensis* Nagao 1936.

Other species: [None.]

Occurrence: Mh7 or Mh6 of Miho Group,
Sachalinskaya Oblast.

Age: Late Cretaceous (Early Santonian or Late
Coniacian).

Known material: Isolated cranial and postcranial
elements representing at least five individuals.

Holotype: Almost complete skeleton including posterior part of skull, atlas, third-seventh cervical
vertebrae, eight dorsals, sacrum, caudal vertebrae,
chevrons, ribs, part of left ilium, (imperfect)
ischia, nearly complete left hindlimb with pes,
distal end of right femur, ossified tendons in dorsal and anterior caudal regions, juvenile.

Diagnosis of genus: [No modern diagnosis published.]

Comments: The genus *Nipponosaurus* was
founded by Nagao (1936) on an almost complete
juvenile skeleton, collected from an unknown horizon (apparently of approximately Campanian age) at
Kawa Kami, Shachalin Island [then a Japanese territory, subsequently part of what had been the Union
of Soviet Socialist Republics], Japan.

Nagao originally diagnosed the monotypic
N. sachalinensis as follows: Relatively small, with
short, deep, somewhat broad skull; frontals with low
swelling apparently representing incipient dome-like
crest [cranial features attributed to immaturity
(Langston 1960; M. K. Brett-Surman, personal communication)].

Later, Rozhdestvensky (1968) augmented
Nagao's diagnosis with postcranial characters not
reported by Nagao, because they pertain to all
lambeosaurines.

Brett-Surman (1975, 1979) referred *N. sachalinensis* to *Jaxartosaurus*. More recently, Brett-Surman
(1989) noted that this referral, not yet certain or
verifiable, should be regarded as provisional.
Although *Nipponosaurus* is still regarded by some
workers as a juvenile *Jaxartosaurus* and both forms
may be synonymous, Brett-Surman (1989) preferred

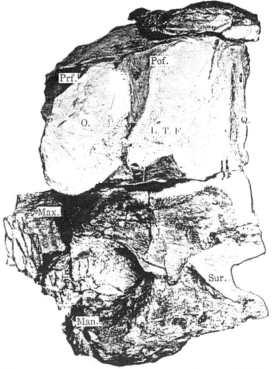

Nipponosaurus sachalinensis, **holotype skull (juvenile), left
lateral view.**

retaining the former taxon until adult specimens are found. Brett-Surman (personal communication 1993) further noted that the type specimen of this taxon should be fully restudied.

Key references: Brett-Surman (1975, 1979, 1989); Nagao (1936); Rozhdestvensky (1968).

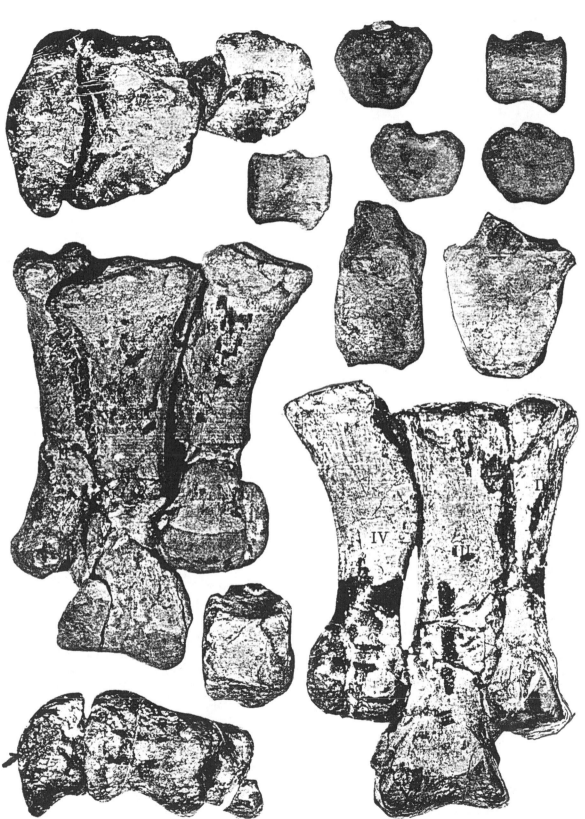

Nipponosaurus sachalinensis, holotype hindfeet elements (juvenile). (After Nagao 1936.)

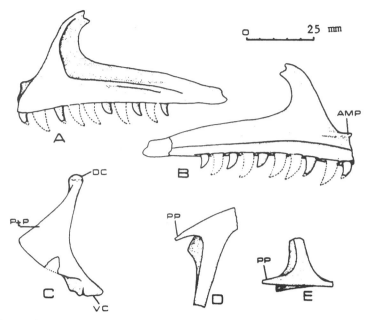

Noasaurus leali, PVL 4061, holotype A.–B. left maxilla in lateral and medial views, C. right quadrate, medial view, D.–E. right squamosal in lateral and dorsal views. (After Bonaparte and Powell 1980.)

NOASAURUS Bonaparte and Powell 1980
Saurischia: Theropoda: Ceratosauria:
 Neoceratosauria: Abelisauroidea.
Name derivation: Spanish (abbreviation) "Noa or NOA [Northwestern Argentina]" + Greek *sauros* = "lizard."
Type species: *N. leali* Bonaparte and Powell 1980.
Other species: [None.]
Occurrence: Lecho Formation, El Brete, Salta, Argentina.
Age: Late Cretaceous (?Late Campanian–Maastrichtian).

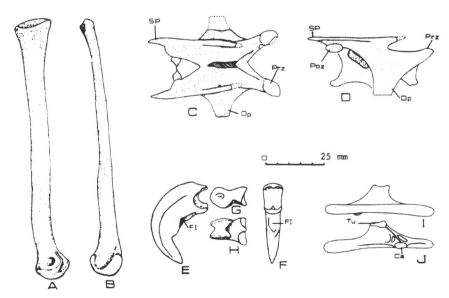

Noasaurus leali, PVL 4061, holotype A.–B. right metatarsal II in medial and ventral views, C.–D. neural arch of cervical vertebra in dorsal and lateral views. E.–F. ?pedal ungual in medial and posterior views, G.–H. ?pedal phalange in medial and posterior views, I.–J. cervical rib in external and medial views. (After Bonaparte and Powell 1980.)

Known material/holotype: PVL 4061, left maxilla, right quadrate, right squamosal, cervical neural arch, dorsal vertebral body, cervical rib, right metatarsal II, pedal phalanx, pedal claw phalanx.

Diagnosis of genus (as for type species): Antorbital fenestra large; cervical neural arches with prominent cranially and caudally directed spines; unguals with flexor pits instead of tubercles (Norman 1990).

Comments: The first supposed "coelurosaur" known from South America, *Noasaurus* was founded upon incomplete remains discovered in an exposure of the Lecho Formation, in El Brete, southern Salta province, Northwestern Argentina (Bonaparte and Powell 1980).

Originally, Bonaparte and Powell diagnosed the monotypic *N. leali* as follows: "Coelurosaur" with maxilla lacking additional preorbital opening or depression, high anteriorly, with sharp edge bordering large preorbital depression; cervical neural arch with anterior and posterior spinous processes; cervical rib with flat lateral surface; metatarsal II longer, more slender, and more in contact with III than in *Deinonychus*; pedal digit II with compressed, recurved ungual phalanx as, or even more than, *Deinonychus*, tendonous insertion in ventral fossa, with wide angle of movement.

As noted by Bonaparte and Powell, the probable second ungual phalanx of the foot has a large, recurved "sickle" claw, perhaps even larger than in *Deinonychus*, the similar claw in *Noasaurus* and dromaeosaurids possibly due to parallel evolution. The long metatarsals suggest a lightly-built running animal. The teeth and form of the hindfoot imply that *Noasaurus* preyed upon rather small animals such as birds and young sauropods,

Because of the difficulty in assessing the affinities of this genus on the basis of the morphology of the maxilla, and with so few skulls known of Cretaceous "coelurosaurs," Bonaparte and Powell placed *Noasaurus* into its own family, Noasauridae (=Noasaurinae Paul 1988).

Bonaparte, Novas and Coria (1990), after comparing abelisaurid *Carnotaurus sastrei* with various other theropods, suggested a monophyletic relationship between the Abeliosauridae and Noasauridae, based upon certain shared characters (including significant reduction of additional preorbital opening; reduction of cervical and neural spines; strong anteriad development of epipophyses; and lateral crest from epipophyses), and recognized that the Abelisauridae and probably Noasauridae may be phylogentically related to the Ceratosauridae.

In a review of problematic "coelurosaurs," Norman (1990) recognized that the theropod group closest to *N. leali* in general form could be the Troodon-

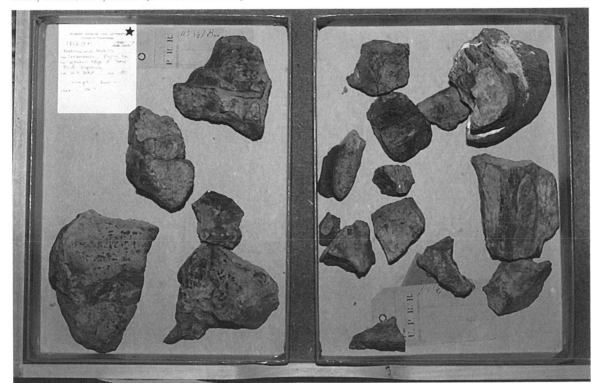

Nodosaurus textilis, YPM 1815, holotype dermal elements.

tidae, but cautioned that the low density of maxillary teeth and unusual form of the ungual phalanx in this species preclude assigning it to that taxon. According to Norman, the imperfect type specimen does not warrant its assignment to a new family, this species' value being a useful geographic record of small Late Cretaceous South American theropods.

More recently, Novas (1992*a*) regarded *Noasaurus* as a ceratosaur, and proposed the new taxon Neoceratosauria (see systematics section) to include the taxa *Ceratosaurus* plus Abelisauridae plus *Noasaurus*.

Key references: Bonaparte, Novas and Coria (1990); Bonaparte and Powell (1980); Norman (1990); Novas (1992*a*).

NODOSAURUS Marsh 1889—(=*Stegopelta*)
Ornithischia: Genasauria: Thyreophora:
    Ankylosauria: Nodosauridae.
Name derivation: Latin *nodus* = "knob" + Greek
    sauros = "lizard."
Type species: *N. textilis* Marsh 1889.
Other species: [None.]
Occurrence: Mowry or Thermopolis Shale,
    Wyoming, Niobrara Chalk Formation, Kansas,
    United States.
Age: Early Cretaceous (Albian–Early Campanian).
Known material: Three fragmentary postcranial
    skeletons with armor.

Dermal scutes and spines of nodosaurid from western Colorado, now referred to the new genus *Mymoorapelta* (see entry).

Nodosaurus textilis, FM UR88, holotype dermal armor of *Stegopelta landerensis.*

Holotype: YPM 1815, partial skeleton including three incomplete dorsal vertebrae with attached ribs and dermal armor, sacrum, 13 caudal vertebrae, ribs with overlaying node-like dermal armor, distal portions of scapular blades, fragments of humeri, incomplete left radius and ulna, parts of manus, ilia with armored "over-sacrum," left femur, left tibia, portion of right femur, large portion of right tibia, incomplete left pes, numerous dermal scutes and spines.

Diagnosis of genus: [No modern diagnosis published].

Comments: Basis for the family Nodosauridae Marsh 1890, the genus *Nodosaurus* was founded on partial postcranial remains (YPM 1815), collected in fragments from [what was believed to be possibly the] Dakota Formation of Albany County, Wyoming.

Marsh (1889*a*) originally regarded the material as belonging to a new genus of stegosaur, having then included all European ankylosaurs within Steg-

osauria, and incorrectly implying that the Nodosauridae was a family of stegosaurs.

In his brief original description of *N. textilis*, Marsh (1889*a*) speculated that the dermal armor closely covered the sides of the body, supported by ribs especially strengthened to accommodate the armor. As some armor was found in position, Marsh (1889*a*) surmised that it was probably arranged in a series of rows. Marsh (1889*a*) noted that dermal ossifications near the head are small, quadrangular in form, and arranged in rows. The external surface of the armor is marked by a texture that appears interwoven.

Marsh (1889*a*) described the forelimbs as massive and powerful, feet having five well-developed digits with relatively narrow terminal phalanges. The total length of *Nodosaurus* was estimated by him to be about 8.8 meters (30 feet) (more recent estimations having shortened the length to approximately 6 meters [over 20 feet] long and about 2.75 meters [more than 9 feet] high at the hips). Lull (1921) attempted the first reconstruction of the skeleton of *Nodosaurus*, with the dorsal region depicted encased in armor. This armor consisted of module-bearing intercostal plates that were separated by rows of smaller plates, oval spined or keeled plates. Lull believed that the armor above the pelvis did not extend above the ilia.

It is not known if *Nodosaurus*, like other nodosaurids, possessed lateral spines.

In a reorganization of the families of Ankylosauria, Coombs (1978*a*) referred the genus *Stegopelta* Williston 1909 to *Nodosaurus*:

The type species *Stegopelta landerensis* was based on a specimen (FM UR88) including fragments of the upper and lower jaws with at least 12 mostly fragmentary teeth, seven imperfect dorsal and two caudal vertebrae, a sacrum, left tibia, distal portion of right tibia, upper and lower ends of right fibula, numerous large metatarsal fragments, some rib fragments, a left ulna, left ilium, incomplete right ilium, right pubis, incomplete left pubis, almost 100 bony scutes, several large plates, spines, and dermal girdles, collected from the Frontier Formation (Cenomanian) of Benton, near Lander, Wyoming.

According to Coombs and Maryańska, the poor type specimen of *N. textilis* may preclude an adequate diagnosis, but the distal limb bones are relatively longer than the proximal elements and the armor is distinct (K. Carpenter, personal communication to Coombs and Maryańska 1990).

Notes: The first dinosaur specimen from Antarctica was discovered in 1986, consisting of partial remains of a small, as yet unnamed nodosaurid. It was collected from the Santa Marta Formation (Upper Cretaceous, tentatively dated Campanian) of James Ross Island, near the tip of the Antarctic Peninsula. The remains also constitute the first ankylosaurian material known from the southern hemisphere, extending the evolution and distribution of this group beyond the northern hemisphere (Gasparini, Oliveri, Scasso and Rinaldi 1987).

What was once regarded as the oldest nodosaurid (now known as anklosaurid) fossils yet known in North America were discovered in the Late Jurassic Morrison Formation (Tithonian–Kimmeridgian) near the central Colorado–Utah border. The discovery was made in September, 1990, during the last day of excavation by the Dinamation International Society Dinosaur Discovery Expedition led by James Kirkland, in cooperation with the Museum of Western Colorado. The find marks the occurrence of ankylosaurs in North America from 20–30 million years earlier than reported previously. To date of this writing, the nodosaurid material recovered from this site includes scutes and two large (and distinctive) lateral spines. Because all of the identified nodosaurid material was found in one area toward the back of the quarry, future excavations may produce more associated remains. The site, called the M & M Quarry (for its discoverers Peter Mygatt and J. D. Moore) and located west of Grand Junction, Colorado, has also yielded numerous well-preserved specimens of other Late Jurassic dinosaurs. It has been interpreted as a waterhole frequented by various kinds of dinosaurs whose carcasses, as evidenced by the scattered distribution of the bones, seem to have been scavenged (see *Mymoorapelta* entry).

Key references: Coombs (1978*a*); Coombs and Maryańska (1990); Lull (1921); Marsh (1889*a*); Williston (1909).

NOTOCERATOPS Tapia 1918 [*nomen dubium*]
Ornithischia *incertae sedis*.
Name derivation: Greek *noton* = "back" + Greek *sauros* = "lizard."
Type species: *N. bonarelli* Tapia 1918 [*nomen dubium*].
Other species: [None.]
Occurrence: [Unnamed Formation], Chubut, Argentina.
Age: Late Cretaceous (?Campanian).

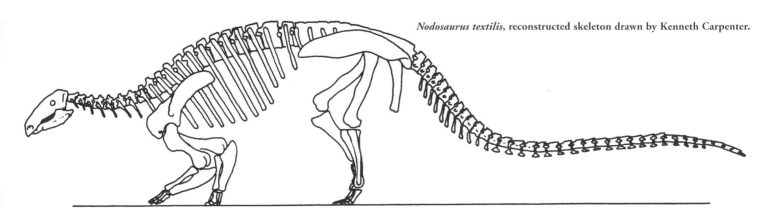

Nodosaurus textilis, reconstructed skeleton drawn by Kenneth Carpenter.

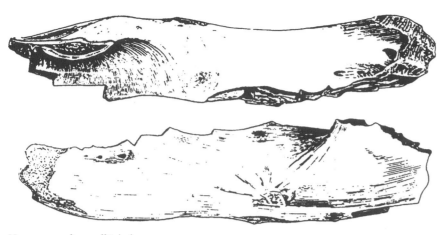

Notoceratops bonarellii, holotype incomplete lower jaw, dorsal and left lateral views. (After Huene 1929.)

Known material/holotype: [?Lost], fragmentary left dentary.

Diagnosis of genus: [None published.]

Comments: The genus *Notoceratops* was founded upon a lower jaw fragment, discovered in 1917 in the Upper Cretaceous of Colhue Huapi, Chubut, Patagonia, Argentina (Tapia 1918).

Tapia did not describe the specimen, but stated that it possessed characters for which the new genus and species *N. bonarelli* should be placed into the ceratopsian family Ceratopsidae.

Huene (1929), after restudying the type specimen, posited that it represented a new and primitive species of ceratopsian. According to Huene, the specimen is distinguished by its small size, measuring only 24.5 centimeters (about 9.5 inches) in length, with an estimated complete length of 30 centimeters (about 11.5 inches). Subsequently, Huene (1956) referred *N. bonarelli* to the Protoceratopsidae.

Bonaparte (1978*b*, 1986*d*) retained *Notoceratops* in the Protoceratopsidae, as representing the only published alleged ceratopsian specimen recorded from South America. The holotype cannot now be found (J. F. Bonaparte, personal communication to Dodson and Currie 1990).

As no other ceratopsians had been reported from South America, Molnar (1980*d*) speculated that *Notoceratops* was actually a hadrosaurid. As pointed out by Brett-Surman (1989), however, Molnar's idea was based on biogeography rather than morphology. With the type specimen lost, and the only available figure of the specimen being an outline drawing that does not give sufficient information for a precise taxonomic determination, Brett-Surman favored regarding, at least until further information is made available, *Notoceratops* as Ceratopsia *incertae sedis*.

There is no other evidence (including that from microfaunae which have yielded evidence of theropods, sauropods, and hadrosaurids) that protoceratopsids or ceratopsids existed in South Amer-

ica. In light of the biogeographic improbability of *Notoceratops* being ceratopsian, and given the possibility of the endemic evolution of unfamiliar or unusual types (*e.g.*, the horned theropod *Carnotaurus*), it may be reasonable to assume that this genus is not ceratopsian (P. Dodson, personal communication 1988, Dodson and Currie 1990).

Key references: Bonaparte (1978*b*, 1986*d*); Brett-Surman (1989); Dodson (1980); Dodson and Currie (1990); Huene (1929, 1956); Molnar (1980*d*); Tapia (1918).

NUROSAURUS Dong and Li [in press]

Saurischia: Sauropodomorpha: Sauropoda: Camarasauridae: Camarasaurinae.

Photo by the author.

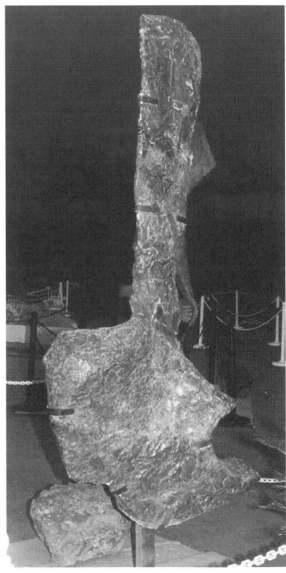

Nurosaurus qoganensis, holotype scapula as displayed at Dinofest International (1996), University of Arizona, Tempe.

Nurosaurus qoganensis, Saurus Corp. somewhat reconstructed skeleton (here labeled *Nuoerosaurus*), at Dinofest International (1996), University of Arizona, Tempe.

Name derivation: "[Oagan] Nur [Salt Mine]" + Greek *sauros* = "lizard."

Type species: *N. qaganensis* Dong 1992.

Other species: [None.]

Occurrence: Qagganur Formation, Inner Mongolia.

Age: Cretaceous.

Known material/holotype: Skeleton.

    Diagnosis: [in press].

    Comments: The genus *Nurosaurus* is known from good skeletal remains collected from the Qagannur (Chagannur) Formation in Inner Mongolia, southeast of Erenhot.

A photograph of the mounted skeleton of this 25-meter long (about 85 feet) genus, displayed at the Inner Mongolian Museum, appeared in the book *Dinosaurian Faunas of China* (Dong 1992). Dong stated that *N. qaganensis* represents "a peculiar, large sauropod."

Another photograph, with the name spelled *Nuoerosaurus chaganensis*, was published in an apparently anonymous dinosaur book published in Japanese by Gakken.

The genus and type species will be formally described by Dong and Li (in press).

Key reference: Dong (1992).

OHMDENOSAURUS Wild 1978

Saurischia: Sauropodomorpha: Sauropoda: ?Vulcanodontidae.

Name derivation: "Ohmden [discovery site]" + Greek *sauros* = "lizard."

Type species: *O. liasicus* Wild 1978.

Other species: [None.]

Occurrence: Poisdonienschiefer, Baden-Württemburg, Germany.

Age: Early Jurassic (Middle Toarcium).

Known material/holotype: Museum of Hauff collection, Holzmaden, right tibia, astragalus, calcaneum, ?sesamoid.

　　Diagnosis of genus (as for type species): Tibia robust, massive, expanded strongly at articular ends, curving laterally, with longitudinal groove; cnemial crest strongly developed; proximal articular end of tibia vertically oriented to shaft; in side view, distal articular end extends to middle of bone and to lateral

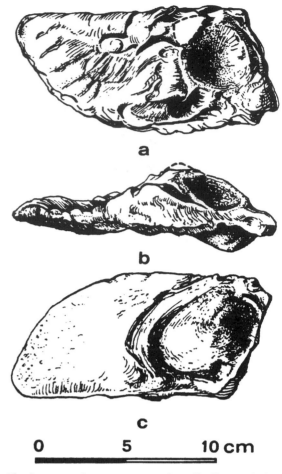

Ohmdenosaurus liasicus, Museum of Hauff collection, holotype right astragalus, in a. dorsal, b. posterior, c. ventral views. (After Wild 1978.)

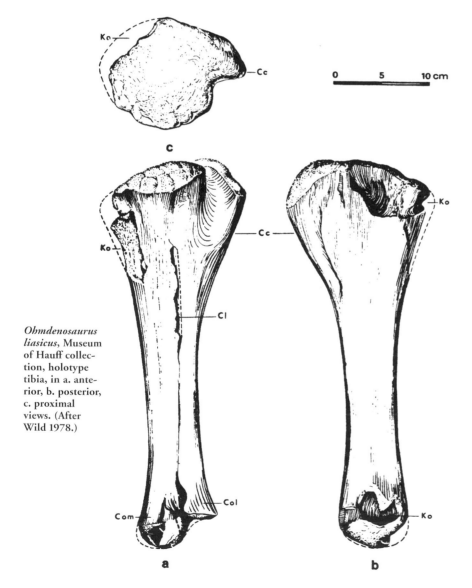

Ohmdenosaurus liasicus, Museum of Hauff collection, holotype tibia, in a. anterior, b. posterior, c. proximal views. (After Wild 1978.)

crest; astragalus flat, "sandal"-shaped, no ascending process; calcaneum small, disc-shaped; ankle joint with ?sesamoid bone; total body length estimated as 3–4 meters (more than 10–over 13.5 feet) (Wild 1978).

　　Comments: One of the earliest apparent sauropods and the first known Upper Liassic dinosaur, the genus *Ohmdenosaurus* was established on limb bone material collected from the Poisdonienschiefer of Ohmden near Holzmaden, Württemberg, [former Federal Republic of] Germany. (The tibia was originally believed to be the humerus of a plesiosaur.)

　　Wild (1978) observed that corrosion marks indicate that the tibia had become dislocated after being imbedded on land or near shore.

　　In his review of the Sauropoda, McIntosh (1990b) tentatively referred this taxon to the Vulcanodontidae, observing that the tibia is quite similar to that of *Vulcanodon*. The astragalus in both genera has the same general shape, although in *O. liasicus* it is more compressed vertically, with a concavity on the ventral surface unknown in any other sauropod astragalus.

　　Key references: McIntosh (1990b); Wild (1978).

OLIGOSAURUS Seeley 1881 [*nomen dubium*] — (See *Rhabdodon*.]

Name derivation: Greek *oligos* = "few" + Greek *sauros* = "lizard."

Type species: *O. adelus* Seeley 1881 [*nomen dubium*].

OMEISAURUS Yang [Young] 1939 —

(=*Zigongosaurus*)

Saurischia: Sauropodomorpha: Sauropoda: Cetiosauridae: Shunosaurinae.

Name derivation: "Omeishan [sacred mountain]" + Greek *sauros* = "lizard."

Type species: *O. junghsiensis* Yang [Young] 1939.

Other species: ?*O. changshouensis* Yang [Young] 1958, *O. fuxiensis* (Hou, Chao and Chu 1976), *O. tianfuensis* He, Li, Cai and Gao 1984, *O. zigongensis* Tanimoto 1988 [*nomen nudum*], *O. luoquanensis* He, Li and Cai 1988.

Occurrence: Shangshaximiao Formation, Xiashaximiao Formation, Sichuan, People's Republic of China.

Age: Late Jurassic.

Known material: About five partial skeletons, two with partial skulls, miscellaneous cranial elements, adult, subadult.

Holotype: IVP AS collection, four cervical, three presacral, and 13 sacral and postsacral vertebrae, eight ribs representing almost entire left side, left scapula (damaged distal portion) and coracoid, complete left humerus, ilia (damaged upper border), almost complete left pubis, proximal end of left femur, complete left fibula, adult.

Diagnosis of genus: Skull moderately high; teeth robust, spatulate, denticles well-developed on anterior edge, poor or absent on posterior edge; ?17 cervical, 12 dorsal, four sacral, and over 36 caudal vertebrae; posterior cervical and anterior dorsal vertebrae with simple, nonbifurcated neural spines; anterior caudals slightly amphicoelous, first caudal rib rather fan-shaped (He, Li and Cai 1988).

Diagnosis of *O. junghsiensis*: Medium-sized sauropod measuring 14 meters (about 47 feet) long; skull high, with moderately developed snout, paired external nares located anteriorly, broad occipital region, and relatively large supratemporal openings; teeth spatulate; four premaxillary, 14 maxillary, and 16 dentary teeth; 17 cervical vertebrae with opisthocoelous centra having rather large pleurocoels; neural spines with well-developed lamellar structure; 13 dorsal and four sacral (five including dorso-sacral) vertebrae, anterior three sacrals with fused spines; caudal vertebrae with unforked chevrons; limb bones rather flat (Dong, Zhou and Zhang 1983).

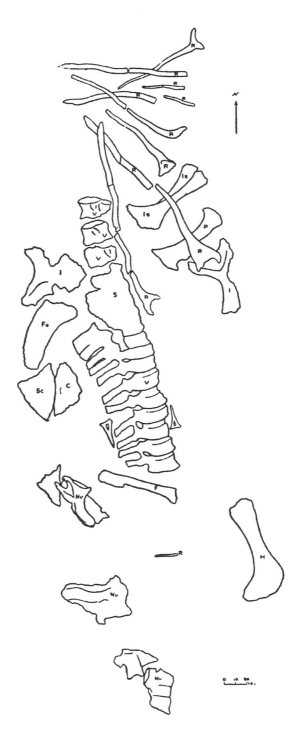

Omeisaurus junghsiensis, IVP AS, holotype skeleton in position as found. (After Yang [Young] 1939.)

Diagnosis of ?*O. changshouensis*: Larger species; tibia and fibula apparently very long proportionately (Yang [Young] 1958).

Diagnosis of *O. tianfuensis*: Large species; skull with height-length ratio of about 1.2 or more; skull wedge-shaped in side view, somewhat oval in dorsal view; supratemporal openings large, elliptical in out-

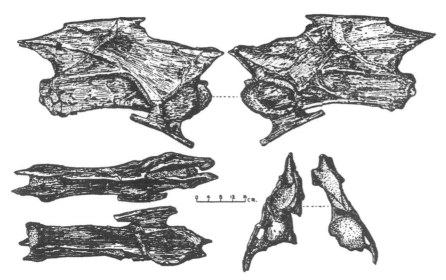

Omeisaurus junghsiensis, IVP AS collection, holotype cervical vertebra, in lateral, dorsal, ventral, anterior, and posterior views. (After Yang [Young] 1939.)

line; naris located in upper lateral, almost middle of skull; intermaxillary foramen; maxilla high, with large ascending process; articular surface of skull and lower jaw below line of dentary series; external mandibular foramen at posteromedial portion of mandible; dentary with high anterior end, equal to two-thirds mandibular length; teeth robust, spatulate, dental formula consisting of four premaxillary, 11 maxillary, and 13–15 dentary teeth; approximately 17 cervical, 12 dorsal, four sacral, and more than 36 caudal vertebrae; cervical vertebrae very long, longest almost three times length of longest dorsal, three and seven tenths average dorsal vertebra length; cervical centra opisthocoelous, each with well-developed pleurocoel

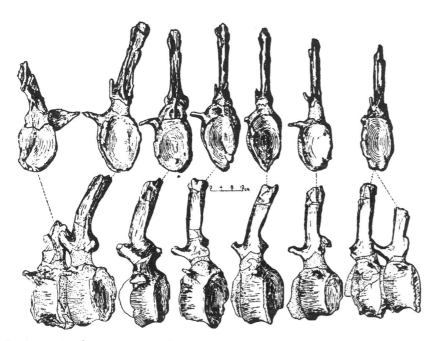

Omeisaurus junghsiensis, IVP AS collection, holotype caudal vertebrae. (After Yang [Young] 1939.)

and ventral keel, each with low, elongated forward and backward neural spine; laminal structure of cervicals developed only on posterior elements; cervical ribs extremely elongated, longest about two and one half times length of longest cervical centrum; dorsal vertebrae opisthocoelous, with well-developed pleurocoels, no bifurcation of neural spines; four co-ossified sacral vertebrae; anterior caudal vertebrae slightly amphicoelous, first with fan-shaped rib, middle caudals with forked chevrons; sternum suboval in outline; clavicle long and spear-shaped; scapula remarkably expanded proximally, markedly obliqued upwards on anterior edge; coracoid almost oval; ilium with robust and medially situated pubic peduncle, poorly-developed ischiadic process; forelimbs four-fifths or more length of hindlimbs, ulna two-thirds or more length of humerus, tibia about two-thirds that of femur; manus and pes with five digits, phalangeal formula of manus 2, 2, ?2, ?2, ?, pes 2, 3, 3, 3, 2; manual digit I and pedal digits I-III with claws (He, Li, Cai and Gao 1984).

Diagnosis of *O. luoquanensis*: Very similar in size and shape to *O. tianfuensis*, differing in following characters: laminae in dorsal vertebrae exceptionally thin; infrapostzygapophysial, infradiapophysial, and infrapostdiapophysial cavities more developed; most anterior caudal spines plate-like, extremely low, broad; humerus remarkably straight, with long, slender shaft rounded in cross-section (He, Li and Cai 1988).

Comments: An extremely long-necked sauropod, *Omeisaurus* was founded upon a partial postcranial skeleton (IVP AS collection) discovered in 1936, just below a hard sandstone cliff at Hsiskuashan, near Junghsien, Szechuan [now Sichuan], China. The first bone noticed was a left femur, after which the sacrum was found still in juxtaposition with the femur, suggesting that a complete skeleton may have been preserved. The position of the bones intimated that the animal's carcass was twisted and dismembered in the water (Yang [formerly known as Young] 1939). The bones were excavated during the summer of that year by Yang Zhungian [Chung-Chien] and Charles L. Camp (Yang 1937*a*).

Originally, Yang (1939) diagnosed *Omeisaurus* as follows: Vertebrae with particularly strong pseudospinous processes, upper border quite short; only three sacral vertebrae, bearing strongly-constructed sacral ribs; anteriormost caudal vertebrae with flattened, fan-like ribs; coracoid very short; scapula with straight border; humerus with rather straight shaft; proximal portion of humerus well palmated, distal portion less so; ilium similar to that of *Euhelopus* [=*Helopus* of his usage], acetabulum more forward, pubic peduncle broad, strong; acetabulum

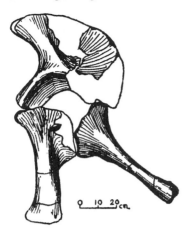

Omeisaurus junghsiensis, IVP AS collection, restored holotype pelvis. (After Yang [Young] 1939.)

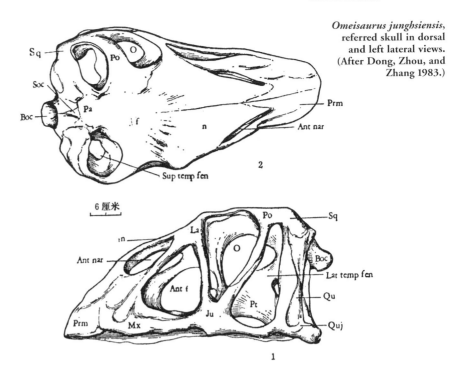

Omeisaurus junghsiensis, referred skull in dorsal and left lateral views. (After Dong, Zhou, and Zhang 1983.)

large, with well-developed wall; pubis with massive shaft, considerably expanded proximal end, moderately expanded distal end; ischium with massive shaft, considerably expanded proximal end, slightly expanded distal end; femur with well-differentiated head and prominent, projecting fourth trochanter.

Yang (1939) found the almost complete pelvic girdle and partially-preserved front and hindlimbs to be most characteristic. Comparing these to those of *Tienshanosaurus* and *Euhelopus*, Yang (1939) found rough differences to warrant the erection of a new genus and species, *O. yunghsiensis* [later commonly spelled *junghsiensis*].

Yang (1939) tentatively referred to type species *O. junghsiensis* a broken tooth found near Chenchia (beds probably Upper Jurassic; see Yang 1958), northeast of the city of Yunghsien, described as very slender, with rounded root, and no accessory cusp or swelling at the lower inner part, and possibly representing a young individual. To this species, Yang (1942*b*) later referred six isolated teeth, a left humerus, and single tooth from Kuangyuan, North Sichuan.

Second species *O. changshouensis* was based on incomplete skeletal remains, including 11 disarticulated cervical and dorsal vertebrae, ?distal portion of right scapula, right coracoid, damaged left humerus, two partly articulated manus bones, broken ischia, right pubis, proximal portion of left femur, almost complete left tibia and fibula, right astragalus (IVPP V930), and ?associated indeterminate remains, from the Early Late Jurassic Shangshaximiao Formation at Moutzenshan, Changshouhsien County, China. Yang (1958; see also Dong, Zhou and Zhang 1983) observed that this species is about as similar to *O. junghsiensis* as to another exceptionally long-necked sauropod, *Mamenchisaurus*, *O. changshouensis* therefore being a problematic species that may or may not belong in *Omeisaurus* (see He, Li, and Cai 1988).

Dong, Zhou and Zhang diagnosed the type species, based on a rather complete composite skeleton (including cranial material) that had been restored from various remains (CV V00260) found at Wujiaba, near Zigong city, and mounted at the Chongqing Municipal Museum.

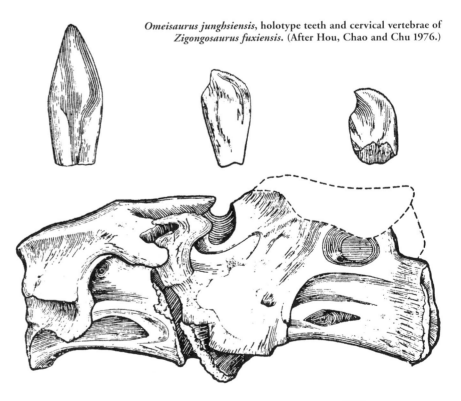

Omeisaurus junghsiensis, holotype teeth and cervical vertebrae of *Zigongosaurus fuxiensis*. (After Hou, Chao and Chu 1976.)

Omeisaurus

Omeisaurus fuxiensis, CV 00261, holotype mandible. (After Dong, Zhou and Zhang 1983.)

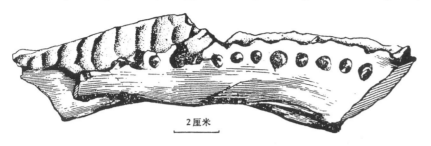

2 厘米

O. tianfuensis, a third species, was based on an incomplete partially articulated skeleton including a skull (CHG T5701), missing lower jaws, recovered from the lower Shanshaximiao Formation, Dashanpu quarry, near Zigong, southeast Sichuan, first described by He, Li, Kui, Cai and Gao (1984). He *et al.* (1984) counted at least ten such individuals (CHG T5701, T5702, T5703, T5704, T5705, *etc.*), perhaps referable to *O. tianfuensis,* from the Dashanpu quarry. Based on these more recently collected remains, He *et al.* (1988) emended the earlier diagnosis (He *et al.* 1984).

Restoring the skeleton of *O. tianfuensis* from various remains collected

from the Dashanpu site, He *et al.* (1988) observed the resemblance of its outline to *Mamenchisaurus hochuanensis*, especially in the especially elongated neck, relatively short trunk, and short fore- and hindlimbs relative to body length. From these similarities, He *et al.* (1988) perceived a close affinity between both species, although the first four dorsal neural spines in *Mamenchisaurus* are divided while those in *Omeisaurus* are not (J. S. McIntosh, personal communication 1989).

From the very long neck, short back and short limbs, He *et al.* (1988) surmised that this species was a rather slow-moving animal that was perhaps better adapted to a somewhat aquatic life style. Owing to the accumulation of a large number of *Omeisaurus* individuals in an area less than 3,000 square meters, they further speculated that this was probably a gregarious dinosaur.

He *et al.* (1988) briefly described an immature specimen (CHG T5710) of *O. tianfuensis* from Dashanpu, consisting of vertebrae (one cervical, five dorsals, two sacrals and six caudals), right scapula, humerus and radius, ilia, left pubis, ischium, femur, and other elements, observing that its total body length was about 6 meters (over 20 feet), about one-third that of adults, that sutures between centra and neural arches are quite clear, and that sacral and caudal vertebrae are not fused respectively with their ribs.

He *et al.* (1988) saw no great variation between the *O. tianfuensis* individuals collected from Dash-

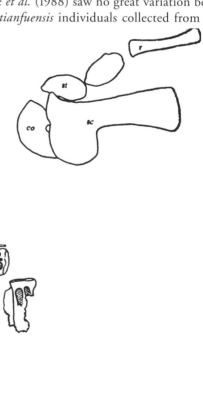

Omeisaurus tianfuensis, CHG T5701, holotype skeleton in position as found. Scale = 80 cm. (After He, Li, Cai and Gao 1984.)

anpu, but did note the following minor differences: 1. Adults measure from 16 to 20 meters (about 54 to nearly 68 feet) in length; 2. some changes exist in size of posttemporal opening and paraoccipital process, and in naris position; 3. some differences exist in the shape of vertebral neural spines and laminal structures; and 4. most individuals have a long symphysis between pubes and ischia, few individuals have a short symphysis.

He *et al.* (1988) based another species, *O. luoquanensis*, on two partial skeletons (CHG V21501) from the Xiashaximiao Formation (Middle Jurassic) at Luoquan village, Zizhong county, Sichuan. The type material includes an imperfect cervical centrum, two cervical spines, 11 dorsal spines, about 20 dorsal ribs, 3 co-ossified sacral spines, 10 sequential proximal caudals, 4 distal caudals, 7 chevrons of proximal caudals, incomplete right scapula, humerus, ilium, pubis, and complete right femur. A referred specimen (CHG V21502) consists of the proximal part of a right scapula, right tibia, and fibula, recovered about 5 meters in horizon higher than the holotype.

In discussing species *O. zigongensis*, Tanimoto (1988) observed that the mounted skeleton on display at the Museum of Natural History, Tainjin, China, has the eleventh and twelfth caudal vertebrae co-ossified, a fairly common sauropod condition, also seen in *Mamenchisaurus* (see *Diplodocus* entry).

New genus and species *Zigongosaurus fuxiensis* Hou, Chao and Chu 1976 was founded on a mandibular fragment with teeth, maxilla, and basioccipital (CV 00261), collected from the Early Late Jurassic of the Shangshaximiao Formation, Sichuan Basin, Wujiaban, Zigong. This taxon was designed by a committee, founded on parts of many individuals, (Mcintosh, personal communication 1987). Dong *et al.* erected new species *O. fuxiensis* upon some incomplete cranial bones, at the same time abandoning *Zigongosaurus* and referring its material to *O. fuxiensis*. However, both *Z. fuxiensis* and *O. fuxiensis* are separate species with distinct type specimens. McIntosh (1990*b*), in his review of the Sauropoda, referred the former species to *O. junghsiensis*.

As noted by McIntosh, *Omeisaurus* may be closely allied with and possibly a descendent of *Datousaurus*, and, when fully described, will be among the best-known sauropods.

Note: Yang (1958) described a broken, spatulate tooth, similar in shape and size to teeth of *Omeisaurus*, plus an indeterminable scapula fragment, discovered in the Outok district, Ikeshaomeng, Southwest Ordos, Inner Mongolia, this material too poor for positive identification.

Key references: Dong, Zhou and Zhang (1983); He, Li, Kui, Cai and Gao (1984); He, Li

and Cai (1988); Hou, Chao and Chu (1956); McIntosh (1990*b*); Yang [Young] (1937*a*, 1939, 1942*b*, 1958).

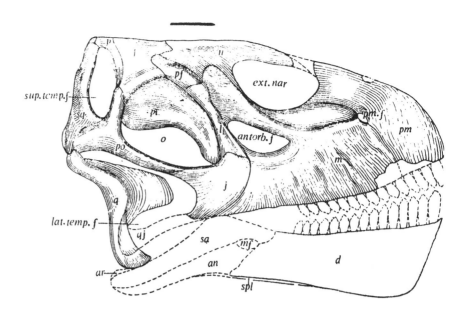

Omeisaurus tianfuensis, CHG T5702, restored partial skull, right lateral view. Scale = 6 cm. (After He, Li, Cai and Gao 1984.)

OMOSAURUS Owen 1875—(Preoccupied, Leidy 1856; see *Dacentrurus*.)
Name derivation: Greek *omos* = "rough" + Greek *sauros* = "lizard."
Type species: *O. armatus* Owen 1875.

Omeisaurus tianfuensis, skeleton on exhibit at the Zigong Dinosaur Museum. (After Dong 1987.)

ONYCHOSAURUS Nopcsa 1902 [*nomen dubium*]—(See *Rhabdodon*.)
Name derivation: Greek *onyx* = "nail" + Greek *sauros* = "lizard."
Type species: *O. hungaricus* Nopcsa 1902 [*nomen dubium*].

OPISTHOCOELICAUDIA Borsuk-Bialynicka 1977
Saurischia: Sauropodomorpha: Sauropoda: ?Camarasauridae: Opisthocoelicaudiinae.
Name derivation: Greek *opisthen* = "backward" + Greek *koelas* = "hollow" + Latin *cauda* = "tail."
Type species: *O. skarzynskii* Borsuk-Bialynicka 1977.
Other species: [None.]
Occurrence: Nemegt Formation, Omnogov, Mongolian People's Republic.
Age: Late Cretaceous (?Late Campanian or Early Maastrichtian).
Known material/holotype: ZPAL MgD-I/48, nearly complete postcranial skeleton lacking cervical series.

Diagnosis of genus (as for type species): Medium-size, straight-backed; centra of dorsal vertebrae not deeply cavernous; dorsal spines divided into two low metapophyses that overhang postzygapophyses; six sacral vertebrae with low spines; second caudo-sacral vertebra fused with ischium; approximately 35 caudal vertebrae lacking pleurocoels, with simple transverse processes and unforked chevrons, chevrons beyond nineteenth caudal; caudals in anterior half of tail opisthocoelous; scapula slightly expanded distally, coracoid subquadrangular; forelimbs about three-fourths length of hindlimbs, humerus about 72 percent length of femur; phalanges of manus probably reduced; ilium with strong anterior flare; ischium, though relatively short element about two-thirds length of pubis, forming greater part of acetabular boundary; pubis with prominence for origin of ambiens [thigh muscle] origin; astra-galus of reduced dimensions; pedal phalangeal formula 2, 2, 2, 1, (?0) (Borsuk-Bialynicka 1977).

Comments: The genus *Opisthocoelicaudia* was founded on an almost complete skeleton (ZPAL MgD-I/48) discovered in 1965 during one of the Polish-Mongolian Paleontological Expeditions, in the Nemegt Formation, Gobi Desert, Mongolia. The unusually high degree of completeness of the specimen was probably due to the remains having been buried before the soft parts of the carcass completely decayed. The head and neck had apparently become separated from the trunk before burial. Traces of gnawing on the bones showed the action of predators or scavengers (Borsuk-Bialynicka 1977).

Borsuk-Bialynicka speculated that the generally streamlined shape implied a possible semiaquatic life style for this genus. Also, the tail is relatively short, more so than that of *Camarasaurus*, and, as evidenced by its unusual articulation and musculature, was carried off the ground in a rather horizontal position. The tail could have been used as a prop, forming a tripod arrangement that allowed the animal to rear up to a bipedal position while feeding on high branches, the massive pelvis and sternal plates probably capable of supporting an occasional bipedal posture. Almost no evidence was found for caudifemoralis muscles that, in most reptiles, connect with the tail and hindlimbs and move the back legs. Apparently, in *Opisthocoelicaudia*, walking was powered by exceptionally strong muscles attached to the posterior portion of the ilium.

Because of similarities between *Opisthocoelicaudia* and *Camarasaurus*, Borsuk-Bialynicka suggested that the former may belong to the Camarasauridae.

Borsuk-Bialynicka argued that neural spine length in sauropods is dependent upon neck and tail length, as well as the degree of backbone curvature. Borsuk-Bialynicka also postulated that, if anterior dorsal vertebrae lack traces of nuchal ligament insertion, then it follows that forked neural spines indicate the neck was carried low or was habitually lowered.

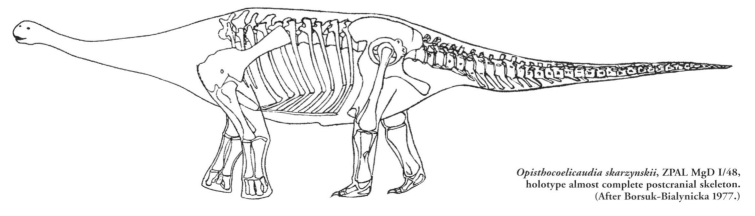

Opisthocoelicaudia skarzynskii, ZPAL MgD I/48, holotype almost complete postcranial skeleton. (After Borsuk-Bialynicka 1977.)

In a review of the Sauropoda, McIntosh (1990*b*) tentatively placed *Opisthocoelicaudia* in the Camarsauridae, at the same time erecting for it new the subfamily Opisthocoelicaudiinae, but cautioned that its relationship to other sauropods is not yet entirely clear. McIntosh observed that the phalangeal formula in this genus represents a greater reduction than in any other known sauropod. Significantly, this genus is an indicator that sauropods other than titanosaurids survived into the Late Cretaceous.

Key references: Borsuk-Bialynicka (1977); McIntosh (1990*b*).

Gervais (1852) later erected the new genus and species combination *Oplosaurus armatus* for this material, after which Lydekker (1890) catalogued the specimen as *Hoplosaurus armatus* [*sic*; error continued by Huene 1932].

Oplosaurus is generally listed as a junior synonym of *Pelorosaurus* (Huene 1932; Romer 1966; Steel 1970; Olshevsky 1978, 1991, 1992). Though *Oplosaurus* is probably congeneric with *Pelorosaurus*, *Eucamerotus* or *Brachiosaurus*, its type material is too inadequate for a positive synonymy, nor are any teeth

OPLOSAURUS Gervais 1852 [*nomen dubium*]—
(=?*Brachiosaurus*, ?*Pelorosaurus*)
Saurischia: Sauropodomorpha: Sauropoda:
Brachiosauridae.
Name derivation: Greek *oplos* = "armed" + Greek *sauros* = "lizard."
Type species: *O. armatus* Gervais 1852 [*nomen dubium*].
Other species: [None.]
Occurrence: Hartwell Clay, Isle of Wight, England.
Age: Early Cretaceous (Valanginian–Barremian).
Known material/holotype: BMNH R964, tooth.
Diagnosis of genus: [None published.]
Comments: The genus *Oplosaurus* was founded upon a single tooth (BMNH R964) collected from the Isle of Wight, England.

Wright (1852) originally described this tooth as very similar to that of *Brachiosaurus*, although from a relatively small individual. Wright did not name the tooth.

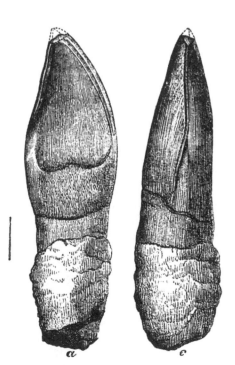

Oplosaurus armatus, BMNH R964, holotype tooth in A. lingual, B. labial, C. edge views. Scale = 1 cm. (After Gervais 1852.)

known in the holotype of *P. conybearei*, reasons for which McIntosh (1990*b*) regarded *Oplosaurus* as a tentative junior synonym of *Pelorosaurus*.

McIntosh described the tooth as follows: Large, spatulate, approximately same size and shape as in *Brachiosaurus*; trace of ridge dies out well up on crown (in *Brachiosaurus*, most teeth have prominent ridge down center of lingual face extending to tip of crown); face of crown concave most of way to tip.

Key references: Gervais (1852); McIntosh (1990*b*); Wright (1852).

ORINOSAURUS   Lydekker 1889 [*nomen dubium*]—(See *Euskelosaurus*.)

Name derivation: Greek *oros* = "mountain" Latin *in* = "in" + Greek *sauros* = "lizard."

Type species: *O. capensis* Lydekker 1889 [*nomen dubium*].

ORNATOTHOLUS   Galton and Sues 1983

Ornithischia: Genasauria: Cerapoda: Marginocephalia: Pachycephalosauria: Pachycephalosauridae.

Name derivation: Latin *ornatus* = "adorned" + Latin *tholus* = "dome."

Type species: *O. browni*, Galton and Sues 1983.

Other species: [None.]

Occurrence: Dinosaur Park Formation, Alberta, Canada.

Age: Late Cretaceous (Late Campanian).

Known material: Dome, three frontals, fused parietals.

Holotype: AMNH 5450, frontoparietal dome.

Photo by the author, courtesy American Museum of Natural History.

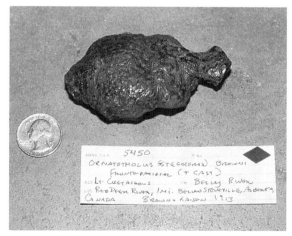

Ornatotholus browni, AMNH 5450, holotype frontoparietal dome of *Stegoceras browni*.

Diagnosis of genus (as for type species): Dome low, divided (in holotype) into frontal and parietal dome shelf by shallow transverse depression; dorsal surfaces of frontal and parietal covered by prominent tubercles (Galton and Sues 1987).

Comments: Marking the first record of a North American relatively "flat-headed" pachycephalosaurid, *Ornatotholus* was founded upon the frontoparietal region of a skull (AMNH 5450), collected in 1913 by Barnum Brown and Peter Kaisen from the Judith River [now Dinosaur Park] Formation, above Red Deer River, near Steveville, Alberta, Canada.

The type specimen was first described and illustrated by Galton (1971) as a ?female *Stegoceras validus* [=validum]. Galton noted the primitive nature of the dome and suggested that it could pertain to a new species. The specimen was then redescribed as the new species *S. browni* by Wall and Galton (1979). Later recognizing that the specimen represented a distinct genus, Galton and Sues (1983) referred it to the new type species *Ornatotholus browni*.

Referred by Galton and Sues to *O. browni* were two Dinosaur Park Formation specimens, a right frontal (RTMP P78.19.4), collected by H. Johnson at White Rock Coulee, Alberta, and an incomplete left frontal (PU 22317), collected by John R. Horner at Sand Creek at Red Deer River, "Steveville."

Originally, Galton and Sues (1983) diagnosed the monotypic *O. browni* as follows: Frontoparietal dome low, divided into frontal and parietal dome by shallow transverse depression; parietal dome slightly lower than frontal dome; supratemporal fossae much larger than in *S. validus*; dorsal surface of frontals (and maybe parietals) with numerous small osseous tubercles.

Later, Sues and Galton (1987) referred to *O. browni* fused parietals (RTMP P82.20.189) and an isolated left frontal (RTMP P81.41.102). As in RTMP P78.19.4, these specimens bear a distinctive ornamentation composed of numerous tubercles, which are partially interconnected in RTMP P82.20.189 and RTMP P81.41.102. Considering also these new specimens, Sues and Galton (1987) slightly emended their earlier diagnosis.

According to Galton and Sues (1983), the flat skull-roof and larger supratemporal fenestrae clearly differentiate *Ornatotholus* from the domed *Stegoceras*, although skulls of both forms are close in length. The coexistence of both relatively flat-roofed and domed pachycephalosaurids in the Dinosaur Park Formation of Alberta is similar to that of flat-roofed *Homalocephale calathocercos* and domed *Prenocephale prenes* from the Nemegt Formation of Mongolia (see Maryańska and Osmólska 1974).

Key references: Galton (1971); Galton and Sues (1983, 1987); Wall and Galton (1979).

ORNITHODESMUS Seeley 1887

Saurischia: Theropoda: Tetanurae: Avetheropoda:
   Coelurosauria: Maniraptora: Arctometatarsalia:
   Bullatosauria: ?Troodontidae.

Name derivation: Greek *ornis* = "bird" + Greek
   desmos = "bond."

Type species: *O. cluniculus* Seeley 1887.

Other species: [None.]

Occurrence: Wealden, Isle of Wight, England.

Age: Lower Cretacetous (Barremian).

Known material: Vertebrae.

Holotype: BMNH R187, six sacral vertebrae.

   Diagnosis of genus (as for type species): All six
sacral vertebrae fully ankylosed at sacrum length of
under 100 millimeters; sacral 6 shorter than 5 (Howse
and Milner 1993).

   Comments: *Ornithodesmus* was first described
as a bird by Seeley (1887*a*), who founded this genus
upon a sacrum (BMNH R187; originally Reverend
William Fox collection), from the late Wealden of
Brook, Isle of Wight, England. According to Seeley,
several other bones [lost] were found with this
sacrum.

   Originally, Seeley described *O. cluniculus* as having sacral vertebrae with modified renal recesses, a
typically avian saddle-shaped intervertebral articulation, and the large number of vertebrae commonly
found in the sacrum in modern birds. As measured
by Seeley, the sacrum is 9.6 centimeters (about 3.75
inches) long.

   Seeley described the sacrum as more similar to
that of birds than dinosaurs or pterosaurs. Seeley concluded that the specimen belonged to a bird that
formed a link with lower avian forms, and was more
closely related to dinosaurs than was any other then
known fossil birds. Hooley (1913) later regarded this
genus as a pterosaur and placed it into its own family Ornithodesmidae. More recently, the holotype
sacrum of *O. cluniculus* was reexamined by Stafford
C. B. Howse and Christopher Bennett, who concluded that it did not resemble the sacrum of any
known pterodactyloid. Howse and Milner (1993)
found BMNH R187 to resemble most closely the
sacrum of troodontid *Saurornithoides junior*, concluding that the Isle of Wight specimen represented
a maniraptoran theropod.

   Owing to the limited nature of holotype
BMNH R187, Howse and Milner could not adequately define *O. cluniculus* within the Troodontidae,
therefore referring this species to that group only tentatively. If a troodontid, *O. cluniculus* represents the
first record of the Troodontidae from the Wealden of
Europe.

   Note: According to Howse and Milner, other
material attributed to *Ornithodesmus*, including the

greater part of a skeleton made the holotype of new
species *O. latidens*, is pterodactyloid and should be
given a new generic name.

   Key references: Howse and Milner (1993); Seeley (1887*a*).

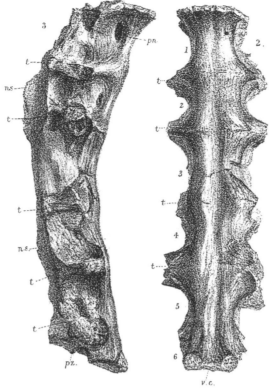

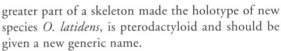

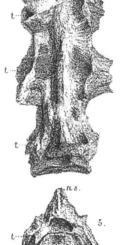

Ornithodesmus cluniculus,
BMNH R187, holotype sacral
vertebrae, in lateral, ventral,
anterior, and dorsal views.
(After Seeley 1887.)

ORNITHOLESTES Osborn 1903

Saurischia: Theropoda: Tetanurae: Avetheropoda:
   Coelurosauria: Maniraptora.

Name derivation: Greek *ornis* = "bird" + Greek
   lestes = "robber."

Type species: *O. hermanni* Osborn 1903.

Other species: [None.]

Occurrence: Morrison Formation, Wyoming, Utah,
   United States.

Age: Late Jurassic–?Early Cretaceous (Kimmeridgian–Tithonian).

Known material: Skeleton, manus.

Holotype: AMNH 619, almost complete skull,
   associated nearly complete postcranial skeleton,
   including 45 vertebrae (three cervicals, 11 dorsals,
   complete sacrum, 27 caudals), complete pelvic
   girdle, parts of both fore- and hindlimbs.

   Diagnosis of genus (as for type species): Small,
1–2 meters (about 3.4–6.8 feet) long; oral margin of
premaxilla short; external nares large; horn or crest
seemingly over external nares, formed by premaxillae and nasals; differentiation of teeth includes con-

Ornitholestes

Photo by R. A. Long and S. P. Welles, courtesy American Museum of Natural History.

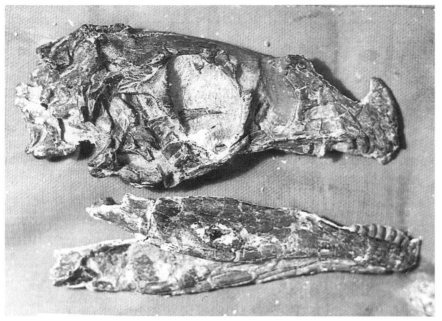

Ornitholestes hermanni,
AMNH 619, holotype skull,
right lateral view.

posterior-caudal vertebrae with greatly elongate zygapophyses.

Accompanying Osborn's original description of the material was a somewhat inaccurate (Osborn 1917) drawing of the reconstructed skeleton, based partly upon Marsh's reconstruction of the prosauropod *Anchisaurus*. Osborn (1903a) estimated the total length of the skeleton to be about 1.75 meters (6 feet).

According to Osborn (1903a), the most distinguishing feature of *Ornitholestes* is the structure of the manus. The hand is narrow, with greatly elongate fingers. Digit II is enlarged by a great elongation of the metacarpals and phalanges, IV is vestigial, and V is wanting. This narrowing of the manus and elongation of digit II indicated to Osborn that *Ornitholestes* had the quick grasping power to catch swift and delicate prey, the manus construction allowing for a relatively strong grip.

Paul (1984), observing an apparent piece of horncore base in the type skull of *O. hermannis*, stated that *Ornitholestes* probably had a horn similar to that of *Proceratosaurus* (although Currie and Zhao 1993a later suggested that the structure in the latter may be a midline crest rather than a horncore). Later, Paul (1988b) argued that both *O. hermanni* and *P. bradleyi* are more similar to one another than previously suspected and belong in their own subfamily, Ornitholestinae. Among the affinities shared by *Ornitholestes* and *Proceratosaurus* observed by Paul (1988b) are: The form of the nasal horn and teeth; maxillary bar (as preserved) in the holotype of *O. hermanni* seemingly flaring upwards in exactly the same place as in *P. bradleyi*; teeth in both forms are rather small and conical, with reduced anterior serrations; tooth rows (especially the dentary sets) not extending as far posteriorly as in most other theropods; short and stout squamosal and quadratojugal process meeting by way of long articulations; short fore-to-aft premaxillae; elongated external nares; and similarly shaped maxilla, preorbital openings, preorbital depression, jugal, and lacrimal.

Paul (1988b) submitted that, if not for the different form of the mandibles in *Ornitholestes* and *Proceratosaurus*, the two forms are similar enough to be congeneric. However, in *Ornitholestes*, the mandibles are deep, the posterior portion long, dentaries short and downcurved; in *Proceratosaurus*, the mandibles are slender, posteriorly short, the dentary long and slightly upcurved. The teeth are more heterodont in *Ornitholestes*.

These differences, according to Paul (1988b), were

ical mesial teeth with reduced marginal serrations, distal crowns laterally compressed, recurved, and serrated blades; dentary tooth row shorter than maxillary tooth row (Norman 1990, modified from Paul 1988b).

Comments: The genus *Ornitholestes* was founded upon a nearly complete skeleton (AMNH 619) recovered from the Morrison Formation, at Bone Cabin Quarry, near Medicine Bow, Wyoming, during the American Museum Expedition of 1900. Referred to the type species, *O. hermanni*, was a complete left manus (AMNH 587). The holotype skeleton was mounted at the American Museum of Natural History.

Osborn (1903a) first diagnosed *Ornitholestes* as follows: Skull with two antorbital openings; four premaxillary and ten maxillary, nonserrate teeth, 12 dentary teeth; sacrum with four firmly coalesced sacral ribs; mid- and

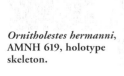

Ornitholestes hermanni,
AMNH 619, holotype
skeleton.

Photo by A. E. Anderson, courtesy Department Library Services, American Museum of Natural History (neg. #35043).

Ornitholestes hermanni, **head restored with horn.**

Illustration by Gregory S. Paul.

sufficient grounds for
maintaining generic separation.

In a review of various problematic "coelurosaurs," Norman (1990*b*) commented that Paul's view on the possible relationships of *Ornitholestes* and *Proceratosaurus* is in advance of a detailed revision of *O. hermanni* being undertaken by John H. Ostrom, and that substantiation will depend upon the results of Ostrom's work.

Onitholestes (like most small theropods) had usually been classified as a coelurosaur. Norman noted that a precise assignment of this genus to any higher-grade taxon below Tetanurae was not possible, with *Ornitholestes* exhibiting these tetanuran features: No fang-like dentary teeth, enlarged and caudally placed maxillary fenestra, maxillary teeth located rostral to orbit, manus measuring two-thirds length of humerus and radius (if the referred manus has been attributed correctly), ischium with obturator process, and femur with wing-like cranial trochanter (if Osborn's interpretation is correct). Matthew and Brown (1922) speculated that the ancestors of tyrannosaurids had the kind of manus structure found in *Ornitholestes*, while the pedal structure was similar to that found in ornithomimids. More recently, Holtz (1994*a*), in a cladistic analysis of various theropod groups, regarded *Ornitholestes* as a maniraptoran coelurosaur and the sister-taxon of all other maniraptorans (including the more derived tyrannosaurids and ornithomimids).

(For the possible occurrence of *Ornitholestes* among the geologically younger [Upper Jurassic] Dry Mesa fauna, see *Coelurus* entry.)

Note: Observing the extreme lightness of the skeleton of *Ornitholestes*, the cursorial structure of the hindlimbs, and apparent balancing function of the tail, Osborn (1903*a*) suggested that this dinosaur may
have been
adapted to hunting
Jurassic birds. Following Osborn's suggestion, artist Charles R. Knight, during the early 1900s, made a drawing of a running *Ornitholestes* in the act of catching an *Archaeopteryx*. Though Osborn later abandoned this notion, the Knight illustration appeared in a wide range of publications, while other artists frequently utilized his theme or even copied from the original drawing. As a result, *Ornitholestes* has traditionally been portrayed capturing its feathered prey, an image that recurs even in modern popular texts about dinosaurs.

Kirkland, Britt, Madsen and Burge (1995) reported a new small theropod (as of this writing neither formally named nor described) known from three partial skeletons, collected from within 50 meters of one another in the basal Cedar Mountain Formation (Lower Cretaceous; Barremian) of Eastern Utah. The specimens include a juvenile (CEUM 5071), with an estimated length of less than 1.5 meters (about 5.1 feet), and two subadults (CEUM 5072 and 5073), less than 3 meters (10 feet), each with much of the tail and gracile hindlimbs preserved. In their preliminary report, Kirkland *et al.* observed these features: Pubic boot seemingly slender and elongate; femur shaft moderately curved mesially; femoral head inclined below greater trochanter; lesser trochanter shorter than greater trochanter; fourth trochanter well developed and proximally positioned; fibular crest long, about one-fourth tibial length; slender fibula tapering and articulating with small,

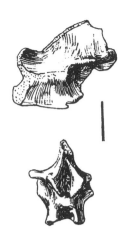

Ornithomimoides barasim-lensis, IM K27/541, holotype partial dorsal vertebra, lateral and posterior views. Scale = 2 cm. (After Huene and Matley 1933.)

laterally thin calcaneum well above end of tibia; ascending process of astragalus one fourth tibial length; proximal metatarsal III laterally constricted between I and IV, these elements in close contact along all but distal portions (as in *Ornitholestes*); phalanges almost as long as metatarsals; unguals long and asymmetric; first manual ungual (unlike *Ornitholestes*) more robust, with more prominent flexor tubercle than other manual unguals.

Key references: Holtz (1994*a*); Matthew and Brown (1922); Norman (1990); Osborn (1903*a*, 1917); Paul (1984, 1988*b*).

ORNITHOMERUS   Seeley 1881 [*nomen dubium*] — (See *Rhabdodon*.)
Name derivation: Greek *ornis* = "bird" + Greek *meros* = "upper thigh."
Type species: *O. gracilis* Seeley 1881 [*nomen dubium*].

ORNITHOMIMIDORUM   Huene 1926 [*nomen oblitum*] — (See *Betasuchus*)
Name derivation: Greek *ornis* + Greek *mimos* = "mimic" + Latin *id* = "it [used in zoology as suffix for family member]" + Latin *orum* = "of [second declension suffix, genitive case]."
Type species: *O. genus b bredai* Huene 1926 [*nomen oblitum*], *O. genus a lonzeensis* Huene 1926 [*nomen oblitum*].

ORNITHOMIMOIDES   Huene 1932 [*nomen dubium*]
Saurischia: Theropoda: Tetanurae *incertae sedis*.
Name derivation: Greek *ornis* = "bird" + Greek *mimos* = "mimic" + Greek *oeides* = "form."

Type species: *O. mobilis* Huene 1932 [*nomen dubium*].
Other species: *O. barasimlensis* Huene 1932 [*nomen dubium*].
Occurrence: Lameta Formation, Madhya Pradesh State, India.
Age: Late Cretaceous (Coniacian–Santonian).
Known material: Vertebrae.
Cotypes: IM K20/610, K20/614B, K27/597, K27/600 and K27/610, five dorsal vertebrae.
Diagnosis of genus: [No modern diagnosis published.]
Comments: The genus *Ornithomimoides* was established upon five dorsal vertebrae (IM K20/610, K20/614B, K27/597, K27/600, and K27/610), collected from the Lameta Formation [Lameta Group] at Bara Simla Hill, in Jubbulpore [now spelled Jabalpur], central province of India (Huene 1932).

Huene (also Huene *see in* Huene and Matley 1933) diagnosed the type species, *O. mobilis,* as follows: Vertebrae large, each about 9 centimeters (almost 3.5 inches) long, fairly elongate; some vertebrae not very constricted at middle, amphicoelous, very broad, with thin walls, posteriorly located pleurocoels; neural arch with very broad diapophysis with rather weak supporting buttress; dorsal spine rising steeply upwards, base barely half as long as vertebra.

Huene (1932) tentatively referred a second species to this genus, *O. barasimiensis*, based on four dorsal vertebrae, which he described as follows: Small, relatively shorter, fuller, and more constricted at middle than in *O. mobilis*; vertebrae about 5 centimeters (approximately 1.95 inches) in length, broad with weak buttresses.

As all of these vertebrae reminded Huene (1932) of the North American forms *Ornithomimus* and *Struthiomimus*, he classified *Ornithomimoides* with the Ornithomimidae.

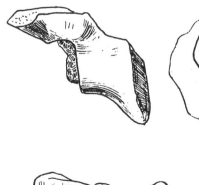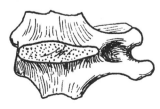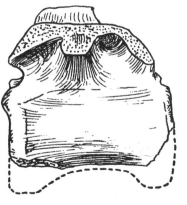

Ornithomimoides mobilis, IM K20/600, cotype dorsal vertebrae, a. lateral, b. anterior views, K20/614, cotype partial dorsal vertebra, c. right lateral, d. dorsal views, K20/610, cotype dorsal vertebra, e. right lateral, f. posterior views. Scale = 2 cm. (After Huene and Matley 1933.)

Molnar (1990) observed that the dorsals have hollow centra and thin walls, and display distinct flanges developed at the articular ends similar to those in *Allosaurus fragilis*.

Key references: Huene (1932); Huene and Matley (1933); Molnar (1990).

ORNITHOMIMUS Marsh 1890—(=*Coelosaurus*; =?*Dromiceiomimus*, ?*Struthiomimus*)

Saurischia: Theropoda: Tetanurae: Avetheropoda: Coelurosauria: Maniraptora: Arctometatarsalia: Bullatosauria: Ornithomimosauria: Ornithomimidae.

Name derivation: Greek *ornis* = "bird" + Greek *mimos* = "mimic."

Type species: *O. velox* Marsh 1890.

Other species: *O. antiquus* (Leidy 1865), ?*O. tenuis* Marsh 1890 [*nomen dubium*], ?*O. sedens* Marsh 1892, *O. edmontonicus* Sternberg 1933.

Occurrence: Denver Formation, Colorado, Kaiparowitz Formation, Utah, Dinosaur Park Formation, Montana, United States; Horseshoe Canyon Formation, Alberta, Canada.

Age: Late Cretaceous (Late Campanian-Late Maastrichtian).

Known material: Hindlimb and foot elements, skull with associated postcrania, two fragmentary postcranial specimens.

Cotypes: YPM 542, distal end of tibia, three left metatarsals, three phalanges of left pedal digit II, YPM 548, left metacarpus.

Diagnosis of genus: Length of presacral vertebral column less than combined length of femur, tibia-astragalus, and metatarsal III; humerus longer than scapula; antebrachium lightly constructed, about half length of femur; metacarpal I longer than II and III, manual digits subequal in length; manual unguals subequal in length, neither heavily recurved nor powerfully constructed; ungual of manual digit III shorter than penultimate phalanx of that digit; antilium relative to femur longer than in *Struthiomimus*, shorter than in *Dromiceiomimus*; tibia and metatarsus shorter relative to femur than in *Struthiomimus* and *Dromiceiomimus* (Russell 1972).

Diagnosis of *O. velox*: Metatarsus unique among ornithomimids in shortness, and in metatarsal II being longer than IV (Russell 1972).

Diagnosis of *O. emontonensis*: Length of presacral vertebral column somewhat less than hindlimb; humerus longer than scapula, antebrachium slender; length of manus about 65 percent femur, equaling that of humerus; metacarpal I longest, adhering to II along entire length; metacarpals II and III of subequal length; all manual digits equal in length, with

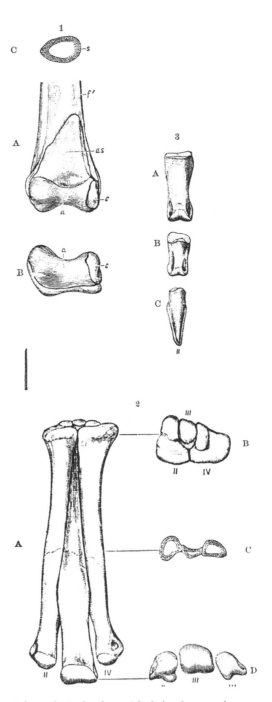

Ornithomimus velox, YPM 542, holotype 1. left tibia, A. anterior view, B. distal end, C. cross-section; 2. left metatarsals, A. anterior view, B. proximal ends, C. cross-section, D. distal ends; 3. phalanges of pedal digit II, same foot, anterior view, A. first phalanx, B. second phalanx, C. third or terminal phalanx. Scale = 3 cm. (After Marsh 1890.)

straight, relatively short (slightly shorter than one-fourth length of manus) unguals, each ungual shorter than penultimate phalanx; flexor tubercles weakly developed; short contact between metatarsals II and IV on flexor side (Barsbold and Osmólska 1990).

Comments: Basis for the family Ornithomimidae Marsh 1890, the genus *Ornithomimus* was founded upon broken hindlimb and foot elements (YPM 542 and 548), found in association with each other and assumed to belong to the same individual. The material was discovered in 1889 by George Cannon, in the Denver Formation, Jefferson County, Colorado.

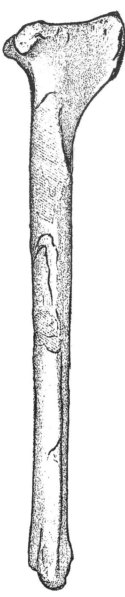

Ornithomimus antiquus, ANSP 9222, holotype tibia of *Coelosaurus antiquus.* (After Leidy 1865.)

Marsh (1890*a*, 1896) originally diagnosed the genus (and type species) as follows: Metatarsus short; metatarsal II longer than IV; astragalus with very large ascending process; tibia and all larger limb bones hollow, thin-walled; fibula slender.

Because of the birdlike structure of the foot, Marsh (1890*a*) first assessed *Ornithomimus* to be an ornithopod. After studying the pelvis of referred species *O. sedens*, Marsh (1892*c*) concluded that *Ornithomimus* was some kind of theropod with a co-ossified ilium, ischium, and pubis, as in *Ceratosaurus*. Later, Marsh (1896) stressed similarities between footbones of *Ornithomimus* and those of an ostrich.

Almost a century after the holotype of *O. velox* was first described, DeCourten and Russell (1985) described a new specimen (MNA Pl.1762A) which they referred to the type species. This specimen, consisting of dorsal, sacral, and caudal vertebrae, shattered pelvic elements, and almost complete left and fragmentary right hindlimb, was discovered by David Jones and collected in 1976 from the Kaiparowits Formation (Gregory and Moore 1931), at the Paria River Amphitheatre in southern Utah. Earlier, DeCourten (1978) had briefly reported this material as documenting the occurrence of ornithomimids in the Kaiparowits Formation.

As noted by DeCourten and Russell, MNA Pl.1762A augmented the current understanding of this species, its osteology comparing favorably with that of other previously described ornithomimids, the major departure being the posterodorsally recurved pubic shaft.

The more complete remains of *O. edmontonicus*, collected from member A of the Horseshoe Canyon Formation above the west bank of Red Deer River, below Munson Ferry, Alberta, Canada, have led to a more complete understanding of *Ornithomimus*. The holotype of this species, discovered in 1931 by Levi Sternberg, consists of an almost complete skeleton (NMC 8632), including fragments of three vertebrae, dorsal and abdominal ribs, proximal ends of scapulae, coracoids and humeri, right forelimb, distal end of the left femur, tibiae-fibulae, right pes, and partial left pes. This material was described by C. M. Sternberg (1933).

Parks (1933) described an almost complete skeleton (ROM 851), including a badly crushed and distorted skull, and lacking the tail, this specimen found within 8 kilometers of the holotype of *O. edmontonicus*. This material was referred by Parks to the genus *Struthiomimus* as new species *S. currelli*, distinguished by its light construction, slender form, and relative dimensions of various bones. Sternberg (1934) considered this species to be a junior synonym of *O. edmontonicus*.

Sternberg (1933) regarded *O. edmontonicus* as a less sturdy animal than *O. velox*, larger and more slender, with an astragalus having a longer and narrower ascending process. Russell, in his review of "ostrich dinosaurs" of western Canada, noted that existing materials do not provide a sufficient basis for separating this species from *O. velox*, suggesting that both species remain distinct based on geographic separation.

Tentative species ?*O. tenuis* was based on the distal half of a left metatarsal III (USNM 5814), collected in 1888 by John Bell Hatcher, from the Judith River [now Dinosaur Park] Formation, on Birch Creek (on Cow Island, Missouri River), Montana. Marsh (1890*a*) diagnosed this species as follows: Metatarsal about twice bulk of *O. velox*, though slenderer medially; metatarsal III more compressed transversely at distal end of shaft; transverse diameter at distal end 30 millimeters (about 1.15 inches), anteroposterior diameter 35 millimeters (about 1.35 inches).

Another species, *O. sedens*, was based on an almost complete sacrum and adjoining pelvic arches, and basal caudal vertebrae, from the Lance Formation, Alkali Creek, Niobrara (formerly Converse) County, Wyoming. This species was first described by Marsh (1892*c*; 1896) as a larger form than *O. velox*. Russell considered the holotype of this species too fragmentary for certain assignment to *Ornithomimus*, *Struthiomimus*, or *Dromiceiomimus*.

As pointed out by Baird and Horner (1979), remains of *Ornithomimus* may have been known, although not as such, before the publication of the name. *Coelosaurus antiquus*, the oldest name for an ornithomimid from Atlantic coastal deposits, had been based on a well-preserved hollow tibia (ANSP 9222) from the greensand of Burlington County, New Jersey, this material described by Leidy (1865). Later, Cope (1868) described *Laelaps macropus* based on foot bones that were actually part of the type specimen of *C. antiquus*.

The name *Coelosaurus* had already been erected by Owen (1854) for a damaged vertebral centrum, although Owen did not assign the genus a specific name. As Leidy's name is a junior homonym of Owen's, Baird and Horner transferred *C. antiquus* to the oldest junior subjective synonym, *Ornithomimus*.

Baird (1986) later referred to *O. antiquus* various specimens collected from the Severn Formation (Middle Maastrichtian; Brouwers and Hazel 1978) in Prince Georges County, Maryland. These include a mutilated left femur (USNM 256614, collected by

Albert C. Myrick, Jr.), with mid-shaft circumference of about 150 millimeters and 7-millimeter wall thickness (see Horner 1979); posterior caudal vertebra (PU 23503, collected by Glenn Medwick), indistinguishable from 22nd and 23rd caudals in *Gallimimus*, centrum 12.5 millimeters high and 13.8 millimeters wide; and small limb-bone fragment (collected by Timothy A. Miller), apparently from a metatarsal shaft or small tibia, from a hollow-boned animal. Other material assigned to this species and reported by Baird include a large caudal vertebra from Burlington County, caudal from Monmouth County, fragmentary tibia shaft from the Navesink of Hop Brook near Holmdel, and partial femur from the Mount Laurel-Wenonah Formation of the Big Brook area. Baird observed that a pedal phalanx, probably of Late Coniacian to Early Campanian age, from Mississippi (see Carpenter 1982*b*), is morphologically identical to, though slightly smaller than, the right third pedal phalanx of *O. antiquus*.

Russell rediagnosed *Ornithomimus*, based on the holotype skeleton of *O. edmontonicus* and referred specimens, including several dorsal ribs, caudal vertebrae, left humerus, radii-ulnae, several metacarpals, phalanges, femora, and tibiae-fibulae (NMC 12441), from the Horseshoe Canyon Formation south of "Steveville," Dinosaur Provincial Park, Alberta, and on the holotype of *S. currelli*.

Ornithomimus has often been considered to be a senior synonym of *Struthiomimus*. Osborn noted that *Ornithomimus* lived significantly later than *Struthiomimus* and had lost the remnant of the fourth toe, a more primitive feature present in the latter genus. Russell recognized both forms as generically separate, distinguishing *Ornithomimus* from *Struthiomimus* by its shorter back, longer forelimbs, form of the manus (including the presence of a small splint of bone articulating with the proximo-internal surface of right metacarpal I), and shorter hindlimbs.

Osborn (1917) believed that dinosaurs like *Ornithomimus*, with their long hindlimbs and rod-like tail balances, were cursorial. Osborn postulated that these animals were basically herbivorous, whereas Gregory (*see in* Osborn) suggested that they were omnivorous. Russell rejected these ideas on the basis of the strongly carnivorous adaptations of other theropods, structure of the skull (including the general shape of the muzzle, recalling the beak in insectivorous birds), weakly-devel-

oped jaw adductor muscles (suggesting a diet of eggs or soft-bodied animals), and complete absence of gastric stones (for grinding vegetable matter) found with remains of this genus and other ornithomimids. Russell also suggested that the hands of *Ornithomimus* were probably utilized in removing light material from food objects resting on the ground, or, as suggested by Gregory, digging.

Notes: Baird (1979) reported various probable ornithomimid specimens from Campanian beds, including a partial metatarsus and anterior caudal centrum (PU 224416, collected by W. Cokeley) from the Merchantville Formation of Delaware (see Baird and Galton 1981); pedal phalanx (A124, collected by Eugene F. Harstein) from the Marshalltown Formation of Delaware; pedal phalanx (ANSP 15319) from the Black Creek Formation of North Carolina (Miller 1967; Baird and Horner 1979); and third phalanx of a left pes from the Mooreville Chalk near Selma, Alabama, figured by Langston (1960) as "Theropoda, genus and species indet."

Russell documented a number of undetermined ornithomimid specimens recovered from Alberta. From the Horseshoe Canyon Formation on Red Deer River, these include distal caudal vertebrae and two pedal phalanges (AMNH 5262); two specimens consisting of pedal elements (AMNH 5264, NMC field number 3, 1916); fragments of tibiae-fibulae, distal ends of left metatarsals, right metatarsal IV, and three pedal phalanges (NMC 12227); and a pelvis (ROM field number 1, 1923); from the "Judith River" [=Dinosaur Park] Formation of Little

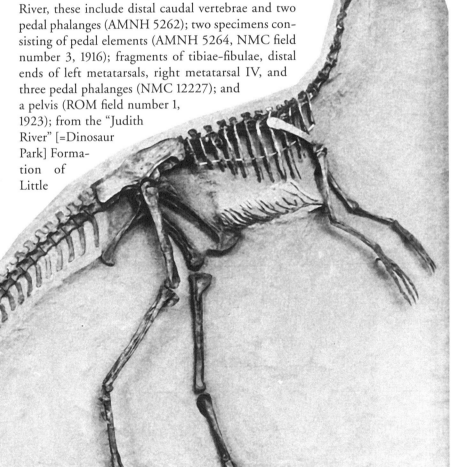

Ornithomimus edmontonicus, ROM 851, holotype skeleton of *Struthiomimus currelli*.
Courtesy Royal Ontario Museum.

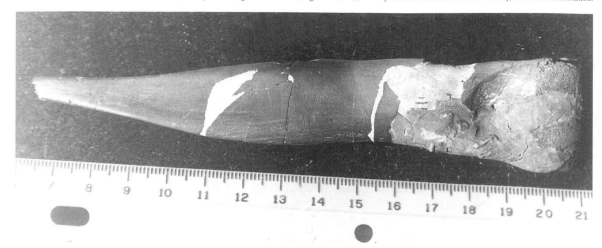

?*Ornithomimus tennuis*, USNM 5814, holotype left metatarsal III.

Sandhill Creek, posterior part of a skeleton (AMNH 5380); from the "Judith River" Formation, Red Deer River, pedal ungual phalanges (AMNH 6175); pedal elements (NMC field number 17, 1913); and various skeletal material (UA field number 21, 1921); from the "Judith River" Formation of Dinosaur Provincial Park, the posterior part of a sacrum and right ilium, acetabular area of a right pubis, and ischia (NMC 12224).

The species *O. grandis* was referred to tyrannosaurid species *Albertosaurus sarcophagus*; *O. minutus* Marsh 1892 referred by Russell to *Dromaeosaurus*; *O. altus* Lambe 1902 was made the type species of *Struthiomimus* by Osborn (1916) and *O. affinis* Gilmore 1920 the type species of *Archaeornithomimus* by Russell; *O. elegans* Parks 1933 was referred to *Elmisaurus* by Currie (1989).

O. lonzeensis (Dollo 1903), originally referred to "genus a" of Huene's (1926*b*) *Ornithomimidorum*, is not an ornithomimid (R. E. Molnar, personal communication 1989).

Key references: Baird (1986): Baird and Galton (1981); Baird and Horner (1979); Barsbold and Osmólska (1990); Cope (1868); DeCourten and Russell (1985); Horner (1979); Langston (1960); Leidy (1865); Marsh (1890*a*, 1892*c*, 1896); Osborn (1917); Owen (1854); Parks (1933); Russell (1972); Sternberg (1933, 1934).

ORNITHOPSIS Seeley 1870 [*nomen dubium*] —
(See *Pelorosaurus*.)
Name derivation: Greek *ornis* = "bird" + Greek *opsis* = "appearance."
Type species: *O. hulkei* Seeley 1870 [*nomen dubium*].

ORNITHOTARSUS Cope 1869 [*nomen dubium*]
Ornithischia: Ornithopoda: Hadrosauridae *incertae sedis*.
Name derivation: Greek *ornis* = "bird" + Greek *tarsos* = "tarsus."
Type species: *O. immanis* Cope 1869 [*nomen dubium*].
Other species: [None.]
Occurrence: Monmouth Formation, New Jersey, United States.
Age: Late Cretaceous (Campanian).

Ornithotarsus immanis, YPM 3221, holotype distal tibia, fibula, and astragalus.

Known material/holotype: YPM 3221, distal ends of left tibia and fibula coossified with astragalus and calcaneum.

Diagnosis of genus: [None published.]

Comments: The genus *Ornithotarsus* was established on hindlimb bones (YPM 3221), collected by Samuel Lockwood from the Lower Cretaceous clays beneath the marl, Monmouth Formation, Raritan Bay, Union east of Keyport, Monmouth County, New Jersey.

The material was described by Cope (1869*a*) as follows: Hindlimb (as preserved) 16 inches (about 43 centimeters) in length; medullary cavity almost filled with cancellous tissue.

Cope believed this specimen pertained to a dinosaur allied with the theropod *Compsognathus*, incorrectly positioning *Ornithotarsus* between the ornithischian *Hadrosaurus* and *Compsognathus*.

Lull and Wright (1942) later commented that the specimen compares quite favorably with the same elements in the plesiotype skeleton (YPM 1190) of "*Anatosaurus*" [=*Edmontosaurus*] mounted at the Yale Peabody Museum of Natural History, the main differences being of size and proportions.

Baird and Horner (1977) regarded *O. immanis* as synonymous with *Hadrosaurus foulkii*. As pointed out later by Brett-Surman (1989), however, this synonymy was based upon biogeography, the structure of holotype of *O. immanis* not allowing identification beyond Hadrosauridae *incertae sedis*.

Key references: Baird and Horner (1977); Brett-Surman (1989); Cope (1869*a*); Lull and Wright (1942).

ORODROMEUS Horner and Weishampel 1988

Ornithischia: Genasauria: Cerapoda: Ornithopoda: Hypsilophodontidae.

Name derivation: Greek *oros* = "[Egg] Mountain" + Greek *dromeus* = "runner."

Type species: *O. makelai* Horner and Weishampel 1988.

Other species: ?*O. minima* (Gilmore 1924).

Occurrence: Two Medicine Formation, Montana, United States, Dinosaur Park Formation, Alberta, Canada.

Age: Late Cretaceous (Late Campanian).

Known material: Three partial skeletons, cranial and postcranial remains, eggs with embryos.

Holotype: MOR 294, articulated, almost complete skull and skeleton missing tail.

Diagnosis of genus (as for type species): Palpebral anchored to postorbital part of posterior margin of orbit; jugal with lateral boss; in side view, maxillary and dentary teeth broadly triangular, often as

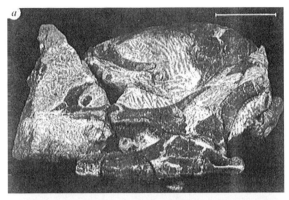

Orodromeus makelai, MOR 294, holotype skull, a. left lateral view, b. MOR 248, left dentary, left lateral view. Scale = a. 2 cm, b. 5 mm. (After Horner and Weishampel 1988.)

wide as high; anterior and posterior area of tooth crown divided equally by rounded apical (primary) ridge; (in adults) anterior and posterior edges of crown with 5–6 denticles of equal size; wrist unfused, formed by radiale, intermedium, ulnare, one distal carpal (Horner and Weishampel 1988).

Diagnosis of ?*O. minima*: Differs from all other known American and Asian ornithopods by very small pes with very slender proportions; absence of vestigial metatarsal V (Russell 1949).

Comments: Among the rarest of dinosaur remains are embryonic specimens, especially those that provide data useful for paleobiological interpretation. Among such finds are the remains of *Orodromeus*, the first hypsilophodontid known from the Campanian of North America.

Before the genus was named, Horner (1982, 1984*a*, 1984*b*) reported clutches of hypsilophodont eggs at the two sites dubbed Egg Mountain and Egg Island (sediments described by Lorenz and Gavin 1984), west of Choteau, Teton County. In the book *Dinosaurs Past and Present*, Horner (1987) chronicled in detail the discovery and collection of the eggs: Discovered in July, 1979, Egg Mountain yielded three hypsilophodont egg clutches, four unidentified eggs (one containing an embryonic skeleton), the hypsilophodont holotype skeleton, and hundreds of hypsilophodont, mammal, and lizard bones. Egg Island, discovered in 1983, yielded three hypsilophodont clutches (one with the 19 eggs). Horner noted that the hypsilophodont skeletal remains, at that time incompletely studied, were generically distinct from all other described hypsilophodonts except the type specimen of *L. minimus*. (See also the book *Digging for Dinosaurs*, by Horner and Gorman 1988, for a chronological account of John R. Horner and Robert Makela's discoveries of the nesting grounds of *Orodromeus*.) Horner and Weishampel diagnosed the monotypic *O. makelai* based on the holotype and referred material.

As described by Horner (1987), the Egg Mountain hypsilophodont eggs, identified as such based on embryonic skeletons found *in situ*, are elongate and ellipsoidal, averaging, when whole, about 17 centimeters (about 6.3 inches) long and 7 centimeters (about 2.75 inches) in greatest latitudinal diameter. Though appearing smooth, the surfaces, revealed under magnification, show numerous parallel, low-relief grooves and ridges occurring on the sides, terminating before reaching apex and nadir. The eggs were laid in a spiral pattern, the clutches apparently originally numbering either 12 or 24 eggs. As most clutches contained a total of 12, Horner postulated that those with double that number might represent communal nests.

The genus *Orodromeus* was founded upon an incomplete skeleton (MOR 294), discovered by Robert Makela in the Two Medicine Formation, Egg Mountain site, Willow Creek Anticline, Teton County, Montana. Referred material includes a clutch of 19 eggs with embryos (MOR 246), hind legs (PU 22412), skeleton (MOR 331), skeleton with skull (MOR 248), and braincase (MOR 403), from the same locality (Horner and Weishampel 1988).

As noted by Horner and Weishampel, hindlimb proportions in *Orodromeus*, from embryo to adult, indicate that this genus was an extremely gracile fast-runner, more so than any other hypsilophodontid save for "*Yandusaurus*" [=*Agillisaurus*] *multidens*. Tooth crowns are quite similar to those in *Lesothosaurus diagnosticus*. Tooth wear suggests a reversion to, or retention of, the primitive high-angle style of chewing in "fabrosaurids."

Horner and Weishampel reported that the epiphyseal surfaces of the limbs in embryos are well formed and made up of calcified cartilage, implying that this genus was a precocious developer, able to seek out its own food almost immediately after hatching. Some bony processes for muscle attachment apparently did not ossify until after the animal hatched and the muscles became active. Denticles found on anterior and posterior borders of the tooth crowns in older individuals were not present during early ontogenetic stages.

From the wealth of information gleaned from the numerous vertebrate and invertebrate remains, in addition to egg, fecal, and other trace-fossil evidence, Horner (1987) envisioned a possible scenario relating to the ecology and general behavior of the faunae inhabiting a dinosaur-nesting site. Included in this scenario were hypsilophodonts that actively tended their nests. Eggs seem to have been arranged so as not to touch one another during incubation. Adult hypsilophodonts may have removed vegetation and sediment from the top portions of the eggs, permitting the relatively large babies to hatch by popping off these tops. As shown above by Horner and Wieshampel, the young were probably capable of precocial activity; however, as Horner (1987) noted, they probably remained together at the nest. At first feeding on adult feces, the young hypsilophodonts then proceeded to eat small plants and insects. They remained under adult protection until large and swift enough to fend for themselves.

According to Sues and Norman (1990) in their review of the Hypsilophodontidae, the tentative species ?*O. minima* may belong to *Orodromeus*, although its type material is too fragmentary for positive identification. This taxon, originally named *Laosaurus minimus* by Gilmore (1924e), was based on a left pes, parts of a hindlimb, and some vertebrae in the Geology department of the University of British Columbia, collected in 1923 by C. H. Crickmay from a heavy-bedded sandstone in the Dinosaur Park Formation (horizon regarded by Gilmore as Lower Cretaceous [Blairmore Formation] age) in Alberta, Canada. Gilmore did not diagnose this species, but justified its validity on the basis of small size, as well as geographic and geologic separation from other described species of "*Laosaurus.*" Russell (1949) regarded this material as pertaining to an undescribed genus too poorly known for further identification.

In a study of dinosaur eggshells from the Two Medicine Formation of Montana, Hirsch and Quinn (1990) observed the following characteristics of eggshells attributed to *O. makelai*: Two distinct shell layers: 1. continuous layer consisting of slender interlocking shell units with prisms; sharp and columnar extinction pattern; restriction of herringbone pattern to column; and 2. thin mammillary layer, one seventh or less of shell thickness; pore canals straight, narrow, about same diameter (angusticanaliculate); shell thickness of 0.8–0.9 millimeters; smooth outer surface with fine longitudinal striations; inner surface with tightly packed mammillae and only a few interstices.

Illustration by Doug Henderson.

Orodromeus makelai, Egg Mountain site, Montana.

Note: Horner (1987) also described a nonhypsilophodont egg from Egg Mountain, oval in shape, about 12 centimeters [over 4.6 inches] long and 6 centimeters [about 2.3 inches] in diameter, with a bumpy surface texture. One such egg contains an embryonic skeleton too small to identify.

Key references: Gilmore (1924e); Hirsch and Quinn (1990); Horner (1982, 1984a, 1984b, 1987); Horner and Weishampel (1988); Russell (1949); Sues and Norman (1990).

OROSAURUS Huxley 1867 [*nomen dubium*] — (Preoccupied, Peters 1862; see *Euskelosaurus*.)
Name derivation: Greek *oros* = "mountain" + Greek *sauros* = "lizard."
Type species: *O. capensis* Steel 1970 [*nomn dubium*].

ORTHOGONIOSAURUS Das-Gupta 1931 [*nomen dubium*]
Saurischia: Theropoda: Tetanurae *incertae sedis*.
Name derivation: Greek *orthos* = "straight" + Greek *gonia* = "angle" + Greek *sauros* = "lizard."
Type species: *O. matleyi* Das-Gupta 1931 [*nomen dubium*].
Other species: ?*O. rawesi* (Lydekker 1890) [*nomen dubium*]).
Occurrence: Lameta Formation, Madhya Pradesh State, India.
Age: Late Cretaceous.
Known material: ?Two teeth.
Holotype: IM collection, isolated tooth.
Diagnosis of genus: [None published.]
Comments: The new type species *Orthogoniosaurus matleyi* was founded upon one rather small,

Orthogoniosaurus matleyi, IM, holotype tooth. Scale = 2 cm. (After Das-Gupta 1931.)

incompletely preserved, isolated tooth (IM collection), discovered in the Upper Cretaceous, green marly clay of the Lameta beds, Bara Simla Hill, Jubbulpore [now Jabalpur], Central India (Das-Gupta 1931).

Das Gupta described the holotype tooth as follows: Rather small, preserved portion about 27 millimeters (about 1.1 inches) long; compressed, with straight and denticulated posterior edge; rather blunt serrations at right angles to edge, running ?entire length; anterior edge convex, not denticulate, exposed face apparently slightly convex.

?*O. rawesi*, originally *Massospondylus rawesi*, was based on a tooth from probably Upper Triassic beds at Takli, near Nagpur, Madhya Pradesh. Sometimes regarded as a species of *Orthogoniosaurus* (Olshevsky 1991, 1992), the specimen is probably nondinosaurian (P. M. Galton, personal communication 1989).

Walker (1964), in reviewing the Lameta Group theropods, regarded the holotype of *O. matleyi* as indeterminate.

The tooth of *Orthogoniosaurus* is similar to posterior maxillary and posterior dentary teeth in both *Tyrannosaurus rex* and *Allosaurus fragilis*. Their similarities have little taxonomical significance, but suggest the *Orthogoniosaurus* tooth is a posterior tooth (R. E. Molnar, personal communication 1989). According to Molnar (1990), while the general form of this tooth is unusual in comparison to most theropod teeth, it is common in both caudal maxillary and dentary teeth, though the lack of mesial serrations is an uncommon feature. The tooth may belong to some other Jabalpur theropod, although its assignment to a taxon above the genus level cannot be substantiated.

Key references: Das-Gupta (1931); Lydekker (1890); Molnar (1990).

ORTHOMERUS Seeley 1883 [*nomen dubium*]—
(=? *Telmatosaurus*)
Ornithischia: Genasauria: Cerapoda: Ornithopoda: Iguanodontia: ?Hadrosauridae *incertae sedis*.
Name derivation: Greek *orthos* = "straight" + Greek *meros* = "upper thigh."
Type species: *O. dolloi* Seeley 1883 [*nomen dubium*].
Other species: ?*O. weberi* Riabinin 1945 [*nomen dubium*].
Occurrence: Maastricht Beds, Province Limburg, Netherlands.
Age: Late Cretaceous (Maastrichtian).
Known material/holotype: BMNH R42955, partial postcranial skeleton including caudal vertebrae, right femur, tibia, incomplete extremities, juvenile.

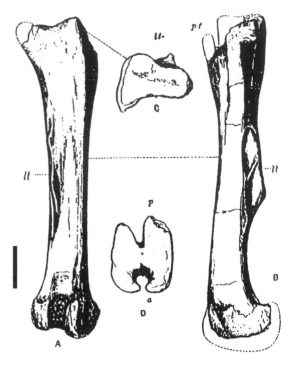

Orthomerus dolloi, BMNH 42955, holotype (juvenile) right femur, A. posterior, B. inner lateral views, C. proximal end (reversed), D. BMNH 42957, referred specimen, distal end. Scale = 5 cm. (After Seeley 1883.)

Diagnosis of genus: [None published.]

Comments: The first European dinosaur to be classified as a hadrosaurid, the genus *Orthomerus* was founded upon incomplete postcranial remains (BMNH R42955), collected from the Upper Cretaceous of Maestrich [now Maastricht], Holland.

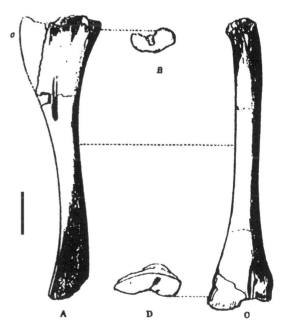

Orthomerus dolloi, B<MH 42955, holotype (juvenile) left tibia, A. outer lateral, C. posterior views, B. proximal end (reversed), D. distal end. Scale = 5 cm. (After Seeley 1883.)

Seeley (1883) described the material as follows: Limb bones relatively straight, femur 50 centimeters (about 19 inches) in length, tibia 27 centimeters (about 10.5 inches).

Orthomerus is usually regarded as senior synonym of *Telmatosaurus* (Lapparent and Lavocat 1955; Romer 1966; Steel 1969). However, as pointed out by Brett-Surman (1989), the type femur of *O. dolloi* lacks any diagnostic features that could ally it with any hadrosaurid (or iguanodontid) lineage. Brett-Surman favored retaining *Orthomerus* in its traditional placing within Iguanodontidae until the taxon can be redefined based upon more complete specimens. Weishampel and Horner (1990), in their review of Hadrosauridae, regarded *Telmatosaurus* as a valid taxon and included *Orthomerus* in a list of hadrosaurids regarded as *nomina dubia*.

Hindlimb material from the Crimea [formerly Union of Soviet Socialist Republic] was referred by Riabinin (1945) to ?*O. weberi*, although there are not sufficient grounds to include them in the genus *Orthomerus* (R. E. Molnar, personal communication).

Key references: Brett-Surman (1989); Riabinin (1945); Seeley (1883); Weishampel and Horner (1990).

OTHNIELIA Galton 1977—(=?*Laosaurus*)
Ornithischia: Genasauria: Cerapoda: Ornithopoda: Hypsilophodontidae.
Name derivation: "Othniel [Charles Marsh]."
Type species: *O. rex* (Marsh 1877).
Other species: [None.]
Occurrence: Morrison Formation, Colorado, Utah, Wyoming, United States.
Age: Late Jurassic–?Early Cretaceous (Late Kimmeridgian–Early Tithonian; ?Neocomian–?Hauterivian).
Known material: Two partial skeletons, postcranial elements, teeth.
Holotype: YPM 1915, femur, other postcranial remains.

Diagnosis of genus (as for type species): At least 14 dentary teeth; maxillary and dentary teeth with prominent bulbous cingulum both medially and laterally; lateral surface of crown deeper than medial, especially for maxillary teeth; in larger teeth, both crown surfaces strongly textured; vertical ridges of subequal size developed to varying degree, one ridge per marginal denticle; eight marginal denticles on each dentary tooth anterior to apical denticle, seven posterior to denticle, with corresponding counts of five and six for maxillary tooth; small cheek teeth with fewer marginal denticles, not textured, with only few vertical ridges; (referred) premaxillary tooth with fine vertical ridges on both lateral and medial surfaces, fine marginal denticles on anterior and posterior edges; dorsal vertebrae with short transverse processes; fifth sacral rib large; humerus with low deltopectoral crest; ilium with deep main body, narrow brevis shelf, ratio posteriorly 2.0; obturator processes at proximal third of ischium; distal half of ischium flattened, blade-like dorsoventrally; femur with deep cleft between lesser and greater trochanters, shallow depression on medial surface of shaft merging with base of fourth trochanter, gently convex anterior edge distally; pedal digit I functional (Galton 1983*b*).

Comments: *Othnielia* was founded on a well-preserved, nearly perfect femur, and other remains (YPM 1915), collected by B. F. Mudge from the Morrison Formation [then "*Atlantosaurus* beds"] at Garden Park, near Cañon City, Colorado. The specimen was originally described by Marsh (1877*d*) representing a new species of *Nanosaurus*, *N. rex*, because of its close agreement to the holotype of type species *N. agilis*.

Marsh originally diagnosed *N. rex* as follows: Small, fox-sized dinosaur; femur most characteristic, greater trochanter and especially third trochanter prominent; fibular ridge well developed, directed outward and backward; walls of femur smooth, cavity very large; 100 millimeters (over 3.75 inches) in length, with greatest antero-posterior diameter 18 millimeters (almost .65 inches).

A well preserved, almost complete skeleton (BYU ESM-163R) of this species, missing the skull and tail, was collected in 1963 by James A. Jensen from the Brushy Basin Member of the Morrison Formation, east of Willow Springs, in Emery County, Utah. The specimen was found in association with skeletal remains of other dinosaurs (*e.g.*, the ornithopod *Camptosaurus*, theropod *Allosaurus*, and sauropod *Camarasaurus*), and also some fragmentary rhynchocephalian remains. The manus was lost prior to excavation due to devastation of the site by amateur fossil collectors (Galton and Jensen 1973*a*).

Galton and Jensen assigned this specimen to the Hypsilophodontidae, observing that all the bones, except for minor differences, are quite similar to those of hypsilophodontids, referring it tentatively to ?*Nanosaurus rex*. According to Galton and Jensen, the femur agrees with that of the holotype of *N. rex* in having a deep cleft between proximal trochanters and in the lack of an anterior intercondylar groove distally. The skeleton closely resembles *Hypsilophodon*, differing in various ways, including cervical vertebrae with proportionally taller neural arches; more robust cervical ribs with capitulum and tuberculum more widely separated; last dorsal and sacral vertebrae with proportionally taller neural spines and arches (more resembling *Dryosaurus lettowvorbecki*); much larger

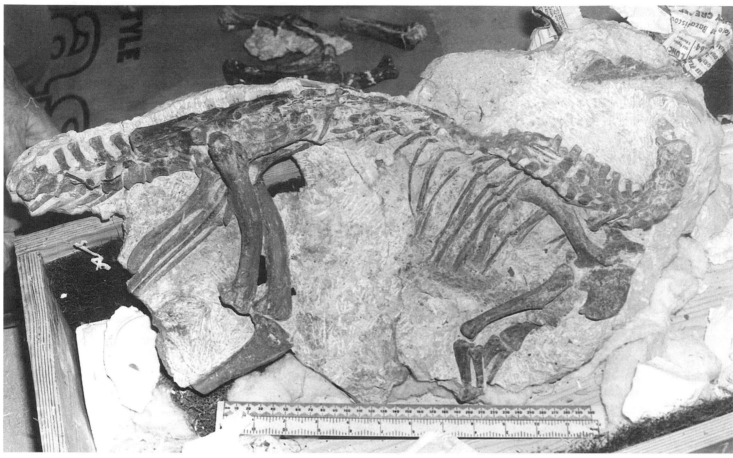

Othnielia rex, BYU ESM-163R, referred postcranial skeleton. (See p. 618, *Nanosaurus* entry for holotype.)

Photo by R. A. Long and S. P. Welles, courtesy Brigham Young University.

first haemal arch; ilium with much broader brevis shelf; ischium with more proximally placed obturator process; astragalus with somewhat higher ascending process; pedal digits more slender.

Galton (1977) later recognized the holotype and referred specimen as generically distinct from *Nanosaurus*, erecting for it the new genus *Othnielia*. *N. agilis* was regarded by Galton as a small "fabrosaurid." As noted by Galton, both *O. rex* and *N. agilis*, with *Dryosaurus altus* and *Camptosaurus dispar*, constitute the four bipedal ornithischians from the Morrison Formation.

Galton (1977) referred to *O. rex* the species *L. gracilis* Marsh 1878, a smaller form based on vertebral centra and parts of the pes (YPM 1875), from Como, Wyoming, and *L. consors* Marsh 1894, a larger form (up to 3.5 meters or almost 12 feet long), based on incomplete skeletal remains (YPM 1882) from Como. Galton later (1983*b*) diagnosed the monotypic *O. rex* based on the holotype, referred specimens YPM 1875, YPM 1882, and an incomplete articulated skeleton (MCZ 4454) found near Willow Springs, Utah.

Later, Jensen (1985*b*) referred to *Othnielia* sp. an

ilium collected by him on the Uncompahgre Upwarp, at the base of the Brushy Basin Member, Morrison Formation (Upper Jurassic [Tithonian]), at Dry Mesa in west central Utah. (Jensen also reported that numerous centra and other random small-bone fragments, belonging to unknown ornithopods or theropods, were also found at this location).

Bakker, Galton, Siegwarth and Filla (1990) removed *Othnielia* from the Hypsilophodontidae, noting that *Hypsilophodon* itself is far more derived (cheek tooth crowns with strong central ridge, accessory ribs greatly reduced in size and number) than the more primitive *Othnielia* (and also *Drinker*) in tooth shape.

Note: According to Sues and Norman (1990) in their review of Hypsilophodontidae, the species tentatively named ?*O. minima*, originally described by Gilmore (1924*e*) as *Laosaurus minimus*, does not belong to *Othnielia* and, though too fragmentary to make a positive identification, probably belongs to *Orodromeus* (see entry).

Key references: Galton (1977, 1983*b*); Galton and Jensen (1973*a*); Jensen (1985*b*); Marsh (1877*d*, 1878*a*, 1894).

OURANOSAURUS Taquet 1976

Ornithischia: Genasauria: Cerapoda: Ornithopoda:
 Iguanodontia: Iguanodontidae.

Name derivation: Touareg *ourane* = "valiant" +
 Greek *sauros* = "lizard."

Type species: *O. nigeriensis* Taquet 1972.

Other species: [None.]

Occurrence: Elrhaz Formation, Agadez, Niger.

Age: Early Cretaceous (Late Aptian).

Known material: Skeleton with skull, skeleton.

Holotype: GDF 300, nearly complete skeleton with
 skull.

Diagnosis of genus (as for type species): Bipedal
iguanodont measuring about 7 meters (almost 24
feet) in length; skull very long, large, relatively deep,
maximum height at rounded dorsal protuberances of
nasals [resembling incipient crest as in the hadrosaur
Prosaurolophus]; muzzle long, slender, terminating in
beak; premaxillaries extremely long, straight, widened
anteriorly, separated posteriorly at contact with
nasals; external nares visible in dorsal view; opening
of convergence between nasal conduits in posterior
part of skull; predentary short, wider than long; maxilla slightly elevated; nasal relatively short; antorbital
fenestrae small; orbit circular in outline, of same
height as inferior temporal opening; posteroexternal

process of squamosal straight and horizontal, slightly
covering paroccipital process; paroccipital process
high, broad, oblique anteriorly; occipital condyle
wide, flat; basipterygoid process directed laterally;
supratemporal openings wide, very divergent anteriorly; dentary deep anteriorly, slightly deep posteriorly,
with well-developed articular process; teeth of iguanodontid type, uniformly covered with enamel, edges
scalloped; 11 cervical, 17 dorsal, six sacral, 40 caudal
vertebrae, dorsal neural spines extremely long; tail
relatively short; humerus long, almost straight; manus
very delicately constructed, phalangeal formula 1-3-
3-3-3 or 4; fifth metacarpal a small spur which does
not diverge laterally; ischium long, straight, distally
enlarged into "foot," obturator process very proximally located, obturator opening very narrow; pubis
very slender, prepubic blade quite deep and developed, pubic bar straight and much shorter than
ischium; ilium slender at preacetabular process, equal
in length to about half entire bone, convex at dorsal
border, rugose at antitrochanter, only slightly deep at
acetabular depression, with slightly marked postacetabular indentation; astragalus with posterior but
no anterior ascending process; pes tridactyl, phalangeal formula 0-3-4-5-0 (Taquet 1976*a*).

Comments: The genus *Ouranosaurus* was
founded upon a well-preserved, nearly complete
skeleton (GDF 300) collected from the Elrhaz Formation, Tégama series (Aptian), at Gadoufaoua, in the Sahara Desert of
Niger, Africa. A paratype
(MNHN GDF 381) con-
sists of another nearly
complete skele-
ton. The finds
(including

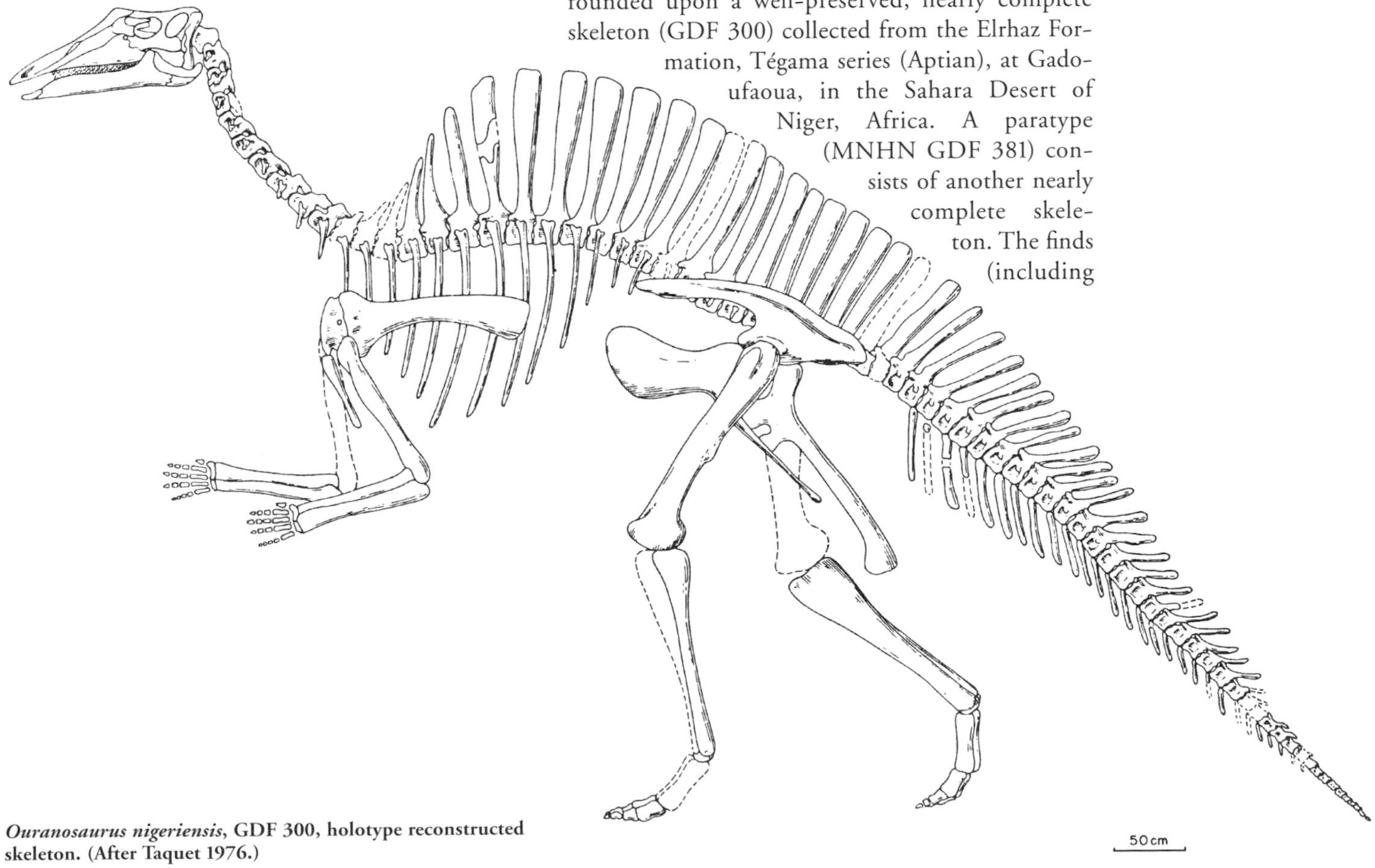

Ouranosaurus nigeriensis, GDF 300, holotype reconstructed
skeleton. (After Taquet 1976.)

50 cm

Ouranosaurus

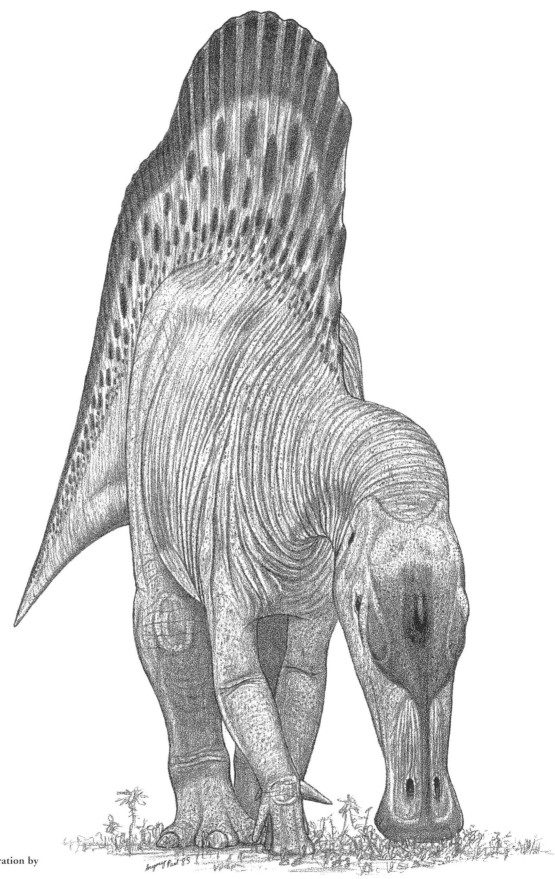

Ouranosaurus nigeriensis, life restoration by
Gregory S. Paul.

dinosaurian and crocodilian material) resulted from expeditions in Niger begun by Philippe Taquet in 1965 (Taquet 1976*a*).

The most characteristic feature of *Ouranosaurus* is the great height of the dorsal neural spines, the longest of which totals about 630 millimeters (about 24 inches), the corresponding centrum only 150 millimeters (about 6.2 inches) high. These spines may have supported a "sail" or the kind of withers found in some present day ungulates.

The possible weight of *Ouranosaurus* may have been about 2.09 metric tons (over 2.3 tons) (G. S. Paul, personal communication 1988).

Note: Buffetaut, Pouit and Taquet (1980) reported an ornithopod tooth resembling those of *Ouranosaurus* and *Iguanodon*. The tooth had been reworked in Miocene marine deposits of Doué-Douces (Main-et-Loire, France). The crown is about 24 millimeters high, width at base about 15 millimeters.

Key references: Taquet (1972, 1975*a*, 1976*a*, 1976*b*).

OVIRAPTOR Osborn 1924—(=*Fenestrosaurus*)

Saurischia: Theropoda: Tetanurae: Avetheropoda: Coelurosauria: Maniraptora: Arctometatarsalia: Oviraptorosauria: Oviraptoridae: Oviraptorinae.

Name derivation: Latin *ovum* = "egg" + Latin *raptor* = "robber."

Type species: *O. philoceratops* Osborn 1924

Other species: *O. mongoliensis* Barsbold 1986.

Occurrence: Djadochta Formation, Khermeen Tsav Formation, Nemegt Formation, Omnogov, Mongolian People's Republic; Ukhaa Tolgod, South Central Mongolia; Bayan Mandahu, Inner Mongolia, People's Republic of China.

Age: Late Cretaceous (Middle–Late Campanian).

Known material: Six skeletons, including partial postcrania with skulls, partial postcrania, skulls, cranial and postcranial fragments, adult; also embryo, eggs, nests.

Holotype: AMNH 6517, skull and jaws, associated cervical vertebrae, greater part of left forelimb.

Diagnosis of genus (as for type species): Nares above antorbital fenestra; antorbital fenestra small relative to orbit; nasal horn or crest; well-developed sagittal crest; mandible with two mandibular fenestrae; process extends from surangular into first mandibular fenestra; depth of mandible highly variable, but jaw articulation becomes displaced ventrally; pectoral girdle with well-developed clavicle (Smith 1993).

Diagnosis of *O. mongoliensis*: Distinguished from *O. philoceratops* by thick, extremely tall, and

Photo by the author, courtesy Royal Tyrrell Museum/Alberta Community Development.

Oviraptor philoceratops, cast of AMNH 6517, holotype skull, left lateral view.

"cupola-shaped" crest extending along upper part of skull from premaxillae to parietals (Barsbold 1986).

Comments: An unusual-looking (and apparently misnamed) theropod, *Oviraptor* was founded on a partial, badly fractured skull with partial postcranial remains (AMNH 6517), collected in July 1923 by George Olsen during the Central Asiatic Expeditions of the American Museum of Natural History, from the Djadochta Formation (Middle-Late Campanian; see Currie 1991; Dong 1993*a*), at a site now known as Bayn Dzak, at Shabarakh Usu, in the southern Gobi Desert of Central Mongolia. The remains (which would be exhibited in 1993 at the American Museum) were preserved in sandstone, found atop a clutch of dinosaur eggs (then presumed to belong to the ceratopsian *Protoceratops*; see entry). In a popular article, Osborn (1924*c*) named this new theropod *Fenestrosaurus philoceratops*, giving no illustration and describing the specimen in one sentence.

The genus was originally diagnosed by Osborn (1924*d*) as follows: Skull extremely abbreviated; cranium longer than facial region; orbit and fenestrations extremely large; eight very large craniofacial and mandibular fenestrations; jaws entirely edentulous [intimating to him relationship to the Ornithomimidae]; interclavicle large; manus with three irregularly-elongated digits, elements of digits not laterally compressed, metacarpals abbreviated.

Osborn (1924*d*) diagnosed the type species, *O. philoceratops*, as follows: Faciocranial ["face" to entire length of skull] index 70 percent; lower jaw with greatly elevated mandibular border and two fenestrae; prominent bony eminence above rostrum; scapula extremely elongate; humerus, ulna, and radius of subequal length; digit II extremely long; I and III comparatively short.

Oviraptor

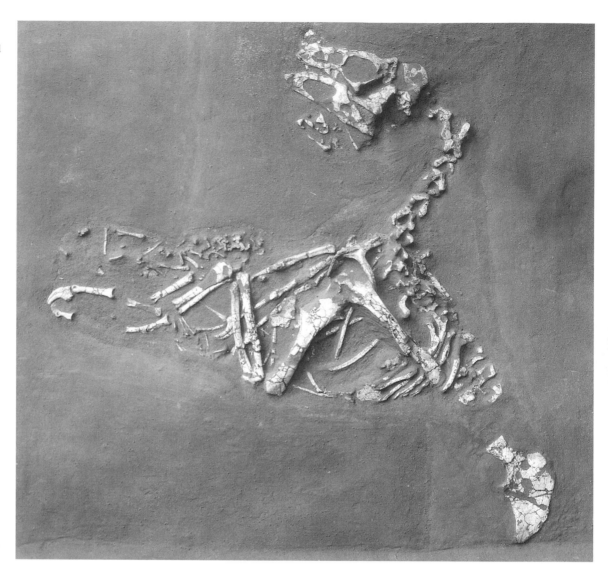

Decades later, Smith (1990, 1993) pointed out that the bone identified by Osborn (1924d) as metacarpal I is actually the first phalanx of digit I.

New *Oviraptor* material was collected during the 1970 and 1971 Polish-Mongolian Paleontological Expeditions to the Gobi Desert in Mongolia. Designated *Oviraptor* sp., the specimens include two skulls and some postcranial fragments (including ZPAL Mg-I/95) from the Khermeen Tsav Formation (?Middle Campanian), plus a fragmentary skull (ZPAL Mg collection) from the Nemegt Formation (?Late Campanian to Early Maastrichtian) (Osmólska 1976).

Based on this material, Osmólska described in detail the skull of *Oviraptor* sp., observing that the palate is unique in its structure among all other known dinosaurs. Its most striking feature is the form of the pterygoids, which are massive bars with their lateral portions turned strongly towards the lower surface. The ectopterygoids are situated parasagittally, joining pterygoids with maxillae medi-ally to the anterior roots of the jugale arches. (In all other known dinosaurs, the ectopterygoids are directed transversely to join pterygoids with jugal arches.) The medial wings of the palatine bones (unlike those in other known dinosaurs) border the chonae posteriorly, forming ventral links between maxillae and ectopterygoids laterally. The cranial bones, especially those of the snout and roof, are very strongly pneumatic. The nasal has a large air chamber that joins with the external naris. Atypically, the olfactory tracks seem to have been quite short. The mandible is similar to that of *Caenagnathus collinsi* and *C. sternbergi*, differing mainly in proportions. These specimens reveal a considerable degree of cranial variation, particularly a prominent hornlike prong. Such variations may have significance on a species level or may be due to ontogenetic changes or sexual dimorphism. Also observed in these specimens was a modified clavicle or collar bone. This avian feature, once believed to be nonexistent in dinosaurs, offers new evidence supporting a dinosaurian ancestry for birds.

A second species, *O. mongoliensis*, was based on an incomplete crested skull (GI 100/32) from the Nemegt Formation of Altan-Ula, Mongolia, this specimen originally identified by Barsbold (1981) as belonging to the genus *Ingenia*. As described by Barsbold (1986), the apex of this nasal crest is above the orbit rather than at the front of the skull (as in the type species). The skull measures approximately 16 centimeters (almost 6.2 inches) in length. The skeleton is somewhat smaller than that of *O. philoceratops*. According to Barsbold *et al.*, the crest may have served as a display structure or been used to aid the animal in passing through obstructions such as vegetation.

Osborn (1924*d*), observing similarities between *Oviraptor* and the toothless ornithomimids, believed that this genus should be classified with the Ornithomimidae, a position it maintained for more than four decades. Osmólska, noting similarities between the lower jaws of *Oviraptor* and *Caenagnathus*, assigned the former to the Caenagnathidae. Barsbold (1976) erected the new taxon Oviraptorosauria to include two families, Caenagnathidae and Oviraptoridae (the latter including *Oviraptor*); subsequently, Barsbold (1981) divided Oviraptoridae into two subfamilies, Oviraptorinae and Ingeniinae.

Oviraptor was a small theropod, the holotype skull of *O. philceratops* measuring 179 millimeters in length (Osborn 1924*d*), ZPAL Mg-I/95 only 98 millimeters long (Osmólska 1976). The jaws were probably covered in life by a horny sheath.

Some workers have speculated on some aspects of the behavior of *Oviraptor*, deduced from its morphology. The beak has suggested to some paleontologists that *Oviraptor* could have been omnivorous, although the jaws and hands, the latter bearing curved claws, seem indicative of a rapacious hunter. That the holotype was discovered atop a nest of fossil eggs suggested to Osborn that this *Oviraptor* individual had been overtaken by a sandstorm while in the act of robbing a nest of its eggs (see below) for consumption. Barsbold later (1986) postulated that *Oviraptor* was an amphibious dinosaur, its muscular tail used for propulsion through water and that its strong jaws were adapted to crushing much harder food than eggs (*e.g.*, mollusks).

In a later review of the Oviraptorosauria, Barsbold, Maryańska and Osmólska (1990) pointed out that the typically cursorial hindlimbs of *Oviraptor* would have allowed for efficient terrestrial locomotion. Smith also (1990, 1993) argued that *Oviraptor* was not amphibious, pointing out that the forelimb and manus were not structurally suited for swimming, the metacarpals being closely appressed and

not splayed for increased surface area (as they are in crocodiles). According to Smith (1990, 1993), *Oviraptor* was a mostly terrestrial animal, though one capable of wading. Also, its large orbit is a primitive feature and not an adaptation for seeing underwater.

Smith (1990, 1993) further argued that *Oviraptor* was not an egg-eater, an omnivore, nor an eater of mollusks, but an herbivore, with leaves being a major part of its diet. The cranium is edentulous and very light, lacking many insertion points for well-developed muscles required for crushing heavy-shelled mollusks, the cranial anatomy also inadequate for active carnivory or scavenging. Smith observed that a powerful shearing mechanism, analogous to that in some derived ceratopsians (*e.g.*, *Triceratops*; see Ostrom 1964*B*), is present in the jaws of *Oviraptor*. This mechanism does not suggest a mollusk-crushing ability, but rather "shearing blades" suited for cutting the fibrous leaves or other vegetable matter available in this dinosaur's environment.

Newer interpretations of the holotype and more recent *Oviraptor* discoveries in Mongolia have led to new incites regarding possible behavior in this dinosaur, as well as the revelation that this dinosaur was seemingly misnamed and wrongly vilified as an egg thief. Osborn (1924*d*) coined the name *O. philoceratops*, meaning "egg stealer with a fondness for ceratopsian eggs." These more recent data, however, imply that the association of the holotype skeleton with eggs suggest not the predation by an "egg rob-

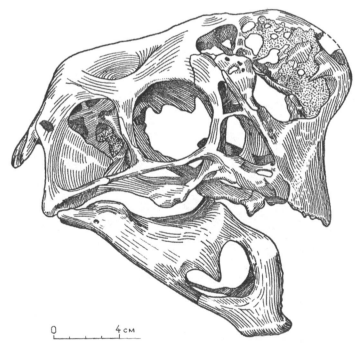

Oviraptor philoceratops, GI 100/42, skull with crest preserved, right lateral view. (After Barsbold 1986.)

ber" of an herbivorous dinosaur's nest, but rather behavior relating to parental care.

Both Elźanowski (1981) and Mikhailov (1991) suspected that the commonly found eggs traditionally referred to *Protoceratops andrewsi* (and those found with the holotype of *O. philoceratops*) were not ceratopsian but theropod eggs (see notes, *Protoceratops* entry). Later, Norell, Clark, Dashzeveg, Barsbold, Chiappe, Davidson, McKenna, Perle and Novacek (1995) identified an oviraptorid embryo inside the kind of egg associated with the holotype of *O. philoceratops*.

With the animal that laid the so-called "*Protoceratops*" eggs unequivocally exposed as *Oviraptor*, Norell, Clark, Chiappe and Dashzeveg (1995) reported a spectacular specimen belonging to the latter genus, collected at Ukhaa Tolgod (Late Cretaceous) in South Central Mongolia, during the 1993 segment of the Mongolian Academy of Sciences/ American Museum of Natural History Paleontological Project. The specimen (IGM 100/979), the partial skeleton of a large *Oviraptor* individual, includes gastralia and ribs, but lacks the skull, vertebrae, tail, dorsal pelvic bones, and the proximal parts of both hindlimbs. According to Norell *et al.,* the specimen exhibits no evidence of transportation after death and was preserved in facies hypothesized to be deposited by large sandstorms. The skeleton was found positioned over an oviraptorid nest in the same posture assumed by many extant birds while brooding. The entire skeleton was collected in a single block, thereby maintaining the spatial relationships definitively.

As pointed out by Norell *et al.,* this specimen represents the most complete and best preserved oviraptorid yet found on a nest (see Dong and Currie, 1995, below), offering the first evidence of the exact position of the skeleton to the nest, described by Norell *et al.* as follows: Hindlimbs tightly folded, feet and lower legs almost parallel to each other; feet atop and adjacent to eggs on inner perimeter of circle defined by nest; pubis lying in direct center of nest, ischia (fused distally) lying more posteriorly atop posteriormost eggs; anteriorly, gastralia just posterior to shoulder girdle lying in contact with eggs; front limbs

Oviraptor philoceratops, life restoration by Brian Franczak.

posteriorly directed, arms wrapped around nest; manual claws directed inward; preserved soft tissue (unusual for sandstone matrices) apparent at tips of manual claws.

Fifteen elongatoolithid eggs were uncovered in IGM 100/979, although Norell *et al.* believe more are present in areas that could not be uncovered without damaging the skeleton, the total number, based upon the spacing between the exposed eggs, estimated to be about 22. As in other oviraptorid nests, the eggs in the Ukhaa Tolgod specimen are arranged in a circular pattern, the broad ends directed toward the center of the nest. Sometimes the eggs are arranged in two levels. The eggs are about 18 centimeters long and 6.5 centimeters wide (measurements possibly influenced by postmortem vertical compression), and are ornamented with small ridges running parallel to the long axes.

According to Norell *et al.,* the occurrence of multiple specimens of large oviraptorids associated with nests suggests that these dinosaurs were the layers of the eggs, and that (like other archosaurs) they habitually stayed near the nests. Considering the near life pose of the IGM 100/979 skeleton, the lack of evidence for postmortem transportation, the definite association of the skeleton with the eggs, the lack of eggs inside the body cavity of the skeleton, and the neat and orderly arrangement of the nest (implying manipulation of the eggs by the parents into a specific configuration, as in extant birds), Norell *et al.* interpreted this specimen as the most compelling to date indicating the "avian type of nesting behavior in oviraptorids" of "sitting on a clutch of eggs in a position homologous to the brooding posture displayed by many modern birds," and "that modern avian brooding behavior evolved long before the origin of modern birds and among non-avian maniraptoran theropods."

In a preliminary report (published before the announcements in the popular press and in the paleontological literature of the specimen from Ukhaa Tolgod), Dong and Currie (1995) reported the discovery of a partial *Oviraptor* skeleton in the Bayan Mandahu (redated by Jerzykiewicz, Currie, Eberth, Johnston, Koster, and Zheng 1993 as Middle–Late Campanian), Inner Mongolia, northern China. According to Dong and Currie (1996), the specimen (IVPP V9608), discovered by the Sino-Canadian Dinosaur Project in 1990, was found squatting atop a nest of elongatoolithid eggs (nest and eggs included as part of the specimen). The cause of death of this *Oviraptor*, based on sedimentologic evidence, seems to have been rapid burial during a sandstorm. Dong and Currie (1995, 1996) noted that, as in similar nests, the eggs were arranged in a circle around an

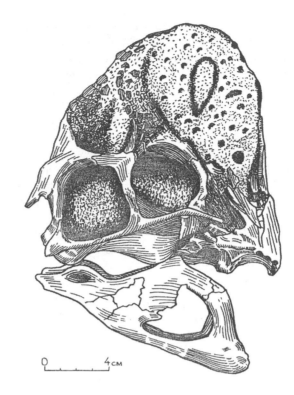

Oviraptor mongoliensis, GI 100/32, holotype skull, right lateral view. (After Barsbold 1986.)

0   4 CM

empty space. The dinosaur's feet were placed in this central space, the hands folded to lay outside the circle of eggs.

Examining the taphonomic evidence of IVPP V9608, Dong and Currie (1996) considered several possible scenarios to explain the association of the theropod skeleton and eggs:

1. The association was coincidental. This idea was deemed unlikely, in that specimens found in this type of bedding at Bayan Mandahu usually occur as untransported, isolated skeletons (Jerzykiewicz *et al.* 1993).

2. The *Oviraptor* was caught while pillaging a nest of eggs (Osborn 1924*d*). However, though just six eggs remain, there is no evidence of preburial destruction of any eggs; and a predatory oviraptorid probably would have eaten or abandoned its food long before it was buried during a sandstorm.

3. The *Oviraptor* was lying on the nest, incubating or protecting the eggs. This hypothesis is supported by the position of the skeleton over the eggs (which have the same size, shape, and shell morphology as those associated with the holotype of *O. philoceratops*) and the fact that the eggs seem to have been laid by a mature animal about the size of the skeleton.

4. The theropod was laying its eggs as it was being buried during the sandstorm. The fact that there is but one layer of eggs supports this idea. However, this theory could not be tested, as too much of the specimen had been lost to erosion.

P

Finding their third scenario to be the most likely, Dong and Currie (1996) further postulated that, like birds, theropods incubated and protected their eggs, and that these instincts were indeed powerful to keep an animal at its nest as it became buried by sand.

From the position of the hind foot in IVPP V9608, and judging from the open centers of this and all other elongatoolithid nests, Dong and Currie (1996) deduced that oviraptorids laid eggs by standing in one place and turning, in one direction, in a circle; the arrangement of the eggs suggested to them that two were laid at a time.

According to Dong and Currie (1996), an *Oviraptor* nest from Bayan Mandahu displayed at the Inner Mongolian (Hohhot) Museum indicates that the mother turned clockwise as she laid her eggs. The first (and lowest) layer of eggs is in a circle with a somewhat wide radius, the spiral tightening as additional layers of eggs were deposited. The lowest-layer eggs slope at a low angle away from the nest's center, the angle increasing at higher levels. This arrangement indicated to Dong and Currie (1996) that "the decrease in radius and the change in angle reflect changes in orientation of the cloaca as the animal rose higher on her hind legs. The hands may have been used to scoop sand onto the eggs as they were laid."

According to Dong and Currie (1996), the above scenario differs from those offered by other workers (*e.g.*, Sabath 1991; Mikhailov, Sabath and Kurzanov 1994), who believed that the eggs were laid with a more vertical orientation and surrounded by vegetation, the eggs supposedly collapsing into a more horizontal orientation as the plant matter decomposed (this hypothesis unable to explain the paired, spiral arrangement of the eggs within the nest).

Key references: Barsbold (1976, 1981, 1986, 1990); Barsbold, Maryańska and Osmólska (1990); Dong and Currie (1995, 1996), Elźanowski (1981); Mikhailov (1991); Norell, Clark, Chiappe, and

Dashzeveg (1995); Norell, Clark, Dashveg, Barsbold, Chiappe, Davidson, McKenna, Perle, and Novacek (1994); Osborn (1924*c*, 1924*d*); Osmólska (1976); Smith (1990, 1993).

PACHYCEPHALOSAURUS   Brown and Schlaikjer 1943—(=*Tylosteus* Leidy 1872 [*nomen oblitum*])

Ornithischia: Genasauria: Cerapoda: Marginocephalia: Pachycephalosauria: Pachycephalosauridae.

Name derivation: Greek *pachys* = "thick" + Greek kephale = "head" + Greek *sauros* = "lizard."

Type species: *P. wyomingensis* (Gilmore 1931).

Other species: [None.]

Occurrence: Lance Formation, Wyoming, Hell Creek Formation, South Dakota, Dinosaur Park Formation, Hell Creek Formation, Montana, United States.

Age: Late Cretaceous (Late Maastrichtian).

Known material: Nearly complete skull, at least three skull fragments.

Holotype: USNM 12031, nearly complete skull.

Diagnosis of genus (as for type species): Large pachycephalosaurid; skull with extremely thickened frontoparietal region, well-developed node-like ornamentation; snout proportionately long, narrow; supratemporal openings entirely closed; quadrate and squamosal fused by sutural contact (Sues and Galton 1987); also, parietosquamosal shelf very narrow or absent (Maryańska 1990).

Comments: *Pachycephalosaurus* is the largest and most derived of the so-called "bone-headed dinosaurs."

Remains now known to belong to *Pachycephalosaurus* were discovered more than seven decades before this genus was named. The first specimen found was a bone fragment (AMNH 8568) secured by Ferdinand Vandiveer Hayden in the "Black Foot country at the head of the Missouri River" (actually the Lance Formation of southeastern Montana.) Baird (1979) found that, on the handwritten label accompanying the specimen, Hayden had given only "Black Foot Country" as its source, Joseph Leidy having added "at the head of the Missouri River." Hayden had been collecting fossils in this region since 1853 and the *Tylosteus* specimen was donated to the Academy of Natural Sciences of Philadelphia in 1867. Utilizing this information as well as various historical data, Baird estimated the date of the fossil's discovery as 1859–60.

Leidy (1872) tentatively identified this specimen as part of the dermal armor of a giant saurian or an armadillo-like animal. Originally, Leidy described the

Photo by D. Baird, courtesy Academy of Natural Sciences of Philadelphia.

Pachycephalosaurus wyomingensis, ANSP 8568, holotype squamosal with node cluster of *Tylosteus ornatus*, three views.

Pachycephalosaurus wyomingensis, AMNH 1696, holotype skull of *P. grangeri*, left lateral view.

specimen as hemivoid, shape, approximately 5.2 centimeters (2 inches) in diameter, concave ventrally, convex dorsally, and covered above by some 15 large "mammillary bosses." He made the specimen the type of new genus and species *Tylosteus ornatus*. In a subsequent description, Leidy (1873) more favored a reptilian origin for this fossil.

(More than a century after it was named, Baird identified the holotype of *T. ornatus* as a squamosal node-cluster of *Pachycephalosaurus*. According to the International Code of Zoological nomenclature, the older name *Tylosteus* has priority over the better known *Pachycephalosaurus*. However, as Baird pointed out, the name *T. ornatus*, a *nomen dubium* based on undiagnostic material with a dubious geographic and stratigraphic source of origin, has not been in use for a half century. Baird 1979, 1983 advocated that *Tylosteus* be suppressed as a *nomen oblitum* in favor of *Pachycephalosaurus*. On December 16, 1985, the International Commission on Zoological Nomenclature ruled in favor of Baird's request. Also, Baird (1979) observed that the boss count on the squamosal is sometimes subjective on the part of the observer, and that the number varies between different *Pacycephalosaurus* individuals.)

Skull material similar to though much larger than that of the allied species, *Stegoceras validum*, was discovered in the 1930s in the Lance Formation of Niobrara County, Wyoming. Gilmore (1931) described this material, which included a cranial dome (USNM 12031), under new name *Troodon* [then *Troödon*] *wyomingensis*.

In 1940, William Winkley discovered a well-preserved, nearly complete skull (AMNH 1696) somewhat resembling that of *S. validum*, though of much larger size. The specimen, missing the lower jaw, was found in the Hell Creek Beds of the Lance Formation, at Powder Hill, north of Ekalaka, Carter County, Montana. Brown and Schlaikjer (1943) described the skull, erecting for it the new genus and species combination, *Pachycephalosaurus grangeri*. (The skull was displayed at the American Museum of Natural History.)

Other Lance Formation material referred to *Pachycephalosaurus* includes a frontoparietal region with attached parts of squamosals (CM 3180), from ?Wyoming, described by Gilmore (1936b), and a right squamosal (YPM 272) found near Lance Creek, Niobrara County, Wyoming.

Originally, Brown and Schlaikjer diagnosed the genus *Pachycephalosaurus* as follows: Moderately large form; skull with low, narrow face; frontoparietal region extremely thickened; node-like ornamentation strongly developed; supratemporal fenestrae entirely enclosed.

Brown and Schlaikjer diagnosed the type species, *P. grangeri*, as follows: Frontoparietal region greatly thickened and vaulted; frontals very deep and narrow at contact with nasals; absence of parietosquamosal shelf; increased extent of skull posterior to occipital condyle.

The holotype skull of *P. grangeris*, as described by Brown and Schlaikjer, measures 62 centimeters (almost 25 inches) in length. It possesses ornamen-

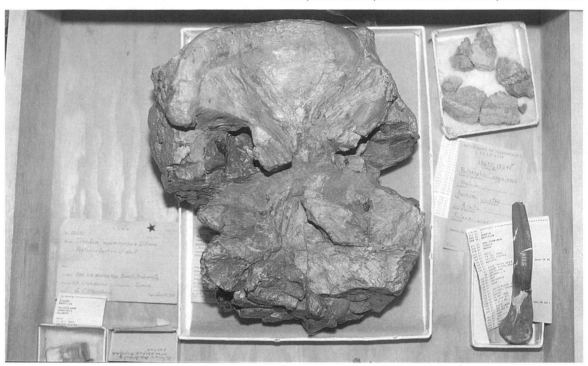

Pachycephalosaurus wyomingensis, USNM 12031, holotype cranial dome of *Troodon wyomingensis.*

tation in the form of bony spikes on the snout, ossifications that may have been utilized in digging up vegetation. The dome measures about 23 centimeters (9 inches) in thickness (see *Stegoceras* entry for possible functions of the pachycephalosaurian dome.)

Gilmore's "*T.*" *wyomingensis* was referred by Brown and Schlaikjer to *Pachycephalosaurus* as the new species *P. wyomingensus,* distinguished by them for the relatively broad and moderately vaulted frontoparietal region, and presence of a parietosquamosal shelf. Brown and Schlaikjer also described a third species, *P. reinheimeri,* based on a frontoparietal mass with attached nasal and squamosal portions (DMNH 469) from the Lance Formation, Corson County, South Dakota.

Various *Pachycephalosaurus* specimens were restudied by Galton (1971a), who concluded that their differences, once thought to have specific importance, may be attributed to sexual dimorphism. Galton suggested that the holotype of *P. grangeri* (with large dome and lack of parieto-squamosal shelf) could represent a male, those of *P. wyomingensis* and *P. reinheimeri* (with low dome and prominent parietosquamosal shelf) females.

In a review of North American pachycephalosaurids, Wall and Galton (1979) described remains of two undetermined species of *Pachycephalosaurus.* The first specimen consists of a dome (BMNH R8648) found in 1916 by Charles M. Sternberg in the Oldman Formation, south of Steveville Ferry, Red Deer River, Alberta. This dome is quite large, with a smooth and rounded dorsal surface. Wall and Galton noted that this is the only *Pachycephalosaurus* specimen not collected from the Lance Formation, which extends the occurrence of this genus to the lower Campanian. The second specimen, a large, very shallow dome (UW 6110), was collected from the Lance Formation of Converse County, Wyoming. This specimen could represent a juvenile *P. wyomingensis,* as well as a new species.

Galton and Sues (1983) rediagnosed the genus based on the holotype (USNM 12031) and referred specimens (AMNH 1696, DMNH 469, ANSP 8568, CM 3180, and YPM 272). Subsequently, Sues and Galton (1987), in their monograph on North American pachycephalosaurs, slightly emended their previous diagnosis of the genus (and type species *P. wyomingensis*).

The discovery by Galton and Sues (1983) of the sutural contact was based upon specimen YPM 272. As observed by Galton and Sues (1983), the squamosal tapers anteriorly and has smooth lateral and medial surfaces that were overlapped by the postorbital. The prominent sutural ridges, apparently for contact with the quadrate, cover the ventral edge of the squamosal. The quadrate was firmly sutured to the ventro-lateral edge of the squamosal, a connection only occurring in one other ornithischian group, the Nodosauridae (see Coombs 1978a). Galton and

Sues added that *Pachycephalosaurus* has the most extensively developed frontoparietal dome of all known pachycephalosaurids.

Investigations by Galton and Sues (1983) of various *Pachycephalosaurus* domes, supplemented in part by a morphometric study of the cranium of *Stegoceras* by Chapman, Galton, Sepkoski and Wall (1981), showed that the holotype of *P. grangeri* represents an adult male and that of *P. reinheimeri* an adult female. Sues and Galton found that the type specimen of *P. wyomingensis* probably represents a subadult male (*contra* Galton 1971*a*), based on the curvature of the dome and the relative small size of the parieto-squamosal shelf. Sues and Galton concluded that all species of *Pachycephalosaurus* are referable to *P. wyomingensis*.

A partial description of the anterior braincase and preliminary examination of change of dome shape with age in *P. wyomingensis* was offered by Giffin (1989*b*), based upon previously undescribed specimens. These specimens include an adult dome (USNM 264304), collected in 1967 by W. J. William from the Hell Creek Formation, and three juvenile domes (CCM 87-1, UCM 42763 and SDSM 54204). Giffin observed that the two morphs of dome shape, recognized in adults by Galton (1971a) and Galton and Sues (1983), are present also in juveniles, domes in juveniles measuring half the length of those in mature adults.

Brown and Schlaikjer originally assigned *Pachycephalosaurus* to the Troodontidae Gilmore 1924, a family that had been established upon the misunderstood taxon "*Troodon*," then embracing a comparatively rare group of ornithischians traditionally included within Ornithopoda. Brown and Schlaikjer did, however, suggest close affinities between pachycephalosaurs and ceratopsians, observing a close resemblance of the postcranial skeleton of *Stegoceras* to that of primitive ceratopsians such as *Protoceratops* (*i.e.,* ventral curve of ilium, alleged ridge-in-groove interzygapophyseal articulations of dorsal vertebrae, and form of vertebrae and ilium; see also Sues and Galton 1987).

Sternberg (1945) renamed this group Pachycephalosauridae, basing it upon the better understood genus *Pachycephalosaurus*. Later, Maryańska and Osmólska (1974) showed that pachycephalosaurids form a separate group distinct from Ornithopoda within Ornithischia, and proposed a list of characteristics that justified the erection of their own "suborder" Pachycephalosauria. According to Maryańska and Osmólska, Pachycephalosauria might also be regarded as an "infraorder" of Ornithopoda. Wall and Galton (1979) regarded pachycephalosaurs as a specialized side branch of the evolution of the Orni-

thopoda. Coombs (1979) noted certain similarities intimating that the Pachycephalosauria is the sistertaxon of Ankylosauria. Sereno (1986) regarded Pachycephalosauria as a valid taxon, adding a few more synapomorphies (including exclusion of premaxillae from margins of internares by maxillae) supporting its relationship as sister-group to the Ceratopsia.

Sues and Galton (1983) argued against earlier classifications that placed Pachycephalosauria within Ornithopoda or closely allied with the Ankylosauria, favoring a tentatively closer relationship between Pachycephalosauria and Ceratopsia, thereby excluding the Pachycephalosauria from Ornithopoda. Both the Pachycephalosauria and Ceratopsia first occur in the Lower Cretaceous, the dichotomy between them having taken place before the Cretaceous. Sereno observed that both groups share an asymmetrical enamel distribution on maxillary and dentary teeth, and (in the pelvis) an entirely open acetabulum and lateral protrusion of the ischiadic peduncle. As pointed out by Sues and Galton, these derived characters, observed by Sereno, are present neither in the primitive ornithischian *Fabrosaurus*, nor in Thyreophora.

Notes: A new large pachycephalosaur, possibly referable to *Pachycephalosaurus*, was discovered by Michael Triebold in the "Sandy Quarry" of the Hell Creek Formation, near Buffalo, South Dakota. The well-preserved, associated but scattered specimen includes a skull and partial postcranial skeleton missing all elements of the shoulder girdles, forelimbs, and hind feet (Russell 1995*b*).

Russell (1995*b*) briefly described this material as follows: Skull about 90 percent of length of type skull of *P. wyomingensis*, narrower than the latter, with

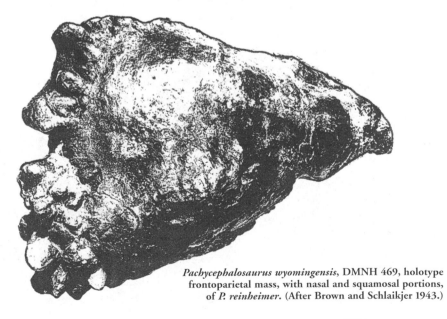

Pachycephalosaurus wyomingensis, DMNH 469, holotype frontoparietal mass, with nasal and squamosal portions, of *P. reinheimer*. (After Brown and Schlaikjer 1943.)

more acuminate cranial "horns"; skull relatively longer than in *S. validum*; at least 19 dentary teeth; atlas-axis articulates with longitudinal axis of skull at about 60-degree angle, as does base of neck with horizontal dorsal column; zygapophyseal facets of vertebrae planar in cervicals, crossed by four longitudinal ridges on dorsals; dorsolateral surfaces of ribs marked by "washboard" of low, irregular ridges; skeletal parts implying reconstructed axial length of 3.4 meters (about 11.5 feet) and height at hips of 1 meter (about 3.75 feet); femoral circumference suggesting weight of live animal to be 260 kilograms (almost 600 pounds); sacrum, ilium, and tibia relatively shorter than in *S. validum*.

If these remains are *Pachycephalosaurus*, they present a visualization of the animal somewhat contrary to earlier conceptions and one that makes the popular idea of head-butting seem unlikely (*i.e.,* body relatively small; head disproportionately large, possessing spikes that project straight back; neck oddly angled).

Key references: Baird (1979, 1983); Chapman , Galton, Sepkoski and Wall (1981); Coombs (1979); Galton (1971*a*); Galton and Sues (1983); Giffin (1989*b*); Gilmore (1931, 1936*b*); Leidy (1872); Maryańska (1990); Maryańska and Osmólska (1974); Russell (1995*b*); Sereno (1986); Sternberg (1945); Sues and Galton (1987); Wall and Galton (1979).

PACHYRHINOSAURUS Sternberg 1950

Ornithischia: Genasauria: Cerapoda: Marginocephalia: Ceratopsia: Neoceratopsia: Ceratopsidae: Centrosaurinae.

Name derivation: Greek *pachys* = "thick" + Greek *rhinos* = "nose" + Greek *sauros* = "lizard."

Type species: *P. canadensis* Sternberg 1950.

Other species: [Unnamed and undescribed.]

Occurrence: Horseshoe Canyon Formation, St. Mary River Formation, Waptiti Formations, Alberta, Canada; Alaska, United States.

Age: Late Cretaceous (Maastrichtian).

Pachycephalosaurus wyomingensis, **life restoration by Brian Franczak.**

Pachyrhinosaurus canadensis, NMC 8867, holotype incomplete skull, right lateral view.

Photo by R. A. Long and S. P. Welles (neg. #73/535-11), reproduced with permission of Canadian Museum of Nature, Ottawa, Canada.

Known material: At least twelve partial skulls, disarticulated cranial and postcranial remains, juvenile, subadult, and adult.

Holotype: NMC 8867, skull missing lower jaws, beak, part of crest.

Diagnosis of genus: Distinguished from all other centrosaurines by shared possession of two derived characters: large Process 2 on posterior parietal margin, and large, laterally directed horns on posterior parietal margin (Sampson 1995).

Comments: The most massive known centrosaurine and most derived ceratopsid, *Pachyrhinosaurus* was founded upon a laterally compressed, incomplete skull (NMC 8867), collected from a sandy clay of the Horseshoe Canyon Formation, at Little Bow River, Carmongay, Alberta, Canada. The anterior part of a second skull (NMC 8866), with right lower jaw, lacking the beak, was found approximately 300 yards away from the holotype. This second specimen, designated the paratype, was the first of the two to be noticed, having been reported sometime before 1945 by J. S. Stewart (Sternberg 1950).

On the basis of both skulls, Sternberg diagnosed the genus (and type species, *P. canadensis*) as follows: Skull large, rectangular, narrowing very rapidly anteriorly to beak; top of skull very broad, thick, flat, or superiorly concave; no horn cores, though broad, flat superior surface, probably was covered by chitinous sheath forming battering ram; vascular markings on exterior surface; sides of nasals coarsely striated; superior surface pitted, suggesting that bone was deposited rapidly; no antorbital fossae; orbits small, circular; frill short, thin, rounded; occipital condyle spherical, pointing downward; jaws short, massive, deep; teeth short, thick, roots partly bifurcated.

In reconstructing the skull, Sternberg estimated the length of the parietals, restoring the frill as rounded and short, with a smooth margin. The mouth was restored as opening only to the beginning of the tooth row. A pouch was shown in the cheek region to retain vegetation as it was shredded by the powerful jaws and fell outside the crushing surface.

Because of the specialized development of the skull, its massive size, and thickness of the nasal boss, Sternberg considered *Pachyrhinosaurus* to be an unusual development of the Late Cretaceous ceratopsians, proposing that it warranted its own family, the Pachyrhinosauridae. More recent evidence implies that *Pachyrhinosaurus* is perhaps not as unusual as Sternberg surmised. In fact, *Pachyrhinosaurus* seems to be rather closely related to the smaller *Centrosaurus*, having, as Sternberg observed, a similar though thinner and shorter squamosal.

Later, Langston (1977) showed that the frill of *Pachyrhinosaurus* did not have a smooth margin (*con-*

tra Sternberg), but, as in *Centrosaurus*, bore prominent spike-like projections.

The presence of a nasofrontal boss in lieu of a nasal horn is an unusual feature in *Pachyrhinosaurus*. Farlow and Dodson (1975) suggested that *Pachyrhinosaurus* utilized this boss in intraspecific shoving matches, as do many artiodactyls. Langston reinforced this idea by showing that the cranial bones in this genus are strongly fused together, an expected condition for such clashes. Currie (in preparation) postulated that the nasal boss may have alternatively functioned as the base of a huge, perhaps keratinized, epidermal horn (see Dodson and Currie 1990).

In 1987, new *Pachyrhinosaurus* material, including two and one half skulls and 278 bones, was collected at Pipestone Creek in southern Alberta under the supervision of Darren Tanke of the Royal Tyrrell Museum of Palaeontology. The animals represented at this site seem to have been victims of a flood (as were 10,000 caribou in Quebec during the early 1980s). The most amazing new feature observed in the Pipestone Creek material was that *Pachyrhinosaurus* bore from one to three straight unicorn-like horns on the middle of its frill.

Tanke (1988) observed that the Pipestone Creek specimens fall into four distinct size classes, ranging from "calf" to about rhinoceros-sized adults. Different skulls display a considerable degree of individual variation in size, shape, and ornamentation. In about half the individuals, the nasal boss has a concave lump, while the other half show a complementary, cup-shaped convex lump, these differences perhaps representing sexual dimorphism. The Pipestone Creek specimens may, according to Tanke, represent a new species of *Pachyrhinosaurus* (see also Sampson 1995).

Based upon more recent studies of this taxon, more, sometimes surprising information may come to light. For example, Sampson, Ryan and Tanke (in press), as well as Currie and colleagues (in preparation), will show that juvenile and subadults of this genus possessed nasal and brow horns that seemingly developed into rugose bosses during ontogeny.

Pachyrhinosaurus remains have also been found on the North Slope of Alaska (W. A. Clemens, personal communication to Dodson and Currie).

Key references: Dodson and Currie (1990); Farlow and Dodson (1975); Langston (1977); Sampson (1995); Sampson, Ryan and Tanke (in press); Sternberg (1950); Tanke (1988).

PACHYSAURISCUS   Kuhn 1959 [*nomen dubium*]—(=*Pachysaurus* Huene1908; = ?*Plateosaurus*)

Saurischia: Sauropodomorpha: Prosauropoda: Plateosauridae.

Name derivation: Greek *pachys* = "thick" + Greek *sauros* = "lizard" + *iscus* = "like."

Type species: *P. ajax* (Huene 1908) [*nomen dubium*].

Other species: *P. magnus* Huene 1908 [*nomen dubium*], *P. reinigeri* (Huene 1908) [*nomen dubium*], ?*P. giganteus* Huene 1932 [*nomen dubium*], *P. wetzelianus* Huene 1932 [*nomen dubium*].

Occurrence: Keuper of Wüstenroth, Württemberg, Germany.

Age: Late Triassic.

Known material: Various partial postcrania specimens.

Holotype: University of Tübingen collection, seventh-thirteenth cervical vertebrae, dorsal vertebrae, scapulacoracoid, humeri, radii, ulnae, part of manus, tibia, fibula, femur fragments.

Diagnosis of genus: [None published].

Comments: The genus now called *Pachysauriscus* was founded upon material originally named *Pachysaurus*.

Huene (1908) described postcranial material (University of Tübingen collection) from the Keuper of Wüstenroth, Löensteinn, Württemberg, Germany, as new genus and species *Pachysaurus ajax*.

P. ajax was described by Huene as follows: Cervical vertebrae robust, 13–14 centimeters (about 5–5.4 inches) in length, last cervical 14 centimeters long with centrum 10 centimeters (about 3.8 inches) high and 13 centimeters wide; dorsal centra divided above arch, 11 centimeters (about 4.4 inches) long, 8 to 12 centimeters (about 3.2 to 4.6 inches) high; first dorsal with ventral longitudinal keel, spine thickened at summit; scapula 55 centimeters (about 21 inches) long; forelimb and manus robust; radius and ulna about 30 centimeters (11.5 inches) long; metacarpal II 12 centimeters long; metacarpal V 5.5–6 centimeters (2.1 to 2.3 inches) long, very strongly constructed.

Huene named a second species, *P. magnus*, based on a humerus, fragmentary shoulder girdle, fragmentary forelimb, carpal, metacarpals, and third sacral vertebra, from the upper Keuper of Brandklinge, in Tübingen, Germany. This species was described by Huene as follows: Third sacral vertebra 11 centimeters (about 4.2 inches) long, centrum 13 centimeters high and spine 31 centimeters (about 12 inches) high; humerus 50 centimeters (over 19 inches) long, greatest proximal width 22 centimeters (about 8.3 inches); metacarpal I 9.5 centimeters (over 3.6 inches) long, 7 centimeters (about 2.7 inches) wide at proximal end; metacarpal II about 12 centimeters long, III 11 centimeters, IV 9.5 centimeters, V 6.5 centimeters (about 2.5 inches), proximal diameter 4 centimeters (about 1.55 inches); metacarpals curved, first most robust, second longest.

Later, Huene (1932) referred to *Pachysaurus* fossils previously described by him (1908) as *Plateosaurus reinigeri*. This material consists of incomplete postcranial remains including about three cervical vertebrae, 15 dorsals, three sacrals, some caudals, a humerus, femur, tibia, and some metatarsals, from the upper Keuper of Württemberg. Huene described this material as follows: Cervical vertebrae about 10 centimeters in length; dorsal vertebrae resembling those of *Plateosaurus*, 8.5 centimeters (about 3.3 inches) long, the last 9 centimeters (almost 3.5 inches); second sacral vertebra most robust, third weakest; first caudal vertebra shorter than dorsals, succeeding caudals about same length as dorsals, last caudal shorter; humerus 40 centimeters (over 15 inches) long, femur 63 centimeters (about 25 inches), tibia 51 centimeters (almost 20 inches); metatarsal I 13 centimeters long, II 20 centimeters (over 7.6 inches), V 10–12 centimeters (Huene 1932).

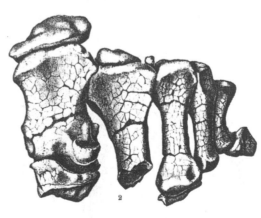

Pachysauriscus ajax, University of Tübingen collection, holotype 1. sacral vertebra (left lateral view), 2. metacarpals, 3. manual phalanx of *Pachysaurus ajax*. Scale = 2 cm. (After Huene 1908.)

Because the recurved teeth in this species were quite similar to those in "*Gresslyosaurus*" [=*Plateosaurus*], Huene (1926*a*) referred the material to that genus as *G. reinigeri*, at the same time abandoning the genus *Pachysaurus*. However, after examination of a skeleton collected from Tübingen from 1921–23, Huene (1932) noted the close relationship of the three "*Pachysaurus*" species and resurrected the name. At the same time Huene (1932) also named two new species, *P. wetzelianus* and ?*P. giganteus*.

The species *P. wetzelianus* was based on eight dorsal vertebrae, three sacrals, 13 articulated caudals, a pair of ribs, distal ends of left humerus, portion of left ilium, ischia, pubes, and almost complete left hindlimb, from the Knollenmergel of Trössingen. Huene (1932) described these remains as follows: Dorsal vertebrae dorsoventrally compressed, longest 15 centimeters (about 5.8 inches); caudal vertebrae

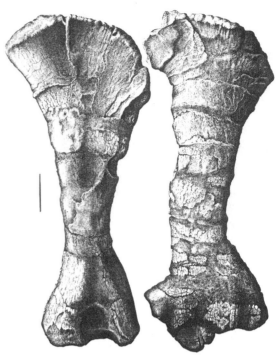

Pachysauriscus ajax, University of Tübingen collection, holotype left humerus (anterior view) and right scapula (lateral view) of *Pachysaurus ajax*. Scale = 4 cm. (After Huene 1908.)

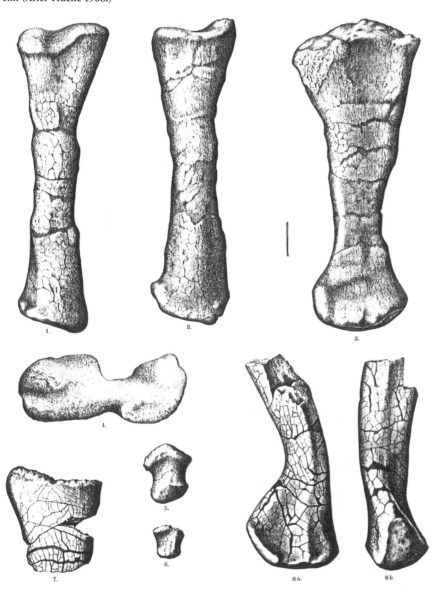

Pachysauriscus ajax, University of Tübingen collection, holotype 1. left radius (lateral view), 2. right radius (medial view), 3. left ulna (antero-lateral view), 4. distal end of left humerus, 5. right metacarpal V, 6. first phalanx of left pedal digit V (anerior view), 7. proximal end of left radius (medial view), 8. distal half of right ulna (a. anterior and b. lateral views) of *Pachysaurus ajax*. Scale = 2 cm. (After Huene 1908.)

approximately 11–10 centimeters long successively, most anterior caudals about 11 centimeters high and 16 centimeters (more than 6 inches) wide; preserved humerus portion resembling that of *P. ajax*; portion of ilium with small proacetabular process; ischia 56 centimeters (about 21 inches) long, concave posteriorly, distal ends thickened; pubes 72 centimeters (about 27 inches) long; femur very slender, strongly sigmoid, 98 centimeters (about 37 inches) long; tibia rather flattened, 79 centimeters (about 30 inches) long; fibula 80 centimeters (over 30 inches) in length, thin, slightly curved; metatarsals very slender, claw like that of *P. reinigeri*.

?*P. giganteus* was based on three (II–IV) long, slender metatarsal elements and an associated phalanx from Trössingen.

As the name *Pachysaurus* proved to be preoccupied (Fitzinger 1843), Kuhn (1959) later proposed the new generic name *Pachysauriscus* to receive the material.

Romer (1956) regarded Huene's *Pachysaurus* as synonymous with "*Gresslyosaurus*" [=*Plateosaurus*]; Lapparent (1955) and White (1973) listed it as a valid genus; some compilers (Olshevsky 1978, 1991, 1992) have regarded *Pachysauriscus* as a junior synonym of *Plateosaurus*. However, the material referred to *Pachysauriscus* is too poor to refer to any other taxon.

Key references: Huene (1908, 1926*a*, 1932).

PACHYSAURUS Huene 1908 [*nomen dubium*]— (Preoccupied, Fitzinger 1843; see *Pachysauriscus*.)

Name derivation: Greek *pachys* = "thick" + Greek *sauros* = "lizard."

Type species: *P. ajax* 1908 [*nomen dubium*].

PACHYSPONDYLUS Owen 1854 [*nomen dubium*]—(See *Massospondylus*.)

Name derivation: Greek *pachys* = "thick" + Greek *spondylos* = "vertebra."

Type species: *P. orpenii* Owen 1854 [*nomen dubium*].

PALAEOSAURISCUS Kuhn 1959 [*nomen dubium*]—(=*Palaeosaurus* Riley and Stutchbury 1836)

Saurischia: Sauropodomorpha: Prosauropoda: Plateosauridae.

Name derivation: Greek *palaios* = "ancient" + Greek *sauros* = "lizard" + *iscus* = "like."

Type species: *P. cylindrodon* (Riley and Stutchbury 1836) [*nomen dubium*].

Other species: [None.]

Occurrence: Dolomitic Conglomerate, Durdham Down, England.

Age: Late Triassic.

Known material: Tooth, associated fragmentary postcranial remains.

Holotype: Bristol Museum collection, tooth.

Diagnosis of genus: [None published.]

Comments: The genus now known as *Palaeosauriscus* was founded upon material originally named *Palaeosaurus*.

The new genus and species, *Palaeosaurus platyodon,* was named by Riley and Stutchbury (1836), founded upon a single worn tooth (Bristol Museum collection) recovered from the Dolomitic Conglomerate of Durdham Down, near Bristol, England. Associated with the tooth were fragments including parts of limb bones.

Riley and Stutchbury described this tooth as broadly lance-shaped and measuring 14 millimeters in length.

As the generic name *Palaeosaurus* was preoccupied (Saint-Hilaire 1833), Kuhn (1959) proposed the new name *Palaeosauriscus* for this material.

Notes: The skeleton (SMNS 12667-8) originally figured in the paleontological literature by Huene (1932) as *Thecodontosaurus diagnosticus*, but usually called *Palaeosaurus diagnosticus*, was renamed *Efraasia diagnostica* by Galton (1973), then later referred by Galton (1985d) to the genus *Sellosaurus*.

Palaeosaurus fraserianus Cope 1878 [*nomen dubium*] has been referred to *Anchisaurus polyzelus*. *P. platyodon* Riley and Stutchbury 1836 and *P. stricklandi* Davies 1881 are nondinosaurian (see Chure and McIntosh 1989).

Key references: Kuhn (1959); Riley and Stutchbury (1836).

PALAEOSAURUS Riley and Stutchbury 1836 [*nomen dubium*]—(Preoccupied, Geoffroy Saint-Hillaire 1831; see *Palaeosauriscus, Sellosaurus*.)

Name derivation: Greek *palaios* = "ancient" + Greek *sauros* = "lizard."

Type species: *P. platyodon* Riley and Stutchbury 1836 [*nomen dubium*].

PALAEOSCINCUS Leidy 1856 [*nomen dubium*]—(=?*Edmontonia*, =?*Panoplosaurus*.

Ornithischia: Thyreophora: Ankylosauria: Nodosauridae.

Name derivation: Greek *palaios* = "ancient" + greek *Scincus* = "[generic name for modern skinks]."

Type species: *P. costatus* Leidy 1856 [*nomen dubium*]

Other species: ?*P. latus* Marsh 1876 [*nomen dubium*].

Occurrence: Judith River Formation, Montana, United States; Dinosaur Park Formation, Alberta, Canada.

Age: Late Cretaceous (Campanian).

Known material: Teeth.

Holotype: ANSP collection, tooth.

Diagnosis for genus: [None published.]

Comments: *Palaeoscincus* (the oldest generic name for a North American ankylosaur) was founded upon a single tooth collected from Judith River [Oldman] Formation at Fort Benton, Montana.

Leidy (1856a) simply described this tooth as having poorly-developed fluting.

In a study of ankylosaurian teeth, Coombs (1990a) stated that the tooth of *P. costatus* is derived from either *Edmontonia longiceps, E. rugosidens*, or *Panoplosaurus mirus*, although no teeth were preserved in the type specimen of the latter species. Comparing *P. costatus* with both species of *Edmontonia*, Coombs found that the type tooth falls within the range of variation of *E. longiceps* and *E. rugosidens*, as well as being quite similar to Lower Cretaceous tooth specimens identified as *Sauropelta "edwardsi"* [=*edwardsorum*]. Unable to refer *P. costatus* to any other taxon, Coombs regarded it as a *nomen dubium*.

Although the type specimen of *P. costatus* is indeterminate, other species have been referred to *Palaeoscincus*: *P. latus* was based on teeth (YPM 4810)

Palaeosauriscus cylindrodon, Bristol Museum, holotype tooth of *Palaeosaurus cylindrodon,* a. lateral view (scale = 1 cm.), b. detail of edge. (After Riley and Stutchbury 1836.)

Palaeosauriscus cylindrodon, Bristol Museum, tooth fragment [originally referred to *Palaeosaurus cylindrodon*]. (After Riley and Stutchbury 1836.)

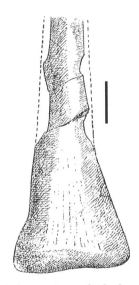

Palaeosauriscus cylindrodon, Bristol Museum, distal half of left femur [originally referred to *Palaeosaurus cylindrodon*]. Scale = 2 cm. (After Riley and Stutchbury 1836.)

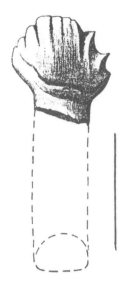

Palaeoscincus costatus, ANSP, holotype partial tooth. Scale = 1 cm. (After Brown 1908.)

with moderately-developed fluting, from the Lance Formation, Peterson's Quarry, Niobrara County, Wyoming, described by Marsh (1892*d*). Coombs regarded this taxon as a *nomen dubium*, noting that the tooth differs in some ways from all other ankylosaurian teeth associated with a skull and could belong to a pachycephalosaur.

Notes: *Palaeoscincus* has generally been depicted in life restorations, published in popular books, as an animal bearing armor plates, lateral spikes, and a clubbed tail. Such traditional illustrations were based on a partial skeleton (AMNH 5665) displayed at the American Museum of Natural History. Although photographs of this specimen have appeared in various technical and popular publications labeled *Palaeoscincus*, Carpenter (1990*a*) identified it as that of the better known nodosaurid *Edmontonia rugosidens*.

The species *P. magoder* [*nomen nudum*] was reported from Germany by E. Hennig (1915*a*) as stegosaurian. Coombs (1990*a*) noted that this taxon is probably a misprint, having appeared without formal description or designated type in a paper reviewing various dinosaur faunas.

Galton and Coombs (1981) referred *P. africanus* Broom 1910 [*nomen dubium*] to the stegosaur *Paranthodon africanus*; *P. asper* Lambe 1902 [*nomen dubium*] and *P. rugosus* Nopcsa 1918 [*sic*] have been referred to *Euoplocephalus tutus*; and *P. rugosidens* Gilmore 1930 was referred by Russell (1940*b*) to *Edmontonia rugosidens*.

Key references: Coombs (1978*a*, 1990*a*); Leidy (1856*a*); Marsh (1876*d*).

Photo by R. A. Long and S. P. Welles (neg. #73/270-11), courtesy Yale Peabody Museum of Natural History.

?Palaeoscincus latus, YPM 4810, holotype tooth.

Photo by R. A. Long and S. P. Welles (neg. #73/536-26), reproduced with permission of Canadian Museum of Nature, Ottawa, Canada.

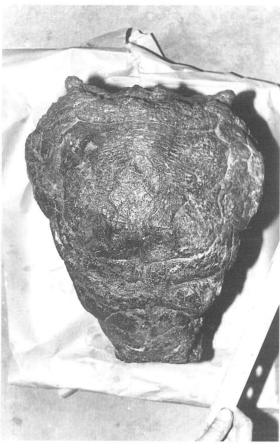

Panoplosaurus mirus, NMC 2759, holotype skull, dorsal view.

PANOPLOSAURUS Lambe 1919—

(=?*Palaeoscincus*)

Ornithischia: Genasauria: Thyreophora: Ankylosauria: Nodosauridae.

Name derivation: Greek *panoplo* = "armored" + Greek *sauros* = "lizard."

Type species: *P. mirus* Lambe 1919.

Other species: [None.]

Occurrence: Dinosaur Park Formation, Alberta, Canada.

Age: Late Cretaceous (Late Campanian).

Known material: Partial skeleton with complete skull, much armor, isolated teeth, postcranial elements, armor.

Holotype: NMC 2759, skull with jaws, atlas, axis, cervical and thoracic vertebrae, at least three cervical ribs, scapulacoracoid, humerus, ulna, radius, three manual digits (in proper relative position to each other), fragment of ilium, part of sacrum, phalanx, two pedal terminal phalanges, metatarsal, dermal armor consisting of about 200 scutes of various sizes (some in proper relative position), numerous ossicles.

Panoplosaurus mirus, life restoration by Brian Franczak.

Diagnosis of genus (as for type species): Skull with snout tapering in dorsal aspect; cranial armor of reniform or "lumpy" type; vomer swolle, grooved; neural pedicles tall, neural spines tall and slender; four coossified sacral vertebrae; scapula and coracoid coossified; ?three manual digits; medial cervical and anterior dorsal armor consisting of transverse bands of paired, low keeled plates, lateral armor a pair of high keeled elongated plates (Carpenter 1990).

Comments: The second ankylosaur to be described from the Oldman Formation [formerly Belly River Series] of Alberta, Canada, the genus *Panoplosaurus* was founded upon incomplete skeletal remains (NMC 2759), discovered in 1917 by Charles M. Sternberg on Red Deer River, Steveville Ferry, Alberta, Canada. About three feet of the vertebral column were found articulated to the skull (Lambe 1919).

Originally, Lambe diagnosed the genus (and type species, *P. mirus*) as follows: Skull depressed, broad posteriorly, ending narrowly and squarely anteriorly, completely enclosed in bony plates and scutes; superior plates of head large; cheek plates; nares lateroterminally located; orbits far back; teeth small; crown laterally compressed, moderately high, on subcylindrical root; transversely twinned, low keeled scutes forming longitudinal dorsal series on neck; main lateral scutes of neck and trunk keeled, arranged in longitudinal rows; scutes of ventral surface small; centra of cervical vertebrae slightly concave at ends; atlas, axis, and third cervical vertebra coossified.

Lambe identified three types of scutes distinctive of definite areas of the body: 1. Large plate-like scutes with a low keel, coossified in transverse pairs (arranged from head backward in longitudinal dorsal series); 2. smaller, various-sized scutes, strongly keeled, from broadly to narrowly suboval in outline, somewhat pointed behind, flat or rather excavated below (laterally on neck, continuing posteriorly on trunk); 3. moderately small, keeled scutes, with thick, swollen base (on throat, passing forward on midline towards chin); 4. small, rather irregular scutes, in close-set longitudinal rows, greater diameter fore and

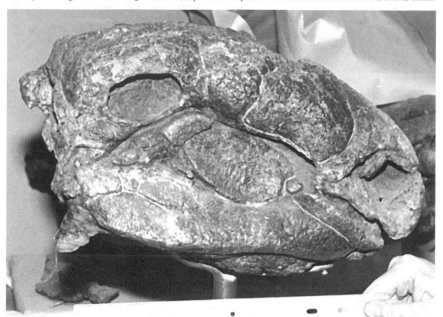

Panoplosaurus mirus, NMC 2759, holotype skull, right lateral view.

aft (latero-ventral position on trunk); 5. small scutes on polygonal outline (along ventral midline, grading outward into lateroventral ones on trunk); 6. rather small, thin, scutes without keels, suboval or subtriangular in shape, often irregular in outline, and thin, generally very small scutes of irregular, broadly suboval, or subcircular outline, with flat lower surface (all apparently from limbs); and 7. irregularly shaped ossicles that grade down to very small size (on neck, laterally on throat, and probably filling smallest interspaces between larger scutes).

Material (PU 21178) collected by Earl Douglass from Lake Basin, near Big Lake, in Stillwater County, near Columbus, Montana, was referred to *Panoplosaurus* sp. by Coombs, (1978a). The remains, described by Horner (1979), includes a robust ulna about 535 millimeters (over 20 inches) long, with maximum width of 186 millimeters (over 7 inches), and distal width of 108 millimeters (over 4 inches); an incomplete humerus, with maximum shaft diameter of 100 millimeters (about 3.8 inches) and deltopectoral width of 218 millimeters (almost 8 inches); and a fragmentary scapula.

Coombs (1978a) synonymized *Panoplosaurus* with *Edmontonia* but did not justify this synonymy. In a paper reviewing ankylosaurian systematics, Carpenter (1990) was of the opinion that both genera are distinct, their generic differences found in cranial armor, palate, vertebrae, ?manus, and body armor. Carpenter's reinstatement of *Panoplosaurus* as a valid genus separate from *Edmontonia* was accepted by Coombs (1990a) in his study of ankylosaurian teeth, and by Coombs and Maryańska (1990) in their review

of the Ankylosauria (wherein they submitted their own revised new diagnosis of *P. mirus*).

In a proposed revision of Upper Cretaceous nodosaurids, Bakker (1988) suggested that the Nodosauridae should be divided into two subfamilies, Panoplosaurinae Nopcsa 1928 and 1929 and Edmontoniinae Russell 1940.

At the same time, Bakker referred a skull (ROM 1215) from Dinosaur Provincial Park, in Alberta, originally described by Gilmore (1930) and later referred by Russell (1940b) to *Edmontonia rugosidens*, to a new species or subspecies of *Panoplosaurus*. (The ROM 1215 specimen comprises a disarticulated partial skeleton including skull with left lower jaw, atlas, axis, a few dorsal and caudal vertebrae, several cervical and dorsal ribs, right scapulacoracoid, ossified intersternal plate, pair of ossified xiphisternals, left ulna, three phalanges, more than 200 scutes, and 30 gastroliths.) Bakker regarded this skull as belonging to an unnamed new species, while Carpenter considered ROM 1215 to belong to *P. mirus*. Also, Carpenter referred to *Panoplosaurus* sp. an uncatalogued (OMNH collection) coossified scapulacoracoid, collected by J. Willis Stovall and Wann Langston, Jr., from the Aguja Formation, Big Bend region of Texas.

Key references: Bakker (1988); Carpenter (1990); Coombs (1978a, 1990a); Coombs and Maryańska (1990); Horner (1979); Lambe (1919); Russell (1940b).

PARANTHODON Nopcsa 1929
Ornithischia: Genasauria: Thyreophora:
  Stegosauria: Stegosauridae.
Name derivation: Greek *para* = "similar" + *Anthodon*.
Type species: *P. africanum* (Broom 1910).
Other species: [None.]
Occurrence: Kirkwood Formation, Cape Province,
  South Africa.
Age: Early Cretaceous (Middle Tithonian–Early
  Valanginian).
Known material/holotype: BMNH R47338,
  incomplete left mandible with teeth.

Diagnosis of genus (as for type species): Snout region characterized by uniquely long, broad, caudal process to premaxilla, maxillary teeth with very large cingulum, and prominent vertical ridges on tooth crown (Galton 1990b).

Comments: The genus *Paranthodon* was founded upon part of lower jaw (BMNH R47338), contained in counterparts of a split mass of matrix, discovered by W. G. Atherstone, and originally attributed to the pareiasaurid *Anthodon* by Owen (1876). The material was found in an unspecified horizon and locality in South Africa, Owen believing this to be a marine formation at Bushman's River.

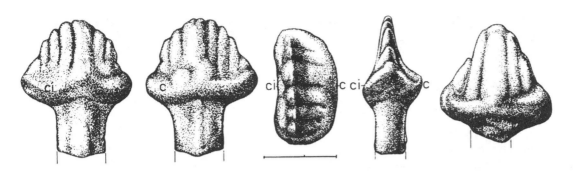

Paranthodon africanus, referred teeth BMNH R4992, from Kirkwood Formation (Lower Cretaceous) of Sunday River, Cape Province, South Africa; first four figures, ?left dentary tooth in lateral, dorsal, and posterior views; last, ?dentary tooth, lateral view. Scale = 10 cm. (After Galton and Coombs, 1981.)

Broom (1905) recognized that these teeth resemble those of dinosaurs and not pareiasaurs. Later, pointing out that Owen's specimen was geologically too late to be a pareiasaur, Broom (1912a) referred the specimen to *Palaeoscincus* as the type of a new species, *P. oweni*. Apparently unaware of Broom's transferral, Nopcsa (1929b) referred the same specimen to the Stegosauria, erecting for it the new genus and species combination, *Paranthodon oweni*.

Coombs (1978a) regarded *Paranthodon* as Ankylosauria *incertae sedis*, after which he (*see in* Olshevsky 1978) established the correct name as *Paranthodon africanus*. Later, Galton and Coombs (1981) removed *Paranthodon* from the Ankylosauria and referred it to the Stegosauria. At the same time, Galton and Coombs determined the correct horizon and locality for the type material as the Kirkwood Formation, Uitenhage Group (Lower Cretaceous, Necomanian; Berriasian or Valanginian), at Bushman's River, Algoa Basin, Cape Province.

Galton and Coombs observed a suite of similarities between the holotype of *P. africanus* and corresponding material in stegosaurs, especially in *Stegosaurus*: In both *Paranthodon* and *Stegosaurus*, the nostrils are entirely enclosed by premaxillae; posterior process of premaxilla is large, overlaps the nasal, and is overlapped by the maxilla; the maxilla has a small posterolateral extension which forms part of the bony secondary palate; nasals and maxillae are not overlain by fused dermal plates (they are in ankylosaurs); and the maxillary tooth row is in line with the lateral edge of the premaxilla (inset medially in ankylosaurs, premaxilla and maxilla forming a wide, almost horizontal shelf lateral to the tooth row).

Based on tooth morphology, Galton and Coombs found *Paranthodon* most similar to *Kentrosaurus*, one of the few stegosaurian forms in which tooth material is known. In both genera, the cingulum has bulbous and rounded vertical ridges. The possibility that these two forms are congeneric, as suggested by Hennig (1924), was discarded by Galton and Coombs, as ridges on the teeth in *Kentrosaurus* are of subequal size and do not curve toward the center as in *Paranthodon*.

Key references: Broom (1905, 1910, 1912a); Coombs (1978a); Galton (1990b); Galton and Coombs (1981); Hennig (1924); Nopcsa (1929b); Olshevsky (1978); Owen 1876).

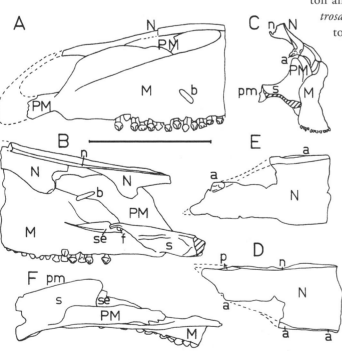

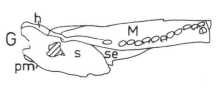

Paranthodon africanus, BMNH 47338, A. left premaxilla and anterior part of maxilla and nasal, lateral view; same as in A., B. medial and C. anterior views; D. anterior portion of left nasal, dorsal view; E. same as in D., ventral view; F. left premaxilla and anterior portion of maxilla, dorsal view; G. same as in F., ventral view; Scale = 3 cm. (After Galton and Coombs, 1981.)

PARARHABDODON   Casanovas-Cladellas, Santafé-Llopis and Isidoro-Llorens 1993
Ornithischia: Genasauria: Cerapoda: Ornithopoda: Iguanodontia *incertae sedis.*
Name derivation: Greek *para* = "similar" + "*Rhabdodon.*"
Type species: *P. isonense* Casanovas-Cladellas, Santafé-Llopis and Isidoro-Llorens 1993.
Other species: [None.]
Occurrence: Yacimiento, Sant Romá d'Abella, Spain, Europe.

Age: Late Cretaceous, Maastrichtian.
Known material: Partial postcranial remains, mostly vertebrae.
Holotype: IPS-SRA 15, almost complete vertebra.

Diagnosis of genus (as for type species): Humerus of medium height, shaft with pronounced curve; slightly slender; ratio of total length to shaft diameter = 6; slight development of distal condyles; ulna with pronounced curvature between proximal epiphysis and shaft; olecranon process anteroposteriorly extended, slightly elevated; proximal area much expanded, as much as transverse processes anteroposteriorly; anterior and middle cervical vertebrae strongly opisthocoelous, very gracile; centrum moderately long, with greatest diameter at apex; neural spine with two symmetrical processes directed anteroposteriorly and dorsoventrally (Casanovas-Cladellas, Santafé-Llopis and Isidoro-Llorens 1993).

Comments: The new type species *Pararhabdodon isonese* was founded upon an almost complete caudal vertebra (IPS-SRA 15), from the middle of the vertebral series, collected from blue-gray sandstone at Yacimiento, Sant Romá d'Abella, Conca de Tremp, Province of Lléida, Spain, this specimen originally referred by Casanovas, Santafé, Sanz and Buscalioni (1987) to the genus *Rhabdodon.* Paratype specimens include a nearly complete left humerus (IPS-SRA 15), proximal fragment of a left ulna (IPS-SRA 16), and an anterior cervical vertebra (IPS-SRA 18). Additional material referred to this species includes an almost complete vertebral centrum (IPS-SRA 7), centra fragments (IPS-SRA 7 and 12), and a dorsal centrum (IPS-SRA 13) (Casanovas-Cladellas *et al.,* 1993). Casanovas-Cladella *et al.* found the remains to be close to those of *Rhabdodon,* but morphologically distinct enough to warrant the erection of a new genus and species for their reception. From radiology and morphology data derived from specimens IPS-SRA 1 and 18, the authors speculated as to the position of these cervical vertebrae, locating them at the 4 to 8 level over a cervical spine of about 10 to 15 cervical vertebrae.

Key reference: Casanovas-Cladellas, Santafé-Llopis and Isidoro-Llorens (1993).

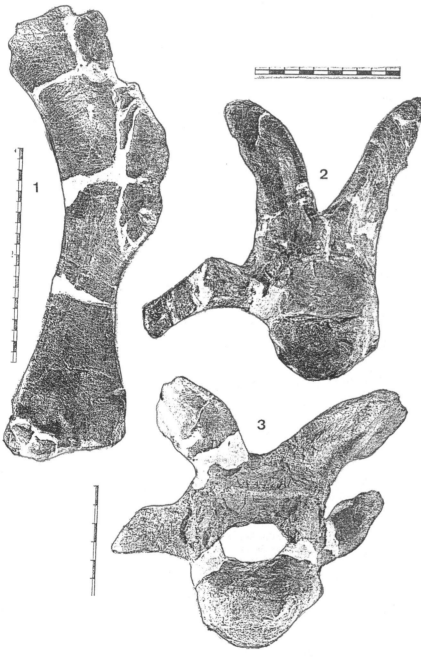

Pararhabdodon isonense, 1. paratype left humerus (IPS-SRA 15), 2. holotype cervical vertebra (IPS-SRA 1), and 3. paratype cervical vertebra (IPS SRA 18). Scale = centimeters. (After Casanovas-Cladellas, Santafe'-llopis and Isidoro-Llorens 1993).

PARASAUROLOPHUS   Parks 1922
Ornithischia: Genasauria: Cerapoda: Ornithopoda: Iguanodontia: Hadrosauridae: Lambeosaurinae.
Name derivation: Greek *para* = "similar" + "*Saurolophus.*"
Type species: *P. walkeri* Parks 1922.
Other species: *P. crytocristatus* Ostrom 1961, *P. tubicen* Wiman 1931.

Parasaurolophus walkeri,
ROM 768, holotype restored
skeleton.

Occurrence: Oldman Formation, Alberta, Canada; ?Hell Creek Formation, Montana, Kirtland Shale, Fruitland Formation, New Mexico, United States.

Age: Late Cretaceous (Late Campanian–Maastrichtian).

Known material: Complete skull and incomplete postcranial skeleton, disarticulated associated skull and postcrania belonging to at least three individuals, fragmentary skull with partial postcrania.

Holotype: ROM 768, skull, postcranial skeleton including trunk, forelimb, pelvis, femur.

Diagnosis of genus: Crest prolonged backward into elongated, curved, parallel-sided apparatus extending beyond rear margin of skull; two hollow parallel tubes within crest, running to posterior end, looping back again; premaxillae forming entire anterior profile of skull including crest; lower branch of premaxilla apparently very short, not transversely expanded; nasal apparently restricted to posterior two-thirds of crest on ventral or posterior portion; muzzle very short, dilated at anterior end; external nares far forward on muzzle; jugal and quadrate bones completely separated by quadratojugal; paroccipital process long; infratemporal fossa narrow for its length, nearly four times long as wide; lower margin of mandible sigmoid but not strongly deflected; edentulous portion of jaws relatively short; scapula very short but wide; forelimb short but relatively stout; spines of seventh and eighth dorsal vertebrae forming V-shape (?pathological) (Lull and Wright 1942).

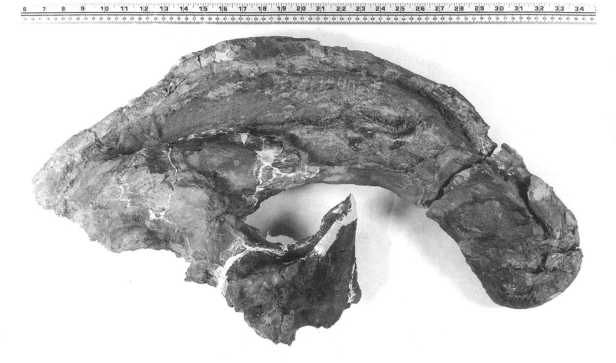

Parasaurolophus cyrtocristatus, FM P27393, holotype partial skull, including crest, left lateral view.

Diagnosis of *P. walkeri*: Posterior end of crest subquadrate in cross-section, anterior end with inferior keel; distal end of crest slightly dilated, with two deep pits; vascular impressions, if present, inconspicuous; ascending process of maxilla broad, contacts lacrimal; lacrimal large, subquadrate, completely excluding premaxilla from orbit; orbit a broad oval, larger than infratemporal fossa, the latter very narrow and longer than orbit; jugal broad, especially posteriorly, apparently excluded by large quadratojugal from contact with quadrate; maxilla massive, with broad ascending process for contact with lacrimal; endulous portion of maxilla short; 31 maxillary and 29 dentary teeth (Lull and Wright 1942).

Diagnosis of *P. tubicen*: Distinguished mostly by its crest, which tapers moreso at distal end than in *P. walkeri*, with acutely rounded terminus (Wiman 1931).

Diagnosis of *P. cyrtocristatus*: Distinguished mostly by form of crest, which is strongly curved downward behind occiput, about one third as long (260 millimeters) as in holotype of *P. walkeri*; postcranial skeleton very similar to that of type species, but with longer limb dimensions (Ostrom 1961*a*)

Comments: The most highly derived lambeosaurine, this rare genus, known from only a small number of specimens, was founded upon an incomplete skeleton (ROM 768; formerly GSC 4578), collected in 1920 by the University of Toronto, from the Oldman Formation (Campanian) [then Belly River Formation], below Sand Creek above Red Deer River, Alberta, Canada. The skeleton was found lying on its left side and was mounted showing the left side for display at the Royal Ontario Museum.

Parks (1922), believing that this form was related to *Saurolophus* because of the latter's superficially similar incipient crest, named the new genus *Parasaurolophus*. However, as later demonstrated by Lull and Wright (1942) in their classic review of North American "duckbilled" dinosaurs, the affinities of *Parasaurolophus* are clearly with such typical lambeosaurines as *Corythosaurus* and *Lambeosaurus*.

Originally, Parks diagnosed *Parasaurolophus* as follows: Body heavy, low-set; head with "very remarkable type of crest." Also, Parks reported the presence of fossilized skin impressions with the usual tuberculated structure, but none of the acorn-like elevations seen in other hadrosaurs, this implying that the skin might have been uniformly tuberculated over the entire body.

Comparing the type species, *P. walkeri*, to other lambeosaurids, Lull and Wright observed that the vertebrae in this species are virtually indistinguishable from those of *Corythosaurus*, although the fifth, sixth, and seventh dorsal spines are remarkably modified (?pathologic). The forelimb in *Parasaurolophus* is more robust than in *Corythosaurus* and *Lambeosaurus*. The manus is relatively shorter than in *Corythosaurus* and the pubis, as preserved, comparatively very short and deep. The skeleton of *Parasaurolophus* is quite

Parasaurolophus walkeri among Dawn Redwoods, the locale being the Oldman Formation during the dry season.

Illustration by Gregory S. Paul.

massive, especially in the shoulder and forelimb areas, suggesting that the animal was comfortable walking on all fours.

Two other species of *Parasaurolophus* have been described, based upon specimens that, along with the holotype of *P. walkeri*, comprise almost all of the known remains pertaining to this genus:

P. tubicen was based on several skull parts collected by Charles H. Sternberg in 1921 from the "Ojo Alamo Member" of the Fruitland Formation of Formation, San Juan County, New Mexico.

P. cyrtocristatus was based on a nearly complete skeleton and fragmentary skull (FM P27393), collected in 1923 from the Fruitland Formation (Early Maastrichtian), near Coal Creek southeast of Tsaya, McKinley County, New Mexico (Ostrom 1961*a*, 1963).

A specimen of *Parasaurolophus*, based upon the distal end of a crest (BYU 2467), collected from the lower third of the Kaiparowits Formation (Late Campanian, contemporary with Fruitland Formation, see Gregory and Moore 1931; see Gunithiominus, Lohrengel 1969, based on palynological evidence, contemporaneous with Lance or Hell Creek Formations, Lohrengel 1969), Garfield County, Utah, was described by Weishampel and Jensen (1979). The specimen is significant as the first generically determinate lambeosaurine from this formation and the first found between Alberta and New Mexico east of the Upper Cretaceous Cordilleran orogenic axis. As internal morphology of the material does not significantly differ from other specimens of this genus, Weishampel and Jensen referred it to *Parasaurolophus* sp.

Weishampel (1981) noted that, among all adult lambeosaurines, the greatest difference in the anatomy of nasal cavity is exhibited between *Parasaurolophus* and other genera. The elongated vestibulum nasi communicates directly with the common median chamber, there is no expanded common median chamber, and the external form of the crest directly reflects its internal anatomy. In other lam-

Courtesy the Field Museum (neg. #GEO-82353).

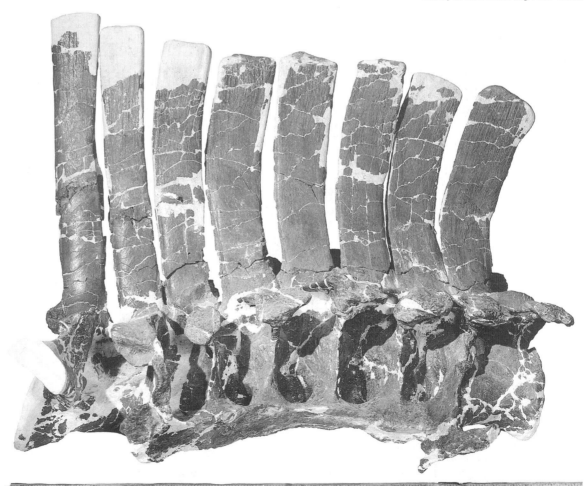

Parasaurolophus cyrtocristatus, FM P27393, holotype sacrum right lateral view.

Parasaurolophus cyrtocristatus, FM P27393, holotype incomplete skeleton, mounted without damage to the specimen, and so that individual bones can be removed for study.

beosaurines, the vestibulum nasi is relatively short, separated from the common median chamber by lateral diverticula, and the expanded common median chamber is topped by a solid "cock's comb."

The most striking feature of *Parasaurolophus* is the crest, the function of which has long been a source of speculation and controversy. Ostrom (1962*a*), in a study of cranial crests in hadrosaurs, detailed the evolution of theories concerning the possible functions of this crest:

Parks, when describing *P. walkeri*, argued that the crest, in life, was joined to the neural spines of the most anterior dorsal vertebra by a strong connection of ligaments or muscles, this attachment supposedly facilitating moving the head. Hence, many early and some recent life restorations of *Parasaurolophus* show a flare of tissue attached to the lower margin of the crest and to the neck. Parks made no mention of the crest being hollow. Ostrom (1962*a*), however, showed that Parks had built his hypothesis on the aberrant form of the sixth and seventh dorsal spines, a condition that seemed to be pathologic, and pointed out that no identifiable ligament or muscle scars are present on the crest of *P. walkeri*. Ostrom (1962*a*) also pointed out that hadrosaurids with much larger heads than *Parasaurolophus* required no such presumed leverage or supporting structures.

Abel (1924) suggested that the crest was a weapon used in intraspecific combat and may also have served an olfactory function. Nopcsa (1929) offered the unpopular theory that only male hadro-

saurs bore crests. Wiman (1931), noting the cavities within the crests, suggested that these hollows were used as resonating chambers for producing loud sounds.

Romer (1933), first in his book *Vertebrate Paleontology*, and later in some popular books about dinosaurs, suggested that the hollow crests had external narial openings to accommodate an aquatic life style, allowing the animal to breathe with the head submerged. As pointed out by Ostrom (1962*a*), however, no such terminal openings are present in *Parasaurolophus*, while those in other forms are seemingly due to incomplete ossifications at bone margins. Wilfarth (1947) suggested that the crest accommodated proboscis muscles, with air conducted down a flexible breathing tube and entering the supposed dorsal nares of the crest to reach, eventually, the mouth and trachea. Wilfarth suggested that this tube, comparable to an elephant's trunk, was prehensile and also utilized in feeding. Ostrom (1962*a*) countered this theory by pointing out that no muscle scars are present on any hadrosaur crests, that trunks in living animals are not used in snorkeling, and (see Sternberg 1939) that a trunk would hardly be functionally advantageous to an animal also equipped with an expanded beak.

Sternberg (1935) and Russell (1946) both believed that the crest served as a trapping device to keep water from entering the narial passages and lungs when the animal was submerged. Russell observed that the shape and curvature of the crest followed the path through which the head must have swung from an elevated to depressed position, thereby remaining in a vertical position regardless of the depth at which the animal was grubbing underwater for food. This implied that, in all positions of submersion, the crest would function at its optimum. Colbert (1945) and Romer expanded on this idea by interpreting the cavities of the crest as air storage chambers that let the animal breathe underwater.

Ostrom (1962a) discounted both of these theories, showing that the structure of the narial passages could not, even at shallow depths, have kept out water, and that the maximum amount of air trapped within the passages would have been inadequate as a reserve air supply. Ostrom (1962a) noted that the most detailed information concerning the possible function of hadrosaur crestal cavities is provided by the holotype of *P. cyrtocristatus*. The paired narial canals extend through the upper half of the crest for its full length, from the external nares to the caudal extremity. There the passages loop downward to the lower half of the crest, then pass forward to the skull roof, joining in a common cavity only at the base of the crest, just above and behind the orbits. Patches of organic material, probably cartilage, are present throughout the matrix of this unpaired chamber and probably represent the remnants of a septum that once divided it. Ostrom proposed that this chamber could have housed the olfactory chambers of the nasal capsule, and that the increased area in olfactory tissue would have served to heighten the dinosaur's

sense of smell. An acute olfactory sense would be an important survival adaptation in an animal lacking any defense weapons, alerting it of impending danger.

Later, Maryańska and Osmólska (1979) postulated that the crests may have housed salt glands which regulated the body's salt balance, a feature found in some modern reptiles.

More recently, other theories regarding the crest have been offered. Dodson (1975), after reviewing numerous lambeosaurine skulls, proposed that differences in crest size and shape could have had ontogenetic and sexual implications. Therefore, according to Dodson (see also Hopson 1975a), *P. walkeri*, with its longer, slightly curved crest, could be male, as can *P. tubicen*, while *P. cyrtocristatus*, with its smaller and more severely curving crest, may be female. Both *P. tubicen* and *P. cyrtocristatus* were considered by Dodson to be junior synonyms of *P. walkeri*. In their review of the Hadrosauridae, Weishampel and Horner (1990) listed both *P. tubicen* and *P. crytocristatus* as valid species.

An adult *Parasaurolophus* weighed approximately 2.47 metric tons (approximately 2.8 tons) (G. S. Paul, personal communication 1988).

Key references: Abel (1924); Colbert (1945); Dodson (1975); Hopson (1975a); Lull and Wright (1942); Maryańska and Osmólska (1979); Nopcsa (1929); Ostrom (1961, 1962a); Parks (1922); Romer (1933); Russell (1946); Sternberg (1935, 1939); Weishampel (1981); Weishampel and Jensen (1979); Wilfarth (1947); Wiman (1931).

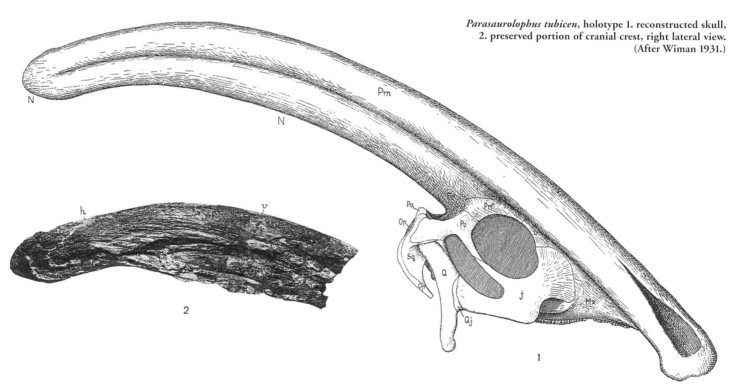

Parasaurolophus tubicen, holotype 1. reconstructed skull, 2. preserved portion of cranial crest, right lateral view. (After Wiman 1931.)

PARKSOSAURUS Sternberg 1937

Ornithischia: Genasauria: Cerapoda: Ornithopoda:
Hypsilophodontidae:

Name derivation: "[William] Parks" + Greek *sauros*
= "lizard."

Type species: *P. warreni* (Parks 1926).

Other species: [None.]

Occurrence: Horseshoe Canyon Formation,
Alberta, Canada.

Age: Late Cretaceous (Early Maastrichtian).

Known material/holotype: ROM 804, incomplete
skull, incomplete postcrania including sternal
ribs, ?sternal plate, scapula, supra-scapula, left
coracoid, left humerus, radius, ulna, sacral
fragments, left ilium, pubis, right ischium, entire
left leg missing two pedal phalanges, most caudal
vertebrae.

   Diagnosis of genus (as for type species): Premaxilla with very deep posterior process; extensive
sutural contact between maxilla and nasal; small oval
antorbital opening; squamosal transversely wide;
well-enamelled surface of cheek tooth with numerous low, rounded ridges (Galton 1995).

   Comments: The first North American hypsilophodont known from a specimen including the
skull, *Parksosaurus* was originally described as a new
species of *Thescelosaurus* by Parks (1926*a*), based on
a skeleton with skull (ROM 804), collected in 1922
from the Edmonton [now Horseshoe Canyon] Formation, near Red Deer River, Alberta, Canada.
Apparently the animal had fallen on its left side, the
head separated from the trunk before burial.

   Parks briefly "diagnosed" this species as follows:
Femur short; tibia long; toes long.

   Also, Parks reported the presence of numerous
broken ossified tendons found in the dorsal, sacral,
and caudal regions of the type specimen. These tendons can be roughly grouped into four bundles, with
a dorsal and ventral bundle on each side: The uppermost bundle of the ventral series arises from the sides
of the centra, passing obliquely down and back. The
bundle of the lower series connects with the chevrons.
The dorsal tendons connect anteriorly with the neural
arches and spines. The tail tendons "[rival] those of
the armoured dinosaurs." The ossifications are quite
even in size, averaging approximately 2 millimeters in
diameter, becoming smaller distally.

   Sternberg (1937), recognizing this material as
representing a new genus, renamed it *Parksosaurus*.
Later, Sternberg (1940*b*) reassigned *Parksosaurus* to
the Hypsilophodontidae, and pointed out that the
femur in this genus is shorter than the tibia, with the
fourth trochanter located above mid-length. (In
Thescelosaurus, the femur is longer than the tibia, the
fourth trochanter below mid-length.)

Parksosaurus warreni, ROM
804, holotype skull of
Thescelosaurus warreni, left
lateral view.

   Parks only described the left side of the skull of
the holotype. Galton (1973*a*), after extensive preparation of the right side, redescribed the skull and
mandible. With the new exposure, Galton recognized
certain cranial elements not described by Parks: The
posterior process of the premaxilla is deep; dorsal end
of the jugal seems expanded anteroposteriorly in a
way unknown in any other ornithopod; pattern of
ridging (lateral for maxillary and medial for dentary)
of the teeth, with low, rounded ridges, seems unique
among all known ornithopods.

   Key references: Galton (1973*a*, 1995); Parks
(1926*a*); Sternberg (1937, 1940*b*).

PARONYCHODON Cope 1876 [*nomen
   dubium*]—(=*Tripriodon, Zapsalis.*)

Saurischia: Theropoda: Tetanurae: Coelurosauria:
   Maniraptora: Dromaeosauridae *incertae sedis*.

Name derivation: Greek *para* = "near" + Greek *onyx*
   = "claw" + Greek *odous* = "tooth."

Type species: *P. lacustris* Cope 1876 [*nomen
   dubium*].

Other species: [None.]

Occurrence: Dinosaur Park Formation, Alberta,
   Canada; Dinosaur Park Formation, Montana,
   "Mesaverde" Formation, Lance Formation,
   Wyoming, Fruitland Formation, New Mexico,
   Laramie Formation, Colorado, Cedar Mountain
   Formation, Dakota Formation, Utah, United
   States.

Age: Late Cretaceous (Cenomanian=Maastrichtian).

Known material: Teeth.

Paronychodon lacustris,
AMNH 3018, holotype tooth.

Paronychodon lacustris,
AMNH 3953, holotype tooth of *Zapsalis abradens.*

Holotype: AMNH 3018, tooth.

Diagnosis of genus: [No modern diagnosis published.]

Comments: The genus *Paronychodon* was established on an incisor-like tooth recovered from the "Judith River" [=Dinosaur Park] Formation ["Fort Union beds"] at Fergus County, Montana.

Cope, who believed the teeth to be mammalian, (1876*a*), diagnosed the genus as follows: Teeth similar to those in some plesiosaurs, crowns subconic, enamel thrown into longitudinal ridges; side of crown convex, other side plane, cross-section semicircular; crown strongly curved.

The type species, *P. lacustris*, was diagnosed by Cope as follows: Anterior and posterior edges of tooth curved, neither acute nor denticulate; flat face with four plicae, two approaching apex; convex face with six keels approaching apex; apex very acute; carinae somewhat obtuse, enamel otherwise smooth.

As measured by Cope, the tooth is 13 millimeters long, anteroposterior diameter 4 millimeters, transverse diameter 2.4 millimeters, crown 10 millimeters in length.

Cope did not figure this material.

Two genera referred to *Paronychodon* were *Zapsalis* and *Tripriodon*: Type species *Zapsalis abradens* Cope 1876 [*nomen dubium*] was based on a worn tooth from the "Judith River" Formation at Fergus County. Estes (1964) regarded the specimen as pertaining to a large individual of *P. lacustris. Tripriodon caperatus* Marsh 1889 was established on teeth from the Laramie Formation of Colorado.

In their study of theropod teeth from the "Judith River" Formation, Currie, Rigby and Sloan (1990) suggested that, as most teeth called "*Paronychodon*" can be referred to other known genera, the name *P. lacustris* be restricted to nonserrate forms, which tend to be more common in Maastrichtian beds and might represent a distinct theropod taxon.

Key references: Cope (1876*a*); Currie, Rigby and Sloan (1990); Estes (1964).

PARROSAURUS Gilmore 1945—(See *Hypsibema*.)
Name derivation: "[Albert] Parr" + Greek *sauros* = "lizard."
Type species: *P. missouriensis* (Gilmore and Stewart 1945).

PATAGOSAURUS Bonaparte 1979
Saurischia: Sauropodomorpha: Sauropoda: Cetiosauridae: Cetiosaurinae.
Name derivation: "Patagonia" + Greek *sauros* = "lizard."

Type species: *P. fariasi* Bonaparte 1979.
Other species: [None.]
Occurrence: Cañodon Carnerro Formation, Chubut, Argentina.
Age: Middle Jurassic (Callovian).
Known material: About 12 skeletons with jaw elements, adult, juvenile.
Holotype: PVL 4170, postcrania including four anterior and three posterior cervical vertebrae, three anterior and five middle to posterior dorsal vertebrae, two dorsal centra, sacrum with five vertebrae, six proximal and series of 12 middle to distal caudal vertebrae, some hemal arches, right ilium, two incomplete ischia, right pubis, proximal portion of right scapula and coracoid, proximal portion of right humerus, right femur, fragments.

Diagnosis of genus (as for type species): Large cetiosaurid with high dorsal vertebrae; posterior dor-

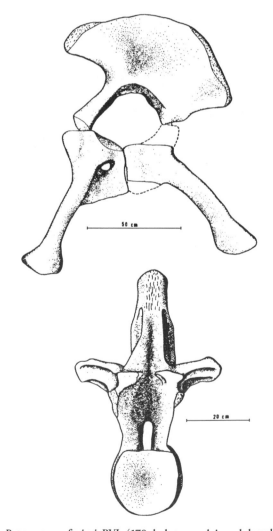

Patagosaurus fariasi, **PVL 4170, holotype pelvis and dorsal vertebra. (After Bonaparte 1979.)**

sals with high neural arches and well-developed spines; pleurocoels of dorsals dorsoventrally oriented as in *Barapasaurus*; anterior and lateral portion of neural arch similar to *Cetiosaurus* and *Barapasaurus*; sacrum with five vertebrae with high neural spines, large expansion of neural canal in second-fourth sacrals; pubis with distal and proximolateral expansions more developed than in *Barapasaurus*, similar though more extended than in *Amygdalodon*; ischium slightly compressed transversally with ventromedial ridge of sublamina type, distinct distal expansion; tibia-femur ratio 1:1.5 in juveniles, 1:1.7 in adults; mandible with weak torsion medially; teeth spatulate, indications of occlusion (Bonaparte 1986b).

Comments: The genus *Patagosaurus* was founded upon a postcranial skeleton (PVL 4170) collected from the Cañadon Asfalto Formation (Callovian) of Argentine Patagonia, South America. Paratype specimens include four neural arches of middle dorsal vertebrae, three dorsal centra, four sacral vertebrae, sacral centrum, three sacral neural arches, one proximal caudal centrum, six middle and posterior caudals, two incomplete neural spines, three hemal arches, six proximal portions of dorsal centra, ilium fragment, right pubis, and two ischia (MACN-CH 935); two cervical centra, anterior dorsal centrum, six neural arches and eight dorsal centra, sacral neural arch, three vertebral centra, two sacral vertebrae, scapula, coracoid, humerus, right radius and ulna, pubis, three metatarsals, two phalanges, and ungual (MACN-CH 932); and an incomplete left mandible,

two cervical centra, anterior dorsal centrum, four neural arches, three dorsal centra, sacral neural arch, pubis, fragment of ilium, femur, and right tibia (MACN-CH 933), from a juvenile individual. Other reported material from Cerro Cóndor, in Chubut, includes a left premaxilla, five articulated cervical vertebrae, two incomplete posterior cervicals, four dorsal vertebrae, anterior dorsal neural arch, dorsal centrum with partial neural arch, fragments of dorsal centra, 17 caudal vertebrae, incomplete right pubis, femur and right tibia (PVL 4076); three dorsal centra, scapula, left humerus, fragment of ischium, and left femur (PVL 4075); six incomplete caudal vertebrae, cervical centrum, scapula, coracoid, and ungual (PVL 4617); and maxillae, five dorsal neural arches, ilium, pubis, ischium, and various fragments (MACN-CH 934), from a juvenile (Bonaparte 1986c).

Originally, Bonaparte (1979) diagnosed *Patagosaurus* as follows: About same size as *Cetiosaurus leedsi*, similar in nonbifurcated cervical neural spines, shallow pleurocoels of dorsal vertebrae, and basic morphology of ilium and ischium.

Because of similarities in vertebrae, pubis, ischium, tarsus, and metacarpals to what is known of these elements in *Cetiosaurus*, Bonaparte (1986a) referred Patagosaurus to the Cetiosauridae. McIntosh (1990b) later placed *Patagosaurus* into the subfamily Cetiosaurinae.

Bonaparte (1980) stated that *Patagosaurus* is the most abundant dinosaurian species of the Cerro Cóndor Local Fauna, that it is a huge form with known

Patagosaurus fariasi, skeleton.

femora measuring as much as 52 centimeters (over 20 inches) in length, and that the few isolated teeth collected are similar to those of *Camarasaurus.*

Later, Bonaparte (1986*c*) completely described the postcranial skeleton of *P. fariasi,* and augmented his original diagnosis based upon the holotype and paratype specimens.

According to Bonaparte (1979), *Patagosaurus* is more derived than *Amygdalodon* in morphology of the vertebrae, but more primitive than *Haplocanthosaurus.* The occurrence of *Patagosaurus* (also the sauropod *Volkheimeria* and theropod *Piatnitzkysaurus*) is significant in providing the first record of a South American assemblage of sauropods and "carnosaurs" of pre–Morrison and Tendaguru age and in supporting the idea that, during the Jurassic, dinosaurs could travel between South America and other continents.

A skeleton of *P. fariasi* has been mounted at the Buenos Aires Museum.

Key references: Bonaparte (1979, 1986*b*, 1990); McIntosh (1990*b*).

PAWPAWSAURUS Lee 1996–(=?Texasetes)
Ornithischia: Genasauria: Thyreophora:
    Ankylosauria: Nodosauridae.
Name derivation: "Paw Paw [Formation]" + Greek *sauros* = "lizard."
Type species: *P. campbelli* Lee 1996.
Other species: [None.]
Occurrence: Paw Paw Formation, Texas, United States.
Age: Late Cretaceous (Late Albian).
Known material: Skull; ?also partial skeleton and postcranial elements, adult and baby.
Holotype: SMU 73202, almost complete skull.
Diagnosis of genus (as for type species): Prevomers having rostral U-shaped ridge that opens pos-

Illustration by Doug Henderson. From *Dinosaurs: A Global View,* by Czerkas and Czerkas, published by Dragon's World Ltd. and its co-edition publishers.

Patagosaurus fariasi group, Middle Jurassic, Argentina.

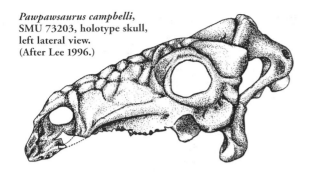

Pawpawsaurus campbelli,
SMU 73203, holotype skull,
left lateral view.
(After Lee 1996.)

teriorly; oval prevomer foramen; lack of sagittal septum (Lee 1996).

Comments: The genus *Pawpawsaurus* was founded upon an isolated skull (SMU 73203) without lower jaws, discovered in 1992 by Cameron Campbell in marine sediments of the Paw Paw Formation (Late Albian), near the top of the Washita Group, in Tarrant County, Texas. The type specimen (originally housed at the Fort Worth Museum of Science and History; see Jacobs 1995) was found on a shallow bottom in a palate-down position, most of its teeth missing, with bony eyelids (the first ever found in a nodosaurid), that were apparently attached to the orbits by ligaments, found nearby. The skull was missing the left paroccipital process and premaxillary bones, these elements subsequently having been found by Robert Reid and John Maurice (Lee 1996).

As measured by Lee, the holotype skull of *P. campbelli* is 250 millimeters (about 9.8 inches) long and 200 millimeters (about 6.8 inches) wide.

Mostly postcranial material from the same formation includes a scapulacoracoid (SMU 73494), humerus and ilia (SMU 73057), a baby (SMU 72444, described by Jacobs, Winkler, Murry and Maurice 1994), and most of a skeleton (USNM 337987, the holotype of Texasetes; see entry), with skull fragments and isolated teeth. According to Lee, although all of these remains apparently belong to a single taxon (and could belong to *Pawpawsaurus*), none can unambiguously be related to the same taxon as SMU 73203 and should, therefore, be regarded as nodosaurid indet.

Lee observed scratch marks on the condyle of the right quadrate and on the anterior end of a humerus, suggesting scavenging, perhaps by sharks and crabs (remains of which are abundant at this site). Oysters apparently made their homes inside the defleshed skull roof and other bones, as oyster remains, small fish teeth, and crab fragments were found filling the matrix of the skull.

In describing the holotype skull of *P. campbelli*, Lee observed features that permitted a revised diagnosis for the cranium of the Nodosauridae, including the following synapomorphies: Palate hourglass-shaped; occipital condyle hemispherical, composed of basioccipital only, set off from braincase on a short neck and angled about 50 degrees downward from line of maxillary tooth row; quadrate angled rostroventrally (Coombs and Maryańska); prominent W-shaped basioccipital tubera; quadrate anteriorly concave, anteroposteriorly flattened; posterior margin of pterygoid transversely continuous and straight, aligned with quadrate shaft. (Lee stated that these synapomorphies are closely related to the downward orientation of the nodosaurid head in life.)

According to Lee, *Pawpawsaurus* may have the most primitive nodosaurid skull, possessing an incomplete septum and no secondary palate (the derived respiratory structure in nodosaurids resulting from the progressive development of the sagittal septum and secondary palate).

In fact, *Pawpawsaurus* seems to be more primitive than the geologically older *Sauropelta*, a nodosaurid from the Cloverly Formation (Late Aptian–Albian) of Montana and Wyoming. However, as Lee pointed out, a progressive incursion of the northern and southern arms of the Western Interior Seaway (Kauffman 1984) occurred during Late Albian times, after which a biogeographic barrier (Winkler, Murry and Jacobs 1989) was established by this seaway during deposition of the Washita Group. *Pawpawsaurus* may be part of an endemic fauna cut off from the Rocky Mountains by that seaway during the Albian.

Key reference: Jacobs (1995); Jacobs, Winkler, Murry and Maurice (1994); Lee (1996).

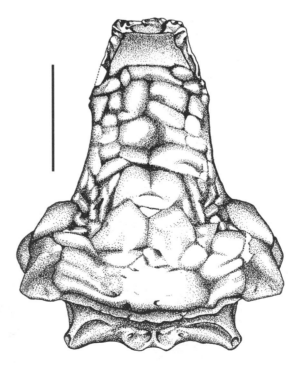

Pawpawsaurus campbelli,
SMU 73203, holotype skull,
dorsal view. Scale = 10 cm.
(After Lee 1996.)

PECTINODON Carpenter 1982—(See *Troodon* Leidy 1856.)

Name derivation: Latin *pectin* = "comb" + Greek *odous* = "tooth."

Type species: *P. bakkeri* Carpenter 1982.

Peishansaurus philemys, holotype (?juvenile), a. lower jaw fragment, b. tooth from same fragment. Scale = 1 cm. (After Bohlin 1953.)

PEISHANSAURUS Bohlin 1953 [*nomen dubium*]

Ornithischia: Thyreophora: ?Ankylosauria: ?Ankylosauridae.

Name derivation: "[Mount] Peishan" + Greek *sauros* = "lizard."

Type species: *P. philemys* Bohlin 1953 [*nomen dubium*].

Other species: [None.]

Occurrence: Minhe Formation, Gansu, People's Republic of China.

Age: Late Cretaceous.

Known material/holotype: IVPP collection (destroyed), anterior end of right lower jaw with tooth, ?juvenile.

Diagnosis of genus: [No modern diagnosis published].

Comments: The genus *Peishansaurus* was established on a fragmentary jaw collected from the Upper Cretaceous of Ehr-Chia-Wu-Tung, West Kansu [now Gansu], China (Bohlin 1953). (The type specimen has "disintegrated"; IVPP, personal communication circa 1976 to W. P. Coombs, Jr.)

Bohlin diagnosed the monotypic *P. philemys* as follows: Jaw strongly curved toward symphysis; narrow surface below alveolar bar faces somewhat upwards on outer surface, much broader lower surface facing downwards and outwards at obtuse angles to that surface; (sufficiently exposed) tooth showing thick, well-defined median ridge, swollen at base, tapering upwards, probably ending in pointed denticle; two anterior and three posterior denticles, two of latter larger, one smaller.

Bohlin noted that the teeth resemble those in the American genus *Ankylosaurus,* but markedly differ in both the number of denticles and the relative size of the main rib. As the five large alveoli of the jaw are out of proportion to their small teeth, Bohlin deduced that the specimen belonged to a very young individual (see Brown and Schlaikjer 1940). Coombs (1971), however, was of the opinion that the jaw may not belong to a juvenile.

According to Coombs and Maryańska (1990) in their review of the Ankylosauria, *P. philemys* is doubtfully ankylosaurian.

Key references: Bohlin (1953); Coombs (1971); Coombs and Maryańska (1990).

Pekinosaurus olseni, YPM 8545, holotype tooth, lingual view. Scale = 1 mm. (After Hunt and Lucas 1994.)

PEKINOSAURUS Hunt and Lucas 1994

Ornithischia *insertae sedis.*

Name derivation: "Pekin [North Carolina; also Pekin Formation]" + Greek *sauros* = "lizard."

Type species: *P. olseni* Hunt and Lucas 1994.

Other species: [None.]

Occurrence: Pekin Formation, North Carolina, United States.

Age: Late Triassic (Upper Carnian).

Known material: Teeth.

Holotype: YPM 8545, dentary/maxillary tooth.

Diagnosis of genus (as for type species): Ornithischian distinguished by very wide and low dentary/maxillary teeth (basal-crown height/length ratio more than 5/5.8 [measured in millimeters]), with no cingulum and relatively short, broad premaxillary teeth (basal-crown width/height ratio more than 2.6/4.0) (Hunt and Lucas 1994).

Comments: The new genus *Pekinosaurus* was founded upon a dentary/maxillary tooth (YPM 8545), collected from rocks in the Pekin Formation (Upper Triassic), east of Pekin, North Carolina. Referred remains from the same locality include a dentary/maxillary tooth and two premaxillary teeth (also catalogued as YPM 8545) (Hunt and Lucas 1994).

As pointed out by Hunt and Lucas, the rocks from which these teeth were recovered, often considered to be of Middle Carnian age, are more likely Late Carnian, based on the presence of the Late Carnian stagonolepidid reptile *Longosuchus* (see Hunt and Lucas 1990).

Key reference: Hunt and Lucas (1984).

PELECANIMIMUS Pérez-Moreno, Sanz, Buscalioni, Moratalla, Ortega and Rasskin-Gutman 1994

Saurischia: Theropoda: Tetanurae: Avetheropoda: Coelurosauria; Maniraptora: Arctometatarsalia: Bullatosauria: Ornithomimosauria *incertae sedis.*

Name derivation: Latin *pelecanus* = "pelican" + Greek *mimos* = "mimic."

Type species: *P. polyodon* Pérez-Moreno, Sanz, Buscalloni, Moratalla, Ortega and Rasskin-Gutman 1994

Other species: [None.]

Occurrence: Calizas de La Huerguina Formation, Cuenca Province, Spain, Europe.

Age: Early Cretaceous (Upper Hauterivian–Lower Barremian).

Known material/holotype: LH 7777, anterior half of skeleton, articulated, including skull, complete cervical and almost complete dorsal vertebral series, ribs, pectoral girdle, sternum, right and almost complete left forelimbs.

Diagnosis of genus (as for type species): Small (2-2,5 meters in length); skull with long, shallow snout (maximum length approximately 4.5 times maximum height); about 220 teeth (7 premaxillary, about 30 maxillary, and about 75 dentary); heterodont; maxillary teeth larger than dentary teeth; teeth unserrated, with constriction between crown and root; no complete interdental plates; maxilla with teeth only in its anterior third, sharp edge in posterior zone; rostral half of lower jaw with straight ventral edge; ulna and radius tightly adhered distally; metacarpal ratio 0.81:1:0.98 Pérez-Moreno, Sanz, Buscalioni, Moratalla, Ortega and Rasskin-Gutman (1994).

As observed by Pérez-Moreno et al., one of the most striking features of the holotype of type species P. polyodon is the dentition, teeth previously reported in otherwise toothless ornithomimosaurs only in the Asian genus Harpymimus (see entry). In fact, Pelecanimimus is unique among known theropods, in having the highest tooth count (about 220) and having maxillary teeth located only in the anterior third of the maxilla, with a sharp edge in the posterior zone.

The authors noted that the morphology of the teeth of this genus is surprisingly similar to those of members of the Troodontidae (including Sinornithoides; see entry), having a basal constriction in the crown and no interdental plates, this suggesting a relationship between the Troodontidae and Ornithomimosauria. However, unlike the teeth of troodontids, those of Pelecanimimus are not serrated.

As described by Pérez-Moreno et al., the teeth in Pelecanimimus have enamel; premaxillary tooth crowns are incisiform and D-shape in cross-section; anterior maxillary teeth are similar to premaxillary teeth, gradually becoming blade-like towards the posterior zone, with mesial and distal carinae; dentary teeth are smaller than upper-jaw teeth (as in troodontids); and anterior teeth have bulky crowns which become smaller and more slender posteriorly.

Pérez-Moreno et al. observed another feature in the type specimen unique to all known ornithomimosaurs—a small prominence, formed by the dorsal part of the lacrimal, over the level of the prefrontal, resembling that in Allosaurus (see entry). The authors pointed out that the hyoid apparatus, preserved in LH 7777 (but rarely in dinosaur specimens), is one-third the length of the skull, V-shaped, with a rostrally directed apex.

In describing the manus, the authors noted a feature unexpected in a primitive ornithomimosaur. As in most derived ornithomimosaurs, its three digits are subequal in length and almost parallel, the hand possibly functioning like a hook (as in Gallimimus and Ornithomimus).

Also, Pérez-Moreno et al. described preserved impressions, probably corresponding to integumentary structures, running below the neck and around the right humerus and elbow, made up of a primary system of subparallel fibres arranged perpendicular to the surface of the bone, and a less conspicuous secondary system which runs parallel to it. Another preserved impression, according to the authors, may correspond to a soft occipital crest.

Generally, the evolution from toothed to the more common toothless condition in ornithomimosaurs has been explained as a probable gradual reduction in number of teeth (see Osmólska and Barsbold 1990). However, Pérez-Moreno et al. postulated that the unusual features of LH 7777 may suggest an alternative evolutionary scenario, possibly based on a functional analysis of increasing numbers of teeth. According to Pérez-Moreno et al., a high number of teeth, with sufficient interdental space and properly placed denticles, would be an adaptation for cutting and ripping (as in troodontids), while a high number with no interdental plates would be a functional counterpart to a beak's cutting edge. In Pelecanimimus, having an increased number of teeth with the spaces between them filled by more teeth, the working effect would be that of a beak. Therefore, the adaptation to a cut-and-rip function gradually evolves to one with a slicing effect and, finally, to the cutting edge common to most ornithomimosaurs. According to Pérez-Moreno et al., the posterior-anterior replacement of teeth by a cutting border on the maxilla of Pelecanimimus illustrates this tendency.

Key references: Osmólska and Barsbold (1990); Pérez-Moreno, Sanz, Buscalioni, Moratalla, Ortega and Rasskin-Gutman (1994).

PELOROSAURUS Mantell 1850 [*nomen dubium*]—(=*Dinodocus, Ornithopsis*; =?*Brachiosaurus*, ?*Ischyrosaurus*, ?*Morinosaurus*, ?*Oplosaurus*)

Saurischia: Sauropodomorpha: Sauropoda: Brachiosauridae.

Name derivation: Greek *pelorious* = "monstrous" + Greek *sauros* = "lizard."

Type species: *P. conybearei* (Melville 1849).

Other species: *P. humerocristatus* (Hulke 1874) [*nomen dubium*], *P. mackesoni* (Owen 1884).

Occurrence: Wealden, Isle of Wight, Sussex, East Sussex, Kent, England; upper Lusitanian, Ourém, Fevenca, Portugal.

Age: Early Cretaceous (Valanginian–Hauterivian–Barremian–Aptian).

Known material: Humerus, caudal vertebrae, pelvis, isolated dorsal vertebrae, other partial remains.

Holotype: BMNH R28626, right humerus.

Diagnosis of genus: [None published.]

Comments: *Pelorosaurus* is historically important as one of the first sauropods to be described from Great Britain; also, discovery of this dinosaur documented the occurrence of the Brachiosauridae in the Lower Cretaceous (Wealden) of England.

Melville (1849) originally described a right humerus (BMNH R28626), lacking the deltoid crest, discovered in 1847 by Peter Fuller in the Wealden sandstone of Tilgate Forest, Cuckfield, Sussex, England, identified as belonging to a new species of *Cetiosaurus*, which he named *C. conybearei*.

The specimen had been in the possession of Gideon Mantell. After Mantell died, the bone was purchased by the British Museum (Natural History) [now Natural History Museum, London]. It was transported to the museum along with some large vertebrae, most of them from the caudal region. Owen (1875), observing that these vertebrae resembled the humerus in color and mineralized condition, also noted that they had been labeled as *Pelorosaurus conybearei* by Mantell, representing a new genus. Owen agreed with Mantell's opinion that the humerus and vertebrae belonged to the same genus and species. According to McIntosh (1990*b*) in his review of the Sauropoda, there is no reason to doubt that these elements belong to the same species, possibly the same individual.

Owen originally described this material as follows: Humerus hollow, somewhat resembling right humerus in crocodiles and alligators; more than 1.3 meters (4.5 feet) in length; proximal end transversely oblong, moderately convex; upper half of posterior portion slightly concave longitudinally; anterior caudal vertebra resembling in proportion that of *Cetiosaurus*, neural spines much longer, neural canal more contracted.

Second species *P. humerocristatus* was based upon a large humerus (BMNH 44635) recovered from the upper Lusitanian of Ourém and Fervenca, Portugal. Originally referred to *Cetiosaurus* as *C. humero-cristatus* Hulke 1874 [*nomen dubium*], this material marked the presence of large sauropods in the area during the Late Jurassic. Huene (1932) referred to this species *Caulodon praecursor* [*nomen dubium*], based on teeth (originally described as *Iguanodon praecursor* by Sauvage 1876) from the Upper Jurassic (Kimmeridge) of France (see *Neosodon* entry).

Other taxa founded upon meager remains collected during the early days of dinosaur research are now generally regarded as junior synonyms of *Peloro-*

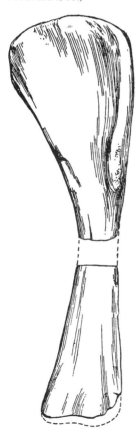

Pelorosaurus mackesoni, BMNH 14695, holotype incomplete humerus of *Dinodocus mackesoni*. (After Woodward 1908.)

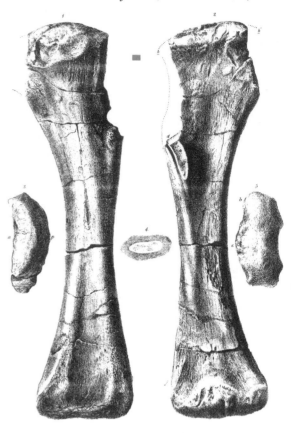

Pelorosaurus conybearei, BMNH R28626, holotype right femur of *Cetiosaurus conybeari*. (After Mantell 1850.)

saurus (see Huene 1932; Lapparent 1955; Romer 1966; Olshevsky 1978, 1991, 1992):

The type species *Ornithopsis hulkei* was founded upon two specimens (BMNH collection)—an imperfectly preserved dorsal centrum collected from the Wealden of Cuckfield, Tilgate, Sussex, England, and an imperfect anterior dorsal vertebra, discovered at an unspecified site in southeastern England (probably the Isle of Wight). This material was described (but not illustrated) by Seeley (1870), who likened the vertebrae to those of pterosaurs and birds, adding that they probably "manifest some affinity with the Dinosaurs." These vertebrae measure, respectively, 23 centimeters (9 inches) and 36 centimeters (14 inches) in length.

Later, Owen (1875) designated these specimens to be holotypes of two new species of *Bothriospondylus*, the first named *B. elongatus*, the second *B. magnus*. Owen (1876) subsequently referred the second specimen (BMNH R28632) to new species *Chondosteosaurus magnus*, after which Hulke (1882) referred it to the second species (see below) established for *Ornithopsis*, *O. eucamerotus*. Later, Lydekker (1888*a*), on verbal authority of Seeley, designated this second specimen to be the type specimen of

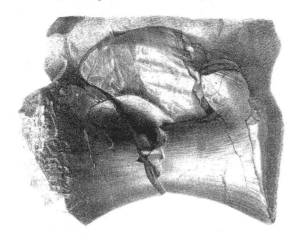

Pelorosaurus conybearei, BMNH collection, holotype dorsal vertebra of *Ornithopsis hulke*. (After Seeley 1870.)

Pelorosaurus humerocristatus, BMNH 44635, holotype humerus of *Cetiosaurus humero-cristatus*. (After Hulke 1874.)

O. hulkei. Both *B. elongatus* and *B. magnus* are sometimes listed (Olshevsky 1978; 1991; 1992) as junior synonyms of *P. conybearei*; however, *B. elongatus* and *B. magnus* are not conspecific, the former having been referred by McIntosh to *P. conybearei*.

?*O. eucamerotus* Hulke 1882 [*nomen dubium*] was based on two ischia and a pubis (BMNH R97) from the Isle of Wight. Though sometimes listed as a junior synonym of *C. gigas* (Olshevsky 1978, 1991, 1992), the only "evidence" supporting this synonymy, according to McIntosh, is that both are Wealden species.

?*O. greppini*, the third species referred to *Ornithopsis*, was based on caudal vertebrae, presacral

vertebral fragments, imperfectly-preserved pelvic elements, and limb bones representing at least two individuals, from the Kimmeridgian of Moutier, Savoy. As described by Huene (1922), these remains belong to a relatively small form, the femur measuring 70 centimeters (about 27 inches) long, the humerus about 60 centimeters (23 inches). Huene (1927) referred this material to the genus *Cetiosaurus*; McIntosh, finding this reference doubtful, referred it to *Cetiosauriscus* as *C. greppini*

The new genus and species combination *Dinodocus mackesoni* was based on a series of broken limb and pelvic bones (BMNH 14695) from the early greensand (Early Cretaceous, Aptian) of Hythe, Kent, England. Owen (1884) found that these fossils, upon reaching the British Museum, were less characteristic than they had seemed to be prior to their extraction from the matrix. Hence, Owen's (1884) published description and drawings of the material do not provide much valuable data; also, the upper half of the left humerus was described as a fractured piece of the ilium, and the lower half as part of a femur.

Pelorosaurus has become a kind of "catch basin" to which has been referred a large amount of European sauropod material, not all of which can justifiably be assigned to this genus. According to McIntosh, *Pelorosaurus* may be synonymous with *Brachiosaurus* or some other genus. However, *Pelorosaurus* and *Brachiosaurus* cannot be separated with certainty from what is now known, especially given the fragmentary nature of the material referred to the former genus; also, the younger age and smaller size

Proximal end of humerus of *Pelorosaurus* sp.

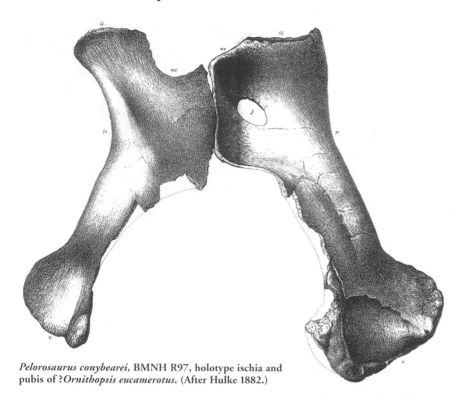

Pelorosaurus conybearei, BMNH R97, holotype ischia and pubis of ?*Ornithopsis eucamerotus*. (After Hulke 1882.)

of *Pelorosaurus* may suggest generic separation, a final verdict pending possible future discoveries.

McIntosh briefly described *Pelorosaurus* as follows: Middle and caudal dorsal vertebrae (those preserved) resembling those of *Brachiosaurus* in having opisthocoelous centra with deep pleurocoels, massive arches with similar laminae, and short massive spines; sacrum closely resembling that of *Brachiosaurus*,

although dorsosacral is not coossified to other four; proximal caudal vertebrae with large centra and short and simple spines, as in *Brachiosaurus*, but centra are relatively slightly shorter, caudal ribs proceeding directly outward instead of outward and backward; chevrons open above hemal canal as in *Brachiosaurus*; humerus long, straight, slender, more expanded proximally than distally, very similar to but slightly more massive than in *Brachiosaurus*; ilia almost identical to those of *Brachiosaurus*, but incomplete blades make bones seem less robust; pubes and ischia resemble those of *Brachiosaurus*, ischia with broad, well-developed head and twisted shaft with ends meeting edge to edge, but with shorter, broader shaft (McIntosh 1990*b*).

Note: *P. becklesii* Mantell 1852 [*nomen dubium*] was based one of the best Wealden specimens, including a left humerus, radius, and ulna (BMNH R1868), from Hastings. Associated with this specimen was a fossilized skin impression revealing a series of convex, boss-like, nonoverlapping hexagonal plates ranging from 9 to 26 millimeters in diameter. This species is sometimes regarded (Olshevsky 1978) as a junior synonym of *Chondosteosaurus gigas*. According to McIntosh, no evidence supports referring *P. becklesii* to any brachiosaurid taxon; this species differs from brachiosaurids in an ulna to humerus ratio of 0.71, and robustness of the ulna.

Key references: Huene (1922, 1927, 1932); Hulke (1874, 1882); Mantell (1852); McIntosh (1990*b*); Melville (1849); Owen (1875, 1884); Sauvage 1876); Seeley (1870).

PENTACERATOPS Osborn 1923

Ornithischia: Genasauria: Cerapoda: Marginocephalia: Ceratopsia: Neoceratopsia: Ceratopsidae: Chasmosaurinae.

Name derivation: Greek *pente* = "five" + Greek *keratos* = "horned" + Greek *ops* = "face."

Type species: *P. sternbergii* Osborn 1923.

Other species: [None.]

Occurrence: Lower-upper Fruitland Formation, lower-upper Kirtland Shale, New Mexico, United States.

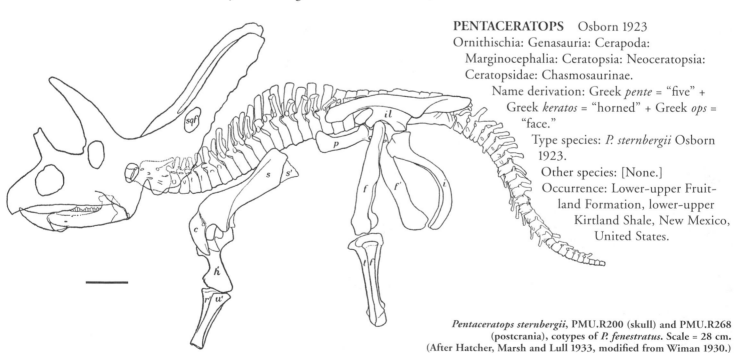

Pentaceratops sternbergii, PMU.R200 (skull) and PMU.R268 (postcrania), cotypes of *P. fenestratus*. Scale = 28 cm. (After Hatcher, Marsh and Lull 1933, modified from Wiman 1930.)

Age: Late Cretaceous (Late Campanian-Early Maastrichtian).

Known material: Eight complete or partial skulls, complete and several incomplete skeletons, numerous fragmentary specimens including cranial and postcranial elements, adults, ?juvenile.

Holotype: AMNH 6325, skull lacking lower jaw, associated partial skeleton.

Diagnosis of genus (as for type species): Large chasmosaurine, with long squamosals having numerous (8--12) pronounced marginal undulations with epoccipitals; parietal slender, with indented medial posterior margin and moderately sized elongate fenestrae; several very large parietal epoccipitals, including pair of upturned epoccipitals on midline dorsal surface of posterior part of parietal; jugals posteriorly directed; large epijugal horncores; supraorbital horncores large, anteriorly curved; rostrum relatively deep (Lehman 1993.)

Comments: The new genus and species combination, *Pentaceratops sternbergii,* was established on an almost complete skull, with partial skeleton (AMNH 6325), collected in 1922 by Charles H. Sternberg, from the Fruitland Formation, in San Juan County, northeast of Tsaya, New Mexico (Osborn 1923*a*).

The name *Pentaceratops* is misleading, however. As in all chasmosaurines, *Pentaceratops* has but three horns, the two supposed additional "horns" being the pronounced epijugals, present in all ceratopsids though not to such a degree of elongation as in this genus. (Other *Pentaceratops* specimens possess jugals of more conservative proportions.)

A second species, *P. fenestratus,* was based on two cotypes, a nearly complete skull lacking the lower jaw (PMU.R200), and an almost complete postcranial skeleton (PMU.R268) questionably associated with that skull, discovered by C. H. Sternberg in the Kirtland Shale, north (Rowe, Colbert and Nations, 1981) of Kimbethoh Wash, San Juan, New Mexico. Wiman (1930) distinguished this species from *P. sternbergi* mostly by geologic separation. Wiman stated that fenestrae are present in the squamosal of *P. fenestratus* and that the epoccipitals are shorter and more numerous than in the type species. Lull (1933) observed that the supposed fenestra is present only in the left squamosal, an indication that this condition is most likely pathologic, perhaps a bone lesion or a wound inflicted by a horn thrust, and that the incom-

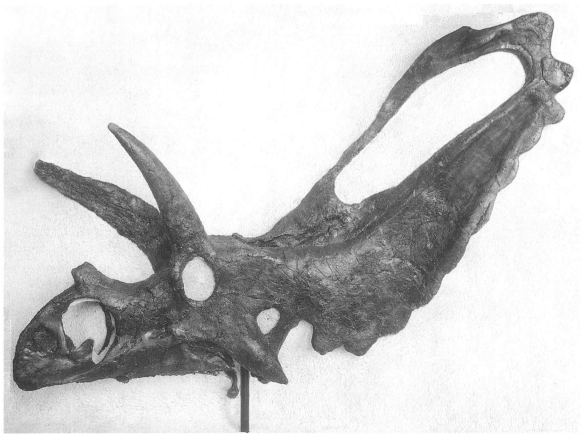

Pentaceratops sternbergii, AMNH 6325, holotype skull, left lateral view.

Courtesy Department Library Services, American Museum of Natural History (neg. #313532).

pleteness of the *Pentaceratops* skull precludes an accurate epoccipital count. Wiman combined both cotypes to create a composite skeletal reconstruction of *P. fenestratus.* Lull (1933), however, questioned the mutual association of the cotypes, noting that neither specimen shares any common bones with the other. Furthermore, since postcranial skeletons of large ceratopsids are virtually indistinguishable from one another, this second specimen could not be positively associated with the first. Dodson and Currie (1990), in their review of the Neoceratopsia, regarded *P. fenestratus* as a junior synonym of the type species.

The discovery of specimen MNA Pl. 174, with a complete frill, jaws, partial vertebral column, and ribs, collected in 1977 near Burnham, New Mexico, and referred to *P.* cf. *sternbergii*, revealed that Osborn's original description of the frill was in error (see Rowe *et. al.*, 1981). In his book, *Dinosaurs: An Illustrated History*, Colbert (1983) reported that this skull was found literally surrounded by fossilized vegetation, including grape leaves, figs, cottonwoods, viburnum, palms, and pines, all suggestive of part of this dinosaur's diet.

Numerous specimens, some fragmentary, have been referred to *Pentaceratops.* Among these, tentatively assigned to *Pentaceratops*, is a squamosal and parietal fragment (UNM-FKK-035) from a juvenile ceratopsian, reported by Thomas M. Lehman to Rowe *et. al.* The material was col-

lected from the De-na-zin Wash in San Juan County. Rowe *et al.* noted that all known *Pentaceratops* material comes from the southwestern San Juan Basin in New Mexico, and that *Pentaceratops* occurs through at least the upper two-thirds of the Fruitland Formation into the Kirtland Shale.

Lehman (1993) later rediagnosed *Pentaceratops*, based upon the earlier collected remains, and also new material referred to *Pentaceratops* cf. *P. sternbergii* (UNM B-1701 and FKK-081) and ?*Pentaceratops* sp. (UNM B-513, B-810a and FKK-035), including skull areas previously unknown. Lehman (1993) described for the first time the braincase of this genus, observing that its structure is similar to that of other chasmosaurines. From this new material, Lehman (1993) found that some apparently adult individuals were substantially smaller than previously reported specimens. Several of these more recently collected specimens were recovered from higher stratigraphic levels than those previously collected. Lehman (1993) determined that the stratigraphic range of *Pentaceratops* spans the Late Campanian to Early Maastrichtian (and not the Late Maastrichtian, as earlier reported, based upon indeterminate specimens referred to this genus).

Lull (1933) observed that *Pentaceratops* resembles both *Chasmosaurus* and *Torosaurus*, agreeing with *Chasmosaurus* in the somewhat short face, longer muzzle, long squamosals, large elongate fontanelles,

Pentaceratops sternbergii, PMU.R200, cotype skull of *P. fenestratus*, left lateral view. Scale = 16 cm. (After Wiman 1930.)

Illustration by Gregory S. Paul.

Pentaceratops sternbergii, restoration depicting theory that ceratopsians could gallop.

and position of the nasal horn, disagreeing in possession of long brow horns; *Pentaceratops* agrees with *Torosaurus* in the short face and elongate frill, but disagrees in ways that may be results of an evolutionary trend (*i.e., Torosaurus* with circular fenestrae, no epoccipitals [as interpreted by Lull and Osborn], reduced epijugals, and smaller nasal horn).

Paul (1987), in the book *Dinosaurs Past and Present*, considered *Pentaceratops* to be a junior synonym of *Chasmosaurus*, but offered no evidence supporting this synonymy. Lehman (1989) maintained that *Pentaceratops* should remain a valid genus because its brow horn cores are curved anteriorly rather than posteriorly (as in the less derived *Chasmosaurus*); parietal has a flattened and plate-like posterior border (squared and bar-like in *Chasmosaurus*); and the adult body size substantially exceeds that of *Chasmosaurus*. Lehman concluded that *Pentaceratops* seems derived from *Chasmosaurus*, the differences between the two forms meriting generic separation. In their review of the Neoceratopsia, Dodson and Currie (1990) acknowledged the possibility that *Pentaceratops* and *Chasmosaurus* may be congeneric.

The most striking feature in *Pentaceratops* is the very large frill. Lull noted that no *Pentaceratops* specimen yet found included a completely preserved frill.

Rowe *et al.* observed that the frill of the holotype of *P. sternbergii* lacks its posterior medial and lateral portions. This specimen, and a second incomplete skull (AMNH 1624) collected in 1923 by C.H. Sternberg from the same locality as the holotype, were exhibited at the American Museum of Natural History, with the missing parts reconstructed in plaster, these restorations hypothetically based upon frills of other genera. (Drawings of these restored skulls have since been prominently figured in the paleontological literature.) As pointed out by Rowe *et. al.*, Osborn's original diagnosis of the frill was based upon the restored holotype.

The *Pentaceratops* frill may have served various functional purposes. Lull (1908) first suggested that the frill served as an expanded frame for the origin of large jaw muscles. Ostrom (1966) demonstrated that the then so-called "long-frilled" ceratopsids [=chasmosaurines], such as *Pentaceratops*, had jaws mechanically inferior to the "short-frilled" forms [=centrosaurines], because of the relative positions of the jaw articulations, height, and position of the coronoid process, and length and position of the tooth row. Ostrom reasoned that "short-frilled" forms compensated for their poorer mechanical arrangement by having a frill structured to support a bulkier M.

adductor mandibulae externus, the only muscle involved with the frill.

Farlow and Dodson (1975) suggested that frills in dinosaurs like *Pentaceratops* served as a frontal threat display, the animals inclining their heads forwards, then perhaps shaking them from side to side. Molnar (1977) observed that the long brow horns in *Pentaceratops* have their axes directed almost through the occipital condyles. This would serve to direct stresses from the horns to the vertebral column during intraspecific combat. Rowe *et al.*, noting that the jaw adductor muscles in *Pentaceratops* were exposed and vulnerable, proposed that such conflicts were probably mostly limited to wrestling and shoving, the brow horns used sparingly to avoid risk of damage to this musculature.

Note: A single incomplete, flattened, epoccipital bone (AMNH 6591), with a bluntly sharpened edge, was collected by George Olsen at Baiying Bologai, Mongolia, in 1925. Provisionally referred to *Pentaceratops* by Gilmore (1933*b*), the specimen has since been identified by Coombs (1987) as ankylosaurian.

Key references: Colbert (1983); Dodson and Currie (1990); Farlow and Dodson (1975); Lehman (1989, 1993); Lull (1908, 1933); Molnar (1977); Osborn (1923*a*); Ostrom (1966); Paul (1987); Rowe, Colbert and Nations (1981); Wiman (1930).

PHAEDROLOSAURUS Dong 1973 [*nomen dubium*]

Saurischia: Theropoda: Tetanurae: Avetheropoda: Coelurosauria: Maniraptora: ?Dromaeosauridae *incertae sedis*.

Name derivation: Greek *phethon* = "shining" + Greek *sauros* = "lizard."

Type species: *P. ilikensis* Dong 1973 [*nomen dubium*].

Other species: [None.]

Occurrence: Lianmugin Formation, Xinjiang Uygur Zizhiqu, People's Republic of China.

Age: Early Cretaceous.

Known material: Tooth, partial postcrania.

Holotype: IVPP V.4024-1, tooth.

Diagnosis of genus (as for type species): Small theropod with short, thick, solid teeth, with small, dense serrations on anterior and posterior margins (Dong 1973).

Comments: The genus *Phaedrolosaurus* was founded upon a complete tooth (IVPP V.4024-1), with a referred pair of tibiofibulae united with astragalus and calcaneum (V.44024-2), from the Lower Cretaceous of Wuerho, Xinjiang, China (Dong Zhiming 1973).

As observed by Dong, these teeth are similar in outline (non–knife shaped and relatively straight) and form to those of the earlier and somewhat smaller North American genus *Deinonychus*, although those in *Phaedrolosaurus* are thicker, shorter, and more solid. Dong speculated that the two genera could be closely related.

Dong surmised that *Phaedrolosaurus* was a rather small, lightly-built, and long-legged theropod.

Note: The tibia referred to *Phaedrolosaurus* appears to be dromaeosaurid, but is longer and more slender than that of *Deinonychus* (R. E. Molnar, personal communication 1989).

Key reference: Dong (1973).

PHUWIANGOSAURUS Martin, Buffetaut and Suteethorn 1994

Saurischia: Sauropodomorpha: Sauropoda *incertae sedis*.

Name derivation: "Phu Wiang [type locality]" + Greek *sauros* = "lizard."

Type species: *P. sirindhornae* Martin, Buffetaut and Suteethorn 1994.

Other species: [None.]

Occurrence: Sao Khua Formation, Khorat group, Phu Wiang, Thailand.

Age: Late Juriassic or Early Cretaceous.

Known material: Abundant [unspecified] incomplete remains, including adults and juveniles.

Holotype: P.W.1-1 to 1-21, partial, partly articulated skeleton, including three cervical and four dorsal vertebrae, several ribs, left scapula, distal end of right scapula, left humerus, part of left ulna, both sides of pelvis, both femora, left fibula, adult.

Diagnosis of genus (as for type species): Middle-sized sauropod (15–20 meters, or approximately 50–64 feet) long; anterior cervical vertebrae with very low and wide neural arch; diapophyses and parapophyses very developed lateroventrally; zygapophyses large, situated low and far from each other, strongly diverging laterally from centrum; neural spine of posterior cervical vertebrae widely bifurcated with no median spine; cervical vertebrae with well-developed system of laminae and cavities; centra of dorsal vertebrae opisthocoelous with deep pleurocoels; posterior dorsals with unforked neural spines; neural spine elongated craniocaudally; diapophyses long, directed more dorsally than laterally, almost reaching level of spine; hyposphene-hypantrum system present; scapula elongate, with lateral ridge of proximal extremity at right angle with shaft, slight distal expansion; humerus similarly expanded at both ends; well-developed anterior blade of ilium; pubic peduncle of ilium straight, long, directed at right angles to direction of blade; ischiatic peduncle of ilium faintly marked; pubis with very open angles between axis of shaft and ischiatic border; caudal border of shaft of ischium with well-marked curvature; femur flattened anteroposteriorly, head located slightly above level of great trochanter; fourth trochanter crest-shaped, situated medially above midlength of shaft; very large lateral epicondyle at distal end of femur; shaft of fibula with slight bend (Martin, Buffetaut and Suteethorn, 1994).

Comments: The new type species *Phuwiangosaurus sirindhornae* was founded upon an incomplete skeleton (P.W.1-1 to P.W.1-21), discovered in 1982 associated with theropod teeth, recovered at Phu Pratu Teema, Phu Wiang National Park, in the Sao Khua Formation (Upper Jurassic or Lower Cretaceous), part of the Khorat Group, at Phu Wiang, in northeastern Thailand. The find constituted the first sauropod remains known in this formation. Sauropod remains have, to date, been collected from 24 local-

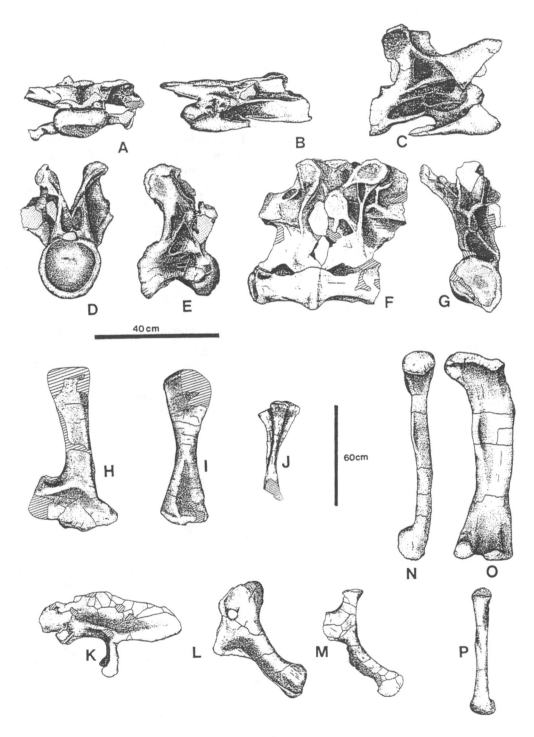

Phuwiangosaurus sirindhornae, holotype, (A-B) P.W. 1-1, anterior cervical vertebra (anterior and lateral views), (C) P.W. 1-2, middle cervical vertebra (lateral), (D-E) P.W. 1-3, posterior cervical vertebra (posterior and lateral), (F-G) P.W. 1-4, dorsal vertebra (lateral and posterior), (H) P.W. 1-7, left scapula (lateral), (I) P.W. 1-8, left humerus (posterior), (J) P.W. 1-9, left ulna (anterolateral), (K) P.W. 1-11, right ilium (lateral), (L) P.W. 1-12, left pubis (medial), (M) P.W. 1-14, left ischium (lateral), (N) P.W. 1-16, left femur (medial), (O) P.W. 1-17, right femur (posterior), and P. P.W. 1-18, left fibula (posterior). (After Martin, Buffetaut and Suteethorn 1994.)

Phyllodon henkeli, MGSP G5, holotype crown of anterior cheek tooth, in a. mesial, b. lingual, c. buccal, and d. distal views. Scale = 28 cm. (After Tulborn 1973.)

ities in Sao Khua deposits, 13 of them in the Phu Wiang area (Martin *et al.,* 1994).

(As noted by Martin *et al.,* the Sao Khua Formation was usually dated as Late Jurassic, based upon its vertebrate fauna [see Buffetaut, Suteethorn, Martin, Chaimanee and Tong-Buffetaut 1993], though more recent palynological data suggest the underlying Phra Wihan Formation is Early Cretaceous [Racey, Love, Canham, Goodall, Polachan and Jones, in press]. As *Phuwiangosaurus* displays advanced characters, Martin *et al.* regarded either dating as consistent with the materials' [and other vertebrae fossils'] occurrence.)

Martin *et al.* reported that other notable sauropod discoveries include seven articulated cervical vertebrae found at another site at Phu Pratu Teema, numerous very small bones of juveniles at several Phu Wiang sites, and a large accumulation of bones representing several individuals at the site of the temple at Phu Pha Ngo in Kalasin Province (Martin, Buffetaut and Suteethorn, 1993).

Comparing the Thai material to other well known sauropods, Martin *et al.* (1994) observed that the former does not exhibit similarities to any sauropod family yet described, and therefore they referred it provisionally to an indeterminate family.

Martin *et al.* (1994) noted that the abundant juvenile specimens correspond to several growth stages, the smallest individuals seemingly less than 2 meters (about 6.8 feet) long and one-half meter (about 1.7 feet) tall, and that some of the characters perceived in the specimens are not unlike those displayed in primitive sauropods. The authors commented that these specimens will be described in more detail at some future date.

Mouret, Heggemann, Gouadain and Krisadasima (1993) concluded from sedimentological data that *Phuwiangosaurus* lived in a floodplain landscape with a low-energy meandering river system, with apparently semi-arid climate, and two distinct seasons.

Key reference: Martin, Buffetaut and Suteethorn (1994).

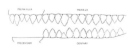

Phyllodon henkeli, reconstructed dentition, left lateral view. (After Thulborn.)

PHYLLODON Thulborn 1973 [*nomen dubium*]
Ornithischia: Genasauria: Cerapoda: Ornithopoda: Hypsilophodontidae.
Name derivation: Greek *phyllon* = "leaf" + Greek *odous* = "tooth."
Type species: *P. henkeli* Thulborn 1973 [*nomen dubium*].
Other species: [None.]
Age: Late Jurassic (Early Kimmeridgian).
Occurrence: [Unnamed formation], Provincia do Beira Litoral, Portugal.
Known material: Teeth.

Holotype: MGSP G5, crown of right dentary tooth.

Diagnosis of genus (as for type species): Dentary teeth lozenge-shaped, higher than long; height of denticulate part of crown greater than of nondenticulate part; marginal denticles bluntly rounded, becoming larger away from cervix, smaller near apex of tooth consisting of three small denticles; crown smooth and convex on both sides, flatter on lateral face; crown without vertical ridges; bulbous cingulum both medially and laterally; medial ridge with finely denticulate dorsal edge passing from lowest marginal denticle across posterior sixth of crown; anterior edge of ventral half of crown transversely convex; (from referred teeth) anterior premaxillary crowns broadly triangular, weakly recurved, without definite marginal denticles; posterior premaxillary-tooth crowns of similar shape, with small denticles on anterior edge, sometimes on posterior margin (Galton 1983*b*).

Comments: The genus *Phyllodon* was founded upon an incomplete dentary tooth (MGSP G5) collected from the lignite marls (Early Kimmeridgian, based on the presence of various characean oogonia plant fossils, including *Porovhara raskyae* and *P. westerbeckensis*; see Kuhn 1968), Guimarota mine, near Leiria, central Portugal. A partatype specimen (MGSP G2) consists of the crown of a left premaxillary tooth. This material was generally well-preserved, but limited by lack in much variation in size and structure (Thulborn 1973*b*).

Originally, Thulborn diagnosed the monotypic *P. henkeli* as follows: Dentition heterodont; tooth crowns fully and uniformly enamelled, bucco-lingually compressed, higher than long, deflected lingually; buccal faces of crowns smooth, convex, sometimes with shallow, divergent furrows; similar lingual surfaces slightly flatter; similarly-shaped anterior premaxillary crowns with small denticles on mesial (and sometimes distal) margin; cheek crowns lozenge-shaped, higher than long, with bluntly rounded denticles directed posteriorly; marginal denticles larger away from cervix, smaller near occlusal tip of crown, latter formed by several small denticles; no definite cingula, although cheek-teeth crowns may bear few small denticles at posterointernal margin.

Given the paucity of the material, Thulborn reconstructed the upper and lower dentition of *Phyllodon* using analogies with other hypsilophodontids, this reconstruction admittedly quite conjectural. The jaws were restored with an edentulous predentary (designed as intermediate in length between those of *Fabrosaurus australis* and *Hypsilophodon foxii*), six somewhat pointed premaxillary teeth, 13 maxillary and 14 dentary teeth, cheek teeth leaf-shaped. Thulborn noted that, among hypsilophodontids, this numbering is quite consistent.

Key references: Galton (1983*b*); Thulborn (1973*b*).

PIATNITZKYSAURUS   Bonaparte 1979

Saurischia: Theropoda: Tetanurae: Avetheropoda: Allosauroidea: Allosauridae.

Name derivation: "[A.] Piatnitzky" + Greek *sauros* = "lizard."

Type species: *P. floresi* Bonaparte 1979.

Other species: [None.]

Occurrence: Cañadon Asfalto Formation, Chubut, Argentina.

Age: Middle Jurassic (Callovian).

Known material: Two fragmentary skulls with associated postcrania.

Holotype: PVL 4073, occipital region of skull, braincase, left frontal, left maxilla, anterior portions of mandibles, axis, 13 presacral vertebrae, anterior and posterior cervical vertebrae, dorsal vertebrae, two anterior caudals, fragments of dorsal centra, scapulae and coracoids, right humerus, left ulna, fragments of ilia, greater portion of pubis and ischia, femora, tibiae, fibulae.

Diagnosis of genus (as for type species): Allosaurid with deep depression between basioccipital condyle and apophyses of opisthotic; braincase similar to that of *Eustreptospondylus*, with more pronounced lateral depressions of basisphenoid and process of laterosphenoid; postcranial characters comparing favorably with *Allosaurus*, scapula and coracoid in *Piatnitzkysaurus* less wide, rather subcircular in outline; pubis with moderate-sized "foot," obturator foramen almost completely surrounded by laminae; ischium more reduced ventrally than in *Allosaurus*; ulna, tibia, and femur more slender than in *Allosaurus*, proportionately more massive than in *Dilophosaurus* (Bonaparte 1986*b*).

Comments: The genus *Piatnitzkysaurus* was founded on most of the associated bones of one individual (PVL 4073), collected from the Callovian-Oxfordian beds of Cañadon Asfalto Formation, Argentine Patagonia, South America. A paratype (MACN CH 895) consists of an incomplete right maxilla, right humerus, proximal half of pubis, ischium, left tibia, left metatarsals II-IV, incomplete sacrum with four vertebrae, two posterior dorsal vertebrae, and two dorsal vertebral centra (Bonaparte 1986*b*).

Piatnitzkysaurus floresi, skeleton including holotype PVL 4073, partial crania and postcrania.

Photo by F. E. Novas, courtesy Buenos Aires Museum.

Piatnitzkysaurus

Piatnitzkysaurus floresi skeleton including holotype PVL 4073, detail of shoulder girdle and frontlimbs.

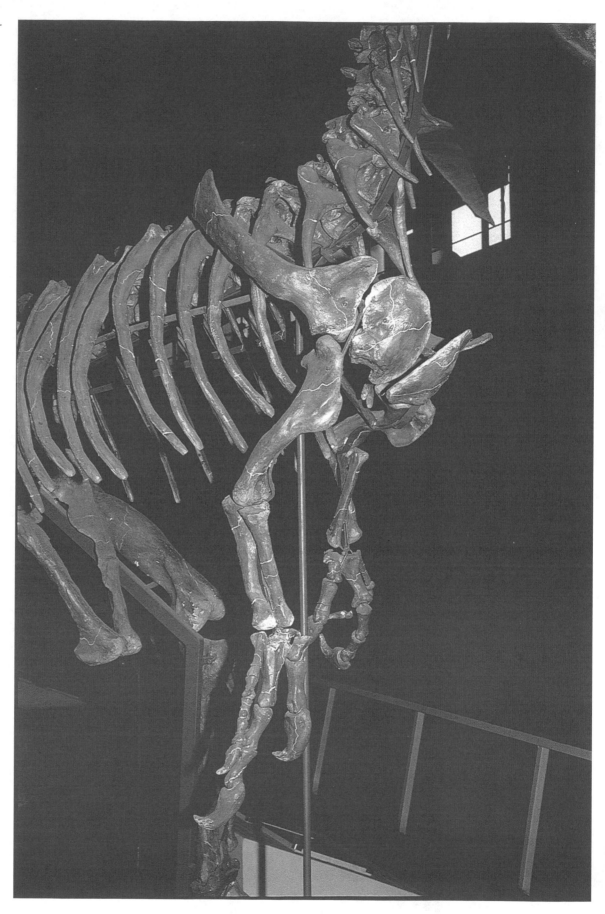

Originally, Bonaparte (1979) briefly diagnosed the monotypic *P. floresi* as follows: Distinguished from *Allosaurus* by more primitive pelvis, smaller pubic "foot," almost entirely bordering obturator foramen; dorsal vertebrae similar to those of *Allosaurus*, differing in ridges on lateral side of neural arches; humerus apparently relatively longer than in *A. fragilis*.

Later, Bonaparte (1986*b*) rediagnosed and fully described this species based on the holotype and paratype specimens.

Bonaparte (1979) noted that the discovery of *Piatnitzkysaurus*, along with two sauropods (*Patagosaurus* and *Volkheimeria*), provides information on a South American sauropod and "carnosaur" dinosaur assemblage predating both Morrison and Tendaguru times. This constitutes the first evidence that the continent was populated by these kinds of dinosaurs during the Callovian-Oxfordian, supporting the theory that a terrestrial interchange of Jurassic fauna was possible between South America and other continents.

Molnar, Kurzanov and Dong regarded *Piatnitzkysaurus* as the earliest known "carnosaur" and possible common ancestor of later "carnosaurs."

Key references: Bonaparte (1979, 1896*b*); Molnar, Kurzanov and Dong (1990).

PICRODON   Seeley 1898 [*nomen dubium*]— (=?*Camelotia*, ?*Plateosaurus*)

Saurischia: Sauropodomopha: Prosauropoda *incertae sedis*.

Name derivation: Greek *pikros* = "bitter" + Greek *odous* = "tooth."

Type species: *P. herveyi* Seeley 1898 [*nomen dubium*].

Other species: [None.]

Occurrence: "Rhaetic" beds, Somerset, England.

Age: Late Triassic.

Known material: Teeth, vertebrae.

Holotype: BMNH R2875, tooth.

Diagnosis of genus: [None published.]

Comments: The genus *Picrodon* was founded upon a single tooth (BMNH R2875), collected from so-called "Rhaetic" beds of Wedmore Hill, Somerset, England.

The tooth was described by Seeley (1898) as follows: Sharply pointed, with oblique serrations; ribbing on lingual side; 20 millimeters (about .75 inches) in length.

Seeley referred to the type species, *P. herveyi*, some dorsal and caudal vertebrae with laterally compressed centra, recovered from the same horizon and locality as the holotype, and a tooth found near Warwick (BMNH collection).

Key reference: Seeley (1898).

PINACOSAURUS   Gilmore 1933—(=*Syrmosaurus*)

Ornithischia: Genasauria: Thyreophora: Ankylosauria: Ankylosauridae.

Name derivation: Greek *pinakos* = "broad" + Greek *sauros* = "lizard."

Type species: *P. grangeri* Gilmore 1933.

Other species: [None.]

Occurrence: Djadochta Formation, Beds of Alag Teg, Omnogov, Mongolian People's Republic; [unnamed formation], Ningxia Huizu Zizhqu, People's Republic of China.

Age: Late Cretaceous (Middle–Late Campanian).

Known material: More than 15 specimens, including one complete and four incomplete skulls, almost complete skeleton with armor, adult, juvenile.

Holotype: AMNH 6523, skull with jaws, dermal bones, adult.

Diagnosis of genus (as for type species): Premaxilla not covered by dermal ossifications; nostril large, oval, facing rostrally, divided by horizontal septum; nasal area (at least in juvenile individuals) with laterally located third opening leading into premaxillary sinus; width of beak slightly more than distance between caudalmost maxillary teeth; mandibular condyle of quadrate below posterior margin of orbit; postcranial bones, especially limbs, relatively slender; manus with five digits, pes four (Coombs and Maryańska 1990).

Comments: *Pinacosaurus* was founded on a badly crushed skull and a few scattered dermal bones (AMNH 6523), collected by Walter Granger from the Djadochta Formation (Middle–Late Campanian; see Currie 1991; Dong 1993*a*) of Shabarakh Usu, in Outer Mongolia (Gilmore 1933*b*).

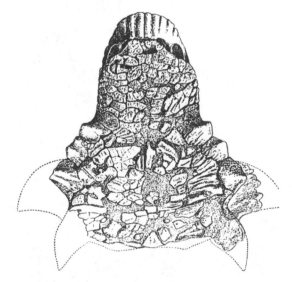

Pinacosaurus grangeri, AMNH 6523, holotype skull, dorsal view. (After Gilmore 1933.)

Pinacosaurus

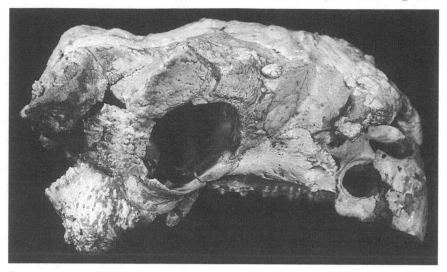

Pinacosaurus grangeri, ZPAL MgD-II/1, skull, (young individual), right lateral view.

Gilmore originally classified *Pinacosaurus* as a nodosaurid (later assigned by Coombs 1978*a* to the Ankylosauridae). As dermal armor was poorly preserved in the type specimen, Gilmore speculated that the body of *Pinacosaurus* was covered with dermal plates, but less massively so than in *Panoplosaurus* [=*Palaeoscincus* of his usage].

With the collection of additional materials from the Djadokhta Formation, including more perfectly preserved skulls and the almost complete, well-pre-

Pinacosaurus grangeri, ZPAL MgD-II/1, skull (young individual), dorsal view.

served postcranial skeleton (ZPAL MgD-II/1) of a young individual, *Pinacosaurus* was redescribed by Maryańska (1977).

In the skull of ZPAL MgD-II/1, Maryańska discovered unusual nasal cavities accommodating thin curved bones similar to turbinal bones in mammals. *Pinacosaurus* and the ankylosaur *Saichania* are the only reptiles, living or extinct, known positively to possess such structures. Maryańska proposed that membranes covered these bones to warm, filter, and moisten incoming air. In their review of the Ankylosauria, Coombs and Maryańska (1990) speculated that these sinuses may also have functioned as a resonating chamber, for housing a variety of glands, and strengthening the skull to compensate for its width and shallowness and almost horizontal orientation of the maxillary shelf, the potential function of these sinuses not mutually exclusive.

ZPAL MgD-11/1 provided new details of the postcrania of *Pinacosaurus,* including the tail. The structure of the caudal vertebrae suggests that the tail could move both vertically and laterally, but only in the proximal part from the third to fourteenth caudals. Vertical movement of the tail was restricted by high neural spines. Fusion between distal vertebral centra suggests that the part of the tail forming the club could not move. Dermal armor in young individual includes both two-layered half rings, cervical and pectoral plates.

According to Maryańska, *Pinacosaurus* is intermediate between the more primitive *Talarurus* and more derived *Saichania*.

The new type species *Syrmosaurus viminicaudus,* founded on an incomplete skeleton (PEN AN SSR 614) from the Early ?Campanian of Mongolia, was described by Maleev (1952*a*) as a fairly conservative ankylosaur, which was the basis for the [abandoned] family Syrmosauridae. Maryańska (1971) showed that this species is a junior synonym of *P. grangeri*.

Notes: Ankylosaurs have generally been regarded as solitary animals (see Dodson 1971; Béland and Russell 1978). That concept was challenged by the discovery (announced in the popular media in mid–August, 1988) of skeletons of five to six *Pinacosaurus* infants by a joint Chinese and Canadian paleontological expedition (Sino-Canadian Dinosaur Project) to Bayan Mandahu, Gobi Desert, Mongolia. The skeletons, each about the size of a sheep, were found under a dune, suggesting that the baby dinosaurs were smothered in a sandstorm. One skeleton was found in a curled-up position.

The name *Viminicaudus* is an error, actually the specific name of *S. viminicaudus,* but used generically by Huene in 1958. Likewise, *Ninghsiasaurus,* a

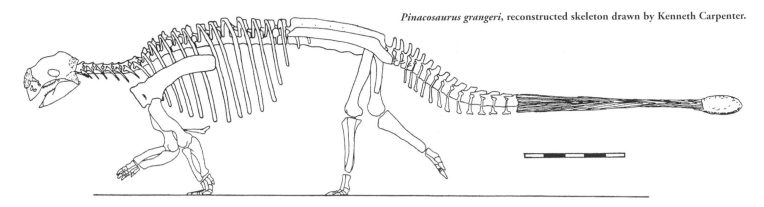

Pinacosaurus grangeri, reconstructed skeleton drawn by Kenneth Carpenter.

similar error made by Yang [formerly Young] in 1965, stems from the junior synonym, *Pinacosaurus ninghsiensis* Yang [*nomen dubium*].

Maryańska (1971, 1977) referred *Syrmosaurus disparoserratus* Maleev 1952 to *Talarurus*, after which Tumanova (1987) made it the type species of a new genus, *Maleevus*.

Key references: Coombs (1978*a*); Coombs and Maryańska (1990); Gilmore (1933*b*); Maleev (1952*a*); Maryańska (1977).

PISANOSAURUS   Casamiquela 1967
Ornithischia *incertae sedis*.
Name derivation: "[Mr.] Pisano's" + Greek *sauros* = "lizard."
Type species: *P. mertii* Casamiquela 1967.
Other species: [None.]
Occurrence: Ischigualasto Formation, La Roja Province, Argentina.
Age: Late Triassic (Middle Carnian).
Known material/holotype: PVL 2577, partial right maxilla with teeth, incomplete right mandibular ramus, parts of three cervical vertebrae, nine incomplete dorsals, rib, rib fragments, right tibia, right fibula with articulated astragalus and calcaneum, tarsal element with metatarsal, two metatarsals with incomplete accompanying digits, indeterminate long-bone fragment.

Diagnosis of genus (as for type species): Acetabulum open; pedicels of ilium short, resulting in low, axially long acetabulum; proximal region of ischia wide, ?larger than that of pubis; metacarpals apparently elongated, measuring about 15 millimeters (Bonaparte 1976).

Comments: The oldest known alleged ornithischian, *Pisanosaurus* was founded upon a weathered fragmentary skeleton (PVL 2577) found by Galileo J. Scaglia, in the Ischigualasto Formation (radiometrically dated as Middle Cranian by Rogers, Swisher, Sereno, Monetta, Forster and Martínez 1993), Agua de Las Catas locality, La Rioja, Argentina (Casamiquela 1967*b*).

The remains were originally described by Casamiquela (1967*b*), who, as noted by Bonaparte (1976), misinterpreted the cervical vertebrae as caudals, and did not describe the incomplete impression of the pelvis, and the body of the sacral vertebrae and three metacarpals.

Casamiquela (1967*b*) originally diagnosed *Pisanosaurus* as follows: Small, bipedal (probably cursorial) form; teeth palisade-like, with no morpho-

Pisanosaurus mertii, PVL 2577, holotype reconstructed partial skeleton. Scale = 8 cm. (After Bonaparte 1976.)

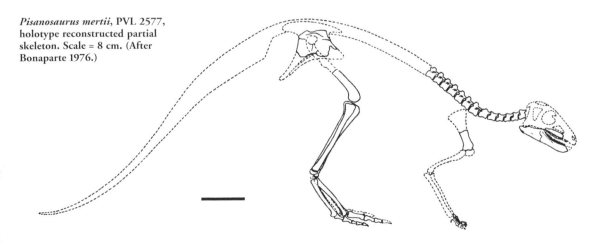

logical differentiation; teeth subcylindrical in alveoli; tooth crowns differentiated; occlusion mechanism; though primitive in some features, lower jaw specialized in low position of fulcrum and pronounced lateral step to inset tooth row.

Casamiquela (1967*b*) placed *Pisanosaurus* into its own family, Pisanosauridae, differentiating this genus from other primitive ornithischians (*i.e.*, *Lycorhinus*, *Geranosaurus*, and *Heterodontosaurus*) mainly by the homodont form of its teeth. Galton (1972, 1973*c*) assigned *Pisanosaurus* to the Hypsilophodontidae as the oldest member of that group, then subsequently (1974) removed it. Bonaparte, observing that both *Pisanosaurus* and *Heterodontosaurus* share basic features in the morphology (subcylindrical and closely packed together) and wear (producing planar or slightly concave occlusal surfaces forming a more or less continuous plane [see below] along the row) of their upper and lower posterior "postcanine" teeth, proposed that *Pisanosaurus* be placed into the Heterodontosauridae. Galton (1986), however, maintained that *Pisanosaurus*, based upon the described material, could just as well be a hypsilophodontid.

In their reassessment of early ornithischians, Weishampel and Witmer (1990*a*) regarded *Pisanosaurus* as certainly a dinosaur (because of its fully "twisted" tibia and the notch in the cranial face of distal tibia for receiving the ascending process of the astragalus). According to Weishampel and Witmer, *Pisanosaurus* is allied with the Ornithischia on the basis of having five sacral vertebrae (suggested by Bonaparte), and because the morphology of its jaws (maxilla and dentary with modest buccal emargination) is that known only in ornithischians. The production of extensive wear between maxillary and dentary teeth is known only in *Pisanosaurus* and some other ornithischians. Weishampel and Witmer noted that *Pisanosaurus* shares synapomorphies with the Ornithischia (see Sereno 1986), including loss of recurvature of maxillary and dentary teeth, separation of tooth crown and root by a "neck," maximal tooth size in middle of tooth row, and dentary forming rostral portion of coronoid process. *Pisanosaurus* is separated from higher ornithischians by its low coronoid process, medial metatarsals overlapping lateral metatarsals, and apex of ascending process of astragalus laterally situated near articulation with calcaneum. For the present, Weishampel and Witmer regarded *Pisanosaurus* as a very primitive member of the ornithischian clade, possibly someday proving to be at the base of the cladogram.

Sereno (1991*a*), in a review of basal ornithischians, noted that Bonaparte had erred in interpreting the wear facets in the teeth of *Pisanosaurus* as forming a continuous occlusal surface as in *Heterodontosaurus*. According to Sereno (1991*a*), the wear facets vary slightly in angle, the adjacent crown margins not squared for close opposition. Sereno (1991*a*) further observed that, in the holotype of *P. mertii*, the skull fragments, pelvis impression, and distal right hind limb could very well belong to a single individual, but speculated that the fragmentary scapula and other associated small postcrania are too small. The cranial remains are clearly ornithischian, the maxilla and dentary, with respect to the presence of well-developed cheek margination, apparently more derived than in *Lesothosaurus diagnosticus*. The tibia and astragalus (recognized by Weishampel and Witmer) are more primitive in structure than in other ornithischians. According to Sereno (1991*a*), *P. mertii*—if crania and postcrania of the holotype are correctly associated—is potentially the sister-taxon to all other ornithischians, underscoring the paucity of ornithischian fossil remains found in Upper Triassic deposits.

According to Bonaparte, *Pisanosaurus* played a role in a fauna dominated by therapsids, a substantial time span allowing for evolution of homodont teeth to produce the caniniform teeth eventually present in *Heterodontosaurus*.

Key references: Bonaparte (1976); Casamiquela (1967*a*, 1967*b*); Galton (1972, 1973*c*, 1974); Sereno (1986, 1991*a*); Weishampel and Witmer (1990*a*).

PIVETEAUSAURUS　Taquet and Welles 1977
Saurischia: Theropoda: ?Tetanurae: ?Eustreptospondylidae.
Name derivation: "[Jean] Piveteau" + Greek *sauros* = "lizard."
Type species: *P. divesensis* Taquet and Welles 1977.
Other species: [None.]
Occurrence: Marnes de Dives, Calvados, France.
Age: Middle Jurassic (Late Callovian).
Known material/holotype: MNHN 1920-7, braincase.

Diagnosis of genus (as for type species): Skull, with large, long parietals; paroccipital processes above occipital condyle, with large and moderately long, tube-like processes; foramen magnum very small; sphenethmoid massive; parasphenoid deep, low, dense; basipterygoid processes short, next to each other (Taquet and Welles 1977).

Comments: In 1923, Piveteau published the figure of a theropod cranium (MNHN 1920-7) that had been collected from the Oxfordian of Vaches Noires, near Dives, Normandy, France.

Later, Walker (1964) erected the new genus and species combination *Eustreptospondylus oxoniensis* to

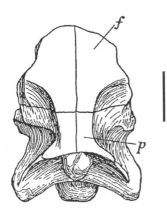

Piveteausaurus divesensis, MNHN 1920-7, holotype braincase of *Eustreptospondylus divesensis*. Scale = 6 cm. (After Piveteau 1923.)

receive a reasonably complete megalosaurid skeleton (UM J13558) from Wolvercot, England. At the same time, Walker referred to *Eustreptospondylus* the cranium figured by Piveteau as the holotype of second species *E. divesensis*. Walker distinguished this species from *E. oxoniensis* on the basis of the more definite anterior contraction of the frontals. For "convenience," Walker also referred to this species various remaining materials from the same region, regarded by previous workers (Cuvier 1836; Nopcsa 1906; Piveteau 1923; Huene 1926c; 1932) as "*Streptospondylus*" *cuvieri*, although none of this material was homogenous with the holotype of *E. divesensis*, nor were they from the same stratigraphic level.

Taquet and Welles (1977), after comparing the holotype of *E. divesensis* with skulls *of Allosaurus, Eustreptospondylus,* and *Ceratosaurus,* recognized Walker's species as representing a new genus, which they named *Piveteausaurus*.

As noted by Kurzanov (1989), the braincase of type species, *P. divesensis,* is markedly similar to that of *Eustreptospondylus oxoniensis* (see also Molnar, Kurzanov and Dong 1990), this suggesting that both species may belong in the same family. Molnar *et al.* theorized that both species could be related to the ancestry of "Carnosauria," though in a way yet to be clarified.

Key references: Cuvier (1836); Huene (1926c, 1932); Kurzanov (1989); Molnar, Kurzanov and Dong (1990); Nopcsa (1906); Piveteau (1923); Taquet and Welles (1977); Walker (1964).

PLATEOSAURAVUS   Huene 1932—(See *Euskelosaurus.*)

Name derivation: *Plateosaurus* + Latin *avus* = "grandfather."

Type species: *P. cullingworthi* (Haughton 1924).

PLATEOSAURUS   Meyer 1837—
(=*Dimodosaurus, Dinosaurus, Gresslyosaurus;* =?*Pachysauriscus*)

Saurischia: Sauropodomorpha: Prosauropoda: Plateosauridae.

Name derivation: Greek *platys* = "flat" + Greek *sauros* = "lizard."

Type species: *P. engelhardti* Meyer 1837.

Other species: [None.]

Occurrence: Knollenmergel, Baden-Württemberg, Niedersachsen, Feurletten, Bavaria, Germany; Knollenmergel, Baselland, Obere Bunte Mergel, Aargau, Switzerland; Marnes irisees supérieures, Jura, [unnamed formation], Doubs, France; Knollenmergel, Magdeburg, Suhl, Germany.

Age: Late Triassic (Late Norian).

Known material: Over 100 skeletons, fragmentary to complete, isolated elements, at least ten skulls, juvenile to adult.

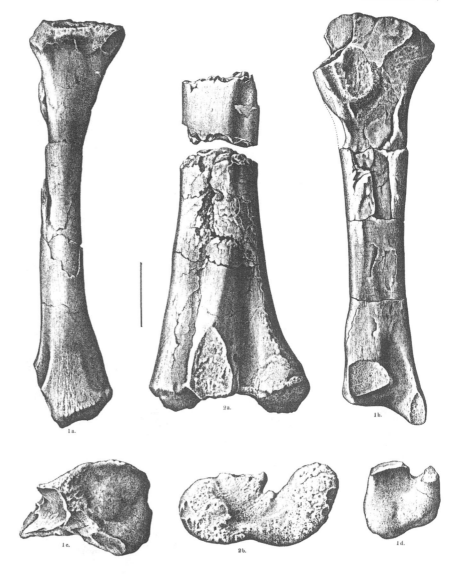

Plateosaurus engelhardti, SMNH, holotype left tibia, 1a. posterior, 1b. lateral, 1c. proximal, 1d. distal views, distal half of left femur, 2a. posterior, 2b. ventral views. Scale = 4 cm. (After Huene 1907–08.)

Plateosaurus

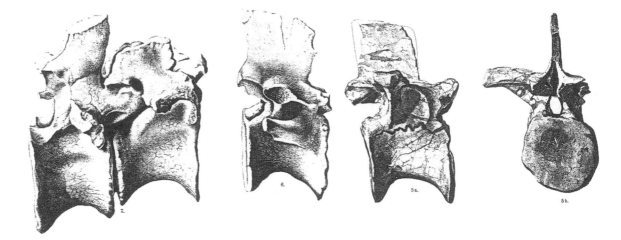

Holotype: SMNS collection, two dorsal vertebrae, sacrum, two caudal vertebrae, pubis, femur, tibia.

Diagnosis of genus (as for type species): Derived characters including tall, narrow skull with elongate snout; maxilla with long lateral lamina and large, triangular medial lamina; transversely broad prefrontal ending near postorbital, frontal contributing small portion of orbital rim (Galton 1990a).

Comments: One of the earliest large dinosaurs, *Plateosaurus* was founded upon a supposed "frontal" [see below] and partial postcranial remains (SMNS collection), collected from the upper red Keuper marls at Heroldsberg, near Nürnberg, Bavaria, [formerly Federal Republic of] Germany. The genus was the basis for the family Plateosauridae Marsh 1895.

Meyer (1837), who did not illustrate the material, originally described *Plateosaurus* as having limbs similar to those of the [rather unrelated] genera *Megalosaurus* and *Iguanodon*, identifying a broad, flat bone as a part of the skull. The latter element was later identified by Huene (1907–8) as a left frontal, then subsequently reidentified by Huene (1932) as a nasal. (In a later detailed study of the cranial anatomy of *Plateosaurus*, Galton 1984a observed that this element does not correspond to any other cranial or postcranial bone, resembling rather a dermal scute; therefore, he removed it from the holotype of *P. engelhardti*.)

Since the early nineteenth century, numerous other prosauropod taxa were described from the Knollenmergel and [abandoned] "Rhaetic" of Germany. Galton (1985d) referred to *P. engelhardti* all of the following that were actually based on prosauropod remains:

Zanclodon quenstedti Koken 1900 was based on an incomplete skeleton, including an articulated series of seven dorsal vertebrae with first and second sacrals, and left pubis, from the upper Keuper of Tübingen; *P. erlenbergiensis* Huene 1908 was based on an incomplete skeleton, including partial skull material, from Halberstadt; *P. ornatus* Huene 1908 [*nomen dubium*] was based on a tooth from the "Rhaetic" of Württemberg; *P. plieningeri* Huene 1908 was based on a skull and incomplete postcranial remains from the upper Keuper of Trössingen; *P. reinigeri* Huene 1908 [*nomen dubium*] was based on incomplete postcranial remains, including cervical and dorsal vertebrae, from the upper Keuper of Württemberg; *P. trossingensis* Fraas 1913 was based on a skeleton from the upper Keuper of Trössingen; and *P. longiceps* Jaekel 1913 was based on postcranial remains.

The type species *Dimodosaurus poligniensis* Pidancet and Chopard 1862 was based on remains of five individuals, collected from the lower half of the *contra-zone* ("Rhaetic"), Poligny, Jura, France. This species was referred by Huene (1907/08) to *P. poligniensis*.

The genus *Gresslyosaurus* was founded on three imperfectly preserved sacral vertebrae (NMB NB1858), proximal end of left tibia (NMB NB1584), incomplete pes including two phalanges (one an ungual), left second metacarpal (NMB NB1875), left metatarsal V (NMB NB1576), and ungual phalanx of left pedal digit IV (NMB NB53), discovered by

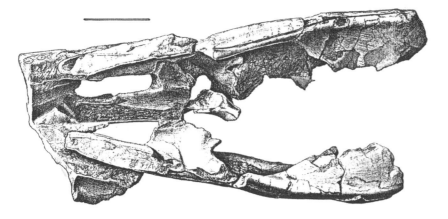

Amanz Gressly in the Upper Keuper von Nieder-Schönthal (Upper Triassic), Knollenmergel, Basel, Switzerland. The material was originally reported (though not described) by Rütimeyer (1856) as new type species *Dinosaurus gresslyi,* the generic name proving to be preoccupied (Waldheim 1847) for a titanosuchian. Galton (1986a) later fully described *Gresslyosaurus* and, after comparing its elements to corresponding bones of larger individuals of *Plateosaurus,* referred the type species *G. ingens* to *P. engelhardti. G. robustus* Huene 1908 [*nomen dubium*], referred by Huene (1932) to *P. robustus,* and *G. torgeri* Jaekel 1913 [*nomen dubium*], referred by Huene (1932) to *P. plieningeri,* were tentatively referred by Galton (1986a) to *P. engelhardti.*

Plateosaurus exhibits the body plan typical of a large (about 8 meters or 26 feet long) prosauropod with its small head, long neck, heavily-built torso, relatively long forelimbs, grasping hands, and strongly developed hindlimbs. Based on one skeleton and parts of another, Huene (1926a) described this genus in detail.

Huene (1926a) reconstructed the skeleton of *Plateosaurus* in a bipedal posture, although the long neck and forelimbs made this stance appear somewhat awkward. Galton (1971b), after reviewing the manus structure and general postcranial morphology of prosauropods, concluded that all prosauropods

Plateosaurus engelhardti, holotype left pes of *Dimodosaurus poligniensis.* Scale = 4 cm. (After Huene 1907–08.)

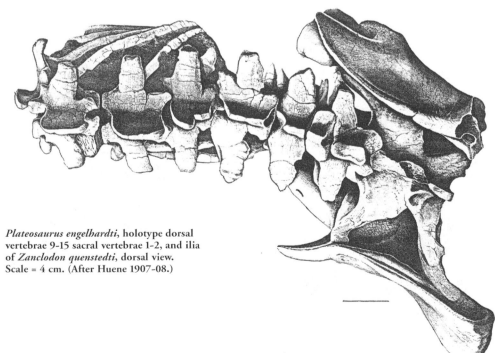

Plateosaurus engelhardti, holotype dorsal vertebrae 9-15 sacral vertebrae 1-2, and ilia of *Zanclodon quenstedti,* dorsal view. Scale = 4 cm. (After Huene 1907-08.)

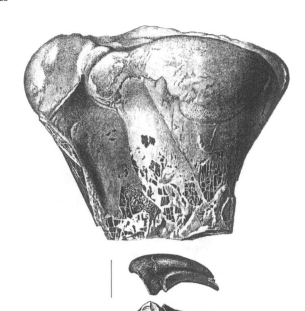

Plateosaurus engelhardti,
holotype proximal end of left
tibia (lateral view) and
phalanx of left pedal digit IV
(medial and ventral views) of
Gresslyosaurus ingens.
Scale = 4 cm. (After Huene
1907–08.)

gen, an almost complete and articulated skull (SMNS 13200) that was part of the holotype of *P. trossingensis* (a *nomen nudum*, described by Huene 1926*a*), and a disarticulated skull (AMNH 6810) collected between 1921 and 1923 by Huene. (A cast of the latter was placed on the mounted skeleton of *Plateosaurus* exhibited at the American Museum of Natural History; see Colbert 1969, 1983).

Galton (1985*d*) interpreted the lower jaw of *Plateosaurus* as incapable of either posterior or anterior movement, demonstrating that the jaws acted as a unit with a hinge-like, open and closing [=orthal] action. Considering the possibility of kinetism in the skull, Galton (1984*a*, 1985*d*) showed that, in adult individuals, the sutures joining various cranial bones are designed to increase firmness between those elements. Galton (1985*d*) concluded that the skull was akinetic; also, that juveniles retained an ancestral kinetism that was lost in adults (suggested earlier by Versluys 1910; Ostrom 1962*b*), due to filling in spaces required for kinesis between the bones, perhaps during allometric bone growth, and to increasing firmness between laterosphenoid and parietal.

Although *Plateosaurus* (and other prosauropods) are generally regarded today as herbivorous, earlier texts sometimes state that this form was either omnivorous or carnivorous. Cooper (1981) resurrected this old notion of meat-eating prosauropods, probably feeding on carrion (see *Massospondylus* entry).

Galton (1984*a*), however, offered the following reasons supporting the idea that prosauropods were strictly vegetarian: 1. Shape of maxillary and dentary teeth crowns (expanded anteroposteriorly, maximum width of crown greater than that of root) is similar

were basically quadrupeds, but suggested that the specialized manus may also have served a function in addition to providing support while walking. Galton (1971*b*) showed that the manus in dinosaurs like *Plateosaurus* was so constructed as to allow digits II–IV to rest on the ground like toes, while the scythe-like claw of digit I was held clear of the ground. This raised claw could have been utilized in raking at vegetation or as a weapon.

The cranial anatomy of *Plateosaurus* was fully described by Galton (1984*a*, 1985*d*), based primarily on two complete skulls from the quarry at Trössin-

Plateosaurus engelhardti, skeleton (skull cast of AMNH 6810).

Plateosaurus engelhardti, skull (cast), left lateral view.

to those of herbivorous "fabrosaurids" (Galton 1978) and the herbivorous lizard *Iguana iguana* (Throckmorton 1976); 2. maxillary and dentary teeth serrations are prominent, set at an approximate 45-degree angle to anterior and posterior cutting edges, as in "fabrosaurids" and *Iguana iguana*; in carnivorous archosaurs, serrations are finer and at right angles to edge; 3. the cutting edges of the crowns are inclined obliquely relative to the long axis of maxilla and dentary, as in *Iguana iguana*; 4. jaw articulation is offset well below line of tooth row, analogous to dorsally offset jaw articulation in herbivorous mammals (Galton 1976a, 1978); 5. lack of wear facets indicate that teeth did not contact each other, the supplementary action of a gastric mill required to break down food (Galton 1976a); and 6. the long neck (as in giraffes) presumably extended vertical feeding range to reach vegetation at higher levels, the small head reducing

its leverage effect on the neck, especially when the neck was held horizontally.

With *Plateosaurus* and other prosauropods viewed as strict herbivores, Galton (1985d) considered the possibility of these animals themselves having cheeks, a feature which would be especially important when feeding on more resistant vegetation. Earlier, Galton (1973b) showed that a prominent and diagonally inclined ridge on the lateral surface of the dentary, passing forwards and downwards from the base of the coronoid eminence, supported the presence of cheeks in most ornithischians. Galton (1985d) later observed a similar although less prominent ridge on the lateral surface of the dentary in *Plateosaurus*, noting that this ridge, absent in all theropods, is not a typical saurischian feature. Galton (1985d) agreed with Paul (1985), who stated that, when cheeks are present, only a few large nerve foramina (instead of a series of many small foramina) are present on the lateral surface of the dentary adjacent to the teeth (as in disarticulated *Plateosaurus* skull specimen AMNH 6810). Galton (1985d) concluded that *Plateosaurus* probably had cheeks that extended anteriorly on the dentary to approximately the middle of the dentary tooth row.

Plateosaurus remains have been found in more than 50 European localities, this genus now the best represented of all prosauropods and most common of all European dinosaurs. Excavations by the Stuttgart Museum für Naturkunde in 1911–12 and Palaeontological Institute of the University of Tübingen, in 1921–23 (also in 1932) at Trössingen, [former Federal Republic of] Germany, retrieved numerous complete

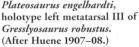

Plateosaurus engelhardti, holotype left metatarsal III of *Gresslyosaurus robustus*. (After Huene 1907–08.)

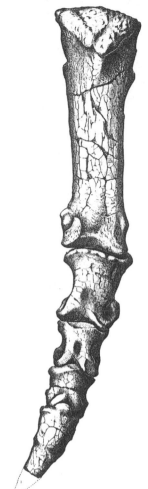

Plateosaurus engelhardti, disarticulated skull elements.

Illustration by Doug Henderson. From *Dinosaurs: A Global View*, by Czerkas and Czerkas, published by Dragon's World Ltd. and its co-edition publishers.

and partial adult and subadult *Plateosaurus* specimens. Huene (1932) described material from the Knollenmergel quarry in Trossingen. Due to the abundance of these specimens, Huene (1926*a*) suggested that *Plateosaurus* may have been a herding creature, possibly undertaking seasonal climatic changes as the animals ranged over this rather arid part of Europe during the Late Triassic; and that the accumulation of remains found at Trössingen resulted from some catastrophe suffered by the herd during migration. Later, Coombs (1990), noting that the stratigraphic distribution of these remains is not consistent (see Weishampel 1984*a*), suggested that the dispersion pattern may have been a combination of both solitary individuals, maybe isolated bulls, and small assemblages, or that herding may have been seasonal rather than permanent.

In an evaluation of the three *Plateosaurus* bone beds (Frick, Trössingen, and Halberstadt), Sander (in press) will note five significant features: 1. Large number of individuals (30–80 known thus far), 2. specimens ranging from individual bones to almost complete skeletons, 3. all reasonably articulated skeletons in upright position, hind legs embedded deepest in rock, 4. carcasses showing typical desiccation pose (neck and tail strongly recurved), and, 5. posterior halves in incomplete skeletons considerably more common than anterior halves. Sander will conclude that these dinosaurs may have perished in mudholes, that the dead animals fell on their sides, and that the anterior parts of the bodies were torn apart by scavenging theropods (which shed teeth) and disarticulated by weathering.

Notes: Following Huene's (1926*a*) reconstruction of the skeleton of *Plateosaurus*, artist Rudolph Zallinger included a life restoration of *Plateosaurus*, reared up on its hind legs, in his Pulitzer Prize–winning mural, painted circa 1940 for the Yale Peabody Museum of Natural History. In the same mural, Zallinger depicted a second and less prominently seen

Plateosaurus down on all fours feeding on vegetation, thereby intimating that the dinosaur was well adapted as both a high and low browser. Due to subsequent numerous reproductions of the preliminary "cartoon" (which Zallinger painted before the execution of the mural), most notably for the fifth installment of "The World We Live In" series in *Life* magazine (September 7, 1953 issue), this restoration was a significant contribution to the public's awareness of *Plateosaurus* as a biped.

Both species *P. stormbergensis* Broom 1915 [*nomen dubium*] and *P. cullingworthi* Haughton 1924 were referred to the genus *Euskelosaurus*.

Key references: Coombs (1990); Cooper (1981); Fraas (1913); Galton (1971*b*, 1984*a*, 1985*d*, 1986*a*, 1990*a*); Huene (1907–8, 1926*a*, 1932); Jaekel (1913); Koken (1900); Meyer (1837); Ostrom (1962*b*); Paul (1985); Pidancet and Chopard (1862); Rütimeyer (1856); Versluys (1910); Weishampel (1984*a*).

PLEUROCOELUS   Marsh 1888—(=*Astrodon*)
Saurischia: Sauropodomorpha: Sauropoda:
   Brachiosauridae.
Name derivation: Greek *pleura* = "side" + Greek
   coelis = "hollow."

Type species: *P. nanus* Marsh 1888.
Other species: *P. valdeni* Lydekker 1889 [*nomen dubium*].
Occurrence: Arundel Formation, Maryland, Paluxy Formation, Glen Rose Formation, Texas, United States; Wealden, East Sussex, Isle of Wight, England; Boca du Chapin, Portugal; ?Niger, West Africa.
Age: Early Cretaceous (Hauterivian–Barremian).
Known material: Isolated remains of more than eight individuals, including cranial elements, tibia, fibula, teeth, dorsal and caudal centra, juvenile to adult.
Holotype: USNM 4968, dorsal and sacral vertebral centra, juvenile.

Diagnosis of genus (as for type species): Maxilla resembling that of *Camarasaurus* more than *Brachiosaurus*, as (missing) dorsal prefrontal process arises much farther forward (suggesting short, high skull of the former); dentary lighter, less deep than in *Camarasaurus*, more resembling *Brachiosaurus*; estimated 9–10 maxillary and 13 dentary teeth; teeth intermediate between spatulate camarasaur-brachiosaur type and slender peg-like *Diplodocus* or *Apatosaurus* type, generally cylindrical, relatively broader than in the latter; vertebral centra opisthocoelous, with huge

Pleurocoelous nanus, (left) USNM 4968, cotype dorsal vertebra, 4969 and 1970, cotype sacral vertebrae, and referred elements (juvenile).

Photo by the author, courtesy National Museum of Natural History, Smithsonian Institution.

Pleurocoelus

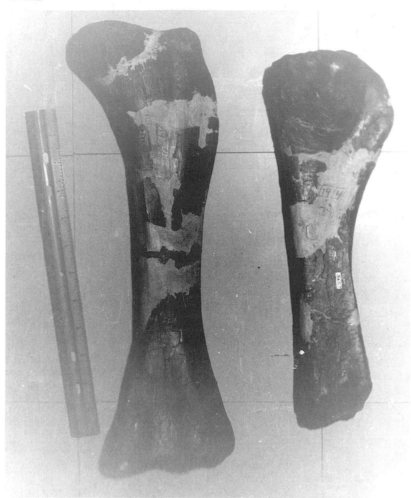

Pleurocoelous nanus, USNM 2263 and 5657, paratype femur and tibia (juvenile).

pleurocoels more strongly developed than in other known forms; cervical centra less elongated than in *Brachiosaurus*; sacral centra relatively elongated and solid, with depression for rib behind articular surface; caudal vertebrae resembling those of *Brachiosaurus*, short procoelous proximal centra with little backward convexity and no pleurocoels, caudal ribs directed caudolaterally and dorsally; neural spines relatively simple, low; most characteristic feature strong development of hyposphene-hypantrum articulation (Langston 1974) typical of sauropod dorsals but not developed in tail of other known forms; middle caudals with neural arch on cranial half of centrum; hemal canal not bridged over in chevrons; backwardly-directed expansion of scapula above glenoid fossa less protruding than in *Brachiosaurus*, distal end less splayed; humerus relatively long and slender, less so than in *Brachiosaurus*, apparently shorter than femur; radius slender, with distal expansion reminiscent of titanosaurids, proximal end not similarly expanded; radius with very sharp edge running down caudal (exterior) face; metacarpals long, slender; femur with prominence on upper lateral margin typical of brachiosaurids and titanosaurids (McIntosh 1990*b*).

Comments: The taxonomic history of *Pleurocoelous* begins with the naming of *Astrodon*, a genus founded upon a single tooth (YPM 798), obtained by a Mr. Tyson from the Arundel Formation (Early Cretaceous, Aptian) of Muirkirk, Prince Georges County, Maryland. The holotype tooth was first reported (though not described) by Johnston (1859), who assigned it a generic but no specific name. The specimen was subsequently described as spoon-shaped by Leidy (1865), who erected upon it the type species *A. johnstoni*.

The genus *Pleurocoelus* was later established upon partial vertebrae (USNM 4968) from a young individual, collected from the Arundel Formation at Muirkirk, Prince Georges County, Maryland.

Marsh (1888*a*) originally diagnosed *Pleurocoelous* as follows: Small sauropod, with rather small skull; teeth similar to those of *Diplodocus*, with shorter roots, more numerous, furnishing entire upper and lower jaws; dentary slender, rounded at symphysis; maxillary less robust than in *Diplodocus* and *Camarasaurus* [=*Morosaurus* of his usage]; cervical vertebrae long, strongly opisthocoelous; dorsal vertebrae with long, deep pleurocoels, somewhat longer than in *Camarasaurus*; sacral vertebrae longer, more solid than in *Camarasaurus*; first caudal centrum very short, with almost amphicoelous articular faces; caudal neural spines transversely compressed; middle and distal caudals relatively short, former bearing neural arch on anterior half of centrum; limb bones resembling those of *Camarasaurus*; toes more slender than in other sauropods, with less robust phalanges (Marsh 1888*a*).

The type species, *P. nanus,* was regarded by Marsh as typical of the genus, diagnosed as follows: Teeth with compressed or flattened crowns; dorsal vertebrae with low neural sutures and elongated excavation in each side of centrum; sacrals solid, with cavity in each side, face for rib in front; anterior caudals with flat articular faces and transversely-compressed neural spines; mid-caudals with neural arch on front half of centrum. The characters of this species suggested to Marsh that *Pleurocoelus* belonged in its own family, which he named Pleurocoelidae.

Marsh observed that *Pleurocoelus* included the smallest sauropod individuals known from North America, measuring approximately 8.8 meters (30 feet) in length (although *P. nanus* represents a juvenile). Marsh envisioned this form as resembling smaller species of *Camarasaurus*, though of slighter

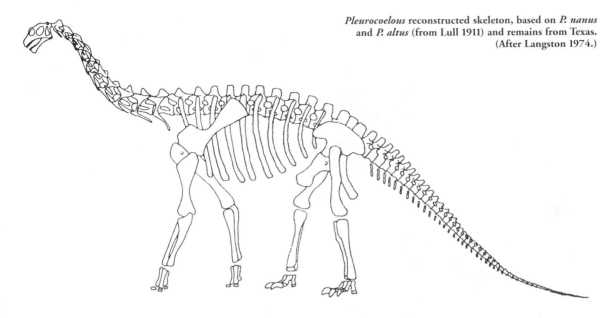

Pleurocoelous reconstructed skeleton, based on *P. nanus* and *P. altus* (from Lull 1911) and remains from Texas. (After Langston 1974.)

and more gracile build, measuring no more than 12–15 feet in length, and with a similar head.

A larger species, *P. altus* Marsh 1888, based on a tibia, and proximal and distal portions of a fibula, from the Arundel Formation of Maryland, is now known to represent an adult *P. nanus*. The skeletal drawing by Lull (1911), labeled *Astrodon nanus*, was based on this material.

Hatcher (1903c), observing striking similarities between the *A. johnstoni* holotype tooth and teeth of *Pleurocoelus nanus*, and pointing out that all related material collected by him came from iron ore beds at essentially or perhaps identically the same horizon and locality, proposed that these two genera be synonymized. *Astrodon* is now generally regarded as a *nomen dubium* abandoned in favor of the name *Pleurocoelous*.

The species *P. valdensis* Lydekker 1889 [*nomen dubium*] was based on two imperfect vertebrae and two teeth from the Wealden of Sussex and Isle of Wight. To this species (as *A. valdensis*) Lapparent and Zbyszewski (1957) referred three teeth from the Aptian of Boca do Chapin, Portugal. Two of these teeth are about 22 centimeters (over 8 inches) long, the third is much narrower.

Gallup (1975) described an articulated leg and pes (PR 977) that he identified as *Pleurocoelus*, collected from the Lower Cretaceous of Texas. As interpreted by Gallup, pedal digit IV bore a small claw, a feature atypical of sauropods.

According to McIntosh (1990b) in a review of the Sauropoda, *P. nanus* probably represents a small Early Cretaceous brachiosaurid survivor.

Teeth similar to YPM 798, from North America and Europe, were later referred to this genus. Lapparent (1960) reported "*Astrodon*" material from the Lower Cretaceous of In Gall, southern Sahara (Niger, West Africa). Galton (1981), however, pointed out that no teeth are known in the African material, and that the only illustrated bone, a small midcaudal vertebra, could belong to a juvenile *Rebbachisaurus tamesnensis* individual.

Notes: the two small vertebral centra (YPM 1908) from the Morrison Formation (Upper Jurassic) of Cañon City, Fremont County, Colorado, described by Marsh (1896) as *P. montanus* [*nomen dubium*] represents a very young *Camarasaurus grandis* (see McIntosh 1991b); *A. pusillus* was identified by Galton and Boine (1980) as stegosaurian, and subsequently referred by Galton (1981c) to *Dacentrurus armatus*.

Pleurocoelus is sometimes identified as the trackmaker of Early Cretaceous (Aptian–Albian) sauropod ichnites (AMNH 3065 and TMM 40638-1) now called *Brontopodus birdi* (named and described by

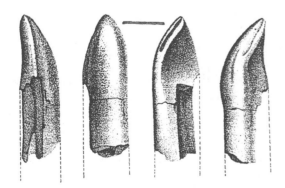

Pleurocoelous altus, YPM 798, holotype tooth of *Astrodon johnstoni*, in lateral, labial, lingual, lateral views. Scale = 1 cm. (After Leidy 1865.)

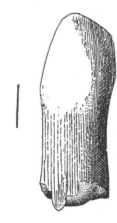

Pleurocoelous valdensis, holotype tooth. Scale = 1 cm. (After Lydekker 1889.)

Pleurocoelus

Fossil collector Roland T. Bird at holotype (AMNH 3065) trackway of *Brontopodus birdi*, attributed to *Pleurocoelous*.

Farlow, Pittman and Hawthorne 1989), discovered by Roland T. Bird in the bed of the Paluxy River, in what is now Dinosaur Valley State Park (Trinity Group, Comanchean Series, lower Glen Rose Limestone) in Glen Rose, Somervell County, Texas (tracks also known from West Verde Creek, extreme northern Medina County, Texas, and Howard County, Arkansas). For decades, these tracks were attributed to a "brontosaur." The most celebrated specimen from this site consists of parallel trackways of a sauropod and large theropod. Langston (1979) and Bird (1985) described the five-month task by Works Progress Administration workers in 1938 of excavating these and other tracks for the Texas Memorial Museum and American Museum of Natural History.

The parallel trackways were prepared by Bird for exhibition at the American Museum, originally displayed along with mounted skeletons of two Late Jurassic Morrison Formation genera, *Apatosaurus* and *Allosaurus*. Generally, these tracks have been interpreted as a record of a theropod pursuing or attacking a sauropod (Bird 1944, 1985; Langston).

Lockley (1986), after examining Bird's unpublished site map (discovered by James O. Farlow, Jr.) and Bird's original photographs and descriptions, pointed out that about a dozen sauropod trackways (Bird 1944) are present, recording the passage of a sauropod herd in the same direction. There are a total of four theropod trackways, one progressing in the opposite direction of the others. To Lockley, this pattern suggested that the carnivores may have followed a herd of sauropods, but that there is no evidence of a "one on one" attack.

Bird (1944) published a map of one Glen Rose site depicting the trackways of 23 sauropods, suggesting that the animals had passed as a single herd. To some authors, this seems evidence of gregarious behavior and apparently indicates the relative positions of adults and subadults when traveling. Bakker (1968) observed that the largest tracks were at the periphery of the herd, suggesting that adults flanked the group, although Ostrom (1972) stated that this interpretation was not clearly evident from Bird's map.

Lockley agreed with Ostrom, suggesting that earlier interpretations did not closely examine relationships of overlapping trackways. The tracks show that some larger individuals passed by first, that the animals were traveling in a series of groups that veered from left to right, and that they were actually following in line.

Pittman (1986) reported an extensive ?sauropod trackway (perhaps referable to *Pleurocoelus*) in the Lower Cretaceous De Queen Formation, discovered in 1983 at Brian Plant Quarry, Howard County, Arkansas. Front tracks are broadly U-shaped with distinct pad impressions, but without claw impressions. Rear tracks are about twice the size of front tracks, with laterally-directed claw marks for digits I–III, a broad pad at fourth position. One trackway site has recorded the movement of about ten dinosaurs across the lime mud surface.

As pointed out by Farlow (1987*b*, 1987*c*), linear or curved grooves sometimes occur with sauropod trackways at Dinosaur Valley State Park and other Texas ichnite sites. Farlow cautioned that these marks should not necessarily be interpreted as tail-drag impressions, as they are often identified. Though not entirely ruling out that interpretation, Farlow noted that the soft carbonate rocks in which Texas dinosaur prints occur readily develop rather linear grooves caused by erosion. These markings are parallel to flows of rivers, the beds of which have preserved these tracks. Making interpretation more difficult is the fact that Paluxy River sauropod trackways are oriented parallel to the direction of flow. Consequently, distinguishing possible tail-drag markings from current scours is difficult.

Paul (1988*a*) estimated that the sauropod that left the Paluxy River tracks weighed about 50 metric tons (more than 56 tons).

As noted by Farlow *et al.*, the name *Brontopodus* was coined by Bird, but never published or defined by him, except in a diagram of the American Museum slab (published by Farlow 1987*b*).

Farlow (1987*b*) noted that, if Gallup's interpretation of the foot of *Pleurocoelus* is correct and if *Pleurocoelus* did make the Glen Rose sauropod tracks, then the footprints suggest that the claw was rather

small or mostly buried in the tissues of the sole of the foot. It must be stressed, however, that almost never can dinosaur footprints be positively identified with any particular genus of dinosaur.

Key references: Bakker (1968); Bird (1944, 1985, 1989); Farlow (1987*b*, 1987*c*); Farlow, Pittman and Hawthorne (1989); Gallup (1975); Galton (1981); Hatcher (1903*c*); Johnston (1859); Langston (1974, 1979); Lapparent (1960); Lapparent and Zbyszewski (1957); Leidy (1865); Lockley (1986); Lull (1911); Lydekker (1889); Marsh (1888*a*, 1896); McIntosh (1990*b*, 1991*b*); Ostrom (1972); Paul (1988*a*); Pittman (1986).

Manus-pes set 52R in type trackway of *Brontopodus birdi*, attributed to *Pleurocoelous*.

PLEUROPELTUS Seeley 1881 [*nomen dubium*]—(See *Danubiosaurus*.)
Name derivation: Greek *pleura* = "side" + Latin *pelta* = "shield."
Type species: *P. suessii* Seeley 1881 [*nomen dubium*].

PODOKESAURUS Talbot 1911—(=?*Coelophysis*, ?*Rioarribasaurus*)
Saurischia: Theropoda *incertae sedis*.
Name derivation: Greek *podokes* = "swift-footed" + Greek *sauros* = "lizard."
Type species: *P. holyokensis* Talbot 1911.
Other species: [None.]
Occurrence: ?Portland Formation, Massachusetts, United States.
Age: Early Jurassic (?Pleinsbachian–Toarcian).
Known material/holotype: [Destroyed; formerly Mount Holyoke College collection], incomplete fragmentary skeleton, including 18 presacral and

Excavation (1938) by Roland T. Bird's American Museum of Natural History crew of Paluxy River trackway apparently recording a large theropod like *Acrocanthosaurus* stalking a sauropod like *Pleurocoelous* (theropod tracks named *Irenesauripus glenrosensis*, sauropod tracks *Brontopodus birdi*).

Podokesaurus

Podokesaurus hollyokensis, holotype incomplete postrcranial skeleton.

13 caudal vertebrae, coracoid, humerus, manus, pelvis, right hind leg, pes,

Diagnosis of genus (as for type species): Smaller than *Rioarribasaurus* [=*Coelophysis* of his usage]; pubis apparently longer than femur; femur shorter than tibia (Colbert 1989).

Comments: Basis for the family Podokesauridae Huene 1914, the genus *Podokesaurus* was founded on an incomplete skeleton measuring about one meter in length, found in a glacial boulder by Mignon Talbot, in the Longmeadow Sandstone, Portland Formation, Newark Supergroup, Holyoke, Hampden County, Massachusetts. The type specimen (museum at Mount Holyoke College, South Hadley, Massachusetts) was destroyed in a fire, though casts exist for study at the Yale Peabody Museum of Natural History and the American Museum of Natural History.

Talbot (1911) briefly described *Podokesaurus* as a "coelurosaurian," with a light and delicate skeletal framework consisting of hollow bones.

Colbert and Baird (1958) observed that the type species *P. holyokensis* was comparable in size to the [then known] smallest specimens of the Triassic Ghost Ranch theropod, "*Coelophysis bauri*" [=*Rioarribasaurus colberti*], and that both species are quite similar in proportions of the lengths of pubis and tibia. The *Podokesaurus* cast suggests an immature "*Coelophysis*" individual, making questionable the validity of *Podokesaurus* as a genus. After further studies of the *Podokesaurus* cast, Colbert (1964) concluded that it represented a juvenile "*Coelophysis*," though a different species, "*C.*" *holyokensis*, distinguished by less elongate neural spines among other slight differences.

Olsen and Galton (1977) redated the *Podokesaurus*-bearing beds as of Lower Jurassic age. In lieu of this redating and noting that the original type specimen of *Podokesaurus* was very incomplete, Colbert (1989) concluded that this genus might best

stand on its own, no attempt being made to resolve its status, though *Podokesaurus* could be congeneric with the Ghost Ranch theropod or Cope's original *Coelophysis* (see entry).

According to Olsen (1980*a*), Padian (1986), Rowe and Gauthier (1990), and Norman (1990), the name *Podokesaurus holyokensis* should be restricted to the type specimen, which, along with the natural casts [see notes below], should be regarded as Theropoda *incertae sedis*. Olsen added that this taxon is best retained as representing a species of small, early theropod whose relationships have not yet been resolved.

Notes: Colbert and Baird reported a "coelurosaurian" dinosaur from the uppermost Triassic of the Connecticut Valley. This record was represented by a sandstone block containing the natural casts of a pubis, tibia, and ribs (BSNH 13656), presented in 1864 by William B. Rogers to the Boston Society of Natural History. The block was apparently collected from the Portland arkose, Newark group, probably from quarries at Portland, Connecticut, across the Connecticut River from Middletown.

The casts were apparently formed after silt entered the bone impressions made in the alluvial plain, after the bones themselves had been swept away by rain. The silt hardened enough to preserve the imprints of the bones. During flooding of the plain by overflowing streams from the east, the impressions were filled with arkosic sand from fault-scarp uplands. This interpretation by Colbert and Baird is in accord with the climate and topography of the Triassic Connecticut Valley as reconstructed by Krynine (1950).

Colbert and Baird described this specimen as follows: Bones representing a small, slender, lightly-built "coelurosaur," comparable in size to largest known "*Coelophysis*" individuals, probably 2.5–3 meters (about 9 feet) from snout to tip of tail; as in "*Coelophysis*," pubis nearly as long as tibia; apparently long pubic symphysis; tibia with long cnemial crest of similar proportions. As the Portland specimen came from a stratigraphic level considerably above the Chinle Formation, Colbert and Baird designated the specimen *Coelophysis* sp., implying either a shifting of the Newark group in Connecticut to a lower position, or extension of the range of this genus to a later and higher limit. Colbert (1989) later doubted the assignment of these bone casts to "*Coelophysis*," as the Portland arkose is now regarded as of Early Jurassic age, based on palynological evidence, implying association with *Podokesaurus*.

Colbert (1970*a*) suggested that variously-sized Connecticut Valley fossil tracks, named *Grallator*, could be logically correlated with bones of "*Coelophysis*." A slab of such footprints in the New York

State Museum represents the only record of dinosaurs in that state (Fisher 1981). The slab was discovered by Paul E. Olsen and Robert Salvia in the Brunswick Formation of the Newark Group, near Nyack, Rockland County, New York.

The Palisades Diabase, a volcanic body within the Newark Group, was dated by Erickson and Culp (1961), utilizing potassium-argon isotope ratios, as originating about the Triassic-Jurassic boundary, 186–196 million years ago. Fisher showed that this diabase, at least in New York State, is geologically younger than the Brunswick Formation. According to Cornet, Traverse and McDonald (1973), fossil pollen evidence from the Hartford Basin in the Connecticut River Valley corresponds with European Jurassic-age pollen. Fisher noted that some structural geologists have advocated a relationship between the Newark and Hartford basins, regarding them, respectively, as west and east flanks of the same upfold or anticline, with the once-intervening redbeds having become eroded. This suggests, according to Fisher, that the Palisades Diabase are of Early Jurassic age, with the Jurassic-Triassic boundary, lying within the Brunswick Formation, about 200 million years old. Given this Jurassic age, *Podokesaurus* rather than *Rioarribasaurus* [=*Coelophysis* of Colbert's usage] might be a more likely trackmaker.

The New York slab bears at least two crossing trackways, one revealing a left foot 13 centimeters (about 5 inches) long and right foot 12 centimeters (over 4.6 inches) long, with strides measuring 49-51 centimeters (about 19-19.5 inches), the other tracks with footprints 14-15 centimeters (almost 5.4-5.8 inches) in length. Fisher pointed out that the disparity in foot size within one individual of walking animals is not unusual and that these tracks suggest an adult trackmaker weighing 45-57 kilograms (100-125 pounds).

Key references: Colbert (1964, 1970a, 1989); Colbert and Baird (1958); Fisher (1981); Norman (1990); Olsen (1980a); Padian (1986); Rowe and Gauthier (1990); Talbot (1911).

POEKILOPLEURON Eudes-Delongchamps 1838
Saurischia: Theropoda: ?Tetanurae: Megalosauridae.
Name derivation: Greek *poikilos* = "various" + Greek *pleura* = "side."
Type species: *P. bucklandii* Eudes-Delongchamps 1838.
Other species: ?*P. schmidti* Kiprijanov 1883 [*nomen dubium*].
Occurrence: Calcaire de Caen, Calvados, France; ?"Sewerische Osteolithe," Kursk.

Age: Middle Jurassic (Early Bathonian).
Known material/holotype: [Destroyed], 21 articulated caudal vertebrae in two articulated series, cervical and numerous dorsal ribs, gastralia, scapula, incomplete limb bones including humerus, radius, ulna, femur, tibia, manual, and pedal bones.

Diagnosis of genus: [No modern diagnosis published.]

Comments: The genus *Poekilopleuron* was founded upon fragmentary postcranial remains collected from the middle Dogger of Maladrerie, near Caen, France. The holotype, one of the first theropod skeletons discovered, was destroyed during World War II.

The material was described by Eudes-Delongchamps (1838), who at first believed it to be referrable to *Megalosaurus*, then later regarded it as generically distinct. Eudes-Delongchamps named the type species *P. bucklandii*, in case future discoveries warranted its referral to *M. bucklandii*.

Poekilopleuron was reassessed and redescribed by Huene (1923), who regarded the genus as representing a rather large species of *Megalosaurus*. Huene suggested that, since the specific names of both species were identical, the species should be more accurately designated *M. poikilopleuron*. Huene distinguished this species mostly by the forelimb, which is very short and heavy, the humerus stout and about half the length of the tibia. Huene stated that both manus and pes have five digits, although, according to Molnar (1990), reexamination of Huene's original illustrations shows no evidence that these are pentadactl. Huene (1926c) stated that Eudes-Delongchamps misidentified the scapula in the type specimen as a pubis, although this identification, according to Molnar, is still not certain.

In their description of the North American theropod *Torvosaurus*, Galton and Jensen (1979) observed various similarities between that genus and the European genera, *Poekilopleuron* and *Megalosaurus*, especially in the morphology of the forelimb and pelvic girdle. Paul (1984) suggested that both forms were congeneric, a synonymy later rejected by Britt (1991) (see *Torvosaurus* entry).

As noted by Molnar, the prominent medial process of the radius and apparent medial process at midlength of metacarpal II are unknown in other theropods; the chevrons display no "carnosaurian" characters and the scapula, if identified correctly, has a broad blade unlike that of any known "carnosaur."

Kurzanov (1990) observed that certain features (caudal vertebrae showing earliest appearance among "carnosaurs" of elongated prezygapophyses; moderately high astragalus with narrow ascending process,

Poekilopleuron bucklandi, holotype humerus. (After Eudes-Delongchamp, 1838.)

with small step on posterior margin, and with low body) in *Poekilopleuron* preclude this taxon's inclusion in the Megalosauridae, indicating affinities with the "Torvosauridae" (=Megalosauridae; see Britt), this genus probably being close to *Erectopus*.

According to Molnar, the species ?*P. schmidtii* (Kiprijanov 1883), represented by pieces of ribs and a poorly-preserved distal tibia, from the "Sewerische Osteolithe" (?Cenomanian to ?Santonian) at Kursk [formerly Union of Soviet Socialist Republics], could belong to any large Late Cretaceous theropod, the tibia not exhibiting the malleolar form characteristic of *P. bucklandii*.

Notes: Molnar (1982*a*) described a theropod caudal vertebra consisting of a centrum with an incomplete arch (NZGS CD1), from the "Mangataniwha Sandstone" (Upper Cretaceous) (Piripauan-Haumurian, corresponding to Campanian-Maastrichtian; see Wellman 1959), valley of the Mangahouanga Stream, tributary of the Te Hoe River, North Island, New Zealand. Molnar described the specimen as resembling caudals of *P. bucklandii*. As similarities exist between this specimen and other caudals, Molnar did not refer it to any genus.

Poikilopleuron [*sic*] *pusillus* Owen 1876 was made the type species of *Aristosuchus* by Seeley (1887) (see *Calamospondylus* entry); *Poicilopleuron* [*sic*] *valens* Leidy 1870 the type species of *Antrodemus valens* by Leidy (1870) (see *Allosaurus* entry).

Key references: Eudes-Delongchamps (1838); Huene (1923); Kiprijanov (1883); Molnar (1982*a*).

POLACANTHOIDES Nopcsa 1929 [*nomen dubium*]—(See *Polacanthus*.)
Name derivation: Greek *poly* = "many" + Greek *akantha* = "spine" + Greek *oeides* = "form."
Type species: *P. ponderosus* Nopcsa 1929 [*nomen dubium*].

POLACANTHUS Owen 1865—
(=*Polacanthoides, Vectensia*)
Ornithischia: Genasauria: Thyreophora: Ankylosauria: Nodosauridae.
Name derivation: Greek *poly* = "many" + Greek *akantha* = "spine."
Type species: *P. foxii* Owen 1865.
Other species: [None].
Occurrence: Wealden Marls (=Wessex Formation), Barnes High, Vectic Formation, Compton Bay beach area, Brixton, Isle of Wight, Bolney, Sussex, England.
Age: Early Cretaceous (Late-Valanginian-Barremian).
Known material: Two partial postcranial skeletons.

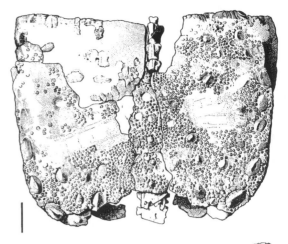

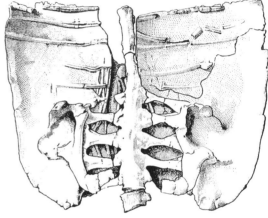

Polacanthus foxi, BMNH R175, holotype sacral shield, dorsal and ventral views. Scale = 3 cm. (After Hulke 1881.)

Holotype: BMNH R175, partial postcranial skeleton.
Diagnosis of genus (as for type species): Moderate- to large-sized nodosaurid; five fused presacral and five fused vertebrae; maximum sacral canal expansion at S2 level (as in the stegosaurs *Stegosaurus* and *Dacentrurus*); five sacral ribs; long posterior dorsal ribs supporting dermal armor and adjoining anterior portion of ilium; ribs dorsally flat, supported by ventral ridge that is T-shaped in cross-section; anterior caudal vertebrae with long lateral processes and thickened neural process with supraspinous notch; caudal-series vertebrae terminating in vertebral-dermal mass having ossified tendon possibly representing primitive tail club; presacral dorsal spines tallest above shoulder region, becoming shorter anteriorly and posteriorly; spines with flattened bases and, in large specimens, dorsal keel twists through almost 90 degrees from base to apex; presacral spines in two rows, lateral to spinal column; presacral "lumbar" region, sacrum, and both ilia covered by large, flat plate of dermal armor that measures about one meter square, this shield ornamented by dorsal ossifications; caudal armor consisting of double row of tall, erect, or short roof-like

plates with rounded and hollow bases, descending in height posteriorly; other armor including rounded, oval or subtriangular ossicles with maximum breadth of 110 millimeters (about 4.4 inches) (Blows 1982).

Comments: In 1843, Lee described and illustrated three pieces of dermal plates which, at the time, could not be referred to any known animal. These fossils were supposedly collected from the "Hastings Sands" of Sandown Bay, Isle of Wight (site correctly identified as the Wealden Marls by Rawson, Curry, Hancock, Neal, Wood and Worsam 1978). Lee reported that the fossils were lost in a hackney coach. Over a century later, Blows (1987) would identify these remains as belonging to the genus *Polacanthus*.

Polacanthus was established on a skeleton (BMNH R175) lacking the skull and forelimbs, collected by William Fox in 1865 from the Wessex Formation (now Wealden Marls) at Barnes High, near Atherfield, Isle of Wight. As these remains included a continuous armored shield (broken up beyond restoration during its extraction from the cliffs), Fox at first assumed them to belong to some huge turtle (Hulke 1881). The new genus and species combination *P. Foxii* [sic] was suggested by Owen (1858) for this material, the discovery announced anonymously by Owen (1865) in *The Illustrated London News*.

In describing the holotype of *P. foxii*, Hulke observed three forms of dermal scutes—simple flat scutes, keeled scutes and spine scutes. The pelvic region is overlaid by a continuous shield ornamented with tubercles. Perceiving no signs of joints, Hulke believed that this covering constituted one large structure. Because the nuchal and scapular regions were unknown in the holotype, Hulke could not ascertain how far anteriorly this "sacral shield" reached. The spines, fewest in number among the dermal ossifications, are asymmetrical and somewhat triangular in shape, shorter ones obtuse, longer spines acute. In the caudal region, there is an upper row and lower row of keeled scutes. From these remains, Hulke envisioned *Polacanthus* as a low-built animal, no longer than about .9 meters (3 feet).

The second Isle of Wight specimen referred to *Polacanthus*, consisting of part of the pelvis with some overlying dermal armor, was described by Lydekker (1891*b*). Seeley (1891*b*) suggested that this specimen might represent a new species, the armor seemingly smooth instead of patterned as in the holotype. Hennig (1924) referred this specimen to a new species, *P. becklesi*, which Blows (1987) later referred to *P. foxii*.

As *Polacanthus* seems to be quite similar to another European ankylosaur, *Hylaeosaurus*, and since the two forms lived at about the same time and in the same place, Coombs (1978*a*) suggested that they were congeneric. However, this assessment was challenged after additional details about *Polacanthus* surfaced with the discovery by William T. Blows, in 1979, of a well-preserved new specimen (BMNH R9293) in the Vectic Formation, Wealden Group, on Compton Bay beach, near Brook, Isle of Wight. This material com-

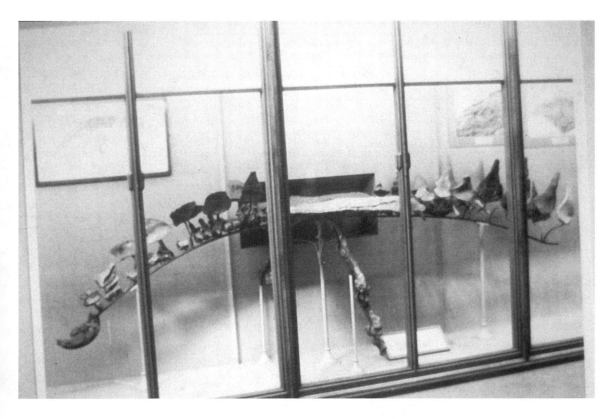

Polacanthus foxii, BMNH R175, holotype skeleton as formerly displayed at the [formerly named] British Museum (Natural History).

Photo courtesy W. T. Blows, J. I. Kirkland and the Natural History Museum, London.

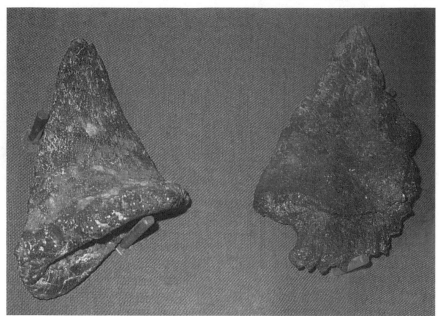

Polacanthus foxi, MIWG, dermal plates.

Polacanthus foxi, BMNH 1107, holotype left scapula of *Polacanthoides ponderosus.* (After Nopcsa 1929.)

prises some 30 elements, including a cranial fragment (?postorbital process), cervical vertebra, four dorsals, two caudals, the sacrum, cervical and dorsal rib, several rib fragments, two ilium fragments, several ischium fragments, four dorsal spines, five caudal plates, two plates of undetermined position, a *Hoplitosaurus*-type plate, several pieces of sacral shield, and numerous dermal ossicles (see Blows 1982). Though less complete than the holotype of *P. foxii*, this specimen was better preserved and, as described by Blows (1982, 1987), displays various elements not previously known. Based upon these specimens (BMNH R175, R9293), and additional fragmentary referred specimens (SMC B53353, B53354-53358, B53588-53591, B53594-53597, and B53372), Blows (1982) published a diagnosis of *P. foxi*.

Contra Coombs, Blows (1987) argued that a separation exists between the geological ranges of both genera, which may be a collecting anomaly, but could also have evolutionary significance, with *Hylaeosaurus* (South East English mainland geology, Wealden Series, Ryzanian to Berremian; see Rawson *et al.* 1978) considerably older than *Polacanthus* (Upper Weald Clay to Hythe Beds). Blows (1987) contended that positive conclusions are difficult to make given the inadequacy of Wealden collecting and the rarity of nodosaurids. Blows (1987) noted osteological differences between both forms, pointing out that no sign of a sacral shield has been found in any specimen of *Hylaeosaurus.* Blows (1987) concluded that *Polacanthus* should be regarded as a separate genus, geologically younger than *Hylaeosaurus*, with a different armor arrangement. In their review of the Ankylosauria, Coombs and

Maryańska (1990) maintained Coombs' earlier contention that *Polacanthus foxii*, as well as *Polacanthoides ponderosus, Vectensia* (based on a single dermal plate from the Isle of Wight; see Delair 1982), and *P. becklesi* were synonymous with *Hylaeosaurus armatus*, the characters listed by Blows (1987) concerning the first two taxa regarded by them as unconvincing for either specific or generic diagnosis.

More recently, after the collection of new material (including remains of *Mymoorapelta*; see entry), *Polacanthus* has generally come to be accepted as a valid genus distinct from *Hylaeosaurus* (Kirkland 1993; Pereda-Suberbiola 1993; Kirkland and Carpenter 1994). Later, Coombs (1995) regarded *Hylaeosaurus* as possibly a junior synonym of *Polacanthus.*

To *Polacanthus*, Blows (1987) referred two other type species, *Polacanthoides ponderosus* and *Hoplitosaurus marshi*: The genus *Polacanthoides* had been founded upon a left tibia (BMNH R1106) and left humerus (BMNH R1107) from Brixton, Isle of Wight, and left scapula (BMNH 2584) from Bolney, Sussex. Lydekker (1888) originally referred these remains to *Hylaeosaurus*, after which Nopcsa (1928a) erected for them the new genus *Polacanthoides*, without adding a specific name. Later, Nopcsa (1929b) introduced the new combination *P. ponderosus.* As Blows (1987) pointed out, the original type material from the Isle of Wight has been lost and the scapula from Bolney is clearly associated with a tibia (BMNH 2615) (Mantell 1841) not mentioned by Nopcsa.

According to Blows (1987), *Polacanthoides* is a *nomen dubium*, differing from *Hylaeosaurus* in the acromion process of the scapula, which is large and flange-like in *Polacanthoides,* but "thumb-like" in the other genus. (Earlier, Coombs 1978a emphasized that the size of the acromion process does not constitute sufficient grounds for establishing a genus. Coombs [personal communication 1988] disagreed with Blows' interpretation that the scapular spine of *H. armatus* is "thumb-like," adding that, if Blows' assessment that the scapula is unique among dinosaurs is correct, then *P. ponderosus* cannot be regarded as a *nomen dubium.*)

Although both *Blows* (1987) and, later, Pereda-Suberbiola (1993) regarded *Hoplitosaurus* as a junior synonym of *Polacanthus*, this synonymy was later rejected by Coombs (1995) (see *Hoplitosaurus* entry).

Notes: Various paleontologists and artists have attempted to make life restorations of *Polacanthus*, based on inadequate fossil material. Nopcsa (1905b) hypothetically restored the skeleton of *P. foxii* after the type material, incorporating various missing features based on the more completely known *Scelidosaurus* and *Stegosaurus*, to which he believed *Polacanthus* was related. Though the long dorsal spines had been scattered in a haphazard position near the rest of the holotype skeleton, Nopcsa positioned them in two upstanding paired rows surmounting the neck and dorsal region. Nopcsa put the sacral shield behind these spikes; following the shield were two rows of small stegosaur-like plates.

Using Nopcsa's reconstruction as a model, artist Neave Parker made a life restoration of *Polacanthus* in the late 1950s for a series of postcards issued by the British Museum (Natural History). Parker's restoration depicts the animal with a *Stegosaurus*-like head and two rows of large paired spines, the two tallest pairs located just behind the shoulder region. First published in the book *Dinosaurs* (Swinton 1962), this restoration, despite its being conjectural, has been the most frequently published restoration of the dinosaur to date and, therefore, has become its standard popular depiction. A more recent life restoration by John Sibbick, executed for Norman's (1985) book *The Illustrated Encyclopedia of Dinosaurs*, shows the spikes protruding almost horizontally from the neck, shoulder, and back areas, the long dorsal spines serving as a frill protecting the animal's flanks and legs.

Key references: Blows (1982, 1987); Bodily (1968, 1969); Coombs (1978a); Coombs and Maryańska (1990); Gilmore (1914b); Hennig (1924); Hulke (1881); Lee (1843); Lucas (1901, 1902); Lydekker (1888, 1891b); Mantell (1841); Nopcsa (1905b, 1928a, 1929b); Owen (1858, 1865); Pereda-Suberbiola (1993); Seeley (1891b).

POLYODONTOSAURUS   Sternberg 1932—(See *Troodon*.)
Name derivation: Greek *poly* = "many" + Greek *odous* = "tooth" + Greek *sauros* = "lizard."
Type species: *P. grandis* Sternberg 1932.

POLYONAX   Cope 1874 [*nomen dubium*]—(=? *Torosaurus*, ? *Triceratops*)
Ornithischia: Genasauria: Cerapoda: Marginocephalia: Ceratopsia: Neoceratopsia: Ceratopsidae: Chasmosaurinae.
Name derivation: Greek *poly* = "many" + Greek *anax* = "master."
Type species: *P. mortuarius* Cope 1874 [*nomen dubium*].
Other species: [None.]
Occurrence: Lance Formation, Colorado, United States.
Age: Late Cretaceous (Maastrichtian).
Known material/holotype: AMNH 3950, three dorsal vertebrae, limb-bone fragments and horn core fragments, subadult.
Diagnosis of genus: [No modern diagnosis published.]

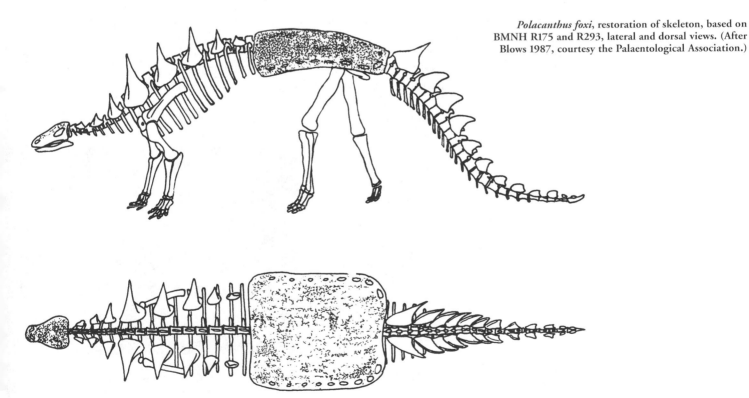

Polacanthus foxi, restoration of skeleton, based on BMNH R175 and R293, lateral and dorsal views. (After Blows 1987, courtesy the Palaentological Association.)

Polyonax mortuarius, AMNH 3950, holotype dorsal vertebrae and horn-core fragments.

Comments: The genus *Polyonax* was established upon fragmentary remains (AMNH 3950) found by Edward Drinker Cope in 1873, in the Laramie Formation (Hatcher, Marsh and Lull 1907), now called the Lance Formation, Colorado.

Polyonax was diagnosed by Cope (1874) as follows: Vertebrae most characteristic, more anterior vertebra shorter than other, with slightly concave articular faces; articular faces of larger vertebra strongly concave; sides of vertebrae concave, neural arches relatively small.

Cope diagnosed the type species *P. mortuarius* as follows: Articular faces of vertebrae deeper than wide, sides smooth, lower face narrowed and probably keeled. [The specific characters observed by Cope are now known to apply to all large ceratopsids.]

Marsh (1896), Cope's professional rival, stated that no evidence existed for separating *Polyonax* from *Agathaumas*. As *Polyonax* was founded on inadequate fragmentary and undiagnostic type material, Hatcher (1896) rejected this taxon as a *nomen nudum*. Generally regarded today as synonymous with *Torosaurus* or *Triceratops*, the *Polyonax* material, lacking as it does a skull, is indeterminate and cannot be definitely assigned to any genus.

Key references: Cope (1874); Hatcher (1896); Marsh (1896).

PRENOCEPHALE Maryańska and Osmólska 1974

Ornithischia: Genasauria: Cerapoda: Marginocephalia: Pachycephalosauria: Pachycephalosauridae.

Name derivation: Greek *prenes* = "inclined" + Greek *cephale* = "head."

Type species: *P. prenes* Maryańska and Osmólska 1974.

Other species: [None.]

Occurrence: Nemegt Formation, Omnogov, Mongolian People's Republic.

Age: Late Cretaceous (?Late Campanian or Early Maastrichtian).

Known material/holotype: ZPAL MgD-I/104, complete skull with teeth but lacking lower jaws, several fragmentary dorsal vertebrae, caudal vertebra, fragmentary dorsal ribs, damaged left femur, right femur missing greater and lesser trochanters and lateral condyle, numerous free caudal tendons.

Diagnosis of genus (as for type species): Prefrontals, supraorbitals, postorbitals, and portion of squamosals incorporated into very high dome; parietosquamosal shelf not developed; supratemporal fenestrae entirely closed; dome surface slightly roughened; row of conspicuous nodes along caudolateral and caudal skull margins (Maryańska 1990).

Comments: The genus *Prenocephale* was established on a perfectly preserved and partial skeleton (ZPAL MgD-I/104), collected during a Polish-Mongolian Paleontological Expedition (Kielan-Jaworoska and Dovchin 1968/1969; Kielan-Jaworoska and Barsbold 1972), from the Nemegt Formation, Nemegt Basin, Gobi Desert, Mongolian People's Republic (Gradziński and Jerzykiewicz 1972).

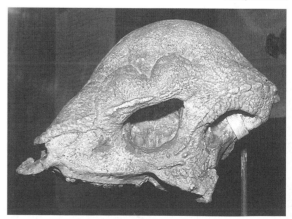

Prenocephale prenes, ZPAL MgD-I/104, holotype skull, left lateral view, in "The Great Russian Dinosaurs" exhibit (1996), Mesa Southwest Museum, Mesa, Arizona.

Maryańska and Osmólska (1974) originally diagnosed the monotypic *P. prenes* as follows: Frontoparietal dome prominent, highest point above postorbital bar; no parietosquamosal shelf; orbit subcircular in outline, with flattened dorsal margin; upper margin of orbit formed by two supraorbital bones, frontal and prefrontal excluded from orbit; postorbital long; long edentulous area separating premaxillary part of snout from maxillary; three incisiform premaxillary teeth with serrated crest developed along posterior faces of crowns; 17 maxillary teeth, crowns small with worn-down ventral edges, arranged in straight line outwardly bent at posterior end; no supratemporal opening; infratemporal opening short, broad; antorbital opening; squamosals strongly swollen, overhanging occipital, central part deeply depressed; foramen magnum small, round; occipital condyle small; basal tuber flat, ventral edge near quadrate wing of pterygoid; basisphenoid deeply wedged dorsally between basal tuber and pterygoids; dome with rough surface, row of nodes developed along posterolateral and posterior margins of skull.

As measured by Maryańska and Osmólska, the length of the skull, from premaxilla to upper end of quadrate, is 218 millimeters (about 8 inches); greatest width of is 169 millimeters (almost 6.5 inches), greatest height 170 millimeters.

Maryańska and Osmólska observed that the pointed nodes are developed in a prominent line along the margin of the cranial roof, becoming less prominent as they pass downwards onto the postorbital bar. A convex ridge is present above the orbit, continuing forwards in the form of separate tubercules along the lateral margin of the nasal. Irregular tubercles completely cover the surface of the external bones (except for the frontoparietal dome).

As noted by Maryańska and Osmólska, the orbits in pachycephalosaurs are very large and deep, with bony walls to protect the eyes. Though the orbits face laterally, they strongly tend to extend the field of vision anteriorly, a tendency climaxed in *Prenocephale*, which also had a very large optic nerve. Vision, with the eyes somewhat forwardly directed, must have played an important role in the lives of such animals.

Key references: Gradziński and Jerzykiewicz (1972); Maryańska (1990); Maryańska and Osmólska (1974).

PRICONODON   Marsh 1888 [*nomen dubium*]
Ornithischia: Genasauria: Thyreophora:
   Ankylosauria: Nodosauridae.
Name derivation: Old English *prica* = "punctured"
   + Greek *odon* = "tooth."

Priconodon crassus, USNM 2135, holotype tooth, a. labial, b. edge, c. lingual views. Scale = 1 cm. (After Marsh 1896.)

Type species: *P. crassus* Marsh 1888 [*nomen dubium*].
Other species: [None.]
Occurrence: Arundel Formation, Maryland, United States.
Age: Early Cretaceous.
Known material/holotype: USNM 2135, tooth.
   Diagnosis of genus: [No modern diagnosis published.]
   Comments: The genus *Priconodon* was founded on a tooth (USNM 2135), recovered from the Arundel Formation of Muirkirk, Prince Georges County, Maryland.
   Marsh (1888a; 1896) described this tooth as follows: Resembles teeth typical of *Stegosaurus* [=*Diracodon* of his usage], with narrow neck, swollen based, flattened crown; differing in serrated edges meeting above at sharp angle rather than forming wide curve at apex (Marsh 1888a, 1896).
   Although Marsh regarded this tooth as stegosaurian, Coombs (1978a) assigned *Priconodon* to the ankylosaurian family Nodosauridae. In their review of the Ankylosauria, Coombs and Maryańska (1990) regarded *P. crassus* as a *nomen dubium*.
   Key references: Coombs (1978a); Coomb and Maryańska (1990); Marsh (1888a, 1896).

PRIODONTOGNATHUS   Seeley 1875 [*nomen dubium*]
Ornithischia: Genasauria: Thyreophora:
   Ankylosauria: ?Nodosauridae.
Name derivation: Greek *prion* = "saw" + Greek *odous* = "tooth" + Greek *gnathos* = "jaw."
Type species: *P. phillipsii* (Seeley 1869) [*nomen dubium*].
Other species: [None.]
Occurrence: ?Lower Calcareous Grit, North Yorkshire, England.
Age: Late Jurassic (?Corallian [Oxfordian]).
Known material: Maxilla, teeth, ?femur.
Holotype: SMC B53408, left maxilla.
   Diagnosis of genus (as for type species): Maxilla with offset anteromedial process fitting into premax-

illa; separate lateral and medial sheets dorsally; 18 large maxillary teeth, with uniformly enamelled and unornamented lateral and medial surfaces; tooth crowns acute, slightly recurved posteriorly; nine acute denticles anteriorly, seven posteriorly; medial cingulum two subcrescents separated by small space, with downward-curving ventral part; numerous fine denticles on ventral edge (Galton 1980b).

Comments: The genus *Priodontognathus* was established on a maxilla (SMC B53408) collected from an unknown locality, probably on the coast of Yorkshire, England (Seeley 1893). Believing the specimen to belong to an iguanodontid, Seeley (1869) originally made it the holotype of a new species of *Iguanodon*, *I. phillipsi*. Later, Seeley (1875b) recog-

nized this specimen as representing a distinct genus, which he named *Priodontognathus*.

Priodontognathus has generally been classified as a stegosaur. However, Galton (1980b) showed that, as in ankylosaurs (Coombs 1971, 1978a), the ventral part of the lateral sheet of the maxilla curves out laterally, forming the base of a horizontal shelf-like area. As teeth in *Priodontognathus* resemble those of the nodosaurids *Priconodon* and *Sauropelta*, Galton tentatively referred the genus to the Nodosauridae.

Seeley (1893) referred a femur to this taxon, although this bone cannot be compared to the holotype.

Key references: Galton (1980b); Seeley (1869, 1893).

Priodontognathus phillipsii, SM B53408, holotype maxilla fragment, 1. external, 2. internal, 3. ventral, 4. dorsal views. Scale = 1.33 cm. (After Seeley 1875.)

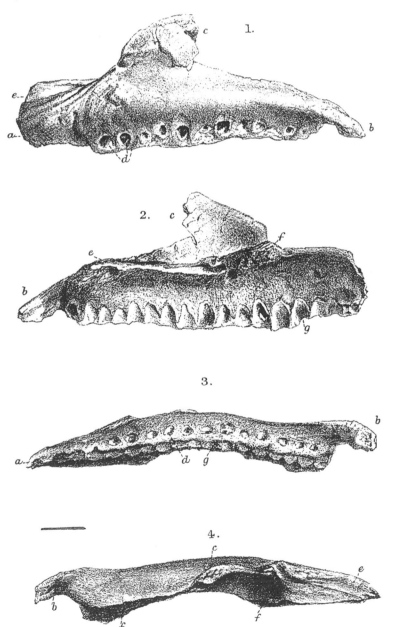

PROBACTROSAURUS Rozhdestvensky 1966

Ornithischia: Genasauria: Cerapoda: Ornithopoda: Iguanodontia.

Name derivation: Greek *pro* = "before" + "*Bactrosaurus*."

Type species: *P. gobiensis* Rozhdestvensky 1966.

Other species: *P. alashanicus* Rozhdestvensky 1966.

Occurrence: Dashuigou Formation, Nei Mongol Zizhiqu, People's Republic of China.

Age: Late Cretaceous (?Cenomanian).

Known material: Skeleton with skull, fragmentary skull, skeleton (subadult).

Holotype: PIN 2232/1, almost complete skeleton.

Diagnosis of genus (as for type species): Medium to large iguanodont, at least 5–6 meters (17–over 20 feet) long; skull slightly elevated in temporal-occipital region, there about as wide as or slightly narrower than in orbital region; occipital margin with relatively shallow depression; height (through orbit) to length of skull ratio about 1.2; quadrate straight, relatively thin; maximum height of maxilla at three-fourths distance from anterior end; tooth rows consisting of both actively shedding and actively replacing rows, with rudimentary third tooth row; at least 23 maxillary and from 21 to 23 dentary teeth; mandibular teeth with one median, strongly-developed crest on crown, two lateral, less-developed crests, anterior crest reaching apex of crown; height to width of crown ratio slightly more than 2.1; six sacral vertebrae, fourth-sixth with median depression ventrally in form of sulcus; sternum with moderately dilated anterior portion occupying about one-fourth length; scapula with dilated proximal end broader than distal end; coracoids not high proximally; humerus with poorly-developed deltopectoral crests usually not reaching middle of shaft, about half as long as scapula, slightly longer than ulna; metacarpals long, rather thin; ilium with narrow, slightly curved

Photo by the author.

Probactrosaurus gobiensis referred skeleton (subadult) in "The Great Russian Dinosaurs" exhibit (1996), Mesa Southwest Museum, Mesa Arizona.

anterior process about 1.5 times length of base, posterior process a subtriangular lobe; prepubis with horizontal and abruptly convex superior margin, maximum width about one-third length; ischium straight, proximal end about one-third as wide as entire length; femur slightly longer than tibia, fourth trochanter at about mid-length; distal condyles of femur not closing foramen dividing them in front, dissimilar, inner condyle noticeably broader; metatarsals relatively long, III less than 2.5 times length of femur (Rozhdestvensky 1966).

Diagnosis of *P. alashanicus*: Distinguished from type species by skull with broader supratemporal depressions and high occiput; clearly expressed distention rising conspicuously above surface of calvaria at frontal-parietal boundary (possibly due to deformation during fossilization); tooth crown elongate; scapula with sharply-dilated proximal end; ilium with curved dorsal surface and strongly-developed postacetabular process; hindlimb bones with dilated epiphyses (Rozhdestvensky 1966).

Comments: The genus *Probactrosaurus* was founded upon a skeleton (PIN 2232/1) discovered in the uppermost bed (Cenomanian, based on morphological affinities of these remains; Rozhdestvensky 1966) of Maortu, Alashan, China. The material was collected during the 1959-1960 Soviet-Chinese Paleontological Expedition (Rozhdestvensky and Chao 1960; Rozhdestvensky 1961). As noted by

Rozhdestvensky (1966), this discovery constituted the first in which iguanodont remains were found with those of hadrosaurid descendents.

Rozhdestvensky (1966) described a second species, *P. alashanicus*, based on the posterior part of a skull (PIN 2232/46), from the same horizon and locality as the type species. Rozhdestvensky (1966) noted that both species resemble one another in general appearance and dimensions.

Rozhdestvensky (1966) suggested that *Probactrosaurus* could have been ancestral to the later hadrosaurid, *Bactrosaurus*. As noted by Rozhdestvensky (1966), *Probactrosaurus* displays such primitive characters typical of the Iguanodontidae as narrow snout, double-layer tooth-row structure, elongate lower jaw, poorly-developed zygomatic bone, no crests on dorsal surface of skull, great dilation of proximal portion of scapula, subtriangular shape of postacetabular lobe of ilium, and lack of suprailiac crest.

Comparing *Probactrosaurus* to *Iguanodon* and *Bactrosaurus*, Rozhdestvensky (1966) concluded that *Probactrosaurus* is morphologically halfway between those two genera, except that its foot is overly long, a feature for which it merits its own generic status. However, as pointed out by Brett-Surman (1989), large feet is a juvenile feature.

In their reassessment of the Iguanodontidae and related ornithopods, Norman and Weishampel (1990)

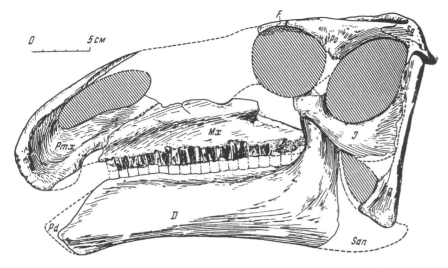

Probactrosaurus gobiensis, PEN AN SSR 2232/1, holotype incomplete skull, left lateral view. (After Rozhdestvensky 1966.)

regarded *Probactrosaurus* as an iguanodontian belonging to its own unnamed family and most closely related to hadrosaurids, sharing with Hadrosauridae a single replacement tooth in each maxillary and dentary tooth family, maxillary teeth with ridges symmetrical on either side of median primary ridge, straight ischium, and loss of metatarsal I.

Key references: Brett-Surman (1989); Norman and Weishampel (1990); Rozhdestvensky (1961, 1966); Rozhdestvensky and Chao (1960).

PROCERATOPS   Lull 1906—(See *Ceratops*).

Name derivation: Greek *pro* = "before" + Greek *keratos* = "horned" + Greek *ops* = "face."
Type species: *P. montanus* (Marsh 1888).

PROCERATOSAURUS   Huene 1926

Saurischia: Theropoda: Tetanurae: Coelurosauria *incertae sedis*.
Name derivation: Greek *pro* = "before" + "*Ceratosaurus.*"
Type species: *P. bradleyi* (Woodward 1910).
Other species: [None.]
Occurrence: Great Oolite, Gloucestershire, England.
Age: Middle Jurassic (Bathonian).
Known material/holotype: BMNH R4860, partial skull with mandibles.

Diagnosis of genus: [No modern diagnosis published.]

Comments: *Proceratosaurus* was originally described by Woodward (1910) as a new species of *Megalosaurus*, which he named *M. bradleyi*, based on a skull (BMNH R4860) discovered in the Great Oolite of Gloucestershire, England.

Woodward distinguished *M. bradleyi* mostly by the presence of a bony nasal horn core, for which he incorrectly assumed that this species was related to the horned *Ceratosaurus*.

Later, Huene (1926*c*, 1926*d*) redescribed the holotype of *M. bradleyi* and attempted to restore the missing upper parts of the skull, at the same time suggesting that the specimen represented a new genus which he named *Proceratosaurus*. Huene (1926*b*) diagnosed the monotypic *P. bradleyi* as follows: Differs markedly from *M. bucklandii, Eustreptospondylus* [=*Streptospondylus* of his usage], and *Allosaurus* [=*Antrodemus* of his usage]; more teeth, four in premaxilla (four preserved, fifth possibly having space behind them), 18 in maxilla (with two gaps); premaxillary teeth with unusual lateral, flat, longitu-

Proceratosaurus bradleyi, BMNH R4860, holotype incomplete skull of *Megalosaurus bradleyi*, left lateral view.

dinal folds, one near top, many others at base; external narial openings differing in shape from megalosaurids and *Ceratosaurus*, shape and breadth of ascending process of maxilla also different; height of preorbital openings much greater than in *Megalosaurus* and *Eustreptospondylus*, orbits and infratemporal openings relatively smaller and narrower; lateral temporal opening apparently relatively broad; squamosal more curved in intertemporal arch than in megalosaurids; quadrate articulation relatively low; skull 26 centimeters (about 10 inches).

Walker (1964) observed that *Proceratosaurus* differs from "carnosaurs" in many features, most markedly in the small size of the skull, anterior triangular extension of maxilla, rounded orbit, apparently small lateral temporal opening, low position of jaw-articulation, slender jaws, rather small teeth, and probably low build of the posterior area of the skull.

Paul (1984) suggested that *Proceratosaurus* and the North American genus *Ornitholestes* form a clade, both possessing nasal horns, and conical, large rooted, poorly-serrated teeth, premaxillary teeth very small; and that both genera form a clade with *Allosaurus*, sharing broad, down- and forward-sloping squamosal-quadratojugal contacts, and metatarsal III L-shaped in proximal view. Later, Paul (1988*b*) suggested that *Proceratosaurus* and *Ornitholestes* are similar enough to be paired within a new subfamily Ornitholestinae, within Allosauridae [these groupings not generally accepted]. In his book, *Predatory Dinosaurs of the World*, Paul (1988*c*) noted that teeth in *Proceratosaurus* show the greatest degree of heterodonty among all known theropod dinosaurs, those in the tips of the jaws much smaller and more conical.

Molnar (1990) later pointed out that the surangular in *P. bradleyi* is shallow (a deep surangular was then regarded as a diagnostic character of "carnosaurs"). More recently, Currie and Zhao (1993*a*) noted that previous assumptions (Woodward 1910; Huene 1926; Paul 1988) that the projection above the narial opening in this genus represents the anteroproximal portion of a horn core (similar to the midline horn in *Ceratosaurus*) are not correct. Currie and Zhao suggested the possibility that this structure in *Proceratosaurus* represents not a nasal horn but rather a midline crest.

Key references: Currie and Zhao (1993*a*); Huene (1926*c*, 1926*d*); Molnar (1990); Paul (1981, 1988*b*, 1988*c*); Walker (1964); Woodward (1910).

PROCHENEOSAURUS Matthew 1920—(See *Corythosaurus, Lambeosaurus*.)
Name derivation: Greek *pro* = "before" + "*Cheneosaurus*."
Type species: *P.* [no type species named] (Parks 1931).

PROCOMPSOGNATHUS Fraas 1913 [*nomen dubium*]—(=?*Pterospondylus*)
Saurischia: Theropoda: Ceratosauria: ?Coelophysoidea.
Name derivation: Greek *pro* = "before" + "*Compsognathus*."
Type species: *P. triassicus* Fraas 1913 [*nomen dubium*].
Other species: [None.]
Occurrence: Mittlerer Stubensandstein, Baden-Württemberg, Germany.
Age: Late Triassic (Middle Norian).
Known material/holotype: SMNS 12591, two cervical, 14 dorsal (with ribs), and 13 caudal vertebrae, right scapulocoracoid, left radius, ulna, incomplete manus, pubes, fragment of ?right ischium, right hindlimb, left femur, fragment of left tibia.

Diagnosis of genus: [No modern diagnosis published.]

Comments: The genus *Procompsognathus* was established upon a partial skeleton (SMNS 12591) [originally including an incomplete skull] contained within three stone blocks, collected during the early 1900s from a sandstone quarry near Plaffenhofen (now Heilbronn), Württemberg, [former Federal Republic of] Germany. The blocks, which contained, respectively, a skull, most postcrania, and anterior caudal vertebrae, were partially prepared by quarry manager Gottlieb Mayer and brought by him to Professor Eberhard Fraas of Stuttgart.

Assuming that the skull belonged with the postcrania, Fraas (1913, 1914) diagnosed the monotypic

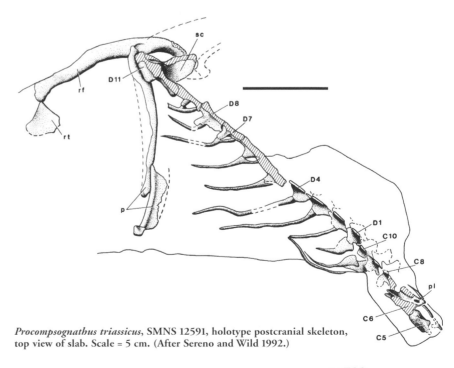

Procompsognathus triassicus, SMNS 12591, holotype postcranial skeleton, top view of slab. Scale = 5 cm. (After Sereno and Wild 1992.)

P. triassicus as follows: Small leaping dinosaur of bird-like construction, resembling *Compsognathus*; skull elongate, low, 8 centimeters (more than 3 inches) long; orbits large, circular in outline; antorbital openings triangular; teeth slightly recurved, sharply pointed; 14 dorsal vertebrae; tibia longer than femur; hindlimb over three times longer than forelimb; manus with five digits, pes three; metatarsals birdlike, long and slender, showing no sign of fusion.

Fraas (1913) did not illustrate the type specimen.

Huene (1921) later published a more detailed description. Subsequently, Huene (1928) placed the genus in its own family, Procompsognathidae. A second specimen (SMNS 12352) contained in two blocks, the remains consisting of the snout of a larger skull and a left manus, was later referred by Huene (1932) to *P. triassicus*.

Ostrom (1978) suggested that *Procompsognathus* might not be a dinosaur, but rather a "pseudosuchian," observing that the pubis lacks the terminal expansion typical of most theropods. After reexami-

nation of the *Procompsognathus* material, Ostrom (1981) listed the following features that suggest affinity with "coelurosaurian" theropods: 1. Slightly bowed, rectangular pubic apron; 2. tridactyl foot, symmetrical about digit III, II and IV shorter than III and of subequal length, partially reflected, distally-situated hallux not contacting tarsus, and digit V reduced to a splint-like remnant of the metatarsal; 3. suggestion of mesotarsal joint; 4. femur with simple planar curve; 5. tibia significantly longer than femur; 6. short, slender radius and ulna; and 7. hollow bones, this latter feature of only doubtful value.

Ostrom (1981) concluded that *Procompsognathus* is a dinosaur closely related to *Coelophysis* and *Halticosaurus*, also noting that its pubis, which is anteroposteriorly compressed and lacks a salient "foot," strikingly resembles that of the small North American ceratosaur, *Segisaurus*.

Ostrom (1981) suggested that Huene's specimen may not be referrable to *Procompsognathus*, noting various perceived differences in the skulls. Also, Huene's specimen is about 50 percent larger than the holotype; and metacarpals II-V are long and of about equal length, making *Procompsognathus* unique among the Theropoda.

Norman (1990) noted that, mostly because of pelvic structure, *Procompsognathus* had been tentatively allied with other Late Triassic/Early Jurassic forms (*e.g.*, *Coelophysis, Syntarsus*, and *Halticosaurus*). Norman pointed out that the structure of the pelvis is also reminiscent of such derived archosaurs as lagosuchids and herrerasaurids. As the supposed diagnostic characters of the pelvis are primitive for all theropods, Norman regarded *P. triassicus* as a *nomen dubium*.

More recently, Sereno and Wild (1992) used cladistic analysis to reevaluate the holotype of *P. triassicus*, discovering the specimen to be a paleontological chimera created by quarrymen from the postcranial skeleton of a *Segisaurus*-like ceratosaurian theropod and skull (as is that of Huene's referred specimen) of the contemporary basal sphenosuchian crocodylomorph, *Saltoposuchus connectens*.

Sereno and Wild restricted the holotype and hypodigm of *P. triassicus* to the articulated postcranial skeleton (SMNS 12591), its theropod status evidenced by these accepted synapomorphies: 1. Low forelimb/hindlimb ratio (reversed in some theropods), 2. short metatarsal I with splint-shaped proximal end articulating against midshaft of II, 3. elongate, curved, splint-shaped metatarsal V, 4. pleurocoel near anterior end of cervical centrum (preserved on the ?fifth cervical), 5. manual digit IV reduced relative to digits I-III, and 6. absence of manual digit V.

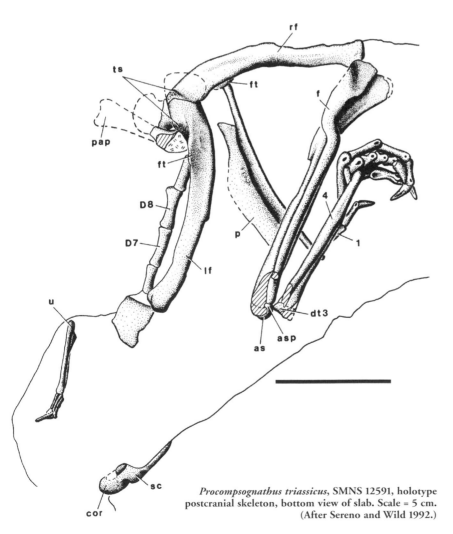

Procompsognathus triassicus, SMNS 12591, holotype postcranial skeleton, bottom view of slab. Scale = 5 cm. (After Sereno and Wild 1992.)

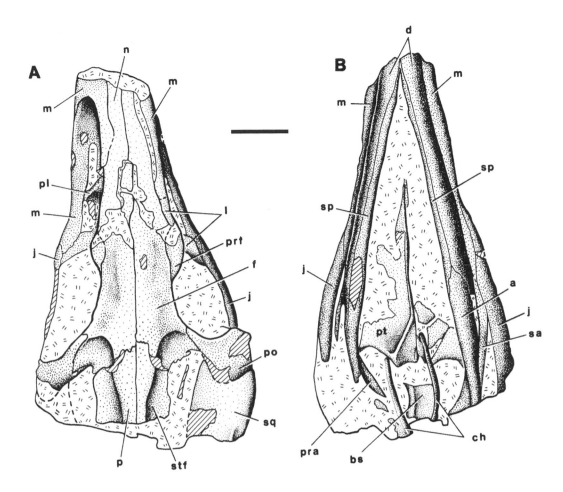

A

B

Skull (SMNS 12591) associated with holotype of *Procompsognathus triassicus*, A. dorsal and B. ventral views. Scale = 1 cm. (After Sereno and Wild 1992.)

Referral by Sereno and Wild of the postcrania to Ceratosauria was based on such features as these: 1. Flattened pubis (as in *Segisaurus*), 2. femur with sigmoid trochanteric shelf (identical to ceratosaurs *Syntarsus* and *Rioarribasaurus* [=*Coelophysis* of their usage]), and 3. coossified astragalocalcaneum. The deep iliac preacetabular process, very well-developed supraacetabular crest, and form of the pubis indicate that *P. triassicus* is not a basal theropod, but rather a derived ceratosaur quite similar to *Rioarribasaurus* and particularly *Segisaurus* (Sereno, in preparation).

However, the taxonomic status of *Procompsognathus* may not be entirely resolved. Chatterjee (1993*b*), in a preliminary report, observed that the skull lacks all the specializations of sphenosuchians, but possesses various theropod synapomorphies (*e.g.*, accessory maxillary fenestra; vomers fused anteriorly; quadrate head received entirely by squamosal without paroccipital contact; laterosphenoid with transpostorbital processes; broad lacrimal exposure on skull roof); and that the otic capsule closely resembles that of *Syntarsus*.

Key references: Chatterjee (1993*b*); Fraas (1913, 1814); Huene (1921, 1928, 1932); Norman (1990); Ostrom (1978, 1981); Sereno and Wild (1992).

PRODEINODON Osborn 1924

Saurischia: Theropoda *incertae sedis*.

Name derivation: Greek *pro* = "before" + "*Deinodon.*"

Type species: *P. mongoliensis* Osborn 1924 [*nomen dubium*].

Other species: ?*P. kwangshiensis* Hou, Yeh and Chao 1975 [*nomen dubium*].

Occurrence: Khukhtekskaya Svita, Ovorokhangai, Mongolian People's Republic; Nei Mongol Zizhiqu, possibly Napai Formation, Guangxi Zhuangzu Zizhiqu, People's Republic of China.

Age: Early Cretaceous (Aptian).

Known material: Isolated teeth.

Holotype: AMNH 6265, upper portion of tooth.

Diagnosis of genus (as for type species): Tooth crown with flattened sides [=quadrate shape], rounded anterior border, compressed posterior border terminating in minutely serrate ridge (Osborn 1924b).

Diagnosis of ?*P. kwangshiensis*: Teeth compressed; anterior edges bending backward; posterior edges straight (Hou, Zhou and Chao 1975).

Comments: The discovery of *Prodeinodon* marked the occurrence of large theropods in the Early Cretaceous of Mongolia.

Photo by R. A. Long and S. P. Welles (neg. #73/407-26), courtesy American Museum of Natural History.

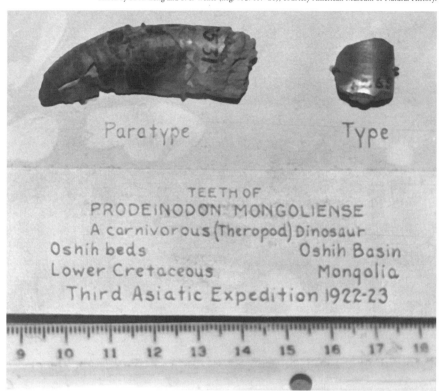

Prodeinodon mongoliensis,
**paratype tooth and AMNH
6265, holotype tooth.**

The genus was founded upon a fragmentary tooth (AMNH 6265), collected by Walter Granger from the Khukhtekskaya Formation (Lower Cretaceous) at Oshih Nuru (Ashile), Red Mesa, Mongolian People's Republic. Granger also collected a complete tooth (AMNH 6531) from the same locality (Osborn 1924b).

Osborn observed that the holotype of *Prodeinodon* most closely agrees in form with that of *Aublysodon.*

To the type species, *P. mongoliensis,* Bohlin (1953) referred a tooth and a large, though fragmentary, ?tibia and ?fibula, collected from Nei Mongol Zizhiqu (Tebch), People's Republic of China. (Due to the extremely cold climate, this material was not collected.)

?*P. kwangshiensis* was described by Hou, Zhou and Chao (1975), this tentative species based on four nondistinctive teeth from Early Cretaceous rocks at Fusui, Kwangshi, People's Republic of China.

Molnar (1990) pointed out that, as *Prodeinodon* is a theropod but otherwise indeterminate, referral of the Chinese material to *Prodeinodon* is highly questionable. Furthermore, the *Prodeinodon* teeth display no characters by which the genus can be referred to any "infraorder." As later pointed out by Okazaki (1992), the tooth of *P. kwangshiensis* is quite different from that of *P. mongoliensis,* but similar to the holotype tooth (KMNH VP 000.016) of the Japanese species, *Wakinosaurus satoi.* Okazaki suggested that future studies of these teeth may show that *P. kwangshiensis* belongs in the genus *Wakinosaurus.*

Key references: Bohlin (1953); Hou, Zhou and Chao (1975); Molnar (1990); Okazaki (1992); Osborn (1924b).

PROSAUROLOPHUS Brown 1916

Ornithischia: Genasauria: Cerapoda:
Ornithopoda: Iguanoidontia: Hadrosauridae:
Hadrosaurinae.
Name derivation: Greek *pro* = "before" +
"*Saurolophus.*"
Type species: *P. maximus* Brown 1916.
Other species: *P. blackfeetensis* Horner 1992.
Occurrence: Oldman Formation, Alberta, Canada;
Two Medicine Formation, Montana, United
States.

Prosaurolophus maximus,
**AMNH 5386, holotype skull,
left lateral view.**

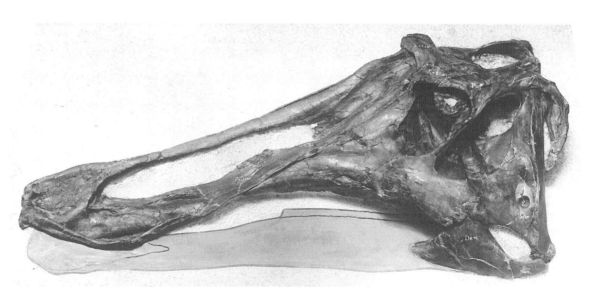

Courtesy Department Library Services,
American Museum of Natural History
(neg. #18553).

Age: Late Cretaceous (Late Campanian).

Known material: At least seven articulated skulls and associated postcrania, representing approximately 25 individuals, partial skull and skeleton, numerous other cranial and postcranial remains.

Holotype: AMNH 5386, incomplete skull with jaws.

Diagnosis of genus: Hadrosaurids with heavily excavated solid nasal crest above anterior margin of orbit (Horner 1992).

Diagnosis of *P. maximus*: Posterior wall of nasal excavation extending lateroventrally onto prefrontal (Horner 1992).

Diagnosis of *P. blackfeetensis*: Nasal excavation formed entirely by nasal, excluding prefrontal and premaxilla; anteroposterior length of nasal crest longer than in type species.

Comments: (Horner 1992), *Prosaurolophus* was founded on a skull (AMNH 5836) collected during the American Museum of Natural History expedition in 1915, from the Oldman Formation [then Belly River Formation], north fork of Sand Creek, below "Steveville Ferry," Red Deer River, Alberta, Canada.

Among the numerous specimens referred to *P. maximus* are two skulls (NMC [formerly GSC] 2277 and 2870), collected by Charles M. Sternberg in 1914 and 1917, southeast of the mouth of Little Sandhill Creek; a skeleton (ROM 787, formerly GSC 4971) lacking only predentary, forelimb digits, and distal extremity of the tail, collected by Levi Sternberg at

Photo by Brown, courtesy Department Library Services, American Museum of Natural History (neg. #18553).

Prosaurolophus maximus, skeleton *in situ*, Alberta, Canada.

Red Deer River for the University of Toronto in 1921; and a skull (USNM 12712) collected by L. Sternberg in 1930, six miles south of "Steveville."

Brown (1916a) originally diagnosed *Prosaurolophus* (and *P. maximus*) as follows: Skull large, high, elongate; short, erect, incipient crest above orbits, formed by prefrontals, frontals, and nasals; frontals

Courtesy Royal Ontario Museum.

Prosaurolophus maximus, ROM 787, skeleton.

Protiguanodon

Prosaurolophus maximus, life restoration by Gregory S. Paul.

Prosaurolophus blackfeetensis, MOR 454, holotype partial skull, left lateral view. Scale bar in centimeters. (After Horner 1992).

not contributing to border of orbit; beak long, spatulate; nasals high posteriorly; lacrimals narrow, low.

As noted by Lull and Wright (1942), the humerus of ROM 787 measures about 532 millimeters (over 20 inches) long, femur 1005 millimeters (about 38 inches), tibia 870 millimeters (over 33 inches) long, hindlimb relatively longer than in *Saurolophus*. Superficially, *Prosaurolophus* resembles *Saurolophus*, although possessing a smaller, shorter bill, and small, spike-like crest.

Horner (1992) named and described a second species, *P. blackfeetensis*, founded upon a partial skull and skeleton (MOR 454) recovered from the Upper Two Medicine Formation, Landslide Butte, Glacier County, Montana. Remains referred to this species include portions of numerous skulls and skeletons (MOR 447, 553).

Key references: Brown (1916a); Horner (1992); Lull and Wright (1942).

PROTIGUANODON   Osborn 1923—(See
   Psittacosaurus.)
Name derivation: Greek *pro* = "before" +
   "*Iguanodon*."
Type species: *P. mongoliensis* Osborn 1923.

PROTOAVIS Chatterjee 1991

Saurischia [provisionally]: ?Theropoda *incertae sedis.*

Name derivation: Greek *protos* = "first" + Latin *avis* = "bird."

Type species: *P. texensis* Chatterjee 1991.

Other species: [None.]

Occurrence: Cooper Member, Upper Dockum Formation, Texas, United States.

Age: Late Triassic (Early Norian).

Known material: Two disarticulated incomplete skulls and skeletons, adult, subadult.

Holotype: TTU P 9200, partial skull, including premaxilla, frontal, parietal, squamosal, lacrimal, quadrate, basioccipital, basisphenoid, alaparasphenoid, supraoccipital, epiotic, exoccipital, opisthotic, prootic, laterosphenoid, dentary, prearticular, articular, portion of angular and surangular, partial postcrania, including two vertebrae, portion of furcula, distal end of scapula, ilium, ischium, portion of pubis, femur, adult.

Diagnosis of genus (as for type species) [as bird]: Skull long, narrow, with sharply tapered snout, relatively deep, expanded temporal region; external naris elliptical, bounded by premaxilla and nasal; maxilla reduced laterally, with large palatal component; antorbital fenestra single, large, triangular; orbit relatively enormous, circular, anteriorly directed (to permit binocular vision); temporal region modified in avian fashion by loss of diapsid arch, postorbital bar, and squamosal-quadratojugal bar, resulting in confluence of supra- and infratemporal fenestrae and orbit; postorbital bone lost; postorbital process formed by frontal and laterosphenoid; squamosal reduced; zygomatic process in squamosal well developed; palate of palaeognathous type; vomers long, narrow, partly fused, meeting maxilla anteriorly and pterygoid posteriorly; palatine fused to pterygoid, not contacting parasphenoid rostrum; choana posteriorly placed, close to basipterygoid articulation; pterygoid highly reduced; ectopterygoid lost; quadrate streptostylic with development of medial orbital process, ventral condylar articulation with pterygoid, lateral cotylus for quadratojugal; prokinetic hinge; skull highly encephalized; cerebellum and cerebrum contacted dorsally, displacing optic lobes ventrally; cerebellar protuberance reflected on external surface of supraoccipital; epiotic on occiput; olfactory lobes reduced; vallecula bordering Wulst; basioccipital horizontal; stapedial fossa containing three foramina (as in birds): fenestra ovalis, fenestra pseudorotunda, and entrance to posterior tympanic recess; large metotic process added to exoccipital; vagus foramen diverted backward; parabasal notch for passage of internal carotid artery; all five tympanic diverticula; anterior and posterior tympanic recesses with developed contralateral communications; Eustachian tube bony; anterior vertical canal highly enlarged, enclosed sagittally in oval tube around deep floccular recess; cochlear recess tubular, elongated; ?predentary; mandibular elements fused posteriorly, compressed laterally; tricondylar articulation between mandible and quadrate; teeth restricted to tip of jaws by loss of posterior teeth; posterior cervical vertebrae heterocoelous; cervical ribs fused in adult; coraco-scapular joint movable; scapula elongated, oriented posteriorly; coracoid strut-like, with prominent acrocoracoid process; furcula present, with large hypocleideum; sternum ossified; humerus with large deltopectoral crest; distal condyles modified in avian fashion, external condyle elongate proximo-distally, internal condyle rounded; carpus with large semilunate carpal, showing single distal facet; Metacarpal with small extensor process; preacetabular ilium elongated to avian dimension; renal fossa; ischium rotated parallel to ilium, fused to it distally; ischiadic fenestra; ischia opened ventrally without symphysis; tibia with internal and external cnemial crests; ankle joint mesotarsal; astragalus and calcaneum fused; ascending process of astragalus with foramen at base; metatarsals appressed together proximally; hallux distally articulated, reversed (Chatterjee 1991).

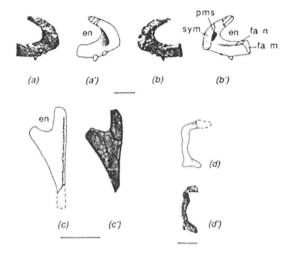

Protoavis texensis, TTU P 9200, holotype dermal roofing bones, a.–a.′, lateral and b.–b.′, medial view of right premaxilla; TTU P 9201, c.–c.′, ventral view of right nasal, small (subadult) individual; TTU P 9200, d.–d.′, medial view of left lacrimal. Scale = 5 cm. (After Chatterjee 1991.)

Protoavis texensis, TTU P 9200, holotype posterior half of skull, left lateral view. Scale = 5 cm. (After Chatterjee 1991.)

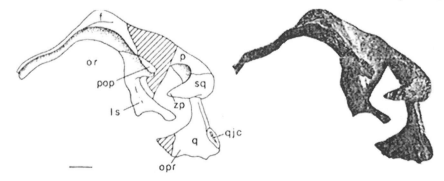

Comments: *Protoavis* is included herein provisionally. The genus was interpreted and described by Chatterjee (1991) as the earliest known "protobird," which he referred to a new "order," Protoaviformes, and new family, Protoavidae. Some workers, however, regard this genus as a small theropod (in the "traditional" sense; see section on *Archeopteryx* and *Mononykus*) rather than a bird.

The genus is known from two specimens found in 1983 in the Post Quarry, on a ranch in the Cooper Member, upper Dockum Formation, southeast of Post, Garza County, Texas. The holotype (TTU P 9200) consists of the partial skull of a large individual, the paratype (TTU P 9201) a partial skull and partial postcranial skeleton of a small individual (including maxilla, nasal, parietal, jugal, quadratojugal, vomer, palatine, pterygoid, quadrate, basioccipital, predentary, portion of dentary, prearticular, articular, portion of angular and surangular, fairly complete vertebral column missing sacrum, scapula, coracoid, humerus, radius, ulna, articulated carpals and metacarpals, phalanges, portion of tibia and fibula, astragalus, calcaneum, metatarsals, and phalanges). The specimens were discovered lying side by side. They were slightly above the bonebed and tightly encased in a mudstone block. Both specimens were the basis for the diagnosis of the genus and type species, as well the two new higher taxa (Chatterjee 1991).

Chatterjee concluded through phylogenetic analysis that theropods shared a common ancestry with birds, but found it indeterminate from the fossil record whether or not the immediate common ancestor was a theropod.

More recently, Currie and Zhao (1993*b*), in a study of a newly collected braincase (RTMP 86.36.475) of *Troodon*, noted that, although *Protoavis* displays characteristics suggesting avian affinities, most of these features can also be found in theropods. Currie and Zhao also pointed out that Chatterjee seems to have misinterpreted some aspects of the anatomy of *Protoavis*.

Comparing the braincases of *Protoavis* and *Troodon*, Currie and Zhao listed numerous similarities between them and found them to be remarkably alike, especially for two animals separated by 160 million years. Currie and Zhao were of the opinion that *Protoavis* possessed but few unique avian characters (*e.g.*, streptostylic quadrate and reduced olfactory lobes), these insufficiently strong to regard *Protoavis* as avian. Furthermore, in at least one feature (*i.e.*, a single exit for the trigeminal), *Protoavis* seems to be less birdlike than *Troodon*.

Note: Prior to the formal description, the name of this genus and photographs of the skeleton appeared in various popular periodicals.

Key reference: Chatterjee (1991); Currie and Zhao (1993*b*).

Protoceratops andrewsi,
AMNH 6251, holotype
incomplete skull (subadult).

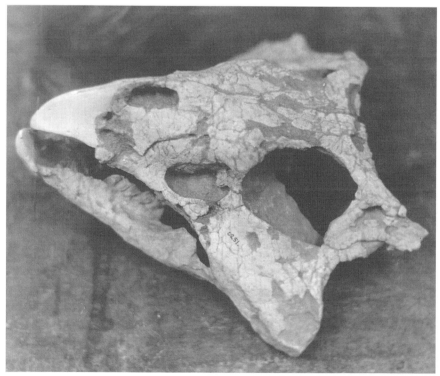

Photo by the author, courtesy American Museum of Natural History.

PROTOCERATOPS Granger and Gregory 1923
Ornithischia: Genasauria: Cerapoda:
  Marginocephalia: Ceratopsia: Neoceratopsia:
  Protoceratopsidae.
Name derivation: Greek *protos* = "first" + Greek
  keratos = "horned" + Greek *ops* = "face."
Type species: *P. andrewsi* Granger and Gregory
  1923.
Other species: [None.]
Occurrence: Djadochta Formation, Beds of
  Toogreeg, ?Beds of Alag Teg, ?Barun Goyot Formation, Omnogov, Bayan Mandahu, Mongolian
  People's Republic; Minhe Formation, Gansu, Nei
  Mongol Zizhiqu, People's Republic of China.
Age: Late Cretaceous (Middle-Late Campanian).
Known material: At least 82 skulls and some skeletons collected, juvenile to adult, ?eggs.
Holotype: AMNH 6251, skull lacking occiput,
  subadult.

Diagnosis of genus (as for type species): Skull hornless, smaller than any [then] known ceratopsian, or [irrelevant] ankylosaur, broadly triangular in dorsal view, wide lateral crests mainly composed of backward-and-downwardly expanded jugals; orbits

Protoceratops andrewsi, FM P14046 skeleton displayed with fossil eggs (FM P12991) possibly belonging to this species.

Courtesy the Field Museum (neg. #GEO81443).

quite large, not surmounted by supraorbital bones or horns; postorbital-squamosal bar narrow; supratemporal openings large; squamosal broadly overlapping enlarged jugal, produced posterosuperiorly, not enlarged; single preorbital fossae much larger than in other ornithischians; premaxillae very large, approaching ceratopsian type as do nasals, pterygoids, internal nares, and quadrates; quadratojugal on medial surface of quadrate; mandibular ramus with about nine teeth [now known to range from seven to 15, depending on size], these relatively large, long-crowned, set far toward midline, worn on buccal sides (Granger and Gregory 1923).

Comments: Although a relatively primitive ceratopsian, *Protoceratops* morphologically establishes the structural pattern of more advanced horned dinosaurs.

The first *Protoceratops* remains were discovered on September 2, 1922, by Walter Granger and his party during the Central Asiatic Expeditions of the American Museum of Natural History. The initial discovery, identified as the bones of a small dinosaur, was made during exploration of the Flaming Cliffs of Djadochta, near Shabarakh Usu [=Bayan Dzak], in Outer Mongolia.

The genus was founded on a nearly complete skull (AMNH 6251), recovered from the Shamo series, Djadochta Formation, of Middle-Late Campanian age (see Currie 1991; Dong 1993a), on the Kwei-wa-ting trail east of Artsa Bogdo, Gobi Desert. Since the discovery of the holotype, much other *Protoceratops* material has been found (not all recovered) at the same locality, including several skeletons, plus at least 73 skulls, the combined remains well representing an ontogeny of this genus from baby to adult.

Granger and Gregory (1923) described these remains and referred *Protoceratops* to its own family, Protoceratopsidae.

Brown and Schlaikjer (1940*b*) noted that one *Protoceratops* specimen (AMNH 6418) seemed, upon initial inspection, to include fossilized integument. This almost complete skeleton was found in a curled-up position with a thin, hard, and wrinkled layer of matrix covering a large part of the skull and jaws. The matrix must have been influenced by the surface form of the original skin. As far as Brown and Schlaikjer could determine, the matrix revealed no trace of skin structure.

The function and evolution of the ceratopsian frill, already well developed in *Protoceratops,* has been a source of conjecture. Superficially, the frill seems to have been an adaptation to protect the shoulder region. However, the large fontanelles in *Protoceratops* made for a rather weakly constructed frill, hardly offering protection. Lull (1933) suggested that the openings in the frill may have provided an area for attachment of large temporal muscles for actuating the jaws. Haas (1955) and Ostrom (1964) sug-

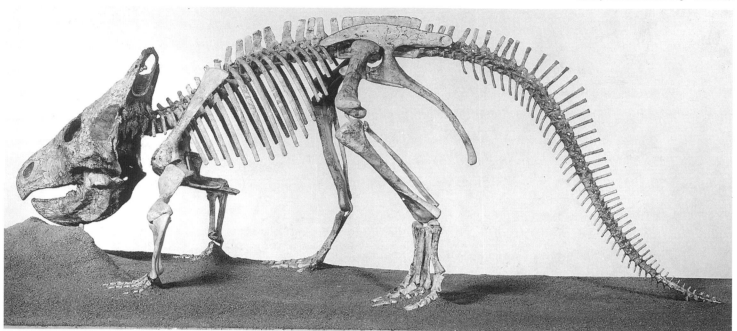

Protoceratops andrewsi, FMNH P14046 skeleton collected in 1926 during the Third Asiatic Expedition of the American Museum of Natural History (co-sponsored by formerly named Field Museum of Natural History).

gested that frill evolution could have been initiated by enlargement of cervical muscles. Jaw muscles would have been attached to the edges of the frill, the large fontanelles lightening the weight of the skull. Haas and Ostrom's idea was later challenged by Dodson and Currie (1990) in their review of the Neoceratopsia. According to Dodson and Currie, this model seems plausible only in *Leptoceratops gracilis*, in which the frill is quite small and supratemporal fenestrae enlarged. In most ceratopsids, these openings are not very spacious, major areas of the parietal exhibiting a vascular texture not compatible with muscle attachment.

Molnar (1977) suggested that evolution of the ceratopsian frill, including that of protoceratopsids, could have been influenced by a display function. According to Molnar, if the frill in *Protoceratops* was used in courtship and threat displays (as proposed by Kurzanov; also Farlow and Dodson 1975), then three conditions would be expected: 1) Evidence for acute vision, 2) evidence of sexual dimorphism in size or shape of frill, 3) and, during evolution, progressive increase in size and ornamentation of the frill. Hopson (1975*a*) noted that the large orbits and sometimes present sclerotic ring in *Protoceratops* indicate large eyes and presumably good vision. Colbert (1948) and Lull and Gray (1949) noted the increase in the frill's relative size during evolution, while Lull (1933) and Colbert also noted the increase in the ornamentation of the frill. Molnar concluded that this evidence supported, at least in part, a display function for the crest.

Gregory and Mook (1925) first suggested that secondary sexual characters existed in protoceratopsids. In their study of structure and relationships of this genus, Brown and Schlaikjer regarded the determination of *Protoceratops* skulls as male or female to be purely conjectural, although they did consider those skulls which, at any growth stage, are most robust and exhibit the most salient growth changes (*e.g.*, widening of frill, development of parieto-frontal depression, increase of facial depth, development of incipient nasal-horn cores, *etc.*) to represent males.

Kurzanov (1972) confirmed such characters in a study of morphological structures of the protoceratopsid skull, this study based on a cast of the plesiotype (AMNH 6408, skull of a small, young, apparently female adult), plus two skulls of *P. andrewsi*, collected by the USSR Academy of Science's paleontological expedition of 1946-1949 to the Mongolian People's Republic. The first (apparently female) skull (PIN 614-6) was collected from the site at Bain-Dzak, the other (apparently male) skull (PIN 3143/4-1) from the site at Tugrikin-Us (Dashzeveg 1963). Kurzanov concluded that the rudimentary nasal horn is entirely absent in adult females, but present in males; the angle of frill elevation in females is no more than 20 degrees, at least 40 degrees in males; in females, the angle of expansion of the frill is no more than 30 degrees, at least 70 degrees in males; and the expansion of the facial part of the skull is no more than 15 degrees in females, at least 40 degrees in males.

Dodson (1976) further investigated both probable sexual dimorphism in the shape and size of the

Protoceratops frill and the feasibility of its having evolved to accommodate the jaw muscles. Dodson based his study on the entire ontogenetic series of skulls (24 reasonably complete) and skeletons in the American Museum of Natural History collection, representing babies to adults.

After subjecting these specimens to formal biometric analysis, Dodson found the characters of the frill to be quite variable and challenged the idea that frills of larger ceratopsians were well designed for origins of the muscles of mastication. Dodson observed that the frill in *Protoceratops* does not seem to increase in relative length during growth, this contrary to Brown and Schlaikjer, who had not themselves studied the entire gamut of American Museum *Protoceratops* specimens. According to Dodson, the coronoid process of the jaw increases in height while elevation of the line of muscle action in the jaw decreases. Accompanying development of the coronoid process is a relative increase in height of both posterior region of skull and frill, changes that tend to negate the mechanical effect of the coronoid process. Also, the thinness of the parietals seems to contradict the theory that the frill evolved to accommodate jaw muscles. Dodson concluded that development of the frill was a significant factor in determining sex, males having a more erect frill, and also prominent snout "bump." Of the studied specimens, eight seemed to

Protoceratops andrewsi, FM P14046, skeleton with eggs possibly belonging to this species.

Courtesy the Field Museum (neg. #GEO81449).

Protoceratops

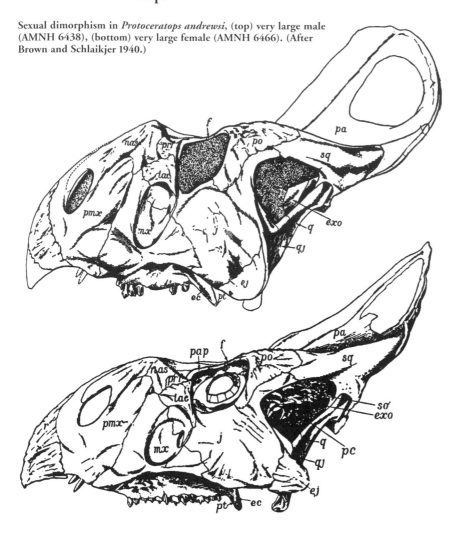

derived ceratopsian *Anchiceratops*, Brown and Schlaikjer found that *Protoceratops* possessed a relatively larger brain than more progressive forms.

Because of the more than 100 specimens collected, *Protoceratops* is one of the best known of all dinosaurs. As Dodson and Currie pointed out, this genus, once considered to be extremely primitive (see Granger and Gregory), is now known to be rather derived within its group, the apparently primitive character of premaxillary teeth now viewed as a secondary specialization. In a report on the morphological and ecological trends in ceratopsian evolution, Dodson (1991) stated that *Protoceratops* is the largest and most derived of a series of basal ceratopsians (including *Psittacosaurus*, *Bagaceratops*, and *Leptoceratops*), and that *Protoceratops* and *Leptoceratops* together form an outgroup to all other ceratopsian taxa.

From the many specimens collected, *Protoceratops* is known to have reached a maximum length of about 2.4 meters (8 feet). Based on a mounted skeleton displayed at the American Museum of Natural History, Colbert (1962) calculated the weight of the living animal to be 177 kilograms (389 pounds).

The tail of *Protoceratops* is relatively long and the feet broadly adapted to quadrupedal locomotion, though Coombs (1978c) suggested that this dinosaur was capable of at least some bipedal movement. Coombs, evaluating the possible cursorial adaptations in various dinosaur groups, observed that *Protoceratops* and the more primitive *Leptoceratops* were probably the swiftest of all known quadrupedal dinosaurs. These two genera display a disparity between forelimbs (with large coracoids and limbbone proportions suggestive of mediportal habits just marginally better than those of large ceratopsians) and hindlimbs (proportionally falling upon the margin of the quadrupedal cursorial range) unique among quadrupedal dinosaurs. In these forms, the structure of the feet (long slender metapodials, short

represent juveniles, eight adult males, seven adult females, and one indeterminate individual, both sexes apparently reaching the same adult size.

Brown and Schlaikjer described an endocranial cast prepared by Otto Falkenbach from a large "male" skull (AMNH 6466). In comparing the cast with that described by Brown (1914a) of the larger and more

Skull ontogeny in *Protoceratops andrewsi*, from infant to adult.

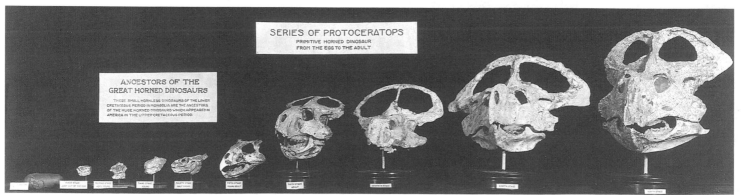

Illustration by Mark Hallett. From *Dinosaurs: A Global View*, by Czerkas and Czerkas, published by Dragon's World Ltd. and its co-edition publishers.

massive propodium, reduced epipodium) are indicative of subcursorial animals. Coombs found these features suggestive of dynamic bipeds comparable to some modern lizards in locomotor behavior.

Jerzykiewicz, Currie, Eberth, Johnston, Koster, and Zheng (1993) reported that a number of articulated *Protoceratops* skeletons discovered in the Bayan Mandahu redbeds and the Djadokhta Formation (both of Campanian age) of Inner Mongolia, People's Republic of China, were found "standing" on their hindlimbs, snouts directed upward, forelimbs tucked at their sides. These poses indicate that the individuals died *in situ*, encased within the surrounding sediment at the time of their deaths, and were not transported, probably perishing while attempting to free themselves from a sandstorm deposit during or just after the storm. Regarding the possibility that these dinosaurs died after burying themselves, Jerzykiewicz *et al.* noted that articulated *Protoceratops* skeletons have only been found in structureless sandstone facies, that all known tetrapod burrowers burrow headfirst and horizontally, and that breathing conditions would be difficult for animals buried "snout up" in loose sand.

Dong and Currie (1993) reported new protoceratopsian specimens collected during the summers of 1988 and 1990 by an expedition of the Sino-Canadian Dinosaur Project (see Currie 1991; Dong 1993*a*), at Bayan Mandahu, west of the Sino-Swedish site of Ulan Tsonchi, near the village of Bayan Tu. This material included embryos, juveniles, and adults represented by 29 skulls ranging in size from 2 centimeters to nearly one meter. Most of these specimens belong to *Protoceratops*, although some represent *Bagaceratops* and *Udanoceratops*.

According to Dong and Currie, the smallest of these fossils—the smallest specimens yet found pertaining to *Protoceratops* and *Bagaceratops*—were not found with fossil eggshell (see notes below), but are small enough to fit within any eggs that have been attributed to protoceratopsids, indicating that these incomplete specimens represent embryos. The smallest of these apparently embryonic specimens (IVPP V10596) has a dentary length of 17 millimeters, which is 6 millimeters shorter than the dentary of the previously published smallest specimen (AMNH 6499) of *Protoceratops*; the estimated body length of the largest of these specimens (IVPP V9606) is less than 25 centimeters. As the latter specimen lacks a nasal horn, it probably belongs to *Protoceratops*.

As pointed out by Dong and Currie, these embryonic specimens reveal that many of the "primitive" characters observed by Maryańska and Osmólska (1975), in listing evolutionary trends of cranial characters of protoceratopsids, are present in all small

Protoceratops andrewsi in combat with *Velociraptor mongoliensis*.

or juvenile specimens. These characters include a relatively short snout, short frill, shallow mandible with straight ventral margin, and poorly developed ridge on the surangular.

Dong and Currie further suggested that the absence of embryos in the thousands of eggs found in Cretaceous sediments of Mongolia and China may have resulted from their destruction by the decomposing contents of the eggs, the embryos preserved only when the eggs were broken and their liquid contents drained.

Notes: Collected during the 1920s, from the same fossil-bearing strata as the commonly found

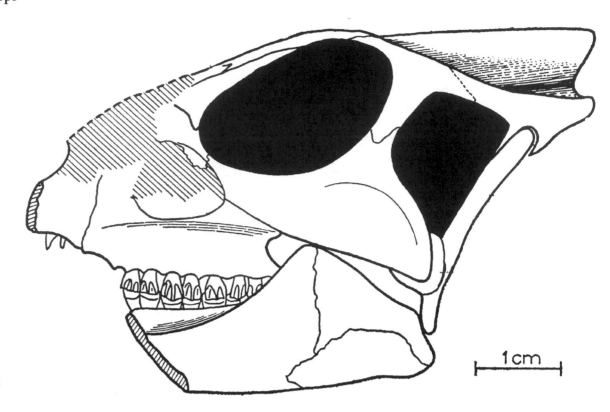

?*Protoceratops kozlowskii*, ZPAL MgD-I/117, holotype incomplete skull (subadult), left lateral view, referred to new genus *Breviceratops* (see entry). (After Maryańska and Osmólska 1975.)

bones of *P. andrewsi*, were nests of eggs originally presumed to have been laid by this species. Roy Chapman Andrews is the name most prominent in the history of the collection of these celebrated eggs. Andrews (1932) claimed that fossilized embryos found within the eggs confirmed identification with *Protoceratops*. Sochava (1972) assigned embryonic remains found in an egg fragment to *Protoceratops*, this identification continuing to appear in the literature (*e.g.*, Kitching 1979). However, as later noted by other workers (Elźanowski 1981; Hirsch 1989), this inference was never unequivocally demonstrated, no positively identifiable embryonic remains having been found in any of these eggs.

The work of collecting these eggs began in 1923, at the Gobi Desert's Flaming Cliffs, by the first of two Central-Asiatic Expeditions of the American Museum of Natural History, a second expedition launched in 1925. Walter Granger (1936) and associates, during an expedition to the Flaming Cliffs the previous year, had found some fossilized eggshells presumed to be those of a large bird. They were collected during the 1923 expedition led by George Olsen. From their elongate shape, the eggs were obviously not avian. Some were about 22 centimeters (8 inches) in length, with wrinkled or pebbly surfaces. They were found in clusters (probably nests) laid in three concentric circles, two of these "nests" (AMNH 6508 and 6631) quite complete. Evidently the egg-layer had dug a hollow in the sand, as do some mod-

ern reptiles, creating a depression into which to deposit the eggs. Each cluster contained some 15 or more eggs. As reported by Brown and Schlaikjer, one nest (AMNH 6508) contained eggs that had been broken before burial; the skeleton (AMNH 6517) of the theropod *Oviraptor* was found lying over this nest, separated from it by only four inches of matrix.

The name *Elongatoolithus* Zhao 1975 was given to these eggs long believed to belong to *Protoceratops*, although this identification was later questioned. Rozhdestvensky (1977), for example, suggested that these eggs might actually be ankylosaurian, based on their size compared with that of adult *Protoceratops* individuals. In more recent years, additional fossil egg material was collected from the Bayn Dzak localities by the Polish-Mongolian Paleontological Expeditions. Although some of this material had been identified as protoceratopsid, the eggs named *Elongatoolithus* were reinterpreted as possibly theropod (see Elźanowski; also Mikhailov 1991).

Sabath (1991), after examining protoceratopsid egg material collected by the Polish-Mongolian Expeditions, concluded that these eggs can be placed into three categories:

1. Larger, smooth-shelled protoceratopsid eggs (ZPAL MgOv-II/2, 2a from Bayn Dzak (Main Field); MgOv-II/3a, 3b from Bayn Dzak (Dashzeveg Sayr); and MgOv-II/20, 21 from Bayn Dzak), described by Sabath as strongly elongate and ovate, with light beige or grayish colored eggshell, no prominent ornamen-

tation; sometimes with faint parallel striation visible in equatorial part of egg; pore openings visible under small magnification; eggshell thickness varying around 0.6 millimeters to twice as much in equatorial area. (Sabath noted that the close oblique or subvertical arrangement of these eggs in the nest seemingly indicates a rather immobile condition until hatching, hence, they were not turned by parents during incubation; possibly they were buried by the female in a deep hole with steep siding, then covered with vegetation; lack of ornament and preserved subvertical orientation may indicate filling the hole with sand.)

2. Smaller, smooth-shelled, ?protoceratopsid eggs (ZPAL MgOv-I/1 from Altan Ula IV; MgOv-I/10 and MgOv-I/25a-b from Khulsan; and MgOv-III/9 from Khermeen Tsav); described by Sabath as elongate of the shape similar to the first kind, although smaller; with thin, smooth angustispherulitic eggshell. (According to Sabath, the very extremely thin eggshell [no more than 0.3 millimeters] is almost never deformed, indicating the eggs were buried in sediment and suggesting a sand-nesting mode.)

3. Prominently ornamented protoceratopsid eggs (ZPAL MgOv-I/4 from Nemegt [Western Sayr]; MgOv-I/5-7, 8a-b, 9a-e, 10a, 12-13, 14a-b, 15a-d, 17, 20, 23-24, 26a-f from Khulsan; MgOv-I/27a-b from Southeast Nemegt; MgOv-II/1a-f from Bayn Dzak; MgOv-II/4, 5a-d, 8, 10, 19, 22 from Bayn Dzak [Main Field]; MgOv-II/23 from Khashaat; MgOv-II/24 from Bayn Dzak [Green Sayr]; and MgOv-III/1-8. 9 from Kermeen Tsav II); described by Sabath as large, asymmetrical and strongly elongated, with linearituberculate ornamentation (consisting of tiny ridges oriented parallel to long axis of egg in equatorial part, meandering to polar area, ornamentation vanishing towards poles); nest, with a diameter of about 0.55 meters, contains about 20 (perhaps up to 30) eggs arranged radially around the center; grayish or beige colored eggshell; eggs often preserved in pairs. (Sabath interpreted "twin" eggs as having been "glued" together from both oviducts during oviposition, the presence of such pairs as fossils possibly being the result of decay of the nest material. The ornament, according to Sabath, suggests a coarser-than-sediment incubation environment and subvertical arrangement of eggs, facilitating convention.)

Mikhailov, in classifying fossil amniotic vertebrates, proposed the following diagnosis of the unnamed egg family to which the protoceratopsid eggs belong, based on a study of parts of eggs and shell fragments (PIN 614 [58, 601, 603], 3142 [415, 429, 447-453, 455, 489, 495, 496], 3143 [121, 122, 123], 4228 1; also GI and ZPAL specimens) collected from six Gobi Desert localities: "Prismatic morphotype; progressively thinning towards equatorial region; angusticanaliculate pore system; surface smooth or with fine linearituberculate ornamentation (fine, long ridges without nodes, variant 2 ...) in the equatorial region (ornamentation not in accordance with the orientation of the accretion lines,

Unidentified fossil eggs (FM P12991) possibly referable to *Protoceratops andrewsi*, collected in Mongolia in 1925, figured by Roy Chapman Andrews (1932).

Courtesy the Field Museum (neg. #50761).

which are horizontal); strongly elongated eggs (slightly asymmetric; elongation—length/breadth = 2.3-2.7); 'thin' eggshell (0.5-1.2 mm), progressively thinning towards equatorial region."

Mikhailov pointed out that, contrary to earlier reports (Sochava 1969), no unquestionably protoceratopsid egg remains have yet been described from China; and that eggshells similar to those of protoceratopsids, with histostructure apparently of a prismatic morphotype, have been described from the Upper Cretaceous of Southern France by Kerourio (1982).

The tentative species ?*P. kozlowskii* was made the type species of a new genus, *Breviceratops*, by Kurzanov (1990).

Key references: Andrews (1932); Brown and Schlaikjer (1940*b*); Colbert (1962); Coombs (1978*c*); Dodson (1976, 1991); Dodson and Currie (1990); Elźanowski (1981); Dong and Currie (1993); Farlow and Dodson (1975); Granger and Gregory (1923); Gray (1949); Gregory and Mook (1925); Haas (1955); Hirsch (1989); Hopson (1975*a*); Jerzykiewicz *et al.* (1993); Kitching (1979); Kurzanov (1972); Lull (1933); Maryańska and Osmólska (1975); Molnar (1977); Ostrom (1964); Sabath (1991); Sochava (1972).

PROTOGNATHOSAURUS Olshevsky 1991—
(=*Protognathus* Zhang)
Saurischia: Prosauropodomorpha: Sauropoda: ?Cetiosauridae.
Name derivation: Greek *protos* = "first" + Greek *gnathos* = "jaw" + Greek *sauros* = "lizard."
Type species: *P. oxyodon* (Zhang 1988).
Other species: [None.]
Occurrence: Shaximiao Formation, Sichuan, China.
Age: Middle Jurassic.
Known material/holotype: CHG CV00732, almost complete dentary.

Diagnosis of genus (as for type species): Dentary thick, heavy, anterior portion spreading forward, upper edge gradually reduced from anterior to posterior, lower border relatively contracted medially; Meckelian canal very deep, long, comparatively close to posteroventral position of internal surface; 19-20 dentary teeth (more than in other sauropods), similar to those in prosauropods, crowns relatively small, slender, rather isodont, sharply-pointed, more or less spatulate and comparatively flat; vertical middle ridge very faint, barely indicated on inner surface of tooth; four-five denticles at anterior and posterior edges of tooth, respectively (Zhang 1988).

Comments: This genus, originally named *Protognathus*, was founded upon a rather complete dentary (CHG CV00732), recovered from the lower Shaximiao Formation (Middle Jurassic), Dashanpu quarry, Zigong, Sichuan, China (Zhang 1988).

According to Zhang, the dentary is approximately 170 millimeters (about 6.6 inches) long and seems to belong to a rather primitive sauropod.

Olshevsky (1991), pointing out that the name *Protognathus* is preoccupied (Basilewsky 1950) for a genus of modern central African beetle, proposed the new generic name *Protognathosaurus*.

Key references: Olshevsky (1991); Zhang (1988).

PROTOGNATHUS Zhang 1988—(Preoccupied, Basilewsky 1950; see *Protognathosaurus*.)
Name derivation: Greek *protos* = "first" + Greek *gnathos* = "jaw."
Type species: *P. oxyodon* Zhang 1988.

PROTOROSAURUS Lambe 1914—
(Preoccupied, Meyer 1830; see *Chasmosaurus*.)
Name derivation: Greek *pro* = "before" + "*Torosaurus*."
Type species: *P. belli* (Lambe 1902).

PSITTACOSAURUS Osborn 1923—
(=*Protiguanodon*.)
Ornithischia: Genasauria: Cerapoda: Marginocephalia: Ceratopsia: Psittacosauridae.
Name derivation: Greek *psittako* = "parrot" + Greek *sauros* = "lizard."
Type species: *P. mongoliensis* Osborn 1923.
Other species: *P. osborni* Young [Yang] 1931, *P. sinensis* Yang [Young] 1958, *P. youngi* Chow 1963, *P. guyangensis* Cheng 1983, *P. xinjiangensis* Sereno and Chao [Zhao] 1988, *P. meileyingensis* Sereno, Zhao, Cheng and Rao 1988, *P. sattayaraki* Buffetaut and Suteethorn (1992), *P. neimongoliensis* Russell and Zhao 1996, *P. ordosensis* Russell and Zhao 1996.
Occurrence: Khuktekskaya Svita [formerly the Oshih Formation], Ovorkhangai, [unnamed formation], Svita, Shinekhuduskaya Svita, Dundgov, Mongolian People's Republic; Jiufotang Formation, Liaoning, ?[unnamed formation], Lisangou Formation, Xinpongnaobao Formation, Nei Mongol, Zizhiqu, Qingshan Formation, Shandong, Lianmugin Formation, Xinjiang, Uygur Zizhiqu, Ejinhoro Formation, Ordos region, Zhidan Group, Luohandong Formation, Bayin Gobi Formation, Inner Mongolia, People's Republic of China; Shestakovskaya Svita, Gorno-Altayaskaya Avtonomnaya Oblast, R.S.F.S.; Khok

Psittacosaurus mongoliensis, AMNH 6254, holotype skeleton, dorsal view.

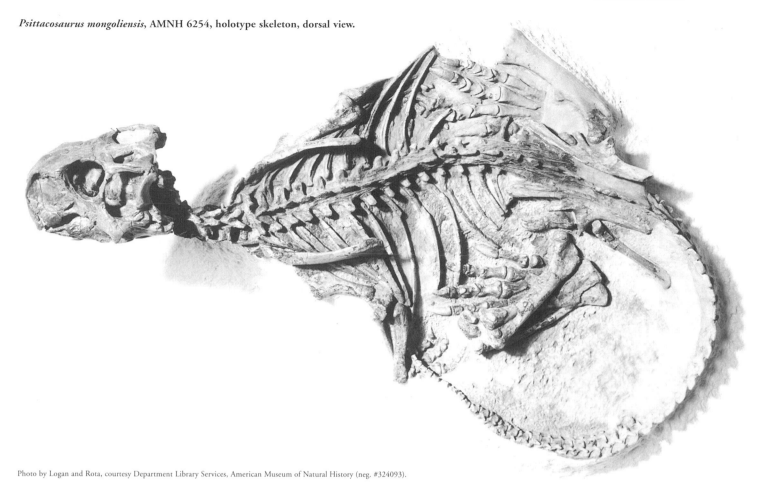

Photo by Logan and Rota, courtesy Department Library Services, American Museum of Natural History (neg. #324093).

Kruat Formation, Ban Dong Bang Noi, Thailand.

Age: Early Cretaceous (Valanginian–?Early Aptian).

Known material: Approximately 160 or more individuals, including articulated skeletons with skulls, complete skulls, partial skeletons, unprepared specimens, fragmentary remains, adults, ?subadults, juveniles.

Holotype: AMNH 6254, skeleton including almost perfect skull with jaws, vertebral column, pelvis, most of limbs.

Diagnosis of genus (as for Psittacosauridae): Preorbital skull segment short (less than 40 percent of skull length); external naris very high on snout; nasal extending rostroventrally below external naris, establishing contact with rostral; caudolateral premaxillary process extremely broad, separating maxilla from external naris by wide margin and extending dorsally to parrot-like rostrum; premaxilla, maxilla, lacrimal, and jugal sutures converging to point on snout; antorbital fenestra and antorbital fossa absent; unossified gap in wall of lacrimal canal; eminence on rim of buccal emargination of maxilla near junction with jugal; pterygoid mandibular ramus elongate; dentary crown with bulbous primary ridge; manual

digit IV with only simplified phalanx; manual digit V absent (Sereno 1990*b*):

Diagnosis of *P. mongoliensis*: Maxillary depression triangular; lateral margin of prefrontal upturned (Sereno 1990*b*).

Diagnosis of *P. osborni*: Approximately half size of *P. mongoliensis*; dentary tooth crowns with strong median ridge; no development of sagittal crest in parietal region (Yang [Young] 1931).

Diagnosis of *P. sinensis*: Smallest known species; skull short, broad, 120 millimeters (over 4.6 inches) long; eight maxillary and nine dentary teeth; nine cervical, 13 dorsal, six sacral, and ?31 caudal vertebrae; tibia considerably longer than femur; gastralia ribs less developed than in *P. mongoliensis* (Yang [Young] 1958*b*); also, small jugal-postorbital horn core on postorbital bar; absence of external mandibular fenestra (Sereno 1990*b*).

Diagnosis of *P. guyangensis*: Distinguished by intermediate size and nine maxillary teeth lacking marked primary ridge (Cheng 1983).

Diagnosis of *P. xinjiangensis*: Jugal horn anteriorly flattened; maxillary crowns with denticulate margin curving posteromedially onto side near base of crown; iliac postacetabular process proportionately

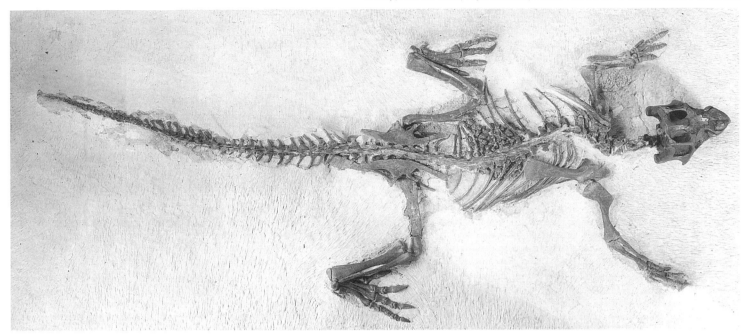

Psittacosaurus mongoliensis, AMNH 6253, holotype skeleton (dorsal view) of *Protiguanodon mongoliensis.*

elongate; ossified dorsal tendons extended onto anterior half of tail (Sereno and Chao 1988).

Diagnosis of *P. meileyingensis:* Distinguished by near-circular profile of skull, also by snout, which is comparatively short rostrocaudally, about 27 percent length of skull (from front of the skull to orbit margin), this percentage smaller than in any other known ornithischian (Sereno 1990*b*).

Diagnosis of *P. sattayaraki:* Dentary with small incipient flange, less developed than in *P. mongoliensis* and *P. meileyingensis;* alveolar edge of dentary strongly convex, more so than in other *Psittacosaurus* species; dentary teeth with five denticles on both sides of median primary ridge (Buffetaut and Suteethorn 1992).

Diagnosis of *P. neimongoliensis:* Frontal narrow (broad in *P. meileyingensis*); anterior ramus from squamosal not reaching anterior wall of supratemporal fenestra (reaches anterior wall in type species, *P. sinensis,* and *P. xinjiangensis*); ischium distinctly longer than femur (shorter than or about equal to femur in type species), distal end of ischium not horizontally flattened (horizontally flattened in type species) (Russell and Zhao 1996).

Diagnosis of *P. ordosensis:* Small, with prominent jugal horns, distinguished from *P. sinensis* in having maxillary dentition arranged in straight line (not medially bowed), jugal horn relatively short, quadrate not strongly emarginate posteriorly, ventrolateral ridge present medially on mandible, lateral mandibular fenestra apparently present, tibia longer (not shorter) than skull, and ratio of lengths of metatarsal I to III approximately 0.7 (not 0.6); differs from *P. xinjiangensis* in having oval (not subcircular) unworn maxillary crowns, maxillary teeth with 8 to 11 relatively large (rather than 14 relatively small) denticles, and shallow sulcus between primary ridge and anterior margin of tooth (rather than flat surface) (Russell and Zhao 1996).

Comments: *Psittacosaurus* is one of the best known of all dinosaurian genera in terms of its number of preserved specimens. Named for its prominent parrot-like beak, this rather small, bipedal genus was founded upon an almost complete skeleton (AMNH 6254) known locally as the "Red Mesa (Oshih) skeleton." The specimen was discovered during the Third Asiatic Expedition of the American Museum of Natural History in 1922, in the "Oshih Formation," Artsa Bogdo basin, Oshih, Mongolian Peoples' Republic. The find was made by the expedition's Mongolian chauffeur, Wong (Osborn 1923*b*).

The holotype skeleton was prepared and mounted at the American Museum of Natural History.

Osborn originally diagnosed the genus (and type species, *P. mongoliensis*) as follows: Skull relatively short, deep, narrow in facial region, broad in cranial region; premaxillary and predentary edentulous; prominent parrot-like rostrum [Osborn not identifying separate rostral bone]; maxillary teeth compressed; external nares small; orbits large; infraorbital region and jaw heavy, with attachments for powerful muscles; jugals with lateral osseous horns; primitive tubercular dermal armature on side of throat region [see below].

As later stated by Sereno (1990*b*) in his review of the Psittacosauridae, the family established upon this genus, the characters of Osborn's diagnosis are now known to apply to all psittacosaurs, or, more generally, to other ornithischians. Sereno, finding no bone structure in cross-sectional examination of the supposed "epidermal ossifications" on the holotype skull of *P. mongoliensis,* correctly identified these structures as sedimentary artifacts (this interpretation also suggested by Granger; *see in* Osborn 1924*a*).

Bohlin (1953) described jaw fragments with teeth, vertebrae, and epiphyses of some limb bones, found scattered in a small river section north of the foot of the Tebch plateau in Mongolia. (The Tebch sequence containing *P. mongoliensis* was later found by Eberth, Russell, Braman and Deini 1993, utilizing new radioisotopic, paleontologic, and palynological data, to be apparently of Barremian or possibly Early Aptian age.) This material apparently represents two individuals, the larger one evidently *P. mongoliensis,* the smaller too poorly preserved for identification.

Sereno speculated that, based upon fore- and hindlimb proportions, *P. mongoliensis* was most likely facultatively bipedal; that forelimb length and structure of manus do not preclude use of the forelimb in locomotion; and that diverging manual digit I suggests that a limited degree of grasping, perhaps for obtaining vegetation, was possible.

Numerous species have been referred to *Psittacosaurus*:

P. osborni Yang [Young] 1931 was based on an incomplete skull with jaws from the Lower Cretaceous of Haratologay, north Gansu [then Kansu], China. As noted by Sereno, small size, one of the features in Yang's (1931) diagnosis of this taxon, is not a sufficient criterion for distinction, while the median ridge on the dentary crowns is now known to occur in all psittacosaurid species.

P. tingi Yang [Young] (1931) was based on two lower jaws and seven teeth, recovered from the same lorizon and locality as *P. osborni*. Yang (1958*c*) later referred *P. tingi* to that species.

P. sinesis Yang [Young] 1958 was based on an almost complete skeleton with well-preserved skull,

Psittacosaurus mongoliensis, life restoration by Brian Franczak.

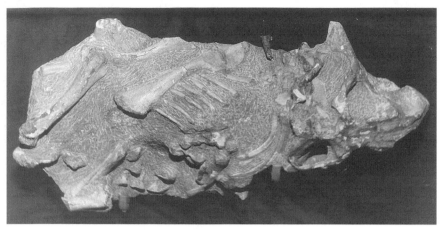

Psittacosaurus youngi, IVPP V8739, skeleton on temporary display at the Museum of Natural History of Los Angeles County.

discovered in the upper Chinshan Beds of Laiyang, Shantung [now Shandong], China.

P. youngi Zhao [formerly Chao] 1962 was based on a well-preserved skull and partial axial skeleton (BPV.149), collected from Laiyang. Sereno observed that this species is very similar to *P. mongoliensis*, indicating that both forms could be conspecific.

P. guyangensis Cheng 1983 was founded on a rostral skull fragment and referred postcranial remains from the Lisangou Formation, Nei Mongol, Zizhqu, People's Republic of China.

P. xinjiangensis Sereno and Zhao [Chao] 1988 is a small species based on a reasonably complete articulated skeleton (IVPP V7698), preserved in a matrix of soft beige sandstone. The type specimen includes the crushed posterior portion of the skull, and is missing both carpi, right and greater part of left manus, hindlimbs beyond proximal ends of tibiae, and most of the tail. The name and a photograph of the holotype first appeared in Dong's (1987) book, *Dinosaurs from China*. The remains were collected in 1964 by the Xinjiang Expedition of the Institute of Vertebrate Paleontology and Paleoanthropology from the ?Lower Cretaceous (tentative dating; Dong 1973) Tugulu Group, Xinjiang Uygur Autonomous

Region, Junggar Basin, Delunshan, northwestern China.

Specimens from the same locality referred to *P. xinjiangensis* include a fragmentary right ilium, left pubis, and possibly associated distal right and left fibulae, a second individual represented by two fragmentary fibulae, and vertebrae from several individuals (IVPP V7701); right and left maxillary fragments, each with five teeth, and an anterior right dentary of similar size but unknown association (IVPP V7702); a left maxillary fragment with unworn replacing crown, and anterior right dentary fragment of similar size but unknown association (IVPP V7703); complete right maxilla with eight alveoli, and unassociated left dentary with one erupting dentary crown (IVPP V7704); fragmentary postcranial remains of several individuals (IVPP field number 64047-6); bone fragments pertaining to several individuals, including two maxillae with teeth, nine jugal horns, articulated basioccipital, basisphenoid, and ventral occipital fragment, dorsal and caudal vertebrae, nine proximal and six distal scapulae, five coracoids, 12 distal humeri, two distal ulnae, one distal radius with articulated radiale, nine proximal and five distal femora, nine proximal and nine distal tibiae (two of the latter with articulated astragali and calcanea), right astragalus, and two right calcanea (IVPP field number 64047). (Zhao [Chao] observed that associated with the specimens of this species were remains of ornithopods, "coelurosaurs," "carnosaurs," pterosaurs, and chelonians.)

Comparing *P. xinjiangensis* to other psittacosaur species, Sereno and Zhao observed it lacks such features diagnostic to other species as the subtriangular antorbital fossa of *P. mongoliensis*, quadrajugal boss and strongly emarginated quadrate shaft of *P. meileyingensis* [see below], and curved tooth row and postorbital-jugal horn core of *P. sinensis*.

P. meileyingensis Sereno, Zhao [Chao], Cheng and Rao 1988 was based on remains including an almost complete skull with articulated lower jaws, and three anterior cervical vertebrae (IVPP V7705), recovered in 1973 by Zhao from the Jiufotang Formation (Lower Cretaceous) of Meileyingze, Liaoning Province, southwest of Chaoyoung, in northeastern China.

Material referred to this species includes the skeleton of an adult smaller individual, including skull missing anterior snout, postero-lateral corner of skull roof, right jugal, and left maxilla, disarticulated right and left mandibular rami lacking symphysial region and predentary, and associated postcrania including two sacral centra, eight articulated caudal vertebrae with chevrons, proximal left scapula, left coracoid, right scapular blade, and almost entire

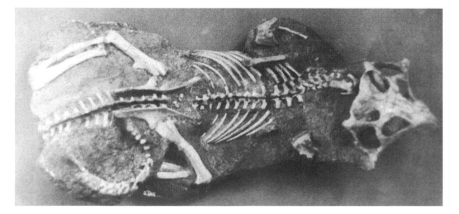

Psittacosaurus sinensis, holotype skeleton, dorsal view. (After Dong 1987.)

left ilium, right ilium lacking ischiac peduncle and postacetabular process, proximal left ischium, proximal left femur, left distal tibia, left proximal and distal tarsals, and left metatarsals I–IV (IG V.330), recovered in 1977 by Cheng in a vicinity of the type locality; fragmentary adult skull with articulated lower jaws, lacking most of snout and skull roof (BNHM BPV.399), weathered juvenile skull with articulated lower jaws (BNHM BPV.400), and very fragmentary, disarticulated adult skull (BNMH BPV.401), all collected from the type locality in 1982 by Rao and Han Zhoukuan. The skull of this species is 11.7 centimeters (about 4.5 inches) in length.

As observed by Sereno *et al.*, the distinct primary ridge on the surface of the lateral maxillary crown is a distinguishing, but variable, characteristic. *P. meileyingensis* lacks such features diagnostic to other *Psittacosaurus* species as the laterally prominent jugal horn in *P. sinensis* and *P. xinjiangensis*, and subtriangular antorbital fossa in *P. mongoliensis*. According to Sereno *et al.*, the prominent laterally projecting jugal horn present in both *P. sinensis* and *P. xinjiangensis*, but absent in *P. mongoliensis* and *P. meileyingensis*, may be indicative of a psittacosaurid subgroup.

P. sattayaraki Buffetaut and Suteethorn 1992, the first *Psittacosaurus* species from Thailand, was based on a well-preserved right dentary (TF 2449*a*) and a referred maxilla fragment (TF 2449*b*), discovered by Nares Sattayarak in the Early Cretaceous (Aptian–Albian) Khok Kruat Formation, Ban Dong Bang Noi, Chaiyaphum Province.

Two *Psittacosaurus* species were named and described by Russell and Zhao (1996), both taxa founded upon material collected during the summers of 1988 and 1989 by field parties of the Sino-Canadian Dinosaur Project, in the Ejinhoro Formation (Dong 1993*c*), in the Ordos region of the Inner Mongolia Autonomous Region (Nei Mongol Zizhiqu):

P. neimongoliensis was established upon an almost complete skeleton (IVPP 12-0888-2), lacking much of the braincase and distal caudal vertebrae, from the Ejinhoro Formation, southeast of Yangpo village, west of Dongsheng, and east of Hangginqi. Referred remains from the same locality include a partial disarticulated skull (IVPP 07-0888-11); centra from one dorsal, six sacral, and 17 associated caudal vertebrae, ilia fragments, a right ischium, and most of right and parts of left hindlimbs (IVPP 12-0888-1); the right lateral margin of a skull and mandible, and anterior part of the skeleton (IVPP-12-0888-3); and three unprepared specimens. Associated fauna includes a partial skeleton of the stegosaur *Wuerhosaurus* (Dong 1993*c*), sauropod teeth (referred to *Chiayüsaurus* sp.), and some pterosaur bones.

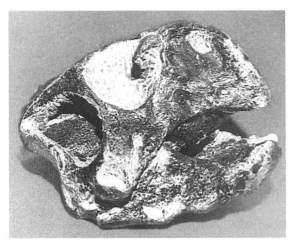

Psittacosaurus meileyingensis, IVPP V7705, holotype skull, right lateral view. (After Dong 1987.)

P. ordosensis was founded upon the ventral half of a skull, lower jaws, and the left crus and foot (IVPP 07-0888-1), collected from the Ejinhoro Formation, near the villages of Huamuxiao (west of Duguijiahan) and Amulonggui. As noted by Russell and Zhao, this skeleton was almost complete when found, but only part of it has been prepared. Referred specimens from the same site include a left jugal and quadrate, two cervical vertebrae, several fragments of vertebrae and ribs, and a left scapula (IVPP 07-0888-5), and also two unprepared specimens. Associated fauna includes a skeleton of the troodontid *Sinornithoides youngi*, a stegosaur tooth, a weathered femoral shaft from a moderately large saurischian (see Russell and Dong 1993*b*), and some pterosaur and turtle bone fragments.

Russell and Zhao noted that the following psittacosaur remains, all designated *Psittacosaurus* sp., were collected from five additional Inner Mongolian

Psittacosaurus xinjiangensis, IVPP V7698, holotype skeleton, dorsal view.

Psittacosaurus sattayaraki, TF 2449a, holotype right dentary in dorsal, medial and lateral views. Scale = 10 mm. (After Buffetaut and Suteethorn, 1992, courtesy the Palaeontological Association.

localities, but are too incomplete and show too meager morphologic detail to establish species:

Fourteen fragmentary specimens pertaining to small (?immature) individuals, from 65 to 77 percent of the linear dimensions of the holotype of *P. neimongoliensis,* were recovered from the Ejinhoro Formation at Alouchaideng, west of Dongsheng. They differ from that species in having a metatarsal I to III length ratio of approximately 0.5 rather than 0.7 (difference possible due to ontogeny). As in *P. neimongoliensis,* there is no depression on the lateral surface of the maxilla.

Three specimens were found in the Zhidan Group (?Ejinhoro Formation), at Ulan Obo, west of Hangginqi and east of the village of Ahlingbola, associated with a fragment of a turtle plastron and a champsosaur vertebra.

Associated remains of at least seven individuals were recovered at Hangginqi (?Ejinhoro Formation), near the villages of Wulahattatu, Argaiwusu, and Gutanwusu.

Two limb elements and a few fragments referred to *Psittacosaurus* sp. were collected from the Luohangdong Formation (Zhidan Group), at Laolonghuozi, east of Deng Kou, associated fossils including remains of fishes, aquatic turtles, champsosaurs, crocodiles, and a few isolated dinosaur bones and teeth.

Two incomplete specimens of *Psittacosaurus* of undetermined species were recovered from the Bayin Gobi Formation (?Albian), near the abandoned village of Elesitai, west of Tukemu village, in the Alashan Desert. Associated fauna includes remains of trionychid and larger turtles, champsosaurs, primitive therizinosaurian dinosaurs, and mammals (Russell and Dong 1993a).

From a cladistic analysis of the various *Psittacosaurus* species (excluding *P. sattayaraki,* whose type material was regarded as too incomplete to confirm its validity as a species), Russell and Zhao concluded "that *P. sinensis, P. ordosensis,* and *P. neimongoliensis* form a cluster of related species that is more closely related to *P. meileyingensis* and *P. xinjiangensis* than to *P. mongoliensis.*

When first describing *Psittacosaurus,* Osborn (1923b) also named and described the new genus and species, *Protiguanodon mongoliense,* based on an almost complete skeleton (AMNH 6253) from the Andai Sair Formation in Mongolia. This skeleton was found lying on its ventral side, the limbs prone. Its total length, as measured by Osborn, is 1350 millimeters (53 inches). For years, the specimen was displayed at the American Museum of Natural History. *Protiguanodon* was regarded as generically distinct from *Psittacosaurus* by Osborn (1923b), who erected for this species the [abandoned] subfamily Protiguanodontinae, which he believed might someday prove to belong to the ornithopod family Iguanodontidae.

Osborn (1923b) listed various "differences" that he believed warranted generic separation between *Psittacosaurus* and *Protiguanodon,* all of which were later shown by Sereno to be invalid or at least highly questionable. The perceived differences between *Psittacosaurus mongoliensis, Protiguanodon mongoliensis,* and various other species of *Psittacosaurus* had been considered by Rozhdestvensky (1955), who concluded that most of them could be attributed to ontogeny and individual variation. Rozhdestvensky regarded *Psittacosaurus mongoliensis* as the senior synonym of *Protiguanodon mongoliensis,* and *P. osborni, P. sinensis,* and *P. youngi* also possibly referable to the type species of *Psittacosaurus.*

Sereno noted that the differences in maxillary tooth crowns perceived by Osborn (1924a) resulted from his inadvertent misidentification of an isolated tooth found associated with the type skeleton of *Protiguanodon mongoliensis,* actually a dentary tooth with characters present in all dentary teeth of *Psittacosaurus mongoliensis.* Osborn's (1924a) misidentification of this tooth can be attributed to the fact that teeth in the holotype of *Psittacosaurus mongoliensis* had not yet been exposed at the time of his writings, and also because maxillary crowns were not preserved in the type specimen of *Protiguanodon mongoliensis.*

Also, Sereno pointed out that the difference in presacral count in both forms, as well as the relative robustness of the bones, could fall within the range of individual variation; that the prepubic process in the type skeleton of *Protiguanodon mongoliensis* seems to have been artificially deepened by postmortem breakage and crushing; and that geographic and stratigraphic separation are not valid criteria for taxonomic distinction. Sereno found that the similarities between *Psittacosaurus mongoliensis* and *Protiguanodon mongoliensis* favored their generic and specific synonymy, but regarded *P. osborni* and *P. sinensis* as valid species, with *P. youngi* possibly conspecific with the very similar *P. sinensis.*

Osborn (1923*b*), referred *Psittacosaurus* to the new family Psittacosauridae, which, because of the presumed armor, he believed represented a group of primitive armored dinosaurs possibly ancestral to Late Cretaceous ankylosaurs. Osborn (1924*a*) later believed psittacosaurids to be primitive iguanodonts belonging to Ornithopoda, mostly because *Psittacosaurus* and "*Protiguanodon*" were bipedal, bipedality then a long-held criterion for inclusion in that group. Maryańska and Osmólska (1974), in removing pachycephalosaurs from Ornithopoda, argued that bipedality alone did not justify this grouping.

Rozhdestvensky (1955, 1960) postulated that psittacosaurid affinities did not lie with the Ornithopoda, but rather the Ceratopsia, a relationship later recognized by various other workers (*e.g.*, Romer 1956; Gregory 1957; Yang [Young] 1958*c*; Colbert 1965; Maryańska and Osmólska 1975). Maryańska and Osmólska (1975) argued that the main criterion for classifying psittacosaurids should be the similar

cranial morphology in this group and ceratopsians, suggested that Osborn (1923*b*, 1924*a*) had misinterpreted the *Psittacosaurus* snout, and posited that *Psittacosaurus* did, in fact, possess a rostral bone (a diagnostic character of Ceratopsia).

Coombs (1980, 1982) concurred with Maryańska and Osmólska, having identified the rostral bone in skulls of juvenile specimens (see below), suggesting that the rostral bone in ceratopsians probably originated as an epidermally induced ossification, the thick and heavily keratinized upper beak eventually deriving from the large, overlying epidermal scale. As the rostral bone in *Psittacosaurus* is poorly defined and fused, in large part, to the premaxillae, this element is not yet an entirely separate bone as in more derived ceratopsians.

Sereno (1986) pointed out that Osborn (1923*b*) had misidentified the rostral bone as the premaxilla. Sereno also noted that the psittacosaurid skull exhibits a suite of characters present in the skulls of all ceratopsians: Triangular shape of the skull in dorsal aspect, tall snout, wide margin of parietal frill, and immobile symphysis of mandible.

Dodson (1991), reporting on the morphological and ecological trends in ceratopsian evolution, suggested that *Psittacosaurus* forms an outgroup to ornithopod, the *Hypsilophodon*, and the primitive ceratopsian *Bagaceratops.*

Osborn (1924*a*) had suggested that the long, laterally directed jugal projection in *Psittacosaurus* may have been utilized in intraspecies combat, one individual laterally swinging its head against another. Molnar (1977) noted that the jugals in this genus are long enough for display purposes, implying that these animals had a good sense of vision. Also, the orbits are sizeable enough to suggest a large eye. According

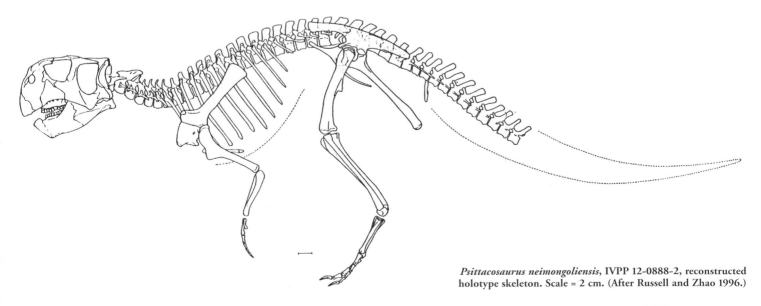

Psittacosaurus neimongoliensis, IVPP 12-0888-2, reconstructed holotype skeleton. Scale = 2 cm. (After Russell and Zhao 1996.)

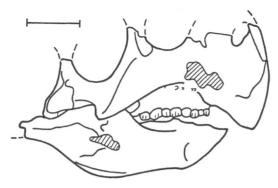

Psittacosaurus ordosensis, IVPP 07-0888-1, holotype incomplete skull, right lateral view. Scale = 2 cm. (After Russell and Zhao 1996.)

to Molnar, if psittacosaurs delivered blows by swinging the head, the cervical muscles would have to be exceptionally developed, a condition suggested by the relatively large muscle scars on the occipital face of the skull.

Coombs (1980, 1982) described remains of two juvenile specimens referred to *P. mongoliensis*, collected during the Third Asiatic Expedition in the "Oshih Formation." The specimens include a skull with partial mandibles (AMNH 6535), and skull, mandibles, cervical, dorsal and caudal vertebrae, ribs, scapulae, coracoid, partial ilium and ischium, humeri, femora, tibiae, fibulae, and almost complete left pes (AMNH 6536). In both specimens, Coombs (1980) identified the rostral bone, noting that this was also present in the *P. mongoliensis* holotype. Tooth wear in these specimens implies a diet of abrasive vegetation, and that hatchlings would have been considerably smaller than these individuals. AMNH 6535 skull measures 28 millimeters (approximately 1.1 inches) in length and AMNH 6536 42 millimeters (about 1.6 inches). Coombs (1980, 1982) estimated the total length of AMNH 6535 as 230–250 millimeters (about 8.6–almost 9.8 inches), both among the smallest dinosaur specimens reported. Among juvenile features (see Brown and Schlaikjer 1940*b*; Maryańska and Osmólska 1975; Dodson 1976) observed by Coombs in these specimens are the very large orbit, relatively large braincase, more curved skull roof, short snout, rostral approaching and possibly contacting maxilla, small and narrow lateral temporal opening, lack of sagittal crest, slender suborbital bar, and small jugal flange.

Because the juveniles had been feeding on abrasive vegetation prior to their deaths, Coombs (1980, 1982) suggested that these dinosaurs were precocial. Juvenile *Psittacosaurus* may not have required parental care, at least in the form of parents offering them transported, premasticated or regurgitated food. However, Coombs (1975, 1982) stressed the danger

in conjuring up mental images comparing the possible relationships between adult and juvenile dinosaurs to those of living animals, particularly mammals and birds, and argued that such behavioral interpretations involving dinosaurs should be made on a case-by-case basis.

More recently, Russell and Zhao speculated that the small brain size of psittacosaurs implies a very restricted behavioral repertoire comparative to that of modern mammals of comparable body size.

Coombs (1980, 1982) noted that the surface area to body mass ratio of *Psittacosaurus* juveniles would promote heat loss at a considerably higher rate than in adults. As pointed out by Welty (1963, 1988) and Gordon (1968), some modern endotherms are ectothermic at birth, endothermic physiology developing with growth and the consequent more favorable surface area to body mass relationship. Coombs (1980, 1982) concluded that these tiny *Psittacosaurus* individuals were endothermic in the avian or mammalian sense, regardless of physiology of the adults.

In a preliminary study of the Early Cretaceous dinosaur faunas of China, Dong (1993*b*) noted that two separate dinosaur faunas existed in northern and southern Asia. The northern or *Psittacosaurus* fauna is known from the wealth of collections recovered from numerous formations and localities throughout northern China and southern Mongolia. The southern fauna, based upon collections from only a few localities, is poorly known but apparently distinguished by an absence of psittacosaurs. The more recent discovery of *Psittacosaurus* further south in Thailand (see Buffetaut and Suteethorn 1992), however, suggests that the differences between northern and southern Chinese faunas are probably ecological in nature, reflecting differences in climate and vegetation during the Early Cretaceous.

Recently, Erickson and Tumanova (1995) performing an histological analysis of the major long bones (humeri, femora, and tibiae) of *P. mongoliensis*, and using a growth series representing nine ontogenetic stages, found that these bones in this species "consist of woven-fibered matrices interrupted by annuli of parallel-fibered or lamellar bone." With ontogeny, all of these elements went through comparable shifts in vascularization pattern (from longitudinal to recticular to radial). Not observed by Erickson and Tumanova in these elements were Haversian remodeling, subperiosteal lamellar-zone bone deposition, and fibro-lamellar bone formation, characters typically found in the bones of most dinosaurs. The authors speculated that the bone histology of *P. mongoliensis* is atypical for ceratopsians and possibly unique to this species and, perhaps, the genus.

Erickson and Tumanova postulated that the "surprising increase in bone vascularization with ontogeny may be explained by allometry associated with functional adaptation." Highly vascularized bone is typical of "rapid" bone growth and is usually observed in subadult individuals. The small adult size of this species may have precluded development of Haversian bone. Erickson and Tumanova found it unlikely that the annuli were deposited annually in *P. mongoliensis*, unless this species grew more slowly than other dinosaurs.

As concluded by Erickson and Tumanova, this study shows "that single elements cannot be used to typify the bone histologies of individuals or taxa and that assessments of relative ages using single elements are prone to misinterpretation."

Key references: Bohlin (1953); Brown and Schlaikjer (1940*b*); Buffetaut and Suteethorn (1991, 1992); Cheng (1983); Chow (1963); Coombs (1975, 1980, 1982); Dodson (1991); Dong (1987, 1993*b*); Eberth, Russell, Braman and Deini (1993); Erickson and Tumanova (1995); Maryańska and Osmólska (1975); Molnar (1977); Osborn (1923*b*, 1924*a*); Rozhdestvensky (1955, 1960); Russell and Zhao (1996); Sereno (1986, 1990*b*); Sereno and Chao [Chao] (1988); Sereno, Zhao [Chao], Cheng and Rao (1988); Yang [Young] (1931, 1958*b*).

PTEROPELYX Cope 1889 [*nomen dubium*]— (=See *Corythosaurus*.)
Name derivation: Greek *pteron* = "wing" + Greek *pelyx* = "pelvis."
Type species: *P. grallipes* Cope 1889 [*nomen dubium*].

PTEROSPONDYLUS Jaekel 1913 [*nomen dubium*]—(=?*Procompsognathus*)
Saurischia: Theropoda *incertae sedis*.
Name derivation: Greek *pteron* = "wing" + Greek *spondylos* = "vertebrae."
Type species: *P. trielbae* Jaekel 1913 [*nomen dubium*].
Other species: [None.]
Occurrence: [Unnamed formation], Bezirk Magdeburg, Germany.
Age: Late Triassic.
Known material/holotype: Mid-dorsal vertebra.
Diagnosis of genus: [None published.]
Comments: The genus *Pterospondylus* was founded upon a vertebra, found (within the shell of a Triassic turtle) in the Upper Keuper of Halberstadt, [former German Democratic Republic] Germany.

As pointed out by Ostrom (1981), *Pterospondylus* is sometimes regarded as synonymous with *Procompsognathus* (see Steel 1970) or at least aligned with

it (Huene 1932). However, the specimen is indeterminate and almost twice the size of the comparable bone in *Procompsognathus*. Thus, no conclusive synonomy can be made, this taxon best regarded (see White 1973) as a *nomen dubium*.

Key references: Huene (1932); Jaekel (1913); Ostrom (1981); Steel (1970); White (1973).

QUAESITOSAURUS Kurzanov and Bannikov 1983
Saurischia: Sauropodomorpha: Sauropoda: Diplodocidae: Dicraeosaurinae.
Name derivation: Latin *quaesitus* = "abnormal" + Greek *sauros* = "lizard."
Species: *Q. orientalis* Kurzanov and Bannikov 1983.
Other species: [None.]
Occurrence: Barungoyotskaya Svita [=Barun Goyot Formation], Omnogov, Mongolian People's Republic.
Age: Late Cretaceous (?Late Santonian or Early Campanian).
Known material/holotype: PIN 3906/2, almost complete skull.

Diagnosis of genus (as for type species): Skull high, short, with wide snout; squamosal and quadratojugal not contacting each other; large "resonator" depression on posterior side of quadrate; no evidence

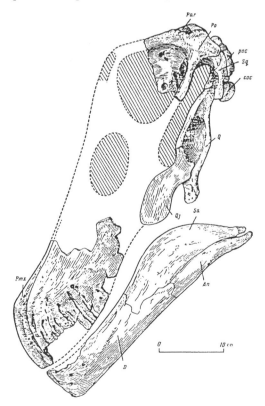

Qaesitosaurus orientalis, PIN 3906/2, holotype reconstructed incomplete skull. (After Kurzanov and Bannikov 1983.)

R

of parietal opening; occipital condyle rounded, below condyle a unique canal passing posteriorly from pituitary depression in base of condyle; nine maxillary teeth; alveolar segment of mandible bending strongly inwards (Kurzanov and Bannikov 1983).

Comments: The genus *Quaesitosaurus* was founded on a skull (PIN 3906/2) discovered during the Combined Soviet-Mongolian Paleontological Expedition to the Barungoyot Formation, in the western part of the Shara-Tsav bluffs, Southeastern Gobi region, Mongolia. The discovery is especially important in that cranial material of Asiatic sauropods is extremely rare, most such dinosaurs known only from isolated teeth and postcranial bone fragments (Kurzanov and Bannikov 1983).

Comparing the skull with those of other known Asiatic sauropods, Kurzanov and Bannikov observed that *Quaesitosaurus* most closely resembles *Nemegtosaurus*, though with a much less narrow snout.

Discussing the abnormally large "resonator" opening of the middle ear, Kurzanov and Bannikov noted that *Quaesitosaurus* most likely had very sensitive hearing, indicating that the animal was mostly terrestrial. However, the musculature and structure of the jaw, with its long facial part, broad scoop, and little worn teeth, are adaptations for the intake of large volumes of soft vegetation, intimating that the animal fed with its head submerged partially in water. The lower jaw is not as developed as the upper and may have been covered in life by a horny layer useful for collecting soft, aquatic vegetation. Kurzanov and Bannikov speculated that *Quaesitosaurus*, because of its unique features, may have lived both on land and in water, but cautioned that this possible lifestyle should not be applied to all sauropods.

In his review of the Sauropoda, McIntosh (1990*b*) observed that the preserved parts of the skull of *Quaesitosaurus* resemble *Nemegtosaurus* in various features (snout broad, quadrate inclined rostroventrally relative to axis of mandible, quadratojugal relatively broad, infratemporal fenestra very narrow, and basipterygoid processes short) and differ in others (snout significantly broader, squamosal shorter and not contacting quadratojugal, no parietal aperture, concavity developed on caudal face of quadrate, nine instead of eight maxillary teeth, longer row of mandibular teeth, and prominent canal opening between basal tubera of basioccipital under condyle, leading to pituitary fossa). Allowing that some differences between the two forms could relate to the state of preservation, the age of the individual, or individual variation, McIntosh referred *Quaesitosaurus* to the diplodocid subfamily Dicraeosaurinae.

Key references: Kurzanov and Bannikov (1983); McIntosh (1990*b*).

RAPATOR Huene 1932 [*nomen dubium*]— (=? *Walgettosuchus*)

Saurischia: Theropoda: ?Tetanurae *incertae sedis*.

Name derivation: Latin *rapere* = "to seize" + Latin *ator* = "one performing."

Type species: *R. ornitholestoides* Huene 1932 [*nomen dubium*].

Other species: [None.]

Occurrence: Griman Creek Formation, New South Wales, Australia.

Age: Early Cretaceous (Albian).

Known material/holotype: BMNH R3718, right metacarpal I.

Diagnosis of genus (as for type species): Metacarpal with exceptionally prolonged posteromedial process known in no other theropod; rather large for "coelurosaur," about 3.5 times larger than in *Ornitholestes* (Huene 1932).

Comments: The genus *Rapator* was established upon a metacarpal (BMNH R3718) recovered from the Lower Cretaceous of Lightning Ridge, New South Wales, Australia.

According to Molnar (1980*b*), the type specimen implies that *Rapator* was a large form about the size of *Allosaurus*. Molnar suggested *Rapator* and *Walgettosuchus* may be congeneric, but reserved making any formal synonymy because the type material belonging to both forms cannot be compared.

Later, Molnar (1990) agreed with Huene that the prominent caudomedial process of the holotype of *R. ornitholestoides*, much stronger than the hardly comparable equivalent in *Ornitholestes hermanni*, is unique among theropods.

Key references: Huene (1932); Molnar (1980*b*, 1990).

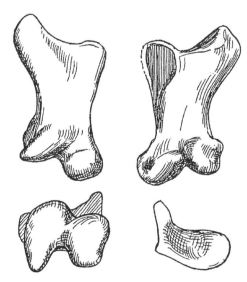

Rapator ornitholestoides, BMNH 3718, holotype metacarpal, four views. (After Huene 1932.)

REBBACHISAURUS   Lavocat 1954

Saurischia: Sauropodomorpha: Sauropoda:
    Diplodocidae: Dicraeosaurinae.

Name derivation: "Rebbach [territory]" + Greek
    sauros = "lizard."

Type species: *R. garasbae* Lavocat 1954.

Other species: *R. tamesnensis* Lapparent 1960.

Occurrence: Tegana Formation, Ksar-es-Souk,
    Morocco; "Continental intercalaire," Adrar,
    Tamenghest, Wargla, Algeria; "Continental
    intercalaire," Medenine, Tunisia; "Continental
    intercalaire," Agadez, Farak Formation, Tahoua,
    Niger.

Age: Early Cretaceous (Albian).

Known material: Postcranial elements, teeth,
    numerous isolated postcranial remains.

Holotype: MNH collection, right scapula, 11
    vertebrae, ten ribs, sacrum, humerus, ?pelvic
    fragments.

    Diagnosis of genus: [No modern diagnosis pub-
lished.]

Diagnosis of *R. garasbae*: [No modern diagnosis published.]

"Diagnosis" of *R. tamesnensis*: Distinguished from *R. garasbae* by different shape of
scapula and shorter dorsal spines (Lapparent
1960)

Comments: The genus *Rebbachisaurus* was
founded upon partial postcranial remains
(MNH collection) discovered in the "Continental intercalaire," Gara Sba, Southern
Morocco (Lavocat 1954).

Lavocat (1954) estimated that the type species,
R. garasbae, attained a length of 20 meters (about 68
feet).

A second species, *R. tamesnensis*, Lapparent 1960
was based upon teeth, vertebrae, limb bones, girdle
bones, and other material from the "Continental
intercalaire" of the central Sahara desert region.

Lapparent (1960) described *R. tamesnensis* as follows: Teeth broadly spatulate; dorsal vertebrae with
much elongated neural spines, posterior dorsal spines
as long as 1.5 meters (over 5 feet); tail long, distal
caudal vertebrae very elongate; fore and hindlimbs
approximately same size; metacarpals over twice
length of metatarsals; pes powerfully built, with massive claws. The total estimated height of the largest
dorsal vertebra is slightly more than 1 meter; humerus
is 123 centimeters (about 47 inches) in length, femur
150 centimeters (about 58 inches).

In his review of the Sauropoda, McIntosh
(1990*b*) regarded *R. garasbae* as distinct from all
known sauropods, briefly describing it as follows:
Caudal dorsal vertebra with enormously elevated
neural spine (most closely resembling twelfth dorsal
in *Dicraeosaurus*); in *Rebbachisaurus* and *Dicraeosaurus*, very thin laminae contributing to neural arch,
especially four laminae of spine; slender transverse
processes of dorsals similarly directed upward and
outward in both genera; (in unprepared sacrum) four
spines ?coalesced; scapular blade broad, distal end
expanding uniquely into broad racket shape. McIntosh questioned whether most of the remains referred

Rebbachisaurus tamesnensis
holotype caudal and dorsal
vertebrae. Scale = 2 cm. (After
Lapparent 1960.)

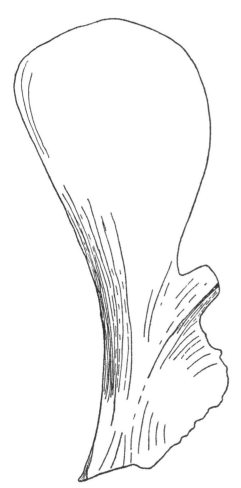

Rebbachisaurus garasbae, MNH, holotype right scapula.
(After Lavocat 1954.)

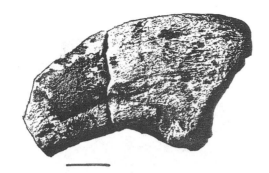

Rebbachisaurus tamesnensis, holotype left pedal ungual. Scale = 2 cm. (After Lapparent 1960.)

to *R. tamesnensis* belong to *Rebacchisaurus*, adding that this material would suggest a form (like *Diplodocus*) with a "whiplash" tail.

Note: Ichnites from the Niger Republic possibly relating to *R. tamesnensis* were reported by Ginsburg, Lapparent, Loiret and Taquet (1966).

Key references: Lapparent (1954, 1960); McIntosh (1990*b*).

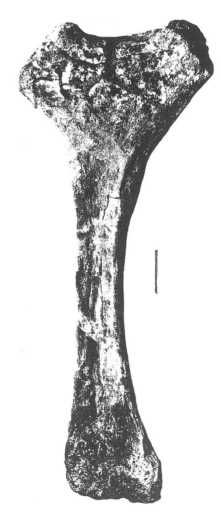

Rebbachisaurus tamesnensis, holotype left ischium. Scale = 5 cm. (After Lapparent 1960.)

REGNOSAURUS   Mantell 1848

Ornithischia: Genasauria: Thyreophora: Stegosauria: Huayangosauridae.

Name derivation: Latin *Regno* [from Regni, ancient tribe that inhabited Sussex County] + Greek *sauros* = "lizard."

Type species: *R. northamptoni* Mantell 1848 [*nomen dubium*].

Other species: [None.]

Occurrence: Wealden, Sussex, England.

Age: Early Cretaceous (Hauterivian–Barremian).

Known material/holotype: BMNH R2422, fragment of right dentary missing tooth crowns.

Diagnosis of genus: [None published.]

Comments: *Regnosaurus* is the first stegosaur found in Europe to be represented by skull material.

As chronicled by Sereno and Upchurch (1995), Mantell (1838) reported the discovery of a small, partial right mandible (BMNH 2422) from the Wealden (Lower Cretaceous) of Cuckfield, Sussex, in northern England, and referred this fossil to the genus *Iguanodon*.

As originally described by Mantell (1848), the fragment possesses a single row of small, closely spaced teeth missing crowns and four successional teeth, showing a total of 18 tooth positions, and a wide lateral shelf. The length of the fragment is 7.6 centimeters (approximately 3 inches), width 4 centimeters (about 1.6 inches). Mantell (1841) noted similarities (absence of tooth alveoli, and ankylosis of teeth to mesial surface of dental parapet, these characters describing a pleurodont dentition) between it and the mandible of the extant lizard *Iguana*.

Owen (1842) recognized the dentition to be thecodont rather than pleurodont and (in 1858) suggested that this specimen belonged to the armored dinosaur *Hylaeosaurus* (in succeeding years, *Regnosaurus* becoming generally regarded as a junior synonym of this genus). Based on a newly discovered *Iguanodon* mandible preserved *in situ* with teeth, recovered from the Wealden of Cuckfield, Mantell (1848) determined that BMNH 2422 was distinct from *Iguanodon* but belonged to the same family, proposing for it the new name *Regnosaurus northamptoni*.

Over the years, *Regnosaurus* has been assigned to various higher taxa, including the Scelidosauridae (Lydekker 1888*b*) and the Ankylosauria (Ostrom 1970). Subsequently, Ostrom (1971) regarded *Regnosaurus* as a *nomen dubium* belonging to the Sauropoda, and probably referable to *Chondrosteosaurus*. Coombs (1978*a*), in his revision of ankylosaurian families, agreed that *Regnosaurus* may not be an ankylosaur.

In a review of the Sauropoda, McIntosh (1990*b*) listed *R. northamptoni* as a tentative junior synonym of the sauropod *Chondostreosaurus gigas*.

Olshevsky and Ford, in a popular article (*The Dinosaur Report,* summer/fall 1993), noted that BMNH 2422 exhibits features consistent with stegosaurs (*e.g.,* slight downward bend of jawline, relative depth of jaw, very gentle inward curvature to tooth row in dorsal view), suggested that this dentary belongs to a primitive stegosaur, and placed it within the family "Dacentruridae" (along with *Dacentrurus* and *Yingshanosaurus*), based on the presence of "small and numerous teeth."

Sereno and Upchurch reexamined BMNH 2422 and pointed out various features that suggest it does not belong to a sauropod. However, Sereno and Upchurch observed one of the autapomorphies (sinuous curve of the tooth row in lateral view; see Sereno 1986) of the ornithischian group "Thyreophoroidea." As *Regnosaurus* possesses neither of two autapomorphies of the Ankylosauria relating to the lower jaw (Coombs 1971; Sereno 1986), Sereno and Upchurch considered the possibility of BMNH 2422 belonging to the Stegosauria, noting the strong similiarity between this specimen and *Huayangosaurus*, a primitive stegosaur from the Middle Jurassic of China.

Sereno and Upchurch suggested that BMNH 2422 represents previously unrecognized remains of a stegosaurian dinosaur, best regarded as Stegosauria gen. et sp. indeterminate, pending further material allowing a definitive diagnosis to be made.

Although Sereno and Upchurch found no evidence supporting Olshevsky and Ford's referral of *Regnosaurus* to the "Dacentruridae" (no cranial remains are known for *Dacentrurus*), they did find it likely that *Regnosaurus* is a relatively primitive stegosaur lacking a derived condition (the "dorsal lamina," a thin plate of bone formed by the dorsal margin of the dentary; Sereno and Dong 1990) present in some members of the Stegosauridae (*e.g., Kentrosaurus, Stegosaurus,* and *Chungkingosaurus*). However, both *Regnosaurus* and *Huayangosaurus* share two derived features not present in other known stegosaurs: 1. prominent ridge on lateral surface of dentary, and 2. deep depression lying immediately below this ridge.

Sereno and Upchurch regarded *Regnosaurus* as a taxon lying outside of the Stegosauridae, possibly the sister-taxon to that group (equivalent to Olshevsky and Ford's interpretation), or as the sister-taxon to all other Stegosauria, or in a trichotomy with *Huayangosaurus* and all other stegosaurs. Four evolutionary steps are required to satisfy all of these topologies: Either the lateral ridge and lateral depression evolved independently in *Regnosaurus* and *Huayangosaurus*, or these features evolved in basal stegosaurians and were subsequently lost in the Stegosauridae. However, only the former two steps are required if *Regno-*

saurus is considered to be the sister-taxon of *Huayangosaurus*. Therefore, in the absence of any contradictory evidence, Sereno and Upchurch found it most parsimonious to regard *Regnosaurus* and *Huayangosaurus* as sister-taxa belonging to the monophyletic group Huayangosauridae. The authors speculated that this unification has potentially interesting implications for faunal exchange between China and western Asia and Europe, *Regnosaurus* perhaps representing a relict population of a group that first appeared during the Middle Jurassic.

Peter M. Galton (personal communication to Sereno and Upchurch) suggested that *Regnosaurus* may, in fact, be referrable to *Huayangosaurus*, no anatomical evidence contradicting this opinion. Sereno and Upchurch found this view unlikely, based on the geographic and stratigraphic locations of these genera, although noting that they may eventually prove to be sister-species of the same genus *Regnosaurus*.

Key references: Coombs (1978*a*); Mantell (1938, 1841, 1848); McIntosh (1990*b*); Ostrom (1970, 1971); Owen (1842, 1858); Sereno and Upchurch (1995).

Revueltosaurus callendri, NMMNH P4957, holotype tooth, internal views. Scale = 22 cm. (After Hunt 1989.)

REVUELTOSAURUS Hunt 1989

?Ornithischia *incertae sedis.*

Name derivation: "Revuelto [Spanish *revuelto* = "revolt"] Creek + Greek *sauros* = "lizard."

Type species: *R. callenderi* Hunt 1989 [*nomen dubium*].

Other species: [None.]

Occurrence: Bull Canyon Formation, New Mexico, United States.

Age: Late Triassic (Early Norian).

Known material: Teeth.

Holotype: NMMNH P4957, tooth.

Diagnosis of genus (as for type species): Large ornithischian distinguished by tall premaxillary teeth (length/height ration = 0.72), with denticulated margins that are slightly recurved and twice the height of dentary/maxillary teeth, with relatively high dentary/maxillary teeth (length/height radio = 0.88) lacking accessory cusps (Hunt and Lucas 1994).

Comments: The genus *Revueltosaurus* was established upon an incisiform tooth (NMMNH P44957) collected from the Bull Canyon Formation of Quay County, New Mexico. Paratypes from the same locality include a dentary/maxillary tooth (NMMNH P 4958) and premaxillary tooth (NMMNH P 4959); referred specimens include 28 premaxillary and dentary/maxillary teeth (NMMNH P 4960) (Hunt 1989).

Hunt (1989) originally diagnosed the monotypic *R. callenderi* as follows: Small herbivorous dinosaur sharing with ornithischians teeth that are low, triangular-shaped in side view, dentary/maxillary teeth not recurved, well-developing necks separating crown from roots (see Sereno 1986); differing from most ornithischians in premaxillary teeth twice the height of maxillary/dentary teeth, from heterodontosaurs in all tooth margins denticulated (see Sereno); unlike "fabrosaurids" (see Galton 1986), teeth lack cingula; unlike *Technosaurus*, lack accessory cusps; unlike other ornithischians, ?premaxillary teeth incisiform (see Sereno).

As no other known ornithischians have anterior teeth (see Sereno 1986), Hunt suggested that *Revueltosaurus* is the sister-taxon of the Ornithischia. Padian (1990) agreed that these teeth are ornithischian and referred to *Revueltosaurus* additional teeth from the Upper Unit of the Petrified Forest Member, Chinle Formation (Late Triassic, Norian), northeastern Arizona. This new material includes three teeth (FMNH PR1697, PR1698, and PR1699) collected in 1983 by John Bolt near Lacey Point, northern end of Petrified Forest National Park.

In a review of basal ornithischians, Sereno (1991) pointed out that, although three tooth forms have been attributed to *R. callenderi*, no supporting evidence was given for their association, the differentiating characters listed in Hunt's diagnosis therefore unconfirmable. According to Sereno (1991), the holotype tooth of *R. callenderi* is spoon-shaped as is the premaxillary tooth of *Lesothosaurus diagnosticus* and many other ornithischians; also, there are more denticles in the tooth crowns of *R. callenderi* than in largest crowns of *L. diagnosticus*, and no prominent basal anterior and posterior denticles and associated ridges, all of these features varying among and, to some extent, within teeth of basal ornithischians. Sereno (1991) questioned Padian's reference of the additional fragmentary crowns to *R. callenderi* and Hunt's proposed sister-taxon assessment of the species. Sereno (1991) concluded that *R. callenderi* is best regarded as a *nomen dubium*, its type and referred material consisting of indeterminate ornithischian remains.

Addressing Sereno's (1991) criticism, Hunt and Lucas maintained that the specimens assigned to this species represent a single taxon because of their large size (being much larger than teeth of other known Triassic ornithischians), the lack of evidence indicating the presence of another ornithischian in this formation, and the fact that all of the specimens described by Hunt (1989) were recovered from the same quarry. Hunt and Lucas also stated that these collected teeth represent dentary/maxillary and premaxillary teeth, and that there is, therefore, no lack of clarity concerning their positions. Furthermore, Hunt and Lucas noted that, given the clear associa-

tion of the specimen referred to *R. callenderi* by Hunt and given that positional data can be inferred, this taxon can be diagnosed by its characters and is therefore not a *nomen dubium*.

According to Hunt and Lucas, the two stratigraphic units (lower part of the Bull Canyon Formation of eastern New Mexico and lower part of the Painted Desert Member of the Petrified Forest Formation in Arizona) which yielded remains of this dinosaur are probably of early Norian age, as suggested by the presence of the phytosaur *Pseudopalatus* and aetosaur *Paratypothorax* (see also Hunt and Lucas 1990).

Key references: Hunt (1989); Hunt and Lucas (1994); Padian (1990); Sereno (1986, 1991).

RHABDODON Matheron 1869—(=*Mochlodon*, *Oligosaurus*, *Onychosaurus*, *Ornithomerus*)

Ornithischia: Genasauria: Cerapoda: Ornithopoda: Iguanodontia *incertae sedis*.

Name derivation: Greek *rhabdos* = "rod" + Greek *odous* = "tooth."

Type species: *R. priscus* Matheron 1869.

Other species: *R. septimanicus* Buffetaut and Le Loeuff 1991 [*nomen dubium*].

Occurrence: Sinpetru Beds, Hunedoara, Romania; Marnes Rouges inférieures, Aude, Grès de Saint-Chinian, Herault, Couches de Rognac, Bouches-du-Rhône, Grès à Reptiles, Var, Grès de Labarre, Arìge, France; [unnamed formation], Soria, Lower "Garumnian" Beds, Lerida, [unnamed formation], Lleida, Spain; Gosau Formation, Niederostereich, Austria.

Age: Late Cretaceous (Campanian–Maastrichtian).

Known material: Disarticulated cranial and postcranial remains, teeth, juvenile to adult.

Holotype: MNHN collection, two jaw fragments, dorsal, two sacral, and two caudal vertebrae, right humerus, proximal portion of right femur, distal end of right tibia.

Diagnosis of genus: Skull simply constructed quadrate, rather primitive mandible with single row of dental alveoli; relatively few teeth; tooth crowns thickly enameled, spatulate, with pronounced median ridge with numerous divergent folds; roots very strong, no tendency to narrow; cervical vertebrae with anteriorly enlarged centra and obliquely backward-

Rhabdodon priscus, Geological Museum, University of Vienna, holotype incomplete femur of *Ornithopsis gracilis*. (After Seeley 1881.)

Rhabdodon priscus, holotype dentary of *Iguanodon suessi*. (After Seeley 1881.)

directed neural spines; middle and posterior caudal vertebrae elongate, laterally compressed; humerus with well-developed deltopectoral crest; pubis relatively large; femur markedly curved, with prominent fourth trochanter forming well-defined ridge (Steel 1969).

Diagnosis of *R. septimanicus*: Dentary with coronoid process in prolongation of alveolar row (process sloping backward much more strongly in many specimens [including type] of *R. priscus*); alveolar row without lateral shelf (present in type species), lateral face of dentary smoothly rounded and not forming angle (as it does in type species); alveolar row markedly curved (curvature less marked in type species) (Buffetaut and Le Loeuff 1991).

Comments: A rather unspecialized, medium-sized ornithopod and the latest known iguanodontian, *Rhabdodon* was founded upon partial postcranial remains (MNHN collection) from the Upper Cretaceous of Bassin-d'Aix, Fuveau, Provence, France.

Seeley (1881) erected the new genus *Mochlodon* to include remains originally named *Iguanodon suessi* [*nomen dubium*], a taxon Bunzel (1871) had based upon a right dentary with teeth from the Gosau Formation of Neue Welt, Austria. Associated with this specimen were two teeth from the upper and lower jaws, belonging to the ?same individual, and, from the same horizon and locality, a parietal and proximal end of a scapula.

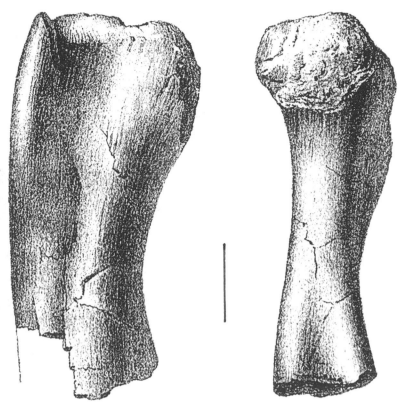

Rhabdodon priscus, MNHN, holotype 1. proximal portion of right femur, anterior and inner views. Scale = 4 cm. (After Matheron 1869.)

Nopcsa (1899) based the new species *M. robustum* [*nomen dubium*] on a lower jaw of stout proportions found in Transylvania, Hungary [now in Romania]. Nopcsa (1902*b*) subsequently referred to *Mochlodon* material including a nasal, maxilla, dentary, articular, quadrate, and upper tooth, collected from Siebenburgen, Transylvania. He did not refer these remains to any species, but observed a similarity between the tooth and teeth of *M. suessi*. A dentary with part of an angular, from the Upper Cretaceous of Comitat Hunyad, Transylvania, had been described previously by Nopcsa (1899) as *Camptosaurus inkeyi*. Later, Nopcsa (1904) referred this specimen to *Mochlodon*. As pointed out by Galton and Powell (1980), this specimen, referred by them to *R. priscus*, was never figured and has apparently been lost.

Nopcsa (1915) later suggested that material referred both to *Rhabdodon* and *Mochlodon* belonged to a single genus, with *Rhabdodon* accepted as the senior synonym by most subsequent workers (Lapparent and Lavocat 1955; Romer 1966; Steel 1969; Olshevsky 1978, 1991, 1992). Also, Nopcsa (1915) suggested that *M. robustum* was conspecific with *R. priscus* and that *R. suessi* should be considered distinct as *R. priscus* var. *suessi*.

Nopcsa (1923) observed that *Rhabdodon* resembles the North American *Camptosaurus* in form of teeth, simplicity of the skull, and size (some adult

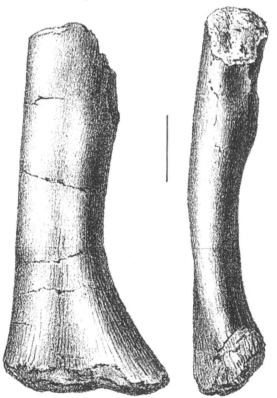

Rhabdodon priscus, MNHN, holotype right humerus, posterior and outer views. Scale = 4 cm. (After Matheron 1869.)

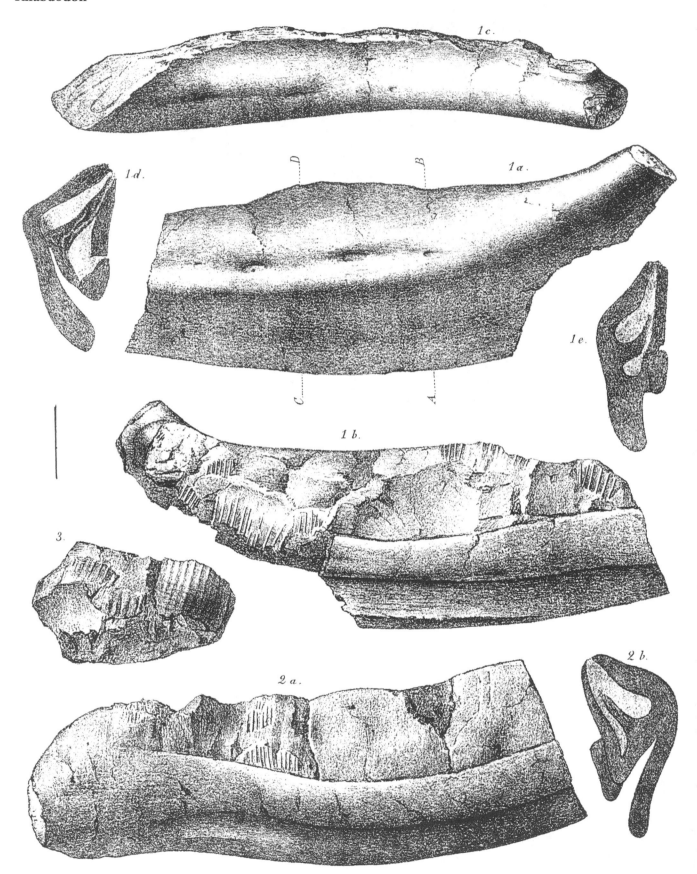

Rhabdodon priscus, MNHN, holotype partial 1. left lower jaw, a. labial and b. lingual views, 2. partial right lower jaw, a. lingual view. Scale = 2 cm. (After Matheron 1869.)

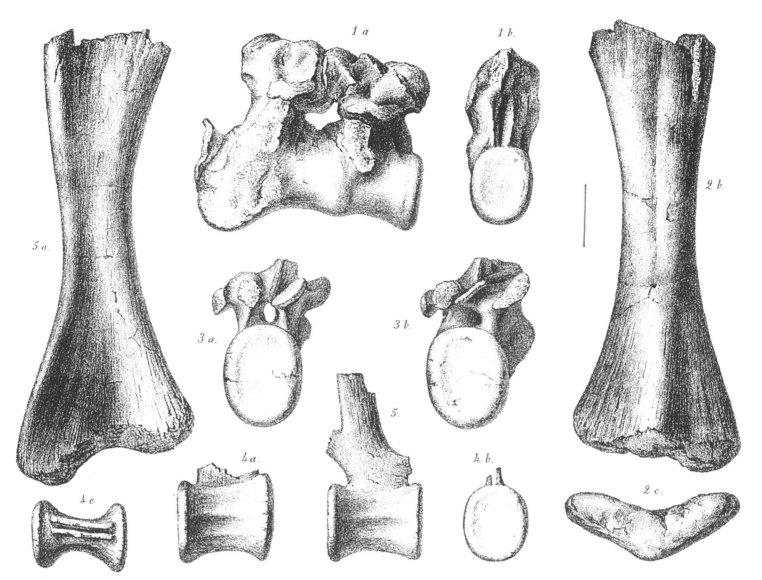

Rhabdodon priscus, MNHN, holotype 1. portion of sacrum, a. right lateral and b. posterior views, 2. right tibia, b. anterior view, 3. dorsal vertebra, a. anterior and b. oblique right views, 4. posterior caudal vertebra, a. right lateral, b. anterior, c. dorsal views, 5. right tibia, posterior view. Scale = 4 cm. (After Matheron 1869.)

Rhabdodon individuals reaching an approximate length of 4 meters [about 13.5 feet]).

Various other taxa have been referred to *Rhabdodon*:

Oligosaurus adelus Seeley 1881 [*nomen dubium*] was based on a specimen from the Gosau Formation (Turonian) of Neue Welt. Bunzel interpreted this specimen as a lacertilian right humerus, after which Seeley identified it as the right scapula of a probable dinosaur.

Ornithomerus gracilis Seeley 1881 [*nomen dubium*] was based on the shaft of a femur (Geological Museum collection, University of Vienna) from the Gosau Formation, Wiener-Neustadt, Austria. Both *O. adelus* and *O. gracilis* (Romer 1956, 1966; Olshevsky 1978, 1991, 1992) are regarded as synonyms of *R. priscus*.

Onychosaurus hungaricus Nopcsa 1902 (junior synonym of *R. priscus*; see Olshevsky 1978, 1991, 1992;

Norman and Weishampel 1990) was founded on remains of two individuals collected from the Upper Cretaceous of Hungary. Bony plates found in the tail region suggested to Nopcsa (1902*a*), who did not figure these remains, that they belonged to an armored dinosaur like *Polacanthus*, the teeth resembling those of *Stegosaurus*.

R. septimanicus Buffetaut and Le Loeuff 1991 was based on an incomplete right dentary (Laboratoire de Paléontologie des Vertébrés collection, Université Paris-VI, number MTL 02) including a partly preserved coronoid process, collected from a layer of course red sandstone of the "Grès a Reptiles," in the continental Upper Cretaceous (Campanian to Maastrichtian) of Montouliers (Hérault). Comparing this specimen to all *Rhabdodon* dentaries in the Marseille (including holotype of *R. priscus*), London and Budapest collections, Buffetaut and Le Loeuff referred it to this genus because of its general morphology and

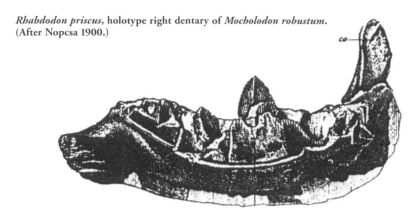

Rhabdodon priscus, holotype right dentary of *Mocholodon robustum*. (After Nopcsa 1900.)

appearance of the teeth, but observed what they believed to be significant differences in the morphology of the dentary's posterior region.

Also, Lapparent (1947) reported teeth, maxillae with teeth, cervical, dorsal, sacral, and caudal vertebrae, limb and pelvic bones, and various fragments referable to *Rhabdodon* from the "Danian" [=Maastrichtian] of central France. Later, Lapparent (1954) described remains from the Upper Cretaceous of Hérault, including ribs and a long bone fragment (collected from Montouliers), and anterior caudal vertebra (from Quarante). *Rhabdodon* material has also been reported from the Upper Cretaceous of Spain (Lapparent and Aguirre 1956; Lapparent, Quintero and Tregueros 1957); from the Danian [=Maastrichtian] of Transylvania (Nopcsa 1915, 1928c); and from Begudian [=Maastrichtian] of Basse-Provence (Dughi and Sirugue 1960).

Although *Rhabdodon* has been generally classified as an iguanodontid, Bartholomai and Molnar (1981) pointed out that the humerus shows a well-developed deltopectoral crest (Lapparent 1947) and less prominent lesser trochanter (Matheron), therefore not meeting Dodson's (1980) criteria for inclusion in the Iguanodontidae. Later studies (see Weishampel and Weishampel 1983; Norman 1984a; Weishampel 1984c; Buffetaut and Le Loeuff) suggest that this taxon might belong in the Hypsilophodontidae. In their review of iguanodontids and related ornithopods, Norman and Weishampel (1990) noted that the affinities of this genus are not currently well understood, with *Rhabdodon* best classified as Iguanodontia *incertae sedis*.

Weishampel, Grigorescu and Norman (1991) reevaluated and redescribed *R. priscus* based upon the existing specimens, including skull material (BMNH R3389, R3393, R3394, R3395, R3396, R3398, R3402, R3411, R4901, R4916, and R5491), and also postcrania (FGGUB 1013, MAFI Ob.3077 and Ob.3078, BMNH R3809, R3810, R3811, R3813,

R3814, R3816, R4900, and MJH 77). Weishampel *et al.* concluded that this taxon shares two synapomorphies with the Hypsilophodontidae (maxillary and dentary teeth with ridges confluent with marginal denticles, maxillary and dentary teeth with cingulum at crown base) and two with the iguanodontian plexus prior to the evolution of hadrosaurids (dentary margins parallel, no premaxillary teeth).

Notes: Bartholomai and Molnar (1981) pointed out that the name *Rhabdodon* is preoccupied [Fleischmann 1831], suggesting that junior subjective synonym *Mochlodon* be used instead. On October 18, 1985, Winand Brinkmann applied to the International Commission on Zoological Nomenclature favoring the retaining of *Rhabdodon* Matheron 1869 and suppression of *Rhabdodon* Fleischmann 1831. In the March 1988 *Bulletin of Zoological Nomenclature*, 45[1], Opinion 1483, the Commission ruled unanimously in favor of Brinkmann's request.

The degree of sloping in MTL 02 is apparently an artifact of preservation, while curvature of the alveolar row could be due to damage; because of the incompleteness of this specimen, the scarcity of *Rhabdodon* material, and extremely wide variation found in all populations of ornithopods, *R. septi-*

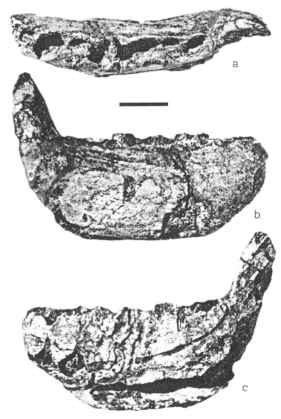

Rhabdodon septimanicus, MTL 02, holotype right dentary, a. dorsal, b. lateral, c. medial views. Scale = 1 cm. (After Buffetaut and Le Loeuff 1991.)

Rhabdodon priscus, life restoration by Brian Franczak.

manicus should be regarded as a *nomen dubium* (M. K. Brett-Surman, personal communication 1991.)

Key references: Bartholomai and Molnar (1981); Buffetaut and Le Loeuff (1991); Dughi and Sirugue (1960); Lapparent (1947); Lapparent and Aguirre (1956); Lapparent, Quintero and Tregueros (1957); Matheron (1869); Nopcsa (1899, 1902*b*, 1915, 1928*c*); Norman (1984*a*); Norman and Weishampel (1990); Seeley (1881); Steel (1969); Weishampel (1984*c*); Weishampel, Grigorescu and Norman (1991); Weishampel and Weishampel (1983).

RHODANOSAURUS Nopcsa 1929 [*nomen dubium*]—(=?"*Struthiosaurus*" [notes])

Ornithischia: Thyreophora: Ankylosauria: Nodosauridae.

Name derivation: Greek *rhos* = "head" + "Danian [age]" + Greek *sauros* = "lizard."

Type species: *R. ludgunensis* Nopcsa 1929 [*nomen dubium*].

Other species: ?*R. alcinus* Seeley 1881.

Occurrence: [Unnamed formation], Département de la Haute-Garonne, Grès de Saint-Chinian,

Rhodanosaurus lugdunensis, Museum de Lyon collection, holotype caudal vertebrae. (After Nopcsa 1929.)

Département de l'Herault, France.

Age: Late Cretaceous (?Maastrichtian).

Known material: Partial postcrania, dermal armor.

Holotype: Museum de Lyon collection, series of caudal vertebrae, portions of limb bones, dermal plates and spines.

Diagnosis of genus: [None published.]

Comments: The genus *Rhodanosaurus* was founded upon postcranial material including vertebrae, limb bones and some well-preserved dermal spines and plates, originally described and referred by Depéret (1900) to the genus *Crataeomus*. The material was collected from the Danian [=Maastrichtian] of Hérault (Quarante and Montouliers), Provence, France.

The new genus and species, *Rhodanosaurus ludgunensis*, was erected for this material by Nopcsa (1929*b*), who, at the same time, referred to it additional fragmentary remains. Nopcsa briefly described this genus as having dermal ossifications including large lateral plates, blunt dorsal plates, and low-sloping tail spines.

To *R. ludgunensis*, Lapparent (1947) referred vertebrae and dermal plates from the "Danian" [Maastrichtian] of central France, material referred by Nopcsa to "*Struthiosaurus*." Coombs (1978*a*) later referred the species ?*R. alcinus*, based upon indeterminate fragments (?two vertebrae and ?two humeri; see Coombs and Maryańska 1990) to the Nodosauridae as a possible junior synonym of "*Struthiosaurus*" *transilvanicus*.

Key references: Coombs (1978*a*); Coombs and Maryańska (1990); Depéret (1900); Lapparent (1947); Nopcsa (1929*b*); Seeley (1881).

RHOETOSAURUS   Longman 1925

Saurischia: Sauropodomorpha: Sauropoda: Cetiosauridae: Shunosaurinae.

Name derivation: Latin *Rhoeteus* = "Trojan" + Greek *sauros* = "lizard."

Type species: *R. brownei* Longman 1925.

Other species: [None.]

Occurrence: ?Injune Creek Beds, Queensland, Australia.

Age: Early Jurassic (?Bajocian).

Known material/holotype: QM F1695 [or F1751], postcrania, mostly including series of 22 mostly fractured vertebrae, fragments representing central portions of femoral shafts, tibia, fibula, many small, shattered pieces of pelvic elements.

Diagnosis of genus (as for type species): Caudal vertebrae amphicoelous; anterior caudals gigantic; caudal centra solid, with expanded elliptical articulating surfaces from which body curves evenly to median construction more pronounced in posterior caudals; centra somewhat laterally compressed; prezygapophyses elongated, with vertical (and not

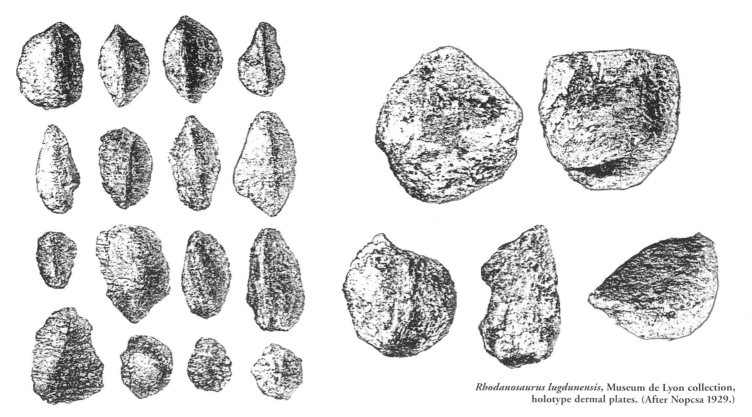

Rhodanosaurus lugdunensis, Museum de Lyon collection, holotype dermal plates. (After Nopcsa 1929.)

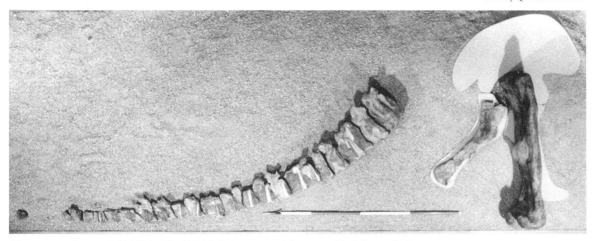

Rhoetosaurus brownei, QM F1695 [or F1751], holotype partial postcranial skeleton. Scale = 1 meter.

obliquely horizontal) articulating surfaces; no postzygapophyses, but well-developed hyposphene; neural spines stout, not greatly elongated; anterior spines subrectangular in side-view outline, oval median recess on posterior margin above junction with somewhat posteriorly projecting hyposphene; inferior border of hyposphene free, articulating between prezygapophyses in hypantrum area and roofing neural canal; anterior chevrons massive, not elongated, intervertebral but not confluent in their attachment, somewhat partly lateral in position, posterior chevrons inferior in position; neural canal of anterior caudals relatively large (Longman 1925).

Comments: *Rhoetosaurus* is historically significant as the first large dinosaur discovered in Australia. The genus was founded upon "Over 100 specimens" (QM F1695; also given as F151) from an incomplete skeleton, discovered in 1924 in the Walloon Series (Jurassic; Jensen 1923), in the Roma district, county of Aberdeen, Durham Downs, Queensland, Australia (Longman 1925).

Longman tentatively assigned *Rhoetosaurus* to the Camarasauridae, envisioning this dinosaur as a bulky quadruped with hindlimbs dominant and a somewhat rigid tail. The length of *Rhoetosaurus* was estimated to be at least 40 feet or over 11.5 meters.

In 1926, Longman visited the locality from which the type remains was retrieved and found additional material including a cervical, at least seven dorsal, four sacral, and six caudal vertebrae, some in juxtaposition, fragments including pieces of the pelvic girdle, and short sections of a massive femur. In describing these newly acquired remains, Longman (1926) observed that a striking feature of the sacral vertebrae is the transverse breadth, which is greater than their length. The pubes are massive and elongated as those in the Camarasauridae, but do not correspond closely with those of other known camarasaurids. The massive femur, similar in main contours to that of *Camarasaurus*, would be almost 1.5 meters (about 5 feet) long if complete. From the collected type material, Longman surmised that his original estimate of the animal's length was probably conservative.

In his review of the Sauropoda, McIntosh (1990*b*) noted that the pubes in *R. brownei* are notable for their large size. McIntosh assigned *Rhoetosaurus* to subfamily Shunosaurinae.

Note: The first attempted life restoration of *R. brownei*, a large oil painting, was prepared Douglas S. Annand under Longman's (1929) direction for display at the Queensland Museum. As the fossil material was incomplete, the painting was largely based on E. S. Christman's sculpture of *Camarasaurus* made for the American Museum of Natural History.

Key references: Longman (1925, 1926, 1929); McIntosh (1990*b*).

RICARDOESTESIA Currie, Rigby and Sloan 1990—(=?*Chirostenotes*, ?*Elmisaurus*)

Saurischia: Theropoda: Tetanurae: Avetheropoda: Coelurosauria: Maniraptora: Arctometatarsalia *incertae sedis*.

Name derivation: "Richard Estes."

Type species: *R. gilmorei* Currie, Rigby and Sloan 1990.

Other species: [None.]

Occurrence: Dinosaur Park Formation, Alberta, Canada.

Age: Late Cretaceous (Early Campanian–Maastrichtian).

Known material/holotype: NMC 343, dentaries, left dentary almost complete, with germ and unerupted teeth.

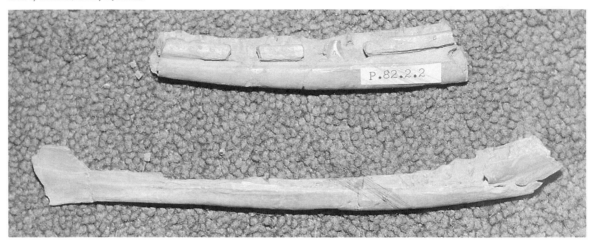

Photo by the author, courtesy P. J. Currie.

Ricardoestesia gilmorei, NMC 343, holotype right (smaller) and left lower jaws.

Diagnosis of genus: Small theropod; jaw elongate, with little lateromedial curvature; 18–19 teeth in each dentary; anterior mandibular teeth relatively straight, with convex posterior outline in side view for at least distal half of tooth; more posterior teeth relatively short, recurved; denticles comparatively shorter than in teeth of any other known "Judithian" theropods, length of 0.15 millimeters; as many as five denticles per millimeter on posterior carina of mandibular teeth (Currie, Rigby and Sloan 1990).

Diagnosis of *R. gilmorei*: Some curvature always present in proximal portion of tooth (in contrast to Maastrichtian teeth referrable to *Ricardoestesia*) (Currie, Rigby and Sloan 1990).

Comments: The genus *Ricardoestesia* was founded upon a pair of small theropod jaws (NMC 343), collected from the "Judith River" [now Dinosaur Park] Formation in what is now Dinosaur Provincial Park, Alberta, Canada. Because they are long and slender, Gilmore (1924) arbitrarily referred these jaws to *Chirostenotes pergracilis*, a species based on a manus found several miles away. Gilmore had hoped that his referral of the jaws to *Chirostenotes* would be confirmed or denied by finding additional fossil materials, a discovery not yet made.

In a study of theropod teeth from the Dinosaur Park Formation, Currie, Rigby and Sloan (1990) pointed out that the dinosaur to which these jaws belong may be synonymous with either elmisaurids *Chirostenotes* or *Elmisaurus* with the potential discovery of more material, but declined to assign the material to Elmisauridae or any other family. As the teeth in NMC 343 are quite distinctive, because other teeth from Dinosaur Provincial Park are referrable to the same species, and to avoid continued confusing and perhaps misleading referral of this specimen to *Chirostenotes*, Currie *et al.* proposed the new genus and species *Ricardoestesia gilmorei* for NMC 343.

Gilmore suggested that each jaw would have contained at least 18 teeth, adding that the number would not have exceeded 20. As Currie *et al.* noted, *R. gilmorei* is distinguished in having more teeth in its jaws than any other known "Judithian" theropod except *Troodon*. Currie *et al.* also conservatively estimated, based upon relative tooth counts in other theropods, that *R. gilmorei* may have had at least three premaxillary teeth and 11 maxillary teeth on each side of the skull, the entire tooth count being from 66 to 90.

To *Ricardoestesia*, Currie *et al.* referred teeth from the Lower Campanian Milk River Formation of Alberta, the Scollard Formation of Alberta, the Frenchman Formation of Saskatchewan, Canada, Hell Creek Formation of Montana, and also the Lance Formation of Wyoming [see below].

Estes (1964) described isolated teeth (AMNH 8113 and 8114) from the Lance Formation (Maastrichtian) of eastern Wyoming that he referred to *Paronychodon lacustris*. Carpenter (1982*a*) reported teeth of baby dinosaurs, collected from the Lance Formation, Wyoming, and from the Hell Creek Formation, which he also referred to *Paronychodon*. These teeth range in size from 1.7 (UCMP 38459) to 4.8 (UCMP 124991) millimeters high, and from 1.3 (UCMP 38459) to 2.3 (UCMP 38459) millimeters wide, are laterally compressed, and have long ridges, parallel to the edges of the crown, covering the flat side. Carpenter noted that the posterior edge may or may not bear serrations. Currie *et al.* suggested that the Maastrichtian teeth, to be described later, may pertain to another species of *Ricardoestesia*. Perplexing was the fact that *Ricardoestesia* teeth have been found in both Lower Campanian and Maastrichtian deposits, but seem virtually absent from the Late Campanian Dinosaur Park and Horseshoe Canyon Formations.

Notes: The name of this genus was misspelled *Richardoestesia* in all but one occurrence in the original description (R. E. Sloan, personal communication to Olshevsky 1992).

Carpenter, in a study of baby dinosaur teeth from the Hell Creek and Lance formations, showed that very young and baby dinosaurs are not as rare in the fossil record as implied by published accounts. Skeletal material of these individuals will always be vulnerable to paleoenvironmental controls, most notably soil drainage and soil pH. Hence, baby-dinosaur remains will always be less common than those of adults, though skeletal material from dinosaur babies may have gone undetected in the field or could be present in unsorted microvertebrates collections. Teeth, however, resist biological destruction. For that reason, Carpenter concluded, perhaps most Lancian and Hell Creek Formation dinosaur babies are known only from teeth.

In a study of more than 500 individual theropod teeth (including those of *R. gilmorei*, cf. *Ricardoestesia*, and *Aublysodon*, wherein the shape of these teeth was compared with canine teeth of mammalian carnivores), Farlow, Brinkman, Abler and Currie (1991) concluded that theropod teeth seem to have been multipurpose implements used in killing prey, cutting flesh and, at least in large "carnosaurs," perhaps breaking bone. Farlow *et al.* found that, in theropods, tooth crown height and tooth mediolateral basal width are linearly (or almost linearly) related to posteroposterior basal length in lateral non-incisiform maxillary and dentary teeth; basal length of an individual tooth serration increases linearly with increasing tooth size; and number of serrations per unit length of tooth carina decreases allometrically with increasing tooth size.

Key references: Carpenter (1982*a*); Currie, Rigby and Sloan (1990); Estes (1964); Farlow, Brinkman, Abler and Currie (1991); Gilmore (1924).

RIOARRIBASAURUS　Hunt and Lucas 1991—
　(=?*Coelophysis*, ?*Podokesaurus*)
Saurischia: Theropoda: Ceratosauria:
　Coelophysoidea.
Name derivation: "Rio Arriba [County, Spanish for 'upper river,' referring to upper Rio Grande region]" + Greek *sauros* = "lizard."
Type species: *R. colberti* Hunt and Lucas (1991).
Other species: [None.]
Occurrence: Chinle Formation, New Mexico, Petrified Forest National Park, Arizona, United States.

Age: Late Triassic (Early Norian).
Known material: Several hundred individuals, including almost complete articulated skeletons, juvenile to adult.
Holotype: AMNH 7224, complete articulated skeleton, adult.

Diagnosis of genus (as for type species): Differing from ceratosaurians *Syntarsus*, *Dilophosaurus*, *Liliensternus*, "*Ceratosaurus*" (see entry), *Segisaurus* and *Sarcosaurus* in lacking two pairs of cervical pleurocoels and large pubic fenestra, from *Dilophosaurus* and *Liliensternus* in having antorbital fenestra more than 25 percent of skull length, and from *Syntarsus* in lacking nasal fenestrae (Lucas and Hunt 1991, based on Rowe 1989, Colbert 1989).

Comments: [This entry discusses the taxon generally known in both the paleontological literature and popular books as *Coelophysis* (see entry). For the present, the newer name *Rioarribasaurus* is valid, although *Coelophysis* may, after this book goes to press, be reinstated; see note below.]

In June of 1947, George Whitaker, an assistant on an American Museum of Natural History expedition led by Edwin H. Colbert, discovered a veritable graveyard of skeletons belonging to a single genus of small theropod at Ghost Ranch (then owned by Arthur N. Pack, now by the Presbyterian Church). The site, located in Rio Arriba County, northwest of Abiquiu, New Mexico, was discovered by Ann and Robert Preston. The actual fossil find was made by Whitaker (see Whitaker and Meyers 1965). The Whitaker quarry, according to Hunt and Lucas (1989*b*, 1991), is included in the Rock Point Member (Late Triassic) of the Chinle Formation, equivalent to the uppermost Church Rock Member of the Chinle in northeastern Arizona.

Over the years, these skeletons have been assigned by Colbert (1947, 1964, 1989) to Cope's genus *Coelophysis* (see entry) and have, due to their abundance and excellent preservation, made this one of the best known of all dinosaurian genera. However, Padian (1986) reviewed the taxonomic status of Cope's *Coelophysis* material and questioned whether or not the Whitaker quarry specimens could, in fact, be referred to that genus.

Hunt and Lucas (1991) regarded *Coelophysis* and its various species as *nomina dubia*, founded upon material that displayed no diagnostic features. Therefore, Hunt and Lucas removed the Ghost Ranch material from *Coelophysis*, erecting for it the new genus and species *Rioarribasaurus colberti*, designating the best skeleton (AMNH 7224) from the Whitaker quarry as the holotype.

Colbert (1961), in his book *Dinosaurs: Their Discovery and Their World* (also Colbert 1989, 1995), related that the Ghost Ranch skeletons were found in great numbers, piled one atop the other. Some are complete, ranking among the most perfect dinosaur specimens ever collected. They range in maturity from juvenile to adult individuals. (In addition to these dinosaur specimens, the Ghost Ranch quarry has also yielded other reptilian remains, including small so-called "thecodontians" and phytosaurs.)

The original diggings at Ghost Ranch continued through two seasons, after which they were closed down. The quarry was reopened in summer 1981 by a joint field party from the Carnegie Museum of Natural History, Museum of Northern Arizona, New Mexico Museum of Natural History, and Yale Peabody Museum of Natural History. After two seasons of excavation, about 15 blocks of fossil materials were removed, some of which were sent to the New Mexico Museum, Peabody Museum, Royal Ontario Museum, Museum of Northern Arizona, Carnegie Museum, and Royal Tyrrell Museum of Paleontology. One block, which stayed in the quarry until 1985, became housed in the Ruth Hall Museum of Paleontology, part of the Florence Ellis Hawley Museum, at Ghost Ranch (Colbert 1989).

From the Whitaker quarry specimens, Colbert (1964) diagnosed and described *Rioarribasaurus* [=*Coelophysis* of his usage] including cranial characters now considered not of diagnostic significance. Padian proposed an updated diagnosis, adapted in part from Colbert's and also from Padian (1982) and Gauthier (1984). Padian's (1986) diagnosis was based upon previously described specimens, and also a pelvis and hindlimbs (UCMP 129618), collected in 1982 in Petrified Forest National Park by a field party sponsored by the Museum of Paleontology of the University of California (Berkeley).

Colbert (1989) fully described the genus in his monograph on *Coelophysis*, his description based upon Cope's original lectotype and syntypes of *Coelophysis* from Cerro Blanco and Arroyo Seco, also numerous bones representing individuals of varying ontogenetic development retrieved from the Ghost Ranch quarry, mostly those in the American Museum of Natural History collection and those collected by the various institutions between 1981 and 1982.

Regarding fragmentary specimens collected from outside the Ghost Ranch quarry ?referrable to *Rioarribasaurus*, Padian (1986) and Colbert (1989) reported remains collected near the Whitaker quarry, also specimens found in 1986 near the "Lot's Wife" rock formation at Petrified Forest National Park, Arizona (a locality dated through palynological evidence as Carnian). According to Colbert (1989), this would indicate that, in at least some of its occurrences, this genus is the oldest known North American dinosaur, perhaps the oldest in the world.

From the many *Rioarribasaurus* specimens retrieved from Ghost Ranch (in collections at the American Museum, Museum of Northern Arizona, Museum of Comparative Zoology, Yale Peabody Museum, and National Museum of Natural History), Colbert (1989) observed a considerable range in size, the largest being two complete articulated adult skeletons (AMNH 7223 and 7224), measuring about 284 and 256 centimeters (approximately 110 and 100 inches), respectively, probably near the top of the growth sequence among adults. The smallest skull from Ghost Ranch measures 8 centimeters (about 3.1 inches), although hatchlings may have been some 2.5 centimeters (less than one inch) long, assuming a tenfold size increase to adult length. Although very small *Rioarribasaurus* skeletons have not yet been found at Ghost Ranch, Colbert (1990) estimated that adults may have grown to as much as 15 times the size of hatchlings. (The smallest skull of this dinosaur yet retrieved from the Ghost Ranch quarry measured less than 2 inches long, but the very fragile condition of the specimen caused it to disintegrate after a couple minutes of exposure to the air; D. D. Gillette and J. L. Gillette, personal communication 1989.)

Padian (1986) noted that various other theropods, including *Podokesaurus* and *Procompsognathus*, and also [nondinosaurian reptile] *Avipes*, are virtually indistinguishable from *Rioarribasaurus* [=*Coelophysis* of his usage] except for differences in size and proportions. Therefore, these and other similar theropod forms are potentially referrable to *Rioarribasaurus*.

Some workers have suggested that the Ghost Ranch theropod is synonymous with *Syntarsus*, a genus known from Zimbabwe, Africa, and recently discovered in the Kayenta Formation. Paul (1988c), in his book *Predatory Dinosaurs of the World*, lumped both forms into *Coelophysis* but did not demonstrate their proposed synonymy (later, Paul 1993 referred the Ghost Ranch theropod to *Syntarsus*). Colbert (1989) stated that, although *Syntarsus* seems to be the dinosaur most closely related to the Ghost Ranch form and that in many instances they share virtually identical anatomical features, the two are not congeneric. Colbert (1989) noted that *Syntarsus* is known from somewhat younger deposits and also listed a suite of significant differences that separate the two forms:

In *Rioarribasaurus* [=*Coelophysis* of his usage], 1. upper tooth row extends to position beneath middle of orbit (to posterior border of antorbital fenestra in *Syntarsus*); 2. 22 to 26 (19 to 20 in *Syntarsus*) maxillary teeth; 3. no nasal fenestra (present in *Syntarsus*); 4. antorbital fenestra less than one-third skull

Photo by Boltin, courtesy Department Library Services, American Museum of Natural History (neg. #329319).

Rioarribasaurus colberti, AMNH 7224, holotype skeleton (lower left) and referred specimen [both originally referred to *Coelophysis bauri*].

length (greater than one-third in *Syntarsus*); 5. post-temporal fenestra persistent (absent in *Syntarsus*); 6. interdental plates absent (present in *Syntarsus*); 7. basiosphenoid relatively short (elongated in *Syntarsus*); 8. no "carnosaur" pocket in pterygoid (present in *Syntarsus*); 9. vomer present (apparently absent in *Syntarsus*); 10. palate not vaulted (vaulted in *Syntarsus*); 11. elongated vacuity (small in *Syntarsus*) anterior to ectopterygoid; 12. anterior palatal vacuity bounded by palatine, vomer, and maxilla (by palatine, pterygoid, and maxilla in *Syntarsus*); 13. 27 (as opposed to 25) dentary teeth; 14. as many as eight (rather than one or two) unopposed maxillary teeth; 15. cervical region comparatively long (shorter in *Syntarsus*); 16. cervical vertebrae not keeled (keeled in *Syntarsus*); 17. hyposphene-hypantrum articulations not seen (present in *Syntarsus*); 18. forelimbs relatively large (comparatively smaller in *Syntarsus*); 19. extended manus longer (equal to or shorter in *Syntarsus*) than radius; 20. pelvic bones persistently separate (coossified in *Syntarsus* adults); 21. iliac blade mostly vertical in position (obliquely expanded in *Syntarsus*); 22. astragalocalcaneum either separate or fused to tibia (variably fused in *Syntarsus*); and 23. ascending process (small in *Syntarsus*) of astragalus variable in development.

Colbert (1989) observed a large degree of variability in skeletal proportions of the Ghost Ranch theropods. Unexpectedly, skulls in younger individuals are proportionately small rather than large (as in most vertebrates). The orbit in smaller individuals is relatively larger, neck somewhat shorter, forelimbs only slightly shorter compared to those of adults. The hindlimbs are already well-developed in young individuals, suggesting that they, adapted for rapid running, might have been more crucial in the struggle to survive than skull size, neck length, or forelimb size.

Colbert (1989) observed other variations, particularly between specimens AMNH 7223 and 7224. AMNH 7223 has a larger skull, longer neck, shorter forelimb, and strongly fused sacral vertebrae (separate in AMNH 7224). These differences could represent sexual dimorphism, although neither specimen has yet been identified as male or female.

Also, Colbert (1989) observed that, while the number of premaxillary teeth remains constant, the number of maxillary teeth can vary from 18 to 26. Fully adult animals may have had a total of from 22 to 25 maxillary teeth, depending on the size and age of the individual.

The great concentration of specimens at the Ghost Ranch quarry might suggest that these individuals fell victim to some local catastrophe. Schwartz (1989; also *see in* Colbert 1989) concluded from the sedimentology, geochemistry, and taphonomy of the quarry that the *Rioarribasaurus* [=*Coelophysis* of her usage] carcasses had been buried in a shallow stream channel by moderately strong currents. These currents transported the remains a short distance to their present location. Since the skeletons are relatively complete and the bones mostly undamaged, the carcasses were probably not exposed on the surface long enough to decay; furthermore, the causes of death and burial could be related. There is no evidence of volcanic ash in or near the quarry. After making a chemical and petrographic analysis of the bone and sediment from the Ghost Ranch quarry, Schwartz then speculated that the many *Rioarribasaurus* individuals preserved there were either the victims of a flood, or may have been killed by arsenic poisoning.

Though Colbert and David D. Gillette independently estimated that the remains of approximately 1,000 individuals of this small dinosaur have, thus far, been removed from the quarry, the total number of individuals preserved at the site may total several thousands (Schwartz and Gillette 1994),

Rioarribasaurus colberti, skull [originally referred to *Coelophysis bauri*] from Ghost Ranch.

Rioarribasaurus remaining the best known of all Triassic theropods.

As noted by Schwartz and Gillette, numerous popular accounts have attributed this mass accumulation of specimens to a scenario involving volcanic activity (see Colbert 1947, 1989). According to this generally accepted idea, all of the Ghost Ranch theropods perished from asphyxiation during a volcanic eruption. Schwartz and Gillette tested this (and other hypotheses) in an attempt to explain this apparent mass death assemblage by recording microstratigraphic data and collecting samples for geochemical analysis at the site.

Schwartz and Gillette pointed out that 25 percent of the *Rioarribasaurus* [=*Coelophysis* of their usage] specimens removed from Ghost Ranch consist of complete (and often articulated) skeletons, with the bones atypically well preserved, and showing little, if any, signs of breakage or weathering, these conditions showing that the remains were buried before the intervention of predators or scavengers, or the results of trampling. Some of the skeletons have been preserved in typical "death poses" (*i.e.*, tails and necks strongly recurved over the main part of the bodies

(Colbert 1989), this condition suggesting that the carcasses became desiccated prior to burial at the site (Weigelt 1989). These features, along with the monospecific fauna and degree of articulation of the skeletons, imply short-term instead of time-averaged, attritional mortality (see also Voorhies 1969; Behrensmeyer 1978; Potts 1986). Furthermore, examination of individual skeletons preserved within two of the bone-filled blocks excavated at Ghost Ranch reveal that most of the specimens tend to be aligned in a preferred direction within the block.

As observed by Schwartz and Gillette, Colbert's (1989) theory that the Ghost Ranch theropods perished during a catastrophic event (*e.g.*, a volcanic eruption) is supported by several sedimentologic and taphonomic features: 1. The preservation of complete skeletons interwoven with other complete specimens, partial skeletons, and isolated bones; 2. specimens are preserved with a relatively uniform style; 3. the deposit preserves a wide range of age suggestive of a population; and, 4. the site is basically monospecific and has preserved numerous specimens, even though this dinosaur was probably not the most abundant terrestrial vertebrate in New Mexico during the Late

Triassic, a time which was otherwise one of comparatively high reptilian diversity.

However, Schwartz and Gillette noted that the Ghost Ranch death assemblage occurs in an overbank sequence comprising three types of deposits (1. "laterally continuous siltstones"; 2. "laterally continuous siltstones with abundant carbonate pebbles and rare mudclasts"; and 3. "laterally restricted, U-shaped siltstones rich in bones, mudclasts, or carbonate pebbles, with scoured lower contacts"), these lithofacies interpreted as "overbank deposits, with continuity and grain size varying with distance from the main channel, current velocity, and source."

According to Schwartz and Gillette, the disarticulation of 70–75 percent of the collected specimens was probably due to a combination of factors, including 1. "brief exposure, desiccation, and disturbance of the remains before final burial," 2. "compaction and root growth after burial," and 3. "fluvial transport of the remains after deposition." The recurved "death pose" of complete skeletons and alignment of the remains further implied that fluvial currents transported the dinosaurs' small, buoyant carcasses to the burial site, a small channel.

In trying to deduce the cause of the dinosaurs' death, Schwartz and Gillette tested various speculations made by previous workers. In addition to Colbert's popular volcanic-eruption scenario, Ratkevich (1976) had proposed that these animals perished from drinking highly alkaline, poisonous water or from floundering in sticky mud, while Bakker (1986) hypothesized that the site represented a "predator trap" not unlike the famous "tar pits" of Rancho La Brea, in Los Angeles, California. Schwartz and Gillette found that neither bentonite nor any other volcanic indicators were present at this stratigraphic level in the Chinle Formation or near the Ghost Ranch quarry, and that iridium levels in the quarry were normal (higher levels being indicative of volcanic activity or asteroid impact); that petrographic and elemental analysis of the Ghost Ranch bones thus far does not reveal any chemistry or paleopathologic condition indicating poisoning or disease; and that the Ghost Ranch accumulation does not fit the predator-trap model exemplified by the La Brea site (*e.g.*, 1. the presence of numerous young, old, and maimed individuals in the deposit; 2. a diverse, commonly herbivore-dominated fauna; 3. randomly oriented and disarticulated specimens due to movement within the enveloping mass and the work of predators and scavengers; and 4. much bone damage from predation and scavenging).

Schwartz and Gillette dismissed the possibility that the Ghost Ranch theropods may have been aggregating at a water hole, like modern predators, either for hunting, eating, or basking, as the only evidence of a food source at the Ghost Ranch quarry are young individuals of the same species. They also considered that these dinosaurs may have been victims of a mass drowning, but noted that fossil assemblages resulting from the same tend to mirror recent assemblages, wherein the victims are mostly herding herbivores (Schaller 1972; Sinclair and Norton-Griffiths 1979; Orr 1970).

Rioarribasaurus colberti, slab of specimens [originally referred to *Coelophysis bauri*] from Ghost Ranch.

Photo by the author, courtesy Royal Tyrrell Museum/Alberta Community Development.

Offering a possible alternative scenario, Schwartz and Gillette observed that the presence of mudcracks, carbonate pebbles (most likely eroded from calcretes), and the recurved (desiccation) "death poses" of some of the Ghost Ranch theropod skeletons are indicative of periodic drying in the quarry sediments and fossils. Furthermore, other workers (Parrish and Peterson 1988; Dubiel 1989) have shown that both wet and dry seasons were part of the climate of the Late Triassic period. Also, the Ghost Ranch assemblage fits three of a suite of criteria proposed by Shipman (1975) and Rogers (1991) for identifying drought assemblages, namely, 1. "aqueous depositional setting," 2. "mono/paucispecific faunal assemblages," and 3. "associated caliche horizons."

Schwartz and Gillette pointed out that drought-induced mortality of recent animals tends to be species-specific because of "ecological segregations and varying susceptibility of different species to adverse conditions" (Hillman and Hillman 1977; Behrensmeyer 1981; Conybeare and Haynes 1984; Haynes 1988), and observed that the Ghost Ranch assemblage reflects this. Also, they noted that modern vertebrates often exhibit increased aggression while existing in stressful situations such as drought (Henshaw 1972), the evidence of cannibalism (Colbert 1989) in *Rioarribasaurus* possibly reflecting this kind of behavior (see below).

Schwartz and Gillette concluded that the thousands of small theropods found at Ghost Ranch probably died during a drought, after which their carcasses were carried downstream by fluvial currents, subsequently clogging and filling in a small channel. There they remained exposed long enough for desiccation to occur, but not long enough for extensive disarticulation, the remains finally becoming covered by silts.

Two adult skeletons from Ghost Ranch included tiny *Rioarribasaurus* skeletons within their body cavities. (One of these small specimens, within AMNH 7224, is not included as part of the holotype). This might suggest that *Rioarribasaurus* was viviparous, the contained remains interpreted as unborn young. However, as Colbert (1961; 1989) observed, these skeletons are fully ossified and quite large for embryos, too large, in fact, to have passed through the posterior opening in the pelvis of the adult. A more feasible explanation for the tiny remains is that *Rioarribasaurus* was cannibalistic. If so, the supposedly ingested bones are remarkably uninjured. This further suggested that *Rioarribasaurus*, like the modern day Komodo dragon lizard, was a compellingly voracious predator that swallowed its prey whole.

As envisioned by Colbert (1989), *Rioarribasaurus* [=*Coelophysis* of his usage] was an active theropod that lived in "upland" environments and fed upon whatever prey it could catch (?including lizard-like procolophonids, eosuchians such as *Icarosaurus* and *Tanytrachelos*, immature metoposaurs, small "thecodontians," and fish). Perhaps its short forelimbs were used extensively in feeding, the large hands and functional clawed digits well adapted for grasping prey. The neck, being long, supple and strong, offered a range of wide action to the jaws, allowing the dinosaur to dart its head in various directions while making its attack. As Colbert (1989) pointed out, *Rioarribasaurus* was not the dominant predator of its time, that role taken by giant rauisuchians (*e.g.*, *Postosuchus*) and phytosaurs (*e.g.*, *Rutiodon*).

Rioarribasaurus may have been a gregarious dinosaur. Colbert (1989) noted that, although carnivores do not usually live in herds, the many *Rioarribasaurus* skeletons found at the Ghost Ranch quarry represent animals ranging from very young individuals to large adults. This concentration of specimens seems indicative of herding, although it might also represent the accumulation of many smaller feeding aggregations. (This idea might contradict the notion of cannibalism, as cannibalism would seem to discourage aggregations of individuals of different ages; R. E. Molnar, personal communication 1990.)

Notes: In Case 2840, in the December 1992 *Bulletin of Zoological Nomenclature*, 49 [4], paleontologists Colbert, Alan J. Charig, Peter Dodson, David D. Gillette, John H. Ostrom, and David B. Weishampel argued that AMNH 7224 should be designated as the neotype of *Coelurus* [=*Coelophysis*] *bauri* Cope 1887, thereby rendering *C. bauri* a senior objective synonym of *R. colberti*, that *Coelophysis* again be the correct name for the Ghost Ranch theropods, and that *Rioarribasaurus* and the binomen *R. colberti* be rejected and considered invalid by the International Commission on Zoological Nomenclature. Since their application, other paleontologists have offered their opinions on this issue, both pro and con, to the ICZN. As of this writing, however, a final decision has not yet been issued by the ICZN regarding this matter. Until the Commission might rule to the contrary, *Rioarribasaurus* remains the official name of the Ghost Ranch theropod.

Colbert and Baird (1958) described a specimen (BSNH 13656), regarded by them as *Coelophysis* sp., consisting of a sandstone slab containing a natural cast of an incomplete tibia, pubis, and rib, collected probably from the Portland arkose of the Newark Supergroup, probably quarries at Portland, Connecticut, across the Connecticut River from Middletown (see *Podokesaurus* entry). According to Rowe and Gauthier (1990), this specimen could belong to

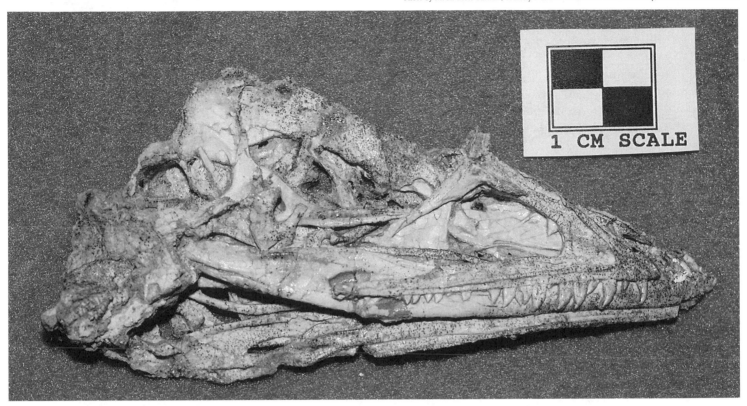

Rioarribasaurus colberti, USNM, skull [originally referred to *Coelophysis bauri*] of baby individual.

Rioarribasaurus [=*Coelophysis* of their usage], although their similarity is restricted to characters present in Theropoda ancestrally.

Padian reported another possible Petrified Forest National Park occurrence of *Rioarribasaurus* from the upper part of the Petrified Forest Member (above Sonsela Sandstone Bed), Chinle Formation, near Lacey Point. The specimen (UCMP 129618) collected from this site exhibits differences from *Rioarribasaurus*. Hunt and Lucas, in evaluating this specimen, noted that UCMP 129618 differs from the Whitaker quarry specimens in having a better development of the posteroventral arch of the ilium; distinct emargination on distal tibia to receive ascending process of astragalus; femur with considerably more offset head, shorter fourth trochanter, and less well-developed trochanteric shelf (character of the Ceratosauria: Gauthier 1986); also a well-developed obturator foramen. According to Hunt and Lucas, the Lacey Point specimen could represent a new genus of ceratosaurian.

Miller, Britt and Stadtman (1986) reported a trackway site discovered in 1982, of Late Triassic or Early Jurassic age, in the Dinosaur Canyon Member, Moenave Formation, Warner Valley, southwesternmost Utah, which include prints of a "coelurosaur" that might represent *Rioarribasaurus* [=*Coelophysis* of their usage], along with those of a possible plateosaurid and probable megalosaurid. These tracks suggest that the animals were walking on damp sediment, most of them in a southwesterly direction.

Other tracks from the Chinle Formation, Petrified Forest National Monument, have also been referred to "*Coelophysis*" [=*Rioarribasaurus*] (Breed and Breed 1972).

Irby (1995) described fossil footprints in five of 34 trackways discovered in 1934 by Roland T. Bird (see Bird 1985) at the Cameron Dinosaur Tracksite, Dinosaur Canyon Member, (Lower Jurassic) Moenave Formation (Irby 1991), in northeastern Arizona. From these five trackways, Irby (1995) named and described *Grallator* (*Anchisauripus*) *madseni*, this new ichnospecies representing small, bipedal dinosaurs. The size and morphology of these prints suggest trackmakers similar to *Rioarribasaurus* [=*Coelophysis* of Irby's usage] and *Syntarsus*.

Irby (1995) observed in these tracks "posterolateral markings, appearing as short, rectilinear grooves projecting from the posterior margins of digit IV." Irby (1995) offered the following working hypotheses as possible explanations for these markings: 1. They were made by the rare feature of the dragging of digit III or of the metatarsus; 2. made by a metatarsal spur (though no data exist suggesting these dinosaurs possessed such spurs; 3. impressions of a rotated digit V (though no data support existence of digit V in body fossils of *Rioarribasaurus* and *Syntarsus*); 4. produced by a feature similar to a horny excrescence or cornified ridge on digito-metatarsal pad IV (G. Demathieu, J. O. Farlow, personal communication to Irby 1995); and, most plausibly, 5. resulted from sexual dimorphism, with only one sex maybe possessing this horny excrescence or cornified ridge (Gierlinski, personal communication to Irby 1995).

Key references: Breed and Breed (1972); Colbert (1947, 1961, 1964, 1989, 1990, 1995); Colbert and Baird (1958); Gauthier (1984, 1986); Hunt and Lucas (1989, 1991); Irby (1995); Miller, Britt and Stadtman (1986); Padian (1982, 1986); Paul (1988*c*); Rowe (1989); Rowe and Gauthier (1990); Whitaker and Meyers (1965).

RIOJASAURUS Bonaparte 1969—(=*Strenusaurus*)
Saurischia: Sauropodomorpha: Prosauropoda: Melanorosauridae.
Name derivation: "[La] Rioja [province, Argentina]" + Greek *sauros* = "lizard."
Type species: *R. incertis* Bonaparte 1969.
Other species: [None.]
Occurrence: Upper Los Colorados Formation, La Rioja, Quebrada del Barro Formation, San Juan, Argentina.
Age: Late Triassic (Norian).
Known material: Over 20 fragmentary to complete skeletons, skull, juvenile to adult.
Holotype: PVL 3808, three dorsal vertebrae.

Diagnosis of genus (as for type species): Cervical vertebrae successively increasing in length and volume; dorsal vertebrae high, with relatively low neural spines; sacral vertebrae and anterior caudals rather robust, latter with high, robust neural spines;

Rioarribasaurus colberti, Ghost Ranch site, Late Cretaceous, New Mexico.

Illustration by Doug Henderson for the Ruth Hall Museum of Paleontology.

Riojasaurus incertus, PVL 3808, holotype left femur, dorsal and medial views, right tibia and astragalus, lateral view. Scale = 10 cm. (After Bonaparte 1969.)

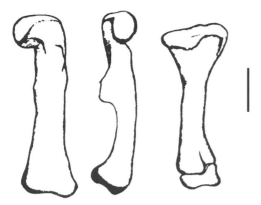

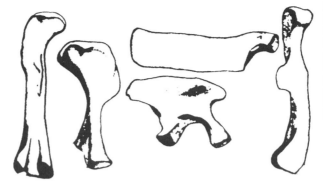

Riojasaurus incertus, PLV 3663, holotype of *Strenusaurus procerus*, left femur, lateral and medial views, right humerus, and right pubis, dorsal views, right ilium, dorsal view. Scale = 6 cm. (After Bonaparte 1969.)

pectoral and pelvic girdles similar to those of *Plateosaurus* and *Massospondylus*, preacetabular process of ilium located higher; humerus rather large and robust, with prominent deltoid crest; femur and tibia similar to, but less robust than, in *Melanorosaurus*; astragalus, calcaneum, and manus similar to *Plateosaurus* and *Massospondylus* (Bonaparte 1972).

Comments: Two new genera from the upper section of the Los Colorados Formation of La Rioja province in northern Argentina were announced by Bonaparte (1967) at the first International Symposium on Gondwana Stratigraphy. Later, Bonaparte (1969) named these genera *Riojasaurus* and *Strenusaurus*, describing them briefly.

The best known melanorosaurid, *Riojasaurus* was founded upon three dorsal vertebrae (PVL 3808), selected as the holotype from remains of several individuals of varying sizes. Other material included three fused sacral vertebrae, two caudals, right ilium, and femora (PVL 3805); five articulated cervical vertebrae and one dorsal vertebra (PVL 3844); distal ends of tibia and fibula joined with astragalus and calca-

neum (PVL 3845); distal ends of tibia and fibula with astragalus in its original position (PVL 3846); left ilium (PVL 3467); left proximally incomplete pubis (PVL 3472); complete left ilium and complete left femur (PVL 3669); complete ischia (PVL 3392); fragments of scapula, coracoid, of proximal ends of humerus and ulna (PVL 3668); fragment of proximal end of humerus (PVL 3478); almost complete left humerus (PVL 3533); three dorsal vertebrae, three incomplete sacrals, one caudal, fragments of scapulae and coracoids, humerus, pubes, tibiae, fibula, and fragment of distal end of femur (PVL 3393); and two cranial fragments from the ?postfrontal region (PVL 3847) (Bonaparte 1972).

As described by Bonaparte (1972), *Riojasaurus* is a quite large and heavily-built prosauropod, attaining a length of up to 11 meters (36 feet). The neck is long and slender, implying that the skull was probably small. The relatively large and robust forelimbs suggested to Bonaparte (1972) a quadrupedal mode of locomotion.

The type species *Strenusaurus procerus*, which Bonaparte (1972) later recognized as synonymous with *Riojasaurus*, was founded upon seven presacral vertebrae, scapulacoracoids, ilium, pubis, humerus, femur, portions of right manus, and fragments of astragalus and tibia (PVL 3663), collected in Argentina.

Bonaparte (1969) referred *Riojasaurus* to the Melanorosauridae. Galton (1985*c*), in his review of the family, agreed with that assessment, pointing out that in both *Melanorosaurus* and *Riojasaurus* the femur is straight in posterior view, with the fourth

Riojasaurus incertus, PLV 3808, holotype left ilium and right ulna, lateral views, left humerus, dorsal view. Scale = 10 cm. (After Bonaparte 1969.)

Riojasaurus incertus, reconstructed skeleton. (After Bonaparte 1978.)

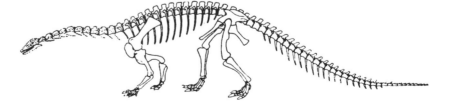

Riojasaurus

Illustration by Gregory S. Paul.

Riojasaurus incertus (background, standing upright), *Riojasuchus tenuisceps* (left, foreground) and *Pseudohesperosuchus.*

trochanter on or near the medial margin of that bone.

Cooper (1980*b*) suggested that *Riojasaurus* was a junior synonym of *Euskelosaurus,* but did not give evidence to support a synonymy. However, as observed by Van Heerden (1979) and later Galton (1985*e*), the femur in *Euskelosaurus* is sigmoidal in posterior view rather than straight as in *Riojasaurus.*

Key references: Bonaparte (1967, 1969, 1972); Cooper (1980*b*); Galton (1985*c*, 1985*e*); Van Heerden (1979).

SAICHANIA Maryańska 1977

Ornithischia: Genasauria: Thyreophora:
Ankylosauria: Ankylosauridae.

Name derivation: Mongolian *saichan* = "beautiful."

Type species: *S. chulsanensis* Maryańska 1977.

Other species: [None.]

Occurrence: Barun Goyot Formation, Red Beds of
Kermeen Tsav, Omnogov, Mongolian People's
Republic.

Age: Late Cretaceous (?Middle Campanian).

Known material: Three specimens, including two
complete skulls, almost complete postcrania,
armor.

Holotype: GI SPS 100/151, skull with jaws,
complete anterior part of postcranial skeleton.

Diagnosis of genus (as for type species): External nares large, oval, rostrally-located, divided by horizontal septum; relatively small number of scutes covering skull roof; well-developed dermal ossifications covering premaxilla; beak with width equal to less than distance between caudalmost maxillary teeth; very low exoccipital; strongly rostrally inclined quadrate fused to paroccipital process; mandibular condyle below middle of orbit; postcranial skeleton very massive; dermal armor covering dorsal and ventral sides of body (unique among known ankylosaurs, though armor of many taxa is not completely known) (Coombs and Maryańska 1990).

Comments: The genus *Saichania* was founded upon a fairly complete skeleton (GI SPS 100/51), collected by the Polish-Mongolian Expeditions of 1963–1971 (see Kielan-Jaworoska and Dovchin 1969; Kielan-Jaworoska and Barsbold 1972; Maryańska 1970, 1971), from the Barun Goyot Formation (?Middle Campanian; Kielan-Jaworoska 1974), Khulsan, Nemegt Basin, Gobi Desert, Mongolia.

Originally, Maryańska (1977) diagnosed the monotypic *S. chulsanensis* as follows: Ankylosaurid attaining length of 7 meters (about 24 feet); nostrils large, oval, located terminally on snout, divided by horizontal septum separating large, suboval, dorsally located foramen of true air passage from ventromedially positioned passage leading to premaxillary sinus; premaxillary part of snout relatively narrow; premaxillae covered partly by well-developed, secondary dermal plates; condyle weakly developed, directed ventrally; epipterygoid; exoccipital low, dorsal portion perpendicular to skull roof, ventral portion strongly deflected anteriorly; quadrate oblique, mandibular cotylus at level of middle part of orbit; orbits closed anteriorly and posteriorly by partly neomorphic bones; skull roof overhanging occipital region; anterior and posterior maxillary shelves of palatal region strongly developed; main body of maxilla surrounding palatal vacuities over small area lat-

erally; width of premaxillary beak almost equal to distance between posteriormost maxillary teeth; one opening for ninth-twelfth nerves; atlas and axis fused; strongly developed, secondary, plate-like intercostal ossifications along latero-ventral area of trunk; limb bones very massive; forelimb strongly flexed; manus with five digits.

Maryańska (1977) noted that *Saichania* differs from the somewhat similar *Pinacosaurus* in these significant ways: In *Saichania*, development of accessory cranial sinuses is more derived, the horizontal septum dividing the external nasal opening depressed; palatal region with a much stronger ossification; paroccipital processes strongly oriented anteriorly; occipital condyle pressed strongly into braincase with

Saichania chulsanensis, life
restoration by Mark Hallett.

From *Dinosaurs: A Global View*, by Czerkas and Czerkas, published by Dragon's World Ltd. and its co-edition publishers.

Saichania

Saichania chulsanensis, GI SPS 100/151, holotype skeleton being excavated during the 1971 Polish-Mongolian Expedition to the Nemegt Basin, Gobi Desert.

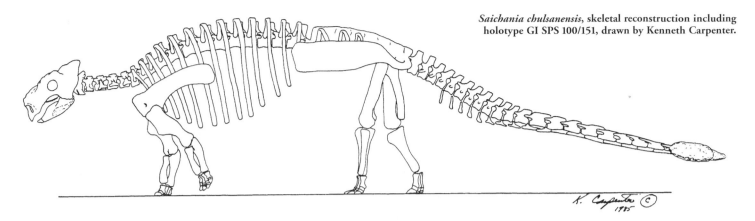

Saichania chulsanensis, skeletal reconstruction including holotype GI SPS 100/151, drawn by Kenneth Carpenter.

no trace of a neck and, when facing ventrally, cannot be seen in dorsal or lateral views; orbit almost entirely closed by well-developed bones in orbital region; quadrate strongly tilted anteriorly, ossified with paroccipital process.

As shown by Maryańska (1977), the pectoral girdle and forelimbs in *Saichania* are the most massive and metacarpals shortest of any known Asian ankylosaurid. The genus is distinct from all ankylosaurids in the unusually strong development of fusion between pectoral girdle and first dorsal rib, additional ossifications in the sternal complex and intercostal plates, coossification of atlas and axis, and fusion of quadrate and paroccipital process. In these latter two features, *Saichania* is similar to some nodosaurids.

Maryańska (1977) referred to *S. chulsanensis* a fragment of skull roof and armor (ZPAL MgD-I/114) from the Upper Cretaceous of Khermeen Tsav II (stratigraphic equivalent of Barun Goyot Formation), Mongolia, and an undescribed, almost complete postcranial skeleton with skull (PIN collection) from the same "formation" and locality.

As observed by Maryańska (1977), *Saichania* and *Pinacosaurus* differ from all other known reptiles, fossil or living, in the structure of their nares and nasal cavities. The nasal cavity of *Saichania* is entirely divided into right and left pairs. Within these passages are thin, curved ossifications resembling the turbinal bones in mammals (in which these bones are covered with membranes that warm, moisten and filter incoming air). Maryańska postulated that dorsal and ventral air passages in ankylosaurids served the same function, the dorsal passage analogous to narial passage in hadrosaurs. Also, in *Saichania*, the smooth surface of the premaxilla, located within the external narial region lateral to the air foramen, may have housed a lateral nasal gland which might also have been present in mammal-like reptiles. A keenly developed sense of smell in ankylosaurs could be related to the relative sluggishness of these animals.

Key references: Coombs and Maryańska (1990); Maryańska (1977).

SALTASAURUS Bonaparte and Powell 1980—
(=*Microcoelus*; =?*Loricosaurus*)
Saurischia: Sauropodomorpha: Sauropoda: Titanosauria: Titanosauridae.
Name derivation: "Salta [province of Northwestern Argentina]" + Greek *sauros* = "lizard."
Type species: *S. loricatus* Bonaparte and Powell 1980.
Other species: ?*S. australis* (Lydekker 1893), ?*S. robustus*.
(Huene 1929).
Occurrence: Lecho Formation, Salta, ?Rio Colorado Formation or Allen Formation, Rio Negro, Argentina.

Saltasaurus loricatus, A. anterior (?3rd) cervical (PVL. 4017-3), B. posterior (12th) cervical (4017-9), C. posterior dorsal (4017-14), D. anterior caudal (4017-23), E. posterior caudal (4017-39) vertebrae. (After Bonaparte and Powell 1980.)

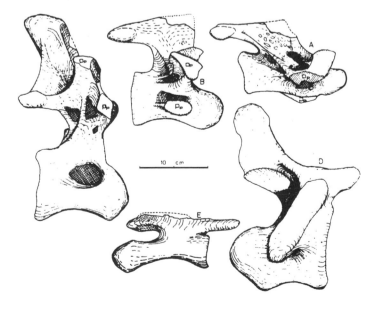

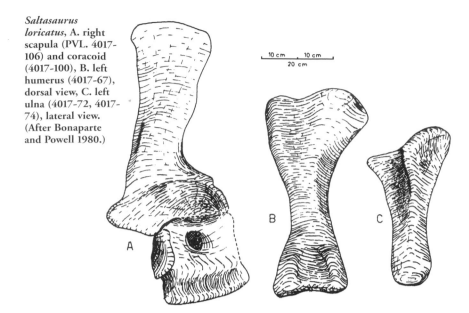

Saltasaurus loricatus, A. right scapula (PVL. 4017-106) and coracoid (4017-100), B. left humerus (4017-67), dorsal view, C. left ulna (4017-72, 4017-74), lateral view. (After Bonaparte and Powell 1980.)

Age: Late Cretaceous (?Early Maastrichtian).
Known material: Partial skeletons of about six individuals, including jaws and armor, miscellaneous postcranial remains of about three individuals, adult, subadult.
Holotype: PVL 4017-92, complete sacrum fused to ilia.

Diagnosis of genus (as for type species): Skull with upper temporal opening more reduced than in *Antarctosaurus*, closed dorsally over coalescence of parietal and frontal; basi-presphenoid complex of triangular outline in ventral view, transversal with narrow base and pronounced saggital crest; *fenestra ovalis* opening accommodating nerves IX-XI; basipterygoid processes united in their proximal portions; basal turberosities fused with basioccipital; cervical vertebrae relatively shorter and wider than in other known titanosaurids; centra of dorsal vertebrae with keels; distal ends of neural spines very thick and round; diapophysis with level dorsal surface at distal end; sacrum with six fused vertebrae, with end articulation convex at anteriorly and posteriorly; first caudal vertebra procoelous; neural spine broad in antero-posterior direction, rather inclined toward posteriorly in early caudals; scapula with prominence near middle of antero-superior border; limb bones relatively short and robust; metacarpals shorter than in *Antarctosaurus*, *Argyrosaurus*, and other titanosaurids; ilium with long preacetabular lamina, curved toward outside; dermal armor integrated by scutes and small rounded intradermical ossicles (Powell 1992).

Comments: The first sauropod known to be armored from substantial fossil evidence, the medium-sized genus *Saltasaurus* was founded on a sacrum fused to both ilia (PVL 4017-92) [not figured by the authors], discovered in an Upper Cretaceous (probably Maastrichtian) exposure of the Lecho Formation, in El Brete, southern Salta province, northwestern Argentina. Referred to the type species *S. loricatus* was a grouping of postcranial remains and osteoderms (PVL 4017), including 67 vertebrae, four scapulae, three coracoids, four sternal plates, sacrum fused to ilia, sacrum, ilium, four incomplete pubes, two ischia, ten humeri, five radii, five ulnae, four femora, three tibiae, three fibulae, ten metacarpals, four metatarsals, a phalange, seven dermal scutes, and four sheets of small dermal ossicles found in natural position (Bonaparte and Powell 1980).

Bonaparte and Powell originally diagnosed the genus (and type species) as follows: Titanosaurid closely related to *Neuquensaurus robustus* [=*Titanosaurus australis* of their usage; see below]; first caudal vertebra procoelian (rather than biconvex); ilia with strongly developed antero-lateral projection; few dermal scutes, thousands of small dermal ossicles (that were distributed in skin).

Because only eight pieces of dermal plates had then been found, Bonaparte and Powell suggested that perhaps only a few of these were present on the living animal, perhaps in the dorsal region. As

Saltasaurus loricatus, reconstruction of skeleton, drawn by Kenneth Carpenter.

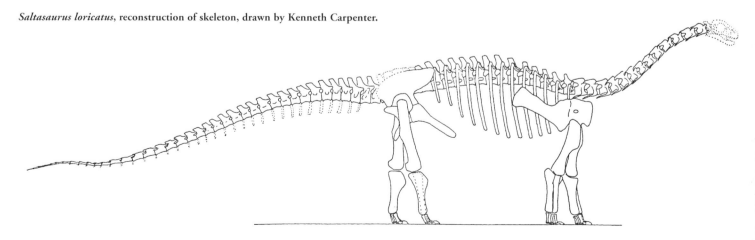

?*Saltasaurus australis*, holotype caudal vertebrae of *Titanosaurus australis*. Scale = 4 cm. (After Lydekker 1893.)

?*Saltasaurus australis*, holotype dorsal vertebra of *Titanosaurus nanus*, left dorsal view. Scale = 2 cm. (After Lydekker 1893.)

described by Bonaparte and Powell, each plate is circular or oval in shape, averaging 10–12 centimeters (about 3.8–4.5 inches) in diameter, with a rugose surface suggesting the attachment of a spike or horny projection. The small, virtually shapeless osteoderms average in size from 6–7 millimeters or less. These number approximately 540 and apparently covered the dorsal and lateral areas of the body.

Powell (1980) described some of the armor referred to *S. loricatus*: The plates (PVL 4017-112/113/114/115/116/134) are rather oval in outline with irregular margins, the dorsal area rough and ornamented with numerous various-sized rugosities. The ossicles (PVL 4017-117/118/119/120) are of various shapes and range from 7 millimeters (about .27 inches)–10 centimeters (about 3.85 inches) in diameter.

Later, Powell (1992) redescribed *S. loricatus* based upon the above remains and a great number of more recently collected osseous elements (CNS-V 10.023 and 10.024) representing adult and subadult individuals, recovered from the Lecho Formation of Salta. At the same time, Powell (1992) used *Saltasaurus* as the basis for a new proposed subfamily, Saltasaurinae.

In his review of the Sauropoda, McIntosh (1990*b*) regarded as tentatively synonymous with *S. loricatus* the species *T. australis* Lydekker 1893 (see *Neuquensaurus* entry, *nomina nuda* section; also see Powell 1992) and *T. robustus* Huene 1929, pointing out that differences between these and the type species, as observed by Bonaparte and Powell, are not of taxonomic significance.

T. australis had been based on a series of large caudal vertebrae mostly pertaining to single individual, fore- and hindlimb bones (including right coracoid and humerus, and right femur), fragments of pectoral and pelvic girdles, and other postcranial bones, collected from the Upper Cretaceous of Neuquen, Argentina. Lydekker designated the caudals as the type specimen, at the same time provisionally referring to this species small cervical vertebrae from a different individual, also collected at Neuquen.

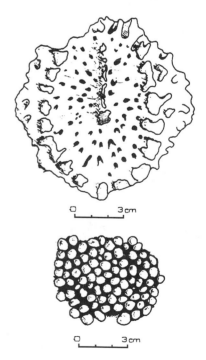

Saltasaurus loricatus, dermal plate (PVL 4017-112, 4017-134), dorsal view, and group of dermal ossicles (4017-118), natural position. (After Bonaparte and Powell 1980.)

Saltasaurus loricatus, A. reconstruction of pelvis (PVL. 4017-92, ilium, 4017-154, 4017-99, ischia, 4017-96, 4017-97, pubes), B. left femur (4017-79), posterior view, C. left tibia (4017-88, 4017-87, right lateral view. (After Bonaparte and Powell 1980.)

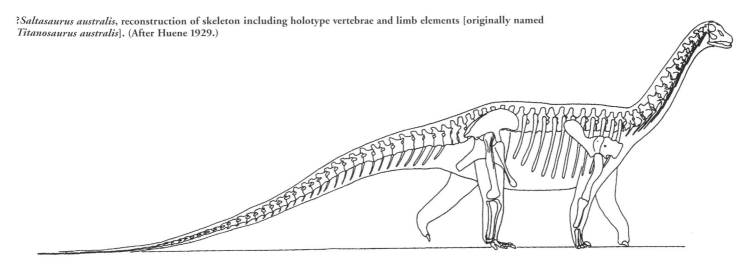

?*Saltasaurus australis*, reconstruction of skeleton including holotype vertebrae and limb elements [originally named *Titanosaurus australis*]. (After Huene 1929.)

Lydekker (1893*b*) diagnosed this species as follows: Distinguished from *T. indicus* by posterior caudal vertebrae with much less marked lateral compression, less distinct anterior facets for chevrons; presacral vertebrae differing from those of other known North American sauropods by lack of pleurocoels; vertebrae pleurocoelous; neural arch far forwards on centrum, lacking spine; anterior caudals resembling posterior ones, but with wide, shorter centra and deeply excavated inferior surfaces; five sacral vertebrae, last resembles anterior caudals, rounded and broad, markedly opisthocoelous; remaining four sacrals much compressed, first rounded, broad; coracoid agreeing in size and form with *Apatosaurus*, scapula rather straight as in that genus; humerus somewhat long, slender, with fairly developed deltoid crest and rounded proximal end with small head; humerus more than 82 centimeters (32 inches) in length, maximum proximal diameter of about 30 centimeters (11.5 inches); ilium apparently low and elongated as in *Apatosaurus*; femur relatively long and slender, about 107 centimeters (41 inches) long.

Huene (1929) reported various round to oval-shaped dermal plates and small, irregularly shaped ossicles found with remains of this species and assumed they pertained to an ankylosaur. However, the more recent discovery of similar plates and ossicles referred to *S. loricatus* has raised the possibility that other or maybe all titanosaurids were similarly armored. The conclusion that ?*S. australis* as well as *Laplatasaurus araukanicus* were probably armored was also reached by Powell (1980) in his review of dermal ossifications found in association with titanosaurid remains.

T. robustus is known from vertebrae and limb elements representing about three individuals.

McIntosh also referred to ?*S. australis* the type species *Microcoelus patagonicus*, which had been founded on an anterior dorsal vertebra, to which was provisionally referred an associated caudal vertebra and humerus, from the Upper Cretaceous (Maastrichtian) of Neuquen, Argentina (Lydekker 1893*b*). Lydekker regarded *M. patagonicus* as a rather small sauropod of uncertain familial standing.

Note: A fragmentary dermal plate had earlier been found in association with incomplete bones of "*Titanosaurus*" *madagascariensis*, suggesting to Deperet (1896) that this species and perhaps other titanosaurids had armor. Huene (1929) reported dermal plates which he believed to belong to *Loricosaurus scultatus* (an apparent sauropod then thought to be an ankylosaur known only from dermal plates) found in 1918 in association with the sauropods "*T.*" *australis*, *T. robustus*, and *L. araukanicus*. Powell, in a review of dermal plates found in association with "*T.*" *australis* and "*T.*" *madagascariensis*, and based on evidence of armor associated with *S. loricatus* remains, postulated that these forms were also armored.

Key references: Bonaparte and Powell (1980); Huene (1929); Lydekker (1893*b*); McIntosh (1990*b*); Powell (1980, 1992).

SALTOPUS Huene 1910 [*nomen dubium*]
?Dinosauria: ?Saurischia: ?Theropoda *incertae sedis*.
Name derivation: Latin *saltus* = "leaping" + Greek *pous* = "foot."
Type species: *S. elginensis* Huene 1910 [*nomen dubium*].
Other species: [None.]
Occurrence: Lossiemouth Sandstone Formation, Grampian, Scotland.
Age: Late Triassic (Carnian–Norian).

Sanpasaurus

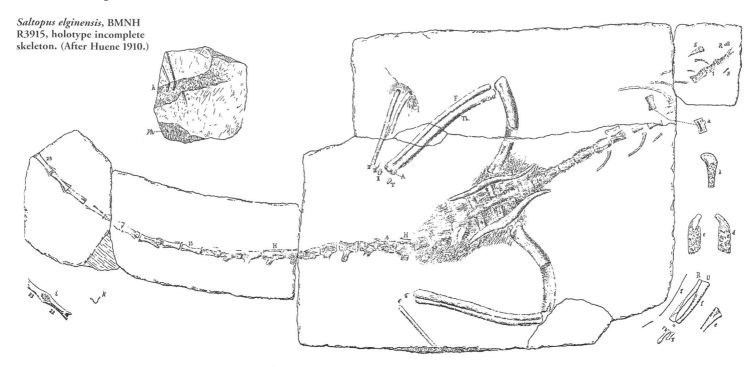

Known material/holotype: BMNH R3915, skeleton including incomplete vertebral column, fourth and fifth metacarpals, pedal phalanx, posterior part of skull.

Diagnosis of genus (as for type species): Very primitive; skull very low and slender; three sacral vertebrae; ilium short; hindlimb with cursorial proportions; metatarsals grouped together for digitigrade stance (typical of but not exclusive to dinosaurs) (Benton and Walker 1985).

Comments: Possibly dinosaurian, the genus *Saltopus* was founded upon a partial skeleton (BMNH R3915) collected from the Lossiemouth Sandstone Formation of Lossiemouth, Elgin, Scotland.

Huene (1910*a*) originally diagnosed *Saltopus* as follows: Tail long, very light, comprising more than 23 caudal vertebrae; forelimb short, about 2.5 centimeters in length; femur markedly curved, 2 centimeters shorter than tibia; metacarpals very much elongate; total length of animal approximately 60 centimeters (about 23 inches).

In an updated diagnosis of the type species *S. elginensis*, Benton and Walker (1985) corrected errors made by Huene.

As assessed by Norman (1990) in his review of problematic "coelurosaurs," *S. elginensis* cannot be unequivocally classified as dinosaurian. The type material is poorly preserved and may belong to a lagosuchid or an early pterosaur. Most prudently, this taxon should be regarded as a *nomen dubium*.

Key references: Benton and Walker (1985); Huene (1910*a*); Norman (1990).

SANPASAURUS Yang [Young] 1944

Dinosauria *incertae sedis*.

Name derivation: "Sanpa [ancient name of "Szechuan" province]" + Greek *sauros* = "lizard."

Type species: *S. yaoi* Yang [Young] 1944.

Other species: [None.]

Occurrence: Kuangyuan Series, Sichuan, People's Republic of China.

Age: Late Jurassic (Tithonian).

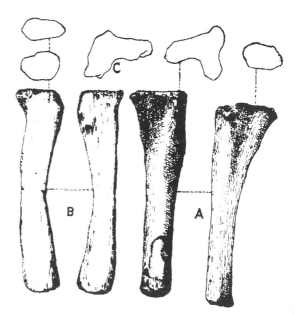

Sanpasaurus yaoi, IVP AS V221-22, holotype A. radius and B. ulna. (After Yang [Young] 1946.)

Known material: Partial postcrania representing several individuals.

Holotype: IVP AS V156, partially articulated skeleton, including 20 isolated vertebrae, scapulae, forelimbs, hindlimb fragments.

Diagnosis of genus: [No modern diagnosis published.]

Comments: The genus *Sanpasaurus* was founded upon an incomplete skeleton (IVP AS V156), in addition to remains of a second individual, discovered in the Kuangyuan Series of Weiyuan, Szechuan [now Sichuan], China. Most of these bones seemingly pertain to the same individual. Specimens tentatively referred to the type species include three or more isolated vertebrae and some broken bones, including a fibula (V221), and cervical vertebra and a few fragments (V222).

These remains were unearthed in 1939 by H. H. Yao of the National Geological Survey of China during geological field work led by T. K. Huang. The fossils, along with remains of other Late Jurassic reptiles, and their labels, reached the Geological Survey's laboratory in a confused state so that the identification given to them might not represent their real association (Yang [formerly published in English-language journals as Young] 1944).

Yang originally diagnosed *Sanpasaurus* as follows: *Camptosaurus* [sic] closely related to Iguanodontidae; vertebrae massive; sacrum apparently not fused; distal end of scapula rather thin; frontlimbs relatively long; ulna and radius facets of humerus not very differentiated from each other; ulna and radius long, slender, ulna slightly longer than radius; femur and fibula relatively tiny; end phalanx of middle toe distinctly curved and depressed (Yang 1944).

Because of perceived similarities between this genus and *Camptosaurus* and *Iguanodon*, Yang assigned *Sanpasaurus* to the Iguanodontidae.

As measured by Yang, the five sacral vertebrae are 420 millimeters (about 16 inches) in length, ulna 420 millimeters, radius 410 millimeters (about 15.75 inches), and fibula 520 millimeters (about 20 inches). From these and other measurements, Yang concluded that *Sanpasaurus* was larger than *Camptosaurus* and decidedly longer than *Iguanodon atherfieldensis*.

Yang also noted that an end phalanx and some phalanges from the Red Beds, below Taanchai limestone near Yunghsien, which Yang (1939) had previously described, probably belong to *S. yaoi*.

If *Sanpasaurus* is an iguanodont, it represents the first certain occurrence of the Iguanodontidae in China based upon good fossil evidence. That assignment was challenged by Rozhdestvensky (1966) in his study of Central Asian iguanodonts. Rozhdestvensky listed various nonornithischian characters of

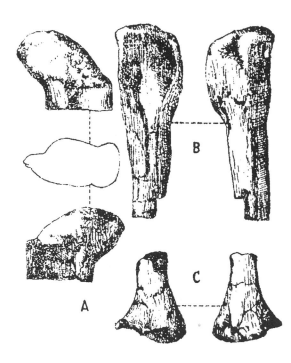

Sanpasaurus yaoi, IVP AS V221-22, holotype A. fragmentary right femur, B. proximal portion of left fibula, C. distal portion of right fibula. (After Yang [Young] 1946.)

the holotype of *S. yaoi*, concluding that *Sanpasaurus* is not an iguanodont but a juvenile sauropod. As the original material from the Weiyuan site had become confused, it is possible that some of the original type material is ornithischian. The scapula is not sauropod, although the forelimb could be (J. S. McIntosh, personal communication 1989).

Notes: Yang (1944) also described an anterior caudal vertebra, distal end of a left femur, left tibia, right fibula, and right pes missing only a few elements (V220). At first considering this material as

Sanpasaurus yaoi, IVP AS V21-22, holotype (clockwise) dorsal ribs, chevron, partial humerus, dorsal vertebrae. (After Yang [Young] 1946.)

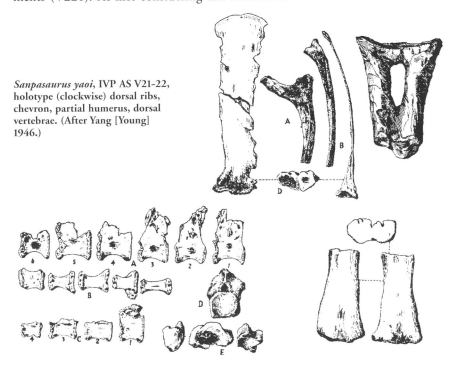

belonging to *S. yaoi*, Yang (1944) then observed that the hind leg in this specimen is relatively shorter than in the type species, and that the phalanges are shorter and broad, not pointed and curved as in *S. yaoi*. As this specimen was not complete enough for assignment to any particular genus, Yang (1944) designated it Gen. indet. *imperfectus*.

Yang (1944) diagnosed this form as follows: Femur rather slender, with small fibular condyle; high protuberance at posterior and lateral proximal end of tibia; tibia, fibula, astragalus, and calcaneum massive; astragalus with distinct ascending process; metatarsal I short, stout, II–IV of subequal length; endphalanges short, broad, of "horseshoe" type.

According to Yang (1944), footprints found by Teilhard de Chardin and Yang (1929) in Upper Jurassic beds in Shenmu, North Shensi, fit well in size with the feet of *Sanpasaurus*.

Key references: Chardin and Yang (1929); McIntosh (1990*b*); Rozhdestvensky (1966); Yang [Young] (1939, 1944).

SARCOLESTES Lydekker 1893

Ornithischia: Genasauria: Thyreophora:
   Ankylosauria: Nodosauridae.

Name derivation: Greek *sarkos* = "flesh" + Greek
   lestes = "robber."

Type species: *S. leedsi* Lydekker 1893.

Other species: [None.]

Occurrence: Lower Oxford Clay, Oxford, England.

Age: Middle Jurassic (Late Callovian).

Known material/holotype: BMNH R2682, two
   portions of left mandibular ramus with teeth.

Diagnosis of genus (as for type species): Teeth relatively small, extending to anterior end of dentary; medial surface of dentary with open Meckelian canal and short spout-like medially projecting process bearing symphysis; crown of first dentary with very fine denticles on anterior edge, other teeth with simple crowns with regular-sized marginal denticles and plain lateral and medial surfaces; dermal plate fused to lateral surface of dentary; coronoid eminence very low; predentary apparently very small; posterodorsal cranial plate with very convex dorsal surface; plate consisting of very dense bone made up of numerous,

closely packed, subvertical bands similar to vertical section of frontoparietal dome of pachycephalosaurid *Stegoceras* (Galton 1983*a*).

Comments: *Sarcolestes*, the oldest known apparent nodosaurid yet described, was founded on a partial lower jaw (BMNH R2682) collected from a brick pit in the Lower Oxford Clay of Fletton, Oxford, near Peterborough, England. Lydekker (1893) incorrectly believed this material belonged to a carnivorous dinosaur (hence, the name) closely related to the prosauropod family Anchisauridae.

Seeley (*see in* Lydekker 1893) provisionally referred *S. leedsi* to the stegosaur "*Omosaurus*" [=*Dacentrurus*]. Romer (1966), believing the Scelidosauridae to represent a family of primitive ankylosaurs, listed *Sarcolestes* as a junior synonym of *Scelidosaurus*. White (1973) transferred *Sarcolestes* to the Stegosauridae. Ostrom (1970) observed that the jaw of *Sarcolestes* is similar to that of the nodosaurid *Sauropelta*.

Galton (1983*a*) pointed out that fusion of a large dermal-bone plate to the lateral surface, with part of the plate projecting below the ventral margin of the lower jaw, is an ankylosaurian feature, and tentatively referred *Sarcolestes* to the Nodosauridae. Subsequently comparing the *Sarcolestes* mandible with those of other ornithischians, Galton (1983*d*) showed that this genus shares characters with the nodosaurids *Silvisaurus* and *Struthiosaurus*. In their review of the Ankylosauria, Coombs and Maryańska (1990) assigned *Sarcolestes* to the Nodosauridae, because the teeth are of large size relative to the mandible, and have basal cingula.

An irregularly-shaped dermal scute from a subadult nodosaurid, collected from the Lower Oxford Clay of St. Ives, Cambridgeshire, was provisionally referred by Galton (1983*a*) to *S. leedsi*. Galton (1983*a*) tentatively identified this scute as the large one covering the frontoparietal region of the skull. Given its similarities to the dome of the pachycephalosaurid *Stegoceras*, the plate, if correctly identified and referred, may have been utilized in some way during intraspecific competition.

Note: An as yet undescribed nodosaurid discovered in 1980, housed at the Institute of Vertebrate Paleontology and Paleoanthropology, Beijing, China, is the earliest ankylosaur yet found. It will be named "Jurassosaurus nedegoapeferkimorum" by Don Lessem of The Dinosaur Society in honor of the motion picture *Jurassic Park* (released in June, 1993) and the film's cast (see *Science* magazine, vol. 258, Dec. 18, 1992).

Key references: Coombs and Maryańska (1990); Galton (1983*a*, 1983*d*); Lydekker (1893); Ostrom (1970); Romer (1966); White (1973).

Sarcolestes leedsi, BMNH R2682, holotype lower jaw. (After Lydekker 1893.)

SARCOSAURUS   Andrews 1921

Saurischia: Theropoda: Ceratosauria *incertae sedis.*

Name derivation: Greek *sarkos* = "flesh" + Greek *sauros* = "lizard."

Type species: *S. woodi* Andrews 1921.

Other species: ?*S. andrewsi* Huene 1932 [*nomen dubium*].

Occurrence: Barrow-on-Soar, Leicestershire, Lias, Warwickshire, England.

Age: Early Jurassic (?Sinemurian–Pleinsbachian).

Known material: Partial postcranial skeleton, fragmentary postcranial remains.

Holotype: BMNH R4840/1, about one half vertebral centrum, portion of neural arch, anterior portion of left ilium united with proximal end of pubis, acetabular region of right ilium joined with portions of proximal ends of pubis and ischium, posterior end of right ilium, poorly-preserved left femur imperfect at both ends.

Diagnosis of genus: [No modern diagnosis published.]

Comments: The genus *Sarcosaurus* was founded on partial postcranial remains (BMNH R4840/1) discovered by S. L. Wood in the Lower Lias, Bucklandi Zone, as Barrow-on-Soar, Leicestershire, England.

Andrews (1921) assigned *Sarcosaurus* to the Megalosauridae, but regarded the remains as distinct enough to warrant its own genus, diagnosing the type species *S. woodi* as follows: Ilium similar to that of *Megalosaurus bucklandi*, but with much narrower preacetabular notch separating anterior lobe from relatively massive pubic process; pubis apparently smaller in proportion to ilium than in more advanced forms; ischium with deep rugose pit (corresponding in position with rugosity in *Ornitholestes*) immediately behind acetabulum; femur rather strongly curved, as a whole, walls very thin; femur (as preserved) 31.5 centimeters (less than 12 inches) in length; vertebral centrum with slightly concave anterior face, almost straight upper border beneath neural canal.

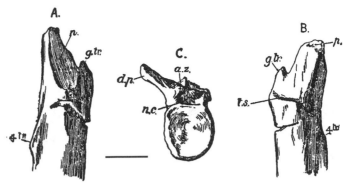

Sarcosaurus woodi, BMNH 4840, holotype distal portion of femur, A. inner and B. outer views, C. incomplete dorsal vertebra, anterior view. Scale = 3 cm. (After Andrews 1921.)

Referred to *S. woodi* were fragmentary remains from the Lower Lias of Wilmcote, Warwickshire, including a dorsal vertebra, dorsal centrum, left pubis fragments, portion of right pubis, imperfect femora, right tibia, proximal portion of left tibia, distal half of fibula, incomplete left metatarsals II-IV, and proximal portion of pedal phalanx.

The species ?*S. andrewsi* [*nomen dubium*] was erected by Huene (1932), based on a fragmentary pelvis, right tibia, and vertebrae from the Lower Lias, Warwickshire, England.

In their review of the Ceratosauria, Rowe and Gauthier (1990) observed that, although belonging to that taxon, *S. woodi* is too incompletely known to position exactly within Ceratosauria. The ilium of *S. woodi* measures approximately 20 centimeters (about 7.75 inches) long, about half that of the ceratosaurs *Dilophosaurus* and the *Rioarribasaurus* [=*Coelophysis* of their usage]-*Syntarsus* group. The firmly-sutured ilium and pubis are indicative of a mature individual and presence of a trochanteric shelf suggest a robust morph; lack of a distinct caudal rim on the M. iliofemoralis of the ilium and lack of an obturator ridge of the femur suggested to Rowe and Gauthier that *Sarcosaurus* lies outside the *Rioarribasaurus-Syntarsus* group.

Rowe and Gauthier suggested that, since *Sarcosaurus* has no apparent diagnostic characters of its own, the generic name be reserved for the original specimen. They also noted that ?*S. andrewsi*, though possibly theropod, preserves no information warranting its referral to *Sarcosaurus* or even to the Ceratosauria, and suggested that this species be best regarded as a *nomen dubium*.

Key references: Andrews (1921); Huene (1932); Rowe and Gauthier (1990).

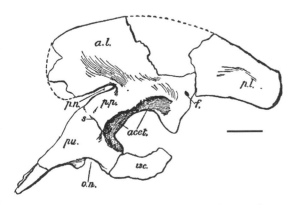

Sarcosaurus woodi, BMNH 4840, holotype pelvis, partly restored from left side. Scale = 3 cm. (After Andrews 1921.)

SAURAECHINODON   Owen 1861—(See *Echinodon*)

Name derivation: Greek *sauros* = "lizard" + Greek *echinos* = "spiky" + Greek *odous* = "tooth."

Type species: *S. becklesii* (Owen 1861).

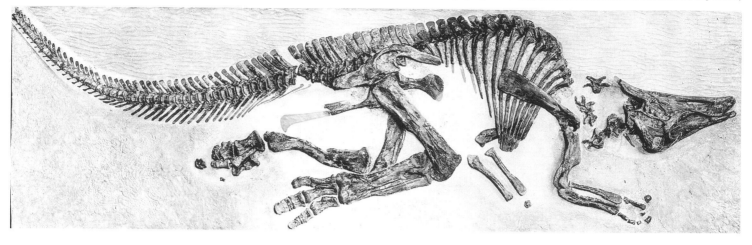

Saurolophus osborni, ANMH 5220, holotype skeleton.

Courtesy Department Library Services, American Museum of Natural History (neg. #34021.)

SAUROLOPHUS   Brown 1912

Ornithischia: Genasauria: Cerapoda: Ornithopoda: Iguanodontia: Hadrosauridae: Hadrosaurinae.

Name derivation: Greek *sauros* = "lizard" + Greek *lophus* = "crest."

Type species: *S. osborni* Brown 1912.

Other species: *S. angustirostris* Rozhdestvensky 1952.

Occurrence: Horseshoe Canyon Formation, Alberta, Canada; Nemegt Formation, Omnogov, White Beds of Khermeen Tsav, Nemegtskaya Svita, Bayankhongor, Mongolian People's Republic; [unnamed formation], Heilungchang, China.

Age: Late Cretaceous, (?Late Campanian–Early Maastrichtian).

Known material: At least 18 specimens, including complete skull and skeleton, two complete skulls, disarticulated crania, skull and postcrania, adult, juvenile.

Holotype: AMNH 5220, nearly complete skeleton with skull, integument.

Diagnosis of genus (as for type species): Skull with long posterior bony crest formed by prolongation of frontal and nasal; lacrimal very long; upper process of premaxilla extending to posterior border of nares; radius and humerus about same length; eight sacral vertebrae; ischium terminating in expanded "foot"; pubis with short anterior expanded blade; ilium strongly arched, anterior process a decurved, thin vertical plate; fourth trochanter of femur below mid-shaft; phalanges of digits II and IV short (Brown 1912*b*). [Note: Brown's characters of pelvis, hindlimb, and toes are now known to apply to all hadrosaurs (Brett-Surman 1989)].

Diagnosis of *S. angustirostris*: Differs primarily from *S. osborni* in narrower skull

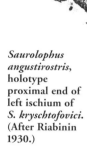

Saurolophus angustirostris, holotype proximal end of left ischium of *S. kryschtofovici.* (After Riabinin 1930.)

and probably longer crest (Rozhdestvensky 1957); also, differs in shorter exterior narial openings, shorter and probably deeper lacrimal, anterior portion of jugal (unlike short, blunt process in *S. osborni*) elongating into long process wedging between maxilla and lacrimal (Maryańska and Osmólska 1981*a*).

Comments: *Saurolophus* is the first Canadian dinosaur known from nearly complete skeletal remains. The specimen (AMNH 5220) was recovered in 1911 by the American Museum of Natural History from the Horseshoe Canyon [then Edmonton] Formation at Tolman Ferry, Red Deer River, Alberta. Also found was a disarticulated skull with jaws (AMNH 6221), designated the paratype. The remains were first reported and holotype skull described in detail by Brown (1912*b*).

After the skeleton was prepared and displayed at the American Museum of Natural History, Brown (1913*b*) diagnosed *Saurolophus* (and type species *S. osborni*) based on the holotype, paratype, and plesiotype, a complete ischium (AMNH 5225) from the same locality.

Saurolophus is a large hadrosaur, its length, based on measurements by Brown (1913*b*) of the holotype skeleton, about 8.4 meters (32 feet). Its weight was approximately 1.9 metric tons (more than 2.1 tons) (G. S. Paul, personal communication 1988).

The most distinguishing feature of *Saurolophus* is the solid crest, which is elevated above the anterior facial angle into a spike-like growth. Brown (1912*b*, 1913*a*), comparing the crest to that of a chameleon, suggested that it served for muscle attachment and that, as in the basilisk lizard, supported a frill. Later, Dodson (1975) suggested that such hadrosaurid crests had significance in sexual identification.

As indicated by the sclerotic ring (the first known in a duck-billed dinosaur) of the holotype skull of *S. osborni*, the eye was considerably smaller than the orbit. Brown (1912*b*) interpreted this ring as having 13 serially-overlapping plates. In a study of the sclerotic ring in *S. osborni* and other duck-billed dinosaurs, Russell (1940*a*) showed that the sclerotic plates, including those in *Saurolophus*, are not serial in one direction, but rather seem to have "one or more segments in which the plates overlap in opposite direction to those in the other segment or segments" (similar to the arrangement in birds, the rhynchocephalian reptile *Sphenodon*, lizards, and other dinosaurs).

Upon *Saurolophus*, Brown (1914) erected the subfamily Saurolophinae to include hadrosaurids bearing a solid rudimentary crest. Brett-Surman (1975, 1979) later observed that all hadrosaurids can be grouped into one of two subfamilies, Hadrosaurinae or Lambeosaurinae, with the Saurolophinae included in the Hadrosaurinae.

The large Mongolian species, *S. angustirostris*, was based on a skeleton excavated by R. Gradiński, J. Kazmierezak, and J. Lefeld (1968–69) from the Nemegt Formation during the 1947–49 Polish-Mongolian Paleontological Expeditions. This skeleton measures some 12 meters (40 feet) long; and there are reports of an even larger specimen from the same region. *S. angustirostris* represents the most abundant Asian hadrosaur remains discovered, known also from the Altan Ula and Tsagan Khushu localities, and seems to have been the dominant Nemegt-Formation herbivore.

Based upon studies of the skull of a young (and smallest known) individual of *S. angustirostris* measuring some 500 millimeters (about 1.7 feet) long and of skulls of other duck-billed dinosaurs, Maryańska and Osmólska (1979) determined that, as in other ornithischians, two supraorbital bones are incorporated into the upper orbital margin of the skull. Maryańska and Osmólska (1979) also suggested that loose supraorbitals are present in both primitive hadrosaurines and in lambeosaurines, while in more advanced hooded lambeosaurines the supraorbitals may have initially been part of the orbital rim, becoming fused with the prefrontal and postorbital bones during ontogeny. From this same, skull Maryańska and Osmólska (1981) showed that the nasal crest is probably hollow, only solid in its thickened end, and suggested that the nasal crest served firstly to enlarge the respiratory surface to the nasal cavity, then had a heat-regulatory function. Also, the somewhat loose joints between many hadrosaurian skull elements, especially between the lower limb of the premaxillary and maxillary bones, served as a kind shock absorber to safeguard the delicate narial structure against harm while the animal was engaged in strong chewing action.

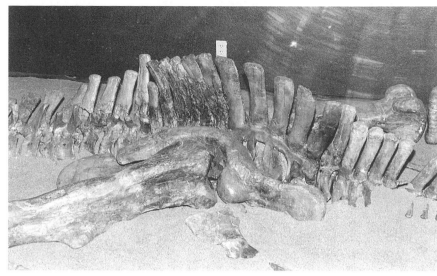

Saurolophus angustirostris, detail of holotype skeleton showing sacrum, pelvic girdle, and left femur, in "The Great Russian Dinosaurs" exhibit (1996), Mesa Southwest Museum, Mesa, Arizona.

Photo by the author.

Another species, *S. kryschtofovici* [*nomen dubium*], was based on the proximal end of a left ischium, found at Beilyie Kruchi, in north Heilungchiang, China, and described by Riabinin (1930*b*). This species is now regarded as synonymous with *S. angustirostris*.

Key references: Brett-Surman (1975, 1979 1989); Brown (1912*b*, 1913*a*, 1913*b*, 1914); Dodson (1975); Gradiński *et al.* (1968-9) Maryańska and Osmólska (1979, 1981*a*); Riabinin (1930*b*); Rozhdestvensky (1952); Russell (1940*a*).

Photo by the author.

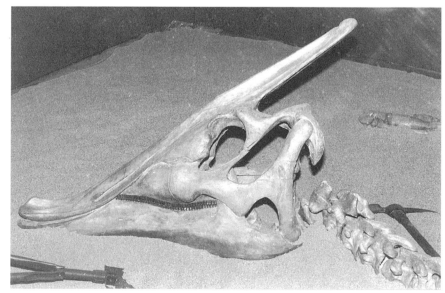

Saurolophus angustirostris skull, middle portion of crest reconstructed, part of holotype skeleton in "The Great Russian Dinosaurs" exhibit (1996), Mesa Southwest Museum, Mesa, Arizona.

Sauropelta edwardsi, AMNH 3032, holotype scutes.

SAUROPELTA Ostrom 1970

Ornithischia: Genasauria: Thyreophora: Ankylosauria: Nodosauridae.

Name derivation: Greek *sauros* = "lizard" + Greek *pelta* = "small shield."

Type species: *S. edwardsorum* Ostrom 1970.

Other species: [None.]

Occurrence: Cloverly Formation, Wyoming, Montana, Cedar Mountan Formation, Utah, United States.

Sauropelta edwardsi, AMNH 3032, holotype scutes.

Age: Early Cretaceous (Late Aptian–Cenomanian).

Known material: Several partial skeletons, crushed skull, numerous postcranial elements, armor plate.

Holotype: AMNH 3032, partial postcranial skeleton.

Diagnosis of genus (as for type species): Characterized by premaxillary teeth, separate atlas and axis, and distinctive armor pattern (Coombs and Maryańska 1990).

Comments: The oldest North American nodosaurid yet found, *Sauropelta* is known from numerous specimens from the Cloverly Formation (defined by Darton 1906; dated as probably Lower Cretaceous [Late Aptian–Early Albian] by Ostrom 1970) of Wyoming and Montana, collected during the 1930s by an American Museum of Natural History expedition headed by Barnum Brown, and during the 1960s by Yale Peabody Museum of Natural History under the direction of John H. Ostrom. The genus was established upon a partial skeleton (AMNH 3032) lacking the skull, which Brown (1933*b*) discovered in Bighorn County, Montana.

A second skeleton (AMNH 3036), the most complete North American nodosaurid specimen, lacks only the skull, neck, anteriormost dorsal vertebrae and their armor, distal portion of the tail, left forelimb, some right manual phalanges, and parts of the left hindlimb. This skeleton, displayed at the American Museum of Natural History, had long remained unnamed. Colbert (1945), in *The Dinosaur Book*, referred to it in a photograph caption as simply "A nodosaur." Colbert (1961) subsequently labeled the same picture *Nodosaurus* in his book, *Dinosaurs: Their Discovery and World*. In *The Dinosaur Dictionary*, Glut (1972) incorrectly captioned that photograph *Peltosaurus* (preoccupied, Cope 1873), the name typed onto the back of the print acquired from the American Museum. As detailed by Chure and McIntosh (1989), who "killed" the name in their bibliography of dinosauria, confusion regarding *Peltosaurus* began after Brown informally proposed a series of names for the various Cloverly dinosaur fauna. Brown neither published these names nor described the dinosaurs, although the names were used in public lectures, on labels for exhibited specimens, in preliminary skeletal reconstructions made under his direction, and on photographs.

Another less complete *in situ* specimen (AMNH 3035) includes an almost complete but crushed skull, a mandible, and cervical armor.

Four decades after the discovery of the original remains, the taxon *Sauropelta* was named by Ostrom (1970). Based on the above material and numerous other referred American Museum and Yale Peabody

Museum specimens, Ostrom described *Sauropelta*, referring it to the [abandoned] family Acanthopholidae Romer 1927.

Ostrom originally diagnosed the genus (and type species *E. edwardsorum*) as follows: Nodosaurid [=Acanthopholid of his usage], with extensive dorsal and flank armor made up of mosaic of large flat and keeled plates interspersed with small plates and irregular ossicles, and flank armor consisting of hollow-based plates that project lateroposteriorly as elongated triangular spines; skull apparently comparatively long, deep, ?narrower than in most other ankylosaurs; lateral temporal openings present, upper opening closed by dermal ossifications; mandible low, with low coronoid process, co-ossified with superficial dermal plate which does not extend onto inferior medial surface; long mandibular tooth row extending almost to symphysis; 25 to 27 mandibular teeth; teeth with laterally compressed crowns triangular in lateral view and denticulate along both anterior and posterior edges; external and internal surfaces generally not ridged or striated, although crown base is irregularly and variably inflated, producing bulbous labial and narrow lingual cingulum, either or both of which may be absent; cervical vertebrae short, wide, massive, width of centrum exceeding length and height, centra faces oval and amphiplatyan; neural canal of cervical vertebrae very large; neural arch low, diapophyses short, massive, laterally projecting, neural spines low, robust, triangular; wide, shallow longitudinal groove bordered laterally by thin, ventrolaterally projecting laminae on inferior surface of centra; long dorsal centra constricted laterally and ventrally at midlength, with circular and amphiplatyan terminal faces; neural arches of dorsal vertebrae high, with high neural canal, diapophyses short, stout, extending up and outward at 50–60 degrees to horizontal; diapophyses and short blade-like neural spines expanded distally, latter both transversely and longitudinally; postzygapophyses overhanging well behind posterior surface of centrum; ribs not fused to vertebrae; proximal caudal centra short, very deep, wide, amphiplatyan, almost circular in end view; transverse processes projecting out and downward proximally from caudals, becoming horizontal posteriorly; caudal neural spines stout, short, much expanded distally; distal caudals elongate, hexagonal in posterior view, with deep, narrow midline groove ventrally (hemal canal); large projectant chevron faces at posterior inferior margins of centra, little or no facets at anterior margins; seven or eight sacral segments; ilia greatly expanded into anterior blades; ischium a simple rod, strongly downcurved distally but with no distal expansion; pubis much reduced to small hook-shaped bone; long hindlimb has long,

Photo by the author, courtesy American Museum of Natural History.

Sauropelta edwardsi, AMNH 3032, holotype scutes.

stout femur, moderately long tibia and fibula; digits of both manus and pes terminating in flat, hoof-like unguals; pedal phalangeal count formula 2-3-4-?5-0.

Sauropelta was regarded by Coombs (1971; 1978*a*) as a typical example of a nodosaurid.

Photo by the author, courtesy American Museum of Natural History.

Sauropelta edwardsi, AMNH 3032, holotype scutes.

Sauropelta

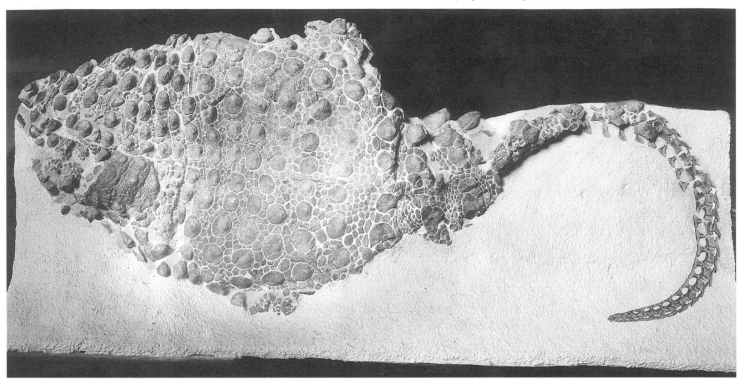

Sauropelta edwardsi, AMNH 3036, referred specimen.

Although various authors and artists have attempted to make skeletal reconstructions and life restorations of *Sauropelta*, the first accurate illustration was that executed by Carpenter (1984c), based on specimens AMNH 3035, 3036 and 3032. Carpenter conservatively estimated a total of 40 caudal vertebrae, which would produce a particularly long tail totaling nearly half the dinosaur's length, stiffened by ossified tendons present from about the seventh dorsal vertebra onward. As the hind legs are longer than forelimbs, the back is arched. The neck is short, shoulder bones and limbs massive, feet short and broad. Dorsally, the neck armor is made up of oval plates. These plates are scooped slightly anterodorsally, posteriorly rising to a low dome. Laterally flanking these plates are large triangular spines with a sharp keel along the anterior edge, increasing in size posteriorly on the neck, largest spines just anterior to the shoulders. Hollow, triangular, dorsoventrally compressed plates constitute the remaining armor, those on the body decreasing in height posteriorly, those across the thighs having low keels, those on the tail becoming shorter posteriorly. Very low cones set in transverse rows cover the body dorsally, separated by irregular ossicles imbedded in the skin to allow lateral body movement. Large, circular, somewhat domed

Sauropelta edwardsi, life restoration by Kenneth Carpenter.

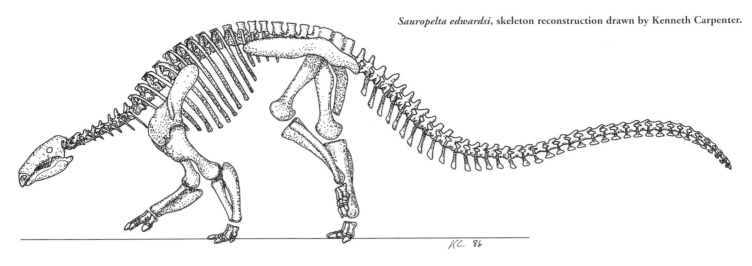

Sauropelta edwardsi, skeleton reconstruction drawn by Kenneth Carpenter.

plates arranged in transverse rows and separated by an interlocking mosaic of irregular scutes, constitute sacral armor. These plates, separated by irregular ossicles, continue onto the dorsal surface of the tail. Carpenter's life restoration of *Sauropelta* depicted the dinosaur as quite large and broad, with robust limbs and short broad feet to bear the animal's weight, the feet near the midline under the body.

Notes: Carpenter speculated that footprints (NMC [formerly GSC] 8556) called *Tetrapodosaurus borealis*, from the Gething member of Bullhead Mountain Formation, Peace River canyon, British Columbia, described as ceratopsian by Sternberg (1932*b*), were made by a nodosaurid. The Gething and Cloverly formations are the same age. Having the same digit count, *Sauropelta* feet quite satisfactorily match the contours of these ichnites. Both front- and hindfeet tracks suggest that they were encased in heavy skin, toes webbed, with an indication of an elephantine pad for cushioning the step in hind impressions.

Olshevsky (1991) pointed out that, since the species *S. edwardsi* was named in honor of two rather than one people, the species name, according to Article 31[a][ii] of the International Code of Zoological Nomenclature, must take the plural-ending spelling, the species corrected to *S. edwardsorum*.

Key references: Brown (1933*b*); Churrie and McIntosh (1989); Coombs (1971, 1978*a*); Coombs and Maryańska (1990); Carpenter (1984*c*); Olshevsky (1991); Ostrom (1970); Sternberg (1932*b*).

SAUROPHAGUS   Ray 1941—(=?*Epantarius*)
Saurischia: Theropoda: Tetanurae: Avetheropoda:
Allosauroidea: Allosauridae.
Name derivation: Greek *sauros* = "lizard" + Greek
phagein = "to eat."

Type species: *S. maximus* Ray 1941.
Other species: [None.]
Occurrence: Morrison Formation, Oklahoma, United States.
Age: Late Jurassic (Kimmeridgian–Tithonian).
Known material/holotype: MUO collection, partial postcrania including femur, claws, representing at least several adult individuals.

Diagnosis of genus: [None published.]

Comments: This very large allosaurid was founded upon partial postcranial remains (MUO collection) recovered from the Brushy Basin Member of the Morrison Formation of Cimmeron County, Oklahoma. *Saurophagus* is sometimes considered to be an invalidly named genus; however, as shown by

Photo by J. S. McIntosh, courtesy University of Oklahoma.

Saurophagus maximus, MUO collection, holotype manual ungual.

Saurophagus maximus. MUO collection, holotype pedal unguals.

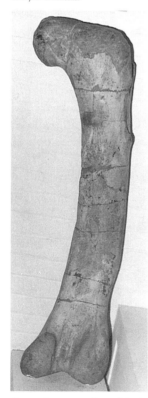

Saurophagus maximus, MUO collection, holotype right femur.

Hunt and Lucas (1987), the description by Ray (1941) of this dinosaur conforms to the rules of scientific nomenclature.

In the past, the type species *S. maximus* has generally been regarded as an unusually big *Allosaurus fragilis* (with a femur measuring approximately 1.2 meters or 4 feet long). The animal may have totaled some 12.5 meters (42 feet) and outweighed the later *Tyrannosaurus.*

In a preliminary report, Chure, Madsen and Britt (1993) noted that *Saurophagus* is a gigantic "carnosaur," with "meat-chopper" chevrons as in tyrannosaurids.

The genus will be renamed *Saurophaganax* by Chure, as the name *Saurophagus* is preoccupied [Swainson 1831].

Key references: Chure, Madsen and Britt (1993); Hunt and Lucas (1987); Ray (1941).

SAUROPLITES Bohlin 1953
Ornithischia: Genasauria: Thyreophora:
    Ankylosauria *incertae sedis.*
Name derivation: Greek *sauro* = "lizard" + Greek
    hoplites = "hoplite [armed foot soldier of ancient
    Greece]."
Type species: *S. scutiger* Bohlin 1953.
Other species: [None.]
Occurrence: [Unnamed formation, Oshih
    equivalent], Nei Mongol Zizhiqu, Mongolian
    People's Republic.
Age: Early Cretaceous.
Known material: Fragmentary postcranial remains.
Holotype: IVPP collection [destroyed], pieces of at
    least seven ribs, partial ?ilium, several complete
    dorsal plates, many plate fragments.

Diagnosis of genus: [None published.]
Comments: The genus *Sauroplites* was established upon fragmentary remains (formerly IVPP collection), collected at Tebch, Kansu [now Gansu], China. The specimen was found by Bent Friis Johansen in a coarse light gray sandstone on the side of a small ravine on the northern slope of the Tebch plateau (Bohlin 1953). The holotype has "disintegrated" (IVPP, personal communication to Coombs, circa 1975).

Bohlin described this material as follows: Ribs with curvature suggesting girth of about 5 meters (almost 17 feet); ischium resembling that of *Pinacosaurus* in relatively broad distal portion; dermal armor consisting of plates more or less circular in outline, marginal zone occupied by pits separated by pronounced ridges; (as indicated by position in which they were found in rock matrix) plates apparently arranged in six longitudinal rows, first, third, and fifth with prominent knobs perhaps supporting low epidermal spines; largest plates seem to follow smaller ones, probably dorsal side of tail covered with such large plates (Bohlin 1953).

Note: Bohlin reported numerous indeterminate dinosaurian fragments from Tsondolein-khuduk, Mongolia. Among these were several indeterminate nodosaurid pieces which were assembled into a reasonably complete dermal plate. The plate resembles those in *Sauroplites,* though with much less pronounced sculpture on the outer surface and apparently without the marginal structure seen in that genus. A fragment of a large, much thicker plate has the same structure as a plate of similar thickness in *Sauroplites.* Bohlin did not speculate as to the identity of this material.

Key reference: Bohlin (1953).

SAURORNITHOIDES Osborn 1924—
    (=*Ornithoides*; =?*Troodon*)
Saurischia: Theropoda: Tetanurae: Avetheropoda:
    Coelurosauria: Maniraptora: Arctometatarsalia:
    Bullatosauria: Troodontidae.
Name derivation: Greek *sauros* = "lizard" + Greek
    ornithoides = "birdlike."
Type species: *S. mongoliensis* Osborn 1924.
Other species: *S. junior* Barsbold 1974.
Occurrence: Djadochta Formation, Nemegt
    Formation, Omnogov, Mongolian People's
    Republic.
Age: Late Cretaceous (?Early Cenomanian–
    Middle–Late Campanian).
Known material: Two skulls with fragmentary
    postcrania.

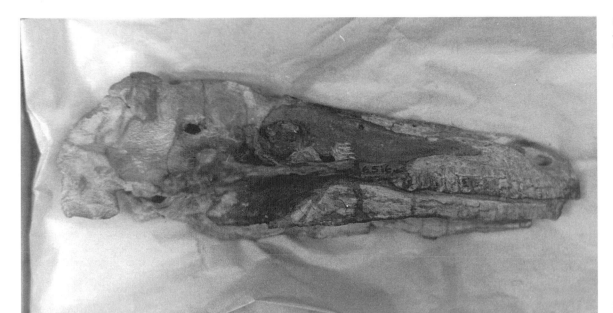

Photo by the author, courtesy American Museum of Natural History.

Holotype: AMNH 6516, skull with jaws, last four dorsal vertebrae, ventral pelvic elements, part of left hind leg.

Diagnosis of genus: Basal tubera weakly-developed; basipterygoid processes laterally directed; supraoccipital rectangular; temporal region somewhat shorter than orbit; pedal digit III strong as IV; second phalanx of pedal digit II half length of first phalanx (Osmólska and Barsbold 1990).

Diagnosis of *S. mongoliensis*: Smaller species; 18 maxillary and 28 dentary teeth (Osmólska and Barsbold 1990).

Diagnosis of *S. junior*: Comparatively large; 20 maxillary and 35 dentary teeth; about 1.3 times larger (skull 280.6 millimeters or about 11 inches long) than *M. mongoliansis* (Barsbold 1974).

Comments: The genus *Saurornithoides* was established on a weather-worn skull with some postcranial remains (AMNH 6516), discovered in 1923 during the Central Asiatic Expedition of the American Museum of Natural History. The material was collected by a worker named Chih, on July 9 of that

year, from a concretion lying on the surface of red sandstone of the Djadocta Formation (?Early Cenomanian; see Currie and Eberth 1993; Middle-Late Campanian; see Currie 1991; Dong 1993*a*), in the Gobi Desert, Central Mongolia. Because of the long and slender rostrum, the skull (put of exhibit at the American Museum in 1993) was originally mistaken for that of a bird (Osborn 1924*d*).

In a popular article, Osborn (1924*c*) named this theropod *Ornithoides oshiensis*, giving the material a single-sentence description, but providing no illustration.

Saurornithoides was subsequently diagnosed by Osborn (1924*d*) as follows: Diapsid and probably theropod reptile, with five cranial fenestrations and one mandibular opening; 19 maxillo-premaxillary teeth, practically homodont, fairly uniform in replacement, serrate only on posterior borders.

Osborn (1924*d*) diagnosed the type species *S. mongoliensis* as follows: Teeth flattened, serrate only on posterior borders, diminishing in size from first premaxillary tooth to fourth, increasing in size from

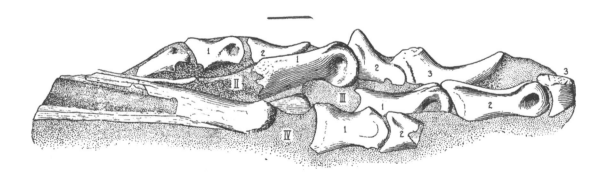

Saurornithoides mongoliensis, AMNH 5616, holotype incomplete left pes, lateral view. Scale = 1 cm. (After Osborn 1924.)

Saurornithoides

Saurornithoides mongoliensis, AMNH 5616, partial skeleton. (After Russell 1972.)

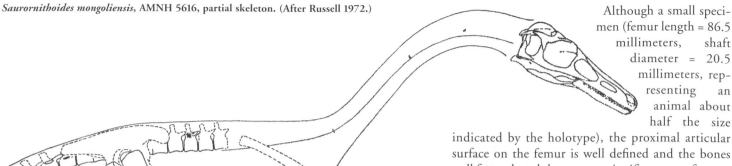

0   10   20mm

Although a small specimen (femur length = 86.5 millimeters, shaft diameter = 20.5 millimeters, representing an animal about half the size indicated by the holotype), the proximal articular surface on the femur is well defined and the bones well formed, and there are no significant gaps for cartilage between the bones. According to Currie and Peng, these features, usually interpreted as signs of maturity, suggest that IVPP V10597 may represent a new troodontid species. However, a juvenile specimen (MOR 430) of *Troodon formusus* shows that the articular surfaces in very young individuals of that species were well formed. Therefore, the degree of ossification cannot be a criterion for indicating maturity in troodontids, nor can size or proportional differences be used to diagnose species in these theropods.

The raptorial digit II is often used as evidence indicating a close relationship between troodontids and dromaeosaurids. However, Currie and Peng noted that there are basic differences in the relative proportions of the phalanges in the second digits in these two theropod groups. In troodontids, phalanx II-1 is longer than II-2 and is almost the length of II-3 (the ungual); in dromaeosaurids, the third (ungual) phalanx is the longest one in pedal digit II, with II-1 and -2 of almost equal length. This suggests (but does not prove) that this feature arose independently in Troodontidae and Dromaeosauridae.

Currie and Peng observed more differences between these two groups in the structure of the hindlimb: (In troodontids) greater (and possibly lesser) trochanter extends dorsally beyond upper margin of femoral head, forming birdlike crista trochanteris; femoral head in proximal aspect almost perpendicular to lateral surface of femur; astragalus with tall ascending process; calcaneum lost as distinct element; metatarsus at least three-fourths length of femur (about half in dromaeosaurids); metatarsal II laterally compressed, flexor surface of proximal end covered by metatarsals II and IV, which contact each other; distal articulatio of metatarsal III extending

first maxillary tooth to tenth; teeth uniform in replacement, closely compacted below; tooth crowns recurved, subacutely pointed.

As measured by Osborn (1924*d*), the holotype skull of *S. mongoliensis* is 192 millimeters (more than 7 inches) long from premaxillaries to basioccipital. Osborn (1924*d*) envisioned this dinosaur as a small, fleet-footed "coelurosaur," swift and raptorial in habit, yet more sluggish than *Velociraptor*, to which it appeared to be remotely related.

Currie and Peng (1993) later described an articulated left hindlimb (IVPP V10597) of *S. mongoliensis*, this specimen including the femur, partial tibia, partial fibula, astragalus, distal tarsals III-IV, metatarsals I-V, and phalanges I-1, II-1, -2, and -3, III-1, -2, and -3, IV-2, -3, -4, and -5, recovered from the Djadokhta Formation equivalent beds (Upper Cretaceous) of Bayan Mandahu, People's Republic of China. The hindlimb was collected during an expedition dispatched in 1988 by the Sino-Canadian Dinosaur Project (see Currie 1991; Dong 1993*a*).

As noted by Currie and Peng, IVPP V10597 offers more information on the anatomy of the leg of *S. mongoliensis* than any other known specimen. The metatarsus shares apomorphies with other troodontids, but is more derived and relatively longer than that of *Troodon*.

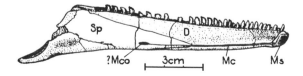

Saurornithoides junior, GI SPS 100-1, holotype anterior part of left lower jaw, lingual view. (After Barsbold 1974.)

posteroproximally into distinctive "tongue"; metatarsal IV most robust bone in metatarsus, almost length of III. Currie and Peng noted that, in the elongation of the metatarsus and reduction of the proximal end of metatarsal III, troodontids are closer to ornithomimids and tyrannosaurids than to dromaeosaurids.

A second species, *S. junior*, was based on an incomplete skull (missing palatal region, quadrates, quadratojugals, left jugal, postorbital, and squamosal) with anterior parts of the lower jaws, sacrum, incomplete series of caudal vertebrae, proximal end of right metatarsus and adjoining tarsals, distal end of right tibia and fibula, and adjoining astragalus and calcaneum (GI SPS 100). These remains were collected in 1964 from the Nemegt Formation (?Late Campanian or Early Maastrichtian), Bugeen Tsav, northwest of the Nemegt Basin, Gobi Desert (Barsbold 1974).

To embrace *Saurornithoides* and the related *Troodon* and "*Stenonychosaurus*" [=*Troodon*], Barsbold erected the family Saurornithoididae; Currie (1987*a*) later resurrected the family Troodontidae, to include Saurornithoididae.

Carpenter (1982*a*) suggested (but did not demonstrate) that the North American *Troodon* [=*Stenonychosaurus* of his usage] is a junior synonym of *Saurornithoides*. Currie (1985), recognizing that both forms are closely related, listed diagnostically significant cranial differences supporting generic separation of these two forms (see also Kurzanov 1976*a*). Subsequently, Currie (1992) stated that, if both *S. mongoliensis* and *S. junior* are valid species, enough cranial differences exist between Asian and North American forms to warrant generic separation, but

noted that the differences between both species of *Saurornithoides* might be due to sexual dimorphism or individual variation. Currie (1992) further suggested that, if both Asian forms proved to be conspecific, the Asian form could be recognized as *Troodon mongoliensis* (see Paul 1988*b*).

Key references: Barsbold (1974); Carpenter (1982*b*); Currie (1985, 1992); Currie and Peng (1993); Kurzanov (1976*a*); Maryańska and Barsbold (1974); Osborn (1924*c*, 1924*d*).

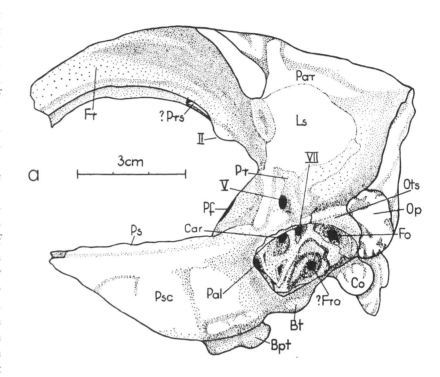

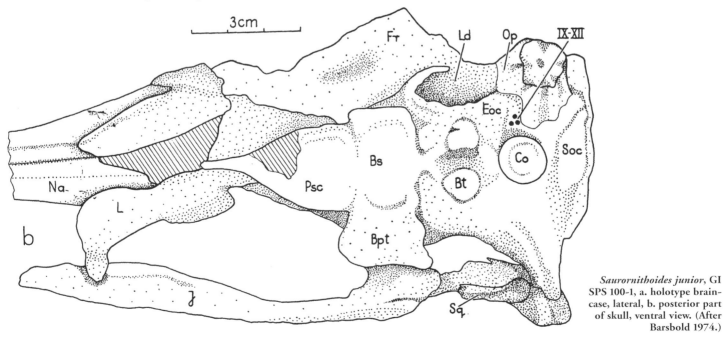

Saurornithoides junior, GI SPS 100-1, a. holotype braincase, lateral, b. posterior part of skull, ventral view. (After Barsbold 1974.)

SAURORNITHOLESTES   Sues 1978—
(=?*Deinonychus*, ?*Velociraptor*)

Saurischia: Theropoda: Tetanurae: Avetheropoda: Coelurosauria: Maniraptora: ?Dromaeosauridae: ?Velociraptorinae.

Name derivation: Greek *sauros* = "lizard" + Greek *ornithos* = "bird" + Greek *lestes* = "robber."

Type species: *S. langstoni* Sues 1987.

Other species: [None.]

Occurrence: Dinosaur Park Formation, Alberta, Canada.

Age: Late Cretaceous (Late Campanian).

Known material: Partial skull and postcrania.

Holotype: PMAA P74.10.5, frontals, left ectopterygoid, left quadrate, two teeth, two vertebrae, gastralia, fragments of thoracic ribs, metacarpal, several phalanges, all unguals of left manus, three isolated prezygapophyses, some very fragmentary indeterminable bones.

Diagnosis of genus (as for type species): Very small, lightly built theropod; frontal triangular (not basin-shaped) between median suture and orbital rim; posterior part of frontal rounded, slightly inflated, lacking frontoparietal crest; lateral walls of anterior part of endocranial cavity flaring out laterally; ectopterygoid with excavated pocket ventrally; teeth with well-developed denticles (from 24 to 26 per 5 millimeters) on posterior carinae, tiny denticles (about 35 per 5 millimeters) on anterior carinae (Sues 1978):

Comments: The genus *Saurornitholestes* was founded on the associated partial remains (PMAA P74.10.5), discovered by Mrs. Victor Vanderloh in the Dinosaur Park Formation at Dinosaur Provincial Park, south-central Alberta, Canada. Referred to *S. langstoni* were three frontals originally regarded by Russell (1969) as indeterminate, including the posterior part of a left frontal (UA 5283), from a site southeast of Dinosaur Provincial Park, and two incomplete left frontals (NMC 12343 and 12354) from Dinosaur Provincial Park (Sues 1978).

Sues erected the new genus *Saurornitholestes* on the basis of differences between this form and other then known "Judithian" theropods of similar size. As noted by Sues, various bits of cranial material, teeth, and postcrania in the holotype of *S. langstoni* are virtually identical to those in the Asian *Velociraptor mongoliensis*.

Paul (1988*b*) observed that the frontal in *S. langstoni*, though possibly more robust, is virtually identical in size and morphology to that of *V. mongoliensis*, and that both species have frontals with a triangular profile that gave the eyes a strong forward orientation. To Paul, this was sufficient grounds to regard *S. langstoni* as a new species of *Velociraptor*, *V. langstoni*, although his synonymy has not been accepted. Also, Paul noticed a unique pattern of sculpture on the frontal of *S. langstoni* at the anterior border of the upper temporal fenestrae, just inside the postorbital articulation, this sculpturing very different from that in *Dromaeosaurus* and *Troodon*.

In a review of the Dromaeosauridae, Ostrom (1990) observed that postcranial remains of *S. langstoni* quite closely resemble *Deinonychus*, cautioning that the absence of characters diagnostic of Dromaeosauridae leaves the assignment of *Saurornitholestes* to that group probable but uncertain.

Saurornitholestes langstoni, PMAA P74.10.5, holotype ectopterygoid, a. dorsal and b. ventral views, c. detail of dorsal surface of pterygoid process. (After Sues 1978.)

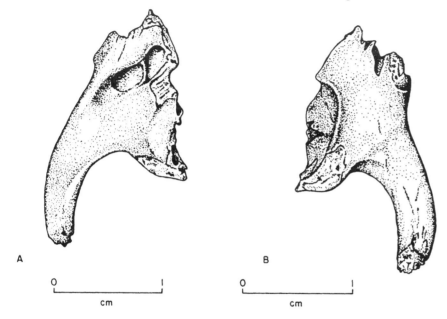

A

cm

B

cm

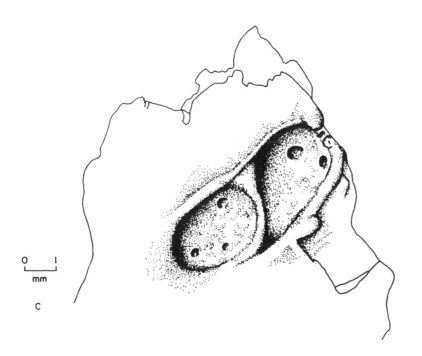

mm

C

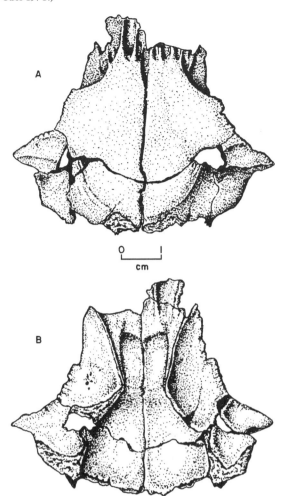

Saurornitholestes langstoni, PMAA P74.10.5, holotype frontal region of skull, a. dorsal and b. ventral views. (After Sues 1978.)

Although strong evidence exists that velociraptorines were active hunters able to attack prey larger than themselves (see Jerzykiewicz, Currie, Eberth, Johnson, Koster and Jia-Jian Zheng 1993), Currie and Jacobsen theorized that the size disparity of *Saurornitholestes*, with an estimated body length of less than 2 meters (about 6.8 feet), and the giant flying reptile represented by RTMP 92.83) is sufficiently great to suggest that the dinosaur could not have killed the pterosaur. In this case, the *Saurornitholestes* may have been scavenging. As the dinosaur scraped the flesh from the pterosaur's carcass, a tooth punctured the tibia and was caught. The twisted nature of the fracture suggested to the authors that the tooth was shattered as the *Saurornitholestes* twisted

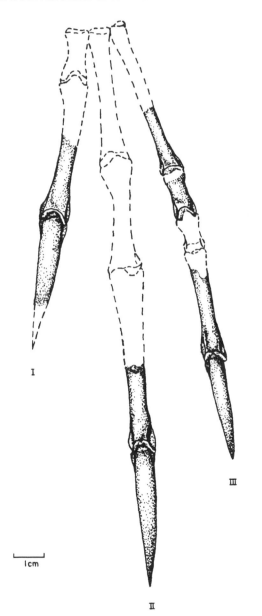

Evidence regarding the diet and possible lifestyle of *Saurornitholestes* surfaced with the discovery, in 1992, of the skeleton (RTMP 92.93) of an azhdarchid pterosaur, found in association with a broken tooth of *S. langstoni*, in white, fine- to medium-grained Upper Cretaceous sediments low in the Dinosaur Park Formation, at Dinosaur Provincial Park, Alberta. The pterosaur was a large yet apparently immature individual with a wingspan of approximately 6 meters (more than 20 feet) (Currie and Jacobsen 1995).

In describing the pterosaur specimen, Currie and Jacobsen observed that the tibia (RTMP 92.83.2) is hollow with walls from 1.0 to 1.5 millimeters thick. The surface of this bone is tooth-marked. Three non-parallel tooth furrows, presumably representing several bites, occur near the distal end of the tibia and measure, respectively, 11.7, 17.3, and 10.4 millimeters. Lodged in the bone is the broken tip of a *Saurornitholestes* tooth measuring 10.8 centimeters from the distal end of the tibia.

Saurornithoides langstoni, PMAA P74.10.5, holotype reconstructed partial left manus. (After Sues 1978.)

its head to pull it from the bone. Though the tibia was thin walled, it must have been quite tough to have broken the tooth, as the teeth of velociraptorines were stronger than most bone. Currie and Jacobsen assumed that the theropod contributed to the scattering of the pterosaur skeleton.

As noted by Currie and Jacobsen, this report constitutes the first known published association of a dinosaur tooth with tooth-marked bone. (J. Brandvold, in a 1993 personal communication to Currie and Jacobsen, reported a tooth-marked hadrosaur bone bearing the tip of a tyrannosaurid tooth, recently found in the Two Medicine Formation of Montana.)

Examining theropod tooth marks on dinosaur bones from the Dinosaur Park Formation of Alberta, Jacobsen (1995) found that 14 percent of all hadrosaur bones were tooth marked; with marks of theropod teeth, the feeding theropod can be identified from family through species levels; and tyrannosaurid tooth marks were present on a variety of prey bones including those of hadrosaurids, ceratopsids, *Saurornitholestes*, and other tyrannosaurids.

Key references: Currie and Jacobsen (1995); Ostrom (1990); Paul (1988*b*); Russell (1969); Sues (1987).

SCELIDOSAURUS Owen 1859

Ornithischia: Genasauria: Thyreophora.

Name derivation: Greek *skelidos* = "rib" + Greek *sauros* = "lizard."

Type species: *S. harrisoni* Owen 1859.

Other species: [None.]

Occurrence: Lower Lias, Charmouth, England; Kayenta Formation, Arizona, United States.

Age: Early Jurassic (Hettangian–Sinemurian).

Known material: Almost complete skeleton, adult; scutes; ?articulated postcranial skeleton, juvenile.

Paralectotype: BMNH R1111, skull with nearly complete articulated postcrania.

Diagnosis of genus: [None published.]

Comments: The genus *Scelidosaurus* was founded by Owen (1859) on the remains of five individuals collected from Charmouth, Dorset, in southern England. These fossils included a left femur fragment (GSM 109560), knee-joint (BMNH 39496), ungual phalanx (GSM 109561), incomplete skull lacking snout (BMNH R1111), remains of a young individual consisting of right femur, tibia, fibula, phalanges, and dorsal centrum (BMNH R6704), and various bones without catalogue numbers, including a vertebral centrum, femur, ?tibia, ?tarsal bone, metatarsal, and phalanges.

Originally, Owen described this material as follows: "Saurian" with hollow limb bones; femur with third inner trochanter; foot bones adapted for terrestrial locomotion.

Owen did not, however, give the genus a specific name. Later, Owen (1861*a*) published the genus and species combination *S. harrisoni* and offered the first detailed description of the material, with emphasis on the skull.

Subsequently, Owen (1862, 1863) redescribed the genus on the basis of the virtually complete postcranial skeleton (BMNH R1111). As the rocks that yielded this specimen were at sea-floor level, Owen (1862) surmised that this individual's carcass had drifted down a river to the sea, where it became bogged down at the bottom. By this time the skin would have so decomposed as to allow gases engendered by putrefaction to escape. Carnivorous fishes and reptiles would have scavenged the remains before the bones entirely sank into the mud.

Lydekker (1889*b*) later designated the knee-joint (BMNH 39496) as the lectotype of *Scelidosaurus*. Newman (1968), however, pointed out that the knee-joint and perhaps the isolated phalanx actually belong to the theropod *Megalosaurus*. The left femur, designated a paratype by Owen (1861*a*), also seems to be megalosaurid, sharing several features (*e.g.*, claw-like phalange) with *M. bucklandi*. With so much confusion surrounding the type material assigned to this taxon, Newman requested that the rules governing scientific nomenclature be waived in this instance, and that the skull with postcranial skeleton (BMNH R1111; now a paralectotype) be established as the new lectotype of this genus [see note below].

Additional information regarding *Scelidosaurus* became available after the discovery of other specimens, including an articulated postcranial juvenile skeleton found in 1985, in Charmouth, by Simon Barnsley, David Costain and Peter Langham. Newman interpreted the right hindlimb bones and vertebral centrum of the juvenile as ornithopod, perhaps belonging to a genus like *Hypsilophodon*. Galton (1975), however, showed that this material agrees with R1111 and should be regarded as a juvenile *Scelidosaurus*. In their review of basal thyreophorans, Coombs, Weishampel and Witmer (1990) regarded this specimen as representing an "Unnamed ?thyreophoran."

Dorsal armor in *Scelidosaurus* was redescribed by Coombs *et al.* as including numerous roughly oval plates with an outer median longitudinal ridge or keel. There are larger plates excavated on the median surface and many smaller plates, some keeled, some merely small nubbins. Armor found *in situ* reveals a pair of unique three-pointed plates just posterior to

Scelidosaurus harrisoni,
**BMNH R1111, almost
complete skeleton.**

the skull, then a longitudinal row of bilateral pairs of plates adjacent to the midline, running from above the atlas down to sacral region, at least two more longitudinal rows of plates more lateral over the thorax, and four longitudinal rows down the tail. Skin impressions found by Barnsley, Costain and Langham indicate that the skin was imbedded by a mosaic of small rounded scales.

Scelidosaurus reached a length of about 4 meters (13.5 feet) and weighed approximately 125 kilograms (275 pounds). Coombs *et al.* judged the animal to be most likely predominantly quadrupedal, based on limb proportions, but surmised that a bipedal or tripodal stance could have been possible.

The classification of *Scelidosaurus* has been debated since its discovery. Traditionally, the genus has been regarded as a primitive stegosaur, with a skull and hips similar to those in stegosaurians. The dermal armor, however, is not unlike that in ankylosaurs. Thulborn (1977), noting similarities in the legs, feet, and tail of *Scelidosaurus* to those in ornithopods, postulated that this was a biped belonging to the Hypsilophodontidae, after which Galton (1980) pointed out that the hind limb-to-trunk ratio in this genus is much less than that for facultatively or fully bipedal ornithopods. In his book *A New Look at the Dinosaurs*, Chairg (1979) commented that *Scelidosaurus* may be neither stegosaur nor ankylosaur. Cooper (1985), in his revised classification of the Ornithischia, placed Scelidosauridae into its own new "infraorder" Scelidosauria. Sereno (1986) put the Scelidosauridae at the base of Thyreophora, as the sister-taxon to Stegosauria and Ankylosauria. Sereno demonstrated the affinities of these groups, noting that the ovate supraorbital bone in the *Scelidosaurus*

skull forms the lateral portion of the orbital roof, excluding the frontal bone from the orbital margin and separating the prefrontal and postorbital. A very similar supraorbital element is present in the stegosaur *Huayangosaurus* and ankylosaur *Pinacosaurus*, but not in other ornithischians, thereby appearing to be a derived character uniting *Scelidosaurus* with both stegosaurs and ankylosaurs. Coombs *et al.* added that *Scelidosaurus* is the sister-group to the stegosaur-ankylosaur clade, identified as such by the presence of distinctive armor, single supraorbital bone in orbital rim, and various cranial details.

The first North American occurrence of *Scelidosaurus* was reported by Padian (1989*a*, 1989*b*), who identified as such parasagittal scutes (MNA V96 and V117, and UCMP 30056) originally assigned to aetosaurs, found in the Glen Canyon Group, Rock Head area of the Kayenta Formation (Early Jurassic), in northern Arizona. The presence of *Scelidosaurus* in North America, known previously only from Jurassic beds, suggests a Jurassic age (Liassic) for at least part of the Glen Canyon Group.

Norman (1985), in his book *The Illustrated Encyclopedia of Dinosaurs*, envisioned *Scelidosaurus* as a somewhat slow-moving creature, relying mostly on its armor for protection against predators, yet with the long tail able to counterbalance the body to allow possible short bipedal runs.

Note: In Case 2857, *Bulletin of Zoological Nomenclature* 49 (4), December, 1992, Alan J. Charig and Bernard H. Newman applied to the International Commission on Zoological Nomenclature to conserve the use of the name *Scelidosaurus harrisonii* for the dinosaur to which it has always been applied, and to designate BMNH R1111 as the new lectotype on which the concept of *Scelidosaurus* has always been based. To date of this writing, the decision of the ICZN is still pending.

Key references: Charig (1979); Coombs, Weishampel and Witmer (1990); Galton (1975); Lydekker (1889*b*); Newman (1968); Norman (1985); Owen (1859, 1861*a*, 1862, 1863); Padian (1989*a*, 1989*b*); Sereno (1986); Thulborn (1977).

SCOLOSAURUS Nopcsa 1928—(See *Euoplocephalus*.)

Name derivation: Greek *scolos* = "thorn" + Greek *sauros* = "lizard."

Type species: *S. cutleri* Nopcsa 1928.

Scutellosaurus lawleri, MNA Pl. 175, tall, narrow "Stegosaur-like" scute. Scale = 2 cm. (After Colbert 1981.)

SCUTELLOSAURUS Colbert 1981

Ornithischia: Genasauria: Thyreophora.

Name derivation: Latin *scutelum* = "little shield" + Greek *sauros* = "lizard."

Type species: *S. lawleri* Colbert 1981

Other species: [None.]

Occurrence: Kayenta Formation, Arizona, United States.

Age: Early Jurassic (Hettangian).

Known material: Fragmentary skull and skeleton representing at least two individuals.

Holotype: NMA Pl.175, partially preserved premaxillae including some erupting teeth, right maxilla with seven erupted teeth and with nasals displaced above lateral surface of maxilla, maxillary fragment, left maxilla with five erupted teeth, fragment of ?paroccipital process of opisthotic, dentaries missing posterior portions, left dentary with 18 erupted teeth, right with ten, 21 presacral vertebral centra, several complete and partial neural arches and spines, five sacral vertebrae, 58 caudal vertebrae with neural arches and several chevrons, incomplete ribs, numerous rib fragments, scapulae, coracoids, partially preserved ilia, several portions of pubes and ischia, humeri, distal end of right radius, proximal and distal ends of left radius and ulna; elements of manus, femora, right tibia, proximal end of right fibula, right astragalus, left tibia, left fibula, ?distal tarsal; various bones of pedes; more than 300 dermal scutes.

Diagnosis of genus (as for type species): Very small ornithischian about same size as *Lesothosaurus*, distinguished by extremely long tail measuring about two and one half times length of presacral series, and by abundance of dermal scutes; predentary probably present; six sharply pointed premaxillary teeth and probably 18 maxillary and dentary teeth, all broadly

triangular in lateral aspect, with denticulated edges; forelimb (including manus) relatively large, more than 50 percent longer than hindlimb; hindlimb relatively short, moreso than sacral series, longer than in *Lesothosaurus* (Colbert 1981*a*).

Comments: An early armored dinosaur, the genus *Scutellosaurus* was founded upon a nearly complete, disarticulated but associated skeleton (NMA Pl.175), collected in 1971 by David Lawler, from the Kayenta Formation (Early Jurassic; see Olsen and Galton 1970; Olsen and Sues 1986, based on fossil material from underlying rocks; Liassic, based on presence of armor scutes belonging to *Scelidosaurus*; Padian 1989*a*), Navajo Indian Reservation, near Rock Head, West Moenkopi Plateau, Ward Terrace, northeast of Flagstaff, Arizona. The paratype (NMA Pl.1752), a less complete skeleton than the holotype, was collected in 1977 by W. Amaral of a Harvard University field party, in the Kayenta Formation, along Gold Wash, northwest of Rock Head, this specimen including four presacral centra, two sacral centra, 44 caudal centra, two scapula fragments, two humerus fragments, two ulna fragments, pelvic fragments, femora and tibiae, calcaneum, distal end of fibula, fragmentary pes, about 15 fragmentary scutes, and unidentified bone fragments (Colbert 1981*a*).

The dermal armor in *Scutellosaurus* is more fully developed than in any other known primitive ornithischian. Colbert counted 304 complete or partial scutes associated with the holotype, surmising that the total number in the living animal would have been even more extensive. Six types of scutes are present, four types grading into each other with no sharp lines of demarcation between them:

Most numerous are scutes resembling broad, flat plates, each asymmetrical in shape and possessing a longitudinal ridge, usually with a slight longitudinal concavity on the ventral surface. The smallest scutes of this category are mere nubbins; the largest are about as long as a presacral vertebra and resembling scutes of *Ankylosaurus* and *Euoplocephalus*. Colbert deduced that these scutes were apparently lateral in their position on the body, the largest set dorsally toward the mid-line, smallest located far down on the dinosaur's flanks; and that they were arranged segmentally with one lateral row positioned above a rib and opposite a vertebra, ranging from largest dorsally to smallest ventrally. These scutes grade into those of the second category.

The second group consists of narrower asymmetrical scutes that are sometimes longer than the largest of the first category. These each have the shape of two long sides that slope up to a ridge forming an apex. Each scute is deeply concave ventrally along a longitudinal axis, its thickness remaining approximately constant. Colbert suggested that these were also laterally situated.

The third grouping consists of asymmetrical scutes that are quite high and broad at the base. Basically dorsally expanded versions of those of the second group, these have a rounded profile in lateral view. Ventrally they are deeply concave longitudinally, with the concavity internally following the scute's external shape. Colbert suggested that these scutes were positioned along the dorsal region on either side of the mid-line.

The fourth group consists of slightly asymmetrical, very tall and narrow scutes that are triangular in lateral aspect. Each of these is individually longer than a single vertebra. With anterior edge longer than posterior edge, the scute slopes back like miniature versions of the large dorsal plates of *Stegosaurus*. Colbert suggested that these scutes were arranged in pairs above the pelvis.

The fifth category is made up of but one rather broad and short scute with two long longitudinal ridges flanking its mid-line. Colbert suggested that this scute was situated on the proximal or medial part of the tail, above the fifteenth caudal vertebra. This scute could have marked the place where (as in modern crocodilians) a double row of tail scutes converged, followed by a single row along the mid-line toward the end of the tail.

The sixth group consists of essentially symmetrical, long, extremely narrow scutes individually the approximate length of a vertebra. Based on the close association in several instances of these scutes with caudal vertebrae, Colbert speculated that they were arranged along the tail's median line, behind the two-ridge arrangement of the fifth group.

The total length of the holotype skeleton is approximately 1.175 meters (4 feet), although other individuals grew much larger. Superficially, this dinosaur, with its rows of armored scutes, probably resembled a smaller version of *Scelidosaurus*.

Colbert speculated that *Scutellosaurus* represented an early stage in the direction of later armored dinosaurs. Noting that Coombs (1978*a*) had stated that the ancestry of ankylosaurs and their connection to other ornithischians (including stegosaurs) remained an open question, Colbert suggested that *Scutellosaurus* could be interpreted as a possible remote ancestor to Jurassic and Cretaceous armored dinosaurs.

Originally, Colbert assigned *Scutellosaurus* to the [abandoned] group Fabrosauridae, regarding it as quite similar to the African *Lesothosaurus*, differing mostly in relative length of the tail, presence of extensive dermal armor, relative length of forelimbs, and shortness of hindlimbs. These differences suggested to Colbert that *Scutellosaurus* was probably only partially bipedal, the scutes weighing down the animal so that it walked efficiently on all fours, becoming bipedal when it ran while counterbalanced by the long tail.

With the discovery of additional *Scutellosaurus* specimens, Sereno (1986) reassessed the systematic position of this genus. Sereno observed that *Scutellosaurus* possesses a buccal emargination along the maxilla, so that the maxillary tooth row is inset medially from the lateral surface of the face, a characteristic of ornithischians more derived than *Lesothosaurus*. *Scutellosaurus* also exhibits characteristics found in later thyreophorans, the most striking being the presence of body armor that would become greatly modified proportionately in stegosaurs and

Scutellosaurus lawleri, MNA Pl. 175, holotype skeleton.

Secernosaurus

Secernosaurus koerneri,
FMNH P13423, holotype ilia.

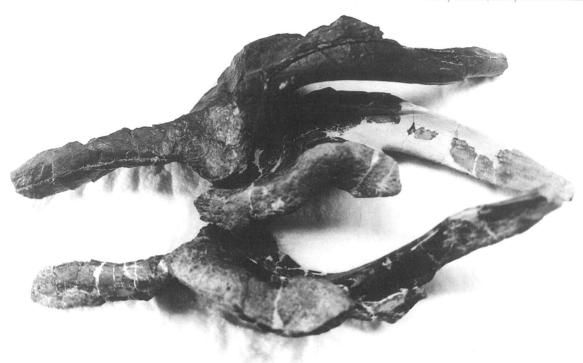

ankylosaurs. According to Sereno, *Lesothosaurus* represents the sister-taxon to other ornithischians. *Scutellosaurus* represents an outgroup to the monophyletic taxon Thyreophora, which includes *Scelidosaurus*, stegosaurs, and ankylosaurs.

Coombs, Weishampel and Witmer (1990), in their review of basal thyreophorans, interpreted *Scutellosaurus* as possibly mostly bipedal, pointing out that the long and slender hindlimbs, compact pes with slender metatarsals, and very long tail all suggest cursorial habits, but also noted that the lengths of femur and metatarsal III relative to that of the tibia are less reflective of such habits, other features (disproportionately long trunk and forelimbs, moderately large manus, wide pelvis, and particularly the dermal armor) suggesting a degree of quadrupedality.

Key references: Colbert (1981*a*); Coombs (1978*a*); Coombs, Weishampel and Witmer (1990); Sereno (1986).

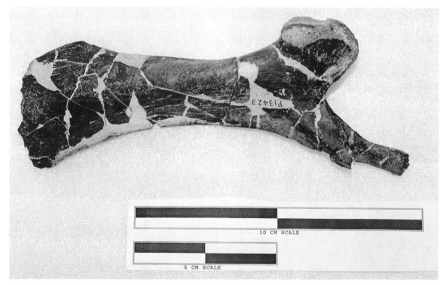

10 CM SCALE

5 CM SCALE

Secernosaurus koerneri, **FMNH P13423, holotype pubis.**

SECERNOSAURUS Brett-Surman 1975

Ornithischia: Genasauria: Cerapoda: Ornithopoda: Iguanodontia: Hadrosauridae.

Name derivation: Latin *secerno* = "severed/divided" + Greek *sauros* = "lizard."

Type species: *S. koerneri* Brett-Surman 1979.

Other species: [None.]

Occurrence: ?Bajo Barreal Formation (="San Jorge" Formation), Alberta, Canada.

Age: Late Cretaceous (?Maastrichtian).

Known material/holotype: FMNH P13423, associated disarticulated partial braincase, caudal vertebrae, scapula, two ilia, prepubis, fibula.

Diagnosis of genus (as for type species): Ilium with postacetabular process greatly deflected dorsomedially and shortened (unlike any other known hadrosaur except *Gilmoreosaurus*); preacetabular process of ilium deflected ventrally at smaller angle than in *Hadrosaurus*; "antitrochanter" (supra-iliac process) comparatively smaller than in hadrosaurids of same size (Brett-Surman 1979).

Comments: A relatively small hadrosaurid, *Secernosaurus* was founded on incomplete remains (FMNH P13423) collected in 1923 by J. B. Abbott for the Field Museum of Natural History [now the Field Museum], from the [then] San Jorge Formation of Rio Chico, Patagonia, Argentina,

As noted by Brett-Surman (1979), this genus was the second hadrosaurid to be found in Gondwana and the first of diagnostic value. The predominance of advanced iguanodontids and primitive hadrosaurids in Laurasia indicates that, by the early Late Cretaceous, duckbilled dinosaurs were present on both of these continents, this not implying that hadrosaurids originated in Laurasia.

Weishampel and Horner (1990), in reviewing the Hadrosauridae, assigned *S. koernieri* to this group but found the type material too poor for referral either to the Hadrosaurinae or Lambeosaurinae.

Key references: Brett-Surman (1979); Weishampel and Horner (1990).

SEGISAURUS   Camp 1936
Saurischia: Theropoda: Ceratosauria:
 Coelophysoidea.

Name derivation: "Segi [Canyon]" + Greek *sauros* = "lizard."

Type species: *S. halli* Camp 1936.
Other species: [None.]
Occurrence: Navajo Sandstone, Arizona, United States.
Age: Early Jurassic (?Sinemurian).
Known material/holotype: UCMP 32101, articulated postcrania including shoulder girdle, two anterior dorsal vertebrae, anterior caudal vertebrae, left humerus, portions of left radius and ulna, ends of two left manual digits, ribs from left side, parasternum, sacrum, pelvis, left hindlimb and pes, parts of right hindlimb and pes, subadult.

Diagnosis of genus (as for type species): Small, tridactyl, with well-developed clavicle; pubis with incomplete obturator notch, lacking expanded terminus; ischium flattened, with completely enclosed fenestra and spatulate distal end; cervical ribs elongate, thread-like; caudal centra solid; midcaudal vertebrae with supplementary anterior spine; humerus 73 percent length of metatarsal III; tibia solid; fibula with slight cavity for marrow; manual digit III slender, compressed, claw closely parallel to larger digit II, claws of both digits almost equal in length; pedal digits I and V vestigial (Camp 1936).

Comments: *Segisaurus* was founded upon an incomplete skeleton (UCMP 32101) discovered on July 27, 1933, by Robert F. Thomas and Max Littlesalt in the Navajo Sandstone (probably Lower Jurassic; Baker, Duane and Reeside 1936), west of Keet Seel Canyon, north branch of Segi Canyon, Navajo Indian Reservation, Arizona. The remains constituted the first vertebrate fossil skeleton recorded from this locality (Camp 1936).

Segisaurus was put into its own [abandoned] family Segisauridae because the bones were interpreted as solid

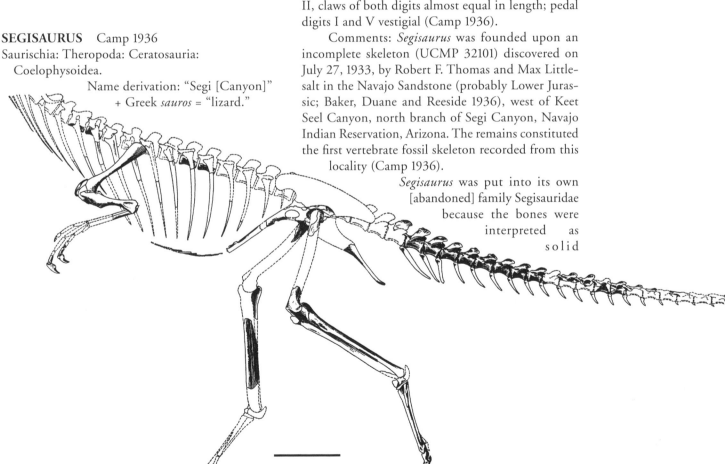

Segisaurus halli, UCMP 32101, holotype restored postcranial subadult skeleton. Scale = 6 cm. (After Camp 1936.)

instead rather than hollow. Welles (1984) questioned that interpretation, suggesting that the specimen is a natural mold. Rowe and Gauthier (1990), in their review of Ceratosauria, confirmed that the preserved material in doubt is almost certainly bone, although the vertebrae and long bones seem to be typically hollow.

Rowe and Gauthier interpreted the holotype of the type species, *S. halli*, as representing a small but robust subadult individual, unique in the possession of a large foramen in the ischium below the acetabulum, with the flattening (?due to crushing) of the shaft of the ischium perhaps also a diagnostic character; also, *Segisaurus* is comparable in size to members of the *Liliensternus-Rioarribasaurus* [=*Coelophysis* of their usage]-*Syntarsus* group and roughly a contemporary of *Syntarsus*.

Noting the articulations of the knee and ankle joints and position (hindlimbs and feet flexed closely underneath body, ribs on left side) in which the skeleton had been found, Camp theorized that *Segisaurus* was capable of squatting on the sand like a setting hen, possibly to elude enemies or as a protection while sleeping against sand blasts during storms. Camp also postulated that the forefoot (as in *Compsognathus*, *Ornitholestes*, and *Struthiomimus*) was adapted to raptorial and grasping habits, fingers perhaps able to rake out burrowing insects or small animals from loose sand. The light construction of the vertebrae, long tail, short body, long pubis and ischium, long hind feet, and powerful tibia and fibula indicated to Camp that *Segisaurus* (and dinosaurs of similar body proportions) were adapted for rapid running and leaping.

Key references: Camp (1936); Rowe and Gauthier (1990); Welles (1984).

SEGNOSAURUS Perle 1979

Saurischia: Theropoda: Tetanurae: ?Coelurosauria: Therizinosauroidea: Therizinosauridae.

Name derivation: Latin *segnis* = "slow" + Greek *sauros* = "lizard."

Type species: *S. galbinensis* Perle 1979.

Segnosaurus ghalbinensis, GI SPS 100/80, holotype mandible. (After Perle 1979.)

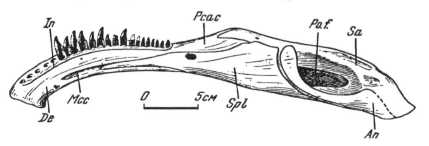

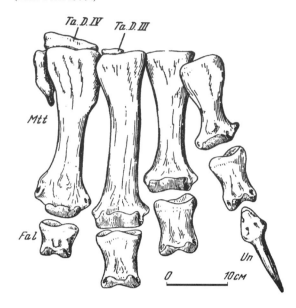

Segnosaurus ghalbinensis, GI SPS 100/82, incomplete pes. (After Perle 1979.)

Other species: [None.]

Occurrence: Baynshirenskaya Svita, Omnogov, Dornogov, Mongolian People's Republic.

Age: Late Cretaceous (?Cenomanian or ?Turonian).

Known material: Three specimens, including mandible, pelvis, hindlimb, scapulacoracoid, partial forelimb.

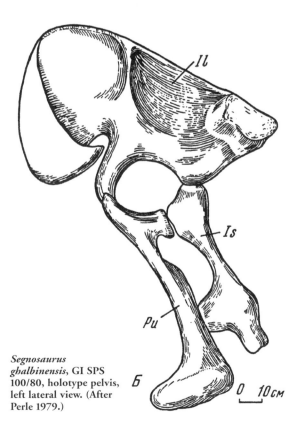

Segnosaurus ghalbinensis, GI SPS 100/80, holotype pelvis, left lateral view. (After Perle 1979.)

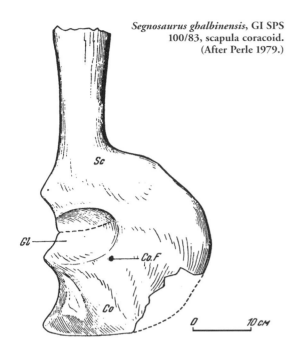

Segnosaurus ghalbinensis, GI SPS 100/83, scapula coracoid. (After Perle 1979.)

well-developed, extending posteriorly below the articulation with the penultimate phalanx, the latter condition found only in *Segnosaurus* among Cretaceous taxa. If correct, this interpretation suggests that therizinosauroids [=segnosaurids of his usage] were not restricted to Asia. However, Currie cautioned that this distinctive articulation may be pathologic, noting that the ungual otherwise resembles the manual ungual of *Chirostenotes*.

Key references: Barsbold and Maryańska (1990); Barsbold and Perle (1980); Gauthier (1986); Perle (1979); Russell and Russell (1993).

SEISMOSAURUS   Gillette 1991

Saurischia: Sauropodomorpha: Sauropoda:
   Diplodocidae: Diplodocinae.
Name derivation: Greek *seismos* = "earthquake" +
   Greek *sauros* = "lizard."
Type species: *S. halli* Gillette 1991.
Other species: [None.]
Occurrence: Morrison Formation, New Mexico,
   United States.
Age: Late Jurassic–?Early Cretaceous.
Known material: Partial postcrania.
Holotype: NMMNH 3690, incomplete, partially
   articulated skeleton, including (to date) one
   isolated and seven articulated dorsal vertebrae,
   articulated ribs, ilia and ischia, pubis, sacrum,
   caudal vertebrae 1-8, 12-16, 20-17, five chevrons,
   230 gastroliths.

Diagnosis of genus (as for type species): Pubis with lower ratio of transverse diameter to anteroposterior diameter than in *Diplodocus* and *Apatosaurus*; transverse diameter of distal expansion and minimum transverse diameter comparatively greater than in other diplodocids; ischium with lower ratio of transverse and anteroposterior diameter to length than in

Holotype: GI SPS 100/80, mandible, disarticulated bones of fore and hindlimb, pelvic girdle, fragmentary vertebral column.

Diagnosis of genus (as for type species): Large segnosaurid; pedal unguals thick (Perle 1979); also, mesial mandibular teeth markedly flattened, slightly recurved; pedal claws moderately compressed transversely (Barsbold and Maryańska 1990).

Comments: Basis for the taxon Segnosauridae [=Therizinosauroidea; see Russell and Dong (1993*a*); Russell and Russell 1993], the genus *Segnosaurus* was founded on partial crania and postcrania (GI SPS 100/80), collected during the Soviet-Mongolian Paleontological Expeditions, from the "Bayan Shireh suite" at Amtgay, southeastern Mongolia. Referred to *S. galbinensis* were a right tibia and fibula (GIN SPS 100/81) from the same horizon and locality; right hindlimb with incomplete pes, rib fragments, ilia, fragmentary ischium, and pubis (GIN SPS 100/82) from Khara Khutul, and left scapulacoracoid, radius, ulna, manual unguals, and cervical fragments (GIN SPS 100/83) (Perle 1979).

Originally, Perle diagnosed the monotypic *S. galbinensis* as follows: Large segnosaurid, with thick, laterally compressed pedal unguals.

Barsbold and Maryańska envisioned dinosaurs like *Segnosaurus* as probably herbivorous, somewhat slow-moving animals having a bulky trunk and short, broad feet.

Note: Currie (1992) reported an isolated ungual (RTMP 79. 15. 1), recovered from the Judith River [now Dinosaur Park] Formation of Alberta, Canada. The specimen is unusual in that the flexor tubercle is

Seismosaurus halli, NMMNH 3690, holotype skeleton, schematic and simplified quarry map (recovered right ribs and distal half of right ischium not shown). (After Gillette 1991.)

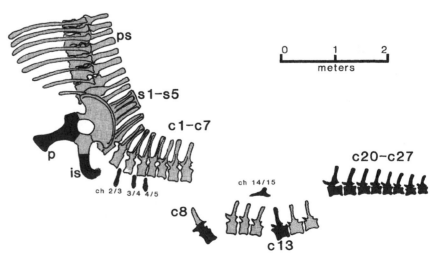

Seismosaurus halli, NMMNH 3690, holotype caudal vertebra 20. (After Gillette 1991.)

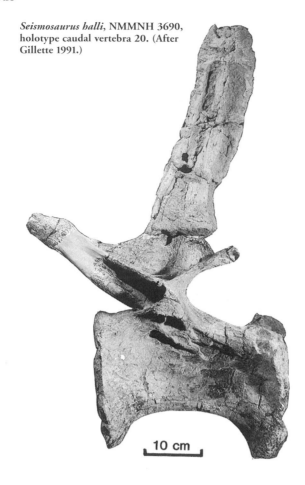

10 cm

taller and more erect, ratio of overall height of vertebra to centra greater; pleurocoels small in or absent from anterior caudals, absent from more distal caudals; anterior chevrons larger than in other diplodocids, expanded distally into paddle-shaped lateral profile; mid-caudal chevrons triangular in side view, larger than in other diplodocids (Gillette 1991).

Comments: The bones of this genus, presently qualifying as the longest dinosaur known, were discovered in 1979 by Arthur Loy, Frank Walker, Jan Cummings and Bill Norlander, who reported them to paleontologist David D. Gillette in 1985 (Gillette 1991).

The as yet unnamed sauropod was first reported in the paleontological literature by Gillette, Gillette and Thomas (1985), and later briefly discussed by Gillette and Schwartz (1986) and Gillette (1987). The giant sauropod's remains had been found in the upper part of the Brushy Basin Member of the Morrison Formation (wholly or partially Cretaceous age; see Kowallis 1986; Kowallis and Heaton 1987; Kowallis, Heaton and Bringhurst 1986; Bowman 1986), at a site west of San Ysidro, Sandoval County, New Mexico. The genus was founded upon an incomplete partially articulated skeleton comprising (to date) one isolated and seven articulated dorsal vertebrae, articulated ribs, ilia and ischia, pubis, sacrum, caudal vertebrae 1-8, 12-16, and 20-27, five chevrons, and 230 gastroliths (NMMNH 3690). Referred material includes the partial shaft of an unidentified limb element (also numbered NMMNH 3690) presumed to belong to the type specimen (Gillette 1991). Some of the vertebrae were first exhibited during the late 1980s at the New Mexico Museum of Natural History.

Seismosaurus halli, NMMNH 3690, holotype left pubis, A. medial, B. lateral views, C. distal extremity, D. x-y cross-section at position shown in B. Scale in B and C = 10 cm. (After Gillette 1991.)

all other known diplodocids; marginal shafts parallel, weakly curved medially; expansion of distal end of shaft relative to minimum diameter greater than in other diplodocids; distal extremity of ischium not fused at midline; caudal vertebrae longer than in other diplodocids, neural spines of median caudals

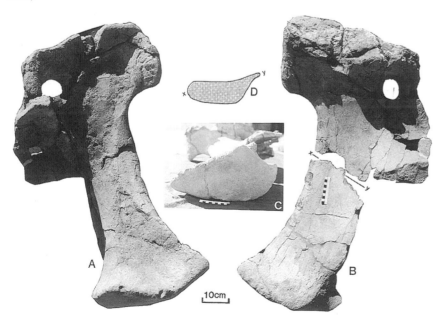

10cm

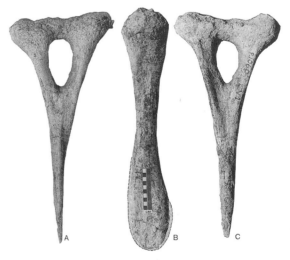

Seismosaurus halli, NMMNH 3690, holotype chevron 2/3, A. anterior, B. left lateral, B. posterior views. Scale = 10 cm. (After Gillette 1991.)

Seismosaurus halli, NMMNH 3690, holotype caudal vertebra 25. (After Gillette 1991.)

Seismosaurus halli, NMMNH 3690, holotype chevron 14/15, A. lateral, B. medial (internal) views. (After Gillette 1991.)

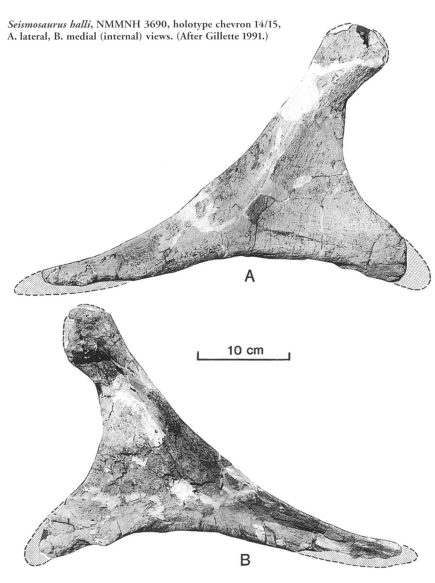

Excavations done through geophysical diffraction tomography (GDT), a quantitative technique for high resolution subsurface imaging, have yielded results suggesting that much of an articulated skeleton may remain to be found (see Gillette, Witten, King, Bechtel and Bechtel 1989). As noted by Gillette

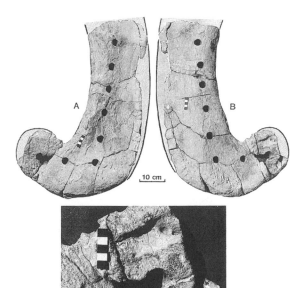

Seismosaurus halli, NMMNH 3690, holotype left ischium, A. medial, B. lateral views, C. detail of distal extremity. Stippling indicates restored edges of bone. Scale in C = 5 cm. (After Gillette 1991.)

(1991), much of the axial skeleton continues into the hill through very hard rock, with several years of excavation and preparation remaining before an osteology of *Seismosaurus* can be published.

From the collected remains, Gillette (1991) estimated the total axial length of *Seismosaurus* to be 39–52 meters (about 135–180 feet). The height dimensions are, however, not much greater than those of *Diplodocus* and *Apatosaurus*. Although good limb bone material has yet to be found, the legs of *Seismosaurus* may have been relatively short (see Gillette and Bechtel 1989), as suggested by the relative short vertical dimensions of the pelvic elements, increased height raising the center of gravity and reducing stability in locomotion.

Gillette, Bechtel and Bechtel (1990) described gastroliths found in two sets within the middle region of this skeleton. Forty gastroliths were located in the pelvic region and 35 in the anterior rib cage, these

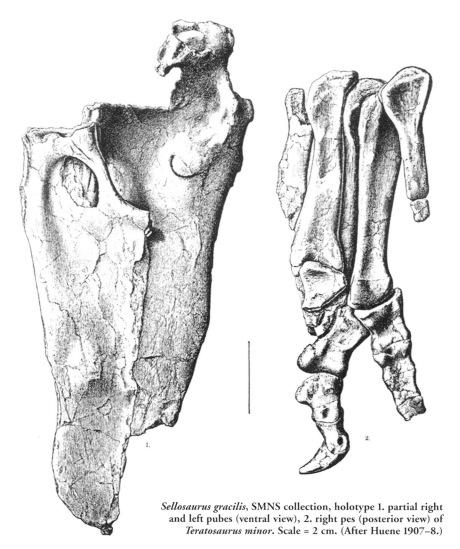

Sellosaurus gracilis, SMNS collection, holotype 1. partial right and left pubes (ventral view), 2. right pes (posterior view) of *Teratosaurus minor*. Scale = 2 cm. (After Huene 1907–8.)

ished surfaces indicate that they remained in both portions of the gut for a relatively long time.

Note: Before the official publication of the generic name, the informal "Seismosaurus" appeared in a number of newspaper articles in 1986, as well as in an article by Anderson for the April 23, 1987, issue of *New Scientist*.

Key references: Gillette (1987, 1991); Gillette and Bechtel (1989); Gillette, Gillette and Thomas (1985); Gillette, Witten, King, Bechtel and Bechtel (1989); Gillette and Schwartz (1986); Gillette, Bechtel and Bechtel (1990).

SELLOSAURUS Huene 1908—(=*Efraasia*)
Saurischia: Sauropodomorpha: Prosauropoda:
    Plateosauridae.
Name derivation: Latin *sella* = "saddle" + Greek
    sauros = "lizard."
Type species: *S. gracilis* Huene 1908.
Other species: [None.]
Occurrence: Unterer and Mittlerer
    Stubensandstein, Baden-Württemberg, Germany.
Age: Late Triassic (Middle Norian).
Known material: Twenty-one partial skeletons,
    isolated elements, three partial skulls, juvenile to
    adult.
Holotype: SMNS collection, two dorsal vertebrae,
    sacrum, most of caudal series, left femur, part of
    fibula.

Diagnosis of genus (as for type species): Slender-footed prosauropod; basipterygoid process of medium length; cervical vertebrae long; dorsal centra low; caudal neural spines with narrow bases; fingers slender, digit II robust and somewhat longer than III; ilium with short anterior process; pubis with closed obturator foramen and apron-shaped distal portion; toes slender, first ungual largest (Galton 1973*b*).

Comments: The new type species *Sellosaurus gracilis* was established on an incomplete postcranial

clusters separated from one another by a barren zone of about two meters. Gillette, Bechtel and Bechtel showed that these regions correspond, respectively, to the gizzard in crocodiles and birds, between stomach and small intestine. They also noted that the rounded shape of the stones and their highly pol-

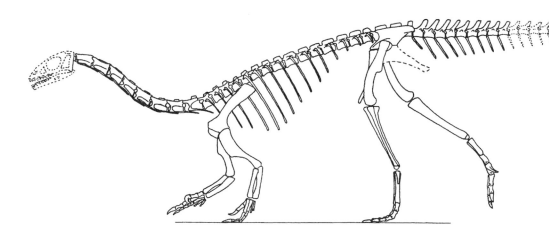

Sellosaurus gracilis, reconstructed skeleton drawn by Kenneth Carpenter.

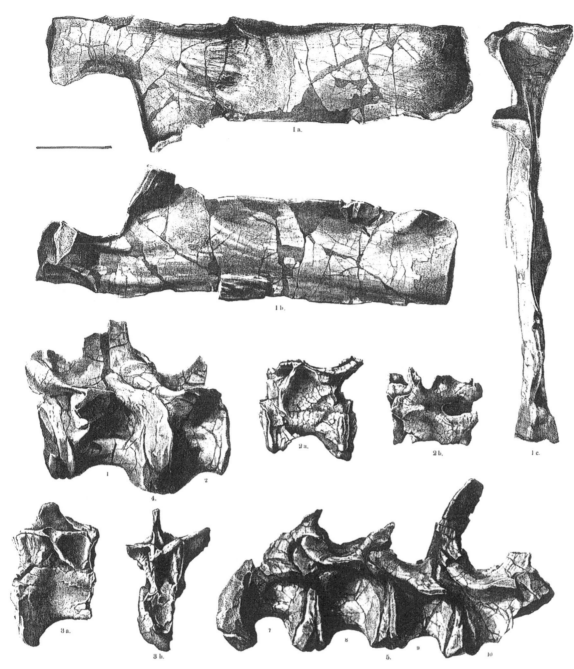

Sellosaurus gracilis, SMNS collection, holotype 1. left pubis, a. dorsal, b. ventral, c. medial views, 2. sixth dorsal vertebra, a. right lateral, b. dorsal views, 3. mid-dorsal vertebra. a. right, b. anterior views, 4. first and second caudal vertebrae, with fragment of third, 5. seventh-tenth caudals. Scale = 4 cm. (After Huene 1907–8.)

skeleton (SMNS collection) recovered from the Middle Stubensandstein (Upper Triassic) of Heslach, Stuttgart, Germany, this material first described by Huene (1907–8).

Later, Eberhard Fraas collected a nearly complete skeleton (SMNS 12667) and parts of a second skeleton (SMNS 12668) from the Burrerschen Quarry near Pfaffenhofen in Nordwurttemberg, [formerly Federal Republic of] Germany. Upon these

remains, Fraas (1913) erected a new species of *Thecodontosaurus*, *T. diagnosticus*. As Fraas did not describe this material, the taxon became a *nomen nudum*. Huene (1932) later described Fraas' material as *Palaeosaurus diagnosticus* Riley and Stutchbury 1836. As the name *Palaeosaurus* proved to be preoccupied (Hillaire 1831), Kuhn (1959) renamed it *Palaeosauriscus*. (The holotypes of both *Palaeosaurus* Riley and Stutchbury 1836 and *Thecodontosaurus* Riley and

Stutchbury 1836 are, respectively, a broken tooth [BM collection] and dentary with teeth [BM 2], with no association between them.)

As teeth have little value in generic identification, Galton (1973*b*) referred Huene's taxon to the new genus *Efraasia* as the new type species *E. diagnostica*. Galton observed that *Efraasia* is quite con-

servative in its anatomy and was an ideal ancestor to the later prosauropod, *Anchisaurus*.

Later recognizing *Sellosaurus* as a valid taxon, Galton (1985*d*) referred *E. diagnostica* to *S. gracilis*. Galton (1985*e*, 1985*f*) showed that the material that had been called "*Efraasia*" actually represented a juvenile individual.

Sellosaurus gracilis, SMNS collection, holotype 1. right ilium with first and second sacral vertebrae, a. anterior, b. posterior, c. right lateral views, 2. proximal half of ischia, a. antero-ventral, b. postero-dorsal views, c. right ischium, right lateral view. Scale = 4 cm. (After Huene 1907–8.)

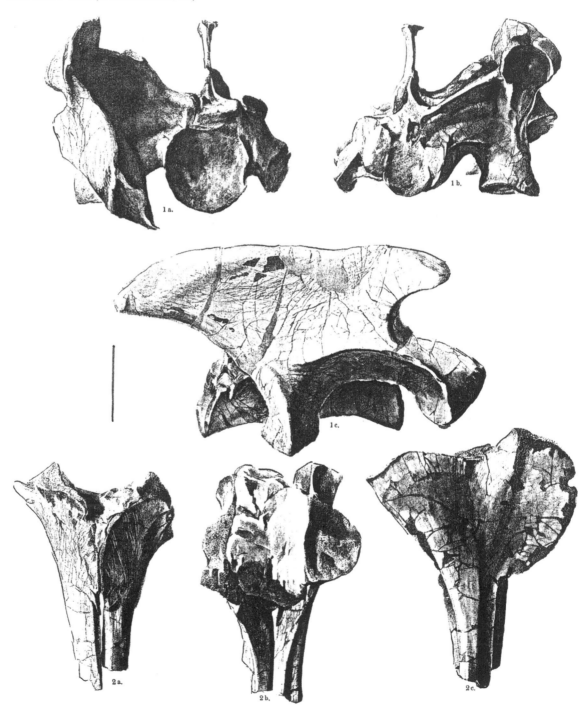

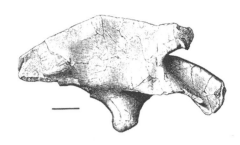

Sellosaurus gracilis, SMNH collection, holotype right ilium of *S. fraasi*. Scale = 1 cm. (After Huene 1907–8.)

To *S. gracilis*, Galton (1985*d*) referred other species from the Stubensandstein of Nordwürttenberg described by Huene (1907-8), including *S. fraasi*, based on incomplete skeletal remains from Pfaffenhofen; *Teratosaurus minor*, based on three dorsal vertebrae, a pubis, femur (measuring 47 centimeters [about 18 inches] long), and right manus, from Pfaffenhofen; and *T. trossingensis*, based on two fragmentary fibulae, a right pes, and most of the tail section, from Trossingen. Galton (1985*d*) also referred to this taxon *Thecodontosaurus hermannianus*, which was based on most of a right maxilla with teeth, from Heslach.

In his review of the Prosauropoda, Galton (1990*a*) noted that the skull of *S. gracilis* exhibits the derived characters of a medium-sized medial lamina to the maxilla and medium-sized lateral lamina to the lacrimal, but lacks several of the derived characters found in *Plateosaurus engelhardti*.

Huene (1932) reported the presence of 14 small, smooth pebbles found in the trunk area of the type specimen of "*T.*" *diagnosticus*, which he identified as gastroliths. Galton (1973*b*, 1990*a*) noted that this identification was reasonable and that such stones, functioning as gastric mills within the stomach, would have compensated for the rather inefficient prosauropod chewing apparatus.

Key references: Fraas (1913); Galton (1973*b*, 1985*d*, 1985*e*, 1985*f*, 1990*a*); Huene (1907–8, 1932); Kuhn (1959).

SHAMOSAURUS Tumanova 1983
Ornithischia: Genasauria: Thyreophora:
  Ankylosauria:
Ankylosauridae.
Name derivation: "Shamo [=Gobi]" + Greek *sauros* = "lizard."
Type species: *S. scutatus* Tumanova 1983.
Other species: [None.]
Occurrence: Kukhteskaya Svita, Dornogov, Ovorkhangai, Mongolian People's Republic.

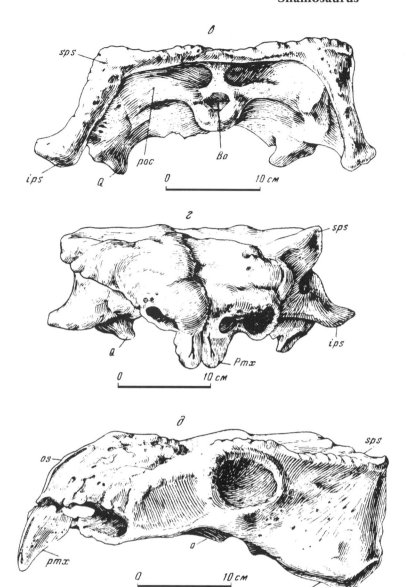

Shamosaurus scutatus, PIN 3779/2, holotype skull, posterior, anterior, left lateral views. (After Tumanova 1983.)

Age: Early Cretaceous (Aptian–Albian).
Known material: Three specimens, including skull, partial skeleton, armor.
Holotype: PIN 3779/2, complete skull with jaw.

Diagnosis of genus (as for type species): Premaxillary beak not covered by dorsal ossifications; laterally facing orbits more rostral than in other ankylosaurids; quadrate weakly inclined rostrally; quadrate condyle positioned behind caudal margin of orbit; slit-like rostrolaterally-facing nostril divided by vertical premaxillary septum; flat caudal part of skull roof with weakly-developed, horn-like dermal projections; occipital condyle extending farther from braincase than in other ankylosaurids; secondary palate with rostral part forming horizontal plate extending caudally from premaxillary to midpoint of maxillary tooth row; relatively long tooth row, equal

Photo by the author.

Shamosaurus scutatus, skull and armor plates, left three-quarter view, in "The Great Russian Dinosaurs" exhibit (1996), Mesa Southwest Museum, Mesa, Arizona.

less than distance between posterior upper teeth; posterior maxillary shelf well-developed; ventral surface of palatines laterally inclined; articulation of mandible far behind posterior border of orbits; occipital surface inclining backwards, occipital condyle ventrally oriented; ventral surface of basioccipital narrow and rounded.

As measured by Tumanova, the skull is 36 centimeters (about 14 inches) in length, 26 centimeters (about 10 inches) wide between orbits, and 37 centimeters (more than 14 inches) between lower postorbital spines.

Tumanova (1985) observed that the skull of *Shamosaurus* most closely resembles that of *Saichania*, both genera having a relatively narrow premaxillary region of the snout, fused quadrates and paroccipital processes, pterygoids fused with braincase, and small interpterygoid vacuity. *Shamosaurus* differs from *Saichania* in that the postorbital osteodermal elements are not shaped like spines, the osterodermal covering does not extend laterally to level of condyle of quadrate, orbits are laterally oriented, and premaxillary region is narrower.

Shamosaurus was placed by Tumanova (1983) into its own subfamily, Shamosaurinae. Because of similarities with *Saichanis*, Tumanova (1985) later referred that genus also to this group. According to Tumanova (1985), the cranial morphology of *Shamosaurus* indicates that this genus is somewhat intermediate between nodosaurids and ankylosaurids. In their review of Ankylosauria, Coombs and Maryańska (1990) did not accept Shamosaurinae as a valid taxon.

Note: *Shamosaurus* is a primitive ankylosaurid, but not exceptionally so, the primitive characters of this taxon being rather subtle and minor (W. P. Coombs, personal communication 1988).

Key references: Coombs and Maryańska (1990); Tumanova (1983, 1985).

to about one half skull length; mandible relatively longer and lower than in other known ankylosaurids (Coombs and Maryańska 1990).

Comments: The earliest Asian and most primitive ankylosaurid known, *Shamosaurus* was founded on a skull (PIN 3779/2), discovered in the Dzunbain suite, Khamryn-Us, south-eastern Gobi, Mongolia, by the Joint Soviet-Mongolian Paleontological Expedition of 1977.

Shamosaurus was originally diagnosed by Tumanova (1983) as follows: Large ankylosaur with cranial roof completely covered with osteodermal scutes, the latter with ornamentation composed of small tubercles; postorbital osteodermal elements not fused into spines; osteodermal elements not covering condyle area of quadrate laterally; orbits at mid-length of skull, almost exactly laterally directed; upper portion of premaxilla covered with osteodermal expansions; anterior part of snout with narrow oval shape, width

SHANSHANOSAURUS   Dong 1977

Saurischia: Theropoda: Tetanurae *incertae sedis*.

Name derivation: "Shanshan [County]" + Greek *sauros* = "lizard."

Type species: *S. huoyanshanensis* Dong 1977.

Other species: [None.]

Occurrence: Subashi Formation, Xinjiang Uygur Ziziqu, People's Republic of China.

Age: Late Cretaceous (?Campanian–Maastrichtian).

Known material/holotype: IVPP V4878, partial skull and associated postcrania.

Diagnosis of genus (as for type species): Small; bones thin-walled; skull small, equal in length to femur; orbit round, larger than first antorbital opening; teeth caniniform, premaxillary teeth with ten-

Shanshanosaurus huoyanshanensis, IVPP V4878, holotype partial skull, left lateral view. (After Dong 1987.)

dency toward incisiform; mandible shallow, with interdental plates and surangular foramen; neck moderately long; pubes with distally expanded "foot"; forelimbs relatively short, humerus approximately one-third length of femur; tibia longer than femur (Dong 1977).

Comments: The genus *Shanshanosaurus* was founded upon an incomplete skull and skeleton (IVPP V4878) collected by the Institute of Vertebrate Palaeontology and Palaeoanthropology, Academia Sinica, expedition of 1964-1966 to the Subash [now Subishi] Formation (based on its dinosaur fauna, estimated as Campanian-Maastrichtian), Turpan basin, Xinjiang [now Sinkiang], People's Republic of China (Dong 1977).

Dong (1977) regarded *Shanshanosaurus* as a probably active and agile dinosaur, which he assigned to its own family, Shanshanosauridae. In his book *Dinosaurs from China*, Dong (1987) stated that the length of *Shanshanosaurus* is 2.5 meters (approximately 8.5 feet).

Paul (1988c), in the book *Predatory Dinosaurs of the World*, synonymized *Shanshanosaurus* with *Aublysodon*. This synonomy was not accepted by Lehman and Carpenter (1990), as Paul did not justify this synonymy.

Molnar (1990), in a review of problematic possible "carnosaurs," observed that *S. huoyanshanensis* shows some "carnosaurian" characters (*e.g.*, narrow scapula with abrupt glenoid expansion, deep surangular), but lacks others (*e.g.*, femoral head not elevated, figured cervical vertebra apparently procoelous). Some

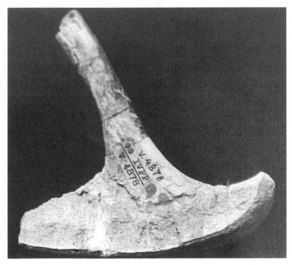

Shanshanosaurus huoyanshanensis, IVPP V4878, holotype pubis. Scale = 2 cm. (After Dong 1987.)

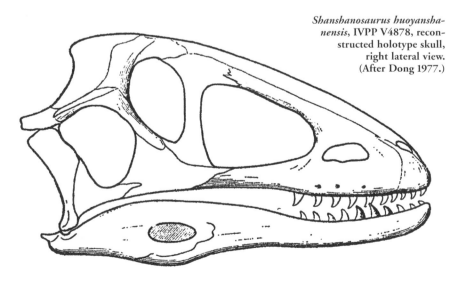

Shanshanosaurus huoyanshanensis, IVPP V4878, reconstructed holotype skull, right lateral view. (After Dong 1977.)

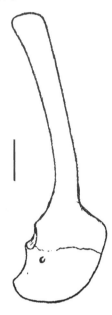

Shanshanosaurus huoyansha-nensis, IVPP V4878, holotype scapulacoracoid. (After Dong 1977.)

features of this species (*e.g.*, surangular foramen, pre-maxillary teeth tending to be incisiform) are also known in dromaeosaurids and (well-developed pubic "foot") in abelisaurids. Molnar found that this combination of features justified Dong's erection of a new family, but cautioned that it was not now possible to assign this group to any higher-level taxon.

Key references: Dong (1977, 1985); Molnar (1990).

SHANTUNGOSAURUS Hu 1973—

(=?*Edmontosaurus*)

Ornithischia: Genasauria: Cerapoda: Ornithopoda: Iguanodontia: Hadrosauridae: Hadrosaurinae.

Name derivation: "Shantung [city]" + Greek *sauros* = "lizard."

Type species: *S. giganteus* Hu 1973.

Other species: [None.]

Occurrence: Wangshi Series, Shandong, People's Republic of China.

Age: Late Cretaceous (?Campanian).

Known material: At least five individuals, including disarticulated cranial and postcranial elements.

Holotype: IG V-1780, cranium, including left quadrate, left and right maxillae, left premaxilla, posterior part of left dentary, right dentary, portion of anterior dentary, most anterior portion of vomer, right jugal.

Diagnosis of genus (as for type species): Gigantic (more than 14 meters, or about 47 feet long); skull rather long, posteriorly high and broad; dentary with from 60 to 63 vertical tooth files, edentulous area rather long; ten sacral vertebrae; longitudinal groove on ventral part of sacrum; ischium straight, long, with very slightly dilated tip at distal end (Hu 1973).

Comments: The largest known hadrosaurid, *Shantungosaurus* was founded upon material discovered in August of 1964 by a field team from the Geological Research Institute, Geological Academy of Science, Ministry of Geology, from beds of the Lower Member of the Wangshi Group (lower Upper Cretaceous, based on lithostratigraphic sequence, lithologic characteristics, and lateral tracing) at Lungkuchian gully, Chucheng County, Shantung [now Shandong] Province, China. The remains were collected from October, 1964 to May, 1968, by the first team and paleontologists from the Geological Museum and Geological Research Institute. The material, collectively weighing some 30 tons, represented at least five individuals (Hu 1973).

Shantungosaurus giganteus, mounted skeleton including restored partial holotype skull IVP V-1780, and referred material, displayed at the Beijing Museum of Natural History.

Courtesy M. K. Brett-Surman.

From the collected material, Hu selected a partial skull (IG V-1780) as the holotype. Paratype specimens include a third cervical vertebra, sacral vertebra, and right ischium. Other remains were used as references.

According to Hu, the collected remains comprised more than enough elements to mount a composite skeleton at the Peking [now Beijing] Museum of Natural History, where it was displayed from April, 1972 to October, 1982. As originally mounted, the skeleton represents a medium-sized adult measuring 14.72 meters (about 51 feet) in length. Larger bones, including a femur reported to be about 2 meters (approximately 6.8 feet) long (within the range of most sauropod femora), belonging to bigger individuals, were not incorporated into the mount. Because the utilized bones represented five individuals with slight variations in size, Hu admitted that some minor errors were probably unavoidable, adding that such errors had no significance in the description of this dinosaur. The restored skeleton is now housed in the Museum of Geology at the Geological Institute of China, Beijing (Hu and Cheng 1988).

Brett-Surman (1989) observed that, with the exception of features related to size (e.g., robustness of bones, number of tooth rows, elongated neural spines, etc.), Shantungosaurus cannot be distinguished from Edmontosaurus. Although this suggests that both forms may be congeneric, Brett-Surman noted that a synonymy cannot now be demonstrated, as only one specimen of Shantungosaurus has yet been published.

S. giganteus is to be redescribed in detail by Hu and Cheng.

Note: Found with the Shantungosaurus material were "carnosaurian" remains including teeth and a metatarsal resembling those of Tyrannosaurus. This suggested to Hu that Shantungosaurus may actually be of latest Cretaceous age, although more conclusive dating for the Wangshih Series requires further investigation.

Key references: Brett-Surman (1989); Hu (1973); Hu and Cheng (1988).

SHUNOSAURUS Dong, Zhow and Chang 1984—(=Shuosaurus)
Saurischia: Sauropodomorpha: Sauropoda: Cetiosauridae: Shunosaurinae.
Name derivation: "Shuo" [old Chinese spelling of Sichuan]" + Greek sauros = "lizard."
Type species: S. lii Dong, Zhow and Chang 1984.
Other species: S. ziliujingensis (anonymous) ?1986 [nomen nudum].
Occurrence: Xiashaximiao Formation, Sichuan, People's Republic of China.

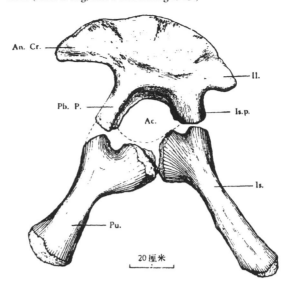

Shunosaurus lii, IVPP V9065, holotype pelvis, left lateral view. (After Dong, Zhou and Zhang 1983.)

Age: Middle Jurassic (Bathonian–Callovian).
Known material: At least 20 skeletons without skulls, ?jaws, adult, subadult.
Type specimen: IVPP V9065, almost complete, articulated postcranial skeleton missing tail.

Diagnosis of genus (as for type species): Medium-size, maximum length of up to 12 meters (more than 40 feet); skull relatively low, rather heavy; skull with length-to-height ratio of about 1.6; external nares in upper anterior part of skull; orbit broad in outline, at mid-posterior part of skull; antorbital and supratemporal openings small, lateral temporal opening long, narrow; quadrate forwardly inclined;

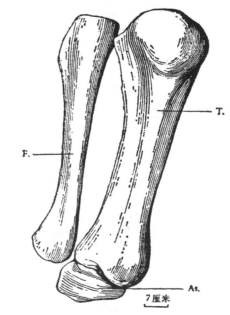

Shunosaurus lii, IVPP V9065, holotype fibula and tibia. (After Dong, Zhou and Zhang 1983.)

Shunosaurus

Shunosaurus lii, IVPP
V9065, holotype humerus.
(After Dong, Zhou and
Zhang 1983.)

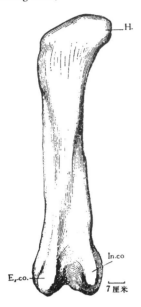

lower jaw relatively solid; mandibular foramen small, at middle or mid-posterior part of ramus; teeth relatively slender, rather spatulate; 4–5 premaxillary, 17–18 maxillary, 18–21 dentary teeth; teeth in upper jaw relatively slender, with convex outer surface and longitudinal depression near posterior keel, very shallow concave inner surface; small feather-like streaks on unworn teeth, resulting in some small denticles along anterior and posterior keels; dentary teeth differing in structure from upper teeth, crowns comparatively flat, inclined toward inside; unworn crowns gently convex on outer surface, relatively even on interior surface, where, having some radiate streaks, there are two-three denticles at anterior and posterior edges, respectively; neck relatively short, with 12 opisthocoelous cervical vertebrae, centra with shallow pleurocoels gradually disappearing from front to back; neural spines of anterior cervicals relatively low; mid-posterior cervicals with higher spines; 13 platycoelous or weakly amphicoelous dorsal vertebrae; cervical vertebrae 1.2 times length of dorsals; anterior dorsal vertebrae lacking pleurocoels, with nonbifurcated, bar-like, upwardly extending neural spines; middle and posterior dorsals relatively high, with comparatively depressed centra, rather high, plate-like neural spines; four sacral vertebrae with rather high, plate-like neural spines, second and third coalesced, first and fourth free; 44 caudal vertebrae, anterior caudals high, short, anterior-middle to mid-posterior caudals becoming moderately cylinder-shaped and faintly amphicoelous, neural spines high, bar-like, becoming reduced to low and plate-like toward posterior part of tail; posterior caudals platycoelous, with small cylindrical centra, low, rod-like neural spines; several of last caudals swollen to form "tail mace" bearing two pairs of small caudal spines (analogous to tail spines in stegosaurs); sternum thick, elliptical; coracoid relatively round; scapula comparatively thick, slender; ilium low, with well-developed pubic peduncle; pubis relatively broad and blade-like, with well-developed pubic foramen; ischium slender, straight; humerus two-thirds length of femur, radius three-fifths length of humerus, tibia approximately three-fifths length of femur; humerus with well-developed deltopectoral crest; three carpal bones; astragalus massive, with relatively high anterior crest; calcaneum small, and flat, circular in dorsal view; metacarpals and metatarsals short, strong; phangeal formula of manus 2, 2, 2, 2, ?2, pes 2, 3, 3, 3, 2 (Zhang 1988).

Battle between
Yangchuanosaurus shangy-ouensis and club-tailed
Shunosaurus lii.

Illustration by Mark Hallett. From *Dinosaurs: A Global View*, by Czerkas and Czerkas, published by Dragon's World Ltd. and its co-edition publishers.

Photo by the author.

Shunosaurus lii, skeleton temporarily displayed at the National Museum of Wales.

Comments: *Shunosaurus,* an unusual sauropod in respect to the tail, was first mentioned (as *Shuosaurus,* a *nomen nudum*), though not described, by Chou in a 1979 article concerning three decades of vertebrate paleontology in China.

The genus was founded upon a postcranial skeleton (IVPP V9065) excavated by students from the Dashanpu quarry (apparently Middle Jurassic), Xiashaximiao Formation, near Zigong, Sichuan Basin, Sichuan Province, China. The material was recovered from 1979–1981 (Dong, Zhou and Zhang 1983; Dong and Tang 1984).

Originally, Dong *et al.* diagnosed the genus (and type species, *S. lii*) as follows: Primitive, medium-sized sauropod; teeth long, slender, spatulate; cervical vertebrae opisthocoelous, with elongate centrum, low neural spine with slight bifurcation on last few spines, small pleurocoels, about 1.5 times length of dorsal vertebrae; dorsals platycoelous, lacking pleurocoels, with high neural spines, reduced lamellar structures on neural arch and spines; presacral vertebrae solidly constructed; sacrum with four coossified vertebrae, with well-developed sacricostal yoke and uncoalesced spines; limb bones columnar, graviportal; pectoral and pelvic girdles typically sauropod in character; femur robust and flatly rounded (similar to *Rhoetosaurus*).

A mounted skeleton of *S. lii* at the Zigong Dinosaur Museum measures about 10 meters (34 feet) in length.

Dong *et al.* hypothesized that *Shunosaurus* was intermediate between prosauropods and Late Jurassic–Late Cretaceous derived sauropods. With the collection of new material, including a skull and caudal vertebrae, Dong and Tang (1984) emended the original diagnosis of the type species.

Dong and Tang noted that *S. lii* is a most abundant species, more than ten skeletons with rather complete skulls and postcranial materials having been collected. At present, *S. lii* seems to be the most com-

Shunosaurus lii, CHG T5403, skull. (After Dong 1987.)

mon Chinese dinosaur, every bone of its skeleton known.

Zhang (1988) reported new material, including the fairly complete skeleton (CHG T5401) of an immature individual and that of a mature individual (CHG T5402), along with a complete skull and lower jaw (CHG T5403), collected by the Dashanpu

Dinosaurian Excavation Team of Zigong from the Dashanpu quarry. The most unexpected skeletal detail revealed by these remains was a tail club possessing a pair of short but prominent spikes, an adaptation not suspected in sauropods. Zhang rediagnosed *S. lii* based on the holotype and these more recently collected referred specimens. Dong (1988) speculated that the club could have been used as a weapon, as in the tail clubs of ankylosaurids.

A second (and apparently somewhat older) species, *S. ziliujingensis* (to be described by Zhang), from the ?Lower Jurassic Ziliujing Formation of the Sichuan Basin, was mentioned but not described in *A Brief Display Introduction of the Zigong Museum*, an anonymously written guidebook pamphlet. The pamphlet, possibly issued in 1986, mentioned that the remains of a subadult of this species was on display.

In his review of the Sauropoda, McIntosh (1990*b*) placed *Shunosaurus* and related genera into the new subfamily Shunosaurinae.

Key references: [Anonymous] ?1986; Dong (1988); Dong and Tang (1983); Dong, Zhow and Chang (1984); Dong, Zhou and Zhang (1983); McIntosh (1990*b*); Zhang (1988).

SHUVOSAURUS Chatterjee 1993

Saurischia: Theropoda: Tetanurae: Avetheropoda: Coelurosauria: Maniraptora: ?Ornithomimosauria.

Name derivation: "Shuvo [Chatterjee, son of author Sankar]" + Greek *sauros* = "lizard."

Type species: *S. inexpectatus* Chatterjee 1993.

Other species: [None.]

Occurrence: Upper Dockum Group, Texas, United States.

Age: Late Triassic (Early Norian).

Known material: Partial cranial and postcranial remains representing at least three juvenile individuals.

Holotype: TTU P 9280, almost complete skull, left lower jaws, dorsal vertebra.

Diagnosis of genus (as for type species and Shuvosauridae): Distinguished from other ornithomimosaurs by this combination of features: external naris small, posteriorly set; premaxillary beak deep dorsoventrally, compact, pointed, hooked; preorbital region short; maxilla relatively small, nasal shorter than frontal, participates in formation of maxillary fenestra; mandibular articulation of quadrate by lateral condyle and medial cotyle; secondary dentary shelf at jaw symphysis (Chatterjee 1993*a*).

Comments: The genus *Shuvosaurus* was established upon a nearly complete skull and a vertebra

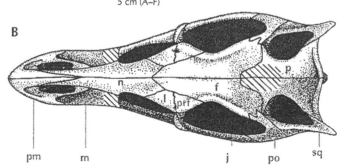

Shuvosaurus inexpectatus, restoration of skull (juvenile), based upon holotype TTU P 9280, A. lateral and B. dorsal views. Scale = 5 cm. (After Chatterjee 1993.)

5 cm (A–F)

(TTU P 9280). Referred material includes the anterior part of two dentaries, left atlantal (or first cervical vertebra) arch, right scapula (TTU P 9281), and a partial skull including premaxillae, frontal, squamosal, "palato-quadrate," braincase, and atlas (TTU P 9282). The material was recovered in 1984 from the Upper Dockum Formation (Triassic red beds), southeast of Post, R C Miller Ranch, Garza County, Texas. As the quarry which yielded these fossils also produced the remains of other kinds of tetrapods (including metoposaurs, brachyiopods, lizards, poposaurs, aetosaurs, phytosaurs, crocodylomorphs, cynodonts, ?mammals, as well as ornithopods and other theropods, these animals may have been died together in a flash flood (Chatterjee 1993).

As measured by Chatterjee, the relatively small skull is 170 millimeters (about 6.6 inches) long, 62 millimeters (about 2.4 inches) wide, and 52 millimeters (about 2 inches) deep; the orbit is enormous (25 percent of the length of the skull), the snout short.

Chatterjee noted that the most unusual feature of the lower mandible is the configuration of the jaw symphysis, wherein a secondary platform is added to accommodate bite force at the front of the jaw. According to Chatterjee, the jaws were particularly designed for dealing with hard foods, the deep and powerful beak associated with strong bite forces. The sharp front part of the beak probably worked like shears for cutting soft food. The back part, however, working with gripping surfaces in the roof and floor of the mouth, was well designed for crushing nuts and seeds. The structure of the beak resulted in a mechanism comparable to a nutcracker, letting the dinosaur crack hard and resistant food and get to the kernels. According to Chatterjee, the animal could have held the food in place at the front of the beak while crushing it. The jaw adductor muscle, because of the short snout and mandible, and the deep pterygoid projecting below the skull margin, would have allowed for greater crushing force at the front of the beak.

Chatterjee placed this genus into its own monotypic family, Shuvosauridae. Because *Shuvosaurus* manifests a suite of characters now perceived only in "ostrich dinosaurs," Chatterjee tentatively referred these new taxa to the Ornithomimosauria (the presence of additional dentary teeth precluding the genus's inclusion in the other established ornithomimosaurian subgroups). These features include the following: Jugal reduced; edentulous jaws; postorbital extended to ventral level of orbit; quadrate strongly inclined, descending anteriorly; lower temporal opening reduced to a vertical slit; upper temporal opening depressed from skull roof to occiput; supraoccipital with dorsolateral concavities.

Furthermore, Chatterjee found *Shuvosaurus*, despite its age, to be quite derived, sharing three synapomorphies with the ornithomimid *Dromiceiomimus*: Frontal participating in formation of orbital rim; lower temporal opening subdivided by forwardly projecting bar of quadratojugal; antorbital fossa extending forward to the premaxillary contact.

Until the discovery of *Shuvosaurus*, the earliest ostrich dinosaurs were known from the Late Jurassic. Chatterjee allowed for a second possible phylogenetic interpretation of this taxon—that it could be an independent Triassic iteration of an ornthiomimosaurian cranial morphology. If, however, this genus is an ornithomimosaur (as its skull characters seem to suggest to Chatterjee), then it is the oldest known member of Ornithomimosauria, extending the range of this group at least 75 million years.

Key reference: Chatterjee (1993a).

SIAMOSAURUS Buffetaut and Ingavat 1986
Saurischia: Theropoda: ?Tetanurae:
   ?Spinosauridae.
Name derivation: "Siam [19th century name of
   Thailand]" + Greek *sauros* = "lizard."
Type species: *S. suteethorni* Buffetaut and Ingavat
   1986.
Other species: [None.]
Occurrence: Sao Khua Formation, Changwat Khon
   Kaen, Thailand.
Age: Late Jurassic.
Known material: Teeth.
Holotype: Department of Mineral Resources TF
   2043a, tooth.

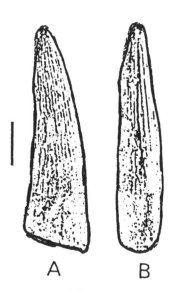

Siamosaurus suteethorni, Department of Mineral Resources TF 2043a, holotype tooth, A. medial and B. anterior views. Scale = 1 cm. (After Buffetaut and Ingavat 1986.)

Diagnosis of genus (as for type species): (Holotype) tooth slightly compressed labiolingually, with oval cross-section (referred teeth almost circular in cross-section); tooth long, relatively straight and slender, with feeble anteroposterior curvature; slight double curvature (not in some other *Siamosaurus* teeth) in anterior and posterior view; crown with rounded tip; fairly distinct anterior and posterior carinae separating labial from lingual surfaces, both equally convex anteroposteriorly; carinae atypically without distinct serrations; marked ridges, extending from base of crown to a point about 5 millimeters from apex, covering surface of enamel on lingual and labial sides, about 15 ridges per side; root hollow, oval in cross-section; no constriction at neck between crown and root; 62.5 millimeters (about 2.4 inches) high (Buffetaut and Ingavat 1986).

Comments: The genus *Siamosaurus* was founded upon an isolated tooth (Department of Mineral Resources, Bangkok, TF 2043a) from the Sao Khua Formation, Khorat Group (Upper Jurassic), Phu Pratu Teema, Phu Wiang, Changwat Khon Kaen, east of Khon Kaen, northern Thailand. Referred material from the same locality includes eight rather well-preserved teeth (TF 2043 b-i), the holotype being the best preserved of this collection (Buffetaut and Ingavat 1986).

Because the teeth of *Siamosaurus* resemble those of *Spinosaurus* (nonserrated carinae, oval cross-section, tall straight crowns), Buffetaut and Ingavat tentatively referred this genus to the Spinosauridae. Because of the faintly compressed and nonserrated form of these teeth, Buffetaut and Ingavat postulated that they were used not for slicing, but rather piercing prey. Observing that these teeth somewhat resemble those in longirostrine crocodilians and plesiosaurs, Buffetaut and Ingavat hypothesized that *Siamosaurus* was a fish-eater, and that this diet necessitated a posture significantly atypical of theropods, one perhaps associated with the elongated neural spines of *Spinosaurus*.

Note: As the teeth are from marine beds, they may derive from a marine reptile rather than a dinosaur (R. E. Molnar, personal communication 1990).

Key reference: Buffetaut and Ingavat (1986).

SIAMOTYRANNUS Buffetaut, Suteethorn and Tong 1996

Saurischia: Theropoda: Tetanurae: Coelurosauria: Maniraptora: Arctometatarsalia: ?Tyrannosauridae.

Name derivation: "Siam [old name of Thailand]" + Greek *tyrannos* = "tyrant."

Type species: *S. isanensis* Buffetaut, Suteethorn and Tong 1996.

Other species: [None.]

Occurrence: Sao Khua Formation, Phu Wiang District, Khon Kaen Province, Thailand.

Age: Early Cretaceous (ante–Albian).

Known material/holotype: PW9-1 (collection of the Department of Mineral Resources, Bangkok), partial skeleton including left half of pelvis, the sacrum, 13 anteriormost caudal vertebrae with several chevrons, and five dorsal vertebrae.

Diagnosis of genus (as for type species): Large theropod (approximately 6.5 meters or about 22.5 feet in length); ilium long and relatively low, anterior blade forming incipient subhorizontal medioventral shelf; pubis with long, straight shaft terminating in a massive distal "boot," the latter more anteriorly than posteriorly developed; pubis without proximolateral crest; obturator foramen of pubis open ventrally, but largely encircled by bony hook; ischium slender, curved, with small but well-defined scar on its proximodorsal edge for insertion of Musculus flexor tibialis internus part 3; anterior caudal vertebrae with tall, slender neural spines; more posterior caudal vertebrae with small dorsal processes on neural arch anterior to main neural spine; anterior chevrons long, straight, slender (Buffetaut, Suteethorn and Tong 1996).

Comments: Possibly the earliest known tyrannosaurid, the genus *Siamotyrannus* was founded on a partial postcranial skeleton (PW9-1) discovered in 1993 by Somchai Triamwichanon of the Department of Mineral Resources, Bangkok, in red sandstones of the Sao Khua Formation, at fossil site Phu Wiang 9, Phu Wiang District, Khon Kaen Province, northeastern Thailand (Buffetaut *et al.,* 1996).

Buffetaut *et al.,* observed in the holotype of type species *S. isanensis* such derived features of the Tyrannosauridae (though less fully developed than in such later taxa as *Tyrannosaurus* and *Albertosaurus*) as the following: Medioventral shelf of anterior wing of ilium (absent in *Allosaurus, Sinraptor,* and other

Drawing by Halyan Tong. (After Buffetaut, Suteethorn and Tong 1996.)

Siamotyrannus isanensis, PW9-1, holotype (reconstructed), a. pelvis, sacrum, and anterior caudal vertebrae (unshaded parts restored), b. ilium (ventral view), c. sacrum (ventral view). Scale = 10 cm.

Jurassic large theropods, but well developed in Late Cretaceous tyrannosaurids); proportions of long and relatively low ilium (like those in tyrannosaurids); iliac blade (higher in allosaurids, sinraptorids, and other Jurassic theropods) showing strong reliefs, including well-marked parallel vertical ridges above acetabulum (similar ridges present in Late Cretaceous tyrannosaurids; Jurassic forms with smoother ilia); position of insertion areas for transverse processes and neural spines of sacral vertebrae in medial surface of ilium (similar to condition in *Albertosaurus* and *Tyrannosaurus*); transverse process of last dorsal vertebra fitting into depression of medial face of ilium, above subhorizontal shelf (corresponding to deep groove on ilia of Late Cretaceous tyrannosaurids); medial brevis shelf relatively narrow posteriorly (as in *Allosaurus* and tyrannosaurids); massive pubic peduncle conspicuously broadens distally (as in *Tyrannosaurus*); prominent supra-acetabular ridge (similar to ridge in later tyrannosaurids) starting from posterior part of pubic peduncle and overhanging ischiadic peduncle; pubis with massive distal "boot," mainly developed anteriorly to shaft ("boot," when present, tending to be more posteriorly developed in large Jurassic theropods); pubic shaft straight (as in *Albertosaurus*, but more slender than in later tyrannosaurids); pubes apparently meeting along part of their length distally (similar to condition in *Albertosaurus*); ischium with slender curved shaft (suggestive of Late Cretaceous tyrannosaurids, particularly *Tyrannosaurus*); well-marked oval scar for insertion of M. flexor tibialis internus part 3 on posterolateral edge of ischium, below contact with ilium (a synapomorphy of an unnamed coelurosaurian taxon comprising Tyrannosauridae and Bullatosauria); shaft of ischium bearing longitudinal ridge (as in *Albertosaurus*); sacrum with five hour-glass shaped vertebrae, with fused centra and neural spines, second and third sacrals with very narrow centra (as in *T. rex*).

The authors also observed various primitive features in this specimen not found in Late Cretaceous tyrannosaurids, including the following: Pubis with well-developed "hook" (Late Cretaceous tyrannosaurids having almost no vestige of a "hook"), which almost encloses an obturator foramen (fully enclosed foramen present in many Jurassic theropods); lack of well-defined anterolateral ridge on anteroproximal edge of pubis (for attachment of ambiens muscle); dorsal vertebrae (from middle part of dorsal series) with hourglass-shaped centra, with dorsal depression on lateral faces (but no pleurocoelic opening as in Late Cretaceous tyrannosaurids); neural spines of preserved fifth to seventh caudal vertebrae tall and slender (more suggestive of *Yangchuanosaurus* and *Allosaurus* than Late Cretaceous tyrannosaurids);

more posterior caudals having lower centra with long neural arch bearing small median spur anterior to main neural spine (condition suggestive of *Allosaurus*).

Buffetaut *et al.,* interpreted *Siamotyrannus* as belonging in the Tyrannosauridae as a primitive member of that group, predating all other known early tyrannosaurids. The authors further speculated that this family (along with such dinosaurian groups as ornithomimosaurs, ceratopsians, and ?hadrosaurs) may have evolved in Asia during a period of relative isolation, while allosaurids were the dominant large theropods in North America, spreading to that continent possibly late in the Early Cretaceous.

Key reference: Buffetaut, Suteethorn and Tong (1996).

SILVISAURUS Eaton 1960

Ornithischa: Genasauria: Thyreophora:
    Ankylosauria: Nodosauridae.

Name derivation: Latin *silva* = "forest" + Greek
    sauros = "lizard."

Type species: *S. condrayi* Eaton 1960.

Other species: [None.]

Occurrence: Dakota Formation, Kansas, United
    States.

Age: Early Cretaceous (Late Aptian–Cenomanian).

Known material/holotype: UKMNH 10296, skull
    with jaws, five cervical vertebrae, five dorsals,
    sacrum, two caudals, numerous dermal elements.

Silvisaurus condrayi,
UKMNH 10296, holotype
skull and dermal armor.

Photo by the author, courtesy University of Kansas Museum of Natural History.

Silvisaurus

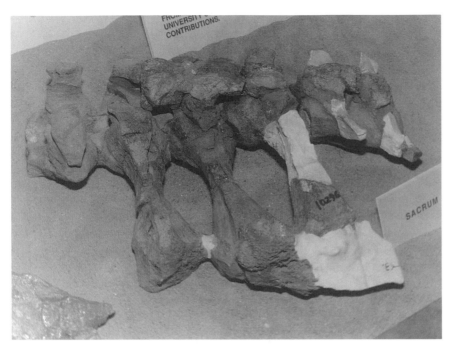

Silvisaurus condrayi,
UKMNH 10296, holotype
sacrum.

Photo by the author, courtesy University of Kansas Museum of Natural History.

Diagnosis of genus (as for type species): Skull approximately three fourths as wide as long; toothed premaxilla and infratemporal fenestra hidden below caudoventrally expanded jugal-quadratojugal-postorbital (condition unique within Nodosauridae) (Coombs and Maryańska 1990).

Comments: The genus *Silvisaurus* was established upon partial skeletal remains (UKMNH 10296) recovered from the Terra Cotta clay member of the Dakota Formation, Ottawa County, Kansas, a locality where dinosaur remains are rare. The material was discovered by Warren H. Condray on his farm, south of the town of Miltonvale. The remains had been partly exposed by a stream bed where they were damaged by stream erosion, weathering, and trampling cattle (Eaton 1960).

Eaton originally diagnosed the monotypic *S. condrayi* as follows: Skull pear-shaped, about three-fourths as wide as long, posterior margins of orbits comprising its greatest width; cranial armor without prominent processes hiding antorbital and temporal openings; pterygoids meeting quadrates, but not fusing with them; palate posteriorly with two deep, elongate clefts, where pterygoids form pair of thin-walled, pouch-like buttresses; occipital condyle slightly decurved; eight or nine bluntly conical, slightly serrate premaxillary teeth without cingulum; 17 or 18 maxillary teeth on either side, with spatulate crowns, margins with seven-nine serrations, grooves extending approximately halfway down flat lateral surfaces; about 27 mandibular teeth similar to maxillary teeth; neck comparatively long; six fused sacral vertebrae with ribs,

presacral rod with five more fused vertebrae; trunk ribs T- or L-shaped in cross-section; dermal armor in sacral region immobile; armor in dorsal region consisting of flattened polygonal or rounded plates; lateral dermal spines borne on tail and part of trunk; overall length of animal about 3.25 meters (11 feet).

According to Eaton, the polygonal and rounded plates seem to have covered the dorsal region in transverse rows. Each row was supported by a pair of dorsally flattened ribs, the areas between the rows either unarmored or bearing small ossicles. Though the preserved armor does not clearly reveal bilateral symmetry, the median scutes were probably supported by neural spines of most vertebrae. An inflexible shield may have been present over presacral and sacral regions. The (preserved) large, crested plates may have been positioned along the shoulders. The strong, curved spine may represent part of a spike in the same series. There is no evidence that the extended caudal ribs supported dermal ossifications.

Eaton noted a number of features that indicate *Silvisaurus* was rather primitive (*e.g.,* presence of premaxillary teeth, nonfusion of pterygoids with quadrates, moderately long neck, and nonfusion of trunk ribs with their corresponding vertebrae) (the latter also a function of ontogeny; W. P. Coombs, Jr., personal communication 1988). Eaton suggested that this genus might have been ancestral to *Edmontonia,* with which it was apparently closely allied (*Edmontonia* differing mostly in a heavier and broader skull, disappearance of pterygo-quadrate joint, and toothless premaxilla), and also to other Late Cretaceous North American ankylosaurs.

Also, Eaton observed close similarities between the braincase and endocranial cavity of *Silvisaurus* and *Stegosaurus,* implying that the Ankylosauria and Stegosauria could be closely related, both stemming from a common, already quadrupedal and armored, Jurassic ancestor (the idea that Stegosauria and Anklosauria share a monophyletic origin was first proposed by Huxley 1867).

Based on a study of the sinus chambers of the skull, Eaton showed that the sinuses in this genus are not simply excavations of otherwise massive bones, but almost balloon-like inflations of the thin pterygoids. These inflations probably served an important function, perhaps that of resonance. Eaton hypothesized that these chambers allowed the passage of air that amplified sound vibrations in the manner of a voice-box, maybe creating a sound of about E or F, four octaves over middle C.

Eaton postulated that *Silvisaurus* lived in a warm-to-temperate deciduous-forest environment.

Key references: Coombs and Maryańska (1990); Eaton (1960).

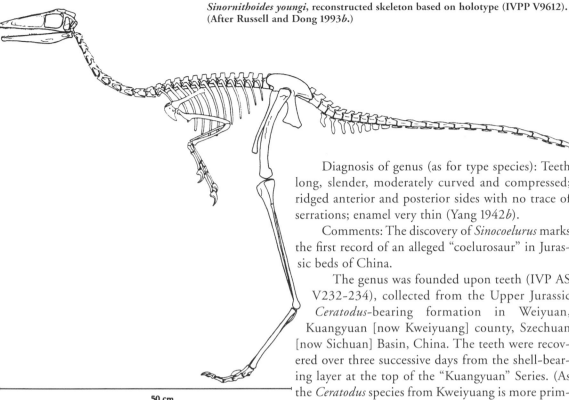

Sinornithoides youngi, reconstructed skeleton based on holotype (IVPP V9612). (After Russell and Dong 1993*b*.)

50 cm

SINOCOELURUS Yang [Young] 1942 [*nomen dubium*]

Saurischia: Theropoda *incertae sedis*.

Name derivation: Greek *Sinai* = "China" + *Coelurus*.

Type species: *S. fragilis* Yang [Young] 1942.

Other species: [None.]

Occurrence: Kyangyan Series, Sichuan, People's Republic of China.

Age: Early or Middle Jurassic.

Known material/holotype: IVP AS V232-234, four isolated teeth.

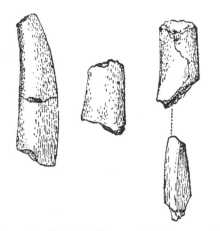

Sinocoelurus fragilis, IVP AS V232-234, holotype teeth. (After Young [Yang] 1942.)

Diagnosis of genus (as for type species): Teeth long, slender, moderately curved and compressed; ridged anterior and posterior sides with no trace of serrations; enamel very thin (Yang 1942*b*).

Comments: The discovery of *Sinocoelurus* marks the first record of an alleged "coelurosaur" in Jurassic beds of China.

The genus was founded upon teeth (IVP AS V232-234), collected from the Upper Jurassic *Ceratodus*-bearing formation in Weiyuan, Kuangyuan [now Kweiyuang] county, Szechuan [now Sichuan] Basin, China. The teeth were recovered over three successive days from the shell-bearing layer at the top of the "Kuangyuan" Series. (As the *Ceratodus* species from Kweiyuang is more primitive than those from the Upper Cretaceous of Egypt, these beds are probably Upper Jurassic.) (Yang [formerly Young] 1942*b*.)

Yang noted that these teeth differ from those of other known "coelurosaurian" genera in lacking serrations. However, *Walkeria* also has nonserrated teeth, and *Siamosaurus* has teeth of the general form of those of *Sinocoelurus* (R. E. Molnar, personal communication 1988).

Type species: *S. fragilis* Yang [Young] 1942 [*nomen dubium*].

SINORNITHOIDES Russell and Dong 1993

Saurischia: Theropoda: Tetanurae: Avetheropoda: Coelurosauria: Maniraptora: Arctometatarsalia: Bullatosauria: Troodontidae.

Name derivation: Latin *Sinae* = "China" + Greek ornithoides = "birdlike" [allusion to Chinese] *Saurornithoides*-like dinosaur].

Type species: *S. youngi* Russell and Dong 1993.

Other species: [None.]

Occurrence: Ordos Basin, Inner Mongolia, People's Republic of China.

Age: Early Cretaceous.

Known material/holotype: IVPP V9612 complete articulated skeleton with skull.

Diagnosis of genus (as for type species): Skull shorter than predicted by lengths of proximal caudal vertebrae and pedal phalanges in *Saurornithoides* by

0.7 factor; nasomaxillary suture inclined at 20-degree angle to alveolar margin of maxilla; temporal region narrower than orbit; vertical plane drawn through orbital rim of frontal intersects vertical plane drawn through midline of skull at 20-degree angle; no evidence of separate ossification lateral to frontal ("prefrontal") on orbital margin; length of tibia exceeding that of femur by 1.4 factor; tip of tongue-like posteroventral extension of distal articular surface of metatarsal III not developed; pedal specializations of *Borogovia* (hyperelongated tibiatarsus, robust digit IV, unrecurved unguals) lacking (Russell and Dong 1993*b*).

Comments: Representing the most complete troodontid specimen yet collected, *Sinornithoides* was established upon a partially eroded skeleton (IVPP V9612), discovered on August 6, 1988, during an expedition of the Sino-Canadian Dinosaur Project (see Currie 1991; Dong 1993*a*), in brick-red sandstone (containing bones of *Psittacosaurus*) west of Muhuaxiao Village, which is west of the town of Duguijiahan, near the northern plain of the Ordos, Inner Mongolia. The skeleton was found buried lying on its stomach, the skull resting on the left shoulder, tail curving to the left (following the arc of a circle with a 24-centimeter diameter, passing under the long axis of the skull, terminating off the right shoulder). Some of the skeleton's more dorsal elements (*e.g.*, right half of skull and braincase, anterior part of neck, dorsal vertebrae except for anteriormost segments, and upper part of iliac blades) had been damaged or destroyed through erosion. Associated remains include turtle and pterosaur bone, the weathered femoral shaft of a moderately large saurischian, a stegosaur tooth, and articulated *Psittacosaurus* specimens with enlarged jugal horns, the latter suggesting a possible late Early Cretaceous age (Russell and Dong 1993*b*).

Russell and Dong described the type species *Sinornithoides youngi* as a one-meter (about 3.4 feet) long theropod, distinguished by a relatively short skull, laterally directed orbital rim, and long hindlimb. In the holotype, Russell and Dong observed details of troodontid morphology previously unknown, including: Quadratic contact with the braincase wall (forming part of a channel leading to the lateral depression); presacral vertebral count possibly similar to most theropods; absence of ossified tendons in the tail; presence of a rod-like clavicle; and absence of sternal ossifications. Sutures of elements between pectoral and pelvic girdles were readily identified in the type specimen, although the degree of ossification of the skeletal parts indicate that this individual was approaching maturity when it died.

Sinosaurus triassicus, IVP AS V34, holotype ?left maxillary fragment, lateral view. (After Yang 1948.)

Sinosaurus triassicus, IVP AS V34, three holotype teeth, two views. (After Yang 1948.)

Russell and Dong noted that this dinosaur is close in morphology to the more fragmentary troodontid specimens described from the Late Cretaceous, an indication that the morphology of this line of animals remained rather stable throughout the Cretaceous.

Key reference: Russell and Dong (1993*b*).

SINOSAURUS Yang [Young] 1948 [*nomen dubium*]

Saurischia: Theropoda *incertas sedis*.

Name derivation: Greek *Sinai* = "China" + Greek *sauros* = "lizard."

Type species: *S. triassicus* Yang [Young] 1948.

Other species: [None.]

Occurrence: Dull Purplish Beds of the Lower Lufeng Series, Yunnan, People's Republic of China.

Age: Early Jurassic.

Known material: Fragmentary jaws, teeth.

Holotype: IVP AS V34, maxillary fragment with teeth.

Diagnosis of genus (as for type species): Gigantic "carnosaur" with high maxilla; teeth with long, massive roots, compressed, sharply pointed, backwardly curving, with fine serrations on anterior and posterior edges (Yang [formerly Young] 1948*a*).

Comments: The genus *Sinosaurus* was founded on a maxillary fragment with teeth (IVP AS V34), with some referred isolated teeth, from the upper Lower Lufeng Series (Hettangian-Pliensbachian) of Lufeng, China (Yang [formerly Young] 1948*a*).

Postcranial remains originally referred to *Sinosaurus* (but not found in association with the type specimen) include a number of articulated neck, dorsal, sacral, and caudal vertebrae, and fore- and hindlimbs. Walker (1948), accepting the jaw bones and teeth as theropod, pointed out that the postcranial material once considered to belong to *Sinosaurus* actually belongs to a prosauropod. Yang (1951), referring more postcranial remains to *Sinosaurus*, concluded that this genus was a carnivorous prosauropod belonging to the Melanorosauridae. Subsequent workers have published mixed opinions as to the classification of this genus. Galton (1985) noted that, if these remains do belong to a melanorosaurid, they constitute the latest known record of the family.

Simmons (1965) later described additional remains referred to the type species *S. triassicus*, including: A fragment of the anterior part of the jaws with teeth (CUP 2097); two isolated teeth; ?dorsal centrum (CUP 2095) and three tooth fragments (CUP 2096) from an unknown locality; teeth (CUP 2001 and 2002) and ?dorsal centrum (CUP 2003) from Hei Koa Peng; and teeth (CUP 2004 and 2005), cervical and two dorsal centra (CUP 2098) from Ta Ti. Simmons noted that similar materials are not known for the type; also, the referred teeth are more greatly compressed than those in known *Sinosaurus* specimens and lack serrations on the anterior trenchant edges.

Cooper (1984) observed that parts of at least nine carnivorous teeth reported by Raath (1972*a*) from Island 126/127, off Bumi Hills, Zimbabwe, in association with the holotype of the sauropod *Vulcanodon karibaensis*, are virtually identical to those of *Sinosaurus* and to other so-called "carnosaur" teeth found with melanorosaurid remains.

Galton later proposed that material assigned to *Sinosaurus triassicus* be restricted to the jaw bones and carnivorous teeth that Yang (1948, 1951) described, suggesting also that this taxon is probably not a dinosaur but rather a rauisuchian "thecodont." In his review of problematic "coelurosaurs," Norman (1990) regarded *S. triassicus* as a *nomen dubium*.

Key references: Cooper (1984); Galton (1985); Raath (1972*a*); Simmons (1965); Walker (1948); Yang [Young] (1948*a*, 1951).

SINRAPTOR Currie and Zhao 1993
Saurischia: Theropoda: Tetanurae: Avetheropoda: Allosauroidea: Sinraptoridae.
Name derivation: Latin *Sinae* = "China" + Latin *raptor* = "robber."
Type species: *S. dongi* Currie and Zhao 1993.
Other species: *S. hepingensis* (Gao 1992).
Occurrence: Sishugou Formation, Xinjiang, Upper Shaximiao Formation, Zigong, Sichuan, People's Republic of China.
Age: Late Jurassic.
Known material: Two incomplete skeletons with skulls, isolated teeth.
Holotype: IVPP 10600, almost complete skull and most of postcranium, missing most of front limbs and part of tail.

Diagnosis of genus: Total skull length and preorbital skull length relatively longer than in *Yangchuanosaurus*, but skull relatively lower; large pneumatopore in jugal; pronounced postorbital rugosity; large lateral temporal fenestra, with relatively long, straight intertemporal bar; very short lateral exposure of intertemporal process of postorbital; palatine pneumatic between internal naris and postpalatine fenestra (Currie and Zhao 1993*a*).

Diagnosis of *S. dongi*: Large theropod more than 7.2 meters long at maturity; quadratojugal process of jugal divided into three prongs; pronounced postorbital rugosity forming lateral margin of relatively large, triangular space on dorsal surface of skull; jugal

ramus of palatine extending ventrally below level of maxillary suture in a distinct process; hollow interior of ectopterygoid confluent with anteroventral pneumatic opening medial to jugal contact; exoccipitals extending ventrally below basal tubera; occipital condyle oriented posteroventrally; inflection in atlas-axis complex bringing vertebral column under back of skull more markedly than in *Yangchuanosaurus*; differs from *S. hepingensis* in having relatively lower, longer premaxilla, more numerous and elaborate accessory pneumatic openings in antorbital fossa, more limited lateral exposure of intertemporal process of postorbital, longer subtemporal bar (Currie and Zhao 1993*a*).

Diagnosis of *S. hepingensis*: Large, 8 meters (over 27 feet) long; skull large, moderately high, 1040 millimeters (3.5 feet) long, 595 millimeters (1.7) feet in height; ratio of length to height of skull (with lower jaw) about 1.75; two antorbital fenestra, first anteroposteriorly elongate and isosceles triangle in outline, second small, quadrilateral in outline; frontal and prefrontal not contributing to upper border of orbit;

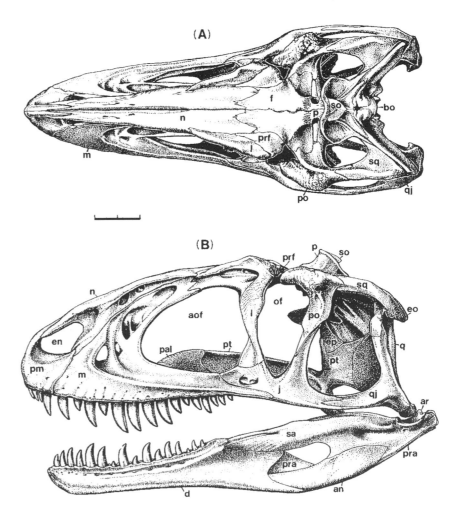

Sinrapter dongi, reconstruction of holotype skull (IVPP 10600), in A. dorsal and B. left lateral views. Scale = 10 cm. (After Currie and Zhao 1993.)

well-developed wing-like plates of parietal; supraoccipital small, narrow; dentary thick, relatively high; mandibular foramen large; teeth relatively small, maxillary teeth relatively thin; four premaxillary, 13–14 maxillary, 16 maxillary teeth; nine opisthocoelous cervical vertebrae; 14 amphiplatyan dorsals, vertebrae relatively shorter than plate-like neural spines; five sacrals, with firmly coossified centra; more than 35 caudals, distal caudals with elongate prezygapophyses; scapular shaft wide; ilium high; pubis with short, wide distal "foot"; ischium with expanded distal end (Gao 1992).

Comments: The genus *Sinraptor* was founded on a nearly complete, well-preserved skeleton with skull (IVPP 10600), discovered in 1987 during an expedition of the Sino-Canadian Dinosaur Project (see Currie 1991; Dong 1993a), in a reddish, cross-bedded, arenaceous siltstone ("interpreted as a sheetwash, ephemeral stream deposit") of the Upper Jurassic Shishugou Formation, above the contact with the Wucaiwan Formation, in the Junggar Basin, northeast of Jiangjunmiao, Xinjiang. The specimen was found lying on its right side, with the right side of the skull, the vertebrae, right hand, and right hindlimb in articulation, much of the left side of the carcass having become disarticulated before burial, teeth of the left mandible having fallen out. Material referred to the type species, *S. dongi,* and collected in 1987-88, includes nine isolated, shed teeth (IVPP collection) recovered from a sauropod (IVPP 87001) found in a quarry less than one kilometer from the holotype (Currie and Zhao 1993a).

As described by the authors, the skull measures 90 centimeters (almost 35 inches) long, with a preorbital length of 52 centimeters (about 20 inches), and height in front of the orbit of 33 centimeters (about 12.5 inches). The entire length of the animal was estimated to be 7.2 meters (about 24 feet), although incomplete fusion of various bones indi-

cates that the individual represented by IVPP 10600 was not fully mature when it died. However, the animal was near maturity, as evidenced by the sternum having been ossified into a single medial element, and the coossification of pubes and ischia.

A second species, *S. hepingensis,* was based on a skull, axial skeleton, pectoral and pelvic girdles, and left femur (ZDM 0024), from the Upper Shaximiao Formation (Upper Jurassic) of Zigong, Sichuan, this material originally described by Gao (1992) as new species *Yangchuanosaurus hepingensis.* As noted by Currie and Zhao, this species shows stronger affinities to *Sinraptor* than to either of the other described species of *Yangchuanosaurus,* although further study of the ZDM 0024 may show that *S. hepingensis* represents a distinct genus.

Comparing *Sinraptor* to other large theropods, Currie and Zhao found that this genus displays the closest similarity to the incompletely known *Yangchuanosaurus,* both genera having been found on the same continent, in beds of equivalent age with similar faunal associations. Therefore, the authors referred both *Sinraptor* and *Yangchuanosaurus* to the new group Sinraptoridae (see introductory chapter).

Currie and Zhao stated that *Sinraptor* can be distinguished from *Yangchuanosaurus* by a relatively longer, lower skull. The occipital condyle has, therefore, rotated ventroposteriorly, and the atlas-axis complex has been modified into a position as much below as behind the condyle, to support the skull better and as a means of shifting the center of gravity nearer the hips. *Sinraptor* also differs from *Yangchuanosaurus* in other features (larger lateral temporal fenestra; intertemporal prong of postorbital covered laterally by squamosal; postorbital rugosity nearly closing gap between lacrimal and postorbital; extra process of jugal contacting quadratojugal).

Note: Tanke and Currie (1995) reported cranial paleopathology consisting of healing or healed

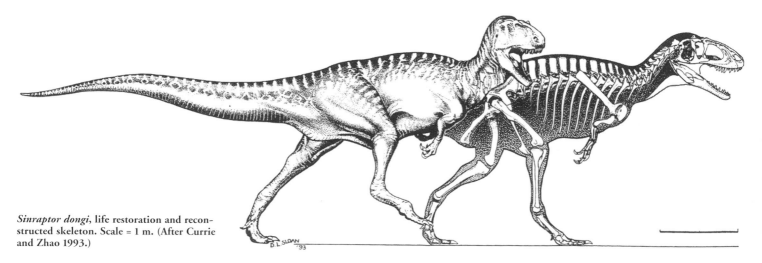

Sinraptor dongi, life restoration and reconstructed skeleton. Scale = 1 m. (After Currie and Zhao 1993.)

toothmarks in the type specimen of *S. dongi* and specimens of *Albertosaurus* sp. These marks are very similar to "alterations seen in classic toothmarked dinosaur bone, but preserve smoothed edges and new reactive bone tissue in the floor of the lesion." Tanke and Currie observed that *Sinraptor* skull elements exhibit various "gently curving tooth drags or gouges, shallow, circular punctures and one fully penetrating lesion." *Albertosaurus* wounds are mostly preserved on dentigerous elements. Generally, these injuries were "in the early stages of repair upon death of the affected individual." Tanke and Currie theorized that the wounds exhibited by these specimens could be attributed to "intraspecific biting behaviors related to territoriality, courtship, defense, feeding, or dominance determination within a grouping."

Key references: Currie and Zhao (1993*a*); Gao (1992); Tanke and Currie (1995).

SPHENOSPONDYLUS Seeley 1883 [*nomen dubium*]—(See *Iguanodon*.)
Name derivation: Greek *sphen* = "wedge" + Greek *spondylos* = "vertebra."
Type species: *S. gracilis* Lydekker 1888 [*nomen dubium*].

SPINOSAURUS Stromer 1915
Saurischia: Theropoda: ?Tetanurae: Spinosauridae.
Name derivation: Latin *spina* = "spine" + Greek *sauros* = "lizard."
Type species: *S. aegyptiacus* Stromer 1915.
Other species: [None.]
Occurrence: Baharija Formation, Marsa Matruh, Egypt.
Age: Late Cretaceous, ?Early Cenomanian.
Known material: Jaw fragments, vertebrae, hindlimb elements.
Holotype: [Formerly IPHG collection; destroyed], anterior portion of lower jaw, maxillary fragment with teeth, two incomplete cervical vertebrae, several dorsal vertebrae, approximately eight caudal centra, ?subadult.

Diagnosis of genus (as for type species): Dentary rather shallow (in preserved anterior portion), becoming higher about mid-length (suggesting that posterior portion was very deep); alveoli circular in cross-section, with no well-defined interdental plates along medial margin of alveoli; teeth straight (rather than curved), unserrated, with long roots; presacral vertebrae opisthocoelous; cervical vertebrae with unusually deep pleurocoels; dorsal vertebrae strongly compressed, 19-21 centimeters (about 7.3–more than 8 inches) long; most conspicuous are greatly elon-

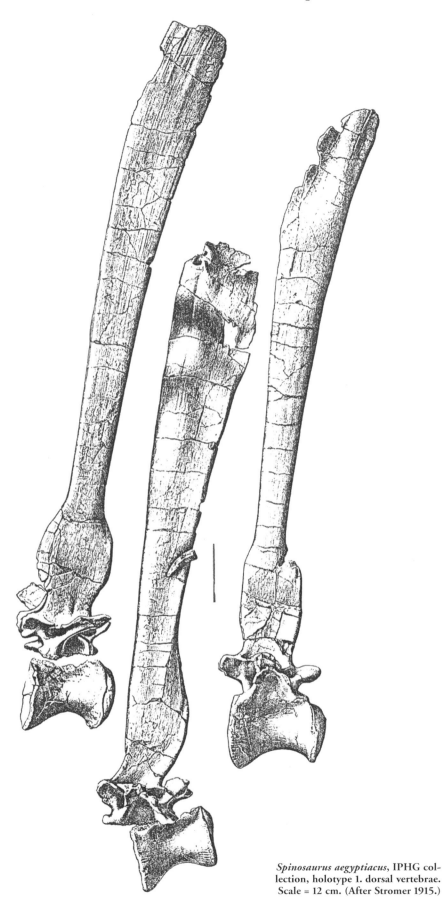

Spinosaurus aegyptiacus, IPHG collection, holotype 1. dorsal vertebrae. Scale = 12 cm. (After Stromer 1915.)

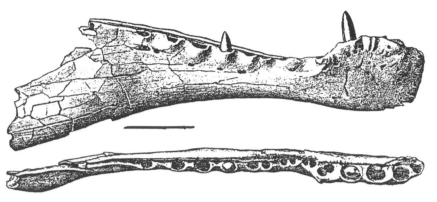

Spinosaurus aegyptiacus, IPHG collection, holotype right mandible, lateral and dorsal views. Scale = 12 cm. (After Stromer 1915.)

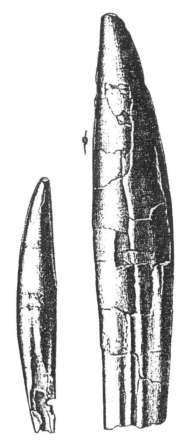

gated dorsal neural spines, (those preserved) 73, 95, 119, 130, 139, and 169 centimeters (about 11, 36.5, 45, 50, 53, and 64 inches) in length; more anterior dorsal neural spines slightly inclined forward, posterior spines backwards; sacral neural spines much shorter (Stromer 1915).

Comments: An unusual and one of the largest known theropods, *Spinosaurus* was founded upon partial cranial and postcranial remains (IPHG collection) recovered from the Baharije Formation of Baharije, Egypt (Stromer 1915). (The type material was allegedly destroyed in Munich in 1944 by a World War II American bombing raid.)

Stromer (1934) later described vertebrae, limb bones, and other fragmentary remains collected from the same formation as the holotype of *S. aegyptiacus*, referring this material to "*Spinosaurus* B," apparently representing a new species. These remains revealed that *Spinosaurus* has relatively long forelimbs and a tridactyl manus, an unusual condition for a large Late Cretaceous theropod.

Stromer (1915) used the genus as the basis for the family Spinosauridae. Walker (1964), in a study on the origin of "carnosaurs," suggested that spinosaurids might have affinities with the Tyrannosauridae as a side branch of that lineage. Kurzanov (1989), in a study on "carnosaurian" origins and evolution, noted that the splenial in *S. aegyptiacus* has an aperture as in tyrannosaurids. In a review of "Carnosauria," Molnar, Kurzanov and Dong (1990) observed that, from the known material, *S. aegyptiacus* displays but one "carnosaurian" feature, *i.e.*, deep extensor groove of femur in specimen "B." In that specimen, chevrons lack cranial processes (then considered to be a diagnostic feature of "Carnosauria"). Molnar *et al.* regarded *Spinosaurus* as possibly "carnosaurian" but not demonstrably so, perhaps derived from *Eustreptospondylus oxoniensis*, in which cranial dorsal vertebrae are also strongly opistocoelus.

Spinosaurus aegyptiacus, IPHG collection, holotype right dorsal rib. Scale = 6 cm. (After Stromer 1915.)

Huene (1932), noting that the dorsal vertebrae in *Tyrannosaurus* only measure 16 centimeters (over 6 inches) long, commented that *Spinosaurus* could have been the largest "beast of prey" that ever lived. Paul (1988*c*), in his book *Predatory Dinosaurs of the World*, regarded *Spinosaurus* as a more lightly-built, gracile animal weighing approximately 4 metric tons (about 4.5 tons), lack of fusion between upper and lower sections of the vertebrae suggesting that the type specimen belongs to an immature individual.

The most striking feature of *Spinosaurus* is the great elongation of the dorsal neural spines, which may in life supported a sail-like membrane resembling the "fin backs" of some Early Permian pelycosaurs (*e.g.*, *Dimetrodon* and *Edaphosaurus*), the function of this "sail" open to speculation (for discussions on possible thermoregulatory functions in pelycosaur dorsal sails, see Rodbard 1949, also Romer 1966). Although it could have served as an identification signal or been utilized in sexual display, it may also, according to Halstead (1975*a*), have functioned as a thermoregulatory device for controlling body temperature in a hot environment. With the body positioned so that the sail could receive the sun's rays, blood circulating through the sail would take in heat to increase body temperature. Turning its side away from the sun, the sail could dissipate heat. (*Ouranosaurus*, an ornithopod from the same age and region, evolved a similar series of less elongated neural spines, intimating parallel development resulting from climatic causes.) The interpretation of these spines as dinosaurian solar panels or radiators may suggest that not all dinosaurs were strictly endothermic.

Note: Buffetaut (1989) described an upper jaw fragment (Georg-August University at Göttingen [then Federal Republic of Germany] collection), which he referred to *Spinosaurus* sp. The specimen was found by him in May, 1988, recovered by H. Alberti from continental red beds referred to the basal Cenomanian (?Upper Albian) near Taouz, in southeastern Morocco. If correctly identified, this constitutes the largest *Spinosaurus* jaw yet collected, tooth crowns ?12 centimeters (approximately 5 inches) in height. From this specimen, Buffetaut determined that the maxilla was low and relatively long, the antorbital opening probably located far backward, jaws crocodile-like, snout rather low and long, contrary to earlier reconstructions. This interpretation suggests that such dinosaurs may have been amphibious, fish-eating animals. According to Charig and Milner (1990), this specimen could belong to a "baryonychid" instead of *Spinosaurus*.

Recently, Russell (1995a) reported the collection of additional *Spinosaurus* remains from the "Grès rouges infracénomaniens" (?Albian) of southern Morocco, this material including a relatively long-necked species, as well as isolated bones of the so-called "*Spinosaurus* B" (Stromer 1934), to be described. (As pointed out by Russell, the "Grès rouges infracénomaniens" contains evidence of one of the most diversified dinosaur assemblages known from Africa, mostly represented by theropods, including the oldest known abelisaurids, then sauropods, including the oldest known African titanosaurids, and also, though uncommonly, ornithischians.)

Key references: Buffetaut (1989); Charig and Milner (1990); Halstead (1975a); Huene (1932); Kurzanov (1989); Molnar, Kurzanov and Dong (1990); Paul (1988c); Russell (1995a); Stromer (1915, 1934); Walker (1964).

SPONDLYOSOMA Huene 1942
?Dinosauria *incertae sedis*.
Name derivation: Greek *spondylous* = "vertebral" + Greek *soma* = "body."
Type species: *S. absconditum* Huene 1942.
Other species: [None.]
Occurrence: Santa Maria Formation, Rio Grande do Sul, Brazil.

Age: Late Triassic (Carnian).
Known material: Fragmentary postcrania, teeth.
Holotype: University of Tübingen collection, two teeth, two cervical, four dorsal, and three sacral vertebrae, scapulae, proximal end of left humerus, distal end of right femur, proximal portion of right pubis.
Diagnosis of genus: [None published.]

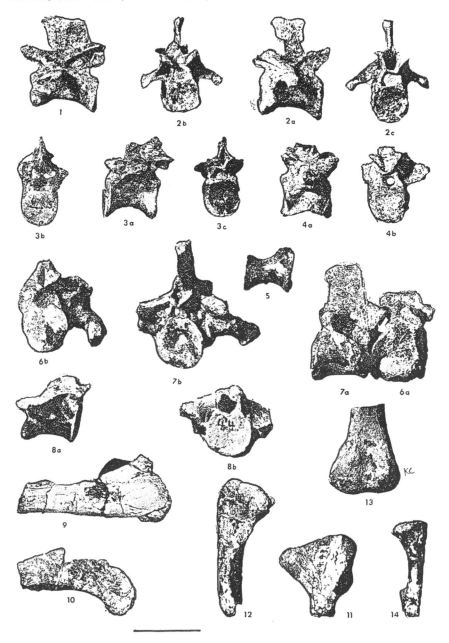

Spondlyosoma absconditum, University of Tübingen, holotype 1. cervical vertebra (lateral view), 2. cervical (a. lateral and b. anterior views), 3. dorsal vertebra (a. lateral, b. anterior, c. posterior views), 4. dorsal (a. right lateral, b. posterior views), 5. dorsal (right lateral view), 6. sacral vertebra I (a. right lateral, b. posterior views), 7. sacral II (a. right lateral, b. posterior views), 8. sacral III (a. right lateral, b. anterior views), 9. distal half of left scapula (lateral view), 10. proximal half of right scapula (lateral view), 11. proximal end of left humerus (anterior view), 12. proximal half of right pubis (medial view), 13. distal end of left femur (posterior view). Scale = 4 cm. (After Huene 1938.)

Comments: The genus *Spondlyosoma* was founded upon fragmentary cranial remains (University of Tübingen collection) retrieved from the Santa Maria Formation (Late Triassic [Carnian]; Anderson and Cruickshank 1978; Anderson 1981; Tucker and Benton 1982; Benton 1983, 1984*a*), Rio Grande do Sul, in southern Brazil. Except for one tooth and a referred vertebra (found at different localities), the material apparently belongs to a single individual. The remains, found associated with those of cynodonts and dicynodonts, were originally described by Huene (1942) as belonging to a primitive prosauropod.

Colbert (1970*b*) observed that *Spondlyosoma* differs from *Staurikosaurus* in the structure of the vertebrae. Galton also noted differences in the pubis (P. M. Galton, personal communication to Sues 1990). Galton and Cluver (1976) removed *Spondlyosoma* from the Prosauropoda and referred it to the "Thecodontia."

Sues (1990), pointing out that dinosaurian affinities of *Spondlyosoma* have yet to be determined, regarded this taxon as ?Dinosauria *incertae sedis*. Galton will redescribe the material assigned to this taxon (Galton, personal communication to Brinkman and Sues 1987 and to Sues 1990).

Key references: Brinkman and Sues (1987); Colbert (1970*b*); Galton and Cluver (1972); Huene (1942); Sues (1990).

STAURIKOSAURUS   Colbert 1970

?Dinosauria: ?Saurischia: Herrerasauridae.

Name derivation: Greek *staurikos* = "cross [Southern Cross star group]" + Greek *sauros* = "lizard."

Type species: *S. pricei* Colbert 1970.

Other species: [None.]

Occurrence: Santa Maria Formation, Rio Grande do Sul, Brazil.

Age: Late Triassic (Middle Carnian).

Known material/holotype: MCZ 1669, skeleton including lower jaws, 20 presacral, three sacral, and 35 caudal vertebrae, pelvis, hindlimbs missing feet.

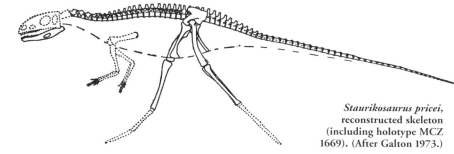

Staurikosaurus pricei, reconstructed skeleton (including holotype MCZ 1669). (After Galton 1973.)

Diagnosis of genus (as for type species): Medium-size (about 2 meters, or almost 7 feet long), bipedal, with slender limb bones; mandible almost as long as femur; dentary fairly deep, but thin, with 13–14 teeth; retroarticular process well developed; 9–10 cervical, 15 dorsal, 2 sacral, and at least 40 caudal vertebrae; cervical centra proportionately short, gently amphicoelous; marked angulation of articular faces occurring on centrum of presumed third cervical; third-fifth cervicals longest; cranial cervical vertebrae lacking epipophyses; dorsal centra slightly amphicoelous, constricted at midlength; V-shaped buttresses supporting well-developed diapophyses; dorsal neural spines short, massive; first sacral vertebra very massive; caudal vertebrae with slightly amphicoelous centra and poorly developed chevron facets; transverse processes developed up to about 20th caudal; scapular blade very slender, not expanded proximally; coracoid large, plate-like; humerus with prominent deltopectoral crest; humeral articular ends distinctly expanded; ilium distinguished from other known dinosaurs (except *Herrerasaurus*) by extensive development of medial wall of acetabulum; iliac blade short, deep, acetabular portion roofed by prominent supraacetabular rim, preacetabular portion of blade deep, postacetabular portion apparently short; pubis long, approximately two-thirds length of femur; pubes contacting each other along extensive median symphysis forming broad "apron"; distal end of pubis expanded craniocaudally; ischium broad proximally, becoming constricted distally to form narrow blade for much of its length; limb bones hollow, with fairly thick walls; femur robust, shaft S-shaped, proximal articular head set off craniomedially at distinct angle, lesser trochanter developed as slight ridge, fourth trochanter prominent, relatively near proximal end of femur, distal femoral condyles at subterminal positions; tibia and fibula slightly longer than femur; tibia robust, straight, bearing distinct cnemial crest, proximal articular end expanded craniocaudally, distal end subcircular in outline and notched for reception of central ascending process of astragalus (Sues 1990).

Comments: One of the earliest apparent dinosaurs, *Staurikosaurus* was founded on a partial skeleton (MCZ 1669) collected from the Santa Maria Formation (of Middle Carnian age; see Rogers, Swisher, Sereno, Monetta, Forster and Martínez 1993).

Colbert (1970*b*) originally referred *Staurikosaurus* to the Palaeosauriscidae [abandoned group of presumed carnivorous prosauropods], diagnosing the genus as a primitive saurischian. Bendetto (1973), emphasizing similarities between *Staurikosaurus* and *Herrerasaurus*, put both genera into the new family Herrerasauridae. Bakker and Galton (1974), com-

Staurikosaurus pricei, life restoration by Gregory S. Paul.

paring *Staurikosaurus* to the prosauropods *Anchisaurus* and *Sellosaurus* [=*Efraasia* of their usage], concluded that *Staurikosaurus* was close to basal saurischian stock and seemingly the earliest known theropod. Emphasizing differences from *Herrerasaurus* and considering *Staurikosaurus* to be sufficiently distinct to warrant its own group, Galton erected for it the family Staurikosauridae.

Reexamining the holotype and noting errors in Colbert's original description, Galton regarded *Staurikosaurus* as a carnivorous saurischian. Galton observed that, although the skull is unknown, the lower jaws indicate a relatively large head. Bakker and Galton suggested that *Staurikosaurus* was a facultatively bipedal, cursorial predator. Brinkman and Sues (1987) later postulated that *Staurikosaurus* and *Herrerasaurus* were successive sister-taxa to a clade consisting of Saurischia and Ornithischia (as defined by Gauthier and Padian), with *Staurikosaurus* the most primitive known representative of the Dinosauria. Accepting the strict definition by Gauthier and Padian of Saurischia as only including Sauropodomorpha and Theropoda, Brinkman and Sues suggested that *Staurikosaurus* and Herrerasauridae be placed within separate and higher taxa indicative of their phylogenetic positions. Later, Sues (1990) maintained that *Staurikosaurus* be separated from Saurischia (as defined by Gauthier 1986), being more primitive than saurischians in the relative elongation of third to fifth cervical vertebrae, absence of intervertebral articulations, and absence of epipophyses on cranial cervical vertebrae. Sues regarded *Staurikosaurus* as the most primitive of all dinosaurs yet

described on the basis of only two sacral vertebrae [now known also in *Herrerasaurus*] and rather circular outline of the distal articular end of the tibia.

Novas (1992) stated that both *Staurikosaurus* and *Herrerasaurus* were obligatory bipeds, measuring from 1–5 meters (about 3.4–17 feet) long, displaying an unusual mixture of both plesiomorphic characters with respect to saurischians and ornithischians, and derived features similar to those in tetanurine theropods. Based upon features found in newly collected specimens of *Herrerasaurus* (see Sereno, Novas, Arcucci and Yu 1988), Novas concluded that *Staurikosaurus* and *Herrerasaurus* uniquely share a suite of nine derived traits that support the monophyletic nature of Herrasauridae (see systematics section) and included both genera in this group. Subsequently, Sereno and Novas (1992) regarded the Herrerasauridae as a group of basal theropods (see *Herrerasaurus* entry).

More recently, Holtz (1995*a*, 1995*b*), in early reports announcing his revision (not yet published) of the Theropoda, stated that herrerasaurids are not theropods, probably not saurischians, and perhaps not dinosaurs at all.

Notes: Case (1927) described an ilium from a dinosaur closely related to *Staurikosaurus*, both, as observed by Parrish (1989), distinguished by a very short and high iliac blade, extremely short posterior blades, and a pubic peduncle that extends further ventrally than the ischiadic.

The partial postcranial skeleton (MCZ 7064) referred by Brinkman and Sues to as cf. *Staurikosaurus* was referred by Novas (1993; see also Sereno 1993; Sereno and Novas 1993) to *Herrerasaurus*.

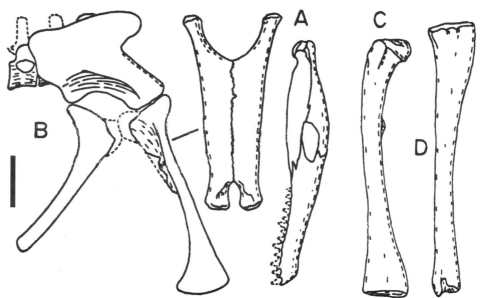

Straurikosaurus pricei, MCZ 1669, holotype A. left mandible, lateral view, B. right pelvic girdle, lateral view, with sacrum and caudal vertebra I, C. femur, anterior view, D. tibia, lateral view. Scale = 4 cm. (After Colbert 1970.)

Key references: Bakker and Galton (1974); Benedetto (1973); Brinkman and Sues (1987); Case (1927); Colbert (1970*b*); Galton (1977*a*); Holtz (1995*a*, 1995*b*); Murry and Long (1989); Novas (1992); Parrish (1989); Sereno, Monetta, Forster and Martínez (1993); Sereno and Novas (1992); Sereno, Novas, Arcucci and Yu (1988); Sues (1990).

STEGOCERAS Lambe 1902—(="*Troodon*" Gilmore 1924)
Ornithischia: Genasauria: Cerapoda:
  Marginocephalia: Pachycephalosauria:
  Pachycephalosauridae.
Name derivation: Greek *stegos* = "roofed" + Greek
  keras = "horn."
Type species: *S. validum* Lambe 1902.
Other species: *S. edmontonense* (Brown and
  Schlaikjer 1943).
Occurrence: Oldman Formation, Horseshoe
  Canyon Formation, Alberta, Canada; Dinosaur
  Park Formation, Hell Creek Formation, Mon-
  tana, United States.
Age: Late Cretaceous (Late
  Campanian–Maastrichtian).
Known material: Complete skull with associated
  partial postcrania, several dozen frontoparietal
  domes, two skull fragments.
Holotype: NMC 515, two frontoparietal fragments.
  Diagnosis of genus: Small to medium size, with
thickened frontoparietal; anteroposterior length of
dome significantly greater than transverse width;
parietosquamosal shelf well developed; supratempo-

ral fenestrae reduced; postorbital lacking prominent tubercles; diastema between premaxillary and maxillary teeth short (Sues and Galton 1987).

Diagnosis of *S. validum*: Well-developed naso-frontal boss laterally delimited on either side by groove (Sues and Galton 1987).

Diagnosis of *S. edmontonense*: Distinguished from *S. validum* by lack of pronounced nasofrontal boss (Sues and Galton 1987).

Comments: The most completely known North American pachycephalosaurid, *Stegoceras* was founded

Pachycephalosaurid frontoparietal, holotype of *Troodon bexelli*. (After Bohlin 1953.)

Stegoceras validum, UA 2, almost complete skull.

upon two well-preserved cranial-dome fragments (NMC 515) collected from the Belly River Series (now Oldman Formation) at Red Deer River, Alberta, Canada. Because of the unusual thickness of these fragments, Lambe (1902) originally believed they belonged to a ceratopsian.

In 1920, George Sternberg discovered a skull and incomplete skeleton (ROM 803) including eight caudal and two dorsal vertebrae, numerous ribs, scapula, coracoid, humerus, ulna, radius, ilium, ischium, femur, tibia, fibula, large portion of the hind foot, and many abdominal ribs. Upon these remains Gilmore (1924*a*) erected the species *Troodon validus*, incorrectly believing that the anterior teeth in this specimen were identical in form to those named *Troodon* [then *Troödon*] *formosus* [now known to be a theropod] by Leidy (1856). As more partial skulls pertaining to Sternberg's species were found during the 1930s and 1940s in Montana, Wyoming, and South Dakota, it became apparent that these thick-skulled animals represented a new genus, as well as a unique group of ornithischians.

Gilmore originally diagnosed the species as follows: Skull thickly developed in fronto-parietal area;

face short, deep; supratemporal fenestrae in process of closure, one side sometimes entirely occluded; ornamentation weakly developed, node-like; premaxilla bearing teeth.

Based on Gilmore's measurements, *S. validum* reached an approximate length of up to 2 meters (about 6.8 feet).

A second species, *S. edmontonensis* [now called *S. edmontonese*], was based upon a worn frontoparietal (NMC 8830) from the Edmonton [now Horseshoe Canyon] Formation of Alberta, originally

Stegoceras validum, NMC 515, holotype frontoparietal dome, lateral view. (After Lambe 1902.)

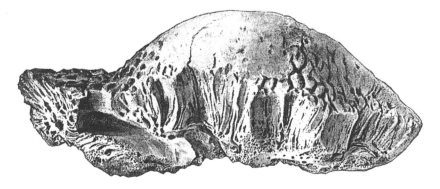

Stegoceras validum, life restoration by Brian Franczak.

Stegoceras edmontonese, NMC 8830, holotype frontoparietal dome. (After Wall and Galton 1979.)

described by Brown and Schlaikjer (1940) as *Troodon edmontonensis.*

Two other species referred to this genus, *S. breve* Lambe 1918, and *S. lambei* Sternberg 1945, the latter based on a well-preserved fronto-parietal segment from the Oldman Formation of South Saskatchewan, Alberta, have been referred to the type species.

The following indeterminate specimens were later referred to *Stegoceras* and described by Wall and Galton (1979): Dome fragment (LACM 15345) from the Hell Creek Formation of Billy Creek, Montana, one of the few specimens reported from the United States; a Hell Creek dome fragment (LACM 64000) from Garfield County, Montana; and a dome fragment (PU 21800) from the Dinosaur Park Formation, south of Chinook, Montana.

Giffin (1989*b*) discovered and collected a well-preserved dome (RTMP 87.113.3) of an adult *S. edmontonense* from the Hell Creek Formation of Carter County, Montana. The specimen, a fronto-parietal, left squamosal, and right postorbital, and with greatest length of 113 millimeters (about 4.25 inches), establishes that this species and the larger *Pachycephalosaurus wyomingensis* could exist sympatrically.

Chapman, Galton, Sepkoski and Wall (1981) performed a morphometric analysis on the cranium of various *Stegoceras* specimens in order to clarify, to an extent, the degree and nature of morphological variation and differentiation within the genus. Utilizing principal component analysis based on dimensions of the dome and braincase of 29 *Stegoceras* specimens, then bivariate methods to examine the ontogenetic basis of morphological differentiation, Chapman *et al.* concluded that the genus is fairly homogenous as a whole regarding gross cranial dimensions. Most common species *S. validum* is heterogeneous consisting of two distinct phenons [=forms]. Although both phenons have domes and braincases of similar shape, these are differentiated by their relative size. In one phenon, size disparity results from a slight increase in growth rate of the dome relative to braincase, perhaps also acquiring a comparatively thicker dome by slight increase in relative growth rate. Based on general morphological similarity, the presumed sympatry and inferred function (head-butting; see below) of the domes, Chapman *et al.* concluded that the phenons constitute a sexual dimorphism in a single species rather than representing distinct species, males identified by relatively larger and thicker domes.

C. M. Sternberg (1970) postulated that, since most *Stegoceras* specimens consist only of the dome with all edges worn smooth as if by the action of rolling down a stream, these animals may have lived in upland areas, their bones having less chance to be buried properly and preserved.

The cranial dome of *Stegoceras* and other pachycephalosaurs may have served a function in head-butting, behavior observed in some present-day animals. This idea was first postulated by Colbert (1955), who interpreted the dome as a battering ram. Galton (1971*a*), elaborating on Colbert's idea, hypothesized that male pachycephalosaurs butted heads during contests involving sexual and social dominance. Indeed, the cranial and postcranial anatomy in *Stegoceras* seemed to support this idea. The skull, thick enough to protect the brain against such clashes, is offset at an angle to the neck. Ossified tendons hold the vertebrae of the back region tightly together. Between vertebrae are specialized articulations that prevent twisting. General skeletal construction seems designed for such violent activity in which one *Stegoceras* individual might position its head face down, keeping neck, back, and tail in a horizontal line, and butt its opponent, the force of impact absorbed by the spine.

Maryańska and Osmólska (1974) agreed with the above scenario, adding that a defensive adaptation such as the dome would be essential in slow-moving animals (*i.e.*, those with femur not shorter than tibia) lacking armor, pointing out that the neck muscles in pachycephalosaurids may have been sufficiently developed to allow such butting.

Further studies regarding the functional morphology of the thickened skull roof in pachycephalosaurids were conducted by Sues (1978), whose conclusions supported the hypothesis that the dome could have served as a battering ram. Utilizing models, Sues determined that forces resulting from impacts as in head-butting could have been transmitted through the unusually well ossified braincase to the occipital condyle, then backwards over the vertebral column. Any lateral flexion of the column during force transmission would be suppressed by the odd tongue-in-groove type of interzygapophyseal articulation in the dorsal vertebrae. Sues suggested that the predominant mode of intraspecific combat was not by ramming animals during high charging velocities (as often depicted by artists), but rather by flank butting. This idea was evidenced by the somewhat thickened nasals and because the potential area for frontal contact in most pachycephalosaurid frontoparietals is slightly convex transversely, the latter indicating that self-correction for mis-aligned heads was not possible.

In a review of the Pachycephalosauria, Maryańska (1990) cited these features reflecting combat habits in pachycephalosaurians: Shortening of basicranium; rostral inclination and vertical expansion of occipital region; tongue-and-groove articulations between zygapophyses; and extremely strong medial extension of caudodorsal wall of acetabulum, for stabilizing the hindlimbs during such combat. (See *Stygimoloch* entry for a different view.)

Stegoceras validum, mounted skeletons.

Courtesy Royal Tyrrell Museum/Alberta Community Development (slide #10.019.05a).

Note: Bohlin (1953) described *Troodon bexelli*, the oldest known Asian pachycephalosaurid species, based on an incomplete and poorly-preserved fronto-parietal from the Upper Cretaceous of Tsondolein-Khuduk, Kansu, China. Bohlin distinguished this species by the outline of the parietal, which is visible in dorsal view. Also, the upper temporal vacuity, which perforates the skull roof as a narrow canal from the temporal fossa upwards and seems to be embraced by parietal processes, apparently does not reach the upper surface, implying to Bohlin that this species was more advanced than some American forms.

As noted by Sues and Galton, the precise stratigraphic age of this specimen has not yet been determined, though the horizon may be older than the Campanian Djadokhta Formation of Mongolia. Sues and Galton observed that the holotype, based on Bohlin's illustrations, differs from *Stegoceras* specimens, and that it should be regarded as an indeterminate pachycephalosaurid, *Stegoceras* apparently restricted to North America. Maryańska (1990) considered Bohlin's species to represent an as yet unnamed pachycephalosaurid genus best called "*Troodon*" *bexelli* for the present, differing significantly from other known forms in 1. its relatively extensive parietosquamosal shelf, 2. closed supratemporal fenestra, and 3. extensive participation of parietal in caudal margin of the skull.

Key references: Bohlin (1953); Brown and Schlaikjer (1943); Chapman, Galton, Sepkoski and Wall (1981); Colbert (1955); Galton (1971*a*); Giffin (1989*b*); Gilmore (1924*a*); Lambe (1902, 1918*b*); Maryańska (1990); Maryańska and Osmólska (1974); Sternberg (1945); Sues (1978); Sues and Galton (1987); Wall and Galton (1979).

STEGOPELTA   Williston, 1905—(See *Nodosaurus*.)
Name derivation: Greek *stegos* = "roofed" + Latin *pelta* = "shield."
Type species: *S. landerensis* Williston 1905.

STEGOSAURIDES   Bohlin 1953 [*nomen dubium*]
Ornithischia: Thyreophora: Ankylosauria *incertae sedis*.
Name derivation: "*Stegosaurus*" [Greek *stegos* = "roofed" + Greek *sauros* = "lizard"] + Greek *oeides* = "having the shape of."
Type species: *S. excavatus* Bohlin 1953 [*nomen dubium*].
Other species: [None.]
Occurrence: Gansu, China.
Age: Late Cretaceous.

Photo by the author, courtesy Royal Tyrrell Museum/Alberta Community Development.

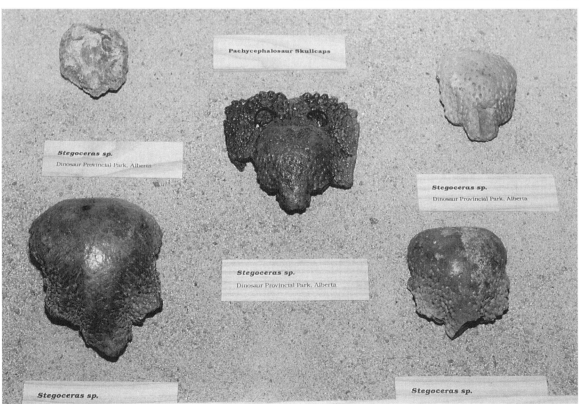

Stegoceras sp., skullcaps, dorsal view.

Known material/holotype: IVPP collection [destroyed], fragmentary remains including two vertebrae, base of dermal spine.

Diagnosis of genus: [No modern diagnosis published.]

Comments: The genus *Stegosaurides* was founded upon a very fragmentary specimen (IVPP collection) recovered from the Upper Cretaceous of Hui-Hui-P'u, in Kansu [now spelled Gansu], northwestern China. Associated with the type material were various fragmentary ribs and other bones. Bohlin (1953), interpreting the armor as of the *Stegosaurus* type, tentatively referred the material to the Stegosauridae. The type material has now "disintegrated" (IVPP, personal communication to W. P. Coombs, Jr., circa 1978).

Bohlin diagnosed the monotypic *S. excavatus* as follows: Vertebrae large, compact, almost cubical, slightly amphicoelous, square in cross-section at middle of centrum and end surfaces, with moderately wide neural canal; dermal spine with asymmetrical basal expansion, slightly convex lower surface, two deep cavities at base separated by narrow lamella, and smooth surface; spine rising from base at about 45-degree angle.

Key reference: Bohlin (1953).

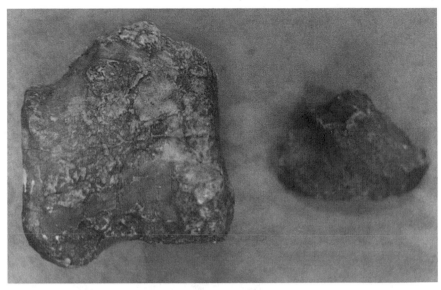

Stegosaurides excavatus, cast of former IVPP collection, holotype vertebra and fragment.

Stegosaurides excavatus, cast of former IVPP collection, holotype dermal armor.

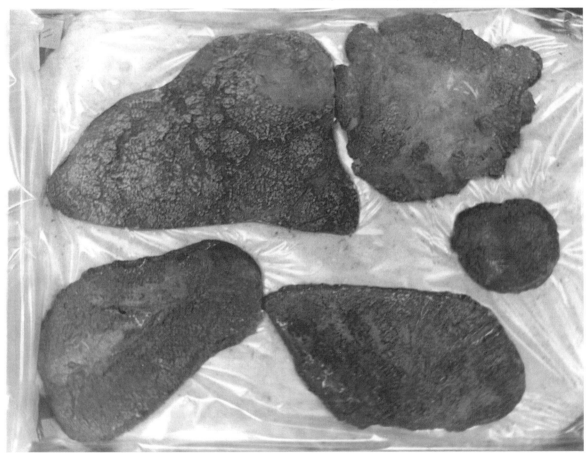

Stegosaurus armatus, referred skeleton.

STEGOSAURUS   Marsh 1877—(=*Diracodon*; =*Hypsirhophus,* in part) Ornithischia: Genasauria: Thyreophora: Stegosauria: Stegosauridae.

Name derivation: Greek *stegos* = "roofed" + Greek *sauros* = "lizard."

Type species: *S. armatus* Marsh 1877.

Other species: ?*S. ungulatus* Marsh 1879, ?*S. affinis* Marsh 1887 [*nomen dubium*], *S. stenops* Marsh 1887, *S. longispinus* Gilmore 1914.

Occurrence: Morrison Formation, Colorado, Wyoming, Utah, United States.

Age: Late Jurassic–?Early Cretaceous (Kimmeridgian–Tithonian; ?Neocomian–?Hauterivian).

Known material: Two complete skeletons with skulls, two partial skeletons, partial postcrania, at least 30 fragmentary postcrania, four braincases, juvenile to adult.

Holotype: YPM 1850, ?complete skeleton.

Diagnosis of genus: Skull characterized by large external nares, long nasals, maxillae, and vomers resulting in elongate snout, jugal with ventral process, vertical lamina lateral to tooth row extending almost to rostral end of dentary, and wide, flat parietal platform between supratemporal fenestrae; sacrum with almost solid dorsal plate; proximal caudal vertebrae with greatly expanded apex to neural spine, transverse process with prominent dorsal process; femur to humerus ratio 180 percent or more; osteoderms mostly consisting of series of thin, very large plates, about equal in length to vertical height (Galton 1990*b*).

Diagnosis of *S. armatus*: [No modern diagnosis published.]

Diagnosis of *S. stenops*: Sacral centra with decided ventral keel; sacral and proximal caudal; neural spines proportionally shorter, with transversely flat tops; middle part of tail bearing plates; two pairs of terminal tail spines (Galton 1990*b*).

Diagnosis of ?*S. ungulatus*: Characterized by broad, rounded sacral centra lacking keel, tall sacral neural spines, dorsally grooved caudals, elongate radius, ulna, and femur, middle part of tail bearing paired caudal spine-plates, four pairs of terminal tail spines (Galton 1990*b*).

Diagnosis of *S. longispinus*: Characterized by two pairs of very elongate tail spines with subequal bases (Galton 1990*b*).

Comments: *Stegosaurus*, on which both the higher taxa Stegosauridae Marsh 1888 and Stegosauria Marsh 1877 were established, is one of that relatively small number of dinosaurian genera best known to the public. Since its discovery, this fascinating animal, largest of all known stegosaurians, has been figured in virtually every popular book about dinosaurs. Its striking appearance, usually depicted in life restorations bearing two alternating rows of roughly triangular dorsal plates and four paired tail spines (or spikes), is immediately recognized by almost anyone with even a modicum of knowledge about extinct animals. Much has been made in the popular press about this dinosaur's alleged "two brains," the brain in the head celebrated as "walnut-sized."

The genus was founded on a large number of elements perhaps totaling a complete skeleton (YPM 1850), collected from the Morrison Formation at Jefferson County, Colorado. Marsh (1877*c*) proposed the name *Stegosaurus armatus* for this material, neither figuring the specimen nor diagnosing the new taxon, at the same time referring it to a new "order," Stegosauria, which also was not defined. Curiously, Marsh (1877*c*) interpreted the limb bones as indicative of an aquatic life style and envisioned *Stegosaurus* as mostly a swimmer.

Marsh (1880), for the first time, diagnosed *Stegosaurus* as follows: All bones solid; femur without third trochanter; crest on outer condyle of femur; tibia firmly coossified with proximal tarsals; fibula with larger extremity below. At the same time and without explanation, Marsh (1880) lowered Stegosauria to a suborder. Teeth described at the same time as belonging to *Stegosaurus* were later correctly identified by Marsh (1883) as those of a sauropod, *Diplodocus*.

To date of this writing, the type species *S. armatus* has not been adequately or formally diagnosed. The holotype was reserved for study by Henry Fairfield Osborn for his planned (but never written) monograph on *Stegosaurus*. As pointed out by Galton (1990*b*) in his review of the Stegosauria, except for two large dorsal plates this specimen has yet to be prepared. Thus, the question of what precisely constitutes the material upon which the genus *Stegosaurus* was founded has not yet been fully answered.

The greatest accumulation of *Stegosaurus* remains was yielded by Quarry 13 in Albany County, near Como Bluff, Wyoming, worked under Marsh's direction by William H. Reed and his team of excavators between 1879 and 1887. More remains were excavated under Marsh by Samuel Wendell Williston between 1877 and 1882, from Quarry 1, at Fremont County, northeast of Canon City, Colorado. The finest *Stegosaurus* specimen ever discovered and described, the holotype of the species *S. stenops* (USNM 4934), was collected from this quarry by M. P. Felch during 1885 and 1886. This remarkable specimen, a so-called "roadkill" representing a medium-sized adult individual, includes the skull (the first and, for more than a century, the only three-dimensional skull known from this genus) and lacks the greater portion of the posterior half of the tail, hindfeet, and some minor elements. The skeleton was

Stegosaurus stenops, USNM 4934, holotype skeleton, exhibited as found in so-called "roadkill" position.

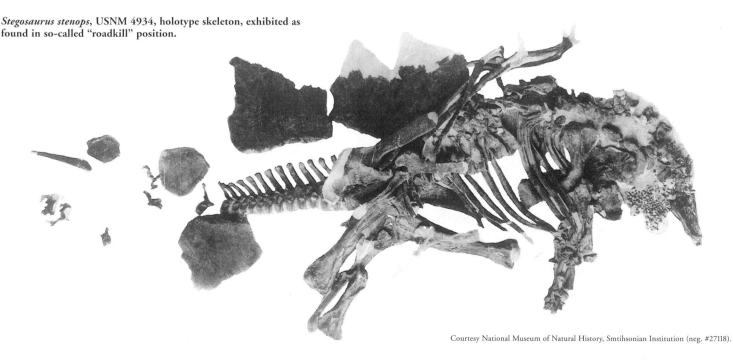

Courtesy National Museum of Natural History, Smtihsonian Institution (neg. #27118).

preserved with vertebral column mostly intact and articulated. Retained *in situ* in their mutual relationships are the animal's dermal plates. The specimen is but slightly disturbed, suggesting that the animal died a natural death. This skeleton was first described, though not in great detail, by Marsh (1887*b*).

In his monograph on armored dinosaurs in the United States National Museum [now National Museum of Natural History], where USNM 4934 is displayed, Gilmore (1914*b*) published a complete description of *S. stenops*. At the same time, Gilmore deduced that the animal must have perished in the water or along the bank of a stream, after which its carcass was swept downstream to become stranded on a river bar, where decomposition and finally fossilization occurred.

The large, robust species *S. ungulatus* was based on various specimens (YPM 1853-1858) described briefly (mostly in pertinent dimensions of various elements) by Marsh (1879*b*), who believed this species might someday prove to be generically distinct from *S. armatus*. Galton agreed that these two forms could be conspecific, although a synonymy should not be made until the type material of *S. armatus* can be sufficiently described. The skeleton of *S. ungulatus*

on display at the Peabody Museum is a composite. Gilmore noted that the unusually long femora give the mounted skeleton added height in the hip region. The mounting also makes the animal appear to be somewhat short. The skeleton, as mounted, measures about 5.8 meters (almost 19.6 feet) long and about 3.5 meters (almost 12 feet) high at the top of the uppermost plate.

Marsh (1887*b*) briefly described two additional large species:

S. duplex was based on a specimen (YPM 1858) comprising the posterior half of a skeleton with no plates or spikes preserved, originally referred to *S. ungulatus*. Lull (1910*b*) later identified the *S. duplex* remains as one of the cotype specimens of *S. ungulatus*.

S. sulcatus was based on four dermal spines, one nuchal dermal plate, one mid-dorsal dermal plate, right humerus, right ulna, radii, forefeet, portions of scapulae, parts of femora, fibula, ischium, and caudal vertebrae, this material collected in 1883 by J. L. Kenney from Quarry 13, Como Bluff, Wyoming. Marsh (1887*b*) then believed that only one pair of spines was present in the type specimen of this species, although Gilmore, in assembling the entire holotype, found the usual two. Marsh (1887*b*)

Stegosaurus stenops, USNM 1851, distal end of tail. (More recently discovered specimens indicate that the spikes were directed off to the sides of the tail.)

Courtesy National Museum of Natural History, Smithsonian Institution (neg. #24559).

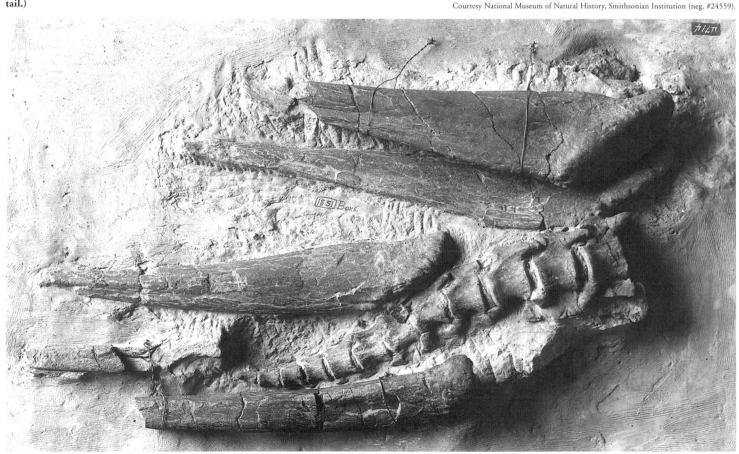

Stegosaurus stenops,
composite skeleton.

observed that the *S. sulcatus* spines were more massive than any yet found. Gilmore observed that the *S. sulcatus* holotype actually represented a quite large and very old individual of *S. ungulatus*. Galton regarded both *S. sulcatus* and *S. duplex* as junior synonyms of *S. armatus*.

The species *S. longispinus* Gilmore 1914 was based on a specimen (UW D54) consisting of 42 vertebrae of all kinds, fragmentary sacrum, several ribs, and four dermal spines (subsequently lost), collected in 1908 by W. H. Reed and A. C. Dart from the Mor-

rison Formation, about 1.5 miles east of Alcova, Natrona County, Wyoming. ?*S. affinis* Marsh 1881 is a somewhat smaller species and, according to Gilmore, inadequately defined. Galton regarded this species as a *nomen dubium*.

Regarding genera now regarded as junior synonyms of *Stegosaurus*, *Hypsirophus* was founded on numerous dorsal and caudal vertebrae (AMNH 5731), some of which actually pertained to the theropod *Allosaurus*. Cope (1878*d*) briefly described the type species, *H. discursus* [*nomen dubium*], then (1879)

Stegosaurus stenops, life restoration by Gregory S. Paul.

second species *H. seelyanus*. Later workers, including Marsh, referred the nontheropod material to *Stegosaurus*. Galton tentatively considered this stegosaurian material as belonging in *S. armatus*.

Diracodon laticeps was based on two imperfect maxillae (YPM 1885) described by Marsh (1881c). All *Diracodon* material comes from Quarry 13, including referred specimens of several individuals. Gilmore noted that the differences between *Diracodon* and *Stegosaurus* are really age features. As caudal vertebrae and spines originally referred to *D. laticeps* are of the same shape and size as those of *Stegosaurus*, Gilmore referred them to *S. stenops*. Bakker (1986) revived the idea that *Stegosaurus* and *Diracodon* are generically distinct, *Stegosaurus* (represented by *S. ungulatus*) having smaller plates and either four or eight tail spikes, *Diracodon* (by *S. stenops*) having

much larger plates and four spikes. This splitting of the two genera has not been generally accepted; *Diracodon* was listed as distinct by Olshevsky (1991), although Galton (1990b) retained *D. laticeps* as a junior synonym of *S. stenops*.

Gilmore authored the first comprehensive osteology of *Stegosaurus*, following studies already performed by Lucas and Lull. Not privy to the type specimen of *S. armatus* housed at the Peabody Museum of Natural History, Gilmore, of necessity, based his work upon the specimens from the two Albany County and Fremont County quarries in the United States National Museum collections, particularly USNM 4934. Other specimens included a complete skull and jaws (USNM 4934), occiput, braincase, and other elements (USNM 6645) referred to *S. stenops*; posterior portion of a skull (USNM 2274) referred to *S. stenops*?; disarticulated skull and portions of lower jaw (USNM 4935), and fragmentary skull with portions of lower jaw (USNM 7637), designated *Stegosaurus* sp.; and the posterior half of a skull (USNM 4936) referred to *S. armatus*. Gilmore observed that the neural spines have distinctly bifurcated summits in the mid-caudal region, this condition present until the 25th or 26th caudal.

The *Stegosaurus* "exoskeleton" (as Gilmore called it) primarily consists of ossicles, plates, and spike-like spines. Gilmore described in detail the osteoderms covering the neck and perhaps the head as small, flattened, angularly rounded, and of irregular sizes, largest about 35 millimeters in diameter. Most of these structures have one flattened side with a sculptured surface. Rugose dermal ossicles (found near or attached to various vertebrae in USNM 4934, but not in other *Stegosaurus* specimens) were also found.

The plates borne on the neck are small, thin and vertically elongate just behind the skull, gradually becoming taller posteriorly. They are flattened only on the external side and slightly convex on the other. Their bases are rugose with an abrupt transverse constriction about 40 millimeters above the basal end (apparently indicating the depth that the plates were imbedded in the skin). There are five nuchal plates in USNM 4934, these wider only in very old individuals.

Succeeding the nuchal plates are larger, more or less oval-shaped plates. These increase rapidly in size and have asymmetrical, transversely expanded bases. These also have a flattened external side and slightly convex interior side. Next are two or more plates of subrectangular outline, rugose bases, showing but slight transverse thickening. There is no apparent differentiation in these plates between exterior and

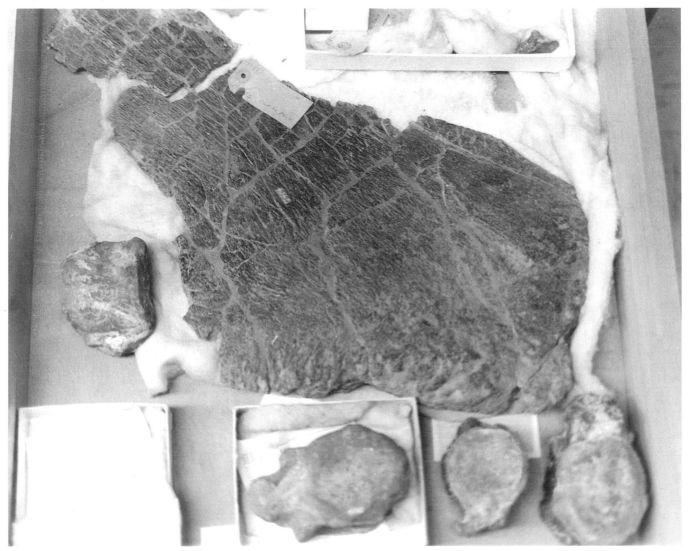

Stegosaurus ungulatus, USNM 7417, plate and vertebral centra, cotype with YPM 1853–1858.

interior surfaces. (Among all the many *Stegosaurus* specimens retrieved from the Cleveland-Lloyd Dinosaur Quarry, within the Brushy Basin member of the Morrison Formation in northeastern Utah, no two corresponding "mirror image" plates nor symmetrical plates have yet been found; J. H. Madsen, Jr., personal communication, 1988.)

Gilmore described the tail spines from a *S. stenops* specimen (USNM 4714) consisting of an articulated series of 44 caudal vertebrae, with the plates of one row and spines preserved in sequential position. The largest plate specimen occupies the same position as the corresponding plate in the *S. stenops* holotype, marking its placement above the base of the tail. Following this plate are three plates of diminishing size. The most distal set of caudal plates are sharp-edged and overhanging. Accounting for interspaces between the plates required for movement of the tail, Gilmore calculated that the remaining articulated caudal vertebrae (to the point where spines begin) could only accommodate three plates, six for both rows, the total number of plates being 20. All plates are marked by vascular grooves.

Marsh (1896) calculated that tail spines ranged in from two to three to four pairs. Lankster (1905), in his book *Extinct Animals*, published without evidence a life restoration of *Stegosaurus* bearing ten spines. Gilmore concluded that, with the possible exception of the species *S. ungulatus*, there are four tail spines, this total based on six specimens in the National Museum collection, particularly USNM 4714 and a tail section (USNM 4288), originally referred by Marsh to *Diracodon laticeps* [see below], with caudals and spikes found in their natural position *in situ*.

Gilmore observed that tail spines vary in size and shape with the individual animal. In all spines examined, the surface of the oblique end is dorsoventrally concave and the base oblique. Bases are very rugose in adults but not so in young individuals. Spines usually taper gradually from base to apex. Their external surfaces are covered with vascular impressions. From evidence exhibited by the two articulated tail specimens, plus 30 spikes representing 10 individuals, Gilmore concluded that anterior spines are always larger than posterior ones and that the anterior pair were more deeply imbedded in the skin. The bases of the posterior pair correspond to the seventh, eighth and ninth caudal vertebrae counting back from the tip of the tail, the anterior pair to the 12th, 13th, and caudals. As shown by the holotype of *S. sulcatus* (USNM 4937), the anterior spines are joined by cartilage at the rugose surface of their bases so that they are directed away from one another to form a widely obtuse angle. This is corroborated in *S. stenops* specimen USNM 4288, in which the distal pair of spines are posteriorly directed.

For more than a century, the position and arrangement of the plates has remained controversial. In making the first pictorial reconstruction of the *Stegosaurus* skeleton, Marsh (1891*a*) arranged the plates in a single row along the median line of the neck, back, and tail. However, this arrangement would have impaired the animal's movement, the plates touching one another as the back and tail articulated. Marsh (1896) subsequently altered this arrangement slightly, pairing the plates on the neck behind the head.

In his book *Animals of the Past*, Lucas (1901*a*) arranged the plates in two paired rows, although in a

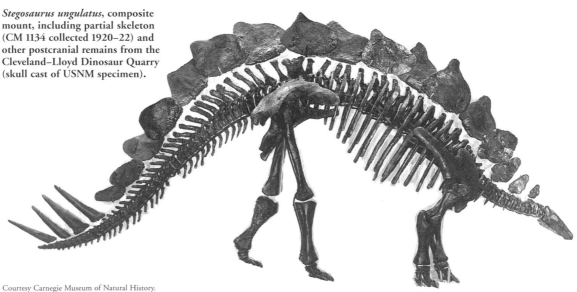

Stegosaurus ungulatus, composite mount, including partial skeleton (CM 1134 collected 1920–22) and other postcranial remains from the Cleveland–Lloyd Dinosaur Quarry (skull cast of USNM specimen).

Courtesy Carnegie Museum of Natural History.

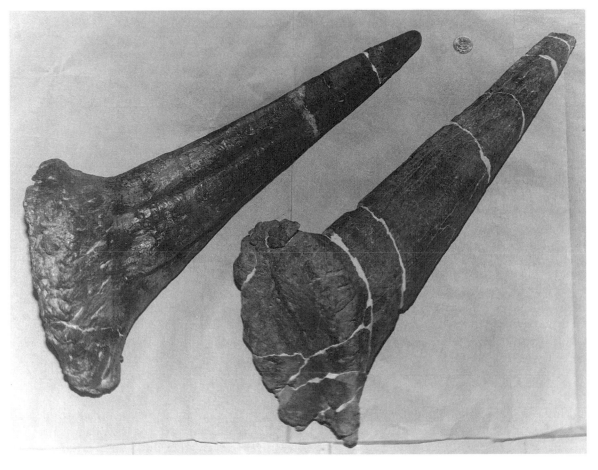

Stegosaurus armatus, USNM, holotype tail spines of *S. sulcatus*.

Photo by the author, courtesy National Museum of Natural History, Smithsonian Institution.

later restoration changed them to a probable alternating position. Gilmore related that Lucas, in an unpublished manuscript, had changed his opinion based upon the excellent holotype of *S. stenops*, the only then known specimen of *Stegosaurus* to indicate the apparent placement the plates had in life.

The 11 preserved plates in this specimen, after becoming dislodged from the skin, had turned back in under the body and neck to form a continuous bony sheet. The three large plates over and posterior to the hip region occupy the same relative positions they had in life, with their bases over their respective neural spines. Lucas confirmed that the plates in this specimen alternated as they lay embedded in the rock matrix and that no two of them are exactly alike in size or shape. Gilmore, agreeing with Lucas, also observed that the asymmetrical dorsal plates would have been inclined slightly outward from the perpendicular when in the skin.

Lull (1910*c*), of the opinion that the plates in USNM 4934 had shifted forward or backward during decomposition or in movement of the rock, mounted the composite skeleton of *S. ungulatus* (including holotype material of this species and also *S. duplex*) at the Peabody Museum with paired plates. Gilmore considered this possibility, then pointed out

that, though some of the plates had fallen to the left and lie beneath the animal, while the posterior plates are approximately in position above the pelvis, all show the same alternating arrangement. Also, plates of one row overlap uniformly with those of the opposite row, the middle point of the underlying plates about in the center of the interspace between the upper plates. The plates must have remained imbedded in the skin until they assumed the position they have in USNM 4934. If shifting had occurred, consistently aligning the plates as they are would have been virtually impossible, the smaller plates having to move but a few inches, the larger at least a foot. There is no evidence, either in skeleton or matrix, that the rock had shifted. Gilmore concluded that the plate arrangement indicated by this specimen was an accurate representation of the position these structures had during life.

Because of the evenness of the bases of the plates anterior to the hips, Gilmore located the two rows fairly close to the midline. If in USNM 4934 there had been a greater space between them as they folded back during decomposition, the bases of one row's plates would project beyond the other's at about equal to the space between the bases during life. USNM 4934 also reveals that the expanded bases of nuchal

Stegosaurus

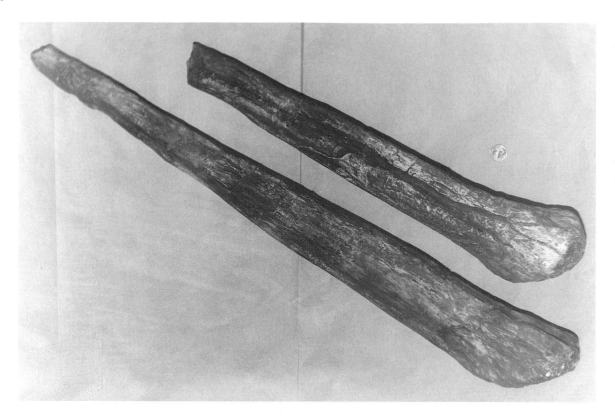

and anterior dorsal plates apparently overlapped the median line of the back, those of one row occupying the interspace of those in the opposing row, so that these plates were very little off the midline. Gilmore favored an erect rather than procumbent position for the plates, pointing out that both surfaces are covered with blood vessels and show no indication of being in contact with the animal's flesh. The extremely rugose bases show an adaptation for insertion into the skin, while in USNM 4934 the plates in the pelvic region were preserved in an erect position.

Gilmore's interpretation of *Stegosaurus* with double rows of alternating plates became generally accepted, although recently there have been detractors.

Czerkas (1987), in the book *Dinosaurs Past and Present*, presented an interpretation of plate arrangement that, in some ways, harkened back to the second depiction proposed by Marsh (1896). Czerkas argued that the plates should be arranged in two closely set alternating rows along the neck, shoulder, and mid-dorsal regions, and in a single row along the remaining dorsal region and down the tail to within proximity of the first pair of spikes. Czerkas posited that the 17 plates in *S. stenops* comprise the entire series; that Marsh (1896) was essentially correct in his single-row arrangement; that Lucas erred in his suggestion of double rows; and that both Lull and Gilmore, following Lucas, incorrectly prompted a misconception that has persisted to this day in our understanding of *Stegosaurus* and of all other known

stegosaurian genera. Galton acknowledged the possibility of Czerkas' interpretation and figured the skeletal reconstruction thusly in his review of the Stegosauria. However, Czerkas' reconstruction allows less room for movement of the animal's back and tail, and may restrict growth of the plates during life, especially if augmented in surface area by horn-like coverings (see Marsh 1896; also, see below).

Additional support for the traditional double-row/alternating plate arrangement surfaced with the discovery, by Donna McKowen in 1978, of an undescribed small, articulated *Stegosaurus* skeleton in the Morrison Formation near Jensen, Utah, south of Dinosaur National Monument, during a field trip of the Vernal Field House of Natural History. Two dermal plates in this specimen were preserved in an overlapping and staggered arrangement.

Yet more recently, another as yet undescribed specimen, an almost complete, articulated "roadkill" skeleton of *S. stenops*, missing parts of the appendicular skeleton, was found by Bryan Small, in the Morrison Formation near Cañon City, Colorado, about 1.25 kilometers northeast of the quarry that yielded the original "roadkill" specimen. Most of the plates were found *in situ*. In a preliminary report, Carpenter and Small (1993) showed that the plates were found basically supporting Gilmore's traditional two-row, alternating arrangement. According to Carpenter and Small, the anteroposterior length of the plate bases extend over several vertebrae, which would have restricted the amount of lateral movement of body and tail, this movement further limited by the alternating plate arrangement. Results of experiments indicated that the plates did not diverge from above the neural spines, but were offset laterally; and that movement would be maximized if the plates were imbedded in a thick skin, the skin able to slide over the muscles (as in crocodiles). Maximum motion would have occurred in the neck, where the plate bases are narrow, and near the end of the tail, just anterior to the first pair of tail spikes; the least amount of side-to-side movement would have been possible at the base of the tail, where the largest and longest plate was present. Carpenter and Small also reported the presence of small keeled discs (measuring 2–5 centimeters across), which were found scattered over the hips and thighs of this specimen.

The function of the plates of *Stegosaurus* has long been a topic for speculation. Marsh (1896) believed the plates served as protective armor and were protected in life by a horny covering, which would have augmented their size and weight. Gilmore subscribed to this idea, not taking into account that, except for the dorsal region, most of the animal's body would have remained unprotected. Also, Gilmore speculated that the plates would have augmented the animal's outline, making it appear larger. Davitashvili (1961) proposed that the plates may have served as sexual-display structures. Returning to the armor notion, Halstead (1975), in the book *The Evolution and Ecology of Dinosaurs*, brought the plates down to a recumbent position lying flat on each side of the backbone, reasoning that thusly oriented they would afford more protection. Continuing the idea that the plates were horn-covered and served as armor, Bakker (1986), in his book *The Dinosaur Heresies*, suggested that muscles in the skin may have given *Stegosaurus* the ability to raise and lower its plates, thereby shielding its hide from attacking predators.

A provocative explanation, departing dramatically from earlier and more conservative theories, was offered by Farlow, Thompson and Rosner (1976).

Skeleton (DINO 2438; originally DNM 2438-2455, 2463-2467, 2474-2547) of juvenile *Stegosaurus* on exhibit at Dinosaur National Monument.

A Rare Specimen

Dissecting a *Stegosaurus* plate, Farlow *et al.* found it not to be solid bone, as expected of armored plating, but honeycombed with foramen that could have housed blood vessels. Blood within the plates suggested that they may have served a heat regulatory function. To test this hypothesis, Farlow *et al.* conducted wind tunnel experiments on finned models in conjunction with internal heat conduction calculations and direct observations of the morphology and internal structure of the plates. Results showed that the plates of *Stegosaurus*, if arranged in two alternating rows, are ideally shaped to dissipate efficiently heat for cooling the animal; acting as solar panels, the plates could also absorb heat from the sun for body warmth. By regulating the flow of blood through its plates, *Stegosaurus* could maintain control over its own body temperature.

Buffrénil, Farlow and Ricqlés (1986) performed further histological examinations of plates, discovering that plate growth proceeded mainly from the basal region, which was firmly imbedded in the animal's thick hide. The plate was held in a more or less erect position by connective fibers, some directly incorporated into the woven bone fabric of the base. Although some workers have maintained that the plates were once covered by horny sheaths (Marsh 1896; Gilmore 1914; Paul 1987), Buffrénil *et al.* found no evidence of such coverings, which, as in certain living animals, should have been deposited in a succession of thick sheets leaving imprints. The network of grooves on the plates could be interpreted as traces of a vascular system in a thin dermis entirely covering each plate (see Galton). Within the plate is a thin wall of incompletely remodeled bone, surrounding a large spongy area containing some large bony "pipes" that probably contained blood vessels. Buffrénil *et al.* found no other direct evidence in the plate interior for an extensive blood vessel system. Their conclusion was that the proposed heat exchange system in *Stegosaurus* was more the role of the skin than the plate itself.

In evaluating various hypotheses attempting to explain plate function, Buffrénil *et al.* rejected ideas that the plates could change their orientation from recumbent to erect or that they served as armor.

Agreeing that the plates could have had more than one function, Buffrénil *et al.* accepted that they were used in display and for enhancement and modification of the animal's size and shape, but maintained that the main function was as part of a thermoregulatory system. As noted by Buffrénil *et al.*, if the plates did regulate temperature, another question is raised regarding dinosaur body heat and metabolism in general. A heat-regulating function is more likely for an ectothermic animal, although this would

not be impossible for an endotherm, suggesting that dinosaurs like *Stegosaurus* were not true endotherms, but, as proposed by Ricqlés (1983) in regards sauropods, mass homeotherms or "incipient endotherms."

Much has been written about the tiny size of the *Stegosaurus* brain, which Marsh (1896) considered to be relatively one of the smallest brains of any known land vertebrate. Certainly its brain seems to have been relatively smaller than in other dinosaurs. According to Gilmore, a cast of the cranial cavity reveals that the small cerebral hemispheres have a transverse diameter just slightly in excess of the medulla oblongata, and that the cerebellum is also quite small, though the optic lobes are strikingly large. Lull estimated the weight of the *Stegosaurus* brain to be about 70 grams (2.5 ounces), cerebrum barely more than one-third the brain's entire weight. By comparison, a modern elephant, an animal smaller than *Stegosaurus*, has a brain approximately 50 times heavier. Lull pointed out that, in addition to the optic lobes, the olfactory portion of the brain is quite large, indicating that the animal's senses of sight and smell were probably well developed.

It was once believed that *Stegosaurus*, to compensate for small brain size, utilized two supposed enlargements (the so-called extra "brains" often referred to in popular books) of its spinal cord, especially in the sacral region, where nerves of the hind legs and tail allegedly met in a network over 20 times more massive than the brain itself. Lull proposed that these perceived enlargements could unburden the brain by assuming control over various body parts. The brachial enlargement supposedly controlled the innervation of the front limbs, the sacral enlargement being the reflex and coordinating center to control the muscles of the huge hindlimbs and powerful spiked tail.

More recently, Giffin (1993) examined the possible causes of extreme sacral neural canal enlargements in stegosaurs (also sauropods) and rejected the notion that such enlargements provided neural supply to the hindquarters. Giffin related the enlargements to the presence of an avian-style glycogen body having a possible role in the synthesis of myelin (a fatty material that forms the medullary sheath of nerve fibres) and to the typical avian enlargement of the neural canal that surrounds the glycogen body. Giffin also showed that such sacral enlargements are restricted to large animals, in which there is a maximal need of enhanced speed of nerve conduction, a function of myelin.

There is little doubt that the spiked tail was utilized as a defensive weapon, swung by powerful tail muscles to lash with deadly impact upon attacking predators like *Allosaurus* and *Ceratosaurus*. Conjuring

Marlene Campnell and assistant uncovering *Stegosaurus* remains in Grand Junction, Colorado.

up hypothetical Late Jurassic scenarios, Gilmore recalled three specimens in which these spines had been injured in life. Two spikes were broken off and had healed; the third (USNM 6646), suffering a different kind of injury, had become curved and thickened in its healing. Gilmore did not believe that the spikes were used as weapons, suggesting that the tail was not constructed to afford the flexibility required to swing it effectively against an active foe.

Contra Gilmore, Bakker argued that the tail's lack of ossified tendons, supple joints of the caudal vertebrae, and atypically strong most distal caudals were all clear adaptations for tail-swinging. According to Bakker, *Stegosaurus* possessed muscle power sufficient to swing its tail, armed with spikes made even longer by horny covering, with enough force to kill even the largest carnivores of its day.

Galton proposed that the tail spines in all stegosaurians were probably used in defense, given the orientation of the spines, and that the animal most likely used the tail with back toward its attacker in the fashion of a modern porcupine.

The adult *Stegosaurus* reached an average length of 7.4 meters (25 feet). Colbert (1962) estimated the weight of the living animal as 1.78 metric tons (1.96 tons), based on the mounted skeleton displayed at the American Museum of Natural History, and on the amount of water displaced by an immersed scale model. Bakker (1987), in *Dinosaurs Past and Present*, estimated the weight of the individual represented by USNM 4934 *S. stenops* as about 2.9 metric tons (3.3 tons) and YPM 1888-1887 *S. ungulatus* about 3.4 metric tons (3.8 tons). Other calculations show that *S. stenops* weighed from about 2.12–3.5 metric tons

Stegosaurus

?Stegosaurid ilium (UVP 5697) from Cleveland-Lloyd Dinosaur Quarry.

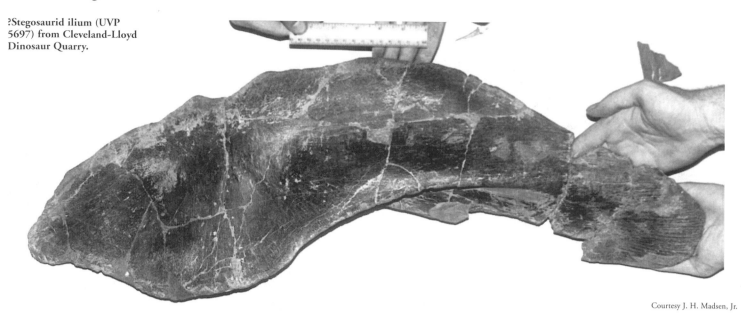

Courtesy J. H. Madsen, Jr.

(over 2.2–nearly 4 tons) (G. S. Paul, personal communication 1988).

Obviously, *Stegosaurus* was not capable of rapid locomotion, the femur being so much longer than the tibia, hindlimb considerably longer than forelimb, both limbs designed for supporting great weight. Early restorations tended to depict the animal with frontlimbs splayed out in lizard fashion, bringing an exaggerated downward slope to the front part of the body, head necessarily low to the ground. This interpretation led to the assumption that *Stegosaurus* was an awkward, ungainly low cropper that fed on cycads, ferns, and other vegetation close to the ground.

Bakker (1986, 1987) resurrected the idea, popular in the late nineteenth century, that *Stegosaurus* could assume a bipedal stance, arguing that the front limbs should not be splayed out, as in most *Stegosaurus* museum mounts, but more or less upright. With this posture, the back does not slope forward but levels off. Vertebral spines at the hips would supply leverage to muscles and ligaments of the back. The large bony flanges at the base of the tail would anchor powerful muscles to brace the body against the ground; chevrons would brace the animal's weight. These adaptations, with the relatively short forelimbs and strength of the hindlimbs, would allow the dinosaur to swing up to rest against its tail in a tripodal stance. Bakker (1986, 1987) concluded that *Stegosaurus* was, in fact, an efficiently designed high feeder. According to Sues (personal communication), however, orientation of the delto-pectoral crest in *Stegosaurus* precludes an entirely upright posture of the front limbs. Regarding feeding habits, Weishampel (1984*b*) suggested that stegosaurs were browsers

that ate foliage, the fleshy parts of bennettitalian inflorescenes, and also the fructiications of the Nilssoniales and Caytoniales plant groups.

Remains of juvenile *Stegosaurus* individuals are rare in the fossil record. The partial skeleton of a juvenile *Stegosaurus* can be seen on display at Dinosaur National Monument, Utah, photographs of which have been published by Hagood (1971) and McIntosh (1977). (Isolated bones of juvenile *Stegosaurus* individuals have been collected from Dinosaur National Monument and Como Bluff.) Galton (1982*b*) described remains of the juvenile, referred to *Stegosaurus* sp., extracted from the lower bone level at the western end of the Monument quarry face by Jim Adams. Although each element was given its own catalogue number (DNM 2438-2443, 2447-2449, 2453, 2455, 2463-2467, 2474, 2544-2547), Galton (1982*b*) preferred to refer to them collectively (as DINO 2438) as all bones are from the same individual. No dermal plates or tail spines were found with these remains.

Based primarily upon the above remains, Galton (1982*b*) observed numerous growth differences between the postcranial elements of juvenile, subadult, and adult *Stegosaurus* individuals, including: 1. Nonfusion of vertebral centrum and neural arch in juveniles, and of sacral ribs to vertebrae and ilium in juveniles and subadults (fused in adults); 2. nonfusion of scapula and coracoid in juveniles (fused in some large individuals; see Gilmore); 3. proportionally more slender and elongate scapulae in juveniles; 4. long bones with smooth surfaces in juveniles (surface markings and irregular and rugose articular ends in subadults and adults); 5. less prominent triceps ridge, supinator ridge and posterior intercondylar groove on humeri of juveniles; 6. small olecranon process of ulna in juveniles (enormous in adults); 7. carpus consisting of four irregularly shaped bones (radiale, intermedium, ulnare, and pisiform) in subadults (two massive block-like bones representing radiale and fused intermedium-ulnarepisiform in adults); 8. much less massive metacarpals in subadults; 9. widest part of first manual ungual phalanx about one-third down from proximal articular end in subadults (at proximal end in adults, just the central part being articular); 10. anterior process of pubis more bar-shaped in juveniles (relatively more expanded vertically and compressed transversely in adults); 11. femur with less spherical head less clearly demarcated from adjacent part of shaft; lesser trochanter a distinct, anteroposteriorly flattened, finger-like process in all but largest femora; shaft lacking longitudinal ossified chords in juveniles (prominent in subadults and adults; Ostrom and McIntosh); 12. distal ends of tibia and fibula not fused to each other or to astragalus in juveniles or subadults (Gilmore), but fused in adults; 13. proximomedial surface of fibula in juveniles that contacts tibia is flat (longitudinally concave in subadults and adults); and, 14. posterodistal surface of fibula merging with shaft in juveniles (demarcated by an obliquely inclined edge against which tibia fitted in subadults and adults).

During the mid–1980s, an incomplete skeleton of *Stegosaurus* (MWC 0081), perhaps representing *S. stenops*, was discovered by Harold Bollan in the Rabbit Valley area along the northern flank of the Uncompahgre Plateau, north of the Colorado River, western Colorado. The specimen, now on display at the Dinosaur Valley exhibit of the Museum of Western Colorado, Grand Junction, includes an articulated forelimb (from scapula to manus) that shows front legs apparently held rather close to body but bent back at the elbow (as in some mammals), two large different-sized plates found *in situ* with lateral edges overlapping, skin patches represented by dermal ossicles, and four tail spines articulated with bases against each other. A fifth tail spine was found near the four articulated spines, suggesting that either this individual bore more than the conventional four spines, or that another *Stegosaurus* individual was present at this site. No other material belonging to an alleged second individual has yet been found (Armstrong, Averett, Averett, McReynolds and Wolny 1987).

Stegosaurus is also known from the Dry Mesa Quarry (Morrison Formation, Upper Jurassic [Tithonian] or Lower Cretaceous [Neocomian or Hauterivian]; see Britt 1991), near the southwest corner of Dry Mesa, west central Colorado.

Stegosaurus is the official state fossil of Colorado.

Notes: Location of the tail spines in USNM 4937 was questioned by Bakker (1988), who interpreted the curvature of their bases as too gentle to fit around the distal tail. Bakker stated that the curvature is, however, wide enough to have fit over the shoulder or at the base of the neck, as in the very large shoulder spines of *Kentrosaurus* and some other stegosaurians, which have expanded bases and seem to have been located in that same area.

Madsen (1976*b*) mentioned an unidentified ankylosaurid from the Cleveland-Lloyd Dinosaur Quarry, based on a supposedly diagnostic ilium (UVP 5697). The specimen may actually pertain to an unusual stegosaur with an ankylosaur-like ilium.

Lucas (1902) made *S. marshi* Lucas 1901 [*nomen dubium*] the type species of the ankylosaurian *Hoplitosaurus*. Hoffstetter (1957) referred *S. priscus* Nopcsa 1911 [*nomen dubium*] to *Lexovisaurus durobrivensis*. *S. madagascariensis* Piviteau 1926 [*nomen dubium*] was shown by Sues (1980) to be nonstegosaurian, probably referrable to the pachycephalosaurid *Majungatholus atopus*.

Key references: Armstrong, Averett, Averett, McReynolds and Wolny (1987); Bakker (1986, 1987, 1988); Buffrénil, Farlow and Ricqlés (1986); Carpenter and Small (1993); Colbert (1962); Cope (1878*d*, 1879); Czerkas (1987); Davittasvili (1961); Farlow, Thompson and Rosner (1976); Galton (1982*b*, 1990*b*); Gilmore (1914*b*); Hagood (1971); Halstead (1975); Lankster (1905); Lucas (1901*a*); Lull (1910*c*); Marsh (1877*b*, 1877*c*, 1879*b*, 1887*b*, 1880, 1881*c*, 1891*a*, 1896); McIntosh (1977); Ostrom and McIntosh (1966); Paul (1987); Steel (1969); Weishampel (1984*b*).

STENONYCHOSAURUS   Sternberg 1932—(See *Troodon*.)
Name derivation: Greek *stenos* = "narrow" + Greek *onychos* = "claw" + Greek *sauros* = "lizard."
Type species: *S. inequalis* Sternberg 1932.

STENOPELIX   Meyer 1857
Ornithischia: Genasauria: Cerapoda: Marginocephalia.
Name derivation: Greek *stenos* = "narrow" + Greek *pelex* = "helmet."
Type species: *S. valdensis* Meyer 1857.
Other species: [None.]
Occurrence: Obernkirchen Sandstein, Niedersachsen, Germany.
Age: Early Cretaceous (Berriasian).
Known material/holotype: GPI 741-2, skeleton including vertebrae (with most caudals), incomplete pelvic girdle, left hindlimb.

Stenopelix

Stenopelix valdensis, GPI 741-2, holotype skeleton. (After Sues and Galton 1982.)

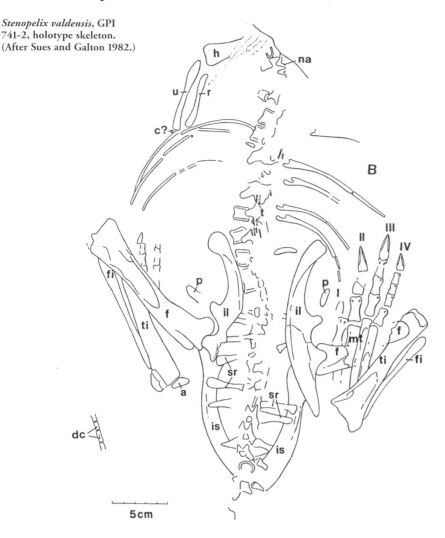

Diagnosis of genus: Humerus with radial condyle smaller than ulnar condyle; ulna with moderately developed olecranon process; pelvis with distinctively long and low ilium, preacetabular process longer than postacetabular; ischium anteroventrally curved, with thickened posterior margin and flattened, blade-like distal portion; lesser trochanter of femur offset from greater trochanter; tibia shorter than femur, with markedly expanded proximal end; fibula thin, slender, shorter than tibia, with sharp medial edge; metatarsals slender, closely applied to one another, III longest and most robust, IV slightly longer than II, I short, phalangeal formula 2-3-4-5-0; ossins (misidentified by Koken 1887 as gastralia) extending horizontally and rather parallel to neural spines; apparently more than six sacral vertebrae; proximal caudal vertebrae apparently with short neural spines and centra about high as long (Sues and Galton 1982).

Diagnosis of *S. valdensis*: Characterized by shortness of tibia relative to femur, and structure of pelvic girdle (Sues and Galton 1982).

Comments: The most completely known dinosaur from the German Wealden, *Stenopelix* was established on an incomplete postcranial skeleton discovered in 1877 in a quarry at Haarl, near Bückeburg (Westphalia), in northwestern [formerly Federal Republic of] Germany. The bones are represented by natural molds in two sandstone slabs. The specimen was originally housed in the Gymnasium Adolfinum at Bückeburg, but has since been transferred to the Geologisch-Paläontogisches Institut of the Georg-August-Universität, Göttingen, cataloged GPI Gö Orig. Nr. 741.

Originally, *Stenopelix* was described by Meyer (1857), who was unable to assign the genus to any particular reptilian group. Huxley (1870*a*), noting that Meyer had misidentified the anterior prolongations of the ilia as pubes, postulated that the affinities of *Stenopelix* were with the ornithischian, *Hypsilophodon*. Koken (1887), recognizing that *Stenopelix* was a dinosaur, considered that it might belong to the Saurischia, but was unable to classify the genus further. Romer (1956) included *Stenopelix* in the Psittacosauridae, after which Maryańska and Osmólska (1974) regarded it as a pachycephalosaurid on the basis of pelvic structure and strong caudal ribs. Galton (*see in* Wall and Galton 1979) announced that he and Sues, after examining latex casts of the holotype, concluded that *Stenopelix* was not a pachycephalosaurid.

According to Sues and Galton (1982), the pelvic structure in *Stenopelix*, especially in form of the ilium and reduced pelvis, conforms to that in the Ceratopsia. *Stenopelix* resembles Psittacosauridae in possession of a low, long ilium with a downward, rather expanded preacetabular region, and resembles Protoceratopsidae in the anteroventral curvature of the ilium. *Stenopelix* differs from both of these taxa in having femur longer than tibia. As the *Stenopelix* holotype lacks any synapomorphies (particularly in regards the skull), Sues and Galton regarded this genus as Ceratopsia *incertae sedis*, noting that it is the first Eurasian record of Ceratopsia, and probably the stratigraphically oldest ceratopsian known thus far.

More recently, the genus was rejected from both the Pachycephalosauria (see Maryańska 1990) and Ceratopsia (Sereno 1990). Dodson (1990*b*) observed that *S. valdensis* exhibits aspects of both Pachycephalosauria and Ceratopsia, but does not seem to belong to either group. According to Dodson, *Stenopelix* may best be regarded as a basal marginocephalian, the sister-taxon of both Pachycephalosauria and Ceratopsia.

Key references: Dodson (1990*b*); Huxley (1870*a*); Koken (1887); Maryańska (1990); Maryańska and Osmólska (1974); Meyer (1857); Sereno (1990); Sues and Galton (1982); Wall and Galton (1979).

STENOTHOLUS Giffin, Gabriel and Johnson 1987—(See *Stygimoloch.*)

Name derivation: Greek *steno* = "narrow" + Greek *tholus* = "dome."

Type species: *S. kohlerorum* Giffin, Gabriel and Johnson 1987.

STEPHANOSAURUS Lambe 1902 [*nomen dubium*]—(See *Lambeosaurus.*)

Name derivation: "Steveville [Ferry, in Alberta]" + Greek *sauros* = "lizard."

Type species: *S. marginatus* Lambe 1902 [*nomen dubium*].

STEREOCEPHALUS Lambe 1902—(Preoccupied, Arribalzaga 1884; see *Euoplocephalus.*)

Name derivation: Greek *stereos* = "solid" + Greek *kephale* = "head."

Type species: *S. tutus* Lambe 1902.

STERRHOLOPHUS Marsh 1891—(See *Triceratops.*)

Name derivation: Greek *sterros* = "solid" + Greek *lophos* = "crest."

Type species: *S. flabellatus* Marsh 1891.

STOKESOSAURUS Madsen 1974

Saurischia: Theropoda: Tetanurae *incertae sedis.*

Name derivation: "[William Lee] Stokes" + Greek *sauros* = "lizard."

Type species: *S. clevelandi* Madsen 1974.

Other species: [None.]

Occurrence: Morrison Formation, Utah, United States.

Age: Late Jurassic–?Early Cretaceous (Kimmeridgian–Tithonian; ?Neocomian–?Hauterivian).

Known material: Ilia, premaxilla.

Holotype: UUVP 2938, left ilium.

Diagnosis of genus (as for type species): Relatively small theropod, with maximum adult length of no more than 4 meters (about 13.5 feet); ilium with distinct median vertical ridge that bridges hood of acetabulum with dorsal margin of the blade; blade extremely thin on either side (Madsen 1974).

Comments: The genus *Stokesosaurus* was founded on a left ilium (UUVP 2938) collected from the Cleveland-Lloyd Quarry, Brushy Basin Member of the Morrison Formation (Stokes 1952), in east central Utah. Referred to *S. clevelandi* was a right ilium (UUVP 2320) 150 percent the size of the holotype, and also a right premaxilla (UUVP 2999).

As measured and described by Madsen (1974), the ilium is 22 centimeters (about 8.4 inches) long and an estimated 11 centimeters (about 4.4 inches) deep, so thin that, posterior to the median ridge, not all of the specimen was preserved. In gross form, the ilium resembles that of a juvenile *Allosaurus* and the tyrannosaurids *Albertosaurus sarcophagus*, *Daspletosaurus torosus*, and *Tyrannosaurus rex*.

The referred premaxilla, morphologically similar to that of *Ceratosaurus*, is unusual in that its length is relatively short (32 millimeters or about 1.3 inches), only about half its depth (60 millimeters or about 2.3 inches), suggesting to Madsen that the snout was

Stokesosaurus clevelandi, UUVP 2938, holotype left ilium. (After Madsen 1974.)

extremely short. Only the second tooth is preserved; it is sub-cylindrical, with serrations on the anterior edge. There are four premaxillary alveoli, which are rounded as in *Allosaurus*. (According to Madsen's 1971 collection notes, the premaxilla was associated with the *Stokesosaurus* material because it did not seem to belong to anything else; R. E. Molnar, personal communication 1987.)

Madsen observed that *Stokesosaurus* differs from such Morrison theropods as *Allosaurus* and *Ceratosaurus* in the structure of the ilium, but displays features suggesting affinities with tyrannosaurids. The median vertical ridge of the ilium, unique among Morrison Formation theropods (though not among all Jurassic ones; see *Iliosuchus* entry, and Galton and Jensen 1979), could foreshadow the rounded vertical ridge (described by Russell 1972) that separates the anterior and posterior heads of the ilio-femoralis in tyrannosaurids. As the four premaxillary teeth in *Stokesosaurus* compare in number to *Daspletosaurus* and *Albertosaurus*, Madsen provisionally assigned *Stokesosaurus* to the Tyrannosauridae as the earliest known tyrannosaurid.

Britt (1991) tentatively referred to *Stokesosaurus* three nonallosaurid, nonceratosaurid caudal vertebrae (BYUVP 5073, 5203, and 8908), apparently from the same individual, recovered from the Dry Mesa Quarry (Morrison Formation, Upper Jurassic [Tithonian] or Lower Cretaceous, [Neocomian or Hauterivian]), near the southwest corner of Dry Mesa, in west central Colorado. Britt noted that this material could also belong to *Marshosaurus* or represent a new genus. If pertaining to either *Stokesosaurus* or *Marshosaurus*, these remains constitute the first specimens attributed to those genera found outside of their type locality.

Key references: Britt (1991); Madsen (1974).

Stokesosaurus clevelandi, UUVP 2999, right premaxilla, medial and lateral views. (After Madsen 1974.)

STRENUSAURUS Bonaparte 1969—(See *Riojasaurus*.)

Name derivation: Latin *strenuus* = "quick" + Greek *sauros* = "lizard."

Type species: *S. procerus* Bonaparte 1969.

STREPTOSPONDYLUS Owen 1842—(Preoccupied, Meyer 1830; see *Eustreptospondylus*.)

Name derivation: Greek *streptos* = "pliant" + Greek *spondylos* = "vertebrae."

Type species: *S. cuvieri* Owen 1842.

STRUTHIOMIMUS Osborn 1917—
(=?*Ornithomimus*)

Saurischia: Theropoda: Tetanurae: Avetheropoda: Coelurosauria: Maniraptora: Arctometatarsalia: Bullatosauria: Ornithomimosauria: Ornithomimidae.

Name derivation: Latin *struthio* = "ostrich" + Greek *mimos* = "mimic."

Type species: *S. altus* (Lambe 1902).

Other species: [None.]

Occurrence: Oldman Formation, Dinosaur Park Formation, Horseshoe Canyon Formation, Alberta, Canada.

Age: Late Cretaceous (Late Campanian).

Known material: Skull and postcrania, two partial skulls with associated fragmentary postcrania, eight incomplete postcrania.

Holotype: NMC 930, distal ends of pubes and ischia, right hindlimb, phalanges of left pes.

Diagnosis of genus (as for type species): Presacral vertebral column longer than hindlimb; scapula longer than humerus; antebrachium robust; radius connecting to ulna by syndesmosis; manus large, powerful, equal in length to humerus, over 70 percent length of femur; metacarpal I shortest and, for more than two-thirds its length, closely applied to II; metacarpal I diverging from rest of metacarpus distally; metacarpals II and III of equal length, digit I shorter than remaining digits, which are of subequal length; unguals very long (about 27 percent length of manus) and, compared to other ornithomimid species, more robust and curved, with well-developed flexor tubercles; second and third pedal unguals longer than respective penultimate phalanges; extensive proximal contact of second and fourth metatarsals on extensor face of metatarsus (Barsbold and Osmólska 1990).

Comments: The most well-known "ostrich dinosaur," *Struthiomimus* was founded upon an incomplete postcranial skeleton (NMC 930), col-

Struthiomimus altus, AMNH 5337, referred skeleton.

lected from member B of the Belly River Series (now Oldman Formation), at Berry Creek, Red Deer River (probably near what is now Dinosaur Provincial Park), in Alberta, Canada. This material was originally described by Lambe (1902) as a species of *Ornithomimus*, which he named *O. altus* (the

Struthiomimus

From *Living with Dinosaurs*, published by Bradbury Press.

Struthiomimus altus, life restoration by Doug Henderson.

holotype of which has become irreparably damaged and is virtually indeterminable; see D. A. Russell 1972, in his review of "ostrich dinosaurs" of Canada).

Since the discovery of this specimen, much well-preserved material pertaining to this species has been collected, particularly an excellent skeleton (AMNH 5339) found during an American Museum of Natural History expedition led by Barnum Brown in the Dinosaur Park Formation, basin of Little Sandhill Creek, Dinosaur Provincial Park. This specimen (mounted at the American Museum), missing only the skull roof and distal end of the tail, remains the most complete and best preserved ornithomimid skeleton ever found in North America.

Osborn (1917) referred this skeleton to *O. altus*; but as AMNH 5339 possessed a rudimentary metatarsal V (lacking in the more derived *Ornithomimus*), Osborn reassigned the specimen to a new genus, *Struthiomimus*.

Originally, Osborn diagnosed *Struthiomimus* as follows: Skull relatively small and edentulous; manus with three fingers of equal length, with elongate and slightly recurved terminal phalanges, first and second metacarpals incipiently coalescent, pollex phalanges separate and divergent; pes with four digits of unequal length, metatarsals II-IV incipiently coalescent, V reduced, digit III relatively elongate.

Osborn speculated that *Struthiomimus* represents a stage of ornithomimid evolution corresponding with the "Judith River" or "Belly River" formation, "*Monoclonius-Ceratops* zone."

Gilmore (1920), finding the grounds for which Osborn separated *Struthiomimus* from *Ornithomimus* insufficient, referred *Struthiomimus* back to *Ornithomimus*, this synonymy having persisted in the literature, as well as popular books, for many years. Russell, however, argued that both forms can be easily separated (see *Ornithomimus* entry).

Judging from specimen AMNH 5339, *Struthiomimus* was an ornithomimid of medium size, measuring about 3-4 meters (10-13 feet) long and about 2.35 meters (8 feet) tall.

As the forelimbs of *Struthiomimus* are reminiscent of those of sloths, Gregory (*see in* Osborn 1917) theorized that this dinosaur may have used them to dig for insects. Osborn, however, found the forelimbs too weak to perform such a task and suggested that *Struthiomimus* was herbivorous, browsing for vegetation, its hands used to bend down branches. Gregory more generalized the dinosaur's diet, suggesting that the animal was an omnivore, subsisting on small vertebrates and larger invertebrates as well as fruits and seeds. Russell later speculated that *Struthiomimus* and other ornithomimids were strictly carnivorous (see *Ornithomimus* entry).

The first complete description of the pectoral girdle and forelimb of *S. altus* was published by Nichols and A. P. Russell (1985), based on an incomplete skeleton including limbs, girdles, gastralia, and fragments of ribs and vertebral column (left forelimb and pectoral girdle completely articulated) from the Oldman Formation of southern Alberta. Nichols and Russell concluded that, based on the structure of the pectoral girdle and forearm, *Struthiomimus* utilized its manus as a hooking and clamping (rather than raking or grasping) device.

The anatomy of *Struthiomimus* suggests that this was a cursorial dinosaur. The stiff tail counterbalanced the body (reduced wings do the same for the ostrich) and stabilized the animal when running and changing direction. Russell, noting the relatively shorter presacral vertebrae, suggested that *Struthiomimus* was less cursorial than either *Ornithomimus* or *Dromiceiomimus*.

Notes: An ungual (NMC 9819), resembling manual digit I of *Struthiomimus*, was collected from the Frenchman Formation of Saskatchewan, Canada, and may, according to Russell, be referrable to that genus.

S. brevetertius Parks 1926 and *S. samueli* Parks 1928 were referred by Russell to the genus *Dromiceiomimus*; *S. currelli* to *O. edmontonicus*.

Key references: Barsbold and Osmólska (1990); Lambe (1902); Nichols and Russell (1985); Osborn (1917); Russell (1972).

STRUTHIOSAURUS Bunzel 1871 [*nomen dubium*] — (Note: "*Struthiosaurus*" [see "notes" below] = *Hoplosaurus*; =?*Crataeomus*, ?*Danubiosaurus*, ?*Leipsanosaurus*, ?*Pleuropeltus*, ?*Rhodanosaurus*)

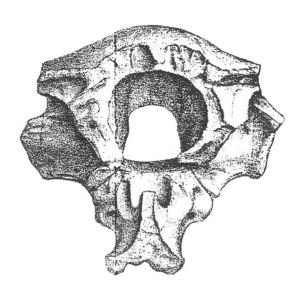

Struthiosaurus austriacus, GIUV collection, holotype fragmentary basicranium. (After Bunzel 1871.)

Ornithischia: Genasauria: Thyreophora: Ankylosauria: Nodosauridae.

Name derivation: Latin *struthio* = "ostrich" + Greek *sauros* = "lizard."

Type species: *S. austriacus* Bunzel 1871 [*nomen dubium*].

Other species: [None; see note below.]

Occurrence: Gosau Formation, Niederöstereich, Austria.

Age: Late Cretaceous (Campanian–Maastrichtian).

Known material: Fragmentary crania, armor.

Holotype: GIUV collection, braincase, caudal scutes.

Diagnosis of genus (as for type species): basisphenoid ventrally projected; cervical vertebrae very elongate; scapula with hook-like acromial; armor distinctive armor (Pereda-Suberbiola and Galton 1992).

Comments: A rather conservative nodosaurid and the smallest known ankylosaur (3 meters or about 10 feet long), *Struthiosaurus* was founded upon the posterior half of a skull and some caudal scutes (GIUV collection), collected from the Gosau Formation, at Niederöstereich, Austria.

Bunzel (1871) originally diagnosed the genus (and type species) as follows: Cranium with somewhat bird-like construction; basicranium completely ossified, rather broad, convex, mildly arched and smooth, no indication of sculpturing.

In their review of the Ankylosauria, Coombs and Maryańska (1990) suggested that the holotype of *S. austriacus* may actually be saurischian because of the saurischian-like feature of a large ventrally projecting basisphenoid, and regarded it as Saurischia *incertae sedis*; in their "carnosaur" review, same volume, Molnar, Kurzanov and Dong (1990) regarded this taxon as "Carnosauria *nomina dubia*."

More recently, Pereda-Suberbolia and Galton (1992) identified the holotype skull as nodosaurid, based on the possession of the following diagnostic characters: Presence of dermal armor co-ossified with skull roof; cranial sutures mostly obliterated; hemispherical occipital condyle formed exclusively by basioccipital, separated from braincase by a distinct neck; paroccipital processes posteroventrally directed, visible in dorsal view; basipterygoid processes rugose.

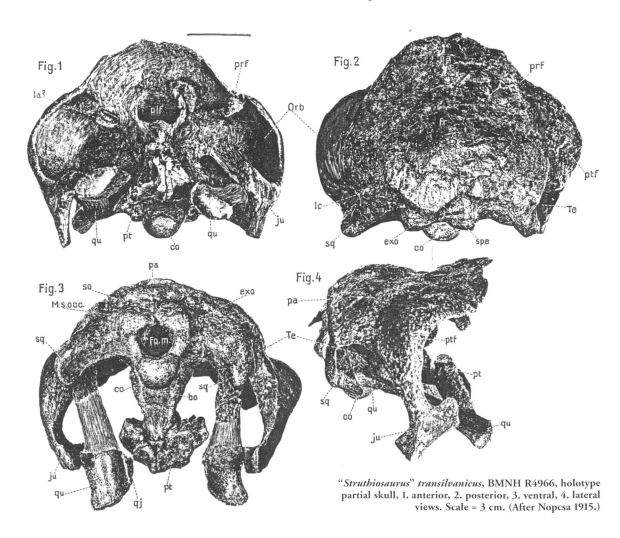

"*Struthiosaurus*" *transilvanicus*, BMNH R4966, holotype partial skull, 1. anterior, 2. posterior, 3. ventral, 4. lateral views. Scale = 3 cm. (After Nopcsa 1915.)

Nopcsa (1923) noted the relatively small size of Transylvanian dinosaurs like *Struthiosaurus*, suggesting that they were probably affected by territorial restrictions, as were mammals of Mediterranean islands during the terminal Tertiary and Quaternary eras. Pereda-Suberbiola (1993), however, pointed out that large dinosaurs have been found in Transylvania, including sauropods exceeding 10 meters (about 35 feet) in length (Le Loeuff, personal communication to Pereda-Suberbiola). Pereda-Suberbiola speculated that the "dwarfism" of Late Cretaceous Transylvanian nodosaurids like *Struthiosaurus* (as well as an unnamed nodosaurid known from disarticulated cranial and postcranial elements [MCNA L.1.A.10-16, T4, L.1.B.10, 18, 91, 102-8] from the Early Maastrichtian, Basque-Cantabric Basin, La`no locality, Trevi`no county, Spain; Pereda-Suberbiola, in press) could be the result of a process of adaptation to an insular environment, with insular nodosaurids possibly having a physiology different from that of their larger relatives. According to Farlow (1987), interspecific differences in body size could correlate with differences in diet and physiology among herbivorous dinosaurs. Pereda-Suberbiola, following Farlow, added that dwarf European nodosaurids may have had a higher metabolism than the larger North American nodosaurids, with also significantly different habitats and behavior.

Notes: A referred species, "*S.*" *transilvanicus*, was based on the posterior portion of the skull, an atlas, dorsal vertebra, caudal vertebra, caudal centrum, nearly complete rib, right scapula, portion of humerus, and various indeterminate fragments (BMNH R4966) from the "Danian" [=Maastrichtian], south of the village of Hateg, Hateg Basin, Judetul Hunedoara, Transylvania, Hungary [now in Romania]. The material was described by Nopcsa (1915), who observed that the skull lacked the linear markings present in the type species. Later, Nopcsa (1929b) published an hypothetical life restoration of this species with a rather birdlike head and a body resembling that of *Hylaeosaurus*.

Nopcsa (1929b) diagnosed this species as follows: Skull small, showing series of linear markings; orbit circular, anterolaterally directed; quadrate slender, inclined forwards, with small articular surface; teeth relatively small, long, laterally compressed, divided into many lobes; mandibular aveolae of sigmoid shape; atlas with "quasicentrum"; cervical vertebrae low, broad; dorsal vertebrae slightly platycoelous; haemopophyses in distal caudals tending to fuse with centrum of preceding vertebra; ribs T-shaped in section near vertebrae, rounded more distally [a common feature in ankylosaurs; W. P. Coombs, Jr., personal communication 1988]; mar-

gins of scapula almost parallel to one another, acromion of scapular spine high, rounded; preacetabular portion of ilium narrow, horizontally directed; femur slightly expanded at extremities; greater and lesser trochanters not separated from femoral head, fourth trochanter forming tuberosity; heavy, rough marking on anterior surface of femur.

As described by Nopcsa (1929b), the armor of this species consists of six different kinds of plates: 1. Paired dermal ossifications, with prominent spine superiorly, and lateral tubercles and scute-like inferior portion (these plates partially surrounding the neck); 2. pair of elongated spines (shoulder area); 3. paired series of posteriorly directed plates (beginning in sacral area and continuing, getting progressively smaller, down length of tail); 4. accessory lateral spines; 5. keeled scutes (extending from shoulders, continuing along flanks and tail area); and 6. very large spines.

Coombs (1978a) noted that this species seems to represent the end of the European lineage of nodosaurids represented by Early Cretaceous forms generally called "*Acanthopholis*," characterized by relatively small size (about one fourth that of North American nodosaurids in linear dimensions), apparent presence of premaxillary teeth, and separate scapula and coracoid. *Contra* Romer (1956, 1966) and Steel (1969), who regarded the Transylvanian form (and *Acanthopholis*) as

"Struthiosaurus" transilvanicus, BMNH R4966, holotype dorsal vertebrae, in anterior, ventral, lateral views. Scale = 3 cm. (After Nopcsa 1915.)

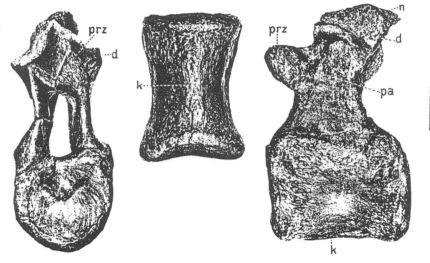

"Struthiosaurus" transilvanicus, BMNH R4966, holotype scapula. Scale = 3 cm. (After Nopcsa 1915.)

more lightly armored than North American forms; Coombs pointed out that all known nodosaurids were armored to approximately the same extent.

This species was regarded by Coombs and Maryańska as an unnamed nodosaurid (see also Weishampel, Grigorescu and Norman 1991) that cannot be referred to *Struthiosaurus*. According to Weishampel *et al.*, "*S.*" *transilvanicus* shares postcranial features with more derived members of the Nodosauridae such as *Sauropelta edwardsorum*, *Panoplosaurus mirus*, and the species of *Edmontonia* (*e.g.*, knob-like scapular spine, angled caudoventrally to form distinct prespinous fossa; typical dermal spines). Contrary to the condition in more derived nodosaurids, the scapula and coracoid in "*S.*" *transilvanicus* are not fused. Although this nonfusion might be interpreted as an immature feature, Coombs and Maryańska reported similar conditions in other adult nodosaurid taxa. Weishampel *et al.* concluded that "*S.*" *transilvanicus* should have primitive status among the Nodosauridae.

To "*S.*" *transilvanicus*, Coombs and Maryańska referred *Danubiosaurus* and *Crataeomus* (see entries), noting that this referral was tentative due to the extremely fragmentary nature of the type specimens of these taxa. *Hoplosaurus ischyrus* Seeley 1881 [*nomen dubium*] (a junior synonym of "*S.*" *transilvanicus*) was founded upon dermal armor (GIUV collection) recovered from the Gosau Formation, Wiener-Neustaadt.

Key references: Bunzel (1871); Coombs (1978*a*); Coombs and Maryańska (1990); Molnar, Kurzanov and Dong (1990); Nopcsa (1915, 1923, 1929*b*); Pereda-Suberbiola (1992); Pereda-Suberbiola and Galton (1992); Romer (1956, 1966); Steel (1969); Weishampel, Grigorescu and Norman (1991).

STYGIMOLOCH Galton and Sues 1983—
(=*Stenotholus*)

Ornithischia: Genasauria: Cerapoda: Marginocephalia: Pachycephalosauria: Pachycephalosauridae.

Name derivation: "Styx [Greek mythology, river of underworld along which dead passed to Hades]" + "Moloch [Old Testament god of Ammonites and Phoenicians]."

Type species: *S. spinifer* Galton and Sues 1983.

Other species: [None.]

Occurrence: Hell Creek Formation, Montana, North Dakota, Lance Formation, Wyoming, United States.

Age: Late Cretaceous (Late Maastrichtian).

Known material: Four skulls, squamosals, three frontoparietal domes with associated postcrania.

Holotype: UCMP 119433, partial left squamosal.

Diagnosis of genus (as for type species): Skull long, narrow, with vaulted frontoparietal dome; prominent squamosal shelf with multiple, large nodes and low-angle spikes; adult intermediate in size between *Stegoceras* and *Pachycephalosaurus* (Goodwin and Johnson 1995).

Comments: The genus *Stygimoloch* was founded upon an incomplete squamosal (UCMP 119433) collected by H. Wagner while part of a field party jointly sponsored by the Natural History Museum of Los Angeles County and University of California Museum of Paleontology, Berkeley. The specimen was found in the Hell Creek Formation of Harbicht Hill South No. 2, McCone County, Montana.

Galton and Sues (1983) originally diagnosed the monotypic *S. spinifer* as follows: Three or four massive horn cores developed on squamosal; squamosal shelf prominent; supratemporal opening developed in some juveniles.

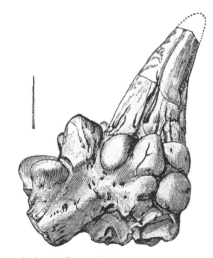

Stygimoloch spinifer, YPM 335, incomplete right squamosal. Scale = 2 cm. (After Marsh 1896.)

As measured by Galton and Sues, the preserved length of the main horn of the squamosal is 100 millimeters (about 30 millimeters missing from the tip). Galton and Sues noted that immediately posterior to the main spine is a smaller posterior spine, while a third spine is located lateral to the second. A system of deep grooves, apparently vascular in nature and similar to those in ceratopsian horn cores, is present on the outer surface of these spines. During life, the spines were apparently covered by a horny sheath, which probably made these structures at least 10 percent longer. More anteriorly, the lateral edge of the third spine originally possessed a linear series of three large nodes, with six other large nodes anterior to the main spine, four contacting its base. A pair of lateral nodes is separated from a medial trio of nodes by a single node. Six small nodes are present anterior to the main spine.

Galton and Sues referred to this species the incomplete right squamosal (YPM 335) of a juvenile, collected by John Bell Hatcher from the Lance Formation, above the mouth of Lance Creek, in Niobrara County, Wyoming. This specimen was originally identified by Marsh (1896) as a dermal ossification of the ceratopsian *Triceratops* (pachycephalosaurs unknown at that time). Marsh incorrectly envisioned the specimen as one of several such elements probably located on the animal's back behind the frill. Hatcher (1907) agreed with Marsh's identification, but theorized that these "dermal ossifications" were located in paired rows at the base of the tail. Lucas (1901*b*) reinterpreted the specimen as the possible dermal spine of the armored "*Stegosaurus*" [=*Hoplitosaurus*] *marshi*, otherwise only known from the Lower Cretaceous. Brown and Schlaikjer (1943) were the first workers to realize the affinities of the specimen, identifying it as a pachycephalosaurid left squamosal, which they referred to *Pachycepahlosaurus* sp. Comparing this specimen with the holotype of *S. spinifer*, Galton and Sues identified the former as a right squamosal.

Later, Sues and Galton (1987) tentatively referred to *S. spinifer* the well-preserved posterodorsal portion of a large pachycephalosaur skull (MPM 7111), associated with bony tubercles, collected from the Hell Creek Formation of Montana. The parietosquamosal shelf is absent and supratemporal fenestrae are obliterated.

The new genus *Stenotholus* was founded upon a well-preserved frontoparietal dome (MPM 7111) with partially preserved occipital and endocranial regions. The holotype was discovered exposed on the surface of the outcrop, underneath a small bench, in the Hell Creek Formation, McCone County, Montana. Collection at the top of the bench also yielded numer-

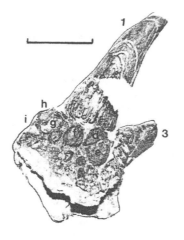
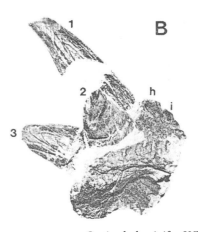

ous pachycephalosaurid skull and sculpture fragments, some of which could be articulated with the type skull. Found near the type specimen were probable hadrosaurid vertebral centra, ribs, and pelvic elements, also some scattered hadrosaurine fragments (Giffin, Gabriel and Johnson 1987).

As measured and described by Giffin *et al.*, the holotype skull (as preserved) is 203 millimeters (about 6.8 inches) long and 144 millimeters (about 5.5 inches) high. The prefrontal bears a sculpture made up of small acute nodes. The postorbital has a dorsal sculpture consisting of small flat nodes.

Giffin *et al.* pointed out notable similarities between the fragmentary sculpture material associated with the holotype of *S. kohleri* and that of isolated squamosals (UCMP 119433 and YPM 335) of *S. spinifer*, the latter two specimens with a major central spine and smaller marginal knobs quite similar to the disarticulated knobs found near the type specimen of *S. kohleri*. Although Giffin *et al.* acknowledged that *Stenotholus* and *Stygimoloch* could be congeneric, they regarded the material pertaining to both

Stygimoloch spinifer, UCMP 110433, holotype left squamosal, anterior and posterior views. Numbers = honrcores, letters = nodes. Scale = 5 cm. (After Galton and Sues 1983.)

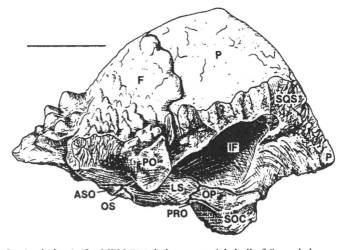

Stygimoloch spinifer, MPM 7111, holotype partial skull of *Stenotholus kohleri*. Scale = 5 cm. (After Giffin, Gabriel and Johnson 1987.)

Stygimoloch

Stygimoloch spinifer skeleton (Triebold Industries cast) at Dinofest International (1996), University of Arizona, Tempe.

forms as too limited to permit a more thorough comparison. (Even as Giffin *et al.*'s paper was in press, Milwaukee Public Museum field crews discovered yet another specimen, a partial pachycephalosaur skull with the narrow dome of *Stenotholus*, found in association with a thorny squamosal of *Stygimoloch*. Comparison of these specimens led Giffin *et al.* to realize that the two forms are congeneric, the results of this comparison presented in a joint paper delivered in September, 1988 at the International Symposium on Vertebrate Behavior as Derived from the Fossil Record, hosted by the Museum of the Rockies, Bozeman, Montana.)

Galton and Sues (1983) interpreted the horn-bearing squamosals as acting in visual display or intraspecific recognition. Perhaps they were utilized

in frontal display as the animal inclined its head forward or nodded or shook it from side to side (see Farlow and Dodson 1975), not unlike the behavior of the modern lizard, *Phrynosoma* (Lynn 1965).

The depiction of pachycephalosaurs (usually *Stegoceras*) butting heads in intraspecific contests has become a clichéd scenario in modern life restorations. More recently, however, this notion of head-butting, at least in regards some genera including *Stygimoloch*, was challenged by Goodwin and Johnson (1995), based on their study of a new skull (MPM 8111) belonging to this genus, recovered from the Hell Creek Formation (Upper Cretaceous) of North Dakota.

Goodwin and Johnson confirmed, for the first time, the orientation of the heavily ornamented parietosquamosal shelf along an unambiguous contact with the frontoparietal suture; observed that the squamosal spikes are parallel to the horizontal plane, extending at a low angle posteriorly from the squamosal; and the laterally constricted cranial dome slopes acutely in anterior view, producing a surface that is not suitable for head-on contact.

According to Goodwin and Johnson, over-extending the neck would have been required for contact with the spikes during head-to-head or head-to-flank encounters. As the cluster of squamosal nodes and spikes is most visible with the head tilted slightly downward, Goodwin and Johnson postulated that they were better suited for display purposes, the deflection of a blow to the head, and for protection of the neck.

Goodwin and Johnson reported that other *Stygimoloch* remains, including two more skulls, two domes, and some associated postcranial material was recovered from the same locality as MPM 8111.

Note: Olshevsky (1991) pointed out that, since *S. kohleri* was named in honor of two persons rather than one, the species name, according to Article 31[a][ii] of the International Code on Zoological Nomenclature, must take plural-ending spelling, the species thereby corrected to *S. kohlerorum*. The ICZN has not yet ruled on this proposed name alteration.

Key references: Galton and Sues (1983); Giffin, Gabriel and Johnson (1987); Goodwin and Johnson (1995); Hatcher (1907); Lucas (1901*b*); Marsh (1896); Olshevsky (1991); Sues and Galton (1987).

STYRACOSAURUS   Lambe 1913—
   (=?*Centrosaurus*)
Ornithischia: Genasauria: Cerapoda:
   Marginocephalia: Ceratopsia: Neoceratopsia:
   Ceratopsidae: Centrosaurinae.
Name derivation: Greek *styrax* = "spiked" + Greek
   sauros = "lizard."
Type species: *S. albertensis* Lambe 1913.
Other species: *S. ovatus* Gilmore 1930.
Occurrence: Oldman Formation, Dinosaur Park
   Formation, Alberta, Canada; Two Medicine For-
   mation, Montana, United States.

Stygimoloch spinifer, life restoration by Brian Franczak.

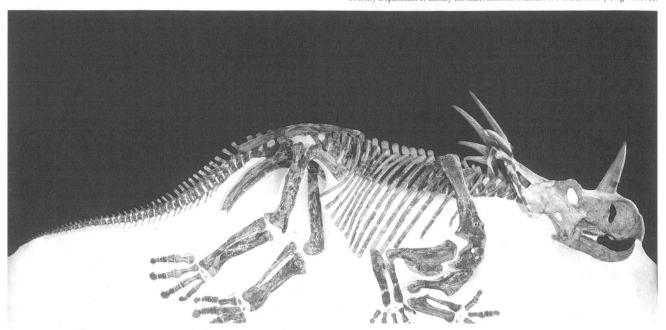

Styracosaurus albertensis, AMNH 5372, holotype skeleton of *S. parksi*.

Age: Late Cretaceous (Late Campanian–Maastrichtian).

Known material: Five skulls, two skeletons, cranial and postcranial material (in bone bed).

Holotype: GSC 344, skull missing part of rostral, barely more than distal half of nasal horn core, portions of spines of parietal crest, and lower jaws.

Diagnosis of genus (as for type species): Characterized by large horn-like processes that project caudally from parietal border (Dodson and Currie 1990).

Diagnosis of *S. ovatus*: Distinguished from *S. albertensis* by features of frill: Third-position frill processes closer at base, converging (diverging in *S. albertensis*) toward their tip; wider separation of first and second processes at base, between them rounded-edged margin of frill (processes in contact in *S. albertensis*); frill with vascular impressions (surface is smooth in type species) [?ontogenetic feature] (Gilmore 1930).

Comments: Well known for its long nasal horn and spiked frill, *Styracosaurus* was founded upon an almost complete skull (GSC 344), collected in 1913 by Charles H. Sternberg from the former "Belly River series," now Oldman Formation, at Red Deer River, Alberta, Canada. (The skull was given an artificial lower jaw, patterned after that of another genus, for display at the National Museum [now National Museum of Natural Science], Ottawa, Canada.)

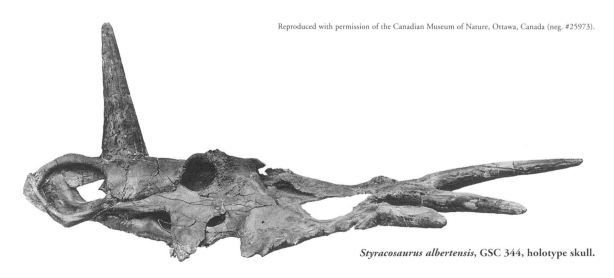

Styracosaurus albertensis, GSC 344, holotype skull.

Styracosaurus ovatus, USNM 11,869, holotype partial frill and other fragmentary remains.

Originally, Lambe (1913) diagnosed the genus (and type species *S. albertensis*) as follows: Skull massive, elongated, pointed at front, greatly extended behind to form neck frill; frill ornamented with long, robust, tapering processes that project obliquely backward and outward from its posterior border; fontanelles of moderate size within coalesced parietals; squamosals somewhat quadrangular, contributing largely in formation of anterior part of frill; postfrontal fontanelle large; supratemporal fossae openings wide posteriorly; nasal horn core large, straight, upright, rising from back of nasals; brow horn cores incipient. [Some of these characters, as the formation of the frill, are now known to apply to all ceratopsids.]

A second species, *S. parksi* Brown and Schlaikjer 1937, was based on a nearly complete skeleton (missing most of the first three coosified cervical vertebrae and distal end of tail) with parts of the skull and left lower jaw (AMNH 5372), collected in summer, 1915 during an American Museum of Natural History field party led by Barnum Brown, from the "Belly River Formation" (now Oldman Formation), near Steveville, Alberta, and displayed at the American Museum of Natural History. The remains were misidentified in the field as a specimen of "*Monoclo-nius*" [=*Centrosaurus*] "because of the extraordinary similarity to that genus as seen in the exposed parts when the skeleton was collected." (Brown and Schlaikjer noted that the type specimen "of the earliest known marsupial, *Eodelphis browni*" was found under the pelvis of this skeleton.) In their review of the Neoceratopsia, Dodson and Currie (1990) regarded *S. parksi* as a junior synonym of *S. albertensis*.

A third species, *S. ovatus,* was based on the posterior portion of a frill and numerous fragments (USNM 11,869), collected in 1928 by George F. Sternberg from the Two Medicine Formation, on the Blackfeet Indian Reservation at Milk River, in Glacier County, Montana.

Styracosaurus attained a length of about 5.25 meters (18 feet). Its weight has been estimated at about 1.8–2.7 metric tons (2–3 tons) (P. Dodson, personal communication 1987).

Various theories have been offered regarding the function of the *Styracosaurus* frill. Lull (1933) observed that the spikes made the head appear to be larger, doubling the length of the frill (certainly an intimidation to carnivorous dinosaurs). As with modern animals having large horns or antlers, the spiked frill would also have provided a striking visual display during intraspecific competition. Moving the head with such an array may have eliminated a need for direct physical combat during contests for sexual or territorial dominance.

Lull observed a number of similarities between *Styracosaurus* and the contemporaneous, closely related *Centrosaurus*, including features of the nasal horn and frill. Dodson (1987) suggested that the differences between *S. albertensis* and *C. nasicornis* might be due to sexual dimorphism, the former species representing the male morph (see *Centrosaurus* entry; also, Dodson and Currie). Later, Dobson (1990) suggested that *Styracosaurus* might represent a species of *Centrosaurus*. Comparing the nasal horn and parietal structures of both genera, Dodson found that, without the processes on the frill, *S. albertensis* is basically indistinguishable from *C. apertus*, adding that no justification exists for maintaining the former as a separate genus.

Once considered a rare genus, *Styracosaurus* is now known from a bone bed discovered in 1984 in the Dinosaur Park Formation at Dinosaur Provincial Park, Alberta (Currie and Dodson 1984). To date of this writing, the bone bed has not been excavated. Currie (1987*b*), in the book *Dinosaurs Past and Present*, related that the bone bed was found in silt stone, suggesting that the individuals contained here perished in a quiet-water environment. Earlier, Sternberg (1970) had suggested that *Styracosaurus* individuals sometimes congregated in swampy areas.

Notes: An apparent new species of *Styracosaurus*, *S. makeli* Czerkas and Czerkas 1990 [*nomen nudum*], collected from the Two Medicine Formation of Montana, was characterized by a forward- and downward-turned nasal horn and a single long epoccipital horn on each parietal. This species was later described by Sampson as a new genus, *Einiosaurus* (see entry).

Olshevsky (1992) pointed out that Barnum Brown had coined the name "Styracosaurus borealis" during the 1930s but never published it, although this combination appears on file photographs of the holotype of *S. parski* at the American Museum of Natural History.

Key references: Brown and Schlaikjer (1937); Currie (1987*b*); Currie and Dodson (1984); Dodson (1987, 1990); Dodson and Currie (1990); Gilmore (1930); Lambe (1913); Lull (1933); Sternberg (1970).

SUPERSAURUS Jensen 1985
Saurischia: Sauropodomorpha: Sauropoda:
    Diplodocidae: Diplodocinae.
Name derivation: "Super [vernacular]" + Greek
    sauros = "lizard."
Species: *S. vivianae* Jensen 1985.

Other species: [None.]
Occurrence: Morrison Formation, Colorado,
    ?Utah, United States.
Age: Early Cretaceous (Hauterivian).
Known material: Partial postcranial remains.
Holotype: BYUVP 5500, right scapulacoracoid.

Diagnosis of genus (as for type species): Scapulacoracoid long, measuring 2.44 meters (8 feet), but not robust; shaft in midsection not severely constricted; distal ends expanded moderately; (as in *Diplodocus*) shallow outward curve in inferior border, near greatest width of scapula at top of transverse ridge, implies ligament origin; inferior border of scapula forming gentle curve from glenoid process to distal end; inferior fossa longer than wide; coracoid subrectangular in lateral outline; ischium very similar to that of *Diplodocus*, with straight (but more robust) shaft; medial caudal vertebrae double-keeled, one with broad central channel, other with transversely thick neural spine dorsoventrally expanded at summit (Jensen 1985*a*); anterior caudal vertebrae having procoelus centra with pronounced posterior ball; lack of supraprezygapophysal laminae; highly rugose, slightly emarginate neural spine; massive neural arch with relatively tiny neural canal; single small pleurocoel; prominent hyposphene (Curtice 1995).

Comments: One of the largest known terrestrial animals, this dinosaur was popularly referred to as "Supersaurus" in an article by J. George in the August, 1973 issue of *Reader's Digest* magazine, after which this informal name became known internationally.

The genus *Supersaurus* was founded upon a scapulacoracoid (BYUVP 5500), discovered by James A. Jensen during the early 1970s and collected by him in 1979, in the Uncompahgre Upwarp, Dry Mesa Quarry, at the base of the Brushy Basin Member of the Morrison Formation (Hauterivian; Britt 1991, based on Kowalis, Heaton and Bringhurst 1986, who used samplings of altered, bentonitic volcanic ash dated by a conventional fission-track method), near Mesa County, west of Delta, Colorado. Referred to *S. vivianae* were a second scapulacoracoid (BYUVP 5501), ischium (BYU 5502), two medial caudal vertebra (BYUVP 5503), and 12 articulated caudal vertebrae (BYUVP 5504) from the same locality. The caudals, found near and parallel to the holotype, were referred in the field to this genus because of their shape and great size, each measuring about 30 centimeters (about 11.5 inches) long, although location does not necessarily imply association due to the extensive fluvial transport of Dry Mesa fossils prior to final burial (Jensen 1985*a*).

Paleontologist and discoverer James A. Jensen with holotype scapulacoracoid (BYUVP 5500) of *Supersaurus viviane*.

Based on the dimensions of the holotype, Jensen, in various popularly published interviews and articles, estimated that *Supersaurus* attained an approximate total length of 25–30 meters (82–98 feet), with a height of 16.5 meters (54 feet), the neck alone measuring almost 15 meters (50 feet) long. As calculated by Paul (1988*a*), the weight of *S. vivianae* was about 50 metric tons (more than 56 tons).

In his review of the Sauropoda, McIntosh (1990*b*) stated that, although but a fraction of the material pertaining to *S. vivianae* has been thus far prepared, bones including the scapula-coracoid, ischium, proximal caudal vertebra, ?caudal cervical, and some distal caudal vertebrae can be reasonably referred to the species. McIntosh observed that the scapula is of the diplodocid type and somewhat resembles that referred to *Amphicoelias*, noting that it is slightly more expanded than in *Diplodocus* and much more so than in *Barosaurus*; the proximal caudal vertebra is similar in both *Supersaurus* and *Barosaurus*; and there is some question as to whether or not Jensen was correct in his observation that the cervical vertebra possessed no pleurocoel, a character which would remove *Supersaurus* from both the Brachiosauridae and the Diplodocidae.

Curtice (1995) reported that three additional anterior caudal vertebrae (BYU 9192, BYU 12369, and BYU 12819), collected from the Dry Mesa Quarry, were assigned to *S. viviane*. According to Curtice, comparison of these bones with anterior caudals of *Diplodocus carnegii* and *Barosaurus lentus* substantiated the validity of *Supersaurus* as a genus and its placement within the Diplodocinae. *Supersaurus* can be separated from *Diplodocus* and *Barosaurus* by such features as these: Lack of extreme emargination atop neural spine; lack of supraprezygapophysal laminae; apparent lack of ventral excavation; small size of pleurocoel. Curtice noted that the presence of a hyposphene on each anterior caudal vertebra is a feature not observed in any other known diplodocid.

Note: An undescribed giant sauropod specimen possibly referable to *Supersaurus* (or to *Ultrasauros*; see entry) was discovered on August 18, 1988, by Brigham Young University field workers Brian Varsey and Cliff Miles, in the same quarry that yielded the holotype specimens of *S. vivianae* and *U. macintoshi*. (It is not possible, however, to refer the material with certainty to either species.) The specimen consists of several sacral vertebrae and a right ilium. According to Wade Miller of the Brigham Young University Geology Department, the pelvis, when freed of the surrounding matrix, will weigh approximately 680 kilograms (1500 pounds) and constitute the largest bone complex yet discovered. Reportedly, the sacrals are extremely tall, measuring about 132 centimeters (52 inches) from the summits of the neural spines to the bottoms of the vertebral centra. Neural spines rise 91 centimeters (3 feet) above the dorsal margin of the ilium. The ilium is 91 centimeters high from pubic peduncle to dorsal margin, 137 centimeters (4.5 feet) long, and 213 centimeters (7 feet) around the circumference of its dorsal margin.

Key references: Curtice (1995); Jensen (1985*a*); McIntosh (1990*b*); Paul (1988*a*).

SYMPHYROPHUS   Cope 1878 [*nomen dubium*]—(See *Camptosaurus*.)
Name derivation: Greek *sympho* = "fused" + Greek *orophe* = "roof" + Greek *os* = [adjectival ending].
Species: *S. musculosus* Cope 1878 [*nomen dubium*].

SYNGONOSAURUS   Seeley 1879 [*nomen dubium*]—(See *Acanthopholis*.)
Name derivation: Greek *syn* = "with" + Greek *gone* = "seed" + Greek *sauros* = "lizard."
Species: *S. macrocercus* Seeley 1879 [*nomen dubium*].

SYNTARSUS   Raath 1969—(=?*Coelophysis*, ?*Halticosaurus*,?*Rioarribasaurus*)
Saurischia: Theropoda: Ceratosauria: Coelophysoidea.
Name derivation: Greek *syn* = "fused" + Greek *tarsus* = "ankle."
Species: *S. rhodesiensis* Raath 1969.
Other species: *S. kayentakatae* Rowe 1989.
Occurrence: Forest Sandstone, Matabeleland North Zimbabwe; Upper Elliot Formation, Cape Province, South Africa; Kayenta Formation, Arizona, United States.
Age: Early Jurassic (Sinemurian–Pliensbachian).
Known material: At least 46 individuals, fully and partially articulated skeletons, juvenile to adult.
Holotype QVM QG/1, almost complete articulated skeleton lacking skull and neck.

Diagnosis of genus (as for type species): Antorbital fenestra elongated to 40 percent skull length; lacrimal with ventral extension overlapping jugal, reaching alveolar margin in condition unlike any other archosaur (from Raath 1977) (Rowe and Gauthier 1990).

Diagnosis of *S. kayentakatae*: Paired crest (no crest on southern African species) on skull roof, crest formed by lacrimal and ?nasals, positioned parasagitally along outer "edges" of skull roof between nares

Illustration by Gregory S. Paul.

Syntarsus rhodesiensis (left) versus *Massospondylus carinatus.*

and orbit; fibula fused to calcaneum in adults (Rowe 1989).

Comments: The genus *Syntarsus* was founded upon most of a well-preserved skeleton (QVM QG/1), discovered in 1963 by a group of boys from North-lea School, Bulawayo, under the direction of Ian K. Stewart, in the Forest Sandstone Formation, Nya-mandhlovu district, Zimbabwe [formerly Rhodesia], in southern Africa. The skeleton was preserved lying on its left side. Michael R. Raath directed the excavation of the skeleton and, on the basis of the structure of the tarsus, named it *Syntarsus* (Raath 1969).

Raath originally diagnosed the genus (and type species, *S. rhodesiensis*) as follows: Small bipedal "coelurosaurian" exhibiting extensive fusion in tarsal region; manus relatively large, well-developed, with three functional digits (I, II and III), digit IV reduced to a metacarpal and single vestigial phalanx, closely apposed in life to third metacarpal; manus raptorial, with well-developed recurved claws and pollex some-what opposable with other fingers; femur with sharply inturned head and distinct "neck"; astragalo-calcaneum with atypical ascending process, fused to tibia; except for fourth free distal tarsal, distal tarsals

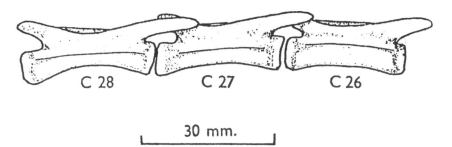

Syntarsus rhodesiensis, QG/1, holotype mid-caudal vertebrae, right lateral view. (After Raath 1969.)

fused to metatarsals; fibula, though free, closely apposed to shaft of tibia and to astragalocalcaneum; calcaneum lacking tuber; metatarsals long, III making up 60 percent length of femur; pes very birdlike, digits II, III, and IV functional; digit I, though complete, highly reduced, aligned in same direction as others, V reduced to splint-like metatarsal; ilium long, blade flared posteriorly, forming wide shallow shelf.

Galton (1971*e*) suggested that the three functional manual digits in the type species could be hyperextended on the metacarpus, and that they rotated laterally around their long axis during flexion, unguals rather laterally directed. This rotation is most

Syntarsus rhodesiensis, QG/1, holotype pelvis and sacrum, left lateral, dorsal, ventral views. (After Raath 1969.)

"100mm"

100 mm

pronounced for the hallux, which was apparently not truly opposable in theropods. Galton concluded that the similarity in form and movement of the hallux in prosauropods and most theropods suggest that the Saurischia is most likely a monophyletic taxon.

As recorded by Rowe (1989), the first North American remains of *Syntarsus* were collected during the summers of 1977–79 by field crews from the Museum of Comparative Zoology, Harvard University, and Museum of Northern Arizona, under the direction of Farish A. Jenkins, Jr., in a survey of the Kayenta Formation (Early Jurassic) vertebrate fauna. Almost 100 specimens were recovered, 14 referable to a new species of *Syntarsus*, in addition to bones from another individual collected in 1982 by James M. Clark and David E. Fastovsky (1986) for the Museum of Paleontology, University of California, Berkeley, and fragmentary remains of two individuals in older MNA collections.

The new species, which Rowe named *S. kayentakatae*, was founded upon a specimen discovered in July, 1977, comprising the skull and partial postcranial skeleton (MNA V2623) of a robust adult individual. The specimen was recovered in June, 1978, by a field party including W. Amaral, Jenkins, Rowe, C. R. Schaff, K. K. Smith and Hans-Dieter Sues, from a quarry in the Kayenta Formation, southwestern side of Sand Mesa, near the southern end of the Adeii Eechii Cliffs, Ward Terrace, Little Colorado River Valley, northeastern Arizona. Referred material includes: (From the quarry that yielded the holotype) remains of at least two adult individuals (MNA and MCZ collections); (from two localities in the Willow Springs area of the Kayenta Formation) fragmentary remains of at least 11 smaller and ?ontogenetically younger individuals (MCZ collection), and a subadult gracile individual, collected by the Berkeley party, represented by several proximal caudal centra, fragmentary left ilium, proximal ends of pubes and femora, and proximal end of a left fibula (UCMP V82309); and two fragmentary specimens (near Rock Head) consisting of a partial left ilium with supraacetabular crest (MNA V100), and weathered fragments of a femur and humerus (MNA V140) apparently belonging to a juvenile.

Comparing *S. kayentakate* to the theropods *S. rhodesiensis*, *Rioarribasaurus colberti* [=*Coelophysis bauri* of his usage], *Liliensternus liliensterni*, *Dilophosaurus wetherilli*, *Ceratosaurus nasicornis*, *Sarcosaurus woodi*, and *Segisaurus halli*, Rowe observed that all of these taxa share certain novel similarities, for which they are now included in the taxon Ceratosauria (Rowe 1988; Rowe and Gauthier 1989). After a cladistic evaluation of these taxa, Rowe concluded that *Dilophosaurus, Liliensternus, Rioarribasaurus,* and

Syntarsus are more closely related to one another than to *C. nasicornis*; *Liliensternus, Rioarribasaurus,* and *Syntarsus* are more closely related to one another than to *Dilophosaurus*; and *C. bauri* and *Syntarsus* are more closely related to one another than to any other theropod.

As pointed out by Raath (1969), the postcranial skeleton of *Syntarsus* is strikingly similar to that of the American genus *Rioarribasaurus* [=*Coelophysis* of his usage]. Paul (1984) regarded these, along with *Halticosaurus*, as congeneric, noting that they share characters of more derived narrow pubes and deep pre-

maxillary-maxillary notches; later Paul (1993) referred *Rioarribasaurus* to senior synonym *Syntarsus*. Raath (1969) noted that the tarsus in *Rioarribasaurus* has a free "cap-like" astragalocalcaneum and does not have the peculiar fusion found in *Syntarsus*. Also, the carpus in the former has no intermedium in the proximal row, while *Syntarsus* retains it.

After examination of the Kayenta material, Rowe (1989) supported generic separation of *Syntarsus* and *Rioarribasaurus*, stating that at least two diagnostic characters distinguish both forms (*i.e.*, nasal fenestra and fusion of proximal ends of metatarsals II and III observable in the holotype of *S. kayentakate*). Also supporting generic separation of *Syntarsus* and *Rioarribsaurus* [=*Coelophysis* of his usage], Colbert (1989, 1990) outlined a suite of differences in skull, manus, and pelvis (see *Rioarribasaurus* entry).

According to Rowe, similarity between the skull crest in *S. kayentakatae* and that of the larger ceratosaurian *D. wetherilli* might suggest that the former could be a juvenile *Dilophosaurus*. Rowe dismissed this notion mainly based on skeletal elements in *S. kayentakatae* indicative of an adult individual; those elements in *D. wetherilli* are not fused, indicating a subadult, although the holotype of this form is twice as large as that of *S. kayentakatae*. Also, *S. kayentakatae* possesses a number of derived characters (including alveolar ridge of maxilla) within Ceratosauria not present in *Dilophosaurus* (see Rowe and Gauthier). Rowe concluded that the evolution of cranial crests within Ceratosauria is most likely due to convergence.

Rowe pointed out that the discovery of *Syntarsus* remains in the Kayenta Formation supports dating that formation as Early Jurassic. As Rowe noted, *Syntarsus* is one of the most derived ceratosaurs, possessing 22 apomorphic character states that evolved after the divergence of Ceratosauria and other theropods from their last common ancestor, *Syntarsus* and *Rioarribasaurus* sharing 20 of these. This suggests that even the earliest known theropods were considerably evolved, contradicting the long-held notion that *Riorribasaurus* was a uniformly primitive genus that gave rise to most other theropod forms.

Raath (1980) reported that, in February 1980, James W. Kitching of the Bernard Price Institute for Palaeontological Research discovered the first South African skeletal remains of *Syntarsus* (and "coelurosaurs") in the Elliott Formation, on a farm near the town of Clocolan. This material (collectively catalogued under temporary BPI [Paleontology] field numbers F7 and F43) consists of disassociated fragmentary postcranial elements from at least eight individuals, including distal ends of femora, proximal end of a tibia, pes fragments, and a cervical and dorsal vertebra.

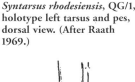

Syntarsus rhodesiensis, QG/1, holotype left tarsus and pes, dorsal view. (After Raath 1969.)

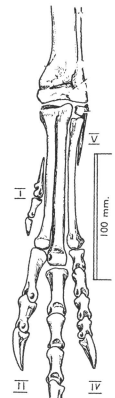

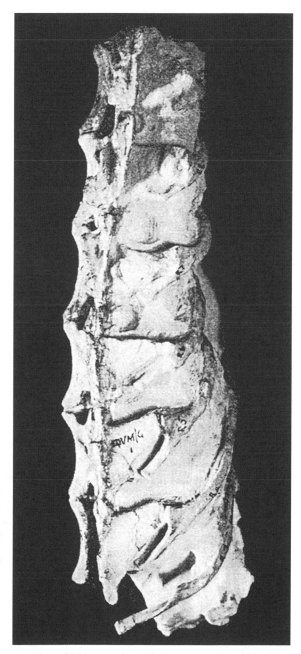

Syntarsus rhodesiensis, QG/1, holotype dorsal vertebrae with ribs, right lateral view. (After Raath 1969.)

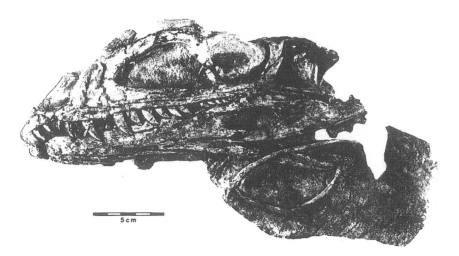

Syntarsus kayentakatae, MNA V2623, holotype skull, left lateral view. (After Rowe 1989.)

Later, Raath (1990) discussed variation in the remains of 30 *S. rhodesiensis* individuals, material that was both excellent in quality and adequate in quantity, recovered from an unusually rich fossiliferous bone bed in the fine-grained aeolian Forest Sandstone Formation of Zimbabwe. Raath (1990) concluded that these remains did not represent different species but a single biological population. Raath (1990) perceived sexual dimorphism between the more common heavier and robust types and less common, lighter and gracile types. Using modern predatory birds as a model, Raath (1990) presumed the more abundant larger forms to be female, the less abundant, gracile forms male. The largest robust forms are approximately 15 percent larger than the largest gracile ones, with robusticity achieved only after the body has reached a size marking the beginning of sexual maturity. All juvenile individuals are gracile.

Raath (1990) allowed for unknown taphonomic biases in the collection from this bone bed, also noting that the extent to which this collection represents the original population is not clear. Nevertheless, Raath (1990) suggested that *Syntarsus* could have been a socially gregarious dinosaur, and that a single catastrophic event may account for the mass death represented in the bonebed.

A glimpse into the environment of *Syntarsus* was provided by other fossil material found with its remains. Raath (1990) reported that found with the Zimbabwe fossils was much prosauropod material, especially that of *Massospondylus carinatus* [=*M. harriesi* of their usage]. Associated with the South African material were remains of *Massospondylus*, the cynodont *Tritylodon*, and other fossil vertebrate material. Raath (1969, 1980) theorized that *Syntarsus* was a desert-dwelling dinosaur, capable (as was *Massospondylus*) of tolerating a wide ecological range, though dependent on the occurrence of surface water.

In his reports on the South African material, Raath (1980; 1990) showed that the Elliot Formation represents an area that was hot and semiarid, bones collected from this locality exhibiting suncracks indicative of hot climate. Raath (1969) concluded that *Syntarsus* was a fully bipedal, lightly-built animal that actively preyed upon (indicated by apparent stomach contents) smaller vertebrates.

Bakker (1975), after an earlier suggestion by Raath (1969), restored *S. rhodesiensis* in life as having feathers for insulation and reflecting the hot sun of the animal's desert environment, though no feather impressions have been found with any specimens of this dinosaur.

Note: Raath (1972) reported footprints attributed to *Syntarsus*, from the Nyamandhlovu Series overlying the Forest Sandstone, near Spring Grange farm.

Key references: Bakker (1975); Clark and Fastovsky (1986); Colbert (1989, 1990); Galton (1971*e*); Paul (1988, 1993); Raath (1969, 1972, 1877, 1980, 1990); Rowe (1989); Rowe and Gauthier (1989).

SYRMOSAURUS Maleev 1952—(See *Pinacosaurus.*)
Name derivation: Greek *syrma* = "something trailed along" + Greek *sauros* = "lizard."
Species: *S. viminocaudus* Maleev 1952.

SZECHUANOSAURUS Yang [Young] 1942 [*nomen dubium*]
Saurischia: Theropoda: Tetanurae: Avetheropoda: Allosauroidea: Allosauridae.
Name derivation: "Szechuan [province]" + Greek *sauros* = "lizard."
Species: *S. campi* Yang [Young] 1942 [*nomen dubium*].
Other species: [None.]
Occurrence: Shangshaximiao Formation, ?Kyanguan Series, Sichuan, Keilozo Formation, Xinjiang Ugyur Zizhiqu, People's Republic of China.
Age: Late Jurassic (Oxfordian–Tithonian).
Known material: Incomplete skeletons, isolated teeth.
Cotypes: IVP AS V235, two broken teeth, V236, broken tooth, V238, fragmentary teeth, V239, almost complete tooth.
Diagnosis of genus (as for type species): Teeth of *Megalosaurus*-type, pointed, moderately curved, distinctly compressed, with anterior and posterior denticulations (Yang [Young] 1942*b*); medium-sized theropod [6 meters or about 20 feet in length], with nine opisthocoelous cervical vertebrae, platycoelous

Photo by M. Tanimoto.

dorsal vertebrae, moderately long forelimb (Dong, Zhou and Zhang, 1983).

Comments: *Szechuanosaurus* was founded on teeth (IVP AS V235-6, V238-9) from the [then unnamed] "*Ceratodus*-bearing formation" [= Shang-shaximiao Formation], (Upper Jurassic), Kuangyuan [now Kweiyuang] county, north Szechuan [now Sichuan] Basin, China (Yang [previously known in English-language publications as Young] 1942*b*).

Camp (1935) described a theropod tooth (UCMP 32102) collected on August 30, 1915, from probable Jurassic beds near Jung Hsien, Szechuan,

Szechuanosaurus

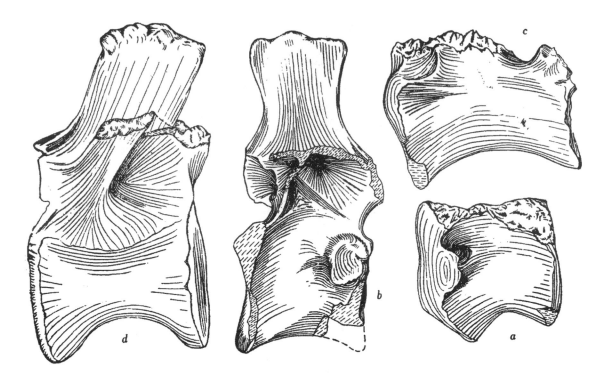

considered to represent an advanced, extremely large megalosaurid. As estimated by Camp, the tooth, if complete, would measure at least 90 millimeters in length. Although this tooth is larger and straighter than the *Szechuanosaurus* type teeth, Yang referred it to *S. campi* because of shared similarities in general structure and form of serrations.

Yang and Sun (1942c) assigned to cf. *S. campi* the anterior portion of a left lower jaw from Ying-choe-shih, Sinkiang. As observed by Molnar (1974), this fragment generally resembles the holotype (LACM 20877) of the North American species *Labocania anomala*.

To the type species *S. campi*, Dong *et al.* (1983) referred a fairly complete skeleton lacking the skull, collected from the early Upper Jurassic of the Shang-shaximiao Formation of the Sichuan Basin, in Wuji-aban, Zigong, China. From this specimen, Dong *et al.* supplemented Yang's original diagnosis and observed that *Szechuanosaurus*, in some ways, resembles *Allosaurus* (*e.g.*, presence of notch on astragalus for calcaneum).

In his book *Dinosaurs from China*, Dong (1987) reported a partial lower jaw, tentatively referred to *S. campi*, from the Late Jurassic Kelaza Formation, Shanshan County, Turpan Basin. The specimen indicates a more robust animal than that indicated by the *S. campi* holotype.

Note: The skull on the mounted skeleton (CV 00214) of *Szechuanosaurus,* displayed at the Zigong Dinosaur Museum, has been greatly restored in plaster and is mostly hypothetical.

Key references: Camp (1935); Dong (1987); Dong, Zhou and Zhang (1983); Molnar (1975); Yang [Young] (1942b); Yang [Young] and Sun (1942e).

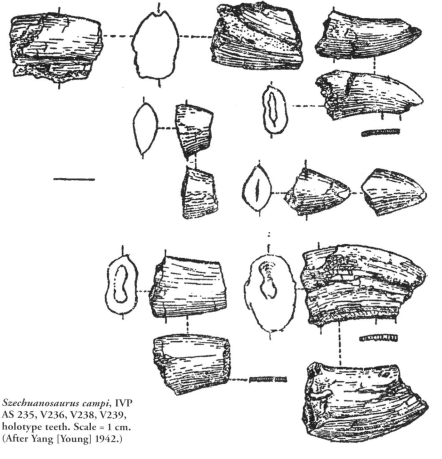

Szechuanosaurus campi, IVP AS 235, V236, V238, V239, holotype teeth. Scale = 1 cm. (After Yang [Young] 1942.)

TALARURUS Maleev 1952—(=?*Amtosaurus*, ?*Maleevus*)

Ornithischia: Genasauria: Thyreophora: Ankylosauria: Ankylosauridae.

Name derivation: Greek *talaros* = "basket" + Greek *ouros*/Latin *urus* = "tail."

Type species: *T. plicatospineus* Maleev 1952.

Other species: [None.]

Occurrence: Baynshirenskaya Svita, Dornogov, Omnogov, Mongolian People's Republic.

Age: Late Cretaceous (Cenomanian–Turonian).

Known material: More than five specimens, including two partial skulls, almost complete skeleton, armor.

Holotype: PIN 557-91, fragmentary skull with posterior part of skull roof, occipital region, basicranium.

Diagnosis of genus (as for type species): Medium-sized ankylosaurid (4–5 meters [about 13.5–16.5 feet] in length), with relatively long, narrow skull (approximately 240 millimeters long, 220 millimeters wide); occipital condyle partially visible in dorsal view (unique among ankylosaurids); maxillary teeth with swollen bases cut on labial side by W-shaped furrows; pentadactyl manus, tetradactyl pes; postcranial bones wide relative to their length; armor plates ribbed; tail club small (Coombs and Maryańska 1990).

Comments: The genus *Talarurus* was founded on a fragmentary skull with partial "postcranial skeleton" (PIN 557-91) collected from the Bayn Shireh "formation" (Maleev 1952*a*; Late Cretaceous [Cenomanian–Early Santonian]; Barsbold 1972), in Eastern Mongolia. Maleev (1956) designated the skeleton

Photo by the author.

Talarurus plicatospineus, mounted composite skeleton, reconstructed with some innaccuracies, left three-quarter view, in "The Great Russian Dinosaurs" exhibit (1996), Mesa Southwest Museum, Mesa, Arizona.

Talarurus plicatospineus, PEN AN SSR 557, holotype dermal scute. (After Maleev 1952.)

and skull fragment as the holotype of type species *T. plicatospineus.*

Reexamination by Maryańska (1977) of the original material, along with other remains of this species in the Palaeontological Institute of the USSR Academy of Sciences collection—including an undescribed incomplete skull with cranial roof, occipital, and braincase (PIN collection) from Bayshin Tsav, and an undescribed maxilla fragment with eight teeth (PIN) from Baga Tarjach—revealed that the "type" represents at least three individuals, and that the chosen cranial fragment pertains to the posterior part of the skull roof. In Maryańska's opinion, only the skull fragment should be regarded as the holotype.

Maleev (1952a) originally diagnosed *Talarurus* as follows: Cervical vertebrae short; dorsal vertebrae long with high centra; nine sacral vertebrae, with transverse processes fused into single unit with sacral ribs; anterior caudal vertebrae short, high, posterior caudals long, low; ribs massive, bent like arch; scapula massive, wide, with strongly bent blade; pes with hoof-like ungual phalanges; ilium wide, long, relatively flat; dermal armor consisting of bony keeled plates (similar to *Euoplocephalus*), 20–50 millimeters thick, joined together by feebly flexible sutures allowing limited movement; lateral margins of carapace and tail with series of symmetrically situated, thick-walled, hollow spines, differing from those in other ankylosaurs by grooved surface.

Coombs (1977a) believed that *Talarurus* could be congeneric with *Euoplocephalus*, though Maryańska disagreed, arguing that the two forms should be regarded as distinct based on proportional and essential anatomical differences. Maryańska showed that *Talarurus* differs from *Euoplocephalus* in the shape of the skull, the structure of palatal region, and in having four pedal digits.

Talarurus is one of the oldest Mongolian ankylosaurids and, as such, shows similarities to nodosaurids, some seemingly primitive characters lost in the Ankylosauridae. As observed by Maryańska, these similarities include a comparatively long skull, subspher-

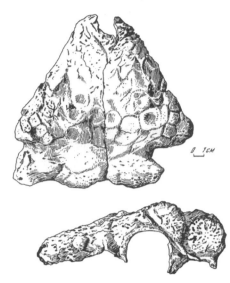

Talarurus plicatospineus, PIN 3780/1, referred skull, dorsal and left lateral views. Scale = 1 cm. (After Tumanova 1983.)

ical occipital condyle, and incomplete coossification of distal caudal vertebrae. Though this may intimate that the Ankylosauridae arose directly from the Nodosauridae, Maryańska cautioned that the data supporting this possibility is insufficient and that new information regarding origins of the more derived group may be supplied after study of a specimen of primitive Early Cretaceous ankylosaur from Khovboor.

Notes: Both *Maleevus* and *Amtosaurus* may be trivial variants on *T. plicatospineus*, at best only marginally justifiable as separate species (W. P. Coombs, Jr., personal communication 1988).

Key references: Coombs (1977a); Coombs and Maryańska (1990); Maleev (1952a, 1956); Maryańska (1977).

TANIUS Wiman 1929
Ornithischia: Genasauria: Cerapoda: Ornithopoda: Iguanodontia: Hadrosauridae: Hadrosaurinae.
Name derivation: "Tan L. [paleontologist]."
Type species: *T. sinensis* Wiman 1929.
Other species: [None.]
Occurrence: Wangshi Series, Shandong, Tsagayanskaya Svita, Heilongjiang, People's Republic of China.
Age: Late Cretaceous (?Maastrichtian).
Known material: Skull and postcranial remains representing at least three individuals.
Holotype: Fragmentary remains including partial skull (missing nasal elements), postcrania including vertebrae, pelvic elements, limb bones.

Diagnosis of genus (as for type species): Skull flat, with no swelling or distal thickening indicated

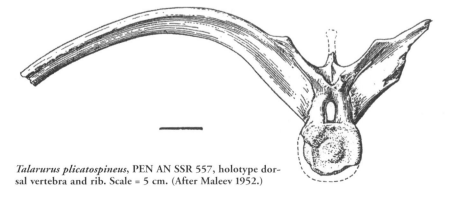

Talarurus plicatospineus, PEN AN SSR 557, holotype dorsal vertebra and rib. Scale = 5 cm. (After Maleev 1952.)

on facial part of braincase, and with anterior-posteriorly elongated supratemporal fossa; preacetabular process of ilium rather straight in lateral aspect (Hu and Cheng 1988).

Comments: The genus *Tanius* was founded upon a fragmentary specimen discovered in 1923 in the Chiangchunting locality, Wangshi [also Wang Shih] Series, Lai Yang Hsien, Shantung [now Shandong], China.

Wiman (1929) originally diagnosed the genus (and type species) as follows: Skull rather low and flat, anterior portion of frontals not enlarged or thickened to support crest; radius longer than humerus; femur about 1 meter (39.37 inches) in length. According to Wiman, this genus is closely related to *Edmontosaurus* [= *Trachodon* of his usage].

As the distal end of the ischium of the holotype is extremely expanded (as in theropods), Hu and Cheng (1988) later removed this element from *Tanius*.

Second species *T. chingkankouensis* was based on bones of more than one individual from the Wangshih series at Hsikou (Chingkankou), Shandong. Found in association with the remains of *Tsintaosaurus*, this material, described by Yang [Young] (1958c), consists of ten dorsal vertebrae, partial dorsal, two sacrals, a right scapula, right ilium, and the distal portion of a right ischium. From these remains, Maryańska and Osmólska (1981) selected the associated ilium and fragmentary ischium (V724) as the lectotype. Found in close proximity of the holotype of *T. sinensis*, these elements could belong to the type species. However, Maryańska and Osmólska preferred keeping the two species separate because of apparent differences in shapes of respective scapulae and antitrochanters of their ilia. This species is now regarded as a junior synonym of *T. sinensis*.

Notes: The species *T. liayangensis* Zhen 1976 was referred by Weishampel and Horner (1990) to *Tsintaosaurus spinorhinus*.

According to Maryańska and Osmólska, a dorsal vertebra with a high neural spine, associated with the holotype of *T. sinensis* and assigned to that species by Wiman, seems to belong to a lambeosaurine.

Key references: Hu and Cheng (1988); Maryańska and Osmólska (1981); Taquet (1991); Wiman (1929).

TARASCOSAURUS Le Loeuff and Buffetaut 1991

Saurischia: Theropoda: Ceratosauria:
  Neoceratosauria: Abelisauroidea: Abelisauridae.
Name derivation: "Tarasque" [legendary dragon-like animal] + Greek *sauros* = "lizard."

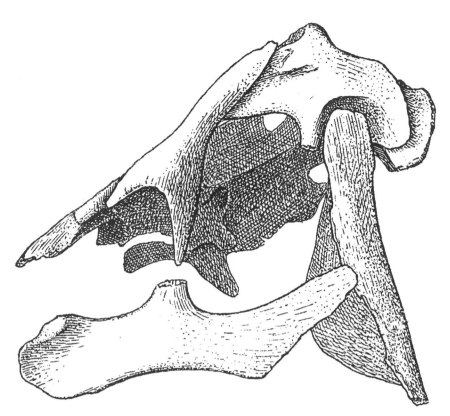

Tanius sinensis, holotype incomplete skull, left lateral view. (After Wiman 1929.)

Type species: *T. salluvicus* Le Loeuff and Buffetaut 1991. Other species: [None.]
Occurrence: Lambeau du Beaussett, France.
Age: Late Cretaceous (Early Campanian [Fuvélien]).
Known material: Femur, vertebrae.
Holotype: FSL 330201, proximal half of left femur.

Diagnosis of genus (as for type species): Small abelisaurid; shaft of femur especially narrow; femoral head directed anteromedially; lesser trochanter projecting beyond boundary of head; foramen underneath lesser trochanter; transverse processes of dorsal vertebrae anteroposteriorly wide; infradiapophyses of dorsal vertebrae blade-like, diverging under diapophyses; hyposphene-hypantrum structure in dorsals; vertebrae very cavernous internally (Loeuff and Buffetaut 1991).

Comments: The first dinosaur described from the Late Cretaceous of the Beausset Syncline, the genus *Tarascosaurus* was founded upon a femur (FSL 330201) collected from Lambeau du Beausset at Bouches-du-Rhône in southern France. A paratype specimen consists of two articulated fragments of dorsal vertebrae (FSL 33020), which may belong to the same individual; referred to the type species was a caudal centrum (FSL 330203) (Le Loeuff and Buffetaut 1991).

According to Le Loeuff and Buffetaut, the occurrence in Europe of an abelisaurid, a kind of theropod

Tarbosaurus

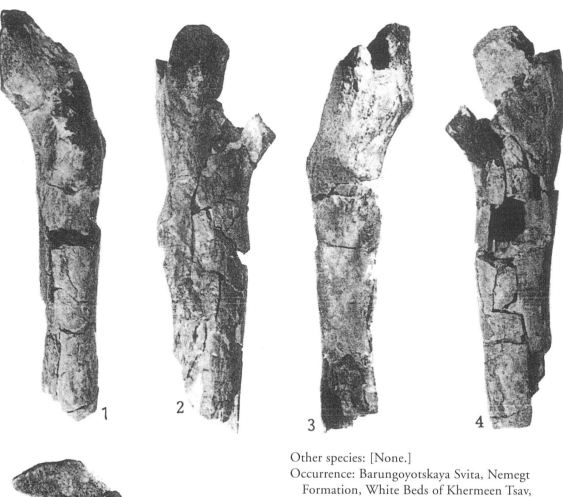

known from South America, India, and Africa, suggests that other Gondwana dinosaurs (*e.g.*, titanosaurid sauropods) might also have lived in Europe during the Late Triassic.

Key reference: Le Loeuff and Buffetaut (1991).

TARBOSAURUS   Maleev 1955—(See *Tyrannosaurus*.)

Name derivation: Greek *tarbo* = "terrible" + Greek *sauros* = "lizard."

Type species: *T. bataar* Maleev 1955.

TARCHIA   Maryańska 1978—(=?*Amtosaurus*)

Ornithischia: Genasauria: Thyreophora: Ankylosauria: Ankylosauridae.

Name derivation: Mongolian *tarchi* = "brain."

Type species: *T. gigantea* (Maleev 1956).

Other species: [None.]

Occurrence: Barungoyotskaya Svita, Nemegt Formation, White Beds of Khermeen Tsav, Omnogov, Bayankhongor, Mongolian People's Republic.

Age: Late Cretaceous (Middle Campanian–Early Maastrichtian).

Known material: Seven specimens, including complete and partial skulls with almost complete postcrania and armor.

Tarchia gigantea, PIN 3142/250, referred skull and lower jaw, left lateral view. (After Tumanova 1983.)

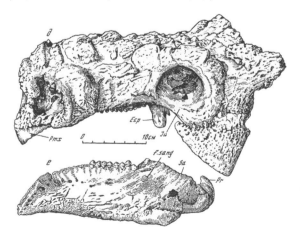

Holotype: ZPAL MgD-I/111, posterior part of skull including skull roof, braincase, occipital.

Diagnosis of genus (as for type species): Premaxilla only partially covered by dermal ossifications; beak equal in width to distance between caudalmost maxillary teeth; premaxillary area of palate of subequal length and width; very high occipital not fused to quadrate; mandibular condyle positioned below caudal part of orbit; pes tetradactyl; tail club large (Coombs and Maryańska 1990).

Comments: The largest and geologically youngest known Mongolian ankylosaurid, *Tarchia* was founded on a partial skull (ZPAL MgD-I/111) discovered during the Polish-Mongolian Paleontological Expeditions to Mongolia of 1963–1971 (Kielan-Jaworoska and Dovchin 1969; Kielan-Jaworoska and Barsbold 1972; Maryańska 1970, 1971), in the Barungoyotskaya Svita [Barun Goyot Formation] (?Middle Campanian; Kielan-Jaworoska 1974), Khulsan, Mongolia (Maryańska 1977).

Originally, Maryańska (1977) diagnosed the monotypic *T. gigantea* as follows: Large ankylosaur; orbits of skull not entirely closed; exoccipital relatively short, high, perpendicular to skull roof; occipital condyle ventro-posteriorly directed; occipital part of skull and occipital condyle partly visible in dorsal aspect; foramen magnum higher than wide; braincase very high; one opening for nerves posterior to foramen ovale.

As described by Maryańska (1977), the skull is about the size of that of *Saichania*, although the braincase is almost twice as high as in that genus.

Maryańska (1977) referred to *Tarchia* the species *Dyoplosaurus giganteus* Maleev 1956 as new species *T. gigantea*, based on caudal vertebrae, metacarpals, and phalanges, and fragments of armor (PIN 551-

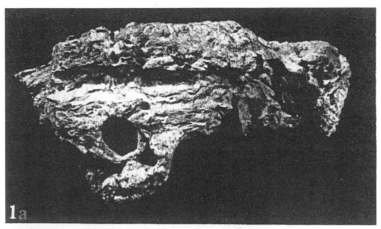

Tarchia gigantea, ZPAL MgD-I/111, holotype damaged posterior part of skull of *T. keilanae*, 1. occipital view, 2. braincase, anteroventral view. (After Maryańska 1977.)

29), from the Nemegt Formation, Altan Ula III, Mongolia. Referred by Maryańska (1977) to this species were a caudal portion including a tail club (ZPAL MgD-I/43; now housed at GI SPS) from the Nemegt Formation, Altan IV; caudal portion of vertebral column with tail club, and armor fragments (ZPAL MgD-I/42); right humerus (ZPAL MgD-I/49) from the same formation and locality; a partial postcranial skeleton (ZPAL MgD-I/113) missing the skull, from Altan III; and an undescribed skeleton with skull (PIN collection), from the upper white beds (stratigraphic equivalent of the Nemegt Formation) of Khermeen Tsav I, Mongolia.

Tumanova (1978) noted that *Tarchia* illustrates the trend in nodosaurid evolution toward increasing massiveness in the skull, achieved by a shortening of the skull relative to its width. In more derived nodosaurids, there is a tendency for fusion of premaxillaries and maxillary shells, resulting in an intensified ossification of the palate. In *Tarchia* (unlike more

Tarchia gigantea, skull (PIN 3142/250) originally referred to *T. kielanae*, in "The Great Russian Dinosaurs" exhibit (1996), Mesa Southwest Museum, Mesa, Arizona.

derived nodosaurids such as *Edmontonia*), the secondary palatine is weakly developed.

T. kielanae Maryańska 1977 was regarded as a junior synonym of *T. gigantea* by Coombs and Maryańska (1990) in their review of the Ankylosauria.

Key references: Coombs and Maryańska (1990); Maleev (1956); Maryańska (1977); Tumanova (1978).

TATISAURUS Simmons 1965
Ornithischia: Genasauria: ?Thyreophora.
Name derivation: "Tati [village in Lufeng Basin]" + Greek *sauros* = "lizard."
Type species: *T. oehleri* Simmons 1965 [*nomen dubium*].
Other species: [None.]

Tatisaurus oehleri, FMNH CUP 2088, holotype jaw, A. medial, B. lateral, C. dorsal views. (After Simmons 1965.)

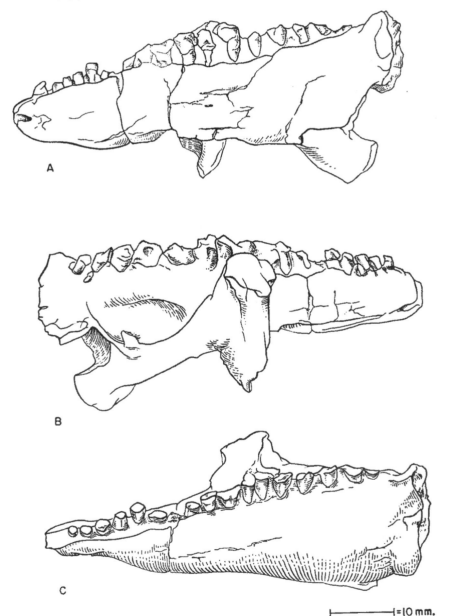

⊢————⊣=10 mm.

Occurrence: Dark Red Beds, Lower Lufeng Series, Yunnan, People's Republic of China.
Age: Early Jurassic.
Known material/holotype: CUP 2088, fragment of left mandible with teeth.

Diagnosis of genus (as for type species): Small ornithischian; anteriorly, mandible low, slender, tapered, anteroventral border bending medially toward symphysis; jaw higher and more convex posteriorly; teeth relatively simple in form, thecodont, overlapping, increasing in size anteriorly to posteriorly; junction of dentary and predentary edentulous [true of all ornithischians] (Simmon 1965); dentigerous margin of mandible sigmoid (Dong 1990*b*).

Comments: The genus *Tatisaurus* was established on a partial mandible (CUP 2088) recovered from the Dark Red Beds, Lower Lufeng Formation (Lufeng Series dated Early Jurassic; Olsen and Galton 1977) Tati village, Lufeng Basin, China (Simmons 1965).

As described by Simmons, the maximum breadth of the jaw is approximately 7.0 millimeters, indicating a possible cheek pouch in life. The dentigerous border of the jaw is higher externally (as in saurischians), but with sigmoid configuration. Functional teeth are worn; crowns are low, rather symetrically triangular, with gently curved or evenly slanted smooth, polished surfaces. Unlike most ornithischians, the lateromedial surfaces of replacement teeth are not fluted. Simmons, believing *Tatisaurus* to be ornithopod, referred it to the Hypsilophodontidae.

Simmons observed that the jaw, with its apparent lack or reduction of a coronoid element and sigmoid character of the dentigerous border and tooth row, resembles that of various ankylosaurs, the teeth and their wear pattern very similar to that of *Struthiosaurus austriacus*. By the Early Jurassic, ornithischians were already diversified; Simmons suggested that *Tatisaurus* could represent an early offshoot from an ankylosaurian line with *Scelidosaurus* at its base.

Dong (1990*b*) regarded *Tatisaurus* as a primitive stegosaur and assigned the genus to the subfamily Huayangosaurinae, because the teeth have features similar to those of *Huayangosaurus*. Reviewing basal thyreophorans, Coombs, Weishampel and Witmer (1990) noted that one feature displayed in *T. oehleri* (*i.e.*, ventral deflection of mesial end of dentary tooth row) is also known in *Scelidosaurus*, stegosaurians, and ankylosaurians and, therefore, provisionally assigned *Tatisaurus* to the Thyreophora.

Key references: Coombs, Weishampel and Witmer (1990); Dong (1990*b*); Simmons (1965).

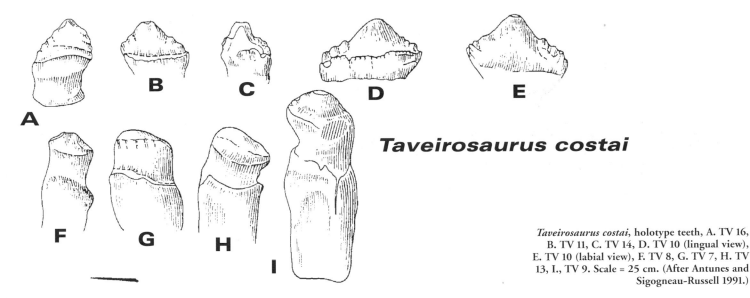

Taveirosaurus costai, holotype teeth, A. TV 16, B. TV 11, C. TV 14, D. TV 10 (lingual view), E. TV 10 (labial view), F. TV 8, G. TV 7, H. TV 13, I., TV 9. Scale = 25 cm. (After Antunes and Sigogneau-Russell 1991.)

TAVEIROSAURUS Antunes and Sigogneau-Russell 1991 [*nomen dubium*]

Ornithischia *incertae sedis.*

Name derivation: "Taveiro [village of the District of Coimbra, Portugal]" + Greek *sauros* = "lizard."

Type species: *T. costai* Antunes and Sigogneau-Russell 1991 [*nomen dubium*].

Other species: [None.]

Occurrence: [Unnamed formation], Taveiro, Portugal.

Age: Late Cretaceous (Maastrichtian).

Known material: Teeth.

Holotype: Centro de Estratigrafia e Paleobiologia da Universidade Nova de Lisboa collection, TV 10, tooth.

Diagnosis of genus (as for type species): Small-sized pachycephalosaur; teeth with low, subtriangular crowns, two to four serrations on edge of crown; labial tooth face convex, lingual face nearly flat and underlined at base by more or less thick cingulum; proximal part of tooth root oval-shaped in cross-section (Antunes and Sigogneau-Russell 1991).

Comments: *Taveirosaurus* was founded upon a tooth (Centro de Estratigrafia e Paleobiologia da Universidade Nova de Lisboa collection, number TV 10) and nine referred teeth (TV 6-9, 11, 13-16), four of the latter with only crowns preserved. They were recovered from the Upper Cretaceous (Maastrichtian) sand and clay at Taveiro, District of Coimbra, Portugal (Antunes and Sigogneau-Russell 1991).

Seeing morphological similarities (*e.g.* contour and number of denticulations) between these teeth and those of *Wannanosaurus*, the authors referred *Taveirosaurus* to the Pachycephalosauria and tentatively to the Homalocephalosauridae. Galton (1996),

however, found them similar to teeth of "fabrosaurids" *Alocodon* and especially *Trimucrodon* (crowns low, asymmetrical, lacking vertical ridges, having few marginal denticles of varying size and prominent ridge forming distinct edge; root in *Taveirosaurus* and *Trimucrodon* narrow close to crown, then widens out, root's maximum width being at middle part and subequal to that of crown).

Large dinosaurs are unknown from the Taveiro locality and from the Maastrichtian locality of Aveiro, Portugal, while a variety of smaller taxa (*e.g.* megalosaurids, dromaeosaurids, troodontids, and indeterminate saurischians and ornithischians) are represented (see *Euronychodon* entry). This implied to Antunes and Sigogneau-Russell that only relatively small dinosaurs persisted in westernmost Europe during the Late Cretaceous, larger forms having already vanished after the Cenomanian transgression that produced more restricted terrestrial areas of availability; and that the final extinction may have been hastened, in part, by faunal impoverishment resulting from this transgression.

Key Reference: Antunes and Sigogneau-Russell (1991); Galton (1996).

TAWASAURUS Yang [Young] 1982 [*nomen dubium*]—(=?*Lufengosaurus*)

Saurischia: Sauropodomorpha: Prosauropoda *incertae sedis.*

Name derivation: "Tawa [now Dawa]" + Greek *sauros* = "lizard."

Type species: *T. minor* Yang [Young] 1982 [*nomen dubium*].

Other species: [None.]

Tawasaurus minor, MG V15, holotype partial skull, right lateral view. (After Dong 1987.)

Occurrence: Lower Lufeng Formation, Yunnan, People's Republic of China.

Age: Late Jurassic (Hettangian-Pliensbachian).

Known material: Partial cranial remains.

Holotype: MG V15, snout region of skull, complete lower jaws, ?hatchling.

Diagnosis of genus: [No modern diagnosis published.]

Comments: The genus *Tawasaurus* was founded upon incomplete cranial remains (MG V15), collected in 1957 by Hu Cheng Zhi of the Museum of Geology, Dawa, from the Lower Lufeng Formation, at Heiguopeng, Dawaxiang, southeast of Lufeng, Yunnan, People's Republic of China. The paratype specimen (MG V11) consists of a damaged skull with lower jaws (Yang [formerly Young] 1982*a*).

Yang diagnosed the monotypic *T. minor* as follows: Skull rather small, no longer than about 35 millimeters (about 1.35 inches) long, with rather short snout; orbits somewhat large, anterior margin of orbit prominently expanded, possibly reaching postero-superior part of preorbital foramen, outline of orbit gently circular; preorbital foramen irregularly triangular in outline, with rather long base; nares about half size of preorbital foramina, platyrectangular in side view; nostrils narrowly separated by premaxilla (upper margin joining nasal on both sides of both nostrils) and maxilla; tiny gap between orbit and preorbital foramen; boundary of junction between orbit and frontal faintly discernible; lacrimal rather large, with nondistinct anteriorly protruding portion; premaxilla very small; mandible very well developed, with very straight basal side; dentary foramina horizontally elliptical; supraangular bone well developed; coronoary very low; about 12 maxillary and five premaxillary teeth; maxillary teeth actutibaculate, with no serrations at margin of crown; premaxillary teeth flat at crown, with small valvular and leaf-like serrations at crown margin; 13–15 marginal serrations on each crown, crown protruding in middle; first to fifth cheek teeth largest of series, fourth premaxillary tooth longest of series; premaxillary teeth with rather acute canine-like crowns, roots subcircular in cross-section, no visibly distinct gaps between them; mandibular teeth circular in cross-section, serrations on crowns smaller than in maxillary teeth

Yang assigned *Tawasaurus* to the [abandoned] ornithishian family Fabrosauridae, believing the genus to be an early form of Late Triassic age. Sun and Cui (1986), in an article about the Lower Lufeng saurischian fauna, stated that Yang's assignment to Ornithischia was questionable, as there is no indication of a diagnostic predentary in the holotype (Dong Z., personal communication to Sun and Cui). Dong (1987) informally described *Tawasaurus* as a small prosauropod measuring no more than one meter (39.37 inches) in length. Galton (1990*a*) referred *T. minor* to the prosauropod *Lufengosaurus hueni*.

In a study on basal ornithischians, Sereno (1991*a*) observed that the holotype and paratype skulls of *T. minor* include such derived characters of prosauropods and segnosaurs as an L-shaped premaxilla-maxilla articulation and posterior premaxillary process that twists into a horizontal plane, and that the holotype features the prosauropod character of a broad ventral process of the nasal. As no discernable autapomorphies are apparent in either specimen, Sereno regarded them as indeterminate prosauropod remains, *T. minor* considered a *nomen dubium*, the material perhaps belonging to a hatchling.

Key reference: Dong (1987); Galton (1990*a*); Sereno (1991*a*); Sun and Cui (1986); Yang [Young] (1982*a*).

TECHNOSAURUS Chatterjee 1984

Ornithischia.

Name derivation: "[Texas] Tech [University]" + Greek *sauros* = "lizard."

Type species: *T. smalli* Chatterjee 1984.

Other species: [None.]

Occurrence: Dockum Formation, Texas, United States.

Age: Late Triassic (Carnian).

Known material: Isolated cranial and postcranial elements.

Holotype: TTU P 9021, right dentary with well-preserved teeth.

Diagnosis of genus (as for type species): Ornithischian distinguished by dentary/maxillary teeth, with anterior and posterior accessory cusps and longitudinal striations in lower area of crown (Hunt and Lucas 1994).

Comments: Perhaps the oldest and most primitive ornithischian known from adequate fossil material, the genus *Technosaurus* was founded upon partial skull and postcranial remains (TTU P 9021) [see below] found during the summer of 1983, in Upper Triassic red mudstone facies of the fluvial Dockum Group, near Post, Garza County, West Texas. (A quarry at the same locality also yielded an assemblage of aetosaurs, poposaurs, tritheledodontids, microsaurs, lizards, pterosaurs, metoposaurs, and parasuchids, the latter two indicating that the Dockum Group is of Carnian–Norian age) (Chatterjee 1988).

Originally, Chatterjee diagnosed the monotypic *T. smalli* as follows: Primitive "fabrosaurid" with skull twice the size of *Lesothosaurus*; teeth heterodont, marginally placed; tooth crown low, with flutings at base, symmetrical in lateral view, entirely enameled, lacking wear facets; premaxillary teeth conical; cheek teeth closely packed with overlap between crown of adjacent tooth; three cusps in crown, lined anteroposteriorly, connected by sharp, denticulated edges, main cusp central, anterior and posterior cusps accessory; no special foramina for replacement teeth; coronoid process high; external mandibular fenestra very large; dorsal vertebrae amphicoelous, with long and compressed transverse processes, paparophysis separated widely from diapophysis; astragalus elongated medio-laterally with ascending process (for locking tibia); tibia with elongated lateral facet and small, concave medial calcanieal facet; ankle joint of "Advanced-Metotarsal" type.

Chatterjee referred *Technosaurus* to the [abandoned; see Weishampel and Witmer (1990*a*)] family "Fabrosauridae," this genus possibly the archetypal ornithischian at the beginning of ornithischian phylogeny. (*Pisanosaurus*, usually regarded as the oldest known alleged ornithischian, is known only from fragmentary material.)

As observed by Weishampel and Witmer, *Technosaurus* retains various primitive characters (*e.g.*, complete premaxillary dental arcade, large external mandibular fenestra, and laterally- located apex of ascending process of astragalus); the teeth are like those of other ornithischians.

In a study of basal ornithischians, Sereno (1991*a*) observed that the holotype of *T. smalli* comprises at least two taxa, neither exhibiting any apomorphic resemblance to *Lesothosaurus diagnosticus*. The holotypic right jaw is seemingly ornithischian, based on tooth form (subtriangular crowns, well-developed neck separating crown and root, imbrication of crown margins in tooth row, increase in tooth size toward posterior center of tooth row; see Sereno 1986) and on posterior dentary teeth inset from the lateral surface (as in other ornithischians) rather than marginal (*con*

tra Chatterjee). As the enamel thickness on each side of the dentary crowns is equal, Sereno regarded this dentary as belonging to a relatively primitive ornithischian best regarded as Ornithischia *incertae sedis*.

Note: Sereno observed that the premaxilla and posterior lower jaw belong to a significantly smaller individual than that represented by the dentary, and that the premaxilla lacks several ornithischian features (*e.g.*, low angle premaxillary secondary palate, rugose anterior premaxillary margin, anterior margin of naris with premaxillary foramen, recurved anterior premaxillary crowns, inset of first premaxillary crown from anterior margin of premaxilla). As the premaxilla exhibits several sauropodomorph and prosauropod-segnosaur synapomorphies (*e.g.*, straight lanceolate crowns, L-shaped premaxilla-maxilla suture), and because the steep, posteriorly-located premaxillary palate and broad sutural surface for the opposing premaxilla are similar to the condition in prosauropods, Sereno tentatively referred this premaxilla to Prosauropoda indet.

Technosaurus smalli, TTU P 9021, holotype premaxilla, a. medial, b. lateral, c. occlusal (diagrammatic) views, right dentary, d. labial and e. lingual views, f. posterior half of left lower jaw, lateral view, g. dorsal vertebra, anterior view, right astragalus, h. anterior and i. posterior views, j. first and second dentary tooth, labial view, k. same, occlusal (diagrammatic) view. (After Chatterjee 1984.)

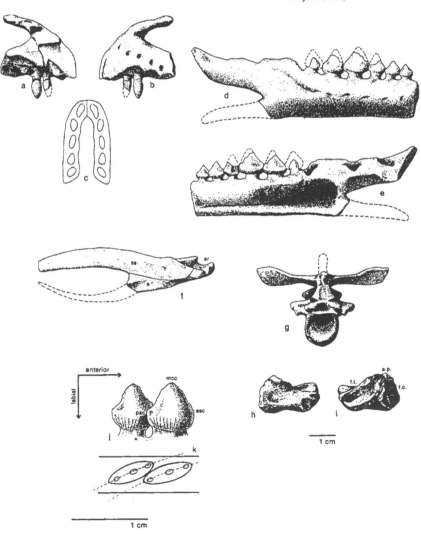

Key references: Chatterjee (1984); Hunt and Lucas (1994); Sereno (1991*a*); Weishampel and Witmer (1990*a*).

TECOVASAURUS   Hunt and Lucas 1994

Ornithischia *insertae sedis*

Name derivation: "Tecovas [Member of Dockum Formation]" + Greek *sauros* = "lizard."

Type species: *T. murryi* Hunt and Lucas 1994

Other species: [None.]

Occurrence: Dockum Formation, Texas, Petrified Forest Formation, Arizona, United States.

Age: Late Triassic (Upper Carnian).

Known material: Dentary/maxillary teeth.

Holotype: NMMNH P-18192, dentary/maxillary tooth.

Diagnosis of genus (as for type species): Ornithischian with low, mesiodistally long and markedly asymmetrical dentary/maxillary crowns, with up to five large denticles on distal margin and up to 12 denticles on steeper-sloping mesial margin; mesial denticles not reaching base of crown; no cingula (Hunt and Lucas 1994).

Comments: The genus *Tecovasaurus* was founded upon a dentary/maxillary tooth (NMMNH P-18192) recovered from the Tecovas Member of the Dockum Formation, Chinle Group (Upper Triassic), in Crosby County, Texas. Referred specimens include four dentary/maxillary teeth (NMMNH P-18193, P-181896 and [tentatively assigned] MNA Pl. 1704) from the same locality, and a dentary/maxillary tooth (NMA Pl. 1699) from the *Placerias* Quarry, lower Blue Mesa Member of the Petrified Forest Formation, Arizona (Hunt and Lucas 1994).

The holotype tooth, as measured by Hunt and Lucas, is 2 millimeters high.

As observed by Hunt and Lucas, tentatively assigned specimen MNA Pl. 1704 differs from other teeth belonging to the type species *T. murryi* in having only four denticles on its anterior margin; it resembles the other teeth in being asymmetrical and recurved, and having a steeper mesial than distal face; also, it has mesial denticles which do not extend to the base of the crown, distal denticles that do, and under five denticles on the distal margin.

Hunt and Lucas noted that the two stratigraphic units which yielded all of the collected *Tecovasaurus* remains contain such diverse tetrapod fauna as the phytosaur *Rutiodon* and stagonolepidid *Stagonolepis*, both fossil reptiles being indicative of latest Carnian age (see Hunt and Lucas 1990).

Key reference: Hunt and Lucas 1994.

Tecovasaurus murryi, NMMNH P-18192, holotype tooth, lingual view. Scale = 1 mm. (After Hunt and Lucas 1994.)

TEINUROSAURUS   Nopcsa 1928 emended 1929

[*nomen dubium*]—(=*Caudocoelus*)

Saurischia: Theropoda *incertae sedis*.

Name derivation: Latin *tendere* = "to stretch" + Greek *sauros* = "lizard."

Type species: *T. sauvagei* (Huene 1932) [*nomen dubium*]. Other species: [None.]

Occurrence: [Unnamed formation], Département du Pas-de-Calais, France.

Age: Late Jurassic (Kimmeridgian).

Known material/type specimen: Museum at "Malm der Gegend von Boulogne-sur-mer" 500 [destroyed], caudal vertebra.

Diagnosis of genus: [None published.]

Comments: In 1897, Sauvage described a caudal vertebra (formerly museum at Boulogne-sur-Mer, no. 500; destroyed during World War II) from Boulogne, France, which he referred to the ornithopod species "*Iguanodon*" [=*Camptosaurus*] *prestwichi*.

Sauvage described this material as follows: Caudal vertebra very elongate, 11 centimeters (about 4.2 inches) in length, centrum 3 centimeters (about 1.15 inches) high and more than 3.5 centimeters (over 1.35 inches) wide; dorsal border (in side view) barely straight; subtle groove along ventral length; posterior end with haemapophysis process (Sauvage 1897).

Nopcsa (1928*c*), recognizing the specimen as a theropod, renamed it *Teinurosaurus*, but failed to assign the genus a specific name. In a footnote (two footnote numbers interchanged due to a printer's error), Nopcsa seemed to imply that the specimen was intended as the basis for new genus *Saurornithoides* (preoccupied, Osborn 1924), this mistake also making it appear that the name *Teinurosaurus* had been proposed by Cope in 1869 to replace Cope's *Deinodon*. Nopcsa (1929*a*) subsequently corrected the first error.

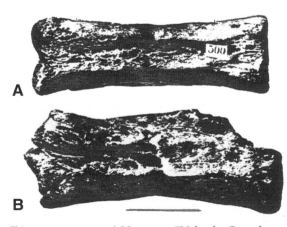

Teinurosaurus sauvagei, Museum at "Malm der Gegend von Boulogne-sur-mer" 500, holotype distal caudal vertebra of *Caudocoelus sauvagei*, A. ventral, B. left lateral views. Scale = 4 cm. (After Huene 1932.)

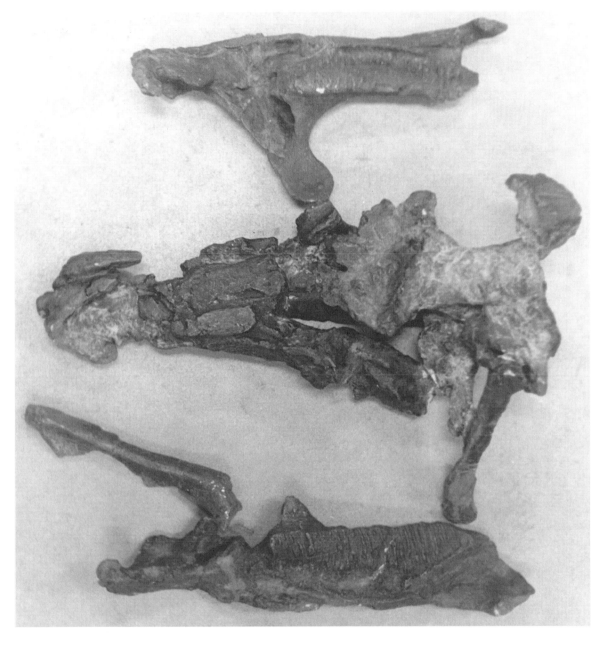

Telmatosaurus transsylvanicus, cast of BMNH B3386, disarticulated holotype skull of *Limnosaurus transsylvanicus*.

Huene (1932), evidently unaware of Nopcsa's correction, renamed the specimen *Caudocoelus sauvagei*. As pointed out by Ostrom (1969*b*), the name *Teinurosaurus* clearly has priority over *Caudocoelus*. Olshevsky (1978), in his compilation of archosaurian taxa, proposed that Nopcsa's original name be reinstated, the new type species combination becoming *Teinurosaurus sauvagei*. This proposal has become accepted by other workers (*e.g.*, Norman 1990).

Huene observed that the type specimen is typical of a "coelurosaurian" distal caudal vertebra, resembling caudals in *Elaphrosaurus*, though with a substantially wider centrum and slightly stronger prezygapophyses. Norman commented that the type material of *T. sauvagei* is definitely theropod, but can-not be further classified, this taxon regarded as a *nomen dubium*.

Key references: Cope (1869); Huene (1932); Nopcsa (1928*c*, 1929*a*); Norman (1990); Olshevsky (1978); Ostrom (1969*b*); Sauvage (1897).

TELMATOSAURUS   Nopcsa 1903—
   (=*Limnosaurus* Nopcsa 1899, *Hecatasaurus*;
   =?*Orthomerus*)
Ornithischia: Genasauria: Cerapoda: Ornithopoda:
   Iguanodontia: Hadrosauridae.
Name derivation: Greek *telmatos* = "marsh" + Greek
   sauros = "lizard."
Type species: *T. transsylvanicus* (Nopcsa 1899).

Telmatosaurus transsylvanicus, life restoration by Brian Franczak.

Other species: ? *T. cantabrigiensis* Lydekker 1888 [*nomen dubium*].

Occurrence: Sinpetru Beds and Densus-Ciula formation, Hateg Basin, Hunedoara, Romania; Grès de Saint-Chinian, Hérault, Grès à Reptiles, Var, France; [unnamed formation], Lleida, Spain.

Age: Late Cretaceous (upper Maastrichtian).

Known material: Five to ten fragmentary skulls, some associated with postcrania, various ages, including articulated and associated cervical, dorsal, sacral, and caudal vertebrae, appendicular elements including scapulacoracoid, humerus, ulna, femur, tibia, pedal elements.

Holotype: BMNH B3386, almost complete skull with lower jaw.

Diagnosis of genus (as for type species): Small-sized (?dwarf) hadrosaurid; caudal ectopterygoidal shelf largel; rostral process of jugal isosceles triangle-shaped; post-metotic braincase relatively long; basipterygoid process relatively large; relatively large scar for *m. protractor pterygoideus* on lateral aspect of basisphenoid; well-developed channel for palatine branch of facial nerve that also accommodates median cerebral vein; absence of diastema between predentary and dentary teeth; femur slightly bowed (Weishampel, Norman and Grigorescu 1993).

Comments: The best known Transylvanian dinosaur and one of the only apparent two known European hadrosaurids (see *Orthomerus* entry), the genus *Telmatosaurus* was founded upon a relatively complete but crushed skull (BMNH B3386) from the Sineptru Beds, south of the village of Hateg, Judetul Hunedoara (Hunedoara County), Transylvania [then part of Hungary], Romania. The remains represented the first fossil vertebrate known found in the Hateg Basin. The specimen was originally described by Nopcsa (1899) as *Limnosaurus transsylvanicus.*

Nopcsa originally diagnosed his new genus as follows: Rather primitive; skull with relatively short snout, narrow, abbreviated premaxilla, no antorbital opening, narrowly proportioned jugal, laterally-compressed teeth; skull about 40 centimeters (15.5 inches) in length; 12 cervical vertebrae with centra wider than deep; no cervical neural spines; caudal spines well developed, backwardly inclined.

As the name *Limnosaurus* was preoccupied (Marsh 1872) for a crocodilian, Nopcsa (1903*b*) subsequently proposed the new name *Telmatosaurus* for this genus, after which Brown (1910) proposed *Hecatasaurus*.

Isolated cervical, dorsal, and caudal vertebrae from the Maastrichtian (Danian) of central France were later referred to *T. transsylvanicus* by Lapparent (1947*b*).

Telmatosaurus is usually regarded as synonymous with *Orthomerus* (Lapparent and Lavocat 1955; Romer 1966; Steel 1969), although there are not sufficient grounds to make a positive synonymy. Brett-Surman (1975, 1989) noted that *Telmatosaurus* should not be referred to *Orthomerus*, the latter founded on a femur belonging to a juvenile individual, an indeterminate form best regarded as *nomen dubium*.

Weishampel and Horner (1990), in their review of hadrosaurids, assigned *Telmatosaurus* to the Hadrosauridae as the most primitive known member of that group, but neither to Hadrosaurinae or Lambeosaurinae. Weishampel, Grigorescu and Norman (1991), in their review and redescription of Transylvanian dinosaurs, noted that *T. transsylvanicus* is one of the smallest (less than 5 meters long, weighing about 500 kilograms, approximately 10 percent the weight of the average-sized contemporary hadrosaurid) duckbilled dinosaurs. The fully adult age of the individuals considered by Weishampel *et al.* was substantiated by fusion of their braincases and verte-

bral structures. Weishampel *et al.* noted that this taxon is one of the best known hadrosaurids, the entire skull and most postcrania represented by a number of various-sized individuals.

As observed by Weishampel *et al.*, *T. transsylvanicus* can be placed at the most primitive level within Hadrosauridae, as one of several hadrosaurid taxa positioned below the clade including hadrosaurines and lambeosaurines, this species lacking various features found in more derived forms (*i.e.,* dentary teeth narrowing, strong median carina developed on dentary teeth, quadrate with narrowing mandibular condyle, premaxilla without strongly serrate oral margin, humerus with strong, angular deltopectoral crest).

Weishampel, Norman and Grigorescu (1993) later redescribed *T. transsylvanicus*, their new diagnosis of this taxon based upon the holotype, and also the referred specimens BMNH R2967, R3387, R3401, R3809, R3828, R3841–3848, R4878, R4897, R4910–4911, R4913–4915, R4973, R5614, R10981, R10983, R11109–R11114, R11539, R11545, FGGUB 1000, 1005–1006, 1008, 1010, 1015, 1018, 1033, 1040, 1051, 1078, MJH 66, 70, MNMB v.60, as well as other isolated elements.

As first observed by Nopcsa (1934), almost all Late Cretaceous animals from Transylvanian sites are considerably smaller than similar animals found elsewhere. Nopcsa (1934) pointed out that these smaller forms were not juveniles, as shown by the degree of fusion of the braincase and vertebrae. Nopcsa (1923, 1934) further pointed out that the Hateg region was

Telmatosaurus transsylvanicus, BMNH B3386, restored holotype skull of *Limnosaurus transsylvanicus*, right lateral view. (After Nopcsa 1900.)

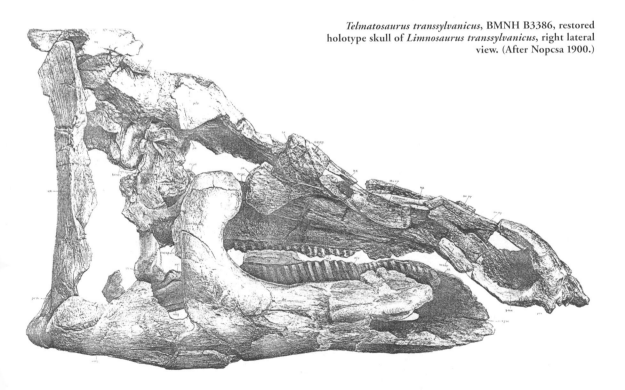

one of many islands making up a trans–European archipelago in the Late Cretaceous and stated that the small size of these animals could be indicative of dwarfism. Weishampel *et al.* (1993) noted that dwarfism should not be unexpected on islands, and that *T. transsylvanicus*, regardless of its small size, appears to be little different ecologically than other, larger iguanodontoidean iguanodontians.

Notes: Paris and Taquet (1973) reported the first discovery in France of a hadrosaurid specimen similar to *T. transsylvanicus*. The specimen, consisting of a scrap of jaw from the Petites Pyrénées of Haute-Garonne, about 4 kilometers (2.49 miles) west of Saint-Martory, expands the distribution of duckbilled dinosaurs in Europe.

Grigorescu, Seclamen, Norman and Weishampel (1990) reported the discovery, by the Universitatea Bucaresti, of 14 fossil eggs, the first from Hateg Basin, found in 1989 at a nesting horizon near the village of Valiora, in Transylvania. Originally believed to belong to the sauropod *Magyarosaurus*, the eggs were reassigned to the Hadrosauridae (most likely *T. transsylvanicus*) by Weishampel *et al.* (1991) based on associated embryonic remains. The eggs were arranged in four linear clutches, with two–four eggs per clutch, approximately 0.5 meters between clutches. If not deformed, the eggs would have been subspherical, measuring about 150 millimeters in diameter, shells about 2.4 millimeters thick and exhibiting a very tuburculated pattern.

Key references: Brett-Surman (1975, 1989); Brown (1910); Grigorescu, Seclamen, Norman and Weishampel (1990); Lapparent (1947*b*); Lapparent and Lavocat (1955); Lydekker (1888); Nopcsa (1899, 1903*b*, 1923, 1934); Paris and Taquet (1973); Romer (1966); Steel (1969); Weishampel and Horner (1990); Weishampel, Grigorescu and Norman (1991); Weishampel, Norman and Grigorescu (1993).

TENONTOSAURUS   Ostrom 1970

Ornithischia, Genasauria, Cerapoda: Ornithopoda: Iguanodontia.

Name derivation: Greek *tenon* = "sinew" + Greek *sauros* = "lizard."

Type species: *T. tilletti* Ostrom 1970.

Other species: [None.]

Occurrence: Cloverly Formation, Montana, Cedar Mountain Formation, Utah, ?Antlers Formation, Oklahoma, ?Antlers Formation, ?Paluxy Formation, Texas, United States.

Age: Early Cretaceous (Late Aptian).

Known material: About 27 skeletons, cranial and postcranial elements, teeth, ?integument, adults, juveniles.

Holotype: AMNH 3040, skeleton lacking skull, pectoral girdle, and cervical vertebrae.

Diagnosis of genus (as for type species): Vertebral count of 12-16-5-60+; tail deep, comprising two-thirds of animal's length; ossified tendons running axially along both sides of dorsal, sacral, and caudal neural spines, and along caudal centra and chevrons; scapula with straight cranial margin; coracoid with strong sternal process, coracoid foramen entirely separated from scapular articulation; forelimb relatively long and robust; humerus dominated by strong, extensive deltopectoral crest; carpus consisting of intermedium, radiale, and ulnare; manus short, broad, phalangeal formula 2-3-3-?1-?1; ilium with long, decurved preacetabular process, dorsally expanded, rugose caudal margin, very narrow brevis shelf; pubis with short, straight pubic rod, obturator foramen closed off from puboischiac suture, and moderately deep, laterally compressed prepubic blade unexpanded at tip; ischium with straight shaft laterally compressed, with tab-like obturator process located one-third down shaft; femur with separate, finger-like lesser trochanter, shallow extensor groove, deep flexor groove; pedal phalangeal formula 2-3-4-5-0, metatarsal V vestigial (Forster 1990*b*).

Comments: The first collected specimen of the genus now known as *Tenontosaurus* was a fragmentary partial skeleton (AMNH 5854) recovered in 1903 at Big Horn County, Montana. In 1931, 1932, 1933, and 1938, Barnum Brown of the American Museum of Natural History led expeditions to Montana, where the partial remains of 18 individuals of the same kind of dinosaur, as well as an incomplete skeleton that would later be designated the holotype (AMNH 3040; see below) of type species *T. tilletti*, were recovered. In 1940, a University of Oklahoma field crew retrieved a nearly complete adult specimen associated with at least four small juveniles, and, in 1948 and 1949, private collector Al Silberling dug out two specimens for Princeton University. As yet unnamed and undescribed, these remains were informally named "Tenantosaurus" [*sic*] by Brown (Forster 1990*b*).

During the 1930s, AMNH 3040, restored, and also a composite skeleton were mounted for exhibit at the American Museum (the former no longer on display). Referred to as simply "camptosaurs," these specimens would not be formally assigned names until the 1960s.

The genus *Tenontosaurus* was founded after numerous additional specimens were found in the Cloverly Formation (defined by Darton 1906; probably Late Aptian–Early Albian), Wheatland County, Montana. The finds were made from 1962–66 by field exploration parties for Yale University's Peabody

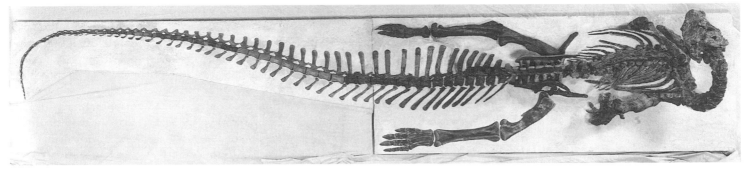

Tenontosaurus tilletti, AMNH 3040, holotype skeleton (restored), dorsal view.

Museum of Natural History, conducted by John H. Ostrom. Ostrom (1970) referred all of these remains to the new genus and species *T. tilletti*, establishing AMNH 3040 as the holotype. Paratype specimens included a partial skeleton (YPM-PU 16338) lacking the skull, pectoral girdle, and cervical vertebrae, and a partial skeleton with skull (YPM 5456).

Ostrom originally defined the monotypic *T. tilletti* as follows: Large, bipedal ornithopod, with moderately deep *Iguanodon*-like skull and extremely long tail; skull with very large external nares, long slit-like antorbital openings, supplementary lateral temporal openings under usual lateral fenestra; orbit subrectangular, larger than either lateral fenestra; premaxilla flaring inferiorly into broad, U-shaped, toothless beak, almost encircling nares; shallow, horseshoe-shaped predentary, with pseudo-tooth projections along dorsal margin opposing beak; coronoid process distinct; mandibles with long, curved retroarticular process; quadrate long, very narrow transversely, with convex posterior margin; process hook-shaped, turning downward at extremity; teeth unilaterally enameled; dentary teeth with very prominent vertical keel; maxillary teeth lacking keels, possessing many nonparallel minor ridges of subequal size; tail reinforced by ossified tendons on both sides of neural spines and chevrons; up to 60 caudal vertebrae, entire series twice or more length of precaudal column; 12 cervical, 16 dorsal, 5 sacral, and at least 59 caudal vertebrae; ischium long, straight, not expanded distally; prepubic blade straight, shallow, parallel-sided, horizontal; postpubic rod long, straight, narrow; ilium with long, narrow, sharply down-turned anterior process and conspicuously concave upper margin; manus very broad, with five flattened metacarpals, phalangeal formula 2-3-3-2-2; manual digits IV and V lacking claw-like unguals; metatarsals I–IV unreduced, V splint-like, phalangeal formula 2-3-4-5-0.

Ostrom calculated the average length of *Tenontosaurus* to be about 6 meters (20 feet).

Ostrom noted that among the collected remains referrable to *T. tilletti* are 26 partial or almost complete skeletons. Eight represent juveniles, most of the others being mature though not fully grown. Forster (1990*b*) added that over 80 specimens, ranging from small juveniles to large adults, have been collected since 1903 from the Cloverly Formation.

The geographic and geologic ranges of *Tenontosaurus* were extended beyond the Big Horn Basin locality by discoveries of extensive fragmentary and poorly represented material in other areas, including the Antler Sands (Late Aptian–Middle Albian) of Oklahoma and Paluxy Formation (Early–Middle Albian) of Texas, representing a ?second species (though, according to Forster 1990*b*, assignment to *Tenontosaurus* cannot be verified until a study of this material is completed), the latter locality also yielding fossilized skin impressions (Langston 1974); Cedar Mountain Formation (Aptian) of Utah and Wayan Group (Albian) of Idaho (Weishampel and Weishampel 1983); ?Arundel Formation (Hauterivian–Aptian) of Maryland; and an unnamed Aptian–Albian unit in Arizona (Langston; Galton and Jensen 1979; Weishampel and Weishampel).

Galton and Jensen referred specimens to *Tenontosaurus* sp., including a nearly complete right femur (UA 22), and two fragments of left femur (UA 23) originally described by Miller (1964), from south of the Empire Mountains, southeast of Tucson, Arizona. The femur measures about 700 millimeters (about 27 inches) in length, the entire animal probably some 5.2 meters (about 18 feet) long.

Also, Galton and Jensen tentatively referred to *Tenontosaurus* an incomplete crown of a right dentary tooth (USNM 244564) from the Arundel Formation, Laurel, Maryland. The specimen hints at a large development of an off-center ridge known only, to date, in lower iguanodontids.

Ostrom referred *Tenontosaurus* to the Iguanodontidae, based upon its large size and general resemblance to *Iguanodon* and *Camptosaurus*. Ostrom (1970) observed that *Tenontosaurus* differs from *Camptosaurus* in a number of features, including possessing a greater number of presacral vertebrae, a much longer tail with ossified rod-like tendons, distinctive pubic elements, less robust limbs, a different manus phalangeal count, different form of metatarsus and tarsus, and numerous cranial characters. The skull resembles that of *Iguanodon* in general form, differing in the lower snout, shallow jugal arch, smaller orbit, larger lateral opening, lack of subsidiary lateral opening, and closer-spaced teeth.

Other workers have suggested that *Tenontosaurus* could be more closely related to hypsilophodontids than iguanodontids (Dodson 1980; Weishampel and Weishampel 1983; Norman 1984a, 1984b). Sereno (1986) argued that *Tenontosaurus* is more closely allied with iguanodonts and hadrosaurs, this genus the basal node of Iguanodontia Dollo 1888 (including, among other taxa, Iguanodontoidea Hay 1902, emended, and Hadrosauroidea Sereno 1986) and the sister-taxon to that iguanodon-hadrosaur clade. Sereno stated that lack of premaxillary teeth, presence of leaf-shaped denticles in cheek teeth, and loss of one phalanx from manual digit III are derived features shared by members of this group but not by heterodontosaurids and hypsilophodontids.

In their review of the Hypsilophodontidae, Sues and Norman (1990) pointed out that *Tenontosaurus* differs from hypsilophodontids in absence of premaxillary teeth, presence of three (instead of four) phalanges in manual digit III, and prepubic process more narrow transversely than deep dorsoventrally, sharing these characters with Iguanodontia, but lacking the other synapomorphies diagnostic for that group. Sues and Norman were of the opinion that *Tenontosaurus* represents an as yet unnamed higher taxon of advanced forms within Ornithopoda.

Forster (1990b) clarified the postcranial osteology of *T. tilletti* with a detailed description based upon the holotype skeleton (AMNH 3040), paratypes (YPM-PU 16338 and YPM 5456), and numerous referred specimens (MCZ 4087, 4166, 4205, 4385, 4388, 4390, 7556–7558; OMNH 10132, 10144; BB 1; YPM-PU 16514; YPM 4882, 4904, 5099, 5117, 5146, 5195, 5299, 5399, 5410, 5411, 5413, 5416, 5417, 5422, 5424, 5426–5428, 5457-5471, 5473–5481, 5483, 5523, 5533-5535; AMNH 3010–3014, 3017, 3020, 3022, 3023, 3031, 3034, 3043–3045, 3050, 3061–3063, and 5854) from the Cloverly Formation.

Reconsidering the systematic assignment of *Tenontosaurus* based upon cladistic analysis, Forster (1990b) stated that referral to the Hypsilophodontidae was based on nine recognized hypsilophodontid characters in the genus (Norman 1986), but considered only one of these characters (presence of ossified hypaxial tendons) as potentially synapomorphic. These tendons (a synapomorphy for hypsilophodontids, derived independently in *Tenontosaurus*) were

explained by Forster (1990b) as a possible example of parallelism or reversal (ornithopod synapomorphy lost in more derived iguanodontians). The other proposed characters were recognized by Forster (1990b) as either plesiomorphic, and having an indeterminable polarity, or as characters not really present in *Tenontosaurus*.

According to Forster (1990b), *Tenontosaurus* shares nine out of the 20 synapomorphies used by Norman (1984a, 1984b) and Sereno (1986) to define the iguanodont-hadrosaur clade: 1. Absence of premaxillary teeth, 2. everted ventral premaxillary margin, 3. maxilla with paired ventral process and new rostroventral process that laps the premaxilla palate ventrally, 4. dentary with parallel dorsal and ventral borders, 5. denticulate predentary margin of bill, 6. teeth leaf-shaped, with denticles, 7. external opening of antorbital fossa small or absent, 8. manual digit III reduced to three phalanges, and, 9. femur with shallow cranial intercondylar groove and deep caudal intercondylar groove. In addition to these characters, Forster (1990b) noted that, in maxillary and dentary teeth of *Tenontosaurus*, enamel is restricted to the distal half of the crowns, another character linking the genus to higher iguanodontians. Forster (1990b) concluded that *Tenontosaurus* is a basal taxon within Iguanodontia (sensu Sereno 1986).

In their evaluation of Lower Cretaceous Cloverly fauna, Dodson, Bakker and Behrensmeyer (1983) observed that highly articulated *Tenontosaurus* remains occur in plant-rich sediments of swampy aspect with remains of turtles and crocodiles, suggesting that this genus preferred a wetter environment.

Forster (1984) noted that the *Tenontosaurus*-bearing units of the Cloverly Formation consist of paleosols indicative of a warm, seasonal climate with a notable rainfall increase through time. Vegetation available to this dinosaur as food consisted mostly of gymnosperms (the gymnospermous community of the Cloverly Formation seemingly consisting mostly of cycads, conifers, ginkos, ferns, and tree ferns), but may have included some of the earliest angiosperms. Apparently a low browser, a large adult *Tenontosaurus* in bipedal posture could crop food at a maximum height of about 3 meters, reaching plants (small- to moderate-sized species and immature individuals of larger species) at relatively low levels, including in its diet leaves, wood, and fruits. Forster (1984) concluded that *Tenontosaurus* was an adaptable animal that thrived in one geographic area for a long temporal span and through marked changes in climate, successfully making the change from drought-prone, semiarid times into and through the more humid, sub-tropical Early Albian.

As the theropod *Deinonychus* (Ostrom 1969a, 1969b, 1969d, 1970) is also known from the Cloverly

Formation, Ostrom speculated that *Tenontosaurus* was probably its frequent prey. This scenario was supported by the presence of isolated *Deinonychus* teeth found in association with *Tenontosaurus* remains at 16 Cloverly Formation sites, almost 20 percent of all collected *Tenontosaurus* material having been found with *Deinonychus* remains. Forster (1984), in a study of the paleoecology of *Tenontosaurus* in the Cloverly Formation of Wyoming and Montana, theorized that a fully grown adult (about four or five times larger than *Deinonychus*) probably passed beyond the predatory abilities of this theropod upon reaching a certain size, leaving *Deinonychus* to prey upon younger individuals. Although most *Tenontosaurus* specimens found associated with *Deinonychus* teeth were in the half-grown range, the largest (AMNH 3040) recovered was also found associated with such teeth, indicating that at least some *Deinonychus* individuals were opportunistic or scavengers.

Earlier evidence for this possible relationship included an uncatalogued *Tenontosaurus* skeleton (listed in Ostrom 1970) discovered at a Yale Peabody Museum locality and a single then-unidentified theropod tooth (now known to be *Deininychus*), the latter found near the remaining dorsal vertebrae during preparation of the specimen. The skeleton, that of a juvenile approximately 2 meters (less than 7 feet) in length and broken up by postmortem diagenetic processes, was intact and in natural articulation except for the missing mid-section, which appeared to have been bitten off by a predator (Ostrom 1963*b*).

Other evidence, collected from another Yale locality and reported by Ostrom (1969*b*), including a series of articulated caudal vertebrae and several isolated proximal caudal and dorsal vertebrae (YPM 5466) of *Tenontosaurus*, and various *Deinonychus* fragments (YPM 5201-5271), suggested not only that *Deinonychus* hunted at least a medium to large *Tenontosaurus*, but did so in a group of not fewer than three, but possibly as many as five or six individuals. Ostrom

(1969) interpreted these remains as those of the smaller carnivores killed by the larger herbivore as the latter defended itself from attack.

New, more compelling evidence regarding the *Tenontosaurus–Deinonychus* relationship, and also of the former's anatomy, was gleaned from the collection of an almost complete, articulated (and best preserved of this genus) skeleton (MOR 682) from a variegated, mostly green-gray mudstone in the Cloverly Formation, north of Bluewater Creek Fish Hatchery, Carbon County, Montana, a Museum of the Rockies locality. The specimen, representing a subadult individual measuring about 4.5 meters (almost 15 feet) in length, includes a complete, medially crushed skull measuring 305 millimeters (almost 12 inches) between premaxilla and occiput and with nasal displaced ventrally, and with the mandibles preserved in articulation. Missing are the left radius and ulna, both hands, and, except for the right femur, both hindlimbs. The complete vertebral column was preserved rotated 90 degrees, with the last dorsal vertebra meeting the first sacral vertebra (Maxwell 1995; Maxwell and Ostrom 1995).

Maxwell and Ostrom (1995) reported that found in close association with MOR 682 were 11 shed *Deinonychus* teeth. These teeth were found in the pelvic region, near the humeri and right femur. According to Maxwell and Ostrom, there is no evidence suggesting that either the skeleton or shed teeth were transported, while the coiling of the *Tenontosaurus* neck and tail in opposing directions discounts the possibility of either being pushed into their final positions by water currents. Discovery of this skeleton, closely associated with the shed teeth of *Deinonychus*, gives evidence supporting the idea that *Deinonychus* was an active predator that hunted in packs, the much larger *Tenontosaurus* being its specific prey.

According to Maxwell and Ostrom, the Museum of the Rockies *Tenontosaurus* may have died

Tenontosaurus tilletti, AMNH 3034, skeleton.

Photo by C. H. Coles, courtesy Department Library Services, American Museum of Natural History (neg. #315987).

on its belly. Probably, the attackers fed upon the freshly killed herbivore, the anterior part of its body dropping to its right side after the predators removed the abdominal flesh, the body being buried shortly afterward. The positioning of the 11 *Deinonychus* teeth found at the Museum of the Rockies site suggested that the attackers concentrated their feeding upon the area close to the right thigh and upper arms. Assuming that the *Tenontosaurus* carcass was not scavenged after the predators abandoned it, Maxwell and Ostrom explained how 11 teeth are somewhat too many for three or four *Deinonychus* to lose while feeding, this suggesting that the *Deinonychus* pack may have comprised as many as six or eight members.

Considering the possibility that MOR 682 represents a *Tenontosaurus* that died of some natural cause other than age, or was killed by just a few *Deinonychus* or by some other larger and as yet undiscovered predator, and was later scavenged by many *Deinonychus*, Maxwell and Ostrom pointed out that attack and feeding by a larger predator would have far more disturbed the carcass, and that scavenging by many smaller individuals would most likely have disrupted the main body of the carcass and disarticulated

the skull, limb girdles, vertebral column, and ribs. It was of Maxwell and Ostrom's opinion that, although no proof existed that the carnivores were only scavenging at the above mentioned sites, the circumstantial evidence supports active predatory behavior instead of scavenging.

As briefly described by Maxwell, MOR 682 shows further examples of variations in cranial anatomy in *Tenontosaurus*, including: 1. Premaxilla edentulous, closes all but most dorsolateral portion of elongate external naris; 2. maxilla overlaps premaxilla-lacrimal junction and defines ventral border of short, slit-like external antorbital fenestra; 3. enlarged rostral maxillary neurovascular foramen present immediately posterior to premaxilla-maxilla junction; 4. orbital opening of nasolacrimal canal formed, in part, by descending process of prefrontal; 5. frontal portion of dorsal orbital rim heavily striated; 6. quadrate almost vertical; 7. foramen magnum (crushed medially) apparently separated from supraoccipitals by stout dorsomedial process of exoccipitals; 8. predentary with single ventral projection; and 9. surangular foramen located far behind surangular-dentary suture. These and other features that

Photo by R. A. Long and S. P. Welles (neg. #73-208A-3), courtesy American Museum of Natural History.

Tenontosaurus tilletti,
AMNH 3034, skeleton.

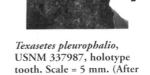

Texasetes pleurophalio, USNM 337987, holotype tooth. Scale = 5 mm. (After Coombs 1995.)

vary between skulls may indicate the presence of more than one species of *Tenontosaurus* in the Cloverly population.

Forster (1990*b*) determined that *Tenontosaurus* was a moderately robust, bipedal animal capable of limited quadrupedal locomotion. The long, deep tail, stiffened by ossified tendons, seems designed to counterbalance the animal's trunk, ossified epaxial tendons keeping the body from sagging over the acetabulum. In the forelimb, the strong deltopectoral crest, short and robust metacarpals, and digits capable of hyperextension are adaptations for quadrupedal standing or walking. Absence of compaction of the proximal metacarpals, great disparity in forelimb and hindlimb lengths, and short forearm and manus indicate that rapid quadrupedal locomotion was not possible. Forster (1990*b*) concluded that *Tenontosaurus* utilized a bipedal stance for more rapid walking, coming down on all fours to stand, walk at a slower pace, or browse on low vegetation.

In briefly discussing juvenile groups in *T. tilletti,* Forster (1990*a*) noted two juvenile groups—the first, comprising a jumble of small weathered skeletons (originally cataloged as AMNH 3019 and 3109; see Dodson 1980; now AMNH 3012, 3022 and 3023) collected in July, 1931, by Brown and Peter Kaisen for the American Museum of Natural History, on Cashen Ranch, Big Horn County, Montana, representing individuals about one-third the size of the largest known adult specimen; the second, collected in 1940 by J. W. Stovall for the University of Oklahoma, Big Hor, representing at least four disassociated skeletons (collectively labeled OMNH 10144). According to W. Langston, Jr. (personal communication to Forster 1990*a*), a field assistant of Stovall during the specimens' excavation, the juvenile material was found beneath a large skeleton. Forster (1990*a*) stated that the presence of both aggregations supports the speculation that *Tenontosaurus* juveniles stayed or congregated in groups for some time after hatching, perhaps enjoying post-hatching parental care not unlike that associated with *Maiasaura* and possibly *Orodromeus.* As no sedimentological information exists from these localities, Forster (1990*a*) could not determine whether either represented a nesting site. Forster (1990*a*) proposed that, given the association of post-hatchling groups with other ornithopod genera, parental care or congregation of juveniles into groups may have constituted common survival behavior among the Ornithopoda.

Notes: Olshevsky (1991) pointed out that, since *T. tilletti* was named in honor of a family rather than an individual, the species name, according to Article 31[a][ii] of the International Code of Zoological Nomenclature, should take plural-ending spelling,

the species thereby corrected to *T. tillettorum.* However, only a ruling of the ICZN can officially change this spelling.

According to Pittman (1986), some of the smaller ornithopod ichnites from the Glen Rose Formation (Late Aptian) of the Gulf Coastal Plain may have been made by *Tenontosaurus.*

Key references: Brown (1933*b*); Dodson (1980); Dodson, Bakker and Behrensmeyer (1983); Farlow (1976); Forster (1984, 1990*a,* 1990*b*); Galton and Jensen (1979); Langston (1974); Maxwell (1995); Maxwell and Ostrom (1995); Miller (1964); Norman (1984*a,* 1984*b,* 1986); Olshevsky (1991); Ostrom (1963*b,* 1969*b,* 1970); Pittman (1986); Sereno (1986); Sues and Norman (1990); Weishampel and Weishampel (1983).

TETRAGONOSAURUS   Parks 1931—(See
    Lambeosaurus.)
Name derivation: Greek *tetra* = "four" + Greek
    gonos = "offspring" + Greek *sauros* = "lizard."
Type species: *T. praeceps* Parks 1931.

Texasetes pleurophalio, USNM 337987, holotype partial right scapulacoracoid. Scale = 5 cm. (After Coombs 1995.)

TEXASETES   Coombs 1995—(=?*Pawpawsaurus*)
Ornithischia: Genasauria: Thyreophora:
    Ankylosauria: Nodosauridae.
Name derivation: "Texas" + *etes* = "dweller."
Type species: *T. pleurophalio* Coombs 1995.
Other species: [None.]
Occurrence: Paw Paw Formation, Texas, United
    States.
Age: Early Cretaceous (Upper Albian).
Known material/holotype: USNM 337987, ?cranial
    fragment, two teeth, five cervical, three sacral,
    and 16 caudal vertebral centra, two partial
    scapulacoracoids, acetabular regions of ilia,
    fragment of ?ischium, proximal and distal ends of
    humeri, femora, and tibiae, proximal ends of
    ulnae and radii, ?distal end of fibula, a few
    indeterminate fragments of long bones, left
    metacarpal IV, left metatarsal IV, three phalanges
    including two unguals, several scraps of armor.

Diagnosis of genus (as for type species): Differs from other primitive nodosaurids (*e.g., Hoplitosaurus marshi, Hylaeosaurus armatus,* and *Polacanthus foxii*) in having finger- or prong-like scapular spine (=acromion or "pseudoacromion" process) that is displaced toward glenoid, and small fossa (=prespinous fossa) developed anterior to confluence of scapular spine with lateral surface of scapular blade; differs from derived nodosaurids (*e.g., Sauropelta, Nodosaurus, Panoplosaurus,* and *Edmontonia*) in retention of splint-like lesser trochanter on femur, and in hav-

Texasetes pleurophalio, USNM 337987, holotype proximal end of left femur, anterior view. Scale = 5 cm. (After Coombs 1995.)

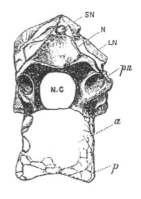

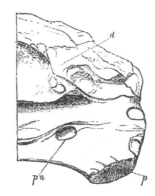

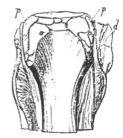

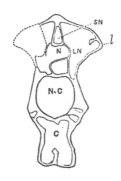

Thecocoelurus daviesi,
BMNH R181, holotype
anterior half of cervical
vertebra, anterior, right
lateral, ventral, polished
cross-section. (After
Seeley 1888.)

ing scapular spine directed at innermost limit of glenoid fossa (Coombs 1995).

Comments: The genus *Texasetes* was founded on a partial skeleton from the Paw Paw (sandy member of the Dennison Formation), Comanche Series, at Blue Mound, Texas. The specimen represents the most complete Early Cretaceous ankylosaur yet recovered from the Gulf Coast area of the United States (Coombs 1995).

With no detailed records exist pertaining to the collection of the holotype, Coombs noted that its preservation was unusual, mostly "in the complete absence of ribs and dearth of vertebrae, the almost complete absence of armor, and the absence of long bone shafts." Finding it questionable that a collector would have retrieved this specimen leaving behind better material, including larger vertebrae and armor, Coombs speculated that processes acting upon the carcass before final burial may have been responsible for its lack of these elements.

According to Coombs, *T. pleurophalio* is an intermediate form between a large number of more derived nodosaurid taxa and a smaller number of more primitive species (most notably, *H. marshi, H. armatus* [including the scapula that was part of the type specimen of *Polacanthoides ponderosus*], and *P. foxii*).

Coombs noted that much of the skeleton of *Texasetes* was buried as a unit in marginal marine sediments, implying that the animal possibly lived in the near-shore area. However, it is probable that the dinosaur lived and died at a more remote inland location, its body transported to the sea before burial via normal stream activity. Coombs cautioned that "emphasis should not be that *Texasetes* was distributed in nearshore environments, but rather that the outermost limit of its terrestrial distribution may have brought it into nearshore areas."

Key references: Coombs (1995).

THECOCOELURUS Huene 1923 [*nomen dubium*] — (=? *Calamospondylus*)
Saurischia: Theropoda *incertae sedis.*
Name derivation: Greek *theka* = "socket" + Greek *koilos* = "hollow."
Type species: *T. daviesi* (Seeley 1888) [*nomen dubium*].
Other species: [None.]
Occurrence: Wealden, Isle of Wight, England.
Age: Lower Cretaceous.
Known material: Vertebrae.
Holotype: BMNH R181, anterior third portion of cervical vertebra.

Diagnosis of genus: [None published.]

Comments: The genus *Thecocoelurus* was founded upon a partial cervical vertebra (BMNH R181), found by William Fox from the Wealden, Isle of Wight. The specimen was originally regarded by Seeley (1882) as representing a new species of *Thecospondylus*, which he named *T. daviesi.*

Seeley (1888) described this species as follows: Centrum laterally compressed, 4 centimeters high; transverse width of neural arch 2–3 centimeters at upper expansion, transverse width at neuro-central suture 1–7 centimeters; height of centrum to neural canal 13 millimeters.

According to Seeley (1888), this specimen (as restored) "indicates a close resemblance and affinity with the cervical vertebra of *Coelurus fragilis* Marsh," but not more than two-thirds (or less) the size of that species.

Huene (1923) considered additional sacral remains from the Wealden, referred by Seeley (1888) to *Thecospondylus*, to be different from the type species of that genus; consequently, he erected for Seeley's material the new genus *Thecocoelurus.*

Although *Thecocoelurus daviesi* is usually regarded as synonymous with *Calamospondylus oweni* (Ostrom 1970), Norman (1990) pointed out that the holotype of *T. daviesi* is not directly comparable to *C. oweni*, this taxon best classified as Theropoda *incertae sedis.*

Key references: Huene (1923); Norman (1990); Ostrom (1970); Seeley (1882, 1888).

THECODONTOSAURUS Riley and Stutchbury 1836

Saurischia: Sauropodomorpha: Prosauropoda: Thecodontosauridae.

Name derivation: Greek *theka* = "socket" + Greek *odous* = "tooth" + Greek *sauros* = "lizard."

Type species: *T. antiquus* Morris 1843.

Other species: ?*T. minor* Haughton 1918.

Occurrence: Magnesian Conglomerate, Avon, England; Fissure Fillings, South Glamorgan, Wales; ?Upper Elliot Formation, Cape Province, South Africa.

Age: Late Triassic (?Norian).

Known material: Over 100 disarticulated elements, skull, partial skeletons, isolated elements, juvenile to adult.

Holotype: Bristol Museum collection [destroyed], imperfect dentary ramus with at least 21 teeth.

Diagnosis of genus (as for type species): Basipterygoid processes elongated; quadrate posteroventrally directed; cervical vertebrae short, dorsal centra high, neural spines of anterior caudals with narrow bases; proximal third of humerus with high deltopectoral crest; first metacarpal slender, digits II and III of subequal length; ilium with short, triangular anterior process (Galton 1973, 1976 [tentatively expanded]).

Comments: The basis for the family Thecodontosauridae Lydekker 1890, *Thecodontosaurus* Riley and Stutchbury 1836 is the earliest and most primitive known prosauropod.

The genus was founded upon an incomplete lower jaw with teeth (Bristol Museum collection), recovered from the Magnesian Conglomerate, Durdham Down, near Bristol, England. Possibly referrable to the type species are remains from the same locality and horizon including a braincase, teeth, vertebrae, ribs, girdle bones, and limbs, including right and left ulnae, radius, left ilium, and a 25.5-centimeter (almost 10 inch) long femur. The original material, not identified by Riley and Stutchbury, was later described by Huene (1907–8, 1914). The type specimen and much of the other material were destroyed in 1940 during a World War II bombing.

Postcranial remains from other localities referred to this genus by Seeley (1859) cannot be positively associated with the holotype. *Thecodontosaurus* has also been reported from North America, Africa and Australia, although they cannot be referred with certainty to this genus. Galton (1973) suggested that the Bristol postcranial remains be retained in *Thecodontosaurus,* as there are no deductive reasons to refer them to any other related genus. Galton (1973, 1976) diagnosed *Thecodontosaurus* based on the holotype and referred specimens.

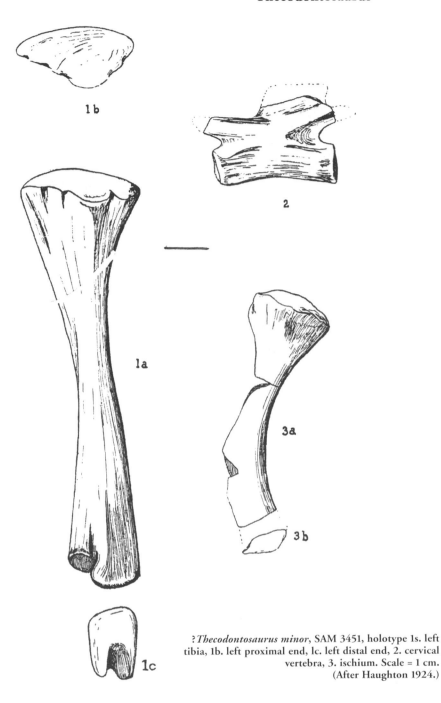

?*Thecodontosaurus minor*, SAM 3451, holotype 1s. left tibia, 1b. left proximal end, 1c. left distal end, 2. cervical vertebra, 3. ischium. Scale = 1 cm. (After Haughton 1924.)

The tentative species ?*T. minor* Haughton 1918 [*nomen dubium*] was based on a left tibia, cervical vertebra, and partial left ischium (SAM 3451) from the Red Beds at Pitsing. Haughton noted that these bones indicate a small individual that could not be identified with any European species, the tibia 109 millimeters long, cervical vertebra 31 millimeters. According to Galton (1976), this species is indeterminate even at the generic level.

In a review of the Prosauropoda, Galton (1990*a*) noted that, among all prosauropods, *Thecodontosaurus* alone is known to have been fully bipedal, the forelimbs about half as long as the hindlimbs (as in other prosauropods), but with proportionally much longer hindlimbs. As other prosauropods have a trunk to hindlimb ratio of 1:1.22–1:1.9 (Galton 1970*a*), that of *Thecodontosaurus* is 1:1.6.

Galton (1990*a*) regarded *Thecodontosaurus* as the sister-taxon of all other prosauropods, sharing all characters diagnostic for Prosauropoda. According to Galton (1990*a*), *Thecodontosaurus* is closer in size and in its bipedality than any other prosauropod to the model of the ancestral saurischian (small, carnivorous, erect-postured, bipedal, and cursorial) envisioned by Gauthier (1986).

Notes: *T. hermannianus* Huene 1908 [*nomen dubium*] was referred by Huene (1932) to *Plateosaurus gracilis*, then by Galton (1985*d*) to *Sellosaurus gracilis*; *T. dubius* Haughton 1924 was referred by Cooper (1981) to *Massospondylus carinatus* [=*M. harriesi* of his usage]; also referred to *M. carinatus* were *T. skirtopodius* (Seeley 1894) and *T. browni* (Seeley 1895).

T. alophos Haughton 1932 was referred by Charig (1967) to the "pseudosuchian" *Teleocrater*. Huene (1932) regarded *T. primus* Huene 1908 as a species of the prolacertiform *Tanystropheus*; Wild (1973) referred it to *Tanystropheus antiquus* and made *T. latespinatus* a junior synonym of *Tanystropheus conspicuus*.

Benton (1986) suggested that *T. latespinatus* Huene 1908, including caudal vertebrae, and *T. subcylindrodon* Huene 1908 [*nomen dubium*], including the distal half of a left femur from Durdham Down, are either prolacertiform or "thecodontian." ?*T. gibbidens* Cope 1878, based on a tooth, belongs to a primitive ornithischian (M. K. Brett-Surman, [personal

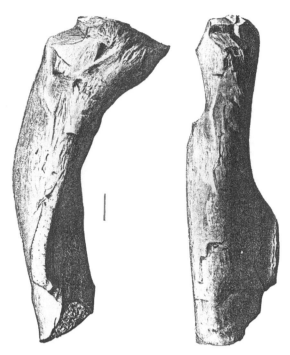

Thecodontosaurus antiquus, Museum of Bristol, No. 68, proximal half of left femur, posterior and lateral views. Scale = 2 cm. (After Huene 1907–08.)

sonal communication 1988) and may be described as a new genus by Olsen and Galton (P. Galton, personal communication to Olshevsky). Galton (1985*c*) noted that ?*T. elizae* (Sauvage 1907) [*nomen dubium*] is non-prosauropod, based on teeth of a carnivorous reptile (theropod, rauisuchid, herrerasaurid, or ornithosuchid).

Key references: Galton (1970*a*, 1973, 1976, 1990*b*); Haughton (1918); Huene (1907–8, 1914); Morris (1843); Riley and Stutchbury (1836); Seeley (1859).

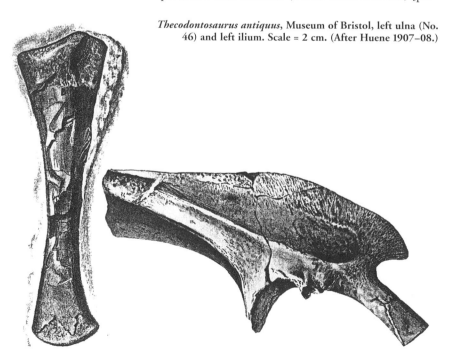

Thecodontosaurus antiquus, Museum of Bristol, left ulna (No. 46) and left ilium. Scale = 2 cm. (After Huene 1907–08.)

THECOSPONDYLUS   Seeley 1882 [*nomen dubium*]—(=?*Calamospondylus*)

Saurischia: Theropoda *incertae sedis*.

Name derivation: Greek *theka* = "socket" + Greek *spondlyos* = "vertebrae."

Type species: *T. horneri* Seeley 1882 [*nomen dubium*].

Other species: [None.]

Occurrence: Wealden, Kent, England.

Age: Lower Cretaceous (Neocomian).

Known material/holotype: BMNH R291, ?natural cast of neural canal of sacrum.

Diagnosis of genus: [None published.]

Comments: The genus *Thecospondylus* was established on a purported internal mold of a sacrum (BMNH R291) collected from Hastings Sand (Neocomian), Southborough, Kent. Though five vertebrae were preserved, fragments of vertebrae at either end of the specimen indicated to Seeley (1882) a total of seven.

As measured by Seeley, the specimen is 60 (about 23 inches) centimeters long, each vertebra 11 centimeters (over 4 inches) long.

T. horneri is generally regarded as a junior synonym of *Calamospondylus oweni* (see Ostrom 1970). However, as Norman (1990) pointed out, the holotype of *T. horneri* is too big to belong to a small form such as *C. oweni*; the specimen is not comparable to the material described as *Calamospondylus*, nor are sacral casts now used as systematic characters.

Key references: Norman (1990); Ostrom (1970); Seeley (1882).

Photo by the author.

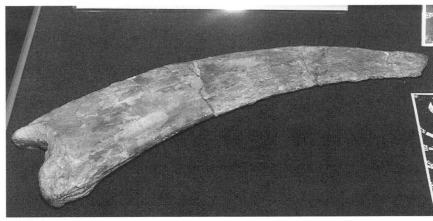

Therizinosaurus cheloniformis claw in "The Great Russian Dinosaurs" exhibit (1996), Mesa Southwest Museum, Mesa, Arizona.

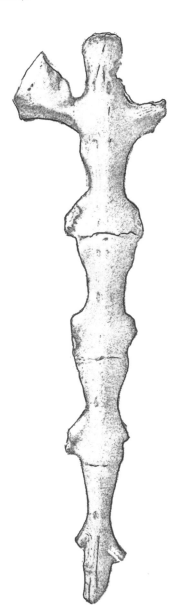

Thecospondylus horneri, BMNH R291, holotype natural cast of neural canal of sacrum. (After Seeley 1882.)

THERIZINOSAURUS   Maleev 1954

Saurischia: Theropoda: Tetanurae: Coelurosauria: ?Maniraptora: Therizinosauroidea: Therizinosauridae.

Name derivation: Greek *therizono* = "scythe" + Greek *sauros* = "lizard."

Type species: *T. cheloniformis* Maleev 1954.

Other species: [None.]

Occurrence: Nemegt Formation, Omnogov, White Beds of Khermeen Tsav, Bayankhongor, Mongolian People's Republic.

Age: Late Cretaceous (?Late Campanian or Early Maastrichtian).

Known material: Forelimb elements.

Holotype: PIN 100/15, manual ungual phalanges.

Diagnosis of genus (as for type species): Gigantic theropods with long forelimbs; humerus not twisted; distal carpals block-like; manus tridactyl; metacarpals of uneven length; unguals long, weakly curved, yet very narrow (Norman 1990).

Comments: Originally described (and depicted in a hypothetical life restoration) by Maleev (1954) as a Mesozoic turtle, *Therizinosaurus* was established on large claws (PIN 100/15) discovered in the southern Gobi Desert, Mongolia, during the 1948 Joint Soviet-Mongolian Paleontological Expedition. (Large flattened ribs found in association with the claws were later identified as sauropod.) Maleev put the genus into its own family, Therizinosauridae.

Other remains attributed to *Therizinosaurus* were found during later expeditions, including additional large claws discovered in 1957 and 1959 in Kazakhstan and Transbaykalia, and, in 1960, material described by Perle (1982), including a tooth, incomplete forelimb, large claw, and partial hindlimbs (including fragments of femur, tibia, astragalus, calcaneum, metatarsals, and pedal digits) with a four-digit foot (GI 100/45), from the White Beds (Nemegtskaya Svita), Khermeen Tsav. This material

Therizinosaurus

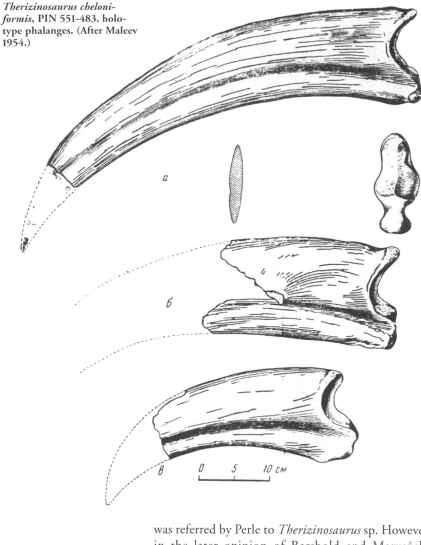

Therizinosaurus cheloniformis, PIN 551-483, holotype phalanges. (After Maleev 1954.)

Because of the unique form of the forelimb, girdle, and unguals, Norman (1990) regarded this genus as Theropoda *incertae sedis*. Later, Russell and Dong (in press) classified *Therizinosaurus* as a descendant of tenaturan theropods on the basis of new, more complete material recovered in 1988 from Aptian–Albian strata in Inner Mongolia.

Russell and Russell (1993) pointed out that, although no large, clawed herbivores inhabit modern terrestrial ecosystems, both *Therizinosaurus* and the mammal *Chalicotherium* evince this adaptation in the past. Russell and Russell considered a "segnosaurian foot" found in the same stratum as the holotype of *T. cheloniformis* to belong to the same specimen as the forelimb. Incorporating elements based upon remains of other taxa (most significantly, the presacral vertebral column, sacrum, and pelvis of the holotype of *Nanshiungosaurus brevispinus*; small, beaked skull based upon *Erlikosaurus andresi*, though entirely edentulous in keeping with the younger age and presumably more specialized morphology), Russell and Russell offered an hypothetical skeletal reconstruction of *Therizinosaurus*, as well as a life restoration depicting the dinosaur as a rather short-tailed, prosauropod-like animal with extremely long forelimbs and fingers, its general shape and posture resembling *Chalicotherium* (body shape of both also recalling that of a gorilla).

Russell and Russell regarded *Therizinosaurus* as a herbivorous theropod which could sit while feeding on foliage from bushes and trees, utilizing broad, powerful hands, capable of rotating, turning, and flexing to some degree, to direct branches and fronds toward its beak. Remains of both *Therizinosaurus* and *Chalicotherium* occur in depositional environments showing evidence of the presence of aborescent vegetation. Both animals were envisioned by Russell and Russell as bipedal foragers. Therefore, both genera were presented as evidence of convergence between dinosaurian and mammalian adaptive radiations, imperfectly expressed in animals of different origins and living at different times.

In preliminary reports, Clark, Novell, Chiappe and Perle (1995) regarded the Therizinosauroidea as a theropod group within the Coelurosauria (as redefined by Gauthier 1986 to include birds, ornithomimosaurs, and various long-armed theropods); and Holtz (1995*a*) proposed that the Oviraptorosauria and Therizinosauroidae constitute a clade within the Coelurosauria.

Key references: Barsbold and Maryańska (1990); Clark, Norell, Chiappe and Perle (1995); Holtz (1995*a*); Maleev (1954); Norman (1990); Paul (1987); Perle (1982); Rozhdestvensky (1970); Russell and Dong (in press); Russell and Russell (1993).

Therizinosaurus cheloniformis, GI 100/15, right scapulacoracoid and forelimb. (After Perle 1982.)

was referred by Perle to *Therizinosaurus* sp. However, in the later opinion of Barsbold and Maryańska (1990), this material is best regarded as "non-theropod" and an indeterminate representative of Segnosauria [=Therizinosauridae], mainly because of the short, broad metatarsus and astragalus with laterally curved ascending process (similar to Mongolian therizinosaurids) (also Paul 1987) [see below].

Rozhdestvensky (1970) identified *Therizinosaurus* as a theropod, but one atypical of Theropoda in the size of its distinguishing foreclaws. These claws are enormous, the largest some 70 centimeters (28 inches) long, considerably longer in life when covered by horny sheath. Rozhdestvensky suggested that this dinosaur fed on insects, using these claws to tear into large anthills.

THESCELOSAURUS   Gilmore 1913

Ornithischia: Genasauria: Cerapoda: Ornithopoda:
    Hypsilophodontidae.

Name derivation: Greek *theskelos* = "marvelous" +
    Greek *sauros* = "lizard."

Type species: *T. neglectus* Gilmore 1913.

Other species: [None.]

Occurrence: Lance Formation, Wyoming, Horse-
    shoe Canyon Formation, Dinosaur Park Forma-
    tion, United States; Scollard Formation, Alberta,
    Frenchman Formation, Saskatchewan, Canada.

Age: Late Cretaceous (Late Maastrichtian).

Known material: About eight partial skeletons,
    cranial and postcranial elements, teeth, vertebrae.

Holotype: USNM 7757, almost complete articulated
    postcranial skeleton, caudal series, other elements.

Diagnosis of genus (as for type species): Well-
enamelled surface of cheek tooth (lateral for maxillary, medially for dentary tooth) with numerous secondary ridges that form two converging crescentic
patterns; surangular with prominent lateral process;
dorsal edge of paroccipital process (opisthotic) adjacent to lateral edge of parietal is indented by deep
excavation that is Y-shaped in dorsal view; wedge-
shaped ventral part of supraoccipital indented by
notch (or pierced by foramen), almost excluded from
dorsal margin of foramen magnum by medial part of
opisthotics (Galton 1995).

Comments: The genus *Thescelosaurus* was
founded on a skeleton (USNM 7757) collected in
July, 1891 by John Bell Hatcher and W. H. Utterback,
from the Lance Formation of Niobrara [then Con-
verse] County, Wyoming. The specimen remained in
its original packing boxes until, years later, it was
studied by Gilmore (1913), who recognized it as representing a new genus and species.

A paratype specimen (USNM 7758), collected
in 1889 by O. A. Peterson, includes a few cervical,
dorsal, and caudal vertebrae, parts of scapulae, ribs,
bones of manus and pes, and portions of limb bones.
Additional specimens include the proximal phalanx
of digit III (USNM 8065), collected by Hatcher in
1890 from Niobrara County; a left scapula and coracoid (USNM 7760), collected by Hatcher in 1891
from Butte County, South Dakota; a cervical centrum (USNM 7761) collected by Hatcher, Sullins and
Surrell in 1891 from "Beecher's Quarry," Niobrara
County; and incomplete skeletons (AMNH 8016,
AMNH 5031, and AMNH 5032) of three individuals collected by Barnum Brown from Dawson
County, Montana.

Originally, *Thescelosaurus* was described briefly
in a preliminary paper by Gilmore (1913), who
mostly focused upon the vertebrae and left scapula
of the paratype, and left forelimb and right hind foot
of the holotype. Gilmore (1915) subsequently
described *Thescelosaurus* in greater detail after complete preparation of the holotype, estimating this
dinosaur to be about 3.5 meters (12 feet) in length
and slightly more than .88 meters (3 feet) high at the
hips.

Comparing forelimb to hindlimb lengths, Gilmore (1913) postulated that *Thescelosaurus* was normally bipedal and referred it to the Camptosauridae.
Later, Gilmore (1915), believing *Thescelosaurus* to have
been a light and agile dinosaur because of the skeleton's construction and the cursorial structure of the
hindlimbs, reassigned the genus to the Hypsilophodontidae.

Gilmore (1915) reported a small, dark colored
area in the holotype, found outside the ribs posterior
to the scapula of the left side, plus a second patch

Thescelosaurus neglectus,
USNM 7757, holotype post-
cranial skeleton (skull
restored).

Courtesy National Museum of Natural History, Smithsonian Institution (neg. #1133).

Thescelosaurus

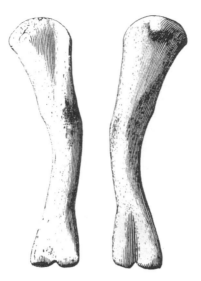

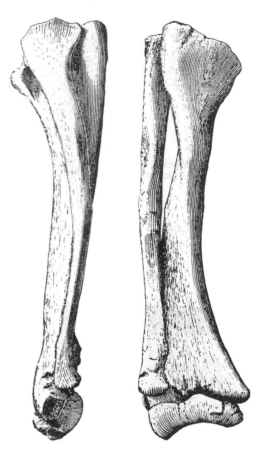

along the outer side of the anterior thoracic vertebrae.
These areas could represent portions of the dinosaur's
carbonized epidermis. They show no evidence of
either a regular pattern or dermal ossifications.
Gilmore (1915) observed that the skin of *Thescelosaurus* was "punctured" rather than scaled, a condition which may be a *post mortem* artifact (M. K.
Brett-Surman, personal communication 1988).

A second species, *T. edmontonensis* Sternberg
1940, was based on a skeleton (GSC 8537) including
the only skull material known from this genus, collected from the ?Upper Edmonton [now Horseshoe
Canyon] Formation, Red Deer River, Alberta,
Canada. Sternberg observed that the skeleton of this
species was generally more massive and the body
broader than in the type species and published a life
restoration depicting *T. edmontonensis* as a substantially heavier animal. Sternberg suggested that *Thes-
colosaurus* be placed in its own subfamily, Thes-
colosaurinae, noting that some of his observed
generic characters might relate to a higher rank than
genus. After reexamining the holotype of *T. edmontonensis*, Galton (1974*b*) suggested that *T. edmontonensis* was a junior synonym of *T. neglectus*, the
differences noted by Sternberg representing either
sexual dimorphism or individual variation (synon-

omy accepted by Sues and Norman 1990 in their
review of the Hypsilophodontidae).

Other material referred to *T. neglectus* includes
a partial skeleton (SMNH P. 1225) from the Frenchman Formation (Late Maastrichtian) at Rocky Creek,
Saskatchewan, Canada, the braincase and endocranial
cast of which was described by Galton (1989).

Galton (1974*b*) noted that, even though
Thescelosaurus retains many primitive features (*e.g.*,
premaxillary teeth; see also below), the genus was
probably less cursorial than other hypsilophodontids
and possibly more quadrupedal than the majority of
ornithopods. Galton (1974*b*) referred *Thescelosaurus*
to the Iguanodontidae as a conservative member of
that family, further suggesting that the genus belongs

Thescelosaurus neglectus, life restoration by Brian Franczak.

in its own group, Thescelosauridae, Galton then regarding Iguanodontidae as including all graviportal ornithopods lacking hadrosaurid skull specializations (a position he has since abandoned). Sereno (1986), and Sues and Norman retained *Thescelosaurus* in the Hypsilophodontidae, based on a number of shared derived skeletal features (*e.g.,* rod-like prepubic process and partially ossified sternal segments). Sues and Norman (1990) also suggested that *Thescelosaurus* may belong to its own subfamily (as proposed by Sternberg).

In a more recent cladistic analysis of this genus, Galton (1995) stated that the skull of *Thescelosaurus* can also be distinguished from other hypsilophodontids by the retention of the following primitive characters: 1. Transverse width of frontal at midorbital level greater than width of frontals across posterior end; and 2. frontal-postorbital suture consisting of interlocking ridges and grooves.

Galton (1995) also noted that the skull of this genus shares the following derived characters with other hypsilophodontids: 1. Raised and rugose area on anterolateral surface of postorbital (opposite to upper half of squamosal process, also in *Orodromeus*); 2. transversely wide squamosal (also in *Parksosaurus*); 3. premaxillary teeth without marginal denticles (also in *Zephyrosaurus*); and 4. primary (apical) vertical ridge of maxillary tooth centrally located on crown (also in *Othnielia*).

Carpenter (1982*a*) referred tiny Lancian teeth to *Thescelosaurus* sp. As described by Carpenter, these teeth are 1.3 (UCMP 124977)–3.2 millimeters (UCMP 124998) high, and 2 (UCMP 124997)–3 millimeters (UCMP 124973) wide, with enamel on one side, resembling miniature versions of cheek teeth figured by Sternberg (1940*b*).

Notes: Sternberg (1937) made *T. warreni* Parks 1926 the type species of a new genus, *Parksosaurus*; tentative species ?*T. garbanii* Morris 1976 was referred by Galton (1995) to a new genus and species, *Bugenasaura infernalis*.

Galton (1995) noted that the dozen teeth referred by Sahni (1972) to *Thescelosaurus*, from the late Campanian of Clambank Hollow, Chouteau County, Montana, belong to *Orodromeus makelai*.

Key references: Carpenter (1982*a*); Galton (1974*b*, 1989, 1995); Gilmore (1913, 1915); Morris (1976); Sereno (1986); Sternberg (1940*b*); Sues and Norman (1990).

THESPESIUS   Leidy 1856 [*nomen dubium*]— (=?*Edmontosaurus*)

Ornithischia: Genasauria: Cerapoda: Ornithopoda: Iguanodontia: Hadrosauridae *incertae sedis*.

Name derivation: Greek *thespesios* = "divine."

Type species: *T. occidentalis* Leidy 1856 [*nomen dubium*].

Other species: [None.]

Occurrence: Lance Formation, South Dakota, United States.

Age: Late Cretaceous (Maastrichtian).

Known material: Miscellaneous postcranial remains.

Cotypes: USNM 219, posterior caudal vertebra, USNM 220, proximal median pedal phalanx, USNM 221, anterior caudal vertebra.

Diagnosis of genus: [None published.]

Comments: *Thespesius*, the first hadrosaurid described from the Lance [then Grand Lignite] Formation, was founded on three cotypes (USNM 219, 220 and 221) collected by Ferdinand Vandiveer Hayden at Grand River, South Dakota. It was also one of the first dinosaurian taxa to be described from North America.

Leidy (1856*a*) described this genus as follows: Gigantic dinosaur; phalanx resembling that of *Iguanodon* and *Hadrosaurus*, is about 13 centimeters (5 inches) long, 11.5 centimeters (4.5 inches) wide at base by about 9.2 centimeters (3.5 inches) thick, 10.4 centimeters (4 inches) wide at distal end by 6.5 centimeters (2.5 inches) thick; vertebrae large, quadrately oval in outline in superior view, notched above, notch corresponding with spinal canal; larger vertebra about 13 centimeters (5 inches) transversely and vertically, smaller almost 12 centimeters (4.5 inches) transversely and vertically.

In their benchmark monograph on North American hadrosaurs, Lull and Wright (1942) commented that the *Thespesius* type material is not sufficiently diagnostic to refer with certainty to any known Lancian species, but observed that the anterior caudal vertebra, in its extreme shortness relative to height, most closely resembles that of "*Anatosaurus edmontoni*" [=*Edmontosaurus annectens*].

According to Brett-Surman (1989), the type material of *T. occidentalis* is not diagnostic even at subfamily level.

Note: *T. edmontoni* Gilmore 1924 and *T. saskatchewanensis* Sternberg 1926 were referred by Lull and Wright to *Anatosaurus*, which were later referred by Brett-Surman (1979) to *Edmontosaurus annectens* and *E. regalis*, respectively.

Key references: Brett-Surman (1975, 1979, 1989); Leidy (1856*a*); Lull and Wright (1942).

Thespesius occidentalis, USNM 219 [8790], anterior caudal vertebra, 220 [8792], proximal median pedal phalanx, 221 [8791], posterior caudal vertebra.

Photo by R. A. Long and S. P. Welles (neg. #73/138-44), courtesy National Museum of Natural History, Smithsonian Institution.

TIANCHISAURUS Dong 1993—(=_Tein-
chisaurus, Tenchisaurus_)
Ornithischia: Genasauria: Thyreophora:
Ankylosauria: Ankylosauridae.
Name derivation: Pinyin Chinese _Tianchi_ =
"Heavenly Pool [_Tian_ = "heaven" + _Chi_ = "pool,"
lake in the Tian Shan Mountains]" + Greek
sauros = "lizard."
Type species: _T. nedegoapeferima_ Dong 1993.
Other species: [None.]
Occurrence: Toutunhe Formation, Xinjiang, China.
Age: Middle Jurassic.
Known material/holotype: IVPP V 10614, skull
fragments, five cervical, six dorsal, seven co-
ossified sacral, and three caudal vertebrae, limb
bone fragments, many scutes, fragmentary
unidentified elements.

Diagnosis of genus (as for type species): Primitive, small (up to 3 meters long) ankylosaur; armor
well developed in shoulder region, many small scutes
in thorax; skull relatively heavy, little wider than in
Scelidosaurus; mandibular thinner than in other
known ankylosaurs, but similar to those in stegosaurs;
intercentrum and arch of atlas not co-ossified with
ribs; dorsal vertebrae amphyplatayan, primitive (for
ankylosaur); dorsal centra and ribs not co-ossified;
seven sacral vertebrae, including two clear dorso-
sacrals and one caudosacral; tail club small, flat; femur

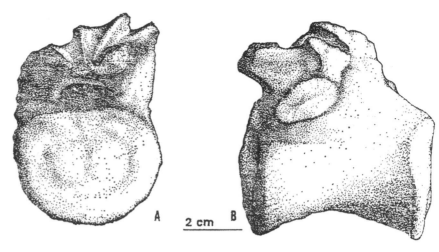

_Tianchisaurus nedegoape-
ferima_, IVPP V 10614, holotype dorsal vertebra. (After
Dong 1993.).

with long, prominent fourth trochanter; metatarsals
I-IV rather primitive for ankylosaur (Dong 1993_d_).

Comments: A small and primitive form, _Tian-
chisaurus_ is significant as the most complete Middle
Jurassic ankylosaur known, and the first to establish
the occurrence of this group of armored dinosaurs in
central Asia at that time. The genus was founded upon
a fragmentary skeleton (IVPP V10614) representing a
single individual, collected in 1974 by students doing
field work for the Geological Department of Xinjiang
University, from a sandstone quarry in the upper part
of the Toutunhe Formation (Middle Jurassic) of the
Sangonghe Valley, on the north slope of Bogda Feng
of the Tian Shan mountains, near the Tianchi lake,
Fukang County, northwest of Urumchi, in Xinjiang,

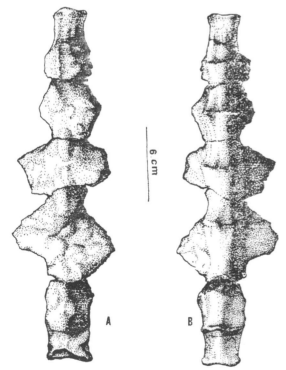

Tianchisaurus nedegoapeferima, IVPP V 10614, holotype
sacrum. (After Dong 1993.)

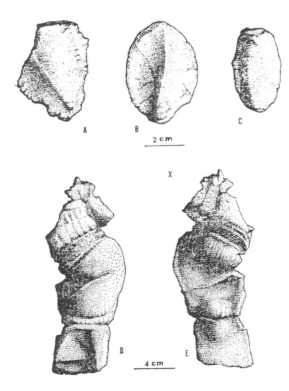

_Tianchisaurus nede-
goapeferima_, IVPP V 10614,
holotype armor plates and
scutes. (After Dong 1993.)

Tianchisaurus nedegoapeferima, IVPP V 10614, holotype first three caudal vertebrae. (After Dong 1993.)

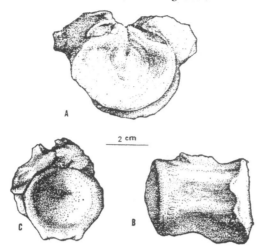

2 cm

China. In 1976, the specimen was sent to the Institute of Vertebrate Paleontology and Palaeoanthropology for identification (associated remains from the same site including two teeth and several limb bones referable to a megalosaurid) (Dong 1993*d*).

Dong noted that the early presence of ankylosaurian fossils on the Euro-Asian continent suggests that this dinosaurian group evolved in this region, perhaps from a small Early Jurassic ornithopod (see Colbert 1981).

Key reference: Dong (1993*d*).

TICHOSTEUS   Cope 1877 [*nomen dubium*]
Dinosauria *incertae sedis*.
Name derivation: Greek *teichos* = "protective wall" + Greek *osteon* = "bone" + Greek *os* = [adjectival ending].
Type species: *T. lucasanus* Cope 1877 [*nomen dubium*].
Other species: *T. aequifacies* Cope 1877 [*nomen dubium*].
Occurrence: Morrison Formation, Colorado, United States.
Age: Late Jurassic (Kimmeridgian–Tithonian).
Known material: Vertebrae.
Holotype: AMNH 5770, vertebral centrum, two fragmentary ?centra.

Diagnosis of genus: [No modern diagnosis published.]

Tichosteus aequifacies, AMNH 5771, holotype vertebral centrum, A. dorsal, B. ?anterior, C. ?left lateral, D. ?posterior, E. ventral views. Scale = 1.50 cm. (After Osborn and Mook 1921.)

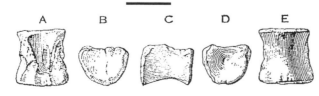

A   B   C   D   E

Tichosteus lucasanus, AMNH 5770, holotype vertebral centrum, A. anterior, B. dorsal, C. lateral views. Scale = 1 cm. (After Osborn and Mook 1921.)

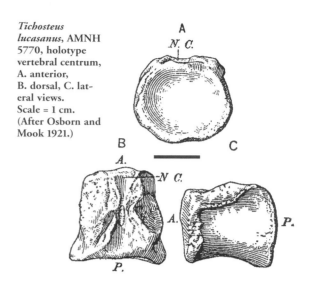

Comments: The genus *Tichosteus* was founded upon vertebrae collected from the uppermost beds of the Morrison Formation, near Canyon City, Colorado. Cope (1877) described these fossils but did not designate any of them as the holotype specimen, nor did he figure the material.

Tichosteus was diagnosed by Cope (1877) as follows: Vertebrae almost amphiplatyan; centrum hollow; neural arch attached by suture; centrum lacking capitular articulation.

Cope diagnosed the type species *T. lucasanus* as follows: Surfaces of vertebrae smooth except for some delicate longitudinal ridges.

From the same locality, a second species, *T. aequifacies*, was based on vertebrae from which Cope (1878*c*) selected the best preserved (?dorsal or ?lumbar [=sacral] vertebra) as the lectotype. Again, Cope (1878*c*) did not figure the remains, diagnosing this species as follows: Centrum inferiorly concave (not laterally compressed), with no processes, .10 centimeters in length.

Osborn and Mook (1921), in their study of Cope's sauropods, deduced that the holotype of *T. lucasanus* apparently consists of one well-preserved vertebral centrum and two fragmentary bones that are apparently also centra (AMNH 5770). Osborn and Mook figured this material.

Cope (1877, 1878*c*) believed that *Tichosteus* was a sauropod, an assessment rejected by Osborn and Mook, who regarded the material as indeterminate and unreferable to any reptilian group. Other authors (Romer 1956, 1966; Steel 1970; Olshevsky 1978) have listed *Tichosteus* as Theropoda *incertae sedis*. More recently, Norman and Weishampel (1990) considered both species of *Tichosteus* to be indeterminate ornithopods possibly related to the Iguanodontidae.

Key references: Cope (1877, 1878*c*); Norman and Weishampel (1990); Osborn and Mook (1921).

TIENSHANOSAURUS   Yang [Young] 1937
Saurischia: Sauropodomorpha: Sauropoda:
  ?Camarasauridae: ?Camarasaurinae.
Name derivation: "Tien Shan [mountain system in
  Asia]" + Greek *sauros* = "lizard."
Type species: *T. chitaiensis* Yang [Young] 1937.
Other species: [None.]
Occurrence: Sishugou Formation, Wucaiwan, Xin-
  jiang, Weiwuer Ziziqu, People's Republic of
  China.
Age: Late Jurassic (Oxfordian).
Known material: Partial postcrania.
Cotypes: IVP AS 40002, three cervical, three dor-
  sal and six caudal vertebrae, broken left coracoid,
  right ilium, distal portion of left pubis, left
  sacrum, IVP AS 40003, broken piece of dorsal
  vertebra, 26 caudal vertebrae, right scapulacora-
  coid, right humerus, proximal end(s) of radius

(or radius and ulna), left ilium (connected to
part of sacrum), left ischium, broken left femur,
proximal portion of tibia, distal portion of
fibula.

Diagnosis of genus: Modest-sized, with rather
short frontlimbs; scapula moderately strong, weakly
expanded distally, scapular shaft subequal in length
to expanded portion plus coracoid; ilium with very
open anterior embayment, pelvic peduncle set forward, acetabulum perforated [true of all dinosaurs],
but with broad, bony marginal area; ischium massive,
but not distally expanded; fourth trochanter of femur
weak (or missing) (Yang 1937*b*).

Comments: *Tienshanosaurus* was the second
Chinese sauropod to be described, the generic name
first mentioned informally by Sven Hedin during the
1920s in reports of new dinosaurs being dug up during his Sino-Swedish expeditions.

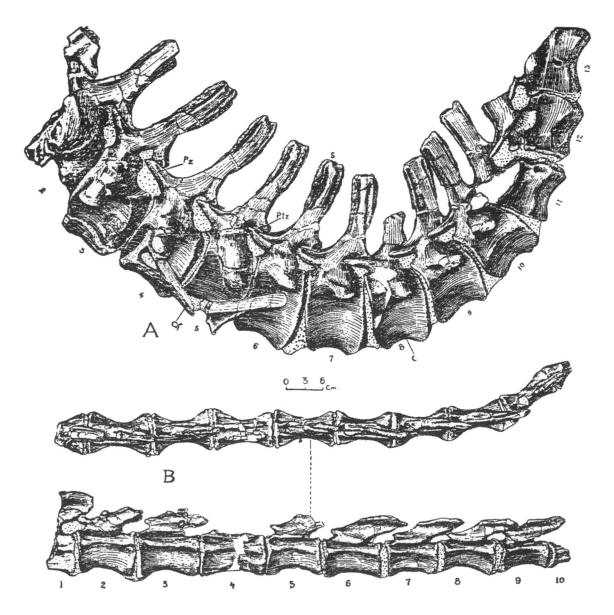

Tienshanosaurus chitaiensis,
IVP AS 40003, cotype caudal
vertebrae. (After Yang
[Young] 1937.)

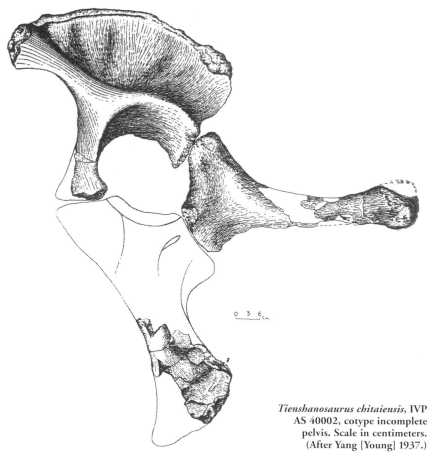

Tienshanosaurus chitaiensis, IVP AS 40002, cotype incomplete pelvis. Scale in centimeters. (After Yang [Young] 1937.)

The genus was established upon an incomplete postcranial skeleton consisting of elements from two specimens (IVP AS 40002 and 40003), collected from probably Late Jurassic beds (Yang [formerly Young] 1958) at Chitai, Sinkiang [now Xinjiang], China. Since both specimens were found in close proximity to each other and neither duplicated elements of the other, it was assumed that they belonged to the same individual (Yang 1937b).

As estimated by Yang (1937b), the length of the complete skeleton would have measured about 10 meters (approximately 34 feet). According to Yang (1937b), most of the preserved remains exhibit a

Tienshanosaurus chitaiensis, reconstructed skeleton including cotypes IVP AS 40002 and 40003. (After Yang [Young] 1937.)

close affinity with *Euhelopus* [=*Helopus* of his usage] *zdanskyi*, another Chinese sauropod. In *Tienshanosaurus*, however, the forelimb seems to have been relatively shorter, as the scapula and humerus are smaller than in *Euhelopus*. From the two specimens, Yang (1937b) reconstructed the skeleton of *T. chitaiensis*, based largely upon a general outline of the skeleton of *Camarasaurus*.

Dong (1990) referred to *Tienshanosaurus* sp. three cervical and 17 caudal vertebrae belonging to a single individual, collected from the Wucaiwan site (?Upper Jurassic), Kelamaili region, Junggar Basin, Xinjiang.

McIntosh (1990b), in a review of the Sauropoda, stated that the relationships of *Tienshanosaurus* are not certain. The long and slender cervical ribs, simple proximal caudal ribs, short distal caudals, and shape of the humerus and ischium suggest that this genus may be a camarasaurid; the scapula suggests affinities with *Apatosaurus*, and bridged-over chevrons a relationship with diplodocids.

Note: Yang (1954) reported a sauropod left scapula, too poor to refer to any genus, collected by T. J. Ting during the Sino-Swedish Expedition in 1930, from about the same horizon from which the *Tienshanosaurus* type material was recovered. Although precise occurrence and stratigraphy are unknown, the fossil came from Toutangho or Toutaoho, Changkehsien, southwest of Urumchi. The scapula is very thick throughout the entire beam. The distal end, unlike that of *Tienshanosaurus*, is not distinctly expanded. A rugosity (unknown in any other sauropod), about 90 millimeters long and 70 millimeters wide on the external side near the proximal expanded portion, is, according to Yang (1954) the result of injury, a healed wound, or pathologic disorder.

Key references: Dong (1990); McIntosh (1990b); Yang [Young] (1937b).

TIMIMUS Rich and Rich 1994
Saurischia: Theropoda: Tetanurae: Coelurosauria: Maniraptora: Arctometatarsalia: Bullatosauria: Ornithomimosauria: Ornithomimidae.
  Name derivation: "Tim [Timothy Rich and Timothy Flannery]" + Greek *mimus* = "mimic" [components combined for alliteration].

Type species: *T. hermani* Rich and Rich 1994.

Other species: [None.]

Occurrence: Otway Group, Dinosaur Cove East, Victoria.

Age: Late Early Cretaceous (Late Aptian–Early Albian).

Known material: Two left femora.

Type specimen: NMV P186303, left femur.

Diagnosis of genus (as for type species): Distinguished from femora of other described ornithomimosaurs by absence of intercondylar groove on extensor (anterior) surface (Rich and Rich 1994).

Comments: The first ornithomimosaur discovered in Australia, the genus *Timimus* was founded upon a left femur (NMV P186303), collected during the early 1990s, from the Ortway Group, Dinosaur Cove East, Victoria. Referred to the type species *T. hermani* was another left femur (NMV P186323), which was found about one meter away from the type specimen (Rich and Rich 1994).

As measured by Rich and Rich, the holotype femur has a length of 440 millimeters, proximal width of 65 millimeters, distal width of 62 millimeters, and distal depth of 40 millimeters; the referred femur measures 195 millimeters in length, with a minimum width of 14 millimeters, proximal width of 25 millimeters, and distal depth of 24 millimeters.

According to the authors, the presence of an ornithomimosaur in the Early Cretaceous of Australia suggests that, although best known from the Late Cretaceous of the Northern Hemisphere, this group of dinosaurs may have had its origins in Gondwana. Furthermore, the lack of an intercondylar groove in the holotype of *T. hermani* indicates that this species is more primitive than other known undoubted ornithomimosaurids.

As noted by Rich and Rich, southern Australia was still adjacent to Antarctica during the Early Cretaceous and at polar latitudes. This location, along with its relative isolation as a peninsula on the eastern part of Gondwana, may, according to the authors, have favored the area as an origin place for "evolutionary novelties" and final haven for groups which, by then, had become extinct in other parts of the world.

Key reference: Rich and Rich (1994).

TITANOSAURUS Lydekker 1877

Saurischia: Sauropodomorpha: Sauropoda: Titanosauria: Titanosauridae.

Name derivation: "Titan ["gigantic," after one of the Titans, a family of primordial Greek gods]" + Greek *sauros* = "lizard."

Type species: *T. indicus* Lydekker 1877.

Other species: *T. blanfordi* Lydekker 1879, *T. nanus* Lydekker 1893, *T. madagascariensis* Depéret 1896, ?*T. lydekkeri* Huene 1929 [*nomen dubium*], ?*T. falloti* Hoffet 1942.

Occurrence: Lameta Formation, Madhya Pradesh, Maharashtra, Aviyalur Group, Tamil Nadu, Pisdura, India; Grès à Reptiles, Var, France; [unnamed formation], Lieda, Spain; Grès de Maevarano, Majunga, Madagascar; [unnamed formation], Khoueng, Laos; ?Wealden, Isle of Wight, England.

Age: Late Cretaceous (Campanian–Late Maastrichtian).

Known material: Isolated postcranial remains, including vertebrae, femur, scute, ?eggs.

Holotype: IM collection, two posterior caudal vertebrae.

Diagnosis of genus: [No modern diagnosis published.]

Comments: *Titanosaurus*, a genus to which many species have been referred (mostly based on quite incomplete remains), was founded upon two posterior caudal vertebrae (IM collection) from the Lameta Formation, at Bara Simla Hill, Jubbulpure [now spelled Jabbalpore], India.

Lydekker (1877, 1893*b*) originally diagnosed the genus (and type species, *T. indicus*) as follows: Large; posterior caudal vertebrae characterized by marked lateral compression of centra, and distinct facets to accommodate articulation with chevrons.

Many species have been referred to *Titanosaurus*: Depéret (1896) described *T. madagascariensis*, based on poorly-preserved material including a

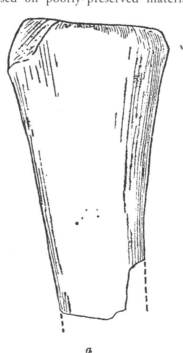
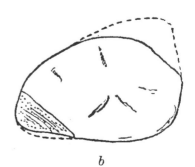

Titanosaurus blanfordi, IM K27/506, holotype probable left metacarpal II, a. anterior, b. dorsal views. Scale = 2 cm. (After Huene and Matley 1933.)

a

b

humerus and two caudal vertebrae, collected from the Upper Cretaceous of Northwest Madagascar. As later redescribed by Huene (1929), the anterior caudal vertebrae are relatively very short, slightly thickened in the middle. Huene referred this species to *Laplatasaurus*, a judgment, according to McIntosh (1990b) in his review of the Sauropoda, that cannot be confirmed.

Included in this species is a large dermal ossification from the same horizon, constituting the first report of sauropod body armor. This element was regarded by Steel (1970) as not of sauropod origin. More recent finds by Bonaparte and Powell (1980), however, have revealed that at least some South American titanosaurids did possess dermal ossifications. On the basis of dermal plates and scutes referred to *Saltasaurus loricatus*, Powell (1980) proposed that other titanosaurids were probably armored (see *Saltasaurus* entry). Possibly referable to *T. madagascariensis* are one sacral and three caudal centra from the Lameta Group of India, described by Huene and Matley (1933), and a caudal vertebra figured by Lydekker (1879) as belonging to *Titanosaurus blanfordi*.

T. nanus was based on two imperfect, apparently associated dorsal vertebrae from Neuquen, Argentina. Lydekker (1893b) provisionally referred these to *Titanosaurus*, but, because of their smaller size, separated them from *T. australis* (tentatively referred by McIntosh, with *T. robustus*, to *Saltasaurus*). Lydekker (1893b) described this species as follows: Dorsal vertebra not unlike that of *T. australis*, though inferior aspect seems less flattened, pleurocoel relatively larger; no traces of rib-facet on anterior border of lamina of arch (suggesting anterior region of dorsal series was articulated as in crocodilians, but with transverse processes) cervical vertebra characterized by extreme expansion and flattening of centrum.

(Though relatively small, these vertebrae were identified by Powell as adult by the absence of any trace of the neuro-central suture.)

T. valdensis Huene 1929 [*nomen dubium*] was based on two incomplete middle caudal vertebrae (BMNH R151) from the Wealden, Isle of Wight. Sometimes regarded as synonymous with *Chondrosteosaurus gigas*, there was no evidence to support a synonymy aside from the fact that both forms occur in the Wealden (J. S. McIntosh, personal communication 1987). This species was referred to the new titanosaurid genus, *Iuticosaurus*.

T. blanfordi Lydekker 1879 [*nomen dubium*] was based upon a caudal vertebra of a young individual from the Lameta beds of Pisdura, Chanda district, India.

As chronicled by Le Loeuff (1993), in 1857 the British Museum (Natural History) (now The Natural History Museum [London]) purchased an incomplete posterior caudal vertebra (BMNH 32390) collected from the Upper Greensand of the Isle of Wight, England. Lydekker (1888a) referred this specimen to *Titanosaurus* sp. b. Huene (1929) later referred this material to a new *Titanosaurus* species, *T. lydekkeri*.

As described by Le Loeuff, this vertebra is strongly procoelous, with neural arch anteriorly inserted on centrum; prezygapophyses extend anteriorly beyond anterior end of sacrum; total length of vertebra, 18 centimeters; centrum, 18 centimeters long. According to Le Loeuff, this species cannot be diagnosed and should provisionally be regarded as a *nomen dubium*.

Despite its name, *Titanosaurus* seems to have been a relatively small sauropod, albeit one heavily constructed, with a wide and sloping head, fairly long front legs, and a long, slender tail.

McIntosh briefly described *Titanosaurus* as follows: Midcaudal vertebrae strongly procoelous, with large distal balls, centra somewhat higher than broad, centra with flattened sides almost rectangular in cross-section; limb bones relatively more slender than in *Alamosaurus* and *Saltasaurus*; radius slender, distal end expanded medially and laterally, distal margin perpendicular to axis; humerus to femur ratio 0.74, tibia to femur 0.65; femur with no trace of lateral prominence.

Notes: Leonardi and Duszczak (1977) described titanosaurid remains from Bauru Formation, in the region of Guararapes, São Paulo. This material, including a diaphysis with the distal epiphysis of a left femur, and part of a left humerus belonging to different individuals, was found at the bottom of a well, about 100 meters above the upper surface of the basaltic lava-flows.

Titanosaurus indicus, IM K20/315, holotype caudal vertebra (12–14), a. right lateral, b. ventral views. Scale = 2 cm. (After Huene and Matley 1933.)

T. montanus Marsh 1877 [*nomen dubium*] was made the type species of *Atlantosaurus*.

According to McIntosh, *T. falloti* Hoffet 1942, based on a robust femur and amphicoelous caudal vertebrae, may belong to another genus in perhaps a different family.

Depéret (1899, 1900) mentioned (but did not describe) various titanosaurid bones, including caudal vertebrae, a femur, and a humerus, collected from several Late Cretaceous (Early Maastrichtian) localities on the Saint-Chinian area (Hérault department) in eastern France. Although Depéret referred these remains (housed at Lyons University) to *Titanosaurus*, Le Loueff regarded them as belonging to undetermined titanosaurids.

Fossil eggs discovered in India were regarded as possibly referable to *Titanosaurus* by Jain (1989). Tiwari (1986) studied fossil eggshell found in 1982 at the Bara Simla Hills in Jabalpore, observing that, in size and internal and external morphology, they exhibit features identical to eggs from France attributed to *Hypselosaurus*. Complete eggs, some in clutches and even a hatchery spread over a 20-square kilometer area, were found in 1983 at Gujarat in the Kheda District. Mohabey (1984) noted that sauropod bones were found in the Kheda beds associated with the eggs; from the same locality, Mathur and Pant (1986) reported several sauropod humeri, with an estimated length of 70–85 centimeters (about 27–32 inches). Given the similarity of both Jabalpore and Kheda eggshell specimens, and the fact that *Titanosaurus* is the most commonly known sauropod from Jabalpore, Jain assigned the eggs to that genus. Subsequently, Mikhailov (1991) referred the eggs from Peninsular India to the egg taxon Megaloolithidae. Jain and Sahni (1985) also described eggs suggesting sauropod affinity from Maharashtra, at Pisdura, possibly assignable to any titanosaurid (*Titanosaurus*, *Antarctosaurus*, and *Laplatasaurus*) known from Pisdura.

Key references: Depéret (1899, 1900); Hoffet (1942); Huene (1929); Huene and Matley (1933); Jain (1989); Jain and Sahni (1985); Leonardi and Duszczak (1977); Lydekker (1877, 1888*a*, 1879, 1893*b*); Mathur and Pant (1986); McIntosh (1990*b*); Mikhailov (1991); Mohabey (1984); Powell (1980); Tiwari (1986).

TOCHISAURUS   Kurzanov and Osmólska 1991
Saurischia: Theropoda: Tetanurae: Avetheropoda: Coelurosauria: Maniraptora: Arctometatarsalia: Bullatosauria: Troodontidae.
Name derivation: Mongolian *toch'* = "ostrich" + Greek *sauros* = "lizard."

Type species: *T. nemegtensis* Kurzanov and Osmólska 1991.
Other species: [None.]
Occurrence: Nemegt Formation, Gobi Desert, Mongolian People's Republic.
Age: Late Cretaceous (Late Campanian or Early Maastrichtian).
Known material/holotype: PIN 551-224, almost complete metatarsus.

Diagnosis of genus (as for type species): Troodontid having long, slender metatarsus with strongly reduced metatarsal II (Kurzanov and Osmólska 1991).

Comments: The genus *Tochisaurus* was established on an almost perfectly preserved metatarsus (PIN 551-224), discovered in 1948 during the Mongolian Paleontological Expedition of the USSR Academy of Sciences, in the Nemegt Formation (upper Campanian or lower Maastrichtian), at Nemegt, Nemegt Basin, southern Gobi Desert. The specimen represents the only complete troodontid metatarsus yet described from Asia, and is the second most complete troodontid metatarsus known (the other being NMC 8539, holotype specimen of the North American "*Stenonychosaurus inequalis*" [=*Troodon formosus*]). The specimen is distinct from the metatarsus of other known Mongolian species and also from that of the Canadian *T. formosus* (Kurzanov and Osmólska 1991).

As measured by Kurzanov and Osmólska, metatarsal II is 222 millimeters long dorsally and 233 millimeters long ventrally, III is 232 millimeters long dorsally, and IV 242 millimeters long dorsally and 252 millimeters long ventrally.

Comparing PIN 551-224 with metatarsi of other troodontid species, Kurzanov and Osmólska observed that the former is most similar to *T. formosus*, the distal articular head of metatarsal II distinctly smaller than the heads of other metatarsals, but noted that proportions in metatarsi of both forms are very different. In general, the metatarsus of *T. nemegtensis* is very slender (that of the Canadian species comparatively stout). Although the digits in *T. nemegtensis* are not known, the overall similarity between metatarsal II in this species to that of *T. formosus* may imply that digit II in the Mongolian form did not generally touch the ground. As the head of this metatarsal is small, Kurzanov and Osmólska surmised that digit II was probably reduced in comparison to that of other known troodontids.

Key reference: Kurzanov and Osmólska (1991).

TOMODON   Leidy 1865 [*nomen dubium*]—
(Preoccupied, Dumeril 1853; see *Diplotomodon*.)

Tochisaurus nemegtensis, PIN 551-224, holotype metatarsus. (After Kurzanov and Osmólska 1991.)

Name derivation: Greek *tomos* = "cutting" + Greek *odous* ="tooth."
Type species: *T. horrificus* Leidy 1865 [*nomen dubium*].

TORNIERIA   Sternfeld 1911—(See *Janenschia*.)
Name derivation: "[Gustav] Tornier."
Type species: *T. robusta* (Fraas 1908).

TOROSAURUS   Marsh 1891—(=?*Agathaumas*, ?*Polyonax*)
Ornithischia: Genasauria: Cerapoda: Marginocephalia: Ceratopsia: Neoceratopsia: Ceratopsidae: Chasmosaurinae.
Name derivation: Greek *toros* = "piercing" + Greek *sauros* = "lizard."
Type species: *T. latus* Marsh 1891.
Other species: [None.]
Occurrence: Lance Formation, Wyoming; Hell Creek Formation, Montana, South Dakota; Laramie Formation, Colorado, North Horn Formation, Utah, Kirtland Shale, New Mexico, Javelina Formation, Texas, United States; Frenchman Formation, Saskatchewan, Canada.
Age: Late Cretaceous (Late Maastrichtian).
Known material: Five partial skulls, isolated cranial material, ?teeth (juvenile).
Holotype: YPM 1830, skull missing lower jaws.

Diagnosis of genus (as for type species): Skull wedge-shaped in dorsal view, with short, pointed facial portion, compressed and forward-directed nasal horn, large supraorbital horns strongly inclined forwardly, long, slender squamosals that diverge rapidly as they extend backward, and parietal crest forming

Torosaurus latus, YPM 1830, holotype skull (restored).

more than half upper surface of skull; crest with two very large, oval-shaped fontanelles in posterior part and two small openings, the latter the ?true supratemporal fossae, between parietal and squamosal, directly behind bases of horncores (Marsh 1891*b*).

Comments: One of the last derived chasmosaurines and the most derived, *Torosaurus* was established on the almost complete skull (YPM 1830) of an old individual, collected by John Bell Hatcher in 1891, from the Lance Formation, near Lightning Creek, in Niobrara County, Wyoming (Hatcher, Marsh and Lull 1907).

Marsh (1891*b*) originally described two species of *Torosaurus*, the type species and the larger *T. gladius*, the latter based on a nearly complete parietal, right squamosal, nasal horn core, brow horn cores, epijugal, occipital condyle, and other cranial fragments (YPM 1831), found in the same horizon as the holotype of *T. latus*. The holotype of this species constitutes the largest skull of any known terrestrial animal, measured by Marsh as about 2.5 meters (8 feet, 5 inches) in length. The frill is immense and the brow horns slender, the latter rising erectly behind the orbits. In restoring the skull of *T. gladius*, Marsh modeled the missing "muzzle" after that of *Triceratops*.

Colbert and Bump (1947) described a smaller *Torosaurus* skull (about 1.5 meters, or 5 feet in length) recovered from the Hell Creek Beds of Harding County, South Dakota, and exhibited at the Academy of Natural Sciences of Philadelphia. Noting that the three known *Torosaurus* skulls were all collected from a relatively restricted geographical area and similar stratigraphic level and that they seemed to exhibit ontogenetic stages rather than specific differences, Colbert and Bump synonymized *T. gladius* with *T. latus*. Also, Colbert and Bump suggested that, during growth, the nasal horn became more prominent, frill progressively longer and losing its upward cur-

Torosaurus latus, YPM 1830, holotype skull (dorsal view). Scale = 20 cm. (After Marsh 1891.)

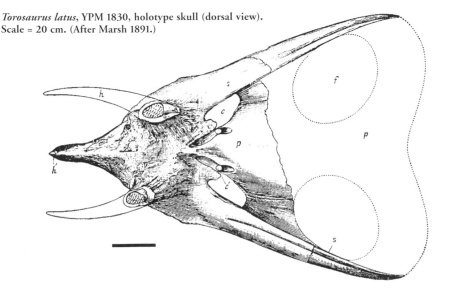

Photo by R. A. Long and S. P. Welles (neg. #73/200-15), courtesy National Museum of Natural History, Smithsonian Institution.

vature, and brow horns longer, more erect, retreating from a position immediately above to behind the orbits.

The species *T. utahensis* was based upon cranial material including a right squamosal, quadrate, quadratojugal, postorbital, brow horn core, postfrontal, lacrimal, jugal, and epijugal (USNM 15583), originally described by Gilmore (1946*b*), who provisionally assigned these remains to *Arrhinoceratops*. The material was collected from the North Horn Formation at North Horn Mountain, Manti National Forest, Emery County, Utah. Material referred to this species from the same locality include the paratype, comprising a right squamosal and posterior part of a parietal (USNM 15875), and an incomplete left parietal (USNM 16573).

With the 1972 discovery of the posterior part of a right parietal (TMM 41480-1) in the Tornillo Group, Big Bend National Park, Brewster County, Texas, Lawson (1976) recognized USNM 15583 and others assigned to ?*Arrhinoceratops utahensis* as referrable to *Torosaurus*, basing this identification on shapes of various ceratopsian frills with fenestrated parietals. As observed by Lawson, these shapes consist of triangular frills (as in *Protoceratops*, *Chasmosaurus*, and *Pentaceratops*), "figure 8" frills (*Brachy-*

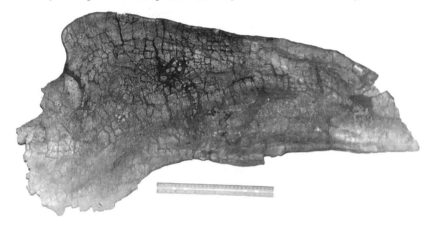

Torosaurus latus, USNM 15875, paratype partial frill.

ceratops, *Monoclonius*, *Styracosaurus*, and apparently *Pachyrhinosaurus*), and broad frills with circular or elliptical openings (*Anchiceratops*, *Arrhinoceratops*, and *Torosaurus*). Both *Anchiceratops* and *Arrhinoceratops* have rectangular frills with well-developed epoccipital processes, while *Torosaurus* has a "heart-shaped" frill with weakly developed epoccipitals, among other differences. According to Lawson, the presence of *T. utahensis* in Texas extends the geographic range of *Torosaurus* and, with other verte-

Torosaurus latus, referred skull.

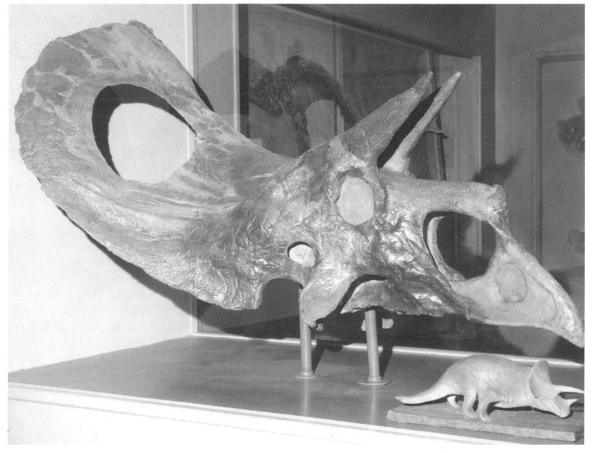

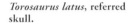

Courtesy Library, The Academy of Natural Sciences of Philadelphia.

Torosaurus

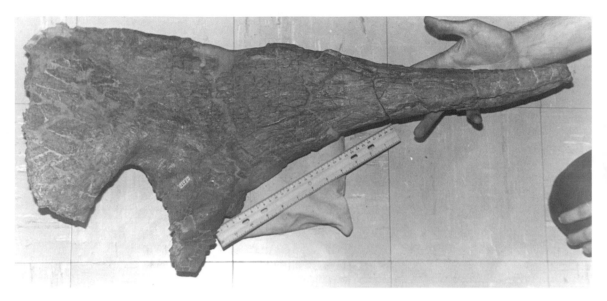

brate and invertebrate fossil remains, indicates a probable Late Maastrichtian age for the Tornillo Group. In their review of the Neoceratopsia, Dodson and Currie (1990) referred *T. utahensis* to the type species.

The most striking feature of the skull of *Torosaurus* is its size, more than half of which consisting of the huge parietal crest. The crest is smooth above and below, with small marginal undulations. The squamosal of the holotype skull (YPM 1831) of *T. gladius* bears three slight undulations, but no certain evidence of epoccipital processes have been found on the frill of any *Torosaurus* skull. Marsh (1892b) theorized that the extreme lightness and great expanse of the skull implied that the frill was entirely encased in integuments with no part free, a curious concept that would have severely limited movement of the head.

Moodie (1930), a specialist on bone disorders, examined the inner surface of the frill in the holotype of *T. latus*. Moodie studied the series of irregularities in the bone and concluded that this individual had suffered from a disease similar to *Multiple Myeloma*. Apparently small cancerous tumors had grown within the bone to create the holes and bumps seen in this specimen.

The only known postcranial remains of *Torosaurus* consist of a few fragmentary limb bones. Nevertheless, Lull (1933), from known skulls and the comparative lengths of other ceratopsids, estimated the total length of an adult *Torosaurus* to be no more than 6.2 meters (21 feet).

Notes: Carpenter (1982a) reported teeth, possibly referable to baby *Torosaurus* or *Triceratops*, from the Lance and Hell Creek formations in Montana and Wyoming. These teeth range from 2 (UCM 43526) to 6 millimeters (UCM 37878) high and 2.5 (UCM 43526) to 4.1 millimeters (UCM 45058) wide. Unlike adult teeth, these have a long, single unbifurcated root, a condition noted by Hatcher *et al.* for young incipient teeth. Carpenter postulated that the teeth probably became bifurcated as the animal matured. One tooth (UCM 45059) is heavily worn; the others have a triangular enameled face with vertical medial ridge and small denticles along the upper edge of the enameled surface.

Ostrom and Wellnhofer (1990) pointed out that *Triceratops* and *Torosaurus*, both elephant-sized herbivores, coexisted in a small geographic area covered by Niobrara County, this bringing up their question of whether the differences between them might constitute sexual dimorphism, with *Torosaurus* the male morph, *Triceratops* female.

Key references: Carpenter (1982a); Colbert and Bumb (1947); Dodson and Currie (1990); Gilmore (1946b); Hatcher, Marsh and Lull (1907); Lehman (1976); Lull (1933); Marsh (1891b, 1892b); Moodie (1930); Ostrom and Wellnhofer (1990).

Torosaurus latus, YPM 1831, restored holotype skull of *T. gladius*, right lateral view. (After Lull 1933.)

TORVOSAURUS Galton and Jensen 1979—
   (=?*Megalosaurus*)
Saurischia: Theropoda: ?Tetanurae: Megalosauridae.
Name derivation: Latin *torvus* = "savage, cruel,
   wild" + Greek *sauros* = "lizard."
Type species: *T. tanneri* Galton and Jensen 1979.
Other species: [None.]
Occurrence: Morrison Formation, Colorado,
   United States.
Age: Late Jurassic or Early Cretaceous (?Tithonian
   or ?Neocomian–?Hauterivian).
Known material: Forelimb elements, partial cranial
   and postcranial material.
Holotype: BYUVP 2002, left and right long bones
   of forelimb.

   Diagnosis of genus (as for type species): Large
(approximately 9 meters or about 31 feet), robust
megalosaurid with moderately long skull with height
equaling about 40 percent length; rostrum especially
narrow; three (?four) premaxillary teeth, 11–probably
13 maxillary teeth, ten–probably 13 dentary teeth;
maxilla dorsoventrally high, with fused interdental
plates making up one-half medial surface of maxillary body; no preantorbital fenestra; cervical vertebrae
strongly opisthocoelous, with ball-like anterior surfaces surrounded by posteriorly sloping rim that takes
up 50 percent of anterior surface, posterior surface
deeply concave; epipophyses long; centra highly excavated, dual chambered; venter strongly V-shaped;
dorsal vertebrae (except posteriormost member)
opisthocoelous, articular ends same form as in cervicals; pleurocoels well developed on anterior members
of series, grading into large, simple lateral excavations on posterior members; fenestrae passing from
side to side through neural arch anterior to hyposphene; thin neural spines with poorly-developed
anterior and posterior supportive laminae; posterior
dorsals with vertically elongate parapophyses; caudal
vertebrae mildly amphicoelous, anterior members
with small, shallow, elongate fossae; posterior chevron
facets much larger than anterior; venters shallowly
grooved; transverse processes long, swept back at
about 35 degrees to axial plane; neural spines narrow,
anterior and posterior margins converging dorsally,
terminating in rounded, expanded apices; transverse
processes and spine intersections straight line uninterrupted by pre- or postzygapophyses; chevrons slender, somewhat rectangular in cross-section; anterior
and posterior surfaces concave except for laterally
compressed distal end, terminating in posteriorly
pointing "foot"; anterior articular surfaces with pair
of digit-like projections; ilia long, low, with height-
to-length index of 29, and with preacetabular notch;
pubes terminating distally in small, slightly expanded
"foot," obturator foramen entirely enclosed; ischia
terminating distally in small, anteroposteriorly
rounded expansion; pubes and ischia of subequal
length, joined mesially by well-developed ventromedian symphysis; forelimb short, humerus-to-radius
index 220; humerus with straight shaft, large delto-

Courtesy J. A. Jensen and Brigham Young University.

Paleontologist James A.
Jensen comparing a humerus
(holotype BYUVP 2002) of
Torvosaurus tanneri with that
of *Allosaurus fragilis*.

Torvosaurus

Torvosaurus tanneri, right premaxilla (BYUVP 4882), left maxilla (BYUVP 9122), left dentary (paratype BYUVP 2003), *Allosaurus fragilis,* left dentary, left lateral views.

pectoral crest; circumference-to-length index 48, tibial circumference-to-length index 47; fibular circumference-to-length index 20; metatarsals robust, with no collateral pits (Britt 1991).

Comments: The genus *Torvosaurus* was founded upon an incomplete forelimb (BYUVP 2002) collected by James A. Jensen from the Upper or Brushy Basin Member of the Morrison Formation, Uncompahgre Upwarp (?Late Jurassic [Tithonian] or Early Cretaceous [Neocomian or Hauterivian]; see Britt 1991; based on Kowalis, Heaton and Bringhurst 1986), Dry Mesa Quarry, Montrose County, western Colorado. Paratype specimens include a left dentary (BYUVP 2003); third, fourth, and fifth cervical vertebrae (BYUVP 2004); seventh cervical (BYUVP 2005); fifth, seventh, tenth, and twelfth dorsal vertebrae (BYUVP 2006-2010); metacarpals I-III (BYUVP 2010-2012); right ilium (BYUVP 2013); pubes (BYUVP 2014); right ischium; right tibia, fibula, astragalas, and calcaneum (BYUVP 2016); right tibia (BYUVP 2017); and left first phalanx of manual digit I (BYUVP 2018) (Galton and Jensen 1979*a*).

Galton and Jensen originally diagnosed the genus (and type species, *T. tanneri*) as follows: (From

Torvosaurus tanneri, BYUVP 4882, right premaxilla, alveolar view.

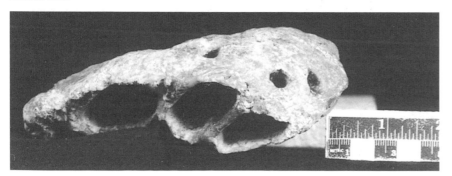

holotype) large, heavily-built theropod, about 10 meters (approximately 34 feet) in length; humerus relatively straight and massive, with a strongly indented head, large deltopectoral crest, broad distal end with squarish radial condyle, small rounded ulnar condyle, large ulnar epicondyle: ratio of maximum length of humerus to maximum proximal and distal widths 2.2 and 2.6; forearm short, ratio of maximum lengths of humerus to radius 2.2; ulna with massive proximal end; (from referred specimens) dentary short, with nine teeth, no Meckelian groove on median surface; centra of third cervical vertebra to mid-dorsal series markedly opisthocoelous, ball-like area delimited by groove from more peripheral anterior surface of centrum; in posterior half of dorsal series, posteroventral surfaces of each pair of transverse processes forming continuous curve that passes through large opening in pillar bearing postzygapophyses and zygosphenes; in last third of dorsal series, superior surfaces of prezygapophyses overlapped behind by expansion from base of laminae of supraprezygapophyses; metacarpal I with square proximolateral corner; first phalanx of digit I stout, short, twisted along its length; metacarpal II short but extremely massive, with 1.5 ratio of maximum length to maximum width; metacarpal III massive (2.2 ratio); ilium heavy, with low dorsal blade that tapers posteriorly to rounded point and wide brevis shelf; acetabulum wide but shallow, with transversely wide distal end to pubic peduncle; pubis and ischium subequal in length; subacetabular region deep, unemarginated, ventromedian symphysis nearly continuous; obturator foramen of pubis terminating in small anteroposteriorly expanded "foot"; indentation in posterior edge of pubis to accommodate corresponding posteriorly bowed, anterior portion of ischium; tibia massive; dorsal process of astragalus triangular in outline, with vertical lateral edge; metatarsus massive.

Originally, Galton and Jensen assigned *Torvosaurus* to the family Megalosauridae.

When laboratory work doubled the number of elements available for study, Jensen (1985*b*) recognized newly revealed diagnostic features in *Torvosaurus* not observed in megalosaurids and, consequently, erected for the genus the new family Torvosauridae. Jensen found that *Torvosaurus* was best characterized as possessing both primitive and derived characteristics, including the prosauropod-like brachyiliac pubis and ischium, and "coelurosaurian"-like dolichoiliac ilium. As already pointed out by Galton and Jensen, this combination had not yet been seen in any other North American theropod, and might possibly be the only such example from any age.

The systematic position of *T. tanneri* was reevaluated by Molnar, Kurzanov and Dong (1990), who noted that *T. tanneri* displays such "carnosaurian" features as enlarged lacrimal apertures, strongly opisthocoelous cervical vertebrae, chevrons with cranially projecting prongs, and ilium with narrow brevis shelf, most other "carnosaurian" features not apparent in the preserved materials. Molnar *et al.* regarded *T. tanneri* as apparently related to "carnosaurian" ancestry, but less closely so than *Eustreptospondylus oxoniensis*.

Galton and Jensen had pointed out that *Torvosaurus* differs from other Morrison theropods mostly in the structure of the forelimb and pelvis, which ally it to the European genera, *Megalosaurus* and *Poekilipleuron*. Kurzanov (1990) observed that *Torvosaurus* resembles *Poekilopleuron* and *Erectopus* in the massiveness of the elements of the extremities and in the very short first phalange of manual digit I, although the combination of dolichoiliac iliac with brachyiliac pubic and ischial bones distinguish *Torvosaurus* from other theropods. Because of similarities between *Torvosaurus, Poekilopleuron,* and some of Buckland's original *Megalosaurus* material, Paul (1984) stated that these forms may be congeneric. Paul noted that these genera are among the most archaic of theropods, all having prosauropod-like hands, pelves with short anterior iliac blades, and short, broad pubes and ischia, and femora with small lesser trochanters. Britt accepted that *Torvosaurus* is vaguely similar to *Poekilipleuron*, but noted that the two forms are clearly not congeneric. Examples of their differences include the form of the humerus, radius, and ulna (see Galton and Jensen), as well of tibia, fibula, astragalus, caudal vertebrae, and chevrons in *Poekilopleuron* (see Eudes-Deslongchamps 1838). Britt allowed for the remote possibility that *Torvosaurus* and *Megalosaurus* are congeneric, any synonymy of the two forms pending possible future studies of European megalosaurids. However, *Torvosaurus* has fused interdental plates, while *Megalosaurus* does not (R. E. Molnar, personal communication 1989).

Britt reported the collection of additional cranial and postcranial elements of *T. tanneri* from the Dry Mesa Quarry. These elements include left and right jugals (BYUVP 4883), a left lacrimal (BYUVP 5286), right postorbital (BYUVP 9249), right premaxilla (BYUVP 4882), right quadrate (BYUVP 5110), first atlas cervical vertebra (BYUVP 4884), third, fifth-eighth cervicals (BYUVP 4860, 2004a-2004d), and first, fourth-seventh, ninth-tenth, twelfth, and fourteenth dorsals (BYUVP 2005, 4998, 9120, 9121, 9090, and 4890). Britt pointed out that the type specimen (BYUVP 2002), as designated by Galton and Jensen, comprises elements not found in articulation. Having little doubt that all of the long bones belong to a single species of *Torvosaurus*, Britt questioned that they represented one individual. Britt chose the best preserved of the humeri, the left humerus (BYUVP 2002), as the holotype. Also, Britt referred to *T. tanneri* a posterior dorsal vertebra (DMNH 2243) collected from Dinosaur National

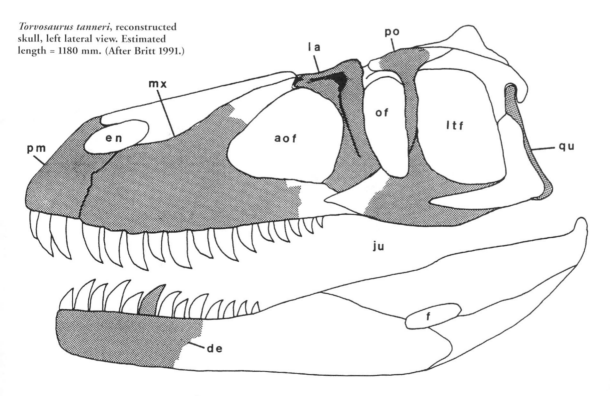

Torvosaurus tanneri, reconstructed skull, left lateral view. Estimated length = 1180 mm. (After Britt 1991.)

Monument Quarry; a tooth (CM 1254) from Charles Whitney Gilmore's Quarry N., Freezout Hills, Carbon County, Wyoming; and a large theropod tooth from Othniel Charles Marsh's Quarry 9, Como Bluff, Wyoming, figured by Lull (1927, plate 16, no specimen number). From the collected material, Britt offered a detailed osteology of *T. tanneri*.

Torvosaurus was regarded by Britt as a megalosaurid based on similarities in the known elements belonging to *T. tanneri* and the holotype (UMO J13506) of *Megalosaurus bucklandi*, at the same time synonomizing Jensen's monogeneric taxon Torvosauridae with Megalosauridae. The ilium of *Megalosaurus* is similar to that of *Torvosaurus* with respective height-to-length indices of 27 and 28; ischia are similar, although that of *Megalosaurus* is more robust, with a sharper ventral deflection at mid-shaft; dentaries are similar, *Megalosaurus* having a height-to-length ratio of 34 for the first nine aveloli, *Torvosaurus* 37. However, the dentary of *Megalosaurus* has a straight ventral margin and pronounced Meckelian groove, that of *Torvosaurus* a curved ventral margin and apparently no groove. Britt also noted similarities between *Torvosaurus* and *Ceratosaurus*, including the form of some cranial elements and ilium.

Notes: Jensen postulated that the Uncompahgre dinosaur fauna demonstrates substantial generic-level evolution in comparison to assemblages of the more familiar Morrison Formation forms, including an increase of at least 100 percent in "carnosaur" genera. According to Jensen, the numerous variations on classical morphology displayed by Uncompahgre forms represent an advanced fauna which superficially look familiar, yet, upon closer examination, reveal substantial differences.

Jensen noted that at least four Uncompahgre theropod genera and more than one unidentified family are known from humeri and caudal vertebrae. Among these specimens is a humerus which has a moderately robust proximal half, straight shaft, moderately expanded proximal articular surfaces and short deltoid crest.

Chure (1995) reported the collection, via screen-washing, of teeth belonging to small (yet more advanced than ceratosaurs) theropods from several localities in the Brushy Basin Member of the Morrison Formation (Late Jurassic; Kimmeridgian), Dinosaur National Monument. According to Chure, these teeth are significant in that most Morrison Formation theropod remains represent large taxa. The tooth crowns exhibit a wide range of curvature, presence or absence of denticles, size and shape of denticles, presence of constriction at the base of the crown, and the degree of mediolateral compression. The crowns generally measure 1 centimeter in height and sometimes .5 centimeters. The diversity in these teeth suggests the presence of several taxa all quite different from the large Morrison theropods *Allosaurus, Ceratosaurus, Marshosaurus,* and *Torvosaurus*; rather, they most closely resemble the teeth of such Cretaceous forms as dromaeosaurids, troodontids, and ornithomimids, groups believed to have originated during the Late Jurassic.

Key references: Britt (1991); Galton and Jensen (1979); Jensen (1985*b*); Kurzanov (1990); Lull (1927); Molnar, Kurzanov and Dong (1990); Paul (1984).

Torvosaurus tanneri wading through a flood.

Illustration by Gregory S. Paul.

TRACHODON   Leidy 1865 [*nomen dubium*]
Ornithischia: Genasauria: Cerapoda:
   Marginocephalia: Ceratopsia *incertae sedis*.
Name derivation: Greek *trachys* = "rough" + Greek
   odous = "tooth."
Type species: *T. mirabilis* Leidy 1865 [*nomen
   dubium*].
Other species: [None.]
Occurrence: Dinosaur Park Formation, Montana,
   United States.
Age: Late Cretaceous (Campanian).
Known material/holotype: ANSP 9260, tooth.

   Diagnosis of genus: [None published.]

   Comments: The name *Trachodon* is ubiquitous in older texts about dinosaurs and regrettably still surfaces in some modern popular writings. Traditionally, *Trachodon* has been portrayed as the classic noncrested "duckbilled dinosaur," supposedly identical to *Edmontosaurus*. The genus was the basis of the [abandoned] hadrosaur family Trachodontidae Brown 1914. However, the true affinities of *Trachodon* are now elsewhere.

   The type species *T. mirabilis* was established on seven worn, unassociated mandibular teeth (ANSP 9260) recovered by Ferdinand Vandiveer Hayden from the "Judith River" Formation, near Judith River, Montana. Hayden collected these specimens among other vertebrate and invertebrate fossils from 1854 to 1856, after having earlier recorded other fossils in this region later identified as hadrosaurid.

   Leidy (1856) originally described these teeth as follows: Tooth shaped like slightly bent hexahedral column, convexly slanting off from summit internally and to base externally; outer surface smooth, with prominent median ridge and subacute lateral borders; inner surface very rugose, with irregular protuberances; base hollow.

   Subsequently, Leidy (1858) described some well-preserved teeth, along with the partial skeleton of *Hadrosaurus foulkii* (ASNP 10005), from the Greensand of New Jersey. Later, Leidy (1865) described this new material more completely.

   As observed by Lambe (1918*a*) and Sternberg (1936) in generally forgotten papers reevaluating the systematic position of *Trachodon*, there has been much confusion between this taxon and *Hadrosaurus*, some workers referring both to the same genus. Among Leidy's cotypes of *T. mirabilis* are a single-rooted hadrosaurid tooth, but also a double-rooted tooth (double roots are a ceratopsian feature; see Hatcher, Marsh and Lull 1907). Realizing that these cotypes were very different, Leidy (1868) proposed that the name *Trachodon* be reserved for the double-rooted tooth, the single-rooted teeth referred to *Hadrosaurus*. Other paleontologists, apparently

unaware of Leidy's abandonment of the name, continued to refer hadrosaurid remains to *Trachodon*.

   Coombs (1988) recommended that *Trachodon mirabilis* be regarded as a *nomen dubium* and, being the oldest available name for any hadrosaurid dinosaur, be used only in historical but not taxonomic discussions.

   Note: Numerous taxa have been assigned to *Trachodon*: *T. atavus* Cope 1871 [*nomen dubium*] and *T. longiceps* Marsh 1890 [*nomen dubium*] have been referred to *Anatotitan copei*; *T. selwyni* Lambe 1902 [*nomen dubium*] was referred to *Edmontosaurus regalis*; *T. cantabrigiensis* Lydekker 1888 [*nomen dubium*] to *?Telmatosaurus cantabrigiensis*; *T. marginatus* Lambe 1902 [*nomen dubium; partim*] to *Gryposaurus notabilis* and *Lambeosaurus lambei*; *T. altidens* Lambe 1902 [*nomen dubium*] to *Corythosaurus casuarius*; and *T. amuerenis* [also known as *T. amurense*] Riabinin 1925 was made type species of "*Mandschurosaurus*" *amurensis* by Riabinin (1930).

   Key references: Coombs (1988); Lambe (1918*a*); Leidy (1856, 1858, 1865, 1868); Sternberg (1936).

Trachodon mirabilis, ANSP 9260, cotype ceratopsian tooth, lateral view. Scale = 1 cm. (After Leidy 1856.)

TRICERATOPS   Marsh 1889—(=*Sterrholophus*, *Ugrosaurus*; =?*Agathaumas*, ?*Polyonax*)
Ornithischia: Genasauria: Cerapoda:
   Marginocephalia: Ceratopsia: Neoceratopsia:
   Ceratopsidae: Chasmosaurinae.
Name derivation: Greek *tri* = "three" + Greek
   keratos = "horn" + Greek *ops* = "face."
Type species: *T. horridus* (Marsh 1889).
Other species: ?*T. alticornis* (Marsh 1887), ?*T. galeus*
   Marsh 1889 [*nomen dubium*], *T. prorsus* Marsh
   1890, ?*T. sulcatus* Marsh 1890 [*nomen dubium*],

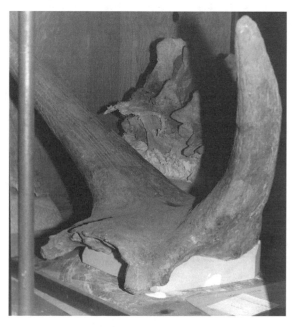

?*Triceratops alticornis* horn-cores (USNM 4739), holotype of *Bison alticornis*, restored by Othniel Charles Marsh to resemble the horns of a bison.

Triceratops horridus, YPM 1823, posterior part of holotype skull of *T. serratus*.

Photo by R. A. Long and S. P. Welles (neg. #73/506-24), courtesy Yale Peabody Museum of Natural History.

?*T. ingens* Lull 1915 [*nomen dubium*], ?*T. maximus* Brown 1933 [*nomen dubium*].

Occurrence: Lance Formation, Evanston Formation, Wyoming; Hell Creek Formation, Montana, South Dakota, Laramie Formation, Colorado, United States; Scollard Formation, Alberta, Frenchman Formation, Saskatchewan, Canada.

Age: Late Cretaceous (Late Maastrichtian).

Known material: Over 50 complete or partial skulls, some partial skeletons, fragmentary cranial elements, adult, subadult, juvenile.

Holotype: YPM 1820, almost complete skull with jaws.

Diagnosis of genus (as for type species): Nasal horn varies from small boss to moderately long horn placed over front of external nares; arched vascular trace across anterior nasal horn; frontal fontanelle either small and circular to absent; frill saddle-shaped, with upturned posterior margin with strong parietal midline ridge that is concave in lateral view; parietals unfenestrated, uniformly and extremely thick (approximate thickness of squamosals); raised vascularized rim present around perimeter of ventral surface of frill; squamosals broad and short relative to other chasmosaurines, with broadly convex lateral margins; epoccipital spanning midline on parietal as well as squamosal parietal suture (Forster 1996*a*, 1996*b*, including autapomorphic characters identified by Hatcher, Marsh and Lull 1907, and Ostrom and Wellnhofer 1986).

Diagnosis of *T. prorsus*: Frontal fontanelle absent; supraorbital horns relatively short, with horn length/basal skull length of 0.61 or less; rostrum relatively deep and short, with convexly rounded rostral margin (Forster 1996*b*).

Comments: *Triceratops*, with its familiar short nasal horn, two long brow horns, and broad frill, is the best known ceratopsian among laymen. The genus was largest of all of these horned dinosaurs (length estimated to be up to 8 or more meters, or over 20 to about 28 feet) and the only one possessing an unfenestrated frill. It was also one of the last

Triceratops horridus, composite skeleton comprising at least four individuals (AMNH 5116, 5039, 5045, 5033), apparently including *Torosaurus* elements.

Courtesy Department Library Services, American Museum of Natural History (neg. #310443).

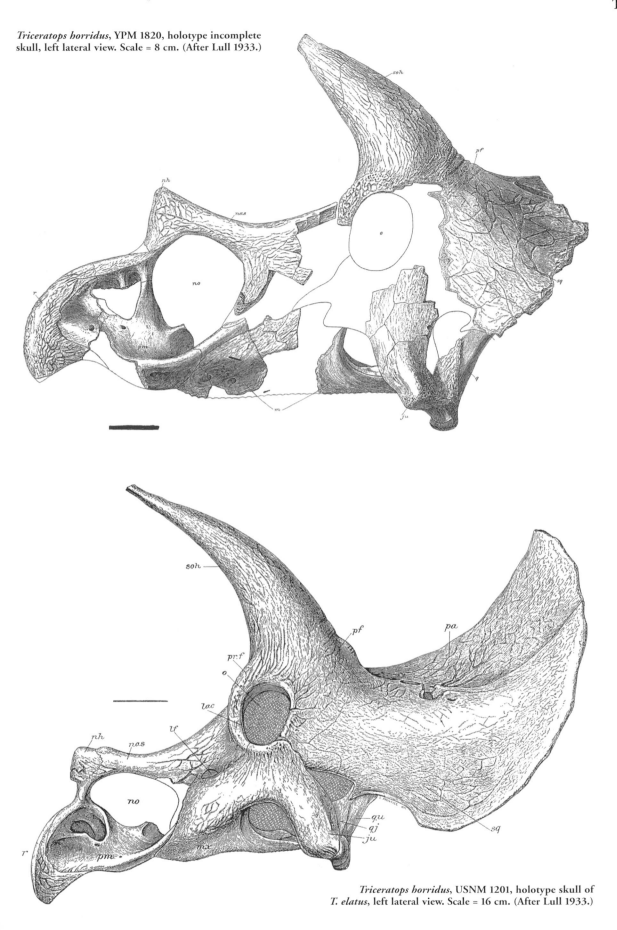

Triceratops horridus, YPM 1820, holotype incomplete skull, left lateral view. Scale = 8 cm. (After Lull 1933.)

Triceratops horridus, USNM 1201, holotype skull of *T. elatus*, left lateral view. Scale = 16 cm. (After Lull 1933.)

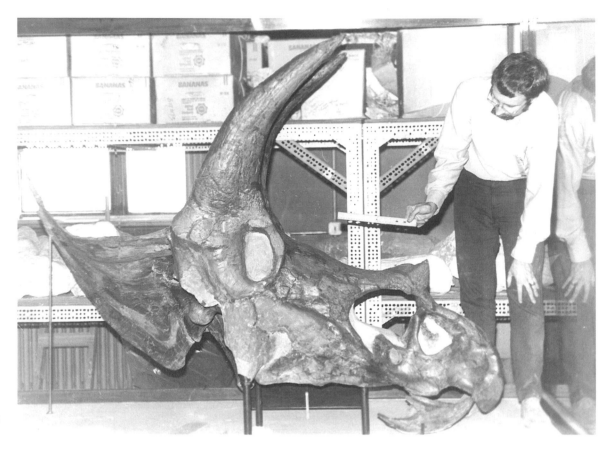

dinosaurian genera, if not the last, to go extinct at the end of the Cretaceous period.

However, before the first publication of that name by Marsh (1889*b*), remains of this dinosaur were already known from various meager remains collected during the early years of North American dinosaur discoveries. Discounting Cope's unde-

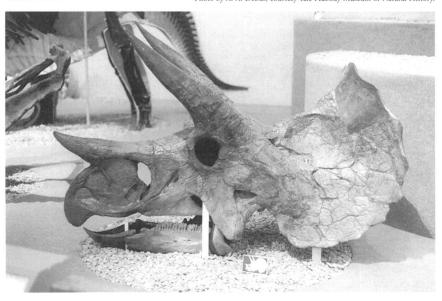

finable and hastily named doubtful genera, *Agathaumas* and *Polyonax*, both of which were founded on fragmentary indeterminate remains, the first definite *Triceratops* specimen collected consists of a pair of large horncores (USNM 4739), discovered in 1887 by George L. Cannon, in the Denver Formation, near Denver, Colorado. Believing the Denver Formation to be Tertiary rather than Cretaceous, Marsh (1887*a*) described these horncores as those of a recently extinct artiodactyl, naming them *Bison alticornis*. In this original description, Marsh (1887*a*) observed that the horncores are long and elevated, unlike the short and transverse horn cores in existing bison, with slender, pointed ends, and large cavities in the base.

Later, Marsh (1889*a*) acknowledged that the Denver beds were actually of Cretaceous age, implying that his *B. alticornis* had been misidentified. At the same time, Marsh (1889*a*) named a new species of another ceratopsian genus, *Ceratops*, designated *C. horridus*, based on the greater part of a skull with jaws (YPM 1820) of an old individual, collected by John Bell Hatcher, C. A. Guernsey, and E. B. Wilson from the Lance Formation, Niobrara County, Wyoming. Marsh (1889*b*) subsequently made *B. alticornis* a species of *Ceratops*, *C. alticornis*, at the same time proposing the new generic name *Triceratops* to

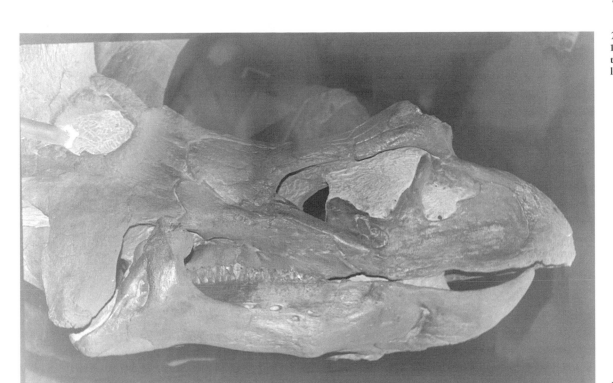

Triceratops horridus, YPM 1823, anterior part of holotype skull of *T. serratus*, right lateral view.

Photo by R. A. Long and S. P. Welles (neg. #73/506-23), courtesy Yale Peabody Museum of Natural History.

embrace the more completely known *C. horridus*, the latter now the type species of *Triceratops*.

Marsh (1889*b*) originally diagnosed the genus *Triceratops* as follows: Two massive brow horns; single smaller horn above snout; maxillaries anteriorly compressed, edentulous; enormous frill extending backward and outward; massive lower jaws united in front by strong beak-like predentary bone. These characters, except those pertaining to the horns, are now known as typical of all ceratopsids.

Not until Hatcher, Marsh and Lull's (1907) classic monograph on the Ceratopsia did Lull make

Triceratops horridus, GSC 8862, holotype partial skull of *T. albertensis*, left lateral view.

Photo by R. A. Long and S. P. Welles (neg. #73/535-9), reproduced with permission of the Canadian Museum of Nature, Ottawa, Canada.

Triceratops horridus, USNM 4720, holotype partial skull of *T. obtusus*, right lateral view.

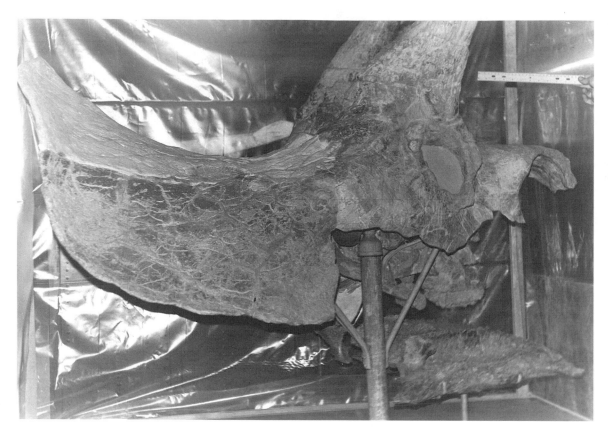

Photo by R. A. Long and S. P. Welles (neg. #73/202-31), courtesy National Museum of Natural History, Smithsonian Institution.

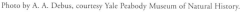

Photo by A. A. Debus, courtesy Yale Peabody Museum of Natural History.

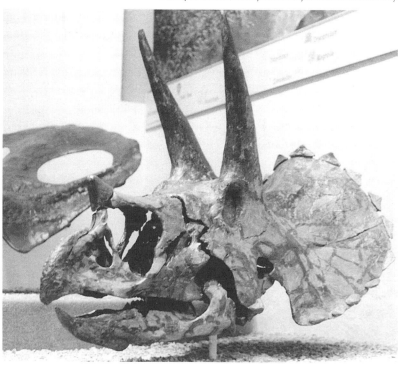

Triceratops horridus, YPM 1821, holotype skull of *Sterrholophus flabellatus*.

C. alticornis a species of *Triceratops*. (In the first modern revision of *Triceratops*, Ostrom and Wellnhofer 1986 stated that *C. alticornis* cannot be referred with certainty to any ceratopsian genus and should be considered a *nomen dubium*.)

Numerous skulls and postcranial remains pertaining to *Triceratops* have been recovered. Brown (1917) reported seeing more than 500 *Triceratops* skulls, most of them incomplete, in the field during seven years of collecting. According to Dodson (1990), however, Brown's estimation is unreliable, as there is a total of about 50 and probably fewer *Triceratops* skulls in museum collections, some reported specimens possibly belonging to *Torosaurus* and other taxa.

Over the decades, various authors have published diagnoses of *Triceratops* (e.g., Hatcher *et al.*; Lull 1933; Steel 1969) though, as pointed out by Ostrom and Wellnhofer, none of these have been adequate, including characters or features applicable to other ceratopsian taxa. Ostrom and Wellnhofer offered the first modern and comprehensive diagnosis of the genus, based on the excellent holotype skull of the species *T. brevicornis* (= *T. prorsus*), and emphasizing variability (especially size and orientation of the horns) in the genus.

The skull of *Triceratops* is enormous, attaining a length of about 2.7 meters (9 feet) in some indi-

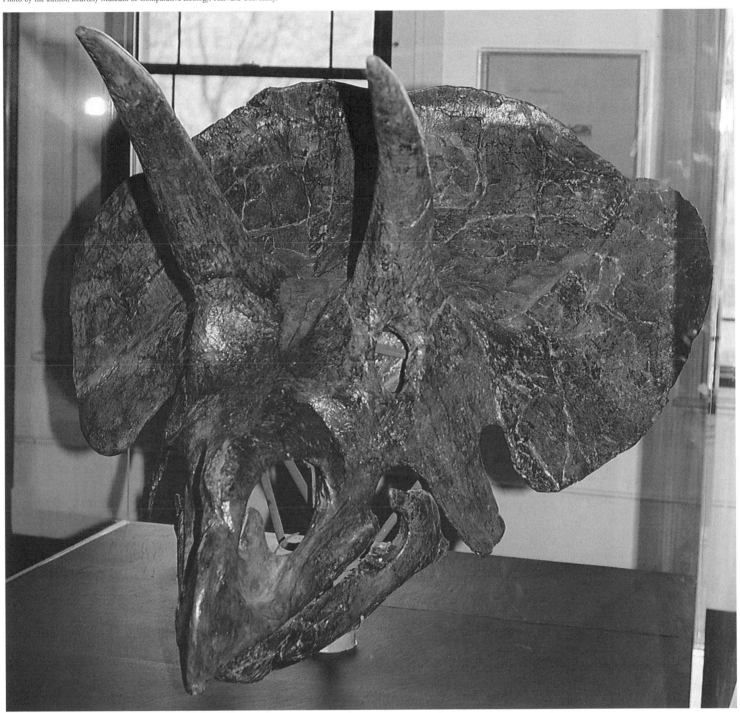

Triceratops horridus, MCZ 1102, holotype skull of *T. eurycephalus*.

viduals. The brow horncores can be as long as 90 centimeters (3 feet), the horny material covering them adding considerably to their length. Lull (1933) noted that the size of the *Triceratops* skull is not necessarily determined by the age of the individual. (Oddly, *Triceratops* skulls from Montana tend to be larger than those from Wyoming.) Lull observed that the muzzle could be short or long, and the frill either broad or relatively narrow, depending on the individual.

Lull also observed that the nasal horn varies in all known *Triceratops* specimens, and that the vascular impressions on the frill's outer surface and facial bones is an ontogentic feature.

Ostrom and Wellnhofer, using various *Triceratops* specimens (AMNH 5883, USNM 4286, and USNM 2410) as examples, agreed with Brown and Schlaikjer (1940*a*) that the nasal horn was suturally joined with the nasals underneath and was an onto-

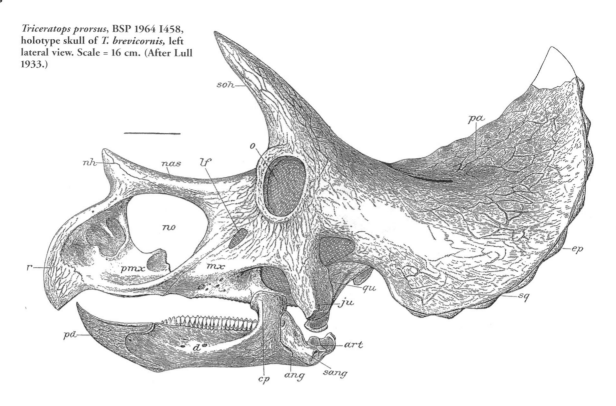

Triceratops prorsus, BSP 1964 I458, holotype skull of *T. brevicornis*, left lateral view. Scale = 16 cm. (After Lull 1933.)

genetically distinct ossification. Some specimens (including USNM 4720 and USNM 2100) feature a broad nasal boss or convexity instead of a horn, possibly providing, as in the modern rhinoceros, a solid foundation for a true horn. In the holotype of the species *T. calicornis* (USNM 4928), the nasal horn is situated atop such a nasal boss. The nasal horn, apparently separated from the nasals by a suture zone, is symmetrical and unpaired, seemingly "clasping" the nasal boss from the front, and shows a unique concave posterior surface. This horn was interpreted by Ostrom and Wellnhofer as developing as a separate epidermal bone growth supported by an expansion of the underlying nasals.

Forster (1996*a*), in a more recent study which yielded new information about the skull of *Tricer-*

Triceratops horridus, USNM 2416, holotype brow horn-core of *T. serratus.*

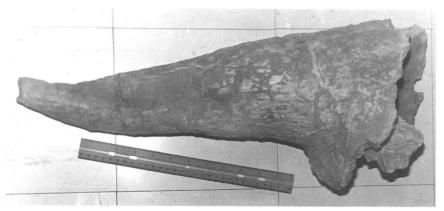

atops, observed a considerable amount of variability in the nasal horns. As stated above, in USNM 4928, the nasals form a large boss with a small, separate epinasal ossification that wraps around its anterior margin. In another specimen (UCMP 113697), the nasal boss is capped by a large, pointed epinasal horn that is partially fused to the nasals. Other specimens (USNM 5741 and 5812) exhibit an epinasal-nasal suture. Juvenile specimen UCMP 136306 possesses a short, blunt epinasal horn with a rugose ventral surface where it apparently attached to the boss. Forster pointed out that, although a separate epinasal boss cannot be distinguished in most *Triceratops* specimens, the presence of an epinasal element is suggested by a rugose overgrowth around the anterior base of the nasal horn and absence of any trace of the anterior nasal-nasal suture (YPM 1822, AMNH 972 and 5116, USNM 101, 4286 and 4928, and CM 1221).

According to Forster, the anterodorsal orbital margin of the skull is formed by the lacrimal and supraorbital, which was fused to the lateral side of the prefrontal, this thick and laterally extensive orbital rim therefore restricting vision forwardly in *Triceratops*. The brain cavity is surrounded completely by an ossified braincase, which is overlain by a deep frontal and cornual sinus complex, these sinuses probably serving as shock absorbers to withstand the stresses encountered by the supraorbital horns during intraspecific conflicts.

A total of 16 species, most of them named and described by Marsh and largely based upon such cra-

Photo by R. A. Long and S. P. Welles (neg. #73/398-30), courtesy American Museum of Natural History.

nial variabilities as ornamental morphology and horn length, have been assigned to *Triceratops*. In addition to 1. *T. alticornis* Marsh 1887 [*nomen dubium*], 2. type species *T. horridus* (Marsh 1889), and 3. the former "*T.*" *hatcheri* [see *Diceratops* entry], these taxa include:

4. *T. flabellatus* Marsh 1889 was based on an incomplete skeleton, including skull with lower jaws, but lacking nasal horn, also with a femur, ilium, ischium, scapula, and some vertebrae (YPM 1821), from a juvenile or adolescent, collected by Hatcher from the Lance Formation, Niobrara County, Wyoming. Marsh (1889*b*) distinguished this species by such features as its fan-shaped frill and large epoccipitals. Subsequently, Marsh (1891) referred this species to the new genus *Sterrholophus*, believing that, during life, the frill's posterior surface was entirely covered with muscles and ligaments for supporting the head. *Sterrholophus* was later synonymized with *Triceratops* by Hatcher *et al.* (1907).

5. ?*T. galeus* Marsh 1889 was based on a small nasal horn core (USNM 2410) apparently from the Denver Formation, near Brighton, Colorado. As the specimen is too poor to refer with certainty to any ceratopsian species, Ostrom and Wellnhofer (1986) designated it a *nomen dubium*. Marsh (1889*b*) described this species as follows: Nasal horn small, distinguished by shape and forwardly-directed orientation (Marsh 1889*b*).

6. *T. serratus* Marsh 1890 was established on a large, well-preserved skull, complete except for nasal horn, including jaws (YPM 1823), collected from the Lance Formation, Niobrara County. The skull was distinguished by a series of bony projections along the median line of the parietal crest, a similar ridge occurring along the squamosals posterior to the postorbital. Though subadult, this skull measures 1.8 meters (about 6 feet) in length.

7. *T. prorsus* Marsh 1890 was established on the complete skull with jaws (YPM 1822) of an aged individual, from Niobrara County, Wyoming. The skull was distinguished by massive horncores, a large, narrow frill with broadly convex squamosals, and a long, anteriorly directed nasal horn. Associated with the skull were six cervical vertebrae.

8. *T. sulcatus* Marsh 1890 [*nomen dubium*] was erected on a poorly-preserved skull, jaws, some vertebrae and limb-bone material (USNM 4276) from a fully adult individual, collected from the Lance Formation of Niobrara County. Marsh (1890*b*) characterized this species by very large, long brow horns; and a deep groove on posterior surface of upper half of horncore. Hatcher *et al.* (1907) challenged the accuracy of Marsh's description of these grooves, concluding that the holotype exhibits no characters of specific distinction.

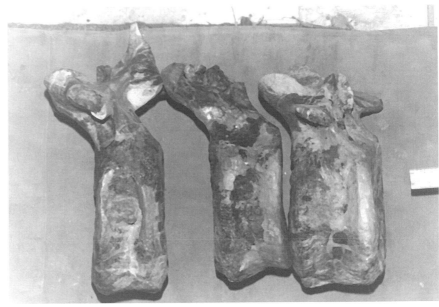

?*Triceratops maximus*, AMNH 5040, holotype vertebrae.

9. *T. elatus* Marsh 1891 was based on the skull (USNM 1201) of a subadult individual from the Lance Formation, Niobrara County, with a high and elongate frill, modest-sized nasal horn, and long, pointed, forward projecting brow horns.

10. *T. calicornis* Marsh 1898 was established on a skull, jaw, and some postcranial remains (USNM 4928) from the Lance Formation of Niobrara County. The nasal horn is dorsally concave and has a horseshoe-shaped dorsal surface.

11. *T. obtusus* Marsh 1898 [*nomen dubium*] was based on a large, nearly complete skull with jaw frag-

?*Triceratops galeus*, USNM 2410, holotype horncores.

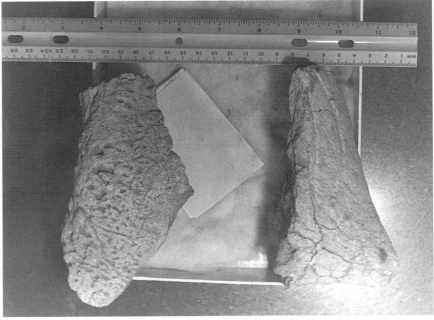

Photo by R. A. Long and S. P. Welles (neg. #73/138-2), courtesy National Museum of Natural History, Smithsonian Institution.

?Triceratops ingens, YPM 2157, holotype rostrum.

horns, short and almost vertical nasal horn, elliptical orbit, and open frontal fontanelle.

13. *?T. ingens*, an unpublished name of Marsh's mentioned by Lull (1915), was based on mostly a large parietal skull and postcranial remains (YPM 1828) collected by Hatcher. Lull (1915a) did not diagnose this species. Ostrom and Wellnhofer regarded it as a *nomen nudum* perhaps not referable to *Triceratops*.

14. *?T. maximus* Brown 1933 [*nomen dubium*] was based on eight separate vertebrae and two anterior caudal vertebrae (AMNH 5040), from the Hell Creek Formation, Garfield County, Montana. Brown (1933a) described this species as follows: Distinguished by great size. As pointed out by Ostrom and Wellnhofer, this specimen, not including skull material, is therefore not assignable to any genus and must be regarded as a *nomen dubium*.

15. *T. eurycephalus* Schlaikjer 1935 was based on an almost complete skull with jaws, also some skeletal fragments (MCZ 1102), recovered from the Torrington member of the Lance Formation, Goshen County, Wyoming. Distinguishing features include the comparatively long frill, short dentary and facial region, elevated orbit, small nose horn, very long and slender brow horns, and separate exits for the left and right olfactory nerves.

16. *T. albertensis* Sternberg 1949 was based on an incomplete left half of a large skull (NMC [formerly GSC] 8862), collected from the Upper member of the Horseshoe Canyon Formation [formerly "Edmonton-B" Member], near Drumheller, Alberta, Canada. Distinguishing features include the high facial region, large antorbital fossa, brow horns vertically directed and located mostly behind the orbits, the not strongly upturned frill, and the long, thick squamosal.

ments, plus a vertebra (USNM 4720), collected by Hatcher from the Lance Formation, Niobrara County. The skull is distinguished by a short, rounded, obtuse nasal horn.

12. *T. brevicornis* Hatcher 1905 was based on a nearly complete skull with lower jaws, an almost complete presacral vertebrae series, and rib and pubic fragments (BSP 1964 I 488; formerly YPM 1834). The specimen was collected in 1891 by Hatcher, W. H. Utterback, A. L. Sullins and T. A. Bostwick from Niobrara [then Converse] County, Wyoming. In 1964, it was transferred to Bayerische Staatssammlung für Paläontologie und Historische Geologie in Munich, Germany (now BSP 1964 I 485). Distinguishing cranial characters include short, stout brow

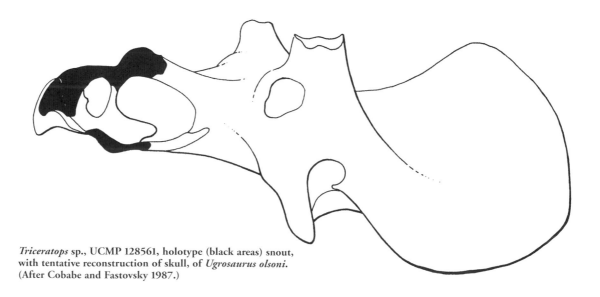

Triceratops sp., UCMP 128561, holotype (black areas) snout, with tentative reconstruction of skull, of *Ugrosaurus olsoni*. (After Cobabe and Fastovsky 1987.)

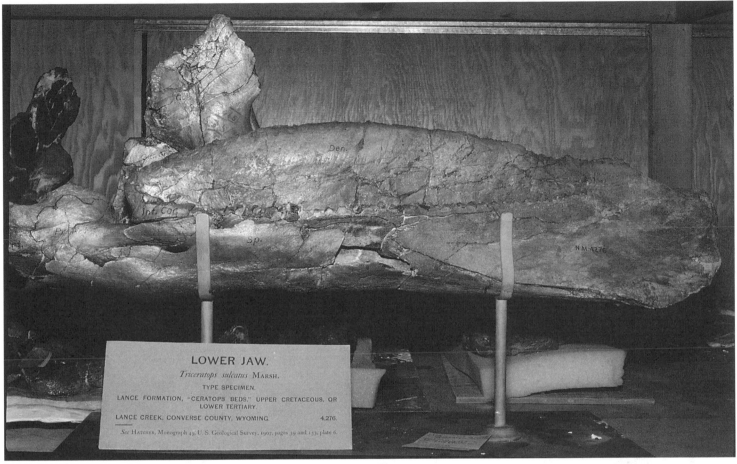

LOWER JAW.

Triceratops sulcatus MARSH.

TYPE SPECIMEN.

LANCE FORMATION, "CERATOPS BEDS," UPPER CRETACEOUS, OR LOWER TERTIARY.

LANCE CREEK, CONVERSE COUNTY, WYOMING. 4,276.

See HATCHER, Monograph 49, U. S. Geological Survey, 1907, pages 39 and 133, plate 6.

?Triceratops sulcatus, USNM 4276, holotype lower jaw.

Ostrom and Wellnhofer questioned the localized occurrence of so many "species" of a genus the size of *Triceratops*, noting for comparison the great intra-specific variation in skulls and horns of African forest and savanna buffalo, *Syncerus caffer caffer*. In reviewing the type specimens of *Triceratops* with their comparable variations and applying to them a modern understanding of the concept of variations within living animal populations, the more modern views of comparative ceratopsian osteology and morphology, and also of the zoogeography of present day large terrestrial animals, Ostrom and Wellnhofer concluded that there is but one valid species of *Triceratops*, the type species *T. horridus*. To *T. horridus* Ostrom and Wellnhofer (excluding *nomina dubia*) referred *T. flabellatus, T. serratus, T. prorsus, T. elatus, T. calicornis, T. brevicornis* and *T. eurycephalus*, with *Diceratops hatcheri, T. obtusus,* and *T. albertensis* probable synonyms, the differences between these taxa attributed to individual variation.

Ostrom and Wellnhofer's consolidation of most *Triceratops* species into one valid taxon was accepted by subsequent workers (*e.g.*, Lehman 1990; Dodson and Currie 1990). Lehman further suggested that some of the proposed species of *Triceratops* could indicate sexual dimorphism, *T. calicornis* and *T. elatus* representing males, *T. brevicornis* and *T. horridus* females (see *Chasmosaurus* entry for Lehman's interpretation of sexual dimorphism in ceratopsians).

More recently, Forster (1996*a*, 1996*b*) analyzed approximately 20 type and nontype *Triceratops* skulls using both cladistic analysis and morphometric shape and analysis. With the results of these studies, Forster weighed the validity of the various species:

In her cladistic analysis (excluding *T. flabellatus, T. obtusus, T. albertensis,* and *T. eurycephalus*, owing to the incompleteness of their holotypes), Forster (1996*b*) found five characters to vary among specimens of *Triceratops*: 1. Contact of the squamosal, jugal, and postorbital above the lower temporal fenestra; 2. supraorbital horn length; 3. closing of the frontal fontanelle; 4. rostrum shape; and 5. nasal horn length. Forster (1996*b*) also noted that brow horns in this genus display a range of variation and slight to marked distortion of these horns are common among specimens as preserved; such variations and distortion is also common in frills. Cladistic analysis indicated that four *Triceratops* specimens (YPM 1822, LACM

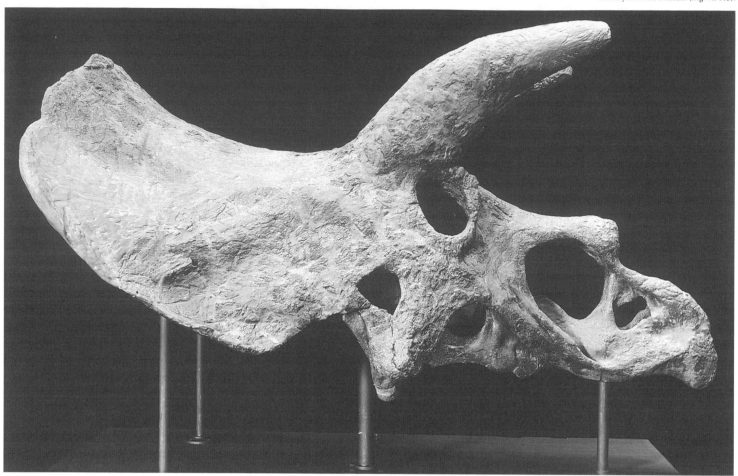

Triceratops horridus, skull (FMNH P12003) originally referred to *T. calicornis*, collected in Montana in 1904 by Elmer S. Riggs for the Field Columbian Museum.

7207, CM 1221, and BSP 1964 I 485, a so-called "*prorsus*" group) are united by characters 2 through 5, derived characters within this group including a closed frontal fontanelle, relatively short brow horns, and a short, convexly rounded rostrum. All other specimens fall within a so-called "*horridus*" group, which retain the primitive states for these characters and display no autapomorphic characters of their own.

Multivariate morphometric shape analysis based upon 14 *Triceratops* skulls (with eight holotypes, including that of *T. flabellatus*) not exhibiting obvious distortions supported the cladistic analysis (separating YPM 1822, LACM 7207, and CM 1221 from the remaining specimens, BSP 1964 I 485 being excluded from this analysis).

Forster (1996b) concluded that the genus *Triceratops* can be divided into two valid species which overlap in geographic and stratigraphic ranges— *T. horridus* (including the junior synonyms *T. flabellatus, T. serratus, T. elatus, T. calicornis,* and *T. obtusus*) and *T. prorsus* (including the junior synonym *T. brevicornis*), with *Diceratops* (see entry) regarded as a

valid genus, *T. ingens* a *nomen nudum*, and the other supposed species of *Triceratops* considered to be *nomina dubia*.

Considering the possibility that these two morphotypes could represent a single sexually dimorphic species, Forster (1996b) pointed out that *T. horridus* specimens greatly outnumber those of *T. prorsus*, an unlikely although not impossible ratio, given possible preservational biases in fossil taxa; also, skull lengths in both morphs broadly overlap, indicating no bimodality that may indicate a size difference between sexes.

Regarding the diet of this genus, Ostrom (1964b), after examining the skulls and jaws of seven *Triceratops* specimens, observed that the dental batteries are highly specialized, elongated, and continuous shearing blades, with no grinding or crushing powers. The jaws and muscles that operated the jaws were structured so as to function as a highly powerful shearing mechanism. The specialized teeth, extremely strong jaws, and their perfected shearing power seemed to exclude ordinary leafy plant tissues, seeds, and fruits from the diet, these foods requiring crushing and grinding abilities that

Triceratops apparently did not possess. Ostrom found it reasonable to suggest a more fibrous diet such as cycad or palm fronds.

Dodson (1991), in a report on morphological and ecological trends in ceratopsian evolution, observed a modest expansion of the jaw muscles onto the base of the *Triceratops* frill. This development compensated for changes in the cheek region that resulted in a relative decrease in size of the adductor chamber for jaw muscles. Dodson (1991) noted that the robust ventral articular condyle in *Triceratops* supports Ostrom's idea that the jaw muscles in this genus were hypertrophied and very strong, but added that the thinness of the dorsal shaft of the quadrate, which seemingly transmitted the masticatory forces of the jaw, suggest the contrary. The jaws of *Triceratops* might not have needed greatly enhanced masticatory forces. The teeth, very robust and showing signs of steady wear, were dominated by orthal shear. According to Dodson (1991), vertical shearing forces, even of fibrous fodder, might not have required augmented masticatory forces.

The frontlimb posture of *Triceratops* and other large ceratopsians has long been a controversial issue, opinions differing on whether these legs should be splayed out (as in most older skeletal reconstructions and life restorations), with elbows angled back (as in some mammals), or straight (as in some modern restorations). In mounting the relatively complete skeleton (USNM 4842) of *T. prorsus* for display at the United States National Museum [now National Museum of Natural History], the front legs were oriented away from the body. Gilmore (1905) commented that, had the legs been straightened, it would have been physically impossible for the animal's head to have reached the ground.

Later, Garstka and Burnham (1995) reported that two recently discovered articulated *Triceratops* speci-

Triceratops horridus, cast of American Museum of Natural History skeleton, mounted with forelimbs slightly bowed, according to the museum label, "enough to lift the beak out of the dirt and let the *Triceratops* pace at a smooth glide."

Photo by Linda Dorman, courtesy The Field Museum (neg. #GN 86416.15).

mens, collected from the Hell Creek Formation of North Dakota, apparently indicate an upright stance, the tendons working as a cantilever support for the vertebral column. According to Garstka and Burnham, one specimen (nicknamed "Willy") reveals an articulated dorsal view with vertebral column and pelvis made rigid by ossified tendons. "Raymond," the second specimen, reveals an articulated lateral view, the position of the glenoid, curve of the coracoid, and flattened, almost straight anterior ribs indicating a narrow chest and upright forelimb. Garstka and Burnham further noted that the position and articulations of manus and pes in the second specimen agree with fossil footprints attributed to ceratopsians from the Laramie Formation of Colorado.

The idea that ceratopsians like *Triceratops* could gallop like a rhinoceros was proposed by Bakker (1968), who argued that the limb bones, despite the short shank, were powerful enough to withstand great forces, and that the long and slender, free-swinging shoulder blades worked independent of the sternal plates with great propulsive force. Coombs (1978c), studying the limbs of dinosaurs in regards to their possibly cursorial adaptations, pointed out that the metacarpals in *Triceratops* are short, massive, and divergently arranged as in graviportal animals, also noting that the mass of this dinosaur exceeded that of the largest modern elephants. *Contra* Bakker, Coombs concluded that such large ceratopsians were rather poor runners on a par with *Hippopotamus*. Ostrom and Wellnhofer added that the vertebrae in the type specimen of *T. brevicornis* are indicative of a stiff-back walking mode and an elephant-like running gait rather than fast gallop, though it was not possible to know for certain whether or not ceratopsians had a rhinoceros-like cursorial ability.

With its great bulk and formidable armature, *Triceratops* might have been a sometimes aggressive animal, perhaps charging large predators as would an enraged rhinoceros. One skull shows a brow horn that had broken off and begun to heal, perhaps after a battle. Foes were apparently not limited to theropods, puncture wounds in some skulls implying intraspecific conflicts, most likely to win mates or establish territory. Rival *Triceratops* may have engaged in such contests by locking horns, then shoving and twisting, protecting themselves with their neck frills.

Lull (1933) classified *Triceratops* as a so-called "short-frilled" ceratopsian, a phylogenetic position it long maintained, despite the short nasal horn and long supraorbital horns characteristic of so-called "long-frilled" forms. Classifying *Triceratops* as a "short-frilled" form, however, left an annoying gap in the fossil record between this genus and geologically younger older members of that grouping. This classification has also left unexplained the supposed evolution of the long nasal and short brow horns in earlier forms to the opposite condition in *Triceratops*. Therefore, modern workers no longer use frill length as a criterion for classifying these dinosaurs, but rather the length of horns, shape of squamosal, and size of squamosal relative to parietal, dividing the Ceratopsidae into the subfamilies Centrosaurinae and Chasmosaurinae, with *Triceratops* regarded as a very late chasmosaurine. Dodson (1991) suggested that the relatively short frill and solid fenestrae, the latter presumably secondarily closed, represent reversals of trends expressed within the Ceratopsidae.

The new genus and species, *Ugrosaurus olsoni*, was founded on a partial snout (including rostral pit, nasal boss, maxillary process of premaxillary), edentulous jaw material, a vertebra, and unidentified ?skull and ?frill fragments (UCMP 128561). The material, some of it showing evidence of contemporaneous water wear, was collected on a ranch in the uppermost exposures of the Hell Creek Formation, at Hell Creek, Garfield County, Montana (Cobabe and Fastovsky 1987). *U. olsoni* was regarded by Lehman, and also by Ostrom and Wellnhofer, as a *nomen dubium*, this taxon having been based on inadequate material. Forster (1993) later referred this species to *Triceratops* sp.

Key references: Bakker (1968); Brown (1917, 1933); Brown and Schlaikjer (1940a); Cobabe and Fastovsky (1987); Dodson (1990, 1991); Dodson and Currie (1990); Forster (1993, 1996a, 1996b); Garstka and Burhman (1995); Gilmore (1905); Hatcher, Marsh and Lull (1907); Lehman (1990); Lull (1915); Marsh (1887a, 1889a, 1889b, 1890); Ostrom (1964b); Ostrom and Wellnhofer (1986).

TRIMUCRODON Thulborn 1973 [*nomen dubium*]

Ornithischia *incertae sedis*.

Name derivation: Greek *tri* = "three" + Latin *mucro* = "point" + Greek *odous* = "tooth."

Type species: *T. cuneatus* Thulborn 1973 [*nomen dubium*].

Other species: [None.]

Occurrence: [Unnamed formation], Província do Estremadura, Portugal.

Age: Late Jurassic (Late Kimmeridgian).

Known material: Three tooth crowns.

Holotype: LPFU collection [no catalog number designated], tooth crown.

Diagnosis of genus (as for type species): Tooth crowns triangular, bucco-lingually compressed, about as long as high, slightly deflected posteriorly; crowns fully and uniformly enamelled, with smooth faces, lingual face slightly flatter than buccal face; mesial and distal edges nearly straight, intersecting at right angles, ornamented with short, blunt denticles that increase in size towards cervix; foremost and hindmost of marginal denticles strongly divergent, salient, sharply pointed (Thulborn 1973*b*).

Comments: The genus *Trimucrodon* was founded upon a single tooth crown (Lehrstuhl für Paläontologie collection, Free University, Berlin) discovered in the marls at the headland of Porto Pinheiro, on the west coast of Portugal. Referred to *T. cuneatus* were two similar crowns from the same locality (Thulborn 1973*b*).

Thulborn regarded *Trimucrodon* as fairly closely related to *Echinodon*, interpreting the cheek teeth in both forms as agreeing in almost every respect (crowns strongly compressed, triangular in profile, with obtuse occlusal tip, fully and uniformly enamelled, tending to slight asymmetry, smooth and featureless surfaces, similar marginal denticulation, almost straight mesial and distal edges ornamented with denticles decreasing in size away from cervix, and enlarged, salient and sharply pointed foremost and hindmost denticles); they differ mainly in style of marginal denticulations (fewer in *Trimucrodon*, stopping well short of occlusal tip of crown, more in *Echinodon*, extending to tip).

Galton (1978), disagreeing with Thulborn's interpretation, suggested that *Trimucrodon* and *Echinodon* are more different than alike, further suggesting that *Trimucrodon* could have descended from a Late Triassic or Early Jurassic dinosaur similar to *Fabrosaurus* or *Lesothosaurus*. [*Echinodon* is now regarded as a ?primitive thyreophoran.]

Weishampel and Witmer (1990*a*), in reviewing various primitive ornithischians, considered *T. cuneatus* and Thulborn's tooth species *Alocodon kuehnei* to be *nomena dubia*, but did not compare these taxa. Sereno (1991), in a review of basal ornithischians, referred both *Trimucrodon* and *Alocodon* to Ornithischia *incertae sedis*, based on ornithischian synapomorphies (low, subtriangular crowns separated from roots by basal constriction and absence of recurvature in maxillary and dentary crowns [see Sereno 1986]).

Key references: Galton (1978); Sereno (1986, 1991); Thulborn (1973*b*); Weishampel and Witmer (1990*a*).

TRIPRIODON Marsh 1889—(See *Paronychodon*.)
Name derivation: Greek *tri* = "three" + priodont [Greek *prion* = "saw" + Greek *odous* = "tooth"].
Type species: *T. capernatum* Marsh 1889 [*nomen dubium*].

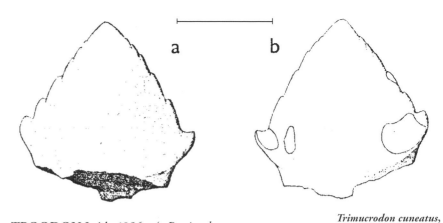

Trimucrodon cuneatus, LPFU, holotype crown of cheek tooth, a. lingual and b. buccal views. Scale = 1 mm. (After Thulborn 1973.)

TROODON Leidy 1856—(=*Pectinodon*, *Polyodontosaurus*, *Stenonychosaurus*; = ?*Saurornithoides*)
Saurischia: Theropoda: Tetanurae: Avetheropoda: Coelurosauria: Maniraptora: Arctometatarsalia: Bullatosauria: Troodontidae.
Name derivation: Greek *troo* = "to wound" + Greek *odous* = "tooth."
Type species: *T. formosus* Leidy 1856.
Other species: *T. asiamericanus* Nessov 1995, *T. isfarensis* Nessov 1995.
Occurrence: Oldman Formation, Horseshoe Canyon Formation, Dinosaur Park Formation, Alberta, Canada; Dinosaur Park Formation, Hell Creek Formation, Montana, Lance Formation, Wyoming, United States; "Northern Eurasia" [*T. asiamericanus* and *T. isfarensis*].
Age: Late Cretaceous (Late Campanian–Early Maastrichtian).
Known material: At least 20 specimens, including fragmentary skulls, fragmentary postcrania, teeth; N 49/12176, holotype tooth of *T. asiamericanus*; N 484/12457, holotype incomplete tooth of *T. isfarensis*, adults, juveniles.
Holotype: ANSP 9259, ?premaxillary or ?anterior maxillary tooth.

Diagnosis of genus (as for type species): Troodontid from "Judith River" [=Oldman], Horseshoe Canyon, and ?Lance Formations of North America, differing from *Saurornithoides junior* and *S. mongoliensis* in following ways: anterior antorbital opening larger in *T. formosus*, implying higher muzzle; sculpturing on nasal process of maxilla not so extensive; temporal region of skull longer relative to length of frontal and size of orbit; no sulcus between parasphenoid capsule and rectangular platform between basipterygoid processes; presphenoid positioned more anteriorly; basioccipital tuberosities more pronounced; middle ear cavity extending farther posteroventrally; symphysial region of lower jaw stronger; denticles at tip of premaxillary, maxillary teeth on anterior carina (Currie 1987*a*); second phalanx of pedal digit II

Troodon formosus, ANSP 9259, holotype tooth, lateral view. (After Russell 1948.)

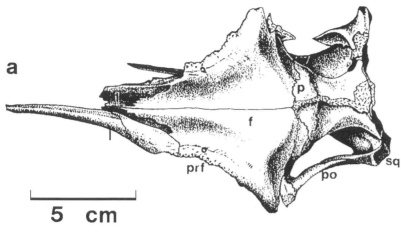

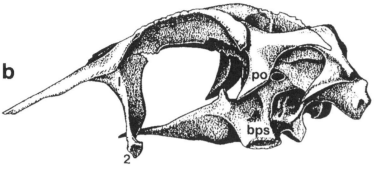

a

b

Troodon formosus, TMP 82.19.23 [originally referred to *Stenonychosaurus inequalis*], partial skull, a. dorsal, b. left lateral views. (After Currie 1985.)

Troodon asiamericanus, N 49/12176, holotype tooth. (After Nessov 1995.)

somewhat longer than half length of first phalanx (Osmólska and Barsbold 1990).

Diagnoses of *T. asiamericanus* and *T. isfarensis*: [Unavailable to date of this writing].

Comments: The taxonomic history of the genus now known to be *Troodon* spans more than a century, during which time it has been known by a variety of generic names. Indeed, some of the fossil material referred to it has been of ornithischian origin.

Troodon [then *Troödon*] was founded on a well-preserved tooth (ANSP 9259) discovered by Ferdinand Hayden in the Belly River [now Oldman] Formation at Judith River, Fergus County, Montana, the naming of new genera based on teeth being a common nineteenth century practice. Leidy (1856*a*) named this tooth *Troodon formosus*, describing it as curved, serrated, and somewhat flattened, but believed it possibly belonged to some huge extinct monitor or other ancient reptile.

More such teeth were found during the early 1900s in the Horseshoe Canyon and Lance formations of Alberta and Wyoming. Nopcsa (1901), Hay (1902), and Hatcher (1905), discoverer of the Wyoming teeth, all suggested that these specimens belonged to a theropod. Gilmore (1924*a*), believing that the *Troodon* teeth pertained to *Stegoceras validus* [=*validum*], a species based on the partial skull of an ornithischian dome-headed dinosaur, synonymized

both genera as *T. validus*. At the same time, Gilmore made *T. validus* the type species of a new family, Troodontidae. For many years the names *Troodon* and *Stegoceras* were confused in popular texts about dinosaurs. Eventually, the theropod affinities of *T. formosus* were recognized by Sternberg (1945), who revived the name *Stegoceras* to receive the ornithischian material.

Troodon became better understood with the discovery of more material originally described as other new genera:

The type species *Stenonychosaurus inequalis* Sternberg 1932 was founded on an eroded, crushed specimen comprising the distal end of a tibia with astragalus, complete left pes, left metacarpal I, distal end of left metacarpal ?II, distal ends of three manual phalanges, and six caudal vertebrae (NMC 8539). The material was collected from the [now] Dinosaur Park Formation, southwest of the mouth of Berry Creek, Red Deer River, Steveville, Alberta. As *Stenonychosaurus* was quite unusual in comparison to other theropods known at that time, particularly in its specialized second toe, Sternberg (1932*a*) regarded this genus as possibly synonymous with *Chirostenotes* and a probable direct descendent of *Ornitholestes*.

D. A. Russell (1969) described the most complete specimen (NMC 12340) of this species, collected from Dinosaur Provincial Park. From this specimen, Russell and Séguin (1982) made the first skeletal reconstruction and life restoration of this dinosaur, basing missing parts on comparative elements of related genera, the skull patterned somewhat after *Saurornithoides*, though broader and shorter, length of the presacral vertebral column tentatively based on vertebral proportions of *Deinonychus*, combined length of six sacral centra based on *Saurornithoides mongoliensis*, and the proximal caudals restored after *Saurornithoides junior*. The forelimb was restored utilizing the humerus-to-ulna ratio of *Deinonychus*, the preserved fragments of phalanges and unguals implying that the hand proportions were some 75 percent those in that genus. The pelvis was restored after *Saurornithoides*, hindlimb bones based on and scaled up from that genus, pes restored after other specimens that had been referred to *Stenonychosaurus*.

Based upon this reconstruction, Russell and Séguin prepared a life-restoration model of the animal following the general body plan of *Saurornithoides*. The eyes are large relative to those in modern tetrapods, with an estimated diameter of 44 millimeters (implying a possible nocturnal lifestyle), and anteromedially inclined (providing stereoscopic vision). From the shape of the ulna, the forearm could apparently be rotated. The hands, patterned after the preserved horny sheaths in *Archaeopteryx lithograph-*

ica and *Compsognathus longipes*, show a third finger that possibly opposed the other two. The frame is lightly-constructed and legs long (suggesting agility). The tail is thin, most flexible at its base (to control angular momentum of the body during quick turns). Each foot bears two raptorial claws, the largest and most formidable being on the second toe. Russell and Séguin pointed out that this form was one of the smallest known Canadian dinosaurs, measuring some 1.75 meters (6 feet) long and weighing about 40 kilograms (almost 90 pounds).

Type species *Polyodontosaurus grandis* Gilmore 1932 was based on a left dentary (GSC 8540) without teeth, collected from the Dinosaur Park Formation, at Berry Creek, Red Deer River. Gilmore (1932) believed this specimen to be lacertalian. It was later recognized as a troodontid theropod by Sternberg (1951*b*), after which Romer (1966) synonymized *Polyodontosaurus* with *Troodon*, which he classified with the Coeluridae.

Type species *Pectinodon bakkeri* Carpenter 1982 was founded on the tooth (UCM 38445) (originally referred to *Saurornithoides* sp. by Estes 1964) of an adult individual, from the Bushy Tailed Blowout, Niobrara County, Wyoming, and three small paratype teeth (UCM 38446, 73098, and 125239) from babies.

More detailed information regarding *Stenonychosaurus* surfaced with the discovery of cranial material including a nearly complete braincase (RTMP 81.22.66), discovered in 1981 by Robin Digby in the Dinosaur Park Formation, in and around Dinosaur Provincial Park, northeast of Brooks, and left dentary with six germ teeth (RTMP 83.12.11) found in 1983 by John R. Horner in the Horseshoe Canyon Formation, near the construction site of the [now Royal] Tyrrell Museum of Paleontology at Drumheller, Alberta. These finds prompted Currie (1985, 1987*a*) to reexamine the relationships of *Troodon* with very similar taxa *Stenonychosaurus, Polyodontosaurus*, and *Pectinodon*.

Russell noted similarities between *Stenonychosaurus* and the Mongolian genus *Saurornithoides*, suggesting that these might be synonymous. Carpenter (1982) and Paul (1984) both agreed with this synonymy, Carpenter creating the new combination *Saurornithoides inequalis*, although this synonymy was not substantiated.

Currie (1985), in describing cranial material assigned to *S. inequalis* in the collections of the American Museum of Natural History, National Museum of Canada, and Royal Tyrrell Museum of Paleontology, concluded that the North American and Mongolian forms, though very similar, are generically distinct. In describing the braincase of *Stenonychosaurus*, Currie postulated that *Stenonychosaurus* had evolved

a larger brain cavity than *Saurornithoides* and more anteriorly positioned olfactory tract. Relative brain size notwithstanding, most features of the braincase in *Stenonychosaurus* appeared to be more derived than those in *Saurornithoides*.

An uncrushed partial foot (RTMP 84.65.1), collected in 1979 by a Provincial Museum of Alberta field party led by Currie from the Dinosaur Park Formation, Dinosaur Provincial Park, revealed additional diagnostic features in metatarsals II and III of *S. inequalis*. As shown by Wilson and Currie (1985), metatarsal II is distinctly compressed, differing from that in dromaeosaurids, elmisaurids, and ornithomimids; and the proximal end of metatarsal III is excluded from the anterior surface of the metatarsus, in anterior view, for almost its entire length. Wilson and Currie noted that this latter condition is unprecedented among theropods.

Currie (1987*a*) later found that the holotype tooth of *T. formosus* shares certain unique diagnostic

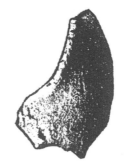

Troodon isfarensis, N 484/ 12457 holotype tooth. (After Nessov 1995.)

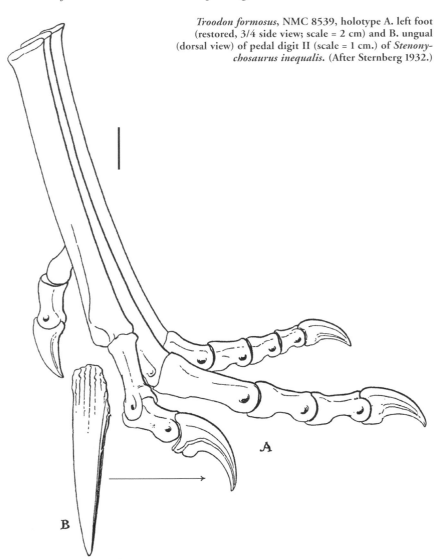

Troodon formosus, NMC 8539, holotype A. left foot (restored, 3/4 side view; scale = 2 cm) and B. ungual (dorsal view) of pedal digit II (scale = 1 cm.) of *Stenonychosaurus inequalis*. (After Sternberg 1932.)

Troodon formosus, UCMP 124990, holotype tooth of *Pectinodon bakkeri*. Scale = 2 mm. (After Carpenter 1982.)

characters with teeth referred to *Stenonychosaurus*, *Polyodontosaurus*, and *Pectinodon*. Although the premaxillary, maxillary, and anterior and posterior dentary teeth in these forms show a considerable degree of variation, they share distinctively characteristic denticles with the type specimen of *T. formosus*. In all of these taxa, denticles are 1. strongly hooked pointing towards the tip of the tooth, 2. larger than those in other theropods, and 3. have a distinctive pit between bases of adjacent denticles.

Because of these shared characters, Currie (1987a) synonymized *T. formosus*, *S. inequalis*, *P. grandis*, and *P. bakkeri*. As *T. formosus* is a valid species with clearly diagnostic characters, and since *Troodon* is the earliest published name relating to this form, Currie (1987a) referred these taxa to that senior synonym. Currie (1992) subsequently observed that, due to slight differences in tooth structure. *P. bakkeri* may eventually prove to be a valid second species of *Troodon*.

Based on the above material and additional specimens, Currie (1987a) published a new diagnosis and description of the genus *Troodon* (and *T. formosus*). All collected from Dinosaur Provincial Park,

this new material includes a partial dentary with three germ teeth (ROM 1445), from Little Sandhill Creek, found by Levi Sternberg in 1935 and described by L. S. Russell (1948); partial dentary with one germ tooth (RTMP 67.14.39) found in 1967 by D. Taylor and J. Poikans, described by Sues (1977); partial edentulous dentary (RTMP 82.16.138) found in 1982 by M. Jasinski; specimen (RTMP 82.19.151) found by P. Harrop in 1982; plus more than 70 isolated teeth from the Horseshoe Canyon and Dinosaur Park formations in the Royal Tyrrell Museum and Canadian Museum of Nature collections.

Based on the dimensions of the braincase, the brain of *Troodon* was sized remarkably large for a dinosaur. Hopson (1980b) estimated its mass to be about 37 grams and D. A. Russell (1969) 45 grams, these estimates suggesting that this was the most intelligent dinosaur yet known (Russell and Séguin approximating its level of intelligence with guinea fowl and bustards, armadillos and opossums, and basal insectivores). Currie (1985) observed that the enlarged middle ear cavity and presence of a periotic sinus system indicate a well-developed hearing sense perhaps capable of detecting low-frequency sounds.

Illustration by Doug Henderson. From *Living with Dinosaurs*, published by Bradbury Press.

Troodon formosus pair with *Orodromeus makelai* hatchling.

However, according to Osmólska and Barsbold (1990) in their review of the Troodontidae, the comparatively narrow olfactory tracts and small external nares suggest a rather inferior sense of smell.

Later, Currie and Zhao (1993*b*) described a well-preserved braincase (RTMP 86.36.457) of *T. formosus*, representing (from its size and degree of fusion of the bones) a mature but not old individual. The specimen was discovered late in July of 1986 by Tang Zhilu, a member of the first collecting party of the Sino-Canadian Dinosaur Project (see Currie 1991; Dong 1993*a*), in Dinosaur Provincial Park, Alberta, Canada.

As noted by Currie and Zhao, this was the first specimen to reveal the internal anatomy of the lower part of the braincase in *T. formosus*. Computerized tomography (CT) scans revealed the nature of the inner ear and course of the pneumatic ducts diverging from the middle ear. Spacious middle ear cavities, such as those in birds of prey, suggested that *Troodon* possessed an excellent sense of hearing possibly including lower-frequency sounds. Currie and Zhao found that the skull of this species seems to possess four of the five periotic pneumatic systems found in bird skulls (anterior tympanic recess, posterior tympanic recess, probably a dorsal tympanic recess, and possibly a pneumatopore in the prootic). Also observed in RTMP 86.36.457 were contralateral connections between the periotic sinuses. These connections may have improved the dinosaur's ability to localize sound (Witmer 1988), but could also have acted as shock absorbers to protect the delicate structures within the inner ear (Smith 1985). The presence of these connections are sometimes used to argue for a close relationship between birds and crocodiles. However, their presence in RTMP 86.36.457 suggested to Currie and Zhao that they appeared more than once in archosaurs, and are plesiomorphic for crocodiles, dinosaurs, and birds.

Currie and Zhao noted that the evidence is strong suggesting that birds derived from theropods, and that examination of specimen RTMP 86.36.457 revealed similarities between troodontids and birds suggesting that these groups of animals are more closely related to each other than to primitive theropods such as *Syntarsus* (*e.g.*, reduction of the basisphenoidal recess; separation of exits of the glossopharyngeal and vagus nerves by a metotic strut; reduction of the crista prootica in favor of an alaparasphenoid; separation of the ophtalmic from maxillo-mandibular branch of trigeminal within the prootic; and physical separation of two functional units of the inner ear). However, Currie and Zhao cautioned that cranial pneumacity

itself cannot be used as a criterion to resolve the relationships of crocodiles, theropods, and birds.

Considering its large brain, stereoscopic vision, and skeletal construction, Russell and Séguin envisioned this dinosaur as a relatively clever, swift-moving and agile hunter that preyed upon active nocturnal mammals of similar brain size, grasping its victims with its specialized hands, then eviscerating them with the talons of the hind feet.

More recently, this use of the feet, generally accepted as a method of killing prey in dromaeosaurids, was questioned regarding troodontids. As pointed out by Osmólska and Barsbold, this specialized digit II is associated with an entirely different, very long and slender metatarsus, and a long, delicate crus. Unlike the condition in dromaeosaurids, the nonginglymoid articular joint between metatarsal II and proximal phalanx of digit II in troontids does not limit excursion of the claw to just a single plane or the range of digit II movements, the force, therefore, exerted on digit II in troodontids being much weaker than in dromaeosaurids. Noting that this claw in troodontid *Borogovia gracilicrus* is straight instead of curved, Osmólska and Barsbold

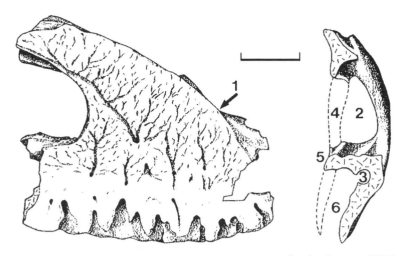

Troodon formosus, NMC 12392 [originally referred to *Stenonychosaurus inequalis*], maxilla, lateral and posterior views. Scale = 1 cm. (After Currie 1985.)

Troodon formosus, reconstructed skeleton [originally referred to *Stenonychosaurus inequalis*].

concluded that pedal digit II in troodontids must have served some purpose other than offense or killing prey.

Note: Russell and Séguin conducted an imaginative and rather provocative experiment regarding *Troodon* [=*Stenonychosaurus* of their usage]. Taking into account the relatively large brain, stereoscopic vision, bipedal stance, and opposable fingers (all suggesting a tendency toward a body plan akin to that of hominids), Russell and Séguin entertained the hypothesis that dinosaurs such as this may have evolved had they survived the Late Cretaceous extinctions. Russell and Séguin's extrapolations produced a hypothetical "dinosauroid," a tailless reptilian creature in superficially humanoid form, with large brain, three-fingered hands, and flat, three-toed feet. This form, whether mammalian or reptilian in nature, might represent a solution to the physical and physiological stresses imposed by a large brain in a terrestrial environment on a vertebrate organism.

Key references: Carpenter (1982); Currie (1987*a*, 1992); Currie and Zhao (1993*b*); Hatcher (1905); Gilmore (1924*a*); Hatcher (1905); Hay (1902); Hopson (1980*b*); Leidy (1956*a*); Nopcsa (1901); Osmólska and Barsbold (1990); Paul (1984); Romer (1966); D. A. Russell (1969); L. S. Russell (1948); D. A. Russell and Séguin (1982); Sternberg (1932*a*, 1945, 1951*b*); Sues (1977); Wilson and Currie (1985).

TSAGANTEGIA Tumanova 1994

Ornithischia: Genasauria: Thyreophora: Ankylosauria: Ankylosauridae.

Name derivation: "Tsagan-Teg [locality]."

Type species: *T. longicranialis* Tumanova 1994.

Other species: [None.]

Occurrence: ?Bayn Shireh Formation, Southeastern Gobi, Mongolia.

Age: Late Cretaceous.

Known material/holotype: GI No. 700/17, skull.

Diagnosis of genus (as for type species): Medium-sized ankylosaurid; skull roof covered with numerous small osteoderms quite distinctly manifested in relief; upper postorbital spines not developed; osteoderms not overhanging occiput; orbits behind level of middle of skull length; osteodermal ring around orbits separated from surrounding osteoderms by distinct groove, ring decreasing size of orbits; promaxillar rostrum trapezial; anterior and posterior maxillary shelves weakly developed; medial part of anterior wall of pterygoids inclined rearward, articulation of basisphenoid with pterygoids sutural; plane of occiput perpendicular to plane of skull roof; lower margin of paroccipital processes bending slightly inward, its distal ends curving somewhat downward; prootic, opisthotic, and exoccipital bones intergrown but with distinct boundaries between them; occipital condyle wide-oval, oriented posteroventrally; quadrate bones intergrown with paroccipital processes; jaw articulation at level of posterior margin of orbit or behind it; ventral surface of basioccipital bearing central depressions, separated by very gentle crests from lateral depressions; cingulum and lingulum of upper-jaw teeth dissected by vertical groove (Tumanova 1994).

Comments: The new genus *Tsagantegia* was established on a well-preserved skull (GI No. 700/17), found in 1983 by the Mesozoic team of the Joint Soviet-Mongolian Paleontological Expedition, at the Tsagan-Teg locality, near the town of Dzun-Bayan (Tumanova 1994), in deposits tentatively identified as the Bayn Shireh Formation (Tumanova 1994).

Tumanova noted that the most diagnostic features of the type species, *T. longicranialis,* were the elongated nasofrontal area, the small orbit and prominent osteodermal ring, and laterally relatively flat skull roof.

Tsagantegia longicraniallis, GI 700/17, holotype skull in dorsal, ventral, anterior, posterior, and lateral views. (After Tumanova 1993.)

Comparing *Tsagantegia* with other ankylosaurs, Tumanova found this genus to be most similar, in general structure and degree of development of osteoderms on the skull roof, to *Shamosaurus* and *Talarurus*; closest to *Shamosaurus* in development of upper postorbital spines (these being more prominent in all other known ankylosaurids); and closest to *Maleevus* in basicranium structure.

Key reference: Tumanova (1994).

TSINTAOSAURUS   Yang [Young] 1958

Ornithischia: Genasauria: Cerapoda: Ornithopoda: Iguanodontia: Hadrosauridae *incertae sedis*.

Name derivation: "Tsingtao [city]" + Greek *sauros* = "lizard."

Type species: *T. spinorhinus* Yang [Young] 1958.

Other species: [None.]

Occurrence: Wangshi Series, Shandong, People's Republic of China.

Age: Late Cretaceous, ?Campanian.

Known material: Isolated cranial and postcranial elements representing at least five individuals.

Holotype: IVP AS V725, posterior part of cranium with nasal process.

Diagnosis of genus (as for type species): [No modern diagnosis published.]

Comments: A problematic genus, *Tsintaosaurus* has long been a familiar hadrosaur pictured in dinosaur books, easily recognized by what was originally interpreted as a long, narrow, vertically-rising cranial crest. The genus was founded on a partial skull including an aberrant nasal process (IVP AS V725), collected from the Wangshih Series, Hsikou, Chingkankou, Laiyang, Shandong. The holotype skull is only tolerably preserved, highly deformed and skewed during fossilization, thereby causing a projection of ventral portions dorsally (see Brett-Surman 1989).

Referred material includes remains of about five individuals, including the posterior part of a second skull (paratype) lacking the nasal process; one right and two left maxillae, right and three left quadrates, nearly complete left premaxilla, various cranial fragments, lower jaws and predentary (apparently part of holotype), incomplete left and right lower jaw, incomplete left dentary, and right and left articular;

Tsintaosaurus spinorhinus, composite skeleton including holotype IVP AS V25], temporarily displayed at the National Museum of Wales.

Photo by the author.

postcranial remains including hypocentrum of the atlas, ten consecutive cervical vertebrae, five sacrals, approximately 59 caudals (most associated with holotype), four scapulae, four coracoids, four sterna, seven humeri, two radii, two ulnae, a few manual elements, four ilia, at least eight ischia, five pubes, four femora, some tibia and fibula fragments, and bones of the pes. Some of these remains (including the heavily restored type skull) were mounted as a composite skeleton, measuring about 7 meters [23 feet] long, at the Institute of Vertebrate Paleontology, Academia Sinica, Beijing (Yang [Young 1958c]).

Based on the type and referred material, Yang originally diagnosed the monotypic *T. spinorhinus* as follows: Nasals forming hollow "tube-like processes," distal extremity enlarged, projecting forward and upward; supratemporal opening wider than long; well-developed transversal ridge above supraoccipital; maxilla with weakly-reflected anterior and lateral margins; 11 cervical, 15 dorsal, probably eight sacral, ?60 caudal vertebrae; sacrals with distinct ventral longitudinal ridge; anterior caudals rather robust; scapula large, with expanded distal portion; upper portion of ilium very arched; distal end of ischium initially "footed"; humerus longer than ulna; femur robust, slightly shorter than tibia; tibial and fibular condyles forming coalesced tendinal canal.

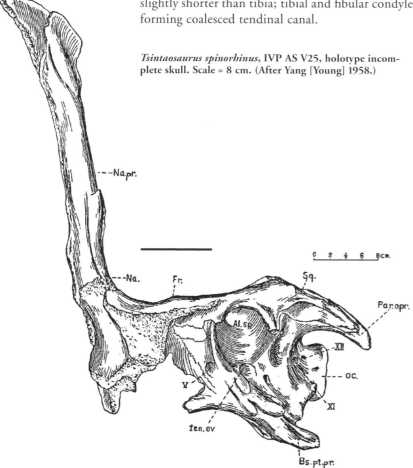

Tsintaosaurus spinorhinus, IVP AS V25, holotype incomplete skull. Scale = 8 cm. (After Yang [Young] 1958.)

Tsintaosaurus spinorhinus, holotype sacral vertebrae of *Tanius laiyangensis*. (After Zhen 1976.)

As the "crest" seemed to Yang to resemble superficially that of *Saurolophus*, he referred *Tsintaosaurus* to the [now abandoned] subfamily Saurolophinae.

The most characteristic feature of *Tsintaosaurus* is the supposed "nasal tube," generally reconstructed as a vertically rising crest projecting perpendicular to the skull outline. The base of this "crest" is reinforced by the swollen anterior portion of the nasal bones and medial part of the prefrontal. The "tube" itself is formed entirely by the nasals and, as restored, measures about 400 millimeters (15.5 inches) in length. Yang observed that the "tube" has an artificial breakage near its base. Life restorations have depicted *Tsintaosaurus* with this "crest" rising straight up from the top of the head, sometimes, as in Yang's original paper, supporting a fleshy membrane.

Some paleontologists have questioned the original interpretation of this "crest." The entire skull, especially the nasal tubes, may have been deformed during preservation, comparison with referred cranial material being difficult in that the "crest" was only preserved in the holotype.

Brett-Surman (1989) observed that the holotype of *T. spinorhinus* more closely resembles the cranial (crest in form of hollow nasals expanded distally, projecting dorso-posteriorly; mandible shorter and wider than in other clades) and postcranial elements in *Parasaurolophus* than in any other genus. Cranially, *Tsintaosaurus* differs from *Parasaurolophus* in having premaxillae that are not expanded and do not override the nasals dorso-posteriorly; postcranially, the two forms differ only in the tarsals, those of *Tsintaosaurus* typical of most hadrosaurids, the tarsus of *Parasaurolophus* unique. Brett-Surman regarded *Tsintaosaurus* as a lambeosaurine because of the form of the pelvis, and noted that the collected material may

Tsintaosaurus spinorhinus,
composite skeleton with
reconstructed holotype skull
(IVP AS V251), temporarily
displayed at the National
Museum of Wales.

be a composite taxon, including elements belonging to the hadrosaurine *Tanius*.

Weishampel and Horner (1990), in their review of the Hadrosauridae, speculated that *T. spinorhinus* could be a chimera, the material consisting both of hadrosaurine (skull-roof-neurocranium material, premaxilla, sacra with ventral groove, and ischia lacking prominent distal expansion) and lambeosaurine (maxilla, quadrates, most of dentaries, ventrally-ridged sacra, prominently footed ischia, and supposed crest fragment) remains, and questioned whether or not the nasal "crest" is really hollow. Weishampel and Horner cited P. Taquet's (personal communication to Weishampel and Horner) suggestion that the so-called "crest" may actually be a misplaced nasal. For these reasons, Weishampel and Horner regarded this genus as Hadrosauridae *incertae sedis*. The species *Tanius laiyangensis* Zhen 1976 was regarded by

Weishampel and Horner as synonymous with *T. spinorhinus*.

More recently, Taquet (1991) noted that the nasals of *T. spinorhinus* should be correctly restored in an antero-ventral position on the maxilla. According to Taquet, *Tsintaosaurus*, restored thusly, becomes a typical hadrosaurine congeneric with *Tanius* and conspecific with *T. sinensis*. Taquet's interpretation of *Tsintaosaurus* as a junior synonym of *Tanius* has not, however, been generally accepted; Buffetaut (in press as of this writing) will demonstrate that Taquet's synonymy is unfounded.

The weight of *Tsintaosaurus*, as estimated by G. S. Paul (personal communication 1988), was about 2.42 metric tons (approximately 2.7 tons).

Key references: Brett-Surman (1989); Taquet (1991); Weishampel and Horner (1990); Yang (1958*c*).

TUGULUSAURUS Dong 1973 [*nomen dubium*]
Saurischia: Theropoda *incertae sedis*.
Name derivation: "Tugulu [Group]" + Greek *sauros* = "lizard."
Type species: *T. faciles* Dong 1973 [*nomen dubium*].
Other species: [None.]
Occurrence: Lianmugin Formation, Xinjiang Uygur Zizhiqu, People's Republic of China.
Age: Early Cretaceous (Neocomian–Albian).
Known material/holotype: IVPP V.4025, four caudal vertebrae, left femur, proximal end of right femur, left radius, astragalus, calcaneum, parts of metatarsus (apparently two distal ends of bones of pedal digit III).

Diagnosis of genus (as for type species): Caudal centrum biconcave, longer than wide, with no keel on ventral surface; left femur hollow, thin-walled, 21 centimeters (about 8 inches) in length; radius expanding triangularly at front and back of proximal end, 23 centimeters (about 8.3 inches long); calcaneum crescent-shaped, tightly joined to astragalus; metatarsal elements typical of *Ornithomimus* in smooth, deeply concave articular surfaces (Dong 1973).

Comments: The genus *Tugulusaurus* was founded upon partial postcranial remains (IVPP V.4025) from the Tugulu Group (Lower Cretaceous) of Xinjian [then Sinkiang], China (Dong 1973). According to Dong (1992), the presence of *Psittacosaurus* confirms that the Tugulu Group is Early Cretaceous, the rich and varied ostracod fauna suggesting a Neocomian-Albian stage.

Note: The femur of *Tugulusaurus* is relatively much longer than in ornithomimids, suggesting that this genus does not belong in the Ornithomimidae (R. E. Molnar, personal communication 1989).

Key references: Dong (1973, 1992).

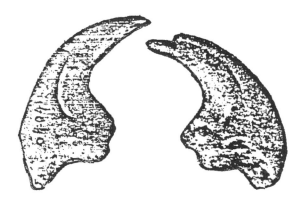

Tugulusaurus facile, IVPP V.4025, holotype pedal unguals. (After Dong 1973.)

TUOJIANGOSAURUS Dong, Li, Zhou and Chang 1977
Ornithischia: Genasauria: Thyreophora: Stegosauria: Stegosauridae.
Name derivation: "Tuojiang River [tributary of Yangtzi in Sichuan Basin]" + Greek *sauros* = "lizard."
Type species: *T. multispinus* Dong, Li, Zhou and Chang 1977.
Other species: [None.]
Occurrence: Shangshaximiao Formation, Sichuan, People's Republic of China.
Age: Late Jurassic (Oxfordian or Kimmeridgian).
Known material: Two partial skeletons.
Holotype: CV 209, almost complete skeleton.

Diagnosis of genus (as for type species): Skull with low, elongate facial region, reduced jugal, three supraorbitals; three pairs of small, elongate, bean-shaped foramina between transverse processes of sacral vertebrae (Dong 1990*b*); neural spines of proximal caudal vertebrae uniquely possessing craniolaterally oriented sheets; dermal ossifications consisting of 17 pairs of symmetrical bony plates and spines, those in neck region spherical, large, high spines in lumbar and sacral regions (Galton 1990*b*).

Comments: The first Asian stegosaur known from nearly complete remains, *Tuojiangosaurus* was founded on a skeleton (CV 209) discovered in 1974 in the early Upper Jurassic Shangshaximiao Formation, near Fushi River, at Wujiabai, Zigong, southwestern Sichuan Province, China. A paratype specimen (CV 210) consists of a partial sacrum (Dong, Zhou, Li and Chang 1977). Dong *et al.* originally diagnosed the monotypic *T. multispinus* as follows: Skull of typically stegosaurian form, with elongate facial region, reduced jugal, two or three supraoccipital elements, occipital part apparently similar to *Kentrosaurus*; teeth more or less spatulate, overlapping one another; about 27 estimated teeth in single functional series in each jaw; five sacral vertebrae, with three pierced openings on back of sacrum; length of femur to humerus ratio 1.57; femur with reduced fourth trochanter at mid-shaft; 17 pairs of symmetrical bony plates and spines, arranged in two dorsal rows from neck to tail.

The skeleton, mounted for display and part of a global traveling exhibit of Chinese dinosaurs, measures 7 meters (about 23.5 feet) in length.

The discovery of another *Tuojiangosaurus* skeleton was reported by Gao, Huang and Zhu (1986), collected from the Upper Jurassic of Sichuan. This find is especially significant in that a pair of "parasacral" spines (see Sereno and Dong 1992) were preserved very near their natural position, the expanded base positioned over the proximal end of the scapula, the spine projecting posterolaterally. Until this dis-

Tuojiangosaurus multispinus, CV 209, holotype skeleton (bottom left) detail of dorsal vertebrae and dermal plates, (top) 3/4 posterior view, (bottom right) 3/4 front view, temporarily displayed at the National Museum of Wales.

Photos by the author.

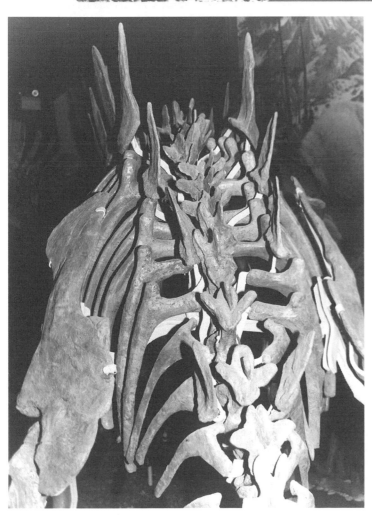

covery, such spines (known also in *Kentrosaurus* and *Huayangosaurus*) were believed to have been located over the hips.

Key references: Dong (1990*b*); Dong, Li, Zhou and Chang (1977); Galton (1990*b*); Gao, Huang and Zhu (1986).

TURANOCERATOPS Nessov and Kaznyshkina 1989 *see in* Nessov, Kaznyshkina and Cherepanov 1989

Ornithischia: Genasauria: Cerapoda: Marginocephalia: Ceratopsia: Neoceratopsia, Ceratopsidae *incertae sedis*.

Name derivation: Persian "Turan [region]" + Greek *keratops* = "horn face."

Type species: *T. tardabilis* Nessov and Kaznyshkina 1989.

Other species: [None.]

Occurrence: Jarakuduk, Russia.

Age: Late Cretaceous (Maastrichtian).

Known material: Partial crania, ?several individuals.

Holotype: Chigr Museum, Leningrad, No. 251/12457, left maxilla.

Diagnosis of genus (as for type species): Nasal horn large, other horns moderate-sized, sharp; rostral bone and jaw low, rostral with dull edge; teeth with divided roots, two per row (Nessov and Kaznyshkina *see in* Nessov, Kaznyshkina and Cherepanov 1989).

Comments: The genus *Turanoceratops* was founded on a jaw (Chigr Museum, No. 251/12457) collected from the Upper Cretaceous of Jarakuduk, Russia. Referred remains from the same locality include three maxillae, five horns, partial scapula (similar to other ceratopsian scapulae), and about 50 teeth (No. 351/310/12457).

As described by Nessov and Kaznyshkina, the jaw, if complete, probably had about 20 teeth. The largest tooth crown is 16.5 millimeters in length. The skull is long anterior to the orbit.

Turanoceratops tardabilis, Chigr Museum 251/12457, holotype left maxilla. (After Nessov and Kaznyshkina 1989.)

Nessov and Kaznyshkina postulated that ceratopsians penetrated western Asia when the climate in that region began to warm, this area becoming the center of development for this group.

Key reference: Nessov and Kaznyshkina *see in* Nessov, Kaznyshkina and Cherepanov (1989).

TYLOCEPHALE Maryańska and Osmólska 1974

Ornithischia: Genasauria: Cerapoda: Marginocephalia: Pachycephalosauria: Pachycephalosauridae.

Name derivation: Greek *tyle* = "swelling on the skin" + Greek *cephale* = "head."

Type species: *T. gilmorei* Maryańska and Osmólska 1974.

Other species: [None.]

Occurrence: Barun Goyot Formation, Omnogov, Mongolian People's Republic.

Age: Late Cretaceous (Middle Campanian).

Known material/holotype: ZPAL MgD-I/105, incomplete skull with several maxillary teeth, incomplete mandible with several teeth.

Diagnosis of genus (as for type species): Skull with strongly elevated dome, highest point located far caudally; postorbitals and supraorbitals incorporated into dome; parietosquamosal shelf very narrow; supratemporal fenestrae probably absent (Maryańska 1990).

Comments: The genus *Tylocephale* was founded by Maryańska and Osmólska (1974) on a damaged incomplete skull (ZPAL MgD-I/105), collected during one of the Polish-Mongolian Paleontological Expeditions (Kielan-Jaworoska and Dovchin 1968/ 1969; Kielan-Jaworoska and Barsbold 1972), from the Barun Goyot Formation, Khulsan, Nemegt Basin, Gobi Desert, Mongolian People's Republic (Gradziński and Jerzykiewicz 1972).

Maryańska and Osmólska originally diagnosed the monotypic *T. gilmorei* as follows: Skull with thickened, highly elevated cranial roof, highest point located far posteriorly; postorbital and both orbitals incorporated into dome; infratemporal openings very long and narrow, almost vertically placed; orbit elongate, oblique, axis long, extending upward and posteriorly; quadrate almost vertical; occipital region narrow, very faintly depressed; tooth-bearing edge of maxilla straight almost to very posterior end; maxillary and mandibulary teeth with large crowns; surface of external bones strongly ornamented, that of dome rough, of jugal at orbital margin and of quadratojugal nearly smooth.

As measured by Maryańska and Osmólska, the skull has a greatest height of 133 millimeters (over 5

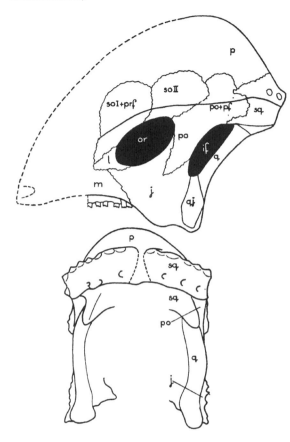

Tylocephale gilmorei, ZPAL MgD-I/105, holotype partial skull, lateral and occipital views. (After Maryańska and Osmólska 1974.)

inches), and a greatest width of 99 millimeters (about 3.8 inches).

Maryańska and Osmólska observed that the ornamentation on the external surface of the supraorbitals and postorbital consists of tubers of moderate size. Large, prominent and irregularly spaced tubers cover the outer surface of the jugal. Eight nodes are present on the squamosal along the posterior margin of the skull roof, and a single large node is below the outermost node of that series. Large nodes continue in a row forwards laterally across squamosal and postorbital, diminishing farther anteriorly, merging as a sharp crest along the supraorbitals. Along the postorbital bar is a not very prominent crest. The skull is unique among known pachycephalosaurids in that the dome elevation can be seen when viewed in posterior aspect.

Key references: Gradziński and Jerzykiewicz (1972); Maryańska (1990); Maryańska and Osmólska (1974).

TYLOSTEUS Leidy 1872 [*nomen oblitum*]—(See *Pachycephalosaurus*.)

Name derivation: Greek *tylos* = "knob" + Greek *osteon* = "bone."
Type species: *T. ornatus* Leidy 1872 [*nomen oblitum*].

TYRANNOSAURUS Osborn 1905—
(=*Dynamosaurus, Jenghiskhan, Manospondylus, Tarbosaurus* =?*Nanotyrannus*)
Saurischia: Theropoda: Tetanurae: Coelurosauria: Maniraptora: Arctometatarsalia: Tyrannosauridae.
Name derivation: Greek *tyrannos* = "tyrant" + Greek *sauros* = "lizard."
Type species: *T. rex* Osborn 1905.
Other species: *T. bataar* Maleev 1955, ?*T. novojilovi* Maleev 1955, ?*T. turpanensis* (Zhai, Zheng and Tong 1978) [*nomen nudum*], ?*T. luanchuanensis* (Dong 1979).
Occurrence: Scollard Formation, Willow Creek Formation, Alberta, Frenchman Formation, Saskatchewan, Canada; Hell Creek South Formation, Livingston Formation, Montana, Hell Creek Formation, South Dakota, Lance Formation, Wyoming, Laramie Formation, Colorado, Javelina Formation, Texas, McRae Formation, New Mexico, United States; Quiba Formation, Henan, Subashi Formation, Xinjiang Uygur Zizhiqu, ?unnamed formation, Heilongjiang, People's Republic of China; Nemegtskaya Svita, White Beds of Khermeen Tsav, Bayankhongor, Nemegt Formation, Omnogov, Mongolian People's Republic.
Age: Late Cretaceous (Early–Late Maastrichtian).
Known material: At least 40 individuals, represented by at least three complete skulls, five partial skulls, skull with partial postcrania, two partial skulls with complete postcrania, at least five skulls with associated postcrania, teeth, some with and associated postcrania, juvenile to adult.
Holotype: CM 9380 [formerly AMNH 973], almost complete skeleton missing most cervical vertebrae, forelimbs, tail.

Diagnosis of genus: Skull (in dorsal view) with muzzle well-differentiated from cranium for well-developed stereoscopic vision; descending process of postorbital extending into orbit; premaxilla contacting nasal below external nares and medial to maxilla (not visible in lateral view); lacrimal horn not developed but rugose, as is dorsal part of postorbital; pro-maxillary fenestra not visible in lateral view; prefrontal forming a wedge between lacrimal and fused frontals; ectopterygoids swollen, with very large sinus opening; front margin of preacetabular blade of ilium with well-developed notch; postacetabular blade slender; wrist consisting of single ele-

Tyrannosaurus rex, CM 9380, holotype skull, heavily restored.

ment; pubic shaft pronouncedly curved (Carpenter 1992).

Diagnosis of *T. rex*: Angular terminating posterior to surangular fenestra, latter much larger than in *T. bataar*; maxilla terminating below lacrimal (Carpenter 1992).

Diagnosis of *T. bataar*: Angular terminating anterior to surangular fenestra, the latter proportionally smaller than in *T. rex* (Carpenter 1992).

Comments: The most famous of all theropods, *Tyrannosaurus*—the celebrated "King Tyrant Lizard"—was among the largest and most powerful terrestrial carnivores of all time.

Remains of *Tyrannosaurus* were known more than two decades before the genus was named. Cope (1892*b*) had described two dorsal vertebrae (AMNH 3982) upon which he erected the new genus and species *Manospondylus gigas*, these having been remains collected from an unspecified locality of the Lance Formation of South Dakota (see Hatcher, Marsh and Lull [1907]). Although the holotype originally consisted of two dorsals, one was lost or mis-

placed by the early 1900s. Cope provisionally assigned this material to the [abandoned] ceratopsian family Agathaumidae.

Cope originally diagnosed *Manospondylus* as follows: Dorsal vertebrae with short anteroposterior length, gently concave articular surfaces, coossified neuropophyses; surfaces of circumference of centrum uninterrupted, except for deep entering fossa at "superior part"; tissue of centrum at borders of articular faces coarsely vascular. Cope diagnosed the type species as follows: Centrum slightly deeper than wide, with smooth lateral surfaces.

The genus *Tyrannosaurus* was founded upon the larger portion of a skeleton (CM 9380; originally AMNH 973), discovered in hard sandstone in 1902 by an American Museum of Natural History expedition led by Barnum Brown, accompanied by Richard Swann Lull, in the Laramie Formation, Hell Creek Beds, Dawson County, Montana, above Fort Pierre. The specimen was excavated in 1902 and 1903 by a field party from the American Museum of Natural History. Additional portions of the skeleton (then

AMNH 973) were collected in 1905 under Brown's direction.

As much of the skeleton, including the skull and jaws, had not yet been prepared, Osborn (1905) only briefly diagnosed the genus (and type species *T. rex*) as follows: Carnivorous dinosaur attaining very large size; humerus assumed to be large and elongate; no evidence of bony dermal armor [reference to ankylosaurian armor incorrectly referred by Osborn to the holotype of *Dynamosaurus imperiosus*; see below].

Osborn noted that, according to calculations made by William Diller Matthew, the total length of the skeleton would be about 39 feet, the skull held about 19 feet off the ground. Osborn (1906) subsequently placed this genus into its own family, Tyrannosauridae, which replaced Deinodontidae Cope 1886, a taxon founded upon type species *Deinodon horridus* (*nomen dubium*).

At the same time that he named and described *T. rex*, Osborn (1905) erected the new genus and species *Dynamosaurus imperiosus*, based on the lower jaws and partial postcrania including vertebrae and ribs (BMNH collection; formerly AMNH 5866), this material recovered by the American Museum of Natural History expedition of 1900 under Brown's supervision, from Seven Mile Creek, north of Cheyenne River, Weston County, Wyoming. Found in association with these remains were numerous irregular bony plates, suggesting to Osborn (1905) that this dinosaur (unlike *T. rex*) was armored. These osteoderms (identified as ankylosaurian by Walker 1964) were believed to have been located on the animal's sides or back. Osborn (1906) later referred *D. imperiosus* to *T. rex*.

(In recent years, some paleontologists have reassessed the validity of *Dynamosaurus*. "Black Beauty," a mounted skeleton of *T. rex* exhibited at the Royal Tyrrell Museum of Palaeontology, was originally labeled *Dynamosaurus*. However, most workers regard *D. imperiosus* as synonymous with *T. rex*, the differences, including fewer mandibular teeth in the former, perhaps attributed to sexual dimorphism.)

In 1908, a more complete skeleton (AMNH 5027) of *T. rex* was collected by the American Museum of Natural History from the same locality as the holotype. This specimen, which included a complete skull distorted on the left side by post-mortem compression, lacked ventral ribs, forearms, and manus. The skeleton was mounted for display at the American Museum with the missing elements cast from the type specimen. Because of its great weight and to make it available for study, the skull was exhibited separately, replaced on the mounted skeleton by a plaster cast.

It was the American Museum's original intent to mount both skeletons in an action pose, as if the animals were about to attack one another. Scaled-down models of these intended mounts were prepared, photographs of them appearing in various publications. In 1941, with the United States entering World War II, the type specimen was bought (for protection) by George H. Clapp, a trustee of the Carnegie Museum of Natural History, to that museum where, the following year, it was mounted for display.

With *Tyrannosaurus* now well known from good fossil remains, Osborn (1917) observed that the remaining dorsal vertebra of Cope's *M. gigas* resembles in size and other characters the posterior cervical or first dorsal vertebra in *T. rex*. As the holotype of *M. gigas* is so incomplete and imperfectly preserved, Osborn (1917) suggested that this fossil should be regarded as indeterminate.

The Asian taxon *Tarbosaurus bataar* Maleev 1955, originally described by Maleev (1955a) as a new species of *Tyrannosaurus* but subsequently referred by Maleev 1955c to new genus *Tarbosaurus*, is now again considered to belong in the genus *Tyrannosaurus* (see below). The type species *T. bataar* was founded on a skeleton (PIN 551-1) missing the right forelimb, collected in 1955 by the Palaeontological Institute of the Academy of Sciences, [then] Union of Soviet Socialist Republics, from the Nemegt Formation, Nemegt, Mongolia. Maleev (1955a, 1955b, 1955c) published brief reports on this species as well as three other new Mongolian tyrannosaurids, which he named *Tarbosaurus efremovi*, *Gorgosaurus lancinator*, and *G. novojilovi*, regarding *T. bataar* as slightly smaller than *Tyrannosaurus*, with a more elongate and less massive

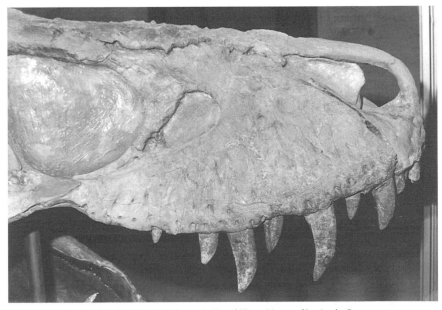

Tyrannosaurus rex, anterior part of skull (LACM 7244/23844), right lateral view.

skull, more laterally compressed teeth, and comparatively shorter forelimbs. Later, Rozhdestvensky (1965), believing the differences between the Mongolian taxa to be ontogenetic with but a single species (intermediate between *Albertosaurus* and *Tyrannosaurus*) represented, referred all four to *T. bataar*.

T. efremovi was based on a skull and postcranial material (PEN AN SSR 551-3) from Tsagan Ula, Mongolia. The type specimen measures 10–12 meters (about 33–39 feet) long, 4.5–5 meters (14.5–16.5 feet) high. The juvenile "*Gorgosaurus*" *lancinator* Maleev 1955 (skull measuring about 74 centimeters or 2.5 feet long) was found at Altan Ula.

Tarbosaurus had generally been regarded as somewhat smaller than *Tyrannosaurus*. One specimen referred to *Tarbosaurus* measures about 6.8 meters (23 feet) long and some 2.8 meters (almost 10 feet) high at the hips, skull approximately 1.15 meters (almost 4 feet) in length, manus over 14 centimeters (5.5 inches) long, though the largest adult individuals may have attained a length of 11.75 meters (40 feet). *Tarbosaurus* had been viewed as the Asian equivalent of *Tyrannosaurus*, the former having a somewhat more pronounced rugosity on the snout. Based on a cast (NMC 10422) of the skull of *T. bataar* specimen PIN 551-3 and morphological data supplied by Rozhdestvensky, Russell regarded *Tarbosaurus* as most closely allied to *Tyrannosaurus*, differ-

ing from the North American genus in that the nasals are less constricted between the lacrimals, the surangular foramen is small, and adult individuals are smaller. Skeletal similarities between *Tarbosaurus* and *Tyrannosaurus* have led some workers to suggest that the differences are too minimal to warrant generic distinction, even given geographical separation. In his book *Predatory Dinosaurs of the World,* Paul (1988*c*) proposed that *Tarbosaurus* be regarded as a subgenus of *Tyrannosaurus,* as *Tyrannosaurus* (*Tarbosaurus*) *bataar.*

More recently, Carpenter (1992) reassessed the figures published by Maleev (1955*a*, 1955*b*), as well as Rozhdestvensky's analysis and photographs of Mongolian tyrannosaurid material. Carpenter observed that, *contra* Rozhdestvensky, the quadratojugal process of the jugal in *T. bataar* reaches the posterior rim of the lateral temporal fenestra (as in *T. rex*); ascending process of jugal in *T. bataar* specimen PIN 551-3 tapers (as in *T. rex* skull LACM 23844), while it is tetragonal in *T. rex* specimen AMNH 5027, illustrating the variability of the shape of this bone; that development of this process into the orbit is variable, PIN 551-1 clearly intermediate in shape between AMNH 5027 and PIN 551-3 (not *Albertosaurus* and *Tyrannosaurus*); and that *Tarbosaurus* is not smaller than the North American form, the holotype skull PIN 551-1 having a premaxillary-to-occipital condyle length of 1220 millimeters (Maleev 1955*a*), that of AMNH 5027 being shorter by 10 millimeters (Osborn 1912*a*). Carpenter referred *Tarbosaurus* to *Tyrannosaurus,* with *T. bataar* accepted as a valid species. (In a review of the Tyrannosauridae published in the Japanese popular magazine, *Dinosaur Frontline,* Olshevsky and Ford 1995 referred *T. bataar* to a new genus, *Jenghiskhan,* named for the Mongol conqueror, Jenghis Khan or Genghis Khan; this referral has not yet been adopted.)

T. bataar is one of the best known tyrannosaurids, remains of at least seven individuals having been collected during the 1955 expedition, with six additional skeletons obtained during the Polish-Mongolian Paleontological Expeditions in 1967, some found in near perfect states of preservation. A number of *T. bataar* skeletons were mounted for display at the Paleontological Museum of the Academy of Sciences in Moscow. These (including excellent juvenile specimen ZPAL MgD-1/3) vary ontogenetically, providing information as to the growth process in tyrannosaurids. Carpenter noted that the general ontogenetic trend in skulls of *T. bataar* "is a deepening of the skull, shortening of the muzzle, and an increase in the rugosity of the region dorsal to the orbit."

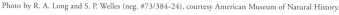
Photo by R. A. Long and S. P. Welles (neg. #73/384-24), courtesy American Museum of Natural History.

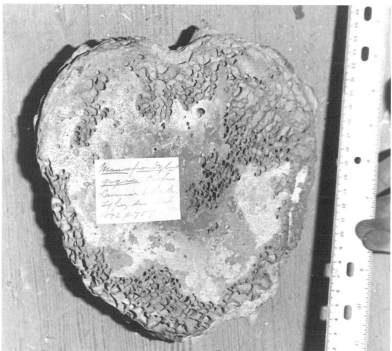

Tyrannosaurus rex, AMNH 3982, holotype centrum of dorsal vertebra of *Manospondylus gigas.*

Skeleton (AMNH 5027) of *Tyrannosaurus rex* as mounted ca. 1915 under Henry Fairfield Osborn's direction, with incorrect upright posture, three-fingered manus, and about 3 meters of extra tail vertebrae. (The skull on this mount is a cast.)

Other species that have been referred to "*Tarbosaurus*" [=*Tyrannosaurus*] include ?*Albertosaurus periculosus* Riabinin 1930 [*nomen dubium*], based on a tooth crown from the Amur River locality in Manchuria, tentatively referred to *T. bataar* by Molnar (1990), regarded by Gilmore (1930) as a *nomen nudum*, having neither specific nor generic distinction, though documenting the occurrence of theropods in the Amur River locality; and *T. luanchuansis*, originally described by Dong (1979) as a new species of *Tyrannosaurus* but generally referred to "*Tarbosaurus*," based on a single tooth (NIGP V4733) and postcranial bones from the Quiba Formation of Songping Valley, Luanchuan County, Henan province, Inner Mongolia, China, with at least four more teeth from that area referred to this species (Dong 1987).

Langston (1965) described the fourth phalanx of pedal digit IV (NMC 9950), part of a badly eroded skeleton reported by Sternberg (1946), from the Horseshoe Canyon Formation, east of Huxley and above Kneehills Tuff, in Alberta, Canada. The specimen measures 53 millimeters (about 2 inches) long

and, at its distal articulation, approximately 80 millimeters (3.1 inches) wide. As the element is relatively larger than the corresponding element in *Albertosaurus* and *Daspletosaurus*, Langston referred it to *Tyrannosaurus*, documenting the occurrence of this genus in upper Edmonton strata. Previously, only the first phalanx of digit IV had been known in *Tyrannosaurus*. In his review of the tyrannosaurids of western Canada, Russell (1970*b*) published a modern diagnosis of *T. rex* based upon the type material, and also various referred specimens including NMC 9950 and also a cervical centrum fragment (NMC 9554), from below and south of the locality that yielded the former specimen. Russell observed that body proportions of *Tyrannosaurus* are similar to *Daspletosaurus* (though about 25 percent larger in the adult), the humerus is more reduced, ilium longer.

In general appearance *Tyrannosaurus* is typical of Tyrannosauridae, but on the family's grandest scale. In his book *The Dinosaurs*, Swinton (1970) commented that the bulk, teeth, and claws in *Tyrannosaurus* could very well have reached maximum development and that the animal's activity would have

Tyrannosaurus rex, BMNH, holotype partial skeleton of *Dynamosaurus imperiosus*.

been less effective if such development had been increased.

The skull of *Tyrannosaurus* is enormous. As measured by Osborn (1906, 1912*a*, 1917), the holotype skull of *T. rex* is 1.3 meters (4 feet) in length (although more recently discovered specimens are considerably larger), containing teeth from nearly 8 to almost 16 centimeters (3–6 inches) long above the bone margin, and about 2.5 centimeters (1 inch) wide. (Current estimates of the length of an average-sized adult settle on about 12 meters [over 40 feet]).

From brain casts made from skulls of *T. rex*, Osborn (1912), and later Hopson (1980*b*), showed that the olfactory tract is long, the pituitary body pendant and "trigger-like," the olfactory region seemingly well-developed.

Swinton noted that the ear structure of *Tyrannosaurus* (and other dinosaurs) is similar to that in crocodiles, dinosaurs apparently having had a well-developed sense of hearing. An efficient ear implies the

possibility of some vocal ability, presumably utilized in recognition of others of its species or to give warning. According to Swinton, *Tyrannosaurus* might be imagined as capable of making a full-throated croaking sound.

Newman (1970) made a study of the stance and locomotion of *Tyrannosaurus* during the mounting of the composite skeleton (including the holotype of *Dynamosaurus imperiosus*) on display at the British Museum (Natural History) [now The Natural History Museum, London]. Newman criticized the skeletal reconstruction of the American Museum of Natural History display specimen as originally restored by Osborn (1917). Newman pointed out that the skull was positioned in such a way that articulation between occipital condyle and atlas would have been severely hindered; that the skull was supported on a well-defined, flexible neck, at a marked angle to the rest of the column; and that, if the dorsal region is rigid and oriented horizontally, the "swan neck" would carry the skull horizontally, giving the head maneuverability and allowing it to reach the ground to feed. With an *Albertosaurus* for comparison, Newman calculated that the tail, with only 20 caudal vertebrae included in American Museum specimen, had been restored too long and should be shortened by some 3.5 meters (12 feet). Newman also stated that the hind legs could not have borne the stresses in walking if the body were oriented so that the tail dragged, and speculated that the weight of the walking animal must have been carried by one leg at a time, the gait most likely sinuous, producing a pigeon-toed waddling as in birds.

A consensus has yet to be reached settling the question of how *Tyrannosaurus* acquired its food. In recent years, as pointed out by Horner (in Horner

and Lessem 1994), scientists and laymen alike have preferred to envision *Tyrannosaurus* as a fierce and active predator.

Farlow (1993) addressed the issue of how some carnivorous dinosaurs like *Tyrannosaurus* attained larger body sizes than the predatory mammals that replaced them, and if, as suggested by some workers (*e.g.*, Lambe 1917*c*; Colinvaux 1978; Halstead and Halstead 1981; Barsbold 1983), theropods achieved huge size by becoming sluggish scavengers.

As cited by Farlow, Colinvaux (1978) had offered the basic premise that loss of energy in the flow from one trophic level to the next (this condition imposed by the second law of thermodynamics) establishes a top limit to the body size and abundance of predatory animals, the supply of energy not stretching to support

Illustration by Gregory S. Paul.

Triceratops horridus (left) attacked by *Tyrannosaurus rex*, the latter portrayed as an active predator.

Tyrannosaurus

Tyrannosaurus rex, cm 9380, restored holotype skeleton mounted in outmoded upright pose.

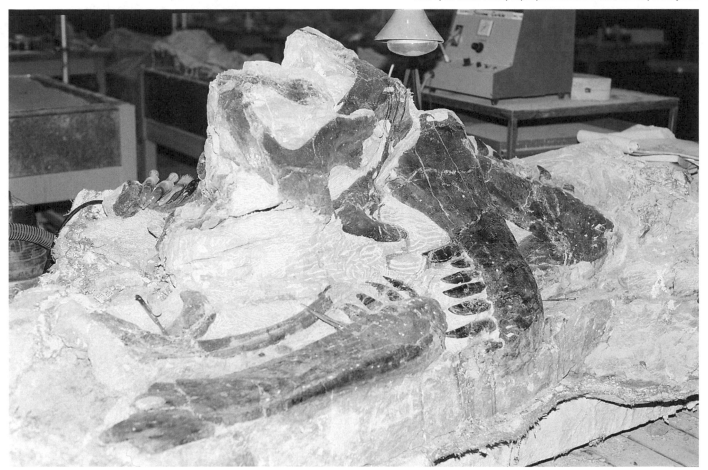

Partially prepared *Tyrannosaurus rex* specimen in the laboratory.

tyrannosaur-sized predators. Today, great white sharks in the sea and tigers on land represent the largest carnivorous animals that the laws of physics allow the Earth to support. Colinvaux concluded that tyrannosaurs maintained great size by consuming the meat of giant prey, but escaped the energy-consuming price of active predation by eating carrion, spending most of their days lying on their bellies conserving energy. The later active mammalian predators could have cleaned up the meat supplies before an animal such as a "sluggish" *Tyrannosaurus* could get at them.

In a publication privately issued in 1996, Stephen Pickering proposed the new species *T.* [*rex*] *stanwinstonorous,* based upon type specimen BHI 2033 and referred specimens BHI 3033, SDSMT 12047, MMS 51-2004, and USNM 358563 and 419706, diagnosed as follows: Reduced nasal rugosities; secondarily reduced postorbital-orbital joint; palatine with no ventral foramina; rostroventral area of pterygoid wing lacking rugosity; rugosity may be visible due to loss of "supradentary"; 6-7 per cent larger body size than *T. bataar* or *T. rex*. To date of this writing, the species has not been adopted.

Farlow rejected the portrayal of giant theropods like *Tyrannosaurus* as simply lethargic scavengers, noting that the skeletal structure of such dinosaurs suggests dynamic bipeds (see below); fossil footprint evidence suggests walking speeds of from 5 to 10 kilometers (about 3.1 to 6.2 miles) per hour, equal to or surpassing the speeds of modern mammals (see also Bakker 1987; Molnar and Farlow 1990); at least medium-sized theropods may have achieved running speeds of up to 40 kilometers (about 24.9 miles) per hour (Farlow 1981); and features of the skull, jaws, and teeth of large theropods suggest dinosaurs like *Tyrannosaurus* were more than merely scavengers (Paul 1988c; Molnar and Farlow 1990; McGowan 1991; Farlow, Brinkman, Abler, and Currie 1991).

Accepting Colinvaux's proposed upper limit to the size of predatory animals, Farlow (1993) noted that an animal's body size can be influenced by a variety of physiological and ecological variables, including "diet, foraging strategy, intraspecific and interspecific competition for food, digestive processes, thermoregulation, intraspecific rivalry for breeding rights, and reproductive dynamics." Also, pointed

Tyrannosaurus

Photo by the author, courtesy Museum of Geology, South Dakota School of Mines and Technology.

Tyrannosaurus rex

The skull of the largest meat-eater to walk the earth. The specimen is the first skull to be found in South Dakota. It was collected during the fall of 1981 from the 64 million year old Hell Creek Formation of Butte County, SD.

Ventral view of skull (SDSMT 12047) of incomplete, immature *Tyrannosaurus rex* skeleton, found by rancher Jennings Flowden in northwestern South Dakota, collected in 1980.

In a private publication of 1996, Stephan Pickering proposed a new (not yet adopted) taxon, *T.* [*rex*] *stanwinstonorus,* based on holotype BHI 2033 and above referred specimen, BHI 3033, MMS 51-2004, and USNM 358563 and 419706, diagnosed thusly: Reduced nasal rugosities; secondarily reduced postorbital-orbital joint; palatine with no ventral foramina; rostroventral area of pterygoid wing lacking rugosity; rugosity may be visible due to loss of "supradentary"; 6-7 per cent larger body size than *T. bataar* or *T. rex.*

out by Paul, some groups of plant-eating mammals have attained the size (1000 kilograms or about 2,240 pounds, or more) of many herbivorous dinosaurs. According to Farlow (1993), the evolution of huge theropods was prompted by more factors than simply the existence of giant-sized prey.

Farlow (1993) reinterpreted Colinvaux's basic premise by considering the constraints that might have prevented predatory mammals from attaining the size of giant theropods, noting the following: Population densities of giant terrestrial predators must be very low to prevent over-eating their food resources; total population sizes must be large enough to eschew chance extinction; "A dinosaur-sized carnivorous mammal would require so large a geographic distribution that this seems to be difficult, or even impossible, to do."

As Farlow (1993) speculated, large carnivorous dinosaurs like *Tyrannosaurus* may have solved the problem of size constraint, not solved by predatory mammals, through one or more factors: 1. Larger population densities of plant-eating dinosaurs than of elephant-sized mammals; 2. rather higher population turnover rates of herbivorous dinosaurs than of large-mammal populations; 3. lower mass-specific food consumption rates of carnivorous dinosaurs than

expected for equally large meat-eating mammals; 4. differences in diet between juvenile and adult theropods; and 5. a higher reproductive potential for egg-laying theropods than in viviparous mammals.

Farlow (1993) concluded that *Tyrannosaurus* and other giant theropods attained their great size through a fortuitous chain of events involving physiological and ecological features in which these animals differed from the mammals that replaced them; and that these theropods must have had some ecological top limit to their body size. Accepting that these theropods attacked live prey when they could do so at minimum self risk, Farlow (1994) did not restrict them to this kind of lifestyle, postulating that they were probably opportunistic meat-eaters, consuming carrion as well as pursuing prey.

Both Houston (1979) and Paul (1988c) suggested that flying animals such as vultures and condors are the only strictly scavenging vertebrates, their soaring ability allowing them to detect dead animals at great distances, covering the ground rapidly and at low energetic cost. Farlow (1994) noted that the tall and bipedal tyrannosaurs, by carrying their heads well off the ground, had an advantage, akin to that of avian scavengers, of spotting dead animals a greater distance away than could be seen by shorter carnivorous animals; that their line of sight to a carcass was less likely to have been obscured by ground vegetation; and that the elevated position of the nostrils could have allowed for the better detection of the smell of carrion than possible for carnivores with nostrils closer to the ground.

Regarding how *Tyrannosaurus* tore off flesh, Coombs observed that teeth in this genus are more rounded and transversely broad in cross-section than in *Allosaurus* and *Albertosaurus*, and that serrations on *Tyrannosaurus* teeth form a faint ridge on a rounded surface instead of sharp cutting edge as in those genera (see Molnar and Farlow). This suggested that, in possessing teeth more like those of a modern killer whale than (as in *Albertosaurus*) those suitable for slicing meat off large carcasses, *Tyrannosaurus* may instead have preyed upon small animals swallowed whole.

Today, *Tyrannosaurus* is generally viewed as an active predator capable of achieving considerable locomotive speed. Bakker (1986), in his book *The Dinosaur Heresies*, estimated this speed to be as high as 45 miles per hour. However, as pointed out by Molnar and Farlow (1990), Bakker did not offer any quantitative argument, but claimed that the hindlimbs in *T. rex* were more massive than those of elephants, and that the large cnemial crest on the tibia accommodated a musculature suggesting cursorial potential. Molnar and Farlow noted that the forceful hindlimb musculature in *T. rex* (and other "carnosaurs") does not necessarily imply great speed, and may have more significance with the bearing of great weight or with the stresses of holding down large prey. According to Molnar and Farlow, regardless of actual speeds, "carnosaurs" were most likely at least as fast or faster than the animals they apparently preyed upon.

More recently, a study involving the body mass, bone "strength indicator," and cursorial potential of *T. rex* was made by Farlow, Smith and Robinson (1995), based on a believed to be accurate 1/20 scale model of *T. rex*, sculpted by one of the authors (Matthew B. Smith), after a fairly complete skeleton (MOR 555; see Horner and Lessem 1993). The skeleton was that of the so-called "gracile morph" of *T. rex*

Tyrannosaurus rex skeleton (cast of AMNH 5627) mounted in correct horizontal pose by paleontologist Kenneth Carpenter.

Photo by the author, courtesy Academy of Natural Sciences of Philadelphia.

(apparently less massive than the other "robust" morph). Basically, by measuring the difference in the model's volume when submerged in water while taking into consideration certain variables (Alexander 1995, 1989), Farlow *et al.* estimated the live mass of the full-sized dinosaur to be approximately 6,000 kilograms (about 6.8 tons).

Farlow *et al.* then estimated Alexander's (1989) "strength indicator," a quantity describing the capacity of a long bone for resisting bending stresses associated with vigorous activity, utilizing calculations made from the preserved long bones, and making assumptions for the slightly crushed femur. Farlow *et al.* estimated the strength indicator for a *T. rex* of the above mass to be about 7.5–9.0 m2/giganewton — higher than that of an African elephant (7.0 m2/giganewton), less than a human being (15 m2/giganewton) and runners like the ostrich (44 m2/giganewton), and less than the white rhinoceros (26 m2/giganewton for an immature female) (for calculations, see Alexander 1985, 1989; Alexander and Pond 1992). In considering the possible running speed of *T. rex*, Farlow *et al.* pointed out that, in mammals and birds, increasing body mass leads to increasingly more erect, less flexed postures for the purpose of maintaining uniform skeletal stresses, resulting "in a lower limb excursion angle for large as opposed to small-bodied species." With body masses exceeding 200 kilograms, more robust elements and a probable decline in sprint speed are also necessary to maintain these stresses, this suggesting that an animal with the mass of "*Tyrannosaurus* is

Tyrannosaurus bataar, PIN 551-1, holotype skull, subsequently named *Tarbosaurus battar*, in "The Great Russian Dinosaurs" exhibit (1996), Mesa Southwest Museum, Mesa, Arizona.

Photo by the author.

unlikely to have been as fast or maneuverable a runner as the best living cursors" or even smaller-bodied theropods.

Farlow *et al.* recalled Hotton's (1980) observation, that the femoral component of the dinosaurian hip joint is cylindrical, rather than spherical as in mammals, suggesting that this construction made dinosaurs less capable than mammals of making adjustments for irregularities of footfall while running; and very large forms such as *Tyrannosaurus* would be presumably more susceptible to this constraint than would smaller theropods. Giant theropods, therefore, could have been restricted in their cursorial abilities to prevent sudden, accidental loadings beyond the handling capacity of the hip joint.

Farlow *et al.* also cited Coombs' (1978) observation that fast-running animals tend to have longer lower than upper limb bones; and that in tyrannosaurids, the tibia/femur and metatarsus/femur length ratios tend to be lower than in smaller, unquestionably cursorial theropods to which they may be related (such ratios sometimes higher in tyrannosaurids than in smaller-bodied members of other, more primitive theropod clades; see Holtz 1994*b*).

Also, Farlow *et al.* considered the consequences of a fast-running *Tyrannosaurus* accidentally falling, a situation which McMahon and Bonner (1983) had described as one of the "most dangerous pieces of bad luck" for a dinosaur of that size (cf. Horner and Lessem 1993). Farlow *et al.* found it reasonable to assume that the more quickly this animal moved, the greater the chance of an error in the way a foot hit the ground, and thus, the greater the risk of falling; and that "whatever the biomechanical limits of the skeleton of *Tyrannosaurus*, the dinosaur may have been loath to attempt sprints during which the risk of falling would have been great."

Falling, according to Farlow *et al.*, would be especially difficult, if not fatal, for a *Tyrannosaurus*. The lower edge of the animal's head was carried about 3.5 meters (about 12 feet) off the ground. Only the hindfoot opposite the one that stumbled, if brought forward quickly enough, might stop an in-progress fall. The very small forelimbs would have been useless in breaking a fall.

Farlow *et al.* calculated various estimates of the impact forces and decelerations that could affect a falling *Tyrannosaurus* in different situations and environments, and concluded that if a 6,000-kilogram individual fell while running at a high speed (20 meters per second), its survival chances would be slim. Even discounting the threat of death, a *Tyrannosaurus* would presumably be cautious about engaging in activity that might result in an injury that

Photo by the author, courtesy American Museum of Natural History.

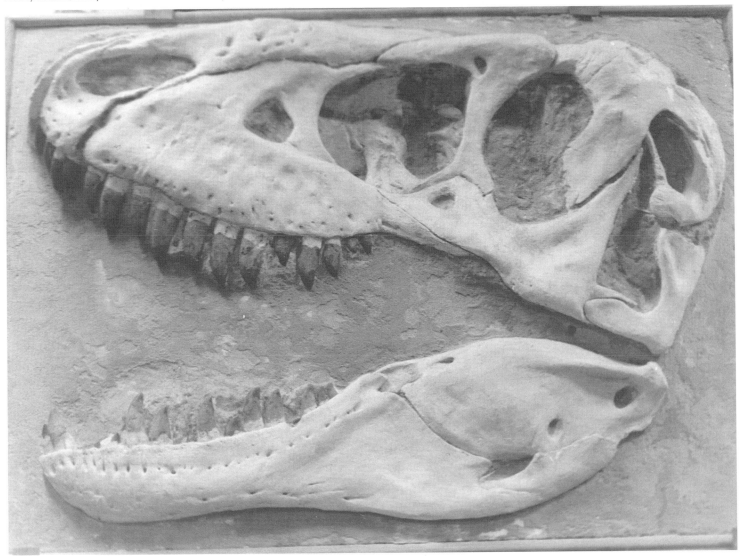

Tyrannosaurus bataar skull (cast), originally referred to *Tarbosaurus bataar*, left lateral view.

would hamper its survival activities. Farlow *et al.* doubted that, even if a *Tyrannosaurus* could run at the unlikely (given the strength indicator value) speed of 20 meters per second, "the benefits of moving at this speed would outweigh the attendant risks."

Taking into consideration mass, strength indicator, and the other above factors, Farlow *et al.* envisioned *Tyrannosaurus* as an active animal for its size, and agreed with Holtz (1994*b*) that it could probably run faster than equally large theropods belonging to other clades. However, they doubted that this dinosaur was as fleet as fast modern cursors, estimating 10 or possibly even 15 meters per second to be a more reasonable sprint speed, and one consistent with currently known theropod trackways (Farlow 1987; Molnar and Farlow 1990; Thulborn 1990). An animal with a hip height of about 3 meters (over 10 feet), running at 20 meters per second, would have had a stride of about 15 meters (more than 50 feet), one not

yet known in the ichnological record. Farlow *et al.* also doubted that adult *Tyrannosaurus* individuals ran with a long suspended phase (both feet simultaneously off the ground during a stride for a significant time), but moved at a fast walk or even a trot. Finally, Farlow *et al.* suspected that, given the consequences of a fall, *Tyrannosaurus* was cautious about when to move at its top speed.

Newman (1970) pointed out that the large scapulae and coracoids must have been associated with strong pectoral muscles and that the humeri, though short, were massive. The forelimbs might then have lifted the chest region from a rest position off the ground. Newman envisioned the animal resting with its head extended, lower jaw on the ground and forelimbs folded; to rise, the animal extended its hindlimbs, body moving forwards to be braked by the forelimbs, hindlimbs continuing to extend and tail depressing as the animal achieved its stance.

Tyrannosaurus bataar, **cast of skeleton of small specimen** [originally referred to *Tarbosaurus bataar*].

Unfortunately, a complete manus belonging to *T. rex* was unknown until relatively recently (although some skeletons of "*Tarbosaurus*" *bataar* clearly showed a two-fingered manus). Osborn's skeletal reconstruction originally showed the manus as tridactyl, an assumption based on the hand of *Allosaurus*, and both Carnegie Museum and American Museum skeletons were originally mounted with three-fingered hands (since corrected). Osborn (1917) agreed that, like the manus of the closely related yet more primitive *Albertosaurus*, the hand of *T. rex* could someday be revealed as functionally didactyl. The forelimbs of *T. rex* were imagined as so short that the fingers could not touch the animal's mouth. Osborn (1906) postulated that these small hands may have been used in grasping prey, or utilized by a male *Tyrannosaurus* to grip a female during mating.

In 1988, Kathy Wankel found some fossil bones on a hillside in the Hell Creek Formation of eastern Montana. Thomas and Kathy Wankel collected some of these remains including a left scapula, humerus, ulna, radius, and partial manus. The fossils were brought to the Museum of the Rockies, in Bozeman, where they were identified by John R. Horner as the first known forearms of *T. rex*. Patrick Leiggi, Robert Harmon and Matthew Smith later found more of the specimen including the skull, cervical and dorsal vertebrae, sacrum, pelvis, hind legs, and ribs (including gastralia). Still undescribed, this is one of the most complete skeletons of *T. rex* yet recovered, including the most complete tail known from this species, and the forelimb material. The latter is exceptionally preserved (showing well-developed muscle scars), comprising shoulder, forearm, and hand. As expected, the manus has two fingers. According to popular accounts, this individual measures 11.5–almost 12 meters (38–40 feet) in length, the tail alone about 6 meters (over 20 feet) long. The specimen was collected by a crew from the Museum of the Rockies led by Horner.

Carpenter and Smith (1995) briefly described the structure and biomechanics of the *T. rex* fore-limb: Forearm small relative to body size, arm and hand with estimated length of approximately 90 centimeters (about 34.5 inches); ulna about 45 percent length of humerus; humerus very massive. Carpenter and Smith rejected earlier notions that the fore-limbs in *T. rex* were used primarily as grapplers in mating or as an aid to get up from a prone position, and argued that they were designed for securing struggling prey during predation. A single arm may have been able to lift more than 450 pounds.

Another *T. rex* specimen, recovered by the Black Hills Institute from a hillside in central South Dakota, apparently includes arms nearly twice as thick as those of the previous specimen. Popular accounts estimate that each of these arms might have been capable of lifting more than 1200 pounds. To date of this writing, this specimen (nicknamed "Sue™") constitutes the largest individual of *T. rex* yet discovered. On May 14, 1992, after various parties claimed ownership of this specimen, it was seized by Federal Bureau of Investigation agents. The skeleton has been stored and currently awaits further legal decisions before the remains can be studied.

The more recently collected *T. rex* skeletons inspired Larson (1994) to pursue a new study of sexual dimorphism in this species. Previously, Carpenter (1990), based on studies of specimens of *T. rex* and the Asian species *T. bataar*, had concluded that the more robust morphotype of this genus was female (contrary to the usually accepted norm that larger and more muscular forms were male, the more gracile forms females) and that the shape of the ischium of the more robust form allowed for a wider passage for laying eggs. Molnar (1991) observed that the presence or lack of a horn-like rugosity on the postorbital bone could have sexual significance, but did not speculate on which sex may have possessed this knob of bone.

After examining 15 significant specimens of *T. rex*, including "Sue™," Larson also noted that they can be divided into two groups—one heavily built or "robust," the other lightly built or "gracile." Larson further observed that certain bones possessed recognizable differences which also fell within these two morphotypes. Among these differences, the "robust" morphotype displayed a wider sacrum and more deeply angled ischium, possible adaptations to provide room for the passage of eggs.

Larson used the seemingly closest living relatives of dinosaurs as models for comparison. Female birds of prey were found to be larger than males of the same species. Larson also noted that (as found by colleague Eberhard Frey of Karslruhe, Germany) in male crocodiles, the first chevron (or hemal arch) of the caudal vertebra is about the same size as the second, while it is only about one-half the size of the second in females. In males, this condition would give more surface area for the attachment of the muscle that allows for the retraction of the animal's "penis"-like reproductive organ; the condition in females would allow more room for the passage of eggs.

Larson found that the dichotomy of first-chevron size seemingly also existed in some mounted skeletons of *T. rex,* the first chevron occurring on different caudal vertebrae in some specimens referred to the same species (although, Larson acknowledged, most descriptive work and restorations were done years ago). Larson observed that, in the more recently recovered, partially articulated gracile *T. rex* specimen (MOR-555), the first and second chevrons are of the same length.

Furthermore, in articulated specimens of the troodontid theropod *Saurornithoides* in the Royal

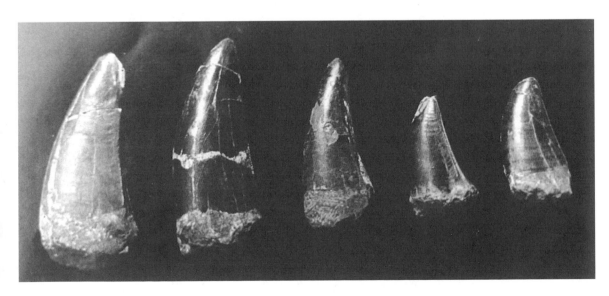

?Tyrannosaurus luanchuanensis, NIGP V4733, holotype teeth. (After Dong 1987.)

Tyrrell Museum of Paleontology, Philip J. Currie (personal communication to Larson) observed that, in the "robust" morphotype, the first chevron is positioned on the rear of the first caudal, and is shorter and more wedge-shaped than the second; in the "gracile" form, the first chevron is on the first caudal (on the rear of the last sacral) vertebrae, and is about the same size and shape as the second.

Larson concluded that *T. rex* males are represented in the fossil record by the more "gracile" morphotype, and that they (as well as other dinosaurs) had an intromittent organ or "penis" similar to that in crocodiles and some birds. Also, Larson believed that two *T. rex* specimens, an adult "male" LACM-28344) and a juvenile (LACM-28345), having been found together in the same excavation, constitute evidence that this species may have been monogamous and probably maintained family groups.

The first record of heme-bearing proteins or hemoglobin breakdown products in extracts of *T. rex* tissues was briefly reported by Schweitzer (1995). As explained by Schweitzer, the amino acid sequence of the protein hemoglobin has been determined for a number of extinct taxa and is, therefore, a useful tool in phylogenetic studies; also, hemoglobin can be an indicator of physiology and metabolic rates. At the core of this protein "is the heme group, a porphyrin ring with one iron atom at its center. This ring structure imparts signatures to heme molecules which are not shared by any other biological or known geological compounds."

Schweitzer made this discovery after five independent lines of study: 1. Signatures from nuclear magnetic resonance, 2. presence of a paramagnetic molecule consistent with heme, 3. UV/vis spectroscopy and 4. HPLC (high performance liquid chromatography) data consistent with Soret absorbence characteristic of this molecule, and 5. resonance raman (RR) profiles consistent with a modified heme structure. Schweitzer concluded that, taken together, "the most parsimonious explanation of the evidence is the presence of blood-derived hemoglobin compounds preserved in these dinosaur tissues."

Notes: *T. lanpingensis* Yeh 1975 [*nomen nudum*], based on a single tooth, with no diagnosis or illustration, is Late Jurassic or Early Cretaceous (Tithonian–Neocomian), therefore not referable to *Tyrannosaurus* (Dong 1992).

Lawson (1976) described a small left maxilla (TMM 41436-1) identified as a ?young *T. rex* individual, discovered in 1970 in the Tornilla Group, Big Bend National Park, Brewster County, Texas. If the specimen does belong to *Tyrannosaurus*, it extends the geographic range of the genus, and also constitutes evidence supporting a Late Maastrichtian age for the

Holotype tooth of *?Albertosaurus periculosus*, tentatively referred to *Tyrannosaurus bataar*. (After Riabinin 1930.)

Tornilla Group (dated Maastrichtian by Maxwell, Lonsdale, Hazzard and Wilson 1967, based on the occurrence of sauropod *Alamosaurus*). According to Carpenter (in press), this specimen does not belong to *Tyrannosaurus*, but some other short-faced theropod.

Lambert (1990) mentioned the unofficially named "Futabasaurus," a large theropod from Japan, regarded as an indeterminate tyrannosaurid by Dong, Hasegawa and Azuma in the guidebook *The Age of Dinosaurs in Japan and China*.

A fossil footprint, measuring nearly 3 feet long and apparently referable to *T. rex*, was found in 1983 by Charles Pillmore, a geologist with the United States Geological Survey, in northern New Mexico. The ichnite will be described by Lockley and co-authors.

Key references: Bakker (1986); Barsbol (1983); Carpenter (1990, 1992); Colbert (1962); Colinveaux (1978); Coombs (1990); Cope (1892*b*); Dong (1979, 1987, 1992); Farlow (1981, 1993, 1994); Farlow, Smith and Robinson (1995); Gilmore (1930); Halstead and Halstead (1981); Hatcher, Marsh and Lull (1907); Hopson (1980*b*); Lambe (1917*c*); Langston (1965); Larson (1994); Lawson (1976); Maleev (1955*a*, 1955*b*, 1955*c*); Molnar (1990, 1991); Molnar and Farlow (1990); Newman (1970); Osborn (1905, 1906, 1912*a*, 1917); Paul (1988*c*); Riabinin (1930); Rozhdestvensky (1965); Russell (1970*b*); Schweitzer (1995); Sternberg (1946); Walker (1964); Zhao (1986).

UDANOCERATOPS   Kurzanov 1992

Ornithischia: Genasauria: Cerapoda: Marginocephalia: Ceratopsia: Neoceratopsia: Protoceratopsidae.

Name derivation: "Udan-Sayr [locality]" + Greek *keratos* = "horned" + Greek *ops* = "face."

Type species: *U. tschizhovi* Kurzanov 1992.

Other species: [None.]

Occurrence: Dzhadokhta Formation, Udan-Sayr, Mongolia, Asia.

Age: Late Cretaceous (Middle–Late Campanian).

Known Material/holotype: GI 3907/11, disarticulated incomplete skull, mostly lacking upper posterior region, partial postcrania.

Diagnosis of genus (as for type species): Very large protoceratopsid, skull 65–70 centimeters long from anterior edge of rostral to posterior end of quadrate; rostral high, narrow, with long posterior process; premaxillaries with wide posterior ascending branch, no teeth; nasal opening high, wide; maxillary shelf sharply manifested, separated from remainder of surface by distinct rugose crest; nasal bones showing no sign of horn development, their dorsal surface smooth, flat, in posterior half forming right angle with lateral surface; jugal bones elongated, occupying almost horizontal

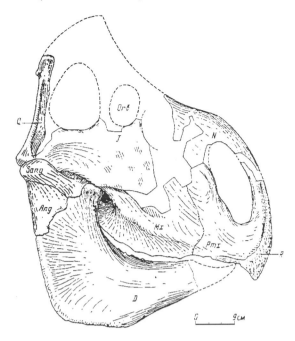

Udanoceratops tschizhovi, GI 3907/11, holotype restored skull. (After Kurzanov 1992.)

position; epijugal absent, but small epijugal process developed on jugal; lateral temporal fossa with horizontal ventral margin; preorbital depression pierced in lower half; quadrate-jugal high, jugal process only slightly manifested; quadrate almost vertically oriented; dentary short, very high in middle, lower margin bending almost at right angles; predentary extending almost to beginning of tooth row, forming long posterior process ending at level of eighth tooth; mandibular shelf with same width along its entire length; retroarticular surface very weakly developed; upper jawbone with 15 teeth, dentary 18; low, narrow "collar" encompassing both "pockets" on crown along upper margin and enamel cover on maxillary teeth; base of central ridge of lower-jaw teeth closer to anterior edge of crown; "masticatory" surface of mandibular teeth strictly vertical; small bony ossifications of various shapes developed (Kurzanov 1992).

Comments: The genus *Udanoceratops* was established upon an incomplete skull with some postcranial remains, collected from a lens of dense, dark gray sandstone in Bed 2 of Dzhadokhta deposits of the Udan-Sayr locality, bordered by the Dzhadokhta and Barun Goyot formations (Middle–Late Campanian; see Currie 1991; Dong 1993*a*), in southern Mongolia, Central Asia. The material was collected in the mid–1980s by a field team of the Joint Soviet-Mongolian Paleontological Expedition. As discovered, the remains were either inside calcareous concretions or mostly covered by a thick calcareous encrustation (Kurzanov 1992).

Reserving a formal description of the postcranial material for a future article, Kurzanov stated that the most characteristic features of these remains included the following: Ilia long, low, with very large, laterally projecting pubic and ischial processes; scapula rather short and wide; coracoid with strongly developed caudal process; extremity bones massive and short.

Kurzanov regarded *Udanoceratops* as a rather primitive protoceratopsid distinguished by its large size, with a short, deep skull. It is primarily distinguished from the previously largest known protoceratopsid, the North American *Montanoceratops*, by the absence of even the slightest development of a nasal horn, in lack of premaxillary teeth, and in having low jugals without epijugals, while exceeding that genus by 1.5 times skull length.

Key reference: Kurzanov (1992).

UGROSAURUS Cobabe and Fastovsky 1987 [*nomen dubium*]—(See *Triceratops*.)
Name derivation: Scandinavian *ugro* = "ugly" + Greek *sauros* = "lizard."
Type species: *U. olsoni* Cobabe and Fastovsky 1987 [*nomen dubium*].

UINTASAURUS Holland 1919—(See *Camarasaurus*.)
Name derivation: "Uinta [Mountains]" + Greek *sauros* = "lizard."
Type species: *U. douglassi* Holland 1919.

ULTRASAUROS Olshevsky 1991—(=*Ultrasaurus* Jensen 1985; =?*Brachiosaurus*.)
Saurischia: Sauropodomorpha: Sauropoda: Brachiosauridae.
Name derivation: Latin *ultra* = "beyond" + Greek *sauros* = "lizard."
Type species: *U. macintoshi* (Jensen 1985).
Other species: [None.]
Occurrence: Morrison Formtion, Colorado, United States.
Age: Late Jurassic (Kimmeridgian-Tithonian).
Known material: Vertebra, scapulacoracoid.
Holotype: BYUVP 4044, dorsal vertebra.

Diagnosis of genus (as for type species): Differs from other brachiosaurids in having scapula with moderately expanded distal end; dorsal vertebrae with anteroposteriorly narrow neural spines; midcervical vertebrae lacking pleurocoels; posterior dorsal vertebrae with high neural spines; anterior caudal vertebrae with high neural spines (Jensen 1985*a*).

Ultrasauros macintoshi,
BYUVP 4044, holotype anterior dorsal vertebra (right lateral view) of *Ultrasaurus
mcintoshi.* Scale = 1 meter.

Photo by J. A. Jensen, courtesy Brigham
Young University.

Diplodocidae on the basis of its bifurcated neural spine and because two diplodocid scapulacoracoids, including the holotype of *Supersaurus vivianae,* were found in the same quarry.

During the late 1970s, these remains were informally called "Ultrasaurus" in both the paleontological literature and popular press, until Jensen officially published the generic name *Ultrasaurus* for the material in 1985. Prior to this publication, Kim (1983), apparently unaware of Jensen's intended naming, described his own fragmentary sauropod specimen under the name *Ultrasaurus* (see *Ultrasaurus* entry, *nomina nuda* section). As Jensen's generic name was then preoccupied, Olshevsky (1991) proposed that *Ultrasauros* (name suggested by Jensen to Olshevsky in a personal communication) be subsituted for this Dry Mesa sauropod.

Paul observed that holotype BYUVP 5000 is very similar to anterior dorsals of *B. altithorax* and, as far as could be determined, belongs to that species. Paul added that the slenderness of the neural spine

Photo by the author, courtesy M. J. Odano and Brigham Young University.

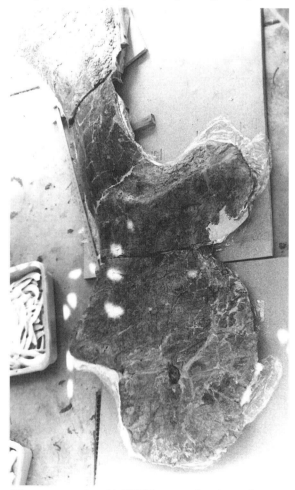

Ultrasauros macintoshi, BYUVP 5001, referred scapulacora-coid. Scale = 1 meter.

Comments: The new genus and species *Ultra-saurus mackintoshi* was founded upon a crushed dorsal vertebra (BYUVP 4044), found in 1979 by James A. Jensen during the filming of a Japanese Television Workshop documentary at the Brushy Basin Member of the Morrison Formation (Upper Jurassic [Tithonian] or Lower Cretaceous [Neocomian or Hauterivian]; see Britt 1991, based on Kowalis, Heaton and Bringhurst 1986), Uncompahgre Upwarp, Dry Mesa Quarry, near Mesa County, west of Delta, Colorado (Jensen 1985*a*).

Misidentified by Jensen as a posterior dorsal (and given incorrect catalog number BYU 5000; J. S. McIntosh, personal communication to Olshevsky 1991), the specimen is actually an anterior dorsal, as exemplified by its transversely narrow neural spine with small head (Paul 1988*a*). Jensen referred to *U. macintoshi* material collected from the same locality including an extremely large (2,690 millimeters or almost 9 feet long) scapulacoracoid (BYUVP 5001), an anterior caudal vertebra (BYU 5002), and a medial cervical vertebra (BYU 5003). Jensen (1987) subsequently acknowledged that he had erred in his identification of the latter specimen, referring it to the suggests that this vertebra should be located anterior to the sixth dorsal, and that the scapula blade is as broad as in some *Brachiosaurus* specimens.

However, Paul's referral of this sauropod to *Brachiosaurus* has not been entirely accepted. Jensen, in a 1988 personal communication to Olshevsky (1991), maintained that the two forms are sufficiently different to warrant generic separation. Olshevskey (1991, 1992), of the opinion that the type vertebra figured by Paul is too dissimilar from dorsal vertebrae of *Brachiosaurus*, kept the two taxa separate.

McIntosh (1990*b*), in his review of the Sauropoda, listed Jensen's *Ultrasaurus* as separate from *Brachiosaurus*, noting that a proper evaluation of this taxon cannot be made until more of its material is prepared. As observed by McIntosh, *U. macintoshi* is a very large brachiosaurid. The dorsal vertebra resembles that of *Brachiosaurus*, but is larger than that of *B. altithorax* or *B. brancai* (perhaps due to its more anterior position in the column). The the scapulacoracoid differs [in unspecified ways] from that of *Brachiosaurus*.

Although it is not unlikely that *Brachiosaurus* and *Ultrasauros* are the same genus, their synonymy has yet to be demonstrated.

Jensen, in various interviews and popular articles, estimated that *Ultrasauros* reached an approximate length of 30 meters (98 feet) and weighed as much as 130 metric ones (70 tons), subsequent writers in popular books raising that weight to an incredible 170 metric tons (190 tons). Paul argued that cross-scaling indicates that the length of the scapulacoracoid of the *B. altithorax* type specimen would have been about the same size as that referred to *U. macintoshi*, and that those of other specimens of the former are almost as large. As calculated by Paul, *Ultrasauros* was not larger than the largest African brachiosaurids.

Key references: Jensen (1985*a*, 1987); McIntosh (1990*b*); Olshevsky (1991); Paul (1988*a*).

UNQUILLOSAURUS   Powell 1979

Saurischia: Theropoda: ?Tetanurae *incertae sedis*.

Name derivation: "Unquillo [name of river]" +
   Greek *sauros* = "lizard."

Type species: *U. ceibalii* Powell 1979.

Other species: [None.]

Occurrence: Los Blanquitos Formation, Salta,
   Argentina.

Age: Late Cretaceous (?Campanian).

Known Material/holotype: PVL 3670-11, left pubis.

   Diagnosis of genus (as for type species): Pubis with furrowed proximal expansion, channel in anterolateral portion, open obturator foramen; exterior

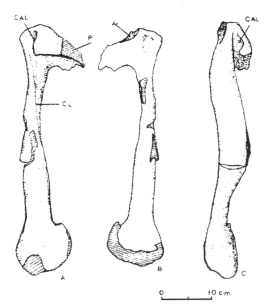

Unquillosaurus ceibalii, PVL 3670-11, holotype left pubis, A. lateral, B. medial, C. antero-dorsal views. (After Powell 1979.)

surface of anterior portion of shaft with prominent longitudinal crest; pubic "foot" lacking anterior projection (Powell 1979).

Comments: *Unquillosaurus* represents the first good postcranial evidence documenting the occurrence of large theropods in northern Argentina. The genus was founded on a pubis (PVL 3670-11), collected from Arroyo Morterito (Los Blanquitos Formation), a stream of the Unquillo river, southern end of La Candelaria Hills, Province of Salta, Argentina (Powell 1979).

As noted by Powell, *Unquillosaurus* is a large theropod perhaps totaling in length 11 meters (36 feet).

Powell observed that the pubis differs from that of most other theropods in the presence of the deep furrow. The pubic "foot" is short as in *Allosaurus*, *Tyrannosaurus*, and *Albertosaurus*. The open obturator foramen is similar to that of *Allosaurus*, *Marshosaurus*, and other theropods.

According to Molnar (1990), *U. ceiballi*, though apparently a valid species, shows no similarity to any known "carnosaur."

Key references: Molnar (1990); Powell (1979).

UTAHRAPTOR   Kirkland, Gaston and Burge
1993

Saurischia: Theropoda: Tetanurae: Avetheropoda:
   Coelurosauria: Maniraptora: Dromaeosauridae:
   Velociraptorinae.

Name derivation: "Utah [state]" + Latin *raptor* =
   "robber."

Utahraptor

Utahraptor ostrommaysi, (top) CEU 184v.86, holotype right pedal ungual II, compared with smaller pedal ungual of *Deinonychus antirrhopus*, (bottom) CEU 184v.294, ?holotype manual ungual I compared with smaller manual ungual of *D. antirrophus*.

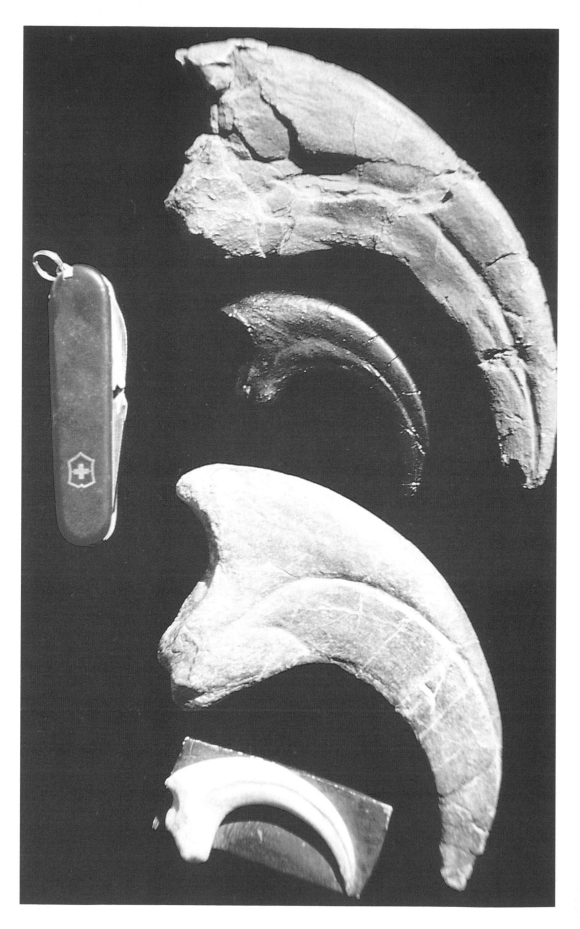

Photo courtesy J. I. Kirkland.

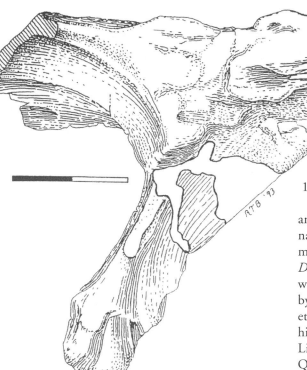

Utahraptor ostrommaysi, CEU 184v.83, right lacrimal, internal view. Scale = 2 cm. (After Kirkland, Gaston and Burge 1993.)

from the Gaston Quarry in the basal Cedar Mountain Formation, in eastern Utah. Referred disarticulated material from the Dalton Well Quarry of the Cedar Mountain Formation include manual unguals I (BYU 13068) and ?II (BYU 9438), midcaudal vertebrae (BYU 9429), and two distal caudal vertebrae (BYU 9435 and 9436) representing one or more moderately large individual(s). (Kirkland, Gaston and Burge 1993).

The discovery of this new dinosaur was first announced in a press release from Dinamation International Society (dated July 14, 1992) as a new dromaeosaurid similar to but apparently twice the size of *Deinonychus*. According to this notice, the material was found in October 1991, through research directed by James I. Kirkland, Dinamation International Society, and Donald Burge, College of Eastern Utah Prehistoric Museum, Price, Utah, and uncovered by Carl Limoni of the Prehistoric Museum, in the Gaston Quarry (Early Cretaceous), eastern Utah. The Gaston Quarry, possibly comparable to Wealden sites on the Isle of Wight, is situated within a 30-million year time interval where there is a data gap about North American dinosaurs, all dinosaur specimens thus far

Type species: *U. ostrommaysi* Kirkland, Gaston and Burge 1993.

Other species: [None.]

Occurrence: Cedar Mountain Formation, Utah, United States.

Age: Early Cretaceous, Barremian.

Known material: Unguals, skull elements, vertebrae.

Holotype: CEU 184v.86, right pedal ungual II, potentially other bones from type locality, including manual ungual I (CEU 184v.294), tibia (CEU 184v.260), lacrimal (CEU 184v.83), premaxilla (CEU 184v.400).

Diagnosis of genus: Manual claws more specialized as cutting blade than in other dromaeosaurs; lachrimal with distinctly parallel mesial and outer sides, giving it elongate subrectangular appearance in dorsal view; premaxilla with base of nasal opening parallel to premaxillary tooth row.

Diagnosis of *U. ostrommaysi*: Same as for genus, except distinguished by very large size (at least 100 percent larger than *Deinonychus*) (Kirkland, Gaston and Burge 1993).

Comments: A very large dromaeosaurid, *Utahraptor* was founded upon associated, disarticulated partial skeletal material (CEU 184v.86, 184v.294, 184v.260, 184v.83, and 184v.400), collected

Photo courtesy J. I. Kirkland.

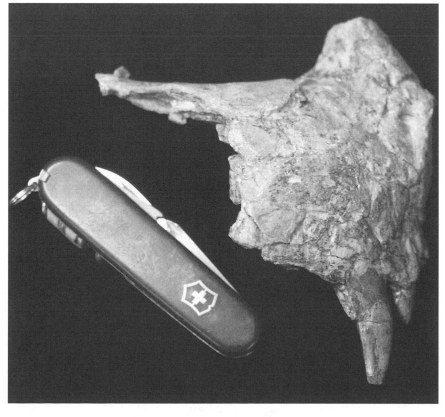

Utahraptor ostrommaysi, CEU 184v.400, premaxilla.

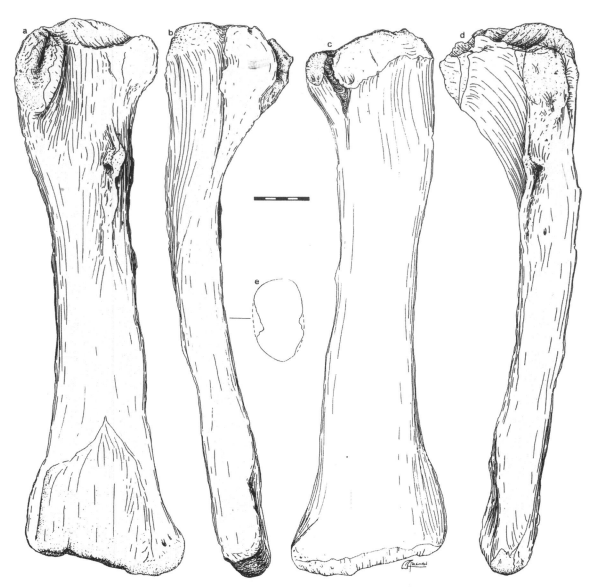

Utahraptor ostrommaysi, CEU 184v.260, ?holotype left tibia, a. anterior, b. medial, c. posterior, d. lateral views, e. cross-section of shaft. Scale = 5 cm. (After Kirkland, Gaston and Burge 1993.)

recovered from this site having been new or poorly known forms.

The collected remains include a very large, thin, deep blade-like manual claw core bone measuring about 24 centimeters (9 inches) in length which, in life, would have been almost 40 centimeters (about 15 inches) long. Kirkland subsequently identified fossil bones of the same age as this new dromaeosaurid in the collections at the Brigham Young Earth Science Museum, Provo, Utah. These bones (BYU 13068, 9438, 9429, 9435, and 9436) were collected in 1975 by Lin Ottinger by a field crew led by James A. Jensen, from a site approximately 25 miles from the Gaston Quarry. The fossils, including leg bones, manual claws, and diagnostic tail bones, show that several different-sized animals, some as large as those col-

lected from the Gaston Quarry, were preserved at the Brigham Young University site.

The remains of *Utahraptor* were exhibited at the Prehistoric Museum.

According to Kirkland *et al.*, *Utahraptor* represents the oldest known dromaeosaurid. It differs from most other described dromaeosaurs in the simple blunt serrations of the premaxillary teeth, similar to those in *Dromaeosaurus*, suggesting that this genus may belong to the Dromaeosaurinae instead of the Velociraptorinae.

Utahraptor was estimated by Kirkland *et al.* to have reached a length of as much as 7 meters (about 24 feet) and weighed almost 500 kilograms (about 1,100 pounds). The authors speculated that the smallest terrestrial vertebrates would have been beneath

this dinosaur's notice, and that a *Utahraptor* pack may have been capable of bringing down a 20-meter (almost 70-foot) long sauropod.

This genus probably closely resembled *Deinonychus*, but with larger, more blade-like manual claws that may have been almost as important as the sickle-like pedal claw in cutting a victim's hide. Kirkland *et al.* noted that smaller dromaeosaurs such as *Deinonychus* and *Velociraptor* most likely used their foreclaws to hold onto prey while they kicked it with their strong hind legs. However, the larger and heavier *Utahraptor* may have been able to kick out at its prey without possibly being thrown off balance by the force of its kick, the more laterally compressed manual claws thereby freed to take on a greater role in the kill. This specialization suggests that *Utahraptor* did not give rise to any other known dromaeosaurs and that an older and smaller form existed that is both ancestral to *Utahraptor* and all other known dromaeosaurids, as well as being closer to the origin of birds.

Kirkland *et al.* interpreted the tibia of *Utahraptor* as subequal in length to the femur (as in other large theropods), perhaps a result of the animal's larger size, suggesting that this genus was proportionally not as swift as *Deinonychus* and *Velociraptor*. The massiveness of this tibia may also reflect the increased strength of the leg utilized in wielding the foot's sickle-claw.

Key reference: Kirkland, Gaston and Burge (1993).

VALDORAPTOR Olshevsky 1991 [*nomen dubium*]

Saurischia: Theropoda: Tetanurae: ?Avetheropoda: ?Allosauroidea: ?Allosauridae.

Name derivation: Latin *valdo* = "Wealden" + Latin *raptor* = "robber."

Type species: *V. oweni* (Lydekker 1889) [*nomen dubium*].

Other species: [None.]

Occurrence: Upper Wealden, West Sussex, England.

Age: Early Cretaceous (Barremian).

Known material/holotype: BMNH R2559, partial left metatarsus.

Diagnosis of genus: [None published.]

Comments: As detailed by Olshevsky (1991), the genus now known as *Valdoraptor* was founded upon a partial left metatarsus (BMNH R2559) from the Upper Wealden of Cuckfield, West Sussex, England. This material was originally described and misidentified by Owen (1857) as a metapodium of the ankylosaur *Hylaeosaurus* and given the incorrect specimen number of R2556.

Hulke (1881) recognized the specimen as belonging to a theropod but did not refer it to any genus. Lydekker (1889*a*), who had already referred most of the Wealden theropod material to *Megalosaurus dunkeri*, redescribed this specimen as pertaining to a new species of *Megalosaurus*, *M. oweni*, misidentifying it as a right metatarsus. (Owen had published a mirror-image figure of the specimen.) Later, Lydekker (1890*a*) referred two additional metatarsals (BMNH R604 and R1525), similar but not identical to those of *M. oweni* and found about 180 yards apart in Hollington Quarry, to *M. dunkeri*, believing them to belong to the same individual. Lydekker (1890*b*) later referred the BMNH Wealden remains to *M. oweni*.

Huene (1926*b*, 1926*c*, 1932) misrepresented the type specimen of *M. oweni* as four metatarsals, an error perpetuated in the paleontological literature by more recent authors, including Steel (1970) and Molnar (1990), both of whom regarded BMNH R604d and R1525 as cotypes of *M. oweni*, overlooking R2559 as the real type specimen.

According to Olshevsky, as the type metatarsus *M. oweni* is more slender and has a proportionately larger and more robust third metatarsal than a metatarsus referred by Phillips (1871) to *M. bucklandii*, the former species should be removed from

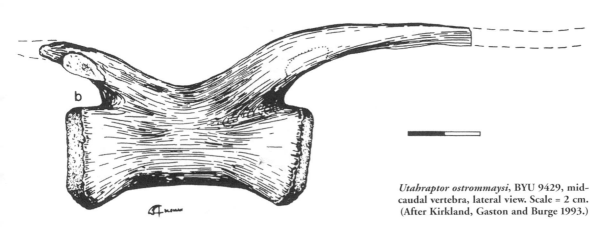

Utahraptor ostrommaysi, BYU 9429, mid-caudal vertebra, lateral view. Scale = 2 cm. (After Kirkland, Gaston and Burge 1993.)

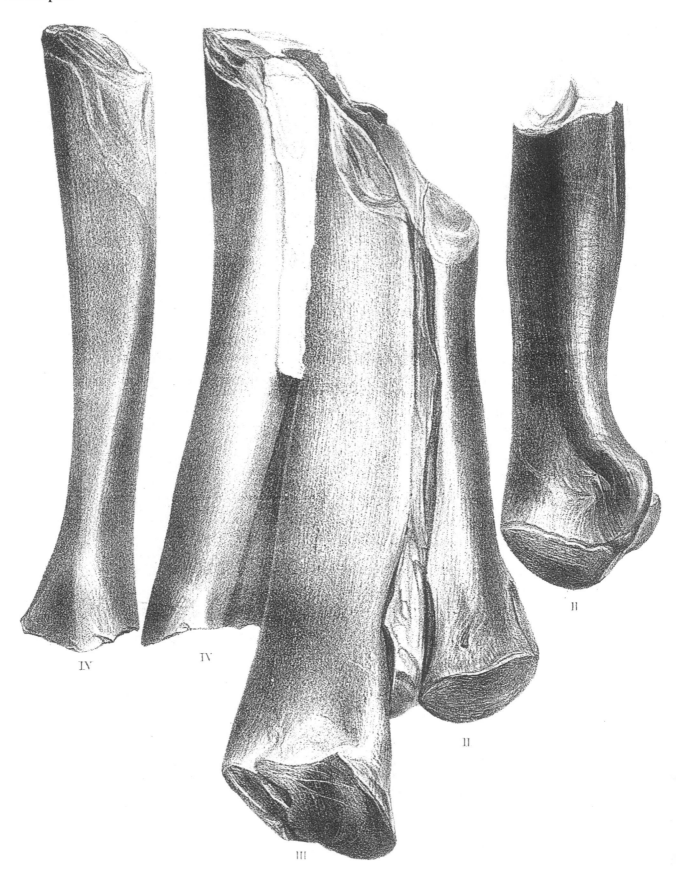

Valdoraptor oweni, BMNH R2559, holotype partial left metatarsus of *Megalosaurus oweni*. (After Lydekker 1889.)

Megalosaurus. As BMNH R2559 shows no signs of having a proximally pinched third metatarsal, Olshevsky tentatively referred the specimen to the Allosauridae, erecting for its reception the new genus *Valdoraptor.*

Key references: Huene (1926*b*, 1926*c*, 1932); Hulke (1881); Lydekker (1889*b*, 1890*a*, 1890*b*); Molnar (1990); Olshevsky (1991); Owen (1857); Steel (1970).

VALDOSAURUS   Galton 1977

Ornithischia: Genasauria: Cerapoda: Ornithopoda: Iguanodontia: Dryosauridae.

Name derivation: Latin *valdo* = "Wealden" + Greek *sauros* = "lizard."

Type species: *V. canaliculatus* (Galton 1975).

Other species: *V. nigeriensis* Galton and Taquet 1982.

Occurrence: Wealden, Isle of Wight, West Sussex, England; Bauxite of Cornet, Romania; El Rhaz Formation, Agadez, Niger.

Age: Early Cretaceous (Berriasian–Barremian, Aptian).

Known material: Femora, postcranial elements, dentary, teeth.

Holotype: BMNH R185 and R167, femora.

Diagnosis of genus: Main body of ilium low, with wide brevis shelf; obturator process of ischium proximally placed; femur with following combination of characters: pendant fourth trochanter well on proximal half of shaft, deep pit medial to fourth trochanter is set well anteriorly on shaft, rod-like lesser trochanter separated from greater trochanter by deep groove, distal end with subsquare medial edges and deep anterior intercondylar groove that may be partly overhung laterally; dentary with 15 teeth (Galton and Taquet 1982).

Diagnosis of *V. canaliculatus*: Proximal end of lesser trochanter of femur level with that of greater trochanter; deep medial pit on shaft merges with base of fourth trochanter (Galton and Taquet 1982).

Diagnosis of *V. nigeriensis*: Proximal end of lesser trochanter of femur below that of greater trochanter; deep medial pit on shaft separated from base of fourth trochanter by raised area (Galton and Taquet 1982).

Comments: The genus *Valdosaurus* was founded upon on a pair of small femora (BMNH R167) recovered from the Wealden (Barremian) of southern England.

Galton (1974*a*), the first author to figure this material, originally considered it to represent a large individual of *Hypsilophodon foxi*. Later, Galton (1975*a*) designated this material the holotype of the

new species *Dryosaurus ? canaliculatus*, after which Galton (1975*b*) referred it to the new genus *Valdosaurus*.

At first, Galton (1974*a*), as had Owen (1864), regarded a complete left dentary (BMNH R180) from the Wealden, Brixton, Isle of Wight, as belonging to a juvenile *Iguanodon*. However, as the posterior dentary teeth are on the antero-medial edge of the coronoid process rather than (as in *Iguanodon*) medial to it, Galton (*see in* Galton and Powell 1980) later referred this specimen to *Valdosaurus*, at the same time referring to this genus an ilium (BMNH R2150) resembling that of *Dryosaurus*, collected from the Wealden of Sussex and figured previously by Lydekker (1888) as *Hylaeosaurus*. Other material referred by Galton (1977*b*) to *V. canaliculatus* includes a left femur (BMNH R167), which Lydekker (1889) had made the holotype of *Camptosaurus valdensis*, and a mandibular ramus (BMNH R180), referred by Lydekker to that species.

A second species, *V. nigeriensis*, was founded upon a left femur (GDF collection), recovered in 1983 by Phillipe Taquet from the upper part of the El Rhaz Formation, Lower Cretaceous (Aptian), Gadoufaoua, region of niveau des Innocents, Republic of Niger.

According to Galton and Taquet, *Valdosaurus* differs primarily from the very similar *Dryosaurus* in having 15 dentary teeth (12 or 13 in *Dryosaurus*), the proportionately deeper and narrower form of the anterior intercondylar groove at the distal end of the femur, and in the lateral overhang of this groove. Galton and Taquet suggested that *Valdosaurus* is a probable descendant of *Dryosaurus*, although there was no way to discern whether the genus was more closely allied with North American species *D. altus* or the East African *D. lettowvorbecki*. Not ruled out was the possibility that *V. canaliculatus* descended from *D. altus*, while *D. nigeriensis* descended from *D. lettowvorbecki*, the similarities between both *Valdosaurus* species then being attributable to parallel evolution in two closely related lineages.

As noted by Galton and Taquet, the occurrence of *Valdosaurus* in both Europe and Africa (also that of *Erectopus* on both continents and *Majungatholus* in the Cretaceous of Madagascar) indicates a possible faunal exchange of dinosaurs via a land connection between Europe and Africa across Tethys, sometime during the Early Cretaceous.

Key references: Galton (1974*a*, 1975*a*, 1975*b*, 1977*b*); Galton and Powell (1980); Galton and Taquet (1982); Lydekker (1888, 1889); Owen (1864).

Valdosaurus canaliculatus, BMNH R185, holotype femur of *Dryosaurus canaliculatus.* Scale = 1 cm. (After Galton 1977.)

VECTISAURUS   Hulke 1879—(See *Iguanodon*.)
Name derivation: Latin *vectis* = "spike" + Greek
  sauros = "lizard."
Type species: *V. valdensis* Hulke 1879.

VELOCIPES   Huene 1932 [*nomen dubium*]
Saurischia: Theropoda *incertae sedis*.
Name derivation: Latin *velocis* = "swift" + Latin *pes*
  = "foot."
Type species: *V. guerichi* Huene 1932 [*nomen
  dubium*].
Other species: [None.]
Occurrence: Lissauer Breccia, Gorny Slask, Poland.
Age: Late Triassic (Late Carnian–Early Norian).
Known material/holotype: Staatsinstitut, proximal
  portion of left ?fibula.

    Diagnosis of genus: [None published.]

    Comments: The genus *Velocipes* was established
upon part of a possible fibula (housed at Staatsinstitut, Hamburg) collected from the Middle Keuper,
Gorny Slask [Schlesien], Poland.

    Huene (1932) described the fragmentary speci-
men as hollow, measuring 17.5 centimeters (about
6.75 inches) long as preserved, perhaps 35 centimeters (about 13.5 inches) when complete, proximal
extremity 4.5 centimeters (over 1.7 inches) in width.

    Finding the type specimen consistent with cor-
responding portions of the fibulae of various
"coelurosaurs," and believing this genus to be quite
similar to *Halticosaurus*, Huene placed *Velocipes* into
the Podokesauridae.

    The holotype of *V. gurichi* is probably too poor
for referral to any particular theropod family (R. E.
Molnar, personal communication 1989). Norman

(1990), in his reevaluation of problematic "coelurosaurs," regarded the material as indeterminate.

    Key references: Huene (1932); Norman (1990).

VELOCIRAPTOR   Osborn 1924—(=*Ovoraptor*;
  =?*Saurornitholestes*)
Saurischia: Theropoda: Tetanurae: Avetheropoda:
  Coelurosauria: Maniraptora: Dromaeosauridae:
  Velociraptorinae.
Name derivation: Latin *velocis* = "swift" + Latin
  raptor = "robber."
Type species: *V. mongoliensis* Osborn 1924.
Other species: [None.]
Occurrence: Djadochta Formation, Beds of
  Toogreeg, Omnogov, Mongolian People's
  Republic; Minhe Formation, Nei Mongol
  Zizhiqu, People's Republic of China.
Age: Late Cretaceous (Middle–Late Campanian).
Known material: Over six partial to complete skulls
  and skeletons, adult, ?babies.
Holotype: AMNH 6515, skull with jaws, manual
  claw with articulated phalanges.

    Diagnosis of genus (as for type species): Skull
small, low; dorsolateral rim of lacrimal smooth; orbit
circular in outline, larger than first antorbital fenestra; supratemporal arcade small; quadratomandibular articulation less depressed below alveolar margin
of jaws than in *Dromaeosaurus*; four premaxillary,
nine maxillary, 14 dentary teeth; carinae symmetrically placed on anterior and posterior edges of dorsal part of tooth crown, position of anterior carina
uncertain nearer base of crown; 38 to 40 denticles per
5 millimeters on anterior carinae, 25 to 26 on posterior carinae; pes similar to that of *Deinonychus* (Colbert and Russell 1969).

    Comments: The genus *Velociraptor* was founded
upon on a skull and a finger with a claw (AMNH
6516), collected in August 1923 by Peter C. Kaisen,
from the Djadochta Formation at Shabarakh Usu, in
[the former] Outer Mongolia. The remains (displayed
at the American Museum of Natural History in 1993)
were found in soft sandstone of early Upper Cretaceous age, lying alongside a skull of the ceratopsian
Protoceratops andrewsi (Osborn 1924*d*).

    In a preliminary report, Osborn (1924*c*) assigned
the name *Ovoraptor djadochtari* [*nomen nudum*] to
the material, giving it a brief one-sentence description but including no illustration.

    Originally, Osborn (1924*d*) diagnosed *Veloci-
raptor* as follows: Skull and jaws diminutive "megalosaurian" type, with abbreviated cranium, elongate
face, very large orbits; four openings in side of skull,
one in jaw; more than three premaxillary teeth, more
than nine maxillary teeth, 14 dentary teeth, all

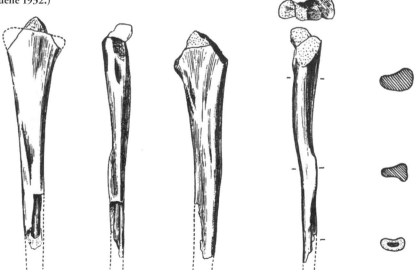

Velocipes gürichi, Staatsinstitut, holotype proximal portion of left ?fibula. (After
Huene 1932.)

Velociraptor mongoliensis, GI 100/25, skeleton (right) found in association with that of *Protoceratops andrewsi* (left) during the 1971 Polish-Mongolian Paleontological Expedition.

recurved, serrate on one or both borders, alternating in replacement.

Osborn (1924*d*) diagnosed the type species, *V. mongoliensis,* as follows: Ungual phalanges very large, laterally compressed, strongly recurved, super-raptorial in type.

As measured by Osborn (1924*d*), the holotype skull is about 176 millimeters (almost 7 inches) long from premaxillaries to occiput, 111 millimeters (about 4.25 inches) from premaxillaries to anterior border of orbits, and 65 millimeters (about 2.5 inches) from anterior border of orbits to occiput; the mandible is 175 millimeters (about 6.8 inches) from tip of dentaries to back of surangular.

Noting that the skull, though small and slender, was of "typical megalosaurian or theropod type," Osborn (1924*d*) incorrectly placed the genus in the Megalosauridae. Interpreting *Velociraptor* as a small yet alert and swift-moving hunter, Osborn (1924*d*) showed that this genus was well adapted for capturing and holding swift-moving, light-weight prey. The phalanges, strongly recurved and laterally compressed, facilitate holding prey, while the long rostrum and wide gape of the jaws suggest that prey could be living and fairly large. Teeth alternate in their replacement, with recurved crowns separated by wide gaps, adaptations for seizing prey.

Colbert and Russell (1969) later referred *Velociraptor* to the family Dromaeosauridae.

Subsequent discoveries showed that *Velociraptor* possessed a sickle-like claw on the second pedal digit. The significance of this claw was not realized until the 1964 discovery of the related *Deinonychus* (see entry), also bearing such a claw. Ostrom (1969) interpreted this claw as a slashing weapon with which dinosaurs such as *Deinonychus* and *Velociraptor* attacked prey.

A remarkable specimen of *V. mongoliensis* was discovered during the 1971 Polish-Mongolian Paleontological Expedition to Toogreeg, Gobi Desert, Mongolia (see Kielan-Jaworoska and Barsbold 1972). This articulated skeleton (GI 100/25) was found with hands and feet grasping a skeleton of *Protoceratops andrewsi*. The original scenario interpreted of these associated specimens was that the two animals had been killed during a death struggle, their supposed simultaneous demise attributed to various possible scenarios (*e.g.*, mutual extermination, drowning, cave or bank collapse, or the accidental death of the theropod while scavenging). The two skeletons seemingly constituted a preserved moment in time representing fossilized predatory behavior.

In a close examination of these skeletons from various perspectives, Unwin, Perle, and Trueman (1995) found the following evidence supporting the hypothesis that both dinosaurs were indeed killed simultaneously: "*Protoceratops* occupies a semi-erect stance, the skull oriented sub-horizontally. The right forelimb of *Velociraptor* is imprisoned within its jaws

and could not have become accidentally lodged in this position. *Velociraptor* lies largely in front of and level with the feet of its prey. The left manus grips the skull of *Protoceratops* while the legs are directed upward so that the pedes are located beneath the neck and thorax." Grain size, texture, and distribution and the thick, structureless nature of the sediment suggested to Unwin *et al.* that the two dinosaurs were smothered by sand during a powerful wind storm.

Unwin *et al.* observed that digits III and IV of the *Velociraptor* were flexed backward, clear of the fully extended sickle claw on digit II. From the preserved evidence, the authors saw *Velociraptor* as an active predator that grasped its prey with its forelimbs, killing its victim by rakes and kicks of the hindlimbs directed at the underside of neck and chest. Unwin *et al.* further speculated that these Mongolian theropods "were aware of *Protoceratops'* crouching behavior during sandstorms and used this to their advantage."

The discovery of these two interlocked skeletons revealed more about the physiology of *Velociraptor* and its possible affinities with other animal groups, as the theropod's skeleton possessed a clavicle or collar bone, a feature shared with birds. As early as the late nineteenth century, Huxley (1868, 1870*b*) noticed the structural similarities between dinosaurs and birds. Heilmann (1926), summarizing the issue of bird origins then known, regarded archosaurs as their most probable ancestors. Though Heilmann agreed that "coelurosaurs" seemed to be likely candidates for bird ancestors, he dismissed the idea on the basis of a supposed lack of a clavicle in dinosaurs. The Gobi Desert discovery of a *Velociraptor* with a collar bone added considerable weight to arguments favoring a dinosaurian ancestry for birds.

Notes: Carpenter reported dentary fragments from the Lance Formation of Wyoming and isolated

Photo by the author, courtesy American Museum of Natural History.

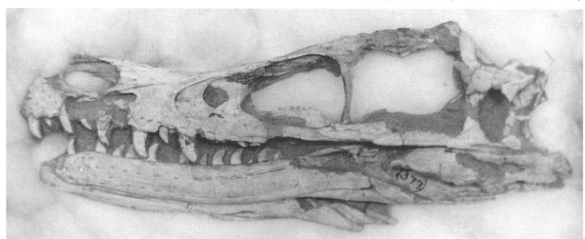

Velociraptor mongoliensis, AMNH 6515, holotype skull and jaws, left lateral view.

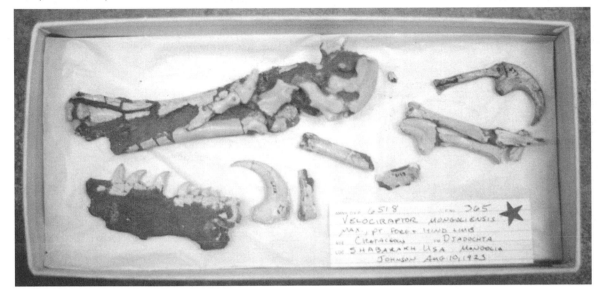

Velociraptor mongoliensis,
AMNH 6518, partial upper
and lower jaws, pedal
elements.

teeth from the Hell Creek Formation of Montana
that may represent baby *Velociraptor* individuals,
though no positive identification was made. The fragments (UW 13684 [UCMP-V5003] and UCMP
125238 [UCMP-V73089]) lack interdental plates,
have inner and outer dental parapets of subequal
height, and have elongated external foramina, features present in the Mongolian genus. Carpenter
observed that the two fragments are seemingly
enough alike to be conspecific. The teeth (UCM
39502 [UCMP-V5711, 45055 [UCMP-V5620],
124983 [UCMP-V73087], 124984 [V-73087], and
124985 [UCMP-V73087]) resemble posterior teeth
in *V. mongoliensis,* being almost as long anteroposteriorly as high, strongly compressed laterally, and
recurved with posterior margin having well-developed serrations. One tooth (UCMP 125238) has 11
serrations per two millimeters on its posterior edge.
These teeth are 1.7–3 millimeters in height and 2–2.2
millimeters in width.

Leonardi and Teruzzi (1993) described (but did
not name) the well-preserved and almost complete
skeleton of a coelurosaurian theropod, found in
Lower Cretaceous rocks of Pietraroia, in the province
of Benevento, Italy. The end of the tail being among
other missing elements, the entire animal, as estimated by Leonardi and Teruzzi, had an approximate
length of 40–50 centimeters (almost 15.5 to more
than 19 inches). The hindfoot displays a "killer claw"
resembling that of *Velociraptor.*

Key references: Carpenter (1982*a*); Colbert and
Russell (1969); Kielan-Jaworoska and Barsbold
(1972); Osborn (1924*c*, 1924*d*); Ostrom (1969, 1990);
Paul (1984*a*, 1987, 1988*b*); Unwin, Perle, and Trueman (1995).

VELOCISAURUS Bonaparte 1991
Saurischia: Theropoda: ?Ceratosauria.
Name derivation: Latin *velocis* = "swift" + Greek
  sauros = "lizard."
Type species: *V. unicus* Bonaparte 1991.
Other species: [None.]

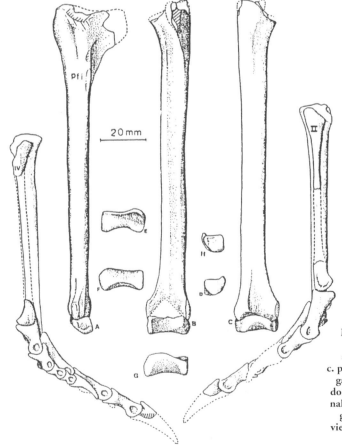

Velocisaurus unicus,
MUCPv 41, holotype
tibia and astragalus,
a. lateral, b. anterior,
c. posterior views; astragalus without anterior
dorsal process, d. inter-
nal, e. dorsal, f. ventral,
g. posterior, h. lateral
views. (After Bonaparte
1991.)

• 973 •

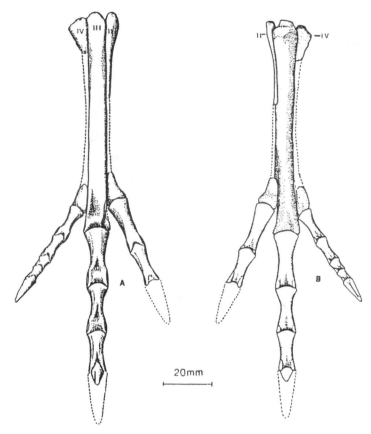

Velocisaurus unicus, MUCPv 41, holotype metatarsus with articulated digits, a. dorsal, b. ventral views. (After Bonaparte 1991.)

Occurrence: Rio Colorado Formation, Coniaciano, Argentina.

Age: Late Cretaceous (Maastrichtian).

Known material/holotype: MUCPv 41, tibia, astragalus, metatarsals II-IV, some partial digits, fragments of metatarsals II and IV, some phalanges.

Diagnosis of genus (as for type species): Small; metatarsus not fused; metatarsal III straight, anterior end entirely exposed where contacting other two metatarsals; metatarsals II and IV relatively average length, but very much reduced; astragalus showing no indication of fusion with tibia; anterior side of astragalus ample, primarily articulating with most distal portion of tibia (Bonaparte 1991).

Comments: The basis for the new monotypic [not generally adopted] family Velocisauridae Bonaparte 1991, *Velocisaurus* was founded upon partial postcranial remains (MUCPv 41) recovered from the inferior member of the Rio Colorado Formation, Neuquén Group, Coniaciano, Argentina (Bonaparte 1991).

Finding the metatarsus most similar to that in ceratosaurians, Bonaparte tentatively referred the Velocisauridae to the Ceratosauria.

Key reference: Bonaparte (1991).

VOLKHEIMERIA Bonaparte 1979

Saurischia: Sauropodomorpha: Sauropoda: Brachiosauridae.

Name derivation: "[Wolfgang] Volkeimer."

Type species: *V. chubutensis* Bonaparte 1979.

Other species: [None.]

Occurrence: Cañodon Asfalto Formation, Chubut, Argentina.

Age: Middle Jurassic (Callovian).

Known material/holotype: Partial skeleton including presacral and sacral vertebrae, incomplete pelvis, femora, tibiae.

Diagnosis of genus (as for type species): Ischium primitive, *Cetiosaurus*-type, with thickening as in *Patagosaurus*; ilium shorter and higher than in *Patagosaurus*, pubis with shorter anterior-posterior proximal region; tibia to femur ratio 1:1.7; dorsal vertebrae (unlike *Patagosaurus* and *Haplocanthosaurus*)

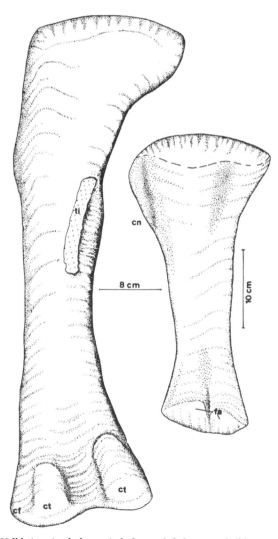

Volkheimeria chubutensis, holotype left femur and tibia. (After Bonaparte 1979.)

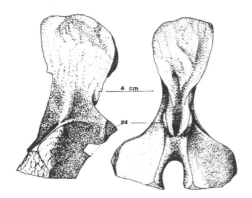

Volkheimeria chubutensis, holotype neural arch of posterior sacral vertebra, lateral and anterior views. (After Bonaparte 1979.)

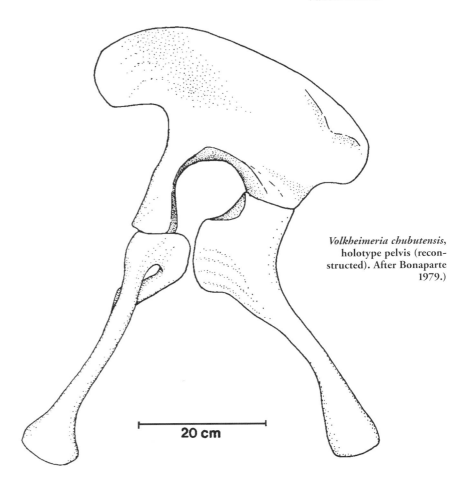

Volkheimeria chubutensis, holotype pelvis (reconstructed). After Bonaparte 1979.)

with very low neural arches and laterally compressed neural spines (Bonaparte 1979).

Comments: The genus *Volkheimeria* was founded upon an incomplete postcranial skeleton collected from Callovian-Oxfordian beds of Argentine Patagonia, South America (Bonaparte 1979).

Bonaparte regarded *Volkheimeria* as more primitive than *Cetiosaurus, Patagosaurus,* and *Haplocanthosaurus.* Comparing *V. chubutensis* with other sauropods, Bonaparte (1980) observed that the dorsal vertebrae in this species differ from those in *P. farasai* in having lower neural arches and laterally compressed neural spines (as in *Bothriospondylus* sp. from the Bathonian of Madagascar). Although related to *Bothriospondylus, V. chubutensis* differs from that form mainly in morphology of the ilium. McIntosh (1990*b*), in his review of the Sauropoda, observed that the low and relatively flat neural spines in the hip region of *Volkeimeria* resemble those of the closely related *Lapparentosaurus.*

As noted by Bonaparte (1979), the discovery of *Volkheimeria* supports the hypothesis that a terrestrial fauna interchange between South America and other continents was feasible during the Jurassic and also (with *Patagosaurus* and the theropod *Piatnitzkysaurus*) establishes the first Jurassic record of an assemblage of pre–Morrison and Tendaguru sauropods and "carnosaurs" in South America.

Key references: Bonaparte (1979, 1980); McIntosh (1990*b*).

VULCANODON Raath 1972
Saurischia: Sauropodomorpha: Sauropoda:
  Vulcanodontidae.
Name derivation: Latin "Vulcanos [Roman god of
  fire]" + Greek *odous* = "tooth."
Type species: *V. karibaensis* Raath 1972.
Other species: [None.]

Occurrence: *Vulcanodon* Beds, Mashonaland North,
  Zimbabwe.
Age: Late Triassic–Early Jurassic (?Hettangian).
Known material: Partial skeleton, scapula.
Holotype: QVM QG24, incomplete skeleton
  including base of right ilium, pubis, ischium,
  parts of three sacral vertebrae, parts of femora,
  left tibia and fibula, tarsus, almost complete left
  pes, 12 anterior caudal vertebrae, right radius and
  ulna, metacarpals, manual phalanges,
  indeterminate fragments (pelvis, sacrum, hind
  leg, and tail in articulation, rest of specimen
  found in association with articulated part).

Diagnosis of genus (as for type species): [No
modern diagnosis published.]

Comments: The genus *Vulcanodon* was founded
on an eroded partial postcranial skeletons (QVM
QG24) [seven teeth originally part of the holotype
were later identified as theropod; see *Sinosaurus* entry]
discovered in 1969 by B. A. Gibson, near the top of
a gritty, current-bedded layer of sandstone overlying
the basal lava flow, Island 126/127, off Bumi Hills,
Zambabwe [formerly Rhodesia]. From the best available
evidence, these "*Vulcanodon* beds" were dated
somewhere between [abandoned name] "Rhaetian"

(uppermost Triassic) and ?Hettangian (lowermost Jurassic). The remains were collected during visits to the site during October 1969, March 1970, and May 1970 (Raath 1972).

In July 1970, Raath and G. Bond briefly reported the discovery of these remains at the Cape Town session of the I.U.G.S. Second Symposium on Gondwana Stratigraphy and Paleontology in South Africa. Later Bond, Wilson and Raath (1970) published their preliminary report on this find.

Originally, Raath diagnosed the monotypic *V. karibaenis* as follows: Large saurischian quadruped with general size and proportions of sauropod, morphologically seemingly intermediate between prosauropods and sauropods, apparently late, derived member of Prosauropoda; primitive features of generalized "carnivorous" teeth, prosauropod-type pubis and ischium, pubes forming transverse distal apron, and ilium apparently of prosauropod type with short anterior process; derived sauropod-like features of solid, robust structure of all limb bones, very long forearm with ulna 106 percent length of tibia, fourth trochanter apparently precisely at midshaft of femur, only proximal tarsals ossified, sacrum probably with more than three sacral vertebrae; pes with well-developed metatarsals; pedal digit I with large sharp claw, II and III terminating in flattened "nail-like" claws.

Raath found the affinities of *Vulcanodon* to be nearest the large prosauropods of South African Red Beds, Chinese Lower Lufeng Series of Yunnan, and "Rhaetic" of Somerset. However, Raath also observed that *Vulcanodon* differs from these forms in having an exceptionally long radius, ulna, and ischium, and a long, straight femur. Therefore, Raath regarded *Vulcanodon* as a specialized melanorosaurid, a prosauropod convergent toward the sauropod condition.

As envisioned by Raath, *Vulcanodon* was a very large animal similar in appearance to sauropods, with plump legs, heavy body, long neck and sauropod-like feet, but an unusually high shoulder.

Later, Cruickshank (1975) and Van Heerden (1978) both regarded *Vulcanodon* as a primitive sauropod.

Cooper (1980) redescribed the ankle of the holotype of *V. karibaensis*, observing that it is fundamentally prosauropodous in structure. The dorsal roller of the astragalus, however, has shifted from ventral to anterior position. Cooper suggested that this shift was related to the acquisition of a plantigrade stance in sauropods, resulting from the stress of great weight. Another sauropod feature of the foot is the absence of distal tarsals, though the functionally obsolete metatarsal V, reduced as much as in the prosauropod *Massospondylus*, is proportionately longer than the others, comparable to that of prosauropod *Plateosaurus*. Cooper argued that the lengthening of metatarsal V could be attributed to the shortening of the others, as similar metatarsal lengths would be advantageous to a plantigrade foot. Acquiring such a stance could also prompt development of subequal metatarsals.

Since discovery of the holotype, remains of a second individual, designated the topotype (QVM QG152), and more material possibly belonging to the holotype, were collected by Bond and Cooper. Based on this new material and the holotype, Cooper (1984) redescribed *Vulcanodon*, arguing that the genus is closest to *Plateosaurus* and *Euskelosaurus* among prosauropods. Cooper (1984) also proposed that *Vulcanodon* should be regarded as the earliest known sauropod because of such sauropodous characters as large size, column-like limbs, length of the forelimbs, pelvic structure, reduced cnemial crest of the tibia, lack of distal tarsals, and the entirely quadrupedal gait.

Cooper (1984) believed *Vulcanodon* to be sufficiently generalized for the Vulcanodontidae to have been ancestral to both the Camarasauridae and Diplodocidae, the genus envisioned as an animal with the basic limb proportions of *Plateosaurus*, but with an unusually longer radius and ulna. The earliest sauropods, then, might have superficially resembled larger, quadrupedal prosauropods, the gigantism of later sauropods possibly evolving to accommodate the harsher climates at the end of the Triassic (see Cooper 1982).

Bonaparte (1986a) noted that the most significant features of *Vulcanodon* are of a sauropod nature, including pubes even more anatomically advanced than in some primitive sauropods; strong, elongate metatarsals almost

Vulcanodon karibaensis, tentative reconstruction including holotype partial skeleton QVM Q624. (After Raath 1972.)

1 metre

as long as the metatarsals; and roughly triangular astragalus in dorsal view, with a wide external side and pointed, narrower internal side. Bonaparte concluded that *Vulcanodon* possessed sufficient primitive and derived characters to be regarded as an early sauropod warranting its own family.

In his review of the Sauropoda, McIntosh (1990*b*) regarded *Vulcanodon* as the earliest and most primitive known sauropod, although Benton (1990) considered this genus to be a derived prosauropod.

McIntosh briefly described *Vulcanodon* as follows: Sacrum narrow; centra of caudal vertebrae amphicoelous, with no pleurocoels, but strongly waisted, containing deep furrow on ventral surface and strong chevron facets at both ends; transverse processes directed outward, also backward and slightly downward; scapula with proximal end apparently less expanded than in other primitive sauropods; frontlimb bones very slender (but typically sauropod); metacarpus only one-third length of radius; pelvis primitive; pubes resembling those of prosauropods, shafts twisted to form transverse apron (similar to but more primitive than in *Barapasaurus*); ischium long, straight, much longer than pubis, shaft expanding gently but continuously to distal end, which meets its mate side by side (reminiscent of diplodocids); femur unique among sauropods in retention of reduced but well-marked lesser trochanter; fourth trochanter more prominent than in later forms; tibia to femur ratio relatively small, 0.58 [see Raath 1972]; ulna to tibia ratio large, 1.04; astragalus large; calcaneum prominent; metatarsal III longest, 32 percent length of tibia (much longer than in any other sauropod).

As pointed out by Cooper (1984), the holotype of *V. karibaenis* was found in a bedded siltstone/sandstone sequence cut by a river channel. The carcass may have been rafted to the excavation site, or perhaps the individual was on the banks of a temporary stream or wadi flowing into a desert when it died. This environment was not known for peat swamps rich in aquatic vegetation and thus constituted evidence refuting the old notion that a sauropod's large size was an adaptation for an aquatic lifestyle, the water supposedly supporting its heavy body.

Note: Raath suggested that fossil footprints, known from several sites in Lesotho and attributed to sauropods, could be those of a dinosaur like *Vulcanodon*. These tracks include that referred to as the "Soebeng Track" by Charig, Attridge and Crompton (1965), identified by Ellenberger (1970) as *Deuterosauropodopus*.

Key references: Benton (1990); Bonaparte (1986*a*); Bond, Wilson and Raath (1970); Cooper (1980, 1982, 1984); Cruickshank (1975); McIntosh (1990*b*); Raath (1972); Van Heerden (1978).

WAKINOSAURUS Okazaki 1992
Saurischia: Theropoda: ?Tetanurae:
  ?Megalosauridae.
Name derivation: "Wakino [Subroup]" + Greek
  sauros = "lizard."
Type species: *W. satoi* Okazaki 1992.
Other species: [None.]
Occurrence: Sengoku Formation, Miyata-machi,
  Japan.
Age: Early Cretaceous (Neocomian).
Known material/holotype: KMNH VP 000,016,
  tooth missing about half of apex.

Diagnosis of genus (as for type species): Tooth with large, compressed, blade-like crown, longitudinal striations on surface, fine serrations on both anterior and posterior cutting edges (Okazaki 1992).

Comments: One of the only dinosaurs known from Japan, *Wakinosaurus* was founded upon a large incomplete tooth (KMNH VP 000,016) discovered on February 9, 1990, by Masahiro Sato, in rock from a river bed in the Sengoku Formation, Wakino Subgroup, Lower Cretaceous (Neocomian) Kwanmon Group, Sengokukyo, Miyata-machi, Kurate Gun, Fukuoka Prefecture, northern Kyushu, Japan. The discovery marked the first occurrence of fossil reptilian remains, excluding a few turtle and crocodile specimens, from the Cretaceous Kwanmon Group (Yoshihiko Okazaki [1992]). The specimen was collected from a medium-grained sandstone to coarse shale including abundant fossils of the freshwater gastropod *Brotiopsis* sp. and numerous carapace fragments of the turtle *Adocus* sp. (Okazaki 1990*a*; see also Okazaki 1990*b*; Sato 1990).

As described by Okazaki (1992), the tooth has more than 100 serrations throughout the preserved anterior cutting edge, this portion measuring approximately 45 millimeters. There are 12 serrations on the preserved (about 5 millimeters) posterior cutting

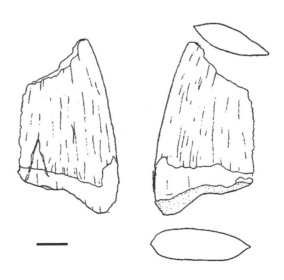

Wakinosaurus satoi, KMNH VP 000,016, holotype incomplete tooth, buccal and lingual sides. Scale = 1 cm. (After Okazaki 1992.)

edge. The serrations are present only near the cutting edge and are not deeply sculptured on the surface. As preserved, the tooth is 57.4 millimeters in height, the crown 50 millimeters. The thickness at the middle is 8.5 millimeters, at the base 10.4 millimeters, width of the base 32.8 millimeters.

Okazaki (1992) pointed out that the diagnostic characters of the holotype tooth are known only separately in other theropod species, and observed that the specimen most closely corresponds to the Chinese species, ?*Prodeinodon kwangshiensis*, which has a compressed crown and backwardly bent anterior end, but rather straight posterior edge (see Hou, Yeh and Zhao 1975). According to Okazaki (1992), *P. kwangshiensis* is quite different from the Mongolian *P. mongoliensis*, type species of *Prodeinodon*. Okazaki suggested that, perhaps after future studies, *P. kwangshiensis* may prove to belong in the genus *Wakinosaurus*.

Okazaki (1992) tentatively referred *Wakinosaurus* to the Megalosauridae.

Key reference: Okazaki (1990*a*, 1990*b*, 1992); Sato (1990).

WALGETTOSUCHUS   Huene 1932 [*nomen dubium*] — (=?*Rapator*)

Saurischia: Theropoda: Tetanurae *incertae sedis*.

Name derivation: "Walgett [town in New South Wales]" + *souchos* = "crocodile."

Type species: *W. woodwardi* Huene 1932 [*nomen dubium*].

Other species: [None.]

Occurrence: Griman Creek Formation, New South Wales, Australia.

Age: Early Cretaceous (Aptian).

Known material/holotype: BMNH R3717, incomplete distal caudal centrum.

Diagnosis of genus: [None published.]

Comments: The genus *Walgettosuchus* was established on an isolated, almost featureless vertebral centrum (BMNH R3717), collected from the Griman Creek Formation, at Lightning Ridge, New South Wales, Australia.

As measured by Huene (1932), the specimen is 6.3 centimeters (about 2.4 inches) long; posterior articular surface 17 millimeters (about .65 inches) high; 21 millimeters (about .78 inches) wide.

Huene suggested that, if more material were available, *Walgettosuchus* might prove to be generically identical to other Lightning Ridge "coelurosaurs" (*i.e.*, *Rapator*).

Apparently, Huene erred in stating that the centrum is flattened dorsoventrally (unlike other known theropods), while the neural spine is long (R. E. Mol-

nar, personal communication 1988). According to Molnar (1990), Huene's reasons for believing that the caudal had possessed elongate prezygapophyses are not known. Molnar (1980*b*) regarded the holotype of *Walgettosuchus* as indeterminate, matched by caudals of at least three theropod families (Allosauridae, Coeluridae, and Ornithomimidae).

Key references: Huene (1932); Molnar (1980*b*, 1990).

WALKERIA   Chatterjee 1986

Dinosauria *incertae sedis*.

Name derivation: "[Alick D.] Walker."

Type species: *W. maleriensis* Chatterjee 1986.

Other species: [None.]

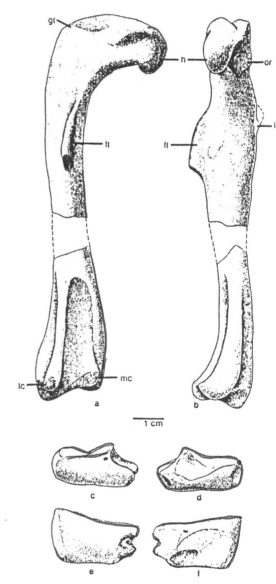

Walkeria maleriensis, ISI R 306, holotype femur, a. posterior, b. medial views, left astragalus, c. anterior, d. posterior, e. distal, f. proximal views. (After Chatterjee 1986.)

Walgettosuchus woodwardi, BMNH R3717, holotype caudal vertebra. (After Huene 1932.)

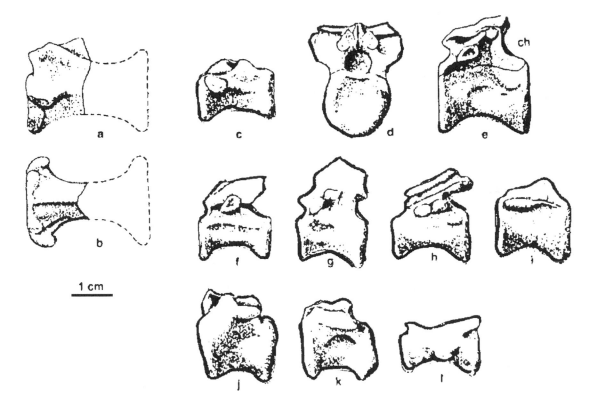

Walkeria maleriensis, ISI R 306, holotype vertebrae, a., b., cervicals, c.-j., dorsals, k., l., caudals, ch. chonoses (juvenile). (After Chatterjee 1986.)

Occurrence: Maleri Formation, Andrhra Pradesh, India.

Age: Late Triassic (Carnian–Middle Norian).

Known material/holotype: ISI R 306, partial skull, several vertebrae, femur, astragalus, juvenile.

Diagnosis of genus (as for type species): Small theropod distinguished from other contemporary forms by absence of ridge below antorbital fenestra, long dentary symphysis, unserrated teeth, conical and procumbent mesial dentary teeth, open astragalocalcaneal joint, and excavation of bases of dorsal neural arches (Norman 1990).

Comments: The earliest and most primitive dinosaur yet recovered from Asia, the genus *Walkeria* was founded on partial skeletal remains (ISI R 306), found in 1974 by Sankar Chatterjee in red mudstone facies of the fluvial Maleri Formation (Upper Triassic), Gondwana Supergroup, near Nennal Village, Adilabad District, Prandhita-Godavari Valley, India. The discovery constituted the first dinosaur known from the Maleri Formation, which has been rich in remains of rhynchosaurs, parasuchids, metoposaurs, aetosaurs, traversodonts, and protorosaurs, taxa identified in the Dockum fauna of North America (Chatterjee 1987).

Originally, Chatterjee diagnosed the monotypic *W. maleriensis* as follows: Skull with narrow, tapering snout; premaxilla loosely attached to maxilla, gap between them; maxilla lacking longitudinal "alveolar ridge" above dental border; dentary with external longitudinal "alveolar groove" and long symphysis; teeth unserrated; anterior teeth conical, posterior teeth laterally compressed; neural arches hollowed out by "chonoses"; femur with highly expanded proximal head and pronounced fourth trochanter; astragalus and calcaneum separate.

Chatterjee pointed out that the occurrence of *Walkeria* in association with taxa identified with Dockum fauna indicates a close faunal link between India and Laurasia, and postulated that the Late Triassic faunal route between India and North America was via northern Africa.

In a review of problematic "coelurosaurs," Norman (1990) stated that this species shows no particularly strong affinities with other known theropods below characters diagnostic to Theropoda. Novas (1992) regarded *Walkeria* as unable to be classified beyond Dinosauria *incertae sedis*.

Key references: Chatterjee (1986); Norman (1990); Novas (1992).

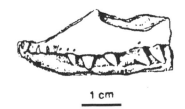

Walkeria maleriensis, ISI R 306, holotype partial skull and jaw (juvenile). (After Chatterjee 1986.)

WANNANOSAURUS Hou 1977

Ornithischia: Genasauria: Cerapoda:
   Marginocepalia: Pachycephalosauria:
   Homalocephalidae.

Name derivation: "Wannan [locality]" + Greek
   sauros = "lizard."

Type species: *W. yansiensis* Hou 1977.

Other species: [None.]

Occurrence: Xiaoyan Formation, Anhui, People's
   Republic of China.

Age: Late Cretaceous (Campanian).

Known material/holotype: Partial skull roof,
   mandible, femur, tibia, rib head, other
   fragments.

Diagnosis of genus (as for type species): Small,
primitive pachycephalosaur, with completely flattened
cranial roof, large supratemporal fenestrae; frontoparietal thick; small, densely arranged bony
processes forming ornamentation on external surface
of crania; parietosquamosal shelf not extending posteriorly; occipital region and quadrate sloping slightly
antero-ventrally; tooth row of lower jaw long, more
than half length along ventral margin; posterior portion of lower jaw thin, with broad base and prominent

retroarticular process; tooth crowns serrated (Hou
1977).

Comments: Morphologically the most primitive known homalocephid genus, *Wannanosaurus* was
established on an incomplete skull and fragmentary
postcranial remains collected from the Xiaoyan Formation, near Yansi, Xuancheng County, Anhui
Province, China (Hou 1977).

As measured by Hou, the femur of *Wannanosaurus* is approximately 8 centimeters (3.1 inches)
long, tibia about 8.8 centimeters (3.75 inches), with
the total length of the animal estimated at less than
1 meter (39.37 inches).

Sereno (1986), envisioning a sequence of pachycephalosaurian evolution, proposed that *Wannanosaurus* may be the most primitive of all known pachycephalosaurs (although Sues and Galton 1987 had
suggested that *Yaverlandia* may be even more primitive). All other pachycephalosaurs possess the more
advanced features of a transversely broadened postorbital bar, and linear row of five-seven tubercles that
project from the posterior margin of the squamosal.
Sereno also noted that all known pachycephalosaurs,
except *Wannanosaurus* and *Goyocephale*, have the

Wannanosaurus yansiensis, holotype
skull and lower jaw, left lateral view.
(After Hou 1977.)

more derived character of relatively smaller supratemporal openings.

In reviewing the Pachycephalosauria, Maryańska (1990) observed that the holotype of *W. yansiensis*, though quite small, most likely represents an adult individual, as evidenced by the obliterated sutures on the skull roof; also, the pattern of skull roof ornamentation in *W. yansiensis* is granulated instead of pitted (as in *Homalocephale calathocercos* and *Goyocephale lattimorei*).

Key references: Hou (1977); Maryańska (1990); Sereno (1986).

WUERHOSAURUS   Dong 1973

Ornithischia: Genasauria: Thyreophora:
   Stegosauria: Stegosauridae.
Name derivation: "Wuerho [town in Xinjiang]" +
   Greek *sauros* = "lizard."
Type species: *W. homheni* Dong 1973.
Other species: *W. ordosensis* Dong 1993.
Occurrence: Lianmuging Formation, Xinjiang
   Uygur Zizhiqu, People's Republic of China, Ejin-
   horo Formation, Ordos Basin, Inner Mongolia.
Age: Early Cretaceous (?Valanginian–Albanian).
Known material: Partial postcrania, partial
   skeleton, dermal plate, vertebra, representing
   three individuals.
Holotype: IVPP V4006, vertebrae, sacrum, four
   relatively complete ribs, right scapulacoracoid,
   humerus, ilium, pubes, complete dorsal dermal
   plate, partial plate.

Diagnosis of genus: Differs from all other stegosaurs in having only 11 dorsal vertebrae; neural canal of dorsals small, not enlarged (Dong 1993*c*).

Diagnosis of *W. homheni*: Large stegosaur, 7–8 meters long (approximately 23.5 to 27 feet) in length,

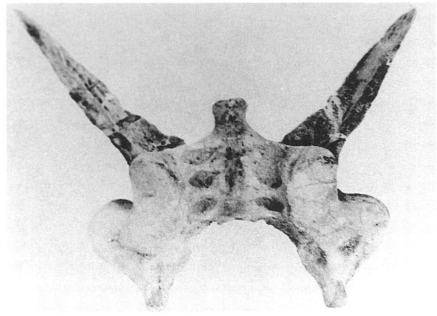

Wuerhosaurus homheni,
IVPP V4006, holotype pelvis.
(After Dong 1987.)

similar to *Stegosaurus* in that neural spine of anterior caudal vertebra is three times height of centrum, with convex dorsal surface; fenestrae present between sacral ribs; sacral processes entirely closed; humeral length to iliac length ratio 1.3; ilia differing from those of *Stegosaurus* in anterior processes separated by wide angle; dermal plates large, long, somewhat low in side view (Dong 1990*b*).

Diagnosis of *W. ordosensis*: Medium-sized, lightly-built, total body length about 4.5 meters; in contrast with *W. homheni*, centra of anterior caudal vertebrae lightly built with thin neural spines; top of neural spine of first caudal vertebra not expanded transversely, not gently curved dorsally (Dong 1993*c*).

Comments: The first positively identified Cretaceous stegosaur, *Wuerhosaurus* was founded upon a

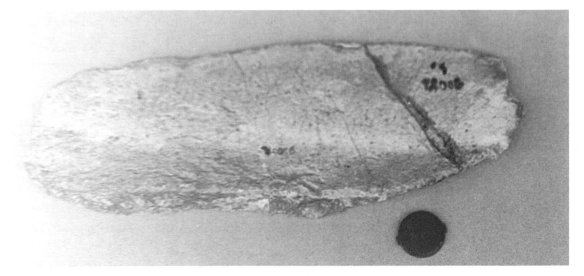

Wuerhosaurus homheni, IVPP
V4006, holotype dermal plate.
(After Dong 1987.)

Wuerhosaurus

partial postcranial skeleton (IVPP V4006) collected from the Urhe region (Lower Cretaceous) of the Junggar Basin in northwestern China. A fragmentary paratype (IVPP V4007) consists of three caudal vertebrae (Dong 1973).

Originally, Dong diagnosed the new genus and species *W. homheni* as follows: Caudal centrum longer than wide, flat, round, with inconspicuous longitudinal ridge on ventral surface; neural arch high, neural foramen large, round, neural spine large, high (higher than in other known stegosaurs); scapula thickened at center, becoming thinner at both margins; coracoid flat, rounded; humerus short, thick, robust, extremities twisted (closely resembling that of *Stegosaurus*); ilium with very long and widespread anterior process and short, wide posterior process extending slightly downward; pubes long, slender, with wide, flat anterior process and club-shaped posterior process; ischium (from referred specimen) relatively thick, proximal end forming posterior margin of acetabulum, distal end rather large and thick; one of two preserved dermal plates rather low and sickle-shaped, with wide, rugose base; plate becoming gradually thinner away from base, upper margin a sharp surface; other plate with various interlaced longitudinal osseous patterns that strengthen plate.

Comparing *Wuerhosaurus* to the North American *Stegosaurus*, Dong noted that the vertebrae and pelvis are quite similar in both forms, except for the enlargement of the protruding angle of the anterior process of the pelvic girdle in *Wuerhosaurus*. Apparently the humerus is comparatively shorter in *Wuerhosaurus*. The tight unification of scapula and coracoid, relatively slender and weak pubis, and thick, strong ischium suggest that *Wuerhosaurus* is more

derived than *Stegosaurus*. Dong also commented that features of the plates are conspicuously different from those of the North American genus.

Dong (1993c) later named and described a second species of this genus, *W. ordosensis*, which represents the first occurrence of a Lower Cretaceous stegosaur from Inner Mongolia, and the only one for which an articulated series of dorsal vertebrae is known. This species was founded upon an incomplete skeleton (IVPP V6877), including a series of three cervical, 11 dorsal, five sacral, and five caudal vertebrae, cervical, dorsal, and sacral ribs, right ilium. The type specimen was collected during an expedition of the Sino-Canadian Dinosaur Project (see Currie 1991; Dong 1993a) from the Ejinhoro Formation, near Yang-paul Village, in Ordos Basin. Referred material from the same locality includes a dorsal plate (IVPP V6878) and dorsal vertebra (IVPP V6879) (Dong 1993c).

According to Dong, the low number of dorsal vertebrae in *W. ordosensis* may have either generic or specific significance, as no specimen of the type species *W. homheni* has a preserved dorsal series (Dong 1990). Also, the anterior five caudal vertebrae in *W. ordosensis* seem to be different from those of Jurassic stegosaurs in that the centra are small and light, rather than large and massive.

In a review of Cretaceous stegosaurs, Galton (1981a) observed that bones of *Wuerhosaurus* are similar to corresponding bones in *Lexovisaurus*, *Kentrosaurus*, and *Stegosaurus*. Apparently *Wuerhosaurus* superficially resembled *Stegosaurus*, although with comparatively shorter frontlimbs and lower plates.

Key references: Dong (1973; 1990b, 1993c); Galton (1981a).

WYLEYIA Harrison and Walker 1973 [*nomen dubium*]

?Saurischia: ?Theropoda *incertae sedis*.

Name derivation: "[J. F.] Wyley."

Type species: *W. valdensis* Harrison and Walker 1973 [*nomen dubium*].

Other species: [None.]

Occurrence: Wealden, West Sussex, England.

Age: Early Cretaceous (Barremian).

Known material/holotype: BMNH R3658, proximal portion of right humerus.

Diagnosis of genus (as for type species): Humerus similar to but smaller than that of (birds) *Archaeopteryx* and *Ichthyornis*; proximal end of humerus relatively smooth and flattened; deltoid crest extending for almost one-third length, apparently making slight angle with plane of proximal palmar surface; palmar surface of crest with small longitudinal ridge on distal half, small curved depression at distal end; no sign of prominent bicipital surface; bicipital crest large, relatively thick, rounded along internal edge; ligamental furrow just below head on palmar surface; shaft curved with some torsion (?result of crushing), becoming wider distally; impression for brachialis anticus muscle very deep, broad (half width of shaft), elongated, nearer external side of shaft (Harrison and Walker 1973).

Comments: The genus *Wyleyia* was established upon a partial humerus (BMNH R3658) discovered in 1964 by J. F. Wyley, in the Weald Clay, Henfield, West Sussex, England.

Harrison and Walker (1973) observed that the specimen was reminiscent of an advanced archosaur. However, after comparing the holotype with humeri of small dinosaurs (*i.e.*, *Deinonychus* and *Hypsilophodon*) and pterosaurs, they concluded that the remains were those of a bird, listing five characters apparent in the holotype regarded as particularly avian: 1. Transverse ligamental furrow on palmar surface just below articular area of proximal end; 2. large, very thin, blade-like deltoid crest; 3. indication of capital groove on "elbow" surface; 4. slender, hollow, thin-walled shaft; and 5. distinct groove (brachial depression) for insertion of the brachialis anticus muscle. Although Harrison and Walker found that the humerus of *Wyleyia* compared most favorably with *Archaeopteryx* and *Ichthyornis*, they did not find that to be sufficient grounds for assigning the genus either to Archaopterygiformes or Ichthyornithiformes, preferring to regard the new form as *incertae sedis*.

Contra Harrison and Walker, Brodkorb (1978) stated that the humerus is almost surely reptilian, the epiphysis unfused or eroded. If reptilian, the specimen represents a small theropod dinosaur.

In reassessing various problematic "coelurosaurs," Norman (1990) pointed out that Harrison and Walker's comparison of *W. valdensis* mostly with *Deinonychus* is not comprehensive, and that, considering the lack of clearly diagnostic avian characters of the proximal end of the humerus and in lack of avian pneumatic openings in the humeral shaft, the type material seems to be theropod. Norman commented that the poorly preserved state of this material warrants its being regarded as a *nomen dubium*.

Key references: Brodkin (1978); Harrison and Walker (1973); Norman (1990).

XENOTARSOSAURUS Martínez, Giménez, Rodríguez and Bochatey 1986

Saurischia: Theropoda: Ceratosauria: Neoceratosauria: ?Abelisauridae: ?Abelisauridae.

Name derivation: Greek *xenos* = "strange" + Greek *tarsos* = "tarsus [ankle bones]" + Greek *sauros* = "lizard."

Type species: *X. bonapartei* Martínez, Giménez, Rodríguez and Bochatey 1986.

Other species: [None.]

Occurrence: Bajo Barreal Formation, Chubut, Argentina.

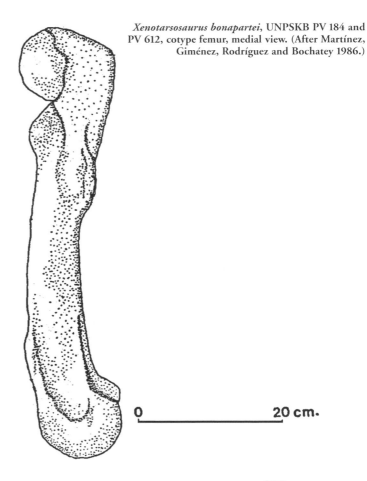

Xenotarsosaurus bonapartei, UNPSKB PV 184 and PV 612, cotype femur, medial view. (After Martínez, Giménez, Rodríguez and Bochatey 1986.)

0   20 cm.

Xiaosaurus

Xenotarsosaurus bonapartei, UNPSKB PV 184 and PV 612, cotype tibia, fibula and astragalus, anterior view. (After Martínez, Giménez, Rodríguez and Bochatey 1986.)

0 [_____] 20 cm.

Age: Late Cretaceous (?Campanian).
Known material/cotypes: UNPSJB PV 184 and PV 612, two cervical-dorsal vertebrae, femur, tibia, fibula, astragalocalcaneum.

Diagnosis of genus (as for type species): Medium-sized "carnosaur"; centra of anterior dorsal vertebrae wider than high, anterior surface concave, not flat (as in *Carnotaurus sastrei*); neural arch higher and neural canal deeper than in *C. sastrei*; femur very similar to that of *C. sastrei*, with trochanter shelf, tibia with less robust proximal portion than in that species, with excavation in base of cnemial crest; fibula and tibia joined into tight contact with indications that strong ligaments were once present; astragalus and calcaneum fused together and to tibia; zone of contact between astragalus and tibia not visible from behind; fibula much compressed latero-medially; femur to tibia ratio 1:0.94 (Martínez, Giménez, Rodríguez and Bochatey 1986).

Comments: The genus *Xenotarsosaurus* was founded upon partial postcranial remains (UNPSJB PV 184 and PV 612) collected from the upper part of the lower member of the Bajo Barreal Formation of Chubut, Argentina (Martínez, Giménez, Rodríguez and Bochatey 1986).

Because of similarities in the type specimen to the abelisaurid *Carnotaurus sastrei*, Martínez *et al.* referred this genus to the Abelisauridae. The authors also noted affinities (based mostly on proportions of anterior dorsal vertebrae, similar lesser trochanter and base of femur, fused astragalus and calcaneum, and contact of tibia with fibula) with the North American *Ceratosaurus nasicornis*, suggesting a relationship with the monotypic Ceratosauridae (see also Rowe and Gauthier 1990).

Key reference: Martínez, Giménez, Rodríguez and Bochatey (1986).

XIAOSAURUS Dong and Tang 1983 [*nomen dubium*] — (=?*Yandusaurus*)
Ornithischia *insertae sedis*.
Name derivation: Chinese "xiao" = "small" + Greek *sauros* = "lizard."
Type species: *X. dashanpensis* Dong and Tang 1983 [*nomen dubium*].
Other species: [None.]
Occurrence: Xiashaximiao Formation, Sichuan, People's Republic of China.
Age: Middle Jurassic (Callovian).
Known material: Teeth, vertebrae, humerus, hindlimb, phalanges, ribs, other remains.
Holotype: IVPP V.6730A, maxillary fragment with first tooth intact, two cervical and four caudal vertebrae, humerus, complete hindlimb.

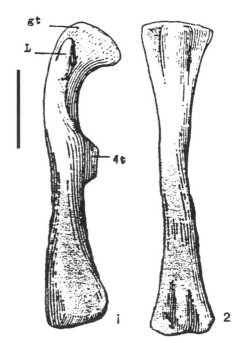

Xiaosaurus dashanpensis, IVPP V.6730A, holotype left femur, 1. anterior and 2. lateral views. Scale = 3 cm. (After Dong and Tang 1983.)

Diagnosis of genus (as for type species): Small cursorial "ornithopod" measuring about one meter (about 3.4 feet) in length; skull rather high, with preorbital foramen; premaxillary teeth; teeth in single row, laterally compressed, enamelled, asymmetrical on both interior and exterior surfaces, denticulate mesially and distally, with flat crowns showing no wear on surface, conical roots; fourth trochanter resembling fan-shaped crest on proximal half of femur; tibia longer than femur; metatarsal III more than 60 percent length of femur; ratio of tibial length plus third metatarsal III to femur approximately 1.09 (Dong and Tang 1983).

Comments: The genus *Xiaosaurus* was established upon rather well-preserved but fragmentary remains (IVPP V.6730A) discovered during field work of 1979–1980, at Dashanpu, in Zigong City, Sichuan Province, China. Referred material includes a complete right femur, dorsal vertebra, two connected sacral vertebrae, ribs, phalanges, and other remains (IVPP V.67303). The material was collected by Xiao-zhong and other paleontologists from Zigong Museum of Salt History (Dong and Tang 1983).

According to Dong and Tang, this genus might represent a transitional form between *Lesothosaurus* and *Hypsilophodon*, although better skull material of *Xiaosaurus* must be obtained and more research

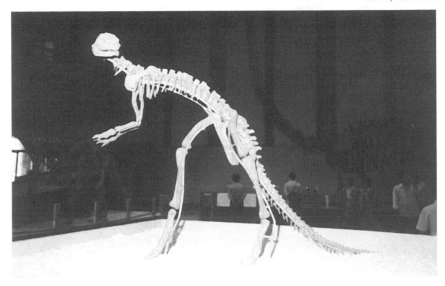

Xiaosaurus dashanpensis, skeleton mounted at the Zigong Dinosaur Museum.

conducted before such a determination can be made.

In his book *Dinosaurs from China*, Dong (1987) stated that *X. dashanpensis* and *"Yandusaurus"* [=*Agilisaurus*] *multidens* were conspecific without providing evidence for synonymy. Weishampel and Witmer (1990*a*), in reassessing various primitive ornithischians, regarded *X. dashanpensis* as a *nomen dubium*. In a study of basal ornithischians, Sereno (1991) stated that the type material of this species is certainly ornithischian; that the long symmetrical metatarsal V does not resemble that in other dinosaurs (and might be misidentified); also that the holotype exhibits no apparent diagnostic characters, nor have any been described. For the latter reasons, Sereno regarded the holotype as indeterminate ornithischian remains.

Key references: Dong (1987); Dong and Tang (1983); Sereno (1991); Weishampel and Witmer (1990*a*).

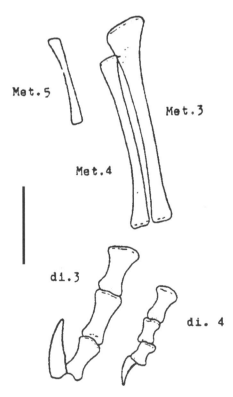

Xiaosaurus dashanpensis, IVPP V.6730A, holotype hindfoot. Scale = 2 cm. (After Dong and Tang 1983.)

XUANHANOSAURUS   Dong 1984

Saurischia: Theropoda: ?Tetanurae: ?Megalosauridae.

Name derivation: "Xhuanhan [County]" + Greek *sauros* = "lizard."

Type species: *X. qilixianensis* Dong 1984.

Other species: [None.]

Occurrence: Xiashaximiao Formation, Sichuan, People's Republic of China.

Age: Middle Jurassic (Bathonian–Callovian).

Xuanhanosaurus

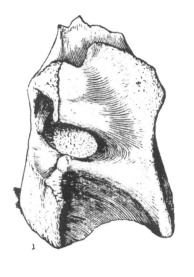

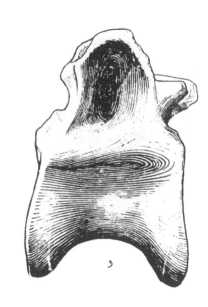

Xuanosaurus qilixiaensis, IVP AS V6729, holotype vertebrae. Scale = 2 cm. (After Dong 1984.)

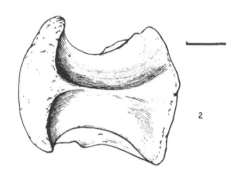

Xuanosaurus qilixiaensis, IVP AS V6729, holotype scapulacoracoid (scale = 2 cm.), humerus, radius, ulna (scale = 3 cm.). (After Dong 1984.)

Known material/holotype: IVP AS V6729, vertebrae, scapulacoracoid, humerus, radius, ulna, manus.

Diagnosis of genus (as for type species): Medium size; extremely conservative "carnosaur," total body length approximately 6 meters (more than 20 feet); forearm relatively long and massive; humerus straight, with medial deltopectoral crest; 1.3 ratio of maximum length of humerus to radius; metacarpal III relatively massive, IV short, light (Dong 1984).

Comments: The genus *Xuanhanosaurus* was established on partial postcranial remains (IVP AS V6729) discovered in the lower Xiashaximiao Formation of Xhuanhan County, Sichuan Basin, People's Republic of China (Dong 1984).

Dong classified *Xuanhanosaurus* as a megalosaurid, envisioning it as a quadruped because of forelimb length, and, hence, rather primitive. Molnar (1990) noted that the relationship between such an apparently primitive taxon and other better-known theropods is uncertain. Britt (1991) later stated that *Xuanhanosaurus* appears to be a true megalosaurid, as evidenced by its caudal vertebra with a strongly keeled venter (as in some cervical and almost all dorsal vertebrae in the megalosaurid *Torvosaurus*), and by the straight-shaft humerus (as in *Torvosaurus* and other megalosaurids).

Key references: Britt (1991); Dong (1984); Molnar (1990).

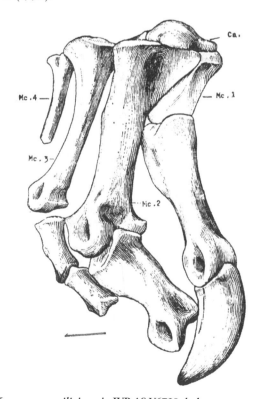

Xuanosaurus qilixiaensis, IVP AS V6729, holotype manus. Scale = 2 cm. (After Dong 1984.)

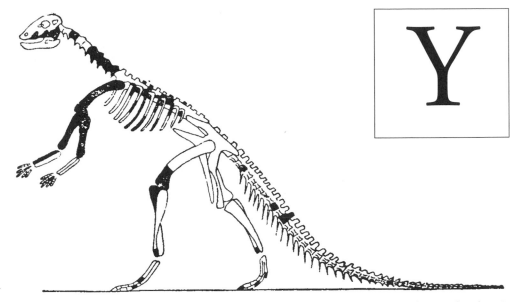

YALEOSAURUS   Huene 1932—(See *Anchisaurus.*)

Name derivation: "Yale [University]" + Greek *sauros* = "lizard."

Type species: *Y. colurus* (Marsh 1891).

YANDUSAURUS   He 1979—

(=?*Xiaosaurus*)

Ornithischia: Genasauria: Cerapoda: Ornithopoda: Hypsilophodontidae.

Name derivation: "Yandum [town]" + Greek *sauros* = "lizard."

Type species: *Y. hongheensis* He 1979.

Other species: [None.]

Occurrence: Xiashaximiao Formation, Sichuan, People's Republic of China.

Age: Middle Jurassic (Bathonian–Callovian).

Known material: Two almost complete skeletons with skulls.

Holotype: T720501, incomplete skeleton including nearly complete maxilla with teeth, cervical, dorsal, and caudal vertebrae, left scapula, humeri, ulna, distal portion of left femur, fragments of hindlimbs and pedes.

Diagnosis of genus (as for type species): Medium size; maxilla slightly triangular; maxilla with 12 teeth, tooth crown evidently higher on outer surface where grooves are almost parallel; cervical vertebrae flat, concave, weakly developed, dorsals rather flat; scapula of medium width, middle outer portion more robust; coracoid rather pentagonal; posterior portion of humerus greatly curved like arc, with triangular thickening about mid-length; humerus and scapula about equal length; ulna relatively short, less than two-thirds length of humerus; distal end of femur with no groove in front view, inner surface of femur distinctly larger than outer (He 1979).

Comments: The genus *Yandusaurus* was founded upon incomplete skeletal remains (T720501) collected from the Hung Hok Region, east suburb of Chi-Kung, Zigong, in Sichuan [then Szechuan] province, China (He 1979).

He estimated that the maxilla, when complete, was more than 120 millimeters (over 4.6 inches) in length.

Note: Second species *Y. multidens* was referred by Peng (1992) to the new genus *Agilisaurus*.

Key reference: He (1979).

Yandusaurus hongheensis, reconstructed skeleton including holotype T720501. (After He 1979.)

Yandusaurus hongheensis, T720501, holotype maxilla. (After He 1979.)

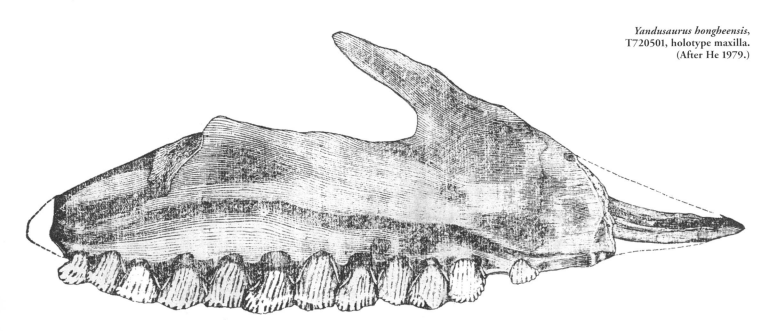

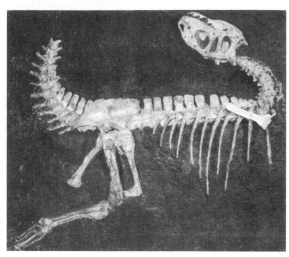

Yangchuanosaurus shangyuensis, CV 00215, holotype skeleton (?juvenile), displayed at the Chongqing Natural History Museum of Sichuan.

Yangchuanosaurus shangyuensis, CV 00215, holotype skull (?juvenile) left lateral view. (After Dong 1987.)

YANGCHUANOSAURUS   Dong, Li, Zhou and Chang 1978

Saurischia: Theropoda: Tetanurae: Avetheropoda: Allosauroidea: Sinraptoridae.

Name derivation: "Yangchuan [District of Szechuan Province]" + Greek *sauros* = "lizard."

Type species: *Y. shangyouensis* Dong, Li, Zhou and Chang 1978.

Other species: *Y. magnus* Dong, Zhou and Zhang 1983.

Occurrence: Shangshaximiao Formation, Sichuan, People's Republic of China.

Age: Late Jurassic.

Known material: Almost complete skeleton, partial skeleton including skull, vertebrae, pelvis, femur, ?juvenile, adult.

Holotype: CV 00215, almost articulated complete skeleton missing forelimbs, distal caudal vertebrae, ?juvenile.

Diagnosis of genus (as for type species): Large megalosaurid, skull 81 centimeters (almost 32 inches) long, 52 centimeters (about 20 inches) high, with two antorbital openings; teeth moderately compressed, denticulation; four premaxillary, 14 maxillary, 14–16 dentary teeth; ten cervical, 13 dorsal, and five sacral vertebrae, latter with firmly coossified centra, last four sacrals with fused neural spines; ilium low; pubis "footed" (Dong, Zhou and Zhang 1983).

Diagnosis of *Y. magnus*: Huge megalosaurid, estimated length 10 meters (about 34 feet), with heavily-built skull measuring 111 centimeters (about 43 inches) in length, 70 centimeters (about 27 inches) high (Dong *et al.* 1983).

Comments: The genus *Yangchuanosaurus* was founded upon an almost complete skeleton (CV 00215) collected from the early Upper Jurassic of the Shangshaximiao Formation, in Yangchuan County, Sichuan [formerly Szechuan] Province, Sichuan Basin, China (Dong, Chang, Li and Zhou 1978).

Originally, Dong *et al.* briefly diagnosed the genus (and type species, *Y. shangyouensis*) as follows:

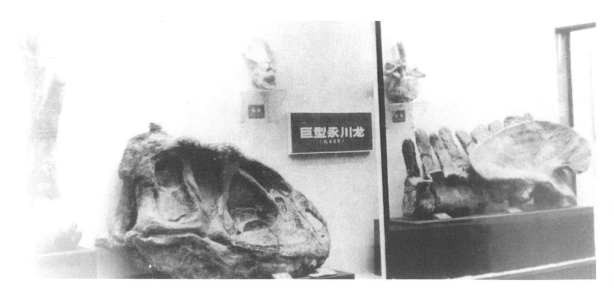

Yangchuanosaurus magnus, holotype femur, skull, vertebrae, sacrum with right ilium. (After Dong 1987.)

Large theropod; four premaxillary, 14–15 dentary, and 14–15 maxillary teeth; ten cervical, 13 dorsal, and five sacral vertebrae.

Kurzanov (1989) later pointed out that *Y. shangyouensis* is the earliest ?"carnosaur" known from a preserved skull.

Dong, Zhou and Zhang (1983) described a second species, *Y. magnus*, based on an incomplete skull with mandible, three cervical, two dorsal and six caudal vertebrae, and complete pelvic girdle (CV V00216), from the early Upper Jurassic, Shangshaximiao Formation, on the outskirts of Yangchuan. As noted by Dong *et al.* (1983), *Y. magnus* is among the largest known members of the Megalosauridae. A second skeleton referred to this species, not yet formally described, was figured by Dong (1987) in his book *Dinosaurs from China*. The skull of this huge specimen measures 110 centimeters (almost 43 inches) in length.

Dong *et al.* (1978) referred *Yangchuanosaurus* to the Megalosauridae. *Yangchuanosaurus* seems to have the same general skeletal proportions as *Allosaurus*, the skull similar to that genus, but with a relatively shorter snout, apparently slenderer teeth, and fewer premaxillary, dentary, and maxillary teeth (R. E. Molnar, personal communication 1989). A double horn-like ridge on the nasal bones suggests a possible cranial crest. As in allosaurids, the upper temporal fossae merge above the parietals (see Kurzanov 1989).

As observed by Molnar, Kurzanov and Dong (1990) in their review of "Carnosauria" [as then understood], *Yangchuanosaurus* exhibits these "carnosaurian" features: Enlarged lacrimal aperture, reduced axial neural spine, ilium with narrow brevis shelf, and femur with wing-like lesser trochanter. The shallow surangular is a "noncarnosaurian" character, although, according to Molnar *et al.*, this seems to be a plesiomorphic feature that does not remove the genus from a position in or near "carnosaurian" ancestry.

Note: Paul (1988*c*), in his book *Predatory Dinosaurs of the World*, stated that *Y. shangyouensis*

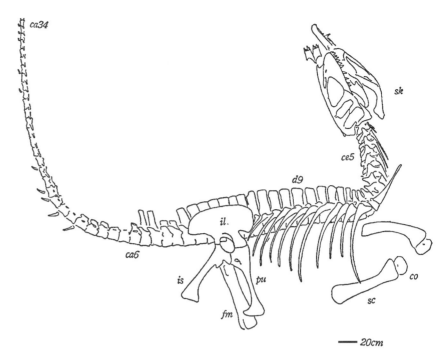

Yangchuanosaurus hepingensis, holotype incomplete skeleton, referred to *Sinraptor* (see entry). (After Gao 1992.)

and *Y. magnus* are conspecific (both species having been referred by him without compelling evidence to *Metriacanthosaurus*), the former supposedly representing a juvenile as evidenced by the poorly ossified ilium, tibia, and other bones.

The species *Y. hepingensis* Gao 1992 was referred by Currie and Zhao (993*a*) to the genus *Sinraptor*.

Key references: Dong (1987); Dong, Chang, Li and Zhou (1978); Dong, Zhou and Zhang (1983); Kurzanov (1989); Molnar, Kurzanov and Dong (1990).

YAVERLANDIA Galton 1971
Ornithischia: Genasauria: Cerapoda:
   Marginocephalia: Pachycephalosauria:
   Pachycephalosauridae.
Name derivation: "Yaverland [Battery]."
Type species: *Y. bitholus* Galton 1971.
Other species: [None.]
Occurrence: Wealden Marls, Isle of Wight,
   England.
Age: Early Cretaceous (Barremian).
Known material/holotype: MIWG 1530, frontal
   region of skull cap.

Diagnosis of genus (as for type species): Skull cap thickened with two small domes, one to each frontal; dorsal surface of skull cap pitted; prefrontal not excluding frontal from rim of orbit; postorbital not constricting in any way supratemporal fenestra (Galton 1971*a*).

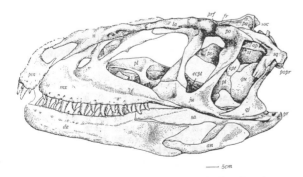

Yangchuanosaurus hepingensis, holotype skull, referred to *Sinraptor* (see entry). (After Gao 1992.)

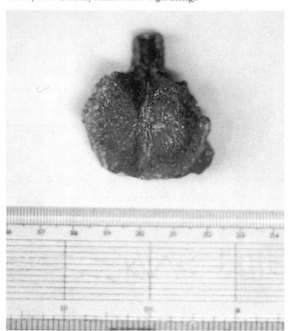

Yaverlandia bitholus, MIWG 1530, holotype frontal region of skull, dorsal view.

Comments: Stratigraphically the oldest known pachycephalosaurid and the only one having two domes, the genus *Yaverlandia* was founded on part of a thickened skull cap (MIWG 1530) discovered in the Wealden Marls (Lower Cretaceous), Upper Silty Bed north of the sea wall below Yaverland Battery, Sandown, Isle of Wight. Although the holotype had been mentioned more than once in the literature during the 1930s (including Swinton 1936, in an article about the Isle of Wight dinosaur fauna), it was not named, described, or figured until Galton (1971*a*) recognized it as representing a primitive pachycephalosaurid.

The skull cap is very small, measured by Galton as 45 millimeters in length and 47 millimeters in maximum width.

Comparing *Yaverlandia* with other ornithischians, Galton suggested that this genus was ancestral to *Stegoceras* and more derived *Pachycephalosaurus*. However, except for its thickening, the skull roof of *Yaverlandia* more closely resembles that of Jurassic hypsilophodontids such as *Hypsilophodon*.

Galton observed the following primitive characters in *Yaverlandia*: 1. Small size with no visible sutures, indicating an adult, frontals less than two-fifths as wide as in *Stegoceras*; 2. frontal region showing just small thickening with small dome to each frontal; 3. depressions on dorsal surface much less marked than in *Stegoceras*, with no well-defined grooves; 4. olfactory lobes probably not ventrally enclosed by bone; 5. large supratemporal opening not constricted by postorbital; 6. orbit partially visible in dorsal aspect; and 7. frontal not excluded from lateral orbital margin by prefrontal, which does not contact postorbital. According to Galton, in characters 1, 3 and 5, changes from *Yaverlandia* to *Stegoceras* continue on to the more derived *Pachycephalosaurus*.

Based on the thickening pattern of the skull roof, Sues and Galton (1987) hypothesized a structural sequence from *Yaverlandia* to *Pachycephalosaurus* and *Prenocephale*: In *Yaverlandia*, the frontals exhibit a dome-like thickening; in *Majungatholus*, there is a single massive frontal dome, olfactory lobes ventrally enclosed in bone, olfactory tracts (much as in other pachycephalosaurids) sloping downward relative to cerebrum; and in *Ornatotholus*, both frontals and parietals display a thickening, the holotype (AMNH 5450) retaining separate frontal and parietal domes. In more derived pachycephalosaurids, the fronto-parietal dome is more developed and involved with the nasals and medial portions of the postorbitals, the interfrontal and frontal-parietal sutures are obliterated, and the supratemporal fossae (in adults) are either very small or closed. In the derived pachycephalosaurids *Stegoceras* and *Tylocephale*, there are no distinct palpebral (supraorbital) I nor prominent tubercles on the postorbital. In the yet more derived *Pachycephalosaurus* and *Prenocephale*, the frontoparietal dome is greatly expanded posteriorly and includes postorbitals and squamosals; lateral and posterior shelves have been eliminated; (in adults) supratemporal fenestrae are closed; and prominent tubercles are present on the nasals.

Hopson (1979), in a paleoneurological study, questioned the pachycephalosaurid status of *Yaverlandia*. Giffin (1989) revived this question, pointing out that, although the cerebrum to orbits relationship in this genus is similar to that in other pachycephalosaurs, almost every other character shows marked differences. These differences, according to Giffin, do not pertain to the size or relative extent of the dome in *Yaverlandia*, as the endocrania in larger and smaller genera, both flat- and dome-headed forms, show typical pachycephalosaur characteristics (many observed by Hopson). Giffin stated that, if *Yaverlandia* belongs in the Pachycephalosauria, the endocranial characters typical of later pachycephalosaur genera had not yet evolved in this primitive form.

More recently, in a review of the Pachycephalosauria, Maryańska (1990) put *Y. bitholus* into the Pachycephalosauridae based on two characters not found in any other ornithischians, 1. thickening on the skull roof, and 2. textured nature of its dorsal surface.

Key references: Galton (1971*a*); Giffin (1989); Hopson (1979); Maryańska (1990); Sues and Galton (1987); Swinton (1936).

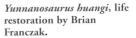

Yunnanosaurus huangi, life
restoration by Brian
Franczak.

YUNNANOSAURUS Yang [Young] 1942
Saurischia: Sauropodomorpha: Prosauropoda:
  Yunnanosauridae.
Name derivation: "Yunnan [province]" + Greek
  sauros = "lizard."
Type species: *Y. huangi* Yang [Young] 1942.
Other species: [None.]
Occurrence: Upper Lower Lufeng Series, Yunnan,
  People's Republic of China.
Age: Early Jurassic (Hettangian–Pliensbachian).
Known material: More than 20 partial to complete
  skeletons, two skulls, juvenile to adult.
Holotype: IVP AS V20, incomplete skeleton with
  skull and lower jaw, ?juvenile.

Diagnosis of genus (as for type species): Skull
proportionately tall, narrow; primitive characters
of skull including short snout, small external
nares, low dorsal maxillary process, narrow
lacrimal, large antorbital opening, and jaw articulation just slightly below maxillary tooth row
line; derived characters (also in *Lufengosaurus* and
Plateosaurus) including long, transversely wide
prefrontal and (relative to all prosauropods) transversely asymmetrical teeth with few marginal serrations and prominent wear features (Galton
1990*a*).

Comments: Basis for the family Yunnanosauridae Yang [formerly Young] 1942, the genus *Yunnanosaurus* was founded upon a skeleton (IVP AS V20)

discovered in the Dark Red Beds, Lower Lufeng
Series, of Huangchiatien, China.

Yang [Young] (1942*a*), observing that the postcranial skeleton was similar to that of *Lufengosaurus
hueni*, distinguished the type species *Y. huangi* primarily by the shape of the skull and teeth, and differences in proportions of the postcrania, these features
suggesting a juvenile individual.

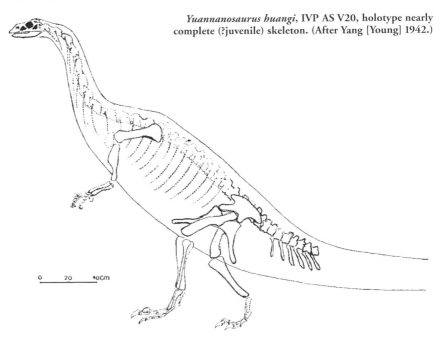

Yuannanosaurus huangi, IVP AS V20, holotype nearly
complete (?juvenile) skeleton. (After Yang [Young] 1942.)

Z

Later, Yang (1951) described a second species, *Y. robustus*, based on a fragmentary skull and incomplete postcranial skeleton from the same locality and horizon as *Y. huangi*, indicating an animal twice as large as the type species. Galton (1990a), in a review of the Prosauropoda, regarded this taxon as conspecific with *Y. huangi*.

Key references: Galton (1990a); Yang [Young] (1942a, 1951).

ZAPSALIS Cope 1876 [*nomen dubium*]—(See *Paronychodon*.}
Name derivation: Greek *za* = "very" + Greek *psalis* = "cutting shears."
Type species: *Z. abradens* Cope 1876 [*nomen dubium*].

ZEPHYROSAURUS Sues 1980
Ornithischia: Genasauria: Cerapoda: Ornithopoda: Hypsilophodontidae.
Name derivation: Greek *zephuros* = "west wind" + Greek *sauros* = "lizard."
Type species: *Z. schaffi* Sues 1980.
Other species: [None.]
Occurrence: Cloverly Formation, Montana, United States.
Age: Early Cretaceous (Late Aptian).
Known material/holotype: MCZ 4392, incomplete skull including excellently-preserved braincase and mandibular fragments, five vertebral centra, incomplete neural arches, numerous rib fragments.

Diagnosis of genus (as for type species): Dental formula consisting of five premaxillary and 14–15 maxillary teeth, step separating former from latter; both sides of crowns of maxillary and dentary teeth with numerous vertical ridges, crowns of maxillary teeth without sharp edges; maxilla with small boss on the lateral surface near anterior end; frontals relatively narrow; central portion or postorbital inflated; supraorbital short, massive; jugal with prominent, posterolaterally-projecting boss; quadrate with distinct dorsal cotylus, offset from pterygoid flange (Sues 1980b).

Comments: The genus *Zephyrosaurus* was founded upon a partial skull and some postcranial elements (MCZ 4392) belonging to the same individual, collected in 1975 by C. R. Schaff, from a red-brown silty sandstone of the Cloverly Formation, at Wolf Creek Canyon, Carbon County, Montana (Sues 1980b).

Sues stated that *Zephyrosaurus* represents a previously unknown hypsilophodontid lineage distinct from that represented by *Hypsilopodon*: and that *Zephyrosaurus* has a premaxilla structured similar to that of *Hypsilophodon* (but different from that of *Parksosaurus*), and shares with that genus such plesiomorphous characters as the presence of five teeth in each premaxilla and the complete dorsal separation of external nares by an internarial bar formed by the anterior premaxillary processes.

As shown by Sues, *Zephyrosaurus* differs from *Hypsilophodon* as follows: Slope of anterior margin of premaxilla steeper; crowns of premaxillary teeth lacking sharp edges; supraorbital shorter, seemingly occupying more dorsal position; postorbital with inflated central portion, anterior margin projecting into orbit; combined maximum width of frontals about equal to half their length (two-thirds of length in *Hypsilophodon* and *Parksosaurus*); jugal with boss; dorsal head of quadrate offset from pterygoid; and dentary teeth crowns apparently more symmetrical than maxillary crowns.

According to Sues, there is anatomical evidence in the skull of *Zephyrosaurus* that suggests possible cranial kinesis involving movement 1. of the braincase relative to the skull roof, 2. for a mesokinetic junction between frontal and parietal, and 3. for rotation of the maxillae (1. and 2. were postulated earlier by Galton 1974a for *Hypsilophodon*).

Sues pointed out that (as in *Hypsilophodon*; see Galton 1974a, 1983b) a small, laterally directed frontal peg fits into a small pit on the articular surface of the postorbital. These pegs allowed rotation at the frontal-parietal junction, if the parietal served as a mesokinetic junction with the axis of rotation passing through the pegs. The frontal-parietal suture is somewhat straight and the sutural surface rather smooth. The anterolateral portion of the parietal fits into a concavity on the posterior surfaces of frontal and postorbital, possibly ensuring close contact between frontal, parietal, and postorbital during hinge movements at the mesokinetic junction.

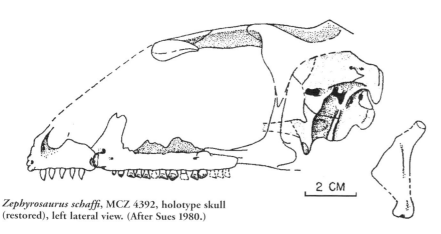

Zephyrosaurus schaffi, MCZ 4392, holotype skull (restored), left lateral view. (After Sues 1980.)

2 CM

Sues observed that the maxilla has a rounded anterior process that fits into a medial groove of the premaxilla and that there is no firm maxilla-jugal sutural junction, these features implying that the maxilla was probably capable of a slight amount of rotation about its longitudinal axis.

Wear facets on the maxillary teeth (and on maxillary and dentary teeth of *Hypsilophodon*), slightly concave transversely, suggested to Sues a certain amount of rotation of both upper and lower jaws. Galton (1983*b*) added that open-and-close jaw movements combined with slight mediolateral rotation were apparently also employed in *Zephyrosaurus*, *Hypsilophodon*, and *Dryosaurus*.

Key reference: Sues (1980*b*).

ZIGONGOSAURUS Hou, Chao and Chu 1976—(See *Omeisaurus*.)
Name derivation: "Zigong [city]" + Greek *sauros* = "lizard."
Type species: *Z. fuxiensis* Hou, Chao and Chu 1976.

ZIZHONGOSAURUS Dong, Zhou and Zhang 1983
Saurischia: Sauropodomorpha: Sauropoda: Vulcanodontidae.
Name derivation: "Zizhong [county]" + Greek *sauros* = "lizard."
Type species: *Z. chuanchensis* Dong, Zhou and Zhang 1983.

Other species: [None.]
Occurrence: Da'znhai Formation, Sichuan, People's Republic of China.
Age: Early Jurassic.
Known material/holotype: IVPP V9067, dorsal vertebra neural spine, distal end of pubis, fragmentary humerus.

Diagnosis of genus (as for type species): Small, primitive; dorsal vertebral spine high, broadening transversely; pubis plate-like, with some features reminiscent of prosauropod condition; forelimb rather long; humerus straight, round in cross-section (Dong, Zhou and Zhang 1983).

Comments: The genus *Zizhongosaurus* was founded upon partial postcrania (IVPP V9067) collected from the S Da'znhai Formation ("Rhaetic"-Lias, comparable to Lower Lufeng Series), of Luanshai, Zizhong County, Sichuan Basin, China (Dong Zhou, and Zhang 1983).

Dong *et al.* observed that *Z. chuanchensis* somewhat resembles the Indian sauropod *Barapasaurus* in diagnostic characters.

McIntosh (1990*b*), in his review of the Sauropoda, assigned *Z. chuanchengensis* to the Vulcanodontidae, noting that the dorsal spine is of moderate height and undivided, and that the diapophyses are stout and directed laterally. McIntosh commented that this is an important taxon, documenting the occurrence of a primitive sauropod in the Lower Jurassic of China.

Key references: Dong, Zhou and Zhang (1983); McIntosh (1990*b*)

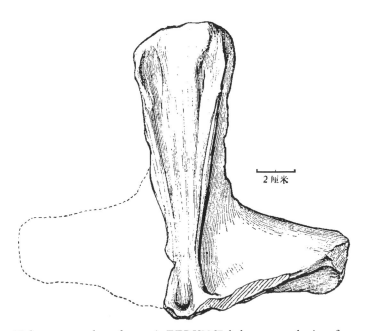

Zizhongosaurus chuanchengensis, IVPP V9067, holotype neural spine of dorsal vertebra. (After Dong, Zhou and Zhang 1983.)

IV: Nomina Nuda

Listed herein are doubtful genera that have appeared in the literature (*e.g.*, faunal lists, notes on taxa to be described), but without proper description following the rules for naming a new taxon. Some were described without a designated type species or holotype, and each is therefore regarded as a *nomen nudum* (*i.e.*, "naked name"). These genera have also appeared in other lists of taxa (*e.g.*, Olshevsky 1991, 1992); some may be formally redescribed at a future date, or preferably renamed:

CHANGDUSAURUS   Zhao 1986 [*nomen nudum*]

Ornithischia: Genasauria: Thyreophora: Stegosauria: Stegosauridae.

Name derivation: "Changdu [Basin, in Tibet]" + Greek *sauros* = "lizard."

Type species: *C. laminaplacodus* Zhao 1986 [*nomen nudum*].

Occurrence: China.

Age: Late Jurassic.

Comments: Name "*Changtusaurus*" first published by Zhao [formerly Chao] (1983*a*), then noted as representing an intermediate stegosaurid. *Changdusaurus* (and type species *C. laminaplacodus*) subsequently mentioned in article by Zhao (1986*a*) about Jurassic reptiles of China.

Key references: Zhao (1983*a*, 1986*a*).

CHAOYOUNGOSAURUS   Zhao 1983 [*nomen nudum*]

Ornithischia: Genasauria: Cerapoda: Marginocephalia: Pachycephalosauria.

Name derivation: "Chaoyoung [city in northeastern China]" + Greek *sauros* = "lizard."

Type species: *C. liaosiensis* Zhao 1986 [*nomen nudum*].

Age: Late Jurassic.

Comments: Generic name first published by Zhao (1983*a*), who proposed that it establish new ornithischian "superfamily" Chaoyoungosauridea (not internationally adopted); characterized as including small transitional ornithischians, with massive and strongly-developed jugal arch, three-lobed teeth with low crowns, weak and canini-form premaxillary teeth. *Chaoyoungosaurus* and superfamily regarded by Zhao as "proto-psitta-cosaurids," belonging to Pachycephalosauria, evolving from dinosaurs such as or similar to *Heterodontosaurus*. Type species *C. liaosiensis* later mentioned in article by Zhao (1986*a*) about Jurassic reptiles of China.

Key references: Zhao (1983*a*, 1986*a*).

CHINSHAKIANGOSAURUS   Zhao 1986 [*nomen nudum*]

Saurischia: Sauropodomorpha: Sauropoda *incertae sedis*.

Name derivation: "Chinshakiang [place in China]" + Greek *sauros* = "lizard."

Type species: *C. zhongheensis* Zhao 1986 [*nomen nudum*].

Age: Late Jurassic.

Known material: Femur.

Comments: Genus and type species, *C. chunghoensis,* mentioned by Yeh (1975). Same species altered by Zhao (1986*a*) to *C. zhonghonensis* (with more correct Chinese spelling) mentioned in article about Jurassic reptiles of China, with photograph of femur.

Key reference: Yeh (1975); Zhao (1986*a*).

DACHUNGOSAURUS   Zhao 1986 [*nomen nudum*]

Saurischia: Sauropodomorpha *incertae sedis*.

Name derivation: "Dachung [place in China]" + Greek *sauros* = "lizard."

Type species: *D. yunnanensis* Zhao (1986) [*nomen nudum*].

Occurrence: China.

Age: Jurassic.

Known material: Incomplete skeleton.

Comments: Genus and type species mentioned by Zhao [Chao] (1986*a*) in article about Jurassic reptiles of China, with photograph of incomplete skeleton *in situ* including vertebrae, ribs, and limb bones.

Key reference: Zhao (1986*a*).

DAMALASAURUS   Zhao 1983 [*nomen nudum*]

Saurischia: Sauropodomorpha: Sauropoda *incertae sedis*.

Name derivation: "Damal [place in China]" + Greek *sauros* = "lizard."

Type species: *D. magnus* Zhao [*nomen nudum*].

Occurrence: China.

Age: Middle Jurassic.

Comments: Genus considered by Zhao [Chao] (1983*a*) to be primitive sauropod. In subsequent article about Jurassic reptiles of China, type species *D. magnus* named by Zhao (1986*a*), referred to in photograph caption as *D. lati-costalis*.

Key references: Zhao (1983*a*, 1986*a*).

DANDAKOSAURUS   Yadagiri ?1989 [*nomen nudum*]

Saurischia: Theropoda *incertae sedis*.

Name derivation: "Dandak [place in China]" + Greek *sauros* = "lizard."

Type species: *D. indicus* Yadagiri 1990 [*nomen nudem*].

Occurrence: Kota Formation, Andhra Pradesh, India.

Age: Early Jurassic.

Comments: One of two Indian "carnosaurs" first reported by Yadagiri (1979) from Kota-Maleri beds, Kota Formation, Andhra Pradesh. In *Geological Survey of India Annual General Report* for 1982-83, 117 (p. 223); type species *D. indicus* announced as designation of new "carnosaurian dinosaur" with "certain similarities with 'Sinosaurus triassicus'."

Key reference: Yadagiri (1979).

DIDANODON   Osborn 1902 [*nomen nudum*]—(See *Lambeosaurus*.)

Name derivation: Greek *di* = "two" + Latin *danio* = "[fish]" + Greek *odous* = "tooth."

Type species: *D. altus* Osborn 1902 [*nomen nudum*].

DORYPHOSAURUS   Nopcsa 1916 [*nomen nudum*]—(See *Kentrosaurus*.)

Name derivation: Greek *dory* = "spear" Greek *phora* = "producing" + Greek *sauros* = "lizard."

Type species: *D. aethiopicus* (Hennig 1915) [*nomen nudum*].

EOLOSAURUS   Bonaparte 1986 [*nomen nudum*]—(See *Aeolosaurus*.)

Name derivation: "Aeolus [in Greek mythology, god of winds]" + Greek *sauros* = "lizard."

Type species: *E. rionegrinus* Bonaparte 1986 [*nomen nudum*].

KOREANOSAURUS   Kim 1979 [*nomen nudum*]—(=?*Deinonychus*)

Saurischia: Theropoda: Tetanurae: Avetheropoda: Coelurosauria: Maniraptora: Dromaeosauridae: ?Velociraptorinae.

Name derivation: "Korea" + Greek *sauros* = "lizard."

Occurrence: Korea.

Age: Late Cretaceous.

Known material: Femur.

Holotype: Femur.

Comments: Referred by Kim (1979) to Deinodontidae; then tentatively referred by Kim (1983) to Hypsilophodontidae; Kim later stated that genus may be synonymous with *Deinonychus* (H. M. Kim, personal communication to Olshevsky 1986).

Key references: Kim (1979, 1983).

KUNMINGOSAURUS   Zhao 1986 [*nomen nudum*]

Saurischia: Sauropodomorpha: Sauropoda *incertae sedis*.

Name derivation: "Kunming [place in China]" + Greek *sauros* = "lizard."

Type species: *K. wudingi* Zhao 1986 [*nomen nudum*].

Other species: [None.]

Occurrence: Yunnan, China.

Age: Early Jurassic.

Known material: Partial skeleton.

Comments: Apparently primitive sauropod, genus mentioned, but not described, in article by Zhao (1986a) about Jurassic system of China. Type species *K. utdingensis* given in plate caption depicting partial mounted skeleton, including pelvis, hindlimb, and at least anterior part of tail. "Complete" (possibly restored) skeleton displayed at "The Age of Dinosaurs in Japan and China" touring exhibit from China. Entire mounted skeleton (skull sculpted) shown in photograph in Dong, Hasegawa and Azuma's (1990) dinosaur exhibition guidebook, *The Age of Dinosaurs in Japan and China*. Referred to by Dong (personal communication to Olshevsky 1991) as "shunosaurid."

Key reference: Zhao (1986).

LANCANGOSAURUS   Dong, Zhou and Zhang 1983 [*nomen nudum*]—(See *Datousaurus*.)

LANCANJIANGOSAURUS   Zhao 1986 [*nomen nudum*]

Saurischia: Sauropodomorpha: Sauropoda *incertae sedis*.

Name derivation: "Lancangian [place in China]" + Greek *sauros* = "lizard."

Type species: *L. cahuensis* Zhao 1986 [*nomen nudum*].

Occurrence: China.

Age: Late Jurassic.

Comments: Referred without type species by Zhao [Chao] (1983a) to proposed new superfamily Bothrosauropodoidea, diagnosed as follows: Teeth typically spatulate; inner surface of tooth crown concave, outer surface convex; middle

ridge reduced; serrations increased; postcranial skeleton very massive, strongly constructed; derived features including vertebrae with cavernous pleurocoels, long girdle and limb bones; ilium with strong and massive pubic peduncle; femur straight and massive, with poorly-developed, proximally located fourth trochanter.
L. cahuensis mentioned by Zhao (1986*a*) in article about Jurassic system of China, field photograph showing specimen in rock matrix.
Key references: Zhao (1983*a*, 1986*a*).

LIKHOELESAURUS   Ellenberger 1970 [*nomen nudum*]
Saurischia: ?Theropoda *incertae sedis*.
Name derivation: "Li Khoele [town in Lesotho, South Africa] + Greek *sauros* = "lizard."
Type species: *L. ingens* Ellenberger 1970 [*nomen nudum*].
Occurrence: Lesotho, southern Africa.
Age: Late Triassic.
Known material/holotype: Teeth, ?bones.
Comments: Founded on theropod-like teeth reported by Ellenberger (1970), collected from Li Khoele, Lesotho, resembling teeth of nondinosaurian *Basutodon*, about 70 millimeters (2.7 inches) in length.
Key reference: Ellenberger (1970).

MEGACERVIXOSAURUS   Zhao 1983 [*nomen nudum*]
Saurischia: Sauropodomorpha: Sauropoda: ?Diplodocidae.
Name derivation: Greek *megas* = "large" + Latin *cervix* = "neck" + Greek *sauros* = "lizard."
Type species: *M. tibetensis* Zhao 1986 [*nomen nudum*].
Occurrence: China.
Age: Late Cretaceous.
Comments: Referred by Zhao [Chao] (1983*a*) to proposed new "superfamily" Homalosauropoidea, diagnosed as follows: Teeth peg-like, with long, thin crowns, no serrations, and cylindrical roots; postcranial skeleton advanced, vertebrae with well-developed pleurocoels, posterior cervical and anterior dorsal neural spines bifurcated; sacral centra firmly coossified, anterior and posterior ends projecting markedly; ilium very massive; pubic foramen very large. Type species *M. tibetensis* mentioned by Zhao (1986*b*) in article about Jurassic system of China.
Key references: Zhao (1983*a*, 1986*b*).

MICRODONTOSAURUS   Zhao 1983 [*nomen nudum*]
Saurischia: Sauropodomorpha: Sauropoda *incertae sedis*.
Name derivation: Greek *mikros* = "small" + Greek *odous* = "tooth" + Greek *sauros* = "lizard."
Type species: *M. dayensis* Zhao 1983 [*nomen nudum*].
Occurrence: Asia.
Age: Late Cretaceous.
Comments: Referred by Zhao [Chao] (1983*a*) to Homalosauropodoidea (see *Megacervixosaurus* entry, this section).
Key references: Zhao (1983*a*).

NEUQUENSAURUS   Powell *see in* Bonaparte 1987 [*nomen nudum*] — (=?*Loricosaurus*, ?*Saltasaurus*)
Saurischia: Prosauropodomorpha: Sauropoda: Titanosauria: Titanosauridae.
Name derivation: "Neuquen [city in Argentina]" + Greek *sauros* = "lizard."
Type species: *N. australis* (Lydekker 1893).
Occurrence: Neuquen, Argentina.
Age: Late Cretaceous.
Known material: Incomplete postcranial remains, vertebrae.
Holotype: Caudal vertebrae.
Comments: Generic name first published by Bonaparte (1987); type species *N. australis* by Powell (1987). Description included in Powell's doctoral dissertation. Originally described by Lydekker (1893*b*) as new species of *Titanosaurus*, *T. australis*. Tentatively referred by McIntosh (1990*b*) to *Saltasaurus* (see entry).
Key references: Bonaparte (1987); Lydekker (1893*b*); McIntosh (1990*b*); Powell (1987, 1980).

NGEXISAURUS   Zhao 1983 [*nomen nudum*]
Saurischia: Theropoda: Coelurosauria *incertae sedis*.
Name derivation: "Ngex [place in China]" + Greek *sauros* = "lizard."
Type species: *N. dapukaensis* Zhao 1986 [*nomen nudum*].
Occurrence: China.
Age: Jurassic.
Comments: Genus named by Zhao [Chao] (1983*a*), referred to as "coelurosaur." Type species *N. dapukaensis* named by Zhao (1986*a*) in article about Jurassic system of China.
Key references: Zhao [Chao] (1983*a*, 1986*a*).

NYASAURUS Charig (*see in* Harland *et al.* 1967) [*nomen nudum*]
?Saurischia.
Name derivation: *Nyasa* ["Nyasaland," former name of Malawi] + Greek *sauros* = "lizard."
Type species: *N. cromptoni* Charig 1967 [*nomen nudum*].
Occurrence: Manda Formation, Ruhuhu Basin, Tanzania.
Age: Middle Triassic.
Holotype: [Unspecified material], BMNH collection.
Comments: Regarded by Charig as possibly anchisaurid prosauropod. If dinosaurian, one of earliest of all known dinosaurian genera.
Key Referenece: Charig (*see in* Harland *et al.* 1967) [*nomen nudum*].

ORNITHOIDES Osborn 1924 [*nomen nudum*]—(Preoccupied, Matthew 1903; see *Saurornithoides*.)
Name derivation: Greek *ornis* = "bird" + Latin *oides* = "form."
Type species: *O. oshiensis* Osborn 1924 [*nomen nudum*].

OSHANOSAURUS Zhao 1986 [*nomen nudum*]
Ornithischia: Ornithopoda: ?Heterodontosauridae.
Name derivation: "Oshih [Formation]" + Greek *sauros* = "lizard."
Type species: *O. youngi* Zhao 1986 [*nomen nudum*].
Occurrence: ?Mongolian People's Republic.
Age: Early Jurassic.
Comments: Possibly "geranosaur," named by Zhao (1986*a*) in article about Jurassic system of China.
Key references: Zhao (1986*a*).

OVORAPTOR Osborn 1924 [*nomen nudum*]—(See *Velociraptor*.)
Name derivation: Latin *ovum* = "egg" + Latin *raptor* = "robber."
Type species: *O. djadochtari* Osborn 1924.

ROCCOSAURUS Van Heerden *see in* Anderson and Cruickshank 1978 [*nomen nudum*]
Saurischia: Sauropodomorpha: Prosauropoda: ?Melanorosauridae.
Type species: *R. tetrasacralis* Van Heerden *see in* Kitching and Raath 1984 [*nomen nudum*].
Occurrence: South Africa.
Age: Late Triassic.

Comments: Genus listed by Van Heerden (*see in* Anderson and Cruickshank 1978) in faunal list of southern Africa. Type species *R. tetrasacralis* named by Van Heerden (*see in* Kitching and Raath 1984) in subsequent list. Reportedly four sacral vertebrae and rather sharp teeth.
Key references: Anderson and Cruickshank (1978); Kitching and Raath (1984).

SANGONGHESAURUS Zhao 1983 [*nomen nudum*]
Ornithischia: Genasauria: Thyreophora: Ankylosauria: Ankylosauridae.
Comments: Referred by Zhao [Chao] (1983*a*) to proposed new superfamily Polysacralosauroidea, regarded as belonging to Pachycephalosauria and derived from Middle Jurassic primitive scelidosaurids, diagnosed as follows: Skulls completely or almost entirely covered by dermal ossifications, with closed supratemporal fenestra and no antorbital opening; six to nine sacral vertebrae; well-developed armor on back of neck and trunk and around tail; dorsal armor including large keeled plates, laterally projecting spines, smaller intermediate ossicles.
Key reference: Zhao (1983*a*).

SHUOSAURUS Chow 1979 [*nomen nudum*]—(See *Shunosaurus*.)
Name derivation: "Shuo [old Chinese spelling of Sichuan, province of China]" + Greek *sauros* = "lizard."

TEINCHISAURUS Dong 1992 [*nomen nudum*]—(See *Tianchisaurus*, "genera" section.)
Name derivation: [?Variant or ?misspelling of *Tianchisaurus*.]

TENCHISAURUS [Anonymous] 1981 [*nomen nudum*]—(See *Tianchisaurus*, "genera" section.)
Name derivation: [?Variant or ?misspelling of *Tianchisaurus*.]

THEROSAURUS Fitzinger 1843 [*nomen nudum*]—(See *Iguanodon*.)
Name derivation: Greek *theros* = "summer" + Greek *sauros* = "lizard."
Type species: *T. mantelli* (Meyer 1823).

THOTOBOLOSAURUS Ellenberger 1970 [*nomen nudum*]

Saurischia: Sauropodomorpha *incertae sedis*.

Name derivation: "Thobol" + Greek *sauros* = "lizard."

Type species: *T. mabeatae* Ellenberger 1970 [*nomen nudum*]

Occurrence: Lower Stormberg Series, Lesotho.

Age: Late Triassic (Carnian or Norian).

Comments: Apparently the so-called "Maphutseng dinosaur" mentioned by Crompton and Charig (1965). According to Ellenberger (1970), a large, possibly quadrupedal melanorosaurid very much like true sauropod, corresponding to fossil footprints which Ellenberger named *Pseudotetrasauropus*, latter synonymized with nondinosaurian ichnogenus "*Brachychirotherium.*" [=*Chirotherium*] by Olsen and Galton (1984).

Key references: Crompton and Charig (1965); Ellenberger (1970); Olsen and Galton (1984).

TIANCHUNGOSAURUS Zhao 1983 [*nomen nudum*]

Ornithischia: ?Pachycephalosauria.

Age: Early-Late Jurassic.

Comments: Regarded by Zhao (1983*a*) as very primitive pachycephalosaur; if correct assessment, then notably older than *Yaverlandia*, the most primitive known member of Pachycephalosauria.

Key references: Zhao [Chao] (1983*a*).

ULTRASAURUS Kim 1983 [*nomen nudum*]

Saurischia: Sauropodomorpha: Sauropoda *incertae sedis*.

Name derivation: Latin *ultra* = "beyond" + Greek *sauros* = "lizard."

Type species: *U. tabriensis* Kim 1983 [*nomen dubium*].

Occurrence: Dogyedong Formation, Kyongsang Pukdo, South Korea.

Age: Early Cretaceous.

Known material/Holotype: DGBU 1973, partial ?ulna, partial ?neural spine of caudal vertebra.

Comments: Founded upon large portion of apparent ulna and part of apparent caudal neural spine (DGBU 1973), collected from a cliff in the Gugyedong Formation, Hayang Group, near Bongam Pass, southwest of Tabri station, Geumseong-myeon, Euiseong-gun, North Gyeongsang-do, South Korea. ?Ulna identified by Kim as sauropod mainly because of size, supposedly indicating animal much larger than [then not yet formally named or described] *Supersaurus*. Material reportedly misidentified, representing somewhat smaller sauropod than estimated by Kim.

Notes: Two versions of Kim's 1983 paper issued, the first (apparently an offprint) without specific name designated, the second naming *U. tabriensis*, papers otherwise virtually identical. Not identical with *Ultrasaurus* Jensen 1985.

Key reference: Kim (1983).

VECTENSIA Delair 1982 [*nomen nudum*]

Name derivation: Latin *vector* = "bearer" + Latin *ensis* = "sword."

Key reference: Delair (1982).

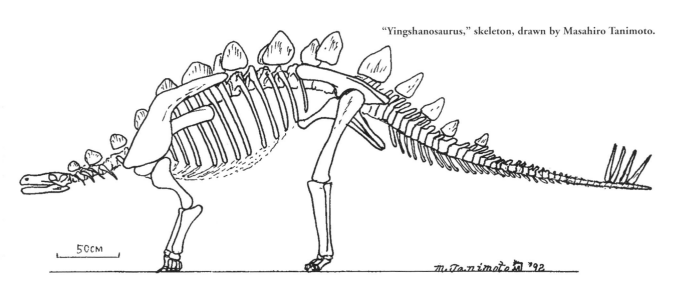

"Yingshanosaurus," skeleton, drawn by Masahiro Tanimoto.

50CM

YINGSHANOSAURUS   Zhou and Tanimoto
[*nomen nudum*]

Ornithischia: Genasauria: Thyreophora:
   Stegosauria: Stegosauridae.

Name derivation: "Yingshan [place in China]" +
   Greek *sauros* = "lizard."

Occurrence: Yingshan, Sichuan Province, China.

Age: Latest Late Jurassic.

Known material/holotype: Almost complete
   skeleton.

Comments: Generic named first mentioned by
   Dong, Zhou and Zhang (1983), and Zhou
   (1983). Mounted skeleton displayed at paleontological exhibitions in Japan (1992–3), total length
   about 5 meters (about 17 feet), with wing-like
   parasacral spines (possibly only present in males).
   Formal description completed but not yet
   published.

Key references: Dong, Zhou and Zhang (1983);
   Zhou (1985).

V: Excluded Genera

This list comprises taxa that have appeared in the paleontological literature and which had been, either in their original or some later publication, classified as dinosaurian genera, although they are generally not now regarded as such. Some names are still valid, such as *Archaeopteryx*; most others are no longer considered valid names.

AACHENOSAURUS Smets 1888
Petrified wood.

AGGIOSAURUS Ambayrac 1913
Crocodile.

ALBISAURUS Fritsch 1905
Non-dinosaurian reptile.

ANKISTRODON Huxley 1865—
(=*Epicampodon*)
"Thecodontian."

ANTHODON Owen 1876
Cotylosaur.

ARCHAEOPTERYX Meyer
1861—(=*Archaeornis*,
Griphosaurus)
Mesozoic bird.

ARCTOSAURUS Adams 1875
Nondinosaurian reptile;
?trilophosaur.

AVALONIA Seeley 1898—(Preoccupied, Walcott 1889; see *Avalonianus*.)

AVALONIANUS Kuhn 1958—
(=*Avalonia*).
"Thecodontian."

AVIPES Huene 1932
Non-dinosaurian reptile.

AVISAURUS Brett-Surman and
Paul 1985
Enantiornithine bird.

BASUTODON Huene 1931
"Thecodontian."

BATHYGNATHUS Leidy 1854
Pelycosaur.

BRASILEOSAURUS Huene 1931
Crocodile.

CHIENKOSAURUS Yang
[Young] 1942—(=*Hsisosuchus*).
Crocodile.

CLADEIDON Owen 1841
"Thecodontian."

CLARENCEA Brink 1959
"Thecodontian."

CLEPSYSAURUS Lea 1853—
(=*Palaeoctonus*, *Suchoprion*)
Phytosaur (crocodile-like
archosaur).

COLONOSAURUS Marsh
1872—(=*Ichthyornis dispar*)
Mesozoic bird.

COSESAURUS Ellenberger and
Villalta 1974
?Megalancosaurid reptile.

CYBELE Reichenbach 1852
Trilobite (invertebrate).

DAKOSAURUS Quenstedt 1856
Crocodile.

DASYGNATHOIDES Kuhn
1877—(See *Ornithosuchus*.)

DASYGNATHUS Huxley 1877—
(See *Ornithosuchus*.)

DEINOSUCHUS Holland
1909—(=*Phobosuchus*)
Crocodile.

DORATODON Seeley 1881—
(=*Crocodilus carcharidens* Bunzel
1871, *Rhadinosaurus*).
Crocodile.

ELOPTERYX Andrews 1913
Mesozoic bird.

EPICAMPODON Huxley
1865—(See *Ankistrodon*.)

EUPODOSAURUS Boulenger
1891
Nothosaur.

GALESAURUS Owen 1859
Procynosuchian reptile.

GOBIPTERYX Elzanowski 1974
Cretaceous bird.

GRACILISUCHUS Romer 1972
"Thecodontian."

GWYNEDDOSAURUS Bock
1945
Lepidosaur.

HALLOPUS Marsh 1881
Crocodile.

HERBSTOSAURUS Casamiquela
1974
Pterosaur

HYPSELORHACHIS Charig
1967
"Thecodontian."

JURAPTERYX Howgate 1985
Mesozoic bird.

LAGERPETON Romer 1971
"Thecodontian."

LAGOSUCHUS Romer 1971
Ornithodiran, pre-dinosaurian archosaur.

LEWISUCHUS Romer 1972
Crocodylotarsan belonging
to unnamed clade near base
of Suchia.

LONGISQUAMA Sharov 1970
Longisquamid reptile.

MACELOGNATHUS Marsh
1884
Crocodile.

MACROSCELOSAURUS Münster (*see in* Meyer 1847)
See *Tanystropheus*.

MEGALANCOSAURUS Calzavara, Muscio and Wild 1980
Megalancosaurid reptile.

MICROSAUROPS Kuhn 1963
"Renaming" of
misprint/nonexistant taxon
"Microsaurus."

MONONYCHUS Perle, Norell,
Chiappe and Clark 1993—(See
Mononykus.)

MONONYKUS Norrell, Chiappe
and Clark 1992—(=*Mononychus*)
Cretaceous flightless bird.

NUTHETES Owen 1854
Non-dinosaurian; ?lepidosaur.

OGLIOSAURUS Seeley 1881
Crocodile.

ORNITHOSUCHUS Newton
1894—(=*Dasygnathoides*, *Dasygnathus*)
"Thecodontian."

PALAEOCTONUS Cope 1877—
(See *Clepsysaurus*.)

PALAEONORNIS Emmons
1857—(=*Rutiodon carolinense*)
Phytosaur

PALAEOPTERYX Jensen 1981
Mesozoic bird.

PNEUMATOARTHRUS Cope
1871—(=*Archelon*?)
Turtle.

POPOSAURUS Mehl 1915
"Thecodontian."

PROCEROSAURUS Huene
1902—(See *Tanystropheus*.)

PSEUDOLAGOSUCHUS Arcucci 1987

Excluded Genera

"Thecodontian."

RACHITREMA   Sauvage 1883—(=?*Merriama*)
Ichthyosaur.

RHADINOSAURUS   Seeley 1881—(See *Doratodon*.)

RHOPALODON   Waldheim 1841
Titanosuchian reptile.

RIOJASUCHUS   Bonaparte 1969
"Thecodontian."

SALTOPOSUCHUS   Huene 1921
"Thecodontian."

SCLEROMOCHLUS   Woodward 1907
"?Thecodontian."

SMILODON   Plieninger 1846—(See *Tanystropheus*.)

SPINOSUCHUS   Huene 1932
"Thecodontian."

STEREOSAURUS   Seeley 1869
Plesiosaur

SUCCINODON   Huene 1941
Filled burrowings of bivalve mollusk *Kuphus*.

SUCHOPRION   Cope 1878—(See *Clepsysaurus*.)

TANYSTROPHEUS   Meyer 1852
Prolacertilian reptile.

TANYSTROSUCHUS   Kuhn 1963
Nondinosaurian reptile.

TAPINOSAURUS   Rabeck 1925
?Plesiosaur

TERATOSAURUS   Meyer 1861
"Thecodontian."

TRIALESTES   Bonaparte 1982—(=*Triassolestes*)
"Thecodontian."

TRIASSOLESTES   Reig 1963—(Preoccupied, Tillyard 1918; see *Trialestes*.)

UNICEROSAURUS   Armstrong 1987
Fish.

VENATIOSUCHUS   Bonaparte 1972
"Thecodontian."

YEZOSAURUS   Obata and Muramoto 1977
Plesiosaur.

ZANCLODON   Plieninger 1846—(See *Tanystropheus*.)

ZATOMUS   Cope 1871
Nondinosaurian reptile.

Restoration by R. Ehrlich of *Tanystropheus longobardicus*, a Middle Triassic prolacertilian. At various times, *Tanystropheus* has been listed as a dinosaur. (After Peyer.)

First complete skeleton (cast of "London specimen," BMNH collection) of *Archaeopteryx lithographica*, a Late Jurassic bird sometimes regarded as a feathered dinosaur (although all birds, extinct and extant, are now generally classified as maniraptoran theropods).

Photo by John Weinstein, courtesy the Field Museum (neg. #GEO85870).

Archaeopteryx lithographica restored as traditionally avian by Arthur Hayward, a paleontologist with The Natural History Museum, London.

Courtesy the Field Museum (neg. #GEO81058).

Excluded Genera

Giant Cretaceous crocodile *Deinosuchus hatcheri*, founded upon fragmentary remains, part of which (including scutes) was considered provisionally to be ankylosaurian, here menacing a young *Chasmosaurus belli*.

Art by Walter Ferguson. Courtesy Department Library Services, American Museum of Natural History (neg. #324784).

Photo by J. Beckett, 1995, courtesy Department Library Services, American Museum of Natural History (neg. #2A21967).

Reconstructed skeleton (cast) of *Monokykus olecrans*, usually classified as a bird, although some paleontologists consider this genus to be a theropod.

Ornithosuchus longidens, a Late Triassic ornithosuchian archosaur once classified as a primitive theropod related to mega-losaurs or the ancestor of "carnosaurs," restored by Neave Parker.

Courtesy Natural History Museum (London) (postcard #G-78).

Courtesy Natural History Museum (London) (postcard #G-87).

Scleromochlus taylori, a Late Triassic pseudosuchian archosaur sometimes regarded as an ancestor to pterosaurs, but once thought of as an ancestral theropod, restored by Neave Parker to suggest the latter.

Occupying an honored place in the Field Museum's Stanley Field Hall since 1956, this skeleton, originally named *Gorcosaurus libratus* and later *Albertosaurus libratus,* looms over that of *Lambeosaurus lambei.* The former may be imagined as gazing toward a future of fascinating new dinosaur discoveries, understandings, and theories—some of them leading to a possible separation, again, of *Gorgosaurus* and *Albertosaurus* (see entry), and also the referral of this skeleton to yet another genus, *Daspletosaurus.* In 1983, both skeletons were moved to the museum's new "DNA to Dinosaurs" exhibit, with *A. libratus* remounted in a modern, more dynamic pose.

A List of Abbreviations

The following list of abbreviations refers to museums and other institutions where fossil specimens are housed:

AC Amherst College Museum, Amherst, Massachusetts

AIS Académie Impériale des Sciences, Belles-Lettres et Arts de Marseille, France

AM Australia Museum, Sydney

AMNH American Museum of Natural History, New York, NY

AMSA Albany Museum, South Africa

ANSP Academy of Natural Sciences of Philadelphia, Pennsylvania

BB Buffalo Bill Museum, Cody, Wyoming

BHI Black Hills Institute, South Dakota

BHM Black Hills Museum of Natural History, Hill City, South Dakota

BM Bristol Museum, England

BMNH The Natural History Museum, London; formerly British Museum (Natural History)

BNHM Beijing Natural History Museum, China

BPI Bernard Price Institute for Palaeontological Research, University of the Witwatersrand, Johannesburg, South Africa

BSNH Boston Society of Natural History, Massachusetts

BSP Bayerische Staatssammlung für Paläontologie und historische Geologie, Munich, Germany

BYU Brigham Young University Vertebrate Paleontology, Provo, Utah

CCG Chengdu College of Geology, China

CCM Carter County Museum, Ekalaka, Montana

CEU College of Eastern Utah Prehistoric Museum, Price, Utah

CM Carnegie Museum, Pittsburgh, Pennsylvania

CMGP Central Museum of Geological Prospecting, St. Petersburg, Russia

CMN Canadian Museum of Nature, Ottawa [see also NMC]

CPS Wyoming-Colorado Paleontographical Society

CS Musée des Dinosaures d'Espéraza (Aude), France

CUP Catholic University of Peking [now Beijing], China

CV Municipal Museum of Chungking, People's Republic of China

DGBU Department of Geology, Busan University, Korea

DINO [formerly **DNM**] Dinosaur National Monument, Jensen, Utah

DMNH Denver Museum of Natural History, Colorado

DPMWA Dorothy Page Museum of Wasilla, Alaska

FGGUB Facultatea de Geologie si Geofisca, Universitatea Bucuresti, Bucharest

FMNH The Field Museum; formerly Field Museum of Natural History, and Chicago Natural History Museum, Chicago, Illinois

FPM Fukuka Prefectural Museum, Fukui, Japan

FSL Collections de la Faculté des Sciences de Lyon, France

FUB Freie Universität, Berlin

GI Geological Institute Section of Palaeontology and Stratigraphy, the Academy of Sciences of the Mongolian People's Republic, Ulan Bator

GIUV Geological Institute, University of Vienna, Austria

GPIT Geological Museum, University of Tübingen, Tanzania

GSC Geological Survey of Canada, Ottawa

GSI Geological Survey of India, Hyderabad

GSM Geologic Museum, Institute of Geologic Sciences, London, England

GSP Geological Survey of Portugal

HGM Hunan Geological Museum, Changsha, China

HMN Humboldt Museum für Naturkunde, East Berlin, Germany

IG Institute of Geology, Beijing, China

IGM Geological Institute, Mongolian Academy of Sciences, Ulaan Baatar, Mongolia

IM Indian Museum, Calcutta, India

IPHG Institut für Paläontologie, Academia Sinica, Beijing, China

IPSN Instituto de Paleontologia de Sabadell, Spain

IRSNB Institut Royal des Sciences Naturelles de Belgique

ISI Indian Statistical Institute, Calcutta

IVPP AS Institute of Vertebrate Paleontology and Paleoanthropology, Academia Sinica, Beijing, China

IZ Institute of Zoology, Academy of Sciences of the Kazakhstan, CLCP, Alma-Ata, Russia

KMNH Kitakyushu Museum of Natural History, Kitakyushu, Japan

KMV Kunming Municipal Museum, Kunming, Yunnan, China

KU [or **KUMNA**] University of Kansas Museum of Natural History, Lawrence

LACM Natural History Museum of Los Angeles County,

A List of Abbreviations

	California; also, Los Angeles County Museum of Natural History
LPFU	Lehrstuhl für Paläontologie, Freie Universitat, Berlin, Germany
LVP-GSC	Laboratory of Vertebrate Paleontology, Geological Survey of China
MACN	Museo Argentino de Ciencias Naturales, Buenos Aires, Argentina
MAFI	Magyar Allami Foldtani Intezet, Budapest
MC	Museo de Cipolleti
MCZ	Museum of Comparative Zoology, Harvard, Cambridge, Massachusetts
MDE	Musée des Dinosaures, Espéraza, France
MDP	Museum de Poligny
MG	Museum of Zoology, China
MGSP	Museum of the Geological Survey of Portugal, Lisbon
MHNN	Musée d'Histoire Naturelle de Normandie, Friadel, Orbec, France
MIWG	Museum of the Isle of Wight Geology, Sandown, England
MJH	Muzeul Judetean Hunedoara, Deva, Romania
MLP	Museo de la Plata, Buenos Aires, Argentina
MNA	Museum of Northern Arizona, Flagstaff
MNHN	Muséum National d'Histoire Naturelle, Paris, France
MNMB	Magyar Nenzeti Múseum, Budapest, Hungary
MOR	Museum of the Rockies, Bozeman, Montana
MPCA	Museuo de Ciencias Naturales, Universidad Nacional del Comahue, Buenos Aires, Neuquén, Argentina (see also MUCP)
MPM	Milwaukee Public Museum, Wisconsin
MSA	Museum of Science and Art, Dublin, Ireland
MUCP	Museo de Ciencias Naturales de la Universidad Nacional del Comahue, Neuquén, Argentina (see also MPCA)
MUO	Stovall Museum of Science and History, University of Oklahoma
MWC	Museum of Western Colorado, Grand Junction
NIGP	Nanking Institute of Geology and Palaeontology, Academia Sinica, China

NMB	Naturhistorisches Museum, Basel, Switzerland
NMBA	National Museum, Buenos Aires, Argentina
NMC	National Museum of Canada, Ottawa [see also CMN]
NMMNH	New Mexico Museum of Natural History and Science, Albuquerque
NMV	National Museum of Victoria, Melbourne, Australia
NMW	Naturhistorisches Museum Wien, Austria
NSM	National Science Museum, Tokyo
OMNH	Oklahoma Museum of Natural History, University of Oklahoma, Norman
OUM	Oxford University Museum, England
PEFO	Petrified Forest, Arizona
PGL	Preussische Geologische Landesanstalt, Berlin, Germany
PIN	Paleontological Institute, Academy of Science, Russia
PMAA	Palaeontological Collections, Provincial Museum and Archives of Alberta, Canada
PMU	Paleontological Museum, Uppsala, Sweden
PU	Princeton University, Princeton, New Jersey
PVL	Paleontologia de Vertebrados de la Fundación Miguel Lillo, Argentina
PVPH	Paleontologa de Vertebrados, Museo del Neuquén, Argentina
P.W.	Paleontological collection, Department of Mineral Resources, Bangkok, Thailand
QG	Queen Victoria Museum, Salisbury, England
QM	Queensland Museum, Australia
QVM	Queen Victoria Museum, Salisbury, Zimbabwe, Rhodesia
RCS	Royal College of Surgeons, London, England
ROM	Royal Ontario Museum, Toronto, Canada
RTMP (formerly **TMP**)	Royal Tyrrell Museum of Paleontology, Drumheller, Alberta, Canada
SAM	South African Museum, Cape Town, South Africa
SDM	Stroud and District Museum, Stroud, Gloucestershire, England

SDSM	South Dakota School of Mines and Technology, Rapid City
SM	Senckenberg Museum, Germany
SMC	Sedgwick Museum, Cambridge, England
SMNS	Staatliches Museum für Naturkunde, Stuttgart, Germany
SMU	Shuler Museum of Paleontology, Southern Methodist University, Dallas, Texas
TMM	Texas Memorial Museum, The University of Texas, Austin
TRM	Transvaal Museum, South Africa
TTU	Texas Tech University Museum, Lubbock
UA	University of Arizona, Tucson
UCDBA	University of Chicago, Department of Biology and Anatomy, Chicago, Illinois
UCL	University College, London, England
UCM	University of Colorado Museum, Boulder
UCMP	University of California Museum of Paleontology, Berkeley
UM	University of Marburg, Germany
UMMP	University of Michigan Museum of Paleontology
UNM	University of New Mexico, Albuquerque
UNPSJB	Universidad Nacional de la Patagonia San Juan Bosco, Argentina
UNT	Universidad Nacional de Tucumn, Argentina
UOM	University of Missouri, Kansas City
USNM	National Museum of Natural History [formerly United States National Museum], Smithsonian Institution, Washington, D.C.
UTEP	Centennial Museum, University of Texas, El Paso
UU	University of Upsala Paleontological Museum, Sweden
UUVP	University of Utah Vertebrate Paleontology Collection, Salt Lake City
UVP	Utah State Vertebrate Paleontology Collection, Salt Lake City
UW	University of Wyoming, Laramie

WAM	Western Australia Museum, Perth
YM	York Museum, York, Yorkshire, England
YPM	Peabody Museum of Natural History, Yale University, New Haven, Connecticut
YPM-PU	Peabody Museum, Yale University, New Haven, Connecticut (originally in the Princeton University collections)
ZDM	Zigong Dinosaur Museum, Zigong, China
ZPAL	Paleobiological Institute of the Polish Academy of Sciences, Warsaw, Poland

Glossary

The following terms are those which appear in the text, but which are not necessarily defined elsewhere in the text. The definitions employed in this glossary were based mostly upon those published in numerous earlier sources, most notably A Dictionary of Scientific Terms *(Kenneth 1960),* The Illustrated Encyclopedia of Dinosaurs *(Norman 1985), and* The Dinosauria *(Weishampel, Dodson and Osmólska 1990), although other sources (including dictionaries of the English language) were also utilized.*

ABERRANT Out of the ordinary; outside the normal range of variation.

ABRADED Worn.

ACETABULUM Cup-shaped socket in the pelvic girdle for the head of the femur.

ACROMIAL Artery, process, or ligament pertaining to the acromion.

ACROMION Ventral prolongation of the scapular spine.

ADDUCTOR Muscle that brings one bony part towards another.

AESTIVATION In some animals, hiding away and becoming dormant during heat and drought period (not the same as hibernation).

ALA Wing-like projection or structure.

ALLOMETRY Change of proportions with growth; study of relative growth.

ALTI-ILIAC Ilium with an extremeley deep, broad anterior and very short posterior wing-like process.

ALVEOLI Pits or sockets on the surface of an organ or a bone.

AMBIENS Thigh muscle.

AMMONITE Any of various invertebrate organisms of the Mesozoic, belonging to the Cephalopoda, having a flat, coiled, and chambered shell.

AMNIOTIC Pertaining to amnion (a foetal membrane of reptiles, birds, and mammals), applied to sac, folds, cavity, and fluids.

AMPHIBIOUS Adapted to live on both land and in water, depending on their ontogenetic stage of development.

AMPHIBIA Group of vertebrates consisting of amphibious tetrapods.

AMPHICOELOUS Concave on both surfaces of vertebral centra.

AMPHYPLATYAN Flat on both ends of vertebral centra.

ANAPSID Reptiles having a skull with no openings behind the orbit.

ANGIOSPERMS Flowering plants, with seeds enclosed in an ovary.

ANKYLOSIS Complete fusion of bone to bone (or other hard parts, as in tooth to bone) to form a single part.

ANGULAR In most vertebrates, a dermal bone in the lower jaw, upon which rest the dentary and splenial bones.

ANTEBRACHIUM Forearm or corresponding portion of a forelimb.

ANTERIOR Near the front end.

ANTORBITAL In front of the orbits.

APICAL At the summit or tip.

APOMORPHY In cladistics, the derived state occurring only within members of an ingroup, when a character exhibits two states within that ingroup.

APPENDICULAR SKELETON That part of the skeleton including the pectoral girdles, forelimbs, pelvic girdles, and hindlimbs.

ARCADE In anatomy, a bony bridge.

ARCHOSAURIA Diapsid group including dinosaurs, pterosaurs, "thecodontians," and crocodiles, defined primarily by the possession of an antorbital fenestra.

ARCTOMETATARSALIAN CONDITION Central metatarsal (III) pinched proximally, therefore obscured from view anteriorly, reduced or excluded from contact with the tibiotarsus.

ARMOR Bony scutes, plates, shields, horns, spikes, and clubs borne by some dinosaurs.

ARTHROPODA Invertebrate phylum consisting of animals with a chitinous exoskeleon and jointed appendages.

ARTICULATED Jointed or joined together.

ASIAMERICA Areas of Asia and America connected by a land bridge formed by the Bering Straits during the Mesozoic.

ASTRAGALUS Larger tarsal bone which mostly articulates with the tibia dorsally and metatarsus ventrally.

ATLAS First cervical vertebra.

AUTAPOMORPHY In cladistics, a character state unique to one taxon.

AXIAL SKELETON That part of the skeleton including the vertebral column and ribs.

AXIS Second cervical vertebra.

BADLANDS Area of barren land heavily roughly eroded by water and wind into ridges, mesas, and peaks.

BASAL Near or at the base of a group.

BASIOCCIPITAL Median bone in the occipital region of the skull, forming at least part of the occipital condyle.

BASIPTERYGOID Process of the basisphenoid contacting the pterygoid.

BASISPHENOID Cranial bone between the basioccipital and presphenoid.

BED In geology, distinct layers of sedimentary rock.

BICONCAVE Concave on both ends.

BIFURCATED Forked; having two prongs or branches.

BIOLOGY Science of life.

BIOTA Flora and fauna of a region.

BIPED Animal that habitually walks on two feet.

BONE BED Mass assemblage of bones at a single site.

BRACHYILIAC Having an anteroposteriorly short ilium.

BRAINCASE Part of the skull enclosing the brain.

BRANCHIAL ARCH Bony or cartilaginous arch on the side of the pharynx, posterior to the hyoid arch.

BREVIS SHELF Median shelf on the postacetabular section of the ilium for the origin of some of the caudifumoralis brevis muscle.

Glossary

BROWSER Animal that feeds on high foliage (*e.g.*, bushes, not grasses).

BUCCAL Pertaining to the cheek; the surface of a tooth toward the cheek or lip.

BUTTRESS Bony structure for reinforcement.

CALCANEUM Smaller tarsal bone, lateral to the astragalus and distal to the fibula.

CALCAREOUS Composed of, containing, or characteristic of calceum carbonate, calcium, or limestone.

CANALICULATE Possessing canals.

CANCELLOUS Made up of lamillae and slender fibres, joining to form a network-like structure.

CANINIFORM Teeth of "canine" form.

CAPITULUM Knob-like swelling at the end of a bone.

CARAPACE Hard outer covering to the body (like a turtle shell).

CARCASS Dead body of an animal.

CARINA On some bones and teeth, a keel-like ridge or edge.

CARNIVORE Flesh-eater.

CARNOSAUR Generally abandoned term referring to what was regarded by Holtz (1994) as a polyphyletic taxon; originally, an informal term referring to most or all large theropods, pertaining to the "infraorder" Carnosauria Huene 1920; as re-defined by Gauthier (1986), and then Molnar, Kurzanov and Dong (1990), a major tetanuran theropod group.

CARTILAGE Transluscent firm and elastic tissue, usually found in connection with bones and on the articular ends of limb bones.

CAUDAL Pertaining to the tail; toward the tail; also, referring to posterior part.

CEMENTUM Substance investing parts of the teeth, chemically and physically allied to bone.

CENTRUM Main body of the vertebra (ventral to the neural chord) from which rise the neural and hemal arches.

CERATOBRANCHIAL Horn-like element of the branchial arch.

CERVICAL Pertaining to the neck.

CERVIX Neck of an organ.

CHELONIA Reptilian group including turtles and tortoises.

CHEVRON Bone that hangs below a caudal vertebra.

CHOANA Funnel-shaped internal nasal opening.

CHONDRIN Gelatinous substance obtained from cartilage.

CINGULUM Girdle-like structure on teeth.

CLADE Monophyletic taxon as diagnosed by synapomorphies.

CLADISTICS Scientific approach in taxonomy to classify groups of organisms in terms of the recency of their last common ancestry.

CLADOGRAM Diagram representing the distribution of shared-derived characters for groupings of organisms.

CLASS In Linnaean classification, a large category below the level of Phylum.

CLASSIFICATION Process of organizing clades into groups related by common descent.

CLAVICLE Collar-bone forming the anterior portion of the shoulder-girdle, found in birds and some dinosaurs.

CNEMIAL CREST Crest along the anterior dorsal margin of the tibia.

COCHLEA Part of the labyrinth of the ear.

COELUROSAUR Formerly, an informal term referring to small theropods, pertaining to the infraorder Coelurosauria Huene 1914, before being reinstated and re-defined by Gauthier and Padian (1986).

COMMON ANCESTOR In cladistics, a taxon exhibiting all synapomorphies of that taxon, but neither autapomorphies nor the synapomorphies at higher levels within that taxon.

COMMUNITY Ecological relationships between a local environment and all its fauna and flora.

CONDYLE Process on a bone utilized in articulation.

CONE (See Mammilla.)

CONGENERIC Belonging to the same genus.

CONIFER Cone-bearing tree.

CONSPECIFIC Belonging to the same species.

CONTINENTAL DRIFT Continents moving on the Earth.

CONVERGENCE Organisms evolving similar appearances due to responses to similar lifestyle demands, though not sharing direct common ancestors.

COPROLITE Fossilized dung.

CORACOID Bone between the scapula and the sternum, participates in the shoulder joint.

CORONOID PROCESS In reptiles, prong-shaped bony process on the lower jaw for the attachment of jaw-closing muscles.

COTYLUS Ball-shaped structure.

COTYPE Additional type specimen, usually collected at the same time and from the same locality as the holotype, or a specimen, along with others, from which the type is defined.

CRANIA (also **CRANIAL SKELETON**) Bones of the skull.

CRANIAL Relating to the cranium; also, referring to anterior part.

CRANIUM Skull, particularly the braincase.

CREST Ridge or rounded area of bone; in hadrosaurids, a rounded area of bone on the upper part of the skull, sometimes containing hollow passages.

CROWN Exposed part of the tooth.

CROWN GROUP All descendants of the closest common ancestor of living forms.

CRUS Shank.

CURSORIAL Running.

CYCAD Flowering gymnosperm prevalent from the Triassic to Early Cretaceous.

DELTOID Thick, triangular muscle covering the shoulder joint.

DELTOPECTORAL CREST Insertion of deltoid and pectoralis muscles on the humerus.

DENTARY Largest bone of the lower jaw, usually bearing teeth.

DENTICLE Small bump-like processes along the edges of teeth.

DENTICULATE Having denticles.

DENTIGEROUS Tooth-bearing.

DENTITION Teeth.

DEPOSIT Accumulation of a substance (*e.g.*, sediment, bones).

DERIVED CHARACTER More specialized character evolved from a simpler, more primitive condition.

DERMAL Pertaining to the skin.

DERMAL ARMOR Platelets or mall plates of bone that grew in the flesh, but were not connected to the skeleton.

DESCRIPTION In paleontology, a detailed verbal representation of material.

DIAGNOSIS Concise statement enumerating the distinctive characters of a particular organism.

DIAPOPHYSIS Lateral or transverse process of the neural arch.

DIAPSID Reptiles with a skull having a pair of openings behind the orbit.

DIASTEMA Toothless space in a jaw, generally between two different kinds of teeth (such as the canine and postcanines in mammals).

DICIDUOUS Teeth that are shed during growth.

DIDACTYL Having two digits.

DIGIT Toe or finger.

DIGITIGRADE   Walking with only the digits touching the ground.

DIMORPHISM   State of having two different forms, usually according to sex.

DISARTICULATED   Pulled apart.

DISPERSAL   In biogeography, spreading out.

DISTAL   End of any structure farthest from the mid-line of an organism, or from the point of attachment; away from the mass of the body; segments of a limb or of elements within a limb; the edge of a tooth away from the symphysis along the tooth row.

DIVERGENCE   In evolution, moving away from a central group or changing in form.

DIVERTICULUM   Sac or tube, blind at distal end, that branches off from a cavity or canal.

DOLICHOILIAC   Having a relatively long ilium.

DORSAL   Relating to the back; toward the back.

ECOSYSTEM   Ecological system formed by interaction of organisms and their environment.

ECOLOGY   Biological study of the relationship between organisms and their environment.

ECTEPICONDYLE   Lateral projection of the distal end of the humerus.

ECTOPTERYGOID   Ventral membrane bone behind the palatine, extending to the quadrate.

ECTOTHERMIC   Relying on external sources of heat to maintain body temperature.

EDENTULOUS   Toothless.

EMBRYO   Young organism in pre-birth stages of development.

ENDOCAST   Fill-in of the brain cavity by sediment, revealing the shape of the brain.

ENDOCHONDRAL   Forming or beginning within the cartilage.

ENDOCRANIAL   Pertaining to the brain cavity.

ENDOTHERMIC   Able to generate body heat internally by means of chemical reactions.

ENTEPICONDYLE   Lower end of the humerus.

ENVIRONMENT   Surroundings in which organisms live.

EPAXIAL   Above the axis; dorsal.

EPICONDYLE   Medial/inner projection at the distal end of the humerus and femur.

EPIJUGAL   Horn-like projection off the jugal in ceratopsians.

EPIPHYSIS   Part or process of a bone formed from a separate center of ossification, later fusing with the bone.

EPIPODIUM   Ridge or fold.

EPOCH   Lesser division of geologic time, part of a period.

EPOCCIPITAL   Small bone located on the edge of the ceratopsian frill.

ERA   Largest division of geologic time.

EROSION   Result of weathering on exposed rocks.

EURAMERICA   Joined areas of Europe and America during the Mesozoic.

EURASIA   Joined area of Europe and Asia.

EVOLUTION   Change in the characteristics of a population of organisms, caused by natural selection over time.

EXOCCIPITAL   Bone of the skull on each side of the foramen magnum.

EXPOSURE   In geology, where rock is exposed due to weathering.

EXTENSOR   Muscle that extends a limb or part of a limb; also used to designate surfaces of a limb, manus, or pes.

EXTINCTION   Termination of a genus or species; having died out.

FABROSAUR   Outmoded term referring to any of a number of basal ornithischians, some possibly related to one another and some not, once regarded as belonging to the [now abandoned] group Fabrosauridae.

FACIES   In geology, one of different types of contemporaneous deposits in a lateral series of deposits; also, the paleontological and lithological makeup of a sedimentary deposit.

FAMILY   In Linnaean classification, a grouping of similar genera.

FAUNA   All the animals of a particular place and time.

FEMUR   Thigh-bone.

FENESTRA   Opening in a bone or between bones.

FIBULA   Smaller, outer shin bone.

FLEXOR   Muscle which bends a joint; also used to designate surfaces of a limb, manus, or pes.

FLORA   All the plants of a particular place and time.

FOLIAGE   Branches, twigs, leaves.

FONTANELLE   Opening on the frill in some ceratopsians.

FORAMEN   Opening through a bone or membraneous structure.

FORAMEN MAGNUM   Opening in the occipital area of the skull through which the spinal cord passes.

FOSSA   Pit or trench-like depression.

FOSSILS   Preserved remains of an animal or plant at least 10,000 years old, usually formed through burial and possibly involving a chemical change; evidence of life in the geological past.

FOSSILIZED   Having become a fossil.

FOVEA   Small pit, fossa, or depression.

FRONTAL   Bone of the skull roof in front of the parietal.

FRONTOPARIETAL   Frontal and parietal bones, usually referring to suture or fusion of both bones.

FUSED   Firmly jointed together (usually when bones grow together).

GAIT   Characteristics of locomotion.

GASTRALIA   Belly ribs.

GASTROLITH   "Stomach" stone swallowed for ballast or to grind up already consumed food.

GENOTYPE   In systematics, the type species of a genus.

GENUS   Group of closely related species.

GEOGRAPHICAL DISTRIBUTION   Localities where animals and plants can be found.

GEOLOGY   Science of the history of the Earth and its fossils.

GINGLYMOID   Hinge joint, or constructed like one.

GINGLYMUS   Articulation constructed to permit motion only in one plane.

GIZZARD   Muscular portion of the stomach utilized in grinding up food.

GLOSSOPHARYNGEAL NERVE   Ninth cranial nerve.

GONDWANA   Prehistoric Southern continent that comprised India and the following Southern Hemisphere landmasses: South America, Africa, Madagascar, Australia, and Antarctica.

GRADE   Paraphyletic taxon as diagnosed by the absence and presence of synapomorphies, delineated based upon morphologic distance.

GRAVIPORTAL   Slow-moving or lumbering.

GRAZER   Animal that feeds on low-lying vegetation (*e.g.*, grasses).

GULAR   In turtles, an anterior unpaired horny shield on the plastron; also refers to the ventral portion of the buccal cavity (birds use gular-flutter to cool off).

GYMNOSPERMS   Generally, non-flowering plants.

HABITAT   Place in which an organism or population of organisms normally lives or occurs.

HAEMAPOPHYSIS   Plate-like or spine-like process of the latero-ventral surfaces of a vertebral centrum.

Glossary

HALLUX   First digit of the pes.

HAMULARIS   Hooked or hook-like.

HEMAL (or HAEMAL)   Pertaining to blood or blood vessels.

HERBIVORE   Plant-eater.

HISTO-   Pertaining to tissue.

HISTOLOGY   Study of the fine structure of body tissues.

HOLOTYPE   Single specimen chosen to designate a new species.

HOMODONT   Having similar teeth throughout.

HOMOPLASY   In cladistics, character incongruence within an arrangement of taxa.

HORIZON   Soil layer formed at a definite time and characterized by definite fossil species.

HUMERUS   Upper arm bone.

HYOID   Pertaining to a bone or series of bones lying at the base of the tongue.

HYPANTRUM   In some reptiles, a notch on vertebrae for articulation with the hyposphene.

HYPAXIAL   Below the vertebral column; ventral.

HYPOSPHENE   In some reptiles, a wedge-shaped process on the neural arch of a vertebra, fitting into the hypantrum.

ICHNITE   Fossil footprint.

ICHTHYOSAURS   Mesozoic marine reptiles with streamlined, dolphin-shaped bodies (not dinosaurs).

ILIO-FEMORALIS   Muscle attached to the ilium and femur.

ILIUM   Dorsal bone of the pelvic arch; hipbone.

IN SITU   Referring to specimens in place in the ground where they are discovered.

INDETERMINATE   Incapable of being defined or classified.

INCISIFORM   Incisor-shaped.

INCISOR   Teeth at the very front of the mouth.

INFERIOR   View from beneath; also, ventral.

INFRAORDER   In Linnaean classification, category between family and suborder.

INFRAPREZYGAPOPHYSAL   Below the prezygapophysis.

INGROUP   In cladistics, a monophyletic grouping of taxa.

INSECTIVOROUS   Insect-eating.

INSTINCT   Unlearned, complex, and normally adaptive innate aspect of behavior.

INTEGUMENT   Outer covering, usually pertaining to skin.

INTERCENTRUM   Second central ring in a vertebra having two vertical rings in each centrum.

INTERMEDIUM   Small bone of the carpus and tarsus.

INTERORBITAL   Between the orbits.

INTRASPECIFIC   Within the same species.

INVERTEBRATE   Animal without a backbone.

IRIDIUM   Element found in meteorites and Earth's core.

ISCHIUM   Ventral and posterior bone of each half of the pelvic girdle.

ISOLATED   Set apart from similar items.

JUGAL   Skull bone between the maxilla and quadrate.

JUNIOR SYNONYM   Taxon suppressed because another name, pertaining to the same fossil materials, was published previously.

KINETIC   In zoology, bones joined together but capable of movement.

LABIAL   Near the lip.

LABYRINTH   Complex internal ear, either bony or membranous.

LACERTILIA   Reptilian suborder comprising lizards.

LACRIMAL   Skull bone contributing to the anterior border of the orbit.

LAGENA   Apical portion of the scala media or cochlear duct.

LAMELLA   Thin scale- or plate-like structure.

LAMINA   Thin sheet or layer.

LATERAL   At the side externally; away from the midline.

LATEROSPHENOID   One of the bones of the braincase.

LAURASIA   Northern supercontinent, including North America, Europe, and parts of Asia.

LECTOTYPE   Specimen chosen from syntypes to re-designate the type of a species.

LEPIDOSAUR   Lizards, snakes, and their close relatives.

LIGAMENT   Strong fibrous band of tissue that support joints between bones, and joins muscles to bones.

LINEAR-   In a line.

LINGUAL   Pertaining to the tongue; the surface of a tooth toward the tongue.

LOCALITY   In geology, named place where specimens have been found.

LONG BONE   Limb bone.

LUMBAR   Pertaining to the region of the loins.

LUNATE   Crescent-shaped.

MALLEUS   Outermost ear-bone in mammals.

MAMILLA (also MAMMILLA)   Nipple-shaped structure.

MAMMILLA   Lower part of an eggshell unit, with a characteristic shape, also called the "cone."

MANUS   Part of the forelimb corresponding to the hand, comprising metacarpals and phalanges.

MARINE   Pertaining to the sea.

MARL   Muddy limestone.

MATRIX   Fossil-embedded rock.

MAXILLA   Usually tooth-bearing principal bone in the upper jaw.

MECKELIAN GROOVE   Groove inside the jaw for Meckel's cartilage and associated vessels/nerves.

MEDIAL   From the inside or inner; toward the midline.

MEDULLA   Central part of a bone or organ.

MESIAL   In middle longitudinal or vertical plane; the edge of a tooth toward the symphysis or premaxillary midline.

METABOLISM   Constructive and destructive chemical changes in the body for maintenance, growth, and repair of an organism.

METACARPUS   Bones of the manus between the wrist and fingers.

METAPHYSIS   Vascular part of the diaphysis that adjoins the epiphyseal cartilage.

METAPODIUM   In tetrapods, the metacarpus and metatarsus.

METATARSUS   Part of the foot between the tarsus and toes.

MIDLINE   Imaginary line extending dorsally along the length of an animal.

MOIETY   Either of two units of equal or indefinite size.

MONOPHYLETIC   Group of taxa including a common ancestor and all of its descendants; derived from a single origin.

MORPHOLOGY   Science of form.

MORPHOTYPE   Type specimen of one form of a polymorphic species.

MOSASAURS   Large Cretaceous marine lizards related to the modern monitor (not dinosaurs).

MUSCULATURE   Arrangement of muscles.

MUZZLE   Anterior part of the head containing the nostrils and jaws.

NARIAL   Pertaining to the nostrils.

NARIS   Nostril opening.

NASAL   Bone near the front of the skull, between the premaxilla and the frontal; also, that which pertains to the nostrils or nose.

NEURAL   Closely connected with nerves or nervous tissues.

NEURAL ARCH   Bony bridge over the passage of the spinal cord.

NEURAL CANAL   Canal formed by neural arch and centrum.

NEURAL SPINE   Spine rising up from the neural arch.

NEUROCENTRA   Type of centrum in primitive vertebrates.

NEUROCRANIUM   Bony or cartilaginous case containing the brain and capsules of special sense organs.

NOMEN DUBIUM   Taxon founded upon material of questionable diagnostic value.

NOMEN NUDUM   Taxon improperly founded without published material, diagnosis, type designation, and figure.

NOMEN OBLITIM   Taxon obsolete from disuse.

NOTOCHORD   Dorsal supporting axis of lowest vertebrates.

NUCHAL   Pertaining to the neck.

OBTURATOR   Pertaining to any structure in the area of the obturator foramen.

OBTURATOR FORAMEN   Oval foramen within the ischium for the passage of the obturator nerve/vessels.

OCCIPUT   Back part of the skull.

OCCIPITAL CONDYLE   Condyle with which the skull moves on the atlas and axis.

OCCLUSAL   Where surfaces of upper and lower teeth touch when the jaws are closed.

ODONTOID   Tooth-like process.

OLECRANON   Process for insertion of the triceps muscle at the proximal end of the ulna.

OLFACTORY   Pertaining to the sense of smell.

OMNIVORE   Animal that eats both plant and animal food.

ONTOGENY   Growth and development of an individual.

OPISTHOCOELOUS   Having the centrum concave posteriorly.

OPISTHOTIC   Inferior posterior bony element of the otic capsule.

OPTIC   Pertaining to vision.

ORBIT   Bony cavity in which the eye is housed.

ORBITOSPHENOID   Paired elements in the skull, located between the presphenoid and frontal.

ORDER   In Linnaean classification, a category including related families within a class.

OROGENIC   Pertaining to the process of mountain building.

OSSEOUS   Resembling or composed of bone.

OSSICLE   Bony platelets set under the skin, serving as secondary armor.

OSSIFY   To change into bone.

OSTEODERM   Bony plates in the skin.

OSTEOLOGY   Part of zoology dealing with the structure and development of bones.

OTIC   Pertaining to the ear.

OUTGROUP   In cladistics, the character state occuring in the nearest relatives of an ingroup.

PACHYDERM   Large, thick-skinned mammal.

PALATE   Roof of the mouth.

PALEOBIOLOGY   Biology of extinct organisms.

PALEOECOLOGY   Study of the relationships between extinct organisms and their paleo-environments.

PALEONTOLOGY   Science of past life, based on the study of fossil and fossil traces.

PALMER   Surface of the manus in contact with the ground.

PALPEBRAL   Small bone located on the rim of the eye socket, often forming a bony eyelid.

PALYNOMORPH   Spores, pollen, and cysts of certain algae.

PANGAEA   Huge supercontinent formed by the collision of all Earth's continents during the Permian period.

PAPILLA   Conical dermal structure constituting the beginning of a feather.

PARASPHENOID   Membrane bone forming the floor of the braincase.

PARATYPE   Specimen used along with the holotype in defining a new species.

PARIETAL BONE   Bone of the skull roof behind the frontal.

PAROCCIPITAL PROCESS   Bony process at the back of the skull.

PARSIMONY   In cladistic analysis, a subjective criterion for selecting taxa, usually that which proposes the least number of homoplasies.

PATHOLOGICAL   Relating to disease.

PECTINEAL   Pertaining to a ridge-line on the femur and the attached pectineus muscle.

PECTORAL   Pertaining to the chest.

PEDICLE   Backward-projecting vertebral process.

PEDUNCLE   Stalk- or stem-like process of a bone.

PELVIC GIRDLE   Hip area of the skeleton, composed of the ilium, ischium, and pubis.

PELYCOSAUR   One of a group of mammal-like reptiles of the Carboniferous and Permian periods, some having dorsal "sails" supported by elongated neural spines (not dinosaurs).

PENTADACTYL   Having five digits.

PERIOD   Division of geologic time, subdivision of an era.

PERIOTIC   Skull bone enclosing parts of membranous labyrinth of the internal ear.

PES   Foot.

PETRIFICATION   Replacement by minerals of a fossilized organism's hard tissues, so that it becomes stone-like.

PHALANGEAL FORMULA   Formula giving the number of phalanges in the digits of the manus and pes.

PHALANX   Segments of digits.

PHENON   Clusters of things with similar shape.

PHYLUM   A group of closely related classes within a kingdom, sharing a basic body plan.

PHYSIOLOGY   Biological study dealing with the functions and activities of organisms.

PHYTOSAUR   Crocodile-like, semi-aquatic archosaurs of the Triassic.

PISCIVORE   Fish-eater.

PISIFORM   Tiny bone in the carpus.

PLANKTON   Generally microscopic plant and animal organisms that drift or float in large masses in fresh or salt water.

PLANTIGRADE   Walking with the entire sole of the foot touching ground.

PLASTRON   Ventral portion of a turtle shell.

PLATE   Piece of bone embedded in the skin.

PLATE TECTONICS   Study of the plates making up the Earth's crust.

PLATYCOELOUS   Condition in which the posterior articular end of a vertebral centrum is flat.

PLESIOMORPHY   In cladistics, the more primitive character state of two that are exhibited within members of an ingroup, while also occurring in the nearest outgroup; a primitive feature.

PLESIOSAUR   One of a group of Mesozoic marine reptiles (not dinosaurs).

PLEUROCOEL   Cavity in the side of a vertebral centrum.

PLICA   Fold of membrane, skin, or lamella.

PNEUMATIC   Bones penetrated by canals and air spaces.

POLLEX   In the manus, the thumb or innermost digit of the normal five.

PORE   Minute opening.

POROUS   Sponge-like.

POSTCRANIA (or **POSTCRANIAL SKELETON**) Skeleton excluding the skull.

POSTZYGAPOPHYSIS Process on the posterior face of the neural arch, for articulation with the vertebra behind it.

POSTURE Walking or standing position.

PREARTICULAR Bone in the lower jaw of primitive tetrapods.

PREDATOR Organism that hunts and eats other organisms.

PREDENTARY BONE In ornithischians, a small crescent-shaped bone located at the tip of the lower jaw.

PREHISTORIC Of, pertaining to, or belonging to a time before recorded history.

PREMAXILLA A usually paired bone at the front of the upper jaw.

PREOCCUPIED In zoological nomenclature, a taxonomic name identical to one published previously by another author.

PREORBITAL Anterior to the orbit (=antorbital).

PRESERVATION General condition of a fossil specimen, referring to its quality and completeness.

PREZYGAPOPHYSIS Process on the anterior face of the neural arch, for articulation with the vertebra in front of it.

PRIORITY Rule in scientific nomenclature stating that, in the case of different taxonomic names given to the same form or groupings of forms, the name published first is valid.

PROCESS In anatomy, a bony projection.

PROOTIC Anterior bone of the otic capsule.

PROVENANCE Place of origin.

PROXIMAL Nearest to the center of the body; toward the mass of the body; segment of a limb or of elements within a limb.

PSEUDOSUCHIAN Old term for a usually bipedal Upper Triassic "thecodontian."

PTEROSAURS Flying reptiles of the Mesozoic, related to dinosaurs.

PTERYGOID Wing-like posterior bone of the palate.

PUBIS Antero-ventral bone of the pelvic girdle.

QUADRATE In birds, reptiles, and amphibians, the bone with which the lower jaw articulates.

QUADRATOJUGAL Bone connecting or overlying the quadrate and jugal.

QUADRATOMANDIBULAR Pertaining to the quadrate and mandible.

QUADRUPED Animal that walks on all four feet.

RADIALE Carpal bone aligned with the radius.

RADIUS Forelimb bone between the humerus and carpals, lying next to the ulna.

RAMUS Branch-like structure.

RATITE One of a group of flightless birds having an unkeeled sternum; also, an eggshell morphotype in which the shell structure is discrete only in the inner one-sixth to one-half of the shell thickness (mammillary layer); most of the eggshell formed of a single, continuous layer.

RECONSTRUCTION Drawn or modeled skeleton or partial skeleton, based upon the original fossil remains, often incorporating other specimens, extrapolation and or knowledge of the more complete remains of other taxa (sometimes used to mean "restoration").

RECTUS CAPITUS A neck muscle.

RECURVED Curved backward.

RELICT Not functional, although originally adaptive.

RESONATOR Device that causes sound to be produced through sympathetic vibrations at specific frequencies.

RESTORATION In paleontology, a drawn or sculpted representation of a fossil organism as it may have appeared in life (sometimes used to mean "reconstruction")

RHYNCHOSAURS Large, squat, beaked, archosaur-like reptiles of the Triassic (not dinosaurs).

RIB Elongate and sometimes curved bone of the trunk, articulating with vertebrae.

RIGOR MORTIS Temporary muscular stiffening after death.

RIMO- With a cleft.

ROSTRAL In ceratopsians, median unpaired bone located at the tip of the upper jaw; also, toward the rostrum or tip of the head.

SACCULUS Small pouch.

SACRAL RIB Rib that connects the sacral vertebrae to the pelvis.

SACRUM Structure formed by the sacral vertebrae and pelvic girdle.

SAGITTAL Pertaining to the midline on the dorsal aspect of the cranium; also, arrow-like.

SAUROPSID All reptiles excluding synapsids.

SCALA Any of three canals in the cochlea of the ear.

SCAVENGER Animal that feeds on dead animal flesh or other decomposing organic matter.

SCLEROTIC RING Ring of a series of overlapping bones around the outside of the eyeball.

SCUTE Horny or bony plate embedded in the skin.

SEDIMENT Deposit of inorganic and or organic particles.

SEDIMENTARY ROCKS Rocks formed from sediments.

SENIOR SYNONYM Taxon having priority over another identically named taxon and regarded as the valid name, because of the former's earlier publication.

SEPTUM Partition separating spaces.

SERRATED Having a notched cutting edge.

SESAMOID Bone developed inside a tendon and near a joint.

SEXUAL DIMORPHISM Marked differences in shape, color, structure, *etc.* between the male and female of the same species.

SHIELD Bony extension of the skull in ceratopsian dinosaurs.

SIGMOID S-shaped.

SINUS Space within a body.

SISTER-GROUP (or **SISTER-TAXON**) Group of organisms descended from the same common ancestor as its closest group.

SPATULATE Spatulate-shaped.

SPECIALIZATION Modification in a particular way.

SPECIES In paleontology, a group of animals with a unique shared morphology; in zoology, a group of naturally interbreeding organisms that do not naturally interbreed with another such group.

SPECIMEN Sample for study.

SPHENETHMOID A principal bone of the ethmoid [regarding bones forming a considerable part of the walls of the nasal cavity] region of the skull.

SPHERULITE Small, usually spheroid, radiating structure.

SPINAL COLUMN Backbone and tail, comprising articulated vertebrae.

SPINAL CHORD Nervous tissue contained in the vertebral or spinal canal.

SPLENIAL BONE Dermal bone in the lower jaw, covering much of Meckel's groove.

SQUAMOSAL In the vertebrate skull, a bone that forms part of the posterior side wall.

STEREOSCOPIC   Pertaining to the ability to see a three-dimensional image.

STERNUM   Breastbone.

STRATIGRAPHY   Study of the pattern of deposition.

STRATUM   Layer of sediment.

SUBFAMILY   In Linnaean classification, a category smaller than a family, including one or more genus.

SUBGENUS   Subtle classification between a genus and a species; a group of related species within a genus.

SUBORDER   In Linnaean classification, a category smaller than an order, larger than an infraorder, including one or more families.

SULCUS   Groove.

SUPERCONTINENT   Large structures formed by the joining of various continental areas.

SUPERORDER   In Linnaean classification, a grouping smaller than a class, including one or more order.

SUPERIOR   View from above; also, dorsal.

SUTURE   Line where bones contact each other.

SYMPHYSIS   Line of junction of two pieces of bone.

SYNAPOMORPHY   Shared/derived feature defining a monophyletic group; unique character shared by two or more taxa.

SYNAPSID   Tetrapods with a skull having one opening behind the eye socket; includes pelycosaurs, therapsids and mammals.

SYNTYPE   When a holotype and paratypes have not been selected, one of a series of specimens used to designate a species.

TAPHONOMY   Study of the processes of burial and fossilization of organisms.

TARSOMETATARSUS   In birds and some dinosaurs, a bone formed by the fusion of the distal row of tarsals with the second to fourth metatarsals.

TARSUS   Ankle bones.

TAXON   Definite unite in the classification of animals and plants.

TAXONOMY   Science of naming and classiying biological organisms.

TERRESTRIAL   Land-dwelling.

TETRADACTYL   Having four digits.

TETRAPOD   Vertebrate with four limbs.

TEXTURE   Sequence of horizontal ultrastructural zones of an eggshell, also called "eggshell unit macrostructure."

THECODONT   Teeth set in sockets.

THECODONTIA   Artificial "order" of early archosaurian reptiles of the Late Permian and Early Triassic, some of which may have been ancestral to dinosaurs, pterosaurs and crocodiles.

THERAPSID   Late Permian and early Mesozoic (Triassic to Middle Jurassic) advanced mammal-like reptile.

THORACIC   Pertaining to the thorax.

THORAX   Part of the body between the neck and abdomen.

TIBIA   Shin bone.

TIBIOTARSUS   In birds and some dinosaurs, the tibial bone to which are fused the proximal tarsals.

TOOTH BATTERY   Set of numerous interlocking teeth arranged to form a grinding or cutting surface.

TRABECULAE   Small sheets of bone.

TRACE FOSSIL   Not the actual remains of an extinct organism, but rather the fossilized record of something left behind by that organism.

TRACKWAY   Series of successive footprints made by a moving animal.

TRANSVERSE PROCESSES   Laterally directed process of the vertebral centrum, for attachment of intervertebral muscles.

TRIDACTYL   Having three digits.

TRIGEMINAL FORAMEN   Opening for the fifth cranial nerve.

TRIPODAL   Stance incorporating and hind feet and tail.

TROCHANTER   Prominence or process on the femur to which muscles are attached.

TROPICAL   Hot and humid area with lush vegetation.

TUBER   Rounded protuberance.

TUBERCLE   Small, rounded protuberance.

TUBERCULATE   Having or resembling tubercles.

TUBERCULOUS   Having many tubercles.

TUBERCULUM   One of the heads of the rib, attaches to the transverse process of the vertebral centrum.

TYPE SPECIMEN   Specimen used to diagnose a new species.

ULNA   In the forearm, the long bone on the medial side, parallel with the radius.

ULNARE   In the proximal row of carpals, the bone at the distal end of the ulna.

UNCINATE PROCESS   In birds and some reptiles, a process on the ribs which overlaps other ribs.

UNGUAL   Phalanx bearing a nail or claw.

UTRICULUS   Membraneous sac of the ear-labyrinth.

VACUITY   Open space.

VAGUS   Tenth cranial nerve.

VARIATION   Range of appearance within a group of organisms.

VARIETY   In biology, a taxonomic category below the species level, comprising naturally occurring or selectively bred individuals having varying characteristics.

VASCULAR   Of or pertaining to the circulatory system.

VENTER   Smooth concave surface; also, abdomen, or a lower abdominal surface.

VENTRAL   From beneath, relating to the belly or venter [abdomen or lower abdominal surface]; toward the belly.

VERTEBRA   Bony segment of the backbone.

VERTEBRATE   Animal with a backbone.

VOLCANISM   Volcanic activity or force.

VOMER   Bone at the front of the palate.

ZOOLOGY   Science dealing with the structure, behavior, functions, classification, evolution and distribution of animals.

ZYGAPOPHYSIS   Bony, usually peg-like process on the neural arch of a vertebra, by which it articulates with other vertebrae.

[Anonymous], ?1986, A Brief Display Introduction of the Zigong Museum, 4 pages.

Abel, Othenio, 1912, *Grundzüge der Palaeobiologie der Wirbeltiere.* Stuttgart: E. Schweizerbart'sche Verlagsbuchhandlung N'a'gele und Dr. Sproesser, 708 pages.

_____, 1922, *Lebensbilder aus der Tierwelt der Vorzeit.* Jena: Gustav Fischer, xiv, 523 pages.

_____, 1924, Die neuen Dinosaurierfunde in der Oberkreide Canadas: *Jahrbuch Naturwissenschaften,* Berlin, 12 (36), pp. 709–716.

_____, 1925, *Geschichte und Methode der Rekonstruktion vorzeitlicher Wirbeltiere.* Jena: Gustav Fischer.

_____, 1926, Die Lebensspuren in der oberen Trias des Connecticuttales: *Amerikafart, Eindrücke, Beobachtungen und Studien eines Naturforschers auf einer Reise nach Nordamerika und Westindien.* Jena: Verlag von Gustav Fisher, pp. 13–55.

Accarie, Hugues, Bernard Beaudoin, Jean Dejax, Gérard Driès, Jean-Guy Michard, and Phillipe Taquet, 1995, Découverte d'un Dinosaure Théropode nouveau (*Genusaurus sisteronis* n.g., n.sp.) dans l'Albien marin de Sisteron (Alpes de Haute-Provence, France) et extension au Crétacé inférieur de la lignée cératosaurienne: *Comptes Rendus des Séances de l'Académie des Sciences,* Paris, 212, Série II a, pp. 327–334.

Adams, A. Leith, 1875, On a fossil saurian vertebra, *Arctosaurus osborni,* from the Arctic regions: *Proceedings of the Royal Irish Academy,* series 2, 2, science, pp. 177–179.

Aiken, W. G., 1961, Geology and paleontology of the Jurassic and Cretaceous of southern Tanganyika: *Bulletin of the Geological Survey of Tanganyika,* 31, pp. 1–144.

Alexander, R. McN., 1976, Estimates of the speeds of dinosaurs: *Nature,* 261, p. 129.

Allen, P., 1955, Age of the Wealden in Northwestern Europe: *Geological Magazine,* 92, pp. 265–281, London.

Alvarez, Luis W., Walter Alvarez, Frank Asaro, and Helen V. Michel, 1980, Extraterrestrial cause for the Cretaceous-Tertiary extinction: *Science,* 209 (4448), pp. 1095–1108.

Alvarez, Walter, Erle G. Kauffman, Finn Surlyk, Luis W. Alvarez, Frank Asaro and Helen V. Michel, 1984, Impact theory of mass extinctions and the invertebrate fossil record: *Science,* 223 (4641), pp. 1135–1141.

_____, 1988, The debate over the Cretaceous-Tertiary boundary: *Global Catastrophes in Earth History:* Abstracts, 1.

Ameghino, Florentino, 1899, Nota preliminar sobre el *Loncosaurus argentinus* un represente de la familia de las Megalosauridae en la República Argentina: *Annales Societas Ciencias,* 47, pp. 61–62.

Anderson, J. F., A. Hall-Martin, and Dale A. Russell, 1985, Long-bone circumference and weight in mammals, birds and dinosaurs: *Journal of Zoology,* London, 207, pp. 53–61.

Anderson, J. M., 1981, World Permo-Triassic correlations: their biostratigraphic basis, *in:* M. H. Cresswell and P. Vella, editors, *Gondwana Five.* Rotterdam: A. A. Balkema, pp. 3–10.

Anderson, J. M., and A. R. I. Cruickshank, 1978, The biostratigraphy of the Permian and Triassic Part 5. A review of the classification and distribution of Permo-Triassic tetrapods: *Palaeontologia Africana,* 21, pp. 15–44.

Andrews, Charles W., 1913, On some bird remains from the Upper Cretaceous of Transylvania: *Geological Magazine,* 5 (10), pp. 193–196.

_____, 1921, On some remains of a theropodous dinosaur from Lower Lias of Barrow-on-Soar: *The Annals and Magazine of Natural History,* 8, 9th series, pp. 570–576.

Andrews, Roy Chapman, 1932, The new conquest of Central Asia: *Natural History of Central Asia,* 1 (1), pp. 1–678.

Antunes, Miguel Telles, 1976, *Dinossáurios Eocretácicos de Lagosteiros.* Lisban: Universidade Nova de Lisboa, Ciencias da Terra, 35 pages.

Antunes, Miguel Telles, and Denise Sigogneau-Russell, 1991, Nouvelles données sur les Dinosaures du Crétacé superieur du Portugal: *Comptes Rendus des Séances de l'Académie des Sciences,* Paris, 212, Série II, pp. 113–119.

Appleby, R. M., Alan J. Charig, C. B. Cox, Kenneth A. Kermack, and L. B. H. Tarlo, 1967, Reptilia: *in* McFarland *et al.,* editors, *The Fossil Record: A Symposium with Documentation.* London: Geological Society, pp. 695–753.

Archibald, J. David, and William A. Clemens, 1982, Late Cretaceous extinctions: *American Scientist,* 80, pp. 377–385.

Arcucci, A., 1986, Nuevos materiales y reinterpretación de *Lagerpeton chanarensis* Romer (Thecodontia, Lagerpetonidae nov.): *Ameghiniana,* 23 (3–4), pp. 233–242.

_____, 1987, Un nuevo Lagosuchidae (Thecodontia-Pseudosuchia) de la fauna de los Chanares (edad Reptil Chanarense, Triásico medio), la Rioja, Argentina: *Ibid.,* 24, pp. 89–94.

Argast, Scott, James O. Farlow, Rose M. Gabet, and Daniel L. Brinkman, 1987, Transport-induced abrasion of fossil reptilian teeth: Implications for the existence of Tertiary dinosaurs in the Hell Creek Formation, Montana: *Geology,* 15, pp. 927–930.

Armstrong, Harley J., Walter R. Averett, Marjorie E. Averett, Elizabeth S. McReynolds, and David G. Wolny, 1987, Mid-Mesozoic paleontology of the Rabbit Valley area, western Colorado, *in:* Walter R. Averett, editor, *Paleontology and Geology of the Dinosaur Triangle, Guidebook for 1987 Field Trip,* pp. 37–43.

Attridge, John A., A. W. Crompton, and Farish A. Jenkins, 1985, The southern African prosauropod *Massospondylus* discovered in North America: *Journal of Vertebrate Paleontology,* 5 (2), pp. 128–132.

Augusta, Joseph, 1960, *Prehistoric Animals.* Translated by Greta Hort. London: Paul Hamlyn Ltd., 171 pages [including (unpaginated) plates].

Averitt, D., J. S. Detterman, J. W. Harshbarger, C. A. Repenning and R. F. Wilson, 1955, Revisions in correlation and nomenclature of Triassic and Jurassic formations in southwestern Utah and northern Arizona: *AAPG Bulletin,* 39, pp. 2515–2524.

Azuma, Yoichi, and Philip J. Currie, 1995, A new giant dromaeosaurid from Japan: *Journal of Vertebrate Paleontology,* Abstracts of Papers, Fifty-fifth Annual Meeting, p. 17A.

Baird, Donald, 1954, *Chirotherium lulli,* a pseudosuchian reptile from New Jersey: *Bulletin of the Museum of Comparative Zoology of Harvard,* 111 (4), pp. 165–192.

_____, 1979, The dome-headed dinosaur *Tylosteus ornatus* Leidy 1872 (Reptilia: Ornithischia: Pachycephalosauridae): *Notulae Naturae of The Academy of Natural Sciences of Philadelphia,* 456, pp. 1–11.

_____, 1983, *Pachycephalosaurus* Brown & Schlaikjer, 1943 and *Troödon wyomingensis* Gilmore, 1931 (Reptilia, Dinosauria): proposed conservation. Z.N.(S)2323: *Bulletin of Zoological Nomenclature,* 40, part. 3, pp. 184–188.

_____, 1986, Upper Cretaceous reptiles from the Severn Formation of Maryland: *The Mosasaur,* 3, pp. 63–85.

Baird, Donald, and Peter M. Galton, 1981, Pterosaur bones from the Upper Cretaceous of Delaware: *Journal of Vertebrate Paleontology,* 1 (1), pp. 67–71.

Baird, Donald, and John R. Horner, 1977, A fresh look at the dinosaurs of New Jersey and Delaware: *New Jersey Academy of Sciences Bulletin,* 22 (2), p. 50.

_____, 1979, Cretaceous Dinosaurs of North Carolina: *Brimleyana,* 2 (1–28), pp. 1–28.

Baker, A. A., C. H. Dane, and J. B. Reeside, Jr., 1936, Correlation of the Jurassic formations of parts of Utah, Arizona, New Mexico, and Colorado: *U. S. Geological Survey Professional Papers,* 183 (5), 66 pages.

Bakker, Robert T., 1968, The superiority of dinosaurs: *Discovery,* 3 (2), pp. 11–22.

_____, 1971, Ecology of the brontosaurs: *Nature,* 229, pp. 172–174.

_____, 1972, Anatomical and ecological evidence of endothermy in dinosaurs: *Ibid.,* 238, pp. 81–85.

_____, 1973, Dinosaur, *in: McGraw-Hill Yearbook of Science and Technology, 1973 Review, 1974 Preview,* pp. 151–155.

_____, 1974, Dinosaur bio-energetics—a reply to Bennett and Dalzell, and Feduccia: *Evolution,* 28, pp. 497–503.

_____, 1975, Dinosaur renaissance: *Scientific American,* April, pp. 58–78.

_____, 1980, Dinosaur trophic dynamics, population structure and physiology, *in:* Roger

Bibliography

D. K. Thomas and Everett C. Olson, editors, *A Cold Look at the Warm Blooded Dinosaurs*, American Association for the Advancement of Science, Selected Symposium, 28.

_____, 1986, *The Dinosaur Heresies: New Theories Unlocking the Mystery of the Dinosaurs and Their Extinction*. New York: William Morrow and Company, 481 pages.

_____, 1987, The return of the dancing dinosaurs, *in*: Sylvia J. Czerkas and Everett C. Olson, editors, *Dinosaurs Past and Present*, Volume 1. Seattle: Natural History Museum of Los Angeles County, in association with University of Washington Press, pp. 38–69.

_____, 1988, Review of the Late Cretaceous nodosaurid Dinosauria, *Denversaurus schlessmania*, a new armor-plated dinosaur from the Latest Cretaceous of South Dakota, the last survivor of the nodosaurians, with comments on stegosaur-nodosaur relationships: *Hunteria*, 1 (3), pp. 3–23.

_____, 1990, *in*: Bakker, A new Latest Jurassic vertebrate fauna, from the highest levels of the Morrison Formation at Como Bluff, Wyoming, with comments on Morrison biochronology, Part I: Biochronology: *Hunteria*, 2 (6), pp. 1–3.

_____, 1992, Inside the head of a tiny *T. rex*: *Discover*, 13 (3), pp. 58–69.

Bakker, Robert T., and Peter M. Galton, 1974, Dinosaur monophyly and a new class of vertebrates: *Nature*, 248, pp. 168–172.

Bakker, Robert T., Peter M. Galton, James Siegwarth, and James Filla, 1990, *in*: Bakker, A new Latest Jurassic vertebrate fauna, from the highest levels of the Morrison Formation at Como Bluff, Wyoming, with comments on Morrison biochronology, Part IV: The dinosaurs: a new *Othnielia*-like hypsilophodontoid: *Hunteria*, 2 (6), pp. 8–13.

Bakker, Robert T., Donald Kralis, James Siegwarth, and James Filla, 1992, *Edmarka rex*, a new, gigantic theropod dinosaur from the middle Morrison Formation, Late Jurassic of the Como Bluff outcrop region: *Hunteria*, 2 (9), pp. 1–24.

Bakker, Robert T., Michael Williams and Philip J. Currie, 1988, *Nanotyrannus*, a new genus of pygmy tyrannosaur, from the Latest Cretaceous of Montana: *Hunteria*, 1 (5), pp. 1–30.

Ballerstedt, M., 1905, Über Saurierfährten der Wealdenformation Bückeburgs: *Die Naturwissenschaften*, new series, 4, pp. 481–485.

Ballou, William H., 1897, Strange creatures of the past: gigantic saurians of the reptilian age: *The Century Illustrated Monthly Magazine*, Nov., pp. 15–23.

Barbarena, M.C., D.C. Araujo, and E.L. Lavina, 1985, Late Permian and Triassic tetrapods of southern Brazil: *National Geographic Research*, 1, pp. 5–20.

Barbour, E. H., 1931, Evidence of dinosaurs in Nebraska: *Nebraska State Museum Bulletin*, 1 (21), pp. 187–190.

Barreto, Claudia, Ralph M. Albrecht, Dale E. Bjorling, John R. Horner, and Norman J. Wilsman, 1993, Evidence of the growth plate and growth of long bones in juvenile dinosaurs: *Science*, 262, pp. 2020–2023.

Barsbold, Rinchen, 1974, Saurornithoididae, a new family of small theropod dinosaurs from Central Asia and North America: *Palaeontologica Polonica*, 30, pp. 5–22.

_____, 1976, New data on *Therizinosaurus* (Therizinosauridae, Theropoda): Paleontology and Biostratigraphy of Mongolia: *The Joint Soviet-Mongolian Paleontological Expedition, Transactions*, 3, pp. 76–92.

_____, 1977, On the evolution of the carnivorous dinosaurs: *Sovmestnaya Sovetsko-Mongol'skaya Paleontologicheskaya Ekspeditsiya Trudy*, 1 (4), pp. 48–56.

_____, 1979, Opisthopubic pelvis in the carnivorous dinosaurs: *Nature*, 279, pp. 792–793.

_____, 1981, Predatory toothless dinosaurs from Mongolia: *Trudy Sovmestnaya Sovetsko-Mongol'skaya Paleontologicheskaya Ekspeditsiya Trudy*, 15, pp. 28–39.

_____, 1983, Carnivorous dinosaurs from the Cretaceous of Mongolia: *The Joint Soviet-Mongolian Palaeontological Expedition, Transactions*, 19, 117 pages.

_____, 1986, [Carnivorous dinosaurs]:Oviraptors, *in*: *Herpetological Investigations in the Mongolian People's Republic, Collected Scientific Transactions of Evolutionary Morphology of the USSR Academy of Sciences*, pp. 210–233.

_____, 1988, Novyy pozdnemelovoy ornithomimid iz MNR: *Palaeontologicheskii Zhurnal*, 1, pp. 122–125. (Translation: A new Late Cretaceous ornithomimid from the Mongolian People's Republic: *Paleontological Journal*, 1, pp. 124–127.)

Barsbold, Rinchen, and Teresa Maryańska, 1990, Segnosauria, *in*: David B. Weishampel, Peter Dodson, and Halszka Osmólska, editors, *The Dinosauria*. Berkeley and Los Angeles: University of California Press, pp. 408–415.

Barsbold, Rinchen, Teresa Maryańska, and Halszka Osmólska, 1990, Oviraptorosauria, *in*: David B. Weishampel, Peter Dodson, and Osmólska, editors, *The Dinosauria*. Berkeley and Los Angeles: University of California Press, pp. 249–258.

Barsbold, Rinchen, and Halszka Osmólska, 1990, Ornithomimosauria, *in*: David B. Weishampel, Peter Dodson, and Osmólska, editors, *The Dinosauria*. Berkeley and Los Angeles: University of California Press, pp. 225–244.

Barsbold, Rinchen, and Altangerel Perle, 1979, The modification of the saurischian pelvis and the parallel development of carnivorous dinosaurs: *Joint Soviet-Mongolian Paleontological Expedition, Transactions*, 8, pp. 39–44.

_____, 1980, Segnosauria, a new infraorder of carnivorous dinosaurs: *Acta Palaeontologica Polonica*, 25 (2), pp. 187–195.

_____, 1983, On the taphonomy of the joint burial of juvenile dinosaurs and some aspects of their ecology: *The Joint Soviet-Mongolian Palaeontological Expedition, Transactions*, 24, pp. 121–125.

_____, 1984, O pervoy nakhodke primitivnogo ornithomimozavra iz mela MNR: *Palaeontologicheskii Zhurnal*, 2, pp. 121–123. (Translation: The first record of a primitive ornithomimosaur from the Cretaceous of Mongolia: *Palaeontological Journal*, pp. 118–120.)

Bartholomai, Alan, and Ralph E. Molnar, 1981, *Muttaburrasaurus*, a new iguanodontid (Ornithischia: Ornithopoda) dinosaur from the Lower Cretaceous of Queensland: *Memoirs of the Queensland Museum*, 20 (2), pp. 319–49.

Baur, G., 1890, A review of the charges against the paleontological department of the U.S. Geological Survey and the defense made by Prof. O.C. Marsh: *American Naturalist*, 24, pp. 298–304.

Behrensmeyer, A. K., 1978, Taxonomic and ecologic information from bone weathering: *Paleobiology*, 4, pp. 160–162.

_____, 1981, Vertebrate paleoecology in a recent East African ecosystem, *in*: J. Gray, A. J. Boucot, and W. B. N. Barry, editors, *Communities of the Past*. Stroudsburg, Pennsylvania: Hutchinson Ross Publishing Company, pp. 591–615.

Béland, P., and Dale A. Russell, 1978, Paleoecology of Dinosaur Provincial Park (Cretaceous), Alberta, interpreted from the distribution of articulated remains: *Canadian Journal of Earth Sciences*, 15, pp. 1012–1024.

Benedetto, J. L., 1973, Herrerasauridae, nueva familia de saurisquios Triásicos: *Ameghiniana*, 10, pp. 89–102.

Bennett, A. F., and W. R. Dawson, 1976, Metabolism, *in*: C. Gans and W. R. Dawson, editors, *Biology of the Reptilia*, 5. London: Academic Press, pp. 127–223.

Benton, Michael J., 1979a, Ecological succession among Late Palaeozoic and Mesozoic tetrapods: *Palaeogeography, Palaeoclimatology, Palaeoecology*, 126, pp. 127–150.

_____, 1979b, Ectothermy and the success of dinosaurs: *Evolution*, 33(3), pp. 983–997.

_____, 1983, Dinosaur success in the Triassic: a noncompetitive ecological model: *The Quarterly Review of Biology*, 58 (1), pp. 29–53.

_____, 1984a, Fossil reptiles from the German Late Triassic and the origin of dinosaurs, *in*: W. E. Reif and F. Westphal, editors, *Third Symposium on Mesozoic Terrestrial Ecosystems, Short Papers*. Tübingen: Attempto Verlag, pp. 13–18.

_____, 1984b, Rauisuchians and the success of dinosaurs: *Nature*, 310, p. 101.

_____, 1985, Classification and phylogeny of the diapsid reptiles: *Zoological Journal of the Linnean Society of London*, 84, pp. 97–164.

_____, 1986a, The late Triassic reptile *Teratosaurus*—a rauisuchian, not a dinosaur: *Paleontology*, 29, part 2, pp. 293–301.

_____, 1986b, Sedimentological use of dinosaurs: *Nature*, 321, p. 732.

_____, 1987, The history of the biosphere: Equilibrium and non-equilibrium models of global diversity: *Trends in Ecology and Evolution*, 2 (6), pp. 153–156.

_____, 1990, Origin and Interrelationships of Dinosaurs, *in*: David B. Weishampel, Peter Dodson, and Halszka Osmólska, editors, *The Dinosauria*. Berkeley and Los Angeles: University of California Press, pp. 11–30.

_____, 1991: *Historical Biology*, 5, p. 263.

_____, 1993, Late Triassic extinctions and the origin of the dinosaurs: *Science*, 260, pp. 769–794.

Benton, Michael J., and Alick D. Walker, 1985, Palaeoecology, taphonomy, and dating of Permo-Triassic reptiles from Elgin, northeast Scotland: *Palaeontology*, 28, pp. 207–234.

Berman, David S, and John S. McIntosh, 1978, Skull and relationships of the Upper Jurassic sauropod *Apatosaurus* (Reptilia, Saurischia): *Bulletin of Carnegie Museum of Natural History*, 8, 35 pages.

Bernier, P., G. Barale, J.-P. Bourseau, E. Buffetaut, G. Demathieu, C. Gaillard, J.-C. Gall, and S. Wenz, 1984, Découverte de pistes de dinosaures sauteurs dans les Calcaires Lithographiques de Cérin (Kimméridgian supérieur, Ain, France)—implications paléoécologiques: *Géobios Mémoires Spéc*, 8, pp. 177–185.

Bidar, Alain, Louis Demay, and Gérard Thomel, 1972, *Compsognathus corallestris* nouvelle espèce de dinosaurien théropode du Portlandien de Canjuers (sud-est de la France): *Extrait des Annales du Museum d'Histoire Naturelle de Nice*, 1 (1), pp. 1–34.

Bien, M. N., 1940, Discovery of Triassic saurischian and primitive mammalian remains at Lufeng, Yunnan: *Bulletin of the Geological Society of China*, 20, 3–4, pp. 225–234.

Bilotte, M., F. Duranthon, P. Clottes, and C. Raynaud, 1986, Gisements de dinosaures de Nord-Est des Pyrénées, *in: Actes du Colloque "Les dinosaures de la Chine à la France,"* Toulose, pp. 151–160.

Bird, Roland T., 1941, A dinosaur walks into the musuem: *Natural History*, 43, pp. 254–261.

_____, 1944, Did *Brontosaurus* walk on land?: *Ibid.*, 53, pp. 61–67.

_____, 1954, We captured a 'live' brontosaur: *National Geographic*, 105, pp. 707–722.

_____, 1985, *Bones for Barnum Brown*, V. Theodore Schreiber, editor. Fort Worth, Texas: Texas Christian University Press, viii, 225 pages.

Blows, William T., 1982, A preliminary account of a new specimen *Polacanthus foxi* (Ankylosauria, Reptilia) from the Wealden of the Isle of Wight: Preceedings, Isle of Wight Natural History Archaeological Society for 1980, 7 (5), pp. 303–306.

_____, 1987, The armoured dinosaur *Polacanthus foxi* from the Lower Cretaceous of the Isle of Wight: *Palaeontology*, 30 (3), pp. 557–580.

Blumberg, B. S., and L. Sokoloff, 1961, Coalescence of caudal vertebrae in the giant dinosaur *Diplodocus*: *Arthritis and Rheumatism*, 4, pp. 592–601.

Bodily, N. M., 1968, An armored dinosaur from the Lower Cretaceous of Utah: M.S. thesis, Department of Geology, Brigham Young University, 40 pages.

_____, 1969, *Ibid.*: Brigham Young University Geological Studies, 16 (3), pp. 35–60.

Bohlin, Birger, 1953, Fossil reptiles from Mongolia and Kansu: *The Sino-Swedish Expedition Publication*, 37 (6), pp. 1–105.

Bonaparte, José F., 1960, Noticia sobre la presencia de restos fósiles de tetrápodos triásicos en los Estratos de Los Colorados (prov. de San Juan): *Acta Geologica Lilloana*, 3, p. 181.

_____, 1967, Dos nuevas "faunas" de reptiles triásicos de Argentina: *Ist International Symposium on Gondwana Stratigraphy*, pp. 283–306.

_____, 1969, Comments on early saurischians: *Zoological Journal of the Linnean Society*, 48, pp. 471–480.

_____, 1972, Los tetrápodos del sector superior de la formación Los Colorados, La Rioja, Argentina (Triásico Superior), 1 Parte: *Opera Lilloana*, 22, pp. 1–183.

_____, 1975a, Nuevos materiales de *Lagasuchus talampayensis* Romer (Thecodontia-Pseudosuchia) y su significado en el origen de los Saurischia. Chanarense inferior, Triásico medio de Argentina: *Acta Geologica Lilloana*, 13 (1), pp. 5–90.

_____, 1975b, Jurassic and Cretaceous terrestrial vertebrates of South America: *National Geographic Society Research Reports*, 1975 Projects, pp. 115–125.

_____, 1976, *Pisanosaurus mertii* Casamiquela and the origin of the Ornithischia: *Journal of Paleontology*, 50, pp. 808–820.

_____, 1978a, *Coloradia brevis* n. g. et n. sp. (Saurischia Prosauropoda), dinosaurio Plateosauridae de la formación los Colorados, Triásico Superior de la Rioja, Argentina: *Ameghiniana*, 15, nos. 3–4, pp. 327–332.

_____, 1978b, El Mesozoico de América del Sur y sus tetrápodos: *Tucuman*, 26, pp. 565–573, Argentina.

_____, 1979a, Faunas y paleobiogeografía de los tetrápodos Mesozoicos de América del Sur: *Ameghiniana*, 16, pp. 217–238.

_____, 1979b, Dinosaurs: a Jurassic assemblage from Patagonia: *Science*, 205, pp. 1377–1378.

_____, 1980, Jurassic tetrapods from South America and dispersal routes, *in*: Louis L. Jacobs, editor, *Aspects of Vertebrate History: Essays in Honor of Edwin Harris Colbert*. Flagstaff: Museum of Northern Arizona Press, pp. 73–98.

_____, 1982, Jurassic and Cretaceous terrestrial vertebrates of South America: *National Geographic Society Research Reports*, 1975 Projects, pp. 115–125.

_____, 1984a, I dinosauria dell'Argentina, *in*: Giancarlo Ligabue, editor, *Sulle Orme dei Dinosauri*. Venice, Italy: Erizzo Editrice, pp. 125–143.

_____, 1984b, Nuevas pruebas de la conexión físca entre Sudamérica y Norteamérica en el Cretácico Tardío (Campaniano): *Actas III Congreso, Argentina Paleontología*, pp. 141–149.

_____, 1985, A Horned Dinosaur from Patagonia: *NGR*, winter, pp. 149–151.

_____, 1986a, The early radiation and phylogenetic relationships of the Jurassic sauropod dinosaurs, based on vertebral anatomy, *in*: Kevin Padian, editor, *The Beginning of the Age of Dinosaurs: Faunal Change across the Triassic-Jurassic Boundary*. New York: Cambridge University Press, pp. 247–258.

_____, 1986b, Les dinosaures (carnosaurs, allosauridés, sauropodes, cétiosauridés) de Jurassic moyen de cerro cóndor (Chubut, Argentine): *Annales de Paléontologie (Vert.-Invert.)*, 72 (3), pp. 247–289.

_____, 1986c, *Ibid*. (part 2), 72 (3), pp. 325–386.

_____, 1986d, History of the terrestrial Cretaceous vertebrates of Gondwana, *in: IV Congresso Argentino de Paleontología y Biostratigrafa, Mendoza*, 2, pp. 63–95.

_____, 1986e, A new and unusual Late Cretaceous mammal from Patagonia: *Journal of Vertebrate Paleontology*, 6 (3), pp. 264–270.

_____, 1987, Late Cretaceous dinosaurs of Laurasia and Gondwana, *in*: Bonaparte and Zophia Kielan-Jaworoska, editors, *4th Symposium on Mesozoic Terrestrial Ecosystems*, pp. 24–29.

_____, 1991, Los vertebrados fósiles de la Formación Río Colorado, de la ciudad de Neuquén y cercanias, Cretácico Superior, Argentina: *Revista del Museo Argentino de Ciencias Naturales (Bernardino Rivadavia), el Instituto Nacional de Investigación de las Ciencias Naturales*, 4 (3), pp. 68–101.

Bonaparte, José F., and G. E. Bossi, 1967, Sobre la presencia de dinosaurios en la Formación Pirgua del Grupo Salta y su significado cronológico: *Acta Geologica Lilloana*, 10 (2), pp. 25–44.

Bonaparte, José F., and Rodolfo A. Coria, 1993, Un nuevo y gigantesco saurópodo titanosaurio de la Formación Río Limay (Albiano-Cenomaniano) de la Provincia del Neuquén, Argentina: *Amedghiniana*, 30 (3), pp. 271–282.

Bonaparte, José F., and Z. B. Gasparini, 1979, Los Saurópodos de los grupos Neuquén y Chubut y sus relaciones cronológicas: *Argentina Geological Congress, VII*, Neuquén 1978, pp. 393–406.

Bonaparte, José F., and Fernando E. Novas, 1985, *Abelisaurus comahuensis*, N.G., N.SP., carnosauria del Cretácio tardío de Patagonia: *Ameghiniana*, 21 (2–4), pp. 259–265.

Bonaparte, José F., Fernando E. Novas, and R. A. Coria, 1990, *Carnotaurus sastrei* Bonaparte, the horned, lightly built carnosaur from the Middle Cretaceous of Patagonia: *Contributions in Science*, 416, pp. 1–42.

Bonaparte, José F., and Jaime E. Powell, 1980, A continental assemblage of tetrapods from the Upper Cretaceous beds of El Brete, northwestern Argentina (Sauropoda-Coelurosauria-Carnosauria-Aves): *Memoires de la Société Geologique de France, Nouvelle Serie*, pp. 19–28.

Bonaparte, José F., and Martin Vince, 1979, El hallazgo del primer nido de dinosaurios Triásicos (Saurischia, Prosauropoda), Triásico Superior de Patagonia, Argentina: *Ameghiniana*, 16, nos. 1–2, pp. 173–182.

Borgomanero, Guido, and Giuseppe Leonardi, 1981, Um ovo de dinossauro de Aix-en-Provence (Franca) e fragmentos de outras provedéncias conservados em Curitiba, Paraná: *Actas 3 Simpium Regionale Geology*, SBG-SP II, pp. 213–225.

Borsuk-Bialynicka, 1977, A new camarasaurid sauropod *Opisthocoelicaudia skarzynskii* gen. n., sp. n. from the Upper Cretaceous of Mongolia: *Palaeontologia Polonica*, 37, 64 pages.

Boslough, M.B., 1987, Quartz grains shape new impact theories: *Geotimes*, 32, pp. 31–33.

Bowman, S. A. B., 1986, Interpretation of the Morrison Formation as a time-transgressive unit: North American Paleontological Convention IV, Boulder, Colorado. Symposium on Stratigraphy and Environments of the Morrison Formation, p. A5.

Brady, L. F., 1935, Preliminary note on the occurrence of a primitive theropod in the Navajo: *American Journal of Science*, 5 (30), pp. 210–215.

Bramwell, C., and G. Whitfield, 1974, Biomechanics of *Pteranodon*: *Philosophical Transactions of the Royal Society of London*, B, 267, pp. 503–581.

Brandvold, Marian, John W. Brandvold, Frank G. Sweeney, and Wesley M. Boyden, 1995, Taphonomy of hadrosaur (Dinosauria: Ornithischia) nesting sites in the Two Medicine Formation provides evidence of behavioral divergence: *Journal of Vertebrate Paleontology*, Abstracts of Papers, Fifty-fifth Annual Meeting, p. 20A.

Branson, E. B., and Maurice G. Mehl, 1932, Footprint records from the Paleozoic and Mesozoic of Missouri, Kansas and Wyoming: *Bulletin of the Geological Society of America*, 43, pp. 383–398.

Breed, C. S., and W. J. Breed, editors, 1972: *Investigations of the Triassic Chinle Forma-*

tion. Flagstaff: Museum of Northern Arizona Press, 47, 103 pages.

Brett, C. Everett, and W. H. Wheeler, 1961, A biostratigraphic evaluation of the Snow Hill Member, Upper Cretaceous of North Carolina: *Southeastern Geology*, 3 (2), pp. 49–132.

Brett-Surman, Michael K. [Keith], 1979, thesis, University of California (Berkeley).

———, 1979, Phylogeny and palaeobiogeography of hadrosaurian dinosaurs: *Nature*, 277 (5697), pp. 560–562.

———, 1980, The Iren Dabasu fauna from Mongolia: *Mesozoic Vertebrate Life*, 1, pp. 19–22.

———, 1989, A revision of the Hadrosauridae (Reptilia: Ornithischia) and their evolution during the Campanian and Maastrichtian, Ph.D. dissertation, Graduate School of Arts and Sciences of The George Washington University, 272 pages.

Brett-Surman, Michael K., and Gregory S. Paul, 1985, A new family of bird-like dinosaurs linking Laurasia and Gondwanaland: *Journal of Vertebrate Paleontology*, 5 (2), pp. 133–138.

Brinkman, Donald B., and Hans-Dieter Sues, 1987, A staurikosaurid dinosaur from the Upper Triassic Ischigualasto Formation of Argentina and the relationships of the Staurikosauridae: *Palaeontology*, 30, part 3, pp. 493–503.

Britt, Brooks B., 1991, Theropods of Dry Mesa Quarry (Morrison Formation, Late Jurassic, Colorado, with emphasis on the osteology of *Torvosaurus tanneri*: *BYU Geological Studies* 1991, 37, pp. 1–72.

———, 1995, The nature and distribution of pneumatic vertebrae in the Theropoda: *Journal of Vertebrate Paleontology*, Abstracts of Papers, Fifty-fifth Annual Meeting, p. 20A.

Brodkorb, Pierce, 1978, Catalogue of fossil birds: *Bulletin Florida State Museum*, 23 (3), pp. 139–228.

Broom, R., 1904, On the occurrence of an opisthocoelian dinosaur (*Algoasaurus bauri*) in the Cretaceous beds of South Africa: *Geological Magazine*, decade 5, 1 (483), pp. 445–447.

———, 1905, Preliminary notice of some new fossil reptiles collected by Mr. Alfred Brown at Aliwal North, South Africa: Rec. Albany Museum, Grahamstown, South Africa, 1, pp. 275–278.

———, 1906, On the South African dinosaur (*Hortalotarsus*): *Transactions of the South African Philosophical Society*, 16, pp. 201–206.

———, 1911, On the dinosaurs of the Stormberg, South Africa: *Annals of the South African Museum*, 7, pp. 291–308.

———, 1912a, Observations on some specimens of South African fossil reptiles preserved in the British Museum: *Transactions of the Royal Society of South Africa*, Capetown, 2, pp. 19–25.

———, 1912b, On the remains of a theropodous dinosaur from the Northern Transvaal: *Transactions of the Geological Survey of South Africa*, pp. 82–83.

———, 1915, Catalogue of the types and figures specimens of fossil vertebrates in the American Museum of Natural History. II. Permian, Triassic and Jurassic reptiles from South Africa: *Bulletin of the American Museum of Natural History*, 25, p. 162.

Brouwers, E. M., and J. E. Hazel, 1978, Ostracoda and correlation of the Severn Forma-

tion (Navarroan; Maastrichtian) of Maryland: *Society of Economic Paleontologists and Mineralogists, Paleontological Monograph 1 (Journal of Paleontology)*, 52 (6), supplement, pp. 1–52.

Brown, Barnum, 1908, The Ankylosauridae, a new family of armored dinosaurs from the Upper Cretaceous: *Bulletin of the American Museum of Natural History*, 24, pp. 187–201.

———, 1910, The Cretaceous Ojo Alamo beds of New Mexico with description of the new dinosaur genus *Kritosaurus*: *Ibid.*, 28, pp. 267–274.

———, 1912, A crested dinosaur from the Edmonton Cretaceous: *Ibid.*, 31, pp. 131–136.

———, 1913a, A new crested dinosaur: *The American Museum Journal*, 13 (1), pp. 139–144.

———, 1913b, The skeleton of *Saurolophus*, a crested duck-billed dinosaur from the Edmonton Cretaceous: *Bulletin of the American Museum of Natural History*, 32, pp. 387–393.

———, 1913c, A new trachodont dinosaur, *Hypacrosaurus*, from the *Edmonton Cretaceous of Alberta*: *Ibid.*, 32, pp. 395–406.

———, 1914a, *Anchiceratops*, a new genus of horned dinosaurs from the Edmonton Cretaceous of Alberta, with discussion of the origin of the ceratopsian crest and the brain casts of *Anchiceratops* and *Trachodon*: *Ibid.*, 33, pp. 539–548.

———, 1914b, A complete skull of *Monoclonius* from the Belly River Cretaceous of Alberta: *Ibid.*, 33, pp. 549–558.

———, 1914c, *Leptoceratops*, a new genus of Ceratopsia from the *Edmonton Cretaceous of Alberta*: *Ibid.*, 33, pp. 567–580.

———, 1914d, *Corythosaurus casuarius*, a new crested dinosaur from the Belly River Cretaceous, with provisional classification of the family Trachodontidae: *Ibid.*, 33, pp. 559–565.

———, 1916a, A new crested trachodont dinosaur, *Prosaurolophus maximus*: *Ibid.*, 35, pp. 701–708.

———, 1916b, *Corythosaurus casuarius* skeleton, musculature and epidermis: *Ibid.*, 35, pp. 709–716.

———, 1917, A complete skeleton of *Monoclonius*, and description of a second skeleton showing skin impressions: *Ibid.*, 37, pp. 281–306.

———, 1933a, A gigantic ceratopsian dinosaur, *Triceratops maximus*, new species: *American Museum of Natural History Novitates*, 649, pp. 1–9.

———, 1933b, Stratigraphy and fauna of the Fuson-Cloverly Formation in Montana, Wyoming and South Dakota (abstract): *Bulletin of the Geological Society of America*, 44, p. 74.

Brown, Barnum, and Erich Maren Schlaikjer, 1937, The skeleton of *Styracosaurus* with the description of a new species: *American Museum Novitates*, 955, pp. 1–12.

———, 1940a, The origin of ceratopsian horncores: *Ibid.*, 1065, pp. 1–7.

———, 1940b, The structure and relationship of *Protoceratops*: *Annals of the New York Academy of Sciences*, 40, pp. 135–266.

———, 1942, The skeleton of *Leptoceratops* with the description of a new species: *American Museum Novitates*, 1169, pp. 1–15.

———, 1943, A study of the troodont dinosaurs with the description of a new

genus and four new species: *Bulletin of the American Museum of Natural History*, 82, pp. 115–150.

Buckland, William, 1824, Notice on the *Megalosaurus* or great fossil lizard of Stonesfield: *Transactions of the Geological Society of London*, Series II, 1, p. 390.

Buckman, J., 1859, On some fossil reptilian eggs from the Great Oolite of Ciren Cester: *Quarterly Journal of the Geological Society of London*, 16, pp. 107–110.

Buffetaut, Éric, 1984, Une vertèbre de Dinosaurien sauropode dans le Crétacé du cap de la Hève (Normandie): *Actes Musée d'Histoire Naturelle de Rouen*, 7, pp. 437–443.

———, 1989, New remains of the enigmatic dinosaur *Spinosaurus* from the Cretaceous of Morocco and the affinities between *Spinosaurus* and *Baryonyx*: *Neus Jahrbuch für Geologie und Paläontologie*, Monatshefte, 1989, 2, pp. 79–87.

Buffetaut, Éric, P. Clottes, G. Cuny, S. Ducrocq, J. Le Loeuff, M. Martin, J. E. Powell, C. Raynaud, and H. Tony, 1989, Les gisements de dinosaures maastrichtiens de la haute vallée de l'Aude (France): premiers résultats des fouilles de 1898: *Comptes Rendus des Séances de l'Académie des Sciences, Paris*, t. 309, pp. 1723–1727.

Buffetaut, Éric, and Rucha Ingavat, 1986, Unusual theropod dinosaur teeth from the Upper Jurassic of Phu Wiang, Northeastern Thailand: *Revue de Paléobiologie*, 3 (2), pp. 217–220.

Buffetaut, Éric, and Jean Le Loeuff, 1991, Une nouvelle espèce de *Rhabdodon* (Dinosauria, Ornithischia) du Crétacé supérieur de l'Hérault (Sud de la France): *Comptes Rendus des Séances de l'Académie des Sciences, Paris*, 312, Série II, pp. 943–948.

Buffetaut, Éric, Patrick Mechin, and Annie Mechin-Salessy, 1988, Un dinosaure théropode d'affinitiés gondwaniennes dans le Crétacé supérieur de Provence: *Comptes Rendus des Séances de l'Académie des Sciences, Paris*, Serie II. pp. 153–158.

Buffetaut, Éric, Daniel Pouit, and Philippe Taquet, 1980, Une dent de Dinosaurien Ornithopode remaniée dans les faluns miocènes de Doué-Douces (Maine-et-Loire): *Compte Rendu Sommaire des Séances de la Société Géologique de France*, 5, pp. 200–202.

Buffetaut, Éric, and Varavudh Suteethorn, 1992, A new species of the ornithischian dinosaur *Psittacosaurus* from the Early Cretaceous of Thailand: *Palaeontology*, 35 (4), pp. 801–812.

———, 1993, The dinosaurs of Thailand: *Journal of the Southeast Asian Earth Society*, 8, pp. 77–82.

Buffetaut, Éric, Varavudh Suteethorn, and Halyan Tong, 1996, The earliest known tyrannosaur from the Lower Cretaceous of Thailand: *Nature*, 381, pp. 689–691.

Buffrénil, V. de, James O. Farlow, and Armand de Ricqlés, 1986, Growth and function of *Stegosaurus* plates: evidence from bone histology: *Paleobiology*, 12 (4), pp. 459–473.

Bunzel, Emanuel, 1871, Die Reptilfauna der Gosau-Formation in der neuen Welt bei Wiener-Neustadt: Abhandlungen der kaiserl. königl. k. k. geolog. Reichsanstalt. Bd. 5, pp. 1–16.

Buscalioni, A. D., F. Ortega, B. P. Pérez-Moreno, B. P., and S. E. Evans, 1996, The Upper Jurassic maniraptoran theropod *Lisboasaurus estesi* (Guimarota, Portugal): *Jour-*

nal of Vertebrate Paleontology, 16 (2), pp. 358–362.

Byrnes, J., 1977, Notes on the Rolling Downs Group in the Milparinka, White Cliffs and Angledool 1 :250 000 sheet areas: *Geological Survey of New South Wales*, Report. GS 1977/005, pp. 1–17.

Cabrera, A., 1947, Un saurópodo nuevo del Jurásico de Patagonia: *Notas del Museo de la Plata*, 12, Paleontology, p.95.

Callison, George, 1987, Fruita: A place for wee fossils, *in*: Walter R. Averett, editor, *Paleontology and Geology of the Dinosaur Triangle, Guidebook for 1987 Field Trip*, pp. 91–96.

Callison, George, and Helen M. Quimby, 1984, Tiny dinosaurs: are they fully grown?: *Journal of Vertebrate Paleontology*, 3 (4), pp. 200–209.

Calvo, Jorge O., and José F. Bonaparte, 1991, *Andesaurus delgadoi* gen et sp. nov. (Saurischia-Sauropoda), Dinosaurio Titanosauridae de la Formación Río Limay (Albiano-Cenomaniano), Neuquén, Argentina: *Ameghiniana*, 28 (3–4), pp. 303–310, Buenos Aires.

Camp, Charles L., 1935, Dinosaur remains from the province of Szechuan, China: University of California Publications, 23 (15), pp. 467–472.

Carpenter, Kenneth, 1982a, Baby dinosaurs from the Late Cretaceous Lance and Hell Creek formations and a description of a new species of theropod: *Contributions to Geology*, 20 (2), pp. 123–134.

_____, 1982b, The oldest Late Cretaceous dinosaurs in North America?: *Mississippi Geology*, 8 (2), pp. 11–17.

_____, 1982c, Skeletal and dermal armor reconstructions of *Euoplocephalus tutus* (Ornithischia: Ankylosauridae) from the late Cretaceous Oldman Formation, Alberta: *Canadian Journal of Earth Sciences*, 19, pp. 689–697.

_____, 1983, Evidence suggesting gradual extinction of Latest Cretaceous dinosaurs: *Naturwissenschaften* 70, pp. 611–612.

_____, 1984, Skeletal reconstruction and life restoration of *Sauropelta* (Ankylosauria: Nodosauridae) from the Cretaceous of North America: *Canadian Journal of Earth Science*, 21, pp. 1491–1498.

_____, 1990, Ankylosaur systematics: example using *Panoplosaurus* and *Edmontonia* (Ankylosauria: Nodosauridae), *in*: Carpenter and Philip J. Currie, editors, *Dinosaur Systematics: Approaches and Perspectives*. Cambridge, New York and Melbourne: Cambridge University Press, pp. 281–299.

_____, 1990a, Variation in *Tyrannosaurus rex*, *in*: Kenneth Carpenter and Philip J. Currie, editors, *Dinosaur Systematics: Approaches and Perspectives*. Cambridge: Cambridge University Press, pp. 141–145.

_____, 1990b, Ankylosaur systematics: example using *Panoplosaurus* and *Edmontonia* (Ankylosauria: Nodosauridae), *in*: Carpenter and Philip J. Currie, editors, *Dinosaur Systematics: Approaches and Perspectives*. Cambridge, New York and Melbourne: Cambridge University Press, pp. 281–299.

_____, 1992, Tyrannosaurids (Dinosauria) of Asia and North America, *in*: Niall J. Mateer and Chen Pei-Ji, editors: *International Symposium on Non-marine Cretaceous Correlation*. Beijing: China Ocean Press, pp. 250–268.

Carpenter, Kenneth, and Brent H. Breithaupt, 1986, Latest Cretaceous occurrence of nodosaurid ankylosaurs (Dinosauria, Ornithischia) in Western North America and the gradual extinction of the dinosaurs: *Journal of Vertebrate Paleontology*, 6 (3), pp. 251–257.

Carpenter, Kenneth, David Dilkes, and David B. Weishampel, 1995, The dinosaurs of the Niobrara Chalk Formation (Upper Cretaceous, Kansas): *Journal of Vertebrate Paleontology*, 15 (2), pp. 275–297.

Carpenter, Kenneth, and Bryan Small, 1993, New evidence for plate arrangement in *Stegosaurus stenops* (Dinosauria): *Journal of Vertebrate Paleontology*, Abstracts of Papers, Fifty-third Annual Meeting, pp. 28A–29A.

Carpenter, Kenneth, and Matthew B. Smith, 1995, Osteology and functional morphology of the forelimb in tyrannosaurids as compared with other theropods (Dinosauria): *Journal of Vertebrate Paleontology*, Abstracts of Papers, Fifty-fifth Annual Meeting, p. 21A.

Carr, Thomas D., 1995, Towards a systematic revision of the Tyrannosauridae from the Judith River Group (Late Campanian) of Alberta: *Journal of Vertebrate Paleontology*, Abstracts of Papers, Fifty-fifth Annual Meeting, p. 21A.

Carroll, Robert T., and Peter M. Galton, 1977, 'Modern' lizard from the Upper Triassic of China: *Nature*, 266, pp. 252–255.

Casamiquela, Rodolfo M., 1963, Consideraciones acerca de *Amygdalodon* Cabrera (Saurópoda, Cetiosauridae) del Jurásico medio de la Patagonia: *Ameghiniana*, 3 (3), pp. 79–95.

_____, 1967a, Materiales adicionales y reinterpretacíin de *Aetosauroides scagliai* (de Ischigualasto, San Juan): Rev. Mus. La Plata (n.s.), Paleontology, 5, pp. 173–196.

_____, 1967b, Un nuevo dinosaurio ornitísquio triásico, (*Pisanosaurus mertii*; Ornithopoda) de la formación Ischigualasto, Argentina: *Ameghiniana*, 5 (2), pp. 47–64.

_____, 1980, La Presencia del genus *Plateosaurus*. Prosaurópoda el Triásico Superior de la Formación El Tranqul Patagonia: Actas 2 Congreso Argentino de Paleontología y Biostratigrafía y 1ero Congreso Latinomericano de Paleontología, Buenos Aires, 1978, 1, pp. 143–159.

Casamiquela, Rodolfo M., and Armando Fasola, 1968, Sobre pisadas de dinosaurios del Cretácico Inferior de Colchagua (Chile): Universidad de Chile, Facultad de Ciencias Físicas y Matemáticas, Departamento de Geología, 30, pp. 5–24.

Casanovas, M. L., J. V. Santafe, J. L. Sanz, and A. D. Buscalioni, 1987, Arcosaurios (Crocodilia, Dinosauria) del Cretácio superior de la Conca de Tremp (Lleida, España): Estudios Geológicos, vol. extraordinario Galve-Tremp, pp. 95–110.

Casanovas-Cladellas, M. L., J. V. Santafé-Llopis, and A. Isidoro-Llorens, 1993, *Pararhabdodon isonense*, n. gen. n. sp. (Dinosauria) Estudio morfológico, radio-tomográfico y consideraciones biomecánicas: *Paleontologia I Evolució*, 26–27, pp. 121–131 (in Spanish).

Case, Ermin J., 1927, The vertebral column of *Coelophysis* Cope: University of Michigan Contributions from the Museum of Geology, 2 (10), pp. 209–222.

Casey, R., 1961, The stratigraphical palaeontology of the Lower Greensand: *Palaeontology*, 3, pp. 487–621.

Chakravarti, D. K., 1934, On a stegosaurian humerus from the Lameta beds of Jubbulpore: *Quarterly Journal, Geological Mining and Metalurgical Society of India*, 6, p. 75.

_____, 1935, Is *Lametasaurus indicus* an armored dinosaur?: *American Journal of Science*, 5 (30), pp. 138–141.

Chanda, S. K., and A. Bhattacharyya, 1966, A re-evaluation of the stratigraphy of the Lameta-Jabalpur contact around Jabalpur: *Journal of the Geological Society of India*, 7, pp. 92–99.

Chang Y.P., and Tung Y.S., 1963, [Subdivision of the "Red Beds" of Nanshiung Basin, Kwantung.]: *Vertebrata PalAsiatica*, 7 (3), pp. 249–262.

Chao, S.T. 1962, A new species of psittacosaurs from Laiyang, Shantung: *Vertebrata PalAsiatica*, 6, pp. 349–360.

Chapman, Ralph E., and Michael K. Brett-Surman, 1990, Morphometric observations on hadrosaurid ornithopods, *in*: Carpenter and Philip J. Currie, editors, *Dinosaur Systematics: Approaches and Perspectives*. Cambridge, New York and Melbourne: Cambridge University Press, pp. 163–177.

Chapman, Ralph E., Peter M. Galton, J. John Sepkoski, Jr., and William P. Wall, 1981, A morphometric study of the pachycephalosaurid dinosaur *Stegoceras*: *Journal of Paleontology*, 55 (3), pp. 608–618.

Charig, Alan J., 1967, Subclass Archosauria, *in*: *The Fossil Record*. Geological Society of London 1967, pp. 708, 718, 725–731.

_____, 1973, Jurassic and Cretaceous dinosaurs, *in*: Hallam, A., editor, *Atlas of Palaeobiogeography*. Amsterdam: Elsevier, pp. 339–352.

_____, 1976, "Dinosaur monophyly and a new class of vertebrates": a critical review: *Linnean Society Symposium*, Series 3, pp. 65–104.

_____, 1978: Report on the British Museum (Natural History) 1975–1977, pp. 20–21.

_____, 1979, *A New Look at the Dinosaurs*. New York: Facts on File, 160 pages.

_____, 1980, A diplodocid sauropod from the Lower Cretaceous of England, *in*: Louis L. Jacobs, editor, *Aspects of Vertebrate History: Essays in Honor of Edwin Harris Colbert*. Flagstaff: Museum of Northern Arizona Press, pp. 231–244.

Charig, Alan J., John Attridge, and A. W. Crompton, 1965, On the origin of the sauropods and the classification of the Saurischia: *Proclamations of the Linnean Society*, 176, pp. 197–221.

Charig, Alan J., and A. W. Crompton, 1974, The alleged synonymy of *Lycorhinus* and *Heterodontosaurus*: *Annals of the South African Museum*, 64, pp. 167–189.

Charig, Alan J., and Angela C. Milner, *Baryonyx*, a remarkable new theropod dinosaur: *Nature*, 324, pp. 359–361.

_____, 1990, The systematic position of *Baryonyx walkeri*, in the light of Gauthier's reclassification of the Teropoda, *in*: Kenneth Carpenter and Philip J. Currie, editors, *Dinosaur Systematics: Approaches and Perspectives*. Cambridge, New York and Melbourne: Cambridge University Press, pp. 127–140.

Chatterjee, Sankar, 1978, *Indosuchus* and *Indosaurus*, Cretaceous carnosaurs from India: *Journal of Paleontology*, 52 (3), pp. 570–580.

_____, 1984, A new ornithischian dinosaur from the Triassic of North America: *Naturwissenschaften*, 71 (630), pp. 630–631.

Bibliography

_____, 1985, *Postosuchus*, a new thecodontian reptile from the Triassic of Texas and the origin of tyrannosaurs: *Philosophical Transactions of the Royal Society of London*, B 309, pp. 395–460.

_____, 1987, A new theropod dinosaur from India with remarks on the Gondwana-Laurasia connection in the Late Triassic, *in*: Garry D. McKenzie, editor, Gondwana Six; Stratigraphy, sedimentology, and paleontology, Geophysical Monograph, 41, pp. 183–189.

_____, 1993a, *Shuvosaurus*, a new theropod: *National Geographic Research & Exploration*, 9 (3), pp. 274–285.

_____, 1993b, *Procompsognathus* from the Triassic of Germany is not a crocodylomorph: *Journal of Vertebrate Paleontology*, Abstracts of Papers, Fifty-third Meeting, p. 29A.

Chen Pei-ji, 1982, Jurassic conchostracans from Mengyin district, Shandong: *Acta Paleontologia Sinica*, 21, pp. 133–139.

Chin, Karen, 1990, Possible herbivorous dinosaur coprolites from the Two Medicine Formation (Late Cretaceous) of Montana: *Journal of Vertebrate Paleontology*, Abstracts of Papers, Fiftieth Annual Meeting, pp. 17A–18A.

Chinsamy, Anusuya, 1995, Ontogenetic changes in the bone histology of the Late Jurassic ornithopod *Dryosaurus lettowvorbecki*: *Journal of Vertebrate Paleontology*, 15 (1), pp. 96–104.

Chure, Daniel J., 1992, Lepidosaurian reptiles from the Brushy Basin Member of the Morrison Formation (Upper Jurassic) of Dinosaur National Monument, Utah and Colorado, USA: *Journal of Vertebrate Paleontology*, Abstracts of Papers, Fifty-second Annual Meeting, p. 24A.

_____, 1994, *Koparion douglassi*, a new dinosaur from the Morrison Formation (Upper Jurassic) of Dinosaur National Monument; the oldest troodontid (Theropoda: Maniraptora): *BYU Geological Studies 1994*, 40, pp. 11–15.

_____, 1995, The teeth of small theropods from the Morrison Formation (Upper Jurassic; Kimmeridgian), Utah: *Journal of Vertebrate Paleontology*, Abstracts of Papers, Fifty-fifth Annual Meeting, p. 23A.

Chure, Daniel J., and George F. Engelmann, 1989, The fauna of the Morrison Formation in Dinosaur National Monument, *in*: J. J. Flynn, editor, Mesozoic/Cenozoic Vertebrate Paleontology: Classic Localities, Contemporary Approaches: 28th International Geological Congress, Field Trip Guidebook T322, pp. 8–14.

Chure, Daniel J., George F. Engelmann, and Scott K. Madsen, 1989, Non-mammalian microvertebrates from the Morrison Formation (Upper Jurassic, Kimmeridgian) of Dinosaur National Monument, Utah-Colorado, USA: *Journal of Vertebrate Paleontology*, Abstracts of Papers, Fiftieth Annual Meeting, pp. 16A–17A.

Chure, Daniel J., James H. Madsen, Jr., and Brooks B. Britt (1993), New data on theropod dinosaurs from the Late Jurassic Morrison Fm (MF): *Journal of Vertebrate Paleontology*, Abstracts of Papers, Fifty-third Annual Meeting, p. 30A.

Chure, Daniel J., and John S. McIntosh, 1989, *A Bibliography of the Dinosauria (Exclusive of the Aves), 1677–1986*. Grand Junction, Colorado: Museum of Western Colorado, *Paleontology Series 1*, 226 pages.

Clark, James M., and David Eliot Fastovsky, 1986, Vertebrate biostratigraphy of the Glen Canyon Group in northern Arizona, *in*: Kevin Padian, editor, *The Beginning of the Age of Dinosaurs*. New York: Cambridge University Press, pp. 285–301.

Clark, James M., Mark N. Norell, Luis M. Chiappe, and Antgerl Perle, 1995, The phylogenetic relationships of "segnosaurs" (Theropoda, Therizinosauridae): *Journal of Vertebrate Paleontology*, Abstracts of Papers, Fifty-fifth Annual Meeting, p. 24A.

Clark, James M., Altangerel Perle, and Michael A. Norell, 1993, The skull of the segnosaurian dinosaur *Erlikosaurus*: *Journal of Vertebrate Paleontology*, Abstracts of Papers, Fifty-third Annual Meeting, pp. 30A–31A.

_____, 1994, The skull of *Erlikosaurus andrewsi*, a Late Cretaceous "segnosaur" (Theropoda: Therizinosauridae) from Mongolia: *American Museum Novitiates*, 3115, 89 pages.

Clayton, R. N., and G. E. Stevens, 1965, Palaeotemperatures of New Zealand belemnites: *Consiglio Nazionale Eelle Ricerche, Laboratorio di Geologia Nucleare*, Pisa, Italy, pp. 1–6.

Clemens, William A., 1986, Evolution of the terrestrial vertebrate fauna during the Cretaceous-Tertiary transition, *in*: Elliot, D.K., editor, *Dynamics of Extinction*. New York: Wiley and Sons.

Clottes, P., and C. Raynaud, 1983, Le gisement à Dinosauriens de Campagne-sur-Aude-Espéraza: observations préliminaires, premiers résultats: *Bull. Soc. Et. Sci. Aude*, 83, pp. 5–14.

Cloudsley-Thompson, J. L., 1972, Temperature regulation in desert reptiles: *Symposium of the Zoological Society of London*, 31, pp. 39–59.

Cobabe, Emily A., and David E. Fastovsky, 1987, *Ugrosaurus olsoni*, a new ceratopsian (Reptilia: Ornithischia) from the Hell Creek Formation of eastern Montana: *Journal of Paleontology*, 61 (1), pp. 148–154.

Colbert, Edwin H. [Harris], 1945, *The Dinosaur Book*. New York: American Museum of Natural History, Man and Nature Publications, 14, 156 pages.

_____, 1947, The little dinosaurs of Ghost Ranch: *Natural History*, 56, pp. 392–399, New York.

_____, 1948a, A hadrosaurian dinosaur from New Jersey: *Academy of Natural Sciences of Philadelphia, Proceedings*, 100, pp. 23–27.

_____, 1948b, Evolution of horned dinosaurs: *Evolution*, 2, pp. 145–163.

_____, 1955, *Evolution of the Vertebrates: A History of the Backboned Animals Through Time*. New York: John Wiley and Sons, xvi, 510 pages.

_____, 1961, *Dinosaurs: Their Discovery and Their World*. New York: E. P. Dutton & Co., xiv, 300 pages.

_____, 1962, The weights of dinosaurs: *American Museum Novitates*, 2076, pp. 1–16.

_____, 1964, The Triassic dinosaur genera *Podokesaurus* and *Coelophysis*: *Ibid.*, 2168, pp. 1–12.

_____, 1965, *The Age of Reptiles*. New York: W. W. Norton & Company, 228 pages.

_____, 1968, *Men and Dinosaurs: The Search in Field and Laboratory*. New York: E. P. Dutton and Company, viii, 283 pages.

_____, 1970a, Fossils of the Connecticut Valley: The Age of Dinosaurs begins (revised edition): State Geological and Natural History Survey of Connecticut, bulletin 96, iv, 32 pages.

_____, 1970b, A saurischian dinosaur from the Triassic of Brazil: *American Museum Novitates*, 2405, 39 pages.

_____, 1973, *Wandering Lands and Animals*. London: Hutchinson & Co., xxi, 325 pages.

_____, 1981a, A primitive ornithischian dinosaur from the Kayenta Formation of Arizona: Museum of Northern Arizona Press, Bulletin Series 53, vii, 61 pages.

_____, 1981b, The Petrified Forest and its vertebrate fauna in Triassic Pangea, *in*: Colbert and R. Roy Johnson, editors, The Petrified Forest Through the Ages, Museum of Northern Arizona Bulletin 54, pp. 33–43.

_____, 1983, *Dinosaurs: An Illustrated History*. Maplewood, New Jersey: Hammond Incorporated, 224 pages.

_____, 1989, The Triassic dinosaur *Coelophysis*: Museum of Northern Arizona Bulletin 57, xv, 160 pages.

_____, 1990, Variation in *Coelophysis bauri*, *in*: Carpenter and Philip J. Currie, editors, *Dinosaur Systematics: Approaches and Perspectives*. Cambridge, New York and Melbourne: Cambridge University Press, pp. 81–90.

_____, 1995, *The Little Dinosaurs of Ghost Ranch*. New York: Columbia University Press, xii, 250 pages.

Colbert, Edwin Harris, and Donald Baird, 1958, Coelurosaur bone casts from the Connecticut Valley Triassic: *American Museum Novitates*, 1901, pp. 1–11.

Colbert, Edwin H., and J. D. Bump, 1947, A skull of *Torosaurus* from South Dakota and a revision of the genus: Academy of Natural Sciences of Philadelphia, Proceedings, 99, pp. 93–106.

Colbert, Edwin H., R. B. Cowles, and C. M. Bogert, 1946, Temperature tolerances in the American alligator and their bearing on the habits, evolution, and extinction of the dinosaurs: *Bulletin of the American Museum of Natural History*, 86, pp. 327–374.

Colbert, Edwin H., and Joseph T. Gregory, 1957, Correlation of continental Triassic sediments by vertebrate fossils: *Bulletin of the Geological Society of America*, 68, pp. 1456–1467.

Colbert, Edwin H., and Dale A. Russell, 1969, The small Cretaceous dinosaur *Dromaeosaurus*: *American Museum Novitiates*, 2380, pp. 145–162.

Colinvaux, P., 1878, *Why Big, Fierce Animals Are Rare: An Ecologist's Perspective*. Princeton, New Jersey: Princeton University Press, 256 pages.

Collot, Louis Marie-Francois, 1891, Description du terrane Crétacé dans une parte de la basse: *Provence Bulletin Société Géologique*, France, 3 (19), pp. 39–92.

Conybeare, A., and G. Haynes, 1984, Observations on elephant mortality and bones in water holes: *Quaternary Research*, 22, pp. 189–200.

Coombs, Walter P., Jr., 1971, The Ankylosauria. Ph.D. thesis, Columbia University, New York: 487 pages.

_____, 1972, The bony eyelid of *Euoplocephalus* (Reptilia, Ornithischia): *Journal of Paleontology*, 46, pp. 637–650.

_____, 1975, Sauropod habits and habitats: *Palaeogeography, Palaeoclimatology, Palaeoecology*, 17, pp. 1–33.

_____, 1978a, The families of the ornithischian dinosaur order Ankylosauria: *Paleontology*, 21, part 1, pp. 143–170.

_____, 1978b, An endocranial cast of *Euoplocephalus* (Reptilia, Ornithischia), Palaeontographica, 161, pp. 176–182.

_____, 1978c, Theoretical aspects of cursorial adaptations in dinosaurs: *The Quarterly Review of Biology*, 53, pp. 393–418.

_____, 1979, Osteology and myology of the hindlimb in the Ankylosauria (Reptilia, Ornithischia): *Journal of Paleontology*, 46, pp. 637–650.

_____, 1980a, Juvenile ceratopsians from Mongolia—the smallest known dinosaur specimens: *Nature*, 283 (5745), pp. 380–381.

_____, 1980b, Swimming ability of carnivorous dinosaurs: *Science*, 207, pp. 1198–1200.

_____, 1982, Juvenile specimens of the ornithischian dinosaur *Psittacosaurus*: *Palaeontology*, 25, part 1, pp. 89–107.

_____, 1986, A juvenile ankylosaur referrable to the genus *Euoplocephalus* (Reptilia, Ornithischia): *Journal of Paleontology*, 6 (2), pp. 162–173.

_____, 1988, The status of the dinosaurian genus *Diclonius* and the taxonomic utility of hadrosaurian teeth: *Journal of Paleontology*, 62 (5), pp. 812–817.

_____, 1989, Modern analogs for dinosaur nesting and parental behavior, *in*: James O. Farlow, editor, Paleobiology of the dinosaurs: *Geological Society of America Special Papers*, 238, pp. 21–54.

_____, 1990a, Teeth and taxonomy in ankylosaurs, *in*: Carpenter and Philip J. Currie, editors, *Dinosaur Systematics: Approaches and Perspectives*. Cambridge, New York and Melbourne: Cambridge University Press, pp. 269–279.

_____, 1990b, Behavior patterns of dinosaurs, *in*: David B. Weishampel, Peter Dodson, and Halszka Osmólska, editors, *The Dinosauria*. Berkeley and Los Angeles: University of California Press, pp. 32–42.

_____, 1995, A new nodosaurid (Dinosauria: Ornithischia) from the Lower Cretaceous of Texas: *Journal of Vertebrate Paleontology*, 15 (2), pp. 298–312.

_____, 1995, Ankylosaurian tail clubs of middle Campanian to early Maastrichtian age from western North America, with description of a tiny club from Alberta and discussion of tail orientation and tail club function: *Canadian Journal of Earth Sciences*, 32, pp. 902–912.

Coombs, Walter P., Jr., and Peter M. Galton, 1988, *Dysganus*, an indeterminate ceratopsian dinosaur: *Journal of Paleontology*, 62 (5), pp. 818–821.

Coombs, Walter P., Jr., and Teresa Maryańska, 1990, Ankylosauria, *in*: David B. Weishampel, Peter Dodson, and Halszka Osmólska, editors, *The Dinosauria*. Berkeley and Los Angeles: University of California Press, pp. 456–483.

Coombs, Walter P., Jr., and Ralph E. Molnar, 1981, Sauropoda (Reptilia, Saurischia) from the Cretaceous of Queensland: *Memoirs of the Queensland Museum*, 20, pp. 351–373.

Coombs, Walter P., Jr., David B. Weishampel, and Lawrence M. Witmer, 1990, Basal Thyreophora, *in*: Weishampel, Peter Dodson, and Halszka Osmólska, editors, *The Dinosauria*. Berkeley and Los Angeles: University of California Press, pp. 427–434.

Cooper, Michael R., 1980a, The prosauropod ankle and dinosaur phylogeny: *South African Journal of Science*, 86, pp. 176–178.

_____, 1980b, The first record of the prosauropod dinosaur *Euskelosaurus* from Zimbabwe: *Arnoldia* (Zimbabwe), 9 (3), pp. 1–17.

_____, 1981, The prosauropod dinosaur *Massospondylus carinatus* Owen from Zimbabwe: its biology, mode of life and phylogenetic significance: *Occasional Papers of the National Museums and Monuments*, B., Natural Science, Bulawayo, 6 (10), pp. 689–840.

_____, 1982, A mid–Permian to earliest Jurassic tetrapod biostratigraphy and its significance: *Arnoldia* (Zimbabwe), 9 (7), pp. 77–104.

_____, 1984, A reassessment of *Vulcanodon karibaensis* Raath (Dinosauria: Saurischia) and the origin of the Sauropoda: *Palaeontologia Africana*, 25, pp. 203–231.

_____, 1985, A revision of the ornithischian dinosaur *Kangnasaurus coeztzeei* Haughton, with a classification of the Ornithischia: *Annals of the South African Museum*, 95, pp. 281–317.

Cope, Edward Drinker, 1866, Remarks on dinosaur remains from New Jersey, Academy of Natural Sciences of Philadelphia, Proceedings, June, pp. 275–279.

_____, 1868, On the genus *Laelaps*: *American Journal of Science*, 2 (66), pp. 415–417.

_____, 1869a, [Remarks on *Holops brevispinus*, *Ornithotarsus immanis* and *Macrosaurus proriger*]: *Academy of Natural Sciences of Philadelphia, Proceedings*, 21, p. 123.

_____, 1869b, [Remarks on *Eschrichtius polyporus*, *Hypsibema crassicauda*, *Hadrosaurus tripos*, and *Polydectes biturgidus*]: *Ibid.*, 21, p. 192.

_____, 1870, Synopsis of the extinct Batrachia, Reptilia and Aves of North America: *Transactions of the American Philosophical Society*, 14, pp. 1–252.

_____, 1871, Supplement to the synopsis of the extinct Batrachia and Reptilia of North America: *American Philosophical Society, Proceedings*, 12 (86), pp. 41–52.

_____, 1872, Review of Professor Marsh's paper of May, 1872; corrections of questions of nomenclature and discovery: *Ibid.*, (separata August 12).

_____, 1874a, Report on the stratigraphy and Pliocene vertebrate paleontology of northern Colorado: *United States Geological and Geographical Survey Territories*, Bulletin 1, series 1, pp. 9–28.

_____, 1874b, Review of the Vertebrata of the Cretaceous period found west of the Mississippi River: *Ibid.*, Bulletin 2, series 1, pp. 3–48.

_____, 1875a, The vertebrata of the Cretaceous formation of the West: *Report of the United States Geological Survey of the Territories*, II, pp. 53–65.

_____, 1875b, On the transition beds of the Saskatchewan district: *Academy of Natural Sciences of Philadelphia, Proceedings*, 27, pp. 9–10.

_____, 1876a, Descriptions of some vertebrate remains from the Fort Union beds of Montana: *Ibid.*, 28, pp. 248–262.

_____, 1876b, On some extinct reptiles and Batrachia from the Judith River and Fox Hills Beds of Montana: *Ibid.*, pp. 340–359.

_____, 1877a, On a gigantic saurian from the Dakota epoch of Colorado: *Paleontology Bulletin*, 27, pp. 5–10.

_____, 1877b, On *Amphicoelias*, a genus of Saurians from the Dakota Epoch of Colorado: *Paleontology Bulletin*, 27, pp. 1–5.

_____, 1877c, On reptilian remains from the Dakota beds of Colorado: *American Philosophical Society, Proceedings*, 17, pp. 193–196.

_____, 1877d, On the carnivorous dinosaur from the Dakota beds of Colorado: *Bulletin of the United States Geological Survey Territories*, 3, pp. 805–806.

_____, 1877e, On a dinosaurian from the Trias of Utah: *American Philosophical Society, Proceedings*, 16 (99), pp. 579–584.

_____, 1878a, On the saurians recently discovered in the Dakota beds of Colorado: *American Naturalist*, 12, p. 82.

_____, 1878b, On the Vertebrata of the Dakota Epoch of Colorado: *Paleontology Bulletin*, 28, pp. 233–247.

_____, 1878c, Descriptions of new extinct Vertebrata from the Upper Tertiary and Dakota Formations: *United States Geological and Geographical Survey, Territories*, 4 (2), p. 392.

_____, 1878d, A new genus of Dinosauria from Colorado: *American Naturalist*, 12, pp. 188–189.

_____, 1878e, A new opisthocoelous dinosaur: *Ibid.*, p. 406.

_____, 1878f, A new species of *Amphicoelias*: *Ibid.*, pp. 563–565.

_____, 1878g, On some saurians found in the Triassic of Pennsylvania by C. M. Wheatley: *Paleontological Bulletin*, 28, pp. 231–232 (also *Proceedings of the American Philosophical Society*, XVII, pp. 231–232).

_____, 1879, New Jurassic Dinosauria: *Ibid.*, 13, pp. 402–404.

_____, 1883, The structure and appearance of a Laramie dinosaurian: *Ibid.*, 17, pp. 774–777.

_____, 1884, Marsh on *Diplodocus*: *Ibid.*, 18, p. 526.

_____, 1887a, The dinosaurian genus *Coelurus*: *American Naturalist*, vol. 21, pp. 367–369.

_____, 1887b, A contribution to the history of the Vertebrata of the Trias of North America: *American Philosophical Society, Proceedings*, 24 (126), pp. 209–228.

_____, 1889a, The horned dinosaurs of the Laramie: *American Naturalist*, 23, pp. 715–717.

_____, 1889b, Notes on the Dinosauria of the Laramie: *Ibid.*, 23, pp. 904–906.

_____, 1890, Note on the teeth mentioned by Professor Marsh: *American Naturalist*, 24, p. 571.

_____, 1892a, On the skull of the dinosaurian *Laelaps incrassatus* Cope: *American Philosophical Society, Proceedings*, 30, pp. 240–245.

_____, 1892b, Fourth note on the Dinosauria of the Laramie: *American Naturalist*, 26, pp. 756–758.

Corla, Rodolfo A., and Leonardo Salgado, 1995, A new giant carnivorous dinosaur from the Cretaceous of Patagonia: *Nature*, 377, pp. 224–226.

Cornet, Bruce, Alfred Traverse, and Nicholas G. McDonald, 1973, Fossil spores, pollen, and fishes from Connecticut indicate early Jurassic age for part of Newark Group: *Science*, 182, pp. 1243–1247.

Corro, Guillermo del, 1966, Un nuevo dinosaurio carnívoro del Chubut: *Museo Argentino de Ciencias Naturales "Bernardino Rivadaria," Communicaciones Paleontología*, 1 (1), pp. 1–14.

Bibliography

_____, 1974, Un nuevo dinosaurio megalo-saurio (carnosaurio) del Cretáceo de Chubut (Argentina): *Ibid.,* pp. 37–44.

_____, 1975, Un nuevo saurópodo del Creta-cio Superior: *Actas 1 Congress Argentina, Paleontology and Biostratigraphy,* 2, pp. 229–240.

Cousins, R., G. Breton, R. Fournier, and J.-P. Watte, 1989, Dinosaur egg-laying and nest-ing: the case of an Upper Maastrichtian site at Rennes-Le-Chateau (Aude, France): *His-torical Biology,* 2 (2), pp. 157–167.

Cox, C. B., 1974, Vertebrate palaeodistribu-tional patterns and continental drift: *Journal of Biogeography,* 1, pp. 75–94.

Cracraft, Joel, 1971, Caenagnathiformes, Cre-taceous birds convergent in jaw mechanism of dicynodont reptiles: *Journal of Paleontol-ogy,* 45 (5), pp. 805–809.

Creisler, Benjamin S., 1992, Why *Monoclonius* Cope was not named for its horn: The ety-mologies of Cope's dinosaurs: *Journal of Vertebrate Paleontology,* 12 (3), pp. 313–317.

Crompton, A. W., 1968, In search of the "insignificant": *Discovery,* 3, pp. 23–32.

Crompton, A. W., and John Attridge, 1986, Masticatory apparatus of the larger herbivores during Late Triassic and Early Jurassic times, *in:* Kevin Padian, editor, *The Beginning of the Age of Dinosaurs: Faunal Change Across the Triassic-Jurassic Boundary.* New York: Cam-bridge University Press, pp. 223–236.

Crompton, A. W., and Alan J. Charig, 1962, A new ornithischian from the Upper Triassic of South Africa: *Nature,* London, 196, pp. 1074–1077.

Cruickshank, A. R. I., 1975, The origin of sauropod dinosaurs: *South African Journal of Science,* 71, pp. 89–90.

_____, 1979, The ankle joint in some early archosaurs: *Ibid.,* 75, pp. 168–178.

Cruickshank, A. R. I., and Michael J. Benton, 1985, Archosaur ankles and relationships of the thecodontian and dinosaurian reptiles: *Nature,* 317, pp. 715–717.

Cuny, Gilles, and Peter M. Galton, 1993, Revi-sion of the Airel dinosaur from the Triassic-Jurassic boundary (Normandy, France): *Neus Jahrbuch Fuer Geologie und Paläontologie Abhandlungen,* 187 (3), pp. 261–288.

Currey, J. D., 1960, Differences in the blood-supply of bone of different histological types: *Quarterly Journal of Microscopic Science,* 101, pp. 351–370.

Currie, Philip J. [John], 1980, Mesozoic ver-tebrate life in Alberta and British Columbia: *Mesozoic Vertebrate Life,* 1 (1), pp. 27–40.

_____, 1985, Cranial anatomy of *Stenony-chosaurus inequalis* (Saurischia, Theropoda) and its bearing on the origin of birds: *Cana-dian Journal of Earth Sciences,* 22, pp. 1643–1658.

_____, 1987a, Bird-like characteristics of the jaws and teeth of troodontid theropods (Dinosauria, Saurischia): *Journal of Vertebrate Paleontology,* 7 (1), pp. 72–81.

_____, 1987b, New approaches to studying dinosaurs in Dinosaur Provincial Park, *in:* Sylvia J. Czerkas and Everett C. Olson, edi-tors, *Dinosaurs Past and Present.* Seattle: Nat-ural History Museum of Los Angeles County, in association with University of Washington Press, pp. 100–117.

_____, 1987c, Theropods of the Judith River Formation of Dinosaur Provincial Park, Alberta, *in:* Currie, and E. H. Koster, editors, Fourth Symposium on Mesozoic Terrestrial Ecosystems, Short Papers, Tyrrell Museum of Paleontology, Drumheller, Alberta, pp. 52–60.

_____, 1989, The first record of *Elmisaurus* (Saurischia, Theropoda) from North Amer-ica: *Canadian Journal of Earth Sciences,* 26 (6), pp. 1319–1324.

_____, 1990, Elmisauridae, *in:* David B. Weis-hampel, Peter Dodson, and Halszka Osmól-ska, editors, *The Dinosauria.* Berkeley and Los Angeles: University of California Press, pp. 245–248.

_____, 1991, The Sino/Canadian Dinosaur Expeditions: *Geotimes,* April, pp. 18–21.

_____, 1992, Saurischian dinosaurs of the Late Cretaceous of Asia and North America, *in:* Niall J. Mateer and Chen Pei-Ji, editors, *Aspects of Nonmarine Cretaceous Geology.* Bei-jing: China Ocean Press, pp. 237–249.

_____, 1995, New information on the anat-omy and relationships of *Dromaeosaurus albertensis* (Dinosauria: Theropoda): *Journal of Vertebrate Paleontology,* 15 (3), pp. 576–591.

_____, 1995, Phylogeny and systematics of theropods (Dinosauria): *Journal of Verte-brate Paleontology,* Abstracts of Papers, Fifty-fifth Annual Meeting, 25A.

Currie, Philip J., and Peter Dodson, 1984, Mass death of a herd of Ceratopsian dino-saurs: Third Symposium on Mesozoic Ter-restrial Ecosystems, Short Papers, edited by W. E. Reif and F. Westphal, Tübingen (Attempto Verlag), pp. 61–66.

Currie, Philip J., and David A. Eberth, 1993, Palaeontology, sedimentology and palaeo-ecology of the Iren Dabasu Formation (Upper Cretaceous), Inner Mongolia, Peo-ple's Republic of China: *Cretaceous Research* (1993), pp. 127–144.

Currie, Philip J., Stephen J. Godfrey and Lev Nessov, 1993, New caenagnathid (Dino-sauria: Theropoda) specimens from the Upper Cretaceous of North America and Asia: *Canadian Journal of Earth Sciences,* 30 (10–11), pp. 2255–2272.

Currie, Philip J., and Aase Roland Jacobsen, 1995, An azhdarchid pterosaur eaten by a velociraptorine theropod: *Canadian Journal of Earth Sciences,* 32, pp. 922–925.

Currie, Philip J., Gregory C. Nadon, and Mar-tin G. Lockley, 1991, Dinosaur footprints with skin impressions from the Cretaceous of Alberta and Colorado: *Canadian Journal of Earth Sciences,* 28, pp. 102–115.

Currie, Philip J., and Jiang-Hua Peng, 1993, A juvenile specimen of *Saurornithoides mon-goliensis* from the Upper Cretaceous of northern China: *Canadian Journal of Earth Sciences,* 30 (10–11), pp. 2224–2230.

Currie, Philip J., J. Keith Rigby, Jr., and Robert E. Sloan, 1990, *in:* Carpenter and Philip J. Currie, editors, *Dinosaur Systematics: Approaches and Perspectives.* Cambridge, New York and Melbourne: Cambridge University Press, pp. 107–125.

Currie, Philip J., and Dale A. Russell, 1988, Osteology and relationships of *Chirostenotes pergracilis* (Saurischia, Theropoda) from the Judith River (Oldman) Formation of Alberta, Canada: *Canadian Journal of Earth Sciences,* 25, pp. 972–986.

Currie, Philip J., and Xi-Jin Zhao, 1993a, A new carnosaur (Dinosauria, Theropoda) from the Jurassic of Xinjiang, People's Republic of China: *Canadian Journal of Earth Sciences,* 30 (10–11), pp. 2037–2081.

_____, 1993b, A new troodontid (Dinosauria, Theropoda) braincase from the Dinosaur Park Formation (Campanian) of Alberta: *Ibid.,* pp. 2231–2247.

Curtice, Brian D., 1995, A description of the anterior caudal vertebrae of *Supersaurus vivianae*: *Journal of Vertebrate Paleontology,* Abstracts of Papers, Fifty-fifth Annual Meet-ing, p. 25A.

Cuvier, Georges, 1812, *Recherches sur les osse-ments fossiles,* Paris.

Czerkas, Stephen A., 1987, A reevaluation of the plate arrangement on *Stegosaurus stenops,* *in:* Sylvia J. Czerkas and Everett C. Olson, editors, *Dinosaurs Past and Present,* Volume II. Seattle: Natural History Museum of Los Angeles County, in association with Univer-sity of Washington Press, pp. 82–99.

_____, 1992, Discovery of dermal spines reveals a new look for sauropod dinosaurs: *Geology,* 20, pp. 1068–1070.

_____, 1993, Frills and goosenecks: *Journal of Vertebrate Paleontology,* Abstracts of Papers, Fifty-third Annual Meeting, p. 32A.

Czerkas, Sylvia J., and Stephen A. Czerkas, 1990, *Dinosaurs: A Global View.* Surrey, United Kingdom: Dragon's World, 247 pages.

Das-Gupta, H. C., 1931, On a new theropod dinosaur (*Orthogoniosaurus matleyi* n.g. et. n.sp.) from the Lameta beds of Jubbulpore: *Journal of the Asiatic Society of Bengal,* (N.S.), 26 (20), pp. 367–369.

Dames, W., 1884, *Megalosaurus Dunkeri:* Gesellschaft Naturforschender Freunde, Ber-lin, Stizungsber, 187 pages.

Darton, N. H., 1906, Geology of the Bighorn Mountains: *United States Geological Profes-sional Papers,* 51, pp. 1–129.

David, T. E. E., 1950, *The geology of the Com-monwealth of Australia,* 1. London: Edward Arnold, 747 pages.

Davitashvili, L., 1961 [*The Theory of Sexual Selection*]. Moscow: U.S.S.R. Academy of Sciences, 538 pages.

DeCourten, Frank L., 1978, Non-marine flora and fauna from the Kaiparowits Formation (Upper Cretaceous) of the Paria River Amphitheater, southwestern Utah: *Geologi-cal Society of America Abstracts with Programs,* 10 (3), p. 102.

DeCourten, Frank L., and Dale A. Russell, 1985, A specimen of *Ornithomimus velox* (Theropoda, Ornithomimidae) from the ter-minal Cretaceous Kaiparowits Formation of Southern Utah: *Journal of Paleontology,* 59 (5), pp. 1091–1099.

Deeming, D. Charles, and David M. Unwin, 1993, Fossil embryos and neonates: are they what we want them to be?: *Journal of Verte-brate Paleontology,* Abstracts of Papers, Fifty-third Annual Meeting, p. 32A.

Delair, Justin B., 1959, The Mesozoic reptiles of Dorset: *Proceedings of the Dorset Natural History Archaeological Society,* 81, pp. 52–90.

_____, 1973, The dinosaurs of Wiltshire: *The Wiltshire Archaeological and Natural History Magazine,* 68, pp. 1–7.

_____, 1982, Notes on an armored dinosaur from Barnes High, Isle of Wight: *Proceed-ings of the Isle of Wight Natural History and Archaeological Society,* 7, pp. 297–302.

Demathieu, Georges, and Hartmut Haubold, 1978, Du problème de l'origine des dino-sauriens d'après les données de l'ichnologie du Trias: *Géobios,* 11 (3), pp. 409–412.

Denton, Robert K., Jr., 1990, A revision of the theropod *Dryptosaurus* (*Laelaps*) *aquilungius*

(Cope 1869): *Journal of Vertebrate Paleontology*, Abstracts of Papers, Fiftieth Annual Meeting, p. 20A.

Depéret, Charles, 1896, Note sur les dinosauriens sauropodes et théropodes du Crétacé supérieur de Madagascar: *Bulletin, Société Géologique de France*, Series 3, 24, pp. 176–194.

_____, 1900, Note sur de nouveaus dinosauriens du Crétacé supérieur de la Monyagne-Noire: *Ibid.*, 3rd series, 28, p. 530.

Depéret, Charles, and J. Savornin, 1927, La faune de Reptiles et de Poissons albiens de Timimoun (Sahara algérien): *Bulletin, Société Géologique de France*, Series 4, 27, p 257.

Derstler, Kraig, 1995, The Dragons Grave: an *Edmontosaurus* bonebed containing theropod egg shells and juveniles, Lance Formation (Uppermost Cretaceous), Niobrara County, Wyoming: *Journal of Vertebrate Paleontology*, Abstracts of Papers, Fifty-fifth Annual Meeting, p. 26A.

Desmond, Adrian J., 1976, *The Hot-Blooded Dinosaurs: A Revolution in Paleontology*. New York: The Dial Press/James Wade, 1976, 238 pages.

Dettmann, M. E., 1973, Angiospermous pollen from Albian to Turonian sediments of eastern Australia: *Special Publications of the Geological Society of Australia*, 4, pp. 3–34.

Dodson, Peter, 1971, Sedimentology and taphonomy of the Oldman Formation (Campanian), Dinosaur Provincial Park, Alberta (Canada): *Palaeogeography, Palaeoclimatology, Palaeoecology*, 10, pp. 21–74.

_____, 1974, Dinosaurs as dinosaurs: *Evolution*, 28, pp. 494–497.

_____, 1975, Taxonomic implications of relative growth in lambeosaurine hadrosaurs: *Systematic Zoology*, 24, pp. 37–54.

_____, 1976, Quantitative aspects of relative growth and sexual dimorphism in *Protocerratops*: *Journal of Paleontology*, 50, pp. 929–940.

_____, 1980, Comparative osteology of the American ornithopods *Camptosaurus* and *Tenontosaurus*: *Mémoires de la Société Géologique de France* (ns), 59, pp. 81–85.

_____, 1984a, Small Judithian ceratopsids, Montana and Alberta, *in* W.-E. Reif and F. Wetphal, editors, Third Symposium on Mesozoic Terrestrial Ecosystems, Short Papers, Atempto Verlag, Tübingen, pp. 73–78.

_____, 1984b, International *Archaeopteryx* Conference: *Journal of Vertebrate Paleontology*, 5(2), pp. 177–179 (reprinted in: The Mosasaur, 2, pp. 164–166).

_____, 1986, *Avaceratops lammersi*: a new ceratopsid from the Judith River Formation of Montana: *Academy of Natural Sciences of Philadelphia, Proceedings*, 138 (2), pp. 305–317.

_____, 1987, Dinosaur Systematics Symposium, Tyrrell Museum of Paleontology, Drumheller, Alberta, June 2–5, 1986 (review): *Journal of Paleontology*, 7 (1), pp. 106–108.

_____, 1990a, Dinosaur Extinction, *in*: David B. Weishampel, Dodson, and Halszka Osmólska, editors, *The Dinosauria*. Berkeley and Los Angeles: University of California Press, pp. 55–62.

_____, 1990b, Marginocephalia, *Ibid.*, pp. 562–563.

_____, 1990c, Ceratopsia, *Ibid.*, p. 578.

_____, 1990d, On the status of the ceratopsids *Monoclonius* and *Centrosaurus*, *in*: Kenneth Carpenter and Philip J. Currie, editors, *Dinosaur Systematics: Approaches and Perspectives*. Cambridge, New York and Melbourne: Cambridge University Press, pp. 231–243.

_____, 1991, Morphological and ecological trends in the evolution of ceratopsian dinosaurs, *in*: Zofia Kielan-Jaworoska, Natascha Heintz, and Hans Arne Nakrem, editors, Fifth Symposium on Mesozoic Terrestrial Ecosystems and Biota, Extended Abstracts: Contributions from the Paleontological Museum, University of Oslo, 36, pp. 17–18.

_____, 1995, Reviews, *Dinosaur Eggs and Babies*: *Journal of Vertebrate Paleontology*, 15 (4), pp. 863–866.

Dodson, Peter, Robert T. Bakker, and Anna K. Behrensmeyer, 1983, Paleocology of the dinosaur-bearing Morrison Formation: *National Geographic Society Research Reports*, 15, pp. 145–156.

Dodson, Peter, and Philip J. Currie, 1988, The smallest ceratopsid skull—Judith River Formation of Alberta: *Canadian Journal of Earth Sciences*, 25 (6), pp. 926–930.

_____, 1990, Neoceratopsia, *in*: David B. Weishampel, Dodson, and Halszka Osmólska, editors, *The Dinosauria*. Berkeley and Los Angeles: University of California Press, pp. 593–618.

Dollo, Louis, 1882, Première note sur les dinosauriens de Bernissart: *Bulletin du Musée Royale d'Histoire Naturelle de Belgique*, 1, pp. 161–180.

_____, 1883, Note sur les restes de dinosauriens rencontrés dans le Crétacé Supérieur de la Belgique: *Ibid.*, 2, pp. 205–221.

_____, 1906, Les allures des Iguanodons, d'après les empreintes des pieds et de la queue: *Bulletin de Biologie*, France-Belgique, 40 (series 5, 9), pp 1–12.

Dong Zhim-Ming [formerly Zhiming], 1973, Reports of paleontological expedition to Sinkiang (II), Pterosaurian fauna from Wuerho, Sinkiang: *Memoirs of the Institute of Vertebrate Paleontology and Paleoanthropology Academia Sinica*, 11, pp. 45–52.

_____, 1977, On the dinosaurian remains from Turpan, Xinjiang: *Vertebrata PalAsiatica*, 15 (1), pp. 59–66.

_____, 1978, A new genus of pachycephalosauria from Laiyang, Shantung: *Ibid.*, 16 (4), pp. 225–226.

_____, 1979, Cretaceous dinosaur of Hunnan, *in*: *Mesozoic-Cenozoic Redbeds of Huanan*. Nanking Institute of Geology and Palaeontology, Academia Sinica, Chi-Ming-Ssu, Nanking, People's Republic of China, pp. 342–350.

_____, 1983, Reports of Paleontological Expedition to Sinkiang (II), Pterosaurian fauna from Wuerho, Sinkiang: *Memoirs of the Institute of Vertebrate Paleontology and Paleoanthropology Academia Sinica*, 11, pp. 45–52.

_____, 1984, A new theropod dinosaur from the Middle Jurassic of Sichuan: *Vertebrata PalAsiatica*, 22 (3), pp. 213–218.

_____, 1987a, [Untitled], *in*: Zhao Xijin, et al., editors, *Stratigraphy and Vertebrate Fossils of Xinjiang*. Beijing: IVPP publication, July, 1987, pp. 28–30.

_____, 1987b, *Dinosaurs from China*. Beijing: China Ocean Press, 114 pages.

_____, 1988, [Bony tail club: defensive weapon of sauropod dinosaurs]: *Hua Shi*, 55, 31 pages.

_____, 1989, On a small ornithopod (*Gongbusaurus wucaiwanensis* sp. nov.) from Kelamaili, Junggar Basin, Xinjiang, China: *Vertebrata PalAsiatica*, 27 (2), pp. 140–146.

_____, 1990a, On remains of the sauropods from Kelamaili Region, Junggar Basin, Xinjiang, China: *Vertebrata PalAsiatica*, 28 (1), pp. 43–58.

_____, 1990b, Stegosaurs of Asia, *in*: Kenneth Carpenter and Philip J. Currie, editors, *Dinosaur Systematics: Approaches and Perspectives*. Cambridge, New York and Melbourne: Cambridge University Press, pp. 255–268.

_____, 1992, *Dinosaurian Faunas of China*. Beijing: China Ocean Press, and Berlin: Springer-Verlag, xiii, 188 pages.

_____, 1993a, The field activities of the Sino-Canadian Dinosaur Project in China, 1987–1990: *Canadian Journal of Earth Sciences*, 30 (10–11), pp. 1997–2001.

_____, 1993b, Early Cretaceous dinosaur faunas in China: an introduction: *Ibid.*, pp. 2096–2100.

_____, 1993c, A new species of stegosaur (Dinosauria) from the Ordos Basin, Inner Mongolia, People's Republic of China: *Ibid.*, pp. 2174–2176.

_____, 1993d, An ankylosaur (ornithischian dinosaur) from the Middle Jurassic of the Junggar Basin, China: *Vertebrata PalAsiatica*, 31 (4), pp. 257–266.

Dong Zhi-Ming, and Philip J. Currie, 1993, Protoceratopsian embryos from Inner Mongolia, People's Republic of China: *Canadian Journal of Earth Sciences*, 30 (10–11), pp. 2248–2254.

_____, 1995, On the discovery of an oviraptorid skeleton on a nest of eggs: *Journal of Vertebrate Paleontology*, Abstracts of Papers, Fifty-fifth Annual Meeting, p. 26A.

_____, 1996, On the discovery of an oviraptorid skeleton on a nest of eggs at Bayan Mandahu, Inner Mongolia, People's Republic of China: *Canadian Journal of Earth Sciences*, 33, pp. 631–636.

Dong Zhi-Ming, Y. Hasagawa, and Y. Azuma, 1990, *The Age of Dinosaurs in Japan and China*. Fukui, Japan: Fukui Prefectural Museum, 65 pages.

Dong Zhi-Ming [formerly Zhiming], Y. H. Zhang, X. Li., and S. W. Zhou, 1978, Note on a new carnosaur *Yangchuanosaurus shangyuensis* gen. et. sp. nov. from the Jurassic of Yangchuan District, Sichuan Province. Kexue Tongbao, 23, pp. 298–302.

Dong Zhi-Ming [formerly Zhiming], Shi-wu Zhou, Xuan-min Li and Yihong Chang, 1977, On the stegosaurian remains from Zigong (Tzekung), Sichuan Province: *Vertebrata PalAsiatica*, 15, pp. 307–312.

Dong Zhi-Ming [formerly Zhiming] and Tang Zilu, 1983, Note on the new Mid-Jurassic ornithopod from Sichuan Basin, China: *Vertebrata PalAsiatica*, 21 (2), pp. 168–172.

Dong Zhi-Ming [formerly Zhiming], Zhou Shiwu and Zhang Zicheng, 1983, The dinosaurian remains from Sichuan Basin, China: *Paleontologia Sinica*, whole number 162, New Series C, 23, pp. 1–145.

Dong Zhi-Ming [formerly Zhiming] and Tang Zilu, 1984, Note on a new mid-Jurassic Sauropod (*Datousaurus bashanensis* gen. et sp. nov.) from Sichuan Basin, China: *Vertebrata PalAsiatica*, 22 (1), pp. 69–75.

Bibliography

_____, 1985, A new mid–Jurassic theropod (*Gasosaurus constructus* gen. et. sp. nov.) from Dashanpu, Zigong, Sichuan Province, China: *Ibid.,* 23 (1), pp. 79–83.

Dong Zhi-Ming [formerly Zhiming], Tang Zilu and Zhou Shiwu, 1982, Note on the new mid–Jurassic stegosaur from Sichuan Basin, China: *Vertebrata PalAsiatica,* 20, pp. 83–87.

Drinnan, A.N., and T.C. Chambers, 1986, Flora of the lower Koonwarra fossil bed (Korumburra Group), South Gippsland, Victoria: *Association of Australasian Palaeontologists Memoir:* 3, p. 77.

Dubiel, R. F., 1989, Depositional and climatic setting of the Upper Triassic Chinle Formation, Colorado Plateau, *in:* Spencer G. Lucas and Adrian P. Hunt, editors, *Dawn of the Age of Dinosaurs in the American Southwest.* Albuquerque: New Mexico Museum of Natural History, pp. 171–187.

Dughi, Raymond, and Francois Sirugue, 1960, Les Dinosaures vivaient en Basse-Provence au Maestrichtien (Bégudien): *Comptes Rendus des Séances de l'Académie des Sciences,* 251 (21), pp. 2387–2388.

Dunham, A. E., K. L. Overall, W. P. Porter, and Catherine A. Forster, 1989, Implications of ecological energetics and biophysical and developmental constraints for life history variation in dinosaurs, *in:* James O. Farlow, editor, *Paleobiology of the Dinosaurs,* Geological Society of America Special Papers, 238, pp. 1–19.

Dutuit, Jean-Michel, 1972, Découverte d'un Dinosaure ornithischien dans le Trias supérieur de l'Atlas occidental marocain: *Comptes Rendus des Séances de l'Académie des Sciences,* Série D, 275, pp. 2841–2844.

Eaton, Jeffrey G., James I. Kirkland, and Kentaro Doi, 1989, Evidence of reworked Cretaceous fossils and their bearing on the existence of Tertiary dinosaurs: *Palaios,* 4, pp. 281–284.

Eaton, Theodore H., Jr., 1960, A new armored dinosaur from the Cretaceous of Kansas: *Vertebrata,* article 8, pp. 1–24.

Eberth, David A., Philip J. Currie, and D. Braman, 1988, Small theropod quarry, *in: Paleoecology of Upper Cretaceous Judith River Formation at Dinosaur Provincial Park, Alberta, Canada,* Stop number 6 of Field Trip "B" (October 12, 1988) of the Society of Vertebrate Paleontology 48th Annual Meeting, *Occasional Paper of the Tyrrell Museum of Paleontology,* 7, pp. 27–31.

Eberth, David A., and Anthony P. Hamblin, 1993, Tectonic, stratigraphic, and sedimentologic significance of a regional discontinuity in the upper Judith River Group (Belly River Wedge) of southern Alberta, Saskatchewan, and Northern Montana: *Canadian Journal of Earth Sciences,* 30, pp. 174–200.

Eberth, David A., D. A. Russell, D. R. Braman, and A. L. Deino, 1993, The age of the dinosaur-bearing sediments at Tebch, Inner Mongolia, People's Republic of China: *Canadian Journal of Earth Sciences,* 30 (10–11), pp. 2101–2106.

Ellenberger, Paul, 1970, Les niveaux paléontologiques de première apparition des Mammifères primordiaux en Afrique du Sud et leur ichnologie—Establissement de zones stratigraphiques détaillées dans le Stormberg du Lesotho (Afrique de Sud) (Trias Supérieur à Jurassique): Proceedings, Second Gondwana Symposium, I.U.G.S. Commission on Stratigraphy, South Africa, July-August, pp. 340–370.

Elżanowski, Andrzei, 1974, Results of the Polish-Mongolian Palaeontological Expeditions, part V. Preliminary note on the palaeognathous bird from the Upper Cretaceous of Mongolia: *Palaeontologia Polonica,* 30, pp. 103–109.

_____, 1976, Palaeognathous bird from the Cretaceous of Central Asia: *Nature,* 264 (4), pp. 51–53.

_____, 1981, Embryonic bird skeletons from the Late Cretaceous of Mongolia, *in:* Zofia Jaworoska, editor, Results of the Polish-Mongolian Palaeontological Expeditions, part IX: Palaeontologia Polonica, 42, pp. 147–179.

_____, 1995, Cranial evidence for the avian relationships of Oviraptorosauria: *Journal of Vertebrate Paleontology,* Abstracts of Papers, Fifty-fifth Annual Meeting, p. 27A.

Elżanowski, Andrzei, and Peter Wellnhofer, 1992, A new link between theropods and birds from the Cretaceous of Mongolia: *Nature,* 359, pp. 821–823.

Embleton, B.J.J., and M.W. McElhinny, 1982, Marine magnetic anomalies, palaeomagnetism and the drift history of Gondwanaland: *Earth and Planetary Science Letters,* 58, pp. 141–150.

Engelmann, George F., Daniel J. Chure, and Scott K. Madsen, 1989, A mammalian fauna from the Jurassic Morrison Formation of Dinosaur National Monument: *Journal of Vertebrate Paleontology,* Abstracts of Papers, Fiftieth Annual Meeting, p. 19A.

Engelmann, George F., N. S. Greenwald, George Callison, and Daniel J. Chure, 1990, Cranial and dental morphology of a late Jurassic multituberculate mammal from the Morrison Formation: *Journal of Vertebrate Paleontology,* Abstracts of Papers, Fifty-first Annual Meeting, p. 22A.

Enlow, D. H., and S. O. Brown, 1956, A comparative histological study of fossil and recent bone tissue, Part I: *Texas Journal of Science,* 8, pp. 405–443.

_____, 1957, A comparative histological study of fossil and recent bone tissue, Part II: *Ibid.,* 9, pp. 186–214.

_____, 1958, A comparative histological study of fossil and recent bone tissue, Part III: *Ibid.,* 10, pp. 187–230.

Erben, H. K., J. Hoefs, and K. H. Wedepohl, 1979, Paleontological and isotopic studies of eggshells from a declining dinosaur species: *Paleobiology,* 5 (4), pp. 380–414.

Erickson, G. P., and J. L. Kulp, 1961, Potassium-argon measurements on the Pallisades sill, New Jersey: *Geological Society of America,* bulletin 72, pp. 649–652.

Erickson, Gregory M., and Tatyana Tumanova, 1995, Histological variation through ontogeny in the long bones of *Psittacosaurus mongoliensis: Journal of Vertebrate Paleontology,* Abstracts of Papers, Fifty-fifth Annual Meeting, p. 28A.

Erve, A. van, and B. A. R. Mohr, 1988, Palynological investigations of the Late Jurassic microflora from the vertebrate locality Guimarota coal mine (Leiria, Central Portugal): *Neues Jahrbuch für Geologie und Paläontologie, Monatshefte,* 1988, pp. 246–262.

Estes, Richard D., 1964, Fossil vertebrates from the Late Cretaceous Lance Formation, eastern Wyoming: University of California, *Publications in Geological Sciences,* 49, 180 pages.

_____, 1983, Sauria terrestria, Amphibisbaenia, *in:* Peter Wellnhofer, editor, *Handbuch der Paläoherpetologie* Teil 10A. Stuttgart, Germany: Gustav Fischer, pp. 1–249.

Estes, Richard D., and B. Sanchiz, 1982, Early Cretaceous lower vertebrates from Galve (Teruel), Spain: *Journal of Vertebrate Paleontology,* 2, pp. 21–39.

Evans, Susan E., 1984, The classification of the Lepidosauria: *Zoological Journal of the Linnean Society of London,* 82, pp. 87–100.

_____, 1988, The early history and relationships of the Diapsida, *in:* Michael J. Benton, editor, *The Phylogeny and Classification of the Tetrapods,* Vol. I. Systematics Association Special Volume 35A, pp. 221–260.

Evans, Susan E., and Andrew R. Milner, 1989, *Fulengia,* a supposed early lizard reinterpreted as a prosauropod dinosaur: *Paleontology,* 32, pp. 223–230.

Farlow, James O., 1976, Speculations about the diet and foraging behavior of large carnivorous dinosaurs: *American Midland Naturalist,* 95 (1), pp. 186–191.

_____, 1980, Predator/prey biomass ratios, community food webs and the interpretation of dinosaur physiology, *in:* Roger D. K. Thomas and Everett C. Olson, editors, *A Cold Look at the Warm Blooded Dinosaurs,* American Association for the Advancement of Science, Selected Symposium 28.

_____, 1981, Estimates of dinosaur speeds from a new trackway site in Texas: *Nature,* 294, pp. 747–748.

_____, 1987, *Lower Cretaceous Dinosaur Tracks, Paluxy River Valley, Texas.* Waco, Texas: Baylor University, 50 pages.

_____, 1987a, Speculations about the diet and digestive physiology of hebivorous dinosaurs: *Paleobiology,* 13 (1), pp. 60–72.

_____, 1987b, *Lower Cretaceous Dinosaur Tracks, Paluxy River Valley, Texas.* Waco, Texas: Baylor University, 50 pages.

_____, 1987c, A Guide to Lower Cretaceous dinosaur Footprints and Tracksites of the Paluxy River Valley, Somerville County, Texas, South-Central Meeting, Geological Society of America, Baylor University, 1987, 5o pages.

_____, 1990, Dinosaur energetics and thermal biology, *in:* David B. Weishampel, Peter Dodson, and Halszka Osmólska, editors, *The Dinosauria.* Berkeley and Los Angeles: University of California Press, pp. 43–55.

_____, 1992, Sauropod tracks and trackmakers: integrating the ichnological and skeletal records: *Zubía,* 10, pp. 89–138.

_____, 1993, On the rareness of big, fierce animals: speculations about the body sizes, population densities, and geographic ranges of predatory mammals and large carnivorous dinosaurs: *American Journal of Science,* 293-A, pp. 167–199.

_____, 1994, Speculations about the carrion-locating ability of tyrannosaurs: *Historical Biology,* 7, pp. 159–165.

Farlow, James O., Daniel L. Brinkman, William L. Abler, and Philip J. Currie, 1991, Size, shape, and serration density of theropod dinosaur lateral teeth: *Modern Geology,* 16, pp. 161–198.

Farlow, James O., and Peter Dodson, 1975, The behavioral significance of frill and horn morphology in ceratopsian dinosaurs: *Evolution,* 29, pp. 353–361.

Farlow, James O., Jeffrey G. Pittman, and J. Michael Hawthorne, 1989, *Brontopodus birdi*, Lower Cretaceous sauropod footprints from the U.S. Gulf Coastal Plain, *in*: David D. Gillette and Martin G. Lockley, editors, *Dinosaur Tracks and Traces*. Cambridge, England: Cambridge University Press, pp. 371–394.

Farlow, James O., Matt B. Smith, and John M. Robinson, 1995, Body mass, bone "strength indicator," and cursorial potential of *Tyrannosaurus rex*: *Journal of Vertebrate Paleontology*, 15 (4), pp. 713–725.

Farlow, James O., Carl V. Thompson, and Daniel E. Rosner (1976), Plates of the dinosaur *Stegosaurus*: forced convection heat loss fins?: *Science*, 192, pp. 1123–1125.

Farris, J. S., 1974, Formal definitions of paraphyly and polyphyly: *Systematic Zoology*, 23, pp. 548–554.

Filla, B. James, and Pat D. Redman, 1994, *Apatosaurus yahnahpin*: a preliminary description of a new species of diplodocid dinosaur from the Late Jurassic Morrison Formation of southern Wyoming, the first sauropod dinosaur found with a complete set of "belly ribs": Forty-Fourth Annual Field Conference—*1994 Wyoming Geological Association Guidebook*, pp. 159–175.

Fiorillo, Anthony R., 1987, Significance of juvenile dinosaurs from Careless Creek Quarry (Judith River Formation), Wheatland County, Montana, *in*: Philip J. Currie and E. H. Koster, editors, Fourth Symposium on Mesozoic Terrestrial Ecosystems, Short Papers, Drumheller, Alberta: *Occasional Papers of the Tyrrell Museum of Paleontology*, 3, pp. 88–95.

_____, 1990, The first occurrence of hadrosaur (Dinosauria) remains from the marine Claggett Formation, Late Cretaceous of south-central Montana: *Journal of Vertebrate Paleontology*, 10 (4), pp. 515–517.

_____, 1991, Dental microwear on the teeth of *Camarasaurus* and *Diplodocus*: implications for sauropod paleoecology, *in*: Zophia Kielan-Jaworoska, Natascha Heintz, and Hans Arne Nakrem, editors, Fifth Symposium on Mesozoic Terrestrial Ecosystems and Biota, Extended Abstracts: Contributions from the Paleontological Museum, University of Oslo, 364, pp. 23–24.

Fisher, Donald W., 1981, The world of *Coelophysis*—a New York dinosaur of 200 million years ago: New York State Museum and Science Service, Geological Survey, circular 49, vi, 22 pages. Fitzinger, L.J., 1843, Systema reptilium. Vienna, 106 pages.

Forster, Catherine A., 1984, The paleoecology of the ornithopod dinosaur *Tenontosaurus tilletti* from the Cloverly Formation, Big Horn Basin of Wyoming and Montana: *The Mosasaur*, 2, pp. 151–163.

_____, 1990a, Evidence for juvenile groups in the ornithopod dinosaur *Tenontosaurus tilletti* Ostrom: *Journal of Paleontology*, 64 (1), pp. 164–165.

_____, 1990b, The postcranial skeleton of the ornithopod dinosaur *Tenontosaurus tilletti*: *Journal of Vertebrate Paleontology*, 10 (3), pp. 273–294.

_____, 1993, Taxonomic validity of the ceratopsid dinosaur *Ugrosaurus olsoni* (Cobabe and Fastovsky): *Journal of Paleontology*, 66 (2), pp. 316–8.

_____, 1996a, New information on the skull of *Triceratops*: *Journal of Vertebrate Paleontology*, 16 (2), pp. 246–258.

_____, 1996b, The fragmentation of Gondwana: using dinosaurs to test biogeographic hypotheses, *in*: John E. Repetski, editor, Sixth North American Paleontological Convention, Abstracts of Papers, p. 127.

_____, 1996b, Species resolution in *Triceratops*: cladistic and morphometric approaches: *Ibid.*, pp. 259–270.

Forster, Catherine A., and C. F. Ross, 1995, New dinosaur material and paleoenvironment of the Early Cretaceous Kirkwood Formation, Algoa Basin, South Africa: *Journal of Vertebrate Paleontology*, Abstracts of Papers, Fifty-fifth Annual Meeting, p. 29A.

Forster, Catherine A., Paul C. Sereno, Thomas W. Evans, and Timothy Rowe, 1992, A complete skull of *Chasmosaurus mariscalensis* (Dinosauria: Ceratopsidae) from the Aguja Formation (late Campanian) of West Texas: *Journal of Vertebrate Paleontology*, 13 (2), pp. 161–170.

Foster, John R., 1995, Allometric and taxonomic limb bone robustness variability in some sauropod dinosaurs: *Journal of Vertebrate Paleontology*, Abstracts of Papers, Fifty-fifth Annual Meeting, p. 29A.

Fox, William, 1866, Another new Wealden reptile: *The Athenaeum*, 2014, p. 740. (Reprinted *in*: *Geological Magazine*, 3, p. 383.)

Fraas, Eberhard, 1908, Ostafrikanische Dinosaurier: *Palaeontographica*, 15, pp. 105–144.

_____, 1913, Die neusten Dinosaurierfunde der schwabischen Trias: *Die Naturwissenschaften*, 1 (45), pp. 1097–1100.

_____, 1914, Die neusten Dinosaurierfunde in der Schwäbischen Trias: *Verhandlungen der Deutschen Naturforschender Gesellschaft Arzte*, Vienna, 85, pp. 125–132.

Fraser, Nicholas C., and Kevin Padian, 1995, Possible basal dinosaur remains from Britain and the diagnosis of the Dinosauria: *Journal of Vertebrate Paleontology*, Abstracts of Papers, Fifty-fifth Annual Meeting, p. 30A.

Friese, H., 1972, *Die Dinosaurierfährten von Barkhausen im Wiehengebirge*. Bad Essen, Germany: Wittlager Heimathefte, 21 pages.

Fritsch [Fric], Anton, 1893, Studien im Gebiete der Böhmischen Kreideformation, Palaeontologische Untersuchungen der einzelnen Schichten: *Archiv der Naturwissenschaften Landesdurchforschung von Böhmen*, 9 (1).

_____, 1905, Synopsis der Saurier der böhm Kreiderformation: *Sitzungsberichte der Königl. Böhmischen Gesellschaft der Wissenschaften, Mathematisch-Naturwissenschaftliche Classe*, pp. 1–7.

_____, 1911, Studien im Gebiete der Böhmischen Kreideformation, Ergänzung zu Band I, Illustriertes Verzeichnis der Petrefacten der Cenomanen Korycaner Schichten: *Archiv für die Naturwissenschaftliche Landesdurchforschung von Bömen*, 15 (1).

Fritz, Sandy, 1988, *Tyrannosaurus* sex: a love tail: *Omni*, 10 (5), pp. 64–68, 78.

Frohawk, F. W., 1905, The attitude of *Diplodocus carnegiei*: *The Field*, 106, p. 388.

Gabunia, L. K., 1951, O sledakh dinozavrov iz nizhnemelovykh otlozhenii Zapadnof Gruzii: *Dokladi Akademii Nauk S.S.S.R.*, 71, pp. 209–222.

Gallup, Marc R., 1975, Lower Cretaceous dinosaurs and associated vertebrates from North-Central Texas in the Field Museum of Natural History: Master's thesis, University of Texas, 159 pages.

_____, 1989, Functional morphology of the hindfoot of the Texas sauropod *Pleurocoelus* sp. indet., *in*: James O. Farlow, editor, *Paleobiology of the Dinosaurs: Geological Society of America Special Paper* 238, pp. 71–74.

Galton, Peter M., 1970, The posture of hadrosaurian dinosaurs: *Journal of Paleontology*, 44 (3), pp. 464–473.

_____, 1971a, A primitive dome-headed dinosaur (Ornithischia: Pachycephalosauridae) from the Lower Cretaceous of England and the function of the dome of pachycephalosaurids: *Journal of Paleontology*, 45 (1), pp. 40–47.

_____, 1971b, The prosauropod dinosaur *Ammosaurus*, the crocodile *Protosuchus*, and their bearing on the age of the Navajo Sandstone of northeastern Arizona: *Ibid.*, 45 (5), pp. 781–795.

_____, 1971c, *Hypsilophodon*, the cursorial non-arboreal dinosaur: *Nature*, 231 (5299), pp. 159–161.

_____, 1971d, The mode of life of *Hypsilophodon*, the supposedly arboreal ornithopod dinosaur: *Lethaia*, 4 (4), pp. 453–465.

_____, 1971e, Manus movements of the coelurosaurian dinosaur *Syntarsus* and the opposability of the theropod helix: *Arnoldia*, 5 (15), 15, pp. 1–8.

_____, 1972, Classification and evolution of ornithopod dinosaurs: *Nature*, 239 (5373), pp. 464–466.

_____, 1973a, Redescription of the skull and mandible of *Parksosaurus* from the Late Cretaceous with comments on the family Hypsilophodontidae (Ornithischia): *Life Science Contributions*, Royal Ontario Museum, 89, pp. 1–21.

_____, 1973b, On the anatomy and relationships of *Efraasia diagnostica* (Huene) n. gen., a prosauropod dinosaur (Reptilia: Saurischia) from the Upper Triassic of Germany: *Paläontraphica Zeitschrift* 47 (5), pp. 229–255.

_____ 1973c, The cheek of ornithischian dinosaurs: *Lethalia*, 6, pp. 67–89.

_____, 1973d, A femur of a small theropod dinosaur from the Lower Cretaceous of England: *Journal of Paleontology*, 47 (5), pp. 996–997.

_____, 1974a, The ornithischian dinosaur *Hypsilophodon* from the Wealden of the Isle of Wight: *Bulletin, British Museum of Natural History (Geology)*, 25 (1), pp. 1–152c.

_____, 1974b, Notes on *Thescelosaurus*, a conservative ornithopod dinosaur from the Upper Cretaceous of North America, with comments on Ornithopod classification: *Journal of Paleontology*, 48 (5), pp. 1048–1067.

_____, 1975, English hypsilophodontid dinosaurs (Reptilia: Ornithischia): *Palaeontology*, 18 (4), pp. 741–752.

_____, 1976a, Prosauropod dinosaurs (Reptilia: Saurischia) of North America: Postilla, Peabody Museum of Natural History, 169, 98 pages.

_____, 1976b, (Short communication) *Iliosuchus*, a Jurassic dinosaur from Oxfordshire and Utah: *Palaeontology*, 19, (3), pp. 587–589.

_____, 1976c, The dinosaur *Vectisaurus valdensis* (Ornithischia: Iguanodontidae) from the Lower Cretaceous of England: *Journal of Paleontology*, 50 (5), pp. 976–984.

_____, 1977a, On *Staurikosaurus pricei*, an early saurischian dinosaur from the Triassic

Bibliography

of Brazil, with notes on the Herrerasauridae and Poposauridae: *Paläontographica Zeitschrift*, 51 (3–4), pp. 234–245.

_____, 1977*b*, The ornithopod dinosaur *Dryosaurus* and a Laurasia-Gondwanaland connection in the Upper Jurassic: *Nature*, 268 (5617), pp. 230–232.

_____, 1978, Fabrosauridae, the basal family of ornithischian dinosaurs (Reptilia: Ornithopoda), Paläontographica Zeitschrift, 52 (1–2), pp. 138–159.

_____, 1980*a*, Partial skeleton of *Dracopelta zbyszewskii* n. gen. and n. sp., an ankylosaurian dinosaur from the upper Jurassic of Portugal: *Géobios*, 13 (3), pp. 451–457.

_____, 1980*b*, Armored dinosaurs (Ornithischia: Ankylosauria) from the Middle and Upper Jurassic of England: *Ibid.*, 13 (6), pp. 825–837.

_____, 1980*c*, European Jurassic ornithopod dinosaurs of the families Hypsilophodontidae and Camptosauridae: *Neus Jahrbuch Fuer Geologie und Paläontologie Abhandlungen*, 160 (1), pp. 73–95.

_____, 1981*a*, *Craterosaurus pottenensis* Seeley, a stegosaurian dinosaur from the Lower Cretaceous, with a review of Cretaceous stegosaurs: *Ibid.*, 161 (1), pp. 28–46.

_____, 1981*b*, *Dryosaurus*, a hypsilophodontid dinsoaur from the Upper Jurassic of North America and Africa: *Paläontographica Zeitschrift*, 55, pp. 271–312.

_____, 1981*c*, A juvenile stegosaurian dinosaur, "*Astrodon pusillus*," from the Upper Jurassic of Portugal, with comments on Upper Jurassic and Lower Cretaceous biogeography: *Journal of Vertebrate Paleontology*, 1 (3–4), pp. 245–256.

_____, 1982*a*, The postcranial anatomy of Stegosaurian Dinosaur *Kentrosaurus* from the Upper Jurassic of Tanzania, East Africa: *Geologica et Palaeontologica*, 15, pp. 139–160.

_____, 1982*b*, Juveniles of the stegosaurian dinosaur *Stegosaurus* from the Upper Jurassic of North America: *Ibid.*, 2 (1), pp. 47–62.

_____, 1982*c*, *Elaphrosaurus*, an ornithomimid dinosaur from the Upper Jurassic of North America and Africa: *Palaontologische Zeitschrift*, 56, pp. 265–275.

_____, 1983*a*, *Sarcolestes leedsi* Lydekker, an ankylosaurian dinosaur from the middle Jurassic of England: *Neus Jahrbuch Fuer Geologie und Paläontollogie Montsah*, Pt. 3, pp. 141–155.

_____, 1983*b*, The cranial anatomy of *Dryosaurus*, a hypsilophodontid dinosaur from the Upper Jurassic of North America and East Africa, with a review of hypsilophodontids from the Upper Jurassic of North America: *Geologica et Palaeontologica*, 17, pp. 207–243.

_____, 1983*c*, Armored dinosaurs (Ornithischia: Ankylosauria) from the Middle and Upper Jurassic of Europe: *Palaeontographica*, A 182, pp. 1–25.

_____, 1984, Cranial anatomy of the prosauropod dinosaur *Plateosaurus* from the Knollenmergel (Middle Keuper, Upper Triassic) of Germany. I. Two complete skulls from Trossingen/Wurt. with comment on the diet: *Geologica et Palaeontologica*, 18, pp. 139–171.

_____, 1985*a*, The diet of prosauropod dinosaurs from the late Triassic and early Jurassic: *Lethaia*, 15, pp. 105–123.

_____, 1985*b*, British plated dinosaurs (Ornithischia, Stegosauridae): *Journal of Vertebrate Paleontology*, 5 (3), pp. 211–254.

_____, 1985*c*, Notes on the Melanorosauridae, a family of large prosauropod dinosaurs (Saurischia: Sauropodomorpha): *Géobios*, 18 (5), pp. 671–676.

_____, 1985*d*, Cranial anatomy of the prosauropod dinosaur *Plateosaurus* from the Knollenmergel (Middle Keuper, Upper Triassic) of Germany. II. All the cranial material and details on soft-part anatomy: *Geologica et Palaeontologica*, 19, pp. 119–159.

_____, 1985*e*, The poposaurid thecodontian *Teratosaurus suevicus* V. Meyer, plus referred specimens mostly based on prosauropod dinosaurs, from the Middle Stubensandstein (Upper Triassic) of Nordwurttemberg, West Germany: *Stuttgarter Beitr. Naturk. (B)*, 116, pp. 1–29.

_____, 1985*f*, Cranial anatomy of the prosauropod dinosaur *Sellosaurus* from the Upper Triassic of Nordwurttemberg, West Germany: *Ibid.*, 118, pp. 1–39.

_____, 1986*a*, Prosauropod dinosaur *Plateosaurus* (=*Gresslyosaurus*) (Saurischia: Sauropodomorpha) from the Upper Triassic of Switzerland: *Geologica et Palaeontologica*, 20, pp. 167–183.

_____, 1986*b*, Herbivorous adaptations of Late Triassic and Early Jurassic dinosaurs, *in*: Kevin Padian, editor, *The Beginning of the Age of Dinosaurs: Faunal Change Across the Triassic-Jurassic Boundary*. New York: Cambridge University Press, pp. 203–221.

_____, 1989, Crania and endocranial casts from ornithopod dinosaurs of the families Dryosauridae and Hypsilophodontidae (Reptilia: Ornithischia): *Geologica et Palaeontologica*, 23, pp. 217–239.

_____, 1990*a*, Basal Sauropodomorpha—Prosauropoda, *in*: David B. Weishampel, Peter Dodson and Halszka Osmólska, editors, *The Dinosauria*. Berkeley and Los Angeles: University of California Press, pp. 320–344.

_____, 1990*b*, Stegosauria, *Ibid.*, pp. 435–455.

_____, 1995, The species of the basal hypsilophodontid dinosaur *Thescelosaurus* Gilmore (Ornithischia: Ornithopoda) from the Late Cretaceous of North America: *Neus Jahrbuch für Geologie und Paläontologie, Abhandlungen*, 198(3), pp. 297–311, Stuttgart.

_____, 1996, Notes on Dinosauria from the Upper Cretaceous of Portugal: *Neus Jahrbuch für Geologie und Paläontologie, Monatshefte*, H. 2, pp. 83–90, Stuttgart.

Galton, Peter M., and G. Boine, 1980, A stegosaurian dinosaur femur from the Kimmeridgian Beds (Upper Jurassic) of the Cap de la Heve, Normandy: *Bulletin Trimestriel de la Société Géologique de Normandie et des Amis du Museum du Havre*, 67 (4), pp. 31–35.

Galton, Peter M., Roger Brun, and Michel Riolt, 1980, Skeleton of the stegosaurian dinosaur *Lexovisaurus* from the lower part of Middle Callovian (Middle Jurassic) of Argences (Calvados), Normandy: *Ibid.*, 67 (4), pp. 39–53.

Galton, Peter M., and M. A. Cluver, 1976, *Anchisaurus capensis* (Broom) and a revision of the Anchisauridae (Reptilia, Saurischia): *Annals of the South African Museum*, 69 (6), pp. 121–159.

Galton, Peter M., and Walter P. Coombs, Jr., 1981, *Paranthodon africanus* (Broom), a stegosaurian dinosaur from the Lower Cretaceous of South Africa: *Géobios*, 14(3), pp. 299–309.

Galton, Peter M., and James A. Jensen, 1973*a*, Skeleton of a hypsilophodontid dinosaur (*Nanosaurus* [?] *rex*) from the Upper Jurassic of Utah: *Brigham Young University Geology Studies*, 20 (4), pp. 137–157.

_____, 1973*b*, Small bones of the hylsilophodontid dinosaur *Dryosaurus altus* from the Upper Jurassic of Colorado: *Great Britain Naturalist*, 33 (2), pp. 129–132.

_____, 1975, *Hypsilophodon* and *Iguanodon* from the Lower Cretaceous of North America: *Nature*, 257 (5528), pp. 668–669.

_____, 1979*a*, A new large theropod dinosaur from the Upper Jurassic of Colorado: *Brigham Young University Geology Studies*, 26 (2), pp. 1–12.

_____, 1979*b*, Remains of ornithopod dinosaurs from the Lower Cretaceous of North America: *Ibid.*, 25 (3), pp. 1–10.

Galton, Peter M., and H. Phillip Powell, 1980, The ornithischian dinosaur *Camptosaurus prestwichii* from the Upper Jurassic of England: *Paleontology*, 23 (2), pp. 411–443.

_____, 1983, Stegosaurian dinosaurs from the Bathonian (Middle Jurassic) of England, the earliest record of the family Stegosauridae: *Géobios*, 16 (2), pp. 219–229.

Galton, Peter M., and Hans-Dieter Sues, 1983, New data on pachycephalosaurid dinosaurs (Reptilia: Ornithischia) from North America: *Canadian Journal of Earth Sciences*, 20, pp. 462–472.

Galton, Peter M., and Phillipe Taquet, 1982, *Valdosaurus*, a hypsilophodontid dinosaur from the Lower Cretaceous of Europe and Africa: *Géobios*, 15 (2), pp. 147–157.

Galton, Peter M., and Jacques Van Heerden, 1985, Partial hindlimb of *Bilkanasaurus cromptoni* n. gen. and n. sp., representing a new family of prosauropod dinosaurs from the Upper Triassic of South Africa: Géobios—Mémoires spéciaux, 18 (4), pp. 509–516.

Gangloff, Roland A., 1995, *Edmontonia* sp., The first record of an ankylosaur from Alaska: *Journal of Vertebrate Paleontology*, 15 (1), pp. 195–200.

Gao R., Huang D., and Zhu S., 1986, [Materials of shoulder spines of stegosaurs from Zigong.]: *Vertebrata PalAsiatica*, 24, pp. 78–79.

Gao, Y. H., 1992, *Yangchuanosaurus hepingensis*—a new species of carnosaur from Zigong, Sichuan: *Vertebrata PalAsiatica*, 30, pp. 313–324.

Garstka, William R., and David A. Burnham, 1995, Posture and stance in *Triceratops*: evidence of digitigrade manus and cantilever vertebral column: *Journal of Vertebrate Paleontology*, Abstracts of Papers, Fifty-fifth Annual Meeting, p. 31A.

Gasparini, Z., E. Olivero, R. Scasco, and C. Rinaldi, 1987, Un Ankylosaurio (Reptilia. Ornithischia) Campanico en el Continente Antartico: *Anais do X Congresso Brasileiro de Paleontologia*, Rio de Janeiro, 19-25 de Julho, 1987, pp. 131–141.

Gauffre, Francis-Xavier, 1993*a*, The prosauropod dinosaur *Azendohsaurus laaroussii* from the Upper Triassic of Morocco: *Palaeontology*, 36 (4), pp. 897–908.

_____, 1993*b*, The most recent Melanorosaurid (Saurischia, Prosauropoda), Lower Jurassic of Lesotho, with remarks on the prosauropod phylogeny: *Neus Jahrbuch für*

Geologie und Paläontologie, Monatshefte, 11, pp. 648–654, Stuttgart.

Gauthier, Jacques A., 1984, A cladistic analysis of the higher systematic categories of the Diapsida: Ph.D. Thesis, Department of Paleontology, University of California, Berkeley, 565 pages (no. 85-12825, University Microfilms, Ann Arbor, Michigan).

_____, 1986, Saurischian monophyly and the origin of birds, *in:* Kevin Padian, editor, *The Origin of Birds and the Evolution of Flight.* Memoirs of the California Academy of Sciences, 8, pp. 1–55.

Gauthier, J. A., and Kevin Padian, 1985, Phylogenetic, functional, and aerodynamic analyses of the origin of birds and their flight, *in:* Max K. Hecht, John H. Ostrom, G. Viohl and Peter Wellnhoffer, editors, *The Beginnings of Birds.* Eichstätt: Freunde des Jura-Museums, pp. 185–197.

Geiger, M. E., and C. A. Hopping, 1968, Triassic stratigraphy of the southern North Sea Basin: *Philosophical Transactions of the Royal Society of London,* B, 254, pp. 1–36.

Geist, N. R., and T. D. Jones, 1995, Long bone epiphyseal structure in juvenile ratites, crocodilians and dinosaurs: *Journal of Vertebrate Paleontology,* Abstracts of Papers, Fifty-fifth Annual Meeting, p. 31A.

Gemmellaro, M., 1921, Rettili maëstrichtane d'Egitto: *Giornale di Scienze Naturali ad Economiche,* Palermo, 32, pp. 339–351.

Gervais, Charles, 1852, *Zoologie et Paléontologie Français (Animaux Vertébrés).* Paris, volume I, iv, 271 pages (text); volume II (explanation of plates); volume III (plates).

Giffin, Emily B., 1989*a,* Pachycephalosaur-paleonuerology (Archosauria: Ornithopoda): *Journal of Vertebrate Paleontology,* 9 (1), pp. 67–77.

_____, 1989*b,* Notes on pachycephalosaurs (Ornithischia): *Journal of Paleontology,* 63 (4), pp. 525–529.

Giffin, Emily B., Diane L. Gabriel, and Rolfe E. Johnson, A new pachycephalosaurid skull (Ornithischia) from the Cretaceous Hell Creek Formation of Montana: *Journal of Vertebrate Paleontology,* 7 (4), pp. 398–407.

Gillette, David D., 1987, A giant sauropod from the Jackpile SS Member of the Morrison Formation: *Journal of Vertebrate Paleontology,* 7 (supplement to 3), pp. 16–17.

_____, 1991, *Seismosaurus halli,* gen. et sp. nov., a new sauropod dinosaur from the Morrison Formation (Upper Jurassic/Lower Cretaceous) of New Mexico, USA: *Ibid.,* 11 (4), pp. 417–433.

_____, 1993, Type locality and stratigraphic position of *Dystrophaeus viaemalae* Cope 1879, the earliest sauropod dinosaur in North America: *Journal of Vertebrate Paleontology,* Abstracts of Papers, Fifty-third Annual Meeting, p. 37A.

Gillette, David D., J. Lynette Gillette, and David A. Thomas, 1985, A diplodocine dinosaur from the Morrison Formation of New Mexico: *Annual Symposium on Southwestern Geology and Paleontology,* Museum of Northern Arizona, p.4.

Gillette, David D., and Hildy Schwartz, 1986, A new giant sauropod from the Morrison Formation, Upper Jurassic, of New Mexico: *Abstracts, North American Paleontological Convention IV,* pp. 16A–17A.

Gillette, David G., Alan Witten, Wendell C. King, Jozef Sypniewski, J. Wilson Bechtel and Peggy Bechtel, 1989, Geophysical diffraction tomography at the "Seismosaurus" sauropod site in central New Mexico, *in:* Jeffrey G. Eaton, Grace V. Irby and Michael Morales, editors, *Abstracts of the Symposium on Southwestern Geology and Paleontology,* 1989, p.10.

Gillette, J. Lynette, Francis A. Barnes, David D. Gillette, and John S. McIntosh, 1989, The type locality and stratigraphic position of *Dystrophaeus viamalae* Cope 1877 (Dinosauria, Sauropoda), *in:* Jeffrey G. Eaton, Grace V. Irby, and Michael Morales, editors, *Abstracts of the Symposium on Southwestern Geology and Paleontology,* 1989, p. 11.

Gilmore, Charles Whitney, 1905, The mounted skeleton of *Triceratops prorsus: Proceedings of the United States National Museum,* 29 (1426), pp. 433–435.

_____, 1906, Notes on some recent additions to the exhibition series of vertebrate fossils: *Ibid.,* 30 (1460), pp. 607–611.

_____, 1907, The type of the Jurassic reptile *Morosaurus agilis* redescribed, with a note on *Camptosaurus: Ibid.,* 32 (1519), pp. 151–165.

_____, 1909*a,* Osteology of the Jurassic reptile *Camptosaurus* with a revision of the species of the genus, and description of two new species: *Ibid.,* 36, pp. 197–332.

_____, 1909*b,* A new rhynchocephalian reptile from the Jurassic of Wyoming, with notes on the fauna of "Quarry 9": *Ibid.,* 37, pp. 35–42.

_____, 1913, A new dinosaur from the Lance Formation of Wyoming: *Smithsonian Miscellaneous Collections,* 61 (5), pp. 1–5.

_____, 1914*a,* A new ceratopsian dinosaur from the Upper Cretaceous of Montana, with note on *Hypacrosaurus: Ibid.,* 63 (3), pp. 1–10.

_____, 1914*b,* Osteology of the armored Dinosauria in the United States National Museum, with special reference to the genus *Stegosaurus: Memoirs of the United States National Museum,* 89, pp. 1–316.

_____, 1915, Osteology of *Thescelosaurus,* an orthopodous dinosaur from the Lance Formation of Wyoming: *Proceedings of the United States National Museum,* 49, pp. 591–616.

_____, 1917, *Brachyceratops,* a ceratopsian dinosaur from the Two Medicine Formation of Montana: *United States Geological Survey Professional Paper,* 103, pp. 1–45.

_____, 1919, A new restoration of *Triceratops,* with notes on the osteology of the genus: *Proceedings of the United States National Museum,* 55, pp. 97–112.

_____, 1920, Osteology of the carnivorous dinosauria in the United States National Museum, with special reference to the genera *Antrodemus (Allosaurus)* and *Ceratosaurus: Bulletin of the United States National Museum,* 110, pp. 1–154.

_____, 1922, A new sauropod dinosaur from the Ojo Alamo Formation of New Mexico: *Smithsonian Miscellaneous Collections,* 72 (14), 9 pages.

_____, 1923, A new species of *Corythosaurus,* with notes on other Belly River Dinosauria: *Canadian Field-Naturalist,* 37 (3), pp. 46–52.

_____, 1924*a,* On *Troodon validus.* An ornithopodus dinosaur from the Belly River Cretaceous of Alberta, Canada: *University of Alberta Bulletin,* Department of Geology, 1, pp. 1–43.

_____, 1924*b,* A new coelurid dinosaur from the Belly River Cretaceous of Alberta: *Geological Survey of Canada, Department of Mines, Bulletin 38,* Geological Series, 43, pp. 1–12.

_____, 1924*c,* A new species of hadrosaurian dinosaur from the Edmonton Formation (Cretaceous) of Alberta: *Ibid.,* 38 (43), pp. 13–26.

_____, 1924*d,* On the genus *Stephanosaurus,* with a description of the type specimen of *Lambeosaurus lambei* Parks: *Ibid.,* 43 (38), pp. 29–45.

_____, 1924*e,* On the skull and skeleton of *Hypacrosaurus,* a helmet-crested dinosaur from the Edmonton Cretaceous of Alberta: *Ibid.,* 43, (38), pp. 49–64.

_____, 1924*f,* A new species of *Laosaurus,* an ornithischian dinosaur from the Cretaceous of Alberta: *Transactions of the Royal Society of Canada,* section 4, 3rd series, 18, pp. 3–6.

_____, 1925*a,* A nearly complete articulated skeleton of *Camarasaurus,* a saurischian dinosaur from the Dinosaur National Monument: *Proceedings of the United States National Museum,* 81 (18), pp. 1–21.

_____, 1925*b,* Osteology of ornithopodous dinosaurs from the Dinosaur National Monument, Utah: *Memoirs of the Carnegie Museum,* 10, pp. 385–409.

_____, 1930, On dinosaurian reptiles from the Two Medicine Formation of Montana: *Proceedings of the United States National Museum,* 77 (16), pp. 1–39.

_____, 1931, A new species of troodont dinosaur from the Lance Formation of Wyoming: *Ibid.,* 79 (9), pp. 1–6.

_____, 1932, A new fossil lizard from the Belly River Formation of Alberta, Canada: *Transactions of the Royal Society of Canada,* 26 (series 3, section 4), pp. 117–120.

_____, 1933*a,* On the dinosaurian fauna from the Iren Dabasu Formation: *Bulletin of the American Museum of Natural History,* 67 (2), pp. 2–78.

_____, 1933*b,* Two new dinosaurian reptiles from Mongolia with notes on some fragmentary specimens: *American Museum Novitates,* 679, pp. 1–20.

_____, 1936*a,* Osteology of *Apatosaurus,* with special reference to specimens in the Carnegie Museum: *Memoirs of the Carnegie Museum,* 11, pp. 175–300.

_____, 1936*b,* Remarks on a skull cap of the genus *Troödon: Annals of the Carnegie Museum,* 25, pp. 109–112.

_____, 1939, Ceratopsian dinosaurs from the Two Medicine Formation, Upper Cretaceous of Montana: *Proceedings of the United States National Museum,* 87 (3066), pp. 1–18.

_____, 1945, *Parrosaurus,* n. name, replacing *Neosaurus* Gilmore, 1945: *Journal of Paleontology,* 19, p. 540.

_____, 1946*a,* A new carnivorous dinosaur from the Lance Formation of Montana: *Smithsonian Miscellaneous Collections,* 106 (13), 19 pages.

_____, 1946*b,* Reptilian fauna of the North Horn Formation of Central Utah: *United States Geological Survey Professional Paper,* 210-C, pp. 29–53.

Gilmore, Charles Whitney, and D. R. Stewart, 1945, A new sauropod dinosaur from the Upper Cretaceous of Missouri: *Journal of Paleontology,* 19, pp. 23–29.

Ginsburg, Léonard, 1964, Decouvert d'un Scelidosaurien (Dinosaure ornithischien)

Bibliography

dans le Trias supérieur du Basutoland: *Comptes Rendus des Séances de l'Académie des Sciences*, 258, pp. 2366–2368.

Ginsburg, Léonard, Albert F. de Lapparent, Bernard Loiret, and Phillipe Taquet, 1966, Empreintes de pas de vertébrés tétrapodes dans le séries continentales a l'Ouest d'Agades (République du Niger): *Comptes Rendus des Séances de l'Académie des Sciences*, 263, pp. 28–31.

Glut, Donald F., 1972, *The Dinosaur Dictionary*. Secaucus, New Jersey: Citadel Press, 217 pages.

———, 1982, *The New Dinosaur Dictionary*. Secaucus, New Jersey: Citadel Press, 288 pages [reissued 1992 as *The Complete Dinosaur Dictionary*].

Godfrey, Stephen J., and Robert Holmes, 1995, Cranial morphology and systematics of *Chasmosaurus* (Dinosauria: Ceratopsidae): *Journal of Vertebrate Paleontology*, 15 (4), pp. 726–742.

Goodwin, Mark B., and Rolf E. Johnson, 1995, A new skull of the pachycephalosaur *Stygimoloch* casts doubt on head butting behavior: *Journal of Vertebrate Paleontology*, Abstracts of Papers, Fifty-fifth Annual Meeting, p. 32A.

Gordon, M. S., 1968, *Animal Function: Principles and Adaptations*. New York: Macmillan Co., pp. 344–347.

Gow, Christopher E., 1975, A new heterodontosaurid from the Redbeds of South Africa showing clear evidence of tooth replacement: *Zoological Journal of the Linnean Society*, 57, pp. 335–339.

———, 1981, Taxonomy of the Fabrosauridae (Reptilia, Ornithischia) and the *Lesothosaurus* myth: *South African Journal of Science*, 77, p. 43.

Gradziński, R., and T. Jerzykiewicz, 1972, Additional geographical and geological data from the Polish-Mongolian Palaeontological Expeditions. Results of the Polish-Mongolian Expeditions, Part IV: *Palaeontologia Polonica*, 27, pp. 17–32.

Gradziński, R., J. Kazmierczak, and J. Lefeld, 1968/1969, Geographical and geological data of the Polish-Mongolian Palaeontological Expeditions. Results of the Polish-Mongolian Expeditions, Part I: *Palaeontologia Polonica*, 19, pp. 33–82.

Granger, Walter, and C. P. Berkey, 1922, Discovery of Cretaceous and older Tertiary strata in Mongolia: *American Museum Novitates*, 42, 7 pages.

Granger, Walter, and William King Gregory, 1923, *Protoceratops andrewsi*, a Pre-Ceratopsian dinosaur from Mongolia: *American Museum Novitates*, 72, pp. 1–9.

Grantz, A., 1961, Geologic map and cross sections of the Anchorage (D-2) Quadrangle, Alaska: U.S. Geological Survey MAP, pp. 1–342.

Gregory, H. E., 1917, Geology of the Navajo country: *United States Geological Survey Professional Paper*, 93, pp. 1–161.

Gregory, H. E., and R. C. Moore, 1931, The Kaiparowits region. A geographic and geologic reconnaissance of part of Utah and Arizona: *United States Geological Survey Professional Paper*, 164, 116 pages.

Gregory, William King, 1951, *Evolution Emerging*. New York: Macmillan Co., volume, 1, xxvi, 736 pages, volume 2, viii, 1013 pages.

Gregory, William King, and Charles C. Mook, 1925, On *Protoceratops*, a primitive ceratop-

sian dinosaur from the Lower Cretaceous of Mongolia: *American Museum Novitates*, 156, pp. 1–9.

Greppin, J. B., 1870, Description géologique du Jura Bernois et de quelques districts adjacents: *Matériaux pour la Carte géologique de la Suisse*, p. 339, Berne.

Grigorescu, Dan, M. Seclamen, David B. Norman, and David B. Weishampel, 1990, Dinosaur eggs from Romania: *Nature*, 346, p. 417.

Gross, W., 1934, Die Typen des mikroskopischen Knochenbaues bei fossilen Stegocephalen und Reptilien: *Anatomi Zeitschrift* 103, pp. 731–764.

Gurich, G., 1926, Über Saurier-Färten aus dem Etjo-Sandstein von Südwestafrika: *Paläontographica Zeitschrift*, 8, pp. 112–120.

Haas, George, 1955, The jaw musculature in *Protoceratops* and in other ceratopsians: *American Museum Novitates*, 1729, pp. 1–24.

———, 1969, On the jaw muscles of ankylosaurs: *Ibid.*, 2399, pp. 1–11.

Hagood, Allen, 1971, *Dinosaur: The Story Behind the Scenery*. Las Vegas: K. C. Publications, 32 pages.

Hall, Jean P., 1993, A juvenile hadrosaurid from New Mexico: *Journal of Vertebrate Paleontology*, 13 (3), pp. 376–369.

Halstead, L. B., 1975*a*, *The Evolution and Ecology of the Dinosaurs*. London: Peter Lowe, 116 pages.

———, 1975*b*, Temperatures rise over hot-blooded dinosaurs: *Sunday Times*, Dec. 7, p. 13.

———, 1976, Dinosaur teleology: Nature, 260, pp. 559–560.

Halstead, L. B., and J. B. Halstead, 1981, *Dinosaurs*. Dorset, England: Blanford Books, Ltd., 170 pages.

Hammer, William R., and William J. Hickerson, 1993, A new Jurassic dinosaur fauna from Antarctica: *Journal of Vertebrate Paleontology*, Abstracts of Papers, Fifty-third Annual Meeting, p. 40A.

———, 1994, A crested theropod dinosaur from Antarctica: *Science*, 264, pp. 828–830.

Hanai, Tetsuro, I. Obata, and I. Hayami, 1968, Notes on the Cretaceous Miyako Group, Northeast Japan: *Memoirs of the Natural Science Museum*, Tokyo, 1, pp. 20–28.

Harland, Walter Brian, 1967, The fossil record: a symposium with documentation jointly sponsored by the Geological Society of London and the Palaeontological Association.

Harland, Walter, R. L. Armstrong, A. V. Cox, L. E. Craig, A. G. Smith, and D. G. Smith, 1990, *A Geologic Time Scale 1989*. Cambridge, England: Cambridge University Press, xv, 263 pages.

Harland, Walter Brian, A. V. Cox, P. G. Llewellyn, A. G. Smith, and R. Walters, 1989, *A Geologic Time Scale*. Cambridge, England: Cambridge University Press, 131 pages.

Harrison, C. J. O., and Cyril A. Walker, 1973, *Wyleia*: a new bird humerus from the Lower Cretaceous of England: *Palaeontology*, 16 (4), pp. 721–728.

———, 1975, The Brachynemidae, a new family of owls from the U. Cretaceous of Romania: *Ibid.*, 16 (4), pp. 563–570.

Hasegawa, Yoshikazu, Tetsuro Hanai, and Tomoki Kase, 1982, The vertebrate fossil

from the Lower Cretaceous in Moshi, Iwaizumi, Iwate, Japan: *Abstracts of the Annual Meeting of the Paleontological Society of Japan at Chiba University*.

Hasegawa, Yoshikazu, Makoto Manabe, Tetsuro Hanai, Tomoki Kase, and Tatsuo Oji, 1991, A diplodocid dinosaur from the Early Cretaceous Miyako Group of Japan: *Bulletin of the Science Museum*, Tokyo, Series C, 17 (1), pp. 1–9.

Hatcher, John Bell, 1896, Some localities for Laramie mammals and horned dinosaurs: *American Naturalist*, 30, pp. 112–120.

———, 1901, *Diplodocus* (Marsh): its osteology, taxonomy, and probable habits, with a restoration of the skeleton: *Memoirs of the Carnegie Museum*, 1 (1), pp. 1–61.

———, 1903*a*, A new sauropod dinosaur from the Jurassic of Colorado: *Proceedings of the Biological Society of Washington*, 16, pp. 1–2.

———, 1903*b*, Osteology of *Haplocanthosaurus*, with description of new species and remarks on probable habits of the Sauropoda, and the age and origin of the *Atlantosaurus* beds: *Memoirs of the Carnegie Museum*, 2, pp. 1–75.

———, 1903*c*, Discovery of remains of *Astrodon* (*Pleurocoelus*) in the *Atlantosaurus* beds of Wyoming: *Annals of the Carnegie Museum*, 2, pp. 9–14.

———, 1905*a*, Vertebrate fauna (of the Judith River beds): *Bulletin of the United States Geological Survey*, 257, pp. 67–103.

———, 1905*b*, Two new Ceratopsia from the Laramie of Converse County, Wyoming: *American Journal of Science*, 4th series, 20, pp. 413–422.

Hatcher, John Bell, Othniel Charles Marsh, and Richard Swann Lull, 1907, The Ceratopsia: *Monographs of the United States Geological Survey*, 49, pp. i–xxx, 1–198.

Hattin, D. E., 1982, Stratigraphy and depositional environment of Smoky Hill Chalk Member, Niobrara Chalk (Upper Cretaceous) of the type area, western Kansas: *Bulletin of the Geological Survey of Kansas*, 225, pp. 1–108.

Haubold, Hartmut, 1969, Die Evolution der Archosaurier in der Trias, aus der Sicht ihrer Fährten: *Hercynia*, 6, pp. 90–106.

———, 1971, Ichnia Amphibiorum et Reptiliorum Fossilium, *in*: Oskar Kuhn, editor, *Handbuch der Paläoherpetologie*, 18. Stuttgart: G. Fischer, viii, 124 pages.

———, 1984, *Saurierfährten*. Wittenberg Lutherstadt: A. Ziemsen Verlag, Die Neue Brehm-Bücherei, 231 pages.

———, 1990, Ein neuer Dinosaurier (Ornithischia, Thyreophora) aus dem unteren Jura des Nördlichen mitteleuropa: *Revue de Paléobiologie*, 9 (1), pp 149–177, Geneva.

Haughton, Sidney H., 1918, A new dinosaur from the Stormberg Beds of South Africa: *Annals of the Magazine of Natural History*, 9 (2), pp. 468–469.

———, 1924, The fauna and stratigraphy of the Stormberg Series: *Annals of the South African Museum*, 12, pp. 323–497.

Hay, Oliver P., 1902, Bibliography and catalogue of the fossil vertebrates of North America: *United States Geological Survey*, Bulletin 179.

———, 1908*a*, On the habits and the pose of the sauropodous dinosaurs, especially *Diplodocus*: *American Naturalist*, 42, pp. 672–681.

_____, 1908*b*, On certain genera and species of carnivorous dinosaurs, with special reference to *Ceratosaurus nasicornis* Marsh: *Proceedings of the United States National Museum*, 35 (1684), pp. 351–366.

_____, 1930, Second bibliography and catalogue of the fossil Vertebrata of North America, volume II: *Publications of the Carnegie Institute of Washington*, 390, xiv, 1074 pages.

Haynes, G., 1988, Mass deaths and serial predation: comparative taphonomic studies of modern large mammal death sites: *Journal of Archaeological Science*, 15, pp. 219–235.

He Xinlu, 1979, [A new discovered ornithopod dinosaur—*Yandusaurus* from Zigong, Sichuan]: *Contribution to International Exchange of Geology*, Part 2, Stratigraphy and Paleontology, Geological Publishing House, Beijing, pp. 116–123.

_____, 1984, The vertebrate fossils of Sichuan: Sichuan Scientific and Technological Publishing House, 168 pages.

He Xinlu, and Cai Kaiji, 1983, A new species of *Yandusaurus* (hypsilophodont dinosaur) from the Middle Jurassic of Dashanpu, Zigong, Sichuan: *Journal of Chengdu College of Geology 1983 Supplement 1*, pp. 5–14.

_____, 1984, *The Middle Jurassic Dinosaurian Fauna from Dashanpu, Zigong, Sichuan*, volume 1, The Ornithopod Dinosaurs. Chengdu, 71 pages.

He Xinlu, Li Kui and Cai Kaiji, 1988, *The Middle Jurassic dinosaur fauna from Dashanpu, Zigong, Sichuan*, volume IV, The Sauropod Dinosaurs (II): Sichuan Publishing House of Science and Technology, Chengdu, pp. 114–133.

He Xinlu, Li Kui, Cai Kaiji, and Gao Yuhui, 1984, *Omeisaurus tianfuensis*—a new species of *Omeisaurus* from Dashanpu, Zigong, Sichuan: *Journal of Chengdu College of Geology*, 2, pp. 15–32.

Heaton, M. J., 1972, The palatal structure of some Canadian Hadrosauridae (Reptilia: Ornithischia): *Canadian Journal of Earth Sciences*, 9 (2), pp. 185–205.

Heaton, R. L., 1950, Late Paleozoic and Mesozoic history of Colorado and adjacent areas: *American Association of Petroleum Geologists Bulletin*, 34, pp. 1659–1698.

Heilmann, Gerhard, 1926, *The Origin of Birds*. London: Witherby, 208 pages.

Hendricks, Alfred, 1980, Die Saurierfährte von Münchchagen bei Rehburg-Loccum (NW-Deutschland): *Abhandlungen aus dem Landemuseum für Naturkunde zu Münster in Westfalen*, 43 (2), pp. 3–22.

_____, 1981, Die Saurierfährte von Münchehagen bei Rehburg-Loccum (NW-Deutschland): *Ibid.*, 43, pp. 1–22.

Hennig, Edwin, 1915*a*, Stegosauria: Fossilium Catalogus, I.—Animalia, part 9, pp. 1–15, Berlin.

_____, 1915*b*, *Kentrosaurus aethiopicus*, der Stegosauride des Tendaguru: *Sonder-Abdruck aus den Sitzungsberichten der Gesellschaft Naturforschender Freunde*, Berlin 14, pp. 219–247.

_____, 1916, *Kentrurosaurus*, non *Doryphosaurus*: Centralblatt für Mineralogie, Geologie und Paläontologie 1916, p.578.

_____, 1924, *Kentrurosaurus aethiopicus* die Stegosaurier-Funde vom Tendaguru, Deutsch-Ostrafrika: *Palaeontographica*, Supplement 7, pp. 103–153.

Hennig, Willi, 1966, *Phylogenetic Systematics*. Urbana, Illinois: University of Illinois Press.

Heron, S. Duncan, Jr., and W. H. Wheeler, 1964, The Cretaceous formations along the Cape Fear River, North Carolina: *Atlantic Coastal Plain Geological Association, Field Conference Guidebook*, 5, pp. 1–55.

Hill, D., G. Playford and J. T. Woods, 1968, Cretaceous fossils of Queensland: *Palaeontographical Society*, Brisbane, 35 pages.

Hillman, J. C., and A. K. K. Hillman, 1977, Mortality of wildlife in Nairobi National Park, during the drought of 1973-1974: *East African Wildlife Journal*, 15, pp. 1–18.

Hirsch, Karl F., 1989, Interpretations of Cretaceous and Pre-Cretaceous eggs and shell fragments, *in*: David D. Gillette and Martin G. Lockley, editors, *Dinosaur Tracks and Traces*. Cambridge, England: Cambridge University Press, pp. 89–97.

Hirsch, Karl F., and Betty Quinn, 1990, Eggs and eggshell fragments from the Upper Cretaceous Two Medicine Formation of Montana: *Journal of Vertebrate Paleontology*, 10 (4), pp. 491–511.

Hitchcock, Charles H., 1858*a*, An attempt to discriminate and describe the animals that made the fossil footprints of the United States and especially of New England: *American Academy of Arts and Sciences*, series 2, 3, pp. 129–256.

_____, 1858*b*, *Ichnology of New England. A report on the sandstone of the Connecticut Valley, especially its fossil footmarks.* Boston: Wright and Potter, 220 pages.

Hoffet, J. H., 1937, Sur le crétacé du Bas-Laos: *Comptes Rendus des Séances de l'Académie des Sciences*, 204, pp. 1439–1441.

_____, 1942, Description de quelques ossements du Sënoniene du Bas-Laos. C. R. Cons. Rech. Sci. Indochine 1942, pp. 49–57.

Hoffstetter, Robert, 1957, Quelques observations sur les stegosaurines: *Muséum National d'Histoire Naturelle*, Paris, Bulletin, 2 (29), pp. 537–547.

Hoffstetter, Robert, and Roger Brun, 1956, Un dinosaurien stegosaurine dans le Callovien du Calvados: *Comptes Rendus des Séances de l'Académie des Sciences*, 243, pp. 1651–1653.

_____, 1958, Note complémentaire sur la découverte d'un dinosaurien stegosaurine dans le Callovien d'Argences (Calvados): *Revue des Sociétés Savantes de Haute-Normandie*, (Sci.), 9, pp. 69–78.

Holder, M. J., and David B. Norman, 1986, Kreide-Dinosaurier im Sauerland: Naturwissenschaften, 73, pp. 109–116.

Holl, Friedrich, 1829, *Handbuch der Petrifaktenkunde*, volume 1. Quedlinburg, 232 pages.

Holland, William J., 1906, The osteology of *Diplodocus* Marsh: *Memoirs of the Carnegie Museum*, 2, pp. 225–264.

_____, 1910, A review of some recent criticisms of the restorations of sauropod dinosaurs existing in the museums of the United States, with special reference to *Diplodocus carnegii* in the Carnegie Museum: *American Naturalist*, 44, pp. 259–283.

_____, 1915*a*, Heads and tails; a few notes relating to the structure of the sauropod dinosaurs: *Annals of the Carnegie Museum*, 9, pp. 273–278.

_____, 1915*b*, A new species of *Apatosaurus*: *Ibid.*, 10, pp. 143–145.

_____, 1924*a*, The skull of *Diplodocus*: *Memoirs of the Carnegie Museum*, 9, pp. 397–403.

_____, 1924*b*, Description of type of *Uintasaurus douglassi* Holland: *Annals of the Carnegie Museum*, 15, pp. 119–138.

Holtz, Jr., Thomas R., 1994, The phylogenetic position of the Tyrannosauridae: implications for theropod systematics: *Journal of Paleontology*, 68 (5), pp. 1100–111.

_____, 1994*b*, The arctometatarsalian pes, an unusual structure of the metatarsus of Cretaceous Theropoda (Dinosauria: Saurischia): *Journal of Vertebrate Paleontology* 14 (4), pp. 480–519.

_____, 1995*a*, A new phylogeny of the Theropoda: *Journal of Vertebrate Paleontology*, Abstracts of Papers, Fifty-fifth Annual Meeting, p. 35A.

_____, 1995*b*, Definition and diagnosis of Theropoda and related taxa: *Ibid.*, p. 35A.

Hooley, R. W., 1912, On the discovery of the remains of *Iguanodon mantelli* in the Wealden beds of Brightstone Bay, Isle of Wight: *Geological Magazine*, 5 (9), pp. 444–449.

_____, 1913, Skeleton of *Ornithodesmus latidens*: *Quarterly Journal of the Geological Society*, 69.

_____, 1917, On the integument of *Iguanodon bernissartensis*, Boulenger, and of *Morosaurus becklesii*, Mantell: *Ibid.*, 6 (4), pp. 148–150.

_____, 1925, On the skeleton of *Iguanodon atherfieldensis* sp. nov. from the Wealden Shales of Athefield (Isle of Wight): *Quarterly Journal of the Geological Society of London*, 81, pp. 1–61.

Hopson, James A., 1975*a*, The evolution of cranial display structures in hadrosaurian dinosaurs: *Paleobiology*, 1 (1), pp. 21–43.

_____, 1975*b*, On the generic separation of the ornithischian dinosaurs *Lychorhinus* [*sic*] and *Heterodontosaurus* from the Stormberg Series (Upper Triassic) of South Africa: *South African Journal of Science*, 71, pp. 302–305.

_____, 1977, Relative brain size and behavior in archosaurian reptiles: *Annual Review of Ecology and Systematics*, 8, pp. 429–448.

_____, 1979, Paleoneurology, *in*: C. Gans, R. C. Northcutt and P. Ulinski, editors, *Biology of the Reptilia*, 9. New York and London: Academic Press, pp. 39–146.

_____, 1980*a*, Tooth function and replacement in early Mesozoic ornithischian dinosaurs: implications for aestivation: *Lethaia*, 13, pp. 93–105.

_____, 1980*b*, Relative brain size in dinosaurs: Implications for endothermy, *in*: D.K. Thomas and Everett C. Olson, editors, *A Cold Look at the Warm-Blooded Dinosaurs, American Association for the Advancement of Science, Selected Symposium*, 28, pp. 287–310.

Horne, Gregory S., 1994, A mid–Cretaceous ornithopod from Central Honduras: *Journal of Vertebrate Paleontology*, 14 (1), pp. 147–150.

Horner, John R., 1979, Upper Cretaceous dinosaurs from the Bearpaw Shale (marine) of south-central Montana with a checklist of Upper Cretaceous dinosaur remains from marine sediments in North America: *Journal of Paleontology*, 53 (3), pp. 566–577.

_____, 1982, Evidence of colonial nesting and 'site fidelity' among ornithischian dinosaurs: *Nature*, 297 (5868), pp. 675–676.

_____, 1983, Cranial osteology and morphology of the type specimen *Maiasaura peeblesorum* (Ornithischia: Hadrosauridae), with discussion of its phylogenetic position: *Journal of Vertebrate Paleontology*, 3 (1): 29–83, pp. 29–38.

Bibliography

———, 1984a, The nesting behavior of dinosaurs: *Scientific American*, 250 (4), pp. 130–137.

———, 1984b, Three ecologically distinct vertebrate faunal communities from the Late Cretaceous Two Medicine Formation of Montana, with discussion of the evolutionary pressures induced by interior seaway fluctuations, *in: Montana Geological Field Conference, Northwestern Montana*, pp. 229–303.

———, 1984c, A "segmented" epidermal tail frill in a species of hadrosaurian dinosaur: *Journal of Paleontology*, 58 (1), pp. 270–271.

———, 1985, Evidence for polyphyletic organization of the Hadrosauridae (Ornithischia): *Proceedings of the Pacific Division, American Association of Advanced Science*, 4, pp. 31–32.

———, 1987, Ecologic and behaviorial implications derived from a dinosaur nesting site, *in*: Sylvia J. Czerkas and Everett C. Olson, editors, *Dinosaurs Past and Present*, Volume II. Seattle: Natural History Museum of Los Angeles County, in association with University of Washington Press, pp. 50–63.

———, 1988, A new hadrosaur (Reptilia, Ornithischia) from the Upper Cretaceous Judith River Formation of Montana: *Journal of Vertebrate Paleontology*, 8 (3), pp. 314–321.

———, 1990, Evidence of diphyletic origination of the hadrosaurian (Reptilia: Ornithischia) dinosaurs, *in*: Kenneth Carpenter and Philip J. Currie, editors, *Dinosaur Systematics: Approaches and Perspectives*. Cambridge, New York and Melbourne: Cambridge University Press, pp. 179–187.

———, and James Gorman, 1988, *Digging Dinosaurs*. New York: Workman Publishing, 210 pages.

———, 1992, Cranial morphology of *Prosaurolophus* (Ornithischia: Hadrosauridae) with descriptions of two new hadrosaurid species and an evaluation of hadrosaurid phylogenetic relationships: *Museum of the Rockies Occasional Paper No. 2*, 120 pages.

———, 1995, Morphology and function of the enclosed narial chambers of lambeosaurid dinosaurs: *Journal of Vertebrate Paleontology*, Abstracts of Papers, Fifty-fifth Annual Meeting, p. 36A.

Horner, John R., and Philip J. Currie, 1994, Embryonic and neonatal morphology and ontogeny of a new species of *Hypacrosaurus* (Ornithischia: Lambeosauridae) from Montana and Alberta, *in*: Kenneth Carpenter, Karl F. Hirsch, and John R. Horner, editors, *Dinosaur Eggs and Babies*. New York: Cambridge University Press, pp. 312–336.

Horner, John R., and Don Lessem, 1993, *The Complete T. rex*. New York: Simon and Schuster, 239 pages.

Horner, John R., and Robert Makela, 1979, Nest of juveniles provides evidence of family structure among dinosaurs: *Nature*, 282 (5736), pp. 296–298.

Horner, John R., David J. Varicchio, and Mark B. Goodwin, 1992, Marine transgressions and the evolution of Cretaceous dinosaurs: *Nature*, 358, pp. 59–61.

Horner, John R., and David B. Weishampel, 1988, A comparative embryological study of two ornithischian dinosaurs: *Nature*, 332, pp. 256–257.

Hotton, Nicholas III, 1963, *Dinosaurs*. New York: Pyramid Books, 192 pages.

———, 1980, An alternative to dinosaur endothermy; the happy wanderers, *in*: Roger D. K. Thomas and Everett C. Olson, editors, *A Cold Look at the Warm Blooded Dinosaurs*. American Association for the Advancement of Science, Selected Symposium, pp. 311–350.

Hou Lian-hai, A new primitive pachycephalosauria from Anhui, China: *Vertebrata PalAsiatica*, 15 (3), pp. 198–202.

Hou Lian-hai, Yeh H.K., and Chou Minchen, 1975, Fossil reptiles from Fusui, Kwangshi: *Vertebrata PalAsiatica*, 13 (1), pp. 23–33.

Houston, D. C., 1979, The adaptations of scavengers, *in*: A. R. E. Sinclair and M. Norton-Griffiths, editors, *Serengeti: Dynamics of an Ecosystem*. Chicago: University of Chicago Press, pp. 263–286.

Howgate, M. E., 1984, The teeth of *Archaeopteryx* and a reinterpretation of the Eichstatt specimen: *Zoological Journal of the Linnean Society*, 82, pp. 159–175.

Howse, Stafford C. B., and Andrew R. Milner, 1993, *Ornithodesmus*—a maniraptoran theropod dinosaur from the lower Cretaceous of the Isle of Wight, England: *Palaeontology*, 36 (2), pp. 425–437.

Hu Cheng-Chin, 1974, Shantung Chucheng geesing yadze long hwashih (translation: A new hadrosaur from the Cretaceous of Chucheng, Shantung): *Acta Geologica Sinica*, 2, pp. 179–206.

Hu Chengzhi and Cheng Zhengwu, 1988, New progress in the restudy on *Shantungosaurus giganteus*: *Bulletin of the Chinese Academy of Geological Sciences*, pp. 251–258, Beijing.

Hu Show-yung, 1964, Carnosaurian remains from Alashan, Inner Mongolia: *Vertebrata PalAsiatica*, 8 (1), pp. 42–63.

Hu S.J., 1993, A new Theropoda (*Dilophosaurus sinensis*, sp.n.) from Yunnan, China: *Vertebrata PalAsiatica*, 31, pp. 56–69.

Huckreide, R., 1982, Die unterkratazische Karsthöhlen-Füllung von Nehden in Sauerland. 1. Geologische, paläozoologische und paläobotanische Befunde und Datierung: *Geologica et Palaeontologica*, 16, pp. 183–242.

Huene, Friedrich von, 1901, Der vermutliche Hautpanzer des *Compsognathus longipes* Wagner: *Neus Jahrbuch Fuer Mineralologie, Geologie und Paläontologie*, 1901, 1 (1), pp. 157–160.

———, 1906, Ueber die Dinosaurier der Aussereuropaeischen Trias: *Ibid.* (N. F.), 8 (12), pp. 99–156.

———, 1907–08, Die Dinosaurier der europäischen Triasformation mit Berucksichtigung der europaischen Vorkommisse: *Geologische und Paläontologische Abhandlungen*, Jena, Supplement 1, 419 pages.

———, 1910a, Ein primitiver Dinosaurier aus der mittleren Trias von Elgin: *Geologie und Paläontologie Abhandl.* 8, pp. 317–322.

———, 1910b, Uber den ältesten Rest von *Omosaurus* (*Dacentrurus*) im englischen Dogger: *Neus Jahrbuch Fuer Mineralogie, Geologie und Paläontologie*, Stuttgart, 1910, pp. 75–78.

———, 1914, Saurischia et Ornithischia Triadica ("Dinosauria" Triadica), *in: Fossilium Catalogus I. Animalia*, 4, pp. 1–21.

———, 1915, On reptiles of the New Mexican Trias in the Cope collection: *Bulletin of the American Museum of Natural History*, 34, pp. 485–507.

———, 1920, Bermerkungen zur Systematik und Stammesgeschichte einiger Reptilien: *Zeitschrift Fuer Indukt. Abstammungslehre und Vererbungslehre*, 24, pp. 162–166.

———, 1921, Neue Pseudosuchier und Coelurosaurier aus dem württembergischen Keuper: *Paläonttologica Zhurnal*, 11, pp. 329–403.

———, 1922, Über einem Sauropodem im oberen Malm des Berner Jura: *Eclogae Geologicae Helvetiae*, 17 (1), pp. 80–94.

———, 1923, Carnivorous Saurischia in Europe since the Triassic: *Bulletin of the Geological Society of America*, 34, pp. 449–458.

———, 1925, Eine neue Rekonstruktion von *Compsognathus*: *Centralblatt für Mineralogie, Geologie und Paläontologie*, Abstract B., p. 157.

———, 1926a, Vollständige Osteologie eines Plateosauriden aus dem schwäbischen Keuper: *Geologische und Palaeontologische Abhandlungen, neue Folge*, 15 [der ganzen Reihe Band 19] (2), pp. 139–179.

———, 1926b, The carnivorous Saurischia in the Jura and Cretaceous formations principally in Europe: *Revista Museo de La Plata*, 29, pp. 35–114.

———, 1926c, On several known and unknown reptiles of the order Saurischia from England and France: *The Annals and Magazine of Natural History*, 17, 9th series, pp. 473–489.

———, 1927, Short review of the present knowledge of the Sauropoda: *Memoirs of the Queensland Museum*, 9, pp. 121–126.

———, 1928, KurzeUbersicht über die Saurischia und ihre natürlichen Zusammenhänge: *Paläontographica Zeitschrift*, 11, pp. 269–273.

———, 1929, Los Saurisquios y Ornitisquios del Cretáceo Argentina: *Anales Museo de La Plata*, 3, Serie 2a., 196 pages.

———, 1931, Verischiedene mesozoische Wiebeltierreste aus Südamerika: *Neus Jahrbuch Fuer Mineralogie, Geologie und Paläontologie*, Abt. B., 66, pp. 181–198.

———, 1932, Die fossile Reptil-Ordnung Saurischia, ihre Entwicklung und Geschichte: *Monographien zur Geologie und Palaeontologie*, series 1, 4, 361 pages.

———, 1934, Ein neuer Coelurosaurier in der thüringischen Trias: *Paläontologische Zeitschrift* 1935, 16, pp. 10–170.

———, 1941, Die Tetrapoden-Fárten im Toskanischen Verrucano und ihre Bedeutung: *Neus Jahrd. Miner. Geol. Paläont. Beilbd.* 1941, Abt. B, 86, pp. 1–34.

———, 1942, *Die fossilen Reptilien des südamerikanischen* Gondwanalandes. Ergebnisse der Sauriergrabungen in Südbrasilien 1928/29. Munich: *Beck'sche Verlagbuchhandlung*, viii, 332 pages.

———, 1956, *Palaontologie und Phylogenie der Niederen Tetrapoden*. Jena: Gustav Fischer, xii, 716 pages.

Huene, Friedrich von, and Charles Alfred Matley, 1933, The Cretaceous Saurischia and Ornithischia of the Central Provinces of India: *Paleontologica Indica*, 21 (1), pp. 1–74.

Hughes, N. F., 1958, Palaeontological evidence for the age of the English Wealden: *Geological Magazine*, 95, pp. 41–49, London.

Hulke, James W., 1869, Note on a large saurian humerus from the Kimmeridge Clay of the Dorset Coast: *Proceedings of the Geological Society of London*, June 23, pp. 386–389.

———, 1874, Note on a very large saurian limb-bone adapted for progression upon land, from the Kimmeridge Clay of Weymouth, Dorset: *Geological Society of London Quarterly Journal*, 30, pp. 16–17.

_____, 1879, *Vectisaurus valdensis*, a new Wealden dinosaur: *Ibid.*, 35, pp. 421–424.

_____, 1880, *Iguanodon prestwichii*, a new species from the Kimmeridge Clay founded on numerous fossil remains lately discovered at Cumnor, near Oxford: *Ibid.*, 36, pp. 433–456.

_____, 1881, *Polacanthus Foxii* a large undescribed dinosaur from the Wealden Formation in the Isle of Wight: *Philosophical Transactions of the Royal Society*, 172, pp. 653–662.

_____, 1882, Note on the os pubis and ischium of *Ornithopsis eucamerotus*: *Quarterly Journal of the Geological Society of London*, 38, pp. 135–144.

_____, 1883, An attempt at a complete osteology of *Hypsilophodon foxii*: *Philosophical Transactions of the Royal Society of London*, 173, p. 1035.

_____, 1887, Note on some dinosaurian remains in the collection of A. Leeds, Esq. of Eyebury, Northamptonshire: *Quarterly Journal of the Geological Society of London*, 43, pp. 695–702.

Hunt, Adrian P., A new ?ornithischian dinosaur from the Bull Canyon Formation (Upper Triassic) of east-central New Mexico, *in*: Spencer G. Lucas and Hunt, editors, *The Dawn of the Age of Dinosaurs in the American Southwest*. Albuquerque: New Mexico Museum of Natural History, pp. 355–358.

Hunt, Adrian P., and Spencer G. Lucas, 1989*a*, Late Triassic vertebrate localities in New Mexico, *in*: Lucas and Hunt, editors, *Dawn of the Age of Dinosaurs in the American Southwest*. Albuquerque: New Mexico Museum of Natural History, pp. 72–101.

_____, 1989*b*, Stratigraphy and vertebrate biochronology of Upper Triassic strata in the Chama basin, north-central New Mexico: *Abstracts, Symposium of Southwestern Geology and Paleontology*, 15, Flagstaff, Arizona.

_____, 1991, *Rioarribasaurus*, a new name for a Late Triassic dinosaur from New Mexico (USA): *Paläontraphica Zeitschrift* 65 (1/2), pp. 191–198.

_____, 1992, Stratigraphy, paleontology and age of the Fruitland and Kirtland Formations (Upper Cretaceous), San Juan Basin, New Mexico: *New Mexico Geological Society, Guidebook* 43, pp. 217–239.

_____, 1993, Cretaceous vertebrates of New Mexico: *Vertebrate Paleontology in New Mexico, New Mexico Museum of Natural History and Science*, Bulletin 2, pp. 76–91.

_____, 1994, Ornithischian dinosaurs from the Upper Triassic of the United States, *in*: Nicholas C. Fraser and Hans-Dieter Sues, editors, *In the Shadow of the Dinosaurs, Early Mesozoic Tetrapods*. New York: Cambridge University Press, pp. 227–241.

Huxley, Thomas Henry, 1866, On some remains of large dinosaurian reptiles from the Stormberg Mountains: *Quarterly Journal of the Geological Society of London*, 23, pp. 1–6.

_____, 1867*a*, On some remains of large dinosaurian reptiles from the Stormberg Mountains, South Africa: *Ibid.*, 23, pp. 1–6.

_____, 1867*b*, On *Acanthopholis horridus*, a new reptile from the chalk marl. *Geological Magazine*, 4, p.65.

_____, 1868*a*, On the animals which are most nearly intermediate between birds and reptiles: *Annals of the Magazine of Natural History*, 4 (2) pp. 66–75, London.

_____, 1868*b*, Remarks on *Archaeopteryx lithographica*: *Ibid.*, 4 (1), pp. 220–224 (reprinted in *Proclamations of the Royal Society of London*, 16, pp. 243–248).

_____, 1869, On *Hypsilophodon*, a new genus of Dinosauria: *Geological Magazine*, 6, p. 573.

_____, 1870*a*, On *Hypsilophodon foxii*, a new dinosaurian from the Wealden of the Isle of Wight: *Quarterly Journal of the Geological Society of London*, 26, pp. 3–12.

_____, 1870*b*, Further evidence of the affinity between the dinosaurian reptiles and birds: *Ibid.*, pp. 12–31.

Idnurm, M., 1985, Late Mesozoic and Cenozoic palaeomagnetism of Australia—I. A redetermined apparent polar wander path: *Geophysical Journal of the Royal Astronomical Society*, 83, pp. 399–418.

Irby, Grace V., 1991, Posterolateral (?) "halluxlike" impressions on dinosaur tracks, Lower Jurassic Moenave Formation, northeastern Arizona: *Journal of Vertebrate Paleontology*, Abstracts of Papers, Fifty-first Annual Meeting, p. 38A.

_____, 1995, Posterolateral markings on dinosaur tracks, Cameron Dinosaur Tracksite, Lower Jurassic Moenave Formation, northeastern Arizona: *Journal of Paleontology*, 69 (4), pp. 779–784.

Jacobs, Louis, 1995, *Lone Star Dinosaurs*. College Station, Texas: Texas A & M University Press, xiv, 160 pages.

Jacobs, Louis L., Dale A. Winkler, William R. Downs, and Elizabeth M. Gomani, 1993, New material of an Early Cretaceous titanosaurid sauropod dinosaur from Malawi: *Palaeontology*, 36 (3), pp. 523–534.

Jacobs, Louis L., David A. Winkler, Phillip A. Murry, and J. M. Maurice, 1994, A nodosaurid scutelling from the Texas shore of the Western Interior Seaway, *in*: Kenneth Carpenter, Karl F. Hirsch, and John R. Horner, editors, *Dinosaur Eggs and Babies*. Cambridge: Cambridge University Press, pp. 337–346.

Jacobsen, A. R., 1995, Ecological interpretation based on theropod tooth marks: feeding behaviors of carnivorous dinosaurs: *Journal of Vertebrate Paleontology*, Abstracts of Papers, Fifty-fifth Annual Meeting, p. 37A.

Jain, Sohan L., 1973, New specimens of Lower Jurassic holostean fishes from India: *Palaeontology*, 16, pp. 149–177.

_____, 1989, Recent dinosaur discoveries in India, including eggshells, nests and coprolites, *in*: David D. Gillette and Martin G. Lockley, editors, *Dinosaur Tracks and Traces*. Cambridge, England: Cambridge University Press, pp. 100–108.

Jain, Sohan L., T.S. Kutty, Tapan Roy-Chowdhury, and Sankar Chatterjee, 1975, The sauropod dinosaur from Lower Jurassic Kota Formation on India: *Proclamantions of the Royal Society of London*, A, 188, pp. 221–228.

Jain, Sohan L., P. L. Robinson, and Tapan K. Roy-Chowdhury, 1962, A new vertebrate fauna from the early Jurassic of the Deccan, India: *Nature*, 194 (4830), pp. 755–757.

Jain, Sohan, and A. Sahni, 1985, Dinosaurian egg shell fragments from the Lameta Formation at Pisdura, Chandrapur District, Maha-

rastra: *Geoscience Journal*, 6 (2), pp. 211–220.

Janensch, Werner, 1914, Ueberischt ueber der Wirbeltierfauna der Tendaguru-Schichten: *Archiv f. Biontologie*, Berlin, III, 1 (1), pp. 82–83, 86–98.

_____, 1920, Über *Elaphrosaurus bambergi* und die Megalosaurier aus den Tendaguru-Schichten Deutsch-Ostafrikas: *Sitzungsberichte der Gesellschaft Naturforschender Freunde zu Berlin* 1920, pp. 225–235.

_____, 1922, Das Handskelett von *Gigantosaurus* and *Brachiosaurus brancai* aus den Tendaguru-Schichten Deutsch-Ostafrika: *Centralblatt für Mineralogie, Geologie und Paläontologie*, 1922, pp. 464–480.

_____, 1925, Die Coelurosaurier und Theropoden der Tendaguru-Schichten Deutsch-Ostafrikas: *Palaeontographica*, Supplement 7, pp. 7–50.

_____, 1929, Die Wirbelsäule der Gattung *Dicraeosaurus*: *Ibid.*, pp. 39–133.

_____, 1961, Die Gliedmaszen und Gliedmaszengürtel der Sauropoden der Tendaguru-Schichten: *Ibid.*, 7 (1), teil 3, lief. 4, pp. 177–235.

Janis, Christine, 1988, As estimation of tooth volume and hypsodonty indices in ungulate mammals, and correlation of these factors with dietary preference, *in*: D. E. Russell, J.-P. Santoro, and D. Sigigneau-Russell, editors, *Teeth Revisited: Proceedings VIIth International Symposium on Dental Morphology*. Memoires du Museum National d'Histoire Naturelle, Paris C 53, pp. 367–387.

Jenny, J., A. Le Marrec, and M. Monbaron, 1981, Les couches rouges du Jurassique moyen du Haut Atlas central (Maroc): correlations lithostratigraphiques, éléments de datations et cadre tectono-sédimentaire: *Bulletin, Société Géologique de France, Paris*, 7, t. 23 (6), pp. 627–639.

Jensen, Herald Ingemann, 1923, The geology of the Cairns Hinterland and other parts of North Queensland: *Proceedings of the Linnean Society of New South Wales*, 58, p. 154.

Jensen, James A., 1985*a*, Three new sauropod dinosaurs from the Upper Jurassic of Colorado: *Great Basin Naturalist*, 45 (4), pp. 697–709.

_____, 1985*b*, Uncompahgre dinosaur fauna: a preliminary report: *Ibid.*, 45 (4), pp. 710–720.

_____, 1987, New brachiosaur material from the Late Jurassic of Utah and Colorado: *Ibid.*, 47 (4), pp. 592–608.

_____, 1988, A fourth new sauropod dinosaur from the Upper Jurassic of the Colorado Plateau and sauropod bipedalism: *Ibid.*, 48 (2), pp. 121–145.

Jensen, James A., and Kevin Padian, 1989, Small pterosaurs and dinosaurs from the Uncompahgre fauna (Brushy Basin Member, Morrison Formation: ?Tithonian), Late Jurassic, Western Colorado: *Journal of Paleontology*, 63 (3), pp. 364–373.

Jerison, H. J., 1973, *Evolution of the Brain and Intelligence*. New York: Academic Press, 496 pages.

Jerzykiewicz, T., P. J. Currie, D. A. Eberth, P. A. Johnson, E. H. Koster and Jia-Jian Zheng, 1993, Djadokhta Formation correlative strata in Chinese Inner Mongolia: an overview of the stratigraphy, sedimentary geology, and paleontology and comparisons with the type locality in the pre–Altai Gobi:

Canadian Journal of Earth Sciences, 30 (10–11), pp. 2180–2195.

Johnston, Christopher, 1859, (Comments on *Astrodon*): *American Journal of Dental Science*, 9, p. 341.

Jones, D. L., 1963, Upper Cretaceous (Campanian and Maastrichtian) ammonites from southern Alaska: *Journal of Paleontology*, 53, pp. 566–577.

Jurscak, Tiberiu, and Elisabeto Popa, 1985, Pterosaurians from the Upper Cretaceous of Cornet, Roumania, in: Wolf-Ernest Reif and Frank Westphal, editors, *Third Symposium on Mesozoic Terrestrial Ecosystems*, Short Papers. Tubingen GmbH: ATTEMPTO Verlag, pp. 117–119.

Kauffman, E. G., 1984, Paleobiogeography and evolutionary response dynamic in the Cretaceous Western Interior Seaway of North America, in: G. E. Westermann, editor, *Jurassic-Cretaceous Biochronology and Paleogeography of North America. Geological Association of Canada Special Paper* 27, Waterloo, pp. 273–306.

Kaye, John M., and Dale A. Russell, 1973, The oldest record of hadrosaurian dinosaurs in North America: *Journal of Paleontology*, 47 (1), pp. 91–93.

Kenneth, J. H., *A Dictionary of Scientific Terms* by I. F. Henderson and W. D. Henderson, seventh edition. Edinburgh: Oliver and Boyd, xv, 595 pages.

Kermack, Kenneth A., 1951, A note on the habits of the sauropods: *Annals of the Magazine of Natural History*, 12 (4), pp. 830–832.

Kerourio, Ph., 1981, Nouvelles observations sur le mode de ponte chez les dinosauriens du Crétacé terminal du Midi de la France: *Compte Rendu Sommaire des Séances de la Société Géologique de France*, 1956, pp. 261–23 (1), pp. 25–28.

Kielan-Jaworoska, Zofia, 1974, Multituberculate succession in the Late Cretaceous of the Gobi Desert (Mongolia). Results of the Polish-Molgolian Palaeontological Expeditions, V: *Palaeontologia Polonica*, 30, pp. 23–44.

Kielan-Jaworoska, Zofia, and Rinchen Barsbold, 1972, Results of the Polish-Mongolian Paleontological Expedition, Part IV: *Paleontologia Polonica*, 27, pp. 5–13, Warsaw.

Kielan-Jaworoska, Zofia, and N. Dovchin, 1968/1969, Narrative of the Polish-Mongolian Paleontological Expeditions 1963–1965, in: Kielan-Jaworoska, editor, Results of the Polish-Mongolian Paleontological Expeditions, *Ibid.*, 19, pp. 7–30.

_____, 1986/1969, Narrative of the Polish-Mongolian Paleontological Expeditions, Part I: *Palaeontologia Polonica*, 19, pp. 7–30, Warsaw.

Kim, Haang Mook, 1983, [Cretaceous dinosaurs from Korea]: *Journal of the Geological Society of Korea*, 19 (3), pp. 115–126. [Note: There are two versions of this paper. The first, apparently an offprint, does not give the specific name; the second, apparently the published version, does.]

Kirkland, James Ian, 1993, Polacanthid nodosaurs from the Upper Jurassic and Lower Cretaceous of the east-central Colorado plateau: *Journal of Vertebrate Paleontology*, Abstracts of Papers, Fifty-third Annual Meeting, pp. 44A–45A.

Kirkland, James I., Brooks B. Britt, Scott Madsen, and Donald Burge, 1995, A small thero-

pod from the basal Cedar Mountain Formation (Lower Cretaceous, Barremian) of Eastern Utah: *Journal of Vertebrate Paleontology*, Abstracts of Papers, Fifty-fifth Annual Meeting, p. 39A.

Kirkland, James I., and Kenneth Carpenter, 1994, North America's first pre–Cretaceous ankylosaur (Dinosauria) from the Upper Jurassic Morrison Formation of Western Colorado: *BYU Geology Studies* 1994, 40, pp. 25–42.

Kirkland, James I., Kenneth Carpenter, and Donald Burge, 1991, A nodosaur with a distinct sacral shield of fused armor from the Lower Cretaceous of eastern Utah: *Journal of Vertebrate Paleontology*, Abstracts of Papers, Fifty-first Annual Meeting, 40A.

Kirkland, James I., Robert Gaston, and Donald Burge, 1993, A large dromaeosaur (Theropoda) from the Lower Cretaceous of Eastern Utah: *Hunteria*, 2 (10), pp. 1–16.

Kitching, J. W., 1979, Preliminary report on a clutch of six dinosaurian eggs from the Upper Triassic Elliott Formation, northern Orange Free State: *Palaeontologia Africana*, 22, pp. 41–45.

Kitching, J. W., and Michael R. Raath, 1984, Fossils from the Elliot and Clarens Formations (Karoo Sequence) of the northeastern Cape, Orange Free State and Lesotho, and a suggested biozonation based on tetrapods: *Palaeontologia Africana*, 25, pp. 111–125.

Koken, E., 1887, Die Dinosaurier, Crocodilien und Sauropterygier des norddeutschen Wealden: *Geologische und Paläontologische Abhandlungen*, 3, pp. 309–419.

Konishi, M., and J. D. Pettigrew, 1981, Some observations on the visual system of the oilbird (*Steatornis caripensis*): *National Geographic Research Rept. 1975*, pp. 439–449.

Kordos, Laszló 1983, Fontosabb szórványletek a máfi Gerinces-Gyüjteményében (8. közlemény) [Major finds of scattered fossils in the palaeovertebrate collection of the Hungarian Geological Institute [Communication 8]: *A Magyar Állami Földtani Intézet évi Jelentése Az* 1981, Évröl, pp. 503–511.

Kossmatt, Franz, 1895, Untensuchungen uber die sub-Indesche Kreide-Formation, Beitz: *Paleontologie und Geologische Osterungarns*, 9, pp. 97–203.

Kowallis, B. J., 1986, Fission track dating of bentonites and bentonitic mudstones from the Morrison Formation, Utah and Colorado: *North American Paleontological Convention IV, Boulder, Colorado. Symposium on Stratigraphy and Environments of the Morrison Formation*, p. A26.

Kowallis, B. J., and J. S. Heaton, 1987, Fission-track dating of bentonites and bentonitic mudstones from the Morrison Formation in central Utah: *Geology*, 15, pp. 1148–1142.

Kowallis, B. J., J. S. Heaton, and K. Bringhurst, 1986, Fission-track dates of volcanically derived sedimentary rocks: *Geology*, 14, pp. 19–22.

Krausel, Richard, 1922, Die Nahrung von *Trachodon*: *Paláontologische Zeitschrift* 4, p.80.

Krynine, P. D., 1950, Petrology, stratigraphy and origin of the Triassic sedimentary rocks of Connecticut: *Bulletin, Connecticut Geological and Natural History Survey*, 73, 248 pages.

Kuhn, Oskar, 1939, Saurischia, in: W. Quenstedt, editor, *Fossilium Catalogus I: Animalia*, part 87, Munich, 124 pages.

_____, 1958, *Die Fährten der vorzeitlichen Amphibien und Reptilien*. Bamberg, 64 pages.

_____, 1959, Ein neuer Microsaurier aus dem deutschen Rotliegenden: *Neus Jahrbuch Fuer Geologie und Paläontologie, Montsah*, 9, pp. 242–246.

_____, 1961, *Die Familien der rezenten und fossilen Amphibien und Reptilien*. Bamberg: Meisenbach, 79 pages.

_____, 1963, *Fossilium Catalogus I: Animalia*, part 104, Sauria (Supplementum I), 176 pages.

_____, 1965, *Fossilium Catalogus I: Animalia*, part 109, Saurischia (Supplementum I), 94 pages.

_____, 1968, Contribugan para a Fauna do Kimmeridgian do Mina de Lignito Gulmarota (Leiria, Portugal). Le Crocodilien *Machimosaurus*: Memoria Servi͵cos Geológicos de Portugal, 14 (N.S.), pp. 21–53.

Kurzanov, Seriozha [Sergei] M., 1972, Sexual dimorphism in protoceratopsians, translated from O polovum dimorphizme protoseratopsov: *Palaeontologicheskii Zhurnal*, 1, pp. 104–112.

_____, 1976a, [Structure of the braincase of the carnosaur *Itemirus* gen. nov. and some questions of cranial anatomy of dinosaurs.]: *Ibid.*, 1976, 3, pp. 127–137 (reprinted and translated in *Paleontological Journal*, 10 [3], pp. 361–369, 1976).

_____, 1976b, New Late Mesozoic carnosaur from Nogon-Tsav, Mongolia: *Paleontology and Biostratigraphy of Mongolia*, The Joint Soviet-Mongolian Paleontological Expedition, Transactions, 3, pp. 93–104.

_____, 1981, Some unusual theropods from the Upper Cretaceous in Mongolia. In: *Iskopayemyye pozvonochnyye Mongolii (Fossil Vertebrates of Mongolia), Trudy-Sovmestnaya Sovetsko-Mongolskaya Paleontologicheskaya Ekspeditsiya*, 15, pp. 39–49.

_____, 1983, New data on the pelvic structure of *Avimimus*: *Paleontological Journal*, 4, pp. 110–111. Translated from: Novyye dannyye o stroyenii taza avimimusa: *Palaeontologicheskii Zhurnal*, 4, pp. 115–16.

_____, 1989, The origin and evolution of the dinosaurian infraaorder Carnosauria: *Paleontological Journal*, 4, pp. 1–11 (translated from: O proiskhozhdenii i evolyutsii infraotryada dinozavrov Carnosauria: *Ibid.*, 4, pp. 3–14, 1989).

_____, 1990, Novyy rod protoceratopsid iz pozdnego mela Mongolii: *Paleontologicheskii Zhurnal*, 4, pp. 91–97. (Translation: A new Late Cretaceous protoceratopsid genus from Mongolia: *Paleontological Journal*, 24 [4], pp. 85–91).

_____, 1992, A giant protoceratopsid from the Upper Cretaceous of Mongolia: *Palaontological Polonica*, 3, pp 81–93 (Translated in: *Paleontological Journal*, 26 [3], pp. 103–116).

Kurzanov, Seriozha M., and A. F. Bannikov, 1983, [A new sauropod from the Upper Cretaceous of Mongolia]: *Ibid.*, 1983, 2, pp. 90–96 (reprinted in: *Paleontological Journal*, 2, pp. 91–97).

Kurzanov, Sergei M., and Halszka Osmóska, 1991, *Tochisaurus nemegtensis* gen. et sp. n., a new troodontid (Dinosauria, Theropoda) from Mongolia: *Acta Palaeontologica Polonica*, 36 (1), pp. 69–76.

Kurzanov, Seriozha M., and T. A. Tumanova, 1978, [Endocranium structure of some Mongolian ankylosaurs]: *Palaeontologicheskii*

Zhurnal, 1978, 3, pp. 90–96 (translated in: *Paleontological Journal*, 12 [3], pp. 369–374).

Lambe, Lawrence M. 1902, On Vertebrata of the Mid-Cretaceous of the North West Territory. 2. New genera and species from the Belly River Series (Mid-Cretaceous): *Geological Survey of Canada, Contributions to Canadian Paleontology*, 3, part 2, pp. 23–81.

———, 1903, The lower jaw of *Dryptosaurus incrassatus* (Cope): *Ottawa Naturalist*, 17, pp. 133–139.

———, 1904a, On the squamoso-parietal crest of two species of horned dinosaurs from the Cretaceous of Alberta: *Ibid.*, 18, pp. 81–84.

———, 1904b, On the squamosa-parietal crest of the horned dinosaurs *Centrosaurus apertus* and *Monoclonius canadensis* from the Cretaceous of Alberta: *Transactions of the Royal Society of Canada*, 2 (10), pp. 3–12.

———, 1904c, On *Dryptosaurus incrassatus* (Cope), from the Edmonton Series of the North West Territory: *Geological Survey of Canada, Contributions to Canadian Paleontology*, 3, pp. 1–27.

———, 1910, Note on the parietal crest of *Centrosaurus apertus*, and a proposed new generic name for *Stereocephalus tutus*: *Ottawa Naturalist*, 24, pp. 149–151.

———, 1913, A new genus and species of Ceratopsia from the Belly River Formation of Alberta: *Ibid.*, 27, pp. 109–116.

———, 1914a, On the fore-limb of a carnivorous dinosaur from the Belly River Formation of Alberta, and a new genus of Ceratopsia from the same horizon, with remarks on the integument of some Cretaceous herbivorous dinosaurs: *Ibid.*, 27 (10), pp. 129–135.

———, 1914b, On *Gryposaurus notabilis*, a new genus and species of trachodont dinosaur from the Belly River Formation of Alberta, with a description of the skull of *Chasmosaurus belli*: *Ibid.*, 27 (11), pp. 145–155.

———, 1914c, On a new genus and species of carnivorous dinosaur from the Belly River Formation of Alberta, with a description of the skull of *Stephanosaurus marginatus* from the same horizon: *Ibid.*, 28, pp. 13–20.

———, 1915, On *Eoceratops canadensis*, gen. nov., with remarks on other genera of Cretaceous horned dinosaurs: *Canada Geological Survey, Museum Bulletin*, 12, Geological series, 24, pp. 1–49.

———, 1917a, On *Cheneosaurus tolmanensis*, a new genus and species of trachodont dinosaur from the Edmonton Cretaceous of Alberta: *The Ottawa Naturalist*, 30 (10), pp. 117–123.

———, 1917b, A new genus and species of crestless hadrosaur from the Edmonton Formation of Alberta: *Ibid.*, 31 (7), pp. 65–73.

———, 1917c, The Cretaceous theropodous dinosaur *Gorgosaurus*: *Canada Department of Mines, Geological Survey, Memoir 100*, pp. 1–84.

———, 1918a, On the genus *Trachodon* of Leidy: *Ottawa Naturalist*, 31, pp. 135–139.

———, 1918b, The Cretaceous genus *Stegoceras* typifying a new family referred provisionally to the Stegosauria: *Transactions of the Royal Society of Canada* (series 3), 12, pp. 23–36.

———, 1919, Description of a new genus and species (*Panoplosaurus mirus*) of armored dinosaur from the Belly River Beds of Alberta: *Transactions of the Royal Society of Canada*, 13, pp. 39–50.

Lambert, David, 1983, *A Field Guide to Dinosaurs*. New York: Avon Books, 256 pages.

———, and the Diagram Group, 1990, *Dinosaur Data Book*. Oxford: Facts on File; New York: Avon, 320 pages.

Lambert, Roger, 1942, État actuel de nos connaissances sur la géologie de la république orientale de l'Uruguay: *American Scientific Congress*, Eighth, Washington, D.C., 1940, Proceedings, 4, pp. 573–576.

Lambrecht, Kámán, 1933, *Handbuch der Palaeornithologie*. Berlin: Gebrüder Borntraeger, xix, 1024 pages.

Langston, Wann, Jr., 1960, The vertebrate fauna of the Selma Formation of Alabama, Part VI, The dinosaurs: Fieldiana: *Geological Memoirs*, 3 (6), pp. 313–363.

———, 1965, Pre-Cenozoic vertebrate paleontology in Alberta: its past and future, *in*: *Vertebrate Paleontology* in Alberta, University of Alberta, Edmonton, pp. 9–31.

———, 1974, Non-mammalian Comanchean tetrapods: *Geoscience and Man*, 3, pp. 77–102.

———, 1975, The ceratopsian dinosaurs and associated lower vertebrates from the St. Mary Formation (Maestrichtian) at Scabby Butte, southern Alberta: *Canadian Journal of Earth Sciences*, 12, pp. 1576–1608.

Lankester, E. Ray, 1905, *Extinct Animals*. New York: Holt & Co., 331 pages.

Lapparent, Albert F. de, 1943, Les dinosauriens jurassiques de Damparis (Jura). *Mémoires de la Société Géologique de France* (Nouvelle Série), s.), 21 mem., 47, pp. 1–21.

———, 1946, Présence de Dinosaurien sauropode dans l'Albien du Bray: *Annales de la Société Géologique du Nord*, 66, pp. 236–243.

———, 1947a, Présence d'un dinosaurien sauropode dans l'Albien du Pays de Bray: *Annales de la Société Géologique du Nord*, 66, pp. 236–243.

———, 1947b, Les dinosauriens du crétacé supérieur du Midi de la France: *Mémoires de la Société Géologique de France (Nouvelle Série)*, 56, pp. 1–54.

———, 1951, Découverte de Dinosauriens associés à une faune de Reptiles et de Poissons, dans le Crétacé inférieur de l'Extrême Sud Tunisien: *Comptes Rendus des Séances de l'Académie des Sciences*, 232, p. 1430.

———, 1952, État actuel de nos connaissances sur la stratigraphie, la paléontologie et la tectonique des "Grès de Nubie." *XIXe International Geological Congress*, Algeria, 21, p. 113.

———, 1954, Nouvelle révision des gisements à Dinosauriens de la région de Saint-Chinan (Hérault): *Bulletin, Société Géologique de France*, 6 (4), pp. 409–413.

———, 1957, The Cretaceous dinosaurs of Africa and India: *Journal of the Palaeontological Society of India, Lucknow*, 2, pp. 109–112.

———, 1960a, Les dinosauriens du "Continental Intercalaire" du Sahara Central: *Mémoires de la Société Géologique de France (Nouvelle Série)*, 88A, 56 pages.

———, 1960b, Los dos Dinosaurios de Galve: *Teruel*, 24, pp. 1–21.

———, 1962, Footprints of dinosaurs in the Lower Cretaceous of Vestspitsbergen—Svalbard: Arbok Norsk Polarinstitutt, 1960, pp. 13–21.

Lapparent, Albert F. de, and Emiliano Aguirre, 1956, Présence de Dinosauriens dans le Crétacé supérieur du bassin de Tremp (Province de Lérida, España): *Compte Rendu Sommaire des Séances de la Société Géologique de France*, 1956, pp. 261–262.

Lapparent, Albert F. de, and René Lavocat, 1955, Dinosauriens, *in*: Jean Piveteau, editor, *Traité de Paléontologie*. Paris: Masson et. Cie, pp. 785–962.

Lapparent, Albert F. de, I. Quintero, and E. Triguero, 1957, Descubrimientos de huesos de dinosaurios en el Cretáceo terminal de Cubilla (Provincia de Soria): *Notas y Comunicaciones de Instituto Geológico y Minero de España*, 45, pp. 59–63.

Lapparent, Albert F. de, and Nowgol Sadat, 1975, Une trace de pas de Dinosaure dans le Lias de l'Elbourz, en Iran. Conséquences de cette découverte: *Comptes Rendus des Séances de l'Académie des Sciences, Paris, Série D*, 280, pp. 161–163.

Lapparent, Albert F. de, and Georges Zbyszewski, 1957, Les dinosauriens du Portugal: 2, 63 pages.

Larson, Peter L., *Tyrannosaurus sex*: Forty-Fourth Annual Field Conference—1994 Wyoming Geological Association Guidebook, pp. 147–157.

Larsonneur, C., and A. F. de Lapparent, 1966, Un dinosaurien carnivore, *Halticosaurus*, dans le Rehien d'Airel (Manche): *Bulletin of the Linnean Society, Normandie*, 10 (7), pp. 108–116.

Lavocat, René, 1954, Sur les Dinosauriens du continental intercalaire des Kem-Kemm de la Daoura: *Comptes Rendus 19th International Geological Congress*, 1952, Part 15 (3), pp. 65–68.

———, 1955a, Sur un membre antérieur du Dinosaurien sauropode *Bothriospondylus* Owen, recueilli à Madagascar: *Comptes Rendus des Séances de l'Académie des Sciences*, 240, p. 1795.

———, 1955b, Sur une portion de mandibule de théropode provenant du Crétacé Supérieur de Madagascar: *Bulletin, Muséum National d'Histoire Naturelle*, 2, pp. 256–259.

Lawson, Douglas A., 1976, *Tyrannosaurus* and *Torosaurus*, Maestrichtian dinosaurs from Trans-Pecos, Texas: *Journal of Paleontology*, 50 (1), pp. 158–164.

Le Loeuff, Jean, 1991, Les vertébrés maastrichtiens du Mas d'Azil (Arige, France): étude préliminaire de la collection Pouech: *Revue Paléobiologie*, Genève, 10, pp. 61–67.

———, 1993, European titanosaurids: *Revue de Palóbiologie*, 7, pp. 105–117.

Le Loeuff, Jean, and Éric Buffetaut, 1991, *Tarascosaurus salluvicus* nov. gen., nov. sp., dinosaure théropode du Crétacé Supérieur du sud de la France: *Géobios*, 24 (5), pp. 585–594.

Lee, J. E., 1843, Notice of saurian dermal plates fro the Wealden of the Isle of Wight: *Annals of the Magazine of Natural History*, 2, pp. 5–7.

Lee, Yuong-Nam, 1996, A new nodosaurid ankylosaur (Dinosauria: Ornithischia) from the Paw Paw Formation (Late Albian) of Texas: *Journal of Vertebrate Paleontology*, 16 (2), pp. 232–245.

Lehman, Thomas M., 1981, The Alamo Wash local fauna: a new look at the old Ojo Alamo fauna, *in*: Spencer G. Lucas, Keith Rigby, and B. Kues, editors: *Advances in San Juan Basin Paleontology*. Albuquerque: University of New Mexico Press, pp. 189–221.

———, 1987, Late Maastrichtian paleoenvironments and dinosaur biogeography in the Western Interior of North America: *Palaeo-*

Bibliography

geography, *Palaeoclimatology and Palaeoecology*, 60, pp. 189–217.

———, 1989, *Chasmosaurus mariscalensis*, sp. nov., a new ceratopsian dinosaur from Texas: *Journal of Vertebrate Paleontology*, 9 (2), pp. 137–162.

———, 1990, The ceratopsian subfamily Chasmosaurinae: sexual dimorphism and systematics, *in*: Kenneth Carpenter and Philip J. Currie, editors, *Dinosaur Systematics: Approaches and Perspectives*. Cambridge, New York and Melbourne: Cambridge University Press, pp. 211–229.

———, 1993, New data on the ceratopsian dinosaur *Pentaceratops sternbergii* Osborn from New Mexico: *Journal of Paleontology*, 67 (2), pp. 279–288.

Lehman, Thomas M., and Kenneth Carpenter, 1990, A partial skeleton of the tyrannosaurid dinosaur *Aublysodon* from the Upper Cretaceous of New Mexico: *Journal of Paleontology*, 64 (6), pp. 1026–1032.

Leidy, Joseph, 1856a, Notices of remains of extinct reptiles and fishes, discovered by Dr. F. V. Hayden in the Bad Lands of Judith River, Nebraska Territory: *Proceedings of the Academy of Natural Sciences of Philadelphia*, 8, pp. 72–73.

———, 1856b, Notices of remains of extinct reptiles and fishes, discovered by Dr. F. V. Hayden in the Bad Lands of Judith River, Nebraska Territory: *Ibid.*, 10, pp. 213–218.

———, 1859a, *Hadrosaurus foulkii*, a new saurian from the Cretaceous of New Jersey, related to the *Iguanodon*: *Ibid.*, 10, pp. 213–218.

———, 1860, Extinct vertebrata from the Judith River and Great Lignite Formations of Nebraska: *Ibid.*, 11, pp. 139–154.

———, 1865, Memoir on the extinct reptiles of the Cretaceous Formations of the United States: *Smithsonian Contributions to Knowledge*, 14 (6), pp. 1–135.

———, 1868a, Remarks on a jaw fragment of *Megalosaurus*: *Academy of Natural Sciences of Philadelphia, Proceedings*, 20, pp. 197–200.

———, 1868b, Remarks on *Conosaurus* of Gibbes: *Ibid.*, 20, pp. 200–202.

———, 1870, (Proposal of *Poicilopleuron valens*): *Ibid.*, 22, pp. 3–4.

———, 1872, Remarks on some extinct vertebrates: *Ibid.*, 1872, pp. 38–40.

———, 1873 (Proposal of *Antrodemus valens*), Contributions to the extinct vertebrate fauna of the western territories: *Report of the U.S. Geological Survey of the Territories*, I, pp. 14–358.

Lemmrich, W., 1931, Der Scleralring der Vögel: *Jenaische Zeitschrift Naturwiss*, 65, pp. 514–586.

Lemonick, Michael D., 1996, Big, fast and vicious: *Time*, May 27, p. 45.

Leonardi, Giuseppe, and Sergio C. Duszczak, 1977, Ocorrência de Titanosaurinae (Sauropoda, Atlantosauridae) na Formação Bauru (Cretáceo Superior) em Guararapes, São Paulo: *Actas o Simpósio de Geologia Regional—Societas Brasiliero Geologia*, 1977, September, pp. 396–403.

Leonardi, Giuseppe, and Giorgio Teruzzi, 1993, Prima segnalazione di uno scheletro fossile di dinosauro (Theropoda, Coelurosauria) in Italy (Cretacico di Pietraroia, Benevento): *Paleocronache*, I, pp. 7–14.

Lim Seong-Kyu, Yang Seong Yang and Martin G. Lockley, 1989, Large dinosaur footprint assemblages from the Cretaceous Jindong Formation of Korea, *in*: David D. Gillette and Martin G. Lockley, editors, *Dinosaur Tracks and Traces*. Cambridge, England: Cambridge University Press, pp. 333–336.

Lindholm, R. C., 1979, Geologic history of and stratigraphy of the Triassic-Jurassic Culpeper basin, Virginia: *Geological Society of America Bulletin*, 90 (11), pp. 1995–1997, 111702–111736.

Litwin, R.R., 1986, The palynostratigraphy and age of the Chinle and Moenave formations, southwestern USA [PhD. dissertation]: College Park, Pennsylvania State University, 265 pages.

Lockley, Martin G., 1986, Dinosaur tracksites: *University of Colorado at Denver Geology Department Magazine, Special Issue 1*, 56 pages.

———, 1989, Summary and prospectus, *in*: David D. Gillete and Lockley, editors, *Dinosaur Tracks and Traces*. New York: Cambridge University Press, pp. 41–447.

Lockley, Martin G., B. H. Young and Kenneth Carpenter, 1983, Hadrosaur locomotion and herding behavior: Evidence from the Mesa Verde Formation Grand Mesa Coalfield, Colorado: *Mountain Geology*, 20, pp. 5–13.

Lohrengel, C. F., II, 1969, Palynology of the Kaiparowits Formation, Garfield County, Utah: *Brigham Young University Geology Studies*, 16 (3), pp. 61–180.

Long, Robert A., and Rose Houk, 1988, *Dawn of the Dinosaurs: The Triassic in Petrified Forest*, illustrated by Doug Henderson. Petrified Forest, Arizona: Petrified Forest Museum Association, 96 pages.

Long, Robert A., and Phillip A. Murry, 1995, Late Triassic (Carnian and Norian) tetrapods from the Southwestern United States: *New Mexico Museum of Natural History and Science, Bulletin 4*.

Longman, Heber A., 1925, A giant dinosaur from Durham Downs, Queensland: *Memoirs of the Queensland Museum*, 8, part 3, pp. 183–194.

———, 1927, The giant dinosaur: *Rhoetosaurus brownei*: *Ibid.*, 9, part 1, pp. 1–18.

———, 1929, Palaeontological notes: *Ibid.*, 9, pp. 249–250.

———, 1933, A new dinosaur from the Queensland Cretaceous: *Ibid.*, 10, pp. 131–144.

Lorenz, J. C., and W. Gavin, 1984, Geology of the Two Medicine Formation and the sedimentology of a dinosaur nesting ground, *in*: *Montana Geological Society 1984 Field Conference, Northwestern Montana*, pp. 175–186.

Lucas, Frederic A., 1901a, *Animals of the Past*. New York: McClure, Phillips and Co., xx, 258 pages.

———, 1901b, A new dinosaur, *Stegosaurus marshi*, from the Lower Cretaceous of South Dakota: *Proceedings, United States National Museum*, 23, pp. 591–592.

———, 1902, Paleontological notes: The generic name *Omosaurus*: *Science* (new series), 16, p. 435.

Lucas, Spencer G., 1981, Dinosaur communities of the San Juan Basin: a case for lateral variations in the composition of Late Cretaceous dinosaur communities, *in*: Lucas, Keith Rigby, and B. Kues, editors: *Advances in San Juan Basin Paleontology*. Albuquerque: University of New Mexico Press, pp. 337–393.

Lucas, Spencer G., and Adrian P. Hunt, 1989, *Alamosaurus* and the sauropod hiatus in the Cretaceous of the North American Western Interior, *in*: James O. Farlow, editor, *Paleobiology of the Dinosaurs, Geological Society of America Special Paper 238*, pp. 75–86.

———, 1989, Dolores Formation should be abandoned for Upper Triassic strata in southwestern Colorado, *in*: Jeffrey Eaton, Grace V. Irby and Michael Morales, editors, *Abstracts of the Symposium on Southwestern Geology and Paleontology*, p. 17.

———, 1992a, Triassic stratigraphy and paleontology; Chama basin and adjacent areas, north-central New Mexico, *in*: S. G. Lucas, B. S. Kues, T. E. Williamson, and A. P. Hunt, editors, *San Juan Basin IV*. Socorro: New Mexico Geological Society, pp. 151–172.

———, 1992b, Stratigraphy, paleontology and age of the Fruitland and Kirtland Formations (Upper Cretaceous), San Juan Basin, New Mexico: *New Mexico Geological Society, Guidebook 43*, pp. 217–239.

Lull, Richard Swann, 1904, The dinosaur *Trachodon annectens*: *Smithsonian Miscellaneous Collections*, 45, pp. 317–320.

———, 1905, Restoration of the horned dinosaur *Diceratops*: *American Journal of Science*, Series 4, 20, pp. 420–422.

———, 1906, A new name for the dinosaurian genus *Ceratops*: *Ibid.*, 21, p. 124.

———, 1908, The cranial musculature and origin of the frill in the ceratopsian dinosaurs: *Ibid.*, 25, pp. 387–399.

———, 1910a, Dinosaurian distribution: *Ibid.*, 29 (169), pp. 1–39.

———, 1910b, The armor of *Stegosaurus*: *Ibid.*, 29, pp. 201–210.

———, 1910c, *Stegosaurus ungulatus* Marsh, recently mounted at the Peabody Museum of Yale University: *Ibid.*, 30, pp. 361–377.

———, 1911, The Reptilia of the Arundel Formation: *Maryland Geological Survey*, Lower Cretaceous, pp. 183–188.

———, 1912, The life of the Connecticut Trias: *American Journal of Science*, Series 4, 33, pp. 397–422.

———, 1915a, The mammals and horned dinosaurs of the Lance Formation of Niobrara County, Wyoming: *Ibid.*, 40, pp. 319–348.

———, 1915b, Sauropoda and Stegosauria of the Morrison of North America compared with those of Europe and eastern Africa: *Bulletin of the Geological Society of America*, 26, pp. 323–334.

———, 1919, The sauropod dinosaur *Barosaurus* Marsh: Redescription of the type specimen in the Peabody Museum, Yale University: *Memoirs of the Connecticut Academy of Arts and Sciences*, 6, 42 pages.

———, 1921, The Cretaceous armored dinosaur *Nodosaurus textilis* Marsh: *American Journal of Science*, Series 5, 1, pp. 97–126.

———, 1927, *Organic Evolution*. New York: MacMillan, 729 pages.

———, 1933, A revision of the Ceratopsia or horned dinosaurs: *Memoirs of the Peabody Museum of Natural History*, 3 (3), pp. 1–135.

Lull, Richard Swann, and Nelda E. Wright, 1942, Hadrosaurian dinosaurs of North America: *Geological Society of America, Special Papers*, 40, 242 pages.

Lydekker, Richard, 1879, Indian Pre-Tertiary Vertebrata. Part 3. Fossil Reptilia and Batrachia: *Palaeontologica Indica*, Series 4, 1 (3), 36 pages.

———, 1887, On certain dinosaurian vertebrae from the Cretaceous of India and the

Isle of Wight: *Natural History*, 1, London, pp. 1–303.

_____, 1888a, Catalogue of Fossil Reptilia and *Amphibia*, Part 1., London, 309 pages.

_____, 1888b, Note on a new Wealden iguanodont and other dinosaurs: *Quarterly Journal of the Geological Society of London*, 44, pp. 46–61.

_____, 1889a, On the remains and affinities of five genera of Mesozoic reptiles: *Ibid.*, 45, pp. 41–59.

_____, 1889b, Catalogue of the Fossil Reptilia and Amphibia in the British Museum (Natural History), part 1. London.

_____, 1890a, Contributions to our knowledge of the dinosaurs of the Wealden and the Sauropteryigians of the Purbeck and Oxford Clay: *Quarterly Journal of the Geological Society of London*, 46, pp. 36–53.

_____, 1890b, Catalogue of the Fossil Reptilia and Amphibia in the British Museum, Part 4. London: British Museum of Natural History, 295 pages.

_____, 1891a, On certain ornithosaurian and dinosaurian remains: *Quarterly Journal of the Geological Society of London*, 67, pp. 41–44.

_____, 1893a, On the jaw of a new carnivorous dinosaur from the Oxford Clay of Peterborough: *Ibid.*, 49, pp. 284–287.

_____, 1893b, Contributions to a knowledge of the fossil vertebrates of Argentina. I. The dinosaurs of Patagonia: *Annales del Museo de La Plata, Palaeontologia Argentina* II pp. 1–14.

_____, 1895, On bones of a sauropod dinosaur from Madagascar: *Quarterly Journal of the Geological Society of London*, 44, pp. 46–61.

Lynn, R. T., 1965, A comparative study of display in *Phynosoma* (Iguanidae): *Southwestern Naturalist*, 10, pp. 25–30.

McGinnis, Helen J. 1982, *Carnegie's Dinosaurs: A Comprehensive Guide to Dinosaur Hall at Carnegie Museum of Natural History, Carnegie Institute*. Pittsburgh, Pennsylvania: The Board of Trustees, Carnegie Institute, 199 pages.

McIntosh, John S., 1971, *Dinosaur National Monument*. San Diego: Constellation Phoenix, Inc., 42 pages.

_____, 1990a, Species determination in sauropod dinosaurs with tentative suggestions for their classification, *in*: Carpenter and Philip J. Currie, editors, *Dinosaur Systematics: Approaches and Perspectives*. Cambridge, New York and Melbourne: Cambridge University Press, pp. 53–69.

_____, 1990b, Sauropoda, *in*: David B. Weishampel, Peter Dodson, and Halszka Osmólska, editors, *The Dinosauria*. Berkeley and Los Angeles: University of California Press, pp. 345401.

McIntosh, John S., Walter P. Coombs, and Dale A. Russell, 1992, A new diplodocid sauropod (Dinosauria) from Wyoming, U.S.A.: *Journal of Vertebrate Paleontology*, 12 (2), pp. 1558–167.

McIntosh, John S., and Michael E. Williams, 1988, A new species of sauropod dinosaur, *Haplocanthosaurus delfsi* sp. nov., from the Upper Jurassic Morrison Fm. of Colorado: *Kirtlandia*, 43, pp. 2–26.

McKenzie, D. B., 1972, Tidal sand flat deposits in Lower Cretaceous, Dakota Group near Denver, Colorado: *Mountain Geology*, 9, pp. 269–277.

McKnight, C. L., S. A. Graham, A. R. Carroll, Q. Gan, D. L. Dilcher, Zhao, M., and Liang, Y. H., 1990, Fluvial sedimentology of an Upper Jurassic petrified forest assemblage, Sishu Formation, Junggar Basin, Xinjiang, China: *Palaeogeography, Palaeoclimatology, Palaeoecology*, 79, pp. 1–9.

McLaren, D.J., 1988, Rare events in geology: *Eos*, 69, pp. 24–25.

McNab, Brian K., and Walter Auffenberg, 1976, The effect of large body size on the temperature regulation of the Komodo dragon, *Varanus komodensis*: *Comparative Biochemistry and Physiology*, 55, pp. 345–350.

McWhae, J. R. H., P. E. Playford, A. W. Lindner, B. F. Glenister, and B. E. Balme, 1958, The stratigraphy of Western Australia: *Journal of the Geological Society of Australia*, 4, pp. 1–161.

Mader, Bryn J., and Robert L. Bradley, 1989, A redescription and revised diagnosis of the syntypes of the Mongolian tyrannosaur *Alectrosaurus olseni*: *Journal of Vertebrate Paleontology*, 9 (1), pp. 41–55.

Madsen, James H., Jr., 1974, A new theropod dinosaur from the Upper Jurassic of Utah: *Journal of Paleontology*, 48 (1), pp. 27–31.

_____, 1976a, *Allosaurus fragilis*: a revised Osteology: *Utah Geological and Mineral Survey*, a division of the Utah Department of Natural Resources, 109, xii, 163 pages.

_____, 1976b, A second new theropod dinosaur from the Late Jurassic of East Central Utah: *Utah Geology*, 3 (1), pp. 51–60.

Maleev, Eugene Alexandrovich, 1952a, A new ankylosaur from the Upper Cretaceous of Mongolia: *Reports of the Academy of Sciences of U.S.S.R.*, 87 (2), pp. 273–276.

_____, 1952b, [A new ankylosaur from the Upper Cretaceous of Mongolia.]: *Dokladi Akademii Nauk S.S.S.R.*, 87 (2), pp. 273–276.

_____, 1954, [A new tortoise-like saurian from Mongolia.]: *Priroda* 1954, 3, pp. 106–108.

_____, 1955a, [Carnivorous dinosaurs of Mongolia.]: *Piroda*, June, 112–115.

_____, 1955b, [Gigantic carnivorous dinosaurs of Mongolia]: *Dokladi Akademii Nauk S.S.S.R.*, 104 (4), pp. 634–637.

_____, 1955c, [New carnivorous dinosaurs from the Upper Cretaceous of Mongolia.]: *Ibid.*, 104 (5), pp. 779–782.

_____, 1974, Giant carnosaurs of the family Tyrannosauridae: Trudy Sovmestnaya Sovetsko-Mongolskaya Paleontologicheskaya Ekspeditsiya, 1, pp. 132–191. (In Russian.)

Mantell, Gideon Algernon, 1825, Notice on the *Iguanodon*, a newly discovered fossil reptile, from the sandstone of Tilgate Forest, in Sussex: *Philosophical Transactions, Royal Society*, 115, pp. 179–186.

_____, 1833, *Geology of the South East of England*. London, xix, 415 pages.

_____, 1834, Discovery of the bones of the *Iguanodon* in a quarry of Kentish Rag (a limestone belonging to the Lower Greensand Formation) near Maidstone, Kent: *Edinburgh New Philosophical Journal*, 17, pp. 200–201.

_____, 1838, *Wonders of Geology*. London.

_____, 1841, Memoir on a portion of the lower jaw of the *Iguanodon*, and on the remains of the *Hylaeosaurus* and other saurians, discovered in the strata of the Tilgate Forest, in Sussex: *Philosophical Transactions of the Royal Society of London*, pp. 131–151.

_____, 1848, On the structure of the jaws and teeth of the *Iguanodon*: *Ibid.*, 138, pp. 183–202.

_____, 1850: On the *Pelorosaurus*; an undescribed gigantic terrestrial reptile, whose remains are associated with those of the *Iguanodon* and other saurians in the strata of the Tilgate Forest, in Sussex: *Ibid.*, 140, pp. 379–390.

Marinescu, Florian, 1989, Lentila de bauxita 204 de la Brusturi-Cornet (Jud. Bihor), zacamînt fosilifer cu dinozauri: *Ocrotirea Naturii si a Mediului Înconjurator [Extras]*, 33 (2), pp. 125–132.

Marsh, Othniel Charles, 1870, [Remarks on *Hadrosaurus minor, Mosasaurus crassidens, Leiodon laticaudus, Baptosaurus,* and *Rhinoceros matutinus*], Proceedings of the Academy of Natural Sciences, 1870, 22, pp. 2–3.

_____, 1872, Notice of a new species of *Hadrosaurus*: *American Journal of Science*, Series 3, 3, p. 301.

_____, 1877a, Notice of a new and gigantic dinosaur: *Ibid.*, 14, pp. 87–88.

_____, 1877b, Notice of some new vertebrate fossils: *Ibid.*, 14, pp. 249–256.

_____, 1877c, A new order of extinct Reptilia (Stegosauria) from the Jurassic of the Rocky Mountains: *Ibid.*, 14, pp. 513–514.

_____, 1877d, Notice of new dinosaurian reptiles from the Jurassic formations: *Ibid.*, 14 (53), pp. 514–516.

_____, 1878a, Notice of new dinosaurian reptiles: *Ibid.*, 15, pp. 241–244.

_____, 1878b, Principal characters of American Jurassic dinosaurs, Part II: *Ibid.*, 21, pp. 411–416.

_____, 1879a, Principal characters of American Jurassic dinosaurs: *Ibid.*, 17 (97), pp. 86–92.

_____, 1879b, Notice of new Jurassic reptiles: *Ibid.*, 18, pp. 501–505.

_____, 1880, Principal characters of American Jurassic dinosaurs, part 3: *Ibid.*, 18, p. 504.

_____, 1881a, Principal characters of American Jurassic dinosaurs, part 4. Spinal cord, pelvis and limbs of *Stegosaurus*: *Ibid.*, 21, pp. 167–170.

_____, 1881b, A new order of extinct Jurassic reptiles (Coeluria): *Ibid.*, 21, pp. 339–340.

_____, 1881c, Principal characters of American Jurassic dinosaurs, part 6: *Ibid.*, 21, pp. 417–423.

_____, 1882, Classification of the Dinosauria: *Ibid.*, 4 (23), pp. 81–86.

_____, 1883, Principal characters of American Jurassic dinosaurs, part 6. Restoration of *Brontosaurus*: *Ibid.*, 26, pp. 81–85.

_____, 1884a, Principal characters of American Jurassic dinosaurs, Part II, Diplodocidae, a new family of the Sauropoda: *Ibid.*, 27, pp. 161–168.

_____, 1884b, Principal characters of American Jurassic dinosaurs, the order Theropoda: *Ibid.*, 27 (38), pp. 329–341.

_____, 1885, Names of extinct reptiles: *Ibid.*, 29, p. 169.

_____, 1887a, Notice of new fossil mammals: *Ibid.*, 34 (202), pp. 323–331.

_____, 1887b, Principal characters of American Jurassic dinosaurs, pt. 9. The skull and dermal armor of *Stegosaurus*. *Ibid.*, 34, pp. 413–417.

_____, 1888a, Notice of a new genus of Sauropoda and other new dinosaurs from the Potomac Formation: *Ibid.*, 35, pp. 93–94.

_____, 1888b, A new family of horned Dinosauria, from the Cretaceous: *Ibid.*, 36, pp. 477–478.

_____, 1889*a*, Notice of new American Dinosauria: *Ibid.,* 37, pp. 331–336.

_____, 1889*b*, Notice of gigantic horned Dinosauria from the Cretaceous: *Ibid.,* 38, pp. 173–175.

_____, 1889*c*, Skull of the gigantic Ceratopsidae: *Ibid.,* 38, pp. 501–506.

_____, 1890*a*, Description of new dinosaurian reptiles: *Ibid.,* 39, pp. 81–86.

_____, 1890*b*, Additional characters of the Ceratopsidae, with notice of new Cretaceous dinosaurs: *Ibid.,* 39, pp. 418–426.

_____, 1891*a*, Restoration of *Stegosaurus: Ibid.,* 42, pp. 179–181.

_____, 1891*b*, Notice of new vertebrate fossils: *Ibid.,* 42, pp. 265–269.

_____, 1892*a*, Notes on Triassic Dinosauria: *Ibid.,* 43, pp. 543–546.

_____, 1892*b*, The skull of *Torosaurus: Ibid.,* 43, pp. 81–84.

_____, 1892*c*, Notice of new reptiles from the Laramie Formation: *Ibid.,* 43, pp. 449–453.

_____, 1892*d*, Notes on Mesozoic vertebrate fossils: *Ibid.,* 44, pp. 171–176.

_____, 1892*e*, Restorations of *Claosaurus* and *Ceratosaurus*. Restoration of *Mastodon americanus: Ibid.,* 64, pp. 23–350.

_____, 1894, The typical Ornithopoda of the American Jurassic: *Ibid.,* 48, pp. 86–90.

_____, 1895, Restoration of some European dinosaurs with suggestions as to their place among the Reptilia: *Ibid.,* 3 (50), pp. 407–412.

_____, 1896, The Dinosaurs of North America: *Sixteenth Annual Report of the U. S. Geological Survey,* 1, pp. 133–415.

_____, 1898, New species of Ceratopsia: *American Journal of Science,* Series 4, 6, p. 92.

Martill, D. M., 1993, Fossils of the Santana and Crato Formations, Brazil: *Paleontological Association, Field Guides to Fossils,* 5.

Martill, D. M., A. R. I. Cruickshank, E. Frey, P. G. Small, and M. Clarke, 1996, A new crested maniraptoran dinosaur from the Santana Formation (Lower Cretaceous) of Brazil: *Journal of the Geological Society,* London, 153, pp. 5–8.

Martin, Valérie, Eric Buffetaut, and Varavudh Suteethorn, 1994, A new genus of sauropod dinosaur from the Sao Khua Formation (Late Jurassic or Early Cretaceous) of northeastern Thailand: *Comptes Rendus des Séances de l'Académie des Sciences, Paris,* t. 319, série II, pp. 1085–1092.

Martínez, Rubén, Olga Giménez, Jorge Rodríguez, and Graciela Bochatey, 1986, *Xenotarsosaurus bonapartei* nov. gen. et sp. (Carnosauria, Abelisauridae), un nuevo terópoda de la Formación Bajo Barreal Chubut, Argentina: *IV Congreso Argentino de Paleontoliga y Bioestratigrafia, Actas,* 2, pp. 23–31.

Martinson, G. G., V. G. Nikitin, L. S. Teplova, and I. V. Vasil'yev, 1966, Stratigraphy and correlation of the Cretaceous continental deposits in the Aral region: *Sovetskoe Geologiya 4,* pp. 92–103.

Maryańska, Teresa, 1969, Remains of armoured dinosaurs from the uppermost Cretaceous in Nemegt Basin, Gobi Desert: *Palaeontologica Polonica,* 21, pp. 22–43.

_____, 1970, Uppermost Cretaceous remains of armoured dinosaurs from Nemegt Basin, Gobi Desert. Results of the Polish-Mongolian Palaeontological Expedition II: *Ibid.,* 21, pp. 23–32.

_____, 1971, New data on the skull of *Pinacosaurus grangeri* (Ankylosauria). Results of the Polish-Mongolian Palaeontological Expeditions—Part III: *Ibid.,* 25, pp. 45–53.

_____, 1977, Ankylosauridae (Dinosauria) from Mongolia. Results of the Polish-Mongolian Palaeontological Expeditions—Part VII: *Ibid.,* 37, pp. 85–151.

_____, 1990, Pachycephalosauria, *in:* David B. Weishampel, Peter Dodson, and Halszka Osmólska, editors, *The Dinosauria.* Berkeley and Los Angeles: University of California Press, pp. 564–577.

Maryańska, Teresa, and Halszka Osmólska, 1974, Pachycephalosauria, a new suborder of ornithischian dinosaurs. Results of the Polish-Mongolian Palaeontological Expeditions—Part V: *Ibid.,* 30, pp. 45–102.

_____, 1975, Results of the Polish-Mongolian palaeontological expeditions, Part VI. Protoceratopsidae (Dinosauria) of Asia: *Ibid.,* 33, pp. 133–182.

_____, 1979, Aspects of hadrosaurian cranial anatomy: *Lethaia,* 12, pp. 265–273.

_____, 1981*a,* Cranial anatomy of *Saurolophus angustirostris* with comments on the Asian Hadrosauridae (Dinosauria): *Palaeontologica Polonica,* 42, pp. 5–24.

_____, 1981*b,* First lambeosaurine dinosaur from the Nemegt Formation, Upper Cretaceous, Mongolia: *Acta Palaeontological Polonica,* 26 (3–4), pp. 243–255.

_____, 1984, Phylogenetic classification of ornithischian dinosaurs: *27th International Geological Congress,* 1, pp. 286–287.

_____, 1985, On ornithischian phylogeny: *Acta Palaeontologica Polonica,* 46, pp. 137–150.

Masriera, A., and J. Ullastre, 1988, Nuevos datos sobre las capas maestrichtienses con *Septorella:* su presencia al norte del Montsec (Pirineo catalán): *Acta Geologica Hispanica,* 23, pp. 71–77.

Mateer, Niall J., 1987, A new report of a theropod dinosaur from South Africa: *Palaeontology,* 30, Part 1, pp. 141–145.

Mateer, Niall J., and John S. McIntosh, 1985, A new reconstruction of the skull of *Euhelopus zdanskyi* (Saurischia: Sauropoda): *Bulletin of the Geological Institutions of the University of Uppsala,* (new series), 11, pp. 124–132.

Matheron, M. Philippe, 1869, Notices sur les reptiles fossiles des dépôts flu crétacés du bassin à lignite de Fuveau: *Mémoires de l'Académie Impériale des Sciences, Belles-Lettres et Arts de Marseille,* pp. 1–39.

Mathur, U.B., and S.C. Pant, 1986, Sauropod dinosaur humeri from Lameta Group (Upper Cretaceous-?Palaeocene) of Kheda District, Gujarat: *Journal of the Palaeontological Society of India,* 31, pp. 22–25.

Matley, Charles A., 1921, On the stratigraphy, fossils and geological relationships of the Lameta beds of Jubbulpore: *Records of the Geological Survey of India,* 53, pp. 152.

_____, 1923, Note on an armoured dinosaur from the Lameta beds of Jubbulpore: *Ibid.,* 55, pp. 105–109.

Matthew, William Diller, 1920, Canadian dinosaurs: *Natural History,* 20 (5), pp. 1–162.

Matthew, William Diller, and Barnum Brown, 1922, The family Deinodontidae, with notice of a new genus from the Cretaceous of Alberta: *Bulletin of the American Museum of Natural History,* 46, pp. 367–385.

_____, 1923, Preliminary notices of skeletons and skulls of Deinodontidae from the Cretaceous of Alberta: *American Museum Novitates,* 30, pp. 1–10.

Maxwell, R. A., J. T. Lonsdale, R. T. Hazzard, and J. A. Wilson, 1967, Geology of the Big Bend National Park, Brewster County, Texas: *University of Texas, Bureau of Economic Geology Publication,* 7611, 320 pages.

Maxwell, W. Desmond, 1995, Cranial osteology of *Tenontosaurus* (Dinosauria: Ornithischia): *Journal of Vertebrate Paleontology,* Abstracts of Papers, Fifty-fifth Annual Meeting, p. 44A.

Maxwell, W. Desmond, and John R. Horner, 1994, Neonate dinosaurian remains and dinosaurian eggshell from the Cloverly Fomation, Montana: *Journal of Vertebrate Paleontology,* 14 (1), pp. 143–146.

Maxwell, W. Desmond, and John H. Ostrom, 1995, Taphonomy and paleobiological implications of *Tenontosaurus-Deinonychus* associations: *Journal of Vertebrate Paleontology,* 15 (4), pp. 707–712.

May, John, *The Day of the Dinosaur.* New York: Park South Books, 193 pages.

Mayr, F. X., 1973, Ein neuer *Archaeopteryx* Fund: *Paläontolgische Zeitschrift,* 47, pp. 17–24.

Mehl, Maurice G., 1931, Additions to the vertebrate record of the Dakota Sandstone: *American Journal of Science,* 21, pp. 441–452.

Melville, A. G., 1849, Notes on the vertebral column of the *Iguanodon: Philosophical Transactions of the Royal Society of London,* 139, pp. 285–300.

Mensink, Hans, and Dorothee Mertmann, 1984, Dinosaurier-Fährten (*Gigantosauropus asturiensis* n. g. n. sp.; *Hispanosauropus hauboldi* n. g. n. sp.) im Jura Asturiens bei La Griega und Ribadesella (Spanien): *Neus Jahrbuch für Geologie und Paläontologie, Montsah,* pp. 405–415.

Meyer, Hermann von, 1832, *Paleologica zur Geschichte der Erde und ihrer Geschöpfe,* pages, 560, Frankfurt-am-Main.

_____, 1837, Briefliche Mittelung an Prof. Bronn über *Plateosaurus englehardti: Neus Jahrbuch für Geololgie und Paläontologie,* 1837, pp. 314–316.

_____, 1857, *Stenopelix valdensis* aus der Wealdon-Formation Deutschland's: *Paleontographica,* 7, pp. 25–34.

_____, 1859, *Stenopelix valdensis* aus der Wealden-Formation Deutschland's: *Ibid.,* 7, pp. 25–34.

_____, 1861*a,* Reptilien aus dem Stubensandstein des oberen Keupers: *Ibid.,* 7, pp. 253–346.

_____, 1861*b, Archaeopteryx lithographica* (Vogel-Feder) und *Pterodactylus* von Solnhofen: *Neus Jahrb. Min. Geol. Paläont.,* pp. 678–679, Stuttgart.

Meyer, Larry L., D-day on the Painted Desert: *Arizona Highways,* 26 (7), pp. 2–13.

Mezzalira, Sergio, 1966, Os fosseis do Estado de São Paulo: *Estado São Paulo, Secretaria da Agricultura, Instituto Geográfico e Geológico,* 45, pp. 91–96.

Mikhailov, Konstantin E., 1991, Classification of fossil eggshells of amniotic vertebrates: *Acta Palaeontologica,* 36 (2), pp. 193–238, Warsaw.

Mikhailov, Konstantin E., K. Sabath, and Sergei Kurzanov, 1994, Eggs and nests from the Cretaceous of Mongolia, *in:* Kenneth Carpenter, Karl F. Hirsch, and John R.

Horner, editors, *Dinosaur Eggs and Babies.* Cambridge: Cambridge University Press, pp. 88–115.

Miller, Halsey W., Jr., 1964, Cretaceous dinosaurian remains from southern Arizona: *Journal of Paleontology*, 38, pp. 378–384.

———, 1967, Cretaceous vertebrates from Phoebus Landing, North Carolina: *J. Elisha Mitchell Scientific Society*, 84 (4), pp. 467–471.

Miller, Wade E., John S. McIntosh, Kenneth L. Stadtman, and David D. Gillette, 1992, Rediscription of a new species of *Camarasaurus: Caramasaurus lewisi* (Jensen): *Journal of Vertebrate Paleontology*, Abstracts of Papers, Fifty-second Annual Meeting, pp. 43A–44A.

Milner, Andrew R., and Susan E. Evans, 1991, The Upper Jurassic diapsid *Lisbosaurus estesi*—a maniraptoran theropod: *Palaeontology*, 34 (3), pp. 503–513.

Milner, Andrew R., and David B. Norman, 1984, The biogeography of advanced ornithopod dinosaurs (Archosauria: Ornithischia)—a cladistic-vicariance model, *in*: W.E. Reif, and F. Westphal, editors, *Third Symposium on Mesozoic Terrestrial Ecosystems. Short Papers*. Tübingen GmbH: Attempto Verlag, vii, pp. 145–150.

Milner, Angela C., 1993, Ground rules for early birds: *Nature*, 362, p. 589.

Mohr, B. A. R., 1989, New palynological information on the age and environment of Late Jurassic and Early Cretaceous vertebrate localities of the Iberian Peninsula (eastern Spain and Portugal): *Berliner geowissenschaftliche Abhandlung, Reihe A*, 106, pp. 291–301.

Mohr, B. A. R., and D. Schmidt, 1988, The Oxfordian/Kimmeridgian boundary in the region of Porto de Mós (Central Portugal): stratigraphy, facies and palynology: *Neus Jahrbuch für Geologie und Paläontologie, Abhandlungen*, 176, pp. 245–267.

Molnar, Ralph E., 1974, A distinctive theropod dinosaur from the Upper Cretaceous of Baja California (Mexico): *Journal of Paleontology*, 48 (5), pp. 1009–1017.

———, 1977, Analogies in the evolution of combat and display structures in ornithopods and ungulates: *Evolutionary Theory*, 3, pp. 165–190.

———, 1978, A new theropod dinosaur from the Upper Cretaceous of central Montana: *Journal of Paleontology*, 52 (1), pp. 73–82.

———, 1980a, An ankylosaur (Ornithischia: Reptilia) from the Lower Cretaceous of southern Queensland: *Memoirs of the Queensland Museum*, 20 (1), pp. 77–87.

———, 1980b, Reflections on the Mesozoic of Australia: *Mesozoic Vertebrate Life*, 1, pp. 47–60.

———, 1980c, An albertosaur from the Hell Creek Formation of Montana: *Journal of Paleontology*, 54 (1), pp. 102–108.

———, 1980d, Australian late Mesozoic terrestrial tetrapods: some implications: *Mémoires de la Société Géologique de France, Paris (Nouvelle Série)*, 59, pp. 131–143.

———, 1981, A dinosaur from New Zealand, *in*: M. M. Creswell and P. Vella, editors, *Gondwana Five*. Rotterdam: pp. 91–96.

———, 1982a, A dinosaur from New Zealand *in*: M. M. Cresswell, and P. Vella, editors, *Gondwana Five*, Selected papers and abstracts of papers presented at the Fifth International Gondwana Symposium, pp. 91–96.

———, 1982b, A catalogue of fossil amphibians and reptiles in Queensland: *Memoirs of the Queensland Museum*, 20 (3), pp. 613–633.

———, 1989, Terrestrial tetrapods in Cretaceous Antarctica, *in*: J. A. Crame, editor, *Origins and Evolution of the Antarctic Biota*, Geological Society Special Publication, 47, pp. 131–140.

———, 1990, Problematic Theropoda: "carnosaurs," *in*: David B. Weishampel, Peter Dodson, and Halszka Osmólska, editors, *The Dinosauria*. Berkeley and Los Angeles: University of California Press, pp. 306–317.

———, 1991, The cranial morphology of *Tyrannosaurus rex*: *Paleontographica*, 217, pp. 137–176, Stuttgart.

Molnar, Ralph E., and Kenneth Carpenter, 1990, The Jordan theropod (Maastrichtian. Montana, U.S.A.) referred to the genus *Aublysodon*: Geobios, 22, pp. 445–4544.

Molnar, Ralph E., and James O. Farlow, 1990, Carnosaur Paleobiology, *in*: David B. Weishampel, Peter Dodson, and Halszka Osmólska, editors, *The Dinosauria*. Berkeley and Los Angeles: University of California Press, pp. 210–224.

Molnar, Ralph E., and E. Frey, 1987, The paravertebral elements of the Australian ankylosaur *Minmi* (Reptilia: Ornithischia, Cretaceous): *Neus Jahrbuch Fuer Geologie und Paläontologie Abhandlungen*, 175 (1), pp. 19–37, Stuttgart.

Molnar, Ralph E., and Peter M. Galton, 1986, Hypsilophodontid dinosaurs from Lightning Ridge, New South Wales, Australia: *Géobios*, 19 (2), pp. 231–239.

Molnar, Ralph E., Seriozha M. Kurzanov, and Dong Zhi-Ming [formerly Zhiming], 1990, Carnosauria, *in*: David B. Weishampel, Peter Dodson, and Halszka Osmólska, editors, *The Dinosauria*. Berkeley and Los Angeles: University of California Press, pp. 169–209.

Molnar, Ralph E., and Neville S. Pledge, 1980, A new theropod dinosaur from South Australia: *Alcheringa*, 4, pp. 281–287.

Molnar, Ralph E., Timothy F. Flannery, and Thomas H. V. Rich, 1980, An allosaurid theropod dinosaur from the Early Cretaceous of Victoria, Australia: *Alcheringa*, pp. 141–146.

———, 1985, Aussie *Allosaurus* after all: *Journal of Paleontology*, 59 (6), pp. 1511–1513.

Molnar, Ralph E., and Margaret O'Reagan, Dinosaur extinctions: *Australian Natural History*, 22 (12), pp. 561–570.

Mones, A., 1980, Nuevos elementos de la paleoherpetofauna del Uruguay (Crocodilia y Dinosauria): *Actas I Congress Latinoamerica Paleontológica, Buenos Aires*, 1978, 1, pp. 165–177.

Moodie, Roy L., 1923, *Paleopathology: An Introduction to the Study of Ancient Evidence of Disease.* Urbana, Illinois: University of Chicago Press 567 pages.

———, 1930, The dinosaurs of Wyoming: *Wyoming Geological Survey*, Bulletin No. 22, xiii, 119 pages.

Mook, Charles Craig, 1914, Notes on *Camarasaurus* Cope: *Annals of the New York Academy of Science*, 24, pp. 19–22.

———, 1917, Criteria for the determination of species in the Sauropoda, with description of a new species of *Apatosaurus: Bulletin of the American Museum of Natural History*, 38, pp. 335–360.

Moore, P. R., 1987, Stratigraphy and structure of the Te Hoe-Waiau River area, western Hawkes Bay: *New Zealand Geological Survey, Recollections*, 18, pp. 4–12.

Moraes, L. J., de, 1924, *Serras e Montanhas do Nordeste.* Brazil: *Insp. Obr. Contra Seccas, Publ. S.I.L.*, 58, xi, 224 pages.

Morell, Virginia, 1987, The birth of a heresy: *Discover*, 8 (3), pp. 26–50.

———, 1994, New African dinosaurs give an Old World a novel look: *Science*, 266, 14 October 1994, pp. 219–220.

Morris, William J., 1970, Hadrosaurian dinosaur bills—morphology and function: *Contributions in Science*, 193, pp. 1–14.

———, 1978, *Hypacrosaurus altispinus*? Brown from the Two Medicine Formation, Montana a taxonomically indeterminate specimen: *Journal of Paleontology*, 52 (1), pp. 200–205.

———, 1981, A new species of Hadrosaurian dinosaur from the Upper Cretaceous of Baja California—?*Lambeosaurus laticaudus: Ibid.*, 55 (2), pp. 453–462.

———, 1982, Terrestrial avian fossils from Mesozoic strata, Baja California, 1973: *National Geographic Society Research Reports*, 14, pp. 487–489.

Mouret, C., H. Heggemann, J. Gouadain, and S. Krisadasima, 1993, Geological history of the siliciclastic Mesozoic strata of the Khorat Group, in the Phu Wiang range area, northeastern Thailand, *in*: T. Thanasutipitak, editor, *Biostratigraphy of Mainland Southeast Asia.* Thailand: Chiang Mai University, 1, pp. 23–49.

Moussaye, M. de la, 1885, Sur une dent de *Neosodon*, trouvée dans les sables ferruginaux de Wimille: *Bulletin, Société Géologique de France*, 3 (13), pp. 51–53.

Murry, Phillip A., and Robert A. Long, 1989, Geology and paleontology of the Chinle Formation, Petrified Forest National Park and vicinity, Arizona and a discussion of vertebrate fossils of the southwestern Upper Triassic, *in*: Spencer G. Lucas and Adrian Hunt, editors, *Dawn of the Age of Dinosaurs in the American Southwest*. Albuquerque: New Mexico Museum of Natural History, pp. 29–64.

Mygatt, Peter, 1991, The Mygatt-Moore Quarry, Rabbit Valley, Mesa County, Colorado, *in*: W. R. Averett, editor, *Guidebook for Dinosaur Quarries and Tracksites Tour, Western Colorado and Eastern Utah.* Grand Junction, Colorado: Grand Junction Geological Society, pp. 57–58.

Nagao, Takumi, 1936, *Nipponosaurus sachalinensis*, a new genus and species of trachodont dinosaur from Japanese Saghalien: *Journal of the Faculty Science, University Hokkaido, Geology and Minerology*, 3 (2), pp. 185–220.

Nessov, Lev A., 1995, Dinosaurs of Northern Eurasia: new data about assemblages, ecology and paleobiogeography [translation], 156 pages.

Nessov, L. A., L. F. Kaznyshkina, and G. O. Cherepanov, 1989, Mesozoic dinosaurs (ceratopsians) and crocodilians of Central Asia, *in*: T. N. Bogdanova and L. I. Khozatsky, editors, *Proceedings of the 33rd Session of the All-Union Paleontological Society: Theoretical and Applied Aspects of Modern Paleontology.* U.S.S.R., pp. 144–154.

Newman, Barney H., 1968, The Jurassic dinosaur *Scelidosaurus harrisoni*, Owen: *Paleontology*, 11, Part 1, pp. 40–43.

———, 1970, Stance and gait in the flesh-eating *Tyrannosaurus: Biological Journal of the Linnean Society*, 2, pp. 119–123.

Bibliography

Newton, Edwin Tully, 1892, Note on an iguanodont tooth from the Lower Chalk ("Totternhoe stone"), near Hitchin: *Geological Magazine*, 3 (9), pp. 49–50.

———, 1899, On a Megalosaurid jaw from Rhaetic beds near Bridgend (Glamorganshire): *Quarterly Journal of the Geological Society of London*, 55, pp. 89–96.

Nichols, D.J., D.M. Jarzen, C.J. Orth, and P.Q. Oliver, 1986, Palynological and iridium anomalies at the Cretaceous-Tertiary boundary, South-Central Saskatchewan: *Science*, 231, pp. 714–717.

Nichols, Elizabeth L., and Anthony P. Russell, 1981, A new specimen of *Struthiomimus altus* from Alberta, with comments on the classifactory characters of ornithomimids: *Canadian Journal of Earth Sciences*, 18, pp. 518–526.

———, 1985, Structure and function of the pectoral girdle and forelimb of *Struthiomimus altus* (Theropoda: Ornithomimidae): *Palaeontology*, 28, part 4, pp. 643–677.

Nikitin, V. G., and I. V. Vasil'yev, 1977, Assemblages of plant fossils in the Upper Cretaceous deposits of the Turanian Plate: *Izvestiya Akademic Nauk S.S.S.R. Seriya Geologickestkaya, Alma Ata*, 8, pp. 53–60.

Nopcsa, Baron Franz [also Ferencz, Francis] (von Felsö-Szilvás), 1899, Dinosaurierreste aus Siedenburgen (Schädel von *Limnosaurus transsylvanicus* nov. gen. et spec.): *Denkschriften der Akademie der Wissenschaften*, 68, pp. 555–591.

———, 1901, Synopsis und Abstammung dur Dinosaurier: *Foldtani kozlony (Supplement)*, 3, pp. 247–288.

———, 1902a, Notizen über Cretacische Dinosaurier. Pt. 1. Zur Systematischen Stellung von *Struthiosaurus* (*Crataeomus*): *Sitzungsberichte Berlin Klasse Akademie Wissenschaften, Vienna*, 3, (1), pp. 93–103.

———, 1902b, Dinosaurierreste aus Siebenburgen III (weitere Schädelreste von Mochlodon). Mit einem Anhange: Zur Phylogenie der Ornithopodiden: *Denkschriften der Akademie der Wissenschaften, Vienna*, 72, pp. 149–175.

———, 1903a, Neues über *Compsognathus*: *Neus Jahrbuch für Minerologie, Geologie und Paläontologie*, 16 (16), p. 476.

———, 1903b, *Telmatosaurus*, new name for the dinosaur *Limnosaurus*: *Geological Magazine*, 4 (10), p. 94–95.

———, 1904, Dinosaurierreste aus Siebenburgen III (Weitere Schädelreste von *Mocholodon*): *Denkschriften der Akademie der Wissenschaften, Vienna*, 74, pp. 229–264.

———, 1905a, Notes on British dinosaurs, Part I: *Hypsilophodon*: *Geological Magazine*, 5 (2), pp. 203–208.

———, 1905b, Notes on British dinosaurs, Part II: *Polacanthus*: *Ibid.*, 2 (2), pp. 241–250.

———, 1906, Zur Kenntnis des Genus *Streptospondylus*: *Beitraege zur Paläontologie und Geologie Osterriech-Ungarns und das Orients*, 19, pp. 59–83.

———, 1911a, Notes on British dinosaurs, Part IV: *Stegosaurus priscus* sp. nov.: *Geological Magazine*, (new series), 8, pp. 109–115, 143–153.

———, 1911b, *Omosaurus lennieri*, un nouveau Dinosaurien du Cap de la Heve: *Bulletin Trimestriel de la Société Géologique de Normandie et des Amis du Muséum du Havre* (1910), 30, pp. 23–42.

———, 1912, Notes on British dinosaurs. Part V. *Craterosaurus* (Seeley): *Geological Magazine*, 5 (9), pp. 481–484, London.

———, 1915, Die Dinosaurier der Siebenbürgischen Landesteile Ungarns: *Mitteilungen Des Jahrbuch Ungarischen Geologischen Reichsforschungsanstalt*, 1 (23), pp. 14–15.

———, 1916, *Doryphosaurus* nov. nom. fur *Kentrosaurus* Hennig: *Centralblatt für Mineralogie, Geologie und Paläontologie* pp. 511–512.

———, 1918, *Leipsanosaurus* n. gen. ein neurer Thyreophore aus der Gosau: *Földragzi Közlemenyek, Uj Folyam [New Series]*, 48, pp. 324–328.

———, 1923, On the geological importance of the primitive reptilian fauna in the Uppermost Cretaceous of Hungary: *Quarterly Journal of the Geological Society of London*, 79, pp. 100–116.

———, 1928a, Paleontological notes on reptiles: *Geologica Hungerica*, 1 (1), pp. 1–84.

———, 1928b, Dinosaurriereste aus Siebenburgen, IV. Die Wirbelsäule von *Rhabdodon* und *Orthomerus*: *Ibid.*, 4, pp. 273–302.

———, 1928c, The genera of reptiles: *Palaeobiologica*, 1, pp. 163–188.

———, 1929a, Sexual differences in ornithopodous dinosaurs: *Ibid.*, 2, pp. 187–201.

———, 1929b, Dinosaurierreste aus Siebenburgen: *Geologica Hungarica*, 4, pp. 1–76.

———, 1933, On the histology of the ribs in immature and half-grown trachodont dinosaurs: *Proclamations of the Zoological Society of London*, 1933, pp. 221–223.

———, 1934, The influence of geological and climatological factors on the distribution of non-marine fossil reptiles and Stegocephalia: *Quarterly Journal of the Geological Society of London*, 90, pp. 76–140.

Norell, Mark, Luis Chiappe, and James Clark, 1993, New limb on the avian family tree: *Natural History*, 9, pp. 38–43.

Norell, Mark A., James M. Clark, Luis M. Chiappe, and Demberelyn Dashzeveg, 1995, A nesting dinosaur: *Nature*, 378, pp. 774–776.

Norell, Mark A., James M. Clark, Demberelynin Dashveg, Rinchen Barsbold, Luis M. Chiappe, Amy R. Davidson, Malcolm C. McKenna, Altangerel Perle, and Michael J. Novacek, 1994, A theropod dinosaur embryo and the affinities of the Flaming Cliffs dinosaur eggs: *Science*, 266, pp. 779–882.

Norman, David Bruce, 1977, On the anatomy of the ornithischian dinosaur *Iguanodon*. Ph.D. thesis, University of London.

———, 1980, On the ornithischian dinosaur *Iguanodon bernissartensis* of Bernissart (Belgium): *Institut Royale des Sciences Naturelles de Belgique, Mémoire* 178, 105 pages.

———, 1984a, On the cranial morphology and evolution of ornithopod dinosaurs: *Symposium of the Zoological Society of London* 1984, pp. 521–547.

———, 1984b, A systematic reappraisal of the reptile order Ornithischia, in: W.-E. Reif, and F. Westphal, editors, Third Symposium on Mesozoic Terrestrial Ecosystems. Tübingen, West Germany: Attempto Verlag, Tübingen University Press, pp. 157–162.

———, 1985, *The Illustrated Encyclopedia of Dinosaurs: An Original and Compelling Insight into Life in the Dinosaur Kingdom*. New York: Crescent Books (Crown Publishers, Inc.), 208 pages.

———, 1986, On the anatomy of *Iguanodon atherfieldensis* (Ornithischia: Ornithopoda): *Bulletin, Institut Royale d'Histoire Naturelle de Belgique*, 56, pp. pp. 281–372.

———, 1987, A mass-accumulation of vertebrates from the Lower Cretaceous of Nehden (Sauerland), West Germany: *Proclamations of the Royal Society of London*, B 230, pp. 215–155.

———, 1990, Problematic Theropoda: "coelurosaurs," in: David B. Weishampel, Peter Dodson, and Halszka Osmólska, editors, *The Dinosauria*. Berkeley and Los Angeles: University of California Press, pp. 280–305.

Norman, David B., and David B. Weishampel, 1990, Iguanodontidae and related ornithopods, in: Weishampel, Peter Dodson, and Halszka Osmólska, editors, *The Dinosauria*. Berkeley and Los Angeles: University of California Press, pp. 510–533.

Novas, Fernando E'., 1986, Un probable terópodo (Saurischia) de la Formación Ischigualasto (Triásico Superior), San Juan, Argentina: *IV Congreso Argentino de Paleontología y Biostratigrafía, Mendoza*, 23–27 (2), pp. 1–6.

———, 1992a, El más antiguo passeriformes, Aves, de América del Sur, in: J. L. Sanz and A. D. Buscalioni, editors, *Los Dinosaurios y su entorno biótico*. Spain: Actas del Segundo Curso de Paleontológica en Cuenca, Instituto "Juan de Valdés: *Exmo. Ayuntamiento de Cuenca*, pp. 126–163.

———, 1992b, Phylogenetic relationships of the basal dinosaurs, the Herrerasauridae: *Palaeontology*, 35, Part 1, pp. 51–62.

———, 1993, New information on the systematics and postcranial skeleton of *Herrerasaurus ischigualastensis* (Theropoda: Herrerasauridae) from the Ischigualasto Formation (Upper Triassic) of Argentina: *Journal of Vertebrate Paleontology*, 13 (4), pp. 400–423.

Nowiński, Aleksander, 1971, *Nemegtosaurus mongoliensis* n. gen., n. sp. (Sauropoda) from the Uppermost Cretaceous of Mongolia. Results of the Polish-Mongolian Palaeontological Expeditions—Part III: *Palaeontologia Polonica*, 25, pp. 57–81, Warsaw.

Obata, I, and T. Matsumoto, 1977, Correlation of the Lower Cretaceous formations in Japan: *Science Report of the Department of Geology, Kyushu University*, 12 (3), pp. 165–179.

Officer, C.B., A. Hallam, C.L. Drake, and J.D. Devine, 1987, Late Cretaceous and paroxymal Cretaceous/Tertiary extinctions: *Nature*, 326, pp. 143–149.

Ogier, A., 1975, Etude de nouveaux ossements de *Bothriospondylus* (Sauropode) d'un gisement du Bathonien de Madagascar: *Doctoral Thesis*. (3e.cycle). Université Paris VI.

Okazaki, Yoshihiko, 1990a, Cretaceous chelonian fossils from the Kwanmon Group: *Abstracts, 1990 Annual Meeting, Palaeontological Society of Japan*, p. 78.

———, 1990b, A discovery of a dinosaur fossil from the Kwanmon Group: *Abstracts, 139th Regular Meeting, Palaeontological Society of Japan*, p. 37.

———, 1992, A new genus and species of carnivorous dinosaur from the Lower Cretaceous Kwanmon Group, Northern Kyushu: *Bulletin of the Kitakyushu Museum of Natural History*, 11, pp. 87–90.

Olsen, Paul E., 1980a, A comparison of the vertebrate assemblages from the Newark and Hartford Basins (early Mesozoic, Newark Supergroup) of eastern North America, in:

Louis L. Jacobs, editor, *Aspects of Vertebrate History*, Museum of Northern Arizona, Flagstaff, pp. 35–54.

_____, 1980*b*, Fossil great lakes of the Newark Supergroup, *in*: W. Manspeizer, editor, *Field Studies of New Jersey Geology and Guide to Field Trips*, 52nd Annual Meeting, New York State Geological Association, Newark College of Arts and Sciences, pp. 352–398.

Olsen, Paul E., and Peter M. Galton, 1977, Triassic-Jurassic tetrapod extinctions: are they real?: *Science*, 197, pp. 983–986.

_____, 1984, A review of the reptile and amphibian assemblages from the Stormberg Series of southern Africa, with special emphasis on the footprints and the age of the Stormberg: *Paleont. Afr., Johannesburg*, 25, pp. 87–109.

Olsen, Paul E., N.H. Shubin, and M.H. Anders, 1987, New early Jurassic tetrapod assemblages constrain Triassic-Jurassic tetrapod extinction event: *Science* 237, pp. 1025–1029.

Olsen, Paul E., and Hans-Dieter Sues, 1986, Correlation of continental Late Triassic and Early Jurassic sediments, and patterns of the Triassic-Jurassic tetrapod transition, *in*: Kevin Padian, editor, *The Beginning of the Age of Dinosaurs*. New York: Cambridge University Press, pp. 321–351.

Olshevsky, George, 1978, The Archosauria (excluding the Crocodylia): *Mesozoic Meanderings*, 1, 49 pages.

_____, 1991, A revision of the parainfraclass Archosauria Cope 1869, excluding the advanced Crocodylia: *Ibid.*, iv, 196 pages.

_____, 1992, Ibid [second printing], iv, 268 pages.

Olshevsky, George, and Tracy L. Ford, 1993, The origin and evolution of the stegosaurs: *Gakken Mook*, 4, pp. 65–103 (in Japanese).

_____, 1995, The origin and evolution of the tyrannosaurids, part 1: *Dinosaur Frontline*, 9, pp. 92–119. (In Japanese.)

Orr, R. T., 1970, *Animals in Migration*. London: Macmillan Company, 303 pages.

Osborn, Henry Fairfield, 1898, Additional characters of the great herbivorous dinosaur *Camarasaurus*: *Bulletin of the American Museum of Natural History*, 10, pp. 219–253.

_____, 1899, A skeleton of *Diplodocus*: *Memoirs of the American Museum of Natural History*, 1, pp. 191–214.

_____, 1903*a*, *Ornitholestes hermanni*, a new compsognathoid dinosaur from the Upper Jurassic: *Bulletin of the American Museum of Natural History*, 19, pp. 459–464.

_____, 1903*b*, The Skull of *Creosaurus*: *Ibid.*, 19 (31), p. 697–701.

_____, 1905, *Tyrannosaurus* and other Cretaceous carnivorous dinosaurs: *Ibid.*, 21, p. 261.

_____, 1906, *Tyrannosaurus*, Upper Cretaceous carnivorous dinosaur (second communication): *Ibid.*, 22, pp. 281–296.

_____, 1912*a*, Crania of *Tyrannosaurus* and *Allosaurus*: *American Museum of Natural History Memoirs, new series*, 1, pp. 1–30.

_____, 1912*b*, Integument of the iguanodont dinosaur *Trachodon*: *Ibid.*, 1, pp. 33–54.

_____, 1915, The dinosaurs of the Bone Cabin Quarry, *in*: Matthew, William Diller, 1915, *Dinosaurs*. New York: American Museum of Natural History, pp. 131–152.

_____, 1917, Skeletal adaptations in *Ornitholestes, Struthiomimus* and *Tyrannosaurus*: *Bulletin of the American Museum of Natural History*, 35, pp. 733–771.

_____, 1923*a*, A new genus of Ceratopsia from New Mexico, *Pentaceratops sternbergii*: *American Museum Novitates*, 93, p.3.

_____, 1923*b*, Two Lower Cretaceous dinosaurs of Mongolia: *Ibid.*, 95, 10 pages.

_____, 1924*a*, *Psittacosaurus* and *Protiguanodon*: two Lower Cretaceous iguanodonts from Mongolia: *Ibid.*, 127, pp. 1–16.

_____, 1924*b*, Sauropoda and Theropoda of the Lower Cretaceous of Mongolia: *Ibid.*, 128, pp. 1–7.

_____, 1924*c*, The discovery of an unknown continent: *Natural History*, 24, pp. 133–149.

_____, 1924*d*, Three new Theropoda, *Protoceratops* zone, central Mongolia: *Ibid.*, 144, pp. 1–12.

Osborn, Henry Fairfield, and Charles Craig Mook, 1921, *Camarasaurus, Amphicoelias*, and other sauropods of Cope: *American Museum of Natural History, Memoirs,* New Series, 3, part 3, pp. 247–387.

Osmólska, Halszka, 1976, New light on the skull anatomy and systematic position of *Oviraptor*: *Nature*, 262A (5570), pp. 683–684.

_____, 1980, The Late Cretaceous vertebrate assemblage of the Gobi Desert (Mongolia): *Mémoires de la Société Géologique de France (Nouvelle Série)*, 59 (139), pp. 145–150.

_____, 1981, Coossified tarsometatarsi in theropod dinosaurs and their bearing on the problem of bird origins: *Palaeontologia Polonica*, 42, pp. 79–95.

_____, 1982, *Hulsanpes perlei* n.g. n.sp. (Deinonychosauria, Saurischia, Dinosauria) from the Upper Cretaceous Barun Goyot Formation of Mongolia: *Neus Jahrbuch für Geologie und Paläontologie, Montsah*, 7, pp. 440–448.

_____, 1987, *Borogovia gracilicrus* gen. et sp. n., a new Troodontid dinosaur from the Late Cretaceous of Mongolia: *Palaeontologica Palonica*, 32 (1–2), pp. 133–150.

_____, 1990, Theropoda, *in*: David B. Weishampel, Peter Dodson, and Osmólska, editors, *The Dinosauria*. Berkeley and Los Angeles: University of California Press, pp. 148–150.

Osmólska, Halszka, and Rinchen Barsbold, 1990, Troodontidae, *in*: David B. Weishampel, Peter Dodson and Osmólska, editors, *The Dinosauria*. Berkeley and Los Angeles: University of California Press, pp. 259–268.

Osmólska, Halszka, and Ewa Roniewicz, 1969, Deinocheiridae, a new family of theropod dinosaurs: *Paleontologia Palonica*, 21, pp. 5–19.

Osmólska, Halszka, Ewa Roniewicz, and Rinchen Barsbold, 1972, A new dinosaur, *Gallimimus bullatus* n. gen., n. sp. (Ornithomimidae) from the Upper Cretaceous of Mongolia: *Palaeontologia Polonica*, 27, pp. 103–143.

Ostrom, John H., 1961*a*, A new species of hadrosaurian dinosaur from the Createceous of New Mexico: *Journal of Paleontology*, 35 (3), pp. 575–577.

_____, 1961*b*, Cranial morphology of the hadrosaurian dinosaurs of North America: *Bulletin of the American Museum of Natural History, new series*, 3, pp. 33–186.

_____, 1962*a*, The cranial crests of hadrosaurian dinosaurs: *Postilla, Peabody Museum of Natural History*, 62, 29 pages.

_____, 1962*b*, On the constrictor dorsalis muscles of *Sphenodon*: *Copeia*, 1962, pp. 732–735.

_____, 1963, *Parasaurolophus cyrtocristatus*, a crested hadrosaurian dinosaur from New Mexico: *Chicago Natural History Museum, Fieldiana*, 14 (8), pp. 143–168.

_____, 1963*b*, Ornithopod discovery from the Clovery Formation: *Bulletin, Society of Vertebrate Paleontology*, 67, p. 19.

_____, 1964*a*, The systematic position of *Hadrosaurus (Ceratops) paucidens* Marsh: *Journal of Paleontology*, 38 (1), pp. 130–134.

_____, 1964*b*, A functional analysis of jaw mechanics in the dinosaur *Triceratops*: *Postilla, Peabody Museum of Natural History*, 88, 35 pages.

_____, 1964*c*, A reconsideration of the paleoecology of hadrosaurian dinosaurs: *American Journal of Science*, 262, pp. 975–997.

_____, 1966, Functional morphology and evolution of the ceratopsian dinosaurs: *Evolution*, 20, pp. 290–308.

_____, 1969*a*, A new theropod dinosaur from the Lower Cretaceous of Montana: *Postilla, Peabody Museum of Natural History*, 128, pp. 1–17.

_____, 1969*b*, Osteology of *Deinonychus antirrhopus*, an unusual theropod from the Lower Cretaceous of Montana: *Bulletin of the Peabody Museum of Natural History*, 30, pp. 1–165.

_____, 1969*c*, Terrestrial vertebrates as indicators of Mesozoic climates: *Proceedings of the North American Paleontological Convention*, pp. 347–376.

_____, 1969*d*, Terrible claw: *Discovery*, 5 (1), pp. 1–9.

_____, 1970, Stratigraphy and paleontology of the Cloverly Formation (Lower Cretaceous) of the Bighorn Basin area, Wyoming and Montana: *Bulletin of the Peabody Museum of Natural History, Yale University*, 35, 234 pages.

_____, 1972, Were some dinosaurs gregarious?: *Palaeogeography, Paleoclimatology, Paleoecology*, 11 (4), pp. 287–301.

_____, 1973, On the origin of *Archaeopteryx* and the ancestry of birds: *Colloques Internationaux du Centre National de la Recherche Scientifique*, 218, Problèmes Actuels de Paléontologie (évolution des Vertébrés), pp. 519–532.

_____, 1974, The pectoral girdle and forelimb function of *Deinonychus* (Reptilia: Saurischia): A correction: *Postilla, Peabody Museum of Natural History*, 165, pp. 1–11.

_____, 1975*a*, The origin of birds: *Annual Review, Earth Planetary Sciences*, 3, pp. 55–77.

_____, 1975*b*, On the origin of *Archaeopteryx* and the ancestry of birds: *Centre National de la Recherche Scientifique*, 218, pp. 519–532.

_____, 1976, On a new specimen of the Lower Cretaceous theropod dinosaur *Deinonychus antirrhopus*: *Breviora, Museum of Comparative Zoology*, 439, pp. 1–21.

_____, 1978*a*, *Leptoceratops gracilis* from the "Lance" Formation of Wyoming: *Journal of Paleontology*, 52 (3), pp. 697–704.

_____, 1978*b*, The osteology of *Compsognathus longipes* Wagner: *Zitteliana, Abhandlungen der Bayerischen Staatssammlung für Paläontologie und historische Geologie (München)*, 4, pp. 73–118.

_____, 1978*c*, Startling finds prompt ... a new look at dinosaurs: *National Geographic*, 154, pp. 152–185.

Bibliography

_____, 1980a, The evidence for endothermy in dinosaurs, *in*: Roger D. K. Thomas and Everett C. Olson, editors, *A Cold Look at the Warm Blooded Dinosaurs, American Association for the Advancement of Science, Selected Symposium* 28, pp. 15–60.

_____, 1980b *Coelurus* and *Ornitholestes*: are they the same?, *in*: Louis Jacobs, editor, *Aspects of Vertebrate History*. Flagstaff: Museum of Northern Arizona Press, pp. 245–256.

_____, 1981, *Procompsognathus*—theropod or thecodont?: *Palaeontographica, Absract A,* 175 (4–6), pp. 179–195.

_____, 1985, The meaning of *Archaeopteryx*, *in*: M. K. Hecht, John H. Ostrom, and Peter Wellnhofer, editors: *The Beginnings of Birds*. Freunde des Jura–Museums Eichstätt, pp. 161–176.

_____, 1990, Dromaeosauridae, *in*: David B. Weishampel, Peter Dodson, and Halszka Osmólska, editors, *The Dinosauria*. Berkeley and Los Angeles: University of California Press, pp. 269–279.

Ostrom, John H., and John S. McIntosh, 1966, *Marsh's Dinosaurs: The Collections from Como Bluff*. New Haven: Yale University Press, 338 pages.

Ostrom, John H., and Peter Wellnhofer, 1986, The Munich specimen of *Triceratops* with a revision of the genus: *Zitteliana Abandlungen der Bayerischen Staatssammlung für Paläontologie und historische Geologie:* 14, pp. 111–158.

_____, 1990, *Triceratops*: an example of flawed systematics, *in*: Kenneth Carpenter and Philip J. Currie, editors, *Dinosaur Systematics: Approaches and Perspectives*. Cambridge, New York and Melbourne: Cambridge University Press, pp. 245–254.

Ota, Y., 1953, Geological study on the late Mesozoic System in Northern Kyushu. (1) On the Mesozoic System in Mt. Kasagi district (so-called Wakino district), Kurate-gun, Fukuoka Prefecture: *Bulletin, Fukuoka Gakugei University,* 2, pp. 206–213) (in Japanese).

Owen, Richard, 1841, Report on British fossil reptiles, part II: *Report of the British Association for the Advancement of Science,* 11, pp. 60–204.

_____, 1842a, Second rapport sur le reptiles fossiles de le Grande Bretagne: *L'Institut,* pp. 11–14.

_____, 1842b, Report on British fossil reptiles: *Report of the British Association for the Advancement of Science,* 11, pp. 60–204 (1841), (reprinted in: *Edinburgh New Philosophical Journal,* 33, pp. 65–88).

_____, 1854, *Descriptive Catalogue of the Fossil Organic Remains of Reptilia and Pisces Contained in the Museum of the Royal College of Surgeons of England*. London: Taylor & Francis, 1854, xix, 184 pages.

_____, 1856, Monograph on the fossil Reptilia of the Wealden Formations, Part III, *Megalosaurus bucklandi*: *Palaeontographical Society (Monograph),* 26 pages.

_____, 1858, Monograph on the fossil Reptilia of the Wealden and Purbeck Formations, Part IV, Dinosauria (*Hylaeosaurus*), *Ibid.,* 26 pages.

_____, 1859, Supplement (No. II) to the Monograph on the fossil Reptilia of the Wealden and Purbeck Formations: *Ibid.,* 44 pages.

_____, 1861a, A monograph on a fossil dinosaur (*Scelidosaurus harrisoni* Owen) of the Lower Lias: *Ibid.,* 1, pp. 1–14.

_____, 1861b, Monograph on the fossil Reptilia of the Wealden and Purbeck formations, part 5: Lacertilia (*Nuthetes, etc.*) (Purbeck): *Ibid.,* 12, pp. 31–39.

_____, 1862, Monographs on the British Fossil Reptilia from the Oolitic Formations, Part Second, Containing *Scelidosaurus harrisoni* and *Pliosaurus grandis, Ibid.,* 26 pages.

_____, 1863, The Fossil Reptilia of the Liassic Formations: *Ibid.,* 2, pp. 1–26.

_____, 1864, Monograph on the fossil Reptilia of the Wealden and Purbeck Formations, SupplementIII, Dinosauria (*Iguanodon*) [Wealden], *Ibid.,* 16, pp. 19–21.

_____, 1865, A new Wealden dragon. Order Sauria, family Dinosaurian; genus, *Polacanthus*; species *foxii*: *Illustrated London News,* 47, p. 270.

_____, 1874, Monograph of the fossil Reptilia of the Wealden and Purbeck Formations. Supplement 5. Dinosauria (*Iguanodon*) (Wealden): *Palaeontographical Society, (Monograph)*, pp. 1–18.

_____, 1875, Monographs on the British fossil Reptilia of the Mesozoic Formations, Part II (Genera *Bothriospondylus, Cetiosaurus, Omosaurus*): *Ibid.,* pp. 1–93.

_____, 1876, A monograph on the fossil Reptilia of the Wealden and Purbeck Formations, Supplement No. VII, Crocodilia (*Poikilpleuron*) and Dinosauria? (*Chondrosteosaurus*), [Wealden]: *Ibid.,* pp. 1–7.

_____, 1879, Monograph on the fossil Reptilia of the Wealden and Purbeck formations. Supplement 9. Crocodilia: *Ibid.,* 33, pp. 1–19.

_____, 1884, *A history of British fossil reptiles.* Palaeontographical Society, 4 volumes (a compilation of memoirs of the Palaeontographical Society, with a new prefaces and other revisions, including new taxa).

Padian, Kevin, 1982, Macroevolution and the origin of major adaptations: vertebrate flight as a paradigm for the analysis of patterns: *3rd North American Paleontological Convention Proceedings,* 2, pp. 387–392.

_____, 1986, On the type material of *Coelophysis* Cope (Saurischia: Theropoda) and a new specimen from the Petrified Forest of Arizona (Late Triassic: Chinle Formation), *in*: Kevin Padian, editor, *The Beginning of the Age of Dinosaurs: Faunal Change Across the Triassic-Jurassic Boundary*. New York: Cambridge University Press, pp. 45–60.

_____, 1989a, Did "thecodontians" survive the Triassic?, *in*: Spencer G. Lucas and Adrian P. Hunt, editors, *Dawn of the Age of Dinosaurs in the American Southwest*. Albuquerque: New Mexico Museum of Natural History, pp. 401–414.

_____, 1989b, Presence of the dinosaur *Scelidosaurus* indicates Jurassic age for the Kayenta Formation (Glen Canyon Group, northern Arizona): *Geology* (in press).

_____, 1990, The ornithischian form genus *Revueltosaurus* from the Petrified Forest of Arizona (Late Triassic: Norian; Chinle Formation): *Journal of Vertebrate Paleontology,* 10 (2), pp. 268–269.

Paladino, Frank V., Peter Dodson, Joel K. Hammond, and James R. Spotila, 1989, Temperature-dependent sex determination in dinosaurs? Implications for population dynamics and extinction, *in*: James O. Farlow, editor, *Paleobiology of the Dinosaurs, Boulder, Colorado*: Geological Society of America Special Paper 238, pp. 63–70.

Paris, Jean-Pierre, and Phillipe Taquet, 1973, Découverte d'un fragment de dentaire d'hadrosaurien (Reptile Dinosaurien) dans le Crétacé supérieur des Petites Pyrénées (Haute-Garonne): *Bulletin du Muséum National d'Histoire Naturelle, Paris,* 3rd series, 130, pp. 17–27.

Parkinson, James, 1822, *Outlines of Orcyctology: An Introduction to the Study of Fossil Organic Remains, Especially Those Found in the British Strata*. London: viii, 350 pages.

Parks, William A., 1919, Preliminary description of a new species of trachodont dinosaur of the genus *Kritosaurus. Kritosaurus incurvimanus: Transactions of the Royal Society of Canada,* Series 3, 13 (4), pp. 51–59.

_____, 1920, The osteology of the trachodont dinosaur *Kritosaurus incurvimanus: University of Toronto Studies, Geological Series* 11, pp. 1–74.

_____, 1922, *Parasaurolophus walkeri*, a new genus and species of crested trachodont dinosaur: *Ibid., Geological Series* 13, pp. 1–32.

_____, 1923, *Corythosaurus intermedius*, a new species of trachodont dinosaur: *Ibid., Geological Series* 15, pp. 1–57.

_____, 1924, *Dyoplosaurus acutosquameus*, a new genus and species of armoured dinosaur; and notes on a skeleton of *Prosaurolophus maximus: Ibid., Geological Series* 18, pp. 1–35.

_____, 1925, *Arrhinoceratops brachyops*, a new genus and species of Ceratopsia from the Edmonton Formation of Alberta: *Ibid., Geological Series* 19, pp. 5–15.

_____, 1926a, *Thescelosaurus warreni* a new species of ornithopodous dinosaur from the Edmonton Formation of Alberta: *Ibid., Geological Series* 19, 42 pages.

_____, 1926b, *Struthiomimus brevetertius*—a new species of dinosaur from the Edmonton Formation of Alberta: *Transactions of the Royal Society of Canada,* Series 3, 20, section 4, pp. 65–70.

_____, 1928a, *Albertosaurus arctunguis*, a new species of therapodous dinosaur from the Edmonton Formation of Alberta: *University of Toronto Studies, Geological Series,* 25, pp. 1–42.

_____, 1928b, *Struthiomimus samueli*, a new species of Ornithomimidae from the Belly River Formation of Alberta: *University of Toronto Studies, Geological Series* 26, 24 pages.

_____, 1931, A new genus and two new species of trachodont dinosaurs from the Belly River Formation of Alberta: *Ibid., Geological Series* 31, pp. 1–11.

_____, 1933, New species of dinosaurs and turtles from the Upper Cretaceous formations of Alberta: *Ibid., Geological Series* 34, pp. 3–33.

_____, 1935, New species of trachodont dinosaurs from the Cretaceous formations of Alberta, with notes on other species: *Ibid., Geological Series* 37, pp. 1–45.

Parrish, J. Michael, 1986, Locomotor adaptations in the hindlimb and pelvis of the Thecodontia: *Huntaria,* 1, pp. 1–35.

_____, 1989, Late Triassic tetrapods of the North American Southwest, *in*: Spencer G. Lucas and Adrian P. Hunt, editors, *Dawn of the Age of Dinosaurs in the American Southwest*. Albuquerque: New Mexico Museum of Natural History, pp. 360–374.

Parrish, J. Michael, and Kenneth Carpenter, 1989, A new vertebrate fauna from the

Dockum Formation (Late Triassic) of eastern New Mexico, *in*: Kevin Padian, editor, *The Beginning of the Age of Dinosaurs: Faunal Change Across the Triassic-Jurassic Boundary*. New York: Cambridge University Press, pp. 151–160.

Parrish, Michael J., and F. Peterson, 1988, Wind directions predicted from global circulation models and wind directions determined from eolian sandstones of the western United States—a comparison: *Sedimentary Geology*, 56, pp. 261–282.

Pasch, Anne D., and Kevin C. May, 1995, The significance of a new hadrosaur (Hadrosauridae) from the Matanuska Formation (Cretaceous) in Southcentral Alaska: *Journal of Vertebrate Paleontology*, Abstracts of Papers, Fifty-fifth Annual Meeting, p. 48A.

Paul, Gregory S., 1984*a*, The archosaurs: a phylogenetic study, *in*: W.E. Reif and F. Westphal, editors: *Third Symposium on Mesozoic Terrestrial Ecosystems, Short Papers*, Tübingen: Attempto Verlag, pp. 175–180.

———, 1984*b*, The segnosaurian dinosaurs: relics of the prosauropod-ornithischian transition?: *Journal of Vertebrate Paleontology*, 4 (4), pp. 507–515.

———, 1987, The science and art of restoring the life appearance of dinosaurs and their relatives, *in*: Sylvia J. Czerkas and Everett C. Olson, editors, *Dinosaurs Past and Present*, Volume II. Seattle: Natural History Museum of Los Angeles/University of Washington Press, pp. 4–49.

———, 1988*a*, The brachiosaur giants of the Morrison and Tendaguru with a description of a new subgenus, *Giraffatitan*, and a comparison of the world's largest dinosaurs: *Hunteria*, 3 (3), pp. 1–14.

———, 1988*b*, The small predatory dinosaurs of the mid–Mesozoic: The horned theropods of the Morrison and Great Oolite—*Ornitholestes* and *Proceratosaurus*—and the sickle-claw theropods of the Cloverly, Djadokhta and Judith River—*Deinonychus*, *Velociraptor* and *Saurornitholestes*: *Ibid.*, 2 (4), pp. 1–9.

———, 1988*c*, *Predatory Dinosaurs of the World*. New York: Simon and Schuster, 403 pages.

———, 1989, Giant meteor impacts and great eruptions: dinosaur killers?: *BioScience*, 39 (3), pp. 162–172.

———, 1993, Are *Syntarsus* and the Whitaker Quarry theropod the same genus?, *in*: Spencer G. Lucas and Michael Morales, editors, *The Nonmarine Triassic*, Bulletin 3, New Mexico Museum of Natural History and Science, pp. 397–402.

Peczkis, Jan, 1994, Implications of body-mass estimates for dinosaurs: *Journal of Vertebrate Paleontology*, 14 (4) pp. 520–533.

Peng Guangzhao, 1990, [Jurassic ornithopod *Agilisaurus louderbacki* . . .]: *Vertebra Pal-Asiatica*, 2, pp. 19–27.

———, 1992, Jurassic Ornithopod *Agilisaurus louderbacki* (Ornithopoda: Fabrosauridae) from Zigong, Sichuan, China: *Ibid.*, 30 (1), pp. 39–53.

Penkalski, Paul G., 1993, The morphology of *Avaceratops lammersi*, a primitive ceratopsid from the Campanian of Montana: *Journal of Vertebrate Paleontology*, Abstracts of Papers, Fifty-third Annual Meeting, p. 52A.

Pereda-Suberbiola, Javier, 1992, A revised census of European Late Cretaceous nodosaurids (Ornithischia: Ankylosauria): last

occurrence and possible extinction scenarios: *Terra Nova*, 4, pp. 641–648.

———, 1993, Un nodosaurids (Onrithischia: Ankylosauria) dans le Crétacé supérieur de Lao, Bassin Basco-Cantabrique: *Paleontologia Paleontologia i Evolució*.

———, and Peter M. Galton, 1992, On the taxonomic status of the dinosaur *Struthiosaurus austriacus* Bunzel from the Late Cretaceous of Austria: *CRAS*, 315, pp. 4275–4280.

Pérez-Moreno, Bernardino, José Luis Sanz, Angela D. Buscalloni, José J. Moratalla, Francisco Ortéga and Diego Rasskin-Gutman, 1994, A unique multitoothed ornithomimosaur dinosaur from the Lower Cretaceous of Spain: *Nature*, 370, pp. 363–367.

Perle, Altangerel, 1977, On the first discovery of *Alectrosaurus* from the Late Cretaceous of Mongolia: *Problems of Mongolian Geology*, 3, pp. 104–113.

———, 1979, Segnosauridae—a new family of theropods from the Late Cretaceous of Mongolia: *Joint Soviet-Mongolian Paleontological Expedition, Transactions*, 8, pp. 45–55.

———, 1981*a*, A new segnosaurid from the Upper Cretaceous of Mongolia: *Ibid.*, 15, pp. 28–39.

———, 1981*b*, [On the discovery of the hindfoot of *Therizinosaurus* sp. from the Upper Cretaceous of Mongolia.]: *Problems of Mongolian Geology*, 5, pp. 94–98.

Perle, Altangerel, Theresa Maryańska, and Halszka Osmólska, 1983, *Goyocephale lattimorei* gen. et sp. n., a new flat-headed pachycephalosaur (Ornithischia, Dinosauria) from the Upper Cretaceous of Mongolia: *Acta Palaeontologica Polonica*, 27, pp. 115–127.

Perle, Altangerel, Mark A. Norell, Luis M. Chiappe, and James M. Clark, 1993, Flightless bird from the Cretaceous of Mongolia: *Nature* 362, pp. 623–626.

Peterson, O. A., and Charles Whitney Gilmore, 1902 *Elosaurus parvus*, a new genus and species of Sauropoda: *Annals of the Carnegie Museum*, 1, pp. 490–499.

Pettigrew, J. D., 1986, The evolution of binocular vision, *in*: Pettigrew, K. J. Sanderson and W. R. Lewick, editors, *Visual Neuroscience*. New York: Cambridge University Press, pp. 208–222.

Peyer, Bernard, 1931, Die Triasfauna der Tessinger Kalkalpen, II: *Tanystropheus longobardicus* bass. sp.: *Abhknolungen der Schweizerischen Paläontologischen Gesellschaft, Band L*.

Phillips, John, 1871, *Geology of Oxford and the Valley of the Thames*. Oxford, England: Clarendon Press, xxiv, 523 pages.

Pillmore, C.L., R.H. Tschudy, C.J. Orth, J.S. Gilmore, and J.D. Knight, 1984, Geologic framework of non-marine Cretaceous-Tertiary boundary sites, Raton Basin, New Mexico and Colorado: *Science*, 223, pp. 1180–1183.

Pittman, Jeffrey G., 1984, Geology of the De Queen Formation of Arkansas: *Gulf Coast Association of Geological Societies Transactions*, 34, pp. 201–209.

———, 1986*a*, Correlation of dinosaur trackway horizons in the Cretaceous of the Gulf Coastal Plain of North America, *in*: David D. Gillette, editor, *First International Symposium on Dinosaur Tracks and Traces* (abstracts with program), Albuquerque, p. 23.

———, 1986*b*, A new sauropod dinosaur trackway in the Lower Cretaceous of Arkansas, *Ibid.*, p. 23.

Piveteau, Jean, 1923, L'arrière-crâne d'un dinosaurien carnivore de l'Oxfordien de Dives: *Annales de Paléontologie*, 12, pp. 1–11.

———, 1926, Contribution à l'étude de formations lagunaires du Nord-Quest de Madagascar: *Bulletin du Muséum National d'Histoire Naturelle, Paris*, 4 (26), pp. 33–38.

Platt, Joshua, 1759, An account of the fossil thigh bone of a huge animal, dug up at Stonesfield near Woodstock in Oxfordshire: *Philosophical Transactions of the Royal Society*, 50, pp. 524–27.

Pombeckj, Josef F., 1922, Diskussion zu den Vorträgen R. Kraüsel und F. Versluys: *Paläontologische Zeitschrift*, 4, pp. 87–90.

Potts, R., 1986, Temporal span of bone accumulations of Olduvai Gorge and implications of early hominid foraging behavior: *Paleobiology*, 12, pp. 25–31.

Pouech, J. J., 1881*a*, Sur un nouveau gisement de reptiles fossiles dans l'Ariège: *Bulletin Société Géologique*, France, 3 (9), pp. 15–16.

———, 1881*b*, Sur un ossement fossiles supposé appartenir à un mammifère, trouvé dans les grès crétacés du Mas (Arièges): *Ibid.*, 3 (9), pp. 88–90.

Powell, Jaime Eduardo, 1979, Sobre una asociación de dinosaurios y otras evidencias de vertebrados del Cretácio Superior de la región de la Candelaria, Prov. de Salta, Argentina: *Ameghiniana*, 16 (1–2), pp. 191–204.

———, 1980, Sobre la presencia de una aramadura dérmica en algunos dinosaurios titanosauridos: *Acta Geológica Lilloana*, 15 (2), pp. 41–47.

———, 1986*a*, Revisión de los Titanosauridos de América del Sur. Tésis Doctoral inédita Fac. de Ciencias Exactas y Naturales, Universidad Nacional de Tucumán, Argentina, 472 pages.

———, 1986*b*, The Late Cretaceous fauna of Los Alamitos, Patagonia, Argentina: *Revista del Museo Argentino de Ciencias Naturales (Bernardino Rivadavia) e Instituto Nacional de Investigación de las Ciencias Naturales*, 3(3), pp. 147–153.

———, 1987, Hallazgo de un dinosaurio hadrosaurido (Ornithishia, Ornithopoda) en la Formación Allen (Cretácio Superior) en Salitral Moreno, Provincia de Río Negro, Argentina, *in*: Florencio G. Aceñolaza, chairperson, *Actas del Décimo congreso geológico argentin, Actas del Congreso Geológico Argentino*, 10 (3), pp. 149–152.

———, 1990, *Epachthosaurus sciuttoi* (gen. et sp. nov.) un dinosaurio sauropodo del Cretácico de Patagonia (Provincia de Chubut, Argentina): *V Congreso Argentino de Paleontología y Bioestratigrafía, Tucumán, 1990*, Actas 1, pp. 123–128.

———, 1992, Osteologia de *Saltasaurus loricatus* (Sauropodo-Titanosauridae) del Cretácico Superior del Noroeste argentino, *in*: J. L. Sanz and A. D. Buscalioni, editors, *Los dinosaurios y su entorno biótico*. Spain: Actas del Segundo Curso de Paleontológica en Cuenca, Instituto "Juan de Valdés: Exmo. Ayuntamiento de Cuenca*, pp. 165–230.

Pyatkov, K. K., I. A. Pyanovskaya, A. K. Bukharin and Yu. K. Bykovsky, 1967, Geological structure of the Central Kyzylkum sands: *Tashkent, FAN Press*, pp. 1–177.

Quirk, Susan, and Michael Archer, editors, 1983, *Prehistoric Animals of Australia*. Sydney, Australia: The Australian Museum, 80 pages.

Raath, Michael A., 1969, A new coelurosaurian dinosaur from the Forest Sandstone of Rhodesia: *Arnoldia* (Rhodesia), 4 (28), pp. 1–25.

_____, 1972*a*, First record of dinosaur footprints from Rhodesia: *Ibid.,* 5 (27), 5 pages.

_____, 1972*b*, Fossil vertebrate studies in Rhodesia: a new dinosaur (Reptilia: Saurischia) from near the Trias-Jurassic boundary: *Ibid.,* 5 (30), pp. 1–37.

_____, 1977, The anatomy of the Triassic theropod *Syntarsus rhodesiensis* (Saurischia: Podokesauridae) and a consideration of its biology. Ph.D. dissertation, Rhodes University, Grahamstown, South Africa.

_____, 1980, The theropod dinosaur *Syntarsus* (Saurischia: Podokesauridae) discovered in South Africa: *South African Journal of Science,* 76, pp. 375–376.

_____, 1990, Morphological variation in small theropods and its meaning in systematics: evidence from *Syntarsus rhodesiensis, in:* Kenneth Carpenter and Philip J. Currie, editors, *Dinosaur Systematics: Approaches and Perspectives.* Cambridge, New York and Melbourne: Cambridge University Press, pp. 91–105.

Racey, A., M. A. Love, A. C. Canham, J. G. S. Goodall, S. Polachan, and P. D. Jones (in press), Stratigraphy and reservoir potential of the Mesozoic Khorat Group, North Eastern Thailand: part 1, Stratigraphy and Sedimentary Evolution: *Journal of Petroleum Geology.*

Rage, Jean-Claude, 1978, Une connexion continentale entre Amérique du Nord et Amérique Sud au Crétacé supérieur? L'example des vertébrés continentaux: *Comptes rendus sommaires des séances de la Société géologique de France,* 6, pp. 281–285.

_____, 1981, Les continents péri-atlantiques au Crétacé supérieur: Migrations des faunes continentales et problèmes paléogéographiques: *Cretaceous Research,* 2, pp. 65–84.

_____, 1986, South American/North American terrestrial interchanges in the latest Cretaceous: short comments on Brett-Surman and Paul (1985), with additional data: *Journal of Vertebrate Paleontology,* 6 (4), pp. 382–383.

Rama Rao, L., 1956, Recent contributions to our knowledge of the Cretaceous rocks of South India: *Proceedings of the Indian Academy of Sciences,* 44 (4), section B, pp. 185–245.

Ratkevich, Ronald Paul, 1976, *Dinosaurs of the Southwest.* Albuquerque: University of New Mexico Press, 115 pages.

Rauhut, Oliver W. M., 1995, Zur systematischen Stellung der afrikanischen Theropoden *Carcharodontosaurus* Stromer 1931 und *Bahariasaurus* Stromer 1934: *Berliner geowissenschaftliche Abhandlung,* E16, pp. 357–375.

Rauhut, Oliver W. M., and Christa Werner, 1995, First record of the family Dromaeosauridae (Dinosauria: Theropoda) in the Cretaceous of Gondwana (Wadi Milk Formation, northern Sudan): *Palaontologische Zeitschrift,* 69, 3/4, pp. 475–489, Berlin.

Rawson, P. F., D. Curry, F. C. Dilley, J. M. Hancock, J. M. Kennedy, J. W. Neal, C. J. Wood, and B. C. Worsam, 1978, A correlation of Cretaceous rocks in the British Isles: *Special Reports, Geological Society of Soc. London,* 9, 70 pages.

Rehnelt, K., 1950, Ein Beitrag über Färtenspuren im unteren Gipskeuper von Beyreuth: *Beircht der Naturwissenschaftlichen Gesellschaft, Bayreuth,* pp. 27–36.

Reid, Robin E. H., 1984, The histology of dinosaurian bone, and its possible bearing on dinosaurian physiology: *Symposium of the Zoological Society of London,* 52, pp. 629–663.

Reig, Osvaldo A., 1959, Primeros datos descriptivos sobre nuevos reptiles arcosaurios del Triásico de Ischigualasto (San Juan, Argentina): *Revista Asociación Geológica Argentina,* 13, pp. 257–270.

_____, 1963, La presencia de dinosaurios saurisquios en los "Estratos de Ischigualasto" (Mesotriásico Superior) de la provincias de San Juan y La Rioja (República Argentina): *Ameghiniana,* 3 (1), pp. 3–20.

Resnick, D., and G. Niwayama, 1988, *Diagnosis of Bone and Joint Disorders.* Philadelphia: Saunders, 3227 pages.

Reuben, J. A., Andrew Leitch, and Willem J. Hillenius, 1995, Respiratory turbinates and the metabolic status of some theropod dinosaurs and *Archaeopteryx: Journal of Vertebrate Paleontology,* Abstracts of Papers, Fifty-fifth Annual Meeting, p. 50A.

Riabinin, Anatoly Nikolaenvich, N., 1925, [A mounted skeleton of the gigantic reptile *Trachodon amurense,* nov. sp.]: *Izvest. Geol. Kom.* [*Museum of the Geological Commiittee*], 44 (1), pp. 1–12.

_____, 1930*a*, [*Mandschurosaurus amurensis,* nov. gen., nov. sp., a hadrosaurian dinosur from the Upper Cretaceous of Amur River]: *Mémoir II, Société Paléontologique de Russie.*

_____, 1930*b*, [On the age and fauna of the dinosaur beds on the Amur River]: *Mémoir, Société Mineral Russia 2* (59), pp. 41–51.

_____, 1931, [Two vertebrae a dinosaur from the Lower Cretaceous of the Trans-Caspian steppes.]: [English Summary] Zapiski Vsesoyunznogo Mineralogicheskogo Obschestva, 60 (1), pp. 110–113.

_____, 1939, Fauna pozbonochnykh iz verkhnego mela Yuzhnogo Kazakhstana: Trudy TsNIGRI, 118 (Fauna of Vertebrates of the Upper Cretaceous Period of Southern Kazakhstan: *Trudy of the Central Scientific Research Institute of Prospecting for Nonferrous, Rare and Noble Metals).*

Rich, Patricia V., Thomas H. V. Rich, B. E. Wagstaff, J. McEwen Mason, C. B. Douthitt, R. T. Gregory, and E. A. Felton, 1988, Evidence for low temperatures and biologic diversity in Cretaceous high latitudes of Australia: *Science,* 242, pp. 1403–1406.

Rich, Thomas H., Ralph E. Molnar, and Patricia V. Rich, 1983, Fossil Vertebrates from the Late Jurassic or Early Cretaceous Kirkwood Formation, Algoa Basin, southern Africa: *Transactions of the Geological Society of South Africa,* 86, pp. 281–291.

Rich, Thomas H. V., and Patricia [Vickers-] Rich, 1988, A juvenile dinosaur brain from Australia: *National Geographic Research,* 4 (2), p. 148.

_____, 1989, Polar dinosaurs and biotas of the Early Cretaceous of Southeastern Australia: *Ibid.,* 5 (1) pp. 15–53.

_____, 1994, Neoceratopsians and ornithomimosaurs: dinosaurs of Gondwana origin?: *Research & Exploration,* 10 (1), pp. 129–131.

Ricqlès, Armand J. de, 1974, Evolution of endothermy: histological evidence: *Evolutionary Theory,* 1, pp. 51–80.

_____, 1975, Recherches paléohistologiques sur les os longs des Tétrapodes. VII: Sur la classification, la signification fonctionelle et l'histoire de tissus osseux des Tétrapodes. Première partie: structures: *Annales de Paléontologie* (Vert.), 611, pp. 49–129.

_____, 1976, On bone histology of fossil and living reptiles, with comments on its functional and evolutionary significance, *in*: A. d'A. Bellairs and C. B. Cox, editors, *Morphology and Biology of Reptiles (Linnean Society of London Symposium 3).* London: Academic Press, pp. 123–150.

_____, 1980, Tissue structure of dinosaur bone. Functional significance and possible relation to dinosaur physiology, *in*: Roger D. K. Thomas and Everett C. Olson, editors, *A Cold Look at the Warm Blooded Dinosaurs. Selected Symposium of the American Association for the Advancement of Science.* Boulder, Colorado: Westview Press, pp. 103–139.

Rigby, J. Keith, Jr., K.R. Newman, J. Smit, S. Van der Kaars, Robert E. Sloan and J. Keith Rigby, 1987, Dinosaurs from the Paleocene part of the Hell Creek Formation, McCone County, Montana: *Palaios,* 2, pp. 296–302.

Riggs, Elmer S., 1901, The fore leg and pectoral girdle of *Morosaurus,* with a note on the genus *Camarosaurus: Field Columbian Museum, Geological Series 1,* 10, pp. 275–281.

_____, 1903*a*, *Brachiosaurus altithorax,* the largest known dinosaur: *American Journal of Science,* Series 4, 15, pp. 299–306.

_____, 1903*b*, Structure and relationships of opisthocoelian dinosaurs. Part I, *Apatosaurus* Marsh: *Field Columbian Museum, Geological Series 2,* 4, pp. 165–196.

_____, 1904, Structure and relationships of opisthocoelian dinosaurs. Part II, the Brachiosauridae: *Ibid., Geological Series 2,* 6, pp. 229–247.

Riley, H., and S. Stutchbury, 1836, A description of various fossil remains of three distinct saurian animals discovered in the autumn of 1834, in the Magnesian Conglomerate on Durdham Down, near Bristol: *Proclamations of the Geological Society of London,* 2, pp. 397–399.

Rodbard, S., 1949, On the dorsal sail of *Dimetrodon: Copeia* 1949, p. 224.

Rogers, Raymond Robert, 1990, The taphonomy of a *Centrosaurus* (Reptilia: Ornithischia) bone bed (Campanian), Dinosaur Provincial Park, Alberta, Canada: M.Sc. dissertation, University of Calgary, Alberta, 521 pages.

_____, 1991, Taphonomy of three dinosaur bone beds in the Upper Cretaceous Two Medicine Formation of northwestern Montana: evidence for drought-related mortality: *Palaios,* 5, pp. 394–413.

Rogers, Raymond R., Carl C. Swisher III, Paul C. Sereno, Alfredo M. Monetta, Catherine A. Forster, and Ricardo N. Martinez, 1993, The Ischigualasto tetrapod assemblage (Late Triassic, Argentina) and 40Ar/39Ar dating of dinosaur origins: *Science.* 260, pp. 794–797.

Rohrer, W. L., and R. Konizeski, 1960, On the occurrence of *Edmontosaurus* in the Hell Creek Formation of Montana: *Journal of Paleontology,* 34 (3), pp. 464–466.

Romer, Alfred Sherwood, 1927, The pelvic musculature of ornithischian dinosaurs: *Acta Zoologica,* 8, pp. 225–275.

_____, 1933, *Vertebrate Paleontology.* Chicago: University of Chicago Press, 491 pages.

_____, 1965, *Osteology of the Reptiles*. Chicago: University of Chicago Press, xxii, 772 pages.

_____, 1966, *Vertebrate Paleontology*. Chicago: University of Chicago Press, Third Edition, vii, 468 pages.

_____, 1968, *Notes and Comments on Vertebrate Paleontology*. Chicago: University of Chicago Press, 304 pages.

_____, 1971, The Chañares (Argentina) Triassic fauna. X. Two new but incompletely known long-limbed pseudosuchians: *Breviora*, 378, pp. 1–22.

_____, 1972a, *Lewisuchus admixtus*, gen. et. sp. nov., a further thecodont from the Chanares beds: *Ibid.*, 390, pp. 1–13.

_____, 1972b, The Chañares (Argentina) Triassic reptile fauna. XVI. Thecodont classification: *Ibid.*, 395, pp. 1–24.

Rosenzweig, M. L., 1966, Community structure in sympatric carnivores: *Journal of Mammalogy*, 47, pp. 602–612.

Rothschild, Bruce M., 1982, *Rheumatology: A Primary Care*. New York: Yorke Medical Press, 416 pages.

_____, 1987, Diffuse idiopathic skeletal hyperostosis as reflected in the paleontologic record: dinosaurs and early mammals: *Seminars in Arthritis and Rheumatism*, 27, pp. 119–125.

Rothschild, Bruce M., and David S Berman, 1991, Fusion of caudal vertebrae in Late Jurassic sauropods: *Journal of Vertebrate Paleontology*, 11 (1), pp. 29–36.

Rowe, Timothy, 1989, A new species of theropod dinosaur *Syntarsus* from the Early Jurassic Kayenta Formation of Arizona: *Journal of Vertebrate Paleontology*, 9 (2), pp. 125–136.

Rowe, Timothy, Edwin H. Colbert, and Dale J. Nations, 1981, The occurrence of *Pentaceratops* with a description of its frill: *Advances in San Juan Basin Paleontology*, 48 pages.

Rowe, Timothy, and J.A. Gauthier, 1990, Ceratosauria, in: David B. Weishampel, Peter Dodson, and Halszka Osmólska, editors, *The Dinosauria*. Berkeley and Los Angeles: University of California Press, pp. 151–167.

Roxo, M.G. de Oliviera, 1929, *Pequenos guias da Colecão de Paleontologia do Museu Nacional*: 11. Crocodilianos. Rio de Janeiro: Ed. Mendoca. Machado & Cia., pp. 1–25.

Rozhdestvensky, A. K., 1952, [The discovery of iguanodonts in Mongolian.]: *Dokladi Akademii Nauk S.S.S.R.*, 84, pp. 1243–1246.

_____, 1955, [New data concerning psittacosaurs—Cretaceous ornithopods.]: *Voprosy Geologii Azii*, 2, pp. 783–788.

_____, 1957, [A duck-billed dinosaur, a sauroloph from the Upper Cretaceous of Mongolia.]: *Vertebrata PalAsiatica*, 1 (2), pp. 129–149.

_____, 1960, [The locality of Lower Cretaceous dinosaurs in Khuzbass]: *Paleontologicheskii Zhurnal*, 2, p. 165.

_____, 1961, Polevyy issledovaniya Sovetsko-Kitayskoy paleontologicheskoy ekspeditsii AN SSSR i AN Kitaya v 1960 g (Field investigations of the 1960 Soviet-Chinese paleontological expedition): *Ibid.*, 1, pp. 170–174.

_____, 1965, Growth changes in Asian dinosaurs and some problems of their taxonomy: *Ibid.*, 1965, 3, pp. 95–105.

_____, 1966, Novye iguanodonty iz Tsentral'noi Azii. Filogeneticheskie i taksonomicheskie vzaimootnosheniya poznik Iguanodontidae i rannikh Hadrosauridae: *Ibid.*, 3, pp. 103–116. (New iguanodonts from Central Asia. Phylogenetic and taxonomic relationships of late Iguanodontidae and early Hadrosauridae: *Palaeontological Journal*, 3, pp. 103–116.)

_____, 1968, [Hadrosaurs of Kazakhstan.], in: *Upper Paleozoic and Mesozoic Amphibians and Reptiles of the USSR*. Nauka, Moscow, pp. 97–141.

_____, 1970, Giant claws of enigmatic Mesozoic reptiles: *Paleontological Journal*, 1, pp. 117–125. (Translated from O gigantskikh kogtevykh falangakh zapadochnykh reptiliy mezozoya: *Paleontologicheskii Zhurnal*, 1, pp. 131–141.)

_____, 1977, The study of dinosaurs in Asia: *Journal of the Palaeontological Society of India*, 20, pp. 102–119.

Rozhdestvensky, A. K., and M. Chao, 1960, O rabote Sovetsko-Kitayskoy paleontologicheskoy ekspeditsii AN SSSR i AN Kitaya v 1959 g (Work of the 1960 Soviet-Chinese paleontological expedition): *Paläontologische Zeitschrift*, 1, pp. 142–147.

Russell, Dale A., 1969, A new specimen of *Stenonychosaurus* from the Oldman Formation (Cretaceous) of Alberta: *Canadian Journal of Earth Sciences*, 6, pp. 596–612.

_____, 1970a, A skeletal reconstruction of *Leptoceratops gracilis* from the upper Edmonton Formation (Cretaceous) of Alberta: *Ibid.*, 7 (1), pp. 181–184.

_____, 1970b, Tyrannosaurs from the Late Cretaceous of western Canada: *National Museum of Natural Sciences, Publications in Paleontology*, 1, viii, 34 pages.

_____, 1972, Ostrich dinosaurs from the Late Cretaceous of western Canada: *Canadian Journal of Earth Sciences*, 9 (375), pp. 375–402.

_____, 1976, A census of dinosaur specimens collected in Western Canada: *National Museum of Canada Natural History Papers*, 36, 13 pages.

_____, 1977, *A Vanished World: The Dinosaurs of Western Canada*. Ottawa: National Museums of Canada, 142 pages.

_____, 1984a, Terminal Cretaceous extinctions of large reptiles, in: W.A. Berggren and J.A. Van Couvering, editors, *Catastrophes and Earth History*. Princeton, New Jersey: Cambridge University Press, pp. 383–384.

_____, 1984b, The gradual decline of dinosaurs—fact or fallacy?: *Nature*, 307, pp. 360–361.

_____, 1984c, A check list of the families and genera of North American dinosaurs: *Syllogeus*, 53, National Museums of Canada, National Museum of Natural Science, 35 pages.

_____, 1985, A check-list of the families and genera of North American dinosaurs: *Syllogeus*, 53, pp. 1–35.

_____, 1987, Models and paintings of North American dinosaurs, in: Sylvia J. Czerkas and Everett C. Olson, editors, *Dinosaurs Past and Present*, Volume I. Seattle: Natural History Museum of Los Angeles County in association with University of Washington Press, pp. 114–131.

_____, 1993, The role of Central Asia in dinosaurian biogeography: *Canadian Journal of Earth Sciences*, 30 (10–11), pp. 2002–2012.

_____, 1995a, Isolated dinosaur bones from the middle Cretaceous of the Tafilalt, Morocco: *Journal of Vertebrate Paleontology*, Abstracts of Papers, Fifty-fifth Annual Meeting, p. 50A.

_____, 1995b, An associated skeleton of a large pachycephalosaur from the Hell Creek Formation: *Journal of Vertebrate Paleontology*, Abstracts of Papers, Fifty-fifth Annual Meeting, p. 51A.

Russell, Dale A., and P. Béland, 1976, Running dinosaurs: *Nature*, 264, p. 486.

Russell, Dale A., P. Béland and John S. McIntosh, 1980, Paleoecology of the dinosaurs of Tendaguru (Tanzania): *Mémoires de la Société Géologique de France (Nouvelle Serié)*, 59 (139), pp. 169–176.

Russell, Dale A., and T. Potter Chamney (1967), Notes on the biostratigraphy of dinosaurian and microfossil faunas in the Edmonton Formation (Cretaceous), Alberta: *National Museum of Canada Natural History Papers*, 35, 22 pages.

Russell, Dale A., and Dong Zhi-Ming, 1993a, The affinities of a new theropod from the Alxa Desert, Inner Mongolia, People's Republic of China: *Canadian Journal of Earth Sciences*, 30 (10–11), pp. 2107–2127.

_____, 1993b, A nearly complete skeleton of a new troodontid dinosaur from the Early Cretaceous of the Ordos Basin, Inner Mongolia, People's Republic of China: *Ibid.*, pp. 2163–2173.

Russell, Dale A., and Donald Russell, 1993, Mammal-dinosaur convergence: *National Geographic Research & Exploration*, 9 (1), pp. 70–79.

Russell, Dale A., and R. Sëguin, 1982, Reconstruction of the small Cretaceous theropod *Stenonychosaurus inequalis* and a hypothetical dinosauroid: *Syllogeus*, 37, 43 pages.

Russell, Dale A., and Xi-Jin, 1996, New psittacosaur occurrences in Inner Mongolia: *Canadian Journal of Earth Sciences*, 33, pp. 637–648.

Russell, Dale A., and Zhong Zheng, 1993, A large mamenchisaurid from the Junggar Basin, Xinjiang, People's Republic of China: *Canadian Journal of Earth Sciences*, 30 (10–11), pp. 2082–2095.

Russell, Loris S., 1940a, The sclerotic ring in the Hadrosauridae: Published by the Royal Ontario Museum, Toronto, Canada, ll pages.

_____, 1940b, *Edmontonia rugosidens* (Gilmore), an armored dinosaur from the Belly River series of Alberta: University of Toronto Studies, Geology Series 43, pp. 3–28.

_____, 1946, The crest of the dinosaur *Parasaurolophus*: Royal Ontario Museum, Paleontology Contributions, ll, pp. 1–5.

_____, 1948, The dentary of *Troödon*, a genus of theropod dinosaur: *Journal of Paleontology*, 22, pp. 625–629.

_____, 1949, The relationships of the Alberta Cretaceous dinosaur "*Laosaurus*" *minimus* Gilmore: *Ibid.*, 23 (5), pp. 518–520.

_____, 1964, Cretaceous non-marine faunas of northwestern North America: *Royal Ontario Museum, Life Science Contribution*, 61, pp. 1–24.

_____, 1970, Correlation of the Upper Cretaceous Montana Group between southern Alberta and Montana: *Canadian Journal of Earth Sciences*, 7, pp. 1099–1108.

Rütimeyer, Ludwig, 1856, Reptiles fossiles du Jura: *Archives des Sciences Physiques et Naturelles*, 33, p. 53.

Bibliography

_____, 1857, Ueber die im Keuper zu Liestal bei Basel aufgefundenen Reptilien-Reste von *Belodon*: *Neus Jahrbuch für Minerologie, Geologie und Paläontologie,* 1857, pp. 141–152.

Ryan, Michael J., J. G. Bell, and D. A. Eberth, 1995, Taphonomy of a hadrosaur (Ornithischia: Hadrosauridae) bone bed from the Horseshoe Canyon Formation (early Maastrichtian), Alberta, Canada: *Journal of Vertebrate Paleontology,* Abstracts of Papers, Fifty-fifth Annual Meeting, p. 51A.

Sabath, K., 1991, Upper Cretaceous amniotic eggs from the Gobi Desert: *Paleontologica Polonica,* 36, pp. 151–192.

Sahni, Ashok, 1972, The vertebrate fauna of the Judith River Formation, Montana: *Bulletin of the American Museum of Natural History,* 147, pp. 321–412.

Saito, T., T. Yamanoi, and K. Kaiho, 1986, End-Cretaceous devastation of terrestrial flora in the boreal Far East: *Nature,* 323, pp. 253–255.

Saitta, David, 1995, Crocodilian and avian homologies to the functional morphology of *Allosaurus fragilis: Journal of Vertebrate Paleontology,* Abstracts of Papers, Fifty-fifth Annual Meeting, p. 51A.

Salgado, Leonardo, and José F. Bonaparte, 1991, Un nuevo sauropodo Dicraeosauridae, *Amargasaurus cazui* gen. et sp. nov., de la Formación la Amarga, Neocomiano de la Provincia del Neuquén, Argentina: *Ameghiniana,* 28 (3–4), pp. 333–346, Buenos Aires.

Salgado, Leonardo, and Rodolfo A. Coria, 1993, El género *Aeolosaurus* (Sauropoda, Titanosauridae) en la Formación Allen (Campaniano-Maastrichtiano) de la provincia de Río Negro, Argentina; *Ameghiniana,* 30 (2), pp. 119–128.

Sampson, Scott D., 1995, Two new horned dinosaurs from the upper Cretaceous Two Medicine Formation of Montana; with a phylogenetic analysis of the Centrosaurinae (Ornithischia: Ceratopsidae): *Journal of Vertebrate Paleontology,* 15 (4), pp. 743–760.

Sampson, Scott D., Catherine A. Forster, David W. Krause, Peter Dodson, and Florent Ravoavy, 1996, New dinosaur discoveries from the Late Cretaceous of Madagascar: Implications for Gondwanan Biogeography, *in:* John E. Repetski, editor, *Sixth North American Paleontological Convention,* Abstracts of Papers, p. 336.

Sampson, Scott D., Michael J. Ryan, and Darren H. Tanke (in press), Craniofacial ontogeny in centrosaurine dinosaurs (Ornithischia: Ceratopsidae): taxonomic and behavioral implications: *Zoological Journal of the Linnean Society.*

Santa Luca, Albert P., 1980, The postcranial skeleton of *Heterodontosaurus tucki* (Reptilia, Ornithischia) from the Stormberg of South Africa: *Annals of the South African Musuem,* 79 (7), pp. 159–211.

_____, 1984, Postcranial remains of Fabrosauridae (Reptilia: Ornithischia) from the Stormberg of South Africa: *Paleontologia Africana,* 25, pp. 151–180.

Santa Luca, Albert P., A. W. Crompton, and Alan J. Charig, 1976, A complete skeleton of the Late Triassic ornithischian *Heterodontosaurus tucki: Nature,* 264, pp. 324–328.

Santafé, J. V., M. L. Casanovas, J. L. Sanz and S. Calzada, 1982, Geología y paleontología (Dinosaurios) de las Capas rojas de Morella (Castellón, España). Diputación Provincial de Castellón y Diputación de Barcelona, 169 pages.

Sanz, J. L., 1983, A nodosaurid ankylosaur from the Lower Cretaceous of Salas de los Infantes (Province of Burgos, Spain): *Géobios,* 16, pp. 615–621.

Sanz, J. L., A. D. Buscalioni, M.-L. Casanovas, and J.-L. Santafé 1987, Dinosaurios del Cretácico Inferior de Galve (Teruel, España): *Estudios Geológicos, vol. extr. Galve-Tremp* (1987), pp. 45–64.

Sanz, J. L., M. L. Casanovas, and J. V. Santafé, 1984, Iguanodóntidos (Reptilia, Ornithopoda) del yacimiento del Cretácio inferior de San Cristobal (Galve, Teruel): *Acta Geologica Hispanica,* 19, pp. 171–176.

Sanz, J. L., J.-V. Santafé, and L. Casanovas, 1983, Wealden ornithopod dinosaur *Hypsilophodon* from the Capas Rojas Formation (Lower Aptian, Lower Cretaceous) of Morella, Castellón, Spain: *Journal of Vertebrate Paleontology,* 3 (1), pp. 39–42.

Sarjeant, William A. S., 1974, A history and bibliography of the study of fossil vertebrate footprints in the British Isles: *Palaeogeography, Palaeoclimatology, Palaeoecology,* 18 (4), ii, 160 pages.

Sastry, M. V. A., B. R. J. Rao, and V. D. Mamgain, 1969, Biostratigraphy zonation of the Upper Cretaceous formation of Trichinopoly district, South India: *Memoirs of the Geological Society of India,* 2, pp. 10–17.

Sato, M., 1990, Long-awaited dinosaur fossil—Wakinosatoryu—: *Watashitachino-Shizenshi,* 34, pp. 3–5.

Sattler, Helen Roney, 1983, *The Illustrated Dinosaur Dictionary.* New York: Lothrop, Lee & Shepard Books, 315 pages.

Sauvage, E., 1874, Les dinosauriens et les crocodiliens des terrains Jurassiques de Boulogne-sur-Mer: *Mémoires de la Société Géologique de France,* second series, 10, pp. 2–16.

_____, 1876, Note sur les reptiles fossiles: *Bulletin du Muséum National d'Histoire Naturelle, Paris,* 3 (4), pp. 438–439.

_____, 1882, Recherches sur les Reptiles trouvés dans le Gault de l'est du basin de Paris: *Mémoires de la Société Géologique de France,* second series, 3 (4), pp. 4–41.

_____, 1888, Sur les reptiles trouvés dans le Portlandien supérieur de Boulogne-sur-mer: *Bulletin du Muséum National d'Histoire Naturelle, Paris,* 3 (16), p. 626.

_____, 1896, Les crocodiliens et les dinosauriens des terrains mésozoique du Portugal: *Ibid.,* 3 (24), pp. 46–48.

_____, 1897, Notes sur les reptiles fossiles: *Ibid.,* 3 (25), pp. 864–875.

Schaller, G. B., 1972, *The Serengeti Lion.* Chicago: University of Chicago Press, 480 pages.

Schlaikjer, Erich M., 1935, Contributions to the stratigraphy and paleontology of the Goshen Hole area, Wyoming. II The Torrington member of the Lance Formation and a study of a new *Triceratops: Bulletin of the Museum of Comparative Zoology,* Harvard, 76, pp. 31–68.

Schubert, Charles, 1918, Age of the American Morrison and East African *Tendaguru* Formations: *Bulletin of the Geological Society of America,* 29, pp. 245–280.

Schwartz, Hilde L., 1989, Chemical and petrographic analysis of bone and sediment from the *Coelophysis* quarry, Ghost Ranch, New Mexico, *in:* Jeffrey G. Eaton, Grace V. Irby and Michael Morales, editors, *Abstracts of the Symposium on Southwestern Geology and Paleontology,* 1989, p. 23.

Schwartz, Hilde L., and David D. Gillette, 1994, Geology and taphonomy of the *Coelophysis* Quarry, Upper Triassic Chinle Formation, Ghost Ranch, New Mexico: *Journal of Paleontology,* 68 (5), pp. 1118–1130.

Sciutto, J. C., 1981, Geología del Codo del Río Senguerr, Chubut, Argentina: *VIII Congreso Argentina, Actas 3,* pp. 203–219.

Seeley, Harry Govier, 1869, *Index to the fossil remains of* Aves, Ornithosauria *and* Reptilia *from the Secondary Strata*: Cambridge University Press, Cambridge, 143 pages.

_____, 1870, On *Ornithopsis,* a gigantic animal of the Pterodactyl kind from the Wealden: *Annals of the Magazine of Natural History,* 4 (5), 283 pages.

_____, 1871, On *Acantopholis platypus* (Seeley), a pachypod from the Cambridge Upper Greensand: *Ibid.,* 4 (8), pp. 305–318.

_____, 1874, On the base of a large lacertian cranium from the Potton Sands, presumably dinosaurian: *Quarterly Journal of the Geological Society of London,* 30, pp. 690–692.

_____, 1875a, On the femur of *Cryptosaurus eumerus* Seeley, a dinosaur from the Oxford Clay of Great Gransden: *Ibid.,* 31, pp. 149–151.

_____, 1875b, On the maxillary bone of a new dinosaur (*Priodontognathus phillipsi*) contained in the Woodwardian Museum of the University of Cambridge: *Ibid.,* 31, pp. 439–443.

_____, 1876, On *Macrurosaurus semnus* (Seeley), a long-tailed animal with procoelous vertebrae from the Cambridge Upper Greensand, preserved in the Woodwardian Museum of the University of Cambridge: *Quarterly Journal of the Geological Society of London,* 32, pp. 440–444.

_____, 1879, On the Dinosauria of the Cambridge Greensand: *Ibid.,* 35, pp. 591–636.

_____, 1881, On the reptile fauna of the Gosau Formation preserved in the Geological Museum of the University of Vienna: *Ibid.,* 37, pp. 619–707.

_____, 1882, On *Thecospondylus horneri,* a new dinosaur from the Hastings sand, indicated by a sacrum and neural canal of the sacral region: *Ibid.,* 38, pp. 457–460.

_____, 1883, On the Dinosauria of the Maestricht beds: *Ibid.,* 39, pp. 426–253.

_____, 1887a, On *Patricosaurus merocratus,* Seeley, a lizard from the Cambridge Greensand, preserved in the Woodwardian Museum of the University of Cambridge: *Ibid.,* pp. 216–220.

_____, 1887b, On *Aristosuchus pussilus* (Owen), being further notes on the fossils described by Sir R. Owen as *Poikilopleuron pussilus,* Owen: *Ibid.,* 43, pp. 221–228.

_____, 1888, On *Thecospondylus daviesi* (Seeley), with some remarks on the classification of the Dinosauria: *Geological Society of London, Quarterly Journal,* 44, pp. 79–87.

_____, 1889, Note on the pelvis of *Ornithopsis: Ibid.,* 45, pp. 391–397.

_____, 1891a, On *Agrosaurus macgillivrayi,* a saurischian reptile from the N.E. coast of Australia: *Queensland Journal of Geology, Society of London,* 47, pp. 164–165.

_____, 1891b, On the pubis of *Polacanthus foxi: Ibid.,* 48, pp. 81–85.

_____, 1893, On *Omosaurus phillipsii: Annual Report, Yorkshire Philosophical Society,* 1892, pp. 52–57.

———, 1894a, On *Euskelosaurus brownii* (Huxley): *Annals of the Magazine of Natural History*, 14 (6), pp. 411–419.

———, 1894b, On *Hortalotarsus skirtopodous*, a new saurischian fossil from Barkly East, Cape Colony: *Ibid.*, 6 (16), pp. 411–419.

———, 1895, On *Thecodontosaurus* and *Palaeosaurus*: *Ibid.*, 6, (15), pp. 144–163.

———, 1898, On large terrestrial saurians from the Rhaetic beds of Wedmore Hill, described as *Avalonia sanfordi* and *Picrodon herveyi*: *Geological Magazine*, 4 (5), p. 106.

———, 1901 (*in* von Huene, F.), *Centralblatt fr Mineralogie, Geologie und Palontologie 1901*, p.718.

Sereno, Paul C., 1984, The phylogeny of the Ornithischia: a reappraisal, *in*: W. Reif and F. Westphal, editors, *Third Symposium on Mesozoic Terrestrial Ecosystems, Short Papers*, Attempto Verlag, Tübingen University Press, pp. 219–226.

———, 1986, Phylogeny of the bird-hipped dinosaurs (order Ornithischia): *National Geographic Research*, 2, pp. 234–256.

———, 1990a, Clades and grades in dinosaur systematics, *in*: Kenneth Carpenter and Philip J. Currie, editors, *Dinosaur Systematics: Approaches and Perspectives*. Cambridge and New York: Cambridge University Press, xiii, 318 pages.

———, 1990b, Psittacosauridae, *in*: David B. Weishampel, Peter Dodson, and Halszka Osmlska, editors, *The Dinosauria*. Berkeley and Los Angeles: University of California Press, pp. 579–592.

———, 1991a, *Lesothosaurus*, "Fabrosaurids," and the early evolution of Ornithischia: *Journal of Vertebrate Paleontology*, 11 (2), pp. 168–197.

———, 1991b, Basal archosaurs: phylogenetic relationships and functional implications: *Society of Vertebrate Paleontology Memoir 2*, pp. 1–53.

———, 1993, The pectoral girdle and forelimb of the basal theropod *Herrerasaurus ischigualastensis*: *Journal of Vertebrate Paleontology*, 13 (4), pp. 425–450.

Sereno, Paul C., Didier B. Dutheil, M. Iarochene, Hans C. E. Larsson, Gabrielle H. Lyon, Paul M. Magwene, Christian A. Sidor, David J. Varracchio, and Jeffrey A. Wilson, 1996, Predatory dinosaurs from the Sahara and Late Cretaceous faunal differentiation: *Science*, 272, pp. 996–990.

Sereno, Paul C., Catherine A. Forster, Raymond R. Rogers, and Alfredo M. Monetta, 1993: *Nature*, 361, p.64.

Sereno, Paul C., and Fernando E. Novas, 1992, The complete skull and skeleton of an early dinosaur: *Science*, 258, November 13, pp. 1137–1140.

———, 1993, The skull and neck of the basal theropod *Herrerasaurus ischigualastensis*: *Journal of Vertebrate Paleontology*, 13 (4), pp. 451–476.

Sereno, Paul C., Fernando Novas, A. Arcucci, and C. Yu, 1988, New evidence on dinosaur and mammal origins from the Ischigualasto Formation (Upper Triassic, Argentina): *Journal of Vertebrate Paleontology*, 8, 3A.

Sereno, Paul C., Chao Shichin [Zhao Xijin], and Rao Chenggang, 1988, *Psittacosaurus meileyingensis* (Ornithischia: Ceratopsia), a new psittacosaur from the Lower Cretaceous of Northeastern China: *Journal of Vertebrate Paleontology*, 8 (4), pp. 366–377.

Sereno, Paul C., and Chao Shichin [Zhao Xijin], 1988, *Psittacosaurus xinjiangensis* (Ornithischia: Ceratopsia), a new psittacosaur from the Lower Cretaceous of Northwestern China: *Journal of Vertebrate Paleontology*, 8 (4), pp. 353–356.

Sereno, Paul C., and Paul Upchurch, 1995, *Regnosaurus northamptoni*, a stegosaurian dinosaur from the Lower Cretaceous of southern England: *Geological Magazine*, 132 (2), pp. 213–222.

Sereno, Paul C., and Rupert Wild, 1992, *Procompsognathus*: theropod, "thecodont" or both?": *Journal of Vertebrate Paleontology*, 12 (4), pp. 435–458.

Sereno, Paul C., Jeffrey A. Wilson, Hans C. E. Larsson, Didier B. Dutheil, and Hans-Dieter Sues, 1994, Early Cretaceous dinosaurs from the Sahara: *Science*, 266, 14 October 1994, pp. 267–271.

Sereno, Paul C., and Dong Zhi-Ming [formerly Zhiming], 1992, The skull of the basal stegosaur *Huayangosaurus taibaii* and a cladistic diagnosis of Stegosauria: *Journal of Vertebrate Paleontology*, 12 (3), pp. 318–343.

Seymour, R. S., 1976, Dinosaurs, endothermy and blood pressure: *Nature*, 262, pp. 207–208.

Shepherd, Jeffrey D., Peter M. Galton, and James A. Jensen, 1977, Additional specimens of the hypsilophodontid dinosaur *Dryosaurus altus* from the Upper Jurassic of western North America: *Brigham Young University Geology Studies*, 24 (2), pp. 11–15.

Shipman, Pat, 1975, Implications of drought for vertebrate fossil assemblages: *Nature*, 257, pp. 667–668.

Shuler, Ellis W., 1917, Dinosaur tracks in the Glen Rose limestone near Glen Rose: *American Journal of Science*, 44, pp. 294–298.

———, 1935, Dinosaur track mounted in the bandstand at Glen Rose, Texas: *Field and Laboratory*, 4, pp. 9–13.

Simmons, David J., 1965, The non-therapsid reptiles of the Lufeng Basin, Yunnan, China: *Fieldiana*, 15 (1), 93 pages.

Simpson, George Gaylord, 1942, The beginnings of vertebrate paleontology in North America: *Proceedings of the American Pilosophical Society*, 86 (1), pp. 130–188.

Sinclair, A. R. E., and M. Norton-Griffiths, 1979, *Serengeti: Dynamics of an Ecosystem*. Chicago: University of Chicago Press, 389 pages.

Sloan, Robert E., 1970, Cretaceous and Paleocene terrestrial communities of western North America: *Proceedings, North American Paleontological Convention*, I, pp. 427–453.

Sloan, Robert E., J. Keith Rigby, Leigh M. Van Valen, and Diane L. Gabriel, 1986, Gradual extinction of dinosaurs and the simultaneous radiation of ungulate mammals in the Hell Creek Formation of McCone County, Montana: *Science*, 232, pp. 629–633.

Smith, C. A., 1985, Inner ear, *in*: A. S. King and J. McLelland, editors, *Form and Function in Birds*. London: Academic Press, pp. 273–310.

Smith, David Kenneth, 1990, Osteology of *Oviraptor philoceratops*, a possible herbivorous theropod from the Upper Cretaceous of Mongolia: *Journal of Vertebrate Paleontology*, Abstracts of Papers, Fiftieth Annual Meeting, p. 42A.

———, 1993, The type specimen of *Oviraptor philoceratops*, a theropod dinosaur from the Upper Cretaceous of Mongolia: *Neus Jahrbuch für Geologie und Paläontologie Abhandlungen*, 186 (3), pp. 365–388.

Smith, David, and Peter M. Galton, 1990, Osteology of *Archaeornithomimus asiaticus* (Upper Cretaceous, Iren Dabasu Formation, People's Republic of China): *Journal of Vertebrate Paleontology*, 10 (2), pp. 255–265.

Smith, N., 1820, Fossil bones found in red sandstone: *American Journal of Science*, 2, pp. 146–147.

Sochava, A. V., 1969, Dinosaur eggs from the Upper Cretaceous of the Gobi Desert: *Paleontology Journal*, 4, pp. 517–527 [English edition].

———, 1972, The skeleton of an embryo in a dinosaur egg: *Ibid.*, 4, pp. 527–531 [English edition].

Sohn, I.G., 1979, Nonmarine ostracodes in the Lakota Formation (Lower Cretaceous) from South Dakota and Wyoming: *U.S. Geological Survey Professional Paper 1069*, pp. 1–22.

Spotila, James R., Michael P. O'Connor, Peter Dodson, and Frank V. Paladino, 1991, Hot and cold running dinosaurs: Body size, metabolism and migration: *Modern Geology*, 16, pp. 203–227.

Steel, Rodney, 1969, Ornithischia, *in*: Oskar Kuhn, editor, *Handbuch der Palaeoherpetologie*, part 15. Stuttgart: Gustav Fischer Verlag, 87 pages.

———, 1970, Saurischia, *in*: Oskar Kuhn, editor, *Ibid.*, Part 14, 87 pages.

———, 1973, Crocodylia, *in*: *Das Tierreich*, 16 (16). Stuttgart: Gustav Fischer Verlag, 116 pages.

Sternberg, Charles H., 1929, Fossil monsters I have hunted: *Popular Science*, 115 (6), pp. 56–57, 139–140.

Sternberg, Charles M., 1926a, Notes on the Edmonton Formation of Alberta: *Canadian Field Naturalist*, 50, pp. 102–104.

———, 1926b, Dinosaur tracks from the Edmonton Formation of Alberta: *Canadian Geological Survey, Bulletin*, 44, pp. 85–87.

———, 1928, A new armored dinosaur from the Edmonton Formation of Alberta: *Transactions of the Royal Society of Canada*, 22, pp. 93–106.

———, 1929, A new species of horned dinosaur from the Upper Cretaceous of Alberta: *Geological Survey of Canada*, Bulletin, 54, pp. 34–37.

———, 1932a, Two new theropod dinosaurs from the Belly River Formation of Alberta: *Canadian Field Naturalist*, 56 (5), pp. 99–105.

———, 1932b, Dinosaur tracks from the Peace River, British Columbia, *in*: *Annual report 1930, National Museum of Canada*, pp. 59–85.

———, 1933, A new *Ornithomimus* with complete abdominal cuirass: *Canadian Field Naturalist*, 47 (5), pp. 79–83.

———, 1935, Hooded hadrosaurs of the Belly River series of the Upper Cretaceous: a comparison, with descriptions of new species: *Canada, Department of Mines, Natural Museum Bulletin*, 77, Geological Series 52, pp. 1–37.

———, 1936, The systematic position of *Trachodon*: *Journal of Paleontology*, 10 (7), pp. 652–655.

———, 1937, (abstract): *Geological Society of America Proceedings for 1936*, p. 375.

———, 1938, *Monoclonius*, from southeastern Alberta, compared with *Centrosaurus*: *Journal of Paleontology*, 12, pp. 284–286.

Bibliography

_____, 1939, Were there proboscis-bearing dinosaurs? Discussion of cranial protuberances in the Hadrosauridae: *Annals and Magazine of Natural History*, Series 11, 3, pp. 556–560.

_____, 1940a, Ceratopsidae from Alberta: *Journal of Paleontology*, 14, pp. 468–480.

_____, 1940b, *Thescelosaurus edmontonensis* n. sp., and the classification of the Hypsilophodontidae: *Ibid.*, 14, pp. 481–494.

_____, 1945, Pachycephalosauridae proposed for the dome-headed dinosaurs, *Stegoceras lambei*, n. sp., described: *Ibid.*, 19, pp. 534–538.

_____, 1946, Canadian dinosaurs: *Bulletin of the National Museum of Canada*, 103, pp. 1–20.

_____, 1949, The Edmonton fauna and description of a new *Triceratops* from the Upper Edmonton member; phylogeny of the Ceratopsidae: *Ibid.*, 113, pp. 35–46.

_____, 1950, *Pachyrhinosaurus canadensis*, representing a new family of the Ceratopsia, from southern Alberta: *Annual Report of the National Museum for the Fiscal Year 1948-1949*, Bulletin, 118, pp. 109–120.

_____, 1951a, Complete skeleton of *Leptoceratops gracilis* Brown from the Upper Edmonton member on Red Deer River, Alberta: *Ibid.*, 1949-1950, Bulletin, 123, pp. 225–255.

_____, 1951b, The lizard *Chamops* from the Wapiti Formation of northern Alberta: *Polyodontosaurus grandis* not a lizard: *Bulletin of the National Museum of Canada*, 123, pp. 256–258.

_____, 1956, A juvenile hadrosaur from the Oldman Formation of southern Alberta: *Ibid.*, 136, pp. 120–122.

_____, 1963, Early discoveries of dinosaurs: *Natural History Papers, National Museum of Canada*, 21, pp. 1–4.

_____, 1965, New restoration of hadrosaurian dinosaur: *Natural History Papers, National Museum of Canada*, 30, 5 pages.

_____, 1970, Comments on dinosaurian preservation in the Cretaceous of Alberta and Wyoming: *National Museums of Canada, Publications in Paleontology*, 4, 9 pages.

Sternberg, R. M., 1940, A toothless bird from the Cretaceous of Alberta: *Journal of Paleontology*, 14 (1), pp. 81–85.

Sternfield, R., 1911, Zur Nomenklatur der Gattung *Gigantosaurus*: *Sitzungberichte der Gesellschaft Naturforschender Freunde zu Berlin*, 398 pages.

Stevens, G. R., 1985, Lands in collision: *New Zealand Geologic Survey*, Wellington.

Stigler, Robert, 1911, Die Kraft unserer Inspirationsmuskulatur: *Pflger's Archiv fr Physiologie*, 139, pp. 234–254.

Stipanicic, P.N., F. Rodrigo, O.L. Baulies, and C.G. Martínez, 1968, Las formaciones presenonianas en el denominado Macizo Nordpatagónico y regiones adyacentes: *Revista Asociación Geológica Argentina, Contributions*, Paper 50, 23 pages.

Stokes, William Lee, 1952, Lower Cretaceous in Colorado Plateau: *American Association of Petroleum Geologists Bulletin 36*, pp. 1766–1776.

_____, 1985, *The Cleveland-Lloyd Dinosaur Quarry—Window to the Past*. Washington, D. C.: U.S. Government Printing Office, 27 pages.

Stovall, J. Willis, 1938, The Morrison of Oklahoma and its dinosaurs: *Journal of Geology*, 46, pp. 583–600.

Stovall, J. Willis, and Wann Langston, Jr., 1950, *Acrocanthosaurus atokensis*, a new genus and species of Lower Cretaceous Theropoda from Oklahoma: *The American Midland Naturalist*, 43 (3), pp. 696–728.

Stoyanow, A. A., 1949, Lower Cretaceous stratigraphy in southeastern Arizona: *Geological Society of America, Memoirs*, 38, pp. 1–26.

Stromer, Ernst, 1915, Ergebnisseder Forschungsreisen Prof.E. Stromers in den Wsten gyptens. II. Wirbeltierreste der Baharije-Stufe (unterstes Cenoman). III. Das Original des Theropoden *Spinosaurus aegyptiacus*n.g.n.sp.: *Abhandlungen der Bayerischen Akademie der Wissenschaften*, 18 (3), pp. 1–32.

_____, 1931, Wirbeltierreste de Baharijestufe (unterstes Cenoman). 10. Ein Skelettrest von *Carcharodontosaurus* nov. gen: *Ibid.*, 9, pp. 1–23.

_____, 1932, Wirbeltier-Reste der Baharije-Stufe, 11: Sauropoda: *Ibid.*, 10, pp. 1–20.

_____, 1934, Ergebnisse der Forschungsreisen Prof. E. Stromer in den Wsten gyptens. II: Wirbeltier-Reste der Baharije-Stufe unterestes (Cenoman). 13. Dinosauria: *Ibid.*, 22, pp. 1–79.

Struckmann, C., 1880, Vorlufige Nachricht ber das Vorkommen grosser vogelhnlicher Tierfhrten (Ornithoidichnites) im Hastingssandstein von Bad Rehburg bei Hannover: *Neus Jahrbuch Fuer Minerologie, Geologie und Palontologie*, 1, pp. 125–128, Stuttgart.

Sues, Hans-Dieter, 1977, Dentaries of small theropods from the Judith River Formation (Campanian) of Alberta, Canada: *Canadian Journal of Earth Sciences*, 14, pp. 587–592.

_____, 1978, A new small theropod dinosaur from the Judith River (Campanian) of Alberta: *Zoological Journal of the Linnean Society*, 62, pp. 381–400.

_____, 1980a, A pachycephalosaurid dinosaur from the Upper Cretaceous of Madagascar and its paleobiogeographical implications: *Journal of Paleontology*, 54 (5), pp. 954–962.

_____, 1980b, Anatomy and relationships of a new hypsilophodontid dinosaur from the Lower Cretaceous of North America: *Palaeontographica*, 169 (1–3), pp. 51–72.

_____, 1983, Functional morphology of the dome in pachycephalosaurid dinosaurs: *Neus Jahrbuch für Geologie und Paläontologie, Montsah*, 8, pp. 459–472.

_____, 1990, *Staurikosaurus* and Herrerasauridae, *in*: David B. Weishampel, Peter Dodson, and Halszka Osmlska, editors, *The Dinosauria*. Berkeley and Los Angeles: University of California Press, pp. 143–150.

Sues, Hans-Dieter, and Peter M. Galton, 1982, The systematic position of *Stenopelix valdensis* (Reptilia: Ornithischia) from the Wealden of North-western Germany: *Palaeontographica*, Abstract A, 178 (4–6), pp. 183–190.

_____, 1987, Anatomy and classification of the North American Pachycephalosauria (Dinosauria: Ornithischia): *Palaeontographica*, Abstract A, 198, pp. 1–40.

Sues, Hans-Dieter, and David B. Norman, 1990, Hypsilophodontidae, *Tenontosaurus*, Dryosauridae, *in*: David B. Weishampel, Peter Dodson, and Halszka Osmlska, editors, *The Dinosauria*. Berkeley and Los Angeles: University of California Press, pp. 498–509.

Sues, Hans-Dieter, and Philippe Taquet, 1979, A pachycephalosaurid dinosaur from Madagascar and a Laurasia-Gondwanaland connection in the Cretaceous: *Nature*, 279, pp. 633–635.

Sun, A. L., and K. H. Cui, 1986, A brief introduction to the Lower Lufeng saurischian fauna (Lower Jurassic: Lufeng, Yunnan, People's Republic of China, *in*: Kevin Padian, editor, *The Beginning of the Age of Dinosaurs: Faunal Change Across the Triassic-Jurassic Boundary*. New York: Cambridge University Press, pp. 275–278.

Suslov, Yu. V., and Shilin, P. V., 1982, A hadrosaur from the northeastern Aral region: *Palaeontologicheskii Zhurnal*, 1, pp. 131–135.

Swinton, W. E., 1936, The dinosaurs of the Isle of Wight: *Proclamations of the Geological Association of London*, 47, pp. 204–220.

_____, 1962, *Dinosaurs*. London: Trustees of the British Museum (Natural History), xiii, 44 pages.

_____, 1970, *The Dinosaurs*. London: George Allen & Unwin, 331 pages.

Tanimoto, Masahiro, 1988, [Sauropods of Sichuan Basin (I)]: *Kaseki no Tomo [Publication of the Tokai Fossil Society]*, 32, pp. 9–16, Nagoya.

Tanke, Darren H., and Philip J. Currie, 1995, Intraspecific behavior inferred from toothmark trauma on skulls and teeth of large carnosaurs (Dinosauria): *Journal of Vertebrate Paleontology*, Abstracts of Papers, Fifty-fifth Annual Meeting, p. 55A.

Tapia, Augusto., 1918. Resúmenes de otras communicaciones: *Physis*, 4, pp. 369–370.

Taquet, Philippe, 1976a, Géologie et Paléontologie du Gisement de Gadoufaoua (Aptien du Niger): Cahiers de Paléontologie. Paris: *Editions du Centre National de la Recherche Scientifique*, 191 pages.

_____, 1976b, Remarques sur l'évolution des iguanodontids et l'origine des hadrosaurids: *Colloque International C.N.R.S.*, Paris, 218, pp. 503–511.

_____, 1984, Une curieuse spécialisation du crâne de certains dinosauriens carnivores du Crétacé le meseau long et étroit des Spinosaurids: *Comptes Rendus des Séances de l'Académie des Sciences*, 299 II (5), pp. 217–222.

_____, 1985, Two new Jurassic specimens of coelurosaurs (Dinosauria), *in*: M.K. Hecht, John H. Ostrom, G. Viohl, and Peter Wellnhoffer, editors, *The Beginning of Birds. Proceedings of the International Archaeopteryx Conference, Eichstatt, 1984*. Willibaldsburg: Jura-Museums Eichstatt, pp. 229–232.

_____, 1991, The status of *Tsintaosaurus spinorhinus* Young, 1958 (Dinosauria), *in*: Zofia Kielan-Jaworoska, Natascha Heintz, and Hans Arne Nakrem, editors: *Fifth Symposium on Mesozoic Ecosystems and Biota, Extended Abstracts*, Oslo, 364, pp. 63–64.

Taquet, Philippe, and Samuel Paul Welles, 1977, Redescription du crâne de dinosaure theropode de Dives (Normandie): *Annales de Paléontologie (Vertébrés)*, 63 (2), pp. 191–206.

Tasnda Kubacska, A., 1967, Dinoszaurusz lbnyomok haznkban: *let s Tud*, 24, pp. 1118–1121.

_____, 1968, Az let fejldse kpekben: *Gondolat Kiad*. 115 pages.

_____, 1970, riasok birodalma: *Mra Kiad*, pp. 113–121. Budapest.

Taylor, A., 1862, On the footprints of an *Iguanodon*, lately found at Hastings: *Quarterly*

Journal of the Geological Society of London, 18, pp. 247–253.

Thommasi, 1886, Note paleontologiche: *Bollottino della Societa Geolica Italiano,* 4, pp. 199–222.

Throckmorton, Gaylor S., 1976, Oral food processing in two herbivorous lizards, *Iguana iguana* (Iguanidae) and *Uromastix aegyptus* (Agamidae): *Journal of Morphology,* 148, pp. 363–390.

Thulborn, Richard A., 1970a, The skull of *Fabrosaurus australis,* a Triassic ornithischian dinosaur: *Palaeontology,* 13, part 3, pp. 414–432.

———, 1970b, The systematic position of the Triassic ornithischian dinosaur *Lycorhinus angustidens: Zoological Journal of the Linnean Society,* 49, pp. 235–245.

———, 1971, Tooth wear and jaw action in the Triassic ornithischian dinosaur *Fabrosaurus: Journal of Zoology,* 164, pp. 165–179.

———, 1972, The post-cranial skeleton of the Triassic ornithischian dinosaur *Fabrosaurus australis: Palaeontology,* 15, part 1, pp. 29–60.

———, 1973a, Thermoregulation in dinosaurs: *Nature,* 245, pp. 51–52.

———, 1973b, Teeth of ornithischian dinosaurs from the Upper Jurassic of Portugal with description of a hypsilophodontid (*Phyllodon henkeli* gen. et sp. nov.) from the Guimarota Lignite: *Memoria Servicos Geologicos de Portugal (new series),* 22, pp. 89–134.

———, 1974, A new heterodontosaurid dinosaur (Reptilia: Ornithischia) from the Upper Triassic Red Beds of Lesotho: *Zoological Journal of the Linnean Society,* 55, pp. 151–175.

———, 1977, Relationships of the Lower Jurassic dinosaur *Scelidosaurus harrisonii: Journal of Paleontology,* 51 (4), pp. 725–739.

———, 1978, Aestivation among ornithopod dinosaurs of the African Trias: *Lethaia,* 3, pp. 185–198.

———, 1984, The avian relationships of *Archaeopteryx* and the origin of birds: *Zoological Journal of the Linnean Society,* 82, pp. 119–158.

Tracy, C. R., 1976, Tyrannosaurs: evidence for endothermy?: *American Naturalist,* 110, pp. 1105–1106.

Trexler, David, 1995, Preliminary work on a recently discovered ceratopsian (Dinosauria: Ceratopsidae) bonebed from the Judith River Formation of Montana suggests remains are of *Ceratops montanus* Marsh: *Journal of Vertebrate Paleontology,* Abstracts of Papers, Fifty-fifth Annual Meeting, p. 57A.

Tschudy, R.H., C.L. Pillmore, C.J. Orth, J.S. Gilmore, and J.D. Knight, 1984, Disruption of the terrestrial plant ecosystem at the Cretaceous-Tertiary boundary, Western Interior: *Science,* 225, pp. 1030–1032.

Tschudy, R.H., and B.D. Tschudy, 1986, Extinction and survival of plant life following the Cretaceous-Tertiary boundary event, Western Interior, North America: *Geology,* 14, pp. 667–670.

Tucker, Maurice E., and Michael J. Benton, 1982, Triassic environments, climates and reptile evolution: *Palaeogeography, Palaeoclimatology, Palaeoecology,* 40, pp. 361–379.

Tumanova, T. A., 1978, New data on the ankylosaur *Tarchia gigantea:* Palaeontologicheskii Zhurnal, 4, pp. 92–100.

———, 1983, [The first ankylosaurs from the Lower Cretaceous of Mongolia.]: *Joint Soviet-Mongolian Palaeontological Expedition, Transactions,* 24, pp. 110–128.

———, 1986, Cranial morphology of the ankylosaur *Shamosaurus scutatus* from the Lower Cretaceous of Mongolia, *in:* Actes du Colloque "*Les Dinosaures de la Chine à la France.*" Muséum d'Histoire Naturelle, Toulouse, 2–6, pp. 73–79.

———, 1987, The armored dinosaurs of Mongolia, The Joint Soviet-Mongolian Paleontological Expedition: *Mockba "Hayka," Transaction,* 32, pp. 3–80.

———, 1993, O novom pantsironom dinozavre iz Yugo-Vostochnoy Gobi: *Palaeontologicheskii Zhurnal,* 2, pp. 92–98. (Translation: A new armored dinosaur from Southeastern Gobi: *Paleontological Journal,* 27 [2], pp. 119–125.)

Tyson, Helen, 1981, The structure and relationship of the horned dinosaur *Arrhinoceratops* Parks (Ornithischia: Ceratopsidae): *Canadian Journal of Earth Sciences,* 18, pp. 1241–1247.

Unwin, David M., Altangerel Perle, and C. Trueman, 1995, *Protoceratops* and *Velociraptor* preserved in association: evidence for predatory behavior in dromaeosaurid dinosaurs: *Journal of Vertebrate Paleontology,* Abstracts of Papers, Fifty-fifth Annual Meeting, pp. 57A–58A.

Van Beneden, P. J., 1878, Sur la découverte de reptiles fossiles gigantesques dans le charbonnage de Bernissart, près de Pruwelz: *Bulletin, Institut Royale d'Histoire Naturelle de Belgique,* 3 (1), pp. 1–19.

Van Heerden, Jacques, 1978, *Herrerasaurus* and the origin of sauropod dinosaurs: *South African Journal of Science,* 74, pp. 187–189.

———, 1979, The morphology and taxonomy of *Euskelosaurus* (Reptilia: Saurischia: Later Triassic) from South Africa: *Navorsinge van die Nasionale Museum,* 4 (2), pp. 21–84.

Van Hoepen, E. C. N., 1916, Des ouderdom der Transvaalische Kar-olagen: *Verhandelingen Geologisch-Mijinbouwkunoig Genootschap voor Nederland en Kolonien, Geologische Series,* 3, p. 107.

———, 1920, Contributions to the knowledge of the reptiles of the Karroo Formation: *Annals of the Transvaal Museum,* 7, part 2, pp. 6–140.

Van Valen, Leigh M., 1984, Catastrophes, expectations, and the evidence: *Paleobiology,* 10, pp. 121–137.

Van Valen, Leigh M., and Robert E. Sloan, 1977, Ecology and extinction of the dinosaurs: *Evolutionary Theory,* 2, pp. 37–64.

Versluys, Jan, 1910, Streptostylie bei Dinosaurien, nebst Bemerkun gen ber die Verwandtschaft der Vgel und Dinosaurier: *Zoologie Jahrbuch (Anat.)* 30, pp. 175–260.

Vianey-Liaud, M., S. L. Jain, and A. Sahni, 1988, Dinosaur eggshells (Saurischia) from the Late Cretaceous Intertrappean and Lameta Formations (Deccan, India): *Journal of Vertebrate Paleontology,* 7 (4), pp. 408–424.

Vickers-Rich, Patricia, and Thomas Hewitt Rich, 1993, Australia's polar dinosaurs: *Scientific American,* 269 (1), pp. 50–55.

Villatte, J., Phillipe Tacuet, and M. Bilotte, 1986, Nouveaux restes de dinosauriens dans le Crétacé terminal de l'anticlinal de la Dreuilhe. Etat des connaissance dans le domains sous-pyrénéen, *in:* Actes du Colloque "*Les Dinosaures de la Chine à la France.*"

Muséum d'Histoire Naturelle, Toulouse, pp. 89–98.

Vine, R. R., and R. W. Day, 1965, Nomenclature of the Rolling Downs Group, northern Eromanga Basin, Queensland: *Queensland Government Mineral Journal,* 66, pp. 416–421.

Vine, R. R., R. W. Day, E. N. Milligan, D. J. Casey, M. C. Galloway, and N. F. Exon, 1967, Revision of the nomenclature of the Rolling Downs Group in the Eromanga and Surat Basin: *Queensland Government Mineral Journal,* 68, pp. 144–151.

Virchow, Hans, 1919, Atlas und Epistrophaus bei den Schildkrten: *Sitzungberichte der Gesellschaft Naturforschender Freunde,* 1919, 15, pp. 303–332.

Voorhies, M. R., 1969, Taphonomy and population dynamics of an Early Pliocene vertebrate fauna, Knox County, Nebraska: *University of Wyoming, Contributions to Geology, Special Paper 1,* 69 pages.

Voss-Foucart, M.F., 1968, Paloprotines des coquilles fossiles d'oeufs de dinosauriens du Crétacé suprieur de Provence: *Comparative Biochemistry and Physiology,* 24, pp. 31–36.

Wagner, Andreas, 1861, Neue Beitrge zur Kenntnis der urweltlichen Fauna des lithographischen Schiefers; V. *Compsognathus longipes* Wagn.: *Abhandlungen bayerische Akadademie der Wissenschaftenlicen,* 9, pp. 30–38.

Wagstaff, Barbara E., and Jennifer M. Mason, 1989, Palynological dating of Lower Cretaceous coastal vertebrate localities, Victoria, Australia: *National Geographic Research,* 5 (1), pp. 54–63.

Waldman, W., 1969, On an immature specimen of *Kritosaurus notabilis* (Lambe), (Ornithischia: Hadrosauridae) from the Upper Cretaceous of Alberta, Canada: *Canadian Journal of Earth Sciences,* 6 (4), pp. 569–576.

———, 1974, Megalosaurids from the Bajocian (Middle Jurassic) of Dorset: *Palaeontology,* 17, pp. 325–339.

Walker, Alick D., 1964, Triassic reptiles from the Elgin area, *Ornithosuchus* and the origin of carnosaurs: *Philosophical Transactions of the Royal Society of London,* Series B, 248, pp. 53–134.

———, 1977, Evolution of the pelvis in birds and dinosaurs, *in:* S. M. Andrews, R. S. Milles, A. D. Walker, editors, *Problems in Vertebrate Evolution, Linnean Society Symposium,* 4, pp. 319–358.

Walker, Cyril, 1981, A new subclass of birds from the Cretaceous of South America: *Nature,* 292, pp. 51–53.

Walker, E. P., 1968, *Mammals of the World.* Baltimore: Johns Hopkins University Press, 1500 pages (2 volumes).

Wall, William P., and Peter M. Galton, 1979, Notes on pachycephalosaurid dinosaurs (Reptilia: Ornithischia) from North America, with comments on their status as ornithopods: *Canadian Journal of Earth Sciences,* 16 (6), pp. 1176–1186.

Watson, D. M. S., 1930, [untitled]: *Isle of Wight Natural History Society, Proceedings,* 2, p. 60.

Weems, Robert E., 1987, A Late Triassic footprint fauna from the Culpeper Basin northern Virginia (U.S.A.): *Transactions of the American Philosophical Society,* 77, part 1, pp. 1–79.

Weigelt, J., 1989, *Recent Vertebrate Carcasses and Their Paleobiological Implications.* Chicago: University of Chicago Press, 188 pages.

Weishampel, David B., 1981, The nasal cavity of lambeosaurine hadrosaurids (Reptilia: Ornithischia): comparative anatomy and homologies: *Journal of Paleontology*, 55 (5), pp. 1046–1057.

_____, 1984*a*, Trössingen: E. Fraas, F. von Huene, R. Seeman and the "Schwbische Lindwurm" *Plateosaurus*, in: W.E. Reif and F. Westphal, editors, *Third Symposium on Mesozoic Terrestrial Ecosystems, Short Papers*. Tübingen, Germany: Attempto Verlag, pp. 249–253.

_____, 1984*b*, Interactions between Mesozoic plants and vertebrates: Fructifications and seed predation: *Neus Jahrbuch Fuer Geolologie und Palontologie Abhandlungen*, 167, pp. 224–250.

_____, 1984*c*, Evolution of jaw mechanisms in ornithopod dinosaurs: *Advances in Anatomy and Cell Biology*, 87, pp. 1–109.

_____, 1990*a*, Dinosaurian distribution, in: Weishampel, Peter Dodson, and Halszka Osmlska, editors, *The Dinosauria*. Berkeley and Los Angeles: University of California Press, pp. 63–139.

_____, 1990*b*, Ornithopoda, in: *Ibid.*, pp. 484–485.

Weishampel, David B., and Philip R. Bjork, 1989, The first indisputable remains of *Iguanodon* (Ornithischia: Ornithopoda) from North America: *Iguanodon lakotaensis*, sp. nov.: *Journal of Vertebrate Paleontology*, 9 (1), pp. 56–66.

Weishampel, David B., Peter Dodson, and Halszka Osmlska, 1990, *The Dinosauria*. Berkeley and Los Angeles: University of California Press, xvi, 733 pages.

Weishampel, David B., Dan Grigorescu, and David B. Norman, 1991, The dinosaurs of Translyvania: *National Geographic Research & Exploration*, 7 (2), pp. 196–215.

Weishampel, David B., and John R. Horner, 1986, The hadrosaurid dinosaurs from the Iren Dabasu fauna (People's Republic of China, late Cretaceous): *Journal of Vertebrate Paleontology*, 6 (1), pp. 38–45.

_____, 1990, Hadrosauridae, in: Weishampel, Peter Dodson, and Halszka Osmlska, editors, *The Dinosauria*. Berkeley and Los Angeles: University of California Press, pp. 534–561.

Weishampel, David B., and James A. Jensen, 1979, *Parasaurolophus* (Reptilia: Hadrosauridae) from Utah: *Journal of Paleontology*, 53 (6), pp. 1422–1427.

Weishampel, David B., David B. Norman, and Dan Grigorescu, 1993, *Telmatosaurus transsylvanicus* from the Late Cretaceous of Romania: the most basal hadrosaurid dinosaur: *Palaeontology*, 36 (2), pp. 361–385.

Weishampel, David B., and Weishampel, Judith B., 1983, Annotated localities of ornithopod dinosaurs: Implications to Mesozoic paleobiogeography: *The Mosasaur*, 1, pp. 43–87.

Weishampel, David B., and Lawrence M. Witmer, 1990*a*, *Lesothosaurus, Pisanosaurus*, and *Technosaurus*, in: Weishampel, Peter Dodson, and Halszka Osmlska, editors, *The Dinosauria*. Berkeley and Los Angeles: University of California Press, pp. 416–426.

_____, 1990*b*, Heterodontosauridae, *Ibid.*, pp. 486–497.

Welles, Samuel Paul, 1952, A review of the North American Cretaceous elasmosaurs:

University of California Publications in Geological Science, 29 (3).

_____, 1964, New Jurassic dinosaur from the Kayenta Formation of Arizona: *Bulletin of the Geological Society of America*, 65, pp. 591–598.

_____, 1970, *Dilophosaurus* (Reptilia: Saurischia), a new name for a dinosaur: *Paleontological Notes, Museum of Paleontology, University of California, Berkeley*, 44 (5), p. 989.

_____, 1971, Dinosaur footprints from the Kayenta Formation of Northern Arizona: *Plateau*, 44 (1), pp. 27–38.

_____, 1983*a*, *Allosaurus* (Saurischia, Theropoda) not yet in Australia: *Journal of Paleontology*, 57 (2), pp. 196–197.

_____, 1983*b*, Two centers of ossification in a theropod astragalus: *Ibid.*, 57 (2), p. 401.

_____, 1984, *Dilophosaurus wetherilli* (Dinosauria, Theropoda) osteology and comparisions: *Palaeontographica*, Abstract. 5, 185, pp. 85–180.

Welles, Samuel P., and Long, Robert A., 1974, The tarsus of theropod dinosaurs: *Annals of the South African Museum*, 64, pp. 191–218.

Wellman, H. W., 1959, Divisions of the New Zealand Cretaceous: *Transactions of the Royal Society of New Zealand*, 87, pp. 99–163.

Wellnhofer, Peter, 1991, *The Illustrated Encyclopedia of Pterosaurs*. New York: Crescent Books, 192 pages.

_____, 1993, Das siebte Exemplar von *Archaeopteryx* aus den Solnhofener Schichten: *Archaeopteryx*, 11, pp. 1–47, Eichsttt.

Welty, J. C., 1963, *The Life of Birds*. New York: Alfred A. Knopf, xiii, 546 pages.

_____, 1988, *Ibid.*, 4th edition. New York: Saunders College Publishers.

Werner, Christa, 1993, Late Cretaceous continental vertebrate faunas of Niger and northern Sudan, in: U. Thorweihe and H. Schandermeier, editors, *Geoscientific Research in Northeast Africa*. Rotterdam: Balkema, pp. 401–405.

_____, 1994*a*, Die kontinentale Wirbeltierfauna aus der unteren Oberkreide des Sudan (Wadi Milk Formation, Sudan): *Berliner geowissenschaftliche Abhandlungen*, E, 13, pp. 221–249, Berlin.

_____, 1994*b*, Der erste Nachweiss von Gymnophionen (Amphibia) in der Kreide (Wadi Milk Formation, Sudan): *Neus Jahrbuch für Geologie und Paläontologie*, Monatshefte 1994, 10, pp. 633–640, Stuttgart.

Wetmore, A., 1960, A classification for the birds of the world: *Smithsonian Miscellaneous Collections*, 139, pp. 1–37.

Whitaker, George O., and J. Myers, 1965, *Dinosaur Hunt*. New York: Harcourt, Brace and World, 94 pages.

White, Theodore E., 1958, The braincase of *Camarasaurus lentus* (Marsh): *Journal of Paleontology*, 32, pp. 477–494.

_____, 1973, Catalogue of the genera of dinosaurs: *Annals of Carnegie Museum*, 44, pp. 117–155.

Wieland, G. R., 1903, Notes on the marine turtle *Archelon*. I. On the structure of the carapace; II. Associated fossils: *American Journal of Science*, Series 4, 15 (87), pp. 211–216.

_____, 1909, A new armored saurian from the Niobrara: *Ibid.*, 27, pp. 250–252.

Wiffen, Joan, and Ralph E. Molnar, 1989, An Upper Cretaceous ornithopod from New Zealand: *Geobios*, 22 (4), pp. 531–536.

Wild, Rupert, 1973, Die Triasfauna der Tessiner Kalkalpen. XXIV. *Tanystropheus longobardi-*

cus (Bassani) Neue Ergebnisse: *Schweizerischen Palontologischen Gesellschaft*, 94, pp. 1–162.

_____, 1991, *Janenschia* n. g. *robusta* (E. Fraas 1908) pro *Tornieria robusta* (E. Fraas 1908) (Reptilia, Saurischia, Sauropodomorpha): *Stuttgarter Beitrge zur Naturkunde*, Serie B (Geologie und Palontologie). 173 (4), pp. 1–4.

Wilfarth, Martin, 1938, Gab es rsseltragende Dinosaurier?: *Zeitschrift Deutsch. Geol. Ges.*, 90 (2), pp. 88–100.

_____, 1947, Russeltragende Dinosaurier: *Orion (Munich)*, 2, pp. 525–532.

Williams, Michael E., 1982, Paleontological displays of the Cleveland Museum of Natural History: *Fossils Quarterly*, 1, pp. 20–26.

Williston, Samuel Wendell, 1905, A new armored dinosaur from the Upper Cretaceous of Wyoming: *Science*, 22, pp. 503–504.

_____, 1914, *Water Reptiles of the Past and Present*. Chicago: University of Chicago Press, 251 pages.

Wilson, Michael Clayton, and Philip J. Currie, 1985, *Stenonychosaurus inequalis* (Saurischia: Theropoda) from the Judith River (Oldman) Formation of Alberta: new findings on metatarsal structure: *Canadian Journal of Earth Sciences*, 22 (12), pp. 1813–1817.

Wiman, Carl, 1929, Die Kreide-Dinosaurier aus Shantung: *Palaeontologia Sinica*, 6, pp. 1–67, Peking.

_____, 1930, Uber Ceratopsia aus der Oberon Kreide in New Mexico: *Nova Acta Regia Societas Scientarum Upsaliensis*, Series 4, 7 (2), pp. 1–19.

_____, 1931, *Parasaurolophus tubicen*, n. sp. aus der Kreide in New Mexico: *Ibid.*, 7 (5), pp. 1–11.

Winkler, David A., Phillip A. Murry, and Louis L. Jacobs, 1989, Vertebrate paleontology of the Trinity Group, Lower Cretaceous of central Texas, in: D. A. Winkler, P. A. Murry, and L. L. Jacobs, editors, *Field Guide to the Vertebrate Paleontology of the Trinity Group, Lower Cretaceous of Central Texas*. Field Guide for the 49th Annual Meeting of the Society of Vertebrate Paleontology, Institute for the Study of Earth and Man, Southern Methodist University, Dallas, pp. 1–22.

Witmer, Lawrence M., 1988, Mechanisms of sound localization in some fossil archosaurs: *Journal of Vertebrate Paleontology*, 8, 29A.

_____, 1991, Perspectives on avian origins, in: H. P. Schultze and L. Trueb, *Origins of the Higher Groups of Tetrapods*. Ithaca, New York: Cornell University Press, pp. 427–466.

Woodward, Arthur A. Smith, 1901, On some extinct reptiles from Patagonia of the genera *Miolina, Dinilysia* and *Genyodectes*: *Proclamations of the Zoological Society of London*, pp. 179–182.

_____, 1905, On parts of the skeleton of *Cetiosaurus leedsii*, a sauropodous dinosaur from the Oxford Clay of Peterborough: *Ibid.*, pp. 232–243.

_____, 1910, On a skull of *Megalosaurus* from the Great Oolite of Minchinhampton (Gloucestershire): *Quarterly Journal of the Geological Society of London*, 66, pp. 111–115.

Wright, Thomas, 1852, Contributions to the paleontology of the Isle of Wight: *Annals of the Magazine of Natural History*, 2 (10), pp. 87–93 [reprinted in: *Proclamations of the Cotteswold Naturalist Field Club*, 1, pp. 229–234 (1853)].

Wyman, J., 1855, Notice of fossil bones from the red sandstone of the Connecticut River Valley: *American Journal of Science*, 2 (20), pp. 394–397.

Yadagiri, P., 1988, A new sauropod *Kotasaurus yamanpalliensis* from Lower Jurassic Kota Formation of India: *Records of the Geological Survey of India*, 11 (3–8), pp. 102–127.

Yadagiri, P., and K. Ayyasami, 1979, A new stegosaurian dinosaur from the Upper Cretaceous sediments of south India: *Journal of the Geological Society of India*, 20, pp. 521–530.

_____, 1989, A carnosaurian dinosaur from the Kallamedu Formation (Maastrichtian horizon), Tamilnadu: *Geological Society of India Special Publication*, 11, pp. 523–528.

Yadagiri, P., K. N. Prasad, and P. P. Satsangi, 1980, Sauropod dinosaur from Kota Formation of Pranhita-Godavari Valley, India: *Proceedings of the IV International Gondwana Symposium, India*, pp. 199–203.

Yang Zhungjian [Young Chung-Chien], 1931, On some new dinosaurs from western Suiyan, Inner Mongolia: *Bulletin of the Geological Society of China*, 11, pp. 159–266.

_____, 1935, Dinosaurian remains from Mengyin, Shantung: *Ibid.*, 14, pp. 519–533, Peiping.

_____, 1937a, New Triassic reptiles and Cretaceous reptiles in China: *Ibid.*, 17 (1), pp. 113–118.

_____, 1937b, A new dinosaur from Sinkiang, *Palaeontologica Sineca*, New Series C., 105 (2), pp. 1–23.

_____, 1939, On a new Sauropoda, with notes on other fragmentary reptiles from Szechuan: *Bulletin of the Geological Society of China*, 19 (3), pp. 299–315.

_____, 1940, Preliminary note on the Lufeng vertebrate fossils: *Ibid.*, 20 (3–4), pp. 235–240.

_____, 1941a, A complete osteology of *Lufengosaurus hueni* Yang [Young] (gen. et. sp. nov.): *Palaeontologica Sineca*, new series G, 7, whole series number 121, pp. x–53.

_____, 1941b, *Gyposaurus sinensis* Tang [Young] (sp. nov.), a new Prosauropoda from the Upper Triassic Beds at Lufeng, Yunnan: *Bulletin of the Geological Society of China*, 21 (2–4), pp. 205–253.

_____, 1942a, *Yunnanosaurus huangi* Yang [Young] (get. et sp. nov.), a new Prosauropoda from the Red Beds at Lufeng, Yunnan: *Ibid.*, 22 (1–2), pp. 63–104.

_____, 1942b, Fossil vertebrates from Kuangyuan, N. Szechuan, China: *Ibid.*, 22 (3–4), pp. 293–309.

_____, 1944, On the reptilian remains from Weiyuan, Szechuan, China: *Ibid.*, 24 (3–4), pp. 187–209.

_____, 1946, The Triassic vertebrate remains of China: *American Museum Novitates*, 1324, 4 pages.

_____, 1947, On *Lufengosaurus magnus* Yang [Young] (sp. nov.) and additional finds of *Lufengosaurus hueni* Yang [Young]: *Palaeontologica Sinica*, New Series C., 12, Whole Series number 132, pp. x–53.

_____, 1948a, On two new saurischians from Lufeng, Yunnan: *Bulletin of the Geological Society of China, Peking*, 28, pp. 75–90.

_____, 1948b, Further notes on *Gyposaurus sinensis* Yang [Young]: *Ibid.*, 28 (1–2), pp. 91–103.

_____, 1951, The Lufeng saurischian fauna of China: *Palaeontologica Sinica*, 134, pp. 1–96.

_____, 1954a, Fossil reptilian eggs from Layang, Shantung, China: *Scienta Sinica*, 3 (4), pp. 523–545 (translated in English and reprinted in *Acta Palaeontologica Sinica*, 2 [4], pp. 371–388).

_____, 1954b, On a new sauropod from Yiping, Szechuan, China: *Scientia Sinica*, 3, pp. 491–504.

_____, 1958a, The first record of dinosaurian remains from Shansi: *Vertebrata PalAsiatica*, 2 (4), pp. 231–236.

_____, 1958b, New sauropods from China: *Ibid.*, 2 (1), 28 pages.

_____, 1958c, The dinosaurian remains of Laiyang, Shantung: *Palaeontologica Sinica*, 16, Whole Number 142, pp. 51–138.

_____, 1959a, On a new stegosaurian remain from Szechuan, China: *Vertebrata PalAsiatica*, 3 (1), pp. 1–8.

_____, 1959b, On a new fossil egg from Laiyang, Shantung: *Ibid.*, 3 (1), pp. 34–35.

_____, 1974, New discoveries on therapsids from Lufeng, Yunnan: *Ibid.*, 12 (2), pp. 111–114.

_____, 1982a, A new ornithopod from Lufeng, Yunnan: *Selected Works of Yang Zhunjian (Young Chung-Chien)*: Science Press, Beijing, pp. 29–35.

_____, 1982b, On a new genus of dinosaur from Lufeng, Yunnan: *Ibid.*, pp. 38–42.

Yang Zhungjian, Bien M.N. and Mi T.H., 1972, *Mamenchisaurus* from Ho Chuan: *Chin. Sci. Inst. Vert. Pal. Paleoantro.*, Monograph Series A 8, 30 pages.

Yang Zhungjian, and A.-L. Sun, 1957, Note on a fragmentary carnosaurian mandible from Turfan, Sinkiang: *Vertebrata PalAsiatica*, 1, pp. 159–162.

Yang, Zhungian [Young Chung-Chien], and X. J. Zhao, 1972, *Mamenchisaurus hochuanensis*: Institute of Vertebrate Paleontology and Paleoanthropology, Monograph Series A, No. 8 (in Chinese).

Yarborough, V. L., 1995, Removal of *Acrocanthosaurus* bones from calcite cemented siliceous sandstone using diamond saws: *Journal of Vertebrate Paleontology*, Abstracts of Papers, Fifty-fifth Annual Meeting, p. 61A.

Yeh H. K., 1975, *Mesozoic Redbeds of Yunnan*. Beijing: *Academica Sinica*.

Yen Teng-Chien, 1952, Molluscan fauna of the Morrison Formation: *United States Geological Survey Professional Paper*, 233-B, pp. 21–51.

Young Chung-Chien. *See* Yang Zhungjian.

Zborzewski, Adalbert, 1834, Aperçu de recherches physiques rationelles sur les nouvelles curiosités podolie-volyniennes, et sur leurs rapports géologiques avec les autres localités: *Bulletin de la Société des Naturalistes et des Archobugues de l'Ain*, 7, pp. 224–254.

Zeng, X., 1982, *Fossil Handbook of Hunan Province*. Geology Bureau of Hunan Province.

Zhang Yihong, 1988, *The Middle Jurassic dinosaur fauna from Dashanpu, Zigong, Sichuan, Vol. I: Sauropod Dinosaurs (I)*: Chengdu, China: Sichuan Publishing House of Science and Technology. pp. 75–81.

Zhao, Xin Jin [formerly Zhao Xijin], 1980, [Mesozoic vertebrate-bearing beds and stratigraphy of northern Xinjiang: Report of Paleontological Expedition to Xinjiang IV.]: *Memoirs, Institute of Vertebrate Paleontology and Palaeoanthropology*, 15, pp. 1–119.

_____, 1986a, The Jurassic Reptilia: *Stratigraphy of China*, 11 (The Jurassic System of China), pp. 286–347.

_____, 1986b, Reptilia: *Ibid.*, 12 (The Cretaceous System of China), pp. 66–299.

Zhao, Xijin, 1993, A new Mid-Jurassic sauropod (*Klamelisaurus gobiensis* gen. et sp. nov.) from Xinjiang, China: *Vertebrata PalAsiatica*, 31 (4), pp. 132–138.

Zhao, Xi-Jin [formerly Zhao Xijin], and Philip J. Currie, 1993, A large crested theropod from the Jurassic of Xinjiang, People's Republic of China: *Canadian Journal of Earth Sciences*, 30 (10–11), pp. 2027–2036.

Zhao Zikui, Ye Jie, Li Humaei, Zhao Zhenhua and Zan Zheng, 1990, Extinction of the dinosaurs across the Cretaceous-Tertiary boundary in Nanxiong Basin, Guangdong Province: *Vertebrata PalAsiatica*, 19 (1), pp. 13–20.

Zhen Shounan, Zhen B.M., Niall J. Mateer, and Spencer G. Lucas, 1985, The Mesozoic reptiles of China: *Bulletin, Geological Institute, University of Uppsala, N.A.*, 11, pp. 130–150.

Zhou Ming-Zhen [formerly Minchen Chow], 1980, Vertebrate paleontology in China (1949–1979): *Vertebrata PalAsiatica*, 17 (4), pp. 263–276.

Zhou Shiwu, 1983, A nearly complete skeleton of a stegosaur from the Middle Jurassic of Dashanpu, Zigong, Sichuan: *Journal of Chengdu College of Geology*, 1983 supplement, 1, pp. 15–26.

_____, 1984, *The Middle Jurassic Dinosaurian Fauna from Dashanpu, Sichuan, 2, Stegosaurs*: Chengdu, China: Sichuan Scientific and Technological Publishing House, 51 pages.

Index

This index includes dinosaurian and some nondinosaurian genera and species; some unofficial names of dinosaurs; selected authors, discoverers, and other persons; selected institutions, organizations, stratigraphic horizons, localities, sites, symposia, and miscellaneous places; and relevant topics that appear in the text and picture captions.

Junior synonyms are cross-referenced to the currently and most widely accepted senior synonym. Page numbers set in *italics* indicate subjects shown or implied in illustrations, or names and topics mentioned or implied in picture captions or credits. Not indexed are dinosaurian taxa above the level of genus, the majority of misspelled taxa that have been published in the paleontological literature or popular texts, and institutions referred to only as abbreviations used to designate catalogue numbers for fossil specimens.

Index

Index

Index

Index

Index